Using Computers
A Gateway to Information
AND
Microsoft Works 3.0 for Windows

Gary B. Shelly
Thomas J. Cashman
Gloria A. Waggoner
William C. Waggoner

Contributing Authors
Misty E. Vermaat
Tim J. Walker

boyd & fraser publishing company

An International Thomson Publishing Company

Danvers • Albany • Bonn • Boston • Cincinnati • Detroit • London • Madrid • Melbourne
Mexico City • New York • Paris • San Francisco • Singapore • Tokyo • Toronto • Washington

SHELLY
CASHMAN
SERIES®

Special thanks go to the following reviewers of *Using Computers: A Gateway to Information*.

Paula Bell, Lock Haven University; **Catherine J. Brotherton**, Riverside Community College; **Deborah Fansler**, Purdue University Calumet; **Kenneth Frizane**, Oakton Community College; **E. Colin Ikei**, Long Beach City College; **Gary L. Margot**, Ashland University; **Harry J. Rosenblatt**, College of the Albemarle; **Althea Stevens**, Mid-Plains Community College, McDonald/Belton Campus; and **Mike Waggoner**, Educational Consultant.

© 1995 boyd & fraser publishing company
One Corporate Place • Ferncroft Village
Danvers, Massachusetts 01923

International Thomson Publishing
boyd & fraser publishing company is an ITP company.
The ITP trademark is used under license.

Printed in the United States of America

For more information, contact boyd & fraser publishing company:

boyd & fraser publishing company
One Corporate Place • Ferncroft Village
Danvers, Massachusetts 01923 USA

International Thomson Publishing Europe
Berkshire House 168-173
High Holborn
London, WC1V 7AA, England

Thomas Nelson Australia
102 Dodds Street
South Melbourne 3205
Victoria, Australia

Nelson Canada
1120 Birchmont Road
Scarborough, Ontario
Canada M1K 5G4

International Thomson Editores
Campose Eliseos 385, Piso 7
Col. Polanco
11560 Mexico D.F. Mexico

International Thomson Publishing GmbH
Konigswinterer Strasse 418
53227 Bonn, Germany

International Thomson Publishing Asia
221 Henderson Road
#05-10 Henderson Building
Singapore 0315

International Thomson Publishing Japan
Hirakawacho Kyowa Building, 3F
2-2-1 Hirakawacho
Chiyoda-ku, Tokyo 102, Japan

ISBN 0-7895-0311-5 (perfect bound)

ISBN 0-7895-0312-3 (spiral bound)

2 3 4 5 6 7 8 9 10   BC   9 8 7 6 5

Contents in Brief

Contents
Using Computers: A Gateway to Information
AND
Microsoft Works 3.0 for Windows

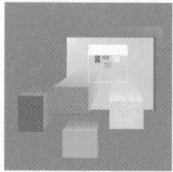

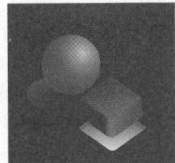

CHAPTER THREE

3

Input to the Computer

CHAPTER FOUR

4

The System Unit

SPECIAL FEATURE

The Internet   **7.43**

8   CHAPTER EIGHT

Operating Systems and System Software

SPECIAL FEATURE

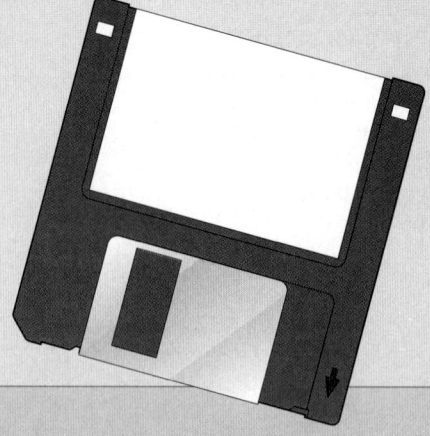

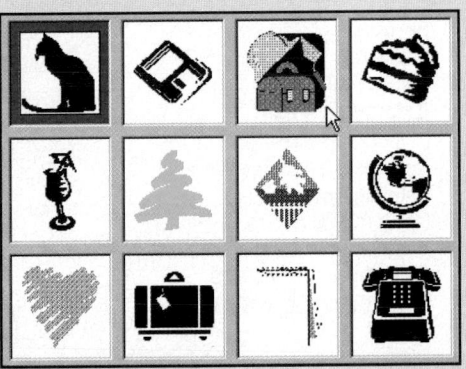

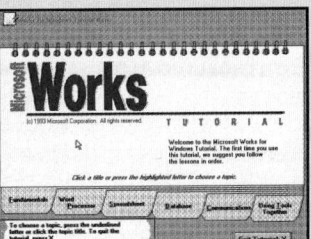

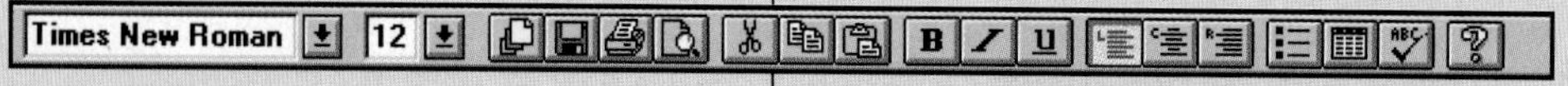
Times New Roman
12

Working with Multiple Documents	W2.44
Quitting Works	W2.45
Creating Custom Templates	**W2.45**
Using Custom Templates	W2.47
Project Summary	**W2.49**
Key Terms	**W2.49**
Quick Reference	**W2.50**
Student Assignments	**W2.50**
Computer Laboratory Exercises	**W2.54**
Computer Laboratory Assignments	**W2.57**

▶ Project Three
Writing and Editing a Research Report with Tables — W3.2

Objectives	**W3.2**
Introduction	**W3.2**
Project Three	**W3.3**
Formatting Standards for the Research Report	W3.4
Starting Works	W3.4
Setting Margins and Controlling the Placement of Footnotes	**W3.5**
Using the Scroll Bar	W3.8
Typing the Research Report	**W3.8**
Headers and Footers	W3.9
Header and Footer Codes	W3.11
Entering Text	W3.11
Centering the Report Title	W3.12
Indenting Paragraphs	W3.13
Entering Text	W3.14
Creating Footnotes	W3.15
Using a Footnote WorksWizard	W3.15
Indenting and Double-Spacing Footnotes	W3.19
Closing the Footnote Pane	W3.20
Saving the Document	W3.21
Entering Text	W3.22
Automatic Page Break	W3.23
Inserting a Manual Page Break and Formatting the Footnotes Page	W3.23

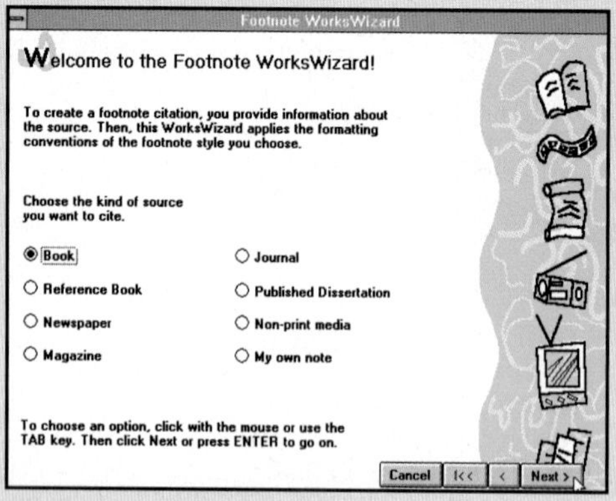
Footnote WorksWizard
Welcome to the Footnote WorksWizard!
To create a footnote citation, you provide information about the source. Then, this WorksWizard applies the formatting conventions of the footnote style you choose.
Choose the kind of source you want to cite.
Book
Journal
Reference Book
Published Dissertation
Newspaper
Non-print media
Magazine
My own note
To choose an option, click with the mouse or use the TAB key. Then click Next or press ENTER to go on.
Cancel
Next >

Editing the Research Report	**W3.25**
Using the Go To Command	W3.26
Using the Find Command	W3.27
Using the Replace Command	W3.29
Undo Editing Command	W3.32
Redo Command	W3.33
Moving Words, Sentences, or Paragraphs	W3.33
Using Drag and Drop to Move Text	W3.33
Copying Data in a Word Processing Document	W3.36
Undoing a Drag-and-Drop Operation	W3.36
Using the Thesaurus	W3.3
Counting Words	W3.3

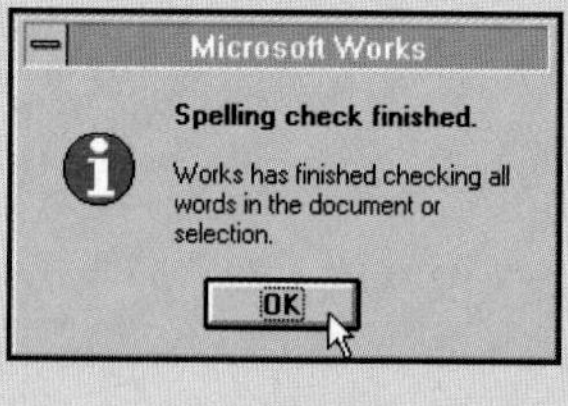
Microsoft Works
Spelling check finished.
Works has finished checking all words in the document or selection.
OK

Checking Spelling, Saving, and Printing the Research Report	W3.3
Tables in Word Processing Documents	**W3.4**
Creating the Table	W3.4
Enlarging the Table	W3.4
Increasing Row Height	W3.4
Changing Column Width	W3.4
Entering Data into the Spreadsheet Table	W3.3
Correcting a Mistake While Typing	W3.5
Entering Row Titles	W3.5
Entering Numeric Data in the Spreadsheet Table	W3.5
Formatting the Spreadsheet Table	W3.5
Removing the Gridlines	W3.5
Adding Borders to the Spreadsheet Table	W3.5
Exiting the Spreadsheet Tool	W3.5
Objects and Object Linking and Embedding (OLE) 2.0	**W3.5**
Project Summary	**W3.6**
Key Terms	**W3.6**
Quick Reference	**W3.6**
Student Assignments	**W3.6**
Computer Laboratory Exercises	**W3.6**
Computer Laboratory Assignments	**W3.6**

▶ Project Four
Building a Spreadsheet — W4.2

Objectives	**W4.2**
Introduction	**W4.2**
The Works Spreadsheet and Charting Tool	**W4.2**
Project Four	**W4.5**
Spreadsheet Preparation Steps	W4.4
Starting the Works Spreadsheet	**W4.4**

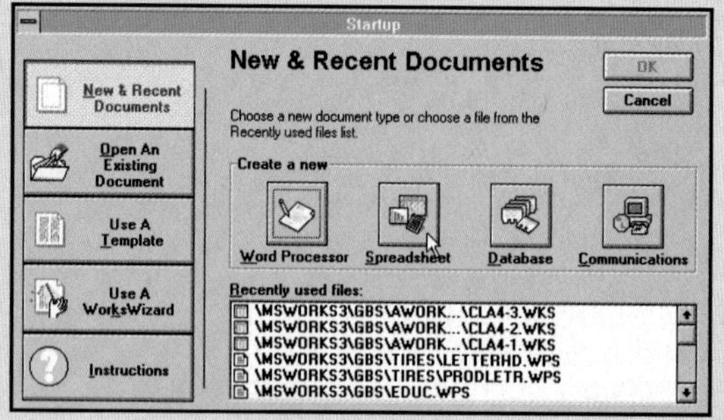
Startup
New & Recent Documents
New & Recent Documents
Open An Existing Document
Use A Template
Use A WorksWizard
Instructions
OK
Cancel
Choose a new document type or choose a file from the Recently used files list.
Create a new
Word Processor
Spreadsheet
Database
Communications
Recently used files:

The Spreadsheet	**W4.6**
Cell, Highlighted Cell, and Mouse Pointer	W4.6
Spreadsheet Window	W4.7
Menu Bar, Toolbar, Formula Bar, and Status Bar	W4.8
Highlighting a Cell	**W4.9**
Entering Text	**W4.9**
Entering the Spreadsheet Title	W4.9
Correcting a Mistake While Typing	W4.11
Entering Column Titles	W4.11
Using the Fill Series Command	W4.12
Entering Row Titles	W4.14
Entering Numbers	**W4.15**
Calculating a Sum	**W4.18**

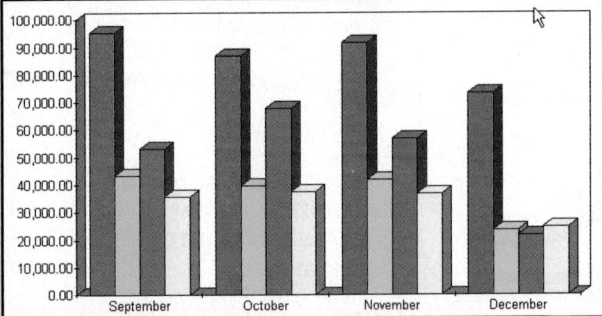

PROJECT FIVE
Formulas, Sorting and Charting W5.2

Investment Club Report

Stock	Purchase Date	Shares	Purchase Price	Cost	Current Price	Current Value	Gain/Loss
AT&T	3/24/94	500	50.00	25,000.00	60.00	30,000.00	5,000.00
Boeing	1/23/94	300	49.50	14,850.00	56.25	16,875.00	2,025.00
Chrysler	3/22/94	300	60.00	18,000.00	68.00	20,400.00	2,400.00
IBM	4/18/94	400	55.00	22,000.00	50.00	20,000.00	(2,000.00)
Lotus	5/21/94	200	70.00	14,000.00	75.00	15,000.00	1,000.00
Microsoft	4/24/94	400	82.00	32,800.00	94.50	37,800.00	5,000.00
Philip Morris	1/17/94	200	50.00	10,000.00	60.00	12,000.00	2,000.00
Xerox	2/28/94	200	98.00	19,600.00	80.00	16,000.00	(3,600.00)

Portfolio Performance

Total Current Value	168,075.00
Total Cost	156,250.00
Net Gain/Loss	11,825.00
Percentage Gain/Loss	7.57%

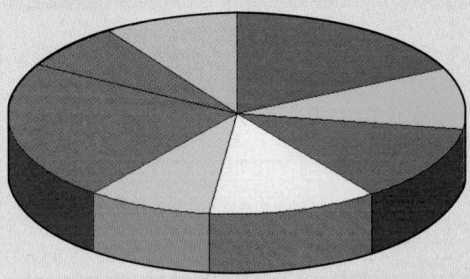

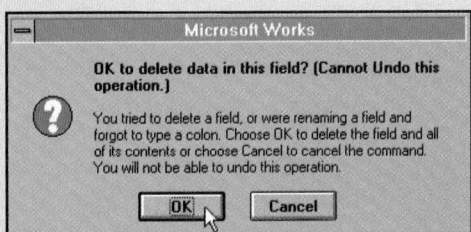

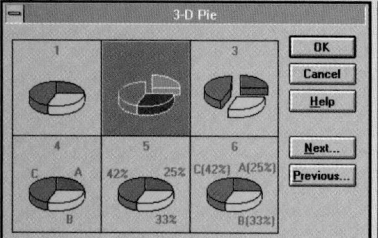 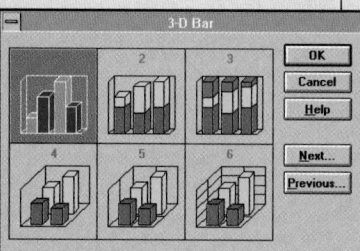

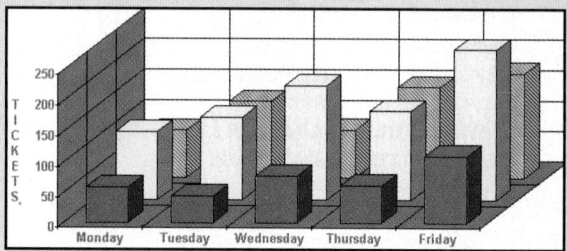

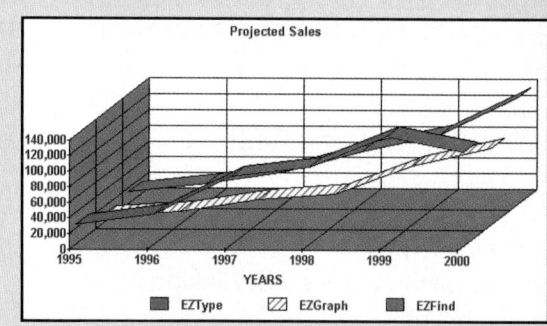

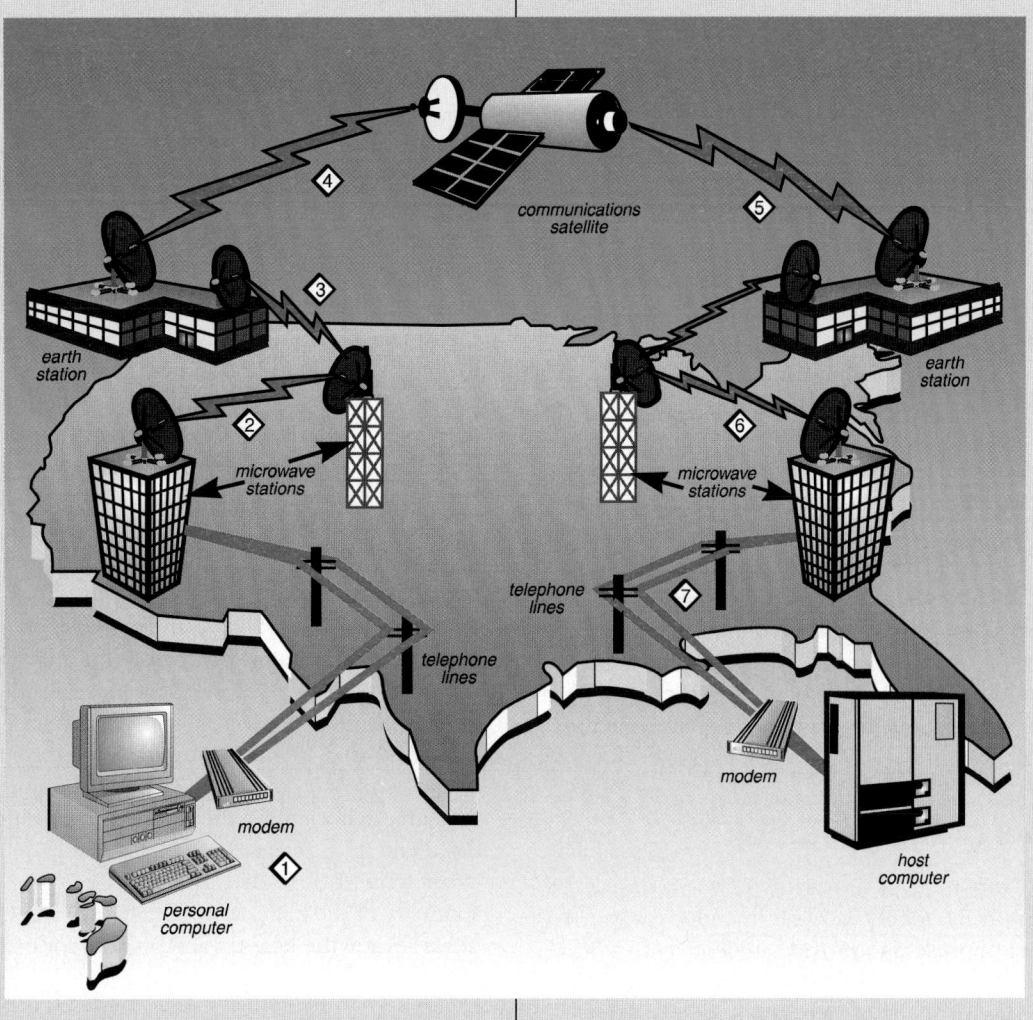

Preface

This Shelly Cashman Series textbook, provides an up-to-date coverage of computers, their uses, and the methods of using a computer. When preparing this book, our single guiding thought was: The book must be relevant to the world of computers today.

Toward that end, with our previous bestsellers as a base, we reviewed each and every aspect of the computer industry to ferret out the essential knowledge a student requires for a well-rounded understanding of using a computer as a tool to produce useful information, whether it be in the home, small business, or large business environments, with special emphasis on personal computer hardware and software.

As a result, this book was developed with five goals in mind: The material must

- represent the latest in computer technology, particularly with respect to personal computer hardware and software.
- recognize that personal computers have become the backbone of the computer industry and emphasize their use as both stand-alone devices and networked devices.
- focus on using the computer as a productivity tool.
- present the material in an interesting, exciting manner with a format that invites the student to learn. This includes new, color photographs and unique, state-of-the-art drawings that augment the text material.
- provide exercises and lab assignments that allow the student to interact with a computer and actually learn by using the computer.

Merely explaining topics without allowing a student to interact with a computer, however, would deprive the student of an essential experience. Therefore, at the end of each of the first eight chapters, we have included a series of *In the Lab* exercises that direct the student to use a computer to learn Microsoft Windows and DOS. In addition, a series of special Shelly Cashman Series Interactive Labs allow students to learn computer skills and gain computer knowledge in an online, interactive setting.

Each of the sections of the book, together with the extraordinary instructor's materials, are explained in the following paragraphs.

Objective of the Textbook

Using Computers: A Gateway to Information and Microsoft Works 3.0 for Windows is intended for use in a course whose purpose is to provide students with a firm foundation in computer technology, computer nomenclature, and the use of Microsoft Works 3.0 for Windows.

When a student has completed a course using this book, he or she will have an understanding of computers, computer technology, computer hardware and software, and how computers can be used to produce meaningful information using Microsoft Works 3.0 for Windows.

Chapter Organization of *Using Computers: A Gateway to Information*

Each of the first eight chapters within the book is organized to present the optimum amount of material in the most effective manner possible. The text is presented in concise, clearly identified sections and subsections so the student is easily guided through the chapter. Figures (pictures and drawings) are visually separated from the text so the student can read without being encumbered by confusing text, graphics, arrows, and drawings.

Each chapter is organized into the following sections:

- **Objectives**   The objectives for the chapter are clearly stated on the first page of the chapter so the student has an overview of the subject matter.
- **Chapter Introduction**   Each chapter has an introduction that briefs the student on the material within the chapter and the reason the material in the chapter is important.
- **Chapter Text, Pictures, and Drawings**   The major learning material in the chapter is presented as text, pictures, and drawings. The pictures have been chosen for their pedagogical value and provide a valuable addition that allows students to see the actual hardware, software, and other subjects described in the text. The drawings, created with the latest state-of-the-art drawing capabilities of computers, specifically illustrate concepts that are understood more easily through the use of drawings. The combination of drawings and pictures used in this book sets a new standard for computer textbooks.
- **Computers at Work**   At the end of each chapter, an example of computers being used for interesting applications is presented. These examples illustrate points made within the chapter.
- **In the Future**   This feature, which appears at the end of each chapter, points out an application or applications that will occur in the future using technology discussed in the chapter.
- **What You Should Know**   This clear, step-by-step summary of the material in the chapter will help students review the chapter and prepare for examinations.

Contents of *Using Computers: A Gateway to Information*

An explanation of each of the first eight chapters in this book follows:

Chapter 1 – An Overview of Computer Concepts   Introduces the student to the fundamentals of a computer, including the information processing cycle. When the student completes the chapter, he or she will have a firm understanding of the basics of computer processing and will be ready for the more in-depth treatment of subjects in subsequent chapters.

Chapter 2 – Computer Software Applications: User Tools   Provides a complete explanation of application software available on computers, with an emphasis on personal computer software that students are likely to use. Numerous examples of the use of software such as word processing, spreadsheets, database, presentation graphics, data communications, electronic mail, and others are included.

Chapter 3 – Input to the Computer   Presents the manner in which data is entered into the computer for processing, with primary attention to personal computers. In addition to the keyboard and mouse, pointing devices, scanners, voice input, and other means of entering data into personal computers is closely examined.

Chapter 4 – The System Unit   Offers a detailed look inside the system unit. Topics include the motherboard, processors, memory, ports, and other elements that make a personal computer run.

Chapter 5 – Output from the Computer Explores the many means for obtaining useful information from a computer, including printers, display devices, voice output, and plotters. Included is an explanation of the types of output from personal computers, such as reports, graphics, audio output, video output, multimedia, and virtual reality.

Chapter 6 – Secondary Storage   Discusses the manner in which data is stored on a computer. Included are diskettes, hard disk, and cartridge tape systems, among others, together with an explanation of such storage issues as defragmentation and compression.

Chapter 7 – Communications and Networks Covers communications and networks from a user's perspective. All important subjects are explained, with a special emphasis on local area networks and personal computers.

- **Terms to Remember**   This listing of the key terms found in the chapter together with the page on which the terms are defined will aid students in mastering the chapter material. A complete summary of all key terms in the book, together with their definitions, appear in the Index at the end of the book.
- **Test Your Knowledge**   Fill-in and short answer questions, together with a figure from the chapter that must be labeled, help focus the student when reviewing the material within the chapter.
- **Points to Ponder**   The computer industry is not without its controversial issues. At the end of each chapter, six scenarios are presented that challenge the student to critically examine the computer industry and rethink his or her perspective of technology in society.
- **Out and About**   Computers are found everywhere. This section, appearing at the end of each chapter, provides multiple projects that send the student out of the classroom and into the world where interesting discoveries about computers will take place.
- **In the Lab**   Students must interact with and use a computer to complete their introduction to computers. At the end of each chapter, a series of lab exercises are presented for student use. These Labs are:
  - **Windows Labs**   Beginning with the simplest exercises within Microsoft Windows, students are led through a series of activities that, by the end of the book, will enable them to be proficient in using Windows.
  - **DOS Labs**   As with Windows, students are given a set of exercises that will lead to proficiency in using DOS commands by the end of the course.
  - **Online Labs**   Online Labs introduce students to the many online services available when using a personal computer and a modem. This series of exercises at the end of each chapter directs students to use and interact with one or more online services.
  - **Shelly Cashman Series Interactive Labs**   These unique exercises, developed specifically for this book, are hands-on exercises that use the computer to teach about the computer. The Labs are described in detail on page xxiv.

This chapter organization and the material presented provide an in-depth treatment of introductory computer subjects. Students will finish the course with a complete understanding of computers and how to use computers.

Chapter 8 – Operating Systems and System Software   Teaches students about operating systems such as DOS, OS/2, and Windows. A clear explanation of difficult subjects such as multitasking and multiprocessing contributes to a student's overall understanding.

Special Features   Within the book, the special features sections provide an in-depth look at certain aspects of computers. The four special features are:
- The Evolution of the Computer Industry
- Making a Computer Chip
- The Internet
- How to Purchase, Install, and Maintain a Personal Computer

These contents, together with *In the Lab* and other projects within this book, present a thorough course on computers and computer usage.

Contents of *Microsoft Works 3.0 for Windows*

The *Microsoft Works 3.0 for Windows* portion of this book consists of two projects on Microsoft Windows 3.1, twelve projects on Microsoft Works 3.0 for Windows, and one appendix. Because the textbook uses a project-oriented approach to teach Works, each major unit of study is called a project. Within each project, the techniques to create or otherwise process one or more word processing documents, spreadsheets, or databases are explained and illustrated. Each project is based upon a realistic application to which the student can relate. The following paragraphs summarize the contents of the major sections of this portion of the textbook.

Using Microsoft Windows 3.1

- **Project 1 – An Introduction to Windows**   The first project introduces the students to Windows concepts, Windows terminology, and how to communicate with Windows using the mouse and keyboard. Topics include starting and exiting Windows; opening group windows; maximizing windows; scrolling; selecting menus; choosing a command from a menu; starting and exiting Windows applications; obtaining online Help; and responding to dialog boxes.

- **Project 2 – Disk and File Management**   The second project introduces the students to File Manager. Topics include formatting a diskette; copying a group of files; renaming and deleting files; searching for help topics; activating, resizing, and closing a group window; switching between applications; and minimizing an application window to an application icon.

Microsoft Works 3.0 for Windows

- **Project 1 – Creating a Document**   Introduces the Word Processor tool, illustrates entering and correcting data, centering data, shows methods for changing type font and style, print preview, opening and editing a word processor document, and Works online Help. The project also includes inserting clip art into a document. Windows allows you to easily and quickly change fonts or insert clip art, demonstrating tasks that in a DOS environment could be difficult to do are done simply in a Windows environment.

- **Project 2 – Creating a Business Letter and Resume**   Illustrates the methods for preparing a letter and resume. Included are techniques for developing a letterhead using WorksWizard, setting margins and tabs, hanging indents, spelling checker, working with multiple documents, text alignment, text formatting, and creating special effects such as paragraph borders. The use of a Works AutoStart Template is used when creating the resume.

- **Project 3 – Writing and Editing a Research Report with Tables**   Demonstrates the preparation of a research report. Setting margins, headers and footers, double-spacing, first-line indent marker, footnotes (endnotes), multiple-page reports, moving words, sentences, and paragraphs, finding text, replacing text, the Works thesaurus, counting words, and techniques for handling larger documents are covered. The report is written using standards from the Modern Language Association of America (MLA). Footnotes are created using a WorksWizard. The table incorporated into the research report is created using a spreadsheet table and OLE 2.0.

- **Project 4 – Building a Spreadsheet**   Introduces the Works Spreadsheet tool. The project includes entering text and numeric values, summing columns and rows using Autosum, copying cells, formatting a spreadsheet (bolding, increasing font size, coloring text and cells, using the AutoFormat feature, changing column widths, adding borders to cells, centering text, removing gridlines, Currency format, and Comma format), saving a spreadsheet, printing a spreadsheet, charting the data in the spreadsheet using a 3-D Bar chart, opening a spreadsheet file, and correcting errors within the spreadsheet.

- **Project 5 – Formulas, Sorting and Charting**
Further explains spreadsheets by introducing entering
and copying formulas, summing and analyzing data,
additional spreadsheet formatting, sorting spreadsheet
data, print preview, printing in landscape page orientation, changing spreadsheet font size, charting spreadsheet data in a 3-D Pie chart, adding and formatting
chart titles, and printing a chart.

- **Project 6 – What-If Analysis, Functions, and
Absolute Cell References**   Places an emphasis on
using spreadsheets for management-decision making by
illustrating the what-if capabilities of the spreadsheet.
Covers and illustrates the use of dates in a spreadsheet,
the Fill Series command, copying numeric cell contents
using a formula, rounding and the Round function,
rounding discrepancies, relative, absolute, and mixed
cell references, and modifying a spreadsheet by inserting rows and columns.

- **Project 7 – Creating a Database**   Introduces the
Works Database tool by creating an investment club
database. The Form view of the database is explained.
The Form view title is created using WordArt, then
fields are entered on the form in Form view. The database is saved. The database title is formatted and clip
art is inserted. The fields in the database are then positioned on the form by dragging fields in Form view. The
fields and labels are formatted. Data is then entered into
the database and formatted. List view is then explained,
and the database is formatted in List view. The database
is saved and then is printed in both Form view and,
using landscape orientation, in List view.

- **Project 8 – Maintaining a Database**   Covers maintaining the database in both Form view and List view,
including adding new records to the database, deleting
records from the database, changing data in database
records, and changing the structure of the database by
inserting fields, deleting fields, renaming fields, resizing
fields, and entering fields containing formulas. The
Form view of the database is reformatted by deleting
some fields and moving other fields to produce a
different database used to generate a different report.

- **Project 9 – Queries and Reports**   Presents techniques for querying the database and developing
reports from the database. Queries using the Create
New Query command and the use of the New Query
dialog box are explained. The various criteria for
queries, including using multiple fields, conditional

operators, and logical operators are explained. Reports
generated from the database include a report with a listing of the database, a report with summary totals, and a
report requiring the sorting of data in the database.

- **Project 10 – Integrating the Microsoft Works Tools**
Uses all three Works tools (Word Processor, Spreadsheet, and Database) in an integrated project to create a
form letter that includes both a spreadsheet and a chart
from the spreadsheet in the letter. A database provides
the names of the individuals to whom the letter is sent
and other data that is incorporated into the letter. The
project includes inserting special characters, inserting
placeholders, creating and entering a table, setting
borders for the table, linking and sizing a spreadsheet
chart in the word processing document, linking a
spreadsheet to a word processing document, inserting
headers, printing form letters, and creating mailing
labels.

- **Project 11 – Speadsheet Charting**   Provides
in-depth explanations of charting techniques, building
on the charting skills taught earlier in the spreadsheet
projects. Emphasis is placed on choosing the correct
chart type for the data to be charted. Charts covered
include 3-D Pie charts, Bar charts, 3-D Bar charts, Line
charts, Stacked Line charts, 3-D Area charts, Combination charts, and X-Y (Scatter) charts. The following
topics are explained: adding and formatting data labels,
adding formatted titles and subtitles, adding borders,
print preview and printing a chart, understanding
charting terms, adding category labels, adding legends,
changing chart colors and patterns, adding a right
vertical axis, naming a chart, altering the vertical axis
scale, and mixed values on the vertical axis scales. Also
introduced is the use of Microsoft Draw.

- **Project 12 – Using the Communications Tools**
Provides an introduction to basic data communication
concepts, explains the purpose and use of modems,
and introduces students to widely used communications services. The Works Communications tool is then
explained and the steps to access a local bulletin board
system are detailed. The project then illustrates how
students may access and navigate Internet to obtain
information from NASA through the resources of the
Yale University library.

- **Appendix A – Works Functions**   A summary of
the functions available in Works and an example of
their use.

Microsoft Works End-of-Project Student Activities

Each project within the Microsoft Works portion of this textbook ends with a multitude of student activities to further assist learning. These activities include:

- A list of key terms for review

- A Quick Reference that lists the ways to carry out a task using the mouse, menu, or keyboard shortcuts

- True/False and Multiple Choice questions to test the student's knowledge of the project material that are useful for in-class review.

- A total of six written and fill-in types of student assignments for homework and classroom discussion.

- Three Computer Laboratory Exercises, including one emphasizing the Help menu, that require the student, using a computer and the Student Diskette provided with the textbook, to complete tasks related to the project just studied to assist in mastering important Works commands and techniques.

- Four Computer Laboratory Assignments that require the student to develop a complete application using a computer and Microsoft Works 3.0 for Windows, with the assignments varying in difficulty from an application quite similar to the project in the book to those requiring the use of the creative skills of the student.

Instructor's Support Package

The most comprehensive instructor's support package ever developed accompanies *Using Computers: A Gateway to Information* and *Microsoft Works 3.0 for Windows*. The elements of this package are as follows:

- **Annotated Instructor's Edition (AIE)**   The AIE for the *Using Computers: A Gateway to Information* portion of this textbook is designed to assist you with your lectures by suggesting transparencies to use, summarizing key points, proposing pertinent questions, offering important tips, and incorporating the answers to the student activities.

- **Multimedia Lecture Presentation System**   The multimedia lecture presentation system was prepared specifically for use with the *Using Computers: A Gateway to Information* portion of this textbook. The system was developed using Microsoft PowerPoint 4 for Windows. The multimedia lecture presentation system is available on CD-ROM or diskette. The CD-ROM version includes chapter highlights, pictures, and more than one hour of video clips. The pictures and video clips can be viewed during lecture at the discretion of the instructor. The diskette version includes chapter highlights and fewer pictures. The Microsoft PowerPoint presentation viewer is included with both versions so an instructor does not need PowerPoint on his or her computer. The source files of the presentation are supplied, however, so instructors who have Microsoft PowerPoint 4 for Windows on their computers can customize the presentation to meet their students' needs.

- **Instructor's Materials**   The instructor's materials include the following:
  - Detailed lesson plans, including objectives, overviews, and lecture outlines with transparency references for each illustration in each chapter of the book
  - A test bank of True/False, Multiple Choice, and Fill-in questions
  - A lesson plans and test bank diskette, called ElecMan, that includes the detailed lesson plans and test bank for customizing to each instructor's needs
  - Answers to all student activities
  - Illustrations for every screen in the *Microsoft Works* portion of this book are available on CD-ROM – for selection and display in a lecture or to print and make transparencies
  - Black and white transparency masters for every figure in the first eight chapters and actual color transparencies of selected drawings for use in lectures
  - A lab solutions diskette that contains all the answers to the *In the Lab* exercises in the book

- **Computer-Based LCD Lecture Success System**
The Shelly Cashman Series proudly presents the finest
LCD learning material available in textbook publishing.
The Lecture Success System diskette, together with a
personal computer and LCD technology, are used in
lieu of transparencies. The system enables you to
explain and illustrate the step-by-step, screen-by-screen
development of a project in the textbook without
entering large amounts of data, thereby improving your
students' grasp of the material. The Lecture Success
System leads to a smooth, easy, error-free lecture.

     The Lecture Success System diskette comes with
files that correspond to key figures in the book. You
load the files that pertain to a project and display them
as needed. If the students want to see a series of steps a
second time, simply reopen the file you want to start
with and redo the steps. This presentation system is
available to adopters without charge.
- **Video Tapes to Augment Lectures**   Complimentary
selections from three series, *Computer Applications*,
The Machine That Changed the World, and *The
Computer Revolution*, are available to qualified
adopters of *Using Computers: A Gateway to
Information*.
- **MicroExam IV**   MicroExam IV, a computerized test-
generating system, is available free to adopters of any
Shelly Cashman Series textbook. It includes all the
questions from the test bank previously described.
MicroExam IV is an easy-to-use, menu-driven software
package that provides instructors with testing flexibility
and allows customizing of testing documents.
- **NetTest IV**   NetTest IV, available at no cost, allows
instructors to take a MicroExam IV file made up of
True/False and Multiple Choice questions and proctor a
paperless examination in a network environment. The
same questions display in a different order on each
personal computer in the network. Students have the
option of instantaneous feedback. Tests are electronically graded, and an item analysis is produced.

Student Study Guide

This highly popular supplement contains
completely new student activities to help solidify the
concepts and techniques presented in the text. The Study
Guide compliments the end-of-chapter material with short
answer, fill-in, and matching questions and other
challenging exercises.

Acknowledgments

The Shelly Cashman Series would not be the
success it is without the contributions of outstanding
publishing professionals. First, and foremost, among them
is Becky Herrington, director of production and designer.
She is the heart and soul of the Shelly Cashman Series, and
it is only through her leadership, dedication, and untiring
efforts that superior products are produced.

Under Becky's direction, the following individuals
made significant contributions to these books: Ginny
Harvey, series administrator and manuscript editor; Peter
Schiller, production manager; Ken Russo, senior illustrator
and cover art; Mike Bodnar, Greg Herrington and Dave
Bonnewitz, illustrators; Jeanne Black, Betty Hopkins,
and Michele Todd, typographers; Tracy Murphy, series
coordinator; Sue Sebok and Melissa Dowling LaRoe, copy
editors; Marilyn Martin and Nancy Lamm, proofreaders;
Sarah Evertson and Sarah Bendersky, photo researchers;
Marilyn Martin, photo credits; Christina Haley, indexer;
Henry Blackham, cover and opener photography; and
Dennis Woelky, glass etchings.

Our sincere thanks go to Dennis Tani, who together
with Becky Herrington, designed *Using Computers: A
Gateway to Information*. In addition, Dennis performed
all the layout and typography, executed the magnificent
drawings contained in this book, designed the cover,
and survived an impossible schedule with goodwill and
amazing patience. We salute Dennis's work.

The efforts of our contributing authors helped make
this book extraordinary. As always, special recognition for
a job well-done must go to Jim Quasney, who quarter-
backed this book from its beginning to its final form.
Thanks to Tom Walker, president and CEO of boyd &
fraser publishing company, for his vision and support of
this product.

We hope you find using this book an enriching and
rewarding experience.

Gary B. Shelly
Thomas J. Cashman
Gloria A. Waggoner
William C. Waggoner

Shelly Cashman Series – Traditionally Bound Textbooks

The Shelly Cashman Series presents both Windows- and DOS-based personal computer applications in a variety of traditionally bound textbooks, as shown in the table below. For more information, see your ITP representative or call 1-800-423-0563.

COMPUTERS	
Computers	Using Computers: A Gateway to Information
	Using Computers: A Gateway to Information, Brief Edition
Computers and Windows Applications	Using Computers: A Gateway to Information, Brief Edition and Microsoft Office: Introductory Concepts and Techniques (also available in spiral bound)
	Using Computers: A Gateway to Information, Brief Edition and Works 3.0 (also available in spiral bound)
	Complete Computer Concepts and Microsoft Works 2.0 (also available in spiral bound)
Computers and DOS Applications	Complete Computer Concepts and WordPerfect 5.1, Lotus 1-2-3 Release 2.2, and dBASE IV Version 1.1 (also available in spiral bound)
	Complete Computer Concepts and WordPerfect 5.1, Lotus 1-2-3 Release 2.2, and dBASE III PLUS (also available in spiral bound)
Computers and Programming	Using Computers: A Gateway to Information and Programming in QuickBASIC
	Using Computers: A Gateway to Information and Programming in Microsoft BASIC
WINDOWS APPLICATIONS	
Integrated Packages	Microsoft Office: Introductory Concepts and Techniques (also available in spiral bound)
	Microsoft Office: Advanced Concepts and Techniques (also available in spiral bound)
	Microsoft Works 3.0 (also available in spiral bound)
	Microsoft Works 2.0 (also available in spiral bound)
Windows	Microsoft Windows 3.1 Introductory Concepts and Techniques
	Microsoft Windows 3.1 Complete Concepts and Techniques
Windows Applications	Microsoft Word 2.0, Microsoft Excel 4, and Paradox 1.0 (also available in spiral bound)
Word Processing	Microsoft Word 6* • Microsoft Word 2.0
	WordPerfect 6.1* • WordPerfect 6* • WordPerfect 5.2
Spreadsheets	Microsoft Excel 5* • Microsoft Excel 4
	Lotus 1-2-3 Release 5* • Lotus 1-2-3 Release 4*
	Quattro Pro 6 •Quattro Pro 5
Database Management	Paradox 5 • Paradox 4.5 • Paradox 1.0
	Microsoft Access 2*
Presentation Graphics	Microsoft PowerPoint 4*
DOS APPLICATIONS	
Operating Systems	DOS 6 Introductory Concepts and Techniques
	DOS 6 and Microsoft Windows 3.1 Introductory Concepts and Techniques
Integrated Package	Microsoft Works 3.0 (also available in spiral bound)
DOS Applications	WordPerfect 5.1, Lotus 1-2-3 Release 2.2, and dBASE IV Version 1.1 (also available in spiral bound)
	WordPerfect 5.1, Lotus 1-2-3 Release 2.2, and dBASE III PLUS (also available in spiral bound)
Word Processing	WordPerfect 6.0
	WordPerfect 5.1 Step-by-Step Function Key Edition
	WordPerfect 5.1
	WordPerfect 5.1 Function Key Edition
	WordPerfect 4.2 (with Educational Software)
	WordStar 6.0 (with Educational Software)
Spreadsheets	Lotus 1-2-3 Release 4 • Lotus 1-2-3 Release 2.4 • Lotus 1-2-3 Release 2.3
	Lotus 1-2-3 Release 2.2 • Lotus 1-2-3 Release 2.01
	Quattro Pro 3.0
	Quattro with 1-2-3 Menus (with Educational Software)
Database Management	dBASE 5
	dBASE IV Version 1.1
	dBASE III PLUS (with Educational Software)
	Paradox 4.5
	Paradox 3.5 (with Educational Software)
PROGRAMMING AND NETWORKING	
Programming	Microsoft Visual Basic 3.0 for Windows*
	Microsoft BASIC
	QBasic
Networking	Novell Netware for Users
Internet	The Internet: Introductory Concepts and Techniques (UNIX Version)
	The Internet: Introductory Concepts and Techniques (Mosaic Version)

*Also available as a Double Diamond Edition, which is a shortened version of the complete book

Shelly Cashman Series – **Custom Edition** Program

If you do not find a Shelly Cashman Series traditionally bound textbook to fit your needs, boyd & fraser's unique **Custom Edition** program allows you to choose from a number of options and create a textbook perfectly suited to your course. The customized materials are available in a variety of binding styles, including boyd & fraser's patented **Custom Edition** kit, spiral bound, and notebook bound. Features of the **Custom Edition** program are:

- Textbooks that match the content of your course
- Windows- and DOS-based materials for the latest versions of personal computer applications software
- Shelly Cashman Series quality, with the same full-color materials and Shelly Cashman Series pedagogy found in the traditionally bound books
- Affordable pricing so your students receive the **Custom Edition** at a cost similar to that of traditionally bound books

The table on the right summarizes the available materials. For more information, see your ITP representative or call 1-800-423-0563.

COMPUTERS	
Computers	Using Computers: A Gateway to Information
	Using Computers: A Gateway to Information, Brief Edition
	Introduction to Computers (32-page)
OPERATING SYSTEMS	
Windows	Microsoft Windows 3.1 Introductory Concepts and Techniques
	Microsoft Windows 3.1 Complete Concepts and Techniques
DOS	Introduction to DOS 6 (using DOS prompt)
	Introduction to DOS 5.0 (using DOS shell)
	Introduction to DOS 5.0 or earlier (using DOS prompt)
WINDOWS APPLICATIONS	
Integrated Packages	Microsoft Works 3.0
	Microsoft Works 2.0
Microsoft Office	Using Microsoft Office (16-page)
	Object Linking and Embedding (OLE) (32-page)
Word Processing	Microsoft Word 6*
	Microsoft Word 2.0
	WordPerfect 6.1*
	WordPerfect 6*
	WordPerfect 5.2
Spreadsheets	Microsoft Excel 5*
	Microsoft Excel 4
	Lotus 1-2-3 Release 5*
	Lotus 1-2-3 Release 4*
	Quattro Pro 6
	Quattro Pro 5
Database Management	Paradox 5
	Paradox 4.5
	Paradox 1.0
	Microsoft Access 2*
Presentation Graphics	Microsoft PowerPoint 4*
DOS APPLICATIONS	
Integrated Package	Microsoft Works 3.0
Word Processing	WordPerfect 6.0
	WordPerfect 5.1 Step-by-Step Function Key Edition
	WordPerfect 5.1
	WordPerfect 5.1 Function Key Edition
	Microsoft Word 5.0
	WordPerfect 4.2
	WordStar 6.0
Spreadsheets	Lotus 1-2-3 Release 4
	Lotus 1-2-3 Release 2.4
	Lotus 1-2-3 Release 2.3
	Lotus 1-2-3 Release 2.2
	Lotus 1-2-3 Release 2.01
	Quattro Pro 3.0
	Quattro with 1-2-3 Menus
Database Management	dBASE 5
	dBASE IV Version 1.1
	dBASE III PLUS
	Paradox 4.5
	Paradox 3.5
PROGRAMMING AND NETWORKING	
Programming	Microsoft Visual Basic 3.0 for Windows*
	Microsoft BASIC
	QBasic
Networking	Novell Netware for Users
Internet	The Internet: Introductory Concepts and Techniques (UNIX Version)
	The Internet: Introductory Concepts and Techniques (Mosaic Version)

* Also available as a mini-module

In the Lab Exercises
with Shelly Cashman Series Interactive Labs

Each of the first eight chapters in this book concludes with a hands-on exercise section titled *In the Lab*, which consists of Windows, DOS, and Shelly Cashman Series Interactive Labs. The purpose of these Labs is to allow students to use computers so they learn firsthand how computers work. The Labs solidify and reinforce the computer concepts presented in each chapter in a way

unparalleled in previous computer textbooks. Students completing these labs will have a firm understanding of how to use computers with both DOS and Windows.

Of particular interest are the Shelly Cashman Series Interactive Labs (below), which help students gain a better understanding of a specific subject covered in a chapter.

Shelly Cashman Series Interactive Labs

Lab	Function	Page
Using the Mouse	Master how to use a mouse. The Lab includes pointing, clicking, double-clicking, and dragging.	1.30
Using the Keyboard	Learn how to use the keyboard. The Lab discusses different categories of keys, including the edit keys, function keys, ESC, CTRL, and ALT keys, and how to press keys simultaneously.	1.30
Scanning Documents	Understand how document scanners work.	3.30
Understanding the Motherboard	Step through the components of the motherboard and build one by adding components. The Lab shows how different motherboard configurations affect the overall speed of a computer.	4.33
Setting Up to Print	See how information flows from the system unit to the printer and how drivers, fonts, and physical connections play a role in generating a printout.	5.36
Configuring Your Display	Recognize the different monitor configurations available, including screen size, display cards, and number of colors.	5.36
Maintaining Your Hard Drive	Understand how files are stored on disk, what causes fragmentation, and how to maintain an efficient hard drive.	6.33
Connecting to the Internet	Learn how a computer is connected to the Internet. The Lab presents using the Internet to access information.	7.41
Evaluating Operating Systems	Evaluate the advantages and disadvantages of different categories of operating systems.	8.27
Working at Your Computer	Learn the basic ergonomic principles that prevent back and neck pain, eye strain, and other computer-related ailments.	8.27

CHAPTER ONE

An Overview of Computer Concepts

1

Objectives

After completing this chapter, you will be able to:

- Define computer and information literacy

- Explain the four operations of the information processing cycle: input, process, output, and storage

- Explain how speed, reliability and storage make computers powerful tools

- Identify the major components of a computer

- Identify the categories of computers

- Explain the difference between system software and application software

- Describe how the six elements of an information system work together

Computers play a key role in how individuals work and how they live. Today, even the smallest organizations have computers to help them operate more efficiently. Computers also affect people's lives in many unseen ways. Buying groceries at the supermarket, using an automated teller machine, or making a long-distance phone call all require using computers.

As they have for a number of years, personal computers continue to make an increasing impact on our lives. At home, at work, and in the field, these small systems help us do our work faster, more accurately, and in some cases, in ways that previously would not have been possible.

Computer and Information Literacy

Today, most people believe that knowing how to use a computer, especially a personal computer, is a basic skill necessary to succeed in business or to function effectively in society. Given the increasing use and availability of computer systems, such knowledge will continue to be an essential skill. Is just knowing how to use a computer, sometimes called **computer literacy**, enough? Many people now believe that a person should be *information literate* as well as *computer literate*. **Information literacy** is defined as knowing how to find, analyze, and use information. It is the ability to gather information from multiple sources, select the relevant material, and organize it into a form that will allow you to make a decision or take a specific action. For example, in shopping for a new car, one approach would be to visit several car dealers and talk to the salespeople about features of the model car in which you are interested. You can take written notes but your information will be limited to what you are told. An information literate person, however, will obtain relevant information about specific vehicles from a variety of sources before making any purchase decision. Such information might include vehicle list price, dealer cost, available options, repair history, and whether or not there have been any recalls. This type of information is available in several consumer-oriented publications and automobile magazines. With these facts, the car buyer is able to make a more informed decision on what car to buy (or not buy). How then do computers relate to information literacy?

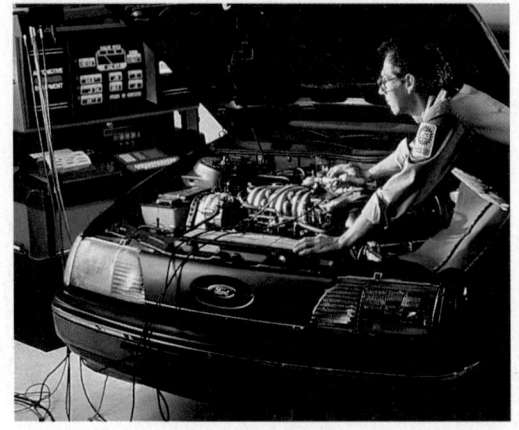

They relate because increasingly, information on cars and other products, as well as information on finances, upcoming events, travel, and weather, is available from information sources that can be accessed using computers. With communications equipment and software, computers can connect with information sources around the world. Using a computer allows you to obtain up-to-date information in a fast, efficient, and cost-effective manner. Computers have become the tools people use to access and manage information.

The purpose of this book is to give you the knowledge you need to understand how computers work and how computers are used by people and organizations to gather and analyze information to make better decisions.

Chapter 1 gives you an overview of computer concepts. You will begin to learn what a computer is, how it processes data into information, and what elements are necessary for a successful information system. You will also begin to develop a basic vocabulary of computer terminology. While you are reading, remember that this chapter is an overview and that many of the terms and concepts that are introduced will be discussed in more detail in later chapters. *Figure1-1* shows a variety of computers including personal computers and their applications. As you can see, the use of computer technology is widespread in our world. New uses for computers and improvements to existing technology are continually being developed. Computers affect your life every day and will continue to do so in the future. Learning about computers and their applications will help you to function more effectively in the world.

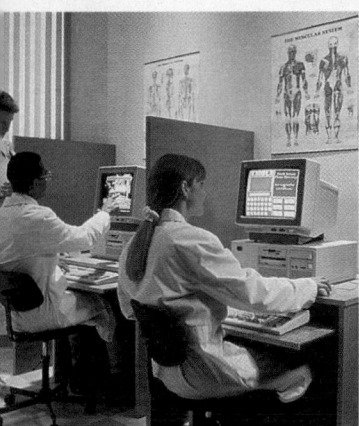

Figure1-1
Computers being used in a wide variety of applications and professions; new applications are being developed every day.

What Is a Computer?

The most obvious question related to understanding computers and their impact on our lives is, "What is a computer?" A **computer** is an electronic device, operating under the control of instructions stored in its own memory unit, that can accept data (input), process data arithmetically and logically, produce output from the processing, and store the results for future use. While broader definitions of a computer exist, this definition includes a wide range of devices with various capabilities. For example, the tiny microprocessor shown in *Figure 1-2* can be called a computer. Generally, the term is used to describe a collection of devices that function together to process data. An example of the devices that make up a computer is shown in *Figure 1-3*.

What Does a Computer Do?

Whether small or large, computers can perform four general operations. These operations comprise the **information processing cycle** and are: input, process, output, and storage. Collectively, these operations describe the procedures that a computer performs to process data into information and store it for future use.

All computer processing requires data. **Data** refers to the raw facts, including numbers, words, images, and sounds, given to a computer during the input operation. In the processing phase, the computer manipulates the data to create information. **Information** refers to data that has been processed into a meaningul and useful form. The production of information by processing data on a computer is called **information processing,** or sometimes **data processing** (DP). During the output operation, the information created is put

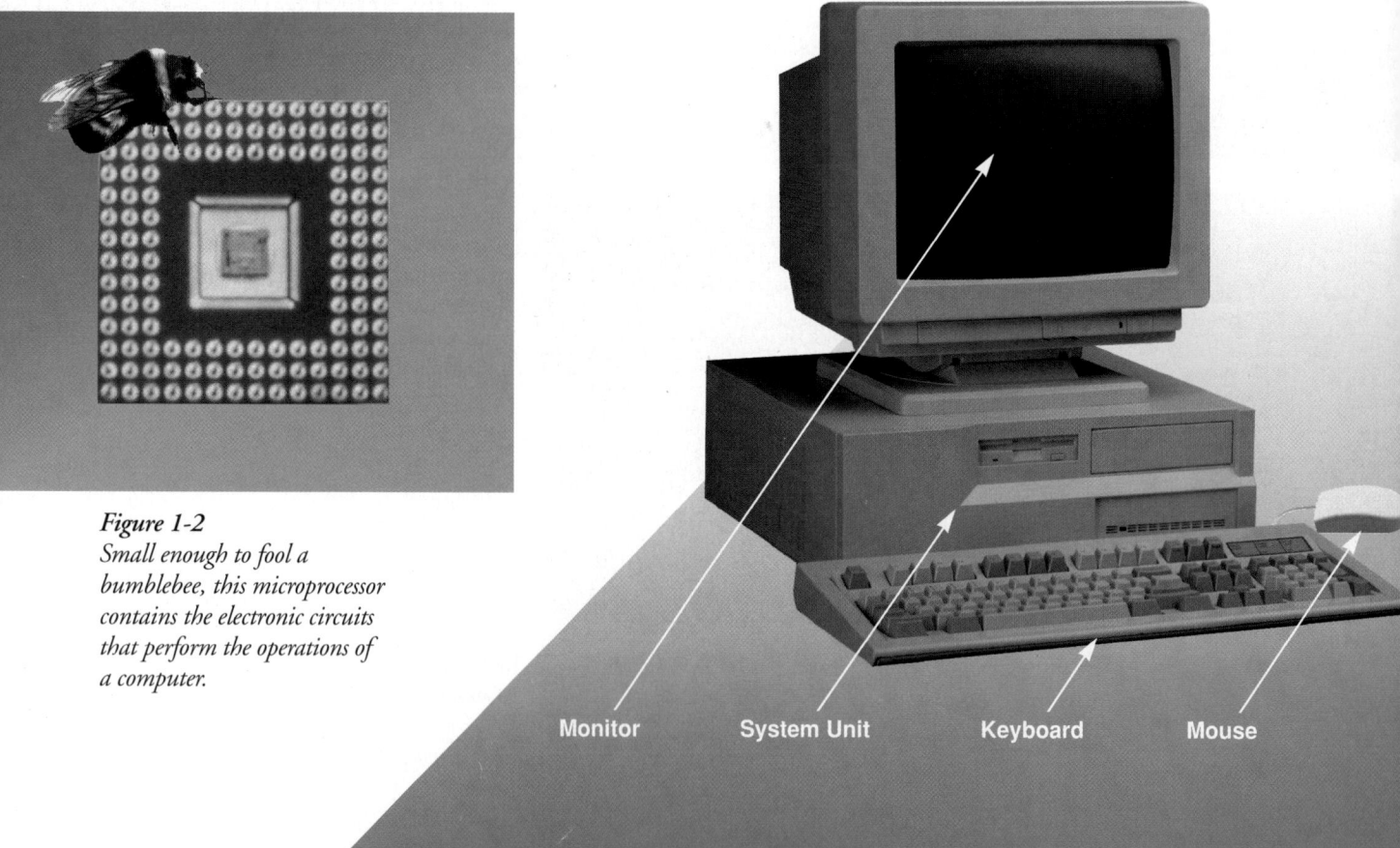

Figure 1-2
Small enough to fool a bumblebee, this microprocessor contains the electronic circuits that perform the operations of a computer.

Monitor   System Unit   Keyboard   Mouse

Figure 1-3
Devices that comprise a personal computer system.

into some form, such as a printed report, that people can use. The information can also be stored electronically for future use.

The people who either use the computer directly or use the information it provides are called **computer users**, **end users**, or **users**. *Figure 1-4* shows a computer user and demonstrates how the four operations of the information processing cycle can occur on a personal computer. (1) The computer user inputs data by pressing the keys on the keyboard. (2) The data is then processed by the device called the system unit. (3) The output, or results, from the processing are displayed on the screen of the monitor or printed on the printer, providing information to the user. (4) Finally, the output is stored on a disk for future reference.

Why Is a Computer so Powerful?

The input, process, output, and storage operations that a computer performs may seem very basic and simple. However, the computer's power derives from its capability to perform these operations with speed and reliability and to store large amounts of data and information.

Speed

In a computer, operations occur through the use of electronic circuits contained on small chips as shown in

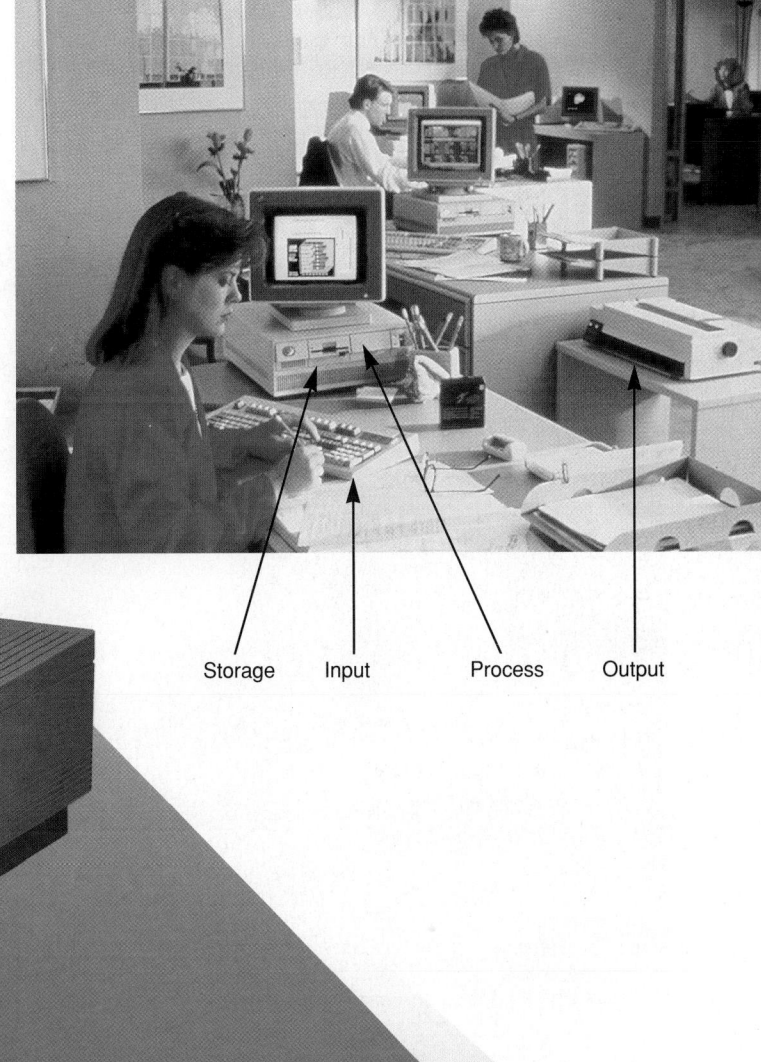

Figure 1-4 ▶
The use of this personal computer illustrates the four operations of the information processing cycle: input, process, output, and storage.

Storage   Input   Process   Output

Printer

Figure 1-5 When data flows along these circuits it travels at close to the speed of light. This allows processing to be accomplished in billionths of a second.

Reliability

The electronic components in modern computers are very reliable and seldom fail. In fact, most reports about computer errors are usually traced to other causes, often human mistakes. The high reliability of the components enables the computer to produce accurate results on a consistent basis.

Storage

Computers can store enormous amounts of data and keep that data readily available for processing. Using modern storage methods, the data can be quickly retrieved and processed and then re-stored for future use.

The speed, reliability, and storage capabilities of the computer make it a powerful tool for information processing.

How Does a Computer Know What to Do?

For a computer to perform the operations in the information processing cycle, it must be given a detailed set of instructions that tell it exactly what to do. These instructions are called a **computer program**, **program instructions**, or **software**.

Before the information processing cycle for a specific job begins, the computer program corresponding to that job is loaded into the computer's memory. Once the program is loaded, the computer can begin to process data by executing the program's first instruction. The computer executes one program instruction after another until the job is complete.

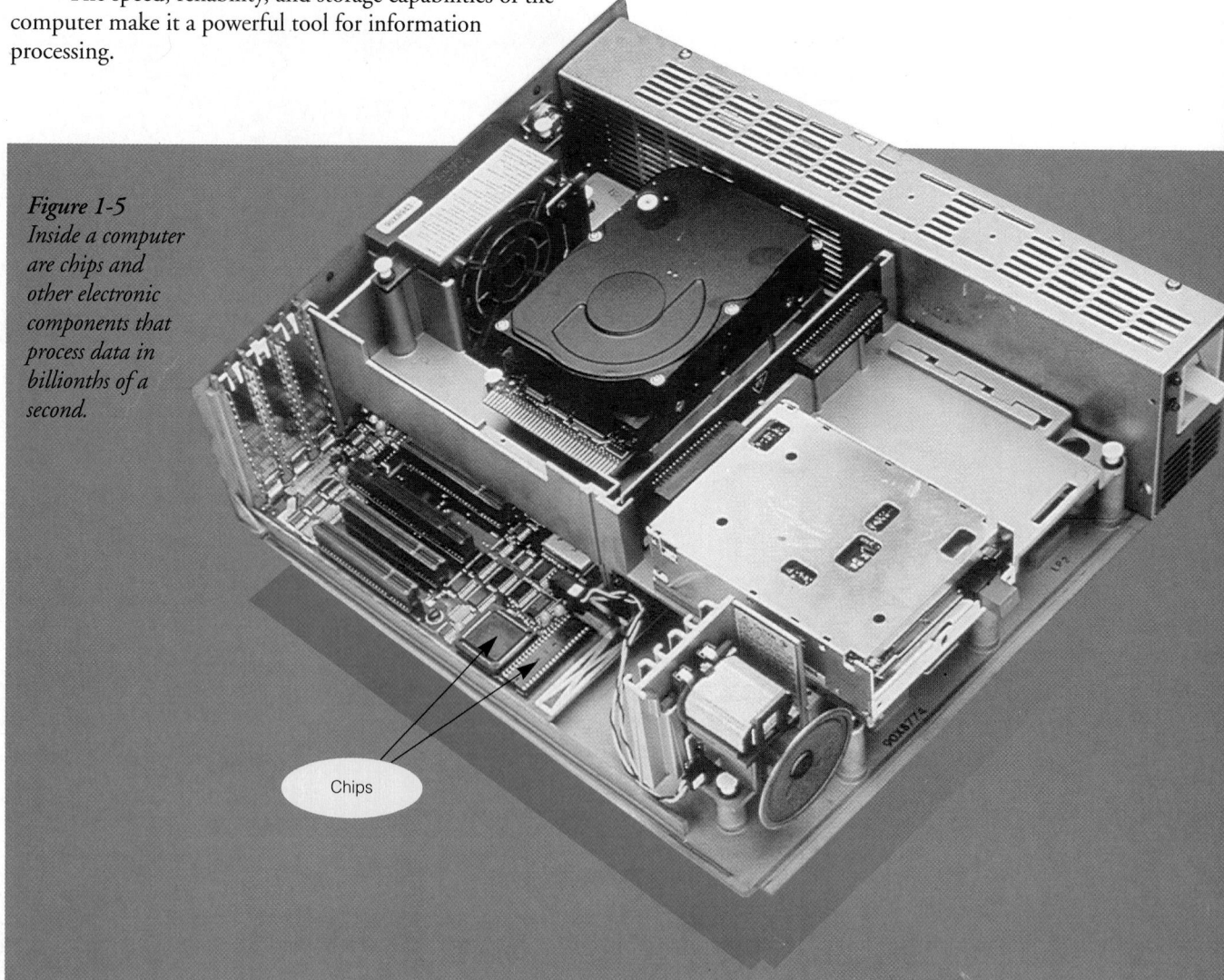

Figure 1-5
Inside a computer are chips and other electronic components that process data in billionths of a second.

Chips

The Information Processing Cycle

Your understanding of the information processing cycle introduced in this chapter is fundamental to understanding computers and how they process data into information. To review, the information processing cycle consists of four operations. They are: input, process, output, and storage.

The first three of these operations, **input**, **process**, and **output**, describe the procedures that a computer performs to process data into information. The fourth operation, **storage**, describes a computer's electronic storage capability. As you learn more about computers, you will see that these four operations apply to both the computer equipment and the computer software. The equipment, or devices, of a computer are classified according to the operations they perform. Computer software is made up of instructions that describe how the operations are to be performed.

What Are the Components of a Computer?

Data is processed by specific equipment that is often called computer **hardware**. This equipment consists of: input devices, a system unit, output devices, and secondary storage devices *(Figure 1-6)*.

Input Devices

Input devices are used to enter data into a computer. Two common input devices shown in *Figure 1-7* on the next page are the keyboard and the mouse. As the data is entered on the **keyboard**, it is temporarily stored in the computer's memory and displayed on the screen of the monitor. A **mouse** is a type of pointing device used to select processing options or information displayed on the screen. The mouse is used to move a small symbol that appears on the screen. This symbol, called a **mouse pointer** or **pointer**, can be many shapes but is often in the shape of an arrow.

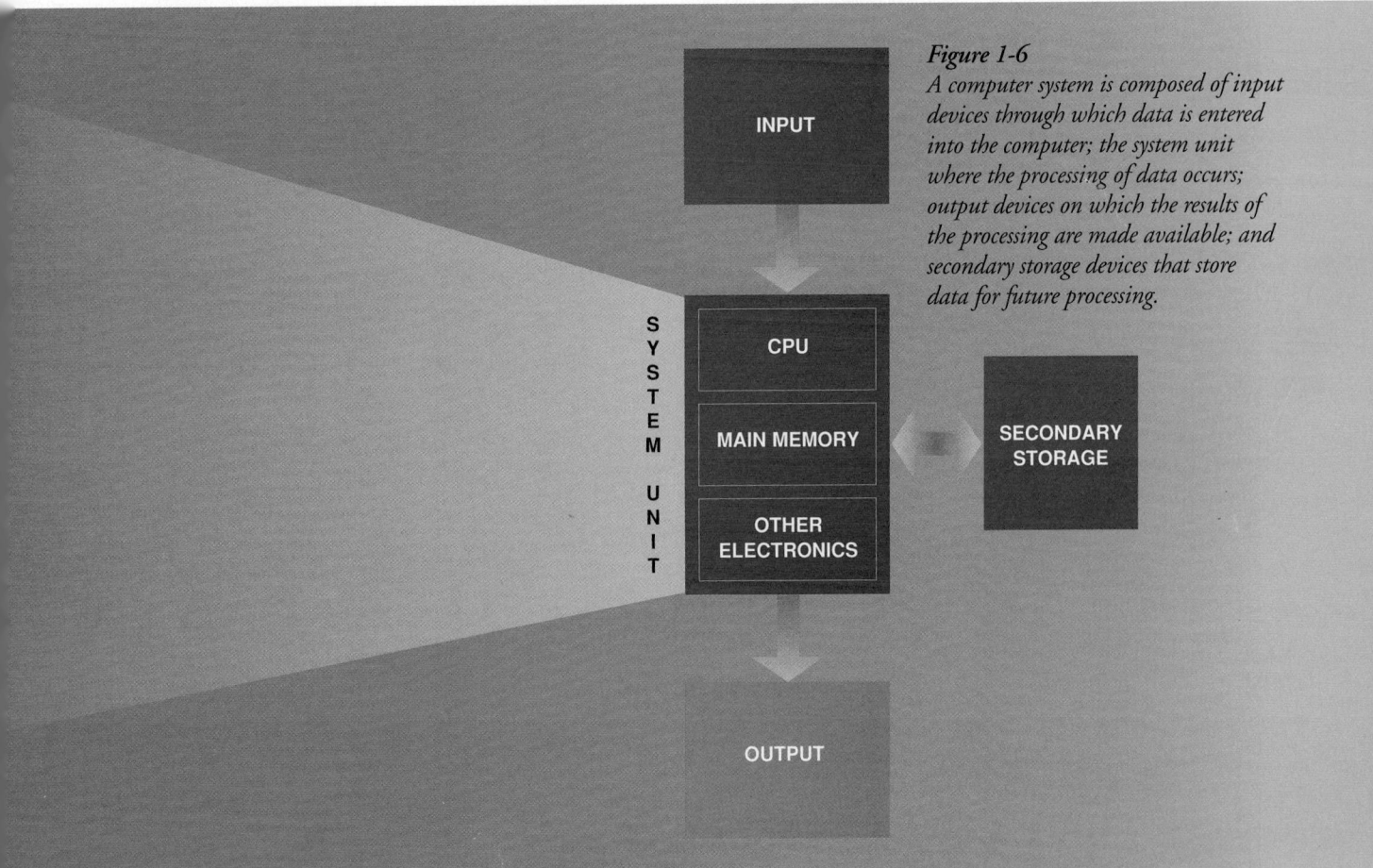

Figure 1-6
A computer system is composed of input devices through which data is entered into the computer; the system unit where the processing of data occurs; output devices on which the results of the processing are made available; and secondary storage devices that store data for future processing.

System Unit

Figure 1-6 on the previous page and *Figure 1-7* show the **system unit** of a computer, which contains the electronic circuits that actually cause the processing of data to occur. The system unit includes the central processing unit, main memory, and other electronic components. The **central processing unit** (CPU) contains a **control unit** that executes the program instructions and an **arithmetic/logic unit** (ALU) that performs math and logic operations. **Arithmetic operations** include numeric calculations such as addition, subtraction, multiplication, and division. Comparisons of data to see if one value is greater than, equal to, or less than another are called **logical operations.**

Main memory, also called RAM (**Random Access Memory**) or **primary storage**, temporarily stores data and program instructions when they are being processed.

Other electronics include components that work with the input, output, and storage devices and optional components that enable the computer to communicate with other computers.

Output Devices

Output from a computer can be presented in many forms. The two most commonly used **output devices** are the **printer** and the **monitor** shown in *Figure 1-7.* Other frequently used names for the monitor are the **screen**, or the CRT, which stands for **cathode ray tube.**

Figure 1-7
The components of a personal computer system perform the four operations of the information processing cycle.

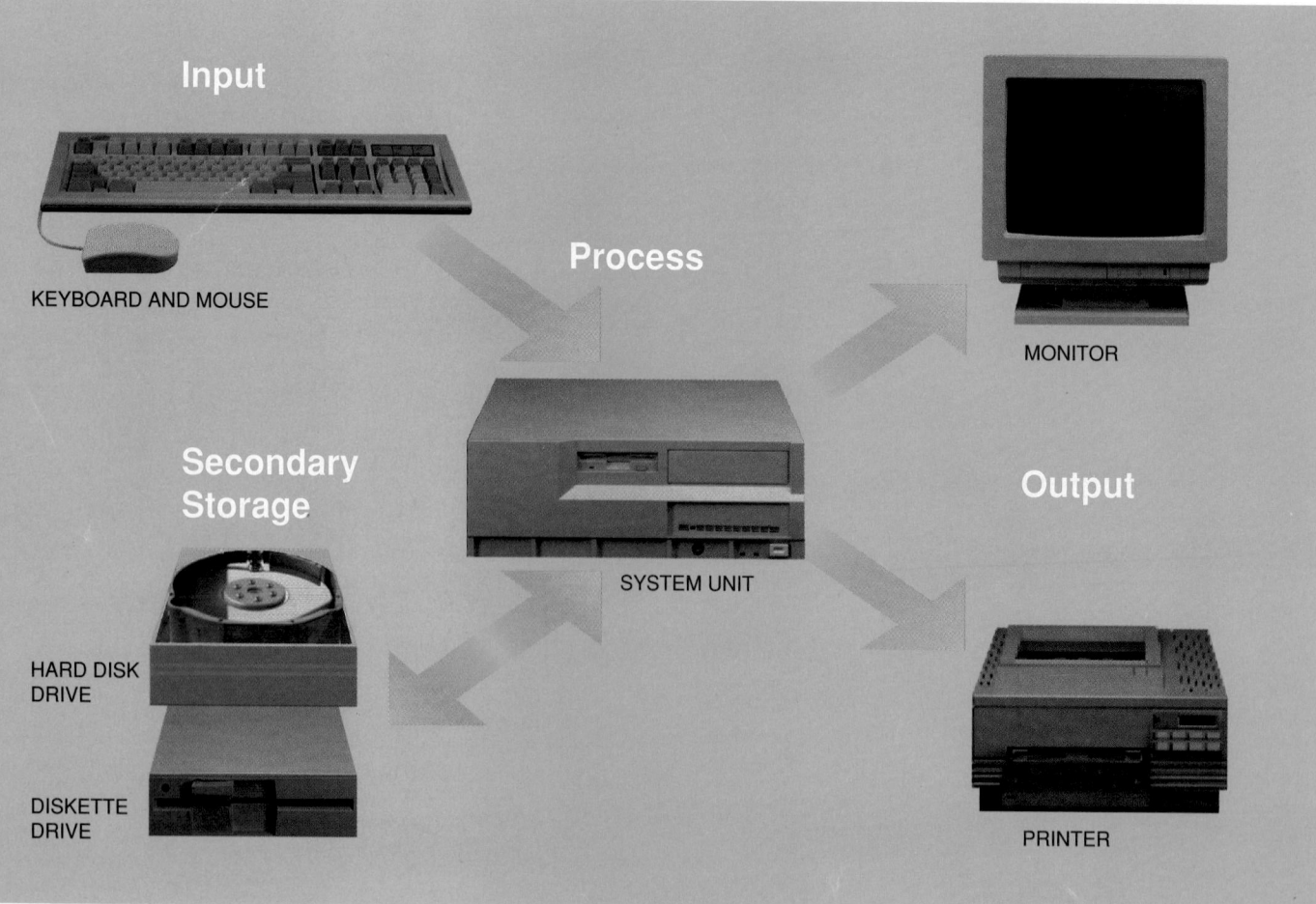

Secondary Storage Devices

Secondary storage devices, sometimes called **auxiliary storage devices,** shown in *Figure 1-7,* store instructions and data when they are not being used by the system unit. A common secondary storage device on personal computers is a diskette drive, which stores data as magnetic areas on a small plastic disk called a **diskette.** Another secondary storage device is called a hard disk drive. **Hard disk** drives contain nonremovable disks and provide larger storage capacities than diskettes.

As you can see, each component shown in *Figure 1-7* plays an important role in information processing. Collectively, this equipment is called a **computer system,** or simply a computer. The term computer is also used to refer to the system unit where the actual processing of data occurs. The input devices, output devices, and secondary storage devices that surround the system unit are sometimes referred to as **peripheral devices.**

Categories of Computers

Figure 1-8 shows the following five major categories of computers: personal computers, servers, minicomputers, mainframe computers, and supercomputers.

Computers are generally classified according to their size, speed, processing capabilities, and price. However, rapid changes in technology make firm definitions of these categories difficult. This year's speed, performance, and price classification of a mainframe might fit next year's classification of a minicomputer. Even though they are not firmly defined, the categories are frequently used and should be generally understood.

CATEGORY	PHYSICAL SIZE	SPEED*	NUMBER OF ONLINE USERS	GENERAL PRICE RANGE
Personal Computer	Hand-held to desktop or tower	1 to 100 MIPS	Usually a single user	Hundreds to several thousand $
Server	Tower or small cabinet	25 to 200 MIPS	2 to 1,000 users	$5,000 to $150,000
Minicomputer	Small cabinet to several large cabinets	Hundreds of MIPS	2 to 4,000 users	$15,000 to several hundred thousand $
Mainframe	Partial to full room of equipment	Hundreds of MIPS	Hundreds to thousands of users	$300,000 to several million $
Supercomputer	Full room of equipment	Thousands of MIPS	Hundreds of users	Several million $ and up

speed rated in MIPS; each MIP equals one million instructions per second.

Figure 1-8
This table summarizes some of the differences between the categories of computers. Because of rapid changes in technology, these should be considered general guidelines only.

Personal Computers

Personal computers (PCs), shown in *Figure 1-9,* also called **microcomputers** or **micros**, are the small systems that have become so widely used. Classifications within this category include hand-held, palmtop, notebook, subnotebook, laptop, pen, desktop, tower, and workstation. Hand-held, palmtop, notebook, subnotebook, laptop, and pen computers are considered portable computers. Depending on their size and features, personal computer prices range from several hundred to several thousand dollars. The most expensive personal computers are generally under $10,000.

Hand-held computers *(Figure 1-9a)* are usually designed for a specific purpose such as meter reading or inventory counting and are used by workers who are on their feet instead of sitting at a desk.

Palmtop computers *(Figure 1-9b)* often have several built-in or interchangeable personal information management functions such as a calendar to keep track of meetings and

events, an address and phone file, and a task list of things to do. Some palmtop computers also have limited capabilities to write correspondence and perform financial analysis. Palmtop computers do not have disk storage devices and usually have a nonstandard keyboard, meaning that the keys are not arranged like a typewriter.

Notebook computers *(Figure 1-9c)* are small enough to be carried in a briefcase but are often transported in their own carrying case. Notebooks are general-purpose computers in that they can run most application software packages. They have standard keyboards and usually have at least one disk drive for storage. Notebooks usually weigh between four and eight pounds.

Subnotebook computers *(Figure 1-9d)* are smaller versions of notebook computers and generally weigh less than four pounds. To save weight and space, some subnotebooks do not have disk drives and use special-purpose memory cards for storage.

Figure 1-9
Personal computers come in many shapes and sizes. Shown in these photos are
(a) hand-held,
(b) palmtop,
(c) notebook,
(d) subnotebook,
(e) laptop,
(f) pen,
(g) personal digital assistant (PDA),
(h) desktop,
(i) tower, and
(j) workstation.

1-9a

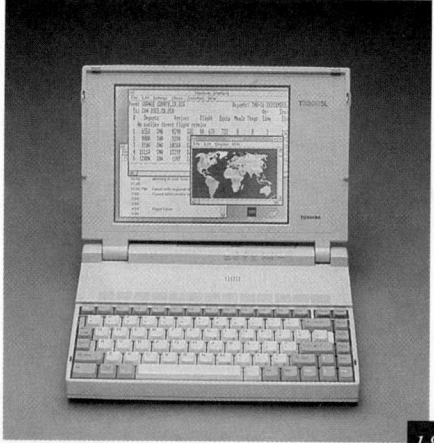
1-9c

1-9b

1-9d

Laptop computers *(Figure 1-9e)* are larger versions of notebook computers that weigh between eight and fifteen pounds. The extra weight comes primarily from large-capacity disk storage devices and larger display screens.

Pen computers *(Figure 1-9f)* are specialized portable computers that use a pen-like device to enter data. Sometimes the pen is used to write information on a special input screen and sometimes it is used as a pointing device to select a processing choice presented on the screen. Pen systems have successfully replaced many applications that previously required the user to fill out a form or checklist. The unique feature about pen systems is the special software that allows the system to recognize handwritten input. One type of small pen input system is called a **personal digital assistant** (PDA) or **personal communicator**. These hand-held devices are designed for workers on the go and often have built-in communications capabilities that allow the PDA to use voice, fax, or data communications. Apple's Newton PDA *(Figure 1-9g)* has built-in intelligence that assists the user in making entries.

Desktop computers *(Figure 1-9h)* are the most common type of personal computer and are designed to fit conveniently on the surface of a desk or workspace. Desktop computers have separate display screens.

Tower computers *(Figure 1-9i)* are personal computers in an upright case. A full-size tower case provides more room for expanding the system and adding optional equipment. The most powerful personal computers are sometimes only available in tower cases. A mini-tower case, approximately half the size of a full tower case, usually has less expansion room than a desktop computer but takes up less room.

Workstations *(Figure l-9j)* are expensive high-end personal computers that have powerful calculating and graphics capabilities. Workstations are frequently used by engineers to aid in product design and testing. The term workstation is sometimes used to refer to a personal computer or terminal connected to a network.

1-9e

1-9g

1-9i

1-9f

1-9h

1-9j

Servers

Server computers, shown in *Figure 1-10,* are designed to support a computer network that allows users to share files, applications software, and hardware such as printers. The term server really describes how a computer is used. Technically, the term could be applied to any of the other categories of computers if they were used to support a network of other computers. However, in recent years manufacturers have built computers specifically designed for network use and the term server is becoming widely used to describe this type of computer. Server computers usually have the following characteristics:

- designed to be connected to one or more networks
- most powerful CPUs available
- capability to add more than one CPU to divide the processing tasks (one manufacturer's server can use up to 32 CPUs)
- large memory capacity
- large disk storage capacity, usually comprised of numerous small disks instead of several large disks
- high-speed internal and external communications

Small servers look like high-end personal computers and are priced in the $5,000 to $20,000 range. The most powerful servers look and function more like minicomputers and are priced as high as $150,000.

Minicomputers

Minicomputers, shown in *Figure 1-11,* are more powerful than personal computers and can support a number of users performing different tasks. Originally developed to perform specific tasks such as engineering calculations, their use grew rapidly as their performance and capabilities increased. Today, many businesses and other organizations use minicomputers for their information processing requirements. These systems can cost from approximately $15,000 up to several hundred thousand dollars. The most powerful minicomputers are called superminicomputers.

Figure 1-11
Minicomputers can perform many of the functions of a mainframe computer but on a smaller scale.

Figure 1-10
Server computers are designed to support a network of other computers. Servers allow the other computers to share data, applications software, and hardware resources such as printers. Small servers are simply powerful personal computers dedicated to a server function. The most powerful servers, however, are more like minicomputers. High-end servers contain multiple CPUs, numerous large-capacity disk drives, and large amounts of memory.

Figure 1-12
Mainframe computers are large, powerful machines that can handle many users concurrently and process large volumes of data.

Mainframe Computers

Mainframe computers, shown in *Figure 1-12*, are large systems that can handle hundreds of users, store large amounts of data, and process transactions at a very high rate. Mainframes usually require a specialized environment including separate air conditioning, cooling, and electrical power. Raised flooring is often built to accommodate the many cables connecting the system components underneath. The price range for mainframes is from several hundred thousand dollars to several million dollars.

Supercomputers

Supercomputers, shown in *Figure 1-13*, are the most powerful category of computers and, accordingly, the most expensive. The capability of these systems to process hundreds of millions of instructions per second is used for such applications as weather forecasting, engineering design and testing, space exploration, and other jobs requiring long, complex calculations *(Figure 1-14)*. These machines cost several million dollars.

Computers of all categories, especially personal computers, are sometimes connected to form **networks** that allow users to share data and computing resources such as software, printers, and storage devices.

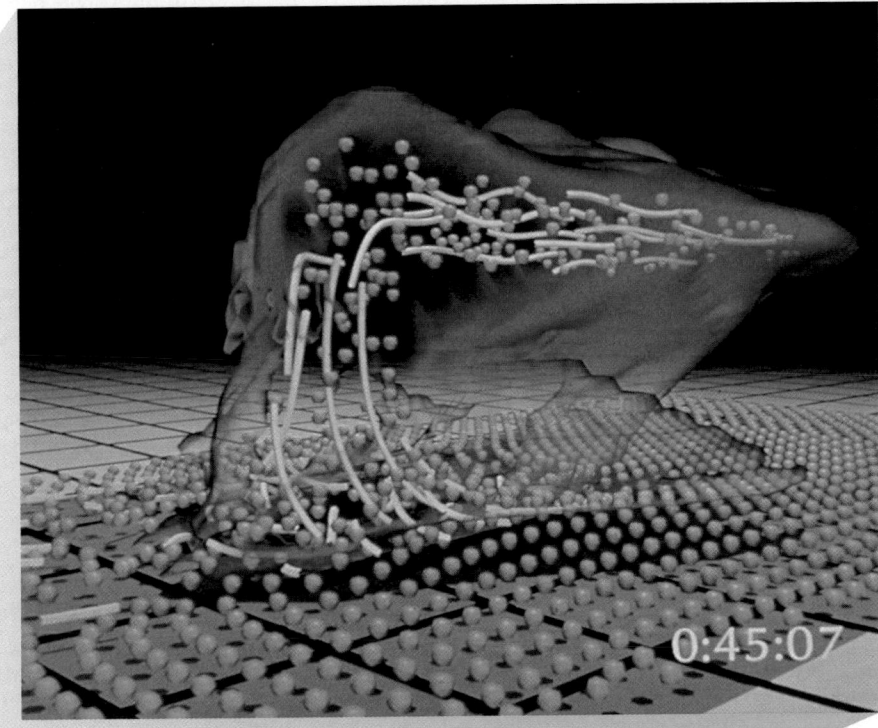

Figure 1-14
This simulated weather pattern was calculated on a supercomputer.

Figure 1-13
Supercomputers are the most powerful and expensive computers.

Computer Software

As mentioned previously, a computer is directed by a series of instructions called a computer program *(Figure 1-15)* that specifies the sequence of operations the computer will perform. To do this, the program must be loaded into the main memory of the computer. Computer programs are commonly referred to as computer software. Many instructions can be used to direct a computer to perform a specific task. For example, some instructions allow data to be entered from a keyboard and stored in main memory; some instructions allow data in main memory to be used in calculations such as adding a series of numbers to obtain a total; some instructions compare two values stored in main memory and direct the computer to perform alternative operations based on the results of the comparison; and some instructions direct the computer to print a report, display information on the screen, draw a color graph on a screen, or store data on a disk.

Most computer programs are written by people with specialized training. These people, called **computer programmers**, write the instructions necessary to direct the computer to process data into information. The instructions must be placed in the correct sequence so the desired results will occur.

Complex programs may require hundreds or even thousands of program instructions. Programmers often follow a plan developed by a **systems analyst** who works with both the user and the programmer to determine and design the desired output of the program.

Computer software is the key to productive use of computers. With the correct software, a computer can become a valuable tool. Software can be categorized into two types: system software and application software.

System Software and Application Software

System software consists of programs that are related to controlling the actual operations of the computer equipment. An important part of the system software is a set of programs called the operating system. The instructions in the **operating system** tell the computer how to perform functions such as how to load, store, and execute an application program and how to transfer data between the input/output devices and main memory. For a computer to operate, an operating system must be stored in the main memory of the computer. Each time a computer is turned on, or restarted, the operating

Figure 1-15
A computer program contains instructions that specify the sequence of operations to be performed. This program is written in a language called QuickBASIC. The program prompts the user for data and then calculates and prints a sales commission amount.

Program

```
REM Program 1-15
REM Determining a Salesperson's Commission
REM Dave Brame, CIS 204, Div. 01
REM September 30, 1996
REM **************************************
REM Clear Screen
CLS
REM Request Data from Operator
INPUT "Commission rate =====> ", Rate
INPUT "Week 1 sales ========> ", Week1
INPUT "Week 2 sales ========> ", Week2
INPUT "Return sales ========> ", Returns
REM Calculate the Earned Commission
Commission = Rate * (Week1 + Week2 - Returns)
REM Display the Earned Commission
PRINT
PRINT "Earned commission ===>"; Commission
END


[run]
```

Results

```
Commission rate =====> 0.15
Week 1 sales ========> 1200
Week 2 sales ========> 1500
Return sales ========> 75

Earned commission ===> 393.75
```

system is loaded into the computer and stored in the computer's main memory. Many different operating systems are available for computers. Today, many computers use what is called an **operating environment** that works with the operating system to make the computer system easier to use. Operating environments have a **graphical user interface** (GUI) that provides visual clues such as symbols, called icons, to help the user. Each **icon** represents an application software package, such as word processing, or a file or document where data is stored. Microsoft Windows *(Figure 1-16)* is a graphical user interface that works with the DOS operating system. DOS, which stands for disk operating system, is the most commonly used operating system on personal computers. Apple Macintosh computers also have a graphical user interface built into the Macintosh operating system.

Application software consists of programs that tell a computer how to produce information. When you think of the different ways that people use computers in their careers or in their personal lives, you are thinking of examples of application software. Business, scientific, and educational programs are all examples of application software.

Application Software Packages

Most end users do not write their own programs. In some corporations, the information processing department develops custom software programs for unique company applications. Programs required for common business and personal applications can be purchased from software vendors or stores that sell computer products *(Figure 1-17)*. Purchased programs are often referred to as **application software packages**, or simply **software packages**.

Personal Computer Application Software Packages

Personal computer users often use application software packages. Some of the most widely used packages are word processing, desktop publishing, electronic spreadsheet, presentation graphics, database, communications, and electronic mail.

Figure 1-16
A graphical user interface, such as Microsoft Windows, makes the computer easier to use. The small pictures, or symbols, on the main part of the screen are called icons. The icons represent different processing options, such as word processing or electronic spreadsheet applications, the user can choose.

Figure 1-17
Many programs commonly required for business and personal applications can be purchased from computer stores.

What Are the Elements of an Information System?

Obtaining useful and timely information from computer processing requires more than just the equipment and software described so far. Other elements required for successful information processing include accurate data, trained information systems personnel, knowledgeable users, and documented procedures. Together these elements are referred to as an **information system** *(Figure 1-18).*

For an information system to provide accurate, timely, and useful information, each element in the system must be strong and all of the elements must work together. The equipment must be reliable and capable of handling the expected work load. The software must have been carefully developed and tested, and the data entered to be processed must be accurate. If the data is incorrect, the resulting information produced from it will be incorrect. Properly trained information systems personnel are required to run most medium and large computer systems. Even small networks of personal computers usually have a system administrator to manage the system. Users are sometimes overlooked as an important element of an information system, but with expanding computer use, users are taking increasing responsibility for the successful operation of information systems. This includes responsibility for the accuracy of both the input and output. In addition, users are taking a more active role in the development of computer applications. They work closely with information systems department personnel in the development of computer applications that relate to their areas of work. Finally, all information processing applications should have documented procedures covering not only the computer operations but any other related procedures as well.

Figure 1-18

An information system requires computer equipment; software that runs on the equipment; data the computer processes; people including both computer personnel who manage the equipment and users who use the information the equipment produces; and finally procedures, that help the entire system run efficiently.

Connectivity

Connectivity refers to the capability to connect a computer to other computers. The connection may be temporary, such as when a computer is connected to an online information service provider, or permanent such as when a computer is connected to a network of other computers. Connectivity has had a significant impact on the way people use computers *(Figure 1-19)*. For many years, computers were used as stand-alone devices, limited to the hardware and software resources contained in that computer. However, stand-alone computers are becoming the exception. One study found that most business computers are connected to other computers as part of a network. Even home computers are increasingly used to access other computers to transfer data or to obtain information on practically any subject. You may have heard about the *Information Highway,* the United States government's plan to bring information access into the home of every citizen. This ambitious plan will create a high-speed network that will allow people, with a computer, to access government information and other information and entertainment services. Many people believe that the computer will eventually be used for all forms of communication; written, visual, and sound.

An Example of How One Company Uses Computers

To show you how a typical mid-sized company might use computers, this section will take you on a visual and narrative tour of Hayden Corporation, an automobile parts manufacturer. All of the computers at Hayden are joined together in a network that allows the computer users to communicate with one another and share information.

Receptionist

One of the things you notice when you enter the main lobby of Hayden is the computer sitting on the receptionist's desk *(Figure 1-20)*. Outside calls are answered by the receptionist who transfers them to the appropriate employee. If an employee doesn't answer his or her phone, the receptionist can use the computer to determine the location of the employee. When employees leave their work area for a meeting, lunch, or to travel away from the office, they record their destination or reason for being away using their computer terminal. An employee can also record any special instructions to the receptionist, such as when he or she will return or to hold calls. If a caller wants to leave a voice message, the company phone system, which also uses a computer, can record the message and play it back for the employee when he or she returns or calls in for messages.

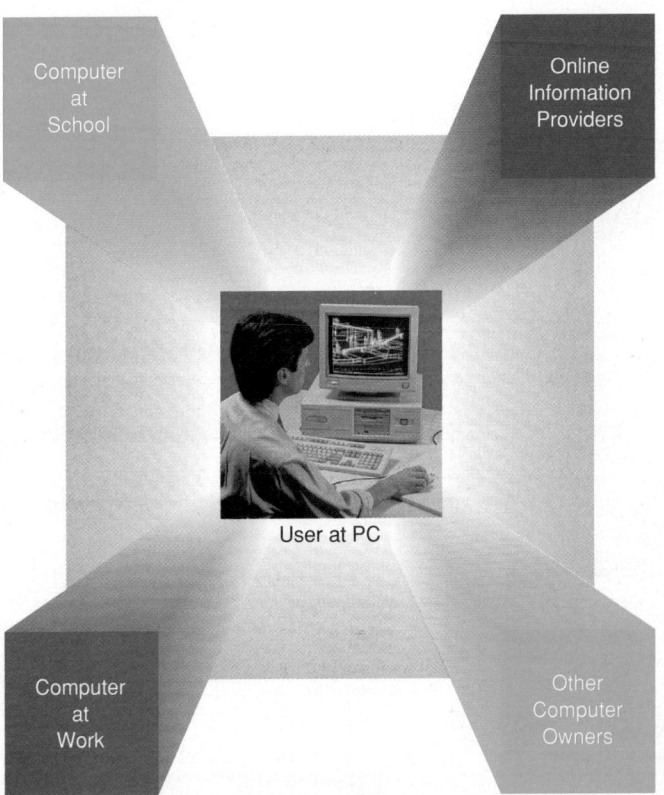

Figure 1-19
Increasingly, computers are connected to other computers to share data and information.

Figure 1-20 The receptionist uses the computer system to locate employees away from their desks, to record messages, and to help with general correspondence.

Sales

The Hayden sales department consists of two groups; in-house sales representatives that handle phone-in and mail-in sales orders and the field sales force that makes sales calls at customer locations. The in-house sales staff use headset phones *(Figure 1-21)* so their hands are free to use their computer keyboards. Using the computer while they are on the phone with a customer allows them to check product availability and the customer's credit status. A computer program also recommends products that compliment the products ordered by the customer and displays information on special product promotions. Field sales force representatives use notebook computers and special communications equipment and software to communicate with the Hayden main office. As with the in-house sales staff, they also can check product availability and customer credit status. If they receive a customer order, they can enter it into the Hayden computer system while they are still at the customer site. In addition, the field sales representatives can use the electronic mail capability to check for or send messages.

Marketing

The marketing department uses the computer system for a number of purposes. Desktop publishing, drawing, and graphics software is used to develop all marketing literature *(Figure 1-22)*. Product brochures, print advertising, and product packaging are all produced in-house, saving considerable time and money. The customer service representatives all have computer terminals that allow them to record a variety of customer inquiries. Recording the nature of each customer service inquiry provides for better follow-up (less chance of forgetting an unresolved inquiry) and enables the company to summarize and review why customers are calling. This helps the company identify and resolve potential problems at an early stage. The marketing department also uses a calendar program to schedule product promotions and attendance at trade shows *(Figure 1-23)*.

Figure 1-21
Order entry personnel use the computer to check if the products requested by the customer are in stock. The system automatically displays additional products the customer might need and information on special product promotions.

Figure 1-22
Many companies now use desktop publishing and drawing software packages to create product literature and advertising materials.

Figure 1-23
Calendar programs help users plan their schedules.

Shipping and Receiving

The shipping and receiving department uses the computer system to enter transactions that keep Hayden's inventory records accurate *(Figure 1-24)*. Inventory receipts are first checked against computer records to make sure that Hayden receives only what was ordered. If the received goods match what was ordered, only a single entry has to be made to update the on-hand inventory and purchasing records. Shipping transactions are also efficient. If all requested items were in stock, only a single entry is required to decrease the inventory and create the information that will be used to prepare the billing invoice. Shipping information such as the method and time of shipment can be added to the transaction record so the computer system can be used to provide up-to-the-minute status of the customer's order.

Manufacturing

The manufacturing department uses the computer to schedule production and to record the costs of the items produced. Special manufacturing software matches the availability of production resources such as people, machines, and material against the desired product output. This information allows Hayden to efficiently schedule production and tells them when and how much to buy of the raw materials they need to produce their products *(Figure 1-25)*. Actual labor, material, and machine usage is recorded on the manufacturing floor using special terminals designed to be used in industrial environments *(Figure 1-26)*. This information is automatically entered into the computer system to update inventory, production, payroll, and cost accounting records.

Figure 1-25
Special software helps the company manufacture products.

Figure 1-24
Computers help companies keep accurate inventory records.

Figure 1-26
Some computer terminals have been specially designed to withstand the heat, dust, and other conditions of a factory floor.

Engineering

The engineering department uses computer-aided design (CAD) software to design new products *(Figure 1-27)*. CAD software allows the engineers to design and review three-dimensional models of new products on the computer before expensive molds are required. If a design is approved, the CAD software can automatically produce a list of the required parts.

Accounting

The accounting department is one of the largest computer system users. Many of the accounting records are the result of transactions entered in the user departments, such as shipping and receiving and manufacturing. These records are used to pay vendor invoices, bill customers for product sales, and to process the Hayden employee payroll *(Figure 1-28)*. The accounting transactions are automatically summarized to produce Hayden's financial statements that are used internally to monitor financial performance and given to outside organizations such as banks.

Human Resources

The human resources department uses the computer system to keep track of information on existing, past, and potential employees *(Figure 1-29)*. Besides the standard information required for payroll and employee benefits, the system keeps track of employees job skills and training. This information enables the human resource department to review the records of existing employees first when a new job becomes available.

Information Systems

A primary responsibility of the information systems department is to keep the existing system running and to

Figure 1-27
Computer-aided design (CAD) software is used to design new products. As with word processing software, CAD programs make the design process easier by allowing the user to make many changes until they are satisfied.

Figure 1-28
Accounting departments were one of the first users of computer systems and still rely heavily on computers to summarize the numerous financial transactions.

Figure 1-29
Human resource departments use computers to keep track of past, present, and potential employees.

determine when and if new equipment or software is required. To help answer these questions, the information systems personnel use diagnostic and performance measurement software that tells them how much the system is being used and if system problems are being encountered *(Figure 1-30)*. A systems analyst works with users to design custom software for user applications for which application software packages do not exist. A computer programmer uses the design to write the program instructions necessary to produce the desired processing results and output.

Executive

The senior management staff of Hayden Corporation (the president and three vice presidents) use the computer for an executive information system (EIS). The EIS summarizes information such as actual sales, order backlog, number of employees, cash on hand, and other performance measures into both a numeric and graphic display *(Figure 1-31)*. The EIS is specifically designed for executives who do not regularly work with computers and who only want to see summarized information.

Summary of How One Company Uses Computers

The computer applications just discussed are only some of the many potential uses of a computer within Hayden Corporation. In addition, employees in each of the departments would use the computer for preparing correspondence, project and task management, budgeting, and sending messages via electronic mail.

As you can see in the Hayden Corporation example, computers are used throughout an organization. Employees use computers to perform a variety of tasks related to their job area. Because of the widespread use of computers, most organizations prefer to hire employees with computer experience and knowledge.

Summary of an Overview of Computer Concepts

This chapter presented a broad introduction to concepts and terminology related to computers. You now have a basic understanding of what a computer is, how it processes data into information, and what elements are necessary for a successful information system. You also have seen some examples of different types of computers and how they are used. Reading the overview of computer concepts in Chapter 1 will help you to more easily understand topics as they are presented in more detail in following chapters.

Figure 1-30
Information system personnel check on how much the computer system is being used with performance measurement software.

Figure 1-31
Executive information system (EIS) software usually includes graphics to convey information to users who do not frequently use the computer and who want summarized information.

COMPUTERS AT WORK

Carnegie Mellon University: Information at Your Dorm Room

Students at Carnegie Mellon University (CMU) can access the latest in research reference materials from the comfort of their dorm rooms. CMU has long been recognized as a leader in computer science education and their Library Information System (LIS) is one of the first decentralized electronic library applications. Using nearly any type of personal computer, CMU's 5,000 students can log into a network that provides information from numerous journals on computer science, artificial intelligence, and other subjects. Eventually, CMU plans on having more than 600 journals available for review online. Some publishers, however, have been reluctant to permit their material to be added to the system. These publishers are concerned about improper use of their materials and loss of subscription revenue. But with the strong overall trend towards electronic publishing, CMU officials are confident that these issues will eventually be resolved. Students without their own personal computers can use systems in the library and at several other locations around the campus. The LIS runs on a campus-wide network supported by seven server computers. Future plans for the LIS include additional server computers, a natural language interface that will make the system easier to use, and expansion of the network to include outside resources such as commercial online services and the Internet.

Figure 1-32

IN THE FUTURE

Information Appliances

Many believe that today's personal computer will evolve into an information appliance. This device will serve as a master control for all your home systems as well as allow you to access and process information from around the world.

Numerous changes will have to take place before any one device can control so many aspects of daily life, but the trend in that direction seems to be firmly established. For one thing, computers can handle different types of information more easily than ever before. Originally limited to text and numbers, computers can now handle sound, sophisticated color graphics, and still images. Movie-length, full-motion video will be available in the near future. Entertainment, hardware, software, and communications companies are forming partnerships to provide video entertainment to individuals on demand. This merging of industries and products is sometimes referred to as digital convergence, the conversion of all types of data into digital input that can be processed and stored by a computer. All forms of voice communications are now heavily computerized, including wireless communication from almost any location on earth.

Even everyday household appliances such as washers, driers, and refrigerators are becoming smarter. These and many other products now use embedded computer chips to help them work more efficiently. Eventually, these embedded computers will be capable of communicating with and be controlled by computers. This will enable you to start dinner and turn on the home air-conditioning before you leave the office; if you work in an office, that is. Another change computers have enabled is working away from the office. With existing communications capabilities, many people work at home and commute to the office electronically.

Can you imagine having to use a remote control to visually search through the 500 or more TV channels that will be available or to look through the directories of five online databases to find information on a single topic? New ways of presenting information will be developed so users can quickly make informed selections from expanded information choices. Smart software will be developed that will perform the necessary research to meet our information requests. Computers will undoubtedly be used to help users sort through all of the information, entertainment, and communications options.

Figure 1-33

File   Edit   Section   Page   Tools   Options   Help

What You Should Know

1. **Computer literacy** is knowing how to use a computer and **information literacy** is knowing how to find, analyze, and use information.

2. A **computer** is an electronic device, operating under the control of instructions stored in its own memory unit, that can accept data (input), process data arithmetically and logically, produce output from the processing, and store the results for future use.

3. The **information processing cycle** is composed of four general operations: input, process, output, and storage.

4. All computer processing requires **data**–raw facts, including numbers, words, images, and sounds, given to a computer during the input operation. In the processing phase, the computer manipulates data to create **infor-mation**–data that has been processed into a form that has meaning and is useful.

5. **Information processing**, sometimes called **data process-ing** (DP), is the production of information by processing data on a computer.

6. People who either use the computer directly or use the information it provides are called **computer users**, **end users**, or **users**.

7. A computer's power derives from its capability to perform input, process, output, and storage operations with speed and reliability and to store large amounts of information.

8. A **computer program**, also called **program instructions** or **software**, is a detailed set of instructions that tell a computer exactly what to do.

9. The first three operations of the information processing cycle, **input**, **process**, and **output**, describe the procedures that a computer performs to process data into informa-tion. The fourth operation, **storage**, describes a computer's electronic storage capability.

10. Data is processed by specific equipment that is often called computer **hardware**.

11. **Input devices** are used to enter data into a computer. Two common input devices are the **keyboard** and the **mouse**. The mouse is used to move a small symbol, called a **mouse pointer** or **pointer**, that appears on the computer screen.

12. A computer's **system unit** contains the electronic circuits that actually cause the processing of data to occur. The system unit includes the central processing unit, main memory, and other electronic components.

13. The **central processing unit** (CPU) contains a **control unit** that executes the program instructions and an **arithmetic/logic unit** (ALU) that performs math and logic operations. **Arithmetic operations** include numeric calculations such as addition, subtraction, multiplica-tion, and division. **Logical operations** are comparisons of data to see if one value is greater than, less than, or equal to another.

14. **Main memory**, also called **RAM** (**Random Access Memory**) or **primary storage**, temporarily stores data and program instructions when they are being processed.

15. **Output devices** present the output from a computer. The two most commonly used output devices are the **printer** and the **monitor**, also called the **screen** or the CRT (which stands for **cathode ray tube**).

16. **Secondary storage devices**, or **auxiliary storage devices**, store instructions and data when they are not being used by the system unit. Common secondary storage devices on personal computers store data as magnetic areas on a **diskette** or **hard disk**.

17. Collectively, the equipment that performs the four operations of the information processing cycle is called a **computer system.** The input devices, output devices, and secondary storage devices that surround the system unit are sometimes referred to as **peripheral devices**.

18. The five major categories of computers are: personal computers, servers, minicomputers, mainframe computers, and supercomputers. Computers are generally classified according to their size, speed, processing capabilities, and price.

19. **Personal computers**, also called **microcomputers** or **micros**, are the small systems that have become so widely used in recent years. Depending on their size and features, personal computer prices range from several hundred to several thousand dollars. Classifications within this category include **hand-held computers**, **palmtop computers**, **notebook computers**, **subnotebook computers**, **laptop computers**, **pen computers**, (such as a **personal digital assistant** (PDA) or **personal communicator**), **desktop computers**, **tower computers**, and **workstations**.

20. **Server** computers are designed to support a computer network that allows users to share files, applications software, and hardware. Small servers look like high-end personal computers and are priced in the $5,000 to $20,000 range, while the most powerful servers look and function more like minicomputers and are priced as high as $150,000.

21. **Minicomputers** are more powerful than personal computers and can support a number of users performing different tasks. These systems cost from approximately $15,000 to several hundred thousand dollars.

22. **Mainframe** computers are large systems that can handle hundreds of users, store large amounts of data, and process transactions at a very high rate. The price range for mainframes is from several hundred thousand dollars to several million dollars.

23. **Supercomputers**, the most powerful category of computers and, accordingly, the most expensive, are capable of processing hundreds of millions of instructions per second. These machines cost several million dollars.

24. Computers of all categories, especially personal computers, are sometimes connected to form **networks** that allow users to share data and computer resources.

25. Computer programs, commonly referred to as computer software, specify the sequence of operations the computer will perform. **Computer programmers** write the instructions (computer programs) necessary to direct the computer to process data into information. Programmers often follow a plan developed by a **systems analyst**, who works with both the user and the programmer to determine and design the desired output of the program.

26. **System software** consists of programs that are related to controlling the actual operations of the computer equipment. The instructions in the **operating system**, a component of system software, tell the computer how to perform functions such as how to load, store, and execute an application program and how to transfer data between the input/output devices and main memory.

27. Today, many computers use an **operating environment** that works with the operating system to make the computer easier to use. Operating environments have a **graphical user interface** (GUI) that provides visual clues, such as symbols called icons, to help the user. Each **icon** represents an application software package or a file or document where data is stored.

28. **Application software** consists of programs that tell a computer how to produce information. Programs required for common business and personal applications can be purchased from software vendors or stores that sell computer products. Purchased programs are often referred to as **application software packages** or simply **software packages**. Some of the more widely used packages for personal computer users are: word processing, desktop publishing, electronic spreadsheet, presentation graphics, database, communications, and electronic mail software.

29. In addition to a computer system and software, other elements required for successful information processing include accurate data, trained information systems personnel, knowledgeable users, and documented procedures. Together these elements are referred to as an **information system**.

30. **Connectivity** refers to the capability to connect a computer to other computers. The connection may be temporary or permanent.

31. A typical mid-sized company might use computers in a variety of areas, including: the receptionist, sales department, marketing department, shipping and receiving department, manufacturing department, engineering department, accounting department, human resources department, information systems department, and executive level.

32. Because of the widespread use of computers, most organizations prefer to hire employees with computer experience and knowledge.

File   Edit   Section   Page   Tools   Options   Help

Terms to Remember

arithmetic/logic unit (ALU) (1.8)
application software (1.15)
application software package (1.15)
arithmetic/logic unit (ALU) (1.8)
arithmetic operation (1.8)
auxiliary storage device (1.9)

cathode ray tube (CRT) (1.8)
central processing unit (CPU) (1.8)
computer (1.4)
computer literacy (1.2)
computer program (1.6)
computer programmer (1.14)
computer system (1.9)
computer users (1.5)
connectivity (1.17)
control unit (1.8)
CPU (central processing unit) (1.8)
CRT (cathode ray tube) (1.8)

data (1.4)
data processing (DP) (1.5)
desktop computer (1.11)
diskette (1.9)
DP (data processing) (1.5)

end users (1.5)

graphical user interface (GUI) (1.15)
GUI (graphical user interface) (1.15)

hand-held computers (1.10)
hard disk (1.9)
hardware (1.7)

icon (1.15)
information (1.4)
information literacy (1.2)
information processing (1.5)
information processing cycle (1.4)
information system (1.16)
input (1.7)
input device (1.7)

keyboard (1.7)

laptop computer (1.11)
logical operation (1.8)

main memory (1.8)
mainframe (1.13)
micro (1.10)
microcomputer (1.10)
minicomputer (1.12)
monitor (1.8)
mouse (1.7)
mouse pointer (1.7)

network (1.13)
notebook computer (1.10)

operating environment (1.15)
operating system (1.14)
output (1.7)
output device (1.8)

palmtop computer (1.10)
PC (personal computer) (1.10)
PDA (personal digital assistant) (1.11)
pen computer (1.11)
peripheral device (1.9)
personal communicator (1.11)
personal computer (PC) (1.10)
personal digital assistant (PDA) (1.11)
pointer (1.7)
primary storage (1.8)
printer (1.8)
process (1.7)
program instructions (1.6)

RAM (Random Access Memory) (1.8)
Random Access Memory (RAM) (1.8)

screen (1.8)
secondary storage device (1.9)
server (1.12)
software (1.6)
software package (1.15)
storage (1.7)
subnotebook computer (1.10)
supercomputer (1.13)
system software (1.14)
system unit (1.8)
systems analyst (1.14)

tower computer (1.11)

users (1.5)

workstation (1.11)

le   Edit   Section   Page   Tools   Options   Help

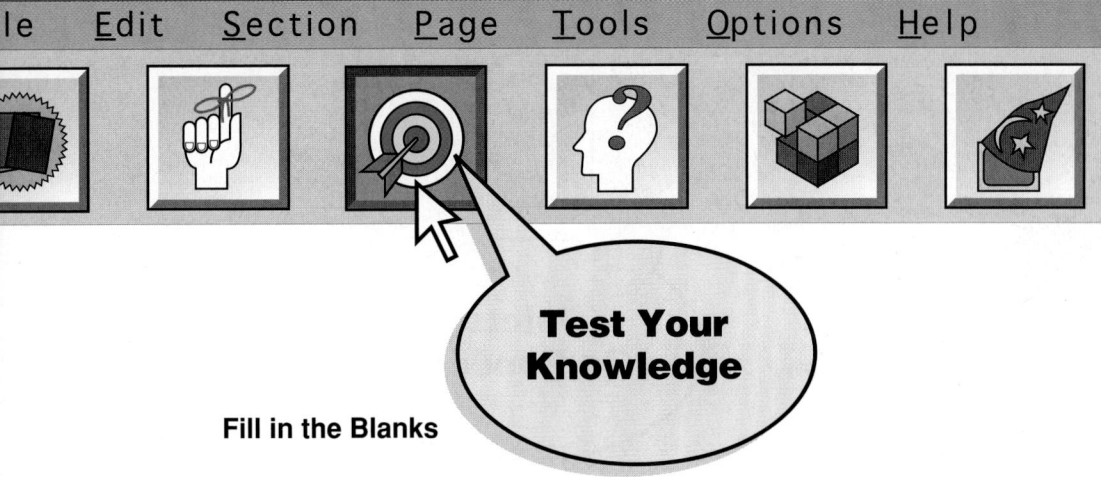

Test Your Knowledge

Fill in the Blanks

1. A(n) _____ is an electronic device, operating under the control of instructions stored in its memory unit, that can accept input, process the input arithmetically and logically, produce output from the processing, and store the results for future use.

2. The four operations of the information processing cycle are: _____, _____, _____, and _____.

3. During information processing, the computer manipulates _____–raw facts given to a computer during the input operation–to create _____–input that has been converted into a form that has meaning and is useful.

4. The central processing unit (CPU) contains a(n) _____ that executes program instructions and a(n) _____ that performs math and logic operations.

5. Collectively, the equipment that performs the four operations of the information processing cycle is called a(n) _____, and the input devices, output devices, and secondary storage devices that surround the system unit are referred to as _____.

Short Answer

1. What is the difference between computer literacy and information literacy? How do computers relate to information literacy?

2. What three characteristics make the computer such a powerful tool? Describe each.

3. How are computers generally classified? What are the five major categories of computers? Briefly describe each. Why is it difficult to make firm definitions of these categories?

4. What is computer software? How is system software different from application software?

5. What is an information system? How do the six elements of an information system work together?

Label the Figure

Instructions: The figure below represents a computer system. In the spaces provided, label the components of the system.

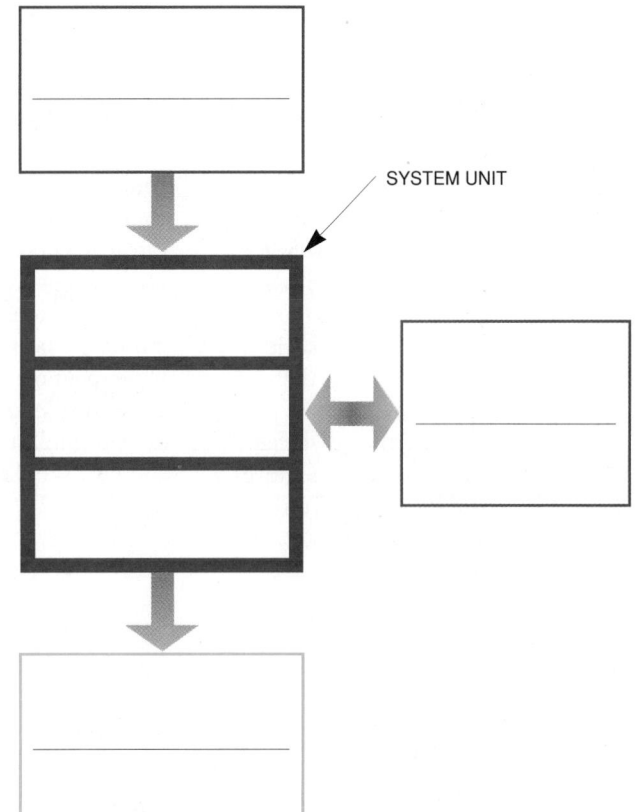

SYSTEM UNIT

File   Edit   Section   Page   Tools   Options   Help

Points to Ponder

1

Cynics once said that it's not *what* you know, it's *who* you know that is important. With the increasing emphasis on information literacy, however, it might be argued that now it's not *what* you know, it's *how you can find out* that is most significant. What do you think? What changes, if any, should schools make to better address information literacy? How should computers be used in schools to enhance information literacy?

2

Some technological innovations, such as the telephone and the automobile, have had a significant impact on society at large, in both positive ways and negative ways. Together with a classmate, present a debate on the ways computers have affected society. One of you should argue that the impact of computers has been primarily positive and the other that the impact has been primarily negative. When the debate is over, and your classmates have had their say, see if you can reach a consensus on whether, overall, society is better off, or worse off, with the proliferation of computers.

3

Despite the reliability of computers, everyone has heard of "computer errors." Describe a situation you are familiar with (either through reading or personal experience) in which a "computer error" occurred. Who, or what, do you feel was responsible for the error? What steps do you think could be taken to ensure that the error does not happen again?

4

Your school has been given a grant to purchase a supercomputer, a mainframe computer, several mini-computers, and a number of personal computers. How do you think each category of computer would be best used in your school? Who should have access to each computer? If the money for personal computers had to be spent on three different types of personal computers, what kind do you think should be purchased and how should they be used?

5

This chapter describes how computers are used in the Hayden Corporation, an automobile manufacturer. You have been hired as a consultant to the Hayden Corporation and asked to provide a worst-case and a best-case scenario. If, due to financial difficulties, the computers in one part of the organization have to be moved to another department, which part of the organization do you feel could best withstand the loss? Why? If, as a result of increased profits, the Hayden Corporation is able to purchase additional computer equipment, where should the equipment go to most benefit the corporation as a whole? Why?

6

From the timeline presented following this chapter, you can see that many of the most notable developments in the computer industry took place over the past thirty years. Draw a hypothetical timeline that chronicles the computer industry over the next twenty years. On your timeline, place and describe at least six developments you think will have a significant impact on the computer industry during the next two decades.

le   Edit   Section   Page   Tools   Options   Help

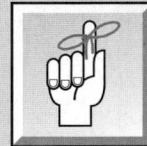
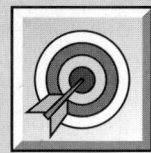

Out and About

1. Visit a library or book store and examine at least three different current magazines aimed at computer users. Write down the name of all three magazines and make a list of the titles of articles in each. Look at the advertisements. What is the most expensive computer equipment advertised? What is the least expensive? What, in your opinion, is the most unusual computer equipment advertised? Do you think each magazine is intended for a particular type of computer user? Why or why not?

2. Interview a person who uses a computer every day at work, and prepare a report on that person's feelings about computers. Some of the questions you might ask are: How is the computer used? Did the person feel any anxiety when first confronted with the computer? What type of computer training did the individual receive? How does the computer make this person's job easier? How does the computer make this person's job more difficult? What kind of computer education would this individual recommend to students interested in going into the same field?

3. Visit a computer vendor and interview the manager or a salesperson. Based on your interview, prepare a report on the demographics of the typical computer buyer at that store. Find the answers to such questions as: What gender are most computer purchasers? In what age range are the buyers? What is their average age? What seems to be the characteristic educational level of a computer buyer? Approximately what is their average income? Why do most purchasers buy a computer?

4. Rent a videotape in which a computer plays a major part–some examples are *2001: A Space Odyssey, War Games,* and *Short Circuit.* Watch the videotape, then prepare a report on how the movie makers view computers. What part did the computer play in the movie? In general, was the computer a hero, a villain, or simply the tool of a human character? Why? What was the theme of the movie? What role, if any, did the computer play in promoting the theme?

5. Prepare a detailed report on one of the individuals or events depicted on the timeline following this chapter. Describe the impact the individual or event has had on the computer industry. How do you think the computer industry would be different if the individual had never existed or if the event had never taken place?

6. Visit a store that sells computer software and examine the application software packages. Make a list of at least five application packages you would like to have on your personal computer. Most application software is written for a specific operating system (system software). Write down the name of the operating system with which each of the application packages you selected is designed to work. If one (or more) of your applications does not work with the same operating system as the others, try to locate a similar application package. Your goal is to find five application packages that all work with the same operating system. Make a list of your final five application packages, and note the operating system that they all use. What features, if any, did you have to give up to find five applications that use the same operating system?

File   Edit   Section   Page   Tools   Options   Help

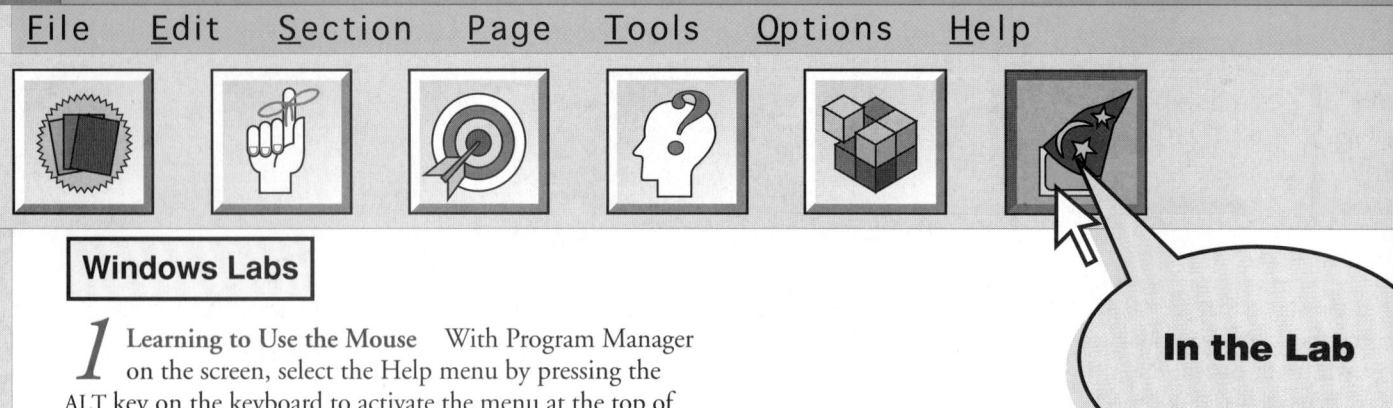

In the Lab

Windows Labs

1 **Learning to Use the Mouse**   With Program Manager on the screen, select the Help menu by pressing the ALT key on the keyboard to activate the menu at the top of the screen and typing the letter H for Help. From the Help menu, choose the Windows Tutorial command by pressing the DOWN ARROW key to highlight it and then press the ENTER key. Windows welcomes you to the tutorial and then displays instructions *(Figure 1-34)*. Type M to begin the mouse lesson. As you move through the mouse lesson, do the following on a sheet of paper: (1) define the terms point, click, double-click, and drag; (2) explain how you would move the mouse pointer to the right if the mouse is on the edge of the right side of your desk. Exit the tutorial by pressing the ESC key and typing the letter Y.

2 **Shelly Cashman Series Mouse Lab**   With Program Manager on the screen, look for the Shelly Cashman Series Labs group window *(Figure 1-36)*. If you do not see it, hold down the CTRL key and press function key F6 until the Shelly Cashman Series Labs group icon is highlighted *(Figure 1-35)*. Release both keys and press the ENTER key. Use the arrow keys to highlight the Shelly Cashman Series program-item icon *(Figure 1-36)*. Press the ENTER key. When the Shelly Cashman Series Labs screen displays *(Figure 1-37)*, use the UP ARROW and DOWN ARROW keys to highlight Using the Mouse. Press the ENTER key. When the introductory screen appears, carefully read the objectives. With your printer turned on, press the P key on the keyboard to print the questions for the Mouse Lab. Fill out the top of the Questions sheet and answer the questions as you step through the Mouse Lab.

3 **Shelly Cashman Series Keyboard Lab**   Follow the instructions in Windows Lab 2 to display the Shelly Cashman Series Labs screen *(Figure 1-37)*. Select Using the Keyboard by pointing to it and clicking the left mouse button. When the initial Keyboard Lab screen displays, carefully read the objectives. With your printer turned on, point to the Print Questions button and click the left mouse button. Fill out the top of the Questions sheet and answer the questions as you step through the Keyboard Lab.

4 **Learning the Basics of Microsoft Windows**   With Program Manager on the screen, point to Help on the menu bar and click the left mouse button. Point to the Windows Tutorial command on the Help menu and click the left mouse button. Windows welcomes you to the tutorial and then displays instructions *(Figure 1-34)*. Type W to begin the Windows Basics lesson. Click the Instructions button and read the instructions. Click the Return to the Tutorial button. Click the Continue button to begin the Windows Basics lesson. As you move through the Windows Basics lesson, use paper and pencil to do the following: (1) describe how to open a group window; (2) name the icons in the Accessories group window; (3) describe how to start an application; (4) describe how to enlarge a window so it fills the computer screen; (5) describe how to resize a window; (6) list the

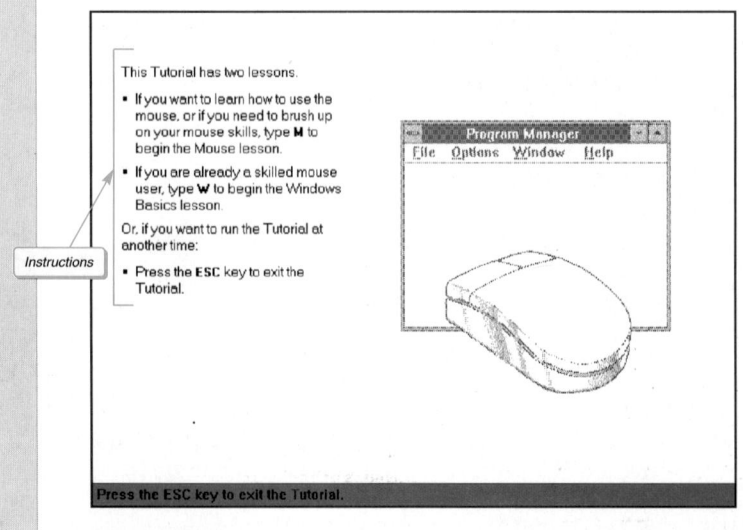

Figure 1-34

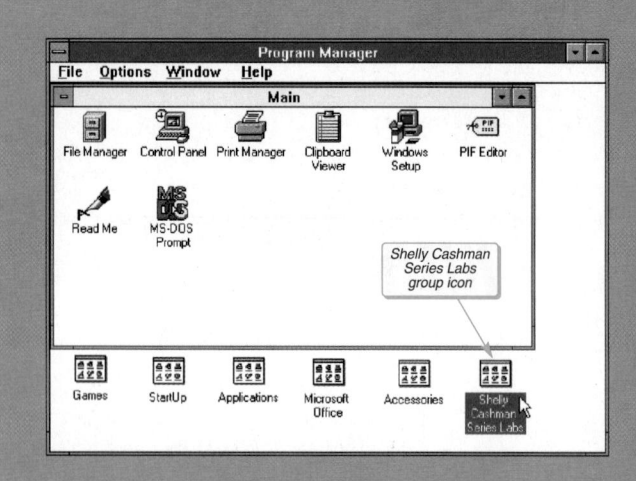

Figure 1-35

commands on the File menu; (7) list the ingredients in the recipe you displayed; (8) name the number of calories in a Strawberry Yogurt Sundae with 2 scoops and nuts; (9) describe how to close an application window. Exit the tutorial.

5 **Improving Your Mouse Skills**   With Program Manager on the screen, double-click the Games group icon to open the Games group window. In the Games group window, double-click the Solitaire program-item icon. When the Solitaire application displays, click its Maximize button. Select the Help menu in the Solitaire window and choose the Contents command. One by one, click the green Help topics to learn how to play Solitaire; then print each Help topic by choosing the Print Topic command from the File menu. To return to the Contents window and select another Help topic, choose the Back button. To close the Solitaire Help window, double-click its Control-menu box. Play the game of Solitaire. To quit Solitaire, double-click the Solitaire window's Control-menu box. Close the Games group window by double-clicking its Control-menu box.

DOS Labs

1 **Booting and Rebooting a Personal Computer** With your computer turned off, **cold boot** it by turning the power switch on. Once the computer is operational, perform a **warm boot** by holding down the CTRL and ALT keys, pressing the DELETE key, and then releasing all three keys. If your computer has a reset button on the system unit, press and then release it to perform a warm boot. Answer the following questions: (1) Which boot process takes longer? (2) Why isn't there just one key on the keyboard to reboot your computer? (3) Why would you warm boot a computer?

2 **Executing a Program**   Obtain information from your instructor on how to change to the directory on your computer containing the TALRCALC.EXE program. At the DOS prompt, type talrcalc and press the ENTER key. Type John and press the ENTER key. Type 36 and press the ENTER key. Type 196 and press the ENTER key. Ready your printer. Press the PRINT SCREEN key to print the results. Answer the following: (1) What was the input for this program and what hardware was used to accomplish the input? (2) What was the output for this program and what hardware was used for the output? (3) Between the input and the output, what took place to produce the output? Run the program again using these values: Sandy, 28, 140. Print the results.

Online Lab

1 **Information About Online Services**   Following is a list of online services and telephone numbers: Prodigy Service, (800) 776-3449; Genie Online Services, (800) 638-9636; Delphi, (800) 695-4005; CompuServe, (800) 848-8199; and America Online, (800) 827-6364. Call each service to compare monthly rates and hours of free connect time per month. Request a membership kit from any two services.

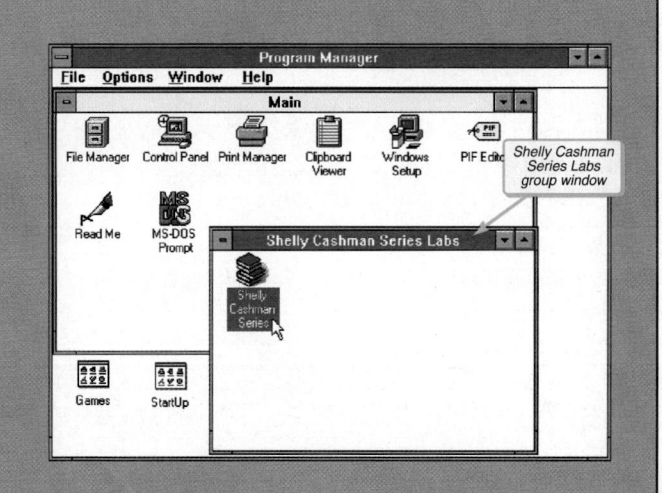

Figure 1-36

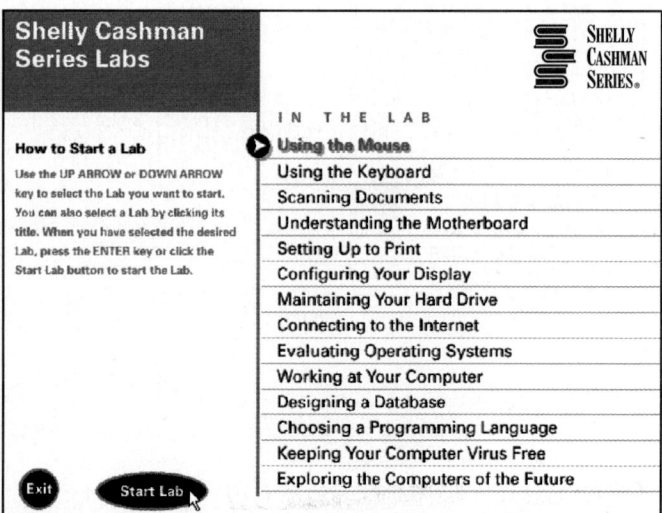

Figure 1-37

The electronic computer industry began more than fifty years ago.

1937

1943

Dr. John V. Atanasoff and his assistant Clifford Berry designed and began to build the first electronic digital computer during the winter of 1937-38. Their machine, the Atanasoff-Berry-Computer, or ABC, provided the foundation for the next advances in electronic digital computers.

During the years 1943 to 1946, Dr. John W Mauchly and J. Presper Eckert, Jr. complete the ENIAC (Electronic Numerical Integrato and Computer), the first large-scale electron digital computer. The ENIAC weighed thirt tons, contained 18,000 vacuum tubes, and occupied a thirty-by-fifty-foot space.

1952

1953

In 1952, Dr. Grace Hopper, a mathematician and commodore in the U.S. Navy, wrote a paper describing how to program a computer with symbolic notation instead of the detailed machine language that had been used.

Dr. Hopper was instrumental in developing high-level languages such as COBOL, a business application language introduced in 1960. COBOL uses English-like phrases and runs on most computers, making it one of the more widely used languages in the world.

The IBM model 650 was one of the first widely used computer systems. Originally, IBM planned to produce only 50 machines, but the system was so successful that eventually it manufactured more than 1,000.

Core memory, developed in the early 1950s, provided much larger storage capacities and greater reliability than vacuum tube memory.

This timeline summarizes the major events in the evolution of the computer industry.

1945   1951   1952

Dr. John von Neumann is credited with writing a brilliant report in 1945 describing several new hardware concepts and the use of stored programs. His breakthrough laid the foundation for the digital computers that have since been built.

J. Presper Eckert, Jr., standing left, explains the operations of the UNIVAC I to newsman Walter Cronkite, right. This machine was the first commercially available electronic digital computer.

In 1951-52, after much discussion, IBM decided to add computers to its line of business equipment products. This led IBM to become a dominant force in the computer industry.

Public awareness of computers increased when, in 1951, the UNIVAC I, after analyzing only 5% of the tallied vote, correctly predicted that Dwight D. Eisenhower would win the presidential election.

1957   1958   1959

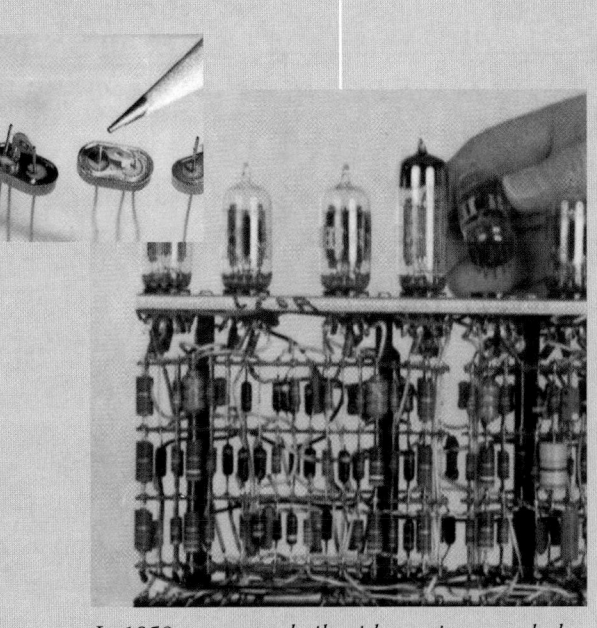

FORTRAN (FORmula TRANslator) was introduced in 1957, proving that efficient, easy-to-use programming languages could be developed. FORTRAN is still in use.

In 1958, computers built with transistors marked the beginning of the second generation of computer hardware. Previous computers built with vacuum tubes were first-generation machines.

By 1959, more than 200 programming languages had been created.

1960 1964 1965

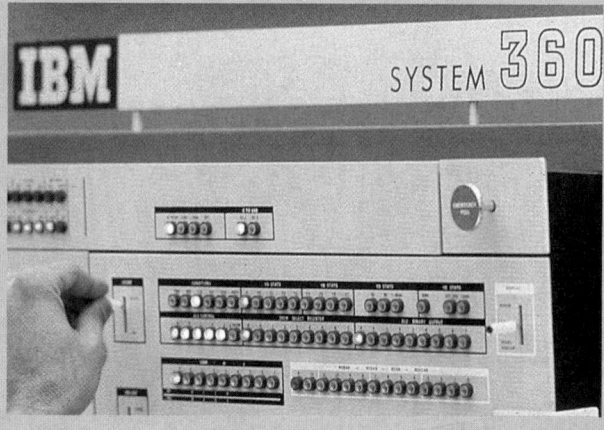

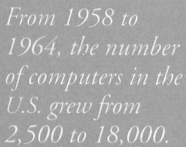

From 1958 to 1964, the number of computers in the U.S. grew from 2,500 to 18,000.

Third-generation computers, with their controlling circuitry stored on chips, were introduced in 1964. The IBM System/360 computers were the first third-generation machines.

In 1965, Dr. John Kemeny of Dartmouth led the development of the BASIC programming language. BASIC is still widely used on personal computers.

1969 1970 1975

In 1969, under pressure from the industry, IBM announced that some of its software would be priced separately from the computer hardware. This "unbundling" allowed software firms to emerge in the industry.

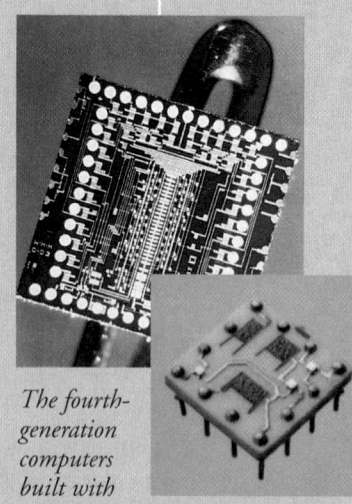

The fourth-generation computers built with chips that used LSI (large-scale integration) arrived in 1970. The chips used in 1965 contained as many as 1,000 circuits. By 1970, the LSI chip contained as many as 15,000.

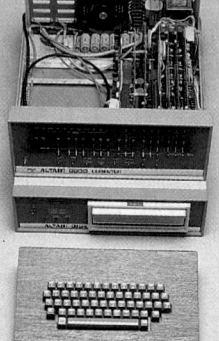

The MITS, Inc. Altair computer, sold in kits for less than $400, was the first commercially successful microcomputer.

ETHERNET, developed at Xerox PARC (Palo Alto Research Center) by Robert Metcalfe, was the first local area network (LAN). Originally designed to link minicomputers, ETHERNET was later extended to personal computers. The LAN allows computers to communicate and share software, data, and peripherals such as printers.

1967   1968   1969

Digital
Equipment
Corporation
(DEC)
introduced
the first
minicomputer
in 1965.

The software industry
emerged in the 1960s.
In 1968, Computer
Science Corporation
became the first software
company to be listed
on the New York
Stock Exchange.

PASCAL, a structured programming
language, was developed by Swiss
computer scientist Niklaus Wirth
between 1967 and 1971.

In 1969, Dr. Ted Hoff of Intel Corporation
developed a microprocessor, or
microprogrammmable computer chip,
the Intel 4004.

1976   1979

The first public
online information
services, CompuServe
and the Source,
were founded.

In 1976, Steve Wozniak
and Steve Jobs built the
first Apple
computer.

The VisiCalc spreadsheet program written
by Bob Frankston and Dan Bricklin was
introduced in 1979. This product was
originally written to run on Apple II
computers. Together, VisiCalc and Apple II
computers rapidly became successful. Most
people consider VisiCalc to be the singlemost
important reason why personal computers
gained acceptance in the business world.

1980

In 1980, IBM offered Microsoft Corporation's founder, Bill Gates, the opportunity to develop the operating system for the soon-to-be announced IBM personal computer. With the development of MS-DOS, Microsoft achieved tremendous growth and success.

1981

The IBM PC was introduced in 1981, signaling IBM's entrance into the personal computer marketplace. The IBM PC quickly garnered the largest share of the personal computer market and became the personal computer of choice in business.

1982

More than 300,00[personal computers were sold in 1981. In 1982, the numl[jumped to 3,275,0[

1984

Apple introduced the Macintosh computer, which incorporated a unique graphical interface, making it easy to learn.

1987

Several personal computers utilizing the powerful Intel 80386 microprocessor were introduced in 1987. These machines handled processing that previously only large systems could handle.

1983

...stead of choosing a ...rson for its annual ...ard, TIME magazine ...med the computer ...Machine of the Year" ...r 1982. This event ...knowledged the ...pact of the computer ...society.

The Lotus 1-2-3 integrated software package, developed by Mitch Kapor, was introduced in 1983. It combined spreadsheet, graphics, and database programs in one package.

1984

IBM introduced a personal computer, called the PC AT, that used the Intel 80286 microprocessor.

1989

...he Intel 486 became the world's ...st 1,000,000 transistor ...icroprocessor. It crammed 1.2 ...illion transistors on a sliver of ...licon that measured .4" x .6" and ...ecuted instructions at 15 MIPS ...illion instructions per second) — ...ur times as fast as its predecessor, ...e 80386 chip. The 80 designation ...ed with previous Intel chips, such ...the 80386 and 80286, was ...opped with the 486.

1990

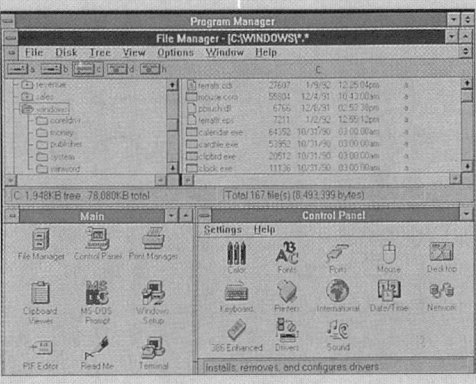

Microsoft released Windows 3.0, a substantially enhanced version of its Windows graphical user interface first introduced in 1985. The software allowed users to run multiple applications on a personal computer and more easily move data from one application to another. The package became an instant success, selling hundreds of thousands of copies.

By 1990, more than 54 million computers were in use in the United States.

1991

The High Performance Computing and Communications (HPCC) initiative, sponsored by U.S. Senator Al Gore, proposed the building of a high-speed network, or digital highway, to connect government research laboratories.

1992

Apple introduced a personal digital assistant (PDA) called the Newton MessagePad. This 7 1/4 -by-4 1/2 -inch personal computer incorporates a pen interface and wireless communications.

1993

Several companies introduced computer systems using the Pentium microprocessor from Intel. The Pentium chip is the successor to the Intel 486 microprocessor. It contains 3.1 million transistors and is able to perform 112 million instructions per second (MIPS).

1993

The Energy Star program, endorsed by the Environmental Protection Agency (EPA), encouraged manufacturers to build computer equipment that meets strict power consumption guidelines. Manufacturers meeting the guidelines can then display the Energy Star logo on their products.

The scope of the network proposed in the 1991 HPCC initiative was significantly expanded to the National Information Infrastructure (NII). The NII is envisioned as a broadband digital network allowing universal access and providing information services, such as government data, training, and medical services, to everyone.

1994

"**WE** are crossing a technology threshold that will forever change the way we learn, work, socialize and shop. It will affect all of us, and businesses of every type, in ways far more pervasive than most people realize."

Bill Gates
COMDEX '94

Estimates indicated that more than 16 million personal computers were sold worldwide in 1994 alone.

Approximately 13 million Americans gained access to online information services. More than 8 million had access to the Internet.

CHAPTER TWO

Computer Software Applications: User Tools

2

Objectives

After completing this chapter, you will be able to:

- Identify the most widely used personal computer software applications

- Describe productivity software

- Define and describe a user interface and a graphical user interface

- Explain the key features of each of the major applications

- Explain the advantages of integrated software

- List and describe learning aids and support tools that help users to use personal computer software applications

Today, understanding the applications commonly used on personal computers is considered a part of being computer literate. In fact, a working knowledge of at least some of these applications is now considered by many employers to be a required skill. Because of this, personal computer software applications are discussed early in this book. Learning about each of the most widely used applications will help you understand how people use personal computers in our modern world. Before discussing the applications, the user interface is explained. The user interface controls how the user works with the software and applies to all the applications. After learning about individual applications, you will learn about integrated software; the combination of several applications into a single software package. Finally, some of the aids and tools that are available to help you learn and use software applications are discussed.

Productivity Software

*T*his chapter will introduce you to nine widely used personal computer software applications:
- Word processing
- Desktop publishing
- Spreadsheet
- Database
- Presentation graphics
- Communications
- Electronic mail
- Personal information management
- Project management

These software applications are used by a wide range of organizations and individuals. Because these applications help people perform their work more efficiently, they are sometimes referred to as **productivity software**.

Although these applications are discussed as they are used on personal computers, they are actually available on computers of all sizes. The concepts you will learn about each application package on personal computers will also apply if you are working on a larger system.

User Interface

To more easily learn about productivity software, you need to understand some of the features of a user interface. A **user interface** is the way the user tells the software what to do and the way the computer displays information and processing options to the user. One of the most common user interfaces is the graphical user interface (GUI). The **graphical user interface**, or GUI (pronounced gooey), combines text and graphics to make the software easier to use. Graphical user interfaces include several common features such as windows, icons, menus, and buttons.

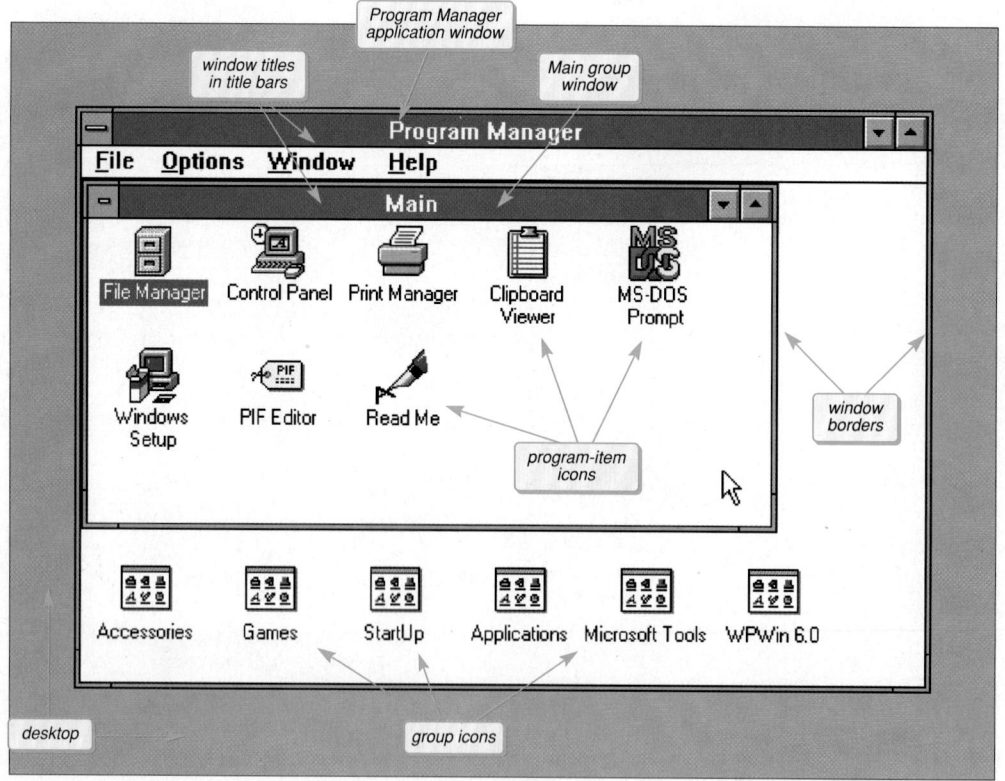

Figure 2-1

Two key features of a graphical user interface (GUI) are windows and icons. Windows are rectangular areas that present information. Icons are symbols that represent processing options or documents. In this screen, there are two windows open; the larger Program Manager window and the smaller Main window contained within the Program Manager window. Several windows can be open at the same time and moved from back to front so all information on a window can be seen. Each of the group icons at the bottom of the screen can be opened into a window such as the Main window.

A **window** is a rectangular area of the screen that is used to present information *(Figure 2-1)*. They are called windows because of their capability to see into another part of a program. Many people consider windows to be like multiple sheets of paper on top of a desk. In the same way that each piece of paper on the desk contains different information, each window on the screen contains different information. Just as papers can be moved from the bottom of a pile to the top of the desk when they are needed, windows can be created on a screen and moved around to show information when it is needed. The term Windows, with a capital W, refers to **Microsoft Windows**, the most popular graphical user interface for personal computers.

Icons are pictures or symbols that are used to represent processing options, such as an application or a program, or documents, such as a letter or spreadsheet *(Figure 2-1)*.

A **menu** is a list of options from which the user can choose. In a graphical user interface, menus often contain a list of related commands. **Commands** are instructions that cause the computer software to perform a specific action. For example, the menu shown in *Figure 2-2* lists commands related to files. Using this menu, the user can work with files by choosing the Open, Move, Copy, or Delete command.

A **button** is an icon (usually a rectangular or circular shape) that causes a specific action to take place. Buttons are selected using a pointing device such as a mouse but can also be activated by using the keyboard. In *Figure 2-3*, the buttons shown are used to control printing a document.

The features of a user interface make it easier for the user to communicate with the computer. You will see examples of these features and how they are used as you learn about the various personal computer applications.

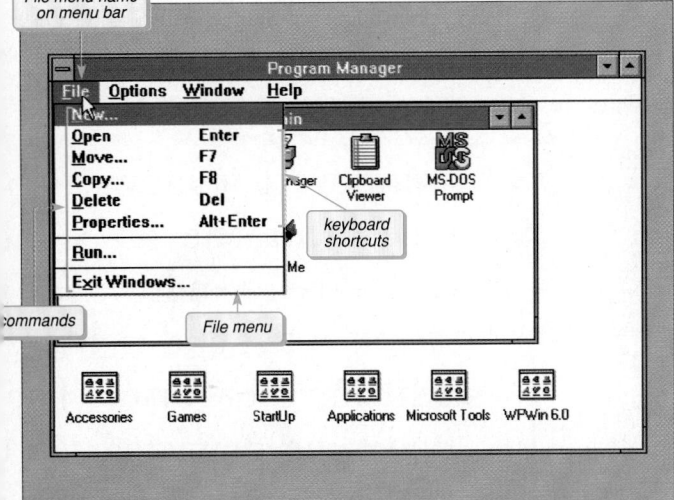

Figure 2-2
A menu is a list of options from which the user can choose. The menu shown on this screen lists commands for file operations. The commands can be chosen with a pointing device or by pressing the keys listed to the right of the commands.

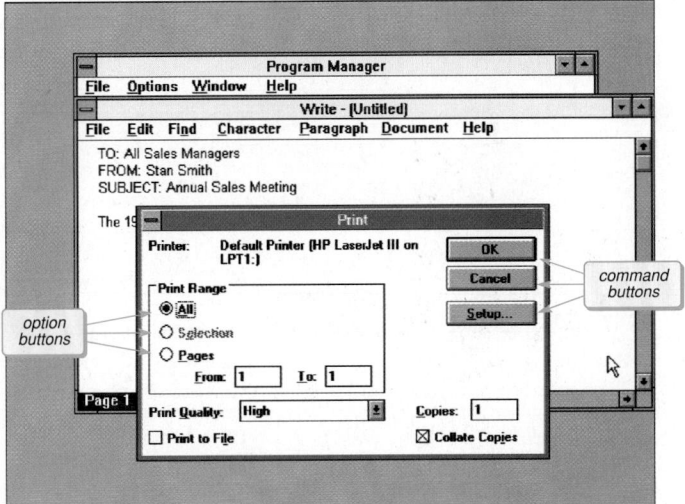

Figure 2-3
A button is an icon that causes a specific action to take place. This screen contains two types of buttons. Option buttons modify the action that will take place. In this example, the option buttons determine what pages are printed. Command buttons start a specific action.

Word Processing Software

The most widely used computer application is word processing. **Word processing software** enables a computer to produce or modify documents that consist primarily of text. Millions of people use word processing software every day to create letters, memos, reports, and other documents. A major advantage of using word processing to produce a document is the capability to easily change what has been done. Because the document is stored electronically, you can add, delete, or rearrange words, sentences, or entire sections. The document can be printed as many times as you like with each copy looking as good as the first. With older methods such as using a typewriter, making changes and reprinting a document take much more time. Using word processing software is also an efficient way of storing documents because many documents can be stored on a disk or diskette. If computers are connected in a network, stored documents can be shared among users.

Today, most people perform word processing using personal computers or larger computer systems such as minicomputers or mainframes. These computers are also used for other applications. **Dedicated word processing systems**, used only for word processing, also exist.

Producing a document using word processing usually consists of four steps: creating, editing, formatting, and printing. A fifth step, saving the document, should be performed frequently throughout the process so work will not be lost.

frequently throughout the

Creating

Creating a word pro
text, usually by using the k
features used during the cr
scrolling, and moving the c
- Word Wrap. **Word wrap**
  when the text reaches a d
  such as the right-hand m
  user can continue typing
  return or line feed key.
- Scrolling. **Scrolling** is the
  so the user can view any
  documents as having bee
  paper *(Figure 2-4)*. The s
  window that allows a po
  The document can be mo
  the screen window. For v
  scrolled left and right, as
- Moving the Cursor. The
  underline character, recta
  where on the screen the

cursor control keys, on th
character or line at a time
movement is repeated un
efficient ways to move the
using the Page Up and Pa

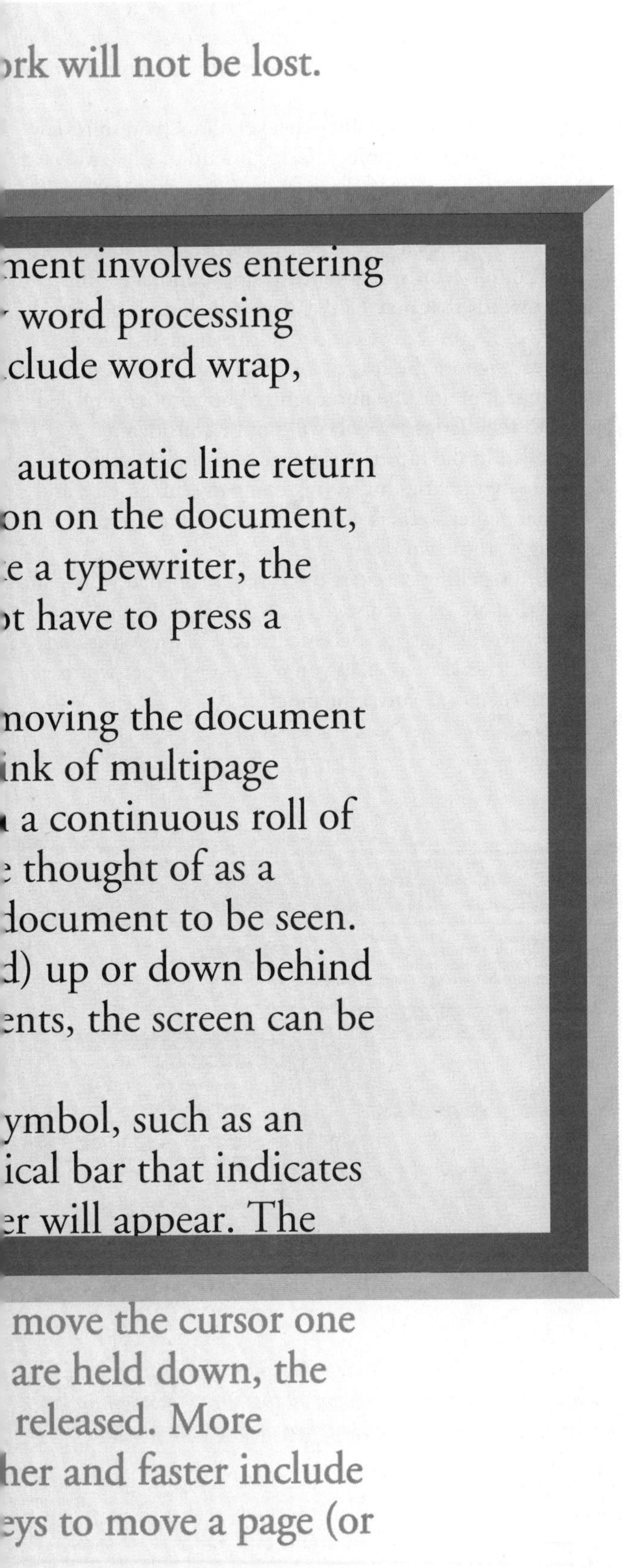

Creating

Creating a word processing document involves entering text, usually by using the keyboard. Key word processing features used during the creating step include word wrap, scrolling, and moving the cursor.

- Word Wrap. **Word wrap** provides an automatic line return when the text reaches a certain position on the document, such as the right-hand margin. Unlike a typewriter, the user can continue typing and does not have to press a return or line feed key.
- Scrolling. **Scrolling** is the process of moving the document so the user can view any portion. Think of multipage documents as having been created on a continuous roll of paper *(Figure 2-4)*. The screen can be thought of as a window that allows a portion of the document to be seen. The document can be moved (scrolled) up or down behind the screen window. For wide documents, the screen can be scrolled left and right, as well.
- Moving the Cursor. The **cursor** is a symbol, such as an underline character, rectangle, or vertical bar that indicates where on the screen the next character will appear. The cursor is moved by using the mouse or keyboard. The cursor control keys, on the keyboard, move the cursor one character or line at a time. If the keys are held down, the movement is repeated until the key is released. More efficient ways to move the cursor farther and faster include using the Page Up and Page Down keys to move a page (or screen) at a time and the Home and End keys to move to the beginning or end of a line. Other key combinations can be used to move to the beginning of words, paragraphs, or the start or end of the document.

Figure 2-4

Scrolling is the process of moving the document so the portion you want to see is displayed on the screen. It's as if the document had been created on a continuous roll of paper. The limited size of the screen only allows you to see a portion of the document. The document can be moved (scrolled) up or down and right or left so any portion of the document that will fit on one screen can be seen.

rk will not be lost.

ment involves entering
word processing
clude word wrap,

automatic line return
on on the document,
e a typewriter, the
ot have to press a

noving the document
ink of multipage
a continuous roll of
e thought of as a
ocument to be seen.
d) up or down behind
ents, the screen can be

ymbol, such as an
ical bar that indicates
er will appear. The

move the cursor one
are held down, the
released. More
her and faster include
eys to move a page (or

Editing

Editing is the process of making changes in the content of a document. Word processing editing features include cutting, copying, and pasting, inserting and deleting, and searching and replacing. Advanced editing features include spell checking, using a thesaurus, and grammar checking.

- Cut, Copy, and Paste. To **cut** involves removing a portion of the document and electronically storing it in a temporary location called the **Clipboard.** Whatever is on the Clipboard can be placed somewhere else in the document by giving a **paste** command. When you **copy,** a portion of the document is duplicated.
- Insert and Delete. When you **insert,** you add text to a document. When you **delete,** you remove text. Most word processors are normally in the *insert mode,* meaning that as you type, any existing text is pushed down the page to make room for the new text. However, word processors can be placed in a *typeover mode* (also called *overtype mode*), where new text replaces any existing text.

- Search. The **search** feature lets you find all occurrences of a particular character, word, or combination of words. Search can be used in combination with **replace** to substitute new letters or words for the old.
- Spelling Checker. A **spelling checker** allows you to review individual words, sections of a document, or the entire document for correct spelling. Words are compared to an electronic dictionary included in the word processing software. Some spelling checker dictionaries contain more than 120,000 words. If a match is not found, a list of similar words that may be the correct spelling is displayed *(Figure 2-5).* You can select one of the suggested words displayed, ignore the suggestions and leave the word unchanged, or add the unrecognized but properly spelled word to the dictionary so it will not be considered misspelled in the future. Many users customize their software dictionaries by adding company, street, city, and personal names so the software can check the correct spelling of those words.

While spelling checkers can catch misspelled words and words that are repeated such as *the the,* they cannot identify words that are used incorrectly. A thesaurus and grammar checker will help you to choose proper words and use them in a correct manner.

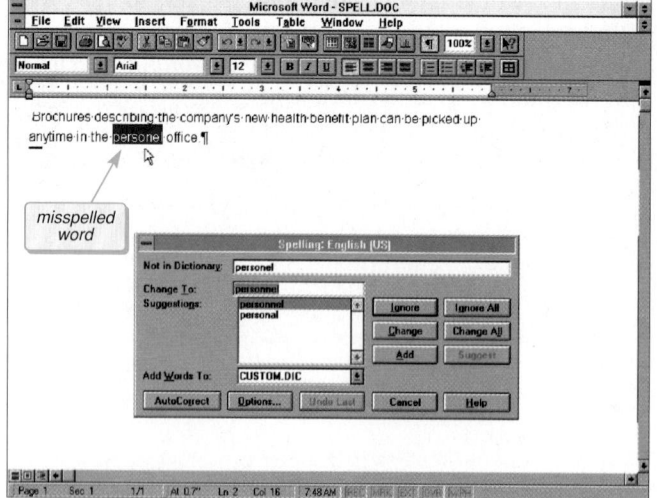

Figure 2-5
A spelling checker identifies words that do not match entries in the spelling checker dictionary. Alternative words are suggested and can be substituted for the unidentified word.

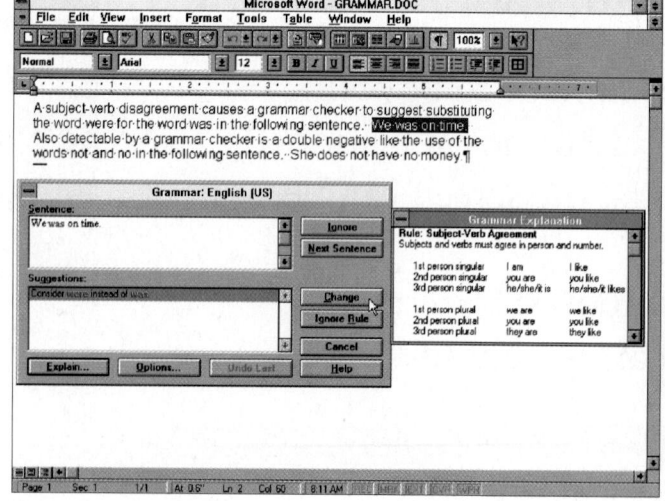

Figure 2-6
Grammar checking software identifies grammar, writing style, and sentence structure errors. As shown on this screen, most grammar checkers offer a possible solution when they detect a problem.

- Thesaurus. A **thesaurus** allows you to look up synonyms for words in a document while you are using your word processor. Using a thesaurus is similar to using a spelling checker. When you want to look up a synonym for a word, you place the cursor on the word to check, and activate the thesaurus with either a keyboard command or by using a pointing device. The thesaurus software displays a list of possible synonyms. If you find a word you would rather use, you select the desired word from the list and the software automatically incorporates it in the document by replacing the previous word.
- Grammar Checker. A **grammar checker** is used to check for grammar, writing style, and sentence structure errors *(Figure 2-6)*. This software can check documents for excessive use of a word or phrase, identify sentences that are too long, and find words that are used out of context such as *four* example.

Formatting

To **format** means to change the appearance of a document. Formatting is important because the overall look of a document can significantly affect its capability to communicate. For documents being sent to clients, it is not unusual to spend more time formatting the document than in entering the text. Word processing features that can be used to format a document include the following *(see Figure 2-7)*:
- Typeface, Font, and Style. A **typeface** is a specific set of characters that are designed the same. Helvetica and Times New Roman are examples of typefaces. The size of a typeface is measured in points. Each **point** is approximately 1/72 of an inch. The text you are reading in this book is ten point type. A specific combination of typeface and point size is called a **font,** though it is common to hear and read of typefaces being called fonts. A particular **style**, such as **bold**, *italics,* or underlining, can be applied to a font to make it stand out.

Figure 2-7
Examples of word processing formatting features.

Formatting Example ◄── header appears at top of every page	date (and time) can appear in header or footer ──► April 20, 1995		
TYPEFACES & STYLES *different typefaces and styles: bold, underline, and italics*	**Chicago** **Chicago Bold**	Helvetica <u>Helvetica Underlined</u>	Times Roman *Times Roman Italicized*
POINT SIZES *different point sizes can be used to make type larger or smaller*	6 point 8 point 10 point **12 point** **14 point** 20 point 30 point 50 point		
COLUMNS & JUSTIFICATION *four columns with different justifications*	This is an example of left justification. Notice how the words at the beginning of each line are aligned with the left column margin.	This is an example of full justification. The spacing between words is adjusted so that the words at the beginning and the end of the lines are aligned with the left and right column margins.	This is an example of center justification. The words are centered in the column. — This is an example of right justification. Only the words at the end of each line are aligned with the column margin.
TABLES & GRAPHICS *three-column table can be moved as a single object* *shading applied to every other row with border around table*	Part Number / Description / Price A101 widget $ 9.95 B202 gizmo $ 14.95 C303 thingee $ 19.95 D404 doodad $ 24.95		graphic can be placed anywhere on page
Computer Concepts ◄── footer appears at bottom of every page	automatic page number can appear anywhere in header or footer ──► 1		

- Margins and Justification. **Margins** specify the space in the border of a page and include the left, right, bottom, and top margin. **Justification**, also called **alignment**, deals with how text is positioned in relation to a fixed reference point, usually a right or left margin. **Full justification** aligns text with both the left and right margins. Left justification and right justification align with the left and right margins only. Centered justification divides the text equally on either side of a reference point, usually the center of the page.
- Spacing. **Spacing** deals with how far apart individual letters (horizontal spacing) and lines of text (vertical spacing) are placed. With **monospacing**, each character takes up the same amount of space. With **proportional spacing**, wide characters, such as a W or M, are given more space than narrow characters, such as an I. **Line spacing** increases the distance from the bottom of one line to the bottom of the next line. Single and double line spacing are the most common, but exact distances can also be specified in some word processing software.
- Columns, Tables, and Graphics. Most word processors can arrange text in two or more columns, like a newspaper or magazine. The text from the bottom of one column automatically flows to the top of the next column. Tables are a way of organizing information in rows and columns. Word processors that support tables enable the user to easily add and change table information and move the entire table as a single item, instead of as individual lines of text. Although word processors are primarily designed to work with text, most can now incorporate graphics such as drawings and pictures. Some graphics are included in word processing packages, however, graphic items are usually created in separate applications and imported (brought into) the word processing document.
- Borders and Shading. Borders and shading can be used to emphasize or highlight sections of a word processing document. A **border** is a decorative line or box that is used with text, graphics, or tables. **Shading** darkens the background area of a section of a document or table. Colors can be used for borders and shading but will print as black or gray unless you have a color printer.

Portrait Orientation

MEMORANDUM

TO: All Village Creek Employees

FROM: Christine Reddings, Training Supervi...

DATE: December 1, 1995

SUBJECT: **Computer Training Seminars**

On Monday, January 2, 1996, we will begin using new versions ...
cessing and electronic spreadsheet software. To prepare you fo...
we are offering the following training seminars.

Word Processing *(December 8, 1995, 1:00 p.m. - 4:30 p.m.)*

This seminar focuses on the new word processor features. Thro...
and hands-on exercises, you will create, edit, format, save and ...
Bring a blank formatted disk to the seminar.

Electronic Spreadsheets *(December 12, 1995, 8:00 a.m. - 11.*

This seminar addresses the new features of the electronic sprea...
ware. During the session, you will build worksheets with calculat...
graphs. Bring a blank formatted disk to the seminar.

Integrating Your Software *(December 15, 1995, 2:00 p.m. - 4.*

This seminar illustrates how to merge worksheet data and graph...
processing documents. Bring a disk containing one word proces...
one electronic spreadsheet file.

These training seminars will be held in Room C-312. Once you h...
selections(s), please check with your supervisor and then call m...
290 to make a reservation.

Landscape Orientation

Village Creek Industries
Personnel Database

Last Name	First Name	Hire Date	Age	Gender	Education	Department	Title	Salary
Hoika	Janice	11/12/71	60	F	BS	R&D	Engineer	52,500
Webb	Marci	2/4/95	34	F	AAS	Computer	Programmer	36,500
Ling	Jodi	2/26/92	25	F	MS	Computer	Analyst	47,400
Webster	Jeffrey	5/22/84	47	M	AAS	R&D	Technician	36,250
Sabol	Lisa	7/15/94	52	F	BS	Marketing	Manager	47,500
Chin	Ben	1/5/89	22	M	HS	Administration	Clerk	18,500
Brown	Jeremiah	9/4/87	29	M	PhD	R&D	Engineer	48,900
Sobalski	Joseph	9/2376	44	M	BS	Marketing	Telemarketer	29,700
Raih	Niki	5/18/79	36	F	AAS	Administration	Receptionist	24,300
Nyguen	Sue	1/17/82	32	F	BS	Computer	Programmer	43,200
Stephens	James	6/22/84	31	M	HS	Mail Room	Clerk	17,400
Rae	Amy	11/26/92	57	F	MS	Production	Manager	52,200
McCarthy	Kevin	1/11/80	62	M	MA	Personnel	Director	57,600
Dolar	Laura	11/2/85	46	F	AA	Production	Supervisor	46,000

Figure 2-8
Most correspondence is printed in portrait orientation; printing across the narrower portion of a sheet of paper. In landscape orientation, the printing goes across the wider portion of the paper.

- Page Numbers, Headers, and Footers. Most word processors can automatically apply page numbers to any location on the page. Page numbers can be started at a particular number and can appear in a font different from the main body of text. **Headers** and **footers** allow you to place the same information at the top or bottom of each page. A company name, report title, date, or page number are examples of items that may appear in a header or footer.
- Style Sheets. A **style sheet** lets you save font and format information so it can be applied to new documents. A style sheet can save you considerable time if you use different formatting techniques on frequently created documents. Company letterhead, a memorandum, or a report that is prepared each month are examples of items that could use style sheets.

Printing

Most word processors give the user many options other than printing a single copy of the entire document.

- Number of Copies and Pages. The capability to print individual pages and a range of pages (for example, pages 2 through 7) is usually available. In addition, the user can specify how many copies are to be printed.
- Portrait and Landscape. **Portrait** printing means that the paper is taller than it is wide. Most letters are printed in portrait orientation. **Landscape** printing means that the paper is wider than it is tall. Tables with a large number of columns are often printed in landscape orientation. See *Figure 2-8* for examples.
- Print Preview. **Print preview** *(Figure 2-9)* allows the user to see on the screen how the document will look when it is printed. In print preview you can see one or more pages. Even though the text may be too small to read, you can review the overall appearance and decide if the page needs additional formatting.

With the features available in word processing packages, users can easily and efficiently create professional looking documents. Packages such as WordPerfect and Microsoft Word may contain enough features to satisfy the desktop publishing needs of many users. However, the document design capabilities of desktop publishing packages still exceed the capabilities of word processing software.

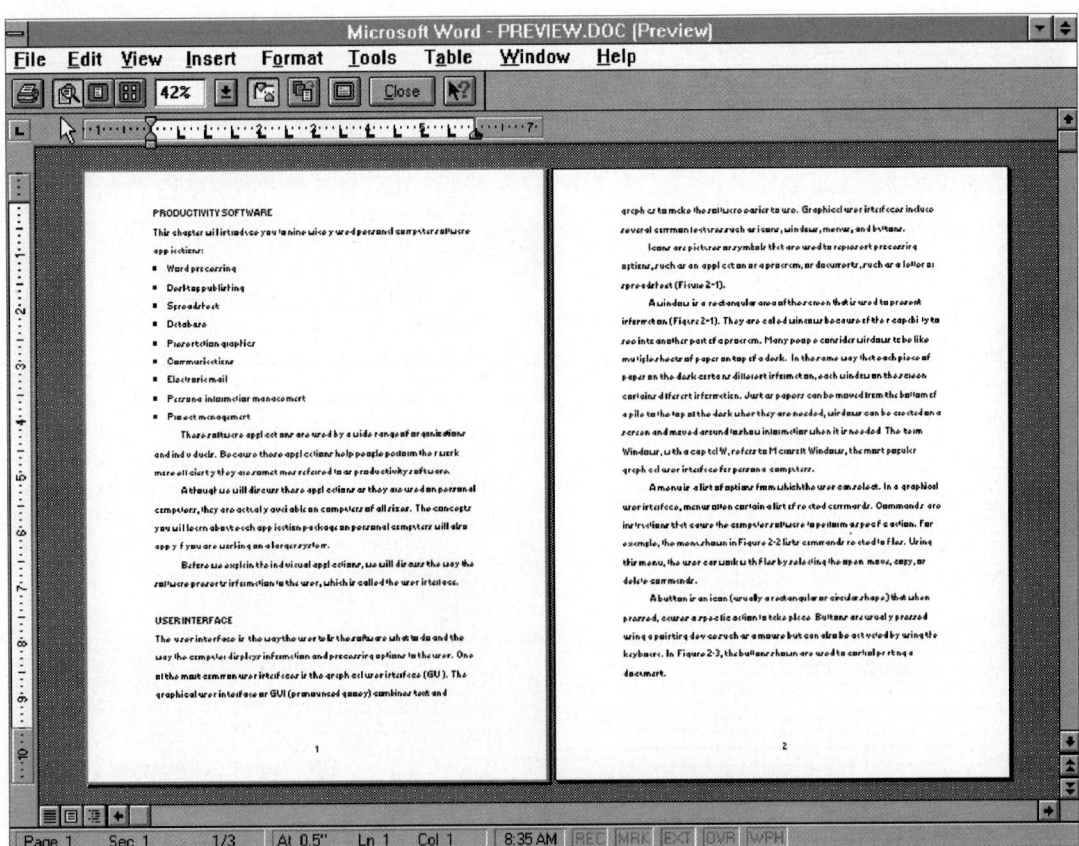

Figure 2-9
Print preview allows you to see on the screen how the document will look when it is printed. This feature helps you decide if the overall appearance of the document is acceptable or if the document needs more formatting.

Desktop Publishing Software

Desktop publishing (DTP) software allows users to design and produce professional looking documents that contain both text and graphics *(Figure 2-10)*. Examples of such documents include newsletters, marketing literature, technical manuals, and annual reports. Documents of this type were previously created by slower, more expensive traditional publishing methods such as typesetting.

Whereas word processing software is designed to manipulate text, DTP software focuses on page composition and layout. **Page composition and layout**, sometimes called **page makeup**, is the process of arranging text and graphics on a document page. The text and graphics used by a DTP program are frequently imported from other software packages. For example, because text manipulation capabilities of word processing packages exceed those offered in DTP packages, text is usually created with a word processor and then transferred into the desktop publishing package. Graphics objects, such as illustrations, and photographs, are also imported from other software packages. Illustration software that is designed for use by artists, such as Corel Draw and Aldus Freehand, is often used to create graphics for DTP documents.

Business\Credit   Business\Globe   Business\File

Business\Head   Business\Dice

Figure 2-11
Clip art consists of previously created illustrations that can be added to documents. Clip art usually comes in collections of individual images that are grouped by type. These clip art examples are from a business collection.

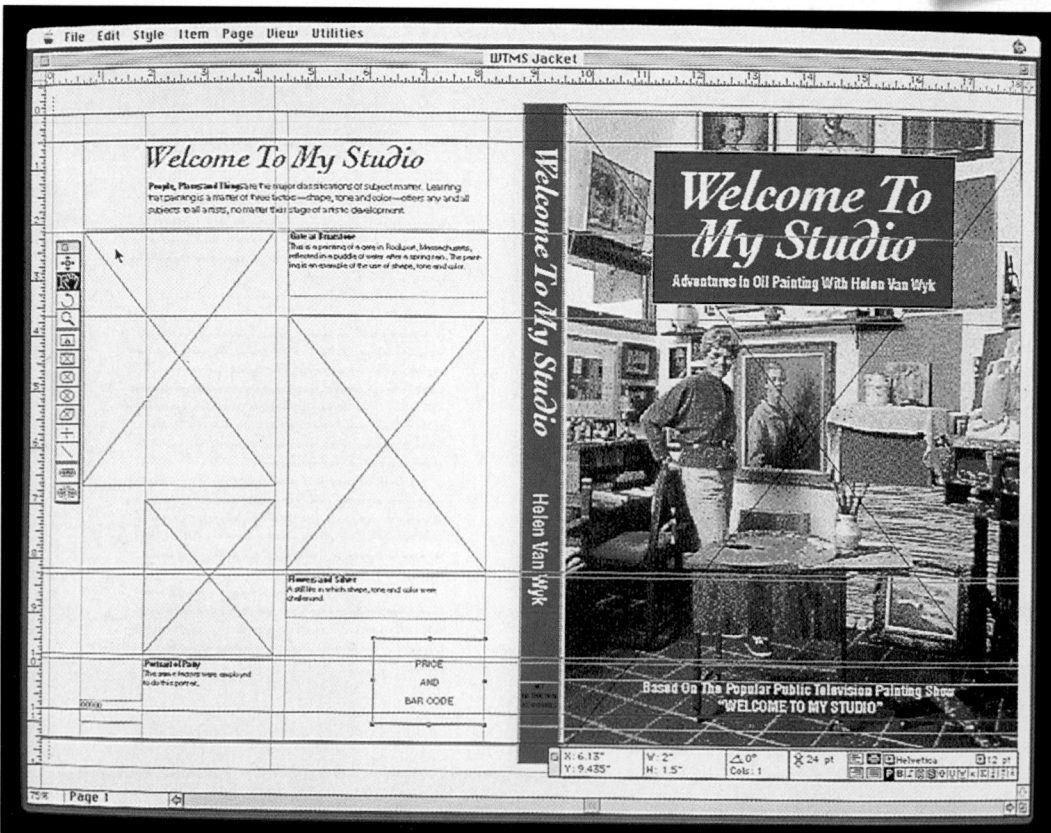

Figure 2-10
Desktop publishing software is used to create professional looking documents that combine text, graphics, illustrations, and photographs.

In addition, DTP documents often make use of previously created art, called **clip art**, that is sold in collections. Collections of clip art contain several hundred to several thousand images grouped by type, such as holidays, vehicles, or people. *Figure 2-11* shows examples of different clip art. Input devices, called scanners, can also be used to import photographs and art into DTP documents.

To aid the user in the process of page layout and design, all DTP programs display information on the screen exactly as it will look when printed. This capability is called WYSIWYG (pronounced whiz-e-wig). **WYSIWYG** is an acronym for What You See Is What You Get. Although many application programs now offer the WYSIWYG feature, DTP software packages were among the first.

Some of the other page composition and layout features that distinguish DTP software include the following (some of these features are illustrated in *Figure 2-12*):

- Capability to increase or decrease the size of graphic objects
- Capability to rotate text and graphics objects
- Backgrounds of different shades, colors, and textures
- Large page sizes (up to 18" by 24")
- Capability to flow text around irregularly shaped objects

- Capability to easily add or delete entire columns or pages
- Rulers and guides for aligning text and graphics
- Precise horizontal and vertical spacing control
- Color control

The capability to print DTP documents relies on a page definition language. A **page definition language**, such as **PostScript**, describes the document to be printed in language the printer can understand. The printer, which includes a page definition language translator, interprets the instructions and prints the document. Using a page definition language enables a DTP document created on one computer system to be printed on another computer with a different printer, as long as the second printer has a compatible page definition language.

With desktop publishing, users can now create professional looking documents on their own computers and produce work that previously could only be done by graphic artists. By using desktop publishing, both the cost and time of producing quality documents is significantly decreased. Popular desktop publishing packages include PageMaker, QuarkXpress, and Corel Ventura.

Figure 2-12
Some of the features available in the PageMaker desktop publishing software package are shown in this screen.

Spreadsheet Software

Spreadsheet software allows you to organize numeric data in a worksheet or table format called an **electronic spreadsheet** or **spreadsheet**. Manual methods, those done by hand, have long been used to organize numeric data in this manner *(Figure 2-13)*. You will see that the data in an electronic spreadsheet is organized in the same manner as it is in a manual spreadsheet. Within a spreadsheet, data is organized vertically in **columns** and horizontally in **rows**. Columns are usually identified by a letter and rows by a number. The intersection where a column and row meet is called a **cell** *(Figure 2-14)*. Cells are named by their location in the spreadsheet. In *Figure 2-14,* the cursor is on cell C2, the intersection of column C and row 2.

Cells may contain three types of data: labels (text), values (numbers), and formulas. The text, or **labels**, as they are called, identify the data and help document the worksheet.

Good spreadsheets contain descriptive labels. The rest of the cells in a spreadsheet may appear to contain numbers, or **values**. However, some of the cells actually contain formulas. The **formulas** perform calculations on the data in the spreadsheet and display the resulting value in the cell containing the formula. Formulas can be created by the user or can use functions that come with the spreadsheet software. **Functions** are stored formulas that perform common calculations, such as adding a range of cells, or generating a value such as the time or date. *Figure 2-15* is a list of functions found in most spreadsheet packages.

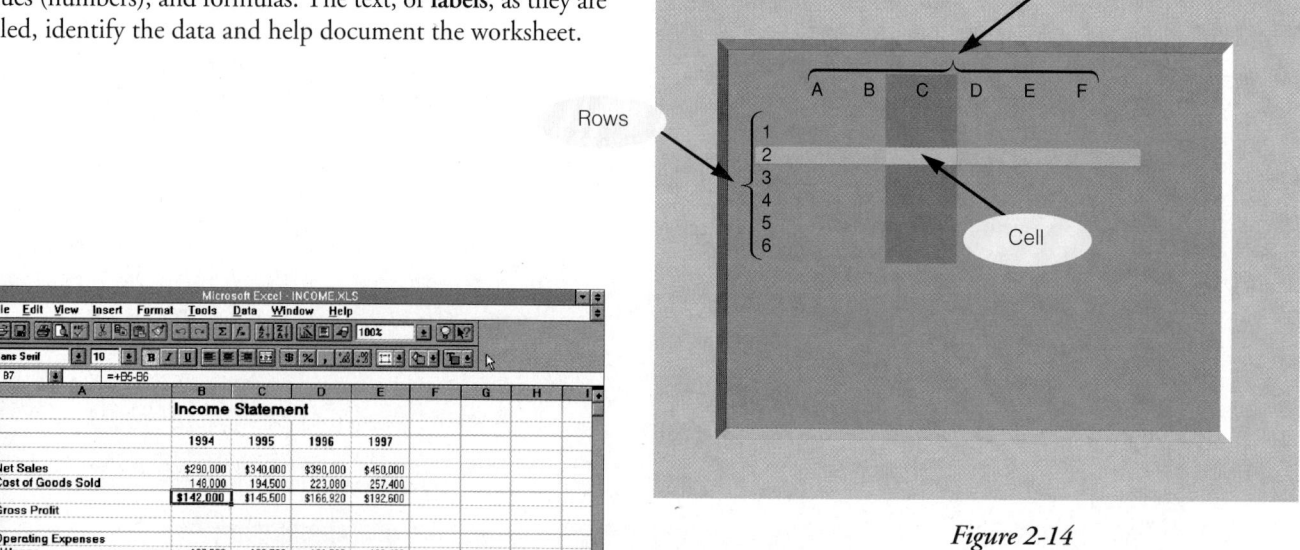

Figure 2-14
In a spreadsheet, columns refer to the vertical lines of data and rows refer to the horizontal lines of data. Columns are identified by letters and rows are identified by numbers. The intersection of a column and row is called a cell.

Figure 2-13
The electronic spreadsheet above still uses the column and row format of the manual spreadsheet on the right.

By developing a simple spreadsheet to calculate the profit and profit % from three months of revenues and costs, you will see how a spreadsheet works. As shown in *Figure 2-16*, the first step in creating the spreadsheet is to enter the labels, or titles. These should be short but descriptive, to help you organize the layout of the data in your spreadsheet.

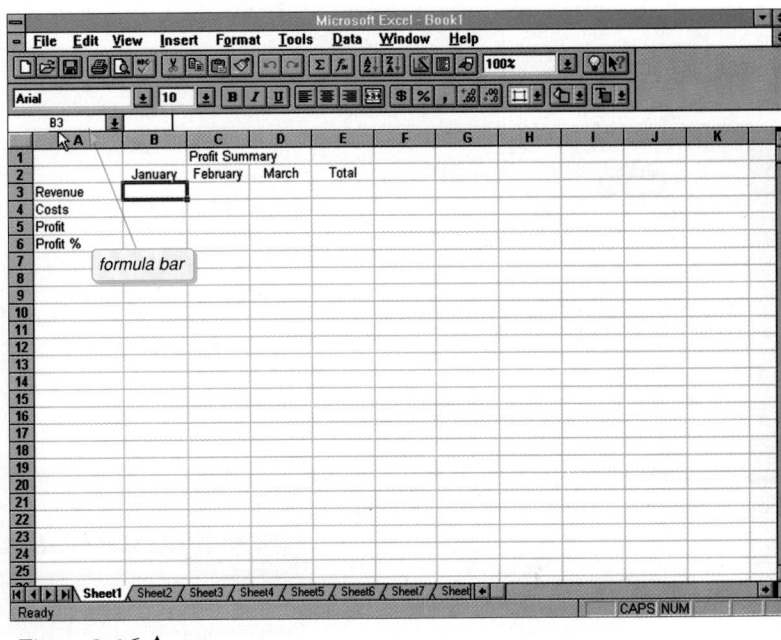

Figure 2-15 ▼
Spreadsheet functions are predefined formulas that perform calculations or return information based on given data. This is just a partial list of some of the more common functions. Probably the most often used function is SUM, which is used to add a range of numbers.

Figure 2-16 ▲
Labels such as January, February, Revenue, and Costs are entered in the spreadsheet to identify columns and rows of data. The formula bar shows the address and contents of the active cell. Here, the active cell is B3 (column B, row 3). Nothing has been entered for this cell, so the formula bar shows only the cell address.

SPREADSHEET FUNCTIONS

FINANCIAL

FV (rate, number of periods, payment)	Calculates the future value of an investment.
NPV (rate, range)	Calculates the net present value of an investment.
PMT (rate, number of periods, present value)	Calculates the periodic payment for an annuity.
PV (rate, number of periods, payment)	Calculates the present value of an investment.
RATE (number of periods, payment, present value)	Calculates the periodic interest rate of an annuity.

DAY & TIME

DATE	Returns the current date.
NOW	Returns the current date and time.
TIME	Returns the current time.

MATHEMATICAL

ABS (number)	Returns the absolute value of a number.
INT (number)	Rounds a number down to the nearest integer.
LN (number)	Calculates the natural logarithm of a number.
LOG (number, base)	Calculates the logarithm of a number to a specified base.
ROUND (number, number of digits)	Rounds a number to a specified number of digits.
SQRT (number)	Calculates the square root of a number.
SUM (range)	Calculates the total of a range of numbers.

STATISTICAL

AVERAGE (range)	Calculates the average value of a range of numbers.
COUNT (range)	Counts how many cells in the range have entries.
MAX (range)	Returns the maximum value in a range.
MIN (range)	Returns the minimum value in a range.
STDEV (range)	Calculates the standard deviation of a range of numbers.

LOGICAL

IF (logical test, value if true, value if false).	Performs a test and returns one value if test is true and another value if test is false.

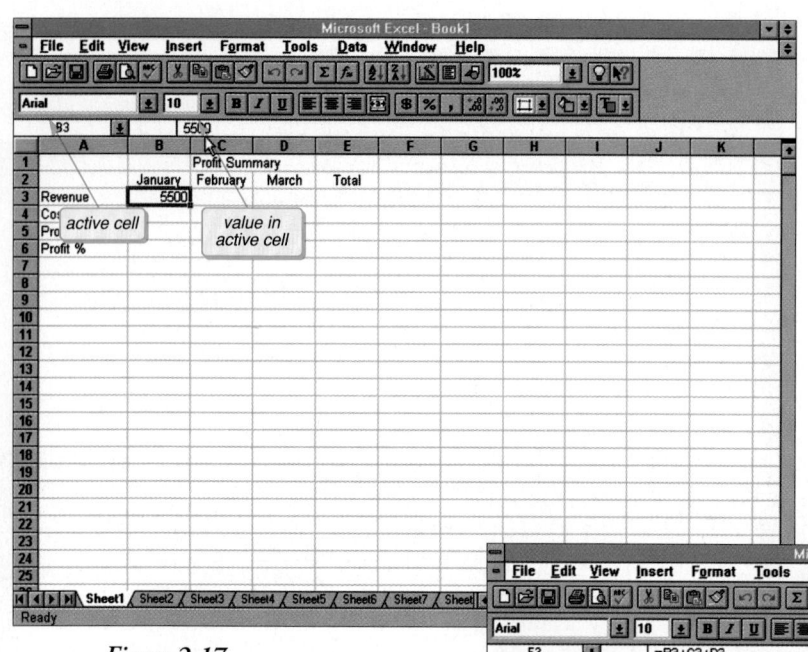

The next step is to enter the data, or numbers, in the body of the spreadsheet (*Figure 2-17*). The final step is to enter the formulas that calculate the totals. For some spreadsheets, formulas are entered before the data.

In a manual spreadsheet, you would have to calculate each of the totals by hand or with your calculator. In an electronic spreadsheet, you simply enter a formula into the cell where the total is to appear. The total is calculated and displayed automatically (*Figure 2-18*).

Once a formula is entered into a cell, it can be copied to any other cell that requires a similar formula. Usually when a formula is copied, the cell references are automatically updated to reflect the new location. For example, in *Figure 2-19*, when the formula is copied from cell E5 to cell E6, the formula changes from

Figure 2-17
The value 5500 is entered and stored in cell B3. The formula bar now displays both the active cell address and the cell value.

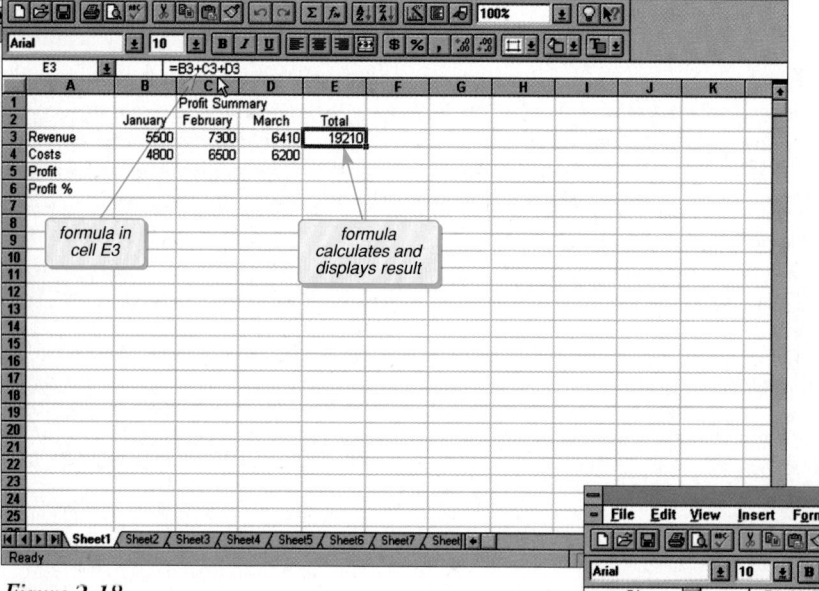

Figure 2-18
The remaining values are entered in cells C3, D3, B4, C4, and D4. A formula is entered in cell E3. The formula specifies that cell E3 is to be the sum of the values in cells B3, C3, and D3. Cell E3 displays the numeric sum. The formula bar at the top of the screen, however, shows the formula that calculates the value in that cell.

Figure 2-19
The formula required for cell E4 is similar to the one for cell E3; it totals the amounts in the three previous columns. When the formula is copied from cell E3 to cell E4, the software automatically changes the cell references from B3, C3, and D3 to B4, C4, and D4.

B5+C5+D5 to B6+C6+D6. This automatic updating of the formula is called **relative referencing**.

If you are going to copy a formula but always want the formula to refer to the same cell location, you would use **absolute referencing**. For example, if you had a single tax rate that was going to be used to calculate taxes on the amounts in more than one cell, you would make an absolute reference to the cell containing the tax rate. To make a cell an absolute reference, you place a dollar sign in front of the column and row. E5 in a formula would be an absolute reference to cell E5. As the formula is copied, the formula calculations are performed automatically. After entering the remaining formulas, the spreadsheet is complete *(Figure 2-20)*.

One of the more powerful features of the electronic spreadsheet occurs when the data in a spreadsheet changes. To appreciate the capabilities of spreadsheet software, consider how a change is handled in a manual system. When a value in a manual spreadsheet changes, you must erase it and write a new value into the cell. You must also erase all cells that contain calculations referring to the value that

changed and then you must recalculate these cells and enter the new result. For example, the row totals and column totals would be updated to reflect changes to any values within their areas. In a large manual spreadsheet, accurately posting changes and updating the values affected would be time consuming and new errors could be introduced. But posting changes on an electronic spreadsheet is easy. You change data in a cell by simply entering in the new value. All other values that are affected are updated automatically. *Figure 2-21* shows that if you change the value in cell C3 from 7300 to 8000, five other cell values will automatically change. On a computer, the updating happens almost instantly.

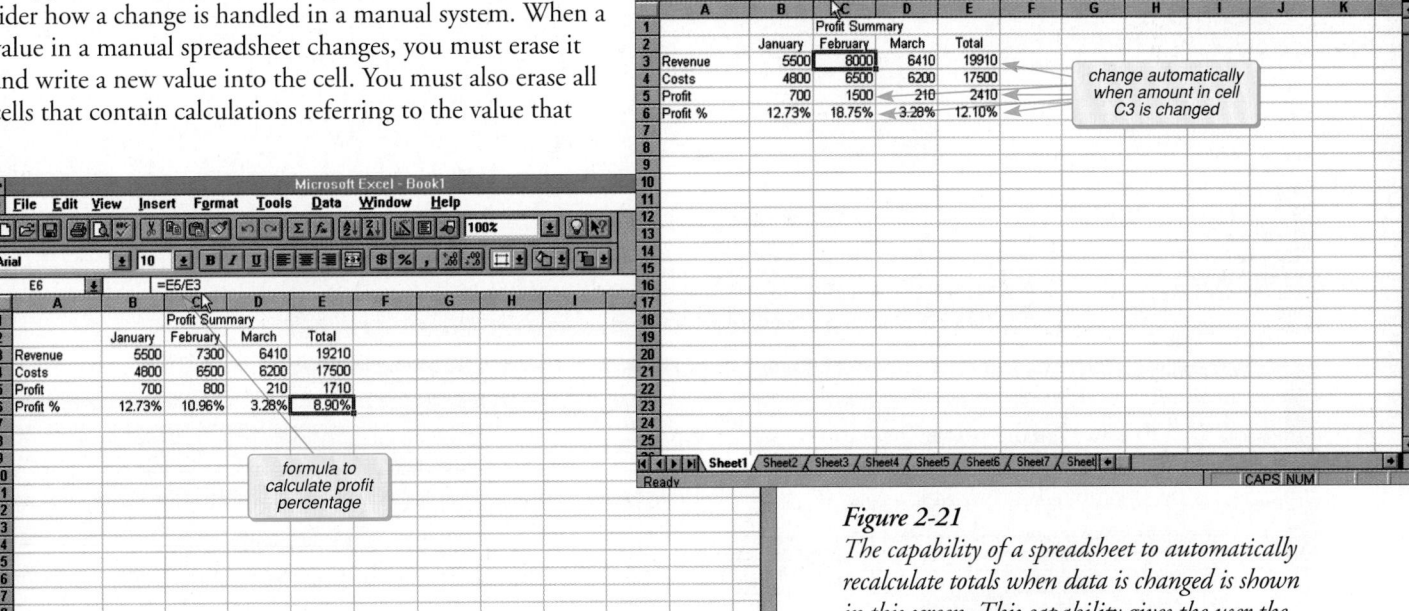

Figure 2-21
The capability of a spreadsheet to automatically recalculate totals when data is changed is shown in this screen. This capability gives the user the ability to quickly see the total impact of changing one or more numbers in a spreadsheet. Using the spreadsheet shown in Figure 2-20, one number was changed; the Revenue amount for February. This one change results in five numbers automatically recalculating in the spreadsheet.

Figure 2-20
In the completed spreadsheet, the value in cell E6 is derived from the formula in the formula bar, which specifies that the value in cell E5 is to be divided by the value in cell E3 (the slash character indicates division).

A spreadsheet's capability to recalculate when data is changed makes it a valuable tool for decision making. This capability is sometimes called **what-if analysis** because the results of different assumptions ("what-if we changed this ...") can be quickly seen.

A standard feature of spreadsheet packages is the capability to create **charts** that graphically present the relationship of numerical data. Visual representation of data in charts often makes it easier to analyze and interpret information. The types of charts provided by spreadsheet packages are sometimes called **analytical graphics** or **business graphics** because they are primarily used for the analysis of numerical data by businesses. *Figure 2-22* shows the chart types offered in one spreadsheet package.

Most of these charts are variations on three basic chart types; line charts, bar charts and pie charts. **Line charts** are effective for showing a trend as indicated by a rising or falling line. If the area below or above a line is filled in with a color or pattern, it is called an area chart. **Bar charts** display bars of various lengths to show the relationship of data *(Figure 2-23)*. The bars can be horizontal, vertical (sometimes called columns), or stacked one on top of the other. **Pie charts**, so called because they look like a pie cut into pieces, are effective for showing the relationship of parts to a whole. Pie charts are often used for budget presentations to show how much each part of the budget is a percentage of the total. To improve their appearance, most charts can be displayed or printed in a three-dimensional (3-D) format.

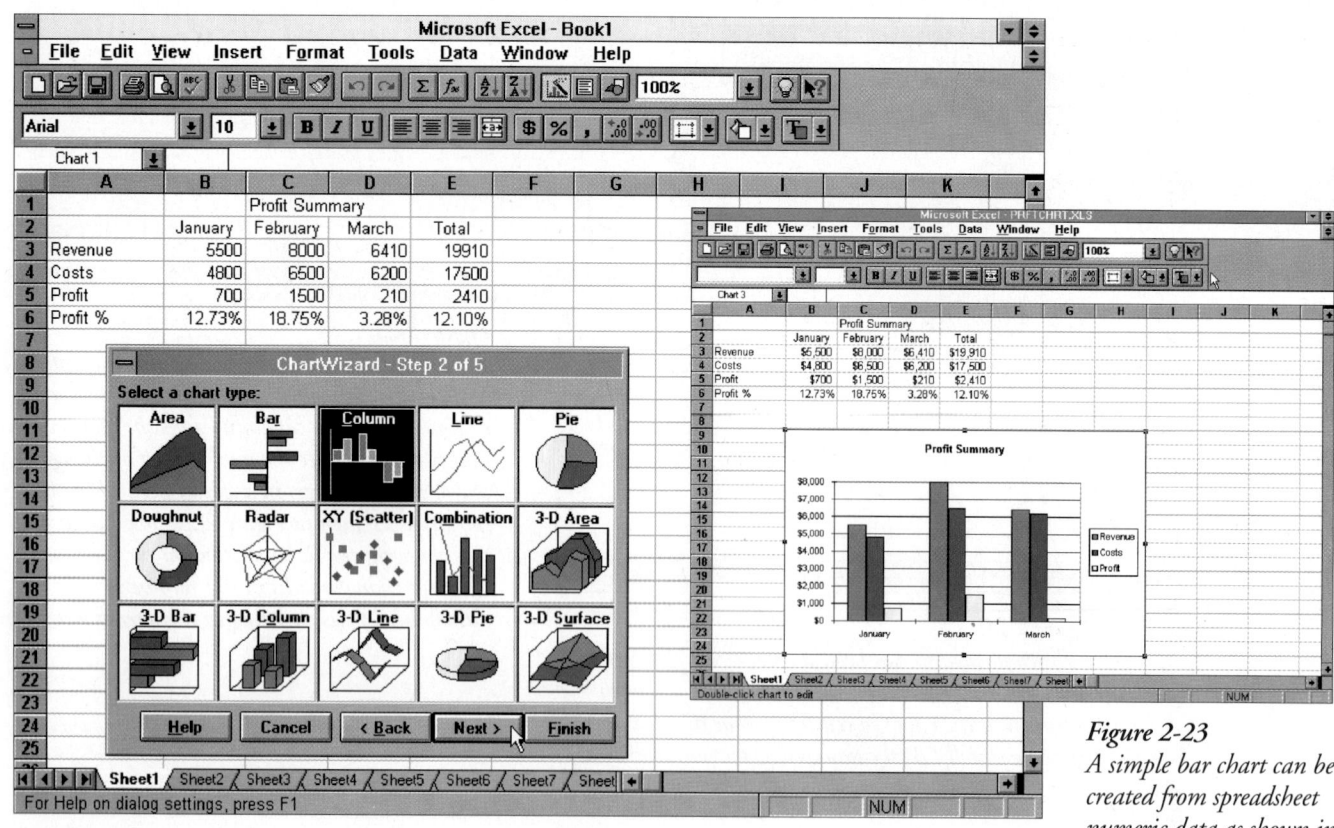

Figure 2-22
Spreadsheet data can be used to create numerous types of charts. This screen shows 15 types of charts that are available with the Microsoft Excel spreadsheet package.

Figure 2-23
A simple bar chart can be created from spreadsheet numeric data as shown in this Excel screen.

Besides the capability to manipulate numbers, spread-sheet packages have many formatting features that can improve the overall appearance of the data. These include typefaces, sizes, and styles, borders and lines, and shading and colors to highlight data. *Figure 2-24* shows the spreadsheet with some of these features added.

Spreadsheets are one of the most popular software packages and have been adapted to a wide range of business and nonbusiness applications. Some of the popular packages used today are Lotus 1-2-3, Microsoft Excel, and Quattro Pro.

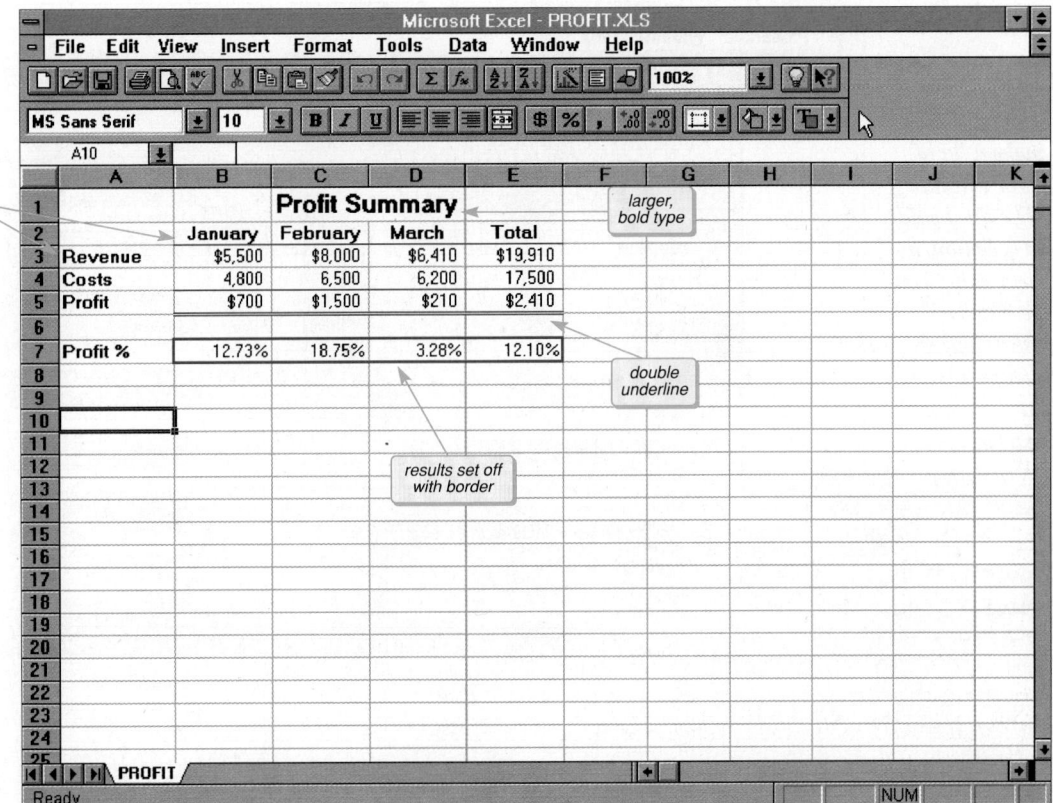

Figure 2-24
This formatted spreadsheet shows how the formatting features improve the appearance of a document.

Database Software

A **database** refers to a collection of data that is stored in files. **Database software** allows you to create a database and to retrieve, manipulate, and update the data that you store in it. In a manual system *(Figure 2-25)*, data is recorded on paper and stored in a filing cabinet. In a database on the computer, the data will be stored in an electronic format on a secondary storage device such as a disk.

When you use a database, you need to be familiar with the terms file, record, and field. Just as in a manual system, the word **file** is a collection of related data that is organized in records. Each **record** contains a collection of related facts called **fields**. For example, an address file might consist of records containing name and address information. All the data that relates to one name would be considered a record. Each fact, such as the street address or phone number, is called a field.

The screens in *Figures 2-26* through *2-29* present the development of a database containing information about the members of a school band booster club. The booster club members donate money to help fund band activities. Besides keeping track of each member's name, address, and phone number, the band director wants to record the amount of money donated and the date the money was received.

A good way to begin creating a database is to make a list of the information you want to record. Each item that you want to keep track of will become a field in the database. Each field should be given a unique name that is short but descriptive. For example, the field name for a member's last name could be LNAME. The field name for a member's first

Figure 2-25
A database is similar to a manual system; related data items are stored in files.

Figure 2-26
One of the first steps in creating a database is to make a list of the items that will be included in the database. The list should include the item description, a short, one-word field name that will be used by the database, the length of the item, and the data type. Most databases allow you to add or delete fields after the database is created.

Band Booster Club

Item	Field Name	Length	Type
last name	LNAME	15	Alphanumeric
first name	FNAME	15	"
street	STREET	20	"
city	CITY	15	"
state	STATE	2	"
zip	ZIP	10	"
phone	PHONE	8	"
amount donated	AMOUNT	10	Currency
date paid	PAYDATE	8	Date
comments	COMMENTS	–	Memo

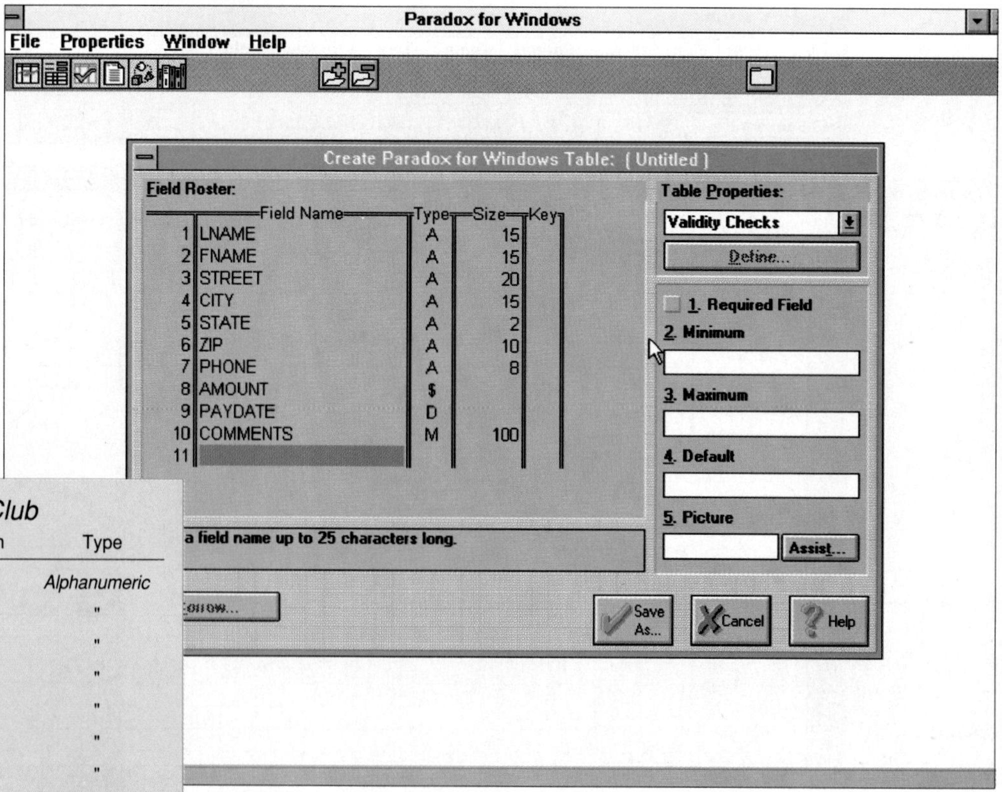

Paradox for Windows

File   Properties   Window   Help

Create Paradox for Windows Table: (Untitled)

Field Roster:

	Field Name	Type	Size	Key
1	LNAME	A	15	
2	FNAME	A	15	
3	STREET	A	20	
4	CITY	A	15	
5	STATE	A	2	
6	ZIP	A	10	
7	PHONE	A	8	
8	AMOUNT	$		
9	PAYDATE	D		
10	COMMENTS	M	100	
11				

Table Properties:

Validity Checks

Define...

1. Required Field

2. Minimum

3. Maximum

4. Default

5. Picture

Assist...

a field name up to 25 characters long.

Save As...   Cancel   Help

Figure 2-27
Fields are entered in the Paradox for Windows database.

name could be FNAME. Additional information that needs to be decided is the length of each field and the type of information that each field will contain. The type of information could be any of the following:

- **Alphanumeric** – letters, numbers, or special characters
- **Numeric** – numbers only
- **Currency** – dollar and cents amounts
- **Date** – month, day, and year information
- **Memo** – free form text of any type or length

A list of the information necessary for the band booster club is shown in *Figure 2-26*.

Each database program differs slightly in how it requires the user to enter the file and field information. A field entry screen from the Paradox for Windows database software package is shown in *Figure 2-27*.

After the database structure is created by defining the fields, individual database records can be entered. Usually, they are entered one at a time by using the keyboard. However, most database programs also have the capability to import data from other files. The information specified for each field helps the user in entering the data. For example, designating the DATE PAID field as a date field prevents

the user from entering anything other than a valid date. Comparing data entered against a predefined format or value is called **validation** and is an important feature of database programs. *Figure 2-28* shows the entry screen for the band booster club data.

After the records are entered, the database can be used to produce information. All or some of the records can be selected and arranged in the order specified by the user. This is one of the most powerful features of a database; the capability to retrieve database information based on criteria specified by the user. For example, suppose the band director wanted to personally call and thank all the booster club members who donated more than $100. A report, called a **query** could be produced that listed the members names, phone numbers, and the amounts and dates donated. An example of such a report is shown in *Figure 2-29*.

As shown in the band boosters club example, database software assists users in creating files and storing, manipulating, and retrieving data. Popular software packages that perform these functions include dBASE, FoxPro, Microsoft Access, and Paradox.

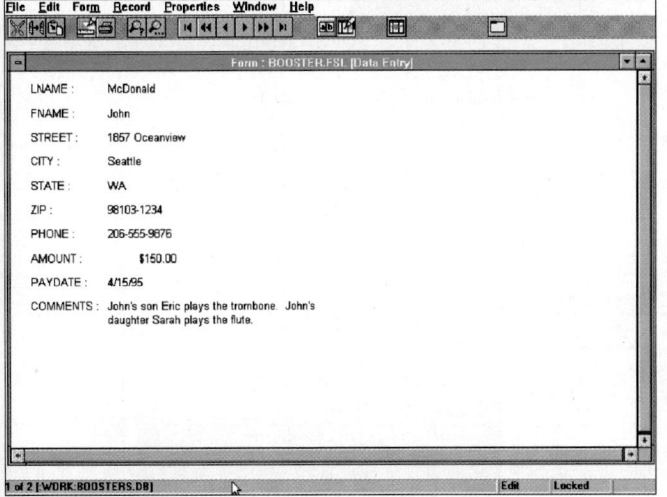

Figure 2-28
Once the database fields are defined, data can be entered. Most database programs automatically create a data entry form based on information that was entered for the fields. This Paradox for Windows data entry form lists each of the database fields in the order they were entered. Advanced database features can be used to design more complex data entry forms.

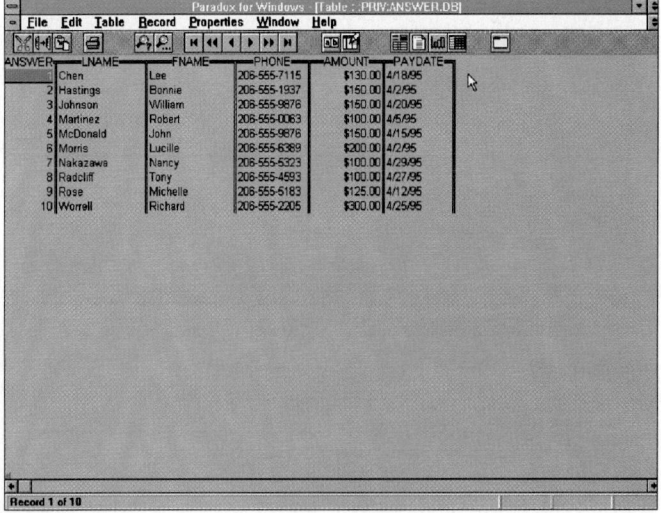

Figure 2-29
Database software packages can produce reports based on criteria specified by the user. For example, this screen shows the result of a request, called a query, that specified the name and phone number of each booster club member that contributed $100 or more. The amount and date of the contribution were also requested. The results of the query can be displayed on the screen or printed.

Presentation Graphics Software

Presentation graphics software allows the user to create documents, called **slides**, that are used in making presentations before a group *(Figure 2-30)*. The slides can be displayed on a large monitor or projected on a screen. Presentation graphics goes beyond analytical graphics by offering the user a wider choice of presentation features. Some of the features included with most presentation graphics packages include:
- Numerous chart types
- Three-dimensional effects for charts, text, and graphics
- Special effects such as shading, shadows, and textures
- Color control that includes preestablished groups of complementary colors for backgrounds, lines and text, shadows, fills, and accents
- Image libraries that include clip art graphics that can be incorporated into the slides; the image libraries are usually business oriented and include illustrations of factories, people, money, and other business-related art

Besides the slides, presentation graphics packages create several other documents that can be used in a presentation *(Figure 2-31)*. *Outlines* include only the text from each slide, usually the slide title and the key points. A *notes page* is used

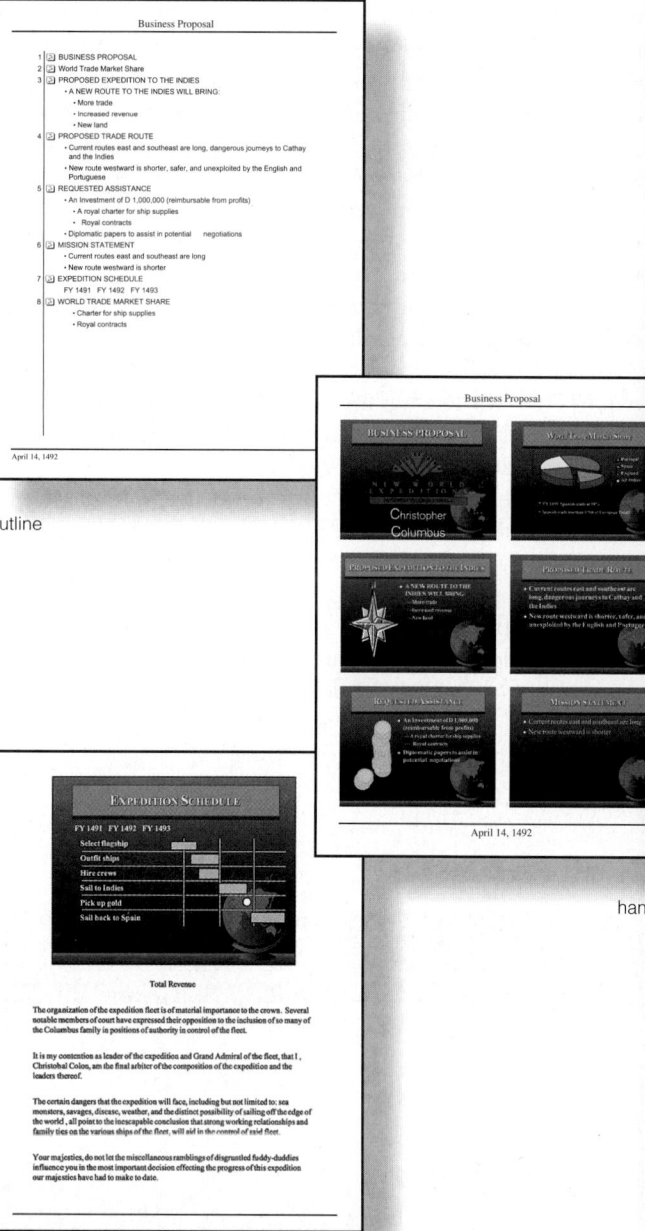

outline

han

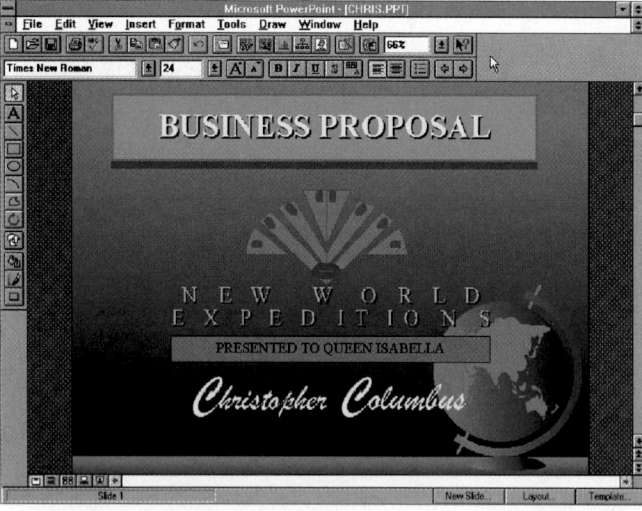

Figure 2-30
Presentation graphics software is used to prepare slides used in making presentations. The slides can be displayed on a computer, projected on a screen, or printed and handed out. The presentation graphics software includes many features to control graphics objects and color to make the slides more visually interesting.

notes page

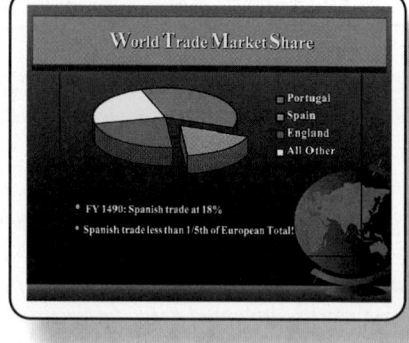

transparency

Figure 2-31
Documents that can be created with presentation software packages.

by the speaker making the presentation and includes a picture of the slide and any notes the speaker wants to see when he or she is discussing the slide. Audience *handouts* include images of two or more slides on a page that can be given to people who attended the presentation.

To help organize and present the slides, presentation graphics packages include slide sorters. A slide sorter presents a screen view similar to how 35mm slides would look on a photographer's light table *(Figure 2-32)*. By using a mouse or other pointing device, the user can arrange the slides in any order. When the slides are arranged in the proper order, they can be displayed one at a time by clicking the mouse or using the keyboard. The presenter can also set up the slides to be automatically displayed with a predetermined time delay between each slide. Special effects can also be applied to the transition between each slide. For example, one slide might slowly dissolve as the other slide comes into view.

Using presentation graphics software allows you to efficiently create professional quality presentations that help communicate information more effectively. Studies have shown that people are more likely to remember information they have seen as well as heard and that they recall 25% more information when it is presented in color. Popular presentation graphics packages include Microsoft PowerPoint, Aldus Persuasion, Lotus Freelance Graphics, and SPC Harvard Graphics.

Figure 2-32
This slide sorter screen shows a miniature version of each slide. Using a pointing device or the keyboard, the slides can be rearranged to change their order of presentation.

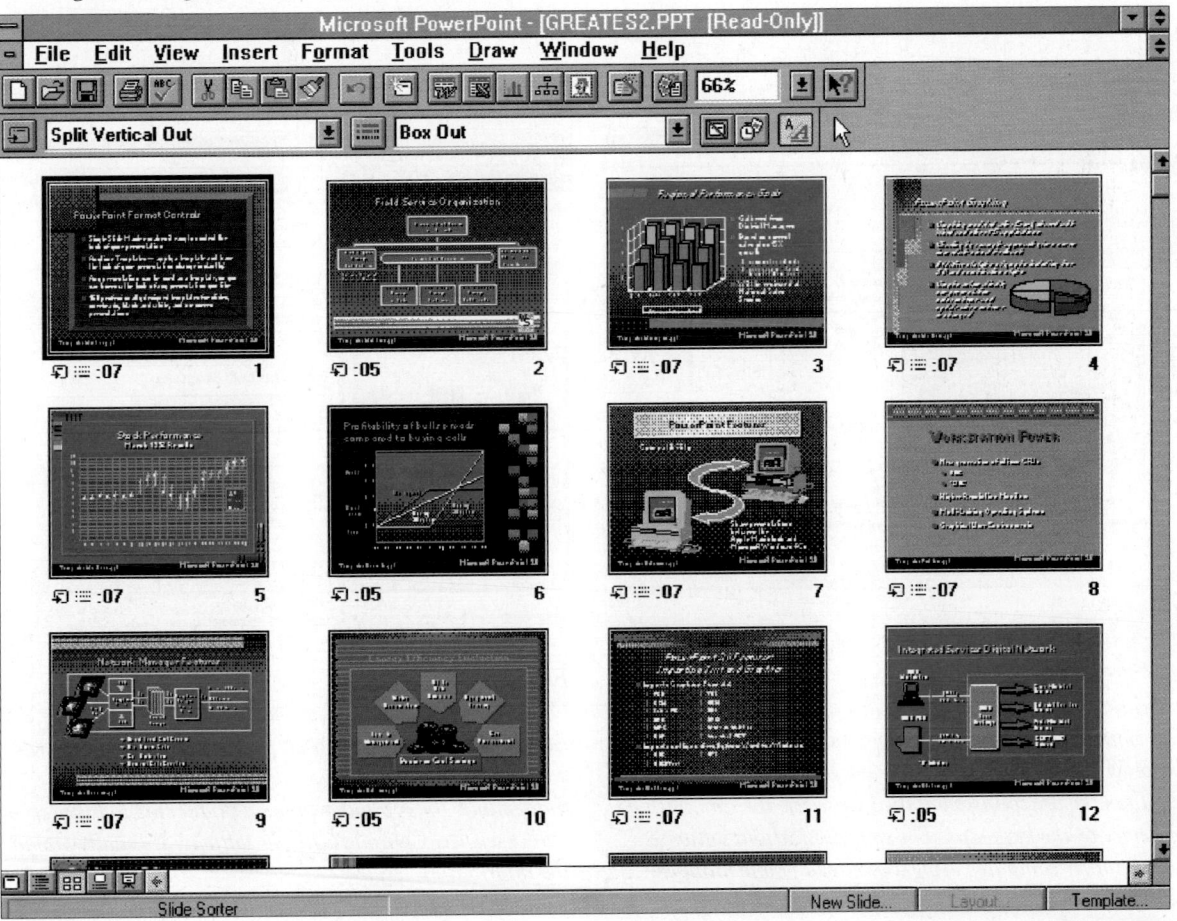

Data Communications Software

Data communications software is used to transmit data from one computer to another. For two computers to communicate, they each must have data communications software, data communications equipment, and be connected by some type of link such as a telephone line. Features that most data communications software packages include are:

- A dialing directory of phone numbers that can be used to automatically connect with other computer systems *(Figure 2-33)*
- Automatic redial that lets the user set the number of times the computer will keep trying to connect with another computer if the line is busy; a time delay between call attempts can also be set
- Automatic answer if another user tries to call your computer
- The capability to send or receive one or more data files

Communications software is frequently used by employees that are away from the office. Using communications software (and sometimes other packages such as E-mail), remote employees can check their messages, send messages to other employees, check the quantity of inventory on hand, and enter orders that they have just received from customers.

Communications software is also used to access online services for news, weather, financial, and travel information. Online service companies such as Prodigy and America Online provide a wide range of information for a small monthly fee *(Figure 2-34)*. Other service companies provide detailed information in subject areas such as medicine, finance, or specific industries. Shopping is also available from several services. Online shoppers can read a description and, in some cases, see a picture of a product on their screen. Using a credit card, the product can be ordered. More banks are now offering online banking. The user can review recent financial transactions, transfer money from one account to another, and even pay bills using his or her computer. All of these activities are made possible through the use of data communications software. Popular communications software packages are Crosstalk and Procomm Plus.

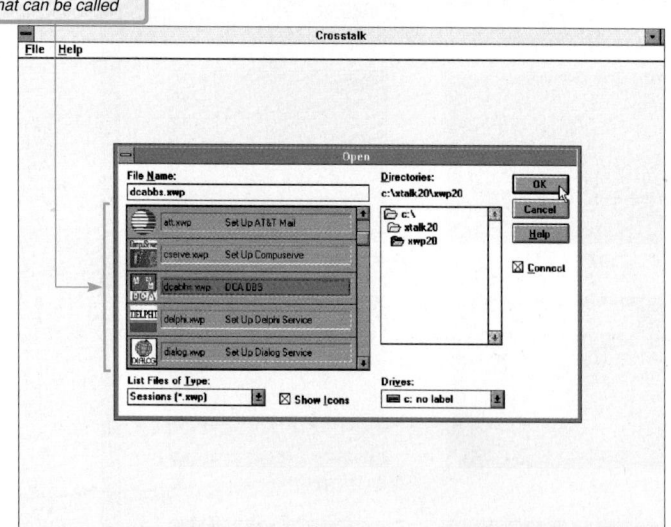

each icon represents
a remote computer
that can be called

Figure 2-33
Communications programs include dialing directories that make it easier to connect with other computers. In this screen from Crosstalk for Windows, each icon represents a computer that can be called. To make the connection, the user selects the icon with a pointing device or the keyboard. The communications software then dials the other computer using a prestored phone number and establishes the connection.

Figure 2-34
Online information services such as America Online offer a wide variety of information to their subscribers. The user needs to have a computer and a modem, a piece of communications equipment that enables the computer to use a phone line to connect to the online service. Communications software is usually provided by the information service.

Electronic Mail Software

Electronic mail software, also called **E-mail,** allows users to send messages to and receive messages from other computer users *(Figure 2-35).* The other users may be on the same computer network or on a separate computer system reached through the use of communications equipment and software. Each E-mail user has a mailbox and an address to which the mail can be sent. To make the sending of messages efficient, E-mail software allows the user to send a single message to a distribution list consisting of two or more individuals. The E-mail software takes care of copying the message and routing it to each person on the distribution list. For example, a message sent to the Department Supervisors distribution list would be routed to each of the department supervisors. E-mail systems usually have a mail waiting alert that notifies a user through a message or sound that a message is waiting to be read even if the user is working in another application.

Although E-mail is primarily used within private organizations, several communications companies (such as MCI) and online services providers (such as Prodigy and America Online) have established public E-mail facilities. For a small monthly fee, users can receive mail from and send mail to other users of the service. E-mail can be especially useful to people whose job keeps them away from the office. Remote workers can dial into their E-mail and send and receive messages at any time of the day. Because of its widespread use, informal rules, called E-mail etiquette, have been developed. These mostly common-sense rules include:

- Keep messages short and to the point.
- Avoid using E-mail for trivia, gossip, or other nonessential communications.
- Keep the distribution list to a minimum.
- Avoid using all capital letters – it is considered the same as yelling.
- It's okay (OK) for you (u) to (2) abbreviate as long as the abbreviation can be easily understood.
- Make the subject as meaningful as possible. Many E-mail systems list a summary of the mail and only show the subject, date, and sender.
- Read your mail regularly and clear messages that are no longer needed.

Popular E-mail packages are Microsoft Mail, Lotus CC:Mail, and Da Vinci eMAIL.

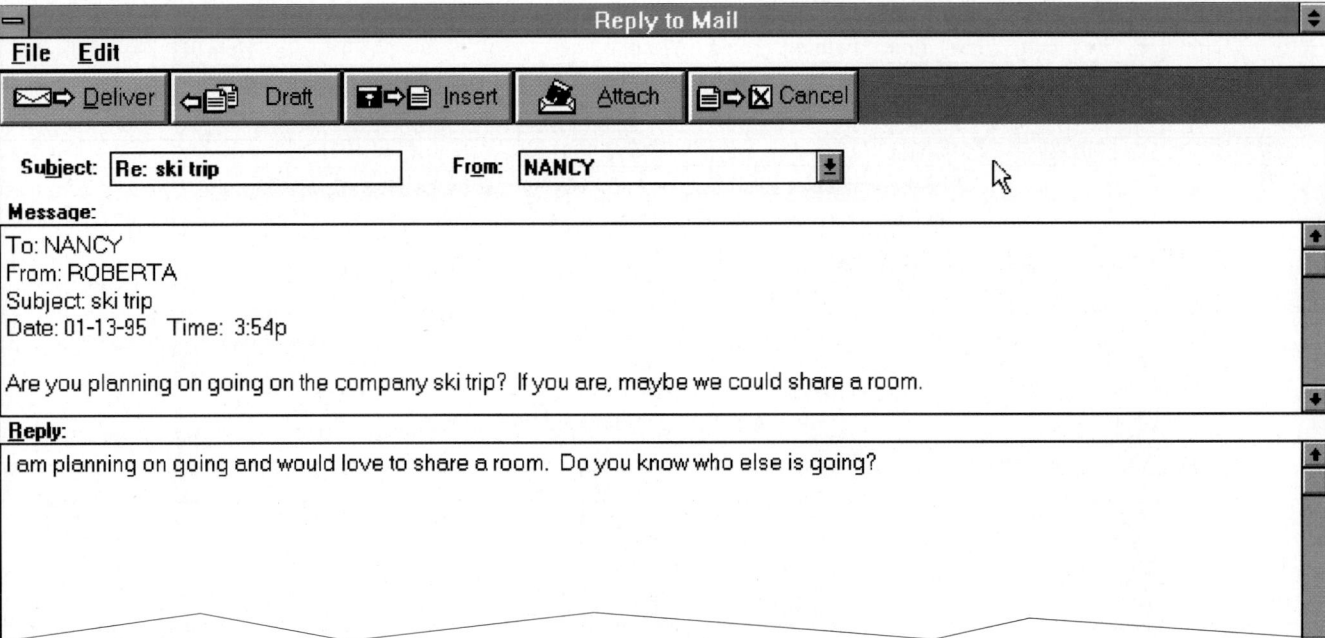

Figure 2-35
Electronic mail allows users to send and receive messages with other computer users. Each user has an electronic mail box to which messages are sent. This screen shows how a user can add a reply to a received message and then send the reply back to the person who sent the original message.

Personal Information Management

Personal information management (PIM) software helps users keep track of the miscellaneous bits of personal information that each of us deals with every day. This information can take many forms: notes to ourselves or from others, phone messages, notes about a current or future project, appointments, and so on. Programs that keep track of this type of information, such as electronic calendars, have been in existence for some time. In recent years, however, such programs have been combined so one package can keep track of all of a user's personal information.

Because of the many types of information that these programs can manage, it is difficult to precisely define personal information software. However, the category can be applied to programs that offer any of the following capabilities: appointment calendars, outliners, electronic notepads, data managers, and text retrieval. Some personal information software packages also include communications software capabilities such as phone dialers and electronic mail.

Appointment calendars allow you to schedule activities for a particular day and time *(Figure 2-36)*. Most of them will warn you if two activities are scheduled for the same time. Outliners allow you to *rough out* an idea by constructing and reorganizing an outline of important points and subpoints. Electronic notepads allow the user to record comments and assign them to one or more categories that can be used to retrieve the comments. Data managers are simple file management systems that allow the input, update, and retrieval of related records such as name and address lists or phone numbers. Text retrieval provides the capability to search files for specific words or phrases such as *Sales Meeting*. Two popular personal information management packages are Ecco and Commence.

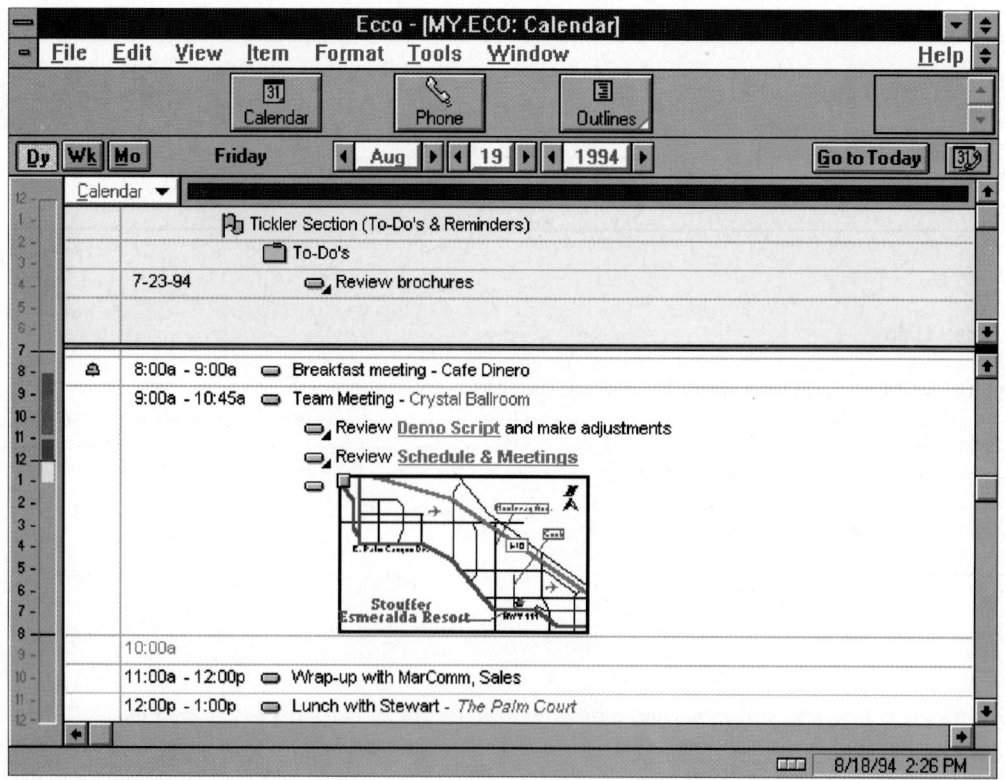

Figure 2-36
Personal information management (PIM) software helps organize and keep track of the many different types of information that people encounter each day. This screen shows the ECCO PIM software. In addition to text, graphics objects, such as the map, can be inserted in the calendar portion of the software.

Project Management

Project management software allows users to plan, schedule, track, and analyze the events, resources, and costs of a project *(Figure 2-37)*. For example, a construction company might use this type of software to manage the building of an apartment complex or a campaign manager might use it to coordinate the many activities of a politician running for office. The value of project management software is that it provides a method for managers to control and manage the variables of a project to help ensure that the project will be completed on time and within budget. Popular project management packages include Timeline and Microsoft Project.

Integrated Software

Software packages such as databases and electronic spreadsheets are generally used independently of each other; but what if you wanted to place information from a database into a spreadsheet? The data in the database would have to be reentered in the spreadsheet. This would be time consuming and errors could be introduced as you reentered the data. The inability of separate programs to easily communicate with one another and use a common set of data has been overcome through the use of integrated software.

Integrated software refers to packages that combine applications such as word processing, spreadsheet, and database into a single, easy-to-use set of programs. Many integrated packages also include communications capabilities. The applications that are included in integrated packages are designed to have a consistent command and menu structure. For example, the command to print a document looks and works the same in each of the integrated applications. Besides a consistent look and feel, a key feature of integrated packages is their capability to pass data quickly and easily from one application to another. For example, revenue and cost information from a database on daily sales could be

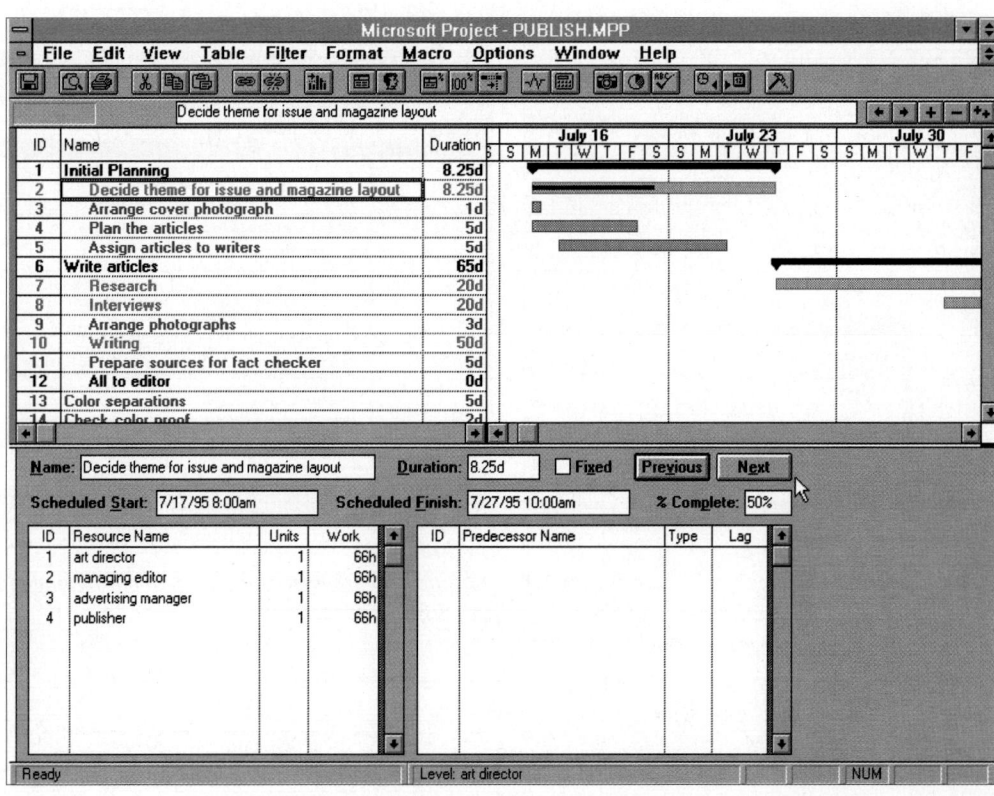

Figure 2-37
Project management software helps you plan and keep track of the tasks and resources necessary to complete a project. This screen shows part of a project plan for publishing a magazine. The most important tasks are listed in red. The bars in the upper right corner, called a Gantt chart, graphically indicate the duration of each task. The bottom portion of the screen identifies the resources required for the highlighted task; in this case, the hours needed from specific individuals.

quickly loaded into a spreadsheet. The spreadsheet could be used to calculate gross profits. Once the calculations are completed, all or a portion of the spreadsheet data can be passed to the word processing application to create a narrative report.

In their early days, integrated packages were criticized as being a collection of good but not great applications. To some extent this is still true. Users who need the most powerful word processor or spreadsheet will probably not be satisfied with the capabilities of an integrated application. For many users, however, the capabilities of today's integrated applications more than meet their needs. Besides the advantages of working well together, integrated applications are less expensive than buying comparable applications separately. Two popular integrated software packages are Microsoft Works and ClarisWorks.

Similar to integrated software are software **suites**; individual applications packaged in the same box and sold for a price that is significantly less than buying the applications individually. Although the use of suites was originally just a pricing strategy, it is becoming more and more like integrated software. First the individual packages were just bundled together for a good price; now they are being modified to work better together and offer the same command and menu structures. For the developer, the advantages of products that look and work the same include shorter development and training time, and easier customer support. Another advantage is that customers who have learned one application package are more likely to buy a second package if they know it works in a similar manner. Popular software suites include Microsoft Office, Lotus SmartSuite, and Novell PerfectOffice.

Figure 2-38
Four ways to learn application software packages.

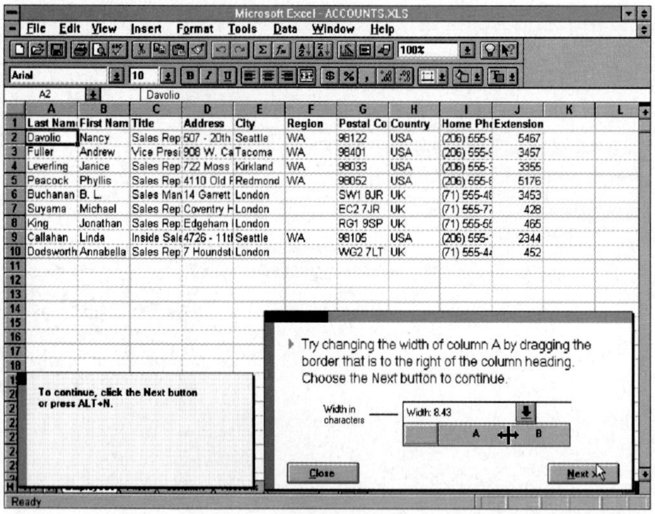

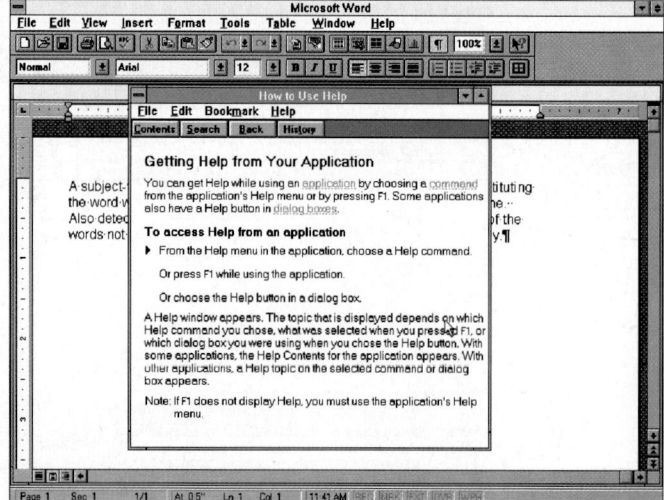

Figure 2-38a
Software tutorials help you learn an application while using the actual software on your computer. This screen shows how the Microsoft Excel tutorial teaches how to change the width of a column in a spreadsheet.

Figure 2-38b
Online help provides assistance without having to leave your application.

Learning Aids and Support Tools for Application Users

Learning to use an application software package involves time and practice. In addition to taking a class to learn how to use a software application, several learning aids and support tools are available to help you including: tutorials, online help, trade books, and keyboard templates *(Figure 2-38)*.

Tutorials are step-by-step instructions using real examples that show you how to use an application. Some tutorials are written manuals, but more tutorials are software based, allowing you to use your computer to learn about a package.

Online help refers to additional instructions that are available within the application. In most packages, a function key is reserved for the help feature. When you are using an application and have a question, pressing the designated *help* key will temporarily overlay your work on the screen with information on how to use the package. When you are finished using the help feature, pressing another key allows you to return to your work.

The documentation that accompanies software packages is frequently organized as reference material. This makes it very useful once you know how to use a package, but difficult to use when you are first learning it. For this reason, many **trade books** are available to help users learn to use the features of personal computer application packages. These books can be found where software is sold and are usually carried in regular bookstores.

Keyboard templates are plastic sheets that fit around a portion of your keyboard. The keyboard commands to select the various features of the application programs are printed on the template. Having a guide to the commands readily available is helpful for both beginners and experienced users. Many application software packages include keyboard templates.

Summary of Personal Computer Software Applications

In this chapter, you have learned about user interfaces and several widely used personal computer applications. The chapter covered the learning aids and support tools available for applications software. Knowledge about these topics increases your computer literacy and helps you to understand how personal computers are being used.

Figure 2-38c
Trade books are available for all popular software applications.

Figure 2-38d
Keyboard templates give you quick reference to software commands.

COMPUTERS AT WORK

Productivity Software Use High in Business

According to a recent report, more than $2 billion of productivity software applications are sold each year. By far, the largest user of this software is business, although home use is increasing. In a survey of 1,000 large businesses, nearly 100% of the companies said they used word processing and spreadsheet software. Close behind at approximately 95% are four applications; database, presentation graphics, communications, and electronic mail. Rounding out the applications were desktop publishing at 84%, project management at 72%, and personal information management at 48%. A survey of smaller businesses ranked the applications in the same order with slightly lower percentages. These results make it clear that productivity software is an essential part of business. Companies and individuals are turning to these software applications to work efficiently and become more productive. Project management is one of the fastest growing applications. Nowadays, practically every manager is a project manager. Likewise, many individuals are now using personal information management (PIM) software to manage their day-to-day activities.

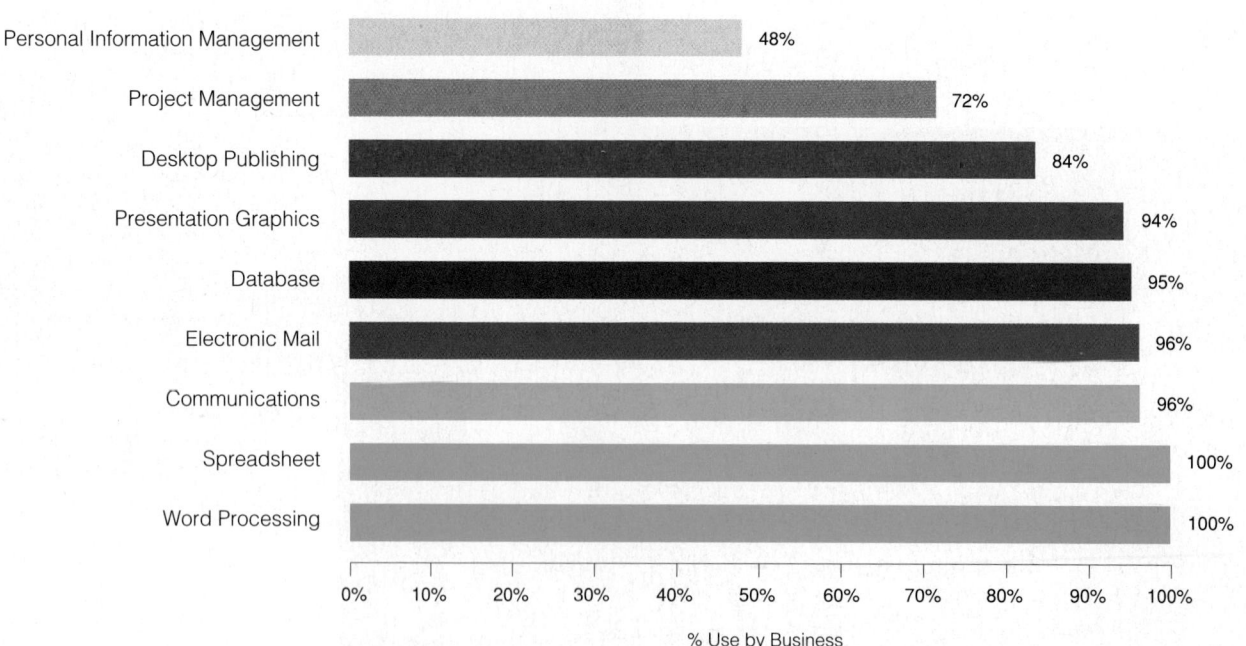

Productivity Software Use

Category	%
Personal Information Management	48%
Project Management	72%
Desktop Publishing	84%
Presentation Graphics	94%
Database	95%
Electronic Mail	96%
Communications	96%
Spreadsheet	100%
Word Processing	100%

% Use by Business

Figure 2-39

IN THE FUTURE

Will There Eventually Be Only One Software Superapplication?

Some people believe that individual software applications such as word processing and spreadsheets will eventually be replaced by a single *super*application that has the combined features of today's separate packages. They believe that the current software applications technology will become more standardized and thus easier to use for different document tasks. Some describe this evolution as a switch from application-oriented computing to document-oriented computing. The idea is that you shouldn't have to worry about what your document might contain before you start working on it. Even though the document may contain text, graphics, a spreadsheet, a chart, sound, or video, the necessary tools should be available as you need them.

Many worry that the trend toward superapplications will lead to less competition in the productivity software industry. Individual application developers will have a hard time competing against suites of applications that offer the user a common interface and one-call support. However, others see a continuing market for applications and individual tools that can be integrated with the superapplication. The same standardization that will enable the individual applications to be combined will enable independent developers to create tools that can replace or be added to the tools of the superapplication. For example, an artist may want a more powerful illustration tool than the one that comes with the superapplication. A salesperson who calls on five customers per day may want a more powerful personal information manager than a salesperson who makes one sales call per week. Other tools, such as a dictionary or a thesaurus, may be customized for specific professions such as law or medicine.

The trend toward the so-called superapplication was started with integrated software. Software suites with common toolbars and menus are the second step. How long will it be before we see ads for DocumentPerfect 1.0?

"To laugh often and love much; to win the respect of intelligent persons and the affection of children; to earn the approbation of honest critics and to endure the betrayal of false friends; to appreciate beauty; to find the best in others; to give of one's self; to leave the world a bit better, whether by a healthy child, a garden patch, or a redeemed social condition; to have played and laughed with exultation; to know that even one life has breathed easier because you have lived – this is to have succeeded."

Ralph Waldo Emerson

620,701
143,142
1,658,654
345,682

2,768,1

Figure 2-40

What You Should Know

1. Applications that help people perform their work more efficiently are sometimes referred to as **productivity software**.

2. A **user interface** is the way the user tells the software what to do and the way the computer displays information and processing options to the user. A **graphical user interface** (GUI) combines text and graphics to make software easier to use. Graphical user interfaces include several common features such as icons, windows, menus, and buttons.

3. **Icons** are pictures, or symbols, used to represent processing options. A **window** is a rectangular area of the screen that is used to present information. The term Windows refers to **Microsoft Windows**, the most popular graphical user interface for personal computers. A **menu** is a list of options from which the user can choose. In a graphical user interface, menus often contain a list of related **commands**, or instructions, that cause the computer software to perform a specific action. A **button** is an icon that, when selected, causes a specific action to take place.

4. **Word processing** involves the use of a computer to produce or modify documents that consist primarily of text. Although most people perform word processing using personal computers or larger computer systems that can also be used for other applications, **dedicated word processing systems**, that can only be used for word processing, also exist.

5. Producing a document using word processing usually involves the following steps: creating, editing, formatting, printing, and saving.

6. Creating a word processing document entails entering text, usually by using the keyboard. Key word processing features used during this step include **word wrap**, **scrolling**, and moving the **cursor**.

7. **Editing** is the process of making changes in the content of a document. Word processing editing features include **cut** (which electronically places text in a temporary storage location called the **Clipboard**), **paste**, **copy**, **insert**, **delete**, **search**, and **replace**. Other editing features include using a **spelling checker**, **thesaurus**, and **grammar checker**.

8. To **format** means to change the appearance of a document. Word processing features that can be used to format a document include **fonts**, a specific combination of **typeface** and **point** size, and **styles**, such as **bold**, *italic*, or <u>underline</u>. Formatting can also involve setting **margins**, changing **justification** or **alignment**, using **full justification**, altering the **spacing** between characters (using **monospacing** or **proportional spacing**), and adjusting **line spacing**. Most word processors can arrange text in columns, organize information in tables, and incorporate graphics. Word processors can also use a **border** or **shading**, and create **headers** and **footers**. A **style sheet** lets you save font and format information so it can be applied to new documents.

9. Most word processors give the user many printing options including number and copies of pages, **portrait** or **landscape orientation**, and **print preview**.

10. **Desktop publishing** (DTP) software allows users to design and produce professional looking documents that contain both text and graphics.

11. DTP software focuses on **page composition** and **layout**, sometimes called **page makeup**, which is the process of arranging text and graphics on a document page. The text and graphics used by a DTP program are frequently imported from other software packages. DTP documents often make use of previously created art, called **clip art**.

12. All DTP programs display information on the screen exactly as it will look when printed, a capability called WYSIWYG (an acronym from What You See Is What You Get).

13. The capability to print DTP documents relies on a **page definition language**, such as **PostScript**, which describes the document to be printed in language the printer can understand.

14. **Spreadsheet software** allows you to organize numeric data in a worksheet or table format called an **electronic spreadsheet** or **spreadsheet**.

15. Within a spreadsheet, data is organized vertically in **columns** and horizontally in **rows**. The intersection where a column and row meet is called a **cell**.

16. Cells may contain three types of data: **labels** (text), **values** (numbers), and **formulas** that perform calculations on the data in the spreadsheet and display the resulting value. **Functions** are stored formulas that perform common calculations. When formulas are copied to another cell, the formula can be automatically updated to the new location (**relative referencing**) or continue to refer to the same cell locations (**absolute referencing**).

17. A spreadsheet's capability to recalculate when data is changed, sometimes called **what-if analysis**, makes it a valuable tool for decision making.

18. A standard feature of spreadsheet packages is the capability to turn numeric data into a **chart** that graphically shows the relationship of numerical data. The types of charts provided by spreadsheet packages are sometimes called **analytical graphics** or **business graphics**, and most are variations on three basic chart types: **line charts**, **bar charts**, and **pie charts**.

19. A **database** refers to a collection of data that is stored in files. **Database software** allows you to create a database and to retrieve, manipulate, and update the data that you store in it.

20. A **file** is a collection of related data that is organized in records. Each **record** contains a collection of related facts called **fields**. A field can contain any of the following types of information: **alphanumeric**, **numeric**, **currency**, **date**, or **memo**.

21. Comparing data entered against a predefined format is called **validation** and is an important feature of database programs.

22. The capability to retrieve database information in a report, called a **query**, based on criteria specified by the user is one of the more powerful features of a database.

23. **Presentation graphics software** allows the user to create documents called **slides** that are used in making presentations before a group to help communicate information more effectively.

24. Some of the features included with most presentation graphics packages include: numerous chart types, three-dimensional effects, special effects, color control, and image libraries. In addition to slides, presentation graphics packages create outlines, notes pages, and audience handouts. Presentation graphics packages also include slide sorters to help organize and present the slides.

25. **Data communications software** is used to transmit data from one computer to another. Features that most data communications software packages include are: a dialing directory of phone numbers, automatic redial, automatic answer, and the capability to send or receive one or more data files.

26. Communications software is frequently used by employees who are away from the office. It is also used to access online services for news, weather, financial, and travel information.

27. **Electronic mail software**, also called **E-mail**, allows users to send messages to and receive messages from other computer users. Although E-mail is primarily used within private organizations, several communications companies and online services have established public E-mail capabilities.

28. **Personal information management** (PIM) **software** helps users keep track of the miscellaneous bits of personal information that each of us deals with every day. The category can be applied to programs that offer any of the following capabilities: appointment calendars, outliners, electronic notepads, data managers, and text retrieval.

29. **Project management software** allows users to plan, schedule, track, and analyze the events, resources, and costs of a project.

30. **Integrated software** refers to packages that combine applications such as word processing, spreadsheet, and database into a single, easy-to-use set of programs. The applications have a consistent look and feel and the capability to pass data quickly from one application to another. Similar to integrated software are software **suites**; individual applications packaged in the same box and sold for a price that is significantly less than buying the applications individually.

31. Several learning aids and support tools are available to help you learn to use an application package including: **tutorials**, **online help**, **trade books**, and **keyboard templates**.

File   Edit   Section   Page   Tools   Options   Help

Terms to Remember

absolute referencing (2.15)
alignment (2.8)
analytical graphics (2.16)

bar chart (2.16)
bold (2.7)
border (2.8)
business graphics (2.16)
button (2.3)

cell (2.12)
chart (2.16)
clip art (2.11)
Clipboard (2.6)
column (2.12)
command (2.3)
copy (2.6)
currency (2.19)
cursor (2.5)
cut (2.6)

data communications software (2.22)
database (2.18)
database software (2.18)
date (2.19)
dedicated word processing system
    (2.4)
delete (2.6)
desktop publishing (DTP)
    software (2.10)

E-mail (2.23)
editing (2.6)
electronic mail software (2.23)
electronic spreadsheet (2.12)

field (2.18)
file (2.18)
font (2.7)
footer (2.9)
format (2.7)
formula (2.12)

full justification (2.8)
functions (2.12)

grammar checker (2.7)
graphical user interface (GUI) (2.2)

header (2.9)

icon (2.3)
insert (2.6)
integrated software (2.25)

justification (2.8)

keyboard template (2.27)

label (2.12)
landscape (2.9)
line chart (2.16)
line spacing (2.8)

margins (2.8)
memo (2.19)
menu (2.3)
Microsoft Windows (2.3)
monospacing (2.8)

numeric (2.19)

online help (2.27)

page composition and layout (2.10)
page definition language (2.11)
page makeup (2.10)
paste (2.6)
personal information management
    (PIM) software (2.24)
pie chart (2.16)
point (2.7)
portrait (2.9)
PostScript (2.11)
presentation graphics software (2.20)

print preview (2.9)
productivity software (2.2)
project management software (2.25)
proportional spacing (2.8)

query (2.19)

record (2.18)
relative referencing (2.15)
replace (2.6)
row (2.12)

scrolling (2.5)
search (2.6)
shade (2.8)
slides (2.20)
spacing (2.8)
spelling checker (2.6)
spreadsheet (2.12)
spreadsheet software (2.12)
style (2.7)
style sheet (2.9)
suites (2.26)

thesaurus (2.7)
trade books (2.27)
tutorials (2.27)
typeface (2.7)

user interface (2.2)

validation (2.19)
values (2.12)

what-if analysis (2.16)
window (2.3)
word processing software (2.4)
word wrap (2.4)
WYSIWYG (2.11)

le   Edit   Section   Page   Tools   Options   Help

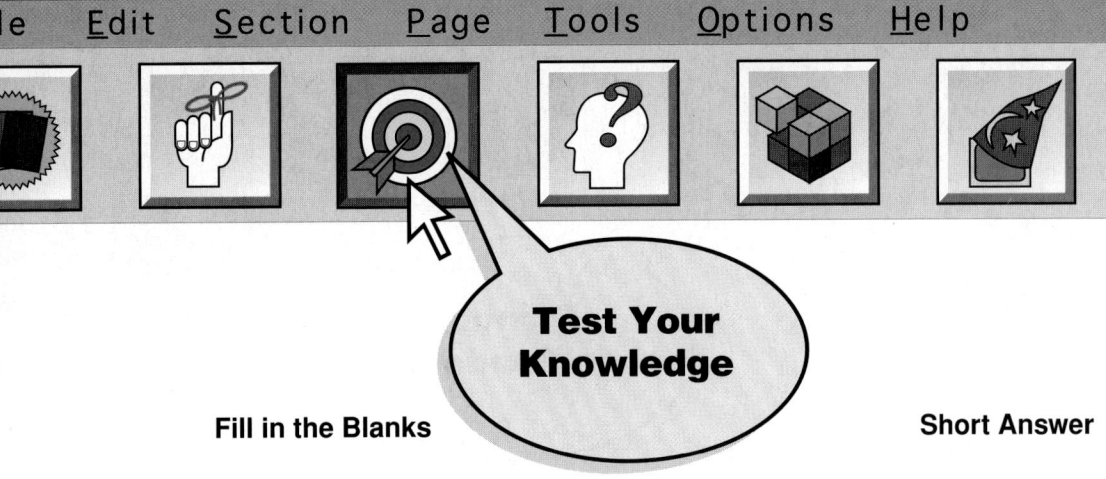

Test Your Knowledge

Fill in the Blanks

1. The nine most widely used personal computer software packages are: _____, _____, _____, _____, _____, _____, _____, _____, and _____.

2. Applications that help people perform their work more efficiently are sometimes referred to as _____.

3. A(n) _____ is the way the user tells the software what to do and the way the computer displays information and processing options to the user.

4. _____ refers to packages that combine applications such as word processing, spreadsheet, and database into a single, easy-to-use set of programs.

5. Four learning aids and support tools available for application users are: _____, _____, _____, and _____.

Short Answer

1. What is productivity software? Briefly explain why each of the nine widely used personal computer software applications described in this chapter can be considered productivity software.

2. What is a graphical user interface (GUI)? Describe the several common features included in most graphical user interfaces.

3. How is word processing software different from desktop publishing software (DTP)? Describe some of the major features of each type of software. In what way are word processing software and desktop publishing software used together?

4. What is the purpose of spreadsheet software? Briefly describe an electronic spreadsheet. How can a spreadsheet be a valuable tool for business decision making?

5. How is presentation graphics similar to analytical graphics? How are they different? Briefly describe the materials that can be created with presentation graphics packages. In what way do presentation graphics packages help communicate information more effectively?

Label the Figure

Instructions: The figure on the right shows Productivity Software Use. In the spaces provided label the bars.

_____
_____
_____
_____
_____
_____
_____
_____
_____

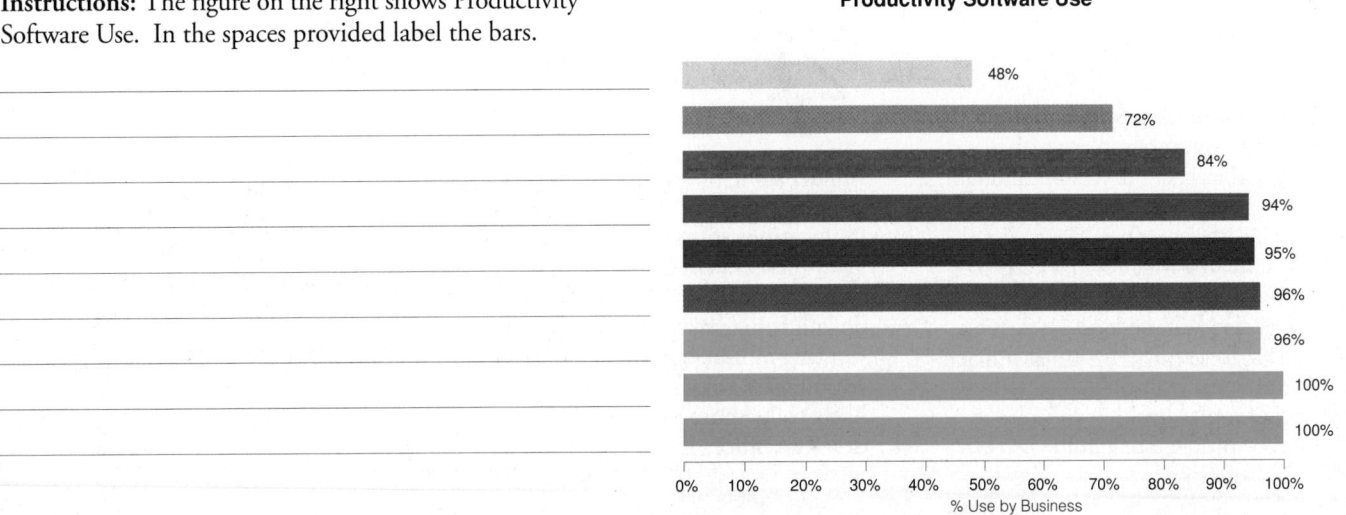

Productivity Software Use

48%
72%
84%
94%
95%
96%
96%
100%
100%

0% 10% 20% 30% 40% 50% 60% 70% 80% 90% 100%
% Use by Business

File   Edit   Section   Page   Tools   Options   Help

Points to Ponder

1

Many people believe that word processing software greatly improves the quality of written material by making it easier to create, edit, and print documents. Some word processing software even provides templates—patterns or blueprints for a document—that can be used to produce reports, memos, cover letters, resumes, legal pleadings, even letters to mom! Yet, other people argue that word processing software has become a crutch, making it unnecessary for students to learn the rudiments and nuances of language. These people feel that much of the work produced with word processors is indeed "processed," lacking the beauty, artistry, and individuality of great literature. What effect do you think word processing software has on written communication? Does it result in better work or simply more correct mediocre work? What word processing features, if any, do you feel are particularly valuable to an author?

2

Johann Guttenberg's invention of printing from moveable type had a profound impact on Western thought, making books that were previously available only to a privileged elite accessible to a much wider audience, thereby facilitating the distribution of knowledge. Will desktop publishing (DTP) software have a similar impact? Will previously unpublished writers use desktop publishing software to produce professional looking works

that are widely circulated? What effect, if any, do you think desktop publishing will have on the ability of people to produce and gain access to material that reflects unconventional, or not generally accepted, ideas?

3

Your Aunt Agatha has offered to buy you some computer software for your birthday. Because she places a great deal of importance on organization (her socks are stored in alphabetical order by color), she will purchase only database software or personal information management software. How could you use both types of software now? How could you use both types of software in the future? If Aunt Agatha asks you which type of software you would rather have, what would you answer? Why?

4

An increasing number of employees are working at home, using data communications software to transmit data from their personal computer to a computer in the central office. What do you think are the advantages of working at home? What are the disadvantages? Do you feel a worker is likely to be more productive at home or in the office? If you could attend

school at home, communicating with your teachers through your personal computer, would you? Why or why not?

5

A woman was once fired when she used her office electronic mail system to complain about her boss. Although she felt her E-mail conversations were private and would not be monitored, she learned, to her chagrin, that she was wrong. Do you think employers have the right to "listen in" to electronic mail conversations? Why or why not? If you "overheard" a fellow employee criticizing your boss on her E-mail system, would you tell your boss? What if you heard the same employee planning a theft of company products? Where do you draw the line?

6

One of the catch phrases in education today is "learning styles," the belief that different people learn things best in different ways. How do you learn things most effectively? Of the four learning aids described in this chapter (tutorials, online help, trade books, and keyboard templates), which fit your learning style best? Why?

le   Edit   Section   Page   Tools   Options   Help

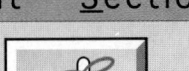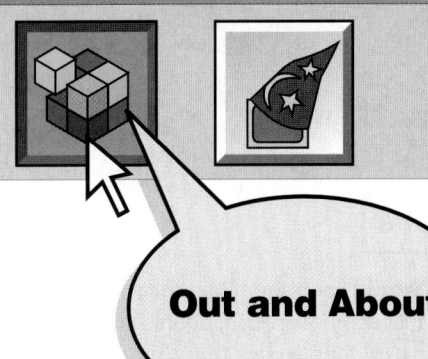

Out and About

1. Unlike a graphical user interface, which combines text and graphics, a text interface uses only text, or commands, to communicate with the computer. Many software packages have one version written for use with a graphical user interface (such as Microsoft Windows) and another written for use with a text interface (such as DOS). Visit a computer store and find a software package that has a version written for both types of interfaces (such as WordPerfect for Windows and WordPerfect for DOS). Try out each version. How are they similar? How are they different? Which version is easier to learn? Why? If you were going to buy this software package, would you buy the version used with the graphical user interface or the version used with the text interface? Why?

2. Interview someone who regularly uses one of the productivity tools discussed in this chapter in the course of his or her work to find out his or her feelings about the software. For what purpose is the software used? Why does this person use the particular software package? What does he or she like about the software? What does the individual dislike? How did the person learn to use the software? If free to choose another software package to perform the same task, would this person choose one? Why or why not?

3. Many bookstores and software vendors carry trade books that can help users learn the features of personal computer application packages. Pick a productivity tool, such as spreadsheet software, and visit a bookstore or software vendor to survey the trade books on that tool. For what particular spreadsheet package (e.g., Lotus 1-2-3, Excel, or Quattro Pro) are the most titles available? How difficult do you think it would be to learn each software package using the available trade books? Which trade book do you think is the best? Why? If you were going to purchase a software package solely on the basis of the available trade books, which package would you buy? Why?

4. Make a list of the features listed in this chapter that are provided by word processing or spreadsheet software. Visit a computer vendor and compare two word processing or spreadsheet packages in terms of the features you have listed. Which package is easier to learn? Why? Once you have learned it, which package allows you to do more? If you were to purchase one of the two packages, which would you buy? Why?

5. Do some research on presentations. Make a list of the characteristics of effective presentations, in order from most important to least important. Which of these characteristics can be enhanced through the use of presentation graphics software? How much of a difference in the overall quality of a presentation do you think presentation graphics software can make? Do you think presentation graphics are more helpful in certain presentations than in others? If you had to give a presentation on your favorite subject, would you like to use presentation graphics software? Why or why not?

6. Uncle Ulysses has agreed to buy you an integrated software package of your choice. Visit a software vendor and compare integrated software packages. Which would you ask Uncle Ulysses to buy? Why? If Uncle Ullysses is willing to buy any applications, or a software suite, that are the same price or less than the integrated software package, which would you prefer? Why?

File   Edit   Section   Page   Tools   Options   Help

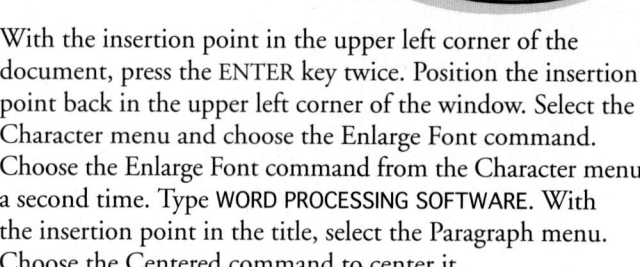

In the Lab

Windows Labs

1 **Creating a Word Processing Document** With Program Manager on the screen, double-click the Accessories group icon ▦. Double-click the Write program-item icon ✐ to start the Write application. Click the Maximize button in the upper right corner of the Write window to maximize it. Type the first three paragraphs on page 2.4 under the heading Word Processing Software as shown in *Figure 2-41*. To indent the first line of each paragraph, press the TAB key. Only press the ENTER key to begin a new paragraph. Do not bold any words in the paragraphs. At the end of the third paragraph, press the ENTER key twice and type your name.

To make corrections in your document, use the mouse to move the I-beam to the location of the error; then click the mouse to move the insertion point to the error. To erase to the left of the insertion point, press the BACKSPACE key; to erase to the right of the insertion point, press the DELETE key. To insert character(s), move the insertion point immediately to the left of the point of insertion and begin typing.

When your document is correct, save it by inserting a formatted diskette in drive A, choosing the Save command from the File menu, typing a:win2-1 and choosing the OK button. With your printer turned on, print the document by choosing the Print command from the File menu. Close Write by double-clicking its Control-menu box.

2 **Formatting a Word Processing Document** Start Write as described in Windows Lab 1 and insert your formatted diskette in drive A. Open the document you created in Windows Lab 1 by choosing the Open command from the File menu, typing a:win2-1 in the File Name box, and choosing the OK button. Maximize the Write window.

With the insertion point in the upper left corner of the document, press the ENTER key twice. Position the insertion point back in the upper left corner of the window. Select the Character menu and choose the Enlarge Font command. Choose the Enlarge Font command from the Character menu a second time. Type WORD PROCESSING SOFTWARE. With the insertion point in the title, select the Paragraph menu. Choose the Centered command to center it.

Drag the mouse over the first three words (Word processing software) in the second sentence. Select the Character menu and choose the Bold command. Drag the mouse from the first character in the first paragraph through the last character in the last paragraph to highlight the three paragraphs of text. Select the Paragraph menu and choose the Double Space command to double-space the document *(Figure 2-42)*. Click anywhere in the document to remove the highlight. Practice using the scroll bar to scroll through the document.

Save the document by choosing the Save As command from the File menu. When the Save As dialog box displays, type a:win2-2 in the File Name box and choose the OK button. Print the document. Close Write by double-clicking its Control-menu box.

3 **Creating a Drawing** With Program Manager on the screen, double-click the Accessories group icon. Double-click the Paintbrush program-item icon 🎨. Maximize

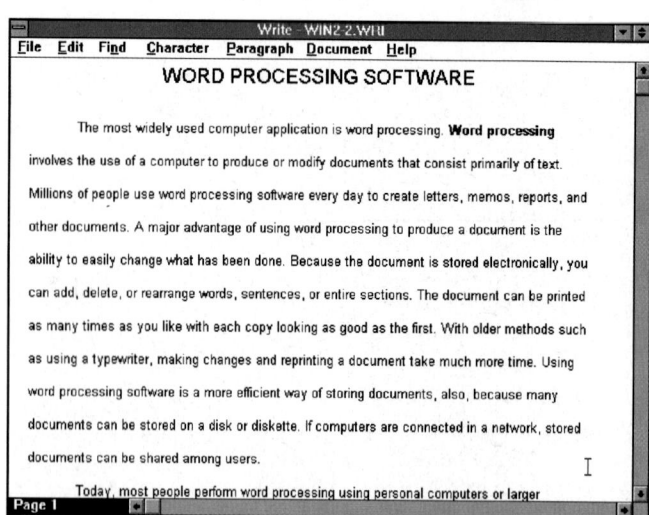

Figure 2-41

Figure 2-42

the Paintbrush window.

Change the background color to royal blue by pointing to the color royal blue in the palette at the bottom of the Paintbrush window and clicking the *right* mouse button. Change the foreground color to yellow by pointing to the color yellow in the palette and clicking the *left* mouse button. Select the File menu and choose the New command. The screen is now royal blue; the drawing you make will be in yellow.

Click the Brush tool 🖌. Move the mouse pointer into the blue window. Use the mouse pointer to write your name in cursive so it is similar to *Figure 2-43.* Drag the mouse through your entire name, or release the mouse in between each character. If you make a mistake, choose the Undo command from the Edit menu to erase your last draw.

Save the drawing to your diskette in drive A by choosing the Save command from the File menu. Type a:win2-3 in the File Name box. What extension does Paintbrush attach to its files? Print the drawing by choosing the Print command from the File menu. Close Paintbrush by double-clicking its Control-menu box.

4 **Using Help**   With Program Manager on the screen, select the Help menu and choose the How to Use Help command. Read the contents of the window *(Figure 2-44).* Print the contents of the window by choosing the Print Topic command from the File menu. Point to the word *topic,* which has a green dotted underline beneath it and click. What is the definition of the word *topic*? Click the Help Basics topic. Read and print the contents of the Help Basics window. Click the Back button. Close the Help window by double-clicking its Control-menu box.

DOS Labs

1 **Creating a Text Document**   At the DOS prompt, type edit and press the ENTER key. Press the ESC key when the Welcome message appears. Type the title and first three paragraphs on page 2.4. Press the ENTER key at the end of each line on page 2.4. Press the ENTER key twice between paragraphs. At the end of the third paragraph, press the ENTER key twice and type your name. To make corrections, use the arrow keys to move the cursor to the error. To erase to the left of the cursor, press the BACKSPACE key; to erase to the right of the cursor, press the DELETE key. When your document is correct, insert a formatted diskette in drive A. Press the ALT key to activate the menu. Type F for File menu and S for Save. In the Save As dialog box, type a:dos2-1 as the filename. Press the ENTER key. Print the document by choosing the Print command on the File menu. Choose the Exit command on the File menu.

2 **Using FastHelp**   At the DOS prompt, type fasthelp and press the ENTER key to display a list of DOS commands and their descriptions. Press the ENTER key to continue through the list. Answer these questions: (1) What is the description of FASTHELP? FORMAT? MORE? (2) Using FastHelp, how do you obtain more information on a specific command?

Online Lab

1 **Viewing an Art Gallery**   Using one of the two online services you selected in Chapter 1, connect to the service and perform the following tasks: (1) Search the online service for an Art or Graphics Gallery. (2) As you view the artwork, make a list of the titles of the artwork and the artists.

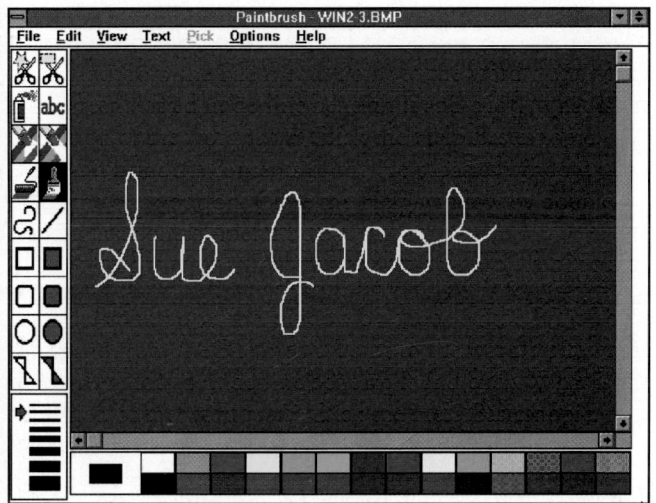

Figure 2-43

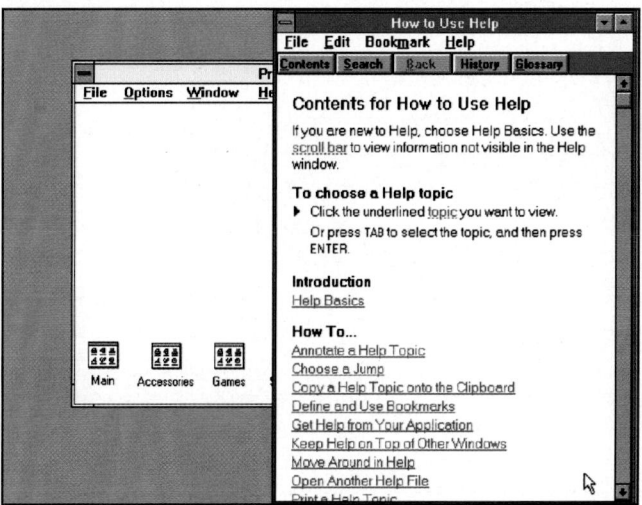

Figure 2-44

Input to the Computer

3

The information processing cycle is basic to all computers, large or small. It is important that you understand this cycle, for much of your success in understanding computers and what they do depends on having an understanding or feeling for the movement of data as it flows through the information processing cycle and becomes information. This chapter discusses the information processing cycle and describes some of the devices used for input. Certain devices that can be used for both input and storage, such as disk and tape drives, are covered in the chapter on secondary storage.

Objectives

After completing this chapter, you will be able to:

- Review the four operations of the information processing cycle: input, process, output, and storage

- Define the four types of input and how the computer uses each type

- Describe the standard features of keyboards, and explain how to use the cursor control and function keys

- Explain how a mouse works and how it is used

- Describe several input devices other than the keyboard and mouse

- Explain the three types of terminals and how they are used

- Explain multimedia input devices

- Describe procedures used to ensure data accuracy

Overview of the Information Processing Cycle

As you saw in Chapter 1, the information processing cycle consists of four operations: input, processing, output, and storage *(Figure 3-1)*. Regardless of the size and type of computer, these operations process data into a meaningful form called information.

The operations in the information processing cycle are carried out through the combined use of computer equipment, also called computer hardware, and computer software. The computer software, or programs, contain instructions that direct the computer equipment to perform the tasks necessary to process data into information. In the information processing cycle, the input operation must take place before any data can be processed and any information produced and stored.

Figure 3-1
A computer consists of input devices, the system unit, output devices, and secondary storage devices. This equipment, or hardware, is used to perform the operations of the information processing cycle.

What Is Input?

Input refers to the process of entering data, programs, commands, and user responses into main memory. Input also refers to the media (e.g., disks, tapes, documents) that contain these input types. These four types of input are used by a computer in the following ways:

- **Data** refers to the raw facts, including numbers, letters, words, images, and sounds that a computer receives during the input operation and processes to produce information. Although technically speaking, a single item of data should be called a *datum,* it is common and accepted usage to use the word data to represent both singular and plural. Data must be entered and stored in main memory for processing to occur. Data is the most common type of input.
- **Programs** are instructions that direct the computer to perform the necessary operations to process data into information. The program that is loaded and stored in main memory determines the processing that the computer will perform. When a program is first created it is usually input by using a keyboard. Once the program has been entered and stored on secondary storage, it can be transferred to main memory by a command.

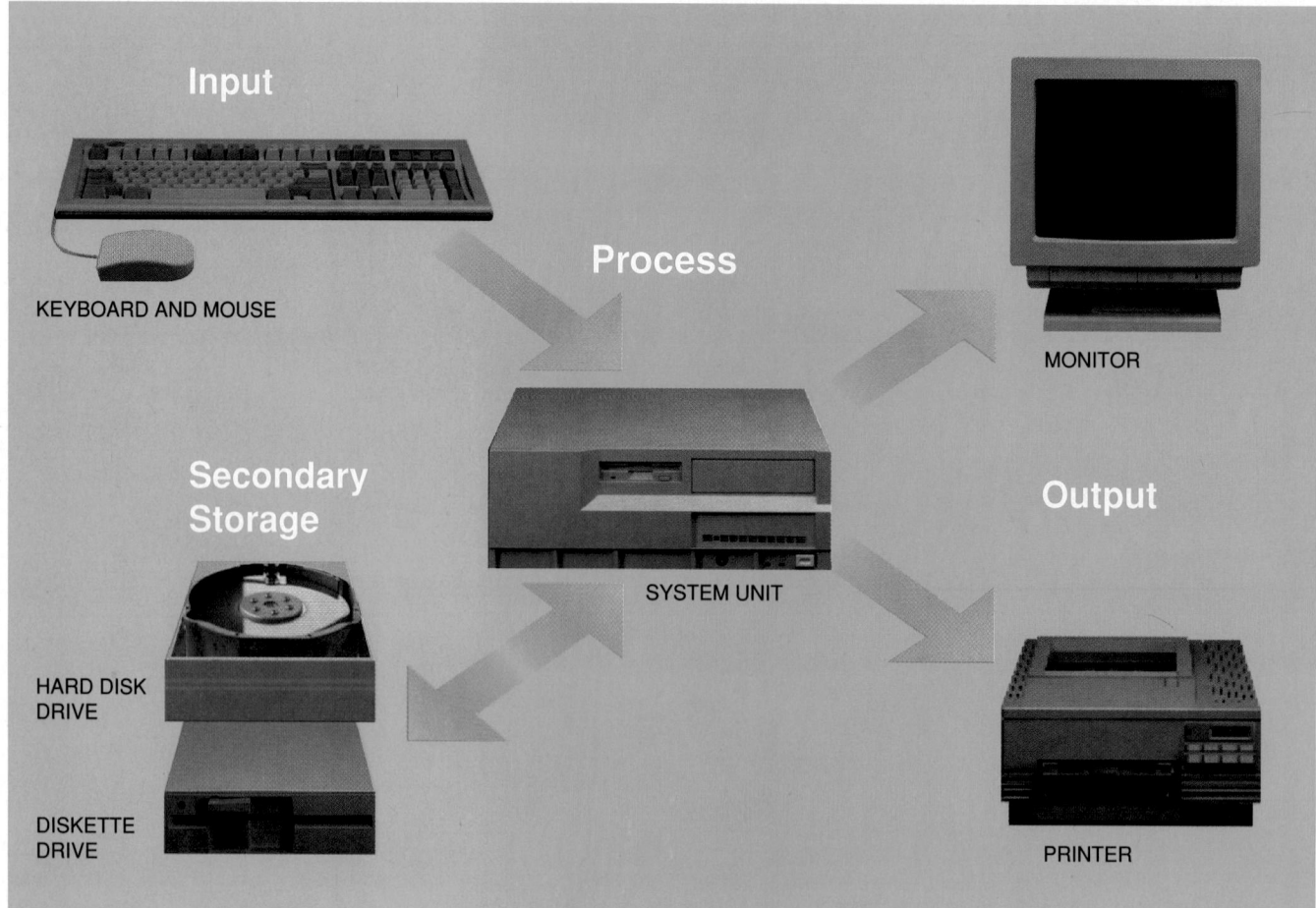

Input
KEYBOARD AND MOUSE

Process

Secondary Storage

SYSTEM UNIT

HARD DISK DRIVE

DISKETTE DRIVE

MONITOR

Output

PRINTER

- **Commands** are key words and phrases that the user inputs to direct the computer to perform certain activities. Commands are usually either entered from the keyboard or selected from a list.
- **User responses** refer to the data that a user inputs to respond to a question or message from the software. One of the most common responses is to answer "Yes" or "No" to a question. Based on the answer, the computer program will perform specific actions. For example, typing the letter Y in response to the message, Do you want to save this file?, will result in the file being saved (written) to the secondary storage device.

The Keyboard

The **keyboard** is the most commonly used input device. Users input data to a computer by pressing the keys on the keyboard. Keyboards are connected to other devices that have screens such as a personal computer or a terminal. As the user enters data through the keyboard, the data displays on the screen.

Keyboards are usually similar to the one shown in *Figure 3-2.* The alphabetic keys are arranged like those on a typewriter. A **numeric keypad** is located on the right-hand side of most keyboards. The numeric keys are arranged in an adding machine or calculator format to allow you to enter numeric data rapidly.

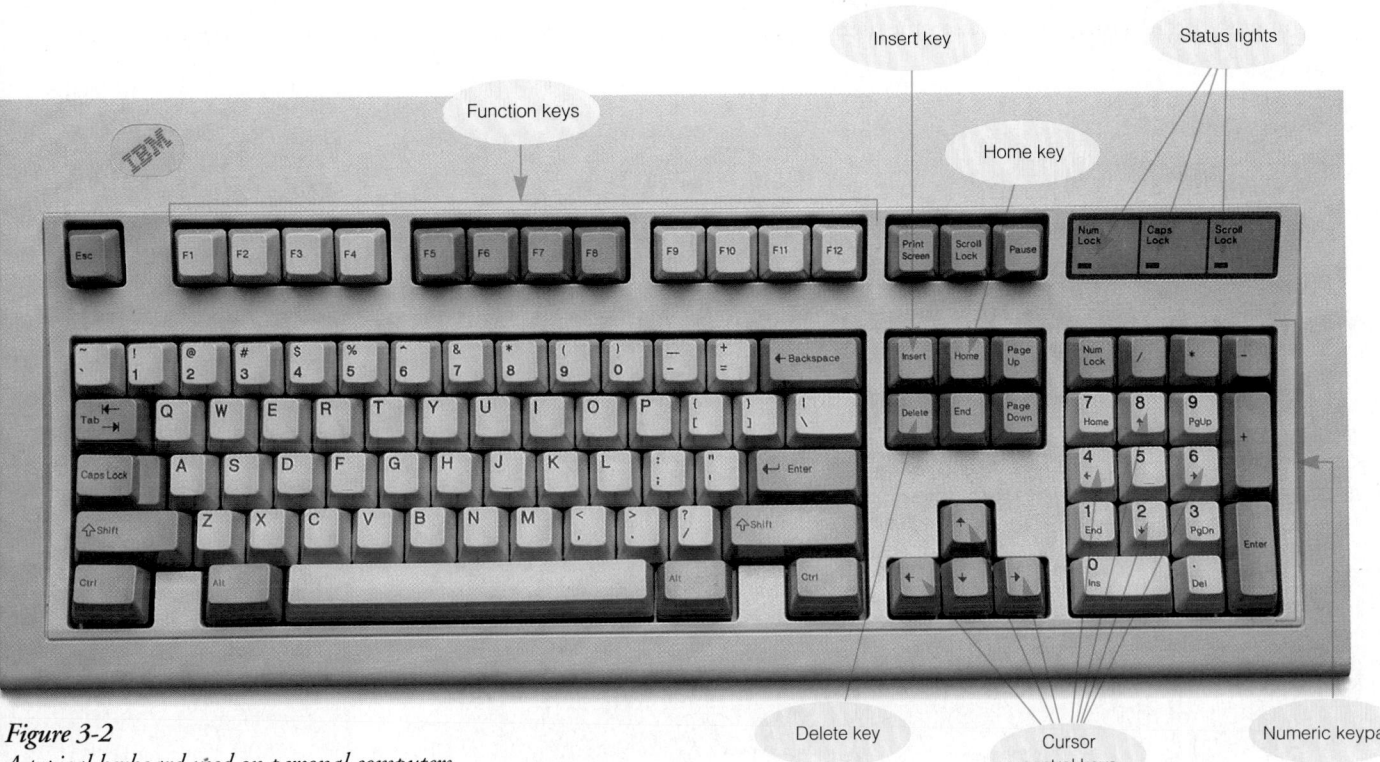

Figure 3-2
A typical keyboard used on personal computers.

Keyboards also contain keys that can be used to position the cursor on the screen. A **cursor** is a symbol, such as an underline character, rectangle, or vertical bar, that indicates where on the screen the next character entered will appear. The keys that move the cursor are called **arrow keys or cursor control keys**. Cursor control keys have an UP ARROW (↑), a DOWN ARROW (↓), a LEFT ARROW (←), and a RIGHT ARROW (→). When you press any of these keys, the cursor moves one space in the same direction as the arrow. In addition, many keyboards contain other cursor control keys, such as the HOME key, which when you press it can send the cursor to a beginning location such as the upper left position of the screen or document. The numeric keypad can also be used to move the cursor. With most keys, if you hold them down they will automatically start to repeat.

Some computer keyboards also contain keys that can alter or edit the text displayed on the screen. For example, the INSERT and DELETE keys allow characters to be inserted into or deleted from data displayed on the screen.

Function keys are keys that can be programmed to accomplish certain tasks that will assist the user. For example,

a function key may be programmed for use as a help key when using software such as a word processor. Whenever the function key is pressed, messages will appear that give helpful information about how to use the word processing software. Function keys can also save keystrokes. Sometimes several keystrokes are required to accomplish a certain task, for example, printing a document. Some application software packages are written so the user can either enter the individual keystrokes or press a function key and obtain the same result.

Status lights in the upper right corner of the keyboard indicate if the numeric keypad, capital letters, and scroll locks are turned on.

The ESCAPE (ESC) key is often used by computer software to cancel an instruction or exit from a situation. The use of the ESC key varies among software packages.

The disadvantage of using a keyboard as an input device is that training is required to use it efficiently. Users who lack typing ability are at a disadvantage because of the time they spend looking for the appropriate keys. While other input devices are appropriate in some situations, users should be encouraged to develop their keyboard skills.

Pointing Devices

Pointing devices allow the user to control an on-screen symbol called the **mouse pointer**, or **pointer**, that is usually represented by an arrow-shaped marker (↖). The pointing device is used to move the cursor to a particular location on the screen or to select available software options.

Mouse

The mouse is a unique device used with personal computers and some computer terminals to select processing options or information displayed on the screen. A **mouse** is a small, lightweight input device that easily fits in the palm of your hand *(Figure 3-3)*. You move the device across a flat surface such as a desktop to control the movement of the pointer on a screen.

The mouse is usually attached to the computer by a cable but wireless mouse devices also exist. On the bottom of the mouse is a device, usually a small ball, that senses the movement of the mouse. Electronic circuits in the mouse translate the movement of the mouse into signals that are sent to the computer. The computer uses the mouse signals to move the pointer on the screen in the same direction as the mouse *(Figure 3-4)*. When you move the mouse left on the surface of the table or desk, the pointer moves left on the screen. When you move the mouse right, the pointer moves right, and so on.

On top of the mouse are one or more buttons. By using the mouse to move the pointer on the screen and pressing the buttons on the mouse, you can perform actions such as making menu selections, editing a word processing document, and moving data from one location on the screen to another.

The primary advantage of a mouse is that it is easy to use. With a little practice, a person can use a mouse to point to locations on the screen just as easily as using a finger.

There are two disadvantages of the mouse. The first is that it requires empty desk space where it can be moved about. The second disadvantage is that the user must remove a hand from the keyboard and place it on the mouse whenever the pointer is to be moved or a command is to be given.

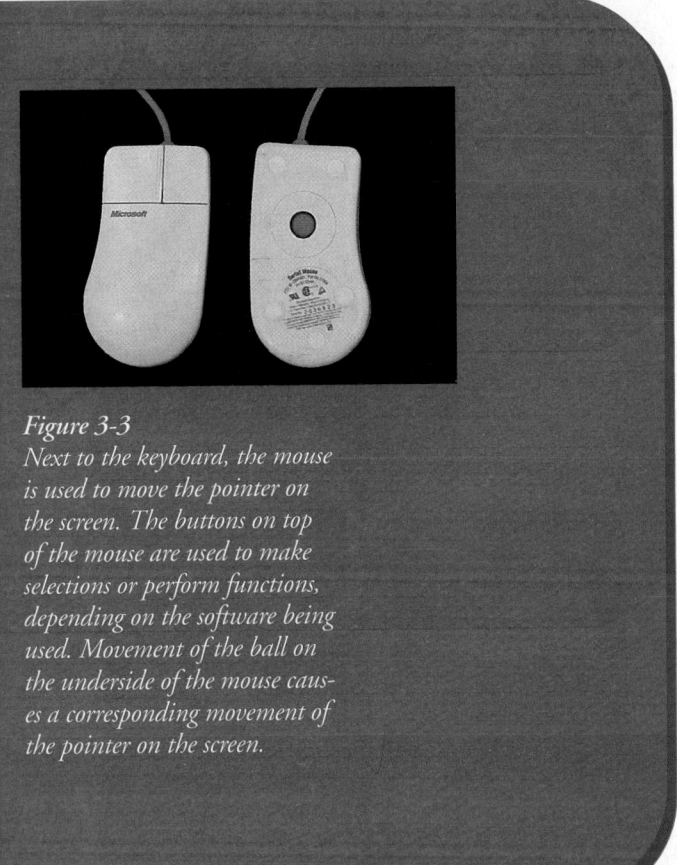

Figure 3-3
Next to the keyboard, the mouse is used to move the pointer on the screen. The buttons on top of the mouse are used to make selections or perform functions, depending on the software being used. Movement of the ball on the underside of the mouse causes a corresponding movement of the pointer on the screen.

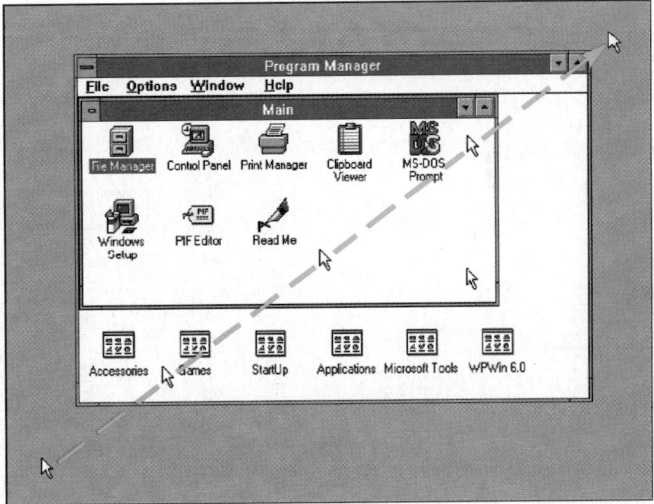

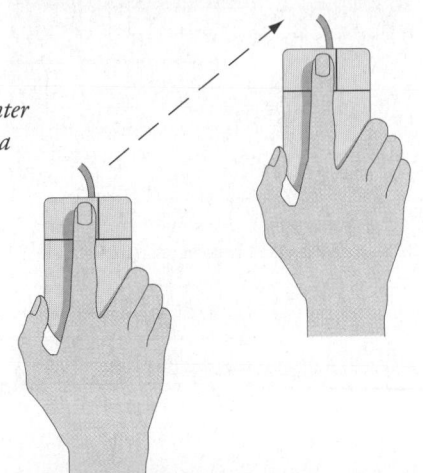

Figure 3-4
As the mouse is moved diagonally across a flat surface, the mouse pointer on the screen moves in a similar direction.

Trackball

A **trackball** is a pointing device like a mouse only with the ball on the top of the device instead of the bottom *(Figure 3-5)*. To move the pointer with a trackball, all you have to do is rotate the ball in the desired direction. With a mouse, you have to move the entire device. To accommodate movement with both the fingers and palms of a hand, the ball on top of a trackball is usually larger than the ball on the bottom of a mouse. The main advantage of a trackball over a mouse is that it doesn't require clear desk space. Smaller trackball units have been designed for use on portable computers *(Figure 3-6)*.

Joystick

A **joystick** uses the movement of a vertical stem to direct the pointer. A full-size joystick, often used with computer games, is usually large enough for the user's hand to wrap around it *(Figure 3-7)*. Full-size joysticks usually have buttons you press to activate certain events, depending on the software. Much smaller joysticks, without buttons, have been incorporated into some portable computers *(Figure 3-8)*. The small joysticks look like a long pencil eraser stuck between the keys. Pressure on the joystick from the user's finger causes the pointer to move.

Figure 3-7
Joysticks are often used with computer games to control the actions of a vehicle or player.

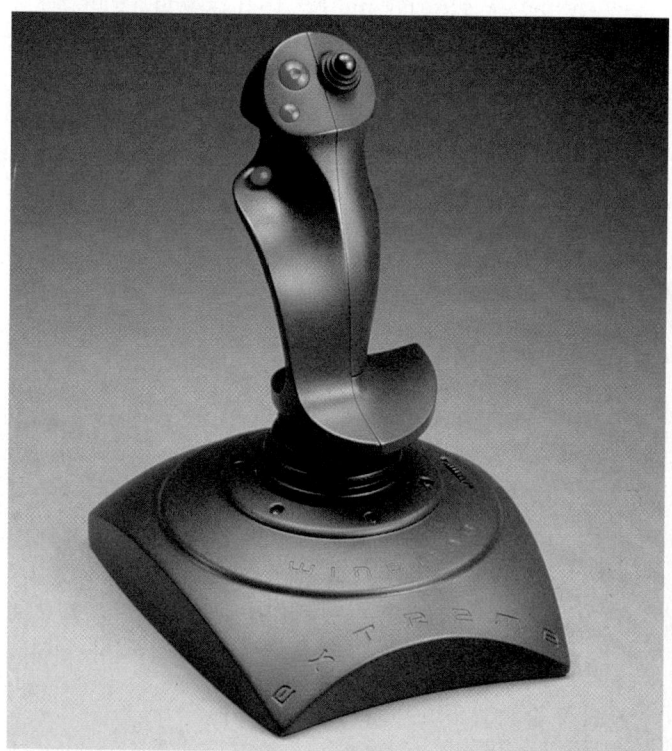

Figure 3-5
The trackball is like a mouse turned upside down. The user rotates the ball to move the cursor and then presses one of the keys shown at the top of the trackball.

Figure 3-6
Smaller trackball units are often used on portable computers. They are attached to the side of the computer as shown on this Texas Instruments Notebook computer. Sometimes they are built into the computer case.

Figure 3-8
IBM has incorporated a type of joystick, called a trackpoint, into their line of portable computers.

Pen Input Devices

Pen input devices have become increasingly popular in recent years and may eventually be part of most, if not all, computers. Almost all of the personal digital assistant (PDA) class of personal computers use a pen. One advantage is that people who have never used a computer adapt naturally to using a pen as an input device *(Figure 3-9)*.

Pen input devices allow the user to use the pen in three ways; to input data using hand-written characters and shapes the computer can recognize, as a pointing device like a mouse to select items on the screen, and to gesture, which is a way of issuing commands.

Pen computers use special hardware and software to interpret the movement of the pen. When the pen touches the screen, it causes two layers of electrically conductive material to make contact. The computer determines the coordinates for the contact point and darkens that location on the screen. The darkened area on the screen is referred to as **ink**. Hand-written characters are converted into computer text by software that matches the shape of the hand-written character to a database of known shapes. If the software cannot recognize a particular letter, it asks the user to identify it. Most **hand-writing recognition software** can be taught to recognize an individual's unique style of writing. In addition to working with character input, graphic recognition software used on pen input devices improves drawings by cleaning up uneven lines. Wavy lines can be straightened and circles can be made perfectly round. Perhaps the most natural use of the pen is as a pointing device. When used this way, the pen functions as a mouse. Pressing the pen against the screen once or twice is the same as using the buttons on a mouse.

Gestures are special symbols made with the pen that issue a command such as delete text. As shown in *Figure 3-10*, many gestures are identical to those used for manual text editing. Gestures can be more efficient than using a mouse or keyboard because they not only identify where you want to make a change but also the type of change to be made.

Pen input devices have already been adapted to many applications that were previously not computerized. Any application where a form has to be filled out is a candidate for a pen input device. One of the largest markets for pen input devices is mobile workers, who spend most of their time away from their desks or offices.

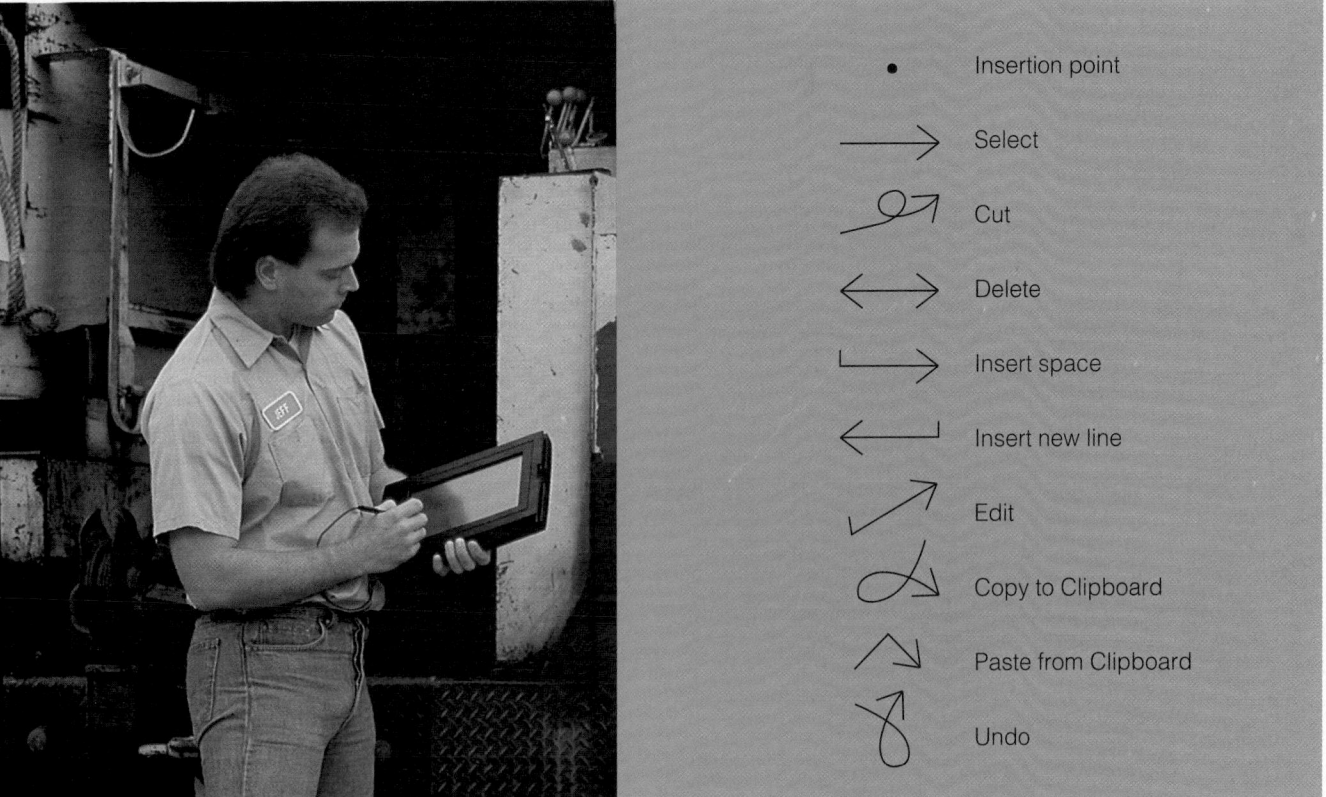

•	Insertion point
→	Select
	Cut
←→	Delete
	Insert space
	Insert new line
	Edit
	Copy to Clipboard
	Paste from Clipboard
	Undo

Figure 3-9
Pen input systems allow the user to use a pen to enter data or select processing options without using a keyboard. This method is easy to learn by individuals who have worked with a pencil and paper.

Figure 3-10
Gestures are a way of issuing commands with a pen. Gestures not only tell what you want done but also where you want to make a change. The arrows indicate the direction of the pen movement.

Touch Screen

A **touch screen** allows users to touch areas of the screen to enter data. They let the user interact with a computer by the touch of a finger rather than typing on a keyboard or moving a mouse. The user enters data by touching words or numbers or locations identified on the screen.

Several electronic techniques change a touch on the screen into electronic signals that are interpreted by the computer software. One technique uses beams of infrared light projected across the surface of the screen. A finger or other object touching the screen interrupts the beams, generating an electronic signal. This signal identifies the location on the screen where the touch occurred. The software interprets the signal and performs the required function.

Touch screens are not used to enter large amounts of data. They are used, however, for applications where the user must issue a command to the software to perform a particular task or must choose from a list of options. Touch screens have been successfully installed in kiosks used to provide information in hotels, airports, and other public locations *(Figure 3-11)*.

There are both advantages and disadvantages to touch screens. A significant advantage is that they are very natural to use; that is, people are used to pointing to things. With touch screens, users can point to indicate the processing they want performed by the computer. In addition, touch screens are usually easy for the user to learn. As quickly as pointing a finger, the user's request is processed. There are some disadvantages to touch screens. First, the resolution of the touching area is not precise. Thus, while a user can point to a box or a fairly large area on the screen and the electronics can determine the location of the touch, it is difficult to point to a single character in a word processing application, for example, and indicate that the character should be deleted. In cases such as these, a keyboard or mouse is easier to use. A second disadvantage is that after a period of reaching for the screen, the user's arm could become tired.

Figure 3-11
Touch screens are frequently used for information kiosks. Users touch the screen and receive information about the chosen topic.

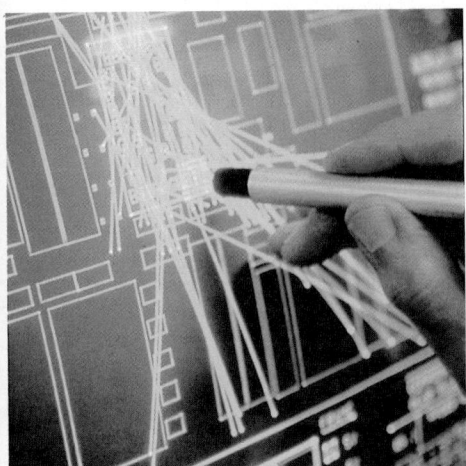

Figure 3-12
The light pen can be used to make selections or to draw directly on the screen. A light cell in the tip of the pen can detect where on the screen the pen is touching. Light pens are often used in engineering applications.

Light Pen

A **light pen** is used by touching it on the display screen to create or modify graphics *(Figure 3-12)*. A light cell in the tip of the pen senses light from the screen to determine the pen's location. The light pen can be used to select processing options or to draw on the screen.

Digitizer

A **digitizer** converts points, lines, and curves from a sketch, drawing, or photograph to digital signals and transmits them to a computer *(Figure 3-13)*. The user indicates the data to be input by pressing one or more buttons on the hand-held digitizer device.

Graphics Tablet

A **graphics tablet** works in a manner similar to a digitizer, but it also contains unique characters and commands that can be automatically generated by the person using the tablet *(Figure 3-14)*.

Figure 3-14
The color template on the graphics tablet allows the user to select processing options by placing a hand-held device over the appropriate location on the tablet and pressing a button.

Figure 3-13
Digitizers are used to create original drawings or to trace and reproduce existing drawings. When buttons on the hand-held device are pushed, the location on the drawing is input to the computer. Special software can link the points together to create a drawing that can be modified.

Source Data Automation

Source data automation refers to procedures and equipment designed to make the input process more efficient by eliminating the manual entry of data. Instead of a person entering data using a keyboard, source data automation equipment captures data directly from its original form such as an invoice or an inventory tag. The original form is called a **source document**. In addition to making the input process more efficient, source data automation usually results in a higher input accuracy rate. The following section describes some of the equipment used for source data automation, which is sometimes called **source data collection**.

Image Scanner

An **image scanner**, sometimes called a **page scanner**, is an input device that electronically captures an entire page of text or images such as photographs or art work *(Figure 3-15)*. The scanner converts the text or image on the original document into digital information that can be stored on a disk and processed by the computer. The digitized information can be printed or displayed separately or merged into another document such as a newsletter. Hand-held devices that scan a portion of a page are also available *(Figure 3-16)* as well as color scanners.

Image processing systems use scanners to capture and electronically file documents such as legal documents or documents with signatures or drawings. These systems are like electronic filing cabinets that allow users to rapidly access and review exact reproductions of the original documents *(Figure 3-17)*.

Figure 3-15
The scanner inputs text, graphics, or photographs for use in word processing or desktop publishing applications.

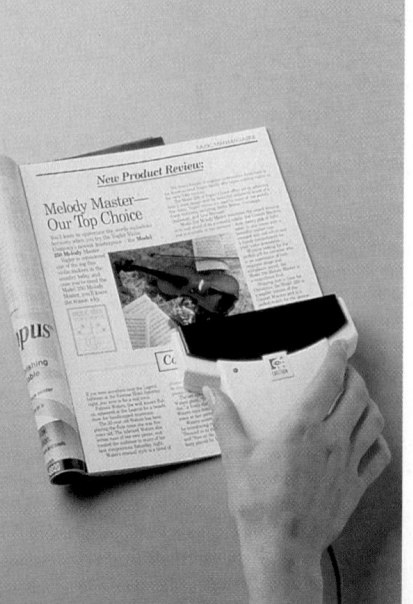

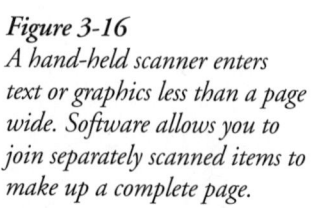

Figure 3-16
A hand-held scanner enters text or graphics less than a page wide. Software allows you to join separately scanned items to make up a complete page.

Figure 3-17
Image processing systems record and store an exact copy of a document. These systems are often used by insurance companies that may need to refer to any of hundreds of thousands of documents.

Optical Recognition

Optical recognition devices use a light source to read codes, marks, and characters and convert them into digital data that can be processed by a computer.

OPTICAL CODES

Optical codes use a pattern or symbols to represent data. The most common optical code is the bar code. A **bar code** consists of a set of vertical lines and spaces of different widths. The bar code is usually either printed on the product package or attached to the product with a label or tag. The bar code reader uses the light pattern from the bar code lines to identify the item. Of the several different types of bar codes, the most familiar is the **universal product code** (UPC). The UPC bar code, used for grocery and retail items, can be translated into a ten-digit number that identifies the product manufacturer and product number *(Figure 3-18)*.

Optical code scanning equipment includes light guns that are aimed at the code and wands that are passed over the code. Grocery stores often use stationary units set in a counter. *Figure 3-19* shows several different types of bar code readers.

Figure 3-18
Bar codes are a type of optical code found on most grocery and retail items. The universal product code (UPC) bar code is the most common. The numbers printed at the bottom identify the manufacturer and the product and can be used to input the item if the bar code reader fails.

Figure 3-19
Three different types of bar code readers are shown here: a hand-held gun, a hand-held wand, and a stationary reader set in the counter of a grocery store.

OPTICAL MARK RECOGNITION

Optical mark recognition (OMR) devices are often used to process questionnaires or test answer sheets *(Figure 3-20)*. Carefully placed marks on the form indicate responses to questions that are read and interpreted by a computer program.

OPTICAL CHARACTER RECOGNITION

Optical character recognition (OCR) devices are scanners that read typewritten, computer-printed, and in some cases hand-printed characters from ordinary documents. OCR devices range from large machines that automatically read thousands of documents per minute to hand-held wands.

An OCR device scans the shape of a character, compares it with a predefined shape stored in memory, and converts the character into the corresponding computer code. The standard OCR typeface, called OCR-A is illustrated in *Figure 3-21.* The characters are read easily by both people and machines. OCR-B is a set of standard characters widely used in Europe and Japan.

OCR is frequently used for **turn-around documents**, documents designed to be returned *(turned around)* to the organization that created them. Examples of such documents are billing statements from credit card companies and department stores. The portion of the statement that you send back with your payment has your account number, total balance, and payment information printed in optical characters.

Figure 3-20
Optical mark recognition devices are often used for processing questionnaires and test answer sheets. For test scores, the reader marks the incorrect answers and reports the number of correct answers and the average score of all tests.

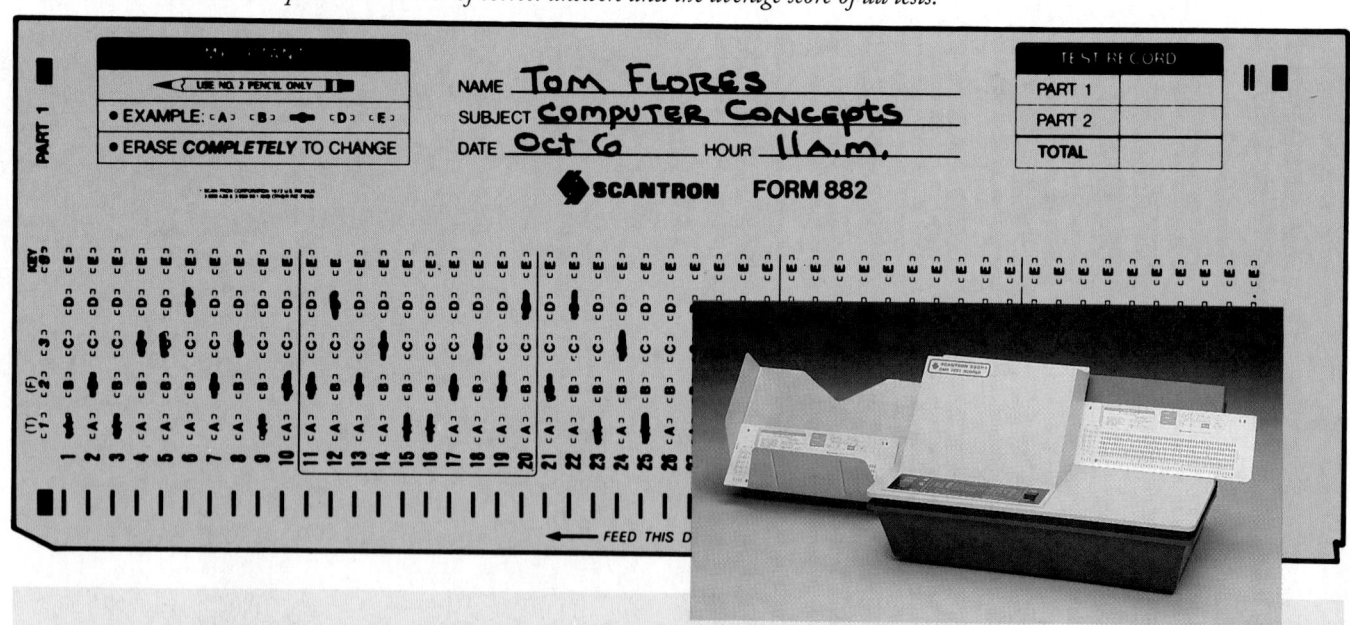

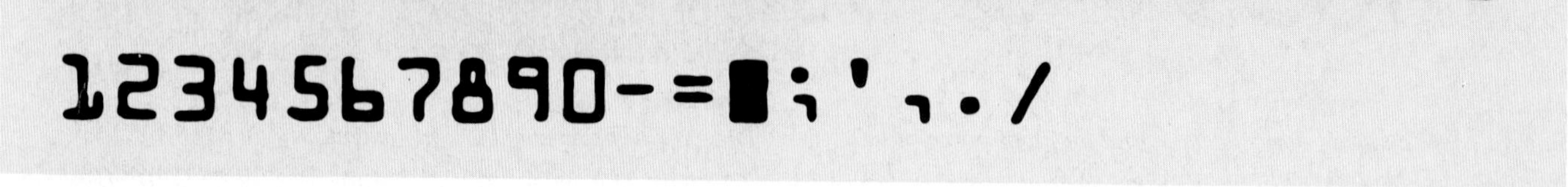

Figure 3-21
In this portion of the OCR-A character set, notice how the characters B and 8 and S and 5 and the number 0 and the letter O are designed differently. Thus, the reading device can easily distinguish between them.

OCR SOFTWARE

OCR **software** is used with image scanners to convert text images into data that can be processed by word processing software. OCR software works as follows: First the entire page of text is scanned. At this point, the page is considered a single graphic image, just like a picture, and individual words are not identified. Next, the software tries to identify individual letters and words. *Figure 3-22* shows how one OCR software package displays the status during this process. Modern OCR software has a very high success rate and can usually identify more than 98% of the scanned material. Finally, the OCR software displays the text that it could not identify. When the user makes the final corrections, the document may be saved in the word processing format of the user's choice.

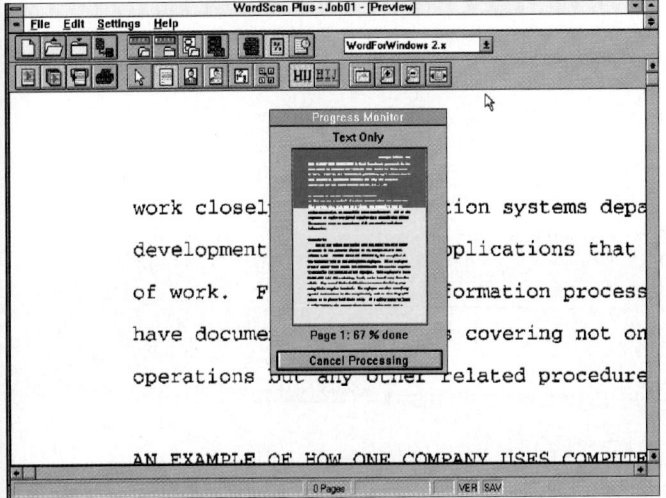

Magnetic Ink Character Recognition (MICR)

Magnetic ink character recognition (MICR) characters use a special ink that is magnetized during processing. MICR is used almost exclusively by the banking industry for processing checks. Blank (unused) checks already have the bank code, account number, and check number printed in MICR characters across the bottom. When the check is processed by the bank, the amount of the check is also printed in the lower right corner *(Figure 3-23)*. Together, this information is read by MICR reader-sorter machines (*Figure 3-24* on the next page) as part of the check-clearing process.

Figure 3-22 ◄
OCR software in the process of converting a page of scanned text into data that can be input to word processing software is shown in this screen. The entire page of text was converted in less than one minute; much faster than the text could be entered using the keyboard.

Figure 3-23 ▼
The MICR characters printed along the bottom edge indicate the bank, account number, and amount of the check. The amount in the lower right corner is added after the check is cashed. The other MICR numbers are preprinted on the check.

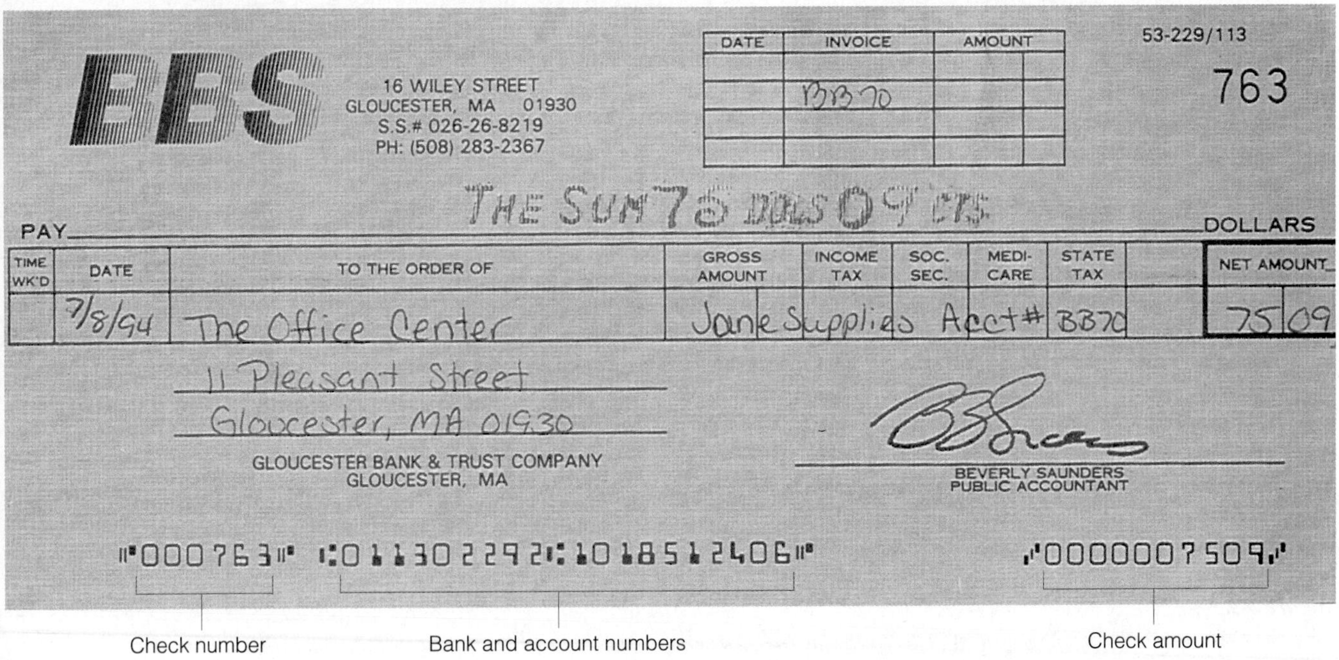

Data Collection Devices

Data collection devices are designed and used for obtaining data at the site where the transaction or event being reported takes place. Oftentimes, data collection equipment is used in factories, warehouses, or other locations where heat, humidity, and cleanliness are difficult to control *(Figure 3-25)*. Data collection equipment must be rugged and easy to use because it is often operated by persons whose primary task is not entering data.

Figure 3-24
This MICR reader-sorter can process more than a thousand documents per minute. After the documents are read, they are sorted into the vertical bins on the right side of the machine. The reader-sorter is connected to a computer so the data is input as the documents are read.

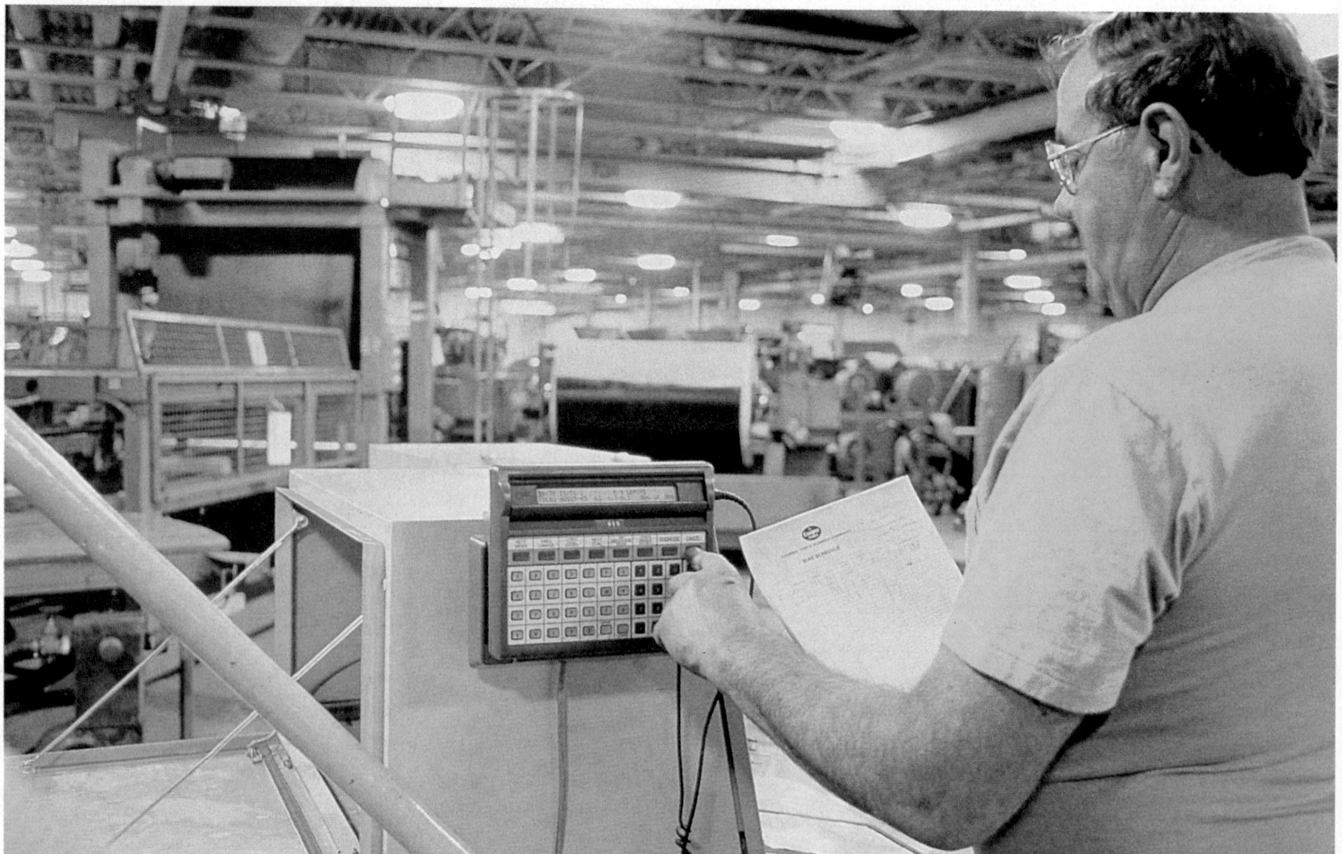

Figure 3-25
Data collection devices are often used in factories and warehouses where heat, humidity, and cleanliness are difficult to control.

Terminals

Terminals, sometimes called **display terminals,** or **video display terminals** (VDTs), consist of a keyboard and a screen. Terminals differ from monitors that only have a viewing screen and no keyboard.

A **dumb terminal** consists of a keyboard and a display screen that are used to enter and transmit data to or receive and display data from a computer to which it is connected. A dumb terminal has no independent processing capability or secondary storage and cannot function as a stand-alone device *(Figure 3-26).* Dumb terminals are often connected to minicomputers, mainframes, or supercomputers.

Intelligent terminals have built-in processing capabilities and often contain not only the keyboard and screen but also secondary storage devices such as disk drives. Because of their built-in capabilities, these terminals can perform limited processing tasks when they are not communicating directly with the central computer. Intelligent terminals are also known as **programmable terminals** or **smart terminals** because they can be programmed by the user to perform

many basic tasks, including arithmetic and logic operations. Personal computers are frequently used as intelligent terminals when they are connected to larger computers.

Special-purpose terminals perform specific jobs and contain features uniquely designed for use in a particular industry. The special-purpose terminal shown in *Figure 3-27* is called a point-of-sale terminal. **Point-of-sale (POS) terminals** allow data to be entered at the time and place where the transaction with a customer occurs, such as in fast-food restaurants or hotels, for example. Point-of-sale terminals serve as input to computers located at the place of business or elsewhere. The data entered is used to maintain sales records, update inventory, make automatic calculations such as sales tax, verify credit, and perform other activities associated with the sales transactions and critical to running the business. Point-of-sale terminals are designed to be easy to operate, requiring little technical knowledge. As shown in *Figure 3-27,* the keys are labeled to assist the user.

Figure 3-26
Dumb terminals have no independent processing capability and cannot function as a stand-alone device. They are usually connected to larger computer systems.

Figure 3-27
Point-of-sale terminals are usually designed for a specific type of business such as a restaurant, hotel, or retail store. Keys are labeled to assist the user in recording transactions.

Multimedia Input Devices

Multimedia is the combination of sound and images with text and graphics. To capture sound and image data, special input devices are required. For personal computers, these input devices consist primarily of electronics contained on a separate card, such as a **sound card** or **video card**, that is installed in the computer.

Sound Input

Sounds are usually recorded with a microphone connected to the sound card or by directly connecting a sound device such as an electronic music keyboard to the sound card. Sound editing software *(Figure 3-28)* allows the user to change the sound after it is recorded.

Voice Input

Voice input, sometimes referred to as speech or voice recognition, allows the user to enter data and issue commands to the computer with spoken words. Some experts think that voice input may eventually be the most common way to operate a computer. Their belief is based on the fact that people can speak much faster than they can type (approximately 200 words per minute speaking and only 40 words per minute for the average typist). In addition, speaking is a more natural means of communicating than using a keyboard, which takes some time to learn.

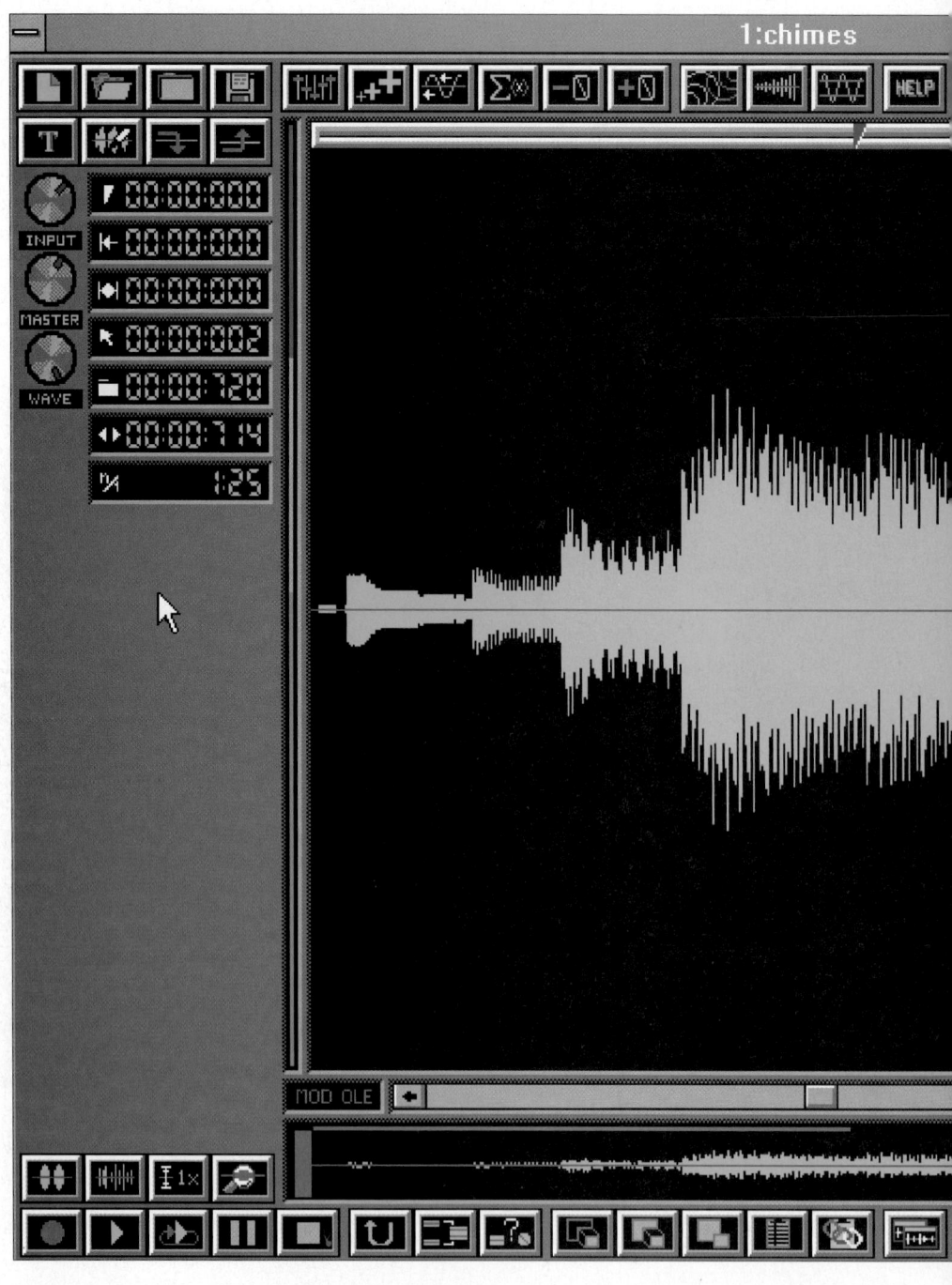

Figure 3-28
Sound editing software allows the user to change sounds that have been digitally recorded. Sounds can be duplicated, speeded up, slowed down, or have special effects such as echo or fade added. This screen represents the sound of chimes.

Four areas where voice input is used are data entry, command and control, speaker recognition, and speech to text.

In many voice data entry applications, it is as if the user is verbally filling out a form. Standard questions are verbally completed, usually with a limited number of acceptable responses. For example, voice data entry systems are used for product inspections in manufacturing companies. Instead of manually recording data or using a keyboard, the inspector dictates the completed product information into a microphone.

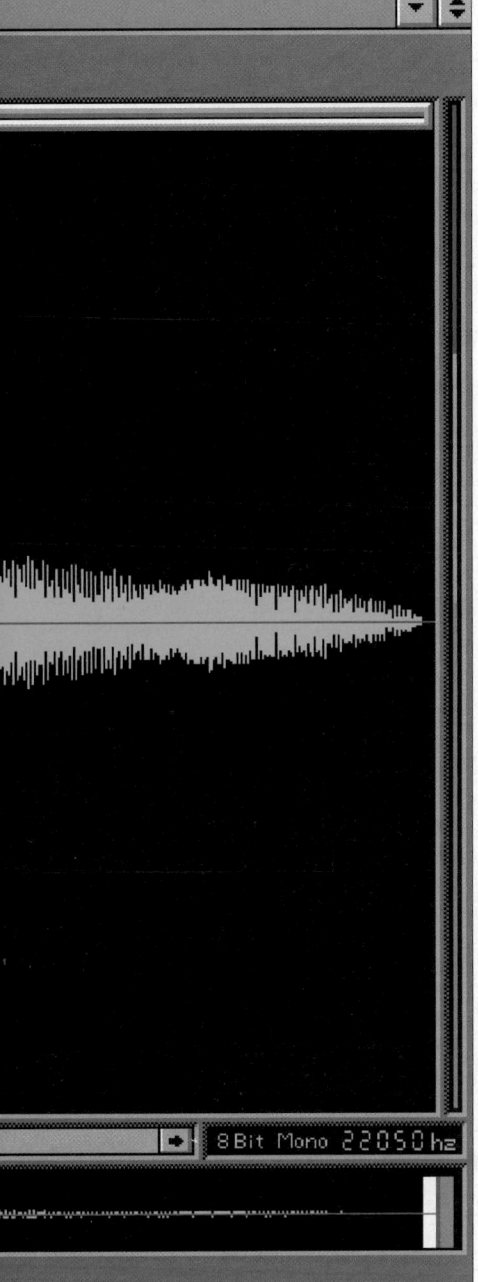

This is especially efficient when the inspector's hands and eyes must stay focused on the item being inspected.

Command and control applications use a limited vocabulary of words that cause the computer to perform a specific action such as *save* or *print* a document. Command and control applications are also used to operate certain types of industrial machinery.

Speaker recognition applications are usually security oriented such as restricting physical access to a particular area. Unless a person's voice matches a previously recorded pattern, he or she is denied entry. This type of application has been used in banks, government installations, and other high security locations.

Speech-to-text applications offer the most possibility for the widespread use of voice input. With speech-to-text applications, spoken words are immediately translated into computer text and usually displayed on the screen. One area where speech-to-text applications have been implemented is in medical reporting. Many health professionals now use speech-to-text systems to input the numerous reports that must be maintained on patients *(Figure 3-29)*.

Figure 3-29
Many health care professionals use speech-to-text systems to record information while they are working.

Most voice input systems use a combination of hardware and software to convert spoken words into data the computer can process. The conversion process used by one voice input system developer, shown in *Figure 3-30,* is as follows:

1. The user's voice, consisting of sound waves, is converted into digital form by **digital signal processing** (DSP) circuits that are usually on a separate board added to the computer.
2. The digitized voice input is compared against patterns stored in the voice system's database.
3. Grammar rules are used to resolve possible word conflicts. Based on how a word was used, the computer can usually identify the correct word in cases of words that sound alike such as to, too, and two.
4. Unrecognized words are presented to the user to identify.

With many voice input systems, especially the lower cost systems with limited vocabularies, the user has to train the system to recognize his or her voice. For each of the words in the vocabulary, the user speaks the word. After each word has been spoken several times, the system develops a digital pattern for the word that can be stored on secondary storage. When the user later speaks a word to the system to request a particular action, the system compares the word to the words that were previously entered. When it finds a match, the software performs the activity associated with the word. Such systems are referred to as **speaker dependent** because each person who wants to use the system has to train it to his or her voice. With larger vocabulary systems containing up to 50,000 words, training on individual words is not practical. Instead, developers include multiple patterns, called **voice templates** for each word. These templates include male and female voices as well as regional accents. These systems are called **speaker independent** because most users will not have to train the system to their speech pattern.

Figure 3-30
This diagram shows how one speech recognition company, Kurzweil AI, Inc., converts spoken words to computer input.

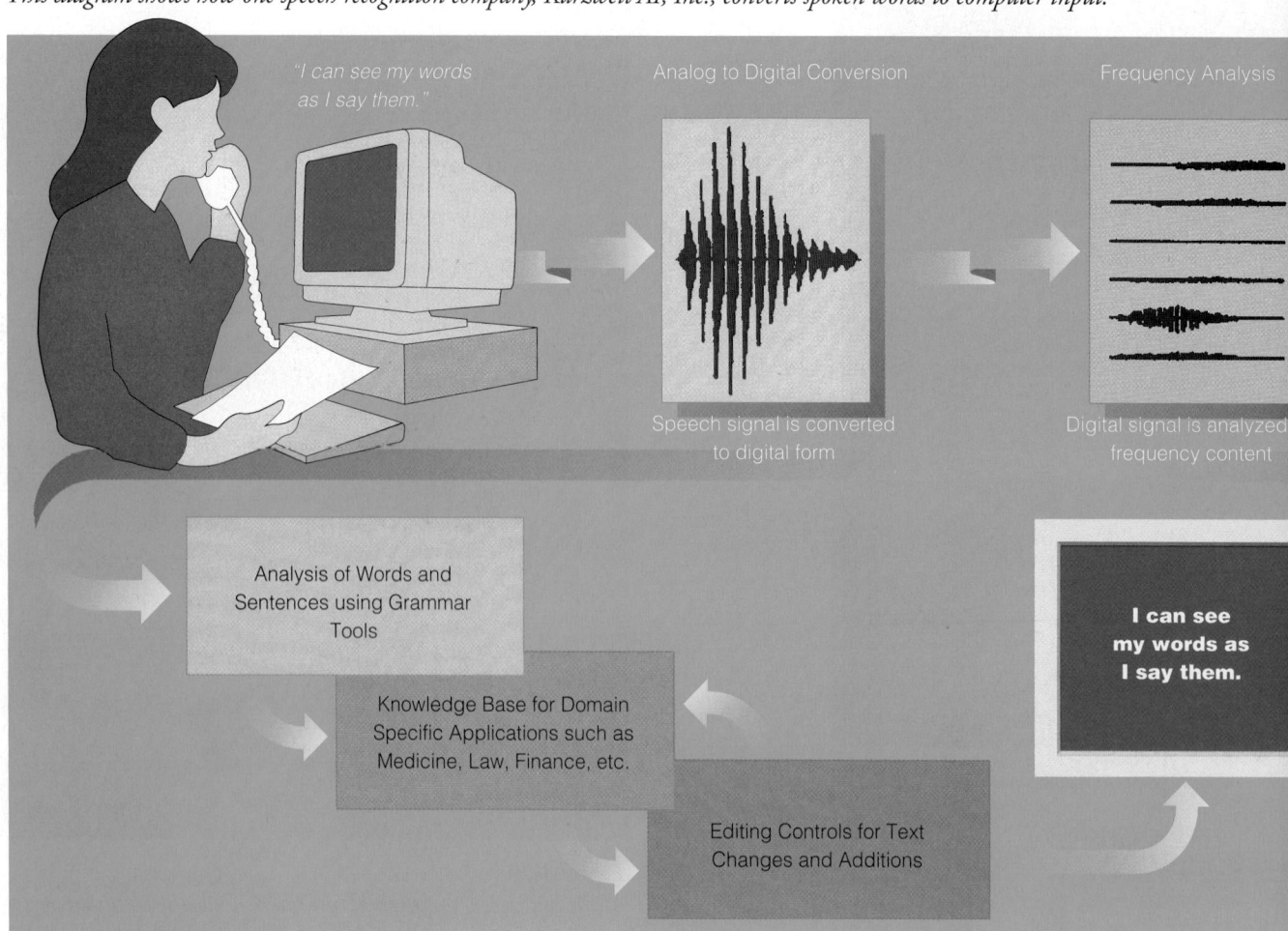

Most speech-to-text systems in use today use **discrete speech recognition** that requires the user to pause slightly between each word. **Continuous speech recognition** systems that allow the user to speak in a flowing conversational tone are not yet widely used because they require more complex software and hardware to separate and make sense of the words. Low cost continuous speech recognition systems are expected to be available for personal computers by the year 2000.

Beyond continuous voice recognition is what is called natural language voice interface. A **natural language voice interface** allows the user to ask a question and have the computer not only convert the question to understandable words but interpret the question and give an appropriate response. For example, think how powerful and easy it would be to use a system if you could simply ask, "How soon can we ship 200 red stainless steel widgets to Boston?" Think about how many different pieces of information the computer might have to pull together to generate a correct response. Such natural language voice recognition systems are not commercially available now but are being developed using powerful computers and sophisticated software.

Digital Camera

Digital cameras record photographs in the form of digital data that can be stored on a computer. No chemical based film is used. Some digital cameras are portable and look similar to traditional film cameras. Other digital cameras are stationary and are connected directly to a computer *(Figure 3-31)*.

Figure 3-31
The digital camera is used to record digital photographs of documents, products, or people. The camera is connected to a video board installed in the computer.

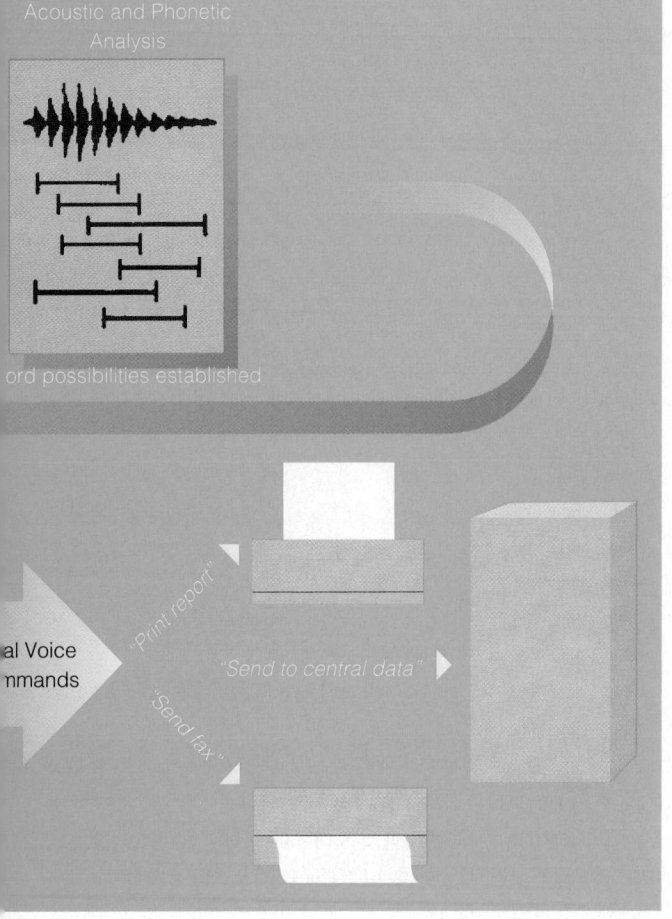

Many companies use digital cameras to record images of their products for computer based catalogs or to record photos of their employees for personnel records *(Figure 3-32).*

Video Input

Video material is input to the computer using a video camera or a video recorder using previously recorded material. Video data requires tremendous amounts of storage space, which is why video segments in personal computer applications are often limited to only a few seconds. Improvements in video electronics and software and larger capacity storage devices will enable movie length video data to eventually become available. Video applications currently under development include video repair manuals. Rather that just looking at a photo or diagram, the user could view narrated video segments on how to disassemble and repair a piece of equipment.

The input devices discussed in this chapter are summarized in *Figure 3-33.* When any of these devices are used to input data, it is important that the data is entered accurately. Various procedures are used to help ensure data accuracy.

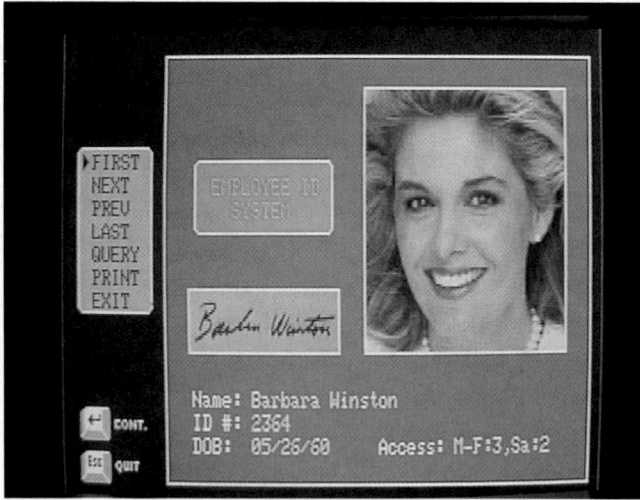

Figure 3-32
Digital cameras are often used to record photographs of employees that are added to their computer-based personnel records.

Figure 3-33
A summary of some of the more common input devices.

Data Accuracy

The procedures developed for controlling input are important because accurate data must be entered into a computer to ensure data integrity. Inaccurate information caused by inaccurate data is often worse than no information at all. The computer jargon term **GIGO** states this point very well; it stands for *Garbage In, Garbage Out.*

Because users are often interacting directly with the computer during the input process, procedures and documentation must be quite clear. Computer programs and procedures must be designed to check for accurate data and should specify the steps to take if the data is not valid. Although different applications will have specific criteria for validating input data, several tests can be performed before the data is processed by the computer. Some of these tests are:

- Tests for data type and format – If data should be of a particular type, such as alphabetic or numeric, then it should be tested for that. Often, a data type test is combined with a data format test. For example, in the United States, the ZIP postal code should either be five digits alone or five digits followed by a dash followed by four digits. Unless the data fits one of those two formats, it should be rejected.

DEVICE	DESCRIPTION
Keyboard	Most commonly used input device; special keys may include numeric keypad, cursor control keys, and function keys
Mouse or Trackball	Used to move pointer and select options
Joystick	Stem device often used as input device for games
Pen Input	Uses pen to input and edit data and select processing options
Touch Screen	User interacts with computer by touching screen with finger
Light Pen	Used to select options or draw on screen
Digitizer	Used to enter or edit drawings
Graphic Tablet	Digitizer with special processing options built into tablet
Image Scanner	Converts text, graphics, or photos into digital input
Optical Recognition	Uses light source to read codes, marks, and characters
MICR	Used in banking to read magnetic ink characters on checks
Data Collection	Used in factories and warehouses to input data at source
Sound Input	Converts sound into digital data
Voice Input	Converts speech into digital data
Digital Camera	Captures digital image of subject or object
Video Input	Converts video into digital data

- Tests for data reasonableness – A reasonableness check ensures that the data entered is within normal or accepted boundaries. For example, suppose no employee within a company is authorized to work more than 80 hours per week. If the value entered in the hours worked field is greater than 80, the value in the field would be indicated as a probable error.
- Tests for data consistency – In some cases, data entered cannot, by itself, be found to be invalid. If, however, the data is examined in relation to other data entered for the same transaction, discrepancies might be found. For example, in a hotel reservation system, both the check-in and check-out dates are entered. Each date should be checked to make sure it is valid. In addition, the check-out date should be later than the check-in date. If the check-out date is earlier than the check-in date, an error has been made when entering one of the dates *(Figure 3-34)*.
- Tests for transcription and transposition errors – The possibility always exists that an operator will make an error when entering data. A **transcription error** occurs when an error is made in copying the values from a source document. For example, if the operator keys the customer number

7165 when the proper number is 7765, the operator has made a transcription error. A **transposition error** happens when the operator switches two numbers. Such an error has occurred when the number 7765 is entered as 7756. Transcription and transposition errors are often difficult to detect. Usually, some other piece of information must be checked to verify that the data entered is correct. For example, when entering a customer number, the user should verify that the corresponding customer name is correct before proceeding.

Summary of Input to the Computer

Chapter 3 presented an overview of the information processing cycle and discussed how data is organized. Also discussed were the four types of input and a variety of input devices. Procedures used to ensure data accuracy were presented and explained. After reading this chapter, you should have a better overall understanding of computer input.

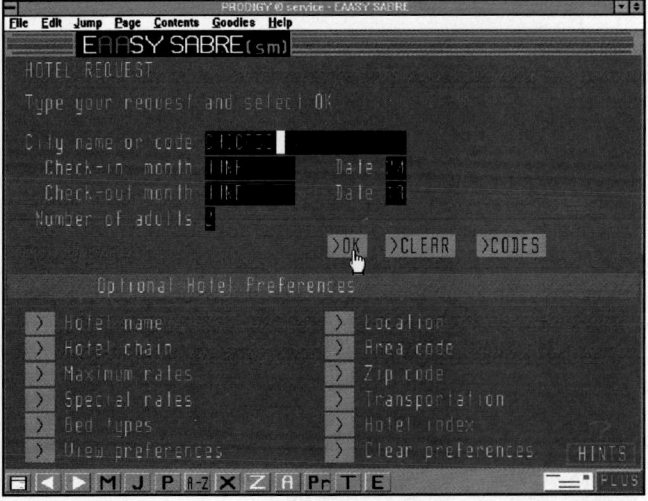 

Figure 3-34
One way to check for data accuracy is to compare one piece of data with another and look for logical errors. In this example of a hotel reservation system, the system compared the check-out date with the check-in date. Because the check-out date was earlier than the check-in date, an error message was displayed and the user was asked to reenter the dates.

COMPUTERS AT WORK

Helping People with Special Needs

For physically challenged and disabled individuals, working with standard computers may be either difficult or impossible. Fortunately, special software and hardware, called adaptive, or assistive, technology enables many of these individuals to use computers productively and independently.

Adaptive technology covers a wide range of hardware and software products that help the user make the computer meet his or her special needs. For people with motor disabilities who cannot use a standard keyboard, there are a number of alternative input devices. Most of these devices involve the use of a switch that is controlled by any reliable muscle. One type of switch is even activated by breathing into a tube. The switches are used with special software to select commands or input characters. For those who cannot use their muscles to activate switches, a system exists that is controlled by eye movement. Called Eyegaze, the system uses a camera mounted on the computer and directed at one of the user's eyes. Using the movement of the user's eye, software determines where on the screen the user is looking to within $1/4$ inch accuracy. To activate a choice on the screen, the user has to stare at it for approximately $1/4$ second.

For blind individuals, voice recognition programs allow for verbal input. Software is also available that converts text to Braille and sends it to Braille printers. Both blind and nonverbal individuals use speech synthesis equipment to convert text documents into spoken words. For people with limited vision, several programs are available that magnify information on the screen.

The use of adaptive technology received further encouragement when the Americans with Disabilities Act (ADA) was enacted. Since 1994, the ADA requires that all companies with 15 or more employees make reasonable attempts to accommodate the needs of workers with physical challenges. Many employers are complying with the legislation through the use of personal computers and adaptive technology software and equipment.

Figure 3-35

IN THE FUTURE

"Computer, tell me the status of . . ."

In many science fiction stories, humans have conversations with computers. The human speaks in a natural, conversational tone and the computer responds in a similar manner, sometimes asking questions to clarify the human's statement or request. Many experts believe that this type of natural language interface will one day become the way humans interact with a computer. To provide this capability, however, much more powerful and faster computers will have to be developed. In addition, voice recognition software will have to be significantly improved.

To understand human speech, a computer has to go through four steps: sound analysis, word recognition, sentence or thought construction, and statement context. Sound analysis is the easiest part. Sound waves are converted into the smallest units of speech, called phonemes. During word recognition, the phonemes are joined together to form words. This can be a difficult task because conversational speech often runs one word into another. The problem becomes more difficult during sentence and thought construction. During this process, the identified words are joined together to make a logical statement. As your high school English teacher may have told you, people do not always speak or write in a logical manner using correct grammar. Statement context involves using past statements to provide information about a current statement. For example, say an airline reservation agent told you there were no flights available on the day you wanted to leave, June 20. If you said, "How about the next day?", the computer should know that you now want to check the flights on June 21.

Some experts think that significant breakthroughs in natural speech recognition are just a few years away. Others think that easy to use systems will not be available until after the year 2000. The optimists, however, are already talking about the next human interface challenge; how to read lips!

Do you remember *HAL*, the computer in the movie *2001: A Space Odyssey*?

Figure 3-36

File   Edit   Section   Page   Tools   Options   Help

What You Should Know

1. The input operation must take place before any data can be processed and any information produced and stored. **Input** refers to the process of entering data, programs, commands, and user responses into main memory.

2. **Data** refers to the raw facts, including numbers, letters, words, images, and sounds a computer receives during the input operation and processes to produce information. **Programs** are instructions that direct the computer to perform the necessary operations to process data into information. **Commands** are key words and phrases the user inputs to direct the computer to perform certain activities. **User responses** refer to the data a user inputs to respond to a question or message from the software.

3. The **keyboard** is the most commonly used input device. The alphabetic keys are arranged like those on a typewriter, and a **numeric keypad** is located on the right-hand side of most keyboards. A **cursor** is a symbol that indicates where the next character typed will appear on the screen. Other keyboard keys include the **arrow keys** or **cursor control keys**, and **function keys**.

4. Pointing devices allow the user to control an on-screen symbol called the **mouse pointer** or **pointer** that is usually represented by an arrow-shaped marker.

5. A **mouse** is a small, lightweight input device that easily fits in the palm of your hand. Moving the mouse across a flat surface controls the movement of the pointer on the screen, and the buttons on top of the mouse can be used to select options displayed on the screen.

6. A **trackball** is a pointing device like a mouse only with the ball on top of the device instead of on the bottom.

7. A **joystick** uses the movement of a vertical stem to direct the pointer.

8. **Pen input devices** allow the user to use the pen in three ways; to input data using hand-written characters and shapes the computer can recognize, as a pointing device like a mouse to select items on the screen, and to gesture, which is a way of issuing commands. When the pen touches the screen, the computer darkens that location. The darkened area is referred to as **ink**.

9. Most **handwriting recognition software** can be taught to recognize an individual's unique style of writing. **Gestures** are special symbols made with the pen that issue a command.

10. A **touch screen** allows users to touch areas of the screen to enter data. A **light pen** is used by touching it on the display screen to create or modify graphics. A **digitizer** converts points, lines, and curves from a sketch, drawing, or photograph to digital impulses and transmits them to a computer. A **graphics tablet** works in a manner similar to a digitizer, but it also contains unique characters and commands that can be automatically generated by the person using the tablet.

11. **Source data automation**, sometimes called **source data collection**, refers to procedures and equipment designed to make the input process more efficient by eliminating the manual entry of data. Data is captured directly from its original form, called a **source document**.

12. An **image scanner**, sometimes called a **page scanner**, is an input device that electronically captures an entire page of text or images, such as photographs or art work. **Image processing systems** use scanners to capture and electronically file documents.

13. **Optical recognition** devices use a light source to read codes, marks, and characters and convert them into digital data that can be processed by a computer.

14. **Optical codes** use a pattern or symbols to represent data. A **bar code**, the most common optical code, consists of a set of vertical lines and spaces of different widths. There are several different types of bar codes, but the most familiar is the **universal product code** (UPC) used for grocery and retail items.

15. **Optical mark recognition** (OMR) devices can read carefully placed marks on specially designed documents such as questionnaires or test answer sheets.

16. **Optical character recognition** (OCR) devices are scanners that read typewritten, computer-printed, and in some cases hand-printed characters from ordinary documents. OCR is frequently used for **turn-around documents** that are designed to be returned to the organization that created them.

17. **OCR software** is used with image scanners to convert text images into data that can be processed by word processing software.

18. **Magnetic ink character recognition** (MICR) characters use a special ink that can be magnetized during processing. MICR is used almost exclusively by the banking industry for processing checks.

19. **Data collection devices** are designed and used for obtaining data at the site where the transaction or event being reported takes place. They are often used in rugged locations, such as factories or warehouses, and operated by persons whose primary task is not entering data.

20. Terminals, sometimes called **display terminals** or **video display terminals** (VDTs), consist of a keyboard and a screen. A **dumb terminal** can be used to enter and transmit data to or receive data from a computer to which it is connected. It has no independent processing capability or secondary storage and cannot function as a stand-alone device. **Intelligent terminals**, also known as **programmable terminals** or **smart terminals**, have built-in processing capabilities, can be programmed by the user to perform many basic tasks, and often contain secondary storage devices. **Point-of-sale** (POS) terminals are special-purpose terminals that allow data to be entered at the time and place where the transaction with a customer occurs.

21. **Multimedia** is the combination of sound and images with text and graphics. Personal computers use special input devices consisting primarily of electronics contained on a separate card, such as a **sound card** or **video card**, that are installed in the computer to capture sound and image data.

22. Sounds are usually recorded by connecting a microphone or electronic music keyboard to the sound card. **Voice input** allows the user to enter data and issue commands to the computer with spoken words. The user's voice, consisting of sound waves, is converted into digital form by **digital signal processing** (DSP) circuits. Four areas where voice input is used are data entry, command and control, speaker recognition, and speech-to-text.

23. Voice input systems that must be trained to the voice of each person who wants to use the system are referred to as **speaker dependent**. Voice input systems that contain **voice templates** for each word are called **speaker independent**, because most users will not have to train the system to their speech pattern.

24. Most speech-to-text systems in use today use **discrete speech recognition** that requires the user to pause slightly between each word. **Continuous speech recognition** systems allow the user to speak in a flowing conversational tone but are not yet widely used. A **natural language voice interface** allows the user to ask a question and have the computer not only convert the question to understandable words but to interpret the question and give an appropriate response.

25. **Digital cameras** record photographs in the form of digital data that can be stored on a computer.

26. Video material is input to the computer with a video camera or a video recorder using previously recorded material. Video data requires tremendous amounts of storage space.

27. Inaccurate information caused by inaccurate data is often worse than no information at all. The computer jargon **GIGO** states this very well; it stands for *Garbage In, Garbage Out*.

28. Several tests can be performed to validate data before it is processed by the computer. Some of these enable tests for data type and format, tests for data reasonableness, tests for data consistency, and tests for source errors (errors made in copying values from made by document) and **transposition errors** (errors made by switching two numbers).

File   Edit   Section   Page   Tools   Options   Help

Terms to Remember

arrow keys (3.4)

bar code (3.11)

commands (3.2)
continuous speed recognition (3.19)
cursor (3.4)
cursor control keys (3.4)

data (3.3)
data collection devices (3.14)
digital camera (3.19)
digital signal processing (DSP) (3.18)
digitizer (3.9)
discrete speech recognition (3.19)
display terminals (3.15)
dumb terminals (3.15)

function keys (3.4)

gestures (3.7)
GIGO (Garbage In, Garbage Out) (3.20)
graphics tablet (3.9)

handwriting recognition software (3.7)

image processing systems (3.10)
image scanner (3.10)
ink (3.7)
input (3.2)
intelligent terminals (3.15)

joystick (3.6)

keyboard (3.3)

light pen (3.9)

magnetic ink character recognition
   (MICR) (3.13)
mouse (3.5)
mouse pointer (3.5)
multimedia (3.16)

natural language voice interface (3.19)
numeric keypad (3.3)

OCR software (3.13)
optical character recognition
   (OCR) (3.12)
optical codes (3.11)
optical mark recognition (OMR) (3.12)
optical recognition (3.11)

page scanner (3.10)
pen input devices (3.7)
point-of-sale (POS) terminals (3.15)
pointer (3.5)
programmable terminals (3.15)
programs (3.2)

smart terminals (3.15)
sound card (3.16)
source data automation (3.10)
source data collection (3.10)
source document (3.10)
speaker dependent (3.18)
speaker independent (3.18)

touch screen (3.8)
trackball (3.6)
transcription error (3.21)
transposition error (3.21)
turn-around documents (3.12)

universal product code (UPC) (3.11)
user responses (3.3)

video card (3.16)
video display terminals (VDT) (3.15)
voice input (3.16)
voice templates (3.18)

le   Edit   Section   Page   Tools   Options   Help

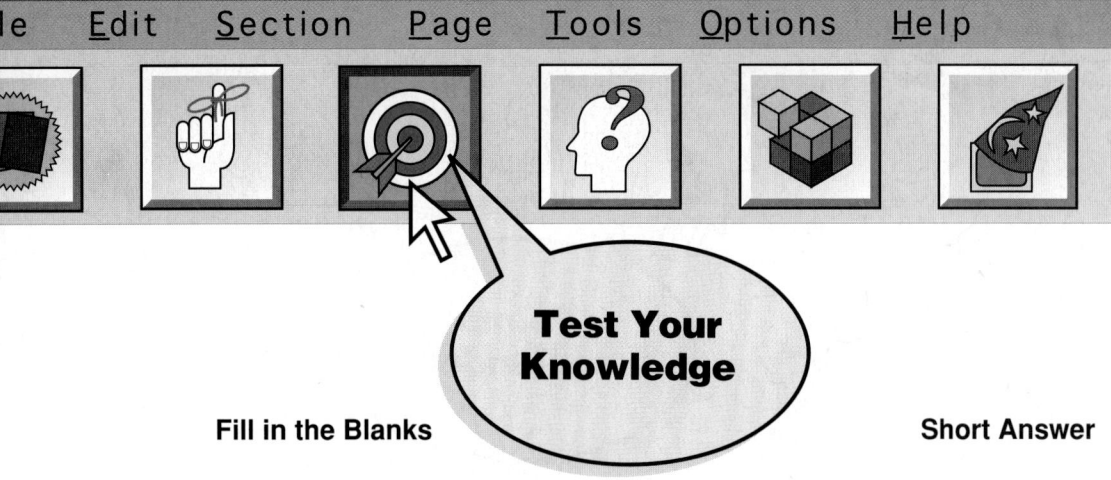

Test Your Knowledge

Fill in the Blanks

1. The information processing cycle consists of four operations: _____, _____, _____, and _____.

2. In the information processing cycle, the _____ operation must take place before any data can be processed and any information produced and stored.

3. A(n) _____ is a pointing device that, by moving it across a flat surface and pressing buttons, can be used to move the pointer and select options on the screen.

4. Three types of terminals are: _____, which can be used to enter, transmit, receive, or display data but have no independent processing capability; _____, which have built-in processing capabilities and often contain disk drives and printers; and _____, which allow data to be entered at the time and place where the transaction with a customer occurs.

5. _____ is the combination of sound and images with text and graphics.

Short Answer

1. What is input? List the four types of input and briefly describe how the computer uses each type.

2. Although a computer keyboard is similar to a typewriter keyboard, a computer keyboard also has keys that are not found on the keyboard of a traditional typewriter. What are some of these keys? For what purpose are these keys used?

3. How are a mouse, trackball, and joystick similar? How are they different? What is the primary advantage of a mouse? What are the disadvantages? What advantage does a trackball have over a mouse?

4. What is a terminal? How is a dumb terminal different from an intelligent terminal? How is a point-of-sale terminal used?

5. Why is data accuracy important? What does the computer jargon term GIGO mean? Briefly describe three tests for data accuracy that can be performed before the data is processed by the computer.

Label the Figure

Instructions: The examples below show gestures; special symbols made with pen input devices. In the spaces provided, list the command issued for each gesture.

Gesture	Command	Gesture	Command
•	_____	⟵	_____
→	_____	↗	_____
⟋	_____	⟋	_____
⟷	_____	⟍↗	_____
⟼	_____	⟋	_____

File   Edit   Section   Page   Tools   Options   Help

Points to Ponder

1

The traditional arrangement of letters on a keyboard is sometimes called the QWERTY layout. The name QWERTY comes from the first six keys in the top row of letters. This layout was initially adopted by early typewriters to place the most commonly used letters in locations that were not easily reached, to slow typists down and prevent keys from jamming. Although keys jamming is no longer a problem, most keyboards still use the same design today. A different key arrangement, called the Dvorak layout, places the most commonly used letters on the home row, the row on which your fingers rest. What are the advantages of the Dvorak layout? What are the disadvantages? If a typist was trained to use both keyboard layouts, which do you think would result in faster data input? Why? Will the Dvorak layout ever be widely accepted? Why or why not?

2

At one time, the keyboard was the only means of inputting data into a computer. Although the keyboard remains the most commonly used input device, the mouse has also become almost essential; many makers of computer software require the use of a mouse with their application packages. What does the future of input devices hold? Thirty years from now, will a different pointing device be more popular than the mouse? Will the keyboard be replaced by another input device? Why? Will any input device become an historical oddity, seen only in museums? Why?

3

Pen input devices have been adapted to many applications and are currently being used by sales representatives, delivery services, nurses and doctors, and inventory takers. In what way do you think pen input devices are particularly useful in each of these fields? List some other areas that you feel could use pen input devices and briefly describe how they could be used in each. Do you think a pen input device would be valuable to a student? Why or why not?

4

A recent controversy in one county in New York state involved the use of optical code scanners in grocery stores. Scanners were being used at the check-out counters to determine the price of each purchase and, although prices were indicated on the grocery shelves, they were not marked on individual grocery items. Consumer groups argued that the shelf price tags were hard to read and not having price stickers on each item made it difficult to compare prices. In addition, they claimed that the databases from which the scanners obtained prices were not always accurate and frequently were not updated to reflect sale prices. The grocery stores maintained that the labor involved in individual item pricing would add to the item's cost, and that most of the time their scanned prices were accurate. What do you think? Should grocery stores be required to put a price on each individual item? Why or why not? Can you think of any other way to answer consumer concerns?

5

Although computers have become widespread, many people are still intimidated when forced to input data into a computer. Of the input devices discussed in this chapter, which do you feel would be the easiest to use for someone who is uncomfortable with computers? Why? Which input device do you think requires the most training? If a school decided every student must learn to use one input device, which device do you think should be taught? Why?

6

All input devices require some form of human interaction. A keyboard requires a great deal of human interaction because someone inputting data must not only read the data accurately but also locate and press the correct keys. In contrast, an optical code scanner requires a minimum of human interaction because the user need only pass the optical code in front of the scanner. Keeping in mind the tests described in this chapter, what impact do you think the degree of human interaction has on data accuracy? Why? List at least five input devices in order, from those that require the most human interaction to those that require the least human interaction. Which input devices do you think result in the most accurate input of data? Why?

le   Edit   Section   Page   Tools   Options   Help

Out and About

1. Although all computer keyboards may seem alike, the placement of special keys, the space between keys, the feel of the keys, and the noise produced when a key is pressed may vary. Visit a computer vendor and try at least three different types of computer keyboards. Evaluate each keyboard in terms of the suggested characteristics. Which keyboard do you like best? Why? Which keyboard do you like least? Why?

2. Visit a firm or organization that uses computers. Talk with a person involved with computer operations to find out what types of input devices are used. For what purpose is each device used? Has the firm or organization ever experienced problems as a result of inaccurate data being entered into the computer? If so, what kinds of problems? What measures were taken to insure that the problems did not happen again?

3. The wide range of input devices available for computers has helped many physically challenged individuals. Use a library to research the types of input devices that have helped people facing physical challenges. What types of input devices have been used? What input devices have been particularly helpful for people with specific physical disabilities?

4. Optical code scanners are used by retail stores, supermarkets, and libraries. Visit an organization that uses optical code scanners to find out how the scanners are used. What types of information are they able to record? How is the information used? In what way does the information obtained through the use of scanners benefit the organization or the organization's clientele? Were they able to keep track of the same information before they used scanners? Why or why not?

5. Visit a local bank and ask an employee about ATM (automatic teller machine) terminals. How are they used? What kind of information do they obtain? What security measures are provided? What precautions does the bank suggest to ATM users? Has the bank ever had any trouble with their ATMs? If so, what? After interviewing the bank employee, decide whether you think an ATM is a dumb terminal or an intelligent terminal. Why?

6. Visit a computer vendor and select a personal computer system displayed in the store. Make a list of the input devices that can be used with that personal computer, and provide a price for each input device. If you were to purchase that personal computer, which input device or devices would you want to purchase right away? Why? Which input devices do you think you might purchase at a later date? Why? Are there any available input devices that you think you would never buy? Why?

File Edit Section Page Tools Options Help

 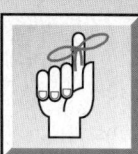    

In the Lab

Windows Labs

1 **Displaying Your System Configuration**   With Program Manager on the screen, double-click the Main group icon. In the Main group window, double-click the Windows Setup program-item icon. Write down the type of display, keyboard, and mouse your computer has. Close Windows Setup by double-clicking its Control-menu box.

2 **Customizing the Mouse**   With Program Manager on the screen, double-click the Main group icon. In the Main group window, double-click the Control Panel program-item icon. In the Control Panel window, double-click the Mouse icon. In your Mouse dialog box, which may be similar to *Figure 3-37,* click the Help button. Read and print all of the Help topics about the Mouse dialog box. To return to the original Help window, click the Back button. Close the Help window.

Test each of the options in the Mouse dialog box. For example, on the Double Click Speed scroll bar, drag the scroll box to Slow. Double-click the Test box to test the speed. A successful double-click reverses the color in the Test box. Test other speeds. Answer the following questions: (1) Why would you want to switch the left and right (primary and secondary) mouse buttons? (2) What are mouse trails? (3) How do you adjust the speed of the mouse? Choose the OK button in the Mouse dialog box. Close Control Panel.

3 **Shelly Cashman Series Input Lab**   Follow the instructions in Windows Lab 2 on page 1.30 to display the Shelly Cashman Series Labs screen. Select Scanning Documents and choose the Start Lab button. When the initial screen displays, carefully read the objectives. With your printer turned on, point to the Print Questions button and click the left mouse button. Fill out the top of the Questions sheet and answer the questions as you step through the Input Lab.

4 **Scanning a Photograph**   Bring a 3 1/2" x 5" (or larger) picture of yourself or family members to class. Ask your instructor for assistance in scanning the photograph to create a digital version on your diskette using the first four characters of your last name as the filename. With Program Manager on the screen, double-click the Accessories group icon. Double-click the Paintbrush program-item icon. Use the Open command on the File menu to open the file containing your picture. Your Paintbrush window should be similar to the one shown in *Figure 3-38.* Print the picture using the Print command on the File menu. For extra credit, autograph your picture in Paintbrush and print it. Do not save the autographed picture to your diskette. Close Paintbrush.

5 **Using the Mouse and Keyboard to Interact with an Online Program**   Obtain information from your instructor on the location (path) of the file LOANCALC.EXE. With Program Manager on the screen, select the File menu and choose the Run command. In the Command Line text box, type the path and filename loancalc. For example, type c:\sclabs\loancalc as shown in *Figure 3-39.* Press the ENTER key. The Loan Payment Calculator window displays on the

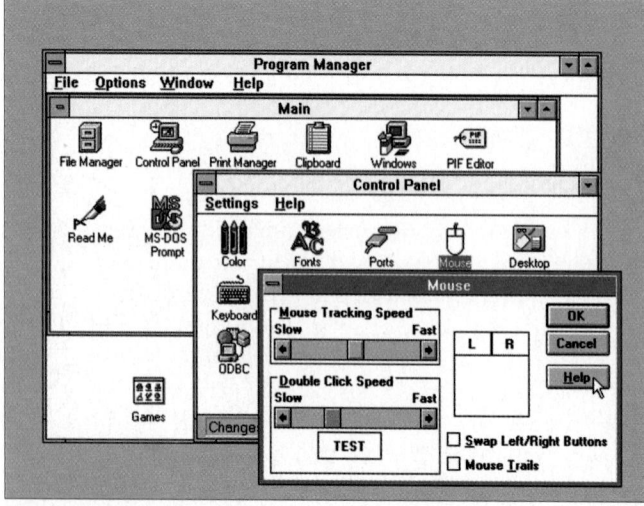

Figure 3-37

Figure 3-38

screen. Type 100000 in the LOAN AMOUNT box. Click the YEARS right scroll arrow or drag the scroll box until the YEARS equals 15. Click the APR right scroll arrow or drag the scroll box until the APR equals 9.75. Click the Calculate button. Note the monthly payment and sum of all payments made *(Figure 3-40)*. Click the Clear button. What is the monthly payment and sum of payments for each of these loan amounts, years, and APRs? (1) 15000, 5, 6.25; (2) 55000, 30, 10.25; (3) 162500, 30, 8; (4) 75550, 15, 9.25; and (5) 9750, 3, 7.5. Click the About button. Who wrote this program? Choose the OK button. Close the Loan Payment Calculator.

6 **More About Using Help** With Program Manager on the screen, select the Help menu and choose the How to Use Help command. One at a time, click the last five topics listed in green at the bottom of the window. Read and print each one. Click the Back button to return to the How to Use Help window. Close the How to Use Help window.

DOS Labs

1 **Using Doskey** At the DOS prompt, type doskey and press the ENTER key. Type dir and press the ENTER key. When the DOS prompt appears again, press the UP ARROW key to recall the dir command and press the ENTER key. Type ver and press the ENTER key. Press the UP ARROW key three times to display one at a time the sequence of commands executed. What is the purpose of the DOSKEY command?

2 **Using the Numeric Keypad to Enter Data** Obtain information from your instructor on how to change to the directory on your computer containing the LOANPAY.EXE

program. At the DOS prompt, type loanpay and press the ENTER key. Press the NUM LOCK key on the numeric keypad to turn on Num Lock. When you are prompted, enter 10500 for the loan amount, 11.5 for the rate, and 4.5 for the years using the numeric keypad. What input device did you use to enter the data? List the input prompts, corresponding data items, and output results for the loan program.

3 **Using Help** At the DOS prompt, type help and press the ENTER key. Press F1 to display the How to Use MS-DOS Help window. Read the contents of the window. Print the contents of the window by pressing the ALT key to activate the menu bar, typing F to display the File menu, and typing P to choose the Print command. Finally, press the ENTER key when the Print dialog box displays. With the cursor on the first Help topic, press the ENTER key. Read and print the information. Press ALT+B to return to the prior Help window. One by one, select and print each remaining topic to learn how to use Help. Exit the Help window by selecting the File menu and choosing the Exit command.

Online Lab

1 **Weather Information** Using one of the two online services you selected in Chapter 1, connect to the service and perform the following tasks: (1) Search the online service for Weather Information. (2) Display the United States weather map. Write down the weather information for your part of the country. (3) Display and write down the weather information for Anchorage, AK; Chicago, IL; Los Angeles, CA; Maui, HI; New York, NY; and the city you live in, or one nearby.

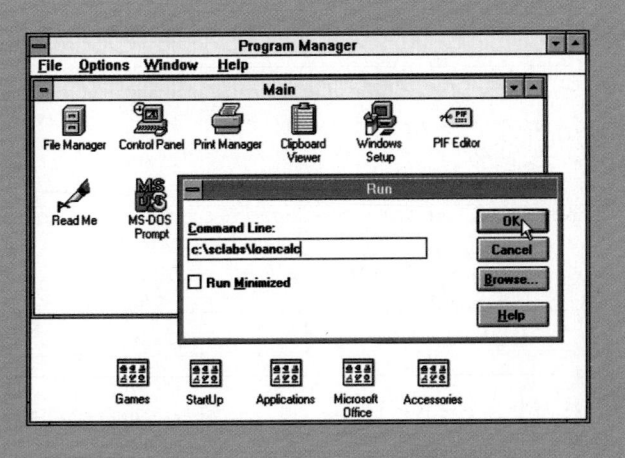

Figure 3-39

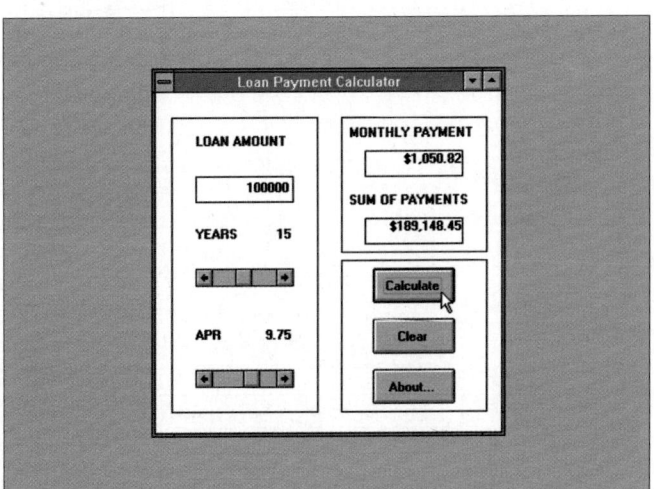

Figure 3-40

The System Unit

Objectives

After completing this chapter, you will be able to:

- Define a bit and describe how a series of bits in a byte is used to represent data

- Discuss how the ASCII and EBCDIC codes represent characters

- Identify the components of the system unit and describe their use

- Describe how the CPU uses the four steps of the machine cycle to process data

- Describe the primary use and characteristics of RAM and ROM memory

- Explain the difference between parallel and serial ports

- Describe a machine language instruction and the instruction set of a computer

- Describe various types of processing including pipe-lining, parallel processing, and neural networks

- Convert numbers between the decimal, binary, and hexadecimal number systems

The information processing cycle consists of input, processing, output, and storage operations. When an input operation is completed and both a program and data are stored in main memory, processing operations can begin. During these operations, the system unit executes, or performs, the program instructions and processes the data into information.

Chapter 4 examines the components of the system unit, describes how main memory stores programs and data, and discusses the sequence of operations that occurs when instructions are executed on a computer. These topics are followed by a discussion of types of processing and number systems.

What Is the System Unit?

*T*he term computer is usually used to describe the collection of devices that perform the information processing cycle. This term is also used more specifically to describe the system unit, because this is where the *computing* actually occurs *(Figure 4-1)*. It is in the **system unit** that the computer program instructions are executed and the data is manipulated. The system unit contains the central processing unit, or CPU, main memory, and other electronics *(Figure 4-2)*. To better understand how the system unit processes data, an explanation of how data is represented electronically follows.

How Data Is Represented Electronically

Most computers are **digital computers**, meaning that the data they process, whether it be text, sound, graphics, or video, is first converted into a digital (numeric) value. Converting data into a digital form is called **digitizing**. Other types of computers, called **analog computers**, are designed to process continuously variable data, such as electrical voltage.

You may be thinking that the digital values used by a computer are the numbers 0 through 9. In fact, only the numbers 0 and 1 are used. A 0 is used to represent the electronic state of *off* and a 1 is used to represent the electronic state of *on*. Each off or on digital value is called a **bit**, the smallest unit of data handled by a computer. Bit is short for *bi*nary dig*it*. The binary number system represents quantities by using only two numbers, 0 and 1 *(Figure 4-3)*.

By itself, a bit cannot represent much data. In a group of eight bits, called a **byte**, 256 different possibilities can be represented by using all the combinations of 0s and 1s. This provides enough combinations so a unique code can be assigned to each of the characters that are commonly used, such as the numbers 0 through 9, the uppercase and lowercase

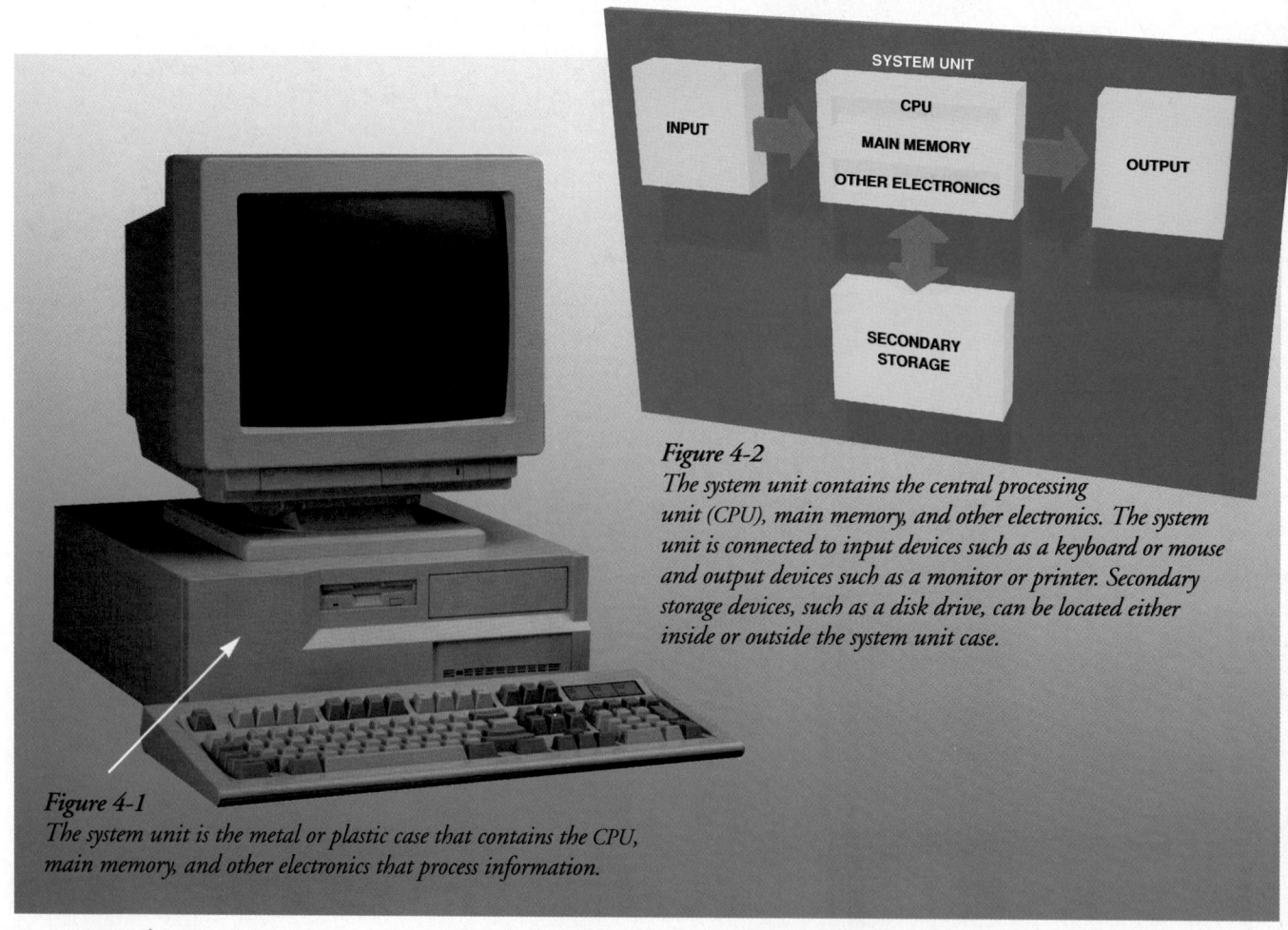

Figure 4-2
The system unit contains the central processing unit (CPU), main memory, and other electronics. The system unit is connected to input devices such as a keyboard or mouse and output devices such as a monitor or printer. Secondary storage devices, such as a disk drive, can be located either inside or outside the system unit case.

Figure 4-1
The system unit is the metal or plastic case that contains the CPU, main memory, and other electronics that process information.

alphabet, foreign characters that require special accent marks such as umlauts (¨) and tildes (˜), and special characters such as punctuation marks *(Figure 4-4)*. Several different coding schemes are used on computers.

ASCII and EBCDIC

Two popular codes that represent characters in memory and on secondary storage are the ASCII and EBCDIC codes. The **American Standard Code for Information Interchange**, called **ASCII** (pronounced ask-ee), is the most widely used coding system to represent data. Originally a seven-bit code, ASCII has been expanded to an eight-bit code. ASCII is used on personal computers and minicomputers. The **Extended Binary Coded Decimal Interchange Code**, or EBCDIC (pronounced eb-see-dick) is used primarily on mainframe computers. *Figure 4-5* summarizes these codes. Notice how the combination of bits, represented in binary, is unique for each character.

BINARY NUMBER	0	1
BIT	○	●
STATUS	OFF	ON

Figure 4-3
A bit, the smallest unit of data handled by a computer, can either be off or on. The binary numbers 0 and 1 are used to represent off and on, respectively.

0	1	0	0	0	0	0	1
○	●	○	○	○	○	○	●

8–BIT BYTE

Figure 4-4
A graphic representation of an eight-bit byte with two bits on and six bits off. The off bits (open circles) are represented by the binary number 0 and the on bits (solid circles) are represented by the binary number 1. This combination of bits represents the letter A using the ASCII code.

SYMBOL	ASCII	EBCDIC
0	01100000	11110000
1	01100001	11110001
2	01100010	11110010
3	01100011	11110011
4	01100100	11110100
5	01100101	11110101
6	01100110	11110110
7	01100111	11110111
8	01101000	11111000
9	01101001	11111001
A	01000001	11000001
B	01000010	11000010
C	01000011	11000011
D	01000100	11000100
E	01000101	11000101
F	01000110	11000110
G	01000111	11000111
H	01001000	11001000
I	01001001	11001001
J	01001010	11010001
K	01001011	11010010
L	01001100	11010011
M	01001101	11010100
N	01001110	11010101
O	01001111	11010110
P	01010000	11010111
Q	01010001	11011000
R	01010010	11011001
S	01010011	11100010
T	01010100	11100011
U	01010101	11100100
V	01010110	11100101
W	01010111	11100110
X	01011000	11100111
Y	01011001	11101000
Z	01011010	11101001
!	00100001	01011010
"	00100010	01111111
#	00100011	01111011
$	00100100	01011011
%	00100101	01101100
&	00100110	01010000
(	00101000	01001101
)	00101001	01011101
*	00101010	01011100
+	00101011	01001110

Figure 4-5
Numeric, uppercase alphabetic, and several special characters as they are represented in ASCII and EBCDIC. Each character is represented in binary using a unique ordering of zeros and ones.

When the ASCII or EBCDIC code is used, each character that is represented is stored in one byte of memory. There are also other binary formats, sometimes used by the computer to represent numeric data. For example, a computer may store, or *pack,* two numeric characters in one byte of memory. These binary formats are used by the computer to increase storage and processing efficiency.

Parity

Regardless of whether ASCII, EBCDIC, or other binary methods are used to represent characters in main memory, it is important that the characters be stored accurately. For each byte of memory, most computers have at least one extra bit, called a **parity bit**, that is used by the computer for error checking. A parity bit can detect if one of the bits in a byte has been accidentally changed. While such errors are rare, they can occur because of voltage fluctuations, static electricity, or a memory failure.

Computers are either odd or even parity machines. In computers with **odd parity**, the total number of *on* bits in the byte (including the parity bit) must be an odd number *(Figure 4-6)*. In computers with **even parity**, the total number of *on* bits must be an even number. Parity is checked by the computer each time a memory location is used. When data is moved from one location to another in main memory, the parity bits of both the sending and receiving locations are compared to see if they are the same. If the system detects a difference or if the wrong number of bits is on (e.g., an even number in a system with odd parity), an error message displays. Some computers use multiple parity bits that enable them to detect and correct a single-bit error and detect multiple-bit errors.

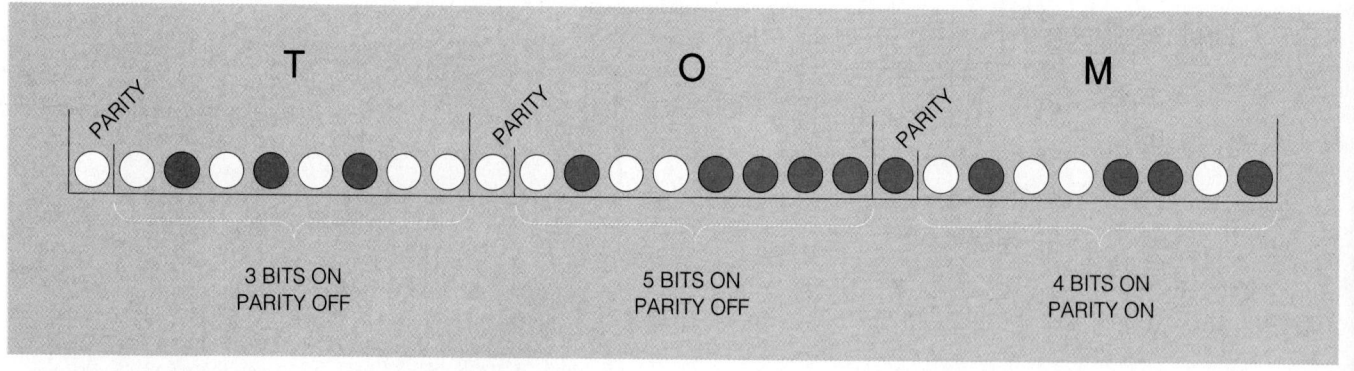

Figure 4-6
In a computer with odd parity, the parity bit is turned on or off to make the total number of on bits (including the parity bit) an odd number. Here, the letters T and O have an odd number of bits so the parity bits are left off. The number of bits for the letter M is even, so in order to achieve parity, the parity bit is turned on.

The Components of the System Unit

The components of the system unit are usually contained in a metal or plastic case. For personal computers, all system unit components are usually in a single box. For larger and more powerful computers, the components may be housed in several cabinets. The components considered part of the system unit and discussed in the following sections include: the motherboard, the microprocessor and CPU, upgrade sockets, memory, coprocessors, buses, expansion slots, ports and connectors, bays, the power supply, and sound components *(Figure 4-7)*.

Figure 4-7
The components of the system unit are usually inside a plastic or metal case. This illustration shows how some of the components might be arranged on a typical PC.

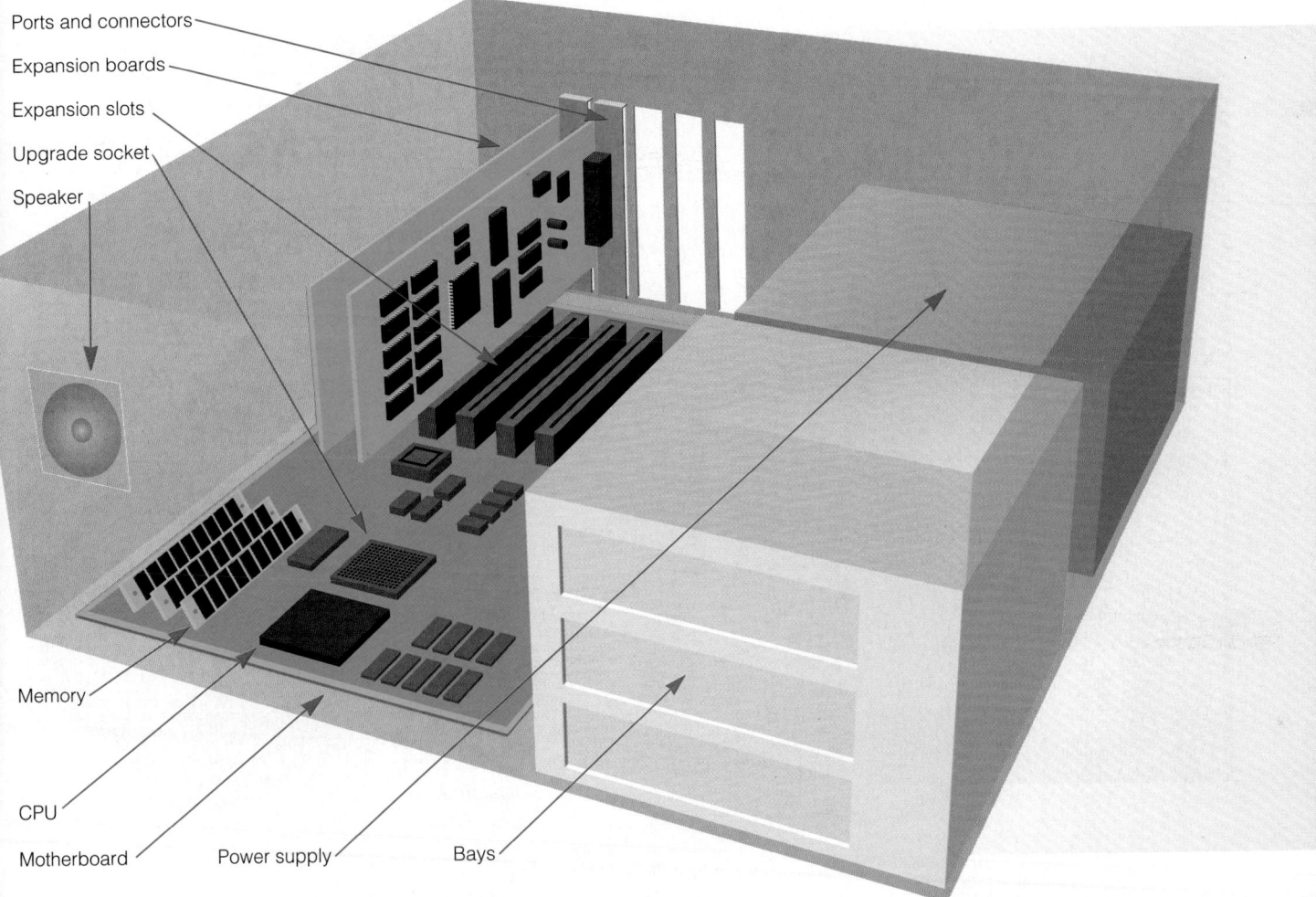

Ports and connectors

Expansion boards

Expansion slots

Upgrade socket

Speaker

Memory

CPU

Motherboard

Power supply

Bays

Motherboard

The **motherboard**, sometimes called the **main board** or **system board**, is a circuit board that contains most of the electronic components of the system unit. *Figure 4-8* shows a photograph of a personal computer motherboard. One of the main components on the motherboard is the microprocessor.

Figure 4-8
The main circuit board (motherboard) of a personal computer.

Microprocessor and the CPU

On a personal computer, the CPU or central processing unit, is contained on a single integrated circuit called a **microprocessor** *(Figure 4-9)* that is located on the motherboard. An **integrated circuit**, also called a **chip** or an **IC**, is a complete electronic circuit that has been etched on a small slice of nonconducting material such as silicon. For mainframe and supercomputers, the CPU consists of one or more circuit boards *(Figure 4-10)*.

The **central processing unit** (CPU) contains the control unit and the arithmetic/logic unit. These two components work together using the program and data stored in main memory to perform the processing operations.

Control Unit

The control unit can be thought of as the *brain* of the computer. Just as the human brain controls the body, the control unit *controls* the computer. The **control unit** operates by repeating the following four operations, called the **machine cycle** *(Figure 4-11):* fetching, decoding, executing, and storing. **Fetching** means obtaining the next program

◄ *Figure 4-9*
A Pentium microprocessor from Intel Corporation. The microprocessor circuits are located in the center. Small gold wires lead from the circuits to the pins that fit in the microprocessor socket on the motherboard. The pins provide an electronic connection to different parts of the computer.

Figure 4-10 ►
With PCs, the CPU is contained in a single microprocessor chip. With larger computers, the CPU operations are split among several chips and sometimes more than one circuit board.

instruction from main memory. **Decoding** is translating the program instruction into the commands the computer can process. **Executing** refers to the actual processing of the computer commands, and **storing** takes place when the result of the instruction is written to main memory.

System Clock

The control unit utilizes the **system clock** to synchronize, or control the timing of, all computer operations. The system clock generates electronic pulses at a fixed rate, measured in **megahertz** (abbreviated **MHz**). One megahertz equals one million pulses per second. The speed of the system clock varies among computers. Some personal computers can operate at speeds in excess of 100 megahertz.

Arithmetic/Logic Unit

The second part of the CPU is the **arithmetic/logic unit** (**ALU**). This unit contains the electronic circuitry necessary to perform arithmetic and logical operations on data. **Arithmetic operations** include addition, subtraction, multiplication, and division. **Logical operations** consist of comparing one data

item to another to determine if the first data item is *greater than, equal to,* or *less than* the other. Based on the result of the comparison, different processing may occur. For example, two part numbers in different records can be compared. If they are equal, the part quantity in one record can be added to the quantity in the other record. If they are not equal, the quantities would not be added.

Registers

Both the control unit and the ALU contain **registers**, temporary storage locations for specific types of data. Separate registers exist for the current program instruction, the address of the next instruction, and the values of data being processed.

Word Size

One aspect of the CPU that affects the speed of a computer is the word size. The **word size** is the number of bits the CPU processes at one time. The word size of a machine is measured in bits. CPUs can have 8-bit, 16-bit, 32-bit, or 64-bit word sizes. A CPU with a 16-bit word size can manipulate

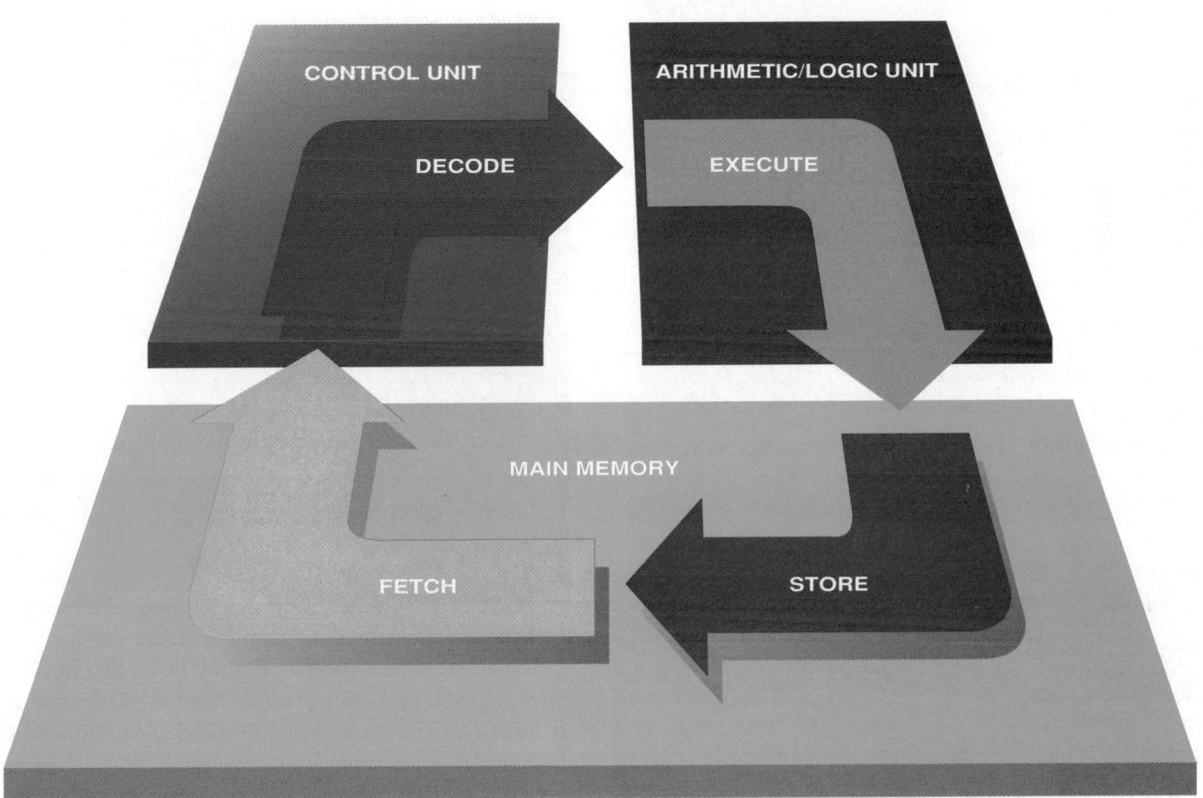

Figure 4-11
The machine cycle consists of four steps; fetching the next instruction, decoding the instruction, executing the instruction, and storing the result. Fetching and decoding are called the instruction cycle. Executing and storing are called the execution cycle.

16 bits at a time. Sometimes, the word size of a computer is given in bytes instead of bits. For example, a word size of 16 bits may be expressed as a word size of two bytes because there are eight bits in a byte. The larger the word size of the CPU, the faster the capability of the computer to process data.

Microprocessor Comparison

Personal computer microprocessors are most often identified by their model number or model name. *Figure 4-12a* summarizes some of the microprocessors currently in use. Microprocessors made by Intel come in several versions designated by letters after the processor name. *Figure 4-12b* explains the differences. Also, when discussing the three Intel processors prior to the Pentium, the "80" in the name/model number is usually not referred to. For example, the 80486 processor is usually referred to as a 486 processor.

Name	Date	Manufacturer	Word Size	Bus Width	Clock Speed (Mhz)	MIPS*
Pentium	1993	Intel	64	64	60-100	112
80486DX	1989	Intel	32	32	25-66	20-54
80386DX	1985	Intel	32	32	16-33	5.5-11.4
80286	1982	Intel	16	16	8-12	1.2-1.7
PowerPC	1994	Motorola	64	64	66-80	>100
68040	1989	Motorola	32	32	25-40	15-35
68030	1987	Motorola	32	32	16-50	12
68020	1984	Motorola	32	32	16-33	5.5
Alpha AXP	1993	Digital	64	64	150	275

MIPS: millions of instructions per second

Figure 4-12a
A comparison of some of the more widely used microprocessors.

486DX4	Internal speed of chip is three times faster than the speed at which the chip communicates with the rest of the system.
486DX2	Internal speed of chip is two times faster than the speed at which the chip communicates with the rest of the system.
486SX	Does not have internal math coprocessor like 486DX models. Slower and less expensive than DX models.
386SX	32-bit word length but only 16-bit data bus. Slower and less expensive than 386DX.
SL	Low voltage version of 386 and 486 chip. Used primarily in portable computers to extend battery life.

Figure 4-12b
Different versions of Intel microprocessors.

Upgrade Sockets

Some motherboards contain empty sockets, called **upgrade sockets** *(Figure 4-13)*, that can be used to install more powerful CPUs or additional memory.

The CPU upgrade sockets enable a user to install a more powerful microprocessor and obtain increased performance without having to buy an entirely new system. With a CPU upgrade socket, the old microprocessor does not have to be removed. When the new microprocessor is installed, the old microprocessor is automatically disabled. Many, but not all, systems can install a more powerful microprocessor even if they do not have a separate CPU upgrade socket. For these systems, the old microprocessor is removed and replaced with the new microprocessor.

ZIF socket

Figure 4-13
This motherboard includes an upgrade socket that can accept a more powerful Intel microprocessor. This particular type of socket is called a zero insertion force (ZIF) socket. The ZIF socket uses a lever to clamp down on the microprocessor pins and makes the installation of the chip easier. Other types of upgrade sockets require the microprocessor pins to be forced into the socket.

Memory

Memory refers to integrated circuits that store program instructions and data that can be retrieved. Memory chips are installed in the system unit and also on circuit boards that control other computer devices such as printers. The two most common types of memory chips are Random Access Memory (RAM) and Read Only Memory (ROM).

Random Access Memory

Random access memory, or **RAM**, is the name given to the integrated circuits, or chips, that are used for main memory. **Main memory**, or **primary storage**, stores three items: the operating system and other system software that direct and coordinate the computer equipment; the application program instructions that direct the work to be done; and the data currently being processed by the application programs. Data and programs are transferred into and out of RAM, and data stored in RAM is manipulated by computer program instructions.

The basic unit of memory is a byte, which you recall consists of eight bits. Just as a house on a street has a unique address that indicates its location on the street, each byte in the main memory of a computer has an address that indicates its location in memory *(Figure 4-14)*. The number that indicates the location of a byte in memory is called a **memory address**. Whenever the computer references a byte, it does so by using the memory address, or location, of that byte.

The size of main memory is measured in either kilobytes or megabytes. A **kilobyte** (abbreviated as **K** or **KB**) is equal to 1,024 bytes, but for discussion purposes, is usually rounded to 1,000 bytes. A **megabyte** (abbreviated as **MB**) is approximately one million bytes. These terms are also used when discussing the storage capacity of other devices such as disk drives.

RAM memory is said to be **volatile** because the programs and data stored in RAM are erased when the power to the computer is turned off. As long as the power remains on,

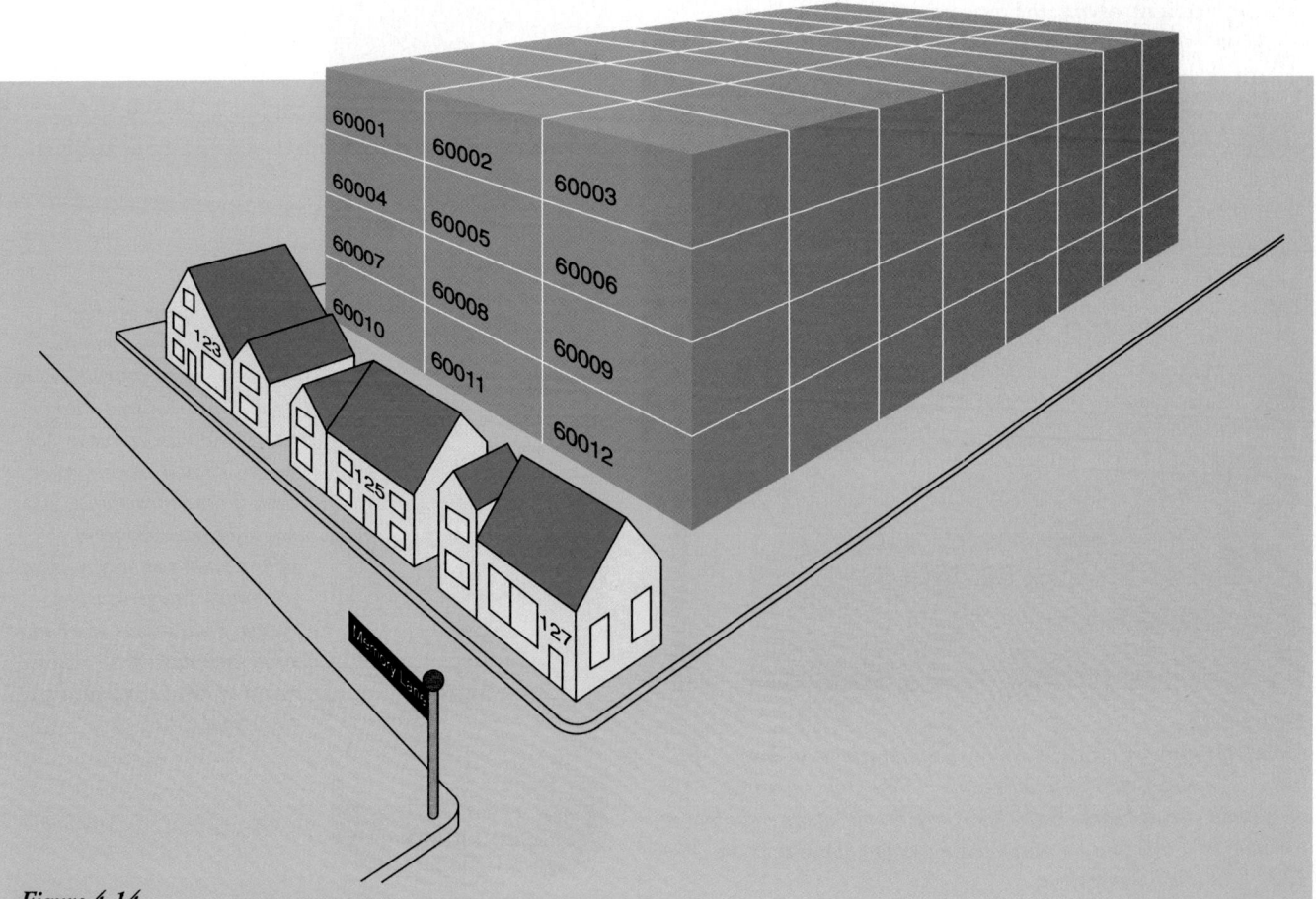

Figure 4-14
Just as each house on a street has its own address, each byte in main memory is identified by a unique address.

the programs and data stored in RAM will remain intact until they are replaced by other programs and data. Programs and data that are needed for future use must be transferred from RAM to secondary storage before the power is turned off. A relatively new type of memory called **flash RAM** or **flash memory** can retain data even when the power is turned off. Flash memory is sometimes used instead of a disk drive in small portable computers.

Today, most RAM memory is installed by using a **SIMM** (single in-line memory module). As shown in *Figure 4-15,* a SIMM is a small circuit board that holds multiple RAM chips. Common SIMM sizes are 1, 2, 4, 8, and 16 megabytes of memory. A SIMM is installed directly on the motherboard.

Some computers improve their processing efficiency by using a limited amount of high-speed RAM memory between the CPU and main memory *(Figure 4-16)*. High-speed memory used in this manner is called **cache memory** (pronounced cash). Cache memory is used to store the most frequently used instructions and data. When the processor needs the next program instruction or data, it first checks the cache memory. If the required instruction or data is present in cache (called a *cache hit*), the processor will execute faster

than if the instruction or data has to be retrieved from the slower main memory.

As shown in *Figure 4-17,* memory on personal computers can be divided into four areas. **Conventional memory** is located in the first 640K of RAM and is used for the operating system, programs, and data. **Upper memory** is located between 640K and 1MB of RAM and is used for programs that control input and output devices and other computer hardware. **Extended memory** consists of all memory above 1MB and is used for programs and data. Not all programs are written to use extended memory. Older programs, including many games, must run in conventional memory space or use expanded memory. **Expanded memory** consists of up to 32MB of memory on a memory expansion board. A separate program called an *expanded memory manager* is used to access this memory 16K at a time and transfer the data into upper memory. Newer computers use extended memory and do not have expanded memory.

Figure 4-15
Most RAM memory is installed using a SIMM (single in-line memory module). SIMMs usually contain nine chips mounted on a small circuit board. Each chip represents one of the eight bit positions in a byte plus the parity bit. Common SIMM sizes are 1, 2, 4, 8, and 16 megabytes.

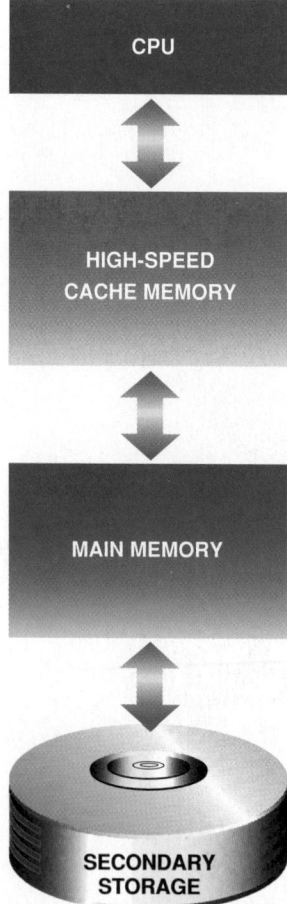

Figure 4-16
Some computers use high-speed cache memory to store frequently used instructions or data. If the required data or instructions are in cache, the processing will execute faster than if the instruction or data has to be retrieved from slower main memory or from secondary storage. Cache memory can consist of separate chips mounted on the motherboard or can be included in the actual CPU.

Read Only Memory

Read only memory (ROM) is the name given to chips that store information or instructions that do not change. For example, ROM is used to store the start up instructions and data used when a computer is first turned on. With ROM, data is permanently recorded in the memory when it is manufactured. ROM memory is described as **nonvolatile** because it retains its contents even when the power is turned off. The data or programs that are stored in ROM can be read and used, but cannot be altered, hence the name *read only*. Many of the special-purpose computers used in automobiles, appliances, and so on use small amounts of ROM to store instructions that will be executed repeatedly. Instructions that are stored in ROM memory are called **firmware** or **microcode**.

Memory Speed

Because of different manufacturing techniques and materials, some types of memory are faster than others. The speed of memory is measured in **nanoseconds**, one billionth of a second. Main memory is comprised of **dynamic RAM (DRAM)** chips that have access speeds of 50 to 100 nanoseconds. RAM cache memory is faster and is comprised of **static RAM (SRAM)** chips with access times of 10 to 50 nanoseconds. Static RAM chips are not used for main memory because they are larger than dynamic RAM chips and because they cost significantly more to manufacture. Registers designed into the CPU chip are the fastest type of memory with access times of 1 to 10 nanoseconds. ROM memory has access times between 50 and 250 nanoseconds. For comparison purposes, accessing data on a fast hard disk takes between 10 and 20 milliseconds. One **millisecond** is a thousandth of a second. Thus, accessing information in memory with a 70 nanosecond access time is 2,500 times faster than accessing data on a hard disk with a 15 millisecond access time.

Figure 4-17
Memory allocation on a personal computer.

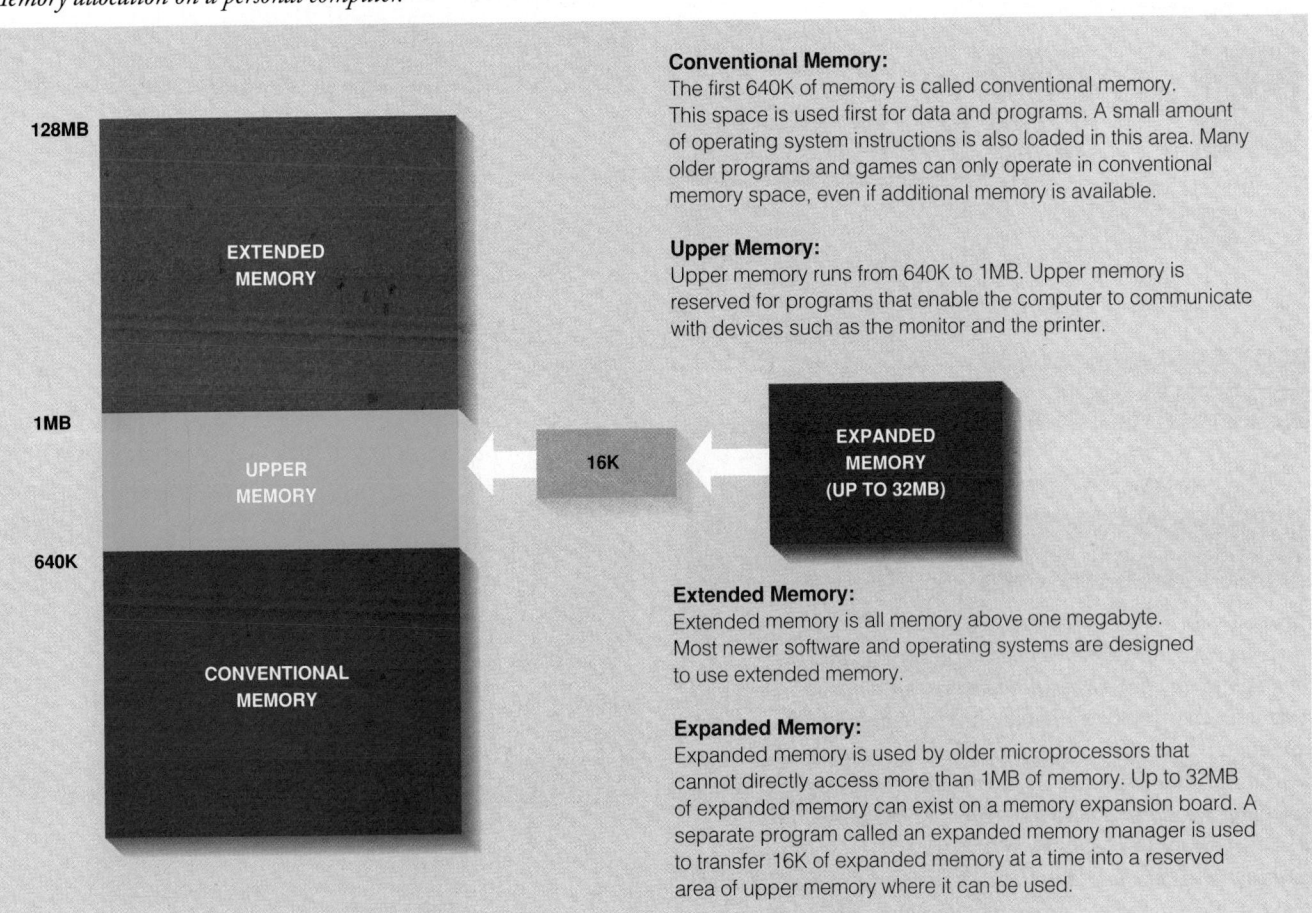

Conventional Memory:
The first 640K of memory is called conventional memory. This space is used first for data and programs. A small amount of operating system instructions is also loaded in this area. Many older programs and games can only operate in conventional memory space, even if additional memory is available.

Upper Memory:
Upper memory runs from 640K to 1MB. Upper memory is reserved for programs that enable the computer to communicate with devices such as the monitor and the printer.

Extended Memory:
Extended memory is all memory above one megabyte. Most newer software and operating systems are designed to use extended memory.

Expanded Memory:
Expanded memory is used by older microprocessors that cannot directly access more than 1MB of memory. Up to 32MB of expanded memory can exist on a memory expansion board. A separate program called an expanded memory manager is used to transfer 16K of expanded memory at a time into a reserved area of upper memory where it can be used.

Coprocessors

One way computers increase their productivity is the use of a **coprocessor**, a special microprocessor chip or circuit board designed to perform a specific task. For example, math coprocessors can be added to computers to greatly speed up the processing of numeric calculations. Other types of coprocessors are used to speed up the display of graphics and for communications. Some computers have coprocessors designed into the CPU.

Buses

As previously explained, computers store and process data as a series of electronic bits. These bits are transferred internally within the circuitry of the computer along paths capable of transmitting electrical impulses. Sometimes these paths are actual wires and sometimes they are etched lines on the circuit board or within the CPU chip itself. Any path along which bits are transmitted is called a **bus**. Buses are used to transfer bits from input devices to memory, from memory to the CPU, from the CPU to memory, and from memory to output devices. Separate buses are used for memory addresses, control signals, and data. One type of bus is called an expansion bus.

An **expansion bus** carries the data to and from the expansion slots *(Figure 4-18)*. Personal computers can have different types of expansion buses. Some computers have more than one type present. It is important to know the type of expansion buses on your computer because some devices

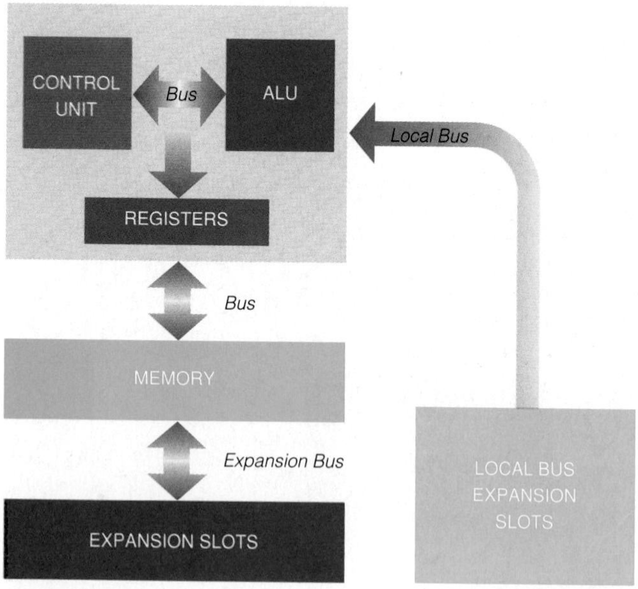

Figure 4-18
Buses are electrical pathways that carry bits from one part of the computer to another. Different buses exist for data, addresses, and control signals. The expansion bus carries data to and from the expansion boards that control peripheral devices and other components used by the computer. Some computers have a special type of expansion bus called a local bus. The local bus communicates directly with the CPU at a much faster rate than the standard expansion bus. The local bus is used for devices that require large amounts of data quickly such as monitors and disk drives.

Figure 4-19
Types of expansion buses found on personal computers.

BUS NAME	TYPE	BITS
XT	standard	8
ISA	standard	16
EISA	standard	32
MCA	standard	16 or 32
VESA or VL	local	32
PCI	local	32 or 64
NuBus	standard	32

are designed to work with only one bus type. Most expansion buses connect directly to RAM. To obtain faster performance, some expansion buses bypass RAM and connect directly to the CPU. An expansion bus that connects directly to the CPU is called a **local bus**. *Figure 4-19* lists the most common expansion bus types on personal computers.

Buses can transfer multiples of eight bits at a time. A 16-bit bus has 16 lines and can transmit 16 bits at a time. On a 32-bit bus, bits can be moved from place to place 32 bits at a time, and on a 64-bit bus, bits are moved 64 bits at a time. The larger the number of bits that are handled by a bus, the faster the computer can transfer data. For example, assume a number in memory occupies four eight-bit bytes. With a 16-bit bus, two steps would be required to transfer the data from memory to the CPU because on the 16-bit bus, the data in two eight-bit bytes would be transferred in an individual step. On a 32-bit bus, the entire four bytes could be transferred at one time. The fewer number of transfer steps required, the faster the transfer of data.

Expansion Slots

An **expansion slot** is a socket designed to hold the circuit board for a device, such as a tape drive or sound card, that adds capability to the computer system. The circuit board for the add-on device is called an **expansion board**. Expansion boards are sometimes called **expansion cards**, **controller cards**, **adapter cards**, or **interface cards**. The expansion card is usually connected to the device it controls by a cable. The socket that holds the card is connected to the expansion bus that transmits data to memory or the CPU. *Figure 4-20* shows an expansion board being placed in an expansion slot on a personal computer motherboard.

A special type of expansion slot is the PCMCIA slot. PCMCIA stands for Personal Computer Memory Card International Association. This group has defined standards for a thin credit card-sized device that can be inserted into a personal computer *(Figure 4-21)*. **PCMCIA cards** are used for additional memory, storage, and communications.

DESCRIPTION

Developed for original IBM PC

Industry Standard Architecture, sometimes called AT bus

Extended Industry Standard Architecture developed by IBM clone manufacturers; backward compatible with ISA bus (ISA cards can run in EISA bus)

Micro Channel Architecture developed by IBM for high-end PS/2 systems

Local bus standard developed by Video Electronics Standards Association

Peripheral Component Interconnect local bus standard developed by Intel

High performance expansion bus used in Apple Macintosh computers

Figure 4-20
An expansion board being inserted into an expansion slot on the motherboard of a personal computer.

Figure 4-21
PCMCIA cards are not much bigger than a credit card and fit in a small slot, usually on the side of a computer. PCMCIA cards are used for additional memory, storage, and communications. Because of their small size, PCMCIA cards are often used on portable computers. The card shown in this photo is a fax/data modem that can be connected to a phone line.

Ports and Connectors

A **port** is a socket used to connect the system unit to a peripheral device such as a printer or a modem. Most of the time, ports are on the back of the system unit *(Figure 4-22)* but they can also be on the front. Ports have different types of couplers, called **connectors**, that are used to attach cables to the peripheral devices. A matching connector is on the end of the cable that attaches to the port. Most connectors are available in two genders – male or female. Male connectors have one or more exposed pins, like the end of an electrical cord you plug into the wall. Female connectors have matching receptacles to accept the pins, like an electrical wall outlet. *Figure 4-23* shows the different type of connectors you may find on a system unit. Ports can either be parallel or serial.

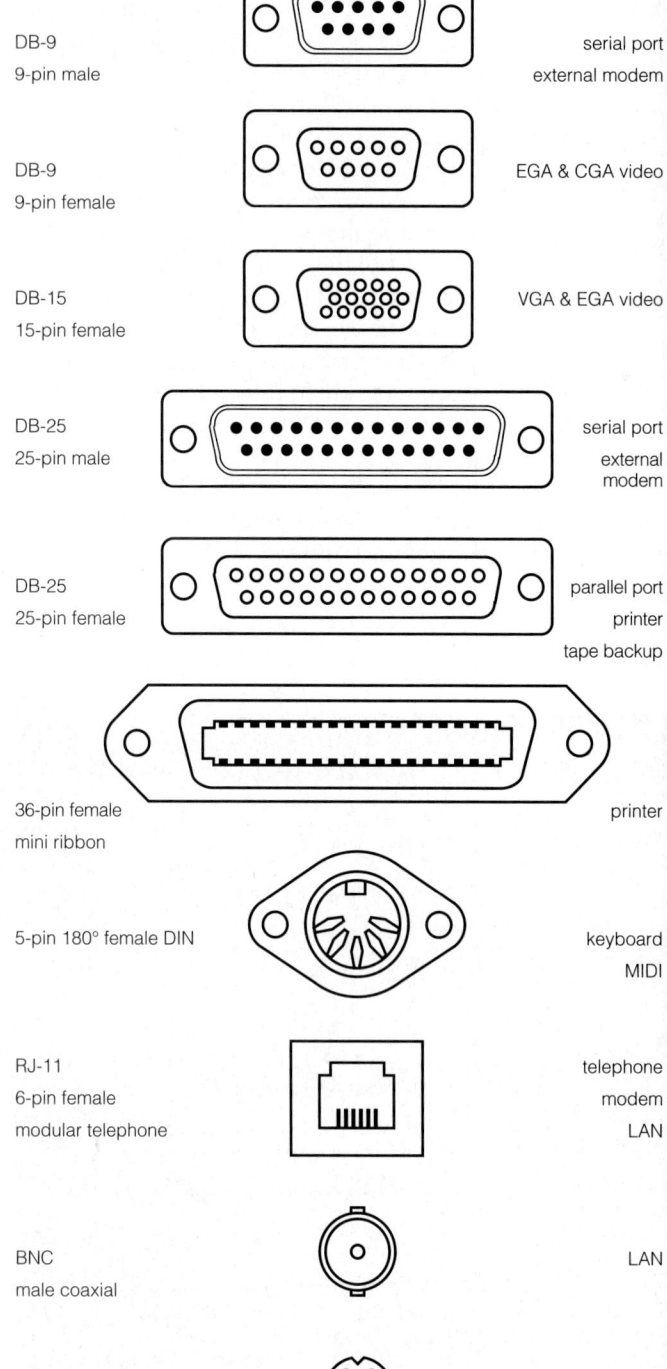

CONNECTORS

TYPE		USE
DB-9 9-pin male		serial port external modem
DB-9 9-pin female		EGA & CGA video
DB-15 15-pin female		VGA & EGA video
DB-25 25-pin male		serial port external modem
DB-25 25-pin female		parallel port printer tape backup
36-pin female mini ribbon		printer
5-pin 180° female DIN		keyboard MIDI
RJ-11 6-pin female modular telephone		telephone modem LAN
BNC male coaxial		LAN
6-pin male mini DIN		mouse keyboard

Figure 4-22
Ports are sockets used for cables that connect the system unit with devices such as a mouse, keyboard, and printer. Usually, ports are on the back of the system unit.

Figure 4-23
Examples of different types of connectors used to connect devices to the system unit. Adapters are available to join one type of connector with another.

Parallel Ports

Parallel ports are most often used to connect devices that send or receive large amounts of data such as printers or disk and tape drives. **Parallel ports** transfer eight bits (one byte) at a time using a cable that has eight data lines *(Figure 4-24)*. The electrical signals in a parallel cable tend to interfere with one another over a long distance and therefore, parallel cables are usually limited to 50 feet. Personal computer parallel cables are usually six to ten feet long. A special type of parallel port is the SCSI (pronounced scuzzy) port. SCSI stands for small computer system interface. A **SCSI port** can be used to attach up to seven different devices to a single port. The devices must be designed to connect to the SCSI port.

Serial Ports

A **serial port** transmits data one bit at a time *(Figure 4-25)* and is considerably slower than a parallel port. Cables connecting serial ports are smaller than parallel cables and do not generate as much electrical interference. Because of this, serial port cables can be up to 1,000 feet long. Serial ports are used for the mouse, the keyboard, and communication devices such as a modem. A special type of serial port is a MIDI (pronounced *midd-dee*) port. MIDI stands for musical instrument digital interface. A **MIDI port** is a serial port designed to be connected to a musical device such as an electronic keyboard or a music synthesizer.

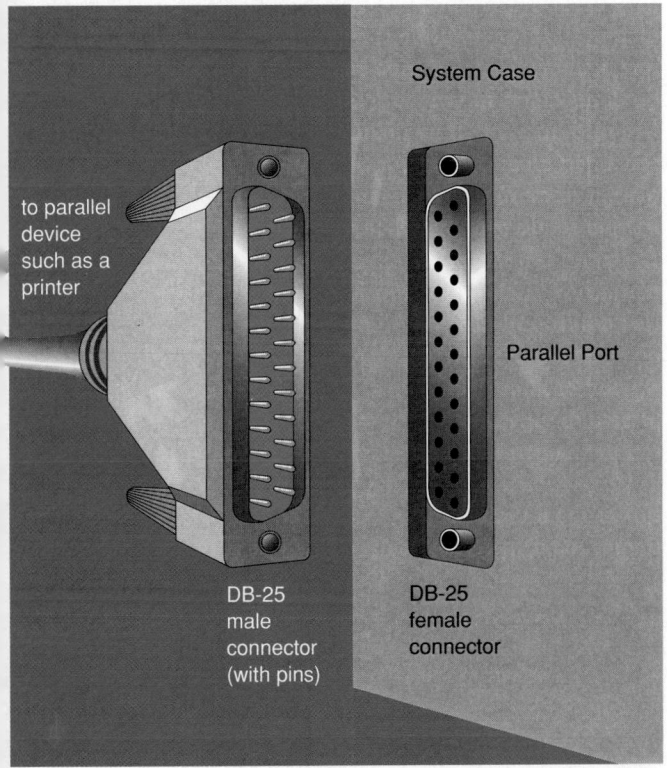

Figure 4-24
Parallel ports transfer eight bits at a time using a cable with eight data lines.

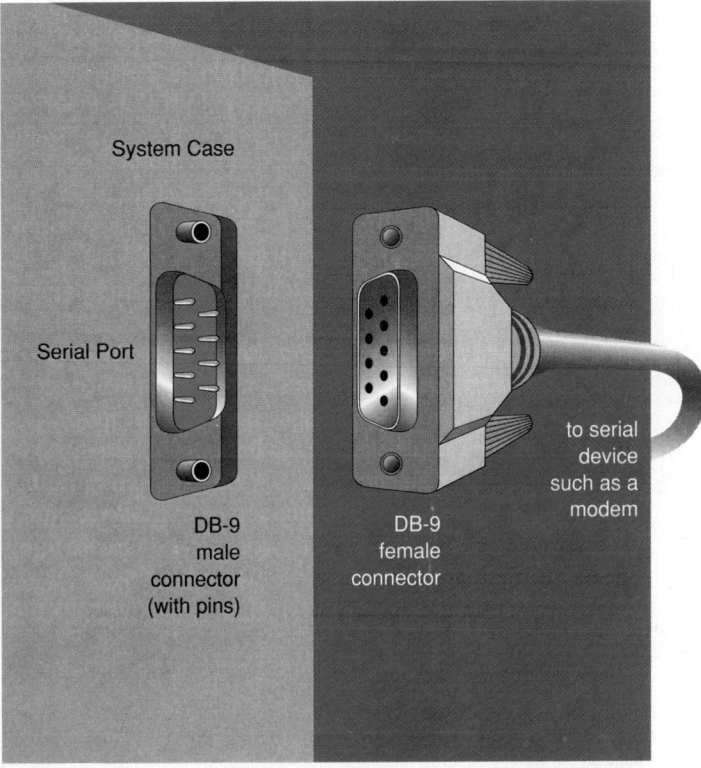

Figure 4-25
Serial ports transfer only one bit at a time and are slower than parallel ports. Separate data lines are used to transmit and receive data. Pin 2 is used to receive data and pin 3 is used to send data.

Bays

A **bay** is an open area inside the system unit used to install additional equipment. Because they are often used for disk and tape drives, these spaces are also called **drive bays**. Mounting brackets called **rails** are sometimes required to install a device in a bay. Two or more bays side by side or on top of one another are called a **cage**. *Figure 4-26* shows a personal computer with a three-bay cage. *External bays* have one end adjacent to an opening in the case. External bays are used for devices that require loading and unloading of storage media such as diskettes, tapes, and CD-ROMs. *Internal bays* are not accessible from outside the case and are used for hard disk drives.

Power Supply

The **power supply** converts the wall outlet electricity (115-120 volts AC) to the lower voltages (5 to 12 volts DC) used by the computer. The power supply also has a fan that provides airflow inside the system unit to help cool the components. The humming noise you hear when you turn on a computer is usually the power supply fan. Personal computer power supplies are rated by wattage and range from 100 to 250 watts. Higher wattage power supplies can support more electronic equipment.

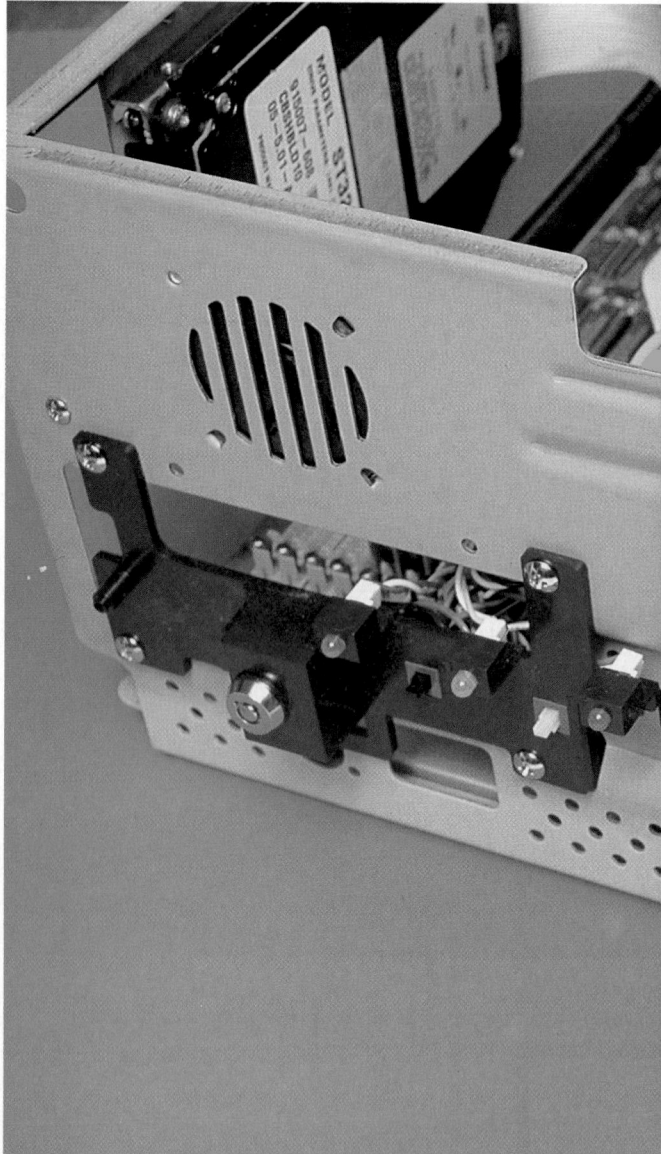

Figure 4-26
Bays, also called drive bays, are usually located beside or on top of one another. Each bay is approximately 1 3/4 inches high by 6 inches wide by 8 inches deep. Two or more bays together are called a cage.

Sound Components

Most personal computers have the capability to generate sounds through a small speaker housed within the system unit. Software allows users to generate a variety of sounds including music and voice. Some computers also have built-in microphones that allow users to record voice messages and other sounds. As you will see in the chapter on output devices, many users enhance the sound-generating capabilities of their systems by installing expansion boards, called sound boards, and by attaching higher quality speakers to their systems.

Summary of the Components of the System Unit

The previous sections have presented information about the various components of the system unit. You should now be able to identify these components and have a more complete understanding about how they operate. The next section will explain how the system unit processes data by executing machine language instructions.

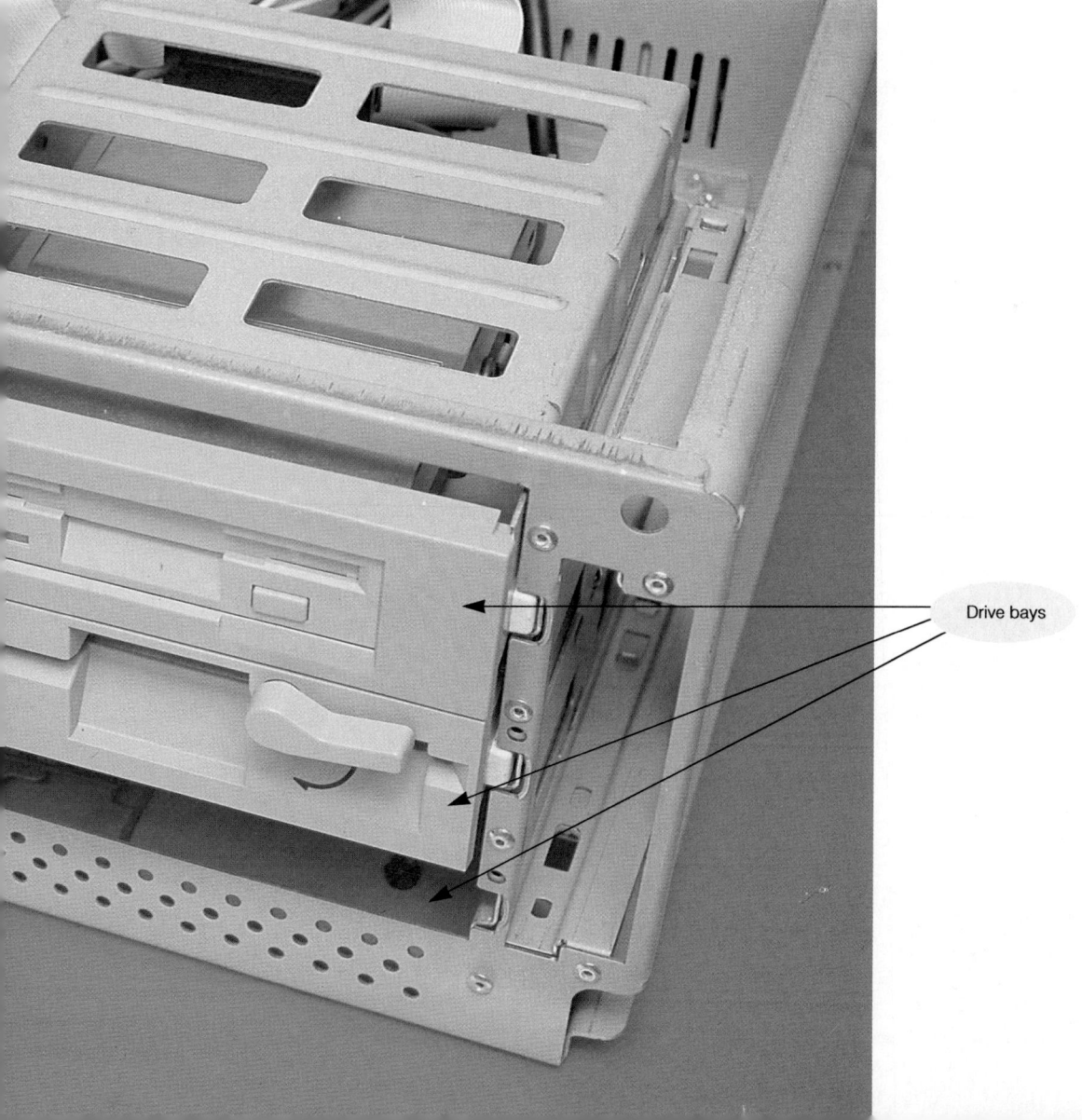

Drive bays

Machine Language Instructions

The system unit gets its directions from programs permanently stored in ROM or temporarily stored in RAM. To execute, program instructions must be in a form, called machine language instructions, the CPU can understand. A **machine language instruction** is binary data that the electronic circuits in the CPU can interpret and convert into one or more of the commands in the computer's instruction set. The **instruction set** contains commands, such as ADD or MOVE, that the computer's circuits can directly perform. Most computers have hundreds of commands in their instruction sets and are referred to as **CISC** computers, standing for *complex instruction set computing* (or *computers*). Studies have shown, however, that as much as 80% of the processing is performed by a small number of frequently used instructions. Based on these findings, some manufacturers have designed CPUs based on RISC technology. **RISC**, which stands for *reduced instruction set computing* (or *computers*), involves reducing the instructions to only those that are most frequently used. Because a RISC computer is designed to execute the frequently used instructions, overall processing capability, or throughput, is increased.

A machine language instruction is composed of two parts. The first part is called an operation code or opcode for short. An **operation code** tells the computer what to do and matches one of the commands in the instruction set. The second part of the machine language instruction is an operand. An **operand** specifies the data or the location of the data that will be used by the instruction. A machine language instruction may have zero to three operands. *Figure 4-27* shows an example of a machine language instruction that adds the number 32 to a register in the CPU.

In the early days, computers actually had to be programmed in machine language instructions using mechanical switches to represent each binary bit. Today, program instructions are written in a readable form using a variety of programming languages. The program instructions are then converted by the computer into machine language instructions. Programming languages and conversion methods are discussed in the chapter on programming languages.

MACHINE LANGUAGE INSTRUCTION		
opcode	operand 1	operand 2
00000101	00100000	00000000
Addition command	the value 32	data register in CPU

Figure 4-27
A PC machine language instruction consists of an operation code (opcode) and up to three operands. This machine language instruction adds the value 32 to a register.

Types of Processing

The number of machine language instructions a computer processes in one second is one way of rating the speed of computers. One **MIPS** equals one million instructions per second. Powerful personal computers today are rated at more than 100 MIPS. Another way of rating computer speed is the number of floating-point operations. Floating-point operations are a type of mathematical calculation. The term **megaflop** (**MFLOPS**) is used for millions of floating-point operations per second. **Gigaflop** (**GFLOPS**) is used for billions of floating-point operations per second. Giga is a prefix indicating billion.

In the discussions thus far, the emphasis has focused on computers with single CPUs processing one instruction at a time. The following section presents variations from this approach.

Pipelining

In most CPUs, the system waits until an instruction completes all four stages of the machine cycle (fetch, decode, execute, and store) before beginning to work on the next instruction. With **pipelining**, a new instruction is started as soon as the preceding instruction moves to the next stage. The result is faster throughput, because by the time the first instruction is in the fourth and final stage of the machine cycle, three other instructions have started to be processed (*Figure 4-28*). Some CPUs, such as the Intel Pentium, have two or more pipelines that can simultaneously process instructions.

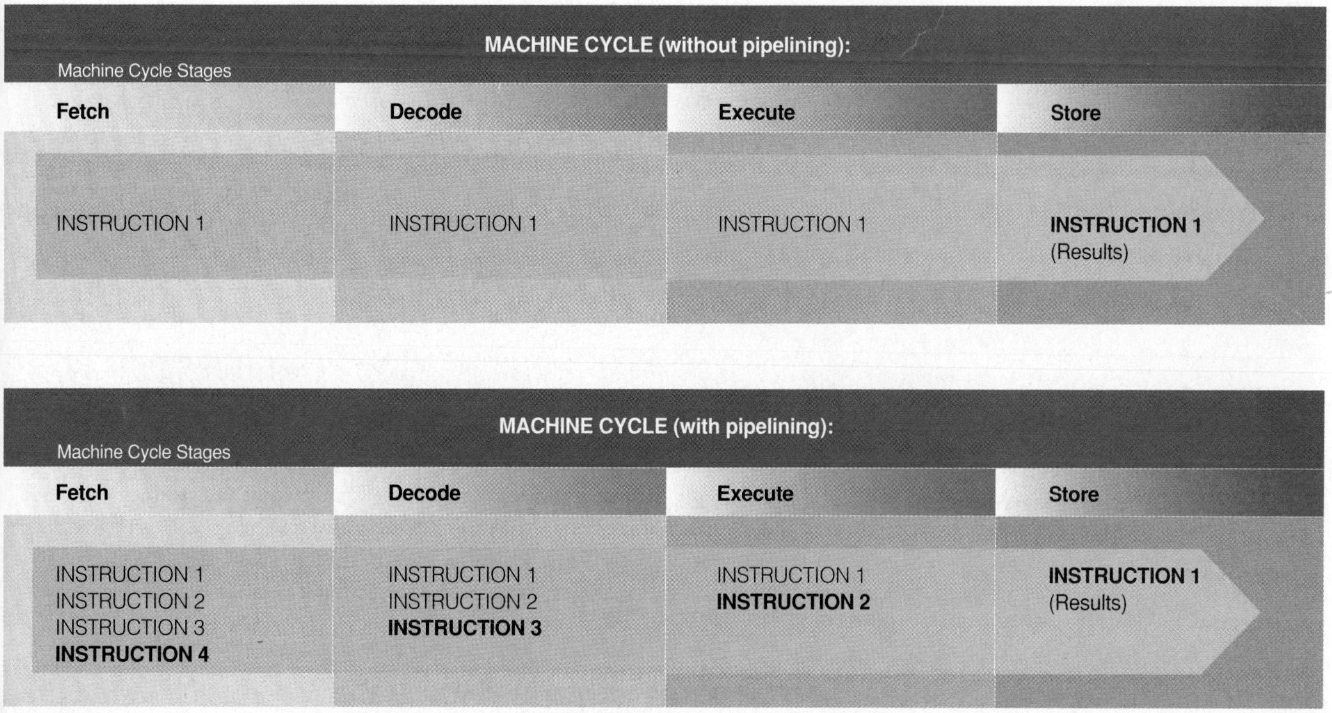

Figure 4-28
Without pipelining, an instruction moves through the complete machine cycle before the next instruction is started. With pipelining, the CPU starts working on another instruction each time the preceding instruction moves to the next stage of the machine cycle. As shown in the illustration for pipelining, by the time the first instruction has reached the fourth stage of the machine cycle, the next three instructions have started the cycle. Some CPUs have more than one pipeline.

Parallel Processing

Most computers contain one central processing unit (CPU) that processes a single instruction at a time. When one instruction is finished, the CPU begins execution of the next instruction, and so on until the program is completed. This method is known as **serial processing**. **Parallel processing** involves the use of multiple CPUs, each with its own memory. Parallel processors divide up a problem so multiple CPUs can work on their assigned portion of the problem simultaneously *(Figure 4-29)*. As you might expect, parallel processors require special software that can recognize how to divide up problems and bring the results back together again. Parallel processors are often used in supercomputers. **Massively parallel processors** (MPP) use hundreds or thousands of microprocessor CPUs to perform calculations.

Neural Network Computers

Neural network computers use specially designed circuits to simulate the way the human brain processes information, learns, and remembers. Neural network chips form a interconnected system of processors that learn to associate the relative strength or weakness of inputs with specific results (output). Neural network computers are used in applications such as pattern recognition to correctly guess the identity of an object when only hazy or partial information is available. Other applications that use neural network computers are speech recognition and speech synthesis.

Figure 4-29
Parallel processors have multiple CPUs that can divide up parts of the same job or work on different jobs at the same time. Special software is required to divide up the tasks and bring the results together.

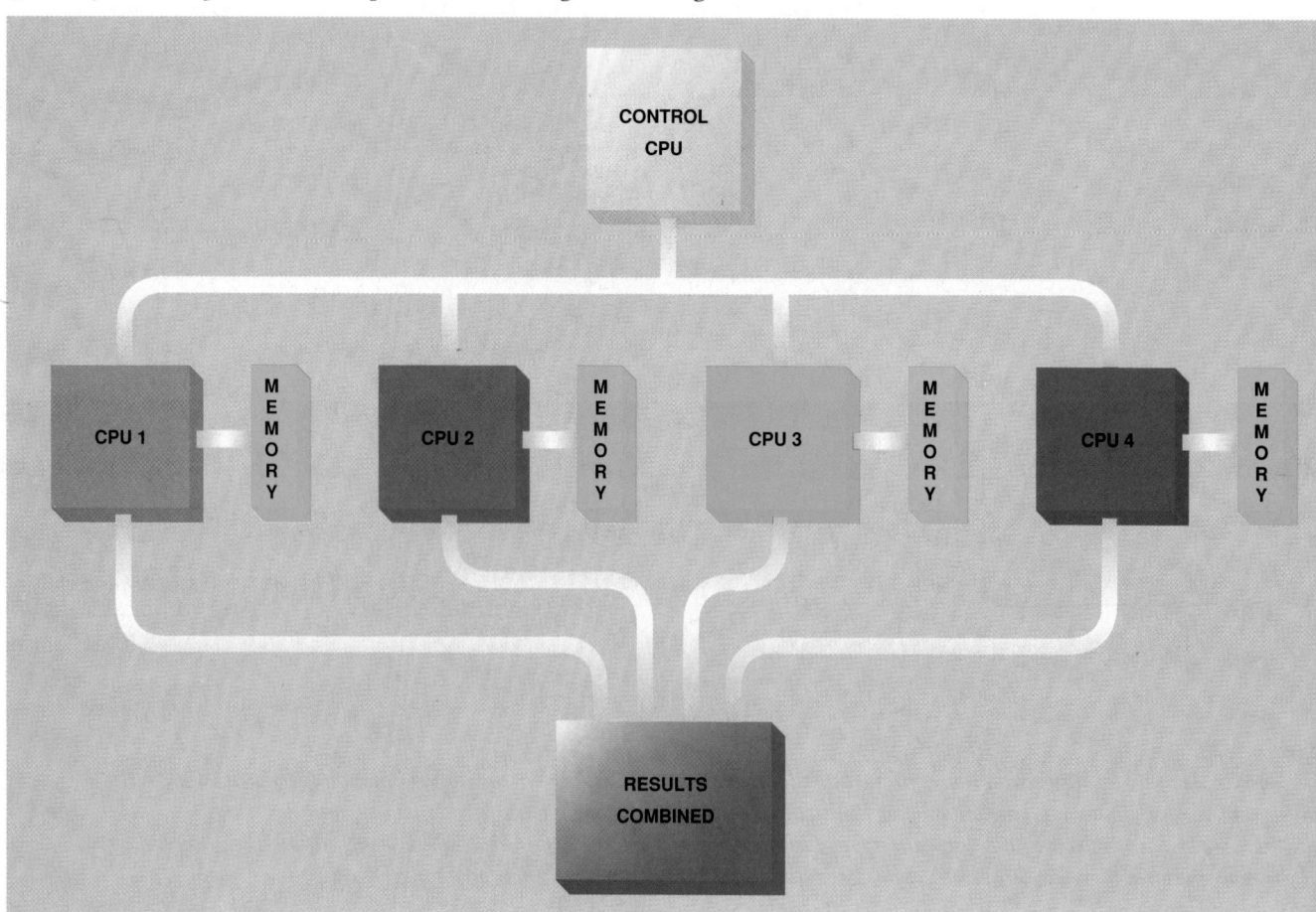

Number Systems

This section describes the number systems that are used with computers. Whereas thorough knowledge of this subject is required for technical computer personnel, a general understanding of number systems and how they relate to computers is all most users need.

As you have seen, the binary (base 2) number system is used to represent the electronic status of the bits in main memory. It is also used for other purposes such as addressing the memory locations. Another number system that is commonly used with computers is **hexadecimal** (base 16). *Figure 4-30* shows how the decimal values 0 through 15 are represented in binary and hexadecimal.

The mathematical principles that apply to the binary and hexadecimal number systems are the same as those that apply to the decimal number system. To help you better understand these principles, this section starts with the familiar decimal system, then progresses to the binary and hexadecimal number systems.

Decimal Number System

The decimal number system is a base 10 number system (*deci* means ten). The *base* of a number system indicates how many symbols are used in it. Decimal uses 10 symbols, 0 through 9. Each of the symbols in the number system has a value associated with it. For example, you know that 3 represents a quantity of three and 5 represents a quantity of five. The decimal number system is also a *positional* number system. This means that in a number such as 143, each position in the number has a value associated with it. When you look at the decimal number 143, you know that the 3 is in the ones, or units, position and represents three ones or (3 x 1); the 4 is in the tens position and represents four tens or (4 x 10); and the 1 is in the hundreds position and represents one hundred or (1 x 100). The number 143 is the sum of the values in each position of the number (100 + 40 + 3 = 143). The chart in *Figure 4-31* shows how the positional values (hundreds, tens, and units) for a number system can be calculated. Starting on the right and working to the left, the base of the number system, in this case 10, is raised to consecutive powers. The value 10^0, or 1, is the positional value for the units position. The value 10^1, or 10, is the positional value for the tens position. The value 10^2, or 100, is the positional value for the hundreds position. These calculations are a mathematical way of determining the place values in a number system.

DECIMAL	BINARY	HEXADECIMAL
0	0000	0
1	0001	1
2	0010	2
3	0011	3
4	0100	4
5	0101	5
6	0110	6
7	0111	7
8	1000	8
9	1001	9
10	1010	A
11	1011	B
12	1100	C
13	1101	D
14	1110	E
15	1111	F

Figure 4-30
The binary and hexadecimal representation of decimal numbers 0 through 15 are shown in this chart. Notice how letters represent the numbers 10 through 15 in the hexadecimal representation.

power of 10	10^2	10^1	10^0
positional value	100	10	1
number	1	4	3

$(1 \times 10^2) + (4 \times 10^1) + (3 \times 10^0) =$

$(1 \times 100) + (4 \times 10) + (3 \times 1) =$

$100 + 40 + 3 = 143$

Figure 4-31
The positional values in the decimal number 143 are shown in this chart.

When you use number systems other than decimal, the same principles apply. The base of the number system indicates the number of symbols that are used, and each position in a number system has a value associated with it. The positional value can be calculated by raising the base of the number system to consecutive powers beginning with zero.

Binary Number System

As previously discussed, binary is a base 2 number system (*bi* means two), and the symbols that are used are 0 and 1. Just as each position in a decimal number has a place value associated with it, so does each position in a binary number. To determine the place values for binary, the base of the number system, in this case 2, is raised to consecutive powers (*Figure 4-32*). To construct a binary number, you place ones in the positions where the corresponding values add up to the quantity you want to represent; you place zeros in the other positions. For example, the binary place values are 8, 4, 2, and 1, and the binary number 1001 has ones in the positions for the values 8 and 1 and zeros in the positions for 4 and 2. Therefore, the quantity represented by binary 1001 is 9 (8 + 0 + 0 + 1).

Hexadecimal Number System

Many computers use a base 16 number system called hexadecimal. The hexadecimal number system uses 16 symbols to represent values. These include the symbols 0 through 9 and A through F (*Figure 4-30* on the previous page). The mathematical principles previously discussed also apply to hexadecimal (*Figure 4-33*).

The primary reason why the hexadecimal number system is used with computers is because it can represent binary values in a more compact form and because the conversion between the binary and the hexadecimal number systems is very efficient. An eight-digit binary number can be represented by a two-digit hexadecimal number. For example, in the ASCII code, the character M is represented as 01001101. This value can be represented in hexadecimal as 4D. One way to convert this binary number to a hexadecimal number is to divide the binary number (from right to left) into groups of four digits; calculate the value of each group; and then change any two-digit values (10 through 15) into the symbols A through F that are used in hexadecimal (*Figure 4-34*).

power of 2	2^3	2^2	2^1	2^0
positional value	8	4	2	1
binary	1	0	0	1

$(1 \times 2^3) + (0 \times 2^2) + (0 \times 2^1) + (1 \times 2^0) =$

$(1 \times 8) + (0 \times 4) + (0 \times 2) + (1 \times 1) =$

$8 + 0 + 0 + 1 = 9$

Figure 4-32
Each positional value in a binary number represents a consecutive power of two. Using the positional values, the binary number 1001 can be converted to the decimal number 9.

power of 16	16^1	16^0
positional value	16	1
hexadecimal	A	5

$(10 \times 16^1) + (5 \times 16^0) =$

$(10 \times 16) + (5 \times 1) =$

$160 + 5 = 165$

Figure 4-33
Conversion of the hexadecimal number A5 to the decimal number 165. Notice that the value 10 is substituted for the A during calculations.

Summary of the System Unit

This chapter examined various aspects of the system unit including its components, how programs and data are stored, and how the processor executes program instructions to process data into information. You have also studied various methods of processing and learned about the various number systems used with computers. Knowing this material will increase your overall understanding of how processing occurs on a computer.

Summary of Number Systems

As mentioned at the beginning of the section on number systems, binary and hexadecimal are used primarily by technical computer personnel. A general user does not need a complete understanding of numbering systems. The concepts that you should remember about number systems are that binary is used to represent the electronic status of the bits in main memory and auxiliary storage. Hexadecimal is used to represent binary in a more compact form.

positional value	8421	8421
binary	0100	1101
decimal	4	13
hexadecimal	4	D

Figure 4-34
Conversion of the ASCII code 01001101 for the letter M to the hexadecimal value 4D. Each group of four binary digits is converted to a hexadecimal symbol.

COMPUTERS AT WORK

Unparalleled Performance from Parallel Processors

One way of obtaining improved computer performance is by using more than one CPU. The theory is simple; if one CPU can do a job in one hour, then two CPUs could do the job in 30 minutes, four CPUs in 15 minutes, 60 CPUs in 1 minute, and so on. Although the results aren't as direct as the example (twice the CPUs does not reduce the time in half), significant improvements in performance can be obtained if the work to be done is divided into separate parts that can be worked on simultaneously. Some applications using this approach have been implemented on parallel processors for some time. These applications include automobile crash simulation and weather forecasting. With automobile crash simulation, parallel processors measure the impact and damage at multiple points on the automobile at the same time *(Figure 4-35)*. With weather forecasting, the effect of simultaneous temperature and pressure changes is calculated. Parallel processors are also being applied to commercial applications in several ways. Large-scale parallel processors are being applied to database searches. Kmart, WalMart, and

Mervyn's are three retailers that use large parallel processors to sort through millions of transactions in hours to spot sales patterns and trends. For this type of application, the database can be divided among the number of processors available. On a mainframe, the same sales analysis application could take days. On a smaller scale, multiple processors are being implemented at the PC level. The most powerful server computers usually have four or more CPUs to handle the network requirements of up to several thousand users. Microprocessor designers are also incorporating parallel processor designs into the CPU itself. For example, Intel has plans to have four separate but linked CPUs in the chip it plans to build sometime around the year 2000 (see **IN THE FUTURE** on the next page). Existing microprocessor chips, such as the Intel Pentium, have some parts, but not all, of the CPU duplicated. Eventually, all computers will have multiple CPUs working in parallel to produce faster results than any single CPU system.

Figure 4-35

IN THE FUTURE

2,000 MIPS by the Year 2000

By the year 2000, Intel, the world's largest manufacturer of microprocessors, predicts it will have a CPU chip that can perform 2,000 MIPS; 2 billion instructions per second. This is almost ten times faster than microprocessor CPUs currently available. To reach this performance level, Intel will have to continue to pack more transistors onto the slice of silicon that becomes the heart of the microprocessor. Intel's Pentium processor has 3.3 million transistors. Their next generation processor, dubbed the P6, is predicted to have between 6 and 8 million transistors. The 2,000 MIPS processor will have between 50 and 100 million transistors spread among four integrated CPUs. To reach this level of transistor density, the size of the transistors will have to shrink below one-tenth of a micron. A micron is one-millionth of a meter. Current microprocessors have transistor sizes approximately six- to eight-tenths of a micron. For comparison purposes, an average human hair is 75 microns, or approximately 100 times the size of current microprocessor transistors. The clock speed of the microprocessor will also have to improve, probably to about 250 megahertz (each megahertz is one million cycles per second). Current microprocessors run at about 100 to 150 megahertz.

To reach these levels of transistor density and clock speed, microprocessor chip advances will have to continue to meet the prediction of Intel founder Gordon Moore. In 1965, Moore predicted that transistor density, and thus relative computing power, would double every 18 to 24 months. Called Moore's Law, this prediction has so far been amazingly accurate (see *Figure 4-36*). To reach Intel's goal of the 2,000 MIPS chip by the year 2000, the law will have to hold true for a few more years.

MOORE'S LAW

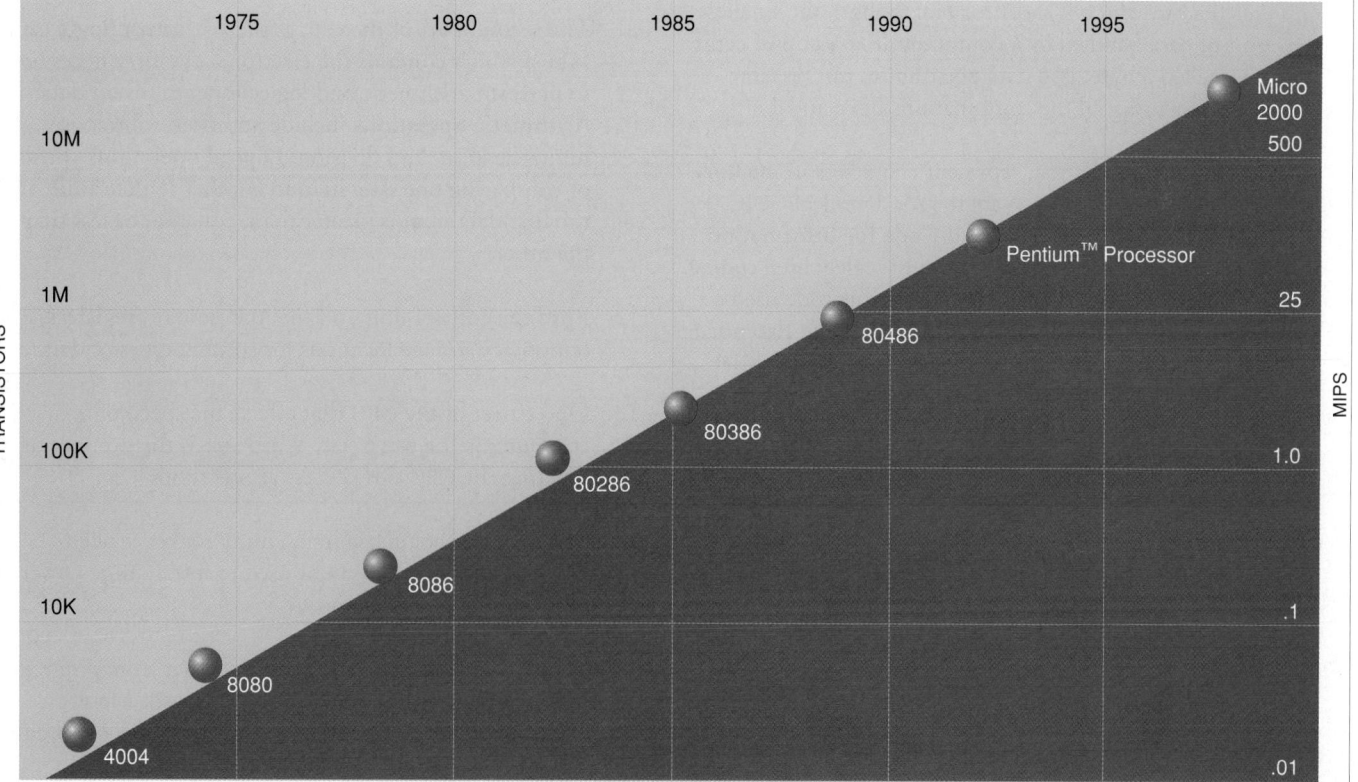

Figure 4-36

File   Edit   Section   Page   Tools   Options   Help

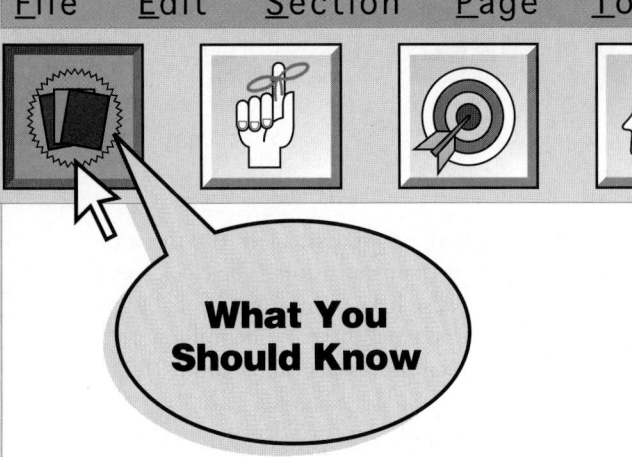

What You Should Know

1. It is in the **system unit** that the computer program instructions are executed and the data is manipulated. The system unit contains the central processing unit, or CPU, main memory, and other electronics.

2. Most computers are **digital computers**, meaning that the data they process is first converted into a digital (numeric) value. Converting data into digital form is called **digitizing**. Other types of computers, called **analog computers**, are designed to process variable data.

3. The digital values used by a computer are 0 (to represent the electronic state of *off*) and 1 (to represent the electronic state of *on*). Each off or on digital value is called a **bit**, which is short for *bi*nary dig*it,* the smallest unit of data handled by a computer. In a group of eight bits, called a **byte**, 256 data possibilities can be represented by using all the combinations of 0s and 1s.

4. Two popular codes that represent characters in memory and on secondary storage are the ASCII and EBCDIC codes. The **American Standard Code for Information Interchange**, called ASCII, is the most widely used coding system to represent data. It is an eight-bit code used on personal computers and minicomputers. The **Extended Binary Coded Decimal Interchange Code**, or EBCDIC, is used primarily on mainframe computers.

5. For each byte of memory, most computers have at least one extra bit, called a **parity bit**, that is used by the computer for error checking. In computers with **odd parity**, the total number of on bits must be an odd number. In computers with **even parity**, the total number of on bits must be an even number.

6. The components considered part of the system unit include: the motherboard, the microprocessor and CPU, upgrade sockets, memory, coprocessors, buses, expansion slots, ports and connectors, bays, the power supply, and sound components.

7. The **motherboard**, sometimes called the **main board** or **system board**, is a circuit board that contains most of the electronic components of the system unit.

8. On a personal computer, the CPU, or central processing unit, is contained on a single integrated circuit, called a **microprocessor**, that is located on the motherboard. An **integrated circuit**, also called a **chip** or an **IC**, is a complete electronic circuit that has been etched on a small slice of semiconducting material. The **central processing unit** (CPU) contains the control unit and the arithmetic/logic unit.

9. The **control unit** operates by repeating four operations, called the **machine cycle: fetching, decoding, executing,** and **storing**.

10. The control unit utilizes the **system clock** to synchronize all computer operations. The system clock generates electronic pulses at a fixed rate, measured in **megahertz (MHz)**.

11. The second part of the CPU is the **arithmetic/logic unit (ALU)**, which contains the electronic circuitry necessary to perform arithmetic and logical operations on data. **Arithmetic operations** include addition, subtraction, multiplication, and division. **Logical operations** consist of comparing one data item to another to determine if the first data item is greater than, equal to, or less than the other.

12. Both the control unit and the ALU contain **registers**, temporary storage locations for specific types of data.

13. One aspect of the CPU that affects the speed of a computer is the word size. **Word size** is the number of bits that the CPU can process at one time.

14. Some motherboards contain empty sockets, called **upgrade sockets**, that can be used to install more powerful CPUs or additional memory.

15. Memory refers to integrated circuits that store program instructions and data that can be retrieved. Memory chips are installed in the system unit and also on circuit boards that control other computer devices.

16. **Random access memory**, or **RAM**, is the name given to the integrated circuits, or chips, that are used for main memory. **Main memory**, or **primary storage**, stores three items: the operating system and other system software, the application program instructions, and the data currently being processed. The number that indicates the location of a byte in memory is called a **memory address**. The size of main memory is measured in **kilobytes** (**K** or **KB**) or **megabytes** (**MB**).

17. RAM memory is said to be **volatile** because the programs and data stored in RAM are erased when the power to the computer is turned off. A relatively new type of memory called **flash RAM**, or **flash memory**, retains data even when the power is turned off.

18. Today, most RAM memory is installed by using a **SIMM** (single in-line memory module). Some computers improve their processing efficiency by using a limited amount of high-speed RAM memory, called **cache memory**, between the CPU and main memory to store the most frequently used program instructions or data. Memory on personal computers can be divided into four areas: **conventional memory**, **upper memory**, **extended memory**, and **expanded memory**.

19. **Read only memory** (**ROM**) is the name given to chips that store information or instructions that do not change. ROM memory is described as **nonvolatile** because it retains its contents even when the power is turned off. Instructions that are stored in ROM memory are called **firmware** or **microcode**.

20. The speed of memory is measured in **nanoseconds**, one billionth of a second. Main memory is comprised of **dynamic RAM** (**DRAM**) chips that have access speeds of 50 to 100 nanoseconds. RAM cache memory is faster and is comprised of **static RAM** (**SRAM**) chips with access times of 10 to 50 nanoseconds. Registers designed into the CPU chip are the fastest type of memory with access times of 1 to 10 nanoseconds. ROM memory has access times between 50 and 250 nanoseconds. Accessing data on a fast hard disk drive takes between 10 and 20 **milliseconds** (a thousandth of a second).

21. One way computers can increase their productivity is through the use of a **coprocessor**, a special microprocessor chip or circuit board designed to perform a specific task.

22. Bits are transferred internally within the circuitry of the computer along paths capable of transmitting electrical impulses. Any path along which bits are transmitted is called a **bus**. An **expansion bus** carries data to and from the expansion slots. An expansion bus that connects directly to the CPU is called a **local bus**. Buses can transfer multiples of eight bits at a time.

23. An **expansion slot** is a socket designed to hold the circuit board for a device that adds capability to the computer system. The circuit board for the add-on device is called an **expansion board**. Expansion boards are also sometimes called **expansion cards**, **controller cards**, **adapter cards**, or **interface cards**. **PCMCIA cards** are used for additional memory, storage, and communications.

24. A **port** is a socket used to connect the system unit to a peripheral device such as a printer or a modem. Ports have different types of couplers, called **connectors**, that are used to attach cables to the peripheral devices. **Parallel ports** transfer eight bits (one byte) at a time using a cable that has eight data lines. These ports are most often used to connect devices that send or receive large amounts of data, such as printers or disk and tape drives. A **SCSI port** is a special type of parallel port that attaches up to seven devices to a single port. **Serial ports** transmit data one bit at a time and are considerably slower than parallel ports. These ports are used for the mouse, the keyboard, and communication devices such as a modem. A **MIDI port** is a special type of serial port designed to be connected to a musical device such as an electronic keyboard or music synthesizer.

25. A **bay** is an open area inside the system unit used to install additional equipment. Because they are often used for disk and tape drives, these spaces are also called **drive bays**. Mounting brackets, called **rails**, are sometimes required to install a device in a bay. Two or more bays side by side or on top of one another are called a **cage**.

26. The **power supply** converts the wall outlet electricity (115-120 volts AC) to the lower voltages (5 to 12 volts DC) used by the computer. The power supply also has a fan to help cool the system unit components. Personal computer power supplies range from 100 to 250 watts.

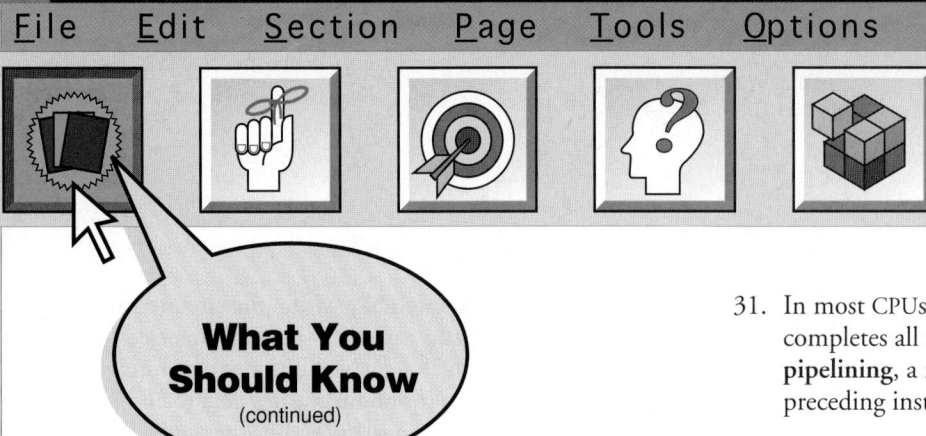

What You Should Know
(continued)

27. Most personal computers can generate sounds through a small speaker housed within the system unit. Some computers also have built-in microphones that allow users to record voice messages and other sounds.

28. A **machine language instruction** is binary data that the electronic circuits in the CPU can interpret and convert into one or more commands in the computer's instruction set. The **instruction set** contains commands that the computer's circuits can directly perform. Most computers have hundreds of commands in their instruction set and are referred to as **CISC** computers, standing for *complex instruction set computing* (or *computers*). Some manufacturers have designed CPUs based on **RISC** technology, *or reduced instruction set computing* (or *computers*), which involves reducing the instructions to only those that are most frequently used, thus increasing overall processing capability.

29. The first part of a machine language instruction, called an **operation code**, tells the computer what to do and matches one of the commands in the instruction set. The second part of a machine language instruction, called an **operand**, specifies the data that will be used by the instruction. Although in the early days computers actually had to be programmed in machine language instructions, today program instructions are written in a readable form using a variety of programming languages.

30. The number of machine language instructions that a computer can process in one second is one way of rating the speed of computers. Powerful personal computers today are rated at more than 100 **MIPS** (million instructions per second). Another way of rating computer speed is the number of floating-point operations (a type of mathematical calculation). The term **megaflop** (**MFLOPS**) is used for millions of floating-point operations per second, and **gigaflop** (**GFLOPS**) is used for billions of floating-point operations per second.

31. In most CPUs, the system waits until an instruction completes all four stages of the machine cycle. With **pipelining**, a new instruction is started as soon as the preceding instruction moves to the next stage.

32. Most computers use a method known as **serial processing** in which one central CPU processes a single instruction at a time until the instruction is finished, then begins execution of the next instruction, and so on until the program is completed. **Parallel processing** involves the use of multiple CPUs, each with its own memory. Parallel processors, often used in supercomputers, divide up a problem so multiple CPUs can work on their assigned portion of the problem simultaneously. **Massively parallel processors** (MPP) use hundreds or thousands of microprocessor CPUs to perform calculations.

33. **Neural network computers** use specifically designed circuits to simulate the way the human brain processes information.

34. The binary (base 2) number system is used to represent the electronic status of the bits in main memory and secondary storage. The **hexadecimal** (base 16) number system, another number system commonly used with computers, represents binary in a more compact form. The mathematical principles that apply to the binary and hexadecimal number systems are the same as those that apply to the decimal system. The *base* of the number system indicates how many symbols are used in it. Each system is also a *positional* number system, meaning that every position in the number has a value associated with it.

le   Edit   Section   Page   Tools   Options   Help

Terms to Remember

adapter cards (4.13)
American Standard Code for
    Information Interchange
    (ASCII) (4.3)
Analog computers (4.2)
arithmetic operations (4.7)
arithmetic/logic unit (ALU) (4.7)
ASCII (4.3)

bay (4.6)
bit (4.2)
bus (4.12)
byte (4.2)

cache memory (4.10)
cage (4.16)
central processing unit (CPU) (4.6)
chip (4.6)
CISC (4.18)
connectors (4.14)
control unit (4.6)
controller cards (4.13)
conventional memory (4.10)
coprocessor (4.12)

decoding (4.7)
digital computers (4.2)
digitizing (4.2)
drive bays (4.16)
dynamic RAM (DRAM) (4.11)

EBCDIC (4.3)
even parity (4.4)
executing (4.7)
expanded memory (4.10)
expansion board (4.13)
expansion bus (4.12)
expansion cards (4.13)
expansion slot (4.13)
Extendend Binary Coded Decimal
    Interchange Code (EBCDIC) (4.3)
extended memory (4.10)

fetching (4.6)
firmware (4.11)
flash memory (4.10)
flash RAM (4.10)

gigaflop (GFLOPS) (4.19)

hexadecimal (4.21)

IC (4.6)
instruction set (4.18)
integrated circuit (4.6)
interface cards (4.13)

kilobyte (K or KB) (4.9)

local bus (4.13)
logical operations (4.7)

machine cycle (4.6)
machine language instruction (4.18)
main board (4.6)
main memory (4.9)
massively parallel processors
    (MPP) (4.20)
megabyte (MB) (4.9)
megaflop (MFLOPS) (4.19)
megahertz (MHz) (4.7)
memory address (4.9)
microcode (4.11)
microprocessor (4.6)
MIDI port (4.15)
millisecond (4.11)
MIPS (4.19)
motherboard (4.6)

nanoseconds (4.11)
neural network computers (4.20)
nonvolatile (4.11)

odd parity (4.4)
operand (4.18)
operation code (4.18)

parallel ports (4.15)
parallel processing (4.20)
parity bit (4.4)
PCMCIA cards (4.13)
pipelining (4.19)
port (4.14)
power supply (4.16)
primary storage (4.9)

rails (4.16)
RAM (4.9)
random access memory (RAM) (4.9)
read only memory (ROM) (4.11)
registers (4.7)
RISC (4.18)

SCSI port (4.15)
serial port (4.15)
serial processing (4.20)
SIMM (4.10)
static RAM (SRAM) (4.11)
storing (4.7)
system board (4.6)
system clock (4.7)
system unit (4.2)

upgrade sockets (4.8)
upper memory (4.10)

volatile (4.9)

word size (4.7)

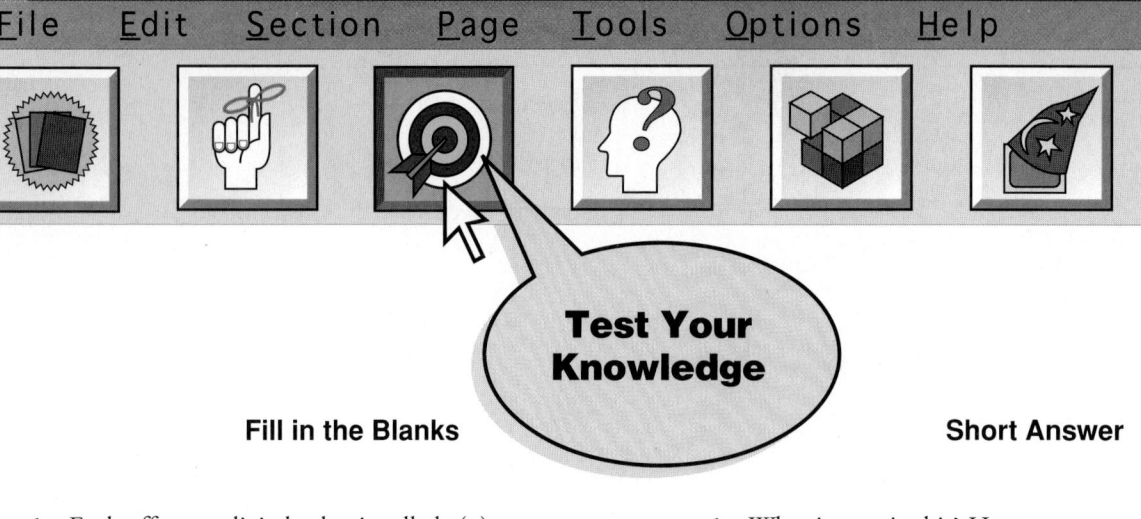

Test Your Knowledge

Fill in the Blanks

1. Each off or on digital value is called a(n) _____, and a group of eight off or on digital values, called a(n) _____, can represent 256 different data possibilities.

2. _____, the most widely used coding system to represent data, is used primarily on personal computers and minicomputers, while _____ is a coding system used primarily on mainframe computers.

3. The four steps of the machine cycle are: _____, _____, _____, and _____.

4. The two parts of a machine language instruction are a(n) _____ that tells the computer what to do and matches one of the commands in the instruction set and a(n) _____ that specifies the data or location of the data that will be used by the instruction.

5. The decimal number _____ can be written as 1101 in the binary number system and as _____ in the hexadecimal number system.

Short Answer

1. What is a parity bit? How are computers with odd parity different from computers with even parity? How are parity bits used to detect if one of the bits in a byte has been accidentally changed when data is moved from one location to another in main memory?

2. How is RAM memory different from ROM memory? For what purpose is each primarily used? What is flash RAM, or flash memory? What is cache memory?

3. How are parallel ports different from serial ports? For what devices are each type of port used? What is a SCSI port? What is a MIDI port?

4. What is an instruction set? How are CISC computers different from computers using RISC technology? Why does RISC technology increase overall processing capability?

5. What is pipelining? How is serial processing different from parallel processing? In what type of computer are parallel processors often used? What is a neural network computer?

Label the Figure

Instructions: Label the parts of the system unit in the spaces provided in the figure below.

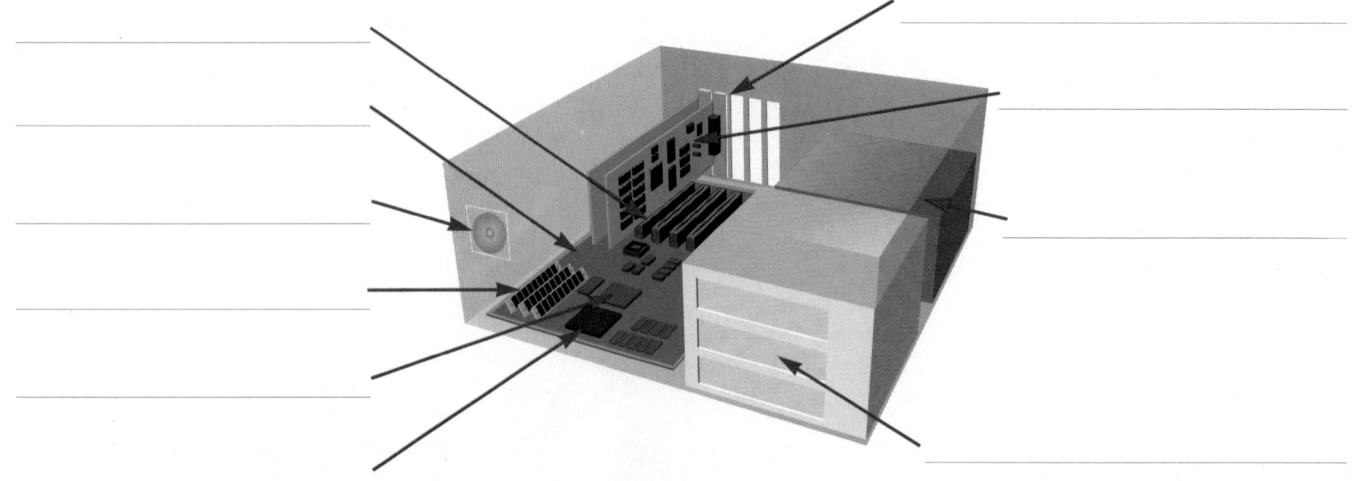

le   Edit   Section   Page   Tools   Options   Help

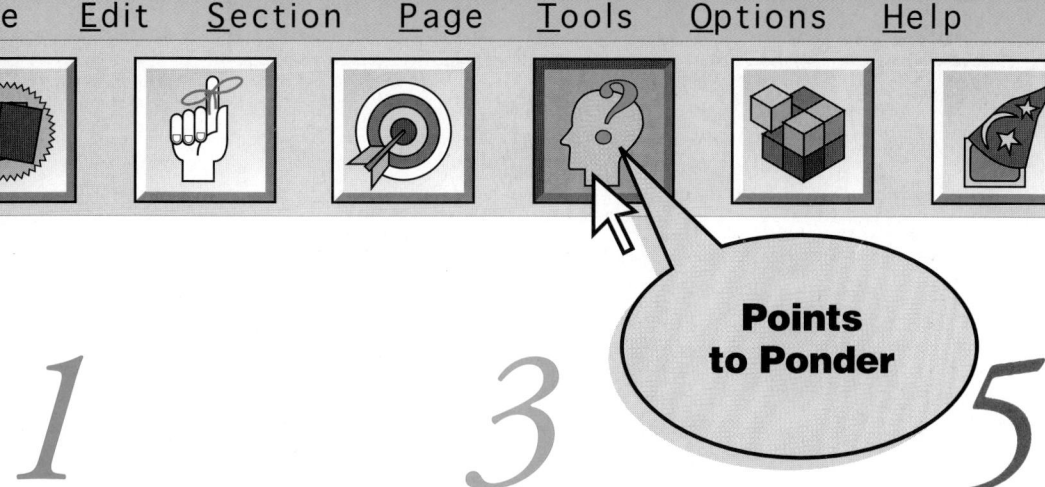

Points to Ponder

1

Although the four operations in the machine cycle may seem new to you, in a sense you carry out these same operations each time you complete certain ordinary tasks. Think of a simple task in which you perform operations analogous to those in the machine cycle. Explain what parts of accomplishing the task would be considered fetching, decoding, executing, and storing.

2

Some of the terms in this chapter have another meaning in a different context. For example, a bus, any path along which bits are transmitted, can also be defined as a large, motor-driven passenger vehicle. In this case the meanings are similar because one involves the transfer of bits and the other the transfer of people. List some other terms in this chapter that have more than one meaning. Give both meanings. If the meanings are similar, explain how.

3

ENIAC, the first computer, filled an entire room, yet it was less powerful than today's laptop computers. As the processing power and memory of personal computers increases (during the 1980s, the power of PCs expanded tenfold, and over the past twenty years, the capacity of RAM has more than doubled every two years), it is becoming increasingly difficult to define "personal computer," and to separate it from its larger cousins. How do you define personal computer? Do you think your definition will still be valid twenty years from now? Why or why not?

4

Consider the differences between RAM and ROM. In terms of your own memory, what kind of information do you have in your "RAM" memory? What kind of information do you have in your "ROM" memory? What information, if any, do you have stored in your "cache" memory?

5

As a general marketing rule, higher quality results in higher prices. Computers appear to challenge this rule, however, as they become more powerful, smaller, faster, and *less* expensive. An Atari 800 purchased at a computer store in the early 1980s for more than $1,000 could, by the mid-1980s, be replaced by one bought at a toy store for about $70. What do you think will be the impact of the decline in the price of computers? Who will be using computers in the future? What effect will the greater affordability of computers have on education?

6

Because the instruction sets, or microcode, used with IBM computers are completely different from those used with Apple computers, unless special enhancements are made, software that is written for an IBM personal computer cannot be used on an Apple Macintosh computer. Recently, however, under an agreement with IBM and Apple, Motorola has created a new processor, called the PowerPC. This chip will enable IBM and Apple to produce software that takes advantage of each other's applications. IBM systems will be able to run Macintosh applications, and Macintosh systems will be able to run IBM software. Who will benefit from this new chip? Why? Will anyone be harmed by this new development? Why or why not?

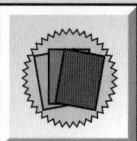
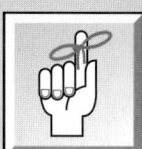

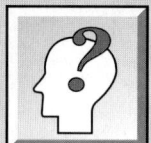

Out and About

1. If you own a personal computer or have access to a personal computer, take the cover off the system unit. Make a sketch of the system unit and try to identify as many components of the system unit as you can. Be careful not to touch any of the components. By referring to the computer's *User Guide,* list the computer's specification for some of the components described in this chapter (for example, CPU, CPU speed, bus speed, cache, RAM type, RAM capacity, expansion slots, and power supply).

2. Make a copy of an advertisement in a newspaper or magazine for a personal computer. Highlight any terms in the advertisement that were discussed in this chapter. List the terms, and explain the meaning of each.

3. Visit a computer vendor and compare one of its less expensive personal computer systems to one of its more expensive computer systems. Make a table that shows the differences between their system units (type of microprocessor, RAM capacity, and so on). Do you think the differences justify the discrepancy in price? Why or why not? Are there any other factors (such as included software) that might also affect the price disparity?

4. Two of the earliest computers were the ENIAC (an acronym for Electronic Numerical Integrator and Computer) and UNIVAC I. Both of these computers were enormous – ENIAC filled an entire room and UNIVAC I weighed 16,000 pounds! Visit a library to research these early computers. What were their components? In what ways were they different from today's personal computers? What technological developments have led to laptop computers that have greater capabilities than either the ENIAC or the UNIVAC I?

5. It is sometimes said that, "Software drives hardware." Although this statement has several interpretations, when purchasing a personal computer, it means that the system unit and peripheral devices (hardware) you buy must be capable of running the application programs (software) in which you are interested. Visit a store that sells computer software and make a list of the application programs you would like now and those you may want in the future. Examine the software packages and note the system requirements. On the basis of your findings, what are the minimum system requirements you would demand in a personal computer?

6. The semiconductor industry continues to develop and introduce new microprocessor and memory chips. Using current computer magazines, explore the most recent advances in microchip technology. What are the latest advances? Where are they being made? How do you think these advances will affect the development of personal computers over the next decade? What impact, if any, will these advances have on the way computers are used?

ile   Edit   Section   Page   Tools   Options   Help

 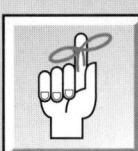   

In the Lab

Windows Labs

1 **Setting the Date and Time**   With Program Manager on the screen, double-click the Main group icon. In the Main group window, double-click the Control Panel program-item icon. In the Control Panel window, double-click the Date/Time icon 🔳. In the Date & Time dialog box *(Figure 4-37)*, click the Help button. Read and print the Date/Time information. Close the Help window.

Practice changing the system date and time. Answer the following questions: (1) How do you change the system date? (2) How do you change the system time? (3) What applications use the system date and time? Choose the Cancel button in the Date & Time dialog box. Close the Control Panel window by double-clicking its Control-menu box.

2 **Using Clock**   With Program Manager on the screen, double-click the Accessories group icon. Double-click the Clock program-item icon 🕐 to start the Clock application. Perform the following tasks: (1) Use the mouse to resize the Clock window to the size shown in *Figure 4-38.* (2) Select the Settings menu and choose the Analog command. Select the Settings menu and choose the Digital command. (3) Select the Settings menu and choose the Seconds command. (4) Select the Settings menu and choose the Date command. Select the Settings menu and choose the No Title command. (5) Double-click inside the Clock window to redisplay the title bar. Select the Settings menu and choose the Set Font command. (6) In the Font dialog box, click a variety of fonts in the Font list box; notice the selected font displays in the Sample area. Select a font and choose the OK button. (7) Click the Minimize button in the Clock window. Double-click the Clock icon to display it in normal size.

(8) Describe the function of all the commands in the Settings menu. (9) In *Figure 4-36,* which Clock settings are selected? Close Clock.

3 **Shelly Cashman Series Motherboard Lab**   Follow the instructions in Windows Lab 2 in Chapter 1 on page 1.30 to display the Shelly Cashman Series Labs screen Select Understanding the Motherboard and choose the Start Lab button. When the initial screen displays, carefully read the objectives. With your printer turned on, point to the Print Questions button and click the left mouse button. Fill out the top of the Questions sheet and answer the questions as you step through the Motherboard Lab.

4 **Using Calculator to Perform Number System Conversion**   With Program Manager on the screen, double-click the Accessories group icon. Double-click the Calculator program-item icon ⌨ to start the Calculator application. Perform the following tasks: (1) Select the View menu and choose the Scientific command to display the scientific calculator *(Figure 4-39* on the next page). (2) Click the Dec option button to select base 10. Enter 16384 by clicking the numeric buttons. Click the Hex option button. What number displays? Click the Bin option button. What number displays? (3) Convert the following base 10 (decimal) numbers to hexadecimal and binary: 7, 16, 32, 64, 4096, and

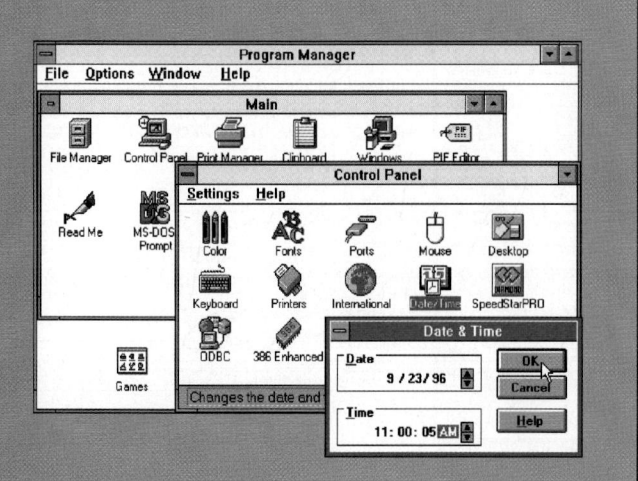

Figure 4-37

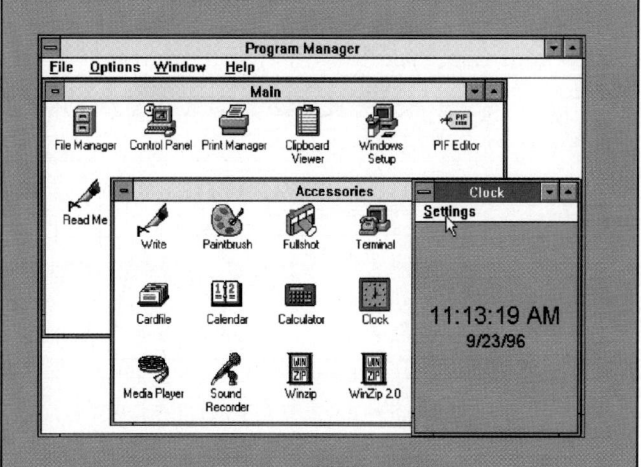

Figure 4-38

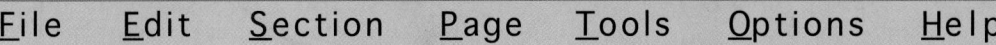

 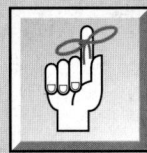 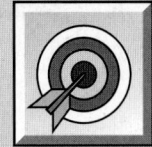   

In the Lab (continued)

8192. (4) Convert the following base 2 (binary) numbers to decimal and hexadecimal: 100, 11111111, 1010, and 100000111000111. (5) Convert the following base 16 (hexadecimal) numbers to decimal and binary: 64, 3AB, BBB, 49C2, FFFF, ACDB12, and 32AC. Close Calculator.

5 **Using Help**　With Program Manager on the screen, select the Help menu and choose the About Program Manager command. To whom is Windows 3.1 licensed? How much memory is free on your system? What percentage of system resources is free? Choose the OK button.

Select the Help menu and choose the Contents command. When the Program Manager Help window displays *(Figure 4-40)*, print the contents of the window by choosing the Print Topic command from the File menu.

DOS Labs

1 **Setting the Date and Time**　At the DOS prompt, type cls and press the ENTER key to clear the screen. Type date and press the ENTER key. At the Enter new date (mm-dd-yy) prompt, type 11-5-98 and press the ENTER key. Type date and press the ENTER key. What date displays as the current date? At the Enter new date (mm-dd-yy) prompt, enter today's date and press the ENTER key. Press the PRINT SCREEN key.

At the DOS prompt, type cls and press the ENTER key. Type time and press the ENTER key. At the Enter new time prompt, type 14:40 and press the ENTER key. Type time and press the ENTER key. What time displays as the current time?

At the Enter new time prompt, enter the current time and press the ENTER key. Press the PRINT SCREEN key.

2 **Checking Memory**　Type cls and press the ENTER key. Type mem and press the ENTER key to display memory information. Press the PRINT SCREEN key. How much of each of these types of memory is on your system: conventional, upper, reserved (adapter), extended, and total? How much expanded memory is on your system? If there is none designated, indicate none. What is the largest executable program size?

3 **Using Help**　At the DOS prompt, type help mem and press the ENTER key to display help about the MEM command. Read and print the information. Read and print the information for the Notes jump topic and the Examples jump topic. Exit the Help window.

Online Lab

1 **Electronic Job Hunting**　Using one of the two online services you selected in Chapter 1, connect to the service and perform the following tasks: (1) Search the online service for job listings. (2) Search the list for Programming positions and write down three openings in your area of the country. (3) Search the list for job openings for your major, and write down three openings in your area of the country. (4) **Extra Credit:** Use electronic mail to enter your resume on the online service. Be advised, you may be contacted.

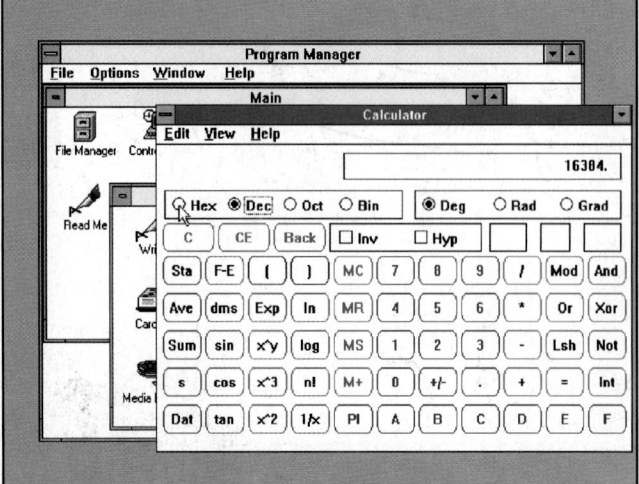

Figure 4-39

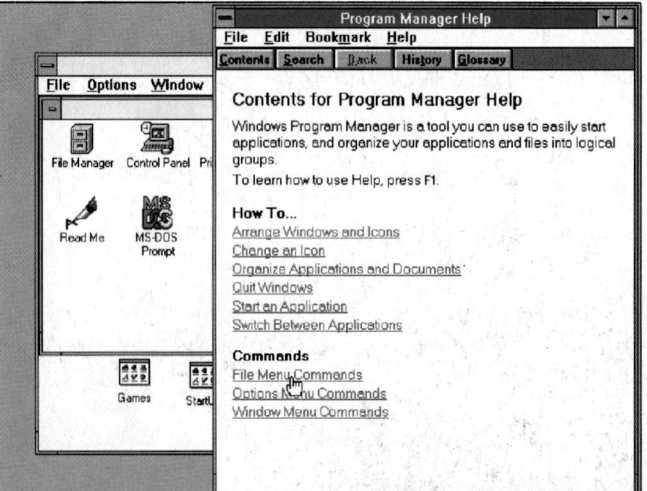

Figure 4-40

Making a Computer Chip

A computer chip is made by building layers of electronic pathways and connections using conducting and non-conducting materials on a surface of silicon. The combination of these materials into specific patterns forms microscopic electronic components such as transistors, diodes, resistors, and capacitors; the basic building blocks of electronic circuits. Connected together on a chip, these components are referred to as an integrated circuit. The application of the conducting and non-conducting materials to the silicon base is done through a series of technically sophisticated chemical and photographic processes. Some of the manufacturing steps are shown in the following photographs.

A computer chip begins with a design developed by engineers using a computer aided circuit design program (1). In order to better review the design, greatly enlarged printouts are prepared. Some chips only take a month or two to design while others may take a year or more. A separate design is required for each layer of the chip. Most chips have at least four to six layers but some have up to fifteen.

Although other materials can be used, the most common raw material used to make chips is silicon crystals (2) that have been refined from quartz rocks. The silicon crystals are melted and formed into a cylinder five to ten inches in diameter and several feet long (3). After being smoothed, the silicon ingot is sliced into wafers four to eight inches in diameter and 4/1000 of an inch thick.

Much of the chip manufacturing process is performed in special laboratories called clean rooms. Because even the smallest particle of dust can ruin a chip, the clean rooms are kept 1000 times cleaner than a hospital operating room. People who work in these facilities must wear special protective clothing called bunny suits (4). Before entering the manufacturing area, the workers remove any dust on their suits in an air shower (5).

After the wafer has been polished and sterilized, it is cleaned in a chemical bath. Because the chemicals used in the cleaning process are dangerous, this step is usually performed

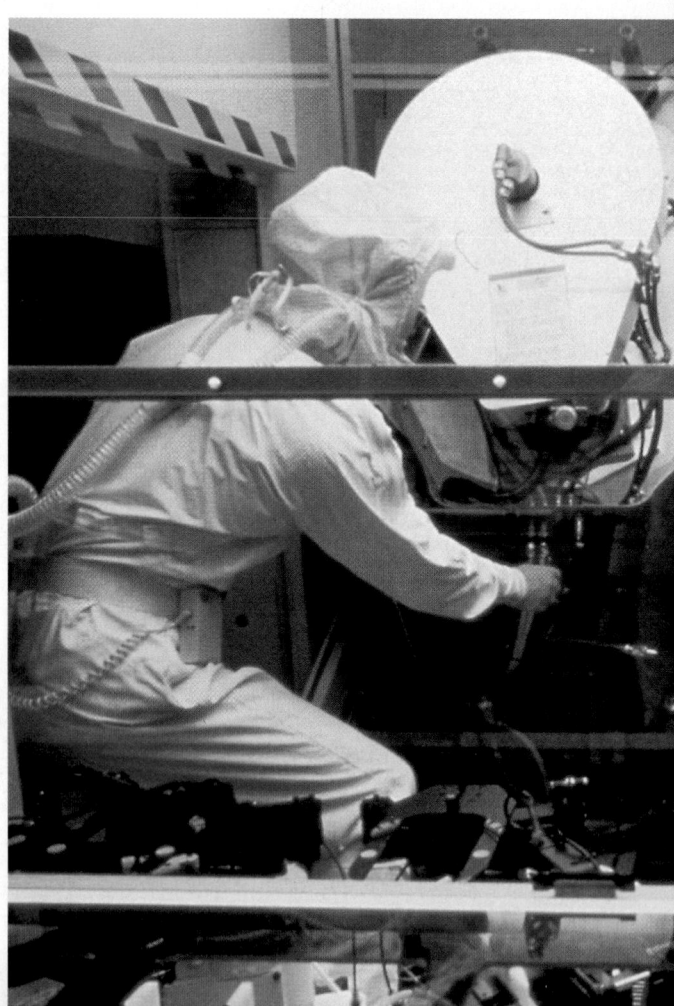

6

7

by a robot (6). After cleaning, the wafers are placed in a diffusion oven where the first layer of material is added to the wafer surface (7). Other materials, called dopants, are added to the surface of the wafer in a process called ion implantation (8). The dopants create areas that will conduct electricity. Channels in these layers of materials are removed in a process called etching. Before etching, a soft gelatin-like emulsion called photoresist is added to the wafer. During photolithography (9), an image of the chip design, called a mask, is used as a negative. The photoresist is exposed to the mask using ultraviolet light. Ultraviolet light is used because its short wavelength can reproduce very small details on the wafer. Up to 100 images of the chip design are exposed on a single wafer. The photoresist exposed to the ultraviolet light becomes hard and the photoresist covered by the chip design on the mask remains soft. The soft photoresist and some of the surface materials are etched away with hot gases leaving what will become the circuit pathways (10). The process of adding material and photoresist to the wafer, exposing it to ultraviolet light, and etching away the unexposed surface, is repeated using a different mask for each layer of the circuit.

8

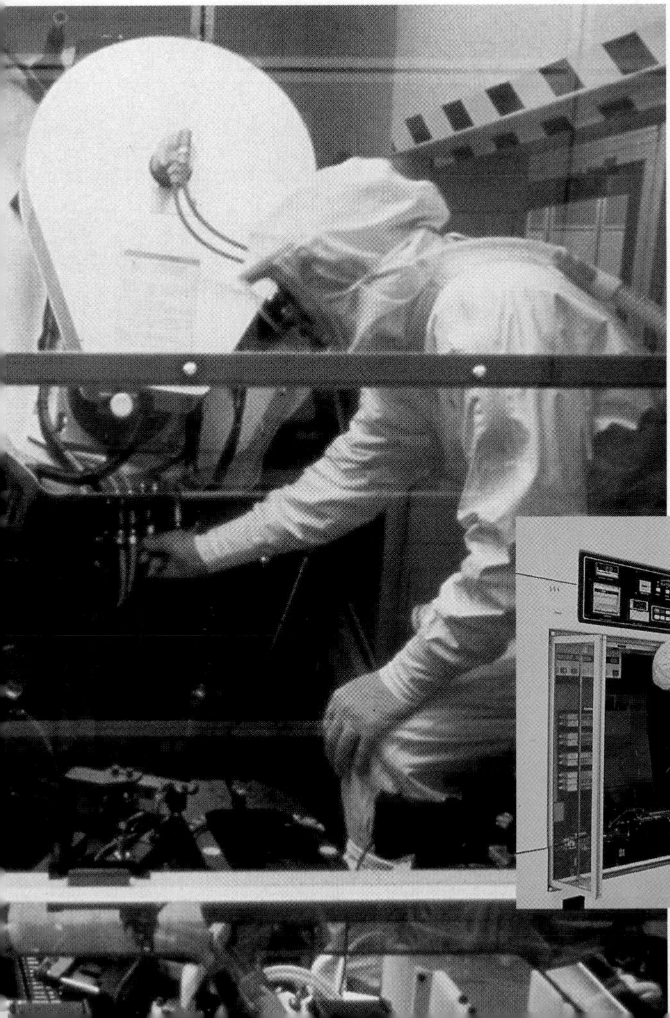

10

9

11

After all circuit layers have been added, individual chips on the wafer are tested by a machine that uses probes to apply electrical current to the chip circuits (11). In a process called dicing, the wafers are cut with a diamond saw (12) into individual chips called die (13). Die that have passed all tests are placed in a ceramic or plastic case called a package (14). Circuits on the chip are connected to pins on the package using gold wires (15). Gold is used because it conducts electricity well and does not corrode. The pins connect the chip to a socket on a circuit board (16).

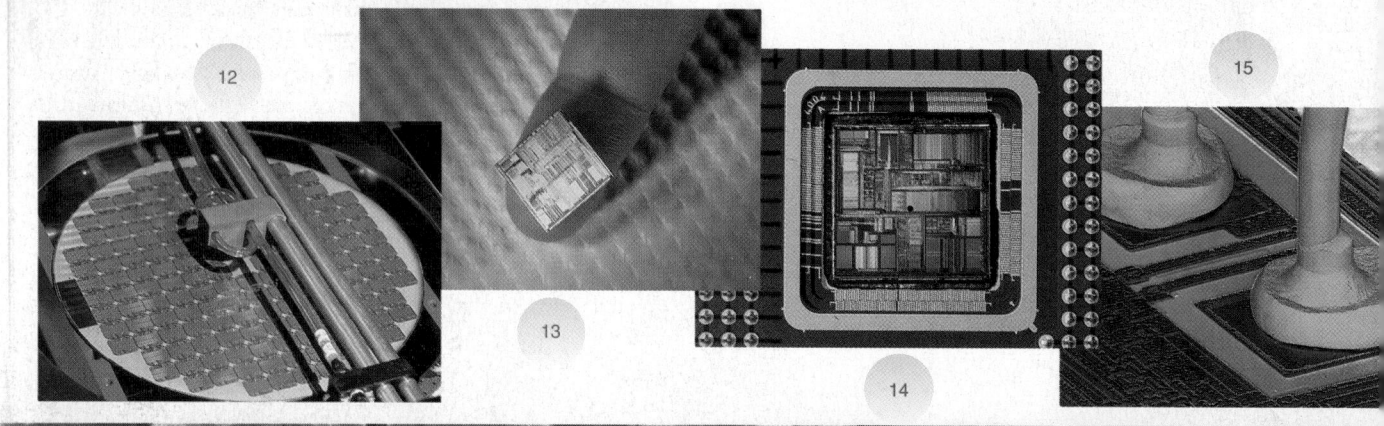

12

13

14

15

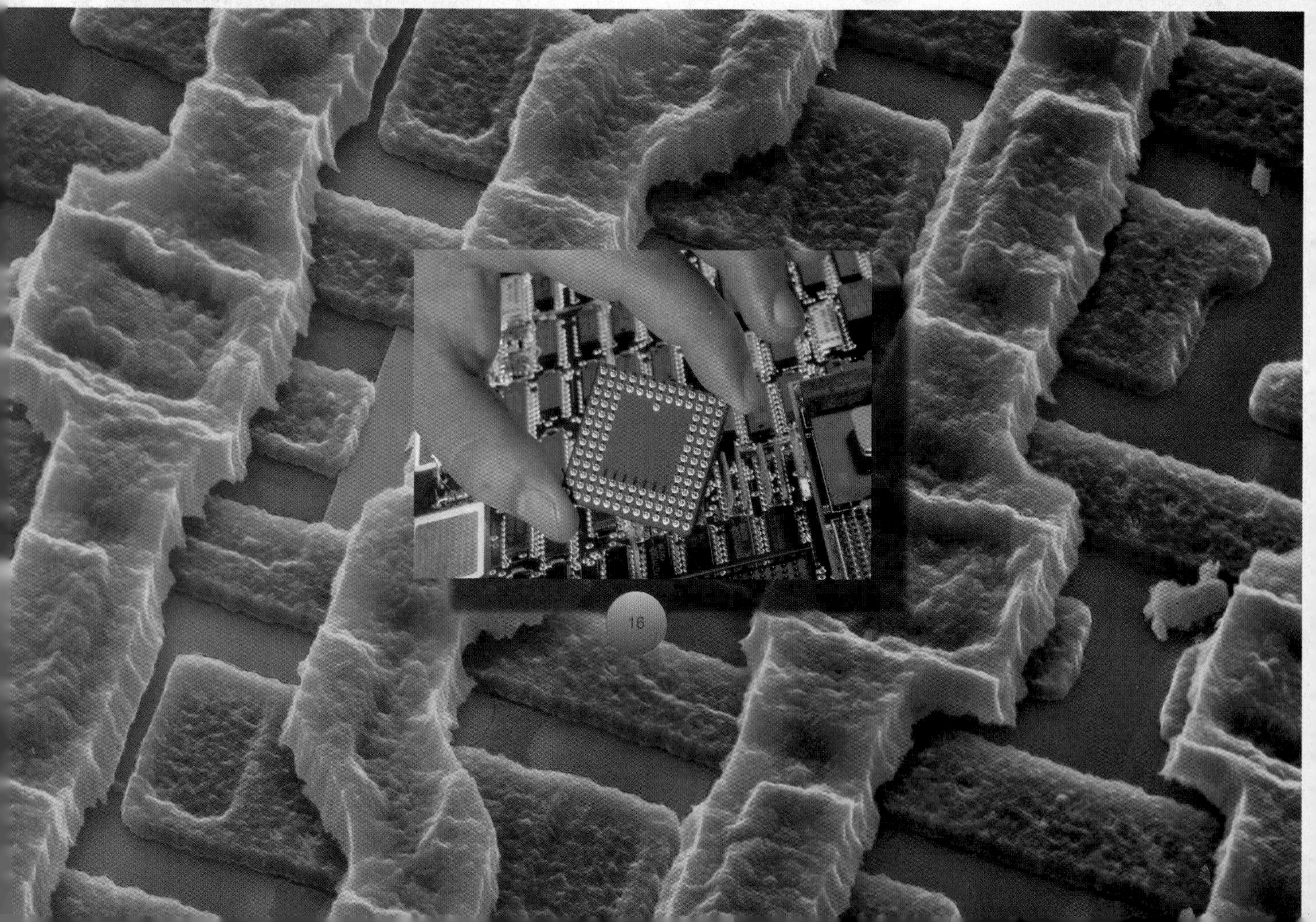

16

CHAPTER FIVE

Output from the Computer

Objectives

After completing this chapter, you will be able to:

- Define the term output

- Describe different types of printed output

- Describe multimedia and virtual reality output

- Explain the difference between impact and nonimpact printers

- Identify different types of display devices

- Explain how images are displayed on a screen

- List and describe other types of output devices used with computers

Output is the way the computer communicates with the user. Most people are familiar with computer printouts and information displayed on a screen, but computer output can take many other forms, as well. This chapter discusses different types of output and the devices computers use to produce output.

What Is Output?

Output is data that has been processed into a useful form called information that can be used by a person or a machine. Output used by a machine, such as a disk or tape file, is usually an intermediate result that eventually will be processed into output that can be used by people.

The type of output generated from the computer depends on the needs of the user and the hardware and software that are used. Two common types of output are reports and graphics. These types of output can be printed on a printer or displayed on a screen. Output that is printed is called **hard copy** and output that is displayed on a screen is called **soft copy**. Other types of output include audio (sound), video (visual images), multimedia, and virtual reality. Multimedia is an exciting method of communicating information that combines several types of output. Virtual reality also combines different types of output to create a simulated, three-dimensional environment that the user can experience using special equipment. Each of these types of output is discussed in the following sections.

Reports

A **report** is information presented in an organized form. Most people think of reports as items printed on paper or displayed on a screen. For example, word processing documents can be considered reports. Information printed on forms such as invoices or payroll checks can also be considered types of reports. One way to classify reports is by who uses them. An **internal report** is used by individuals in the performance of their jobs. For example, a daily sales report that is distributed to sales personnel is an internal report because it is used only by personnel within the organization. An **external report** is used outside the organization. Sales invoices that are printed and mailed to customers are external reports.

Reports can also be classified by the way they present information. The four types of common reports are: narrative reports, detail reports, summary reports, and exception reports.

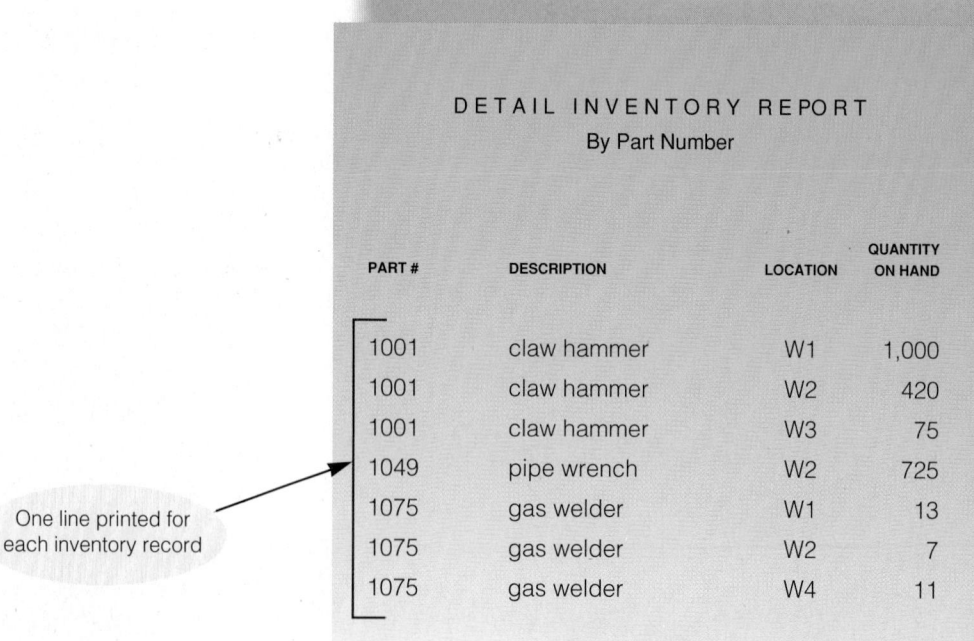

Figure 5-1
The data for this detail report was obtained from each inventory record.

Narrative reports may contain some graphic or numeric information but are primarily text-based reports. These reports, usually prepared with word processing software, include the various types of correspondence commonly used in business such as memos, letters, and sales proposals.

Detail, summary, and exception reports are primarily used to organize and present numeric-based information.

In a **detail report,** each line on the report usually corresponds to one record that has been processed. Detail reports contain a great deal of information and can be quite lengthy. They are usually required by individuals who need access to the day-to-day information that reflects the operating status of the organization. For example, people in the warehouse of a hardware distributor should have access to the location and number of units on hand for each product. The Detail Inventory Report in *Figure 5-1* contains a line for each warehouse location for each part number. Separate inventory records exist for each line on the report.

As the name implies, a **summary report** summarizes data. It contains totals for certain values found in the input records. The report shown in *Figure 5-2* contains a summary of the total quantity on hand for each part. The information on the summary report consists of totals for each part from the information contained in the detail report in *Figure 5-1*. Detail reports frequently contain more information than most managers have time to review. With a summary report, however, a manager can quickly review information in summarized form.

An **exception report** contains information that is outside of *normal* user-specified values or conditions, called the *exception criteria*. Records meeting this criteria are an *exception* to the majority of the data. For example, if an organization wants to know when to reorder inventory items to avoid running out of stock, it would design an exception report. The report would tell which inventory items fell below the reorder points and therefore need to be ordered. An example of such a report is shown in *Figure 5-3*.

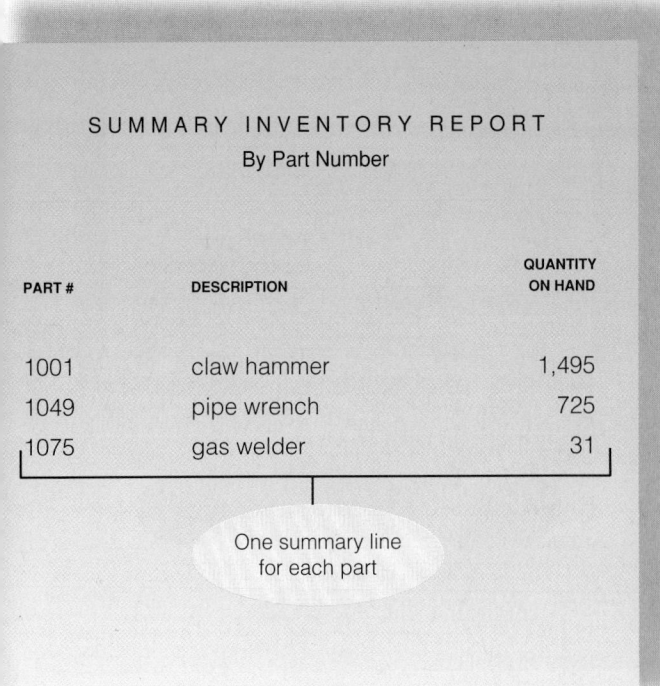
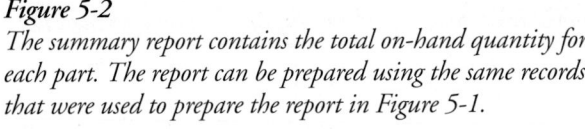

Figure 5-2
The summary report contains the total on-hand quantity for each part. The report can be prepared using the same records that were used to prepare the report in Figure 5-1.

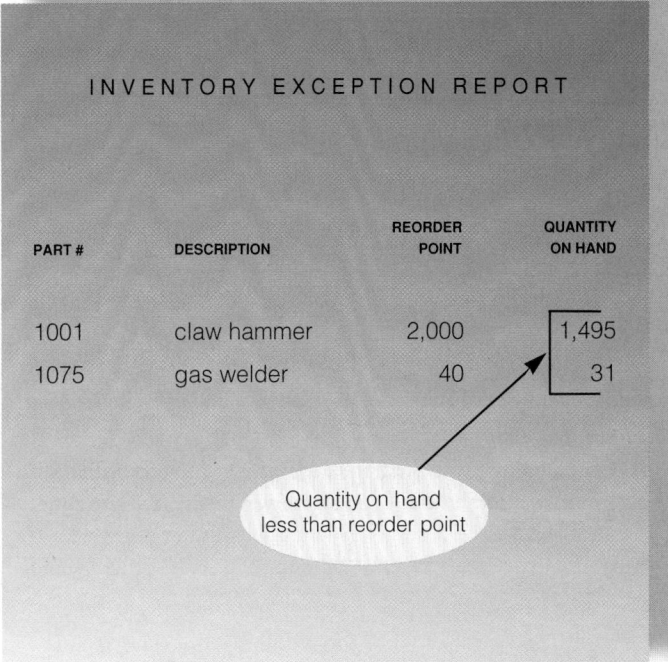

Figure 5-3
The exception report lists inventory items with an on-hand quantity below their reorder points. These parts could have been selected from thousands of inventory records. Only these items met the user's exception criteria.

Exception reports help users focus on situations that may require immediate decisions or specific actions. The advantage of exception reports is that they save time and money. In a large department store, for example, there may be more than 100,000 inventory items. A detail report containing all inventory items could be longer than 2,000 pages. To search through the report to determine the items whose on-hand quantity was less than the reorder point would be a difficult and time-consuming task. The exception report, however, could select these items, which might number 100 to 200, and place them on a two- to four-page report that could be reviewed in just a few minutes.

Reports are also sometimes classified by how often they are produced. **Periodic reports**, also called **scheduled reports**, are produced on a regular basis such as daily, weekly, monthly, or yearly. **On-demand reports** are created whenever they are needed for information that is not required on a scheduled basis.

Graphics

Computer graphics are any nontext pictorial information. One of the early uses of computer graphics was for charts to help analyze numeric information. Charts are now widely used in spreadsheet and presentation graphics software packages *(Figure 5-4)*. In recent years, computer graphics have gone far beyond charting capabilities. **Computer drawing programs** and **computer paint programs** allow an artistic user to create stunning looking works of art. These programs are frequently used for developing advertising and other marketing materials *(Figure 5-5)*. Clip art and photographs are also considered types of computer graphics.

Audio Output

Audio output, sometimes called **audio response**, consists of sounds, including words and music, produced by the computer. An audio output device on a computer is

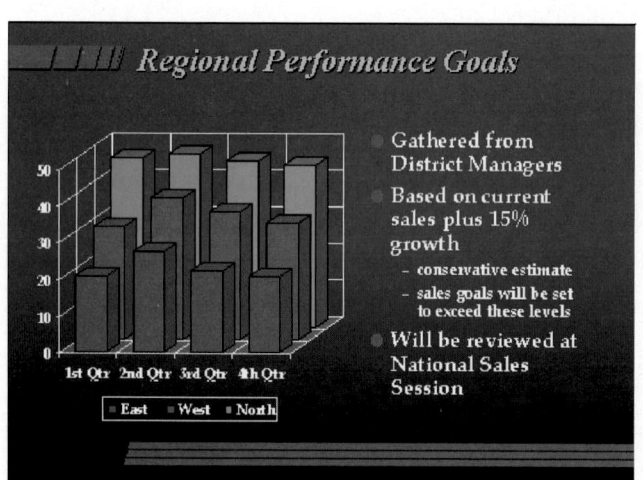

Figure 5-4
A presentation graphics slide is an example of graphics output that combines text, charts based on numeric data, and art.

Figure 5-5
Computer drawing and paint programs are often used by professional artists to create advertising and marketing materials.

a speaker. Most personal computers come with a small speaker (approximately two inches) that is usually located behind an opening on the front or side of the system unit case. Increasingly, personal computer users are adding higher quality stereo speakers to their systems *(Figure 5-6)*. The stereo speakers connect to a port on a sound card that works with sound, voice, and music software.

Video Output

Video output consists of visual images that have been captured with a video input device, such as a VCR or camera, digitized, and directed to an output device such as a computer monitor *(Figure 5-7)*. As was mentioned in Chapter 3, some video input devices can digitize the image as it is captured. Video output can also be directed to a television monitor. Because standard televisions are not designed to handle a computer's digital signals, the video output has to be converted to an analog signal that can be displayed by the television. **High definition television** (HDTV) sets are designed for digital signals and may eventually replace computer monitors.

Multimedia

Multimedia is the combination of text, graphics, video, and sound. Some people have described it as a combination of traditional text-based computers and television. Multimedia is really more than just a combination of these previously separate information elements. Multimedia is different because it usually gives the user options on the amount of material to review and the sequence in which the material will be reviewed. For example, a typical multimedia presentation will display text material along with one or more photos or graphic images. Some sound or voice narration may also be provided. In addition, the screen will usually show icons that represent additional material, such as pictures, sounds, animation, or maps, that the user can also choose to review. Most multimedia presentations use a technique, called **hypermedia**, that allows the user to quickly move to related subject areas. An example of these features can be seen in *Figures 5-8* and *5-9* on the next page; screens from Microsoft's multimedia encyclopedia, Encarta. *Figure 5-8* shows text information about the famous jazz musician, Duke Ellington. The small icons at the top of the text material indicate there is an image item (represented by

Figure 5-6
To fully experience computer audio output, many users are adding or purchasing systems with stereo speakers.

Figure 5-7
Use of video output is like a video telephone system; it allows company employees to see the coworker with whom they are talking.

the camera- shaped icon) and a sound item (represented by the speaker- shaped icon) that can also be reviewed. To see or hear these items, the user selects the icon with the mouse. To see related topics, the user can choose the See Also button at the bottom of the screen. When this is done, a list of the topics is presented *(Figure 5-9)*. The user can move directly to any of these topics by selecting one with the mouse.

The Microsoft Encarta multimedia encyclopedia, like most multimedia products available today, is stored on a CD-ROM disk. This type of storage device is required because of the large amounts of data that most multimedia applications require. For example, the Encarta encyclopedia takes more than 550MB of storage space. Full-motion video, which is used sparingly in most multimedia presentations today, can require more than 2 gigabytes of storage for each minute of video. These storage requirements can be reduced

through the use of data compression techniques.

Currently, multimedia applications are primarily used in four areas; education, training, entertainment, and information. Information applications include multimedia kiosks that can be found in museums, airports, and hotels *(Figure 5-10)*. Eventually, multimedia techniques will be incorporated into most all software applications.

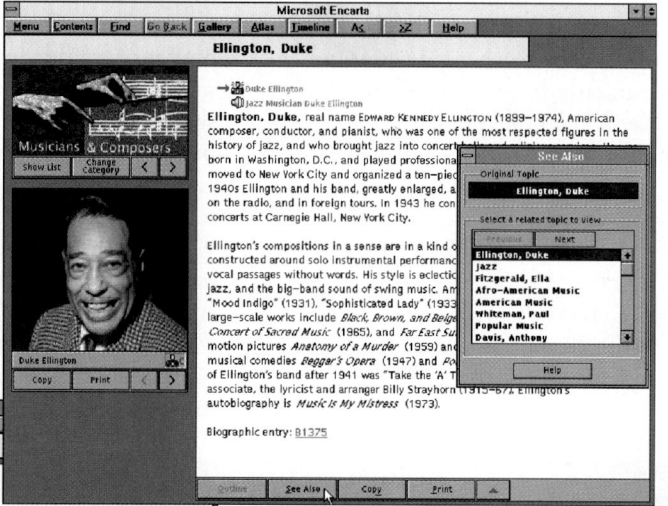

Figure 5-9
When the user chooses the See Also button at the bottom of the screen, a list of related topics is displayed. The user can move directly to any of these topics by selecting one of them with a pointing device.

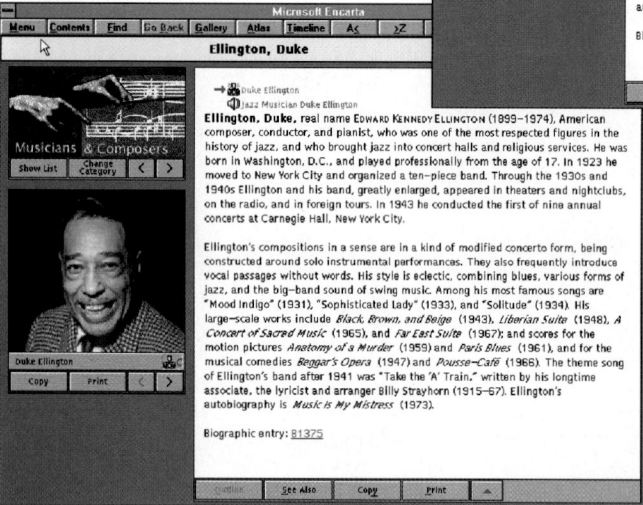

Figure 5-8
The Microsoft Encarta multimedia encyclopedia offers text, graphics, sound, and animation. Clicking the camera-shaped icon at the top of the text displays a photograph of jazz musician Duke Ellington. Clicking the speaker-shaped icon below the camera plays a portion of one of Ellington's compositions.

Figure 5-10
Coca-Cola uses multimedia kiosks to present information on their products and history at their Atlanta visitors center. Multimedia information kiosks are becoming a frequent site in hotels, museums, airports, and other locations where infrequent visitors need to obtain information.

Figure 5-11
One of the first practical applications of virtual reality software was in the architectural profession. Architects use VR software to create a model of the project on which they are working. Clients can then walk through the virtual project and specify design changes before the project is built.

Virtual Reality

Virtual reality (VR) refers to the use of a computer to create an artificial environment that can be experienced by the computer user. In its simplest form, VR software displays what appears to be a three-dimensional view of a place, such as a landscape or a building, that can be explored by the user. Architects are using such software to show clients what proposed construction or remodeling changes will look like *(Figure 5-11)*. In more advanced forms, VR software requires the user to wear specialized headgear, gloves, and body suits to enhance the experience of the artificial environment *(Figure 5-12)*. The headgear includes displays in front of both eyes that project the artificial environment being experienced by the wearer. The glove and body suit sense the motion and direction of the user. Gloves allow the user to pick up and hold items displayed in the virtual environment. Eventually, experts predict, the body suits will provide tactile feedback so the wearer can experience the touch and feel of the virtual world.

Figure 5-12
The virtual reality body suit, called a "Datasuit" by developer VPL research, allows more than 50 different movements of the wearer to be interpreted by the VR software. The software then manipulates the image in the virtual environment, which is displayed in the headset.

Most experts agree that VR is still in its early stages and that practical applications are just now becoming available. The potential applications of VR, however, have many people excited and have kept millions of dollars flowing into VR research.

The general public's first encounter with VR will likely be through a three-dimensional electronic game. One such game is called Dactyl Nightmare *(Figure 5-13)*. Special visors allow the player to *see* the computer-generated environment. Sensors in the surrounding game machine record movement and direction as the player *walks* around the game's electronic landscape. The object of the game is to use a simulated laser gun to shoot other players before they shoot you. Players also have to avoid being snatched by giant green pterodactyls (prehistoric birds) that can carry them high into the sky before letting them crash to the ground. Because of their high cost (more than $50,000) and the special equipment required, VR games are not spreading across the land as fast as pin ball machines once did. Most major metropolitan U.S. cities, however, now have VR arcades installed or planned for the near future.

Commercial applications of VR include a virtual showroom and a virtual office. The showroom lets customers wander among available products and inspect those they find interesting. In the virtual office, created for an office furniture company, clients can see what their selected furniture will look like and can experiment with different furniture arrangements.

As computing power increases, VR applications will be able to be run on lower cost computers. This in turn will increase the number of commercial VR applications and make VR technology available for a wider number of users.

A variety of devices produce the output created in the information processing cycle. The following sections describe the devices most commonly used.

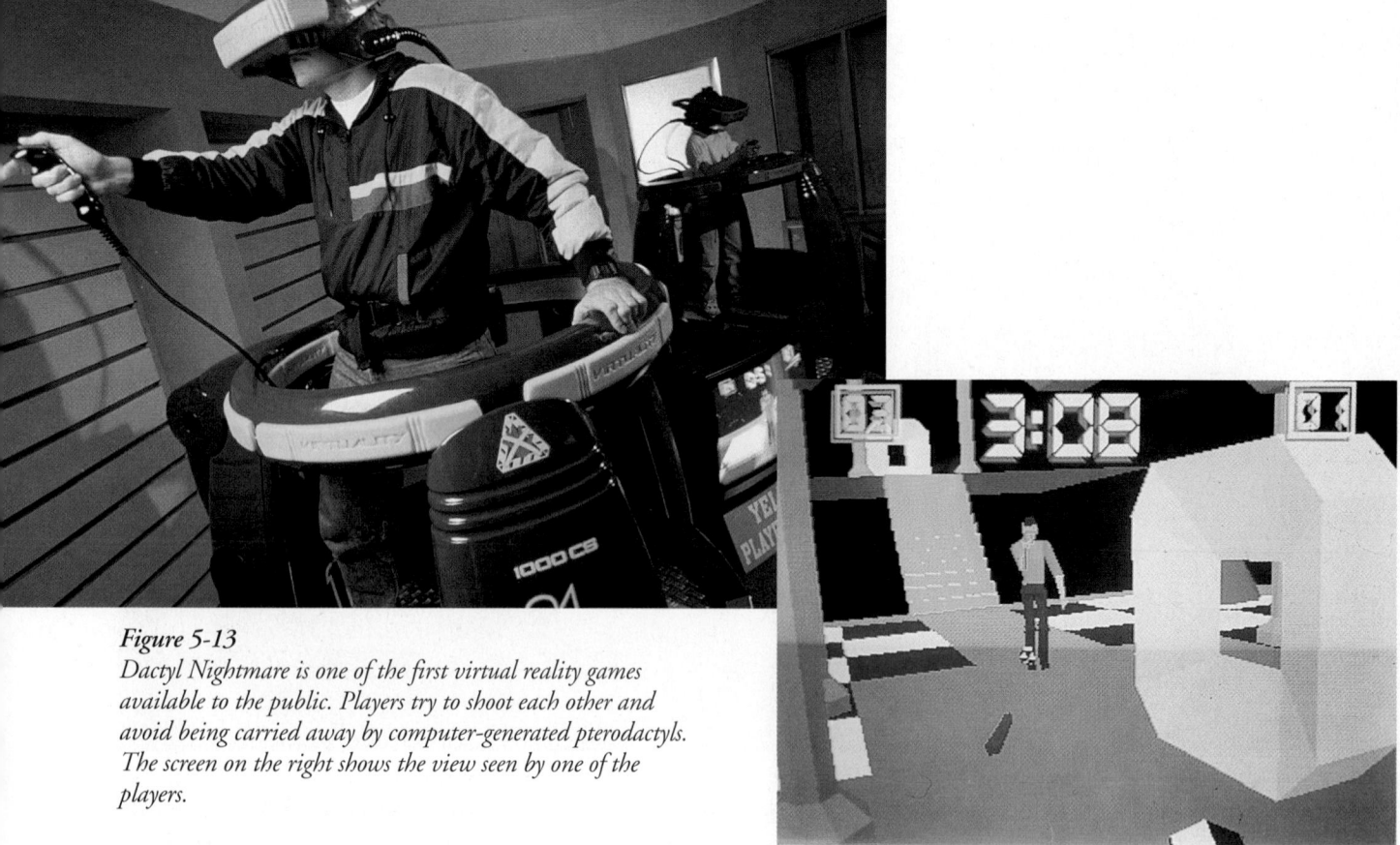

Figure 5-13
Dactyl Nightmare is one of the first virtual reality games available to the public. Players try to shoot each other and avoid being carried away by computer-generated pterodactyls. The screen on the right shows the view seen by one of the players.

Printers

Printing requirements vary greatly among computer users. For example, home computer users may only print a hundred pages or fewer a week. Small business computer users may print several hundred pages a day. Users of mainframe computers, such as large utility companies that send printed bills to hundreds of thousands of customers each month, need printers that are capable of printing thousands of pages per hour. These different needs have resulted in the development of printers with varying speeds, capabilities, and printing methods. Generally, printers can be classified into two groups, impact or nonimpact, based on how they transfer characters to the paper.

Impact Printers

Impact printers transfer the image onto paper by some type of printing mechanism striking the paper, ribbon, and character together. One technique is front striking in which the printing mechanism that forms the character strikes a ribbon against the paper from the front to form an image. This is similar to the method used on typewriters. The second technique utilizes a hammer striking device. The ribbon and paper are struck against the character from the back by a hammer to form the image on the paper *(Figure 5-14)*.

Most impact printers use continuous-form paper. The pages of **continuous-form paper** are connected together for a continuous flow through the printer *(Figure 5-15)*. The advantage of continuous-form paper is that it need not be changed frequently; thousands of pages come connected together. Some impact printers use single-sheet paper. The advantage of using single-sheet paper is that different types of paper, such as letterhead, can be quickly changed.

Figure 5-14
Impact printers operate in one of two ways; front striking or hammer striking.

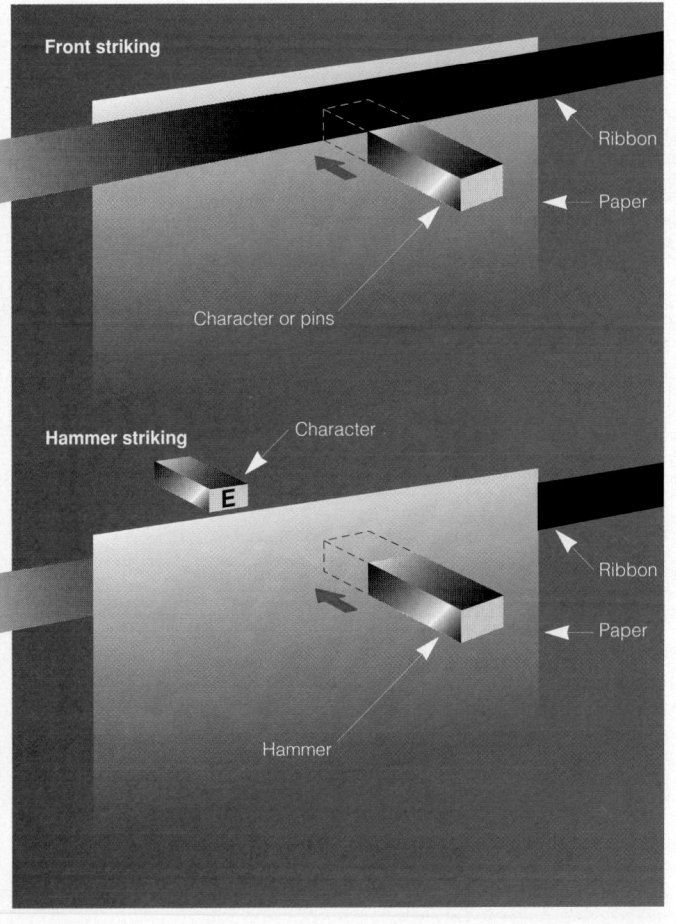

Figure 5-15
Sheets of continuous-form paper are connected together. Small holes on the sides of the paper allow sprockets to pull the paper through the printer. Perforations between each sheet allow the pages to be easily separated.

Dot Matrix Printers

A **dot matrix printer** produces printed images by striking wire pins against an inked ribbon. Its print head consists of a series of small tubes containing wire pins that, when pressed against a ribbon and paper, print small dots. The pins are activated by electromagnets that are arranged in a circular pattern. The combination of small dots printed closely together forms the character *(Figure 5-16)*. Dot matrix printers are used extensively because they are versatile and relatively inexpensive. The printer shown in *Figure 5-17* is a dot matrix printer used with personal computers. *Figure 5-18* shows a dot matrix printer frequently used with larger systems.

To print a character using a dot matrix printer, the character stored in main memory is sent to the printer's electronic circuitry. The printer circuitry activates the pins in the print head that correspond to the pattern of the character to be printed. The selected pins strike the ribbon and paper and print the character. Most dot matrix printers used with personal computers have a single print head that moves

across the page. Dot matrix printers used with larger computers usually have fixed print mechanisms at each print position and can print an entire line at one time. Because the individual pins of a dot matrix printer can be activated, a dot matrix printer can be used to print expanded (larger than normal) and condensed (smaller than normal) characters and graphics.

Dot matrix printers can contain a varying number of pins, depending on the manufacturer and the printer model. Print heads consisting of 9 and 24 pins (two vertical rows of 12) are most common. *Figure 5-19* illustrates the formation of the letter E using a nine-pin dot matrix printer.

The speed of impact printers with movable print heads is rated in **characters per second (cps)**. Depending on the printer model, this speed varies between 50 and 300 cps. The speed of impact printers that print one line at a time is rated in **lines per minute (lpm)**. High-speed dot matrix printers can print up to 1,200 lpm. The speeds quoted by dot matrix printer manufacturers are usually for what is called draft-quality printing. **Draft-quality** printing uses the minimum

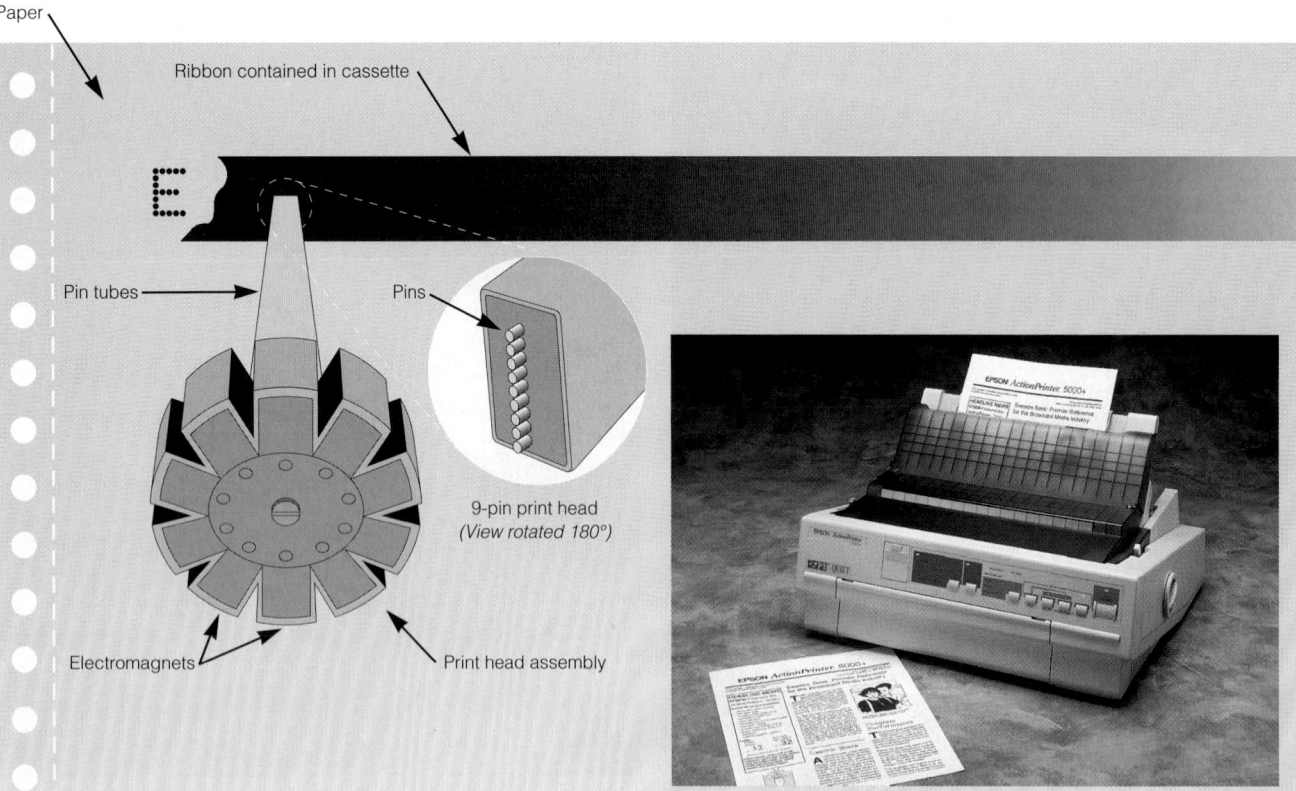

Paper

Ribbon contained in cassette

Pin tubes

Pins

9-pin print head
(View rotated 180°)

Electromagnets

Print head assembly

Figure 5-16
The print head assembly for a dot matrix printer consists of a series of pins that are fired at the paper by electromagnets. When activated, the pins push the ribbon into the paper forming an image made up of small dots.

Figure 5-17
Many different types of small dot matrix printers are available for use with personal computers.

number of dots to form a character and achieve the fastest printing speed. Draft quality is fine for internal reports but is not adequate for sending printed material to customers or other outsiders. To achieve a sharper, higher quality look, called **letter quality** (LQ) or **near letter quality** (NLQ), the printer overlaps the printed dots. Nine-pin print heads accomplish the overlapping by printing the line twice. The character is slightly offset during the second printing. This results in the appearance of solid characters *(Figure 5-20)*. Twenty-four-pin printers can accomplish the overlapping on a single pass because their multiple rows of pins are slightly offset *(Figure 5-21)*.

Dot matrix printers with movable print heads are designed to print in a **bidirectional** manner. That is, the print head, the device that contains the mechanism for transferring the character to the paper, can print as it moves from left to right and from right to left. The printer does this by storing the next line to be printed in its memory and then

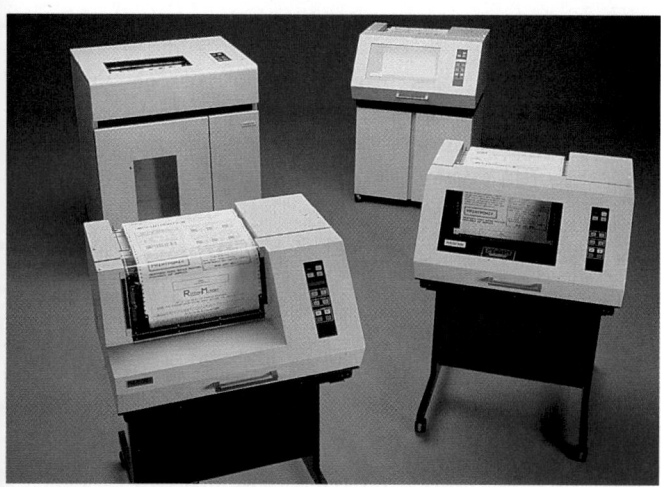

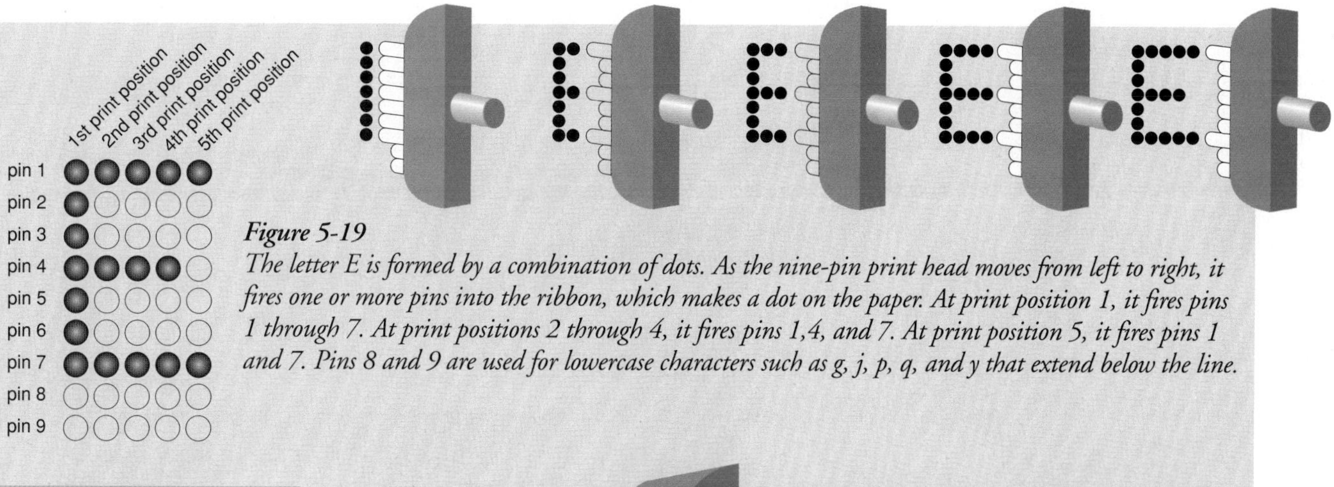

Figure 5-18
Dot matrix printers used with larger systems often have print heads at each print position that allow them to print an entire line at a time.

Figure 5-19
The letter E is formed by a combination of dots. As the nine-pin print head moves from left to right, it fires one or more pins into the ribbon, which makes a dot on the paper. At print position 1, it fires pins 1 through 7. At print positions 2 through 4, it fires pins 1,4, and 7. At print position 5, it fires pins 1 and 7. Pins 8 and 9 are used for lowercase characters such as g, j, p, q, and y that extend below the line.

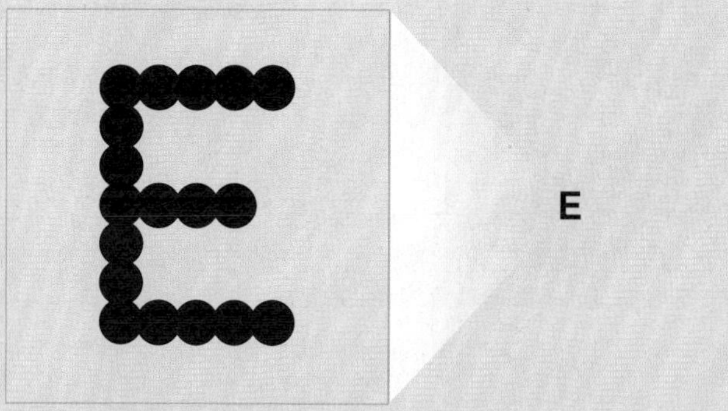

Figure 5-20
Overlapping the printed dots gives the appearance of a more solid-looking character that is easier to read.

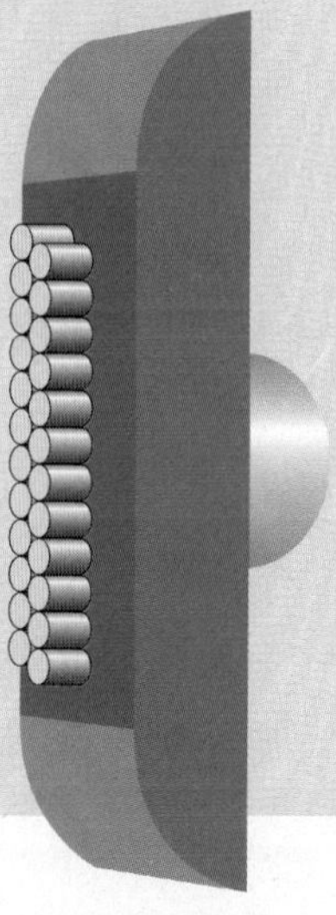

Figure 5-21
The two rows of pins on this 24-pin dot matrix print head are slightly offset (one is higher than the other) so they will overlap and produce a more solid-looking character or a smoother line.

printing the line forward or backward as needed. Bidirectional printing greatly increases the speed of the printer.

The feed mechanism determines how the paper moves through the printer. Two types of feed mechanisms found on dot matrix printers are tractor feed and friction feed. **Tractor feed mechanisms** transport continuous-form paper through the printer by using sprockets, which are small protruding prongs of plastic or metal that fit into holes on each side of the paper. Where it is necessary to feed single sheets of paper into the printer, **friction feed mechanisms** are used. As the name implies, paper is moved through friction feed printers by pressure on the paper and the carriage, as it is on a typewriter. As the carriage rotates, the paper moves through the printer.

Dot matrix printers are built with a standard, medium, or wide carriage. A standard carriage printer can accommodate paper up to 8 $\frac{1}{2}$ inches wide. A medium carriage can accommodate paper up to 11 inches wide, and a wide carriage printer can accommodate paper up to 14 inches wide.

Some dot matrix printers can print in multiple colors using ribbons that contain the colors red, yellow, and blue in addition to the standard black. Color output is obtained by repeated printing and repositioning of the paper, print head, and ribbon. Such printers can be useful in printing graphs and charts, but other types of color printers offer a higher quality of color output.

Dot matrix printers range in cost from less than $200 for small desktop units to more than $10,000 for heavy-use business models. Most dot matrix printers are available for less than $1,000.

Band and Chain Printers

Band and chain printers are used for high-volume output on large computer systems. **Band printers** use a horizontal, rotating band containing numbers, letters of the alphabet, and selected special characters. The characters are struck by hammers located at each print position behind the paper and ribbon to create a line of print on the paper *(Figure 5-22)*.

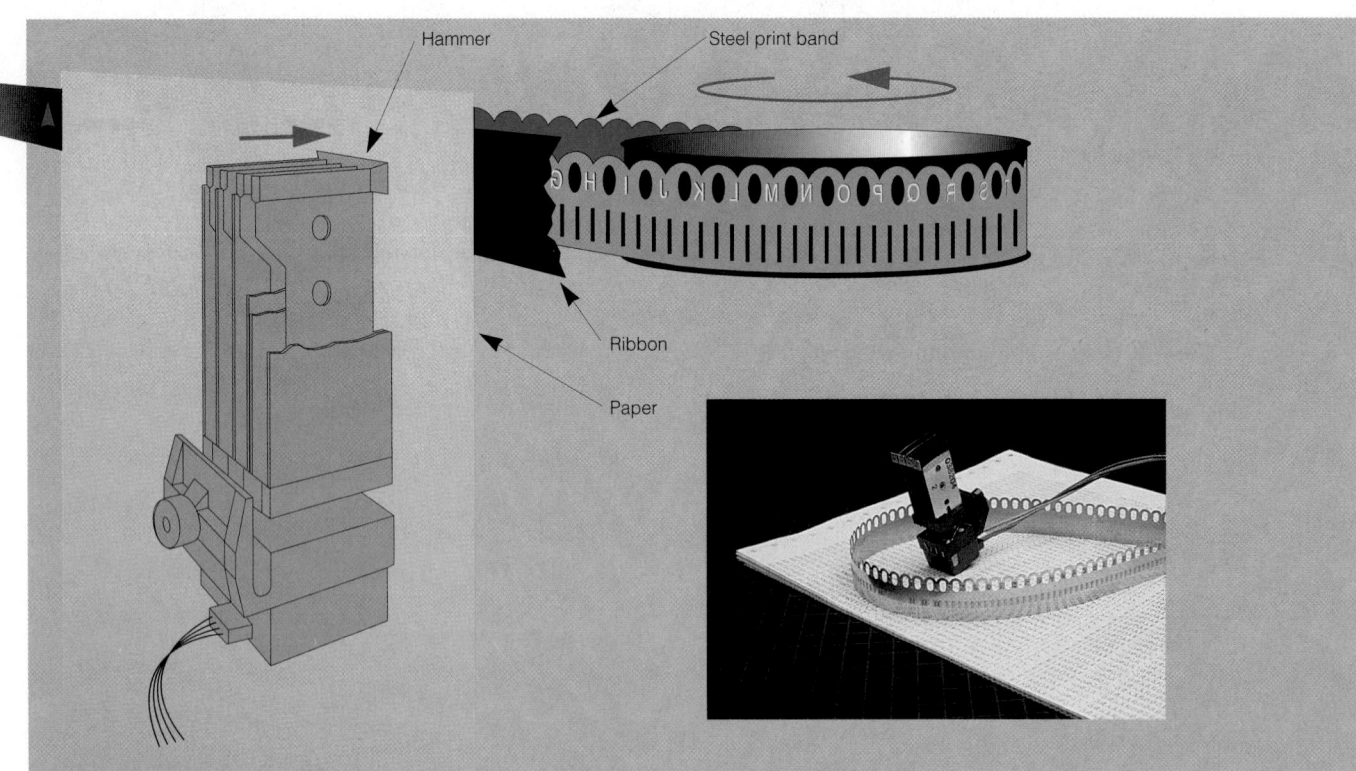

Figure 5-22
A band printer uses a metal band that contains solid characters. When the character to be printed on the band comes by, print hammers strike the paper and the ribbon forcing them into the band to print the character.

Interchangeable type bands with different fonts can be used on band printers. A band printer can produce up to six carbon copies, has good print quality, high reliability, and depending on the manufacturer and model of the printer, can print in the range of 600 to 2,000 lines per minute.

The **chain printer** is similar to a band printer and contains characters on a rotating chain *(Figure 5-23)*. The chain consists of a series of type slugs that contains the character set. The character set on the type slugs is repeated two or more times on the chain mechanism. The chain rotates at a very high speed. Each possible print position has a hammer that can strike against the back of the paper, forcing the paper and ribbon against the character on the chain. As the chain rotates, the hammer strikes when the character to be printed is in the proper position.

The chain printer produces good print quality up to 3,000 lines per minute.

Nonimpact Printers

Nonimpact printing means that printing occurs without having a mechanism striking against a sheet of paper. For example, ink is sprayed against the paper or heat and pressure is used to fuse a fine black powder into the shape of a character.

Just as there are a variety of impact printers, there are also a variety of nonimpact printers. Ink-jet, small page printers, and thermal printers are frequently used on personal computers and small minicomputers. Medium- and high-speed page printers are used on minicomputers, mainframes, and supercomputers. The following sections discuss the various types of nonimpact printers.

Ink-Jet Printers

An **ink-jet printer** sprays tiny drops of ink onto the paper. The print head of an ink-jet printer contains a nozzle with anywhere from 50 to more than 100 small holes *(Figure 5-24)*. Although there are many more of them, the ink holes in the nozzle are similar to the individual pins on a dot matrix

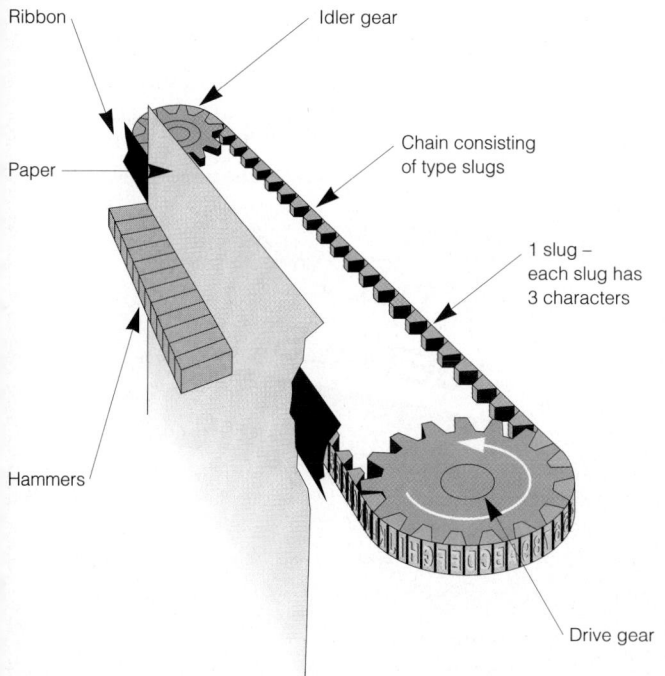

Ribbon Idler gear

Paper

Chain consisting of type slugs

1 slug – each slug has 3 characters

Hammers

Drive gear

Figure 5-23
The chain printer contains a complete set of characters on several sections of a chain that rotates at a high constant speed. Print hammers are located at each horizontal print position. The paper and ribbon are located between the hammers and the chain. As the chain rotates, the hammers fire when the proper characters are in front of their print positions.

Figure 5-24
The print head of an ink-jet printer contains many tiny holes that act as nozzles to spray drops of ink onto the paper.

printer. Just as any combination of dot matrix pins can be activated, ink can be propelled by heat or pressure through any combination of the nozzle holes to form a character or image on the paper. Ink-jet printers produce high-quality print and graphics and are quiet because the paper is not struck as it is by dot matrix printers. Good quality, single-sheet paper is usually used with ink-jet printers. Lower quality paper can be too soft and cause the ink to bleed. Transparency sheets can also be used. Ink-jet printers print at rates from 30 to 150 cps. Color ink-jet printers are also available *(Figure 5-25)*.

Page Printers

The **page printer** is a nonimpact printer that operates similar to a copying machine. The page printer converts data from the computer into light that is directed to a positively charged revolving drum. Each position on the drum touched by the light becomes negatively charged and attracts the toner (powdered ink). The toner is transferred onto the paper and then fused to the paper by heat and pressure. Several methods are used to direct light to the photosensitive drum and create the text or image that will be transferred to the paper. **Laser printers** use a laser beam aimed at the drum by a spinning mirror *(Figure 5-26)*.

Other page printers use light emitting diode (LED) arrays or liquid crystal shutters (LCS). With these methods, the light can expose thousands of individual points on the drum. Although the light exposure methods of LED and LCS printers are different from laser printers, they are often referred to and classified with laser printers. All page printers produce high-quality text and graphics suitable for business correspondence *(Figure 5-27)*. Color laser printers are available but are very expensive and not yet widely used.

An advantage of page printers is that they usually come with a large number of built-in fonts. As you recall from Chapter 2, a font is a specific combination of *typeface,* such as Courier, and *point size,* the height of the type. Although different fonts can be produced using software, documents using a printer's built-in fonts print faster.

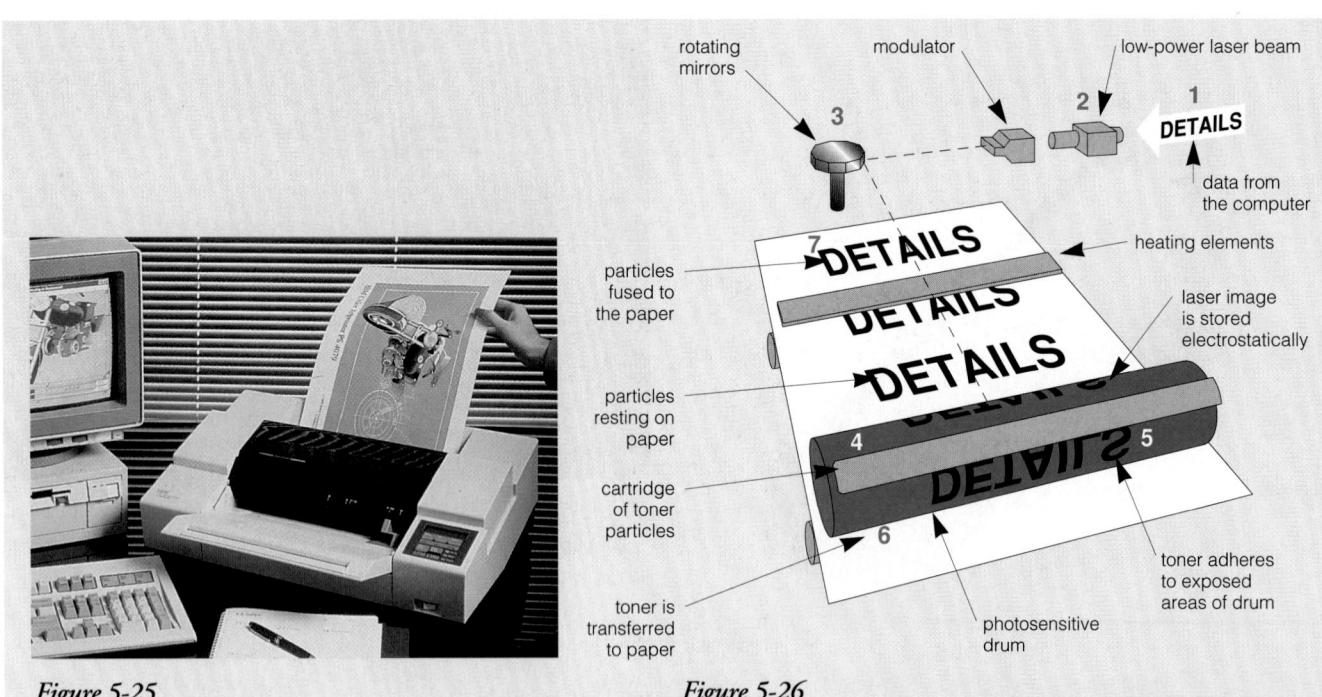

Figure 5-25
A color ink-jet printer.

Figure 5-26
Laser printers use a process similar to a copying machine. Data from the computer, such as the word DETAILS (1), is converted into a laser beam (2) that is directed by a mirror (3) to a photosensitive drum (4). The areas on the drum touched by the laser attract toner particles (5) that are transferred to the paper (6). The toner is fused to the paper with heat and pressure (7).

Page printers are rated by their speed and resolution. Speed is measured in **pages per minute (ppm).** Page printers used with individual personal computers range from 4 to 12 ppm and start at less than $500. Page printers supporting multiple users on a network or larger computer range from 16 to 50 ppm and cost from $10,000 to $100,000. High-speed page printers costing as much as several hundred thousand dollars can produce output at the rate of several hundred pages per minute *(Figure 5-28)*. Page printer resolution is measured by the number of **dots per inch (dpi)** that can be printed. The more dots, the sharper the image. The resolution of page printers ranges from 240 to 1200 dpi with most printers currently offering 300 or 600 dpi. Page printers usually use individual sheets of paper stored in a removable tray that slides into the printer case. Some page printers have trays that can accommodate different-sized paper while others require separate trays for letter and legal paper. Most page printers have a manual feed slot where individual sheets can be inserted. Transparencies and envelopes can also be printed on page printers.

Thermal Printers

Thermal printers, sometimes called **thermal-transfer printers**, use heat to transfer colored inks from ink sheets onto the printing surface *(Figure 5-29 on the next page)*. Thermal printers can work with plain paper but produce the best results when higher quality, smooth paper or plastic transparencies are used. A special type of thermal printer using a method called **dye diffusion** uses chemically treated paper to obtain color print quality equal to glossy magazines. Dye diffusion actually varies the color intensity of each dot placed on the page. Most color printers merely alter the pattern of red, blue, yellow, and black dots to create the illusion of different colors. Thermal printers produce output at the rate of one to two pages per minute.

Figure 5-27
Page printers such as the laser printer can produce high-quality text or graphics output.

Figure 5-28
High speed laser printers can operate at speeds greater than 200 pages per minute. These printing systems can cost more than $200,000.

Other Types of Printers

In addition to the printers just discussed, there are a number of printers developed for special purposes. These include single label printers, bar code label printers, and portable printers. *Figure 5-30* shows examples of these printers.

Figure 5-29
Thermal-transfer printers are used to produce high-quality color output.

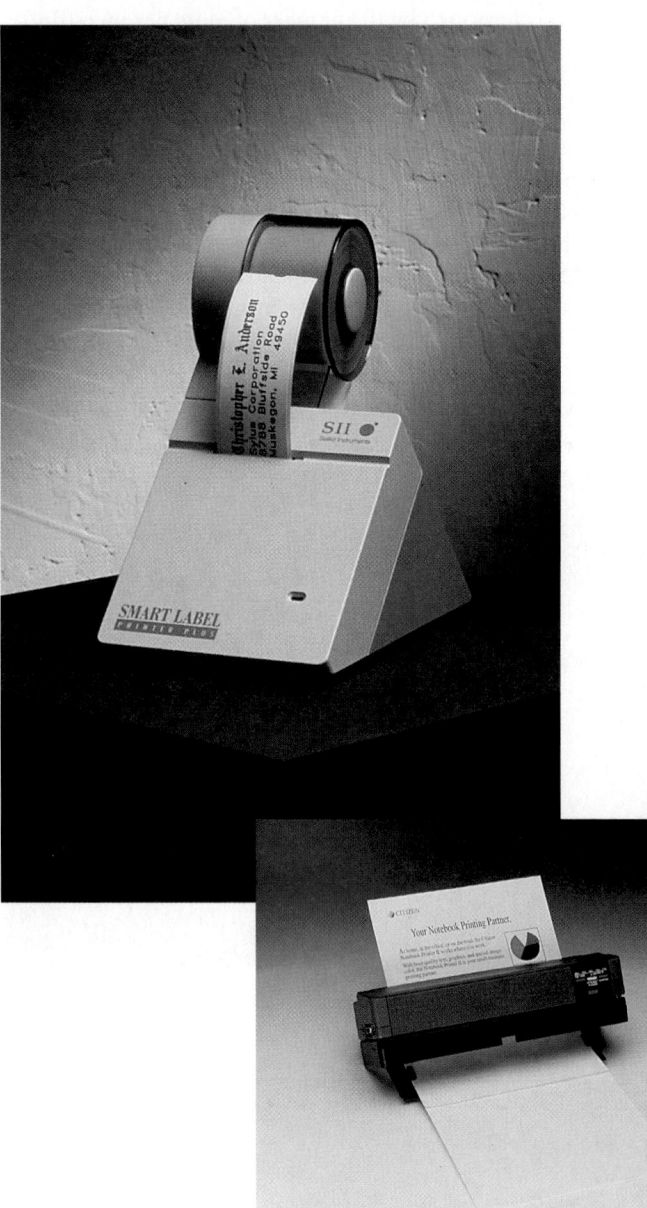

Figure 5-30
Other types of printers, from left to right, include a bar code label printer, a single label printer, and a portable printer designed for use with portable computers.

Summary of Impact and Nonimpact Printers

Impact and nonimpact methods of printing each have advantages and disadvantages. Impact printing can be noisy because the paper is struck when printing occurs. Because the paper is struck, specially treated multipart paper can be used to create multiple copies of a report at one time, such as an invoice, that is routed to different people. Nonimpact printers are quiet, produce high-quality output, and have become the standard for business correspondence. They do not strike the paper, however, and can therefore create only one printed copy at a time. If additional copies are needed, they must each be printed separately. Color output is more attractive, but is slower and more expensive than black and white output for all printer types.

Considerations in Choosing a Printer

In addition to understanding the features and capabilities of the various types of printers that are available, you must consider several other factors before choosing a printer. These include factors such as how much output will be produced and who will use the output. Considering these and the other factors stated in *Figure 5-31* will help you to choose a printer to meet your needs.

Figure 5-31
Questions to consider when choosing a printer.

QUESTION	EXPLANATION
How much output will be produced?	Desktop printers are not designed for continous use. More than several hundred pages a day requires a commercial (business) grade printer. Check a printer's **duty cycle,** the recommended maximum number of copies per month and **mean time between failures (MTBF),** the estimated time the before a component needs service.
What type of output will be produced?	Make a list of the types of output that will be produced (e.g., reports, transparencies, labels, charts, graphics) and match this list with printer capabilities.
Who will use the output?	Internal-only reports can be prepared on fast, draft-quality printers. External correspondence requires the letter-quality output of a nonimpact printer.
Where will the output be produced?	If the output will be produced at the user's desk or in an open office environment, a sound enclosure may be required to reduce printer noise.
Are multiple copies required?	Only impact printers can produce multiple copies on a single pass.
Is color required?	Color can enhance a document, but color printers are slower and cost more.
Are different fonts needed?	Most, but not all, printers have some built-in fonts. Page printers usually offer the most choices. Software-based fonts are also available.
Where will the printer be located?	Printers close (within 25 feet) to a computer use a faster parallel interface. Printers farther away will use a slower interface or use network cabling.

Display Devices

A **display device** is the visual output device of a computer. The most common type of display device is a monitor. A **monitor** looks like a television and consists of a display surface, called a screen, and a plastic or metal case to house the electrical components. A monitor often has a swivel base that allows the angle of the screen surface to be adjusted. The term **screen** is used to refer to both the surface of any display device and to any type of display device. A **video display terminal** (VDT) is a type of display device that also includes a keyboard. VDTs, also called dumb terminals, are usually connected to larger systems such as minicomputers or mainframes. An older term sometimes used to refer to monitor or VDT display devices is CRT. A **CRT**, which stands for **cathode ray tube**, is actually the large tube inside a monitor or VDT. The front part of the tube is the display surface or screen.

The most widely used monitors are equivalent in size to a 14- to 17-inch television screen. Monitors designed for use with desktop publishing, graphics, or engineering applications come in even larger sizes that can display full-size images of one or sometimes two 8 1/2 by 11-inch pages of data. One company even makes a monitor that can be tilted 90 degrees to display either long or wide pages or two pages side by side *(Figure 5-32)*.

Resolution

The **resolution**, or clarity, of the image on the monitor depends on the number of individual dots displayed on the monitor and the distance between each dot. Each dot that can be illuminated is called a **picture element**, or **pixel**. The pixels are illuminated to form an image on the screen *(Figure 5-33)*. The distance between each pixel is called the **dot pitch**. The greater the number of pixels and the closer they are, the better the monitor resolution. The resolution of a monitor is important, especially when the monitor will be used to display graphics or other nontext information.

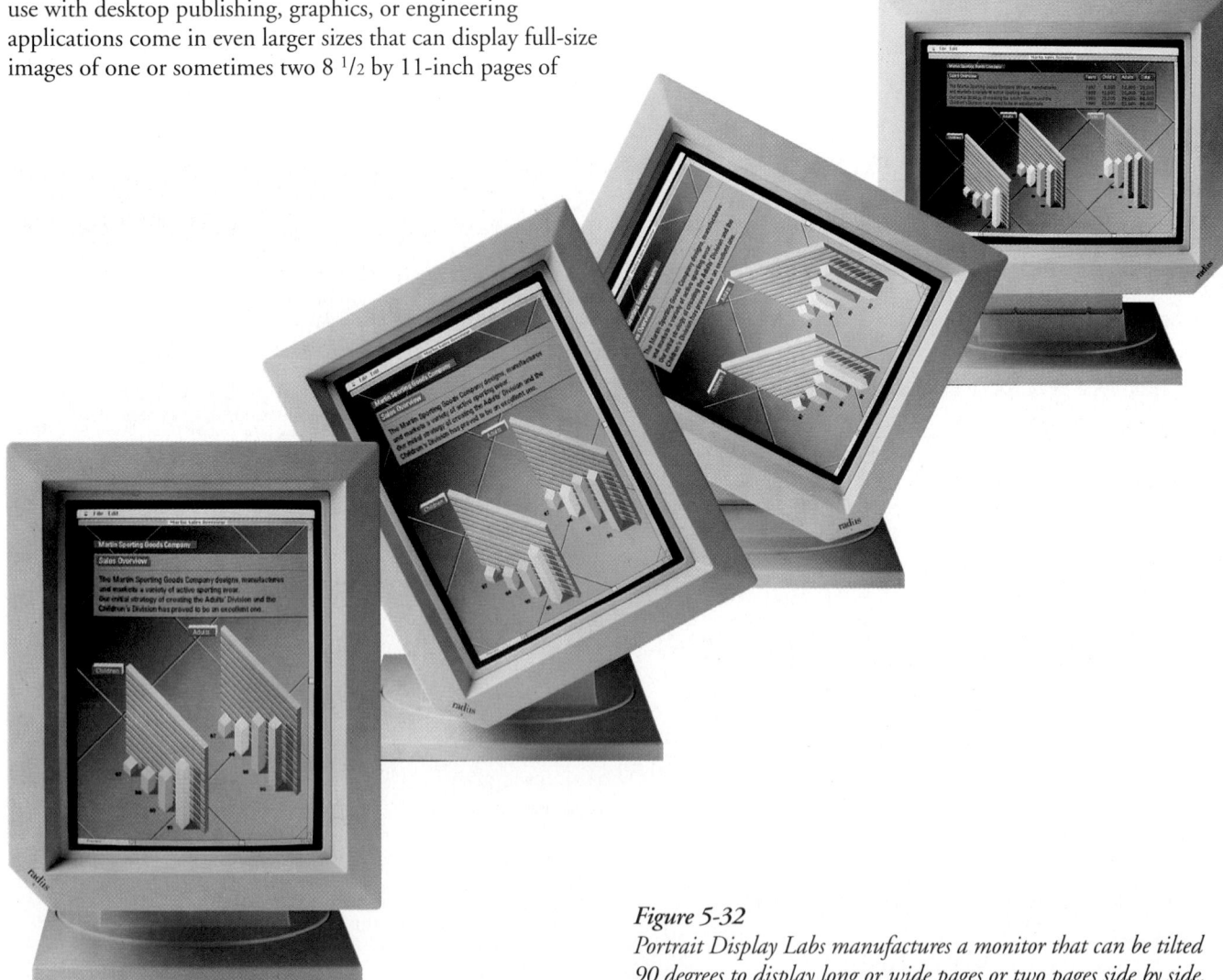

Figure 5-32
Portrait Display Labs manufactures a monitor that can be tilted 90 degrees to display long or wide pages or two pages side by side.

Figure 5-33
The word "pixel" shown here is made up of individual picture elements (pixels) as they would be displayed on a bit-mapped screen. Each pixel can be turned on or off to form an image on the screen.

Monitors used for graphics are called **dot-addressable displays** or **bit-mapped displays**. On these monitors, the number of addressable locations on the monitor corresponds to the number of pixels, or dots, that can be illuminated. The number of pixels that is actually displayed is determined by a combination of the software in the computer, the capability of the video adapter board in the computer, and the monitor itself. High-resolution display devices can produce an image that is almost equivalent to the quality of a photograph *(Figure 5-34)*.

Several video graphics standards have been developed, including CGA (Color Graphics Adapter), EGA (Enhanced Graphics Adapter), VGA (Video Graphics Array), and super VGA (SVGA). The term super VGA is often used for any resolution beyond 640 x 480. As shown in *Figure 5-35,* each standard provides for a different number of pixels and colors. Some manufacturers offer even higher resolution monitors. The resolution of most monitors sold for personal computer systems is SVGA.

Figure 5-34
High-resolution display devices can produce images that are equivalent to the quality of a photograph. These devices are often used in graphic arts, engineering, and scientific applications.

Standard	Year	Resolution (W x H)	Available Colors	Maximum Displayed Colors
CGA	1981	640 x 200	16	4
Hercules	1982	720 x 348	None	None
EGA	1984	640 x 480	64	16
VGA	1986	640 x 480	262,144	256
Super VGA	1988	800 x 600 to 1600 x 1200	16.7 million	16.7 million

Figure 5-35
A summary of the more widely used video graphics standards for display screens.

Each of the video graphics standards have a specific frequency or rate at which the video signals are sent to the monitor. Some monitors are designed to only work at a particular frequency and video standard. Other monitors, called **multiscanning** or **multisync monitors**, are designed to work within a range of frequencies and thus can work with different standards and video adapters.

Color Monitors

A **color monitor** can display text or graphics in color *(Figure 5-36)*. Color monitors are widely used with all types of computers because of reduced prices and because much of today's software is written to display information in color. Although some color monitors are capable of displaying millions of colors, the human eye cannot distinguish the differences. Most PC color monitors display up to 256 colors at one time.

Monochrome Monitors

Monochrome monitors display a single color such as white, green, or amber characters on a black background *(Figure 5-37)* or black characters on a white background. Monochrome monitors are less expensive than color monitors and are often used by businesses for word processing, order entry, and other applications that do not require color. Using a technique known as gray scaling, some monochrome monitors can display good-quality graphic images. **Gray scaling** involves converting an image into pixels that are different shades of gray like a black and white photograph.

Flat Panel Displays

A **flat panel display** is a thin display screen that does not use cathode ray tube (CRT) technology. Flat panel displays are most often used in portable computers but larger units that can mount on a wall or other structure are also available.

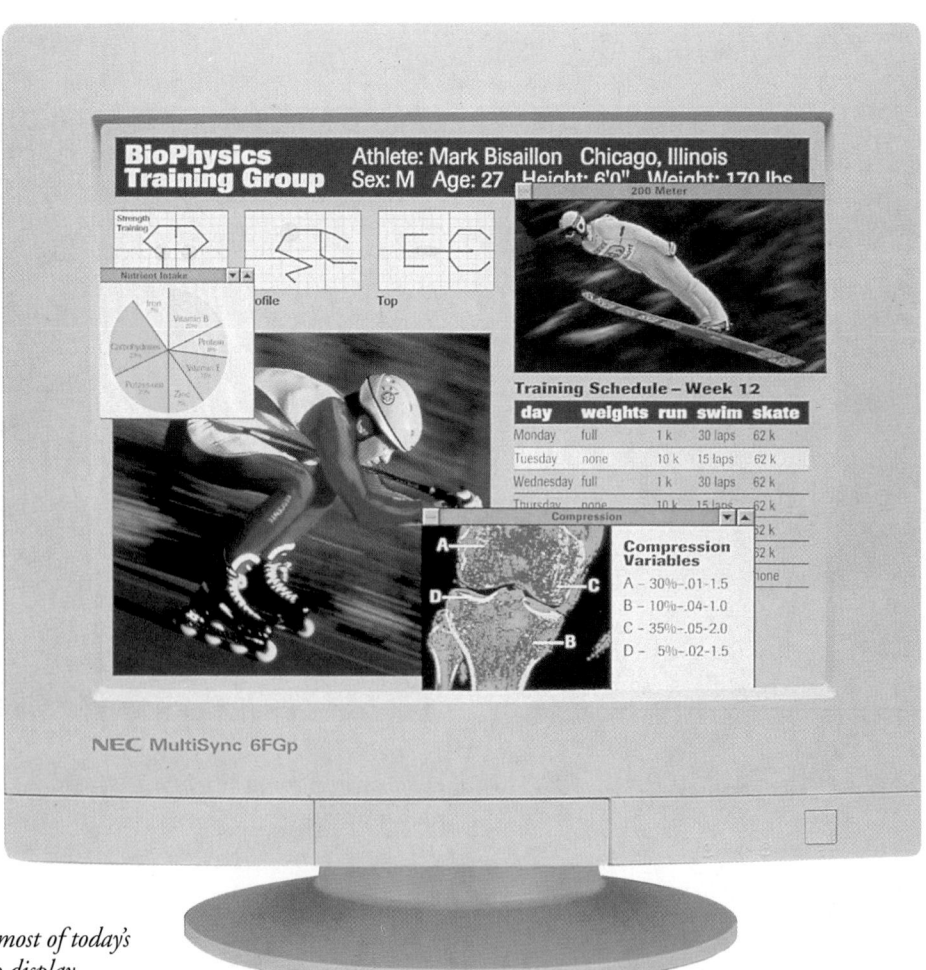

Figure 5-36
Color monitors are widely used because most of today's software is written to display information in color.

Two common types of technology used for flat panel displays are liquid crystal display (LCD) and gas plasma *(Figure 5-38)*.

In a **liquid crystal display** (LCD), a liquid crystal is deposited between two sheets of polarizing material. When an electrical current passes between crossing wires, the liquid crystals are aligned so light cannot shine through, producing an image on the screen. LCD technology is also commonly used in digital watches, clocks, and calculators. **Active matrix** LCD screens use individual transistors to control each crystal cell. **Passive matrix** LCD screens use fewer transistors; one for each row and column. Active matrix displays cost more but display a sharper, brighter picture (Figure 5-39).

Gas plasma screens substitute a neon gas for the liquid crystal material. Any locations on a grid of horizontal and vertical electrodes can be turned on to cause the neon gas to glow and produce the pixels that form an image. Gas plasma screens offer better resolution than LCD screens but are more expensive.

Figure 5-38
Flat panel displays are most often used on portable computers. The system on the left uses a liquid crystal display (LCD) and the system on the right uses a gas plasma display.

Figure 5-37
Monochrome monitors display a single color against a solid background.

Figure 5-39
Active matrix LCD screens produce the best color resolution by using individual transistors to control each crystal cell.

How Images Are Displayed on a Monitor

Most monitors used with personal computers and terminals use cathode ray tube (CRT) technology. When these monitors produce an image, the following steps occur *(Figure 5-40)*:

1. The image to be displayed on the monitor is sent electronically from the CPU to the video circuits to the cathode ray tube.
2. An electron gun at the rear of the tube generates an electron beam towards the screen. The beam passes through holes in a metal screen called the *shadow mask.* The shadow mask helps align the beam so it hits the correct dot on the screen. The screen is coated with phosphor, a substance that glows when it is struck by the electron beam.
3. The yoke, which generates an electromagnetic field, moves the electron beam across and down the screen. **Interlaced monitors** illuminate every other line and then return to the top to illuminate the lines they skipped. **Noninterlaced monitors** illuminate the entire screen more quickly in a single pass. The speed at which the entire screen is redrawn is called the **refresh rate**.
4. The illuminated phosphors create an image on the screen.

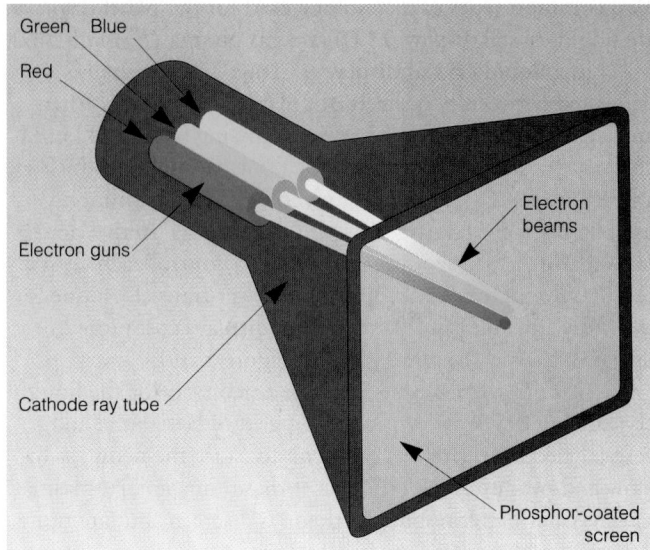

Figure 5-41
Each pixel on a color monitor screen is made up of three colored (red, green, and blue) phosphor dots. These dots can be turned on individually or in combinations to display a wide range of colors.

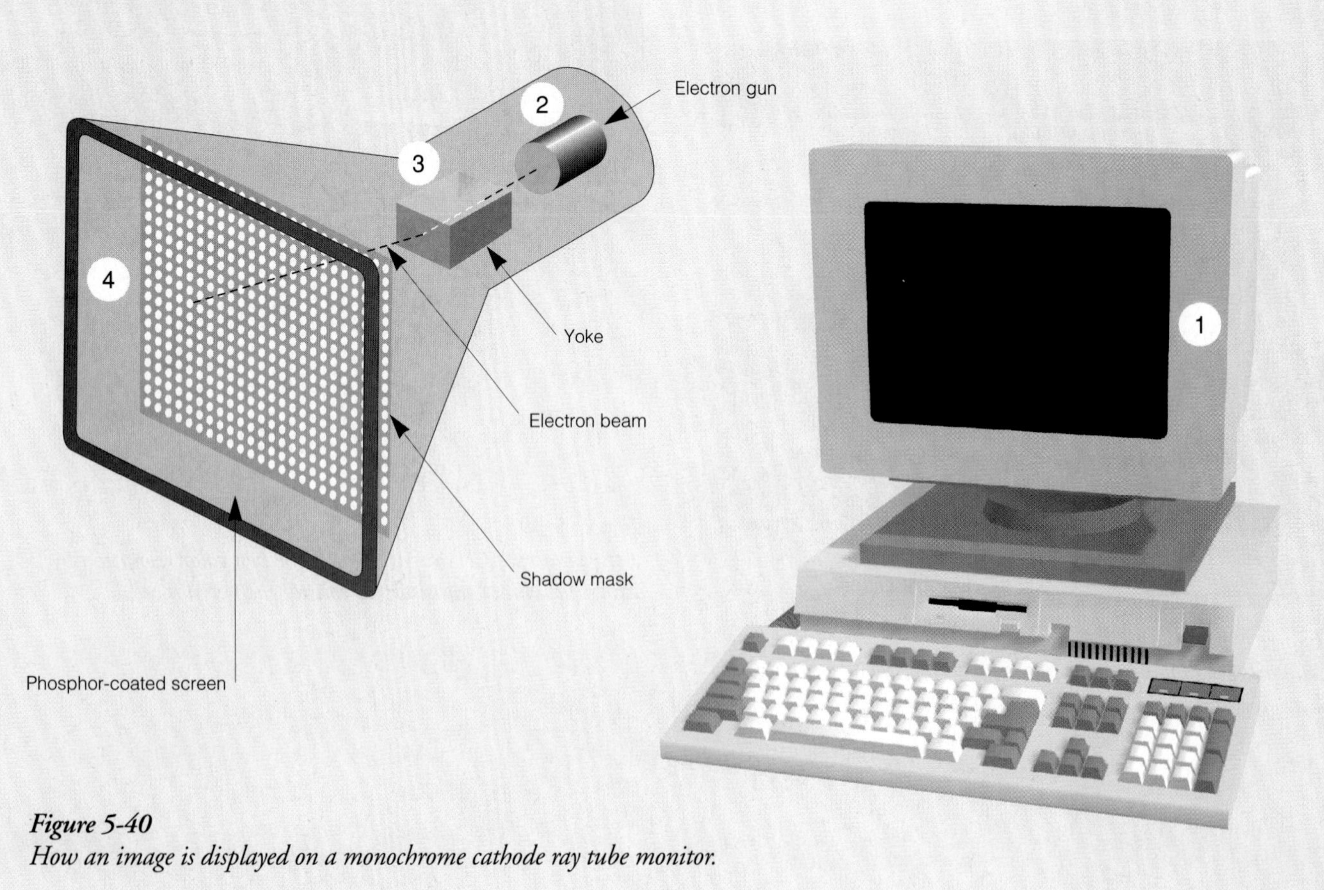

Figure 5-40
How an image is displayed on a monochrome cathode ray tube monitor.

How Color Is Produced

To show color on a screen, each pixel must have three colored phosphor dots. These dots are the additive primary colors red, green, and blue *(Figure 5-41)*. A separate electron gun is used for each color. In the simplest combinations, eight colors can be generated – black (no color), red only, blue only, green only, magenta (red and blue), yellow (red and green), blue-green (blue and green), and white (red, blue, and green together). By varying the intensity of the electron beam striking the phosphors, and making some colored dots glow more than others, many more colors can be generated.

Other Output Devices

Although printers and display devices provide the majority of computer output, other devices are available for particular uses and applications. These include data projectors, plotters, computer output microfilm devices, and voice output devices.

Data Projectors

A variety of devices are available to take the image that displays on a computer screen and project it so it can be clearly seen by a room full of people. Smaller, lower cost units, called **projection panels**, use liquid crystal display (LCD) technology and are designed to be placed on top of an overhead projector *(Figure 5-42)*.

Larger, more expensive units use technology similar to large-screen projection TV sets; separate red, green, and blue beams of light are focused onto the screen (*Figure 5-43* on the next page). The projection panels are easily portable and, depending on the overhead projector with which they are used, can be located at different distances from the projection screen. The three-beam projectors must be focused and aligned for a specific distance and thus once installed, are usually not moved.

Figure 5-42
Projection panels are used together with overhead projectors to display computer screen images to a room full of people.

Plotters

A **plotter** is an output device used to produce high-quality line drawings such as building plans, charts, or circuit diagrams. These drawings can be quite large; some plotters are designed to handle paper up to 40 inches by 48 inches, much larger than would fit in a standard printer. Plotters can be classified by the way they create the drawing. The two types are pen plotters and electrostatic plotters.

As the name implies, **pen plotters** create images on a sheet of paper by moving one or more pens over the surface of the paper or by moving the paper under the tip of the pens.

Two different kinds of pen plotters are flatbed plotters and drum plotters. When a **flatbed plotter** is used to plot, or draw, the pen or pens are instructed by the software to move to the down position so the pen contacts the flat surface of the paper. Further instructions then direct the movement of the pens to create the image. Most flatbed plotters have one or more pens of varying colors or widths. The plotter shown in *Figure 5-44* is a flatbed plotter used to create color drawings.

A **drum plotter** uses a rotating drum, or cylinder, over which drawing pens are mounted. The pens can move to the left and right as the drum rotates, creating an image *(Figure 5-45)*. An advantage of the drum plotter is that the length of the plot is virtually unlimited because roll paper can be used. The width of the plot is limited by the width of the drum.

With an **electrostatic plotter,** the paper moves under a row of wires (called styli) that can be turned on to create an electrostatic charge on the paper. The paper then passes through a developer and the drawing emerges where the charged wires touched the paper. The electrostatic printer image is composed of a series of very small dots, resulting in relatively high-quality output. In addition, the speed of electrostatic plotting is faster than with pen plotters.

Computer Output Microfilm

Computer output microfilm (COM) is an output technique that records output from a computer as microscopic images on roll or sheet film *(Figure 5-46)*. The images stored on COM are the same as the images that would be printed on paper. The COM recording process reduces characters 24, 42,

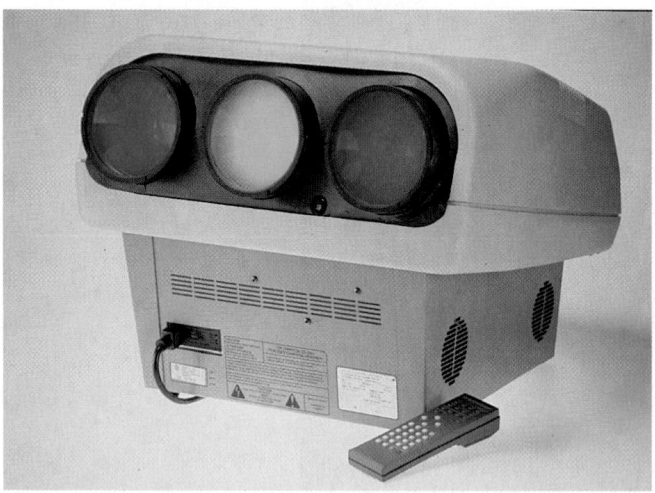

Figure 5-43
The data projector uses three separate red, green, and blue beams to project data onto a screen. Single beam projectors are also available.

Figure 5-44
A color flatbed plotter.

or 48 times smaller than would be produced on a printer. The information is then recorded on sheet film called **microfiche** or on 16mm, 35mm, or 105mm roll film.

Microfilm has several advantages over printed reports or other storage media for certain applications. Some of these advantages are:

1. Data can be recorded on the film faster than printers; up to 30,000 lines per minute.
2. Costs for recording the data are lower. Studies have shown that microfilm can be as little as one-tenth the cost of printing a report.
3. Less space is required to store microfilm than printed materials. Microfilm that weighs one ounce can store the equivalent of 10 pounds of paper.
4. The cost to store a megabyte of information is less on microfilm than it is on disk.

To access data stored on microfilm, a variety of readers are available. They utilize indexing techniques to provide a quick reference to the data. Some microfilm readers can perform automatic data lookup, called **computer-assisted retrieval (CAR)**, under the control of an attached computer. With the indexing software and hardware now available for microfilm, a user can usually locate any piece of data in a database in less than 10 seconds, at a far lower cost per inquiry than using an online inquiry system consisting of a computer system that stores the data on a hard disk.

Voice Output

Another important means of generating output from a computer is voice output. **Voice output** consists of spoken words that are conveyed to the user from the computer. Thus, instead of reading words on a printed report or monitor, the user hears the words over earphones, the telephone, or other devices from which sound can be generated.

The data that produces voice output is usually created in one of two ways. First, a person can talk into a device that will encode the words in a digital pattern. For example, the words, *The number is,* can be spoken into a microphone, and the computer software can assign a digital pattern to the words. The digital data is then stored on a disk. At a later time, the data can be retrieved from the disk and translated back from digital data into voice, so the person listening will actually hear the words.

Figure 5-45
A drum plotter can handle larger paper sizes than a flatbed plotter.

Figure 5-46
Microfilm is often used for reports that must be kept on file but do not have to be referred to frequently.

A second type of voice generation is called voice synthesis. **Voice synthesis** can transform words stored in main memory into speech. The words are analyzed by a program that examines the letters stored in memory and generates sounds for the letter combinations. The software can apply rules of intonation and stress to make it sound as though a person were speaking. The speech is then projected over speakers attached to the computer.

You may have heard voice output used by the telephone company for giving number information. Automobile and vending machine manufacturers are also incorporating voice output into their products. The potential for this type of output is great and it will continue to be incorporated in products and services in the future.

Summary of Output from the Computer

The output step of the information processing cycle uses a variety of devices to provide users with information. The equipment discussed in this chapter, including printers, display devices, and other output devices are summarized in *Figure 5-47.*

OUTPUT DEVICE		DESCRIPTION
Speakers		Used for audio (sound) output.
Printers – Impact	Dot matrix	Prints text and graphics using small dots.
	Band	High-speed rotating band text-only printer.
	Chain	High-speed rotating chain text-only printer.
Printers – Nonimpact	Ink-jet	Sprays tiny drops of ink onto a page to form text and graphics. Prints quietly. Inexpensive color printer.
	Page (laser)	Works like a copying machine. Produces very high quality text and graphics.
	Thermal	Uses heat to produce high-quality color output.
Display Devices	Color monitors	Can display multiple colors to enhance information.
	Monochrome monitors	Displays one color on solid background. Less expensive than color.
	LCD	Flat panel liquid crystal display used for laptops. Available in color.
	Gas plasma	High-resolution flat panel display.
Data Projectors		Projects display screen image to a group.
Plotters		Produces hard-copy graphic output. Some can handle large paper sizes.
COM		Stores reduced-size image on sheet or roll film.
Voice		Communicates information to user in the form of speech.

Figure 5-47
A summary of the more common output devices.

COMPUTERS AT WORK

NoteStation – The Key to Getting the Right Music

Musicians and vocalists who purchase sheet music often have a problem finding music in the key that matches their instruments or vocal ranges. Traditionally printed sheet music usually comes in only one key. If the key is not right, the music must be transposed (converted) into another key. Transposing takes additional time and usually costs money if done by someone else. However, a company in California, using computers and multimedia software, appears to have solved the problem.

In combination with computer maker IBM, MusicWriter, Inc. of Los Gatos, California has developed NoteStation, a stand-alone multimedia kiosk that can generate sheet music in any key for more than 3,000 song titles. The potential sheet music buyer uses the NoteStation touch screen display to browse through the available songs by title, artist, style, or composer *(Figure 5-48)*. The system can even find songs if only a portion of the title is known. Once a song is selected, the sheet music is displayed on the screen. If desired, the customer can play a portion of the song. If the key is not right, it can be changed and the song played again. When the customer is happy with the music in his or her chosen key, the sheet music is printed on a laser printer or saved as a MIDI file on a diskette.

The advantages of NoteStation to musicians and vocalists are obvious. They can get their music in the key they want and listen to it before they buy it. If they are not exactly sure of what they want, using the computer to search through the song titles is much easier than leafing through pages of sheet music or a printed catalog. For the music stores where most NoteStations are installed, there are also numerous advantages. The music stores no longer have to order, stock, and inventory individual pieces of sheet music. Unless they run out of printer paper, they are never out of stock of any piece of music. The NoteStation kiosk takes a fraction of the space previously devoted to sheet music. The number of song titles available increases each month when the stores receive a new CD-ROM to load in the kiosk.

The NoteStation kiosk has significance beyond music publishing. The NoteStation is one of the first examples of what is called **point-of-sale manufacturing;** allowing the customer to design, manufacture, and purchase the product on the spot. The kiosk has become the showroom, warehouse, and manufacturing plant all rolled into a single unit that takes up fewer than 10 square feet of floor space. Eventually, this concept will be applied to many consumer products.

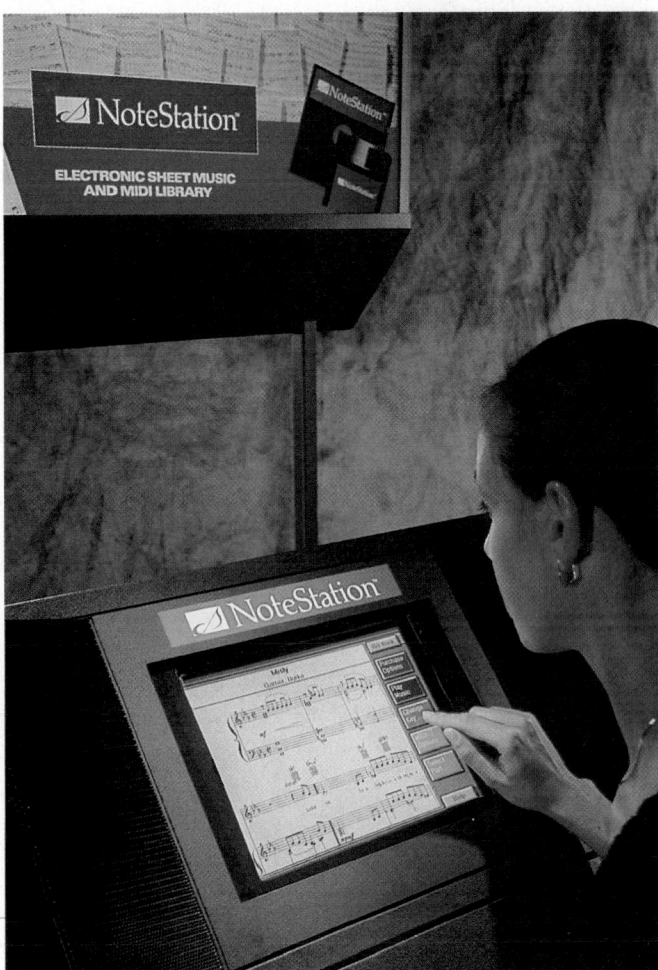

Figure 5-48

IN THE FUTURE

Virtual Reality   Beyond Entertainment

Most articles on virtual reality quickly move to discussions of games and rides designed to thrill the participants. Clearly, entertainment is the driving force behind most of today's VR applications. Many believe that VR will eventually have numerous practical applications that go beyond using a simulated laser gun to blast your opponent before he or she blasts you. The following discusses some of the probable future VR applications in training, medicine, and manufacturing.

Training

For some time, virtual reality like simulations have been used to train operators of expensive equipment such as airplanes and ships. In recent years, VR simulators have been developed for less expensive and complicated equipment such as trucks and construction equipment. The logical progression of this trend is that eventually, all products will come with VR training material that will help the user quickly and safely learn to use the equipment. For example, power tools such as a circular saw or electric drill could come with VR training materials that will enable the owner to saw or drill wood and build a project before attempting to use the real equipment.

Medicine

Medicine is another area where VR development work now being done may eventually be used on a widespread basis. To date, most of the VR work in medicine has involved learning systems. Different parts of the human anatomy have been digitized so students can use computer images to explore the body. Some work is already being done on using VR to simulate surgery. Portions of virtual bodies with internal organs and body fluids have been developed for these applications. Eventually, complete virtual patients will be developed to train medical personnel on all aspects of health care from initial consultation to post-operative recovery.

Manufacturing

Manufacturing companies are also experimenting with VR to improve design, production, and maintenance activities. VR prototypes will enable companies and prospective customers to evaluate designs before actual models are built. VR prototypes can also be used for repeated product testing. Manufacturing processes from welding to installing a nut and bolt can be tested for feasibility before production lines are built. Boeing is currently using a process closely related to VR called *augmented reality* to assist in manufacturing jumbo jets. Unlike VR, which creates a simulated scene, **augmented reality** superimposes information on a real scene. In Boeing's case, manufacturing procedures such as how to connect electrical wires in a plane are projected onto special glasses worn by the worker. The worker can see both the wiring diagram and the actual area of the plane where the wires are to be connected. Eventually, all equipment repair manuals might be available for such projected display as you work on the equipment.

All of the probable commercial applications of VR just discussed are either in limited use or under development. However, it may take years before they are widely used. In the meantime, there is this great VR game that you really should experience. Each player has a laser gun and the object of the game is . . .

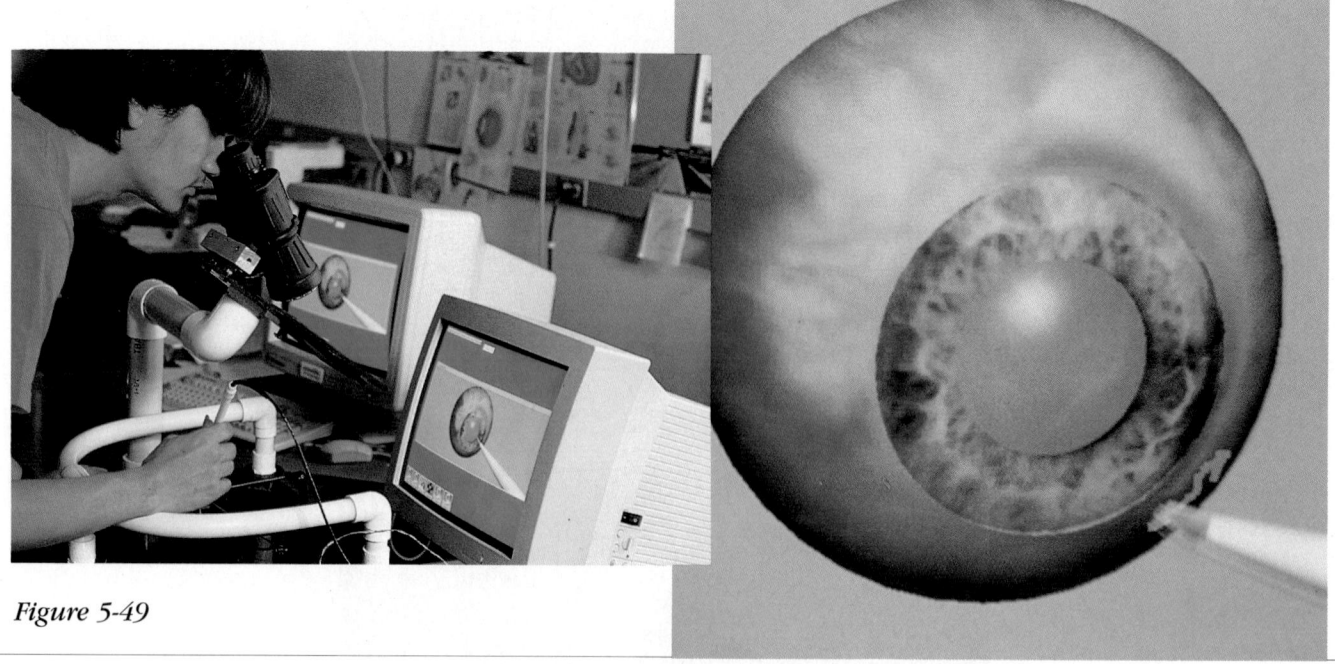

Figure 5-49

What You Should Know

1. **Output** is data that has been processed into a useful form called information that can be used by a person or a machine. Output that is printed is called **hard copy**, and output that is displayed on a screen is called **soft copy**.

2. A **report** is information presented in an organized form. An **internal report** is used by individuals in the performance of their jobs. An **external report** is used outside the organization. The four common types of reports are: **narrative reports**, **detail reports**, **summary reports**, and **exception reports**. **Periodic reports**, also called **scheduled reports**, are produced on a regular basis. **On-demand reports** are created whenever they are needed for information that is not required on a scheduled basis.

3. **Computer graphics** are any non-text pictorial information. **Computer drawing programs** and **computer paint programs** allow an artistic user to create stunning looking works of art.

4. **Audio output**, sometimes called **audio response**, consists of sounds, including words and music, produced by the computer.

5. **Video output** consists of visual images that have been captured with a video input device, such as a VCR or camera, digitized, and directed to an output device such as a computer monitor. **High definition television** (HDTV) sets are designed for digital signals and may eventually replace computer monitors.

6. **Multimedia** is the combination of text, graphics, video, and sound. Most multimedia presentations use a technique called **hypermedia** that allows the user to quickly move to related subject areas. Because of the large amounts of data that multimedia applications require, most multimedia products available today are stored on CD-ROM disks.

7. **Virtual reality** (**VR**) refers to the use of a computer to create an artificial environment that can be experienced by the computer user. In its simplest form, VR software can display what appears to be a three-dimensional view of a place that can be explored by the user. In more advanced forms, VR software requires the user to wear specialized headgear, gloves, and body suits to enhance the experience of the artificial environment.

8. Generally, printers can be classified into two groups, impact or nonimpact, based on how they transfer characters to the paper.

9. **Impact printers** transfer the image onto paper by some type of printing mechanism striking the paper, ribbon, and character together. Most impact printers use **continuous-form paper**, which has pages that are connected together for a continuous flow through the printer.

10. A **dot matrix printer** produces printed images by striking wire pins against an inked ribbon. Most dot matrix printers used with personal computers have a single print head that moves across the page. Dot matrix printers used with larger computers have fixed print mechanisms at each print position and can print an entire line at a time.

11. The speed of impact printers with movable print heads is rated in **characters per second** (**cps**). The speed of impact printers that print one line at a time is rated in **lines per minute** (**lpm**). The speeds quoted by dot matrix printer manufacturers are usually for draft-quality printing. **Draft-quality** printing uses the minimum number of dots to form a character and achieve the fastest printing speed. To achieve a sharper, higher quality look, called **letter quality** (**LQ**) or **near letter quality** (**NLQ**), the printer overlaps printed dots.

12. Dot matrix printers with movable print heads are designed to print in a **bidirectional** manner; that is, the print head can print as it moves from left to right, and from right to left. Two types of paper feed mechanisms found on dot matrix printers are **tractor feed mechanisms** and **friction feed mechanisms**.

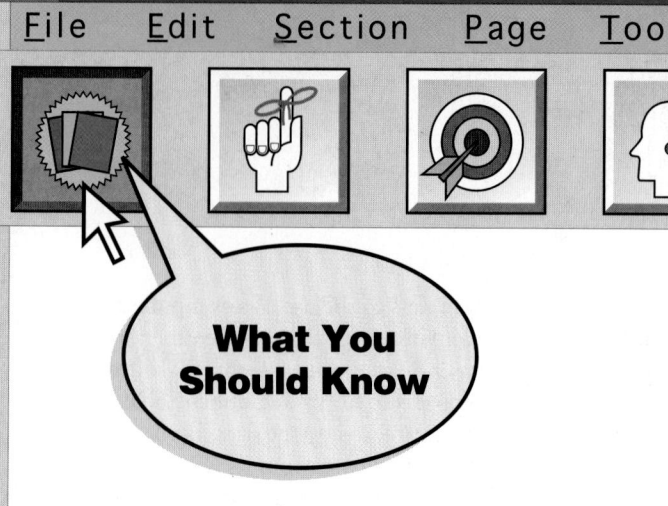

What You Should Know

13. Some dot matrix printers can print in multiple colors. Most dot matrix printers are available for less than $1,000.

14. Band and chain printers are impact printers used for high-volume output on large computer systems. **Band printers** use a horizontal, rotating band containing numbers, letters of the alphabet, and selected special characters. The **chain printer** is similar to a band printer and contains characters on a rotating chain.

15. **Nonimpact printing** means that printing occurs without having a mechanism striking against a sheet of paper.

16. An **ink-jet printer** sprays tiny drops of ink onto the paper. The **page printer** is a nonimpact printer that operates similar to a copying machine. Data is converted into light that is directed to a revolving drum. Each position on the drum touched by light attracts the toner (powdered ink) that is transferred onto the paper and then fused to the paper by heat and pressure. **Laser printers** use a laser beam aimed at the drum by a spinning mirror.

17. Page printers are rated by their speed and resolution. Speed is measured in **pages per minute (ppm)**. Page printer resolution is measured by the number of **dots per inch (dpi)** that can be printed.

18. **Thermal printers**, sometimes called **thermal transfer printers**, use heat to transfer colored inks from ink sheets onto the printing surface. A special type of thermal printer using a method called **dye diffusion** uses chemically treated paper to obtain color print quality equal to glossy magazines.

19. A number of printers have been developed for special purposes, including single label printers, bar code label printers, and portable printers.

20. A **display device** is the visual output device of a computer. A **monitor** looks like a television and consists of a display surface, called a screen, and a plastic or metal case to house the electrical components. The term **screen** is used to refer to both the surface of any display device and to any type of display device. A **video display terminal (VDT)** is a type of display device that also includes a keyboard. **CRT**, which stands for **cathode ray tube**, is an older term sometimes used to refer to monitor or VDT display devices. CRT is actually the large tube inside a monitor or VDT.

21. **The resolution**, or clarity, of the image on a monitor depends on the number of individual dots that are displayed on the monitor and the distance between each dot. Each dot that can be illuminated is called a **picture element,** or **pixel**. The distance between each pixel is called the **dot pitch**.

22. Monitors used for graphics are called **dot-addressable displays** or **bit-mapped displays**. Several video graphics standards have been developed, including CGA (Color Graphics Adapter), EGA (Enhanced Graphics Adapter), VGA (Video Graphics Array), and super VGA (SVGA). Some monitors are designed to only work with a particular frequency and video standard. Other monitors, called **multiscanning** or **multisync monitors**, are designed to work within a range of frequencies and thus can work with different standards and video adapters.

23. A **color monitor** can display text or graphics in color. **Monochrome monitors** display a single color such as white, green, or amber characters on a black background, or black characters on a white background. Using a technique known as **gray scaling**, which involves converting an image into pixels that are different shades of gray like a black and white photograph, some monochrome monitors can display good quality graphic images.

24. A **flat panel display** is a thin display screen that does not use cathode ray tube (CRT) technology. In a **liquid crystal display** (LCD), a liquid crystal is deposited between two sheets of polarizing material. When an electrical current passes between crossing wires, the liquid crystals are aligned so light cannot shine through, producing an image on the screen. **Active matrix** LCD screens use individual transistors to control each crystal cell. **Passive matrix** LCD screens use fewer transistors; one for each row and column. **Gas plasma** screens substitute a neon gas for the liquid crystal material.

25. Most monitors used with personal computers and terminals use cathode ray tube (CRT) technology. An electron gun at the rear of the tube generates an electron beam toward the phosphor-coated screen, which glows when it is struck by the electron beam. **Interlaced monitors** illuminate every other line and then return to the top of the screen to illuminate the lines they skipped. **Noninterlaced monitors** illuminate the entire screen in a single pass. The speed at which the entire screen is redrawn is called the **refresh rate**. To show color on a screen, each pixel must have three colored phosphor dots (red, green, and blue). By varying the intensity of the electron beam striking the phosphors, many colors can be generated.

26. **Projection panels** use liquid crystal display (LCD) technology and are designed to be placed on top of an overhead projector.

27. A **plotter** is an output device used to produce high-quality line drawings such as building plans, charts, or circuit diagrams. **Pen plotters** create images on a sheet of paper by moving one or more pens over the surface of the paper or by moving the paper under the tip of the pens. When a **flatbed plotter** is used to plot, or draw, the pen or pens are instructed by the software to move to the down position so the pen contacts the flat surface of the paper. A **drum plotter** uses a rotating drum, or cylinder, over which drawing pens are mounted. With an **electrostatic plotter,** the paper moves under a row of wires (called styli) that can be turned on to create an electrostatic charge on the paper.

28. **Computer output microfilm** (COM) is an output technique that records output from a computer as microscopic images on sheet film, called **microfiche** or on rolls of film. Some microfilm readers can perform automatic data lookup, called **computer-assisted retrieval** (CAR).

29. **Voice output** consists of spoken words that are conveyed to the user from the computer. **Voice synthesis** can transform words stored in main memory into speech.

File   Edit   Section   Page   Tools   Options   Help

Terms to Remember

active matrix (5.21)
audio output (5.4)
audio response (5.4)
augmented reality (5.28)

band printers (5.12)
bidirectional (5.11)
bit-mapped displays (5.19)

cathode ray tube (CRT) (5.18)
chain printers (5.13)
characters per second (cps) (5.10)
color monitor (5.20)
computer-assisted retrieval
    (CAR) (5.25)
computer drawing programs (5.4)
computer graphics (5.4)
computer output microfilm
    (COM) (5.24)
computer paint programs (5.4)
continuous-form paper (5.9)
CRT (5.18)

detail report (5.3)
display device (5.18)
dot matrix printer (5.10)
dot pitch (5.18)
dot-addressable displays (5.19)
dots per inch (dpi) (5.15)
draft quality (5.10)
drum plotter (5.24)
dye diffusion (5.15)

electronic plotter (5.24)
exception report (5.3)
external report (5.3)

flat panel display (5.20)
flatbed plotters (5.24)
friction feed mechanisms (5.12)

gas plasma (5.21)
gray scaling (5.20)

hard copy (5.2)
high definition television
    (HDTV) (5.5)
hypermedia (5.5)

impact printers (5.9)
ink-jet printer (5.13)
interlaced monitors (5.22)
internal report (5.2)

laser printers (5.14)
letter quality (5.11)
lines per minute (lpm) (5.10)
liquid crystal display (LCD) (5.21)

microfiche (5.25)
monitor (5.18)
monochrome monitors (5.20)
multimedia (5.5)
multiscanning (5.20)
multisync monitors (5.20)

narrative reports (5.3)
near letter quality (5.11)
nonimpact printing (5.13)
noninterlaced monitors (5.22)

on-demand reports (5.4)
output (5.2)

page printer (5.14)
pages per minute (ppm) (5.15)
passive matrix (5.21)
pen plotters (5.24)
periodic reports (5.4)
picture element (5.18)
pixel (5.18)
plotter (5.24)
point-of-sale manufacturing (5.27)
projection panels (5.23)

refresh rate (5.22)
report (5.2)
resolution (5.18)

scheduled reports (5.4)
screen (5.18)
soft copy (5.2)
summary report (5.3)

thermal printers (5.15)
thermal transfer printers (5.15)
tractor feed mechanisms (5.12)

video display terminal (VDT) (5.18)
video output (5.5)
virtual reality (VR) (5.7)
voice output (5.25)
voice synthesis (5.26)

le   Edit   Section   Page   Tools   Options   Help

Test Your Knowledge

Fill in the Blanks

1. _____ is data that has been processed into a useful form called information that can be used by a person or a machine.

2. Output that is printed is called _____, and output that is displayed on the screen is called _____.

3. _____ is the combination of text, graphics, video, and sound; most presentations of this type use a technique called _____ that allows the user to quickly move to related subject areas.

4. Generally, printers can be classified into two groups, _____ or _____, based on how they transfer characters to the paper.

5. Three different types of display devices are: _____, which display text and graphics in color; _____, which display a single color on a black or white background; and _____, which are thin display screens that do not use cathode ray tube (CRT) technology.

Short Answer

1. What is a report? How is an internal report different from an external report? How is a periodic report different from an on-demand report?

2. How is multimedia more than just a combination of traditional text-based computers and television? Why are most multimedia products available today stored on CD-ROM disks? In what four areas are multimedia applications primarily used?

3. How are impact printers different from nonimpact printers? Give at least two examples of each type of printer. What are the advantages and disadvantages of each printing method?

4. How are images displayed on a monitor that uses cathode ray tube (CRT) technology? How is color produced?

5. Although printers and display devices provide the majority of computer output, other devices are available for particular uses and applications. List at least three output devices other than printers or display devices. Briefly describe each.

Label the Figure

Instructions: Identify the parts of the monochrome cathode ray tube monitor shown in the figure below.

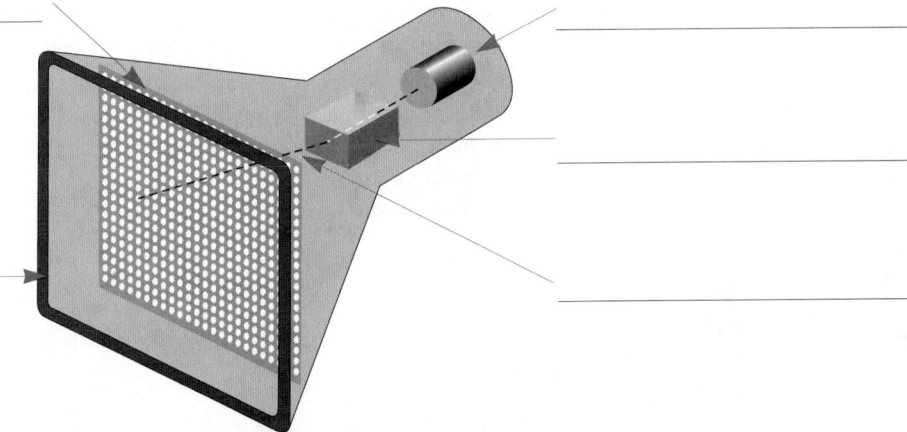

File   Edit   Section   Page   Tools   Options   Help

Points to Ponder

1

Reports can be classified by the way they present information. The four common types of reports are narrative reports, detail reports, summary reports, and exception reports. During your lifetime, you have probably given all of these reports, in either written or oral form. Describe a circumstance in which you offered each type of report.

2

Computer graphics and audio output are assuming increasingly important roles in art and music. Computer drawing programs and computer paint programs make it easy to draw perfect circles, three-dimensional figures, and arresting images. Electronic music technology enables a single person to produce sounds that once required a room full of musicians. What changes, if any, do you foresee in art or music as a result of these technologies? Do you think people who use computers to create graphic images or musical pieces should be called artists or musicians? Why or why not?

3

Some people believe that multimedia will revolutionize the way information is presented and the way people learn. It has even been predicted that eventually books will only be found in museums and antique stores. Do you think that multimedia will eventually replace all books, or certain types of books? Why or why not? What advantages, if any, do books have over multimedia?

4

Virtual reality (VR) software is currently being used to show clients proposed architectural changes, to allow customers to wander among available products in a virtual showroom or virtual office, and in three-dimensional electronic games. As computing power increases, and VR applications are able to run on lower cost computers, even more VR applications and VR technology will be available for a wider number of users. Think of at least three areas in which you think virtual reality software could be effectively employed. Describe how VR applications could be used in each.

5

When computers were first used in business, some people predicted the paperless office; a place where most documents would only exist electronically in the computer database. Many people now feel, however, that the widespread use of computers has actually elevated the quantity of paper used. Why do you think word processing software, spreadsheet programs, and low-cost printers might have increased the paperwork in the typical office? What steps could be taken to decrease the amount of paperwork?

6

Today, nearly all personal computers use two output devices – a monitor and a printer. Do you think these two output devices will still be the most popular twenty-five years from now? Why or why not? What other types of output devices do you think many personal computers will utilize? Why?

le   Edit   Section   Page   Tools   Options   Help

Out and About

1. Figure 5-31 on page 5.17 offers several questions to be considered when choosing a printer. List the questions posed in Figure 5-31 and answer each according to your current needs. Then, visit a computer store and find at least two printers that fit your requirements. Write down the name of each printer and note its advantages and disadvantages. If you were going to purchase one of these printers, which would you buy? Why?

2. Unlike ordinary television, which uses analog signals, high definition television (HDTV) sets are designed for digital signals. This results in clearer, sharper pictures and makes HDTV sets compatible with other digital technologies such as computers. Visit a library and research HDTV. How is analog technology different from digital technology? Will the development of HDTV be as significant as the introduction of color television approximately thirty years ago? What effect will the evolution of HDTV have on the computer industry?

3. Locate an organization that uses plotters. Possible users include architectural firms, electrical contractors, and a city planning department. Arrange to interview someone in the organization. Find out the purposes for which the plotter is used, what kind of plotter is used, and the advantages (or disadvantages) of using a plotter over creating a drawing by hand. If possible, ask to see a demonstration of the plotter's capabilities.

4. Examine the classified advertisement section of a newspaper or computer magazine. List all of the used computer output devices available. Which type of output device is most prevalent? Why? Choose two output devices in which you might be interested. Note the features and price of each. Would you consider purchasing either of these devices? Why or why not?

5. Contact a library or business that uses computer output microfilm (COM). Interview someone in the library or business to find out why COM is used. What advantages does computer output microfilm have over printed storage media? What are the disadvantages? How is the information accessed? Is the system capable of performing computer-assisted retrieval (CAR)?

6. Visit a computer vendor and obtain information about the highest and lowest priced monitors. Record the names of the monitors, their costs, and the features available with each. Do you think the more expensive monitor is worth the difference in price? Why or why not? Examine a portable computer that uses a flat panel display. What type of screen is it (LCD or gas plasma)? How does its image compare with the least expensive CRT monitor? How does it compare with the most expensive CRT monitor?

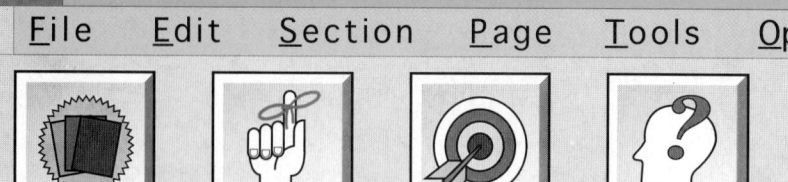

In the Lab

Windows Labs

1 **Using a Screen Saver** A screen saver, such as those shown in *Figures 5-50* and *5-51,* displays when you are not actively using Windows. Later, when you press a key on the keyboard or move the mouse, the screen saver disappears from the screen. To activate or modify a screen saver, make sure Program Manager displays on the screen. Then, double-click the Main group icon. In the Main group window, double-click the Control Panel program-item icon. In the Control Panel window, double-click the Desktop icon. Perform the following tasks: (1) Click the Help button. Obtain and write down the definition of screen saver. (2) Select the Screen Savers Help topic. Read and print the information. (3) Close the Help window. (4) In the Screen Saver area, click the Name drop-down list box arrow. Select Flying Windows. Click the Test button to display a sample of the screen saver *(Figure 5-50).* Click the left mouse button. (5) Select Mystify. Click the Test button to display a sample of the screen saver *(Figure 5-51).* Click the left mouse button. Choose the OK button. (6) Close the Control Panel window by double-clicking its Control-menu box.

2 **Changing Desktop Colors** With Program Manager on the screen, double-click the Main group icon. In the Main group window, double-click the Control Panel program-item icon. In the Control Panel window, double-click the Color icon. In the Color dialog box, perform the following tasks: (1) Click the Help button. Click the Color Schemes and Sample Screen buttons and write down the definitions. Close the Help window. (2) Click the Color Schemes drop-down list box arrow. Select Hotdog Stand. Notice the Sample Screen displays the Hotdog Stand color *(Figure 5-52).* (3) Practice selecting other color schemes. Choose the OK button

in the Color dialog box. (4) Close the Control Panel window by double-clicking its Control-menu box.

3 **Shelly Cashman Series Printer Lab** instructions in Windows Lab 2 in Chapter 1 on page 1.30 to display the Shelly Cashman Series Labs window. Select Setting Up to Print and choose the Start Lab button. When the initial screen displays, carefully read the objectives. With your printer turned on, point to the Print Questions button and click the left mouse button. Fill out the top of the Questions sheet and answer the questions as you step through the Lab.

4 **Shelly Cashman Series Monitor Lab** Follow the instructions in Windows Lab 2 in Chapter 1 on page 1.30 to display the Shelly Cashman Series Labs window. Select Configuring Your Display and choose the Start Lab button. When the initial screen displays, carefully read the objectives. With your printer turned on, point to the Print Questions button and click the left mouse button. Fill out the top of the Questions sheet and answer the questions as you step through the Lab.

5 **Printing a Document Using File Manager and Print Manager** With Program Manager on the screen, double-click the Main group icon. In the Main group window, double-click the Print Manager program-item icon. Perform the

Figure 5-50

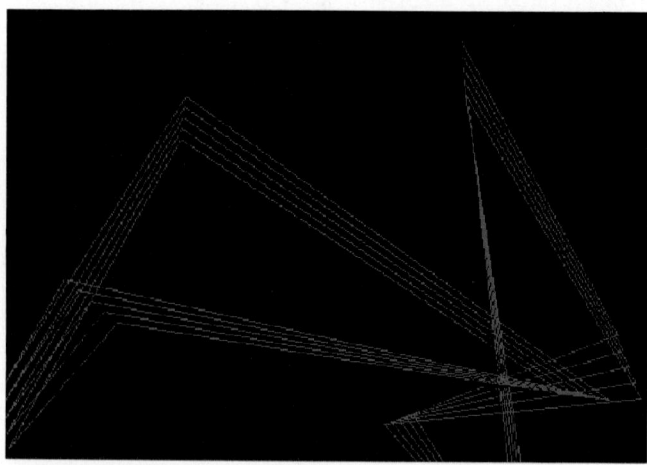

Figure 5-51

following tasks: (1) Minimize the Print Manager window by clicking the Minimize button in the upper right corner of the window. In the Main group window, double-click the File Manager program-item icon 🖳. If the File Manager window is maximized, restore it. If necessary, resize the File Manager window so you can see the Print Manager icon at the bottom of your desktop. (2) Insert your diskette with the file win2-2.wri into drive A. Click the drive A icon 📁 in the File Manager window to display files on drive A in the directory window. If you do not see the file win2-2.wri, obtain a copy of it from your instructor. (3) Select the file win2-2.wri by clicking it *(Figure 5-53)*. To print the selected file, drag it down to the Print Manager icon and release the mouse button when the mouse pointer changes to a sheet of paper. Choose the OK button in the Print dialog box. (4) Close File Manager. Click the Print Manager program-item icon and choose Close from the Control menu.

6 Using Help to Understand Print Manager   With Program Manager on the screen, double-click the Main group icon. In the Main group window, double-click the Print Manager program-item icon. Perform the following tasks: (1) Select the Print Manager Help menu and choose the Contents command. Read and print the information. (2) Select the What Is Print Manager? Help topic. Read and print the information. (3) Click the Back button. Select the Print Your Documents Help topic. Read and print this Help topic and all associated topics on this screen. Close the Help window. Close Print Manager.

DOS Labs

1 Displaying File Contents   Insert your diskette containing DOS Lab 2-1 into drive A. At the DOS prompt, type type a:dos2-1 | more and press the ENTER key. Press the PRINT SCREEN key. Press ENTER to see the next screen.

2 Printing File Contents   Insert your diskette containing DOS Lab 2-1 into drive A. At the DOS prompt, type print a:dos2-1 and press the ENTER key twice to print it.

3 Redirecting Output   Insert a formatted diskette into drive A. At the DOS prompt, type dir > a:dos5-3.txt and press the ENTER key. Did the directory display on the screen? At the DOS prompt, type print a:dos5-3.txt and press the ENTER key. What is the function of the > symbol?

4 Using Help   At the DOS prompt, type help and press the ENTER key. Type t to move the cursor to the Help topics beginning with the letter T. Use the arrow keys to move the cursor to <Type> and press the ENTER key. Read and then print the information by pressing ALT, F, P, ENTER.

Online Lab

1 Perusing Advice Columns   Using one of the two online services you selected in Chapter 1, connect to the service and perform the following tasks: (1) Search the online service for Advice columns. (2) Write down the names of the available Advice columnists. (3) Read and print three Advice columns.

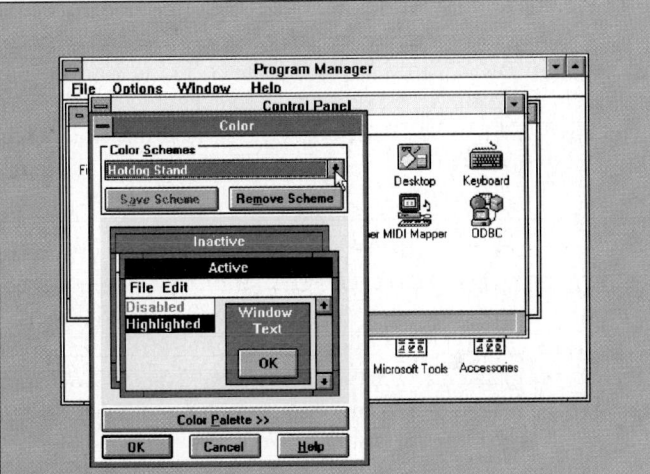

Figure 5-52

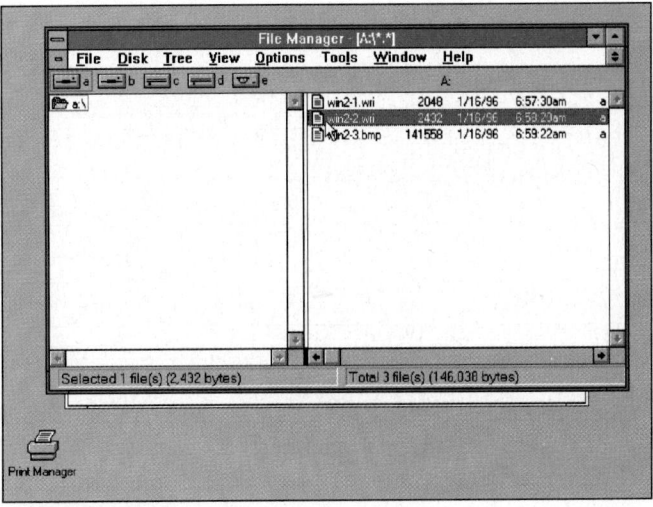

Figure 5-53

Secondary Storage

Objectives

After completing this chapter, you will be able to:

- Define secondary storage

- Identify the primary devices used for secondary storage

- Explain how data is stored on diskettes and hard disks

- Describe how data stored on diskettes can be protected

- Explain how magnetic tape storage is used with computers

- Describe four other forms of secondary storage: PC cards, optical disks, solid-state devices, and mass storage devices

- Describe how special-purpose storage devices such as smart cards are used

Storage is the fourth and final operation in the information processing cycle. Chapter 6 explains storage operations and the various types of secondary storage devices used with computers. Combining what you learn about storage with your knowledge of input, processing, and output will allow you to complete your understanding of the information processing cycle.

What Is Secondary Storage?

*I*t is important to understand the difference between how a computer uses main memory and how it uses secondary storage. As you have seen, main memory, also called primary storage or ram, temporarily stores programs and data that are being processed. **Secondary storage**, also called **auxiliary storage**, stores programs and data when they are not being processed, just as a filing cabinet is used in an office to store records. Records that are not being used are kept in the filing cabinet until they are needed. In the same way, data and programs that are not being used on a computer are kept in secondary storage until they are needed.

Most secondary storage devices provide a more permanent form of storage than main memory because they are nonvolatile, that is, data and programs stored on secondary storage devices are retained when the power is turned off. Main memory is volatile, which means that when power is turned off, whatever is stored in main memory is erased.

Secondary storage devices can be used as both input and output devices. When they are used to receive data processed by the computer, they are functioning as output devices. When some of their stored data is transferred to the computer for processing, they are functioning as input devices.

User secondary storage needs can vary greatly. Personal computer users may find the amount of data to be stored to be relatively small. For example, the names, addresses, and telephone numbers of several hundred friends or customers of a small business might require only 20,000 bytes of secondary storage (200 records x 100 characters per record). Users of large computers, such as banks or insurance companies, however, may need secondary storage devices that can store billions of characters. To meet the different needs of users, a variety of storage devices are available. *Figure 6-1* shows how different types of storage devices compare in terms of cost and speed. The secondary storage devices named in the pyramid are discussed in this chapter.

Figure 6-1
The pyramid chart compares the different types of computer storage. Main memory (primary storage) is the fastest but is also the most expensive and therefore uneconomical to use for all storage requirements. Secondary storage devices are less expensive per megabyte stored but are not as fast. Many computer systems have two or more types of secondary storage devices.

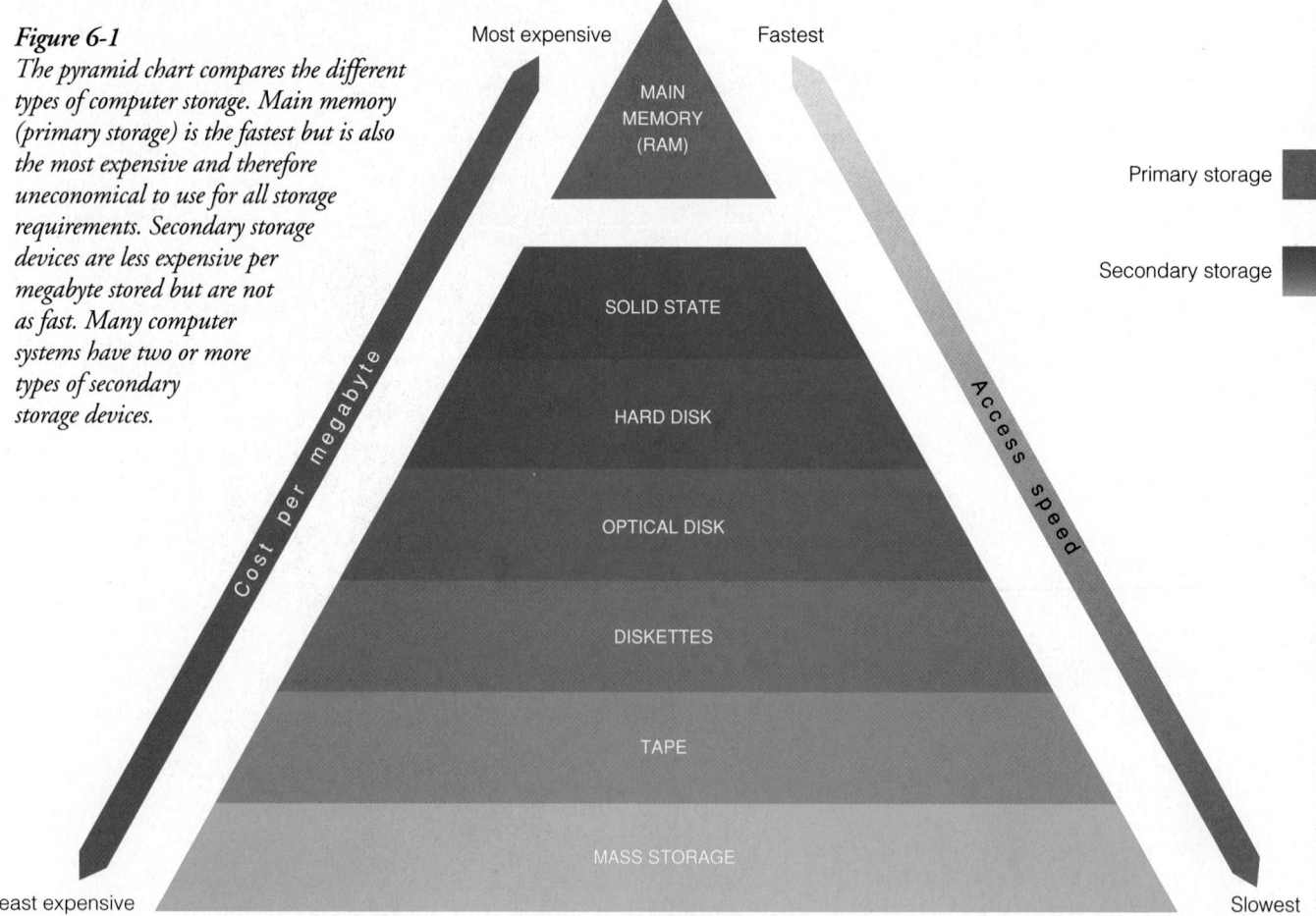

Magnetic Disk Storage

Magnetic disk is the most widely used storage medium for all types of computers. A **magnetic disk** consists of a round platter whose surface is covered with a magnetic material. Information can be recorded on or read from the magnetic surface. Magnetic disk offers high storage capacity, reliability, and the capability to directly access stored data. Magnetic disk types include diskettes, hard disks, and removable disk cartridges.

Diskettes

A **diskette** consists of a circular piece of thin mylar plastic (the actual disk), which is coated with an oxide material similar to that used on recording tape. In the early 1970s, IBM introduced the diskette as a new type of secondary storage. These diskettes were eight inches in diameter and were thin and flexible. Because they were flexible, they were often called **floppy disks**, or *floppies,* terms that are still used. Today, diskettes are used as a principal secondary storage medium for personal computers. This type of storage is convenient, reliable, and inexpensive.

Diskettes are available in two different sizes; $3^1/_2$ inch and $5^1/_4$ inch *(Figure 6-2)*. The size indicates the diameter (width) of the diskette.

Figure 6-2
The most commonly used diskettes are the $3^1/_2$" (above) and the $5^1/_4$" (left).

On a 3^1/$_2$-inch diskette, the circular piece of plastic is enclosed in a rigid plastic shell and a piece of metal called the shutter covers the reading and writing area. Paper liners help keep the recording surfaces clean *(Figure 6-3)*. When the 3^1/$_2$-inch diskette is inserted into a disk drive *(Figure 6-4)*, the drive slides the shutter to the side to expose a portion of both sides of the recording surface.

On a 5^1/$_4$-inch diskette, the circular piece of plastic is enclosed in a flexible, square protective jacket. The jacket has an opening on each side so that a portion of the diskette's surfaces are exposed for reading and writing as shown in *Figure 6-5*.

FORMATTING: PREPARING A DISKETTE FOR USE

Before a diskette can be used for secondary storage, it must be formatted. The **formatting** process prepares the diskette so it can store data and includes defining the tracks, cylinders, and sectors on the surfaces of a diskette *(Figure 6-6)*.

A **track** is a narrow recording band forming a full circle around the diskette. A **cylinder** is defined as all tracks of the same number. For example, track 0 on side 1 of the diskette and track 0 on side 2 of the diskette would be called cylinder 0. A **sector** is a pie-shaped section of the diskette. The term sector is more frequently used to refer to a track sector, a section of track within a sector. Each track sector holds 512 bytes. For reading and writing purposes, track sectors are grouped into clusters. A **cluster** consists of two to eight track sectors (the number varies depending on the operating system). A cluster is the smallest unit of diskette space used to store data. Even if a file consisted of only a few characters, one cluster would be used for storage. Each cluster can only hold data from one file, but a file can be made up of many clusters. The number of tracks and sectors created on a

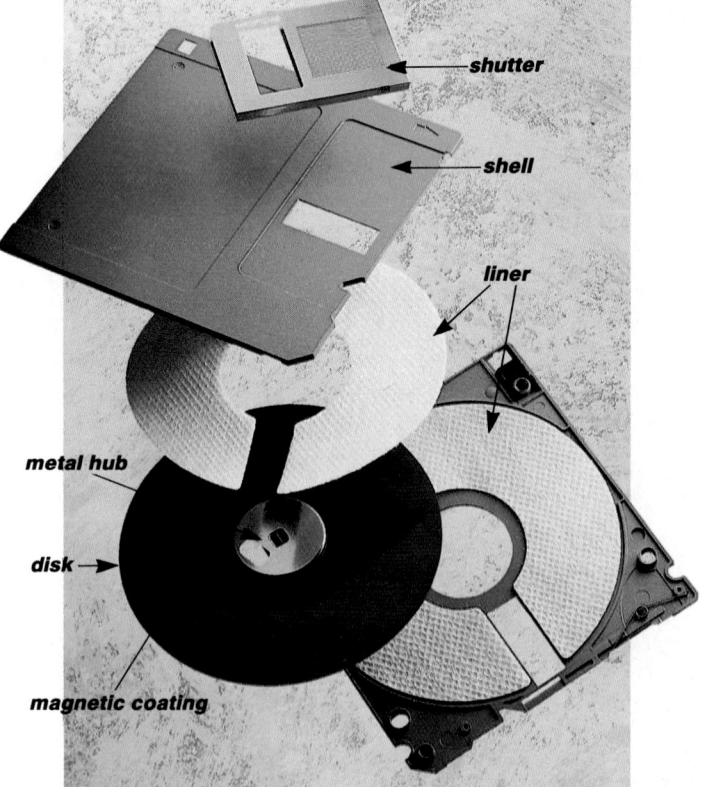

shutter

shell

liner

metal hub

disk

magnetic coating

Figure 6-3
In a 3 ^{1}/$_2$" diskette, the flexible plastic disk is enclosed between two liners that clean the disk surface of any microscopic debris and help to disperse static electricity. The outside cover is made of a rigid plastic material, and the recording window is covered by a metal shutter that slides to the side when the disk is inserted into the disk drive.

Figure 6-4
A user inserts a diskette into the disk drive of an IBM personal computer.

diskette when it is formatted varies based on the capacity of the diskette, the capabilities of the diskette drive being used, and the specifications in the operating system software that does the formatting. 5¹/₄-inch diskettes are formatted with 40 or 80 tracks and 9 or 15 sectors on the surface of the diskette. 3¹/₂-inch diskettes are usually formatted with 80 tracks and either 9, 18, or 36 sectors on each side.

In addition to defining the diskette surface, the formatting process erases any data that is on the diskette, analyzes the diskette surface for any defective spots, and establishes a directory that will be used to record information about files stored on the diskette. On personal computers using the DOS operating system, the directory is called the file allocation table. The **file allocation table** (FAT) file stores the file-name, file size, the time and date the file was last changed,

and the cluster number where the file begins. The FAT file also keeps track of unused clusters and is used when the computer writes new files to the diskette. When you instruct the computer to list the files on a diskette, the information comes from the FAT file.

To protect data from being accidentally erased during formatting or other writing operations, diskettes have write-protection features. A 5¹/₄-inch diskette has a write-protect notch. This notch is located on the side of the diskette. To prevent writing to a diskette, you cover this notch with a small piece of removable tape. Before writing data onto a diskette, the diskette drive checks the notch. If the notch is open, the drive will proceed to write on the diskette. If the

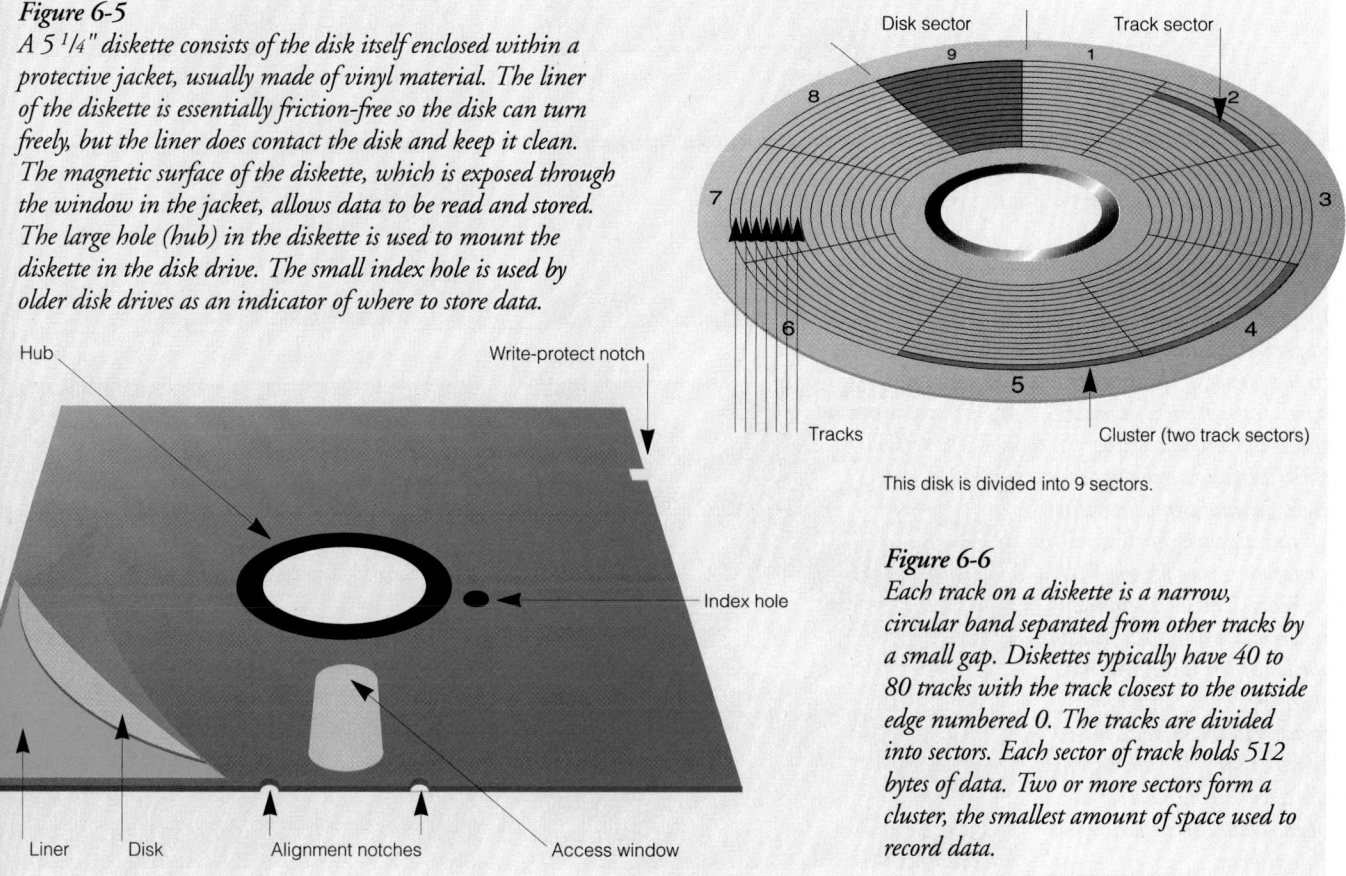

Figure 6-5
A 5 ¹/₄" diskette consists of the disk itself enclosed within a protective jacket, usually made of vinyl material. The liner of the diskette is essentially friction-free so the disk can turn freely, but the liner does contact the disk and keep it clean. The magnetic surface of the diskette, which is exposed through the window in the jacket, allows data to be read and stored. The large hole (hub) in the diskette is used to mount the diskette in the disk drive. The small index hole is used by older disk drives as an indicator of where to store data.

Hub

Write-protect notch

Index hole

Liner Disk Alignment notches Access window

Disk sector Track sector

Tracks Cluster (two track sectors)

This disk is divided into 9 sectors.

Figure 6-6
Each track on a diskette is a narrow, circular band separated from other tracks by a small gap. Diskettes typically have 40 to 80 tracks with the track closest to the outside edge numbered 0. The tracks are divided into sectors. Each sector of track holds 512 bytes of data. Two or more sectors form a cluster, the smallest amount of space used to record data.

notch is covered, the diskette drive will not write on the diskette *(Figure 6-7)*. On 3¹/₂-inch diskettes, the situation is reversed. Instead of a write-protect notch, there is a small window in the corner of the diskette. A piece of plastic in the window can be moved to open and close the window. If the write-protect window is closed, the drive can write on the diskette. If the window is open, the drive will not write on the diskette.

DISKETTE STORAGE CAPACITY

The amount of data you can store on a diskette depends on two factors: (1) the recording density; and (2) the number of tracks on the diskette.

The **recording density** is the number of bits that can be recorded on one inch of track on the diskette. This measurement is referred to as **bits per inch (bpi)**. The higher the recording density, the higher the storage capacity of the diskette. Most drives store the same amount of data on the longer outside tracks as they do on the shorter inside tracks. Thus, the bpi is measured on the innermost track where it is highest. Some newer drives use a different method. **Multiple zone recording** (MZR) records data at the same density on all

tracks. This means that the longer tracks closer to the outside edge of the disk can contain extra sectors. Each time a track becomes long enough to accept it, another sector is added.

The second factor that influences the amount of data that can be stored on a diskette is the number of tracks onto which data can be recorded. This measurement is referred to as **tracks per inch (tpi)**. As you learned earlier in this chapter, the number of tracks depends on the size of the diskette, the drive being used, and how the diskette was formatted.

The capacity of diskettes varies and increases every two or three years as manufacturers develop new ways of recording data more densely. Commonly used diskettes are referred to as either double-density or high-density. Older **single-density** diskettes that could only be written on one side are no longer used. **Double-density (DD) diskettes** can store 360K for a 5¹/₄-inch diskette and 720K for a 3¹/₂-inch diskette. **High-density (HD) diskettes** can store 1.2 megabytes (million characters) on a 5¹/₄-inch diskette and 1.44 megabytes on a 3¹/₂-inch diskette. **Extended-density (ED)** 3¹/₂-inch diskettes that can store 2.88 megabytes are also starting to be used. Even though it is smaller in size, a 3¹/₂-inch diskette can hold more data than a 5¹/₄-inch diskette because it has a higher recording density.

Figure 6-7
Data cannot be written on the 3 ¹/₂" diskette on the upper left because the window in the corner of the diskette is open. A small piece of plastic covers the window of the 3 ¹/₂" diskette on the upper right, so data can be written on this diskette. The reverse situation is true for the 5 ¹/₄" diskettes. The write-protect notch of the 5 ¹/₄" diskette on the lower left is covered and, therefore, data cannot be written to the diskette. The notch of the 5 ¹/₄" diskette on the lower right, however, is open. Data can be written to this diskette.

A special type of diskette, called a **floptical** diskette, combines optical and magnetic technology to achieve even higher storage rates (currently up to 21 megabytes) on what is basically a $3^1/2$-inch diskette. A floptical disk drive uses a low-power laser to read grooves that have been permanently engraved in the diskette recording surface. The grooves allow closely spaced recording and higher bpi and tpi densities. Another advantage of a floptical drive is that it can also read double- and high-density $3^1/2$-inch diskettes.

STORING DATA ON A DISKETTE

Regardless of the type of diskette or how it is formatted, the method of storing data on a diskette is essentially the same. When a $3^1/2$-inch diskette is inserted into a diskette drive, the notches in the metal hub are engaged by a shaft connected to the drive motor *(Figure 6-8)*.

When you read from or write to a diskette, the motor spins the circular plastic recording surface at approximately 360 revolutions per minute. When you are not reading or writing, the disk does not spin. A lever opens the shutter to expose a portion of the plastic recording surface. Data is stored on tracks of the disk, using the same code, such as

ASCII, that is used to store the data in main memory. To do this, a recording mechanism in the drive called the **read/write head** rests on the top and bottom surface of the rotating diskette, generating electronic impulses. The electronic impulses change the magnetic polarity, or alignment, of magnetic areas along a track on the disk. The plus or minus polarity represents the 1 or 0 bits being recorded. To access different tracks on the diskette, the drive moves the read/write head from track to track. When reading data from the diskette, the read/write head senses the magnetic areas that are recorded on the diskette along the various tracks and transfers the data to main memory. When writing data to the diskette, the read/write head transfers data from main memory and stores it as magnetic areas on the tracks on the recording surface.

Data stored in sectors on a diskette must be retrieved and placed in main memory to be processed. The time required to access and retrieve the data is called the **access time**.

The access time for a diskette drive depends on three factors:
1. **Seek time**, the time it takes to position the read/write head over the proper track.

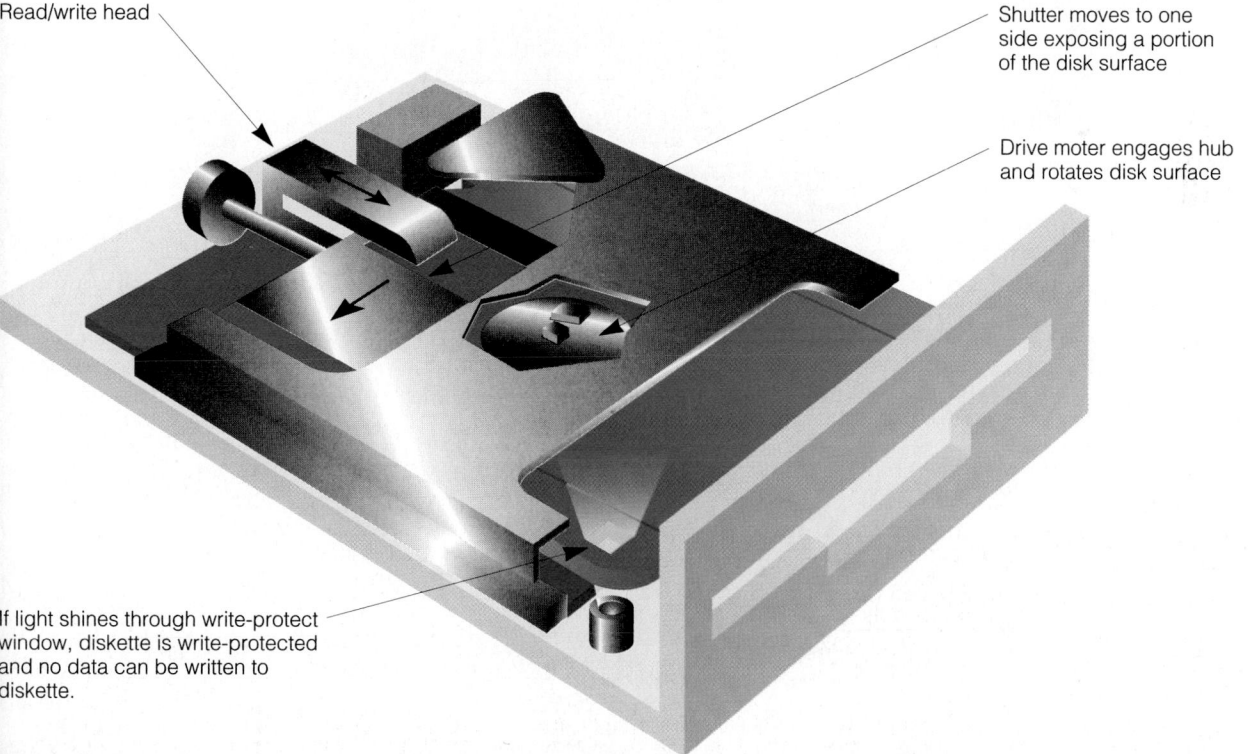

Read/write head

Shutter moves to one side exposing a portion of the disk surface

Drive moter engages hub and rotates disk surface

If light shines through write-protect window, diskette is write-protected and no data can be written to diskette.

Figure 6-8
When you insert a $3^1/2$" diskette in a drive, the notches in the metal hub are engaged by a drive motor shaft. A lever moves the shutter to one side so a portion of the disk surfaces are exposed. When you read from or write to a diskette, the shaft spins the disk at approximately 360 rpm. Read/write heads above and below the recording surface move in and out to read or write data.

2. **Rotational delay** (also called **latency**), the time it takes for the sector containing the data to rotate under the read/write head.
3. **Data transfer rate**, the time required to transfer the data from the disk to main memory.

The access time for diskettes varies from about 175 milliseconds (one millisecond equals $^1/_{1000}$ of one second) to approximately 300 milliseconds. What this means to the user is that, on the average, data stored in a single sector on a diskette can be retrieved in approximately $^1/_5$ to $^1/_3$ of one second.

THE CARE OF DISKETTES

With reasonable care, diskettes provide an inexpensive and reliable form of storage. In handling diskettes, you should take care to avoid exposing them to heat, cold, magnetic fields, and contaminated environments such as dust, smoke, or salt air. One advantage of the $3^1/_2$-inch diskette is that its rigid plastic cover provides more protection for the data stored on

the plastic disk inside than the flexible cover on a $5^1/_4$-inch diskette. *Figure 6-9* shows you ways to properly care for your diskettes. Because the read/write head actually comes in contact with the diskette surface, wear takes place and the diskette will eventually become unreadable. To protect against loss, you should copy data onto other diskettes.

Hard Disks

Hard disks provide larger and faster secondary storage capabilities than diskettes. **Hard disks** consist of one or more rigid platters coated with an oxide material that allows data to be magnetically recorded on the surface of the platters *(Figure 6-10)*. The platters are usually made of aluminum but some newer disks use glass or ceramic materials. Most hard disks are permanently mounted inside the computer and are not removable like diskettes. On hard disks, the platters, the read/write heads, and the mechanism for moving the heads across the surface of the disk are enclosed in an airtight, sealed case. This helps to ensure a clean environment for the disk.

Figure 6-9
Guidelines for the proper care of diskettes.

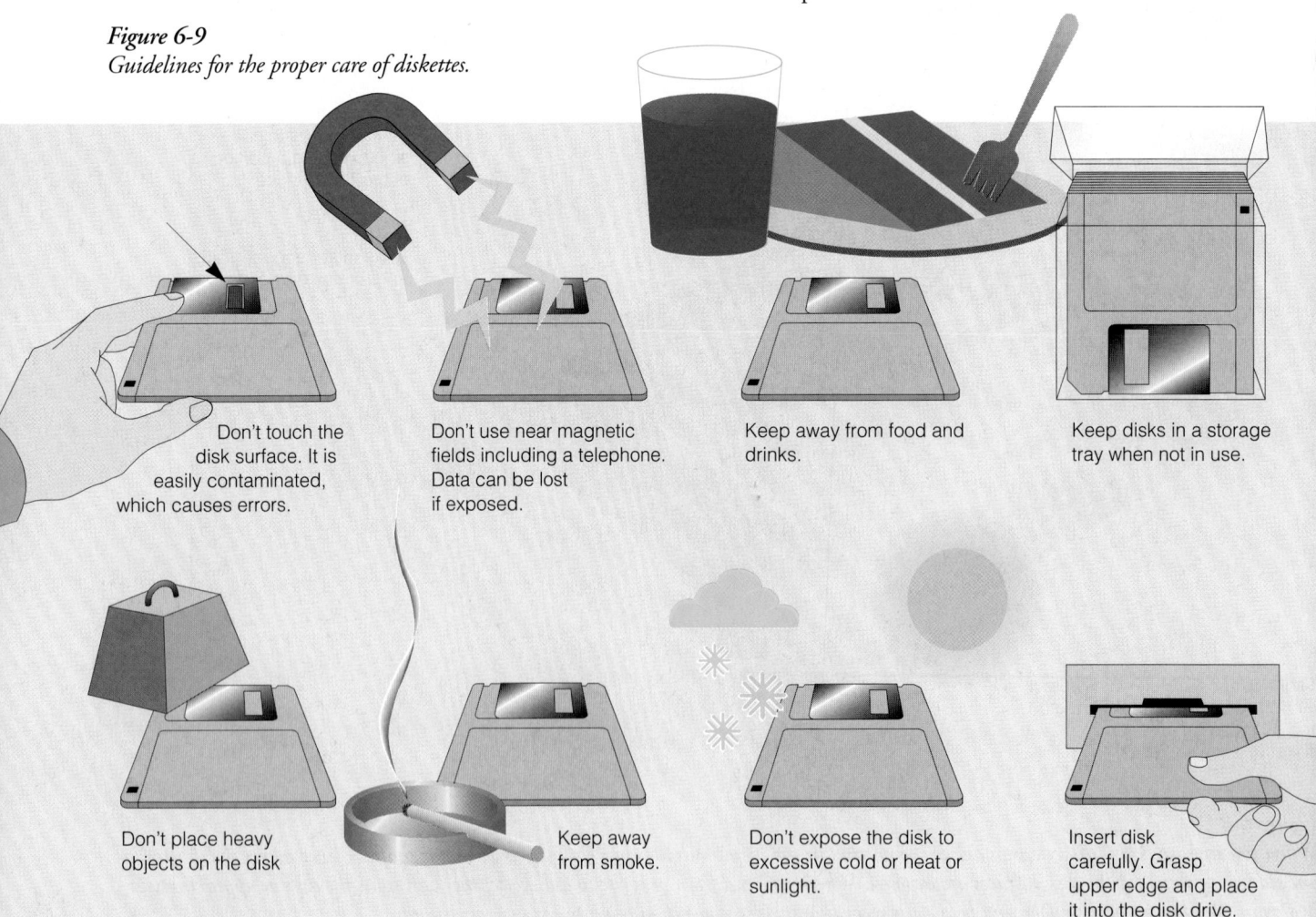

Don't touch the disk surface. It is easily contaminated, which causes errors.

Don't use near magnetic fields including a telephone. Data can be lost if exposed.

Keep away from food and drinks.

Keep disks in a storage tray when not in use.

Don't place heavy objects on the disk

Keep away from smoke.

Don't expose the disk to excessive cold or heat or sunlight.

Insert disk carefully. Grasp upper edge and place it into the disk drive.

On minicomputers and mainframes, hard disks are sometimes called **fixed disks** because they cannot be removed like diskettes. They are also referred to as **direct-access storage devices** (DASD). These hard disks are often larger versions of the hard disks used on personal computers and can be either mounted in the same cabinet as the computer or enclosed in their own stand-alone cabinet *(Figure 6-11)*.

While most personal computers are limited to two to four disk drives, minicomputers can support 8 to 16 disk devices, and mainframe computers can support more than 100 high-speed disk devices.

HARD DISK STORAGE CAPACITY

Hard disks contain a spindle on which one or more disk platters are mounted *(Figure 6-12* on the next page). Each surface of a platter can be used to store data. Thus, if one platter is used in the drive, two surfaces are available for data. If two platters are used, four surfaces are available for data, and so on. Naturally, the more platters, the more data that can be stored on the drive. Like a diskette, hard disks must be formatted before they can be used to store data. Before a hard disk is formatted, it can be divided into separate areas called

partitions. Each partition can function as if it were a separate disk. Partitions are sometimes used to separate different types or classes of items such as programs and data or data from different organizations such as subsidiary companies. Separate partitions are also sometimes used for different operating systems. On personal computers, hard disk partitions are usually given letter identifiers, starting with the letter C. The letters A and B are reserved for diskette drives.

Access time for a hard disk is between ten and twenty milliseconds. This is significantly faster than for a diskette because of two reasons. First, a hard disk spins ten to twenty times faster than a diskette drive. Second, a hard disk is always spinning, whereas a diskette only starts spinning when a read or write command is received.

The storage capacity of hard drives is measured in megabytes or millions of bytes of storage. Common sizes for personal computers range from 100MB to 500MB of storage and even larger sizes are available. Each 10MB of storage is equivalent to approximately 5,000 printed pages, assuming approximately 2,000 characters per page.

Figure 6-10
A hard disk consists of one or more disk platters. Each side of the platter is coated with an oxide substance that allows data to be magnetically stored.

Figure 6-11
A high-speed, high-capacity fixed disk drive in a stand-alone cabinet.

Some disk devices used on large computers can store billions of bytes of information *(Figure 6-13)*. A billion bytes of information is called a **gigabyte**.

STORING DATA ON A HARD DISK

Storing data on hard disks is similar to storing data on diskettes. Hard disks rotate at a high rate of speed, usually 3,600 to 7,200 revolutions per minute. Hard disk read/write heads are attached to **access arms** that swing out over the disk surface to the correct track. The read/write heads float on a cushion of air and do not actually touch the surface of the disk. The distance between the head and the surface varies from approximately ten to twenty millionths of an inch. As shown in *Figure 6-14,* the close tolerance leaves no room for any type of contamination. If some form of contamination is introduced or if the alignment of the read/write heads is altered by something accidentally jarring the computer, the disk head can collide with and damage the disk surface, causing a loss of data. This event is known as a **head crash**. Because of the time needed to repair the disk and to reconstruct the data that was lost, head crashes can be extremely costly to users in terms of both time and money.

Depending on the type of disk drive, data is physically organized in one of two ways. One way is the sector method and the other is the cylinder method.

The **sector method** for physically organizing data on hard disks is similar to the method used for diskettes. Each track on the disk surface is divided into sectors. Each sector can contain a specified number of bytes. Data is referenced by indicating the surface, track, and sector where the data is stored.

With the **cylinder method**, all tracks of the same number on each recording surface are considered part of the same cylinder *(Figure 6-15)*. For example, the fifth track on all surfaces would be considered part of cylinder five. All twentieth tracks would be part of cylinder twenty, and so on. When the computer requests data from a disk using the cylinder method, it must specify the cylinder, recording surface, and record number. Because the access arms containing the read/write heads all move together, they are always over the same track on all surfaces. Thus, using the cylinder method to record data *down* the disk surfaces reduces the movement of the read/write head during both reading and writing of data.

Figure 6-13
The IBM 3390 disk drive is used on mainframe computer systems. Each drive, shown here being assembled during manufacturing, can hold 22.7 billion bytes of data.

Figure 6-12
A hard disk with its protective cover removed. The access arm and read/write head over the top platter can be clearly seen. Each platter surface, top and bottom, has an access arm and read/write head.

Some computers improve the apparent speed at which data is transferred to and from a disk by using disk cache. Similar in concept to the RAM cache memory described in Chapter 4, **disk cache** is an area of memory set aside for data most often read from the disk. Every time the computer requests data from the disk, disk cache software looks first for the data in the disk cache memory area. If the requested data is in disk cache, it is immediately transferred to the CPU and the slower disk read operation is avoided. Disk cache memory is updated every time a disk read takes place. In addition to the data requested from the disk, disk cache software also reads adjacent clusters on the assumption that they may be needed next. Disk cache software also makes disk write operations more efficient by temporarily holding data to be written until the CPU is not busy. Microsoft includes a disk cache program called SMARTDrive with the Windows and the DOS operating systems.

The flow of data to and from the hard disk is managed by electronic circuits called the hard disk controller. Sometimes the controller is a separate board in an expansion slot and sometimes the controller is part of the disk drive itself.

On personal computers, two types of controllers are most common, IDE and SCSI. **Integrated Drive Electronics** (IDE) controllers can operate one or two hard disk drives. Most motherboards have built-in IDE connectors that use a cable to attach directly to the disk drive. IDE controllers can transfer data to the disk at a rate of up to 8MB per second. SCSI, pronounced *scuzzy*, stands for **Small Computer System Interface**. SCSI controllers can support seven disk drives or any mix up to seven SCSI devices. SCSI devices are connected to each other in a chain with a cable between each device. SCSI controllers are faster than IDE controllers and can support up to 100MB per second transfer rates. SCSI controllers usually consist of a circuit board mounted in an expansion slot.

Data Compression

One way of storing more data on a disk is to use data compression. **Data compression** reduces the storage requirements of data by substituting codes for repeating patterns of data. For example, consider the familiar Ben Franklin saying, "Early to bed, early to rise, makes a man healthy, wealthy,

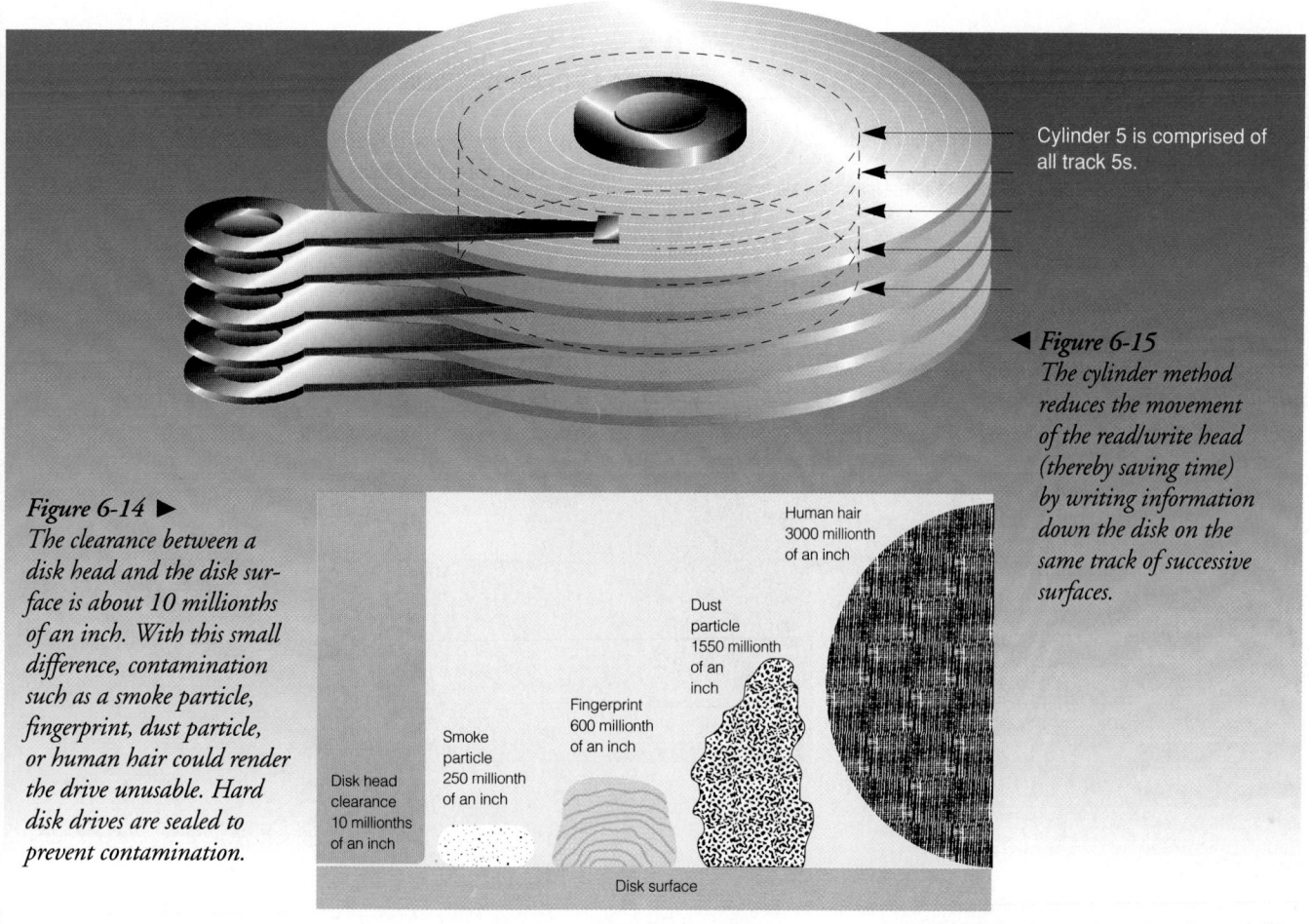

Cylinder 5 is comprised of all track 5s.

◀ *Figure 6-15*
The cylinder method reduces the movement of the read/write head (thereby saving time) by writing information down the disk on the same track of successive surfaces.

Figure 6-14 ▶
The clearance between a disk head and the disk surface is about 10 millionths of an inch. With this small difference, contamination such as a smoke particle, fingerprint, dust particle, or human hair could render the drive unusable. Hard disk drives are sealed to prevent contamination.

Human hair
3000 millionth
of an inch

Dust
particle
1550 millionth
of an
inch

Fingerprint
600 millionth
of an inch

Smoke
particle
250 millionth
of an inch

Disk head
clearance
10 millionths
of an inch

Disk surface

and wise." Including punctuation, this phrase includes 56 characters. As shown in *Figure 6-16,* by substituting special characters for repeating patterns, the original phrase can be compressed to only 30 characters; a reduction of 46%. Compression is most often stated as a ratio of the size of the original uncompressed data divided by the size of the compressed data. In the *Figure 6-16* example, this would be a compression ratio of 1.9 to 1 (56 divided by 30). The codes substituted for the repeating patterns are filed in a table when the data is compressed. This substitution table is used to restore the compressed data to its original form when necessary.

The type of compression just described is called *lossless compression* because no data is lost in the process. Lossless compression works best for text and numeric data that cannot afford to lose any data. Compression ratios for lossless compression average 2 to 1 (the size of the data is reduced 50%). Other compression methods, called *lossy compression,* give up some accuracy for higher compression ratios (up to 200 to 1). Lossy compression methods are typically used to compress video images and sound. Video and sound can both have data removed without a noticeable reduction in the overall quality of the output. Lossy compression is usually accomplished with special hardware such as a video or sound expansion board.

Many manufacturers of complex software programs, such as word processing and spreadsheets, use compression methods to reduce the number of disks that are needed to distribute their products. Utility programs loaded with the software expand the software files as they are loaded on the user's system.

Some file compression programs, such as PKZIP, compress and uncompress data as directed by the user. Disk compression programs, such as Stacker, can be installed to automatically keep all files on a hard disk compressed until they are needed for processing.

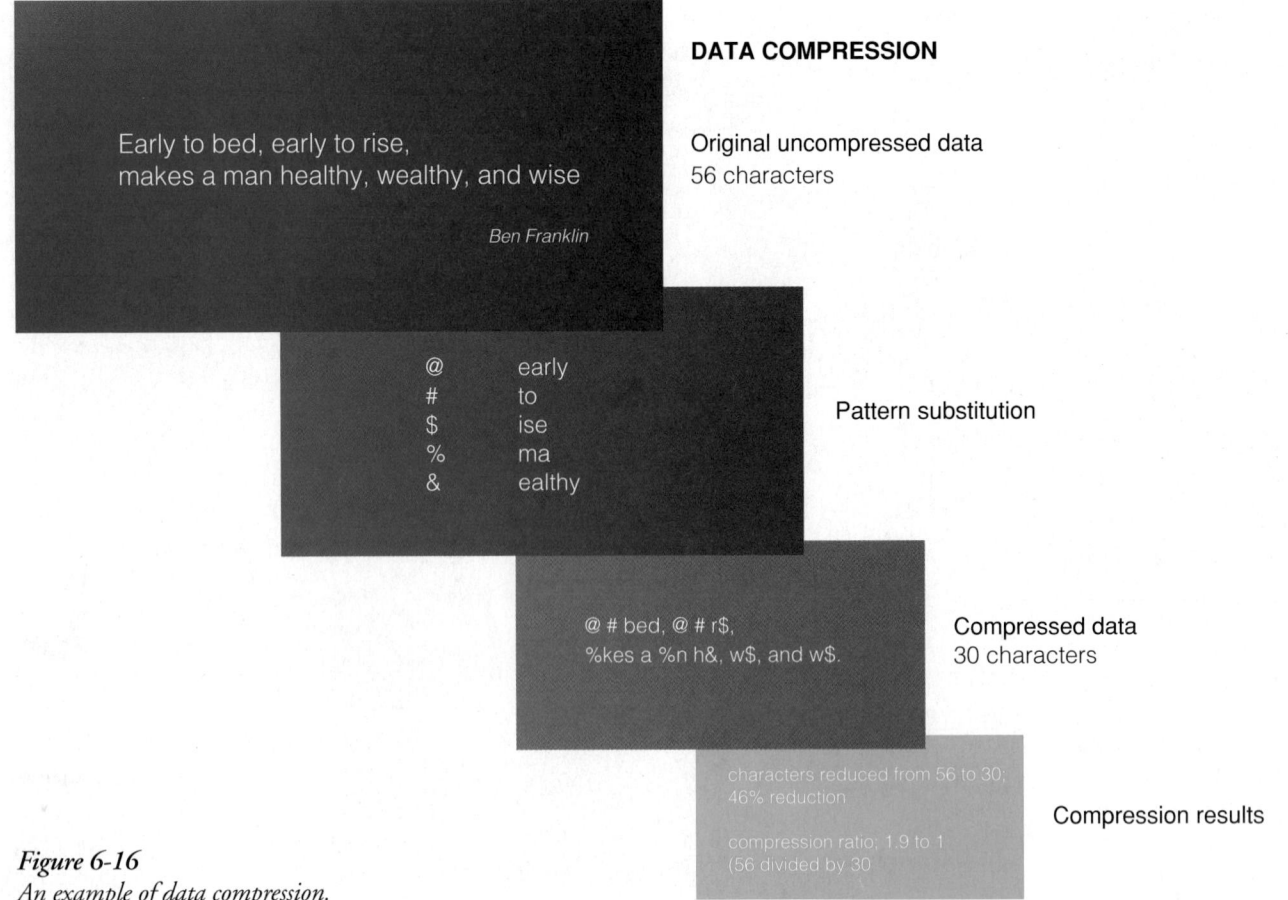

Figure 6-16
An example of data compression.

RAID

As computers became faster, writing data to and reading data from increasingly larger disks became a bottleneck. Computers spent a large percentage of time waiting for data to go to or come from the disk drive. Rather than trying to build even larger and faster disk drives, some disk manufacturers began to connect multiple smaller disks into an integrated unit that acted like it was a single large disk drive. A group of integrated small disks is called a **RAID**, which stands for **redundant array of inexpensive disks**. RAID technology can be implemented in several ways called *RAID levels*.

In the simplest RAID method, called RAID level 1, one backup disk exists for each data disk *(Figure 6-17)*. Each backup disk contains the same information as its corresponding data disk. If the data disk fails, the backup disk becomes the data disk. Because the disks contain duplicate information, RAID level 1 is sometimes called **disk mirroring**.

RAID levels beyond level 1 all spread data across more than one drive. Dividing a logical piece of data, such as a record, word, or character, into smaller parts and writing those parts on multiple drives is called **striping** *(Figure 6-18)*. Some RAID levels call for a separate disk, called a parity or check disk, to keep track of information that can be used to recreate data if one of the data disks malfunctions. Other RAID levels store the parity information on the data disk. This parity information is an important part of RAID technology. It allows the system to rebuild, sometimes automatically, any information that is damaged on one of the data disks.

RAID disks offer a number of advantages over single large disks (called SLEDs for single large expensive disks). Because multiple read or write operations can take place at the same time, data can be read from or written to RAID disks faster. The biggest advantage, however, is the reduced risk of losing data. The capability to rebuild any damaged data is important to organizations that cannot afford to be without the information stored on their disks.

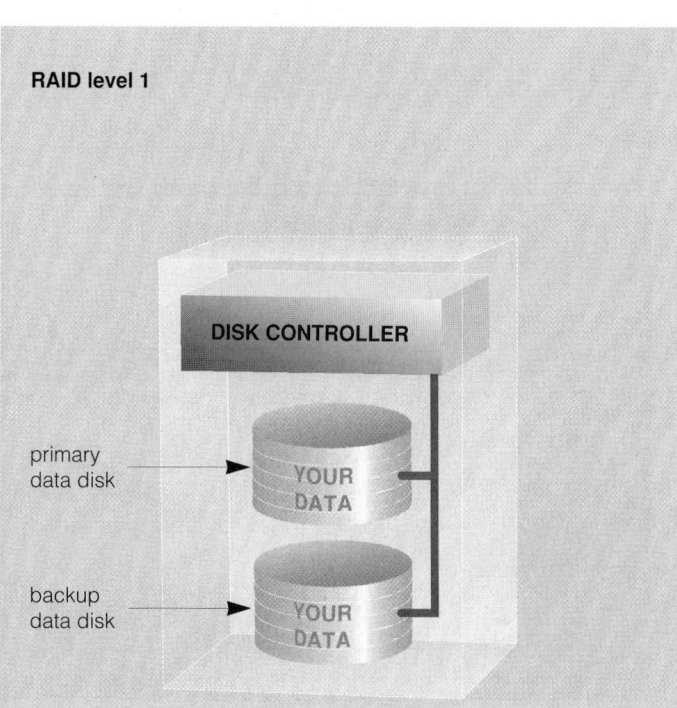

Figure 6-17
In RAID level 1, called disk mirroring, a backup disk exists for each data disk.

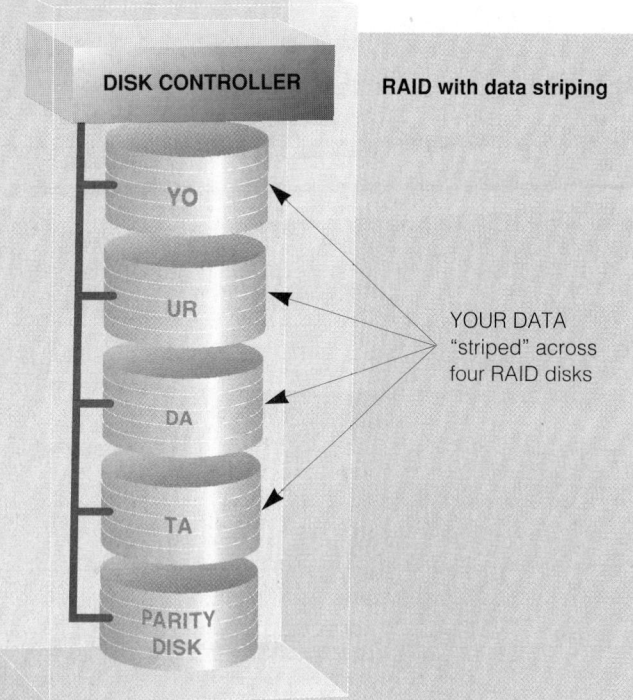

Figure 6-18
In RAID levels beyond level 1, data to be stored is divided into parts and written across several disks. This process is called striping. Some RAID levels call for additional parity disks that keep track of information to be used to recreate information if one of the data disks malfunctions.

Other Types of Hard Disks

Other devices that use hard disk technology are presented in this section. These include disk cartridges, hard cards, and removable disks.

DISK CARTRIDGES

Another variation of disk storage available for use with personal computers is the removable disk cartridge. **Disk cartridges**, which can be inserted and removed from a computer *(Figure 6-19)*, offer the storage and fast access features of hard disks and the portability of diskettes. Disk cartridges are often used when data security is an issue. At the end of a work session, the disk cartridge can be removed and locked up, leaving no data on the computer.

One unique type of disk cartridge is called a Bernoulli disk. The **Bernoulli disk cartridge** works with a special drive

unit that uses a cushion of air to keep the flexible disk surface from touching the read/write head. The flexible disk surface reduces the chance of a head crash but does cause the cartridges to eventually wear out.

HARD CARDS

One option for installing a hard disk in a personal computer is a hard card. The **hard card** is a circuit board that has a hard disk built onto it. Hard cards provide an easy way to expand the storage capacity of a personal computer because the board can be installed into an expansion slot of the computer *(Figure 6-20)*. Because of lower prices on larger capacity disk drives, hard cards are not used as much as they once were.

REMOVABLE DISKS

Removable disk devices consist of the drive unit, which is usually in its own cabinet, and the removable recording media, called a **disk pack**. Removable disk packs consist of multiple metal platters that could record from 10 to 300 megabytes of data. Removable disk units were introduced in

Figure 6-19
A removable hard disk cartridge allows a user to remove and transport the entire hard disk from computer to computer or to lock it up in a safe.

Figure 6-20
A hard card is a hard disk drive on a circuit board that can be mounted in a computer's expansion slot.

the early 1960s and for nearly 20 years were the most prevalent type of disk storage on minicomputers and mainframes. During the 1980s, however, removable disks began to be replaced by hard fixed disks that offered larger storage capacities and higher reliability.

Maintaining Data Stored on a Disk

To prevent the loss of disk data, two procedures should be performed on a regular basis; backup and defragmentation.

BACKUP

Backup means creating a copy of important programs and data. To backup diskettes, simply copy the data on one diskette to another diskette. Diskettes are also commonly used to backup at least some of the data stored on a hard disk of a personal computer. Because hard disks can store large quantities of data (up to a gigabyte) diskettes are often used just to backup important files. Magnetic tape, another form of secondary storage, is commonly used to backup data stored on large-capacity hard disks.

DEFRAGMENTATION

When data is stored on a disk, it is placed in the first available clusters. The computer tries to place the data in clusters that are *contiguous* (all in a row), but contiguous clusters may not be available. When a file is stored in clusters that are not next to each other, the file is said to be **fragmented.** The term fragmented is also used to describe the condition of a disk drive that has many files stored in non-contiguous clusters *(Figure 6-21)*. Fragmentation causes the computer to run slower because reading data from the disk takes longer than if the data were all in one location. To solve this problem, the disk must be defragmented. **Defragmentation** reorganizes the data stored on the disk so files are located in contiguous clusters. Defragmentation programs are available as separate programs or as part of system utility packages. Some operating systems also contain defragmentation programs.

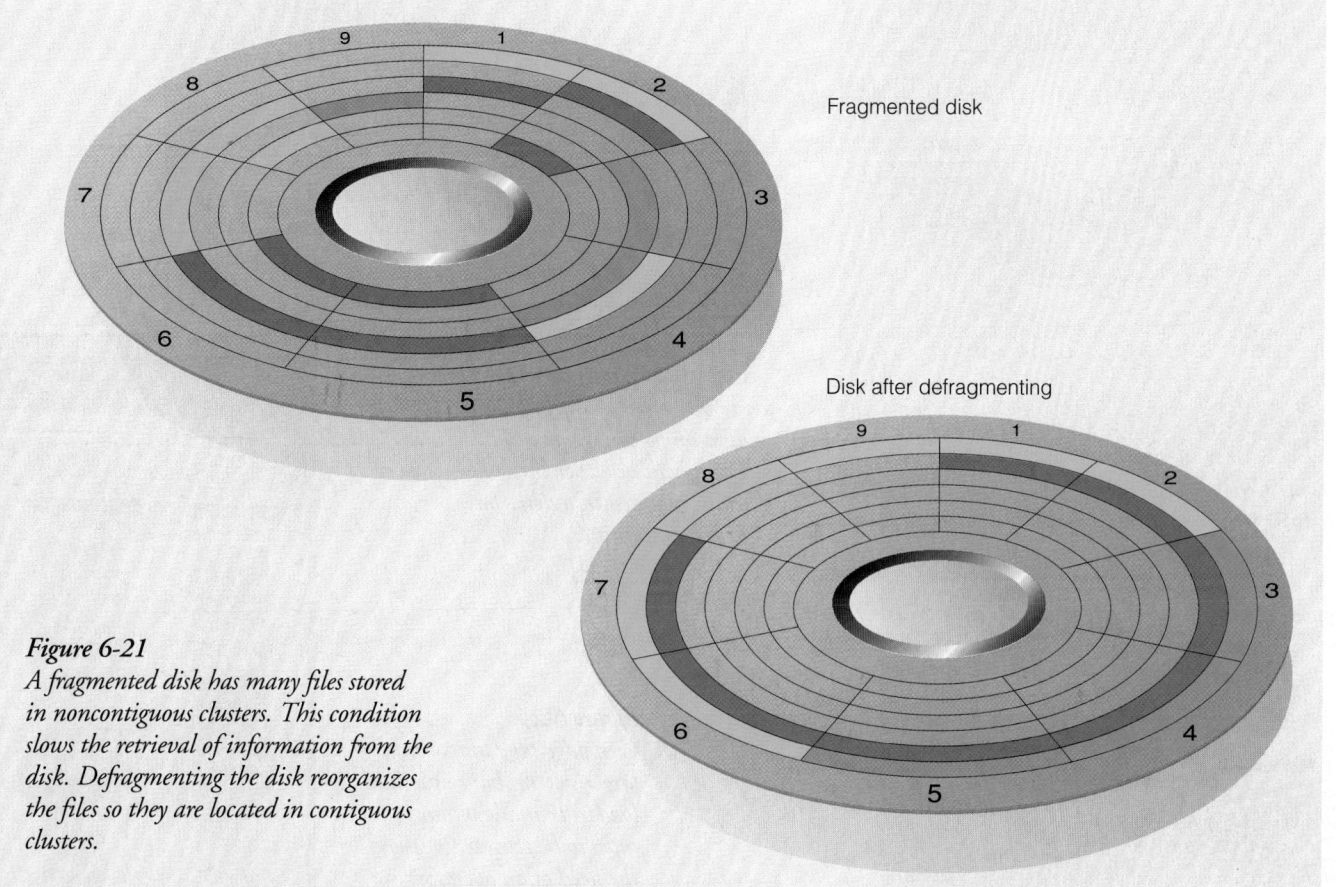

Fragmented disk

Disk after defragmenting

Figure 6-21
A fragmented disk has many files stored in noncontiguous clusters. This condition slows the retrieval of information from the disk. Defragmenting the disk reorganizes the files so they are located in contiguous clusters.

Magnetic Tape

During the 1950s and early 1960s, prior to the introduction of removable disk pack drives, magnetic tape was the primary method of storing large amounts of data. Today, even though tape is no longer used as the primary method of secondary storage, it still functions as a cost-effective way to store data that does not have to be accessed immediately. In addition, tape serves as the primary means of backup for most medium and large systems and is often used to transfer data from one system to another.

Magnetic tape consists of a thin ribbon of plastic. The tape is coated on one side with a material that can be magnetized to record the bit patterns that represent data. The most common types of magnetic tape devices are cartridge and reel-to-reel. Cartridge tape varies from ¹/₄- or ¹/₂-inch wide, and reel-to-reel tape is ¹/₂-inch wide *(Figure 6-22)*.

Cartridge Tape Devices

A **cartridge tape** contains magnetic recording tape in a small rectangular plastic housing. One quarter-inch wide tape in cartridges slightly larger than audio tapes are frequently used for backup on personal computers. Faster and higher storage capacity ¹/₂-inch cartridge tapes are increasingly replacing reel-to-reel tape devices on minicomputers and mainframes. For personal computers, cartridge tape units are designed to be internally mounted in a bay or in a separate external cabinet *(Figure 6-23)*.

Figure 6-22
One-half inch reel tape (top) and magnetic tape cartridge (bottom).

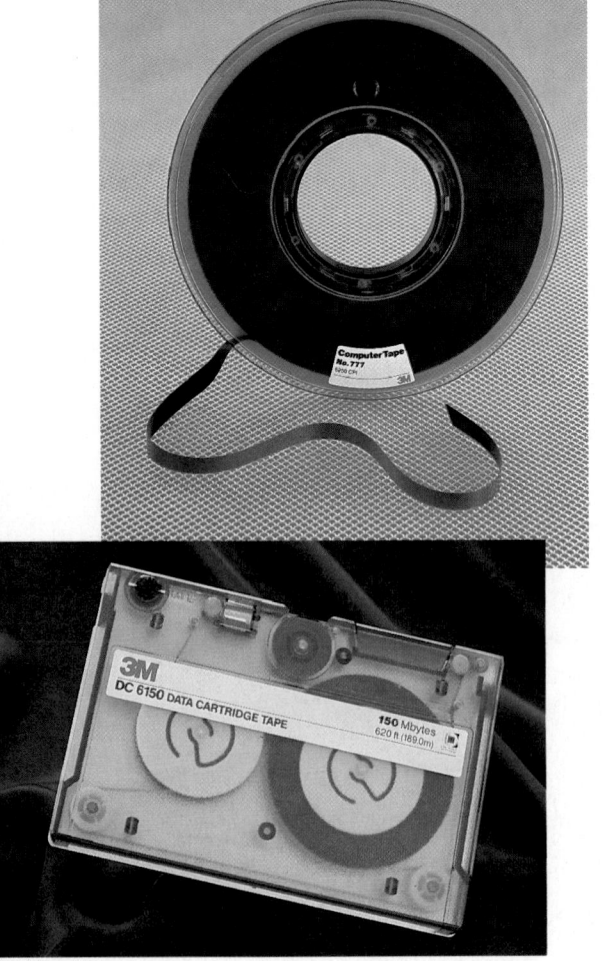

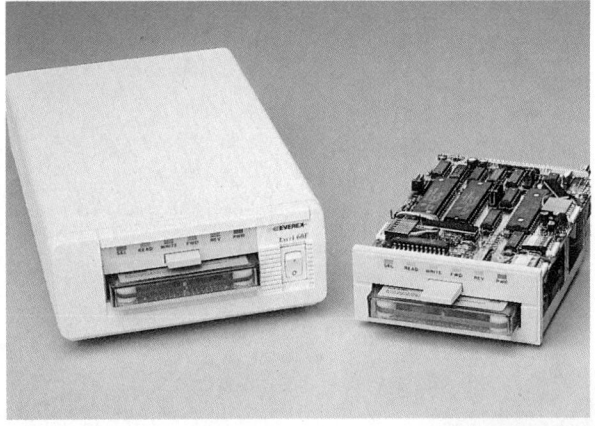

Figure 6-23
One-quarter inch cartridge tapes are often used to backup hard disks on personal computers. Drives can be either internal units mounted in a drive bay or external units.

Figure 6-24
Cartridge tape units used for larger systems have automatic loaders that allow multiple tapes to be recorded without the need of an operator.

For larger systems, cartridge tapes are usually mounted in their own cabinet. Cartridge tapes for larger systems are designed so multiple tapes can be automatically loaded and unloaded, allowing tape storage operations to take place unattended *(Figure 6-24)*.

Reel-to-Reel Tape Devices

Reel-to-reel tape devices use two reels: a supply reel to hold the tape that will be read from or written to, and the take-up reel to temporarily hold portions of the supply reel tape as it is being processed. As the tape moves from one reel to another, it passes over a read/write head, an electromagnetic device that can read or write data on the tape. At the completion of processing, tape on the take-up reel is wound back onto the supply reel.

Older style tape units used vertical cabinets with vacuum columns that held five or six feet of slack tape to prevent breaking during sudden start or stop operations.

Newer style tape units *(Figure 6-25)* allow a tape to be inserted through a slot opening similar to the way videotapes are loaded in a videocassette recorder. This front-loading tape drive takes less space and can be cabinet mounted. The drive automatically threads the end of the tape onto an internal take-up reel. Because of their size and cost, reel-to-reel tape drives are used almost exclusively on minicomputer and mainframe systems.

Reels of tape usually come in lengths of 300 to 3,600 feet and can store up to 200 megabytes of data.

Storing Data on Magnetic Tape

Tape is considered a **sequential storage** media because the computer must record and read tape records one after another. For example, to read the 1,000th record on a tape, the tape drive must first pass over the previous 999 records.

Figure 6-25
Newer style ¹/2" inch tape drives allow the user to slide the tape into a slot at the front of the unit. The drive automatically threads the tape onto an internal take-up reel.

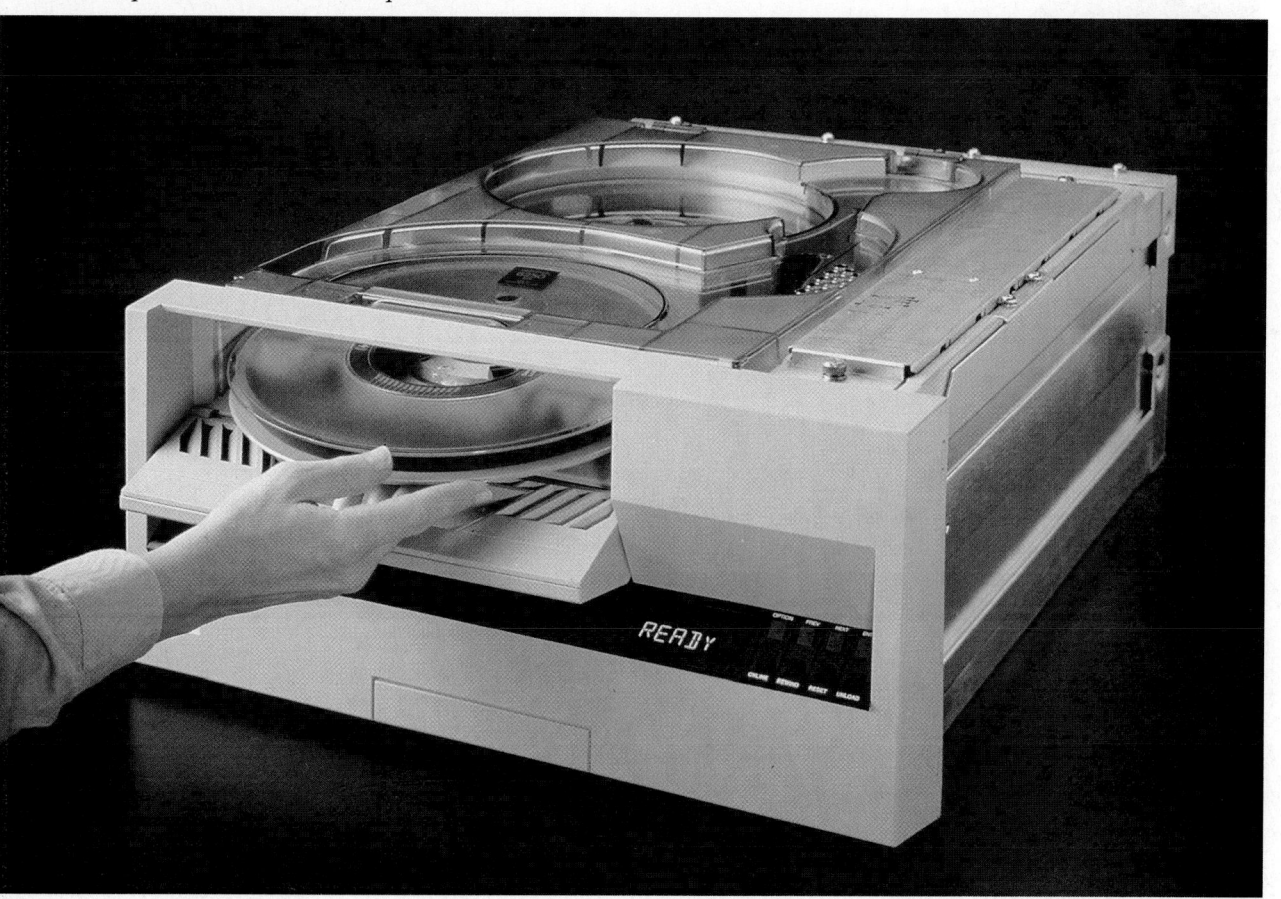

Binary codes, such as ASCII and EBCDIC, are used to represent data stored on magnetic tape. Within a code, each character is represented by a unique combination of bits. The bits are stored on tape in the form of magnetic areas *(Figure 6-26)*. The magnetic areas are organized into rows, called channels, that run the length of the tape. A combination of bits in a vertical column (one from each channel) is used to represent a character. An additional bit is used as a parity bit for error checking.

Tape density is the number of bits that can be stored on an inch of tape. As on disk drives, tape density is expressed in bits per inch, or bpi. Commonly used tape densities are 800, 1,600, 3,200 and 6,250 bpi. Some of the newer cartridge tape devices can record at densities higher than 60,000 bpi. The higher the density, the more data that can be stored on a tape.

Some tape drives can operate in a high-speed streaming mode used to backup and restore hard disk drives. In the **streaming mode**, the tape records data in exactly the same byte-by-byte order as it appears on the hard disk. When used to restore a hard disk, the data recorded on the tape in the streaming mode is used to recreate all the data on the hard disk. The advantage of streaming is that it is faster than normal tape operations and thus data can be recorded in less time. The disadvantage is that the streaming method cannot be used to selectively record or restore an individual file.

Another method of storing large amounts of data on tape is **digital audio tape** (DAT). DAT uses **helical scan technology** to write data at much higher densities across the tape at an angle instead of down the length of the tape *(Figure 6-27)*. Using this method, tape densities can be as high as 61,000 bpi.

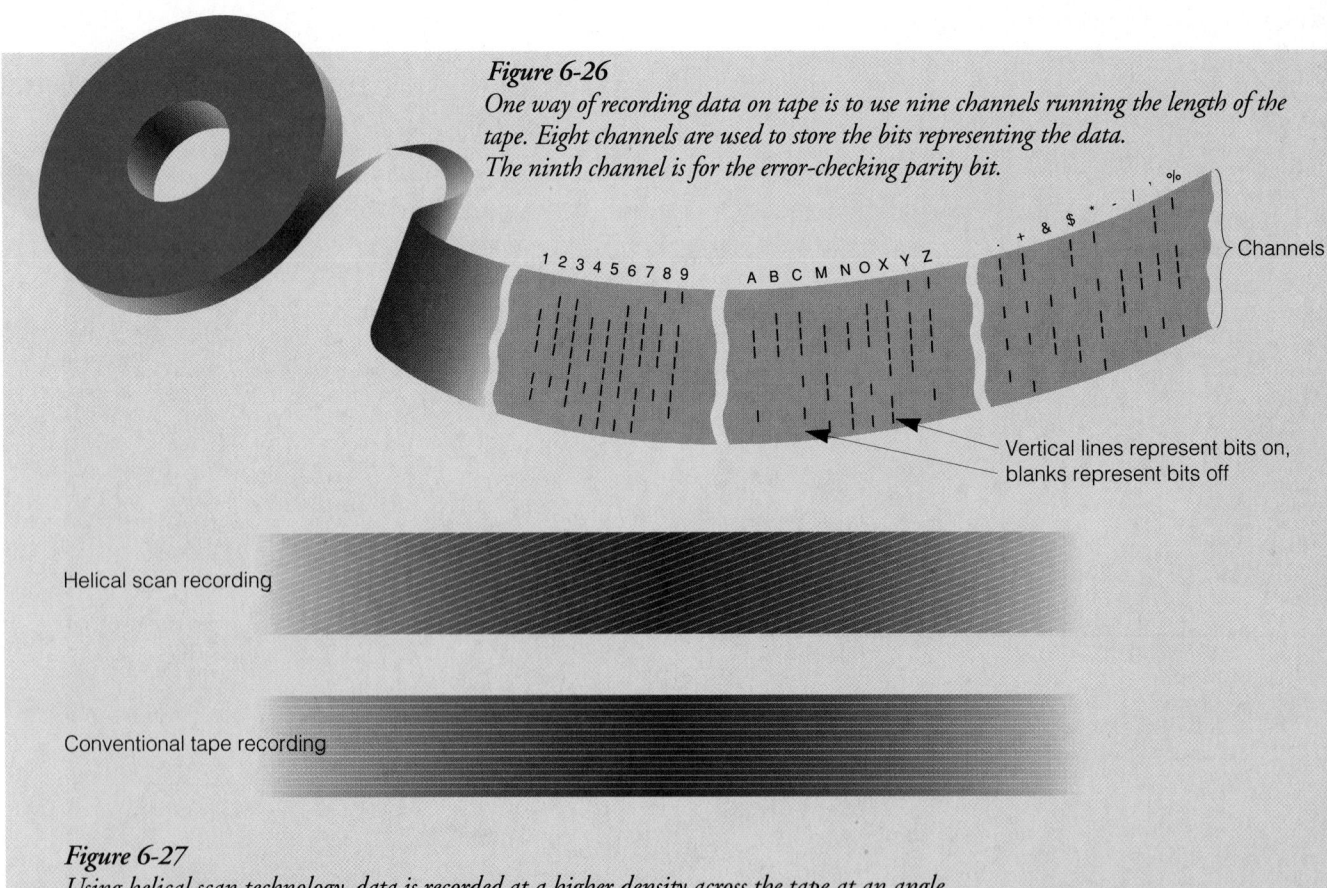

Figure 6-26
One way of recording data on tape is to use nine channels running the length of the tape. Eight channels are used to store the bits representing the data. The ninth channel is for the error-checking parity bit.

Channels

Vertical lines represent bits on, blanks represent bits off

Helical scan recording

Conventional tape recording

Figure 6-27
Using helical scan technology, data is recorded at a higher density across the tape at an angle. Conventional tape drives record data in channels running the length of the tape.

Other Forms of Secondary Storage

The conventional disk and tape devices just described comprise the majority of secondary storage devices and media, but other means for storing data are sometimes used. These include PC cards, optical disks, solid-state devices, and mass storage devices.

PC Cards

PC cards are small, credit card-sized cards that fit into PCMCIA expansion slots. You may recall from Chapter 4 that PCMCIA stands for the Personal Computer Memory Card International Association, the group that develops standards for the cards. Different versions and sizes of the cards are used for storage, communications, and additional memory.

Most often, PC cards are used on portable computers, but they can be incorporated into desktop systems as well. Although they are only 10.5mm thick (about .4 inch), PC cards used for storage contain small rotating disk drives 1.3 inches in diameter that can contain more than 200 megabytes of data *(Figure 6-28)*.

The storage cards can be useful for people who work with more than one computer or who have to share a computer with others. Their data can be maintained on a PC storage card and kept with them.

Optical Disks

Enormous quantities of information are stored on **optical disks** by using a laser to burn microscopic holes on the surface of a hard plastic disk.

A lower power laser reads the disk by reflecting light off the disk surface. The reflected light is converted into a series of bits that the computer can process *(Figure 6-29)*.

Figure 6-28
Type III PC cards are used for small removable disk drives that can hold over 200 megabytes of data.

Figure 6-29
To record data on an optical disk, a high-power laser heats the surface and makes a microscopic pit. To read data, a low-power laser light is reflected from the smooth unpitted areas and is interpreted as 1 bit. The pitted areas do not reflect the laser beam and are interpreted as 0 bits.

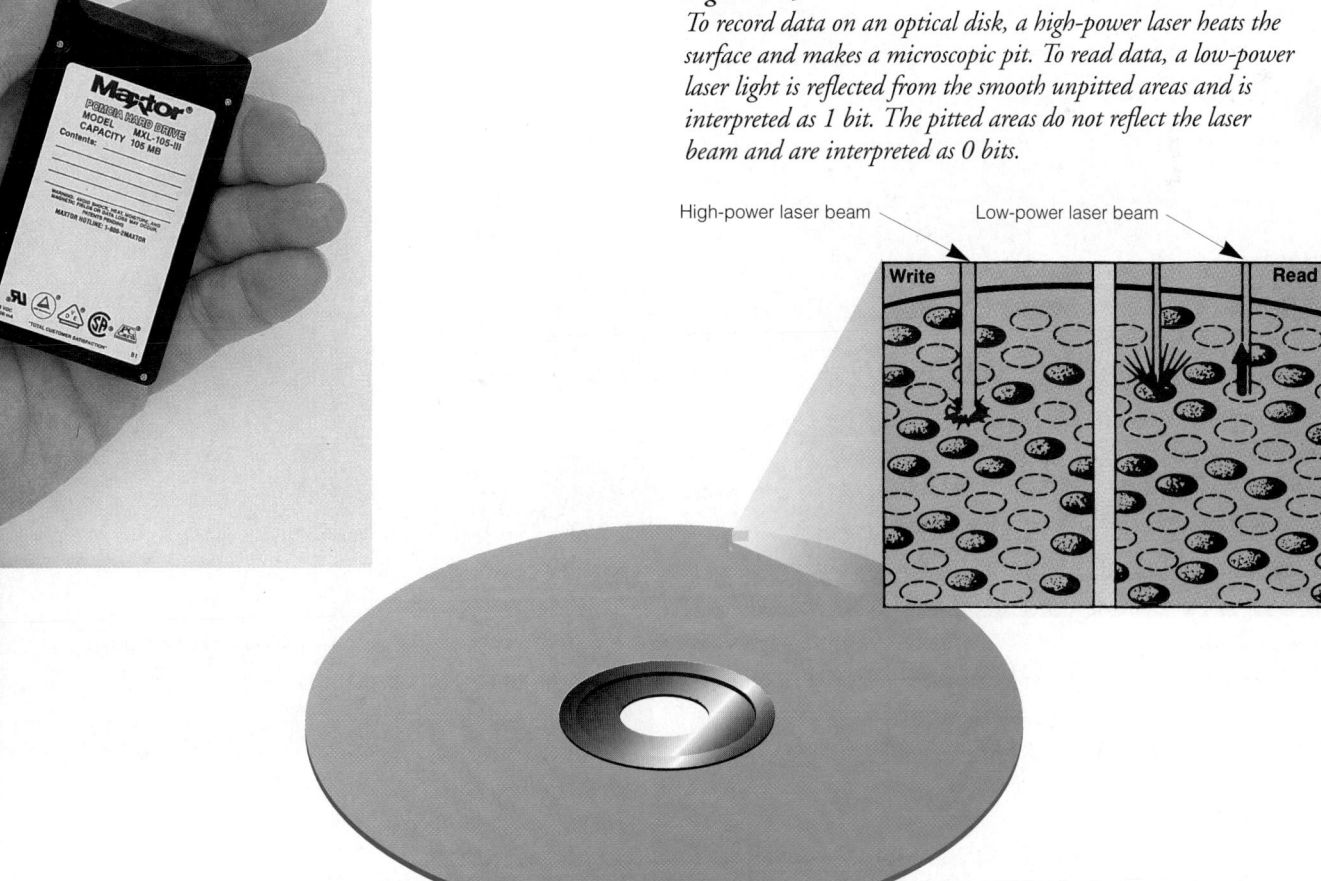

High-power laser beam   Low-power laser beam

Write   Read

A full-size, 14-inch optical disk can store 6.8 billion bytes of information. Up to 150 of these disks can be installed in automated disk library systems (called jukeboxes) that provide more than one trillion bytes (called a **terabyte**) of online storage. The smaller disks, just under five inches in diameter, can store more than 800 million bytes, or approximately 550 times the data that can be stored on a high-density 3^1/$_2$-inch diskette. That is enough space to store approximately 400,000 pages of typed data.

The smaller optical disk is called a **CD-ROM**, an acronym for compact disk read-only memory *(Figure 6-30)*. They use the same laser technology used for the CD-ROM disks that have become popular for recorded music. In fact, if a computer is equipped with a CD-ROM drive, a sound card, and speakers, audio CD-ROM disks can be played.

CD-ROM drives are often advertised as double-, triple-, or quadruple-speed drives. The ratings refer to how fast the drive can transfer data in relation to a standard established for CD-ROM drives used for multimedia applications. The original standard established a minimum transfer rate of 150 kilobytes per second (kbps). A double-speed drive can transfer data at 300 kbps, a triple-speed drive at 450 kbps, and a quadruple-speed drive at 600 kbps.

Most optical disks are prerecorded and cannot be modified by the user. These disks are used for applications such as an auto parts catalog where the information is changed only occasionally, such as once a month, and a new updated optical disk is created. Optical disk devices that provide for one-time recording are called **WORM** devices, an acronym for *write once, read many*. Erasable optical disk drives are just starting to be used. The most common erasable optical drives use **magneto-optical technology**, in which a magnetic field changes the polarity of a spot on the disk that has been heated by a laser.

Figure 6-30
A CD-ROM can store hundreds of times the information as can be stored on a diskette of similar size. Many reference materials, such as encyclopedias, catalogs, and even phone books, are now published on CD-ROM instead of paper.

Figure 6-31
Solid-state storage devices use rows of RAM chips to emulate a conventional rotating disk drive. This solid-state device can transfer data 15 to 20 times faster than a rotating disk system.

Because of their tremendous storage capacities, entire catalogs or reference materials can be stored on a single optical disk. Some people predict that optical disks will someday replace data now stored on film such as microfiche.

Solid-State Storage Devices

To the computer, solid-state storage devices act just like disk drives, only faster. As their name suggests, they contain no moving parts, only electronic circuits. **Solid-state storage devices** *(Figure 6-31)* use the latest in random access memory (RAM) technology to provide high-speed data access and retrieval. Rows of RAM chips provide megabytes of memory that can be accessed much faster than the fastest conventional disk drives. Solid-state storage devices are significantly more expensive than conventional disk drives offering the same

storage capacity. Unlike disk or tape systems, solid-state storage devices are volatile; if they lose power their contents are lost. For this reason, these devices are usually attached to emergency power backup systems.

Mass Storage Devices

Mass storage devices provide automated retrieval of data from a library of storage media such as tape or data cartridges. Mass storage is ideal for extremely large databases that require all information to be readily accessible even though any one portion of the database may be infrequently required. Mass storage systems take less room than conventional tape storage and can retrieve and begin accessing records within seconds. *Figure 6-32* shows a mass storage system that uses tape cartridges.

Figure 6-32
The inside of an automated mass storage system that uses tape cartridges. A robot arm with a camera mounted on top accesses and loads any one of thousands of tape cartridges in an average of 1½ seconds. Each cartridge is a 4" x 4" square and about 1" thick and can hold up to 200 megabytes of data. The tapes are stored in a circular cabinet referred to as a silo.

CHAPTER

SECONDARY

STORAGE

Special-Purpose Storage Devices

Several devices have been developed for special-purpose storage applications. Three of these are memory buttons, smart cards, and optical memory cards.

Memory buttons are small storage devices about the size of a dime that look like watch batteries *(Figure 6-33)*. The buttons can currently hold up to 8,000 characters of information but storage capacities are increasing rapidly. To read or update information in the button, the user touches the button with a small, pen-like probe attached to a hand-held terminal. An audible sound is generated to indicate that the read or write operation has been completed. The buttons are used in applications where information about an item must travel with the item. Examples are laboratory samples, shipping containers, and rental equipment.

Figure 6-34
Smart cards are credit card-sized devices that contain a microprocessor in the left center of the card. The microprocessor can store up to 128,000 bits of information.

Figure 6-33
Memory buttons can hold up to 8,000 characters of information. The buttons are used in applications where information about an item must travel with the item. The buttons can be read or updated using a hand-held device.

Figure 6-35
The optical card can store up to 1,600 pages of information and images. It is the size and thickness of a credit card.

Smart cards are the same size and thickness of a credit card and contain a thin microprocessor capable of storing recorded information *(Figure 6-34)*. When it is inserted into compatible equipment, the information on the smart card can be read and, if necessary, updated. A current user of smart cards is the U. S. Marine Corps, who issues the cards to recruits instead of cash. Each time a recruit uses the card, the transaction amount is subtracted from the previous balance. Other uses of the card include employee time and attendance tracking (instead of time cards) and security applications where detailed information about the card holder is stored in the card.

Optical memory cards can store up to 1,600 pages of text or images on a device the size of a credit card *(Figure 6-35)*. Applications include automobile records and the recording of personal and health-care data.

Summary of Secondary Storage

Secondary storage is used to store programs and data that are not currently being processed by the computer. This chapter discussed the various types of secondary storage used with computers. The chart in *Figure 6-36* provides a summary of the secondary storage devices covered. What you have learned about these devices and storage operations in general can now be added to what you have learned about the input, processing, and output operations to complete your understanding of the information processing cycle.

TYPE	DEVICE	DESCRIPTION
Magnetic Disk	Diskette	Thin, portable plastic storage media that is reliable and low cost.
	Hard disk	Fixed platter storage media that provides large storage capacity and fast access.
	RAID	Multiple small disks integrated into a single unit.
	Disk cartridge	Portable disk unit that provides security.
	Hard card	Hard disk on expansion slot circuit board.
	Removable disk	Older style disk unit with removable disk packs.
Magnetic Tape	Cartridge tape	Tape enclosed in rectangular plastic housing.
	Reel tape	$1/2$-inch tape on 300 to 3,600 foot reel.
Other Storage Devices	PC card	Removable 1.3-inch disks used on portable computers.
	Optical disk	High capacity disks use laser to read and record data.
	Solid-state	Simulate disks using RAM chips to provide high-speed access.
	Mass storage	Automated retrieval of storage media such as tape or data cartridges.
Special-Purpose Devices	Memory button	Stores data on chip in small metal cannister.
	Smart card	Thin microprocessor stores data in credit card-sized holder.
	Optical card	Text and images stored in credit card-sized holder.

Figure 6-36
A summary of secondary storage devices.

COMPUTERS AT WORK

American Express Opts for Optical Storage

American Express' billing operation was once drowning in a sea of paperwork. The AMEX Travel Related Services Company (TRS) was one of the last large credit card operations that still included the actual charge receipts with the monthly statement sent to the cardholder. That meant that each day, several million charge documents had to be processed and temporarily stored until the card holder's bill was prepared. The paper system was prone to errors and at one time, nearly 200 people were assigned to tracking down missing receipts. TRS could have eliminated the receipts like most charge card processors, but they felt that including the receipts was a service to their cardholders.

TRS solved their paperwork problem by implementing the world's largest transaction processing system using optical storage. With the new system, paper charge slips are handled only once when an image of the receipt is captured and stored on a write-once read-many (WORM) optical disk.

After they are recorded, the paper receipts are destroyed. Each 12-inch disk can store 100,000 images; the equivalent of six filing cabinets of paper. In a typical year, more than 5,000 WORM disks are used. At the time the image is captured, billing information is also recorded. When it is time to prepare a cardholder's monthly billing statement, the images are electronically sorted and printed along with the statement giving the cardholder written proof of the charge.

Not only does the system offer a unique service to the cardholders, but it costs TRS less than their previous way of processing receipts; nearly 25% less, according to TRS estimates. As their slogan says about their card, "don't leave home without it;" but as far as charge receipts go, don't worry, they'll send them to you in the mail.

Figure 6-37

IN THE FUTURE

Memory Cubes

In the not-too-distant future, you may be able to fit the equivalent of a small library in the palm of your hand. Professor Peter Rentzepis at the University of California Irvine campus has patented a laser device capable of recording 6.5 trillion bits of information on a piece of plastic the size of a sugar cube. That is roughly equal to one million novels.

The plastic cube is made of commercially available polystyrene plastic that has been chemically treated *(Figure 6-38)*. To record data, a single laser beam is split in two and directed toward the cube at right angles. Where the laser beams meet, the plastic molecules are altered and the color changes from clear to blue. Blue molecules are considered 1 bit and the clear, unaltered plastic molecules are considered 0 bits. To read information, a different colored laser beam is used. The reading laser beam only interacts with the blue molecules making them briefly emit a red light. Sensors read the red light and transmit a 1 bit to the computer.

Several obstacles need to be overcome before the memory cubes become commercially feasible. The first challenge is the size of the equipment necessary to record and read the cubes.

The smallest size so far is approximately one foot square. This may not seem that big but it is still much too large for the fastest growing segment of the computer market; personal computers. The second challenge is even more formidable; heat. Currently, the cubes need to stay at very low temperatures to retain their stored information. If the cubes are left at room temperature, they lose their information in a few hours. Even when they are cooled with liquid nitrogen, they only retain their data for a few months. These challenges are worth pursuing however, because of the memory cube's potential. In addition to storing tremendous amounts of data in a small space, the cubes are inexpensive and, unlike disk drives, have no moving parts.

Figure 6-38

File　　Edit　　Section　　Page　　Tools　　Options　　Help

What You Should Know

1. Main memory, also called primary storage, temporarily stores programs and data that are being processed. **Secondary storage**, also called **auxiliary storage**, stores programs and data when they are not being processed.

2. Most secondary storage devices provide a more permanent form of storage than main memory because they are nonvolatile; that is, data and programs stored on secondary storage devices are retained when the power is turned off. Secondary storage devices are used as both input and output devices. To meet the different needs of users, a variety of secondary storage devices are available.

3. A **magnetic disk** consists of a round platter whose surface is covered with a magnetic material. Magnetic disk offers high storage capacity, reliability, and the capability to directly access stored data. Several types of magnetic disk include diskettes, hard disks, and removable disk cartridges.

4. A **diskette** consists of a circular piece of thin mylar plastic (the actual disk), which is coated with an oxide material similar to that used on recording tape. Because the original diskettes were flexible, they were often called **floppy disks**, or *floppies,* terms that are still used. Because they are convenient, reliable, and inexpensive, diskettes are used as a principal secondary storage medium for personal computers. Diskettes are available in two different sizes (diameters); 3 1/2 inches and 5 1/4 inches.

5. Before a diskette can be used for secondary storage, it must be formatted. The **formatting** process prepares the diskette so that it can store data and includes defining the tracks, cylinders, and sectors on the surfaces of a diskette. A **track** is a narrow recording band forming a full circle around the diskette. A **cylinder** is defined as all tracks of the same number. A **sector** is a pie-shaped section of the diskette. A **cluster**, the smallest unit of diskette space used to hold data, consists of two to eight

track sectors. The formatting process also erases any data on the diskette, analyzes the diskette surface for any defective spots, and establishes a directory that will be used to record information about files stored on the diskette. On personal computers using the DOS operating system, the directory is called the **file allocation table** (**FAT**).

6. The amount of data you can store on a diskette depends on two factors: (1) the recording density; and (2) the number of tracks on the diskette.

7. The **recording density** is the number of bits that can be recorded on one inch of track on the diskette. This measurement is referred to as **bits per inch (bpi)**. Most drives store the same amount of data on the longer outside tracks as they do on the shorter inside tracks. Some newer drives, however, use **multiple zone recording** (**MZR**), which records data at the same density on all tracks, so the longer tracks can contain extra sectors.

8. The measurement of the number of tracks onto which data can be recorded is referred to as **tracks per inch (tpi)**. This number depends on the size of the diskette, the drive being used, and how the diskette was formatted.

9. Older **single-density** diskettes that could only be written on one side are no longer used. **Double-density** (DD) **diskettes** can store 360K for a 5 1/4-inch diskette and 720K for a 3 1/2-inch diskette. **High-density** (HD) **diskettes** can store 1.2 megabytes (million characters) on a 5 1/4-inch diskette and 1.44 megabytes on a 3 1/2-inch diskette. **Extended-density** (ED) 3 1/2-inch diskettes that can store 2.88 megabytes are also starting to be used. A **floptical diskette** combines optical and magnetic technology to achieve even higher storage rates.

10. When you read from or write to a diskette, a motor spins the circular plastic recording surface at approximately 360 revolutions per minute. A recording mechanism in the drive called the **read/write head** rests on the top and bottom surface of the rotating diskette, generating electronic impulses. The electronic impulses change the polarity, or alignment, of magnetic areas along a track on the disk.

11. When reading data from a diskette, the read/write head senses the magnetic areas that are recorded on the diskette along various tracks and transfers the data into main memory. The time required to access and retrieve data is called the access time. The access time for a diskette depends on three factors: **seek time, rotational delay** (also called **latency**), and **data transfer rate**.

12. With reasonable care, diskettes provide an inexpensive and reliable form of storage. Wear does take place, however, and a diskette will eventually become unreadable. To protect against loss, data should be copied onto other diskettes.

13. Hard disks provide larger and faster secondary storage capabilities than diskettes. **Hard disks** consist of rigid platters coated with an oxide material that allows data to be magnetically recorded on the surface of the platters. Most hard disks are permanently mounted inside the computer and are not removable like diskettes.

14. On minicomputers and mainframes, hard disks are sometimes called **fixed disks** because they cannot be removed like diskettes. They are also referred to as **direct-access storage devices (DASD)**.

15. Hard disks contain a spindle on which one or more disk platters are mounted. Like a diskette, hard disks must be formatted before they can be used to store data. Before a hard disk is formatted, it can be divided into separate areas called **partitions**, each of which can function as if it were a separate disk.

16. The storage capacity of hard drives is measured in megabytes, or millions of bytes, of storage. Some disk devices can store billions of bytes of information, called a **gigabyte**.

17. Storing data on hard disks is similar to storing data on diskettes. Hard disk read/write heads are attached to **access arms** that swing out over the disk surface to the correct track. The read/write heads float on a cushion of air and do not actually touch the surface of the disk. If some form of contamination is introduced or if the alignment of the read/write head is altered by something jarring the computer, the disk head can collide with and damage the surface of the disk. This event is known as a **head crash** and causes a loss of data.

18. Depending on the type of disk drive, data is physically organized in two ways. The **sector method** for physically organizing data on hard disks is similar to the method used for diskettes. With the **cylinder method**, all tracks of the same number on each recording surface are considered part of the same cylinder.

19. Some computers improve the apparent speed at which data is transferred to and from a disk by using a **disk cache**, an area of memory set aside for data most often read from the disk.

20. The flow of data to and from the hard disk is managed by electronic circuits called the hard disk controller. **Integrated Drive Electronics** (IDE) controllers can operate one or two disk drives. SCSI (**Small Computer System Interface**) controllers can support seven disk drives or any mix of up to seven SCSI devices.

21. **Data compression** reduces the storage requirements of data by substituting codes for repeating patterns of data. Compression ratios for *lossless compression,* in which no data is lost, average 2 to 1. *Lossy compression* gives up some accuracy for higher compression ratios (up to 200 to 1).

22. A group of integrated small disks is called a **RAID**, which stands for **redundant array of inexpensive disks**. In the simplest RAID method, called RAID level 1, one backup disk exists for each data disk. Because disks contain duplicate information, RAID level 1 is sometimes called **disk mirroring**. RAID levels beyond level 1 all spread data across more than one drive. Dividing a logical piece of data into smaller parts and writing those parts on multiple drives is called **striping**.

23. **Disk cartridges**, which can be inserted and removed from a computer, offer the storage and fast access features of hard disks and the portability of diskettes. The **Bernoulli disk cartridge** works with a special drive unit that uses a cushion of air to keep the flexible disk surface from touching the read/write head.

24. The **hard card** is a circuit board that has a hard disk built onto it. Hard cards provide an easy way to expand the storage capacity of a personal computer because the board can be installed into an expansion slot of the computer.

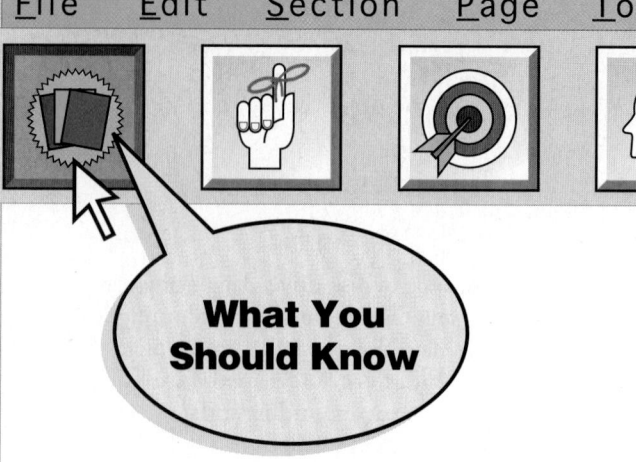

What You Should Know

25. **Removable disk devices** consist of the drive unit, which is usually in its own cabinet, and the removable recording media, called a **disk pack**.

26. To prevent the loss of disk data, two procedures should be performed on a regular basis; backup and defragmentation. **Backup** means creating a copy of important programs and data. When a file is stored in clusters that are not next to each other, the file is said to be **fragmented**. **Defragmentation** reorganizes the data stored on the disk so files are located in contiguous clusters.

27. **Magnetic tape** consists of a thin ribbon of plastic coated on one side with a material that can be magnetized to record the bit patterns that represent data. At one time the primary method of storing large amounts of data, magnetic tape still functions as a cost-effective way to store data that does not have to be accessed immediately, serves as the primary means of backup for most medium and large systems, and is often used to transfer data from one system to another.

28. A **cartridge tape** contains magnetic recording tape in a small, rectangular plastic housing. **Reel-to-reel tape devices** use two reels: a supply reel to hold the tape that will be read from or written to, and the take-up reel to temporarily hold portions of the supply reel tape as it is being processed.

29. Tape is considered a **sequential storage** media because the computer must record and read tape records one after another. **Tape density** is the number of bits that can be stored on an inch of tape. Some tape drives can operate in a high-speed streaming mode used to backup and restore hard disk drives. In the **streaming mode**, the tape records data in exactly the same byte-by-byte order as it appears on the hard disk. Another method of storing large amounts of data on tape is **digital audio tape (DAT)**. DAT uses **helical scan technology** to write data at much higher densities across the tape at an angle instead of down the length of the tape.

30. **PC cards** are small, credit card-sized cards that fit into PCMCIA expansion slots. Although they are only 10.5mm thick (about .4 inch), PC cards used for storage contain small rotating disk drives 1.3 inches in diameter that can contain over 200 megabytes of data.

31. Enormous quantities of information are stored on **optical disks** by using a laser to burn microscopic holes on the surface of a hard plastic disk. Up to 150 of these disks can be installed in automated disk libraries (called jukeboxes) that provide more than one trillion bytes (called a **terabyte**) of online storage. A smaller optical disk is called a **CD-ROM**, an acronym for compact disk-read only memory. Most optical disks are prerecorded and cannot be modified by the user. Optical disk devices that provide for one-time recording are called **WORM** devices, an acronym for write once, read many. The most common erasable optical devices use **magneto-optical technology**, in which a magnetic field changes the polarity of a spot on the disk that has been heated by a laser.

32. Solid-state storage devices contain no moving parts, only electronic circuits. **Solid-state storage devices** use the latest in random access memory (RAM) technology to provide high-speed data access and retrieval.

33. **Mass storage devices** provide automated retrieval of data from a library of storage media such as tape or data cartridges.

34. Several devices have been developed for special-purpose storage applications. **Memory buttons** are small storage devices about the size of a dime that look like watch batteries. The buttons are used in applications where information about an item must travel with the item. **Smart cards** are the same size and thickness of a credit card and contain a thin microprocessor capable of storing recorded information. Smart cards are used for employee time and attendance tracking and security applications where detailed information about the card holder is stored in the card. **Optical memory cards** can store up to 1,600 pages of text or images on a device the size of a credit card. Applications include automobile records and the recording of personal and health-care data.

le   **E**dit   **S**ection   **P**age   **T**ools   **O**ptions   **H**elp

Terms to Remember

access arms (6.10)
access time (6.7)
auxiliary storage (6.2)

backup (6.15)
Bernoulli disk cartridge (6.14)
bits per inch (bpi) (6.6)

cartridge tape (6.16)
CD-ROM (6.20)
cluster (6.4)
cylinder (6.4)
cylinder method (610)

data compression (6.11)
data transfer rate (6.8)
defragmentation (6.15)
digital audio tape (DAT) (6.18)
direct-access storage devices
    (DASD) (6.9)
disk cache (6.11)
disk cartridges (6.14)
disk mirroring (6.13)
disk pack (6.14)
diskette (6.3)
double-density (DD) diskettes (6.6)

extended-density (ED) diskettes (6.6)

file allocation table (FAT) (6.5)
fixed disks (6.9)
floppy disks (6.3)
floptical (6.7)
formatting (6.4)
fragmented (6.15)

gigabyte (6.10)

hard card (6.14)
hard disks (6.8)
head crash (6.10)
helical scan technology (6.18)
high-density (HD) diskettes (6.6)

Integrated Drive Electronics
    (IDE) (6.11)

latency (6.8)

magnetic disk (6.3)
magnetic tape (6.16)
magneto-optical technology (6.20)
mass storage devices (6.21)
memory buttons (6.21)
multiple zone recording (MZR) (6.6)

optical disks (6.19)
optical memory cards (6.22)

partitions (6.9)
PC cards (6.19)

RAID (6.13)
read/write head (6.7)
recording density (6.6)
redundant array of inexpensive disks
    (RAID) (6.13)
reel-to-reel tape devices (6.17)
removable disk (6.14)
rotational delay (6.8)

SCSI (6.11)
secondary storage (6.2)
sector (6.4)
sector method (6.10)
seek time (6.7)
sequential storage (6.17)
single-density (6.6)
Small Computer System Interface
    (SCSI) (6.11)
smart cards (6.22)
solid-state storage (6.21)
streaming mode (6.18)
striping (6.13)

tape density (6.18)
terabyte (6.20)
track (6.4)
tracks per inch (tpi) (6.6)

WORM (6.20)

File   Edit   Section   Page   Tools   Options   Help

Test Your Knowledge

Fill in the Blanks

1. _____ stores programs and data when they are not being processed.

2. A(n) _____ the most widely used storage medium for all types of computers, consists of a round platter whose surface is covered with a magnetic material.

3. _____, which consists of a thin ribbon of plastic, functions as a cost-effective way to store data that does not have to be accessed immediately.

4. Enormous quantities of information are stored on _____ by using a laser to burn microscopic holes on the surface of a hard plastic disk.

5. _____, which contain only electronic circuits, use the latest in random access memory (RAM) technology to provide megabytes of memory that can be accessed much faster than conventional disk drives.

Short Answer

1. How is data written to and read from a diskette?

2. What is access time? On what three factors does access time depend? Briefly explain each. Why is access time significantly faster for a hard disk than for a diskette?

3. What is data compression? How is lossless compression different from lossy compression? For what kind of data is each type of compression used?

4. What two procedures should be performed on a regular basis to prevent the loss of disk data? Explain each.

5. What do memory buttons, smart cards, and optical memory cards have in common? How are they different? For what purpose is each used?

Label the Figure

Instructions: Write the appropriate secondary storage device in each level of the pyramid chart shown below.

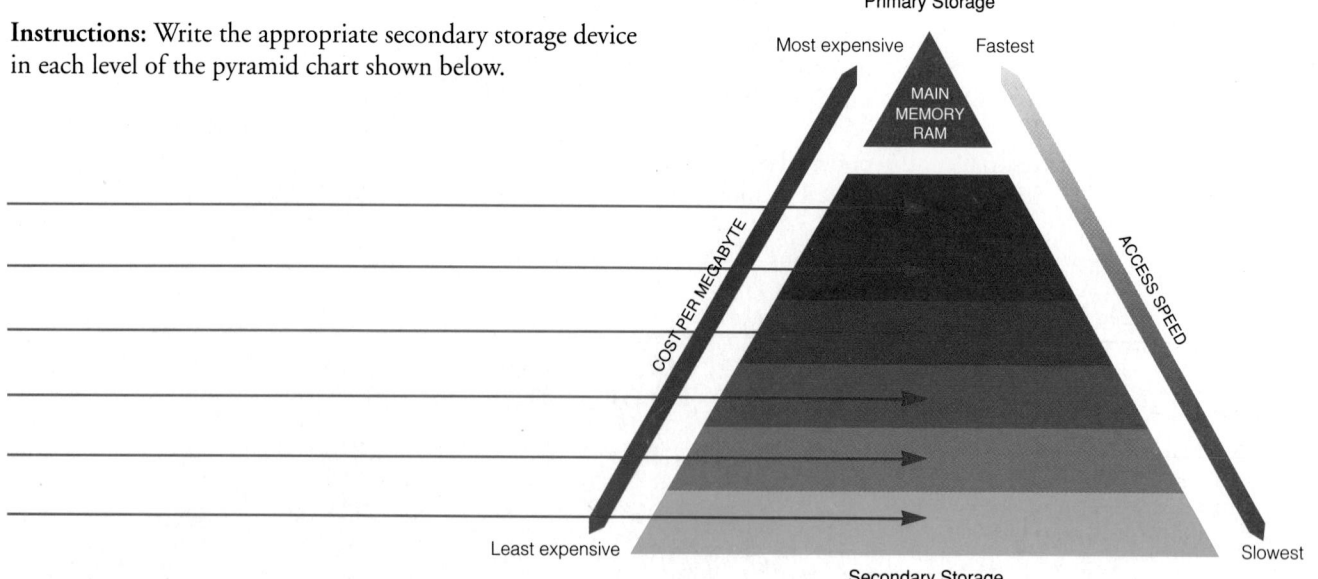

le   Edit   Section   Page   Tools   Options   Help

Points to Ponder

1

Magnetic disks are called direct-access storage devices because a computer system can go directly to a desired piece of data. Magnetic tape, on the other hand, is called a sequential access storage device because data must be read in sequence, one piece of data after another. Although magnetic tape is slower than magnetic disks, it is less expensive and well-suited for certain applications such as providing a backup. Think of at least one other business application for which a sequential access storage device, such as magnetic tape, is ideal. Explain why magnetic tape is appropriate for the application. Think of at least one business application for which magnetic tape is unsuitable. Explain why.

2

Instead of supplying potential customers with printed brochures, a few companies now provide a marketing diskette or CD-ROM that can be used by customers with personal computers. Some automobile manufacturers provide a marketing diskette or CD-ROM that lets PC users "walk around and kick the tires" of a vehicle by furnishing photographs, statistics, option packages, and pricing information. A personal computer video game is even supplied that allows buyers to "test drive" a vehicle by participating in a wildlife photo safari. Think of another product that you could market. What kind of information would you provide? Do you think potential sales of the product would justify the cost of producing the diskette or CD-ROM? Why or why not?

3

Some CD-ROM disks contain interactive children's "books." Using these disks, a computer can read the story in several different languages, reread selected passages, show the book's illustrations, allow children to ask questions about what is on the screen, and even reveal surprises when children use a mouse to click some part of a picture. Discuss the advantages and disadvantages of these CD-ROM disks compared to watching a television program or hearing a story read by someone else.

4

The National Gallery of Art in Washington, D.C. has recorded its entire collection on an optical disk, including works that, because of space limitations, are not normally displayed. The images on the disk offer startling clarity – even brush strokes are visible. Users of the disk can almost instantaneously display any work in the collection, locate works based on a wide range of criteria (artist, nationality, period, and so on), and magnify portions of a work on the screen. The optical disk is being made available to schools around the country. Why do you think optical disk was chosen to store the gallery's collection instead of some other secondary storage medium such as magnetic disk or magnetic tape? In what school classes do you think the disk will be used? How? As more museums take advantage of optical disk technology, do you think museum attendance will decline? Why or why not?

5

Despite the risk of data loss, a study has shown that less than 35 percent of all companies, and less than 20 percent of small companies, have backup policies. Of companies that do have backup policies, more than one-quarter had experienced a computer crash in the past. It is estimated that data loss costs American companies approximately $4 billion each year. Why do you think so few companies backup their data? If you were the CEO of a large company, what backup policy would you establish? How would you make sure your policy was carried out?

6

Recently out of college, you have just been hired by Wiley's Widgets, LTD. Although Wiley's Widgets uses computers to produce letters, memorandums, and spreadsheets, much to your surprise, you find that all of the employee, customer, and inventory records are stored on paper in file cabinets. Your coworkers tell you that this is the way Wiley's Widgets has kept its records since the company was founded in 1865, and that old Mr. Wiley hates change. One day as you are riding the elevator up to your office, you bump into Mr. Wiley and mention the benefits of saving records using some form of computer secondary storage. Mr. Wiley is intrigued and wants to hear more. Write a memo to Mr. Wiley describing the advantages and, because Mr. Wiley is no fool, any disadvantages in using some type of secondary storage to store company records. What form of secondary storage would you recommend? Why?

File   Edit   Section   Page   Tools   Options   Help

 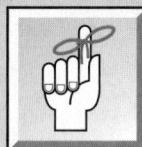  

Out and About

1. Some organizations, such as insurance companies, banks, libraries, and college registrars, are *information-intensive,* meaning that they must keep track of and manipulate large amounts of data. Visit an information-intensive organization and interview someone responsible for maintaining the organization's data. What are the organization's storage requirements? What type of secondary storage medium is used? Why? Have there ever been any problems with secondary storage? If so, how were the problems remedied? What type of backup procedures are employed?

2. The price of diskettes varies depending on such things as diskette size, recording density, the diskette manufacturer, and whether or not the diskette is already formatted for an Apple or IBM-compatible personal computer. Visit a store that sells computer supplies and compare the price of the least expensive diskettes to the price of the most expensive diskettes. What factors account for the difference in price? Which diskettes are recommended by the store's salesperson? Why? If you were buying diskettes for your own personal computer, which ones would you purchase? Why?

3. Because many companies store large amounts of information on hard disks that are permanently mounted inside the computer, the problem of data security has become an important issue. No companies can afford to have sensitive information on customers or product development stolen by industrial spies or dissatisfied employees. Visit a large firm and interview an employee on data security. How are records protected? Who has access to sensitive data? Have there ever been problems with data security? If so, what measures have been taken to make sure the problems do not recur?

4. As a result of the expanding storage requirements of some software and graphic files, new technologies are being developed that offer even greater secondary storage. These technologies include flash memory cards, glass disks, glass-ceramic disks, and "wet" hard drives. Using current computer magazines, prepare a report on one or more of these new technologies. What does the technology entail? What benefits does it offer? Why? When is the technology likely to be available for general use?

5. Visit a computer store and obtain information on the different types of hard disk drives available for personal computers. Summarize your findings and include data on price, storage capacity, and access speed. Calculate the cost per megabyte of storage for each drive. If you have a personal computer, which type of hard disk drive do you think is best suited for your current needs? Do you think the same disk drive will be adequate five years from now? Why or why not?

6. Many people feel that we have only begun to take advantage of smart card technology. In addition to the uses described in this chapter, smart cards that store the medical histories of the cardholders are being tested in New York, and smart cards have taken the place of food stamps for some residents of Dayton, Ohio. Visit a library and research smart cards. How much information can they contain? How do they work? In what applications have they been used? Why? How may smart cards be used in the future?

le   Edit   Section   Page   Tools   Options   Help

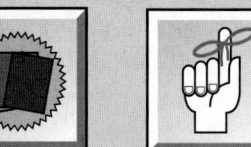    

In the Lab

Windows Labs

1 **Formatting a Diskette**   With Program Manager on the screen, double-click the Main group icon. Double-click the File Manager program-item icon. Click the Maximize button to maximize the window. Insert a diskette into drive A other than the one you used in earlier Labs. (*Caution:* Formatting erases all information on a diskette.) Select the Disk menu and choose Format Disk. If necessary, change the displayed capacity of the diskette (see page 6.6) by clicking the Capacity drop-down list box arrow and selecting the appropriate capacity from the list. Choose the OK button. If a confirmation dialog box displays, choose the Yes button. As Windows formats the diskette, it displays a percentage complete message *(Figure 6-39)*. When the formatting process is complete, Windows displays a Format Complete dialog box. Choose the No button in this dialog box. Remove the diskette from drive A. Put your name on a label and place it on the diskette. Close File Manager by clicking its Control-menu box.

2 **Managing Files on a Disk**   Open the File Manager window as described above in Windows Lab 1. Maximize the File Manager window. Perform the following tasks: (1) Insert the diskette containing your Windows Labs from previous chapters into drive A. Click the drive A icon in the File Manager window to display files on drive A in the directory window. If you do not see your windows labs, click the subdirectory name containing these files. Select the file win2-2.wri by clicking it. If you do not have a copy of win2-2.wri, ask your instructor for a copy. (2) Select the File menu and choose the Copy command. In the Copy dialog box, type win2-2a.wri and choose the OK button. Notice that win2-2a.wri, an exact copy of win2-2.wri, now displays in the

directory window *(Figure 6-40)*. (3) Select the file win2-2a.wri by clicking it. Select the File menu and choose the Rename command. In the Rename dialog box, type win6-2.wri and choose the OK button. Notice that the name of win2-2a.wri has changed to win6-2.wri in the directory window *(Figure 6-41* on the next page). (4) Select the file win6-2.wri by clicking it. Select the File menu and choose the Print command. Choose the OK button in each Print dialog box that displays. (5) Select the file win6-2.wri by clicking it. Select the File menu and choose the Delete command. In the Delete dialog box, choose the OK button. Choose the Yes button in the Confirm File Delete dialog box. Notice that the file win6-2.wri is no longer in the directory window. (6) Select the File menu and choose the Undelete command to display the Microsoft Undelete dialog box. Click the filename ?IN6-2.WRI to select it *(Figure 6-42* on the next page). Click the Undelete button ⬜ . Type w as the first character of the filename and choose the OK button. Close the Microsoft Undelete dialog box. Notice that the file win6-2.wri once again displays in the directory window. Close File Manager by clicking its Control-menu box.

3 **Shelly Cashman Series Secondary Storage Lab**   Follow the instructions in Windows Lab 2 in Chapter 1 on page 1.30 to display the Shelly Cashman Series Labs screen.

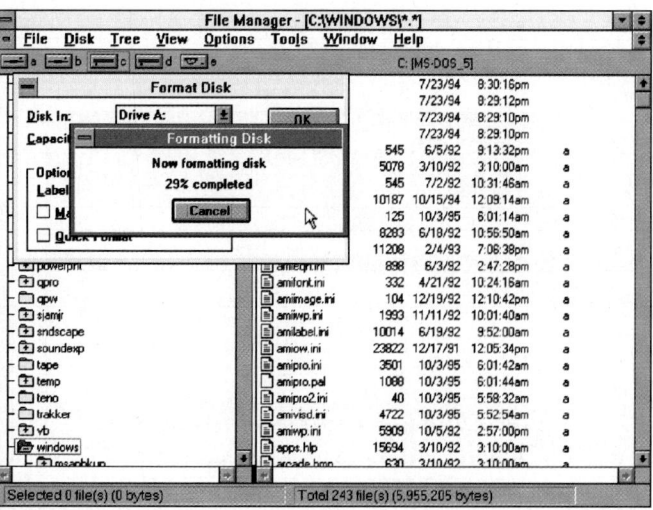

Figure 6-39

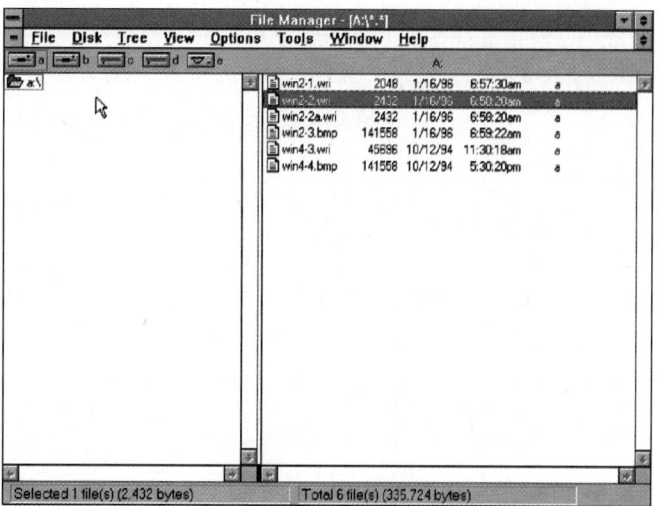

Figure 6-40

File   Edit   Section   Page   Tools   Options   Help

In the Lab (continued)

Select Secondary Storage by pointing to it and clicking the left mouse button. When the initial Secondary Storage Lab screen displays, carefully read the objectives. With your printer turned on, point to the Print Questions button and click the left mouse button. Fill out the top of the Questions sheet and answer the questions as you step through the Secondary Storage Lab.

4 **Using File Manager Help** Open File Manager and maximize its window as described in Windows Lab 1 on the previous page. Select the Help menu and choose the Search for Help on command. Perform the following tasks: (1) Type changing drives and press the ENTER key twice. Read and print the information. Choose the Search button. (2) Repeat the procedure in Step 1 for these topics: selecting files, copying files, renaming files, deleting files, and formatting disks. Close the Help window. Close File Manager.

DOS Labs

1 **Formatting a Diskette** Determine the byte capacity of your diskette; that is, it is either 360K, 720K, 1.2M, or 1.44M (see page 6.6). At the DOS prompt, type format a:/f:nnnn, where nnnn is the capacity of the diskette in kilobytes or megabytes. Press the ENTER key. Insert a diskette into drive A other than the one you used in earlier Labs and press the ENTER key. (*Caution:* Formatting erases all information on a diskette.) As DOS formats the diskette, it displays a percent complete message. Enter your last name as the volume label. When prompted to format another diskette, type n and press the ENTER key. Remove the diskette, put your name on a label and place it on the diskette.

2 **Managing Files on a Disk** Insert the diskette containing your DOS Labs into drive A. At the DOS prompt, perform the following tasks: (1) Type a: and press the ENTER key to change the default to drive A. (2) Type dir and press the ENTER key. Press PRINT SCREEN to print the screen. (3) Type copy dos2-1 dos 2-1a and press the ENTER key to make a copy of the source file. If you do not have a copy of dos2-1, ask your instructor for a copy. (4) Type ren dos2-1a dos6-2 and press the ENTER key to rename the file. (5) Print the file dos6-2 by typing print dos6-2 and pressing the ENTER key twice. (6) Type del dos6-2 and press the ENTER key to remove the file. Type dir and press ENTER to view the file names. (7) Type undelete and press ENTER. At the Undelete prompt for the file ?OS6-2, type y and then type d as the first character of the filename. Type dir and press the ENTER key to view the file names. Press the PRINT SCREEN key.

3 **Using the Question Mark to Obtain Help** Clear the screen. Type copy /? and press the ENTER key to display help on the COPY command. Press PRINT SCREEN. Use this same technique to obtain help on: REN, DEL, UNDELETE, and FORMAT. Print each command's help.

Online Lab

1 **Using an Electronic Encyclopedia** Using one of the two online services you selected in Chapter 1, connect to the service and perform the following tasks: (1) Search the online service for the Encyclopedia section. (2) Select a topic related to computers or the use of computers in your field of study and print the information.

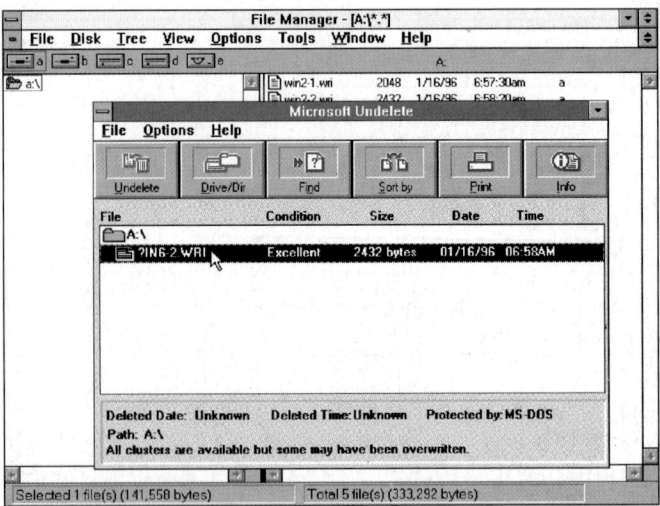

Figure 6-41   *Figure 6-42*

Communications and Networks

7

Objectives

After completing this chapter, you will be able to:

- Describe several examples of how communications technology is used

- Define the term communications

- Describe the basic components of a communications system

- Describe the various transmission media used for communications channels

- Describe the different types of line configurations

- Describe how data is transmitted

- Identify and explain the communications equipment used in a communications system

- Describe the functions performed by communications software

- Explain the two major categories of networks, and describe three common network configurations

- Describe how bridges and gateways are used to connect networks

Computers are well recognized as important computing devices. They should also be recognized as important communications devices. It is now possible for a computer to communicate with other computers anywhere in the world. This capability, sometimes referred to as connectivity, allows users to quickly and directly access data and information that otherwise would have been unavailable or that probably would have taken considerable time to acquire. Banks, retail stores, airlines, hotels, and many other businesses use computers for communications purposes. Personal computer users communicate with other personal computer users. They can also access special databases available on larger computers to quickly and conveniently obtain information such as weather reports, stock market data, airline schedules, news stories, or even theater and movie reviews.

This chapter provides an overview of communications with an emphasis on the communication of data and information. The chapter explains some of the terminology, equipment, procedures, and applications that relate to computers and their use as communications devices. How computers can be joined together into computer networks is discussed. Networks multiply the power of individual computers by allowing users to communicate and share hardware, software, and information.

Examples of How Communications Is Used

*T*he ability to instantly and accurately communicate information is changing the way people do business and interact with each other. Advances in communications software and hardware now allow people to easily transmit voice and data communications around the world. The following applications rely on communications technology:

- Electronic mail
- Voice mail
- Teleconferencing
- FAX
- Groupware
- Telecommuting
- Electronic data interchange (EDI)
- Global positioning systems (GPS)
- Bulletin board systems (BBS)
- Online services

Electronic Mail

Electronic mail, also described in detail in Chapter 2, is the capability to use computers to transmit messages to and receive messages from other computer users. The other users may be on the same computer network or on a separate computer system reached through the use of communications equipment. Each E-mail user has an address to which mail can be sent. The address acts as a mailbox and accumulates messages. Most E-mail programs support distribution lists that send messages to several individuals at the same time.

Many organizations with internal computer networks provide E-mail for employees. Online service providers such as Prodigy and America Online also offer E-mail capabilities.

Voice Mail

Voice mail can be considered verbal electronic mail. Made possible by the latest computerized telephone systems, voice mail reduces the problem of telephone tag, where two people trying to reach each other wind up leaving a series of messages to please call back. With voice mail, the caller can leave a message, similar to leaving a message on an answering machine. The difference between voice mail and an answering machine is that with a voice mail system the caller's message is digitized so it can be stored on a disk like other computer data. This allows the party who was called to hear the message later (by converting it to an audio form) and also, if desired, add a reply or additional comments and forward the message to someone else who has access to the system.

Teleconferencing

Teleconferencing once meant three or more people sharing a phone conversation. Today, however, **teleconferencing** usually means video conferencing, the use of computers and television cameras to transmit video images and the sound of the participant(s) to a remote location that has compatible equipment *(Figure 7-1)*. Special software and equipment is used to digitize and compress the video image so it can be transmitted along with the audio over standard communications channels. Although the video image is not as clear for moving objects as commercial television, it does contribute to the discussion and is adequate for nonmoving objects such as charts and graphs. Video conferencing was originally developed for larger groups of people who had to use a room specially outfitted with video conferencing equipment. More recently, desktop video equipment has been developed to allow individual users to visually communicate with other people within their building or at remote locations *(Figure 7-2)*.

Figure 7-1
Video conferencing is used to transmit and receive video and audio signals over standard communications channels. This meeting is being transmitted to a video conference center at another location. The people at the other location are also being recorded and transmitted and can be seen on the TV monitor.

Figure 7-2
Desktop video conferencing equipment allows individual users to communicate with other employees on their computer network. Some systems can also connect to remote locations.

FAX

Facsimile, or **FAX,** equipment is used to transmit a reproduced image of a document over phone lines *(Figure 7-3).* The document can contain text or graphics, can be hand-written, or be a photograph. FAX machines optically scan the document and convert the image into digitized data that is transmitted over a phone line. A FAX machine at the receiving end converts the digitized data back into its original image. FAX equipment is available as stand-alone machines or as part of data communications equipment called modems that are discussed later in this chapter. Using FAX software, the FAX modems can directly transmit computer-prepared documents or documents that have been digitized with the use of a scanner. FAX equipment is having an increasing impact on the way people transmit documents. Many documents that were previously sent through the mail are now sent by FAX. With the speed and convenience of a phone call, a document sent by FAX can be transmitted anywhere in the world.

Groupware

Groupware is a loosely defined term applied to software that helps multiple users work together by sharing information.

Groupware is part of a broad concept called **workgroup technology** that includes equipment and software that help group members communicate and manage their activities.

Some software applications discussed separately in this section, including E-mail and video conferencing, can also be considered groupware. Other groupware applications include:
- **Group Editing**   The capability for multiple users to revise a document with each set of revisions separately identified.
- **Group Scheduling**   A group calendar that tracks the time commitments of multiple users and helps schedule meetings when necessary.
- **Group Decision Support**   A decision support system that relies on the input of multiple users.
- **Workflow Software**   Software that automates repetitive processes such as processing an insurance claim, in which multiple persons must review and approve a document.

One of the more widely used groupware packages is Lotus Notes *(Figure 7-4).* Notes uses a shared database approach to groupware. In addition, Notes offers E-mail and a programming language that can be used to develop customized groupware applications.

Figure 7-3
A facsimile (FAX) machine can send and receive copies of documents to and from any location where there is phone service and another FAX machine.

Figure 7-4
Notes from Lotus Corporation is one of the most widely used groupware packages. Notes allows users to share information and work together on documents. Notes also includes E-mail capabilities.

Groupware and workgroup technology are still relatively new ideas and, other than E-mail, are not yet widely used. The need for small staffs to work quickly and efficiently on changing job assignments will, however, increase the use of groupware.

Telecommuting

Telecommuting refers to the capability of individuals to work at home and communicate with their offices by using personal computers and communications channels. With a personal computer, an employee can access the main computer at the office. He or she can read and answer electronic mail. An employee can access databases and can transmit completed projects. Some predict that by the year 2000, ten percent of the work force will be telecommuters. Telecommuting provides flexibility, allowing companies and employees to increase productivity and, at the same time, meet the needs

of individual employees. Some of the advantages of telecommuting include reducing the time used to commute to the office each week; eliminating the need to travel during poor weather conditions; providing a convenient and comfortable work environment for disabled employees or workers recovering from injuries or illnesses; and allowing employees to combine work with personal responsibilities such as child care.

Electronic Data Interchange (EDI)

Electronic data interchange (EDI) is the capability to electronically transfer documents from one business to another. EDI is frequently used by large companies for routine transactions such as purchase orders and billing. In some businesses, such as the automotive industry, EDI is the standard way of doing repeat business with suppliers. EDI offers a number of

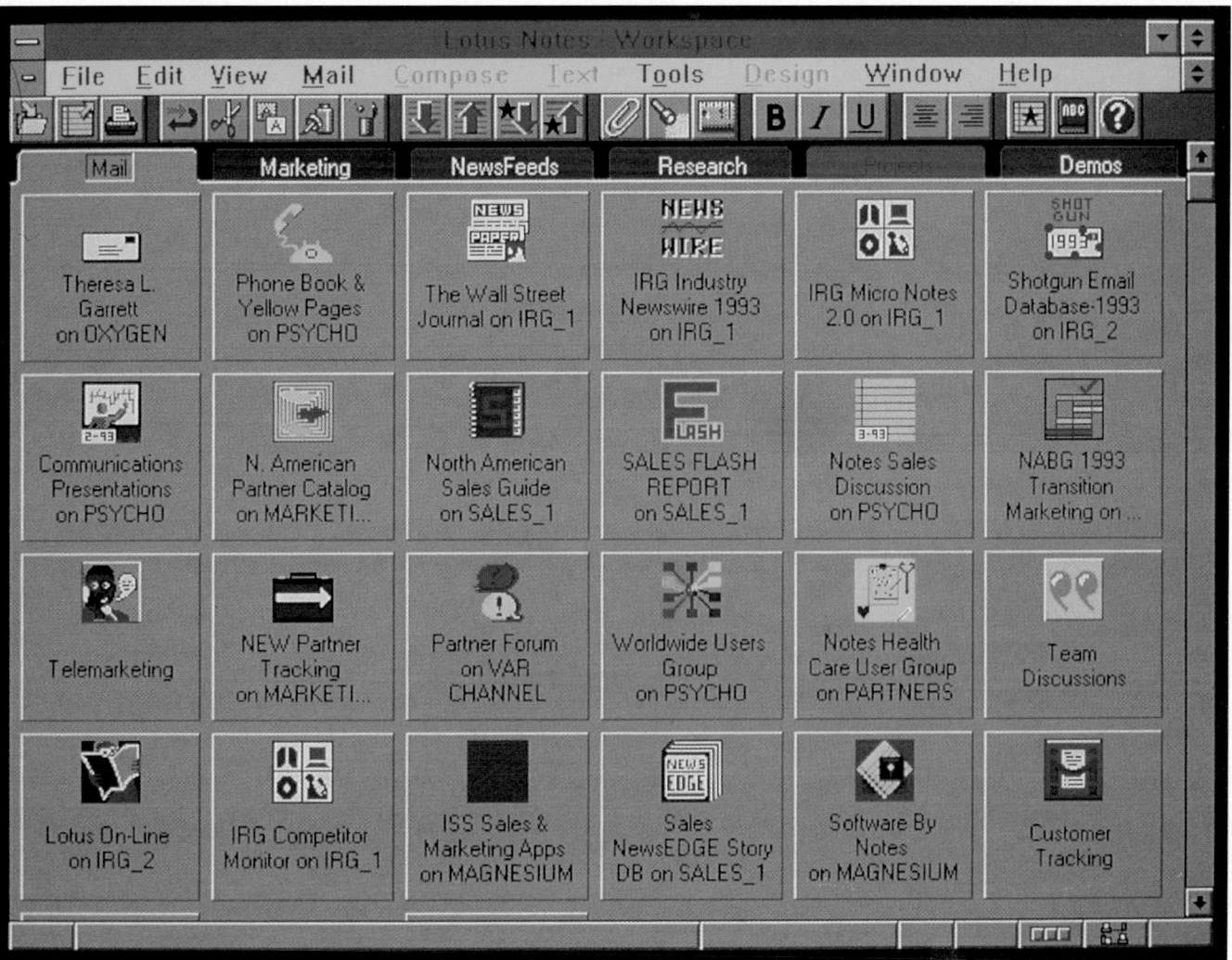

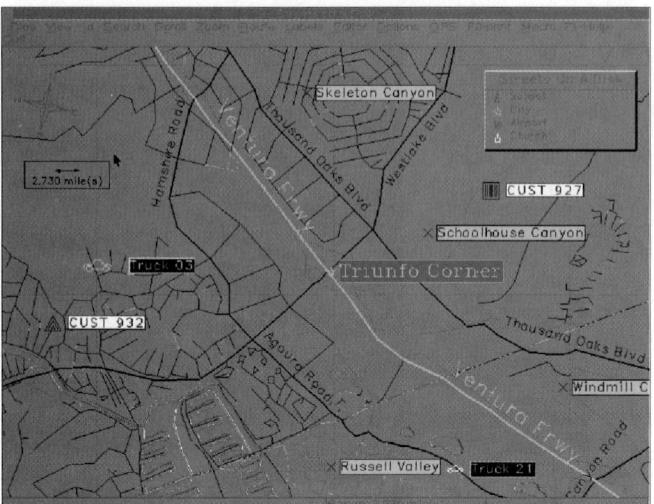

Figure 7-5
Satellite mapping software works with global positioning system (GPS) equipment to help users locate their exact location on a displayed map. Maps are available for most metropolitan areas.

advantages over paper documents, including the following:

- Lower transaction costs
- Reduced time to transmit documents
- Reduced data entry errors because data need not be reentered at the receiving end
- Reduced paper flow

Some companies have developed sophisticated EDI applications where orders from a customer are automatically created based on sales or inventory levels, transmitted to a vendor electronically, and shipped to the customer without any human intervention.

Global Positioning Systems (GPS)

A **global positioning system** (GPS) uses satellites to determine the geographic location of earth-based GPS equipment. Depending on the equipment used, a GPS system can be accurate up to 100 feet. GPS systems are often used for tracking and navigation of all types of vehicles; cars, trucks,

BBS	MODEM NUMBER	DESCRIPTION	LOCATION
America's Suggestion Box	516-471-8625	Collects and distributes consumer feedback	Ronkonkoma, NY
Automobile Consumer Services	513-624-0552	New and used car pricing reports	Cincinnati, OH
Boardwatch	303-973-4222	Lists of BBSs maintained by Boardwatch magazine	Denver, CO
BMUG BBS	510-849-2684	Macintosh support and information	Berkeley, CA
Exec PC	414-789-4210	Largest BBS in United States	Elm Grove, WI
FEDLINK ALIXII	202-707-4888	US government information	Washington, D.C.
NASA Spacelink	205-895-0028	NASA space information and history	Huntsville, AL
SBA Online	800-697-4636	Advice for small business owners	Washington, D.C.
The Well	415-332-6106	Whole Earth conferencing system	Sausalito, CA
WeatherBank	800-827-2727	Weather forecasts for any city	SaltLake City, UT

Figure 7-6
A partial list of the major bulletin boards in the United States.

boats, and planes. Small GPS systems have even been designed for use in portable personal computers. A number of companies have developed map software to work with GPS systems *(Figure 7-5)*. The map software can either be used by itself to find locations or to measure distances between two points. When the software is used with GPS equipment, the user's exact location and direction of travel is displayed on the map.

Bulletin Board Systems (BBS)

A **bulletin board system** (BBS) allows users to communicate with one another and share information *(Figure 7-6)*. While some bulletin boards provide specific services such as buying and selling used computer equipment, many bulletin boards function as electronic clubs for special-interest groups and are used to share information about hobbies as diverse as stamp collecting, music, genealogy, and astronomy. Some BBSs are strictly social; users meet new friends and conduct conversations by entering messages through their keyboards. Many hardware and software vendors have set up BBSs to provide online support for their products.

Online Services

Online services, sometimes called **information services**, include information and services provided to users who subscribe to the service for a fee. Typically, the user accesses the services by using communications equipment and software to temporarily connect to the service provider's computer. Services that are available include electronic banking, shopping, news, weather, hotel and airline reservations, and investment information. Some online services provide very specific information such as stock market data. Other online services, such as Prodigy *(Figure 7-7)* and America Online, provide a wide variety of information. *Figure 7-8* is a list of major online service providers.

Figure 7-7
The Prodigy online information service offers the latest news, weather, sports, and financial information along with shopping, entertainment, and electronic mail.

NAME	DESCRIPTION	PHONE
America Online	Fastest growing provider; news, weather, shopping, finance, travel, and more	800-827-6364
Prodigy	Largest online provider; news, weather, shopping, finance, travel, and more	800-776-3449
CompuServe	Most comprehensive of all services; business oriented	800-848-8199
Delphi	Internet access and services	800-695-4005
GEnie	News plus professional and technical databases	800-638-9636
Imagination	Games and entertainment	800-743-7721
eWorld	General-interest service started by Apple	800-775-4556
Dow Jones	Finance and business news	800-522-3567

Figure 7-8
The names and information phone numbers of major online information service providers.

What Is Communications?

Communications, sometimes called **data communications**, refers to the transmission of data and information over a communications channel, such as a standard telephone line, between one computer or terminal and another computer. Other terms such as telecommunications and teleprocessing are also used to describe communications.

Telecommunications describes any type of long-distance communications including television signals. **Teleprocessing** refers to the use of a terminal or a computer and communications equipment to access computers and computer files located elsewhere. As communications technology continues to advance, the distinction between these terms is blurred. Therefore, most people refer to the process of transmitting data or information of any type as data communications, or simply communications.

A Communications System Model

Figure 7-9 shows the basic model for a communications system. This model consists of the following equipment:
- A computer or a terminal
- Communications equipment that sends (and can usually receive) data
- The communications channel over which the data is sent
- Communications equipment that receives (and can usually send) data
- Another computer

The basic model also includes communications software. If two computers are communicating with each other, compatible communications software is required on each system. If a computer is communicating with a terminal, communications are directed either by a separate program running on the computer or by the computer operating system. A **communications channel**, also called a **communications line**, **communications link**, or **data link**, is the path the data follows as it is transmitted from the sending equipment to the receiving equipment in a communications system. These channels are made up of one or more transmission media.

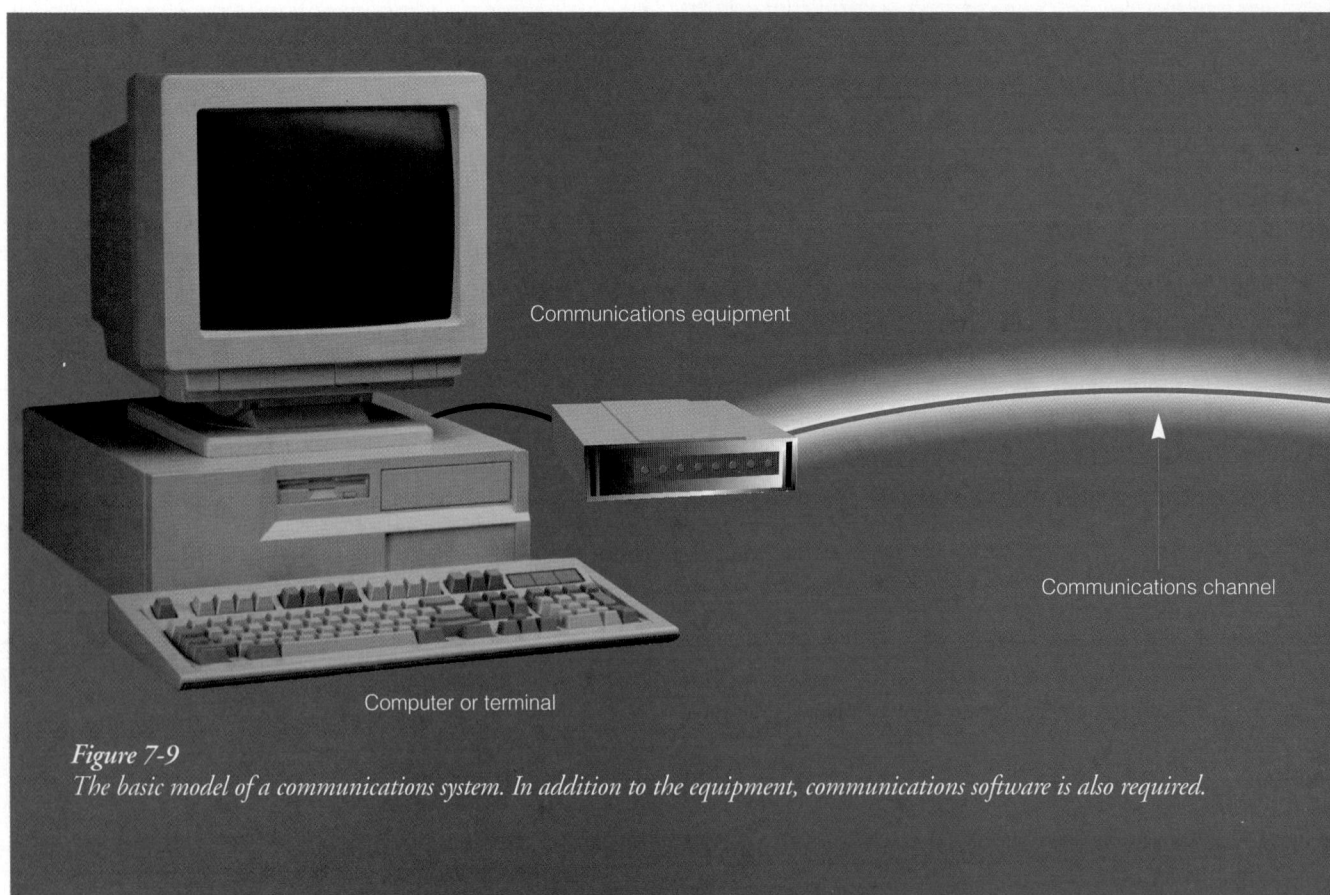

Communications equipment

Communications channel

Computer or terminal

Figure 7-9
The basic model of a communications system. In addition to the equipment, communications software is also required.

Transmission Media

Transmission media are the materials or technologies that are used to establish the communications channel. Two types of transmission media include those that use some type of physical cabling and those that use wireless technology. Cabling media include twisted pair wire, coaxial cable, and fiber-optics cable. Wireless technology includes microwaves, radio waves, or light waves.

Twisted Pair Wire

Twisted pair wire *(Figure 7-10)* consists of pairs of copper wires that are twisted together. To insulate and identify the wires, each wire is covered with a thin layer of colored plastic. Twisted pair wire is commonly used for telephone lines and to connect personal computers with one another. It is an inexpensive transmission medium, and it can be easily strung from one location to another. A disadvantage of twisted pair wire is that it can be affected by outside electrical interference generated by machines such as fans or air conditioners. While this interference may be acceptable on a voice call, it can garble the data as it is sent over the line, causing transmission errors to occur.

Coaxial Cable

A **coaxial cable** is a high-quality communications line used in offices, and it can be laid underground or underwater. Coaxial cable consists of a copper wire conductor surrounded by a nonconducting insulator that is in turn surrounded by a woven metal outer conductor, and finally a plastic outer coating *(Figure 7-11)*. Because of its more heavily insulated construction, coaxial cable is not susceptible to electrical interference and can transmit data at higher data rates over longer distances than twisted pair wire.

The two types of coaxial cable, named for the transmission techniques they support, are baseband and broadband. **Baseband** coaxial cable carries one signal at a time. The signal, however, can travel very fast – in the area of ten million bits per second for the first 1,000 feet. The speed drops significantly as the length of the cable increases, and special equipment is needed to amplify (boost) the signal if it is transmitted more than approximately one mile.

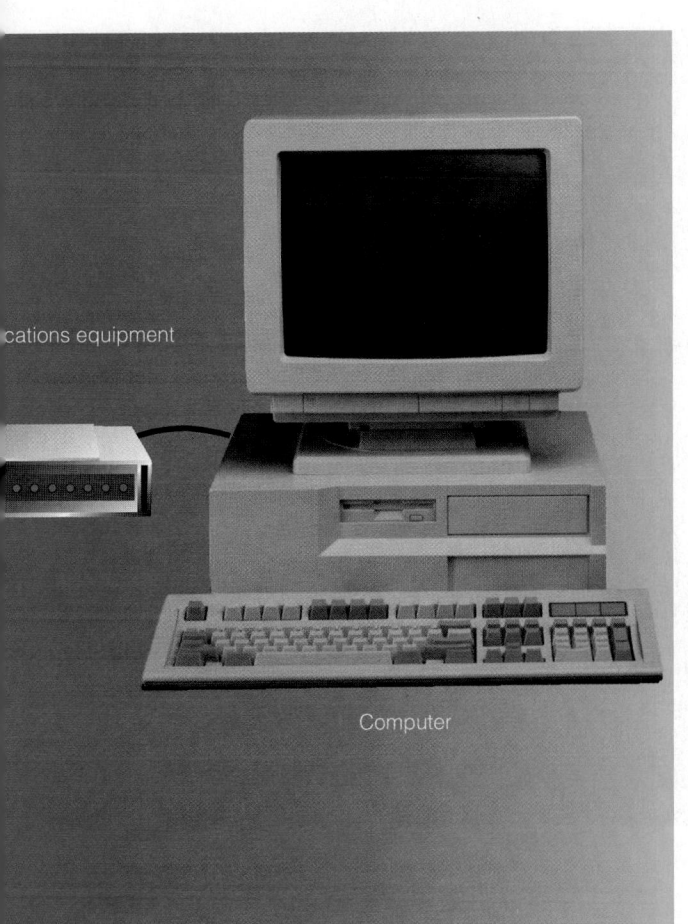

cations equipment

Computer

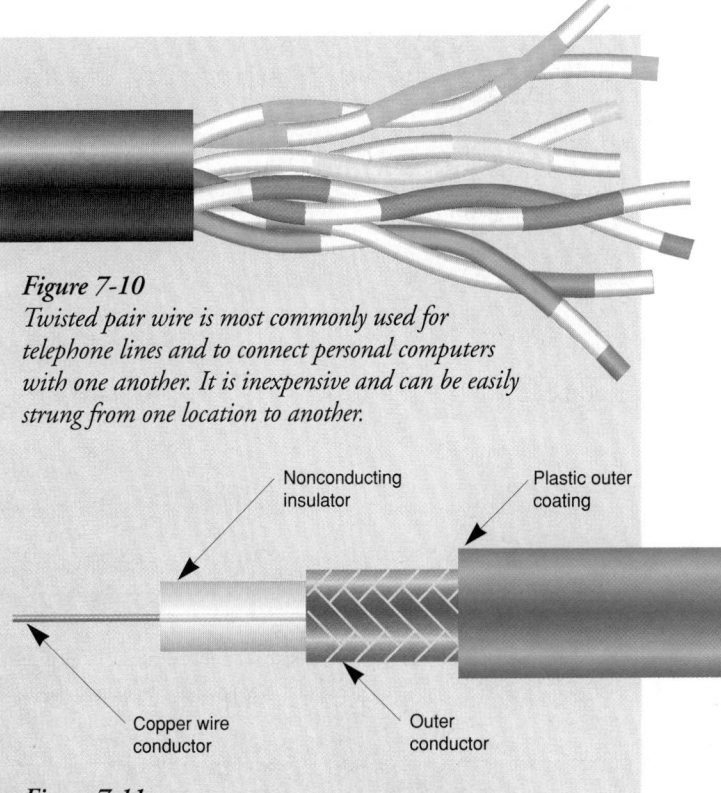

Figure 7-10
Twisted pair wire is most commonly used for telephone lines and to connect personal computers with one another. It is inexpensive and can be easily strung from one location to another.

Nonconducting insulator

Plastic outer coating

Copper wire conductor

Outer conductor

Figure 7-11
On coaxial cable, data travels through the copper wire conductor. The outer conductor is made of woven metal mesh that acts as an electrical ground.

Broadband coaxial cable can carry multiple signals at one time. It is similar to cable TV where a single cable offers a number of channels to the user. A particular advantage of broadband channels is that data, audio, and video transmission can occur over the same line.

Fiber Optics

Fiber-optics cable uses smooth, hair-thin strands of glass to conduct light with high efficiency *(Figure 7-12)*. The major advantages of fiber optics over wire cables include substantial weight and size savings and increased speed of transmission. Another advantage is that fiber-optic cable is not affected by electrical and magnetic fields. A single fiber-optic cable can carry several hundred thousand voice communications simultaneously. The disadvantages of fiber-optic cable are that it is more expensive than twisted pair or coaxial cable and it is more difficult to install and modify than metal wiring. Fiber optics is frequently being used in new voice and data installations.

Figure 7-12
The fiber-optic cable (right) can transmit as much information as the 1,500-pair copper-wire cable (left).

Figure 7-13
The round antenna on this tower is used for microwave transmission. Microwave transmission is limited to line-of-sight. Antennas are usually placed 25 to 75 miles apart.

Microwave Transmission

Microwaves are radio waves that can be used to provide high-speed transmission of both voice and data. Data is transmitted through the air from one microwave station to another in a manner similar to the way radio signals are transmitted *(Figure 7-13)*. A disadvantage of microwaves is that they are limited to line-of-sight transmission. This means that microwaves must be transmitted in a straight line and that there can be no obstructions, such as buildings or mountains, between microwave stations. For this reason, microwave stations are characterized by antennas positioned on tops of buildings, towers, or mountains.

Satellite Transmission

Communications satellites receive microwave signals from earth, amplify the signals, and retransmit the signals back to earth. The microwave signals used by satellites are generally of a higher frequency than the signals used by terrestrial (earth-based) microwave equipment. **Earth stations** *(Figure 7-14)* are communications facilities that use large,

dish-shaped antennas to transmit and receive data from satellites. The transmission *to* the satellite is called an **uplink** and the transmission *from* the satellite to a receiving earth station is called a **downlink**.

Many businesses with operations in multiple locations are now using private satellite systems to communicate information. If only a limited amount of information needs to be transmitted each day, such as daily sales results from a retail store, a small dish-shaped antenna can be used. **Very small aperture terminal** (VSAT) antenna measuring only one to three meters in size can transmit up to 19,200 bits per second. Higher speeds require larger antenna. The use of a private satellite using a VSAT antenna can be as low as $200 per month.

Communications satellites are usually placed about 22,300 miles above the earth in a **geosynchronous orbit** *(Figure 7-15)*. This means that the satellite is placed in an orbit where it rotates with the earth, so the same antennas on earth that are used to send and receive signals can remain fixed on the satellite at all times.

Figure 7-14
Earth stations use large, dish-shaped antennas to communicate with satellites.

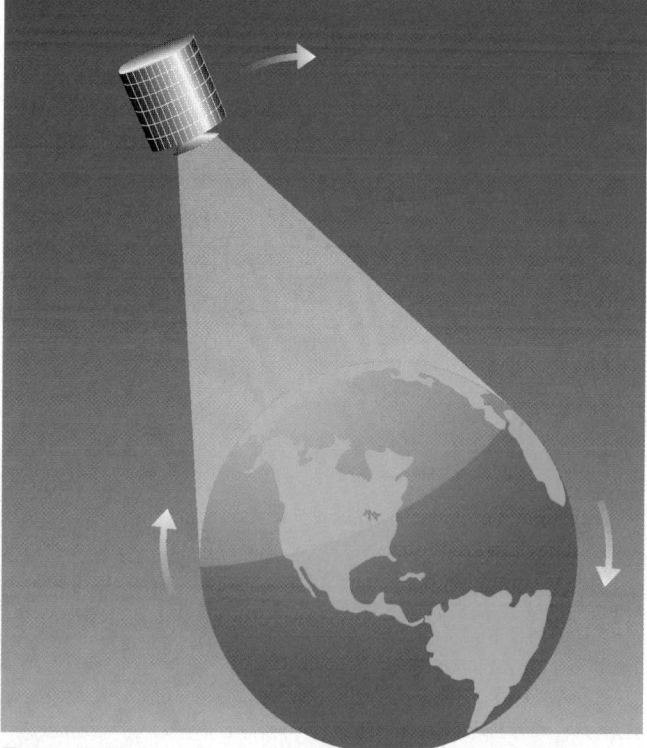

Figure 7-15
Communications satellites are placed in geosynchronous orbits approximately 22,300 miles above the earth. Geosynchronous means that the orbit of the satellite matches the rotation of the earth so the satellite is always above the same spot on the earth.

Several groups are planning on launching a series of low earth orbit (LEO) satellites between 1996 and 1998. For example, Motorola plans on launching 66 satellites as part of their Iridium system that will offer inexpensive, two-way voice and data communications from any spot on the globe. Because they will orbit only 400 to 500 miles above the earth, the LEO satellites will not be as expensive to build or launch as geosynchronous satellites. The closer distance will also mean that earth-based phones and other satellite communications equipment will not have to be as powerful.

Wireless Transmission

Wireless transmission uses one of three techniques to transmit data: light beams, radio waves, or carrier-connect radio, which uses the existing electrical wiring of a building to act as an antenna. These methods are sometimes used by companies to connect devices that are in the same general area such as an office or business park. For example, the unit shown in *Figure 7-16* uses light beams to transmit or receive data over a distance up to 70 feet. Local wireless systems offer design flexibility and portability but provide slower transmission speed than wired connections.

For longer distances, radio-wave wireless systems are becoming widely used. Motorola sells time on its ARDIS network that contains more than 1,100 base radio stations serving more than 8,000 cities in 50 states. Potential users include companies with large numbers of service personnel who need access to their company's computer data when they are at a customer site. For example, a repair technician may need to know the nearest location of a particular part. Using a portable radio data terminal *(Figure 7-17)* the technician could access the company's inventory database and obtain information about the availability of the required part.

A wireless device available to the general public that offers many of the same advantages as private radio networks is a cellular telephone. A **cellular telephone** uses radio waves to communicate with a local antenna assigned to a specific geographic area called a cell *(Figure 7-18)*. Cellular phones are often used in automobiles. As a cellular telephone user travels

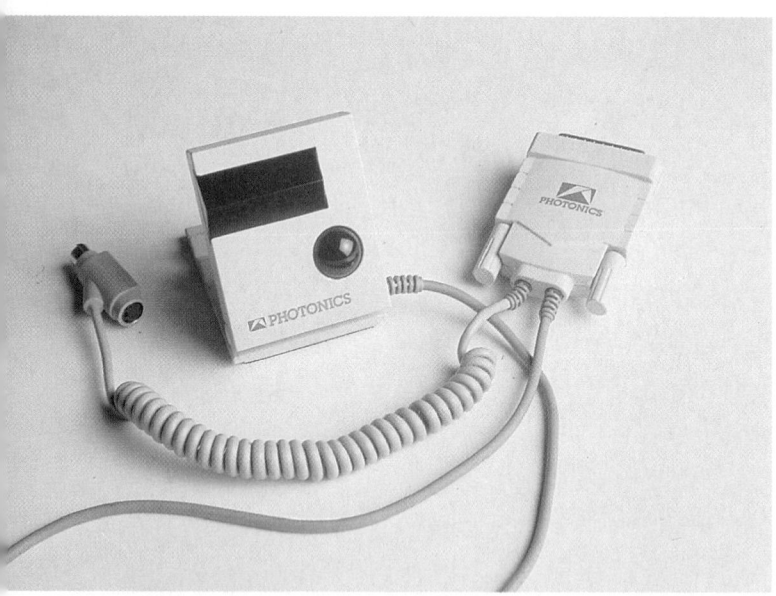

Figure 7-16
This wireless communication device from Photonics Corp. transmits data by bouncing infrared light beams off reflective surfaces such as a ceiling or a wall. The unit can also receive reflected light signals and convert them back to data. The device can transmit one million bits of data per second and has a range of thirty feet.

Figure 7-17
The portable terminal uses radio waves to communicate with a base radio station that is connected to a host computer. Using such a terminal, service technicians can instantly inquire as to the availability of repair parts.

from one cell to another, a computer that monitors the activity in each cell switches the conversation from one radio channel to another. By switching channels in this manner, the same channel can be used by another caller in a nonadjacent cell. Individual cells range from one to ten miles in width and use between 50 and 75 radio channels. Cellular telephone channels can be used for both voice and data transmission.

An Example of a Communications Channel

When data is transmitted over long distances, several different transmission media are generally used to make a complete communications channel. *Figure 7-19* on the next page illustrates how some of the various transmission media could be used to transmit data from a personal computer on the West Coast of the United States to a large computer on the East Coast. An example of the steps that could occur are as follows:

1. An entry is made on the personal computer. The data is sent over telephone lines from the computer to a microwave station.

2. The data is then transmitted from one microwave station to another.
3. The data is transmitted from the last microwave station to an earth station.
4. The earth station transmits the data to the communications satellite.
5. The satellite relays the data to another earth station on the other side of the country.
6. The data received at the earth station is transmitted to microwave stations.
7. The data is sent by telephone lines to the large computer.

This entire transmission process would take less than one second. Not all data transmission is as complex as this example, but such sophisticated communications systems do exist to meet the needs of some users.

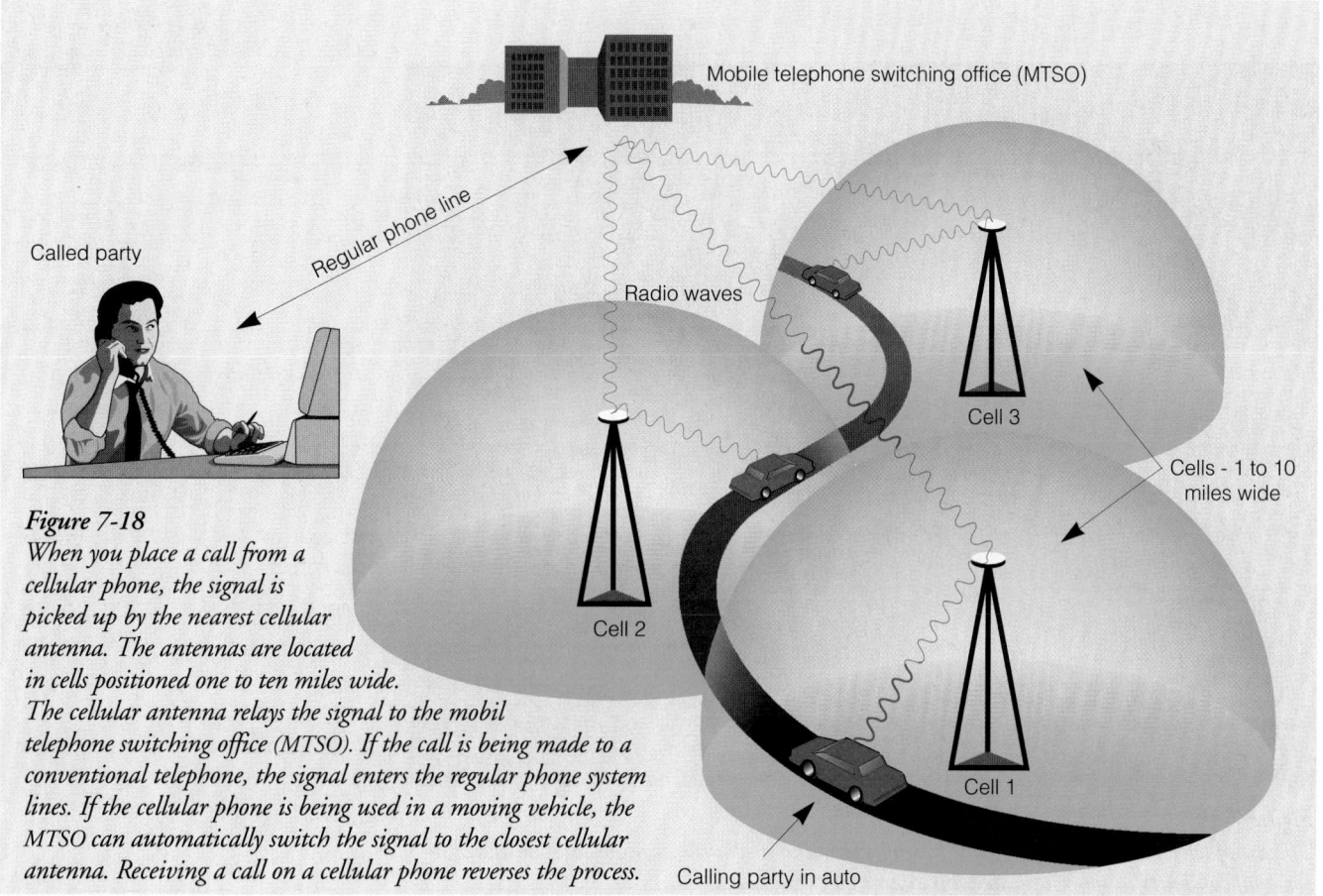

Mobile telephone switching office (MTSO)

Called party

Regular phone line

Radio waves

Cell 3

Cells - 1 to 10 miles wide

Cell 2

Cell 1

Calling party in auto

Figure 7-18
When you place a call from a cellular phone, the signal is picked up by the nearest cellular antenna. The antennas are located in cells positioned one to ten miles wide. The cellular antenna relays the signal to the mobil telephone switching office (MTSO). If the call is being made to a conventional telephone, the signal enters the regular phone system lines. If the cellular phone is being used in a moving vehicle, the MTSO can automatically switch the signal to the closest cellular antenna. Receiving a call on a cellular phone reverses the process.

Line Configurations

Two major **line configurations** (types of line connections) commonly used in communications are point-to-point lines and multidrop, or multipoint, lines.

Point-to-Point Lines

A **point-to-point line** is a direct line between a sending and a receiving device. It may be one of two types: a switched line or a dedicated line *(Figure 7-20)*.

SWITCHED LINE

A **switched line** uses a regular telephone line to establish a communications connection. Each time a connection is made, the line to be used for the call is selected by the telephone company switching stations (hence the name switched line). Using a switched line for communicating data is the same process as one person using a telephone to call another person. The communications equipment at the sending end dials the telephone number of the communications equipment at the receiving end. When the communications equipment at the receiving end answers the call, a connection is established and data can be transmitted. The process of establishing the communications connection is sometimes referred to as the

handshake. When the transmission of data is complete, the communications equipment at either end terminates the call by hanging up and the line is disconnected.

An advantage of using switched lines is that a connection can be made between any two locations that have telephone service and communications equipment. For example, a personal computer could dial one computer to get information about the weather and then hang up and place a second call to another computer to get information about the stock market. A disadvantage of a switched line is that the quality of the line cannot be controlled because the line is chosen at random by the telephone company switching equipment. The cost of a switched line is the same for data communications as for a regular telephone call.

DEDICATED LINE

A **dedicated line** is a line connection that is always established (unlike the switched line where the line connection is reestablished each time it is used). The communications device at one end is always connected to the device at the other end. A user can create his or her own dedicated line connection by running a wire or cable between two points, such as between two offices or buildings, or the dedicated line can be provided

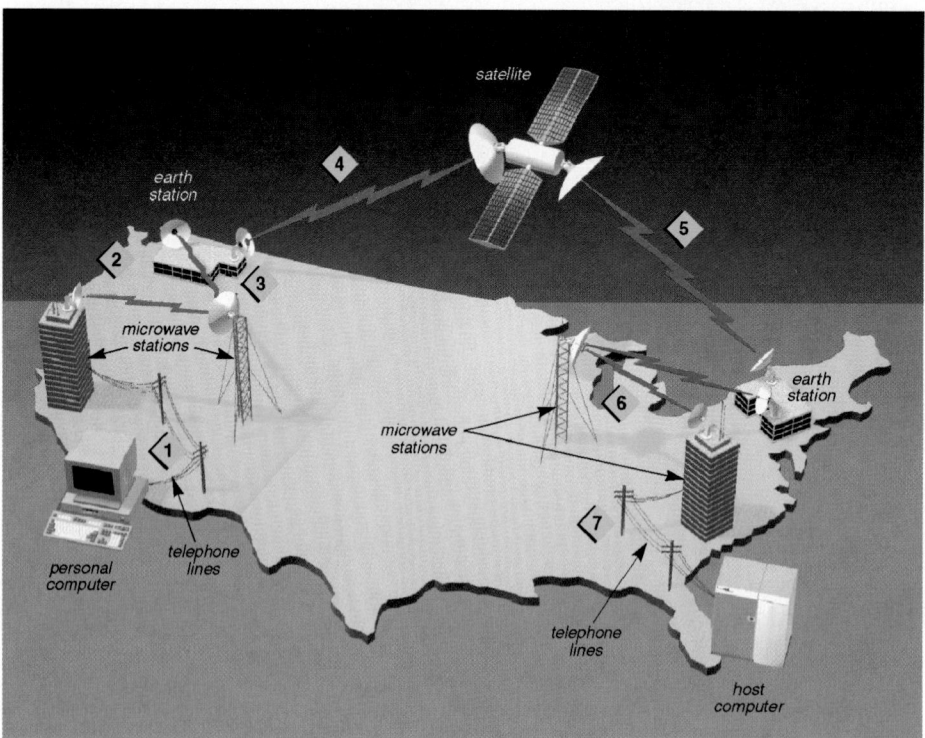

Figure 7-19
The use of telephone wires, microwave transmission, and a communications satellite allows a personal computer to communicate with a large host computer.

by an outside organization such as a telephone company or some other communications service company. If the dedicated line is provided by an outside organization, it is sometimes called a **leased line,** or a **private line.** The quality and consistency of the connection is better than on a switched line because a dedicated line is always established. Use of dedicated lines provided by outside organizations are usually charged on a flat-fee basis, which is a fixed amount each month regardless of how much time the line is actually used to transmit data. The cost of dedicated lines varies based on the distance between the two connected points and, sometimes, the speed at which data will be transmitted.

Multidrop Lines

The second major line configuration is called a **multidrop line,** or **multipoint line.** This type of line configuration is commonly used to connect multiple devices, such as terminals or personal computers, on a single line to a main computer, sometimes called a **host computer** *(Figure 7-21).*

For example, a ticket agent could use a terminal to enter an inquiry requesting flight information from a database

stored on a main computer. While the request is being transmitted to the main computer, other terminals on the line are not able to transmit data. The time required for the data to be transmitted to the main computer, however, is short – most likely less than one second. As soon as the inquiry is received by the computer, a second terminal can send an inquiry. With such short delays, it appears to the users that no other terminals are using the line, even though multiple terminals may be sharing the same line.

The number of terminals to be placed on one line is a decision made by the designer of the system based on the anticipated amount of traffic on the line. For example, 100 or more terminals could be contained on a single line, provided each one would send only short messages, such as inquiries, and each terminal would use the communications line only a few hours per day. But if longer messages, such as reports, were required and if the terminals were to be used almost continuously, the number of terminals on one line would have to be smaller.

A leased line is almost always used for multidrop line configurations. The use of multidrop lines can decrease line costs considerably because one line is used by many terminals.

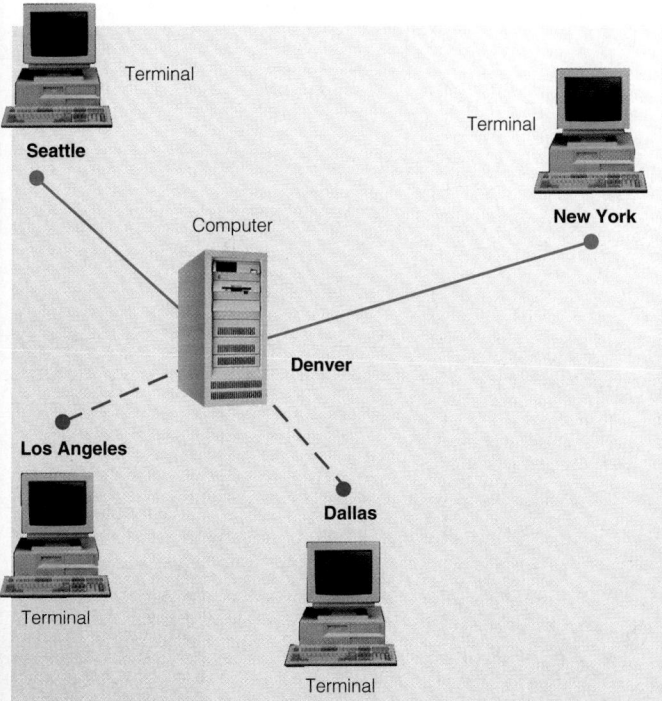

Figure 7-20
A point-to-point line configuration using both switched telephone (dial-up) lines (– – – –) and dedicated lines (———) are connected to a computer in Denver. The dedicated lines are always connected, whereas the switched lines have to be connected each time they are used.

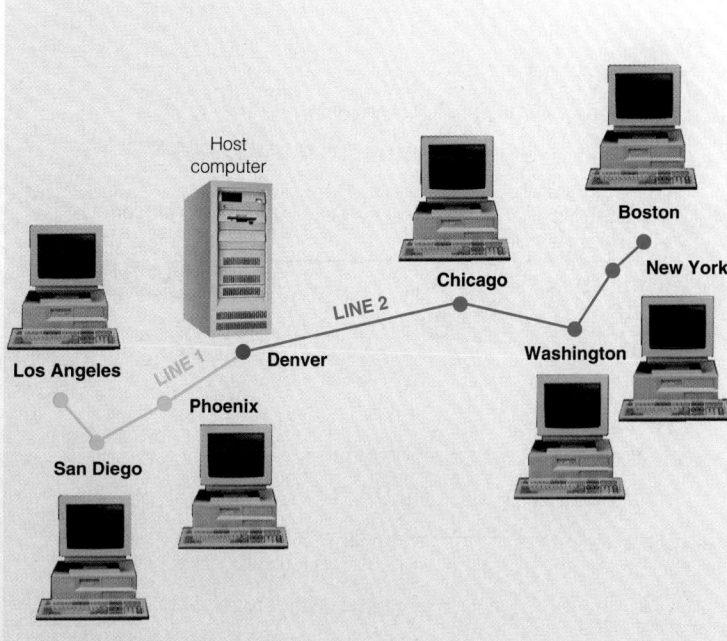

Figure 7-21
Two multidrop lines connect several cities with a computer in Denver. Each line is shared by terminals at several locations. Multidrop line configurations are less expensive than individual lines to each remote location.

Characteristics of Communications Channels

The communications channels just described can be categorized by a number of characteristics including the type of signal, transmission mode, transmission direction, and transmission rate.

Types of Signals: Digital and Analog

Computer equipment is designed to process data as **digital signals**, which are individual electrical pulses that represent the bits that are grouped together to form characters. Telephone equipment was originally designed to carry only voice transmission, which is comprised of a continuous electrical wave called an **analog signal** *(Figure 7-22)*. Thus, a special piece of equipment called a *modem* is required to convert the digital signals to analog signals so telephone lines can carry data. Modems are discussed in more detail later in this chapter.

To provide better communications services, telephone companies are now offering **digital data service**, communications channels specifically designed to carry digital instead of voice signals. Digital data service is available within and between all major metropolitan areas and provides higher speed and lower error rates than voice lines. Modems are not needed with digital data service; instead, users connect to the communications line through a device called a **digital service unit** (DSU).

Transmission Modes: Asynchronous and Synchronous

In **asynchronous transmission mode** *(Figure 7-23)*, individual bytes (made up of bits) are transmitted at irregular intervals, such as when a user enters data. To distinguish where one byte stops and another starts, the asynchronous transmission mode uses a start and a stop bit. An additional bit, called a *parity bit*, is sometimes included at the end of each byte. As you learned in the discussion of memory in Chapter 4, parity bits are used for error checking and they detect if one of the data bits has been changed during transmission. The asynchronous transmission mode is used for lower speed data transmission and is used with most communications equipment designed for personal computers.

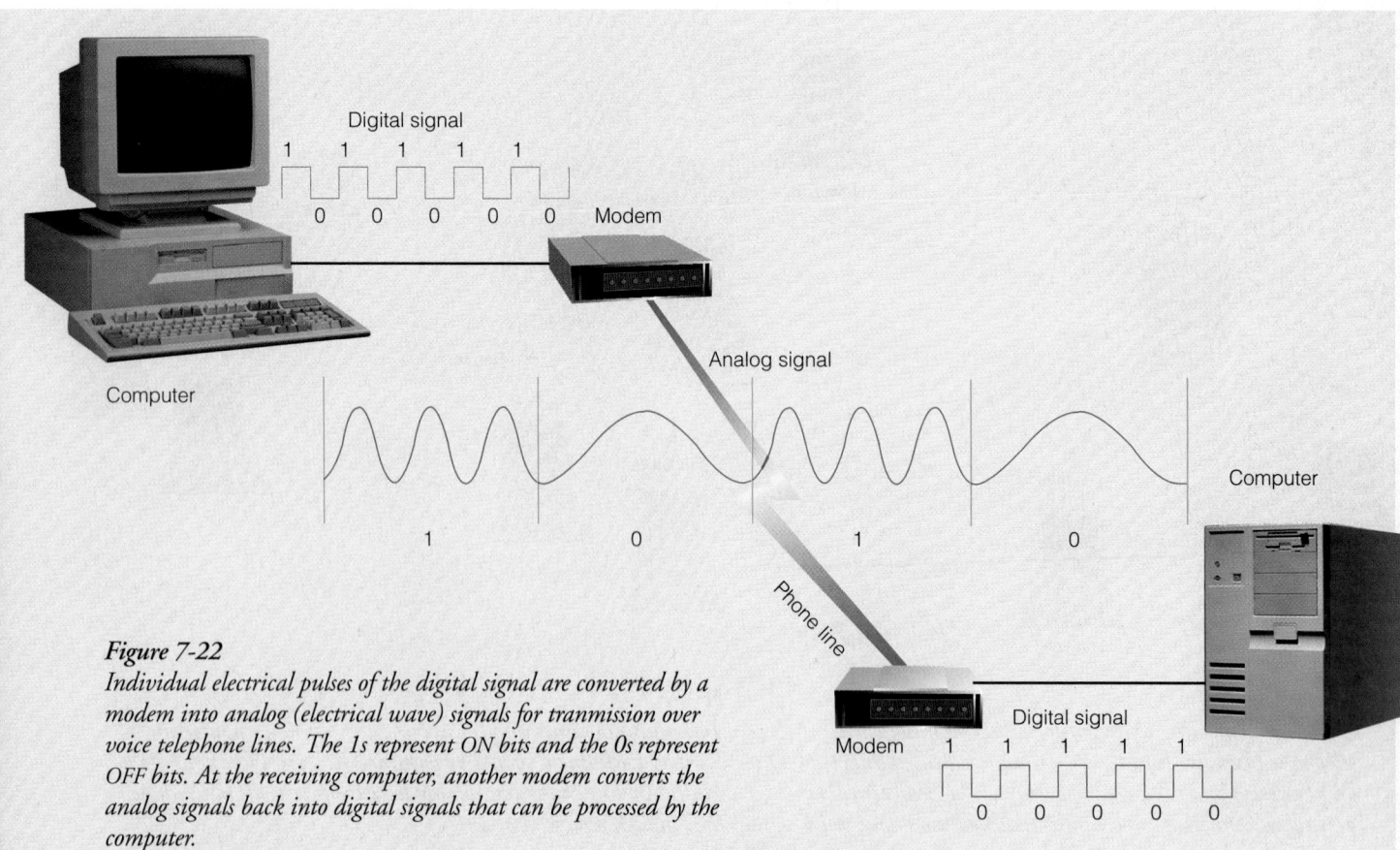

Figure 7-22
Individual electrical pulses of the digital signal are converted by a modem into analog (electrical wave) signals for tranmission over voice telephone lines. The 1s represent ON bits and the 0s represent OFF bits. At the receiving computer, another modem converts the analog signals back into digital signals that can be processed by the computer.

In the **synchronous transmission mode** *(Figure 7-23)*, large blocks of data are transmitted at regular intervals. Timing signals synchronize the communications equipment at both the sending and receiving ends and eliminate the need for start and stop bits for each byte. Error-check bits and start and stop bytes, called sync bytes, are also transmitted. Synchronous transmission requires more sophisticated and expensive equipment but it does give much higher speeds and accuracy than asynchronous transmission.

Direction of Transmission: Simplex, Half-Duplex, and Full-Duplex

The direction of data transmission is classified as either simplex, half-duplex, or full-duplex *(Figure 7-24)*. In **simplex transmission**, data flows in one direction only. Simplex is used only when the sending device, such as a temperature sensor, never requires a response from the computer. For example, if a computer is used to control the temperature of a building, numerous sensors are placed throughout it. Each sensor is connected to the computer with a simplex transmission line because the computer only needs to receive data from the temperature sensors and does not need to send data back to the sensors.

In **half-duplex transmission**, data can flow in both directions but in only one direction at a time. An example is a citizens band radio. The user can talk or listen but not do both at the same time.

In **full-duplex transmission**, data can be sent in both directions at the same time. A normal telephone line is an example of full-duplex transmission. Both parties can talk at the same time. Full-duplex transmission is used for most interactive computer applications and for computer-to-computer data transmission.

Transmission Rate

The transmission rate of a communications channel is determined by its bandwidth and its speed. The **bandwidth** is the range of frequencies that a channel can carry. Because transmitted data can be assigned to different frequencies, the wider the bandwidth, the more frequencies. Thus, more data can be transmitted at the same time.

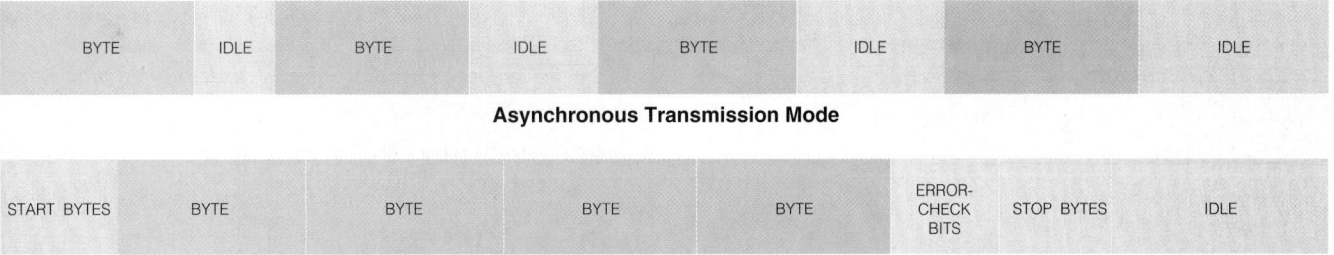

BYTE	IDLE	BYTE	IDLE	BYTE	IDLE	BYTE	IDLE

Asynchronous Transmission Mode

START BYTES	BYTE	BYTE	BYTE	BYTE	ERROR-CHECK BITS	STOP BYTES	IDLE

Synchronous Transmission Mode

Figure 7-23
In asynchronous transmission mode, individual bytes are transmitted. Each byte has start, stop, and error-check bits.
In synchronous transmission mode, multiple bytes are sent in a block with start bytes at the beginning of the block and error-check bits and stop bytes at the end of the block. Synchronous transmission is faster and more accurate.

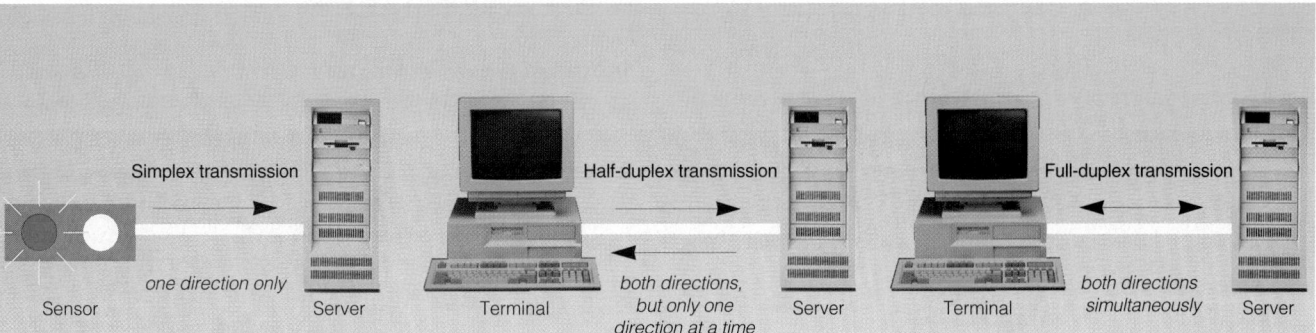

Simplex transmission — one direction only — Sensor → Server

Half-duplex transmission — both directions, but only one direction at a time — Terminal → Server

Full-duplex transmission — both directions simultaneously — Terminal ↔ Server

Figure 7-24
Simplex transmission allows data to flow in one direction only. Half-duplex transmission allows data to flow in both directions but not at the same time. Full-duplex transmission allows data to flow in both directions simultaneously.

The speed at which data is transmitted is usually expressed as bits per second or as a baud rate. **Bits per second (bps)** is the number of bits that can be transmitted in one second. Using a 10-bit byte to represent a character (7 data bits, 1 start, 1 stop, and 1 parity bit), a 9,600 bps transmission would transmit 960 characters per second. At this rate, a 20-page, single-spaced report that has an average of 3,000 characters per page would be transmitted in a little more than one minute. The **baud rate** is the number of times per second that the signal being transmitted changes. With each change, one or more bits can be transmitted. At speeds up to 2,400 bps, usually only one bit is transmitted per signal change and, thus, the bits per second and the baud rate are the same. To achieve speeds in excess of 2,400 bps, more than one bit is transmitted with each signal change and, thus, the bps will exceed the baud rate. *Figure 7-25* shows the range of transmission rates that can be achieved with different media. Each year, communications companies invent ways to increase these rates.

Communications Equipment

If a terminal or a personal computer is within approximately 1,000 feet of another computer, the two devices can usually be directly connected by a cable. At distances of more than 1,000 feet, however, the electrical signal weakens to the point that some type of special communications equipment is required to increase or change the signal to transmit it farther. A variety of communications equipment exists to perform this task, but the equipment that a user is most likely to encounter is a modem, a multiplexor, and a front-end processor. Computers that are connected to a network, which are discussed later in this chapter, usually require a network interface card.

Modems

A **modem** converts the digital signals of a terminal or computer to analog signals that are transmitted over a communications channel. It also converts analog signals it receives into digital signals that are used by a terminal or computer. The word modem comes from a combination of the words *mo*dulate, which means to change into a sound or analog signal, and *dem*odulate, which means to convert an analog signal into a digital signal. A modem is needed at both the sending and receiving ends of a communications channel.

MEDIA	RATE*
Twisted pair wire (voice-grade phone line)	300 bps to 28.8 Kbps
Twisted pair wire (direct connection)	1 to 10 Mbps
Coaxial cable	1 to 20 Mbps
Fiber-optic cable	up to 200 Mbps
Terrestial microwave	1.544 Mbps
Satellite microwave	64 to 512 Kbps
Wireless (radio wave)	4.8 to 19.2 Kbps

*RATE:	bps	bits per second
	Kbps	kilo (thousand) bits per second
	Mbps	mega (million) bits per second

Figure 7-25
Transmission rates of different media.

Figure 7-26
An external modem is connected to a terminal or computer and to a telephone outlet.

Figure 7-27
An internal modem is mounted inside a personal computer.

An **external modem** *(Figure 7-26)* is a separate, or stand-alone, device that is attached to the computer or terminal by a cable and to the telephone outlet by a standard telephone cord. An advantage of an external modem is that it can be easily moved from one terminal or computer to another.

An **internal modem** *(Figure 7-27)* is a circuit board installed inside a computer or terminal. Internal modems are generally less expensive than comparable external modems but once installed, they are not as easy to move.

Modems can transmit data at rates from 300 to 38,400 bits per second (bps). Most personal computers would use a modem between 2,400 and 14,400 bps. Business or heavier volume users would use faster and more expensive modems.

Multiplexors

A **multiplexor,** sometimes referred to as a MUX, combines more than one input signal into a single stream of data that can be transmitted over a communications channel *(Figure 7-28)*. The multiplexor at the sending end codes each character it receives with an identifier that is used by the multiplexor at the receiving end to separate the combined data stream into its original parts. A multiplexor may be connected to a separate

modem or may have a modem built in. By combining the individual data streams into one, a multiplexor increases the efficiency of communications and saves the cost of individual communications channels.

Front-End Processors

A **front-end processor** is a computer that is dedicated to handling the communications requirements of a larger computer. Relieved of these tasks, the larger computer is then dedicated to processing data, while the front-end processor communicates the data. Tasks that the front-end processor would handle include **polling** (checking the connected terminals or computers to see if they have data to send), error checking and correction, and access security to make sure that a connected device or the user of the connected device is authorized to access the computer.

Network Interface Cards

A **network interface card** (NIC) fits in an expansion slot of a computer and attaches to the cable or wireless technology used to connect the devices in the network. The NIC has circuits that coordinate the transmission, receipt, and error checking of transmitted data.

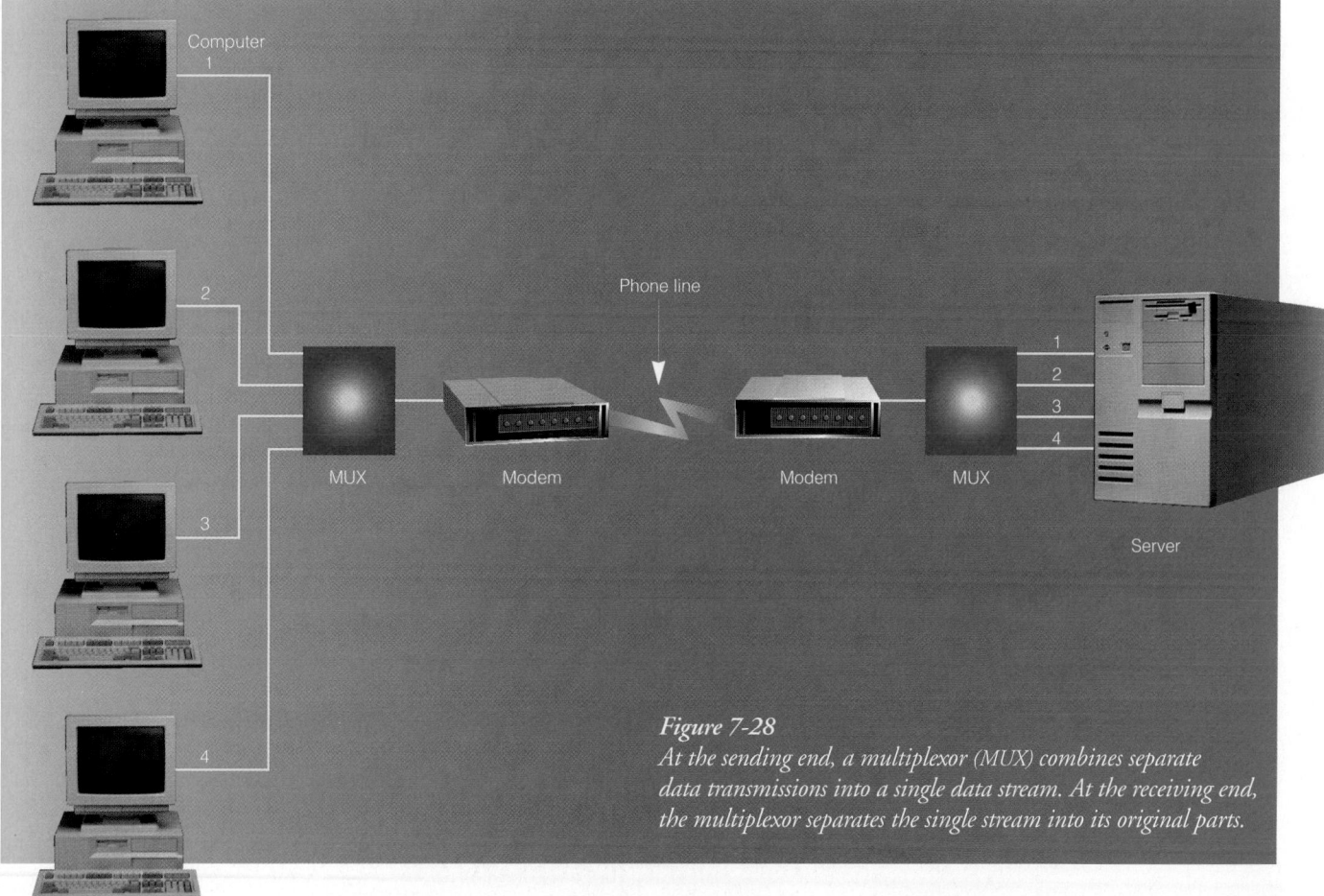

Figure 7-28
At the sending end, a multiplexor (MUX) combines separate data transmissions into a single data stream. At the receiving end, the multiplexor separates the single stream into its original parts.

Communications Software

Sometimes communications equipment is preprogrammed to accomplish its designed communications tasks. Other times, the user must load a program before transmitting data. These programs, referred to as **communications software,** can perform a number of tasks including dialing (if a switched telephone line is used), file transfer, terminal emulation, and data encryption.

Dialing software allows you to store, review, select, and dial telephone numbers of computers that can be called. The software provides a variety of meaningful messages to assist you in establishing a connection before transmitting data. For example, a person using a personal computer and a modem at home to communicate with a computer at the office could use dialing software to establish the communications connection. The software would display the office computer's telephone number on the user's personal computer screen. The user would enter the appropriate command for the dialing software to begin dialing the office computer and to establish a connection. During the 10 or 15 seconds of this process, the software would display messages to indicate specifically what was happening, such as "DIALING," "CARRIER DETECT" (which means that the office computer has

answered), and "CONNECTED" (to indicate that the communications connection has been established and data transmission can begin).

File transfer software allows you to move one or more files from one system to another. Generally, you have to load the file transfer software on both the sending and receiving computers.

Terminal emulation software allows a personal computer to imitate or appear to be a specific type of terminal, so the personal computer can connect to another, usually larger, computer *(Figure 7-29)*. Most minicomputers and mainframes are designed to work with terminals that have specific characteristics such as speed and parity. Terminal emulation software performs the necessary speed and parity conversion.

Data encryption protects confidential data during transmission. **Data encryption** is the conversion of data at the sending end into an unrecognizable string of characters or bits and the reconversion of the data at the receiving end. Without knowing how the data was encrypted, someone who intercepted the transmitted data would have a difficult time determining what the data meant.

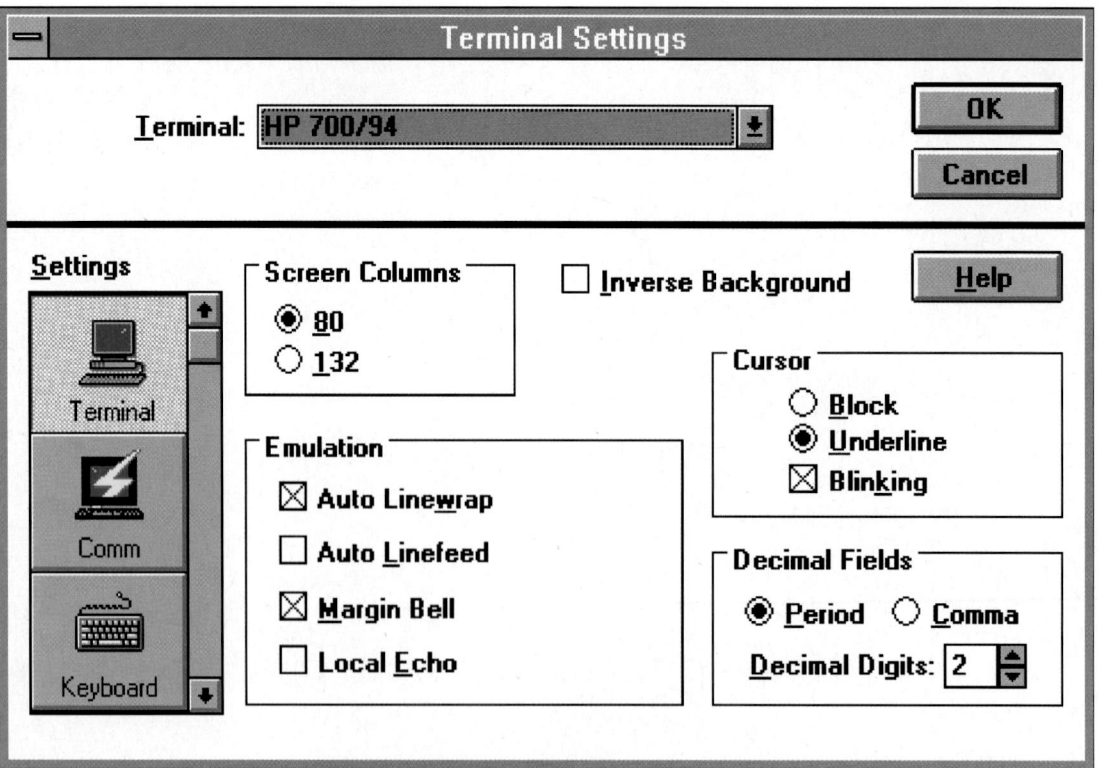

Figure 7-29
Terminal emulation software makes a personal computer function as if it were a particular type of terminal. Terminal emulation software is often used to allow PCs to communicate with larger systems such as minicomputers or mainframes. This screen, from Crosstalk for Windows, shows how a personal computer is set up to emulate a Hewlett-Packard (HP) model 700/94 terminal.

Communications Protocols

Communications software is written to work with one or more protocols. A **protocol** is a set of rules and procedures for exchanging information between computers. Protocols define how the communications link is established, how information is transmitted, and how errors are detected and corrected. Using the same protocol, different types and makes of computers can communicate with each other. Over the years, numerous protocols have been developed. The table shown in *Figure 7-30* lists some of the more widely used protocols. Today, however, there are strong efforts to establish standards that all computer and communications equipment manufacturers will follow. The International Standards Organization (ISO) based in Geneva, Switzerland has defined a set of communications protocols called the **Open Systems Interconnection** (OSI) model. The OSI model has been endorsed by the United Nations.

Communications Networks

A communications **network** is a collection of terminals, computers, and other equipment that uses communications channels to share data, information, hardware, and software. Networks can be classified as either local area networks or wide area networks.

Local Area Networks (LANs)

A **local area network,** or LAN, is a privately owned communications network that covers a limited geographic area such as a school computer laboratory, an office, a building, or a group of buildings.

The LAN consists of a communications channel that connects either a series of computer terminals together with a minicomputer or, more commonly, a group of personal computers to one another. Very sophisticated LANs can connect a variety of office devices such as word processing equipment, computer terminals, video equipment, and personal computers.

Three common applications of local area networks are hardware, software, and information resource sharing. **Hardware resource sharing** allows each personal computer in the network to access and use devices that would be too expensive to provide for each user or would not be justified for each

PROTOCOL	DESCRIPTION
Ethernet	One of the most widely used protocols for LANS
Token ring	Uses an electronic token to avoid transmission conflict by only allowing one device to transmit at at time
PowerTalk	Links Apple Macintosh computers
FDDI	Fiber Distributed Data Interface; high-speed fiber-optic protocol
SNA	System Network Architecture; primarily used to link large systems
TCP/IP	Transmission Control Protocol/Internet Protocol; used on the Internet
X.25	International standard for packet switching
ATM	Asynchronous Transfer Mode; recently developed protocol for transmitting voice, data, and video over any type of media
IPX	Used on Novell Netware networks
Xmodem	PC protocol that uses 128-byte blocks
Ymodem	PC protocol that uses 1,024-byte blocks
Zmodem	PC protocol that uses 512-byte blocks
Kermit	PC protocol that uses variable-length blocks

Figure 7-30
Some of the more commonly used communications protocols. Protocols specify the procedures that are used during transmission.

user because of only occasional use. For example, when a number of personal computers are used on the network, each may need to use a laser printer. Using a LAN, a laser printer could be purchased and made a part of the network. Whenever a user of a personal computer on the network needed the laser printer, it could be accessed over the network. *Figure 7-31* depicts a simple local area network consisting of four personal computers linked together by a cable. Three of the personal computers (computer 1 in the sales and marketing department, computer 2 in the accounting department, and computer 3 in the personnel department) are available for use at all times. Computer 4 is used as a **server**, a computer dedicated to handling the communications needs of the other computers in the network. The users of this LAN have connected the laser printer to the server. Using the LAN, all computers and the server can use the printer. In small networks, the server computer can also be used to run applications, along with the other computers on the network. In large networks, the server is usually dedicated to providing network services such as hardware, software, and information resource sharing.

Software resource sharing consists of storing frequently used software on the hard disk of the server so the software can be accessed by multiple users. Sharing software is a common practice for both in-house and commercial software. Many software vendors now sell a network version of their software. When a commercial software package is accessed by many users, it is sometimes necessary to obtain a special agreement from the software vendor called a **site license**. The site license fee is usually based on the number of computers on the network and is less than if individual copies of the software package were purchased for each computer.

Information resource sharing allows anyone using a personal computer on the local area network to access data stored on any other computer in the network. In actual practice, hardware resource sharing and information resource sharing are often combined. For example, in *Figure 7-31,* the daily sales records could be stored on the hard disk associated with the server unit personal computer. Anyone needing access to the sales records could use this information resource. The capability to access and store data on common secondary storage is an important feature of many local area networks.

Information resource sharing is usually provided by using either the file-server or client-server method. Using the

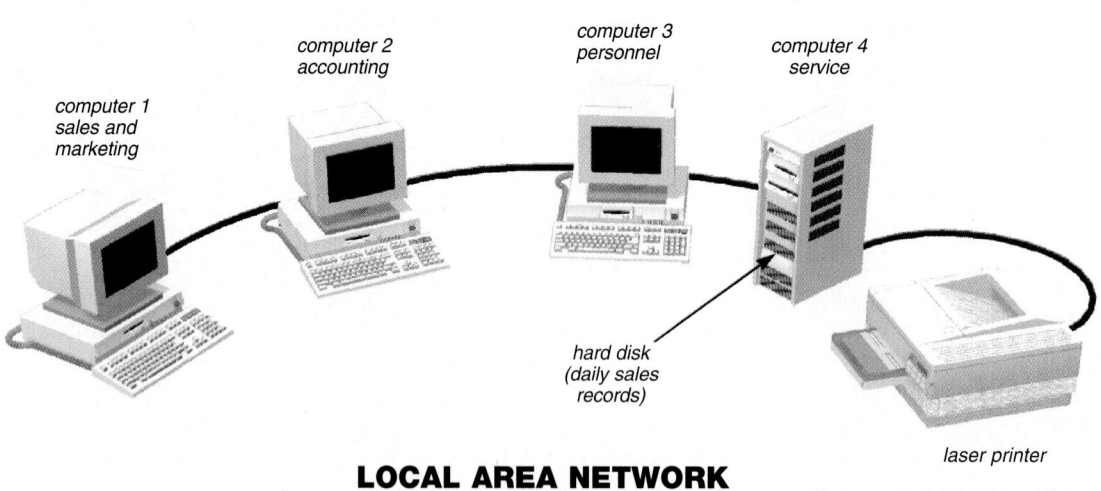

computer 1
sales and
marketing

computer 2
accounting

computer 3
personnel

computer 4
service

hard disk
(daily sales
records)

laser printer

LOCAL AREA NETWORK

Figure 7-31
A local area network (LAN) consists of multiple personal computers or terminals connected to one another. The LAN allows users to share hardware and information.

file-server method, the server sends an entire file at a time. The requesting computer then performs the processing. With the **client-server** method, as much processing as possible is done on the server system before data is transmitted.

Figure 7-32 illustrates how the two methods would process a request for information stored on the server system for customers with balances over $1,000. With the file-server method, the user transmits a request for the customer file to the server unit (1). The server unit locates the customer file (2) and transmits the entire file to the requesting computer (3). The requesting computer selects customers with balances over $1,000 and prepares the report (4).

With the client-server method, the user transmits a request for customers with a balance over $1,000 to the server unit (1). The server unit selects the customer records that meet the criteria (2) and transmits the selected records to the requesting computer (3). The requesting computer prepares the report (4). The client-server method greatly reduces the amount of data sent over a network but requires a more powerful server system.

A local area network does not have to use a single server computer. A **peer-to-peer network** allows any computer to share the software, data, or hardware (such as a printer) located on any other computer in the network. Peer-to-peer networks are appropriate for a small number of users who primarily work on their own computers and only occasionally need to use the resources of other computers.

Simple peer-to-peer networks need a minimum amount of software to manage their activities. Often the necessary software is provided by the manufacturer of the network interface cards or other hardware used to link the networked systems. Artisoft's LANtastic, Microsoft's Windows for Workgroups, and Apple's AppleTalk are examples of peer-to-peer network software. Client-server networks, however, need more sophisticated software, called a network operating system, to keep them running efficiently. A **network operating system** (**NOS**) is software that allows a user to manage the resources of a computer network. The NOS runs on the server computer in addition to the client operating systems, such as DOS, Windows, or OS/2, that run on the individual computers that make up the network. A NOS usually provides the following capabilities:

- **Administration**   Adding, deleting, and organizing client users and performing maintenance tasks such as backup.

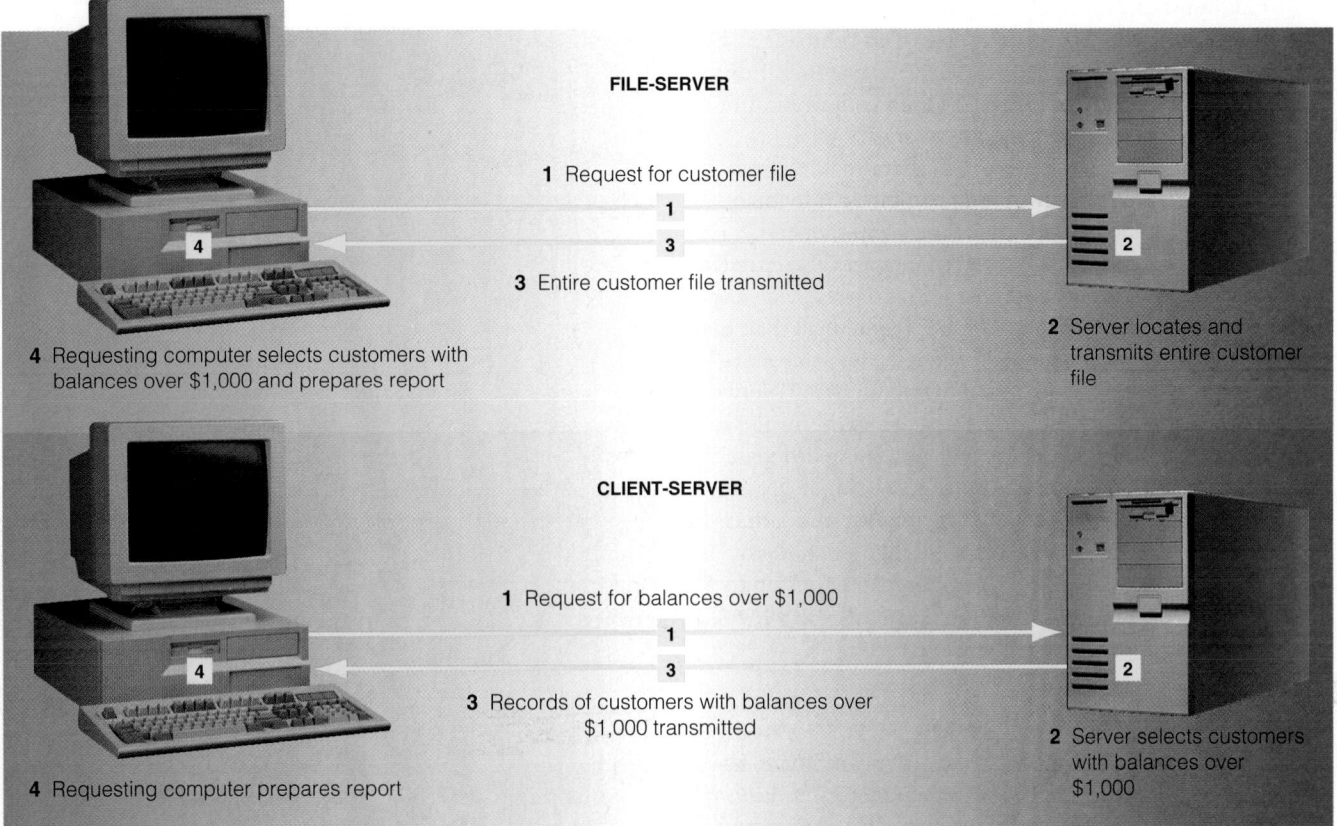

Figure 7-32
A request for information about customers with balances over $1,000 would be processed differently by file-server and client-server networks.

- **File Management**   The capability to quickly locate and transfer files from the server to the client computers.
- **Printer Management**   The capability to prioritize print jobs and direct reports to specific printers on the network.
- **Security**   The capability to restrict access to network resources. Novell's Netware, Microsoft's Advanced NT Server, and IBM's LAN Server are examples of network operating systems.

Wide Area Networks (WANs)

A **wide area network**, or WAN, is geographic in scope (as opposed to local) and uses telephone lines, microwaves, satellites, or a combination of communications channels. A wide area network limited to the area surrounding a city is sometimes referred to as a **metropolitan area network**, or MAN. Public wide area network companies include so-called **common carriers** such as the telephone companies. Telephone company deregulation has encouraged a number of companies to build their own wide area networks. For example, EDS has built one of the larger private communications networks *(Figure 7-33)* to handle the needs of its computer services business and the needs of its parent company, General Motors.

Communications companies, such as MCI, have built WANs to compete with other communications companies. Companies called **value-added carriers** lease channels from the common carriers to provide specialized communications services referred to as **value-added networks** (VANs). For example, Tymnet, Inc. operates a VAN that provides packet-switching services. **Packet-switching** combines individual packets of information from various users and transmits them together over a high-speed channel. The messages are separated and distributed over lower speed channels at the receiving end. Sharing the high-speed channel is more economical than each user having their own high-speed channel. Most common carriers are now offering **Integrated Services Digital Network** (ISDN) services. ISDN is an international standard for the digital transmission of both voice and data using different channels and communications companies. Using ISDN lines, data can be transmitted over one or more separate channels at 64,000 bits per second. Future plans for ISDN include the use of fiber-optic cable that will allow transmission rates up to 2.2 billion bits per second. These higher speeds will allow full-motion video images to be transmitted.

Figure 7-33
The control room for EDSNET, the private communications network of Electronic Data Systems Corporation (EDS). The network was built by EDS spanning a three-year period and with a cost of more than $1 billion. The network provides communications for EDS, its computer services customers, and its parent company, General Motors.

The Internet

The largest and best known wide area network is the Internet. The **Internet** is a worldwide network of computer networks. It is difficult to give numbers for the size of the Internet because of its rapid growth. In late 1994, it was estimated that the Internet consisted of the following:
- 30 million users worldwide
- Users located in 100 countries
- 20,000 member organizations
- 21,000 connected networks
- 2 million connected computers

Because of its tremendous size and number of users, some have called the Internet a "virtual community." The Internet was originally started in 1969 as a way of linking government researchers at four universities. Other university and private research sites were added over the years. The Internet really started to grow in the late 1980s when a number of public and private networks were joined together with the National Science Foundation network. Since 1988, the Internet has doubled in size every year. Some of the services and resources available on the Internet include the following:

- **Electronic mail** E-mail can be sent anywhere in the world to users with an Internet address. Addresses can be obtained free of charge.
- **File transfer** Thousands of files on countless subjects are available for transfer.
- **Database search** More than 200 universities and several public libraries have their databases online and available for review. Internet offers several tools for finding information on a particular subject.
- **Remote logon** The capability to run a program located on another computer.
- **Discussion and news groups** Thousands of discussion topics currently exist, or you can start your own on a subject of interest.
- **Games** A variety of single and multiple player games.

Students can usually gain access to the Internet through one of their school's computer systems. Most colleges and universities have access. Individuals can gain access through many of the online service providers. Businesses or other organizations that want to regularly use the Internet can obtain direct connection rights. For further examples of using the Internet, see page 7.43.

Network Configurations

The configuration, or physical layout, of the equipment in a communications network is called **topology**. Communications networks are usually configured in one or a combination of three patterns. These configurations are star, bus, and ring networks. Although these configurations can be used with wide area networks, they are illustrated here with local area networks. Devices connected to a network, such as terminals, printers, or other computers, are referred to as **nodes**.

Star Network

A **star network** contains a central computer and one or more terminals or personal computers connected to it, forming a star. A pure star network consists of only point-to-point lines between the terminals and the computer, but most star networks, such as the one shown on the next page in *Figure 7-34,* include both point-to-point lines and multidrop lines. A star network configuration is often used when the central

computer contains all the data required to process the input from the terminals, such as an airline reservation system. For example, if inquiries are being processed in the star network, all the data to answer the inquiry would be contained in the database stored on the central computer.

A star network can be relatively efficient and close control can be kept over the data processed on the network. Its major disadvantage is that the entire network is dependent on the central computer and the associated hardware and software. If any of these elements fail, the entire network is disabled. Therefore, in most large star networks, backup computer systems are available in case the primary system fails.

Bus Network

When a **bus network** is used, all the devices in the network are connected to and share a single cable. Information is transmitted in either direction from any one personal computer to another. Any message can be directed to a specific device. An advantage of the bus network is that devices can be attached or detached from the network at any point without disturbing the rest of the network. In addition, if one computer on the network fails, this does not affect the other users of the network. *Figure 7-31* on page 7.22 illustrates a simple bus network.

Ring Network

A **ring network** does not use a centralized host computer. Instead, a circle of computers communicate with one another *(Figure 7-35)*. A ring network can be useful when the processing is not done at a central site, but at local sites. For example, computers could be located in three departments: accounting, personnel, and shipping and receiving. The computers in each of these departments could perform the processing required for each of the departments. On occasion, however, the computer in the shipping and receiving department could communicate with the computer in the accounting department to update certain data stored on the accounting department computer. Data travels around a ring network in one direction

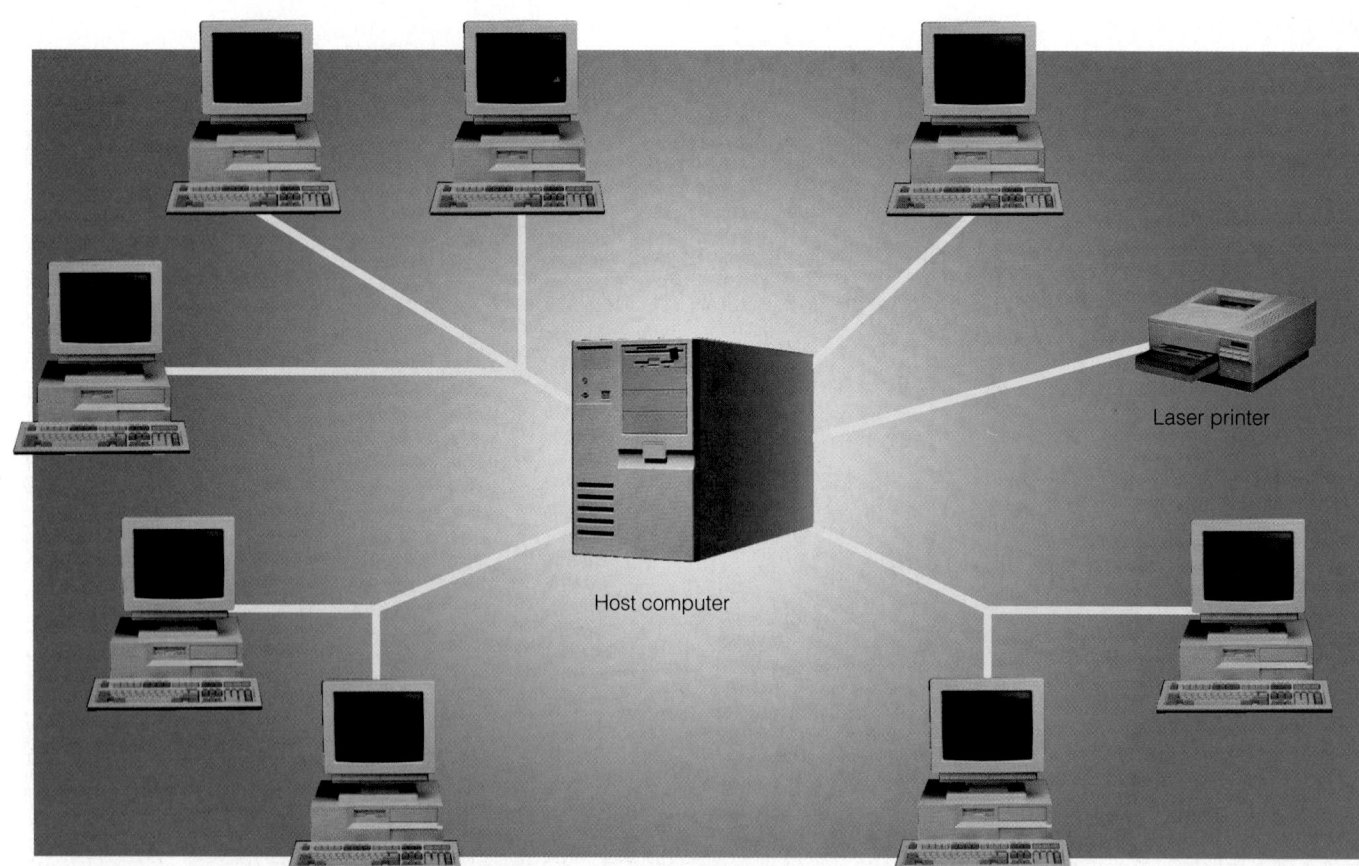

Laser printer

Host computer

Figure 7-34
A star network contains a single, centralized host computer with which all the terminals or personal computers in the network communicate. Both point-to-point and multidrop lines can be used in a star network.

only and passes through each node. Thus, one disadvantage of a ring network is that if one node fails, the entire network fails because the data does not get past the failed node. An advantage of a ring network is that less cable is usually needed than for a star network and therefore network cabling costs are lower.

A common type of ring network is called a token ring network. A **token ring network** constantly circulates an electronic signal, called a token, around the network. Devices on the network that want to send a message take the token and attach it to their data. When it is attached to data, the token is not available for other devices to use. When data is delivered to its destination, the data is replaced with an acknowledgment that the data was received. When the original sending device receives the token and the acknowledgment, the token is again made available for other devices to use.

Connecting Networks

Certain circumstances require you to connect separate networks. You do this by using gateways, bridges, and routers. A **gateway** is a combination of hardware and software that allows users on one network to access the resources on a *different* type of network. For example, a gateway could be used to connect a local area network of personal computers to a mainframe computer network. A **bridge** is a combination of hardware and software used to connect *similar* networks. For example, if a company had similar but separate local area networks of personal computers in its accounting and marketing departments, the networks could be connected with a bridge. In this example, using a bridge makes more sense than joining all the personal computers together in one large network because the individual departments only occasionally need to access information on the other network. A router is used when several networks are connected together. A **router** is an intelligent network-connecting device that can route communications traffic directly to the appropriate network. In the case of a partial network failure, routers are smart enough to determine alternate routes.

Laser printer

Figure 7-35
In a ring network, all computers are connected in a continous loop. Data flows around the ring in one direction only.

An Example of a Communications Network

The diagram in *Figure 7-36* illustrates how two personal computer networks and a mainframe computer can be connected to share information with each other and with outside sources.

The marketing department operates a bus network of four personal computers (1). Frequently used marketing data and programs are stored in the server unit (2). The personal computers in the marketing department share a laser printer (3). A modem (4) is attached to the marketing server unit so outside sales representatives can use a dial telephone line (5) to call the marketing system and obtain product price information.

The administration department operates a bus network of three personal computers (6). As with the marketing network, common data and programs are stored on a server unit (7) and the administration personal computers share a laser printer (8). Because the administration department sometimes needs information from the marketing system, the two similar networks are connected with a LAN bridge (9). The bridge allows users on either network to access data or programs on the other network.

Administration department users sometimes need information from the company's mainframe computer system (10). They can access the mainframe through the use of a gateway (11) that allows different types of network systems to be connected. All communications with the mainframe computer are controlled by a front-end processor (12). A dial telephone line (13) connected to a modem (14) allows remote users to call the mainframe and allows mainframe users to call other computers. A leased telephone line (15) and a modem (16) are used for a permanent connection to

1 MARKETING PC NETWORK

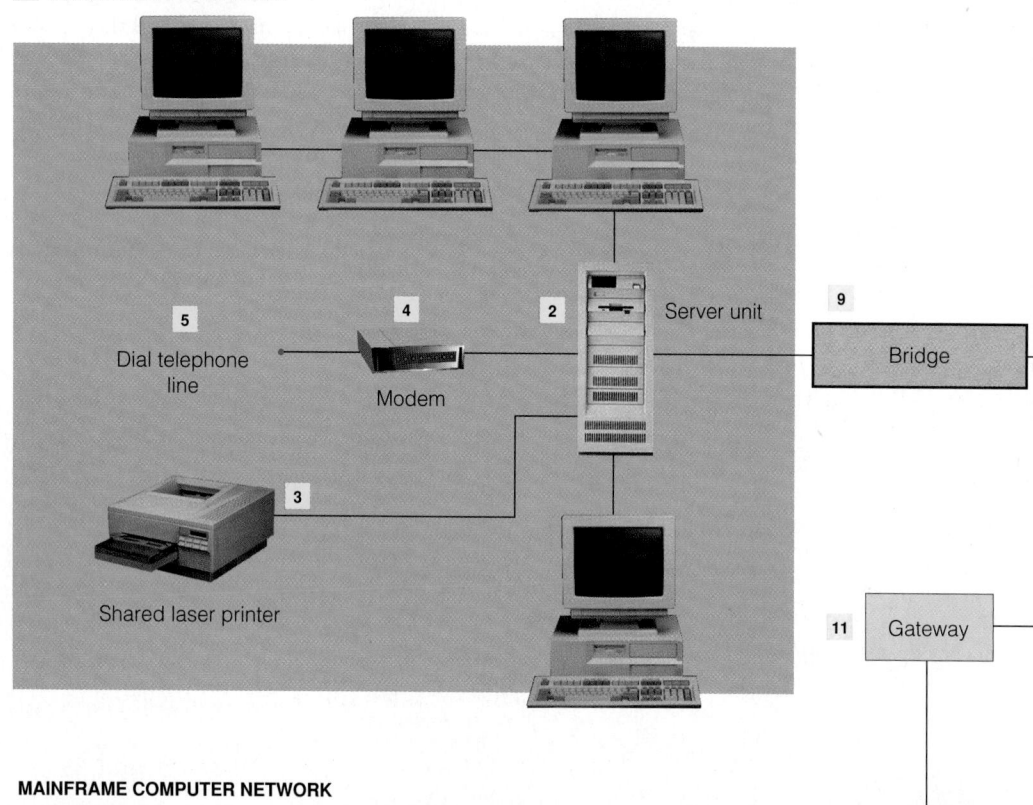

MAINFRAME COMPUTER NETWORK

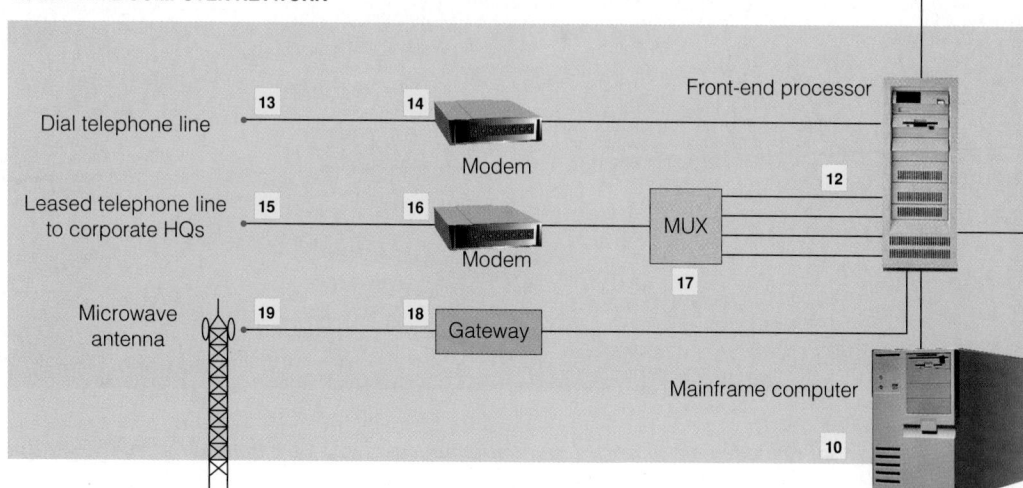

Summary of Communications and Networks

the computer at the corporate headquarters, several hundred miles away. The leased line can carry the signals of up to four different users. The signals are separated by the use of a multiplexor (MUX) (17). A gateway (18) connects the front-end processor and mainframe system to a microwave antenna (19) on the roof of the building. The microwave antenna sends and receives data from a computer at the manufacturing plant located two miles away. The front-end processor also controls mainframe computer terminals located throughout the company (20).

Communications will continue to affect how people work and how they use computers. Individuals and organizations are no longer limited to local data resources but instead, with communications capabilities, they can obtain information from anywhere in the world at electronic speed. With communications technology rapidly changing, today's businesses are challenged to find ways to adapt the technology to provide better products and services for their customers and make their operations more efficient. Networks are one way that organizations are making individual computers more powerful. By joining individual computers into networks, computing resources are expanded and the ability of individuals to communicate with each other is increased. For individuals, the new technology offers increased access to worldwide information and services and provides new opportunities in business and education.

6   ADMINISTRATION PC NETWORK

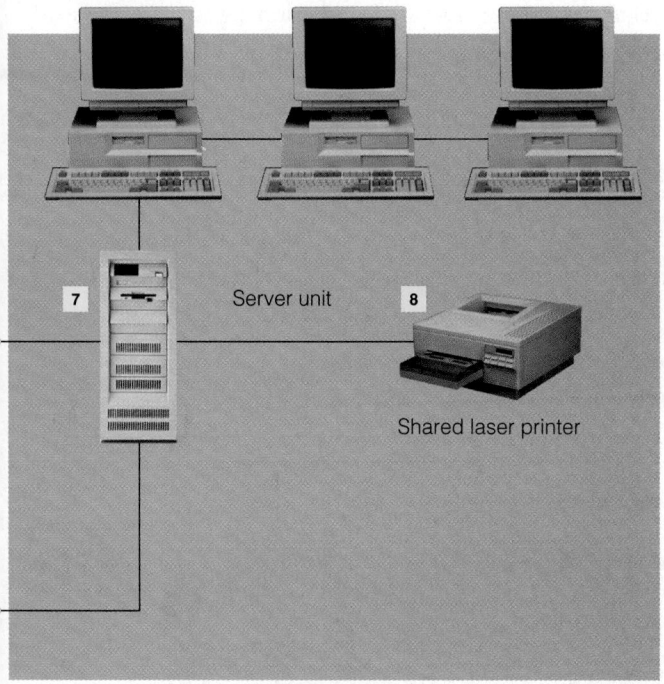

7   Server unit   **8**

Shared laser printer

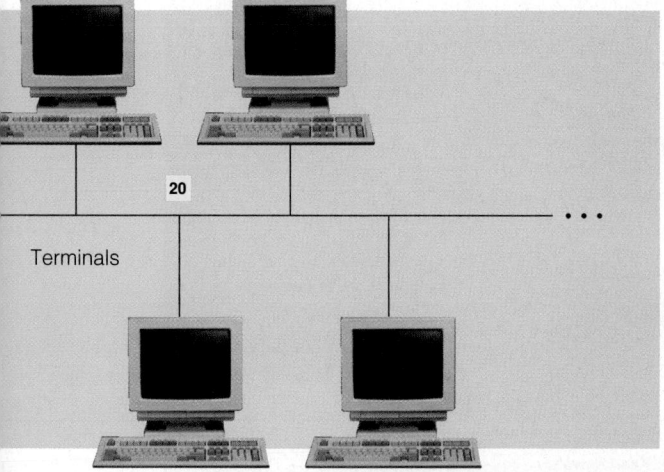

20

Terminals

Figure 7-36
The two personal computer networks are connected together with a bridge. A gateway is used to connect the administration personal computer network with the mainframe. All communications with the mainframe are controlled by a separate computer called a front-end processor. Modems are used to connect the networks to leased and dial telephone lines.

COMPUTERS AT WORK

Satellites Help Track Moving Vans

Have you ever stayed around the house or apartment all day waiting for an item to be delivered by truck? When you call the trucking company, all they can tell you is, "the truck is on the way!" This is not the case with North American Van Lines. If you ship your items with North American, they can tell you the exact location of their trucks within 1,000 feet. North American, the fifth largest trucking company in the United States, has outfitted its trucks with a two-way satellite communications system manufactured by Qualcomm of San Diego, California. Besides being able to pinpoint the location of its trucks, North American can instantly communicate with the drivers. There is no longer a wait until the driver pulls off the road to call in. The two-way communication feature allows North American to direct its drivers to pick up additional cargo as they pass through an area. Before they had the systems, drivers might have driven

through an area not knowing that a load was waiting. The system offers benefits to the drivers, as well. If a driver runs into trouble because of bad weather or a mechanical breakdown, he or she can send a message to the home office in Indiana *(Figure 7-36)*. Even if the truck is in the middle of a snow storm on a stretch of deserted highway, the message will get through instantly. The system has even been used to dispatch emergency help to the scenes of accidents. Like many other business systems that have been computerized, the benefits of the North American Van Lines system may one day be made directly available to North American customers. North American is considering allowing its regular customers who frequently ship high-tech cargo such as computers and medical equipment to directly access the tracking system.

Figure 7-36

IN THE FUTURE

The Information Superhighway

Many believe that the path to the future may be along what has been called the **Information Superhighway;** a nationwide and eventually worldwide network of information and services. Originally proposed as part of the 1991 High Performance Computing and Communications (HPCC) initiative, the scope of the U.S. network was expanded in 1993 as part of the **National Information Infrastructure (NII).** The NII is envisioned as a high-speed digital network that will make information services, training, education, medical services, and government data available to everyone, including individuals as well as businesses and larger organizations. Universal access is one of the key principles of NII.

Some of the preliminary work on a nationwide network is already being accomplished by private organizations such as cable TV and telephone companies. This is consistent with the NII plan to allow private companies to construct and operate much of the network. The U.S. government's challenge is to provide guidelines, standards, and incentives to make sure that separately constructed parts of the network can communicate with each other and that all individuals have access to the network at a reasonable price. Several other countries have similar nationwide networks planned or under development. Eventually, all these networks could be linked together using software that automatically translates one language into another.

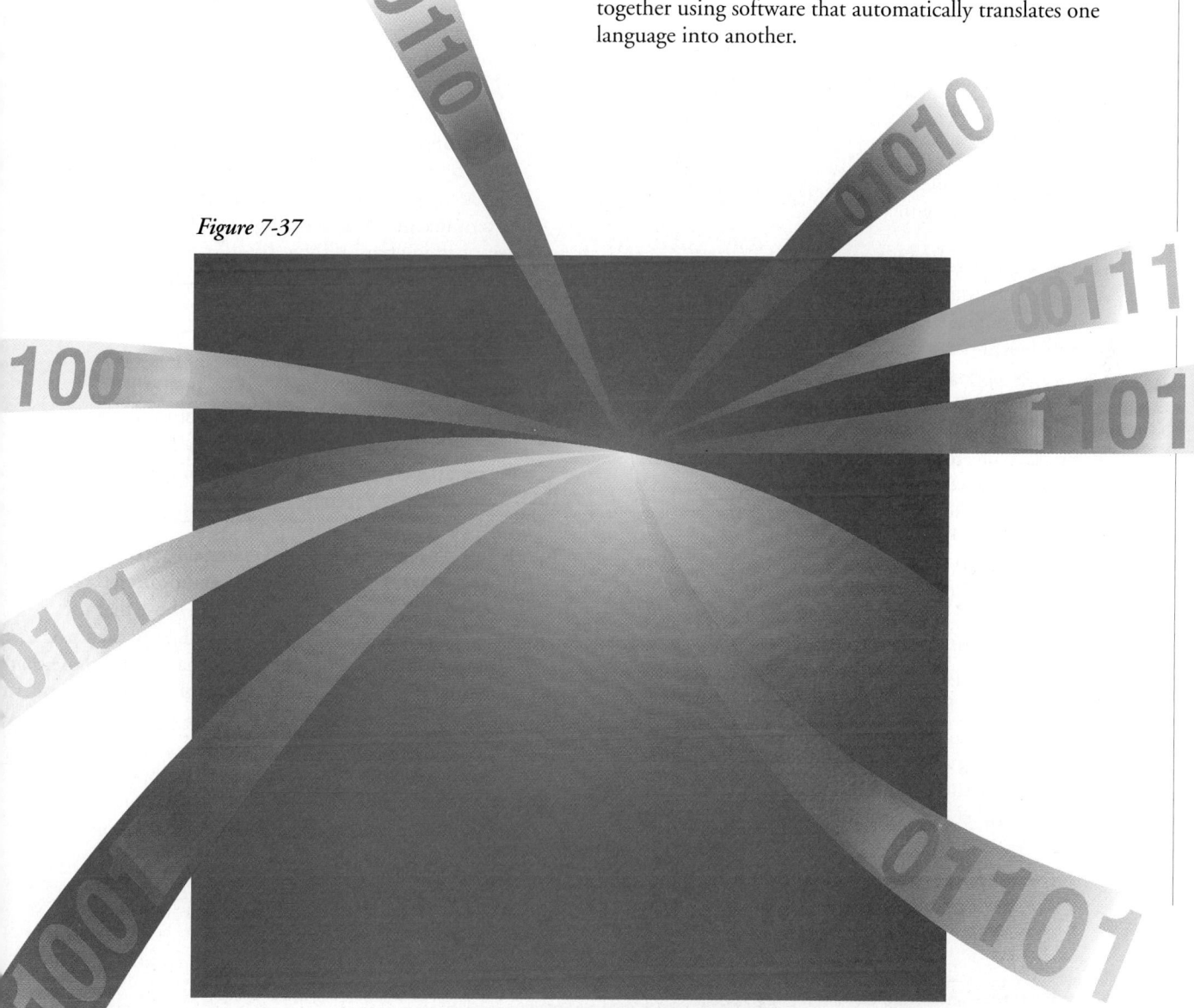

Figure 7-37

File   Edit   Section   Page   Tools   Options   Help

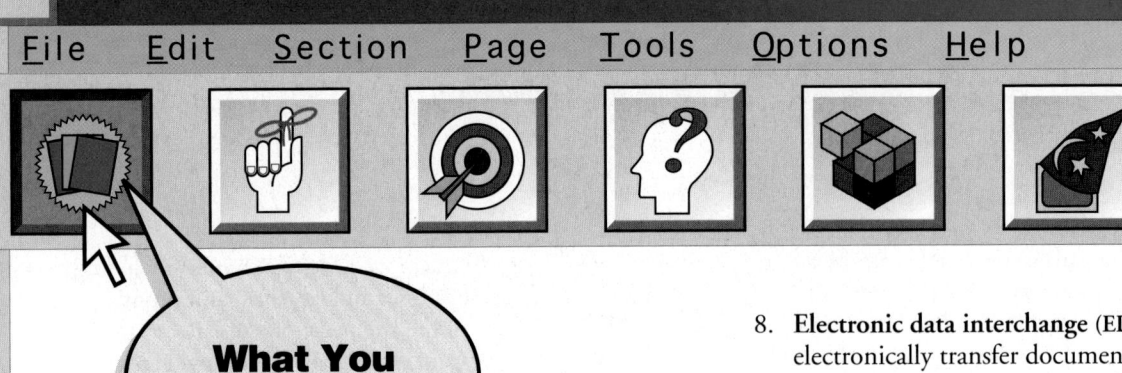

What You Should Know

1. The capability of a computer to communicate with other computers, sometimes called connectivity, allows users to quickly and directly access data and information that otherwise would have been unavailable or that probably would have taken considerable time to acquire.

2. **Electronic mail** is the capability to use computers to transmit messages and receive messages from other computer users.

3. **Voice mail,** which can be considered verbal electronic mail, digitizes a caller's message so it can be stored on disk like other computer data.

4. Today, **teleconferencing** usually means video conferencing, the use of computers and television cameras to transmit video images and the sound of the participant(s) to a remote location that has compatible equipment.

5. **Facsimile,** or FAX, equipment is used to transmit a reproduced image of a document over phone lines. FAX machines convert the image into digitized data that is transmitted and then convert the digitized data back into its original image at the receiving end.

6. **Groupware** is a loosely defined term applied to software that helps multiple users work together by sharing information. Groupware is part of a broad concept called **workgroup technology** that includes equipment and software that help group members communicate and manage their activities.

7. **Telecommuting** refers to the ability of individuals to work at home and communicate with their offices by using personal computers and communications channels.

8. **Electronic data interchange** (EDI) is the capability to electronically transfer documents from one business to another. EDI is frequently used by large companies for routine transactions such as purchase orders and billing.

9. A **global positioning system** (GPS) uses satellites to determine the geographic location of earthbased GPS equipment. GPS systems are often used for tracking and navigation of all types of vehicles.

10. A **bulletin board system** (BBS) allows users to communicate with one another and share information.

11. **Online services,** sometimes called **information services,** include information and services provided to users who subscribe to the service for a fee.

12. **Communications,** sometimes called **data communications,** refers to the transmission of data and information over a communications channel between one computer or terminal and another computer. **Telecommunications** describes any type of long-distance communications including television signals. **Teleprocessing** refers to the use of computers and communications equipment to access computers and computer files located elsewhere.

13. A **communications channel,** also called a **communications line, communications link,** or **data link,** is the path the data follows as it is transmitted from the sending equipment to the receiving equipment in a communications system.

14. **Transmission media** are the materials or technologies that are used to establish the communications channel. Two types of transmission media are those that use some type of physical cabling (including twisted pair wire, coaxial cable, and fiber-optics cable) and those that use wireless technology (including microwaves, radio waves, or light waves).

15. **Twisted pair wire** consists of pairs of copper wires that are twisted together. Twisted pair wire is commonly used for telephone lines and to connect personal computers with one another.

16. A **coaxial cable** is a high-quality, heavily insulated communications line that is used in offices and can be laid underground or underwater. **Baseband** coaxial cable carries one signal at a time. **Broadband** coaxial cable can carry multiple signals at one time.

17. **Fiber-optic** cable uses smooth, hair-thin strands of glass to conduct light with high efficiency. Fiber optics is frequently being used in new voice and data installations.

18. **Microwaves** are radio waves that can be used to provide high-speed transmission of both voice and data. Data is transmitted through the air from one microwave station to another in a manner similar to the way radio signals are transmitted.

19. **Communications satellites** receive microwave signals from earth, amplify the signals, and retransmit the signals back to earth. **Earth stations** are communications facilities that use large, dish-shaped antennas to transmit and receive data from satellites. The transmission *to* the satellite is called an **uplink** and the transmission *from* the satellite to a receiving earth station is called a **down-link**. To transmit a limited amount of information, a small satellite dish can be used. **Very small aperture terminal** (VSAT) antenna measuring only one to three meters in size can transmit up to 19,200 bits per second. Communications satellites are usually positioned about 22,300 miles above the earth in a **geosynchonous orbit**, meaning that the satellite is placed in an orbit where it rotates with the earth.

20. **Wireless transmission** uses one of three techniques to transmit data: light beams, radio waves, or carrier-connect radio. A **cellular telephone** uses radio waves to communicate with a local antenna assigned to a specific geographic area called a cell.

21. Two major **line configurations** (types of line connections) commonly used in communications are point-to-point lines and multidrop, or multipoint, lines.

22. A **point-to-point** line is a direct line between a sending and a receiving device. A **switched line** uses a regular telephone line to establish a communications connection. The process of establishing the communications connection is sometimes referred to as the **handshake**. A **dedicated line** is a line connection that is always established (unlike the switched line where the line connection is reestablished each time it is used). If the dedicated line is provided by an outside organization, it is sometimes called a **leased line**, or a **private line**.

23. The second major line configuration is called a **multidrop**, or **multipoint**, **line**. This type of line configuration is commonly used to connect multiple devices on a single line to a main computer, sometimes called a **host computer**.

24. Communications channels can be categorized by a number of characteristics including the type of signal, transmission mode, transmission direction, and transmission rate.

25. Computer equipment is designed to process data as **digital signals**, which are individual electrical pulses that represent the bits that are grouped together to form characters. Telephone equipment was originally designed to carry only voice transmission, which is comprised of a continuous electrical wave called an **analog signal**. A special piece of equipment called a modem is used to convert between the digital signals and analog signals so that telephone lines can carry data. To provide better communication services, telephone companies are now offering **digital data service** communications channels, which are specifically designed to carry digital instead of voice signals. Modems are not needed with digital data service; instead, users connect to the communications line through a device called a **digital service unit** (DSU).

26. In **asynchronous transmission mode**, individual bytes (made up of bits) are transmitted at irregular intervals, such as when a user enters data. In the **synchronous transmission mode**, large blocks of data are transmitted at regular intervals.

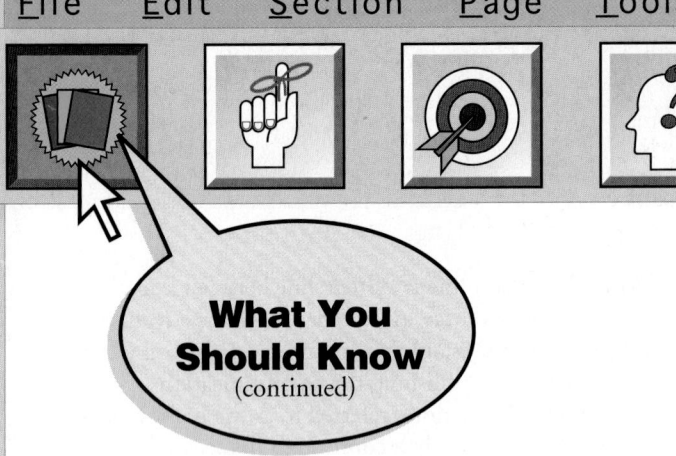

What You Should Know
(continued)

27. In **simplex transmission**, data flows in one direction only. In **half-duplex transmission**, data can flow in both directions but in only one direction at a time. In **full-duplex transmission**, data can be sent in both directions at the same time.

28. The transmission rate of a communications channel is determined by its bandwidth and its speed. The **bandwidth** is the range of frequencies that a channel can carry. The speed at which data is transmitted is usually expressed as **bits per second (bps)**, the number of bits that can be transmitted in one second, or as **baud rate**, the number of times per second the signal being transmitted changes.

29. A variety of communications equipment exists to increase or change a signal to transmit it farther, but the equipment a user is most likely to encounter is a modem, a multiplexor, and a front-end processor. Computers that are connected to a network usually require a network interface card.

30. A **modem** converts the digital signals of a terminal or computer to analog signals that are transmitted over a communications channel. An **external modem** is a separate, or stand-alone, device that is attached to the computer or terminal by a cable and to the telephone outlet by a standard telephone cord. An **internal modem** is a circuit board that is installed inside a computer or terminal.

31. A **multiplexor**, sometimes referred to as a MUX, combines more than one input signal into a single stream of data that can be transmitted over a communications channel, thus increasing the efficiency of communications and saving on the cost of individual communications channels.

32. A **front-end processor** is a computer that is dedicated to handling the communications requirements of a larger computer. Tasks that the front-end processor would handle include **polling** (checking the connected terminals or computers to see if they have data to send), error checking and correction, and access security.

33. A **network interface card** (NIC) fits in an expansion slot of a computer and attaches to the cable or wireless technology used to connect the devices in the network.

34. Programs that a user must load before transmitting data, referred to as **communications software**, can perform a number of tasks. **Dialing software** allows you to store, review, select, and dial telephone numbers of computers that can be called. **File transfer software** allows you to move one or more files from one system to another. **Terminal emulation software** allows a personal computer to imitate or appear to be a specific type of terminal so the personal computer can connect to another usually larger computer. **Data encryption** protects confidential data through the conversion of data at the sending end into an unrecognizable string of characters or bits and the reconversion of the data at the receiving end.

35. A **protocol** is a set of rules and procedures for exchanging information between computers. The International Standards Organization (ISO) based in Geneva, Switzerland has defined a set of communications protocols, called the **Open Systems Interconnection** (OSI) model, which has been endorsed by the United Nations.

36. A communications **network** is a collection of terminals, computers, and other equipment that uses communications channels to share data, information, hardware, and software.

37. A **local area network**, or LAN, is a privately owned communications network that covers a limited geographic area. Three common applications of local area networks are hardware, software, and information resource sharing.

38. **Hardware resource sharing** allows each personal computer in the network to access and use devices that would be too expensive to provide for each user or would not be justified for each user because of only occasional use. A **server** is a computer dedicated to handling the communications needs of the other computers in a network.

39. **Software resource sharing** consists of storing frequently used software on the hard disk of the server so the software can be accessed by multiple users. When a commercial software package is accessed by many users, it is sometimes necessary to obtain a special agreement from the software vendor called a **site license**.

40. **Information resource sharing** allows anyone using a personal computer on the local area network to access data stored on any other computer in the network. Using the **file-server** method, the server sends an entire file at a time and the requesting computer then performs the processing. With the **client-server** method, as much processing as possible is done on the server system before the data is transmitted.

41. A **peer-to-peer network** allows any computer to share software, data, or hardware located on any other computer in the network. A **network operating system (NOS)** is software that allows a user to manage the resources of a computer network.

42. A **wide area network**, or WAN, is geographic in scope (as opposed to local) and uses telephone lines, microwaves, satellites, or a combination of communications channels. A wide area network limited to the area surrounding a city is sometimes referred to as a **metropolitan area network**, or MAN. Public wide area network companies include so-called **common carriers** such as the telephone companies. Companies called **value-added carriers** lease channels from the common carriers to provide specialized communications services referred to as **value-added networks** (VANs). **Packet-switching** combines individual packets of information from various users and transmits them together over a high-speed channel. Most common carriers are now offering **Integrated Services Digital Network** (ISDN) services. ISDN is an international standard for the digital transmission of both voice and data using different channels and communications companies.

43. The largest and best known wide area network is the Internet. The **Internet** is a worldwide network of computer networks.

44. The configuration, or physical layout, of the equipment in a communications network is called **topology**. Devices connected to a network, such as terminals, printers, or other computers, are referred to as **nodes**.

45. A **star network** contains a central computer and one or more terminals or personal computers connected to it, forming a star. A star network configuration is often used when the central computer contains all the data required to process the input from the terminals.

46. When a **bus network** is used, all the devices in the network are connected to and share a single cable. Information is transmitted in either direction from any one personal computer to another.

47. A **ring network** does not use a centralized host computer. Data travels around a ring network in one direction only and passes through each node. A **token ring network** constantly circulates an electronic signal, called a token, around the network. If a device has the token, a message can be sent.

48. A **gateway** is a combination of hardware and software that allows users on one network access to the resources on a *different* type of network. A **bridge** is a combination of hardware and software that is used to connect *similar* networks. A **router** is an intelligent network connecting device that can route communications traffic directly to the appropriate network.

File   Edit   Section   Page   Tools   Options   Help

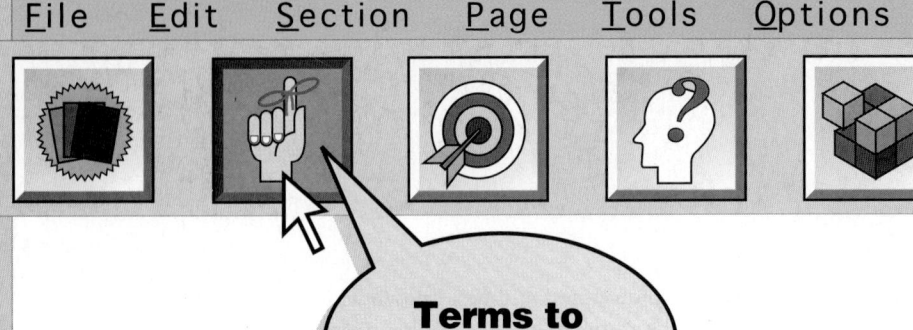

Terms to Remember

analog signal (7.16)
asynchronous transmission mode
   (7.16)

bandwidth (7.17)
baseband (7.9)
baud rate (7.18)
bits per second (bps) (7.18)
bridge (7.27)
broadband (7.10)
bulletin board system (BBS) (7.7)
bus network (7.26)

cellular telephone (7.12)
client-server (7.23)
coaxial cable (7.9)
common carriers (7.24)
communications (7.8)
communications channel (7.8)
communications line (7.8)
communications link (7.8)
communications satellites (7.11)
communications software (7.20)

data communications (7.8)
data encryption (7.20)
data link (7.8)
dedicated line (7.14)
dialing software (7.20)
digital data service (7.16)
digital service unit (DSU) (7.16)
digital signals (7.16)
downlink (7.11)

earth stations (7.11)
electronic data interchange (EDI) (7.5)
electronic mail (7.2)
external modem (7.19)

facsimile (7.4)
FAX (7.4)
fiber optics (7.10)

file-server (7.23)
file transfer software (7.20)
front-end processor (7.19)
full-duplex transmission (7.17)

gateway (7.27)
geosynchronous orbit (7.11)
global positioning system (GPS) (7.6)
groupware (7.4)

half-duplex transmission (7.17)
handshake (7.14)
hardware resource sharing (7.21)
host computer (7.15)

information resource sharing (7.22)
information services (7.7)
information superhighway (7.31)
Integrated Services Digital Network
   (ISDN) (7.24)
internal modem (7.19)
Internet (7.25)

LAN (7.21)
leased line (7.15)
line configurations (7.14)
local area network (LAN) (7.21)

MAN (7.24)
metropolitan area network
   (MAN) (7.24)
microwaves (7.11)
modem (7.18)
multidrop line (7.15)
multiplexor (7.19)
multipoint line (7.15)

National Information Infrastructure
   (NII) (7.31)
network (7.21)
network interface card (NIC) (7.19)
network operating system
   (NOS) (7.23)
nodes (7.26)

online services (7.7)
Open Systems Interconnection
   (OSI) (7.21)

packet-switching (7.24)
peer-to-peer network (7.23)
point-to-point line (7.14)
polling (7.19)
private line (7.15)
protocol (7.21)

ring network (7.27)
router (7.27)

server (7.22)
simplex transmission (7.17)
site license (7.22)
software resource sharing (7.22)
star network (7.26)
switched line (7.14)
synchronous transmission mode (7.17)

telecommunications (7.8)
telecommuting (7.5)
teleconferencing (7.3)
teleprocessing (7.8)
terminal emulation software (7.20)
token ring network (7.27)
topology (7.26)
transmission media (7.9)
twisted pair wire (7.9)

uplink (7.11)

value-added carriers (7.24)
value-added networks (VANs) (7.24)
very small aperture terminal
   (VSAT) (7.11)
voice mail (7.3)

WAN (7.24)
wide area network (WAN) (7.24)
wireless transmission (7.12)
workgroup technology (7.4)

ile   Edit   Section   Page   Tools   Options   Help

Fill in the Blanks

1. _Communication_ refers to the transmission of data and information over a channel such as a telephone line, between one computer and another computer.

2. In _____ transmission mode, individual bytes (made up of bits) are transmitted at irregular intervals, while in _____ transmission mode, large blocks of data are transmitted at regular intervals.

3. The direction of data transmission is classified as either _____ (data flows in one direction only), _____ (data can flow in both directions but in only one direction at a time), or _____ (data can be sent in both directions at the same time).

4. Communications equipment includes a(n) _____, which converts the digital signals of a terminal or computer to analog signals, a(n) _____, which combines more than one input signal into a single stream of data, a(n) _____, which is a computer dedicated to handling the communications requirements of a larger computer, and a(n) _____ that fits in an expansion slot of a computer and attaches to the cable or wireless technology used to connect the devices in a network.

5. A(n) _____ is a combination of hardware and software that allows users on one network to access the resources on a different network, while a(n) _____ is a combination of hardware and software that is used to connect similar networks.

Short Answer

1. List seven examples of how communications technology is used. Briefly describe each.

2. Name three transmission media that use some type of physical cabling. How are they different? Name three transmission media that use wireless technology. How are they different?

3. Two major line configurations commonly used in communications are point-to-point lines and multidrop lines. What are point-to-point lines? How is a switched line different from a dedicated line? What are multidrop lines?

4. What is communications software? Describe four tasks that can be performed by communications software.

5. What is a network? How is a local area network (LAN) different from a wide area network (WAN)? Briefly describe three common network topologies.

Label the Figure

Instructions: Identify the basic components of a communications system shown in the figure below.

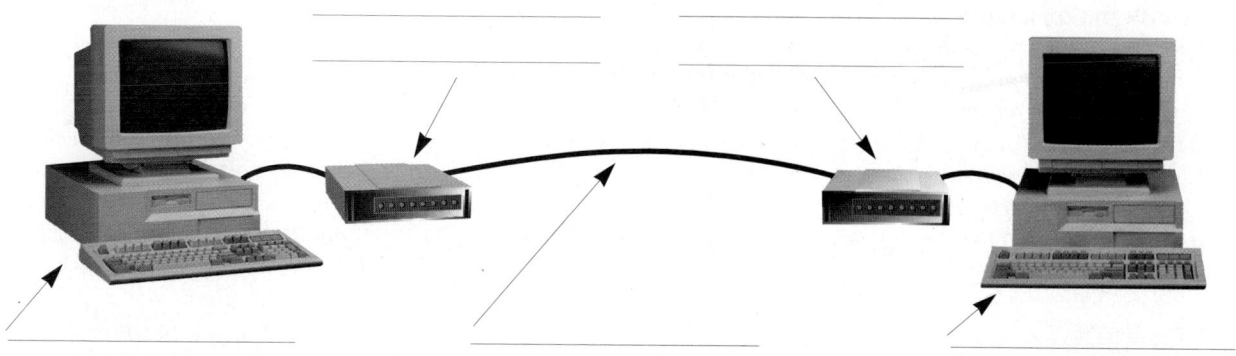

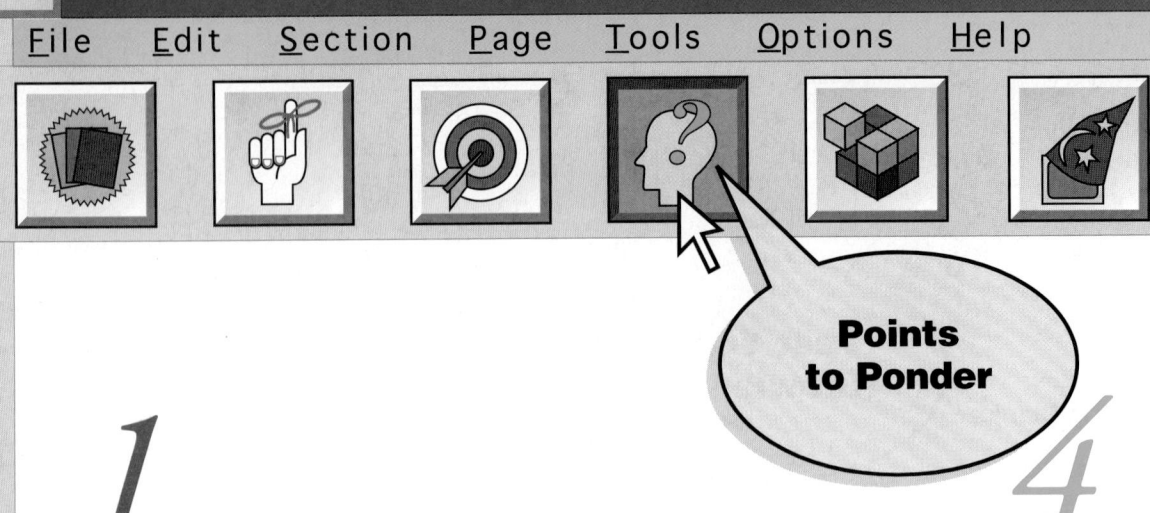

Points to Ponder

1

This chapter describes several applications that rely on communications technology. Which of these applications would you be most likely to use as a college student? Which application do you think you would use in your career? Which application would you be most likely to use for social reasons? Which application do you think will have the greatest impact on society over the next twenty-five years? Explain why you answered each part of this question as you did.

2

Plagiarism is the act of stealing someone else's ideas or words and passing them off as one's own. In ancient Greece, however, "plagiarism" often worked in reverse; in an effort to give his thoughts a wider audience, an unknown author would pass off his own ideas or words as the work of someone famous. Some people feel that the anonymity provided by electronic mail and computerized bulletin board systems will also lead to a wider dissemination of ideas by eliminating biases based on age, gender, race, social class, or cultural origin. Others believe, however, that the high cost of the necessary computer equipment will continue to keep a large percentage of the population silent. What do you think? Will these applications give more people the opportunity to express their views? Why or why not?

3

Computer bulletin board systems (BBSs) have led to some controversies related to the issue of free speech. Police have closed bulletin board systems providing information that could be used to commit crimes, such as telephone codes that can be employed to make free long-distance telephone calls. It is more difficult, however, to control the posting of confidential material, hate messages, and discriminatory correspondence. Bulletin board systems are often available to a large geographic area, and statutes and standards vary from state to state and community to community. Some BBS operators have pulled communications they considered objectionable, but many feel this amounts to censorship. Do you think a bulletin board system operator has the right to control what information is presented? Why or why not? What regulations, if any, do you think should be passed to control the type of material that can be posted on a bulletin board system? Why?

4

The number of employees telecommuting either full or part time in the United States more than doubled from 1988 to 1991 and is expected to double again by 1996. Studies have shown that telecommuting workers are 10 to 20 percent more productive than their office-bound brethren. There are disadvantages to telecommuting, however, including the inability of office managers to oversee workers, the difficulty in conducting spontaneous staff meetings, and a potential loss of "team spirit." Whether or not telecommuting is a success seems to depend primarily on the employee's personality and the employer's ability to make adjustments. What type of personality do you think is necessary for someone to telecommute successfully? What types of adjustments must be made by employers? Given your personality and the career you intend to pursue, do you think you would be a successful telecommuter? Why or why not?

5

During a typical day, you probably encounter communication situations that have distinct directions of transmission. Describe three circumstances you have experienced with different directions of transmission; one in which the direction of communication was comparable to simplex transmission, another in which the direction

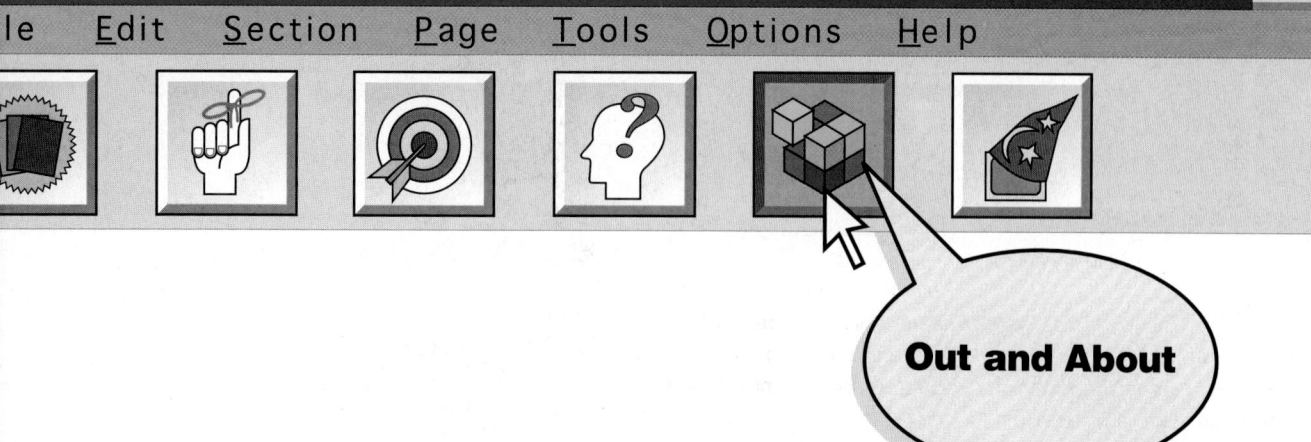

Out and About

of communication was comparable to half-duplex transmission, and a third in which the direction of communication was comparable to full-duplex transmission. Why did you classify each situation as you did? Do you think communication would have been improved if the direction of transmission had been different? Why or why not?

6

Although analog telephone transmissions can be tapped fairly easily, data encryption can make digital telephone transmissions very difficult to tap. So that police can gather the evidence necessary to convict some criminals, the FBI has proposed legislation that would require all providers of electronic communications to use equipment capable of being wiretapped. An encryption standard, the details of which would be available only to law enforcement agencies, has also been presented that would eventually eliminate all other standards. Some businesses and civil liberties groups have objected to the proposals, insisting that wiretapping would become too easy, and there is no guarantee unauthorized government eavesdropping would not take place. What do you think? Should government be allowed to regulate data communications? Why or why not?

1. Many experts feel that online information services will eventually be as much a part of our lives as newspapers, radio, and television are today. Figure 7-8 on page 7.7 furnishes the names of major online information service providers and offers a brief description of each. Call the phone numbers for at least three of the services listed to obtain additional information. What services are offered? Does the service require a particular type of user interface? What is the membership fee? Are there other fees (such as a minimum monthly charge, hourly access fee, or added cost for certain services)? From the information supplied, in which online information service are you most interested? Why?

2. Questions have been raised regarding concerns that cellular telephones cause brain tumors or other health problems. A Florida man has filed a lawsuit, claiming that his wife's death resulted from a brain tumor induced by radiation from her cellular telephone. Although the Cellular Telecommunications Industry Association maintains thousands of studies have been done showing the phones are not hazardous, an advisory group that has reviewed the studies feels they contain data gaps and insufficient evidence. Visit a library and, using current newspapers and periodicals, prepare a report on the health issues related to cellular telephone use. On the basis of your findings, do you think the use of cellular telephones is safe? Why or why not? What additional studies, if any, do you think should be done?

File Edit Section Page Tools Options Help

Out and About

3. Many schools and offices have a network connecting their computers. Locate a school or office that uses a network and talk to someone connected to it about how the network works. What are the advantages of having a network? What are the disadvantages? Find out what type of network (star, bus, ring, or token ring) it is and draw a simple diagram of the network. Why is that network topology used? Have there ever been any problems with the network? If so, would the problems have been avoided with a different network configuration? Is the network connected to another network? If so, how?

4. To take advantage of computerized telecommunications over analog phone lines, a modem is an essential piece of equipment. Visit a computer vendor and compare several modems. List the characteristics of each, including such items as the transmission rate, the cost, and whether it is an internal or external modem. If you have a personal computer, or know what type of personal computer you would like to have, ask a salesperson to recommend a modem for your personal computer. On the basis of the information you have gathered, which modem would you be most likely to purchase? Why?

5. Regardless of your interests, a computer bulletin board system (BBS) probably exists that is tailor-made for you. Currently, there are more than 50,000 public-access bulletin boards in the United States dealing with a wide range of topics, including politics, the environment, sports, religion, alternative lifestyles, music, and business opportunities. Make a list of at least three areas of interest to you. Then, by using a personal computer magazine, contacting a local computer users' group, or telephoning an online information service that offers a BBS, discover the name of a bulletin board system that fits each of your interests. If possible, find out the answers to such questions as: How do you connect to the BBS? Are any fees required? Are electronic mail services offered? Are public domain software and shareware provided that can be downloaded (copied from the BBS) to a personal computer system?

6. Facsimile equipment has become incredibly popular. FAX machines are now an essential piece of equipment for even small businesses, and many people have FAX machines in their homes. As a result, FAX machines are now available at a variety of stores including computer stores, office supply stores, discount stores, electronics stores, and catalog stores. Visit three different types of stores and find FAX machines that offer similar features. Write down the brand name of each machine, the available features, in what store the machine was found, and the cost of each. Ask a salesperson to explain the machine's warranty and the store's service policy. From what you have learned, in which store would you be most likely to purchase a FAX machine? Why?

 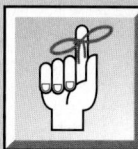    

ile   Edit   Section   Page   Tools   Options   Help

In the Lab

Windows Labs

1 **Understanding the Terminal Window**   With
Program Manager on the screen, double-click the
Accessories group icon. Double-click the Terminal program-
item icon 🖳. Maximize the Terminal window.

Select the Settings menu and choose the Communications command. If all the options are ghosted (dimmed)
in the Communications dialog box, select a connector in
the Connector list box *(Figure 7-38)*. Answer the following
questions: (1) What are the baud rate options? (2) What are
the options for data and stop bits? (3) What are the parity
options? (4) What connectors are in the scrollable list?
Choose the Cancel button. Close Terminal.

2 **Shelly Cashman Series Communications Lab**
Follow the instructions in Windows Lab 2 in Chapter 1
on page 1.30 to display the Shelly Cashman Series Labs
screen. Select Connecting to the Internet by pointing to
it and clicking the left mouse button. When the initial screen
displays, carefully read the objectives. With your printer
turned on, point to the Print Questions button and click
the left mouse button. Fill out the top of the Questions
sheet and answer the questions as you step through the
Communications Lab.

3 **Creating a Text File for File Transfer**   Text files
(also called ASCII files) are often used in online file transfer operations because they can be read by any word processing
package or editor. Many Windows users use Notepad to create
files to upload to a bulletin board or a friend's computer
through the Terminal program.

With Program Manager on the screen, double-click the
Accessories group icon. In the Accessories group window,
double-click the Notepad program-item icon 🗒. Maximize
the Notepad window. Type the first paragraph on page 7.8
under the heading, What Is Communications?, as shown in
Figure 7-39. To indent the first line of the paragraph, press the
SPACEBAR five times. Press the ENTER key at the end of each
line on page 7.8. Use the same error-correction techniques in
Notepad as you used in Write (see Windows Lab 1 in
Chapter 2 on page 2.36). When your document is correct,
save it by choosing the Save command from the File menu,
typing a:win7-3 and choosing the OK button. With your
printer turned on, print the document by choosing the Print
command from the File menu. Close Notepad.

4 **Connecting to a Bulletin Board System**   Turn on
your modem. Open the Terminal window as described
in Windows Lab 1 above. Maximize the Terminal window.
Select the Settings menu and choose the Communications
command. If a connector is not specified, select the
appropriate connector (port). Choose the OK button. Select
the Settings menu and choose the Terminal Preferences command. In the Terminal Font area of the Terminal Preferences
dialog box, enlarge the font size to 14. Choose the OK button.
Select the Settings menu and choose the Phone Number
command. In the Phone Number dialog box, type 1-800-
697-4636 and choose the OK button. Select the Phone menu

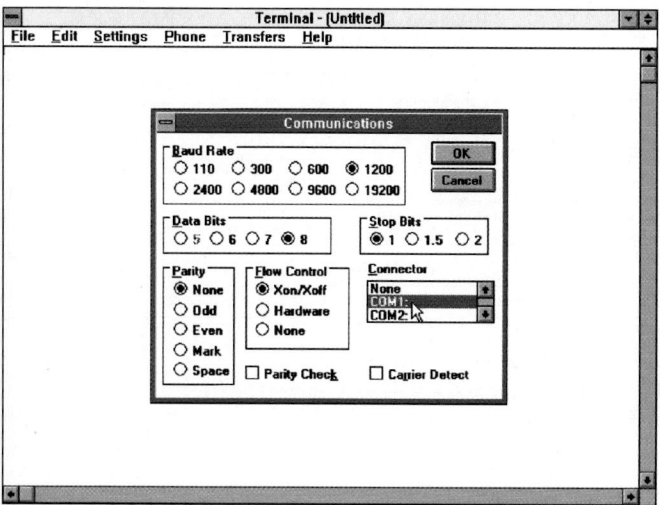

Figure 7-38

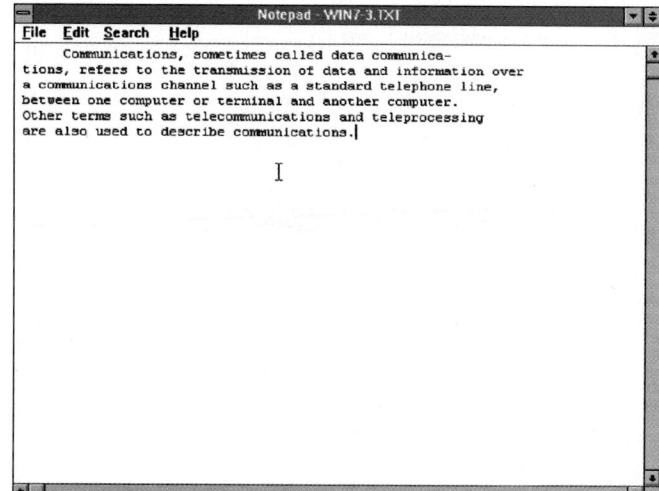

Figure 7-39

File   Edit   Section   Page   Tools   Options   Help

 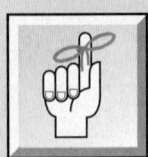    

In the Lab (continued)

and choose the Dial command. While the connection is being established, your computer displays a series of messages *(Figure 7-40)*. What does your system display?

Once you are connected to SBA Online *(Figure 7-41)*, write down your caller number, register yourself, and then use SBA Online to obtain the following information: (1) Identify the purpose of SBA. (2) Discuss one of SBA's programs. (3) List three federal bulletin board systems, along with their Federal Agency, telephone number, and communication speed. (4) List the names and addresses of the senators and representatives in your state. Quit SBA Online. Select the Phone menu and choose Hangup. Close Terminal. Choose the No button to not save settings. Close Accessories.

5 **Using Help**   With Program Manager on the screen, double-click the Main group icon. In the Main group window, double-click the Windows Setup program-item icon. If your system has a network installed, write down its name. Select the Windows Setup Help menu and choose the Contents command. One by one, click the green items below the How To Help topic. Read and print the contents of the windows. After printing each window, click the Back button to return to the Contents window. Close Help. Close Windows Setup.

DOS Labs

1 **Understanding Your System's Configuration**   At the DOS prompt, type msd and press the ENTER key to display the Microsoft Diagnostics (MSD) program. If your system displays a Microsoft Windows message, press the ENTER key.

If your system has a network installed, write down its name. Press N to display the Network window. Write down your station number. Press ENTER. How many COM Ports does your system have? Press C to display the COM Ports window. For each COM port listed, identify its baud rate, number of data bits, and number of stop bits. Press ENTER to return to the MSD screen. Press F3 to exit MSD.

2 **Creating a Brief ASCII File for File Transfer**   At the DOS prompt, type copy con a:dos7-2.txt and press the ENTER key. Type your name and press the ENTER key. Type your course name and press the ENTER key. Press F6. Press the ENTER key. Display the file by typing type a:dos7-2.txt and pressing the ENTER key. Print the file by typing print a:dos7-2.txt and pressing the ENTER key twice.

3 **Using Help**   At the DOS prompt, type help msd and press the ENTER key to display help on the Microsoft Diagnostics program. Read and print the information on the Notes and Examples jump topics. Exit the Help window.

Online Lab

1 **Corresponding via Electronic Mail**   Using one of the two online services you selected in Chapter 1, connect to the service and perform the following tasks: (1) Obtain the account number of a friend or someone on the service who has the same interests as you. (2) Search the service for the Electronic Mail section. Read the policy on electronic mail. (3) Send a message to the person you selected and ask him or her to respond to your message. (4) Later, check for mail. Display and print the message sent back to you.

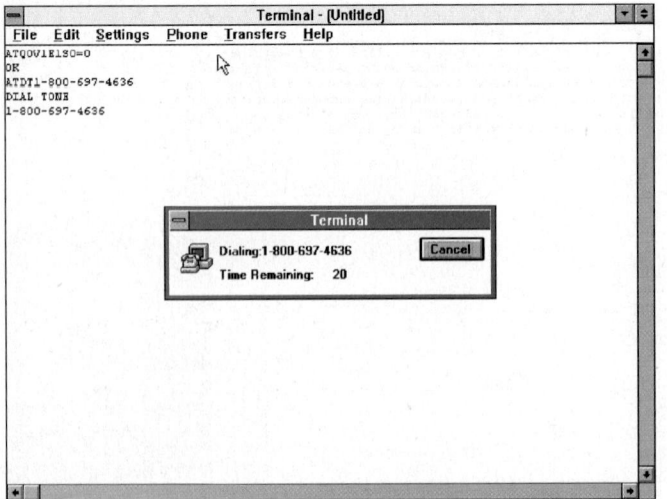

Figure 7-40

Figure 7-41

The Internet

The Internet is a network of networks. It links approximately 30 million people and thousands of organizations worldwide. The number of people using the Internet is growing 5% each month. The Internet is a vast resource of information and services. Some of the things you can do on the Internet are listed on the right.

- Send and receive electronic mail
- Transfer files
- Search databases
- Participate in discussions on particular subjects
- Play games
- Run programs on remote computers
- Order products and services

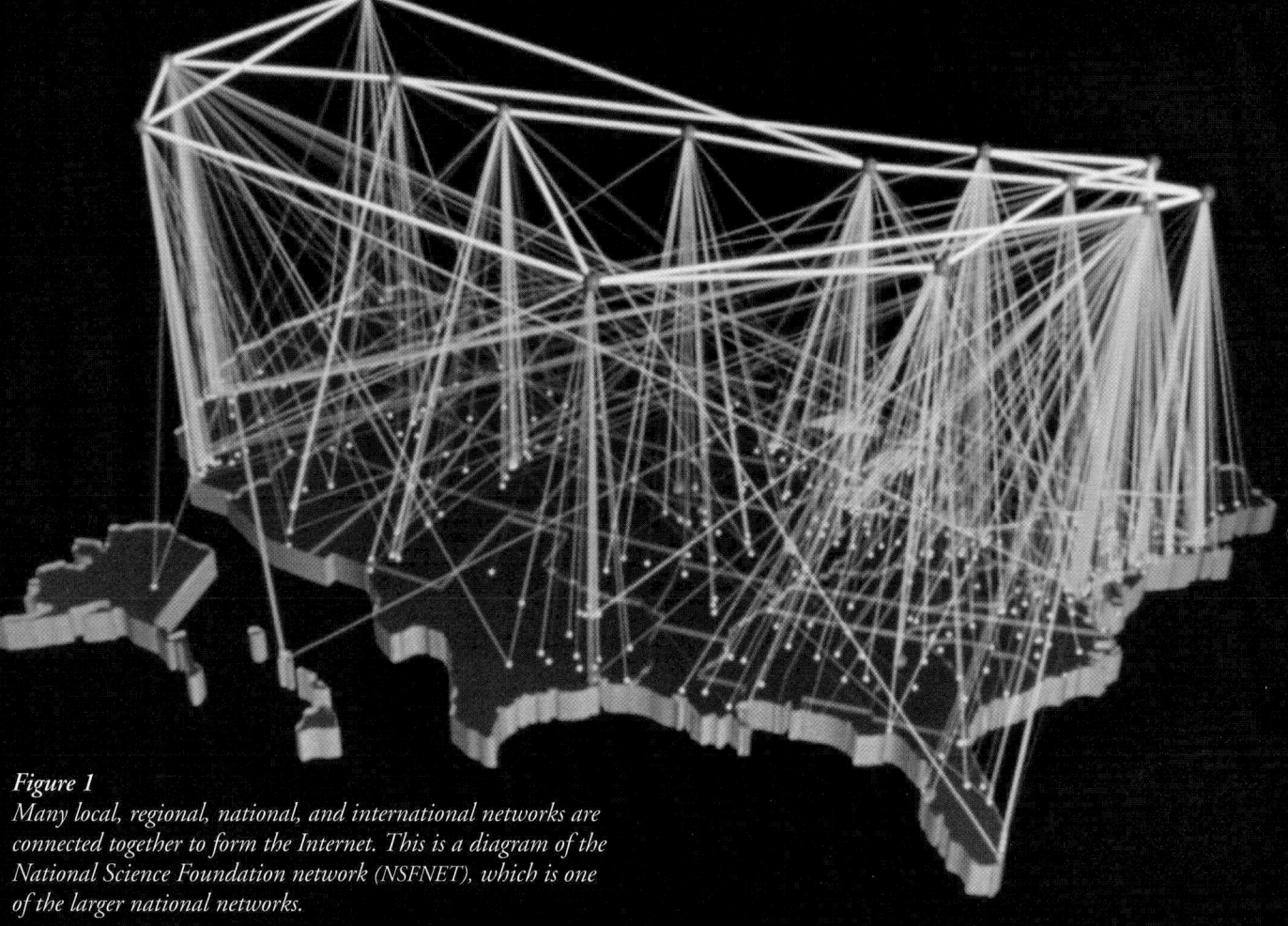

Figure 1
Many local, regional, national, and international networks are connected together to form the Internet. This is a diagram of the National Science Foundation network (NSFNET), which is one of the larger national networks.

- **30 million users**
- **Users located in more than 100 countries**
- **20,000 member organizations**
- **21,000 connected networks**
- **2 million networked computers**
- **Number of users growing at 5% per month**

INTERNET TERMS

ARCHIE	A method of locating files on the Net.
FAQ	Frequently Asked Question. Lists of FAQs help users learn about a particular topic on the Net.
FLAME	Slang term for an aggressive or rude message.
FTP	File Transfer Protocol. Method of transferring files from one computer to another.
GOPHER	A menu-based system for exploring the Net.
IRC	Internet Relay Chat. Interactive discussion among multiple users.
MOSAIC	Graphical user interface that uses hypertext links.
NET	Abbreviation for the Internet.
NEWSGROUPS	Discussion groups on various topics.
PPP	Point-to-Point Protocol. A type of Internet connection.
SLIP	Serial Line Internet Protocol. A type of Internet connection.
SURFING	Slang term for browsing the Net.
TCP/IP	Transmission Control Protocol/Internet Protocol. Primary communications protocol used on the Net.
TELNET	A terminal emulation communications protocol that allows users to login to other computer systems.
URL	Uniform Resource Locator. The Internet address where a document can be found.
USENET	An informal group of systems that exchange news on a variety of topics.
VERONICA	A search tool used with Gopher.
WAIS	Wide Area Information Service. A system for finding information in Net databases.
WWW	World Wide Web. A linked hypertext system used for accessing Net resources.

Figure 2
Common Internet terms.

Figure 3
A quick and easy way to get connected to the Internet is to buy a starter kit such as Internet In A Box. Internet In A Box provides the necessary communications and utility software as well as a guide book of Internet resources.

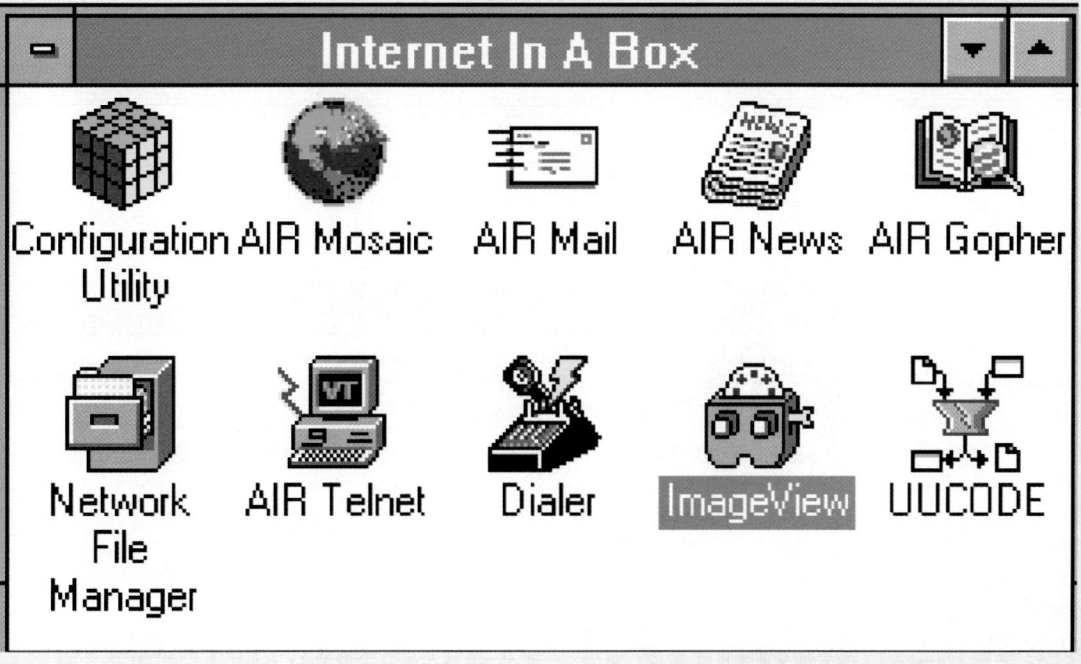

Figure 4
Some portions of the Internet are administered by private companies that provide Internet access and services. This photograph shows the control center of Nearnet, an Internet access provider that serves the northeastern United States.

Figure 5
Sending mail on the Internet is similar to using most electronic mail systems.

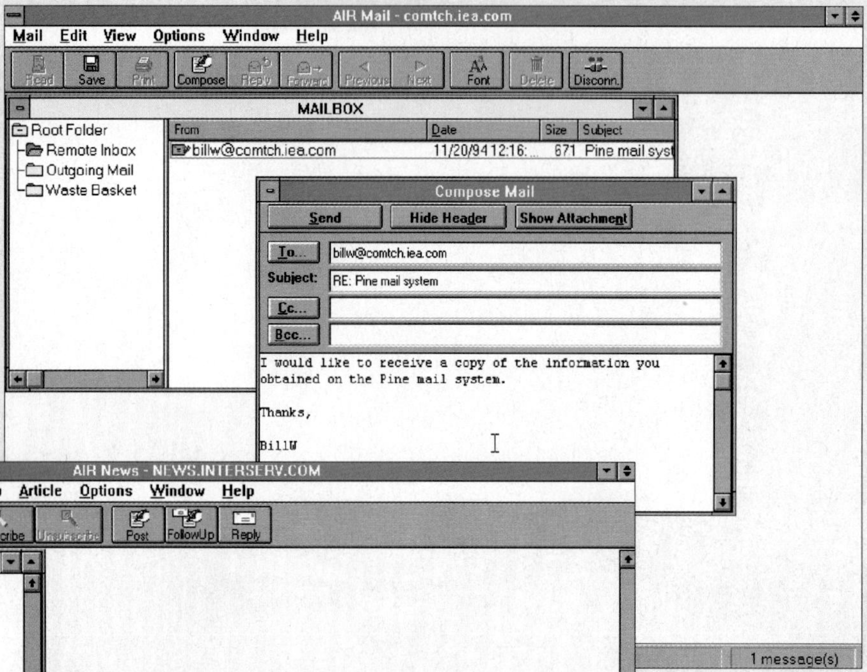

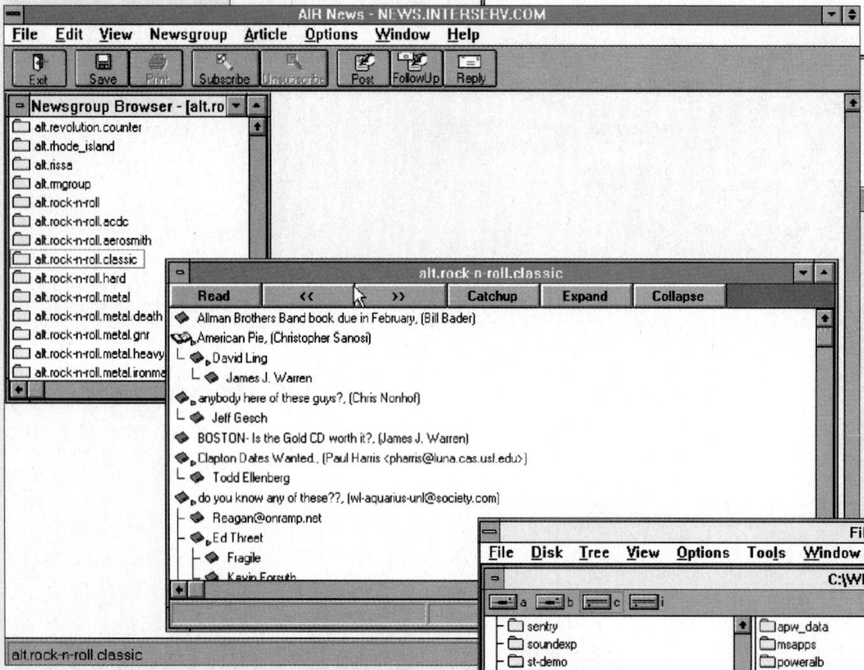

Figure 6
Discussion groups, called newsgroups, exist for thousands of subjects. This screen shows a list of recent messages posted in the classic rock and roll newsgroup. Selecting one of the messages on the list will display the text of the message.

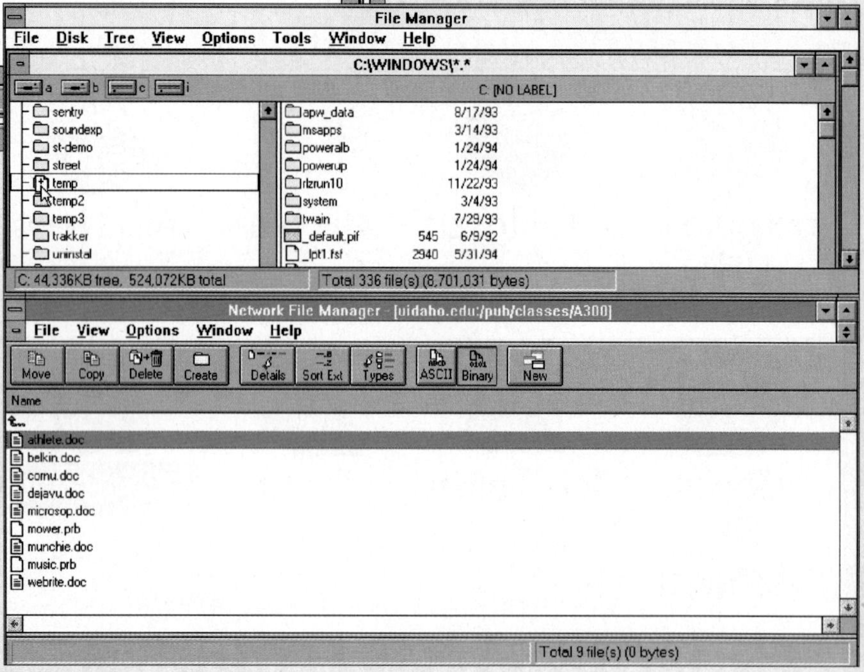

Figure 7
Transferring files on the Internet is easy if you have a graphical user interface as shown in this screen. The chosen file can be dragged from the network file manager in the lower half of the screen to any file directory shown in the file listing in the upper half of the screen. The upper half of the screen shows files on the local system. The bottom half of the screen shows files at the remote Internet location; in this case, the University of Idaho.

Figure 8
A wide variey of information is available on the Internet from government and educational organizations. This screen shows population estimates that are updated monthly by the U.S. Census Bureau.

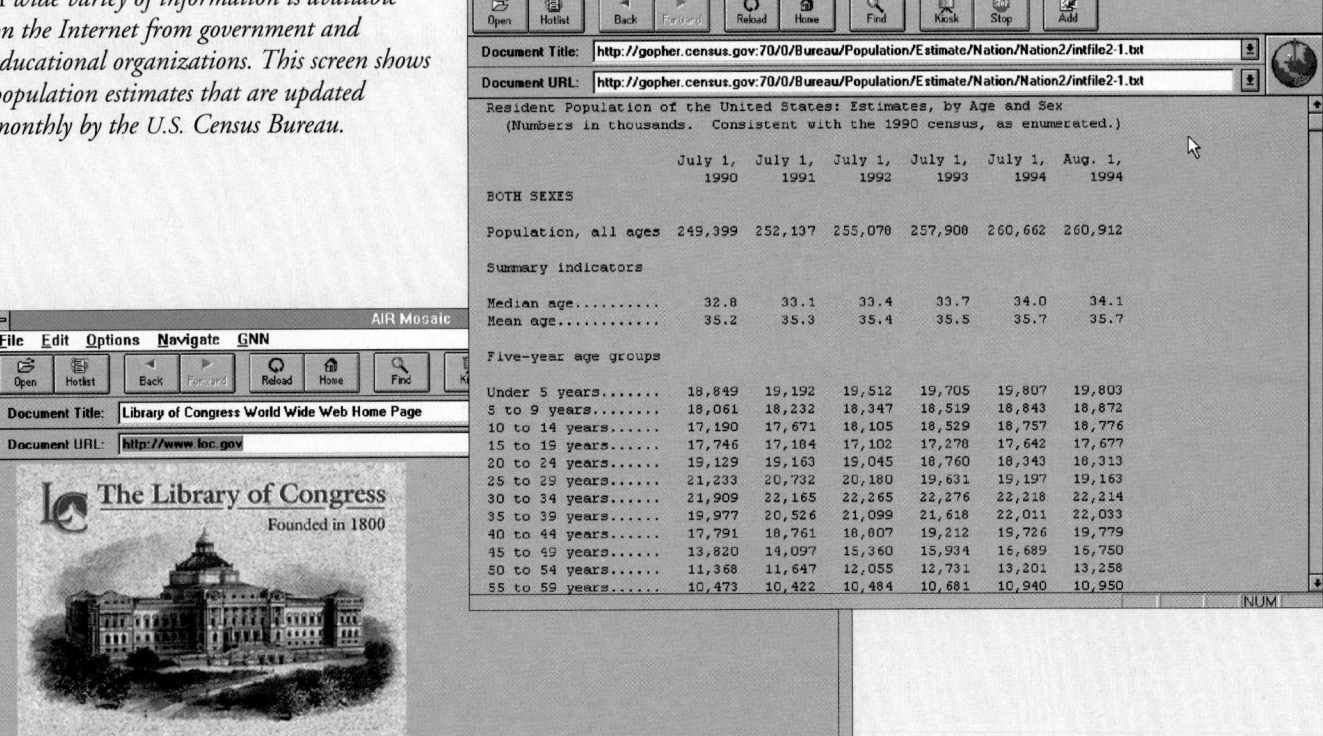

Figure 9
The Library of Congress is another source of research information on many subjects.

Figure 10
A number of employers are now listing job openings and information about their companies on the Internet.

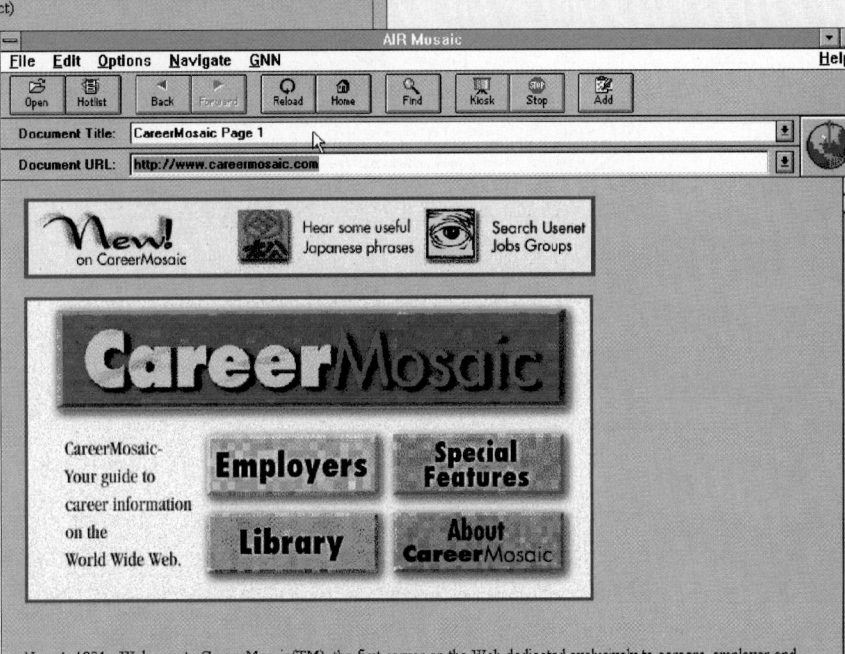

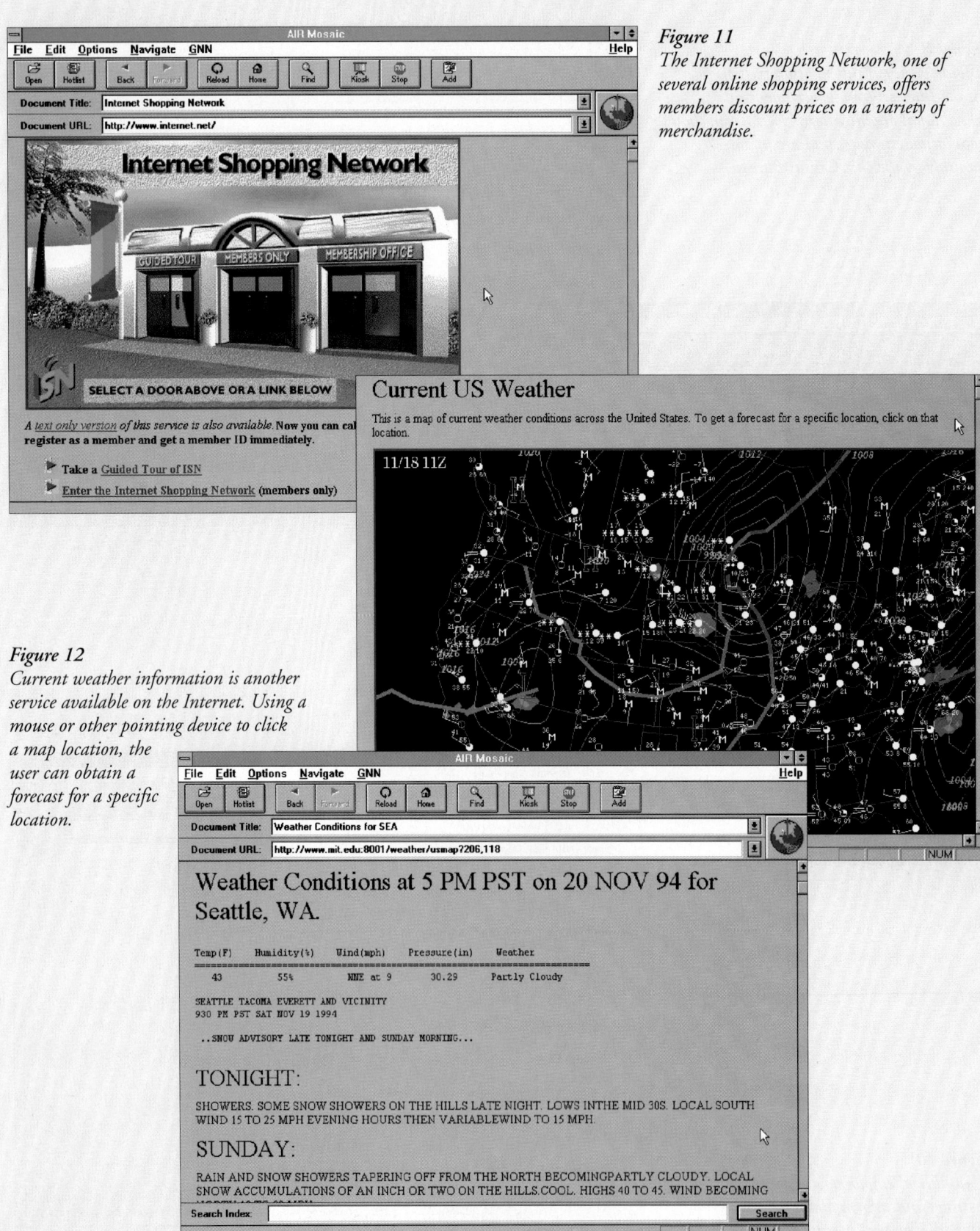

Figure 11
The Internet Shopping Network, one of several online shopping services, offers members discount prices on a variety of merchandise.

Figure 12
Current weather information is another service available on the Internet. Using a mouse or other pointing device to click a map location, the user can obtain a forecast for a specific location.

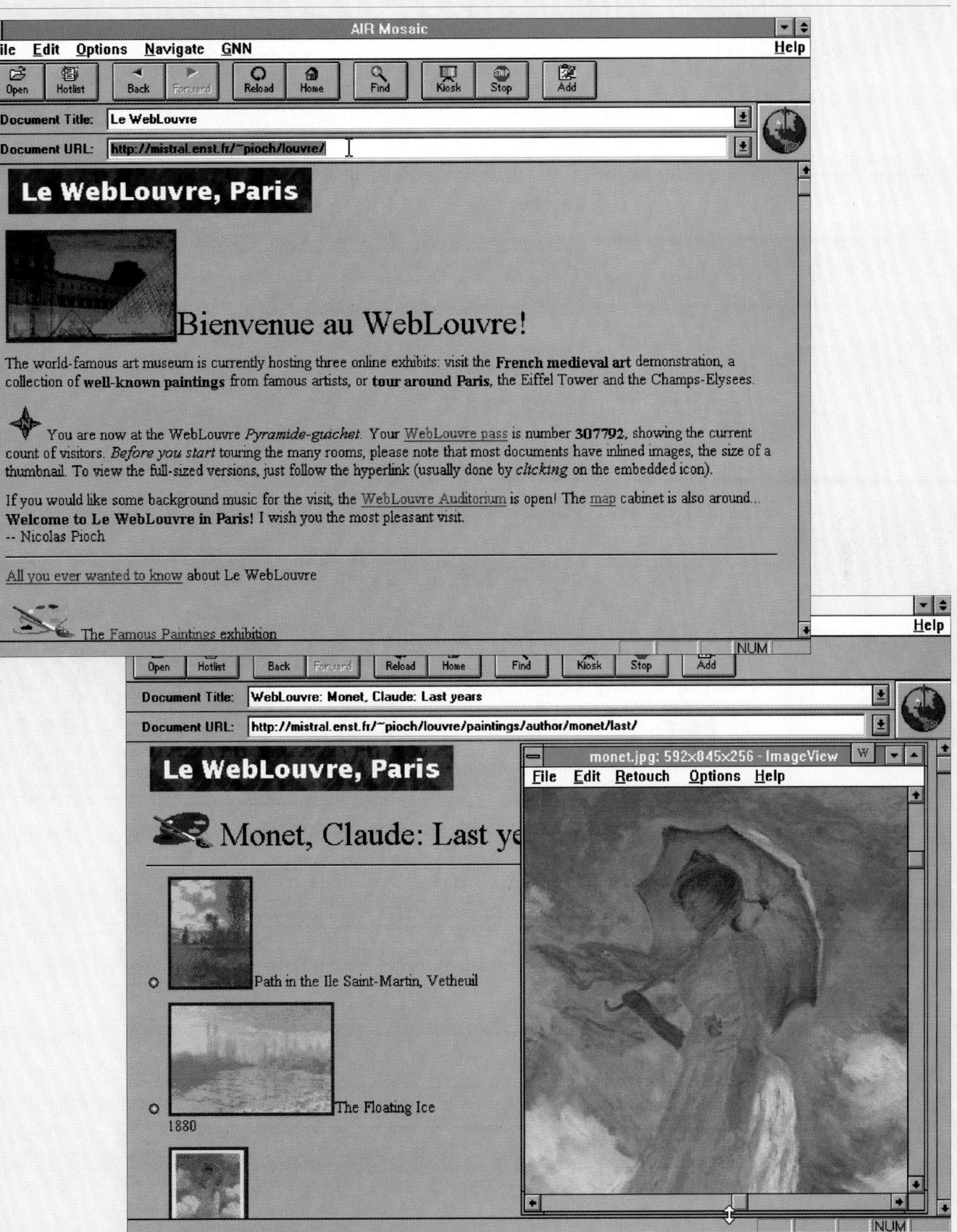

Figure 13
A number of international locations have English language services. These screens above show information
on the Louve Museum in Paris, France. This service resides on a computer in Paris connected to the Internet.
The information includes details on current exhibits and information on famous painters. Digital images of
many of the paintings can be displayed and downloaded.

Figure 14
The White House, home of the United States President, is also connected to the Internet. Electronic visitors can sign the guest book, listen to messages from the President and Vice President, and take a tour.

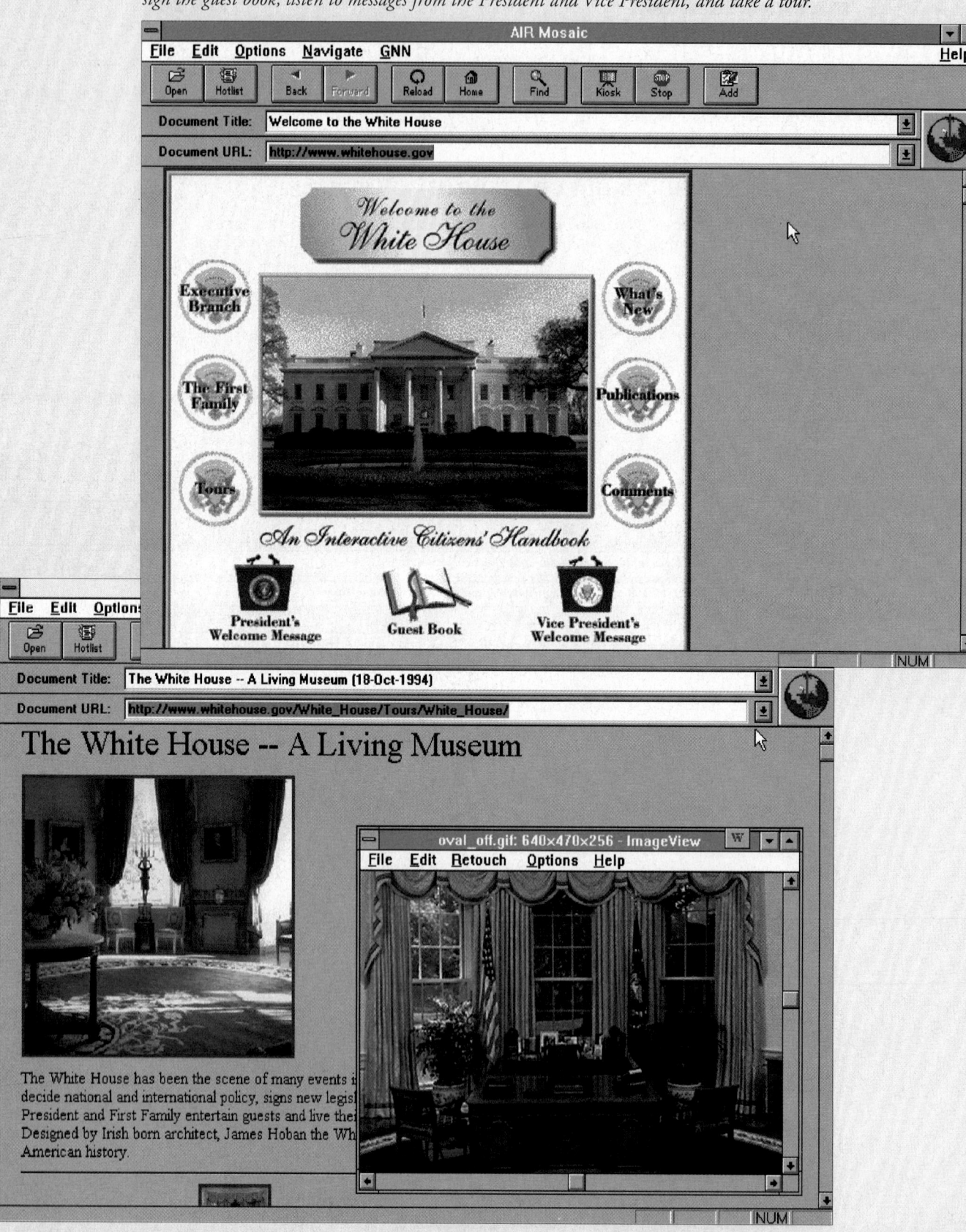

CHAPTER EIGHT

Operating Systems and System Software

8

Objectives

After completing this chapter, you will be able to:

- Describe the three major categories of system software

- Define the term operating system

- Describe the various types of operating systems and explain the differences in their capabilities

- Describe the functions of an operating system, including allocating system resources, monitoring system activities, and disk and file management

- Explain the difference between proprietary and portable operating systems

- Name and briefly describe the major operating systems that are being used today

- Discuss utilities and language translators

When most people think of software they think of application software such as word processing, spreadsheet, and database software. For application software to run on a computer, however, another type of software is needed to interface between the user, the application software, and the equipment. This software consists of programs referred to as the operating system. The operating system is part of what is called system software.

This chapter discusses operating system features of both large and small computer systems. It is important to understand the features of large computer operating systems because these features are steadily being implemented on small systems such as personal computers.

What Is System Software?

System software consists of all the programs including the operating system that are related to controlling the operations of the computer equipment. Some of the functions that system software perform include: starting up the computer; loading, executing, and storing application programs; storing and retrieving files; and performing a variety of functions such as formatting disks, sorting data files, and translating program instructions into machine language. System software can be classified into three major categories; operating systems, utilities, and language translators.

What Is an Operating System?

An **operating system** (OS) consists of one or more programs that control the allocation and usage of hardware resources such as memory, CPU time, disk space, and peripheral devices. These programs function as an interface between the user, the application programs, and the computer equipment *(Figure 8-1)*.

The operating system is usually stored on disk. For a computer to operate, the essential and most frequently used instructions in the operating system must be copied from the disk and stored in the main memory of the computer. This *resident* portion of the operating system is called by many different names: the **supervisor**, **monitor**, **executive**, **master program**, **control program**, or **kernel**. Commands that are included in the resident portion of the operating system are called **internal commands**. The *nonresident* portions of the operating system are called **external commands**. The nonresident portions of the operating system remain on the disk and are available to be loaded into main memory whenever they are needed.

Most operating systems allow the user to give specific instructions to the computer, such as to list all the files on a diskette or to copy a file from one diskette to another. These instructions are called the **command language**. The portion of the operating system that carries out the command language instructions is called the **command language interpreter**.

Figure 8-1
The operating system and other system software programs act as an interface between the user, the application software, and the computer.

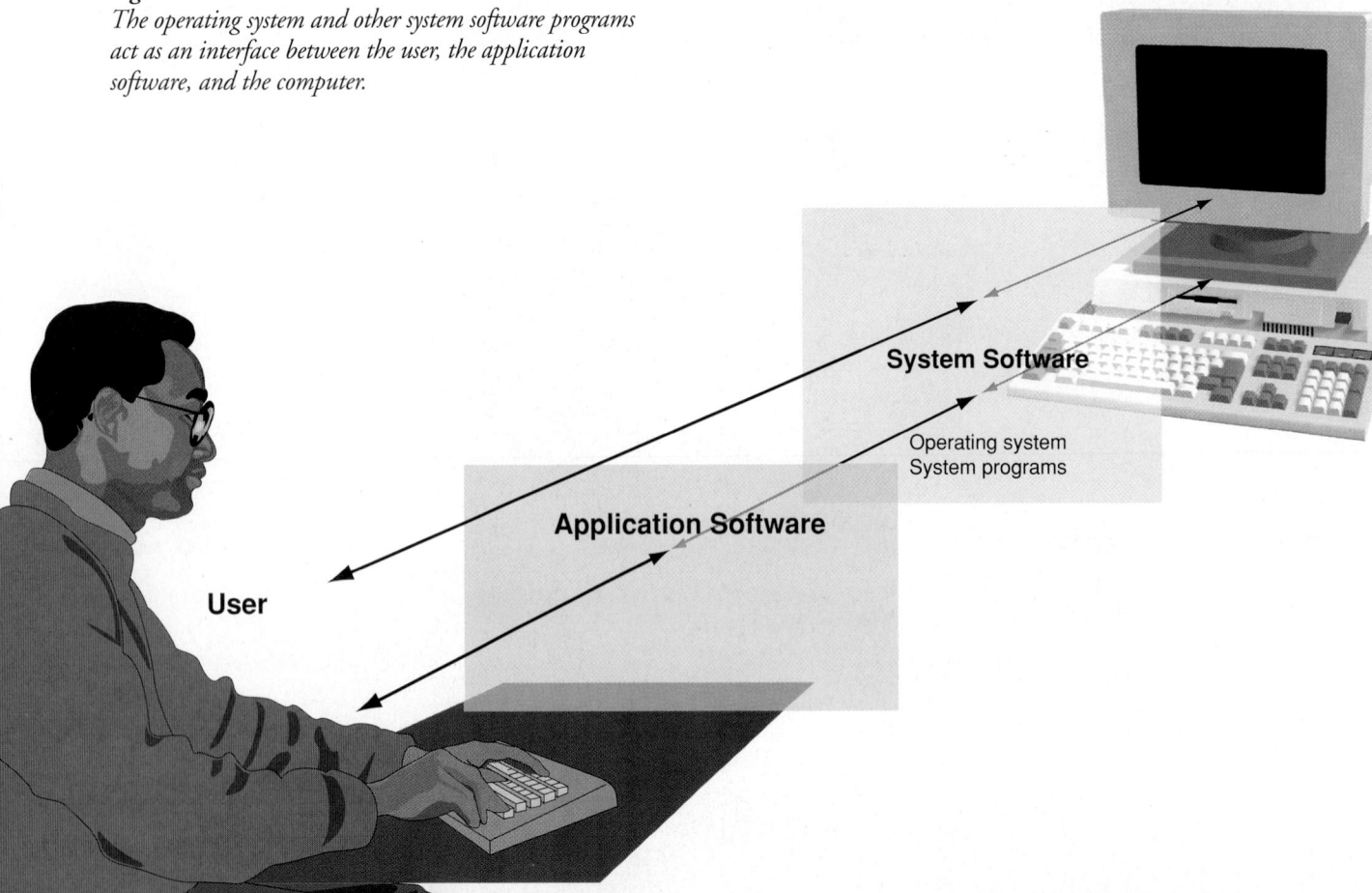

System Software

Operating system
System programs

Application Software

User

Loading an Operating System

The process of loading an operating system into main memory is called **booting** the system. *Figure 8-2* shows information that is displayed during this process. The actual information displayed will vary depending on the make of the computer and the equipment installed. The following steps explain what happens during the boot process on an IBM compatible personal computer that operates using DOS (Disk Operating System).

1. When you turn on your computer, the power supply distributes current to the motherboard and the other devices located in the system unit case.
2. The surge of electricity causes the CPU chip to reset itself and look to the BIOS chip for instructions on how to proceed. BIOS stands for **Basic Input/Output System**. The BIOS is a set of instructions that provides the interface between the operating system and the hardware devices. The BIOS is stored in a read-only memory (ROM) chip.
3. The BIOS chip begins a set of tests to make sure the equipment is working correctly. The tests, called the **POST**, for **Power On Self Test**, check the memory, keyboard, buses, and expansion cards. After some of the early tests are completed, the BIOS instructions are copied into memory where they can be executed faster than in ROM.
4. After the POST tests are successfully completed, the BIOS begins looking for the operating system. Usually, it first looks in diskette drive A. If an operating system disk is not loaded in drive A, the BIOS looks on drive C, the drive letter usually given to the first hard drive.

5. When the BIOS finds the operating system, it begins loading the *resident* portion into memory. For personal computers using a version of DOS, the resident portion is called the *DOS kernel*.
6. The kernel then loads system configuration information. The configuration information is contained in a file called **CONFIG.SYS**. This file tells the computer what devices you are using, such as a mouse, a CD-ROM, a scanner, or other devices. For each of these devices, a device driver program is usually loaded. Device driver programs tell the computer how to communicate with a device.
7. The kernel loads the command language interpreter. On DOS computers, the command language interpreter is called **COMMAND.COM**.
8. COMMAND.COM loads a batch file named **AUTOEXEC.BAT** that performs optional tasks such as telling the system where to look for files (PATH command) and loading programs that you want to run every time you turn on your system, such as certain utility programs.
9. If you haven't specified that the computer immediately start a particular application program, the system displays a **command language prompt** that indicates the system is ready to accept a command from the user. If you always want a particular application program to automatically start during the boot process, such as a word processing program or Microsoft Windows, you include the name of the program as the last line in the AUTOEXEC.BAT file.

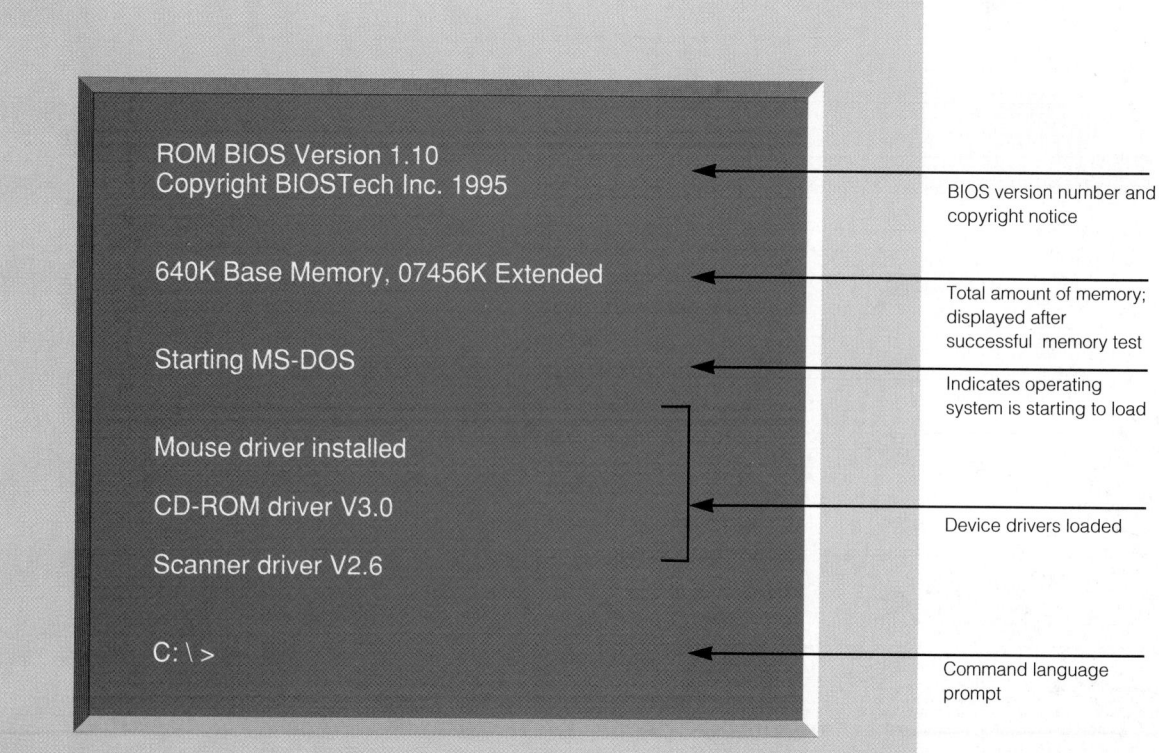

Figure 8-2
An example of information that is displayed during the boot process.

Types of Operating Systems

The types of operating systems include single program, multitasking, multiprocessing, and virtual machine operating systems. These operating systems can be classified by two criteria: (1) whether they allow more than one user to use the computer at the same time and (2) whether they allow more than one program to run at the same time *(Figure 8-3)*.

Single Program

Single program operating systems allow only a single user to run a single program at one time. This was the first type of operating system developed. Older personal computers used this type of operating system. For example, a single program operating system allowed you to load only one application, such as a spreadsheet, into main memory. To work on another application, such as word processing, you would exit the spreadsheet application and load the word processing program into memory.

Multitasking

Multitasking operating systems allow more than one program to run at the same time on one computer. Even though the CPU is only capable of working on one program instruction at a time, its capability to switch back and forth between programs makes it appear as though all programs are running at the same time. For example, with a multitasking operating system, the computer could be performing a complex spreadsheet calculation and at the same time be downloading a file from another computer while the user is writing a memo with the word processing program.

Multitasking operating systems on personal computers can usually support a single user running multiple programs. Multitasking operating systems on some personal computers and most minicomputers and mainframes can support more than one user running more than one program. This version of a multitasking operating system is sometimes called a **timesharing** or **multiuser** operating system. These operating systems also allow more than one user to run the same program. For example, a wholesale distributor may have dozens of terminal operators entering sales orders using the same order entry program on the same computer.

	SINGLE PROGRAM	MULTITASKING	MULTIPROCESSING	VIRTUAL MACHINE
NUMBER OF PROGRAMS RUNNING	One program	More than one program	More than one program each CPU	More than one program on each operating system
NUMBER OF USERS	One user	One or more than one user (timesharing)	More than one user each CPU	More than one user on each operating system

Figure 8-3
Operating systems can be classified by whether they allow more than one user and whether they allow more than one program to be operating at the same time.

Multiprocessing

Computers that have more than one CPU are called **multiprocessors**. A **multiprocessing** operating system coordinates the operations of computers with more than one CPU. Because each CPU in a multiprocessor computer can be executing one program instruction, more than one instruction can be executed simultaneously. Besides providing an increase in performance, most multiprocessors offer another advantage. If one CPU fails, work can be shifted to the remaining CPUs. There are two ways to implement multiprocessing *(Figure 8-4)*. In **asymmetric multiprocessing**, application tasks are assigned to a specific CPU. Each CPU has its own amount of memory. In **symmetric multiprocessing**, application tasks may be assigned to whatever CPU is available. Memory, as needed, is shared among the CPUs. Symmetric multiprocessing is more complex but achieves a higher processing rate because the operating system has more flexibility in assigning tasks to available CPUs.

As mentioned in Chapter 4, some microprocessors have multiple CPUs designed into a single chip. Other multiprocessor systems use physically separate CPUs. Some of the systems with separate CPUs are designed to keep operating even if one of the CPUs fails. **Fault-tolerant computers** are built with redundant components such as memory, input and output controllers, and disk drives. If any one of the components fail, the system can continue to operate with the duplicate component. Fault-tolerant systems are used for airline reservation systems, communications networks, bank teller machines, and other applications where it is important to keep the computer operating at all times.

Virtual Machine

A **virtual machine** (VM) operating system allows a single computer to run two or more different operating systems. The VM operating system allocates system resources such as memory and processing time to each operating system. To users, it appears that they are working on separate systems, hence the term virtual machine. The advantage of this approach is that an organization can run different operating systems (at the same time) that are best suited to different tasks. For example, some operating systems are best for interactive processing and others are best for batch processing. With a VM operating system, both types of operating systems can be run concurrently.

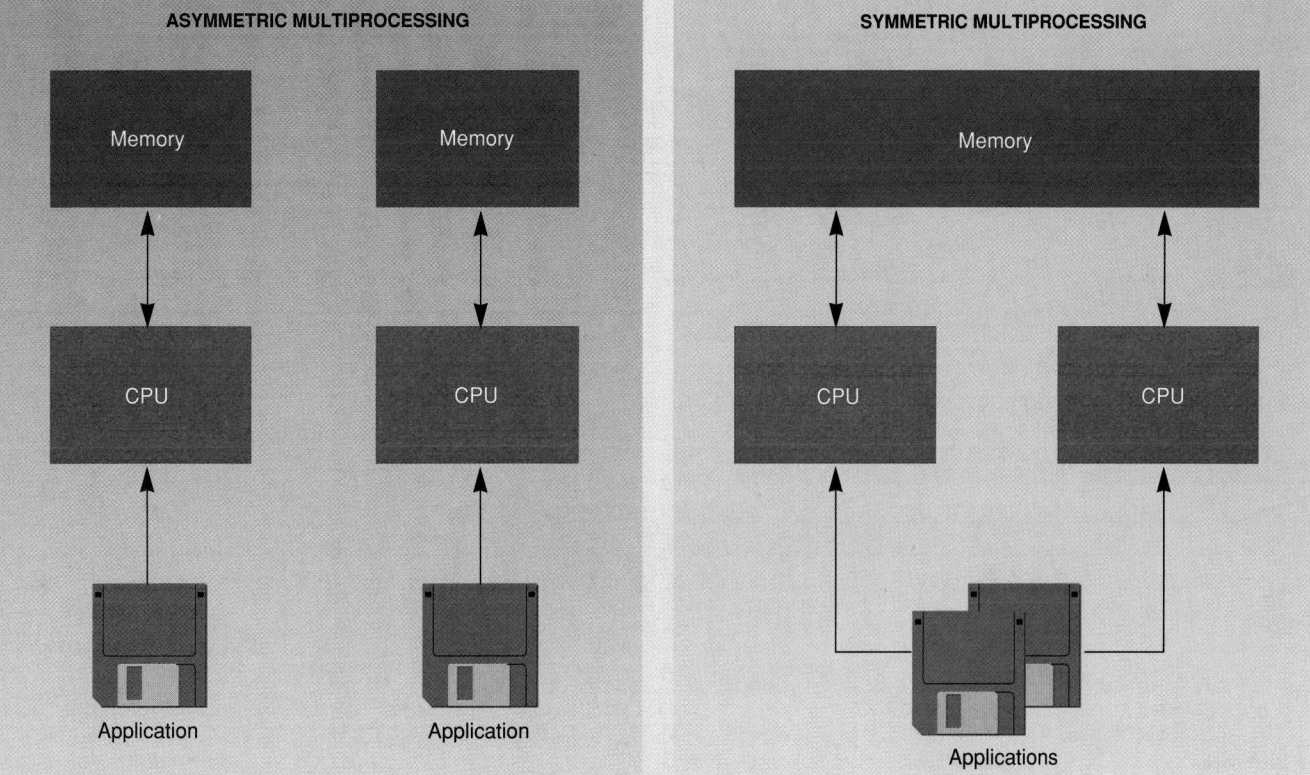

Figure 8-4
In asymmetric multiprocessing, application tasks are assigned to a specific CPU that has its own memory.
In symmetric multiprocessing, application tasks are assigned to any available CPU that shares memory with the other CPUs.

Functions of Operating Systems

The operating system performs a number of functions that allow the user and the application software to interact with the computer. These functions apply to all operating systems but become more complex for operating systems that allow more than one program to run at a time. The functions can be grouped into three types: allocating system resources, monitoring system activities, and disk and file management *(Figure 8-5)*.

Allocating System Resources

The primary function of the operating system is to allocate, or assign, the resources of the computer system. That is, just as a police officer directs traffic, the operating system decides what resource will currently be used and for how long. These resources include the CPU, main memory, and the input and output devices such as disk and tape drives and printers.

CPU MANAGEMENT

Because a CPU can only work on one program instruction at a time, a multitasking operating system must keep switching the CPU among the different instructions of the programs that are waiting to be performed. A common way of allocating CPU processing is time slicing. A **time slice** is a fixed amount of CPU processing time, usually measured in milliseconds (thousandths of a second). With this technique, each user in turn receives a time slice. Because some instructions take less time to execute than others, some users may have more instructions completed in their time slice than other users. When a user's time slice has expired, the operating system directs the CPU to work on another user's program instructions, and the most recent user moves to the end of the line to await the next time slice *(Figure 8-6)*. Unless the system has a heavy work load, however, users may not even be aware that their program has been temporarily set aside. Before they notice a delay, the operating system has allocated them another time slice and their processing continues.

Because some work has a higher priority or is more important than other work, most operating systems have ways to adjust the amount of time slices a user receives, either automatically or based on user-specified criteria. One technique for modifying the number of time slices is to have different priorities assigned to each user. For each time slice received by the lowest priority, the highest priority would receive several consecutive time slices. For example, it would be logical to assign a higher priority to a program that processes

ALLOCATING RESOURCES	MONITORING ACTIVITIES	DISK AND FILE MANAGEMENT
CPU management	System performance	Formatting
Memory management	System security	Copying
Input/output management		Deleting

Figure 8-5
Operating system functions.

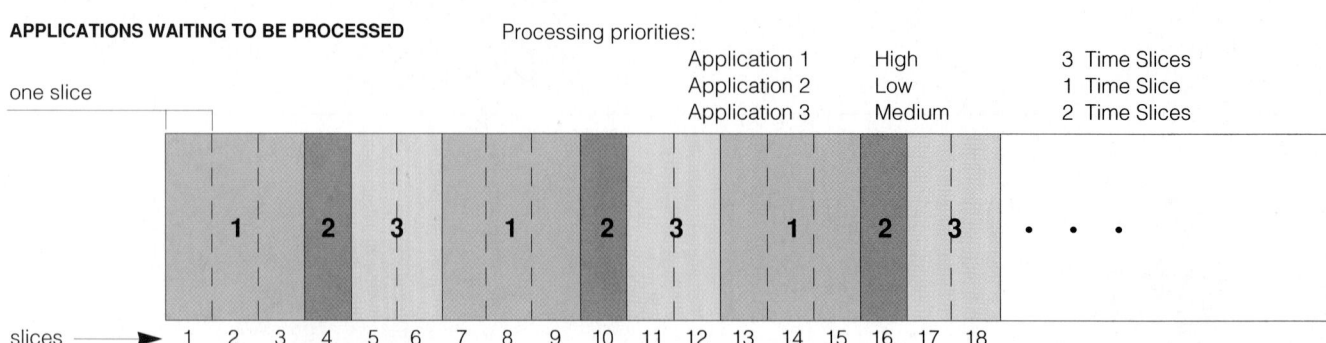

APPLICATIONS WAITING TO BE PROCESSED

Processing priorities:

Application 1	High	3 Time Slices
Application 2	Low	1 Time Slice
Application 3	Medium	2 Time Slices

Figure 8-6
With the time slice method of CPU management, each application is allocated one or more fixed amounts of time called slices. Higher priority (more important) applications receive more consecutive slices than lower priority applications. When its processing time has expired, an application goes to the end of the line until all other applications have received at least one time slice. Here, application 2 is the lowest priority and so receives only one time slice. Application 1 is the highest priority and receives three time slices.

orders and records sales than to an accounting program that could be run at a later time. Another way to allocate time slices is based on the type of work being performed. For example, some operating systems automatically allocate more time slices to interactive processes such as keyboard entry than they do to CPU-only processes such as calculations. This gives a higher priority to users entering data than to a report being printed.

Another way of assigning processing priorities is to designate each job as either foreground or background. **Foreground** jobs receive a higher processing priority and more CPU time. Data entry would be an example of a job that would be classified as a foreground job. **Background** jobs receive a lower processing priority and less CPU time. Printing a report or calculating payroll are examples of jobs that could be classified as background jobs.

MEMORY MANAGEMENT

During processing, items such as the operating system, application program instructions, data waiting to be processed, and work space used for calculations, sorting, and other temporary tasks are stored in main memory. It is the operating system's job to allocate, or assign, each of these items to areas of main memory. Data that has just been read into main memory from an input device or is waiting to be sent to an output device is stored in areas of main memory called **buffers.** The operating system assigns the location of the buffers in main memory and manages the data that is stored in them.

Operating systems allocate at least some portion of memory into fixed areas called **partitions** *(Figure 8-7).* Some operating systems allocate all memory on this basis while others use partitions only for the operating system instructions and buffers.

Another way of allocating memory is called virtual memory management, or virtual storage. **Virtual memory management** increases the effective (or *virtual*) limits of memory by expanding the amount of main memory to include disk space. Without virtual memory management, an entire program must be loaded into main memory during execution. With virtual memory management, only the portion of the program that is currently being used is required to be in main memory. Virtual memory management is used with multitasking operating systems to maximize the number of programs using memory at the same time. The operating system performs

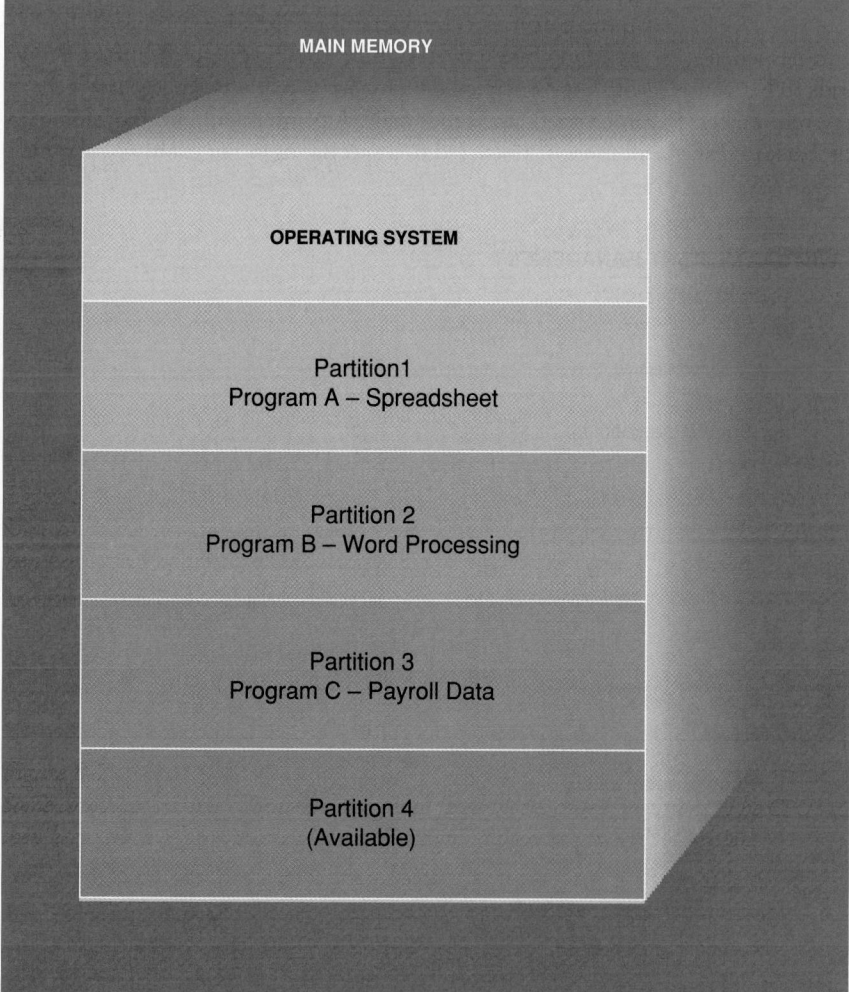

Figure 8-7
Some computer systems allocate memory into fixed blocks called partitions. The CPU then keeps track of programs and data by assigning them to a specific partition.

virtual memory management by transferring data and instructions to and from memory and the disk by using one or both of the two methods, segmentation and paging.

In **segmentation**, programs are divided into logical portions called **segments**. For example, one segment of a program may edit data and another segment may perform a calculation. Because the segments are based on logical portions of a program, some segments are larger than others. When a particular program instruction is required, the segment containing that instruction is transferred from the disk into main memory.

In **paging**, a fixed number of bytes is transferred from the disk each time data or program instructions are required. This fixed amount of data is called a **page**, or a **frame**. The size of a page, generally from 512 to 4,000 bytes, is determined by the operating system. Because a page is a fixed number of bytes, it may not correspond to a logical division of a program like a segment.

In both segmentation and paging, a time comes when memory is full but another page or segment needs to be read into memory. When this occurs, the operating system makes room for the new data or instructions by writing back to disk one or more of the pages or segments currently in memory. This process is referred to as **swapping** *(Figure 8-8)*. The operating system usually chooses the least recently used page or segment to transfer back to disk.

INPUT AND OUTPUT MANAGEMENT

At any given time, more than one input device can be sending data to the computer. At the same time, the CPU could be ready to send data to an output device such as a terminal or printer or a storage device such as a disk. The operating system is responsible for managing these input and output processes.

Some devices, such as a tape drive, are usually allocated to a specific user or application program. This is because tape is a sequential storage medium, and generally it would not make sense to have more than one application writing records to a single tape. Disk drives are usually allocated to all users because the programs and data files that users need are stored on these devices. The operating system keeps track of disk read and write requests, stores these requests in buffers along with the associated data for write requests, and usually processes them sequentially. A printer could be allocated to all users or restricted to a specific user. For example, a printer

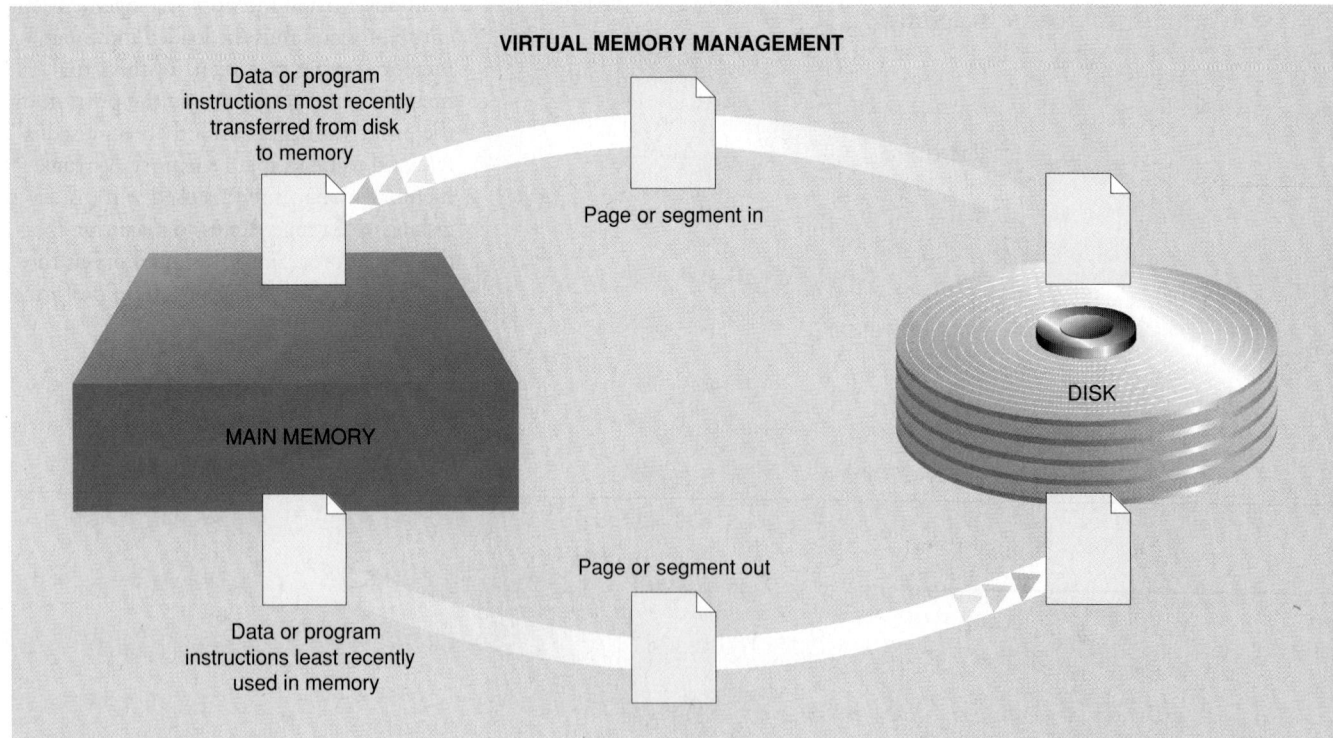

Figure 8-8
With virtual memory management, the operating system expands the amount of main memory to include available disk space. Data and program instructions are transferred to and from memory and disk as required. The segmentation technique transfers logical portions of programs that may be different sizes. The paging technique transfers pages of the same size. To make room for the new page or segment, the least recently used page or segment is swapped, or written back to the disk.

would be restricted to a specific user if the printer was going to be used with preprinted forms such as payroll checks.

Because the printer is a relatively slow device compared to other computer system devices, the technique of spooling is used to increase printer efficiency and reduce the number of printers required. With **spooling** *(Figure 8-9),* a report is first written (saved) to the disk before it is printed. Writing to the disk is much faster than writing to the printer. For example, a report that may take one-half hour to print (depending on the speed of the printer) may take only one minute to write to the disk. After the report is written to the disk, the CPU is available to process other programs. The report saved on the disk can be printed at a later time or, in a multitasking operating system, a print program can be run (at the same time other programs are running) to process the **print spool** (the reports on the disk waiting to be printed).

Because many input and output devices use different commands and control codes to transmit and receive data, programs called **device drivers** are used by the operating system to control these devices. For example, a different device driver would be required for a high-resolution color monitor than for a standard-resolution monochrome monitor. Device drivers are usually supplied with the operating system or by the device manufacturers.

Monitoring System Activities

Another function of the operating system is monitoring the system activity. This includes monitoring system performance and system security.

SYSTEM PERFORMANCE

System performance can be measured in a number of ways but is usually gauged by the user in terms of response time. **Response time** is the amount of time from the moment a user enters data until the computer responds.

Response time can vary based on what the user has entered. If the user is simply entering data into a file, the response time is usually within a second or two. However, if the user has just completed a request for a display of sorted data from several files, the response time could be minutes.

A more precise way of measuring performance is to run a program that is designed to record and report system activity.

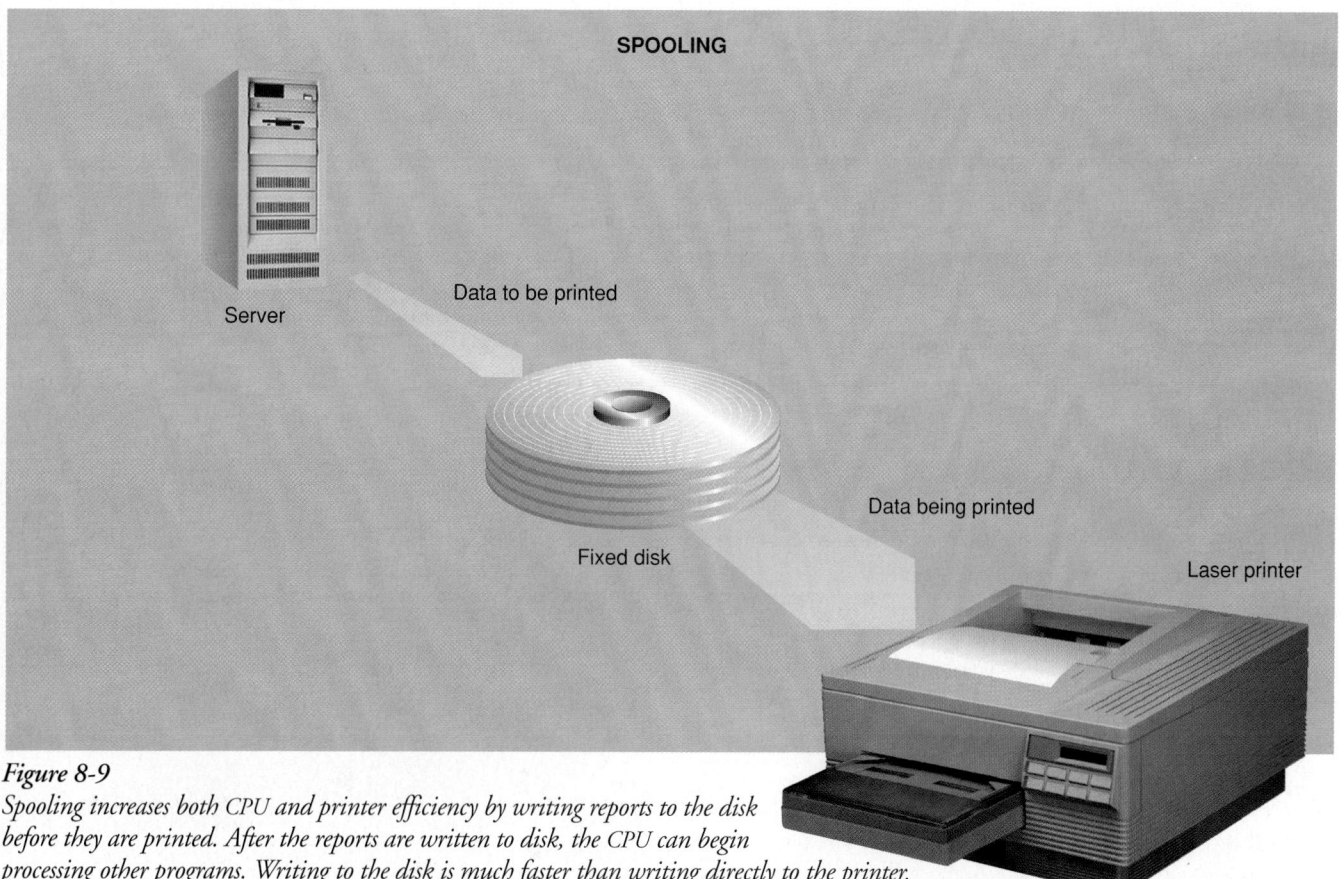

SPOOLING

Server

Data to be printed

Fixed disk

Data being printed

Laser printer

Figure 8-9
Spooling increases both CPU and printer efficiency by writing reports to the disk before they are printed. After the reports are written to disk, the CPU can begin processing other programs. Writing to the disk is much faster than writing directly to the printer.

Among other information, these programs usually report CPU **utilization,** the amount of time that the CPU is working and not idle, waiting for data to process. *Figure 8-10* shows a CPU performance measurement report.

Another measure of performance is to compare the CPU utilization with the disk input and output rate, referred to as disk I/O. How a virtual memory management operating system swaps pages or segments from disk to memory as they are needed was previously discussed. Systems with heavy work loads and insufficient memory or CPU power can get into a situation called **thrashing,** where the system is spending more time moving pages to and from the disk than processing the data. System performance reporting can alert the computer user to this problem.

System Security

Most multiuser operating systems provide for a logon code, a user ID, and a password that must all be entered correctly before a user is allowed to use an application program *(Figure 8-11)*. Each is a word or series of characters. A **logon code** usually identifies the application that will be used, such as accounting, sales, or manufacturing. A **user ID** identifies the user, such as Jeffrey Ryan or Mary Gonzales. The **password** is usually confidential; often it is known only to the user and the computer system administrator. The logon code, user ID, and password must match entries in an authorization file. If they do not match, the user is denied access to the system. Both successful and unsuccessful logon attempts are often recorded in a file so management can review who is using or attempting to use the system. These logs can also be used to allocate computing expenses based on the percentage of system use by an organization's various departments.

Disk and File Management

In addition to allocating system resources and monitoring system activities, most operating systems contain programs that can perform functions related to disk and file management. Some of these functions include formatting disks and diskettes, deleting files from a disk, copying files from one secondary storage device to another, and renaming stored files.

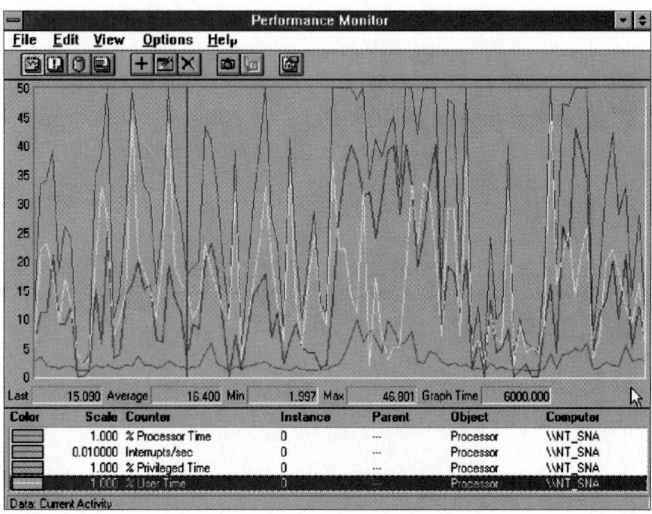

Figure 8-10
System performance measurement programs report the amount of time the CPU is actually working and not waiting to process data.

Figure 8-11
The logon code, user ID, and password must all be entered correctly before the user is allowed to use the computer. Because the password is confidential, it is usually not displayed on the screen when the user enters it.

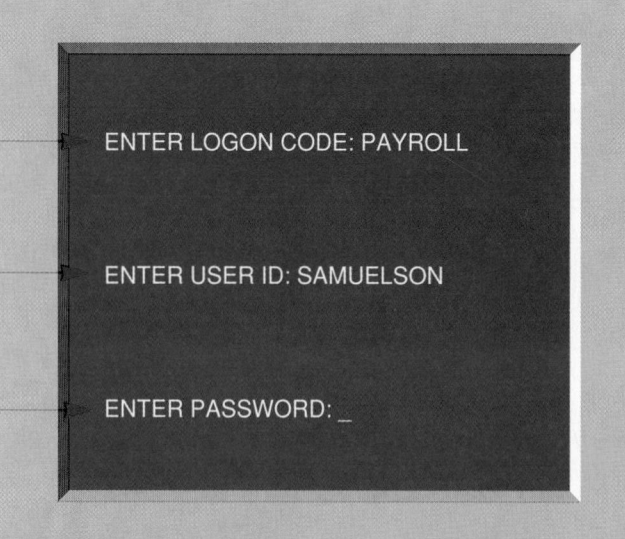

Logon code; usually specifies application to be used

User ID; usually name of user

Password; unique word or combination of characters known only to user

Popular Operating Systems

The first operating systems were developed by manufacturers for the computers in their product line. When the manufacturers came out with another computer or model, they often produced an improved and different operating system. Because programs are designed to be used with a particular operating system, this meant that users who wanted to switch computers, either from one vendor to another or to a different model from the same vendor, would have to convert their existing programs to run under the new operating system. Today, however, the trend is away from operating systems limited to a specific model and toward operating systems that will run on any model by a particular manufacturer.

Going even further, many computer users are supporting the move away from **proprietary operating systems** (meaning privately owned) and toward **portable operating systems** that will run on many manufacturers' computers. The advantage of portable operating systems is that the user is not tied to a particular manufacturer. Using a portable operating system, a user could change computer systems, yet retain existing software and data files, which usually represent a sizable investment in time and money. For example, consider

a small business that purchases a computer system to handle their immediate needs and to provide for several years of anticipated growth. Five years later, the business has reached the capacity of the computer; no more memory or terminals can be added. In addition, the manufacturer of the five-year-old computer does not make a larger or more powerful model. Because the business originally chose a computer that used a portable operating system, it can purchase a more powerful computer from another manufacturer that offers the same portable operating system and continue to use the existing software and data files.

One of the most popular portable operating systems is DOS, which is discussed along with the several other computer operating systems in this section.

DOS

DOS stands for **Disk Operating System,** the most widely used operating system on personal computers. Several slightly different but compatible versions of DOS exist. The two most widely used, MS-DOS and PC-DOS, were both originally developed by Microsoft Corporation in 1981.

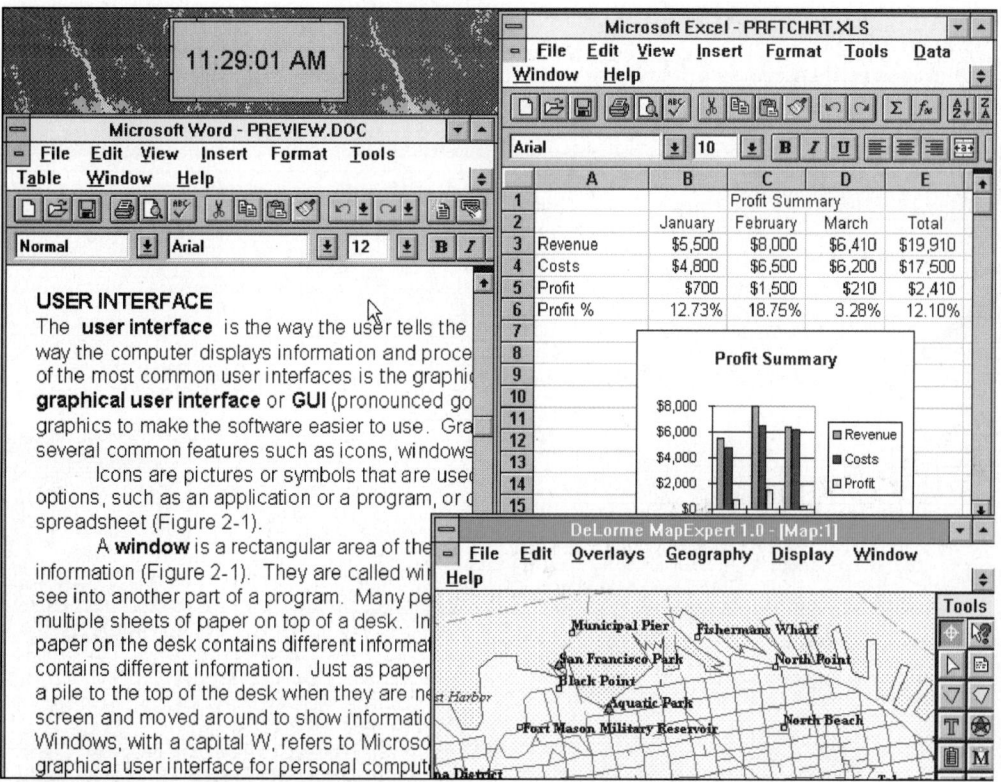

Figure 8-12
The Microsoft Windows operating system provides a graphical user interface that makes computers easy to use. This screen shows three different applications; word processing, spreadsheet, and a map program. Each application is displayed in a window. A digital clock is displayed in the upper left corner.

MS-DOS is marketed directly by Microsoft and is installed on most IBM-compatible personal computer systems. **PC-DOS** was developed by Microsoft for IBM and is installed by IBM on systems that IBM sells. Through the years, DOS has been improved many times. Each new version, called a *release,* has added new features and capabilities. However, DOS remains primarily a single user, single program operating system. Most importantly, DOS is unable to take full advantage of the newer 32-bit microprocessors, but DOS does have a large installed base, estimated at more than 100 million users.

Windows

Microsoft Windows is the most widely used graphical user interface for personal computers (*Figure 8-12* on the previous page). Windows version number 3.1 or below is not technically an operating system, but rather, is a multitasking graphical user interface **operating environment** that runs on DOS-based computers.

Common features of an operating environment (and Windows) include support for use of a mouse, icons, pull-down menus, the capability to have several applications open at the same time, and the capability to easily move data from one application to another. Closely related to operating environments are operating system shell programs. Like an operating environment, a **shell** program acts as an interface between the user and the operating system. Shell programs, however, usually offer a limited number of utility functions such as file maintenance and do not offer application windowing or graphics.

The most recent version of Windows, called Windows 95, does not require DOS and is a true multitasking operating system designed to take advantage of 32-bit microprocessors. Application programs written for prior versions of Windows and DOS can still run under the newer 32-bit version of Windows.

Windows NT

Microsoft Windows NT is a sophisticated version of Windows that is designed for use on client-server computer systems. Like the latest version of Windows, Windows NT is a complete operating system that does not require DOS. Unique features of Windows NT include the following:

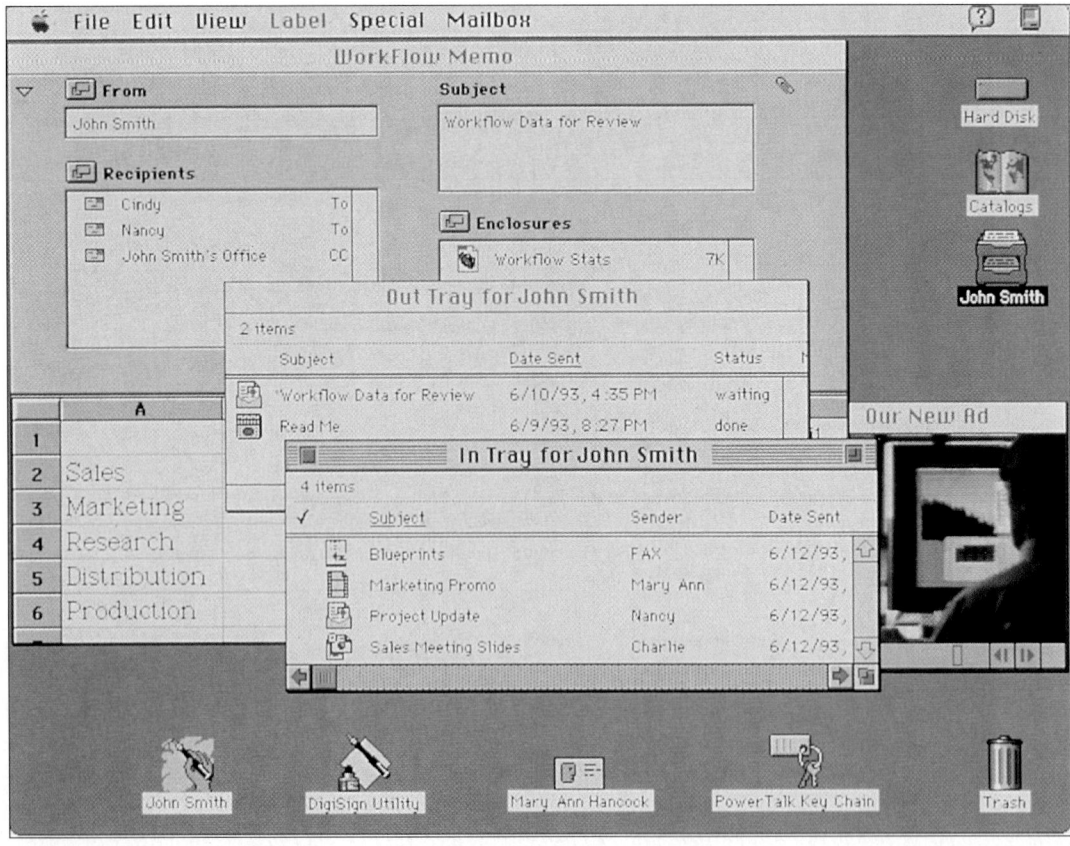

Figure 8-13
Apple's Macintosh operating system offers a graphical user interface and the capability to display information in separate windows.

- Support for most major networking communications protocols
- The capability to run 32-bit application programs
- *User Manager,* a program that creates user accounts and manages system security
- *Performance Monitor,* a program that measures network performance

Because it is more complex than Windows, Windows NT requires significant system resources including 12 to 16 MB of memory and 75 to 100 MB of disk space.

Macintosh

The Apple **Macintosh** multitasking operating system used the first commercially successful graphical user interface when it was released with Macintosh computers in 1984 *(Figure 8-13).* Since then, it has set the standard for operating system ease of use and has been the model for most of the new graphical user interfaces developed for non-Macintosh systems. Distinctive features of the latest version of the operating system, called System 7.5, include built-in networking support, electronic mail, and an extensive step-by-step help system called Apple Guide.

OS/2

OS/2 is IBM's operating system designed to work with 32-bit microprocessors *(Figure 8-14).* Besides being able to run programs written specifically for OS/2, the operating system can also run programs written for DOS or Windows. Like Windows, OS/2 has a graphical user interface. OS/2 is popular with businesses that need a sophisticated operating system to use for day-to-day operations. Several different versions of OS/2 exist, including an entry-level version designed to work on systems with only 4 MB of memory and a more complex version designed to work on servers with multiple processors. The latest version of OS/2 is called OS/2 Warp, version 3.

UNIX

The **UNIX** operating system was developed in the early 1970s by scientists at Bell Laboratories. It was specifically designed to provide a way to manage a variety of scientific and specialized computer applications. Because of federal regulations, Bell Labs (a subsidiary of AT&T) was prohibited from actively promoting UNIX in the commercial marketplace.

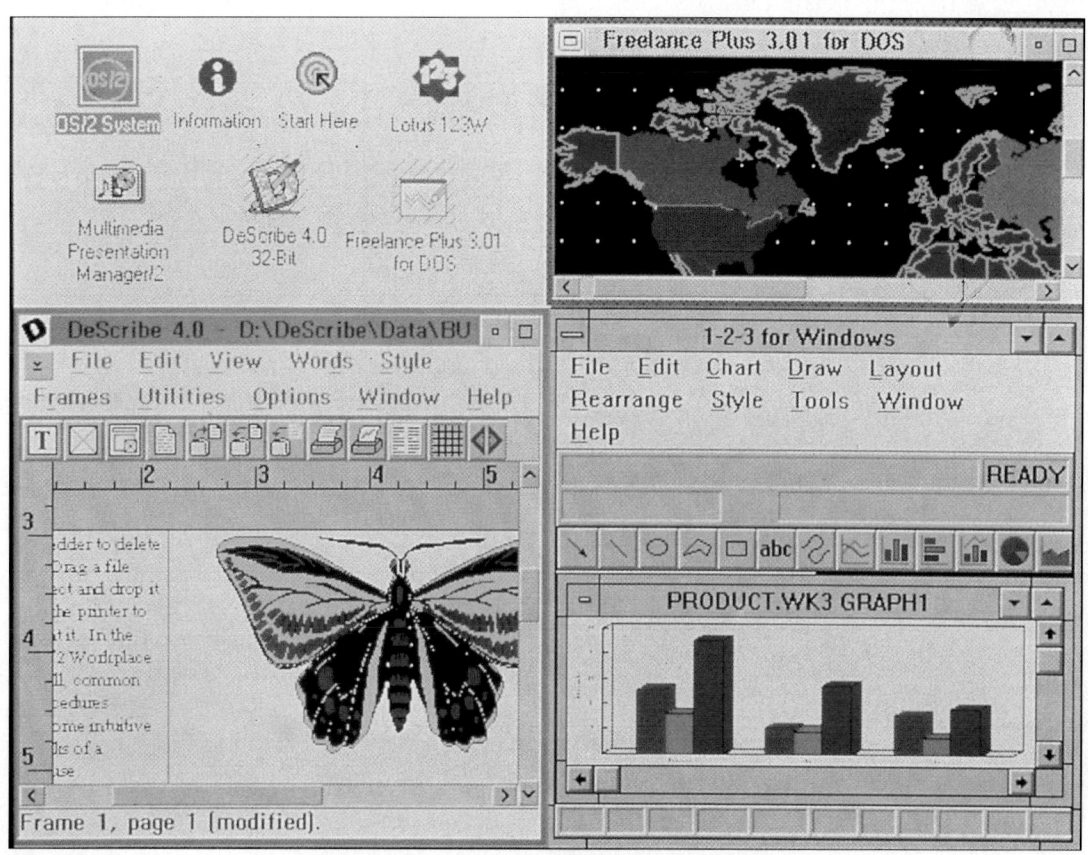

Figure 8-14
IBM's OS/2 operating system takes advantage of the increased processing power of the latest 32-bit microprocessors.

Instead, for a low fee, Bell Labs licensed UNIX to numerous colleges and universities where it obtained a wide following. With the deregulation of the telephone companies in the 1980s, AT&T was allowed to enter the computer system marketplace. With increased promotion and the trend toward portable operating systems, UNIX has aroused tremendous interest. One of the advantages of UNIX is its extensive library of more than 400 instruction modules that can be linked together to perform almost any programming task. Today, most major computer manufacturers offer a multiuser version of the UNIX operating system to run on their computers.

With all its strengths, however, UNIX has not yet obtained success in the commercial business systems marketplace. Some people attribute this to the fact that UNIX has never been considered user friendly. For example, most of the UNIX program modules are identified by obscure names such as MAUS, SHMOP, and BRK. Other critics contend that UNIX lacks the file management capabilities to support the online interactive databases that increasingly more businesses are implementing. With the support of most major computer manufacturers, however, these problems are being worked on, and UNIX may become one of the major operating systems of the coming years.

Figure 8-15
The NextStep operating system from NeXT Computer is designed to help software developers create new applications in significantly less time than using traditional methods and operating systems.

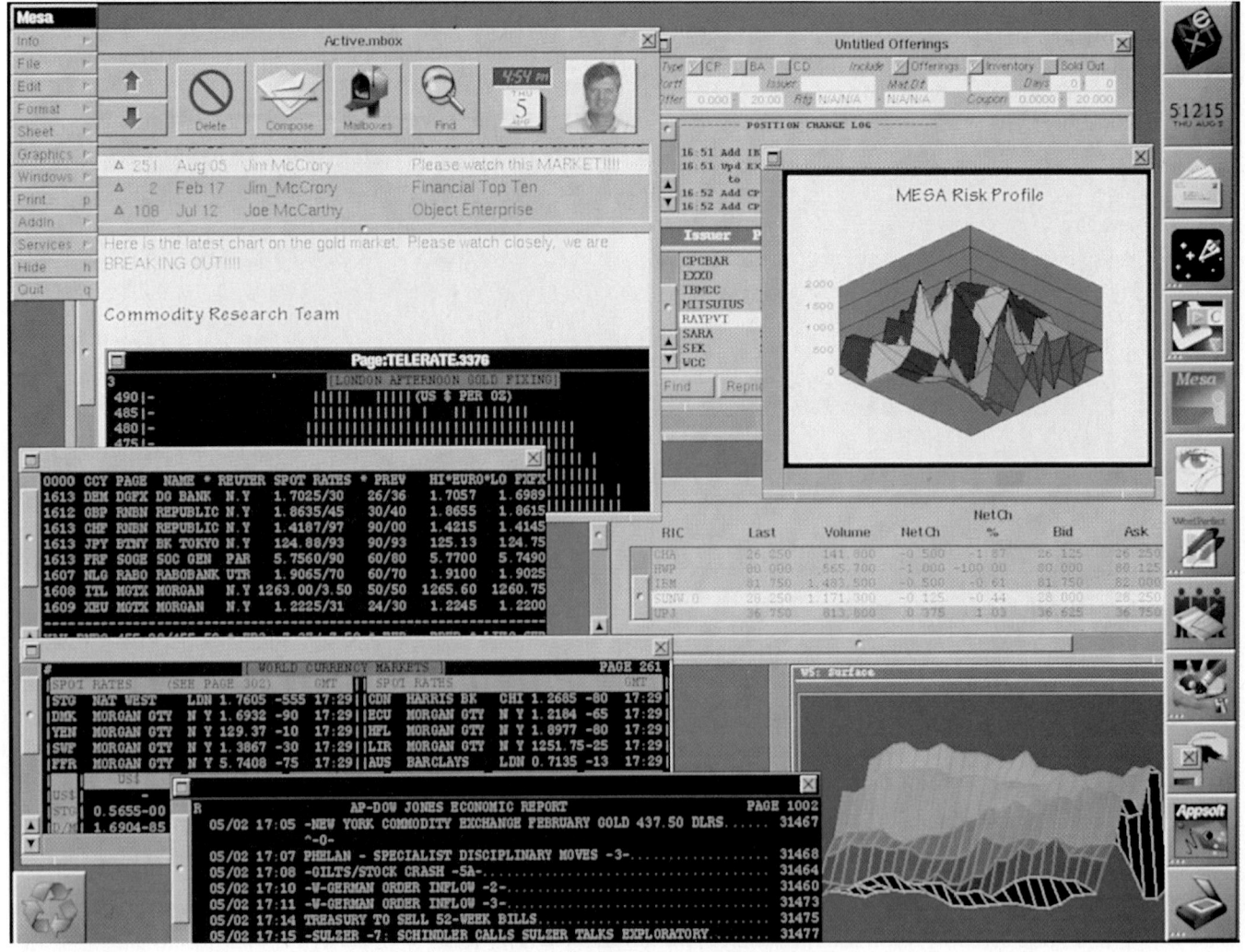

NextStep

The NextStep operating system from NeXT Computer was originally written to operate on the computers they manufactured. In recent years, NeXT has rewritten the operating system to run on Intel and other microprocessors and has stopped manufacturing computers to concentrate on NextStep development and marketing. NextStep is fundamentally different because it is the only object-oriented operating system *(Figure 8-15)*. Objects are a combination of the separate procedures and data that are used by most programs and operating systems. The main impact of object-oriented technology is that programs can be developed in much less time; some say in as little as one-tenth the time of traditional methods. NeXT hopes that NextStep, which has been designed to support object-oriented programming, will appeal to businesses that must develop new applications quickly.

Other Operating Systems

Other popular operating systems exist in addition to those just discussed. Most mainframe operating systems are unique to a particular make of computer or are designed to be compatible with one of IBM's operating systems such as DOS/VS, MVS, or VM, IBM's virtual machine operating system.

Although not yet widely used, the MACH operating system has been called a possible replacement for the increasingly popular UNIX operating system and possibly the standard operating system of the future. Considered a streamlined version of UNIX, MACH has the support of several large governmental and educational organizations. Currently being developed by Carnegie Mellon University, MACH has also been chosen by the Open Software Foundation (OSF), a 170-member organization that is trying to establish an industry-wide operating system standard.

Utilities

Utility programs perform specific tasks related to managing computer resources or files. Many utility programs are included with the operating system. These utility programs usually handle frequently performed tasks such as copying and moving files and formatting disks. Other utility programs are sold separately or in a group with other utility programs that are designed to work together. A brief description of some of the tasks addressed by utility programs follows:

- **File Management**   Listing, editing, copying, moving, and deleting files and directories.
- **Disk Management**   Formatting and defragmenting disks.
- **Memory Management**   Configuring a system to make the most memory available for running application programs. Memory managers do this by moving certain programs, such as device drivers, to other areas of RAM.
- **Backup and Restore**   Backup software allows the user to select one or more files for copying to diskettes or tape. The backup software monitors the copying process and alerts the user if an additional diskette or tape is needed. Restore software reverses the process and allows the user to reinstate files that have been previously copied to disk or tape.
- **Data Recovery**   Data recovery software assists the user in rebuilding files that have been deleted or files that have been damaged.
- **Data Compression**   Reduces the amount of space that a file requires. See Chapter 6 for a discussion on how data compression works.
- **Virus Protection**   A virus is a computer program that is designed to copy itself into other programs and spread through multiple computer systems. Most virus programs cause damage to files on the system where the virus is present. Virus protection programs use a number of methods to prevent virus programs from being loaded on a computer.

Another type of utility program is a screen saver. If the same image is displayed on a monitor for long periods of time, a very dim version of the image can be permanently etched on the monitor screen. A **screen saver** program prevents this problem, called *ghosting*, by dimming the brightness of the screen or displays moving images on the screen. The screen saver program automatically starts if the image on a screen does not change for a certain period of time that can be set by the user. The moving image screen savers are often quite entertaining and allow the user to choose from a variety of images. *Figure 8-16* is an example of a screen saver display.

Language Translators

Special-purpose system software programs called **language translators** are used to convert the programming instructions written by programmers into the machine instructions that a computer can understand. Language translators are written for specific programming languages and computer systems.

Summary of Operating Systems and System Software

System software, including the operating system, utilities, and language translators, are essential parts of a computer system and should be understood by users who want to obtain the maximum benefits from their computers. This is especially true for the latest personal computer operating systems that include features such as virtual memory management and multitasking. Understanding and being able to use these and other features will give users more control over their computer resources.

Figure 8-16
The After Dark screen saver utility program from Berkeley Systems prevents an image from being permanently etched on a monitor screen by displaying entertaining images that move across the screen.

COMPUTERS AT WORK

NextStep: Objects May Be Closer Than They Appear

NeXT Computer believes that its NextStep operating system has a significant advantage that business users will want. So far, the businesses that have tried NextStep think that NeXT is right. NextStep is the only operating system designed to support object-oriented computing. Objects are combinations of data and procedures that are treated separately by traditional operating systems. One advantage of objects is that they are *smart*. Because they contain procedures that specify how they behave in certain situations, much less programming code is required and applications can be developed in a fraction of the time. An example of an object would be an invoice that knows how to print itself. Instead of using a program to specify exactly how to print the invoice data, an invoice object merely has to be sent a message saying, print. Another advantage of objects is that they are reusable. Over time, the user builds a library of objects that can be used to quickly create applications. NeXT claims that with NextStep, applications can be developed in one-fifth to one-tenth the time. Many of their customers have found this to be true.

Chrysler Financial, the financing subsidiary of the Chrysler automobile company, used NextStep to create a system for processing all car loans. They developed their first five applications in four months, less time than it takes to even design most programs. In the next four months, Chrysler Financial developed nineteen more applications. These applications are being used by approximately 3,000 people at 100 financial centers. Another NextStep user, Swiss Bank Corporation, developed a sophisticated options trading system in only two and one-half months.

NeXT believes that three trends will help NextStep become successful in the corporate market:

- The move to client/server computing
- The move to object-oriented computing
- The continued reengineering of major businesses that requires them to develop new ways of processing information

If NeXT is correct, the widespread use of objects may be closer that some people think.

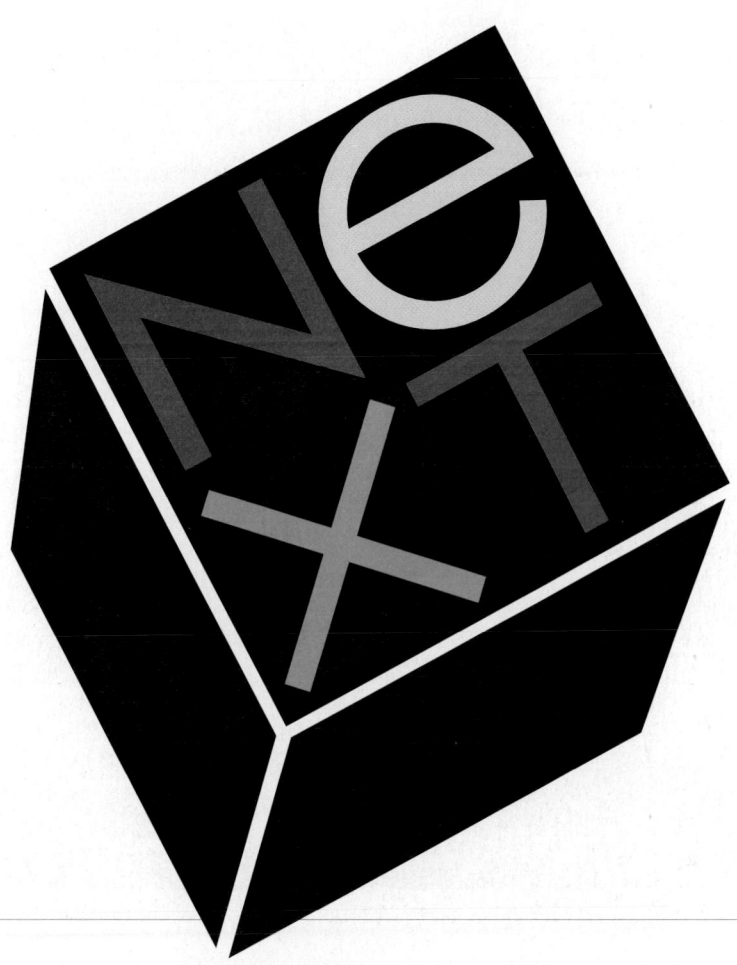

Figure 8-17

IN THE FUTURE

Is There a Future for Utility Software?

Some utility software developers worry about the future of their type of software. Recently, it seems that every time a good utility program is developed, it is not long before a similar utility program shows up as part of one of the major operating systems. When users upgrade to the new version of an operating system and obtain the additional utility programs, they have little, if any, incentive to pay for the utilities separately. Examples of utilities that started out as separate programs but have wound up as part of the operating system include the following:

- Communications
- Memory management
- File management
- Backup and restore
- Disk compression
- Virus protection
- Performance monitoring

To better support the increased use of computer networks, several developers have plans to include features such as network configuration management, network security, and electronic mail in future versions of their operating systems.

As with the consolidation in the application software industry, some worry that the trend of moving utilities into the operating system will lead to less competition and less innovation. Optimistic and confident developers point out that good utility programs will always find a market. Still others suggest that moving utilities into the operating system is a natural evolution with several advantages. They claim that users want to minimize the number of companies they buy products from and, perhaps more importantly, want to minimize the number of companies they have to talk with if something goes wrong.

Figure 8-18

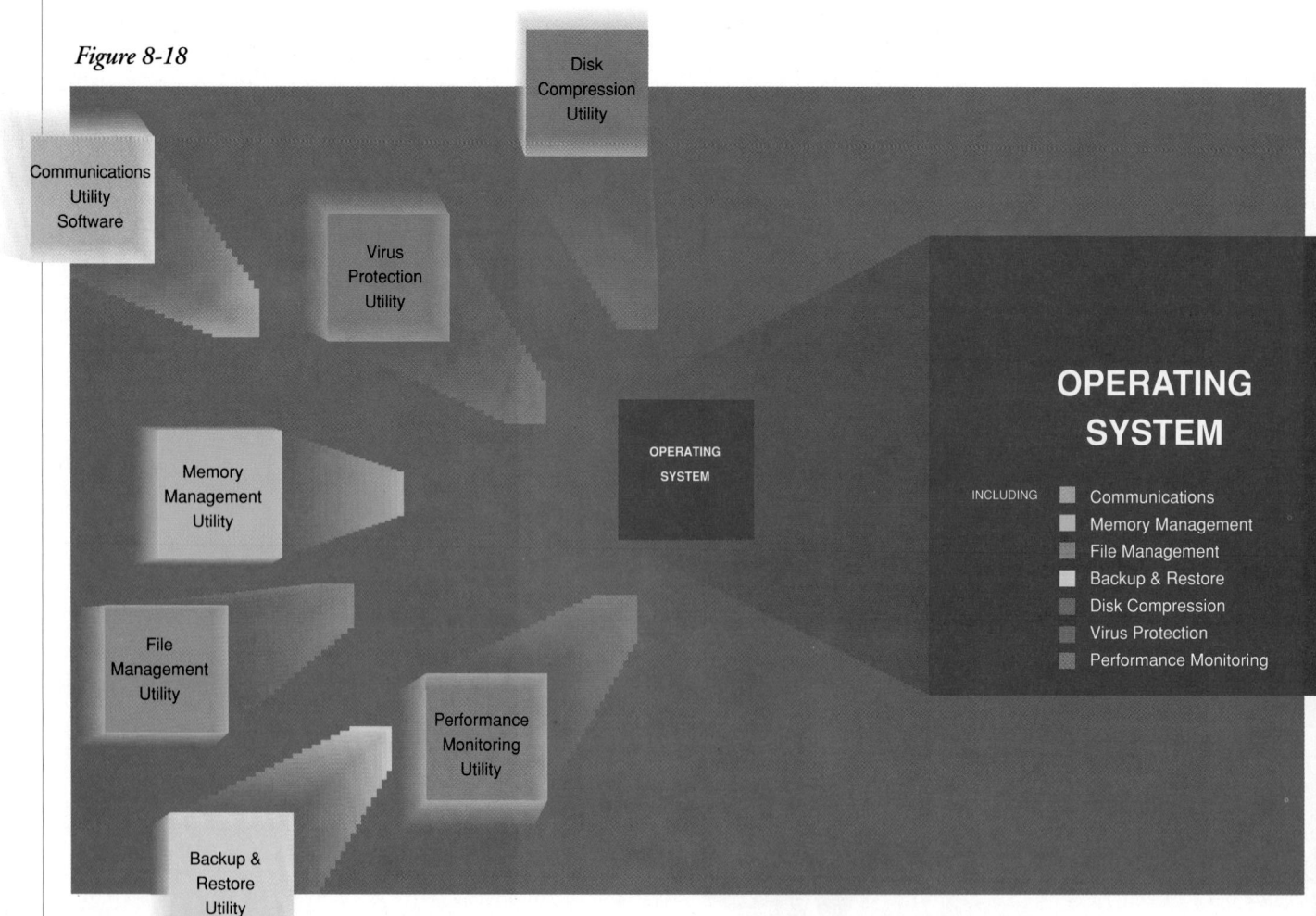

｜e   Edit   Section   Page   Tools   Options   Help

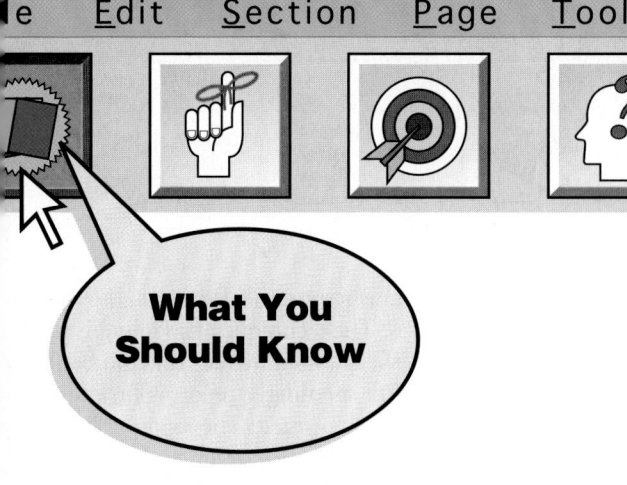

What You Should Know

1. **System software** consists of all the programs, including the operating system, that are related to controlling the operations of the computer equipment. System software can be classified into three major categories; operating systems, utilities, and language translators.

2. An **operating system** (OS) consists of one or more programs that control the allocation of hardware resources such as memory, CPU time, disk space, and peripheral devices. These programs function as an interface between the user, the application programs, and the computer equipment.

3. For a computer to operate, the essential and most frequently used instructions in the operating system must be copied from disk and stored in the main memory of the computer. This *resident* portion of the operating system is called by many different names: the **supervisor**, **monitor**, **executive**, **master program**, **control program**, or **kernel**. Commands that are included in the resident portion of the operating system are called **internal commands**. The *nonresident* portions of the operating system are called **external commands** that remain on disk and are available to be loaded into main memory when needed.

4. Most operating systems allow the user to give specific instructions to the computer. These instructions are called the **command language**. The **command language interpreter** is the portion of the operating system that carries out the command language instructions.

5. The process of loading an operating system into main memory is called **booting** the system. When the computer is turned on, the power supply distributes current to the devices in the system unit. The CPU chip resets itself and looks to the BIOS chip for instructions on how to proceed. The **BIOS**, which stands for **Basic Input/Output System**, is a set of instructions that provides the interface between the operating system and the hardware devices. The BIOS chip runs a series of tests, called the **POST**, for **Power On Self Test**, to make sure the equipment is working correctly. After the POST tests are completed, the BIOS looks for the operating system and begins loading the *resident* portion, called the kernel, into main memory. The kernel then loads the system configuration information, which is contained in a file called **CONFIG.SYS**, that tells the computer what devices you are using. For each device, a device driver program is usually loaded that tells the computer how to communicate with the device. The kernel loads the command language interpreter, called **COMMAND.COM** on DOS computers. COMMAND.COM loads a batch file named **AUTOEXEC.BAT** that performs optional tasks. If you haven't specified that the computer immediately start a particular application program, the system displays a **command language prompt** that indicates the system is ready to accept a command from the user.

6. Operating systems can be classified by two criteria: (1) whether they allow more than one user to use the computer at the same time; and (2) whether they allow more than one program to run at the same time.

7. **Single program** operating systems allow only a single user to run a single program at one time.

8. **Multitasking** operating systems allow more than one program to be run at the same time on one computer. Multitasking operating systems on some personal computers and most minicomputers and mainframes that can support more than one user running multiple programs, are called **timesharing** or **multiuser** operating systems.

9. Computers that have more than one CPU are called **multiprocessors**. A multiprocessing operating system coordinates the operations of computers with more than one CPU. In **asymmetric multiprocessing**, application tasks are assigned to a specific CPU. In **symmetric multiprocessing**, application tasks may be assigned to whatever CPU is available. **Fault-tolerant computers** are built with redundant components and can continue to operate with duplicate components if one of the components fails.

10. A **virtual machine** (VM) operating system allows a single computer to run two or more different operating systems.

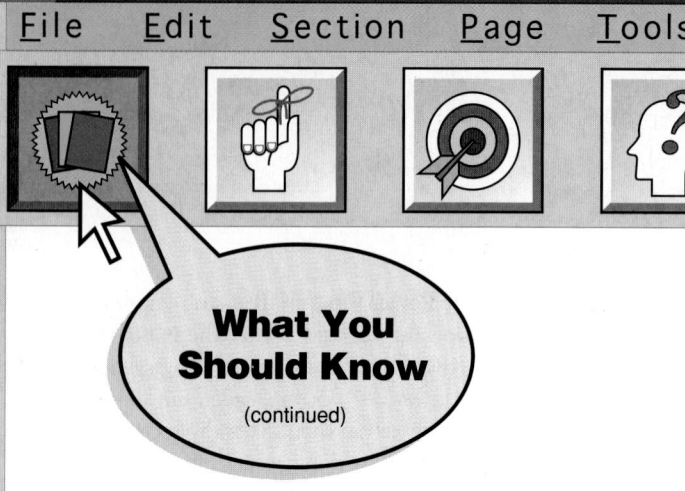

What You Should Know

(continued)

11. The primary function of the operating system is to allocate, or assign, the resources of the computer system. These resources include the CPU, main memory, and the input and output devices.

12. A common way a multitasking operating system allocates CPU processing time is time slicing. A **time slice** is a fixed amount of CPU processing time, usually measured in milliseconds (thousandths of a second). Processing priorities can be assigned by designating each job as either a **foreground** job, which receives a higher priority and more CPU time, or a **background** job, which receives a lower priority and less processing time.

13. It is the operating system's job to allocate, or assign, items to areas of main memory. Data that has just been read into main memory from an input device or is waiting to be sent to an output device is stored in areas of main memory called **buffers**. Operating systems allocate at least some portion of main memory into fixed areas called **partitions**. The effective (or virtual) limits of memory can be increased by **virtual memory management**, which expands the amount of main memory to include disk space. With virtual memory management, only the portion of the program currently being used is required in main memory. In **segmentation**, the operating system performs virtual memory management by dividing programs into logical portions called **segments**. In **paging**, virtual memory management is performed by transferring a fixed number of bytes, called a **page** or a **frame**, from the disk each time data or program instructions are required. The process of making room for new data or instructions by writing back to disk one or more of the segments or pages currently in memory is referred to as **swapping**.

14. The operating system is responsible for managing input and output processes. The technique of spooling is used to increase printer efficiency and reduce the number of printers required. With **spooling**, a report is first written to disk (saved) before it is printed. The report saved on disk can be printed at a later time or, on a multitasking operating system, a print program can be run at the same time other programs are running to process the **print spool** (the reports on the disk waiting to be printed). Because many input and output devices use different commands and control codes to transmit and receive data, programs called **device drivers** are used by the operating system to control these devices.

15. Another function of the operating system is monitoring system activity. This includes monitoring system performance and system security.

16. System performance is usually gauged by the user in terms of **response time**, the amount of time from the moment a user enters data until the computer responds. **CPU utilization** is the amount of time that the CPU is working and not idle, waiting for data to process. Systems with heavy work loads and insufficient memory or CPU power can get into a situation called **thrashing**, where the system is spending more time moving pages to and from the disk than processing data.

17. Most multiuser operating systems monitor system security by providing for a logon code, a user ID, and a password that must all be entered correctly before a user is allowed to use the application program. A **logon code** usually identifies the application that will be used. A **user ID** identifies the user. The **password** is usually confidential; often it is known only to the user and the computer system administrator.

18. In addition to allocating system resources and monitoring system activities, most operating systems contain programs that can perform functions related to disk and file management.

19. Although the first operating systems were developed by manufacturers for computers in their product lines, today the trend is away from operating systems limited to a specific model and toward operating systems that will run on any model by a particular manufacturer. Going even further, many computer users are supporting the move away from **proprietary operating systems** (meaning privately owned) and toward **portable operating systems** that will run on many manufacturers' computers.

20. **DOS** stands for **Disk Operating System**, the most widely used operating system on personal computers. **MS-DOS** is marketed by Microsoft and is installed on most IBM-compatible personal computer systems. **PC-DOS** was developed by Microsoft for IBM and is installed by IBM on systems that IBM sells. Each new version of DOS, called a *release*, has added new features and capabilities.

21. Microsoft Windows is the most widely used graphical user interface for personal computers. Prior versions of Windows (version numbers 3.1 and below) were not technically an operating system, but were actually an **operating environment**, a graphical user interface designed to work in combination with an operating system. Like an operating environment, a **shell** program acts as an interface between the user and the operating system.

22. **Microsoft Windows NT** is a sophisticated version of Windows that is designed for use on client-server computer systems. Like the latest version of Windows (Windows 95), Windows NT is a complete operating system that does not require DOS.

23. The Apple **Macintosh** multitasking operating system used the first commercially successful graphical user interface. It has set the standard for operating system ease of use and has been the model for most of the new graphical user interfaces designed for non-Macintosh systems.

24. **OS/2** is IBM's operating system designed to work with 32-bit microprocessors. The operating system can run programs written for OS/2, DOS, or Windows. OS/2 has a graphical user interface (like Windows).

25. The **UNIX** operating system was developed in the early 1970s by scientists at Bell Laboratories to provide a way to manage a variety of scientific and specialized computer applications. Today, most major computer manufacturers offer a multiuser version of the UNIX operating system to run on their computers.

26. The NextStep operating system, from NeXT Computer, is the only object-oriented operating system. The main impact of object-oriented technology is that programs can be developed in much less time.

27. Other operating systems include mainframe operating systems (unique to a particular machine or designed to be compatible with one of IBM's operating systems) and MACH (considered a streamlined version of UNIX).

28. **Utility programs** perform specific tasks related to managing computer resources or files. These tasks include: file management, disk management, memory management, backup and restore, data recovery, data compression, and virus protection. A **screen saver** program prevents a problem called *ghosting* (having a dim version of a long-displayed image etched on the monitor screen) by dimming the brightness of the screen or displays moving images on the screen.

29. Special-purpose system software programs called **language translators** are used to convert the programming instructions written by programmers into the machine language instructions that a computer can understand.

Terms to Remember

asymmetric multiprocessing (8.5)
AUTOEXEC.BAT (8.3)

background (8.7)
Basic Input/Output System (BIOS)
    (8.3)
BIOS (8.3)
booting (8.3)
buffers (8.7)

command language (8.2)
command language interpreter (8.2)
command language prompt (8.3)
COMMAND.COM (8.3)
CONFIG.SYS (8.3)
control program (8.2)
CPU utilization (8.10)

device driver (8.9)
Disk Operating System (DOS) (8.11)
DOS (8.11)

executive (8.2)
external commands (8.2)

fault-tolerant computers (8.5)
foreground (8.7)
frame (8.8)

internal commands (8.2)

kernel (8.2)

language translators (8.16)
logon code (8.10)

Macintosh (8.13)
master program (8.2)
Microsoft Windows NT (8.12)
monitor (8.2)
MS-DOS (8.12)
multiprocessing (8.5)
multiprocessors (8.5)
multitasking (8.4)
multiuser (8.4)

operating environment (8.12)
operating system (8.2)
OS/2 (8.13)

page (8.8)
paging (8.8)
partitions (8.7)
password (8.10)
PC-DOS (8.12)
portable operating systems (8.11)
POST (8.3)
Power On Self Test (POST) (8.3)
print spool (8.9)
proprietary operating systems (8.11)

response time (8.9)

screen saver (8.16)
segmentation (8.8)
segments (8.8)
shell (8.12)
single program (8.4)
spooling (8.9)
supervisor (8.2)
swapping (8.8)
symmetric multiprocessing (8.5)
system software (8.2)

thrashing (8.10)
time slice (8.6)
timesharing (8.4)

UNIX (8.13)
user ID (8.10)
utility programs (8.15)

virtual machine (VM) (8.5)
virtual memory management (8.7)

le   Edit   Section   Page   Tools   Options   Help

Test Your Knowledge

Fill in the Blanks

1. System software can be classified into three major categories; _OP.STK_ , _L.T_ , and _utilin_ .

2. A(n) _OPS_ consists of one or more programs that manage the operations of a computer.

3. _OS_ is the most widely used operating system on personal computers.

4. The _Unix_ operating system, developed by scientists at Bell Laboratories, was specifically designed to provide a way to manage a variety of scientific and specialized computer applications.

5. Special-purpose system software programs called _compiler vint_ are used to convert the programming instructions written by programmers into machine instructions that a computer can understand.

Short Answer

1. What is a single program operating system? How is a multitasking operating system different from a multi-processing operation system? What is a virtual machine OS?

2. What is virtual memory management? With what types of operating systems is virtual memory management used? Why? How is segmentation different from paging? What is thrashing?

3. How are proprietary operating systems different from portable operating systems? What is the advantage of portable operating systems?

4. What do Microsoft Windows, Windows NT, Macintosh, and OS/2 have in common? How are they different? Why are earlier versions of Windows called operating environments?

5. What are utility programs? What are some of the tasks addressed by utility programs? What is the purpose of a screen saver?

Label the Figure

Instructions: Complete the diagrams to show the two ways in which multiprocessing is implemented.

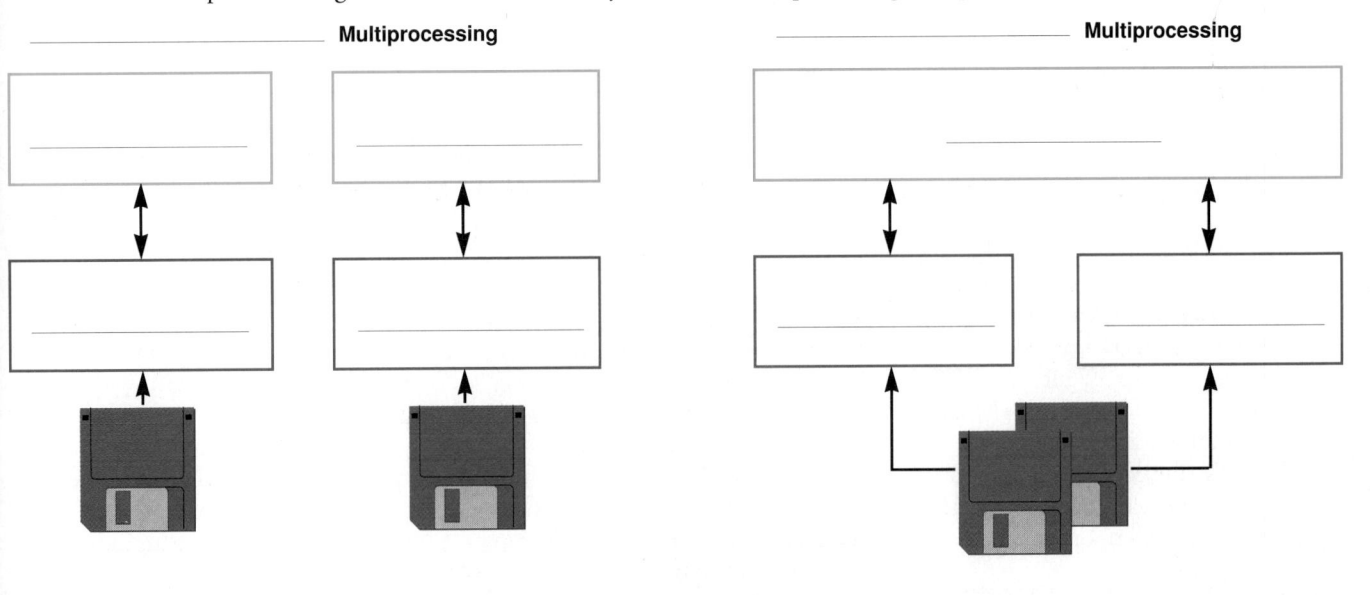

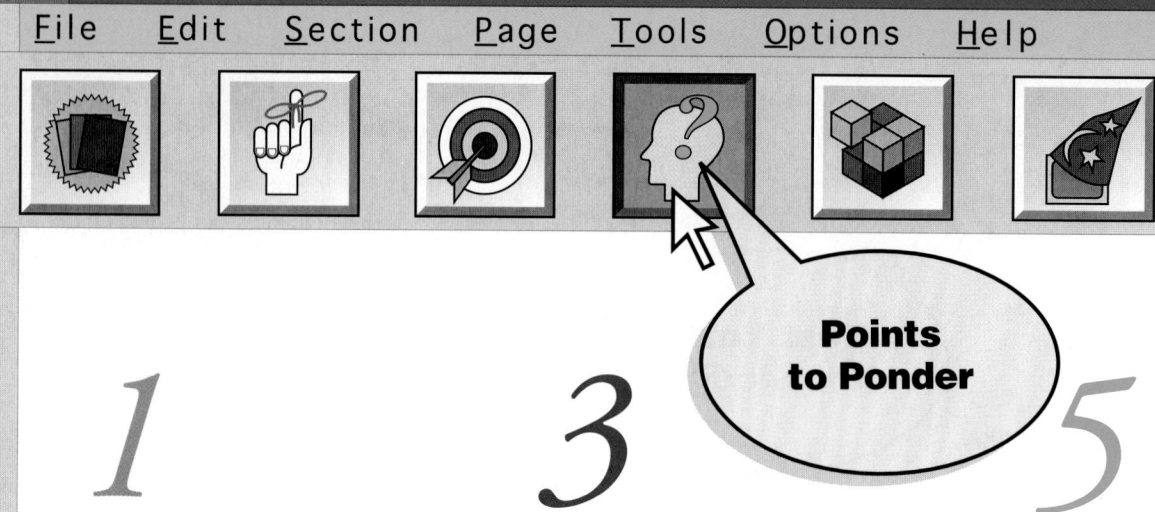

Points to Ponder

1

In its role as an interface between application programs and computer hardware, one of the things an operating system does is provide a common set of computer functions. Some basic tasks need to be accomplished by almost all application programs, such as getting input from the keyboard. The operating system converts an application program's simple instruction to perform a task to the more complex set of instructions the hardware needs to complete the task. Make a list of at least six functions you think must be performed by almost all application programs. Rank your list from the function that you believe is performed most to the function that you believe is performed least. Briefly explain why you ranked the functions as you did.

2

You are the team leader of a group developing a new operating system. As team leader, you are responsible for providing a "vision" of the ideal operating system. Write a description of the perfect operating system. Answer such questions as: What type of operating system (single program, multitasking, multiprocessing, or virtual machine) is it? How does the operating system allocate system resources, monitor system activities, and manage disks and files? What kind of interface does the operating system use? Explain why you think each of the features of your ideal operating system is important.

3

You are the CEO of Computers and Advanced Technology (CAT), a company that specializes in the manufacture of laptop computers (company slogan: "Life is better with a CAT on your lap"). Your research department has just developed a new operating system, the features of which promise to make most other operating systems seem antiquated. Although the operating system was designed specifically to work with CAT laptop computers, your programmers assure you that it can be adapted to work with other personal computers. As CEO, you now have a decision to make. Should the new operating system remain proprietary, possibly enhancing the sale of CAT computers, or should you instruct your programmers to make it portable, thus making it marketable to a wider spectrum of users? Explain your decision.

4

You have been hired as a consultant by a small, family-run printing business that wants to purchase its first personal computers. The company intends to buy twelve PCs and does not plan to obtain any more computers for about five years. Your job is to make a recommendation regarding the type of personal computers the company should purchase and the operating system (DOS, Windows, Windows NT, Macintosh, OS/2, UNIX, or NextStep) it should buy to work with the computers. Write a report to the company giving your recommendations and explaining the reasons behind them.

5

Some of the tasks described in this chapter that are addressed by utility programs include file management, disk management, memory management, backup and restore, data recovery, data compression, virus protection, and screen saver. If you could afford to purchase only four of these utility programs for your personal computer, which would you buy? Why? If you were purchasing utility programs for an entire company, which four do you think are most important? Why? If the utility programs you would buy for your personal computer are not the same as the utility programs you think are most important for a company, briefly explain why the lists are different.

6

The latest in utility programs are intelligent utilities. These utility programs can be customized to fit your needs and will perform a task until you tell it to stop. For example, intelligent utilities can be programmed to turn on your computer at a certain time, automatically backup files you've changed, examine the latest stock prices and advise you when to buy or sell, or even check your calendar and remind you to buy a birthday or anniversary gift for your spouse! If you had an intelligent utility, what types of tasks would you program it to do? What tasks could you program it to do in your chosen career field? As intelligent utilities continue to develop, what effect do you think they will have on an individual's personal and professional life in the future?

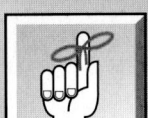

Out and About

1. Using current computer magazines and business publications, research the ways in which one of the operating systems described in this chapter is being used today. What kinds of businesses are using the operating system? Why? How much is the operating system being used by individuals on personal computers? What are the advantages of the operating system? What are the disadvantages? What are the system requirements and price of the operating system? From your research, what do you think is the future of the operating system?

2. Find out the operating system that is used on your, or a friend's, personal computer. What company manufactures the operating system? What type of interface does the operating system use? Does the operating system support multitasking? Refer to the documentation that accompanied the computer or operating system to determine the operating system's version and release number, and the year it was produced. Try to find out when the first version of the operating system was introduced, when the next version is expected, and how much the company charges for upgrades.

3. Locate a department in your school or a local company that uses a mainframe computer. Interview an administrator in charge of the mainframe about the computer's operating system. What operating system is used? How was the operating system chosen? What are the advantages of the operating system? What are the disadvantages? Have there ever been any problems with the operating system? Has the operating system been changed to meet specific needs of the department or company? If so, how? Does the administrator anticipate using the same operating system five years from now? Why or why not?

4. Bill Gates, the founder of Microsoft Corporation, is a modern legend. Gates is one of the wealthiest men in America, and Microsoft is one of the most influential companies in the computer industry. The fascinating story of Bill Gates and Microsoft is told in several books, including: *Hard Drive: Bill Gates and the Making of the Microsoft Empire* (by James Wallace), *Gates* (by Stephen Manes), and *Accidental Empires: How the Boys of Silicon Valley Make Their Millions, Battle Foreign Competition, and Still Can't Get a Date* (by Robert X. Cringely). Read one of these books, or another book on Gates and Microsoft, and write a report on the qualities you think led to the success of Bill Gates and Microsoft.

File   Edit   Section   Page   Tools   Options   Help

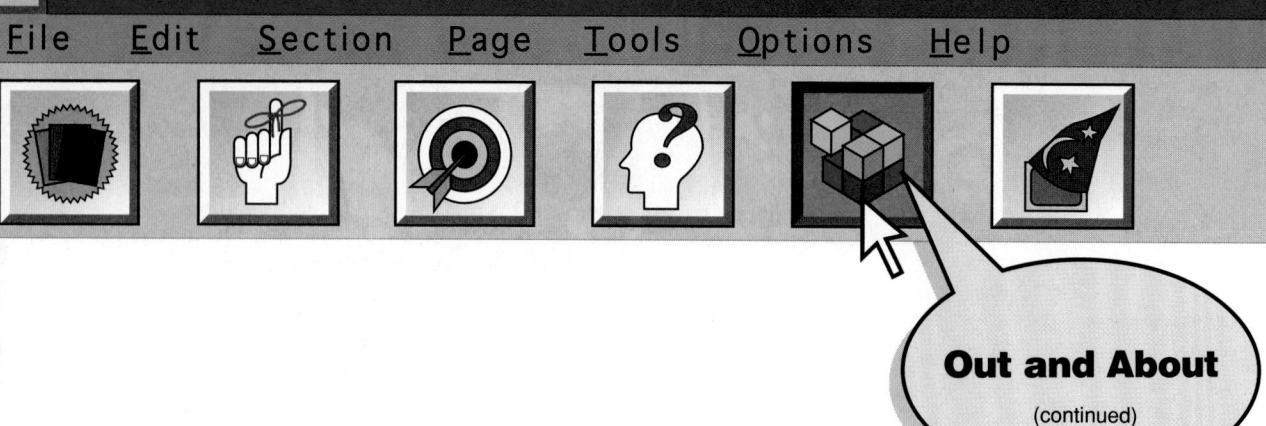

Out and About

(continued)

5. Application programs are designed to be used with specific operating systems. When you purchase software, it is important to read the program's packaging to determine if it is compatible with the operating system on your personal computer. Operating systems undergo frequent revisions, each of which is designated by a version number. A higher version number means a more recent revision (DOS 6.0 is a newer version than DOS 5.0). Usually, operating systems are downwardly compatible, meaning that an application program written for an earlier version of an operating system will work with a later version of the same operating system. Often, however, an application program written for a later version of an operating system will not work correctly with an earlier version. Visit a computer software vendor and find four application programs in which you are interested that require the DOS operating system. Which of the programs could you run on your personal computer if you had DOS 3.3? DOS 5.0? DOS 6.0?

6. Many utility programs are available for users of personal computers. Visit a computer store, or read a computer magazine, and choose two utility programs in which you are interested. Write a review of the two programs. What is the function of each? What are the system requirements? How easy is the program to use? How much does the program cost? In your opinion, is the utility worth the price? Why or why not? If you could buy only one of the utility programs, which would you purchase? Why?

e **E**dit   **S**ection   **P**age   **T**ools   **O**ptions   **H**elp

In the Lab

Windows Labs

1 **Searching for System Files** With Program Manager on the screen, double-click the Main group icon. In the Main group window, double-click the File Manager program-item icon. Maximize the File Manager window. Be sure the directory window in NOT maximized. Select the View menu and choose the By File Type command. If it is not already selected, click the Show Hidden/System Files check box in the By File Type dialog box. Choose the OK button.

Select the File menu and choose the Search command. In the Search dialog box, type *.sys in the Search For text box, type c:\ in the Start From text box, be sure the Search All Subdirectories check box is selected, and choose the OK button to display the Search Results window *(Figure 8-19)*. Scroll through the list of files. Write down the filenames that have a red exclamation point (!) in their icons. Write down the path where the file config.sys is located. Close the Search Results window.

Use the same procedure to search for the filename autoexec.bat, and write down the path where this file is located. Close the Search Results window. Close File Manager.

2 **Shelly Cashman Series System Software Lab** Follow the instructions in Windows Lab 2 in Chapter 1 on page 1.30 to display the Shelly Cashman Series Labs screen. Select Evaluating Operating Systems and choose the Start Lab button. When the initial screen displays, carefully read the objectives. With your printer turned on, point to the Print Questions button and click the left mouse button. Fill out the top of the Questions sheet and answer the questions as you step through the System Software Lab.

3 **Shelly Cashman Series Ergonomics Lab** Follow the instructions in Windows Lab 2 in Chapter 1 on page 1.30 to display the Shelly Cashman Series Labs screen. Select Working at Your Computer and choose the Start Lab button. When the initial screen displays, carefully read the objectives. With your printer turned on, point to the Print Questions button and click the left mouse button. Fill out the top of the Questions sheet and answer the questions as you step through the Ergonomics Lab.

4 **Performing Calculations** With Program Manager on the screen, double-click the Accessories group icon. Double-click the Calculator program-item icon. Select the View menu and choose Standard. Press NUM LOCK. Using the numeric keypad, type 23.65+98.42 and press the ENTER key. The result displays in the Calculator window *(Figure 8-20)*. Press ESC to clear the calculation. You can also use the mouse to enter expressions. Type 4624 and click the sqrt button. Write down the result. Press ESC to clear the calculation. Write down the results of each of these calculations: 2489 divided by 8; 54 multiplied by 78; and 65 minus 423.5. Close Calculator.

5 **Keeping Track of Appointments** With Program Manager on the screen, double-click the Accessories group icon. In the Accessories group window, double-click

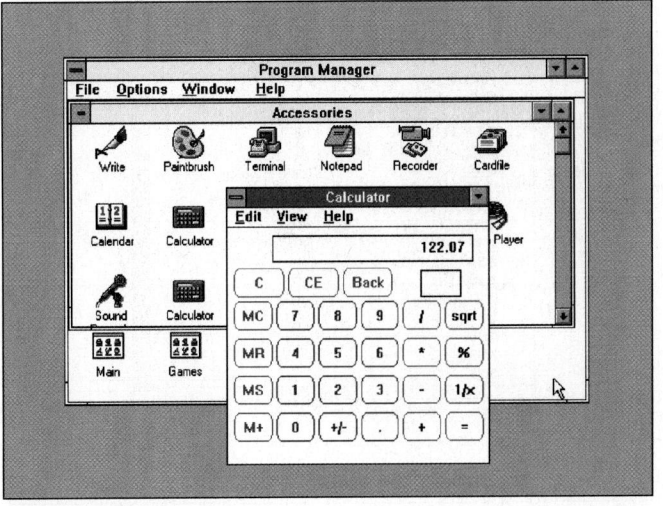

Figure 8-19   *Figure 8-20*

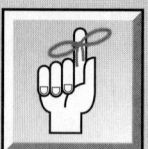

File   Edit   Section   Page   Tools   Options   Help

In the Lab (continued)

the Calendar program-item icon. Maximize the Calendar window. Select the Show menu and choose the Date command. In the Show Date dialog box, type 2-15-96 in the Show Date text box and choose the OK button. Under AM times, click 8:00 and type ENGL 104; click 10:00 and type COM 115; click 12:00 PM and type Meet Sue in Cafeteria (Figure 8-21). Select the Options menu and choose the Special Time command. In the Special Time dialog box, type 3:30 in the Special Time text box and click the PM option button. Choose the Insert button. Type CIS 204. Click the right arrow in the status line, the line below the menu bar, to display 2-16-96. Click 10:00 and type Meet John in Library; click 5:00 and type Pizza Party at Gino's. Click the left arrow in the status line.

Save the appointment book by choosing the Save command from the File menu. Use the filename WIN8-5. Select the File menu and choose the Print command. With 2/15/96 in the From text box, press the TAB key, type 2/16/96 in the To text box and choose the OK button. From the View menu, choose the Month command to display the calendar in month view (Figure 8-22). Close Calendar.

6 Using Help to Switch Between Open Applications
With Program Manager on the screen, select the Help menu and choose the Contents command. Select the Switch Between Applications topic. Read and print the topic contents. With the Help screen still open, click in the Program Manager window to make it active. Open the Write application in the Accessories group. With the Program Manager, Write, and Help windows all open, practice the techniques listed on the Switch Between Applications Help topic. Close the Help window. Close Write.

DOS Labs

1 Displaying the DOS Version and Disk Volume
At the DOS prompt, type cls and press the ENTER key. Type ver and press the ENTER key to display the version of DOS currently loaded into memory. What version of DOS are you using? Type vol and press the ENTER key to display the volume information for the default disk drive. What is the volume label and serial number of the default disk drive? Press the PRINT SCREEN key.

2 Optimizing Your Computer's Memory   Before starting this Lab, check with your instructor. At the DOS prompt, type memmaker and press the ENTER key. Read the welcome screen and press the ENTER key. Choose Express Setup and follow the remaining instructions. When the MemMaker program is finished, write down the free conventional memory both before and after MemMaker. Press the ESC key to undo MemMaker's changes. Press the ENTER key twice.

Online Lab

1 Reviewing Entertainment   Using one of the two online services you selected in Chapter 1, connect to the service and perform the following tasks: (1) Search the online service for the Entertainment section. (2) Locate, display, and print the five best-selling: video movies, nonfiction books, fiction books, and CD albums. (3) Locate, display, and print two Broadway reviews.

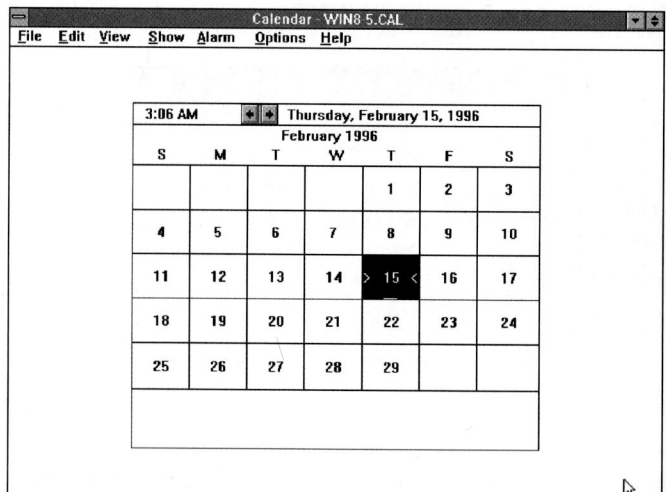

Figure 8-21   Figure 8-22

How to Purchase, Install, and Maintain a Personal Computer

*A*t some point in time, perhaps during this course, you may decide to buy a computer system. It could be your first system or a replacement system. The decision is an important one and will require an investment of both time and money. The following guidelines are presented to help you purchase, install, and maintain your system. The guidelines assume you are purchasing a desktop personal computer, often referred to as a PC. It is further assumed that the computer will be used for home or small business use. Because it is the most widely purchased type of system, some of the guidelines assume an IBM-compatible computer is being purchased. Most of the guidelines however, may be applied to the purchase of any personal computer, including a Macintosh or other non-DOS or non-Windows system. The type of system you purchase should be determined by your software requirements and the need to be compatible with other systems with which you work. Many of the guidelines can also be applied to purchasing a portable computer such as a laptop. A laptop computer may be an appropriate choice if you need computing capability when you travel. Keep in mind, though, that many laptop computer users also have larger capacity desktop systems at home and/or at work. The laptop systems are commonly used for applications such as word processing and electronic mail that the user needs when he or she is traveling.

How to Purchase a Computer System

1 **Determine what applications you will use on your computer.** This decision will guide you as to the type and size of computer. Artists and others who work with graphics will need a larger, better quality monitor and additional disk space.

2 **Choose your software first.** Some packages only run on Macintosh computers, others only on a PC. Certain packages only run under the Windows operating system. In addition, some software requires more memory and disk space than other packages. Most users will want at least word processing and spreadsheet packages. For the most software for the money, consider purchasing an integrated package or a software suite that offers reduced pricing on several applications purchased at the same time. Be sure the software contains the features that are necessary for the work you will be performing.

3 **Be aware of *hidden costs*.** Realize there will be additional costs associated with buying a computer. Such costs may include the following: an additional phone line or outlet to use a modem; computer furniture; consumable supplies such as diskettes and paper; diskette holders; reference manuals on specific software packages; and special training classes you may want to take. Depending on where you buy your computer, the seller may be willing to include some or all of these in the system purchase price.

4 **Buy equipment that meets the *Energy Star* power consumption guidelines.** These guidelines require that computer systems, monitors, and printers reduce electrical consumption if they have not been used for some period of time, usually several minutes. Equipment meeting the guidelines can display the *Energy Star* logo.

5 **Consider buying from local computer dealers, retail stores, or direct mail companies.** Each has certain advantages. The local dealer or retail store can more easily provide hands-on support, if necessary. With a mail-order company, you are usually limited to speaking to someone over the phone. Mail-order companies usually, but not always, offer the lowest prices. The important thing to do when you are shopping for a system is to make sure you are comparing identical or similar configurations. Local companies can be found in the phone book. Call first to see if they sell to individual customers; some sell only or primarily sell to businesses. Phone numbers for mail-order companies can be found in their advertisements that run in PC periodicals. Most libraries subscribe to several of the major PC magazines. If you call a mail-order firm, ask if it has a catalog that can be sent to you. If you do not buy a system right away, call for another catalog; prices and configurations change frequently.

6 **Use a spreadsheet, like the one shown in Figure 1, to compare purchase alternatives.** Use a separate sheet of paper to take notes on each vendor's system and then summarize the information on the spreadsheet.

Figure 1

A spreadsheet is an effective way to summarize and compare the prices and equipment offered by different system vendors. List your desired system in the column labeled Desired. Place descriptions on the lines and enter prices in the boxes.

SYSTEM COST COMPARISON WORKSHEET

		Desired	#1	#2	#3	#4
Base	Mfr					
System	Model					
	Processor	486DX2				
	Speed	66 MHz				
	Power supply	200 watts				
	Expansion slots	5				
	Local bus video	yes				
	Operating System	Windows				
	Price					
Memory	Amount	8 MB				
	Price					
Disk	Mfr					
	Size	>500 MB				
	Price					
Diskette	3 1/2					
	5 1/4					
	Combination	Combo				
Color	Mfr					
Monitor	Model					
	Size	15 inch				
	Resolution	SVGA				
	Dot Pitch	0.28 mm				
	Price					
Sound	Mfr					
Card	Model					
	Price					
Speakers	Mfr					
	Model					
	Size	2 inch				
	Price					
CD-ROM	Mfr					
	Speed	300 kbps				
	Price					
Mouse	Mfr					
	Price					
Fax	Mfr					
Modem	Speeds	14.4/14.4				
	Price					
Printer	Mfr					
	Model					
	Type	ink jet				
	Speed	6 ppm				
	Price					
Surge	Mfr					
Protector	Price					
Tape	Mfr					
Backup	Price					
UPS	Mfr					
	Price					
Other	Sales Tax					
	Shipping					
	1 YR Warranty	standard				
	1 YR On-Site Svc					
	3 YR On-Site Svc					
	TOTAL					
Software	List free software					

7 **Consider more than just price.** Do not necessarily buy the lowest priced system. Consider intangibles such as how long the vendor has been in business, its reputation for quality, and reputation for support.

8 **Do some research.** Talk to friends, coworkers, and teachers. Ask what type of system and software they bought and why. Would they recommend their systems and the companies they bought from? Are they satisfied with their software? Spend some time at the library reviewing computer periodicals. Most have frequent articles that rate systems and software on cost, performance, and support issues.

9 **Look for free software.** Many system vendors now include free software with their systems. Some even let you choose which software you want. Free software only has value, however, if you would have purchased it if it had not come with the computer.

10 **Buy a system compatible with the one you use elsewhere.** If you use a personal computer at work or at some other organization, make sure the computer you buy is compatible. That way, if you need or want to, you can work on projects at home.

11

Consider purchasing an on-site service agreement. If you use your system for business or otherwise cannot afford to be without your computer, consider purchasing an on-site service agreement. Many of the mail-order vendors offer such support through third-party companies. Agreements usually state that a technician will be on-site within 24 hours. Some systems include on-site service for only the first year. It is usually less expensive to extend the service for two or three years when you buy the computer instead of waiting to buy the service agreement later.

12

Use a credit card to purchase your system, if possible. Many credit cards now have purchase-protection benefits that cover you in case of loss or damage to purchased goods. Some also extend the warranty of any products purchased with the card. Paying by credit card also gives you time to install and use the system before you have to pay for it. Finally, if you're dissatisfied with the system and cannot reach an agreement with the seller, paying by credit card gives you certain rights regarding withholding payment until the dispute is resolved. Check your credit card agreement for specific details.

13

Avoid buying the smallest system available. Studies show that many users become dissatisfied because they did not buy a powerful enough system. Plan on buying a system that will last you for at least three years. If you have to buy a smaller system, be sure it can be upgraded with additional memory and devices as your system requirements grow. Consider the entries in the box below as a minimum recommended system. Each of the components are discussed separately in the box to the right.

Base System Components

486DX2 Processor, 66 megahertz
200 watt power supply
340 to 540 MB hard disk drive
8 MB of RAM
3 expansion slots
1 open expansion bay
local bus video card
1 parallel and 2 serial ports
3.5" diskette drive
14" or 15" SVGA color monitor
mouse or other pointing device
enhanced keyboard
ink-jet or dot matrix printer
surge protector
latest version of operating system
FCC Class B approved

Optional Components

5.25" diskette
14.4 fax modem
laser printer
sound card and speakers
CD-ROM drive
tape backup
uninterruptable power supply (UPS)

Processor:
A 486DX2 processor with a speed rating of at least 66 megahertz is needed for today's more sophisticated software, eve word processing software.

Power Supply:
200 watts. If the power supply is too small, it will not be able to support additional expansion cards that you may want to add in the future. The power supply should be UL (Underwriters Laboratory) approved.

Hard Disk:
340 to 540 megabytes (MB). Each new release of software requires more hard disk space. Even with disk compression programs, disk space is used up fast. Start with more disk than you ever think you'll need.

Memory (RAM):
8 megabytes (MB). Like disk space, the new applications demand more memory. It is easier and less expensive to obtain the memory when you buy the system than if you wait until later.

Expansion Slots:
At least three open slots. Expansion slots are needed for scanners, tape drives, video capture boards, and other equipment you may want to add in the future as your needs change and the price of this equipment becomes lower.

Expansion Bay:
At least one open bay. An expansion (drive) bay will let you add another disk o diskette drive, a tape drive, or a CD-ROM drive.

Local Bus Video Card:
Local bus video cards provide faster video performance than video cards that use the slower expansion bus. Make sure the video card has at least 1 MB of memory

Ports:
At least one parallel and two serial ports. The parallel port is used for your printer. The serial ports can be used for additiona printers, external modems, joysticks, a mouse, and some network connections.

Diskette Drives:
Most software is now distributed on 3.5-inch disks. As an option, consider adding

a 5.25-inch diskette to read data and programs stored on that format. The best way to achieve this is to buy a combination diskette drive which is only slightly more expensive than a single 3.5-inch diskette drive. The combination device has both 3.5- and 5.25-inch diskette drives in a single unit.

Color Monitor:
14 or 15 inch. This is one device where it pays to spend a little more money. A 15-inch super VGA (SVGA) monitor with a dot pitch of 0.28 mm or less will display graphics better than a 14-inch model. For health reasons, make sure you pick a low- radiation model. Also, look for a monitor with an antiglare coating on the screen or consider buying an antiglare filter that mounts on the front of the screen.

Pointing Device:
Most systems include a mouse as part of the base package. Some people prefer to use a trackball.

Enhanced Keyboard:
Almost always included with the system. Check to make sure the keyboard is the *enhanced* and not the older *standard* model. The enhanced keyboard is also sometimes called the *101 keyboard* because it has 101 keys (some enhanced keyboards have even more keys).

Printer:
Dot matrix are the lowest cost and most reliable types of printers. However, they do not print graphics as well as an ink-jet printer, which is only slightly more expensive. If you are going to be frequently working with graphics or want the best quality output, choose a laser or other type of page printer.

Surge Protector
A voltage spike can literally destroy your system. It is low-cost insurance to protect

yourself with a surge protector. Do not merely buy a fused multiple-plug outlet from the local hardware store. Buy a surge protector designed for computers with a separate protected jack for your phone (modem) line.

Operating System:
Almost all new systems come with an operating system, but it is not always the most current. Make sure the operating system is the one you want and is the latest version.

FCC Class B approved
The Federal Communications Commission (FCC) provides radio frequency emission standards that computer manufacturers must meet. If a computer does not meet the FCC standards, it could cause interference with radio and television reception. Class B standards apply to computers used in a home. Class A standards apply to a business installation.

Fax Modem:
14.4K speed for both the modem and FAX. Volumes of information are available via online databases. In addition, many software vendors provide assistance and free software upgrades via bulletin boards. For the speed they provide. 14.4K modems are worth the extra money. Facsimile (FAX) capability costs only a few dollars more and gives you more communication options.

Sound Card and Speakers:
Increasingly more software and support materials are incorporating sound.

CD-ROM Drive:
Multimedia is the wave of the future and it requires a CD-ROM drive. Buy a double-speed or faster.

Tape Backup
Larger hard disks make backing up data on diskettes impractical. Internal or external tape backup systems are the most common solution. Some portable units, great if you have more than one system, are designed to connect to your printer port. The small tapes can store the equivalent of hundreds of diskettes.

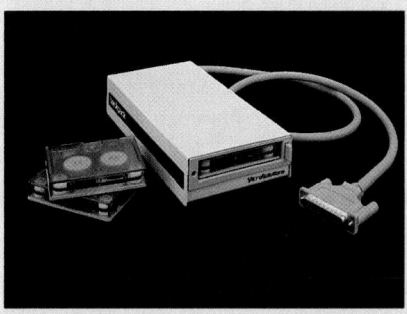

Uninterruptable Power Supply (UPS):
A UPS uses batteries to start or keep your system running if the main electrical power is turned off. The length of time they provide depends on the size of the batteries and the electrical requirements of your system but is usually at least 10 minutes. The idea of a UPS is to give you enough time to save your work. Get a UPS that is rated for your size system.

Remember that the types of applications you want to use on your system will guide you as to the type and size of computer that is right for you. The ideal computer system you choose may differ from the general recommendation presented here. Determine your needs and buy the best system your budget will allow.

How to Install a Computer System

1. Read the installation manuals *before* you start to install your equipment. Many manufacturers include separate installation instructions with their equipment that contain important information. Take the time to read them.

2. Allow for adequate workspace around the computer. A work space of at least two feet by four feet is recommended.

3. Install bookshelves. Bookshelves above and/or to the side of the computer area are useful for keeping manuals and other reference materials handy.

4. Install your computer in a well-designed work area. An applied science called **ergonomics** is devoted to making the equipment people use and the surrounding work area safer and more efficient. Ergonomic studies have shown that the height of your chair, keyboard, monitor, and work surface is important and can affect your health. See *Figure 2* for specific work area guidelines.

5. Use a document holder. To minimize neck and eye strain, obtain a document holder that holds documents at the same height and distance as your computer screen.

6. Provide adequate lighting. Use nonglare bulbs that illuminate your entire work area.

7. While working at your computer, be aware of health issues. See *Figure 3* for a list of computer user health guidelines.

8. Have a phone nearby that can be used while you are sitting at the computer. Having a phone near the computer really helps if you need to call a vendor about a hardware or software problem. Often the vendor support person can talk you through the correction while you are on the phone. To avoid data loss, however, do not place diskettes on the phone or near any other electrical or electronic equipment.

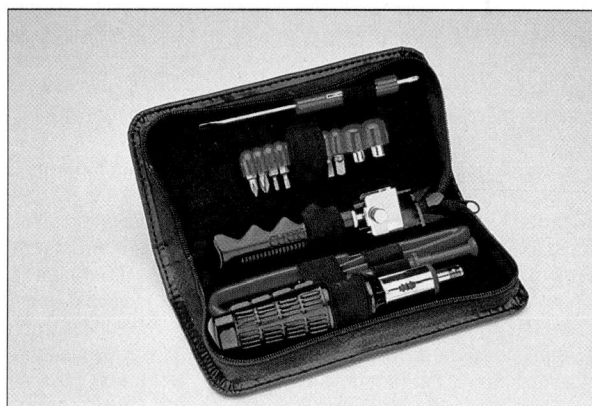

9. Obtain a computer tool set. Computer tool sets are available from computer dealers, office supply stores, and mail-order companies. These sets will have the right size screwdrivers and other tools to work on your system. Get one that comes in a zippered carrying case to keep all the tools together.

10. Save all the paperwork that comes with your system. Keep it in an accessible place with the paperwork from your other computer-related purchases. To keep different-sized documents together, consider putting them in a sealable plastic bag.

11. Record the serial numbers of all your equipment and software. Write the serial numbers on the outside of the manuals that came with the equipment as well as in a single list that contains the serial numbers of all your equipment and software.

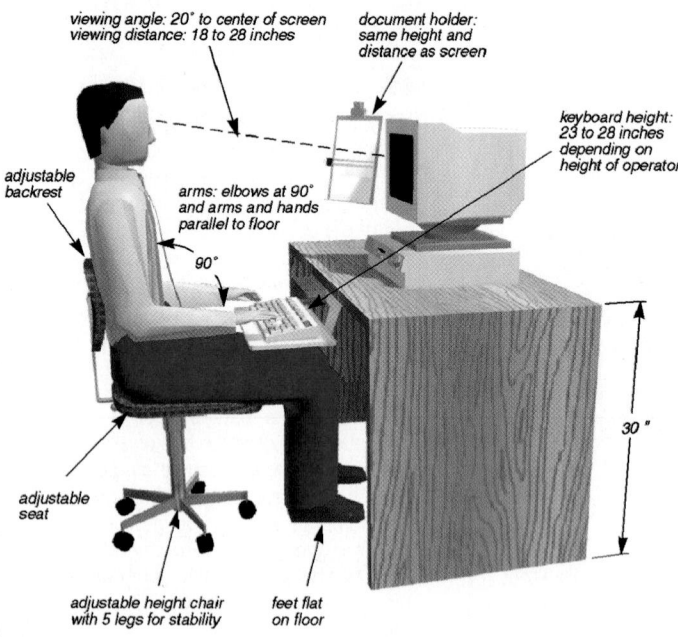

Figure 2
More than anything else, a well-designed work area should be flexible to allow adjustment to the height and build of different individuals. Good lighting and air quality should also be considered

12. Keep the shipping containers and packing materials for all your equipment. This material will come in handy if you have to return your equipment for servicing or have to move it to another location.

Figure 3
All computer users should follow the guidelines below to maintain their health.

Computer User Health Guidelines

1. Work in a well-designed work area. See Figure 2 for guidelines.
2. Alternate work activities to prevent physical and mental fatigue. If possible, change the order of your work to provide some variety.
3. Take frequent breaks. Every 15 minutes look away from the screen to give your eyes a break. At least once per hour, get out of your chair and move around. Every two hours, take at least a 15 minute break.
4. Incorporate hand, arm, and body stretching exercises into your breaks. At lunch, try to get outside and walk.
5. Make sure your computer monitor is designed to minimize electromagnetic radiation (EMR). If it is an older model, consider adding EMR reducing accessories.
6. Try to eliminate or minimize surrounding noise. Noisy environments contribute to stress and tension.
7. If you frequently have to use the phone and the computer at the same time, consider using a telephone headset. Cradling the phone between your head and shoulder can cause muscle strain.
8. Be aware of symptoms of repetitive strain injuries; soreness, pain, numbness, or weakness in neck, shoulders, arms, wrists, and hands. Do not ignore early signs; seek medical advice.

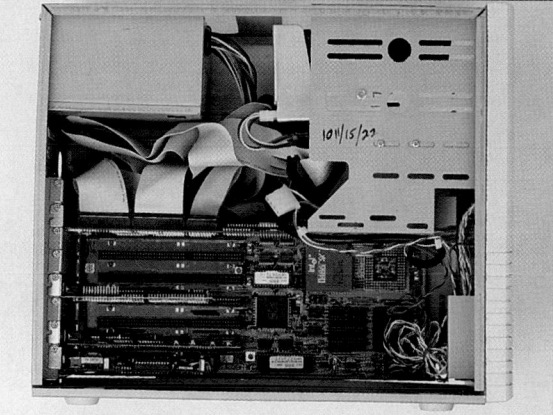

13. Look at the inside of your computer. Before you connect power to your system, remove the computer case cover and visually inspect the internal components. The user manual usually identifies what each component does. Look for any disconnected wires, loose screws or washers, or any other obvious signs of trouble. Be careful not to touch anything inside the case unless you are grounded.

Static electricity can permanently damage the microprocessor chips on the circuit boards. Before you replace the cover, take several photographs of the computer showing the location of the circuit boards. These photos may save you from taking the cover off in the future if you or a vendor has a question about which equipment controller card is installed in which expansion slot. If you don't feel comfortable performing this step by yourself, ask a more experienced computer user to help. If you buy your system from a local dealer, have the dealer perform this step with you.

14. **Identify device connectors.** At the back of your system there are a number of connectors for the printer, the monitor, the mouse, a phone line, and so on. If they are not already identified by the manufacturer, use a marking pen to write the purpose of each connector on the back of the computer case.

15. **Complete and send in your equipment and software registration cards right away.** If you are already entered in the vendors user database, it can save you time when you call in with a support question. Being a registered user also makes you eligible for special pricing on software upgrades.

16. **Install your system in an area where the temperature and humidity can be maintained.** Try to maintain a constant temperature between 60 and 80 degrees Fahrenheit when the computer is operating. High temperatures and humidity can damage electronic components. Be careful when using space heaters; their hot, dry air has been known to cause disk problems.

17. **Keep your computer area clean.** Avoid eating and drinking around the computer. Smoking should be avoided also. Cigarette smoke can quickly cause damage to the diskette drives and diskette surfaces.

18. **Check your home or renters insurance policy.** Some policies have limits on the amount of computer equipment they cover. Other policies do not cover computer equipment at all if it is used for a business (a separate policy is required).

How to Maintain a Computer System

1. **Start a notebook that includes information on your system.** This notebook should be a single source of information about your entire system, both hardware and software. Each time you make a change to your system, adding or removing hardware or software, or when you change system parameters, record the change. Include the following items:

- Serial numbers of all equipment and software.
- Vendor support phone numbers. These numbers are often buried in user manuals. Look up these numbers once and record all of them on a single sheet of paper at the front of your notebook.
- Date and vendor for each equipment and software purchase.
- Print outs for key system files (e.g., autoexec.bat and config.sys).
- Trouble log; a chronological history of any equipment or software problems. This history can be helpful if the problem persists and you have to call for support.
- Notes on discussions with vendor support personnel (can be combined with trouble log). *(Figure 4.)*

2. **Periodically review disk directories and delete unneeded files.** Files have a way of building up and can quickly use up your disk space. If you think you may need a file in the future, back it up to a diskette.

3. **Any time you work inside your computer turn off the power and disconnect the equipment from the power source.** In addition, before you touch anything inside the computer, touch an unpainted metal surface such as the power supply. This will help to discharge any static electricity that could damage internal components.

4. **Reduce the need to clean the inside of your system by keeping the surrounding area dirt and dust free.** Diskette cleaners are available but should be used sparingly (some owners never use them unless they experience diskette problems). If dust builds up inside the computer it should be carefully removed with compressed air and a small vacuum. Don't touch the components with the vacuum.

5. **Back up key files and data.** At a minimum, you should have a system diskette with your **command.com, autoexec.bat,** and **config.sys** files. If your system crashes, these files will help you get going again. In addition, back up any files with a file extension of **.sys.** For Windows systems, all files with a file extension of **.ini** and **.grp** should also be backed up.

6. **Periodically, defragment your hard disk.** Defragmenting your hard disk reorganizes files so they are in contiguous (adjacent) clusters and makes disk operations faster. Defragmentation programs have been known to damage files so make sure your disk is backed up first.

7. **Protect your system from computer viruses.** Computer viruses are programs designed to *infect* computer systems by copying themselves into other computer files. The virus program spreads when the infected files are used by or copied to another system. Virus programs are dangerous because they are often designed to damage the files of the infected system. You can protect yourself from viruses by installing an anti-virus program.

8. **Learn to use system diagnostic programs.** If they did not come with your system, obtain a set. These programs help you identify and possibly solve problems before you call for technical assistance. Some system manufacturers now include diagnostic programs with their systems and ask that you run the programs before you call for help.

PC OWNER'S NOTEBOOK OUTLINE

1. Vendor phone numbers
   Vendor
   City/State
   Product
   Phone #

2. Serial numbers
   Product
   Manufacturer
   Serial #

3. Purchase history
   Date
   Product
   Manufacturer
   Vendor
   Cost

4. Key file listings
   autoexec.bat
   config.sys
   win.ini
   system.ini

5. Trouble log
   Date
   Time
   Problem
   Resolution

6. Support calls
   Date
   Time
   Company
   Contact
   Problem
   Comments

7. Vendor paperwork

Figure 4
This suggested notebook outline to organize important information about your computer should be kept on hand.

INDEX

Absolute referencing: In spreadsheet programs, when a formula is copied to another cell, the formula continues to refer to the same cell locations. **2.15**

Access arm: Contains the read/write heads and moves the heads across the surface of the disk. **6.10**

Access time: The time required to access and retrieve data stored in sectors on a diskette. **6.7**

Active matrix: LCD screens that use individual transistors to control each crystal cell. **5.21**

Adapter cards, *see* **Expansion board**

Adaptive technology, 3.22

Alignment: Formatting text so that characters line up with a margin or tab. **2.8**

American Express, 6.24

American Standard Code For Information Interchange (ASCII): The most widely used coding system to represent data, primarily on personal computers and many minicomputers. **4.3**

Analog computer: Computer designed to process continuously variable data, such as electrical voltage. **4.2**

Analog signal: A signal used on communications lines that consists of a continuous electrical wave. **7.16**

Analytical graphics: The charts provided by spreadsheet packages. **2.16**

Apple computer, development of, 1.35. *See also* **Macintosh**

Application software: Programs that tell a computer how to produce information. **1.15**
purchasing, 8.30
user tools, 2.1-32

Application software packages: Programs purchased from computer stores or software vendors. **1.15**
early development of, 1.36
integrated, 2.25-26
registering, 8.35
superapplications and, 2.29
See also Software

Arithmetic/logic unit (ALU): Part of the CPU that performs arithmetic and logical operations. **1.8, 4.7**

Arithmetic operations: Numeric calculations performed by the arithmetic/logic unit in the CPU, and include addition, subtraction, multiplication, and division. **1.9, 4.7**

Arrow keys: Keys on a keyboard that move the cursor up, down, left, or right on the screen. **3.4**

ASCII, *see* **American Standard Code for Information Interchange**

Assistive technology, 3.22

Asymmetric multiprocessing: Type of processing whereby application tasks are assigned to a specific CPU in computers that have more than one CPU. **8.5**

Asynchronous transmission mode: Data communication method which transmits one character at a time at irregular intervals using start and stop bits. **7.16**

Atanasoff, John V., 1.32

Audio output: Consists of sounds, including words and music, produced by the computer; sometimes called audio response. **5.4-5**

Audio response, *see* **Audio output**

Augmented reality: Used by manufacturing companies; virtual reality simulation that superimposes computer design information on a real scene. The worker wears a special pair of glasses that allow the design to be seen, superimposed on the actual work area. **5.28**

AUTOEXEC.BAT: A batch file loaded by the DOS kernel when the computer is turned on that performs tasks such as telling the system where to look for files (PATH command) and loading programs that the user wants to run every time the system is turned on, such as certain utility programs. **8.3**
backup of, 8.37
printout of, 8.36

Auxiliary storage devices: Devices that store instructions and data when they are not being used by the system unit. **1.9,** 6.2
computer output microfilm and, 5.24-25
See also Storage

Background: Jobs assigned a lower processing priority and less CPU time. Compare with foreground jobs. **8.7**

Backup: Storage method of creating a copy of important programs and data. **6.15**
need for, 8.37
utilities and, 8.15

Band printers: Impact printers that use a horizontal, rotating band, and can print in the range of 600 to 2,000 lines per minute. **5.12**

Bandwidth: The range of frequencies that a communications channel can carry. **7.17**

Bar chart: Chart that displays relationships among data with blocks or bars. **2.16**

Bar code: A type of optical code found on most grocery and retail items, usually scanned to produce price and inventory information about the product. **3.11**

Bar code label printers, 5.16

Base of a number system, 4.21

Baseband: Coaxial cable that can carry one signal at a time at very high rates of speed. **7.9**

BASIC (Beginner's All-purpose Symbolic Instruction Code), development of, 1.34

Basic Input/Output System (BIOS): When the computer is turned on, the CPU chip looks to the BIOS chip for instructions on how to proceed. The instructions provide the interface between the operating system and the hardware devices. **8.3**

Baud rate: The number of times per second that a data communications signal being transmitted changes; with each change, one or more bits can be transmitted. **7.18**

Bay: An open area inside the system unit used to install additional equipment. **4.6, 4.16**
purchasing computers and, 8.32

Bell Laboratories, 8.13

Bernoulli disk cartridge: Disk storage device that works with a special drive unit that uses a cushion of air to keep the flexible disk surface from touching the read/write head. The flexible disk surface reduces the chance of a head crash but does cause the cartridges to eventually wear out. **6.14**

Bidirectional printing: Printing method of dot matrix printers, in which the print head can print while moving in either direction. **5.11**

Binary number system, 4.2, 4.22

BIOS, *see* **Basic Input/Output System**

Bit(s): An element of a byte that can represent one of two values, on or off. There are 8 bits in a byte. **4.2**
parity, 4.4

Bit-mapped displays, *see* **Dot-addressable displays**

Bits per inch (bpi): Number of bits that can be recorded on one inch of track on a diskette. **6.6**

Bits per second (bps): A measure of the speed of data transmission; the number of bits transmitted in one second. **7.18**

Bold: Formatting text so that characters appear thicker and more distinct than surrounding text. **2.7**

Booting: The process of loading an operating system into main memory. **8.3**

Border: A line or lines around text or graphics to distinguish it from the rest of the document. **2.8**

Bricklin, Dan, 1.35

Bridge: A combination of hardware and software that is used to connect similar networks. **7.28**

Broadband: Coaxial cable that can carry multiple signals at one time. **7.10**

Buffers: Areas of memory used to store data that has been read or is waiting to be sent to sent to an output device. **8.7**

Bulletin board systems (BBSs): Allows users to communicate electronically with one another and share information, using personal computers. **7.7**

Bus: Any line that transmits bits between the memory and the input/output devices, and between memory and the CPU. **4.12**
comparison of widths, 4.8
expansion, 4.12
local, 4.13

Business graphics, *see* **Analytical graphics**

Bus network: A communications network in which all the devices are connected to and share a single cable. **7.26**

Button: An icon that, whenselected, causes a specific action to take place. **2.3**

Byte: Each storage location within main memory, identified with a memory address. **4.2**

Cache memory: High-speed RAM memory between the CPU and the main memory that increases processing efficiency. **4.10** *See also* **Disk cache**

Cage: 2 or more bays together. **4.16**

Cartridge tape: Frequently used storage medium for backup on personal computers. **6.16**
purchasing computers and, 8.33

Cathode ray tube (CRT): An output device;monitor. **1.8, 5.18**

CD-ROM (compact disk read-only memory): A small optical disk that uses the same laser technology as audio compact disks. **6.20**
purchasing, 8.33

Cell: The intersection where a row and a column meet on a spreadsheet. **2.12**

Cellular telephone: A wireless telephone available to the general public that uses radio waves to communicate with a local antenna assigned to a specific geographic area called a cell. **7.12**

Central processing unit (CPU): Processing unit containing a control unit that executes program instructions, and an arithmetic/logic unit (ALU) that performs math and logic operations. **1.8, 4.6**
operating system management of, 8.6-7
performance of, 8.9-10
utilization, 8.10

Chain printers: High-speed impact printers that use a rotating chain to print up 3,000 lines per minute of good print quality. **5.13**

Characters per second (cps): Speed measurement of impact printers that have movable print heads. **5.10**

Chart: In spreadsheet program, a graphic representation of the relationship of numeric data. **2.16**

Chip, *see* **Integrated circuit**

CISC (complex instruction set computing): Computers that have hundreds of commands in their instruction sets;describes most computers. **4.18**

Client-server: In information resource sharing on a network, as much processing as possible is done on the server system before data is transmitted to the requesting computer. **7.23**

Clip art: Collections of art that are stored on disks and are designed for use with desktop publishing packages. **2.11**

Clipboard: Temporary storage place for text during cut operations. **2.6**

Clock, *see* **System clock**

Cluster: 2 to 8 track sectors on a diskette; the smallest unit of diskette space used to store data. **6.4**
contiguous, 6.15

Coaxial cable: A high-quality communications line that is used in offices and laid underground and laid underneath the ocean. Coaxial cable consists of a copper wire conductor surrounded by a nonconducting insulator that is in turn surrounded by a woven metal mesh outer conductor, and finally a plastic outer coating. **7.9**

COBOL (COmmon Business Oriented Language), 1.32

Color monitor: Monitor that can display text or graphics in color. **5.20**
method of producing color, 5.23
purchasing, 8.33

Color printers, 5.14, 5.15

Columns: Data that is organized vertically on a spreadsheet. **2.12**

Command(s): In a graphical user interface, instructions for menus that cause the software to perform specific actions. **2.3, 3.2**

COMMAND.COM: The DOS command language interpreter. **8.3**
backup of, 8.37

Command language: Instructions that the operating system allows the user to give to the computer, such as to list all the files on a diskette, or to copy a file from one diskette to another. **8.2**

Command language interpreter: The portion of the operating system that carries out the command language instructions. **8.2**

Command language prompt: Prompt displayed when the computer is turned on that indicates the system is ready to accept a command from the user. **8.3**

Common carriers: Public wide area network companies such as the telephone companies. **7.24**

Communications: The transmission of data and information over a communications channel such as a standard telephone line, between one computer terminal and another

computer. 7.1, **7.8**
bulletin board systems and, 7.6
electronic data interchange and, 7.5-6
electronic mail, 7.2
equipment, 7.18-19
examples of use, 7.2
fax, 7.4
global positioning systems and, 7.6-7
groupware and, 7.4-5
line configurations and, 7.14-15
networks, 7.21-29
online services and, 7.7
protocols, 7.21
software, 7.20
system model, 7.8
telecommuting and, 7.5
teleconferencing, 7.3
transmission media and, 7.8-13
voice mail, 7.3

Communications channel: The link, or path, that the data follows as it is transmitted from the sending equipment to the receiving equipment in a communications system. **7.8**
characteristics of, 7.16-18
example of, 7.13

Communications line, *see* **Communications channel**

Communications link, *see* **Communications channel**

Communications network, *see* **Network**

Communications satellites: Man-made space devices that receive, amplify, and retransmit signals from earth. **7.11**

Communications software: Programs that perform data communications tasks such as dialing, file transfer, terminal emulation, and data encryption. **2.22, 7.20**

Computer(s): An electronic device, operating under the control of instructions stored in its own memory unit, that can accept data (input), that process data arithmetically and logically, produce output from the processing, and store the results for future use. **1.4**
categories of, 1.9-13
components of, 1.7-9
diagnostic programs, 8.37
evolution of industry, 1.32-38
example of use, 1.17-21
fourth-generation, 1.34
host, 7.15
installing, 8.34-35
maintenance of, 8.36-37
operations, 1.4-5
performance of, 8.9-10
purchasing, 8.30-33
reliability, 1.6
speed, 1.5
storage, *see* Storage
third-generation, 1.34
tool set for, 8.34
See also Personal computer(s)

Computer-assisted design (CAD) software, 1.20

External modem: A separate, or stand-alone, device attached to the computer or terminal by a cable and to the telephone outlet by a standard telephone cord. **7.19**

External report: A report used outside the organization. **5.3**

Facsimile, *see* **Fax**

Fault-tolerant computers: Computers built with redundant components to allow processing to continue if any single component fails. **8.5**

Fax (facsimile): Communications method in which equipment is used to transmit a reproduced image of a document over phone lines. The image is scanned and converted into digitized data that is transmitted to a receiving fax machine that converts the digitized data back into its original image. **7.4**
purchasing, 8.33
Federal Communications Commission, 8.33

Fetching: Control unit operation that obtains the next program instruction from main memory. **4.6**

Fiber optics: A technology based on the capability of smooth, hair-thin strand of glass that conduct light waves to rapidly and efficiently transmit data. **7.10**

Fields: A specific item of information, such as a name or Social Security number, in a record of a database file. **2.18**

File(s): A collection of related records. **2.18**
defragmentation of, 6.15
fragmented, 6.15
operating system management of, 8.10
utilities managing, 8.15

File allocation table: On personal computers using the DOS operating system, the file that stores information such as the filename, file size, the time and date the file was last changed, and the cluster numbers where the file begins. **6.5**

File-server: In information resource sharing on a network, allows an entire file to be sent at a time, on request. The requesting computer then performs the processing. **7.23**

File transfer, Internet and, 7.25

File transfer software: Communications software that allows the user to move one or more files from one system to another. The software generally has to be loaded on both the sending and receiving computers. **7.20**

Firmware: Instructions that are stored in ROM memory. Also called microcode. **4.11**

Fixed disks: Hard disks on mini-computers and mainframes. Also called direct-access storage devices. **6.9**

Flash memory: Type of RAM that can retain data even when power is turned off. **4.10**

Flash RAM, *see* **Flash memory**

Flatbed plotter: Plotter in which the pens are instructed by the software to move to the down position so the pen contacts the flat surface of the paper. **5.24**

Flat panel display: Plasma and LCD screens, which do not use the conventional cathode ray tube technology, and are relatively flat. **5.20**

Floppy disks, *see* **Diskettes**

Floptical: Diskette that combines optical and magnetic technology to achieve high storage rates (currently up to 21 megabytes) on what is basically a 3 1/2 inch diskette. **6.6**

Fonts: A specific combination of typeface and point size. **2.7**, 5.14

Footer: In word processing documents, text that is printed at the bottom of every page. **2.9**

Foreground jobs: Assignment of a higher processing priority and more CPU time. Compare with background jobs. **8.7**

Format: Changing the appearance of a document. **2.7**
desktop publishing, 2.10-11
spreadsheet, 2.17
word processing document, 2.7

Formatting: Process that prepares a diskette so that it can store data, and includes defining the tracks, cylinders, and sectors on the surfaces of the diskette. **6.4**

Formulas: Perform calculations on the data on a spreadsheet. **2.12**

FORTRAN (FORmula TRANslator), 1.33

Fourth-generation computers, 1.34

Fragmented: File stored in clusters that are not next to each other; also used to describe the condition of a disk drive that has many files stored in non-contiguous clusters, slowing down the computer's speed. **6.15**

Frame, *see* **Page**

Frankston, Bob, 1.35

Friction feed mechanism: Printing mechanisms that move paper through a printer by pressure between the paper and the carriage. **5.12**

Front-end processor: A computer that is dedicated to handling the communications requirements of a larger computer. **7.19**

Full-duplex transmission: Data transmission method in which data can be sent both directions at the same time. **7.17**

Full justification: Text is aligned with both the left and right margins. **2.8**

Function(s): Stored formulas that perform common calculations in a spreadsheet. **2.12**

Function keys: A set of numerical keys preceded by an "F" included on computer keyboards as a type of user interface. Pressing a function key in an applications program is a shortcut that takes the place of entering a command. **3.4**

Games
Internet and, 7.25
virtual reality and, 5.8

Garbage In, Garbage Out (GIGO): Describes inaccurate information caused by inaccurate data. **3.20**

Gas plasma: Screens that use neon gas deposited between 2 sheets of polarizing material. **5.21**

Gates, Bill, 1.36

Gateway: A combination of hardware and software that allows users on one network to access the resources on a different type of network. **7.28**

Geosynchronous orbit: Orbit about 22,300 miles above the earth that communications satellites are placed in. The satellite rotates with the earth, so that the same dish antennas on earth that are used to send and receive signals can remain fixed on the satellite at all times. **7.11**

Gestures: Special symbols made with pen input device that issue commands to the computer. **3.7**

Gigabyte (GB): A measurement of memory space, equal to a billion bytes. **6.10**

Gigaflops (GFLOPS): Billions of floating-point operations per second. **4.19**

GIGO, *see* **Garbage In, Garbage Out**

Global positioning system (GPS): Communications system that uses satellites to determine the geographic location of earth-based GPS equipment; often used for tracking and navigation of all type of vehicles. **7.6-7**

Grammar checker: Software used to check for grammar, writing style, and sentence structure errors. **2.7**

Graphic(s), multimedia and, 5.5-6

Graphical user interface (GUI): A user interface that provides visual clues, such as symbols called icons, to help the user when entering data or running programs. **1.15**, **2.2**

Graphics tablet: Converts points, lines, and curves from a sketch, drawing, or photograph to digital impulses and transmits them to a computer. It also contains unique characters and commands that can be automatically generated by the person using the tablet. **3.9**

Gray scaling: Used by monochrome monitors to convert an image into pixels that are different shades of gray, like a black and white photograph. **5.20**

Groupware: Software that helps multiple users work together by sharing information. **7.4-5**
GRP file extension, 8.37
GUI, *see* **Graphical user interface**

Half-duplex transmission: Data transmission method in which data can flow in both directions, but in only one direction at a time. **7.17**
Hand-held computers: Small computers used by workers who are on their feet instead of sitting at a desk, such as meter readers or inventory counters. **1.10**
Handouts, presentation graphics and, 2.21
Handshake: The process of establishing the communications connection on a switched line. **7.14**
Handwriting recognition software: Software that can be taught to recognize an individual's unique style of writing. **3.7**
Hard card: A circuit board that has a hard disk built onto it. The board can be installed into expansion slot of a personal computer. **6.14**
Hard copy: Output that is printed. **5.2**
Hard disk/drive: Secondary storage device containing nonremovable disks. **1.9, 6.8**
disk cartridges, 6.14
hard cards, 6.14
maintenance and, 6.15
purchasing computers and, 8.32
removable disks, 6.14
storage capacity, 6.9-10
streaming mode and, 6.18
Hardware: Equipment that processes data, consisting of input devices, a processor unit, output devices, and auxiliary storage units. **1.7**
communications, 7.9-15, 7.18-19
disabled persons and, 3.22
front-end processors, 7.19
input devices, 1.7-9, 3.2-22
installing, 8.34-35
keyboard, 3.3-4
line configurations and, 7.14-15
maintenance of, 8.36
modems, 7.18-19
multimedia, 3.16-20
multiplexors, 7.19
network interface cards, 7.19
output devices, 1.8
pointing devices, 3.5-9
registering, 8.35
secondary storage devices, 1.9, 6.1-25
source data automation and, 3.10-14
system unit, 1.8, 4.5
terminals, 3.15
wireless, 7.12
Hardware resource sharing: Used in local area networks, allowing all network users to access a single piece of equipment rather than each user having to be connected to their own device. **7.21**

Head crash: The disk head collides with and damages the surface of a hard disk, causing a loss of data. The collision is caused if some form of contamination is introduced, or if the alignment of the read/write heads is altered. **6.10**
Header: In word processing documents, text that is printed at the top of every page. **2.9**
Health guidelines, 8.35
Helical scan technology: Used by digital audio tape to write data at high densities across the tape at an angle instead of down the length of the tape. **6.18**
Hexadecimal (base 16): Number system which represents binary in a more compact form. Hexadecimal is used to represent the electronic status of bits in main memory, and addressing the memory locations. **4.21,** 4.22
High definition television (HDTV): Television sets designed to handle a computer's digital signals; may eventually replace computer screens. **5.5**
High-density (HD) diskettes: Diskettes that can store 1.2 megabytes on a 5 1/4 inch diskette and 1.44 megabytes on a 3 1/2 inch diskette. **6.6**
High Performance Computing and Communications (HPCC), 1.38
Hoff, Ted, 1.35
Home, working at, 7.5
Hopper, Grace, 1.32
Host computer: In a data communications system, a main computer that is connected to several devices (such as terminals or personal computers). **7.15**
Hypermedia: Technique used in multimedia presentations that allows the user to quickly move among screens to related subject area, such as pictures, sounds, animation, or maps in computerized encyclopedias. **5.5**

IBM (International Business Machines)
early computer development, 1.32, 1.34
operating systems and, 8.12
personal computers development, 1.36
third-generation computers and, 1.34
virtual machine operating system, 8.15
IC, *see* **Integrated circuit**
Icons: On screen pictures that represent processing options. **1.15, 2.3**
Image on screen, resolution of, 5.18-20
Image processing systems: Use scanners to input and store an image of the source document. These systems are like electronic filing systems. **3.10**
Image scanner, *see* **Page scanner**
Impact printers: Printers that transfer the image onto paper by some type of printing mechanism striking the paper, ribbon, and character together. **5.9**
band, 5.12-13
chain, 5.13
dot matrix, 5.10-12

Information: Data that has been processed into a form that has meaning and is useful. **1.4**
Information appliances, 1.23
Information literacy: Knowing how to find, analyze, and use information. **1.2**
Information processing: The production of information by processing data on a computer, also called data processing (DP), **1.5**
Information processing cycle: Input, process, output, and storage operations. Collectively, these operations describe the procedures that a computer performs to process data into information and store it for future use. **1.4,** 1.7
input and, *see* Input
output and, *see* Output
overview of, 3.2
processing and, 1.7
storage and, *see* Storage
Information resource sharing: Allows local area network users to access the data stored on any other computer in the network. **7.22**
Information services, *see* **Online services**
Information superhighway: A nationwide and eventually worldwide network of information and services. **7.31**
Information system: A collection of elements that provides accurate, timely, and useful information. These elements include: equipment, software, accurate data, trained information systems personnel, knowledgeable users, and documented procedures. **1.16**
Information systems department, 1.21
INI file extension, 8.37
Ink: Describes the darkened location on screen when a pen input device touches it. **3.7**
Ink jet printer: Nonimpact printer that forms characters by using a nozzle that shoots droplets of ink onto the page, producing high-quality print and graphics. **5.13-14**
Input: The process of entering programs, commands, user responses, and data into main memory. Input can also refer to the media (such as disks, tapes, and documents) that contain these input types. **1.7, 3.2-26**
data accuracy and, 3.20-21
disabled persons and, 3.22
keyboard, 3.3-4
multimedia, 3.16-20
operating system managing, 8.8
pointing devices, 3.5-9
source data automation, 3.10-14
terminals, 3.15
Input devices: Hardware used to enter data into a computer. **1.7**
Insert mode, 2.6
Insert text: Add characters to existing text in a word processing document. **2.6**

Optical codes: In source data automation, codes that use a pattern or symbol to represent data, such as a bar code. **3.11**

Optical disks: Storage medium that uses lasers to burn microscopic holes on the surface of a hard plastic disk;able to store enormous quantities of information. **6.19**

Optical mark recognition (OMR): Input devices that are often used to process questionnaires or test answer sheets. Carefully placed marks on the form indicate responses to questions that are read and interpreted by a computer program. **3.12**

Optical memory cards: Storage devices that can store up to 1,600 pages of text or images on a device the size of a credit card. **6.22**

Optical recognition: Devices that use a light source to read codes, marks, and characters and convert them into digital data that an be processed by a computer. **3.11**

OS/2: IBM's operating system designed to work with 32-bit microprocessors. In addition to running programs written specifically for OS/2, the operating system can also run programs written for DOS or Windows. **8.13**

Outlines, presentation graphics and, 2.20

Output: The data that has been processed into a useful form called information that can be used by a person or machine. **1.7, 5.2-32**
audio, 5.4-5, 5.25-26
computer output microfilm, 5.24-25
data projectors, 5.23
display devices, 5.18-23
graphics, 5.4
multimedia, 5.5-6, 5.27
operating system managing, 8.8
plotters, 5.24
printers and, 5.9-17
reports, 5.2-4
types of, 5.2-8
video, 5.5
virtual reality, 5.7-8, 5.28
voice, 5.25-26

Output devices: Most commonly used devices are the printer and the computer screen. **1.8**

Overtype mode, 2.6

Packet switching: In communications networks, individual packets of information from various users are combined and transmitted over a high-speed channel. **7.24**

Page: In virtual memory management, the fixed number of bytes that are transferred from disk to memory each time new data or program instruction are required. **8.8**

Page composition and layout: In desktop publishing, the process of arranging text and graphics on a document page. **2.10**

Page definition language: In desktop publishing, language describing the document to be printed that the printer can understand. **2.11**

Page makeup, *see* **Page composition and layout**

Page printers: Nonimpact printers that operate similar to a copying machine to produce high-quality text and graphic output. **5.14**

Page scanner: An input device that electronically captures an entire page of text or images such as photography or art work. The scanner converts the text or image on the original document into digital information that can be stored on a disk and processed by the computer. **3.10**

Pages per minute (ppm): Measure of the speed of printers that can produce an entire page at one time. **5.15**

Paging: In virtual memory management, a fixed number of bytes (a page) is transferred from disk to memory each time new data or program instructions are required. **8.8**

Palmtop computer: Small computers that often have several built-in or interchangeable personal information management functions, such as a calendar to keep track of meetings and events, and an address and phone file; they do not have disk storage devices and usually have a nonstandard keyboard. **1.10**

Parallel ports: Ports most often used to connect devices that send or receive large amounts of data such as printers or disk and tape drives. **4.15**
purchasing computers and, 8.32

Parallel processing: The use of multiple CPU's, each with their own memory, that work on their assigned portion of a problem simultaneously. **4.20**
applications of, 4.24

Parity bit: One extra bit for each byte that is used for error checking. **4.4**

Partition(s): Portions of memory allocated by operating system into fixed areas. **8.7**

Partitioned disk: Hard disk is divided into separate areas called partitions before it is formatted. **6.9**

PASCAL, 1.35

Passive matrix: LCD screens that use fewer transistors;one for each row and column. **5.21**

Password: A value, such as a word or number, which identifies the user. In multiuser operating systems, the password must be entered correctly before a user is allowed to use an application program. The password is usually confidential. **8.10**

Paste: In word processing operations, an option used after performing either the cut or the copy command, where the text is placed elsewhere in the document. **2.6**

PC cards: Small, credit-card sized cards that fit into PCMCIA expansion slots, used for storage, communications, and additional memory. **6.19**

PC-DOS: Operating system developed by Microsoft Corporation for IBM and is installed by IBM on systems that IBM sells. **8.12**

PCMCIA (Personal Computer Memory Card International Association) cards: A special type of expansion slot that can be inserted into a personal computer, used for additional memory, storage, and communications. The small fitting into the expansion slot, called PC cards, are the size of credit cards. **4.13**

PCs, *see* **Personal computer(s)**

PDA, *see* **Personal digital assistant**

Peer-to-peer network: Local area network that allows any computer to share the software, data, or hardware (such as a printer) located on any other computer in the network. **7.23**

Pen computers: Specialized portable computers that use a pen-like device to enter data. **1.11**

Pen input devices: Allows the user to input hand-printed letters and numbers to record information. **3.7**

Pen plotters: Plotters used to create images on a sheet of paper by moving one or more pens over the surface. **5.24**

Pentium microprocessor, 1.38

Periodic reports: Reports that are produced on a regular basis such as daily, weekly, or monthly. Also called scheduled reports. **5.4**

Peripheral devices: The input devices, output devices, and auxiliary storage units that surround the processing unit. **1.9**

Personal communicator, *see* **Personal digital assistant**

Personal computer(s): The small systems that have become so widely used in recent years. Depending on their size and features, personal computer prices range from several hundred to several thousand dollars. **1.10**
application software packages, 1.15
evolution of, 1.35-38
installation of, 8.34-35
maintenance of, 8.36-37
owner's notebook outline, 8.36
purchasing, 8.30-33
See also Computer(s)

Personal Computer Memory Card International Association, *see* **PCMCIA**

Personal digital assistant (PDA): Small pen input device designed for workers on the go;often has built-in communications capabilities that allow the PDA to use voice, fax, or data communications. **1.11,** 1.38

Utility programs: Programs that perform specific tasks related to managing computer resources or files, and are included with the operating system. Tasks performed include copying and moving files and formatting disks. **8.15**
future of, 8.18

Vacuum tubes, 1.32
Validation: In database programs, the comparison of data entered against a predefined format or value. **2.19**
Value-added carriers: Companies that lease channels from common carriers to provide specialized communications services. **7.24**
Value-added networks: Networks provided by companies that lease channels from common carriers to provide specialized communications services. **7.24**
Values: Numerical data contained in the cells of a spreadsheet. **2.12**
Vendors, 8.30
  support phone numbers, 8.36
Very small aperture terminal (VSAT): Satellite antenna measuring only 1 to 3 meters in size than can transmit up to 19,200 bits of data per second. **7.11**
Video, in multimedia, 5.6
Video card: Multimedia device containing electronics that capture and process video data; installed in the computer. **3.16**
  local bus, 8.32
Video display terminals (VDT), *see* **Display terminals; Screen(s)**
Video output: Output that consists of visual images that have been captured with a video input device, such as a VCR or camera, digitized, and directed to an output device such as a computer monitor. Video output can also be directed to a television monitor. **5.5**
Virtual machine (VM) operating system: Allows a single computer to run two or more different operating systems. **8.5,** 8.15
Virtual memory management: Increases the effective (or virtual) limit of memory by expanding the amount of main memory to include disk space. **8.7**
Virtual reality: The use of a computer to create an artificial environment that can be experienced by the computer user. **5.7**
  commercial applications, 5.8
Viruses, 8.37
VisiCalc, 1.35
Voice, fiber optics and, 7.10
Voice input: Allows the user to enter data and issue commands to the computer with spoken words. **3.16**-20, 3.23, **5.25**

Voice mail: Verbal electronic mail that allows the caller to leave a message via telephone that is digitized so it can be stored on a disk like other computer data, and accessed by the recipient. **7.3**
Voice output: Spoken words that are conveyed to the user from the computer. **5.25**
Voice synthesis: A type of voice generation that can transform words stored in main memory into speech. **5.26**
Voice templates: Used by voice input systems that recognize patterns of sounds. **3.18**
Volatile memory: RAM memory is said to be volatile because the programs and data stored in RAM are erased when the power to the computer is turned off. **4.9**
von Neumann, John, 1.33
WAN, *see* **Wide area network**
What-if analysis: The capability of a spreadsheet to recalculate when data is changed. **2.16**
Wide area network (WAN): A communications network that covers a large geographical area, and uses telephone lines, microwaves, satellites, or a combination of communications channels. **7.24**
Window: A rectangular portion of the screen that is used to display information. **2.3**
Windows, *see* **Microsoft Windows**
Wireless transmission: Used to connect devices that are in the same general area such as an office or business park, using one of three transmission techniques: light beams, radio waves, or carrier-connect radio. **7.12**
Word processing: Computer software used to produce or modify documents that consist primarily of text. **2.4**-9
Word recognition, 3.23
Word size: The number of bits that the CPU can process at one time. **4.7**
Word wrap: An automatic line return that occurs when text reaches a certain position on the word processing document. **2.5**
Workgroup technology: Equipment and software that help group members communicate and manage their activities. **7.4**
Workstations: Expensive high-end personal computers that have powerful calculating and graphics capabilities; frequently used by engineers. **1.11**
WORM (write once, read many): Optical disk devices that provide for one-time recording. **6.20**

WYSIWYG: An acronym for What You See Is What You Get. A feature that allows the user to design on screen an exact image of what a printed page will look like. **2.11**

Zero insertion force socket, 4.8

PHOTO CREDITS

All photographs, unless noted as copyrighted, are provided courtesy of the following companies.

CHAPTER 1 *Figure 1-1,* (top left) International Business Machines Corp.; (center left) International Business Machines Corp.; (bottom left) Contura Corp.; (bottom right) © 1989 Bruce Frisch; *Figure 1-3,* © Henry Blackham: *Figure 1-4,* International Business Machines Corp.; *Figure 1-5,* International Business Machines Corp.; *Figure 1-7,* © Henry Blackham; *Figure 1-9,* (a) Omnidata; (b) Hewlett-Packard Co.; (c) Toshiba America Information Systems, Inc.; (d) Zeos International Ltd.; (e) International Business Machines Corp.; (f) EO Inc.; (g) © Frank Pryor/Apple Computer Inc.; (h) © Mosgrove Photo/Apple Computer Inc.; (i) International Business Machines Corp.; (j) International Business Machines Corp.; *Figure 1-10,* Dell Computer Corp.; *Figure 1-11,* International Business Machines Corp.; *Figure 1-12,* International Business Machines Corp.; *Figure 1-13,* Cray Computer Corp.; *Figure 1-14,* Cray Research; *Figure 1-16,* Microsoft Corp.; *Figure 1-17,* CompUSA Inc.; *Figure 1-21,* Hewlett-Packard Co.; *Figure 1-22,* Hewlett-Packard Co.; *Figure 1-23,* Travel Co.; *Figure 1-24,* International Business Machines Corp.; *Figure 1-25,* International Business Machines Corp.; *Figure 1-26,* International Business Machines Corp.; *Figure 1-27,* International Business Machines Corp.; *Figure 1-28,* © Stacey Pick/Stock/Boston; *Figure 1-29,* Hewlett-Packard Co.; *Figure 1-30,* International Business Machines Corp.; *Figure 1-31,* International Business Machines Corp.; *Figure 1-32,* International Business Machines Corp.; *Figure 1-33,* © Frank Pryor/Apple Computer; *Figures 1-34-1-37,* Microsoft Corp. **TIMELINE** *Page 1.32,* (top left) Iowa State University, News Service Photo Dept.; (top center left) Iowa State University; (top center right) Iowa State University; (top right) University of Pennsylvania Archives; (bottom left) Harvard University Archives; (bottom center left) Dept. of Navy; (bottom center right) Massachusetts Institute of Technology; (bottom right) Dept of Navy; *Page 1.33,* (top left) Institute for Advanced Studies; (top center) UNISYS Corp.; (top right) UNISYS Corp.; (bottom left) Dept. of Navy; (bottom center); Massachusetts Institute of Technology; (bottom right) International Business Machines Corp.; *Page 1.34,* (top left) International Business Machines Corp.; (top right) © Stuart Bratesman; (bottom left) Integrated Circuit Corporation; (bottom center left) International Business Machines Corp.; (bottom center right) Computer Museum; (bottom right) InfoWorld; *Page 1.35,* (top left) Digital Equipment Corp.; (top center left) © Shelly R. Harrison; (top center right) Intel Corp.; (top right) Intel Corp.; (bottom left) Apple Computer, Inc.; (bottom center left) Apple Computer, Inc.; (bottom center right) Apple Computer, Inc.; (bottom right) © Ira Wyman; *Page 1.36,* (top left) Microsoft Corp.; (top right) International Business Machines Corp.; (bottom left) Apple Computer, Inc. (bottom right) Compaq Computer Corp.; *Page 1.37,* (top left) Time Magazine; (top center left) Lotus Development Corp.; (top center right) Lotus Development Corporation; (top right) International Business Machines Corp.; (bottom left) Intel Corp.; (bottom right) Microsoft Corp.; *Page 1.38,* (top left) Apple Computer, Inc.; (top center) Apple Computer, Inc.; (top right) Intel Corp.; (bottom) Environmental Protection Agency (EPA). **CHAPTER 2** *Figures 2-1-2-6, 2-9,* Microsoft Corporation; *Figure 2-10,* © Fredrik D. Bodin/Offshoot; *Figure 2-12,* Aldus Corp.; *Figures 2-13, 2-14, 2-16-2-24,* Microsoft Corp.; *Figure 2-25,* © Curtis Fukuda; *Figures 2-27-2-29,* Borland International, Inc.; *Figures 2-30-2-32,* Microsoft Corp.; *Figure 2-33,* Digital Communications Associates, Inc.; *Figure 2-34,* America Online; *Figure 2-36,* ECCO Software Corp.; *Figure 2-37,* Microsoft Corporation; *Figure 2-38,* (c) © Fredrik D. Bodin; (d) © Fredrik D. Bodin; *Figures 2-41-2-44,* Microsoft Corp. **CHAPTER 3** *Figure 3-1,* © Henry Blackham; *Figure 3-2,* (a) International Business Machines Corp.; (b) International Business Machines Corp.; *Figure 3-3,* (a) © Henry Blackham; (b) © Phil Matt; *Figure 3-4,* Microsoft Corp.; *Figure 3-5,* International Business Machines Corp.; *Figure 3-6,* Texas Instruments Inc./Temelin McClain PR; *Figure 3-7,* Logitech, Inc.; *Figure 3-8,* (a) International Business Machines Corp.; (b) International Business Machines Corp.; *Figure 3-9,* GRID System Corp.; *Figure 3-11,* International Business Machines Corp.; *Figure 3-12,* International Business Machines Corp.; *Figure 3-13,* Compaq Computer Corp.; *Figure 3-14,* Compaq Computer Corp.; *Figure 3-15,* Hewlett-Packard Co.; *Figure 3-16,* Logitech Inc.; *Figure 3-17,* International Business Machines Corp.; *Figure 3-19,* (a) © Ed Kashi/Dell Computer; (b) Hewlett-Packard Co.; (c) © Paul Shambroom/Photo Researchers, Inc.; *Figure 3-20 (right),* Scantron Corp.; *Figure 3-22,* Calera Recognition Systems, Inc.; *Figure 3-23,* © Fredrik D. Bodin; *Figure 3-24,* NCR Corp.; *Figure 3-25,* Cooper Tire, Inc.; *Figure 3-26,* Cimlinc, Inc.; *Figure 3-27,* International Business Machines Corp.; *Figure 3-28,* Creative Labs, Inc.; *Figure 3-29,* Texas Instruments Inc.; *Figure 3-31,* Videolabs Inc.; *Figure 3-32,* © Fredrik D. Bodin, *Figure 3-33,* © Fredrik D. Bodin/Offshoot; *Figure 3-34,* Prodigy; *Figure 3-35,* © Gary Payne/ Liaison International; *Figure 3-36,* Motion Pictures and TV Archives; *Figures 3-37-3-40,* The Image Bank. **CHAPTER 4** *Figure 4-1,* © Henry Blackham; *Figure 4-8,* © Phil Matt; *Figure 4-9,* Intel Corp.; *Figure 4-10,* International Business Machines Corp.; *Figure 4-13,* © Phil Matt; *Figure 4-15,* © Alan L. Detrick; *Figure 4-20,* © Phil Matt, *Figure 4-21,* MegaHertz Corp.; *Figure 4-22,* © Phil Matt; *Figure 4-26,* © Tom Pantages; *Figure 4-35,* Cray Research, Inc. and Paul DuBois, Hermes Engineering NV; *Figures 4-37-4-40,* Microsoft Corp. **MAKING A COMPUTER CHIP** *Page 4.35,* (1) Index Stock Photography; *Page 4.36* (2) © Frank Wing Photographer; (6) Intel Corp.; (7) Intel Corp.; *Page 4.37,* (5) Photo Researchers, Inc.; (9) International Business Machines Corp.; (10) © David Scharf; *Page 4.38,* (11) © L. Manning/Westlight; (12) International Business Machines Corp.; (13) Intel Corp.; (14) © Chuck O'Rear/Westlight; (15) © Photo Researchers; (16) © Pelton & Associates, Inc./Westlight. **CHAPTER 5** *Figure 5-5,* Radius Computer Corp.; *Figure 5-6,* International Business Machines Corp.; *Figure 5-7,* AT&T; *Figures 5-8, 5-9,* Microsoft Corp.; *Figure 5-10,* International Business Machines Corp.; *Figure 5-11,* © Peter Menzel; *Figure 5-12,* © Ed Kashi; *Figure 5-13,* © Gerry Gropp/Sipa Press; *Figure 5-15,* © Eric Futran Photography/Liaison International; *Figure 5-17,* Epson America, Inc.; *Figure 5-18,* Printronix; *Figure 5-24,* Jon Mankin/Mankin Images and Hewlett-Packard Co.; *Figure 5-25,* Lexmark; *Figure 5-27,* Hewlett-Packard Co.; *Figure 5-28,* Siemens Nixdorf Printing Systems; *Figure 5-29,* CalComp Inc.; *Figure 5-30,* (a) Zebra Technologies Corp.; (b) Seiko Corporation; (c) Citizen America Corp.; *Figure 5-32;* Portrait Display Labs, Inc.; *Figure 5-34,* Evans & Sutherland Computer Corp.; *Figure 5-36,* NEC Technologies Inc.; *Figure 5-37,* International Business Machines Corp.; *Figure 5-38,* Toshiba America Information Systems, Inc.; *Figure 5-39,* NEC Corp.; *Figure 5-42,* TRW Inc.; *Figure 5-43,* Electrohome Inc.; *Figure 5-44,* © Dick Luris/Photo Researchers, Inc.; *Figure 5-45,* Hewlett-Packard Co.; *Figure 5-46,* Eastman Kodak Co.; *Figure 5-48,* MusicWriter, Inc.; *Figure 5-49,* © Hank Morgan/Science Photo Library; *Figures 5-50-5-53,* Microsoft Corp. **CHAPTER 6** *Figure 6-2,* © Phil Matt; *Figure 6-3,* © Henry Blackham; *Figure 6-7,* © Phil Matt; *Figure 6-10,* Hewlett-Packard Co.; *Figure 6-11,* International Business Machines Corp.; *Figure 6-12,* Quantum, Inc.; *Figure 6-13,* International Business Machines Corp.; *Figure 6-19,* © Phil Matt; *Figure 6-20,* Quantum, Inc.; *Figure 6-22,* 3M Corp.; *Figure 6-23,* Colorado Memory Systems, a division of Hewlett-Packard Co.; *Figure 6-24,* International Business Machines Corp.; *Figure 6-28,* © Phil Matt; *Figure 6-30,* 3M Corporation; *Figure 6-31,* Symmetrix Inc.; *Figure 6-25,* Hewlett-Packard Co.; *Figure 6-28,* © Phil Matt; *Figure 6-32,* Storage Tek Systems, Inc.; *Figure 6-33,* Dallas Semiconductor; *Figure 6-34,* © Phil Matt; *Figure 6-35,* LaserCard Inc.; *Figure 6-37,* © Phil Matt; *Figure 6-38,* © Kerry Klayman/U. C. Irvine; *Figure 6-39,* © Kerry Klayman/U. C. Irvine; *Figures 6-40-6-43,* Microsoft Corp. **CHAPTER 7** *Figure 7-1,* © The Image Bank; *Figure 7-2,* (b) MCI Telecommunications Corp.; *Figure 7-3,* © Peter Hendrie/The Image Bank; *Figure 7-4,* Lotus Development Corporation; *Figure 7-5,* Klynas Engineering; *Figure 7-7,* Prodigy; *Figure 7-9,* © Henry Blackham; *Figure 7-12,* The Image Bank; *Figure 7-13,* © Don Lowe/Tony Stone Images; *Figure 7-14,* © Jim Zuckerman/Westlight; *Figure 7-16,* Photonics Corp.; *Figure 7-24,* © Henry Blackham; *Figure 7-26,* © Fredrik D. Bodin/Offshoot; *Figure 7-27,* Hayes Microcomputer Products, Inc.; *Figure 7-28,* Photos © Henry Blackham; *Figure 7-29,* Digital Communications Associates, Inc.; *Figure 7-31,* Photos © Henry Blackham; *Figure 7-32,* Photos © Henry Blackham; *Figure 7-33,* EDS Corp.; *Figure 7-34,* Photos © Henry Blackham; *Figure 7-35,* Photos © Henry Blackham; *Figure 7-36,* Photos © Henry Blackham; *Figure 7-37,* North American Van Lines *Figures 7-38-7-42,* Microsoft Corp. **THE INTERNET** *Figure 1,* National Center for SuperComputing Applications at the University of Illinois; *Figure 3,* Internet; *Figure 4,* Bolt, Beranek & Newman, Inc.; *Figures 5-14,* Internet. **CHAPTER 8** *Figure 8-9,* Photos © Henry Blackham; *Figure 8-12,* Microsoft Corp.; *Figure 8-13,* Apple Computer Inc.; *Figure 8-14,* International Business Machines Corp.; *Figure 8-15,* NeXT Computer Corp.; *Figure 8-16,* Berkeley Systems Inc.; *Figure 8-17,* NeXT Computer Corp.; *Figures 8-19-8-22,* Microsoft Corporation. **BUYER'S GUIDE** *Page 8.29,* (a) International Business Machines Corp.; (b) © Phil Matt; (c) © Phil Matt; *Page 8.30,* (a) Environmental Protective Agency (EPA): (b) Dell Computer Corp.: *Page 8.33,* (a) Curtis Manufacturing Co., Inc.; (b) © Phil Matt; (c) American Power Conversion Corp. (APC); (d) MicroSolutions Computer Products, Inc.; *Page 8.34,* Curtis Manufacturing Co., Inc.; *Page 8.35,* © Phil Matt.

W I N D O W S

USING *M*ICROSOFT *W*INDOWS 3.1

_M_ICROSOFT _W_INDOWS 3.1

P R O J E C T O N E

AN INTRODUCTION TO WINDOWS

OBJECTIVES   You will have mastered the material in this project when you can:

▶ Describe a user interface
▶ Describe Microsoft Windows
▶ Identify the elements of a window
▶ Perform the four basic mouse operations of pointing, clicking, double-clicking, and dragging
▶ Correct errors made while performing mouse operations
▶ Understand the keyboard shortcut notation
▶ Select a menu
▶ Choose a command from a menu

▶ Respond to dialog boxes
▶ Start and exit an application
▶ Name a file
▶ Understand directories and subdirectories
▶ Understand directory structures and directory paths
▶ Create, save, open, and print a document
▶ Open, enlarge, and scroll a window
▶ Obtain online Help while using an application

▶ INTRODUCTION

T he most popular and widely used graphical user interface available today is **Microsoft Windows**, or **Windows**. Microsoft Windows allows you to easily communicate with and control your computer. In addition, Microsoft Windows makes it easy to learn the application software installed on your computer, transfer data between the applications, and manage the data created while using an application.

In this project, you learn about user interfaces, the computer hardware and computer software that comprise a user interface, and Microsoft Windows. You use Microsoft Windows to perform the operations of opening a group window, starting and exiting an application, enlarging an application window, entering and editing data within an application, printing a document on the printer, saving a document on disk, opening a document, and obtaining online Help while using an application.

What Is a User Interface?

A **user interface** is the combination of hardware and software that allows the computer user to communicate with and control the computer. Through the user interface, you are able to control the computer, request information from the computer, and respond to messages displayed by the computer. Thus, a user interface provides the means for dialogue between you and the computer.

Hardware and software together form the user interface. Among the hardware associated with a user interface are the CRT screen, keyboard, and mouse (Figure 1-1). The CRT screen displays messages and provides information. You respond by entering data in the form of a command or other response using the keyboard or mouse. Among the responses available to you are responses that specify what application software to run, when to print, and where to store the data for future use.

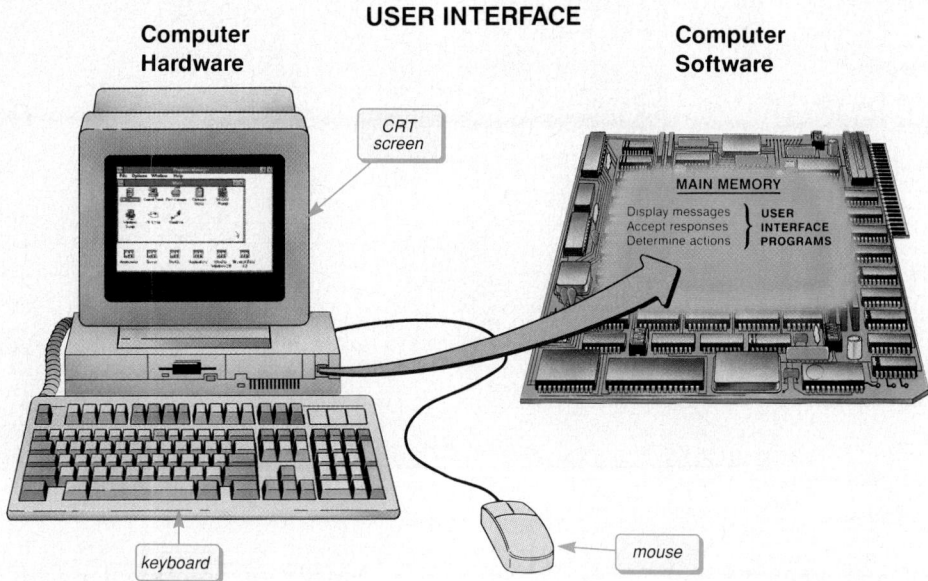

USER INTERFACE   **FIGURE 1-1**

The computer software associated with the user interface are the programs that engage you in dialogue (Figure 1-1). The computer software determines the messages you receive, the manner in which you should respond, and the actions that occur based on your responses. The goal of an effective user interface is to be **user friendly**, meaning the software can be easily used by individuals with limited training. Research studies have indicated that the use of graphics can play an important role in aiding users to effectively interact with a computer. A **graphical user interface**, or **GUI**, is a user interface that displays graphics in addition to text when it communicates with the user.

▶ MICROSOFT WINDOWS

Microsoft Windows, or Windows, the most popular graphical user interface, makes it easy to learn and work with **application software**, which is software that performs an application-related function, such as word processing. Numerous application software packages are available for purchase from retail computer stores, and several applications are included with the Windows interface software. In Windows terminology, these application software packages are referred to as **applications**.

Starting Microsoft Windows

When you turn on the computer, an introductory screen consisting of the Windows logo, Windows name, version number (3.1), and copyright notices displays momentarily (Figure 1-2). Next, a blank screen containing an hourglass icon (⧗) displays (Figure 1-3). The **hourglass icon** indicates that Windows requires a brief interval of time to change the display on the screen, and you should wait until the hourglass icon disappears.

FIGURE 1-2

FIGURE 1-3

Finally, two rectangular areas, or **windows**, display (Figure 1-4). The double-line, or **window border**, surrounding each window determines their shape and size. The horizontal bar at the top of each window, called the **title bar**, contains a **window title** that identifies each window. In Figure 1-4, the Program Manager and Main titles identify each window.

The screen background on which the windows display is called the **desktop**. If your desktop does not look similar to the desktop in Figure 1-4, your instructor will inform you of the modifications necessary to change your desktop.

FIGURE 1-4

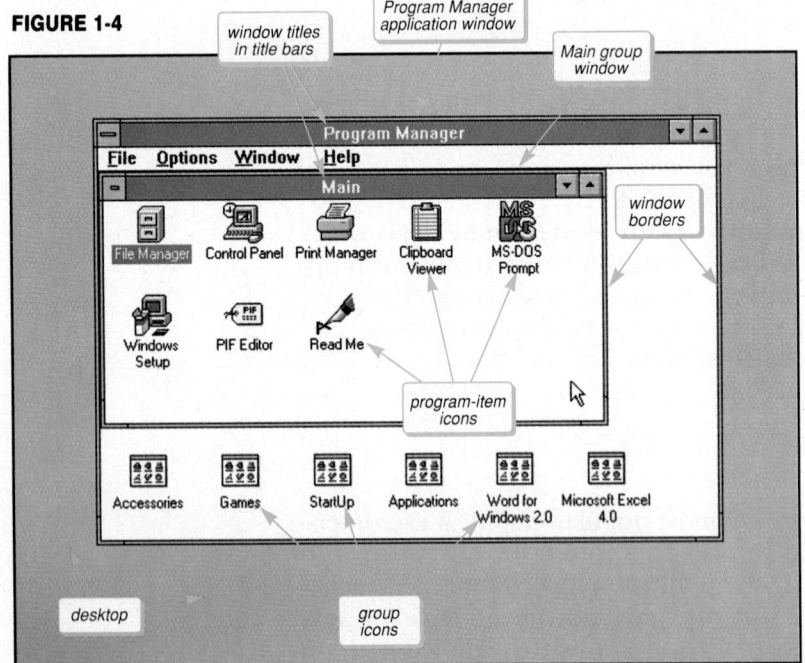

The Program Manager window represents the **Program Manager** application. The Program Manager application starts when you start Windows and is central to the operation of Windows. Program Manager organizes related applications into groups and displays the groups in the Program Manager window. A window that represents an application, such as the Program Manager window, is called an **application window**.

Small pictures, or **icons**, represent an individual application or groups of applications. In Figure 1-4 on the previous page, the Main window contains a group of eight icons (File Manager, Control Panel, Print Manager, Clipboard Viewer, MS-DOS Prompt, Windows Setup, PIF Editor, and Read Me). A window that contains a group of icons, such as the Main window, is called a **group window**. The icons in a group window, called **program-item icons**, each represent an individual application. A name below each program-item icon identifies the application. The program-item icons are unique and, therefore, easily distinguished from each other.

The six icons at the bottom of the Program Manager window in Figure 1-4 on the previous page, (Accessories, Games, StartUp, Applications, Word for Windows 2.0, and Microsoft Excel 4.0), called **group icons**, each represent a group of applications. Group icons are similar in appearance and only the name below the icon distinguishes one icon from another icon. Although the program-item icons of the individual applications in these groups are not visible in Figure 1-4, a method to view these icons will be demonstrated later in this project.

▶ COMMUNICATING WITH MICROSOFT WINDOWS

T he Windows interface software provides the means for dialogue between you and the computer. Part of this dialogue involves requesting information from the computer and responding to messages displayed by the computer. You can request information and respond to messages using either the mouse or keyboard.

The Mouse and Mouse Pointer

A **mouse** is a pointing device commonly used with Windows that is attached to the computer by a cable and contains one or more buttons. The mouse in Figure 1-5 contains two buttons, the left mouse button and the right mouse button. On the bottom of this mouse is a ball (Figure 1-6).

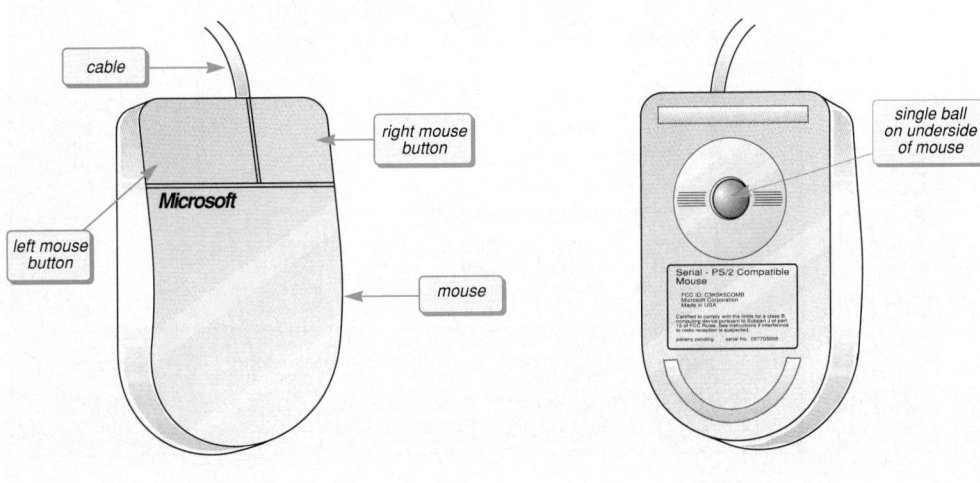

FIGURE 1-5   **FIGURE 1-6**

As you move the mouse across a flat surface (Figure 1-7), the movement of the ball is electronically sensed, and a **mouse pointer** in the shape of a block arrow ( ) moves across the desktop in the same direction.

**Mouse moves
diagonally across
flat surface**

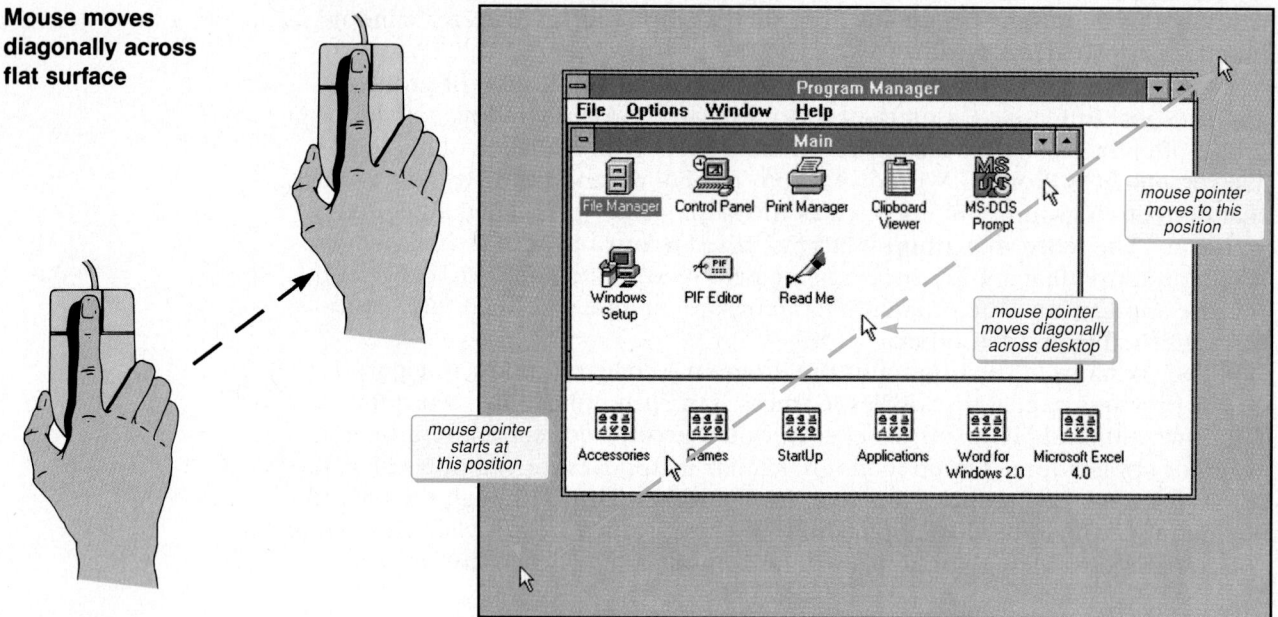

FIGURE 1-7

Mouse Operations

You use the mouse to perform four basic operations: (1) pointing; (2) clicking; (3) double-clicking; and (4) dragging. **Pointing** means moving the mouse across a flat surface until the mouse pointer rests on the item of choice on the desktop. In Figure 1-8, you move the mouse diagonally across a flat surface until the tip of the mouse pointer rests on the Print Manager icon.

**Mouse moves
diagonally**

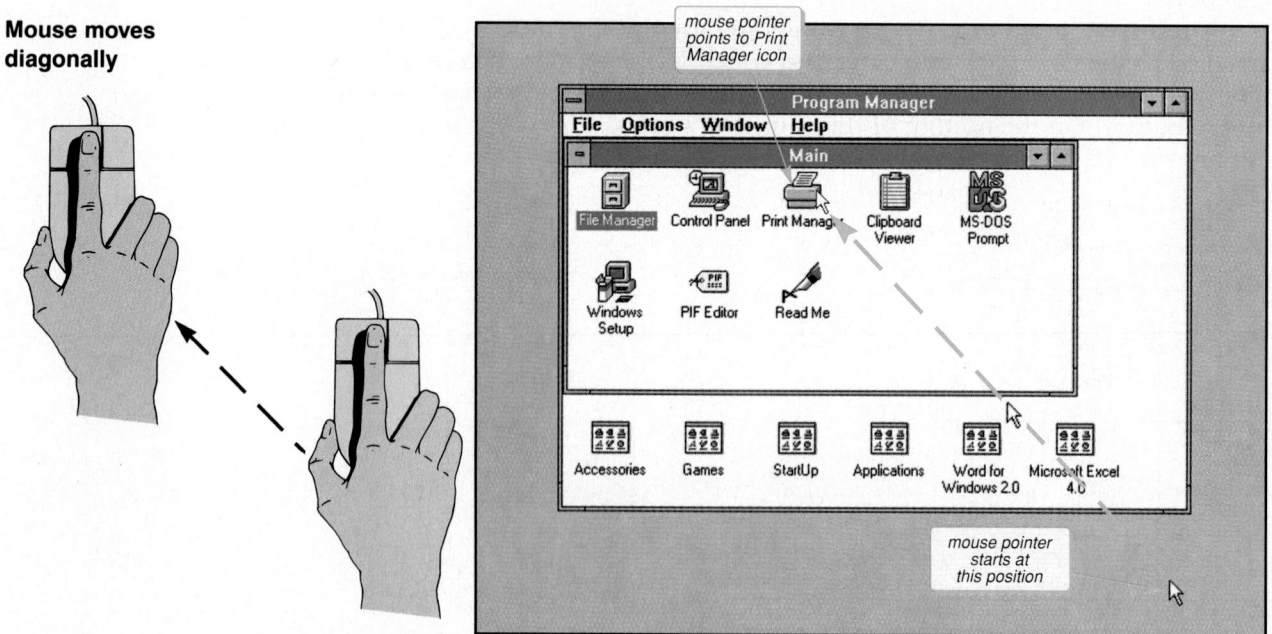

FIGURE 1-8

Clicking means pressing and releasing a mouse button. In most cases, you must point to an item before pressing and releasing a mouse button. In Figure 1-9, you highlight the Print Manager icon by pointing to the Print Manager icon (Step 1) and pressing and releasing the left mouse button (Step 2). These steps are commonly referred to as clicking the Print Manager icon. When you click the Print Manager icon, Windows highlights, or places color behind, the name below the Print Manager icon (Step 3).

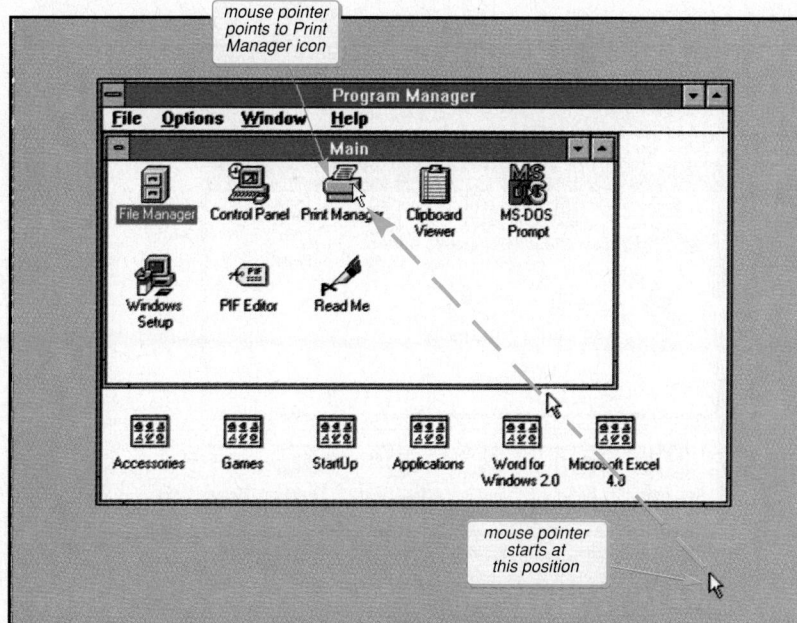

Step 1: Point to the Print Manager icon.

Step 2: Press and release the left mouse button.

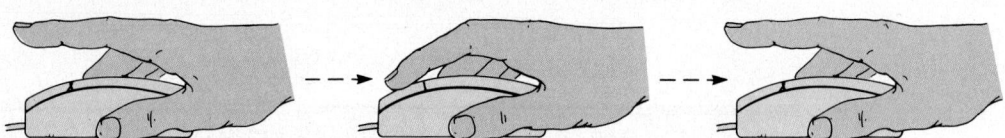

Step 3: Windows highlights the Print Manager name.

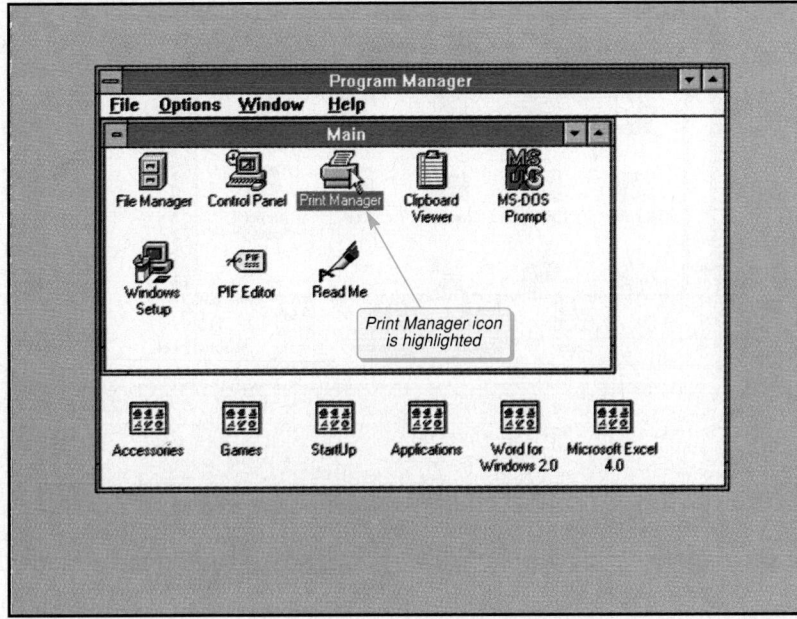

FIGURE 1-9

Double-clicking means quickly pressing and releasing a mouse button twice without moving the mouse. In most cases, you must point to an item before quickly pressing and releasing a mouse button twice. In Figure 1-10, to open the Accessories group window, point to the Accessories icon (Step 1), and quickly press and release the left mouse button twice (Step 2). These steps are commonly referred to as double-clicking the Accessories icon. When you double-click the Accessories icon, Windows opens a group window with the same name (Step 3).

Step 1: Point to the Accessories icon.

Step 2: Quickly press and release the left mouse button twice.

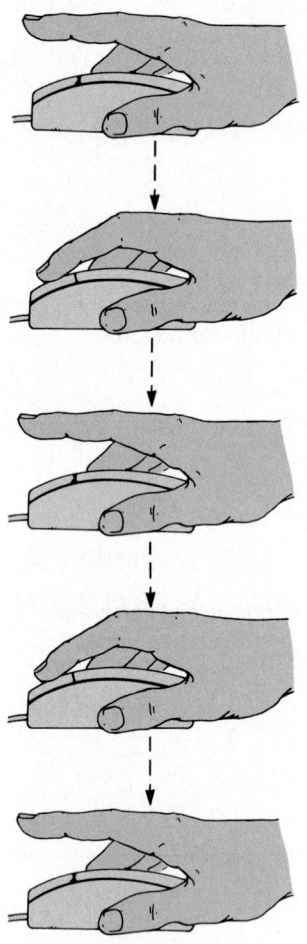

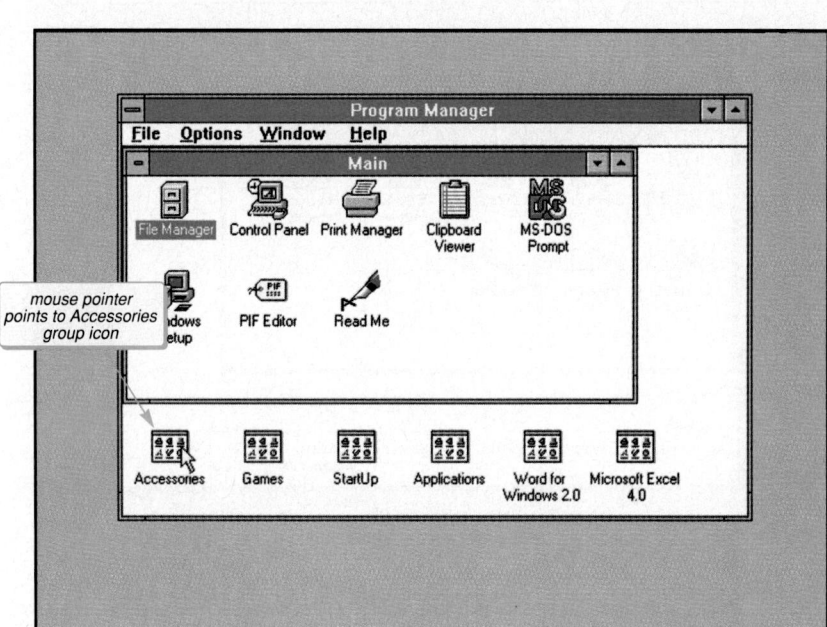

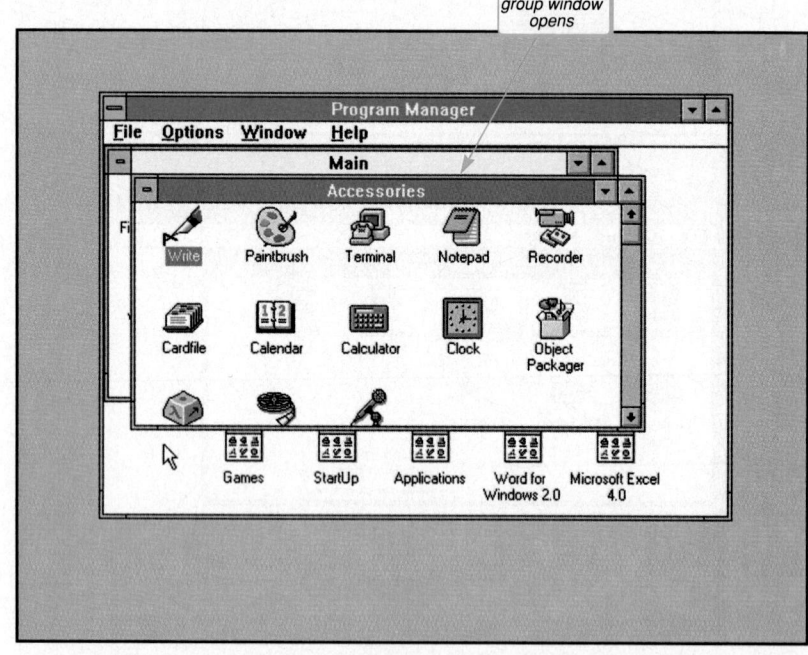

Step 3: Windows opens the Accessories group window.

FIGURE 1-10

Dragging means holding down the left mouse button, moving an item to the desired location, and then releasing the left mouse button. In most cases, you must point to an item before doing this. In Figure 1-11, you move the Control Panel program-item icon by pointing to the Control Panel icon (Step 1), holding down the left mouse button while moving the icon to its new location (Step 2), and releasing the left mouse button (Step 3). These steps are commonly referred to as dragging the Control Panel icon.

In Figure 1-11, the location of the Control Panel program-item icon was moved to rearrange the icons in the Main group window. Dragging has many uses in Windows, as you will see in subsequent examples.

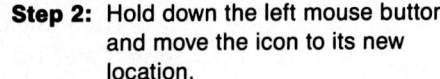

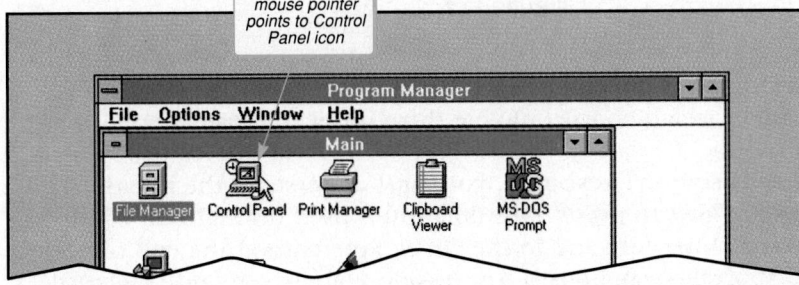

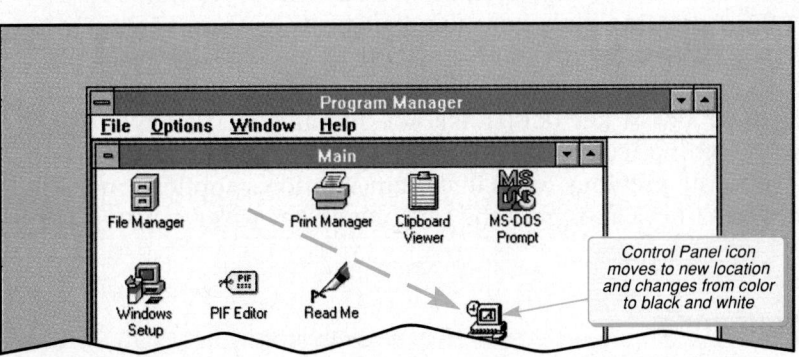

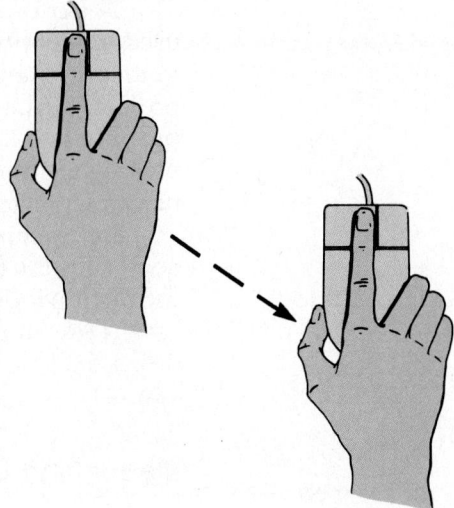

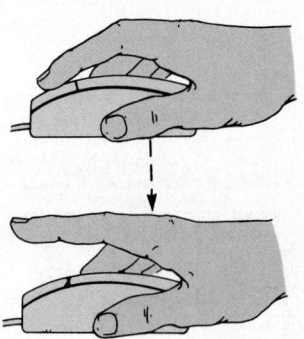

FIGURE 1-11

Step 1: Point to the Control Panel icon.

Step 2: Hold down the left mouse button and move the icon to its new location.

Step 3: Release the left mouse button.

The Keyboard and Keyboard Shortcuts

The **keyboard** is an input device on which you manually key, or type, data. Figure 1-12 on the next page shows the enhanced IBM PS/2 keyboard. Any task you accomplish with a mouse you can also accomplish with the keyboard. Although the choice of whether you use the mouse or keyboard is a matter of personal preference, the mouse is strongly recommended.

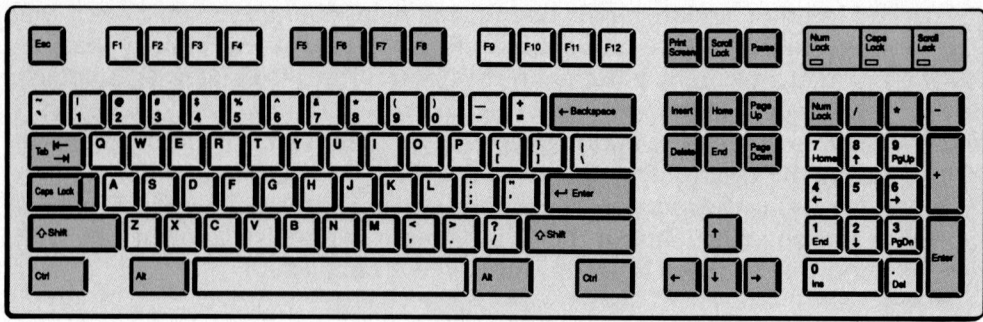

FIGURE 1-12

The Quick Reference at the end of each project provides a list of tasks presented and the manner in which to complete them using a mouse, menu, or keyboard.

To perform tasks using the keyboard, you must understand the notation used to identify which keys to press. This notation is used throughout Windows to identify **keyboard shortcuts** and in the Quick Reference at the end of each project. Keyboard shortcuts can consist of pressing a single key (RIGHT ARROW), pressing two keys simultaneously as shown by two key names separated by a plus sign (CTRL + F6), or pressing three keys simultaneously as shown by three key names separated by plus signs (CTRL + SHIFT + LEFT ARROW).

For example, to move the highlight from one program-item icon to the next you can press the RIGHT ARROW key (RIGHT ARROW). To move the highlight from the Main window to a group icon, hold down the CTRL key and press the F6 key (CTRL + F6). To move to the previous word in certain Windows applications, hold down the CTRL and SHIFT keys and press the LEFT ARROW key (CTRL + SHIFT + LEFT ARROW).

Menus and Commands

A **command** directs the software to perform a specific action, such as printing on the printer or saving data for use at a future time. One method in which you carry out a command is by choosing the command from a list of available commands, called a menu.

Windows organizes related groups of commands into **menus** and assigns a menu name to each menu. The **menu bar**, a horizontal bar below the title bar of an application window, contains a list of the menu names for that application. The menu bar for the Program Manager window in Figure 1-13 contains the following menu names: File, Options, Window, and Help. One letter in each name is underlined.

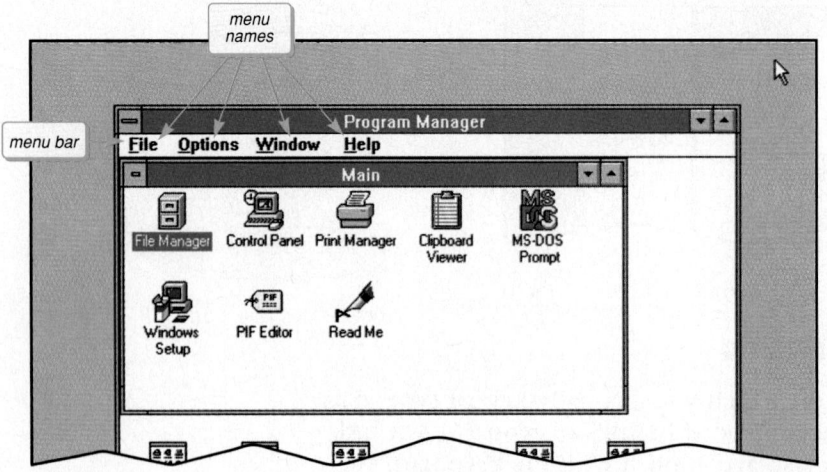

FIGURE 1-13

Selecting a Menu

To display a menu, you select the menu name. **Selecting** means marking an item. In some cases, when you select an item, Windows marks the item with a highlight by placing color behind the item. You select a menu name by pointing to the menu name in the menu bar and pressing the left mouse button (called clicking) or by using the keyboard to press the ALT key and then the keyboard key of the underlined letter in the menu name. Clicking the menu name File in the menu bar or pressing the ALT key and then the F key opens the File menu (Figure 1-14).

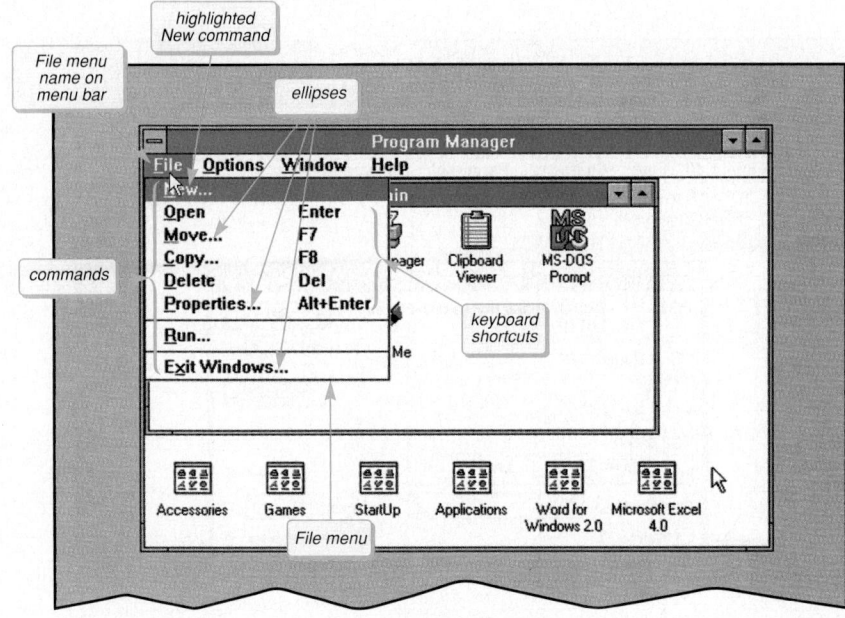

FIGURE 1-14

The File menu in Figure 1-14 contains the following commands: New, Open, Move, Copy, Delete, Properties, Run, and Exit Windows. The first command in the menu (New) is highlighted and a single character in each command is underlined. Some commands (New, Move, Copy, Properties, Run, and Exit Windows) are followed by an ellipsis (...). An **ellipsis** indicates Windows requires more information before executing the command. Commands without an ellipsis, such as the Open command, execute immediately.

Choosing a Command

You **choose** an item to carry out an action. You can choose using a mouse or keyboard. For example, to choose a command using a mouse, either click the command name in the menu or drag the highlight to the command name. To choose a command using the keyboard, either press the keyboard key of the underlined character in the command name or use the Arrow keys to move the highlight to the command name and press the ENTER key.

Some command names are followed by a keyboard shortcut. In Figure 1-14, the Open, Move, Copy, Delete, and Properties command names have keyboard shortcuts. The keyboard shortcut for the Properties command is ALT + ENTER. Holding down the ALT key and then pressing the ENTER key chooses the Properties command without selecting the File menu.

Dialog Boxes

When you choose a command whose command name is followed by an ellipsis (...), Windows opens a dialog box. A **dialog box** is a window that appears when Windows needs to supply information to you or wants you to enter information or select among options.

For example, Windows may inform you that a document is printing on the printer through the use of dialog box; or Windows may ask you whether you want to print all the pages in a printed report or just certain pages in the report.

A dialog box contains a title bar that identifies the name of the dialog box. In Figure 1-15, the name of the dialog box is Print.

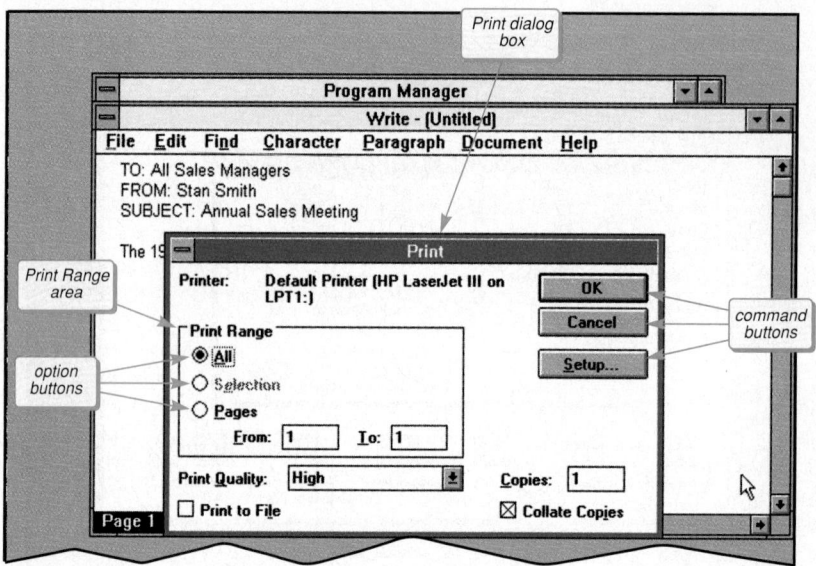

FIGURE 1-15

The types of responses Windows will ask for when working with dialog boxes fall into five categories: (1) Selecting mutually exclusive options; (2) Selecting one or more multiple options; (3) Entering specific information from the keyboard; (4) Selecting one item from a list of items; (5) Choosing a command to be implemented from the dialog box.

Each of these types of responses is discussed in the following paragraphs, together with the method for specifying them.

The Print dialog box in Figure 1-15 opens when you choose the Print command from the File menu of some windows. The Print Range area, defined by the name Print Range and a rectangular box, contains three option buttons.

The **option buttons** give you the choice of printing all pages of a report (All), selected parts of a report (Selection), or certain pages of a report (Pages). The option button containing the black dot (All) is the **selected button**. You can select only one option button at a time. A dimmed option, such as the Selection button, cannot be selected. To select an option button, use the mouse to click the option button or press the TAB key until the area containing the option button is selected and press the Arrow keys to highlight the option button.

The Print dialog box in Figure 1-15 on the previous page also contains the OK, Cancel, and Setup command buttons. **Command buttons** execute an action. The OK button executes the Print command, and the Cancel button cancels the Print command. The Setup button changes the setup of the printer by allowing you to select a printer from a list of printers, select the paper size, etc.

Figure 1-16 illustrates text boxes and check boxes. A **text box** is a rectangular area in which Windows displays text or you enter text. In the Print dialog box in Figure 1-16, the Pages option button is selected, which means only certain pages of a report are to print. You select which pages by entering the first page in the From text box (1) and the last page in the To text box (4). To enter text into a text box, select the text box by clicking it or by pressing the TAB key until the text in the text box is highlighted, and then type the text using the keyboard. The Copies text box in Figure 1-16 contains the number of copies to be printed (3).

FIGURE 1-16

Check boxes represent options you can turn on or off. An X in a check box indicates the option is turned on. To place an X in the box, click the box, or press the TAB key until the Print To File check box is highlighted, and then press SPACEBAR. In Figure 1-16, the Print to File check box, which does not contain an X, indicates the Print to File option is turned off and the pages will print on the printer. The Collate Copies check box, which contains an X, indicates the Collate Copies feature is turned on and the pages will print in collated order.

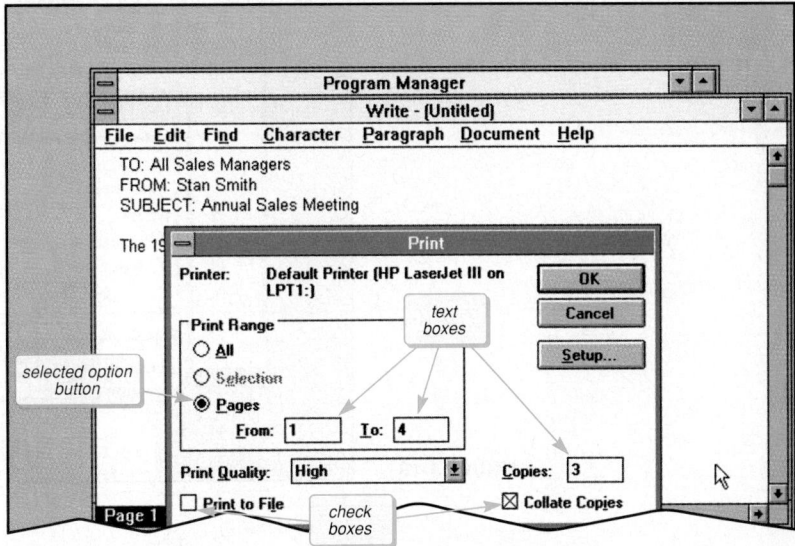

The Print dialog boxes in Figure 1-17 and Figure 1-18 on the next page, illustrate the Print Quality drop-down list box. When first selected, a **drop-down list box** is a rectangular box containing highlighted text and a down arrow box on the right. In Figure 1-17, the highlighted text, or **current selection**, is High.

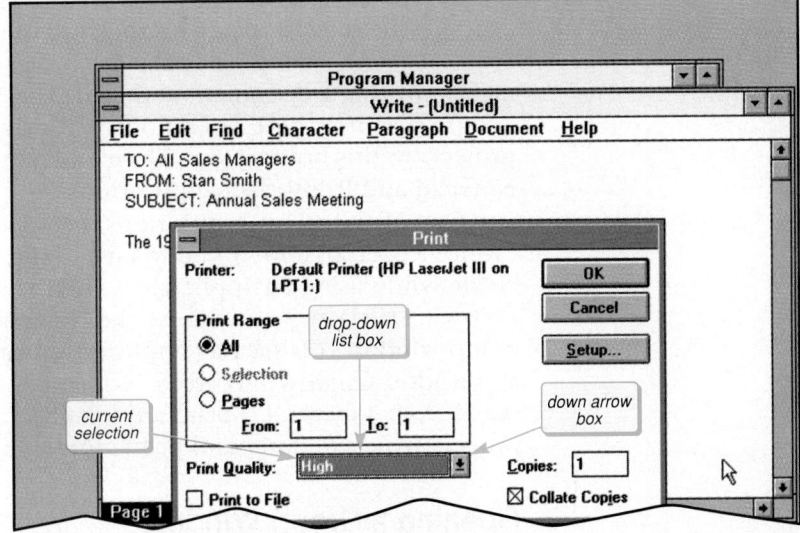

FIGURE 1-17

When you click the down arrow button, the drop-down list in Figure 1-18 appears. The list contains three choices (High, Medium, and Low). The current selection, High, is highlighted. To select from the list, use the mouse to click the selection or press the TAB key until the Print Quality drop-down list box is highlighted, press the DOWN ARROW key to highlight the selection, and then press ALT + UP ARROW or ALT + DOWN ARROW to make the selection.

Windows uses drop-down list boxes when a list of options must be presented but the dialog box is too crowded to contain the entire list. After you make your selection, the list disappears and only the current selection displays.

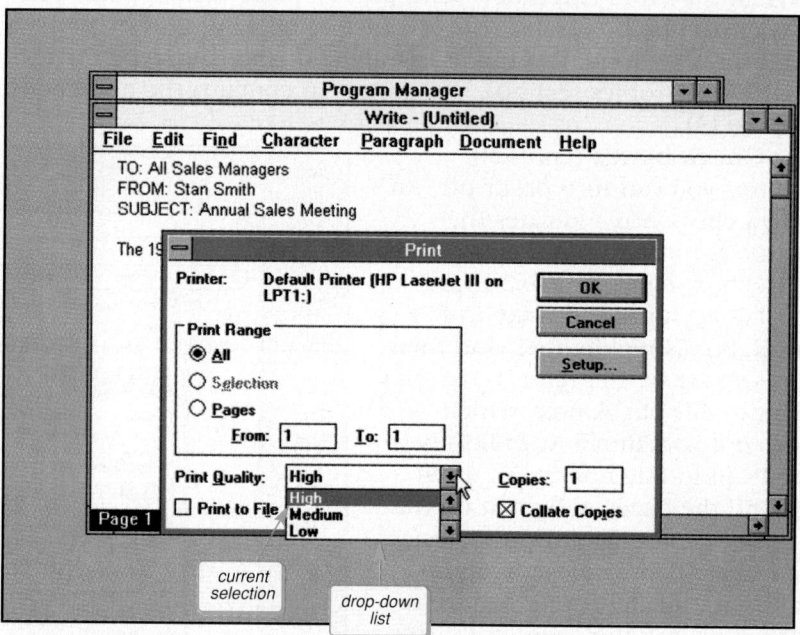

FIGURE 1-18

▶ USING MICROSOFT WINDOWS

T he remainder of this project illustrates how to use Windows to perform the operations of starting and quitting an application, creating a document, saving a document on disk, opening a document, editing a document, printing a document and using the Windows help facility. Understanding how to perform these operations will make completing the remainder of the projects in this book easier. These operations are illustrated by the use of the Notepad and Paintbrush applications.

One of the many applications included with Windows is the Notepad application. **Notepad** allows you to enter, edit, save, and print notes. Items that you create while using an application, such as a note, are called **documents**. In the following section, you will use the Notepad application to learn to (1) open a group window, (2) start an application from a group window, (3) maximize an application window, (4) create a document, (5) select a menu, (6) choose a command from a menu, (7) print a document, and (8) quit an application. In the process, you will enter and print a note.

Opening a Group Window

Each group icon at the bottom of the Program Manager window represents a group window that may contain program-item icons. To open the group window and view the program-item icons in that window use the mouse to point to the group icon and then double-click the left mouse button, as shown in the steps on the next page.

TO OPEN A GROUP WINDOW ▼

STEP 1 ►

Point to the Accessories group icon at the bottom of the Program Manager window.

The mouse pointer points to the Accessories icon (Figure 1-19).

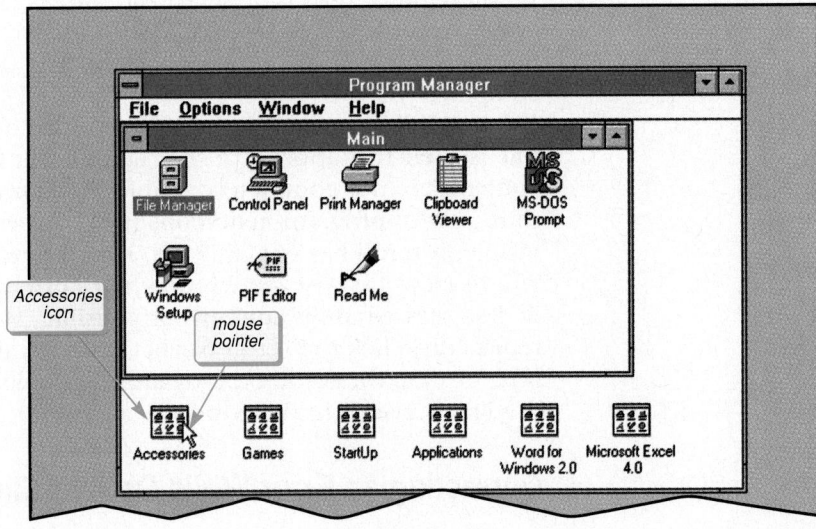

FIGURE 1-19

STEP 2 ►

Double-click the left mouse button.

Windows removes the Accessories icon from the Program Manager window and opens the Accessories group window on top of the Program Manager and Main windows (Figure 1-20). The Accessories window contains the Notepad icon.

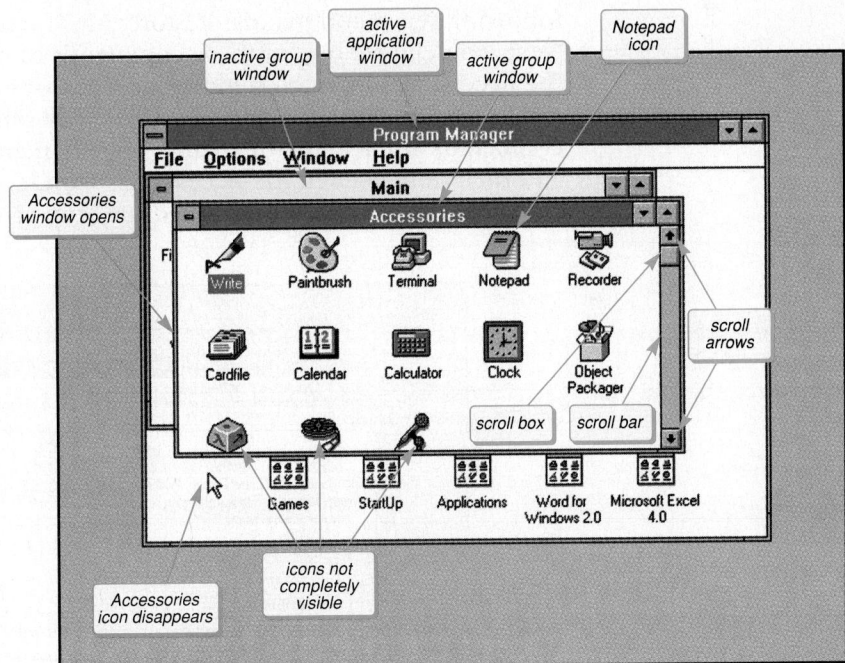

FIGURE 1-20

Opening a group window when one or more group windows are already open in the Program Manager window causes the new group window to display on top of the other group windows. The title bar of the newly opened group window is a different color or intensity than the title bars of the other group windows. This indicates the new group window is the active window. The **active window** is the window currently being used. Only one application window and one group window can be active at the same time. In Figure 1-20 on the previous page, the colors of the title bars indicate that Program Manager is the active application window (green title bar) and the Accessories group window is the active group window (green title bar). The color of the Main window title bar (yellow) indicates the Main window is inactive. The colors may not be the same on the computer you use.

A scroll bar appears on the right edge of the Accessories window. A **scroll bar** is a bar that appears at the right and/or bottom edge of a window whose contents are not completely visible. In Figure 1-20 on the previous page, the third row of program-item icons in the Accessories window is not completely visible. A scroll bar contains two **scroll arrows** and a **scroll box** which enable you to view areas of the window not currently visible. To view areas of the Accessories window not currently visible, you can click the down scroll arrow repeatedly, click the scroll bar between the down scroll arrow and the scroll box, or drag the scroll box toward the down scroll arrow until the area you want to view is visible in the window.

Correcting an Error While Double-Clicking a Group Icon

While double-clicking, it is easy to mistakenly click once instead of double-clicking. When you click a group icon such as the Accessories icon once, the **Control menu** for that icon opens (Figure 1-21). The Control menu contains the following seven commands: Restore, Move, Size, Minimize, Maximize, Close, and Next. You choose one of these commands to carry out an action associated with the Accessories icon. To remove the Control menu and open the Accessories window after clicking the Accessories icon once, you can choose the Restore command; or click any open area outside the menu to remove the Control menu and then double-click the Accessories icon; or simply double-click the Accessories icon as if you had not clicked the icon at all.

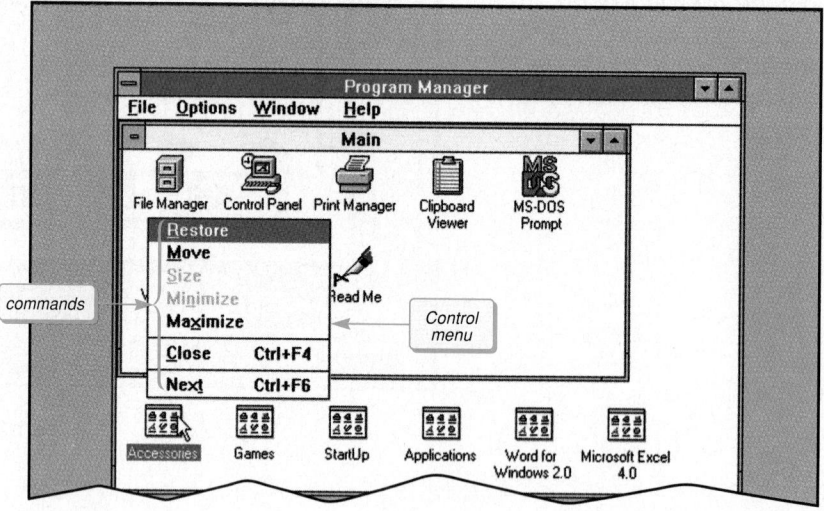

FIGURE 1-21

Starting an Application

Each program-item icon in a group window represents an application. To start an application, double-click the program-item icon. In this project, you want to start the Notepad application. To start the Notepad application, perform the steps on the next page.

TO START AN APPLICATION ▼

STEP 1 ►

Point to the Notepad icon (Figure 1-22).

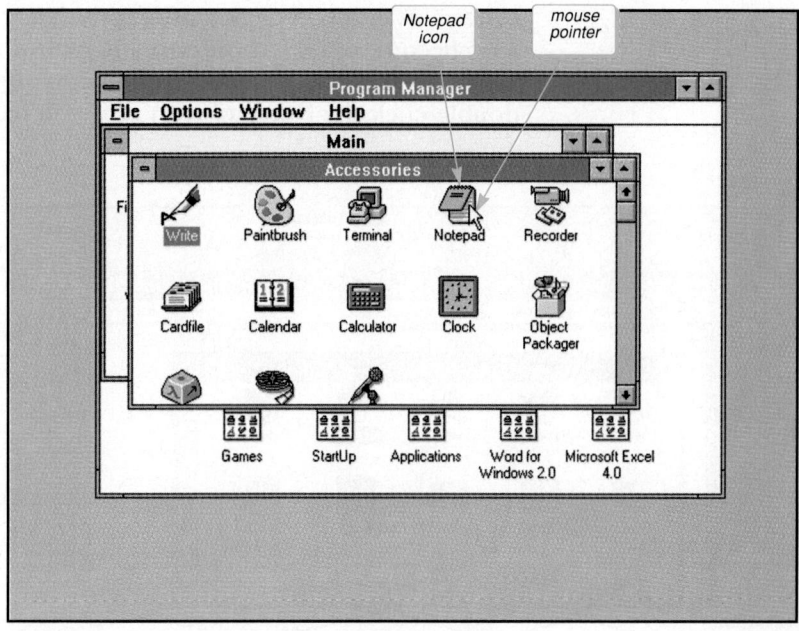

FIGURE 1-22

STEP 2 ►

Double-click the left mouse button.

*Windows opens the Notepad window on the desktop (Figure 1-23). Program Manager becomes the inactive application (yellow title bar) and Notepad is the active application (green title bar). The word Untitled in the window title (Notepad — [Untitled]) indicates a document has not been created and saved on disk. The menu bar contains the following menus: File, Edit, Search, and Help. The area below the menu bar contains an insertion point, mouse pointer, and two scroll bars. The **insertion point** is a flashing vertical line that indicates the point at which text entered from the keyboard will be displayed. When you point to the interior of the Notepad window, the mouse pointer changes from a block arrow to an I-beam (I).*

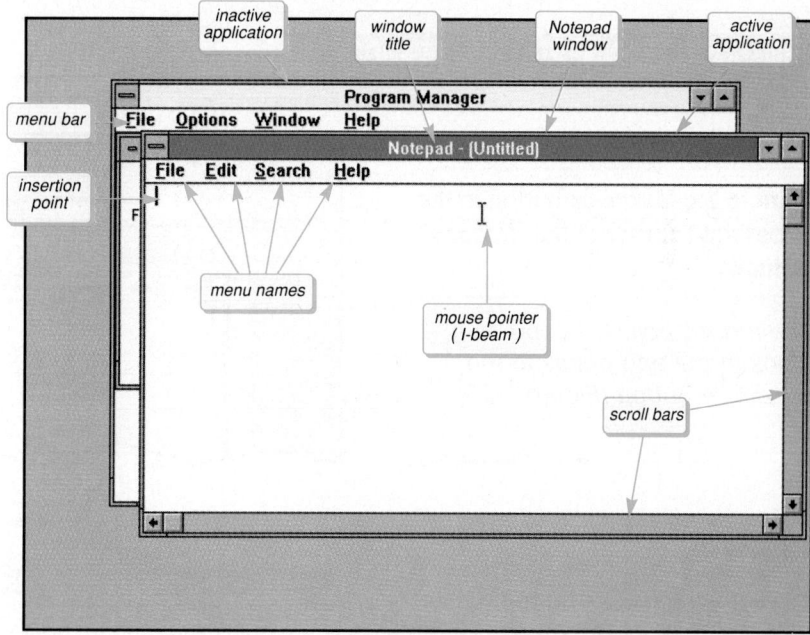

FIGURE 1-23

Correcting an Error While Double-Clicking a Program-Item Icon

While double-clicking a program-item icon you can easily click once instead. When you click a program-item icon such as the Notepad icon once, the icon becomes the **active icon** and Windows highlights the icon name (Figure 1-24). To start the Notepad application after clicking the Notepad icon once, double-click the Notepad icon as if you had not clicked the icon at all.

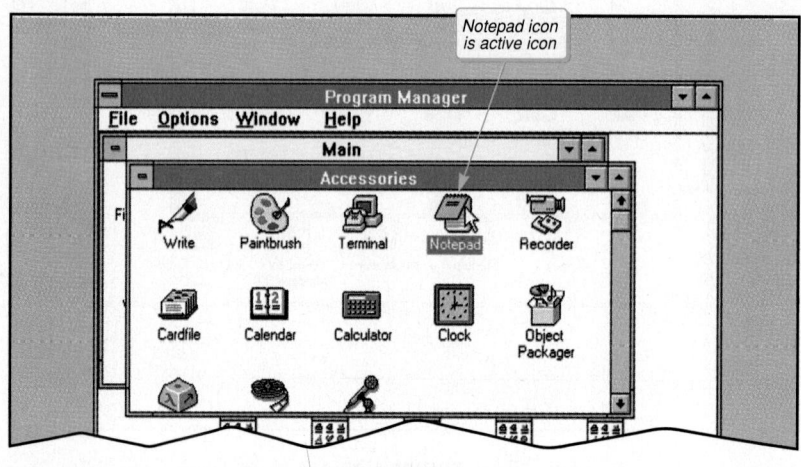

FIGURE 1-24

Maximizing an Application Window

Before you work with an application, maximizing the application window makes it easier to see the contents of the window. You can maximize an application window so the window fills the entire desktop. To maximize an application window to its maximum size, choose the **Maximize button** (▲) by pointing to the Maximize button and clicking the left mouse button. Complete the following steps to maximize the Notepad window.

TO MAXIMIZE AN APPLICATION WINDOW ▼

STEP 1 ▶

Point to the Maximize button in the upper right corner of the Notepad window.

The mouse pointer becomes a block arrow and points to the Maximize button (Figure 1-25).

FIGURE 1-25

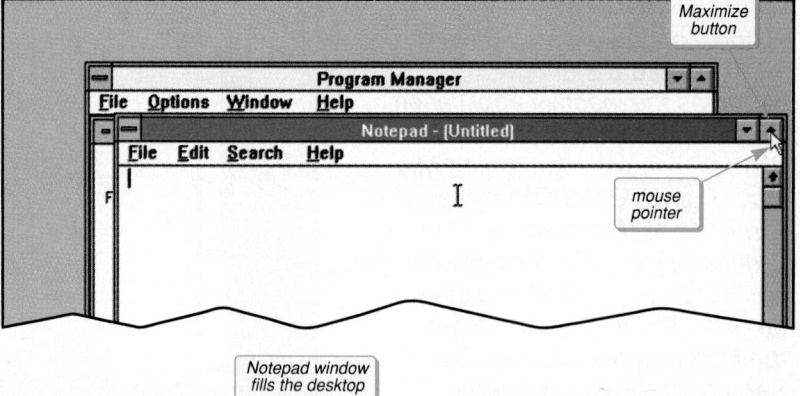

STEP 2 ▶

Click the left mouse button.

The Notepad window fills the desktop (Figure 1-26). The **Restore button** *(◆) replaces the Maximize button at the right side of the title bar. Clicking the Restore button will return the window to its size before maximizing.*

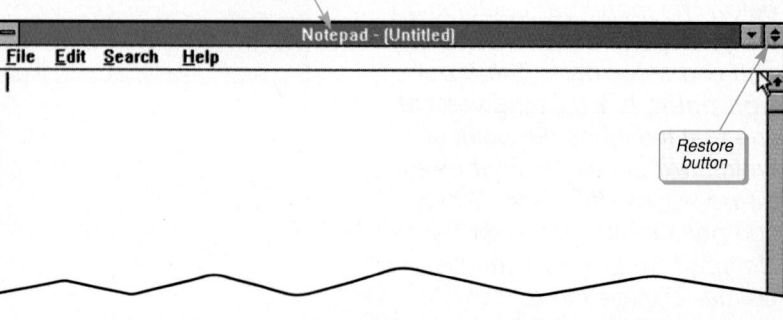

FIGURE 1-26

Creating a Document

To create a document in Notepad, type the text you want to display in the document. After typing a line of text, press the ENTER key to terminate the entry of the line. To create a document, enter the note to the right by performing the steps below.

> Things to do today —
> 1) Take fax\phone to Conway Service Center
> 2) Pick up payroll checks from ADM
> 3) Order 3 boxes of copier paper

TO CREATE A NOTEPAD DOCUMENT ▼

STEP 1 ▶

Type Things to do today – **and press the** ENTER **key.**

The first line of the note is entered and the insertion point appears at the beginning of the next line (Figure 1-27).

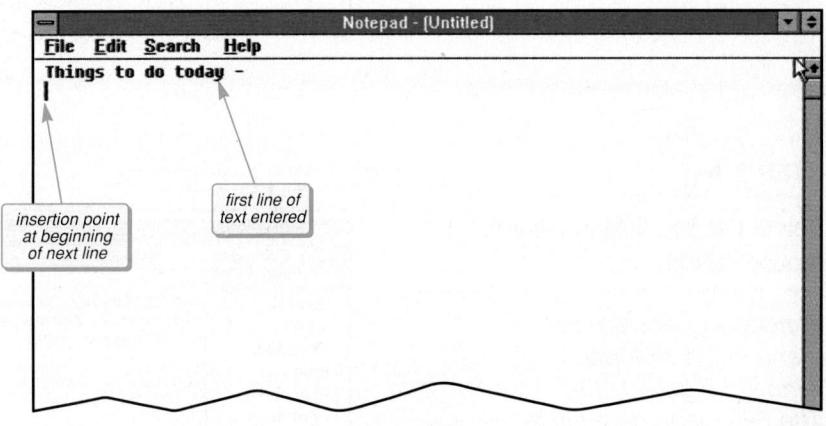

FIGURE 1-27

STEP 2 ▶

Type the remaining lines of the note. Press the ENTER **key after typing each line.**

The remaining lines in the note are entered and the insertion point is located at the beginning of the line following the note (Figure 1-28).

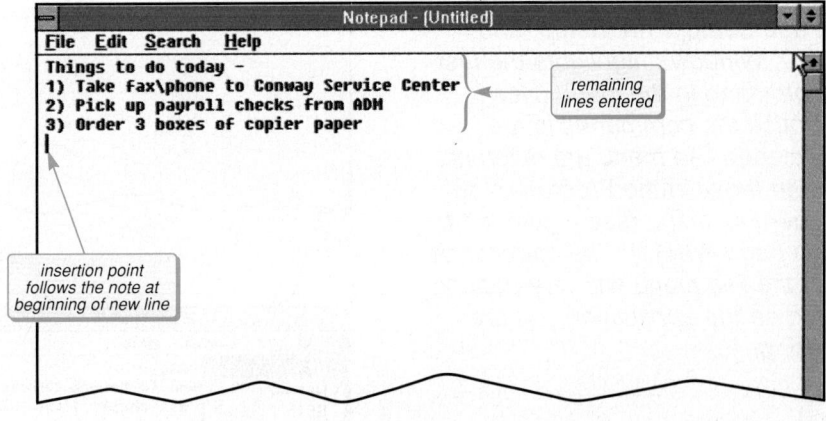

FIGURE 1-28

Printing a Document by Choosing a Command from a Menu

After creating a document, you often print the document on the printer. To print the note, complete the following steps.

TO PRINT A DOCUMENT ▼

STEP 1 ►

Point to File on the Notepad menu bar (Figure 1-29).

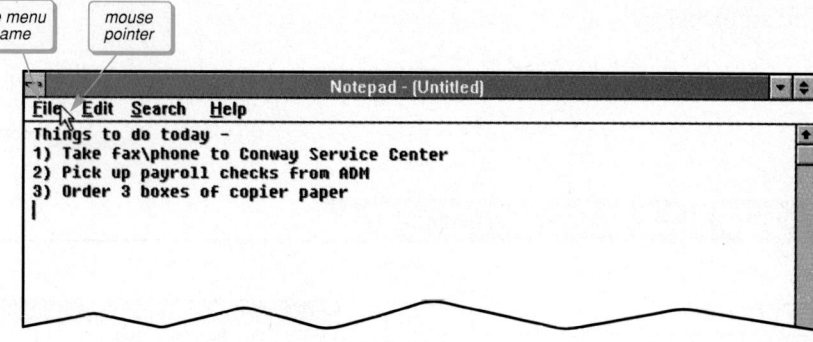

FIGURE 1-29

STEP 2 ►

Select File by clicking the left mouse button.

Windows opens the File menu in the Notepad window (Figure 1-30). The File menu name is highlighted and the File menu contains the following commands: New, Open, Save, Save As, Print, Page Setup, Print Setup, and Exit. Windows highlights the first command in the menu (New). Notice the commands in the Notepad File menu are different than those in the Program Manager File menu (see Figure 1-14 on page WIN11). The commands in the File menu will vary depending on the application you are using.

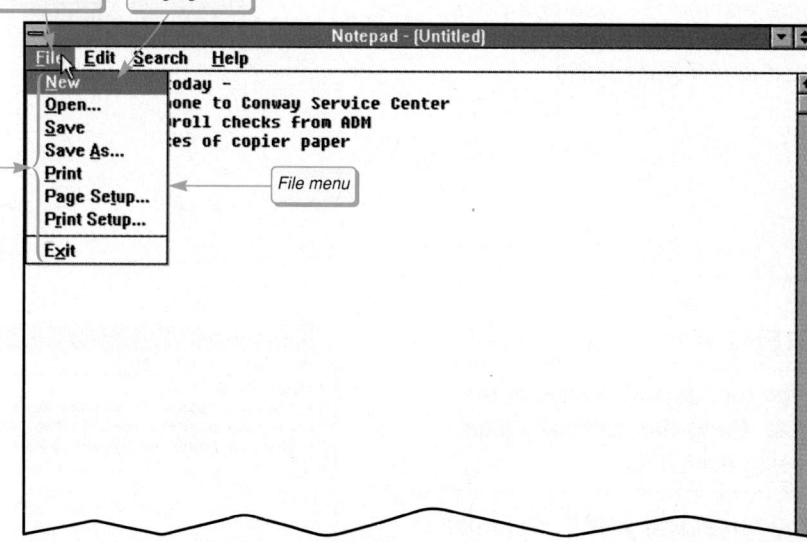

FIGURE 1-30

STEP 3 ►

Point to the Print command.

The mouse pointer points to the Print command (Figure 1-31).

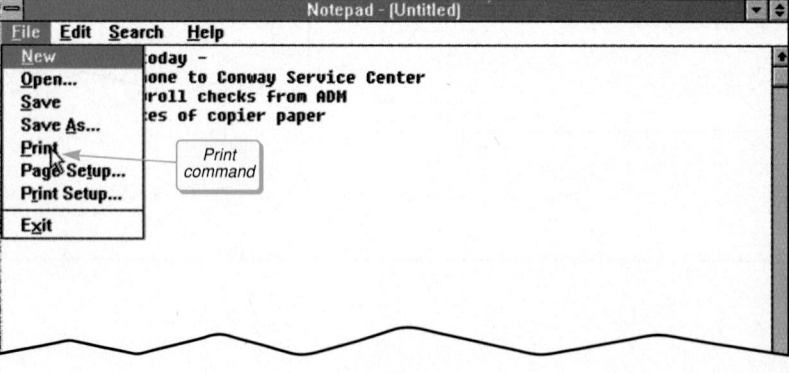

FIGURE 1-31

STEP 4 ▶

Choose the Print command from
the File menu by clicking the left
mouse button.

*Windows momentarily opens the
Notepad dialog box (Figure 1-32).
The dialog box contains the Now
Printing text message and the
Cancel command button
(Cancel). When the Notepad
dialog box closes, Windows
prints the document on the
printer (Figure 1-33).*

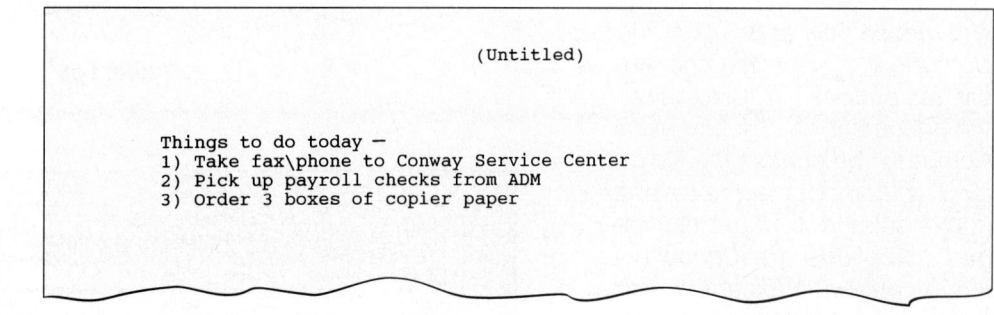

FIGURE 1-32

FIGURE 1-33

Quitting an Application

When you have finished creating and printing the document, quit the application by following the steps below and on the next page.

TO QUIT AN APPLICATION ▼

STEP 1 ▶

Point to File on the Notepad menu
bar (Figure 1-34).

FIGURE 1-34

STEP 2 ▶

Select File by clicking the left
mouse button, and then point to
the Exit command.

*Windows opens the File menu
and the mouse pointer points to
the Exit command (Figure 1-35).*

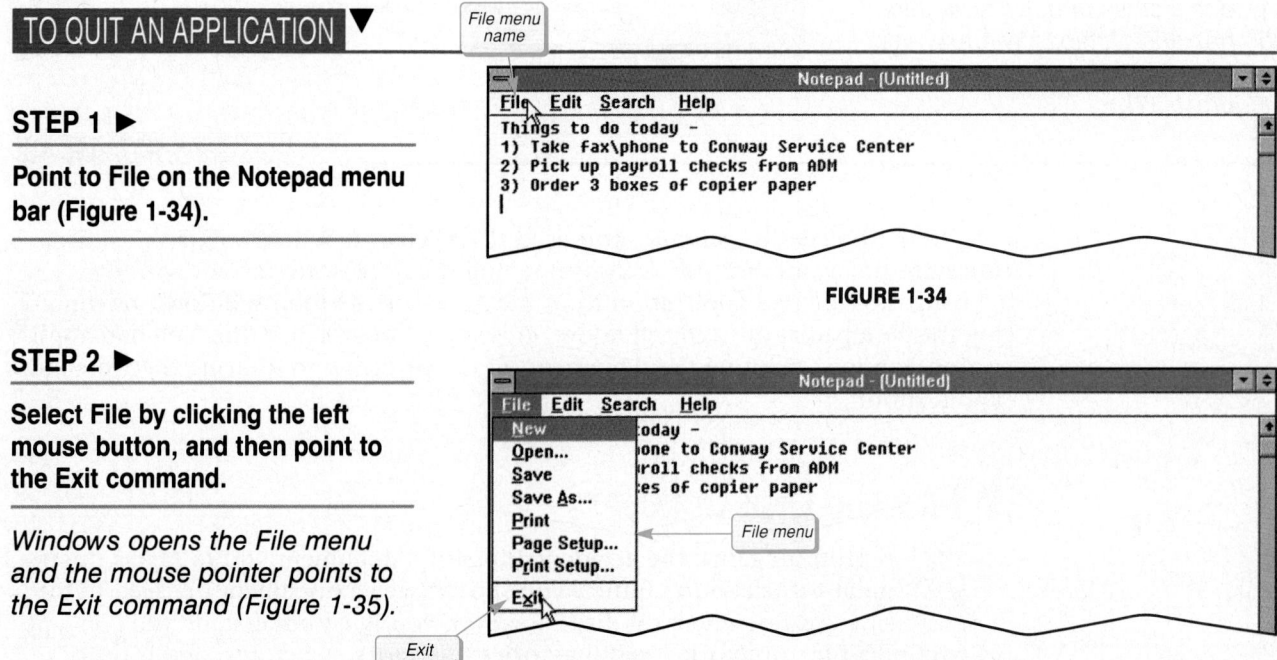

FIGURE 1-35

STEP 3 ▶

Choose the Exit command from the File menu by clicking the left mouse button, and then point to the No button.

Windows opens the Notepad dialog box (Figure 1-36). The dialog box contains the following: The message, The text in the [Untitled] file has changed., the question, Do you want to save the changes?, and the Yes, No, and Cancel command buttons. The mouse pointer points to the No button (No). You choose the Yes button (Yes) to save the document on disk and exit Notepad. You choose the No button if you do not want to save the document and want to exit Notepad. You choose the Cancel button to cancel the Exit command.

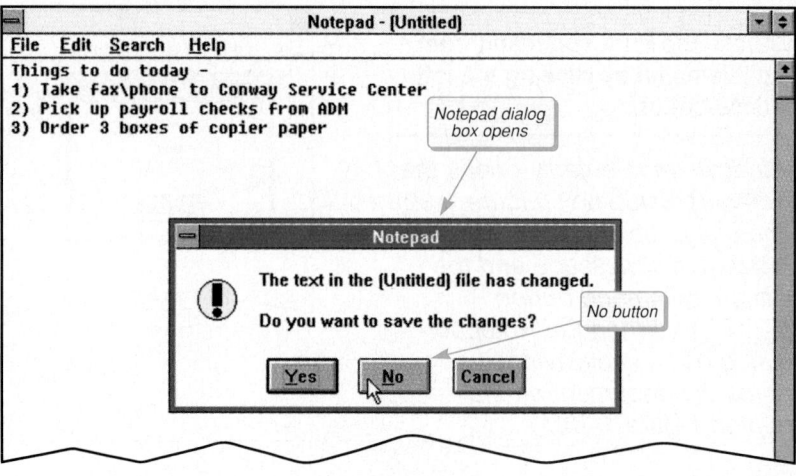

FIGURE 1-36

STEP 4 ▶

Choose the No button by clicking the left mouse button.

Windows closes the Notepad dialog box and Notepad window and exits the Notepad application (Figure 1-37).

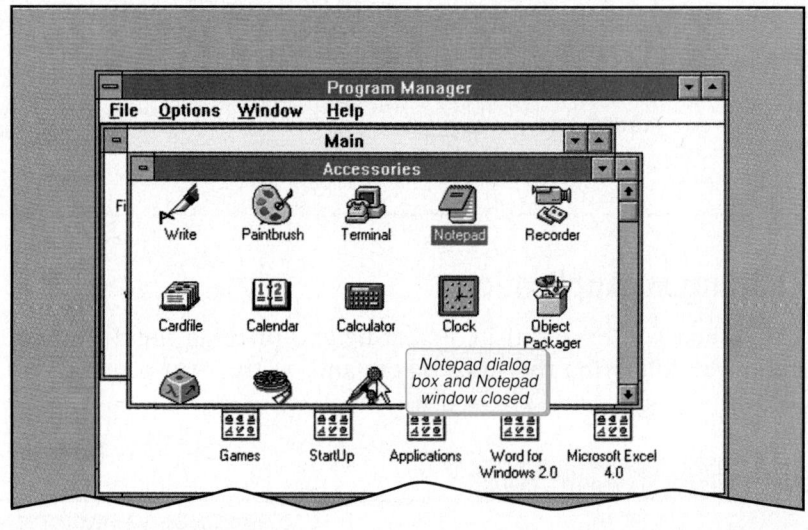

FIGURE 1-37

In the preceding example, you used the Microsoft Windows graphical user interface to accomplish the tasks of opening the Accessories group window, starting the Notepad application from the Accessories group window, maximizing the Notepad application window, creating a document in the Notepad application window, printing the document on the printer, and quitting the Notepad application.

▶ FILE AND DISK CONCEPTS

T o protect against the accidental loss of a document and to save a document for use in the future, you should save a document on disk. Before saving a document on disk, however, you must understand the concepts of naming a file, directories, subdirectories, directory structures, and directory paths. The following section explains these concepts.

Naming a File

When you create a document using an application, the document is stored in main memory. If you quit the application without saving the document on disk, the document is lost. To save the document for future use, you must store the document in a **document file** on the hard disk or on a diskette before quitting the application. Before saving a document, you must assign a name to the document file.

All files are identified on disk by a **filename** and an **extension**. For example, the name SALES.TXT consists of a filename (SALES) and an extension (.TXT). A filename can contain from one to eight characters and the extension begins with a period and can contain from one to three characters. Filenames must start with a letter or number. Any uppercase or lowercase character is valid except a period (.), quotation mark (''), slash (/), backslash (\), brackets ([]), colon (:), semicolon (;), vertical bar (|), equal sign (=), comma (,), or blank space. Filenames cannot be CON, AUX, COM1, COM2, COM3, COM4, LPT1, LPT2, LPT3, PRN, and NUL.

To more easily identify document files on disk, it is convenient to assign the same extension to document files you create with a given application. The Notepad application, for instance, automatically uses the .TXT extension for each document file saved on disk. Typical filenames and extensions of document files saved using Notepad are: SHOPPING.TXT, MECHANIC.TXT, and 1994.TXT.

You can use the asterisk character (*) in place of a filename or extension to refer to a group of files. For example, the asterisk in the expression *.TXT tells Windows to reference any file that contains the .TXT extension, regardless of the filename. This group of files might consist of the HOME.TXT, AUTOPART-.TXT, MARKET.TXT, JONES.TXT, and FRANK.TXT files.

The asterisk in MONTHLY.* tells Windows to reference any file that contains the filename MONTHLY, regardless of the extension. Files in this group might consist of the MONTHLY.TXT, MONTHLY.CAL, and MONTHLY.CRD files.

Directory Structures and Directory Paths

After selecting a name and extension for a file, you must decide which auxiliary storage device (hard disk or diskette) to use and in which directory you want to save the file. A **directory** is an area of a disk created to store related groups of files. When you first prepare a disk for use on a computer, a single directory, called the **root directory**, is created on the disk. You can create **subdirectories** in the root directory to store additional groups of related files. The hard disk in Figure 1-38 contains the root directory and the WINDOWS, MSAPPS, and SYSTEM subdirectories. The WINDOWS, MSAPPS, and SYSTEM subdirectories are created when Windows is installed and contain files related to Windows.

HARD DISK

FIGURE 1-38

Directory Structure	Directory Path
🗁 c:\	C:\
📂 windows	C:\WINDOWS
🗀 msapps	C:\WINDOWS\MSAPPS
🗀 system	C:\WINDOWS\SYSTEM

▶ **TABLE 1-1**

The relationship between the root directory and any subdirectories is called the **directory structure**. Each directory or subdirectory in the directory structure has an associated directory path. The **directory path** is the path Windows follows to find a file in a directory. Table 1-1 contains a graphic representation of the directory structure and the associated paths of drive C.

Each directory and subdirectory on drive C is represented by a file folder icon in the directory structure. The first file folder icon, an unshaded open file folder (🗁), represents the root directory of the current drive (drive C). The c:\ entry to the right of the icon symbolizes the root directory (identified by the \ character) of drive C (c:). The path is C:\. Thus, to find a file in this directory, Windows locates drive C (C:) and the root directory (\) on drive C.

The second icon, a shaded open file folder (📂), represents the current subdirectory. This icon is indented below the first file folder icon because it is a subdirectory. The name of the subdirectory (windows) appears to the right of the shaded file folder icon. Because the WINDOWS subdirectory was created in the root directory, the path for the WINDOWS subdirectory is C:\WINDOWS. To find a file in this subdirectory, Windows locates drive C, locates the root directory on drive C, and then locates the WINDOWS subdirectory in the root directory.

Because the current path is C:\WINDOWS, the file folder icons for both the root directory and WINDOWS subdirectory are open file folders. An open file folder indicates the directory or subdirectory is in the current path. Unopened file folders represent subdirectories not in the current path.

The third and fourth icons in Table 1-1, unopened file folders (🗀), represent the MSAPPS and SYSTEM subdirectories. The unopened file folders indicate these subdirectories are not part of the current path. These file folder icons are indented below the file folder for the WINDOWS subdirectory which means they were created in the WINDOWS subdirectory. The subdirectory names (msapps and system) appear to the right of the file folder icons.

Since the MSAPPS and SYSTEM subdirectories were created in the WINDOWS subdirectory, the paths for these subdirectories are C:\WINDOWS\MSAPPS and C:\WINDOWS\SYSTEM. The second backslash (\) in these paths separates the two subdirectory names. To find a file in these subdirectories, Windows locates drive C, locates the root directory on drive C, then locates the WINDOWS subdirectory in the root directory, and finally locates the MSAPPS or SYSTEM subdirectory in the WINDOWS subdirectory.

Saving a Document on Disk

After entering data into a document, you will often save it on the hard disk or a diskette to protect against accidental loss and to make the document available for use later. In the previous example using the Notepad application, the note was not saved prior to exiting Notepad. Instead of exiting, assume you want to save the document you created. The screen before you begin to save the document is shown in Figure 1-39. To save the document on a diskette in drive A using the filename, agenda, perform the steps that begin at the top of the next page.

FIGURE 1-39

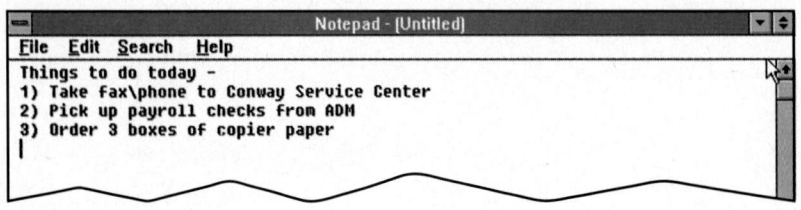

TO SAVE A FILE ▼

STEP 1 ▶

Insert a formatted diskette into drive A (Figure 1-40).

The diskette must be properly formatted before being used to save data. To learn the technique for formatting a diskette see Project 2.

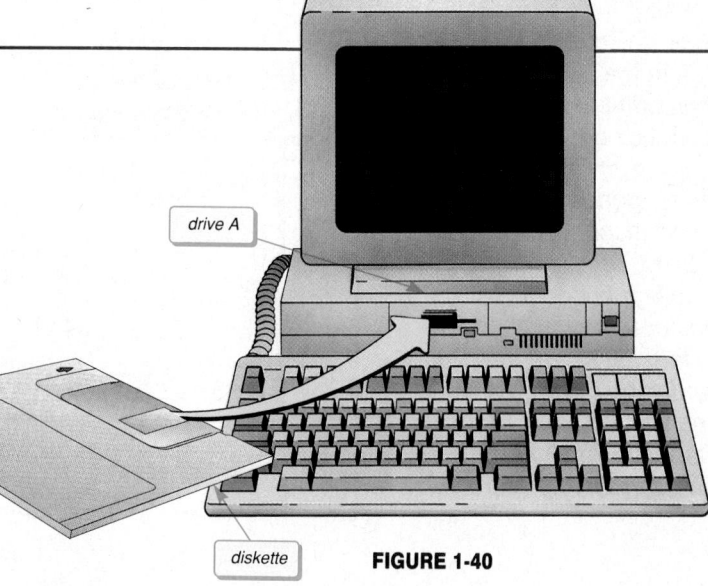

drive A

diskette

FIGURE 1-40

STEP 2 ▶

Select File on the Notepad menu bar, and then point to the Save As command.

Windows opens the File menu in the Notepad window and the mouse pointer points to the Save As command (Figure 1-41). The ellipsis (...) following the Save As command indicates Windows will open a dialog box when you choose this command.

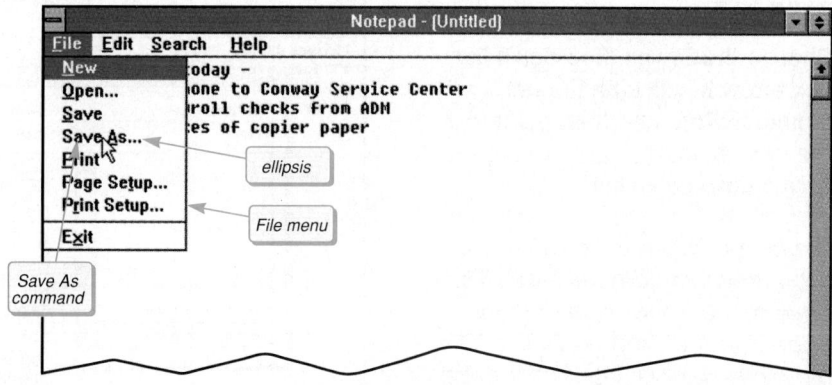

ellipsis

File menu

Save As command

FIGURE 1-41

STEP 3 ▶

Choose the Save As command from the File menu by clicking the left mouse button.

The Save As dialog box opens (Figure 1-42). The File Name text box contains the highlighted *.txt entry. Typing a filename from the keyboard will replace the entire *.txt entry with the filename entered from the keyboard. The current path is c:\windows and the Directories list box contains the directory structure of the current subdirectory (windows). The drive selection in the Drives drop-down list box is c:. The dialog box contains the OK (OK) and Cancel (Cancel) command buttons.

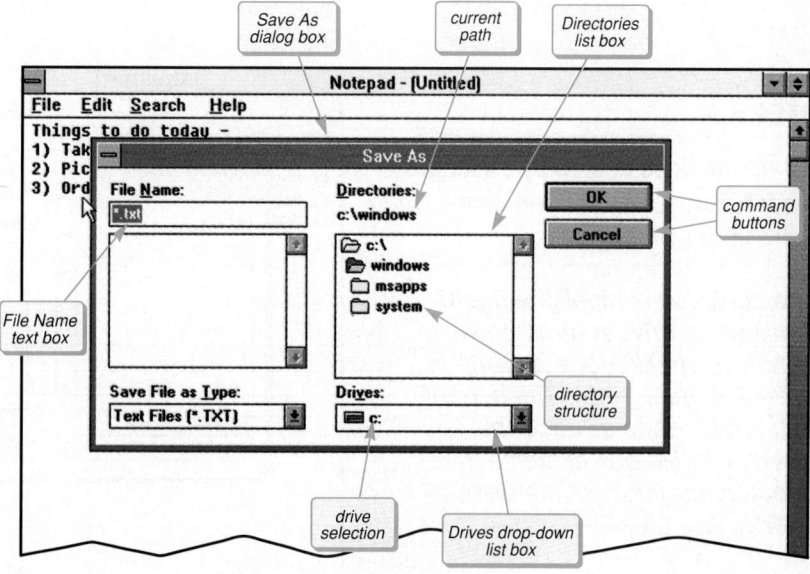

Save As dialog box

current path

Directories list box

File Name text box

command buttons

directory structure

drive selection

Drives drop-down list box

FIGURE 1-42

STEP 4 ▶

Type agenda in the File Name text box, and then point to the Drives drop-down list box arrow.

The filename, agenda, and an insertion point display in the File Name text box (Figure 1-43). When you save this document, Notepad will automatically add the .TXT extension to the agenda filename and save the file on disk using the name AGENDA.TXT. The mouse pointer points to the Drives drop-down list box arrow.

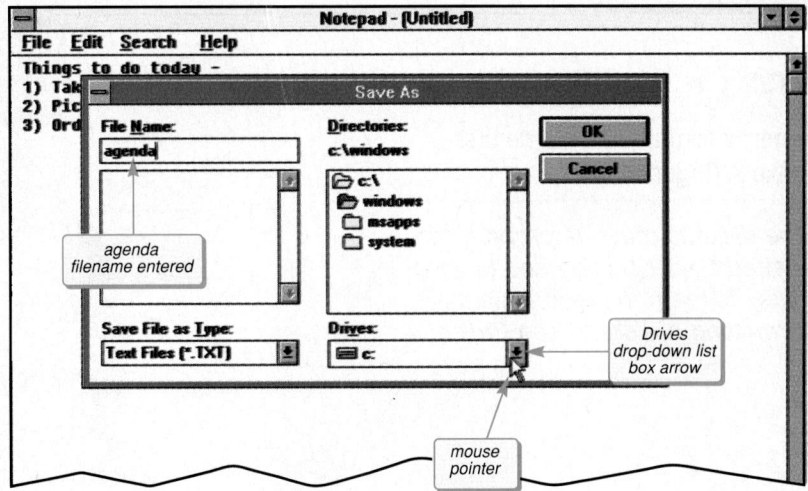

FIGURE 1-43

STEP 5 ▶

Choose the Drives drop-down list box arrow by clicking the left mouse button, and then point to the drive a: icon (🖫) in the Drives drop-down list.

Windows displays the Drives drop-down list (Figure 1-44). The drive a: icon and drive c: icon appear in the drop-down list. The mouse pointer points to the drive a: icon.

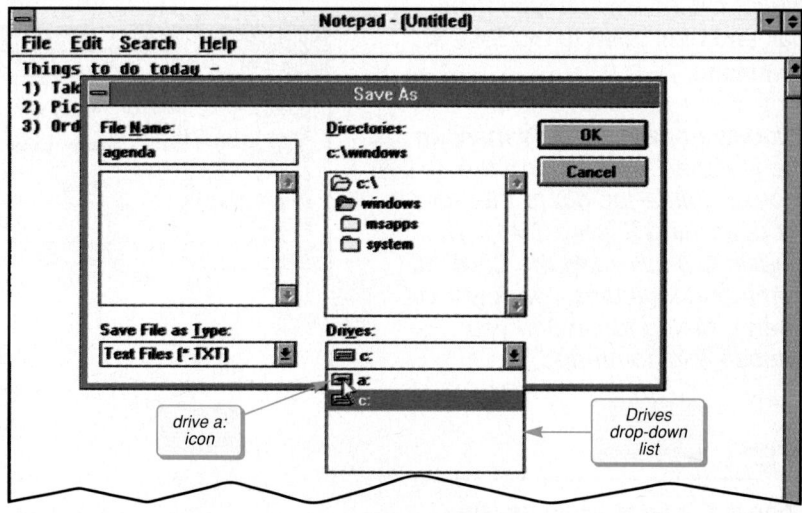

FIGURE 1-44

STEP 6 ▶

Select the drive a: icon by clicking the left mouse button, and then point to the OK button.

The selection is highlighted and the light on drive A turns on while Windows checks for a diskette in drive A (Figure 1-45). The current path changes to a:\ and the Directories list box contains the directory structure of the diskette in drive A.

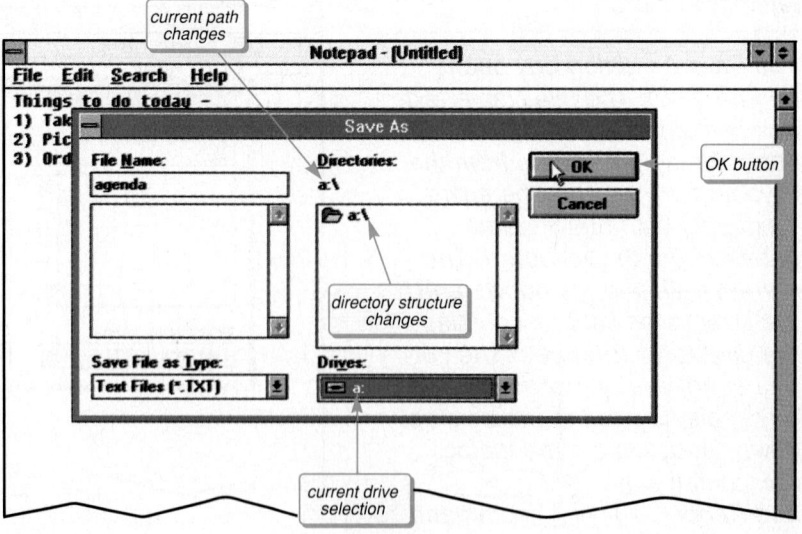

FIGURE 1-45

STEP 7 ►

Choose the OK button in the Save As dialog box by clicking the left mouse button.

Windows closes the Save As dialog box and displays an hourglass icon while saving the AGENDA.TXT document file on the diskette in drive A. After the file is saved, Windows changes the window title of the Notepad window to reflect the name of the AGENDA.TXT file (Figure 1-46).

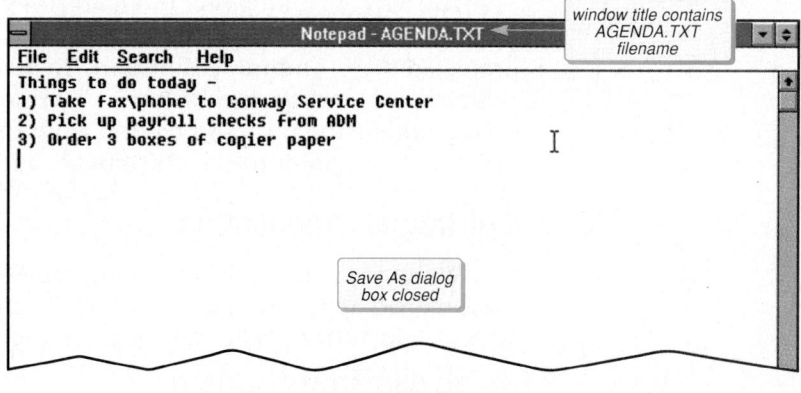

FIGURE 1-46

Correcting Errors Encountered While Saving a Document File

Before you can save a document file on a diskette, you must insert a formatted diskette into the diskette drive. **Formatting** is the process of preparing a diskette for use on a computer by establishing the sectors and cylinders on a disk, analyzing the diskette for defective cylinders, and establishing the root directory. The technique for formatting a diskette is shown in Project 2. If you try to save a file on a diskette and forget to insert a diskette, forget to close the diskette drive door after inserting a diskette, insert an unformatted diskette, or insert a damaged diskette, Windows opens the Save As dialog box in Figure 1-47.

The dialog box contains the messages telling you the condition found and the Retry (Retry) and Cancel buttons. To save a file on the diskette in drive A after receiving this message, insert a formatted diskette into the diskette drive, point to the Retry button, and click the left mouse button.

In addition, you cannot save a document file on a write-protected diskette. A **write-protected diskette** prevents accidentally erasing data stored on the diskette by not letting the disk drive write new data or erase existing data on the diskette. If you try to save a file on a write-protected diskette, Windows opens the Save As dialog box shown in Figure 1-48.

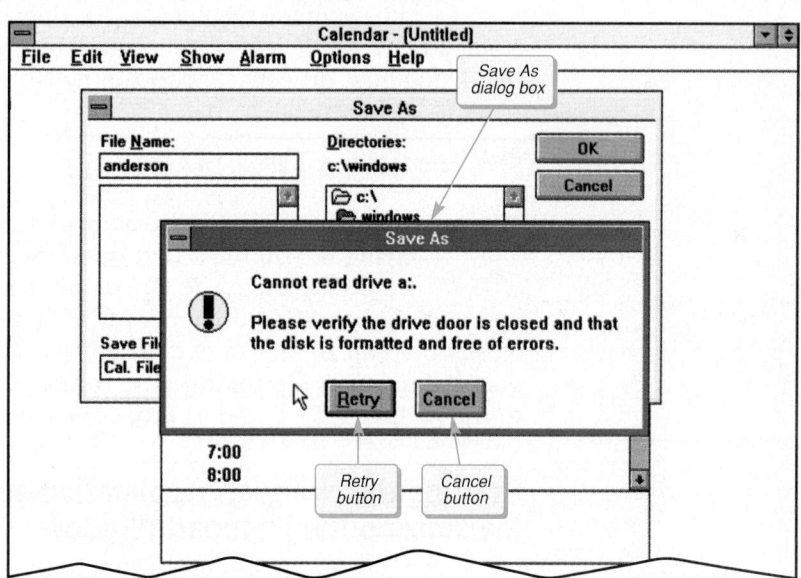

FIGURE 1-47

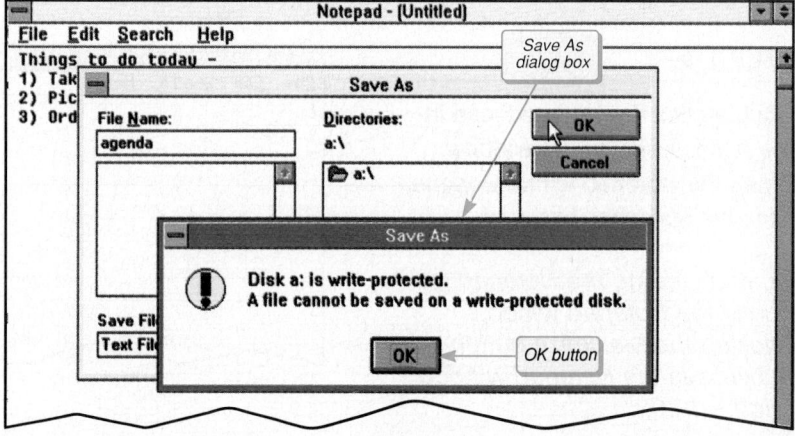

FIGURE 1-48

The Save As dialog box in Figure 1-48 on the previous page contains the messages, Disk a: is write-protected., and, A file cannot be saved on a write-protected disk., and the OK button. To save a file on diskette after inserting a write-protected diskette into drive A, remove the diskette from the diskette drive, remove the write-protection from the diskette, insert the diskette into the diskette drive, point to the OK button, and click the left mouse button.

Quitting an Application

When you have finished saving the AGENDA.TXT file on disk, you can quit the Notepad application as shown in Figure 1-34 through Figure 1-37 on pages WIN21 and WIN22. The steps are summarized below.

TO QUIT AN APPLICATION

Step 1: Point to File on the Notepad menu bar.
Step 2: Select File by clicking the left mouse button, and then point to the Exit command.
Step 3: Choose the Exit command by clicking the left mouse button.

If you have made changes to the document since saving it on the diskette, Notepad will ask if you want to save the changes. If so, choose the Yes button in the dialog box; otherwise, choose the No button.

▶ OPENING A DOCUMENT FILE

C hanges are frequently made to a document saved on disk. To make these changes, you must first open the document file by retrieving the file from disk using the Open command. After modifying the document, you save the modified document file on disk using the Save command. Using the Notepad application, you will learn to (1) open a document file and (2) save an edited document file on diskette. In the process, you will add the following line to the AGENDA.TXT file: 4) Buy copier toner.

Starting the Notepad Application and Maximizing the Notepad Window

To start the Notepad application and maximize the Notepad window, perform the following step.

TO START AN APPLICATION AND MAXIMIZE ITS WINDOW ▼

STEP 1 ▶

Double-click the Notepad icon in the Accessories group window. When the Notepad window opens, click the Maximize button.

Double-clicking the Notepad icon opens the Notepad window. Clicking the Maximize button maximizes the Notepad window (Figure 1-49).

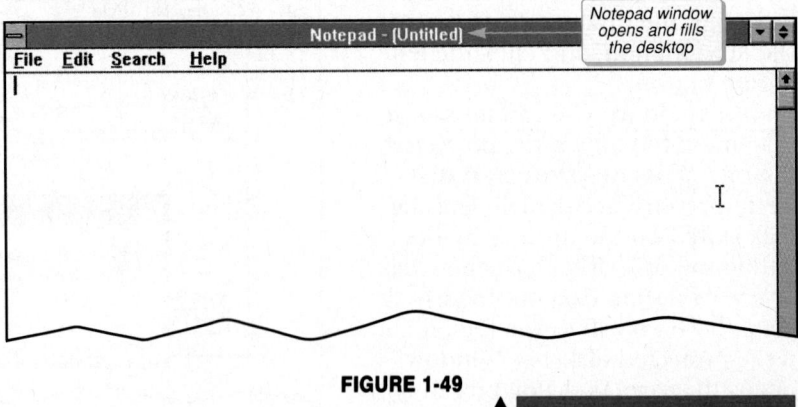

FIGURE 1-49

Opening a Document File

Before you can modify the AGENDA.TXT document, you must open the file from the diskette on which it was stored. To do so, ensure the diskette containing the file is inserted into drive A, then perform the following steps.

TO OPEN A DOCUMENT FILE ▼

STEP 1 ▶

Select File on the menu bar, and then point to the Open command.

Windows opens the File menu and the mouse pointer points to the Open command (Figure 1-50).

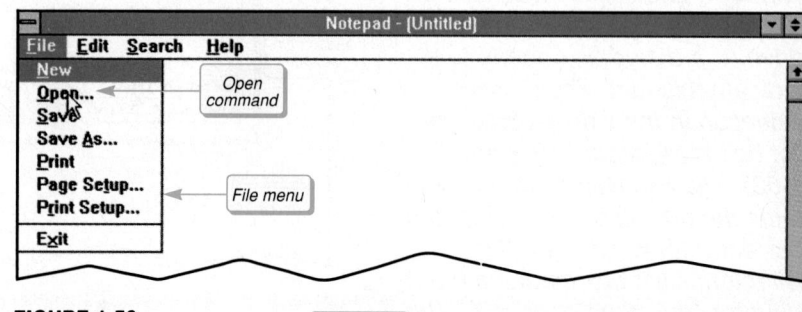

FIGURE 1-50

STEP 2 ▶

Choose the Open command from the File menu by clicking the left mouse button, and then point to the Drives drop-down list box arrow.

The Open dialog box opens (Figure 1-51). The File Name text box contains the *.txt entry and the File Name list box is empty because no files with the .TXT extension appear in the current directory. The current path is c:\windows. The Directories list box contains the directory structure of the current subdirectory (WINDOWS). The selected drive in the Drives drop-down list box is c:. The mouse pointer points to the Drives drop-down list box arrow.

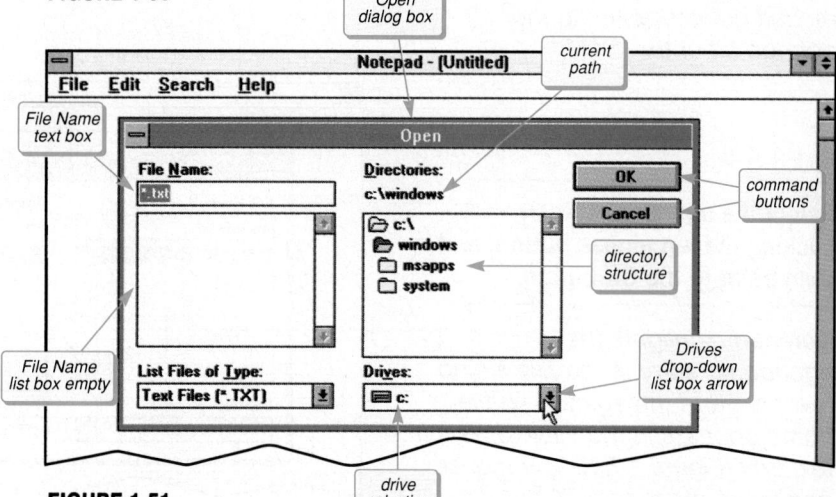

FIGURE 1-51

STEP 3 ▶

Choose the Drives drop-down list box arrow by clicking the left mouse button, and then point to the drive a: icon.

Windows displays the Drives drop-down list (Figure 1-52). The drive a: icon and drive c: icon appear in the drop-down list. The current selection is c:. The mouse pointer points to the drive a: icon.

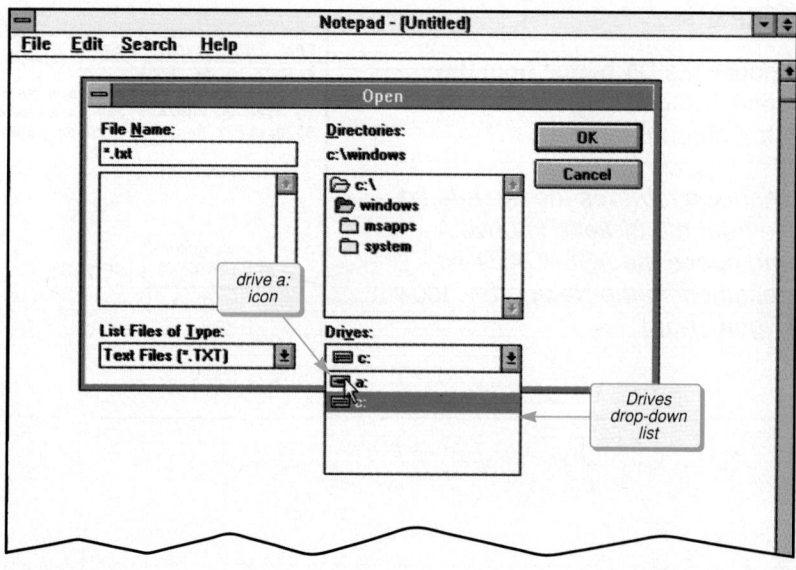

FIGURE 1-52

STEP 4 ▶

Select the drive a: icon by clicking the left mouse button, and then point to the agenda.txt entry in the File Name list box.

The light on drive A turns on, and Windows checks for a diskette in drive A. If there is no diskette in drive A, a dialog box opens to indicate this fact. The current selection in the Drives drop-down list box is highlighted (Figure 1-53). The File Name list box contains the filename agenda.txt, the current path is a:\, and the Directories list box contains the directory structure of drive A. The mouse pointer points to the agenda.txt entry.

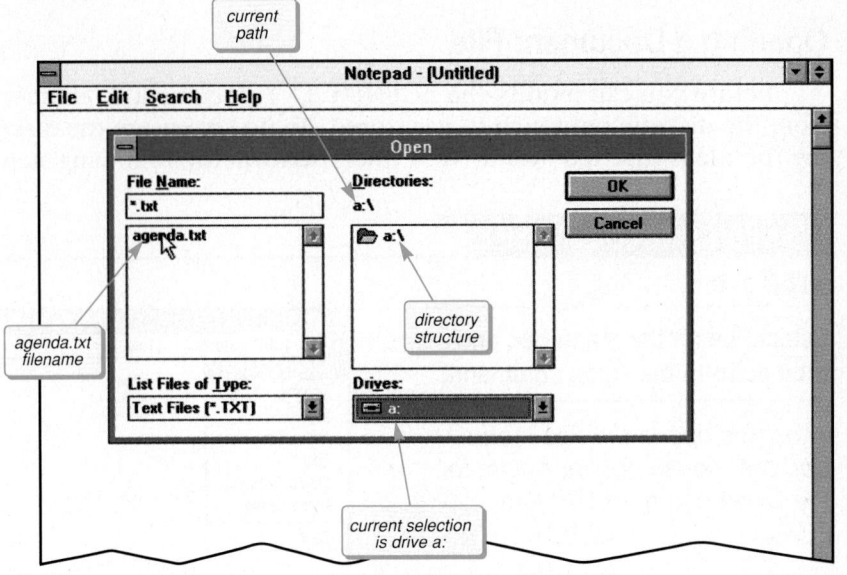

FIGURE 1-53

STEP 5 ▶

Select the agenda.txt file by clicking the left mouse button, and then point to the OK button.

Notepad highlights the agenda.txt entry in the File Name text box, and the agenda.txt filename appears in the File Name text box (Figure 1-54). The mouse pointer points to the OK button.

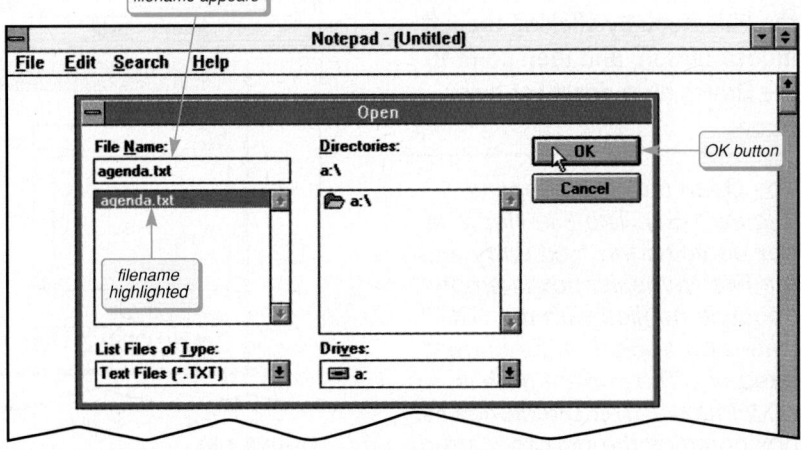

FIGURE 1-54

STEP 6 ▶

Choose the OK button from the Open dialog box by clicking the left mouse button.

Windows retrieves the agenda.txt file from the diskette in drive A and opens the AGENDA.TXT document in the Notepad window (Figure 1-55).

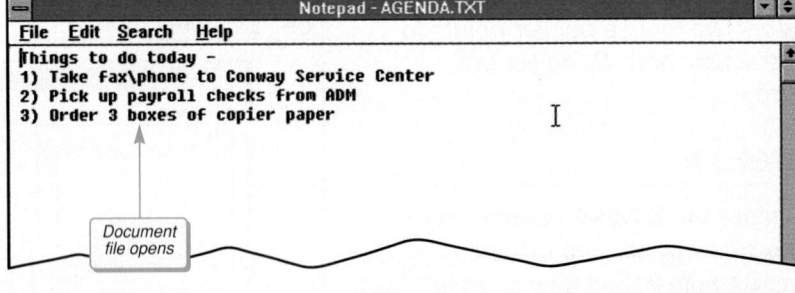

FIGURE 1-55

Editing the Document File

You edit the AGENDA.TXT document file by entering the fourth line of text.

TO EDIT THE DOCUMENT ▼

STEP 1 ▶

Press the DOWN ARROW key four times to position the insertion point, and then type the new line, 4) Buy Copier toner.

The new line appears in the Note-pad document (Figure 1-56).

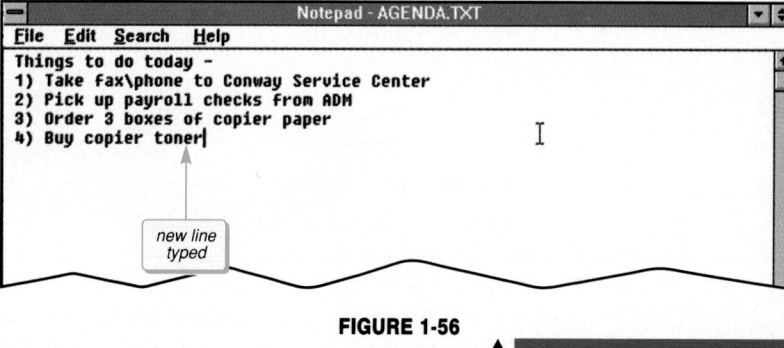

FIGURE 1-56

Saving the Modified Document File

After modifying the AGENDA.TXT document, you should save the modified document on disk using the same AGENDA.TXT filename. To save a modified file on disk, choose the Save command. The Save command differs from the Save As command in that you choose the Save command to save changes to an existing file while you choose the Save As command to name and save a new file or to save an existing file under a new name.

TO SAVE A MODIFIED DOCUMENT FILE ▼

STEP 1 ▶

Select File on the Notepad menu bar, and then point to the Save command.

Windows opens the File menu and the mouse pointer points to the Save command (Figure 1-57).

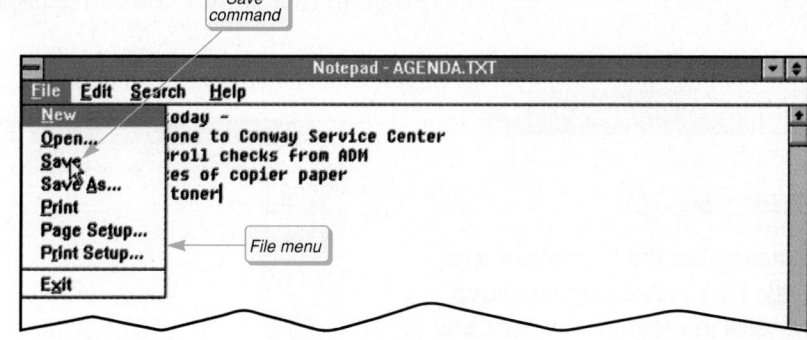

FIGURE 1-57

STEP 2 ▶

Choose the Save command from the File menu by clicking the left mouse button.

Windows closes the File menu, displays the hourglass icon momentarily, and saves the AGENDA.TXT document on the diskette in drive A (Figure 1-58).

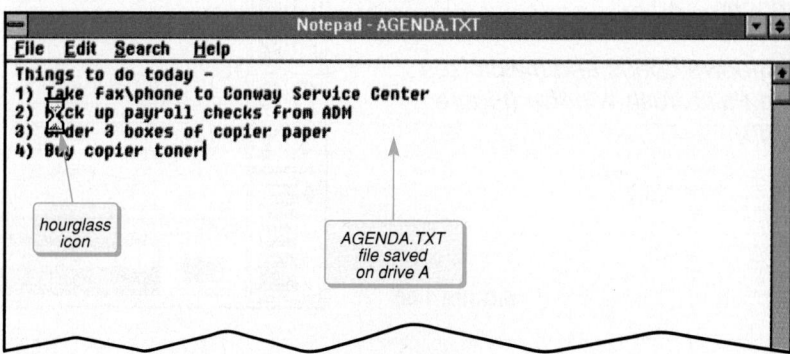

FIGURE 1-58

STEP 3 ▶

Remove the diskette from Drive A (Figure 1-59).

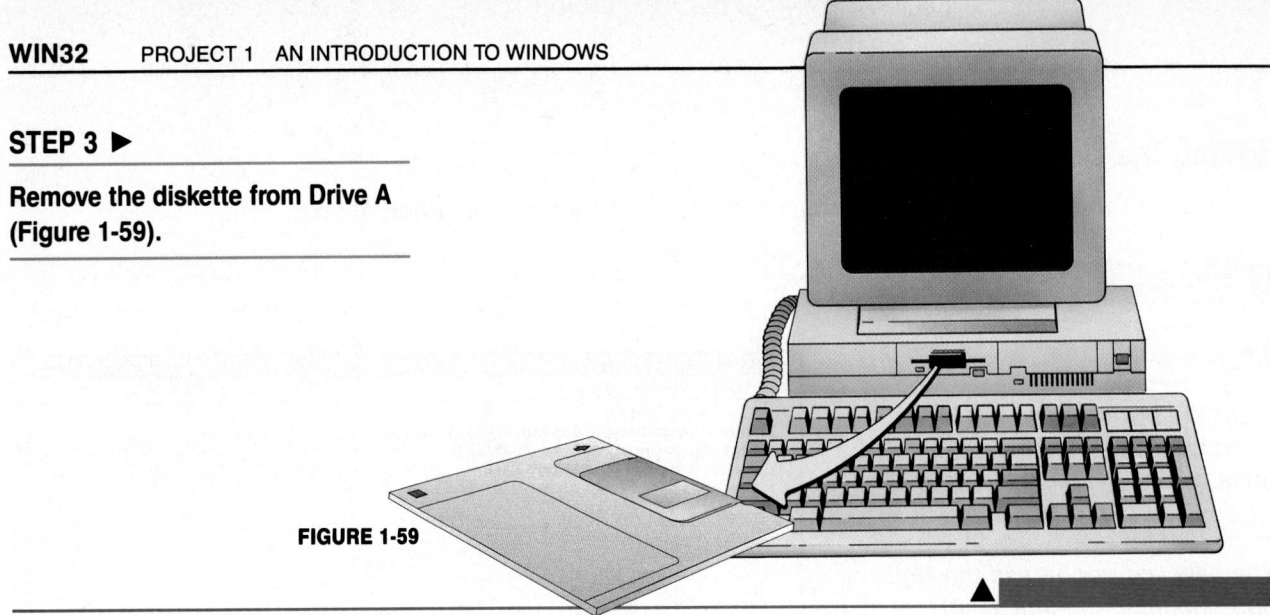

FIGURE 1-59

When you have finished saving the modified AGENDA.TXT file, quit the Notepad application by performing the following steps.

TO QUIT NOTEPAD

Step 1: Select File on the Notepad menu bar.
Step 2: Choose the Exit command.

▶ USING WINDOWS HELP

I f you need help while using an application, you can use Windows online Help. **Online Help** is available for all applications except Clock. To illustrate Windows online Help, you will start the Paintbrush application and obtain help about the commands on the Edit menu. **Paintbrush** is a drawing program that allows you to create, edit, and print full-color illustrations.

TO START AN APPLICATION

STEP 1 ▶

Double-click the Paintbrush icon (🖌) in the Accessories group window in Program Manager, and then click the Maximize button on the Paintbrush — [Untitled] window.

Windows opens and maximizes the Paintbrush window (Figure 1-60).

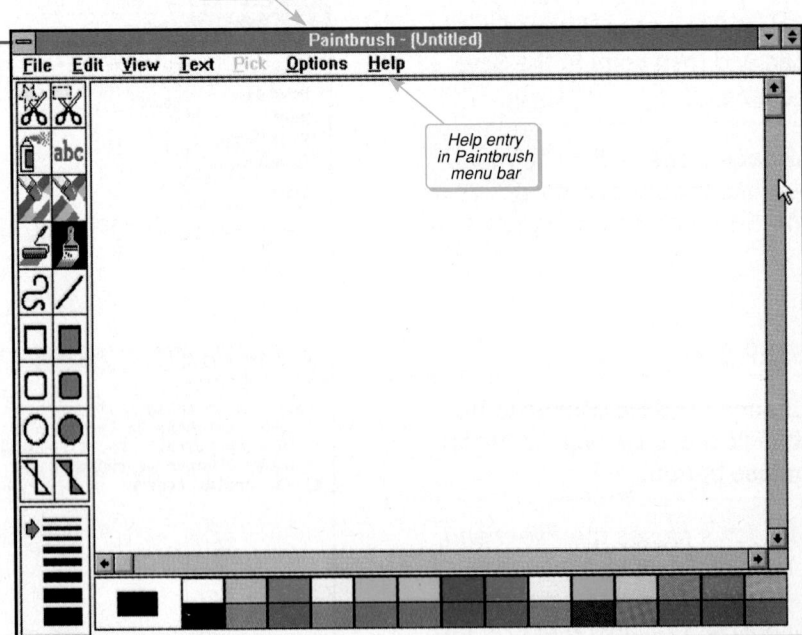

FIGURE 1-60

TO OBTAIN HELP ▼

STEP 1 ▶

Select Help on the Paintbrush menu bar, and then point to the Contents command.

Windows opens the Help menu (Figure 1-61). The Help menu contains four commands. The mouse pointer points to the Contents command.

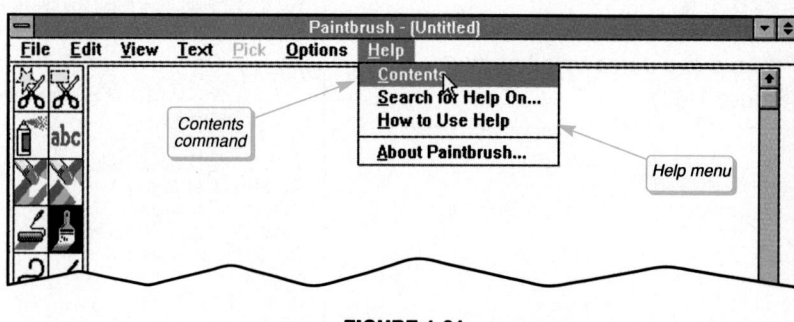

FIGURE 1-61

STEP 2 ▶

Choose the Contents command from the Help menu by clicking the left mouse button. Then click the Maximize button on the Paintbrush Help window.

Windows opens the Paintbrush Help window (Figure 1-62), and when you click the Maximize button, it maximizes the window.

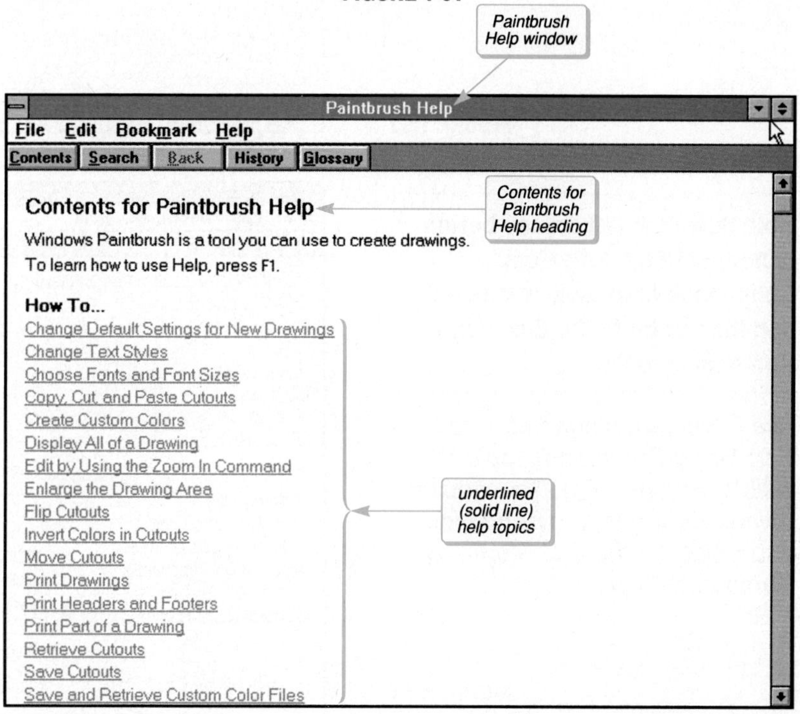

FIGURE 1-62

The Contents for Paintbrush Help screen appears in the window. This screen contains information about the Paintbrush application, how to learn to use online Help (press F1), and an alphabetical list of all help topics for the Paintbrush application. Each **help topic** is underlined with a solid line. The solid line indicates additional information relating to the topic is available. Underlined help topics are called jumps. A **jump** provides a link to viewing information about another help topic or more information about the current topic. A jump may be either text or graphics.

Choosing a Help Topic

To choose an underlined help topic, scroll the help topics to make the help topic you want visible, then point to the help topic and click the left mouse button. When you place the mouse pointer on a help topic, the mouse pointer changes to a hand (🖑). To obtain help about the Edit menu, perform the steps on the next page.

TO CHOOSE A HELP TOPIC ▼

STEP 1 ▶

Point to the down scroll arrow (Figure 1-63).

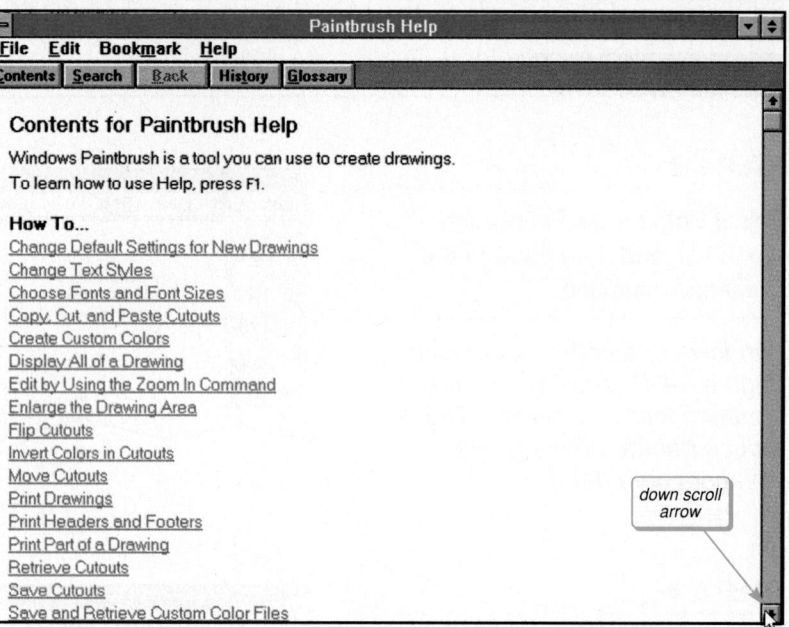

FIGURE 1-63

STEP 2 ▶

Hold down the left mouse button (scroll) until the Edit Menu Commands help topic is visible, and then point to the Edit Menu Commands topic.

The Commands heading and the Edit Menu Commands topic are visible (Figure 1-64). The mouse pointer changes to a hand icon and points to the Edit Menu Commands topic.

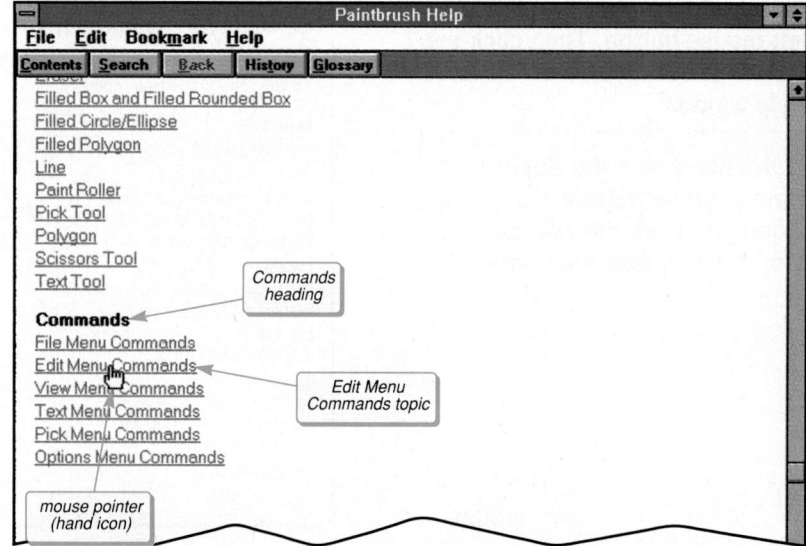

FIGURE 1-64

STEP 3 ▶

Choose the Edit Menu Commands topic by clicking the left mouse button.

The Edit Menu Commands screen contains information about each of the commands in the Edit menu (Figure 1-65). Two terms (scroll bar and cutout) are underlined with a dotted line. Terms underlined with a dotted line have an associated glossary definition. To display a term's glossary definition, point to the term and click the left mouse button.

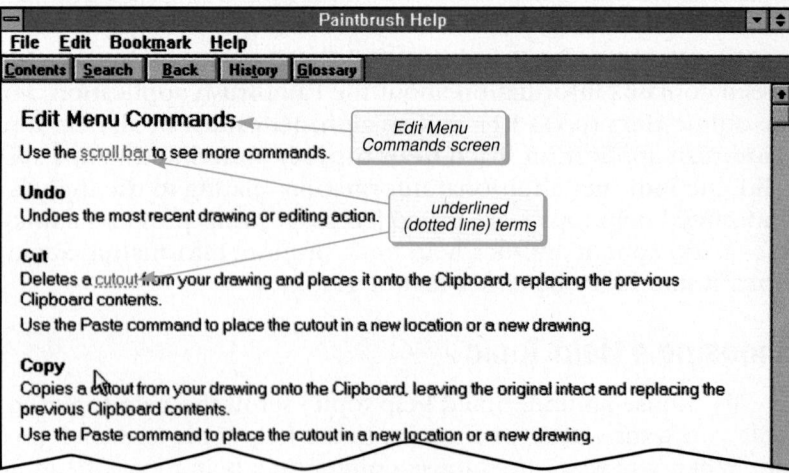

FIGURE 1-65

TO DISPLAY A DEFINITION ▼

STEP 1 ▶

Point to the term, scroll bar.

*The mouse pointer changes to a
hand and points to the term,
scroll bar (Figure 1-66).*

scroll bar
term

Paintbrush Help

File Edit Bookmark Help

Contents | Search | Back | History | Glossary

Edit Menu Commands

Use the scroll bar to see more commands.   mouse
pointer

Undo
Undoes the most recent drawing or editing action.

FIGURE 1-66

STEP 2 ▶

Choose the term, scroll bar, by
clicking the left mouse button.

*Windows opens a **pop-up
window** containing the
glossary definition of the
term, scroll bar (Figure 1-67).*

FIGURE 1-67

Paintbrush Help

File Edit Bookmark Help

Contents | Search | Back | History | Glossary   pop-up
window

Edit Menu Commands

Use the scroll bar to see more commands.

definition
displayed

scroll bar
A bar that appears at the right and/or bottom edge of a window or list box whose contents are
not completely visible. Each scroll bar contains two scroll arrows and a scroll box, which
enable you to scroll through the contents of the window or list box.

Clipboard contents.
Use the Paste command to place the cutout in a new location or a new drawing.

STEP 3 ▶

When you have finished reading
the definition, close the pop-up
window by clicking anywhere on
the screen.

*Windows closes the pop-up win-
dow containing the glossary
definition (Figure 1-68).*

Paintbrush Help

File Edit Bookmark Help

Contents | Search | Back | History | Glossary

Edit Menu Commands

Use the scroll bar to see more commands.

Undo
Undoes the most recent drawing or editing action.   pop-up window
closed

Cut
Deletes a cutout from your drawing and places it onto the Clipboard, replacing the previous
Clipboard contents.
Use the Paste command to place the cutout in a new location or a new drawing.

FIGURE 1-68

Exiting the Online Help and Paintbrush Applications

After obtaining help about the Edit Menu commands, quit Help by choosing
the Exit command from the Help File menu. Then, quit Paintbrush by choosing
the Exit command from the Paintbrush File menu. The steps are summarized
below.

TO QUIT PAINTBRUSH HELP

Step 1: Select File on the Paintbrush Help menu bar.
Step 2: Choose the Exit command.

TO QUIT PAINTBRUSH

Step 1: Select File on the Paintbrush menu bar.
Step 2: Choose the Exit command.

▶ QUITTING WINDOWS

Y ou always want to return the desktop to its original state before beginning your next session with Windows. Therefore, before exiting Windows, you must verify that any changes made to the desktop are not saved when you quit windows.

Verify Changes to the Desktop Will Not be Saved

Because you want to return the desktop to its state before you started Windows, no changes should be saved. The Save Settings on Exit command on the Program Manager Options menu controls whether changes to the desktop are saved or are not saved when you quit Windows. A check mark (✓) preceding the Save Settings on Exit command indicates the command is active and all changes to the layout of the desktop will be saved when you quit Windows. If the command is preceded by a check mark, choose the Save Settings from Exit command by clicking the left mouse button to remove the check mark, so the changes will not be saved. Perform the following steps to verify that changes are not saved to the desktop.

TO VERIFY CHANGES ARE NOT SAVED TO THE DESKTOP ▼

STEP 1 ▶

Select Options on the Program Manager menu bar, and then point to the Save Settings on Exit command.

The Options menu opens (Figure 1-69). A check mark (✓) precedes the Save Settings on Exit command.

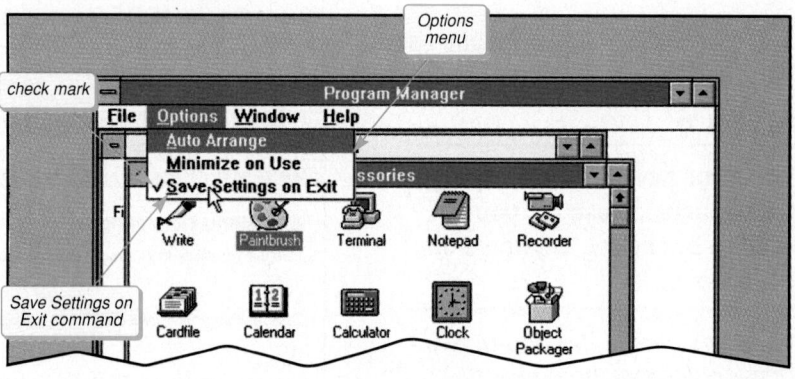

FIGURE 1-69

STEP 2 ▶

To remove the check mark, choose the Save Settings on Exit command from the Options menu by clicking the left mouse button.

Windows closes the Options menu (Figure 1-70). Although not visible in Figure 1-70, the check mark preceding the Save Settings from Exit command has been removed. This means any changes made to the desktop will not be saved when you exit Windows.

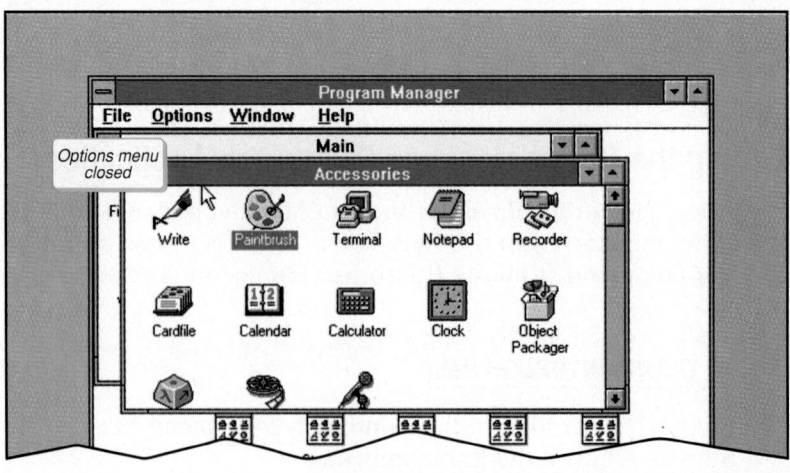

FIGURE 1-70

Quitting Windows Without Saving Changes

After verifying the Save Settings on Exit command is not active, quit Windows by choosing the Exit Windows command from the File menu, as shown below.

TO QUIT WINDOWS ▼

STEP 1 ►

Select File on the Program Manager menu bar, and then point to the Exit Windows command.

Windows opens the File menu and the mouse pointer points to the Exit Windows command (Figure 1-71).

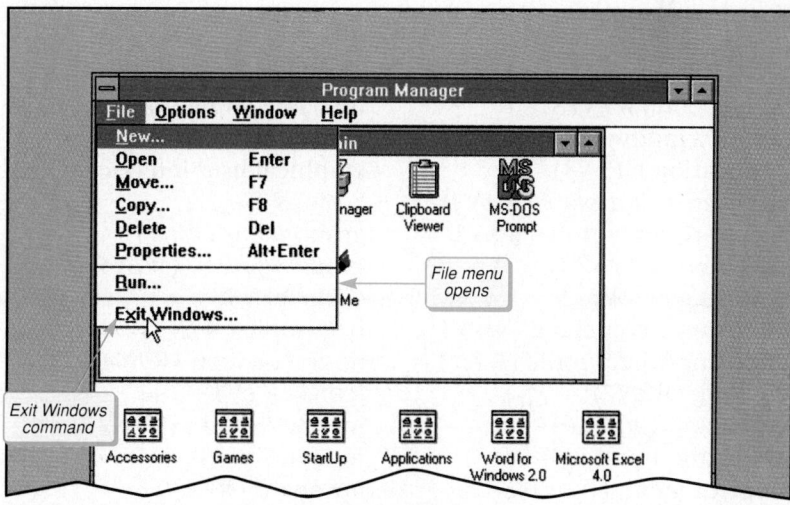

FIGURE 1-71

STEP 2 ►

Choose the Exit Windows command from the File menu by clicking the left mouse button and point to the OK button.

The Exit Windows dialog box opens and contains the message, This will end your Windows session., and the OK and Cancel buttons (Figure 1-72). Choosing the OK button exits Windows. Choosing the Cancel button cancels the exit from Windows and returns you to the Program Manager window. The mouse pointer points to the OK button.

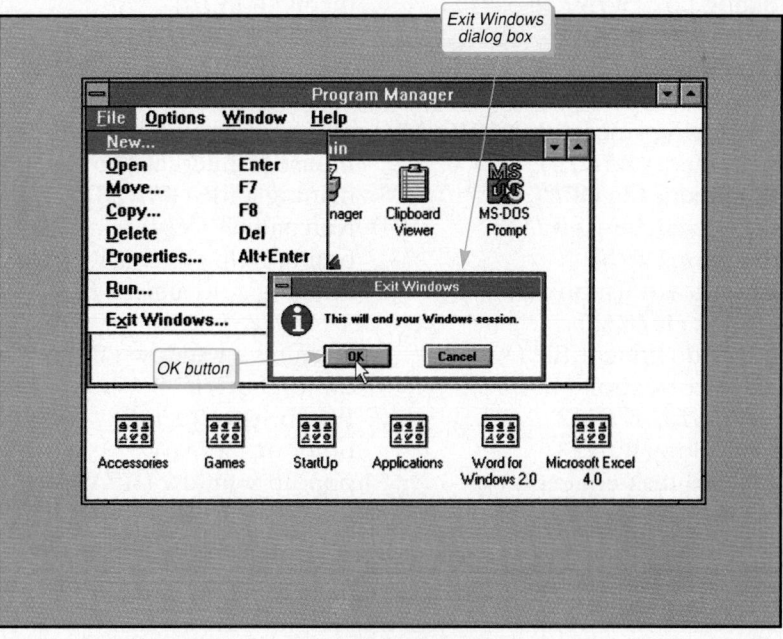

STEP 3 ►

Choose the OK button by clicking the left mouse button.

When you quit Windows, all windows are removed from the desktop and control is returned to the DOS operating system.

FIGURE 1-72

▶ PROJECT SUMMARY

In this project you learned about user interfaces and the Microsoft Windows graphical user interface. You started and exited Windows and learned the parts of a window. You started Notepad, entered and printed a note, edited the note, opened and saved files, and exited the applications. You opened group windows, maximized application windows, and scrolled the windows. You used the mouse to select a menu, choose a command from a menu, and respond to dialog boxes. You used Windows online Help to obtain help about the Paintbrush application.

▶ KEY TERMS

active icon (*WIN18*)
active window (*WIN15*)
application (*WIN3*)
application software (*WIN3*)
application window (*WIN5*)
check box (*WIN13*)
choosing (*WIN11*)
choosing a command (*WIN11*)
choosing a help topic (*WIN33*)
clicking (*WIN7*)
command (*WIN10*)
command button (*WIN13*)
Control menu (*WIN16*)
creating a document (*WIN19*)
current selection (*WIN13*)
desktop (*WIN4*)
dialog box (*WIN12*)
directory (*WIN23*)
directory path (*WIN24*)
directory structure (*WIN24*)
displaying a definition (*WIN35*)
document (*WIN14*)
document file (*WIN23*)
double-clicking (*WIN8*)
dragging (*WIN9*)
drop-down list box (*WIN13*)
ellipsis (*WIN11*)
edit a document file (*WIN31*)
error correction (*WIN16,*
  WIN18, WIN27)
extension (*WIN23*)
file and disk concepts
  (*WIN22–WIN24*)

filename (*WIN23*)
formatting (*WIN27*)
graphical user interface (GUI)
  (*WIN3*)
group icons (*WIN5*)
group window (*WIN5*)
GUI (*WIN3*)
help topic (*WIN33*)
hourglass icon (*WIN4*)
icons (*WIN5*)
insertion point (*WIN17*)
jump (*WIN33*)
keyboard (*WIN9*)
keyboard shortcuts (*WIN10*)
Maximize button (*WIN18*)
maximizing a window (*WIN18*)
menu (*WIN10*)
menu bar (*WIN10*)
Microsoft Windows (*WIN2*)
mouse (*WIN5*)
mouse operations (*WIN6–WIN9*)
mouse pointer (*WIN6*)
naming a file (*WIN23*)
Notepad (*WIN14*)
online Help (*WIN32*)
opening a document file
  (*WIN28*)
opening a window (*WIN14*)
option button (*WIN12*)
Paintbrush (*WIN32*)
pointing (*WIN6*)
pop-up window (*WIN35*)

printing a document (*WIN20*)
Program Manager (*WIN5*)
program-item icons (*WIN5*)
quitting an application (*WIN21,*
  WIN28)
quitting Windows (*WIN36*)
Restore button (*WIN18*)
root directory (*WIN23*)
saving a document (*WIN24*)
saving a modified document file
  (*WIN31*)
scroll arrows (*WIN16*)
scroll bar (*WIN16*)
scroll box (*WIN16*)
selected button (*WIN12*)
selecting (*WIN11*)
selecting a menu (*WIN11*)
starting an application (*WIN16*)
starting Microsoft Windows
  (*WIN4*)
subdirectory (*WIN23*)
text box (*WIN13*)
title bar (*WIN4*)
user friendly (*WIN3*)
user interface (*WIN3*)
using Windows help (*WIN32*)
window (*WIN4*)
window border (*WIN4*)
window title (*WIN4*)
Windows (*WIN2*)
write-protected diskette
  (*WIN27*)

In Microsoft Windows you can accomplish a task in a number of ways. The following table provides a quick reference to each task presented in this project with it available options. The commands listed in the Menu column can be executed using either the keyboard or mouse.

Task	Mouse	Menu	Keyboard Shortcuts
Choose a Command from a menu	Click command name, or drag highlight to command name and release mouse button		Press underlined character; or press arrow keys to select command, and press ENTER
Choose a Help Topic	Click Help topic		Press TAB, ENTER
Display a Definition	Click definition		Press TAB, ENTER
Enlarge an Application Window	Click Maximize button	From Control menu, choose Maximize	
Obtain Online Help		From Help menu, choose Contents	Press F1
Open a Document		From File menu, choose Open	
Open a Group Window	Double-click group icon	From Window menu, choose group window name	Press CTRL + F6 (or CTRL + TAB) to select group icon, and press ENTER
Print a File		From File menu, choose Print	
Quit an Application	Double-click control menu box, click OK button	From File menu, choose Exit	
Quit Windows	Double-click Control menu box, click OK button	From File menu, choose Exit Windows, choose OK button	
Remove a Definition	Click open space on desktop		Press ENTER
Save a Document on Disk		From File menu, choose Save As	
Save an Edited Document on Disk		From File menu, choose Save	
Save Changes when Quitting Windows		From Options menu, choose Save Settings on Exit if no check mark precedes command	
Save No Changes when Quitting Windows		From Options menu, choose Save Settings on Exit if check mark precedes command	
Scroll a Window	Click up or down arrow, drag scroll box, click scroll bar		Press UP or DOWN ARROW
Select a Menu	Click menu name on menu bar		Press ALT + underlined character (or F10 + underlined character)
Start an Application	Double-click program-item icon	From File menu, choose Open	Press arrow keys to select program-item icon, and press ENTER

STUDENT ASSIGNMENT 1
True/False

Instructions: Circle T if the statement is true or F if the statement is false.

T F 1. A user interface is a combination of computer hardware and computer software.
T F 2. Microsoft Windows is a graphical user interface.
T F 3. The Program Manager window is a group window.
T F 4. The desktop is the screen background on which windows are displayed.
T F 5. A menu is a small picture that can represent an application or a group of applications.
T F 6. Clicking means quickly pressing and releasing a mouse button twice without moving the mouse.
T F 7. CTRL + SHIFT + LEFT ARROW is an example of a keyboard shortcut.
T F 8. You can carry out an action in an application by choosing a command from a menu.
T F 9. Selecting means marking an item.
T F 10. Windows opens a dialog box to supply information, allow you to enter information, or select among several options.
T F 11. A program-item icon represents a group of applications.
T F 12. You open a group window by pointing to its icon and double-clicking the left mouse button.
T F 13. A scroll bar allows you to view areas of a window that are not currently visible.
T F 14. Notepad and Paintbrush are applications.
T F 15. Choosing the Restore button maximizes a window to its maximize size.
T F 16. APPLICATION.TXT is a valid name for a document file.
T F 17. The directory structure is the relationship between the root directory and any subdirectories.
T F 18. You save a new document on disk by choosing the Save As command from the File menu.
T F 19. You open a document by choosing the Retrieve command from the File menu.
T F 20. Help is available while using Windows only in the *User's Guide* that accompanies the Windows software.

STUDENT ASSIGNMENT 2
Multiple Choice

Instructions: Circle the correct response.

1. Through a user interface, the user is able to _____.
   a. control the computer
   b. request information from the computer
   c. respond to messages displayed by the computer
   d. all of the above
2. _____ is quickly pressing and releasing a mouse button twice without moving the mouse.
   a. Double-clicking
   b. Clicking
   c. Dragging
   d. Pointing

3. To view the commands in a menu, you _____ the menu name.
   a. choose
   b. maximize
   c. close
   d. select
4. A _____ is a window that displays to supply information, allow you to enter information, or choose among several options.
   a. group window
   b. dialog box
   c. application window
   d. drop-down list box
5. A _____ is a rectangular area in which Windows displays text or you enter text.
   a. dialog box
   b. text box
   c. drop-down list box
   d. list box
6. The title bar of one group window that is a different color or intensity than the title bars of the other group windows indicates a(n) _____ window.
   a. inactive
   b. application
   c. group
   d. active
7. To view an area of a window that is not currently visible in a window, use the _____.
   a. title bar
   b. scroll bar
   c. menu bar
   d. Restore button
8. The _____ menu in the Notepad application contains the Save, Open, and Print commands.
   a. Window
   b. Options
   c. Help
   d. File
9. Before exiting Windows, you should check the _____ command to verify that no changes to the desktop will be saved.
   a. Open
   b. Exit Windows
   c. Save Settings on Exit
   d. Save Changes
10. Online Help is available for all applications except _____.
   a. Program Manager
   b. Calendar
   c. Clock
   d. File Manager

STUDENT ASSIGNMENT 3
Identifying Items in the Program Manager Window

Instructions: On the desktop in Figure SA1-3, arrows point to several items in the Program Manager window. Identify the items in the space provided.

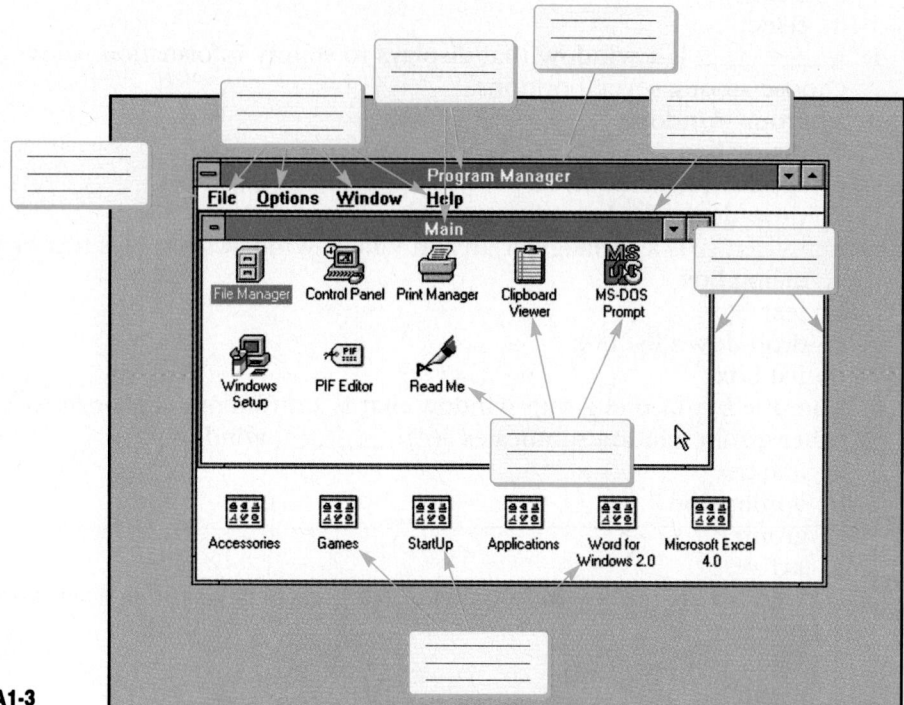

FIGURE SA1-3

STUDENT ASSIGNMENT 4
Starting an Application

Instructions: Using the desktop shown in Figure SA1-4, list the steps in the space provided to open the Accessories window and start the Notepad application.

Step 1: _____

_____

_____

Step 2: _____

_____

_____

Step 3: _____

_____

_____

Step 4: _____

_____

_____

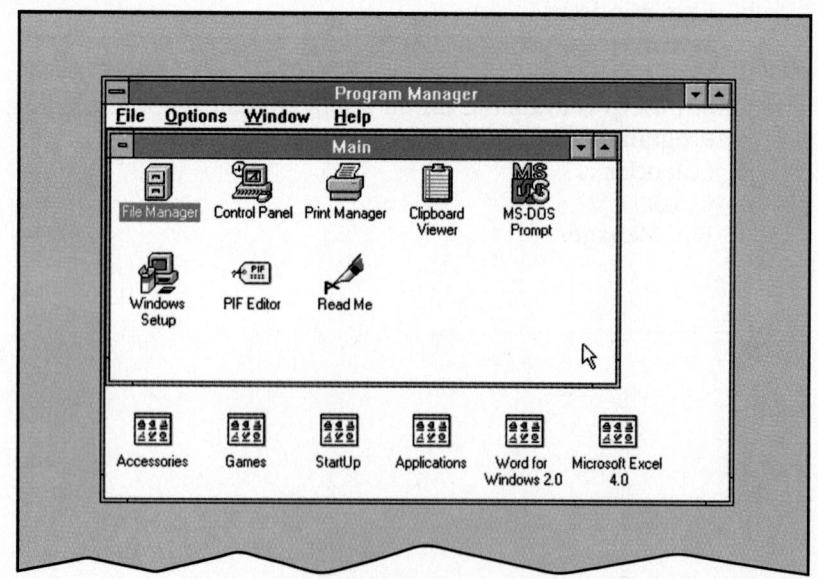

FIGURE SA1-4

COMPUTER LABORATORY EXERCISE 1
Improving Your Mouse Skills

Instructions: Use a computer to perform the following tasks.

1. Start Microsoft Windows.
2. Double-click the Games group icon (📅 Games) to open the Games window if necessary.
3. Double-click the Solitaire program-item icon (🂠).
4. Click the Maximize button to maximize the Solitaire window.
5. From the Help menu in the Solitaire window (Figure CLE1-1), choose the Contents command. One-by-one click on the help topics in green. Double-click on the Control-menu box in the title bar of the Solitaire Help window to close it.
6. Play the game of Solitaire.
7. To quit Solitaire choose the Exit command from the Game menu.

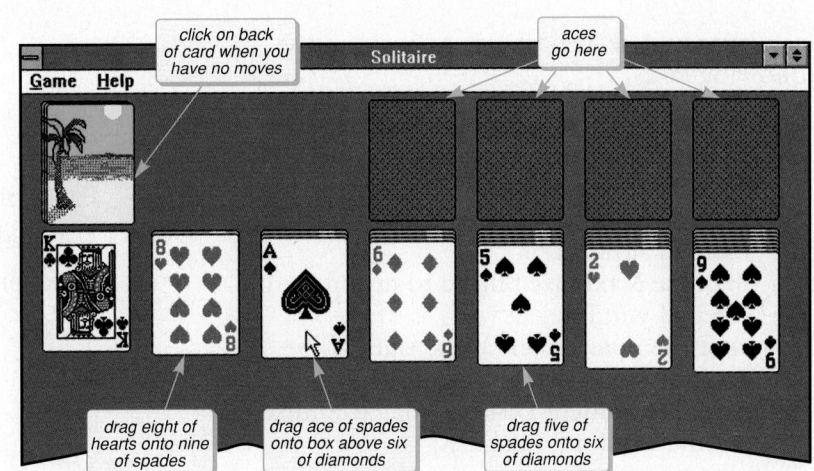

FIGURE CLE1-1

COMPUTER LABORATORY EXERCISE 2
Windows Tutorial

Instructions: Use a computer to perform the following tasks.

1. Start Microsoft Windows.
2. From the Help menu in the Program Manager window, choose the Windows Tutorial command.
3. Type the letter M. Follow the instructions (Figure CLE1-2) to step through the mouse practice lesson. Press the ESC key to exit the tutorial.
4. From the Help menu in the Program Manager window, choose the Windows Tutorial command.

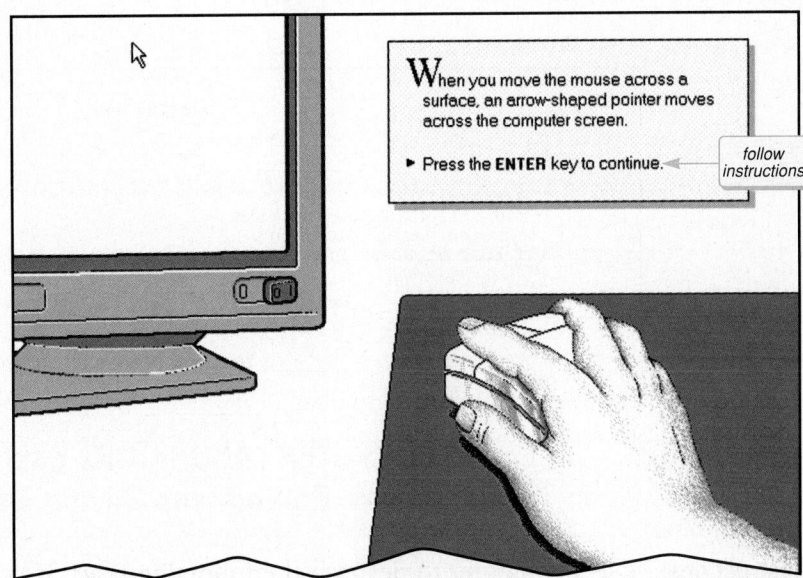

FIGURE CLE1-2

5. Type the letter W. Click the Instructions button (Instructions) and read the information. When you are finished, choose the Return to the Tutorial button (Return to the Tutorial). Next choose the Contents button (Contents) in the lower right corner of the screen.
6. Choose the second item (Starting an Application) from the Contents list. The Windows tutorial will step you through the remaining lessons. Respond as needed to the questions and instructions. Press the ESC key to exit the tutorial.

COMPUTER LABORATORY EXERCISE 3
Creating, Saving, and Printing Documents

Instructions: Use a computer to perform the following tasks.

1. Start Microsoft Windows if necessary.
2. Double-click the Accessories icon to open the Accessories window.
3. Double-click the Notepad icon to start the Notepad application.
4. Click the Maximize button to maximize the Notepad window.
5. Enter the note shown at the right at the insertion point on the screen.
6. Insert the Student Diskette that accompanies this book into drive A.
7. Select the File menu on the Notepad menu bar.
8. Choose the Save As command.
9. Enter grocery in the File Name text box.
10. Change the current selection in the Drives drop-down list box to a:.
11. Click the OK button to save the document on drive A.
12. Select the File menu on the Notepad menu bar.
13. Choose the Print command to print the document on the printer (Figure CLE1-3).
14. Remove the Student Diskette from drive A.
15. Select the File menu on the Notepad menu bar.
16. Choose the Exit command to quit Notepad.

Grocery List —
1/2 Gallon of Low Fat Milk
1 Dozen Medium Size Eggs
1 Loaf of Wheat Bread

```
                              GROCERY.TXT



          Grocery List -
          1/2 Gallon of Low Fat Milk
          1 Dozen Medium Size Eggs
          1 Loaf of Wheat Bread
```

FIGURE CLE1-3

COMPUTER LABORATORY EXERCISE 4
Opening, Editing, and Saving Documents

Instructions: Use a computer to perform the following tasks. If you have questions on how to procede, use the Calendar Help menu.

1. Start Microsoft Windows if necessary.
2. Double-click the Accessories icon to open the Accessories window.
3. Double-click the Calendar icon (🗓) to start the Calendar application.
4. Click the Maximize button to maximize the Calendar window.
5. Insert the Student Diskette that accompanies this book into drive A.
6. Select the File menu on the Calendar menu bar.

7. Choose the Open command.
8. Change the current selection in the Drives drop-down list box to a:.
9. Select the thompson.cal filename in the File Name list box. The THOMPSON.CAL file contains the daily appointments for Mr. Thompson.
10. Click the OK button in the Open dialog box to open the THOMPSON.CAL document. The document on your screen is shown in Figure CLE1-4a.
11. Click the Left or Right Scroll arrow repeatedly to locate the appointments for Thursday, September 29, 1994.
12. Make the changes shown below to the document.

TIME	CHANGE
11:00 AM	Stay at Auto Show one more hour
2:00 PM	Change the Designer's Meeting from 2:00 PM to 3:00 PM
4:00 PM	Remove the Quality Control Meeting

13. Select the File menu on the Calendar menu bar.
14. Choose the Save As command to save the document file on drive A. Use the filename PETER.CAL.
15. Select the File menu on the Calendar menu bar.
16. Choose the Print command.
17. Choose the OK button to print the document on the printer (Figure CLE1-4b).
18. Remove the Student Diskette from drive A.
19. Select the File menu on the Calendar menu bar.
20. Choose the Exit command to quit Calendar.

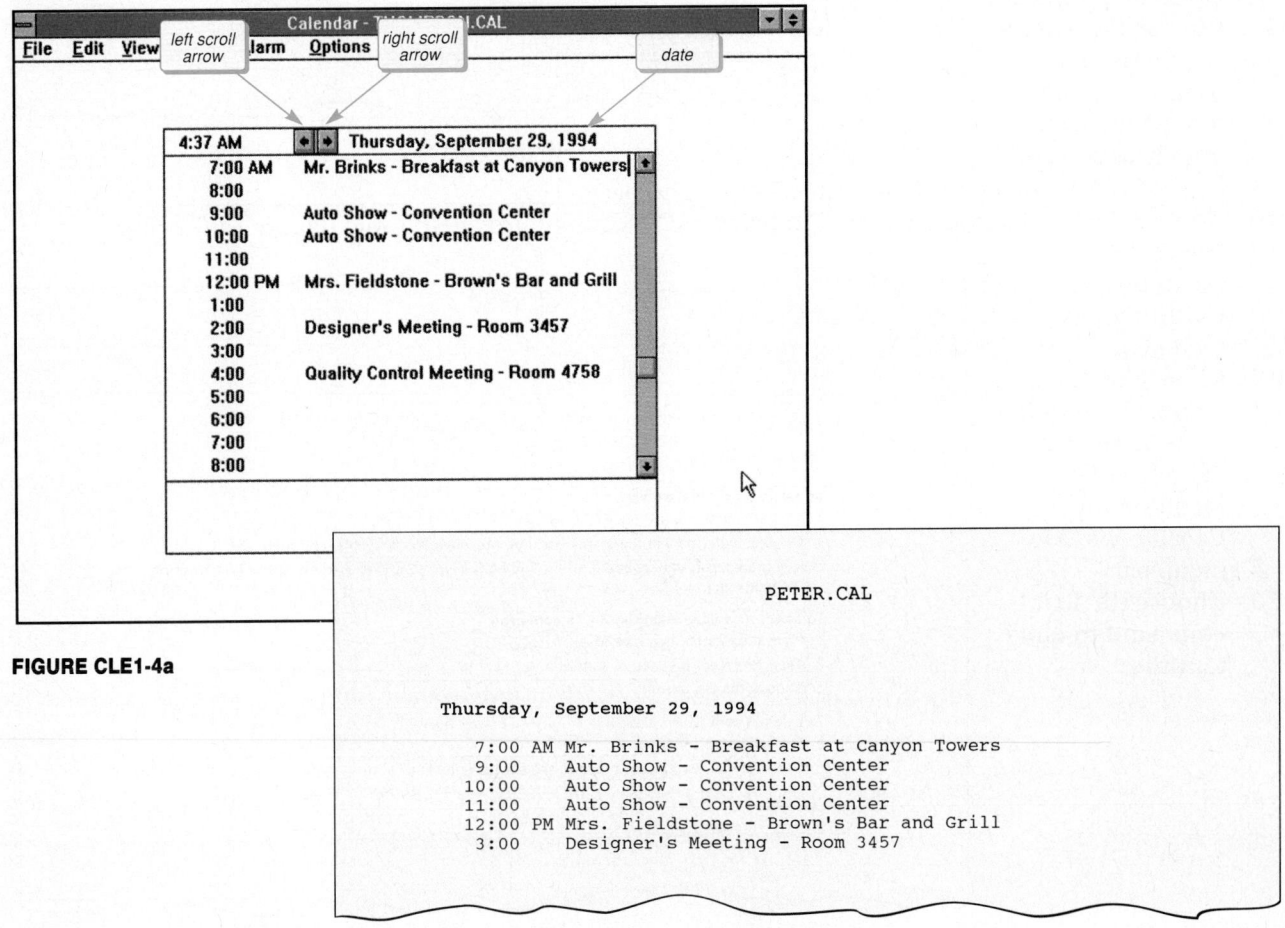

FIGURE CLE1-4a

FIGURE CLE1-4b

COMPUTER LABORATORY EXERCISE 5
Using Online Help

Instructions: Use a computer to perform the following tasks.

1. Start Microsoft Windows if necessary.
2. Double-click the Accessories icon to open the Accessories window.
3. Double-click the Cardfile icon (📒) to start the Cardfile application.
4. Select the Help menu.
5. Choose the Contents command.
6. Click the Maximize button to maximize the Cardfile Help window.
7. Choose the Add More Cards help topic.
8. Select the File menu on the Cardfile Help menu bar.
9. Choose the Print Topic command to print the Adding More Cards help topic on the printer (Figure CLE1-5a).
10. Display the definition of the term, index line.
11. Remove the index line definition from the desktop.
12. Choose the Contents button.
13. Choose the Delete Cards help topic.
14. Choose the Selecting Cards help topic at the bottom of the Deleting Cards screen.

Adding More Cards

Cardfile adds new cards in the correct alphabetic order and scrolls to display the new card at the front.

To add a new card to a file
1 From the Card menu, choose Add.
2 Type the text you want to appear on the index line.
3 Choose the OK button.
4 In the information area, type text.

FIGURE CLE1-5a

---

15. Select the File menu on the Cardfile Help menu bar.
16. Choose the Print Topic command to print the Selecting Cards help topic (Figure CLE 1-5b).
17. Select the File menu on the Cardfile Help menu bar.
18. Choose the Exit command to quit Cardfile Help.
19. Select the File menu on the Cardfile window menu bar.
20. Choose the Exit command to quit Cardfile.

Selecting Cards

To select a card in Card view
▶ Click the card's index line if it is visible.
   Or click the arrows in the status bar until the index line is visible, and then click it.
   If you are using the keyboard, press and hold down CTRL+SHIFT and type the first letter of the index line.

To select a card by using the Go To command
1 From the Search menu, choose Go To.
2 Type text from the card's index line.
3 Choose the OK button.

To select a card in List view
▶ Click the card's index line.
   Or use the arrow keys to move to the card's index line.

See Also
Moving Through a Card File

FIGURE CLE1-5b

MICROSOFT WINDOWS 3.1

PROJECT TWO

▼

DISK AND FILE MANAGEMENT

OBJECTIVES You will have mastered the material in this project when you can:

▸ Identify the elements of the directory tree window
▸ Understand the concepts of diskette size and capacity
▸ Format and copy a diskette
▸ Select and copy one file or a group of files
▸ Change the current drive
▸ Rename or delete a file

▸ Create a backup diskette
▸ Search for help topics using Windows online Help
▸ Switch between applications
▸ Activate, resize, and close a group window
▸ Arrange the icons in a group window
▸ Minimize an application window to an icon

▸ INTRODUCTION

File Manager is an application included with Windows that allows you to organize and work with your hard disk and diskettes and the files on those disks. In this project, you will use File Manager to (1) format a diskette; (2) copy files between the hard disk and a diskette; (3) copy a diskette; (4) rename a file on diskette; and (5) delete a file from diskette.

Formatting a diskette and copying files to a diskette are common operations illustrated in this project that you should understand how to perform. While performing the Computer Laboratory Exercises and the Computer Laboratory Assignments at the end of each application project, you will save documents on a diskette that accompanies this textbook. To prevent the accidental loss of stored documents on a diskette, it is important to periodically make a copy of the entire diskette. A copy of a diskette is called a **backup diskette**. In this project, you will learn how to create a backup diskette to protect against the accidental loss of documents on a diskette.

You will also use Windows online Help in this project. In Project 1, you obtained help by choosing a topic from a list of help topics. In this project, you will use the Search feature to search for help topics.

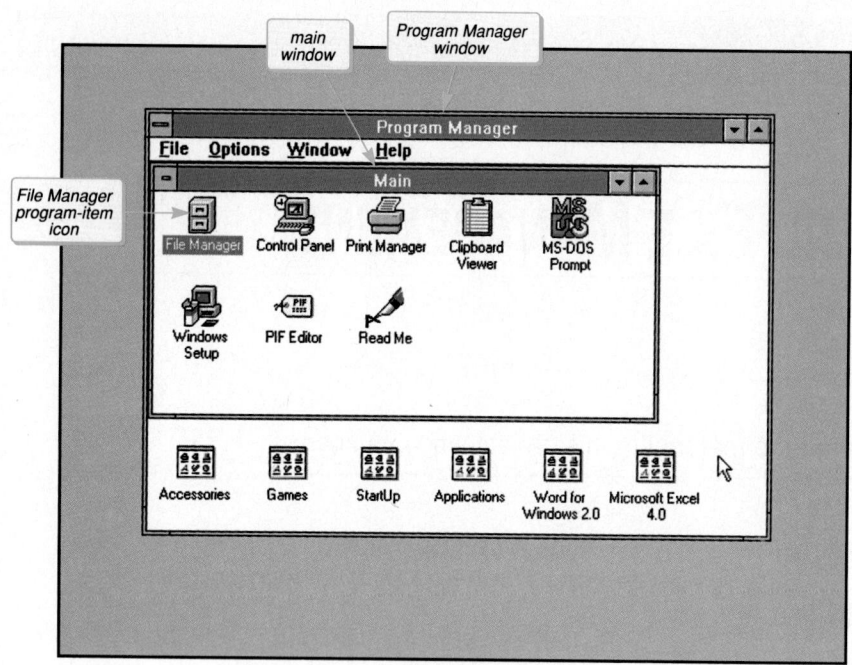

FIGURE 2-1

STARTING WINDOWS

As explained in Project 1, when you turn on the computer, an introductory screen consisting of the Windows logo, Windows name, version number, and copyright notices displays momentarily. Next, a blank screen containing an hourglass icon displays. Finally, the Program Manager and Main windows open on the desktop (Figure 2-1). The File Manager program-item icon displays in the Main window. If your desktop does not look similar to the desktop in Figure 2-1, your instructor will inform you of the modifications necessary to change your desktop.

Starting File Manager and Maximizing the File Manager Window

To start File Manager, double-click the File Manager icon ( ) in the Main window. To maximize the File Manager window, choose the Maximize button on the File Manager window by pointing to the Maximize button and clicking the left mouse button.

TO START AN APPLICATION AND MAXIMIZE ITS WINDOW ▼

STEP 1 ▶

Double-click the File Manager icon in the Main window (see Figure 2-1), then click the Maximize button on the File Manager title bar.

Windows opens and maximizes the File Manager window (Figure 2-2).

FIGURE 2-2

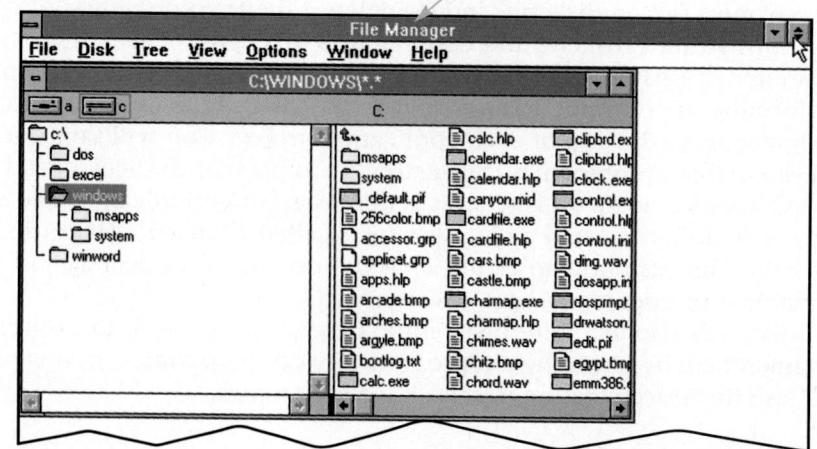

▶ FILE MANAGER

W hen you start File Manager, Windows opens the File Manager window (Figure 2-3). The menu bar contains the File, Disk, Tree, View, Options, Window, and Help menus. These menus contain the commands to organize and work with the disks and the files on those disks.

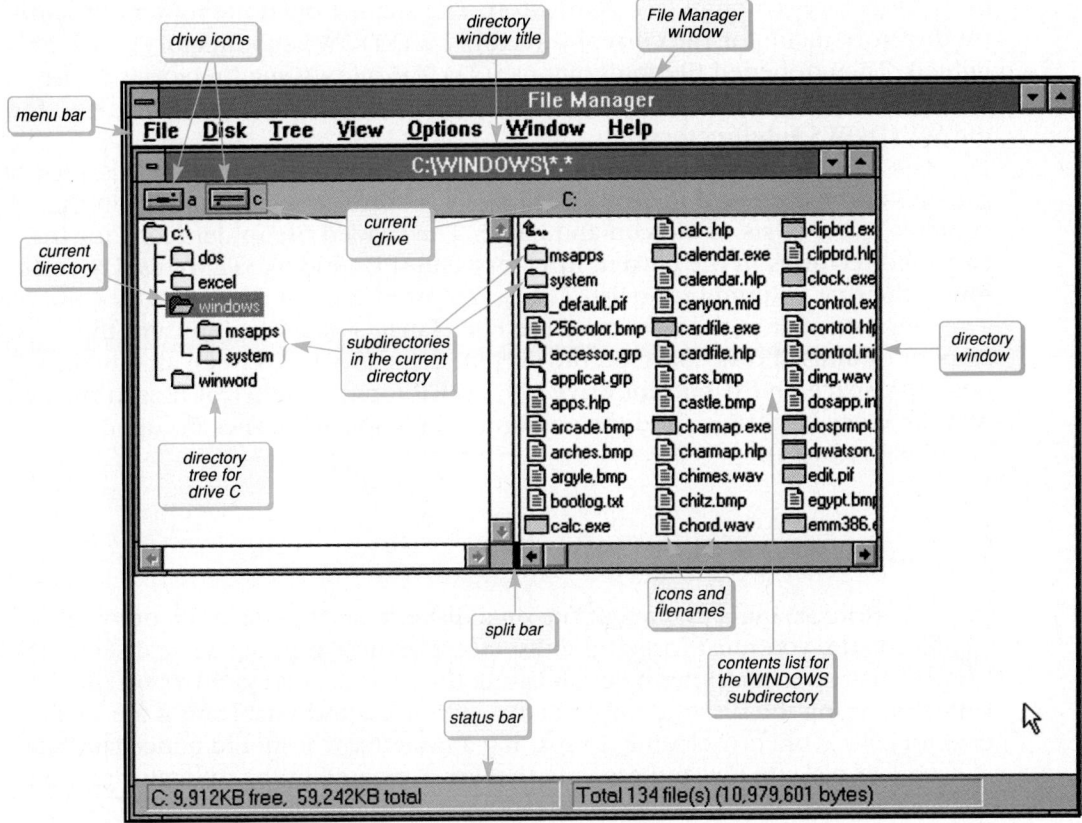

FIGURE 2-3

Below the menu bar is a **directory window** titled C:\WINDOWS*.*. The window title consists of a directory path (C:\WINDOWS), backslash (\), and filename (*.*). The directory path is the path of the current directory on drive C (WINDOWS subdirectory). The backslash separates the path and filename. The filename (*.*) references a group of files whose filename and extension can be any valid filename and extension.

Below the title bar is a horizontal bar that contains two **drive icons**. The drive icons represent the disk drives attached to the computer. The first drive icon (▣ a:) represents drive A (diskette drive) and the second drive icon (▣ c:) represents drive C (hard drive). Depending upon the number of disk drives attached to your computer, there may be more than two drive icons in the horizontal bar. A rectangular box surrounding the drive C icon indicates drive C is the **current drive**. The entry to the right of the icons (C:) also indicates drive C is the current drive.

The directory window is divided into two equal-sized areas. Each area is separated by a split bar. The **directory tree** in the area on the left contains the directory structure. The **directory tree** in the **directory structure** shows the relationship between the root directory and any subdirectories on the current drive (drive C). You can drag the **split bar** to the left or right to change the size of the two areas.

In the left area, a file folder icon represents each directory or subdirectory in the directory structure (see Figure 2-3). The shaded open file folder (🗁) and subdirectory name for the current directory (WINDOWS subdirectory) are highlighted. The unopened file folder icons (🗀) for the two subdirectories in the WINDOWS subdirectory (MSAPPS and SYSTEM) are indented below the icon for the WINDOWS subdirectory.

The area on the right contains the contents list. The **contents list** is a list of the files in the current directory (WINDOWS subdirectory). Each entry in the contents list consists of an icon and name. The shaded file folder icons for the two subdirectories in the current directory (MSAPPS and SYSTEM) display at the top of the first column in the list.

The status bar at the bottom of the File Manager window indicates the amount of unused disk space on the current drive (9,912KB free), amount of total disk space on the current drive (59,242KB total), number of files in the current directory (134 files), and the amount of disk space the files occupy (10,979,601 bytes).

▶ FORMATTING A DISKETTE

Before saving a document file on a diskette or copying a file onto a diskette, you must format the diskette. **Formatting** prepares a diskette for use on a computer by establishing the sectors and cylinders on the diskette, analyzing the diskette for defective cylinders, and establishing the root directory. To avoid errors while formatting a diskette, you should understand the concepts of diskette size and capacity that are explained in the following section.

Diskette Size and Capacity

How a diskette is formatted is determined by the size of the diskette, capacity of the diskette as established by the diskette manufacturer, and capabilities of the disk drive you use to format the diskette. **Diskette size** is the physical size of the diskette. Common diskette sizes are 5 1/4-inch and 3 1/2-inch.

Diskette capacity is the amount of space on the disk, measured in kilobytes (K) or megabytes (MB), available to store data. A diskette's capacity is established by the diskette manufacturer. Common diskette capacities are 360K and 1.2MB for a 5 1/4-inch diskette and 720K and 1.44MB for a 3 1/2-inch diskette.

A diskette drive's capability is established by the diskette drive manufacturer. There are 3 1/2-inch diskette drives that are capable of formatting a diskette with a capacity of 720K or 1.44MB and there are 5 1/4-inch diskette drives capable of formatting a diskette with a capacity of 360K or 1.2MB.

Before formatting a diskette, you must consider two things. First, the diskette drive you use to format a diskette must be capable of formatting the size of diskette you want to format. You can use a 3 1/2-inch diskette drive to format a 3 1/2-inch diskette, but you cannot use a 3 1/2-inch diskette drive to format a

5 1/4-inch diskette. Similarly, you can use a 5 1/4-inch diskette drive to format a 5 1/4-inch diskette, but you cannot use a 5 1/4-inch diskette drive to format a 3 1/2-inch diskette.

Second, the diskette drive you use to format a diskette must be capable of formatting the capacity of the diskette you want to format. A 5 1/4-inch diskette drive capable of formatting 1.2MB diskettes can be used to either format a 360K or 1.2MB diskette. However, because of the differences in the diskette manufacturing process, you cannot use a diskette drive capable of formatting 360K diskettes to format a 1.2MB diskette. A 3 1/2-inch diskette drive capable of formatting 1.44MB diskettes can be used to format either a 720K or 1.44MB diskette. Since the 1.44 MB diskette is manufactured with two square holes in the plastic cover and the 720K diskette is manufactured with only one square hole, you cannot use a diskette drive capable of formatting 720K diskette to format a 1.44MB diskette.

The computer you use to complete this project should have a 3 1/2-inch diskette drive capable of formatting a diskette with 1.44MB of disk storage. Trying to format a 3 1/2-inch diskette with any other diskette drive may result in an error. Typical errors encountered because of incorrect diskette capacity and diskette drive capabilities are explained later in this project. For more information about the diskette drive you will use to complete the projects in this textbook, contact your instructor.

Formatting a Diskette

To store a file on a diskette, the diskette must already be formatted. If the diskette is not formatted, you must format the diskette using File Manager. When formatting a diskette, use either an unformatted diskette or a diskette containing files you no longer need. Do not format the Student Diskette that accompanies this book.

To format a diskette using File Manager, you insert the diskette into the diskette drive, and then choose the **Format Disk command** from the Disk menu. Perform the following steps to format a diskette.

TO FORMAT A DISKETTE ▼

STEP 1

Insert an unformatted diskette or a formatted diskette containing files you no longer need into drive A.

STEP 2 ▶

Select the Disk menu, and then point to the Format Disk command.

Windows opens the Disk menu (Figure 2-4). The mouse pointer points to the Format Disk command.

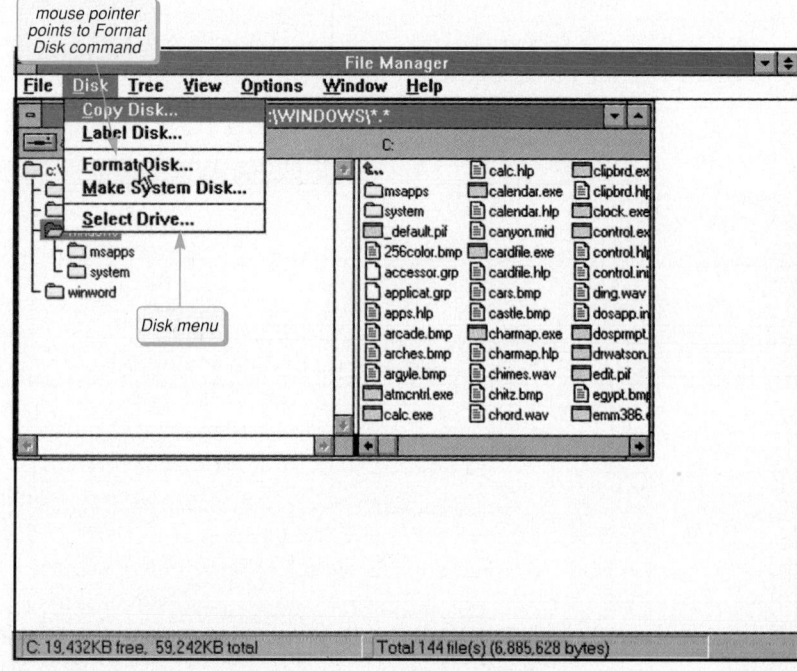

FIGURE 2-4

STEP 3 ▶

Choose the Format Disk command from the Disk menu, and then point to the OK button.

Windows opens the Format Disk dialog box (Figure 2-5). The current selections in the Disk In and Capacity boxes are Drive A: and 1.44 MB, respectively. With these selections, the diskette in drive A will be formatted with a capacity of 1.44MB. The Options list box is not required to format a diskette in this project. The mouse pointer points to the OK button.

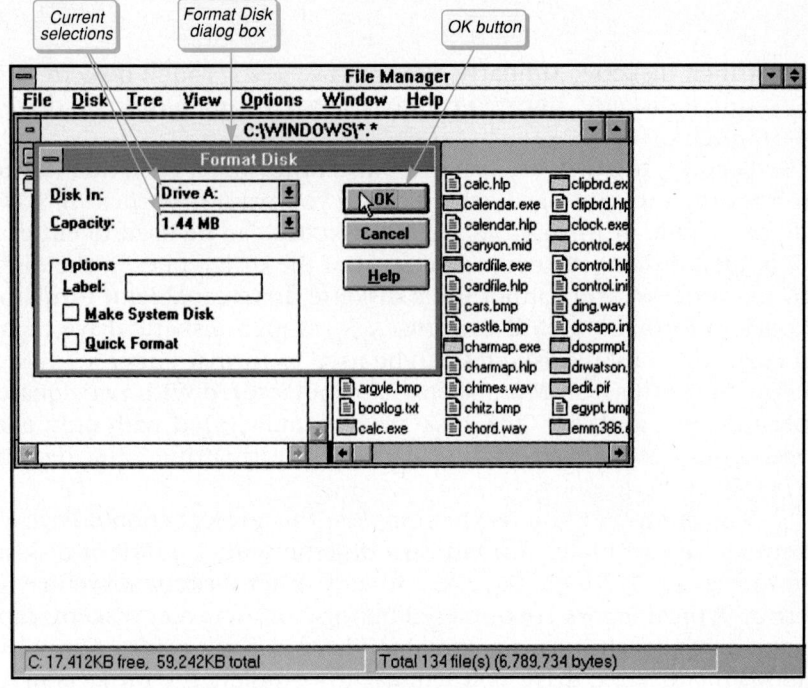

FIGURE 2-5

STEP 4 ▶

Choose the OK button by clicking the left mouse button, and then point to the Yes button.

Windows opens the Confirm Format Disk dialog box (Figure 2-6). This dialog box reminds you that if you continue, Windows will erase all data on the diskette in drive A. The mouse pointer points to the Yes button.

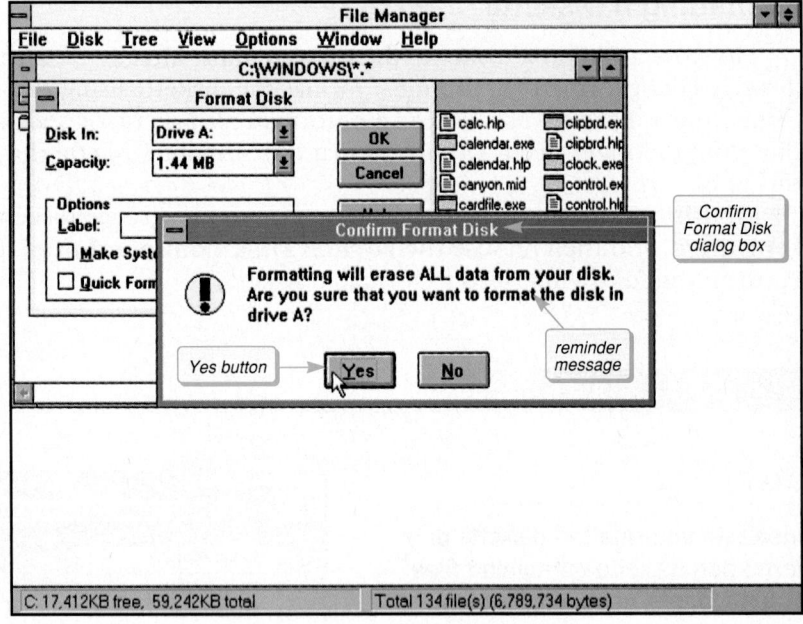

FIGURE 2-6

STEP 5 ▶

Choose the Yes button by clicking the left mouse button.

Windows opens the Formatting Disk dialog box (Figure 2-7). As the formatting process progresses, a value from 1 to 100 indicates what percent of the formatting process is complete. Toward the end of the formatting process, the creating root directory message replaces the 1% completed message to indicate Windows is creating the root directory on the diskette. The formatting process takes approximately two minutes.

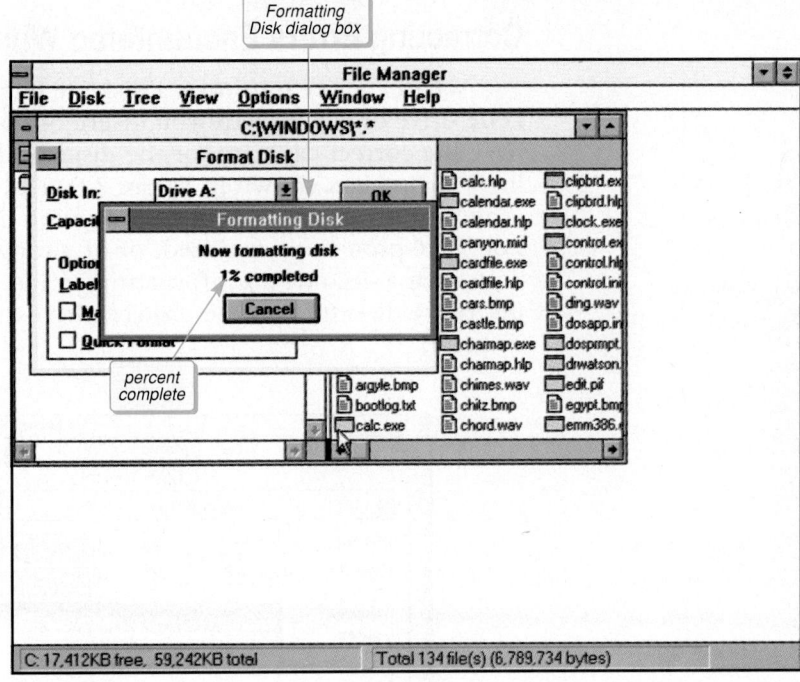

FIGURE 2-7

When the formatting process is complete, Windows opens the Format Complete dialog box (Figure 2-8). The dialog box contains the total disk space (1,457,664 bytes) and available disk space (1,457,664 bytes) of the newly formatted diskette. The values for the total disk space and available disk space in the Format Complete dialog box may be different for your computer.

STEP 6 ▶

Choose the No button by pointing to the No button, and then clicking the left mouse button.

Windows closes the Format Disk and Format Complete dialog boxes.

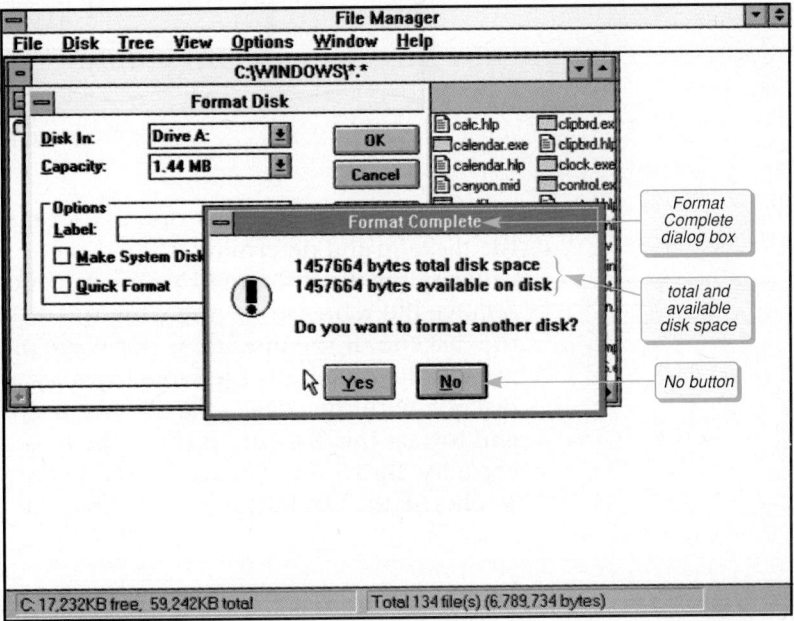

FIGURE 2-8

Correcting Errors Encountered While Formatting a Diskette

When you try to format a diskette but forget to insert a diskette into the diskette drive or the diskette you inserted is write-protected, damaged, or does not have the correct capacity for the diskette drive, Windows opens the Format Disk Error dialog box shown in Figure 2-9. The dialog box contains an error message (Cannot format disk.), a suggested action (Make sure the disk is in the drive and not write-protected, damaged, or of wrong density rating.), and the OK button. To format a diskette after forgetting to insert the diskette into the diskette drive, insert the diskette into the diskette drive, choose the OK button, and format the diskette.

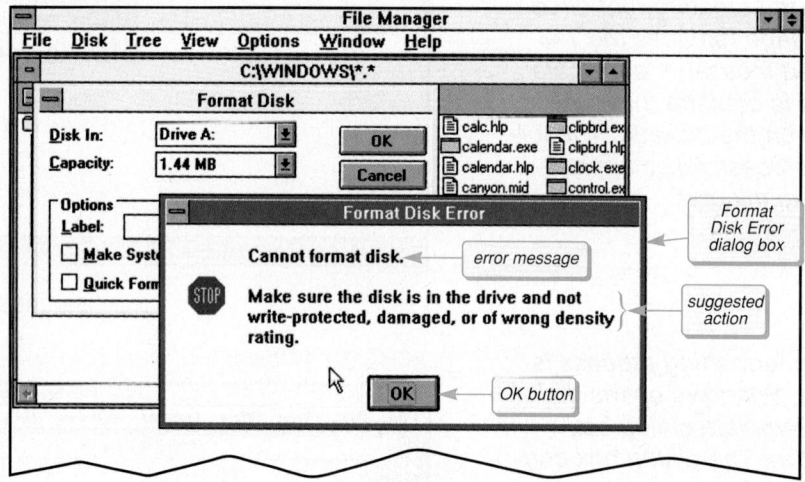

FIGURE 2-9

If the same dialog box opens after inserting a diskette into drive A, remove the diskette and determine if the diskette is write-protected, not the correct capacity for the diskette drive, or damaged. If the diskette is write-protected, remove the write-protection from the diskette, choose the OK button and format the diskette. If the diskette is not write-protected, check the diskette to determine if the diskette is the same capacity as the diskette drive. If it is not, insert a diskette with the correct capacity into the diskette drive, choose the OK button and format the diskette. If the diskette is not write-protected and the correct capacity, throw the damaged diskette away and insert another diskette into drive A, choose the OK button, and format the new diskette.

▶ COPYING FILES TO A DISKETTE

After formatting a diskette, you can save files on the diskette or copy files to the diskette from the hard drive or another diskette. You can easily copy a single file or group of files from one directory to another directory using File Manager. When copying files, the drive and directory containing the files to be copied are called the **source drive** and **source directory**, respectively. The drive and directory to which the files are copied are called the **destination drive** and **destination directory**, respectively.

To copy a file, select the filename in the contents list and drag the high-lighted filename to the destination drive icon or destination directory icon. Groups of files are copied in a similar fashion. You select the filenames in the contents list and drag the highlighted group of filenames to the destination drive or destination directory icon. In this project, you will copy a group of files consisting of the ARCADE.BMP, CARS.BMP, and EGYPT.BMP files from the WINDOWS subdirectory of drive C to the root directory of the diskette that you formatted earlier in this project. Before copying the files, maximize the directory window to make it easier to view the contents of the window.

Maximizing the Directory Window

To enlarge the C:\WINDOWS*.* window, click the Maximize button on the right side of the directory window title bar. When you maximize a directory window, the window fills the File Manager window.

TO MAXIMIZE A DIRECTORY WINDOW ▼

STEP 1 ►

Click the Maximize button on the right side of the C:\WINDOWS*.* window title bar.

The directory window fills the File Manager window (Figure 2-10). Windows changes the File Manager window title to contain the directory window title (File Manager - [C:\WINDOWS*.]) and removes the title bar of the directory tree window. A Restore button displays at the right side of the File Manager menu bar. Clicking the Restore button returns the directory window to its previous size.*

FIGURE 2-10

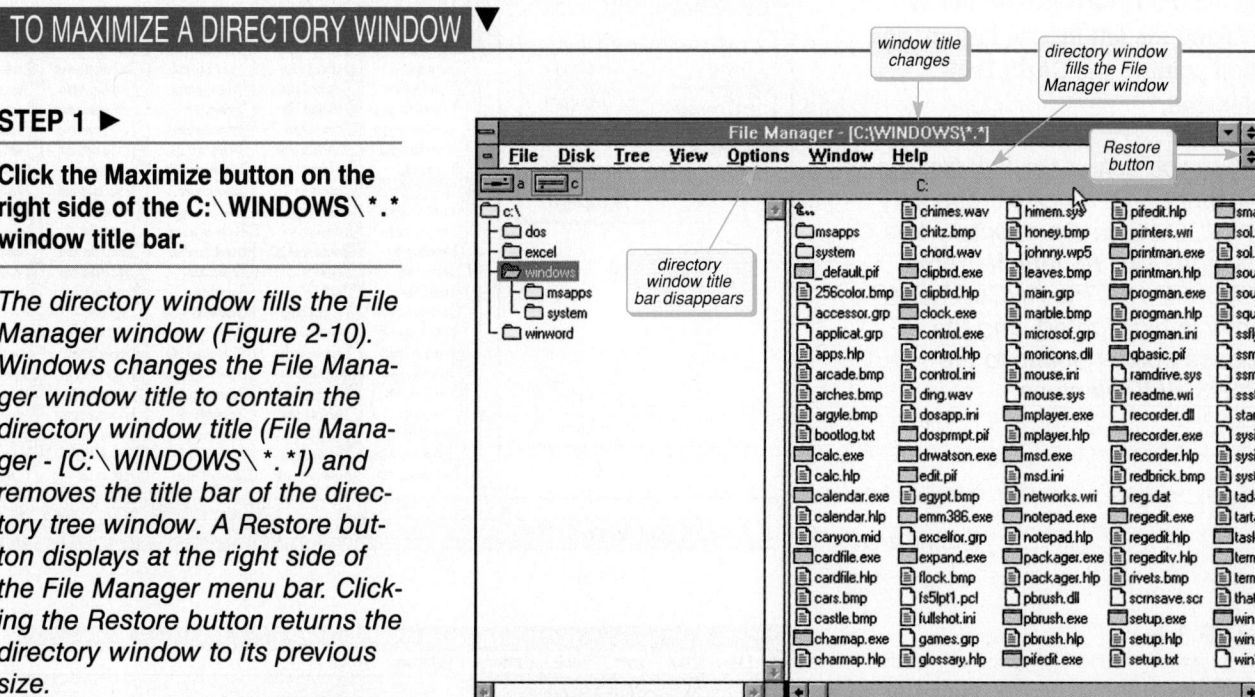

Selecting a Group of Files

Before copying a group of files, you must select (highlight) each file in the contents list. You select the first file in a group of files by pointing to its icon or filename and clicking the left mouse button. You select the remaining files in the group by pointing to each file icon or filename, holding down the CTRL key, clicking the left mouse button, and releasing the CTRL key. The steps on the following pages show how to select the group of files consisting of the ARCADE.BMP, CARS.BMP, and EGYPT.BMP files.

TO SELECT A GROUP OF FILES ▼

STEP 1 ▶

Point to the ARCADE.BMP file-name in the contents list (Figure 2-11).

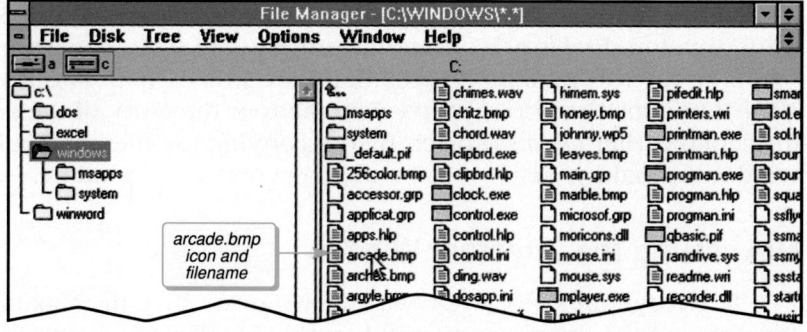

FIGURE 2-11

STEP 2 ▶

Select the ARCADE.BMP file by clicking the left mouse button, and then point to the CARS.BMP filename.

When you select the first file, the highlight on the current directory (WINDOWS) in the directory tree changes to a rectangular box (Figure 2-12). The ARCADE.BMP entry is highlighted, and the mouse pointer points to the CARS.BMP filename.

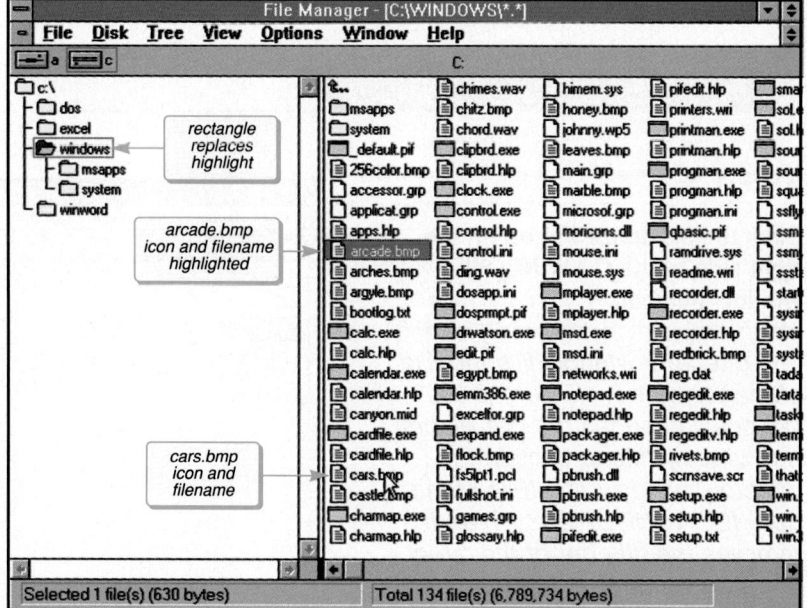

FIGURE 2-12

STEP 3 ▶

Hold down the CTRL key, click the left mouse button, release the CTRL key, and then point to the EGYPT.BMP filename.

Two files, ARCADE.BMP and CARS.BMP are highlighted (Figure 2-13). The mouse pointer points to the EGYPT.BMP filename.

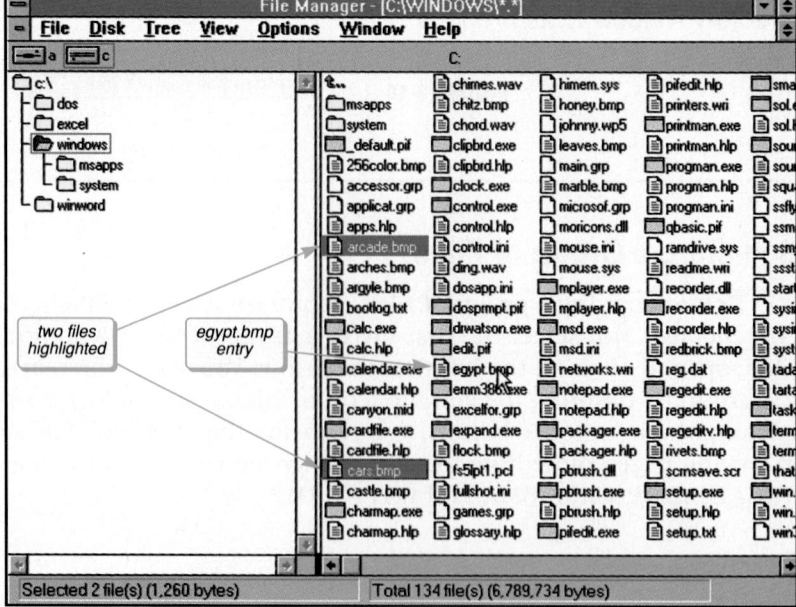

FIGURE 2-13

STEP 4 ▶

Hold down the CTRL key, click the left mouse button, and then release the CTRL key.

The group of files consisting of the ARCADE.BMP, CARS.BMP, and EGYPT.BMP files is highlighted (Figure 2-14).

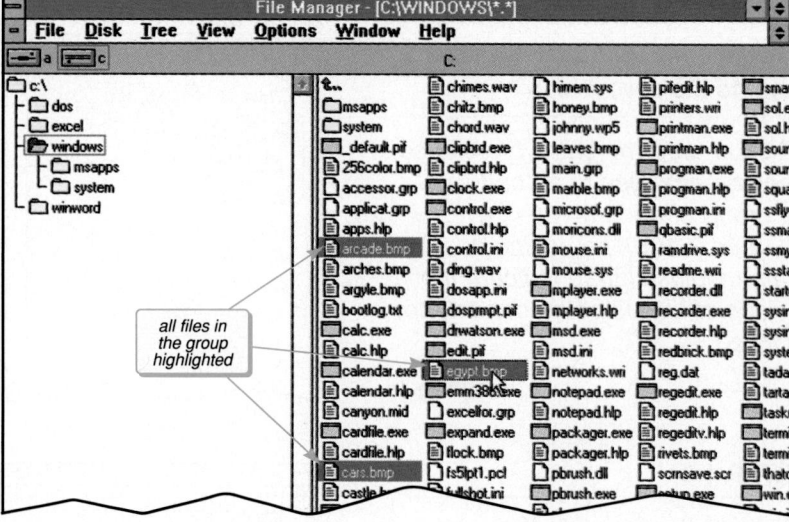

FIGURE 2-14

The ARCADE.BMP, CARS,BMP, and EGYPT.BMP files in Figure 2-14 are not located next to each other (sequentially) in the contents list. To select this group of files you selected the first file by pointing to its filename and clicking the left mouse button. Then, you selected each of the other files by pointing to their filenames, holding down the CTRL key, and clicking the left mouse button. If a group of files is located sequentially in the contents list, you select the group by pointing to the first filename in the list and clicking the left mouse button, and then hold down the SHIFT key, point to the last filename in the group and click the left mouse button.

Copying a Group of Files

After selecting each file in the group, insert the formatted diskette into drive A, and then copy the files to drive A by pointing to any highlighted filename and dragging the filename to the drive A icon.

TO COPY A GROUP OF FILES ▼

STEP 1

Verify that the formatted diskette is in drive A.

STEP 2 ▶

Point to the highlighted ARCADE.BMP entry (Figure 2-15).

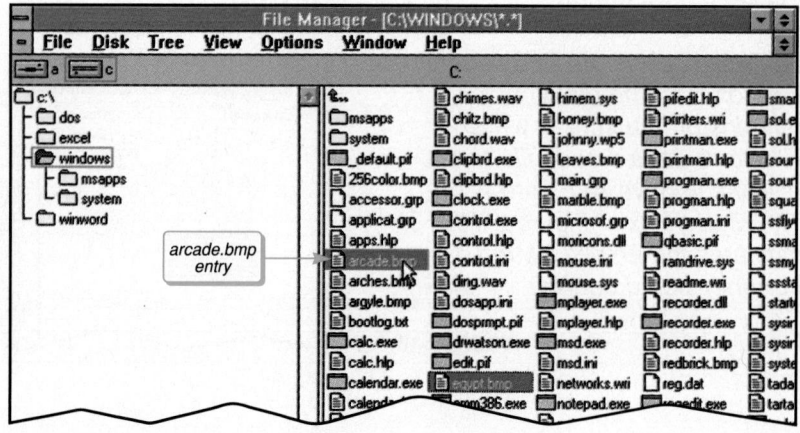

FIGURE 2-15

STEP 3 ▶

Drag the ARCADE.BMP filename over to the drive A icon.

As you drag the entry, the mouse pointer changes to an outline of a group of documents (🗐) (Figure 2-16). The outline contains a plus sign to indicate the group of files is being copied, not moved.

FIGURE 2-16

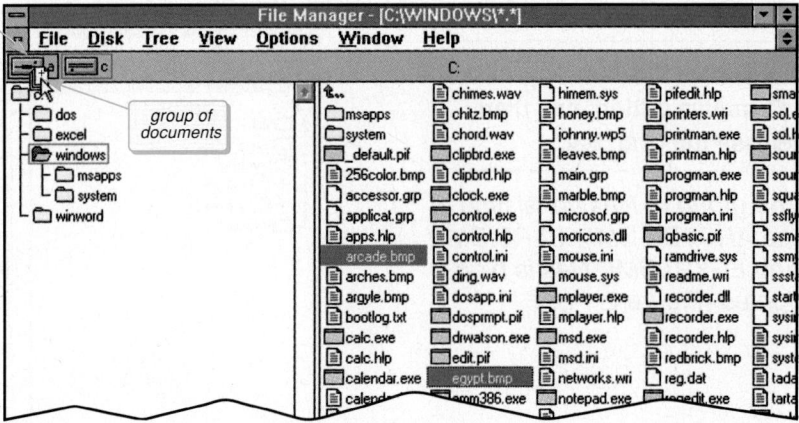

STEP 4 ▶

Release the mouse button, and then point to the Yes button.

Windows opens the Confirm Mouse Operation dialog box (Figure 2-17). The dialog box opens to confirm that you want to copy the files to the root directory of drive A (A:\). The highlight over the CARS.BMP entry is replaced with a dashed rectangular box. The mouse pointer points to the Yes button.

FIGURE 2-17

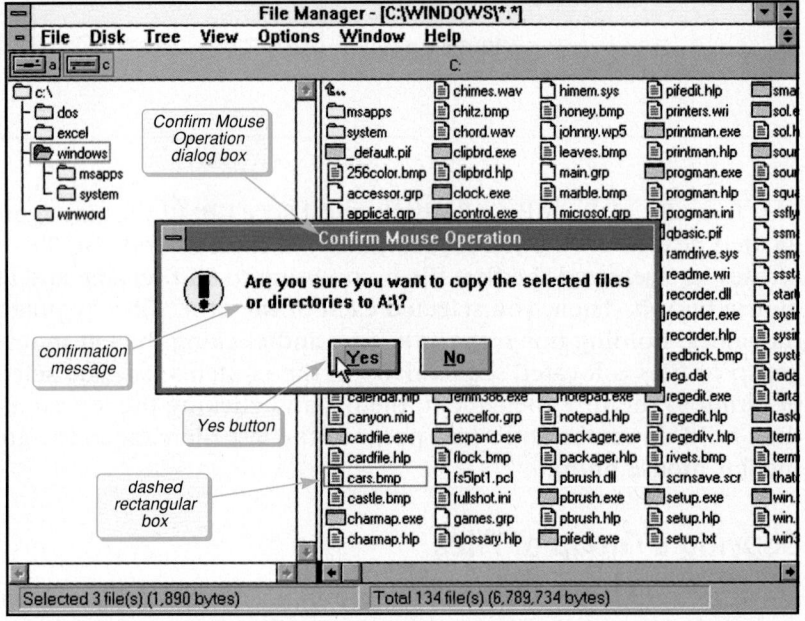

STEP 5 ▶

Choose the Yes button by clicking the left mouse button.

Windows opens the Copying dialog box, and the dialog box remains on the screen while Windows copies each file to the diskette in drive A (Figure 2-18). The dialog box in Figure 2-18 indicates the EGYPT.BMP file is currently being copied.

FIGURE 2-18

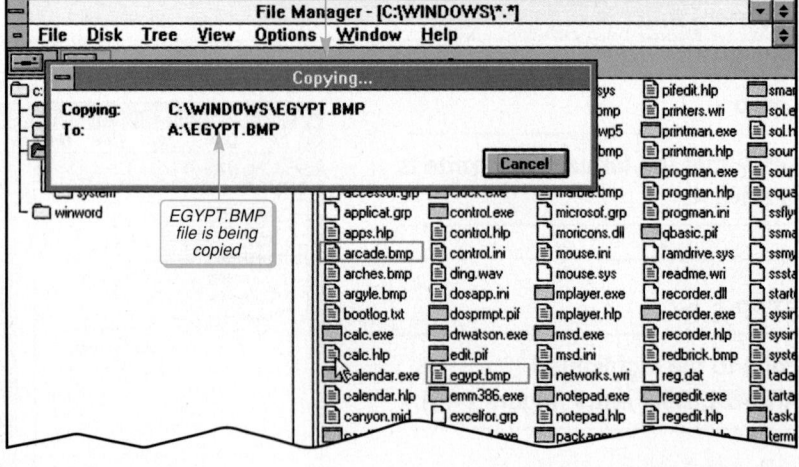

Correcting Errors Encountered While Copying Files

When you try to copy a file to an unformatted diskette, Windows opens the Error Copying File dialog box illustrated in Figure 2-19. The dialog box contains an error message (The disk in drive A is not formatted.), a question (Do you want to format it now?), and the Yes and No buttons. To continue the copy operation, format the diskette by choosing the Yes button. To cancel the copy operation, choose the No button.

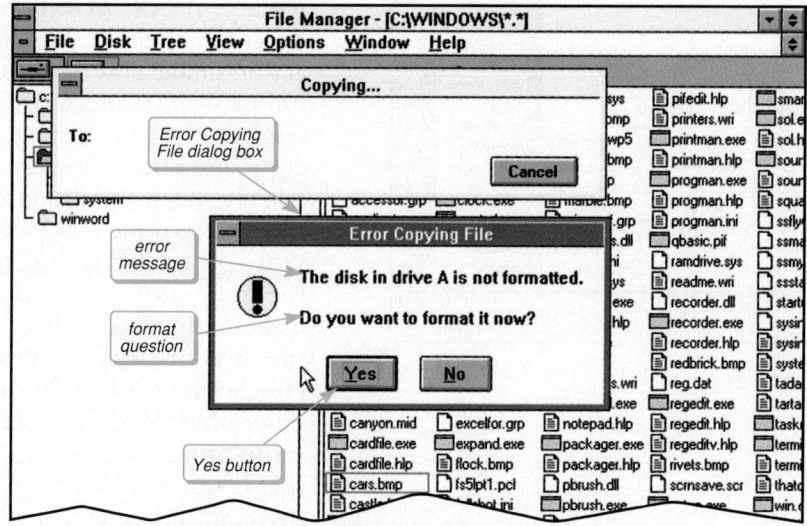

FIGURE 2-19

When you try to copy a file to a diskette but forget to insert a diskette into the diskette drive, Windows opens the Error Copying File dialog box shown in Figure 2-20. The dialog box contains an error message (There is no disk in drive A.), a suggested action (Insert a disk, and then try again.), and the Retry and Cancel buttons. To continue the copy operation, insert a diskette into drive A, and then choose the Retry button.

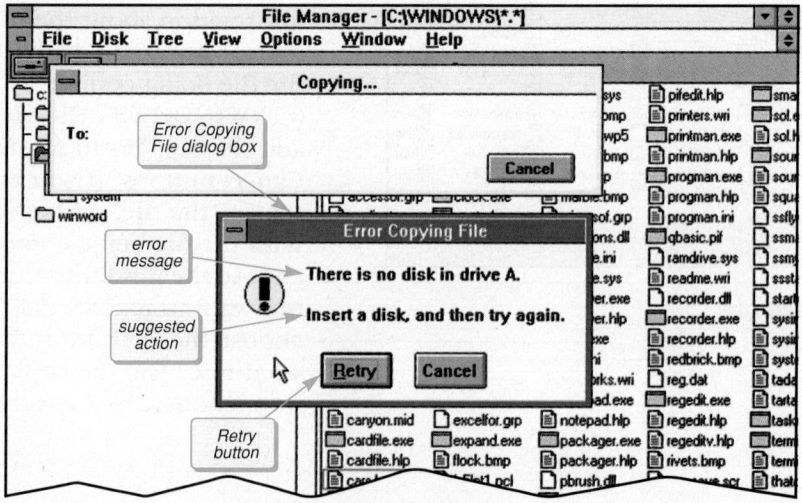

FIGURE 2-20

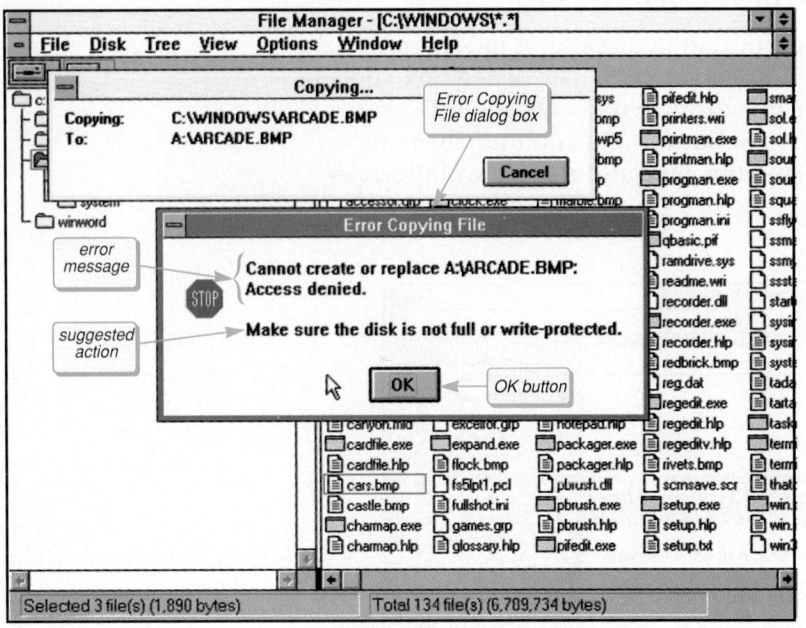

FIGURE 2-21

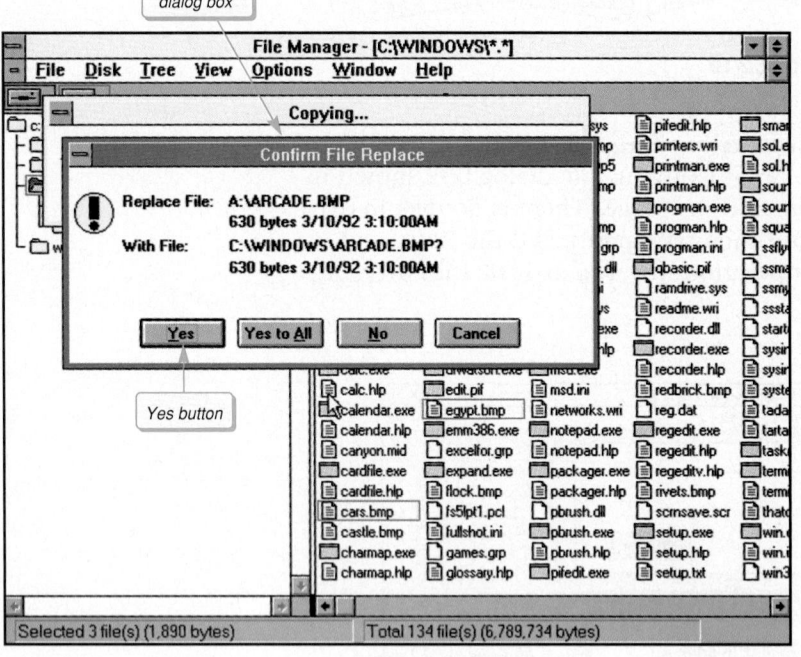

FIGURE 2-22

If you try to copy a file to a diskette that does not have enough room for the file, or you have inserted a write-protected diskette into the diskette drive, Windows opens the Error Copying File dialog box in Figure 2-21. The dialog box contains an error message (**Cannot create or replace A:\ARCADE.BMP: Access denied.**), a suggested action (**Make sure the disk is not full or write-protected.**), and the OK button. To continue with the copy operation, first remove the diskette from the diskette drive. Next, determine if the diskette is write-protected. If it is, remove the write-protection from the diskette, insert the diskette into the diskette drive, and then choose the OK button. If you determine the diskette is not write-protected, insert a diskette that is not full into the diskette drive, and then choose the OK button.

Replacing a File on Disk

If you try to copy a file to a diskette that already contains a file with the same filename and extension, Windows opens the Confirm File Replace dialog box (Figure 2-22). The Confirm File Replace dialog box contains information about the file being replaced (A:\ARCADE.BMP), the file being copied (C:\WINDOWS\ARCADE.BMP), and the Yes, Yes to All, No, and Cancel buttons. If you want to replace the file, on the diskette with the file being copied, choose the Yes button. If you do not want to replace the file choose the No button. If you want to cancel the copy operation, choose the Cancel button.

Changing the Current Drive

After copying a group of files, you should verify the files were copied onto the correct drive and into the correct directory. To view the files on drive A, change the current drive to drive A by pointing to the drive A icon and clicking the left mouse button.

TO CHANGE THE CURRENT DRIVE ▼

STEP 1 ▶

Point to the drive A icon.

The mouse pointer points to the drive A icon and the current drive is drive C (Figure 2-23).

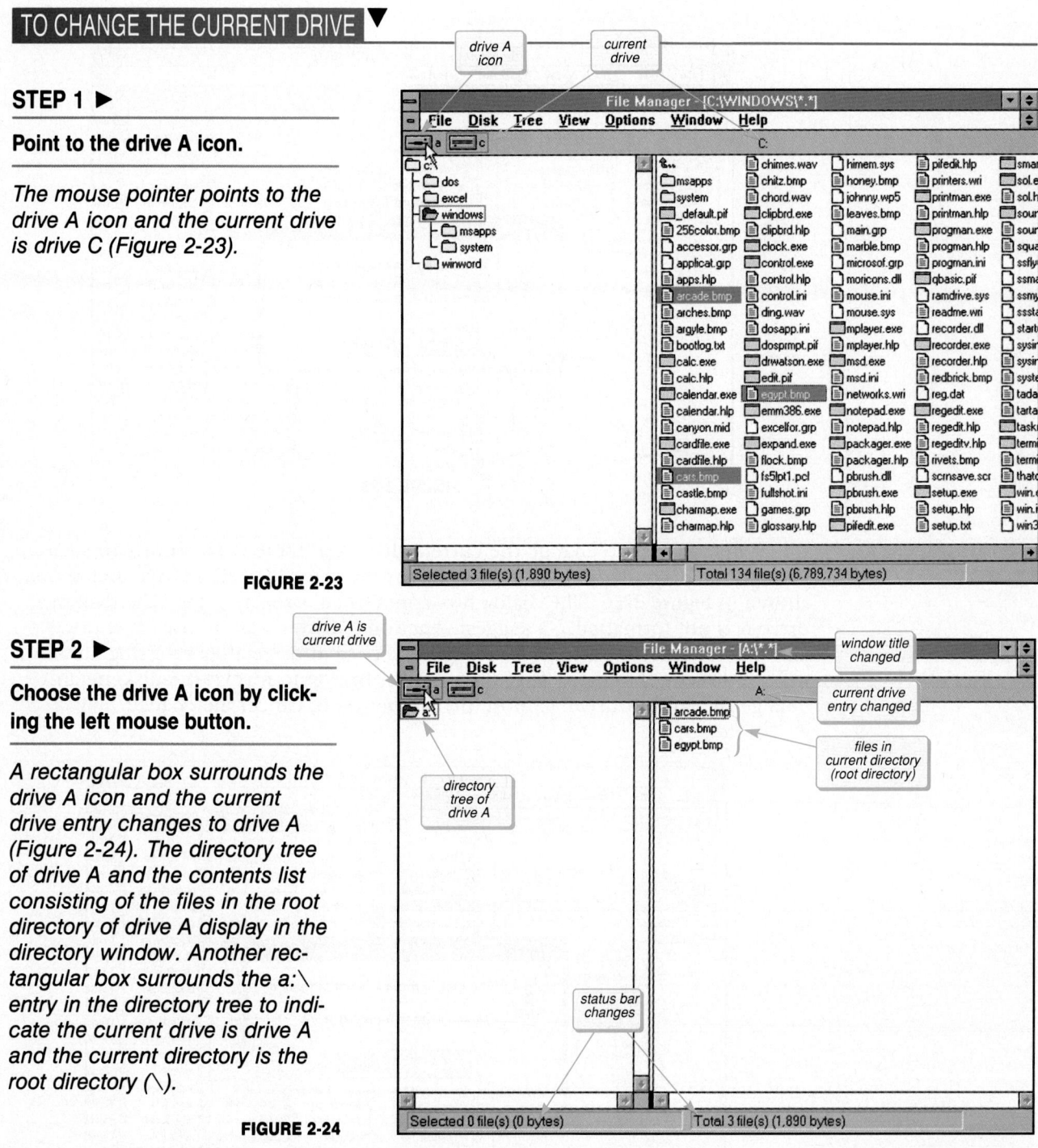

FIGURE 2-23

STEP 2 ▶

Choose the drive A icon by clicking the left mouse button.

A rectangular box surrounds the drive A icon and the current drive entry changes to drive A (Figure 2-24). The directory tree of drive A and the contents list consisting of the files in the root directory of drive A display in the directory window. Another rectangular box surrounds the a:\ entry in the directory tree to indicate the current drive is drive A and the current directory is the root directory (\).

FIGURE 2-24

Correcting Errors Encountered While Changing the Current Drive

When you try to change the current drive before inserting a diskette into the diskette drive, Windows opens the Error Selecting Drive dialog box illustrated in Figure 2-25. The dialog box contains an error message (There is no disk in drive A.), a suggested action (Insert a disk, and then try again.), and the Retry and Cancel buttons. To change the current drive after forgetting to insert a diskette into drive A, insert a diskette into drive A, and choose the Retry button.

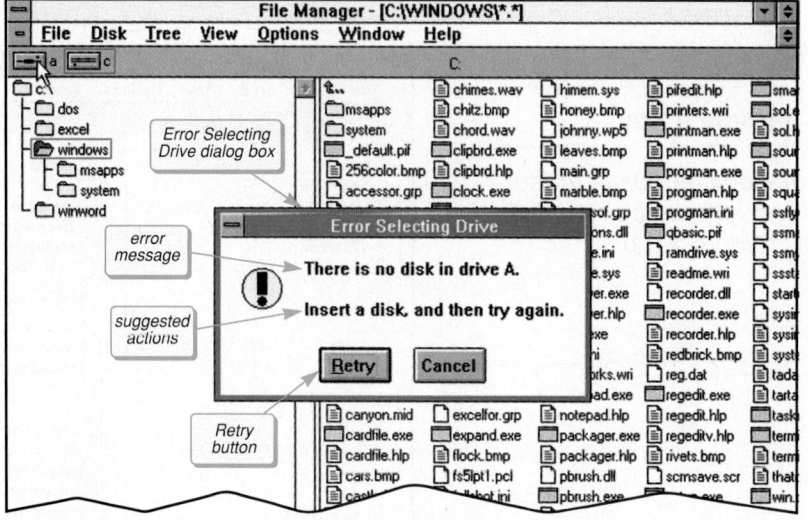

FIGURE 2-25

When you try to change the current drive and there is an unformatted diskette in the diskette drive, Windows opens the Error Selecting Drive dialog box shown in Figure 2-26. The dialog box contains an error message (The disk in drive A is not formatted.), a suggested action (Do you want to format it now?), and the Yes and No buttons. To change the current drive after inserting an unformatted diskette into drive A, choose the Yes button to format the diskette and change the current drive. Choose the No button to cancel the change.

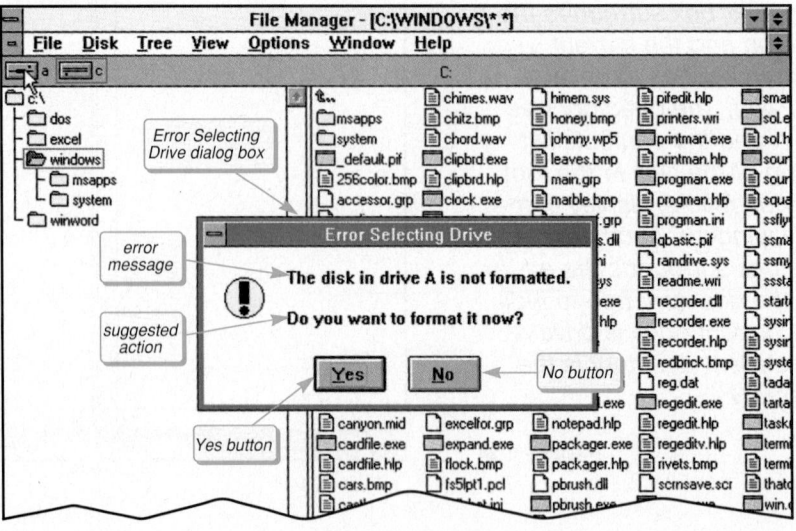

FIGURE 2-26

▶ RENAMING A FILE

S ometimes you may want to rename a file by changing its name or file-name extension. You change the name or extension of a file by selecting the filename in the contents list, choosing the **Rename command** from the File menu, entering the new filename, and choosing the OK button. In this project, you will change the name of the CARS.BMP file on the diskette in drive A to AUTOS.BMP.

TO RENAME A FILE ▼

STEP 1 ▶

Select the CARS.BMP entry by clicking the CARS.BMP filename in the contents list.

The CARS.BMP entry is high-lighted (Figure 2-27).

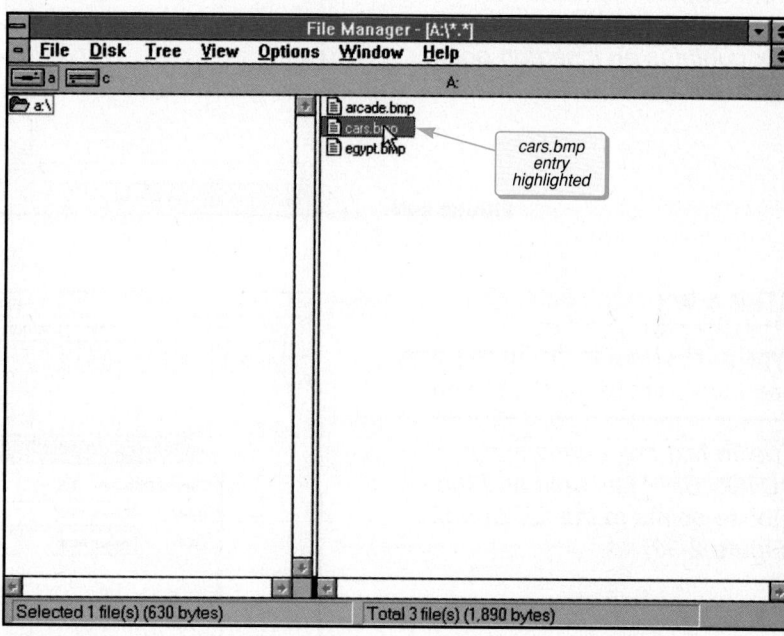

FIGURE 2-27

STEP 2 ▶

Select the File menu, and then point to the Rename command.

Windows opens the File menu (Figure 2-28). The mouse pointer points to the Rename command.

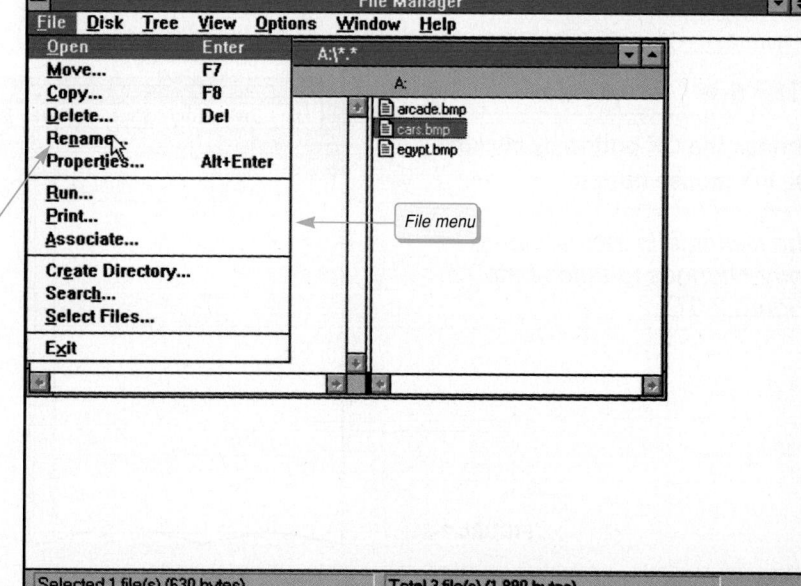

FIGURE 2-28

STEP 3 ▶

Choose the Rename command from the File menu by clicking the left mouse button.

Windows opens the Rename dialog box (Figure 2-29). The dialog box contains the Current Directory : A:\ message, the From and To text boxes, and the OK, Cancel, and Help buttons. The From text box contains the CARS.BMP filename and To text box contains an insertion point.

FIGURE 2-29

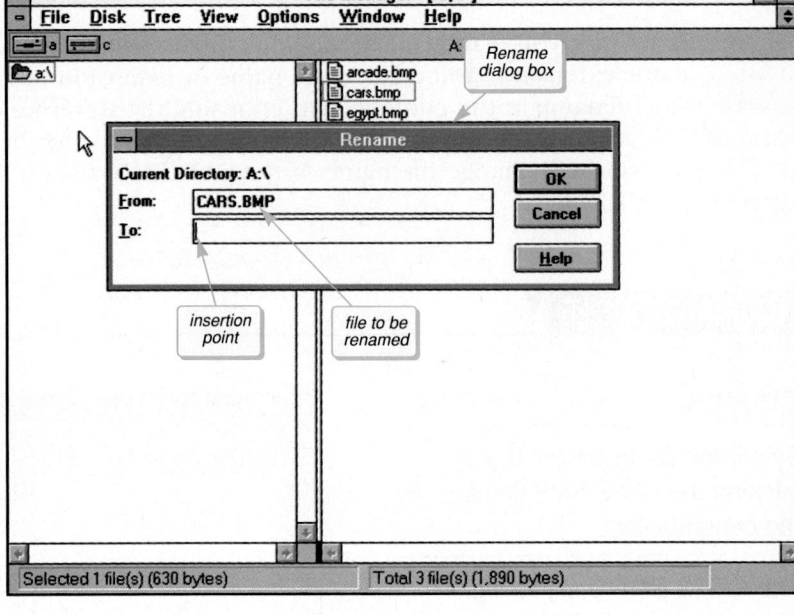

STEP 4 ▶

Type `autos.bmp` **in the To text box, and then point to the OK button.**

The To text box contains the AUTOS.BMP filename and the mouse points to the OK button (Figure 2-30).

FIGURE 2-30

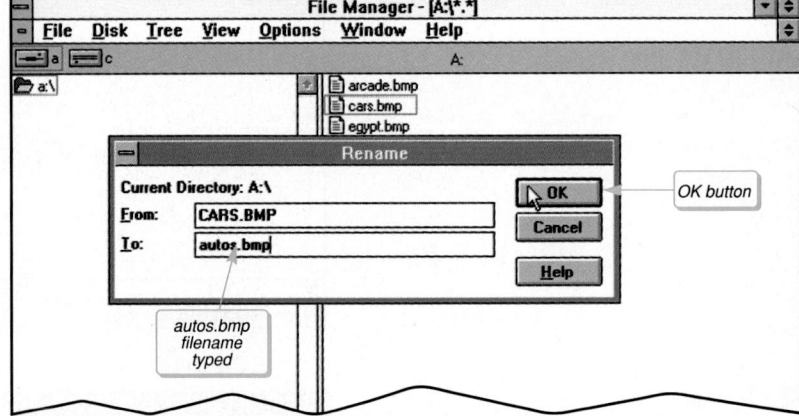

STEP 5 ▶

Choose the OK button by clicking the left mouse button.

The filename in the cars.bmp entry changes to autos.bmp (Figure 2-31).

FIGURE 2-31

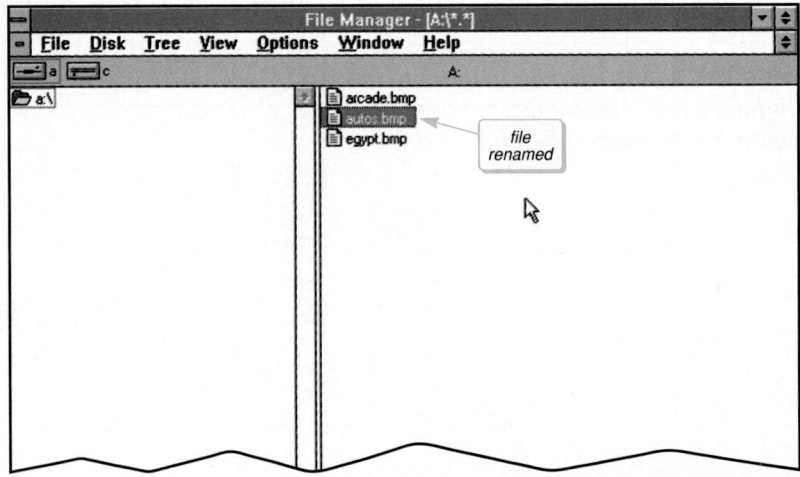

▶ DELETING A FILE

When you no longer need a file, you can delete it by selecting the file-name in the contents list, choosing the **Delete command** from the File menu, choosing the OK button, and then choosing the Yes button. In this project, you will delete the EGYPT.BMP file from the diskette in drive A.

TO DELETE A FILE ▼

STEP 1 ▶

Select the EGYPT.BMP entry.

The EGYPT.BMP entry is high-lighted (Figure 2-32).

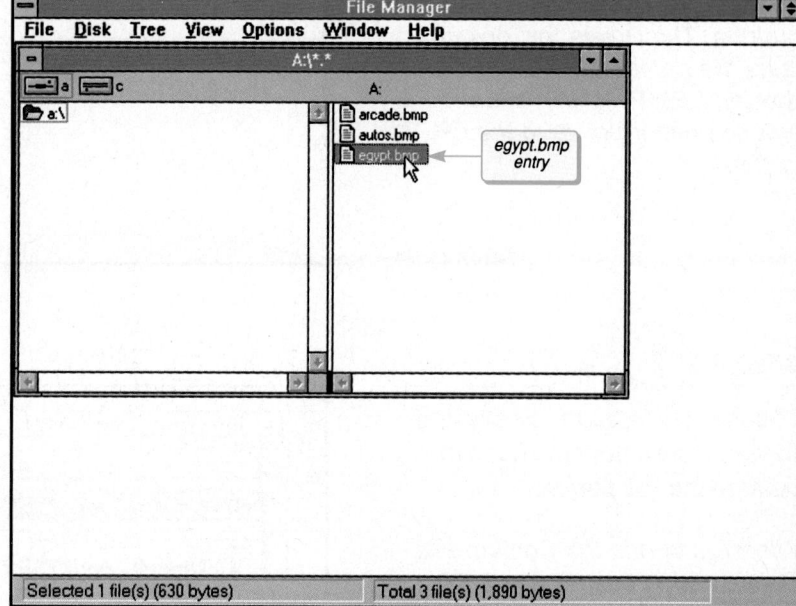

FIGURE 2-32

STEP 2 ▶

Select the File menu from the menu bar, and then point to the Delete command.

Windows opens the File menu (Figure 2-33). The mouse pointer points to the Delete command.

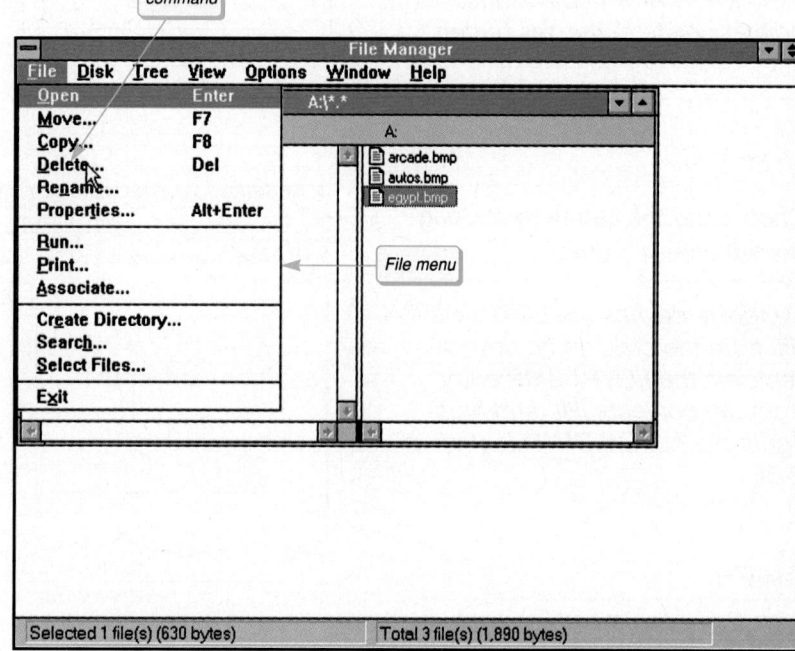

FIGURE 2-33

STEP 3 ▶

Choose the Delete command from the File menu by clicking the left mouse button, and then point to the OK button.

Windows opens the Delete dialog box (Figure 2-34). The dialog box contains the Current Directory: A:\ message, Delete text box, and the OK, Cancel, and Help buttons. The Delete text box contains the name of the file to be deleted (EGYPT.BMP), and the mouse pointer points to the OK button.

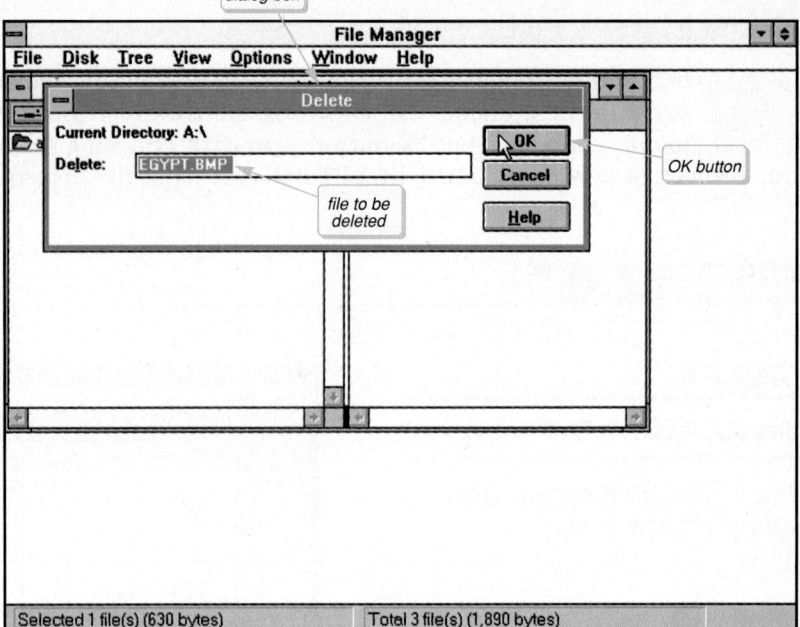

FIGURE 2-34

STEP 4 ▶

Choose the OK button by clicking the left mouse button, and then point to the Yes button.

Windows opens the Confirm File Delete dialog box (Figure 2-35). The dialog box contains the Delete File message and the path and filename of the file to delete (A:\EGYPT.BMP). The mouse pointer points to the Yes button.

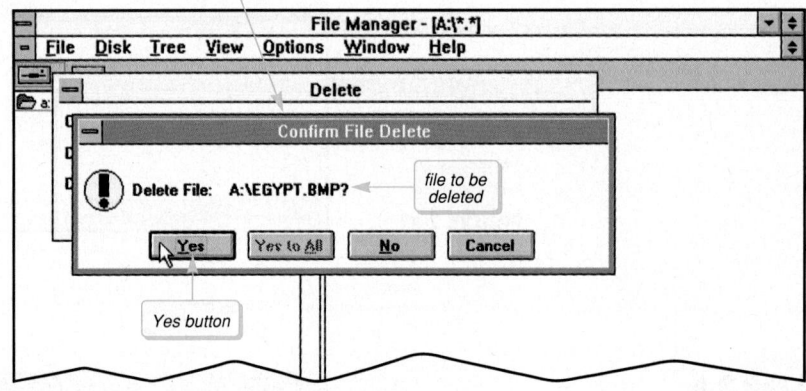

FIGURE 2-35

STEP 5 ▶

Choose the Yes button by clicking the left mouse button.

Windows deletes the EGYPT.BMP file from the diskette on drive A, removes the EGYPT.BMP entry from the contents list, and highlights the AUTOS.BMP file (Figure 2-36).

STEP 6

Remove the diskette from drive A.

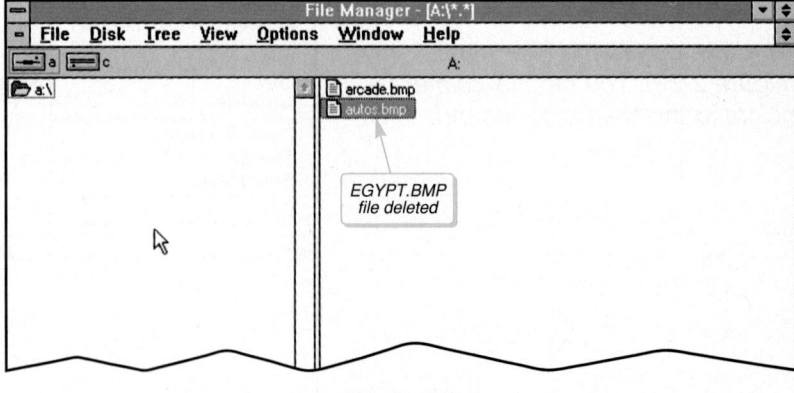

FIGURE 2-36

▶ CREATING A BACKUP DISKETTE

T o prevent accidental loss of a file on a diskette, you should make a backup copy of the diskette. A copy of a diskette made to prevent accidental loss of data is called a **backup diskette**. Always be sure to make backup diskettes before installing software stored on diskettes onto the hard drive.

The first step in creating a backup diskette is to protect the diskette to be copied, or **source diskette**, from accidental erasure by write-protecting the diskette. After write-protecting the source diskette, choose the **Copy Disk command** from the Disk menu to copy the contents of the source diskette to another diskette, called the **destination diskette**. After copying the source diskette to the destination diskette, remove the write-protection from the source diskette and identify the destination diskette by writing a name on the paper label supplied with the diskette and affixing the label to the diskette.

In this project, you will use File Manager to create a backup diskette for a diskette labeled Business Documents. The Business Documents diskette contains valuable business documents that should be backed up to prevent accidental loss. The source diskette will be the Business Documents diskette and the destination diskette will be a formatted diskette that will later be labeled Business Documents Backup. To create a backup diskette, both the Business Documents diskette and the formatted diskette must be the same size and capacity.

File Manager copies a diskette by asking you to insert the source diskette into drive A, reading data from the source diskette into main memory, asking you to insert the destination disk, and then copying the data from main memory to the destination disk. Depending on the size of main memory on your computer, you may have to insert and remove the source and destination diskettes several times before the copy process is complete. The copy process takes about three minutes to complete.

TO COPY A DISKETTE ▼

STEP 1 ▶

Write-protect the Business Documents diskette by opening the write-protect window (Figure 2-37).

Business Documents

write-protect window open means diskette is write-protected

FIGURE 2-37

STEP 2 ▶

Select the Disk menu from the menu bar, and then point to the Copy Disk command.

Windows opens the Disk menu (Figure 2-38). The mouse pointer points to the Copy Disk command.

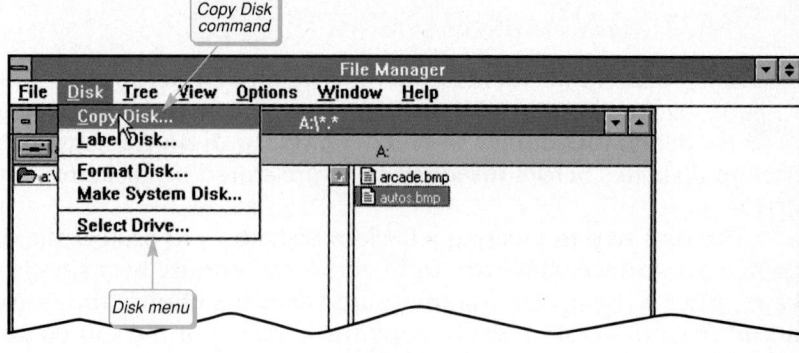

FIGURE 2-38

STEP 3 ▶

Choose the Copy Disk command from the Disk menu by clicking the left mouse button, and then point to the Yes button.

Windows opens the Confirm Copy Disk dialog box (Figure 2-39). The dialog box reminds you that the copy process will erase all data on the destination disk. The mouse pointer points to the Yes button.

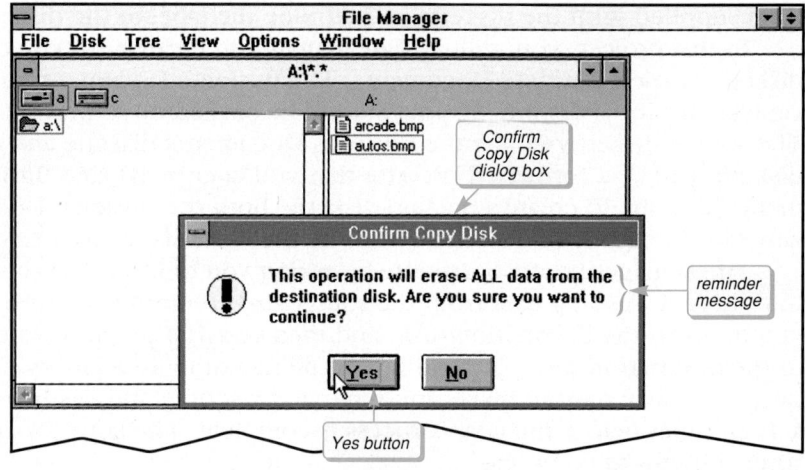

FIGURE 2-39

STEP 4 ▶

Choose the Yes button by clicking the left mouse button, and then point to the OK button.

Windows opens the Copy Disk dialog box (Figure 2-40). The dialog box contains the Insert source disk message and the mouse pointer points to the OK button.

STEP 5 ▶

Insert the source diskette, the Business Documents diskette, into drive A.

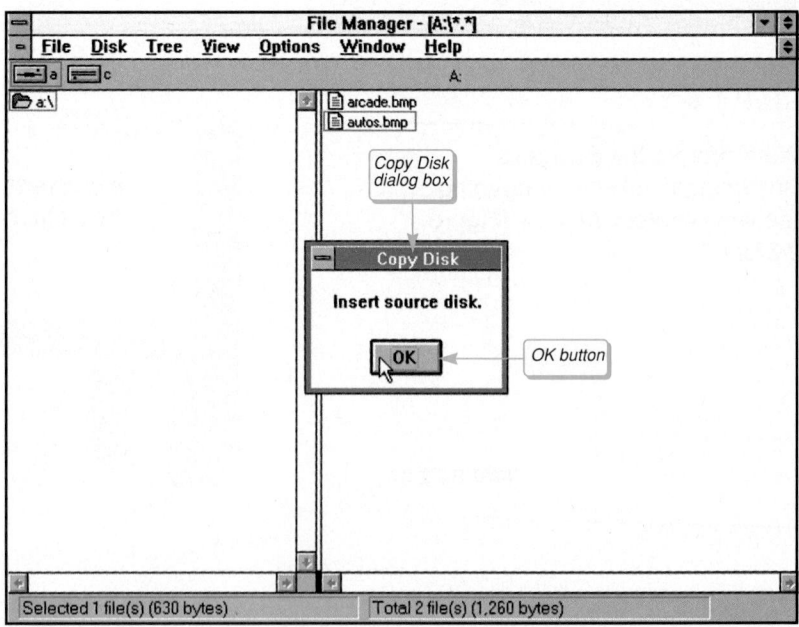

FIGURE 2-40

STEP 6 ▶

Choose the OK button in the Copy Disk dialog box by clicking the left mouse button.

Windows opens the Copying Disk dialog box (Figure 2-41). The dialog box contains the messages, Now Copying disk in Drive A:. and 1% completed. As the copy process progresses, a value from 1 to 100 indicates what percent of the copy process is complete.

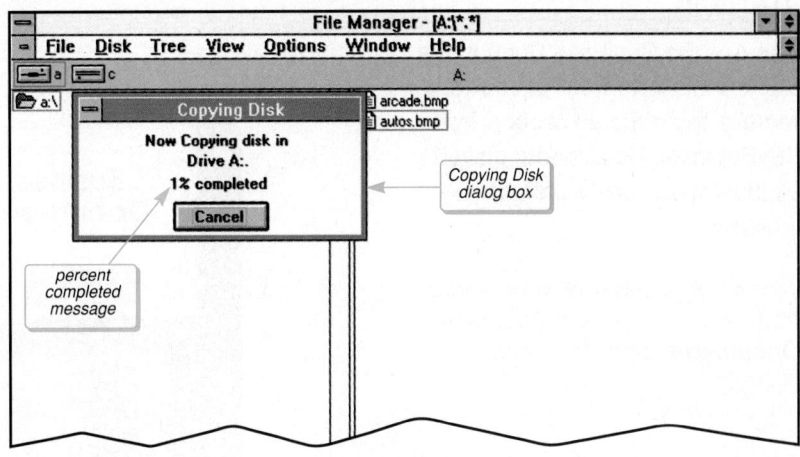

FIGURE 2-41

When as much data from the source diskette as will fit in main memory is copied to main memory, Windows opens the Copy Disk dialog box (Figure 2-42). The dialog box contains the message, Insert destination disk, and the OK button.

STEP 7 ▶

Remove the source diskette (Business Documents diskette) from drive A and insert the destination diskette (Business Documents Backup diskette) into drive A.

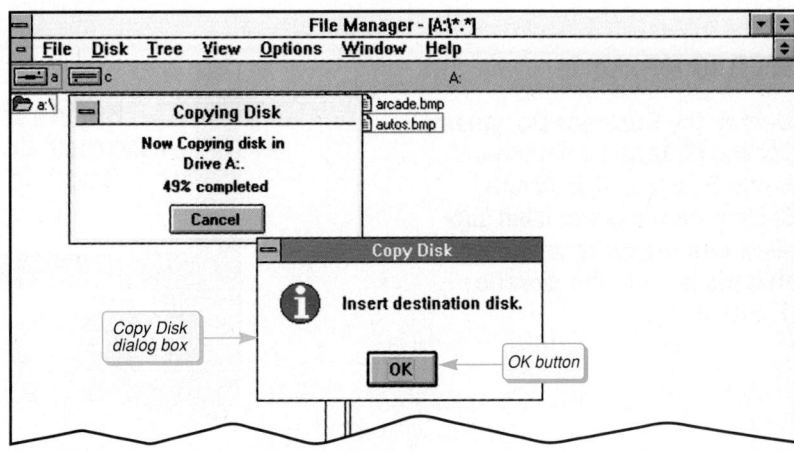

FIGURE 2-42

STEP 8 ▶

Choose the OK button from the Copy Disk dialog box.

Windows opens the Copying Disk dialog box (Figure 2-43). A value from 1 to 100 displays as the data in main memory is copied to the destination disk.

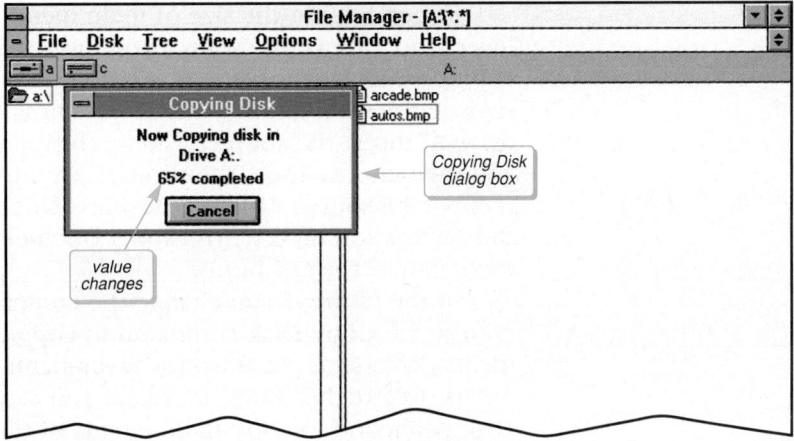

FIGURE 2-43

STEP 9 ▶

Remove the Business Documents Backup diskette from drive A and remove the write-protection from the Business Documents diskette by closing the write-protect window.

The write-protection is removed from the 3 1/2—inch Business Documents diskette (Figure 2-44).

write-protect window closed means you can write to this diskette

Business Documents

FIGURE 2-44

STEP 10 ▶

Identify the Business Documents Backup diskette by writing the words Business Documents Backup on the paper label supplied with the diskette and then affix the label to the diskette (Figure 2-45).

Business Documents Backup

FIGURE 2-45

Depending on the size of main memory on your computer, you may have to insert and remove the source and destination diskettes several times before the copy process is complete. If prompted by Windows to insert the source diskette, remove the destination diskette (Business Documents Backup diskette) from drive A, insert the source diskette (Business Documents diskette) into drive A, and then choose the OK button. If prompted to insert the destination diskette, remove the source diskette (Business Documents diskette) from drive A, insert the destination diskette (Business Documents Backup diskette) into drive A, and then choose the OK button.

In the future if you change the contents of the Business Documents diskette, choose the Copy Disk command to copy the contents of the Business Documents diskette to the Business Documents Backup diskette. If the Business Documents diskette becomes unusable, you can format a diskette, choose the Copy Disk command to copy the contents of the Business Documents Backup diskette (source diskette) to the formatted diskette (destination diskette), label the formatted diskette, Business Documents, and use the new Business Documents diskette in place of the unusable Business Documents diskette.

Correcting Errors Encountered While Copying A Diskette

When you try to copy a disk and forget to insert the source diskette when prompted, insert an unformatted source diskette, forget to insert the destination diskette when prompted, or insert a write-protected destination diskette, Windows opens the Copy Disk Error dialog box illustrated in Figure 2-46. The dialog box contains the Unable to copy disk error message and OK button. To complete the copy process after forgetting to insert a source diskette or inserting an unformatted source diskette, choose the OK button, insert the formatted source diskette into the diskette drive, and choose the **Disk Copy command** to start over the disk copy process. To complete the copy process after forgetting to insert a destination diskette or inserting a write-protected destination diskette, choose the OK button, insert a nonwrite-protected diskette in the diskette drive, and choose the Disk Copy command to start over the disk copy.

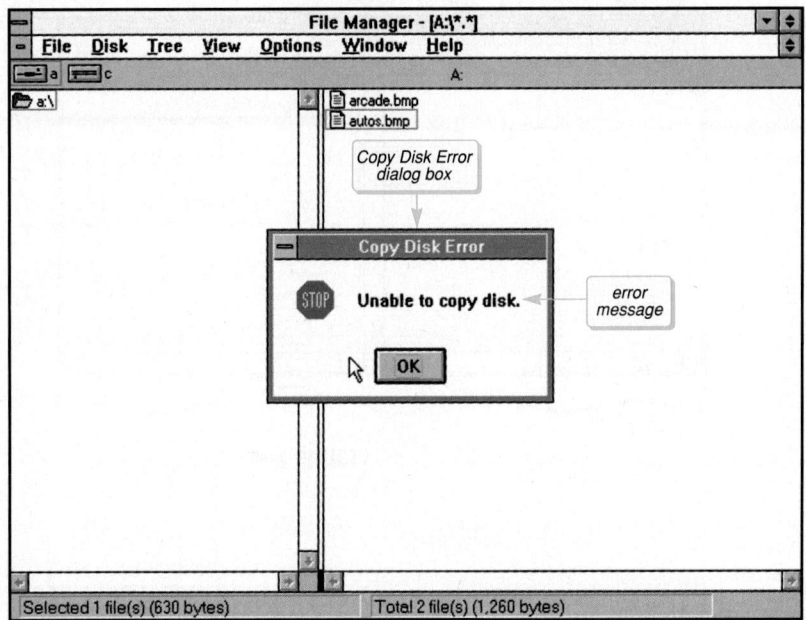

FIGURE 2-46

▶ SEARCHING FOR HELP USING ONLINE HELP

I n Project 1, you obtained help about the Paintbrush application by choosing the Contents command from the Help menu of the Paintbrush window (see pages WIN32 through WIN35). You then chose a topic from a list of help topics on the screen. In addition to choosing a topic from a list of available help topics, you can use the Search feature to search for help topics. In this project, you will use the Search feature to obtain help about copying files and selecting groups of files using the keyboard.

Searching for a Help Topic

In this project, you used a mouse to select and copy a group of files. If you want to obtain information about how to select a group of files using the keyboard instead of the mouse, you can use the Search feature. A search can be performed in one of two ways. The first method allows you to select a search topic from a list of search topics. A list of help topics associated with the search topic displays. You then select a help topic from this list. To begin the search, choose the **Search for Help on command** from the Help menu.

TO SEARCH FOR A HELP TOPIC ▼

STEP 1 ▶

Select the Help menu from the File Manager window menu bar, and then point to the Search for Help on command.

Windows opens the Help menu (Figure 2-47). The mouse pointer points to the Search for Help on command.

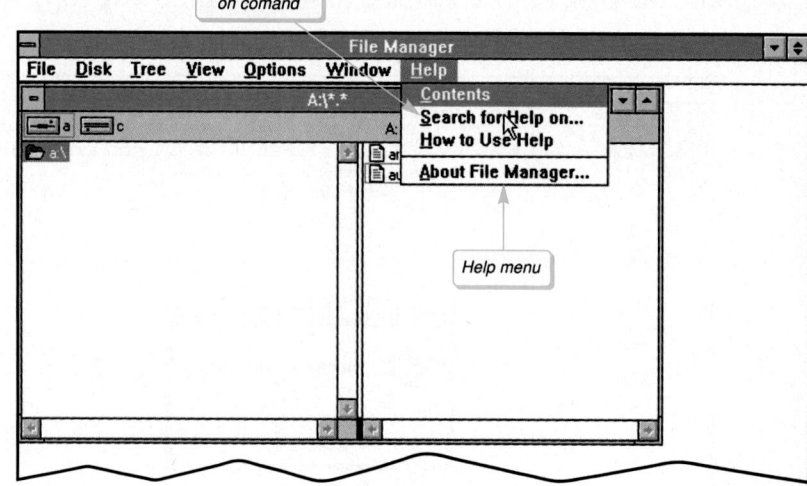

FIGURE 2-47

STEP 2 ▶

Choose the Search for Help on command from the Help menu by clicking the left mouse button.

Windows opens the Search dialog box (Figure 2-48). The dialog box consists of two areas separated by a horizontal line. The top area contains the Search For text box, Search For list box, and Cancel and Show Topics buttons. The Search For list box contains an alphabetical list of search topics. A vertical scroll bar indicates there are more search topics than appear in the list box. The Cancel button cancels the Search operation. The Show Topics button is dimmed and cannot be chosen. The bottom area of the dialog box contains the empty Help Topics list box and the dimmed Go To button.

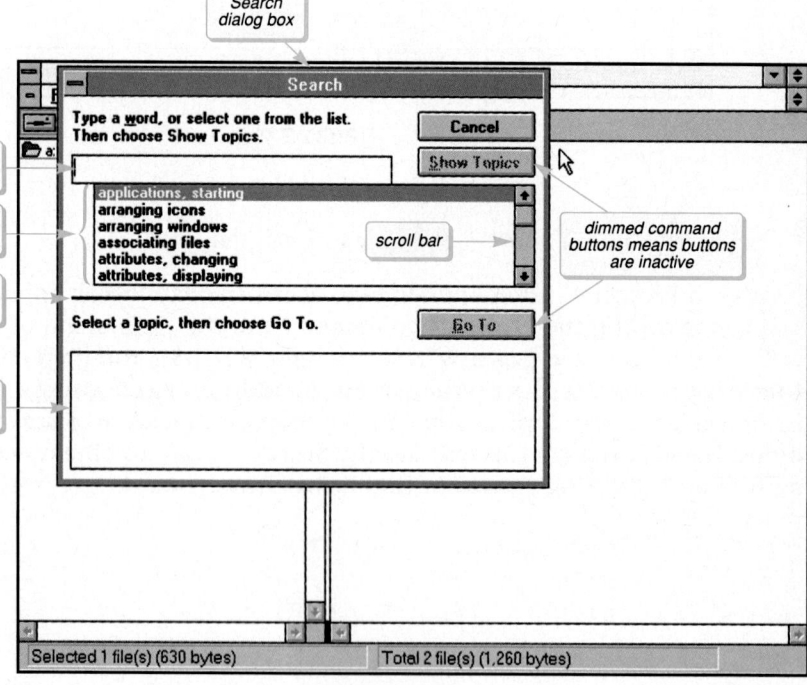

FIGURE 2-48

STEP 3 ▶

Point to the down scroll arrow in the Search For list box (Figure 2-49).

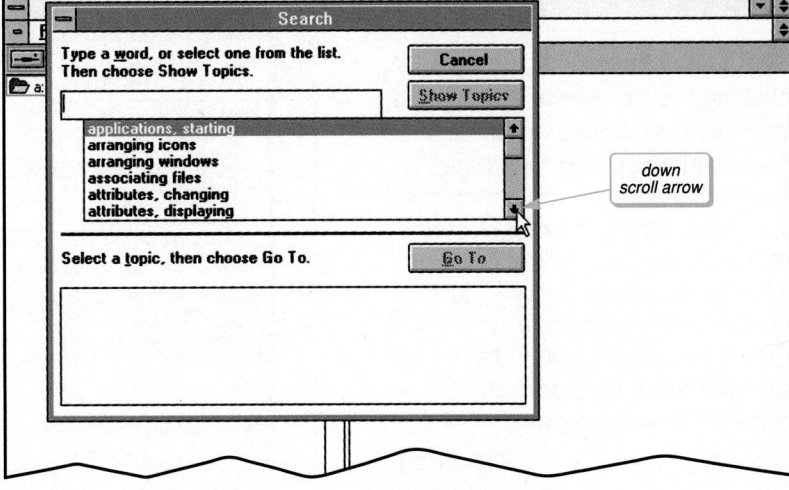

FIGURE 2-49

STEP 4 ▶

Hold down the left mouse button until the selecting files search topic is visible, and then point to the selecting files search topic (Figure 2-50).

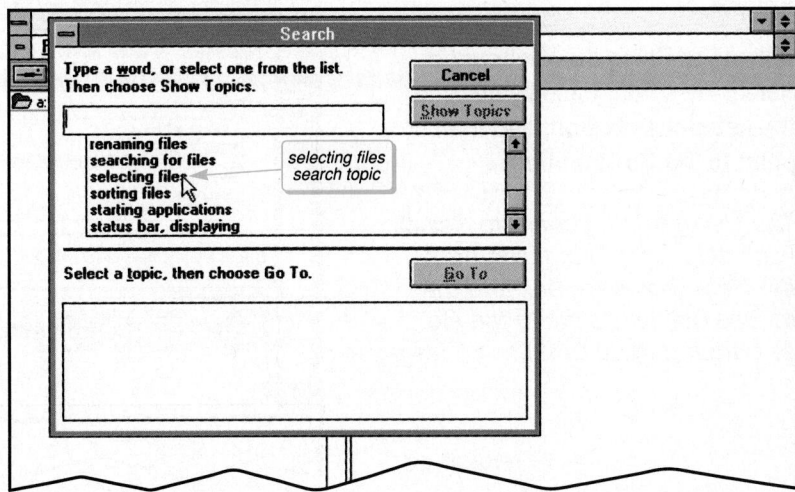

FIGURE 2-50

STEP 5 ▶

Select the selecting files search topic by clicking the left mouse button, and then point to the Show Topics button (Show Topics).

The selecting files search topic is highlighted in the Search For list box and displays in the Search For text box (Figure 2-51). The Show Topics button is no longer dimmed and the mouse pointer points to the Show Topics button.

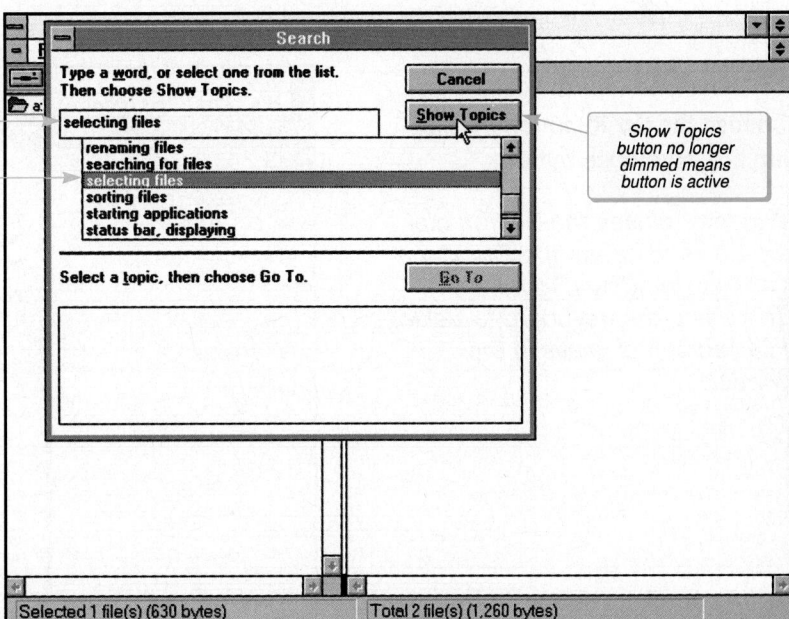

FIGURE 2-51

STEP 6 ▶

Choose the Show Topics button by clicking the left mouse button, and then point to the Using the Keyboard to Select Files help topic.

The Help Topics list box contains four help topics (Figure 2-52). The Go To button (Go To) is no longer dimmed, and the mouse pointer points to the Using the Keyboard to Select Files help topic.

FIGURE 2-52

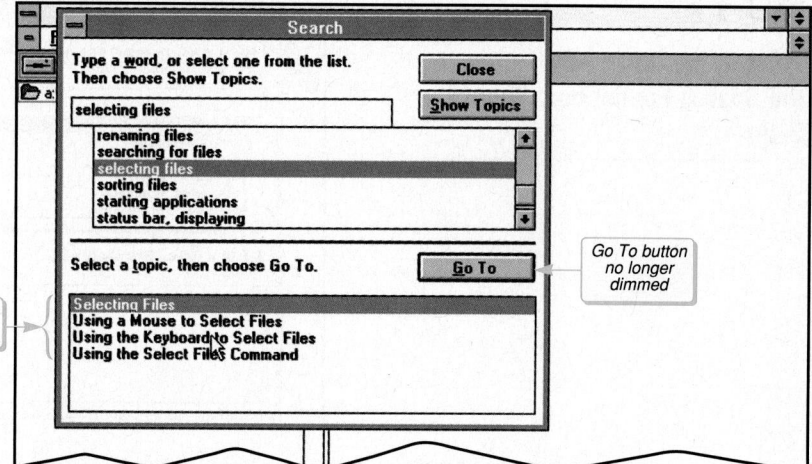

STEP 7 ▶

Select the Using the Keyboard to Select Files help topic by clicking the left mouse button, and then point to the Go To button.

The Using the Keyboard to Select Files help topic is highlighted in the Help Topics list box and the mouse pointer points to the Go To button (Figure 2-53).

FIGURE 2-53

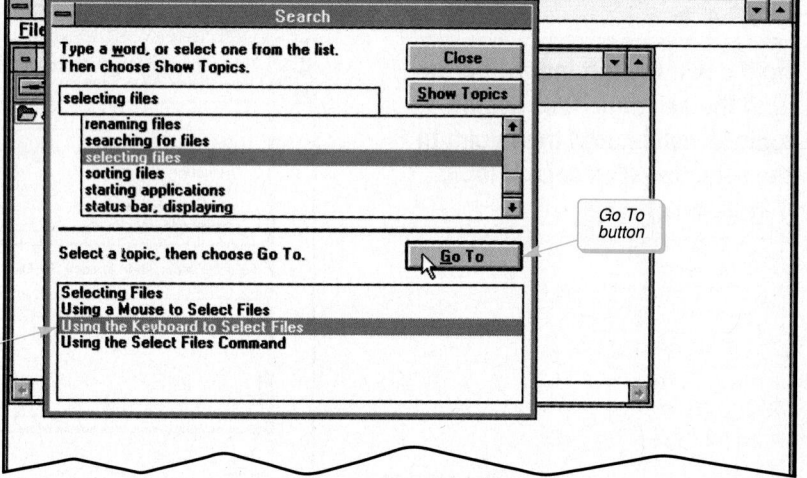

STEP 8 ▶

Choose the Go To button by clicking the left mouse button.

Windows closes the Search dialog box and opens the File Manager Help window (Figure 2-54). The Using the Keyboard to Select Files screen displays in the window.

FIGURE 2-54

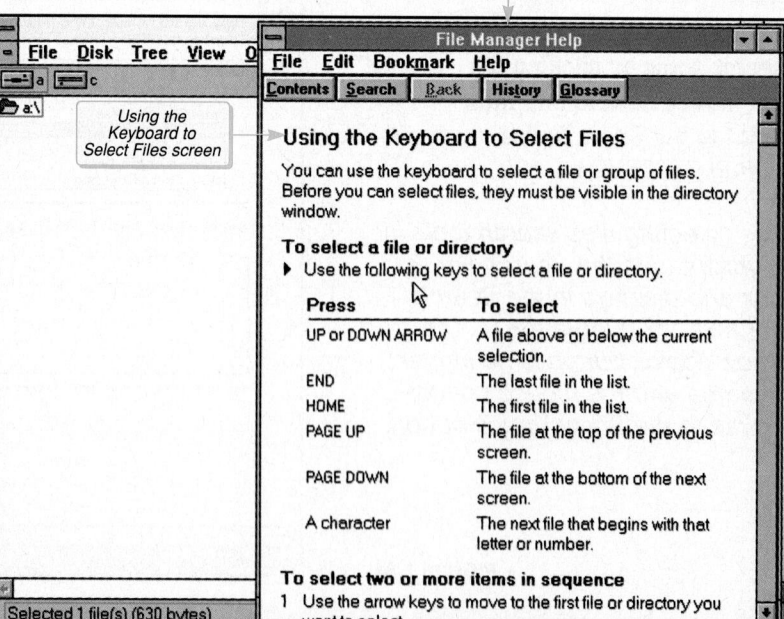

STEP 9 ▶

Click the Maximize button (◆) to maximize the File Manager Help window (Figure 2-55).

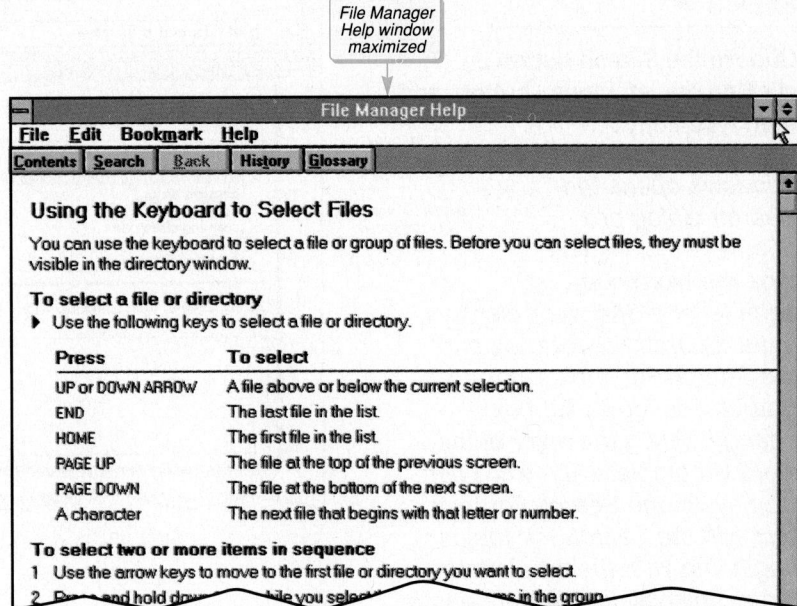

FIGURE 2-55

Searching for Help Using a Word or Phrase

The second method you can use to search for help involves entering a word or phrase to assist the Search feature in finding help related to the word or phrase. In this project, you copied a group of files from the hard disk to a diskette. To obtain additional information about copying files, choose the Search button and type copy from the keyboard.

TO SEARCH FOR A HELP TOPIC ▼

STEP 1 ▶

Point to the Search button (Search) (Figure 2-56).

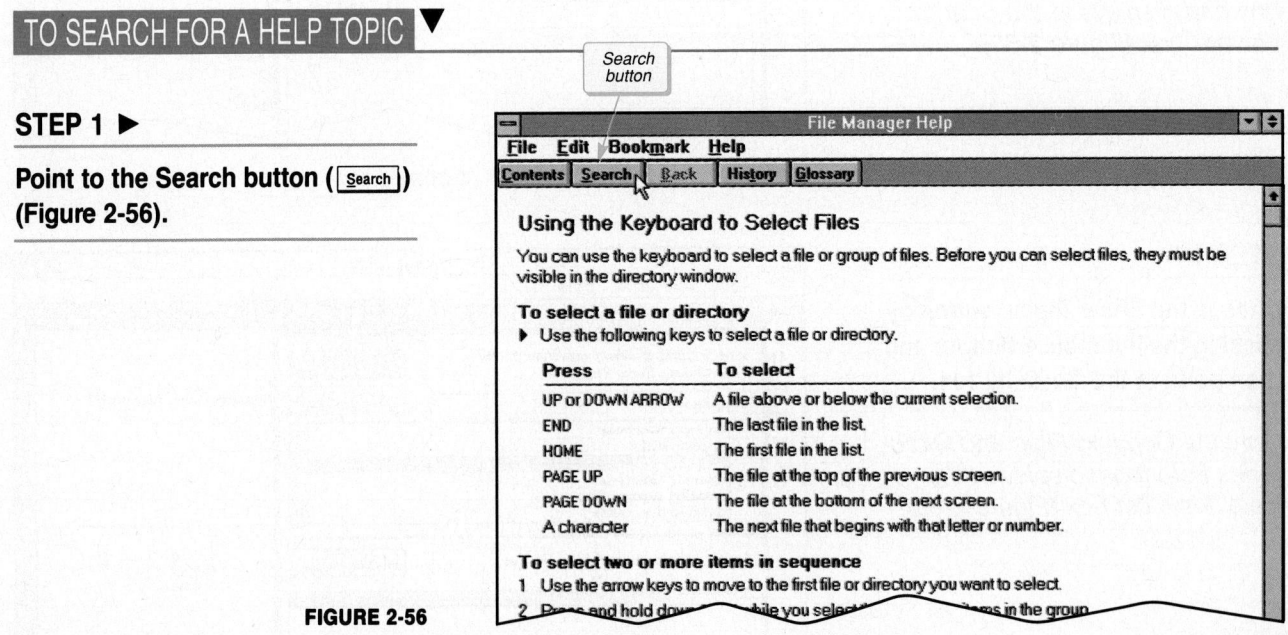

FIGURE 2-56

STEP 2 ▶

Choose the Search button by clicking the left mouse button, and then type copy**.**

Windows opens the Search dialog box (Figure 2-57). As you type the word copy, each letter of the word displays in the Search For text box and the Search For Topics in the Search For Topics list box change. When the entry of the word is complete, the word copy displays in the Search For text box and the Search For topics beginning with the four letters c-o-p-y display first in the Search For list box.

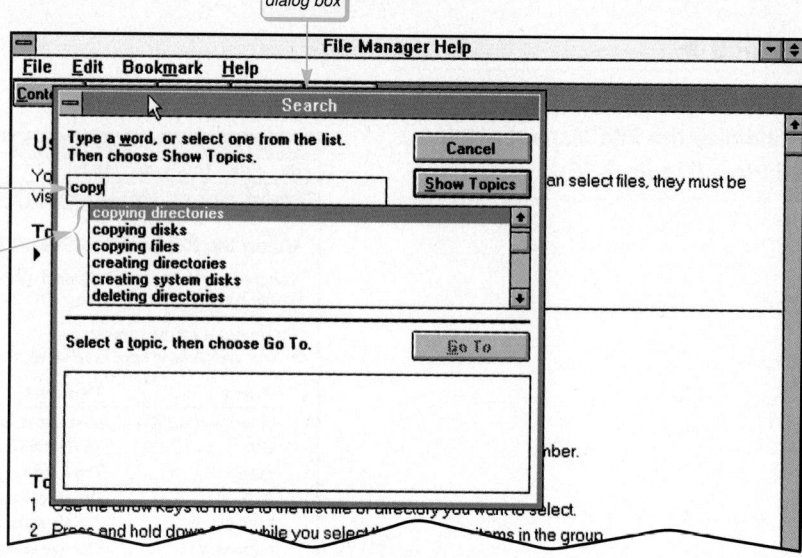

FIGURE 2-57

STEP 3 ▶

Select the copying files search topic by pointing to the topic and clicking the left mouse button, and then point to the Show Topics button.

The copying files search topic is highlighted in the Search For list box and displays in the Search For text box (Figure 2-58).

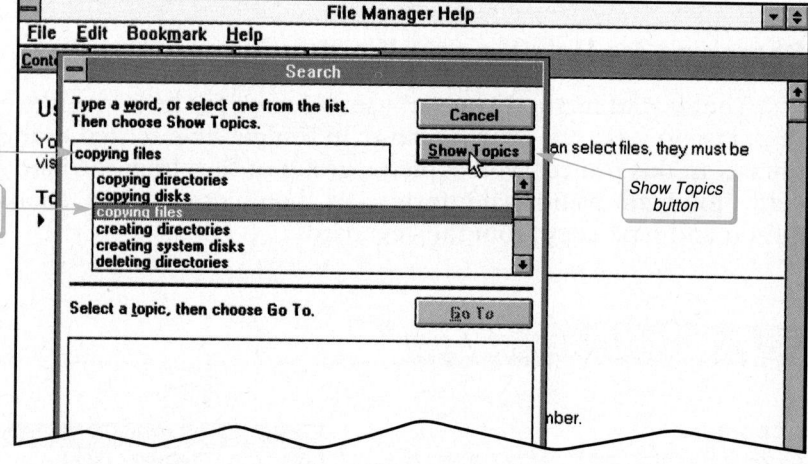

FIGURE 2-58

STEP 4 ▶

Choose the Show Topics button by clicking the left mouse button, and then point to the Go To button.

Only the Copying Files and Directories help topic display in the Help Topic list box (Figure 2-59).

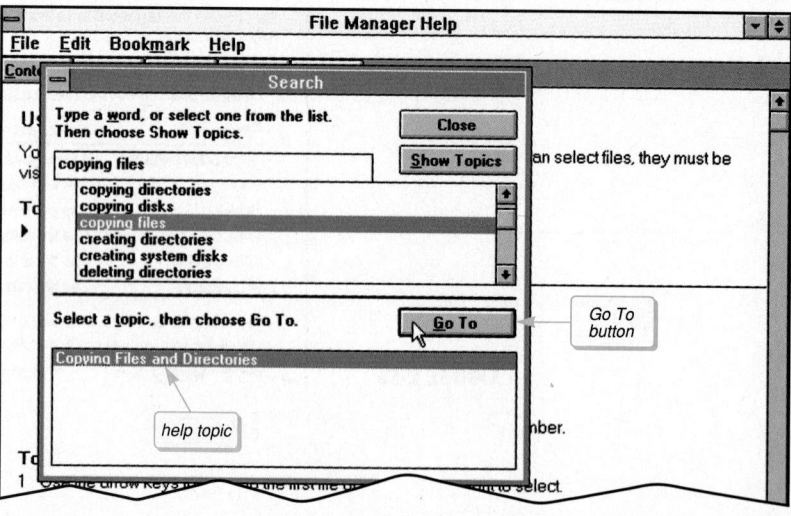

FIGURE 2-59

STEP 5 ►

Choose the Go To button by clicking the left mouse button.

Windows closes the Search dialog box and displays the Copying Files and Directories help screen (Figure 2-60).

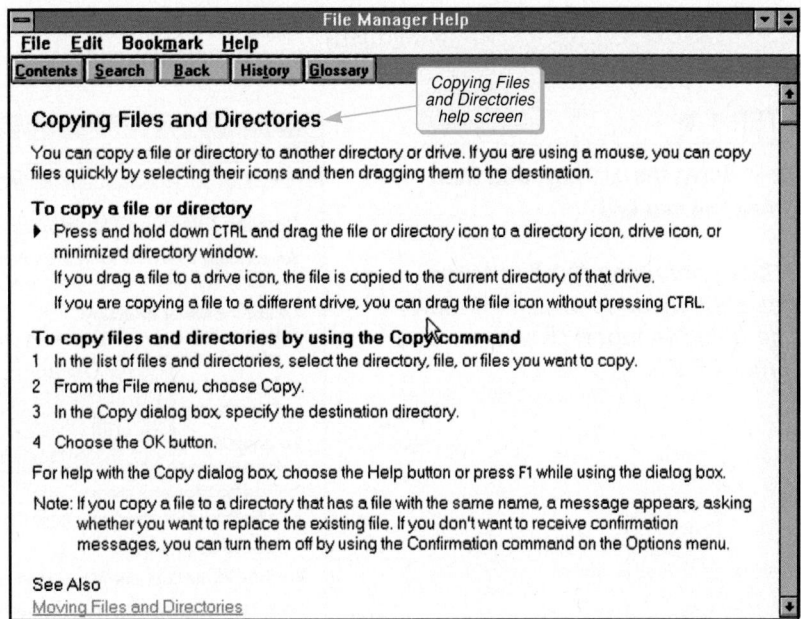

FIGURE 2-60

Quitting File Manager and Online Help

When you finish using File Manager and Windows online Help, you should quit the File Manager Help and File Manager applications. One method of quitting these applications is to first quit the File Manager Help application, and then quit the File Manager application. However, because quitting an application automatically quits the help application associated with that application, you can simply quit the File Manager application to quit both applications. Because the Program Manager and File Manager windows are hidden behind the File Manager Help window (see Figure 2-60), you must move the File Manager window on top of the other windows before quitting File Manager. To do this, you must switch to the File Manager application.

▶ SWITCHING BETWEEN APPLICATIONS

Each time you start an application and maximize its window, its application window displays on top of the other windows on the desktop. To display a hidden application window, you must switch between applications on the desktop using the ALT and TAB keys. To switch to another application, hold down the ALT key, press the TAB key one or more times, and then release the ALT key. Each time you press the TAB key, a box containing an application icon and application window title opens on the desktop. To display the File Manager window, you will have to press the TAB key only once.

TO SWITCH BETWEEN APPLICATIONS ▼

STEP 1 ▶

Hold down the ALT key, and then press the TAB key.

A box containing the File Manager application icon and window title (File Manager) displays (Figure 2-61).

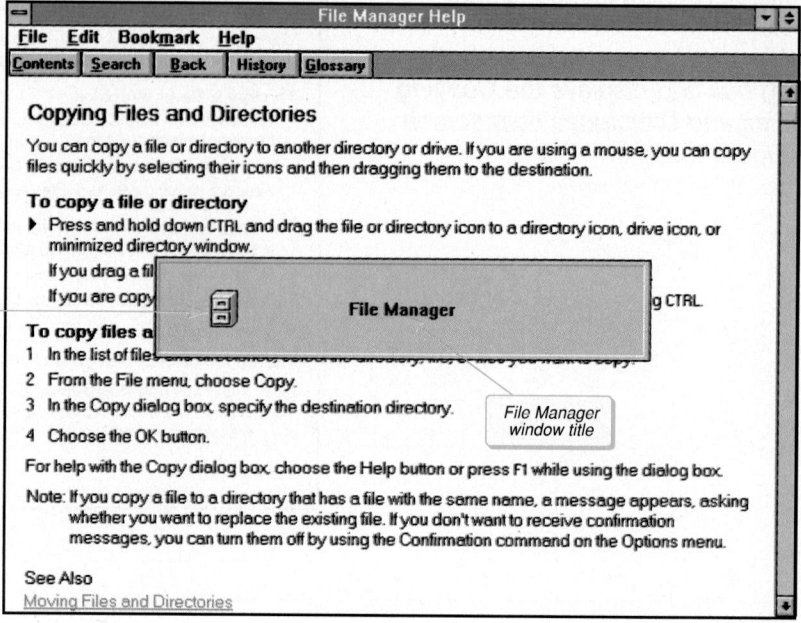

FIGURE 2-61

STEP 2 ▶

Release the ALT key.

The File Manager window moves on top of the other windows on the desktop (Figure 2-62).

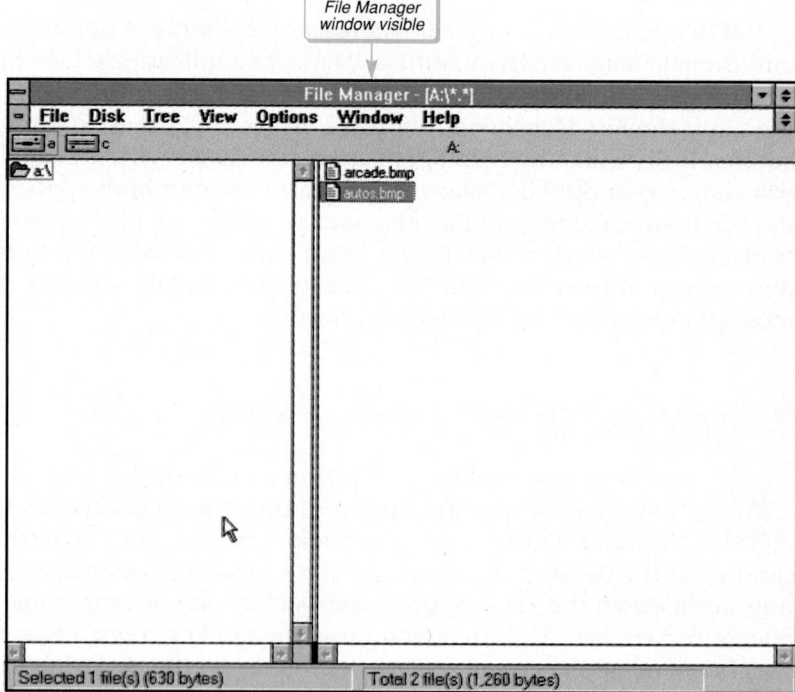

FIGURE 2-62

Verify Changes to the File Manager Window Will Not Be Saved

Because you want to return the File Manager window to its state before you started the application, no changes should be saved. The **Save Settings on Exit command** on the Options menu controls whether changes to the File Manager window are saved or not saved when you quit File Manager. A check mark (✔) preceding the Save Settings on Exit command indicates the command is active and all changes to the layout of the File Manager window will be saved when you quit File Manager. If the command is preceded by a check mark, choose the Save Settings on Exit command by clicking the left mouse button to remove the check mark, so the changes will not be saved. Perform the following steps to verify that changes are not saved to the File Manager window.

TO VERIFY CHANGES WILL NOT BE SAVED ▼

STEP 1 ▶

Select the Options menu from the File Manager menu bar.

The Options menu opens (Figure 2-63). A check mark (✔) precedes the Save Settings on Exit command.

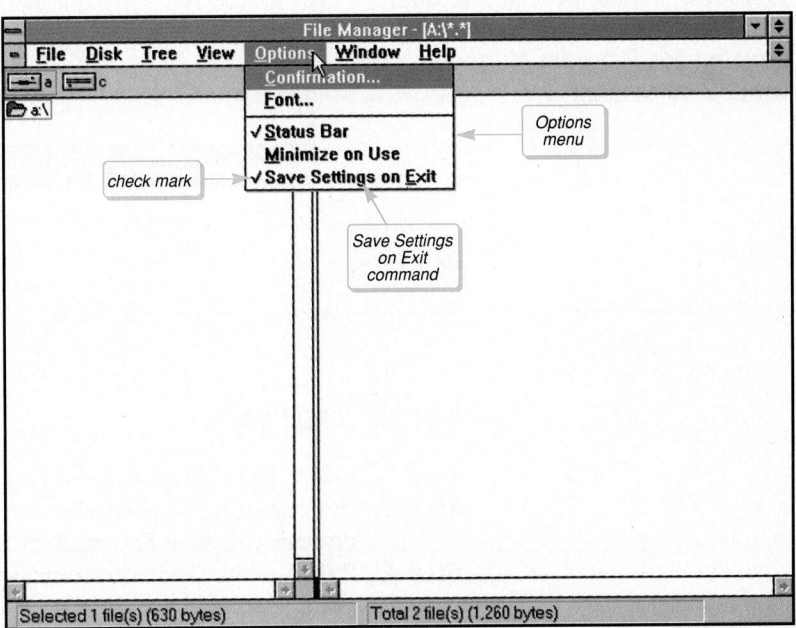

FIGURE 2-63

STEP 2 ▶

To remove the check mark, choose the Save Settings on Exit command from the Options menu by pointing to the Save Settings on Exit command and clicking the left mouse button.

Windows closes the Options menu. Although not visible, the check mark preceding the Save Settings on Exit command has been removed. This means any changes made to the desktop will not be saved when you exit File Manager.

Quitting File Manager

After verifying no changes to the File Manager window will be saved, the Save Settings on Exit command is not active, so you can quit the File Manager application. In Project 1 you chose the Exit command from the File menu to quit an application. In addition to choosing a command from a menu, you can also quit an application by pointing to the **Control-menu box** in the upper left corner of the application window and double-clicking the left mouse button, as shown in the steps on the next page.

TO QUIT AN APPLICATION ▼

STEP 1 ▶

Point to the Control-menu box in the upper left corner of the File Manager window (Figure 2-64).

STEP 2 ▶

Double-click the left mouse button to exit the File Manager application.

Windows closes the File Manager and File Manager Help windows, causing the Program Manager window to display.

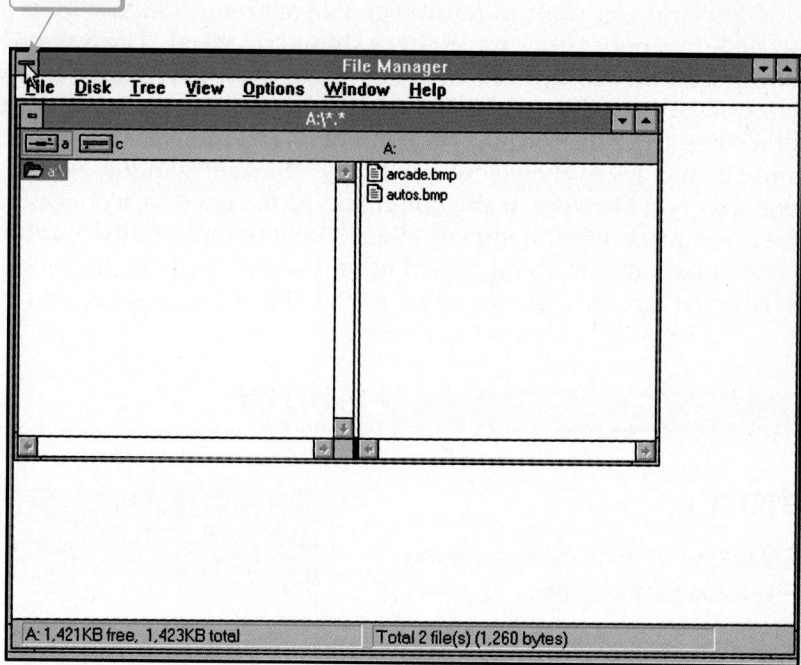

FIGURE 2-64

TO QUIT WINDOWS

Step 1: Select the Options menu from the Program Manager menu bar.
Step 2: If a check mark precedes the Save Settings on Exit command, choose the Save Settings on Exit command.
Step 3: Point to the Control-menu box in the upper left corner of the Program Manager window.
Step 4: Double-click the left mouse button.
Step 5: Choose the OK button to exit Windows.

▶ ADDITIONAL COMMANDS AND CONCEPTS

I n addition to the commands and concepts presented in Project 1 and this project, you should understand how to activate a group window, arrange the program-item icons in a group window, and close a group window. These topics are discussed on the following pages. In addition, methods to resize a window and minimize an application window to an application icon are explained.

Activating a Group Window

Frequently, several group windows are open in the Program Manager window at the same time. In Figure 2-65, two group windows (Main and Accessories) are open. The Accessories window is the active group window, and the inactive Main window is partially hidden behind the Accessories window. To view a group window that is partially hidden, activate the hidden window by selecting the Window menu and then choosing the name of the group window you wish to view.

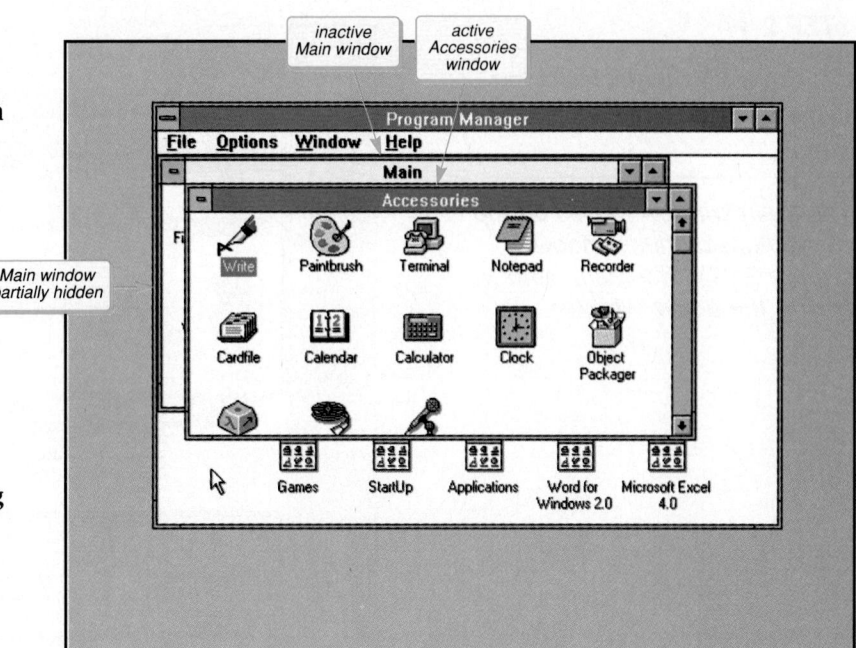

FIGURE 2-65

TO ACTIVATE A GROUP WINDOW ▼

STEP 1 ▶

Select the Window menu from the Program Manager menu bar, and then point to the Main group window name.

The Window menu consists of two areas separated by a horizontal line (Figure 2-66). Below the line is a list of the group windows and group icons in the Program Manager window. Each entry in the list is preceded by a value from one to seven. The number of the active window (Accessories) is preceded by a check mark and the mouse pointer points to the Main group window name.

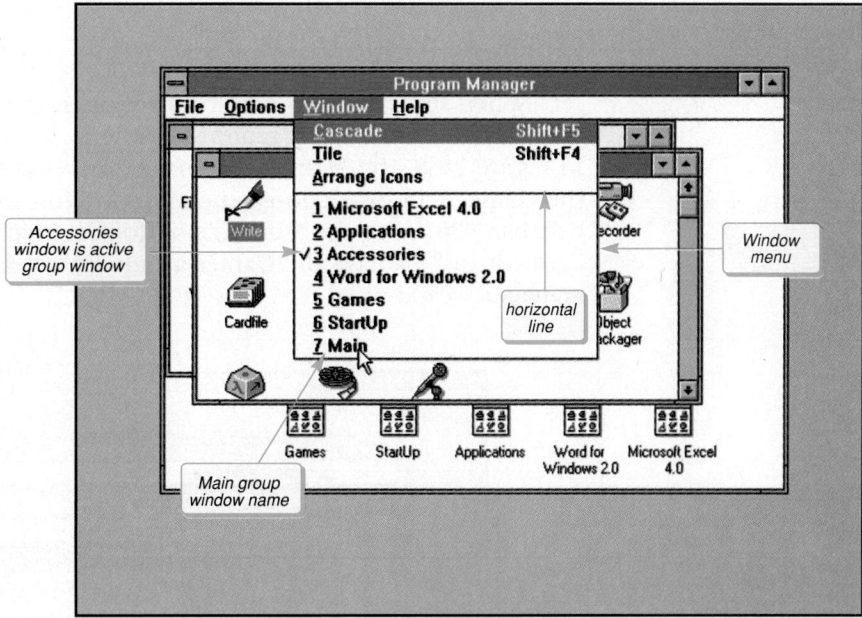

FIGURE 2-66

STEP 2 ▶

Choose the Main group window name by clicking the left mouse button.

The Main window moves on top of the Accessories window (Figure 2-67). The Main window is now the active window.

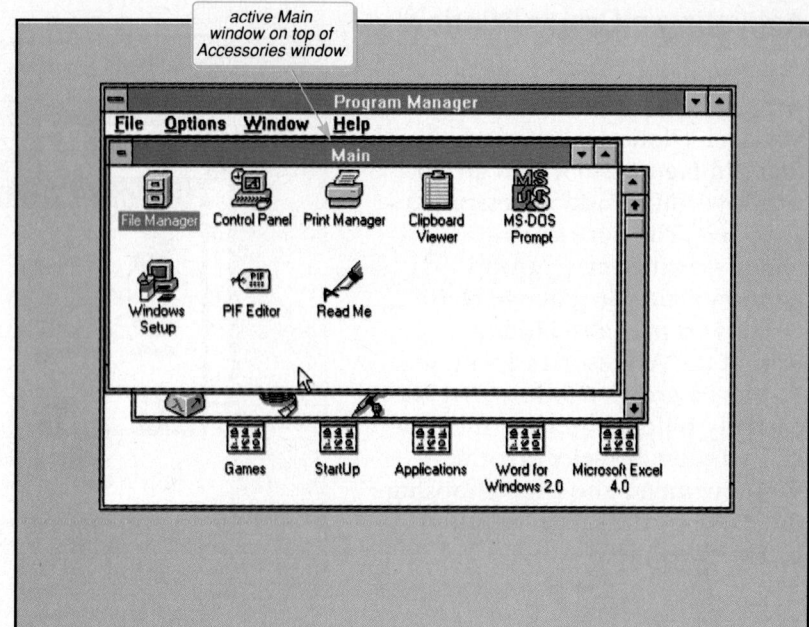

FIGURE 2-67

An alternative method of activating an inactive window is to point to any open area of the window and click the left mouse button. This method cannot be used if the inactive window is completely hidden behind another window.

Closing a Group Window

When several group windows are open in the Program Manager window, you may want to close a group window to reduce the number of open windows. In Figure 2-68, the Main, Accessories, and Games windows are open. To close the Games window, choose the Minimize button on the right side of the Games title bar. Choosing the Minimize button removes the group window from the desktop and displays the Games group icon at the bottom of the Program Manager window.

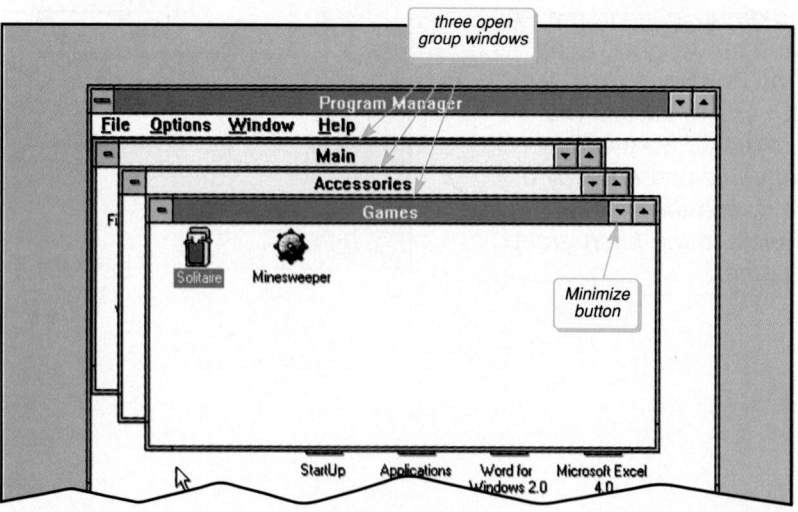

FIGURE 2-68

TO CLOSE A GROUP WINDOW ▼

STEP 1 ▶

Choose the Minimize button (⏷) on the Games title bar.

The Games window closes and the Games icon displays at the bottom edge of the Program Manager window (Figure 2-69).

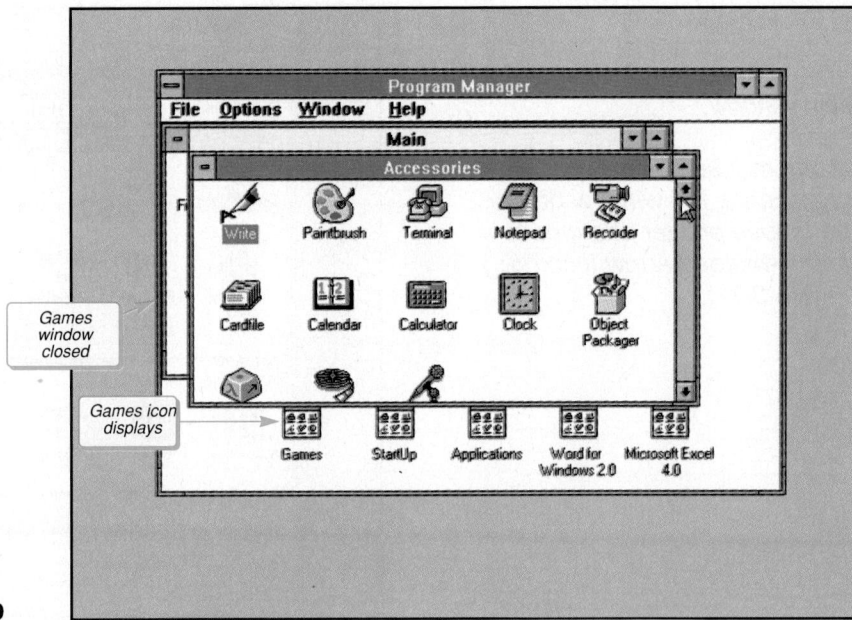

FIGURE 2-69

Resizing a Group Window

When more than six group icons display at the bottom of the Program Manager window, some group icons may not be completely visible. In Figure 2-70, the name of the Microsoft SolutionsSeries icon is partially visible. To make the icon visible, resize the Main window by dragging the bottom window border toward the window title.

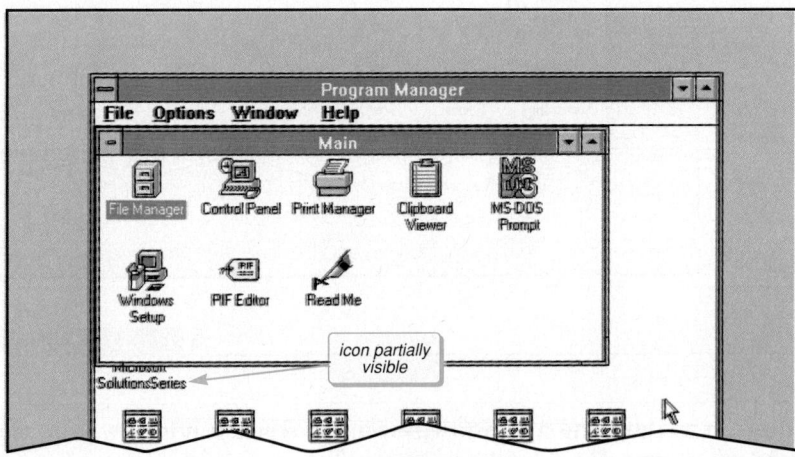

FIGURE 2-70

TO RESIZE A WINDOW ▼

STEP 1 ▶

Point to the bottom border of the Main window.

As the mouse pointer approaches the window border, the mouse pointer changes to a double-headed arrow icon (⇕) (Figure 2-71).

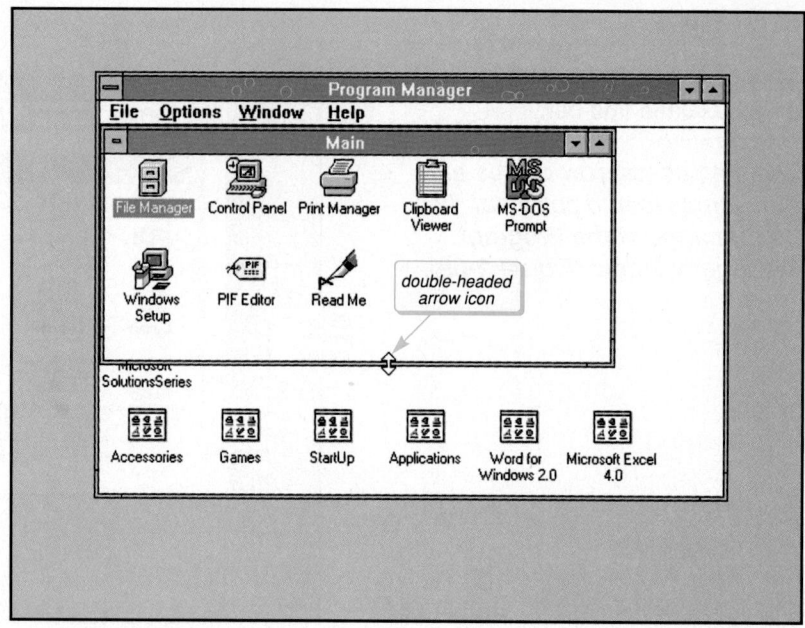

FIGURE 2-71

STEP 2 ▶

Drag the bottom border toward the window title until the Microsoft SolutionsSeries icon is visible.

The Main window changes shape, and the Microsoft SolutionsSeries icon is visible (Figure 2-72).

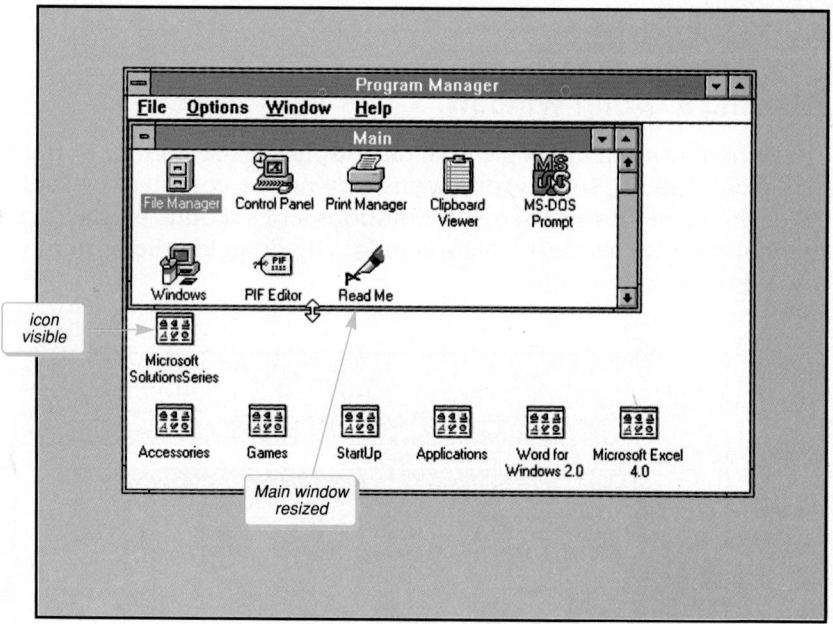

FIGURE 2-72

In addition to dragging a window border to resize a window, you can also drag a window corner to resize the window. By dragging a corner, you can change both the width and length of a window.

Arranging Icons

Occasionally, a program-item icon is either accidentally or intentionally moved within a group window. The result is that the program-item icons are not arranged in an organized fashion in the window. Figure 2-73 shows the eight program-item icons in the Main window. One icon, the File Manager icon, is not aligned with the other icons. As a result, the icons in the Main window appear unorganized. To arrange the icons in the Main window, choose the **Arrange Icons command** from the Window menu.

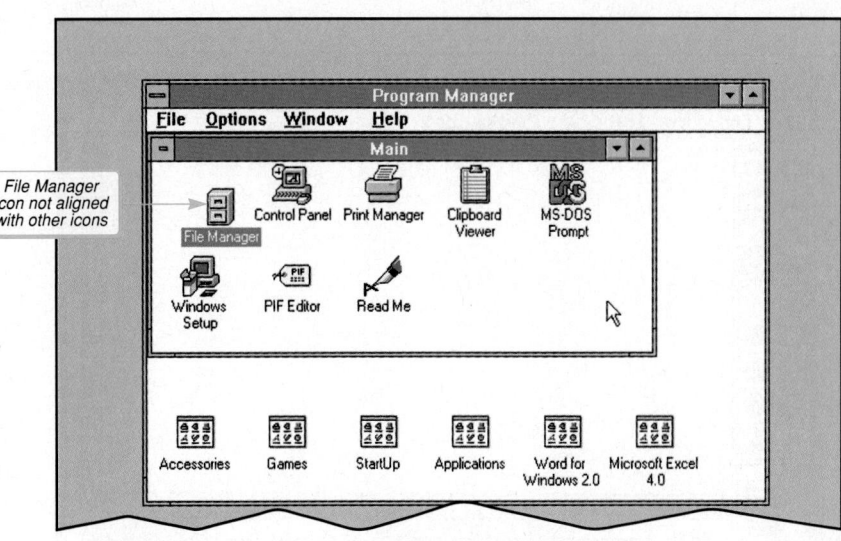

FIGURE 2-73

TO ARRANGE PROGRAM-ITEM ICONS ▼

STEP 1 ▶

Select the Window menu from the Program Manager menu bar, and then point to the Arrange Icons command.

Windows opens the Window menu (Figure 2-74). The mouse pointer points to the Arrange Icons command.

FIGURE 2-74

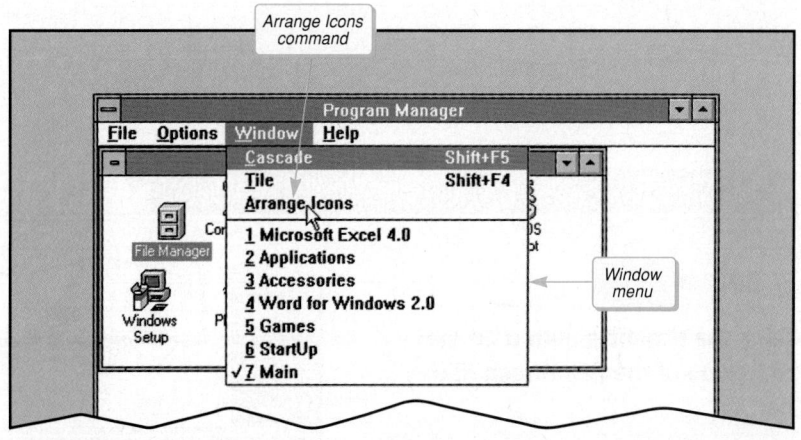

STEP 2 ▶

Choose the Arrange Icons command by clicking the left mouse button.

The icons in the Main window are arranged (Figure 2-75).

FIGURE 2-75

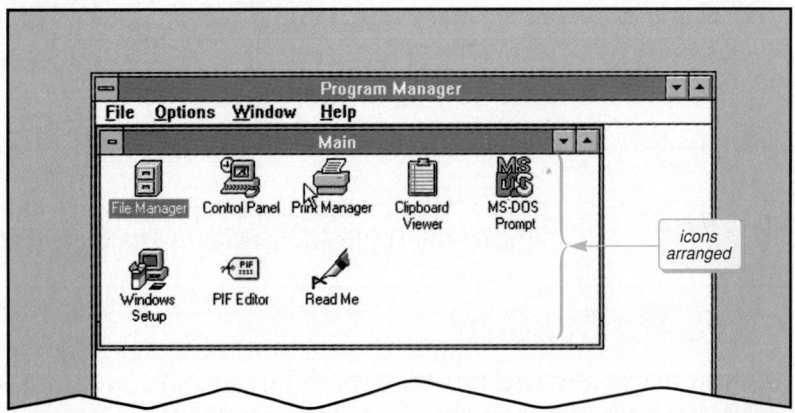

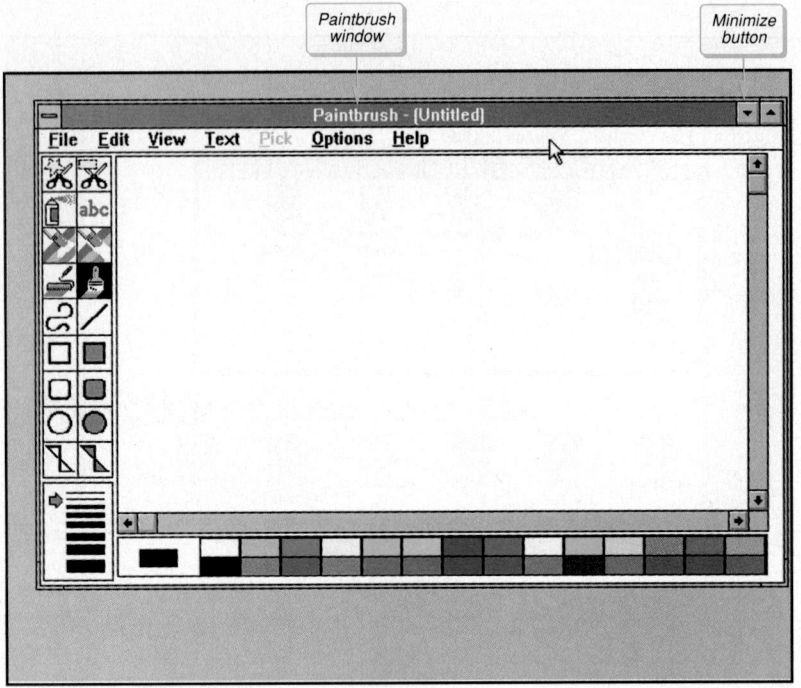

FIGURE 2-76

Minimizing an Application Window to an Icon

When you finish work in an application and there is a possibility of using the application again before quitting Windows, you should minimize the application window to an application icon instead of quitting the application. An **application icon** represents an application that was started and then minimized. Minimizing a window to an application icon saves you the time of starting the application and maximizing its window if you decide to use the application again. In addition, you free space on the desktop without quitting the application. The desktop in Figure 2-76 contains the Paintbrush window. To minimize the Paintbrush window to an application icon, click the Minimize button on the right side of the Paintbrush title bar.

TO MINIMIZE AN APPLICATION WINDOW TO AN ICON ▼

STEP 1 ►

Click the Minimize button on the right side of the Paintbrush title bar.

Windows closes the Paintbrush window and displays the Paintbrush application icon at the bottom of the desktop (Figure 2-77).

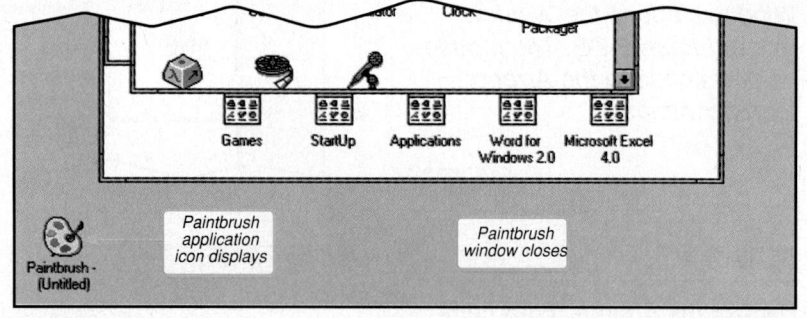

FIGURE 2-77

After minimizing an application window to an application icon, you can start the application again by double-clicking the application icon.

► PROJECT SUMMARY

In this project, you used File Manager to format and copy a diskette, copy a group of files, and rename and delete a file. You searched for help about File Manager using the Search feature of online Help, and you switched between applications on the desktop. In addition, you activated, resized, and closed a group window, arranged the icons in a group window, and minimized an application window to an application icon.

▶ Key Terms

application icon (*WIN86*)
Arrange Icons command
 (*WIN85*)
backup diskette (*WIN47*)
Cascade command (*WIN94*)
contents list (*WIN49*)
Control-menu box (*WIN79*)
Copy Disk command (*WIN67*)
current drive (*WIN48*)
Delete command (*WIN65*)
destination directory (*WIN54*)
destination diskette (*WIN67*)
destination drive (*WIN54*)

directory structure (*WIN49*)
directory tree (*WIN49*)
directory window (*WIN48*)
Disk Copy command (*WIN71*)
Disk menu (*WIN51*)
diskette capacity (*WIN50*)
diskette size (*WIN50*)
drive icon (*WIN48*)
File Manager (*WIN48*)
Format Disk command (*WIN51*)
formatting (*WIN50*)
Help menu (*WIN72*)

Options menu (*WIN79*)
Rename command (*WIN63*)
Save Settings on Exit command
 (*WIN79*)
Search for Help on command
 (*WIN72*)
source directory (*WIN54*)
source diskette (*WIN67*)
source drive (*WIN54*)
split bar (*WIN49*)
Tile command (*WIN94*)
Window menu (*WIN81*)

Q U I C K   R E F E R E N C E

In Windows you can accomplish a task in a number of ways. The following table provides a quick reference to each task presented in the project with its available options. The commands listed in the Menu column can be executed using either the keyboard or mouse.

Task	Mouse	Menu	Keyboard Shortcuts
Activate a Group Window	Click group window	From Window menu, choose window title	
Arrange Program-Item Icons in a Group Window		From Window menu, choose Arrange Icons	
Change the Current Drive	Click drive icon		Press TAB to move highlight to drive icon area, press arrow keys to outline drive icon, and press ENTER
Close a Group Window	Click Minimize button or double-click control-menu box	From Control menu, choose Close	Press CTRL + F4
Copy a Diskette		From Disk menu, choose Copy Disk	
Copy a File or Group of Files	Drag highlighted file-name(s) to destination drive or directory icon	From File menu, choose Copy	
Delete a File		From File menu, choose Delete	Press DEL
Format a Diskette		From Disk menu, choose Format Disk	

(continued)

QUICK REFERENCE (continued)

Task	Mouse	Menu	Keyboard Shortcuts
Maximize a Directory Window	Click Maximize button	From Control menu, choose Maximize	
Minimize an Application Window	Click Minimize button	From Control menu, choose Minimize	Press ALT, SPACE BAR, N
Rename a File		From File menu, choose Rename	
Resize a Window	Drag window border or corner	From Control menu, choose Size	
Save Changes when Quitting File Manager		From Options menu, choose Save Settings on Exit if no check mark precedes command	
Save No Changes when Quitting Windows		From Options menu, choose Save Settings on Exit if check mark precedes command	
Search for a Help Topic		From Help menu, choose Search for Help on	
Select a File in the Contents List	Click the filename		Press arrow keys to outline filename, press SHIFT + F8
Select a Group of Files in the Contents List	Select first file, hold down CTRL key and select other files		Press arrow keys to outline first file, press SHIFT + F8, press arrow keys to outline each additional filename, and press SPACEBAR
Switch between Applications	Click application window		Hold down ALT, press TAB (or ESC), release ALT

S T U D E N T   A S S I G N M E N T S

STUDENT ASSIGNMENT 1
True/False

Instructions: Circle T if the statement is true or F if the statement if false.

T F   1. Formatting prepares a diskette for use on a computer.

T F   2. It is not important to create a backup diskette of the Business Documents diskette.

T F   3. Program Manager is an application you can use to organize and work with your hard disk and diskettes and the files on those disks.

T F   4. A directory window title bar usually contains the current directory path.

T F   5. A directory window consists of a directory tree and contents list.

T F   6. The directory tree contains a list of the files in the current directory.

T F   7. The disk capacity of a 3 1/2-inch diskette is typically 360K or 1.2MB.

T F   8. The source drive is the drive from which files are copied.

T F   9. You select a single file in the contents list by pointing to the filename and clicking the left mouse button.

T F 10. You select a group of files in the contents list by pointing to each filename and clicking the left mouse button.

T F 11. Windows opens the Error Copying File dialog box if you try to copy a file to an unformatted diskette.

T F 12. You change the filename or extension of a file using the Change command.

T F 13. Windows opens the Confirm File Delete dialog box when you try to delete a file.

T F 14. When creating a backup diskette, the disk to receive the copy is the source disk.

T F 15. The first step in creating a backup diskette is to choose the Copy Disk command from the Disk menu.

T F 16. On some computers, you may have to insert and remove the source and destination diskettes several times to copy a diskette.

T F 17. Both the Search for Help on command and the Search button initiate a search for help.

T F 18. An application icon represents an application that was started and then minimized.

T F 19. You hold down the TAB key, press the ALT key, and then release the TAB key to switch between applications on the desktop.

T F 20. An application icon displays on the desktop when you minimize an application window.

STUDENT ASSIGNMENT 2
Multiple Choice

Instructions: Circle the correct response.

1. The _____ application allows you to format a diskette.
   a. Program Manager
   b. File Manager
   c. online Help
   d. Paintbrush

2. The _____ contains the directory structure of the current drive.
   a. contents list
   b. status bar
   c. split bar
   d. directory tree

3. The _____ key is used when selecting a group of files.
   a. CTRL
   b. ALT
   c. TAB
   d. ESC

4. After selecting a group of files, you _____ the group of files to copy the files to a new drive or directory.
   a. click
   b. double-click
   c. drag
   d. none of the above

5. The commands to rename and delete a file are located on the _____ menu.
   a. Window
   b. Options
   c. Disk
   d. File

6. The first step in creating a backup diskette is to _____.
   a. write-protect the destination diskette
   b. choose the Copy command from the Disk menu
   c. write-protect the source diskette
   d. label the destination diskette

STUDENT ASSIGNMENT 2 (continued)

7. When searching for help, the _____ button displays a list of Help topics.
   a. Go To
   b. Topics
   c. Show Topics
   d. Search

8. You use the _____ and _____ keys to switch between applications on the desktop.
   a. ALT, TAB
   b. SHIFT, ALT
   c. ALT, CTRL
   d. ESC, CTRL

9. When you choose a window title from the Window menu, Windows _____ the associated group window.
   a. opens
   b. closes
   c. enlarges
   d. activates

10. To resize a group window, you can use the _____.
    a. title bar
    b. window border
    c. resize command on the Window menu
    d. arrange Icons command on the Options menu

STUDENT ASSIGNMENT 3
Identifying the Parts of a Directory Window

Instructions: On the desktop in Figure SA2-3, arrows point to several items in the C:\WINDOWS*.* directory window. Identify the items in the space provided.

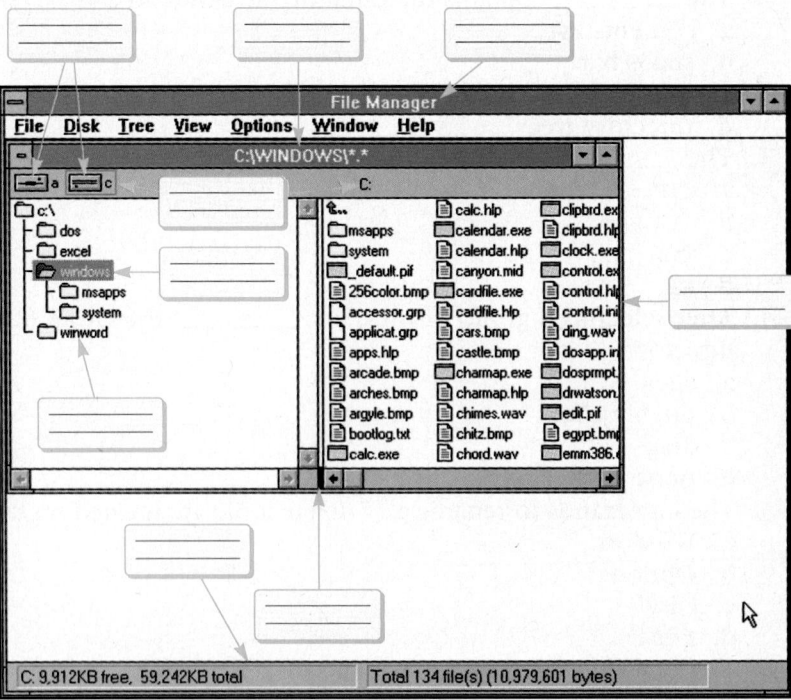

FIGURE SA2-3

STUDENT ASSIGNMENT 4
Selecting a Group of Files

Instructions: Using the desktop in Figure SA2-4, list the steps to select the group of files consisting of the ARCADE.BMP, CARS.BMP, and EGYPT.BMP files in the space provided.

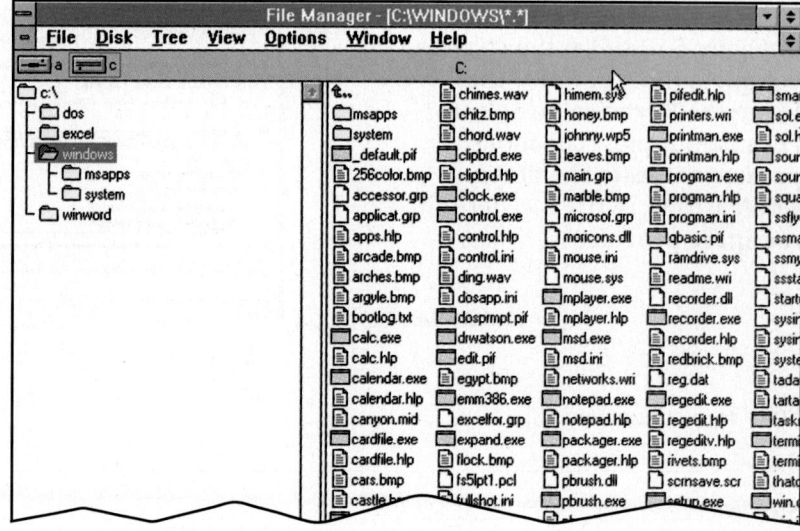

FIGURE SA2-4

Step 1: _____

Step 2: _____

Step 3: _____

Step 4: _____

STUDENT ASSIGNMENT 5
Copying a Group of Files

Instructions: Using the desktop in Figure SA2-5, list the steps to copy the group of files selected in Student Assignment 4 to the root directory of drive A. Write the steps in the space provided.

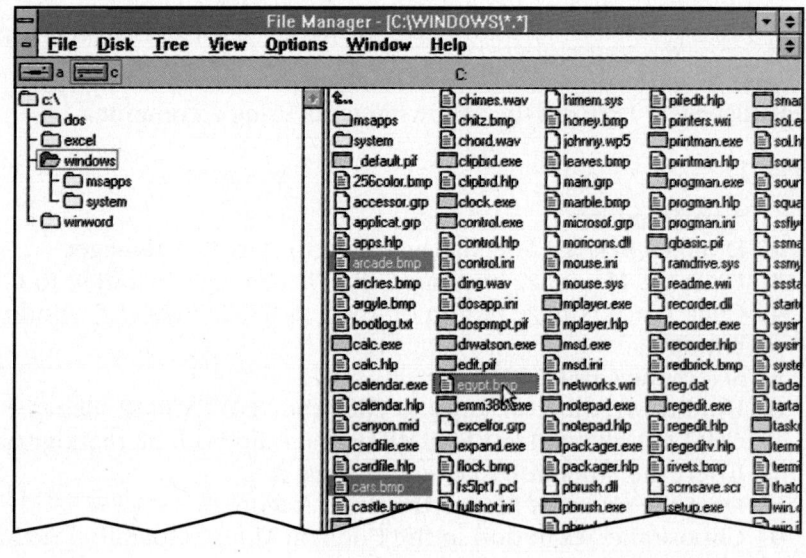

FIGURE SA2-5

Step 1: _____

Step 2: _____

Step 3: _____

Step 4: _____

STUDENT ASSIGNMENT 6
Searching for Help

Instructions: Using the desktop in Figure SA2-6, list the steps to complete the search for the Using the Keyboard to Select Files help topic. The mouse pointer points to the down scroll arrow. Write the steps in the space provided.

FIGURE SA2-6

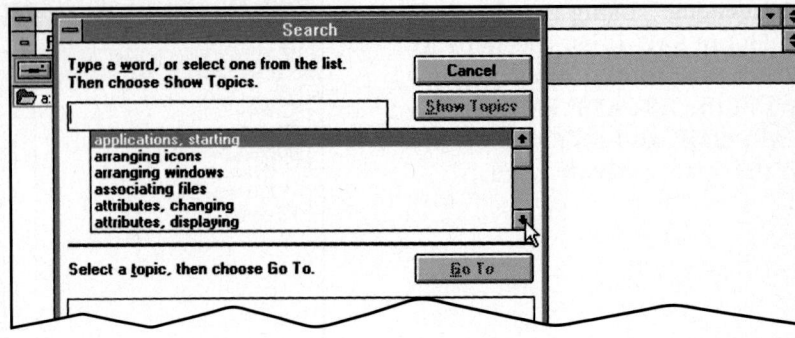

Step 1: _____

Step 2: _____

Step 3: _____

Step 4: _____

Step 5: _____

Step 6: _____

C O M P U T E R   L A B O R A T O R Y   E X E R C I S E S

COMPUTER LABORATORY EXERCISE 1
Selecting and Copying Files

Instructions: Perform the following tasks using a computer.

Part 1:

1. Start Windows.
2. Double-click the File Manager icon to start File Manager.
3. Click the Maximize button on the File Manager window to enlarge the File Manager window.
4. Click the Maximize button on the C:\WINDOWS*.* window to enlarge the C:\WINDOWS*.* window.
5. Select the CHITZ.BMP file.
6. Hold down the CTRL key and click the LEAVES.BMP filename to select the LEAVES.BMP file. The CHITZ.BMP and LEAVES.BMP files should both be highlighted.
7. Insert the Student Diskette into drive A.
8. Drag the group of files to the drive A icon.
9. Choose the Yes button in the Confirm Mouse Operation dialog box.
10. Choose the drive A icon to change the current drive to drive A.
11. Select the CHITZ.BMP file.
12. Choose the Delete command from the File menu.
13. Choose the OK button in the Delete dialog box.
14. Choose the Yes button in the Confirm File Delete dialog box.
15. If the LEAVES.BMP file is not highlighted, select the LEAVES.BMP file.

16. Choose the Rename command from the File menu.
17. Type AUTUMN.BMP in the To text box.
18. Choose the OK button in the Rename dialog box to rename the LEAVES.BMP file.

Part 2:

 1. Hold down the ALT key, press the TAB key, and release the ALT key to switch to the Program Manager application.
 2. Double-click the Accessories icon to open the Accessories window.
 3. Double-click the Paintbrush icon to start Paintbrush.
 4. Click the Maximize button on the Paintbrush window to enlarge the Paintbrush window.
 5. Choose the Open command from the File menu.
 6. Click the Down Arrow button in the Drives drop down list box to display the Drives drop down list.
 7. Select the drive A icon.
 8. Select the AUTUMN.BMP file in the File Name list box.
 9. Choose the OK button to retrieve the AUTUMN.BMP file into Paintbrush.
10. Choose the Print command from the File menu.
11. Click the Draft option button in the Print dialog box.
12. Choose the OK button in the Print dialog box to print the contents of the AUTUMN.BMP file.
13. Remove the Student Diskette from drive A.
14. Choose the Exit command from the File menu to quit Paintbrush.
15. Hold down the ALT key, press the TAB key, and release the ALT key to switch to the File Manager application.
16. Select the Options menu.
17. If a check mark precedes the Save Settings on Exit command, choose the Save Settings on Exit command.
18. Choose the Exit command from the File menu of the File Manager window to quit File Manager.
19. Choose the Exit Windows command from the File menu of the Program Manager window.
20. Click the OK button to quit Windows.

COMPUTER LABORATORY EXERCISE 2
Searching with Online Help

Instructions: Perform the following tasks using a computer.

 1. Start Microsoft Windows.
 2. Double-click the Accessories icon to open the Accessories window.
 3. Double-click the Write icon to start the Write application.
 4. Click the Maximize button on the Write window to enlarge the Write window.
 5. Choose the Search for Help on command from the Help menu.
 6. Scroll the Search For list box to make the cutting text topic visible.
 7. Select the cutting text topic.
 8. Choose the Show Topics button.
 9. Choose the Go To button to display the Copying, Cutting, and Pasting Text topic.
10. Click the Maximize button on the Write Help window to enlarge the window.
11. Choose the Print Topic command from the File menu to print the Copying, Cutting, and Pasting Text topic on the printer.
12. Choose the Search button.
13. Enter the word paste in the Search For list box.
14. Select the Pasting Pictures search topic.
15. Choose the Show Topics button.
16. Choose the Go To button to display the Copying, Cutting, and Pasting Pictures topic.
17. Choose the Print Topic command from the File menu to print the Copying, Cutting, and Pasting Pictures topic on the printer.

COMPUTER LABORATORY EXERCISE 2 (continued)

18. Choose the Exit command from the File menu to quit Write Help.
19. Choose the Exit command from the File menu to quit Write.
20. Select the Options menu.
21. If a check mark precedes the Save Settings on Exit command, choose the Save Settings on Exit command.
22. Choose the Exit Windows command from the File menu.
23. Click the OK button to quit Windows.

COMPUTER LABORATORY EXERCISE 3
Working with Group Windows

Instructions: Perform the following tasks using a computer.

1. Start Windows. The Main window should be open in the Program Manger window.
2. Double-click the Accessories icon to open the Accessories window.
3. Double-click the Games icon to open the Games window.
4. Choose the Accessories window title from the Window menu to activate the Accessories window.
5. Click the Minimize button on the Accessories window to close the Accessories window.
6. Choose the **Tile command** from the Window menu. The Tile command arranges a group of windows so no windows overlap, all windows are visible, and each window occupies an equal portion of the screen.
7. Move and resize the Main and Games windows to resemble the desktop in Figure CLE2-3. To resize a window, drag the window border or corner. To move a group window, drag the window title bar. Choose the Arrange Icons command from the Window menu to arrange the icons in each window.

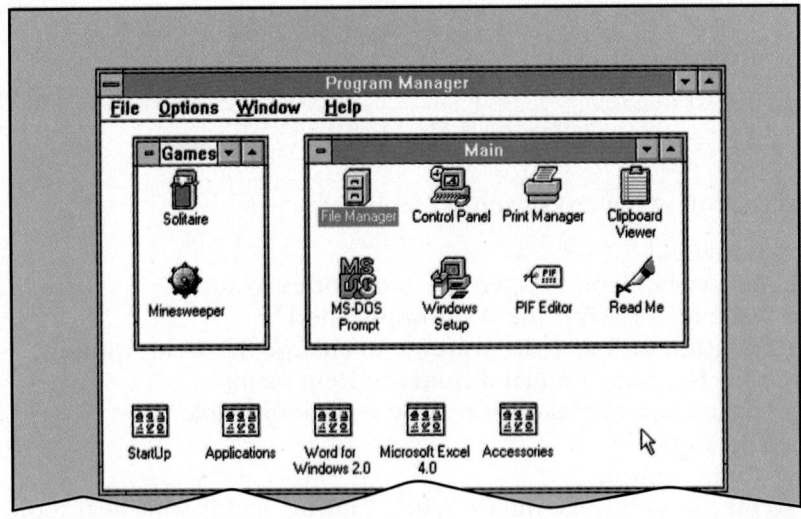

FIGURE CLE2-3

8. Press the PRINTSCREEN key to capture the desktop.
9. Open the Accessories window.
10. Choose the **Cascade command** from the Window menu. The Cascade command arranges a group of windows so the windows overlap and the title bar of each window is visible.
11. Double-click the Paintbrush icon to start Paintbrush.
12. Click the Maximize button on the Paintbrush window to enlarge the Paintbrush window.
13. Choose the Paste command from the Edit menu to place the picture of the desktop in the window.
14. Choose the Print command from the File menu.

15. Click the Draft option button.
16. Choose the OK button in the Print dialog box to print the desktop.
17. Choose the Exit command from the File menu of the Paintbrush window.
18. Choose the No button to not save current changes and quit Paintbrush.
19. Select the Options menu.
20. If a check mark precedes the Save Settings on Exit command, choose the Save Settings on Exit command.
21. Choose the Exit Windows command from the File menu.
22. Click the OK button.

COMPUTER LABORATORY EXERCISE 4
Backing Up Your Student Diskette

Instructions: Perform the following tasks using a computer to back up your Student Diskette.

Part 1:

1. Start Windows.
2. Double-click the File Manager icon to start the File Manager application.
3. Click the Maximize button on the File Manager window to enlarge the File Manager window.
4. Write-protect the Student Diskette.
5. Choose the Copy Disk command from the Disk menu.
6. Choose the Yes button in the Confirm Copy Disk dialog box.
7. Insert the source diskette (Student Diskette) into drive A.
8. Choose the OK button in the Copy Disk dialog box.
9. When prompted, insert the destination diskette (the formatted diskette created in this project) into drive A.
10. Choose the OK button in the Copy Disk dialog box.
11. Insert and remove the source and destination diskette until the copy process is complete.
12. Click the drive A icon to change the current drive to drive A.
13. Press the PRINTSCREEN key to capture the desktop.
14. Select the Options menu on the File Manager menu bar.
15. If a check mark precedes the Save Settings on Exit command, choose the Save Settings on Exit command.
16. Choose the Exit command from the File menu on the File Manager menu bar to quit File Manager.

Part 2:

1. Double-click the Accessories icon to open the Accessories window.
2. Double-click the Paintbrush icon to start Paintbrush.
3. Click the Maximize button to enlarge the Paintbrush window.
4. Choose the Paste command from the Edit menu to place the picture of the desktop in the window.
5. Choose the Print command from the File menu.
6. Click the Draft option button.
7. Choose the OK button in the Print dialog box to print the picture of the desktop on the printer.
8. Choose the Exit command from the File menu.
9. Choose the No button to not save current changes and quit Paintbrush.
10. Select the Options menu.
11. If a check mark precedes the Save Settings on Exit command, choose the Save Settings on Exit command.
12. Choose the Exit Windows command from the File menu of the Program Manager menu bar.
13. Click the OK button to quit Windows.
14. Remove the diskette from drive A.
15. Remove the write-protection from the Student Diskette.

INDEX

Active command, WIN36, WIN79
Active icon, **WIN18**
Active window, **WIN15**–16,
  WIN81–82
ALT key, switching between applications and, WIN77–78
Application(s), **WIN3**
  inactive, WIN17·
  quitting, WIN21–22, WIN28, WIN32,
    WIN79–80
  starting, WIN16–17
  switching between, WIN77–78
Application icon, **WIN86**
Application software, **WIN3**
Application window
  displaying hidden, WIN77–80
  maximizing, WIN18
Arrange Icons command, **WIN85**
Asterisk (*), group of files and, WIN23
Auxiliary storage device, WIN23

Backslash (\), directory and, WIN24,
  WIN48
Backup diskette, **WIN47, WIN67**–71,
  WIN95
Bottom window border, WIN83–84
Buttons, WIN12, WIN13

Calendar application, WIN44–45
Cancel command button, WIN21
Cancel copy operation, WIN60
Cardfile application, WIN46
Cascade command, **WIN94**
Check boxes, **WIN13**
Check mark, active command and,
  WIN36, WIN79
Choosing a command, WIN11
Close, WIN16
Closing
  group window, WIN82–83
  pop-up window, WIN35
Command, **WIN10**
  active, WIN36, WIN79
Command buttons, **WIN13**
Confirm Copy Disk dialog box, WIN68
Confirm File Delete dialog box, WIN66
Confirm File Replace dialog box,
  WIN60
Confirm Format Disk dialog box,
  WIN52
Confirm Mouse Operation dialog box,
  WIN58
Contents command, WIN33
Contents list, **WIN49,** WIN61, WIN63
Control menu, **WIN16**
Control-menu box, WIN79–80
Copy Disk command, **WIN67,** WIN68,
  WIN70
Copy Disk dialog box, WIN68–69
Copy Disk Error dialog box, WIN71
Copying Disk dialog box, WIN69
Copying dialog box, WIN58
Copying files, WIN54–62, WIN71,
  WIN92–93
  searching for help about, WIN75–77
CRT screen, WIN3
CTRL key, selecting files and,
  WIN55–57
Current directory, number of files in,
  WIN49
Current drive, **WIN48**
  changing, WIN61–62
  disk space on, WIN49
Current path, WIN24
Current selection, **WIN13**

Delete command, **WIN65**–66
Delete dialog box, WIN66
Delete text box, WIN66
Desktop, **WIN4,** WIN18, WIN49
Destination directory, **WIN54**
Destination directory icon, WIN55
Destination diskette, **WIN67,** WIN69,
  WIN70
Destination drive, **WIN54**
Destination drive icon, WIN55
Dialog boxes, **WIN12**–14
Directory, **WIN23,** WIN54–55
Directory path, **WIN24,** WIN48
Directory structure, **WIN24, WIN49**
Directory tree, **WIN49,** WIN61
Directory window, **WIN48**–49
  maximizing, WIN55
Disk, replacing file on, WIN60

Disk Copy command, **WIN71**
Disk drives, WIN48
Disk management, WIN47–71
Disk menu
  Copy Disk, WIN67, WIN68, WIN70
  Format Disk, WIN51–53
Diskette, WIN23
  protecting, WIN67
  saving document on, WIN24–28
Diskette capacity, **WIN50**–51
Diskette drive, WIN48, WIN50–51
Diskette size, **WIN50**–51
Document(s), **WIN14**
  creating, WIN19, WIN44
  printing, WIN20–21, WIN44
Document file, **WIN23**
Dragging window border to resize
  window, WIN83–84
Drive, WIN23, WIN48, WIN50–51,
  WIN54, WIN61–62
Drive icons, **WIN48**
Drives drop-down list box, WIN29
Drop-down list box, **WIN13**–14

Editing document file, WIN31,
  WIN44–45
Edit menu, help and, WIN32–34
Ellipsis, commands and, **WIN11,**
  WIN12, WIN25
Error Copying File dialog box, WIN59
Error correction
  changing current drive and, WIN62
  copying files and, WIN59–60, WIN71
  double-clicking group icon and,
    WIN16
  double-clicking program-item icon
    and, WIN18
  saving document file and, WIN27–28
Error Selecting Drive dialog box,
  WIN62
Exit command, WIN21–22, WIN28,
  WIN37
Exiting
  online help, WIN35
  Windows, WIN36–37
Extension, file, **WIN23**

File(s)
  copying to a diskette, WIN54–62
  in current directory, WIN49
  deleting, WIN65–66
  disk space occupied by, WIN49
  editing, WIN31
  naming, WIN23
  opening, WIN28–32
  renaming, WIN63–64
  replacing on disk, WIN60
  saving, WIN31–32
  selecting group of, WIN55–57,
    WIN92–93
File management, WIN47–80
  deleting files, WIN65–66
  formatting diskettes, WIN50–54
File Manager, **WIN47**–49
  quitting, WIN77, WIN79–80
  starting, WIN50
File Manager Help applications,
  quitting, WIN77
File Manager Help window, WIN74–75
File Manager icon, WIN50
File Manager menu bar, WIN48
File Manager window, WIN48, WIN55
  maximizing, WIN50
  saving changes to, WIN79
File menu, WIN25
Filename, **WIN23,** WIN48
  changing, WIN63–64
Filename extension, changing, WIN63
File Name list box, WIN30
File Name text box, WIN25
Format Disk command, **WIN51**–53
Format Disk dialog box, WIN52
Format Disk Error dialog box, WIN54
Formatting a diskette, **WIN27,**
  WIN50–54
  error correction and, WIN54
Formatting Complete dialog box,
  WIN53
Formatting Disk dialog box, WIN53

Games, Solitaire, WIN43
Glossary definition, help and, WIN34
Go To button, WIN74
Graphical user interface (GUI), **WIN3**
Group icons, WIN14

error correction while
  double-clicking, WIN16
Group of files
  copying, WIN57–58, WIN92–93
  selecting, WIN55–57, WIN92–93
Group window(s), WIN81–85,
  WIN94–95
  activating, WIN81–82
  active window, WIN15–16
  closing, WIN82–83
  hidden, WIN81
  opening, WIN14–15
  resizing, WIN83–84

Hard disk, WIN23
Hard drive, WIN48
Help, online, **WIN32**–35, WIN46,
  WIN71–77, WIN93–94
  exiting, WIN35, WIN77
  searching with, WIN71–77,
    WIN93–94
Help menu, WIN33
  Search for Help, WIN72
  Windows Tutorial, WIN43
Help topic, **WIN33**–35
  searching for, WIN47, WIN72–75
Help Topics list box, WIN74

Icon(s)
  active, WIN18
  arranging, WIN85
  Control menu for, WIN16
  drive, **WIN48**
  file folder, WIN24
  minimizing application window to,
    WIN86
Insertion point, **WIN17,** WIN19

Jump, **WIN33**

Keyboard, WIN3, **WIN9**–10
Keyboard shortcuts, **WIN10,** WIN11

Main memory, copying disks and,
  WIN69, WIN70
Maximize, WIN16
  application window, WIN18
  directory window, WIN55
  File Manager Help window, WIN75
  File Manager window, WIN55
  Help window, WIN33
  Notepad window, WIN28
Maximize button, **WIN18,** WIN50,
  WIN55
Menu(s), **WIN10**–11, WIN20–21
Menu bar, **WIN10**
Microsoft Windows, *see* Windows,
  Microsoft
Minimize, WIN16
  application window to an icon,
    WIN86
Minimize button, WIN83, WIN86
Mouse, WIN3, **WIN5**–9
  clicking, WIN7
  double-clicking, WIN8
  double-clicking and error
    correction, WIN16–18
  dragging, WIN9
  pointing with, WIN6
Mouse pointer, **WIN6**
  block arrow, WIN6
  double-headed arrow icon, WIN84
  hand, WIN33
  I-beam, WIN17
Mouse skills exercise, WIN43
Move, WIN16

Naming files, WIN23
Next, WIN16
Notepad application, **WIN14**–22
  quitting, WIN32
  starting, WIN28
Notepad dialog box, WIN21, WIN22
Notepad menu, File, WIN25

Open command, WIN29, WIN44–45
Opening file, WIN28–32
Option(s), turning on or off, WIN13
Option buttons, WIN12
Options menu, Save Settings on Exit,
  WIN36, WIN79, WIN80

Paintbrush application, **WIN32**–34,
  WIN93, WIN94, WIN95
  quitting, WIN35
Phrase, searching for help using,
  WIN75–77

Pop-up window, **WIN35**
Print command, WIN20–21
Print dialog box, WIN12–14
Printing, WIN44
  by choosing command from menu,
    WIN20–21
Program Manager menu, WIN10
Program Manager window, WIN80
  activating group window, WIN81
Program-item icons, WIN14
  double-clicking, WIN16–17
  error correction while
    double-clicking, WIN18

Quitting,
  without saving changes, WIN37

Rename command, **WIN63**–64
Rename dialog box, WIN64
Resizing group window, WIN83–84
Restore, WIN16
Restore button, **WIN18,** WIN55
Retrieving files, WIN29–30
Retry button, WIN59, WIN62
Root directory, **WIN23,** WIN24, WIN49

Save As command, WIN25
Save As dialog box, WIN25, WIN27–29
Save command, WIN31
Save Settings on Exit command,
  WIN36, **WIN79,** WIN80
Saving, WIN24–28, WIN44
  modified document file, WIN31–32
Screen, WIN3, WIN4
Scroll arrows, **WIN16**
Scroll bar, **WIN16**
Scroll box, **WIN16**
Search dialog box, WIN72, WIN76
Search feature, help and, WIN47,
  WIN71–77, WIN93–94
Search for Help on command, **WIN72**
Search topics, WIN72
Selected button, **WIN12**
Selecting a menu, **WIN11**
Selecting files search topic, WIN73
Selection, current, **WIN13**
SHIFT key, selecting group of files and,
  WIN57
Show Topics button, WIN73–74,
  WIN76
Size, Control menu and, WIN16
Size, group window, WIN83–84
Software, user interface and, WIN3
Source directory, **WIN54**
Source diskette, **WIN67,** WIN68–69
Source drive, **WIN54**
Split bar, directory window and,
  WIN49
Status bar, WIN49
Subdirectories, **WIN23,** WIN49

Text box, **WIN13**
Tile command, **WIN94**
Title bar, **WIN4**
  dialog box and, WIN12
Tutorial, WIN43
TXT extension, WIN25–26

User friendly, **WIN3**
User interface, WIN3

Window border, **WIN4**
  dragging to resize window, WIN83–84
Window corner, dragging, WIN84
Window menu, WIN81, WIN85,
  WIN94
Window title, **WIN4**
Windows, **WIN4**
  activating group, WIN81–82
  dialog box and, WIN12
  directory, WIN48–49
  minimizing to icon, WIN86
Windows, Microsoft, WIN2, WIN3
  communicating with, WIN5–14
  mouse operations and, WIN5–9
  quitting, WIN36–37
  starting, WIN4–5, WIN49–50
  tutorial, WIN43
  using, WIN14–22
Word, searching for help using,
  WIN75–77
Write application, WIN93
Write-protect window, WIN70
Write-protected diskette, **WIN27,**
  WIN28, WIN54, WIN60, WIN67,
  WIN70

WIN96

▼

CREATING A DOCUMENT

CREATING A DOCUMENT

You will have mastered the material in this project when you can:

▶ Start Microsoft Works
▶ Start the Word Processor tool
▶ Identify the features of the Works word processing window
▶ Enter text
▶ Highlight a character, word, line, or paragraph
▶ Center one or more words
▶ Change fonts, font sizes, and font styles
▶ Create a bulleted list
▶ Change the color of text

▶ Insert clip art in a document
▶ Use the Print Preview command
▶ Save a document
▶ Print a document
▶ Close a document
▶ Exit Works
▶ Open a document
▶ Delete and insert data
▶ Use online Help
▶ Use Cue Cards
▶ Use the Works Tutorial

▶ INTRODUCTION TO MICROSOFT WORKS FOR WINDOWS

icrosoft Works for Windows is applications software that provides word processing, spreadsheet, database, communications, and drawing capabilities in a single package.

The applications within Microsoft Works for Windows, called **tools**, are briefly described in the following paragraphs.

1. **Word Processor Tool** — You use the Word Processor tool to prepare all forms of personal and business communications, including letters, business and academic reports, and other types of written documents.

2. **Spreadsheet with Charting Tool** — You use the Spreadsheet with Charting tool for applications that require you to enter, calculate, manipulate, and analyze data. With the Charting tool you can display data graphically in the form of charts, such as bar charts and pie charts.

3. **Database with Reporting Tool** — You use the Database with Reporting tool for creating, sorting, retrieving, displaying, and printing data such as names and addresses of friends or customers, company inventories, employee payroll records, or other types of business or personal data. You can use the Database with Reporting tool for virtually any type of record keeping activity that requires you to create, sort, display, retrieve, and print data.

4. **Communications Tool** — The Communications tool, when used with a modem, allows you to communicate computer to computer with other computer users, information services, and special-interest bulletin board services.

5. **Microsoft Draw Tool** — You use the Microsoft Draw tool to create drawings that can be inserted into a Word Processor document or a Database form.

Microsoft Works Accessories

Additional software features, called **accessories**, are a part of the software package that help you work more effectively with the various tools. These accessories include Spelling Checker, which allows you to check the spelling in documents; ClipArt Gallery, which contains illustrations you can insert in documents; a WordArt feature, which allows you to change plain text into artistically designed text; and, Note-It, which allows you to insert pop-up notes in a document. Pop-up notes are notes that can be displayed when needed by the user. Works also provides electronic mail capabilities. These accessories will be explained in detail as they are used throughout the book.

AutoStart Templates and WorksWizards

In addition to the Microsoft Works tools and accessories, Works includes **AutoStart templates** and **WorksWizards** to assist you in using the software. AutoStart templates consist of preformatted documents designed to meet your word processing, spreadsheet, or database needs. For example, Works provides templates that you can use when you need a sales order, a purchase order, a membership roster, or a newsletter. If necessary, you can modify a template to meet specific needs.

WorksWizards permit you to create letterhead stationery, design a database, create footnotes, create a form letter, find files, and similar activities by asking you what you want to do. Based on your responses, WorksWizards perform the task. For example, when creating letterhead stationery, Works will ask if you want to emphasize your name or the name of a company. Based upon your response, the letterhead will be designed for you.

▶ PROJECT ONE

Because word processing is widely used in both the academic and business world, the Word Processor is the first of the Works tools presented. To illustrate the use and power of the Word Processor, the steps necessary to create the document shown on the next page in Figure 1-1 are explained on the following pages. This announcement advertises the opportunities available in Construction Technology at Westlake Career College.

ENROLL NOW

Construction Technology

Westlake Career College offers comprehensive training in the field of Construction Technology.

Courses of study include:

- **Computer-Assisted Design**
- **Residential and Commercial Construction**

For information, contact Janet L. Holiday, Westlake Career College.

CALL (714) 555-2339

FIGURE 1-1

To create the announcement, you must type the text, center selected lines, use several different fonts and font styles, enlarge the fonts, change the font styles to bold, insert an illustration into the document, and display the last line in red. You can easily accomplish these tasks using the Microsoft Works for Windows Word Processor.

▶ STARTING WORKS

T o start Works, Windows must be running and Program Manager must display on the screen. Open the Microsoft Works for Windows group window if necessary. Once the group window is open, complete the following steps.

TO START MICROSOFT WORKS FOR WINDOWS ▼

STEP 1 ▶

Use the mouse to point to the Microsoft Works program-item icon (Figure 1-2).

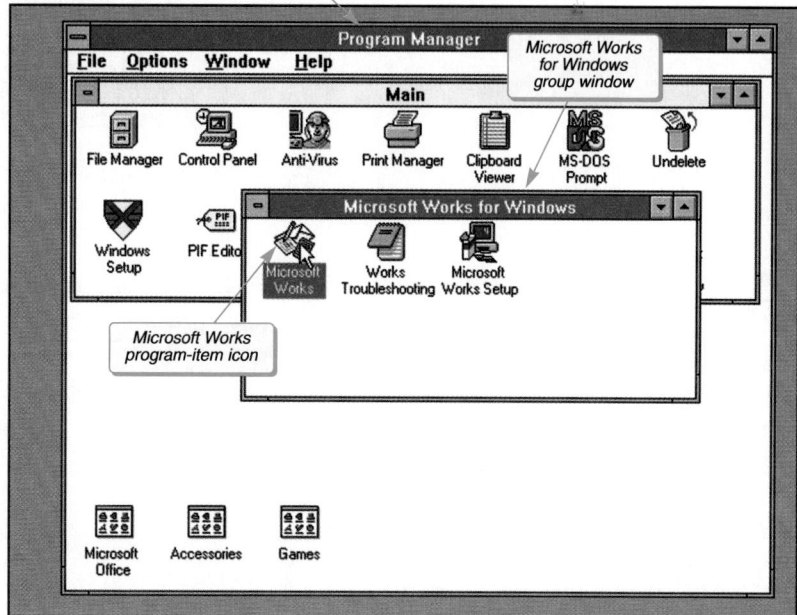

FIGURE 1-2

STEP 2 ▶

Double-click the left mouse button.

Works briefly displays a message on the screen about Works and the software license. Then, the Microsoft Works application window containing a dialog box with the title, Welcome to Microsoft Works, displays (Figure 1-3). The Welcome to Microsoft Works dialog box does not always appear. It will not display if you have previously chosen the Skip Welcome Screen button in the dialog box.

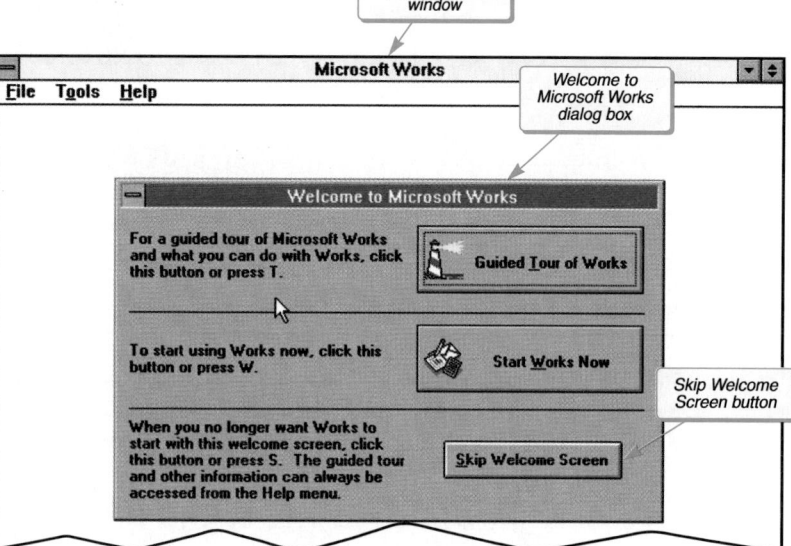

FIGURE 1-3

STEP 3 ▶

Position the mouse pointer on the Start Works Now button (Figure 1-4).

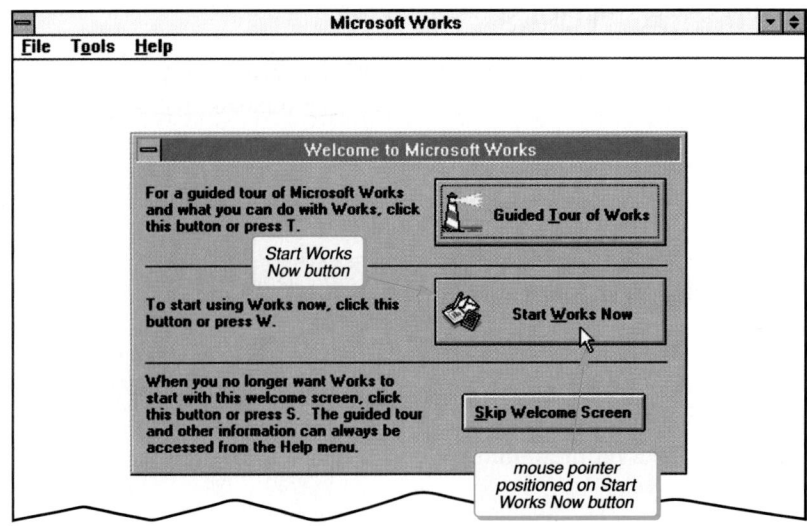

FIGURE 1-4

STEP 4 ▶

Choose the Start Works Now button in the Welcome to Microsoft Works dialog box by clicking the left mouse button.

Works displays the Startup dialog box (Figure 1-5). The buttons in the Startup dialog box allow you to start any of the Works tools, open an existing document, and use a template or WorksWizard.

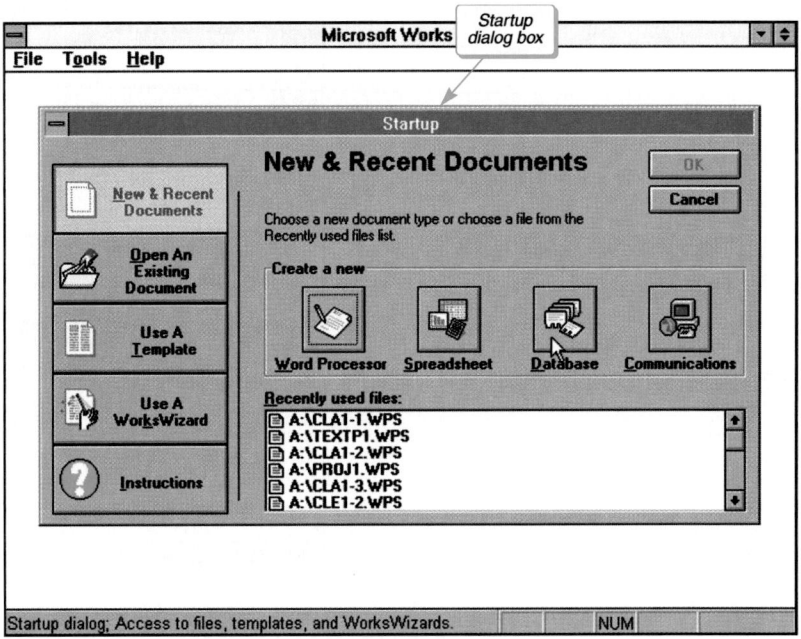

FIGURE 1-5

You have now started Works and are ready to choose the tool you want to use. To create the document in Figure 1-1 on page W1.4, use the Word Processor tool.

▶ STARTING THE WORD PROCESSOR

tart the Word Processor by choosing the appropriate button in the Startup dialog box. The following steps explain this process.

TO START THE WORD PROCESSOR ▼

STEP 1 ►

Point to the Word Processor button
(Figure 1-6).

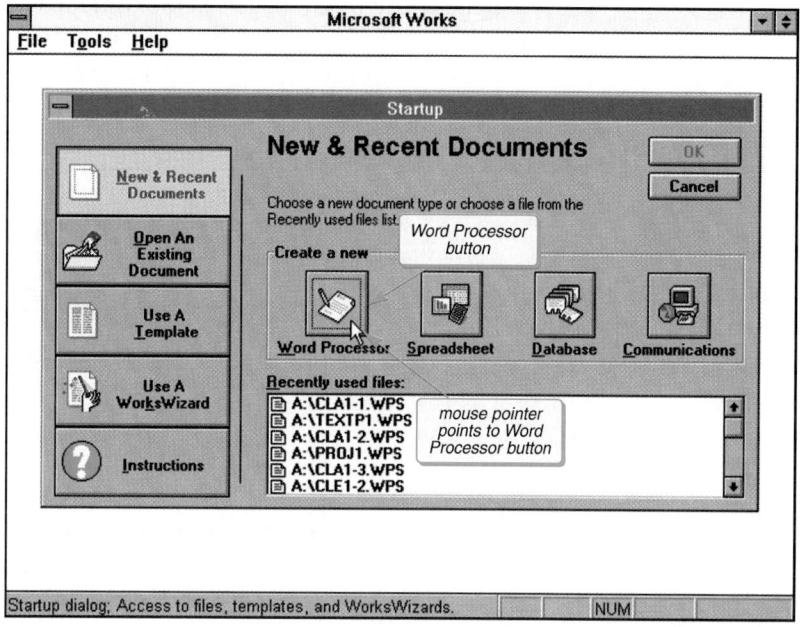

FIGURE 1-6

STEP 2 ►

Choose the Word Processor button
by clicking the left mouse button.

Works displays the Word Processor document window containing the document name, Word1, within the Microsoft Works application window (Figure 1-7).

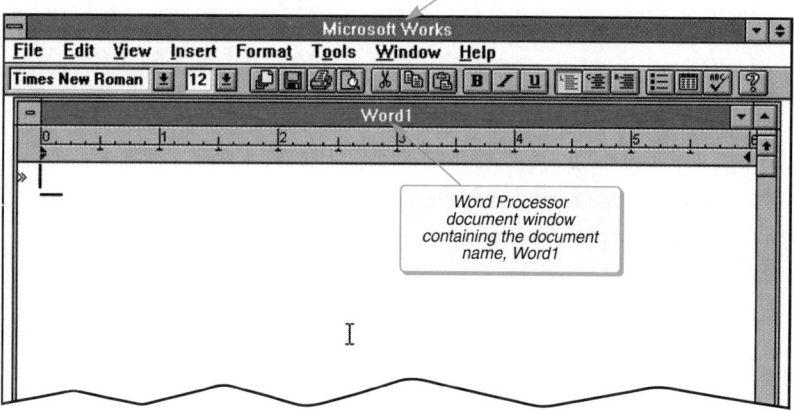

FIGURE 1-7

The large window is the Microsoft Works application window, and the smaller window is the Word Processor document window. The blank area in the document window is the area where Works displays the text as you type. The document window contains the title, Word1. Word1 is the name assigned by Works to the first word processing document you create. Works uses this name until you name the document and save it on disk.

Each window has its own border, title bar, and Minimize, Maximize, or Restore buttons. It is recommended that both the application window and the document window be maximized when you use the Word Processor tool.

Maximizing the Document Window

When you start the Word Processor, the Microsoft Works application window is maximized by default. The document window, however, is not maximized. To maximize the document window, complete the following steps.

TO MAXIMIZE THE DOCUMENT WINDOW ▼

STEP 1 ▶

Point to the Maximize button in the document window (Figure 1-8).

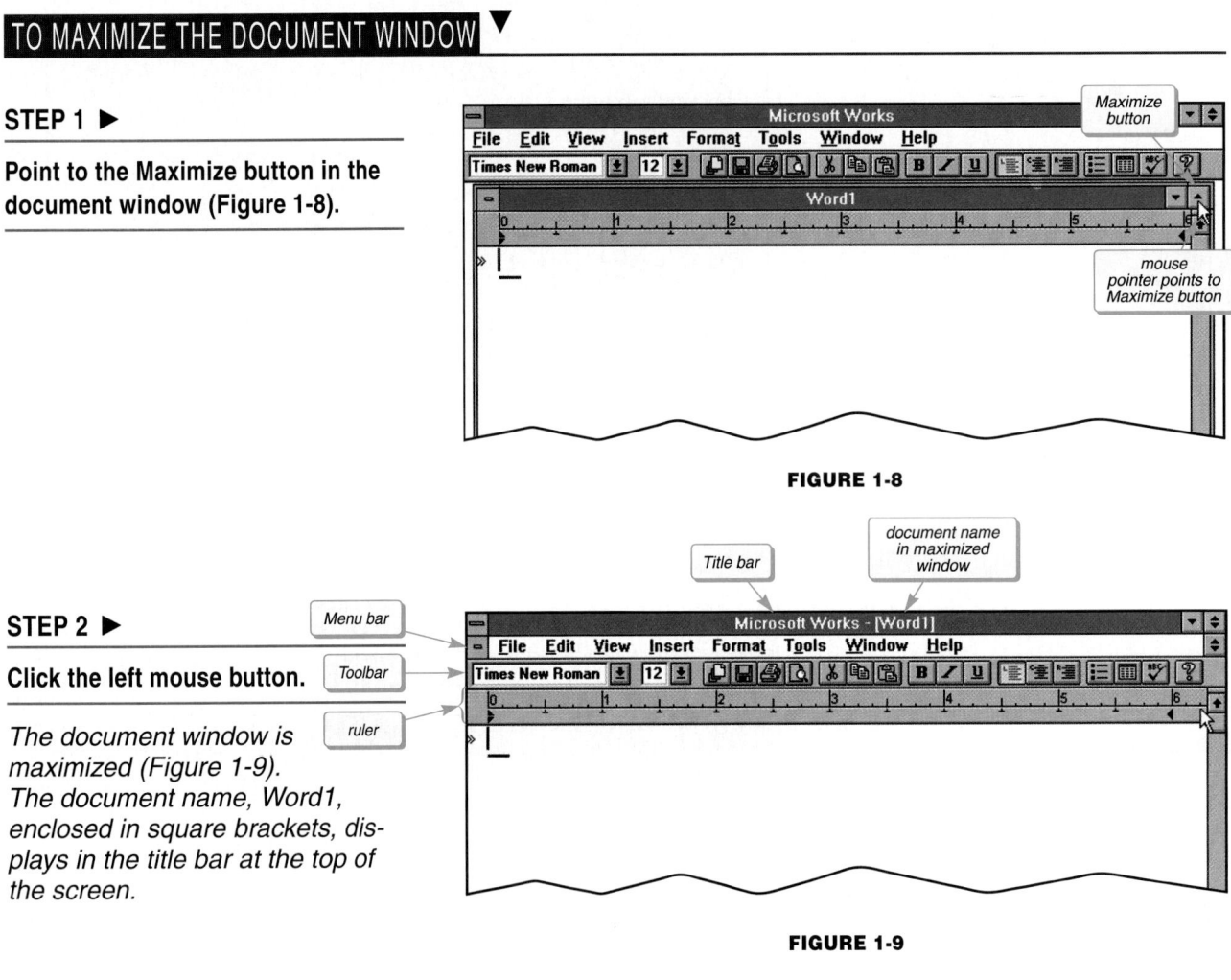

FIGURE 1-8

STEP 2 ▶

Click the left mouse button.

The document window is maximized (Figure 1-9). The document name, Word1, enclosed in square brackets, displays in the title bar at the top of the screen.

FIGURE 1-9

The features of the maximized word processor document window, Word1, the title bar, menu bar, Toolbar, and ruler are explained in the following paragraphs.

▶ THE WORD PROCESSOR WINDOW

The Word Processor window has many of the features common to all window screens. The following section describes these features.

Title Bar

The **title bar** contains the title of the application window, Microsoft Works, and the document name, Word1, enclosed in square brackets.

Menu Bar

The **menu bar** displays menu names. Each menu name represents a menu that contains commands you choose when you open, close, save, or print documents, or otherwise manipulate data in the document you are creating.

Toolbar

The **Toolbar** contains buttons that allow you to perform frequently required tasks more rapidly than when using the commands in the menus. Each button on the Toolbar has a pictorial representation in a small square box that helps you identify its function. Figure 1-10 illustrates the Toolbar and describes the function of each of the buttons. The use of the Toolbar is explained in more detail as you use the buttons in the projects in this book.

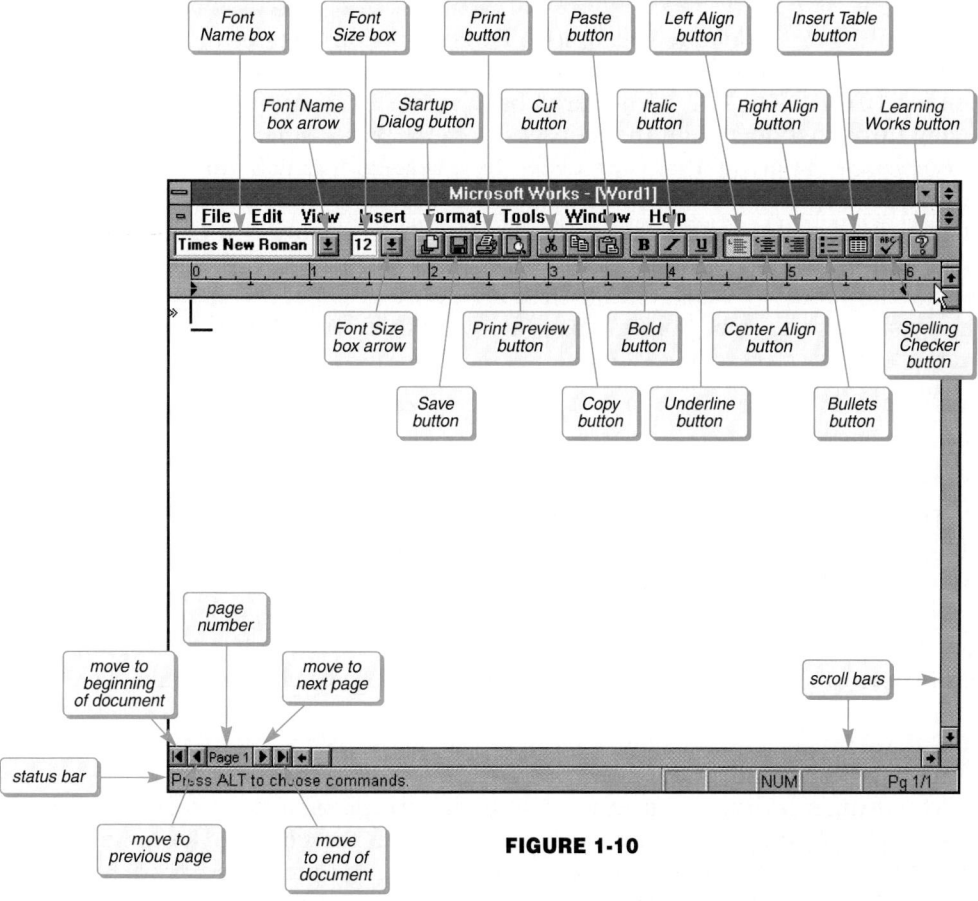

FIGURE 1-10

To choose any of these buttons, position the mouse pointer on the button and click the left mouse button. Any button you choose appears light gray with red letters or icons. When you position the mouse pointer on a button on the Toolbar, a small rectangular box displays that contains a word or words describing the purpose of the button and a more complete description of the button function displays in the status bar. You can control when the Toolbar displays by choosing the **Show Toolbar command** from the **View menu**.

Ruler

The area beneath the Toolbar is called the **ruler** (Figure 1-9 on page W1.8). At the left side of the ruler is a zero. Toward the right side of the ruler is the number six. The numbers in-between show the distance in inches on the document. Thus, a line approximately six inches in length is represented on the screen. As you type characters on the screen, the characters display in the blank area beneath the ruler. By comparing the characters typed to the ruler, it is easy to see the number of inches occupied by the typed characters. You can use the small triangles on the left and right sides of the ruler to control margin settings and paragraph indents. When the ruler is displayed you can change margin and paragraph indents by dragging the small triangles. Tab stops are set by default at each half inch on the ruler and are denoted by the small upside down T characters on the ruler line.

In addition to inches, the ruler can indicate settings in other modes, such as centimeters, through use of the **Options command** on the **Tools menu**. The function of the ruler is explained as you use it in creating documents.

You can control whether the ruler displays by choosing the **Ruler command** from the **View menu**.

Scroll Bars

When the text you enter occupies a length or width greater than the size of the display screen, you can use the **scroll bars** to move through the document (Figure 1-10). The left side of the scroll bar contains page arrows that assist you in moving through a document that consists of more than a single page. Clicking the left pointing page arrow that is preceded by a vertical line will move the insertion point to the beginning of the document. Click the left pointing page arrow without a vertical line to move the insertion point to the beginning of the previous page. Clicking the right pointing page arrow without the vertical line will move the insertion point forward to the beginning of the next page in the document. When you click the right pointing page arrow with a vertical line, the insertion point will move to the end of the document. The page number displays between the page arrows.

Status Bar

The **status bar** is located at the bottom of the screen (Figure 1-10). The left side of the status bar displays comments that assist you in using Works. Keyboard indicators such as NUM display on the right side of the status bar. NUM indicates that Works will display numbers if you press the keys on the numeric keypad that is located to the right of the standard keyboard. The page number and total number of pages in a document display in the lower right corner of the status bar.

Mouse Pointer

The **mouse pointer** is used to point to various parts of the screen and indicates which area of the screen will be affected when you click the left mouse button (Figure 1-11). The mouse pointer changes shape in different parts of the screen. Within the blank area of the screen, called the document workspace, the mouse pointer takes the shape of an **I-beam**. An I-beam is a vertical line with short crossbars on the top and bottom.

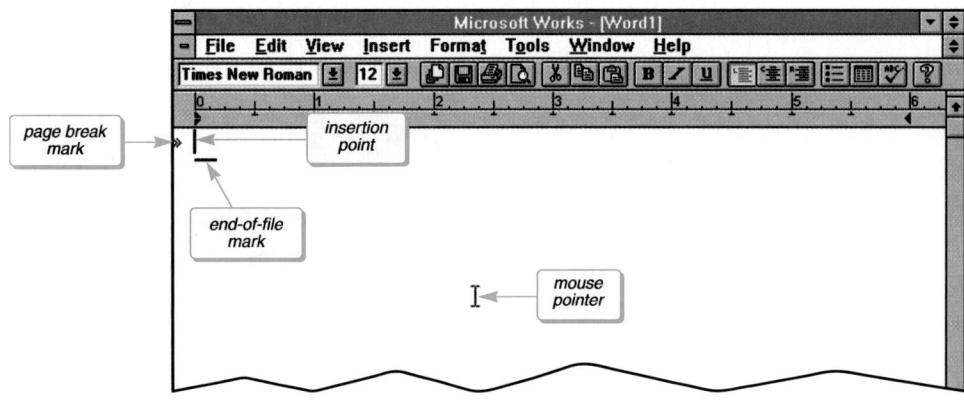

FIGURE 1-11

On the menu bar, the ruler, and the scroll bar areas, the mouse pointer takes the shape of a block arrow. Other forms and uses of the mouse pointer are explained as required in the development of various documents.

Page Break Mark, Insertion Point, and End-of-File Mark

In the upper left corner of the blank workspace, two small arrows, called a chevron character, point to the right. The Chevron character is the **page break mark** that appears on the first line of a new document. The mark also appears in the left margin of the screen when a page break occurs after you have entered a full page of text.

The **insertion point** is a blinking vertical bar that indicates where the next character you type will appear on the screen. The insertion point also indicates the beginning position in a document where you can insert text, delete text, or change the appearance of text. The insertion point is controlled by the movement of the mouse.

The short horizontal line below the insertion point in Figure 1-11 is the **end-of-file mark**. This mark displays as the last character in every document and indicates where the document ends. You can move the insertion point throughout the document you create, but you cannot move it beyond the end-of-file mark.

▶ WORD PROCESSOR DEFAULTS

Before you enter the text to create a document, you should know about the predefined settings for the Word Processor, called **defaults**, that affect the way your screen appears and the way a document prints. Consider the following important defaults.

1. Margins — When printing a document, Works places a one-inch top margin and a one-inch bottom margin on each page. The right and left margins are 1.25 inches each.
2. Spacing — Text is single-spaced.
3. Line Width — Line width is six inches, based upon a paper size of 8.5 inches by 11 inches.
4. Tab Stops — Tab stops are set along the ruler at one-half inch intervals.
5. Default Drive — Drive C, the hard disk, is the default drive for saving and retrieving documents.

You can change these defaults by using the commands from various Works menus.

▶ UNDERSTANDING FONTS, FONT STYLES, AND FONT SIZES

To create the announcement in Figure 1-1 on page W1.4, you must **format** the page. Formatting refers to the process of controlling the appearance of the characters that appear on the screen and in the printed document. With Works you can specify the font, font size, font style and color of one or more characters, words, sentences, or paragraphs in a document.

Fonts

A **font** is a set of characters with a specific design. Each font is identified by a name. Some of the commonly used fonts are **Times New Roman**, **Courier New**, and **Arial** (Figure 1-12).

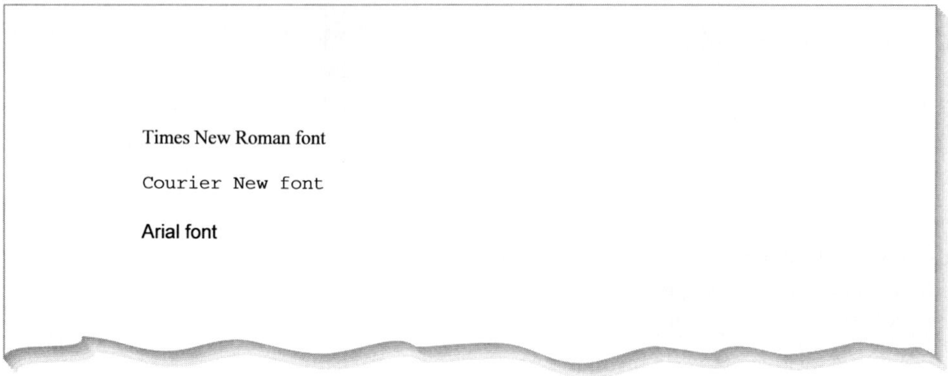

Times New Roman font

Courier New font

Arial font

FIGURE 1-12

Each of the fonts in Figure 1-12 has a unique design. When using Windows 3.1, a variety of fonts become available that you can use with Works.

Most fonts fall into one of two major categories: (1) **serif**, or (2) **sans serif**. Serif fonts have small curved finishing strokes in the characters. The Times New Roman and Courier New fonts are examples of a serif font. Serif fonts are considered easy to read when large blocks of text are involved and are normally used in books and magazines for the main text material.

Sans serif fonts are relatively plain, straight letter forms. The Arial font in Figure 1-12 is a sans serif font. Sans serif fonts are commonly used in headlines and short titles.

Font Style

In Works, **font style** is the term used to describe the special appearance of text and numbers. Widely used font styles include bold, italic, and underlined (Figure 1-13). You can choose bold, italic, and underlined font styles using Toolbar buttons. All three styles can be applied to a set of characters.

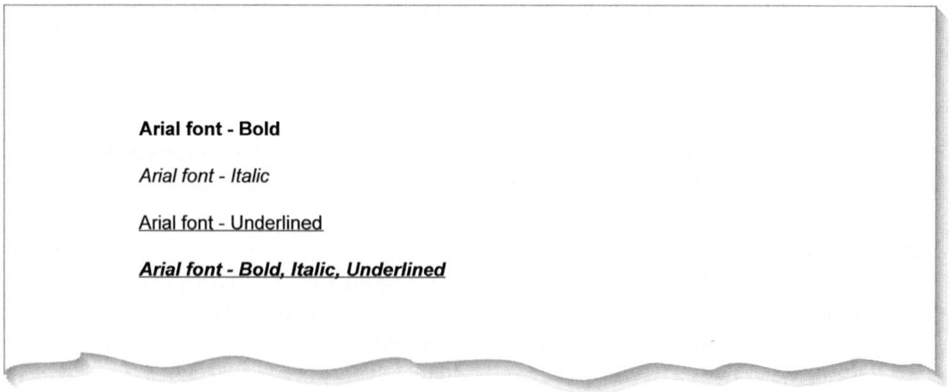

Arial font - Bold

Arial font - Italic

Arial font - Underlined

Arial font - Bold, Italic, Underlined

FIGURE 1-13

Font Sizes

Font sizes are measured in **points**. There are seventy-two points to the inch. Thus, a font size of thirty-six points is approximately one-half inch in height. The measurement is based on measuring from the top of the tallest character in a font (such as a lowercase l) to the bottom of the lowest character (such as a lowercase g which extends below a line). Figure 1-14 illustrates the Arial font in various sizes.

The fonts and font sizes you choose sometimes depends on the printer you are using and the fonts available within your software. Available fonts can vary from system to system. In the Works Word Processor, the default font is 12 point Times New Roman.

Arial font - 12 point

Arial font - 18 point

Arial font - 24 point

Arial font - 36 point

FIGURE 1-14

▶ FORMATTING REQUIREMENTS FOR PROJECT ONE

FIGURE 1-15

T he announcement used in this project is again illustrated in Figure 1-15. Before typing the text, you must understand the fonts, font styles, font sizes, and colors you will use in creating the announcement.

In this document, the first two lines are centered on the page and display using Arial font. The first line displays using 36 point font size, and the second line is 24 point font size. An illustration from the Works ClipArt Gallery is placed after the second heading line. The next two lines are single-spaced and display in 14 point Times New Roman font. These lines are followed by a blank space and then another line displays in 14 point Times New Roman. Next, two of the lines are indented one inch, contain a bullet (a small black circle) before the beginning of each line of text, and display in 18 point Times New Roman font. The line following the bulleted list displays in 14 point Times New Roman. The last line in the document is centered and displays in red using 18 point Arial italic font. The entire document displays in bold.

When you understand the format of the document, you are ready to use the word processing software to create the document.

▶ CREATING A DOCUMENT

T he following list provides an overview of the steps required to create, save, and print the announcement. If you are working on a computer, do not attempt to perform the steps in this list.

1. Type the text line by line.
2. Begin each line at the left margin.
3. Leave one blank line before the illustration, one blank line for the illustration, and one blank line after the illustration.
4. Format the document; that is, center lines, change fonts, font sizes, font styles, and color as required to produce the document.
5. Insert the clip art illustration.
6. Save the document.
7. Print the document.

All Characters Command

When using the Works Word Processor, each time you press a key on the keyboard a character is created, and each character becomes part of the document. For example, pressing the SPACEBAR between words creates a small black dot, called a space mark, in the space between the words. Pressing the ENTER key creates a character called the **paragraph mark**. These characters do not print, but it is recommended that you display these special characters as you type. The following steps explain how to display on the screen all the characters you type.

TO DISPLAY ALL CHARACTERS ▼

STEP 1 ▶

Select the View menu by pointing to the word View in the menu bar and clicking the left mouse button. Then point to the All Characters command.

Works displays the View menu and the mouse pointer is positioned on the All Characters command (Figure 1-16).

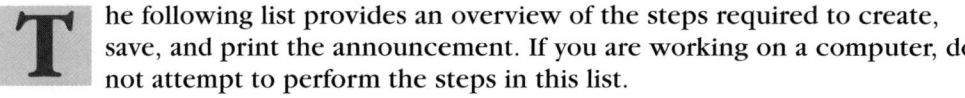

FIGURE 1-16

STEP 2 ▶

Choose the All Characters command from the View menu by clicking the left mouse button.

A paragraph mark now appears after the insertion point (Figure 1-17).

FIGURE 1-17

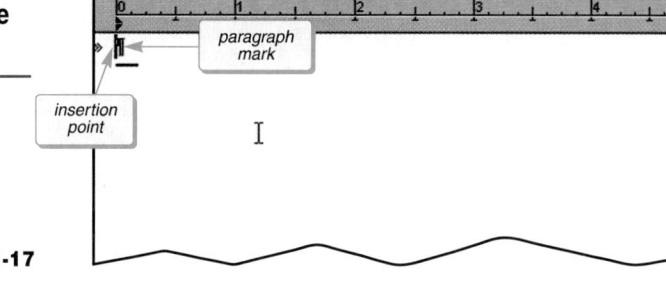

Works automatically inserts a paragraph mark at the end of every document. Because you have not yet entered text, a paragraph mark appears after the insertion point because it is the end of the document at this time. As you type, a small dot appears when you press the SPACEBAR, and a paragraph mark will appear whenever you press the ENTER key.

After you choose the All Characters command, a check mark appears to the left of this command the next time you display the View menu, indicating the command is in effect. Clicking the left mouse button again when pointing to this command will turn off the All Characters command and remove the check mark.

You are now ready to enter the text to create the document.

Entering Text

Perform the following steps to enter the text of the document.

TO ENTER TEXT ▼

STEP 1 ▶

Press the CAPS LOCK key on the keyboard and type the first line of text, ENROLL NOW.

As you type, the characters display in capital letters and the insertion point and paragraph mark move to the right one character at a time (Figure 1-18). If you make an error while typing, press the BACKSPACE key to delete the character or characters that you have just typed and then type the characters correctly.

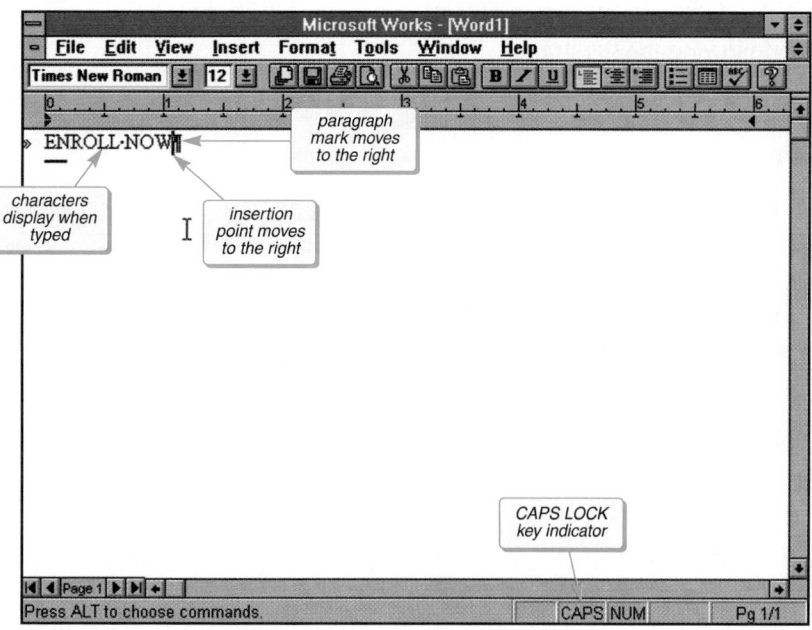

FIGURE 1-18

STEP 2 ▶

Press the ENTER key to end the first line.

When you press the ENTER key, Works inserts a paragraph mark immediately after the last character typed (Figure 1-19). The insertion point moves to the beginning of the next line followed by a paragraph mark, and the end-of-file mark moves down one line.

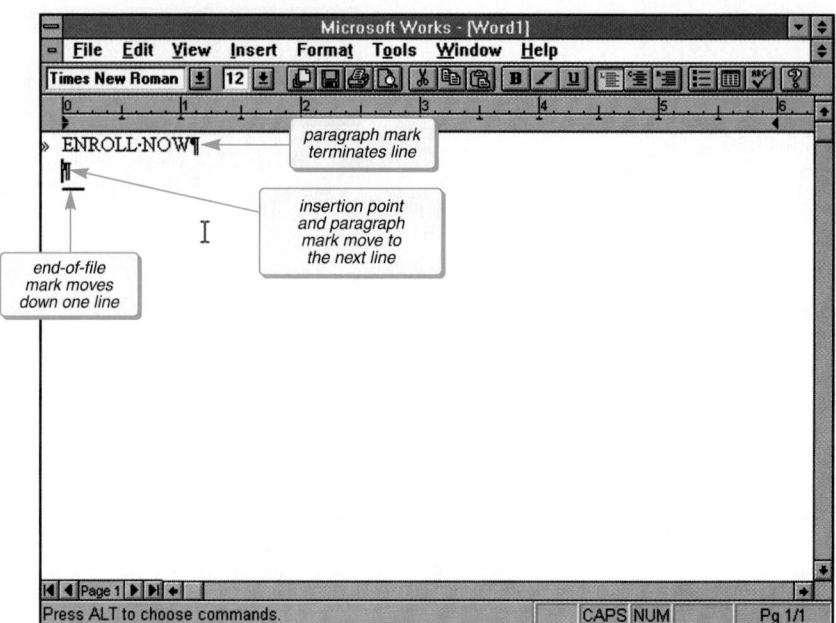

FIGURE 1-19

STEP 3 ▶

Press the ENTER key to create a blank line. Press the CAPS LOCK key to remove this feature. Type the heading line, Construction Technology, and then press the ENTER key once to end the second line of text. Press the ENTER key three more times to create a blank line before the clip art illustration, a line for the illustration, and a blank line following the illustration. The insertion point now displays on the line where you will type the next line of text.

Only one line needs to be allowed for the clip art illustration (Figure 1-20). When Works inserts the illustration in the document, the space is expanded to allow the illustration to be placed between the lines of text. The CAPS LOCK indicator in the status bar is turned off.

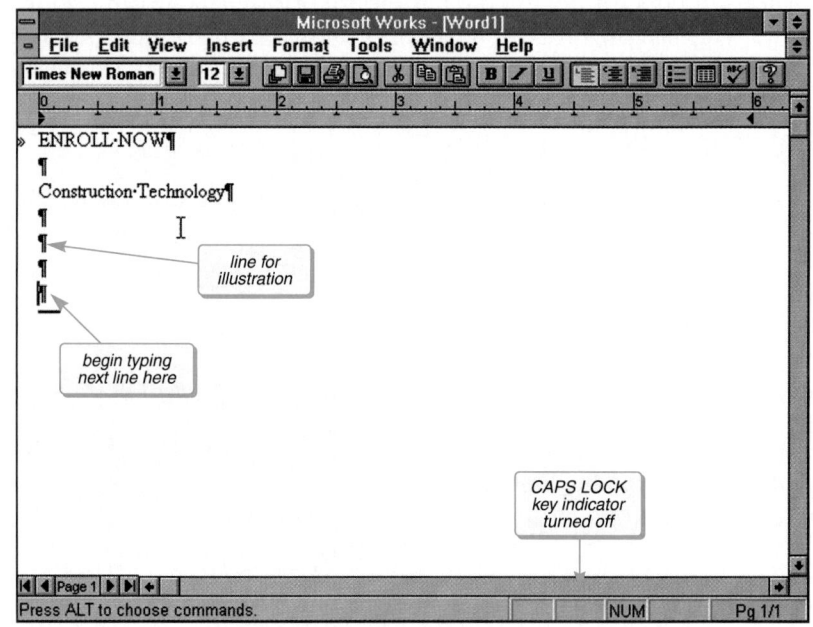

FIGURE 1-20

STEP 4 ▶

Type the remaining lines of text. Do not press the ENTER key at the end of the line beginning with the words, **Westlake Career College. Press the** ENTER **key to end each paragraph.**

The paragraph begin-
ning with the words,
Westlake Career College, displays
after the heading lines (Figure
1-21). You should NOT press the
ENTER *key at the end of the line*
beginning with the words Westlake
Career College because if a word
or words will not fit on a line,
Works automatically places the
word or words on the next line.
This is called **wordwrap***. You*
should press the ENTER *key only at*
the end of each paragraph and to
create blank lines.

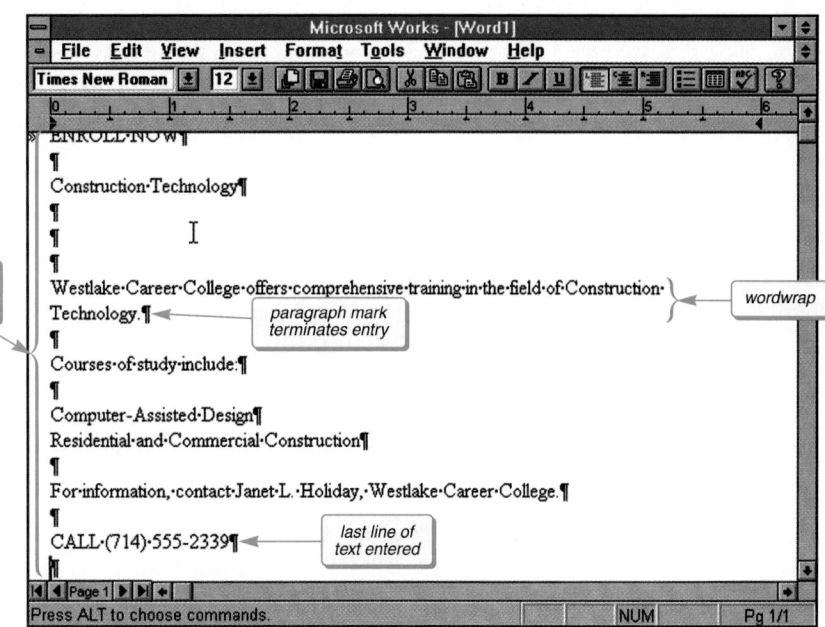

FIGURE 1-21

If the first lines of text scroll off the screen as you enter the data, you can display the top portion of the text by clicking the up scroll arrow on the scroll bar until the text displays. Pressing the CTRL+HOME keys or clicking the beginning of document button on the scroll bar will also move the insertion point to the first character of text in the document.

Wordwrap

It is important to understand what occurs when you type multiple lines such as the two lines in the announcement beginning with the words, Westlake Career College. When typing text that requires more than one line, the insertion point continues to the right margin and then automatically drops down to the beginning of the next line. In addition, when you type a line and a word extends beyond the right margin, the word is automatically placed on the next line. As previously stated, this is called **wordwrap**. Wordwrap is an important feature of the Word Processor because it facilitates rapid entry of data and allows Works to easily rearrange characters, words, and sentences within a paragraph when you make changes.

Paragraph Marks

You should also understand the purpose of the paragraph mark. The term paragraph, when using the Works Word Processor, can mean a single character, a word, a single line, or many sentences. You create a paragraph by pressing the ENTER key. When you are typing and press the ENTER key, Works inserts a paragraph mark after the last character typed.

A paragraph is a section of text treated as a unified group of characters to which various types of formatting can be applied. Once you have established the characteristics of a paragraph, text you add to the paragraph will take on the characteristics of that paragraph.

▶ FORMATTING THE DOCUMENT

The next step in preparing the announcement is to format the document, which involves centering selected lines, specifying the font and font size for each of the lines, and applying the proper font style and color to the lines.

Highlighting Characters, Words, Lines, and Paragraphs

Before you can change the format of a document, you must **highlight** the text you want to change. Highlighted text displays as white text on a black background on the screen. Figure 1-22 illustrates a highlighted word in a sentence.

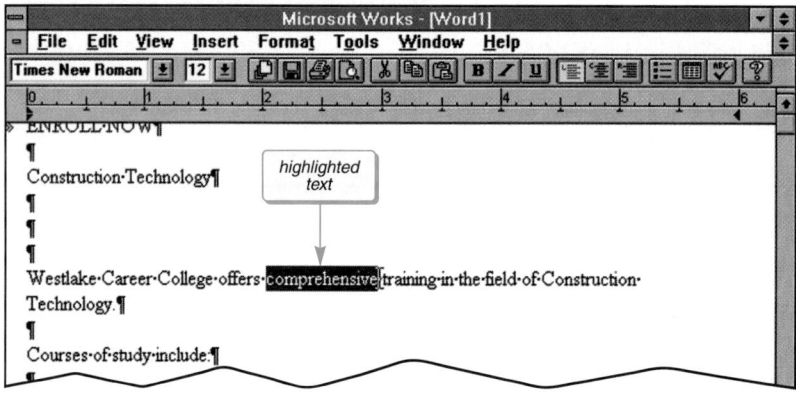

FIGURE 1-22

Works provides a variety of ways to highlight text. One method of highlighting is to move the mouse pointer to the first character of the text to format, hold down the left mouse button, and drag the mouse pointer across the word or words you want to highlight.

Table 1-1 explains other techniques you can use to highlight text.

▶ **TABLE 1-1**

TO HIGHLIGHT	ACTION TO BE PERFORMED
A word	Double-click when the mouse pointer is located anywhere within the word.
A line	Click in the left margin of the document window beside the line. The I-beam pointer changes to a block arrow in this area.
A sentence	Drag the mouse pointer over the sentence or press the CTRL key and click with the mouse pointer located anywhere within the sentence.
A paragraph	Double-click in the left margin of the document window beside the paragraph.
Several lines	Position the mouse pointer in the left margin of the document window and drag the pointer up or down.
An entire document	Hold down the CTRL key and click in the left margin of the document window or choose the Select All command from the Edit menu.

When highlighting more than one word, Works automatically highlights all of the next word as you drag through that word. If you prefer to highlight character by character, you can turn off the Automatic Word Selection feature by removing the X from the Automatic Word Selection check box in the Options dialog box. The Options dialog box can be displayed by choosing the Options command from the Tools menu.

If you have highlighted text and you want to remove the highlighting for any reason, click the mouse when the pointer is located anywhere within the work-space area of the screen. The highlighting will be removed. You may also press any arrow key to remove highlighting.

Centering Paragraphs

The first two lines of the announcement are centered within the margins of the document. You can take several approaches when centering these two lines. You can center one line at a time, or by highlighting both lines, you can center both lines at once with a single click of the mouse button. It is more efficient to center both lines at once, so this approach is illustrated in the following steps.

TO CENTER PARAGRAPHS ▼

STEP 1 ▶

Scroll up so the first line is completely visible on the screen. Position the mouse pointer in the left margin of the document window next to the first line of the paragraphs you want to center.

The mouse pointer becomes the shape of a block arrow pointing to the right (Figure 1-23).

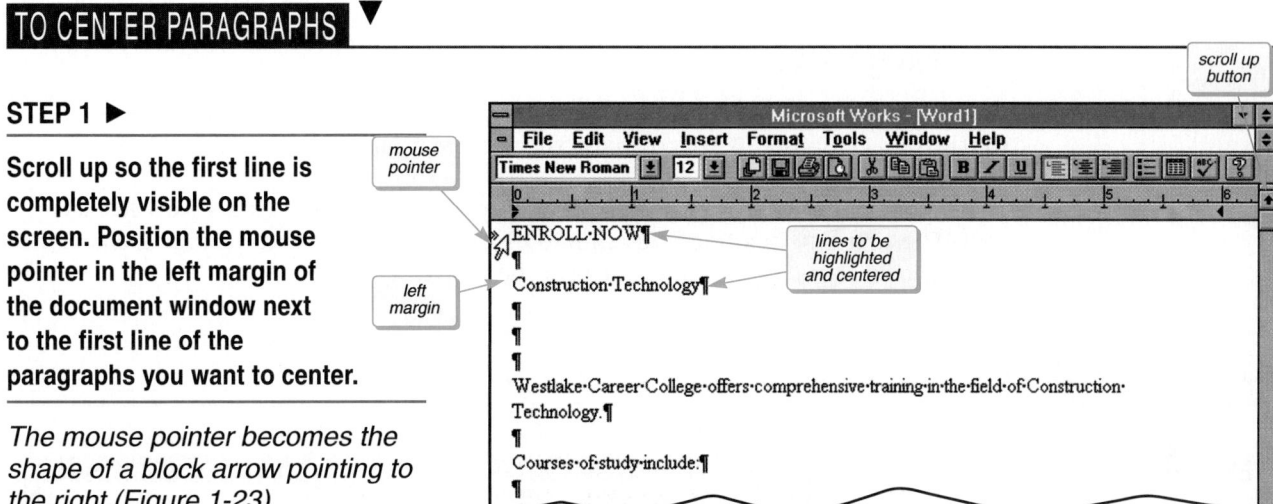

FIGURE 1-23

STEP 2 ▶

Drag the mouse pointer down the left margin of the document window until the lines you want to center are highlighted. Release the left mouse button.

The lines are highlighted (Figure 1-24).

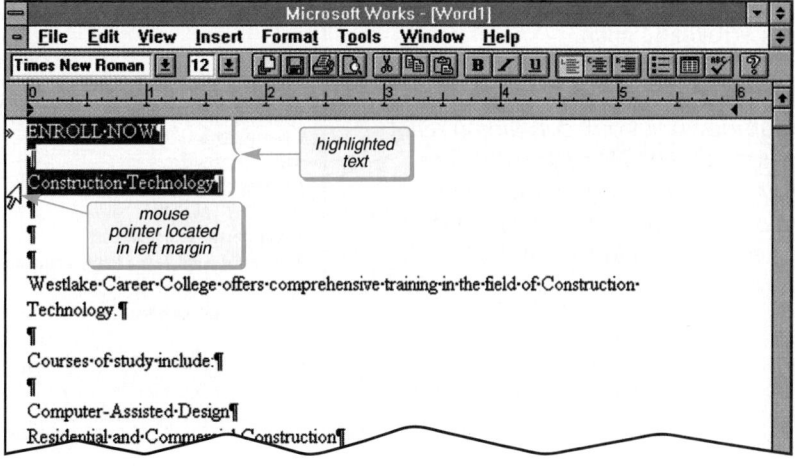

FIGURE 1-24

STEP 3 ▶

Point to the Center Align button on the Toolbar and click.

Works centers the two heading lines between the page margins (Figure 1-25). Notice the letter C and the lines within the Center Align button display in red, indicating the highlighted text is centered.

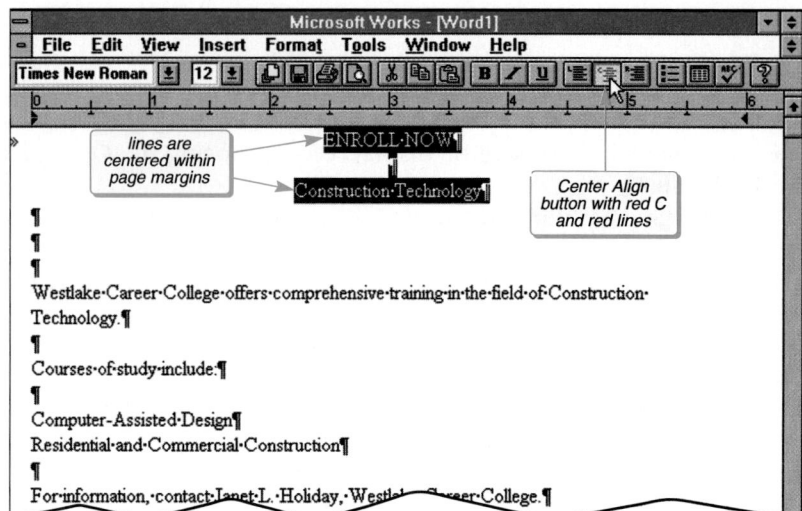

FIGURE 1-25

Changing Fonts

When Works is started, the default font is Times New Roman and the default font size is 12 points. Works displays this information on the left side of the Toolbar.

The text in the announcement now displays in 12 point Times New Roman font. The first two heading lines should display in Arial font. To change from Times New Roman font to Arial font, perform the following steps.

TO CHANGE FONTS ▼

STEP 1 ▶

Highlight the paragraphs you want to change to Arial font. Position the mouse pointer on the Font Name box arrow and click.

Works displays the Font Name drop-down list box containing a list of font names (Figure 1-26). The font names on your computer might be different from the font names shown in Figure 1-26.

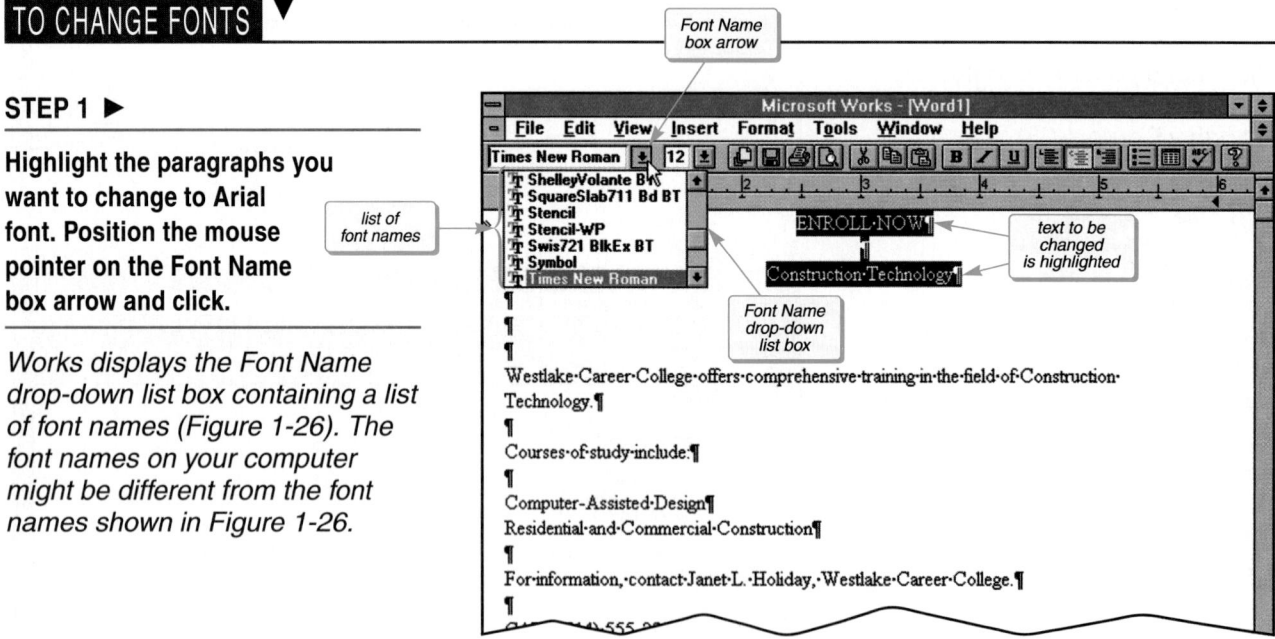

FIGURE 1-26

STEP 2 ▶

Position the mouse pointer on the up scroll arrow and scroll to display additional names until the Arial font name appears in the Font Name drop-down list.

Additional font names display as you scroll through the Font Name drop-down list (Figure 1-27). The Arial font name displays near the top of the list.

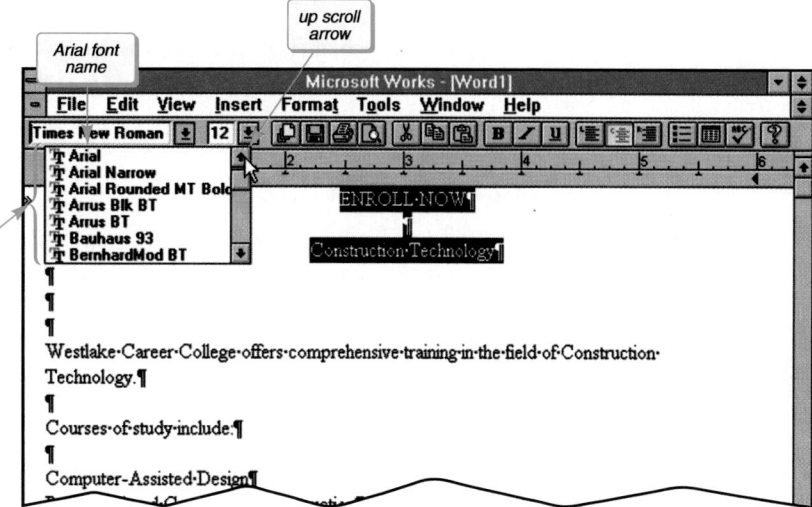

FIGURE 1-27

STEP 3 ▶

Point to the Arial font name in the Font Name drop-down list (Figure 1-28).

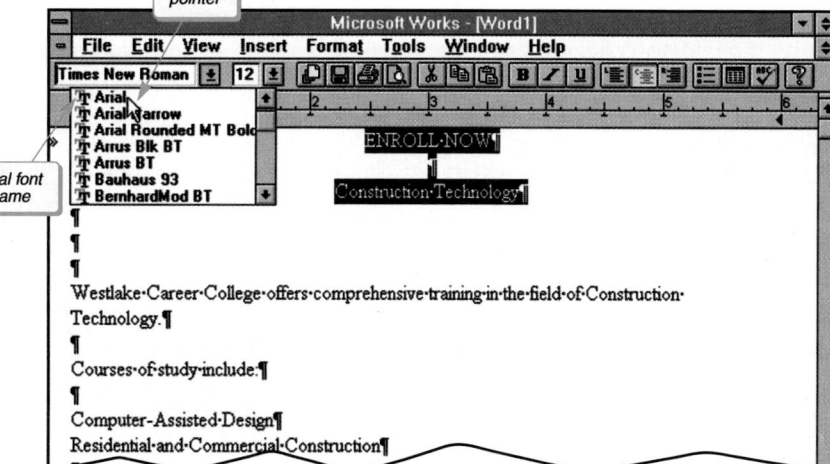

FIGURE 1-28

STEP 4 ▶

Select the Arial font by clicking the left mouse button.

The two heading lines display in Arial font (Figure 1-29). The Arial font name appears in the Font Name box.

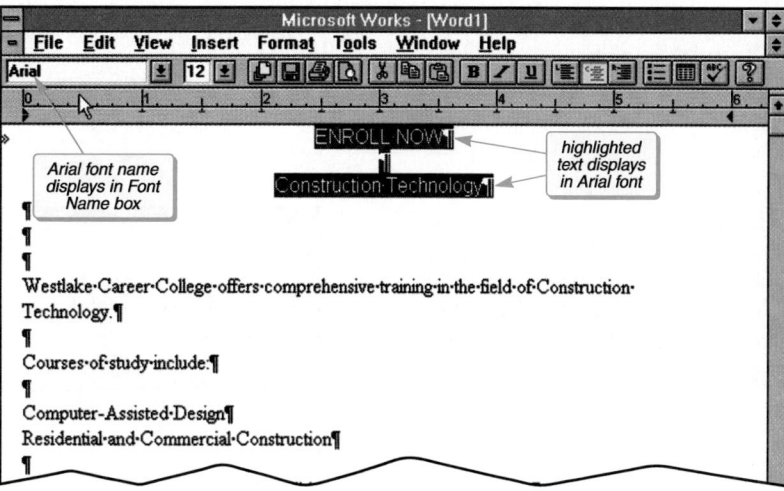

FIGURE 1-29

After choosing the font, the changed lines remain highlighted. To remove the highlighting, click the left mouse button when the mouse is pointing anywhere in the workspace area of the screen.

Changing Font Size

The next step in formatting the document is to change the font size in the heading lines. The words, ENROLL NOW, should display in 36 point size.

TO CHANGE FONT SIZE

STEP 1 ►

Highlight the line of text to enlarge (ENROLL NOW) by positioning the mouse pointer in the left margin of the document window on the same line as the text and clicking the left mouse button.

Works highlights the words, ENROLL NOW (Figure 1-30).

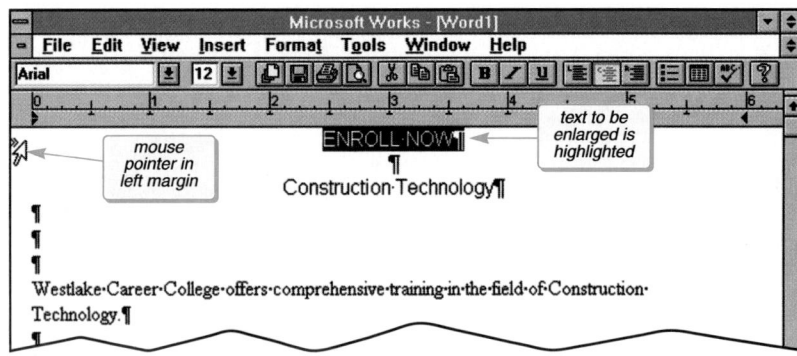

FIGURE 1-30

STEP 2 ►

Point to the Font Size box arrow on the Toolbar and click.

A list of font sizes displays (Figure 1-31). The current font size (12) is highlighted in the list.

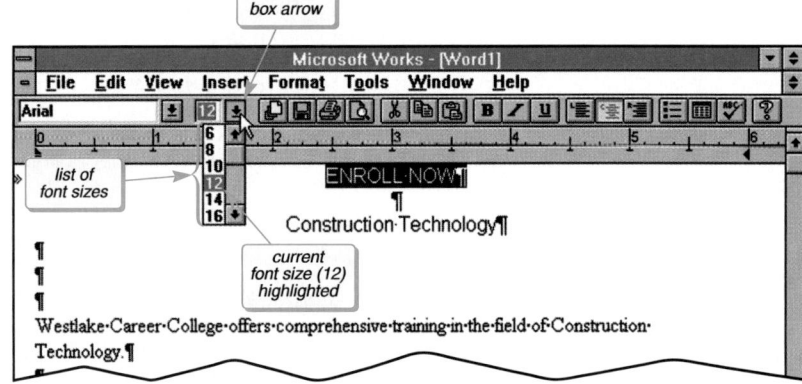

FIGURE 1-31

STEP 3 ►

Point to the down scroll arrow and scroll down to display additional font sizes until 36 is visible (Figure 1-32).

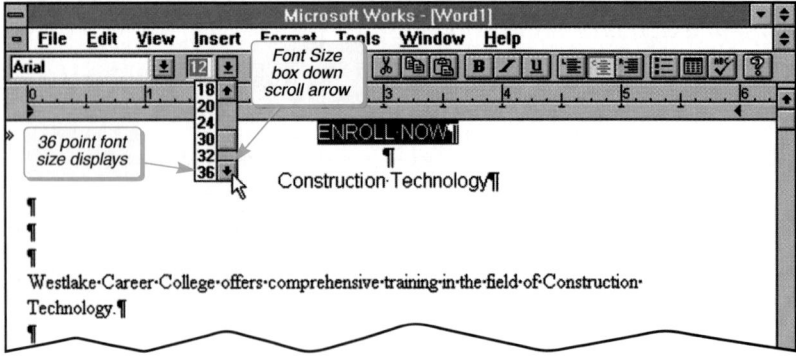

FIGURE 1-32

STEP 4 ▶

Point to the number 36, which indicates 36 point font size (Figure 1-33).

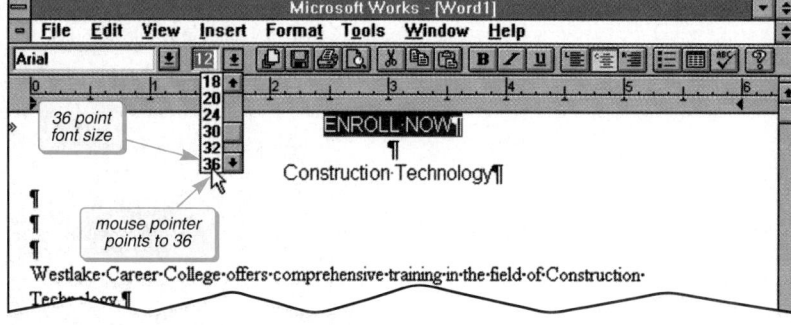

FIGURE 1-33

STEP 5 ▶

Select the number 36 by clicking the left mouse button.

Works changes the first heading line to 36 point Arial font (Figure 1-34). The number 36 displays in the Font Size box on the Toolbar.

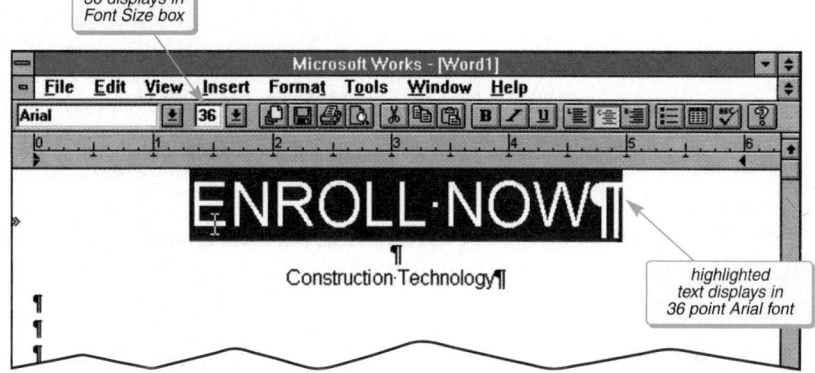

FIGURE 1-34

Formatting the Remaining Heading Lines

The heading line, Construction Technology, should display in 24 point Arial font. Perform the following steps to accomplish this formatting.

TO CHANGE FONT SIZE ▼

STEP 1 ▶

Highlight the line of text to enlarge (Construction Technology) by positioning the mouse pointer in the left margin of the document window on the same line as the text and clicking the left mouse button. Point to the Font Size box arrow on the Toolbar and click. Scroll down if necessary, and then point to the number 24, which indicates 24 point font size.

Works highlights the words, Construction Technology, a list of font sizes displays, and the mouse pointer points to the number 24 in the drop-down list box (Figure 1-35).

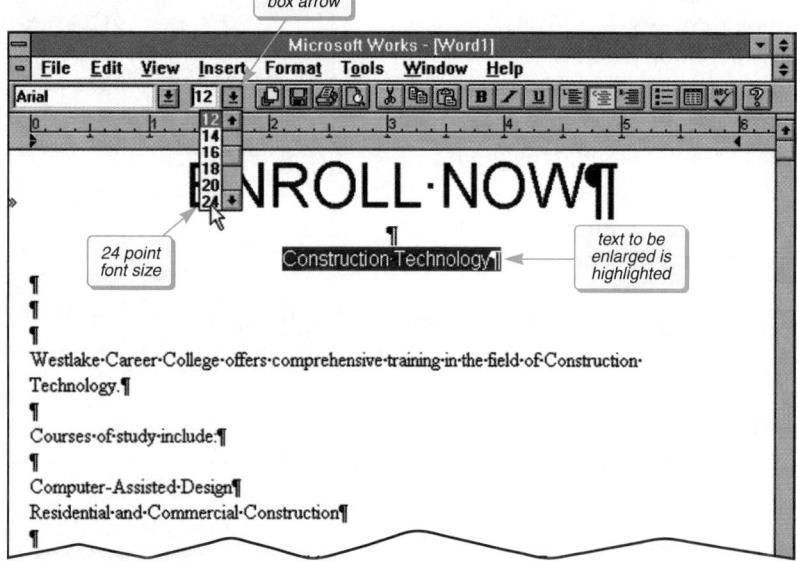

FIGURE 1-35

STEP 2 ▶

Select the number 24 by clicking the left mouse button.

Works changes the second heading line to 24 point Arial font (Figure 1-36). The number 24 displays in the Font Size box on the Toolbar.

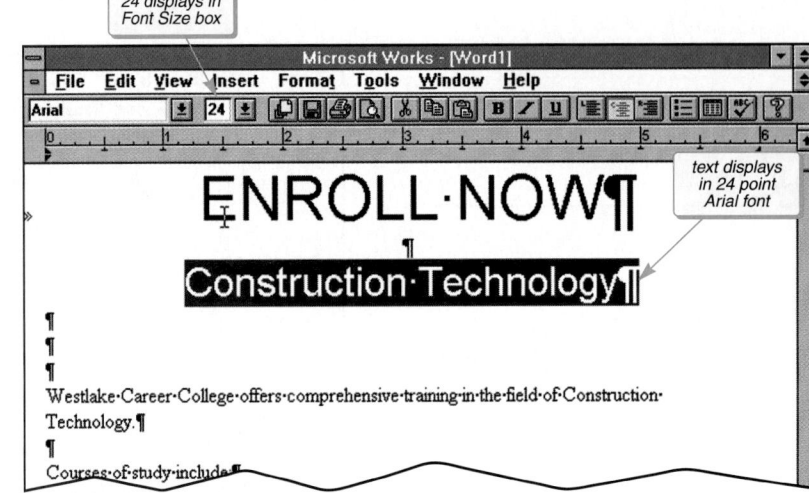

FIGURE 1-36

The heading lines are now formatted in the proper font and font size.

Formatting Additional Text

The three lines following the heading lines are to display in 14 point Times New Roman. Because the default font and font size are 12 point Times New Roman, the only step necessary is to change the font size for the lines to 14 point. To accomplish this formatting, perform the following steps.

TO CHANGE FONT SIZE ▼

STEP 1 ▶

Highlight the next three lines of text by positioning the mouse pointer in the left margin of the document window next to the first word in the next line and dragging the mouse pointer down. Release the left mouse button. Point to the Font Size box arrow on the Toolbar and click. Point to the number 14, which indicates 14 point font size.

Works highlights the three lines, a list of font sizes appears, and the mouse pointer points to the number 14 in the drop-down list box (Figure 1-37).

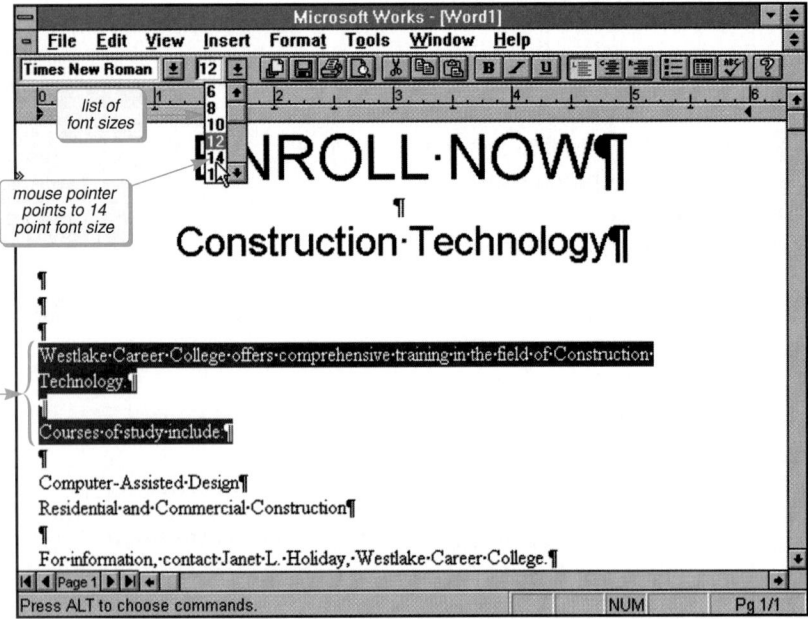

FIGURE 1-37

STEP 2 ▶

Select the number 14 by clicking the left mouse button.

Works changes the three lines to 14 point font size. The number 14 displays in the Font Size box on the Toolbar (Figure 1-38)

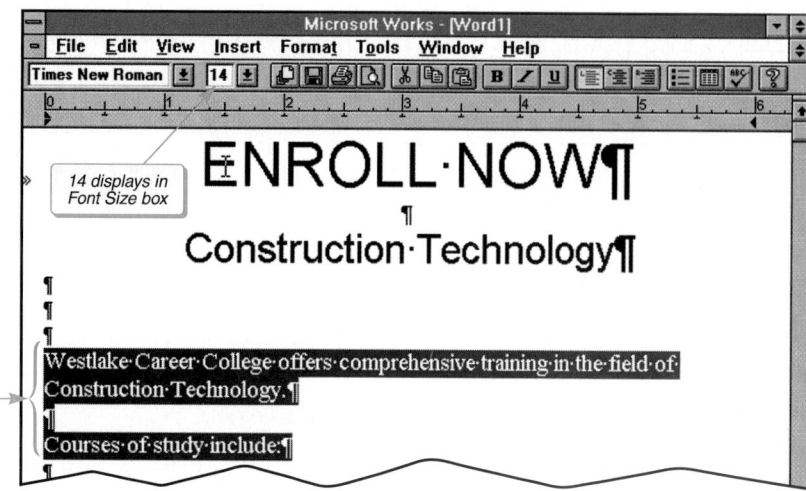

FIGURE 1-38

The first part of the announcement is now formatted with the proper fonts and font sizes.

Creating a Bulleted List

The line containing the words, Computer-Assisted Design, and the line containing the words, Residential and Commercial Construction, are indented one inch from the left margin, appear as a **bulleted list**, and display in 18 point Times New Roman font. A bulleted list consists of a word or words on one or more lines that are preceded by a small black circle or other special character at the beginning of the line. The purpose is to have the list stand out from the rest of the text. To create a bulleted list and increase the point size, perform the following steps.

TO CREATE A BULLETED LIST AND INCREASE FONT POINT SIZE ▼

STEP 1 ▶

Highlight the lines that are to comprise the bulleted list (Figure 1-39).

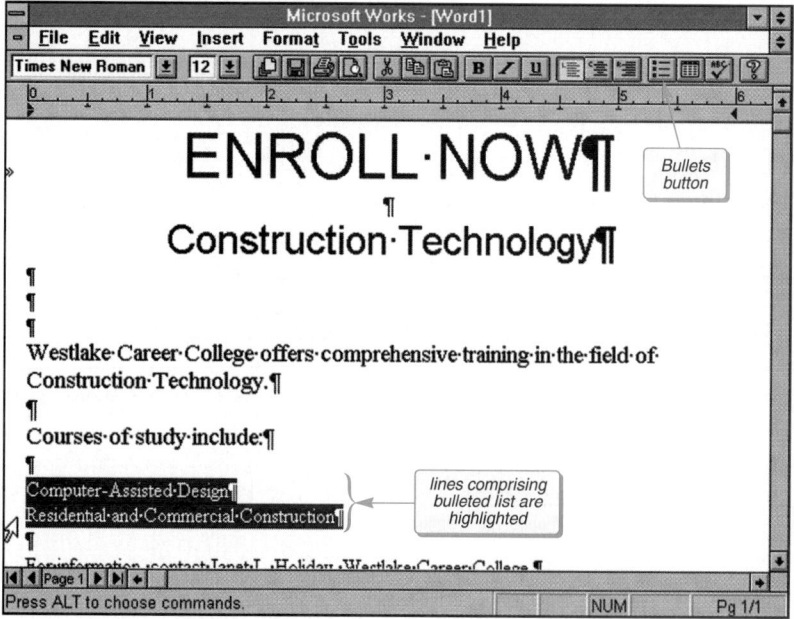

FIGURE 1-39

STEP 2 ▶

Point to the Bullets button on the Toolbar and click.

A small black circle (bullet) displays in front of the text (Figure 1-40). The text moves to the right one-quarter of an inch. The small lower triangle on the left side of the ruler, called the left-margin indent marker, moves to the right one-quarter of an inch.
Although not shown on the screen, a small yellow box below the button displays to tell you the function of the button the mouse pointer points to.

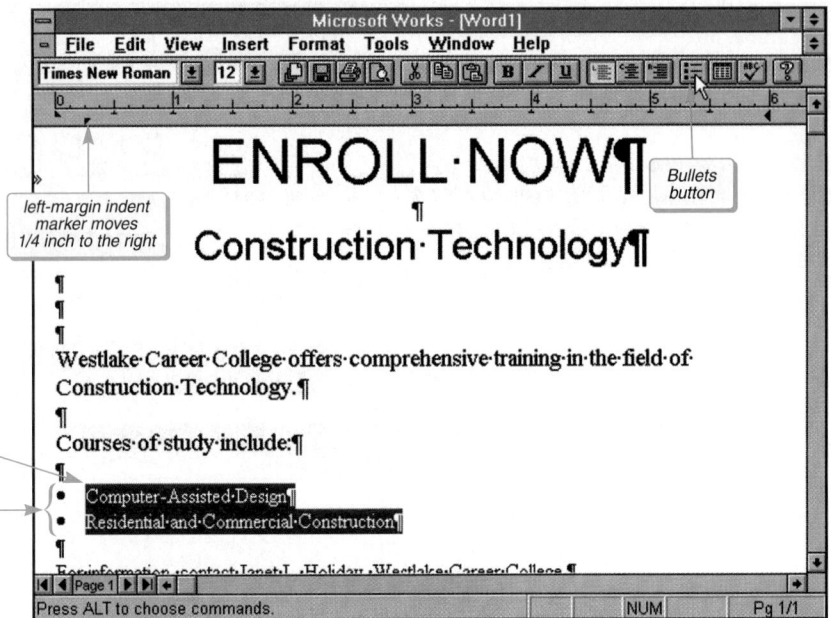

FIGURE 1-40

STEP 3 ▶

Click the Bullets button on the Toolbar again.

The bullets and related text indent an additional one-quarter of an inch (Figure 1-41). The small upper triangle on the left side of the ruler, called the first-line indent marker, moves to the right one-quarter of an inch, and the left-margin indent marker moves to the right an additional one-quarter of an inch.

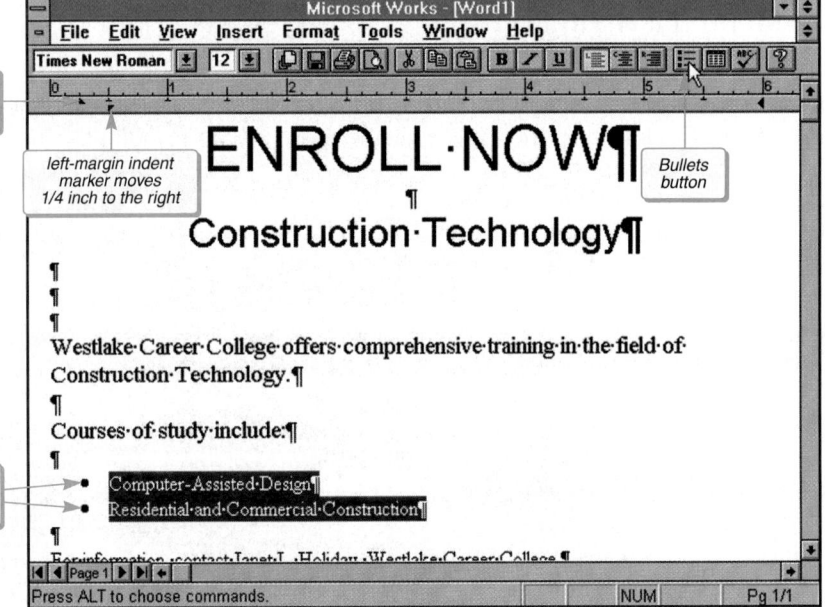

FIGURE 1-41

STEP 4 ▶

Click the Bullets button three times.

The bullets and related text move to the right (Figure 1-42). The bullets now begin at the one-inch mark on the ruler. After clicking the Bullets button the first time, each time you click the Bullets button on the Toolbar, the bullet and text will indent one-quarter of an inch. The bullets are indented one-inch from the left margin. The text begins one and one-quarter inch from the left margin.

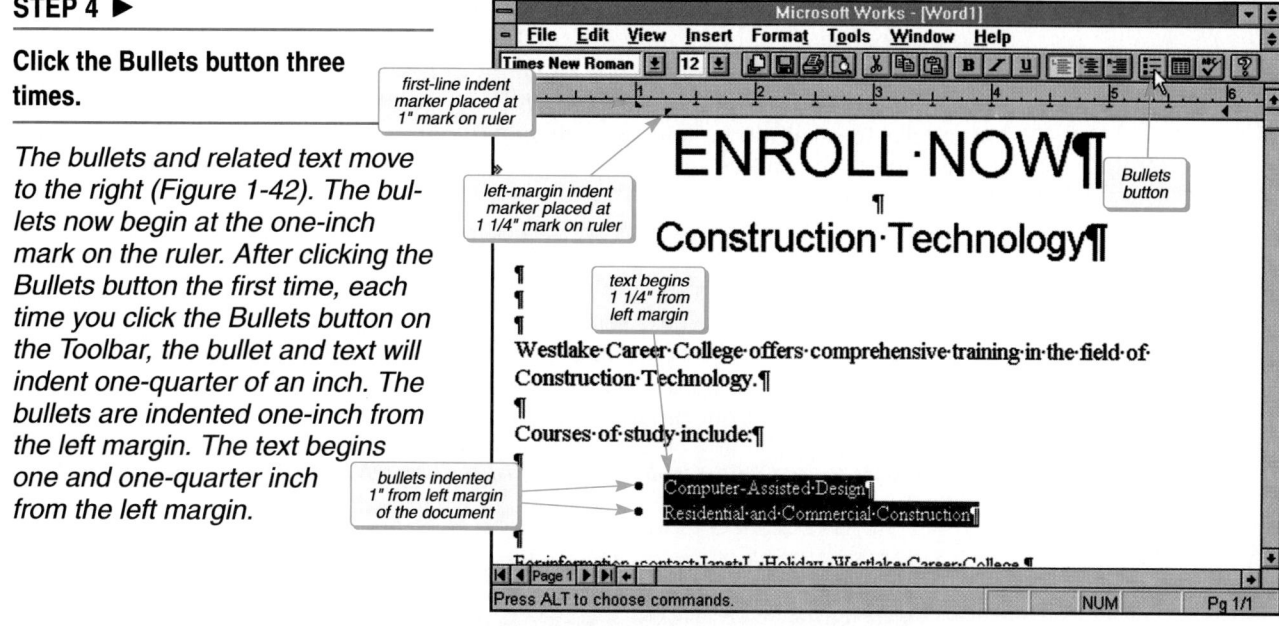

FIGURE 1-42

STEP 5 ▶

Change the font size of the bulleted list to 18 point by selecting the number 18 in the Font Size drop-down list box as explained in previous steps.

The bulleted list displays in 18 point Times New Roman font (Figure 1-43).

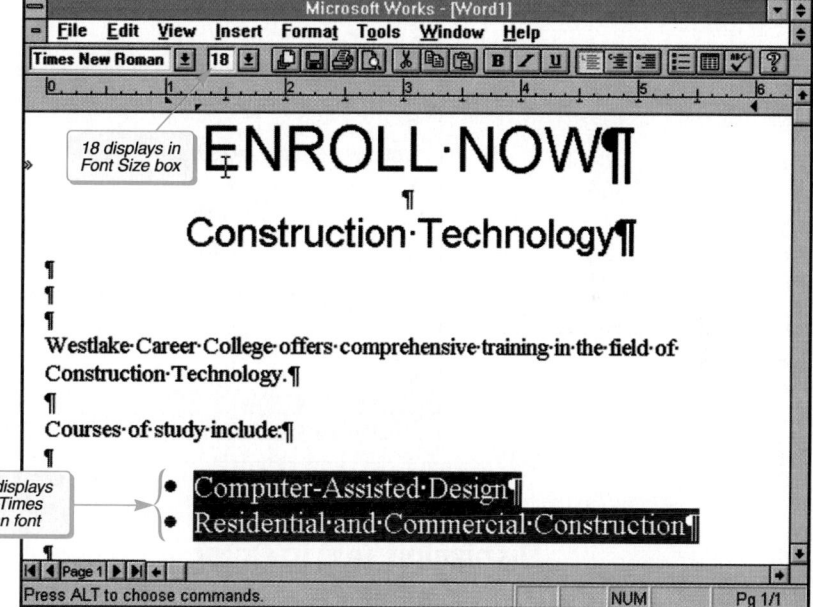

FIGURE 1-43

If you want to change the bulleted list to standard text, highlight the bulleted list and press the CTRL+Q keys, or choose the **Paragraph command** from the **Format menu** and select the Normal option in the Paragraph dialog box that displays.

To remove the highlighting, click the left mouse button with the mouse pointer positioned anywhere in the workspace area.

The document is now formatted with the proper font and font sizes except for the last two lines. The line following the bulleted list should display in 14 point font size. Because the entire document cannot display on the screen at one time due to the enlarged fonts, you must scroll down to display the last lines in the document. To scroll down and then change the next to last line to 14 point font size, complete the following steps.

TO SCROLL DOWN AND CHANGE FONT SIZE

Step 1: Point to the down scroll arrow and scroll until the last lines of the document display on the screen.

Step 2: Highlight the line beginning with the words, "For information,".

Step 3: Click the Font Size box arrow to display the list of font sizes.

Step 4: Select 14 from the list of font sizes.

The next to last line displays in 14 point Times New Roman font (Figure 1-44).

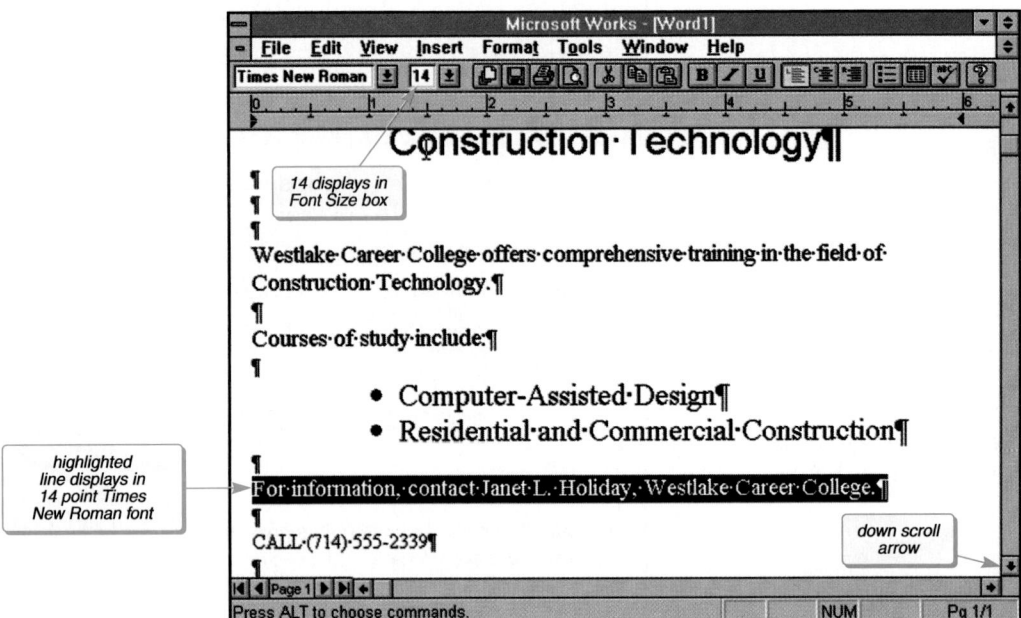

FIGURE 1-44

Displaying Text in Color

The last line is to be centered and displayed in red 18 point Arial italic font. To format this line, use the **Font and Style Command** in the Format menu as shown in the following steps.

TO CHANGE FONT AND FONT SIZE AND DISPLAY TEXT IN COLOR ▼

STEP 1 ▶

Highlight the last line in the document, and click the Center Align button on the Toolbar.

The line is highlighted and centered (Figure 1-45).

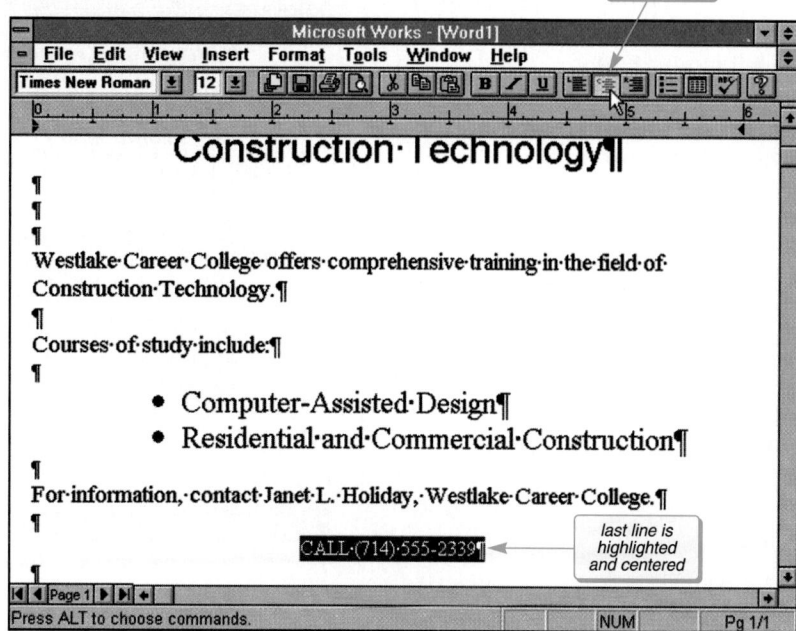

FIGURE 1-45

STEP 2 ▶

Select the Format menu by pointing to the word Format on the menu bar and clicking the left mouse button. Then point to the Font and Style command.

Works displays the Format menu and the mouse pointer is positioned on the Font and Style command (Figure 1-46).

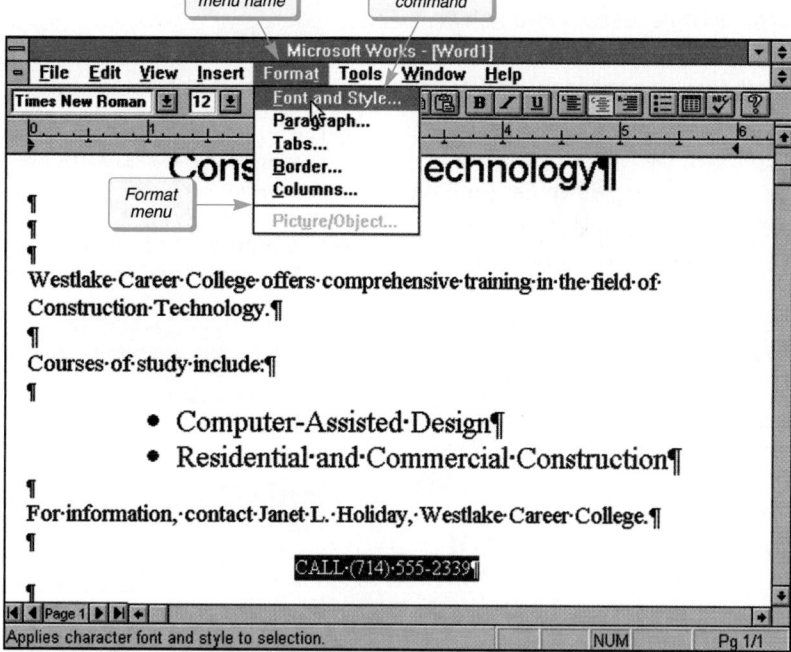

FIGURE 1-46

STEP 3 ▶

Choose the Font and Style command from the Format menu by clicking the left mouse button.

The Font and Style dialog box displays (Figure 1-47).

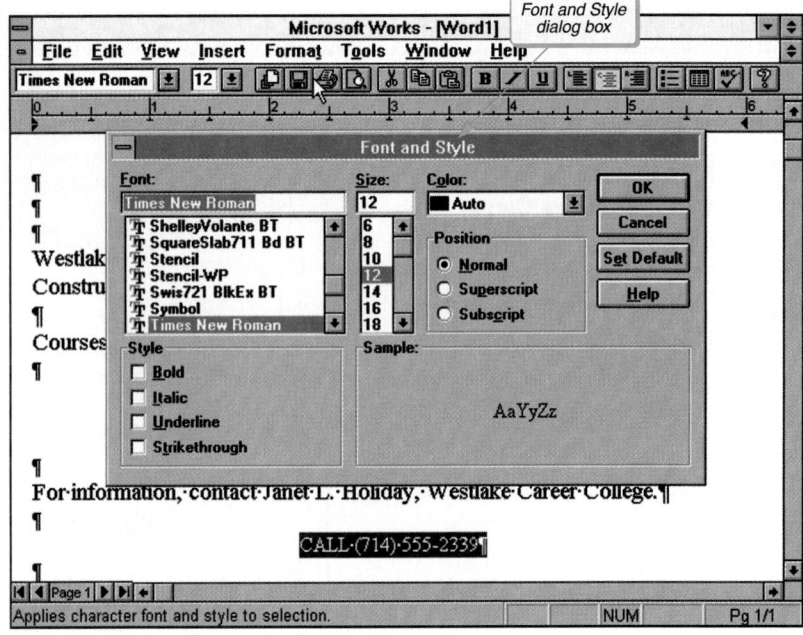

FIGURE 1-47

STEP 4 ▶

In the Font and Style dialog box, scroll up if necessary and select Arial font in the Font box. Then, scroll down if necessary and select 18 in the Size box. Click the Color drop-down list box arrow, scroll through the drop-down list until the Red color box displays, and then point to the Red color box.

In the Font and Style dialog box, Arial is highlighted in the Font list box, 18 is highlighted in Size list box, and the mouse pointer points to the red rectangle in the Color dorp-down list box (Figure 1-48). The text in the Sample area changes to 18 point Arial font.

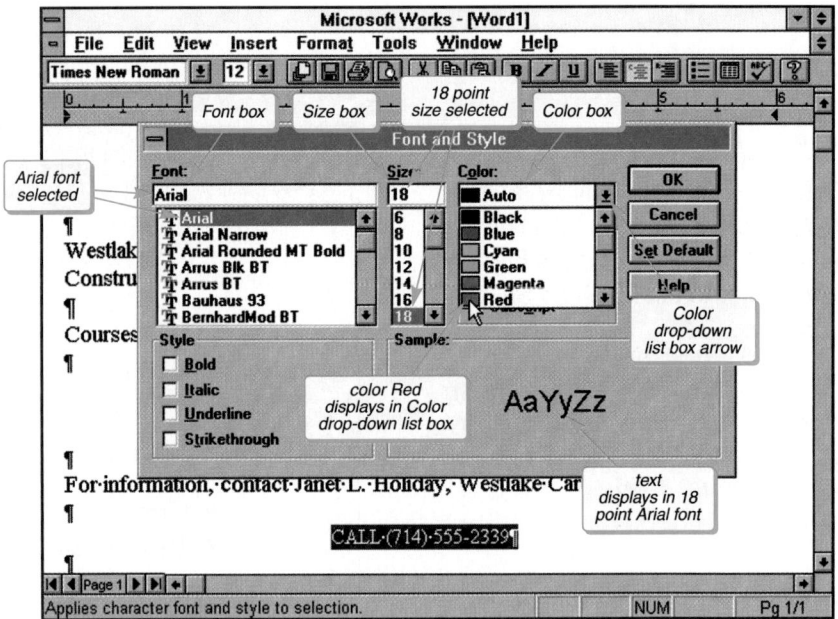

FIGURE 1-48

STEP 5 ▶

Select the color Red by clicking the left mouse button. Click the Italic check box in the Style area of the dialog box.

Text in the Sample area displays as red 18 point Arial italic font (Figure 1-49). An X displays in the Italic check box.

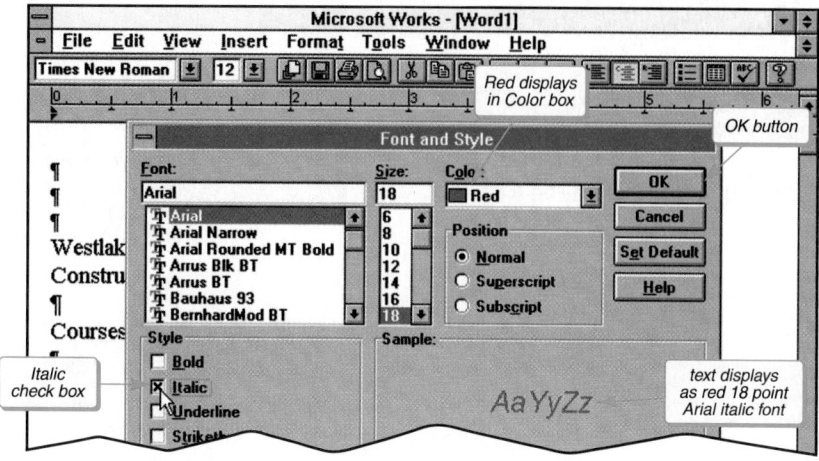

FIGURE 1-49

STEP 6 ▶

Choose the OK button by pointing to and clicking the OK button in the Font and Style dialog box. Click anywhere in the blank workspace area to remove the highlighting.

Works displays the last line in red 18 point Arial italic font (Figure 1-50). The paragraph mark for the next paragraph retains the formatting from the previous paragraph.

FIGURE 1-50

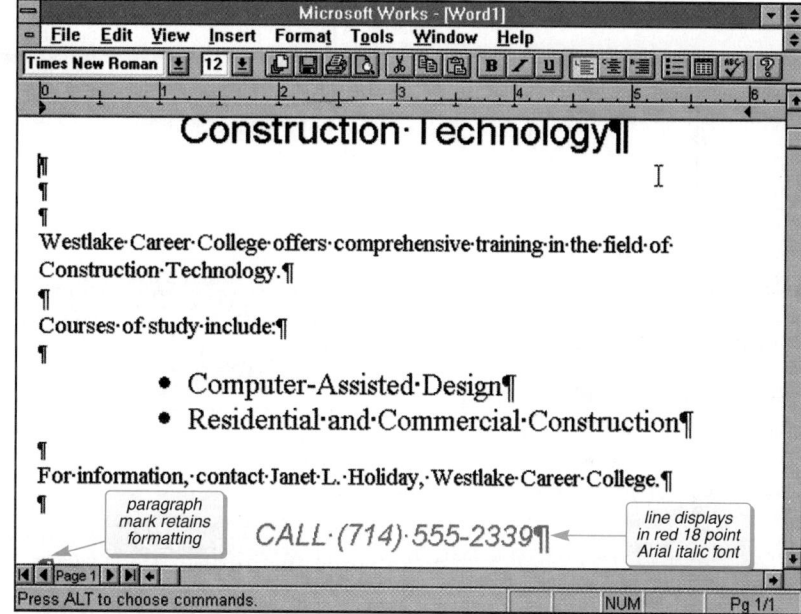

When you format the last paragraph in a document, the formatting remains in place for subsequent paragraphs unless you change it. That is the reason the paragraph mark on the last line in Figure 1-50 displays in red 18 point Arial italic font.

You can use either the buttons on the Toolbar or the Font and Style command from the Format menu when you want to change fonts, font sizes, and font styles. To change the color of text, you must use the Font and Style command from the Format menu and make the appropriate entries in the Font and Style dialog box.

Bold Style

To further emphasize the contents of the announcement, the entire document should display in bold. To do this, you must first highlight the entire document, and then click the Bold button. To display the document in bold, perform the steps on the next page.

TO DISPLAY AN ENTIRE DOCUMENT IN BOLD ▼

STEP 1 ►

Position the mouse pointer in the left margin, hold down the CTRL key, and press the left mouse button.

The entire document is highlighted (Figure 1-51).

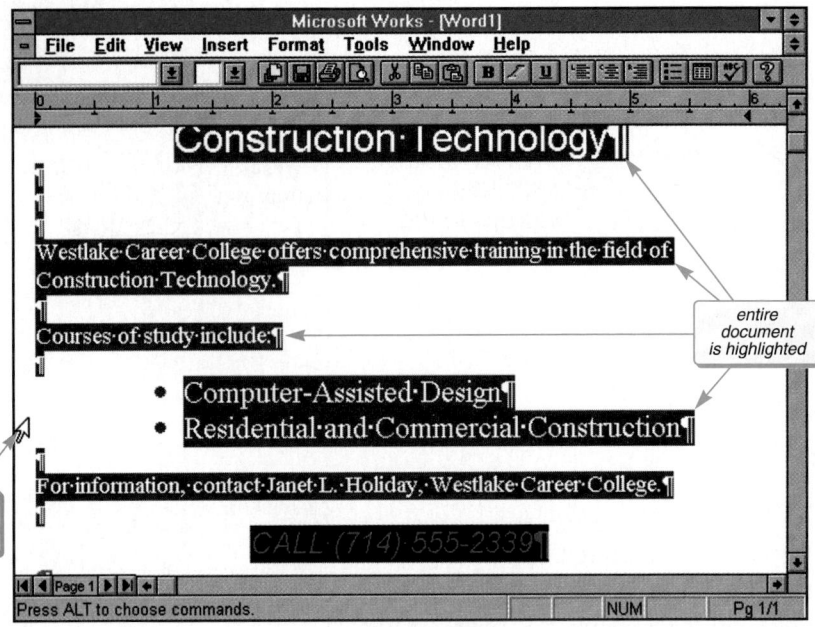

FIGURE 1-51

STEP 2 ►

Click the Bold button on the Toolbar

Works changes all text to bold (Figure 1-52).

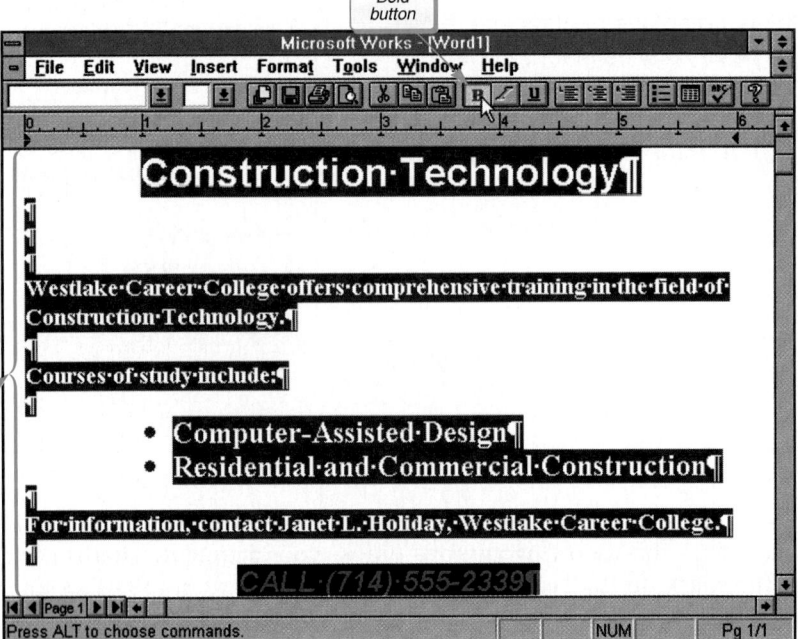

FIGURE 1-52

You can also highlight the entire document by choosing the Select All command from the Edit menu.

The document is now formatted except for the illustration which must be inserted into the document.

▶ USING CLIP ART IN A DOCUMENT

T he next step in preparing the announcement is to insert an illustration related to construction in the document (see Figure 1-1 on page W1.4). To accomplish this, you must use the Microsoft **clip art** (predrawn illustrations) that is available for use as a part of the Word Processor.

Inserting Clip Art in a Word Processing Document

The steps to insert clip art into the announcement are explained below and on the following pages.

TO INSERT CLIP ART INTO A DOCUMENT ▼

STEP 1 ▶

If necessary, click the beginning of document button on the scroll bar to display the top portion of the document on the screen. Move the mouse pointer (I-beam) to the line in the document where you want to place the clip art and click.

The first lines of the document display on the screen and the insertion point is positioned on the line where you will insert the clip art (Figure 1-53).

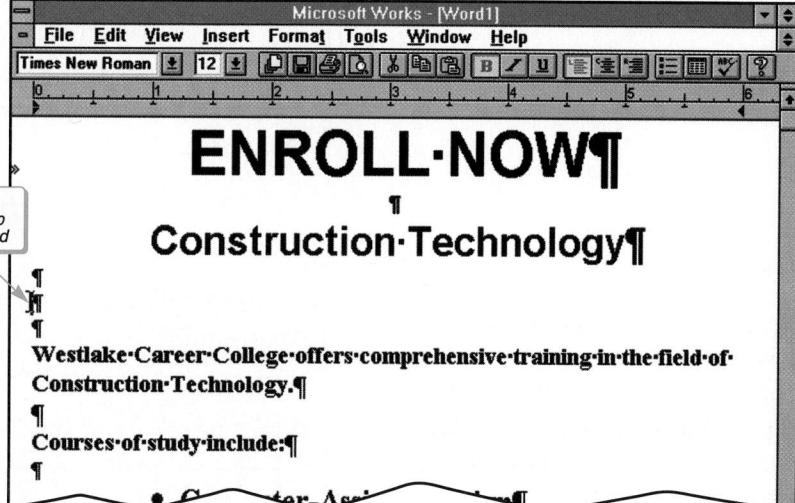

FIGURE 1-53

STEP 2 ▶

Because you want to center the clip art, click the Center Align button on the Toolbar.

Works centers the insertion point and the paragraph mark on the screen (Figure 1-54).

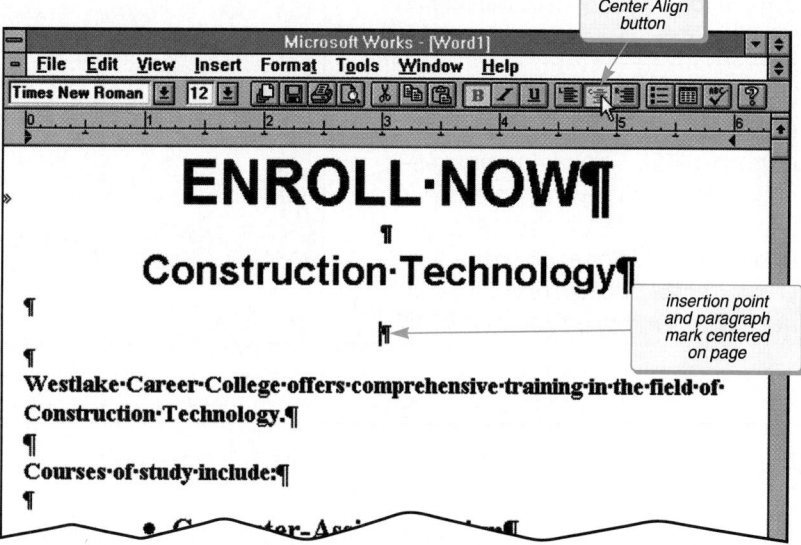

FIGURE 1-54

STEP 3 ►

Select the Insert menu by clicking the word Insert on the menu bar. Point to the Clip Art command.

*Works displays the **Insert menu**. The mouse pointer points to the **ClipArt command** (Figure 1-55).*

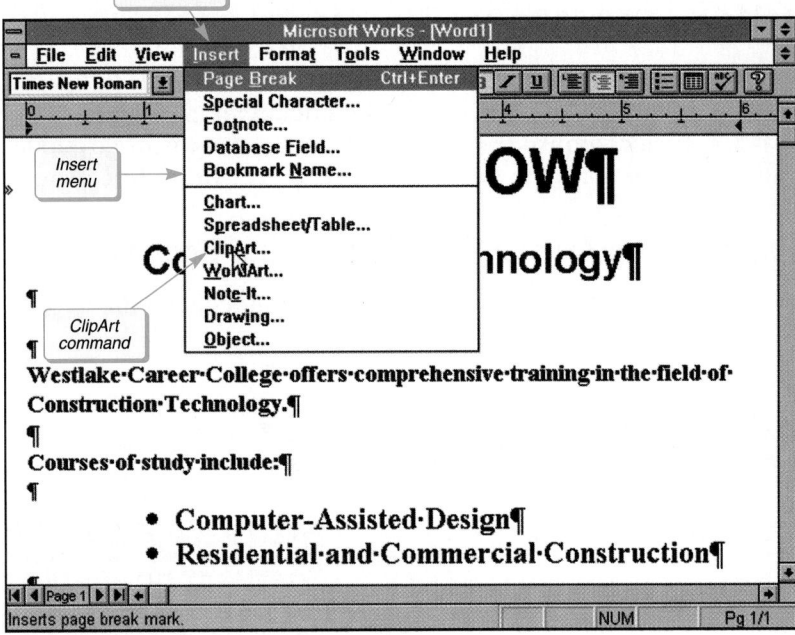

FIGURE 1-55

STEP 4 ►

Choose the ClipArt command from the Insert menu by clicking the left mouse button. When the Microsoft ClipArt Gallery dialog box displays, point to the clip art illustrating the hard hat. The clip art on your computer might appear in a different sequence than shown in Figure 1-56. If so, scroll until the hard hat clip art displays.

*Works displays the **Microsoft ClipArt Gallery dialog box** (Figure 1-56). The dialog box displays clip art that you can place in a document. You can scroll down to display additional clip art and you can click a category name to display a particular type of clip art.*

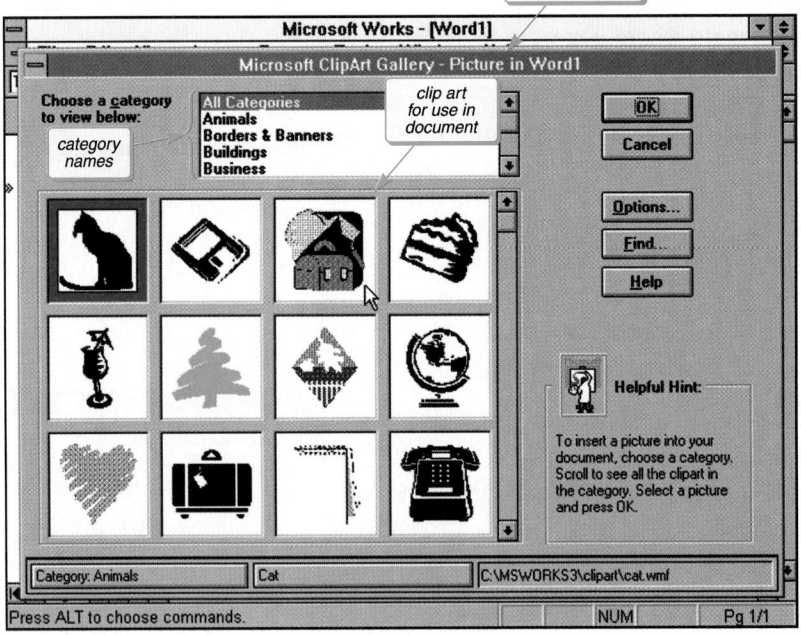

FIGURE 1-56

STEP 5 ▶

Click the left mouse button to highlight the clip art for the document, and then point to the OK button.

The clip art with the illustration of the hard hat and lunch box is highlighted as indicated by the blue outline around the clip art (Figure 1-57). The mouse pointer points to the OK button.

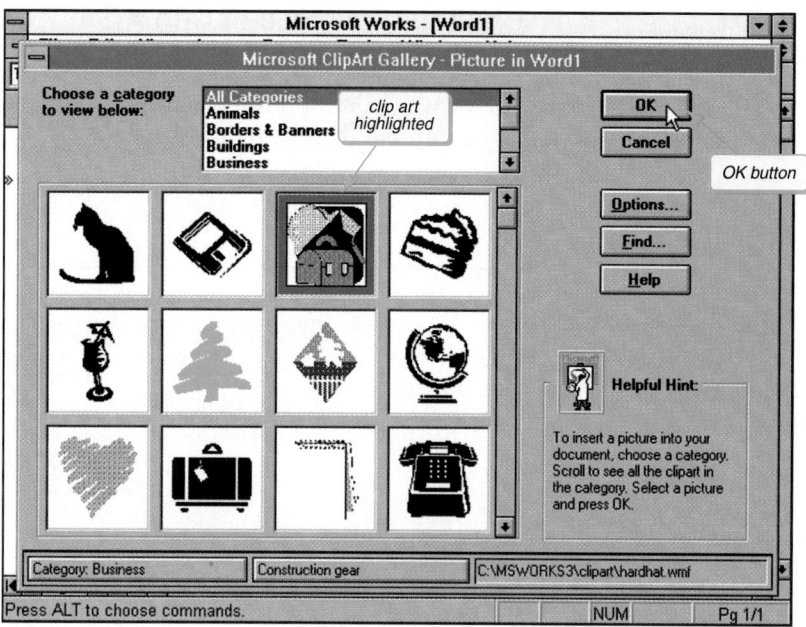

FIGURE 1-57

STEP 6 ▶

Choose the OK button in the Microsoft ClipArt Gallery dialog box.

Works inserts the clip art in the word processing document at the location of the insertion point (Figure 1-58).

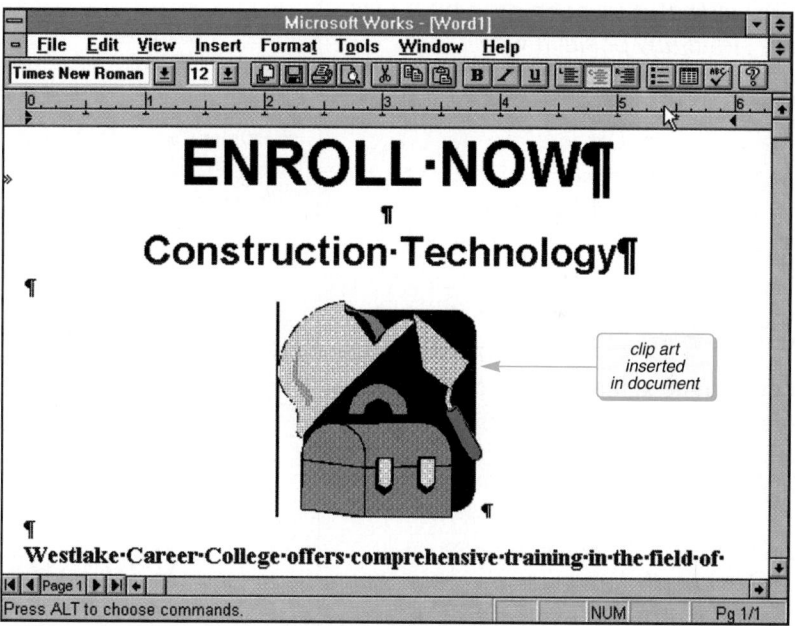

FIGURE 1-58

The Microsoft ClipArt Gallery dialog box that displays on your computer may contain additional images. Many different clip art images may be purchased and added to Works.

The clip art that is placed in the word processing document is called an **object.** Once in the word processing document, the object may be resized, that is made larger or smaller, as required.

Changing the Size of Clip Art

After adding the clip art to the document, the size of the clip art must be changed to correspond to Figure 1-1 on page W1.4. To change the size of the clip art, complete the following steps.

TO RESIZE CLIP ART

STEP 1 ▶

Point to the clip art and click the left mouse button.

*When the clip art object is selected, Works displays the clip art within a rectangular border that contains small dark squares, called **resize handles**, around the border (Figure 1-59). The mouse pointer changes to a block arrow with the word DRAG beneath it. This indicates you can drag the clip art to any position within the document.*

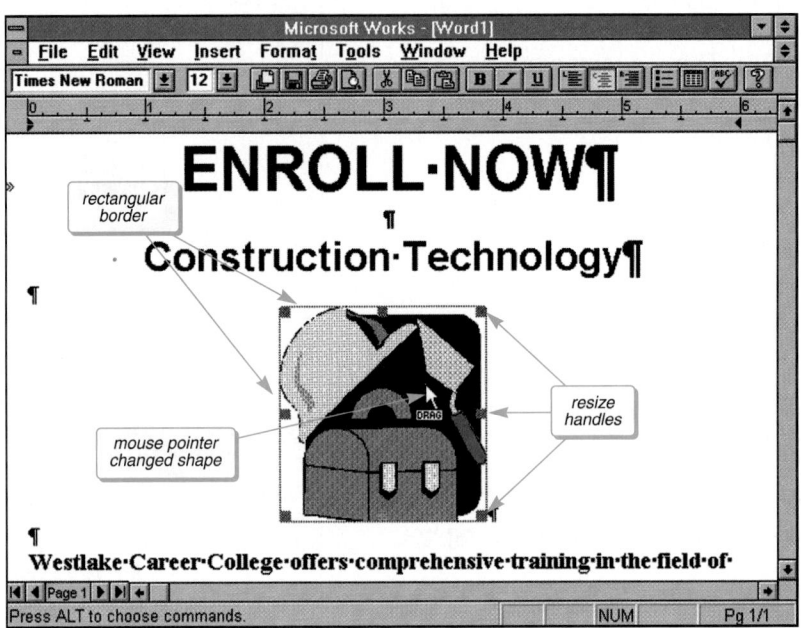

FIGURE 1-59

STEP 2 ▶

Position the mouse pointer over the resize handle in the upper right corner of the border that surrounds the clip art.

Positioning the mouse pointer on a resize handle causes the mouse pointer to change to a small square with a two-headed arrow intersecting the square (Figure 1-60). The word RESIZE displays beneath the square.

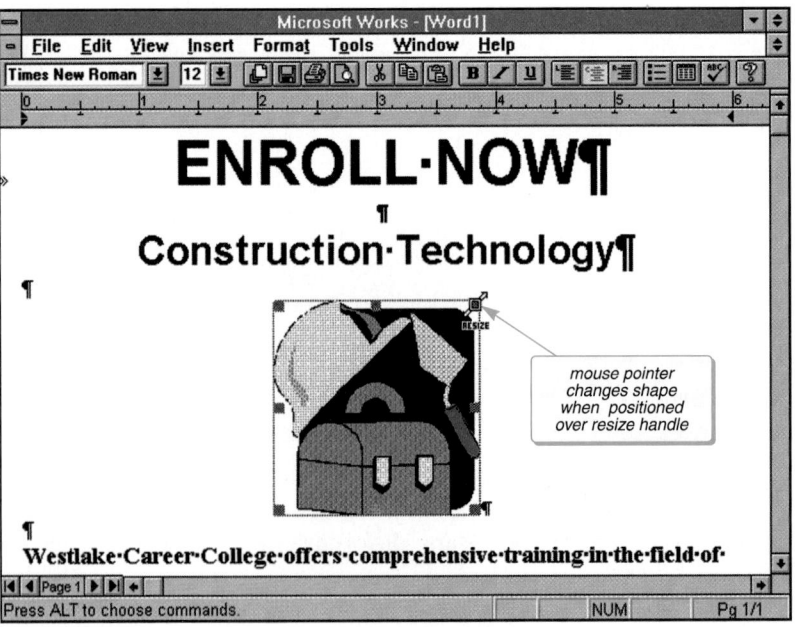

FIGURE 1-60

STEP 3 ▶

With the mouse pointer pointing to the resize handle in the upper right corner of the clip art, drag upward and to the right until the right border displays approximately under the 4 3/4" mark on the ruler.

As you drag upward and to the right, the entire rectangular border around the clip art enlarges (Figure 1-61).

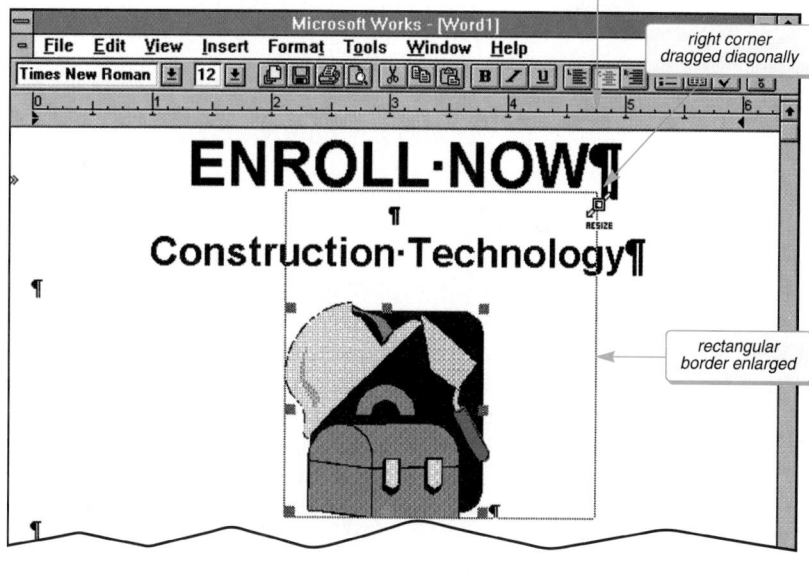

FIGURE 1-61

STEP 4 ▶

Release the left mouse button.

The illustration expands to fill the enlarged rectangular border (Figure 1-62). Works also recenters the enlarged illustration.

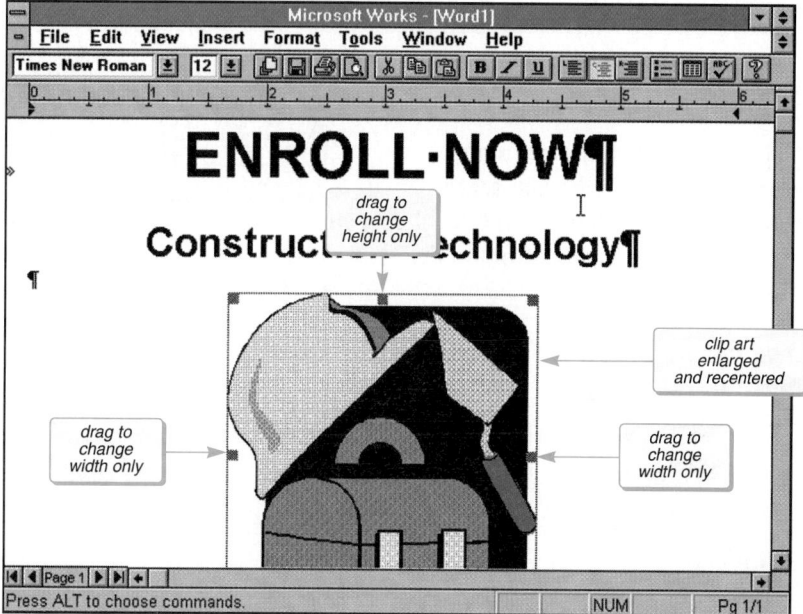

FIGURE 1-62

For objects in a Word Processor document, when you drag one of the corner resize handles, the entire rectangular border increases or decreases proportionately in size. If you drag a resize handle in the middle of a vertical border, only the width of the illustration changes. Similarly, if you drag a resize handle in the middle of a horizontal border, only the height of the illustration changes.

You can precisely set the size of the clip art by selecting the Format menu, choosing the Picture/Object command, choosing the Size tab, and then typing precise measurements or percentages in the dialog box that displays.

If you ever need to clear a clip art image from a Microsoft Works Word Processor document, select the image and then press the DELETE key. You can also select the image and then choose the Clear command from the Edit menu.

If an object has been previously selected, clicking anywhere in the document workspace except the selected object will remove the rectangular border.

▶ SAVING A DOCUMENT

When you create a document, the document is recorded only in your computer's random access memory until you save the document on hard disk or on a diskette. If the computer is turned off or if there is a power loss before you save a document, your work will be lost. You should save all documents either on the hard disk or on a diskette. When saving a document, you must select a **filename**. The filename is the name that is used to reference the file (document) when it is stored on a hard disk or diskette. The filename must be no longer than eight characters. The characters can consist of letters of the alphabet, numbers, and the following special characters: ', @, $, %, &,), (, }, {, -, _, ~, and #.

To save the document created in Project 1 on a diskette in drive A using the filename proj1, insert a diskette in drive A and then perform the following steps.

TO SAVE A DOCUMENT ▼

STEP 1 ▶

Click anywhere in the document workspace except the clip art to remove the highlight around the clip art. Point to the Save button on the Toolbar

The mouse pointer points to the **Save button** *(Figure 1-63).*

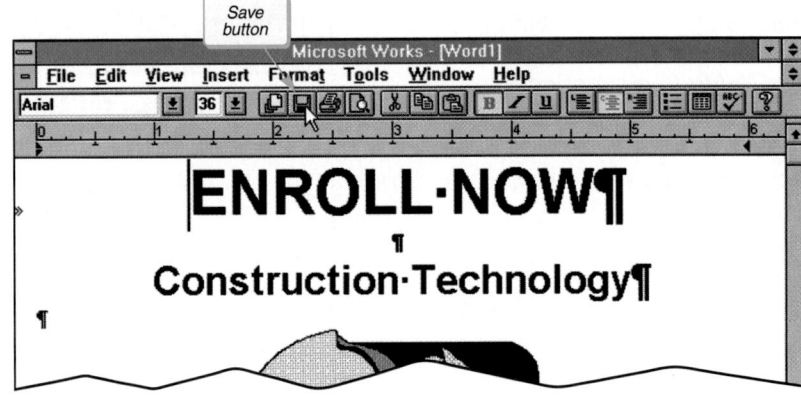

FIGURE 1-63

STEP 2 ▶

Click the Save button on the Toolbar. When the Save As dialog box displays, type `proj1` in the File Name text box. Click the Drives drop-down list box arrow.

The **Save As dialog box** *displays on the screen (Figure 1-64). Initially, word1 displays in the File Name text box but is replaced by proj1 as you type. Drives a:, c:, d:, and i: appear in the Drives drop-down list box. The drives on your computer might be different.*

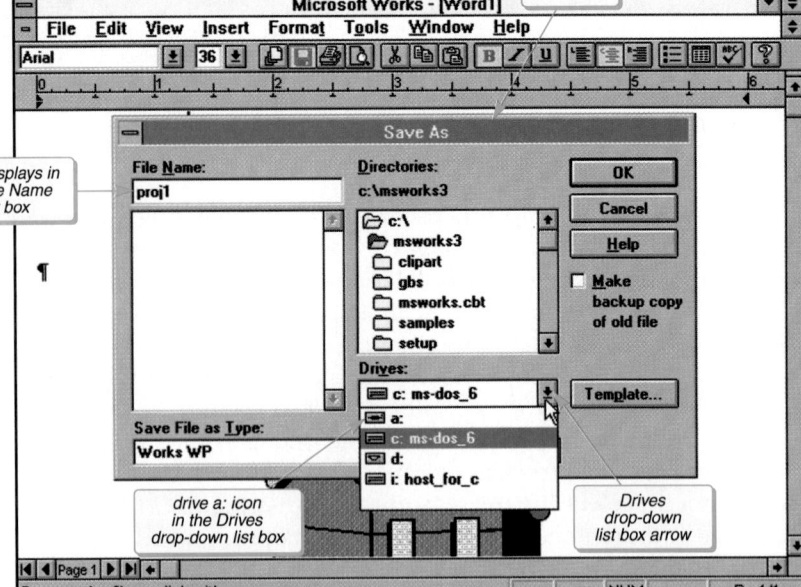

FIGURE 1-64

STEP 3 ▶

Select a: in the Drives drop-down list box by pointing to the drive a: icon and clicking the left mouse button. Point to the OK button.

When you select a: in the Drives drop-down list box, a: is high-lighted and the Directories list box changes to a: (Figure 1-65).

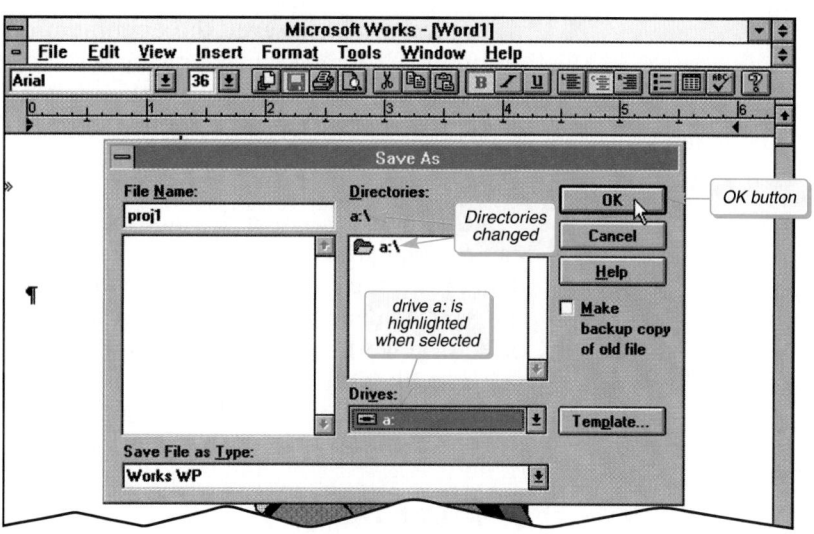

FIGURE 1-65

STEP 4 ▶

Choose the OK button in the Save As dialog box to save the document.

The dialog box disappears and the document remains displayed on the screen (Figure 1-66). The name changes in the title bar from Word1 to the name of the document saved (PROJ1.WPS). Works automatically adds the filename extension, .wps, to the filename.

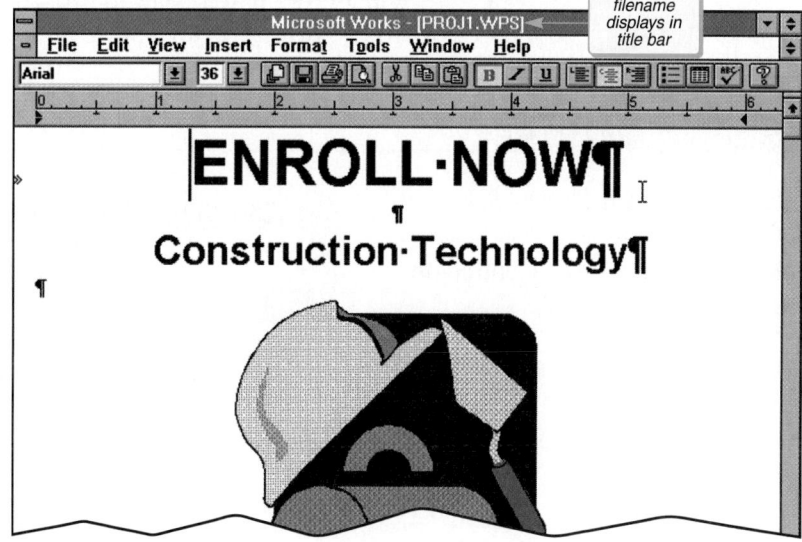

FIGURE 1-66

An alternative method of saving the document in Step 2 is to type a: followed by the filename in the File Name text box (for example, a:proj1), and then choose the OK button.

You may also save documents using the **Save command** and the **Save As command** from the File menu.

When you save a document for the first time, it is necessary to enter a file-name and indicate the drive and subdirectory in which the file will be saved. Whether you use the Save button on the Toolbar, the Save command from the File menu, or the Save As command from the File menu, Works will display the Save As dialog box so you can enter the required information.

Once you have saved the document on disk, however, these commands work differently. When you make changes to an already-saved document and want to save the modified document without changing the filename, use the Save button on the Toolbar or the Save command from the File menu. Works will save the modified document without displaying the Save As dialog box and asking you for a new filename.

If you want to save the modified document using a filename different from the name under which the file is currently saved, then you must use the Save As command from the File menu. When you use the Save As command, Works will display the Save As dialog box and you must then enter the new filename, drive, and sub-directory. Works will save the document using the new filename in the location you specify. Note, however, that the file saved using the old filename still resides on disk. The file using the new name does not replace the file with the old name.

▶ PRINT PREVIEW

A fter you create and save a word processor document, you will often want to print the document. To view the document in the exact form in which it will appear when printed, use the print preview feature of the Word Processor. To use print preview, perform the following steps.

TO USE PRINT PREVIEW ▼

STEP 1 ▶

Point to the Print Preview button on the Toolbar (Figure 1-67).

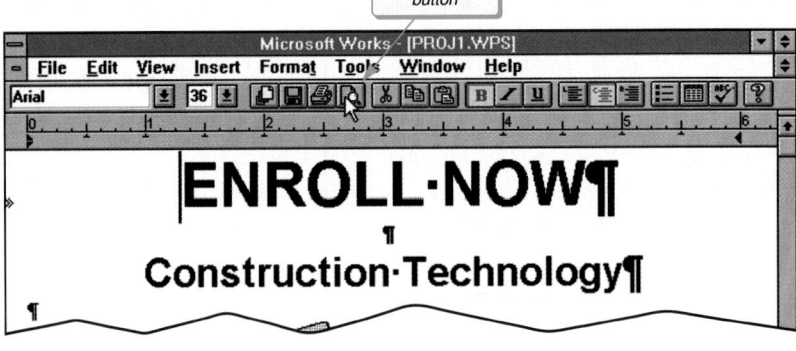

FIGURE 1-67

STEP 2 ▶

Click the Print Preview button on the Toolbar.

Works opens the print preview window, and you can see the entire document as it will print (Figure 1-68).

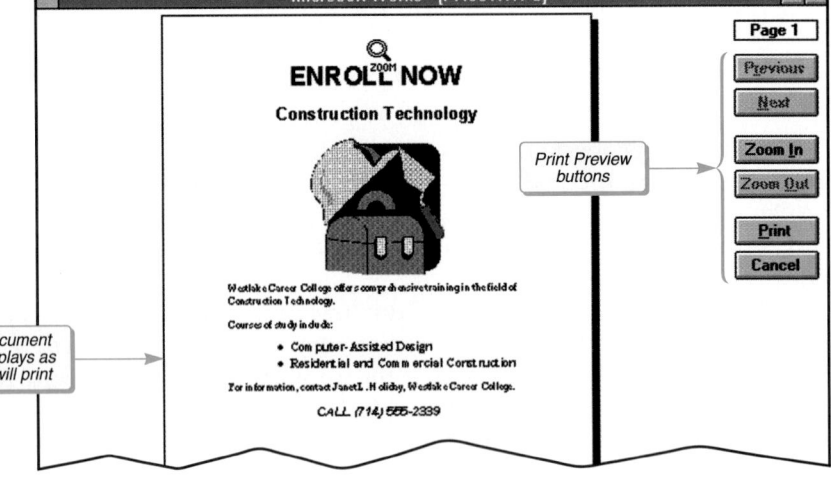

FIGURE 1-68

At the top right side of the window, a box contains the page number of the page displayed. Below the page number box is a series of buttons, called **Print Preview buttons**, you can use to control what you want to display. Clicking the Previous button will display a previous page, if there is one. Clicking the Next button will display the next page, if there is one.

The document image that Works displays is reduced in size. It is possible to enlarge the image. Clicking the Zoom In button once will enlarge the image to approximately one-half the size displayed in the document window where you enter text. Clicking the Zoom In button twice will enlarge the image to the full size displayed in the document window where you enter text. Use the Zoom Out button to reduce the size of the image after you have enlarged it.

Clicking the Print button will cause Works to print the document. Clicking the Cancel button returns you to the document window where you can enter text.

Choosing the **Print Preview command** from the File menu also causes the print preview window to display.

If you position the mouse pointer in the print preview image area, the mouse pointer shape changes to a magnifying glass and you can use the mouse to enlarge the print preview image. Clicking the left mouse button one time will enlarge the image to one-half its normal screen size. Clicking a second time will enlarge the image to approximately full-size. Clicking a third time will reduce the image to its original size as shown in Figure 1-68.

▶ PRINTING A DOCUMENT

T he following steps explain how to print a document that appears in the document window by choosing the **Print command** from the File menu. The Print command available from the File menu should be used the first time you print a document on a given computer to ensure the print options are properly selected.

TO PRINT A DOCUMENT ▼

STEP 1 ▶

Choose the Cancel button in the print preview window to return to the document window. Select the File menu from the menu bar and point to the Print command.

The File menu displays (Figure 1-69). The mouse pointer points to the Print command.

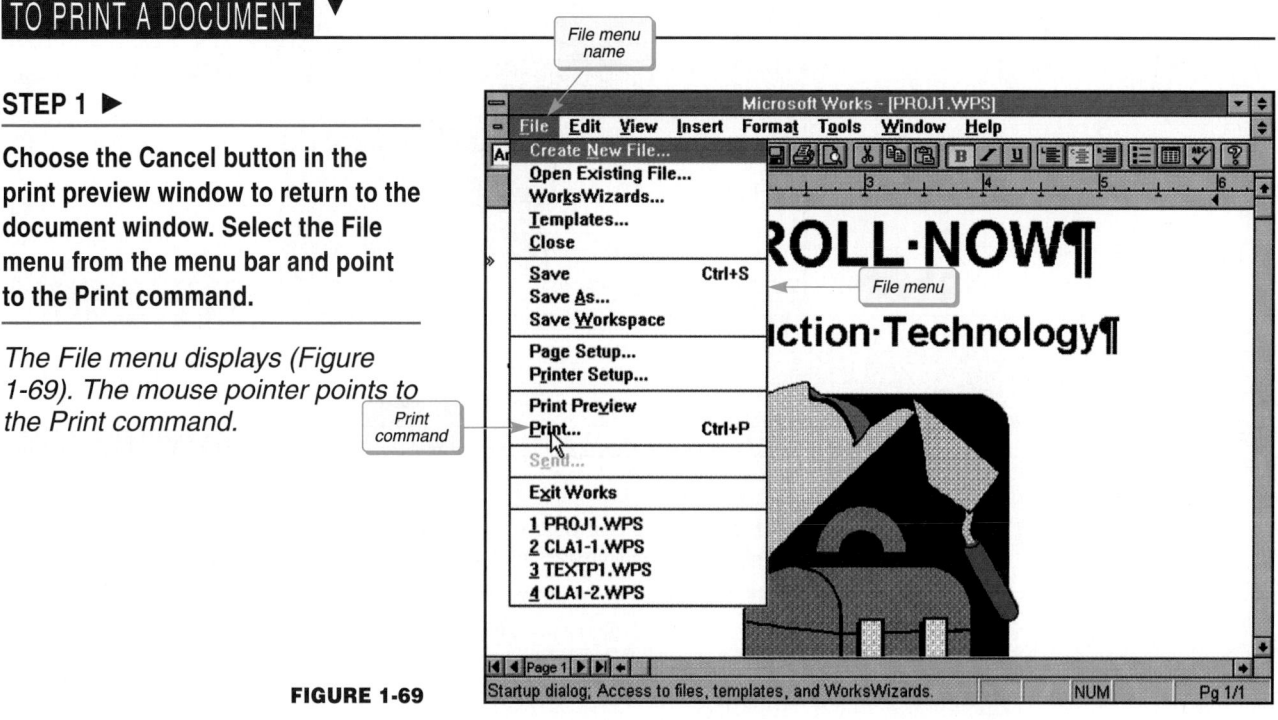

FIGURE 1-69

STEP 2 ▶

Choose the Print command from the File menu. When the Print dialog box displays, point to the OK button.

*The **Print dialog box** displays on the screen (Figure 1-70). Review the Print dialog box to ensure the Number of Copies text box contains 1 and the All option button is selected (a small black circle appears within the All option button when it is selected). This indicates all pages will print. In the What to print area, make sure the Main Document option button is selected.*

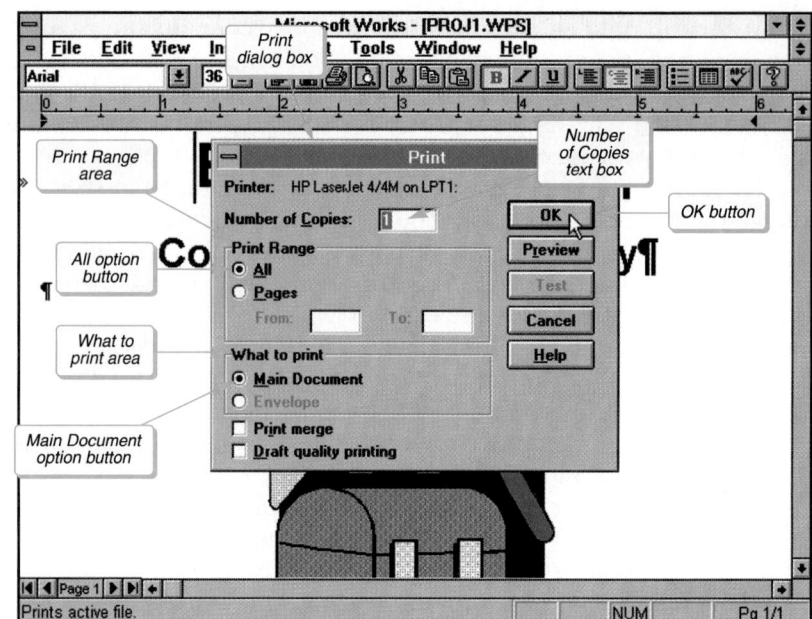

FIGURE 1-70

STEP 3 ▶

Choose the OK button in the Print dialog box.

The Printing dialog box displays a brief message on the screen describing the status of the printing operation (Figure 1-71). The document is then printed on your printer.

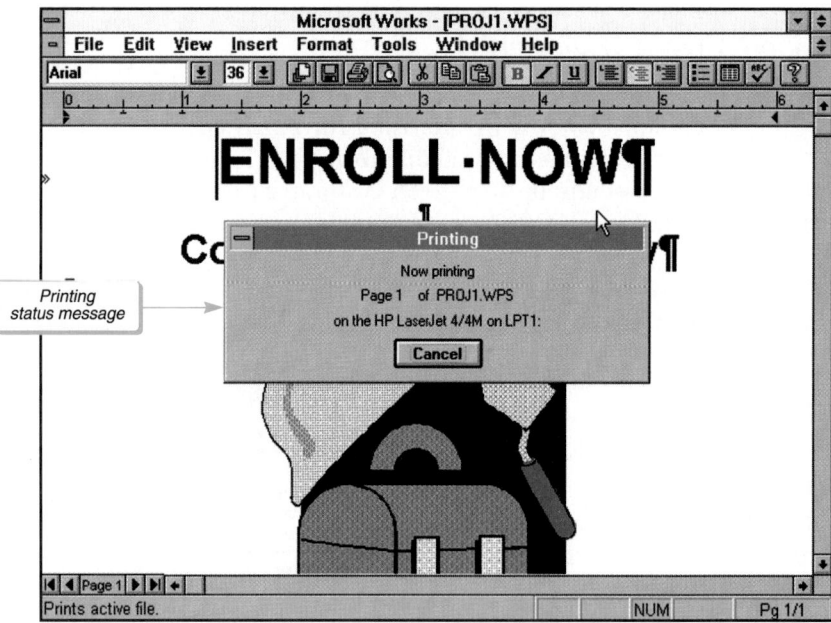

FIGURE 1-71

If you have a color printer, the document will print as illustrated in Figure 1-72. If you do not have a color printer, the document will print in black and white and the clip art appears in shades of gray.

ENROLL NOW

Construction Technology

Westlake Career College offers comprehensive training in the field of Construction Technology.

Courses of study include:

- **Computer-Assisted Design**
- **Residential and Commercial Construction**

For information, contact Janet L. Holiday, Westlake Career College.

CALL (714) 555-2339

FIGURE 1-72

After you have made entries in the Print dialog box to assure that printing will occur as you want, you can use the Print button on the Toolbar to print the document. When you click the Print button on the Toolbar, the Print dialog box will not appear. Printing will occur based on previous entries in the Print dialog box.

▶ CLOSING A DOCUMENT

When you have completed working on a document, normally you will close the document and begin work on another document or quit Works. Closing a document you are working on removes the document from the screen and from random access memory. If you close a document and no other documents are open, Works displays the Startup dialog box, which allows you to continue using Works.

If you make changes to a document and then close it before saving the changed document, Works displays a dialog box asking if you want to save the changes before closing. Choose the Yes button in the dialog box to save changes.

You should close a document when you no longer want to work on that document, but want to continue using Works.

TO CLOSE A DOCUMENT ▼

STEP 1 ▶

Select the File menu from the menu bar and point to the Close command.

*Works displays the File menu and the mouse pointer points to the **Close command** (Figure 1-73).*

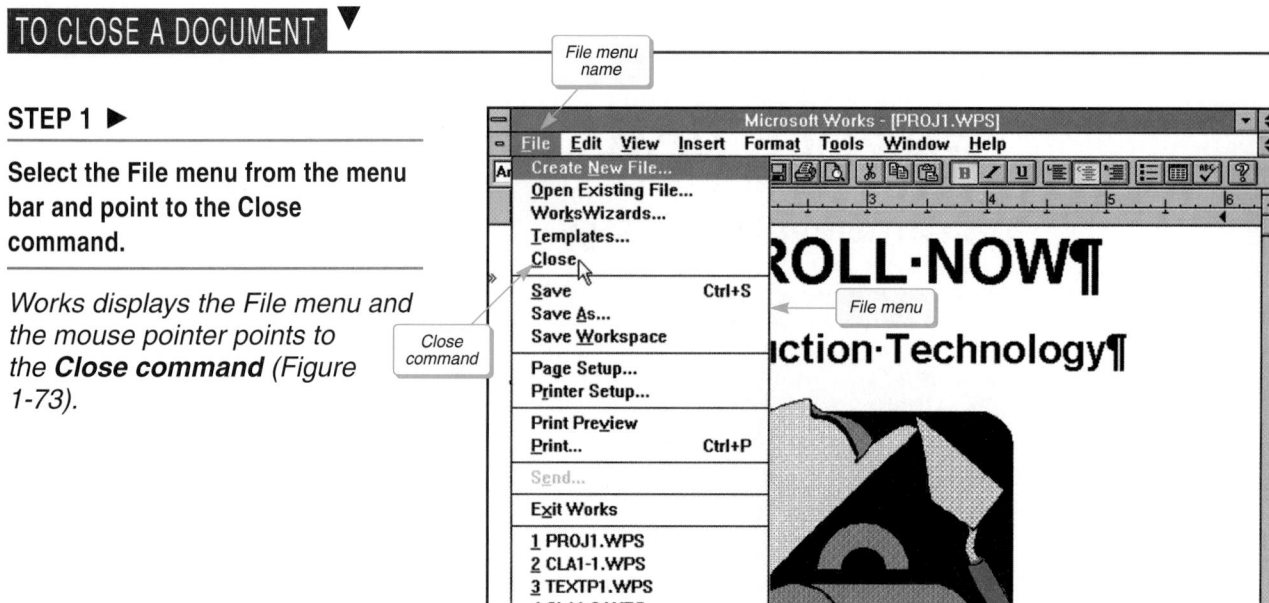

FIGURE 1-73

STEP 2 ▶

Choose the Close command by clicking the left mouse button.

The text on the screen disappears and the Startup dialog box displays, allowing you to continue to use Works (Figure 1-74).

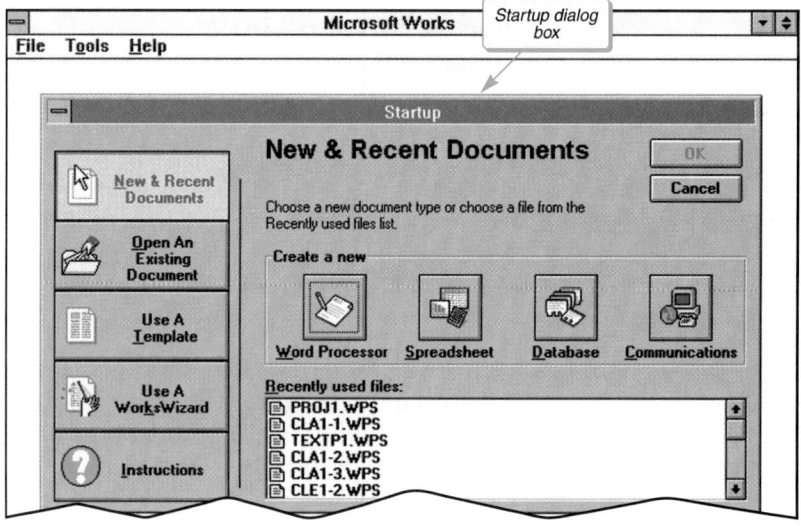

FIGURE 1-74

▶ QUITTING WORKS

I f you are finished using Works, you should quit Works. It is important to quit Works using commands from the menu and not just turn the machine off after completing a document. The following steps explain how to quit Works.

TO QUIT WORKS ▼

STEP 1 ►

Select the File menu from the menu bar and point to the Exit Works command.

Works displays the File menu and the mouse pointer points to the **Exit Works command** *(Figure 1-75).*

STEP 2

Choose the Exit Works command from the File menu by clicking the left mouse button.

FIGURE 1-75

Works is terminated, and the Microsoft Works for Windows group window in Program Manager will again display. If you have made any changes to a document after it has been saved, a dialog box appears asking you if you want to save the changes before exiting. Choose the Yes button in the dialog box to save changes.

You should use the Close command when you have completed a document and desire to continue using Microsoft Works for Windows. You should use the Exit command when you have completed a document and desire to quit Works and will not be working on another application requiring the use of Works at this time.

▶ OPENING A DOCUMENT

Often after creating, saving, and printing a document and exiting Works, you may want to open a document again to make changes to that document. When you do, start Works again. Then open the document to be revised.

Opening a document makes the document available for use or modification. A variety of methods exist for opening a document. One method of opening a document stored on a diskette in drive A is explained in the steps on the next page.

TO OPEN A DOCUMENT ▼

STEP 1 ▶

Start Works as explained on page W1.5. When the Startup dialog box displays, point to the Open An Existing Document button (Figure 1-76).

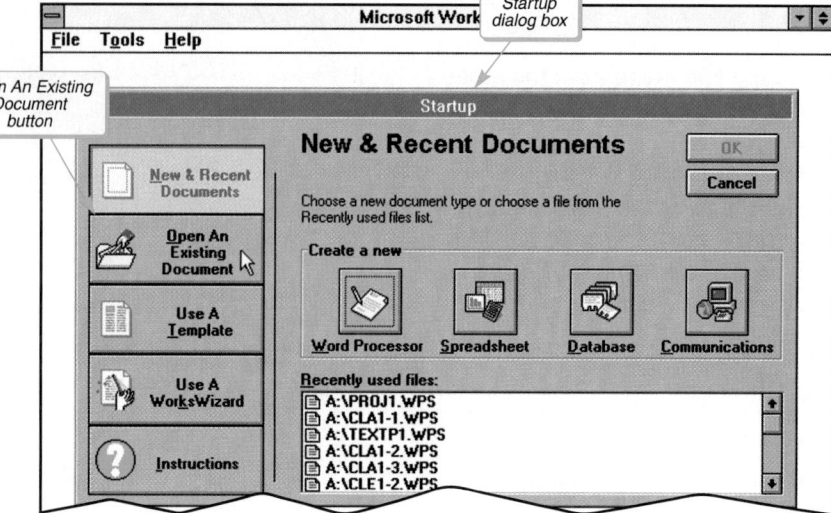

FIGURE 1-76

STEP 2 ▶

Choose the Open An Existing Document button in the Startup dialog box.

*Works displays the **Open dialog box** (Figure 1-77).*

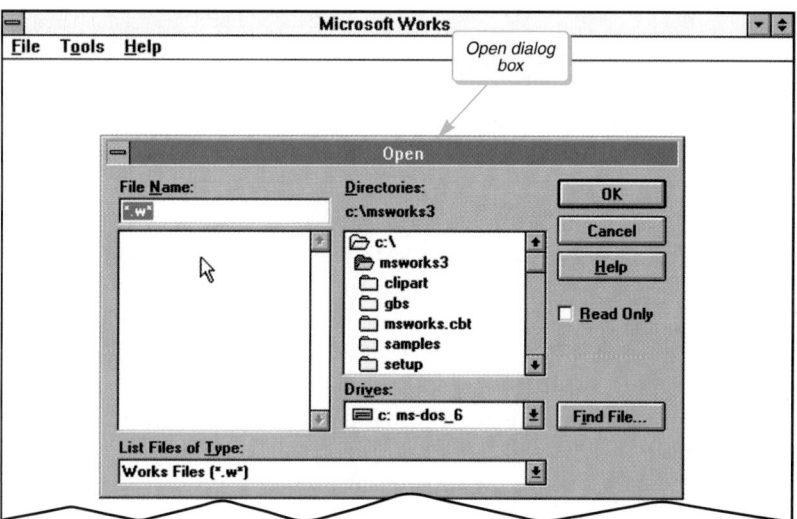

FIGURE 1-77

STEP 3 ▶

Click the Drives drop-down list box arrow and point to the drive a: icon in the Drives drop-down list box (Figure 1-78).

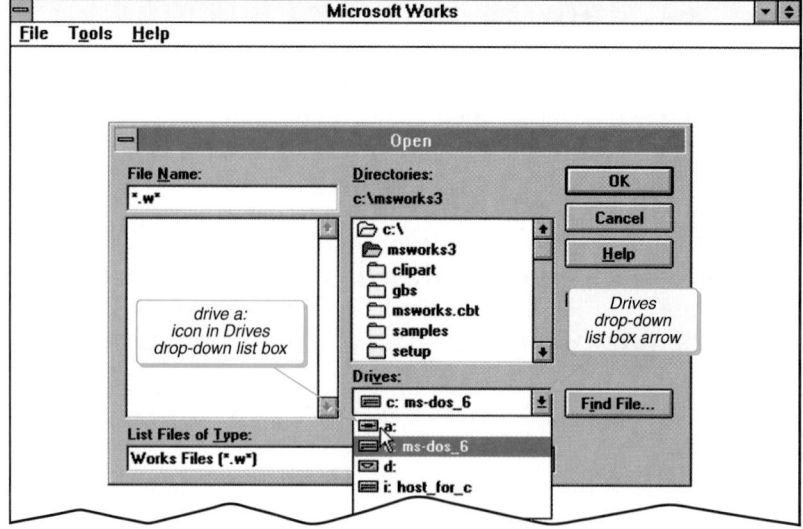

FIGURE 1-78

STEP 4 ►

Select drive a:. Then select proj1.wps by pointing to proj1.wps in the File Name list box and clicking the left mouse button.

Works displays the filenames on drive a: in the File Name list box (Figure 1-79). Selecting proj1.wps in the list places the file-name, proj1.wps, in the File Name text box.

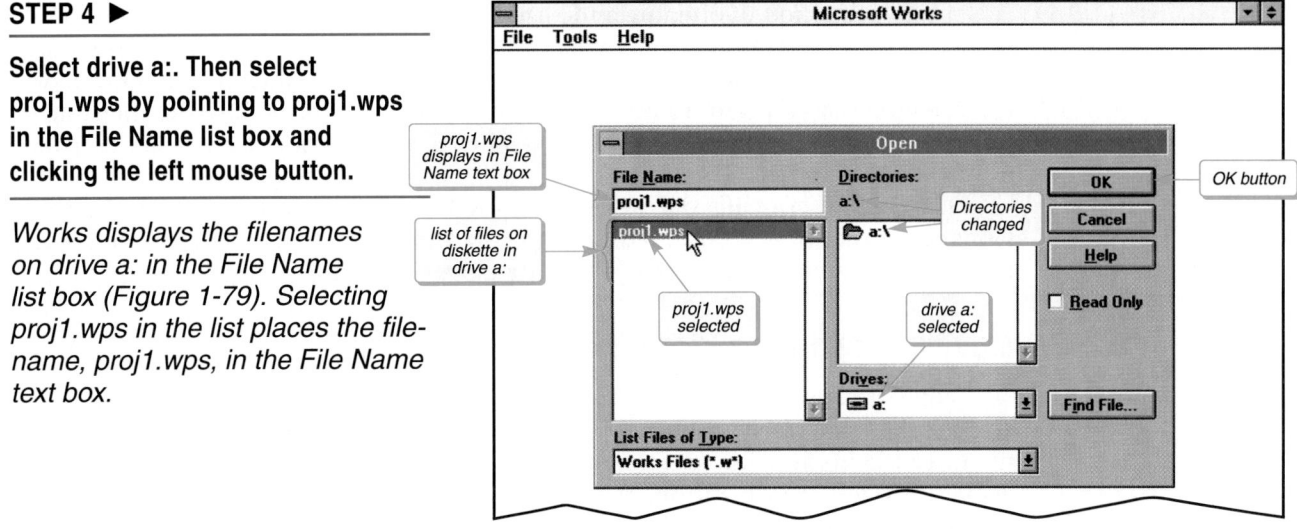

FIGURE 1-79

STEP 5 ►

Choose the OK button in the Open dialog box.

Works displays the document, proj1.wps, on the screen (Figure 1-80). You can revise or print the document as required.

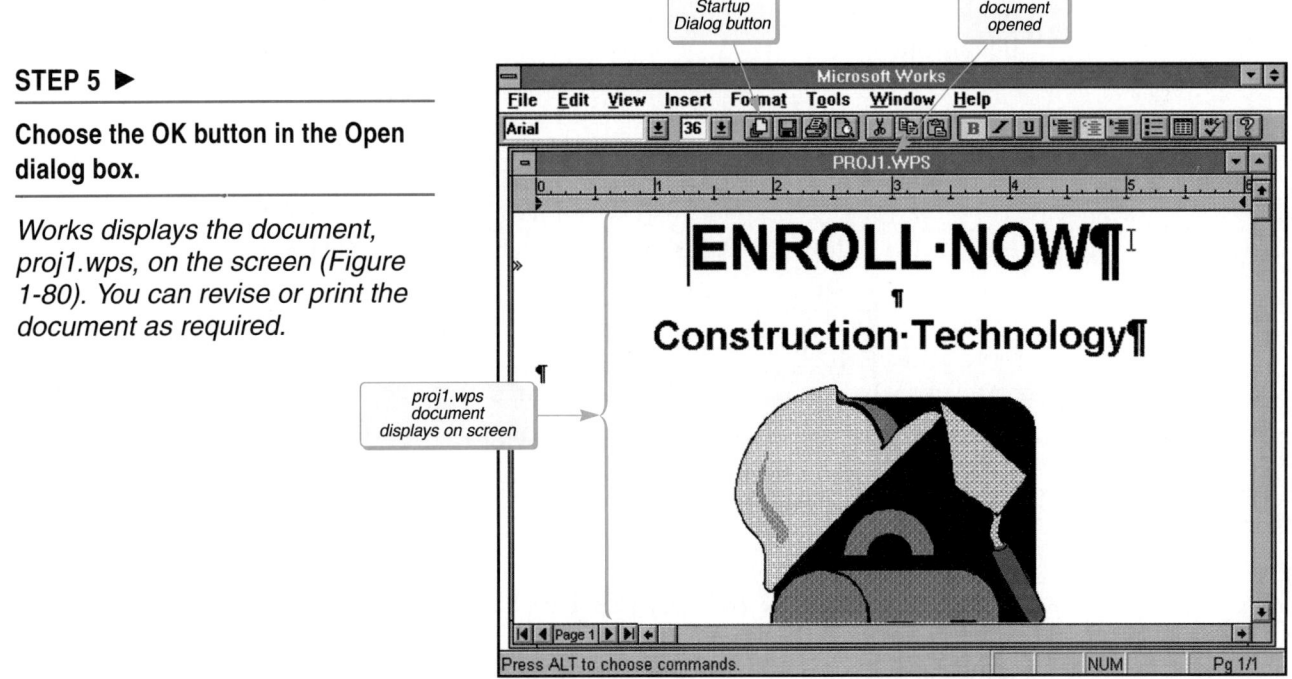

FIGURE 1-80

You can also open a document when the Startup dialog box displays by click-ing the filename in the Recently used files box and choosing the OK button or by double-clicking the appropriate filename in the Recently used files box (see Figure 1-76). If the Startup dialog box is not displayed and you want to open a document, choose the **Open Existing File command** from the File menu. Then follow Steps 3, 4, and 5 in the previous example.

Another method of opening a file uses filenames displayed at the bottom of the File menu (see Figure 1-73 on page W1.44). Works saves the names of the last four documents on which you have worked and lists their names at the bottom of the File menu. If you want to open one of these documents, choose the filename by pointing to the appropriate filename and clicking. The document will open and display on the screen.

The Toolbar contains the **Startup Dialog button** (see Figure 1-80 on the previous page) that you can use to display the Startup dialog box. This is useful if you need to open another document while the current document displays.

Moving Around in a Word Processor Document

When you modify a document, you will often have to place the insertion point at different locations within the document. When using the mouse, you can place the insertion point at any location on the screen by pointing to the location and clicking the left mouse button. To place the insertion point at a location in the document that does not display on the screen, use the scroll bars to move the document until the desired location displays and then point and click the desired location in the document.

In some instances, you might want to use keystrokes to move larger distances in a document. Table 1-2 summarizes useful keystrokes for moving around in a document.

▶ **TABLE 1-2**

TASK	KEYSTROKES
Move to the beginning of a document	CTRL+HOME
Move to the end of a document	CTRL+END
Move up one screen	PAGE UP
Move down one screen	PAGE DOWN
Move to the beginning of a line	HOME
Move to the end of a line	END

You can also use the UP, DOWN, LEFT, and RIGHT ARROW keys to move the insertion point through a document.

▶ DELETING AND INSERTING TEXT IN A DOCUMENT

When modifying a document, you might find it necessary to delete certain characters, words, sentences, or paragraphs or to insert additional characters, words, or paragraphs. You can use a variety of methods to delete and insert text. Table 1-3 summarizes methods of deleting text.

▶ **TABLE 1-3**

METHOD	RESULT
Press the DELETE key	Deletes the character to the right
Press the BACKSPACE key	Deletes the character to the left
Highlight words, sentences, or paragraphs and press the DELETE key or choose the Clear command from the Edit menu	Deletes highlighted information

Inserting Text

The Word Processor is initially set to allow you to insert new text between characters, words, lines, and paragraphs without deleting any of the existing text. To insert text in an existing document, place the insertion point where you want the text to appear and then type. The text to the right of the text you type will be adjusted to accommodate the insertion. For example, to insert the word now before the word offers in the first paragraph of the announcement in Figure 1-1 on page W1.4, place the insertion point in the space before the word offers by pointing and clicking the left mouse button and then type the word now followed by a space. Works inserts the word now in the paragraph.

Overtyping Existing Text

Sometimes you might need to type over existing text. One method of doing this is to press the INSERT key on the keyboard, which causes the letters OVR to display in the status bar, and then type the new text.

When you type, the existing text will be typed over. For example, if a document contains 714, and it should contain 213, position the insertion point immediately to the left of the 7 in 714, press the INSERT key, and type 213. The number 213 will replace the number 714. To remove the overtyping status, press the INSERT key again.

You can also implement overtyping by choosing the **Options command** from the **Tools menu**. When the Options dialog box displays, select the Overtype check box in the In Word Processor area and choose the OK button.

Replacing Text with New Text

Another method you can use to replace existing text with new text is to highlight all the text you want to replace. When you start typing new text, the highlighted text is deleted and the new text takes its place.

Undo Command

You can use the **Undo command** to reverse a typing, editing, or formatting change. For example, if you accidentally delete a paragraph, you can restore the paragraph by immediately choosing the Undo command. The Undo command is effective only if you choose it immediately after making a change and before taking any other action. The Undo command is found on the Edit menu (Figure 1-81).

FIGURE 1-81

Undo Paragraph Formatting

To undo all paragraph formatting changes at any time and revert to the default formatting, highlight the text you want to undo, hold down the CTRL key, and press the letter Q key. For example, if several lines are centered and you no longer want the lines centered, highlight the lines, hold down the CTRL key, and press the Q key. You can also change and undo paragraph formatting by choosing the Paragraph command from the Format menu and making appropriate entries in the Paragraph dialog box that displays.

Undo Font Styles

To undo font styles and revert to the default font and styles, highlight the text you want to undo, hold down the CTRL key, and press the SPACEBAR. For example, if a word displays in italics, bold, and underlined, and you want to remove these font styles from the word, highlight the word, hold down the CTRL key, and press the SPACEBAR. You can also click the Bold, Italic, and Underline buttons on the Toolbar to undo their effect when they have been selected. Another method is to choose the Font and Style command from the Format menu and make appropriate entries in the Font and Style dialog box that displays.

▶ ONLINE HELP

To assist you in learning and referencing Works, Works provides an extensive Help library, Cue Cards, and a Tutorial. You can access these features through the Help menu or by clicking the Learning Works button on the Toolbar. If you have a question about any of the commands, online Help can be very valuable. To learn how to use online Help, perform the following steps.

TO LEARN ONLINE HELP ▼

STEP 1 ▶

Select Help from the menu bar, and then point to the How to Use Help command.

*Works displays the **Help menu** (Figure 1-82). The mouse pointer points to the How to Use Help command.*

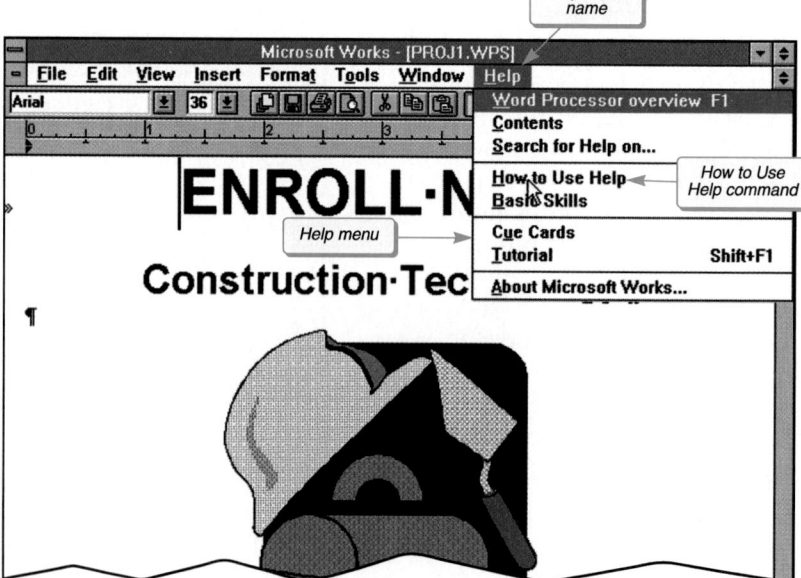

FIGURE 1-82

STEP 2 ▶

Choose the How to Use Help
command from the Help menu by
clicking the left mouse button. Point
to any of the green underlined
topics.

*Works displays the How to Use
Help window (Figure 1-83). When
you point to a green, underlined
topic, the mouse pointer changes
to a hand with a pointing finger.*

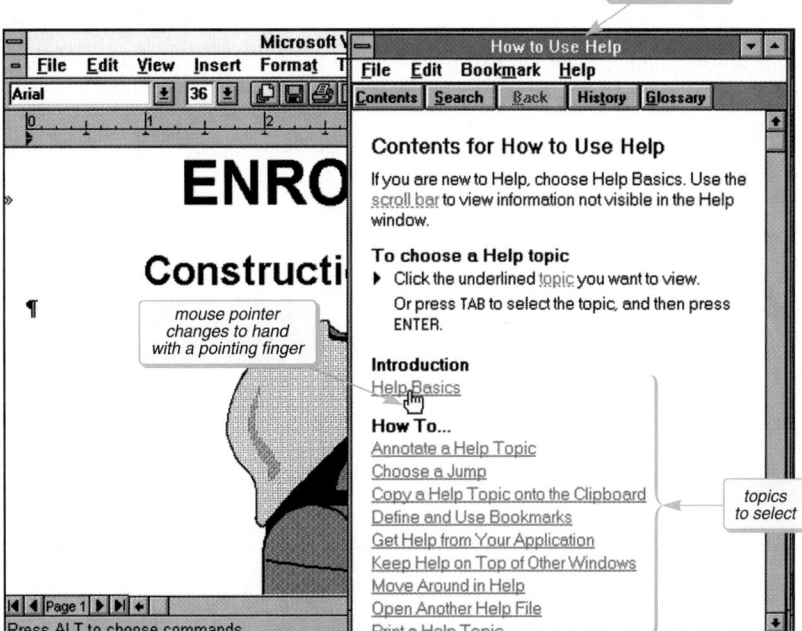

FIGURE 1-83

Reading Contents for How to Use Help provides you with the information you
need to further explore online Help. You can access online Help at any time when
you are creating a document. To return to the document on which you are working, select the Help File menu and choose the Exit command.

▶ CUE CARDS

C **ue Cards** are a help display that appear on the right side of the Works
window. The Cue Cards display contains step-by-step instructions on how
to accomplish basic tasks using Works. Cue Cards overlay the contents of
the application window. You can turn Cue Cards on or off depending upon your
needs. The following steps assume the Cue Cards do not currently display.

TO DISPLAY CUE CARDS ▼

STEP 1 ▶

Select the Help menu from the menu
bar and point to the Cue Cards
command.

*Works displays the Help menu
(Figure 1-84).*

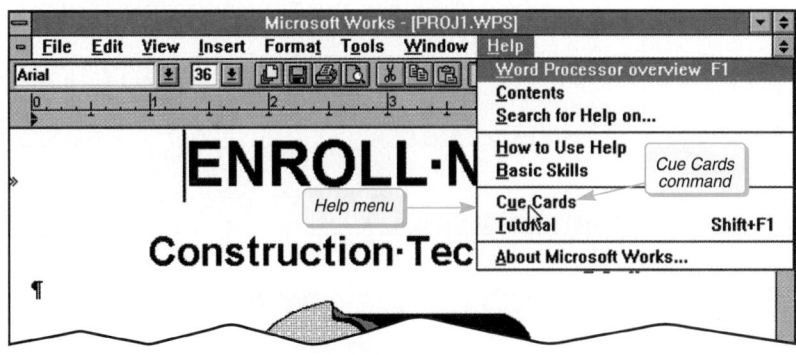

FIGURE 1-84

STEP 2 ▶

Choose the Cue Cards command from the Help menu by clicking the left mouse button.

Works displays the first Cue Card (Figure 1-85).

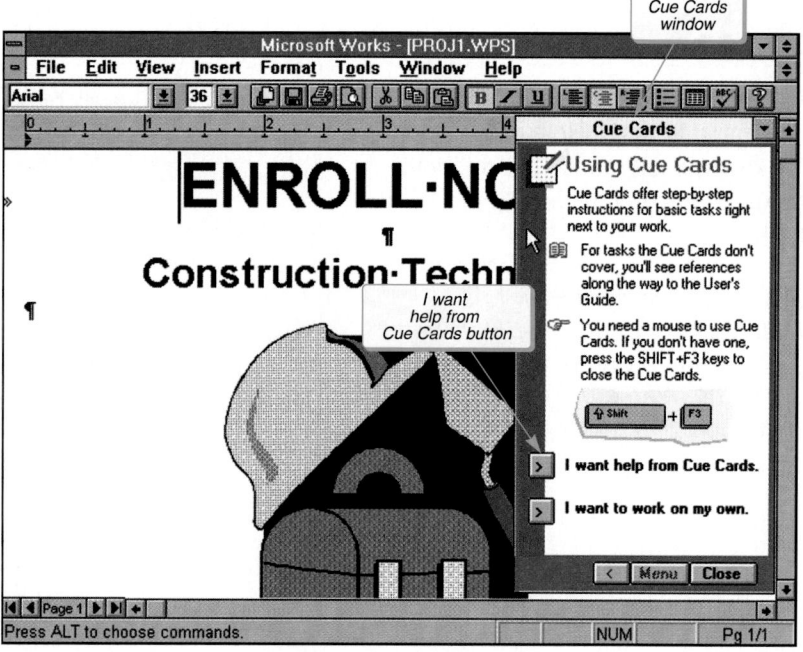

FIGURE 1-85

Click the I want help from Cue Cards button to display an explanation of the help offered by Cue Cards. To remove Cue Cards from the display, choose the Cue Cards command from the Help menu again. You can also control the display of the Cue Cards by using the Learning Works button on the Toolbar.

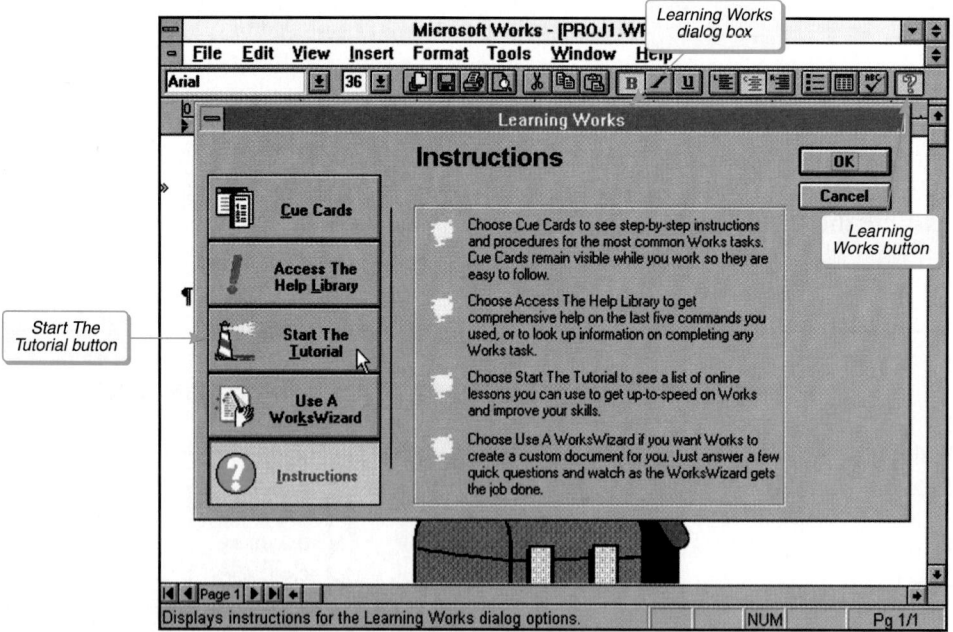

FIGURE 1-86

Learning Works Button

Clicking the Learning Works button on the Toolbar causes the Learning Works dialog box to display (Figure 1-86). You can choose a button in the left side of the dialog box to display Cue Cards, Access The Help Library, Start The Tutorial, Use A Works-Wizard, or obtain Instructions on how to use the Learning Works dialog box.

▶ THE TUTORIAL

T o provide a more structured method of learning about Works, a tutorial is included as a part of the software. You can access the tutorial by choosing the **Tutorial command** from the Help menu or by choosing the Start The Tutorial button in the Learning Works dialog box (see Figure 1-86 on the previous page). When you choose the Tutorial command, the screen shown in Figure 1-87 displays. The tutorial takes you step by step through information that will assist you in mastering many of the Works features .

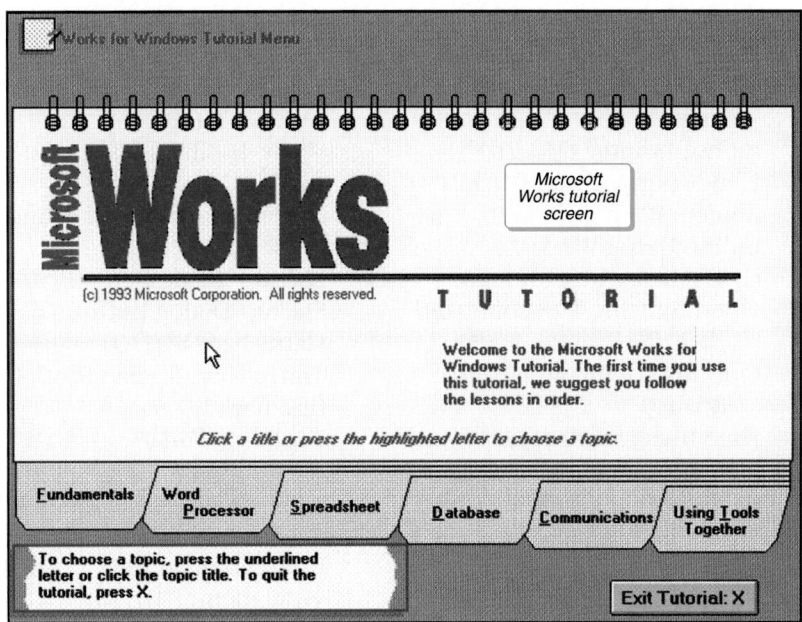

FIGURE 1-87

▶ PROJECT SUMMARY

This project taught you many of the capabilities of the Works Word Processor. Important subject matter included starting Works, entering text, centering text, using fonts, increasing font size, using different font styles, previewing documents, using the Print Preview command, saving a document, closing a document, quitting Works, opening a document, inserting and deleting data, and using online Help and the tutorial. With a knowledge of these features of the Word Processor, you are now capable of creating a variety of documents.

▶ KEY TERMS

accessories *(W1.3)*
All Characters command *(W1.14)*
Arial font *(W1.12)*
AutoStart templates *(W1.3)*
Bold button *(W1.32)*
bulleted list *(W1.25)*
Bullets button *(W1.25)*
Center Align button *(W1.19)*
clip art *(W1.33)*
ClipArt command *(W1.34)*
Close command *(W1.44)*
Communications tool *(W1.3)*
Cue Cards *(W1.51)*
Database with Reporting tool
   (W1.2)
defaults *(W1.11)*
Edit menu *(W1.49)*
end-of-file mark *(W1.11)*
Exit Works command *(W1.45)*
filename *(W1.38)*
font *(W1.12)*
Font and Style command *(W1.29)*
Font Name box arrow *(W1.20)*
Font Size box arrow *(W1.22)*
font sizes *(W1.13)*
font style *(W1.12)*
format *(W1.12)*
Format menu *(W1.20, W1.50)*
Help menu *(W1.50)*
highlight *(W1.18)*

How to Use Help command
   (W1.50)
I-beam *(W1.10)*
insertion point *(W1.11)*
Insert menu *(W1.34)*
Learning Works button *(W1.52)*
menu bar *(W1.9)*
Microsoft ClipArt Gallery dialog
   box *(W1.34)*
Microsoft Draw tool *(W1.3)*
Microsoft Works program-item
   icon *(W1.5)*
mouse pointer *(W1.10)*
New Courier font *(W1.12)*
object *(W1.35)*
online Help *(W1.50)*
Open dialog box *(W1.46)*
Open Existing File command
   (W1.47)
Options command *(W1.10,
   W1.49)*
page break mark *(W1.11)*
Paragraph command *(W1.50)*
paragraph mark *(W1.14, W1.17)*
points *(W1.13)*
Print command *(W1.41)*
Print button *(W1.43)*
Print dialog box *(W1.42*
Print Preview button *(W1.40)*
Print Preview buttons *(W1.41)*

Print Preview command *(W1.41)*
Quit Works *(W1.44)*
resize handles *(W1.36)*
ruler *(W1.10)*
Ruler command *(W1.10)*
sans serif *(W1.12)*
Save As command *(W1.39)*
Save As dialog box *(W1.38)*
Save button *(W1.38)*
Save command *(W1.39)*
scroll bars *(W1.10)*
serif *(W1.12)*
Show Toolbars command
   (W1.10)
Spreadsheet with Charting tool
   (W1.2)
Startup dialog box *(W1.6, W1.44)*
Startup Dialog button *(W1.48)*
status bar *(W1.10)*
Times New Roman font *(W1.12)*
title bar *(W1.9)*
Toolbar *(W1.9)*
tools *(W1.2)*
Tools menu *(W1.10, W1.49)*
Tutorial command *(W1.53)*
Undo command *(W1.49)*
View menu *(W1.10)*
Word Processor tool *(W1.2)*
WorksWizards *(W1.3)*
wordwrap *(W1.17)*

Q U I C K   R E F E R E N C E

In Microsoft Works, you can accomplish a task in a number of ways. The following table provides a quick
reference to each task presented in this project with its available options. The commands listed in the
Menu column can be executed using either the keyboard or mouse.

Task	Mouse	Menu	Keyboard Shortcuts
Apply Bold Format	Click Bold button	From Format menu, choose Font and Style	Press CTRL+B
Apply Italic Format	Click Italic button	From Format menu, choose Font and Style	Press CTRL+I
Apply Underline Format	Click Underline button	From Format menu, choose Font and Style	Press CTRL+U
Center Text	Click Center Align button	From Format menu, choose Paragraph	Press CTRL+E
Clear Clip Art		From Edit menu, choose Clear	Press DELETE with clip art highlighted

Task	Mouse	Menu	Keyboard Shortcuts
Close a Document		From File menu, choose Close	Press CTRL+F4
Highlight an Entire Document	Hold down CTRL and click in left margin	From Edit menu, choose Select All	Press F8 five times
Highlight a Line	Click in left margin beside line		Move insertion point to start of line and press SHIFT+END
Highlight Multiple Lines	Position mouse pointer in left margin and drag up or down		Position insertion point, then hold down SHIFT and press DOWN ARROW or UP ARROW
Highlight a Paragraph	Double-click in left margin beside paragraph		Move insertion point to paragraph and press F8 four times
Highlight a Sentence	Drag mouse pointer over sentence		With insertion point in sentence, press F8 three times
Highlight a Word	Double-click the word		Move insertion point to word and press F8 twice
Open an Existing File	In Startup dialog box, Choose Open An Existing Document button	From File menu, choose Open Existing File	
Open the Font Name Box	Click Font Name box arrow	From Format menu, choose Font and Style	Press CTRL+F
Open the Font Size Box	Click Font Size box arrow	From Format menu, choose Font and Style	Press CTRL+K
Open the Help Menu		Select Help menu	Press F1
Print a Document	Click Print button	From File menu, choose Print	Press CTRL+P
Print Preview	Click Print Preview button	From File menu, choose Print Preview	Press ALT+F+V
Quit Works		From File menu, choose Exit Works or from Control menu, choose Close	Press ALT+F4
Remove a Font Style	Click appropriate Toolbar button	From Format menu, choose Font and Style	Press CTRL+SPACEBAR
Remove a Highlight	Click left mouse button		Press ESC and press arrow key
Remove a Paragraph Style		From Format menu, choose Font and Style	Press CTRL+Q
Save a Document	Click Save button	From File menu, choose Save	Press CTRL+S
Save a Document (New Name)		From File menu, choose Save As	Press CTRL+A
Undo the Last Change		From Edit menu, choose Undo	Press CTRL+Z

STUDENT ASSIGNMENT 1
True/False

Instructions: Circle T if the statement is true or F if the statement is false.

T   F   1. Microsoft Works for Windows provides word processing, spreadsheet, database, communications, and drawing capabilities in a single software package.

T   F   2. To start Microsoft Works for Windows, point to the Microsoft Works program-item icon in the Microsoft Works for Windows group window and click the left mouse button.

T   F   3. The title bar in the document window contains the title of the tool you are using (Word Processor) and the name of the document you are creating.

T   F   4. The Toolbar contains buttons that are used to display specific menus.

T   F   5. The mouse pointer takes the shape of a block arrow as soon as you type the first character.

T   F   6. The insertion point is a blinking vertical bar that indicates where the next character you type will appear on the screen.

T   F   7. With Works, the default font is 12 point Times New Roman.

T   F   8. A font size of 36 points is approximately one inch in height.

T   F   9. With wordwrap, you must press the ENTER key at the end of every line.

T   F   10. To highlight a paragraph to be formatted, click in the left margin beside the paragraph.

T   F   11. To change font size, you must select a command from the File menu.

T   F   12. The Bullets button on the Toolbar is designed to assist you in creating bulleted lists.

T   F   13. You must use print preview to make insertions or deletions in a document.

T   F   14. When saving a document, you must select a filename no longer than eight characters and a filename extension no longer than three characters.

T   F   15. When saving a document for the first time, you must choose the Save As command from the File menu.

T   F   16. When you close a document, you exit Works.

T   F   17. After you have closed a document, use the Open command to make the document available.

T   F   18. Pressing the DELETE key deletes the character to the right of the insertion point.

T   F   19. If you position the insertion point in the middle of a sentence and type, the text you type will replace the existing text to the right of the insertion point.

T   F   20. You can use the Undo command to remove formatting from a document anytime before exiting Works.

STUDENT ASSIGNMENT 2
Multiple Choice

Instructions: Circle the correct response.

1. Microsoft Works for Windows is a software package that contains a _____.
   a. Word Processor tool
   b. Spreadsheet tool
   c. Database tool
   d. all of the above

2. To start Microsoft Works for Windows, _____.
   a. point to the Microsoft Works program-item icon and click the left mouse button
   b. point to the Microsoft Works program-item icon and double-click the left mouse button
   c. point to File Manager and double-click the left mouse button
   d. point to the Open command in the File menu and click the left mouse button
3. When the mouse pointer is located in the document workspace area of the screen, it appears as _____.
   a. an I-beam
   b. a block arrow
   c. a straight vertical bar
   d. a straight horizontal line
4. When the mouse pointer is pointing to a button in the Toolbar, it appears as a(n) _____.
   a. I-beam
   b. block arrow
   c. straight vertical bar
   d. underscore character
5. The All Characters command is used to display _____.
   a. all characters on the printer
   b. special characters, such as paragraph marks, on the printer
   c. special characters, such as paragraph marks, on the screen
   d. both b and c
6. When you type a line of text and a word cannot completely be placed on that line, _____.
   a. press the ENTER key at the end of the line
   b. press the DOWN ARROW key at the end of the line
   c. position the mouse pointer at the beginning of the next line and click
   d. continue typing because Works places the word on the next line using wordwrap
7. Before you can change the format of a paragraph, you must _____.
   a. position the mouse pointer beside the first character in the paragraph to be formatted
   b. underscore the paragraph to be formatted
   c. highlight the paragraph to be formatted
   d. highlight only the first word in the paragraph to be formatted
8. To highlight only a word, _____.
   a. click when the mouse pointer is anywhere within the word
   b. double-click when the mouse pointer is anywhere within the word
   c. double-click the space before the word you want to highlight
   d. click the space before the word you want to highlight
9. To save a document using a filename different from the one you have already used for the document, use the _____ command.
   a. Save
   b. Save As
   c. Close
   d. Exit
10. To delete a paragraph, _____.
    a. point to the left margin and press the DELETE key
    b. point to the paragraph mark and press the DELETE key
    c. highlight the first word in the paragraph and press the DELETE key
    d. highlight the paragraph and press the DELETE key

STUDENT ASSIGNMENT 3
Understanding the Microsoft Works Word Processor Window

Instructions: In Figure SA1-3, a series of arrows points to the major components of the Microsoft Works Word Processor window. Identify the parts of the window in the space provided.

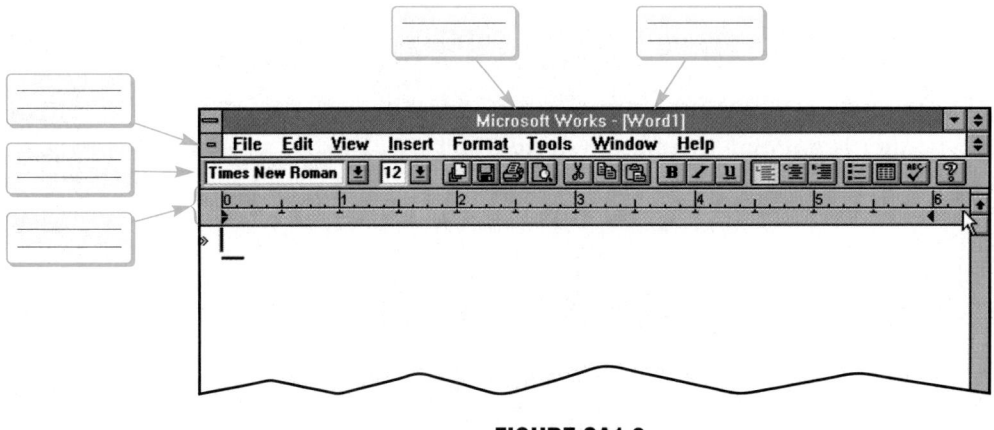

FIGURE SA1-3

STUDENT ASSIGNMENT 4
Understanding the Toolbar

Instructions: In Figure SA1-4, identify each of the elements on the Toolbar in the space provided.

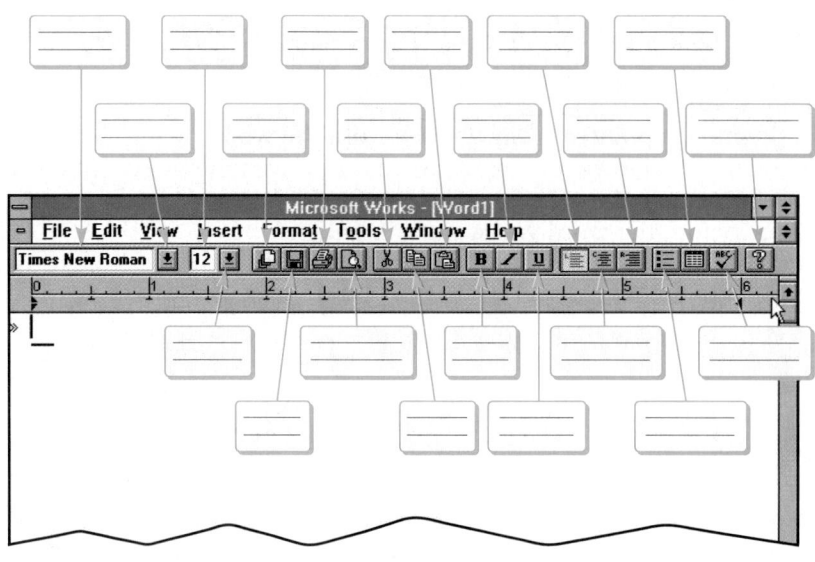

FIGURE SA1-4

STUDENT ASSIGNMENT 5
Highlighting Text

Instructions: List the action to be performed in the space provided.

TO HIGHLIGHT	ACTION TO BE PERFORMED
A word	_____
A line	_____
A sentence	_____
A paragraph	_____
Several lines	_____
An entire document	_____

STUDENT ASSIGNMENT 6
Understanding Methods of Deleting Text

Instructions: Describe the result of the various methods of deleting text in the space provided.

METHOD	RESULT
Press DELETE key	_____
Press BACKSPACE key	_____
Highlight words, sentences, or paragraphs, and then press the DELETE key	_____

C O M P U T E R   L A B O R A T O R Y   E X E R C I S E S

COMPUTER LABORATORY EXERCISE 1
Using the Help Menu

Use your computer to perform the following tasks to obtain experience using online Help.

Part 1 Instructions:

1. Start the Microsoft Works Word Processor tool.
2. Select the Help menu from the menu bar by pointing to Help and clicking the left mouse button.
3. Choose the How to Use Help command by pointing to the How to Use Help command and clicking the left mouse button.
4. A window with the title How to Use Help displays.
5. Read the screen.
6. Select the File menu from the menu bar.
7. Choose the Print Topic command.
8. Works produces a printed copy of the How to Use Help window.

COMPUTER LABORATORY EXERCISE 1 (continued)

Part 2 Instructions:

1. In the lower portion of the How to Use Help window are sections titled, Introduction, How To..., and Commands and Buttons. When the mouse pointer is positioned over a green word in these sections, it displays as a hand with a pointing finger. Position the mouse pointer on the line, Help Basics, and click the left mouse button.
2. Read the screen that Works displays.
3. With the Help Basics topic displaying, position the mouse pointer over the green, underlined word jumps. Click the left mouse button. Works displays a pop-up definition box. Read the information in the box. When you are finished reading, click the left mouse button again.
4. To return to the Contents for How to Use Help screen, click the Back button on the How to Use Help Toolbar.
5. Review other topics that display when you click the topic name.
6. To exit from online Help, select the File menu from the menu bar and choose the Exit command.

COMPUTER LABORATORY EXERCISE 2
Formatting a Word Processing Document

Instructions: Start the Works Word Processor tool. Open the CLE1-2.WPS file on the Student Diskette that accompanies this book. The document is illustrated in Figure CLE1-2. Format the document using the instructions in the text. Refer to Figure 1-15 on page W1.13. Do not insert clip art.

    Save the file using the filename, CLE1-2A.WPS. You will use this file in Computer Laboratory Exercise 3.

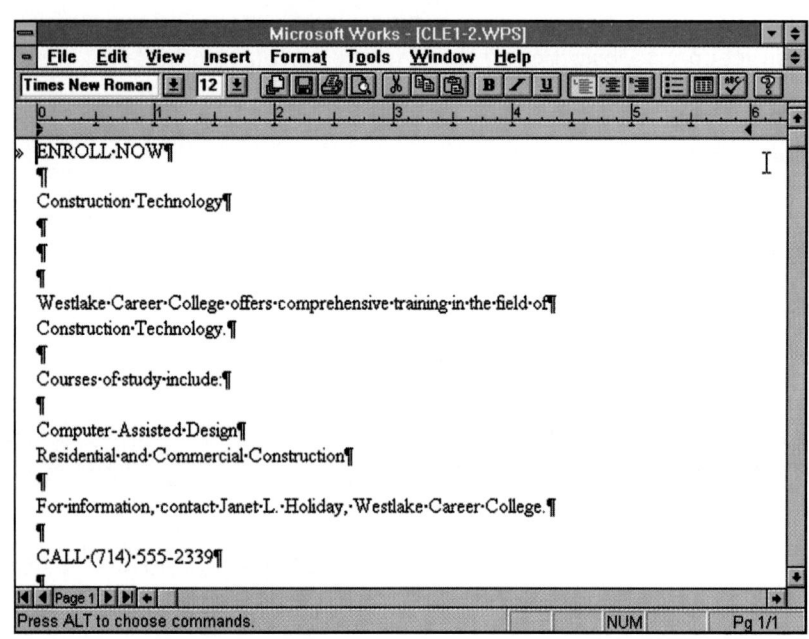

FIGURE CLE1-2

COMPUTER LABORATORY EXERCISE 3
Inserting Clip Art in a Document

Instructions: Open the file named CLE1-2A.WPS that you formatted and saved in Computer Laboratory Exercise 2, and insert the clip art of the hard hat and lunch box from the Microsoft ClipArt Gallery in the document after the third heading line. Follow the step-by-step instructions in the text. After you insert the clip art, obtain a printout of the document and turn it in to your instructor.

COMPUTER LABORATORY ASSIGNMENT 1
Creating a Document

Purpose: To provide experience using the Word Processor to create a document that requires entering text, centering selected lines, changing font sizes and styles, inserting clip art, and saving and printing the document.

Problem: Create the document illustrated in Figure CLA1-1.

SAILING CLUB
Monthly Meeting

Plan to attend the meeting of the Sailing Club on May 1, 1995, in the auditorium of Kennedy College.

Ranger Bruce Wayne will lecture on:

- **Harbor Patrol rules and regulations**
- **Basic sailing techniques**

Please call Leslie Danes, (714) 555-5029, to make your reservation.

Reservations Required

See You There!

FIGURE CLA1-1

(continued)

COMPUTER LABORATORY ASSIGNMENT 1 (continued)

Instructions: Display the first heading line, SAILING CLUB, in 36 point Arial font. Display the second heading line in 24 point Arial font. The picture is clip art from Microsoft ClipArt Gallery. The next three lines display in 14 point Times New Roman font. Display the bulleted list with a one-inch margin in 18 point Times New Roman font. The next line displays in 14 point Times New Roman font. The last two lines display in blue 18 point Arial font. Display the entire document in bold.

After you have typed and formatted the document, save the document on a diskette. Use a filename consisting of the initials of your first and last names followed by the assignment number. Example: TC1-1. Print the document, and then follow directions from your instructor for turning in the assignment.

COMPUTER LABORATORY ASSIGNMENT 2
Creating a Document

Purpose: To provide experience using the Word Processor to create a document that requires entering text, centering selected lines, changing font sizes and styles, inserting clip art, and saving and printing the document.

Problem: Create the document illustrated in Figure CLA1-2.

PACIFIC CRUISE LINE

ADVENTURES

Cruise Hawaii

Plan to attend a lecture presented by a representative of Pacific Cruise Line on October 15, 1995 at 6:00 p.m. in the Civic Center auditorium.

Pacific Cruise Line representative Mary Ann Marshall will explain how to:

- Choose a cruise line
- Select a cabin to meet your needs
- Obtain discount cruise line fares

Call Bill Aims, (714) 555-5027, to make your reservation.

Free Admission

Bring a Friend!

FIGURE CLA1-2

Instructions: Display the first heading line, PACIFIC CRUISE LINE, in 36 point Arial font. Display the second heading line in 24 point Arial font. Choose the illustration from the clip art in the Microsoft ClipArt Gallery. Display the Cruise Hawaii line in 18 point Arial font. The next four lines display in 14 point Times New Roman font. Display the bulleted list with a one-inch margin in 18 point Times New Roman font. The line following the bulleted list displays in 14 point Times New Roman font. The last two lines display in green 18 point Arial font. Display the entire document in bold.

   After you have typed and formatted the document, save the document on a diskette. Use a filename consisting of the initials of your first and last names followed by the assignment number. Example: TC1-2. Print the document, and then follow directions from your instructor for turning in the assignment.

COMPUTER LABORATORY ASSIGNMENT 3
Creating a Document

Purpose: To provide experience using the Word Processor to create a document that requires entering text, centering selected lines, changing font sizes and styles, inserting clip art, and saving and printing the document.

Problem: Snowflake Ski Resort has asked you to prepare the document shown in Figure CLA1-3.

Instructions: Create the document illustrated in Figure CLA1-3 using appropriate fonts, font styles, sizes, and colors.

   After you have typed and formatted the document, save the document on a diskette. Use a filename consisting of the initials of your first and last names followed by the assignment number. Example: TC1-3. Print the document, and then follow directions from your instructor for turning in the assignment.

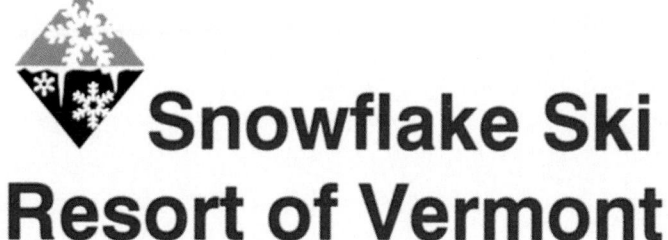

Snowflake Ski Resort of Vermont

Grand Opening

Make your reservation now for the grand opening of Snowflake Ski Resort of Vermont.

Ski slopes are available for skiers and snow boarders with a wide range of skill levels, including:

- **Beginning skiers**
- **Intermediate skiers**
- **Advanced skiers**
- **Extreme skiers**

Reservations are recommended. For additional information, contact Richard L. Burke, (802) 555-2829.

Call Now!

FIGURE CLA1-3

COMPUTER LABORATORY ASSIGNMENT 4
Designing and Creating a Document

Purpose: To provide experience designing and creating a document using the Word Processor that requires entering text, centering selected lines, changing font sizes and styles, inserting clip art, and saving and printing the document.

Problem: Your friend owns a large sailboat that she rents for $75.00 per hour. She has asked you to prepare a brochure that advertises the boat. The name of the company is Yachts For Rent. The telephone number of the company is (714) 555-1718.

Instructions: Design and create a document advertising the boat. Be creative in your design. Use appropriate clip art from the Microsoft ClipArt Gallery.

▼

CREATING A BUSINESS LETTER AND RESUME

CREATING A BUSINESS LETTER AND RESUME

OBJECTIVES   You will have mastered the material in this project when you can:

▸ Explain the parts of a business letter
▸ Explain the spacing used in a business letter
▸ Use a WorksWizard to create a letterhead
▸ Create a business letter
▸ Set margin indents to create a numbered list
▸ Create and use a hanging indent
▸ Use the Works spelling checker
▸ Print a business letter

▸ Open two document windows
▸ Describe the contents of a resume
▸ Use a Works AutoStart template to create a resume
▸ Add information to a Works AutoStart template
▸ Use the Window menu
▸ Create and use a custom template

▶ INTRODUCTION

In Project 1, you learned how to use many features of the Works Word Processor. You learned how to enter text, center text, change fonts, font sizes, font styles, and font colors, and how to insert clip art in a document. You also learned about the Print Preview, Save As, and Print commands, as well as the methods of closing and opening a file and exiting Works. With a knowledge of these word processing techniques and commands, you can create a wide variety of documents.

▶ PROJECT TWO

In Project 2, you will learn how to use a **WorksWizard** to create a letterhead. A **letterhead** is the information appearing at the top of a letter that contains a person's name, address, phone number, and other information. You will also learn how to produce a professional appearing business letter. After producing the letter, you will learn how to use an **AutoStart template** to create a professional resume. A **resume** is a printed document given to potential employers. It contains information about an applicant's educational background, employment experience, and related data. This project presents the Works commands and word processing techniques to create the business letter and resume shown in Figure 2-1.

Mary B. Riley

1191 Walnut Avenue
Anaheim, California 92805

Telephone (714) 555-1219

October 8, 1995

Ms. Beverly A. Thompson
Personnel Director
Haines Accounting Services
441 Commerce Avenue
Los Angeles, CA 90023

Dear Ms. Thompson:

I would like you to consider me for the position of accounting trainee. This employment
opportunity was advertised in the October 5 edition of the <u>Los Angeles Times</u>. I am a
recent graduate of Western State University with a major in Accounting.

While in college I completed 30 units of accounting. Course work included classes in cost
accounting, tax accounting, and managerial accounting. I have also had recent work
experience in the accounting department of Microtech Corporation.

My interest in pursuing a career in the accounting profession and my leadership skills are
reflected in the following accomplishments while attending Western State University:

1. During my two years of college at Western State University, I
   maintained a grade point average of 3.5.

2. I served as President of the Future Accountant's Association for one
   year and was responsible for planning all professional activities.

My resume is enclosed for your review. I will call on October 12, 1995, to set an
appointment for a personal interview.

Sincerely,

Mary B. Riley

FIGURE 2-1

RESUME

Mary B. Riley
1191 Walnut Avenue
Anaheim, California, 92805
(714) 555-1219

OBJECTIVE

To gain employment as an accounting trainee with the potential to work as a staff
accountant in a public accounting firm. I am a detail oriented person with strong
mathematical skills and have a thorough knowledge of spreadsheet software.

WORK HISTORY

**Microtech Corporation, Payroll Clerk. Responsible for the time card records for
over 100 employees**
Summer employment, June 1995 to September 1995
Collected time cards from ten departments, reviewed accuracy of entries and maintained
payroll records for all employees.

**Kroll Company, Accounting Clerk. Responsible for creating daily sales reports
using Microsoft Works spreadsheet software**
Summer employment, June 1994 to September 1994
From information on daily sales invoices created sales reports for management using
spreadsheet software.

**Seaside Inn, Shift Supervisor. Responsible for maintaining records of cash received
from five cashiers at a fast food outlet**
Summer employment, June 1993 to September 1993
Supervised five employees, balanced all cash received, made daily bank deposits of cash
received.

EDUCATION

Bachelor of Arts degree in Accounting, June 1995
Western State University, Los Angeles, California.
1995 - Student of the Year award, Accounting, Western State University.
1994 - 1995, President, Future Accountant's Association, Western State University.

Associate of Arts degree in Business Administration, June 1993
Western Los Angeles Community College, Santa Monica, California.
Graduated with honors.

High School Graduate, college transfer program, June 1991
Santa Monica High School, Santa Monica, California.

AWARDS/COMMUNITY SERVICE

1993 - Volunteer, Legal Aid for the Homeless Association, Los Angeles, California.
1991 - Volunteer, Admissions Clerk, Los Angeles Central Hospital.

The letter in Figure 2-1 is a
response to an advertisement in a
newspaper for an employment
opportunity with a company. The
letter contains a personalized
letterhead. Rather than type the
name and address in a fixed size
type, aligned to the left or right,
with a WorksWizard you can create
attractive, personalized stationery.
In Figure 2-1, the name and the
address and phone number appear
in different font sizes. An additional
enhancement to the appearance of
the letterhead is a double line
beneath the city, state, and zip
code entry.

The resume to accompany the letter is also illustrated in Figure 2-1. A Works AutoStart template designed to assist you in creating a resume is used to produce this document to present to potential employers.

Document Preparation Steps

The general steps to create the letterhead, the business letter, and the resume shown in Figure 2-1 are:

1. Use the Letterhead WorksWizard to create a custom letterhead.
2. Save the letterhead on a diskette using the filename, LETTERHD, and exit Works.
3. When you need to write a letter, retrieve the letterhead file from the diskette so the letterhead will display on the screen.
4. Type the letter.
5. Check the spelling of the letter using the Works spelling checker.
6. Save the letter on a diskette using the filename, COVRLETR.
7. Print the letter.
8. Use a Works AutoStart template to create a resume.
9. Type the information in the resume.
10. Check the spelling of the resume using the Works spelling checker.
11. Save the resume on a diskette using the filename, RESUME1.
12. Print the resume.
13. Use the entries in the Window menu to view either the letter or the resume.

Each of these steps is explained in detail in this project.

▶ FORMAT OF A BUSINESS LETTER

A t the top of the letter is the letterhead. The letterhead contains the name, address, city, state, zip code, and telephone number of the individual creating the letter. In the example in Figure 2-2 on the next page, the letter head was created using a WorksWizard.

The letter is typed beneath the letterhead. A variety of letter styles may be used when creating a business letter. The style illustrated in Figure 2-2 is called a **block letter**. In a block letter, all the components of the letter begin at the left margin except the numbered list of items in the fourth paragraph. Figure 2-2 identifies the components of a basic business letter and the recommended spacing for a long (full page) letter.

A business letter contains the date line at the top of the letter. The next element is the **inside address**. The inside address contains the name of the person to whom the letter is being sent, followed by the person's title, the name of the company, and the address of the company. After the inside address is the **salutation** (Dear Ms. Thompson:). A colon is placed after the name in the salutation.

The next element of the letter is the message, which is called the body of the letter. After the body of the letter is the **complimentary close**, which consists of the word, Sincerely, a comma, three blank lines, and then the name of the individual sending the letter.

The recommended spacing within the letter is also indicated in Figure 2-2. The letter is single-spaced. It is important to follow recommended spacing standards to produce a professional looking letter.

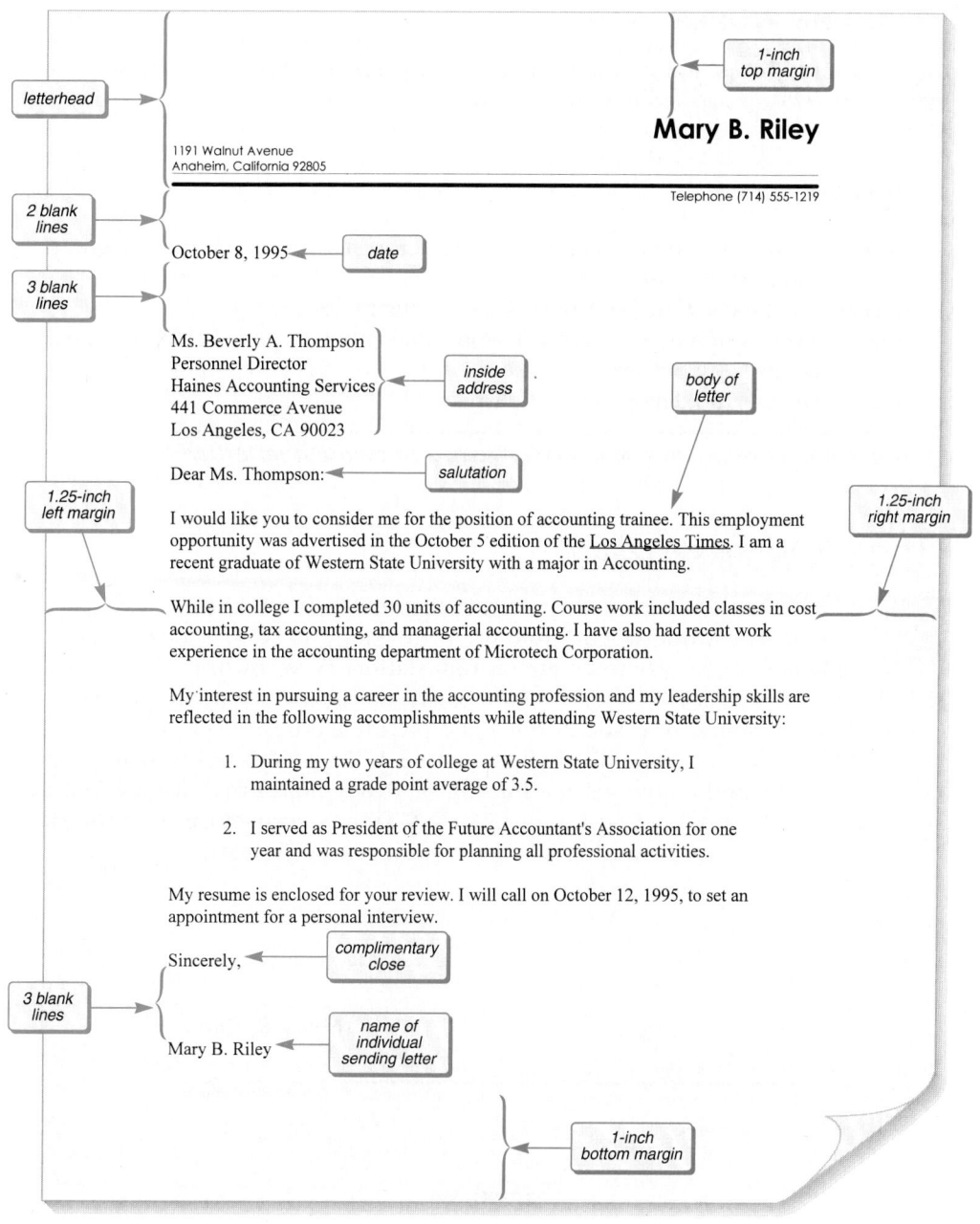

FIGURE 2-2

Page Setup and Margins

When creating a long letter (one full page or more), you should use a line that is six-inches wide. A six-inch wide line means the text you type in the letter will occupy an area six-inches wide. A six-inch wide line requires left and right margins of 1.25 inches on paper 8.5-inches wide. Works provides default values of 1.25 inches for the left and right margins, so no changes need to be made in the left and right margins. The default values for the top and bottom margins are 1 inch. No changes need to be made in these margins when producing a letter, so you are ready to begin. These default values can be reviewed and changed by choosing the **Page Setup Command** from the File Menu. The Page Setup dialog box that displays will contain the page setup values currently in effect.

▶ STARTING WORKS

 o start Works, follow the procedures explained in Project 1. These procedures are summarized below.

TO START WORKS

Step 1: From Program Manager, open the Microsoft Works for Windows group window.
Step 2: Double-click the Microsoft Works program-item icon.
Step 3: If the Welcome to Microsoft Works dialog box appears, click the Start Works Now button.
Step 4: The Startup dialog box will display.

You are now ready to use a WorksWizard to create a letterhead.

▶ USING A WORKSWIZARD

o create the letterhead illustrated in Figure 2-3, you will use a Works-Wizard. The WorksWizard used to create a letterhead provides a quick and convenient way to create custom stationery for business and personal needs. Using the WorksWizard allows you to select your own style of letterhead from six different styles, plus add borders and pictures, if desired. To use the letterhead WorksWizard, you will choose the **Use A WorksWizard button** in the Startup dialog box and follow instructions in the dialog boxes that display. You can also use a WorksWizard by choosing the **WorksWizards command** from the File menu, or by clicking the **Learning Works button** on the Toolbar.

FIGURE 2-3

Perform the following steps to utilize a WorksWizard to create a letterhead.

TO UTILIZE A WORKSWIZARD TO CREATE A LETTERHEAD ▼

STEP 1 ▶

With the Startup dialog box displayed, point to the Use A WorksWizard button on the left side of the dialog box.

The mouse pointer points to the Use A WorksWizard button (Figure 2-4).

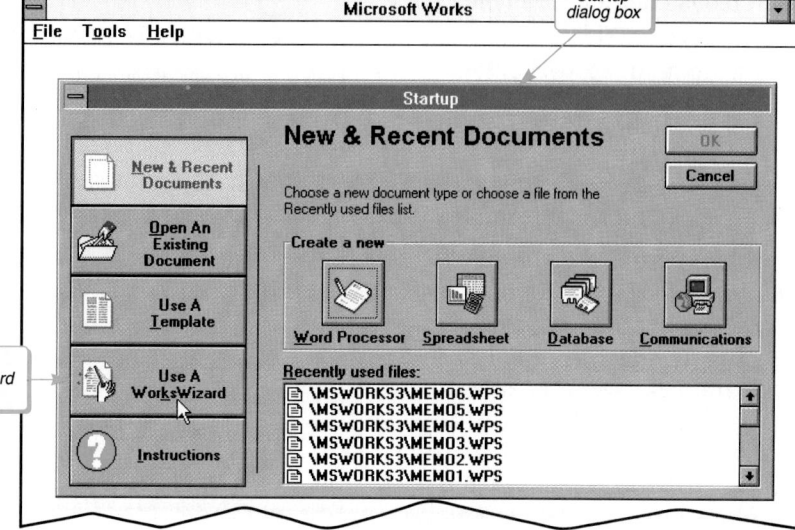

FIGURE 2-4

STEP 2 ▶

Choose the Use A WorksWizard button by clicking the left mouse button. Then point to the word Letterhead in the Choose a WorksWizard list box and click the left mouse button.

The word Letterhead is highlighted in the Choose a WorksWizard list box (Figure 2-5).

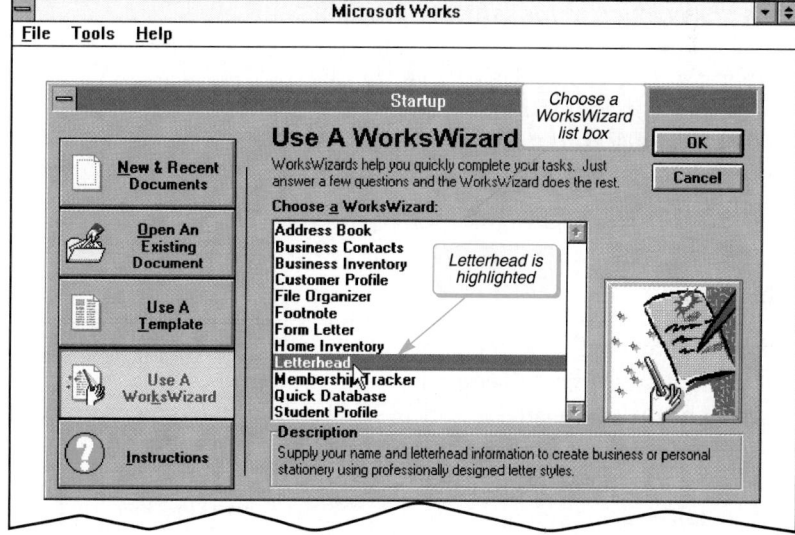

FIGURE 2-5

STEP 3 ▶

Point to the OK button in the Startup dialog box (Figure 2-6).

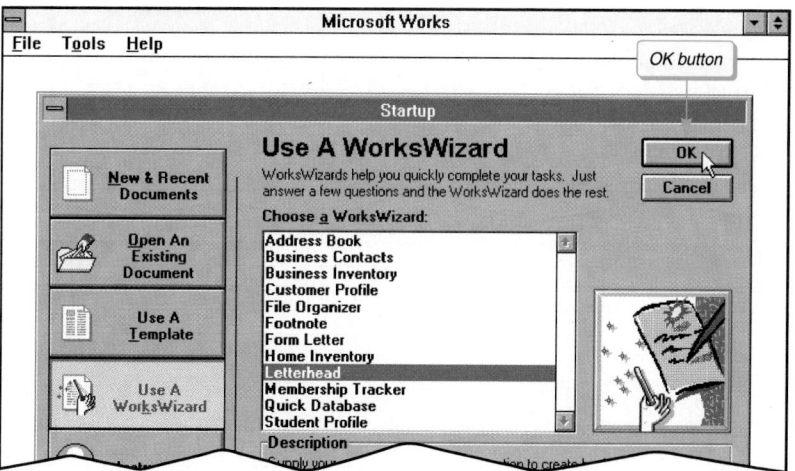

FIGURE 2-6

STEP 4 ▶

Choose the OK button by clicking the left mouse button. When the Letterhead WorksWizard dialog box displays, point to the Next button.

A dialog box with the title Letterhead WorksWizard displays (Figure 2-7). The dialog box provides general information about the WorksWizard. The mouse pointer points to the Next button in the lower right portion of the screen. Choosing this button will display the next WorksWizard dialog box. To the left of the Next button is a button identified by a single arrowhead pointing to the left. Choosing this button will move you to the preceding dialog box. The button with the chevron character pointing to the left preceded by a vertical line is used to move to the first WorksWizard dialog box in a series. Because this is the first WorksWizard dialog box displayed, these buttons are dimmed.

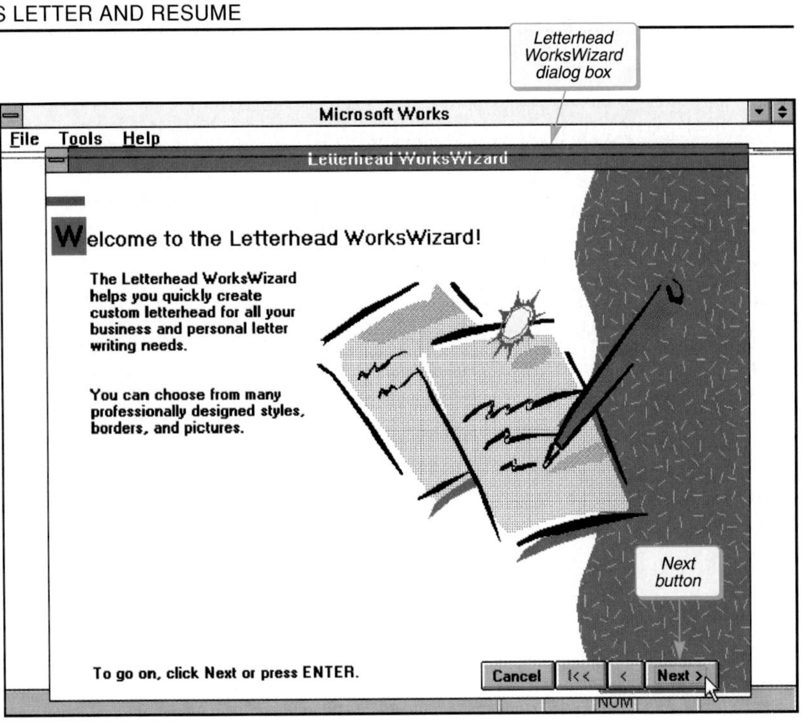

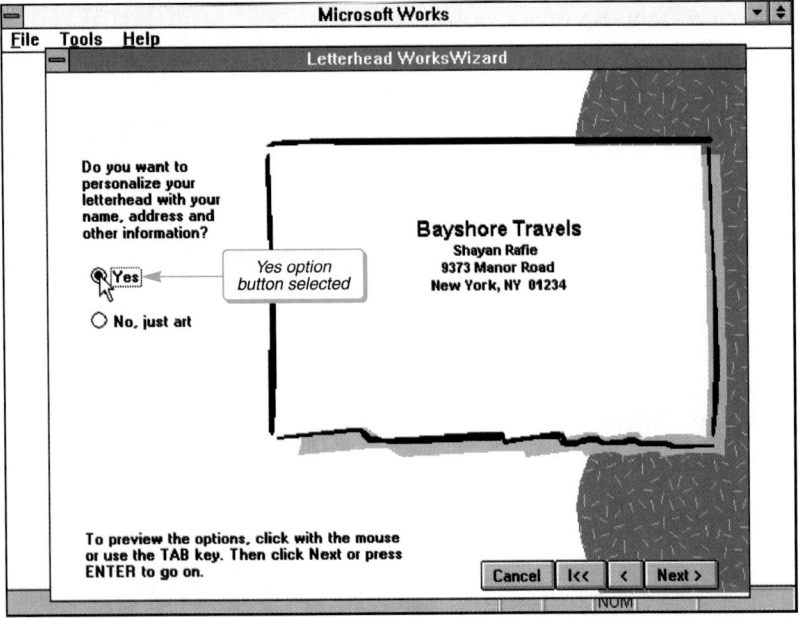

FIGURE 2-7

STEP 5 ▶

Choose the Next button in the first Letterhead WorksWizard dialog box. When the next Letterhead WorksWizard dialog box displays, point to the Yes option button and click the left mouse button.

A new dialog box titled, Letterhead WorksWizard, displays asking Do you want to personalize your letterhead with your name, address and other information? (Figure 2-8). A small dark circle within the option button indicates the Yes option button has been selected.

FIGURE 2-8

STEP 6 ▶

Point to the Next button.

The mouse pointer points to the Next button (Figure 2-9).

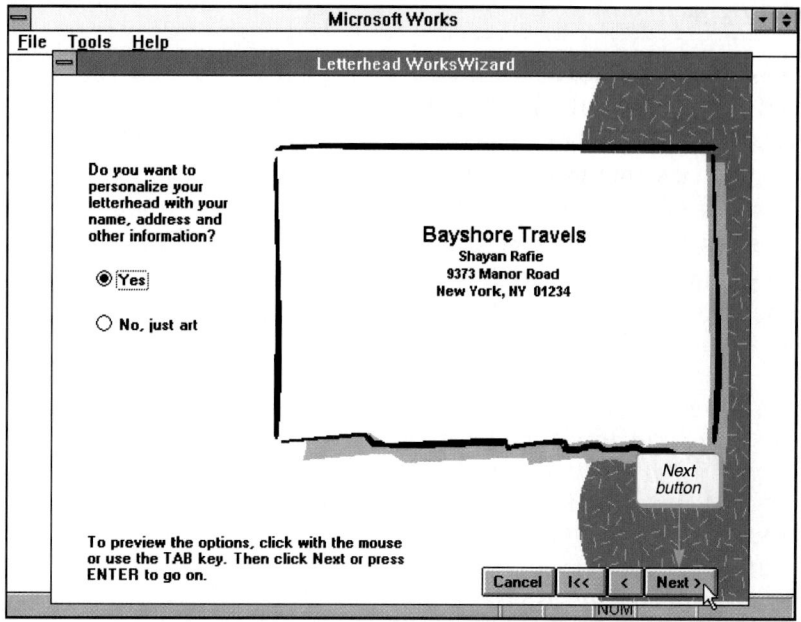

FIGURE 2-9

STEP 7 ▶

Choose the Next button. When the next Letterhead WorksWizard dialog box displays, select the My Name option button and point to the Next button.

A new dialog box displays the question, What do you want your letterhead to emphasize? (Figure 2-10). The My name option button is selected and the mouse pointer points to the Next button.

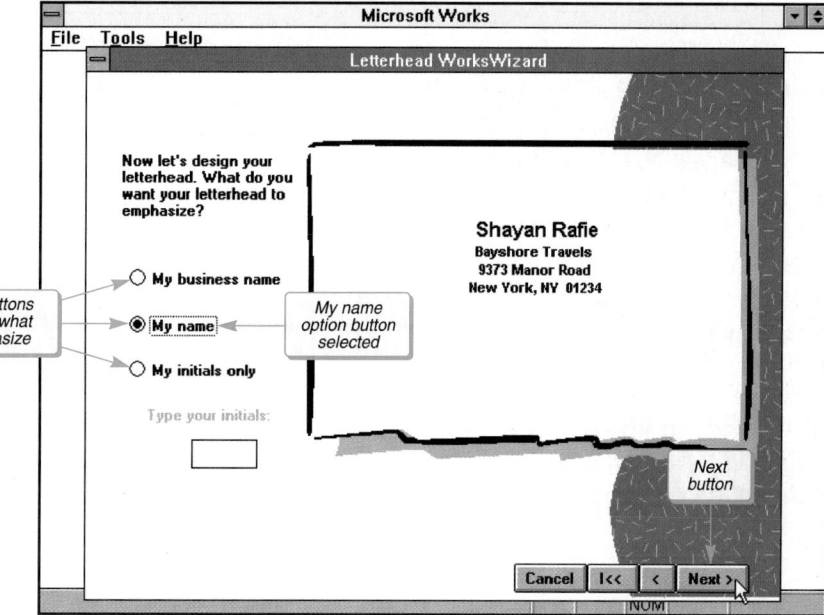

FIGURE 2-10

STEP 8 ▶

Choose the Next button. When the next Letterhead WorksWizard dialog box displays, type Mary B. Riley **in the Your name text box. Press the TAB key to move to the Business name text box. Make no entry in the Business name text box. Press the TAB key again to move to the Address text box.**

A dialog box displays that allows you to enter information that is to appear in the letterhead (Figure 2-11). When you complete typing, the name Mary. B. Riley appears in the Your name text box. The insertion point is positioned in the Address text box.

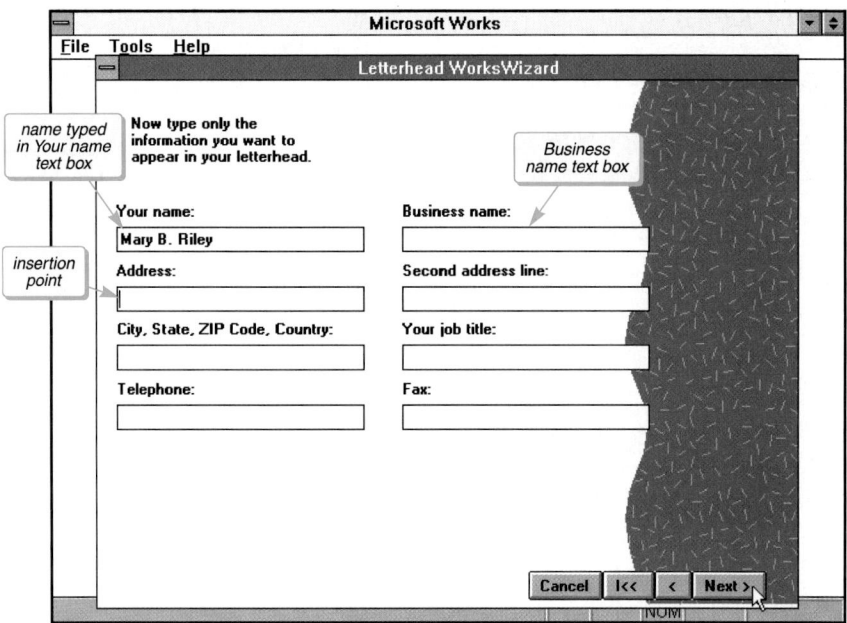

FIGURE 2-11

STEP 9 ▶

Type the proper information in the Address text box, the City, State, ZIP Code, Country text box, and the Telephone text box. Press the TAB key to move the insertion point from one text box to the next. Make no entries In the Second address line text box, the Your job title text box, or the Fax text box. Point to the Next button.

The dialog box contains the information you typed that is to appear in the letterhead (Figure 2-12).

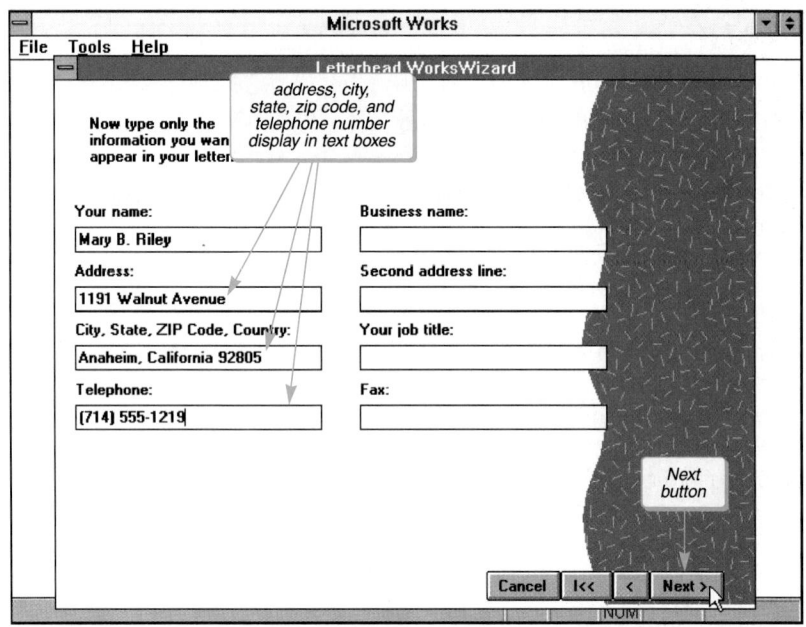

FIGURE 2-12

STEP 10 ▶

Choose the Next button. When the next Letterhead WorksWizard dialog box displays, select the Prestige option button. Point to the Next button.

A dialog box displays that allows you to select one of six letterhead styles (Figure 2-13). You can click each option button to display the styles on the right of the screen. The small dark circle within the Prestige option button indicates you have selected the Prestige style. A sample of the Prestige letterhead style displays on the right of the dialog box. You will have the opportunity later to change the format of the line that displays above the telephone number. The mouse pointer points to the Next button.

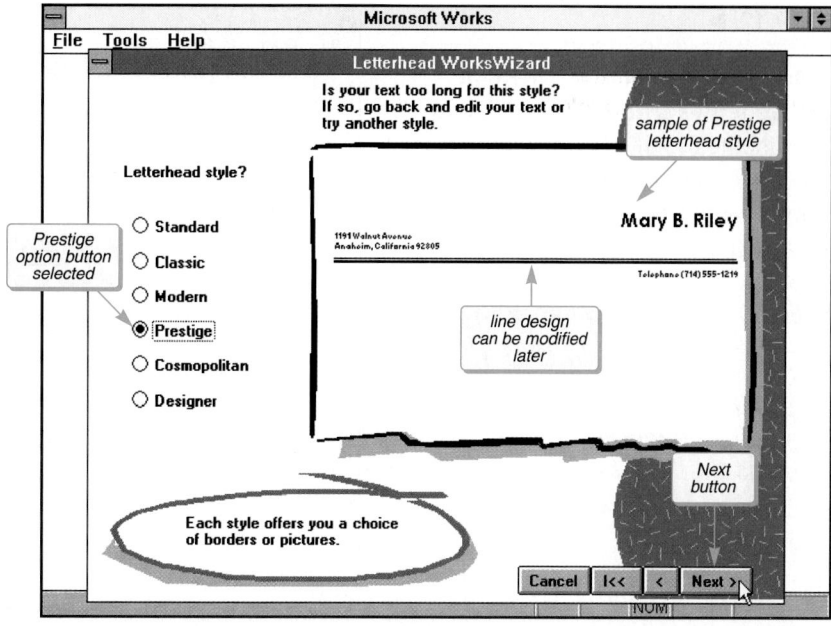

FIGURE 2-13

STEP 11 ▶

Choose the Next button. When the next Letterhead WorksWizard dialog box displays, select the option button adjacent to the double line with the lower line in bold. Point to the Next button.

A dialog box displays that allows you to select one of five line designs (Figure 2-14). The double line with the lower line in bold is selected. A sample of the letterhead, based upon selecting the line design, displays on the right of the screen. The mouse pointer points to the Next button.

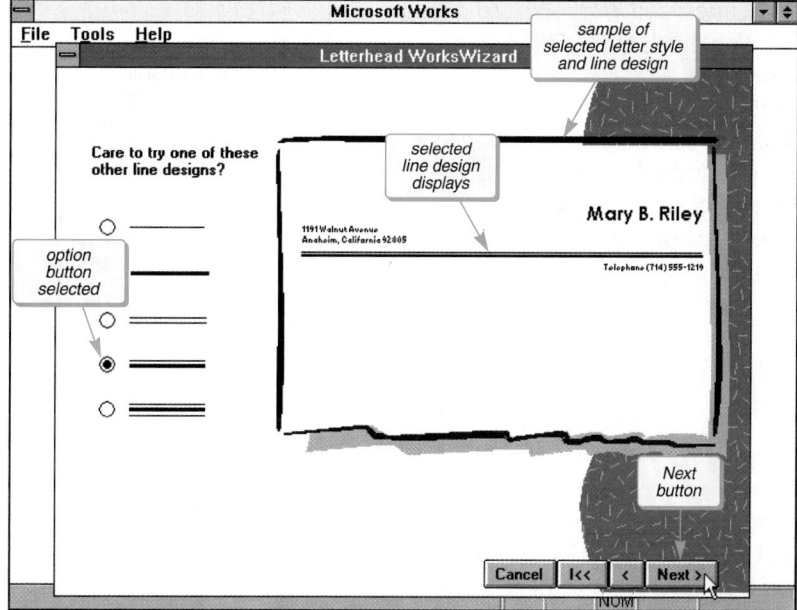

FIGURE 2-14

STEP 12 ▶

Choose the Next button. When the next Letterhead WorksWizard dialog box displays asking if you would like to add a border or picture, select the Neither option button. Point to the Next button.

A dialog box displays that asks, Would you like to add a decorative border or picture? (Figure 2-15). The Neither option button is selected. The mouse pointer points to the Next button.

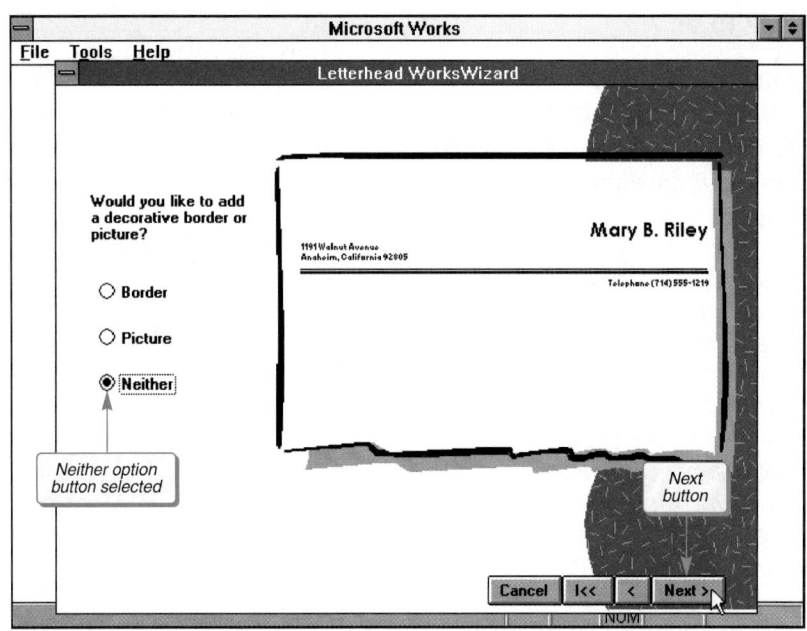

FIGURE 2-15

STEP 13 ▶

Choose the Next button. When the next Letterhead WorksWizard dialog box displays, point to the Create button.

A dialog box displays indicating the letterhead is ready to be created (Figure 2-16). The mouse pointer points to the Create button.

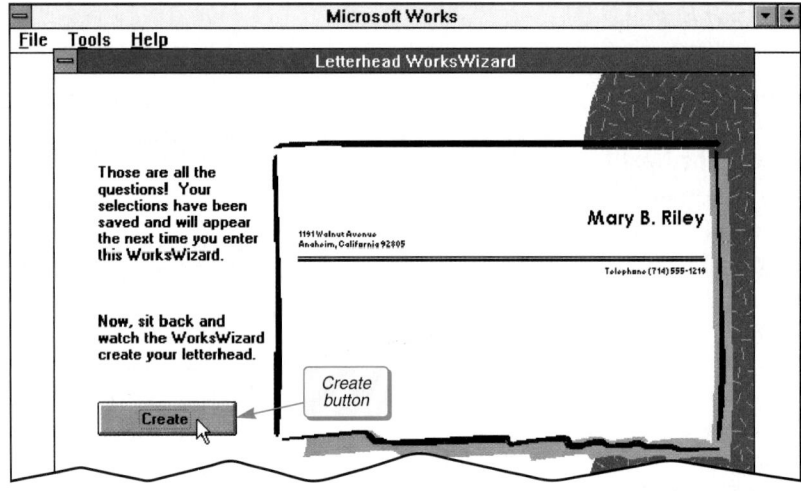

FIGURE 2-16

STEP 14 ▶

Choose the Create button. When the next Letterhead WorksWizard dialog box displays, point to the OK button.

Several screens will momentarily display indicating the letterhead is being created. Then the dialog box displays indicating the letterhead is ready (Figure 2-17). The mouse pointer points to the OK button.

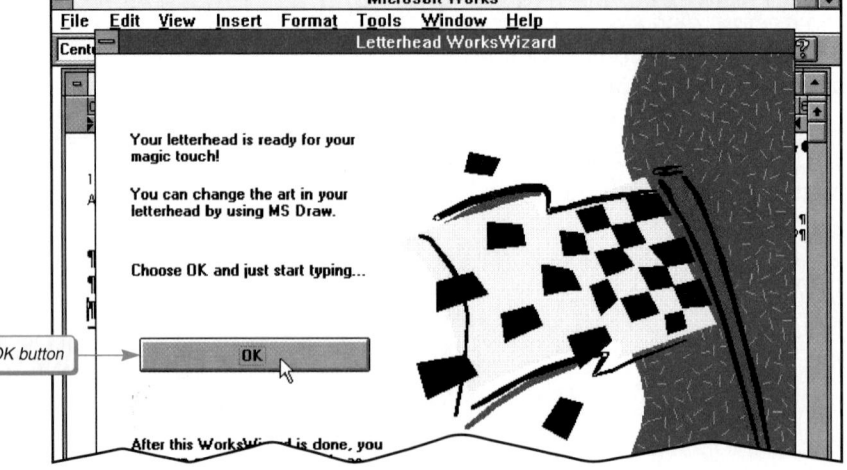

FIGURE 2-17

STEP 15 ►

Choose the OK button. When the Microsoft Works application window and the Word1 document window display, if necessary, maximize the windows and remove the Cue Card.

The letterhead displays in the maximized Word1 document window (Figure 2-18). Works automatically creates two blank lines following the letterhead and positions the insertion point in front of the last paragraph mark beneath the letterhead.

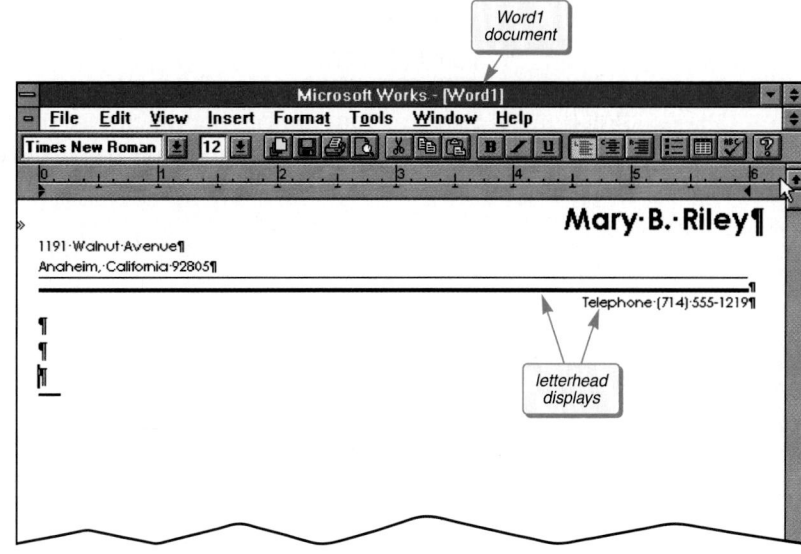

FIGURE 2-18

Saving the Letterhead Document

The next step is to save the letterhead document using the filename LETTERHD. Once you save the letterhead document, you can retrieve it at a later time and use it when typing a letter. The technique for saving a document using the Save command was explained in Project 1 and is summarized below.

TO SAVE THE LETTERHEAD DOCUMENT

Step 1: Point to the Save button on the Toolbar and click the left mouse button.
Step 2: When the Save As dialog box displays, type letterhd in the File Name text box.
Step 3: To save a file on a diskette inserted in drive A, select drive A by clicking the Drives drop-down list box arrow and then clicking the diskette icon that is followed by a:.
Step 4: Choose the OK button in the Save As dialog box.

Works saves the letterhead document on the diskette inserted in drive A using the filename, LETTERHD. The filename, LETTERHD.WPS, displays in the title bar of the document window.

You can use any filename you choose as long as the name follows the rules for constructing a filename as explained in Project 1. The filename LETTERHD was chosen because it represents the content of the document.

Quitting Works

Once you save the letterhead document, you can use the letterhead for all letters you write. If you are not going to use the letterhead immediately, you can quit Works. To quit Works, follow the steps explained in Project 1. These steps are summarized on the next page.

TO QUIT WORKS

Step 1: From the File menu, choose the Exit Works command.
Step 2: If you have made any changes to a document after saving it, a dialog box will display asking if you want to save the changes. Choose the Yes or No button as required.
Step 3: Works returns control to Program Manager.

▶ TYPING THE LETTER

When you are ready to type a letter using the letterhead, you must open the document file with the name LETTERHD. When Works opens the document file, the letterhead displays on the screen. You can then type your letter below the letterhead.

When you finish the letter, the letter displays with the letterhead at the top of the page, followed by the words you typed. You should save the letter using a new filename, such as COVRLETR. At a later time, you can again open the document file named LETTERHD, and use the letterhead for another letter.

The steps to create the letter shown in Figure 2-1 on page W2.3 are explained in detail below and on the following pages.

Starting Works and Opening a Document File

Use the following steps to start Works and open the document file named LETTERHD stored on the diskette in drive A.

TO START WORKS AND OPEN A DOCUMENT FILE ▼

STEP 1 ▶

Start Windows. From the Microsoft Works for Windows group window, double-click the Microsoft Works program-item icon. If the Welcome to Microsoft Works dialog box displays, click the Start Works Now button. The Startup dialog box will display. Point to the Open An Existing Document button.

The Startup dialog box displays (Figure 2-19). The mouse pointer points to the Open An Existing Document button.

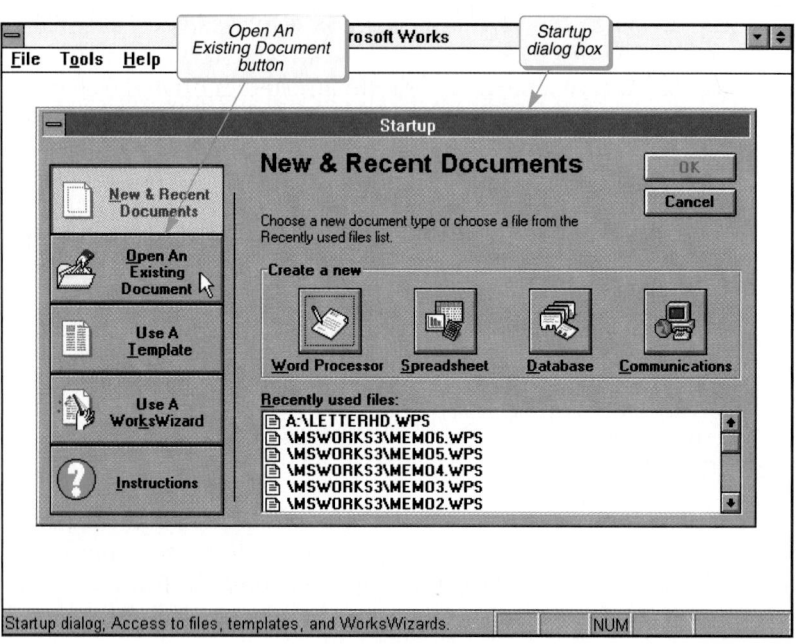

FIGURE 2-19

STEP 2 ▶

Choose the Open An Existing Document button in the Startup dialog box.

*Works displays the **Open dialog box** (Figure 2-20).*

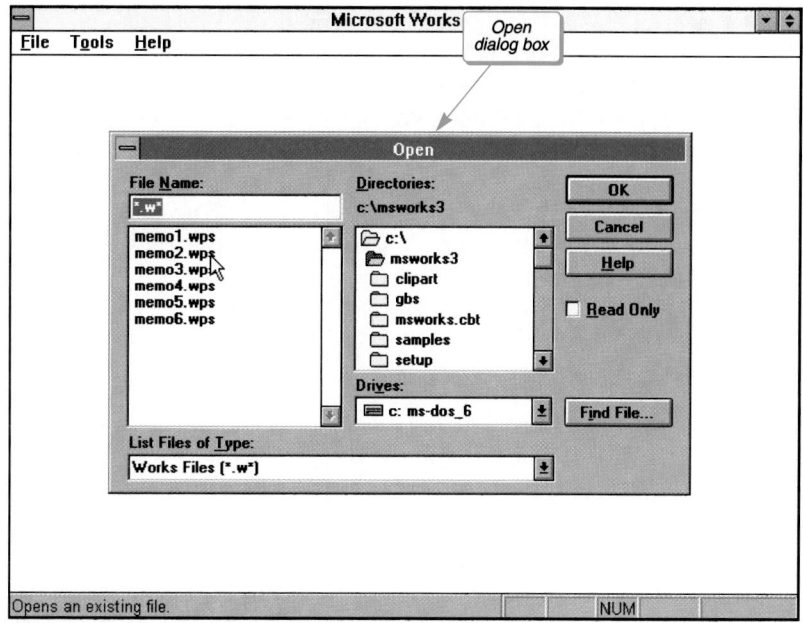

FIGURE 2-20

STEP 3 ▶

If it is necessary to select drive a:, point to the Drives drop-down list box arrow and click. Then select drive a: in the Drives drop-down list box.

Drive a: is selected (Figure 2-21). A list of files on the diskette in drive a: displays in the File Name list box.

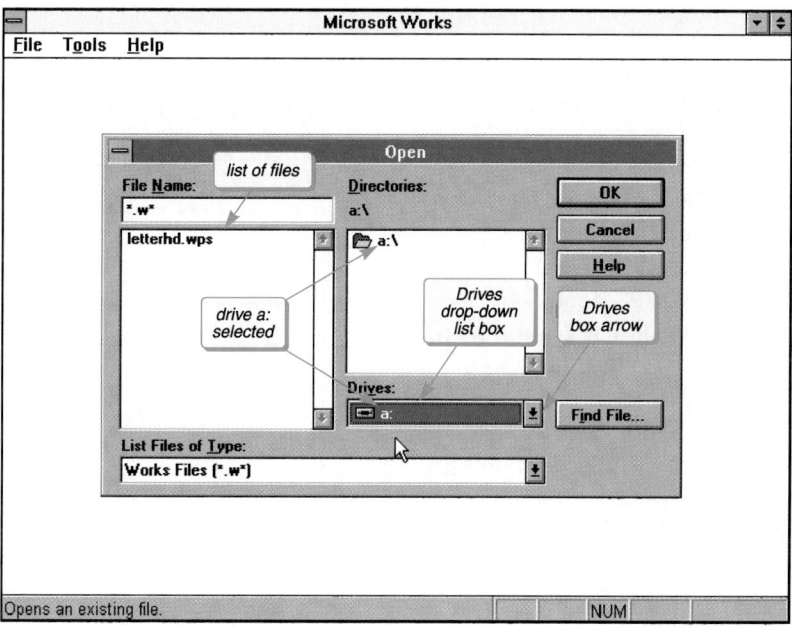

FIGURE 2-21

STEP 4 ▶

Select the filename, letterhd.wps, in the File Name list box by pointing to letterhd.wps and clicking the left mouse button.

The filename, letterhd.wps, displays in the File Name text box (Figure 2-22).

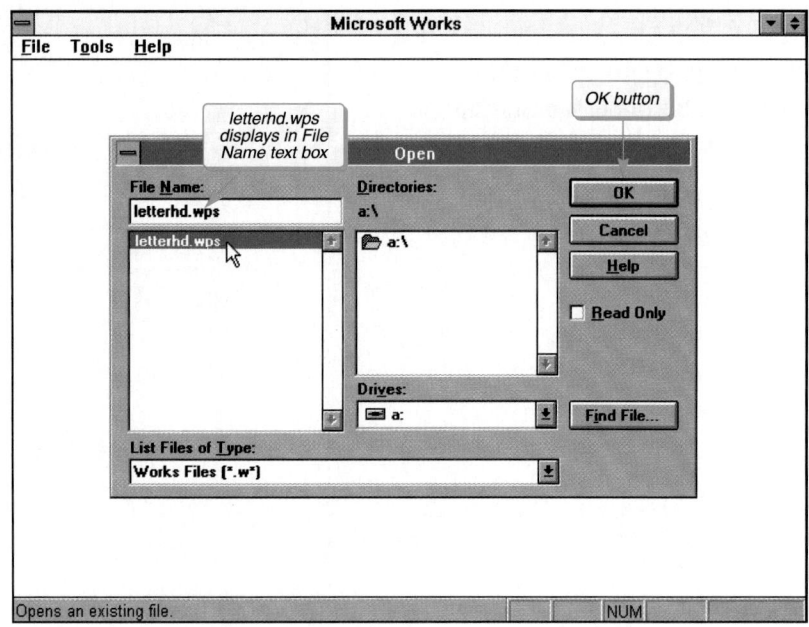

FIGURE 2-22

STEP 5 ▶

Choose the OK button in the Open dialog box. If necessary, maximize the Microsoft Works application window and the LETTERHD.WPS document window. Position the insertion point in front of the third paragraph mark beneath the letterhead.

The letterhead displays on the screen with the filename LETTERHD.WPS in the title bar (Figure 2-23). The insertion point is positioned in front of the third paragraph mark beneath the letterhead.

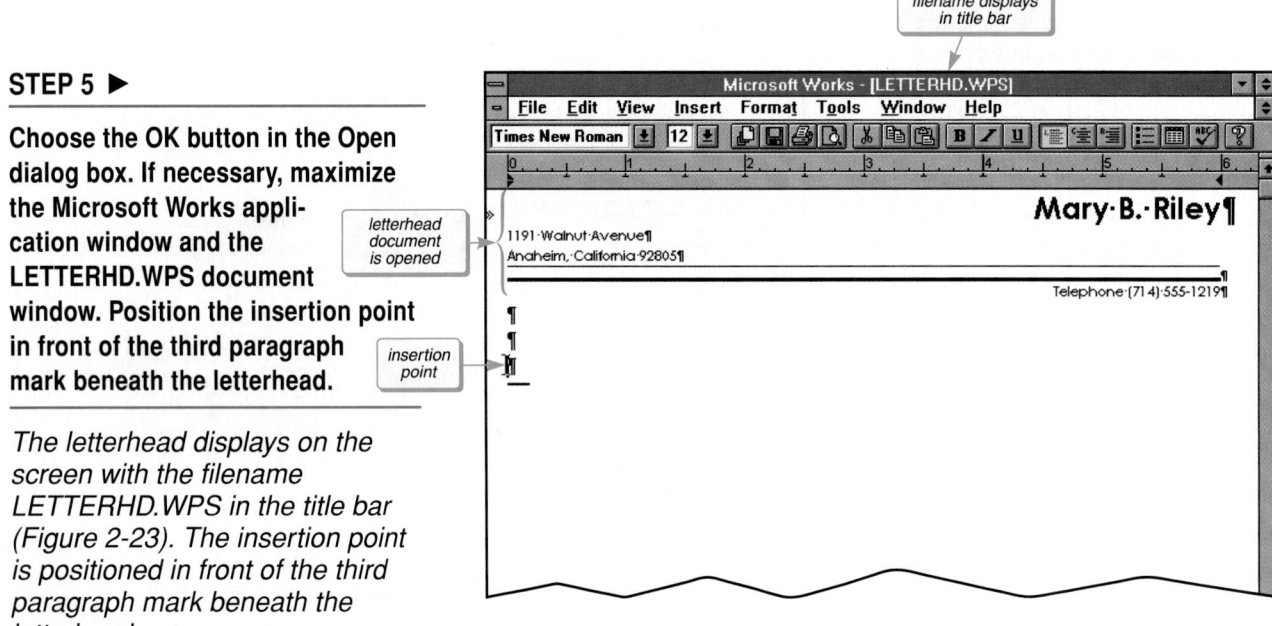

FIGURE 2-23

Following the completion of these steps, you are ready to type the letter beneath the letterhead.

Typing the Date and Inside Address

After you retrieve the letterhead from the diskette, begin typing the letter, as indicated in the following steps (see Figure 2-24).

TO TYPE THE DATE AND INSIDE ADDRESS

Step 1: Type the current date and press the ENTER key four times.
Step 2: Type Ms. Beverly A. Thompson and press the ENTER key one time.
Step 3: Type the title, company name, address, city, state, and zip code as shown in Figure 2-24.
Step 4: Press the ENTER key two times to create a blank line following the inside address.

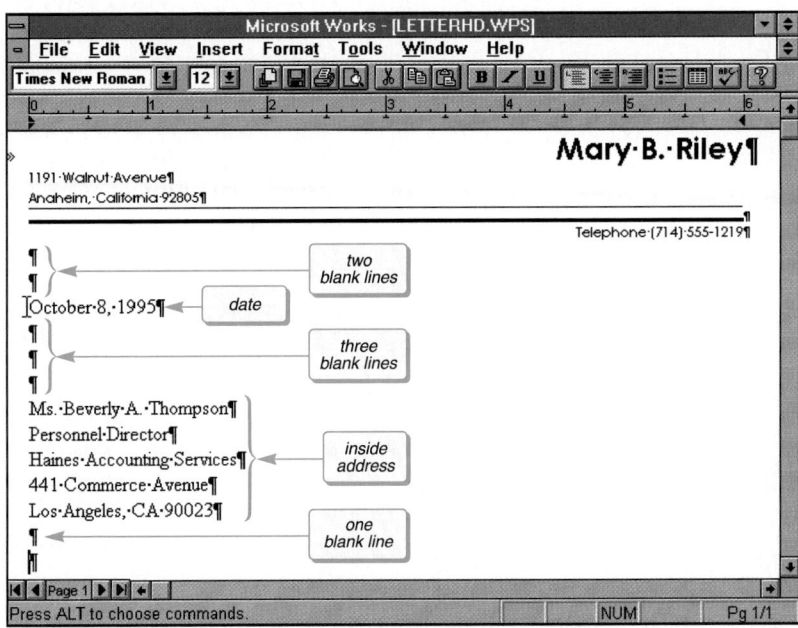

FIGURE 2-24

When typing the date and inside address, pay careful attention to proper spacing. Type the date beginning at the third paragraph mark beneath the letterhead. When typing a full-page letter, insert three blank lines following the date. To create a blank line, press the ENTER key for each blank line you need. For shorter letters you can add additional blank lines after the date to give the letter a balanced appearance on the page. One blank line follows the inside address.

Typing the Salutation

The next step is to type the salutation, as specified in the following steps (see Figure 2-25).

TO TYPE THE SALUTATION

Step 1: Type Dear Ms. Thompson:.
Step 2: Press the ENTER key two times.

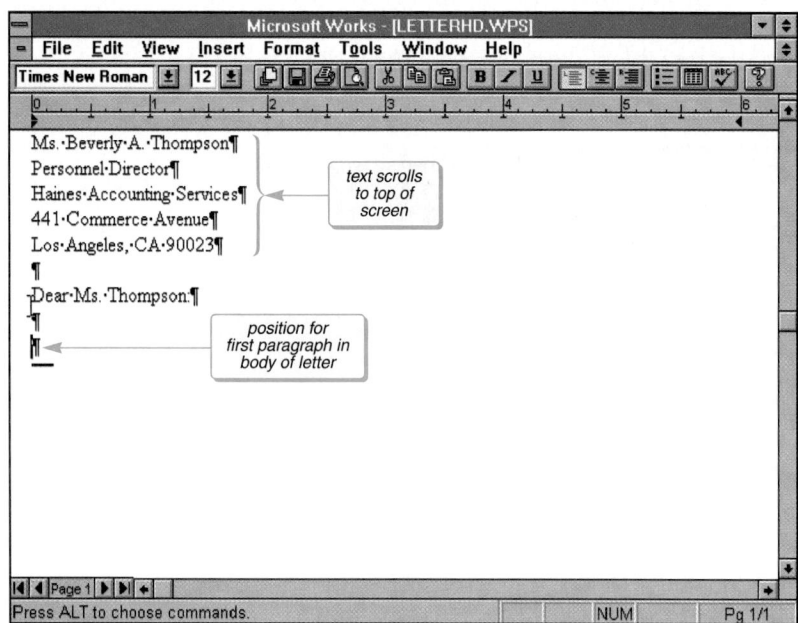

FIGURE 2-25

The letter in this project uses **mixed punctuation**. When using mixed punctuation, place a colon after the salutation (Dear Ms. Thompson:). When you press the ENTER key two times, a paragraph mark displays for the blank line; and the letterhead and the date scroll off the screen, creating a blank area at the bottom of the screen that allows you to see the new data as you type it (Figure 2-25).

Typing the Body of the Letter

Next, type the body of the letter, as specified in the following steps (see Figure 2-26).

TO TYPE THE BODY OF THE LETTER

Step 1: Without indenting, type the first paragraph. Do not press the ENTER key while typing the paragraph.
Step 2: When you reach the words, Los Angeles Times, click the Underline button on the Toolbar.
Step 3: Type Los Angeles Times. Each time you type a letter, Works underlines it.
Step 4: Click the Underline button on the Toolbar again. Works turns off underlining.
Step 5: Type the remainder of the first paragraph.
Step 6: Press the ENTER key two times — once to end the paragraph and once to create a blank line.
Step 7: Type the second and third paragraphs.
Step 8: Scroll the document so the screen displays as shown in Figure 2-26.

A blank line appears between paragraphs. In a block letter, you do not indent paragraphs.

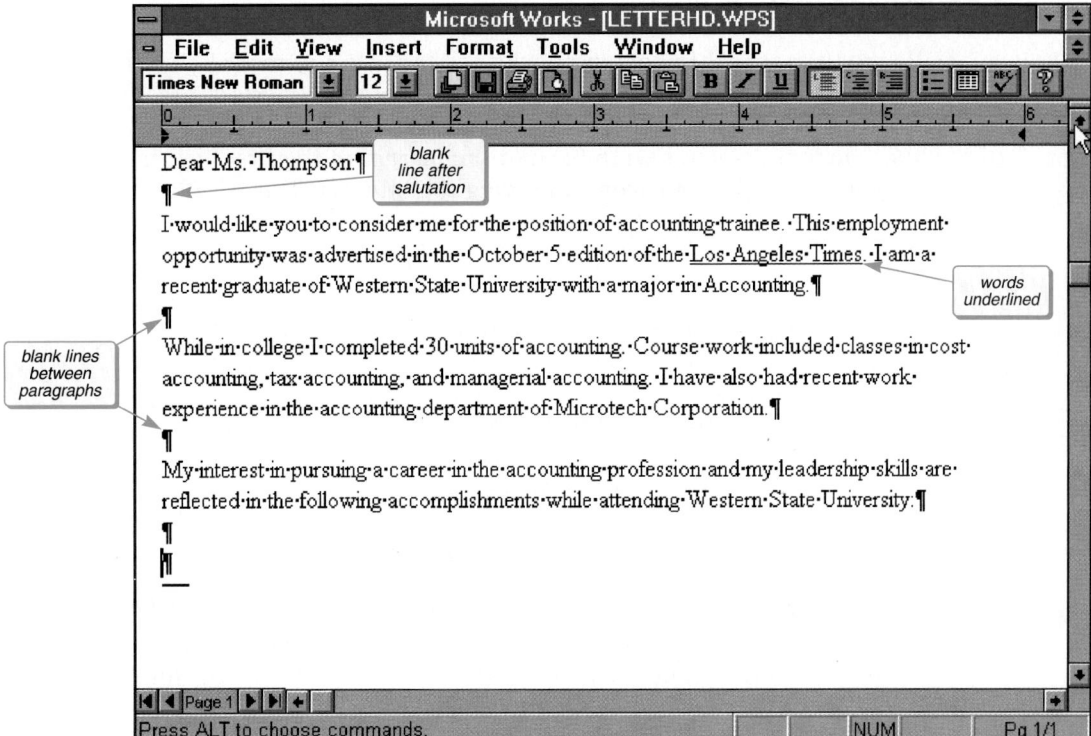

FIGURE 2-26

As you type the body of the letter and the screen fills with text, the inside address, the salutation, and a portion of the body of the letter will scroll off the screen. In Figure 2-26, the up scroll arrow has been used to position the letter so that the salutation displays on the top line of the screen. This has been done so you can easily view the first three paragraphs of the letter.

Differences in Document Displays

The screen shown in Figure 2-26 displays the first paragraphs of the letter. You should be aware that the number of words displayed per line in the document and printed per line on the printer can vary slightly from computer to computer. This occurs because the screen shows text exactly as it will print on your printer and, even though the font and font size are the same, some printers will print a different number of characters per line than other printers. Therefore, do not be concerned if a line on your screen does not correspond exactly to the screen shown in Figure 2-26.

Again, it should be noted that as you type the letter and the screen becomes completely filled with text, Works will automatically scroll the text upward. A portion of the text just typed will continue to display and approximately one-half of the screen will be blank, allowing additional text to be typed and viewed on the screen.

Hanging Indents

Following the first three paragraphs of the letter is a numbered list (Figure 2-27). In a numbered list, you type a number followed by a period, press the TAB **key** to create blank space, and then type the text. When the text reaches the end of the line, the text does not wrap back to the margin of the first line. Instead, it aligns vertically with the first word following the number. This is called a **hanging indent**.

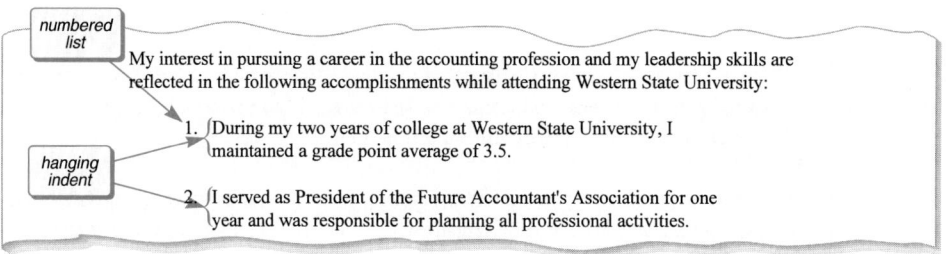

FIGURE 2-27

It is recommended you indent the numbered list one-half inch from the left and right margins, and indent the text one-quarter inch from the beginning of the number.

The following steps explain how to create a hanging indent and the numbered list in the letter using the **first-line indent marker**, the **left-margin indent marker**, and the **right-margin indent marker.**

TO CREATE A HANGING INDENT AND A NUMBERED LIST ▼

STEP 1 ►

Make sure the insertion point is positioned at the location in the letter where you want to type the numbered list. Point to the left-margin indent marker, which is the lower of two triangles on the ruler.

The mouse pointer points to the left-margin indent marker on the ruler (Figure 2-28).

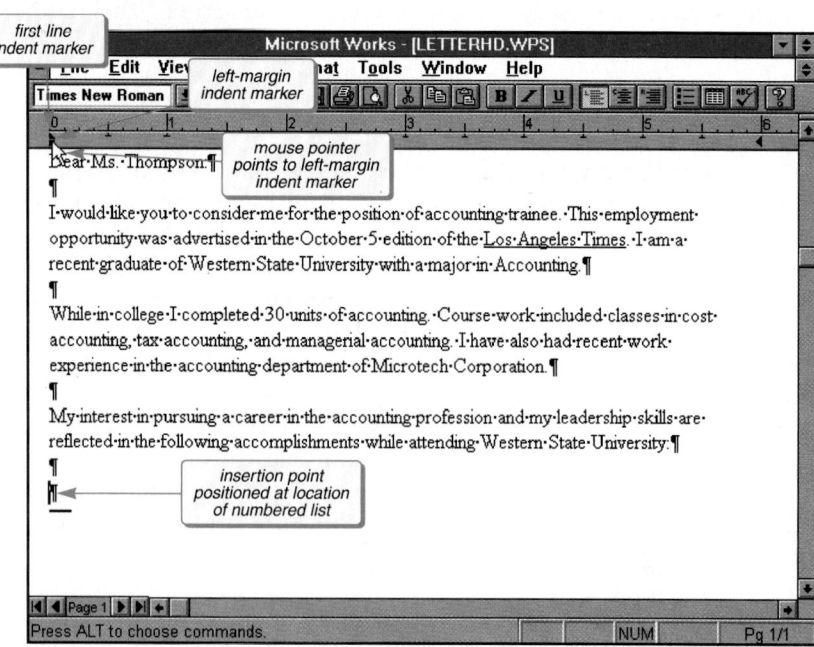

FIGURE 2-28

STEP 2 ▶

Hold down the SHIFT key and drag the left-margin indent marker right to the 3/4-inch mark on the ruler. Then release the left mouse button and the SHIFT key. This establishes the left margin for the text in the numbered list.

The left-margin indent marker is positioned at the 3/4-inch mark on the ruler (Figure 2-29). Holding down the SHIFT key informs Works you want to drag only the left-margin indent marker. If you do not hold down the SHIFT key, both the left-margin indent marker and the first-line indent marker would move.

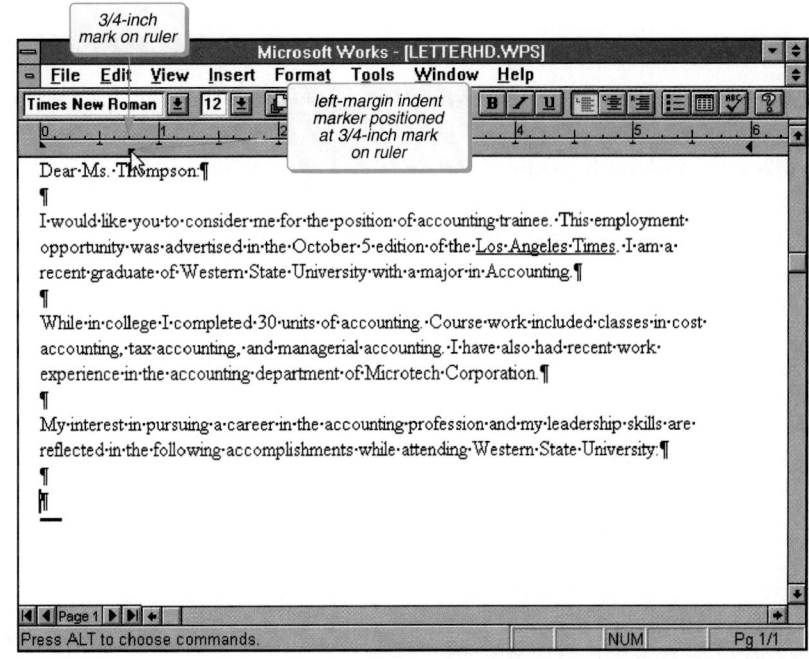

FIGURE 2-29

STEP 3 ▶

Point to the first-line indent marker, which is the upper triangle on the ruler, and drag the first-line indent marker to the 1/2-inch mark on the ruler. This establishes the leftmost position of the numbers in the numbered list.

The left-margin indent marker is set at the 3/4-inch mark and the first-line indent marker is set at the 1/2-inch mark on the ruler (Figure 2-30). The paragraph mark and the insertion point move 1/2 inch to the right.

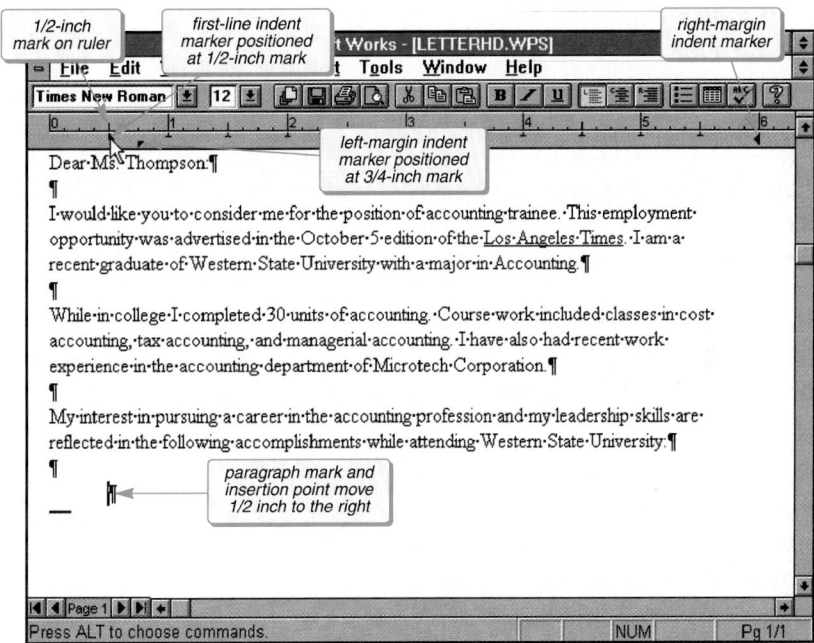

FIGURE 2-30

STEP 4 ▶

Drag the right-margin indent marker from the 6-inch mark to the 5 1/2-inch mark on the ruler. Type 1., press the TAB key, and type the text associated with the number. Press the ENTER key when the paragraph is completed.

The right-margin indent marker is positioned at the 5 1/2-inch mark, which indents the right margin 1/2 inch (Figure 2-31). The number 1 begins 1/2 inch to the right of the 0 position on the ruler. Works inserts an arrow pointing to the right to indicate the TAB key has been pressed. The text begins at the left-margin indent marker (3/4-inch mark). The text on the second line indents automatically to the left-margin indent marker, aligning the text on the first and second lines.

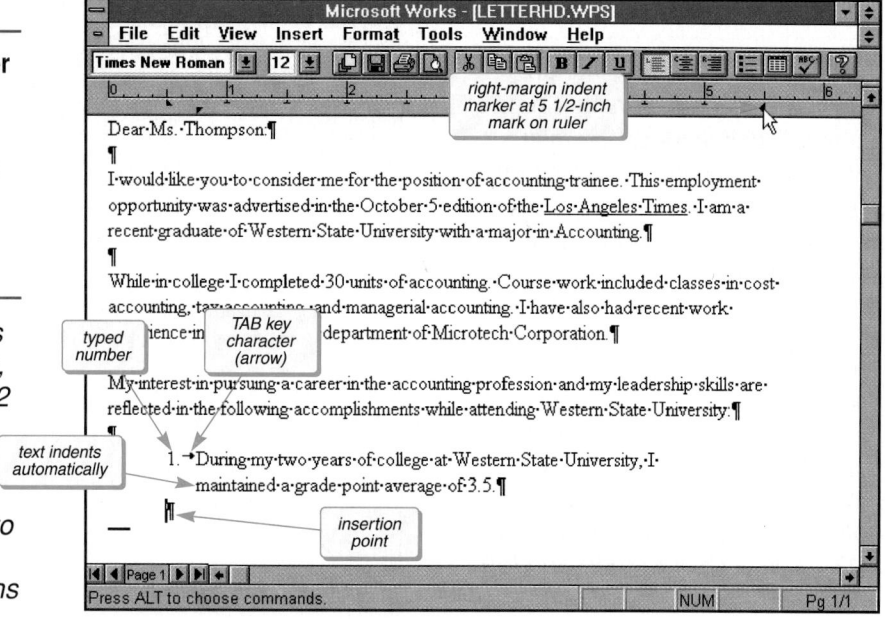

FIGURE 2-31

STEP 5 ▶

Press the ENTER key to create a blank line. Then type the remainder of the numbered list. Press the ENTER key.

The numbered list displays (Figure 2-32). Works indents the insertion point and the paragraph mark following the numbered list. Notice that the insertion point and the paragraph mark are located approximately halfway down the document window, whereas in Figure 2-31, they were located at the bottom of the window. When the insertion point is located on the last line of the window and you type a character, Works automatically scrolls the screen up so approximately one-half of the screen is blank to allow you to add additional text below the existing text.

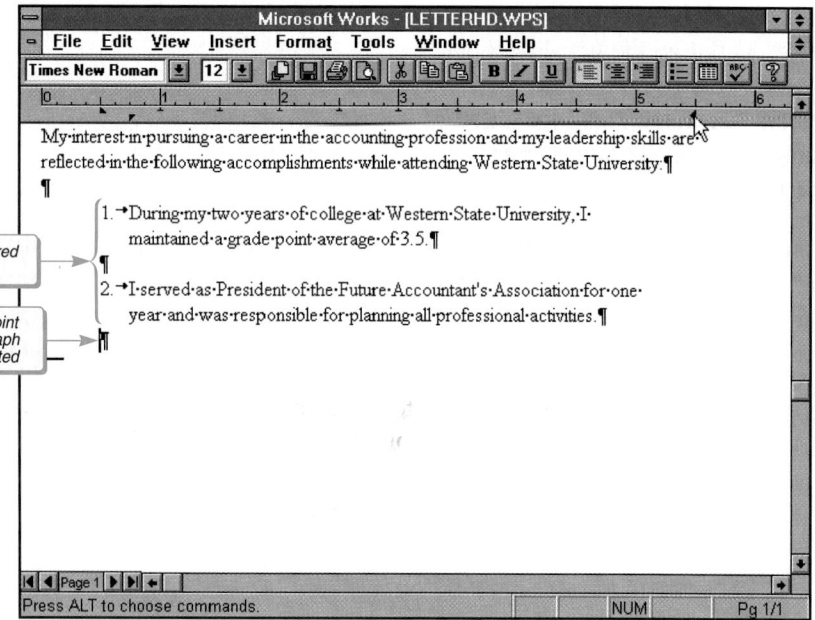

FIGURE 2-32

STEP 6 ▶

To return the left-margin indent marker and the first-line indent marker to the 0-inch position on the ruler and the right-margin indent marker to the 6-inch mark on the ruler, press the CTRL+Q keys.

The left-margin indent marker and the first-line indent marker return to the 0-inch position on the ruler (Figure 2-33). The right-margin indent marker returns to the 6-inch mark on the ruler. The insertion point and the paragraph mark are located at the 0-inch position also.

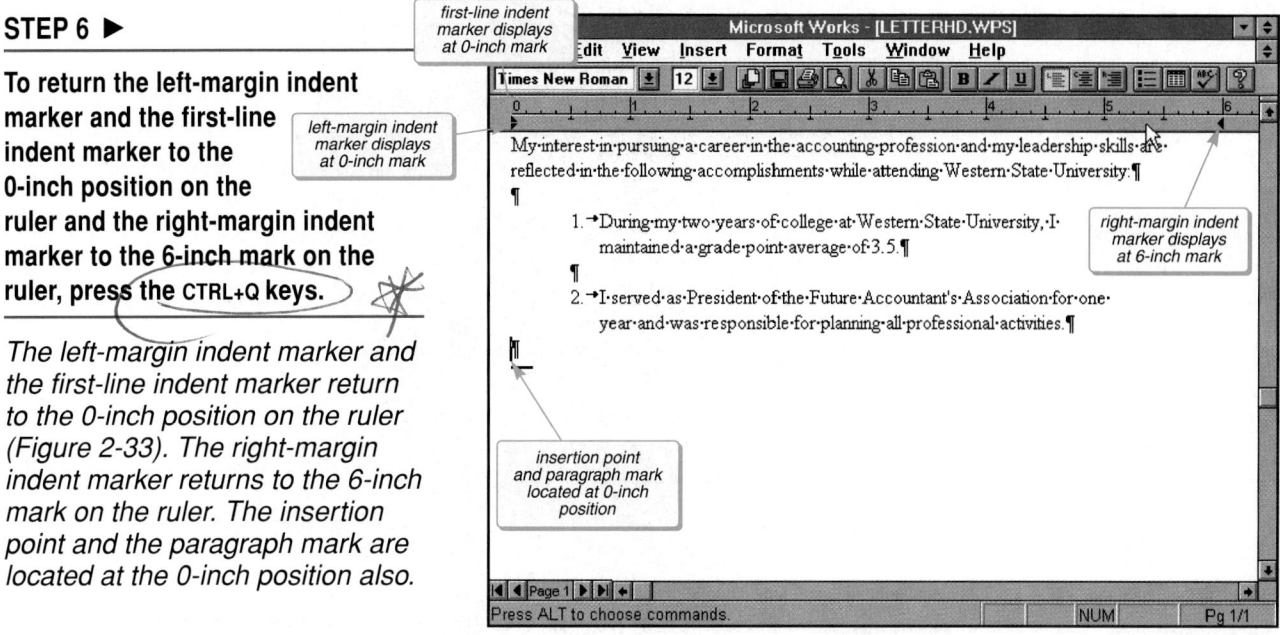

FIGURE 2-33

The formatting accomplished by dragging the indent markers and pressing the CTRL+Q keys also could have been accomplished using the **Paragraph command** from the Format menu and making appropriate entries in the Paragraph dialog box that displays when choosing the Paragraph command.

Use the CTRL+Q key combination any time you want to remove all paragraph formatting from a paragraph at one time.

Completing the Letter

To complete the letter, perform the following steps (see Figure 2-34 on the next page).

TO COMPLETE THE LETTER

Step 1: Press the ENTER key to create a blank line following the numbered list.

Step 2: Type the last paragraph of the letter. Press the ENTER key one time to end the paragraph and a second time to create a blank line.

Step 3: Type Sincerely, and press the ENTER key four times.

Step 4: Type Mary B. Riley and press the ENTER key one time.

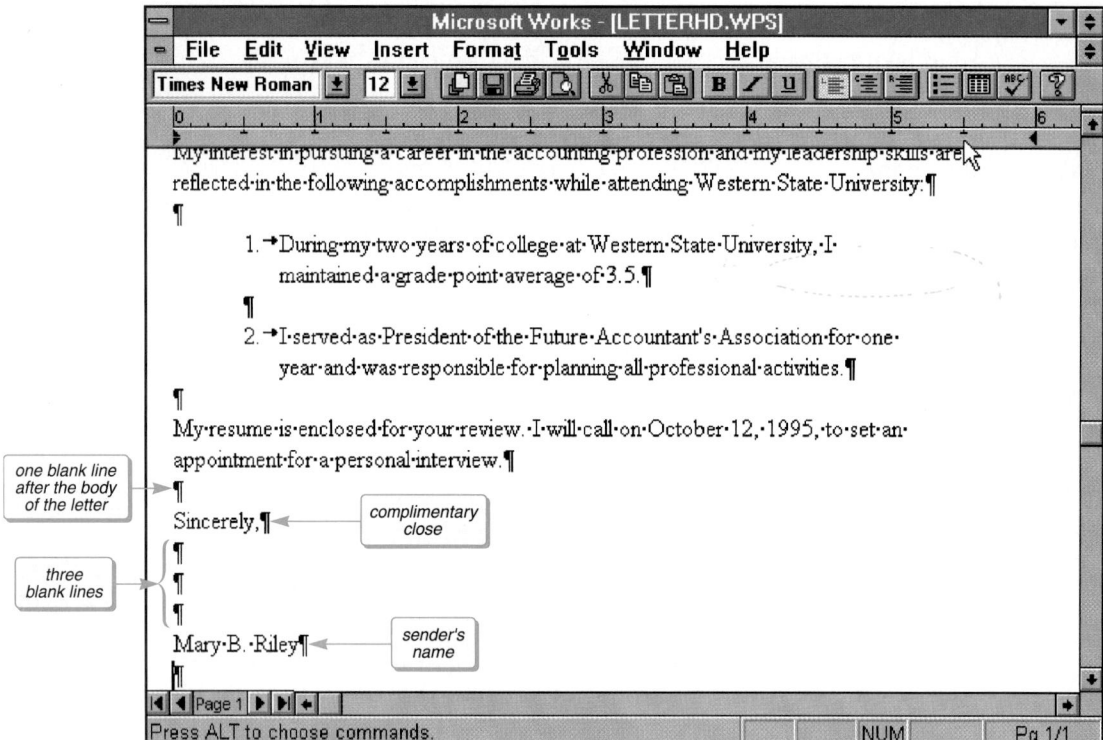

FIGURE 2-34

The numbered list, the last paragraph in the letter, the complimentary close, and the sender's name are illustrated in Figure 2-34. One blank line follows the last line of the body of the letter. Place a comma after the word Sincerely when using mixed punctuation. Three blank lines follow the word Sincerely. Remember to carefully follow these spacing standards when typing business letters.

Using the Spelling Checker

After typing the letter, you should check the document for spelling or typing errors. Works provides the capability of checking the spelling of all words in a document through the use of its spelling checker. To use the spelling checker, you can click the **Spelling Checker button** on the Toolbar. When checking spelling, Works compares the words in a document to the words in a 113,664 word dictionary. When Works finds a word in a document it does not find in the dictionary, Works displays the word in the **Spelling dialog box** and can provide a list of suggested spellings for the word. You can add specialized words to the dictionary if you desire, or you can ignore words that Works identifies as misspelled.

To illustrate the use of the Works spelling checker, the word personnel has been deliberately misspelled as personnell for the following steps only. Perform the following steps to use the spelling checker to find the incorrectly spelled word.

TO CHECK SPELLING ▼

STEP 1 ►

Click the beginning of document button on the scroll bar to position the insertion point at the beginning of the document and then click the Spelling Checker button on the Toolbar.

Works scans the document until it finds a word that is not in the dictionary. Because the last name (Riley) is not in the dictionary, Works highlights the name Riley on the screen and also displays the Spelling dialog box (Figure 2-35). The Change To text box contains the highlighted word, Riley.

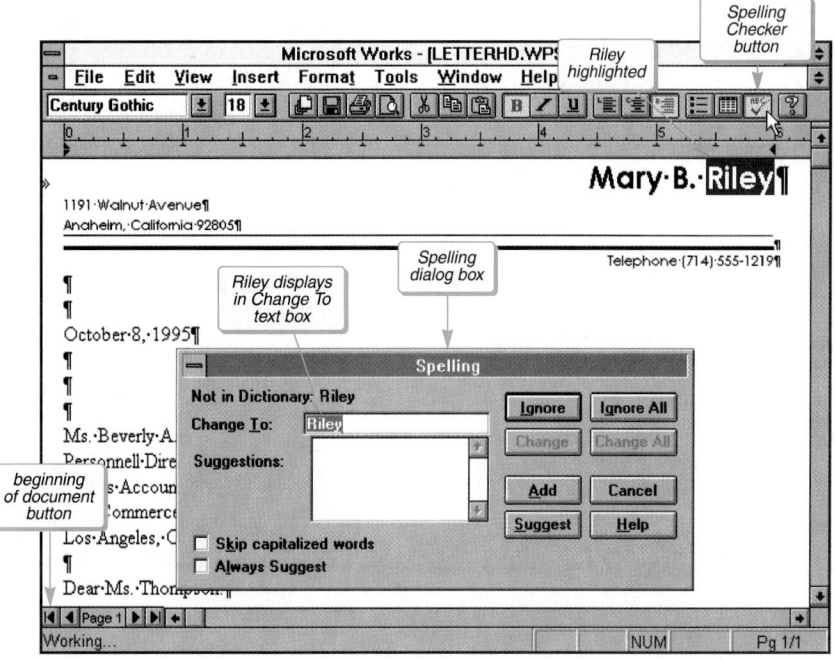

FIGURE 2-35

STEP 2 ►

Because Riley is a last name and this word is not misspelled, point to the Ignore All button in the Spelling dialog box (Figure 2-36).

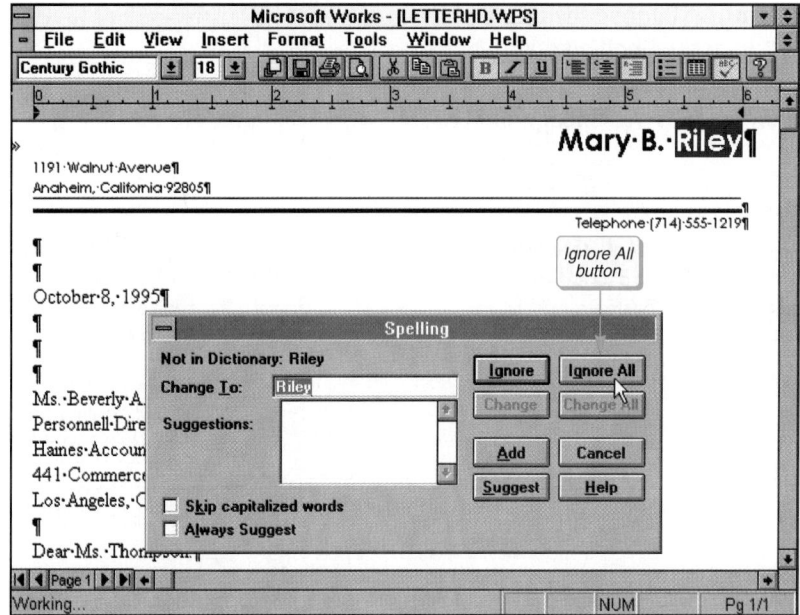

FIGURE 2-36

STEP 3 ►

Choose the Ignore All button in the Spelling dialog box. When Works displays the word Personnell, point to the Suggest button.

Works ignores all future uses of the word Riley. Works continues to search for words not in the dictionary. Additional words not found in the dictionary will include the name Thompson. Choose the Ignore All button to continue. Works highlights the word Personnell in the letter on the screen and displays the word Personnell in the Change To text box (Figure 2-37).

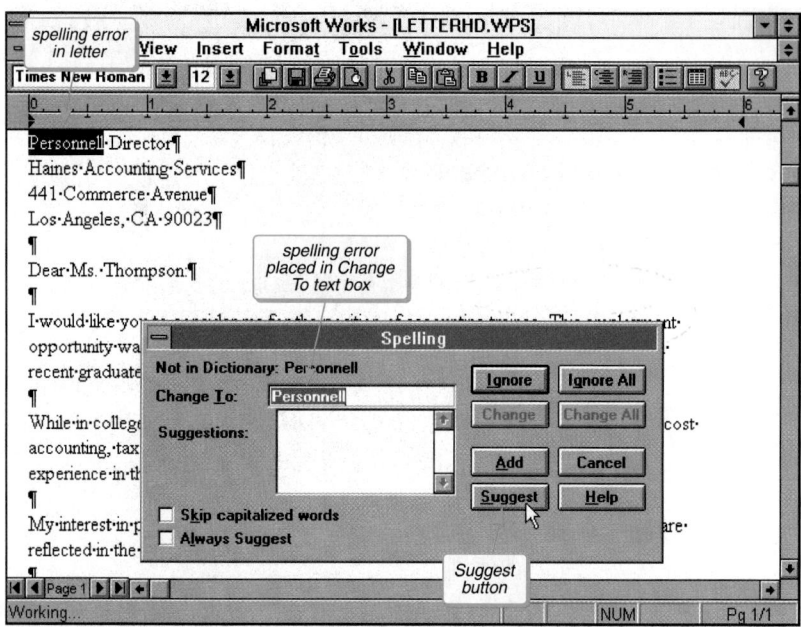

FIGURE 2-37

STEP 4 ►

The word Personnell appears to be in error, so choose the Suggest button in the Spelling dialog box to view Works's suggested spellings. Then point to the Change button.

Works displays suggested spellings for the word Personnell and places the most likely spelling (Personnel) in the Change To text box (Figure 2-38).

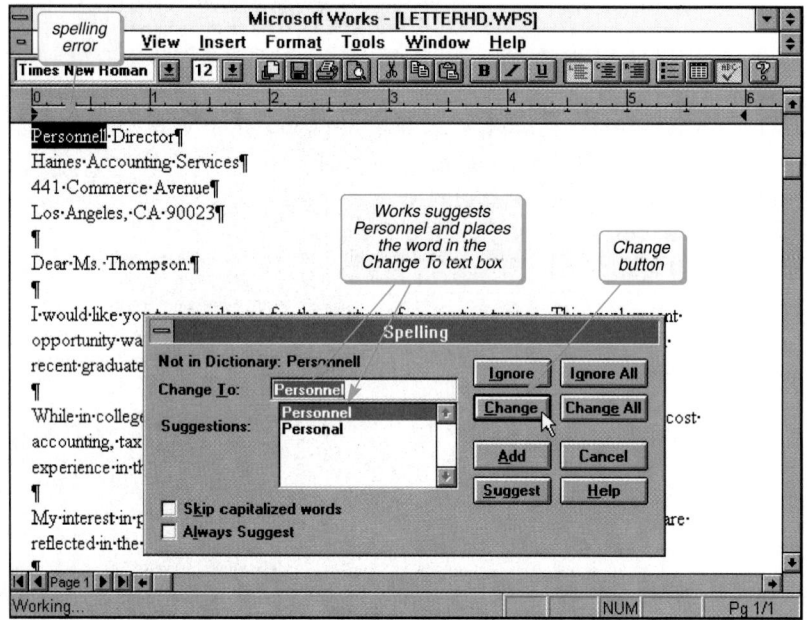

FIGURE 2-38

STEP 5 ▶

To accept the suggested spelling, choose the Change button in the Spelling dialog box.

Works inserts the word Personnel in the letter, and immediately continues checking the spelling of each subsequent word. After checking the entire document, Works displays the Microsoft Works dialog box indicating the spelling check is finished (Figure 2-39).

STEP 6 ▶

Choose the OK button in the dialog box to remove the dialog box from the screen. Click the beginning of document button on the scroll bar to return the letterhead to the top of the screen.

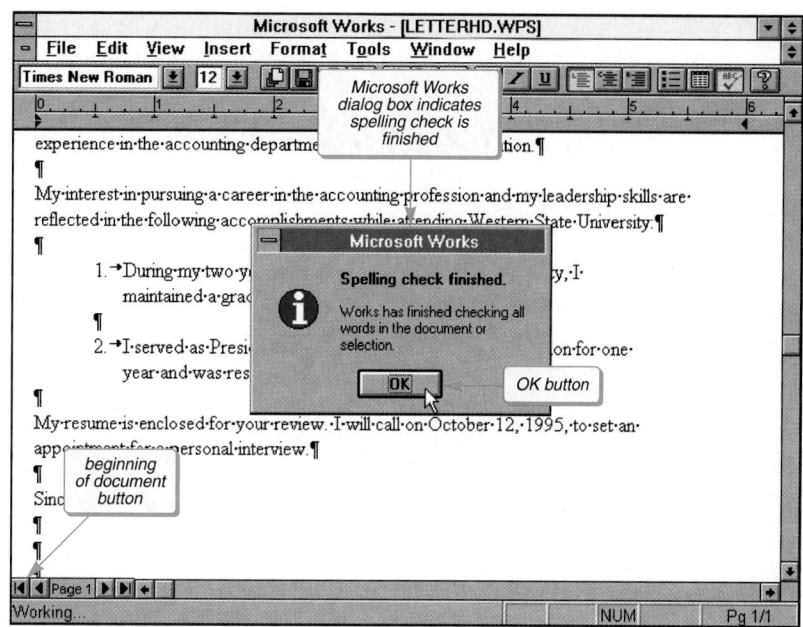

FIGURE 2-39

When using the spelling checker, you can also type a word in the Change To text box to change a highlighted word, or you can correct a word that is placed in the Change To text box by adding or deleting one or more characters.

The spelling checker also looks for repeated words, such as for for, in a document. You can choose either the Ignore button to ignore the repeated words or the Change button to delete the second occurrence of the repeated word.

If you select the Always Suggest check box within the Spelling dialog box (see Figure 2-38), Works will always provide suggested spellings and you will not have to choose the Suggest button for suggestions. If you select the Skip capitalized words check box, the Works spelling checker will ignore words that display in all capital letters.

If you choose the Ignore button for a misspelled word, Works will ignore only that occurrence of the word, while if you choose the Ignore All button, all occurrences of the word will be ignored. Similarly, if you choose the Change button, only that occurrence of the word is changed, while if you choose the Change All button, all occurrences of the word will be changed.

If you want to add a word to the spelling dictionary, choose the Add button when the spelling checker stops on the word.

For most efficient use of the spelling checker you should place the insertion point at the beginning of the document before you begin to check the spelling. If you do not, Works will check the spelling in the document from the insertion point to the end of the document. Then Works will display a dialog box containing the message, "End of document: continue to check spelling from start?" To continue the spelling check from the start, choose the OK button in the dialog box. To terminate the spelling check operation, choose the Cancel button in the dialog box.

In addition to the Spelling Checker button on the Toolbar you can also choose the **Spelling command** from the Tools menu to start the Works spelling checker.

Saving the Letter on Disk

After checking the spelling of the letter, the next step is to save the letter on a diskette inserted in drive A using the filename, COVRLETR. To save the letter using a new filename, you must use the Save As command from the File menu. The steps to save the letter with a new name are summarized below.

TO SAVE THE LETTER WITH A NEW NAME

Step 1: From the File menu, choose the Save As command.
Step 2: In the Save As dialog box, type the filename `covrletr`.
Step 3: Select drive A from the Drives drop-down list box if necessary.
Step 4: Choose the OK button in the Save As dialog box.

The letter displays on the screen with the filename COVRLETR.WPS in the title bar (Figure 2-40).

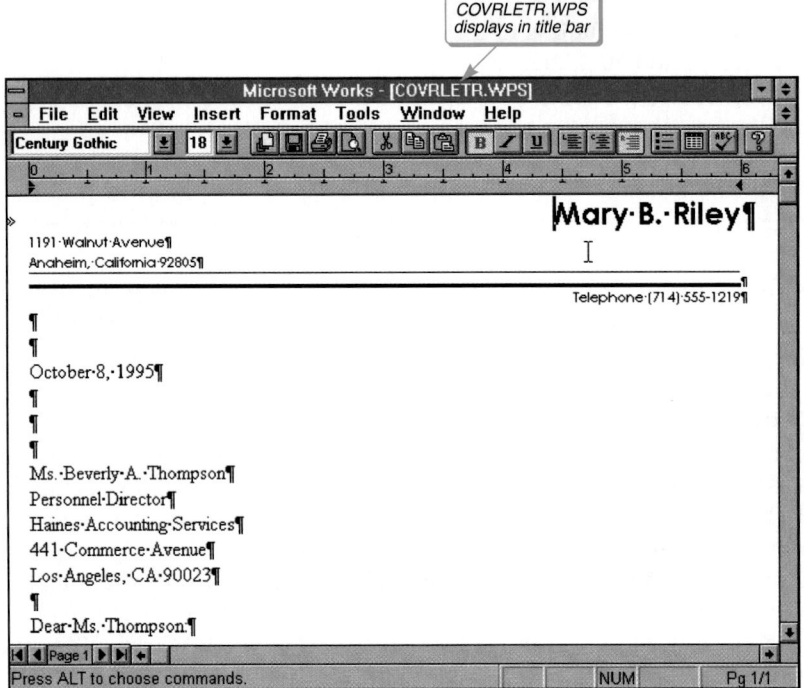

FIGURE 2-40

Printing the Letter

The next step is to print the letter. If the entries you have previously used in the Print dialog box apply to the document you are currently going to print, click the Print button on the Toolbar to print the letter. If you want to display the Print dialog box before printing, you must choose the Print command from the File menu.

TO PRINT THE LETTER

Step 1: Click the Print button on the Toolbar.

The letter will print as shown in Figure 2-1 on page W2.3.

▶ CREATING THE RESUME

A fter typing the letter, checking the spelling, and saving and printing the letter, the next step is to create the resume. Instead of closing the file containing the letter or quitting Works, leave the letter displayed on the screen and proceed to the next step, which involves creating the resume.

With Works for Windows, you can have up to eight documents open at one time. This technique allows you to switch between documents and display them on the screen with a few clicks of the mouse. For example, when creating the resume, you might want to switch to a screen that displays the letter to assist you in creating the resume or you might want to make changes to the letter as you develop the resume. The techniques for creating a resume and switching between open documents (the letter and the resume) are explained on the following pages.

The Resume AutoStart Template

When creating a resume, you can design your own format and use the Word Processor to create the resume, or you can use an AutoStart template. As previously explained, Works provides a number of preformatted documents, called AutoStart templates, to assist you in performing common tasks. One of the AutoStart templates that is provided by Works is the resume AutoStart template. If you are not familiar with the content or format of a resume, the Works resume AutoStart template can be a valuable tool. Figure 2-41 illustrates the resume AutoStart template.

Your Name
Street Address
City, Prov/State, Postal Code
Phone Number

OBJECTIVE

In this section describe the job you are applying for, your employment goals, your personal strengths, reasons why you feel qualified for the position.

WORK HISTORY

Describe your last job (the company, your position, responsibilities, etc.)
Type the beginning and ending dates
Tell about your work and accomplishments.
Describe your job before that
Type the beginning and ending dates
Tell about your work and accomplishments.
And the job before that
Type the beginning and ending dates
Tell about your work and accomplishments.
And the job before that
Type the beginning and ending dates
Tell about your work and accomplishments.

EDUCATION

Latest Certificate or degree
Name of school and accomplishments.
Training before that
Name of school and accomplishments.
Training before that
Name of school and accomplishments.

AWARDS/COMMUNITY SERVICE

Describe personal accomplishments in community clubs, church, service groups, etc.
Other personal accomplishments.
Other personal accomplishments.

FIGURE 2-41

As you can see in Figure 2-41, the AutoStart template consists of preformatted words, lines, and paragraphs that contain a description of the recommended contents of the resume. The fonts, font styles, and font sizes are also predetermined. To use the AutoStart template, highlight the words, lines or paragraphs that explain what the resume is to contain and type the actual information you want to appear in the resume. For example, the first line of the AutoStart template contains the words, *Your Name*. This line should be replaced by the name of the individual creating the resume.

A review of the resume in Figure 2-41 indicates locations for name, street address, city, prov/state, postal code, phone number, Objective (work objective), Work History, Education, and Awards/Community Service.

It is possible to change formatting, such as font style or size, on the AutoStart template, and you can add or delete information as required.

Resume Preparation Steps

To create the resume shown in Figure 2-1 on page W2.3, you should follow these general steps. The detailed explanation for each of the steps is provided on subsequent pages.

1. With the letter displayed on the screen, select the File menu and choose the Templates command.
2. When the Startup dialog box displays, the Use A Template button is selected (recessed) and the characters on it are red.
3. In the drop-down list box listing the Works AutoStart template groups, select the Personal group. Then select the resume AutoStart template and choose the OK button.
4. The resume will display. Highlight each line or paragraph in which you want to enter new information and type the new text.
5. Center and add the word Resume at the top of the page. Use 16 point Times New Roman italic font.
6. Check the resume spelling.
7. Use Print Preview to preview the resume.
8. Save the resume.
9. Print the resume.
10. Switch between the two open documents, if necessary, to review both the letter and resume.
11. Quit Works

Displaying the AutoStart Template

The first step in creating a resume is to display the resume AutoStart template. Assuming you have not yet quit Works and the letter is displayed on the screen, you can display the resume AutoStart template by choosing the Templates command from the File menu and making the appropriate choices in the Startup dialog box that displays. To display the resume AutoStart template, perform the following steps.

TO DISPLAY THE RESUME AUTOSTART TEMPLATE ▼

STEP 1 ▶

Select the File menu and point to the Templates command.

The File menu displays and the mouse pointer points to the Templates command (Figure 2-42).

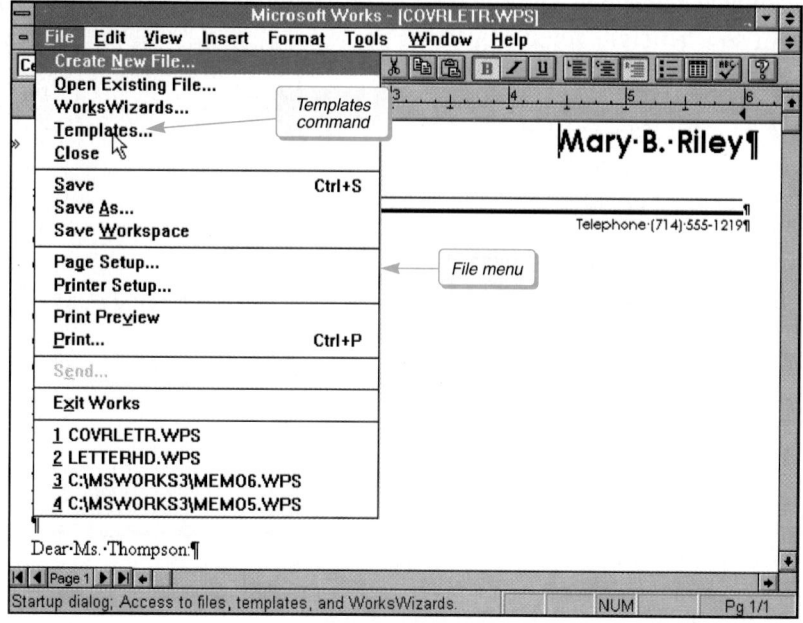

FIGURE 2-42

STEP 2 ▶

Choose the Templates command. When the Startup dialog box displays, point to the Choose a template group drop-down list box arrow.

The Startup dialog box displays with the Use A Template button recessed and the Use A Template message shown (Figure 2-43). The mouse pointer points to the Choose a template group drop-down list box arrow. List boxes display that allow you to choose a category and choose a template. The Show Instructions Cue Cards check box is selected by default.

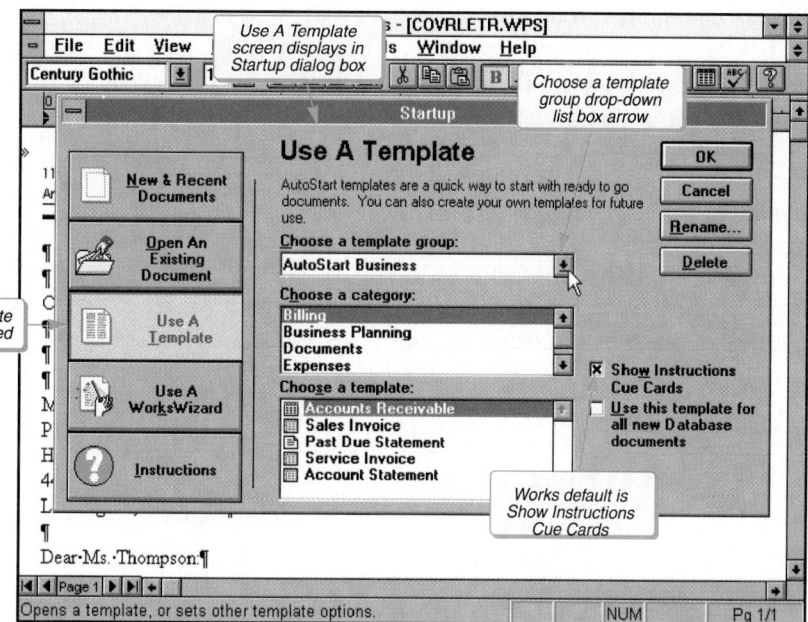

FIGURE 2-43

STEP 3 ▶

Click the left mouse button. When additional selections display in the Choose a template group drop-down list box, point to AutoStart Personal.

A list of AutoStart template groups displays (Figure 2-44). AutoStart Business is highlighted. In the Choose a template list box, Accounts Receivable is highlighted. The resume AutoStart template is not included in this template group, so you must select another group. The mouse pointer points to AutoStart Personal.

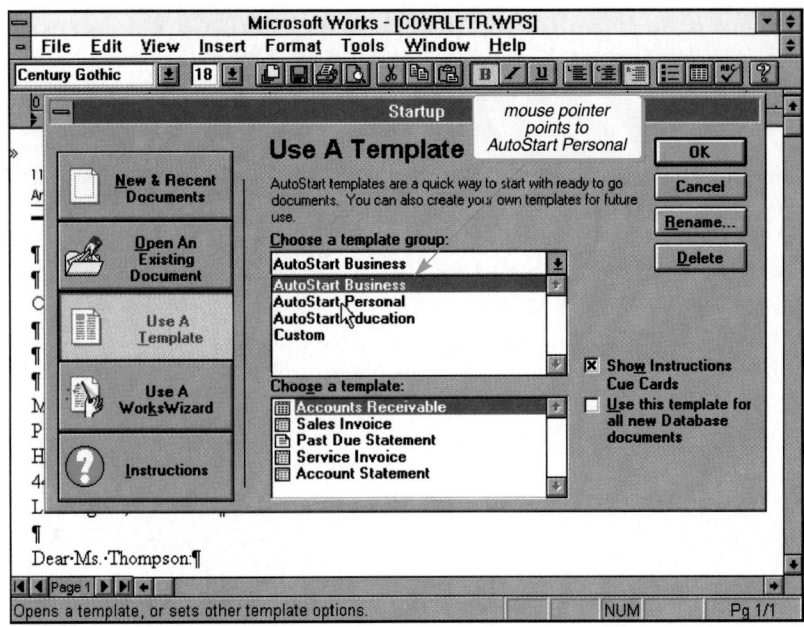

FIGURE 2-44

STEP 4 ▶

Select AutoStart Personal in the Choose a template group drop-down list box by clicking the left mouse button. Point to the word Documents in the Choose a category list box.

The words AutoStart Personal display in the Choose a template group drop-down list box (Figure 2-45). The mouse pointer points to the word Documents in the Choose a category list box.

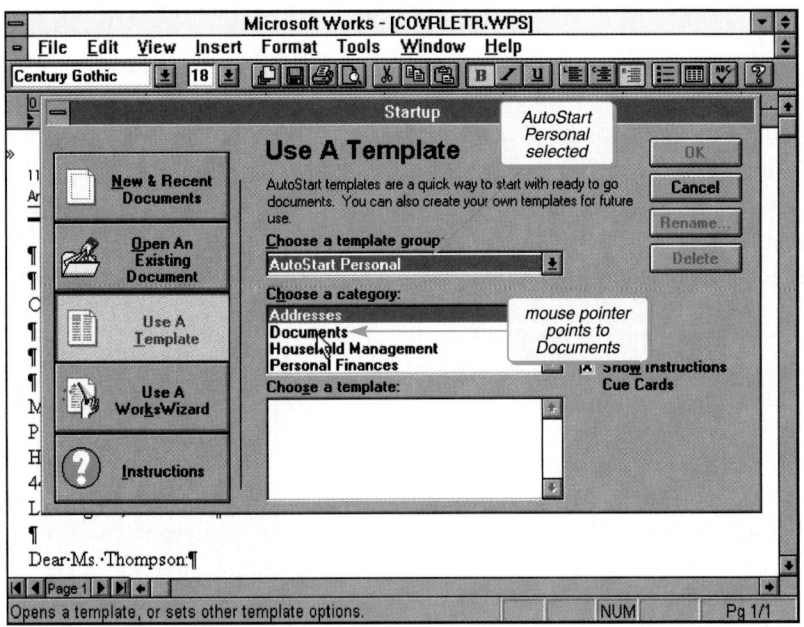

FIGURE 2-45

STEP 5 ▶

Select the word Documents by clicking the left mouse button.

The word Resume displays in the Choose a template list box and is highlighted because it is the only entry in the list (Figure 2-46).

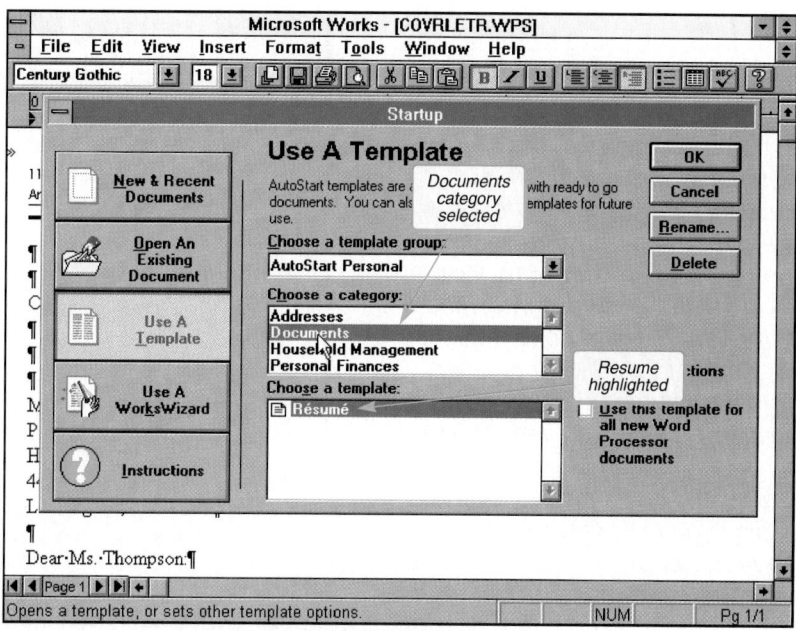

FIGURE 2-46

STEP 6 ▶

Turn off the Show Instructions Cue Cards check box, and point to the OK button.

The Show Instructions Cue Cards check box does not contain an X and the mouse pointer points to the OK button (Figure 2-47).

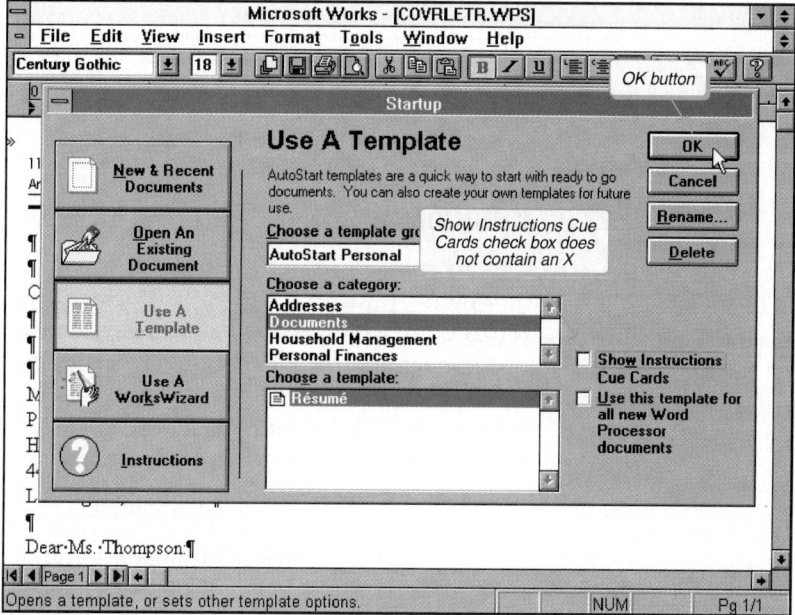

FIGURE 2-47

STEP 7 ▶

Choose the OK button in the Startup dialog box.

*Works displays the resume AutoStart template (Figure 2-48). The ruler of the AutoStart template contains a **right-align tab stop** at the 1 3/4-inch mark as indicated by the arrow with a bottom line pointing to the left. Right-alignment means data typed at the location of the right-align tab stop will be aligned on the rightmost character. Not all of the resume displays on the screen because the right margin is set at the 7-inch mark. The rightmost portion of the screen can be displayed by clicking the right scroll arrow in the lower right corner of the screen.*

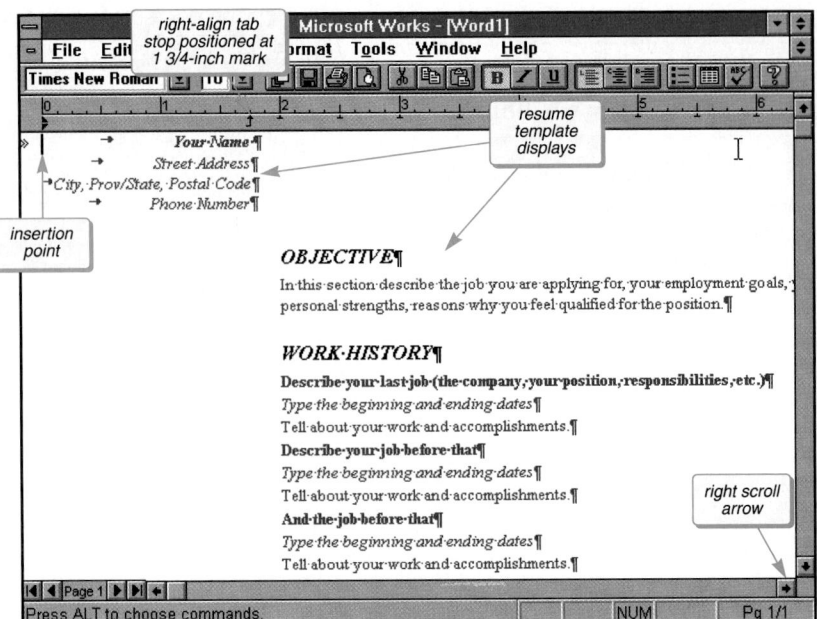

FIGURE 2-48

You are now ready to enter personalized information in the AutoStart template to create the customized resume.

Entering Information in the Resume AutoStart Template

To enter information in the resume template, highlight each line or paragraph in which you want to replace information, and then type the new information to replace the existing text. The easiest way to accomplish this is to use the word processing feature called **typing replaces selection**. Typing replaces selection means when you highlight text and then type, the text you type replaces the highlighted text. This feature, which is, by default, turned on, can be turned on or off by selecting the appropriate check box in the **Options dialog box**. The Options dialog box can be displayed by choosing the **Options command** from the **Tools menu**.

To enter personalized information in the resume AutoStart template, complete the following steps.

TO ENTER INFORMATION IN THE RESUME AUTOSTART TEMPLATE ▼

STEP 1 ►

Position the mouse pointer on the word Your in the first line of the resume template and highlight the line (sentence) by holding down the CTRL key and pressing the left mouse button at the same time. Move the mouse pointer to the right of the paragraph mark so you can easily see the highlighted words.

The words Your Name are highlighted (Figure 2-49). Notice at the top left of the resume template the right pointing arrows, indicating the TAB key has been pressed in the template. By pressing the TAB key and using the right-align tab stop, the first line is right-aligned. Notice also that the tab mark and the paragraph mark on the first line in Figure 2-49 are not highlighted. You should not highlight these marks because if you do, when you type they will be deleted.

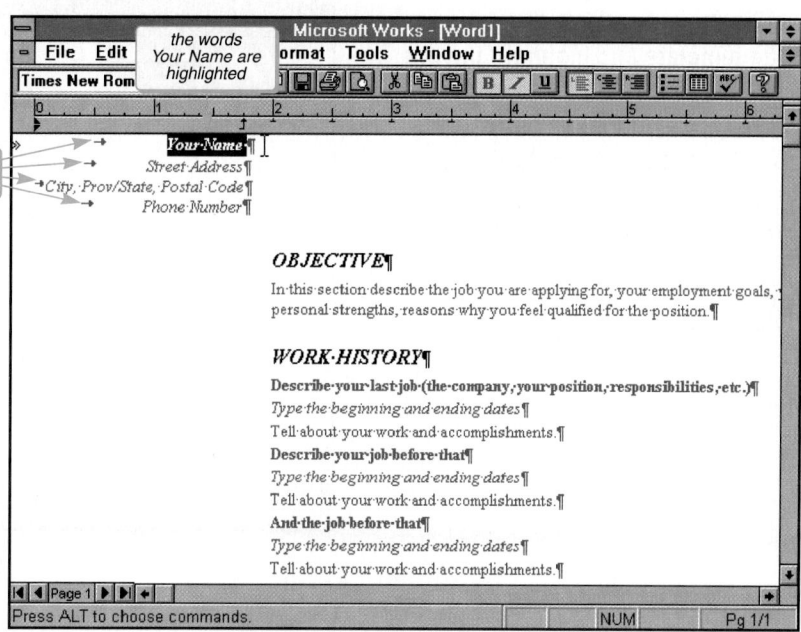

FIGURE 2-49

STEP 2 ►

Type Mary B. Riley.

As you type Mary B. Riley, the words Your Name disappear and are replaced by the words Mary B. Riley (Figure 2-50). The words are right-aligned.

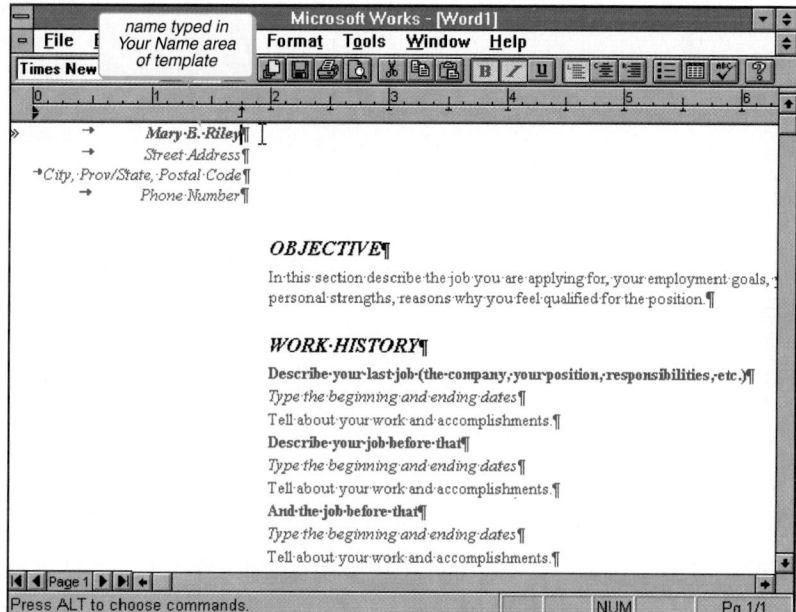

FIGURE 2-50

STEP 3 ▶

Position the mouse pointer on a word in the second line (sentence) of the template and highlight the line by holding down the CTRL key and pressing the left mouse button. Move the mouse pointer to the right of the paragraph mark so you can easily see the highlighted words.

The words Street Address are highlighted (Figure 2-51).

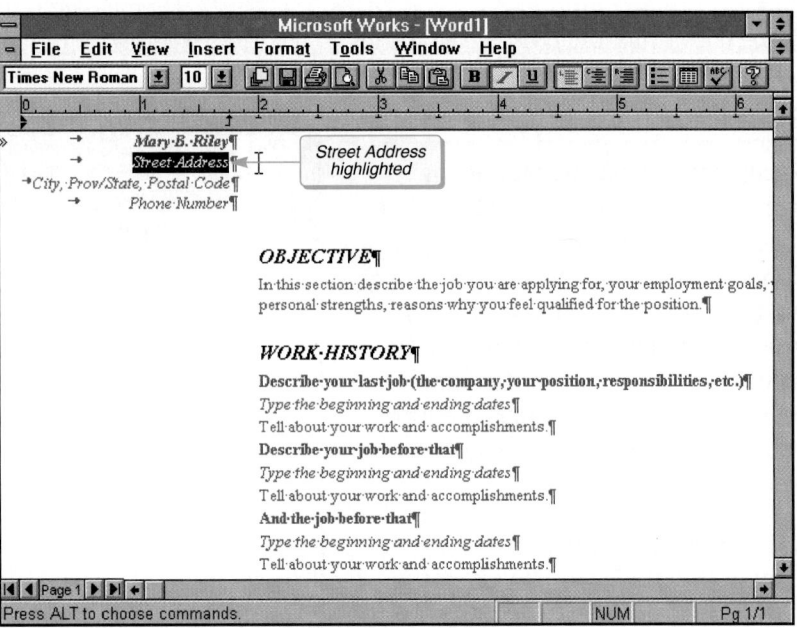

FIGURE 2-51

STEP 4 ▶

Type 1191 Walnut Avenue.

As you type the address, the words Street Address disappear and are replaced by 1191 Walnut Avenue (Figure 2-52). The address is right-aligned.

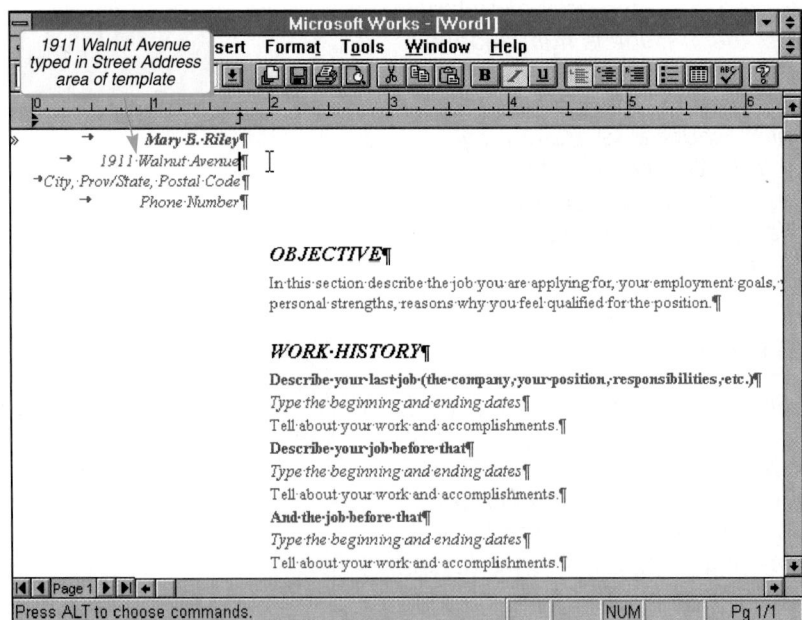

FIGURE 2-52

STEP 5 ▶

Highlight the third line for the City, Prov/State, and Postal Code. Type Anaheim, California 92805. **Highlight the fourth line containing the words Phone Number. Type** (714) 555-1219.

The portion of the resume containing the name, address, city, prov/state, postal code, and phone number is complete (Figure 2-53).

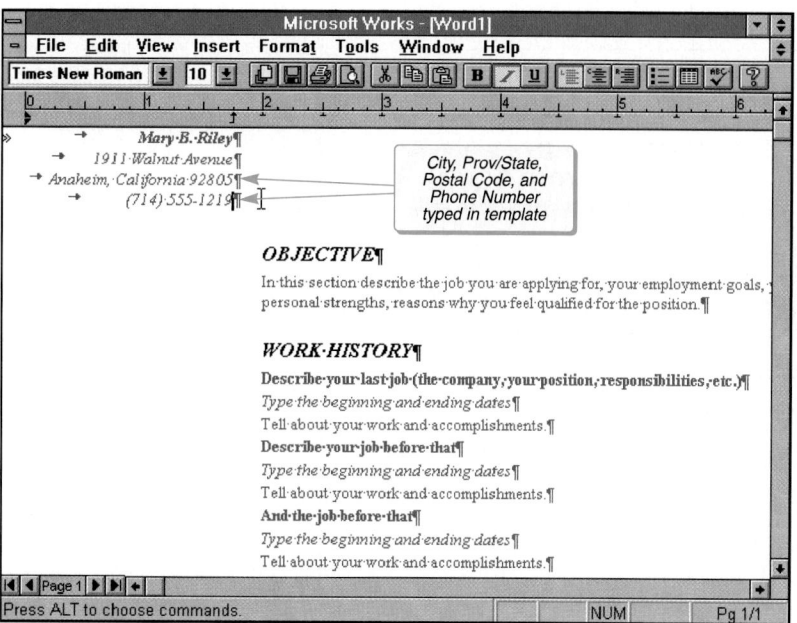

FIGURE 2-53

STEP 6 ▶

Highlight the sentence under the word OBJECTIVE. Move the mouse pointer to the right of the paragraph mark so you can easily see the highlighted words.

On the ruler, the first-line indent marker, the left-margin indent marker and the right-align tab stop are positioned at the 2-inch mark (Figure 2-54). The sentence under the word OBJECTIVE is highlighted.

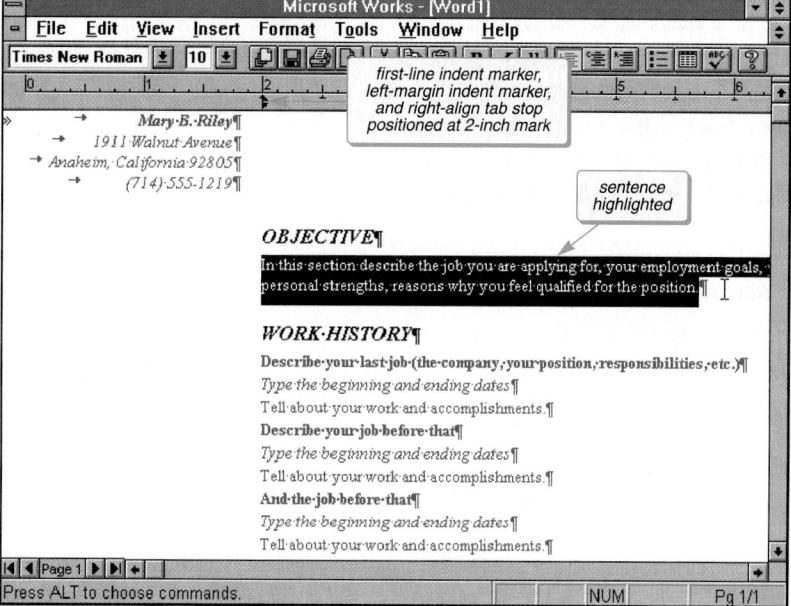

FIGURE 2-54

STEP 7 ►

Type a paragraph explaining Mary B. Riley's employment objective.

As you type, the screen display shifts to the left to display the full width of the paragraph (Figure 2-55). The right-margin indent marker is set at the 7-inch position. The typed paragraph replaces the previous paragraph.

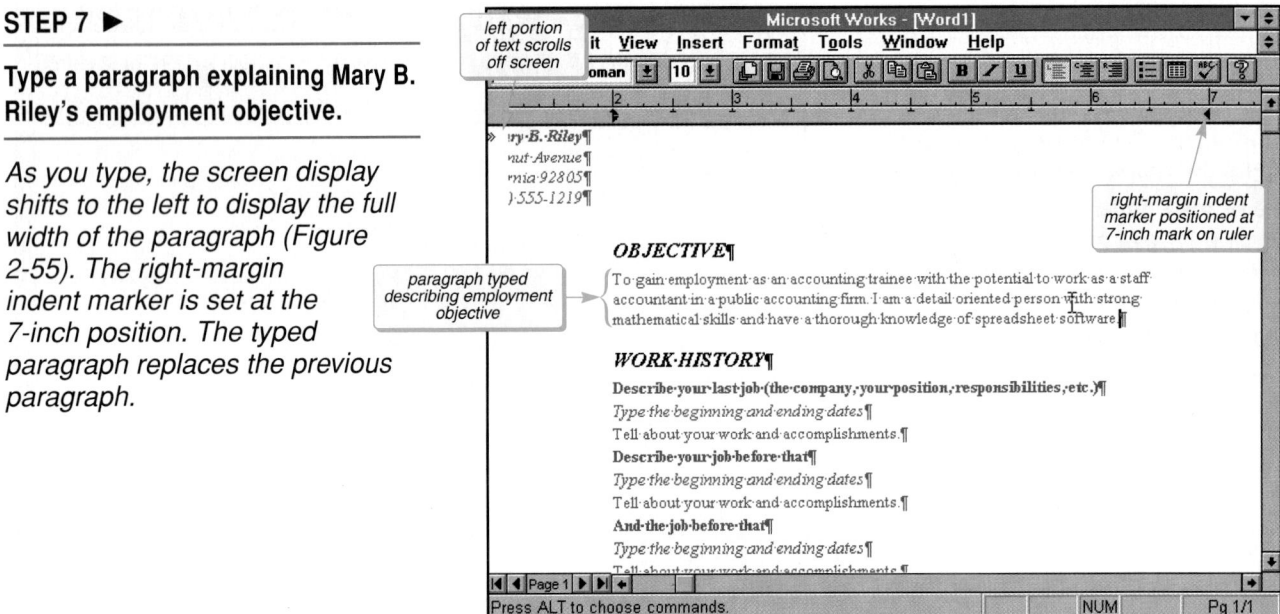

FIGURE 2-55

STEP 8 ►

Highlight the first line (sentence) under the words WORK HISTORY. Move the mouse pointer to the right of the paragraph mark so you can easily see the highlighted words.

The line indicating you are to describe your last job is high-lighted (Figure 2-56).

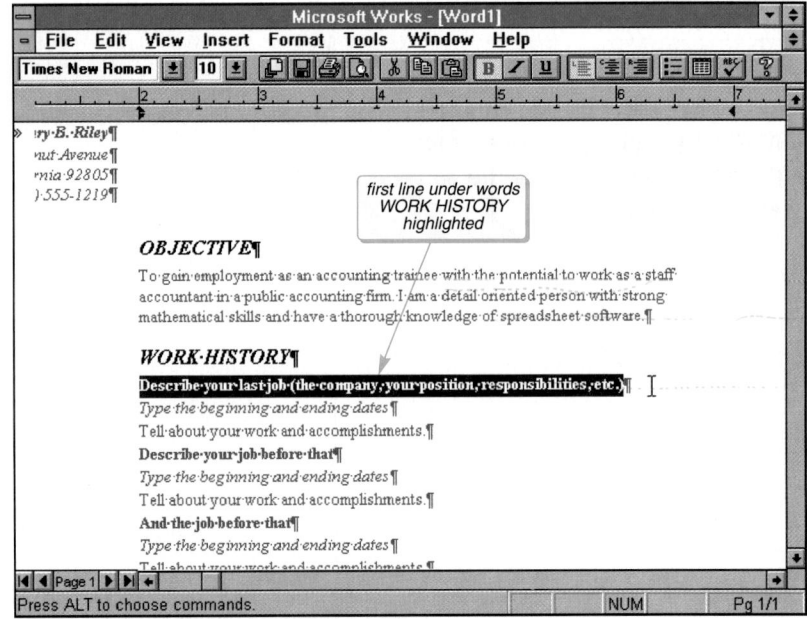

FIGURE 2-56

STEP 9 ▶

Type information concerning Mary B. Riley's last job. Highlight the next line, which indicates you should type the beginning and ending employment dates.

Information concerning Mary's work history displays (Figure 2-57). The next line is highlighted.

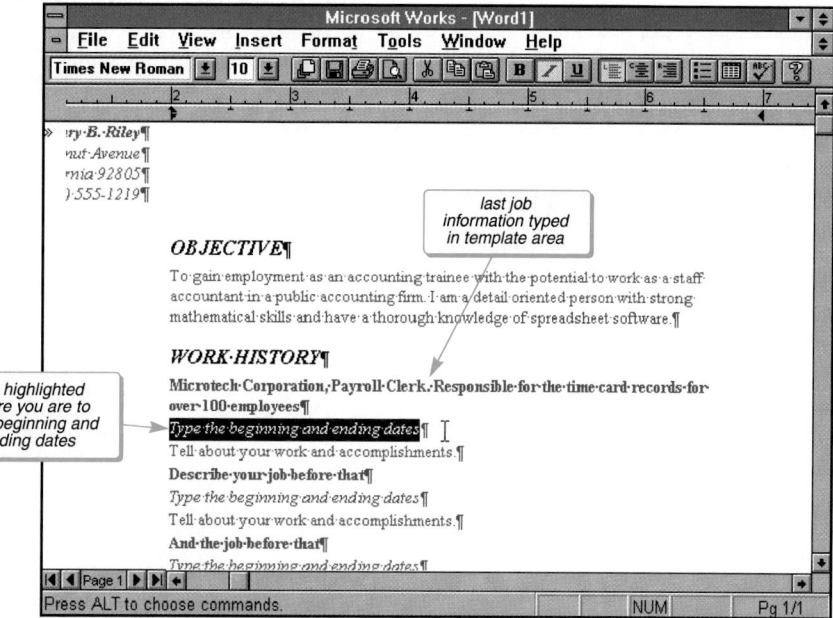

FIGURE 2-57

STEP 10 ▶

Type Mary's beginning and ending employment dates. Highlight the next line and type a paragraph describing Mary's work and accomplishments. When you have completed the paragraph, press the ENTER key. Then highlight the line, Describe your job before that.

The beginning and ending employment dates and the description of Mary's work display (Figure 2-58). Following the work description line, you have inserted a blank line to increase the readability of the resume. Templates can be modified in any way you see fit. The next line is highlighted.

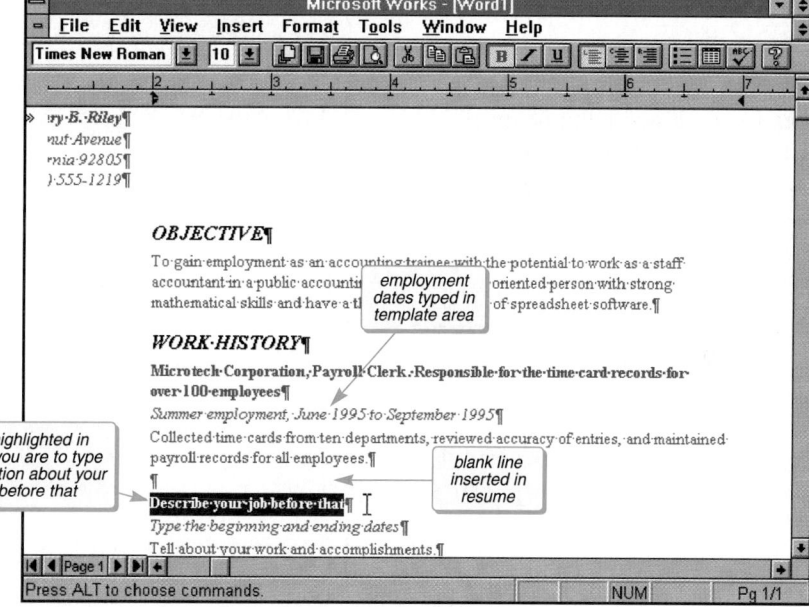

FIGURE 2-58

STEP 11 ▶

Following the techniques previously explained, type remaining entries that tell about Mary's work history. Because she has only had three jobs, the last three lines in the WORK HISTORY portion of the resume must be deleted. Highlight these lines by dragging in the left margin.

As you type, previously entered resume information will scroll off the screen. The last three lines in the WORK HISTORY portion of the resume are highlighted (Figure 2-59).

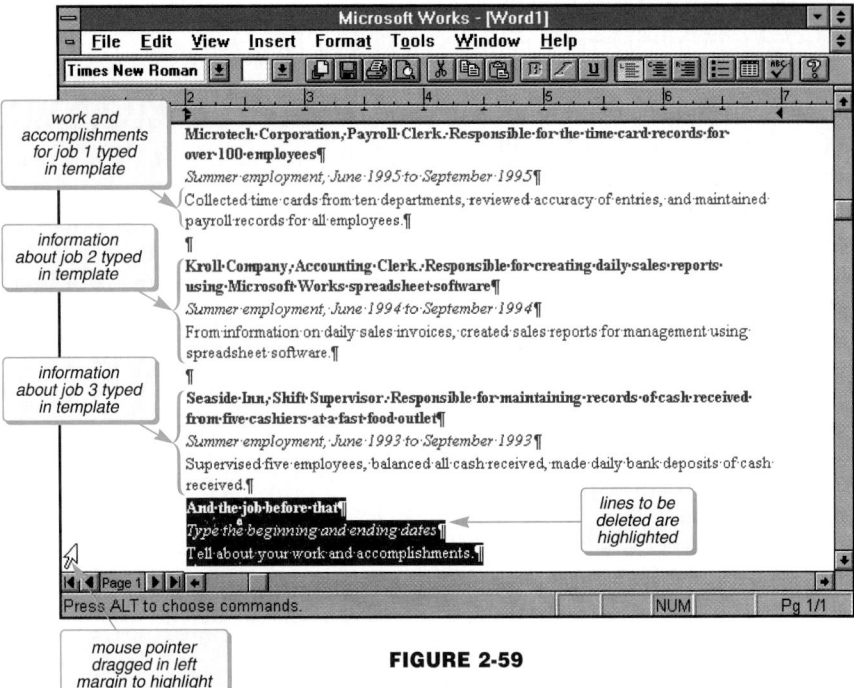

FIGURE 2-59

STEP 12 ▶

Press the DELETE key. Complete the remaining entries in the resume following the techniques previously explained. For the information to enter, reference the resume in Figure 2-1 on page W2.3. After all entries are completed, click the beginning of document button on the scroll bar to return to the beginning of the resume.

The first portion of the resume displays (Figure 2-60).

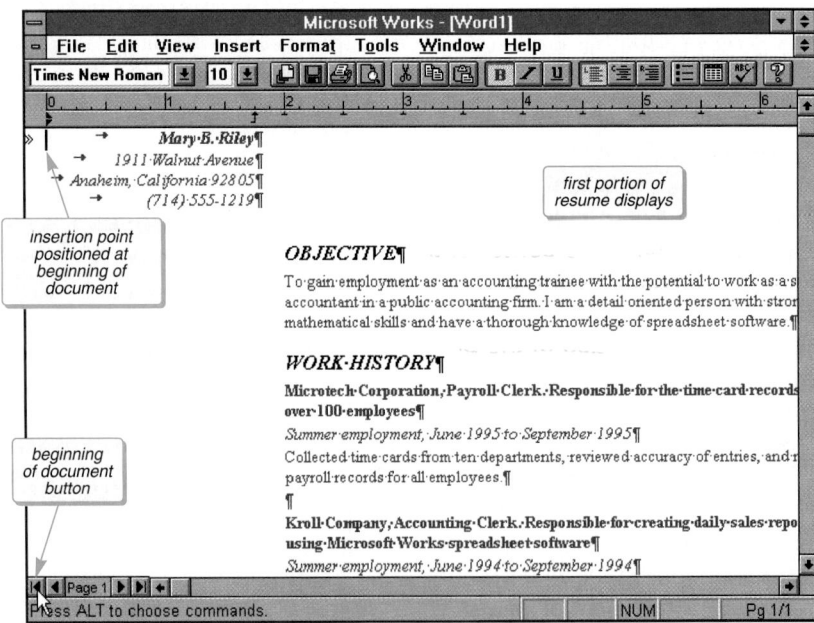

FIGURE 2-60

The resume data has now been completely entered based upon the format of the AutoStart template

Adding a Title to the Resume

In the previous steps, you entered an extra blank line following categories within the resume to make the resume more readable. A template can be modified in any manner you see fit to fill your needs. The template acts only as a starting point. For example, in the resume in Figure 2-1 on page W2.3, the title Resume prints at the top of the document. Because the word Resume is not a part of the template, the word, in 16 point Times New Roman bold italic font, must be added to the document.

Complete the following steps to add the title Resume to the document.

TO ADD INFORMATION TO AN AUTOSTART TEMPLATE ▼

STEP 1 ►

Ensure that the insertion point is positioned at the beginning of the document. Press the ENTER key twice to add two blank lines at the beginning of the document. Position the insertion point in front of the first paragraph mark. Click the Center Align button to center the first paragraph mark.

Two blank lines display at the top of the document (Figure 2-61). The first paragraph mark is positioned at the 3 1/2-inch mark on the ruler, which is the center of the 7-inch line. Notice that the Bold button on the Toolbar is recessed and the B on the face of the button is red in color. This occurs because the first line in the resume is bold, and this characteristic stays with the newly created paragraph marks placed at the top of the screen.

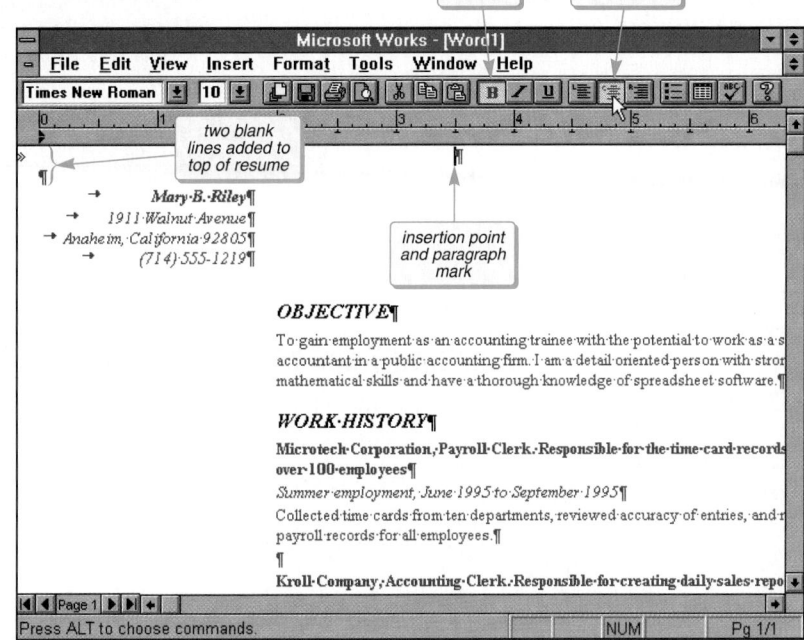

FIGURE 2-61

STEP 2 ▶

**Press the CAPS LOCK key. Type
RESUME. Press the CAPS LOCK key
again. Highlight the word by
positioning the insertion point
within the word and double-clicking
the left mouse button. Change the
font size to 16 point using
techniques previously explained.
Click the Italic button on the Toolbar.**

*The word RESUME displays in 16
point Times New Roman bold italic
font (Figure 2-62).*

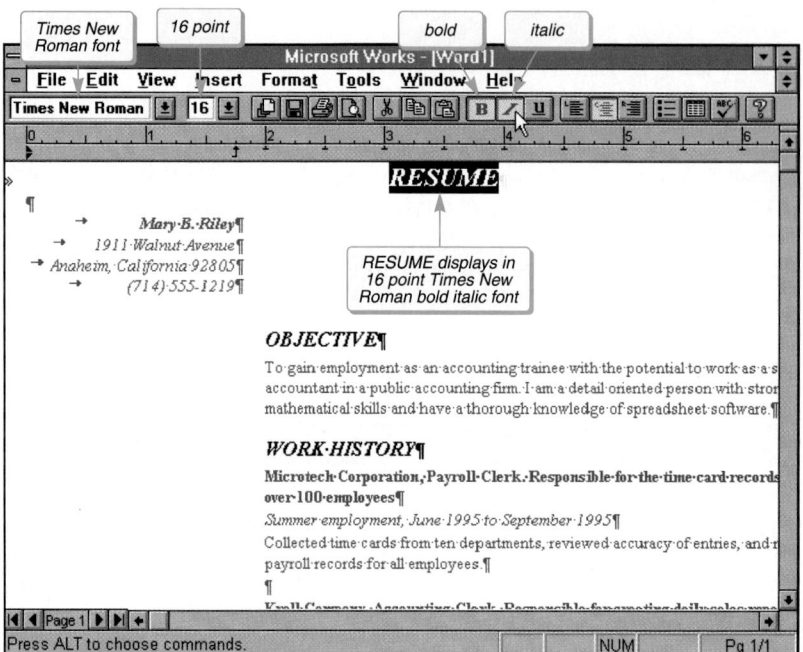

FIGURE 2-62

Checking Spelling and Using Print Preview

The resume is now complete. You should check the spelling of the document using the Works Spelling Checker and make any needed corrections using the steps specified below.

TO CHECK SPELLING

Step 1: Position the insertion point at the beginning of the document.
Step 2: Click the Spelling Checker button on the Toolbar.
Step 3: If the Spelling Checker stops at any words, take the appropriate action to either correct the word or accept the word.
Step 4: When the Microsoft Works dialog box displays telling you the spelling check is finished, click the OK button in the dialog box.

After checking the spelling, use the steps below to preview the completed document to ensure it will print properly.

TO USE PRINT PREVIEW

Step 1: Click the Print Preview button on the Toolbar.
Step 2: If necessary, zoom in on the document to review the document.
Step 3: Click the Cancel button in the Print Preview screen to return to the document.

Saving the Resume Document

After you create the resume, you should save the resume on a diskette. To save the resume, complete the following steps.

TO SAVE THE RESUME

Step 1: Click the Save button on the Toolbar.
Step 2: In the Save As dialog box, type the filename `RESUME1`.
Step 3: Select drive A from the Drives drop-down list box if necessary.
Step 4: Choose the OK button in the Save As dialog box.

Printing the Resume

Printing the resume is the final step in creating the document. If the entries you have previously used in the Print dialog box apply to the resume, complete the following step to print the resume.

TO PRINT THE RESUME

Step 1: Click the Print button on the Toolbar.

The resume will print as formatted. Figure 2-63 illustrates the completed resume.

RESUME

Mary B. Riley
1191 Walnut Avenue
Anaheim, California, 92805
(714) 555-1219

OBJECTIVE

To gain employment as an accounting trainee with the potential to work as a staff accountant in a public accounting firm. I am a detail oriented person with strong mathematical skills and have a thorough knowledge of spreadsheet software.

WORK HISTORY

Microtech Corporation, Payroll Clerk. Responsible for the time card records for over 100 employees
Summer employment, June 1995 to September 1995
Collected time cards from ten departments, reviewed accuracy of entries and maintained payroll records for all employees.

Kroll Company, Accounting Clerk. Responsible for creating daily sales reports using Microsoft Works spreadsheet software
Summer employment, June 1994 to September 1994
From information on daily sales invoices created sales reports for management using spreadsheet software.

Seaside Inn, Shift Supervisor. Responsible for maintaining records of cash received from five cashiers at a fast food outlet
Summer employment, June 1993 to September 1993
Supervised five employees, balanced all cash received, made daily bank deposits of cash received.

EDUCATION

Bachelor of Arts degree in Accounting, June 1995
Western State University, Los Angeles, California.
1995 - Student of the Year award, Accounting, Western State University.
1994 - 1995, President, Future Accountant's Association, Western State University.

Associate of Arts degree in Business Administration, June 1993
Western Los Angeles Community College, Santa Monica, California.
Graduated with honors.

High School Graduate, college transfer program, June 1991
Santa Monica High School, Santa Monica, California.

AWARDS/COMMUNITY SERVICE

1993 - Volunteer, Legal Aid for the Homeless Association, Los Angeles, California.
1991 - Volunteer, Admissions Clerk, Los Angeles Central Hospital.

FIGURE 2-63

If you want to display the Print dialog box to make print control changes before printing, you must use the Print command from the File menu.

Working with Multiple Documents

When you create the resume, you may want to review the letter you wrote regarding the employment opportunity. This can be accomplished by using entries in the **Window menu**. To display the letter again, perform the following steps.

TO VIEW MULTIPLE DOCUMENTS ▼

STEP 1 ►

Select the Window menu and point to COVRLETR.WPS at the bottom of the menu.

Works displays the names of the open documents at the bottom of the Window menu (Figure 2-64).

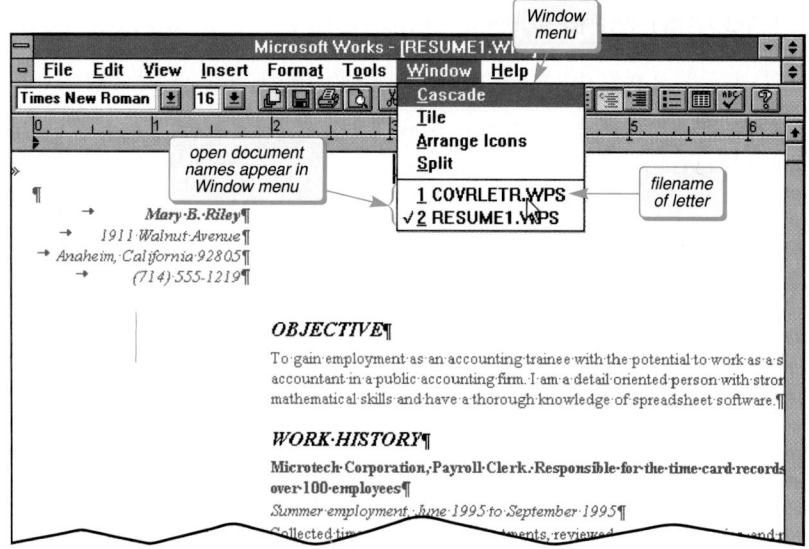

FIGURE 2-64

STEP 2 ►

Choose COVRLETR.WPS by clicking the left mouse button.

Works displays the document, COVRLETR.WPS, which is the letter (Figure 2-65). You may review or change the letter as necessary.

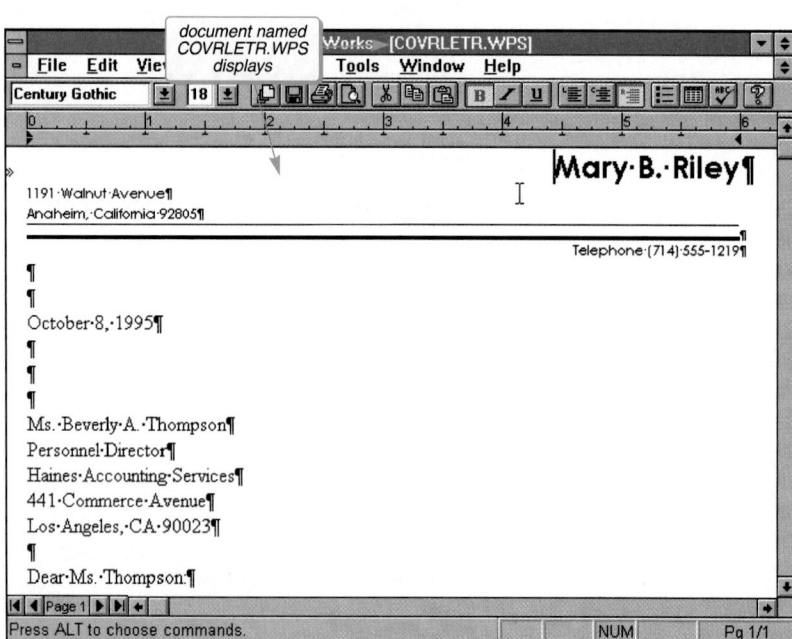

FIGURE 2-65

STEP 3 ►

To display the resume again, select the Window menu and point to RESUME1.WPS.

Works displays the Window menu (Figure 2-66)

STEP 4 ►

Choose RESUME1.WPS by clicking the left mouse button.

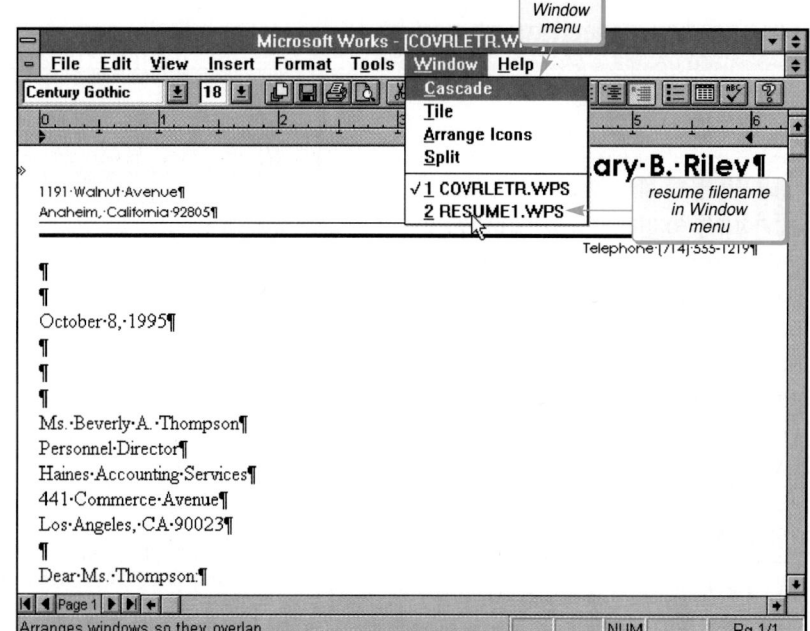

FIGURE 2-66

The resume will again display. The capability to work with multiple documents is an important feature of Works. This feature can be useful when there is a need to quickly review on the screen two or more documents that contain related information.

Quitting Works

After you have saved the letter and the resume and you have printed the letter and the resume, you can quit Works. Complete the following steps to quit Works.

TO QUIT WORKS

Step 1: Select the File menu.
Step 2: Choose the Exit Works command from the File menu.

Control is returned to Program Manager.

► CREATING CUSTOM TEMPLATES

W orks allows you to design and save your own custom templates as well as use those AutoStart templates available within Works. To create a custom template, first prepare a document using the Word Processor until it is exactly as you want. Then, use the Template button in the Save As dialog box to save the document as a template.

To save the letterhead created earlier in this project as a custom template, complete the steps on the next page.

TO CREATE A CUSTOM TEMPLATE ▼

STEP 1 ►

Start Works using the techniques previously explained. When the Startup dialog box displays, choose the Open An Existing Document button and open the LETTERHD.WPS file you saved on a diskette in drive A (see page W2.14 for this open process). After you have opened the file, select the File menu and point to the Save As command.

The LETTERHD.WPS document is open and displays on the screen (Figure 2-67). The File menu is selected and the mouse pointer points to the Save As command.

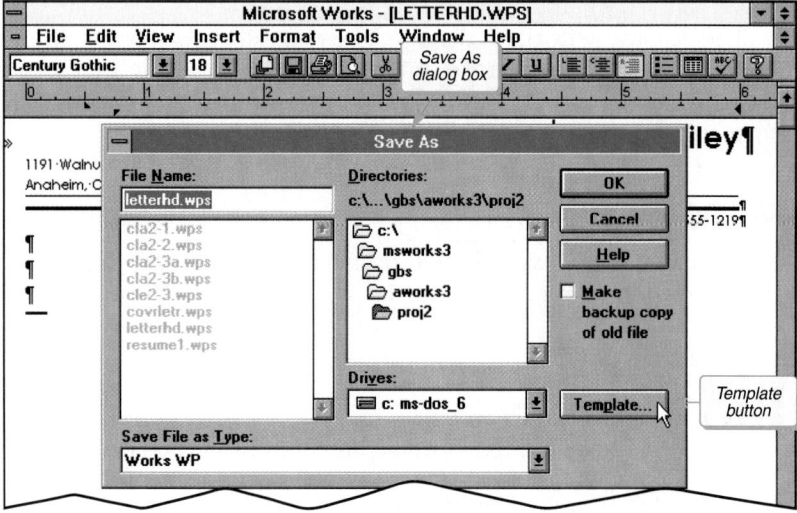

FIGURE 2-67

STEP 2 ►

Choose the Save As command by clicking the left mouse button. When the Save As dialog box displays, point to the Template button.

The Save As dialog box displays and the mouse pointer points to the Template button (Figure 2-68).

FIGURE 2-68

STEP 3 ►

Choose the Template button in the Save As dialog box.

Works displays the Save As Template dialog box (Figure 2-69). The Template Name text box contains no data.

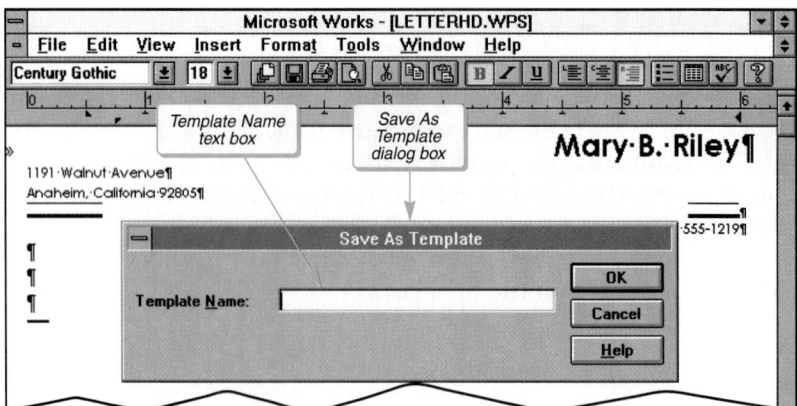

FIGURE 2-69

STEP 4 ▶

Type the name of the template, `letterhead`, and point to the OK button.

The name of the template, letterhead, displays in the Template Name text box (Figure 2-70). The mouse pointer points to the OK button.

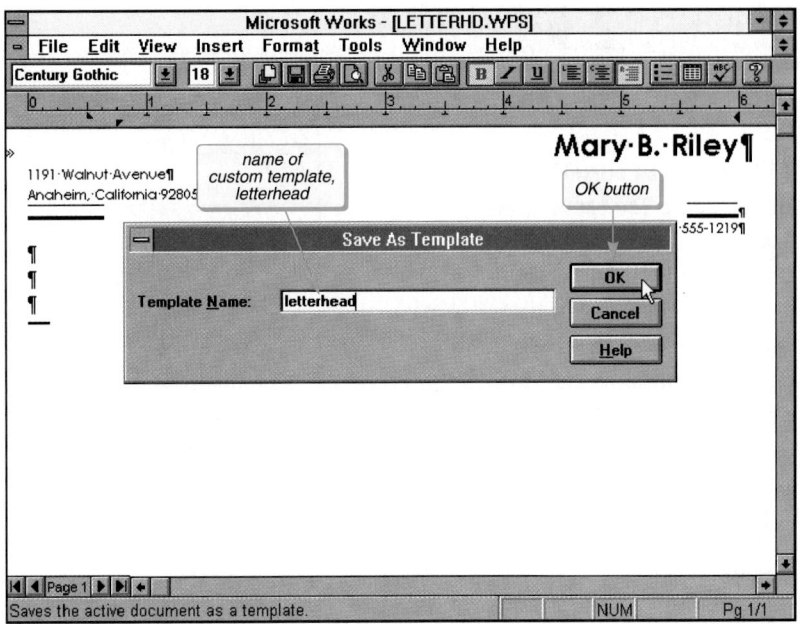

FIGURE 2-70

STEP 5 ▶

Choose the OK button in the Save As Template dialog box.

The template is saved in the Custom template group and control returns to the open document, which is the LETTERHD.WPS document (Figure 2-71). The template is saved on the hard disk drive on which the Works software is saved.

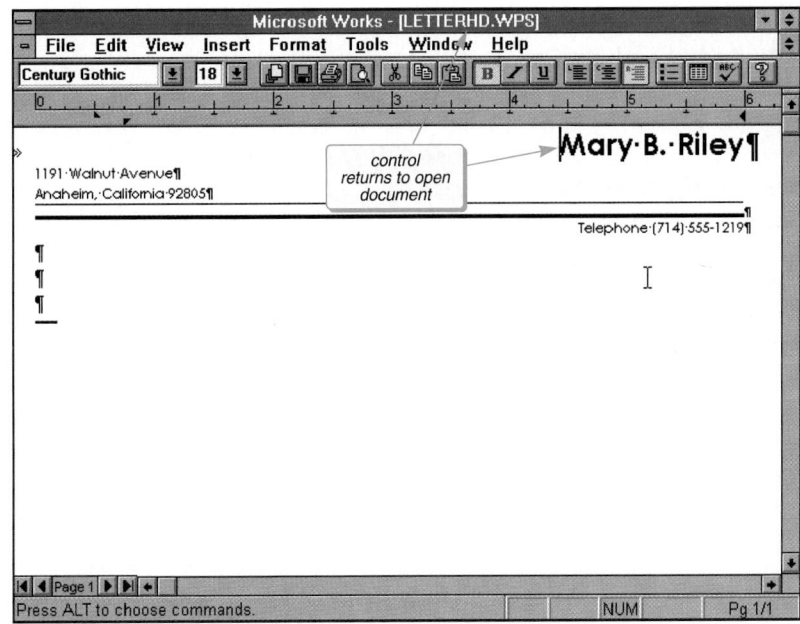

FIGURE 2-71

Using Custom Templates

Once you have created a custom template, you can use it in the same manner as you used the resume AutoStart template provided by Works. To use the letterhead custom template, complete the steps on the next page.

TO USE A CUSTOM TEMPLATE ▼

STEP 1 ▶

If Works is not currently active, start Works using the techniques previously explained. When the Startup dialog box displays, choose the Use A Template button. If Works is currently active, select the File menu and choose the Templates command. Then, click the Choose a template group drop-down list box arrow and point to Custom in the list.

Works displays the Startup dialog box (Figure 2-72). The Use A Template group button is recessed and the text in the button is red. The Choose a template group list displays and the mouse pointer points to Custom.

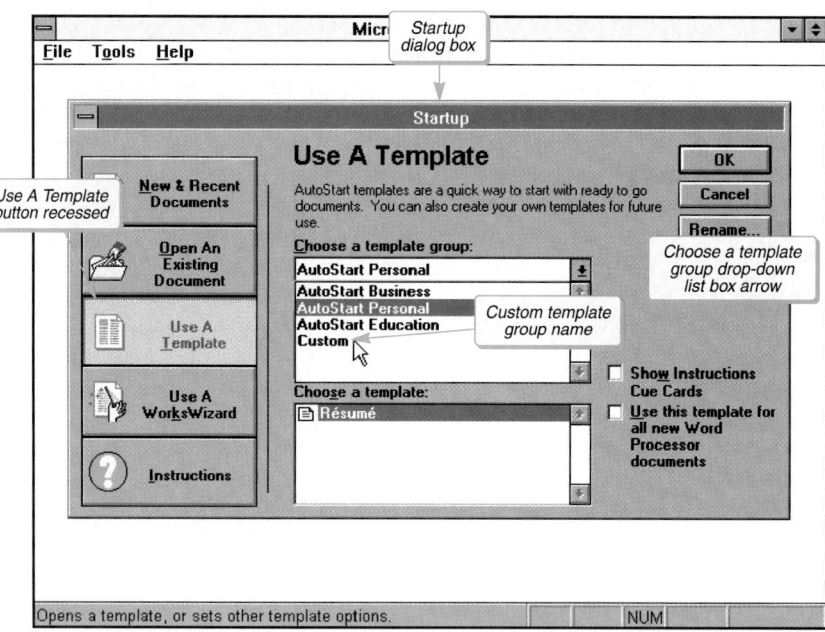

FIGURE 2-72

STEP 2 ▶

Select Custom and point to the OK button in the Startup dialog box.

The Custom group is selected (Figure 2-73). In the Choose a template list, the template name, letterhead, is selected because it is the only custom template. If more than one name appeared in the list, you would have to select a custom template to use.

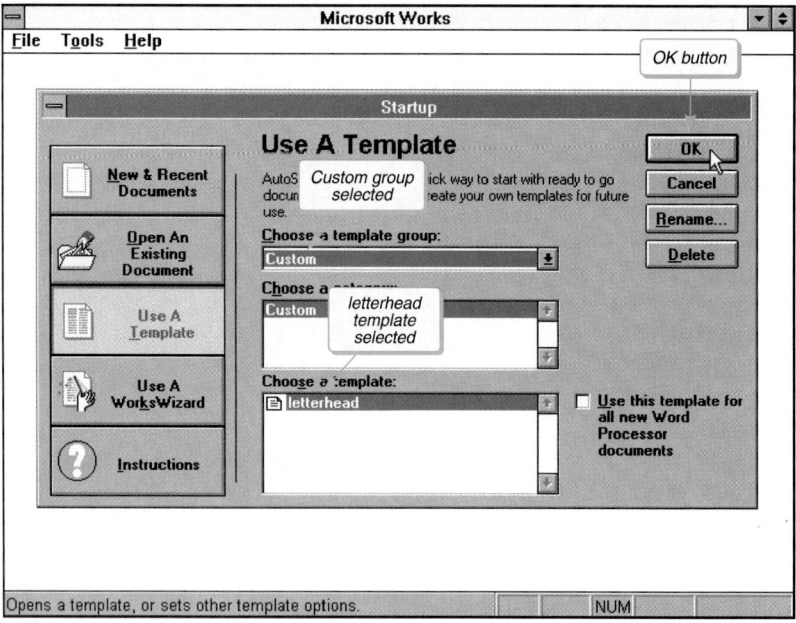

FIGURE 2-73

STEP 3 ▶

Choose the OK button in the Startup dialog box.

The letterhead template displays on the screen (Figure 2-74). Note that the document name is Word1, not LETTERHD.WPS. A template is not the same as a document file.

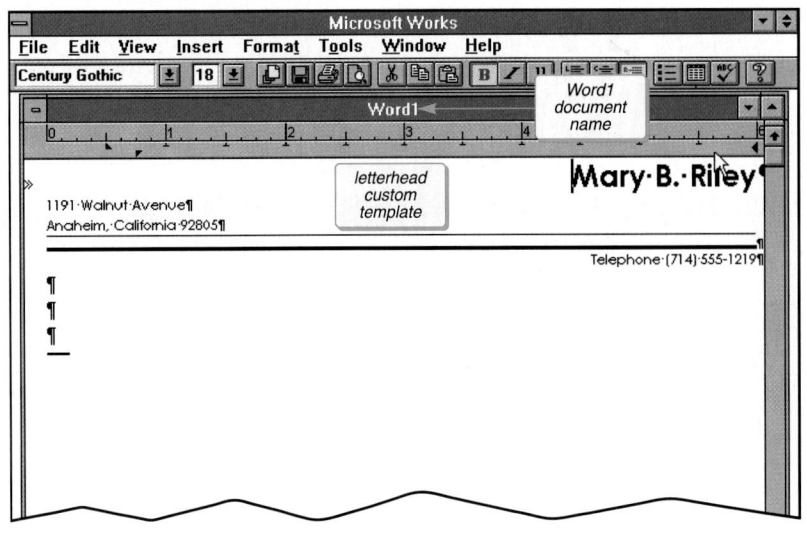

FIGURE 2-74

You can create custom templates for any need you have. Custom templates can also be created for the Spreadsheet and Database tools within Works.

▶ PROJECT SUMMARY

In this project, you learned how to create a business letter and a resume. Using a WorksWizard, you also learned how to design and create a letterhead. In the letter, you learned how to type a numbered list with a hanging indent. This required the use of the left-margin indent marker and the first-line indent marker. To check the spelling of a document, you used the Spelling Checker button on the Toolbar.

Using the steps and techniques presented in this project, you learned how to create a resume using a Works AutoStart template and how to create and use a custom template. In addition, you learned how to view two open documents using the Window menu.

▶ KEY TERMS

AutoStart template *(W2.2)*
block letter *(W2.4)*
complimentary close *(W2.4)*
first-line indent marker *(W2.20)*
hanging indent *(W2.20)*
inside address *(W2.4)*
Learning Works button *(W2.6)*
left-margin indent marker *(W2.20)*
letterhead *(W2.2)*
mixed punctuation *(W2.18)*
Open An Existing Document button *(W2.14)*

Open dialog box *(W2.15)*
Options command *(W2.34)*
Options dialog box *(W2.34)*
Page Setup command *(W2.5)*
Paragraph command *(W2.23)*
resume *(W2.2)*
right-align tab stop *(W2.34)*
right-margin indent marker *(W2.20)*
salutation *(W2.4)*
Spelling Checker button *(W2.24)*
Spelling command *(W2.28)*
Spelling dialog box *(W2.24)*

TAB key *(W2.20)*
Templates command *(W2.31)*
Tools menu *(W2.34)*
typing replaces selection *(W2.34)*
Use A WorksWizard button *(W2.6)*
Window menu *(W2.44)*
WorksWizard *(W2.2)*
WorksWizards command *(W2.6)*

In Microsoft Works, you can accomplish a task in a number of ways. The following table provides a quick reference to each task presented in this project with its available options. The commands listed in the Menu column can be executed using either the keyboard or mouse.

Task	Mouse	Menu	Keyboard Shortcuts
Create a New File		From File menu, choose Create New File	
First-Line Indent	Drag first-line indent marker on ruler	From Format menu, choose Paragraph	
Hanging Indent	Use first-line indent marker/left-margin indent marker	From Format menu, choose Paragraph	Press CTRL+H
Left-Margin Indent	Drag left-margin indent marker on ruler	From Format menu, choose Paragraph	
Right-Align Tab Stop		From Format menu, choose Tabs	
Spelling Checker	Click Spelling Checker button	From Tools menu, choose Spelling	
Switch Between Open Windows		From Window menu, choose a file name at bottom of menu	Press CTRL+F6 or CTRL+SHIFT+F6
Undo Hanging Indent		From Format menu, choose Paragraph	Press CTRL+Q

S T U D E N T   A S S I G N M E N T S

STUDENT ASSIGNMENT 1
True/False

Instructions: Circle T if the statement is true or F if the statement is false.

T F 1. To create a letterhead, you can use a WorksWizard.

T F 2. To create a resume, use a WorksWizard.

T F 3. You should use a six-inch wide line for a long letter.

T F 4. A long letter should use top and bottom margins of 1 inch on paper 11 inches in length.

T F 5. To use a WorksWizard, choose the Use A WorksWizard button in the Startup dialog box.

T F 6. You can open an existing file by clicking the Open An Existing File button in the Welcome to Microsoft Works dialog box.

T F 7. When typing a long letter, insert three blank lines between the date line and the inside address.

T F 8. When using mixed punctuation, place a comma after each line in the inside address.

T F 9. To create a hanging indent, press the TAB key, then begin typing.

T F 10. To set the left-margin indent marker, position the insertion point and click.

W2.50

T F 11. The first-line indent marker is the set of two small triangles on the left side of the ruler.
T F 12. Preset tab stops are set every one inch on the ruler.
T F 13. Use the CTRL+Q key combination any time you want to remove all paragraph formatting from a paragraph at one time.
T F 14. The Spelling command on the Tools menu can be used to cause Works to check the spelling in a document.
T F 15. If Works detects a word that is not in the dictionary, you can ignore all further occurrences of the word in a document by clicking the Ignore All button.
T F 16. The Works Spelling Checker ignores duplicate adjacent words in a document.
T F 17. You can open an AutoStart template by clicking the AutoStart Template button on the Toolbar.
T F 18. Before typing over information in an AutoStart template, you must press the INS key on the keyboard.
T F 19. To move between two open windows, select a filename from the Window menu.
T F 20. When you create a template, Works stores it in the Custom group.

STUDENT ASSIGNMENT 2
Multiple Choice

Instructions: Circle the correct response.

1. To create a letterhead for a letter, you can use _____.
   a. an AutoStart template
   b. a WorksWizard
   c. the Page Setup command from the File menu
   d. the Letterhead check box in the Options dialog box
2. To open a WorksWizard dialog box, _____.
   a. click the Use A WorksWizard button in the Startup dialog box
   b. choose the WorksWizard command from the Format menu
   c. click the Learning Works button on the Toolbar
   d. click the WorksWizard button on the Toolbar
3. When typing a long letter, you should use a six-inch wide line. This requires left and right margins of _____ each when using 8.5-inch wide paper.
   a. six inches
   b. one inch
   c. 1.25 inches
   d. .75 inch
4. One method of creating a hanging indent is to use the _____.
   a. first-line indent marker and the left-margin indent marker on the ruler
   b. first-line indent marker and the right-margin indent marker on the ruler
   c. Page Setup command from the File menu
   d. Printer Setup command from the File menu
5. The first-line indent marker is positioned by _____.
   a. clicking the left mouse button on the ruler
   b. dragging the first-line indent marker on the ruler
   c. choosing the Tabs command from the Format menu
   d. pressing the SHIFT+F keys
6. To check the spelling in a document, use the _____.
   a. Spelling Checker button on the Toolbar
   b. Options command from the Tools menu
   c. CTRL+Q keys
   d. CTRL+S keys

STUDENT ASSIGNMENT 2 (continued)

7. When using the Works spelling checker, a word that is not found in the dictionary can be _____.
   a. ignored
   b. added to the dictionary
   c. changed
   d. all of the above

8. To remove all paragraph formatting, use the _____.
   a. Page Setup command from the File menu
   b. SHIFT+Q keys
   c. SHIFT+ENTER keys
   d. CTRL+Q keys

9. To move between two open windows, _____.
   a. close one file and open another file
   b. choose the Create New File command from the File menu
   c. select the Window menu and choose one of the filenames at the bottom of the menu
   d. choose the Open Existing File command from the File menu

10. To save a custom template, _____.
   a. choose the Save Custom Template command from the File menu
   b. choose the Template button in the Save As dialog box
   c. choose the Use A Template button in the Startup dialog box
   d. choose the Template command from the Tools menu

STUDENT ASSIGNMENT 3
Understanding the Ruler

Instructions: In the spaces provided, identify each of the marks on the ruler in Figure SA2-3.

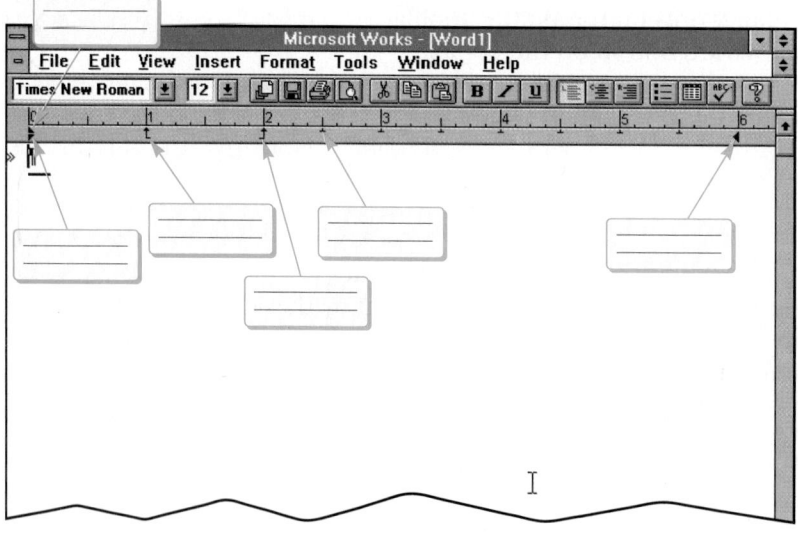

FIGURE SA2-3

STUDENT ASSIGNMENT 4
Understanding Menus and Commands

Instructions: In the spaces provided in the MENU column, write the name of the menu that contains the commands listed in the COMMAND column.

COMMAND   **MENU**

Paragraph command   _____

Page Setup command   _____

Spelling command   _____

Templates command   _____

WorksWizards command   _____

STUDENT ASSIGNMENT 5
Creating a Numbered List

Instructions: In the space provided, explain the steps necessary to create the numbered list in the letter illustrated in Figure SA2-5.

FIGURE SA2-5

Steps: _____

_____

_____

STUDENT ASSIGNMENT 6
Understanding the Works Spelling Checker

Instructions: In the space provided, explain the steps necessary to correct the spelling of the word, Personnell, in the letter shown in Figure SA2-6.

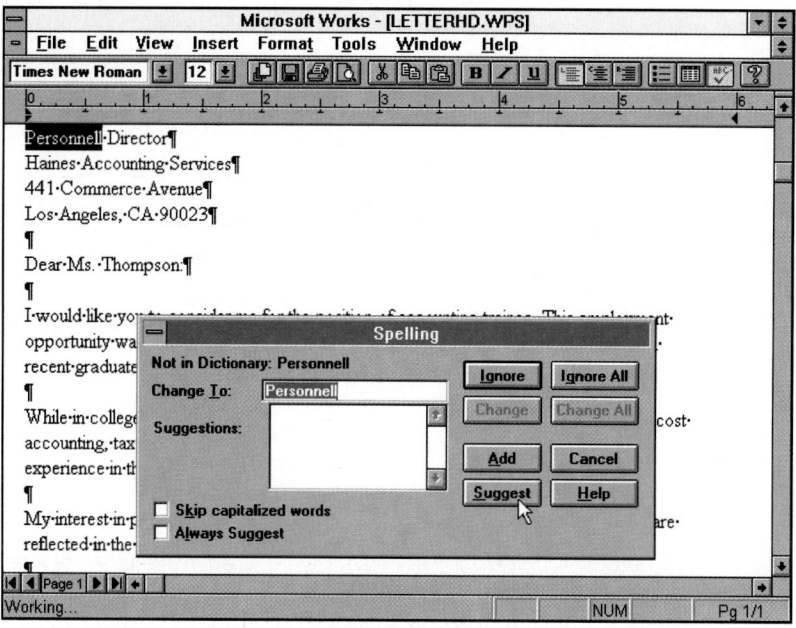

FIGURE SA2-6

Steps: _____

_____

_____

COMPUTER LABORATORY EXERCISES

COMPUTER LABORATORY EXERCISE 1
Using the Help Menu

Instructions: Perform the following tasks using a computer.

1. Start the Microsoft Works Word Processor tool.
2. Select the Help menu.
3. Choose the Contents command from the Help menu.
4. Scroll down to display all of the Reference Information section of the screen. Point to the words Command reference. When pointing to the green, underlined words, the mouse pointer becomes the shape of a hand with a pointing finger. Click the words, Command reference. A screen displays with the title Command reference.

5. On the Command reference screen, point to the words Word Processor and click. A screen displays with the name, Word Processor: Command reference.
6. On the Word Processor: Command reference screen, a list of menu names displays. Click the words Tools menu. Another screen displays with the title, Word Processor: Command reference and displays commands on the Tools menu.
7. Click the words Spelling command.
8. Information displays about the Spelling command.
9. In the space provided, write the purpose of each of the boxes and buttons in the Spelling dialog box.

BOXES AND BUTTONS   **PURPOSE**

Change To   _____

Ignore   _____

Ignore All   _____

Change   _____

Change All   _____

Suggest   _____

Always Suggest   _____

Add   _____

Skip Capitalized Words   _____

Cancel   _____

10. Scroll down. At the bottom of the Spelling command screen, point to the topic, Checking spelling and counting words, and click. Review and print the contents of this screen. Answer the following questions.

    a. How many words are in the dictionary?

    _____

    b. What menu and command should you use to count words in a document?

    _____

11. From the Help File menu, choose the Exit command to return to the Works Word Processor.

COMPUTER LABORATORY EXERCISE 2
Creating A Personal Letterhead

Instructions: Using the WorksWizard, create and print a copy of each of the six styles of letterheads. Select different lines and pictures for each letterhead. Use your name, address, and phone number in each of the examples. Then, design a letterhead that you would like to place on your own personal stationery. Save your personal letterhead as a file on a diskette in drive A. Print your personal letterhead. Turn in a copy of each of the letterheads created to your instructor.

COMPUTER LABORATORY EXERCISE 3
Using the Spelling Checker

Instructions: Start the Works Word Processor tool. Open the CLE2-3.WPS file on the Student Diskette that accompanies this book. This file contains the letter created in Project 2 (see Figure CLE2-3). One or more spelling errors have been incorporated into the letter. Perform the following tasks.

1. Use the spelling checker to check the spelling of the letter.
2. Make corrections as required.
3. Print a copy of the corrected letter.
4. Turn in a printed copy of the incorrect and the corrected letters to your instructor.

Mary B. Riley

1191 Walnut Avenue
Anaheim, California 92805
_____

Telephone (714) 555-1219

October 8, 1995

Ms. Beverly A. Thompson
Personnel Director
Haines Acounting Services
441 Commerce Avenue
Los Angeles, CA 90023

Dear Ms. Thompson:

I would like you to consider me for the position of of accounting trainee. This employment opportunity was advertised in the October 5 edition of the Los Angeles Times. I am a recent graduate of Western State University with a major in Accounting.

While in college I completed 30 units of accounting. Course work included classes in cost accounting, tax accounting, and managerial accounting. I have also had recent work expereince in the accounting department of Microtech Corporation.

My interest in pursueing a career in the accounting profession and my leadership skills are reflected in the following acomplishments while attending Western State University:

1. During my two years of college at Western State University, I maintained a grade point average of 3.5.

2. I served as President of the Future Accountant's Association for one year and was responsible for planing all professional activities.

My resume is enclosed for your review. I will call on October 12, 1995, to set an appointtment for a personel interview.

Sincerely,

Mary B. Riley

FIGURE CLE2-3

COMPUTER LABORATORY ASSIGNMENT 1
Writing a Business Letter

Purpose: To provide experience using a WorksWizard to create a personalized letterhead, saving the letterhead as a Works template or a Works document file, and typing a professional business letter.

Problem: You are to retype the letter shown in Figure CLA2-1 using the Works Word Processor.

Instructions:

1. Create a letterhead using a Works-Wizard. You may use a design similar to that used in Project 2 or you may design your own professional letterhead.
2. Either save the letterhead as a template on the hard disk or as a document file on a diskette, depending on the directions from your instructor. Use a template name or a filename consisting of the initials of your first and last names followed by the assignment number and the letter L. Example: TC2-1L.
3. If you want, exit Works.
4. Start the Works Word Processor, if necessary, and retype the letter in Figure CLA2-1 using 12 point Times New Roman font. Use the letterhead you created in Step 1.

Mr. John N. Michaels
925 Woods Street
Anaheim, CA 92805

November 3, 1995

Ms. Roberta R. Greene
Personnel Director
Burlington Distribution Company
321 Commerce Avenue
Los Angeles, CA 92808

Dear Ms. Greene:

In response to your November 1 advertisement in the Long Beach Times, I would like you to consider me for the position of computer software system specialist.

Although I do not have full-time paid work experience as a software system specialist, I have completed course work in word processing, spreadsheet, and database software while attending South Coast College.

My interest in computers in business is reflected in the following accomplishments while attending South Coast College:

1. I was employed as a student assistant in the personal computer laboratory at South Coast College for one year.
2. I maintained an A average in the five computer software classes I took while attending South Coast College, and I recently completed requirements for a Certificate in Personal Computer Software.

I would like to put my knowledge of computer software to work for your company. Enclosed is my resume for your review. I will call your office on November 10, 1995 to arrange for a personal interview.

Sincerely,

John N. Michaels

FIGURE CLA2-1

COMPUTER LABORATORY ASSIGNMENT 1 (continued)

5. Check the spelling in the letter using the Works spelling checker.
6. Save the letter on a diskette in drive A. Use a filename consisting of the initials of your first and last names followed by the assignment number. Example: TC2-1.
7. Print the letter.
8. Follow directions from your instructor for turning in this assignment.

COMPUTER LABORATORY ASSIGNMENT 2
Writing a Resume

Purpose: To provide experience using an AutoStart template to write a resume.

Problem: Prepare the resume shown in Figure CLA2-2 using an AutoStart template.

Instructions:

1. Revise the resume in Figure CLA 2-2 using the resume AutoStart template provided by Works.
2. Check the spelling of the resume using the Works spelling checker.
3. Save the resume on a diskette in drive A using a filename consisting of the initials of your first and last names followed by the assignment number. Example: TC2-2.
4. Print a copy of the resume.
5. Follow directions from your instructor for turning in this assignment.

```
                                 Resume

John N. Michaels            925 Woods Street, Anaheim,
                               California 92805


Employment Objective        Gain employment as a computer
                               software specialist or trainer

Education                   South Coast College, Computer
                               Technology Major, 1992-94
                            High School Graduate, Yorba Linda
                               High School, 1988-1992

Employment                  South Coast College, Computer
                               Laboratory Assistant, 1993-94.
                               Helped students with
                               computers, installed software,
                               wired the LAN, wrote macros
                               for Excel.
                            Computer Software Store, Retail
                               Sales Representative, Summer,
                               1993. Sold software and
                               hardware, installed computer
                               systems for customers,
                               arranged store inventory.

Award & Honors              Outstanding Student, Computer
                               Technology, South Coast
                               College, 1994
                            Certificate in Personal Computer
                               Software, South Coast College,
                               1994
```

FIGURE CLA2-2

COMPUTER LABORATORY ASSIGNMENT 3
Creating a Letterhead and Writing a Business Letter and Resume

Purpose: To provide experience creating a personalized letterhead and writing a business letter and resume.

Problem: The advertisement shown in Figure CLA2-3a appeared in the October 25 issue of the *Lakewood Press*. You have been asked by a friend to prepare a cover letter and a resume to respond to the employment opportunity advertised in the newspaper. You have been provided with the biographical information shown in Figure CLA2-3b to assist you in preparing the letter and resume.

Help Wanted - Recent college graduate with knowledge of Microsoft Works for Windows to work in training department assisting accounting staff in use of personal computers. Respond to: Ms. Marie D. Rosario, Personnel Director, Maywood Enterprises, P.O. Box 2073, Dana Point, California 92629. Please include resume.

FIGURE CLA2-3a

Sylvia A Goldmeyer

I was born in Santa Rosa, California on September 4, 1972 and attended Lincoln High School, graduating with honors in 1990. My major was business. After graduating from high school, I attended Lakewood College in Long Beach, California. I received an Associate of Arts degree in Accounting in June 1993. I then attended Computer Arts University and graduated with Bachelor of Science degree in Computer Information Systems in June 1995.

While at Lakewood College, I took four courses in accounting. These courses included beginning accounting, intermediate accounting, managerial accounting, and cost accounting. I received A grades in all accounting classes. My minor was Business Information Systems, and I completed 15 units of class work in the use of personal computer software. Course work included the use of Microsoft Works for Windows, which covered word processing, spreadsheet, and database software. I was voted the outstanding accounting student by the Business Administration faculty in June 1994. I also served as President of the Computer Club at Lakewood College in Spring 1994.

At Computer Arts University, I continued my education with courses in programming (Visual Basic), applications software (a variety of applications software packages), systems analysis and design, and a specialized course in teaching computer applications. I completed my degree magna cum laude.

During the summer of 1993, I worked as a payroll clerk for Lakewood Business Services. While employed there, I developed several large spreadsheets for clients to assist the clients in their five year sales projections.

For a reference, please contact Mr. Hubert L. Green, President, Lakewood Business Services, (714) 555-0997.

My current address is 1980 Oak Avenue, Lakewood, CA 92808. My Phone number is (213) 555-4233.

FIGURE CLA2-3b

(continued)

COMPUTER LABORATORY ASSIGNMENT 3 (continued)

Instructions:

1. Create a professional letterhead of your own design.
2. Either save the letterhead as a template on the hard disk or as a document file on a diskette, depending on the directions from your instructor. Use a template name or a filename consisting of the initials of your first and last names followed by the assignment number and the letter L. Example: TC3-3L.
3. Type a letter that includes the letterhead requesting an interview.
4. Check the spelling of the letter using the Works spelling checker.
5. Save the letter on a diskette in drive A using a filename consisting of the initials of your first and last names followed by the assignment number. Example: TC2-3.
6. Print the letter.
7. Create a resume from the available information using the Works resume template. Add a section in the resume to include references.
8. Check the spelling of the resume using the Works spelling checker.
9. Save the resume on a diskette in drive A using a filename consisting of the initials of your first and last names followed by the assignment number and the letter R. Example: TC2-3R.
10. Print the resume.
11. Follow directions from your instructor for turning in this assignment.

COMPUTER LABORATORY ASSIGNMENT 4
Creating a Letterhead and Writing a Business Letter and a Resume

Purpose: To provide experience creating a letterhead, business letter, and resume for personal use.

Problem: Prepare a cover letter and your personal resume for response to an employment opportunity advertised in your local newspaper.

Instructions:

1. Design a professional letterhead for your use containing your name, address, and phone number.
2. After creating the letterhead, save the letterhead as a file on a diskette or as a template on your hard disk.
3. Retrieve the letterhead and type a letter inquiring about a job opportunity advertised in the local paper.
4. Save the letter on a diskette.
5. Print the letter.
6. Using the Works Resume AutoStart template, type a resume based on your own qualifications.
7. Save the resume on a diskette.
8. Print the resume.
9. Follow directions from your instructor for turning in this assignment.

MICROSOFT WORKS 3.0 FOR WINDOWS

PROJECT THREE

▼

WRITING AND EDITING A RESEARCH REPORT WITH TABLES

WRITING AND EDITING A RESEARCH REPORT WITH TABLES

OBJECTIVES You will have mastered the material in this project when you can:

- ▶ Describe the format of a research report
- ▶ Use the Page Setup command
- ▶ Create a report header using the Headers and Footers command
- ▶ Create a footnote using the Footnote WorksWizard
- ▶ Close a footnote pane
- ▶ Insert a page break in a document
- ▶ Use the Go To command

- ▶ Use the Find command
- ▶ Replace a word in a document using the Replace command
- ▶ Use the Undo command
- ▶ Move a paragraph using the drag-and-drop method
- ▶ Use the Thesaurus command
- ▶ Use the Word Count command
- ▶ Create a spreadsheet table using OLE 2.0

▶ INTRODUCTION

I n both the business world and the academic world, writing research reports is an important task. In the business world, you might prepare reports for sales representatives, management personnel, and stockholders. In the academic world, instructors require you to write research reports as a part of course work.

Whether you are preparing a report for the business world or for class work, you should use a standard format, or style, when preparing the report. Specific standards and recommendations for writing research reports have been proposed by various professional associations. The **Modern Language Association of America (MLA)** recommends several styles that you may use when you write research reports. These styles are used by many instructors and schools throughout the United States. Project 3 uses one of the recommended MLA styles. The style used is explained in the following paragraphs.

▶ Project Three

A complete, brief research report entitled Internet is illustrated in Figure 3-1. The research report contains approximately 450 words, requires two pages of text, and includes a table. The third page contains a section entitled NOTES. The references (names of the books or other material) used in preparing the research report are in the NOTES section of the paper. The raised numbers in the text and in the NOTES section are called **superscripts**. The numbers associate portions of the text with the individual references cited on the NOTES page of the research report.

Lopez 3

NOTES

[1] William Masterson, Beginner's Guide to Using Internet (San Francisco: Computer Network Press, 1995) 13-17.

[2] Marilyn Burkenson, "Who Is Using Internet?" Business Network World 17 (July 1995): 22-25.

[3] USA Wireservice, "The New World of Communications," USA Daily 19 May 1995, Evening ed., sec. Business: 12+.

Lopez 2

All types of people use Internet, including students, librarians, scientists, engineers, university researchers, and individuals in governmental agencies. Their purpose is to communicate, exchange ideas, and gain access to knowledge. Internet is now comprised of more than 7,500 networks used by approximately 25 million people each day.[2]

Internet has a variety of uses. The main uses include electronic mail, file transfer from one computer to another, running programs on remote computers, searching files and databases, ...rs.[3]

...5 to the year 2000.

2000
200,000
50,000,000
5,000
100,000,000

...nd schools of all types, even ...ty and benefits, an Internet ...ine.

Lopez 1

Mary B. Lopez

Professor Henry R. Davis

Computer Science 101

October 19, 1995

Internet

Internet is a web of interconnecting computer networks funded by commercial and governmental organizations that allows computer-to-computer communication by millions of users throughout the world. More than one million computers of all sizes are now connected to Internet.

Internet began in 1969 under the name ARPANET. The first system involved four computers designed to demonstrate the feasibility of creating networks that would allow computers to transmit data over communications lines dispersed throughout a wide area. The network was originally designed to support users involved in research for the military. An important goal was to design networks that would not fail.[1]

The four computers forming the original ARPANET were located at the University of California at Santa Barbara, the University of California at Los Angeles, Stanford Research Institute, and the University of Utah. During the 1970s, numerous other computers and networks were added to the system. Some were privately funded and others were funded by the government. Eventually many of the privately and publicly funded networks merged to form a comprehensive interconnected network called Internet. Today, Internet consists of many different intercommunicating networks. Internet now operates in more than 40 countries throughout the world.

Internet services are designed to support scholarly research for individuals, educational institutions, and governmental agencies. Internet may also be used by commercial firms when engaged in open research. As a system, Internet is governed and regulated cooperatively without actual laws. It is operated based on codes of conduct and a common ethic.

FIGURE 3-1

Superscripts and their corresponding references are called **footnotes**. Footnotes may appear at the bottom of the page or footnotes may appear at the end of the document. Footnotes at the end of the document are sometimes called **endnotes.**

In the research report prepared in this project, the footnotes are placed at the end of the document as illustrated in Figure 3-1. This is one of the widely used MLA styles. This MLA style specifies that the title, NOTES, and related references in the form of footnotes be placed on a separate page at the end of the research report.

In this project, you will learn the word processing techniques and Works commands necessary to create the research report in Figure 3-1. You will first create the research report without the table. The table will be added later in the project.

Formatting Standards for the Research Report

When creating the research report, you should follow a number of important standards relating to formatting the document. These standards, specified by the MLA, are described in the following paragraphs and are illustrated in Figure 3-2. Follow these standards when you type the research report:

1. Double-space the research report.
2. Number all pages consecutively in the upper right corner of the manuscript, one-half inch from the top of the page. Type your last name before the page number. Leave one space between your name and the page number. This is called the report **header**.

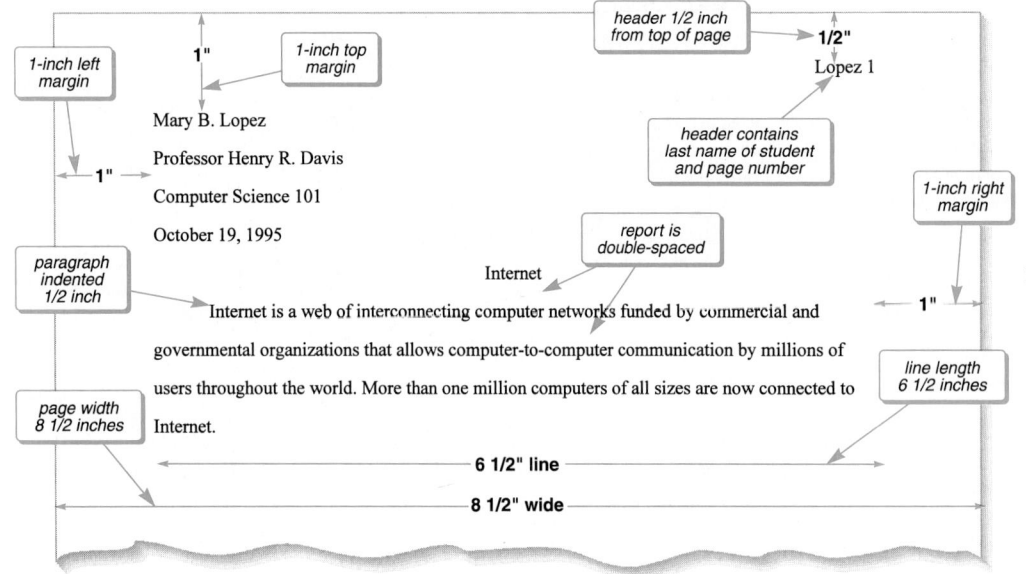

3. A brief research report does not require the use of a title page. Instead, begin one inch down from the top of the first page at the left margin. On separate lines, type your name, the instructor's name, the course title and number, and the date.

FIGURE 3-2

4. Provide a one-inch margin at the bottom of the page.
5. Provide one-inch left and right margins.
6. Indent the first line in a paragraph one-half inch.
7. Single-space after a period when using Times New Roman font or any proportional spacing font.
8. Print the research report on standard-sized paper, 8.5 inches wide by 11 inches long.

Starting Works

To create the research report, start the Works Word Processor using the procedures learned in Project 1 and Project 2. The steps are reviewed on the next page.

TO START WORKS

Step 1: Open the Microsoft Works for Windows group window.
Step 2: Double-click the Microsoft Works program-item icon.
Step 3: If necessary, choose the Start Works Now button, and then choose the
Word Processor button in the Startup dialog box.
Step 4: Maximize the application and document windows.

▶ SETTING MARGINS AND CONTROLLING THE PLACEMENT OF FOOTNOTES

Before typing the research report, you must set margins as specified by the preceding standards and indicate to Works that you want to place the footnotes at the end of the report. These tasks are accomplished using the **Page Setup command** on the File menu.

Works normally provides a one-half inch (.5") header margin, a one-inch top margin, a one-inch bottom margin, a 1.25-inch left margin and a 1.25-inch right margin. These header, top, bottom, left, and right margin sizes are Works default values; that is, the values are set when you start Works.

Because the standards for the research report indicate a one-inch left margin and a one-inch right margin, you must change Works default values. In addition, when you double-space a report, Works inserts a blank line before printing the first line on each page. The blank line occupies approximately .17 inch on the page. Therefore, to obtain a true one-inch top margin, you must specify the top margin as .83 inch. The blank line (.17 inch) and the .83 inch-setting before printing will give you a one-inch top margin. The bottom margin is not affected. To set the margins, perform the following steps.

TO SET MARGINS ▼

STEP 1 ▶

Select the File menu and point to the Page Setup command.

Works displays the File menu (Figure 3-3). The mouse pointer points to the Page Setup command.

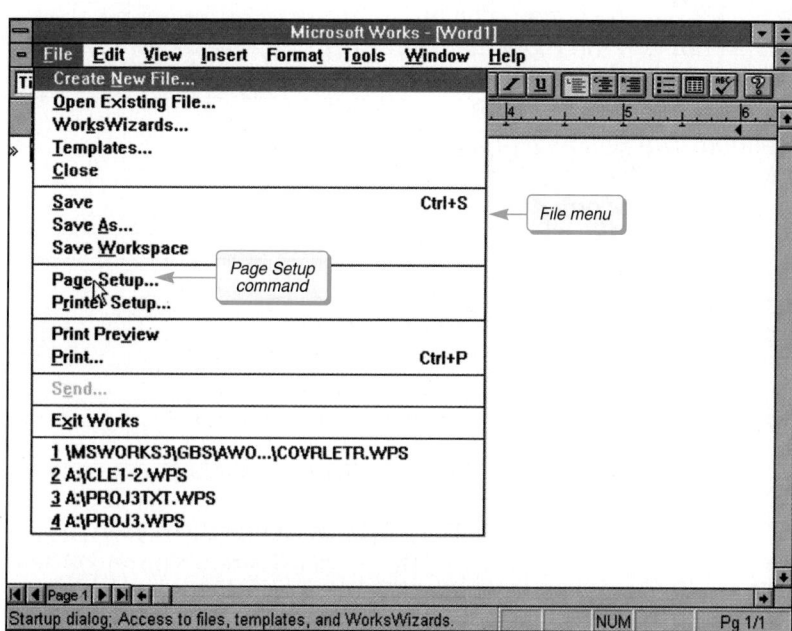

FIGURE 3-3

STEP 2 ►

Choose the Page Setup command from the File menu. If necessary, select the Margins tab in the Page Setup dialog box by clicking it.

Works displays the Margins screen within the Page Setup dialog box (Figure 3-4). Default values for the Top margin, Bottom margin, Left margin, Right margin, Header margin, and Footer margin display in their respective text boxes.

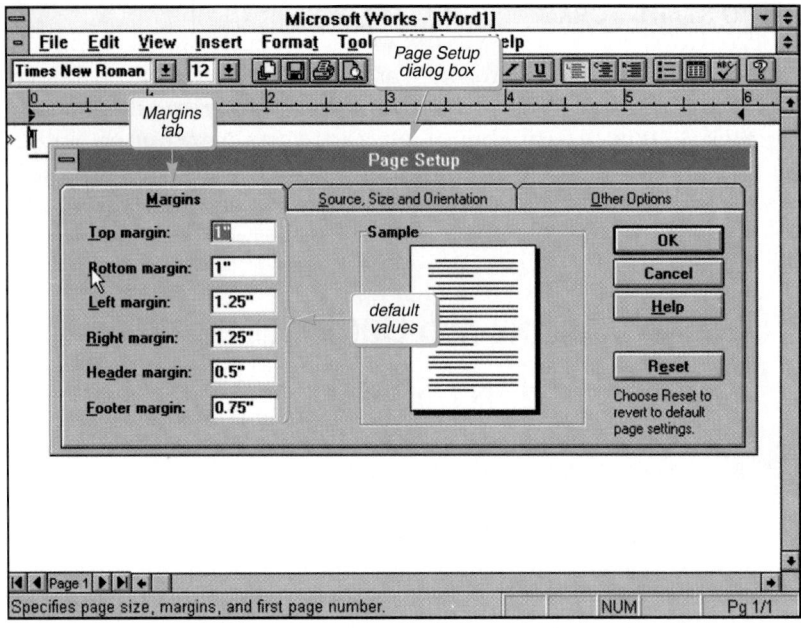

FIGURE 3-4

STEP 3 ►

Type `.83"` in the Top margin text box, press the TAB key two times to move the insertion point to the Left margin text box, and type `1"` in the Left margin text box. Press the TAB key once and type `1"` in the Right margin text box.

The Top margin text box now contains .83", and both the Left margin text box and the Right margin text box contain 1" (Figure 3-5). Other default values are not changed. The Bottom margin text box contains the default value of 1", which is the correct value. The Header margin text box contains 0.5", which is the correct value for a one-half inch top margin for the header.

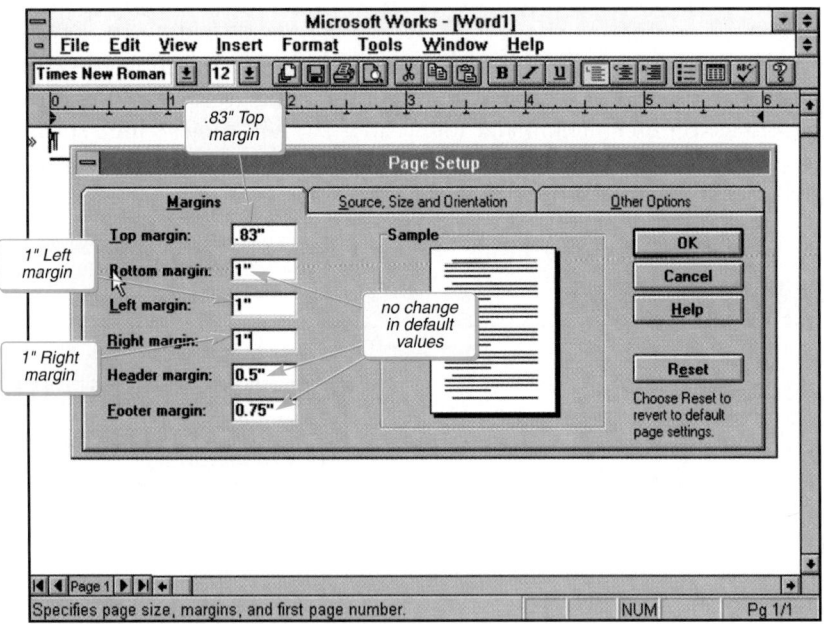

FIGURE 3-5

The Page Setup dialog box contains three separate displays you can select by pointing to and clicking the **tabs** at the top of the screen display within the dialog box. These tabs resemble the tabs on a standard file folder. Selecting the tab that contains the words, Source, Size and Orientation, will cause a screen to display that allows you to specify the paper size and how text will display when printed. Selecting the tab that contains the words, Other Options, will display a screen that allows you to direct Works to print footnotes at the end of the report. The Works default is for footnotes to print at the bottom of the page. The following steps explain how to cause footnotes to print at the end of a document.

TO PRINT FOOTNOTES AT THE END OF A DOCUMENT ▼

STEP 1 ▶

Point to the Other Options tab in the Page Setup dialog box.

The Page Setup dialog box displays on the screen (Figure 3-6). The mouse pointer points to the Other Options tab.

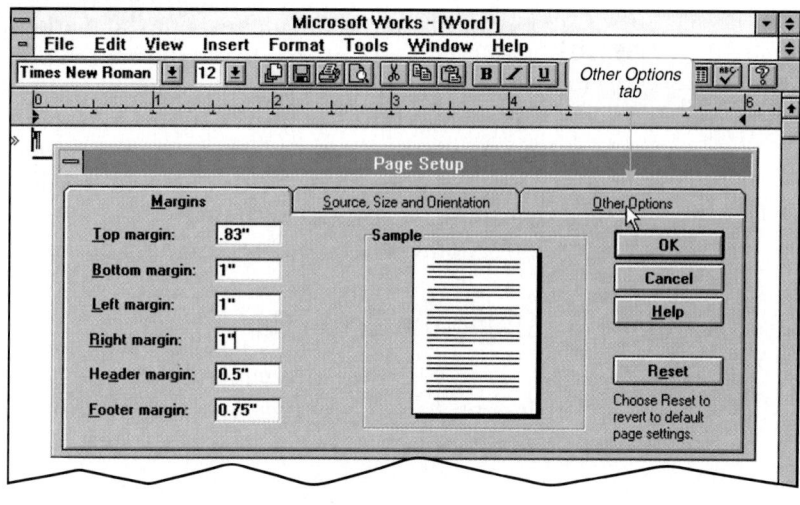

FIGURE 3-6

STEP 2 ▶

Select the Other Options tab by clicking the left mouse button. When the Other Options screen displays within the Page Setup dialog box, select the Print footnotes at end of document check box and point to the OK button.

Works displays the Other Options screen associated with the Other Options tab (Figure 3-7). Selecting the check box causes an X to appear in the Print footnotes at end of document check box. The mouse pointer points to the OK button.

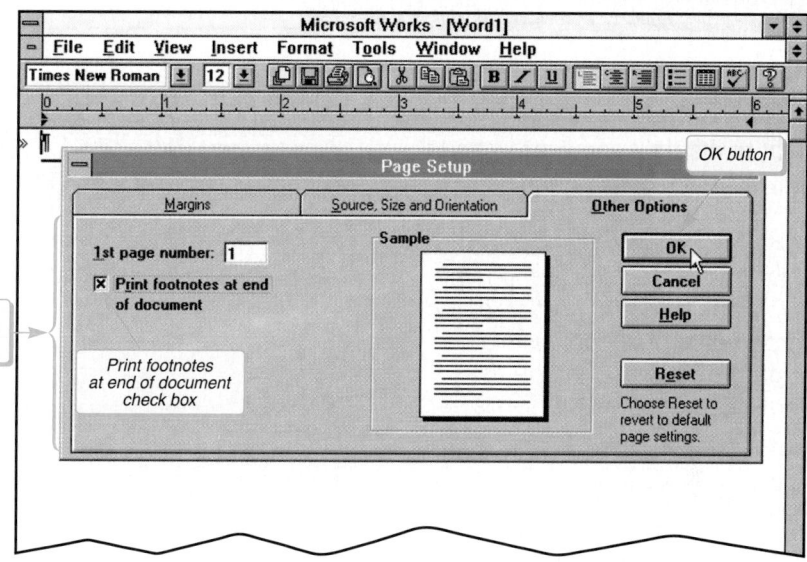

FIGURE 3-7

STEP 3 ▶

Choose the OK button in the Page Setup dialog box.

The Works Word Processor document screen displays; however, the right-margin indent marker is not visible (Figure 3-8).

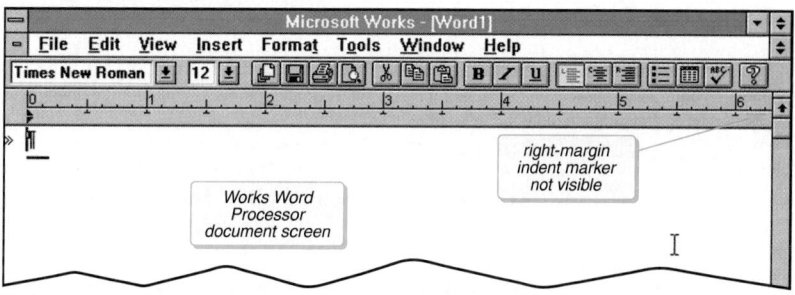

FIGURE 3-8

The right margin is no longer set at 6 inches as in Project 1 and Project 2 because a one-inch left margin and a one-inch right margin (two inches total) provide a 6.5-inch line on an 8.5-inch wide document. Works sets the right-margin indent marker at 6.5 inches, but the marker is not visible on the right side of the screen because of the size of the screen display.

The margin settings you entered in the Margins screen of the Page Setup dialog box and the entry in the Print footnotes at end of document check box in the Other Options screen of the Page Setup dialog box stay in effect when you create the research report. When you save the document and then open the document again, these values continue to be in effect. The original default values will be in effect only when you create a new document.

Using the Scroll Bar

To verify the proper setting of the right margin and to view the right-margin indent marker, you must use the scroll bar and the right scroll arrow at the bottom of the screen.

TO SCROLL THE SCREEN HORIZONTALLY ▼

STEP 1 ▶

Point to the right scroll arrow and click the left mouse button.

The entire screen moves approximately one-half inch to the left, displaying the right portion of the screen previously not visible (Figure 3-9). You can see the right-margin indent marker is set at 6.5 inches.

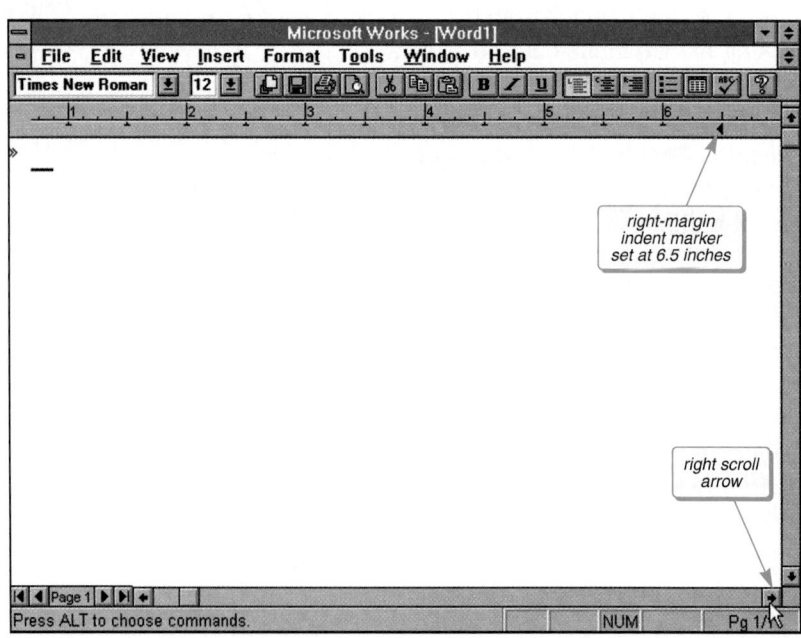

right-margin indent marker set at 6.5 inches

right scroll arrow

FIGURE 3-9

To return the screen to its normal position, position the mouse pointer on the left scroll arrow and click the left mouse button.

▶ TYPING THE RESEARCH REPORT

After setting the margins and the location for printing the footnotes, the next step in preparing the research report is to type the report header. The header consists of the student's last name on the top right side of the page followed by a blank space and then the page number (see Figure 3-2 on page W3.4).

Headers and Footers

A **header** is special text that appears at the top of every printed page in a document. A **footer** is special text that appears at the bottom of every printed page in a document. You use headers and footers to number pages and/or add a title or other types of information to the pages in a document. In the research report, you use a header to identify the student and to number the pages in the report. According to MLA standards, you are to print the header one-half inch from the top of the page. In this document, you are not using a footer. Headers and footers do not display on the screen in Normal view. They appear only on the documents you print or when you choose the Page Layout command from the View menu.

Works provides two types of headers and footers. One is the **paragraph header** or **footer** and the second is the **standard header** or **footer**. A paragraph header or footer allows you to include one or more lines in the header or footer. A standard header or footer contains only one line of text. The research report in this project contains a standard header.

To create the header, you will use the **Headers and Footers command** on the View menu to display the Headers and Footers dialog box. In the dialog box, you will type the entry, &rLopez &p. The entry, &r, is a code instructing Works to right-align the word or words that follow. The student name (Lopez) is followed by a blank space. The &p is a code that directs Works to print the page number.

Follow these steps to create a standard header for the research report.

TO CREATE A STANDARD HEADER ▼

STEP 1 ▶

Select the View menu and point to the Headers and Footers command.

Works displays the View menu (Figure 3-10). The mouse pointer points to the Headers and Footers command.

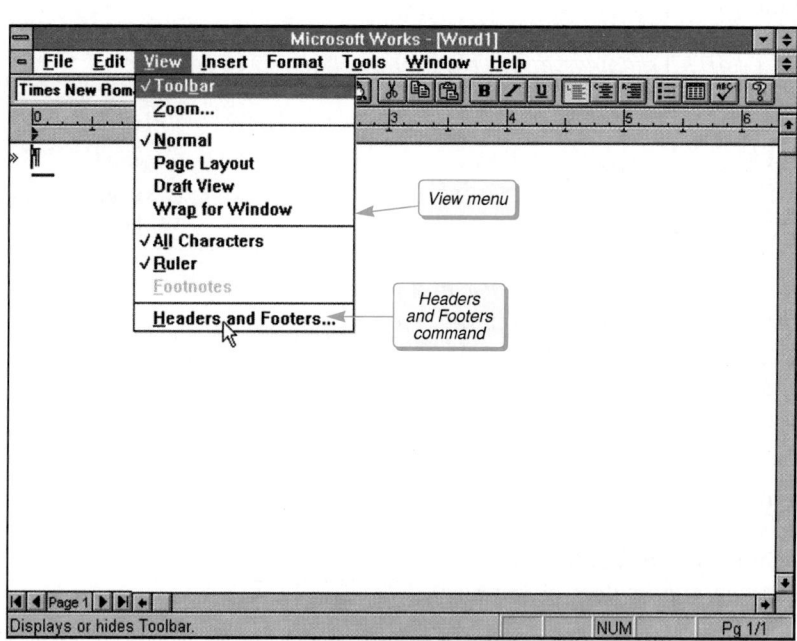

FIGURE 3-10

STEP 2 ▶

Choose the Headers and Footers command from the View menu.

Works displays the Headers and Footers dialog box (Figure 3-11).

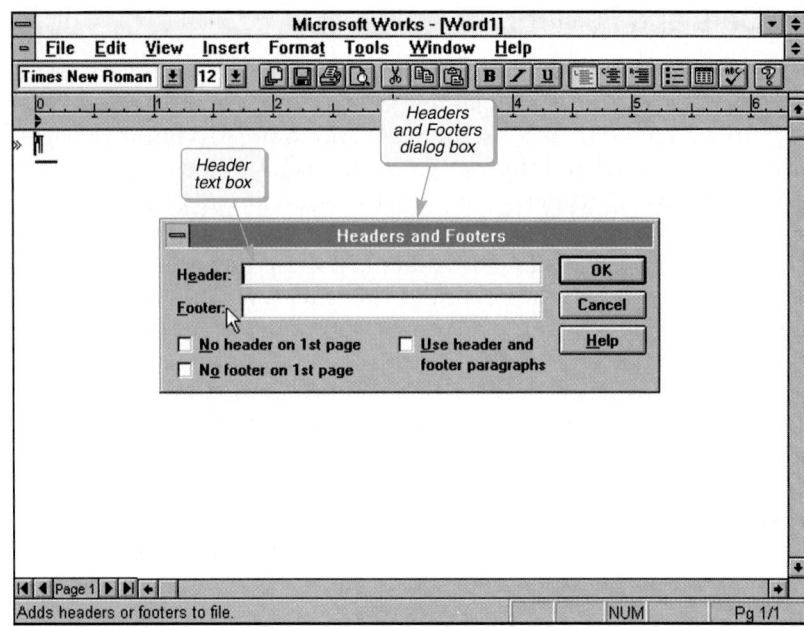

FIGURE 3-11

STEP 3 ▶

Type `&rLopez &p` **in the Header text box, and then point to the OK button.**

&rLopez &p displays in the Header text box (Figure 3-12). If you select the No header on 1st page check box in the Headers and Footers dialog box, an X appears in the box, and the header will not print on the first page. The No footer on 1st page check box operates in a similar manner. To use a paragraph header, select the Use header and footer paragraphs check box.

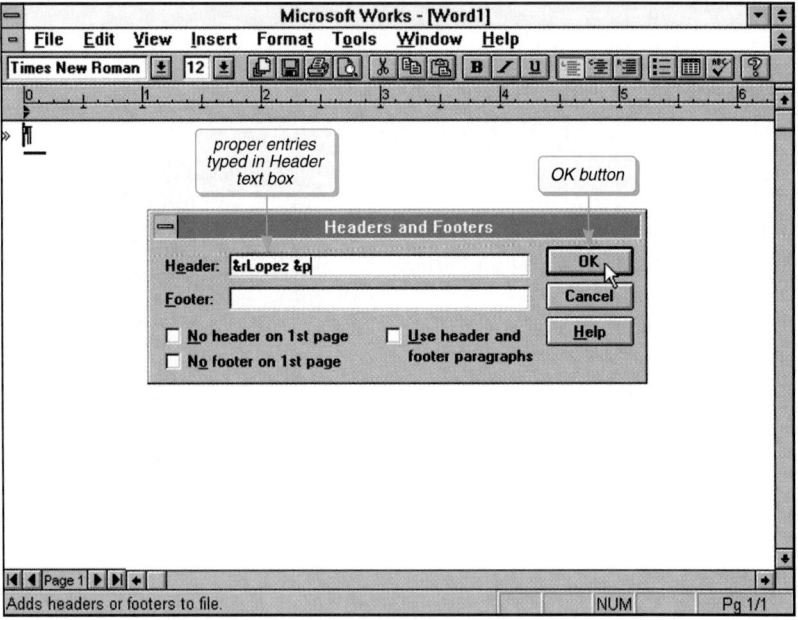

FIGURE 3-12

STEP 4 ▶

Choose the OK button in the Headers and Footers dialog box.

Works returns to the document window. The header information entered into the dialog box will not display on the screen in Normal view but will print one-half inch down from the top of each page when you print the research report.

Header and Footer Codes

Works provides great flexibility in printing information on the header line. Table 3-1 shows the list of codes you can use in the Headers and Footers dialog box to control printing information.

The print date code (&d) prints the date in the form of month/day/year (for example, 10/15/95). The print date in long format code (&n) prints the date in the form of month, day, year (for example, October 15, 1995).

After creating a header, you can use print preview as explained in Project 1 or choose the **Page Layout command** from the View menu to display the header to ensure you have created it correctly.

▸ **TABLE 3-1**

TASK	CODE
Left-align characters that follow	&l
Right-align characters that follow	&r
Center characters that follow	&c
Print page number	&p
Print filename	&f
Print date	&d
Print date in long format	&n
Print time	&t
Print single ampersand	&&

Entering Text

According to the MLA style, the first step in entering the text comprising the research report is to type the name of the student on the first line, followed by the name of the instructor on the second line, the course title on the third line, and the date on the fourth line. Because all lines on the report are double-spaced, you must also specify double-spacing. Perform the following step to accomplish these tasks.

TO DOUBLE-SPACE AND ENTER IDENTIFYING INFORMATION ▼

STEP 1 ▶

Press the CTRL+2 keys to double-space the document. Then type the name of the student on the first line, the name of the instructor on the second line, the course title on the third line, and the date on the fourth line. Press the ENTER key after each line.

The student name displays on the second line of the screen because of the double-space mode (Figure 3-13). The instructor name, course title, and date are double-spaced below the student name. The insertion point is positioned at the left margin of the next double-spaced line.

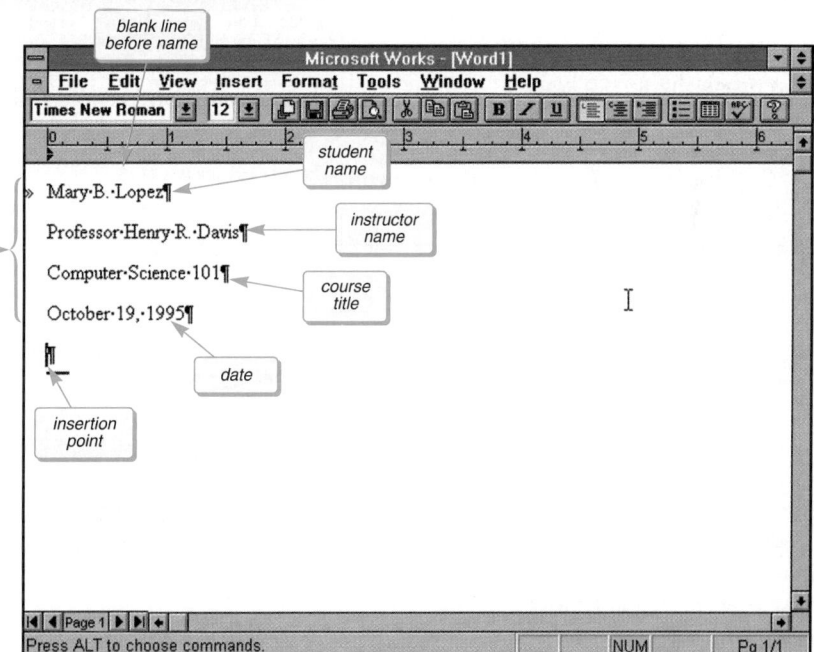

FIGURE 3-13

You can also double-space the lines on the document by choosing the **Paragraph command** from the Format menu and typing 2 in the Between Lines text box that displays on the Breaks and Spacing screen within the Paragraph dialog box.

Centering the Report Title

After typing the heading information, the next step is to type the title of the research report, which is to be centered on the document. To center a single line (the title) on a document, complete the following steps.

TO CENTER A REPORT TITLE ▼

STEP 1 ▶

Click the Center Align button on the Toolbar.

The insertion point and paragraph mark display in the center of the line (Figure 3-14).

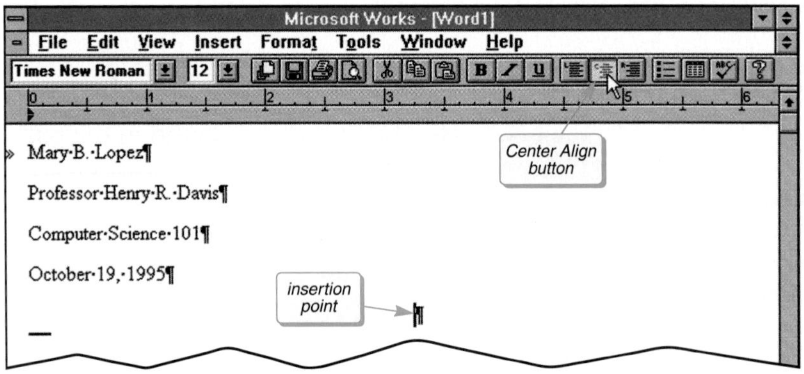

FIGURE 3-14

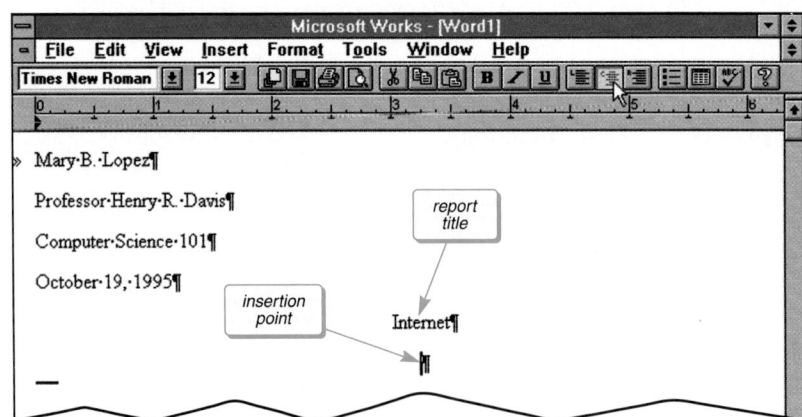

STEP 2 ▶

Type the report title, Internet, **and then press the ENTER key.**

Works centers the title (Figure 3-15). The insertion point remains in the center of the report, double-spaced below the report title.

FIGURE 3-15

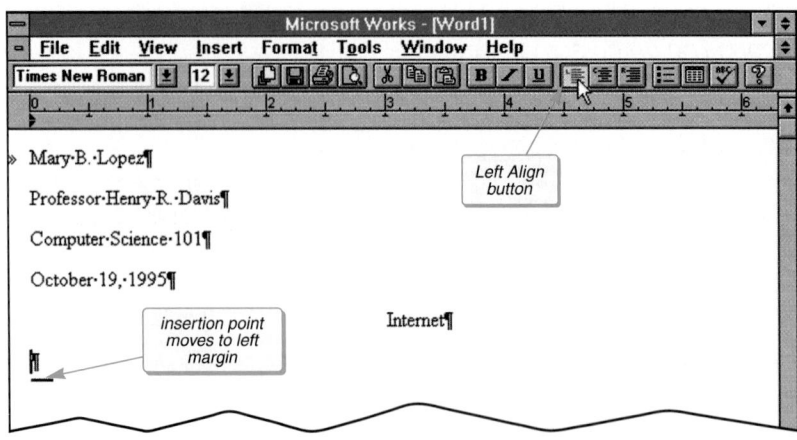

STEP 3 ▶

Click the Left Align button on the Toolbar.

The insertion point moves to the left margin (Figure 3-16).

FIGURE 3-16

Another way to control centering and text alignment is to choose the Paragraph command from the Format menu and make appropriate entries on the Indents and Alignment screen within the Paragraph dialog box that displays.

Indenting Paragraphs

In the report, the first line of each paragraph is indented one-half inch. You can use the TAB key to indent each paragraph, or you can use the Works **first-line indent** feature when there is a need to indent the first line of numerous paragraphs such as in the research report. The following steps explain how to use the first-line indent marker to indent the first line of each paragraph one-half inch from the left margin.

TO USE FIRST-LINE INDENT ▼

STEP 1 ▶

Position the mouse pointer on the first-line indent marker on the ruler (the upper triangle on the left side of the ruler).

The mouse pointer points to the first-line indent marker (Figure 3-17).

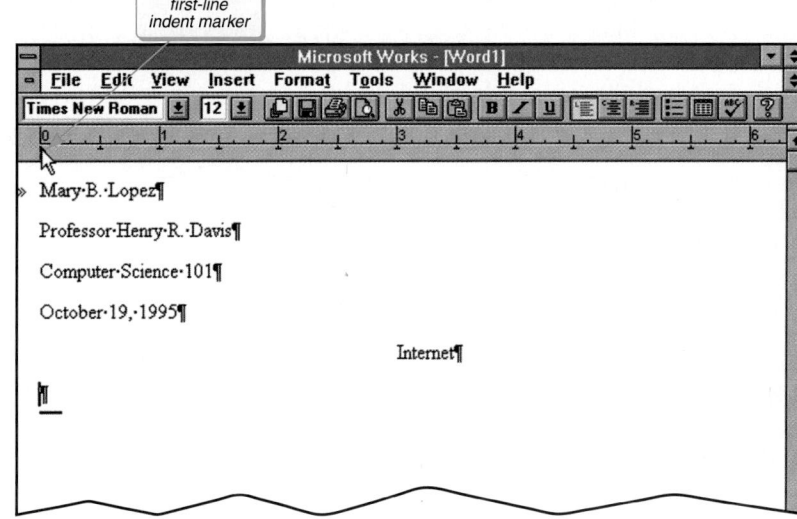

FIGURE 3-17

STEP 2 ▶

Drag the first-line indent marker to the right and position it at the one-half inch mark on the ruler. Then release the left mouse button.

Works indents the insertion point for the first paragraph one-half inch (Figure 3-18).

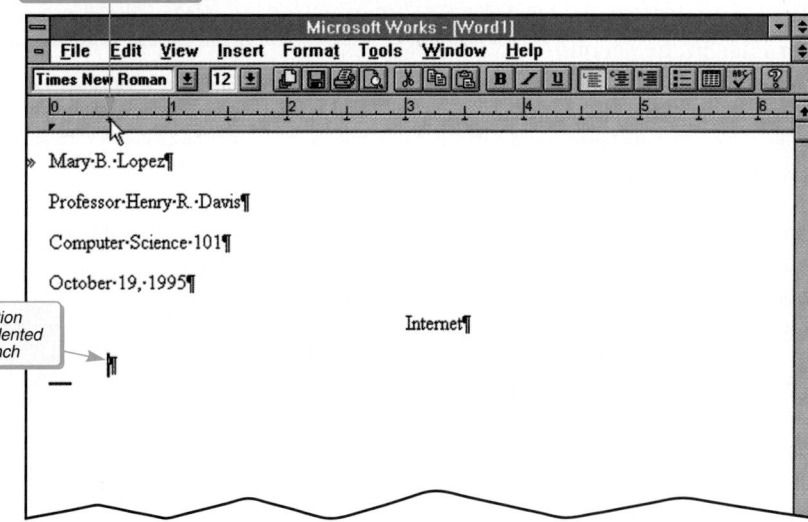

FIGURE 3-18

STEP 3 ▶

Begin typing the report.

As you type the report, the first line of each paragraph will automatically be indented one-half inch after you press the ENTER key (Figure 3-19).

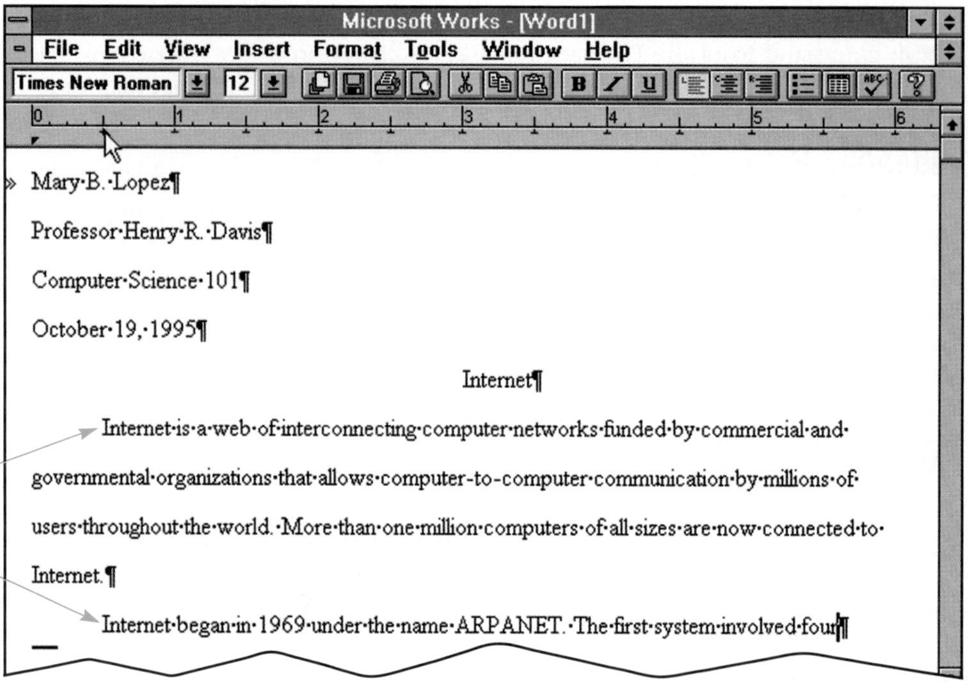

first line of paragraphs automatically indented

FIGURE 3-19

First-line indent can also be specified by choosing the Paragraph command from the Format menu and typing the indent location in the First Line text box on the Indents and Alignment screen within the Paragraph dialog box.

Entering Text

Continue entering text, as specified in the step below (see Figure 3-20).

TO ENTER TEXT

Step 1:
Type the remaining four lines in the second paragraph.

As you continue typing the report and the screen fills with text, the text will scroll upward (Figure 3-20).

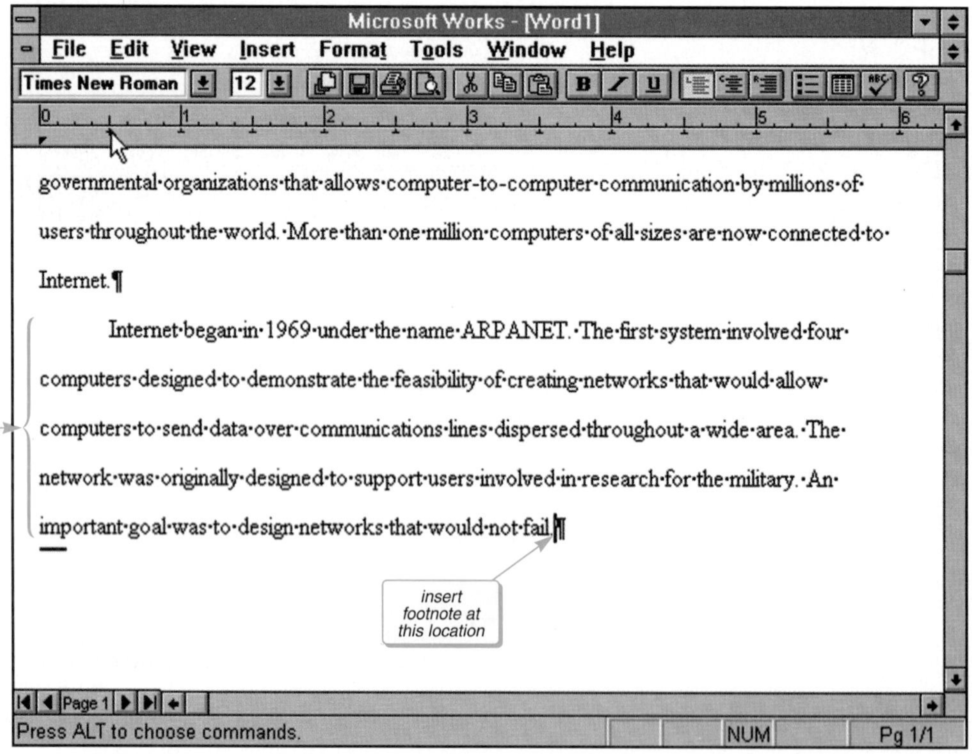

second paragraph in report

insert footnote at this location

FIGURE 3-20

Creating Footnotes

The second paragraph in the research report describes the historical development of Internet. This description was taken from a book that was used as a source of information when preparing the report. When you use information from a book or other reference source, you must identify the source and also credit the author by including a footnote (or endnote) in the report. When you create a footnote, Works places a **footnote reference mark** in your document. The footnote reference mark can be a raised number, called a **superscript**, or you can use other characters, such as an asterisk.

When you create a footnote, Works opens an area at the bottom of the screen called the **footnote pane**. When you use a WorksWizard to create a footnote, Works automatically places the footnote reference mark and the text in the footnote pane; or, if you do not use a WorksWizard, you can type text directly in this footnote pane following the reference mark.

In a research report, the footnote text will vary depending upon whether the reference is a book, newspaper, magazine, or other source. However, the information in the footnote commonly consists of the name of the author of the reference work, the title of the work, the location of the publisher, the publisher, the year of publication of the work, and the page number or numbers you reference in the work (see Figure 3-1 on page W3.3).

Using a Footnote WorksWizard

Works provides a Footnote WorksWizard to assist in creating a footnote in a research report. The Footnote WorksWizard provides the proper format for the footnote as recommended by MLA.

The steps on the following pages explain how to include a footnote (endnote) in a report using the Footnote WorksWizard.

TO CREATE A FOOTNOTE USING A WORKSWIZARD ▼

STEP 1 ▶

Position the insertion point where you want the footnote reference mark to appear. Select the Insert menu and point to the Footnote command.

*The Insert menu displays and the mouse pointer points to the **Footnote command** (Figure 3-21).*

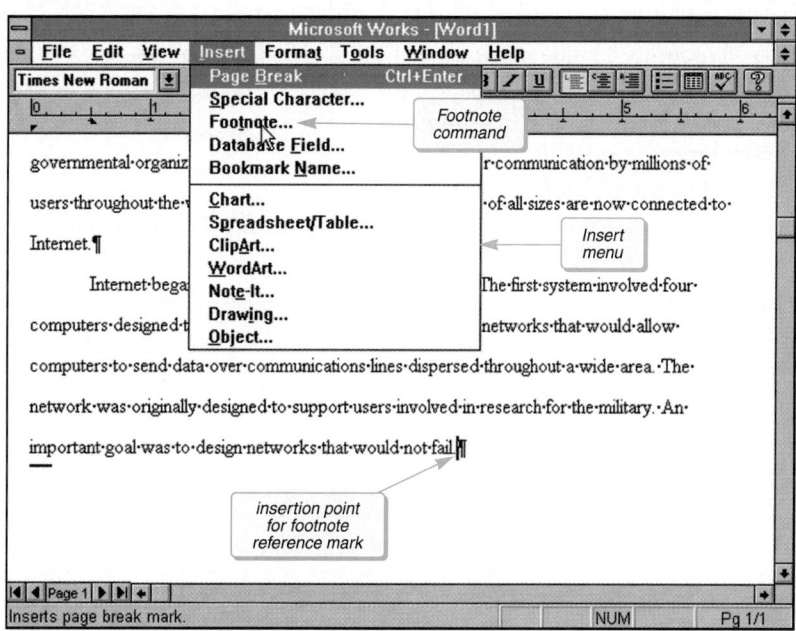

FIGURE 3-21

STEP 2 ▶

Choose the Footnote command from the Insert menu. When the Footnote dialog box displays, select the Numbered option button, if necessary, and then point to the Use WorksWizard button in the dialog box.

Works displays the Footnote dialog box (Figure 3-22). The Numbered option button in the Footnote Type area is selected, as indicated by the dark circle in the button. This is the Works default selection. This selection causes a number to display as the footnote reference mark. The mouse pointer points to the Use Works-Wizard button.

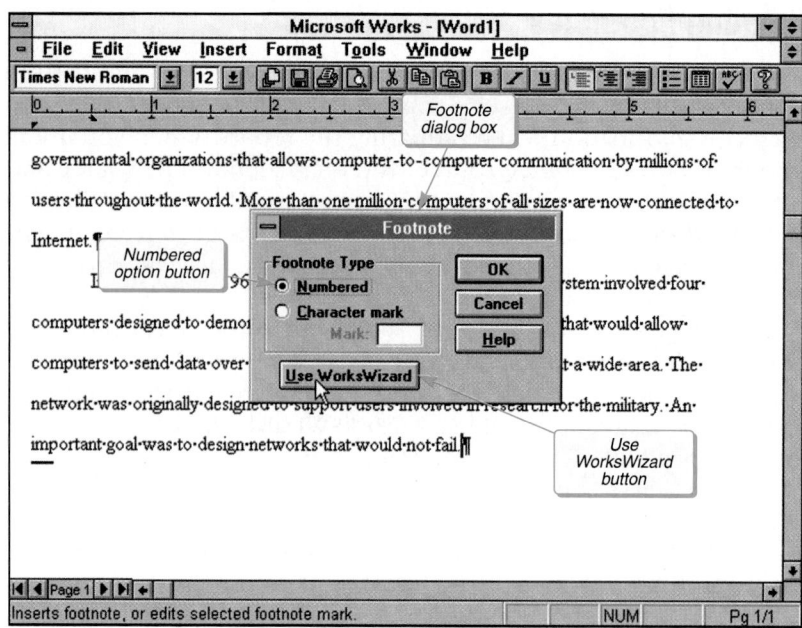

FIGURE 3-22

STEP 3 ▶

Choose the Use WorksWizard button in the Footnote dialog box. When the Footnote WorksWizard dialog box displays, select the Book option button, if necessary, and then point to the Next button.

The first Footnote WorksWizard dialog box displays (Figure 3-23). This dialog box allows you to select the source you want to cite. The Book option button is selected and the mouse pointer points to the Next button. The Book option button is the default selection.

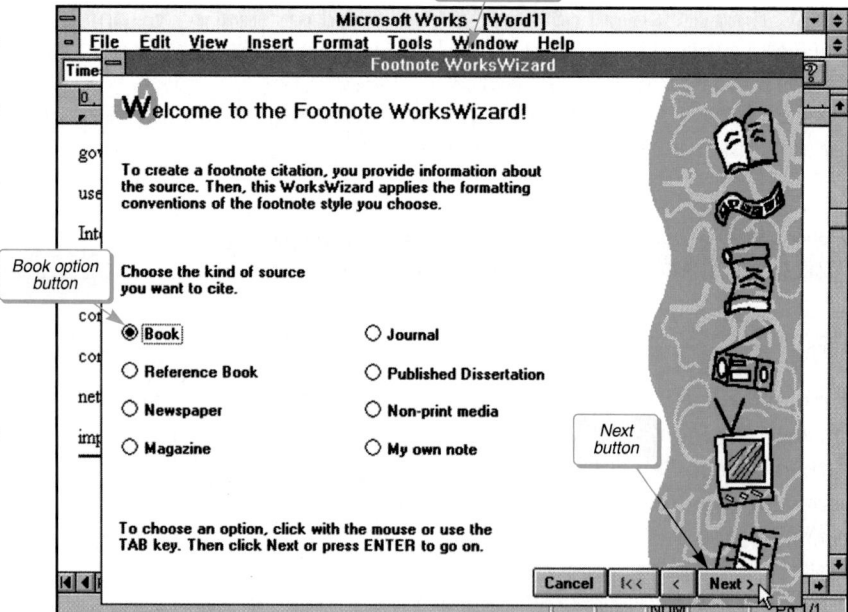

FIGURE 3-23

STEP 4 ▶

Choose the Next button in the first Footnote WorksWizard dialog box. When the next Footnote WorksWizard dialog box displays, type Beginner's Guide to Using Internet, **the title of the book used as reference, in the Title of Book text box.**

The words Beginner's Guide to Using Internet display in the Title of Book text box (Figure 3-24). At the bottom of the dialog box, a Tip section provides instructions for completing entries in each of the text boxes as they are used. These tips should be carefully reviewed because they provide instructions about entering information using the correct research report style.

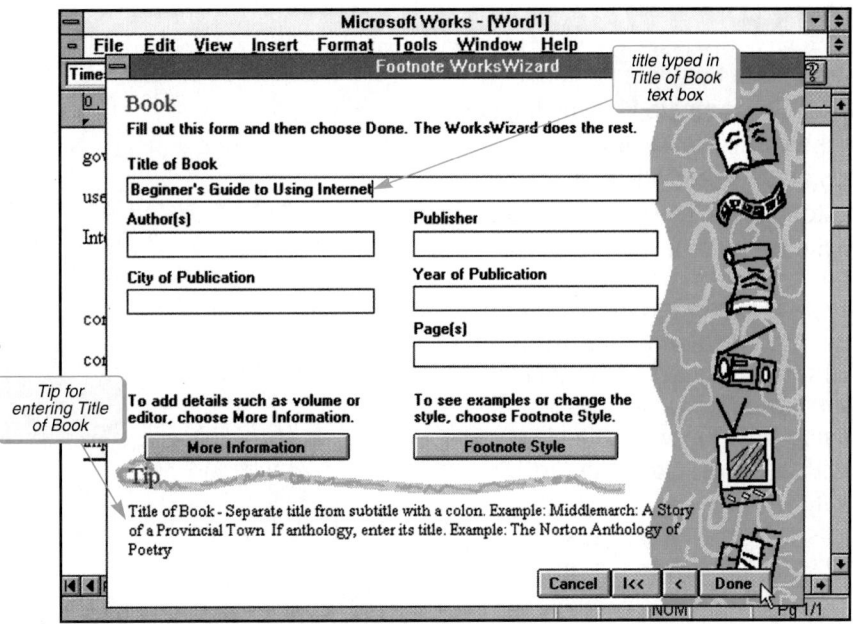

FIGURE 3-24

STEP 5 ▶

Press the TAB key and type the author of the book, William Masterson, **in the Author(s) text box. Press the TAB key and type the publisher,** Computer Network Press, **in the Publisher text box. Press the TAB key and type the city of publication,** San Francisco. **Press the TAB key and type the year of publication,** 1995. **Press the TAB key and type the pages that contain the reference,** 13-17. **Point to the Footnote Style button.**

The information required for the footnote is typed in the Footnote WorksWizard dialog box (Figure 3-25). Pressing the TAB key moves the insertion point from one text box to another. It is important to understand that as the insertion point is placed in each text box, the Tip at the bottom of the Footnote WorksWizard dialog box displays instructions on exactly how to type the entry for that particular text box.

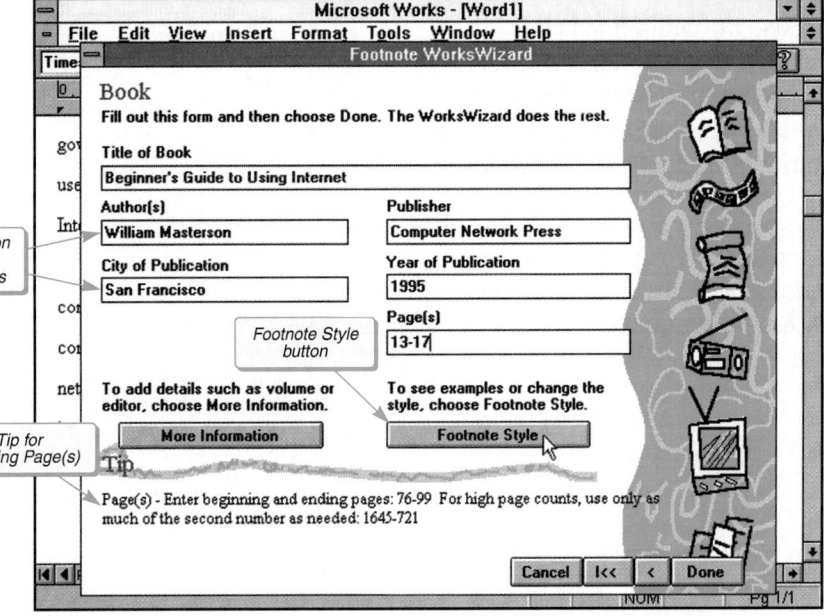

FIGURE 3-25

STEP 6 ▶

Choose the Footnote Style button. When the Footnote Style dialog box displays, select the Modern Language Association option button, if necessary. Then point to the OK button.

An example of the MLA footnote style displays under the words Modern Language Association within the Footnote Style dialog box (Figure 3-26). The mouse pointer points to the OK button.

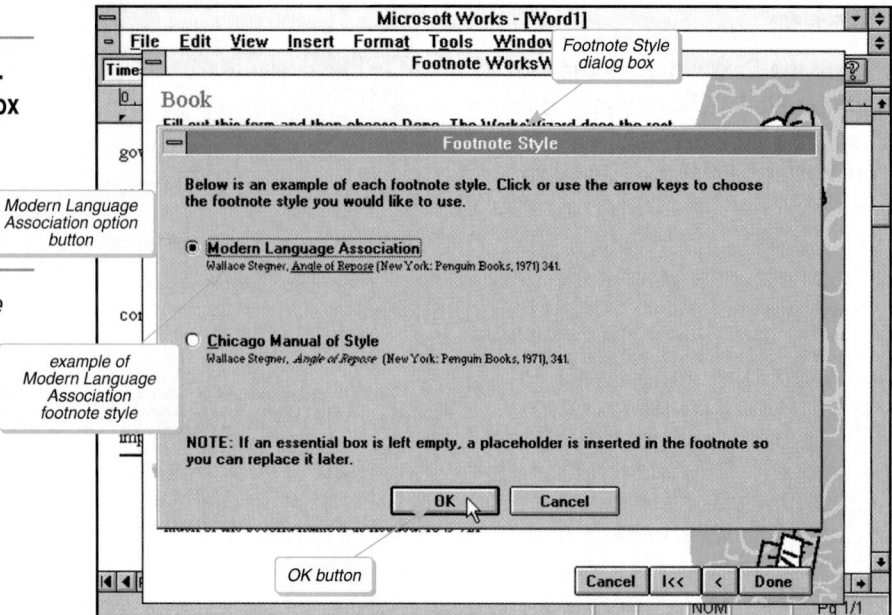

FIGURE 3-26

STEP 7 ▶

Choose the OK button in the Footnote Style dialog box to return to the Footnote WorksWizard dialog box. Point to the Done button in the Footnote WorksWizard dialog box.

The previous Footnote Works-Wizard dialog box displays and the mouse pointer points to the Done button (Figure 3-27).

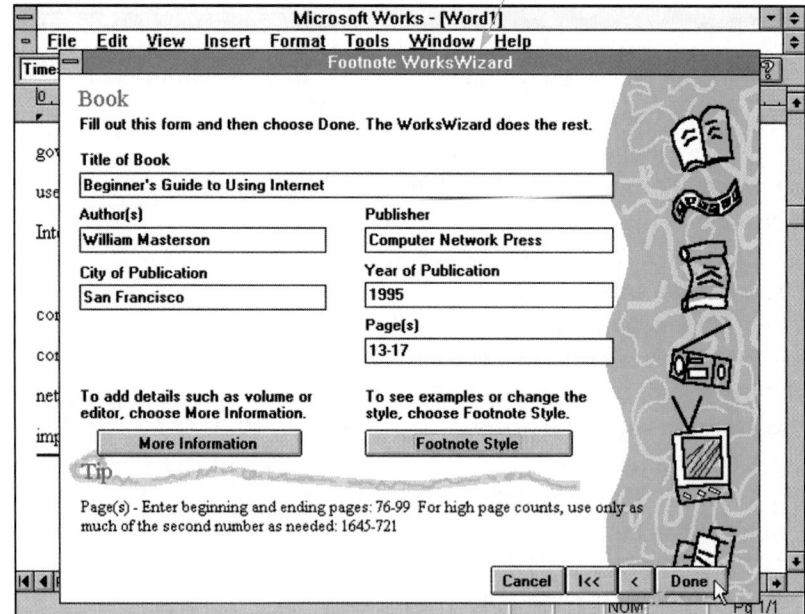

FIGURE 3-27

STEP 8 ▶

Choose the Done button in the Footnote WorksWizard dialog box.

The screen scrolls upward and displays a single line containing footnote reference mark number 1 at the top of the screen (Figure 3-28). The footnote created by Works displays at the bottom of the screen in an area called the **footnote pane**. *The footnote begins with a raised superscript number 1, and is followed by the information comprising the foot-note. Works creates the footnote using the style recommended by MLA. Note that the book title is automatically underlined, and the city, publisher, and year are enclosed in parentheses.*

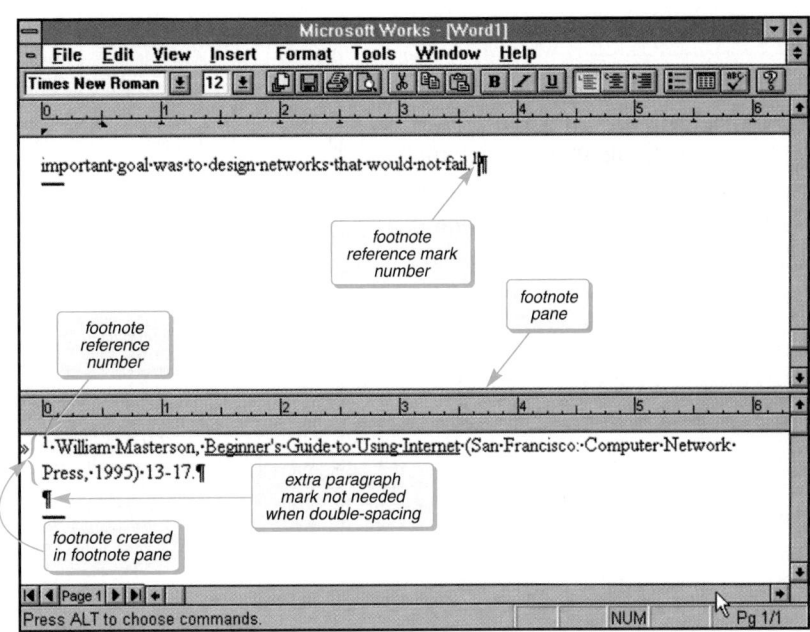

FIGURE 3-28

Indenting and Double-Spacing Footnotes

The Footnote WorksWizard does not indent nor double-space the footnote. Because the footnotes in this report are double-spaced and the first line of the foot-note is indented one-half inch (see Figure 3-1 on page W3.3), additional editing must be performed on the footnote in the footnote pane.

In addition, when double-spacing a footnote, the extra paragraph mark follow-ing the footnote (see Figure 3-28) must be deleted. Complete the following steps to double-space and indent the footnote.

TO DOUBLE-SPACE AND INDENT THE FOOTNOTE ▼

STEP 1 ▶

Delete the extra paragraph mark (blank line) on the line following the footnote by positioning the insertion point at the end of the second line of the footnote, immediately before the paragraph mark. Then press the DELETE key.

The paragraph mark following the footnote is deleted (Figure 3-29). If this is not done, an extra blank line will display when you enter subsequent footnotes. This paragraph mark should remain if you single-space foot-note entries.

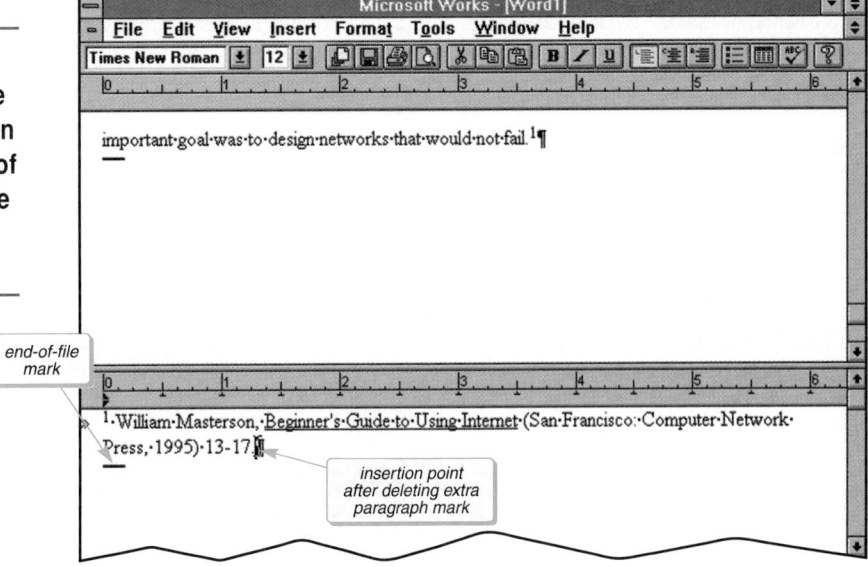

FIGURE 3-29

STEP 2 ▶

Highlight both lines of the footnote and press the CTRL+2 keys to double-space the footnote. Click the beginning of the footnote to remove the highlight. Point to the first-line indent marker on the footnote pane ruler and drag the marker to the one-half inch mark on the ruler.

The first line of the footnote is indented one-half inch and the footnote is double-spaced (Figure 3-30). Notice that a blank line displays above the first line of the footnote in the same manner as when you double-spaced the report.

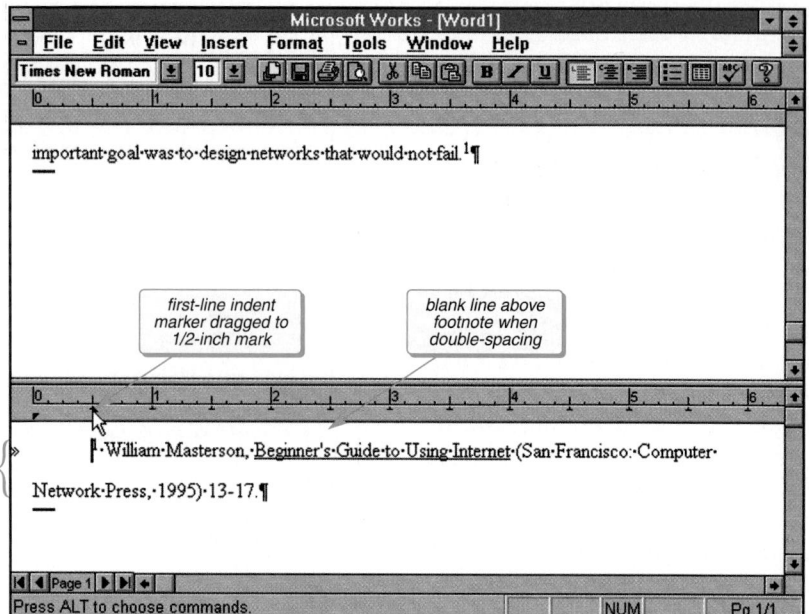

FIGURE 3-30

Each time you create a footnote, it is necessary to perform Step 1 and Step 2 above to properly double-space the footnote and indent the first line of the footnote in the footnote pane.

When a report contains a large numbers of footnotes, the footnotes can be single-spaced. When only a few footnotes appear in the report, it is recommended that the footnotes be double-spaced.

Closing the Footnote Pane

After creating the footnote, you should close the footnote pane. Closing the footnote pane will remove the footnote pane from the screen. Perform the following steps to close the footnote pane.

TO CLOSE THE FOOTNOTE PANE ▼

STEP 1 ▶

Position the mouse pointer on the narrow split bar at the top of the ruler in the footnote pane.

*The mouse pointer becomes an equal sign with small arrows on the top and bottom of the equal sign and displays on the **split bar** (Figure 3-31).*

FIGURE 3-31

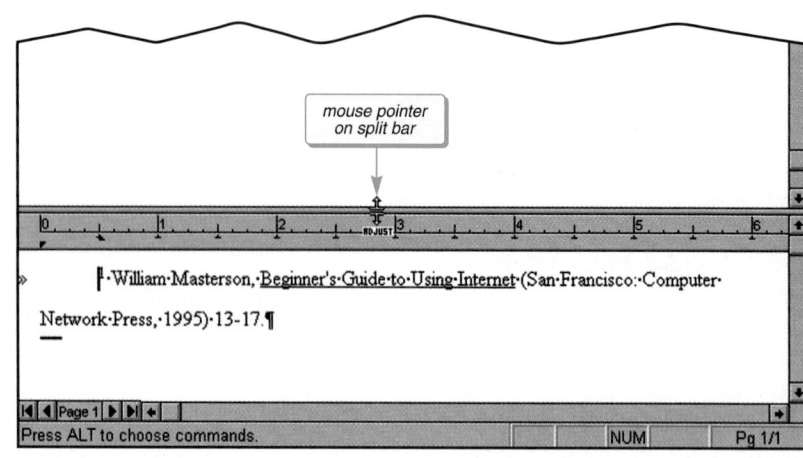

STEP 2 ▶

Double-click the left mouse button.

The footnote pane closes (disappears) and the line of the research report containing the footnote reference mark displays at the top of the screen (Figure 3-32).

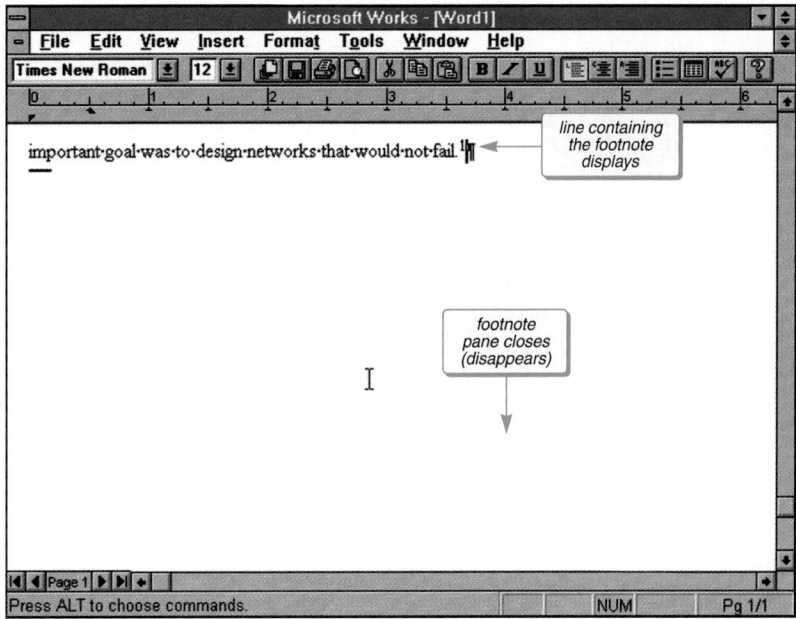

FIGURE 3-32

To view the footnote in the footnote pane, choose the **Footnotes command** from the View menu. When you choose the Footnotes command from the View menu, a checkmark displays beside the command in the View menu. To turn off the Footnotes command, which results in closing the footnote pane, choose the Footnotes command again or double-click the split bar. The checkmark adjacent to the Footnotes command disappears.

To delete a footnote, highlight the footnote reference mark in the document window and press the DELETE key. If there are multiple footnotes, Works renumbers them. To correct a footnote, choose the Footnotes command from the View menu if the footnote pane is closed, move the insertion point to the footnote pane area, and make the correction. To enlarge or resize the footnote pane, position the mouse pointer on the split bar above the footnote pane ruler and drag up or down.

You can also display the footnote by choosing the Page Layout command from the View menu. In page layout mode, the footnote displays as a part of the document instead of inside the footnote pane. You can correct or otherwise change the footnote as required.

Saving the Document

A good practice is to periodically save the information you are typing on a diskette or hard disk to eliminate retyping information in the event of power or computer failure. To save the document on a diskette in drive A using the name PROJ3, complete the steps below.

TO SAVE A DOCUMENT

Step 1: Click the Save button on the Toolbar or choose the Save or Save As command from the File menu.

Step 2: Type the filename, `proj3` in the File Name text box in the Save As dialog box.

Step 3: If necessary, select drive A from the Drives drop-down list box.

Step 4: Choose the OK button in the Save As dialog box.

Entering Text

After creating the first footnote, continue to type the remainder of the research report, as specified below.

TO ENTER TEXT

Step 1:
Type the data shown in Figure 3-33.

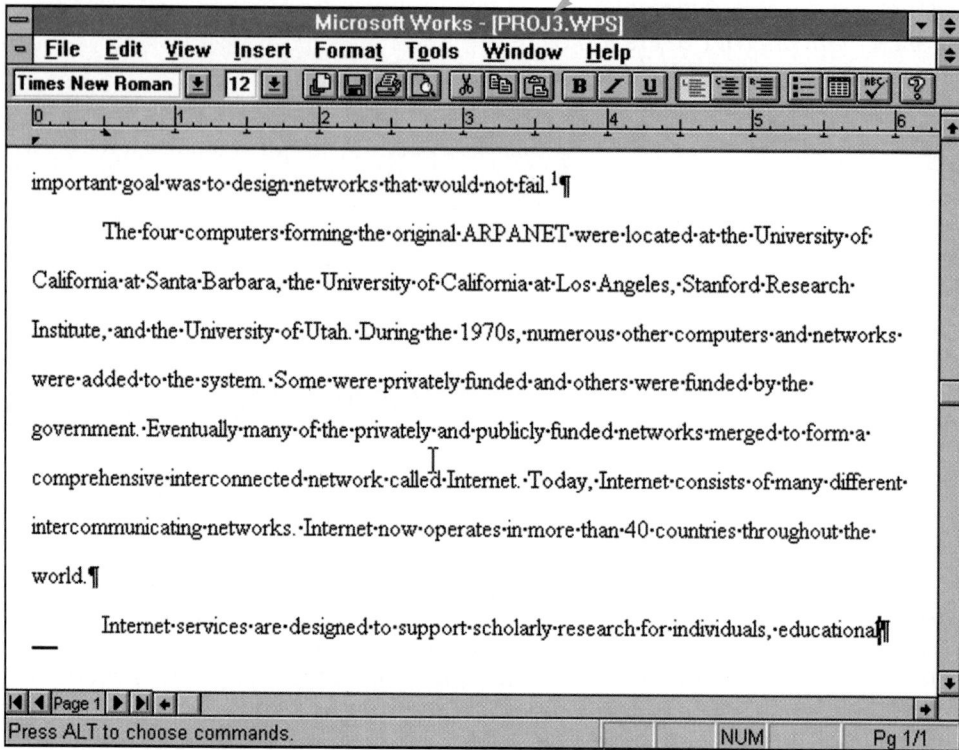

FIGURE 3-33

Step 2:
Type the data shown in Figure 3-34. As you continue typing, the text automatically scrolls upward when the screen fills with text.

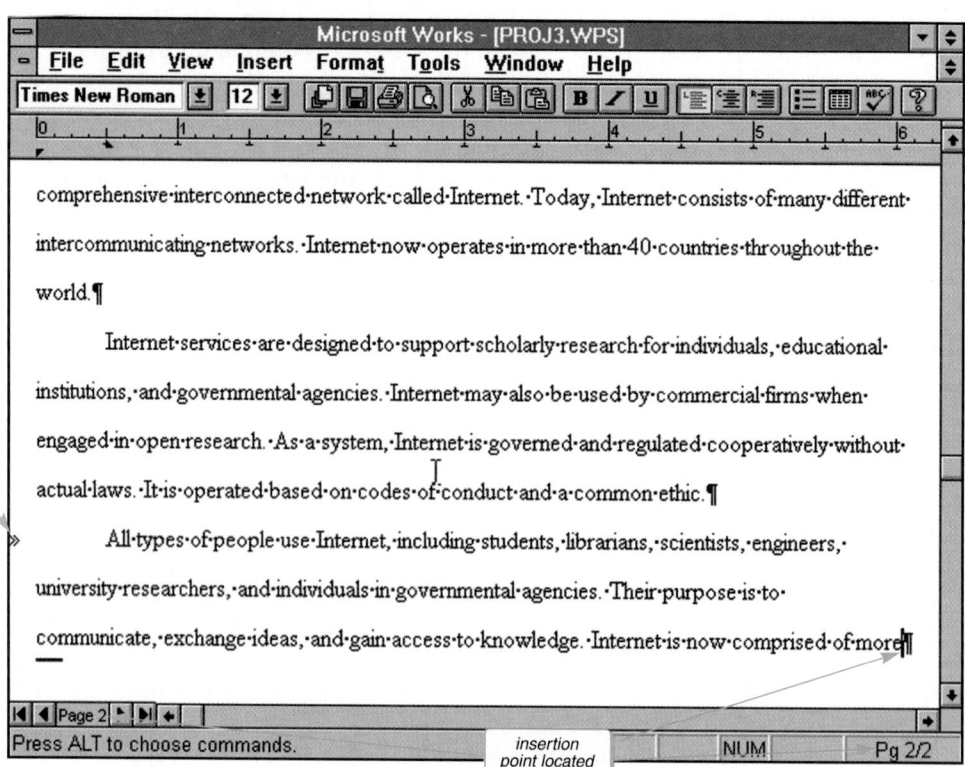

FIGURE 3-34

Step 3: Type the end of the research paper as shown in Figure 3-35, where the paragraphs have been scrolled to display both footnote 2 and footnote 3. Create footnote 2 and footnote 3 using the Footnote WorksWizard as illustrated previously. Footnote 2 is from a journal and footnote 3 is from a newspaper. To obtain the data required for the footnote information, refer to Figure 3-1 on page W3.3. If necessary, when creating footnotes or when viewing footnotes after choosing the Footnotes command from the View menu, use the scroll bar and scroll arrows in the footnote pane to display the footnotes.

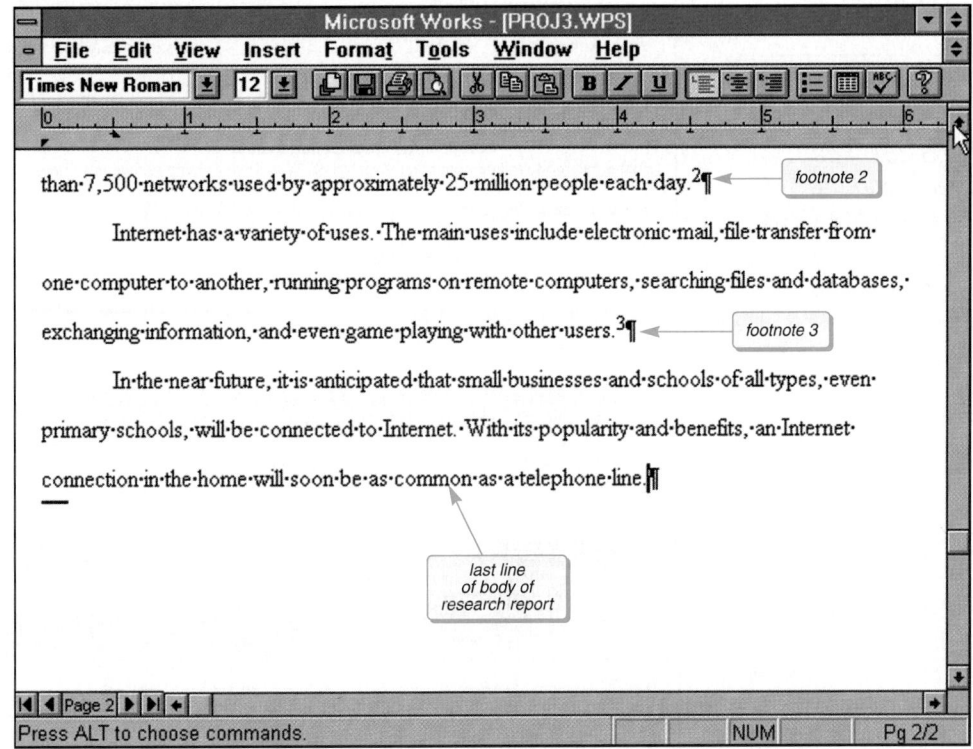

FIGURE 3-35

Automatic Page Break

Works automatically creates a **page break** in a document if you type more information than can fit on one sheet of a printed report. The automatic page break mark displays as a chevron character in the left margin (see Figure 3-34). The line to the right of the page break mark will print as the first line on the next page of the report. You can control where the page break occurs by specifying a value in the Bottom margin text box on the Margins screen within the Page Setup dialog box. The Works default value is a 1-inch bottom margin.

Inserting a Manual Page Break and Formatting the Footnotes Page

According to the MLA style, the footnotes (endnotes) should print on a separate page at the end of the report with the heading, NOTES, centered horizontally on the line. Therefore, to format the footnote page, you must (1) create a manual page break; and (2) center the word NOTES on the separate page. The footnotes will then automatically print after the word NOTES because the word is the last line of the report.

To accomplish these tasks, perform the steps on the next two pages.

TO INSERT A MANUAL PAGE BREAK AND PLACE A WORD ON THE NEW PAGE ▼

STEP 1 ▶

Position the insertion point in the document where you want the page break to occur (after the last line on the report). Select the Insert menu and point to the Page Break command.

*The insertion point is positioned immediately after the last line in the report (Figure 3-36). The Insert menu displays and the mouse pointer points to the **Page Break command.***

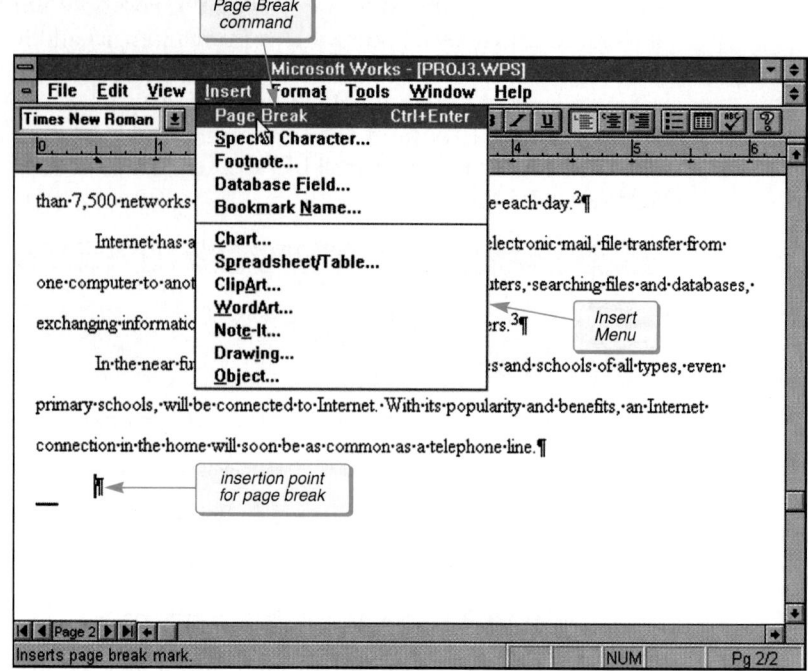

FIGURE 3-36

STEP 2 ▶

Choose the Page Break command from the Insert menu.

A dotted line indicating a manual page break displays on the screen immediately above the insertion point (Figure 3-37). The page break mark displays below the dotted line and the new page number (3) displays in the scroll bar and the status bar.

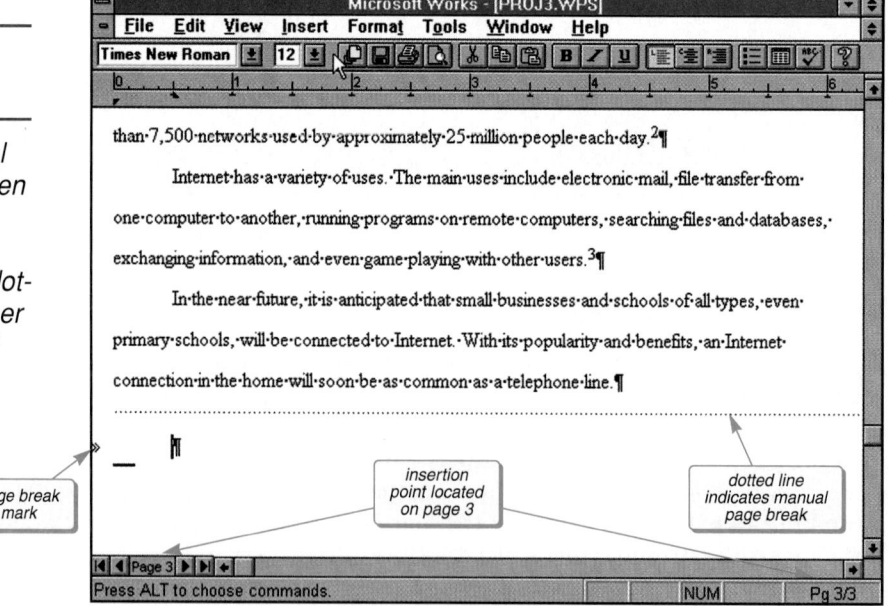

FIGURE 3-37

STEP 3 ▶

Drag the first-line indent marker to the zero position on the ruler. Click the Center Align button on the Toolbar. Type NOTES.

The first-line indent marker is located at the zero position on the ruler (Figure 3-38). The word NOTES displays centered between the document margins.

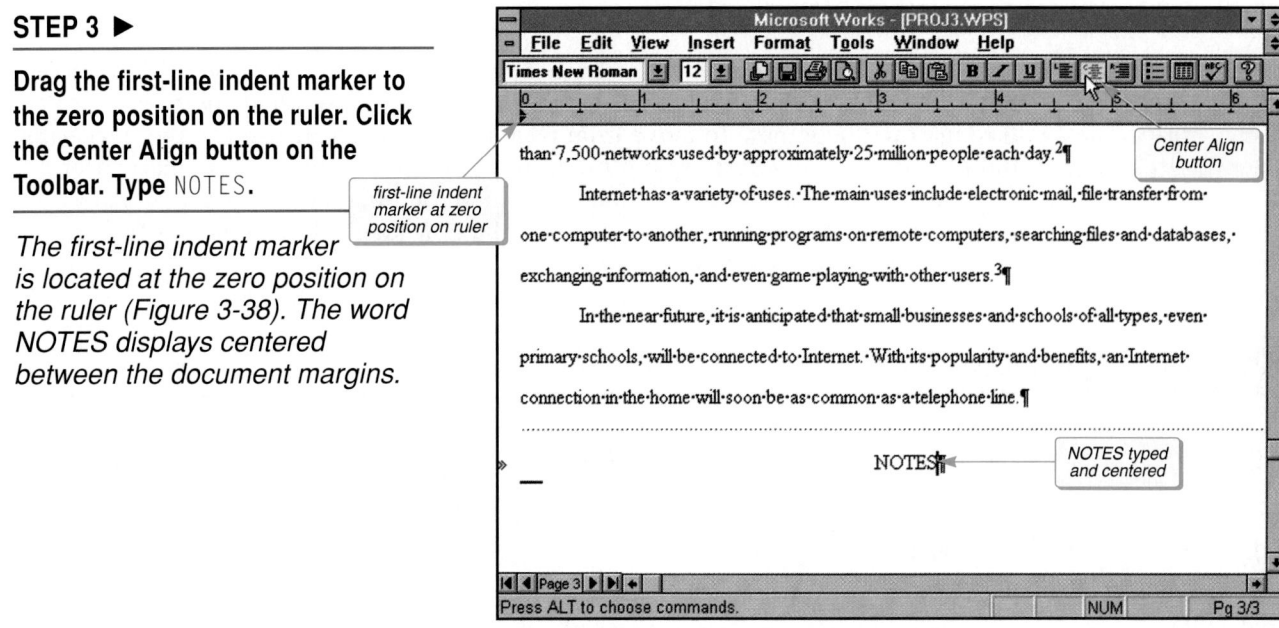

FIGURE 3-38

Rather than using the Page Break command from the Insert menu to insert a manual page break, you can press the CTRL+ENTER keys.

If you insert a page break by mistake, you can delete it by moving the insertion point to the beginning of the line that immediately follows the page break and pressing the BACKSPACE key; or you can highlight the dotted line and press the DELETE key.

When you print the research report, Works places the information in the footnote pane double-spaced below the word NOTES on the last page of the report (see Figure 3-1 on page W3.3).

EDITING THE RESEARCH REPORT

A fter typing the research report, you should save it using the Save button or Save command as previously explained. Next, you should edit the research report; that is, review the report for any additions, deletions, or changes. You can edit the report while it displays on the screen, or you might find it valuable to print a copy of the report and edit the printed copy. When making changes to a report, you might want to move quickly to a certain page on the report or to a certain word or words. You might also have a need to replace certain words in the document, or move words, sentences, or paragraphs. Works provides a number of useful commands to assist you in the performing these editing tasks.

Using the Go To Command

If the insertion point is at the beginning of a document and you want to move to page 2 of the document, you can use the scroll bar or scroll arrow to move through the document. To move from page to page, you can also use the next page button and the previous page button on the scroll bar. Another particularly useful method to move throughout a document when the document consists of many pages is using the **Go To command** from the Edit menu. To use the Go To command, perform the following steps.

TO USE THE GO TO COMMAND ▼

STEP 1 ▶

Position the insertion point at the beginning of the document. Select the Edit menu and point to the Go To command.

Works displays the Edit menu and the mouse pointer points to the Go To command (Figure 3-39).

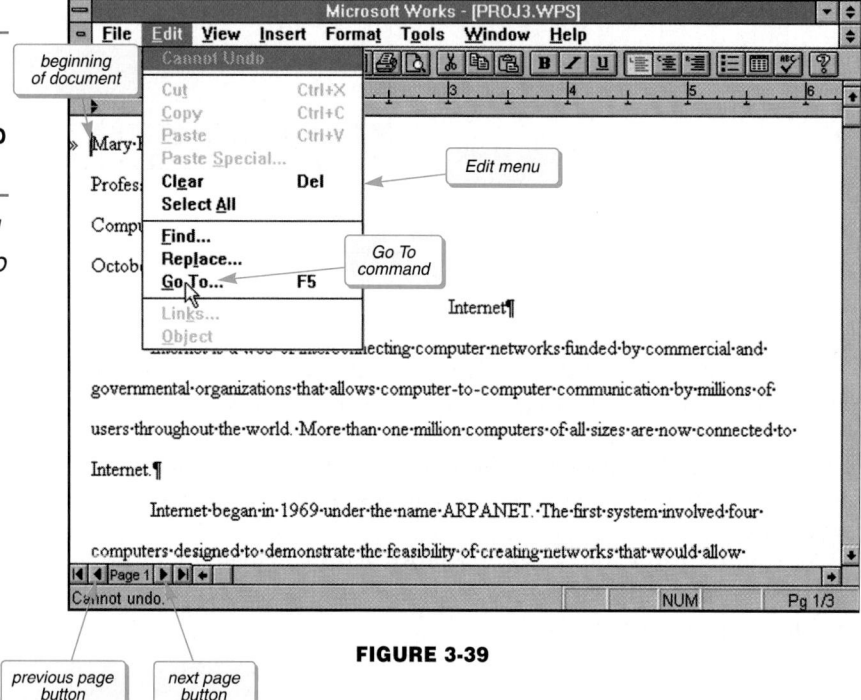

FIGURE 3-39

STEP 2 ▶

Choose the Go To command from the Edit menu. When the Go To dialog box displays, type 2 in the Go to text box, and then point to the OK button.

Works displays the Go To dialog box (Figure 3-40). The number 2 displays in the Go to text box. The mouse pointer points to the OK button.

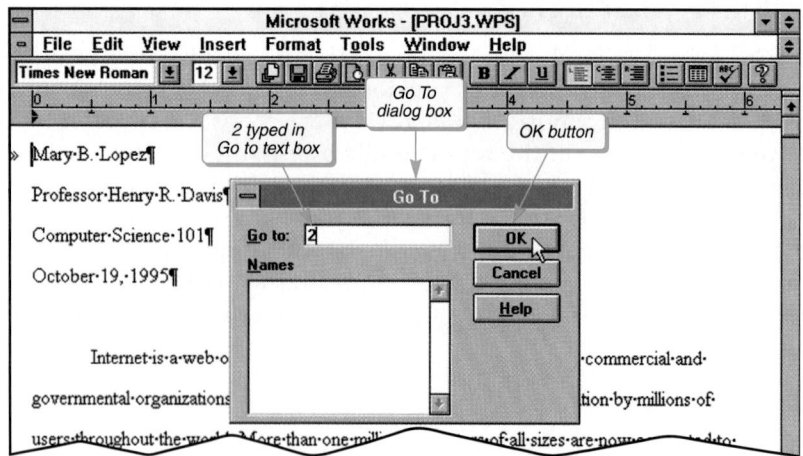

FIGURE 3-40

STEP 3 ►

Choose the OK button in the Go To dialog box.

Page 2 of the research report displays (Figure 3-41). Works places the insertion point at the leftmost position of the first line of page 2 and displays the line at the top of the screen.

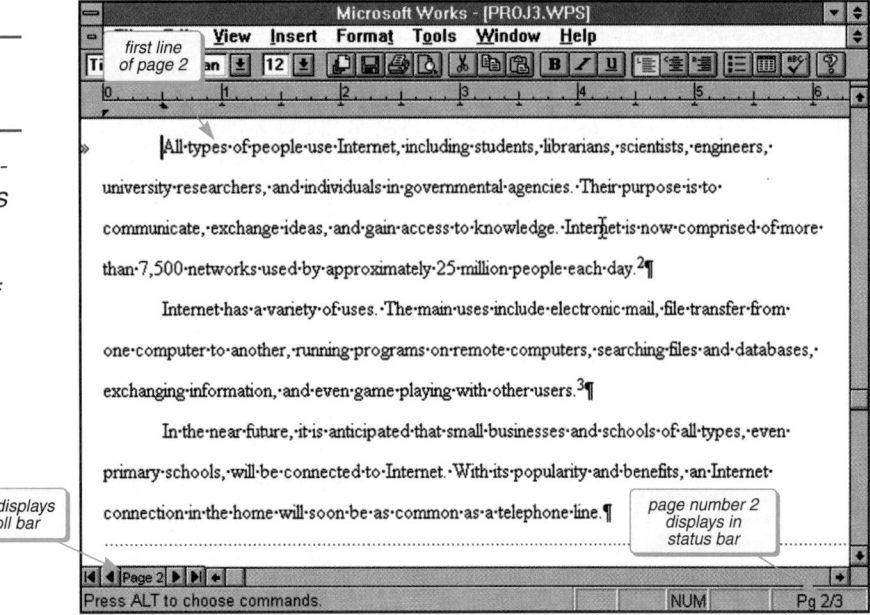

FIGURE 3-41

The Go To command provides a quick way to move to a specific page in a document. Once the page is reached, you can click to move to a specific location in the document, or you can use the scroll bar and scroll arrows or the arrow keys to move through the document to find a specific paragraph.

Using the Find Command

Another command you can use to quickly move to a specific area in a document is the **Find command**. The Find command allows you to specify one or more words you want to locate in a document. In the following example, assume the insertion point is located at the beginning of the document and you want to find the words, electronic mail, which are located somewhere within the research report. To use the Find command, perform the steps on the next two pages.

TO USE THE FIND COMMAND ▼

STEP 1 ▶

Position the insertion point at the beginning of the document. Select the Edit menu and point to the Find command.

Works displays the Edit menu and the mouse pointer points to the Find command (Figure 3-42).

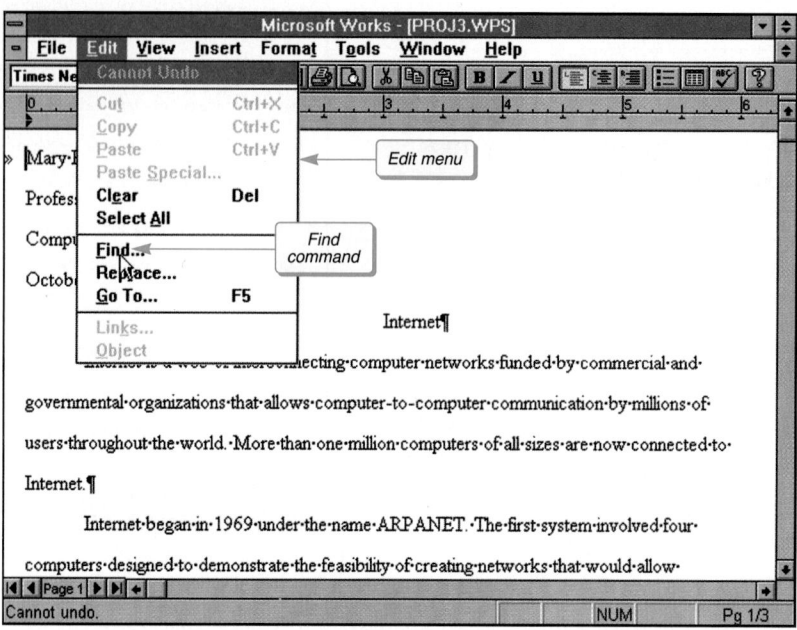

FIGURE 3-42

STEP 2 ▶

Choose the Find command from the Edit menu. When the Find dialog box displays, type electronic mail in the Find What text box. Select the Match Case check box and then point to the Find Next button.

*Works displays the Find dialog box (Figure 3-43). The words, electronic mail, display in the Find What text box. The **Match Case check box** is selected, which means the case of the characters in the document must match the case of the characters you type in the Find What text box. The mouse pointer points to the Find Next button.*

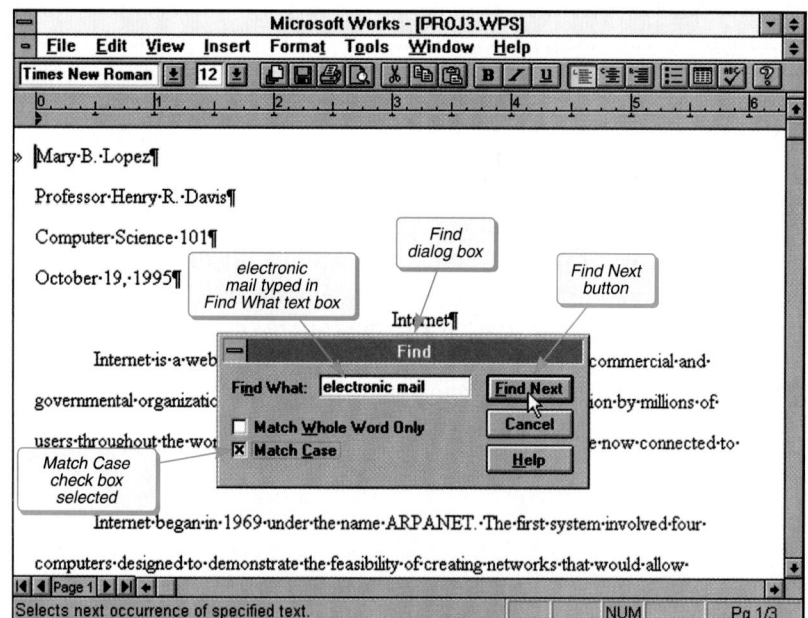

FIGURE 3-43

STEP 3 ▶

Choose the Find Next button in the Find dialog box.

Works locates the first line where the words, electronic mail, occur and highlights the words (Figure 3-44).

STEP 4 ▶

Choose the Find Next button to search for the next occurrence of the words, or choose the Cancel button to exit from the Find dialog box and return to the word processing document. If you choose the Find Next button and no additional occurrence of the words is found, a Microsoft Works dialog box displays indicating the search has reached the end of the document. Choose the OK button in the Microsoft Works dialog box and then choose the Cancel button in the Find dialog box to return to the document.

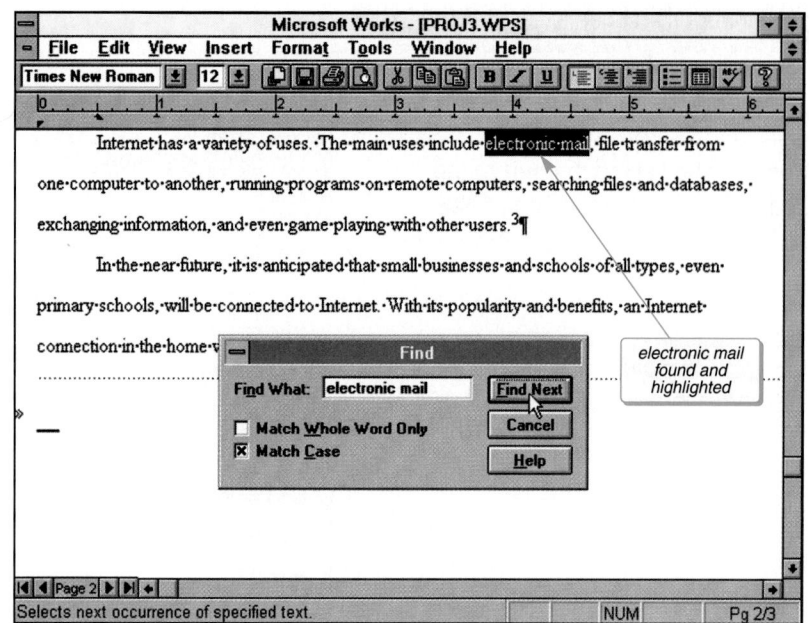

FIGURE 3-44

When you select the Match Case check box, Works matches exactly the case of the characters you type. Case refers to uppercase or lowercase letters of the alphabet. For example, if you type ELECTRONIC MAIL and select the Match Case check box, Works will not find the words, electronic mail. The Find dialog box also contains the **Match Whole Word Only check box**. If you select this box, Works finds only whole words. For example, if you select this box and type Internet Services, Works would find Internet Services but would not find Internet Service.

Using the Replace Command

Another powerful Works editing feature is the **Replace command**. The Replace command searches a document for specified text and replaces it with new text. When using the Replace command, Works searches the text from the insertion point to the end of the document; or, if you highlight text, Works searches only the highlighted portion of the document.

In the research report, assume you would like to replace the abbreviation, ARPANET, with the words, Advanced Research Projects Agency Network. To accomplish this task, use the Replace command as shown in the steps on the next two pages.

TO USE THE REPLACE COMMAND ▼

STEP 1 ▶

Position the insertion point at the beginning of the document. Then, select the Edit menu and point to the Replace command.

Works displays the Edit menu and the mouse pointer points to the Replace command (Figure 3-45).

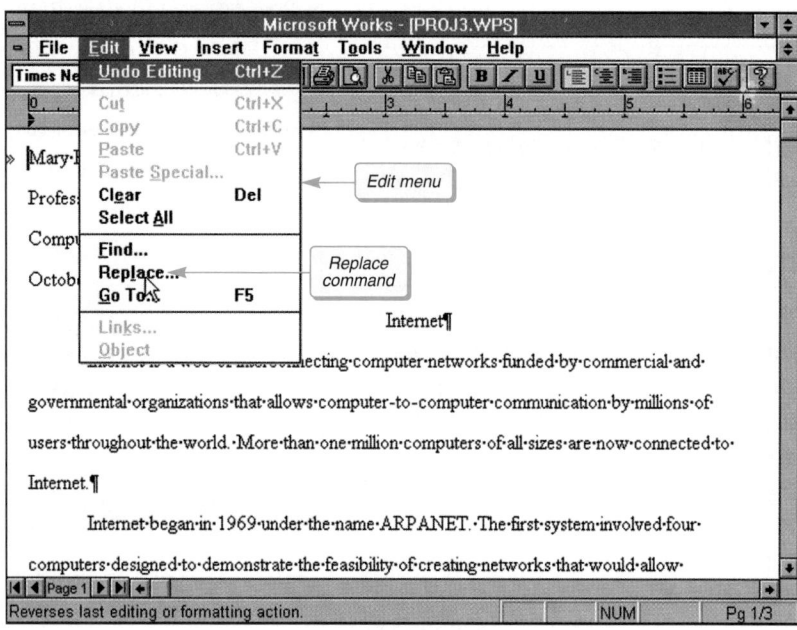

FIGURE 3-45

STEP 2 ▶

Choose the Replace command from the Edit menu. When Works displays the Replace dialog box, type `ARPANET` **in the Find What text box, press the TAB key, and in the Replace With text box, type** `Advanced Research Projects Agency Network`**. Select the Match Case check box and point to the Find Next button.**

Works displays the Replace dialog box (Figure 3-46). The word ARPANET and the words, Advanced Research Projects Agency Network, display in the appropriate text boxes. Only the last portion of the words, Advanced Research Projects Agency Network, displays because the words are too long to fit in the text box. The Match Case check box is selected.

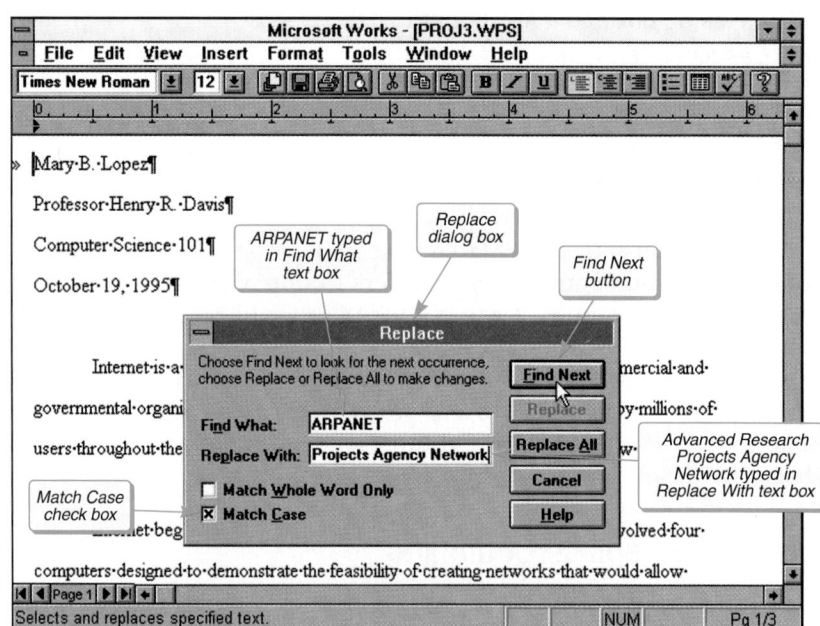

FIGURE 3-46

STEP 3 ▶

Choose the Find Next button in the Replace dialog box. When a match is found, point to the Replace button.

Works highlights the first occurrence of the word ARPANET in the research report (Figure 3-47).

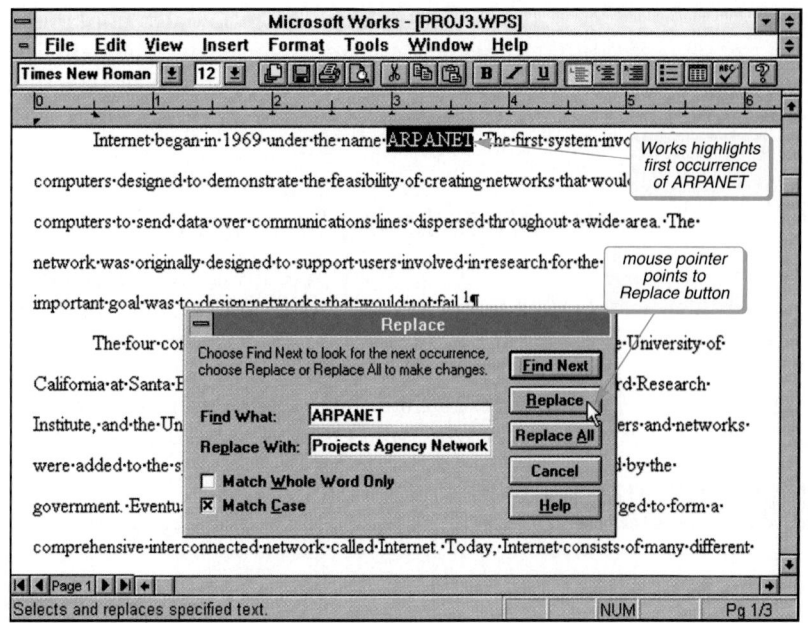

FIGURE 3-47

STEP 4 ▶

Choose the Replace button in the Replace dialog box. When the next occurrence of ARPANET is found, choose the Replace button again. Then choose the Close button.

Works replaces the word ARPANET with the words, Advanced Research Projects Agency Network (Figure 3-48).

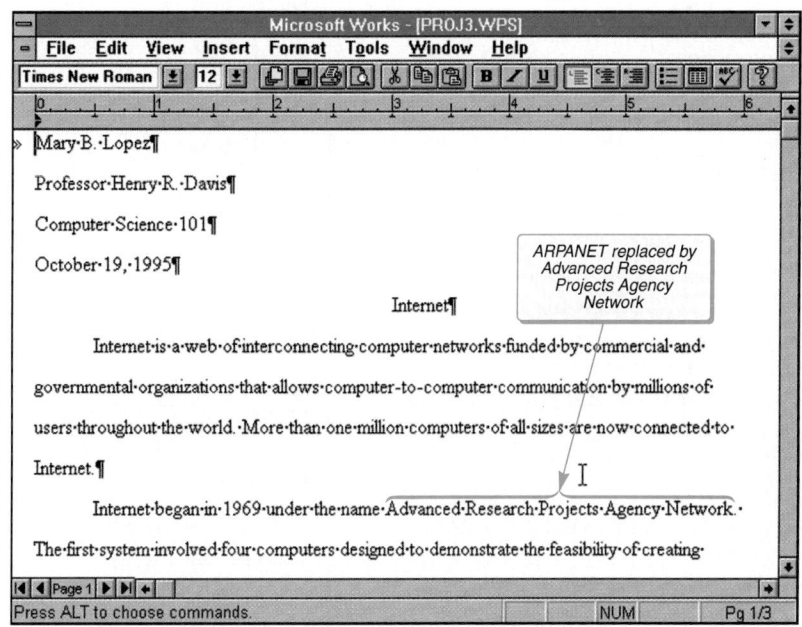

FIGURE 3-48

After Works highlights the first occurrence of the word ARPANET you can replace the word with the text in the Replace With text box by choosing the Replace button, or you can find the next occurrence of the word by choosing the Find Next button. Continue this process until Works returns to the beginning of the document. At any time you can exit from the Replace dialog box by choosing the Close button. Once you replace a word or words, the Cancel button in the Replace dialog box changes to a Close button. When you choose the Close button in the Replace dialog box, the Replace dialog box will be removed from the screen.

The Replace dialog box also contains a Replace All button. If you choose the Replace All button, Works automatically replaces all occurrences of the word in the Find What text box without the need to choose the Replace button each time.

When the Replace All operation is complete, Works displays the page where you began the search.

Undo Editing Command

If you make an editing change in a document and you want to restore the document to its form before the change, Works provides an **Undo Editing command**. This command will allow you to undo the last editing that has taken place on a document. Assume you would like to return the research paper to its original form so the word ARPANET appears where it was previously replaced. Perform the following steps to undo the editing.

TO UNDO EDITING ▼

STEP 1 ►

Select the Edit menu and point to the Undo Editing command.

The Edit menu displays and the mouse pointer points to the Undo Editing command (Figure 3-49).

FIGURE 3-49

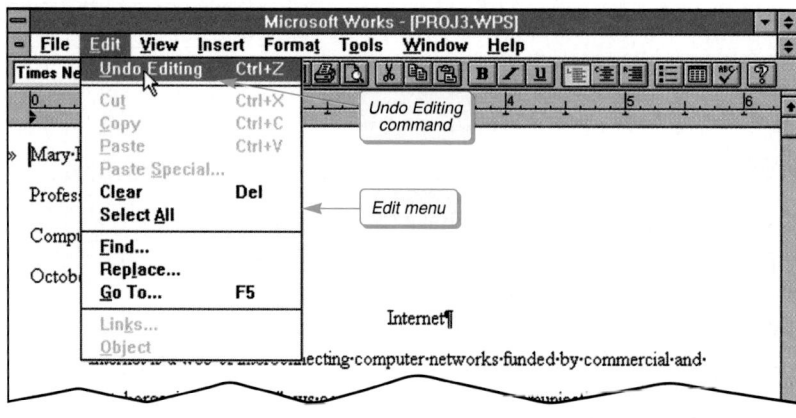

STEP 2 ►

Choose the Undo Editing command from the Edit menu.

Works undoes the editing that was performed and displays the document with the word ARPANET in the second paragraph and wherever else it was replaced (Figure 3-50).

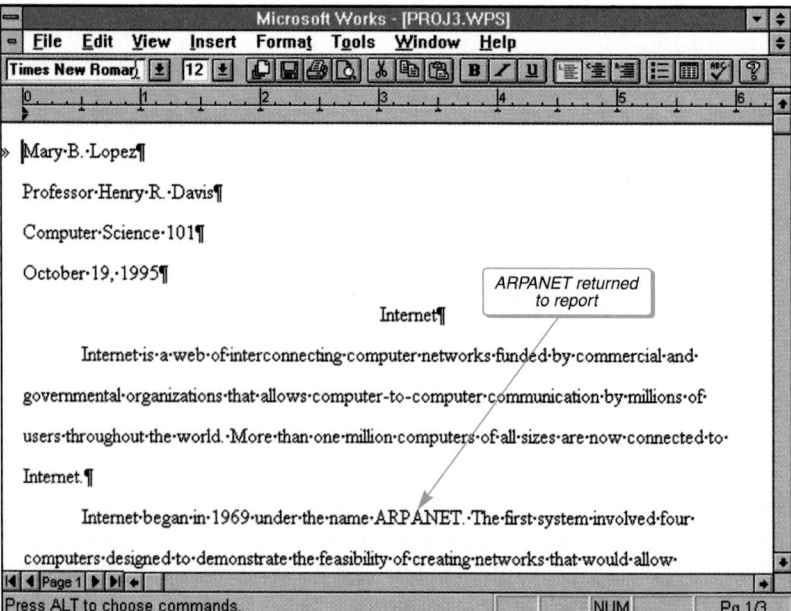

FIGURE 3-50

The Undo Editing command is a useful command and is especially valuable when you delete words or paragraphs accidentally and want to restore the document. Note, however, that you must choose the Undo command from the Edit menu immediately after you have performed the editing, without any intervening operations.

Redo Command

If you Undo an editing operation using the Undo Editing command, you can choose the **Redo Editing command** from the Edit menu to restore the document so it once again contains the editing. The Redo Editing command appears on the Edit menu after the Undo Editing command is used.

Moving Words, Sentences, or Paragraphs

Upon reviewing a document, you might want to move certain text to other locations within the document. With Works, you can move a single character, a single word or words, a sentence or sentences, or one or more paragraphs or sections of text within a document. Works provides three techniques that can be used to move data previously typed in a document.

These techniques are: (1) Use the **Cut button** and **Paste button** on the Toolbar; (2) Use the **Cut command** and **Paste command** from the Edit menu; and (3) Use **drag and drop**.

To use the Cut button and the Paste button to move text, highlight the text you want to move and then click the Cut button on the Toolbar. The text will be removed from the document and will be placed in an area of memory called the **Clipboard.** Then, position the insertion point at the location in the document where you want to place the text you just *cut* from the document and click the Paste button. The text on the Clipboard will be *pasted* into the document at the insertion point.

Instead of the Cut and Paste buttons, you can highlight the text you want to move, choose the Cut command from the Edit menu, position the insertion point where you want to place the text, and choose the Paste command from the Edit menu.

Using Drag and Drop to Move Text

In this project, you will learn to use the drag-and-drop method. The general steps to move text in a document using drag and drop are given below.

1. Highlight the text you want to move.
2. Position the mouse pointer within the highlighted text. The mouse pointer becomes the shape of a block arrow and the word DRAG displays below the arrow.
3. Hold down the left mouse button and drag the mouse pointer and accompanying insertion point to the location where you want to move the text. Release the left mouse button.

To illustrate the drag-and-drop method, assume in the research report you decide to move the second paragraph on page 2 that begins with the words, Internet has, to a location in front of the first paragraph on page 2 that begins with the words, All types (see Figure 3-51).

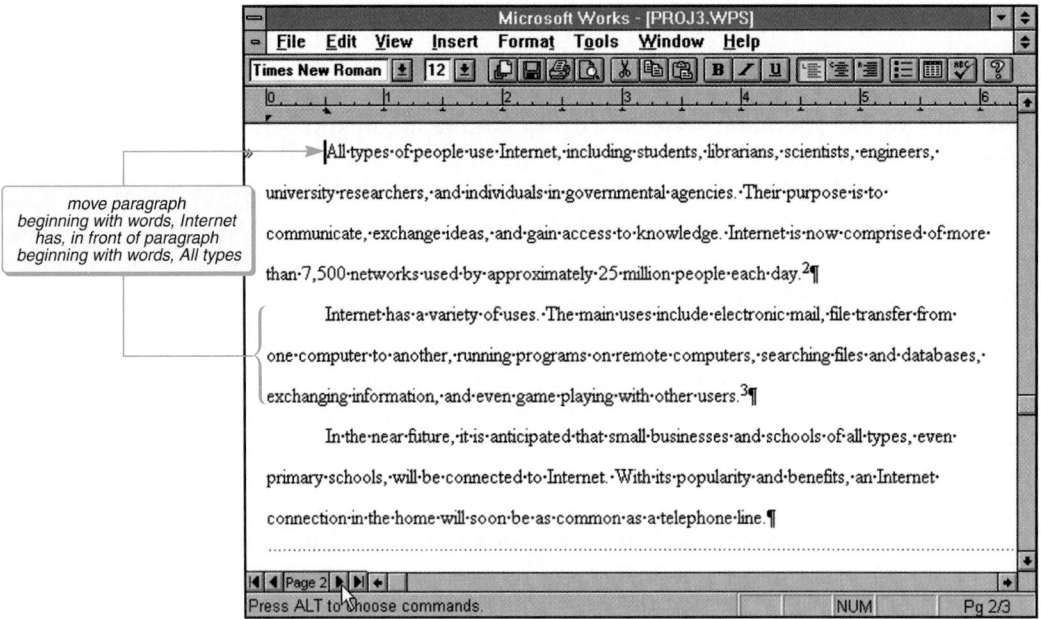

FIGURE 3-51

To move a paragraph using drag and drop, perform the following steps.

TO MOVE TEXT USING DRAG AND DROP ▼

STEP 1 ▶

Position the research report using the scroll arrows, page buttons, or Go To command so the first line of page 2 displays at the top of the screen. Highlight the second paragraph. Position the mouse pointer within the highlighted area of the paragraph.

The second paragraph is highlighted (Figure 3-52). The mouse pointer displays with the word DRAG beneath the arrow.

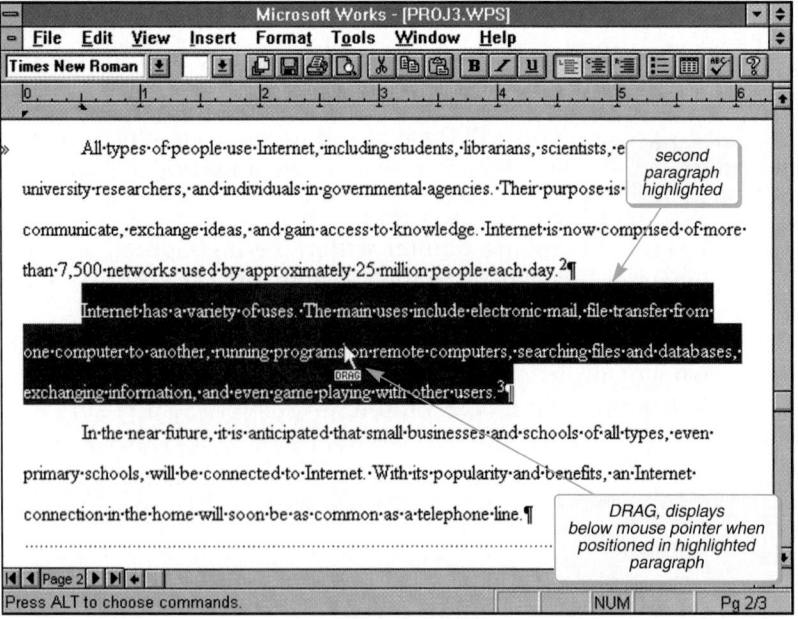

FIGURE 3-52

STEP 2 ▶

Drag upward until the dragged insertion point is positioned just in front of the word All, which is the first word in the first paragraph of the second page.

An insertion point follows the tip of the mouse pointer being dragged (Figure 3-53). The dragged insertion point is positioned in front of the word All, where the highlighted paragraph will be moved.

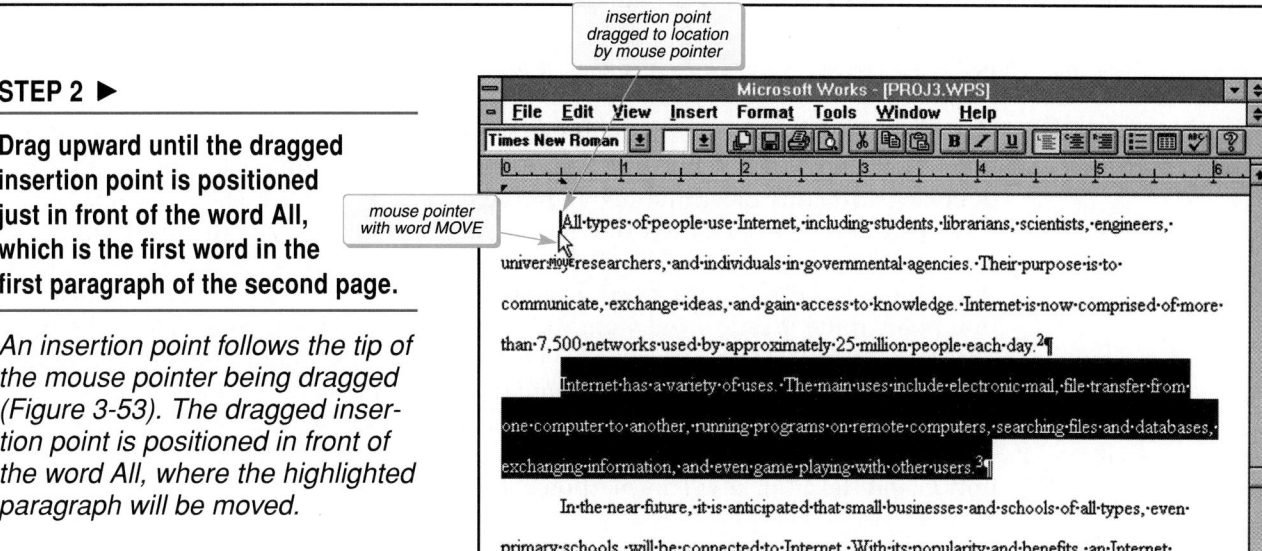

FIGURE 3-53

STEP 3 ▶

Release the left mouse button.

Works moves the highlighted paragraph and places it at the top of page 2 (Figure 3-54). Note that the footnote reference mark numbers have been automatically changed so they are in sequence in the document. The related footnotes in the NOTES section of the report will also be repositioned automatically.

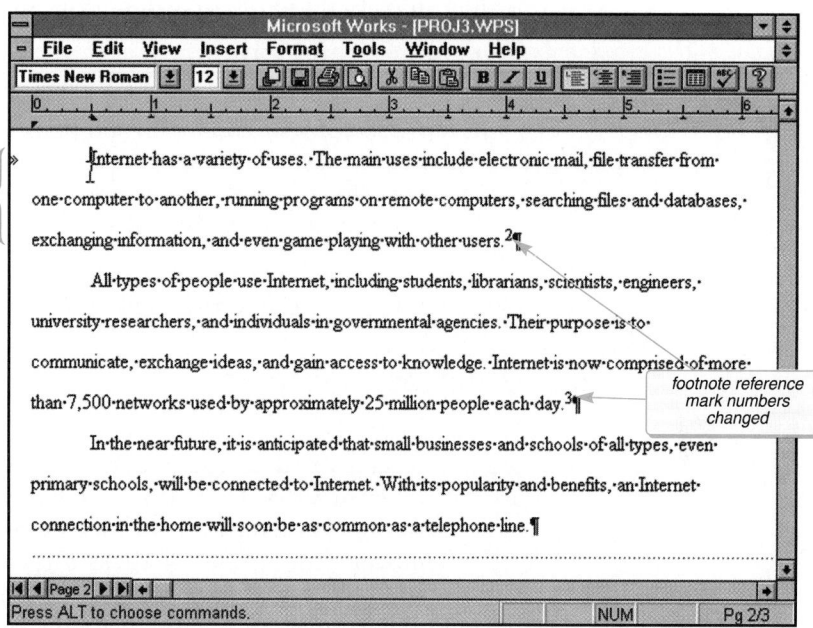

FIGURE 3-54

Drag and drop can be used to move a word or words, lines, sentences, or one or more paragraphs. As previously stated, you can also move words, lines, sentences, or one or more paragraphs using the Cut button and Paste button on the Toolbar, or the Cut command and Paste command from the Edit menu.

Copying Data in a Word Processing Document

In addition to moving text within a word processing document, you can also copy data. Copying data means to duplicate the data at another location within the document. To copy data, first highlight the data to be copied. Then, use one of three methods: (1) Click the Copy button on the Toolbar, place the insertion point at the location you want the copied data to appear, and click the Paste button on the Toolbar; (2) Choose the Copy command from the Edit menu, place the insertion point at the location you want the copied data to appear, and choose the Paste command from the Edit menu; or (3) Position the mouse pointer in the highlighted text, press the CTRL key and at the same time drag the mouse pointer displayed as a block arrow with the word COPY underneath it and the accompanying insertion point to the location you want the copied data to appear. Release the left mouse button and the CTRL key. This method is the drag-and-drop method.

Undoing a Drag-and-Drop Operation

You can undo a move or copy operation by choosing the Undo Drag and Drop command from the Edit menu. For example, in Figure 3-52 through Figure 3-54 on the previous two pages, paragraphs were moved, but the paragraphs in this project should actually remain in their original sequence. Therefore, perform the following steps to undo the drag-and-drop operation.

TO UNDO A DRAG-AND-DROP OPERATION

Step 1: Select the Edit menu and point to the Undo Drag and Drop command.
Step 2: Choose the Undo Drag and Drop command from the Edit menu.
Step 3: The text will appear in the report in the same order as it was prior to the drag-and-drop operation.

For the Undo Drag and Drop command to be effective, the command must be chosen before any other intervening steps occur.

Using the Thesaurus

When writing a research report, you might find instances where you want to replace certain words in the document with words of similar meaning. Such words are called **synonyms**. To do this, you can use the Works **thesaurus**. A thesaurus is a dictionary of synonyms. The Works thesaurus contains 200,000 words.

To illustrate the use of the thesaurus, you are to find a word to replace the word send in the research report. The word send is found in the second paragraph on page 1. To replace the word using the thesaurus, perform the following steps.

TO USE THE THESAURUS ▼

STEP 1 ►

Display page 1 of the research report. Scroll down to display the second paragraph. Highlight the word for which you need a synonym (send), select the Tools menu, and point to the Thesaurus command.

*The word send is highlighted in the research report (Figure 3-55). The mouse pointer points to the **Thesaurus command** on the Tools menu.*

FIGURE 3-55

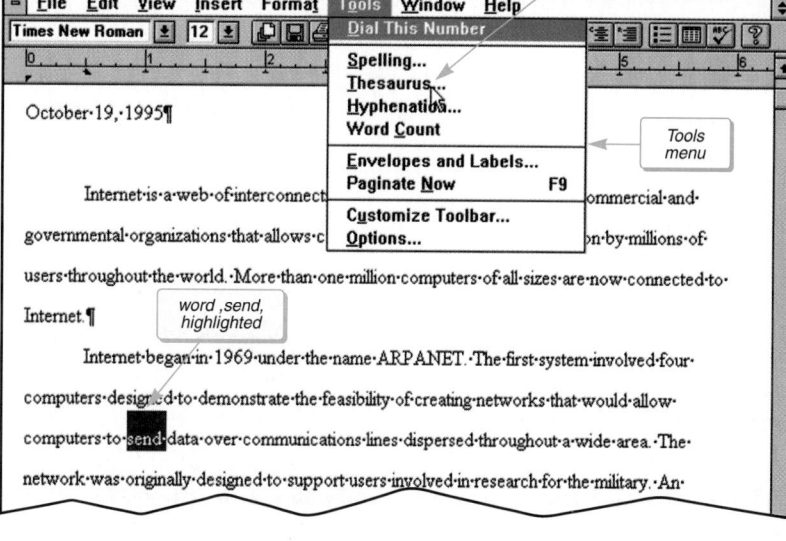

STEP 2 ►

Choose the Thesaurus command. When the Thesaurus dialog box displays, select transmit in the Synonyms box, and point to the Change button.

Works displays the Thesaurus dialog box (Figure 3-56). In the Meanings list box, Works displays a list of meanings of the word send. In the Synonyms list box is a list of synonyms. The word transmit is selected. The mouse pointer points to the Change button.

FIGURE 3-56

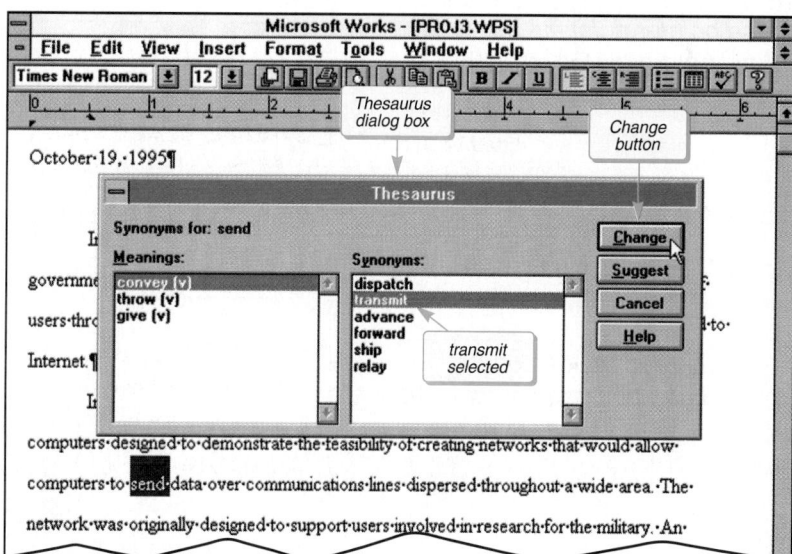

STEP 3 ►

Choose the Change button in the Thesaurus dialog box.

Works replaces the word send in the document with the word transmit (Figure 3-57).

FIGURE 3-57

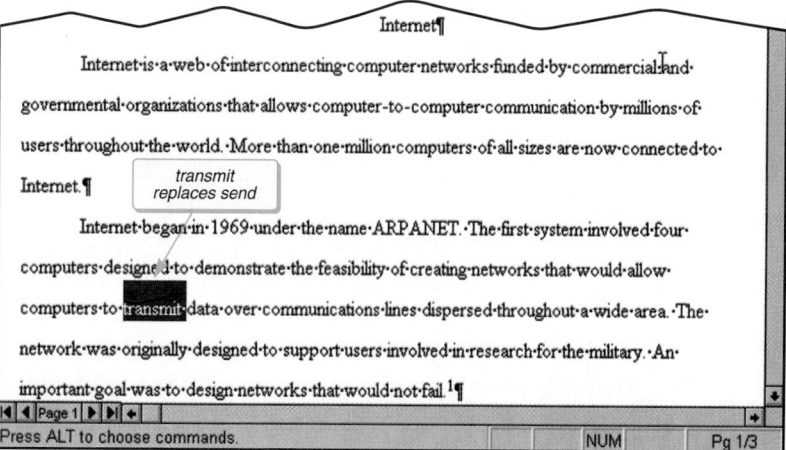

When using the Works thesaurus, you can select words from either the Meanings list box or the Synonyms list box. Clicking the Suggest button in the Thesaurus dialog box will display additional words in the thesaurus.

Counting Words

Works provides the capability to count the number of words in your document. When the words are counted, the count includes the words in the headers, footers, and footnotes. You can also count only the words in a highlighted portion of a document. To count all the words in a document, perform the following steps.

TO USE WORD COUNT ▼

STEP 1 ▶

Position the insertion point anywhere within the document. Select the Tools menu and point to the Word Count command.

The Tools menu displays and the mouse pointer points to the Word Count command (Figure 3-58).

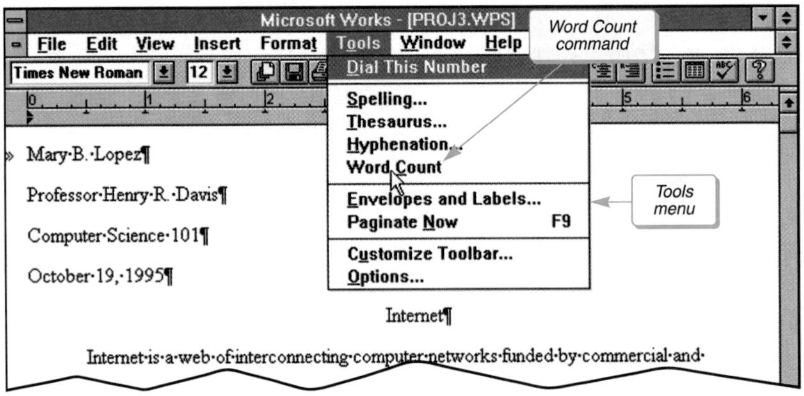

FIGURE 3-58

STEP 2 ▶

Choose the Word Count command from the Tools menu.

Works displays the Microsoft Works dialog box that contains the number of words in the document (Figure 3-59).

STEP 3 ▶

Choose the OK button in the Microsoft Works dialog box to remove the dialog box from the screen.

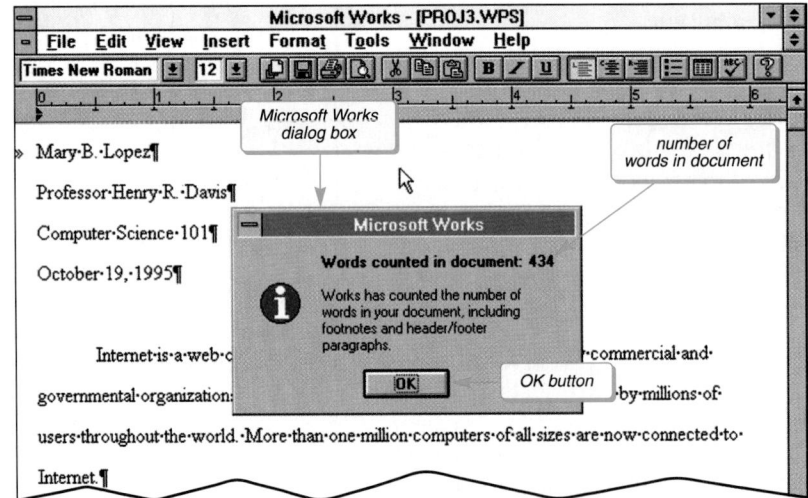

FIGURE 3-59

To count the number of words in the research report excluding the heading information and the footnotes, highlight the entire document beginning with the first paragraph and ending with the last paragraph, and then choose the Word Count command from the Tools menu.

Checking Spelling, Saving, and Printing the Research Report

After you enter and edit the report, check the spelling of the research report using the Check Spelling button on the Toolbar. When you create documents you should, as a final step, check the spelling to ensure no errors have occurred.

After checking the spelling, save the document on a diskette inserted in drive A, and then print the document using the Print button on the Toolbar. The completed research report appears in Figure 3-60.

Lopez 3

NOTES

[1] William Masterson, <u>Beginner's Guide to Using Internet</u> (San Francisco: Computer Network Press, 1995) 13-17.

[2] Marilyn Burkenson, "Who Is Using Internet?" <u>Business Network World</u> 17 (July 1995): 22-25.

[3] USA Wireservice, "The New World of Communications," <u>USA Daily</u> 19 May 1995, Evening ed., sec. Business: 12+.

Lopez 2

All types of people use Internet, including students, librarians, scientists, engineers, university researchers, and individuals in governmental agencies. Their purpose is to communicate, exchange ideas, and gain access to knowledge. Internet is now comprised of more than 7,500 networks used by approximately 25 million people each day.[2]

Internet has a variety of uses. The main uses include electronic mail, file transfer from one computer to another, running programs on remote computers, searching files and databases, exchanging information, and even game playing with other users.[3]

In the near future, it is anticipated that small businesses and schools of all types, even primary schools, will be connected to Internet. With its popularity and benefits, an Internet connection in the home will soon be as common as a telephone line.

Lopez 1

Mary B. Lopez
Professor Henry R. Davis
Computer Science 101
October 19, 1995

Internet

Internet is a web of interconnecting computer networks funded by commercial and governmental organizations that allows computer-to-computer communication by millions of users throughout the world. More than one million computers of all sizes are now connected to Internet.

Internet began in 1969 under the name ARPANET. The first system involved four computers designed to demonstrate the feasibility of creating networks that would allow computers to transmit data over communications lines dispersed throughout a wide area. The network was originally designed to support users involved in research for the military. An important goal was to design networks that would not fail.[1]

The four computers forming the original ARPANET were located at the University of California at Santa Barbara, the University of California at Los Angeles, Stanford Research Institute, and the University of Utah. During the 1970s, numerous other computers and networks were added to the system. Some were privately funded and others were funded by the government. Eventually many of the privately and publicly funded networks merged to form a comprehensive interconnected network called Internet. Today, Internet consists of many different intercommunicating networks. Internet now operates in more than 40 countries throughout the world.

Internet services are designed to support scholarly research for individuals, educational institutions, and governmental agencies. Internet may also be used by commercial firms when engaged in open research. As a system, Internet is governed and regulated cooperatively without actual laws. It is operated based on codes of conduct and a common ethic.

FIGURE 3-60

▶ TABLES IN WORD PROCESSING DOCUMENTS

After reviewing the research report in Figure 3-60, the next step is to add a table to the report to depict the growth predictions for the use of Internet. Tables provide a method of presenting information that may be conveniently displayed in columns and rows. Figure 3-61 illustrates the table.

Table 1

Internet Growth Projections

	1995	2000
Networks	7,500	200,000
Computers	1,000,000	50,000,000
Service Providers	1,000	5,000
Direct Users	25,000,000	100,000,000

FIGURE 3-61

When writing research reports, use the following general guidelines for creating a table.

1. Begin the table with the table heading. The heading should start with the word Table and be followed by the number of the table. The first table should be labeled Table 1.
2. The next line should contain the title of the table.
3. Column headings should appear on the next line, followed by row labels and the data comprising the table.
4. The table should be double-spaced.
5. The columns should be wide enough to display the information in a visually appealing form that can be easily read.
6. The table should be centered horizontally on the document.
7. Immediately under the table title, a single border line should display. A double border line should display beneath the column headings. After the last line in the table, a single border line should display.
8. Three blank lines should separate the table from the text, both at the beginning of the table and at the end of the table.

It is important to follow these guidelines when creating a table for use in a research report.

Creating the Table

Works provides several ways in which you can create a table. One method uses tab stops placed at locations on the ruler to allow information to be typed in columns. The other method uses the **Spreadsheet/Table command** from the Insert menu, the **Object command** from the Insert menu, or the **Insert Table button** on the Toolbar. This method causes a spreadsheet table to be placed within the word processing document. A spreadsheet table provides for entering data in columns and rows. The table in the research report will be created using the spreadsheet table approach together with the Insert Table button on the Toolbar.

Before creating the table, you should determine where in the report the table will be placed and create space for the table. The table in the research report in this project is to be placed following the second paragraph on page 2 and is to be preceded by a sentence explaining the contents of the table.

Thus, the first step in creating a spreadsheet table is to enter an explanatory sentence, create space in the word processing document for the spreadsheet table, and insert the table into the document. To accomplish these tasks, complete the steps below and on the next page.

TO CREATE SPACE FOR A TABLE ▼

STEP 1 ►

Position the text in the document so the last line of the second paragraph on page 2 (the line ending with footnote reference mark number 3) displays at the top of the screen. Then place the insertion point at the end of the line following the footnote reference mark number and press the ENTER key once. Type Table 1 shows the projected growth of Internet from 1995 to the year 2000. **Press the ENTER key once. Move the first-line indent marker to the zero position on the ruler. Press the ENTER key two additional times. Position the insertion point in front of the second paragraph mark and click the Center Align button on the Toolbar. The screen now contains an area for the table.**

The line of text introducing the table displays near the top of the screen (Figure 3-62). The insertion point and paragraph mark for the table are centered in the document. The first paragraph mark provides space before the table. The last paragraph mark provides space after the table.

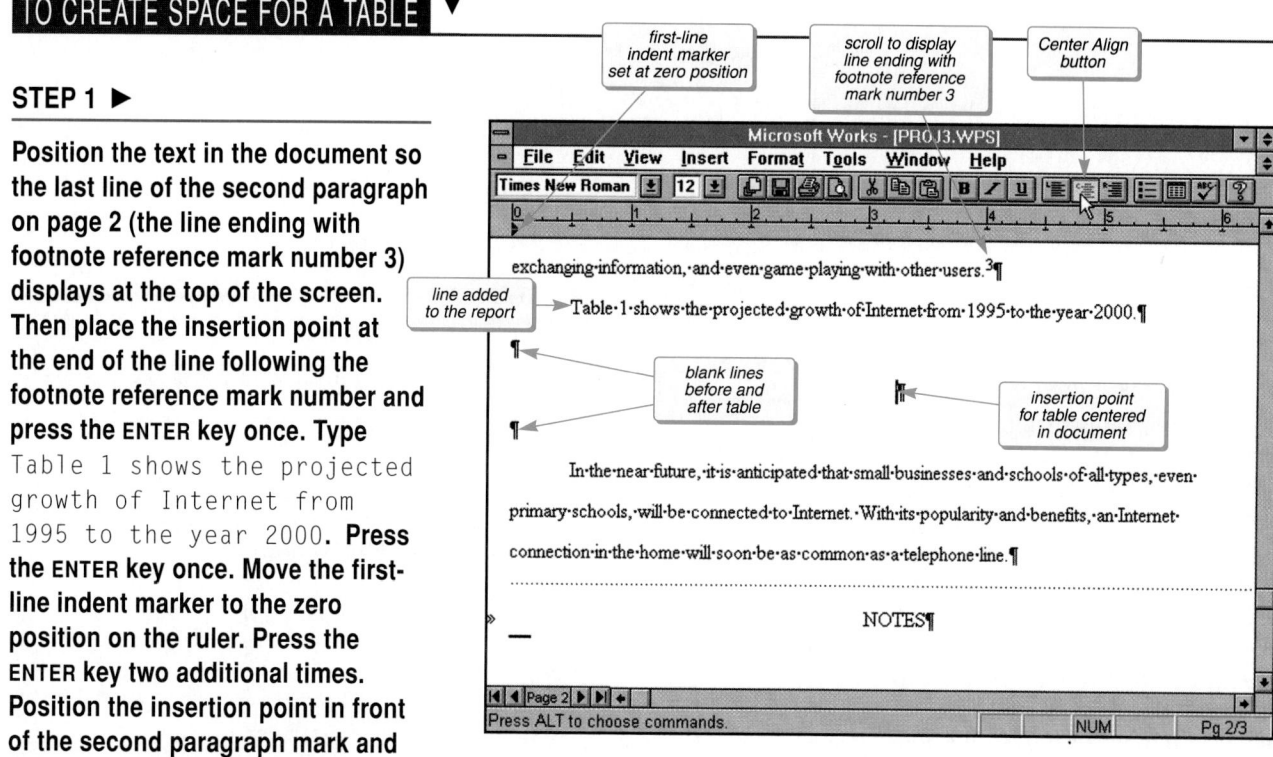

FIGURE 3-62

STEP 2 ▶

Click the Insert Table button on the Toolbar.

The Spreadsheet/Table dialog box displays (Figure 3-63). The New table option button is selected. This is the default selection and should be used because a new table is going to be created.

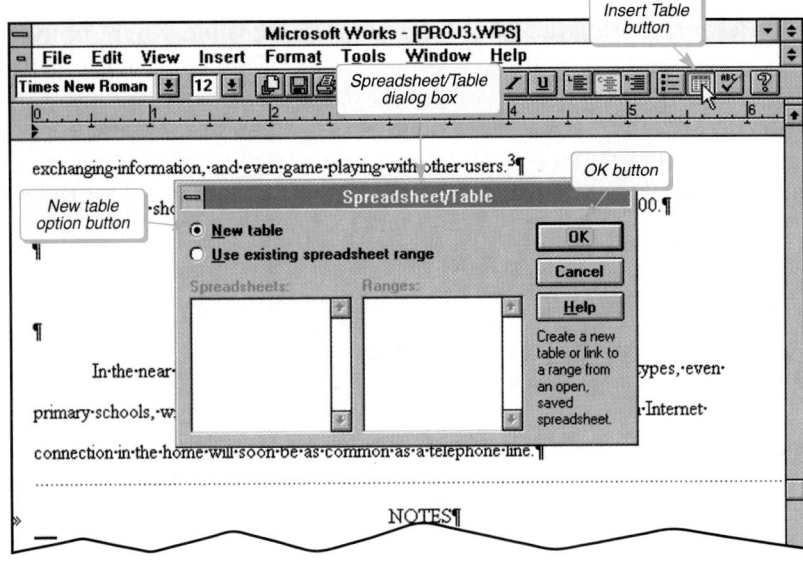

FIGURE 3-63

STEP 3 ▶

Choose the OK button in the Spreadsheet/Table dialog box.

A spreadsheet table displays in the word processing document window (Figure 3-64). The Toolbar changes and displays the buttons associated with a spreadsheet; the Font and Font Size change; and the menu changes to contain the spreadsheet commands. Thus, within the word processing document, you have the capability to use the full power of the Works Spreadsheet to create a table.

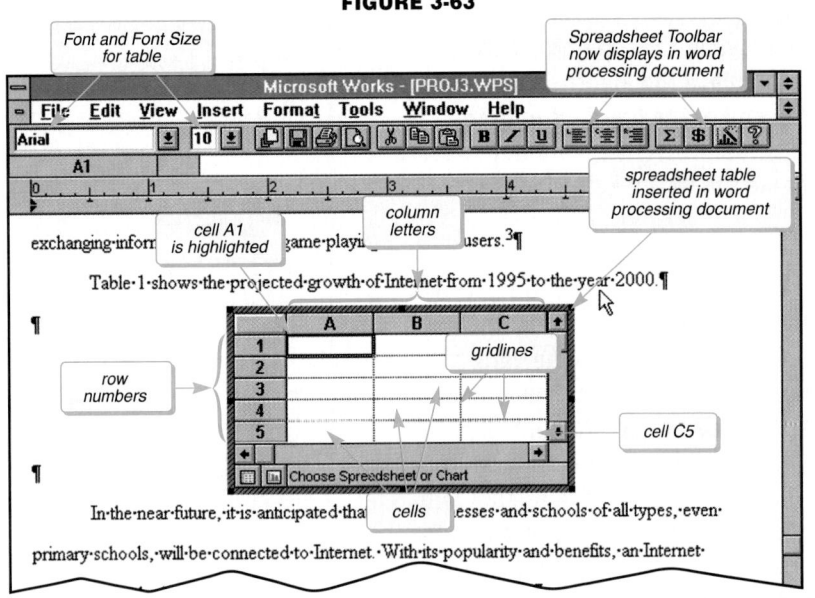

FIGURE 3-64

The spreadsheet table that displays consists of three prealigned **columns**, labeled A, B, and C, and five **rows** labeled 1, 2, 3, 4, and 5. The columns and rows are separated by vertical and horizontal lines called **gridlines**. The gridlines form small rectangular boxes called **cells**. Each cell is referenced by specifying an intersecting column letter and row number. Thus, A1 references the cell in the upper left corner of the spreadsheet table, and C5 references the cell in the lower right corner of the spreadsheet table.

When creating a table, information is entered into specific cells in the spreadsheet table. To enter data into a cell, you must highlight the cell. When you highlight a cell, the cell is outlined by a dark border. In Figure 3-64, cell A1 is highlighted. A variety of ways exist to highlight a cell, including positioning the mouse pointer in the cell and clicking the left mouse button.

Enlarging the Table

The spreadsheet table that displays in the word processing document window contains three columns and five rows. In analyzing the table you are to create as illustrated in Figure 3-61 on page W3.40, you can see there are seven lines of text and/or numbers. Therefore, the number of rows in the table must be increased to seven. To increase the number of rows in a table, complete the following steps.

TO INCREASE THE ROWS IN A SPREADSHEET TABLE ▼

STEP 1 ▶

Click outside the spreadsheet table that displays within the word processing document.

The spreadsheet table with column letters and row numbers disappears from the screen and a table consisting of three columns and five rows displays (Figure 3-65). The table contains no values. Also, the Word Processor Toolbar and menu bar display.

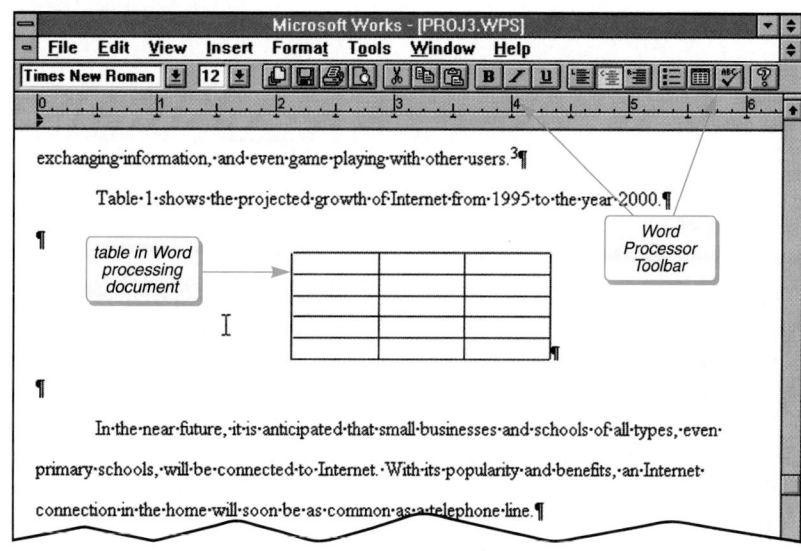

FIGURE 3-65

STEP 2 ▶

Position the mouse pointer in the table and click. Then, position the mouse pointer on the small darkened box in the center of the bottom line of the table. The mouse pointer becomes the shape of a small square with an arrow on the top and bottom of the box and the word RESIZE below it.

*The table displays with dotted lines around the outside border (Figure 3-66). Small darkened boxes, called **resize handles**, appear in each corner and in the center of each of the sides of the table. The table is an **object** in the word processing document. You can move or change the size of an object.*

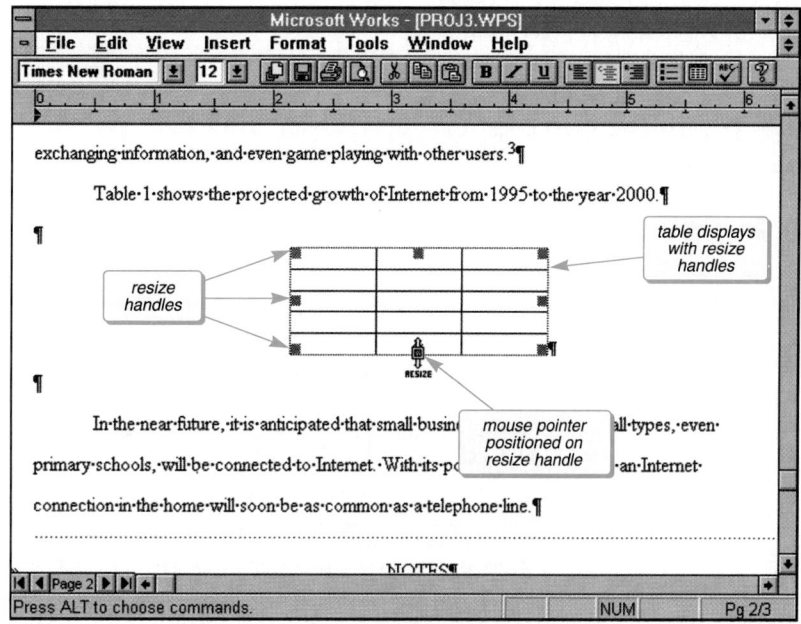

FIGURE 3-66

STEP 3 ▶

Hold down the left mouse button and drag the mouse pointer down approximately the height of two rows. Release the left mouse button.

Works adds two rows to the table to expand it to seven rows (Figure 3-67).

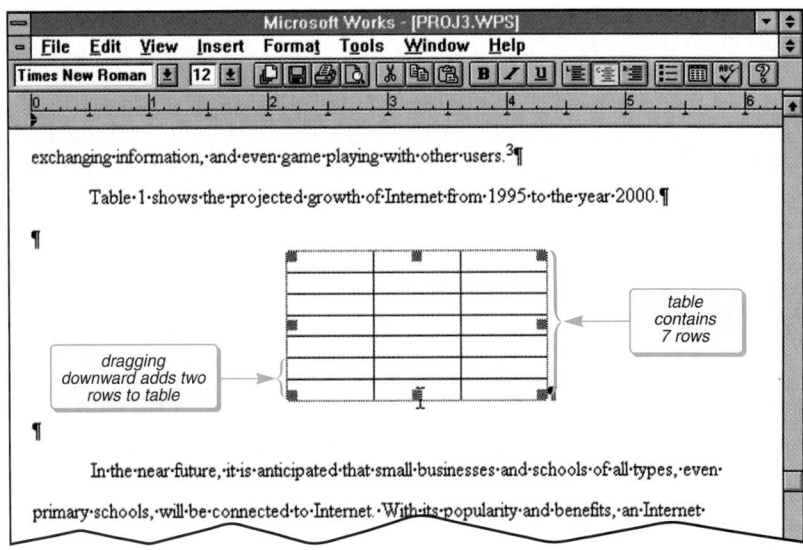

FIGURE 3-67

STEP 4 ▶

With the mouse pointer located anywhere within the table object, double-click the left mouse button to return to the spreadsheet table.

The spreadsheet table that contains column letters and row numbers again displays (Figure 3-68). The spreadsheet table contains seven rows. Cell A1 is the highlighted cell. The mouse pointer becomes the shape of a block plus sign within the spreadsheet table. The Spreadsheet menu bar and Toolbar display.

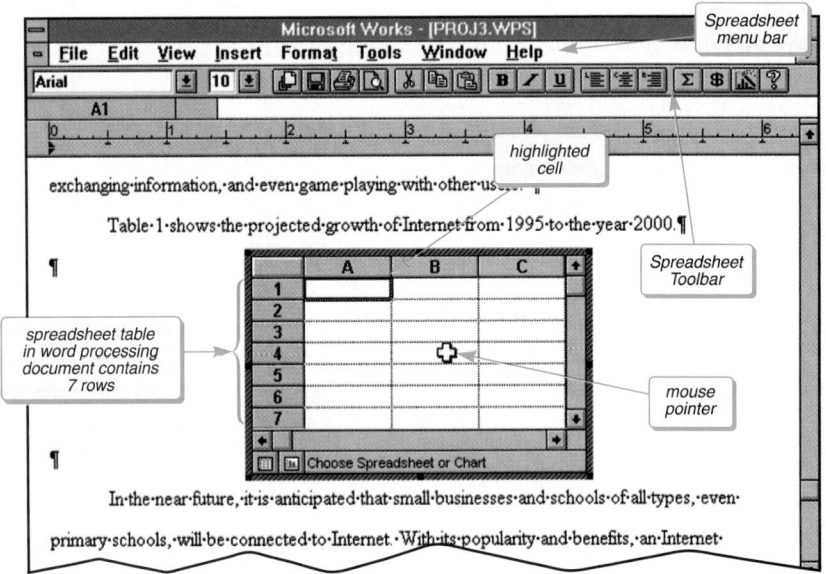

FIGURE 3-68

It is now possible to enter data into the table.

Increasing Row Height

Although it is possible to enter data into the spreadsheet table at this point, the column widths are too small to effectively display the information; and as specified in the guidelines for creating a table, the table should be double-spaced, that is, each line of text should be separated by a blank line. It is recommended, therefore, that before you enter data in the spreadsheet table, you increase the height of each row to effectively create a blank line between each line of text and/or numbers; and, that you increase the width of the columns to produce a table in which the data can be easily read.

To increase the row height to achieve the appearance of double-spacing in the spreadsheet, complete the following steps.

TO INCREASE ROW HEIGHT ▼

STEP 1 ►

Position the mouse pointer in cell A1 and drag down through cell A7.

Cells A1 through A7 are high-lighted (Figure 3-69).

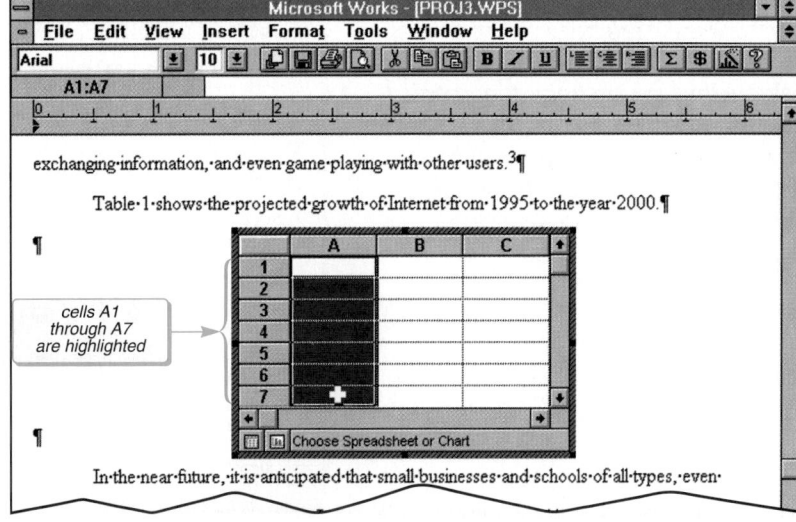

FIGURE 3-69

STEP 2 ►

Select the Format menu and point to the Row Height command.

The Format menu displays and the mouse pointer points to the Row Height command (Figure 3-70). Notice that the Format menu now contains entries pertaining to the spreadsheet/table as opposed to entries for the word processing document.

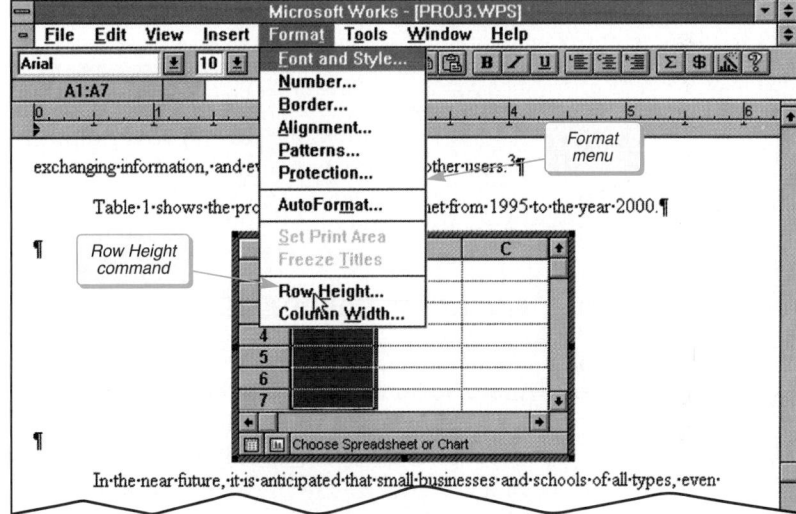

FIGURE 3-70

STEP 3 ►

Choose the Row Height command from the Format menu. When the Row Height dialog box displays, type 24 in the Height text box. Then point to the OK button.

The Row Height dialog box dis-plays (Figure 3-71). Initially, the box contains the number 12. The 12 indicates a standard row height that will properly display 10 point fonts. You double the height of each cell when you type 24 in the Height text box. The mouse pointer points to the OK button.

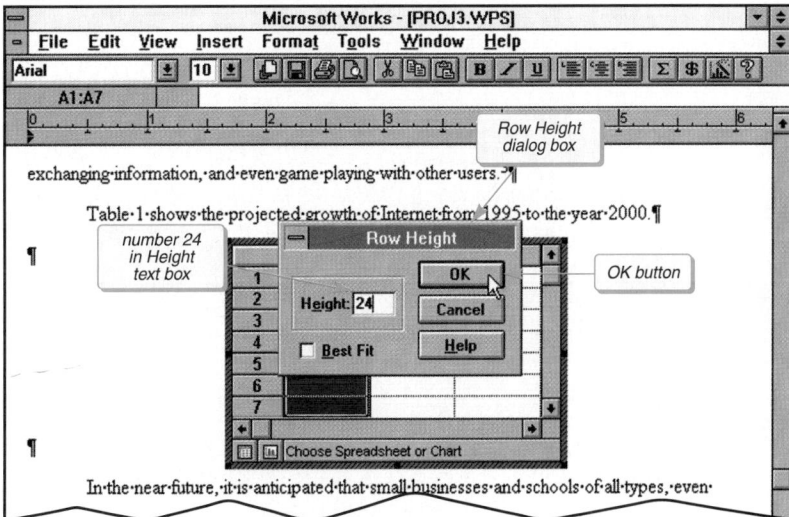

FIGURE 3-71

STEP 4 ▶

Choose the OK button in the Row Height dialog box.

Works displays the spreadsheet table with the row height increased (Figure 3-72). When data is entered in a cell in the spreadsheet table, a blank area will display above each line, as if the table is double-spaced.

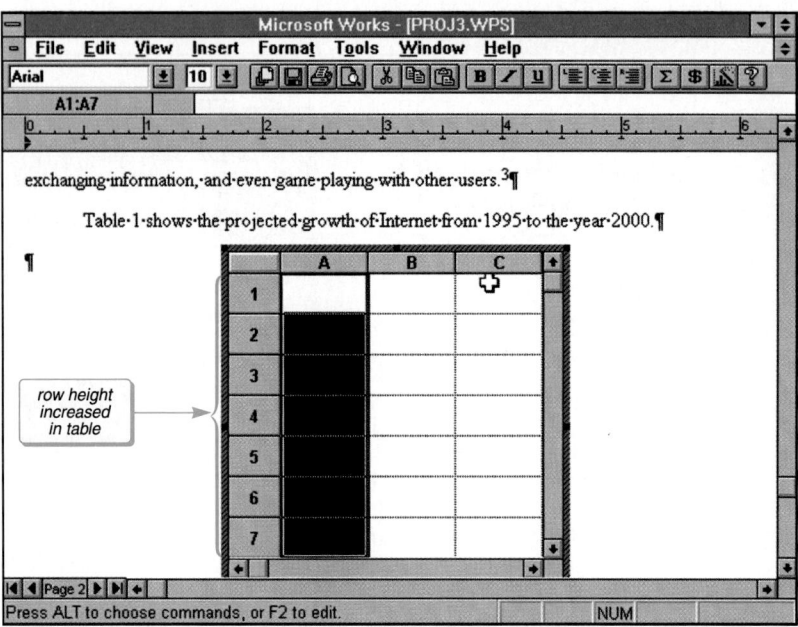

FIGURE 3-72

The default value for the row height is 12. To change back to the default value, you must enter the number 12 in the Height text box in the Row Height dialog box. Click any cell to remove the highlight from cells A1 through A7 in the spreadsheet table.

Changing Column Width

To produce a table where the data is easy to read, the width of the columns must be increased. The default column width is 10. Approximately 9 average-width letters of the alphabet, numbers, or special characters can be placed in a column with a width of 10, although this number may vary based on the characters placed in a column. To allow more characters to be entered and to make the table more readable, the column width of all columns in the table should be increased to 20. To change the width of all columns in the spreadsheet table to 20, perform the following steps.

TO CHANGE COLUMN WIDTH ▼

STEP 1 ▶

To view the entire table on the screen, scroll the spreadsheet table upward by clicking the down scroll arrow in the word processing document window. Drag the mouse pointer across cells A1, B1, and C1 to highlight cells in all three columns of the table. Select the Format menu and point to the Column Width command.

*Cells A1, B1, and C1 are highlighted (Figure 3-73). The Format menu displays and the mouse pointer points to the **Column Width command**.*

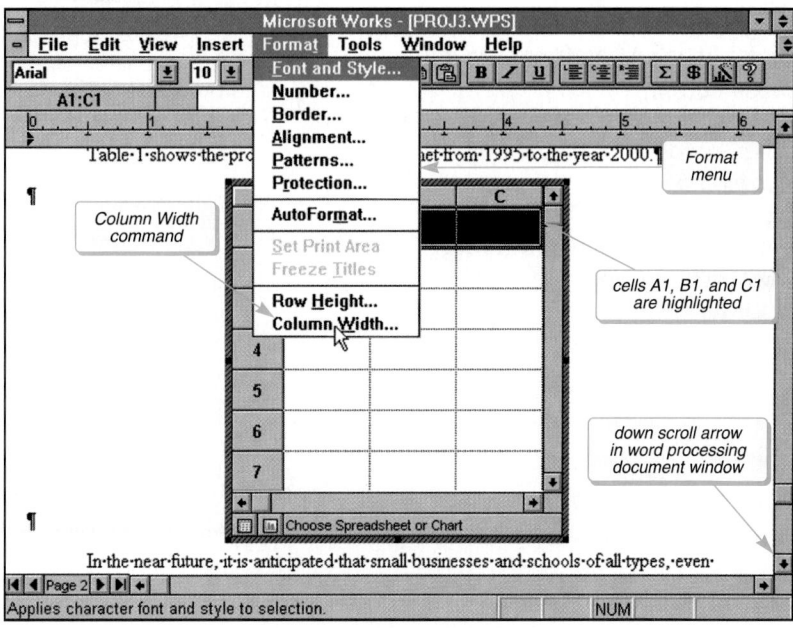

FIGURE 3-73

STEP 2 ▶

Choose the Column Width command from the Format menu. When the Column Width dialog box displays, type 20 in the Width text box and then point to the OK button.

The Column Width dialog box displays (Figure 3-74). The default value in the Width text box (10) has been changed to 20 to double the width of the columns. The mouse pointer points to the OK button.

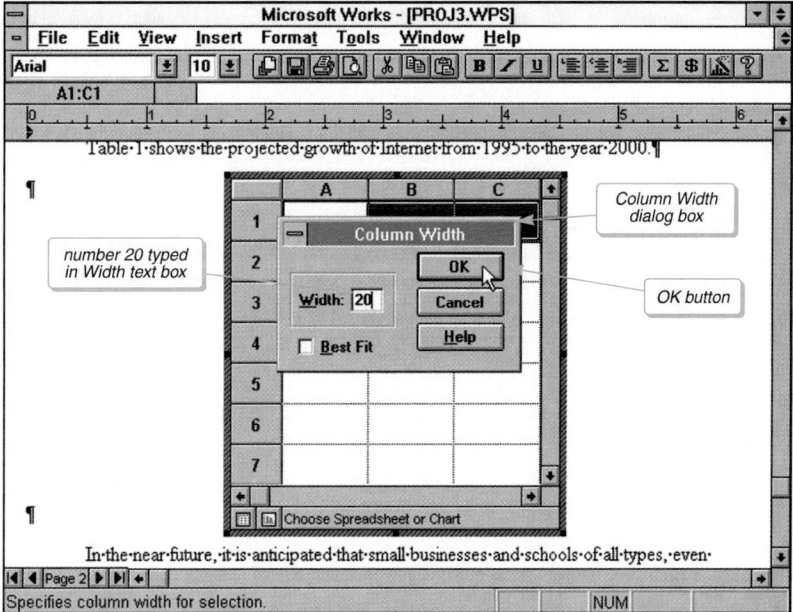

FIGURE 3-74

STEP 3 ▶

Choose the OK button. When the table displays, position the mouse pointer in cell A1 and click the left mouse button.

The spreadsheet table displays with the column widths increased (Figure 3-75). Selecting cell A1 removes the highlight from the other cells.

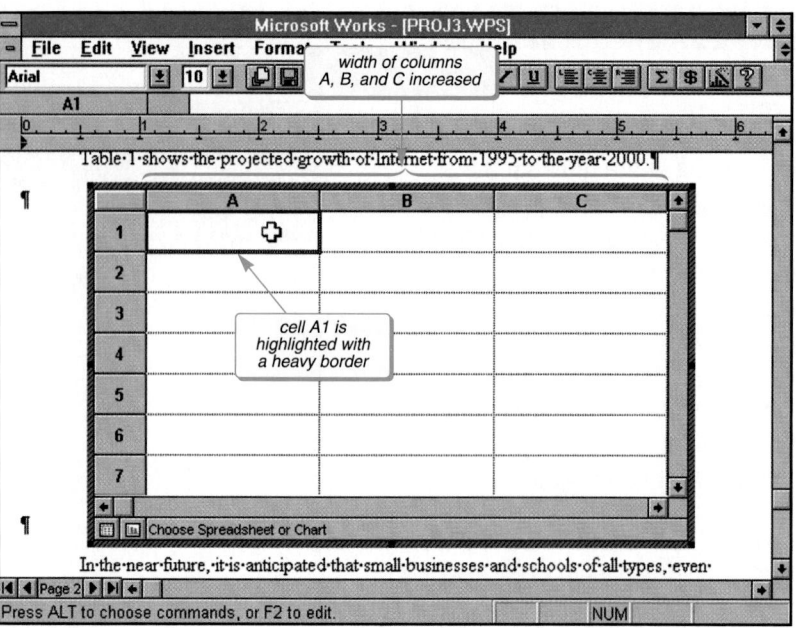

FIGURE 3-75

The new column width was an arbitrary selection to provide space between the columns so data placed in the columns would not have a crowded appearance. All columns do not have to be the same width.

Entering Data into the Spreadsheet Table

The next step is to enter data into the spreadsheet table. This is accomplished by highlighting the cell in which you want to enter data and typing the data. One method to highlight a cell is to position the mouse pointer in the cell and click the left mouse button. An alternative method is to use the arrow keys that are located to the right of the typewriter keys on the keyboard. After you press an arrow key, the adjacent cell in the direction of the arrow on the key becomes the highlighted cell.

To enter the table title and column headings into the spreadsheet table, perform the following steps.

TO ENTER DATA INTO A SPREADSHEET TABLE ▼

STEP 1 ▶

If necessary, highlight cell A1 by pointing to cell A1 and clicking the left mouse button. Type Table 1 in cell A1.

The entry Table 1 displays in cell A1 (Figure 3-76). The highlighted cell reference, A1, displays in the upper left portion of the screen called the **cell reference area**. This area is located in the **formula bar**. Works displays two boxes, one called the Cancel box and the other called the Enter box, in the formula bar. Clicking the Cancel box allows you to cancel an entry. Clicking the Enter box allows you to confirm an entry. All the characters you type display in the formula bar, followed immediately by an insertion point.

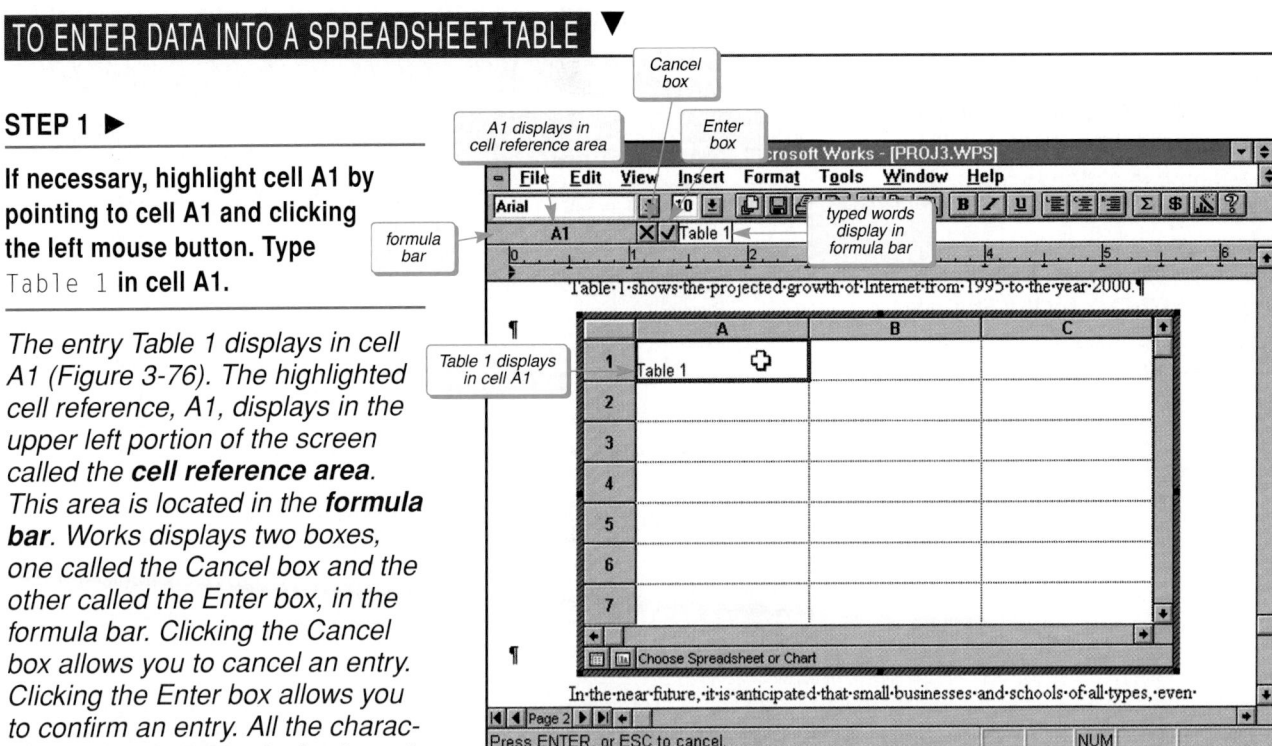

FIGURE 3-76

STEP 2 ▶

Press the DOWN ARROW key, and then type Internet Growth Projections in cell A2. Point to the Enter box in the formula bar.

When you press the DOWN ARROW key, Works confirms the entry in cell A1 and left-aligns the text in cell A1 (Figure 3-77). Because you pressed the DOWN ARROW key, the cell immediately below cell A1, cell A2, becomes the highlighted cell. As you type, the table title displays in cell A2 and in the formula bar. When you type more characters than can display in the cell, only the rightmost characters display in the cell, but all characters display in the formula bar.

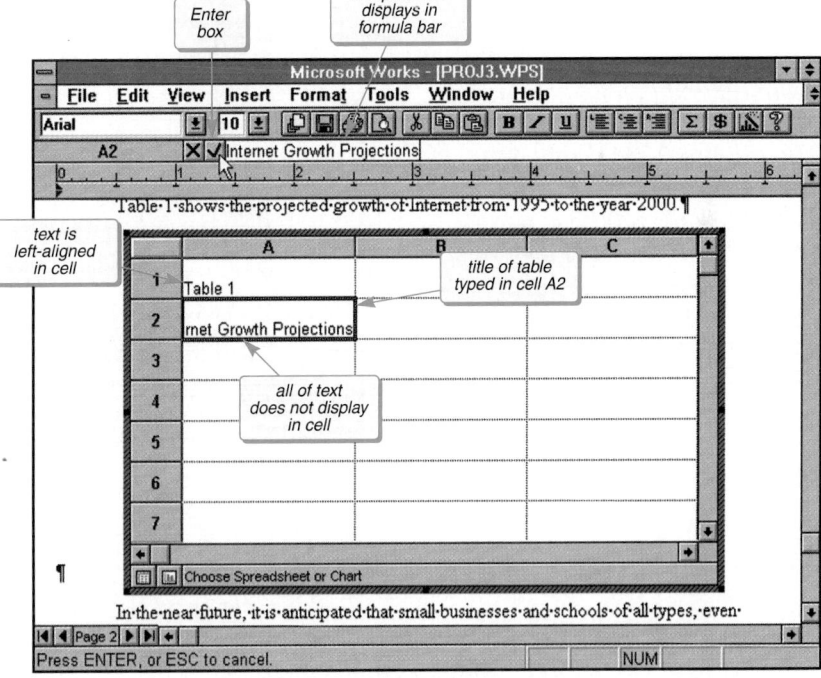

FIGURE 3-77

STEP 3 ▶

Click the Enter box to confirm the entry in cell A2. Then position the mouse pointer in cell B3 and click the left mouse button to highlight cell B3. Type 1995.

Works confirms the entry in cell A2 (Figure 3-78). All the text now displays and it overflows into cell B2. The entry is considered to be in cell A2, however. The column heading, consisting of the year 1995, displays in cell B3.

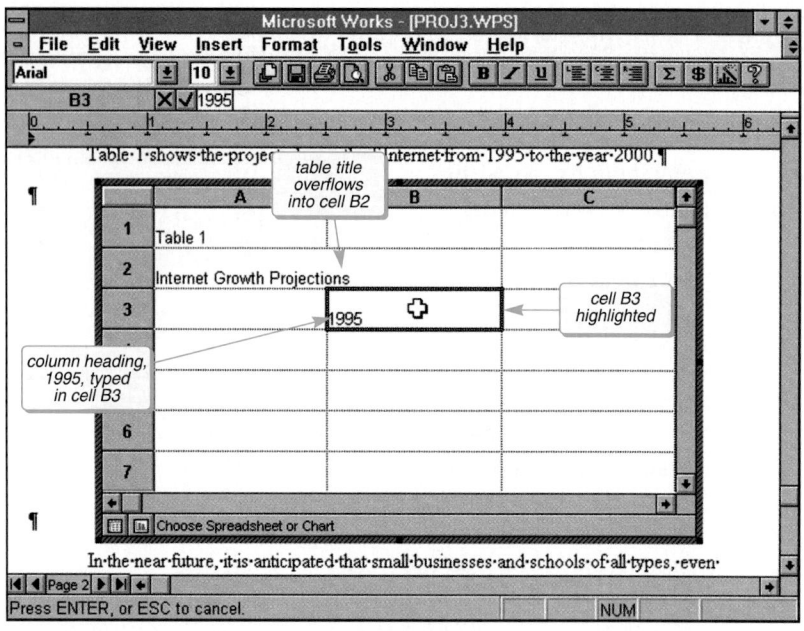

FIGURE 3-78

STEP 4 ▶

Press the RIGHT ARROW key. Type the column heading, 2000, in cell C3. Press the ENTER key.

When you press the RIGHT ARROW key, the entry in cell B3 is confirmed and is right-aligned in cell B3 because 1995 is a numeric value (Figure 3-79). When you press the ENTER key, the data you typed in cell C3 (2000) is confirmed, the data is right-aligned in the cell, and the cell remains highlighted. The entry of the table title and column headings is now complete.

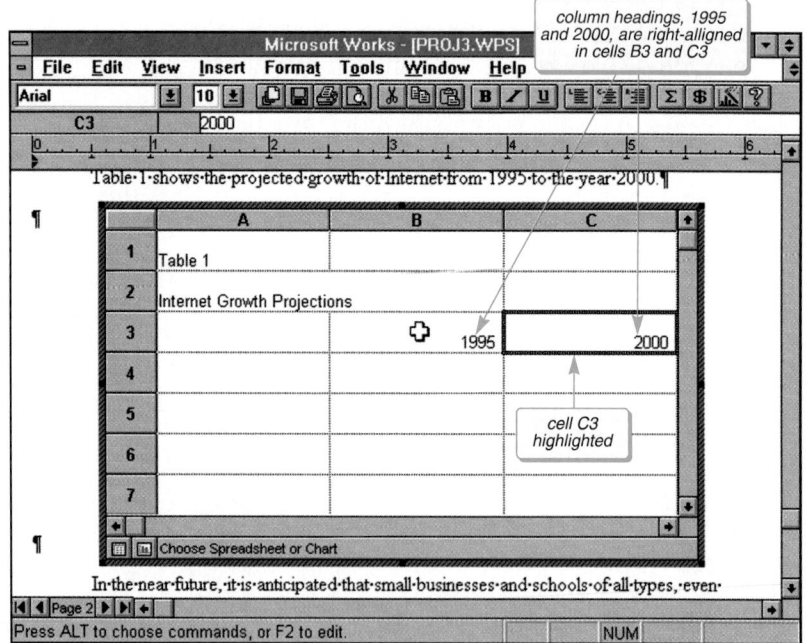

FIGURE 3-79

In the previous examples, three methods were used to confirm an entry in a cell. These methods included using the arrow keys, clicking the Enter box in the formula bar, and pressing the ENTER key. You can also confirm an entry in a cell by positioning the mouse pointer in a cell and clicking the left mouse button.

When you confirm an entry into a cell, a series of events occurs. First, when non-numeric data, called **text**, is confirmed, Works positions the text left-aligned in the highlighted cell. When you confirm the entry of numeric data into a cell, the data is right-aligned in the cell. Second, when text you enter contains more characters than can be displayed in the width of the cell, Works displays the over-flow characters in adjacent cells to the right as long as these adjacent cells contain no data. In Figure 3-78, cell A2 is not wide enough to contain the entire title. Thus, Works displays the overflow characters in cell B2 because it is empty. Third, when you confirm a text or numeric entry into a cell by clicking the Enter box or press-ing the ENTER key, the cell into which the data is entered remains the highlighted cell. When you confirm an entry using the arrow keys, the adjacent cell becomes highlighted.

When you confirm an entry into a cell, use the arrow keys if the next entry is in an adjacent cell. If the next entry is not in an adjacent cell, click the Enter box in the formula bar or press the ENTER key and then use the mouse pointer to high-light the appropriate cell for the next entry.

Correcting a Mistake While Typing

If you type the wrong letter or number and notice the error before confirming the entry, use the BACKSPACE key to erase all the characters back to and including the ones that are wrong. The insertion point will indicate where the next charac-ter you type will display. Then retype the remainder of the entry.

To cancel the entire entry before confirming the entry, click the Cancel box or press the ESC key.

If you see an error in data you have already entered into a cell, highlight the cell and retype the entire entry. To delete data from a cell, highlight the cell and press the DELETE key.

Entering Row Titles

The next step in developing the spreadsheet table is to enter the row titles in cells A4, A5, A6, and A7. This process is similar to entering the column titles. To enter the row titles, perform the steps below and on the next page.

TO ENTER ROW TITLES ▼

STEP 1 ▶

Highlight cell A4 by positioning the mouse pointer in cell A4 and clicking the left mouse button. Type the row title, Networks, and press the DOWN ARROW key.

The word Networks displays in cell A4, and cell A5 is highlighted (Figure 3-80).

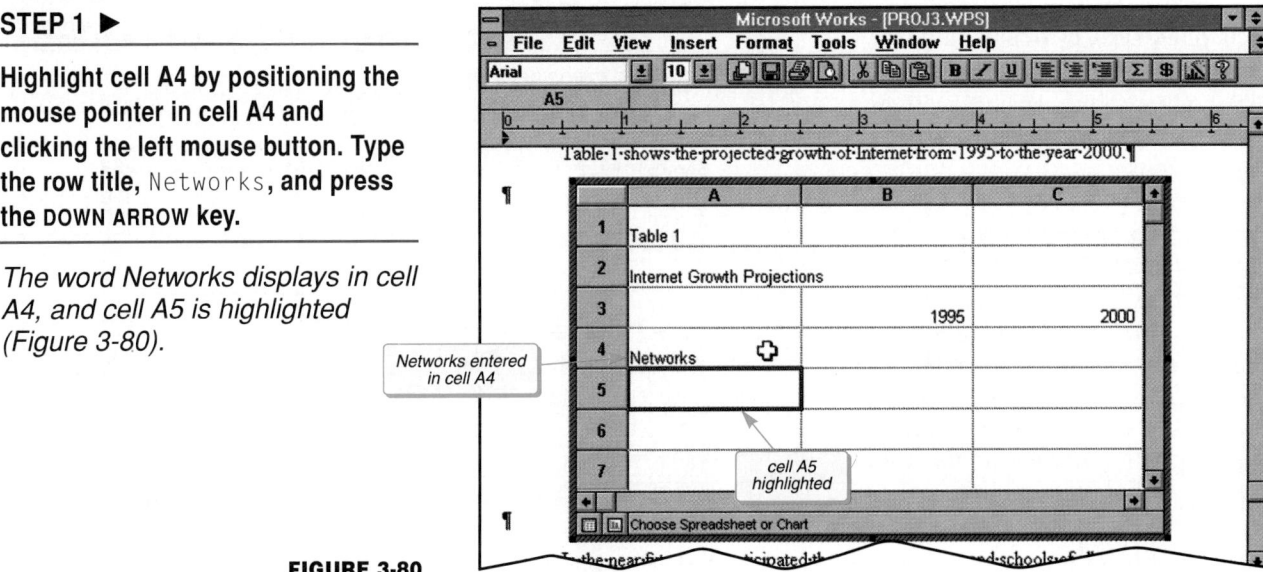

FIGURE 3-80

STEP 2 ▶

Type `Computers` **in cell A5 and press the DOWN ARROW key. Type** `Service Providers` **in cell A6 and press the DOWN ARROW key. Type** `Direct Users` **in cell A7. Confirm the last row title in cell A7 by clicking the Enter box or pressing the ENTER key.**

The row titles display as shown in Figure 3-81. Cell A7 remains highlighted.

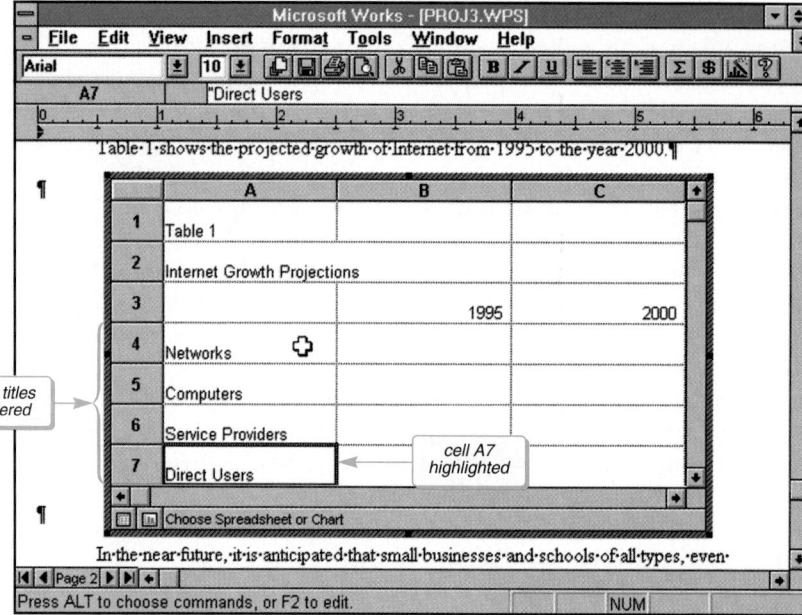

FIGURE 3-81

Entering Numeric Data in the Spreadsheet Table

The next step is to enter the numeric data that comprises the table. Numbers can include the digits zero through nine and any one of the following characters: + - ( ) , / . $ % E e. The E and e are used when performing special types of mathematical operations. If a cell entry contains any other character from the keyboard, Works interprets the entry as text and treats it accordingly.

In the spreadsheet table, you must enter the numbers for the various categories for the year 1995 and the year 2000. Complete the following steps to enter these values one row at a time.

TO ENTER NUMERIC DATA INTO A TABLE ▼

STEP 1 ▶

Highlight cell B4 by positioning the mouse pointer in cell B4 and clicking the left mouse button. Then type `7500`**. Press the RIGHT ARROW key.**

When you type, the number 7500 displays in cell B4 (Figure 3-82). The number is entered without a comma. You will add the comma later when you format the data. Pressing the RIGHT ARROW key confirms the entry in cell B4 and right-aligns the number in the cell. Cell C4 is highlighted.

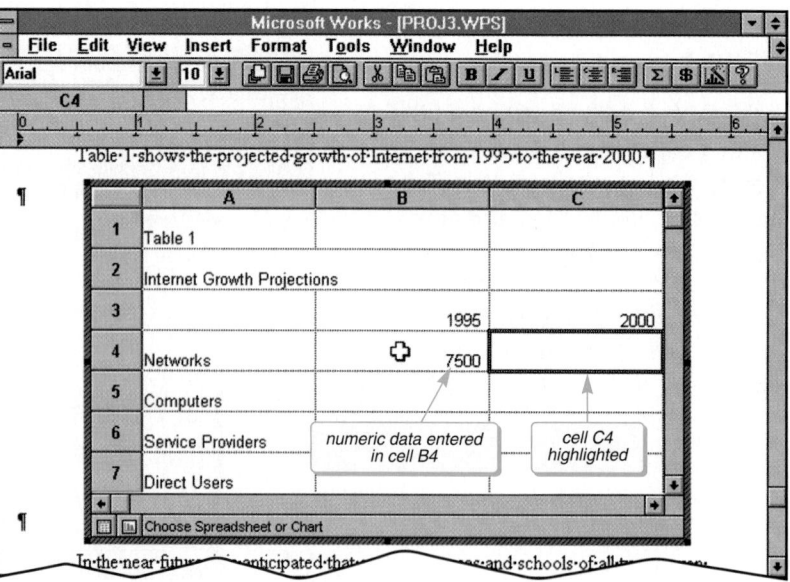

FIGURE 3-82

STEP 2 ▶

Enter 200000 in cell C4. Press the ENTER key or click the Enter box. Highlight each of the remaining cells, one at a time, and enter the appropriate number in each cell using techniques previously explained. After the value is entered in cell C7, press the ENTER key or click the Enter box.

You have now entered all the numbers required for the spreadsheet table (Figure 3-83).

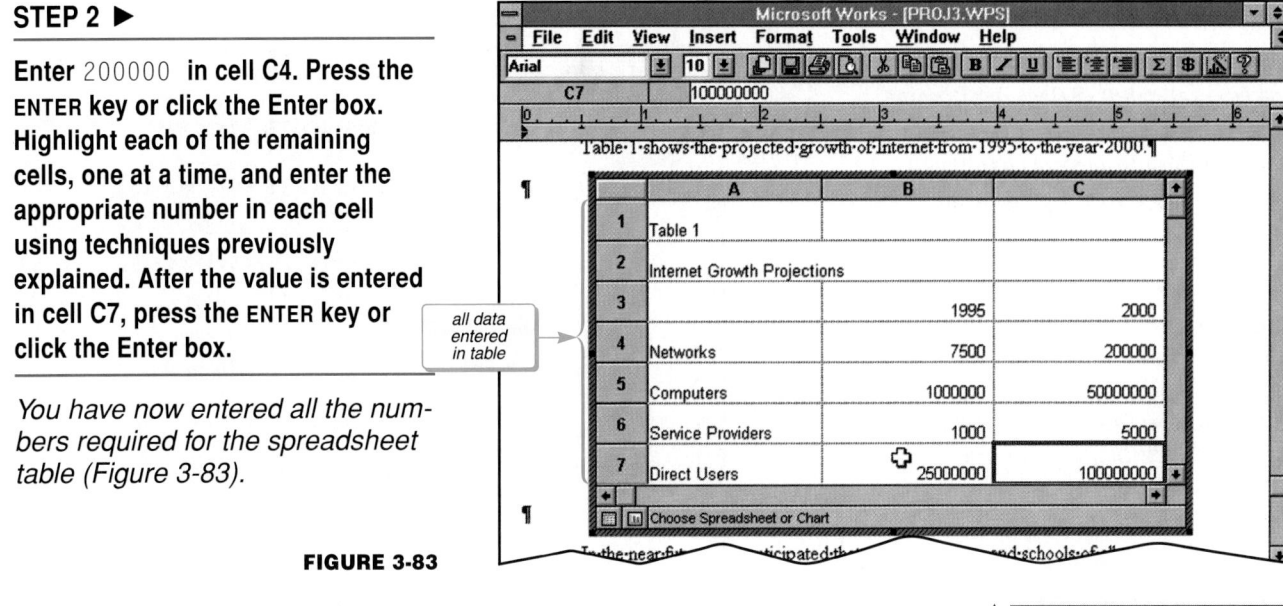

FIGURE 3-83

Formatting the Spreadsheet Table

After typing the information comprising the spreadsheet table, it is frequently desirable to format the table. Formatting involves such tasks as inserting dollar signs, commas, and decimal points in the numeric data entered; changing fonts and font styles and sizes; adding borders; and similar tasks.

In the research report, you should insert commas in the numbers so they are easier to read, add a single border line beneath the table title, add a double border line beneath the column titles, and add a single border line across the width of the table after the last row. This is the style recommended when a table is used in a research report.

Complete the following steps to format the numbers to display with commas.

TO FORMAT NUMBERS WITH COMMAS ▼

STEP 1 ▶

Highlight cell B4 through cell C7 by positioning the mouse pointer in cell B4 and dragging across and down to cell C7. Select the Format menu and point to the Number command.

*Cells B4 through C7 are highlighted (Figure 3-84). The mouse pointer points to the **Number command** on the Format menu.*

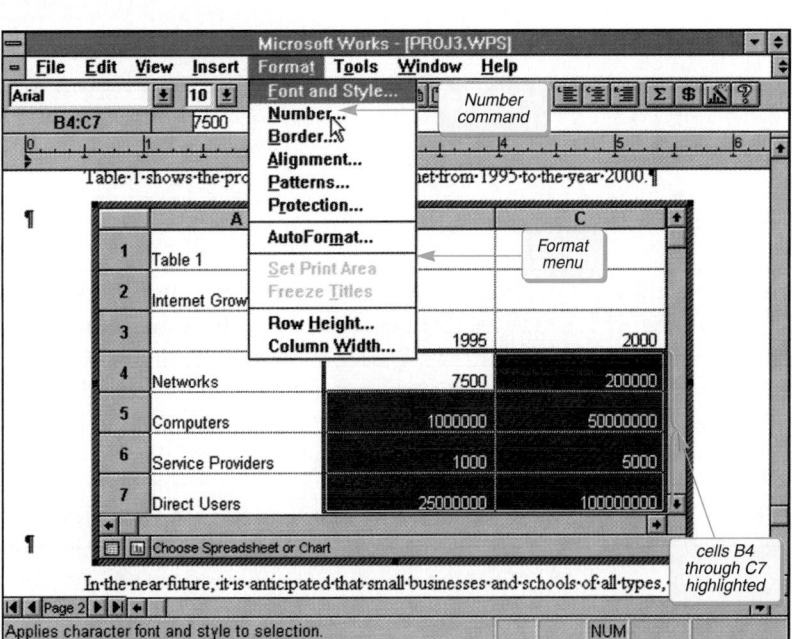

FIGURE 3-84

STEP 2 ▶

Choose the Number command from the Format menu. Select the Comma option button in the Format area. Type 0 in the Number of decimals text box. Point to the OK button.

The Number dialog box displays (Figure 3-85). The Comma option button is selected. The value 0 displays in the Number of decimals text box and the mouse pointer points to the OK button. A sample of the format displays in the Sample area.

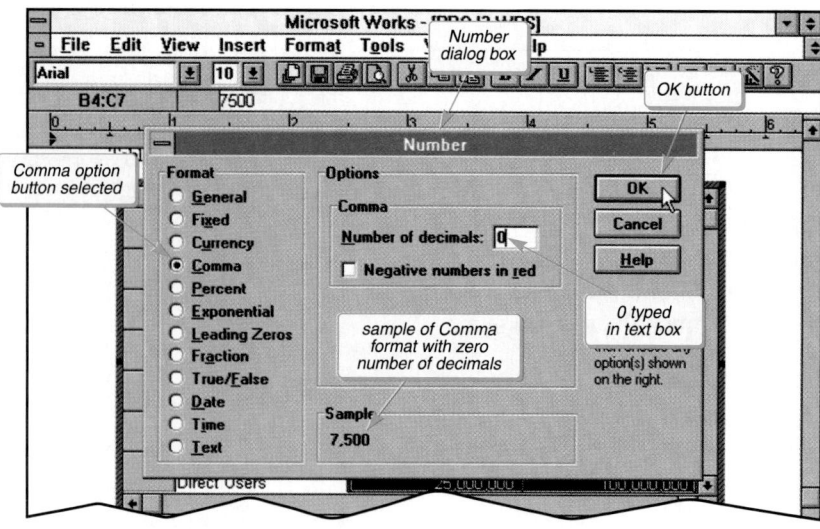

FIGURE 3-85

STEP 3 ▶

Choose the OK button in the Number dialog box. Click any cell in the table to remove the highlight.

The spreadsheet table displays with the numbers formatted using commas (Figure 3-86).

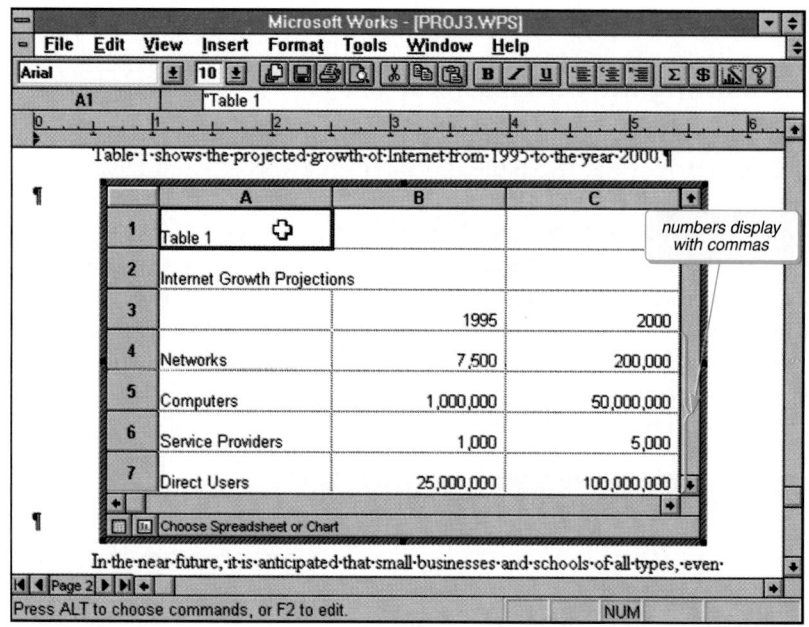

FIGURE 3-86

After inserting commas in the numbers, you are now ready to format the spreadsheet table by adding the required border lines under the titles and after the last row. Before you do this, it is recommended that you remove the gridlines from the screen so the lines will be easier to see.

Removing Gridlines

The dotted lines surrounding each cell are called **gridlines**. It is recommended that you remove the gridlines from the screen when adding other types of lines on the display. To remove the gridlines from the display, complete the following steps.

TO REMOVE GRIDLINES ▼

STEP 1 ►

Select the View menu and point to the Gridlines command.

*The View menu displays (Figure 3-87). The mouse pointer points to the **Gridlines command**. Notice there is a checkmark to the left of the Gridlines command. This indicates gridlines will display.*

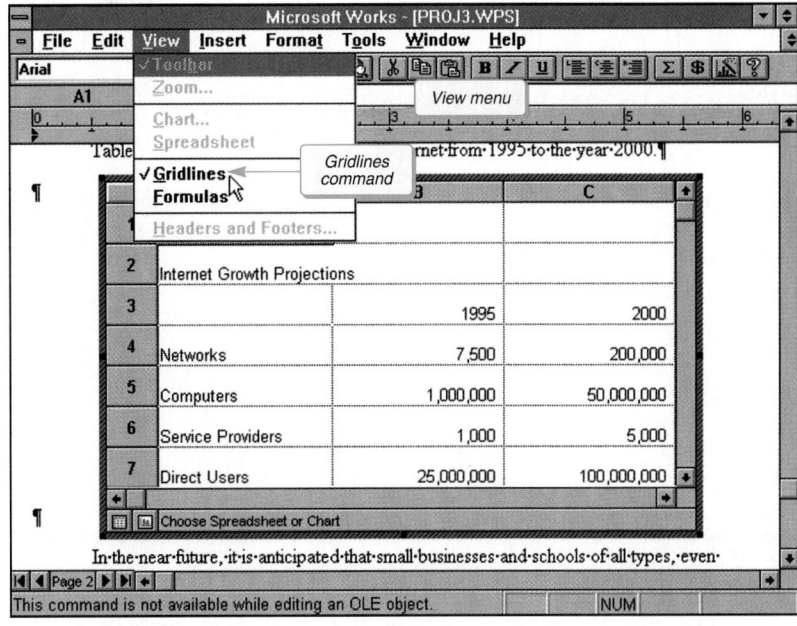

FIGURE 3-87

STEP 2 ►

Choose the Gridlines command from the View menu.

The spreadsheet table displays without the gridlines (Figure 3-88).

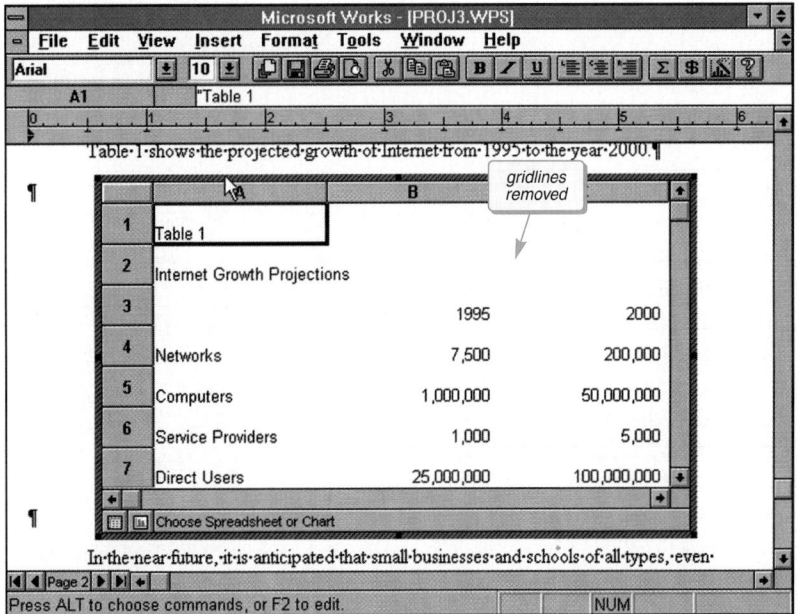

FIGURE 3-88

Adding Borders to the Spreadsheet Table

The final step in creating the spreadsheet table is to add the required borders. To add borders, perform the following steps.

TO ADD BORDERS TO A SPREADSHEET TABLE ▼

STEP 1 ▶

Highlight cells A2, B2, and C2 by positioning the mouse pointer in cell A2 and dragging across through cell C2. Select the Format menu and point to the Border command.

Cells A2, B2, and C2 are highlighted (Figure 3-89). Works displays the Format menu and the mouse pointer points to the **Border command***.*

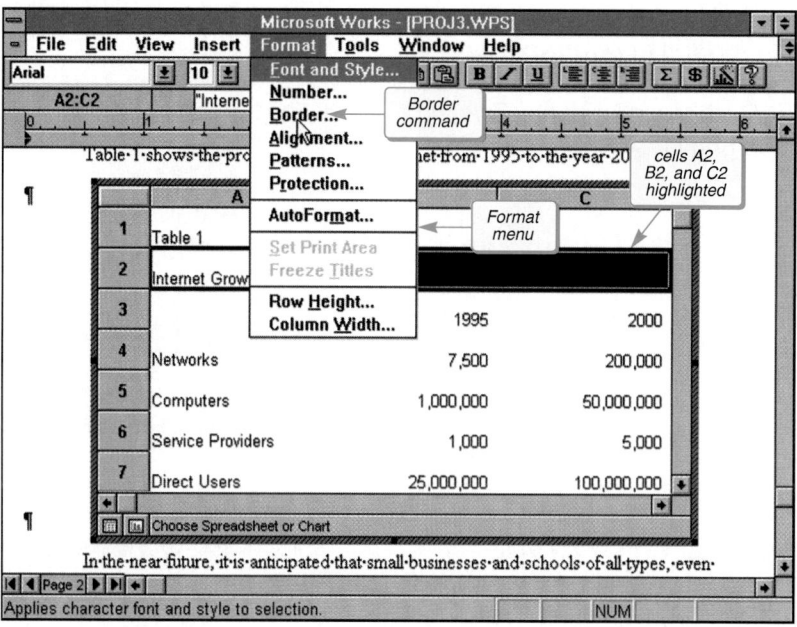

FIGURE 3-89

STEP 2 ▶

Choose the Border command from the Format menu. When the Border dialog box displays, point to the Bottom box in the Border area.

The Border dialog box displays (Figure 3-90). The box containing the narrow line in the Line Style area is selected as indicated by the dark border surrounding the box. This is the Works default selection. A dark border also appears around the Outline box in the Border area. The Outline box is the default selection. The mouse pointer points to the Bottom box.

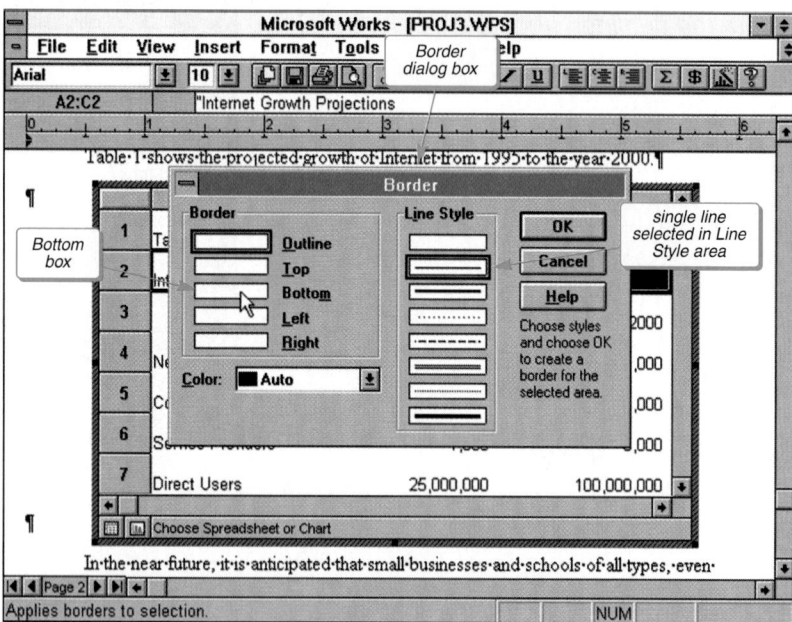

FIGURE 3-90

STEP 3 ▶

Select the Bottom box in the Border area by clicking the left mouse button. Point to the OK button.

The Bottom box is outlined with a dark border and a single narrow line appears within the box (Figure 3-91). This is the line that will display at the bottom of the highlighted cells.

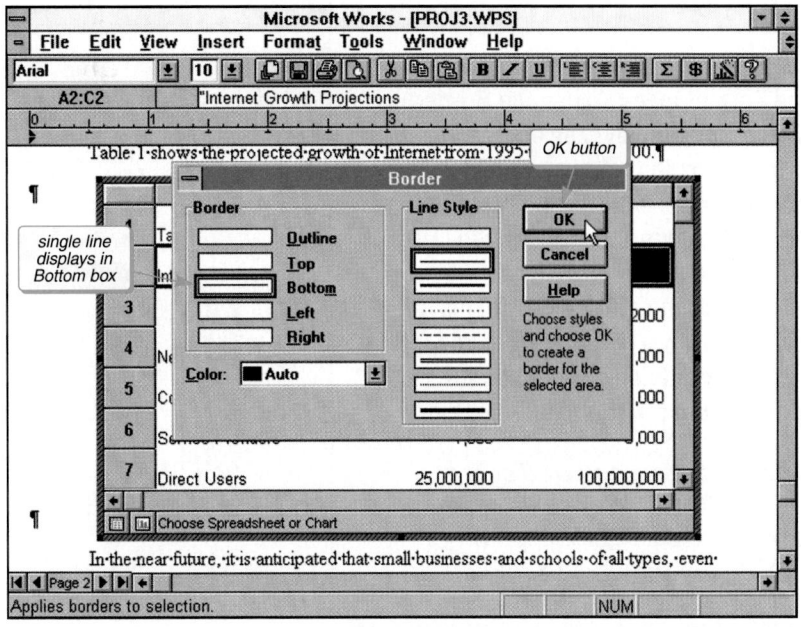

FIGURE 3-91

STEP 4 ▶

Choose the OK button in the Border dialog box. Highlight cells A3, B3, and C3 by positioning the mouse pointer in cell A3 and dragging across through cell C3. Select the Format menu and point to the Border command.

The table displays (Figure 3-92). A single, narrow line displays at the bottom of cells A2, B2, and C2. The single line is difficult to see because of the highlight around cells A3, B3, and C3. Works displays the Format menu and the mouse pointer points to the Border command.

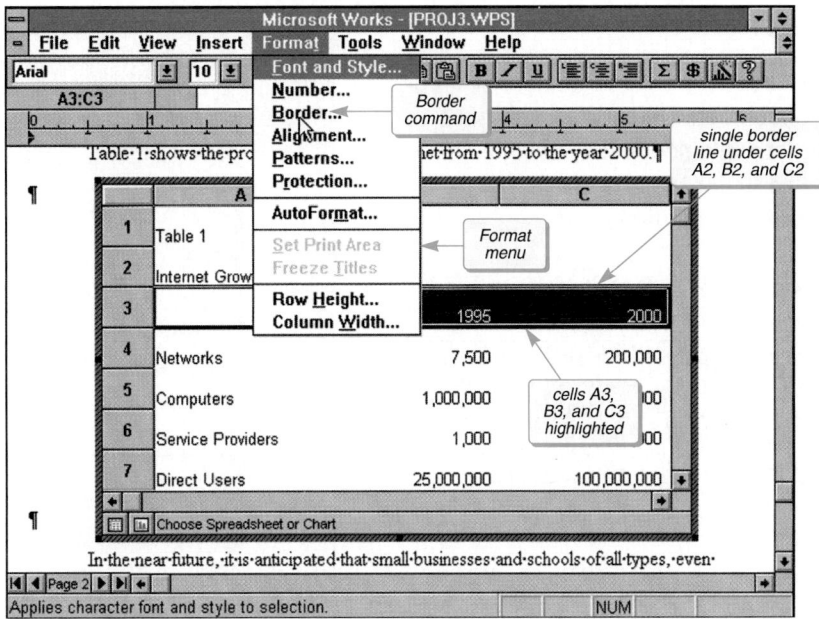

FIGURE 3-92

STEP 5 ▶

Choose the Border command from the Format menu. When the Border dialog box displays, select the Bottom box in the Border area by positioning the mouse pointer in the box and clicking the left mouse button. Select the option box containing the double line in the Line Style area by pointing to the box that contains the double line and clicking the left mouse button.

The Border dialog box displays (Figure 3-93). After selecting the boxes, a dark border appears around the Bottom box and the box contains a double line. A dark border also appears around the Double Line option box.

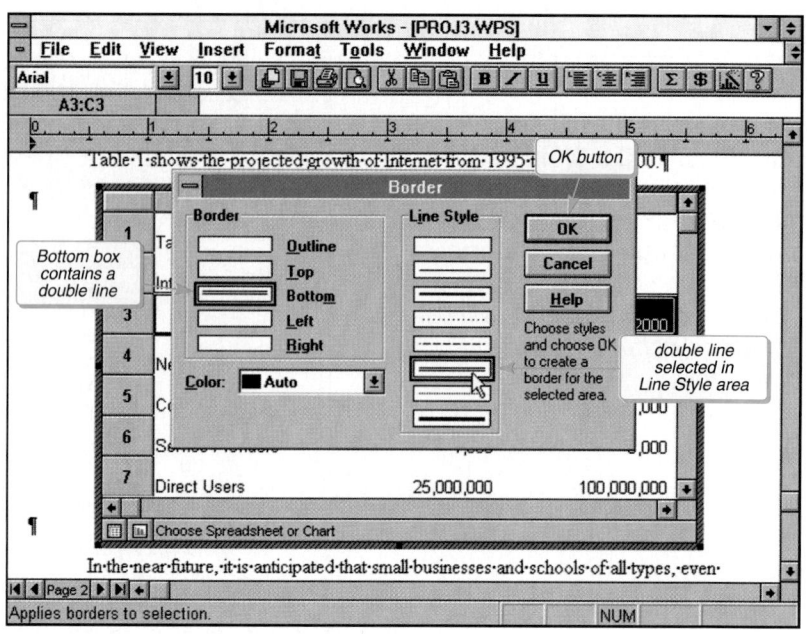

FIGURE 3-93

STEP 6 ▶

Choose the OK button in the Border dialog box. Using the techniques just explained, place a single narrow line under the last row in the spreadsheet table.

The completed spreadsheet table displays in Figure 3-94. A single line appears under the table title. A double line appears under the column titles, and a single line is placed under the last row, although it is difficult to see.

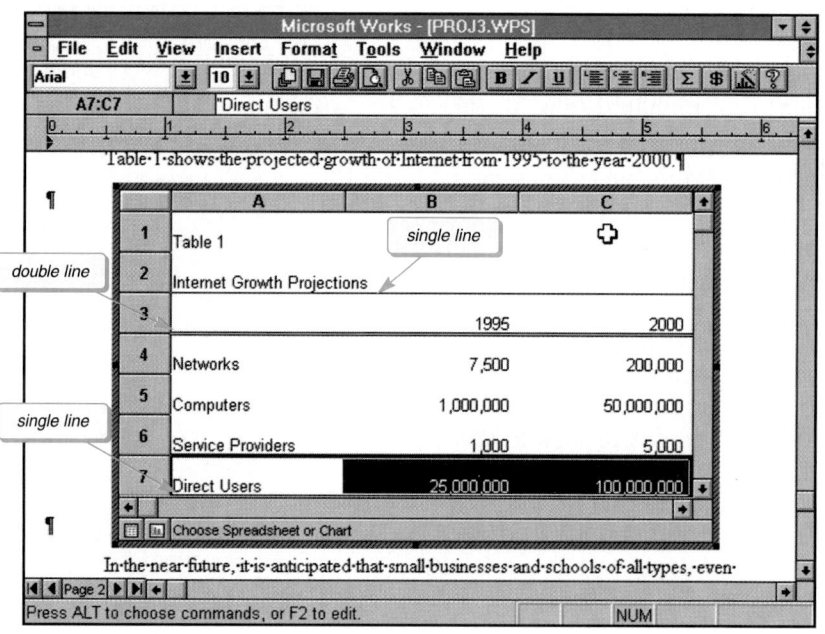

FIGURE 3-94

If you need to delete a selection in the Border area of the Border dialog box, click with the mouse pointer pointing within the box until the box becomes white. When the box is white, the line selection has been deleted.

Exiting the Spreadsheet Tool

While creating the spreadsheet table, you have been using the Works Spreadsheet tool. To exit from the Spreadsheet tool and display the table in the word processing document, complete the following step.

TO EXIT FROM THE SPREADSHEET TOOL ▼

STEP 1 ▶

Click two times in the word processing document to the left of the spreadsheet table.

The spreadsheet disappears and the table in the word processing document displays (Figure 3-95). The insertion point displays adjacent to the table.

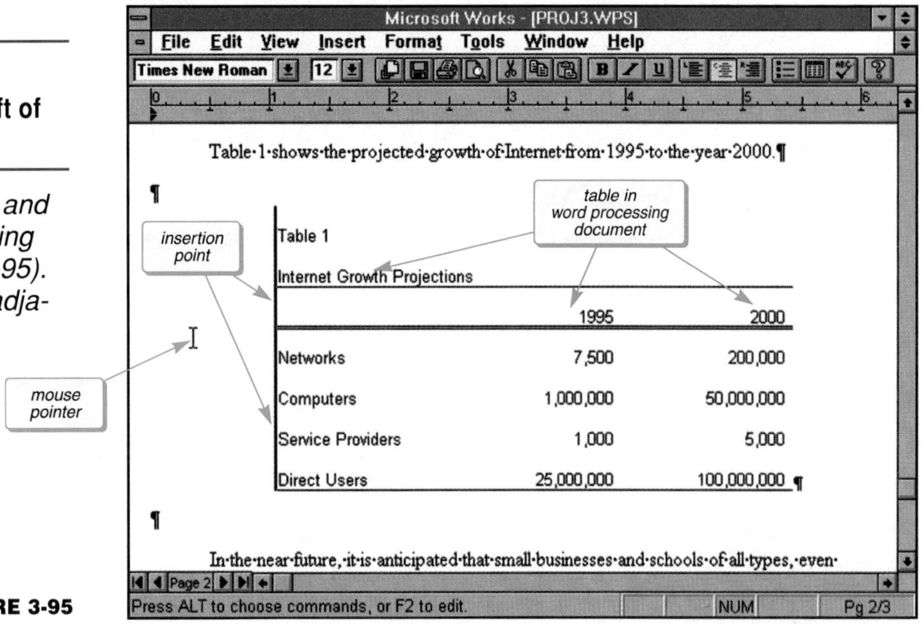

FIGURE 3-95

The research report is now complete with the table as illustrated in Figure 3-1 on page W3.3.

▶ OBJECTS AND OBJECT LINKING AND EMBEDDING (OLE) 2.0

S witching back and forth between the word processing document and the spreadsheet table uses a methodology available in Works 3.0 and Windows 3.1 called **object linking and embedding** (**OLE**, pronounced oh-lay). The version of OLE being used is 2.0. OLE 2.0 allows you to use one software application, such as the spreadsheet application, to create an object that resides within a document created by another software application, such as the word processor. In this case, the spreadsheet application was used to create the spreadsheet table, which is an **object** that resides within the word processing document.

You can highlight an object such as the spreadsheet table at any time by clicking anywhere on the object. When you do so, the object is highlighted with a dotted line around it and resize handles on the corners and sides (see Figure 3-96). When positioned within a highlighted object, the mouse pointer changes to a block arrow with the word DRAG beneath it, indicating you can drag the object to other locations within the word processing document.

FIGURE 3-96

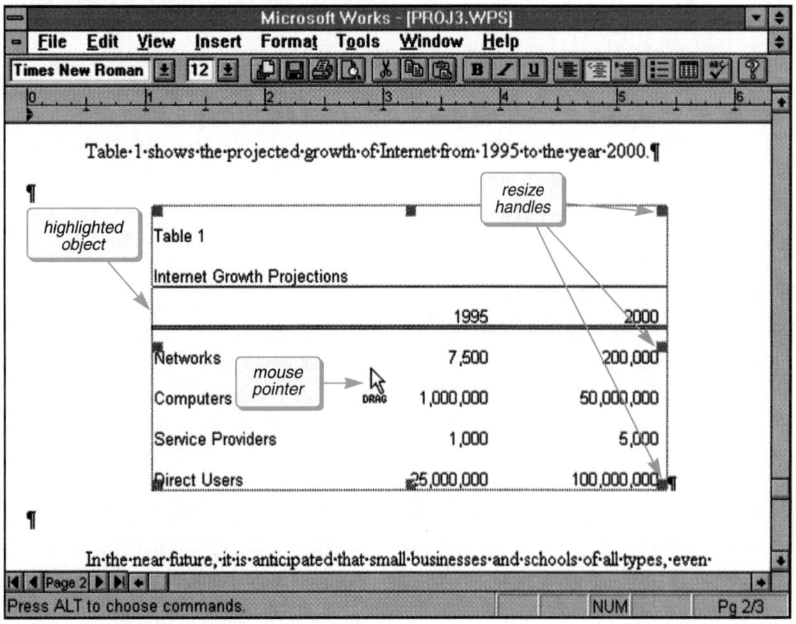

Because the object was created using another software application, in this case the spreadsheet application, you must use that application to make any changes in the object. For example, if you wanted to change the row heading, Networks, to Local and Wide Area Networks, you would have to make the change using the spreadsheet application. To invoke the application used to create an object, such as the spreadsheet application used to create the spreadsheet table, place the mouse pointer anywhere within the object and double-click the left mouse button. The document and the object remain on the screen, but the menu bar and the Toolbar change to the commands and buttons available with the application that created the object. Changing the menu bar and the Toolbar when the object is double-clicked is called visual editing when using OLE 2.0.

After you have made any desired changes, clicking anywhere in the document except on the object will change the menu bar and the Toolbar back to the menu bar and Toolbar of the application that made the document in which the object resides.

When the object is highlighted, it displays with a dotted line and resize handles around it. The object can be resized by dragging the resize handles, as you did earlier in this project.

To delete an object, highlight the object and press the DELETE key on the keyboard or choose the Clear command from the Edit menu.

▶ PROJECT SUMMARY

When you master the skills presented in Project 3, you are capable of writing a research report using the recommended style of the Modern Language Association. In this project, you learned how to set top, bottom, left, and right margins using the Page Setup command from the File menu. Next, you learned to set up a header for each page using the Headers and Footers command from the Edit menu.

When writing the body of the report, you learned how to create a footnote using the Footnote Works-Wizard, and you learned how to create a manual page break.

To assist in editing a research report, you learned the use of the Go To, Find, and Replace commands, and how to use the drag-and-drop method to move a paragraph. You also learned to use the Works thesaurus and how to use the Word Count command from the Tools menu to determine the number of words in a document. To conclude the project, you learned how to incorporate a spreadsheet table in a word processing document using OLE 2.0.

▶ KEY TERMS

Border command *(W3.56)*
cell *(W3.42)*
cell reference area *(W3.42)*
Clipboard *(W3.33)*
column *(W3.42)*
Column Width command *(W3.47)*
Cut button *(W3.33)*
Cut command *(W3.33)*
drag and drop *(W3.33)*
endnotes *(W3.4)*
Find command *(W3.27)*
first-line indent *(W3.14)*
footer *(W3.9)*
footnotes *(W3.4)*
Footnote command *(W3.16)*
footnote pane *(W3.16)*
footnote reference mark *(W3.16)*
Footnotes command (view menu) *(W3.22)*
formula bar *(W3.49)*
Go To command *(W3.26)*

Gridlines command *(W3.55)*
gridlines *(W3.42, W3.54)*
header *(W3.4, W3.9)*
Headers and Footers command *(W3.10)*
Insert Table button *(W3.40)*
Match Case check box *(W3.28)*
Match Whole Word Only check box *(W3.29)*
Modern Language Association of America (MLA) *(W3.2)*
Number command *(W3.53)*
object *(W3.43)*
Object command *(W3.40)*
object linking and embedding (OLE 2.0) *(W3.59)*
page break *(W3.24)*
Page Break command *(W3.24)*
Page Layout command *(W3.11)*
Page Setup command *(W3.5)*
Paste button *(W3.33)*

Paste command *(W3.33)*
Paragraph command *(W3.12)*
paragraph header or footer *(W3.9)*
Redo Editing command *(W3.33)*
Replace command *(W3.29)*
resize handles *(W3.43)*
row *(W3.42)*
Row Height command *(W3.45)*
split bar *(W3.21)*
Spreadsheet/Table command *(W3.40)*
standard header or footer *(W3.9)*
superscript *(W3.3, W3.16)*
synonyms *(W3.36)*
tabs *(W3.7)*
text *(W3.51)*
thesaurus *(W3.36)*
Thesaurus command *(W3.37)*
Undo Editing command *(W3.32)*
Word Count command *(W3.38)*

QUICK REFERENCE

In Microsoft Works, you can accomplish a task in a number of ways. The following table provides a quick reference to each task presented in the project with its available options. The commands listed in the Menu column can be executed using either the keyboard or mouse.

Task	Mouse	Menu	Keyboard Shortcuts
Close a Footnote Pane	Double-click split bar	From View menu, choose Footnotes	
Cut	Click Cut button	From Edit menu, choose Cut	Press CTRL+X or SHIFT+DELETE
Find		From Edit menu, choose Find	
Go To	Point to scroll bar arrows and click	From Edit menu, choose Go To	Press F5
Indent	Drag first-line indent marker on ruler	From Format menu, choose Paragraph	Press TAB
Insert a Header		From View menu, choose Headers and Footers	
Insert a Page Break		From Insert menu, choose Page Break	Press CTRL+ENTER
Insert a Table	Click Insert Table button	From Insert menu, choose Spreadsheet/Table	
Left-Align Text	Click Left-Align button	From Format menu, choose Paragraph	Press CTRL+L
Move to the Beginning of a Document	Drag scroll box or click beginning of document button		Press CTRL+HOME
Move to the End of a Document	Drag scroll box or click end of document button		Press CTRL+END
Open a Footnote Pane		From View menu, choose Footnotes	
Paste	Drag and drop	From Edit menu, choose Paste	Press CTRL+V or SHIFT+INSERT
Place a Footnote		From Insert menu, choose Footnote	
Replace		From Edit menu, choose Replace	
Set the Bottom Margin		From File menu, choose Page Setup	
Set the Header Margin		From File menu, choose Page Setup	
Set Margins	Drag left and right margin indent markers	From File menu, choose Page Setup	
Set the Top Margin		From File menu choose Page Setup	
Use the Thesaurus		From Tools menu, choose Thesaurus	
Word Count		From Tools menu, choose Word Count	

STUDENT ASSIGNMENT 1
True/False

Instructions: Circle T if the statement is true or F if the statement is false.

T F 1. A research report should have a one-inch top margin and a one-inch bottom margin, which are the Works default values for top and bottom margins.

T F 2. To set margins for a page, choose the Page Setup command from the File menu.

T F 3. Set the header margin on a research report at .05 inches.

T F 4. To establish a header for a document, choose the Headers and Footers command from the Edit menu.

T F 5. The entry, &rLopez &page, in the Header text box in the Headers and Footers dialog box will cause the name Lopez followed by the page number to display right-aligned on the screen.

T F 6. It is not possible to have more than one line on a header.

T F 7. You must always press the TAB key to indent paragraphs.

T F 8. The Footnote command will cause any footnotes created to be placed at the end of the document.

T F 9. Using a Footnote WorksWizard is the only way to enter data into a footnote.

T F 10. The only character that may be used to identify a footnote in a report is a raised number called a superscript.

T F 11. When the Footnote command is chosen, a footnote pane opens at the bottom of the screen, where the actual footnote displays.

T F 12. To close the footnote pane, double-click with the mouse pointer located anywhere within the blank area of the footnote pane.

T F 13. To create a manual page break in a report, choose the Page Break command from the Insert menu or press the CTRL+ENTER keys.

T F 14. You can use the Go To command on the Edit menu to quickly move to a specific page of a multiple-page report.

T F 15. You can use the Find command to move to a specific page number in a document by specifying a number in the Find text box.

T F 16. You can use the Works drag-and-drop method to copy a paragraph to another location.

T F 17. The Replace command searches a document for specified text and, when found, replaces the text with new text.

T F 18. The Thesaurus command may be used to check the spelling of a document.

T F 19. Use the Word Count command to count the total number of words in a document including headers, footers, and footnotes.

T F 20. To insert a table in a word processing document, you must choose the Spreadsheet button in the Startup dialog box.

STUDENT ASSIGNMENT 2
Multiple Choice

Instructions: Circle the correct response.

1. To set the top, bottom, left, and right margins in a word processing document, use the _____.
   a. Page Setup command from the File menu
   b. Headers and Footers command from the View menu
   c. Paragraph command from the Format menu
   d. Options command from the Tools menu

2. The Headers and Footers command is found on the _____ menu.
   a. File
   b. Edit
   c. View
   d. Format

3. The entry in the Headers and Footers dialog box to specify printing the page number in the header is _____.
   a. &page
   b. &number
   c. &p
   d. &pp

4. In Normal view, a header created using the Headers and Footers command will _____.
   a. display at the top of each screen unless certain boxes have been selected
   b. display on the screen only when there is a page break mark on the screen
   c. print at the top of each page unless certain boxes have been selected
   d. display on the screen and print at the top of each page unless certain boxes have been selected

5. Dragging the first-line indent marker on the ruler one-half inch to the right will cause _____.
   a. all lines typed to be indented one-half inch
   b. all new sentences to be indented one-half inch
   c. the first line of each paragraph to be indented one-half inch
   d. the first line of each paragraph to be indented one-half inch if you press the TAB key

6. When you choose the Footnote command from the Insert menu, _____.
   a. a footnote pane appears at the top of the screen allowing you to type the footnote
   b. a footnote pane appears at the end of the document allowing you to select a number or a character as a footnote reference mark
   c. a Footnote dialog box displays in the footnote pane
   d. a Footnote dialog box displays in the center of the screen allowing you to select a numbered footnote or a character

7. To cause a manual page break to occur on a document, _____.
   a. choose the Break command from the Insert menu
   b. press CTRL+ENTER
   c. press CRTL+SHIFT
   d. press SHIFT+ENTER

8. The command used to replace one or more words at a time in a document with another word or words is the _____ command.
   a. Find
   b. Go To
   c. Thesaurus
   d. Replace

9. The Works drag-and-drop method may be used to _____.
   a. move text from one location to another location in a document
   b. copy text from one location to the another location in a document with the copied text remaining in its original position
   c. position footnotes at the end of a document
   d. both a and b

10. To create a table in a word processing document, you can use the _____.
    a. Insert Table button on the Toolbar
    b. Spreadsheet/Table command from the Insert menu
    c. Object command from the Insert menu
    d. a, b, and c

STUDENT ASSIGNMENT 3
Locating Commands in Menus

Instructions: In the space provided under the column heading, MENU NAME, fill in the name of the menu associated with the commands in the column on the left.

COMMAND	MENU NAME
Page Setup	_____
Headers and Footers	_____
Footnote	_____
Page Break	_____
Go To	_____
Find	_____
Replace	_____
Thesaurus	_____
Word Count	_____
Spreadsheet/Table	_____

STUDENT ASSIGNMENT 4
Understanding Codes Used with a Header

Instructions: The codes listed can be used when creating a header in a document. In the space provided, explain the purpose of each of the codes.

CODE	PURPOSE
&l	_____
&r	_____
&c	_____
&p	_____
&f	_____
&d	_____
&n	_____
&t	_____
&&	_____

STUDENT ASSIGNMENT 5
Understanding the Find Dialog Box

Instructions: In the space provided in the bubbles, explain what happens if you select the options identified by the pointing arrows in Figure SA3-5.

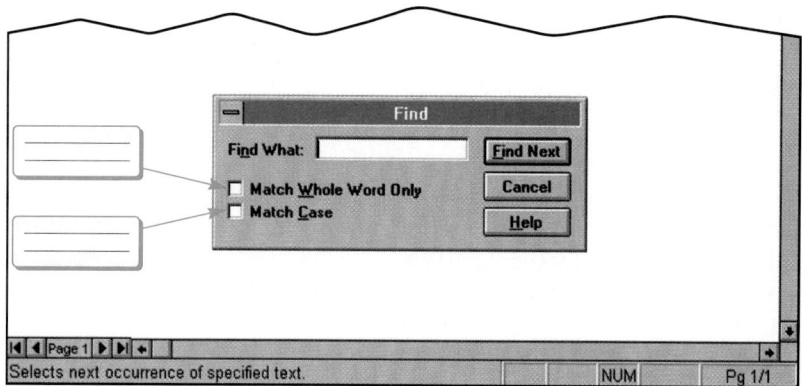

FIGURE SA3-5

STUDENT ASSIGNMENT 6
Moving and Sizing a Table

Instructions: In the space following Figure SA3-6, specify the steps necessary to increase the number of rows in the table to seven, increase the number of columns in the table to five, and move the table up to the second line in the document.

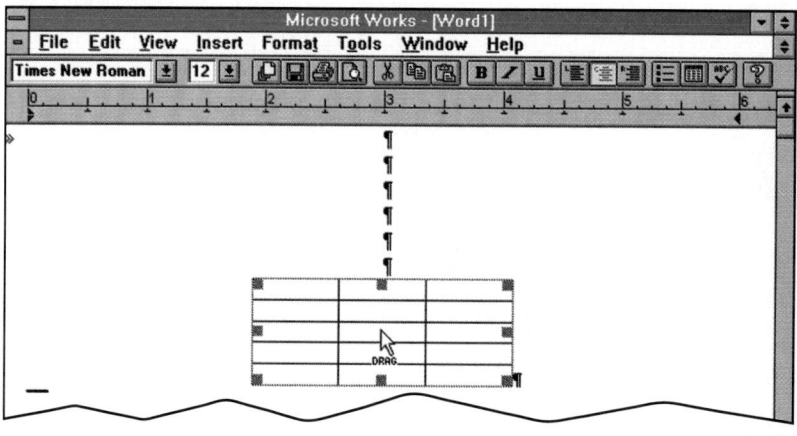

FIGURE SA3-6

Steps: _____

_____

_____

_____

_____

_____

COMPUTER LABORATORY EXERCISE 1
Using the Online Help Search Feature

Instructions: The following instructions provide detailed steps for finding information about the use of the Works drag-and-drop method. Follow each of the instructions and then answer the questions in the space provided.

1. Start Works and the Word Processor tool. Maximize the document window.
2. Select the Help menu and then choose the Search for Help on command.
3. A Search dialog box displays. Type drag in the text box.
4. The words drag and drop are highlighted in a list box. Choose the Show Topics button.
5. A list of topics displays in another list box. The words Copying and moving information using the mouse are highlighted. Choose the Go To button.
6. A screen displays with the title, Copying and moving information using the mouse. From the information on the screen, answer the following questions.
   a. How do you move information within a single Works document?

   _____

   _____

   b. How do you copy information within a single Works document?

   _____

   _____

   c. How do you Undo a drag and drop operation?

   _____

   _____

   d. How do you cancel a drag and drop operation?

   _____

   _____

7. Choose the Exit command from the File Menu to exit from Help.

COMPUTER LABORATORY EXERCISE 2
Using the Word Count Command

Instructions: Start the Works Word Processor. Open the word processing document with the filename CLE3-2.WPS on the Student Diskette that accompanies this book. This file contains the first two paragraphs of the research report created in Project 3. After opening the document, complete the following tasks.

1. Use the Word Count command to count the number of words in the first two paragraphs. Begin the count starting with the report title. How many words are in the first two paragraphs? _____
2. Use the Word Count command to count the number of words in the second paragraph of the report. How many words are in the second paragraph? _____
3. Exit Works.

COMPUTER LABORATORY EXERCISE 3
Using the Replace Command

Instructions: Start the Works Word Processor. Open the word processing document with the filename CLE3-2.WPS on the Student Diskette that accompanies this book. This file contains the first two paragraphs of the research report created in Project 3. After opening the document, complete the following tasks.

Part 1:

1. Follow the steps described in the text and replace all occurrences of the word ARPANET with the words Advanced Research Projects Agency Network.
2. Print a copy of the first page of the research report after the changes have been made. Turn the report into your instructor.

Part 2:

1. Use the Undo Editing command to return the word ARPANET to the report.

Part 3:

1. Using drag and drop, move the last two sentences of the second paragraph to a location immediately following the first sentence in the second paragraph.
2. Print a copy of the first page of the report and turn in a copy to your instructor.
3. Use the Undo Drag and Drop command to undo the move operation.
4. Exit Works.

COMPUTER LABORATORY ASSIGNMENTS

COMPUTER LABORATORY ASSIGNMENT 1
Preparing a Research Report

Part 1:   Typing the Research Report

Purpose: To provide experience using the Word Processor to prepare a multiple-page research report with footnotes at the end of the document.

Problem: You have been asked by a friend to retype the research report in Figure CLA3-1 on the next page using the Modern Language Association's style for writing research reports as illustrated in Project 3 of this book.

Instructions: Type the research report using Times New Roman 12 point font. The student's name is Andrew J. Long. The professor's name is Sidney L. Ranger. The class is Computer Software Applications 101. Use the current date in the report heading.

After you type the research report, save the document on a diskette. Use a filename consisting of the initials of your first and last names followed by the assignment number. Example: TC3-1. Retain the diskette for use in Part 2 of this assignment. Print the research report. Then follow directions from your instructor for turning in the assignment.

Part 2:   Editing the Research Report

Purpose: To provide experience using the Replace command, drag and drop editing, the Thesaurus command, and Word Count command.

(continued)

COMPUTER LABORATORY ASSIGNMENT 1 (continued)

Computer Viruses

The computer virus is a threat to the effective use of computers in homes and businesses. A computer virus is a computer program that is specifically designed to become a part of an operating system or an application program and adversely affect computer processing when executed.[1]

Some viruses are relatively innocuous. One known virus randomly displays on the screen, "I am a computer virus - catch me if you can." In other cases, viruses do considerable harm to a computer system. One type of virus, sometimes referred to as a software bomb, will cause all application programs or data on a disk to be erased when the virus is executed.

Viruses may be activated based upon a date or the time. Viruses of this type allow application programs to execute properly until a predetermined date or time of the day. Then, the virus will execute, causing the program or data to be adversely affected in some manner.

Viruses become a part of software in a number of ways. If your computer is linked to other computers by means of data communication lines, there is a possibility that you may access a program that contains a virus and that virus will be transferred to your computer. If a friend gives you a copy of a program and its source is not known, the program may contain a virus. Once you run the program on your computer, a virus program may be stored on your disk. If you give a copy of the program that contains the virus to another person, the virus is effectively transmitted from one computer to another.

A number of programs on the market can scan software prior to execution to detect virus instructions placed in the software. These are called anti-virus programs.[2]

All programs obtained from any source should be scanned for a virus with an anti-virus program to protect your computer system.

---

1 Charles D. Davis, <u>Introduction To Computer System Security</u> (New York: Computer Press, 1994) 13.

2 John C. Reynolds, <u>Introduction To Telecommunications</u> (San Francisco: Communications Publishing Company, 1994) 56.

FIGURE CLA3-1

Problem: You are to edit the research report you typed in Part 1 of this computer laboratory assignment. Follow the instructions below to edit the report.

Instructions: Use the Replace command to replace the word virus in the research report with the words, computer virus, where appropriate. Use the thesaurus to replace the word innocuous in the second paragraph with a word recommended by the thesaurus. Use drag and drop to place the fourth paragraph in the research report immediately after the first paragraph. Check the spelling of the entire document, and then use the Word Count command to count the number of words in the research report.

   After you edit the research report, save the document on a diskette. Use a filename consisting of the initials of your first and last names followed by the assignment number and the letter A. Example: TC3-1A. Print the research report. Write the total number of words in the research report above the student name on the report. Follow directions from your instructor for turning in the assignment.

Part 3:   Adding a Table

Purpose: To provide experience creating a table in a word processing document.

Problem: You are to insert the following table in the research report.

Computer Viruses

	Virus Name	Effect
1991	Destroyer	Clears data from disk
1992	Screenman	Displays random messages
1993	Time Bomb	Destroys data based on time

Instructions: The table should be inserted after the third paragraph. Include the following sentence before the table: Table 1 lists the first year the computer viruses were found on computer systems, the name of the virus, and the effect of the virus.

   The table should be created in the word processing document using the style presented in Project 3.

   After you add the table to the research report, save the document on a diskette. Use a filename consisting of the initials of your first and last names followed by the assignment number and the letter B. Example: TC3-1B. Print the research report.

   Follow directions from your instructor for turning in the assignment.

COMPUTER LABORATORY ASSIGNMENT 2
Preparing a Research Report

Part 1:   Typing the Research Report

Purpose: To provide experience using the Word Processor to prepare a multiple-page research report with footnotes at the end of the report.

Problem: You have been asked by a friend to retype the research report in Figure CLA3-2 on the next page using the Modern Language Association's style for writing research reports as illustrated in Project 3 of this book.

Instructions: Type the research report using Times New Roman 12 point font. The student's name is Susan L. Tran. The professor's name is Jane E. Evans. The class is Accounting Systems 301. Use the current date in the report heading.

   After you type the research report, save the document on a diskette. Use a filename consisting of the initials of your first and last names followed by the assignment number. Example: TC3-2. Retain the diskette for use in Part 2 of this assignment. Print the research report. Then follow directions from your instructor for turning in the assignment.

(continued)

COMPUTER LABORATORY ASSIGNMENT 2 (continued)

The Accounting Profession

Three major fields of accounting are public accounting, management accounting, and government accounting. Public accountants serve the general public and either own their own businesses or work for public accounting firms. Management accountants are employed by companies to handle financial records. Government accountants maintain records of government agencies and audit private businesses and individuals whose operations are subject to government regulation.1

Accountants normally work in offices, but public accountants and government accountants may visit the offices of clients while consulting or conducting audits. Most accountants work 40 hours per week, although overtime work is often required during tax season. Many accountants are employed in urban areas where accounting firms or regional offices of businesses are concentrated.

It is estimated that there are 975,000 individuals employed in the accounting profession. Approximately 300,000 are Certified Public Accountants. To become a Certified Public Accountant, an individual must pass a rigorous examination administered by various states.2

Most public accounting and business firms require applicants for accounting positions to have at least a bachelor's degree in accounting. A growing number of employers require new accountants to have a knowledge of computers, computer software, and the use of computers in accounting.

Individuals interested in a career in accounting should have an aptitude for mathematics and be able to analyze facts and figures quickly and accurately. Accountants must be able to concentrate for extended periods of time, but should also be good at dealing with people and be able to communicate the results of their work orally and by written correspondence.

Beginning accountants recruited from colleges receive offers in the $25,000 per year range. Salaries for chief financial officers of large corporations can exceed $100,000 per year. Employment opportunities for accountants are expected to grow through the year 2000 because of increased governmental regulations and the key role accountants play in the operation of all businesses.

---

1 Richard A. Warner, Career Opportunities In Business (Los Angeles: Business Press, 1994) 19.

2 Mary B. Allen, Introduction To Business Accounting (Kansas City: Wabash Publishing Company, 1994) 68.

FIGURE CLA3-2

Part 2:   Editing the Report

Purpose: To provide experience using the Replace command, drag and drop, the Thesaurus command, and the Word Count command.

Problem: You are to edit the research report you typed in Part 1 of this computer laboratory assignment. Follow the instructions below to edit the report.

Instructions: Use the Replace command to replace the word computer in the research report with the words, personal computer, where appropriate. Use drag and drop to place the third paragraph in the research report immediately after the first paragraph. Use the thesaurus to replace the word aptitude in the fifth paragraph with a word recommended by the thesaurus. Check the spelling of the entire document, and then use the Word Count command to count the number of words in the research report.

After you edit the research report, save the document on a diskette. Use a filename consisting of the initials of your first and last names followed by the assignment number and the letter A. Example: TC3-2A. Print the research report. Write the total number of words in the research paper above the student name on the report. Follow directions from your instructor for turning in the assignment.

Part 3:   Adding a Table

Purpose: To provide experience creating a table in a word processing document.

Problem: You are to insert the following table in the research report.

Accounting Salaries in Public Accounting Firms

	Minimum	Maximum
Level 1	$24,181.00	$28,654.00
Level 2	$29,747.00	$34,783.00
Level 3	$36,995.00	$48,195.00

Instructions: The table should be inserted after the sixth paragraph. Include the following two sentences before the table: Table 1 lists salary rates in small public accounting firms. The table is listed below.

The table should be created in the word processing document using the style presented in Project 3.

After you add the table to the research report, save the document on a diskette. Use a filename consisting of the initials of your first and last names followed by the assignment number and the letter B. Example: TC3-2B. Print the research report.

Follow directions from your instructor for turning in the assignment.

COMPUTER LABORATORY ASSIGNMENT 3
Preparing a Research Report

Purpose: To provide experience using the Word Processor to prepare a multiple page research report with footnotes at the end of the report.

Problem: The notes in Figure CLA3-3 on the next page represent research on the topic of local area networks. Review the notes, and rearrange and reword the notes if necessary. Then prepare a research report entitled, Local Area Networks. Type the research report using the Modern Language Association's style for writing research reports as illustrated in Project 3 of this book.

(continued)

COMPUTER LABORATORY ASSIGNMENT 3 (continued)

under control of a network operating system that allows communication and the sharing of resources between computer users.

A LAN is not just interconnected computers operating under control of a network operating system. A LAN should be viewed as a system that allows businesses to operate more efficiently by utilizing computer hardware in the most efficient manner possible.

A local area network, abbreviated LAN, commonly consists of a group of personal computers, located relatively close to one another, that are interconnected for the purpose of sharing access to resources such as large disk drives, high speed printers, laser printers or other peripheral devices.

Richard E. Harrison, Introduction to Local Area Networks (San Francisco: Delta Publishing Company 1994) 23

A characteristic of LANs is a relatively limited number of users per LAN. Most LANs support fewer than five people. LANs are expanded by linking these small LANs together, rather than creating very large single networks. A local area network typically is found in a single office, building or a few buildings, such as in an academic environment.

Leslie N. Truman, Telecommunications in Business (New York: Computer Technology Press 1993) 89

Local Area Networks are designed for the purpose of sharing resources. Office workers routinely have access to common paper files such as purchase orders. Each worker does not have his or her own set of files. Similarly, LANs help personal computer users share access to files and programs by storing master copies of these files and programs on one system and allowing other users to access that system. With LANs, provision must be made to manage each user's access to files and programs, and keep track of modifications to shared files.

The first LANs were designed to allow sharing of hard disk drives and printers, because these devices were too expensive to provide for every user.

The first LANs were relatively simple and merely allowed computer users to connect to another computer to share access to high capacity hard disk drives. The computer with the large capacity disk drive was called the disk server. Software on the computer containing the shared disk drive divided the shared hard disk drive into areas called volumes, one for each user. When operating the computer, individuals accessed the hard disk drive as if it were a part of their own computer. These LANs also included a public volume that let users share information. Today, these disk servers are called file servers.

After hard disk drives, most users look to various types of printers as a resource to share. Almost all LANs offer shared access to printers, commonly high speed laser printers, which are relatively expensive to purchase for individual work stations.

Technically, a LAN may be defined as a network of personal computers connected by specific types of cable transmission media and network adapters, operating

FIGURE CLA3-2

Instructions: Type the research report using Times New Roman 12 point font. Use your name, your professor's name, the name of the class in which you are currently enrolled, and the current date in the heading of the report.

Include the following table in the report.

Number of LANs Installed

Type	1994	1995
Value Net	250,000	750,000
Lan Net	375,000	900,000
EZ Net	125,000	650,000

Include the following sentence before the table: Table 1 contains the sales of the leading personal computer local area networks.

After you type the research report, save the report on a diskette. Use a filename consisting of the initials of your first and last names followed by the assignment number. Example: TC3-3. Print the research report, and then follow directions from your instructor for turning in the assignment.

COMPUTER LABORATORY ASSIGNMENT 4
Preparing a Research Report

Purpose: To provide experience creating a multiple-page report based on original research.

Problem: Prepare a report explaining the basic components of a personal computer system. Obtain the information necessary to prepare this research report from any available source material. The research report must be at least 500 words in length. Include a table in the report.

Instructions: You may review the introductory material in this book as a reference. If you use this book as a reference, include this textbook as a reference source when you create footnotes. You must have at least two footnotes in the research report. Type the report according to MLA style. Check the spelling of the entire document. Use the Word Count command to verify the length of the report.

After typing the research report, save the document on a diskette. Use a filename consisting of the initials of your first and last names followed by the assignment number. Example: TC3-4. Print the document, and then follow directions from your instructor for turning in the assignment.

BUILDING A SPREADSHEET

▼

BUILDING A SPREADSHEET

You will have mastered the material in this project when you can:

▸ Start the Microsoft Works Spreadsheet tool
▸ List the steps required to build a spreadsheet
▸ Describe the spreadsheet
▸ Highlight a cell or range of cells
▸ Enter text
▸ Use the Fill Series command
▸ Enter numbers
▸ Use the Autosum button to sum a range of cells in a row or column
▸ Copy a cell to a range of adjacent cells
▸ Format a spreadsheet
▸ Center text in a range of cells

▸ Add color to a spreadsheet
▸ Use the AutoFormat feature
▸ Change column widths
▸ Save a spreadsheet
▸ Print a spreadsheet
▸ Create a 3-D Bar chart
▸ Close a spreadsheet
▸ Quit Works
▸ Open a spreadsheet file
▸ Correct errors in a spreadsheet
▸ Clear cells and clear the entire spreadsheet

▶ THE WORKS SPREADSHEET AND CHARTING TOOL

A spreadsheet is a software tool that is useful when you have a need to enter and calculate data that can be conveniently displayed in rows and columns. The Microsoft Works for Windows Spreadsheet and Charting tool allows you to enter data in a spreadsheet, perform calculations on that data, ask what-if questions regarding the data in the spreadsheet, make decisions based on the results found in a spreadsheet, chart data in the spreadsheet, and share these results with other tools within Works.

As a result of the capabilities of the Works for Windows Spreadsheet tool, you can accomplish such tasks as accounting and record keeping, financial planning and budgeting, sales forecasting and reporting, or keeping track of your basketball team's scoring averages. In addition, once you have determined the information you require, you can present it as a spreadsheet or as a chart in printed reports.

Works also allows you to change data and automatically recalculate your spreadsheets. You can place data in the spreadsheet that simulates given conditions, which you can then test and determine the results. For example, you can enter the monthly payment you want to make on a house and then determine the price of the house you can afford based on various interest rates.

▶ Project Four

T o illustrate the use of the Microsoft Works for Windows Spreadsheet and Charting tool, this section of the book presents a series of projects similar to those you have seen previously for the Works Word Processor. Project 4 uses the Works Spreadsheet tool to produce the spreadsheet, 3-D Bar chart, and printed report shown in Figure 4-1.

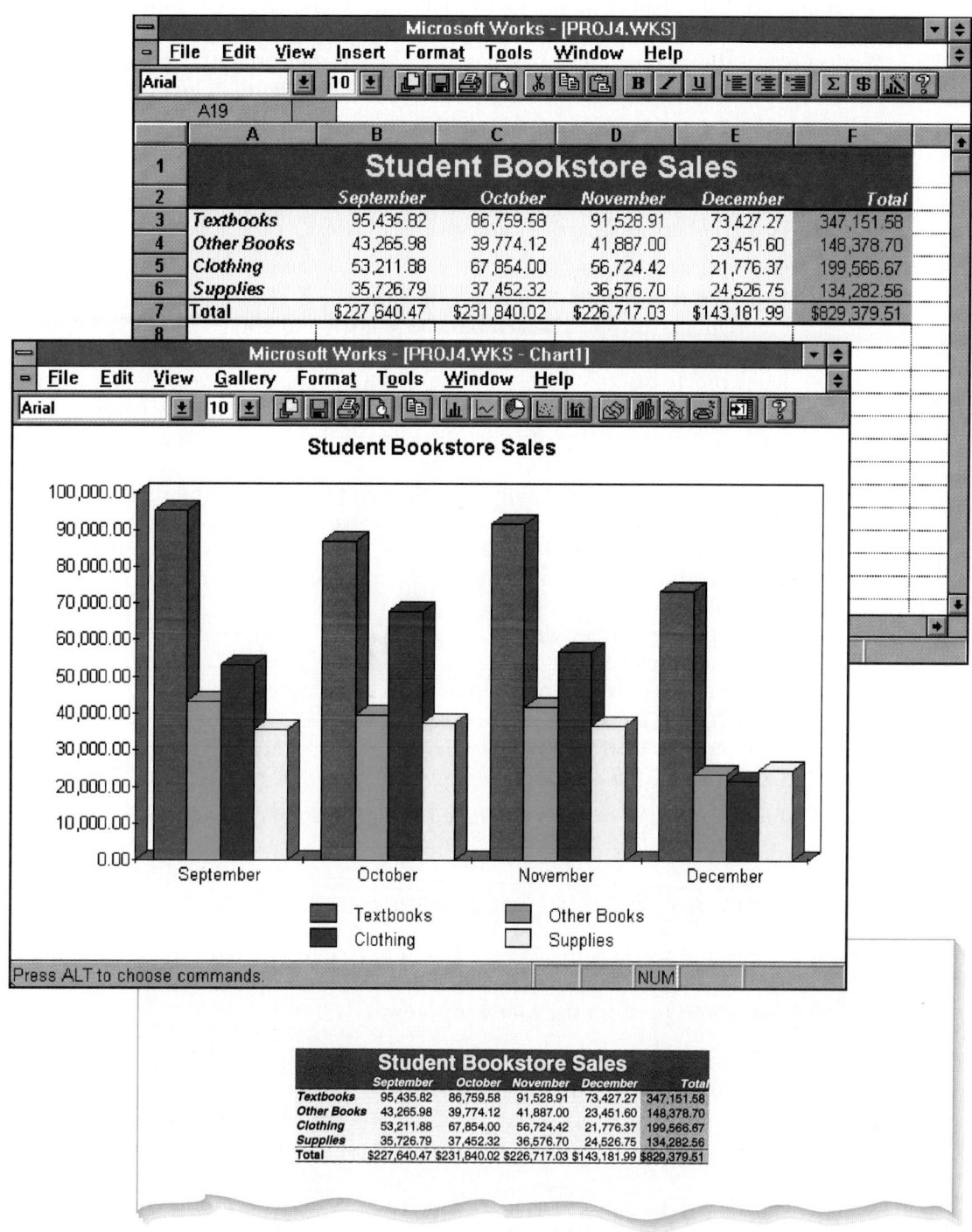

FIGURE 4-1

The spreadsheet and report contain monthly sales for a Student Bookstore for the months of September, October, November, and December. The sales fall into four categories: Textbooks, Other Books, Clothing, and Supplies. Works calculates the total sales for each month, the total sales for each category, and the total sales for all four months. The spreadsheet in this project also demonstrates the use of the various fonts, font sizes, styles, and colors in both the spreadsheet and the report. Proper spreadsheet formatting as shown in this project is an important factor in modern spreadsheet design and reporting.

The Bar chart, called a 3-D Bar chart, displays the sales categories by month. Works creates the 3-D Bar chart based on the data in the spreadsheet. Each category is represented by the color indicated by the chart legend below the chart.

Spreadsheet Preparation Steps

To provide an overview of this project, the general steps to prepare the spreadsheet and chart in Figure 4-1 are specified below.

1. Start the Works Spreadsheet.
2. Enter the report title (Student Bookstore Sales), the column titles (September, October, November, December, and Total), and the row titles (Textbooks, Other Books, Clothing, Supplies, and Total).
3. Enter the Textbooks, Other Books, Clothing, and Supplies sales for each of the four months (September, October, November, and December).
4. Enter the formulas to calculate the sales for each month, for each category of sales, and for the total sales.
5. Format the spreadsheet title, including adding color to the title.
6. Format the body of the spreadsheet. The sales data and category totals are to contain commas and decimal points. The bottom row of numbers, which contains totals, is to display with dollar signs, commas, and decimal points.
7. Save the spreadsheet on disk.
8. Print the spreadsheet.
9. Create the 3-D Bar chart based on data in the spreadsheet.
10. Print the 3-D Bar chart.
11. Save the spreadsheet and chart.
12. Exit Works.

The following pages contain a detailed explanation of each of these steps.

▶ STARTING THE WORKS SPREADSHEET

T o start the Works Spreadsheet, follow the steps you have used in the first three projects to open the Microsoft Works Startup dialog box (Figure 4-2). Then perform the following steps.

TO START THE WORKS SPREADSHEET ▼

STEP 1 ▶

Point to the Spreadsheet button in the Works Startup dialog box (Figure 4-2).

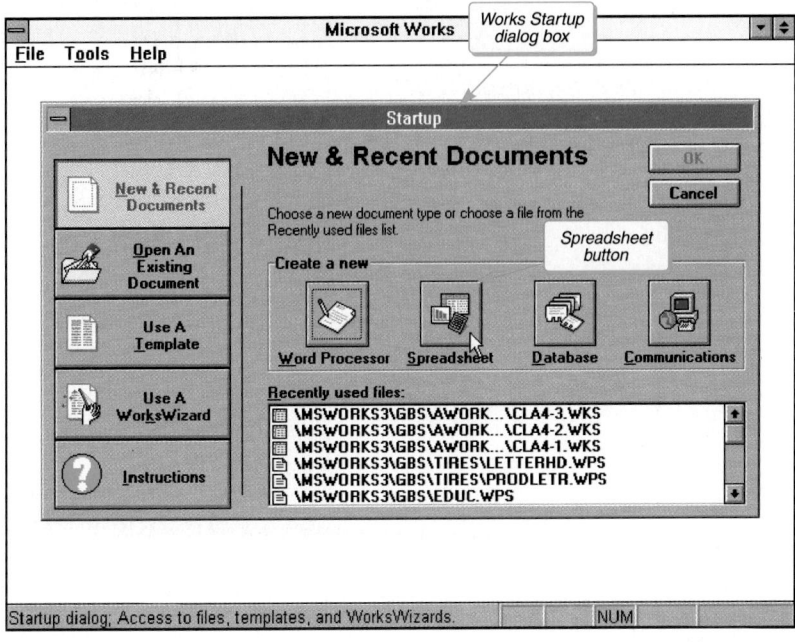

FIGURE 4-2

STEP 2 ▶

Click the left mouse button. When the Microsoft Works window displays, maximize the window if necessary. Then point to the Sheet1 Maximize button.

Works displays an empty spreadsheet entitled Sheet1 (Figure 4-3). The mouse pointer points to the Maximize button.

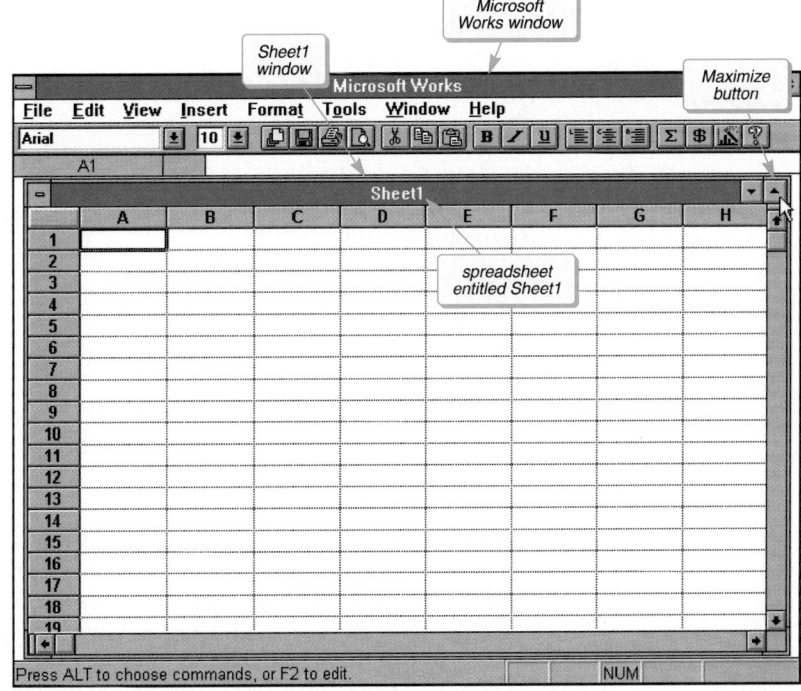

FIGURE 4-3

STEP 3 ▶

Click the left mouse button.

Works maximizes the spreadsheet and places the spreadsheet title, Sheet1, in the main title bar (Figure 4-4).

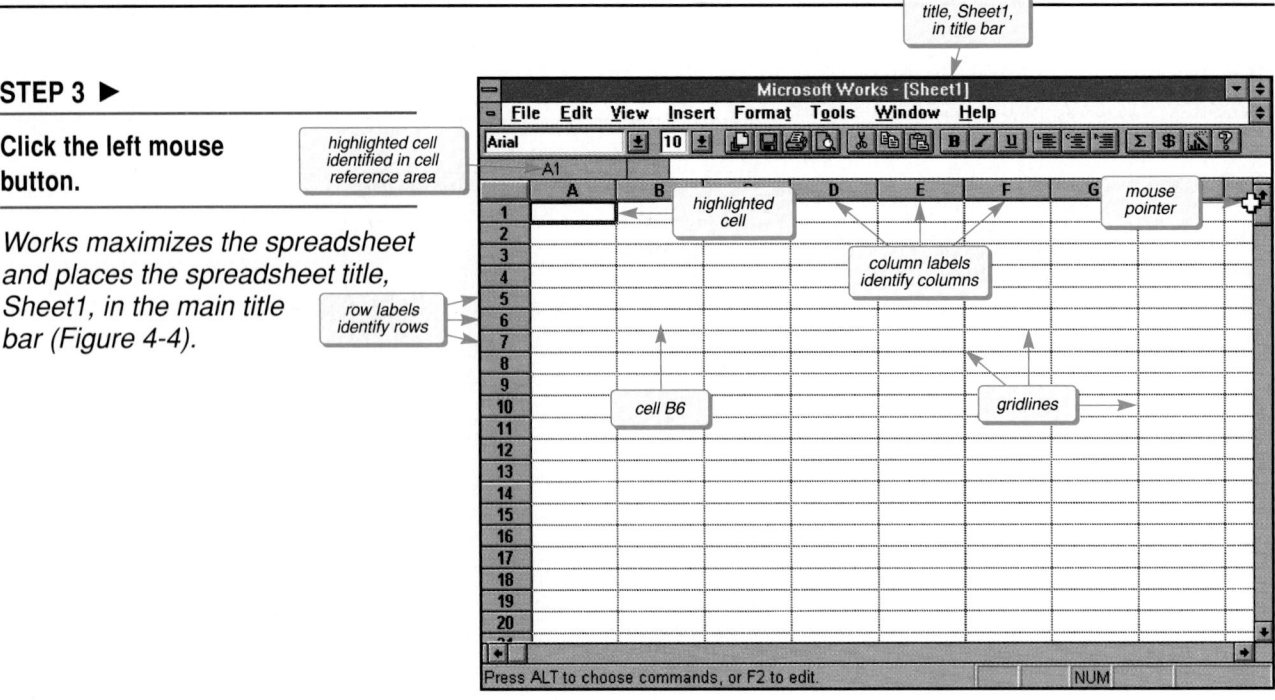

FIGURE 4-4

The following paragraphs describe the elements of the spreadsheet screen identified in Figure 4-4.

▶ THE SPREADSHEET

The spreadsheet is organized into a rectangular grid containing columns (vertical) and rows (horizontal). A **column label**, which is a letter of the alphabet above the grid, identifies each **column**. A **row label**, which is a number down the left side of the grid, identifies each **row**. Eight complete columns (letters A through H) and twenty complete rows (numbered 1 through 20) appear on the screen when the spreadsheet is maximized.

Cell, Highlighted Cell, and Mouse Pointer

The intersection of each column and each row is a **cell**. A cell is the basic unit of a spreadsheet into which you enter data. A cell is referred to by its **cell reference**, which is the coordinate of the intersection of a column and a row. To identify a cell, specify the column label (a letter of the alphabet) first, followed by the row label (a number). For example, cell reference B6 refers to the cell located at the intersection of column B and row 6 (Figure 4-4 on the previous page).

The horizontal and vertical lines on the spreadsheet itself are called **gridlines**. Gridlines are intended to make it easier to see and identify each cell on the spreadsheet. If desired, you can remove the gridlines from the spreadsheet but it is recommended that you use the gridlines in most circumstances.

One cell in the spreadsheet, designated the **highlighted cell**, is the one into which you can enter data. The highlighted cell in Figure 4-4 is cell A1. Works identifies the highlighted cell in two ways. First, Works places a heavy border around it. Second, the cell reference area, which is above the column labels on the left side of the screen, contains the cell reference of the highlighted cell (Figure 4-4).

The **mouse pointer** can become a number of shapes when used with the Works Spreadsheet, depending on the activity in Works and the location of the mouse pointer on the spreadsheet screen. In Figure 4-4, the mouse pointer has the shape of a block plus sign. The mouse pointer normally displays as a block plus sign whenever it is located in a cell on the spreadsheet.

Another common mouse pointer shape is the block arrow. The mouse pointer turns into a block arrow whenever you move it outside the spreadsheet window. Other mouse pointer shapes will be described when they appear on the screen in this and subsequent projects.

Spreadsheet Window

The Works Spreadsheet contains 256 columns and 16,384 rows for a total of 4,194,304 cells. The column labels begin with A and end with IV. The row labels begin with 1 and end with 16384. Only a small fraction of the spreadsheet displays on the screen at one time. You view the portion of the spreadsheet displayed on the screen through the **spreadsheet window** (Figure 4-5). Scroll bars, scroll arrows, and scroll boxes that you can use to move the window around the spreadsheet are located below and to the right of the spreadsheet window.

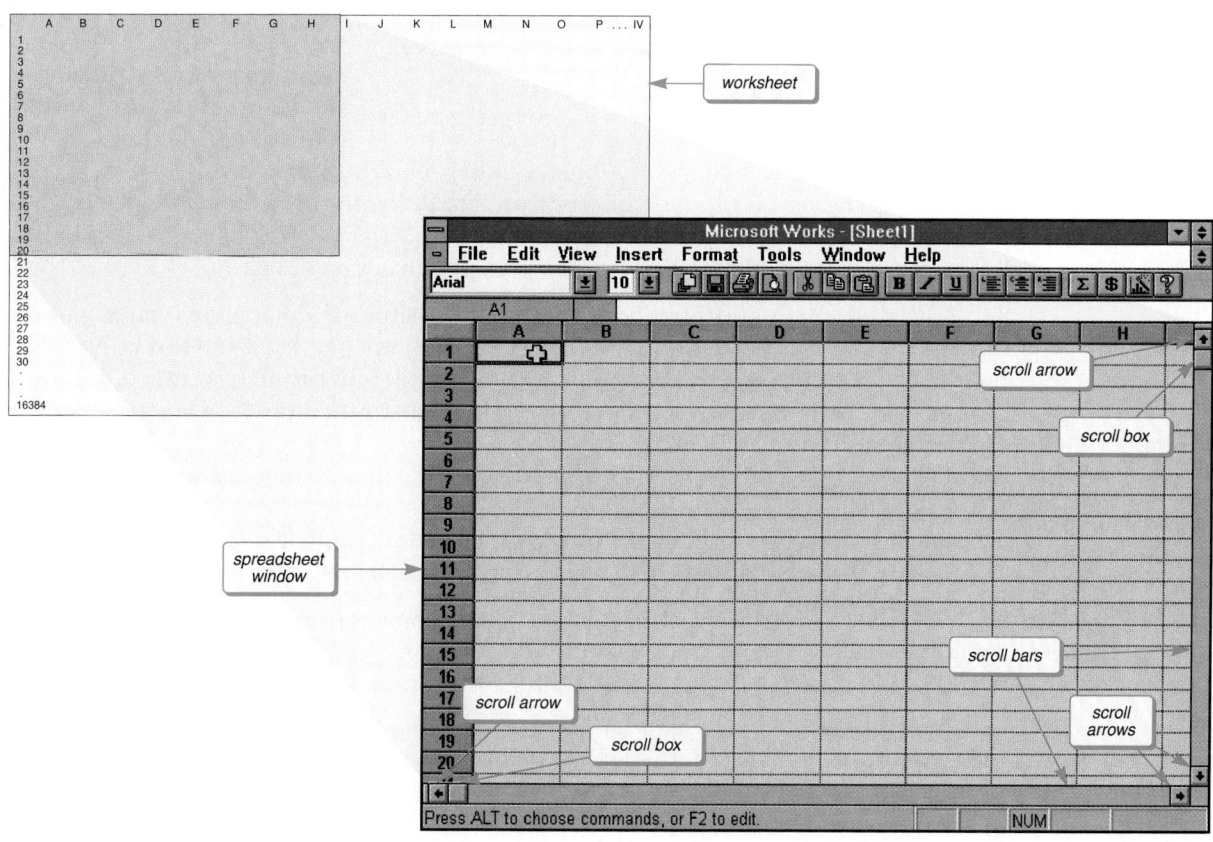

FIGURE 4-5

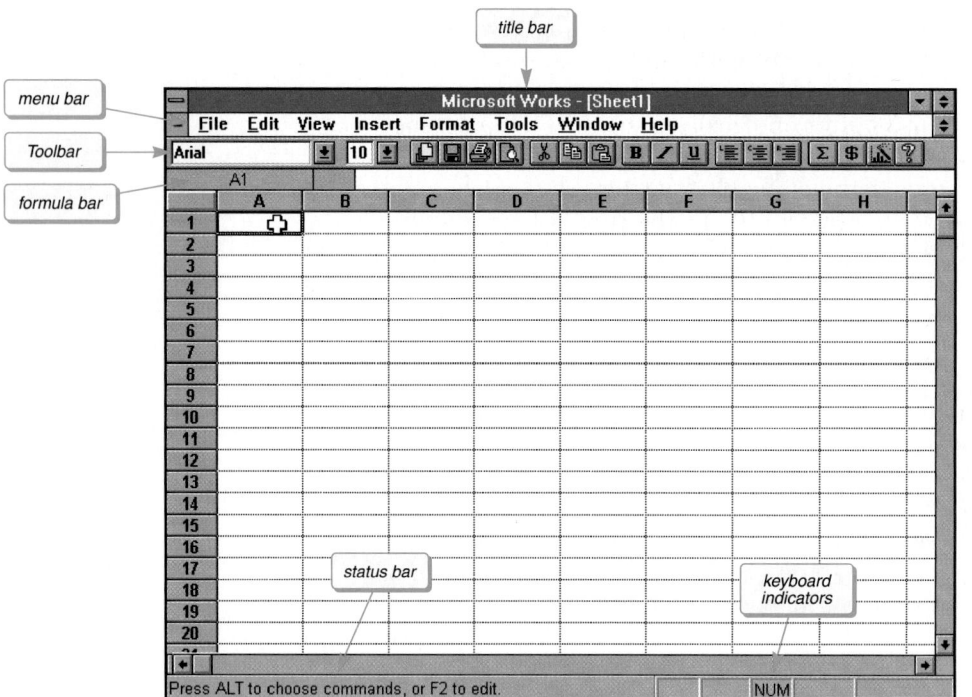

FIGURE 4-6

Menu Bar, Toolbar, Formula Bar, and Status Bar

The menu bar, Toolbar, and formula bar display at the top of the screen just below the title bar (Figure 4-6). The status bar displays at the bottom of the screen.

MENU BAR   The **menu bar** displays the Works Spreadsheet menu names (Figure 4-6). Each menu name represents a menu of commands that can retrieve, save, print, and manipulate data in the spreadsheet. To display a menu such as the File menu or the Edit menu, select the menu name in the manner you learned in *Using Microsoft Windows 3.1.*

The menu bar can change to include other menu names and other menu choices depending on the type of work you are doing in the Works Spreadsheet. For example, if you are working with a chart rather than a spreadsheet, the menu bar consists of a list of menu names for use specifically with charts.

TOOLBAR   The **Toolbar** (Figure 4-6) contains buttons that allow you to perform frequent tasks more quickly than using the menu bar. Each **button** contains a picture that helps you remember its function. If you point to the button, a description of the purpose of the button will display beneath the button in a yellow rectangle and also in the status bar. You click a button to cause a command to execute. Each of the buttons on the Toolbar is explained when used in the projects.

As with the menu bar, Works displays a different Toolbar when you work with charts. The buttons on the Charting Toolbar are explained when charts are used.

FORMULA BAR   Below the Toolbar, Works displays the **formula bar** (Figure 4-6). Data that you type appears in the formula bar. Works also displays the highlighted cell reference in the cell reference area on the left side of the formula bar.

STATUS BAR   The left side of the **status bar** at the bottom of the screen displays brief instructions, a brief description of the currently selected command, a brief description of the function of a Toolbar button, or one or more words describing the current activity in progress.

Keyboard indicators indicating which keys are engaged, such as NUM (Num Lock key active) and CAPS (Caps Lock key active), display in the right side of the status bar within the small rectangular boxes.

▶ HIGHLIGHTING A CELL

To enter data into a cell, you must first **highlight** the cell. The easiest method to highlight a cell is to position the block plus sign mouse pointer in the desired cell and click the left mouse button.

An alternative method is to use the arrow keys that are located to the right of the typewriter keys on the keyboard. After you press an arrow key, the adjacent cell in the direction of the arrow on the key becomes the highlighted cell. You can also use the TAB **key** to move from one cell to another in a row.

You know a cell is highlighted when a heavy border surrounds the cell and the cell reference of the highlighted cell displays in the cell reference area in the formula bar (Figure 4-7).

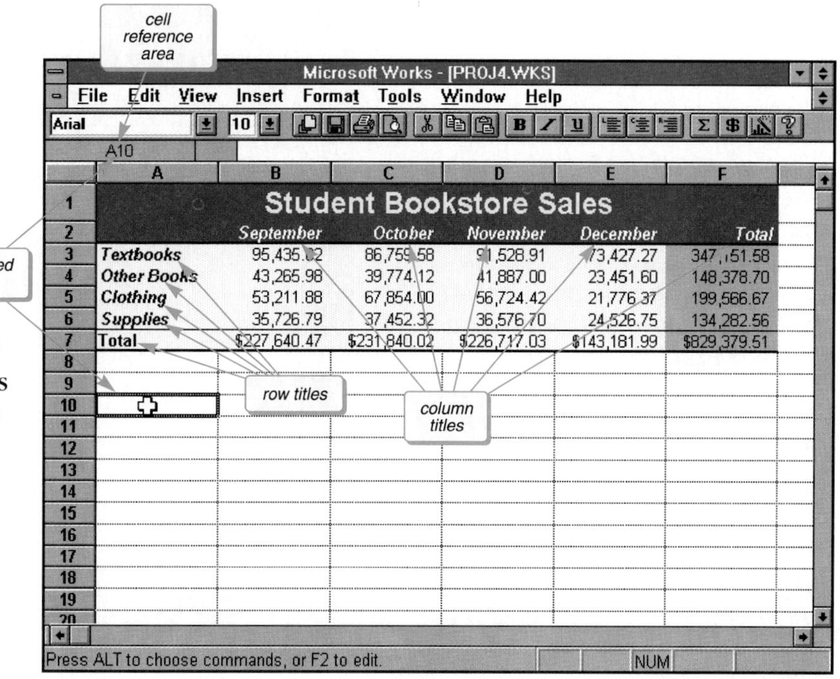

FIGURE 4-7

▶ ENTERING TEXT

In the Works Spreadsheet, any set of characters containing a letter is **text.** Text is used for titles, such as spreadsheet titles, column titles, and row titles. In Project 4 (Figure 4-7), the spreadsheet title, Student Bookstore Sales, identifies the spreadsheet. The column titles consist of the words September, October, November, December, and Total. The row titles (Textbooks, Other Books, Clothing, Supplies, and Total) identify each row in the spreadsheet.

Entering the Spreadsheet Title

Complete the following steps to enter the spreadsheet title into cell A1.

TO ENTER THE SPREADSHEET TITLE ▼

STEP 1 ▶

Highlight cell A1 by pointing to the cell and clicking the left mouse button.

A heavy border surrounds cell A1, and cell A1 displays in the cell reference area in the formula bar (Figure 4-8).

FIGURE 4-8

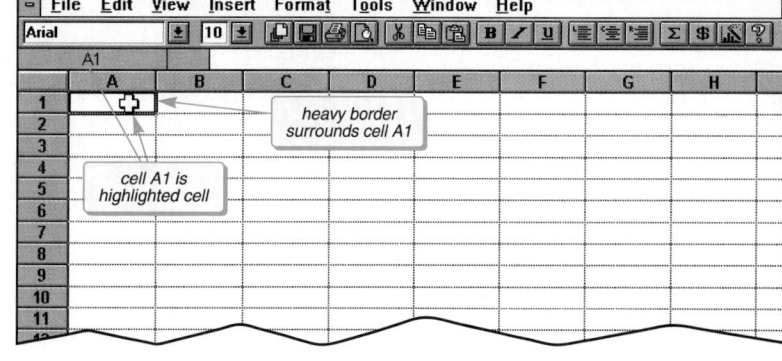

STEP 2 ▶

Type Student Bookstore Sales.

When you type the first character, a new message displays in the status bar (Figure 4-9). Works displays two boxes, one called the **Cancel box** *and the other called the* **Enter box***, in the formula bar. All the characters you type display in the formula bar, followed immediately by a blinking vertical bar called the* **insertion point***. The insertion point indicates where the next character typed will display. As you type, the characters display in the highlighted cell. If you type more characters than can display in the cell, only the last few characters appear.*

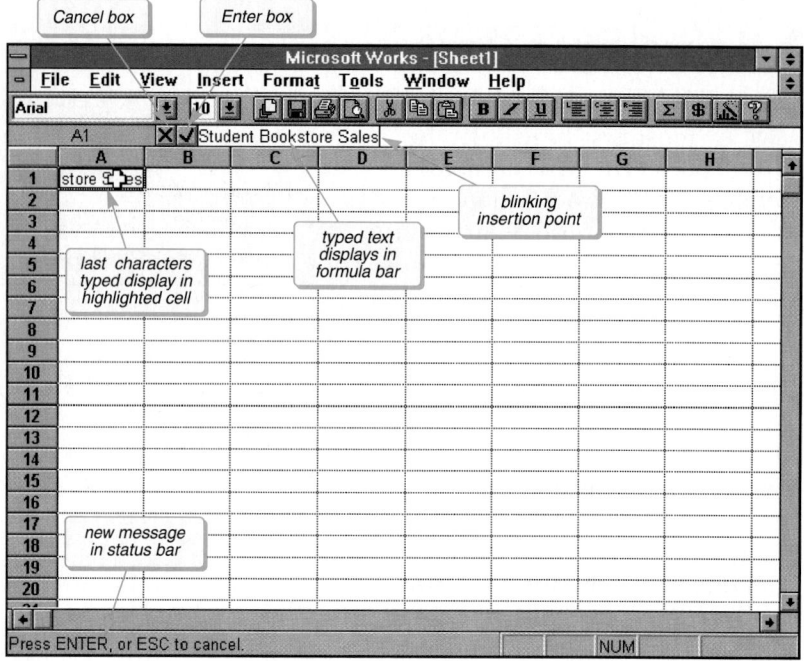

FIGURE 4-9

STEP 3 ▶

After you type the text, point to the Enter box (Figure 4-10).

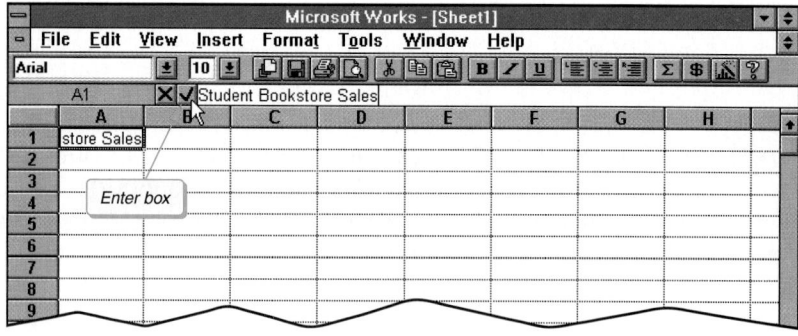

FIGURE 4-10

STEP 4 ▶

Click the Enter box to confirm the entry.

When you confirm the entry, Works enters the text in cell A1 (Figure 4-11).

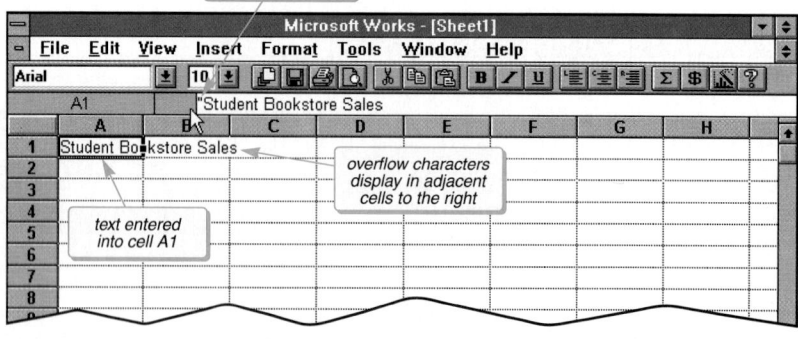

FIGURE 4-11

In the example in Figure 4-11, instead of using the mouse to **confirm the entry**, you can press the ENTER **key** after typing the text. Pressing the ENTER key replaces Step 3 and Step 4.

When you confirm a text entry into a cell, a series of events occurs. First, when text displays in the formula bar, it displays preceded by a **double quotation mark**, which indicates the entry is text and not a number or other value.

Second, Works positions the text **left-aligned** in the highlighted cell. Therefore, the S in the word Student begins in the leftmost position of cell A1.

Third, when the text you enter contains more characters than can be displayed in the width of the cell, Works displays the overflow characters in adjacent cells to the right as long as these adjacent cells contain no data. In Figure 4-11, cell A1 is not wide enough to contain twenty-one characters plus two blank spaces. Thus, Works displays the overflow characters in cells B1 and C1 because they are empty.

Fourth, when you confirm an entry into a cell by clicking the Enter box or pressing the ENTER key, the cell into which the text is entered remains the highlighted cell.

Correcting a Mistake While Typing

If you type the wrong letter and notice the error before clicking the Enter box or pressing the ENTER key, use the BACKSPACE key to erase all the characters back to and including the ones that are wrong. The insertion point will indicate where in the text the next character you type will display. Then retype the remainder of the text entry.

To cancel the entire entry before confirming the entry, click the Cancel box or press the ESC key.

If you see an error in data you have already entered into a cell, highlight the cell and retype the entire entry. Later in this project, additional error-correction techniques are explained.

Entering Column Titles

The next step is to enter the column titles consisting of the words September, October, November, December, and Total. When entering a series of titles consisting of the months of the year, Works allows you to enter only the first three characters of the name of a month. When the entry is confirmed, the name of the entire month will display. For example, when you type Sep in cell B2 and confirm the entry, the word September will display. Works also provides a **Fill Series command**, which, when used with a cell containing a month name, will display subsequent month names in adjacent highlighted cells.

To enter the first **column title**, complete the following steps.

TO ENTER A COLUMN TITLE ▼

STEP 1 ▶

Highlight cell B2 by pointing to the cell and clicking the left mouse button. Then type the column title Sep.

A heavy border surrounds cell B2, and B2 displays in the cell reference area in the formula bar (Figure 4-12). Sep displays in cell B2 and in the formula bar.

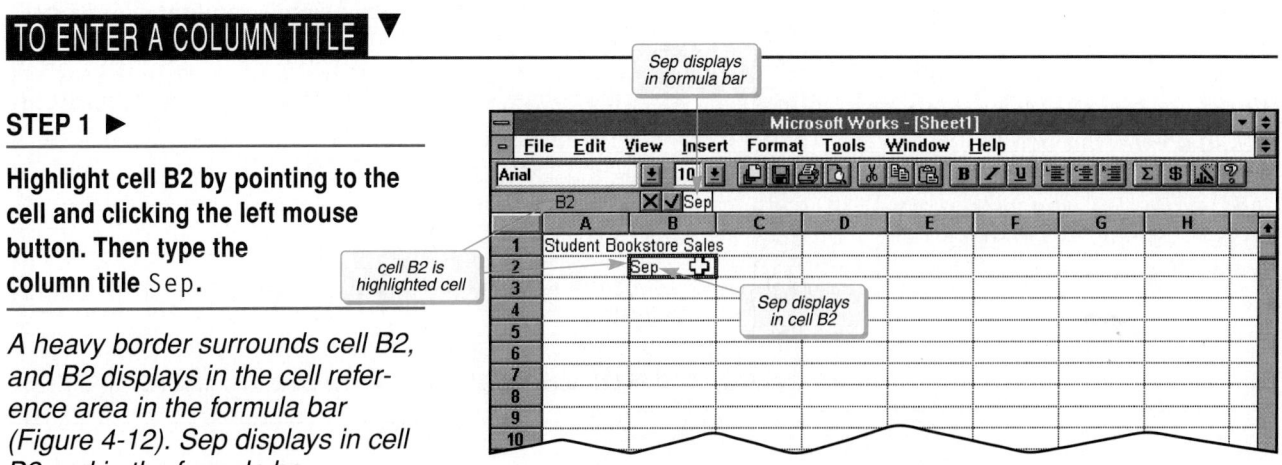

FIGURE 4-12

STEP 2 ▶

Press the ENTER key to confirm Sep as the entry.

September displays in cell B2, because Works recognizes that Sep is the first 3 characters of the month name September (Figure 4-13). Works enters September into cell B2. Because September is considered a date, a double quotation mark does not appear before September in the formula bar.

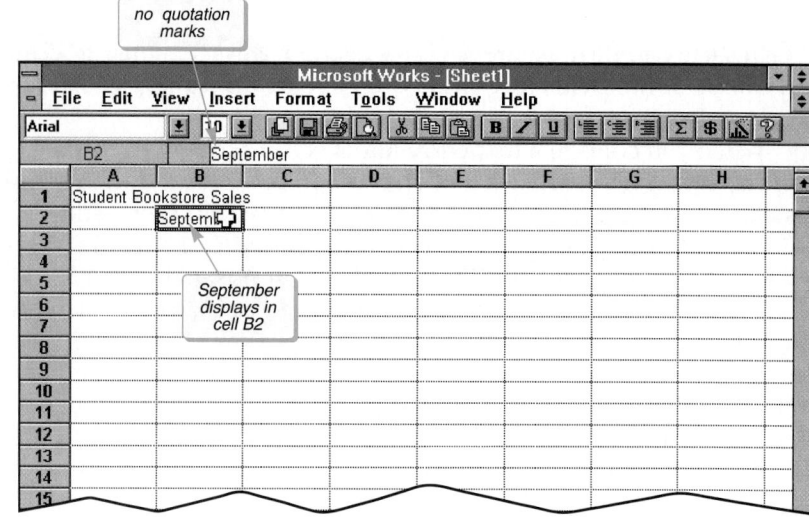

FIGURE 4-13

Using the Fill Series Command

You can use the Fill Series command to enter a series of dates or numbers in a spreadsheet. To use the Fill Series command, you must first highlight the cells that are to contain the dates. You can highlight a series of adjacent cells by dragging the mouse pointer through the cells you want to highlight.

Complete the following steps to use the Fill Series command.

TO USE THE FILL SERIES COMMAND ▼

STEP 1 ▶

Highlight the cell containing the starting month name (B2) and the cells that will contain the subsequent month names (C2, D2, and E2) by dragging the block plus sign mouse pointer through those cells.

When you drag the block plus sign mouse pointer through the cells, Works surrounds one cell by a dark border (B2) and the remaining cells contain a dark background (Figure 4-14).

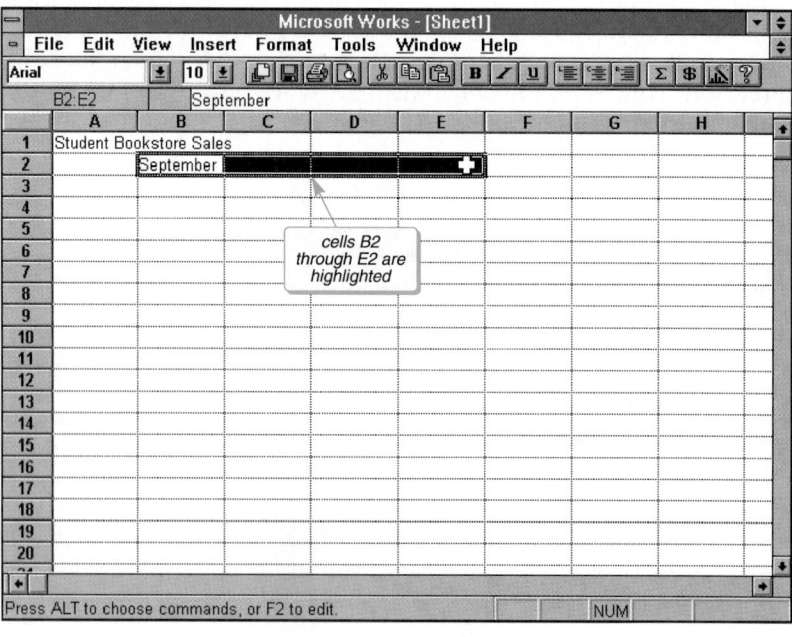

FIGURE 4-14

STEP 2 ▶

Select the Edit menu and point to
the Fill Series command.

*Works displays the **Edit menu** and
the mouse pointer points to the Fill
Series command (Figure 4-15).*

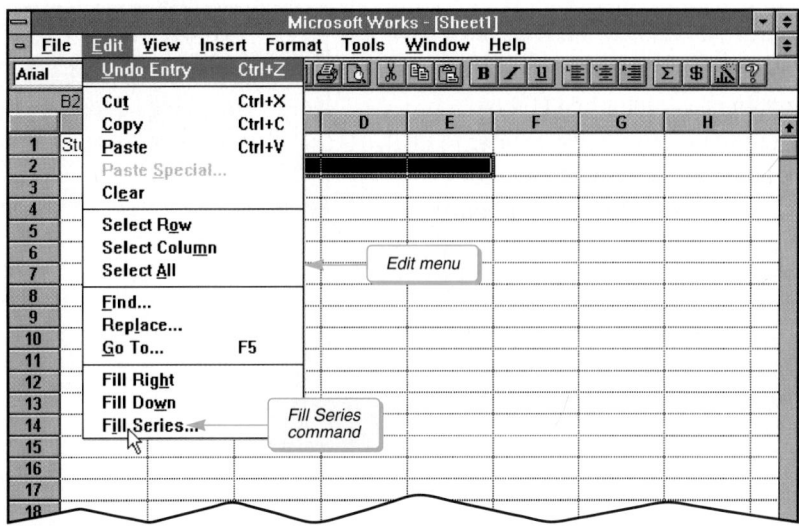

FIGURE 4-15

STEP 3 ▶

Choose the Fill Series command.
When the Fill Series dialog box
displays, select the Month option
button and point to OK button.

*Works displays the Fill Series dia-
log box (Figure 4-16). The Month
option button is selected. The Step
by text box contains a 1 and the
mouse pointer points to the OK
button.*

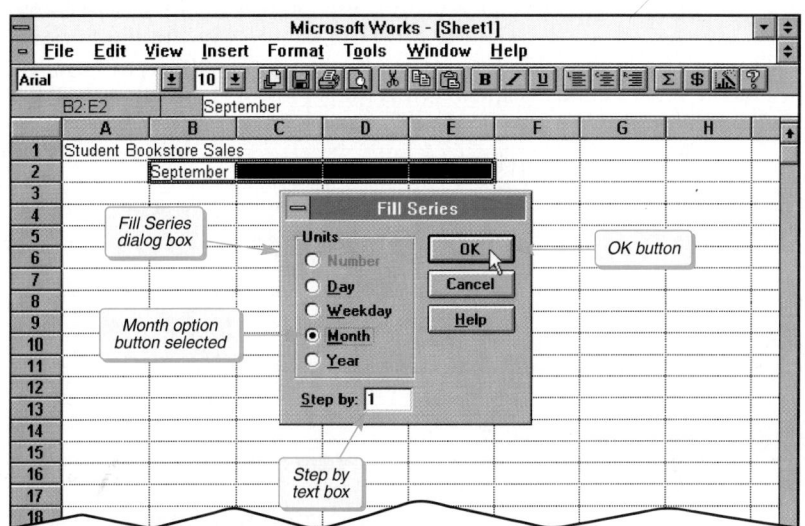

FIGURE 4-16

STEP 4 ▶

Choose the OK button in the Fill
Series dialog box.

*Works fills the highlighted cells
(C2, D2, and E2) with the next
successive month names, that is,
October, November, and December (Figure 4-17). Although difficult
to see because of the length of the
month names, the names are
right-aligned in each cell.*

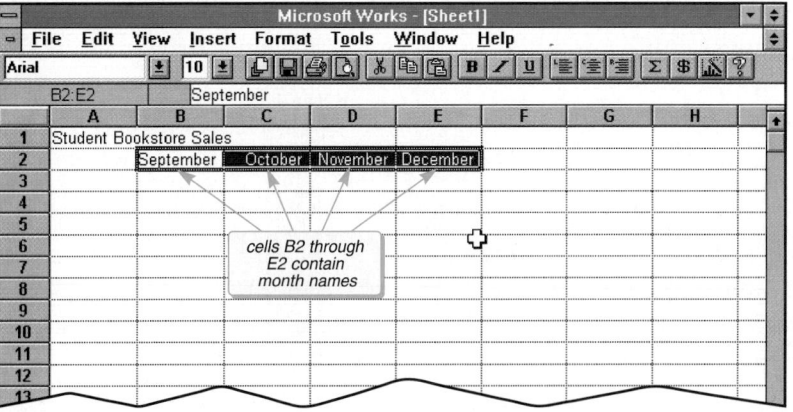

FIGURE 4-17

STEP 5 ▶

To complete the entry of the column headings, highlight cell F2 by positioning the mouse pointer in cell F2 and clicking the left mouse button. Type `Total` and press the ENTER key.

The column titles display in the spreadsheet (Figure 4-18). The word Total is left-aligned in the cell.

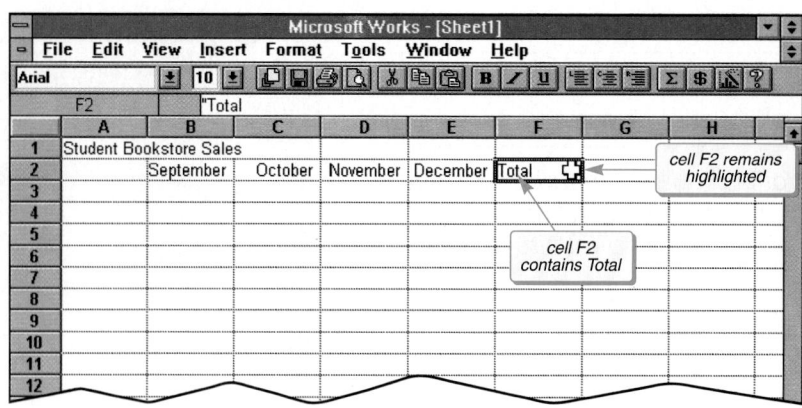

FIGURE 4-18

The Fill series command can also be used to display a sequence of numbers or dates in other formats, as will be seen in subsequent projects.

The Step by text box in the Fill Series dialog box (see Figure 4-16) allows you to increment by a number different from one. If, for example, you enter the value 2 in the Step by text box, the month names will be incremented by 2 and every other month name (September, November, January, March) will be entered in the cells.

Entering Row Titles

The next step in developing the spreadsheet is to enter the row titles in column A. Complete the following steps to enter the row titles.

TO ENTER ROW TITLES ▼

STEP 1 ▶

Highlight cell A3 by positioning the mouse pointer in cell A3 and clicking the left mouse button (Figure 4-19).

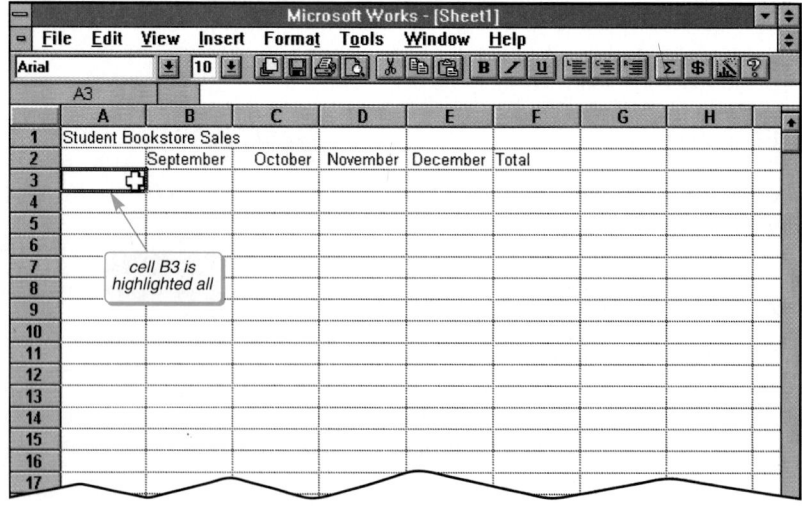

FIGURE 4-19

STEP 2 ▶

Type the row title `Textbooks` and press the DOWN ARROW key.

When you press the DOWN ARROW *key, Works enters the row title, Textbooks, in cell A3 and makes cell A4 the highlighted cell (Figure 4-20).*

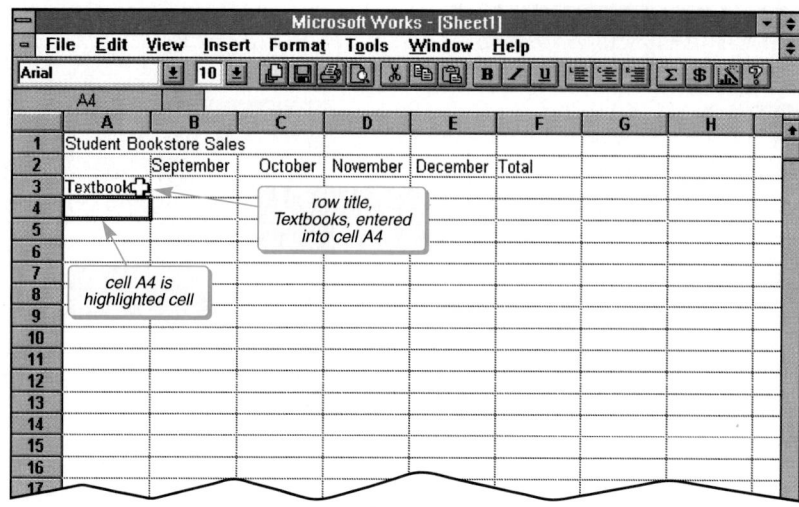

FIGURE 4-20

STEP 3 ▶

Type `Other Books` in cell A4 and press the DOWN ARROW key. Type `Clothing` in cell A5 and press the DOWN ARROW key. Type `Supplies` in cell A6 and press the DOWN ARROW key. Type `Total` in cell A7 and confirm the entry by clicking the Enter box or pressing the ENTER key.

The row titles display as shown in Figure 4-21. The row titles are left-aligned in each cell. Cell A7 is the highlighted cell.

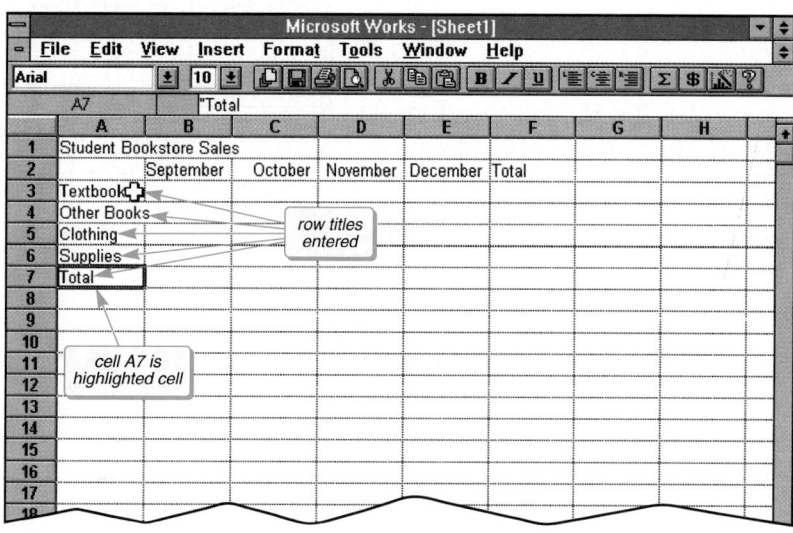

FIGURE 4-21

▶ ENTERING NUMBERS

ou can enter numbers into cells to represent amounts and other numeric values. **Numbers** can include the digits zero through nine and any one of the following characters:

+ - ( ) , . / $ % E e

The use of these characters is explained when they are required in a project. If a cell entry contains any other character from the keyboard, Works interprets the entry as text or a date and treats it accordingly.

In Project 4, you must enter the sales amounts for September, October, November, and December for each of the categories, Textbooks, Other Books, Clothing, and Supplies in rows 3, 4, 5, and 6. The following steps illustrate how to enter these values one row at a time.

TO ENTER NUMERIC DATA ▼

STEP 1 ►

Highlight cell B3 by positioning the
mouse pointer in cell B3 and
clicking the left mouse button
(Figure 4-22).

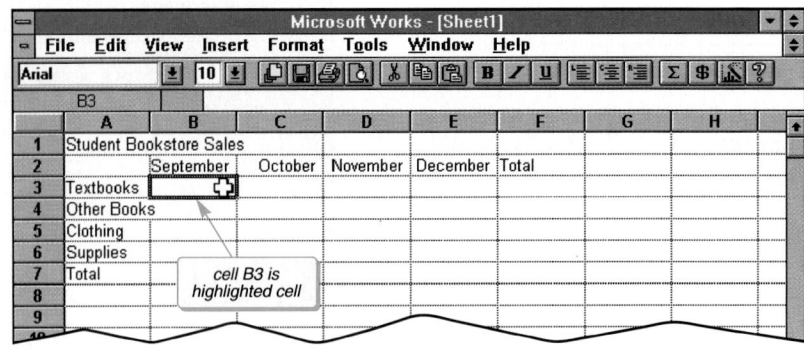

FIGURE 4-22

STEP 2 ►

Type 95435.82.

*The number 95435.82 displays in
the formula bar and in the highlighted cell (Figure 4-23). Enter the
number without a comma. You will
format the numbers in the spreadsheet with commas in a later step.*

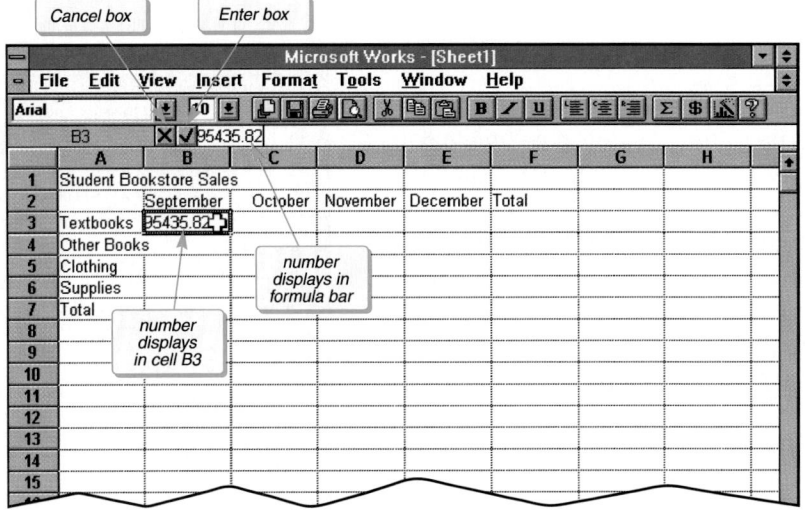

FIGURE 4-23

STEP 3 ►

Press the RIGHT ARROW key.

*Works enters the number
95435.82 into cell B3 and makes
cell C3 the highlighted cell (Figure
4-24).*

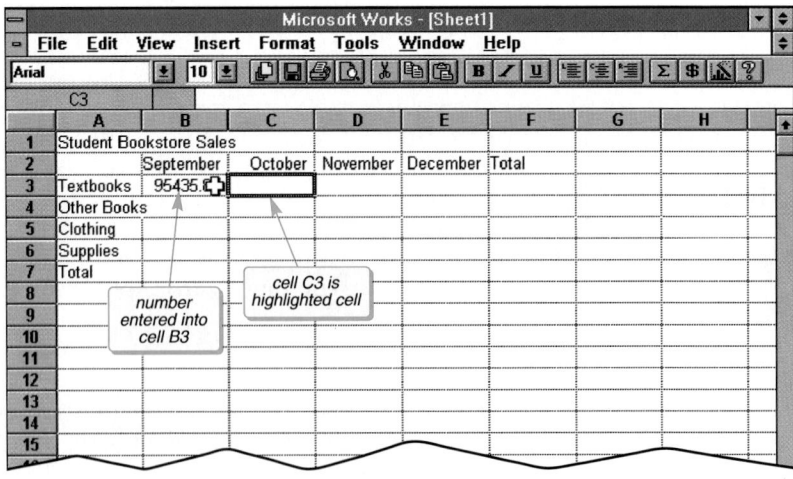

FIGURE 4-24

STEP 4 ▶

Type 86759.58 into cell C3 and press the RIGHT ARROW key. Type 91528.91 into cell D3 and press the RIGHT ARROW key. Type 73427.27 into cell E3 and press the ENTER key.

Row 3 contains the Textbooks sales and cell E3 is highlighted (Figure 4-25).

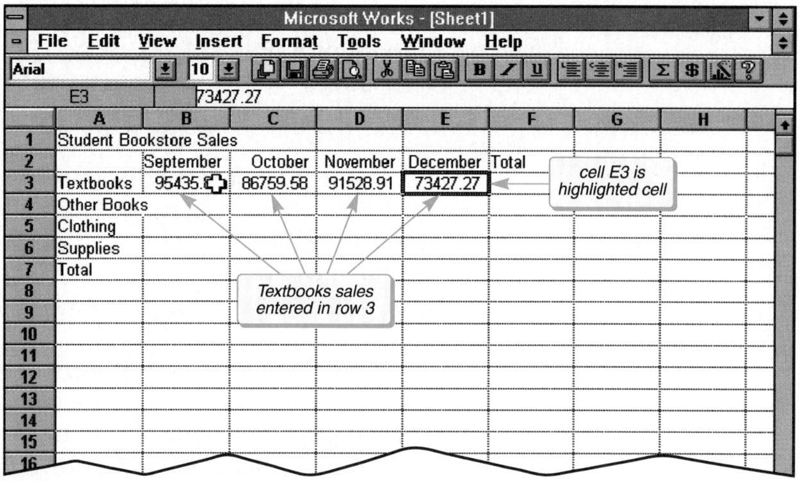

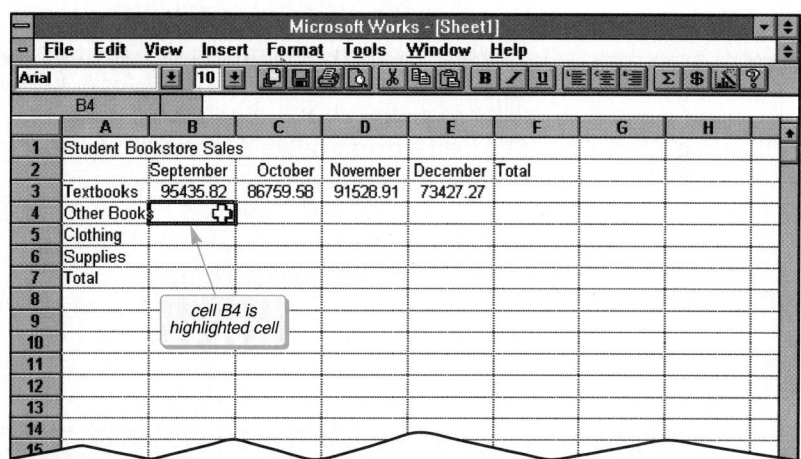

FIGURE 4-25

STEP 5 ▶

Highlight cell B4 by positioning the mouse pointer in cell B4 and clicking the left mouse button (Figure 4-26).

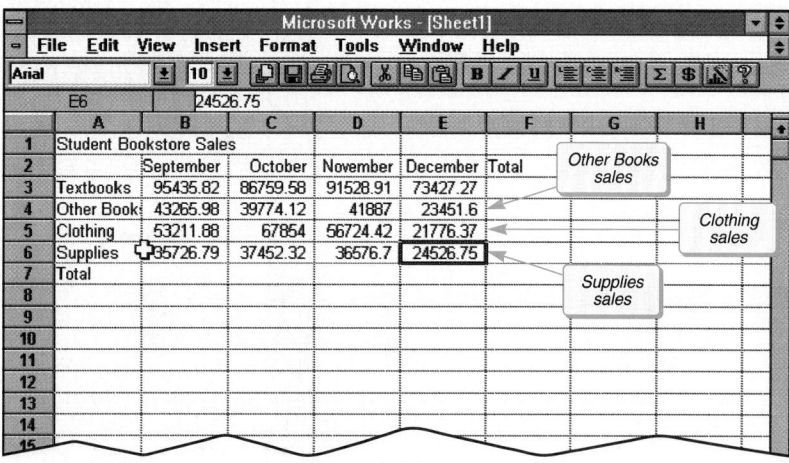

FIGURE 4-26

STEP 6 ▶

Repeat the procedures used in Step 2 through Step 4 to enter the Other Books sales, the Clothing sales, and the Supplies sales.

The Other Books, Clothing, and Supplies sales are entered in rows 4, 5, and 6, respectively (Figure 4-27).

FIGURE 4-27

You have now entered all the numbers required for this spreadsheet. Notice several important points.

First, commas, which are used to separate every third digit to the left of the decimal point, are not required when you enter numbers. You will add them in a later step.

Second, you can enter **whole numbers** without the decimal point and the zeros to the right of the decimal point (cells D4 and C5 in Figure 4-27). If you enter the zeros following the decimal point, they do not display. You will add the decimal point and zeroes in a later step when the numbers are formatted. The same is true when only one digit follows the decimal point (cells E4 and D6 in Figure 4-27).

Third, Works enters numbers **right-aligned** in the cells, which means they occupy the rightmost positions in the cells.

Fourth, Works will calculate the totals in row 7 and column F. The capability of the Works Spreadsheet tool to perform calculations is one of its major features.

▶ CALCULATING A SUM

The next step in creating the Student Bookstore Sales spreadsheet is to calculate the total sales for September. To calculate this value and enter it into cell B7, Works must add the numbers in cells B3, B4, B5, and B6. The **SUM function** available in the Works Spreadsheet tool provides a convenient means to accomplish this task.

To use the SUM function, you must first identify the cell in which the sum will be entered after it is calculated. Then, you can use the **Autosum button** on the Toolbar to actually sum the numbers.

The following steps illustrate how to use the Autosum button to sum the sales for September in cells B3, B4, B5, and B6 and enter the answer in cell B7.

TO SUM A COLUMN OF NUMBERS USING THE AUTOSUM BUTTON ▼

STEP 1 ▶

Highlight the cell that will contain the sum for September – cell B7.

Cell B7 is highlighted (Figure 4-28).

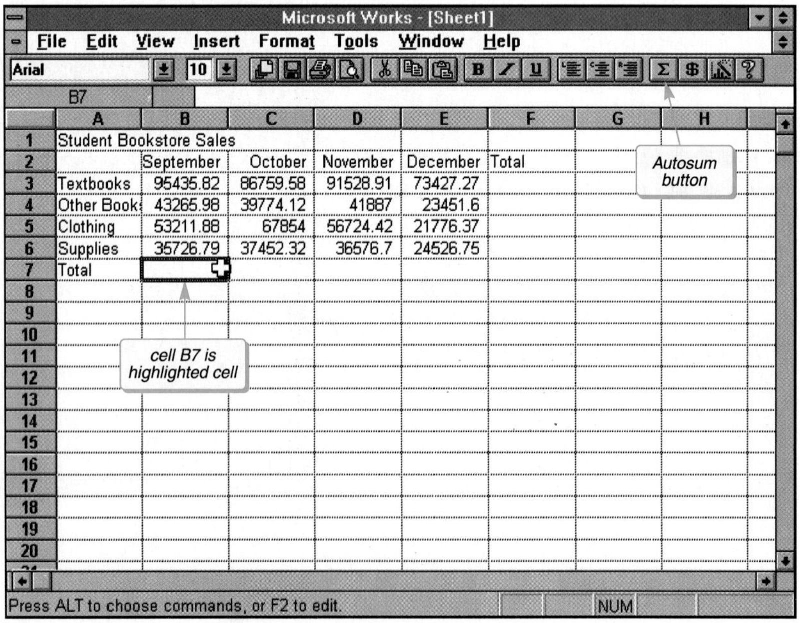

FIGURE 4-28

STEP 2 ▶

Click the Autosum button on the Toolbar.

Works responds by displaying =SUM(B3:B6) in the formula bar and in the highlighted cell (Figure 4-29). The =SUM entry identifies the SUM function. The B3:B6 entry within parentheses following the function name SUM is the way Works identifies cells B3, B4, B5, and B6 as the cells containing the values to be summed. Works also places a dark background behind the proposed cells to sum. The word POINT displays in the status bar.

FIGURE 4-29

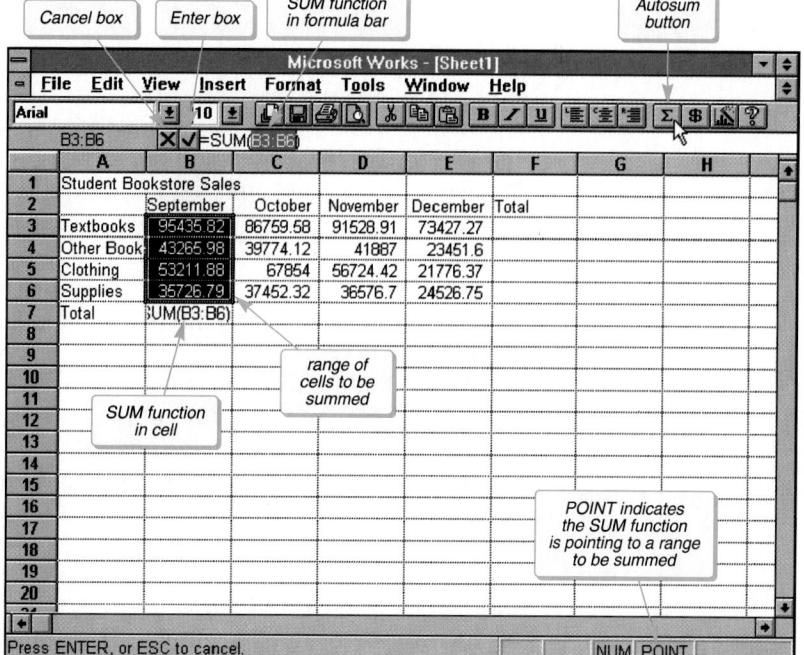

STEP 3 ▶

Point to the Enter box in the formula bar (Figure 4-30)

FIGURE 4-30

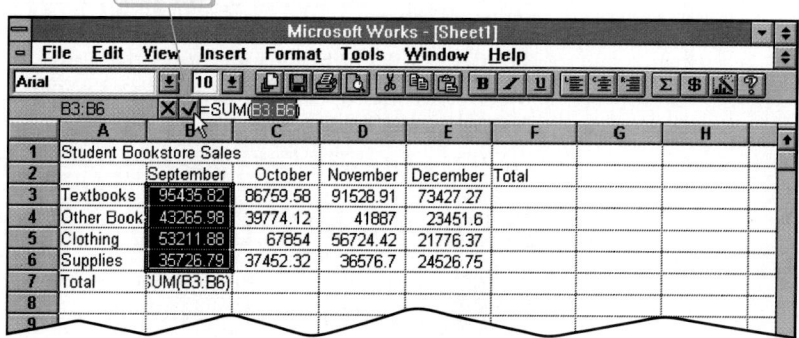

STEP 4 ▶

Click the Enter box in the formula bar.

Works displays the sum of the sales for September (95435.82 + 43265.98 + 53211.88 + 35726.79 = 227640.47) in cell B7 (Figure 4-31). Although the SUM function assigned to cell B7 is not displayed in the cell, it remains in the cell and displays in the formula bar when the cell is highlighted.

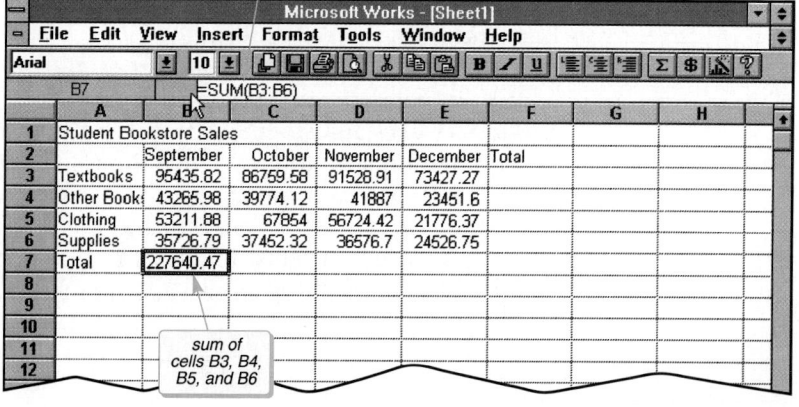

FIGURE 4-31

To display the SUM function in a cell instead of the sum, highlight the cell and click in the formula bar area.

When you enter the SUM function using the Autosum button, Works automatically highlights what it considers to be your choice of the group of cells to sum. The group of cells B3, B4, B5, and B6 is called a range. A **range** is a block of adjacent cells in a spreadsheet. Ranges can be as small as a single cell and as large as an entire spreadsheet. Once you define a range, you can work with all the cells in the range rather than one cell at a time. In Figure 4-29, clicking the Autosum button defines the range, which consists of cells B3 through B6 (designated B3:B6 by Works).

When highlighting the range of cells to sum using the Autosum button, Works first looks for a range with numbers above the highlighted cell, and then to the left. If Works highlights the wrong range, highlight the range designation in the formula bar and then use the mouse to drag the correct range any time prior to clicking the Enter box or pressing the ENTER key. You can also enter the correct range in the formula bar by dragging the mouse pointer over the range specified in the formula bar and then typing the beginning cell reference, a colon (:), and the ending cell reference, followed by clicking the Enter box or pressing the ENTER key. A third method to fix an incorrect range specified by Works is to highlight the first cell in the range, type a colon, highlight the lower cell in the range, and click the Enter box or press the ENTER key.

You can also speed up the entry of the SUM function by clicking the Autosum button a second time instead of moving the pointer and clicking the Enter box. That is, after clicking once and ensuring the correct range is selected, clicking the Autosum button a second time will perform the same task as clicking the Enter box or pressing the ENTER key.

▶ COPYING A CELL TO ADJACENT CELLS

In the Student Bookstore Sales spreadsheet, Works must also calculate the totals for October, November, and December. For the October sales, the total is the sum of the values in the range C3:C6. Similarly, for November sales, the range to sum is D3:D6 and for December sales, the range is E3:E6.

To calculate these sums, you can follow the steps shown in Figures 4-28 through 4-31 on the previous two pages. A more efficient method, however, is to copy the SUM function from cell B7 to the range C7:E7 using the **Fill Right command** from the **Edit menu**.

The copy cannot be an exact duplicate, though, because different columns must be referenced for each respective total. Therefore, when you **copy** cell references, Works adjusts the cell references for each column. As a result, the range in the SUM function in cell C7 will be C3:C6, the range in SUM function in cell D7 will be D3:D6, and the range in SUM function in cell E7 will be E3:E6.

To copy the SUM function and the respective ranges into the adjacent cells in the same row, you must highlight the range you want to copy and then choose the Fill Right command from the Edit menu. Complete the following steps to perform this operation.

TO COPY ONE CELL TO ADJACENT CELLS IN A ROW ▼

STEP 1 ▶

Highlight the cell you want to copy –
cell B7 (Figure 4-32).

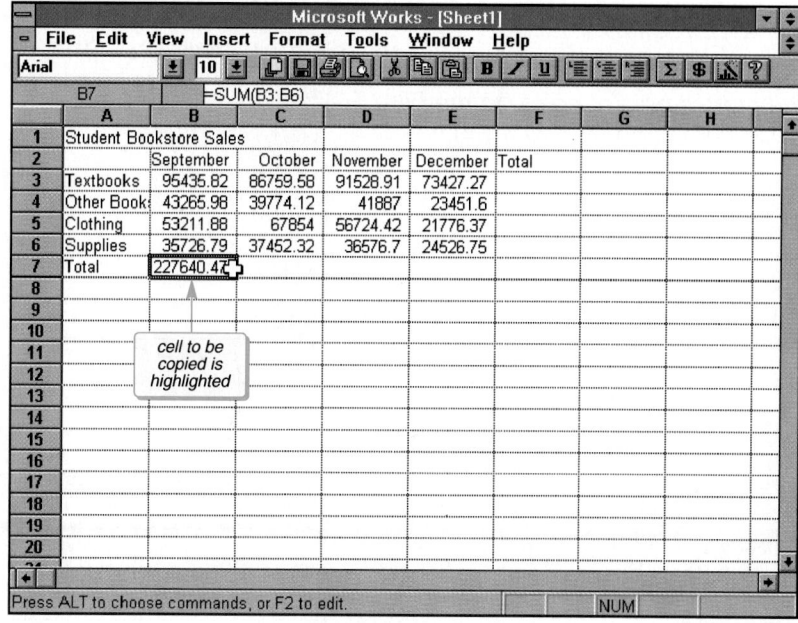

FIGURE 4-32

STEP 2 ▶

Highlight the range you want to copy
into by dragging the block plus sign
mouse pointer from cell B7 through
those cells (cells C7, D7, and E7).

*When you drag the block plus sign
through the cells, Works highlights
each cell with a dark background
(Figure 4-33). When multiple cells
are highlighted, Works surrounds
one cell by a dark border and the
remaining cells in the range have
a dark background.*

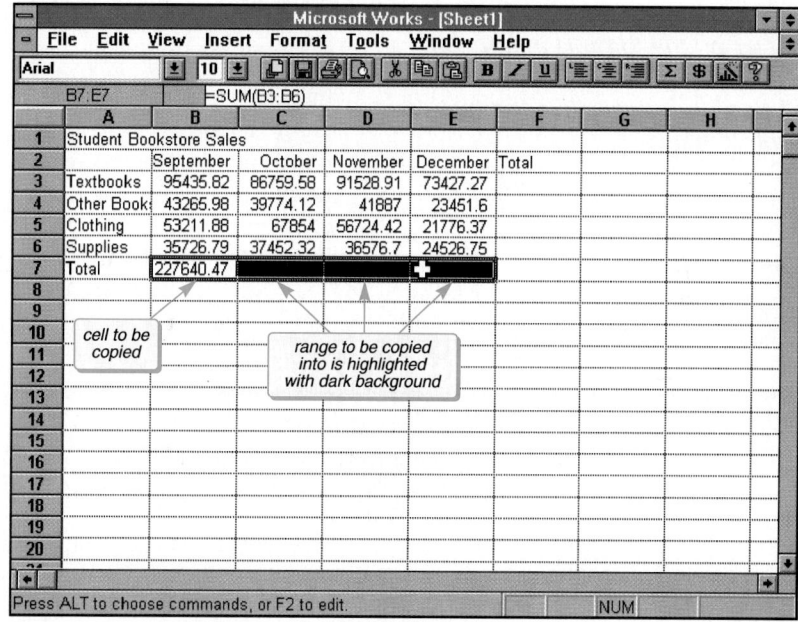

FIGURE 4-33

STEP 3 ▶

Select the Edit menu and point to the Fill Right command.

Works displays the Edit menu and the mouse pointer points to the Fill Right command (Figure 4-34).

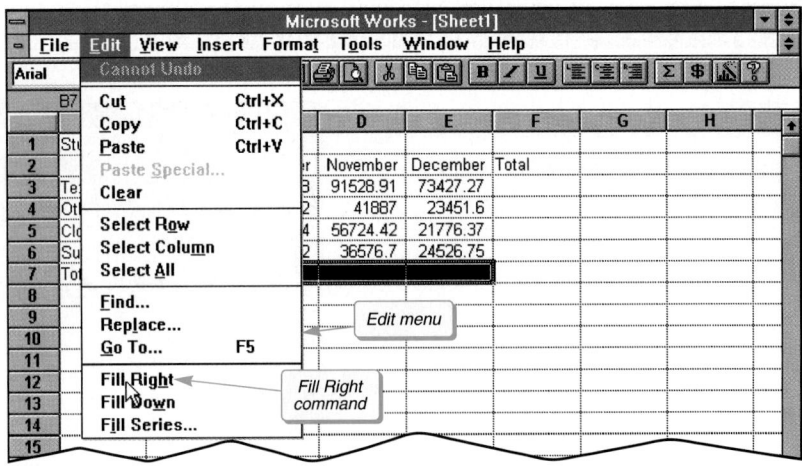

FIGURE 4-34

STEP 4 ▶

Choose the Fill Right command from the Edit menu.

Works copies the SUM formula from cell B7 into the cells within the highlighted range (Figure 4-35). It then performs calculations based on the formula in each of the cells and displays sums in each of the cells within the highlighted range.

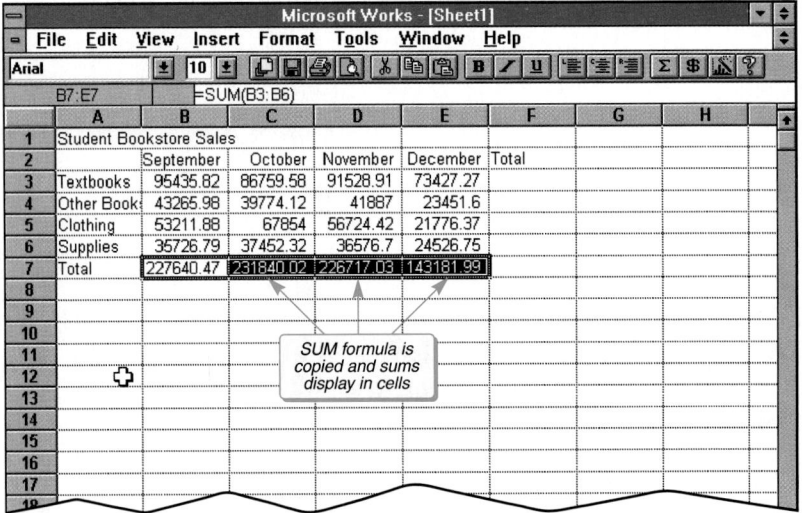

FIGURE 4-35

After Works has copied the contents of a cell into a range, the range remains highlighted. To remove the range highlight, click any cell in the spreadsheet.

▶ SUMMING A ROW TOTAL

The next step in building the Student Bookstore Sales spreadsheet is to total the Textbooks sales, the Other Books sales, the Clothing sales, and the Supplies sales, and then to calculate the total sales for the store. These totals will be entered in column F. The SUM function is used in the same manner as totaling the sales by month in row 7. Perform the steps below to sum the row numbers.

TO SUM A ROW OF NUMBERS USING THE AUTOSUM BUTTON ▼

STEP 1 ▶

Highlight the cell that will contain the total for Textbooks — cell F3.

Cell F3 is highlighted (Figure 4-36).

FIGURE 4-36

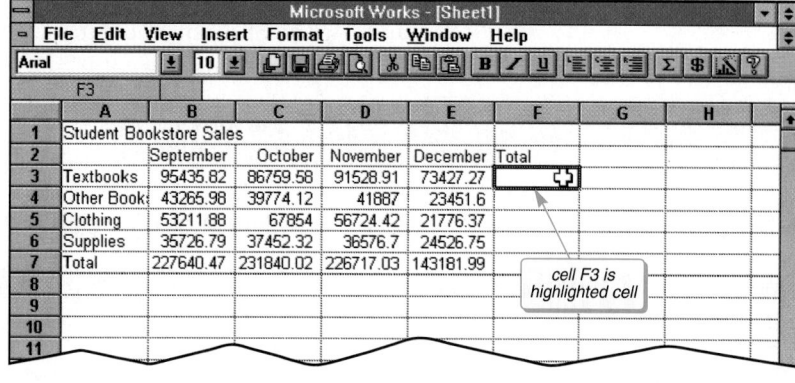

STEP 2 ▶

Click the Autosum button on the Toolbar.

Works responds by displaying =SUM(B3:E3) in the formula bar and in the highlighted cell (Figure 4-37). Works also places a dark background behind the proposed cells to sum. The =SUM entry identifies the SUM function. The B3:E3 entry within parentheses following the function name SUM is the way Works identifies cells B3, C3, D3, and E3 as the cells containing the values to be added.

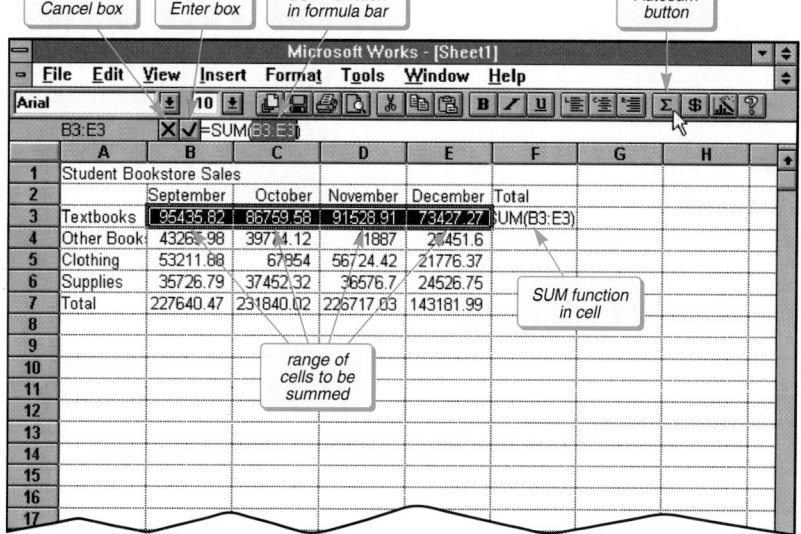

FIGURE 4-37

STEP 3 ▶

Click the Enter box.

Works enters the formula in cell F3, displays the sum in the cell, and displays the SUM function from cell F3 in the formula bar (Figure 4-38).

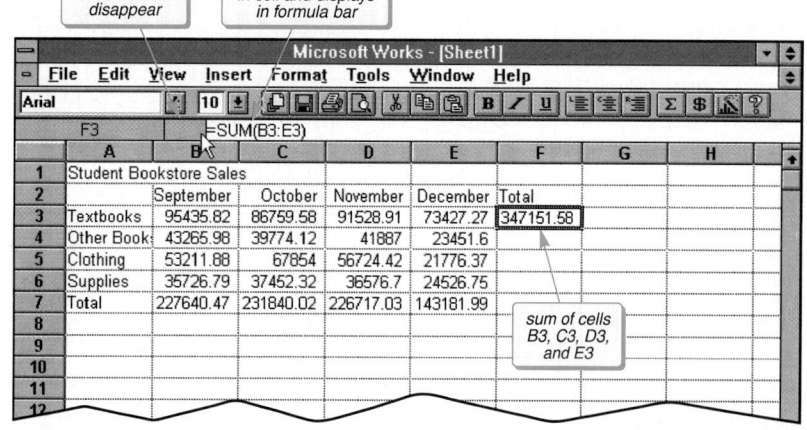

FIGURE 4-38

As noted previously, you can accomplish Step 3 by clicking the Autosum button a second time.

▶ COPYING ADJACENT CELLS IN A COLUMN

 he next task is to copy the SUM function from cell F3 to the range F4:F7 to obtain the total sales for Other Books, Clothing, Supplies, and the total sales for the Student Bookstore. The steps to accomplish this task follow.

TO COPY ONE CELL TO ADJACENT CELLS IN A COLUMN ▼

STEP 1 ▶

Highlight cell F3, if necessary, and drag the range F3:F7.

Works highlights the range F3:F7 (Figure 4-39).

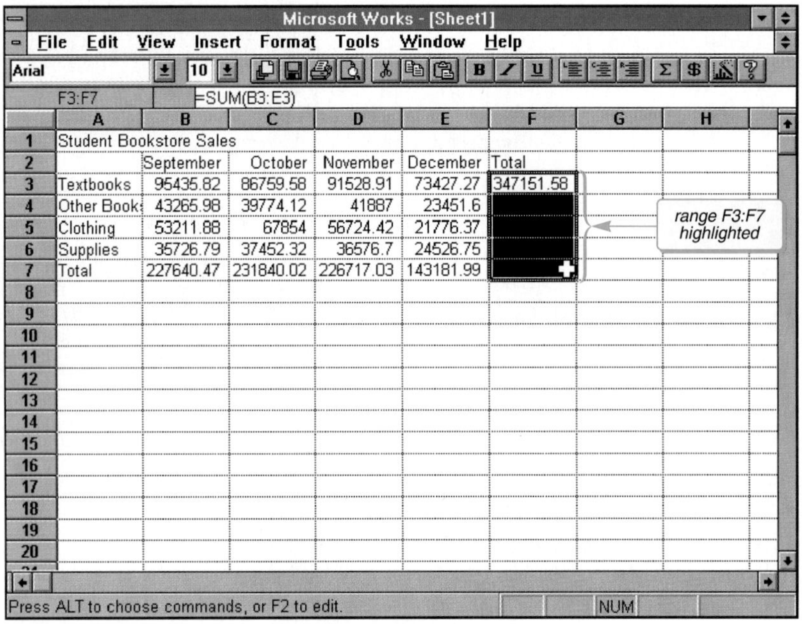

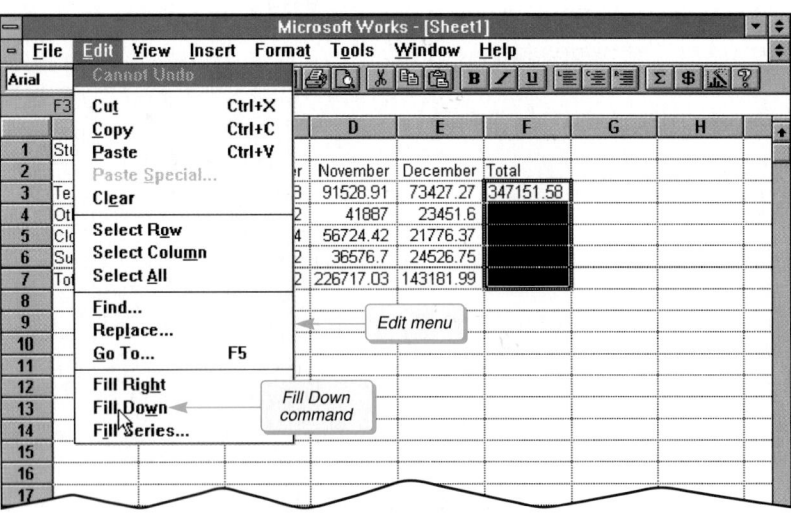

FIGURE 4-39

STEP 2 ▶

Select the Edit menu and point to the Fill Down command.

*The Edit menu displays and the mouse pointer points to the **Fill Down command** (Figure 4-40).*

FIGURE 4-40

STEP 3 ▶

Choose the Fill Down command from the Edit menu.

Works fills the highlighted range with the SUM function and displays the calculated sums in each of the cells (Figure 4-41). When Works copies the function, each range reference in the function is adjusted to reflect the proper rows of numbers to sum.

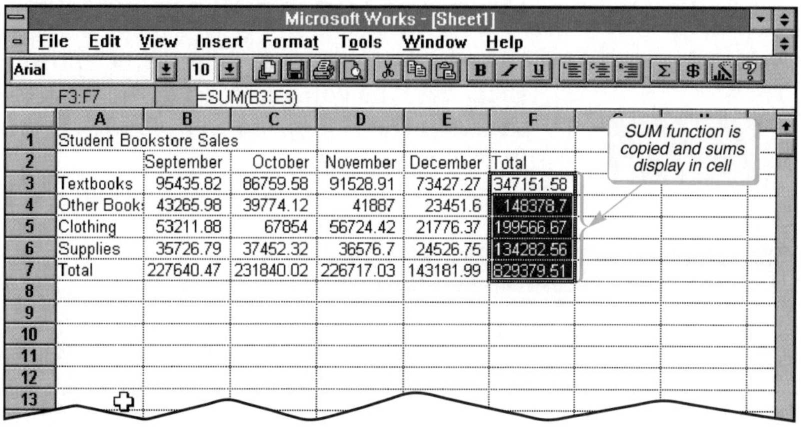

FIGURE 4-41

After Works copies the cell contents, the range F3:F7 remains highlighted. You can remove this highlight by clicking any cell in the spreadsheet.

▶ FORMATTING THE SPREADSHEET

You have now entered all the text, numeric entries, and functions for the spreadsheet. The next step is to format the spreadsheet. You **format a spreadsheet** to emphasize certain entries and make the spreadsheet attractive to view and easy to read and understand.

With Works you have the ability to change fonts, font sizes, and font styles such as bold and italic, and to color the font and cells containing the data in the spreadsheet. On the following pages you will learn to format the spreadsheet in Project 4 as shown in Figure 4-42 and as described in the list.

1. The spreadsheet title displays in yellow 18 point Arial bold font. The cell background is dark red. The title is centered over the columns in the spreadsheet.

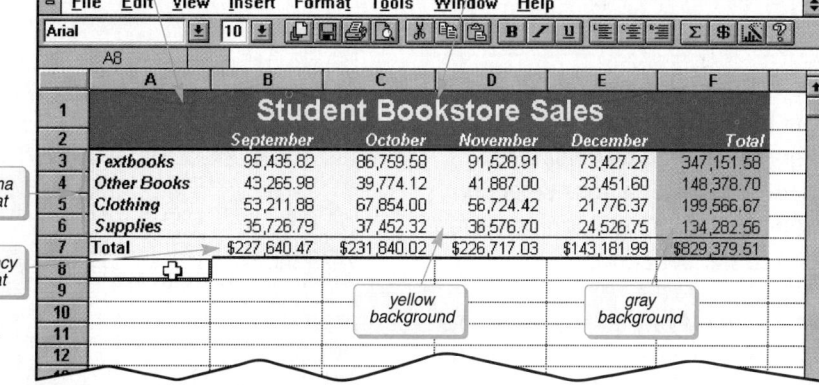

FIGURE 4-42

2. The color of the column titles (dark red), row titles (yellow)and the remainder of the spreadsheet display as illustrated. The fonts, font sizes, styles, and colors are determined by the AutoFormat feature of Works.
3. The sales numbers and the totals for the categories display with commas, decimal points, and two positions to the right of the decimal point.
4. The last line of numbers (the totals) displays in Currency format; that is, each number displays with a dollar sign, a comma if necessary, a decimal point, and two digits to the right of the decimal point.

The following paragraphs explain how to format the spreadsheet.

Centering Text in a Range of Cells

The first step in formatting the spreadsheet is to center the title of the spreadsheet over the columns used in the spreadsheet. This can be accomplished using the **Alignment command** from the Format menu. Complete the following steps to center the title.

TO CENTER TEXT IN A RANGE OF CELLS ▼

STEP 1 ▶

Highlight the range of cells A1:F1. Select the Format menu and point to the Alignment command.

Cells A1 through F1 are highlighted (Figure 4-43). The Format menu displays and the mouse pointer points to the Alignment command.

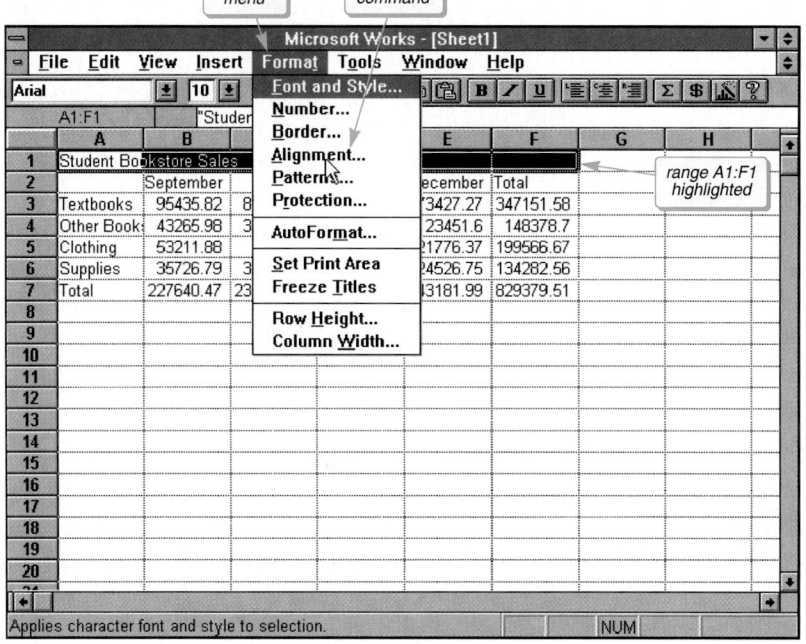

FIGURE 4-43

STEP 2 ▶

Choose the Alignment command from the Format menu. When the Alignment dialog box displays, select the Center across selection option button in the Alignment area. Point to the OK button.

Works displays the Alignment dialog box (Figure 4-44). The Center across selection option button is selected. The mouse pointer points to the OK button.

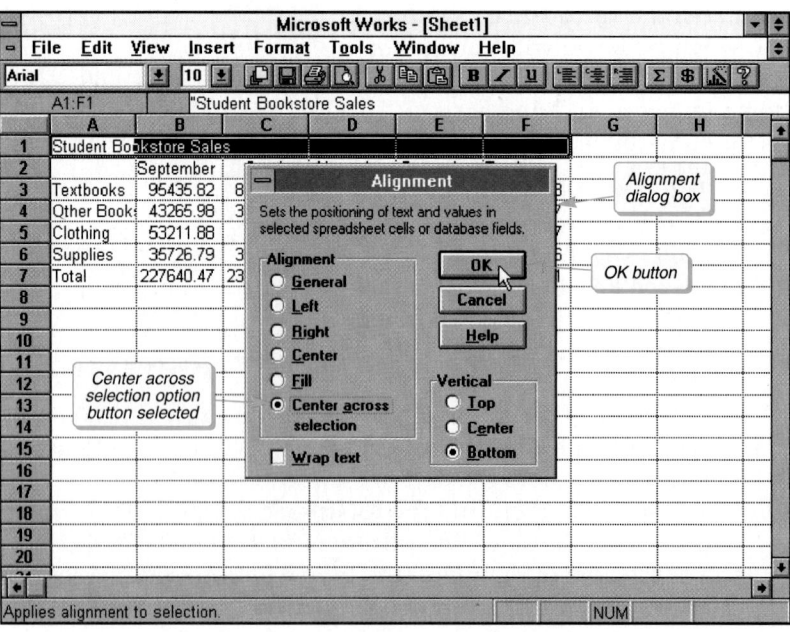

FIGURE 4-44

STEP 3 ▶

Choose the OK button in the Alignment dialog box. Select any cell to remove the highlight so you can easily view the spreadsheet title centered over the columns.

The title is now centered across columns A through F (Figure 4-45). When using the Center across selection option in the Alignment dialog box, vertical gridlines between the cells referenced do not display.

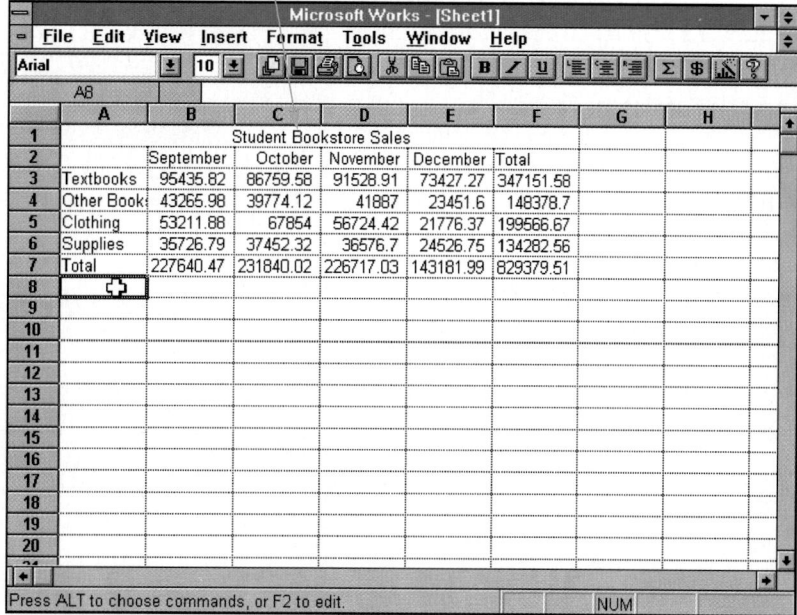

FIGURE 4-45

Changing Font Size, Style, and Color

The next step in formatting the title on the spreadsheet is to change the font size to 18 point, the style to bold, and the color to yellow. The following paragraphs explain the steps necessary to accomplish these tasks.

TO CHANGE FONT SIZE, STYLE, AND COLOR ▼

STEP 1 ▶

Highlight cell A1. Select the Format menu and point to the Font and Style command.

Cell A1 is highlighted (Figure 4-46). Works considers the spreadsheet title to be in cell A1 even though the title is centered across a range of cells. The Format menu displays and the mouse pointer points to the Font and Style command.

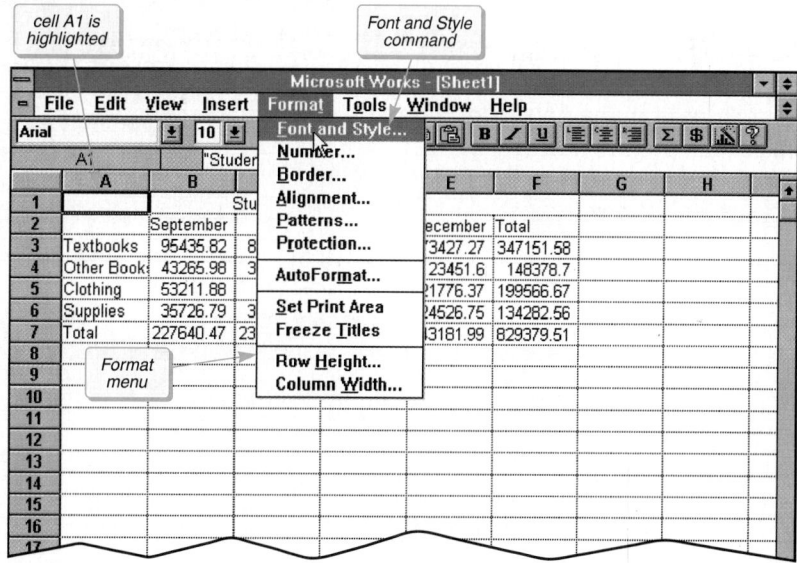

FIGURE 4-46

STEP 2 ►

Choose the Font and Style command from the Format menu.

Works displays the Font and Style dialog box (Figure 4-47). The default values are Arial Font, 10 point Size, Auto Color, and no selections in the Style check boxes. The Sample area displays an example of the text with these options in effect. Auto color displays text in black.

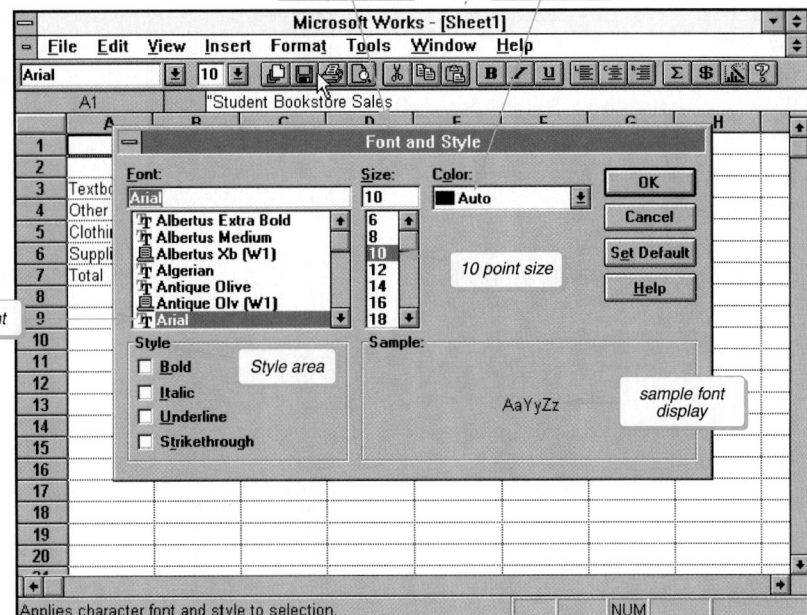

FIGURE 4-47

STEP 3 ►

Select 18 in the Size list box by pointing to the number 18 and clicking the left mouse button. In the Style area, select the Bold check box. Point to the Color drop-down list box arrow.

Works displays a preview of 18 point Arial bold text in the Sample area of the Font and Style dialog box (Figure 4-48). The mouse pointer points to the Color drop-down list box arrow.

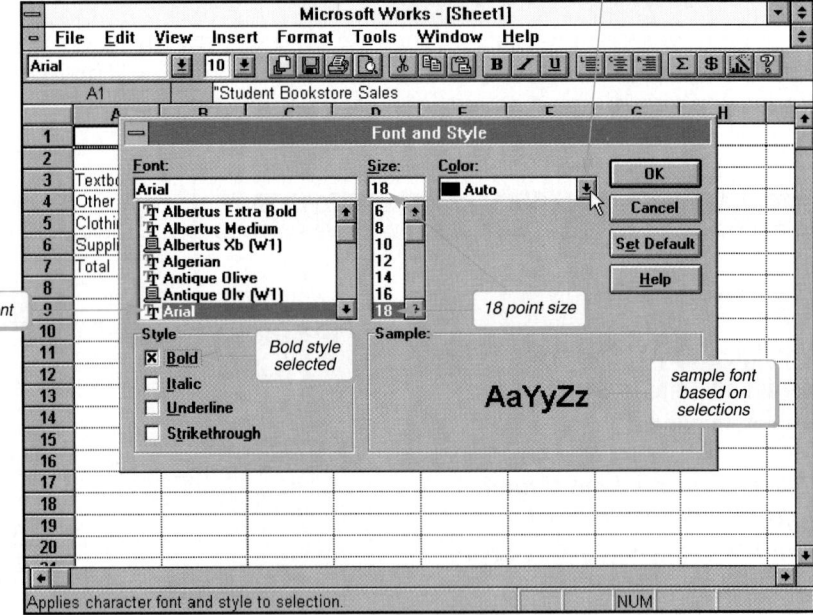

FIGURE 4-48

STEP 4 ►

Click the Color drop-down list box arrow. Scroll down to make the color Yellow visible. Point to the color Yellow.

The Color drop-down list box displays and the mouse pointer points to the color Yellow (Figure 4-49).

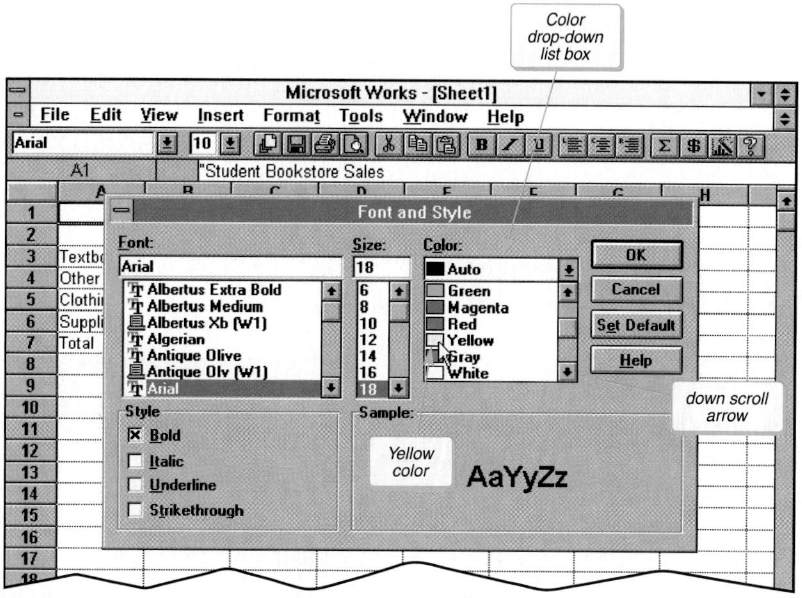

FIGURE 4-49

STEP 5 ►

Select the color Yellow by clicking the left mouse button. Then point to the OK button.

The color yellow and the word Yellow display in the Color drop-down list box (Figure 4-50). The Sample area displays text with the current selections in effect. The mouse pointer points to the OK button.

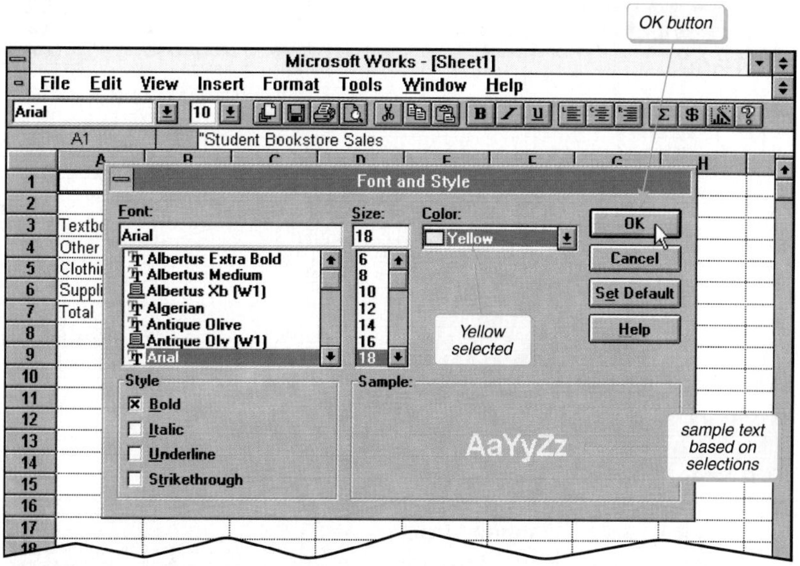

FIGURE 4-50

STEP 6 ►

Choose the OK button in the Font and Style dialog box.

Works displays Student Bookstore Sales in yellow 18 point Arial bold font (Figure 4-51). Notice that when the font size is increased to 18 point, Works automatically increases the height of row 1 so the enlarged text displays properly.

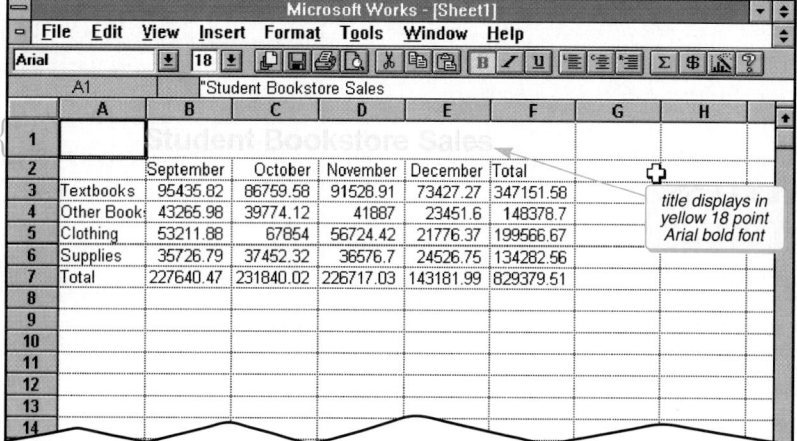

FIGURE 4-51

Adding Color to Cells

Adding color to one or more cells can enhance the appearance of a spreadsheet. In Project 4, the yellow spreadsheet title displays in cells containing a dark red color. To add the dark red color to the cells, complete the following steps.

TO ADD COLOR TO CELLS ▼

STEP 1 ▶

Highlight the range of cells A1:F1. Select the Format menu and point to the Patterns command.

Cells A1 through F1 are highlighted (Figure 4-52). The Format menu is selected and the mouse pointer points to the Patterns command.

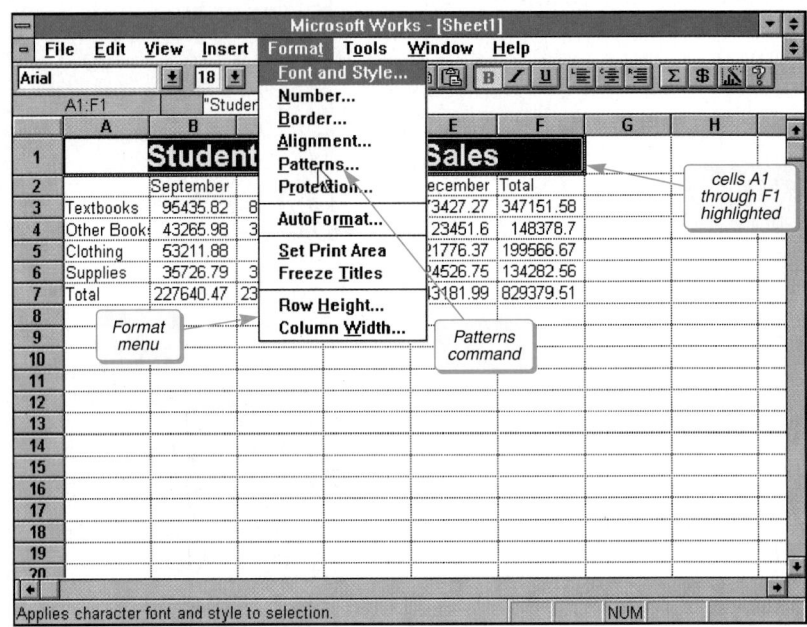

FIGURE 4-52

STEP 2 ▶

Choose the Patterns command from the Format menu. When the Patterns dialog box displays, point to the Pattern drop-down list box arrow.

Works displays the Patterns dialog box (Figure 4-53). The Pattern drop-down list box contains the word None. The mouse pointer points to the drop-down list box arrow.

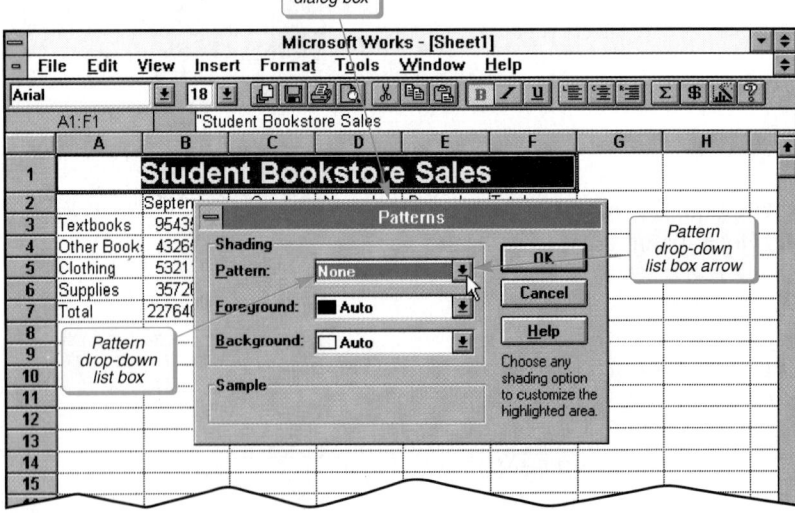

FIGURE 4-53

STEP 3 ▶

Click the Pattern drop-down list box arrow. When the drop-down list box displays, point to the solid pattern.

A series of rectangular boxes display in the drop-down list box (Figure 4-54). The first rectangular box contains the word None. This box is followed by a series of boxes with various patterns you can select. The first pattern below None is the solid pattern. The mouse pointer points to the solid pattern.

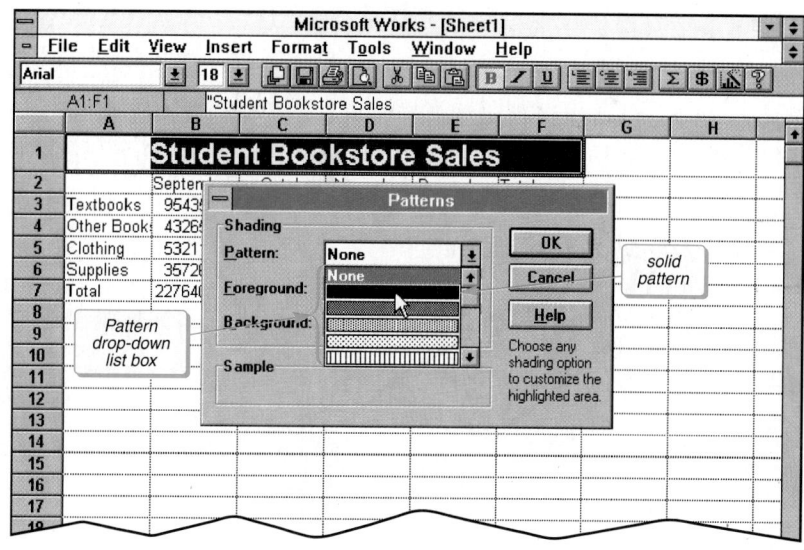

FIGURE 4-54

STEP 4 ▶

Select the solid pattern by clicking the left mouse button. Point to the Foreground drop-down list box arrow.

The Pattern box that contained the word None has been replaced with a solid pattern (Figure 4-55). The mouse pointer points to the Foreground drop-down list box arrow.

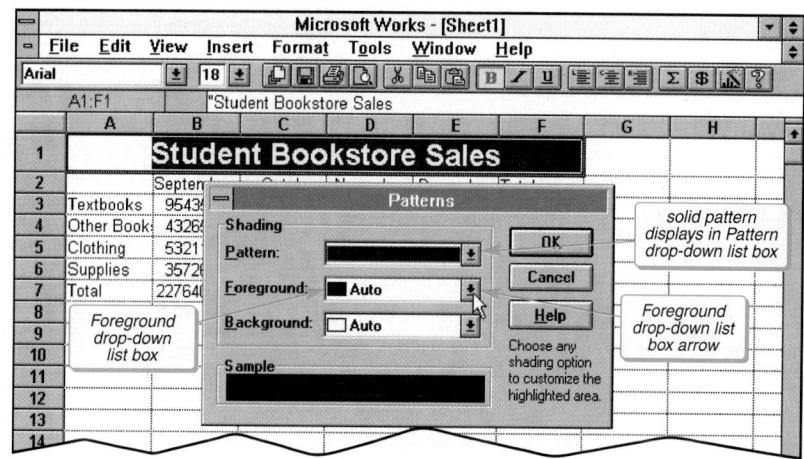

FIGURE 4-55

STEP 5 ▶

Click the Foreground drop-down list box arrow. When the Foreground drop-down list box displays, scroll down and point to Dark Red.

The Foreground drop-down list box displays (Figure 4-56). The Foreground color is the color that will display in the highlighted cells.

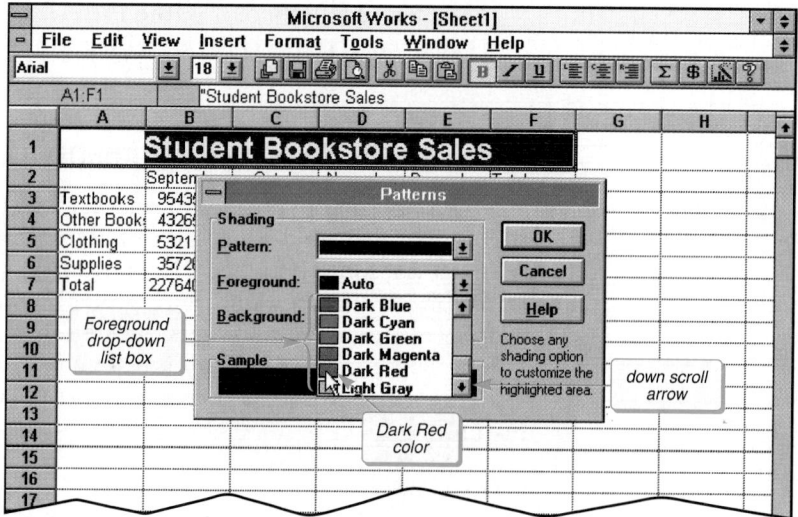

FIGURE 4-56

STEP 6 ►

Click the left mouse button to choose Dark Red in the Foreground drop-down list box. Point to the OK button.

The Foreground drop-down list box contains Dark Red (Figure 4-57). A preview of Solid pattern, Dark Red displays in the Sample area of the Patterns dialog box.

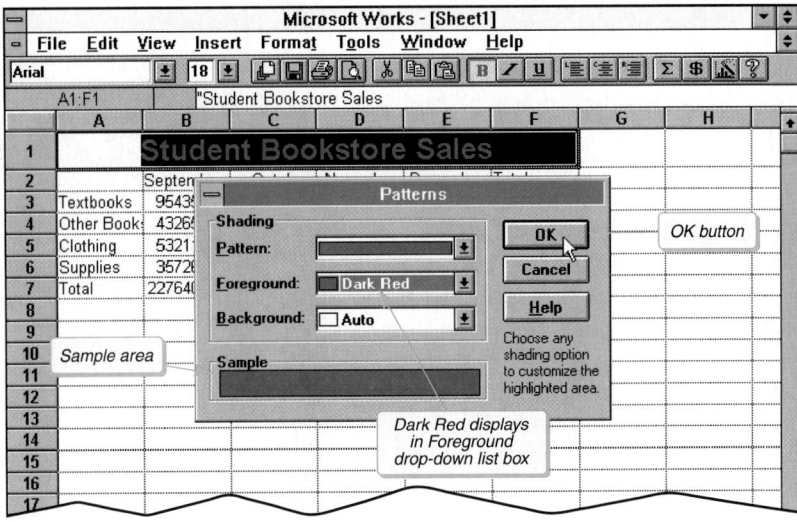

FIGURE 4-57

STEP 7 ►

Choose the OK button in the Patterns dialog box. Click any cell to remove the highlight.

Works displays the foreground color in cells A1 through F1 in dark red (Figure 4-58). The title displays in yellow.

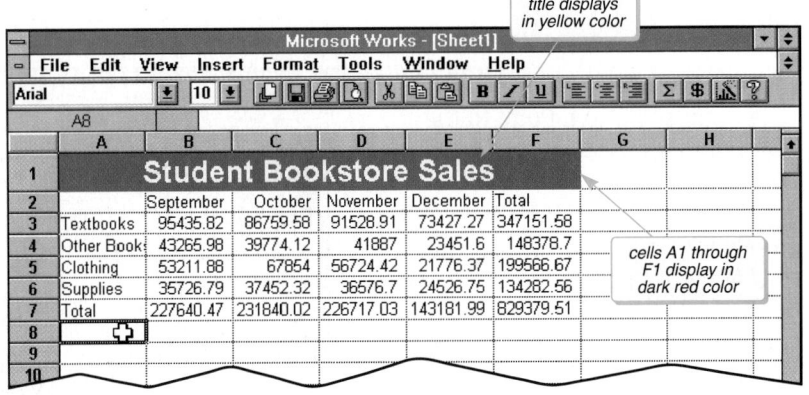

FIGURE 4-58

The background color in the Patterns dialog box can be used when a pattern other than solid is selected. Patterns other than solid may use both a foreground and background color.

Using the AutoFormat Command

Works provides an AutoFormat feature that enables you to format a spreadsheet in a variety of styles without going through a series of individual steps to select color, font and font styles, borders, and so forth. AutoFormat allows you to select one of fourteen different, predefined formats to apply to a spreadsheet. AutoFormat automatically sets the alignment, fonts, patterns, column width, cell height, and borders to match the style option you select.

The steps on the next two pages explain how to use the Works AutoFormat feature.

TO USE AUTOFORMAT ▼

STEP 1 ►

Highlight cells A2:F7 by dragging the mouse pointer from cell A2 through cell F7. Select the Format menu and point to the AutoFormat command.

Cells A2 through F7 are high-lighted (Figure 4-59). The Format menu displays. The mouse pointer points to the AutoFormat command.

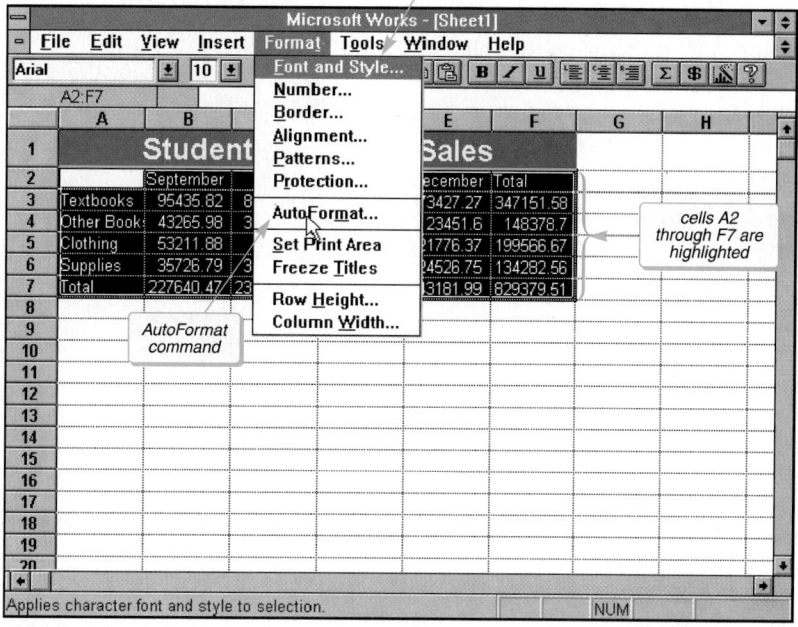

FIGURE 4-59

STEP 2 ►

Choose the AutoFormat command from the Format menu.

Works displays the AutoFormat dialog box (Figure 4-60). The Table Format list box displays a list of preformatted styles. You can click the down scroll arrow to display additional styles. The White on Black style is the default format. A sample of this style displays in the Sample area. The Sample area displays how the highlighted cells in the spreadsheet will display based on the selection in the Table Format list.

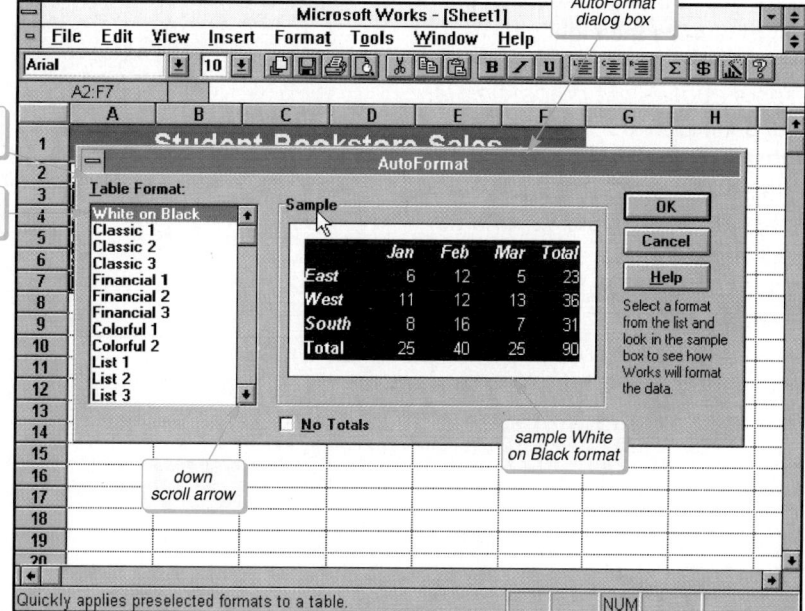

FIGURE 4-60

STEP 3 ▶

From the Table Format list box, select Colorful 2 by pointing to Colorful 2 and clicking the left mouse button. Point to the OK button.

Works displays a sample of Colorful 2 in the Sample area (Figure 4-61).

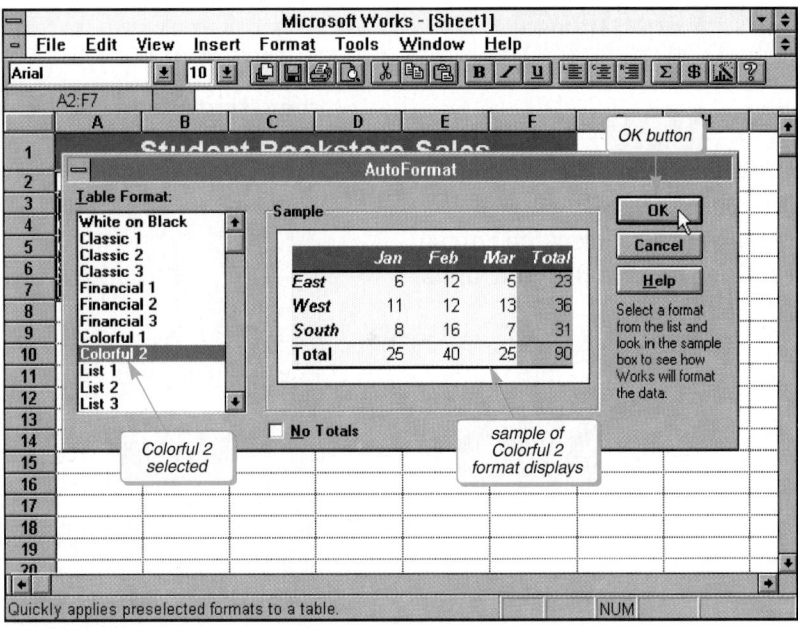

FIGURE 4-61

STEP 4 ▶

Choose the OK button in the AutoFormat dialog box. Click any cell to remove the highlight.

Works applies the predefined format style Colorful 2 to the highlighted spreadsheet (Figure 4-62). The spreadsheet displays with the fonts, font styles, colors, and borders as illustrated. Note that insignificant zeros to the right of a decimal point or to the right of a whole number do not display with the Colorful 2 format.

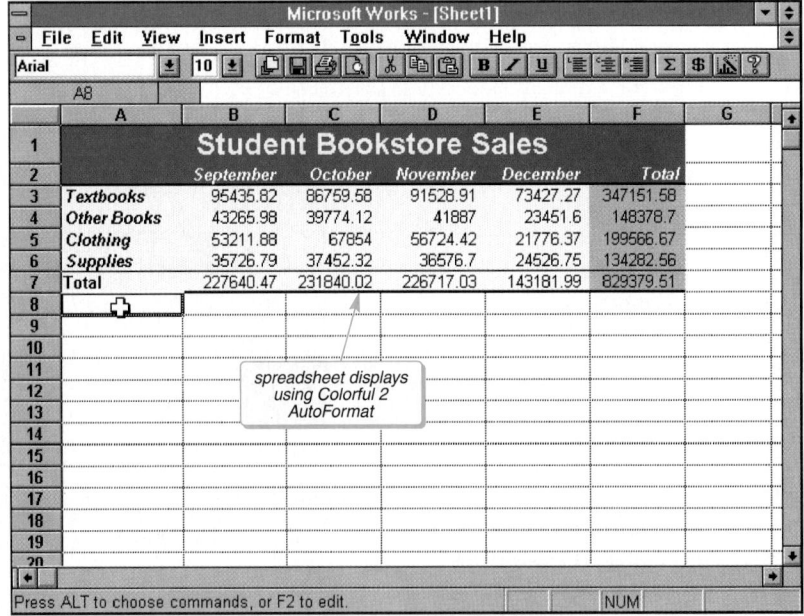

FIGURE 4-62

You can apply additional formatting to the spreadsheet. In Project 4, the numbers in cells B3 through F6 are to contain decimal points and commas if necessary. The numbers in cells B7 through F7 are to contain dollar signs, commas and decimal points. This requires additional formatting.

Comma Format

The numeric values in rows 3, 4, 5, and 6 are to be formatted with commas and two digits to the right of the decimal point. In Works this requires the use of the **Comma format**. When you use the Comma format, by default Works places two digits to the right of the decimal point (including zeroes) and a comma separating every three digits to the left of the decimal point. To format numeric values in the Comma format, complete the following steps.

TO DISPLAY NUMBERS WITH THE COMMA FORMAT ▼

STEP 1 ►

Highlight the range of cells B3:F6 by dragging from cell B3 to cell F6. Select the Format menu and point to the Number command.

*Cells B3 through F6 are highlighted (Figure 4-63). The Format menu displays. The mouse pointer points to the **Number command.***

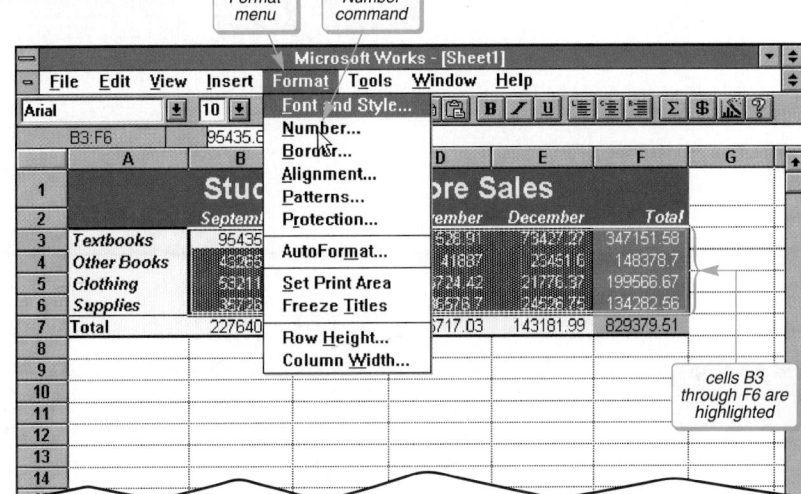

FIGURE 4-63

STEP 2 ►

Choose the Number command from the Format menu. When the Number dialog box displays, select the Comma option button and point to OK button.

The Comma option button is selected and the mouse pointer points to the OK button (Figure 4-64). The value 2, which is the default value, displays in the Number of decimals text box.

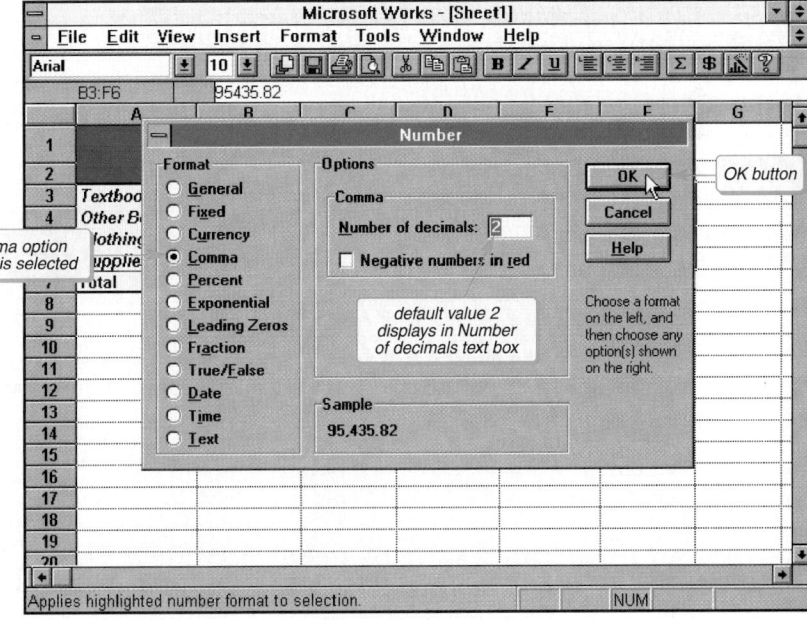

FIGURE 4-64

STEP 3 ▶

Choose the OK button. Click any cell to remove the highlight.

Works formats the range of cells B3:F6 using the Comma format with commas every three digits to the left of the decimal point and two digits to the right of the decimal point (Figure 4-65).

range B3: F6 is formatted with commas and two digits to the right of the decimal point

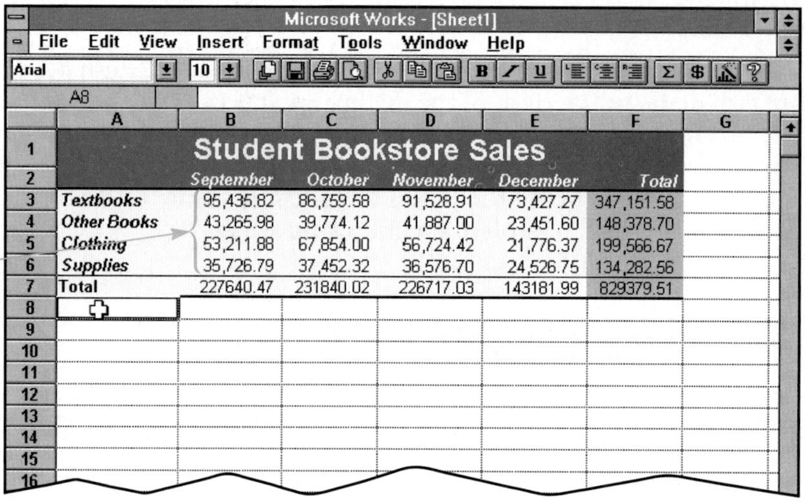

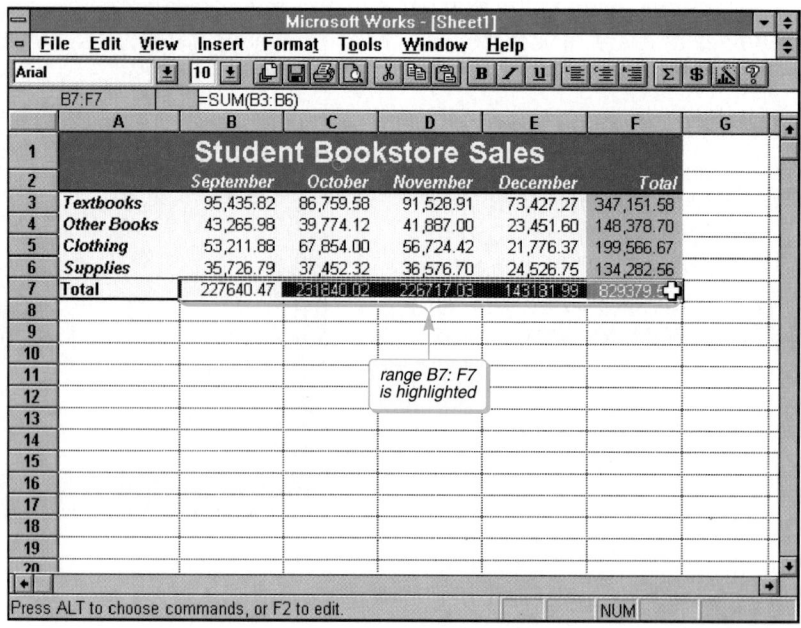

FIGURE 4-65

Currency Format

When you want to include dollar signs, commas and zeroes to the right of the decimal point in the numbers in a spreadsheet, use the **Currency format**. Because this format is commonly used, Works provides a **Currency button** on the Toolbar. There is also a Currency option button in the Numbers dialog box that can be selected. The following steps explain how to display the totals in row 7 in the Currency format.

TO DISPLAY NUMBERS WITH THE CURRENCY FORMAT ▼

STEP 1 ▶

Highlight the range of cells B7:F7.

Cells B7 through F7 are highlighted (Figure 4-66).

range B7: F7 is highlighted

FIGURE 4-66

STEP 2 ►

Click the Currency button on the Toolbar.

Works changes the range of cells B7:F7 to Currency format (Figure 4-67). Dollar signs display to the left of each number in the highlighted cells.

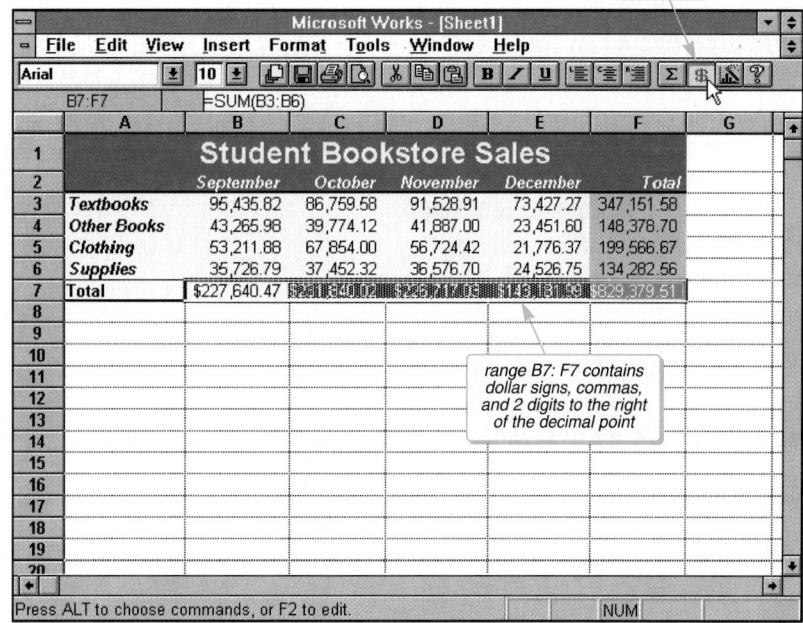

FIGURE 4-67

Changing Column Widths

The next step in formatting the spreadsheet is to change the column widths. The default column width is ten characters. You change column widths for several reasons. First, changing the column width increases the space between each column and often makes the spreadsheet easier to read. Also, in some instances the values you enter into a cell or the values Works calculates in a cell will not fit in a ten character-wide cell. When this occurs, you must change the width of the column to a size that can accommodate the entry in the cell.

The AutoFormat feature changes column width to a best fit to accommodate the numbers in each of the columns. Adding formatting such as the Comma format or the Currency format may require increasing the column width. In this project when the formatting was changed by adding commas, dollar signs, and digits to the right of the decimal point, the columns became too narrow for good readability. Therefore, the column width of columns B through F should be changed to thirteen to improve the readability of the spreadsheet.

Works provides the capability to change each column individually or you can change the width of a group of columns. In the following example, the columns will be changed as a group, which requires highlighting at least one cell in each column to be changed and then choosing the **Column Width command** from the Format menu. To complete the task, perform the following steps on the next page.

TO CHANGE COLUMN WIDTHS ▼

STEP 1 ▶

Drag across the range B3:F3 to highlight a cell in column B through column F. Select the Format menu and point to the Column Width command.

Cells B3 through F3 are highlighted (Figure 4-68). The Format menu displays and the mouse pointer points to the Column Width command.

FIGURE 4-68

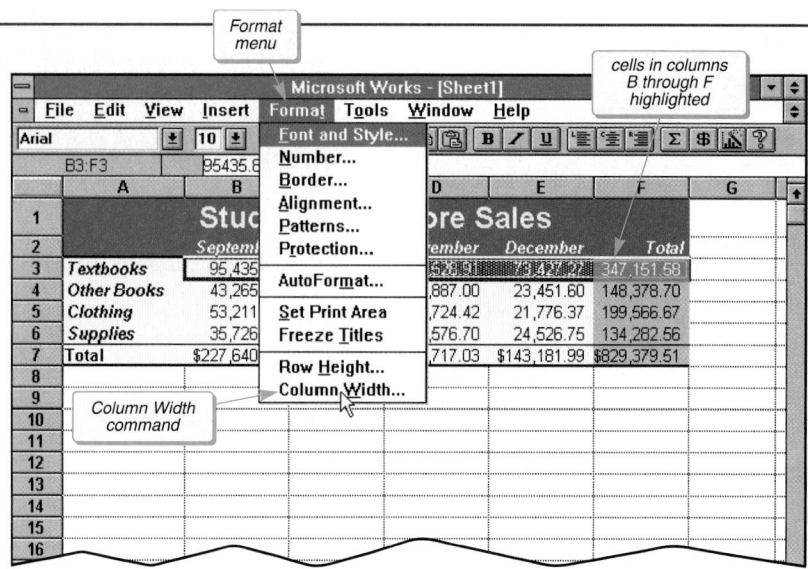

STEP 2 ▶

Choose the Column Width command from the Format menu. When the Column Width dialog box displays, type 13 in the Width text box. Point to the OK button.

Works displays the Column Width dialog box (Figure 4-69). The number 13 has been typed in the Width text box. The mouse pointer points to the OK button.

FIGURE 4-69

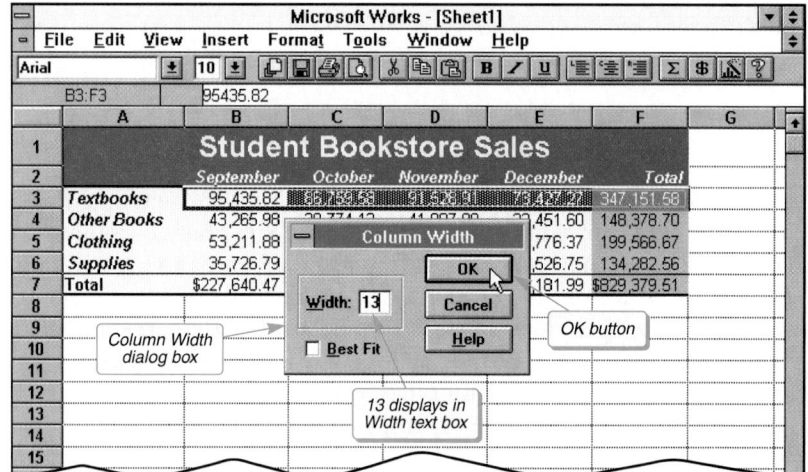

STEP 3 ▶

Choose the OK button in the Column Width dialog box. Click any cell to remove the highlight.

Works makes columns B through F thirteen characters wide (Figure 4-70). Notice columns G and H have moved off the screen.

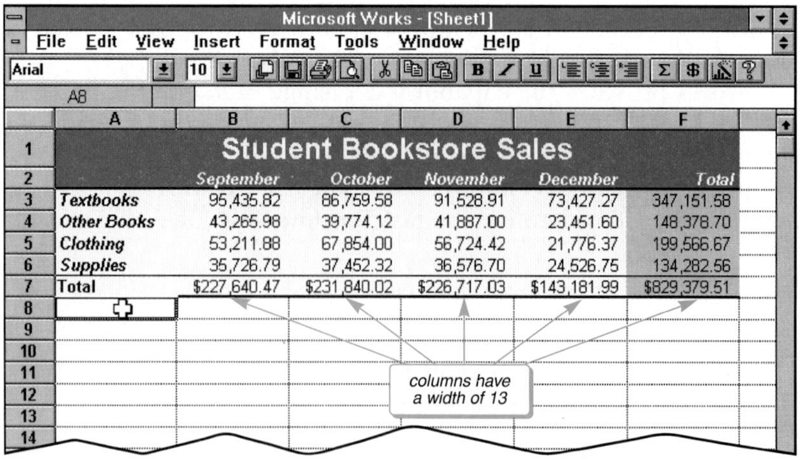

FIGURE 4-70

Works provides a number of methods that can be used to change the column width. To quickly change the width of a single column, place the mouse pointer over the column border (the right or left vertical line in the column label area) and drag. When the column is as large or small as you want, release the left mouse button.

To quickly adjust the column width for best fit, double-click the column letter. This will adjust the column width to fit the longest entry in the column. To obtain best fit you can also select the **Best Fit check box** in the Column Width dialog box.

If, at a later time, you want to change these columns back to the default value or any of the columns in the range to any other size, follow the steps previously explained.

Checking the Spelling on the Spreadsheet

The spreadsheet is now complete. All the data is entered and the formatting is complete. You should now check the spelling on the spreadsheet using the **Spelling command** on the Tools menu. The spelling check feature is the same as used in the word processing projects. To check the spelling, complete the following steps.

TO CHECK SPELLING

Step 1: Select the Tools menu.
Step 2: Choose the Spelling command.
Step 3: If any errors are found, perform the steps to correct the errors.

▶ SAVING A SPREADSHEET

I f you accidentally turn off your computer or if electrical power fails, you will lose all your work on the spreadsheet unless you have saved it on disk. Therefore, after you have worked on a spreadsheet for a period of time, or when you complete the spreadsheet, you should save it on hard disk or a diskette. When saving the spreadsheet for the first time, use the **Save button** on the Toolbar.

You can save a spreadsheet on hard disk or on a diskette. In Project 4, you are to save the spreadsheet on a diskette located in drive A. You can use the procedure explained below, however, for either hard disk or diskette.

TO SAVE A SPREADSHEET ▼

STEP 1 ▶

Point to the Save button on the Toolbar (Figure 4-71).

	A	B	C	D	E	F
1		Student Bookstore Sales				
2		September	October	November	December	Total
3	Textbooks	95,435.82	86,759.58	91,528.91	73,427.27	347,151.58
4	Other Books	43,265.98	39,774.12	41,887.00	23,451.60	148,378.70
5	Clothing	53,211.88	67,854.00	56,724.42	21,776.37	199,566.67
6	Supplies	35,726.79	37,452.32	36,576.70	24,526.75	134,282.56
7	Total	$227,640.47	$231,840.02	$226,717.03	$143,181.99	$829,379.51
8						
9						
10						
11						
12						

FIGURE 4-71

STEP 2 ▶

Click the Save button. When the Save As dialog box displays, type the filename, `proj4`, in the File Name text box. Click the Drives drop-down list box arrow. Select drive a: from the Drives drop-down list box and then point to the OK button.

Works displays the Save As dialog box (Figure 4-72). The filename you type displays in the File Name text box. This is the name Works will use to store the file. Drive a is selected in the Drives drop-down list box. The mouse pointer points to the OK button.

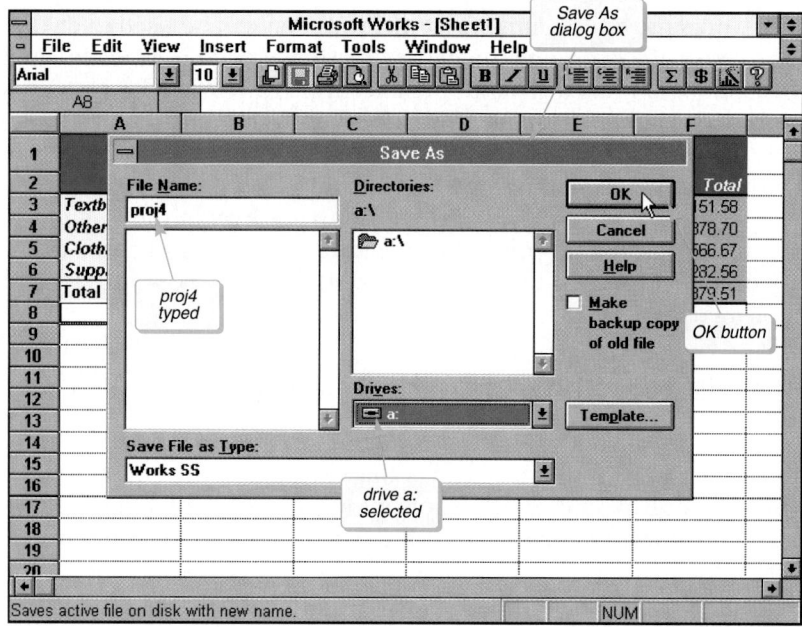

FIGURE 4-72

STEP 3 ▶

Choose the OK button in the Save As dialog box.

Works saves the file on the designated disk drive, drive a, and places the filename in the title bar (Figure 4-73). Works automatically places the file extension .WKS following the filename of spreadsheet files.

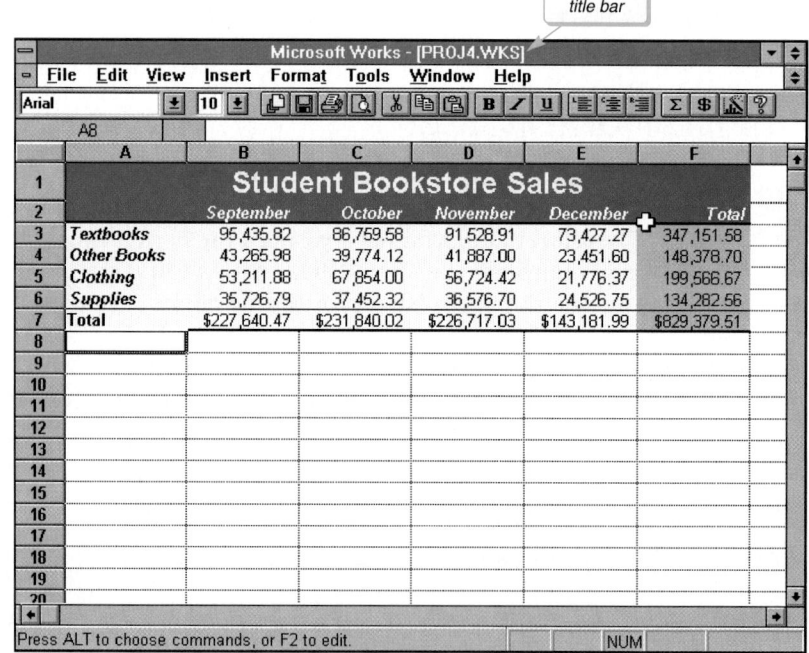

FIGURE 4-73

If, at some future time, you want to save the spreadsheet using a different file name, use the **Save As command** on the File menu.

PRINTING A SPREADSHEET

A fter you save the spreadsheet, the next step is to print the spreadsheet. To print a spreadsheet, choose the **Print command** from the File menu, as explained below.

TO PRINT A SPREADSHEET ▼

STEP 1 ►

Select the File menu and point to the Print command.

Works displays the File menu and the mouse pointer points to the Print command (Figure 4-74).

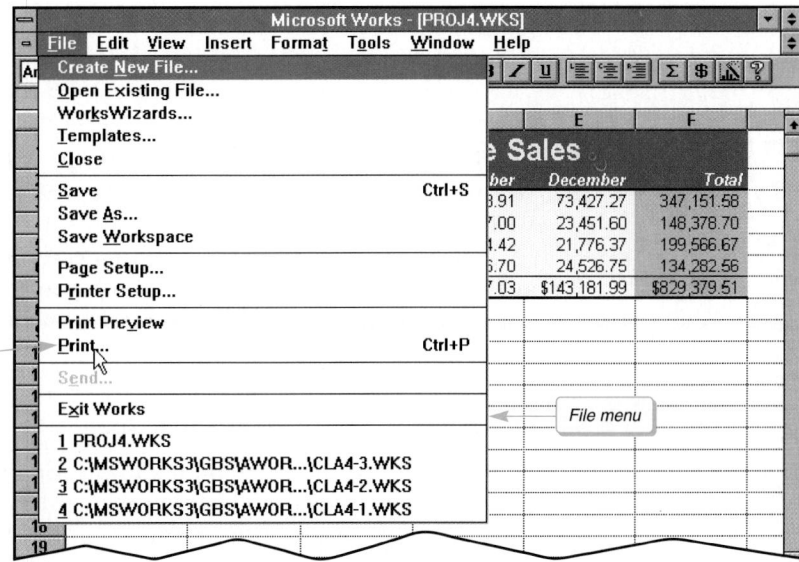

FIGURE 4-74

STEP 2 ►

Choose the Print command from the File menu. When the Print dialog box displays, point to the OK button.

Works displays the Print dialog box (Figure 4-75). The default for the dialog box is that one copy of the spreadsheet is to print and all pages in the document are to print.

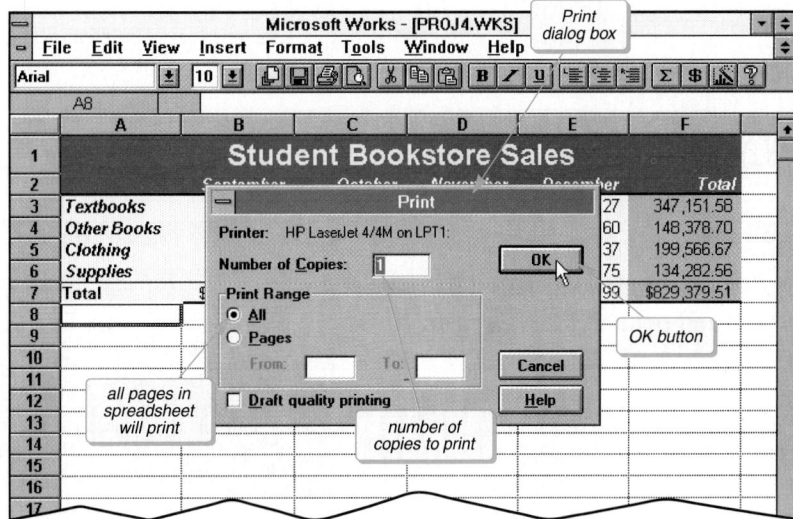

FIGURE 4-75

STEP 3 ▶

Choose the OK button in the Print dialog box.

Works momentarily displays a Printing dialog box. Then, the document is printed on the printer (Figure 4-76).

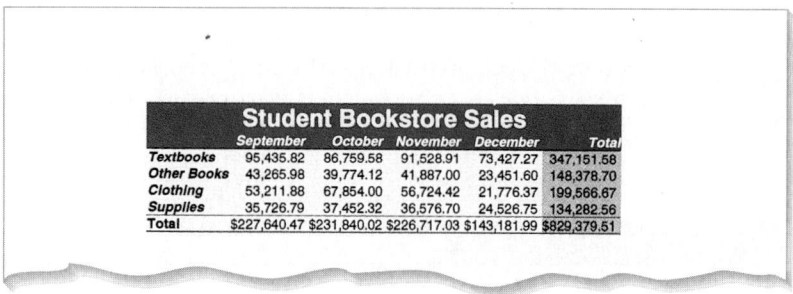

FIGURE 4-76

If a color printer is used, the output will appear as illustrated. If a black and white printer is used, the spreadsheet will print in shades of black, gray, and white.

If you have previously used the Print command and know that proper entries are contained in the Print dialog box, you can click the **Print button** on the Toolbar to cause the spreadsheet to print.

▶ CHARTING A SPREADSHEET

In addition to creating and printing the spreadsheet, Project 4 requires a portion of the data in the spreadsheet to be charted. A **chart** is a graphical representation of the data in the spreadsheet. You are to create a 3-D Bar chart of the sales for September, October, November, and December for each of the four categories (Textbooks, Other Books, Clothing, and Supplies). With a 3-D Bar chart, sales are represented by a series of vertical bars that are shaded to give a three-dimensional effect.

To create the 3-D Bar chart, perform the following steps.

TO CREATE A 3-D BAR CHART ▼

STEP 1 ▶

Highlight the cells to be charted (A2:E6) and point to the New Chart button.

*The highlighted cells include the column titles, the row titles, and the sales for September, October, November, and December (Figure 4-77). The totals are not included because they do not present meaningful comparisons on a Bar chart. The mouse pointer points to the **New Chart button.***

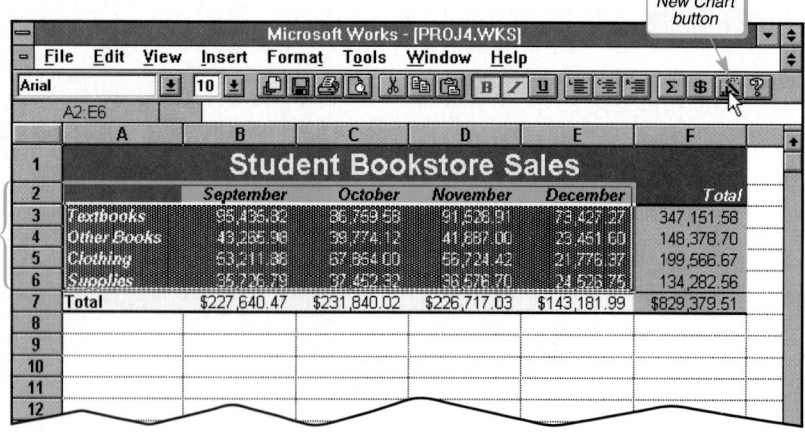

FIGURE 4-77

STEP 2 ▶

Click the New Chart button on the Toolbar. When the New Chart dialog box displays, click the What type of chart do you want? drop-down list box arrow.

Works displays the New Chart dialog box (Figure 4-78). A drop-down list box of chart types displays. The Works default is a Bar chart. A sample of the chart that will display is shown in the lower right portion of the dialog box.

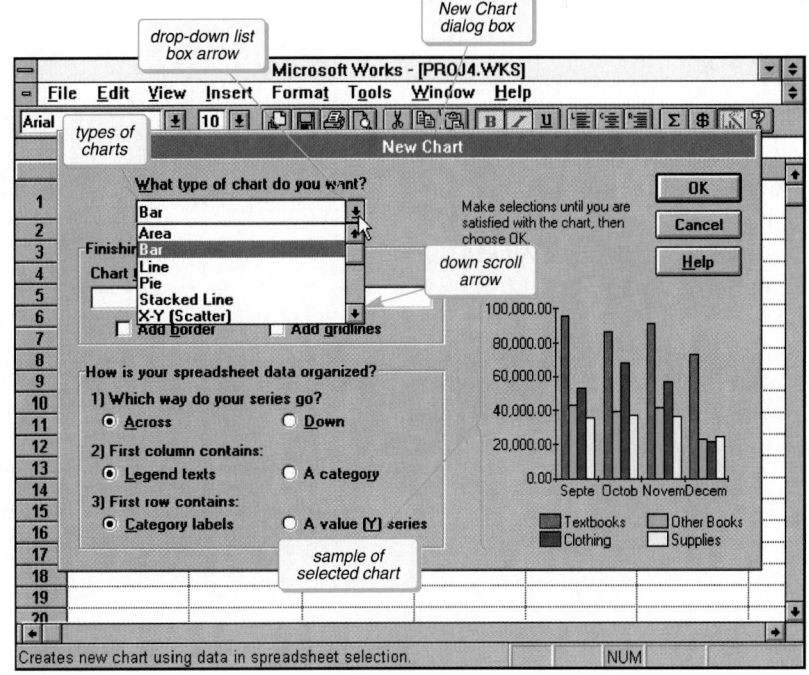

FIGURE 4-78

STEP 3 ▶

Scroll down in the list box until 3-D Bar appears. Point to 3-D Bar.

The mouse pointer points to 3-D Bar in the drop-down list box (Figure 4-79).

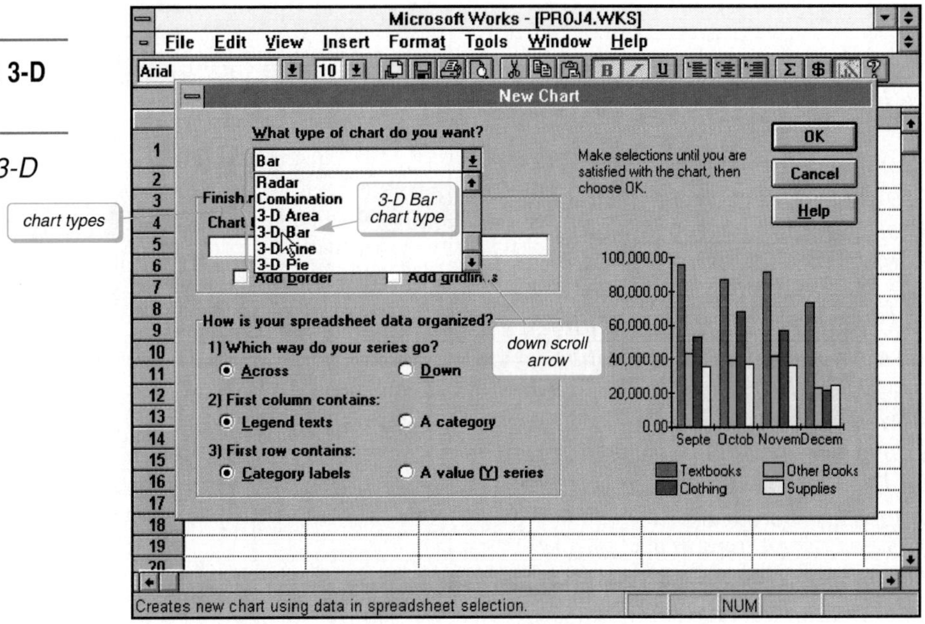

FIGURE 4-79

STEP 4 ▶

Select 3-D Bar in the New Chart dialog box by clicking the left mouse button. Press the TAB key and type Student Bookstore Sales in the Chart title text box. Point to the OK button.

The lower right portion of the New Chart dialog box contains an illustration of the chart that will display (Figure 4-80).

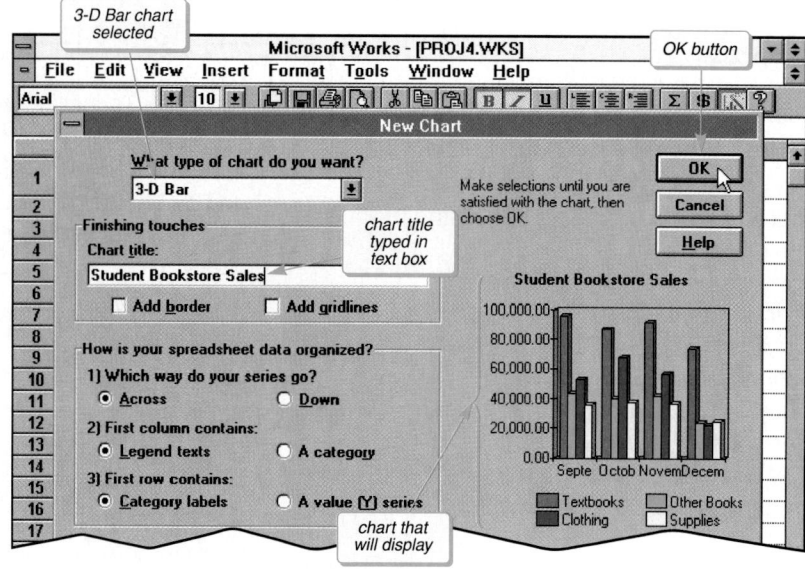

FIGURE 4-80

STEP 5 ▶

Choose the OK button in the New Chart dialog box.

*Works displays the chart with the title PROJ4.WKS - Chart1 in the title bar (Figure 4-81). The cluster of bars for each month (September, October, November, and December) is called a **category**. All the category labels together are called the **category (X) series**. Each bar (red for Textbooks, green for Other Books, blue for Clothing, and yellow for Supplies) represents the sales for each item in the spreadsheet and is called the **Y-series**, or the **value series**. The chart legend indicates the item each color represents.*

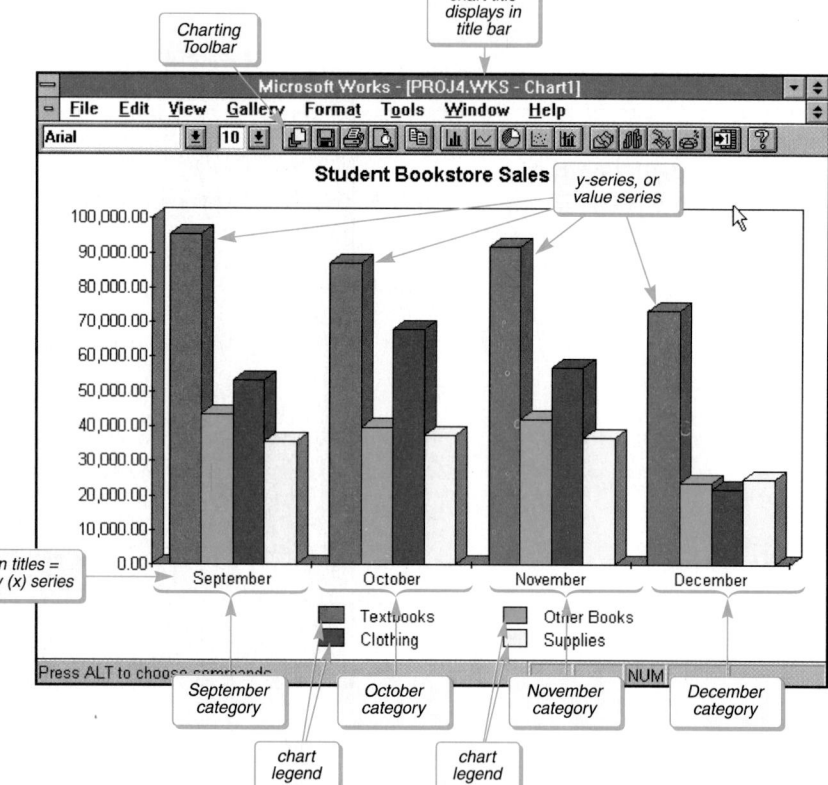

FIGURE 4-81

STEP 6 ▶

To return to the spreadsheet, select the Window menu and point to PROJ4.WKS, the filename of the spreadsheet.

The Window menu displays and lists the open windows in the application (Figure 4-82). The chart is the active window and Works indicates this by the check-mark next to the chart name PROJ4.WKS – Chart 1.

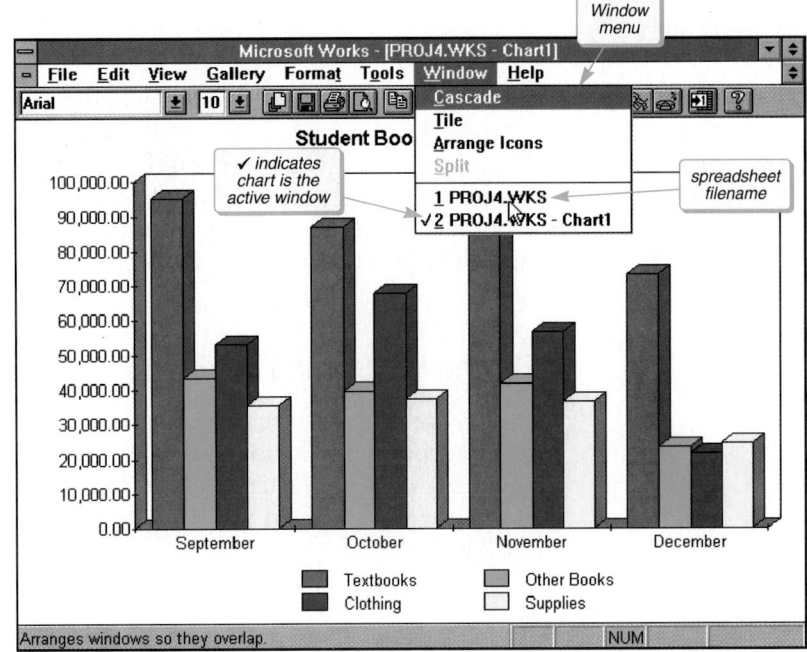

FIGURE 4-82

STEP 7 ▶

Choose the spreadsheet name, PROJ4.WKS, by choosing the name in the Window menu. Click any cell to remove the highlight from the cells.

Works displays the spreadsheet and makes the spreadsheet win-dow the active window (Figure 4-83).

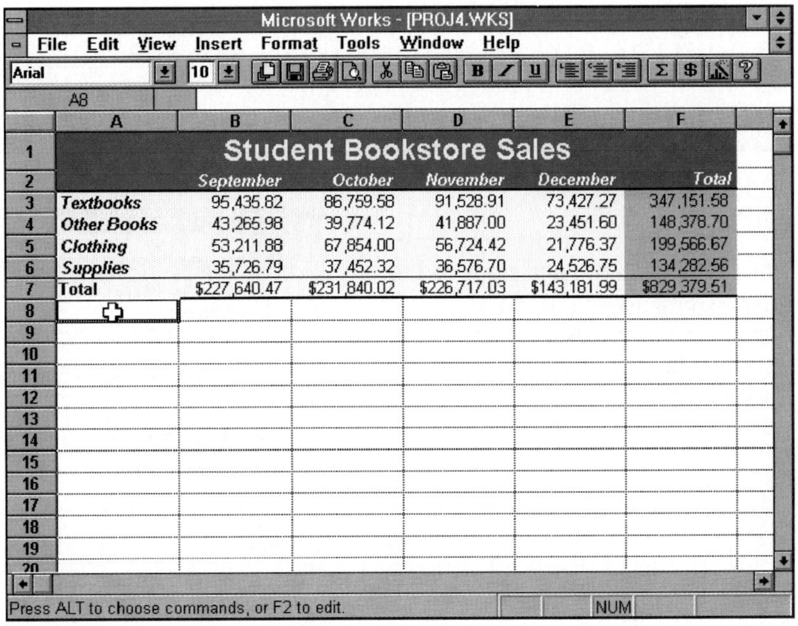

FIGURE 4-83

To move back to the chart window, select the Window menu and choose the chart name. You can also view the chart or spreadsheet by selecting the **View menu** and choosing the **Chart command** or the **Spreadsheet command**.

In addition to the New Chart button on the Toolbar, Works also provides the **Create New Chart command** on the Tools menu that can be used to create a new chart.

Printing the Chart

You can print the chart by clicking the Print button on the Charting Toolbar. By default, Works attempts to fill the entire page with the chart when printing. Therefore, if you want to print a chart with proper proportions, you should first choose the **Page Setup command** from the File menu and select the Other Options tab. In the screen that displays, select the **Full page, keep proportions** option button and choose the OK button. Then click the Print button on the Toolbar.

Saving the Spreadsheet and Chart

If you want to save the chart with the spreadsheet, save the spreadsheet again using techniques previously explained. The chart will be saved with the spreadsheet. To view the chart at a later time (for example, after you have closed the spreadsheet file), open the spreadsheet file and choose the Chart command from the View menu.

▶ CLOSING A SPREADSHEET

 nce you complete the spreadsheet and chart, you can **close the spreadsheet** and work on another spreadsheet or another Works project. To close the spreadsheet, perform the following steps.

TO CLOSE THE SPREADSHEET ▼

STEP 1 ▶

Select the File menu and point to the Close command (Figure 4-84).

STEP 2 ▶

Choose the Close command from the File menu.

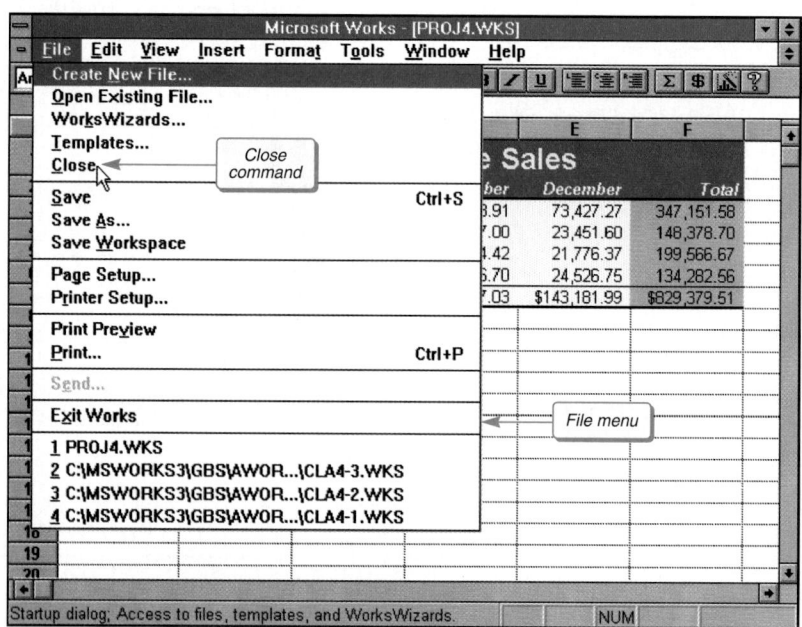

FIGURE 4-84

Works closes the spreadsheet and returns control to the Startup dialog box from which you can choose another Works application.

You can close a chart without closing the entire spreadsheet file by choosing the Close command from the Chart File menu.

If you have made changes to the spreadsheet without saving it after making those changes, Works will present a dialog box when you close the spreadsheet asking if you want to save the file with the changes. If you want to save the file with changes, choose the Yes button, otherwise choose the No button.

Quitting Works

After you have completed all your tasks, you will normally want to **quit Works** and return to Windows Program Manager. To quit Works, do the following:

TO QUIT WORKS ▼

STEP 1 ▶

Select the File menu and point to the Exit Works command (Figure 4-85).

STEP 2 ▶

Choose the Exit Works command from the File menu.

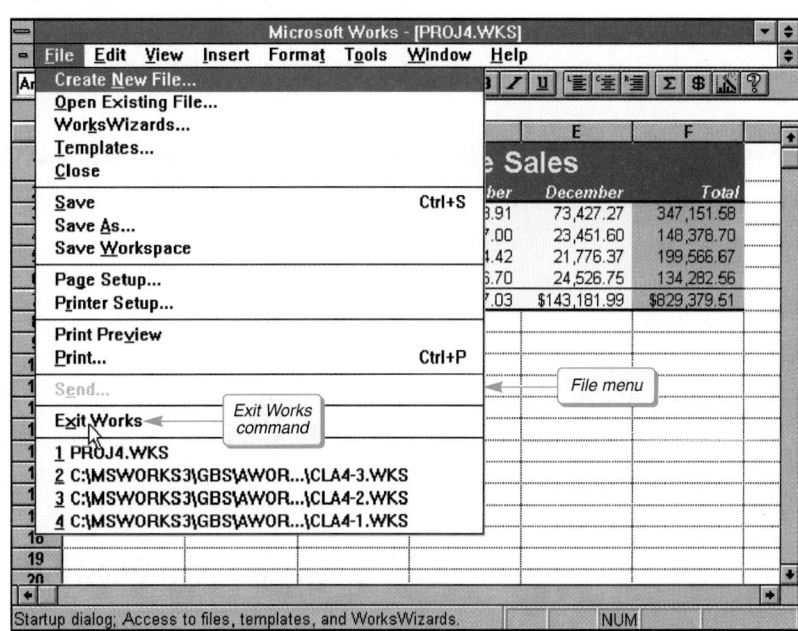

FIGURE 4-85

Works returns control to Windows Program Manager from which you can select other programs or terminate your computer activity.

▶ OPENING A SPREADSHEET FILE

 nce you have saved a spreadsheet on disk, you may need to retrieve the spreadsheet to make changes to it or otherwise process it. To retrieve the spreadsheet, you must open the spreadsheet. **Opening a spreadsheet** means the spreadsheet is retrieved from the disk into main memory. You can use one of the following methods on the next page to open a Works spreadsheet file.

TO OPEN A WORKS SPREADSHEET FILE USING THE STARTUP DIALOG BOX

Step 1: Follow the steps explained in the earlier word processing projects (Projects 1, 2, and 3) to display the Works Startup dialog box.

Step 2: Choose the Open An Existing Document button.

Step 3: When the Open dialog box displays, if necessary select the drive from the Drives drop-down list box and subdirectories from the Directories list box where the spreadsheet file is stored.

Step 4: Select the file you want to open.

Step 5: Choose the OK button in the Open dialog box.

When opening a file from the Startup dialog box, you can also click the filename of the file you want to open in the Recently used files list box.

TO OPEN A WORKS SPREADSHEET FILE USING THE FILE MENU

Step 1: Select the File menu and point to the Open Existing File command.

Step 2: Choose the Open Existing File command from the File menu.

Step 3: If necessary, select the drive from the Drives drop-down list box and the subdirectory from the Directories list box where the file is stored.

Step 4: Select the file you want to open.

Step 5: Choose the OK button in the Open dialog box.

You can also click one of the filenames at the bottom of the File menu to open that file.

▶ CORRECTING ERRORS

When you create a spreadsheet, the possibility exists that you might make an error by entering the wrong text or data in a cell. In addition, it is possible that you must change a value in a cell even though it was correct when you entered it. Works provides several methods for changing data in a spreadsheet and **correcting errors**. These methods are explained below.

Correcting Errors Prior to Entering Data into a Cell

If you notice an error in the formula bar prior to confirming the entry and entering the data into a cell, do one of the following:

1. Use the **BACKSPACE key** to erase back to the error and then type the correct characters; or
2. If the error is too severe, click the Cancel box in the formula bar or press the ESC key to erase the entire entry in the formula bar and reenter the data from the beginning.

Editing Data in a Cell

If you notice an error in the spreadsheet after confirming the entry and entering the data, highlight the cell with the error and use one of the following methods to correct the error.

1. If the entry is short, retype it and click the Enter box or press the ENTER key. The new entry will replace the old entry. Remember that you must highlight the cell containing the error before you begin typing.
2. If the entry in the cell is long and the errors are minor, you may want to edit the entry rather than retype it. To edit an entry in a cell:
   a. Highlight the cell containing the error.
   b. Click the first character in error in the formula bar. Works places the insertion point at the location you clicked in the formula bar.
   c. Make your changes.

When you type characters in the formula bar, Works inserts the character and moves all characters one position to the right.

To delete a character in the formula bar, place the insertion point to the left of the character you want to delete and press the DELETE key, or place the insertion point to the right of the character you want to delete and press the BACKSPACE key.

While the insertion point is located in the formula bar, you might have occasion to move it to various points in the bar. Table 4-1 illustrates the means for moving the insertion point in the formula bar.

▶ **TABLE 4-1**

TASK	MOUSE	KEYBOARD
Move the Insertion Point to the Beginning of Text	Click to left of first character	Press HOME
Move the Insertion Point to the End of Text	Click to right of last character	Press END
Move the Insertion Point One Character to the Left	Click one character to left	Press LEFT ARROW
Move the Insertion Point One Character	Click one character to right	Press RIGHT ARROW
Move the Insertion Point Anywhere in the Formula Bar	Click formula bar at appropriate position	Press LEFT or RIGHT ARROW
Highlight One or Move Characters	Drag mouse pointer over the characters	Press SHIFT+ LEFT ARROW or SHIFT+ RIGHT ARROW
Delete Highlighted Characters	None	Press DELETE

When you are finished editing an entry, click the Enter box or press the ENTER key.

Understanding how to correct errors or change entries in a spreadsheet is an important skill.

Clearing a Cell or Range of Cells

It is not unusual to enter data into the wrong cell or range of cells. In such a case, to correct the error you might want to delete, or clear, the data. Never highlight a cell and press the SPACEBAR to enter a blank character and assume you have cleared the cell. A blank character is text and is different from an empty cell even though the cell may appear empty.

Works provides a variety of methods to clear the contents of a cell or a range of cells. The various methods are explained in the following paragraphs.

TO CLEAR CELL CONTENTS — DELETE KEY

Step 1: Highlight the cell or range of cells.
Step 2: Press the DELETE key.

TO CLEAR CELL CONTENTS — EDIT MENU AND CLEAR COMMAND

Step 1: Highlight the cell or range of cells.
Step 2: From the Edit menu choose the **Clear command**.

TO CLEAR CELL CONTENTS — EDIT MENU AND CUT COMMAND OR CUT BUTTON

Step 1: Highlight the cell or range of cells.
Step 2: From the Edit menu choose the **Cut command**; or click the **Cut button** on the Toolbar.

Each of these methods has differences you should understand. In the first method, when you press the DELETE key the data in the cell or cells is cleared but the formatting remains. Thus, even after you clear the cells using the DELETE key, formatting such as dollar formats, bold, italic, underlining, and so on remain. To clear the formatting, you must individually turn off each of the formatting features or use the Cut command for clearing the cells.

When you use the Edit menu and Clear command, the data in the cell or range of cells is cleared, but the formatting remains. This method has the same effect as using the DELETE key.

When you choose the Cut command from the Edit menu or click the Cut button on the Toolbar, Works clears both the data and the formatting from the cell or range of cells. Actually, the data and the associated formatting are placed on the Windows Clipboard for potential pasting elsewhere, but if you never paste the data into the same or another Works document, in effect the data and formatting have been entirely cleared from the spreadsheet.

Another method of clearing a cell or range of cells after the entry has been confirmed, but not clearing the formatting, is to highlight the cell or range of cells, press the BACKSPACE key, and then press the ENTER key or click the Enter box. If you highlight a range of cells to clear, you must press the keys for each cell in the range.

Clearing the Entire Spreadsheet

Sometimes so many major errors are made with a spreadsheet that it is easier to start over. To clear an entire spreadsheet, follow these steps.

TO CLEAR THE ENTIRE SPREADSHEET

Step 1: Highlight the entire spreadsheet by clicking the box located just above row 1 and immediately to the left of column A, or choose the Select All command from the Edit menu.
Step 2: Follow any of the three methods specified previously to clear the cell contents. The method used should be based upon whether you want the formatting to remain.

An alternative to the previous steps is to choose the Close command from the File menu and not save the spreadsheet. Works closes the spreadsheet. You can then choose the Spreadsheet button in the Startup dialog box to begin working on your new spreadsheet.

▶ PROJECT SUMMARY

In this project, you have learned to start the Microsoft Works Spreadsheet tool, enter both text and numeric data into the spreadsheet, calculate the sum of numeric values in both rows and columns, and copy formulas to adjacent cells in both rows and columns. In addition, you have seen how to display the title centered across columns, display the title with color, and you learned how to use the AutoFormat feature to format a spreadsheet. Using the steps and techniques presented, you changed column widths and formatted numeric data in both the Comma and Currency formats.

Next, you learned to save a spreadsheet, print a spreadsheet, create a chart from spreadsheet data, print the chart, and open a spreadsheet. Finally, after completing the project, you know how to correct errors on the spreadsheet.

▶ KEY TERMS

Alignment command *(W4.26)*
Autosum button *(W4.18)*
BACKSPACE key *(W4.48)*
Best Fit check box *(W4.39)*
button *(W4.8)*
Cancel box *(W4.10)*
category *(W4.44)*
category (X) series *(W4.44)*
cell *(W4.6)*
cell reference *(W4.6)*
chart *(W4.42)*
Chart command *(W4.45)*
Clear command *(W4.49)*
close the spreadsheet *(W4.46)*
column *(W4.6)*
column label *(W4.6)*
column title *(W4.11)*
Column Width command
    (W4.37)
Comma format *(W4.35)*
confirm the entry *(W4.11)*
copy *(W4.20)*
correcting errors *(W4.48)*
Create New Chart command
    (W4.45)

Currency button *(W4.36)*
Currency format *(W4.36)*
Cut button *(W4.50)*
Cut command *(W4.50)*
double quotation mark *(W4.11)*
Edit menu *(W4.13, W4.20)*
Enter box *(W4.10)*
ENTER key *(W4.11)*
Fill Down command *(W4.24)*
Fill Right command *(W4.20)*
Fill Series command *(W4.11)*
format a spreadsheet *(W4.25)*
formula bar *(W4.8)*
Full page, keep proportions
    (W4.46)
gridlines *(W4.6)*
highlight *(W4.9)*
highlighted cell *(W4.6)*
insertion point *(W4.10)*
keyboard indicators *(W4.8)*
left-aligned *(W4.11)*
menu bar *(W4.8)*
mouse pointer *(W4.6)*
New Chart button *(W4.42)*
numbers *(W4.15)*

Number command *(W4.35)*
opening a spreadsheet *(W4.47)*
Page Setup command *(W4.46)*
Patterns command *(W4.30)*
Print button *(W4.42)*
Print command *(W4.41)*
quit Works *(W4.47)*
range *(W4.20)*
right-aligned *(W4.18)*
row *(W4.6)*
row label *(W4.6)*
Save button *(W4.39)*
Save As command *(W4.40)*
Spelling command *(W4.39)*
Spreadsheet command *(W4.45)*
spreadsheet window *(W4.6)*
status bar *(W4.8)*
SUM function *(W4.18)*
TAB key *(W4.9)*
text *(W4.9)*
Toolbar *(W4.9)*
value series *(W4.44)*
View menu *(W4.45)*
whole numbers *(W4.18)*
Y-series *(W4.44)*

QUICK REFERENCE

In Microsoft Works, you can accomplish a task in a number of ways. The following table provides a quick reference to each task presented in this project with its available options. The commands listed in the Menu column can be executed using either the keyboard or mouse.

Task	Mouse	Menu	Keyboard Shortcuts
AutoFormat		From Format menu, choose AutoFormat	
Bold Format	Click Bold button	From Format menu, choose Font and Style	Press CTRL+B
Cancel Data Entry Before Confirming	Click Cancel box		Press ESC
Cancel Range Highlight	Click anywhere in spreadsheet		
Center Text Across Selection		From Format menu, choose Alignment	
Change the Column Width	Drag column separator to desired width	From Format menu, choose Column Width	
Chart a Spreadsheet	Click Chart button	From Tools menu, choose Create New Chart	

(continued)

QUICK REFERENCE (continued)

Task	Mouse	Menu	Keyboard Shortcuts
Clear a Cell		From Edit menu, choose Clear or from Edit menu, choose Cut	Press DELETE
Clear an Entire Spreadsheet		Highlight entire spreadsheet; from Edit menu, choose Clear or from Edit menu, choose Cut	Highlight entire spreadsheet; press DELETE
Close a Spreadsheet		From File menu, choose Close	Press CTRL+F4
Color a Cell		From the Format menu, choose Patterns	
Color Text		From the Format menu, choose Font and Style	
Comma Format		From Format menu, choose Number	Press CTRL+, (comma)
Confirm Data Entry	Click Enter box		Press ENTER or any arrow key
Copy Data or Formula Down		From Edit menu, choose Fill Down	
Copy Data or Formula Right		Form Edit menu, choose Fill Right	
Copy Dates Across		From Edit menu, choose Fill Series	
Currency Format	Click Currency button	From Format menu, choose Number	Press CTRL+4
Edit Data in a Cell	Click formula bar		Press F2
Highlight a Cell	Click the cell		Press any arrow key
Highlight a Column	Click column letter	From Edit menu, choose Select Column	Press SHIFT+F8
Highlight an Entire Spreadsheet	Click box to left of column A and above row 1	From Edit menu, choose Select All	Press CTRL+SHIFT+F8
Highlight a Group of Cells	Drag from upper left to lower right cell		Press F8+arrow (to extend highlight)
Highlight Row	Click row number	From Edit menu, choose Select Row	Press CTRL+F8
Italic Format	Click Italic button	From Format menu, choose Font and Style	Press CTRL+I
Open a Spreadsheet File		From File menu, choose Open Existing File	

Task	Mouse	Menu	Keyboard Shortcuts
Print a Spreadsheet	Click Print button	From File menu, choose Print	Press CTRL+P
Quit Works		From File menu, choose Exit Works or from Control menu, choose Close	Press ALT+F4
Return to a Spreadsheet from a Chart		From Window menu, choose Spreadsheet name or from View menu choose Spreadsheet	Press CTRL+F6
Save a Spreadsheet	Click Save button	From File menu, choose Save	Press CTRL+S
Save a Spreadsheet (with a New Name)		From File menu, choose Save As	CTRL+S
Start Works Spreadsheet	Click Spreadsheet button		Press S
Sum a Column of Numbers	Click Autosum button		Press CTRL+M
Sum a Row of Numbers	Click Autosum button		Press CTRL+M

S T U D E N T   A S S I G N M E N T S

STUDENT ASSIGNMENT 1
True/False

Instructions: Circle T if the statement is true or F if the statement is false.

T F 1. The Works Spreadsheet tool can create a Bar chart based on the data in the spreadsheet.

T F 2. To start the Works Spreadsheet tool, choose Spreadsheet from the Microsoft Works for Windows group window in Program Manager.

T F 3. The intersection of a column and a row is called a cell.

T F 4. Columns are identified by numbers and rows are identified by letters of the alphabet.

T F 5. A highlighted cell is identified by a heavy border around the cell.

T F 6. The Cancel box and the Enter box are displayed in the formula bar.

T F 7. Pressing the ENTER key accomplishes the same task as clicking the Enter box when entering data into a cell.

T F 8. When you enter text, the text is placed in the highlighted cell right-aligned in the cell.

T F 9. To cancel an entry before entering it into a cell, press the ESC key or click the Enter box.

T F 10. When you press the RIGHT ARROW key after typing data in a cell, Works enters the data in the cell to the right of the highlighted cell.

T F 11. Numeric data can be summed using the Autosum button on the Toolbar.

T F 12. To format a number with a dollar sign, comma and decimal point, you must click the Currency button on the Toolbar prior to typing the numeric value.

T F 13. When you use the Autosum button to add numbers, Works highlights what it considers your choice of the group of cells to sum by first looking at the range of numbers above the highlighted cell and then to the right of the highlighted cell.

STUDENT ASSIGNMENT 1 (continued)

T   F   14. When you copy cell references in a formula, Works automatically adjusts the cell references for each new position of the formula.

T   F   15. To copy a formula from one cell to adjacent cells in a column, highlight the cell containing the formula, drag the range into which the formula will be copied, and choose the Fill command from the Edit menu.

T   F   16. To center text across a range of cells, highlight the range of cells where the text must be centered and click the Center Align button on the Toolbar.

T   F   17. To change the spreadsheet title color, use the Font command from the Format menu.

T   F   18. Only numeric values can be included in the spreadsheet range that is charted.

T   F   19. The AutoFormat feature cannot be used to display a dollar sign as part of a numeric value.

T   F   20. Once you have entered data into a cell, the only practical way to change the data is to highlight the cell and retype the data.

STUDENT ASSIGNMENT 2
Multiple Choice

Instructions: Circle the correct response.

1. You can highlight a cell by _____.
    a. clicking the cell while the mouse pointer is in the cell
    b. pressing an arrow key until the desired cell is outlined with a heavy border
    c. both a and b
    d. neither a nor b
2. The column titles, September, October, November, and December can be conveniently placed in a spreadsheet by using the _____ command.
    a. Fill Series
    b. Fill Right
    c. Replace
    d. Select All
3. A _____ is a block of adjacent cells in a spreadsheet.
    a. range
    b. group
    c. highlight
    d. format
4. Clicking the Autosum button two times is the same as _____.
    a. clicking the Autosum button one time and pressing the RIGHT ARROW key
    b. clicking the Autosum button one time and clicking the Enter box
    c. clicking the Autosum button one time
    d. clicking the Autosum button and clicking the Currency button on the Toolbar
5. To change the width of more than one column at a time, you must first _____.
    a. highlight cell A1
    b. highlight any cell in the beginning column
    c. highlight at least one cell in every column you want to change
    d. highlight the entire spreadsheet
6. To remove the highlighting from a group of cells, _____.
    a. click any cell on the spreadsheet
    b. choose the Clear command from the Edit menu
    c. click the Cut button on the Toolbar
    d. press the DELETE key on the keyboard

7. To save your spreadsheet the first time, choose the _____.
   a. Save As button on the Toolbar
   b. Startup button on the Toolbar
   c. Close button on the Toolbar
   d. Save button on the Toolbar
8. To create a chart, highlight the portion of the spreadsheet to be charted and then _____.
   a. choose the New Chart command from the View menu
   b. click the New Chart button on the Toolbar
   c. choose the Options command from the Tools menu
   d. select the Window menu
9. To delete a character in the formula bar, _____.
   a. place the insertion point to the right of the character to delete and press the DELETE key
   b. place the insertion point to the right of the character to delete and press the BACKSPACE key
   c. place the insertion point to the left of the character to delete and press the SPACEBAR
   d. place the insertion point to the left of the character to delete and press the BACKSPACE key
10. To remove the contents and formatting of a highlighted cell, _____.
    a. press the DELETE key
    b. from the Edit menu, choose the Clear command
    c. click the Cut button the Toolbar
    d. from the Edit menu, choose the Delete command

STUDENT ASSIGNMENT 3
Understanding the Works Spreadsheet

Instructions: In the Figure SA4-3, arrows point to the major components of a Works spreadsheet. Identify the various parts of the spreadsheet in the space provided.

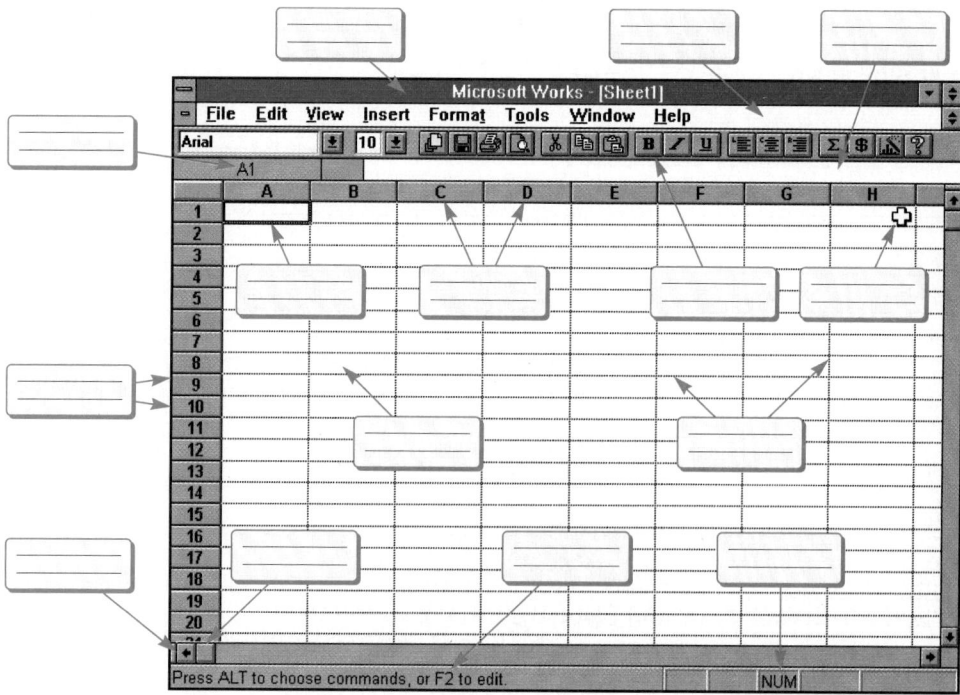

FIGURE SA4-3

STUDENT ASSIGNMENT 4
Understanding the Toolbar

Instructions: Figure SA4-4 shows the Toolbar used with the Works Spreadsheet. Arrows point to selected buttons. In the space provided, briefly explain the function of each of these buttons.

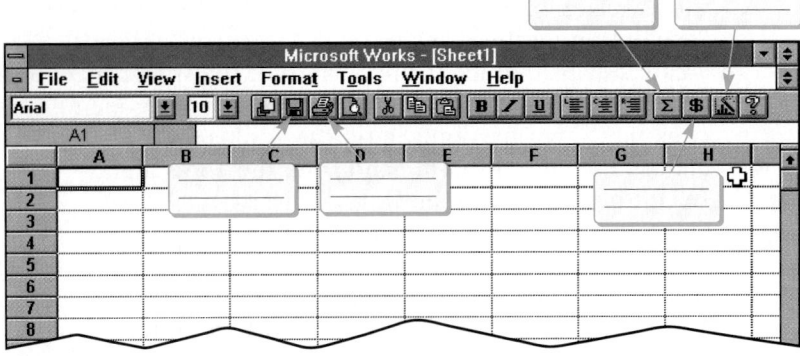

FIGURE SA4-4

STUDENT ASSIGNMENT 5
Summing Values

Instructions: The spreadsheet in Figure SA4-5 contains data but no totals. In the space provided below the spreadsheet, list the steps to accomplish the required tasks.

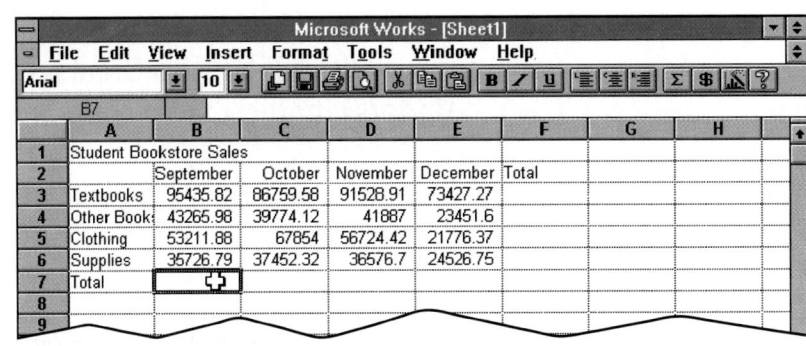

FIGURE SA4-5

Task 1: Sum the values in the September column and place the answer in cell B7.

Steps: _____

_____

_____

_____

Task 2: Sum the values in the October, November, and December columns and place the answers in cells C7, D7, and E7, respectively.

Steps: _____

_____

_____

Task 3: Sum the values in the Textbooks row and place the answer in cell F3.

Steps: _____

_____

_____

Task 4: Sum the values in the Other Books, Clothing, Supplies, and Total rows and place the answers in cells F4, F5, F6, and F7, respectively.

Steps: _____

_____

_____

STUDENT ASSIGNMENT 6
Formatting a Spreadsheet

Instructions: Format the spreadsheet in Figure SA4-6 the same as the spreadsheet in Figure 4-1 in the book. In the space provided below, list the steps to accomplish the required tasks.

FIGURE SA4-6

Task 1: Center the spreadsheet title across the width of the spreadsheet.

Steps: _____

_____

_____

Task 2: Change the title to yellow, 18 point, Arial bold, font.

Steps: _____

_____

_____

Task 3: Change the foreground color in the area containing the title to dark red.

Steps: _____

_____

_____

Task 4: Format the column titles and numeric values using the AutoFormat feature.

Steps: _____

_____

(continued)

STUDENT ASSIGNMENT 6 (continued)

Task 5: Display the numeric values in the sales cells and categories totals cells with a comma and two digits to the right of the decimal point.

Steps: _____

_____

_____

Task 6: Display the numeric values in the bottom total line with dollar signs, commas, and two digits to the right of the decimal point.

Steps: _____

_____

_____

C O M P U T E R   L A B O R A T O R Y   E X E R C I S E S

COMPUTER LABORATORY EXERCISE 1
Using the Help Menu

Instructions: Perform the following tasks using a computer.

1. Start the Microsoft Works Spreadsheet tool.
2. Select the Help menu.
3. Choose the Contents command from the Help menu.
4. When the Works for Windows Help Contents screen displays, click the word Spreadsheet.
5. When the Spreadsheet: Step-by-step help screen displays, click the words, Changing the appearance of your spreadsheet.
6. When the Changing the appearance of your spreadsheet screen displays, click the words, Number formats.
7. When the Number formats screen displays, answer the following questions:
   a. What is the general format? _____

   _____

   b. How is a negative number in the general format displayed? _____

   _____

   c. What does a cell containing ##### mean? _____

   _____

   d. What can you do to display an entire number in a cell when all you see is #####?

   _____

8. Click the Back button on the Toolbar.

9. When the Changing the appearance of your spreadsheet screen displays, click the words, Adjusting spreadsheet column width and answer the following questions.

    a. How can you change the width of all columns on the spreadsheet to a width of 15?

    _____

    b. How can you quickly adjust the column width to fit the longest entry in the column?

    _____

    c. What is the smallest value you can specify for a column width? _____

    d. What is the largest value you can specify for a column width? _____

10. Exit Works Help by choosing the Exit command from the Help File menu.

COMPUTER LABORATORY EXERCISE 2
Correcting a Spreadsheet

Instructions: Start the Works Spreadsheet tool. Open the CLE4-2.WKS file on the Student Diskette that accompanies this book. The spreadsheet is shown in Figure CLE4-2. The spreadsheet is supposed to be exactly the same as the spreadsheet shown in Figure 4-1 on page W4.3 of the book. However, three errors have been incorporated into the CLE4-2.WKS spreadsheet. In the space provided, identify the errors and explain the steps required to correct the errors. Then, correct the errors using your knowledge of the Works Spreadsheet tool and turn in a printed copy of the corrected spreadsheet to your instructor.

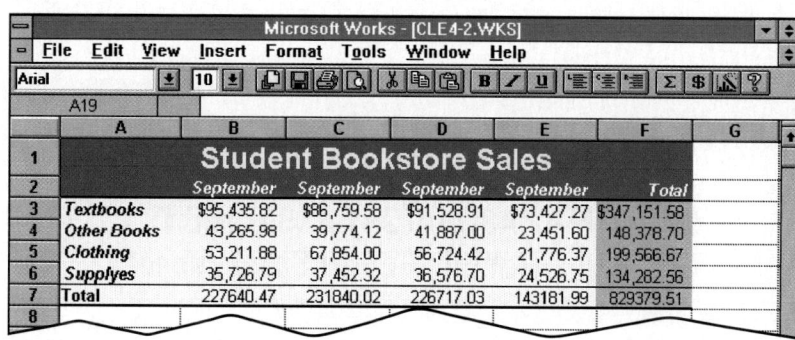

FIGURE CLE4-2

Error number 1: _____

Steps to correct error number 1: _____

_____

Error number 2: _____

Steps to correct error number 2: _____

Error number 3: _____

Steps to correct error number 3: _____

_____

COMPUTER LABORATORY EXERCISE 3
Formatting a Spreadsheet

Instructions: Start the Works Spreadsheet tool. Open the CLE4-3.WKS file on the Student Diskette that accompanies this book. The spreadsheet CLE4-3.WKS is shown in Figure CLE4-3. Format the spreadsheet according to the following directions.

1. Center the spreadsheet title, Student Bookstore Sales, across columns A through F. The Font should display in cyan 18 point Arial bold font. The color in the cell should be solid dark magenta.

2. Format the column titles and remaining portion of the spreadsheet using AutoFormat. Use the Classic 2 format.

3. Format sales numbers and category totals, cells B3 through F6, using the Comma format.

4. Format the bottom total line using the Currency format.

5. Increase the width of columns B through F to 13.

6. Print the formatted spreadsheet.

7. Turn in a copy of the formatted spreadsheet to your instructor.

	Microsoft Works - [CLE4-3.WKS]						
File Edit View Insert Format Tools Window Help							
Arial	± 10 ±				B I U Σ $		
A19							
	A	B	C	D	E	F	G	H
1	Student Bookstore Sales							
2		September	October	November	December	Total		
3	Textbooks	95435.82	86759.58	91528.91	73427.27	347151.58		
4	Other Book	43265.98	39774.12	41887	23451.6	148378.7		
5	Clothing	53211.88	67854	56724.42	21776.37	199566.67		
6	Supplies	35726.79	37452.32	36576.7	24526.75	134282.56		
7	Total	227640.47	231840.02	226717.03	143181.99	829379.51		
8								

FIGURE CLE4-3

COMPUTER LABORATORY ASSIGNMENTS

COMPUTER LABORATORY ASSIGNMENT 1
Creating a Monthly Report Spreadsheet

Purpose: To provide experience using the Works Spreadsheet tool to create a spreadsheet that requires entering text and numbers, centering the title, enlarging and displaying the title in color, calculating sums, using AutoFormat, using Comma and Currency formatting, saving and printing a spreadsheet, and creating and printing a chart.

Problem: Create a spreadsheet and chart for the monthly sales of Judi's Clothes store. The sales are shown in the following table. The spreadsheet and chart are illustrated in Figure CLA4-1.

Instructions:

1. Create a spreadsheet in the format shown using the numbers and text from the table.

2. Calculate the total sales for January, February, March, and April.

3. Calculate the total sales for Dresses, Suits, Lingerie, and Accessories.

4. Calculate the total sales for Judi's Clothes store.

	JANUARY	FEBRUARY	MARCH	APRIL
Dresses	22132.86	31216.00	21389.90	12343.96
Suits	12312.83	15440.20	13222.48	12111.10
Lingerie	8765.99	3242.59	6500.05	5633.16
Accessories	1765.80	2133.32	1998.89	2000.01

5. Format the spreadsheet as shown. Center the title across the columns. The spreadsheet title is to display in yellow 20 point Arial bold font. Display the cells where the title is located in dark red. Use AutoFormat and the Colorful 2 table format for the remaining portion of the spreadsheet. The sales numbers display using the Comma format. The last row containing the total line displays using the Currency format.
6. The column width should be 14 for column A and 13 for columns B through F.
7. Save the spreadsheet you create on a diskette. Use a filename consisting of the initials of your first and last names followed by the assignment number. Example: TC4-1.
8. Print the spreadsheet you create.
9. Create the 3-D Bar chart from the spreadsheet data.
10. Print the 3-D Bar chart.
11. Save the spreadsheet with the chart using the same filename as in step 7.
12. Follow directions from your instructor for turning in this assignment.

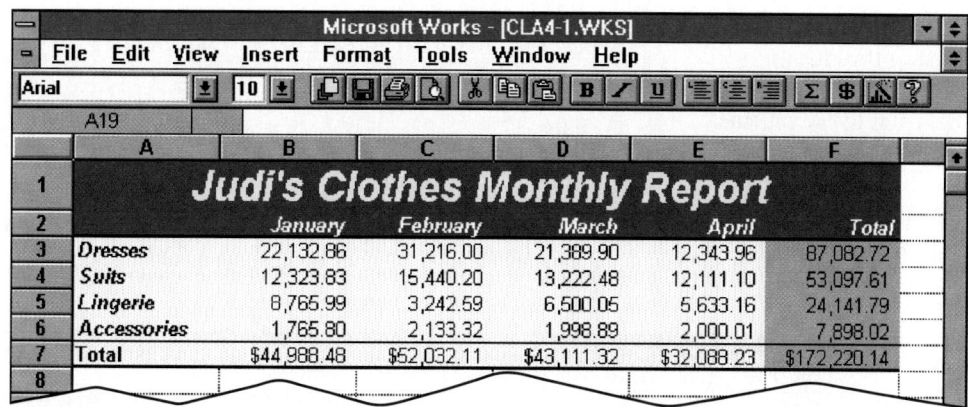

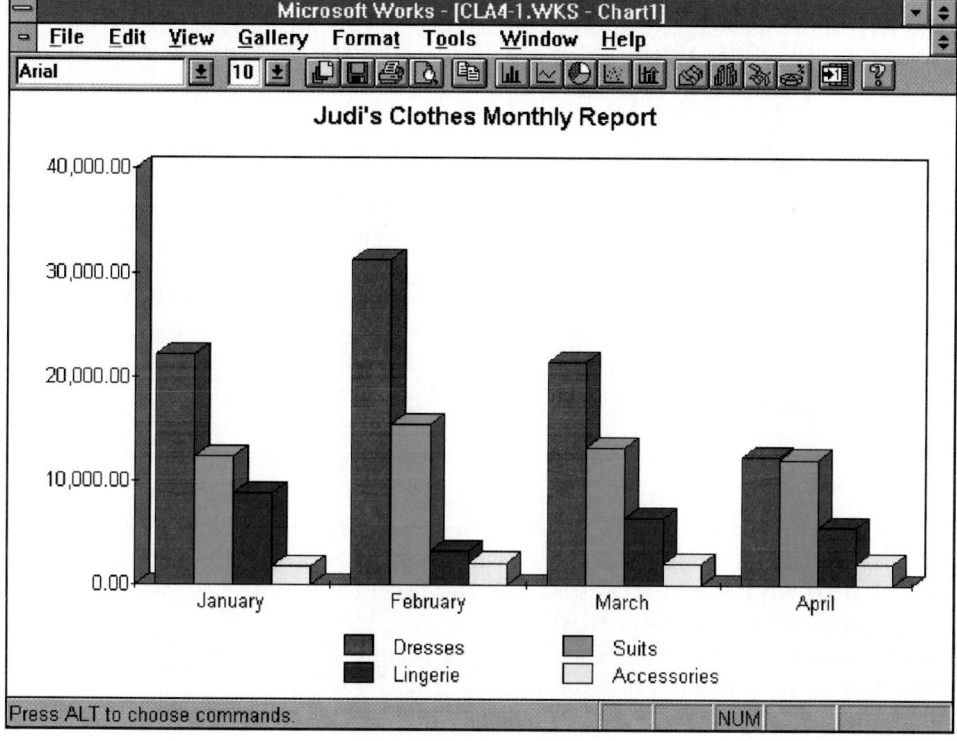

FIGURE CLA4-1

COMPUTER LABORATORY ASSIGNMENT 2
Creating a Phone Calls Spreadsheet

Purpose: To provide experience using the Works Spreadsheet tool to create a spreadsheet that requires entering text and numbers, calculating sums, centering the title, enlarging and displaying the title in color, using AutoFormat, using Comma and Currency formatting, saving and printing a spreadsheet, and creating and printing a chart.

Problem: Create a spreadsheet and chart for a Phone Call survey that was completed in the month of June and July. The data is shown in the table. The spreadsheet and chart are illustrated in Figures CLA4-2a and CLA4-2b.

Instructions:

1. Create a spreadsheet in the format shown using the numbers and text from the table.
2. Calculate the Total In Favor, the Total Against, and the Total No Opinion.
3. Calculate the Total Calls for June 10, June 17, June 24, July 01, and July 08.
4. Calculate the total number of calls for all five weeks.
5. Format the spreadsheet title as shown. The title is 16 point Arial bold italic font. The title displays in white and the color of the cells in which the title displays is dark magenta. Center the title across the columns of the spreadsheet. It is suggested that when you format text in white, you first place a pattern and color in the cell. If you

WEEK ENDING	IN FAVOR	AGAINST	NO OPINION
June 10	231	657	
June 17	567	769	
June 24	378	487	
July 01	363	197	
July 08	633	209	

	A	B	C	D	E	F	G
1		*Phone Calls*					
2	Week Ending	In Favor	Against	No Opinion	Total Calls		
3	June 10	231	657	119	1,007		
4	June 17	567	769	290	1,626		
5	June 24	378	487	211	1,076		
6	July 01	363	197	322	882		
7	July 08	633	209	433	1,275		
8	Totals	2,172	2,319	1,375	5,866		
9							
10							
11							
12							
13							
14							

FIGURE CLA4-2a

display white text in a cell with no color, it will appear as if the cell is blank. Format the remaining portion of the spreadsheet as illustrated. Use AutoFormat with the Classic 2 table format. The text in cell A2 displays in white. Bold the text in cells B2, C2, and D2.

6. Change the column width for all columns to 13.
7. Save the spreadsheet you create on a diskette. Use a filename consisting of the initials of your first and last names followed by the assignment number. Example: TC4-2.
8. Print the spreadsheet you have created.
9. Create the 3-D Bar chart in Figure CLA4-2b from the spreadsheet data.
10. Print the chart.
11. Save the spreadsheet and chart using the same filename as in step 7.
12. Follow directions from your instructor for turning in this assignment.

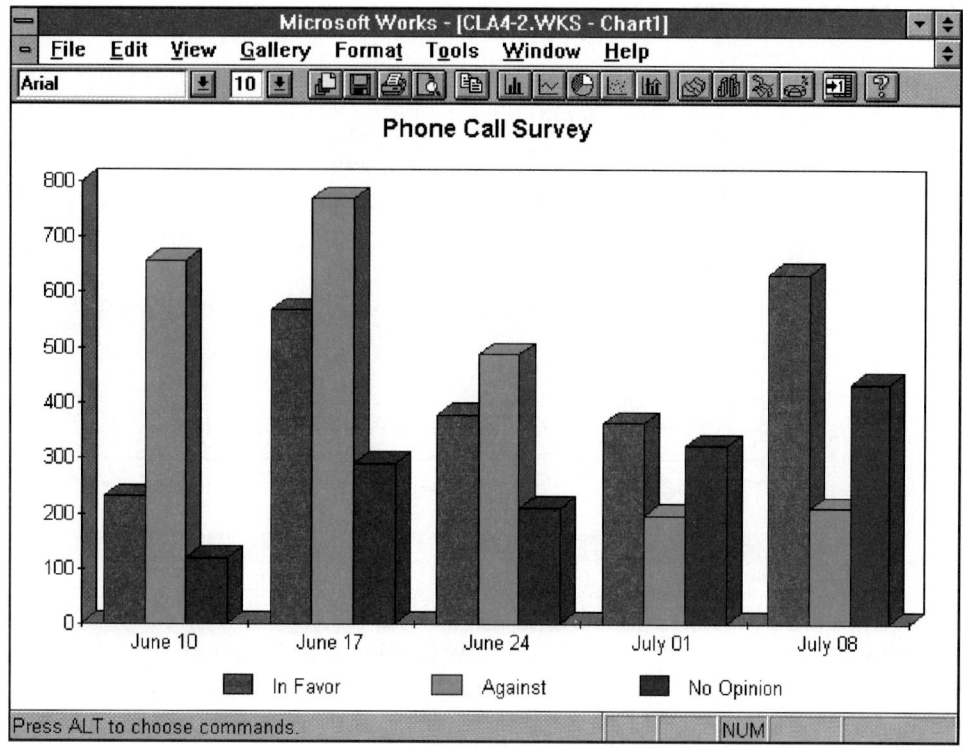

FIGURE CLA4-2b

COMPUTER LABORATORY ASSIGNMENT 3
Creating a Charities Contributions Spreadsheet

Purpose: To provide experience using the Works Spreadsheet tool to create a spreadsheet that requires entering text and numbers, calculating sums, centering the title, enlarging and displaying the title in color, using AutoFormat, using Comma and Currency formatting, saving and printing a spreadsheet, and creating and printing a chart.

Problem: Create a spreadsheet showing the Charities Contributions for the first quarter of the year (January, February, and March). The contributions received are shown in the table below. The spreadsheet and chart are illustrated in Figure CLA4-3 on the next page.

Instructions:

1. Create a spreadsheet in the format shown using the numbers and text from the table.
2. Calculate Totals for January, February, and March.
3. Calculate total contributions for United Way, Red Cross, Boy Scouts, and Girl Scouts.
4. Calculate total contributions.
5. Format the spreadsheet as shown on the next page. The font for the spreadsheet title is 18 point Arial bold. The font for the spreadsheet subtitle is 14 point Arial bold italic underlined. Carefully review each line to determine the required formatting. Use AutoFormat where appropriate when formatting the spreadsheet. Experiment with the pattern selections to obtain the required gray shading in the cells. Column width is 14 for all columns.

CHARITY	JANUARY	FEBRUARY	MARCH
United Way	212879	1232454	2112434
Red Cross	198765	1323298	1765898
Boy Scouts	143442	988769	1009428
Girl Scouts	324344	1000973	776442

(continued)

COMPUTER LABORATORY ASSIGNMENT 3 (continued)

6. Save the spreadsheet you create on a diskette. Use a filename consisting of the initials of your first and last names followed by the assignment number. Example: TC4-3.

7. Print the spreadsheet.

8. Create the 3-D Bar chart from the spreadsheet data. Save the spreadsheet and chart using the same filename as in step 6.

9. Follow directions from your instructor for turning in this assignment.

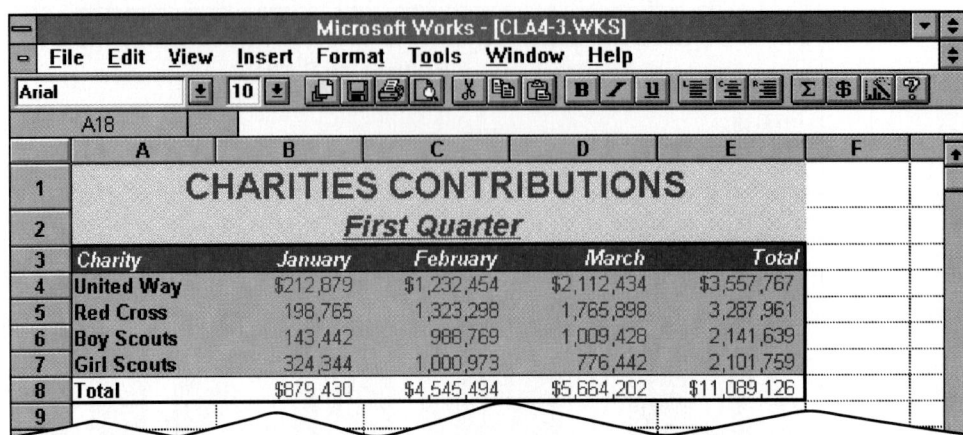

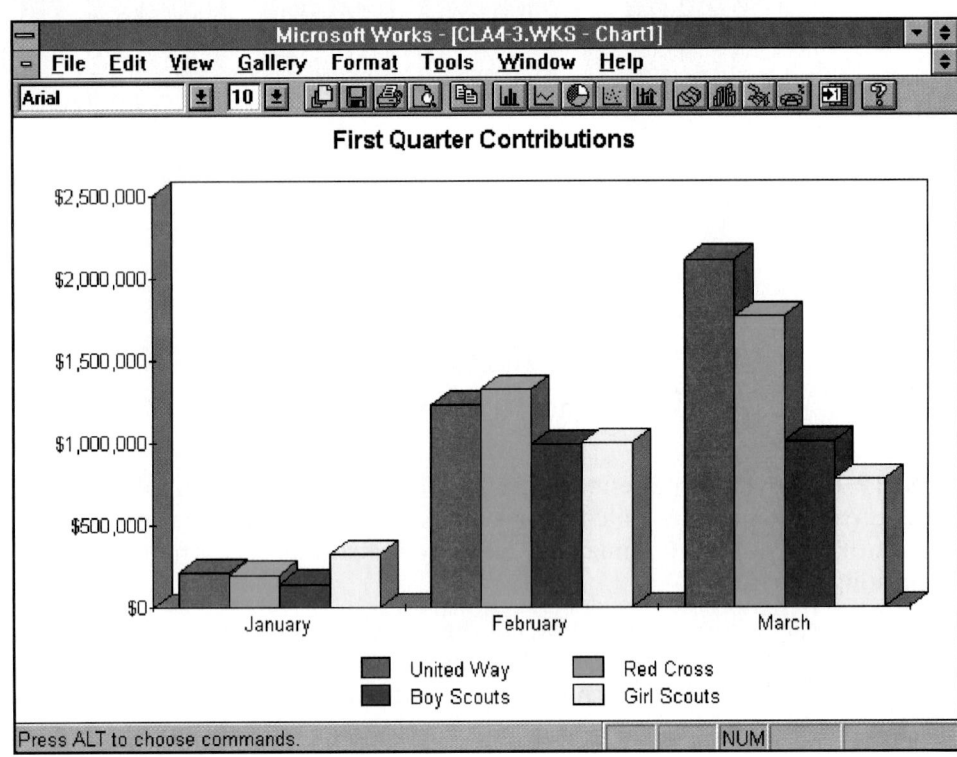

FIGURE CLA4-3

COMPUTER LABORATORY ASSIGNMENT 4
Creating a Student Expenses Spreadsheet

Purpose: To provide experience in planning and creating a spreadsheet using the skills learned in Project 4.

Problem: You are to create a budget for your expenses during the first semester of school, which covers September, October, November, and December. The expenses you have determined are listed in the table below.

EXPENSE	SEPTEMBER	OCTOBER	NOVEMBER	DECEMBER
Room	250	250	250	250
Meals	380	410	460	375
Books	360	40	25	25
Entertainment	100	150	180	50
Automobile	40	50	90	45

Instructions:

Part 1:

 1. Design and create a spreadsheet that contains the data in the table.
 2. On the spreadsheet, calculate the total expenses for September, October, November, and December.
 3. On the spreadsheet, calculate the total expenses for Room, Meals, Books, Entertainment, and Automobile.
 4. On the spreadsheet, calculate the total expenses for the first semester.
 5. Format the spreadsheet appropriately.
 6. Save the spreadsheet you create on a diskette. Use a filename consisting of the initials of your first and last names followed by the assignment number. Example: TC4-4.
 7. Print the spreadsheet you have created.
 8. Create a 3-D Bar chart for all expenses for each month.
 9. Print the 3-D Bar chart. Save the spreadsheet and 3-D Bar chart.
10. Follow directions from your instructor for turning in this assignment.

Part 2:

1. Modify the spreadsheet to prepare a budget for your personal use. Include at least two additional expense items.
2. Follow directions from your instructor for turning in this assignment.

FORMULAS, SORTING AND CHARTING

▼

FORMULAS, SORTING AND CHARTING

OBJECTIVES You will have mastered the material in this project when you can:

▶ Enter row titles
▶ Enter and display row titles using wrap text
▶ Write and enter formulas
▶ Use arithmetic operators in formulas
▶ Use parentheses in formulas
▶ Use the Point mode to enter cell references in formulas
▶ Copy formulas in single and multiple columns
▶ Alter the range of the SUM function
▶ Format a spreadsheet

▶ Change column widths
▶ Add color to a spreadsheet
▶ Sort rows in the spreadsheet
▶ Use Print Preview
▶ Zoom in and out on a print preview page
▶ Print in landscape page orientation
▶ Create a 3-D Pie chart
▶ Add data labels to a chart from nonadjacent columns
▶ Format a chart title and data labels
▶ Save and print a chart

▶ INTRODUCTION

I n Project 4, you learned that a spreadsheet is useful for presenting data and performing calculations. In addition to performing calculations using the SUM function you used in the previous project, Works allows you to perform calculations based upon formulas you enter in selected cells.

The data in the spreadsheet in Project 4 was graphically illustrated using a 3-D Bar chart. Works allows you to graphically display data using many different types of charts. In addition, you can identify a specific order in which the rows in your spreadsheet appear.

▶ PROJECT FIVE

T o illustrate these capabilities, Project 5 produces the spreadsheet, chart, and report shown in Figure 5-1. The spreadsheet contains the stock port-folio of an investment club. The name of the stock, the purchase date, the number of shares purchased, and the purchase price per share of the stock occupy the first four columns. In the fifth column, titled Cost, Works calculates the cost for the shares from a formula that multiplies the number of shares purchased (column C) times the purchase price per share (column D). For example, the investment club bought five hundred shares of AT&T stock at a price of 50.00 per share. The total cost (500 * 50.00) is 25,000.00.

FIGURE 5-1

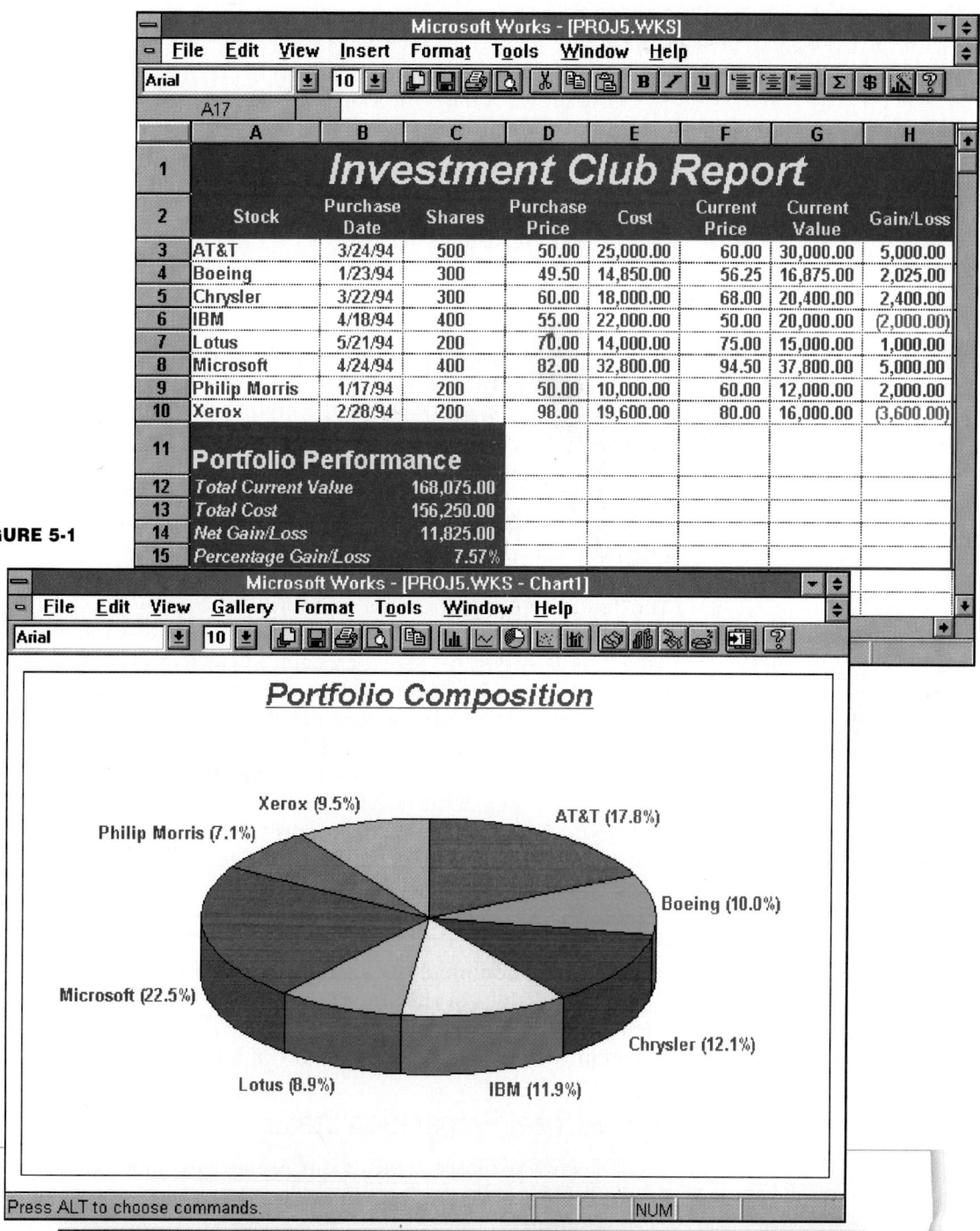

The following represents the spreadsheet content shown in Figure 5-1:

Microsoft Works - [PROJ5.WKS]

File Edit View Insert Format Tools Window Help

Arial   10

A17

Investment Club Report

Stock	Purchase Date	Shares	Purchase Price	Cost	Current Price	Current Value	Gain/Loss
AT&T	3/24/94	500	50.00	25,000.00	60.00	30,000.00	5,000.00
Boeing	1/23/94	300	49.50	14,850.00	56.25	16,875.00	2,025.00
Chrysler	3/22/94	300	60.00	18,000.00	68.00	20,400.00	2,400.00
IBM	4/18/94	400	55.00	22,000.00	50.00	20,000.00	(2,000.00)
Lotus	5/21/94	200	70.00	14,000.00	75.00	15,000.00	1,000.00
Microsoft	4/24/94	400	82.00	32,800.00	94.50	37,800.00	5,000.00
Philip Morris	1/17/94	200	50.00	10,000.00	60.00	12,000.00	2,000.00
Xerox	2/28/94	200	98.00	19,600.00	80.00	16,000.00	(3,600.00)

Portfolio Performance

Total Current Value	168,075.00
Total Cost	156,250.00
Net Gain/Loss	11,825.00
Percentage Gain/Loss	7.57%

Microsoft Works - [PROJ5.WKS - Chart1]

File Edit View Gallery Format Tools Window Help

Arial   10

Portfolio Composition

Xerox (9.5%)
Philip Morris (7.1%)
AT&T (17.8%)
Boeing (10.0%)
Microsoft (22.5%)
Chrysler (12.1%)
Lotus (8.9%)
IBM (11.9%)

Press ALT to choose commands.   NUM

Investment Club Report

Stock	Purchase Date	Shares	Purchase Price	Cost	Current Price	Current Value	Gain/Loss
AT&T	3/24/94	500	50.00	25,000.00	60.00	30,000.00	5,000.00
Boeing	1/23/94	300	49.50	14,850.00	56.25	16,875.00	2,025.00
Chrysler	3/22/94	300	60.00	18,000.00	68.00	20,400.00	2,400.00
IBM	4/18/94	400	55.00	22,000.00	50.00	20,000.00	(2,000.00)
Lotus	5/21/94	200	70.00	14,000.00	75.00	15,000.00	1,000.00
Microsoft	4/24/94	400	82.00	32,800.00	94.50	37,800.00	5,000.00
Philip Morris	1/17/94	200	50.00	10,000.00	60.00	12,000.00	2,000.00
Xerox	2/28/94	200	98.00	19,600.00	80.00	16,000.00	(3,600.00)

Portfolio Performance

Total Current Value	168,075.00
Total Cost	156,250.00
Net Gain/Loss	11,825.00
Percentage Gain/Loss	7.57%

Column F contains the Current Price per share of the stock. For AT&T, the current price per share is 60.00 (cell F3). Works calculates the Current Value (column G) using a formula that multiplies the number of Shares (column C) times the Current Price (column F). The Current Value of the AT&T stock is 30,000.00 (500 * 60.00).

In the spreadsheet in Figure 5-1 on the previous page, both the Purchase Price and the Current Price are fictitious. These values may not be the actual values of the stocks on the dates shown.

When the investment club purchases and holds stock, the Current Value of the stock can increase or decrease from the Cost. If the Current Value is greater than the Cost, the club has realized a gain. If the Current Value goes down and is less than the Cost, the club has suffered a loss. Works calculates the Gain/Loss of a stock (column H) using a formula that subtracts the Cost (column E) from the Current Value (column G). For example, AT&T shows a gain because the Current Value minus the Cost is a positive value (30,000.00 - 25,000.00 = 5,000.00). If a stock has a loss, such as IBM in row 6, the loss displays in red within parentheses.

The box at the bottom of the screen contains the Portfolio Performance. The Total Current Value is the sum of the values in column G. The Total Cost is the sum of the costs in column E. Net Gain/Loss is equal to Total Current Value minus Total Cost. The Percentage Gain/Loss is calculated by a formula that divides the Net Gain/Loss by the Total Cost. In the spreadsheet, Works uses a formula to divide the gain (11,825.00) by the Cost (156,250.00), yielding a Percentage Gain/Loss of 7.57%.

In Figure 5-1, the stocks are displayed in alphabetical order based on the name of the stock. That is, AT&T is first, Boeing is second, Chrysler is third, and so on. When you enter the records, however, you enter them in the sequence of the date they are purchased (column B). Therefore, the first stock you enter is Philip Morris, followed by Boeing, Xerox, and so on. You will use the sorting feature of Works to place the rows in alphabetical order by Stock name.

After you complete the spreadsheet, you will prepare a chart based on the Current Values of the stocks. This chart (Figure 5-1) is a 3-D Pie chart illustrating the percentage of the portfolio each stock represents. A **Pie chart** is commonly used to show percentages of a whole.

Spreadsheet Preparation Steps

To provide an overview of this project, the general steps to prepare the spreadsheet, printed report, and chart in Figure 5-1 are listed below.

1. Start the Works Spreadsheet.
2. Enter the spreadsheet title (Investment Club Report) and the column titles (Stock, Purchase Date, Shares, Purchase Price, Cost, Current Price, Current Value, and Gain/Loss).
3. Enter the Stock name for the first stock, the Purchase Date, the Shares, and the Purchase Price.
4. Enter the formula to calculate the Cost (Shares times Purchase Price).
5. Enter the Current Price.
6. Enter the formula to calculate the Current Value (Shares times Current Price).
7. Enter the formula to calculate Gain/Loss (Current Value minus Cost).
8. Enter the data for the remaining stocks in the report.
9. Copy the formulas for Cost, Current Value, and Gain/Loss for each stock.

10. Enter the titles for the Portfolio Performance section.
11. Enter the formulas to calculate Total Current Value, Total Cost, Net Gain/Loss, and Percentage Gain/Loss.
12. Format the spreadsheet.
13. Save the spreadsheet.
14. Add color to the spreadsheet
15. Print the spreadsheet.
16. Prepare the 3-D Pie chart.
17. Print the 3-D Pie chart.
18. Save the spreadsheet and the 3-D Pie chart.

The following sections contain a detailed explanation of each of these steps.

▶ STARTING THE WORKS SPREADSHEET

o start the Works Spreadsheet, follow the steps used in Project 4. These steps are summarized below.

TO START THE WORKS SPREADSHEET

Step 1: From Program Manager, open the Microsoft Works for Windows group window.

Step 2: Double-click the Microsoft Works program-item icon.

Step 3: If necessary, choose the Start Works Now button and then point to the Spreadsheet button in the Works Startup dialog box.

Step 4: Choose the Spreadsheet button in the Works Startup dialog box.

Step 5: If the Microsoft Works window is not maximized, maximize it.

Step 6: Maximize the Sheet1 window.

▶ ENTERING THE SPREADSHEET TITLE AND COLUMN HEADINGS

omplete the following steps to enter the spreadsheet title and column headings in the spreadsheet.

TO ENTER THE SPREADSHEET TITLE AND COLUMN HEADINGS ▼

STEP 1 ▶

Highlight the cell where you will enter the spreadsheet title – cell A1 (Figure 5-2).

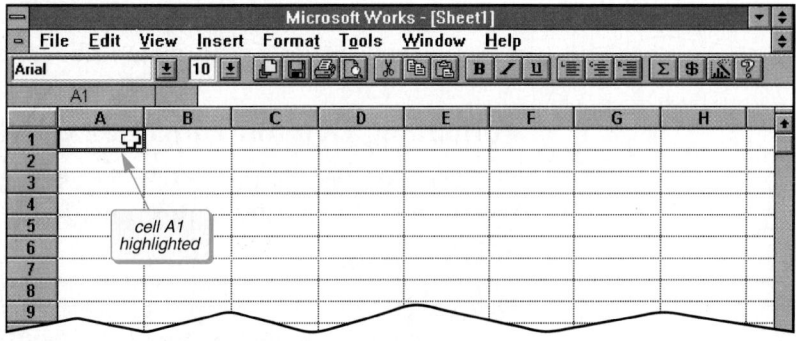

cell A1 highlighted

FIGURE 5-2

STEP 2 ▶

Type the spreadsheet title,
Investment Club Report,
and either press the ENTER key or
click the Enter box to confirm the
entry.

*Works enters the spreadsheet title
into cell A1 (Figure 5-3). The title
overflows into cell B1 because cell
B1 is empty.*

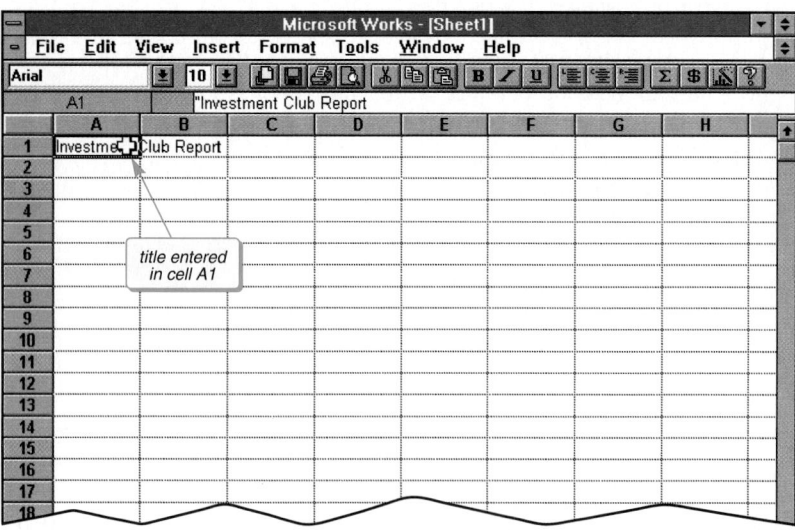

FIGURE 5-3

STEP 3 ▶

Highlight the appropriate cells one
at a time and enter each of the
column titles.

*The column titles are
entered in cells A2 through H2
(Figure 5-4). Column titles that are
too long to display in a cell are
partially hidden behind the adjacent cells to the right.*

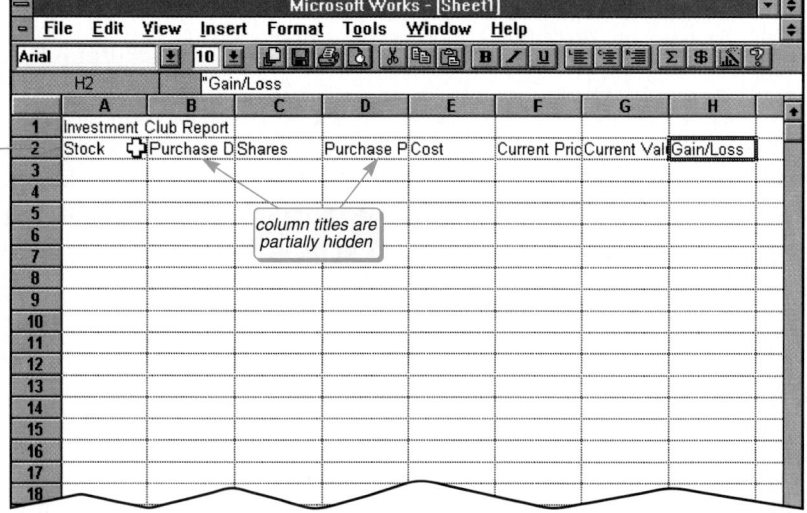

FIGURE 5-4

Some column titles do not completely display in the cells when they are
entered (columns B, D, F, and G in Figure 5-4). Although these column titles do not
completely display, the complete titles are contained within the cells.

Formatting Column Titles Using Wrap Text

Because some of the column titles cannot be read, it is recommended that you
format the column titles at this point so that all of the words in the column titles
display.

One method of formatting cells so all the words in the cell can be read is to
wrap text. When you wrap text, Works fits the words in the cell by increasing the
row height and placing the words on multiple lines within the cell. To format the
column titles using wrap text, complete the following steps.

TO FORMAT CELLS USING WRAP TEXT ▼

STEP 1 ▶

Highlight cells A2 through H2. Select the Format menu and point to the Alignment command.

Cells A2 through H2 are high-lighted (Figure 5-5). The Format menu displays and the mouse pointer points to the Alignment command.

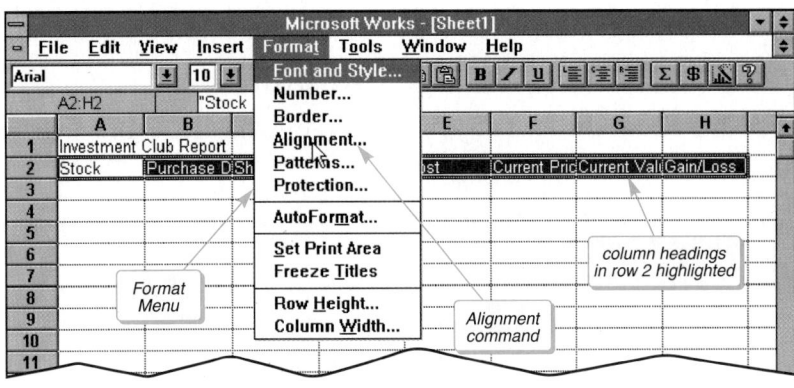

FIGURE 5-5

STEP 2 ▶

Choose the Alignment command. When the Alignment dialog box displays, select the Center option button in the Alignment area, select the Wrap text check box, select the Center option button in the Vertical area, and point to the OK button.

The Center option button in the Alignment area is selected, the Wrap text check box contains an X, the Center option button in the Vertical area is selected, and the mouse pointer points to the OK button (Figure 5-6). The Center option button in the Alignment area directs Works to center the text horizontally within a cell. The Center option button in the Vertical area tells Works to center the text vertically within a cell.

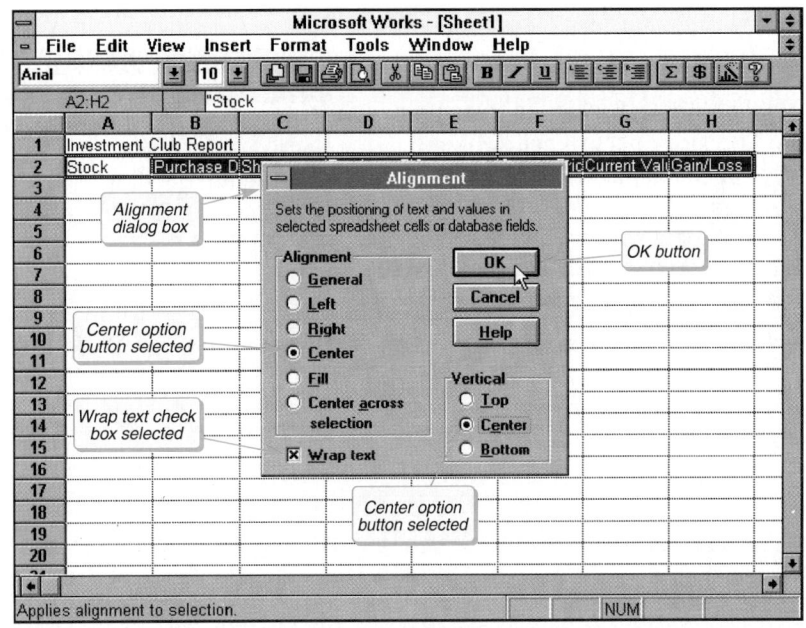

FIGURE 5-6

STEP 4 ▶

Choose the OK button in the Alignment dialog box.

Works displays the column headings centered both vertically and horizontally within the cells (Figure 5-7). Column headings that were too long to display in the cell now display on two lines. Works increases the row height to allow two lines to display.

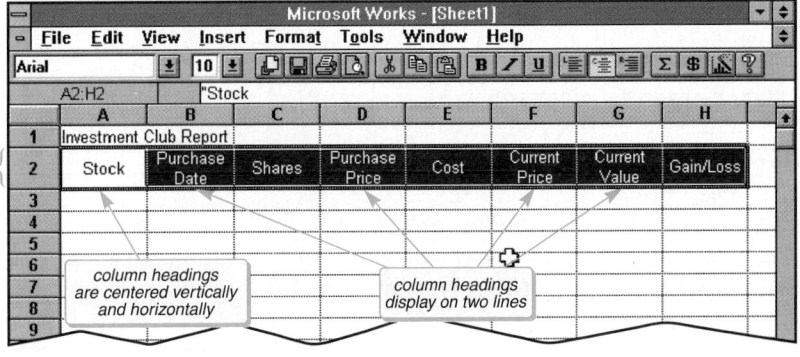

FIGURE 5-7

You can now clearly read each column title, which greatly simplifies entering the data that follows.

▶ ENTERING DATA

After entering the titles, the next step is to enter the data in the spreadsheet. The data consists of text (Stock Name), a date (Purchase Date), numeric data (Shares, Purchase Price, and Current Price), and formulas that calculate Cost, Current Value, and Gain/Loss. You enter data in Purchase Date sequence.

To enter the Stock name, Purchase Date, Shares, and Purchase Price, perform the following steps.

TO ENTER TEXT, DATE, AND NUMERIC DATA ▼

STEP 1 ▶

Highlight the cell which is to contain the first stock name – cell A3 – and type the stock name, Philip Morris.

Works displays the text you type in the formula bar and in the cell (Figure 5-8).

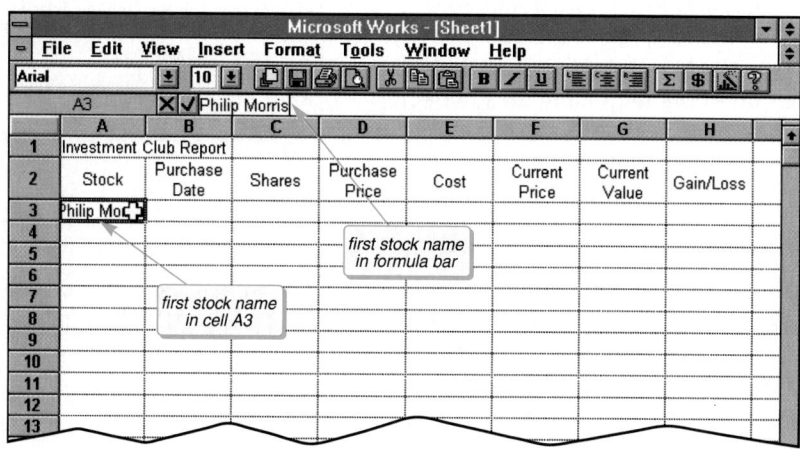

FIGURE 5-8

STEP 2 ▶

Press the RIGHT ARROW key, type the purchase date (1/17/94) in cell B3, press the RIGHT ARROW key, type the number of shares (200) in cell C3, press the RIGHT ARROW key, type the purchase price (50.00) in cell D3, and press the RIGHT ARROW key.

The values you enter are stored in the cells (Figure 5-9). The Purchase Price is not formatted in the Comma format. You will perform this formatting later. Cell E3 is highlighted.

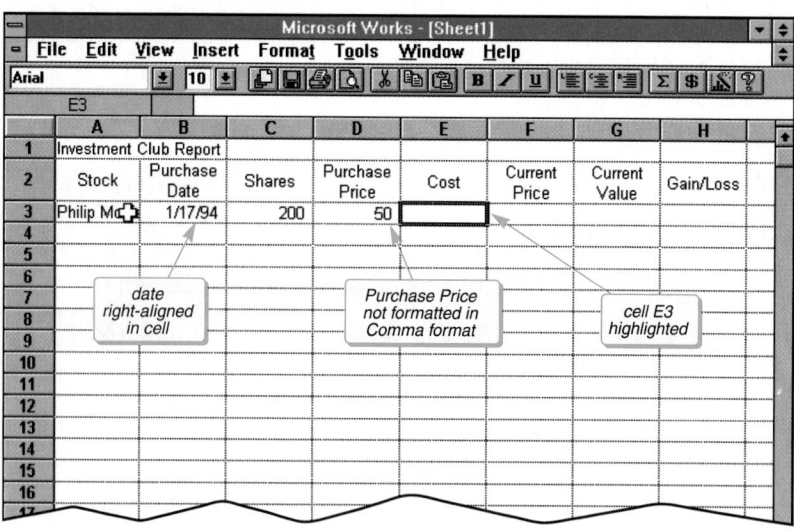

FIGURE 5-9

Works considers a date to be a numeric field and, therefore, stores it right-aligned in cell B3. Because cell D3 is not yet formatted, Works removes the trailing zeros in the value 50.00 and displays only 50.

Entering Formulas

The Cost, Current Value, and Gain/Loss fields in the spreadsheet are calculated based on formulas. Thus, to continue building the spreadsheet, you must enter the formulas in their respective cells.

In Works, a **formula** is an equation that calculates a new value from existing values in cells within the spreadsheet. For example, the Cost is calculated based on the existing values in the Shares column and the Purchase Price column.

A formula always begins with an equal sign. It is followed by a combination of cell references, numbers, operators, and possibly functions such as the SUM function used in Project 4.

In a formula, a **cell reference** identifies a cell that contains data to be used in the formula. For example, when you place the formula =C3*D3 in cell E3, Works will multiply the numeric value in cell C3 by the numeric value in cell D3 and place the product in cell E3. The asterisk (*) in the formula is called an operator. An **operator** specifies the arithmetic operation to be carried out in the formula. You can use five different operators in a formula. These operators are summarized in Table 5-1.

Formulas can contain more than two cell references or numeric values and can also contain multiple operators. For example, the formula =C4*(D4+H9)/F5 is a valid formula. To determine the results of this formula, Works performs the operations within the formula according to standard **algebraic rules**. First, any operation contained within parentheses is performed. Therefore, in the example formula, the first operation is to add the value in cell D4 to the value in cell H9.

Then, exponentiation is performed, followed by any multiplication or division operations. Finally, addition and subtraction are performed. If two or more operators within the formula have the same **order of evaluation**, Works performs the operations from left to right. Thus, in the example formula, Works would multiply the sum of the values in cell D4 and cell H9 by the value in cell C4 and then divide the result by the value in cell F5.

The examples in Table 5-2 further illustrate the way Works evaluates formulas.

When writing formulas, you must take care to ensure the proper calculations are performed. One method to ensure the correct sequence is to use **parentheses**. For example, if a formula in cell K12 was supposed to calculate the average of the values in cells L2, L4, and L6, the formula =L2+L4+L6/3 would not obtain the proper result because Works would first divide the value in cell L6 by 3 and then add the values in L2, L4, and the result of the division.

The correct way to write the formula is =(L2+L4+L6)/3. In this formula, which uses parentheses, Works will first add the values in cells L2, L4, and L6. Then, it will divide the answer by 3, resulting in the average of the three numbers.

Whenever you enter a formula, review the formula carefully to ensure the correct calculation will occur.

▸ **TABLE 5-1**

OPERATOR	FUNCTION
+	Addition
−	Subtraction
*	Multiplication
/	Division
^	Exponentiation

▸ **TABLE 5-2**

CELL VALUES	FORMULA	RESULT
C4=25 D6=5 F12=100	=F12+C4/D6	105
F2=4 H6=8 G8=12	=F2^3/H6+G8	20
E6=9 G13=3 D9=6 E8=2	=(E6+G13)/D9+E8	4

In Project 5, the Cost is calculated by multiplying the number of Shares times the Purchase Price. From the spreadsheet in Figure 5-9 on page W5.8, notice that for Philip Morris, the number of Shares is contained in cell C3 and the Purchase Price is located in cell D3. Therefore, the formula to calculate the Cost is =C3*D3. To enter the formula that calculates Cost, perform the following steps.

TO ENTER A FORMULA ▼

STEP 1 ►

Highlight cell E3, the cell that will contain the formula, and type an equal sign.

Works displays the equal sign in the formula bar and in cell E3 (Figure 5-10). The equal sign informs Works you are entering a formula. The Cancel box and the Enter box display in the formula bar.

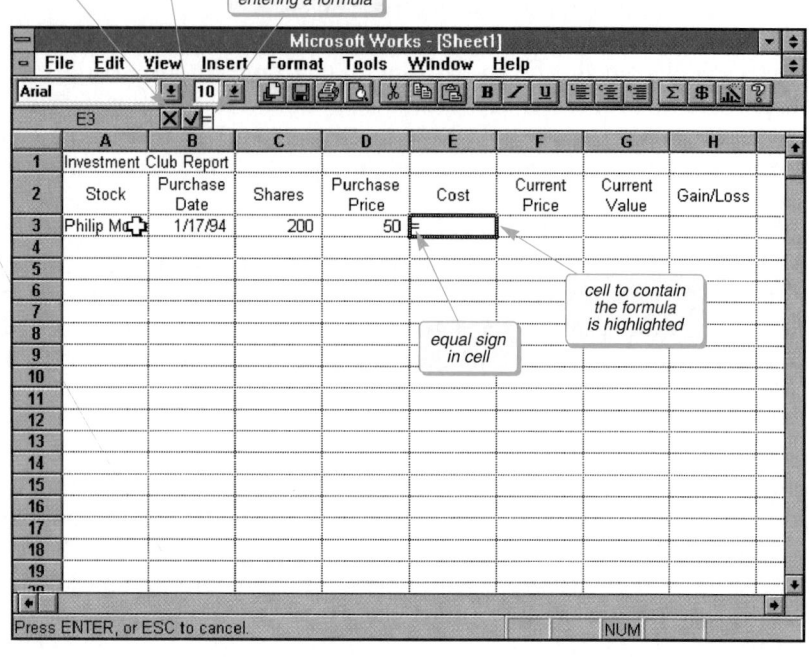

FIGURE 5-10

STEP 2 ►

Highlight the first cell in the formula – cell C3 – by clicking the cell or pressing an arrow key to move to the cell.

*When you highlight the cell, Works places a black background in the cell and also places the cell reference in the formula (Figure 5-11). Works also indicates in the status bar that you are using the **Point mode**, which is the term used when you point to a cell to be included in a formula.*

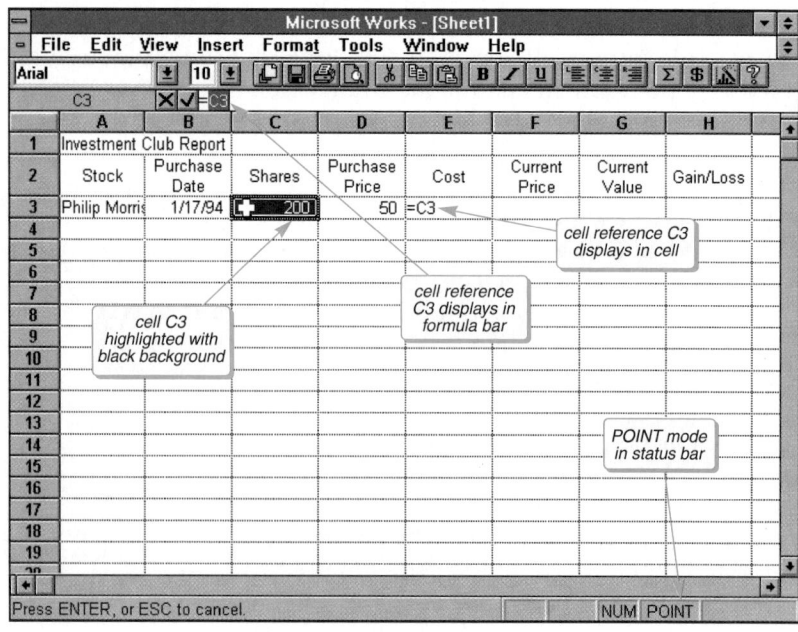

FIGURE 5-11

STEP 3 ►

Type the multiplication operator (*).

Works displays the multiplication operator in both the formula bar and the cell where you are entering the formula (Figure 5-12). In addition, Works removes the temporary highlight from cell C3, which you pointed to, and returns it to the cell that contains the formula.

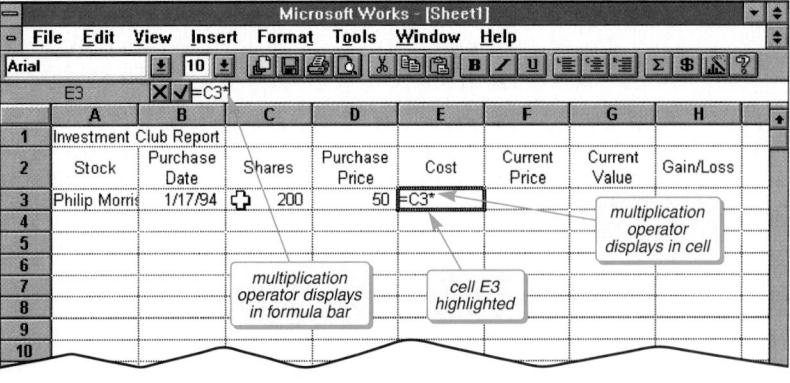

FIGURE 5-12

STEP 4 ►

Highlight the second cell in the formula – cell D3 – by clicking the cell or using an arrow key to move to the cell.

Once again, Works places a black background in the highlighted cell and places the cell reference in the formula in both the formula bar and cell E3 (Figure 5-13).

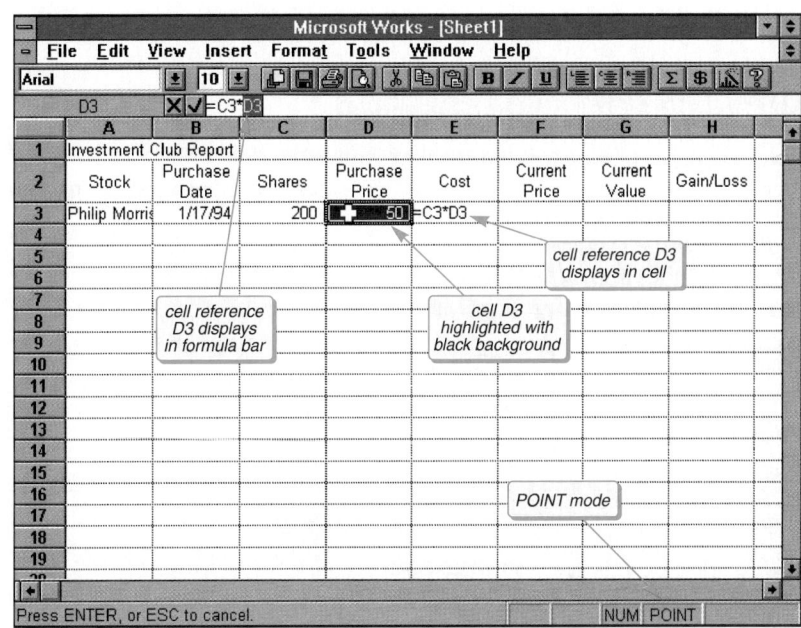

FIGURE 5-13

STEP 5 ►

Enter the formula by clicking the Enter box or pressing the ENTER key.

Works enters the formula into cell E3 and performs the calculation (Figure 5-14). The result of the calculation is 10000, which is the product of 200 (value in cell C3) times 50 (value in cell D3).

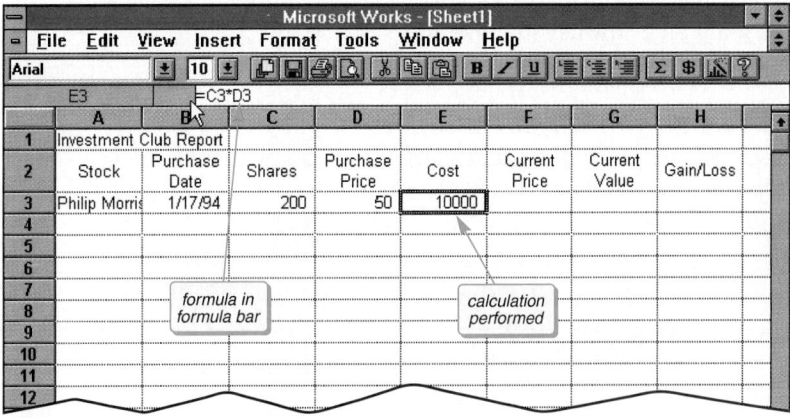

FIGURE 5-14

In the previous steps, you selected the cells used in the formula by highlighting the cell with either the mouse or the arrow keys. Works also allows you to actually type the cell reference when you enter the formula. For example, to enter the formula in cell E3 in the previous illustration, you could type =C3*D3 and then press the RIGHT ARROW key, click the Enter box, or press the ENTER key. This method, however, is prone to error because you might type the incorrect cell reference. It is recommended, therefore, that you use the **pointing method** of identifying cells to enter cell references into a formula because it leads to greater accuracy.

To continue to enter data for the Philip Morris stock, you must enter the Current Price into cell F3 and then enter the formula to calculate the Current Value in cell G3. To calculate the Current Value for Philip Morris, the number of Shares in cell C3 is multiplied by the Current Price in cell F3. Therefore, the formula is =C3*F3. The steps to enter the Current Price and the formula for the Current Value follow.

TO ENTER A VALUE AND A FORMULA ▼

STEP 1 ▶

Highlight cell F3, type the current price for Philip Morris (60), press the RIGHT ARROW key, and type an equal sign.

Works enters the Current Price into cell F3, highlights cell G3, and displays the equal sign in both the formula bar and cell G3 (Figure 5-15).

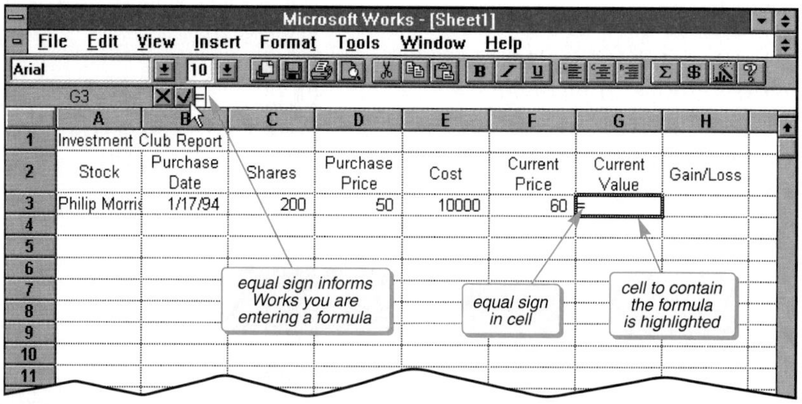

FIGURE 5-15

STEP 2 ▶

Highlight the first cell in the formula – cell C3 – by clicking the cell or pressing an arrow key to move to the cell.

Works highlights cell C3 with a black background and places the cell reference in the formula (Figure 5-16).

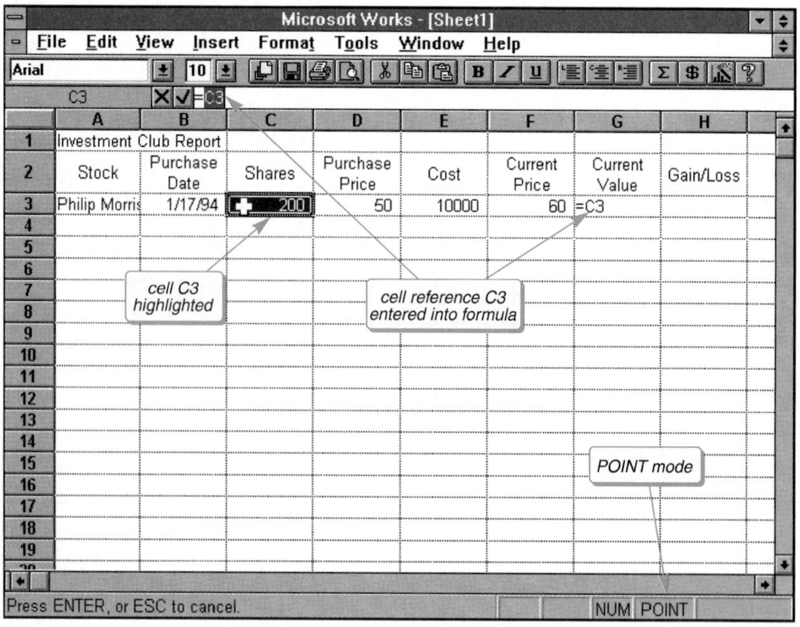

FIGURE 5-16

STEP 3 ▶

Type the multiplication operator (*) and highlight the second cell in the formula – cell F3.

Once again, Works highlights cell F3 with a black background and places the cell reference in the formula (Figure 5-17).

FIGURE 5-17

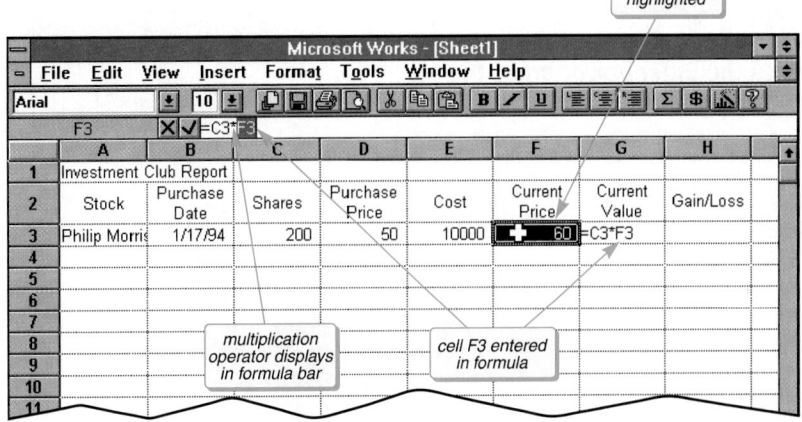

STEP 4 ▶

Enter the formula by clicking the Enter box or pressing the ENTER key.

*Works enters the formula into cell G3, calculates the answer, and displays the answer (200 * 60 = 12000) in cell G3 (Figure 5-18).*

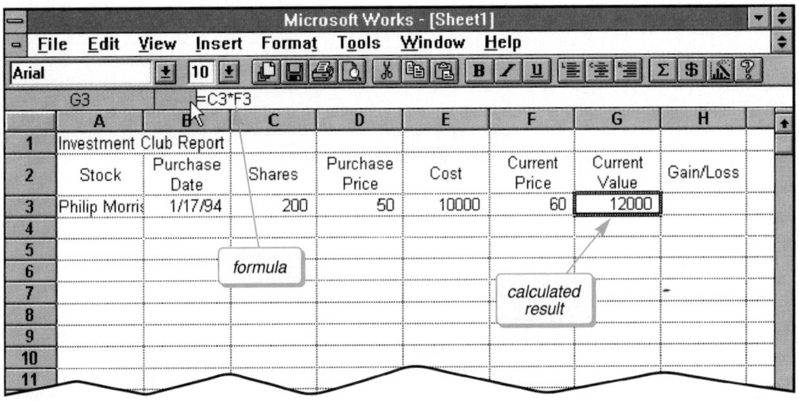

FIGURE 5-18

The last formula you must enter for the first row in the spreadsheet calculates the Gain/Loss of the stock by subtracting the Cost from the Current Value. You should enter this formula, =G3-E3, into cell H3. To enter it, perform the following steps.

TO ENTER A FORMULA ▼

STEP 1 ▶

Highlight cell H3, type an equal sign, highlight cell G3, type a minus sign, and highlight cell E3.

The formula appears in the formula bar and in cell H3 (Figure 5-19).

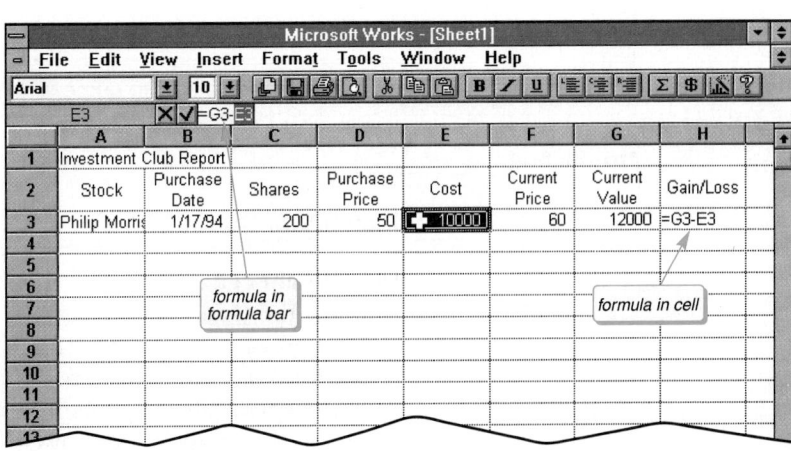

FIGURE 5-19

STEP 2 ▶

Click the Enter box or press the ENTER key.

Works enters the formula into cell H3 and calculates the results (12000-10000=2000) (Figure 5-20).

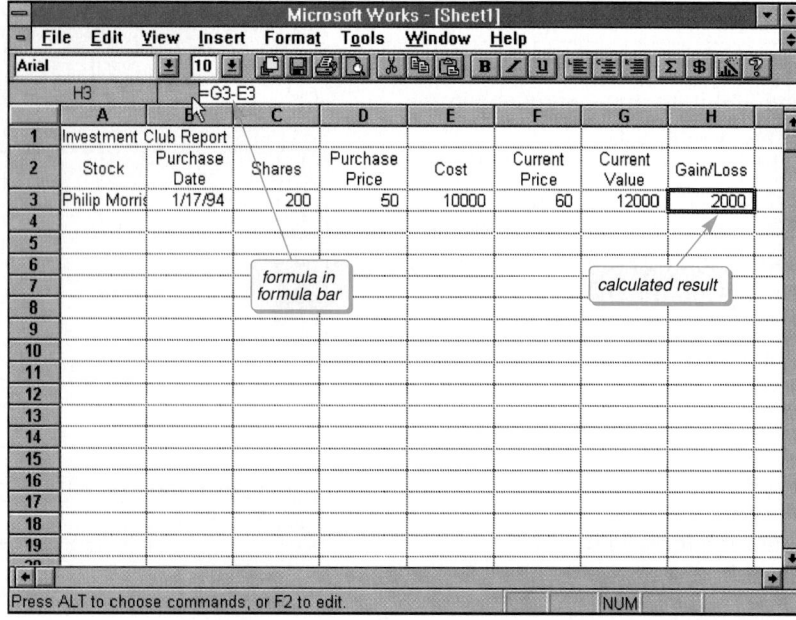

FIGURE 5-20

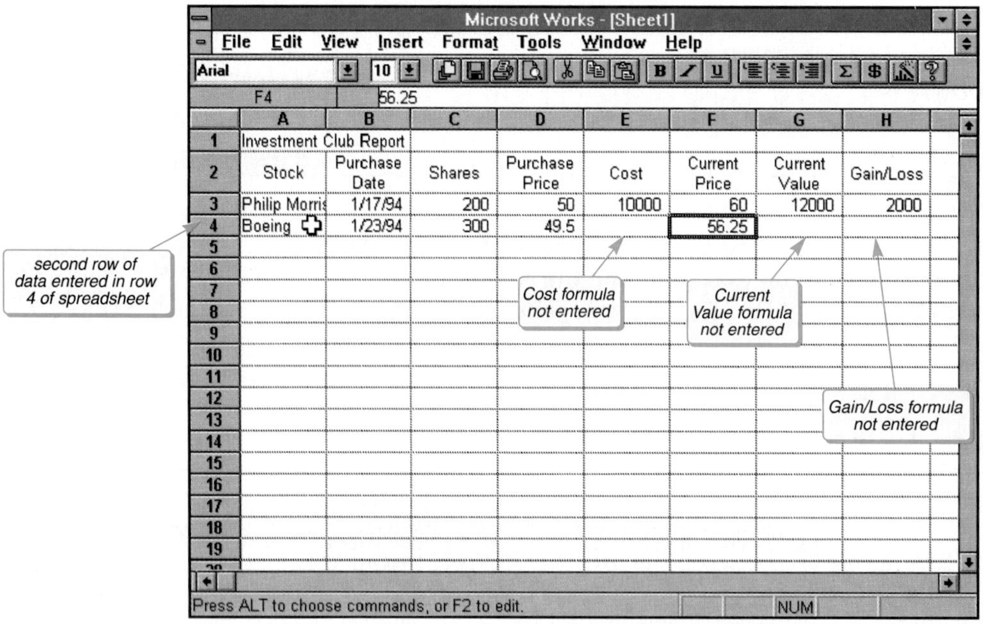

Entering the Spreadsheet Data

After you have entered data for the first stock, Philip Morris, you must enter the data for the next stock into row 4 of the spreadsheet using the same method you used for row 3. After entering the data for row 4, you will enter the data for the remainder of the spreadsheet. To enter the data, complete the following steps (see Figure 5-21 and Figure 5-22).

FIGURE 5-21

TO ENTER SPREADSHEET DATA

Step 1: Highlight cell A4 and type the stock name, `Boeing`.

Step 2: Using the techniques described previously, enter the data in cells B4, C4, D4, and F4 (see Figure 5-21). Do not enter any formulas. You will copy the formulas down from row 3 after you have entered all the other data in the spreadsheet. It is more efficient to copy the formulas all at one time rather than row by row.

Step 3: Enter the data for the subsequent rows (see Figure 5-22). Do not enter the formulas.

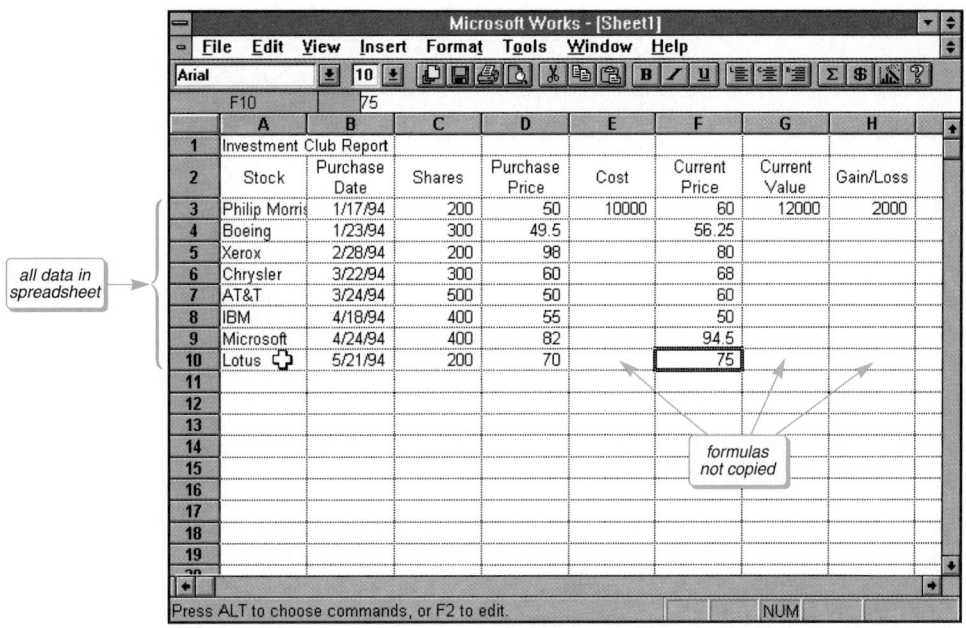

FIGURE 5-22

Copying a Formula

Once the data is in the spreadsheet, you must copy the formulas down columns E, G, and H. You can use the **Fill Down command** from the Edit menu to copy a formula down in a column.

To copy the formula that calculates the Cost, perform the following steps.

TO COPY A FORMULA ▼

STEP 1 ►

Highlight the cell containing the formula to copy – cell E3 – and the range where you want to copy the formula – E4:E10. Then, select the Edit menu and point to the Fill Down command.

Cells E3 through E10 are high-lighted (Figure 5-23). The Edit menu displays and the mouse pointer points to the Fill Down command.

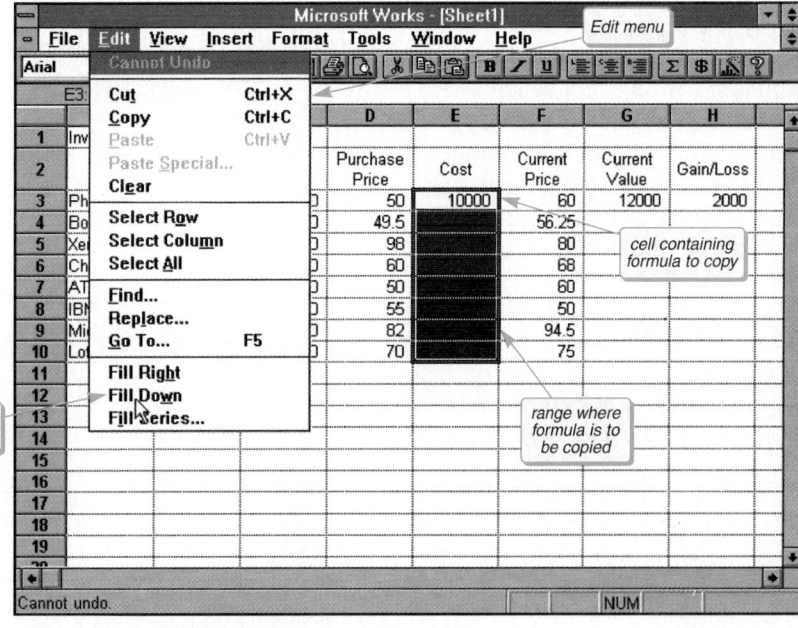

FIGURE 5-23

STEP 2 ▶

Choose the Fill Down command from the Edit menu.

Works copies the formula in cell E3 to the range E4:E10 and displays the calculated results in each of the cells (Figure 5-24). As with the SUM function in Project 4, the cell references for each row change to reflect the correct row. For example, the formula in cell E3 is =C3*D3 and the formula in cell E4 is =C4*D4.

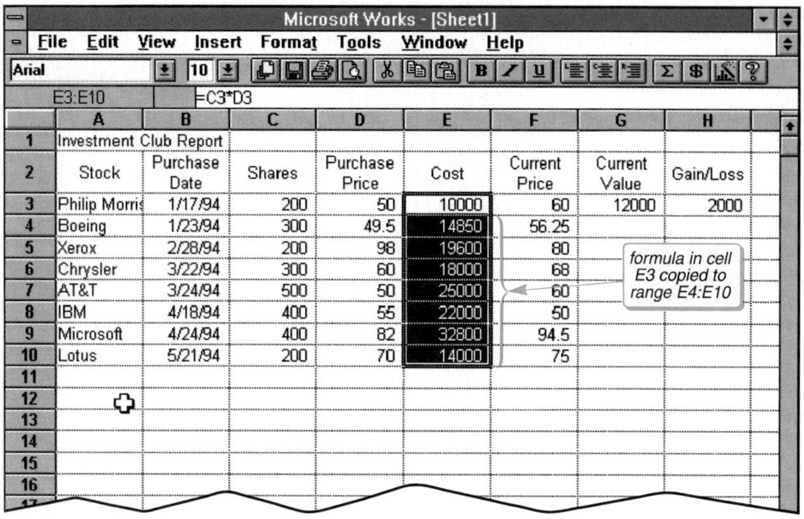

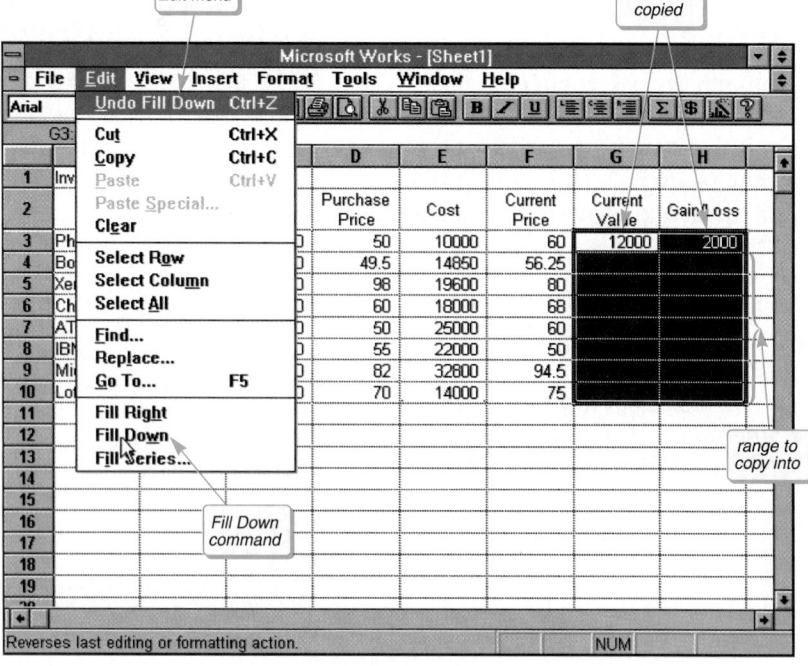

FIGURE 5-24

Copying Multiple Columns

The next step in building the spreadsheet is to copy the Current Value formula in cell G3 to cells G4:G10, and to copy the Gain/Loss formula in cell H3 to cells H4:H10. When you must copy cells in adjacent columns, you can copy the cells all at one time by highlighting multiple columns and using the Fill Down command. Perform the following steps to copy cells in adjacent columns.

TO COPY CELLS IN ADJACENT COLUMNS ▼

STEP 1 ▶

Highlight the adjacent cells containing the formulas to copy – cells G3 and H3 – and the range where you want to copy them – G4:H10. Then, select the Edit menu and point to the Fill Down command.

Cells G3 through G10 and cells H3 through H10 are highlighted (Figure 5-25). The Edit menu displays and the mouse pointer points to the Fill Down command.

FIGURE 5-25

STEP 2 ▶

Choose the Fill Down command from the Edit menu.

Works copies the formulas in each of the cells, G3 and H3, down their respective columns and displays the calculated results in each of the cells (Figure 5-26). The cell references within the cells are modified to reference the proper rows. Thus, cell G4 contains the formula =C4*F4, cell H4 contains the formula =G4-E4, and so on.

FIGURE 5-26

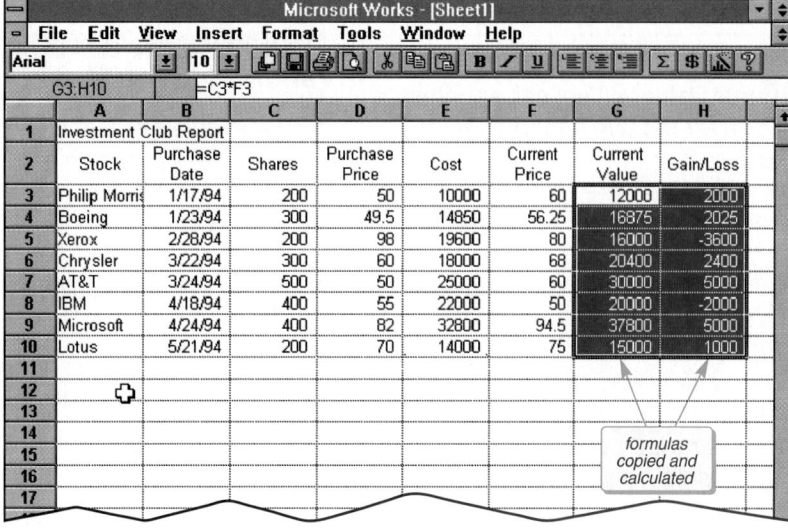

To remove the highlight, click any cell. Notice that when you copy the cells, Works performs the arithmetic in the formulas as part of the copying process, and then displays the results in the cells.

Entering Portfolio Performance Data

The final data entry requirement for the spreadsheet in Project 5 is to enter the Portfolio Performance data. This data includes the Total Current Value of all stocks, the Total Cost of all stocks, the Net Gain/Loss of the stocks, and the Percentage Gain/Loss.

To calculate the Total Current Value of all stocks, use the SUM function to sum the values in the range G3:G10. Similarly, use the SUM function to sum the values in the range E3:E10 to obtain the Total Cost. You obtain the Net Gain/Loss by calculating Total Current Value minus Total Cost (=C12-C13). Finally, determine the Percentage Gain/Loss by dividing the Net Gain/Loss by the Total Cost (=C14/C13).

Perform the following steps to enter the Portfolio Performance titles and the accompanying formulas.

TO ENTER TITLES AND FORMULAS ▼

STEP 1 ▶

Highlight cell A11 and enter Portfolio Performance. **Then, enter** Total Current Value **in cell A12,** Total Cost **in cell A13,** Net Gain/Loss **in cell A14, and** Percentage Gain/Loss **in cell A15 (Figure 5-27).**

FIGURE 5-27

	A	B	C	D	E	F	G	H
1	Investment Club Report							
2	Stock	Purchase Date	Shares	Purchase Price	Cost	Current Price	Current Value	Gain/Loss
3	Philip Morris	1/17/94	200	50	10000	60	12000	2000
4	Boeing	1/23/94	300	49.5	14850	56.25	16875	2025
5	Xerox	2/28/94	200	98	19600	80	16000	-3600
6	Chrysler	3/22/94	300	60	18000	68	20400	2400
7	AT&T	3/24/94	500	50	25000	60	30000	5000
8	IBM	4/18/94	400	55	22000	50	20000	-2000
9	Microsoft	4/24/94	400	82	32800	94.5	37800	5000
10	Lotus	5/21/94	200	70	14000	75	15000	1000
11	Portfolio Performance							
12	Total Current Value				titles entered			
13	Total Cost							
14	Net Gain/Loss							
15	Percentage Gain/Loss							
16								
17								

STEP 2 ▶

Highlight cell C12 where the Total Current Value will appear, and then click the Autosum button on the Toolbar.

When you click the Autosum button, Works chooses the most likely values to sum. In Figure 5-28, Works chose the range C3:C11 because those cells are immediately above cell C12. This is incorrect, however, because the chosen range contains Shares purchased, not Current Values.

FIGURE 5-28

STEP 3 ▶

Highlight the correct range by dragging cells G3:G10.

When you highlight the range G3:G10, Works places the range in the SUM function (Figure 5-29).

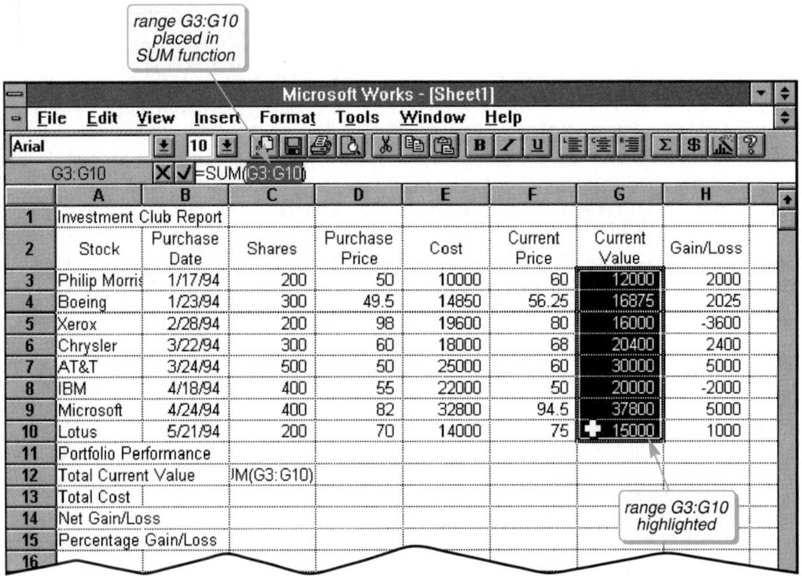

FIGURE 5-29

STEP 4 ▶

Click the Enter box, press the ENTER key, or click the Autosum button a second time.

Works enters the SUM function into cell C12, calculates the sum, and displays the sum in the cell (Figure 5-30).

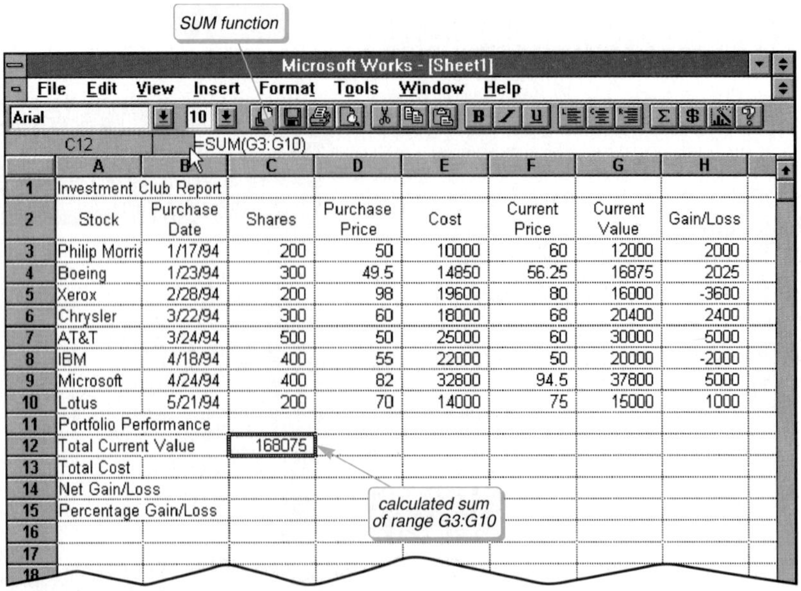

FIGURE 5-30

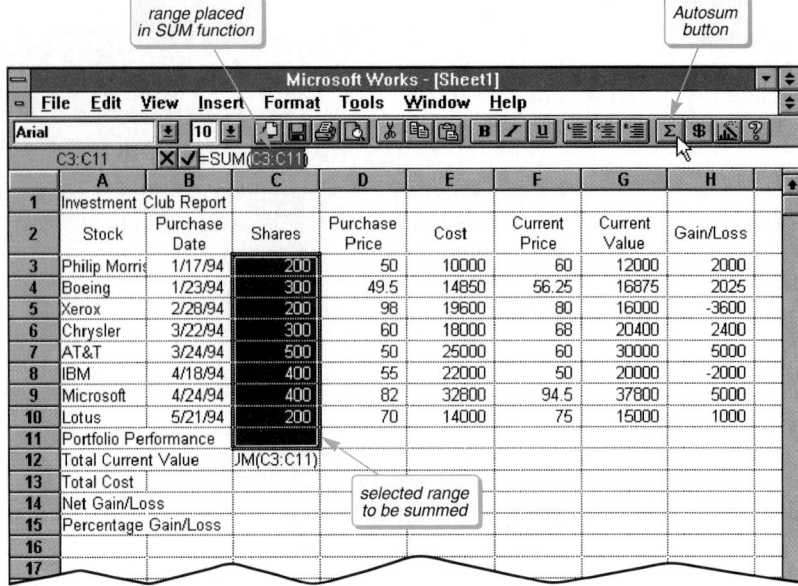

STEP 5 ▶

Highlight cell C13, click the Autosum button on the Toolbar, and highlight the range E3:E10.

The SUM function displays in cell C13 and in the formula bar (Figure 5-31). The range of cells highlighted (E3:E10) contains the values to add to obtain the Total Cost.

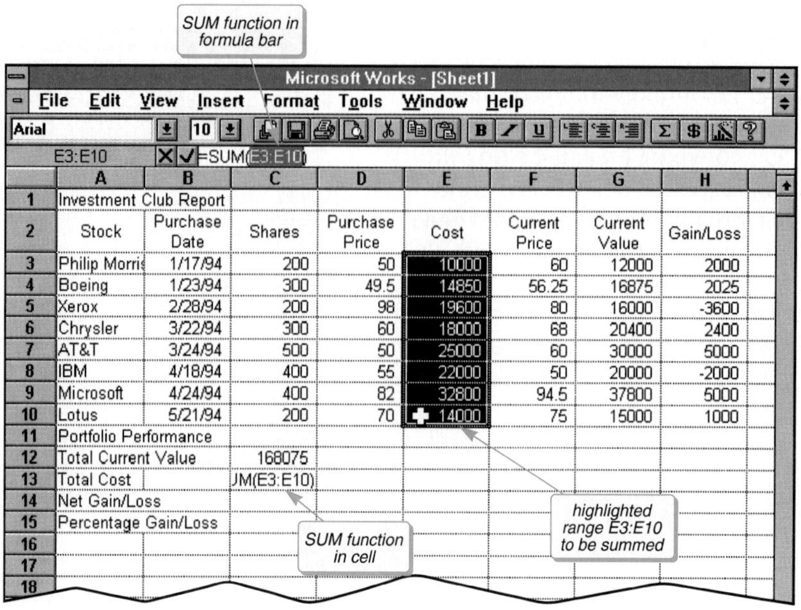

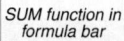

SUM function in formula bar

SUM function in cell

highlighted range E3:E10 to be summed

FIGURE 5-31

STEP 6 ▶

Click the Enter box, press the ENTER key, or click the Autosum button a second time.

Works enters the SUM function into cell C13, calculates the sum of cells E3:E10, and displays the sum in the cell (Figure 5-32).

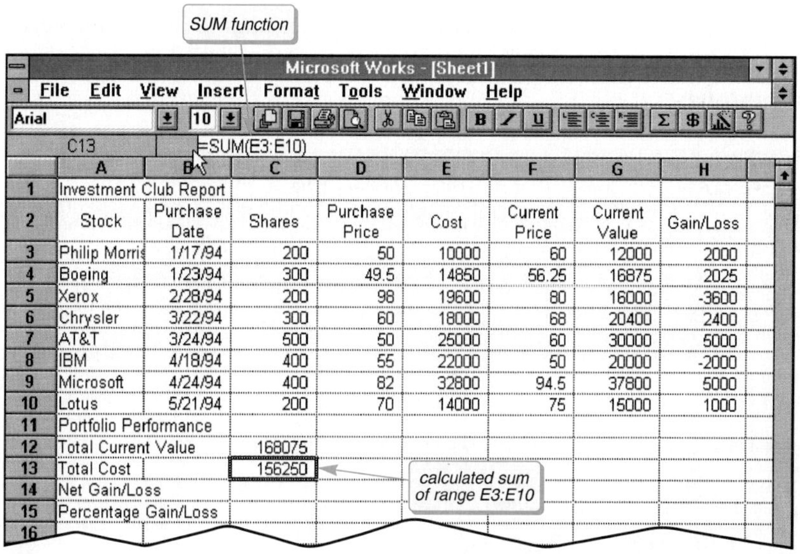

SUM function

calculated sum of range E3:E10

FIGURE 5-32

STEP 7 ▶

Enter the formula for Net Gain/Loss by first highlighting cell C14 and typing an equal sign (=). Then, highlight cell C12, type the subtraction operator (–), highlight cell C13, and click the Enter box or press the ENTER key.

Works enters the net gain/loss in cell C14 (Figure 5-33).

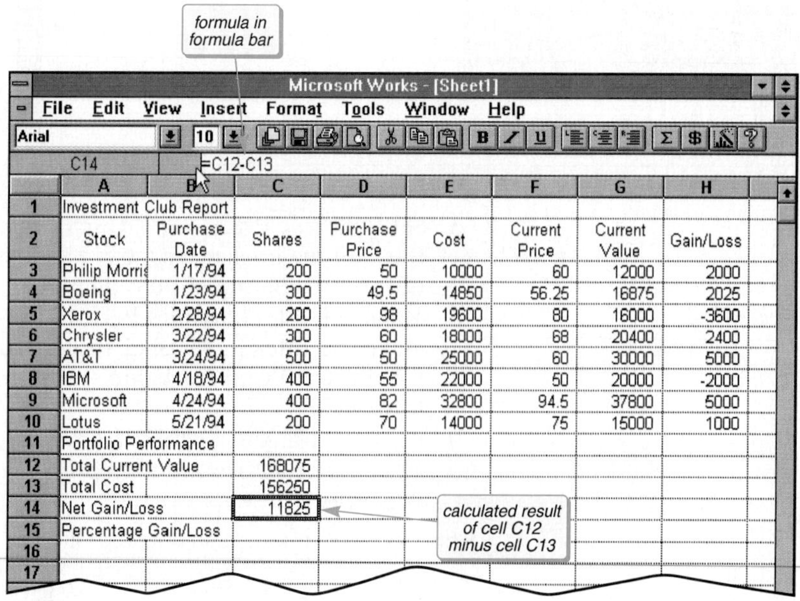

formula in formula bar

calculated result of cell C12 minus cell C13

FIGURE 5-33

STEP 8 ▶

Enter the formula for Percentage
Gain/Loss by first highlighting cell
C15 and typing an equal sign (=).
Then, highlight cell C14, type the
division operator (/), highlight cell
C13, and click the Enter box or
press the ENTER key.

*Works enters the percentage
gain/loss in cell C15 (Figure 5-34).*

FIGURE 5-34

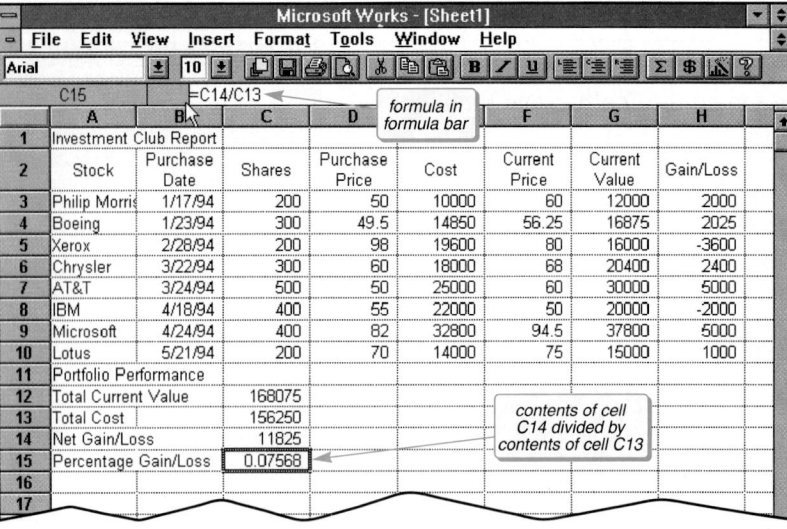

The spreadsheet data is now complete. All the data and formulas are contained within the spreadsheet.

FIGURE 5-35

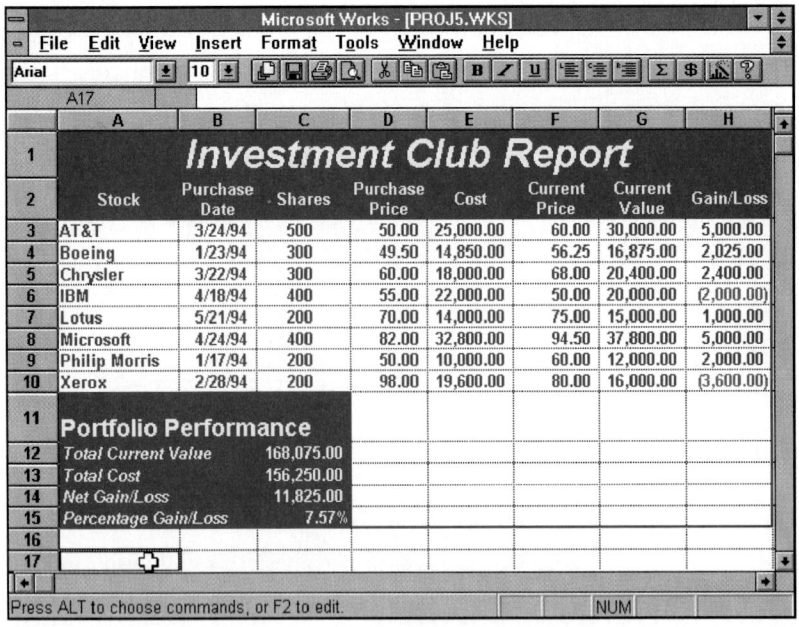

▶ FORMATTING THE SPREADSHEET

The next task is to format the
spreadsheet. The formatted
spreadsheet is shown in
Figure 5-35. The requirements to
complete the formatting are as
follows:

1. Make the entire spreadsheet
bold.
2. Make the spreadsheet title 24
point Arial italic font. Center
the title across the columns.
3. Set the following column
widths: A=14; B=9; C=11;
D=9; E=10; F=10; G=10; and
H=10.
4. Center the number of shares
in column C.
5. Set Purchase Price, Cost, Current Price, Current Value, and Gain/Loss to
the Comma format with two decimal positions. Negative amounts in the
Gain/Loss column should display in red.
6. Make the title, Portfolio Performance, 14 point.
7. Make the titles in rows 12 through 15 in column A italic.
8. Set the Total Current Value, Total Cost and Net Gain/Loss to the Comma
format.
9. Set Percentage Gain/Loss to the Percent format.
10. Place a border around the spreadsheet. Format the spreadsheet in color as
illustrated.

The steps to accomplish this formatting are explained on the following pages.

Making the Entire Spreadsheet Bold

In Project 5, the entire spreadsheet displays in bold. Complete the following step to accomplish this task.

TO MAKE ENTIRE SPREADSHEET BOLD ▼

STEP 1 ▶

Position the mouse pointer in cell A1 and click the left mouse button. Move the mouse pointer to cell H15, hold down the SHIFT key, and click left mouse button. Click the Bold button on the Toolbar.

click here to highlight the entire spreadsheet

Cells A1:H15 are highlighted. When you click the Bold button, Works changes the high-lighted cells to the bold format (Figure 5-36).

the entire spreadsheet displays in bold

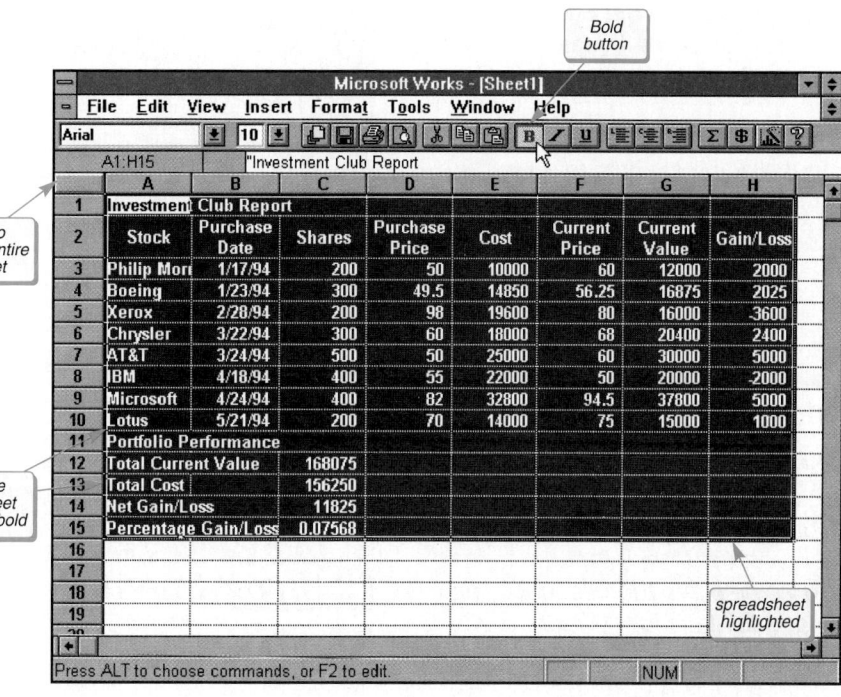

FIGURE 5-36

Works provides a variety of methods to highlight an entire spreadsheet. In addition to holding down the SHIFT key and clicking the upper left and lower right cells of a range, as shown in Figure 5-36, you can highlight the data in the entire spreadsheet by dragging from cell A1 through cell H15. You can highlight the entire spreadsheet, including all blank cells, by choosing the Select All command from the Edit menu or by clicking the box above row 1 and to the left of column A (see Figure 5-36).

Formatting the Spreadsheet Title

The spreadsheet title is to display in 24 point Arial italic font. The title is to be centered across the columns. Complete the steps on the next two pages to accomplish these tasks.

TO FORMAT THE SPREADSHEET TITLE ▼

STEP 1 ▶

Highlight the spreadsheet title by positioning the mouse pointer in cell A1 and clicking the left mouse button. Click the Font Size box arrow, scroll down if necessary, and point to 24 in the drop-down list box.

Cell A1 is highlighted and the mouse pointer points to 24 in the Font Size drop-down list box (Figure 5-37).

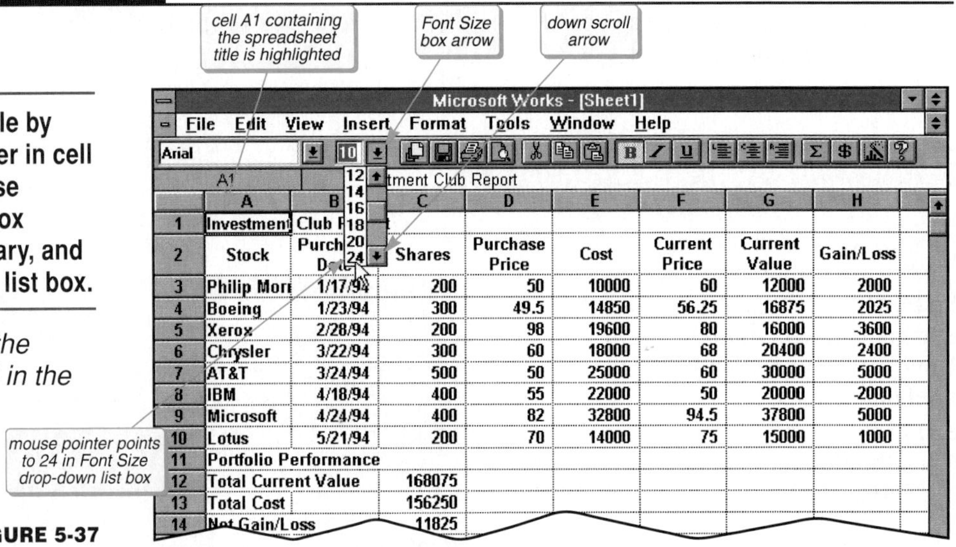

FIGURE 5-37

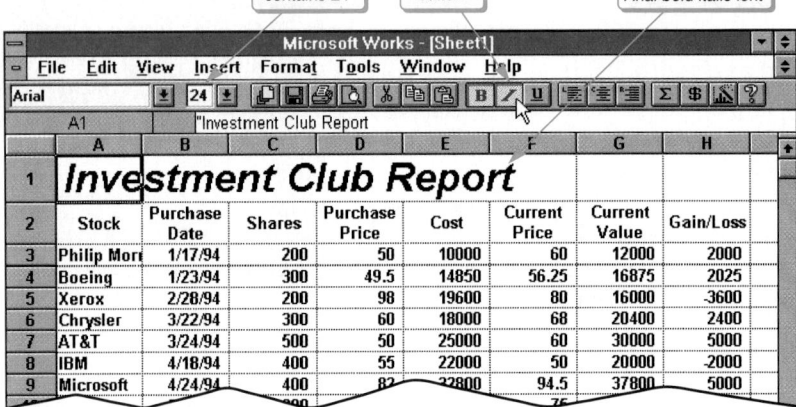

STEP 2 ▶

Select the number 24 by clicking the left mouse button. Then click the Italic button on the Toolbar.

Works displays the title in 24 point Arial bold italic font (Figure 5-38).

FIGURE 5-38

STEP 3 ▶

Highlight cells A1 through H1. Select the Format menu and point to the Alignment command.

*Cells A1 through H1 are highlighted, the Format menu displays, and the mouse pointer points to the **Alignment command** (Figure 5-39).*

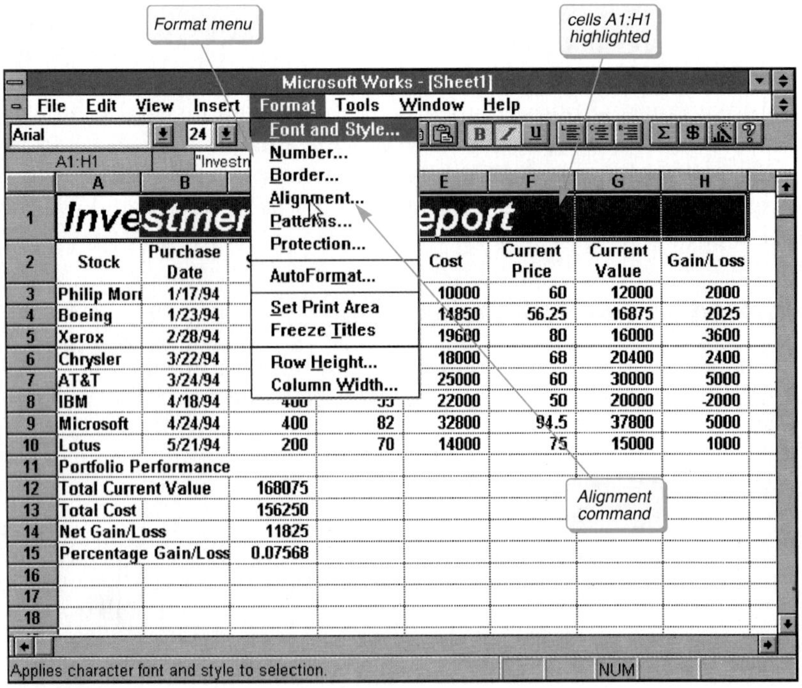

FIGURE 5-39

STEP 4 ▶

Choose the Alignment command from the Format menu. When the Alignment dialog box displays, select the Center across selection option button in the Alignment area and then point to the OK button.

The Alignment dialog box displays, the Center across selection option button is selected, and the mouse pointer points to the OK button (Figure 5-40).

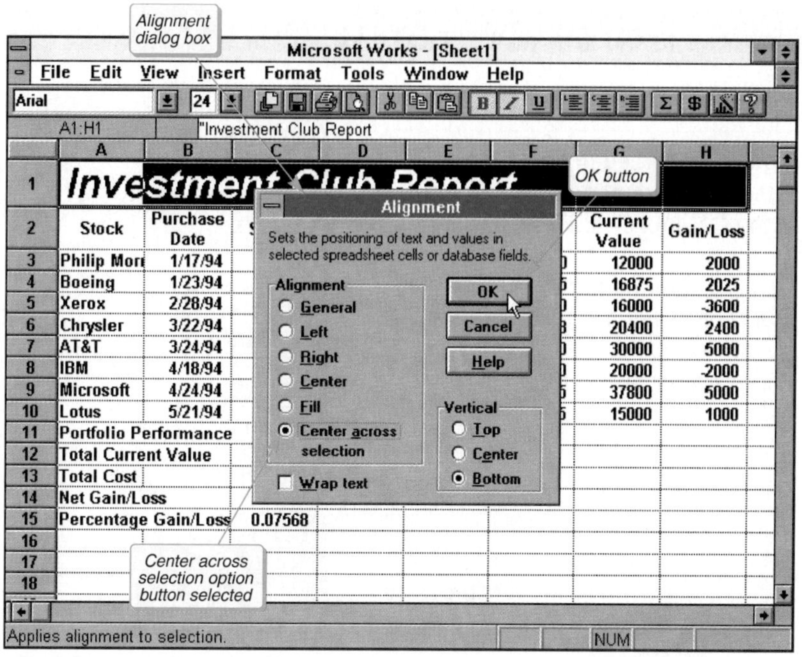

FIGURE 5-40

STEP 5 ▶

Choose the OK button. Then click any cell to remove the highlight.

Works displays the spreadsheet title centered across the columns A through H of the spreadsheet (Figure 5-41). Notice that the vertical gridlines do not display in the area containing the title.

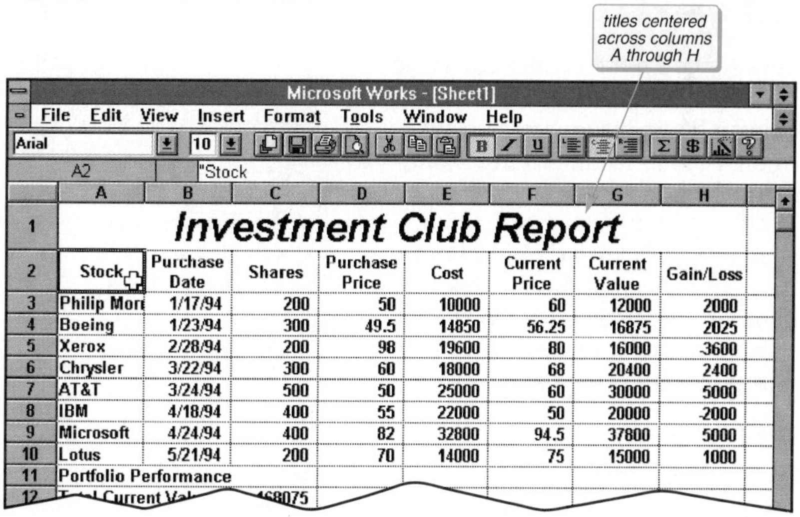

FIGURE 5-41

The column titles were formatted when the titles were entered into the spreadsheet; therefore, the next step is to format the individual columns.

Changing Column Widths and Centering Data in a Column

You change the width of columns for a variety of reasons. You may want to change column width to improve the readability of the spreadsheet, to insure that the columns are wide enough to properly display data after formatting, and sometimes so the entire spreadsheet will display on a single screen.

In Project 5, the width of column A must be increased so the names of all stocks will fully display in the column A. Other columns are changed according to the specifications on page W5.20. Changing column widths is explained in the steps on the next two pages. In addition, the steps also explain how to center data in a selected column.

TO CHANGE COLUMN WIDTHS AND CENTER DATA IN A COLUMN ▼

STEP 1 ▶

Highlight any cell in column A, select the Format menu, and point to the Column Width command.

Cell A2 is highlighted, the Format menu displays, and the mouse pointer points to the Column Width command (Figure 5-42).

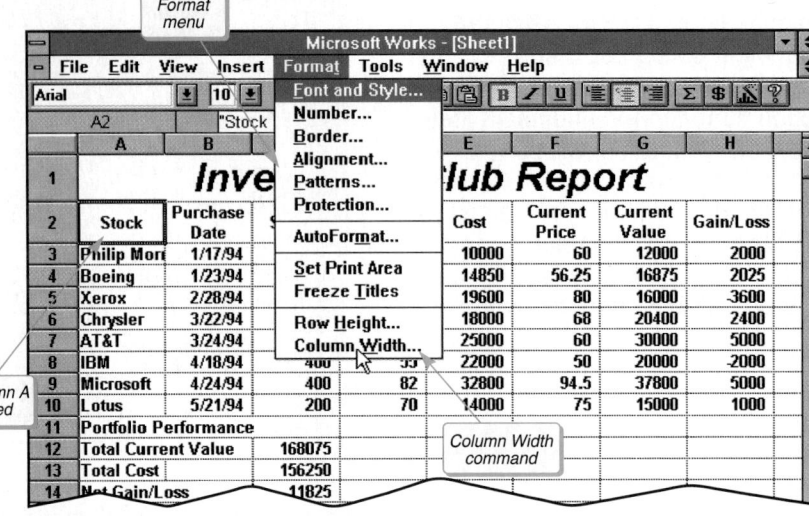

FIGURE 5-42

STEP 2 ▶

Choose the Column Width command from the Format menu. When the Column Width dialog box displays, type 14 in the Width text box. Point to the OK button.

Works displays the Column Width dialog box (Figure 5-43). The number, 14, displays in the Width text box and the mouse pointer points to the OK button.

FIGURE 5-43

STEP 3 ▶

Choose the OK button in the Column Width dialog box.

Works changes the width of column A to 14, and all the stock names fit in the column (Figure 5-44).

STEP 4 ▶

Using the techniques previously explained, change the widths of the remaining columns in the spreadsheet to the sizes specified on page W5.20.

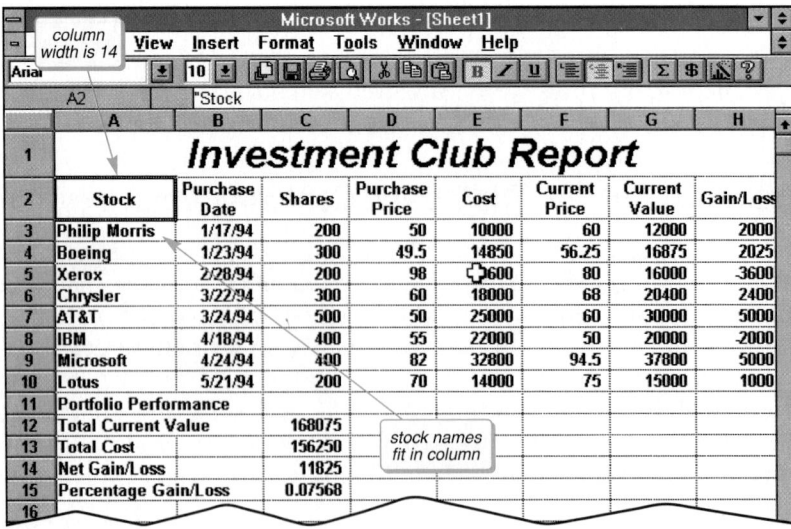

FIGURE 5-44

STEP 5 ▶

To center the number of shares in column C, highlight the range C3:C10 and click the Center Align button on the Toolbar.

Works centers the number of shares in column C (Figure 5-45).

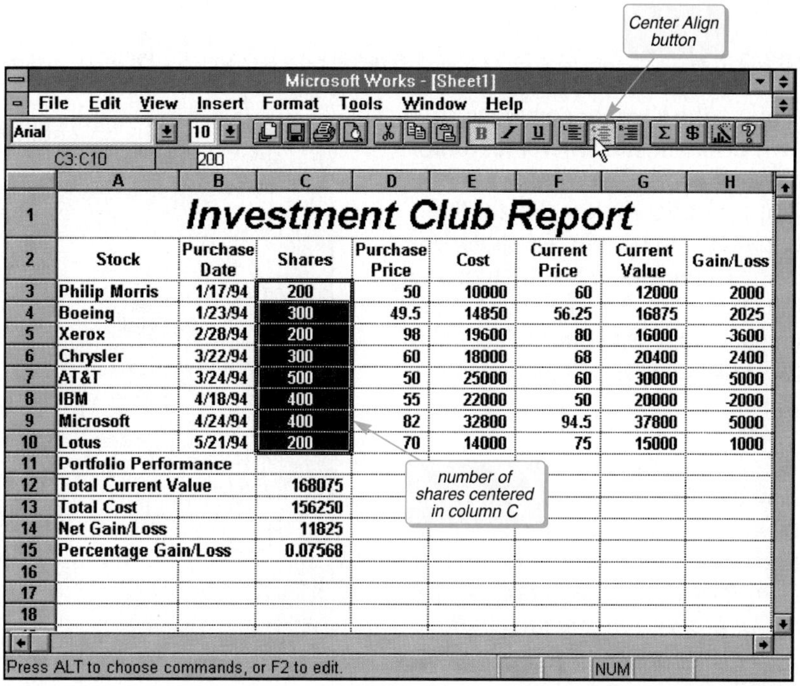

FIGURE 5-45

Formatting Data with the Comma Format

You should now format the numeric data containing dollar amounts in the Comma format. The Comma format will place a comma every third position to the left of the decimal point, and will allow you to specify the number of positions to the right of the decimal point. In addition, any negative numbers should display in red. The following steps explain how to format selected cells using the Comma format.

TO USE THE COMMA FORMAT ▼

STEP 1 ▶

Highlight the range of cells D3:H10. These are the cells you want to format with the Comma format. Select the Format menu and point to the Number command.

*Cells D3:H10 are highlighted, the Format menu displays, and the mouse pointer points to the **Number command** (Figure 5-46).*

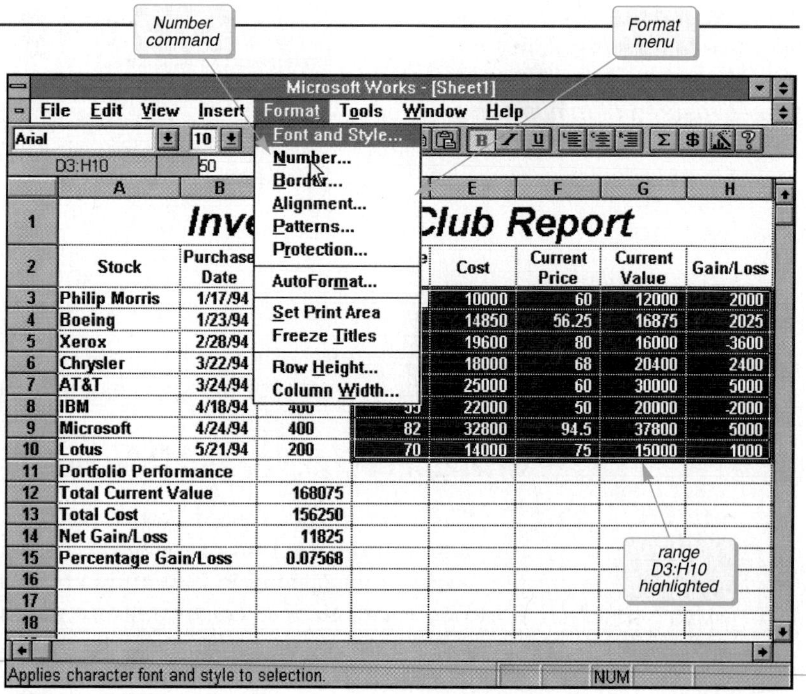

FIGURE 5-46

STEP 2 ▶

Choose the Number command from the Format menu. When the Number dialog box displays, select the Comma option button. Select the Negative numbers in red check box in the Comma area and then point to the OK button. The number 2 should display in the Number of decimals text box because 2 is the default value.

The Number dialog box displays (Figure 5-47). The Comma option button is selected, and an X displays in the Negative numbers in red check box. A sample of the format displays in the Sample area. The mouse pointer points to the OK button.

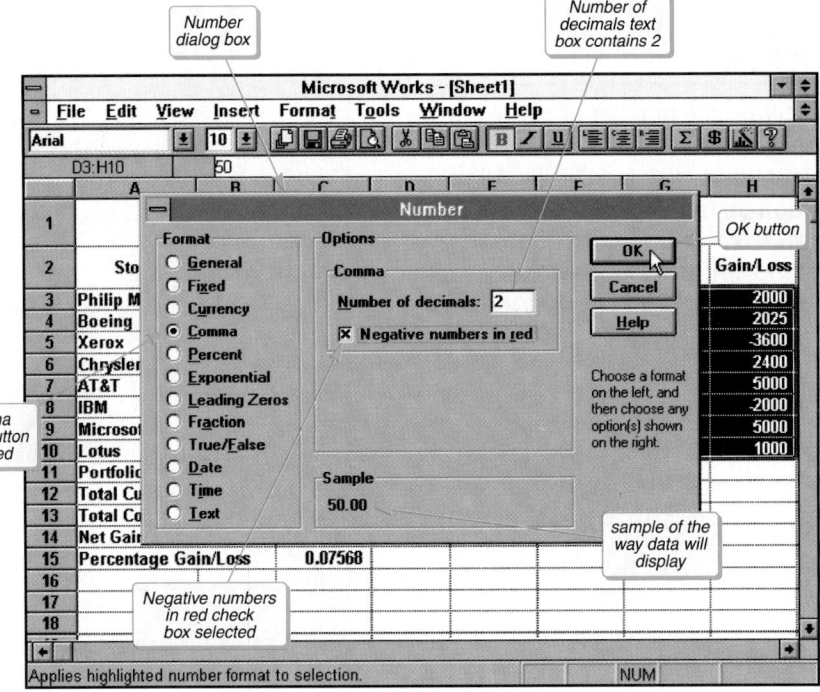

FIGURE 5-47

STEP 3 ▶

Choose the OK button in the Number dialog box. Click any cell to remove the highlight.

Works formats the highlighted range with the Comma format (Figure 5-48). The Comma format displays numeric values with two digits to the right of the decimal point. Notice that Works displays negative values in column H (Gain/Loss) in red with parentheses instead of minus signs.

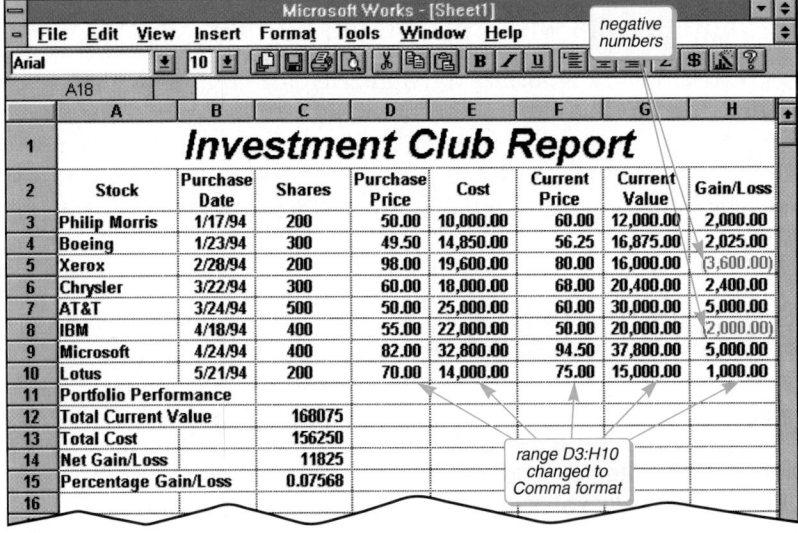

FIGURE 5-48

The first portion of the spreadsheet is now formatted.

Changing Font Size and Row Height

The next step is to format the section of the spreadsheet labeled Portfolio Performance. In this section of the spreadsheet, the words Portfolio Performance display in 14 point Arial bold font and extra blank space appears above the words Portfolio Performance. This requires changing the font size and the row height. To accomplish these tasks, complete the following steps.

TO CHANGE FONT SIZE AND ROW HEIGHT ▼

STEP 1 ▶

Highlight cell A11, point to the Font Size box arrow and click. Point to 14 in the Font Size drop-down list box and click. Position the mouse pointer on the border line that separates row number 11 and row number 12 in the row headings on the left side of the spreadsheet.

The words, Portfolio Performance, display in 14 point Arial bold font (Figure 5-49). The mouse pointer becomes the shape of an equal sign with upward and downward pointing arrows. The word ADJUST displays below the mouse pointer.

14 displays in Font Size box

mouse pointer positioned to adjust row height

Portfolio Performance changed to 14 point

Microsoft Works - [Sheet1]

File Edit View Insert Format Tools Window Help

Arial   14

A11   "Portfolio Performance

Investment Club Report

	Stock	Purchase Date	Shares	Purchase Price	Cost	Current Price	Current Value	Gain/Loss
3	Philip Morris	1/17/94	200	50.00	10,000.00	60.00	12,000.00	2,000.00
4	Boeing	1/23/94	300	49.50	14,850.00	56.25	16,875.00	2,025.00
5	Xerox	2/28/94	200	98.00	19,600.00	80.00	16,000.00	(3,600.00)
6	Chrysler	3/22/94	300	60.00	18,000.00	68.00	20,400.00	2,400.00
7	AT&T	3/24/94	500	50.00	25,000.00	60.00	30,000.00	5,000.00
8	IBM	4/18/94	400	55.00	22,000.00	50.00	20,000.00	(2,000.00)
9	Microsoft	4/24/94	400	82.00	32,800.00	94.50	37,800.00	5,000.00
10	Lotus	5/21/94	200	70.00	14,000.00	75.00	15,000.00	1,000.00
11	**Portfolio Performance**							
12	Total Current Value		168075					
13	Total Cost		156250					
14	Net Gain/Loss		11825					
15	Percentage Gain/Loss		0.07568					

Press ALT to choose commands, or F2 to edit.   NUM

FIGURE 5-49

STEP 2 ▶

Drag the mouse pointer down the height of one row. Release the left mouse button.

Works increases the height of the row, causing a blank space to appear above the words, Portfolio Performance (Figure 5-50).

blank space above title

row height increased

Microsoft Works - [Sheet1]

File Edit View Insert Format Tools Window Help

Arial   14

A11   "Portfolio Performance

Investment Club Report

	Stock	Purchase Date	Shares	Purchase Price	Cost	Current Price	Current Value	Gain/Loss
3	Philip Morris	1/17/94	200	50.00	10,000.00	60.00	12,000.00	2,000.00
4	Boeing	1/23/94	300	49.50	14,850.00	56.25	16,875.00	2,025.00
5	Xerox	2/28/94	200	98.00	19,600.00	80.00	16,000.00	(3,600.00)
6	Chrysler	3/22/94	300	60.00	18,000.00	68.00	20,400.00	2,400.00
7	AT&T	3/24/94	500	50.00	25,000.00	60.00	30,000.00	5,000.00
8	IBM	4/18/94	400	55.00	22,000.00	50.00	20,000.00	(2,000.00)
9	Microsoft	4/24/94	400	82.00	32,800.00	94.50	37,800.00	5,000.00
10	Lotus	5/21/94	200	70.00	14,000.00	75.00	15,000.00	1,000.00
11	**Portfolio Performance**							
12	Total Current Value		168075					
13	Total Cost		156250					
14	Net Gain/Loss		11825					
15	Percentage Gain/Loss		0.07568					

Press ALT to choose commands, or F2 to edit.   NUM

FIGURE 5-50

The formatting of the title of this portion of the spreadsheet is now complete.

Font Style, Comma Format, and Percent Format

To complete the formatting of the spreadsheet, you must change the titles in rows 12 through 15 of column A to italic, format the numbers in cells C12:C14 using the Comma format, and change the number in cell C15 to Percent format. Complete the following step to accomplish these tasks.

TO USE ITALIC STYLE AND NUMBER AND PERCENT FORMATS ▼

STEP 1 ▶

Highlight the range A12:A15 and click the Italic button on the Toolbar. Highlight the range C12:C14. Select the Format menu and choose the Number command. In the Number dialog box, select the Comma option button and then choose the OK button. Highlight cell C15. Select the Format menu and choose the Number command. In the Number dialog box, select the Percent option button and choose the OK button.

The Portfolio Performance section of the spreadsheet is now formatted (Figure 5-51). Notice in cell C15 that when you select the Percent format, the number displays with two digits to the right of the decimal point and Works rounds the number; that is, 0.07568 displays as 7.57%.

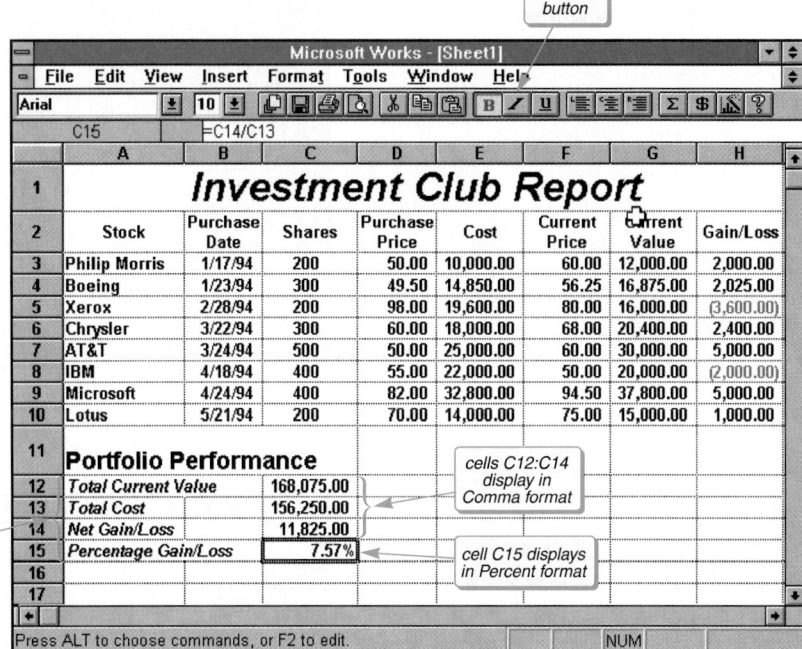

FIGURE 5-51

▶ **SAVING THE SPREADSHEET**

he data in the spreadsheet is complete. You should save the spreadsheet on disk. To save the spreadsheet on drive A using the filename PROJ5, perform the following steps.

TO SAVE THE WORKSHEET

Step 1: Click the Save button on the Toolbar.
Step 2: When the Save As dialog box displays, type `proj5`.
Step 3: Select drive a: from the Drives drop-down list box.
Step 4: Choose the OK button in the Save As dialog box.

▶ ADDING COLOR TO THE SPREADSHEET

T he final task in formatting the spreadsheet is to add color to selected portions of the spreadsheet. Color greatly enhances the impact a spreadsheet can have on those viewing it. In Project 5, the report and column titles are displayed in yellow in cells that are blue (see Figure 5-35 on page W5.20). The stock names and other values in the spreadsheet display in blue, and the Portfolio Performance section matches the spreadsheet title and column titles section. The entire spreadsheet is surrounded by a blue border.

Adding Color to the Spreadsheet Title and Column Titles

In Project 5, the spreadsheet title and the column titles display in yellow. The cells in which the spreadsheet title and the column titles display are blue. Complete the following steps to color the spreadsheet title, column titles, and cells.

TO ADD COLOR TO THE SPREADSHEET TITLE AND COLUMN TITLES ▼

STEP 1 ▶

Highlight cells A1:H2. Select the Format menu and point to the Font and Style command.

*Cells A1:H2 are highlighted, the Format menu is selected, and the mouse pointer points to the **Font and Style command** (Figure 5-52).*

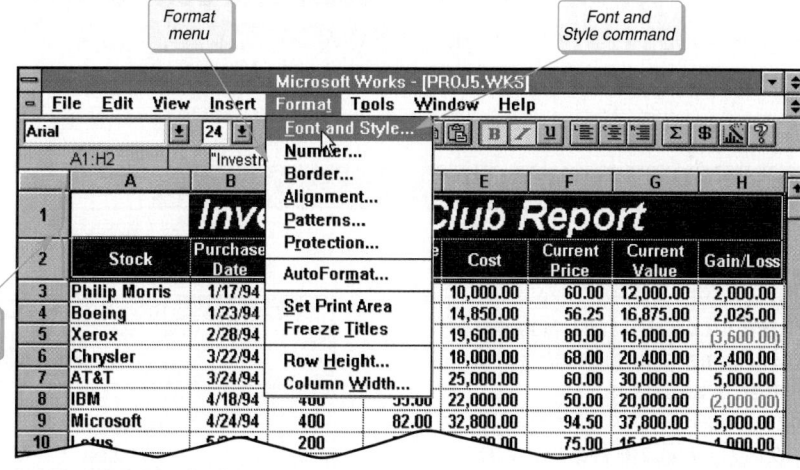

FIGURE 5-52

STEP 2 ▶

Choose the Font and Style command from the Format menu. When the Font and Style dialog box displays, click the Color drop-down list box arrow, scroll down if necessary until Yellow displays, and point to Yellow.

The Font and Style dialog box displays (Figure 5-53). The Color drop-down list box displays. The mouse pointer points to Yellow.

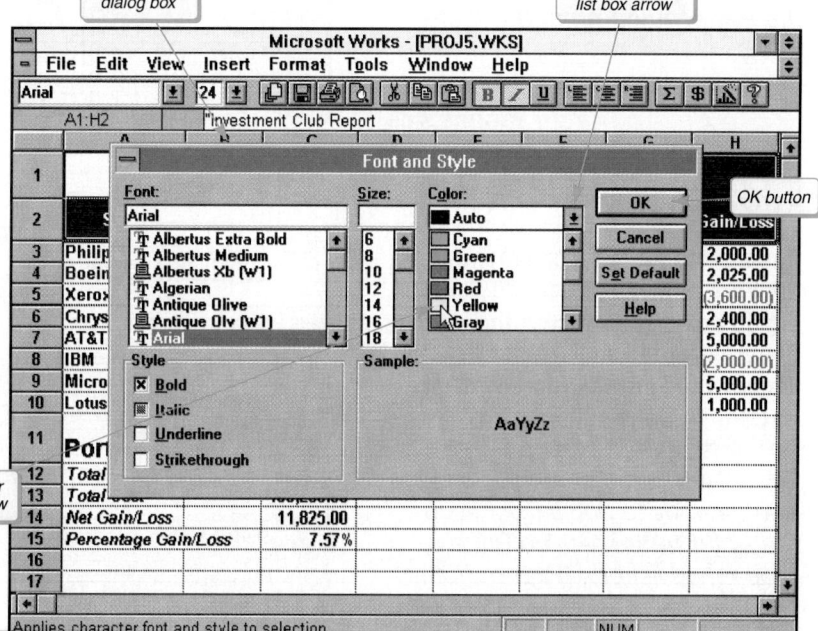

FIGURE 5-53

STEP 3 ▶

Select the color Yellow by clicking the left mouse button. Choose the OK button in the Font and Style dialog box. Click any cell to remove the highlight.

The spreadsheet displays with the spreadsheet title and the column titles in yellow (Figure 5-54).

FIGURE 5-54

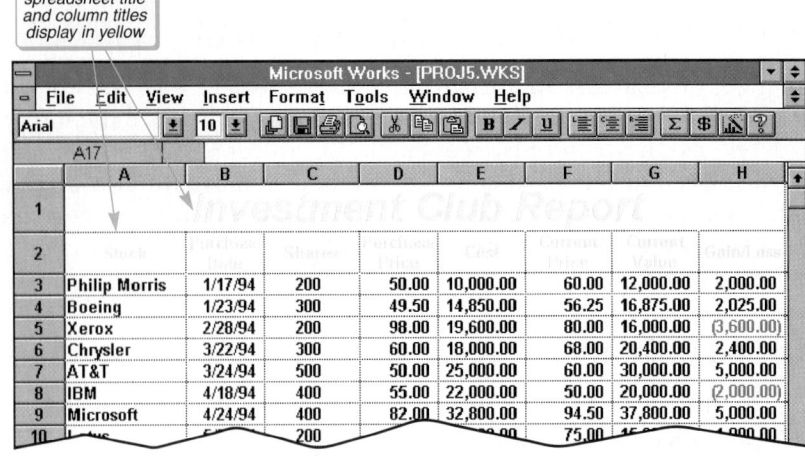

Adding a Pattern and Color to Cells

The next task is to select a pattern and color for cells A1:H2. Perform the following steps to complete this task.

TO USE THE PATTERN COMMAND TO COLOR CELLS ▼

STEP 1 ▶

Highlight cells A1:H2. Select the Format menu and point to the Patterns command.

*Cells A1:H2 are highlighted, the Format menu displays, and the mouse pointer points to the **Patterns command** (Figure 5-55).*

FIGURE 5-55

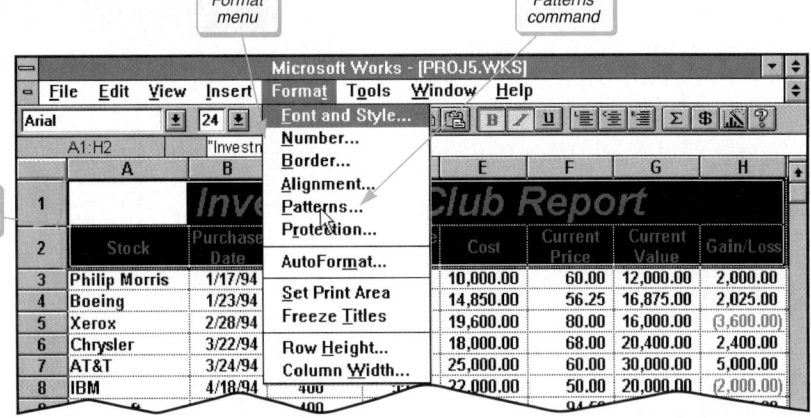

STEP 2 ▶

Choose the Patterns command from the Format menu. When the Patterns dialog box displays, click the Pattern drop-down list box arrow to display the Pattern drop-down list box. Point to the solid pattern.

*The Patterns dialog box displays and the mouse pointer points to the **solid pattern** in the Pattern drop-down list box (Figure 5-56).*

FIGURE 5-56

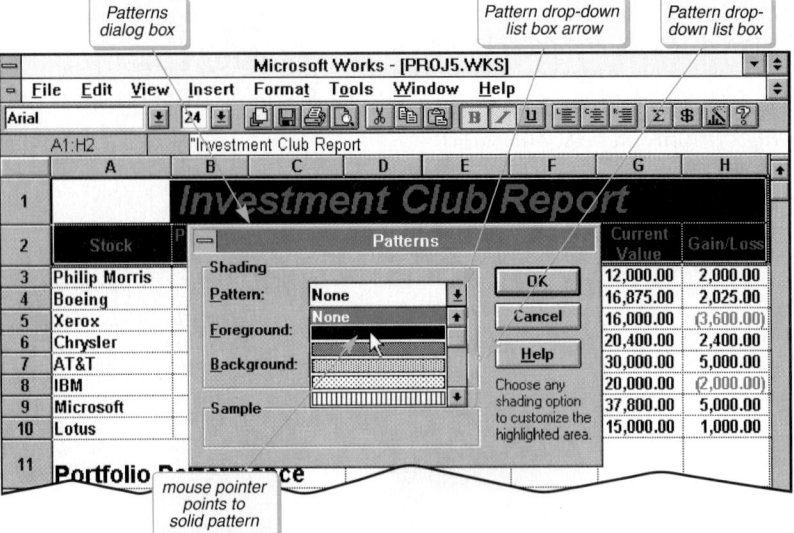

STEP 3 ▶

Select the solid pattern. Click the Foreground drop-down list box arrow. When the drop-down list box displays, point to Blue.

The mouse pointer points to Blue in the Foreground drop-down list box (Figure 5-57).

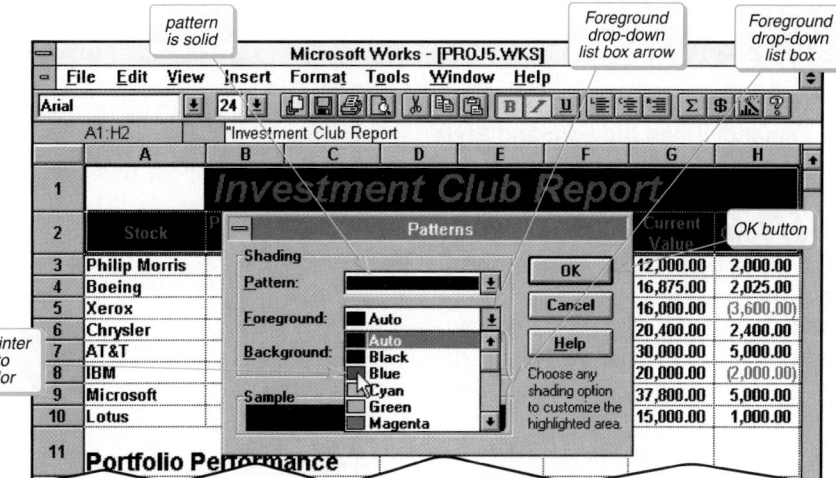

FIGURE 5-57

STEP 4 ▶

Select Blue, and then choose the OK button in the Patterns dialog box. Click any cell to remove the highlight.

Works displays the titles in yellow and the cell color is solid blue (Figure 5-58).

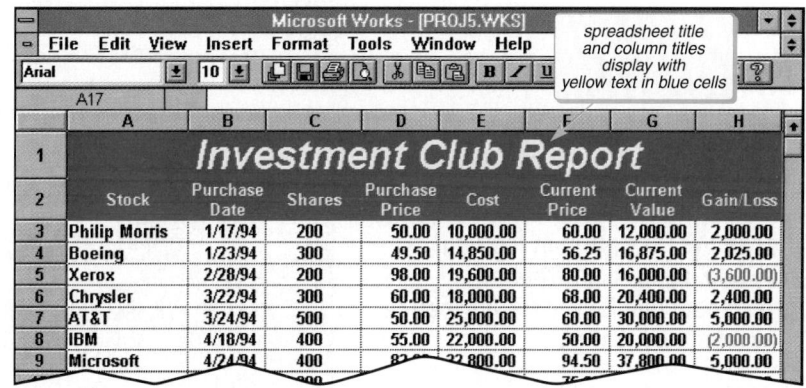

FIGURE 5-58

Displaying Spreadsheet Entries in Color

In Project 5, the text, date, and numbers in rows 3 through 10 display in blue. Perform the following steps to display the entries in blue.

TO DISPLAY SPREADSHEET ENTRIES IN COLOR ▼

STEP 1 ▶

Highlight the range of cells A3:H10. Then, select the Format menu and point to the Font and Style command.

Cells A3:H10 are highlighted, the Format menu displays, and the mouse pointer points to the Font and Style command (Figure 5-59).

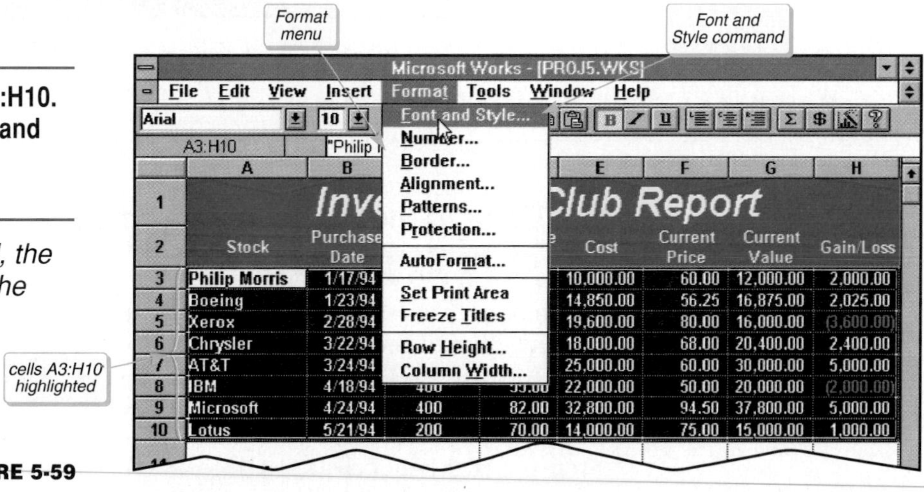

FIGURE 5-59

STEP 2 ▶

Choose the Font and Style command. When the Font and Style dialog box displays, click the Color drop-down list box arrow. When the drop-down list box displays, select the color Blue. Then, point to the OK button.

The Font and Style dialog box displays (Figure 5-60). Blue displays in the Color drop-down list box and in the Sample area. The mouse pointer points to the OK button.

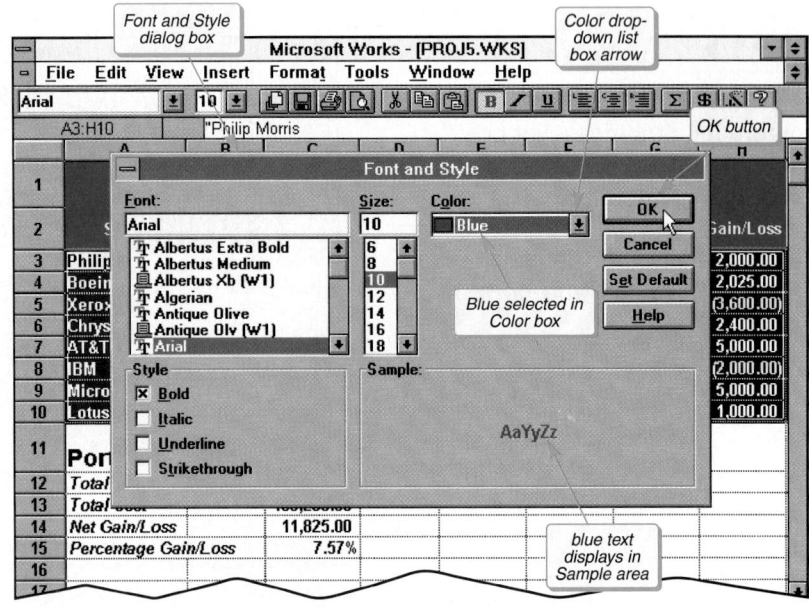

FIGURE 5-60

STEP 3 ▶

Choose the OK button in the Font and Style dialog box. When the spreadsheet displays, click any cell to remove the highlight.

Works displays the text and numbers in the range A3:H10 in blue (Figure 5-61). The negative numbers remain red.

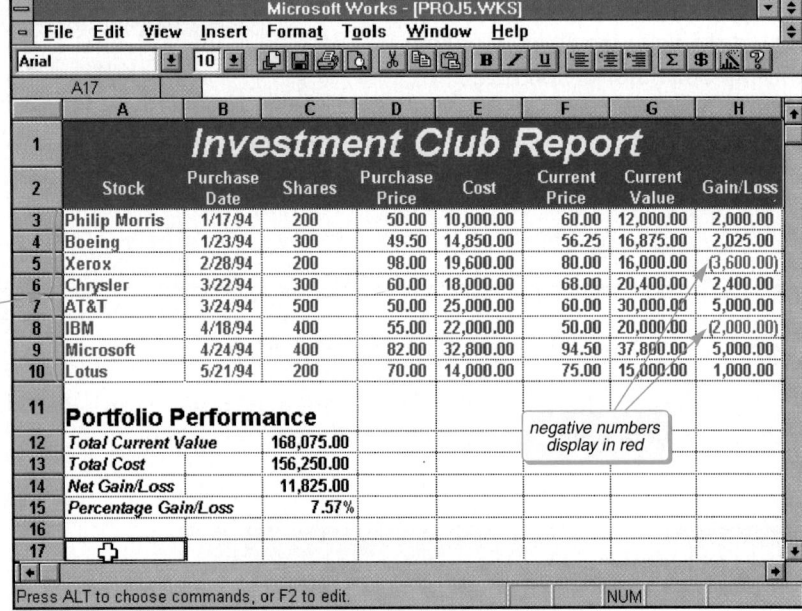

FIGURE 5-61

Adding Color to the Portfolio Performance Section of the Spreadsheet

The next step is to add color to the Portfolio Performance section of the spreadsheet. To add the color, perform the following steps (see Figure 5-62).

TO ADD COLOR TO THE SPREADSHEET

Step 1: Highlight cells A11:C15.
Step 2: Select the Format menu.

Step 3: Choose the Font and Style command.

Step 4: Click the Color drop-down list box arrow.

Step 5: If necessary, scroll down until Yellow displays. Select Yellow.

Step 6: Choose the OK button in the Font and Style dialog box.

Step 7: With cells A11:C15 highlighted, select the Format menu.

Step 8: Choose the Patterns command.

Step 9: Click the Pattern drop-down list box arrow and then select the solid pattern.

Step 10: Click the Foreground drop-down list box arrow.

Step 11: Select Blue from the Foreground drop-down list box.

Step 12: Choose the OK button in the Patterns dialog box.

Step 13: Click any cell to remove the highlight.

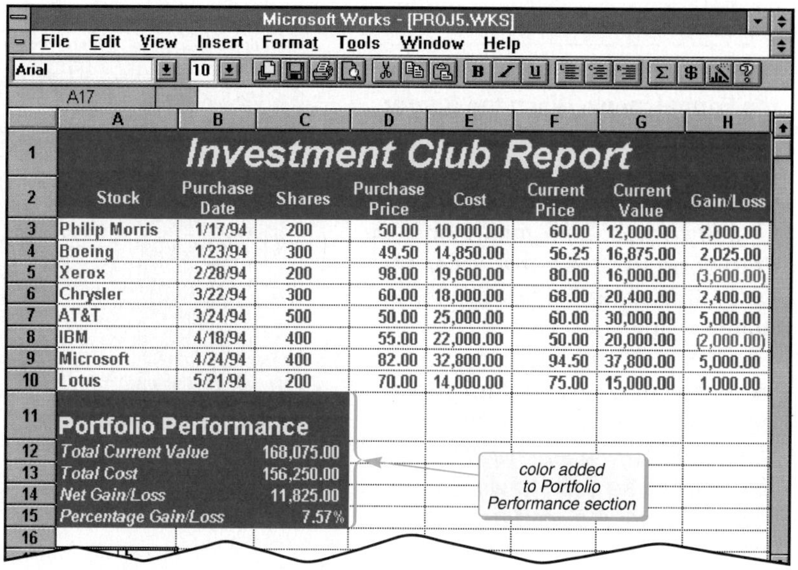

FIGURE 5-62

The Portfolio Performance section of the spreadsheet displays with yellow characters in blue cells (Figure 5-62).

Adding a Border

The final step in formatting the spreadsheet is to outline the entire spreadsheet with a blue border. Perform the following steps to complete this task.

TO ADD A BORDER TO A SPREADSHEET ▼

STEP 1 ▶

Highlight cells A1:H15, select the Format menu, and point to the Border command.

Cells A1:A15 are highlighted and the mouse pointer points to the Border command (Figure 5-63).

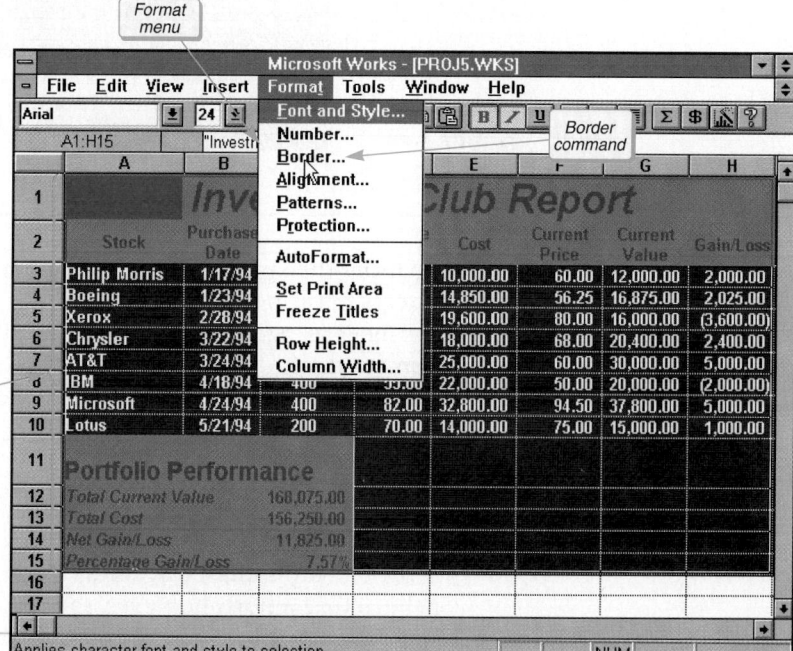

FIGURE 5-63

STEP 2 ▶

Choose the Border command from the Format menu. When the Border dialog box displays, select Outline in the Border area and then select the medium solid line box in the Line Style area. Click the Color drop-down list box arrow. When the Color drop-down list box displays, point to Blue.

Works displays the Border dialog box (Figure 5-64). The Outline selection contains a medium solid line. These selections will cause Works to place a medium solid line outline (border) around the entire highlighted range. The border will be blue.

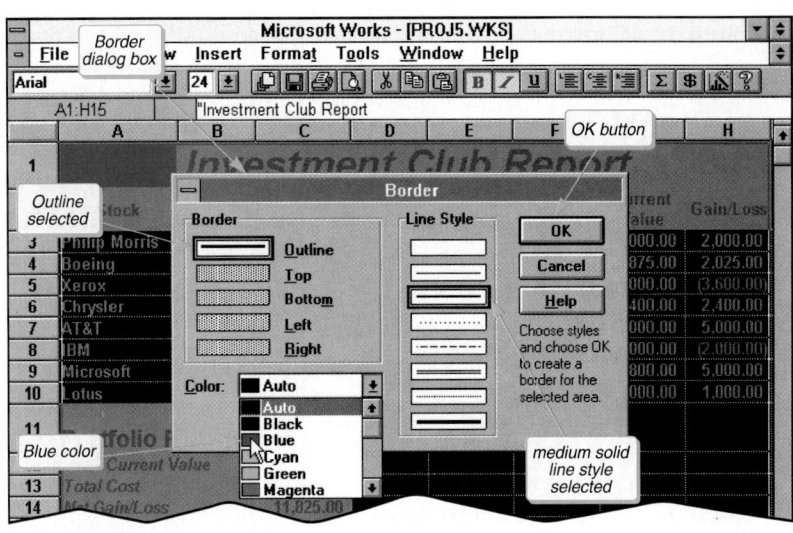

FIGURE 5-64

STEP 3 ▶

Select Blue in the Color drop-down list box. Choose the OK button in the Border dialog box. Click any cell to remove the highlight.

Works places the blue border around the highlighted range (Figure 5-65).

FIGURE 5-65

Formatting the spreadsheet is now complete. When you are sure the spreadsheet appears in proper format and color, it is recommended that you again save the spreadsheet using the same file name. You will now have a spreadsheet saved that is formatted with color.

▶ SORTING ROWS

 ou entered the stocks in the spreadsheet in the sequence of Purchase Date; that is, you entered the stock purchased first (Philip Morris), then the stock purchased second (Boeing), and so on.

For the actual report, however, the stocks appear in alphabetical sequence. This change is shown in Figure 5-66 on the next page.

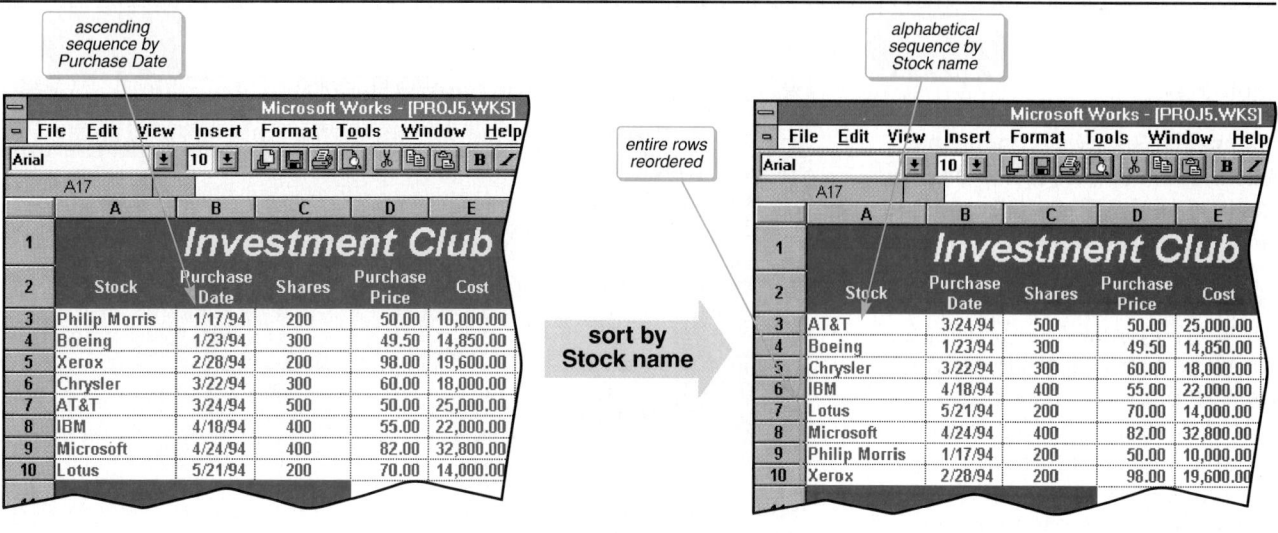

FIGURE 5-66

Notice that Works has not only placed the Stock names in alphabetical sequence, but the entire rows have been reordered as well.

Sorting means placing rows of spreadsheet data in a prescribed sequence. The sequence can be either **ascending**, meaning the records appear from lowest to highest, or **descending**, meaning the records appear from highest to lowest. Table 5-3 illustrates this concept when sorting the Stock names.

Notice that when the names are in ascending sequence, they move from the first letter of the alphabet (A) toward the last letter of the alphabet. In descending sequence, they move from the last of the alphabet to the first of the alphabet.

UNORDERED	ASCENDING	DESCENDING
Philip Morris	AT&T	Xerox
Boeing	Boeing	Philip Morris
Xerox	Chrysler	Microsoft
Chrysler	IBM	Lotus
AT&T	Lotus	IBM
IBM	Microsoft	Chrysler
Microsoft	Philip Morris	Boeing
Lotus	Xerox	AT&T

▶ **TABLE 5-3**

When you sort numbers, ascending sequence moves from the lowest number to the highest number, while a descending sequence moves from the highest number to the lowest number.

To sort the stocks in the Investment Club Report in ascending sequence by Stock name, use the **Sort Rows command** from the Tools menu as shown in the following steps.

TO SORT ROWS ▼

STEP 1 ▶

Highlight the cells containing the values on which to sort – the range A3:A10, select the Tools menu, and point to the Sort Rows command.

By highlighting the range A3:A10, you specify that Works should sort only those rows (Figure 5-67). Therefore, rows 11 through 15, for example, will not be included in the sorting process.

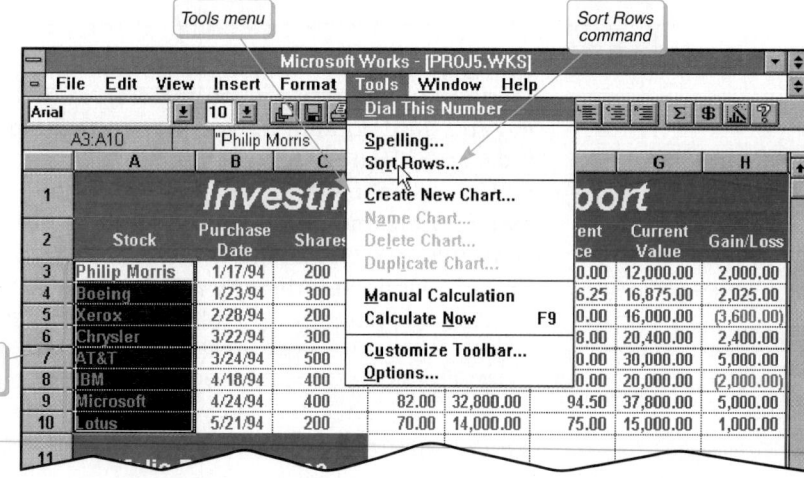

FIGURE 5-67

STEP 2 ▶

Choose the Sort Rows command. When the Sort Rows dialog box displays, review the entries and then point to the OK button.

Works displays the Sort Rows dialog box (Figure 5-68). The 1st Column box specifies the column on which the sort will take place. Column A is specified. This is determined from the highlighted range. You can determine the sort sequence by selecting the Ascend or Descend option button. Ascend is the default selection. No further entries are required.

FIGURE 5-68

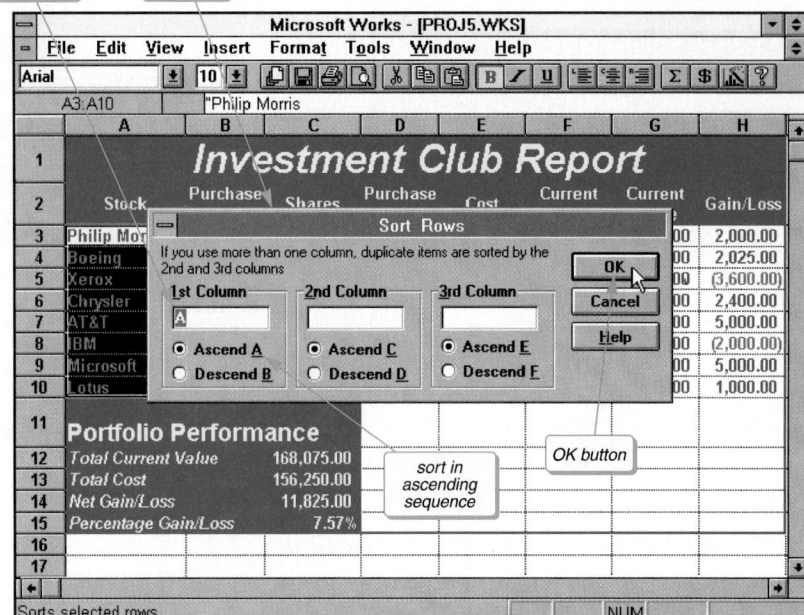

STEP 3 ▶

Choose the OK button. Click any cell to remove the highlight.

Works sorts the highlighted rows into ascending sequence (Figure 5-69). Notice that the data in each of the rows has been resequenced as well so that the correct Purchase Date, Shares, and so on remain with the sorted Stock name.

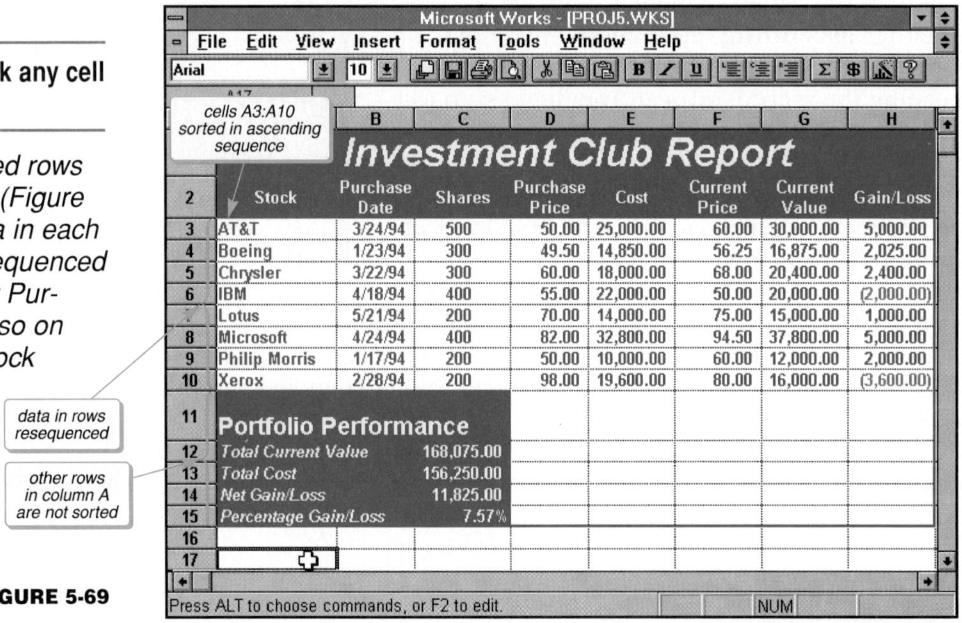

FIGURE 5-69

In the Sort Rows dialog box (Figure 5-68), notice that you can also use a second and third column for sorting. You would use a second or third column if duplicate values are found in the first column and you want to place rows in a particular sequence within the duplicate values. For example, if one column contained state names and another contained city names, to sort the rows on state name and then cities within the state, you would specify the state name column as the 1st Column and the city name column as the 2nd Column.

After sorting, the spreadsheet is complete.

▶ SAVING THE SPREADSHEET

 ou should save the final version of the spreadsheet on disk. To save the spreadsheet, click the Save button on the Toolbar.

▶ PRINT PREVIEW AND PRINTING THE SPREADSHEET

he spreadsheet must be printed in order to be distributed to the investors in the Investment Club. When a spreadsheet contains more than six columns or when you increase the width of the columns, the spreadsheet often will not fit across a piece of paper that is 8.5 inches wide and 11 inches long. To check whether it will fit, the best technique is to use Print Preview. Print Preview allows you to see the exact layout of your printed report prior to actually printing the report. In Project 5, because eight columns are required, print preview should be used to determine if the report will fit on a sheet of paper. To use Print Preview, perform the following steps.

TO USE PRINT PREVIEW ▼

STEP 1 ▶

Point to the Print Preview button on the Toolbar (Figure 5-70).

FIGURE 5-70

STEP 2 ▶

Click the Print Preview button on the Toolbar.

Works displays a full page and the report as it will appear on the page (Figure 5-71). When you move the mouse pointer onto the page, it assumes the shape of a magnifying glass with the word ZOOM beneath the magnifying glass. The display in Figure 5-71 shows the entire page, but it can be difficult to read the actual report. Therefore, you should magnify the report.

FIGURE 5-71

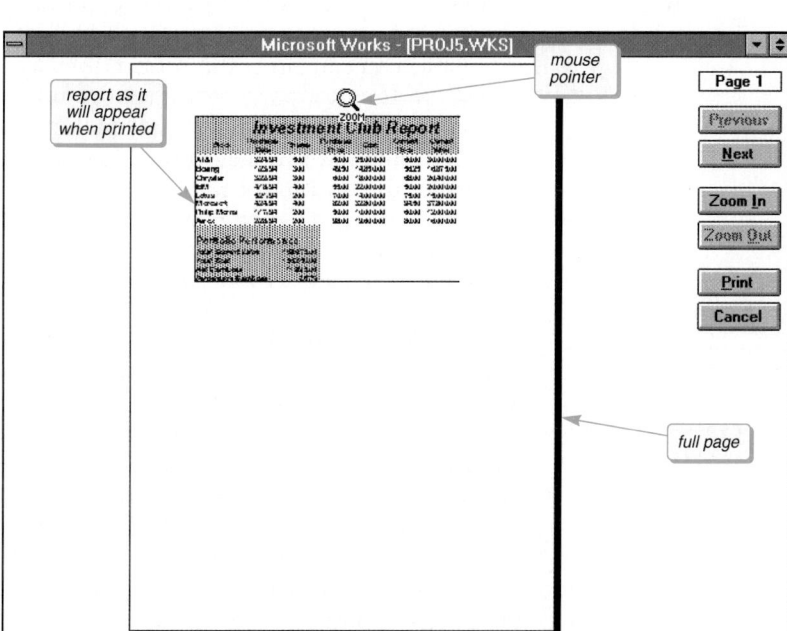

STEP 3 ▶

Click the left mouse button two times.

When you click the mouse button one time, Works magnifies the page to approximately one-half the size it will print. When you click a second time, the page becomes full-size (Figure 5-72). The displayed report does not contain the Gain/Loss column, which means the column will not appear on the printed report.

STEP 4 ▶

To return to the spreadsheet from the Print Preview window, choose the Cancel button.

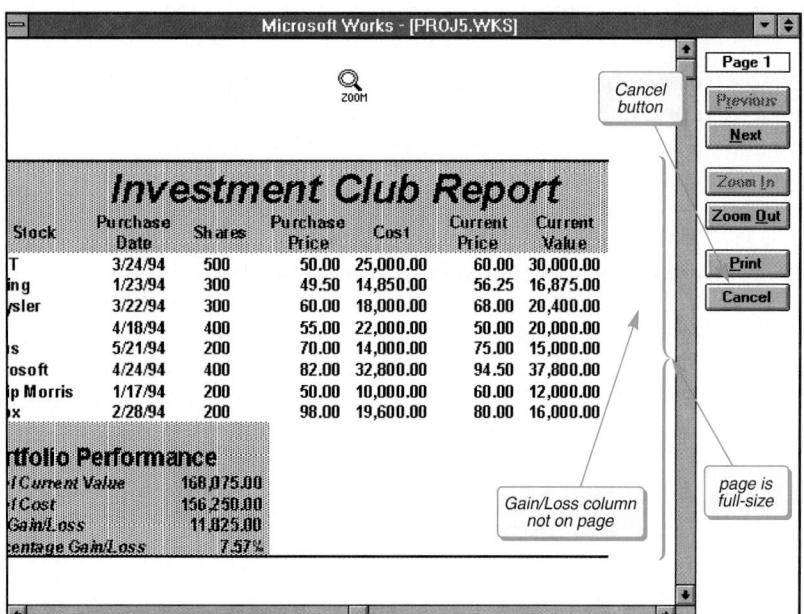

FIGURE 5-72

In the Print Preview window (Figure 5-72), Works provides several buttons. If you click the Next button, you will see the next page in the report. Clicking the Previous button causes Works to display the previous page of the report. The Zoom In and Zoom Out buttons increase or decrease the size of the report in the print preview window the same as clicking the mouse when the mouse pointer is shaped as a magnifying glass on the report. The Print button allows you to print the report directly from the print preview window.

Printing Landscape Reports

Because the Gain/Loss column does not fit on a page with a width of 8.5 inches and a length of 11 inches, you have a number of options you can use to display the report.

First, you can print the report anyway. Works will print column A through column G on the first page of the report and column H on the second page of the report. This is not normally a satisfactory technique.

The second option is to print the spreadsheet across the length of the paper instead of the width of the paper; that is, in effect turn the page ninety degrees so that the paper is 11 inches wide and 8.5 inches in height. When you print a report in this manner, you are using the **landscape** page orientation as opposed to the **portrait** page orientation you use when the printed page is 8.5 inches wide by 11 inches long.

A third technique is to change the entire spreadsheet to a smaller font size. This technique, however, will substantially change the appearance of the report when you have designed the spreadsheet using multiple font sizes.

A fourth technique is to change the right and left margins. The default for the right and left margins is 1.25 inches. Reducing these margins to 1 inch or .5 inch may increase the width to properly display the spreadsheet.

A widely used technique to display spreadsheets that are wider than a standard sheet of paper is to use the landscape orientation. To print in the landscape orientation, you must tell Works to use the landscape orientation instead of the portrait orientation. To accomplish this, perform the following steps.

TO PRINT A REPORT WITH LANDSCAPE ORIENTATION ▼

STEP 1 ▶

Select the File menu and point to the Page Setup command.

*The File menu displays and the mouse pointer points to the **Page Setup command** (Figure 5-73).*

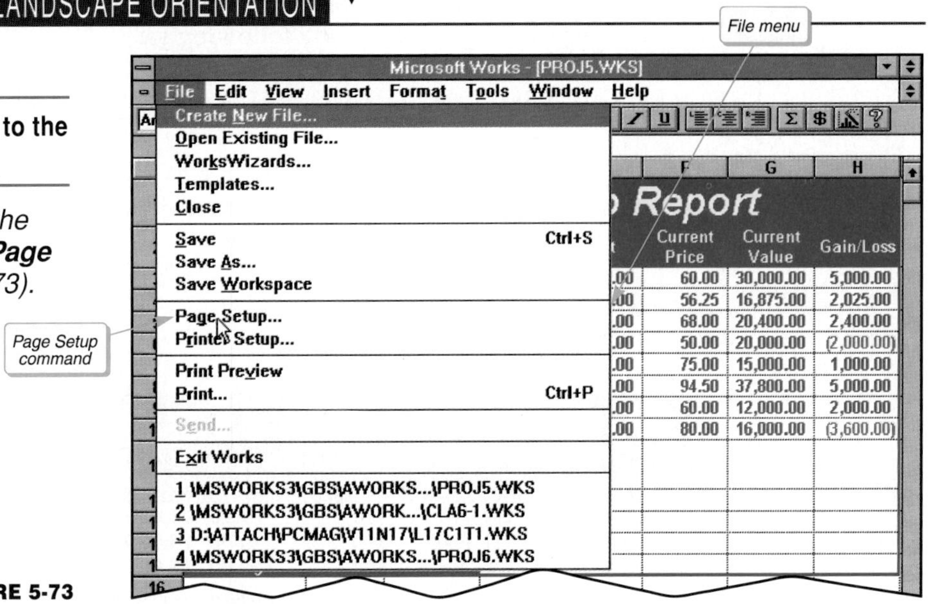

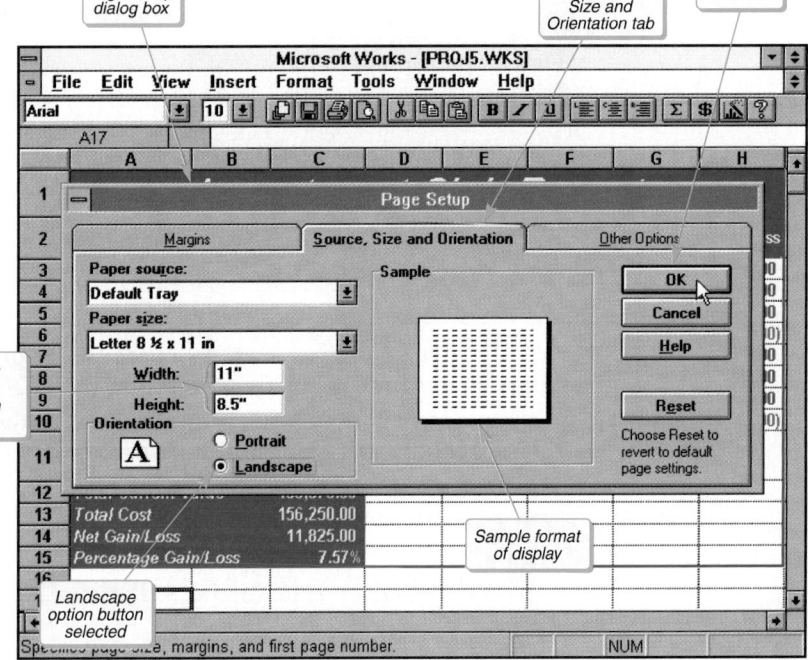

FIGURE 5-73

STEP 2 ▶

Choose the Page Setup command. When the Page Setup dialog box displays, select the Source, Size and Orientation tab. When the Source, Size and Orientation screen displays, select the Landscape option button in the Orientation area. Point to the OK button.

The Page Setup dialog box displays (Figure 5-74). Within the Page Setup dialog box, the Source, Size and Orientation screen displays. The Landscape option button is selected. When you select this option button, Works automatically changes the Width text box to 11" and the Height text box to 8.5". The Sample area changes to illustrate the landscape orientation. The mouse pointer points to the OK button.

FIGURE 5-74

STEP 3 ▶

Choose the OK button in the Page Setup dialog box to return to the spreadsheet.

Works is now set to print the spreadsheet in landscape orientation. To print the spreadsheet, perform the following step.

TO PRINT THE SPREADSHEET IN LANDSCAPE ORIENTATION

Step 1: Click the Print button on the Toolbar.

The landscape report generated is shown in Figure 5-75. Notice that the entire spreadsheet appears on a single page.

Investment Club Report

Stock	Purchase Date	Shares	Purchase Price	Cost	Current Price	Current Value	Gain/Loss
AT&T	3/24/94	500	50.00	25,000.00	60.00	30,000.00	5,000.00
Boeing	1/23/94	300	49.50	14,850.00	56.25	16,875.00	2,025.00
Chrysler	3/22/94	300	60.00	18,000.00	68.00	20,400.00	2,400.00
IBM	4/18/94	400	55.00	22,000.00	50.00	20,000.00	(2,000.00)
Lotus	5/21/94	200	70.00	14,000.00	75.00	15,000.00	1,000.00
Microsoft	4/24/94	400	82.00	32,800.00	94.50	37,800.00	5,000.00
Philip Morris	1/17/94	200	50.00	10,000.00	60.00	12,000.00	2,000.00
Xerox	2/28/94	200	98.00	19,600.00	80.00	16,000.00	(3,600.00)

Portfolio Performance

Total Current Value	168,075.00
Total Cost	156,250.00
Net Gain/Loss	11,825.00
Percentage Gain/Loss	7.57%

FIGURE 5-75

Once you have printed a spreadsheet in the landscape orientation, landscape orientation remains the selection in the Page Setup dialog box for that spreadsheet. Therefore, if you are going to print the spreadsheet again, be aware that the spreadsheet will print in the landscape orientation until you change back to portrait orientation.

▶ CHARTING THE SPREADSHEET

A fter you have printed the spreadsheet, your next task is to create a 3-D Pie chart. In Project 4, you created a 3-D Bar chart from data in adjacent columns. In this project, you will prepare a 3-D Pie chart based on the Current Value in column G and the Stock names in column A (Figure 5-76). Notice that the 3-D Pie chart shows what proportion of the entire stock portfolio each stock's Current Value represents. The name of the stock and the percentage is included on the chart.

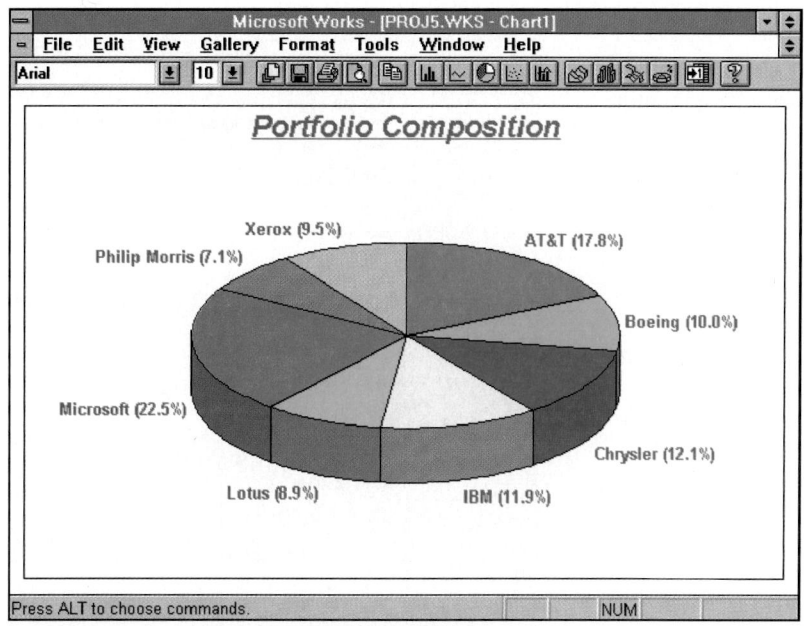

FIGURE 5-76

When you create a chart based on data from nonadjacent columns (column A and column G), you must use a slightly different procedure than when creating a chart from data in adjacent columns.

The procedure is: (1) highlight the range of data in column G to chart; (2) click the New Chart button on the Toolbar; (3) select the 3-D Pie chart; (4) add a chart title and a border; (5) add the labels from column A; and (6) format the chart title and data labels. To create the 3-D Pie chart, perform the following steps.

TO CREATE A PIE CHART FROM NONADJACENT COLUMNS ▼

STEP 1 ►

Highlight the range to chart (cells G3:G10) and point to the New Chart button on the Toolbar (Figure 5-77).

New Chart button

Microsoft Works - [PROJ5.WKS]

File Edit View Insert Format Tools Window Help

Arial   10   B I U   Σ $

G3:G10   =C3*F3

Investment Club Report

	Stock	Purchase Date	Shares	Purchase Price	Cost	Current Price	Current Value	Gain/Loss
3	AT&T	3/24/94	500	50.00	25,000.00	60.00	30,000.00	5,000.00
4	Boeing	1/23/94	300	49.50	14,850.00	56.25	16,875.00	2,025.00
5	Chrysler	3/22/94	300	60.00	18,000.00	68.00	20,400.00	2,400.00
6	IBM	4/18/94	400	55.00	22,000.00	50.00	20,000.00	(2,000.00)
7	Lotus	5/21/94	200	70.00	14,000.00	75.00	15,000.00	1,000.00
8	Microsoft	4/24/94	400	82.00	32,800.00	94.50	37,800.00	5,000.00
9	Philip Morris	1/17/94	200	50.00	10,000.00	60.00	12,000.00	2,000.00
10	Xerox	2/28/94	200	98.00	19,600.00	80.00	16,000.00	(3,600.00)

11	**Portfolio Performance**		
12	*Total Current Value*		168,075.00
13	*Total Cost*		156,250.00
14	*Net Gain/Loss*		11,825.00
15	*Percentage Gain/Loss*		7.57%
16			
17			

range of cells to chart is highlighted

Press ALT to choose commands, or F2 to edit.   NUM

FIGURE 5-77

STEP 2 ▶

Click the New Chart button on the Toolbar. When the New Chart dialog box displays, click the What type of chart do you want? drop-down list box arrow. Scroll down and point to 3-D Pie.

Works displays the New Chart dialog box (Figure 5-78). A drop-down list box displays the types of charts you can select. The mouse pointer points to 3-D Pie.

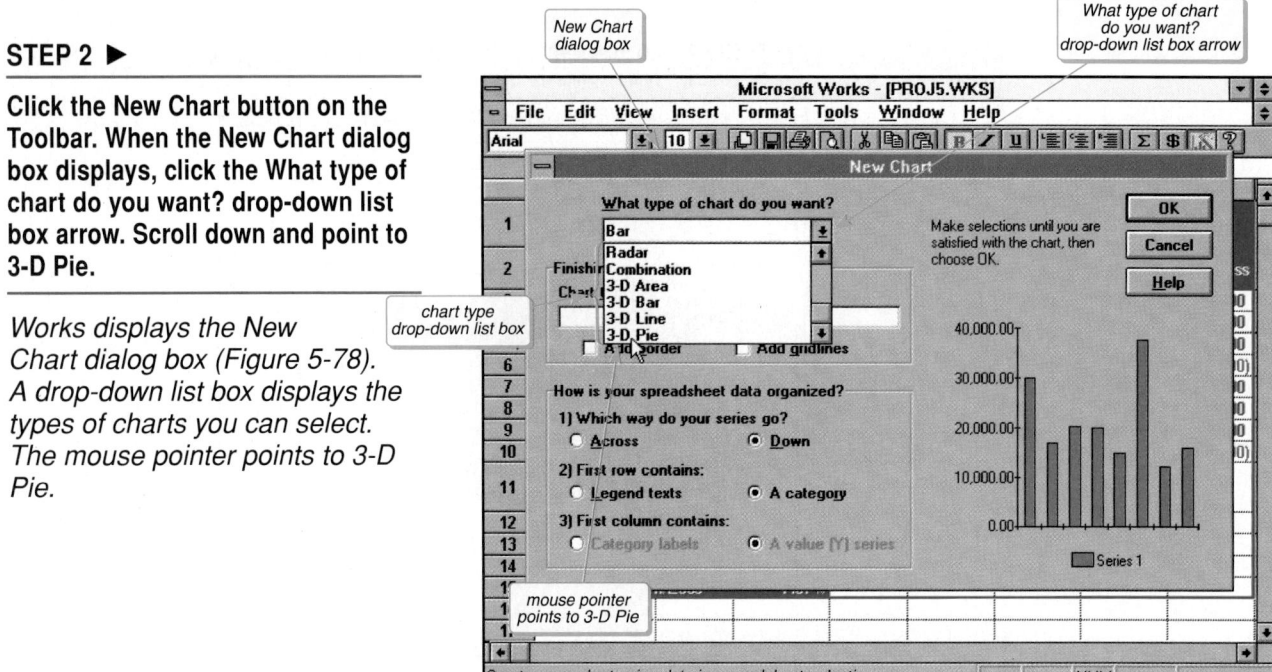

FIGURE 5-78

STEP 3 ▶

Select 3-D Pie from the drop-down list box. Press the TAB key and type Portfolio Composition **in the Chart title text box. Select the Add border check box. Point to the OK button.**

Works enters the words 3-D Pie in the What type of chart do you want? box (Figure 5-79). The words Portfolio Composition display in the Chart title text box. An X displays in the Add border check box. A 3-D Pie chart and the chart title display in the Sample area of the New Chart dialog box. The mouse pointer points to the OK button.

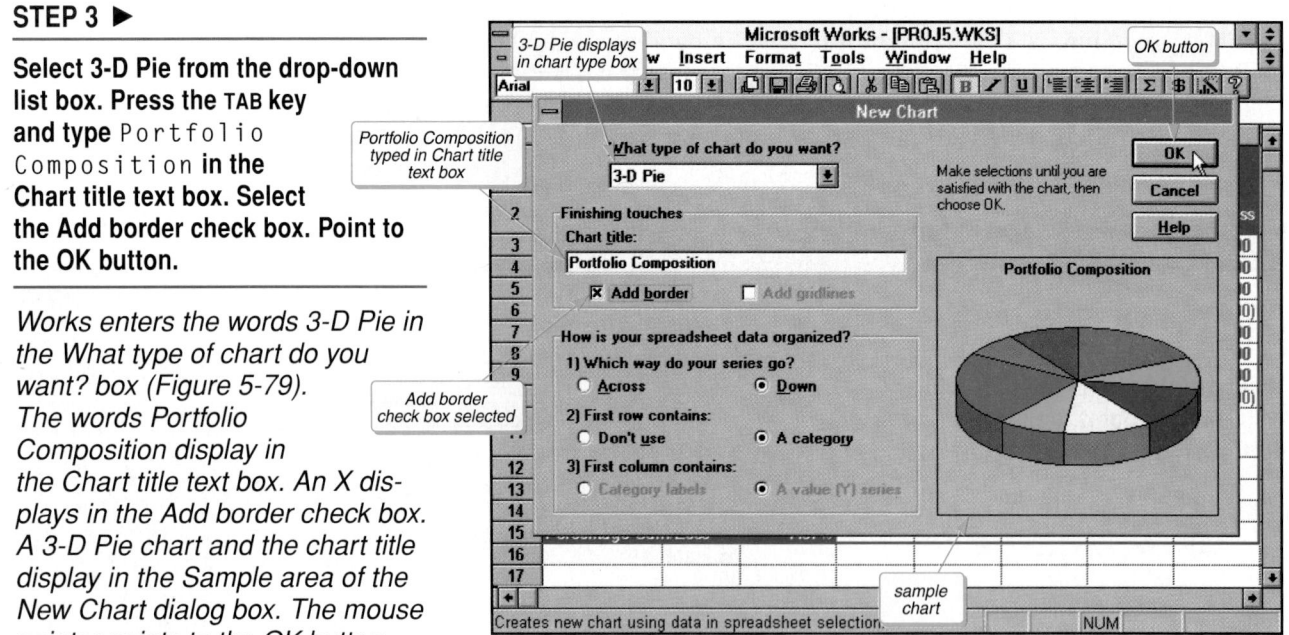

FIGURE 5-79

STEP 4 ▶

Choose the OK button in the New Chart dialog box.

Works displays the 3-D Pie chart (Figure 5-80).

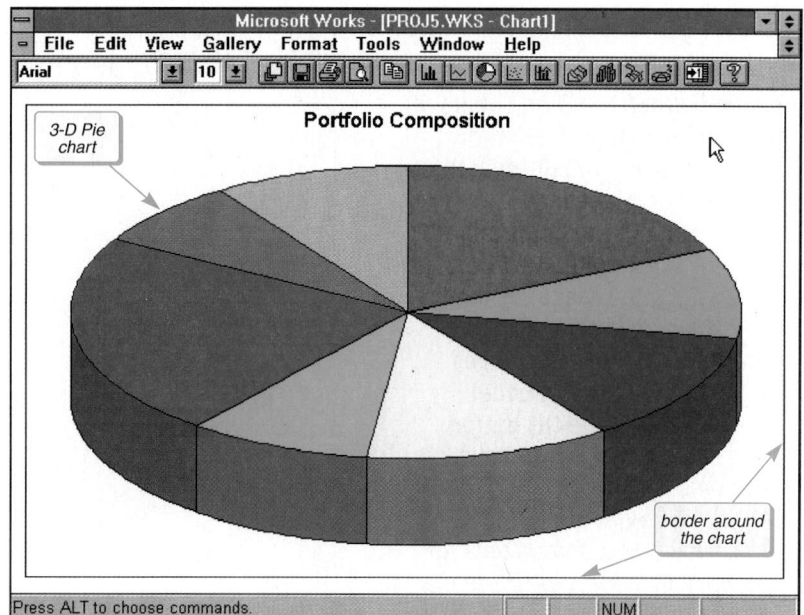

FIGURE 5-80

Adding Data Labels from Nonadjacent Columns

The 3-D Pie chart in Figure 5-80 charts the Current Value for each stock in the portfolio but the chart labels, which include the name of the stock and the percentage that each slice in the Pie chart represents, are not identified on the chart. The name of each corresponding stock is contained in the range A3:A10 of the spreadsheet. To place the Stock names in the range A3:A10 on the chart, and to display a label for the percentage that each slice represents, perform the following steps.

 TO ADD DATA LABELS FROM NONADJACENT COLUMNS ▼

STEP 1 ▶

Select the chart Edit menu and point to the Data Labels command (Figure 5-81).

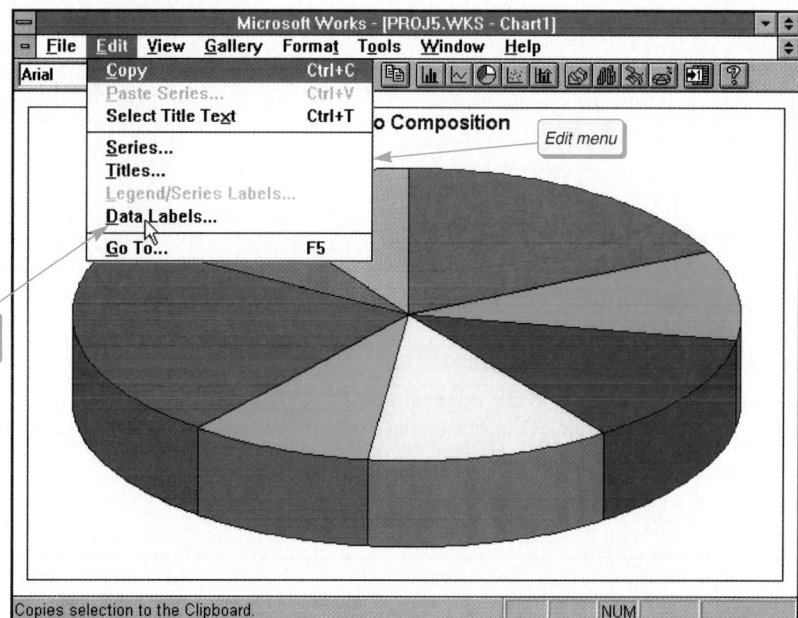

FIGURE 5-81

STEP 2 ▶

Choose the Data Labels command. When the Data Labels dialog box displays, select the Cell Contents option button in the 1st Label area; place the insertion point in the Cell Range text box by clicking the text box; type `A3:A10`**, the range for the Stock names, in the Cell Range text box; select the Percentages option button in the 2nd Label area; and point to the OK button.**

Works displays the Data Labels dialog box (Figure 5-82). Because Works allows two data labels for each entry in a Pie chart, the dialog box contains option buttons for the 1st Label and the 2nd Label. In Project 5, the 1st Label uses Cell Contents (the name of stock) and the second label is for Percentages. When you click the Cell Range text box and type the cell range A3:A10, you tell Works to use the contents of these cells for the 1st data label in the Pie chart.

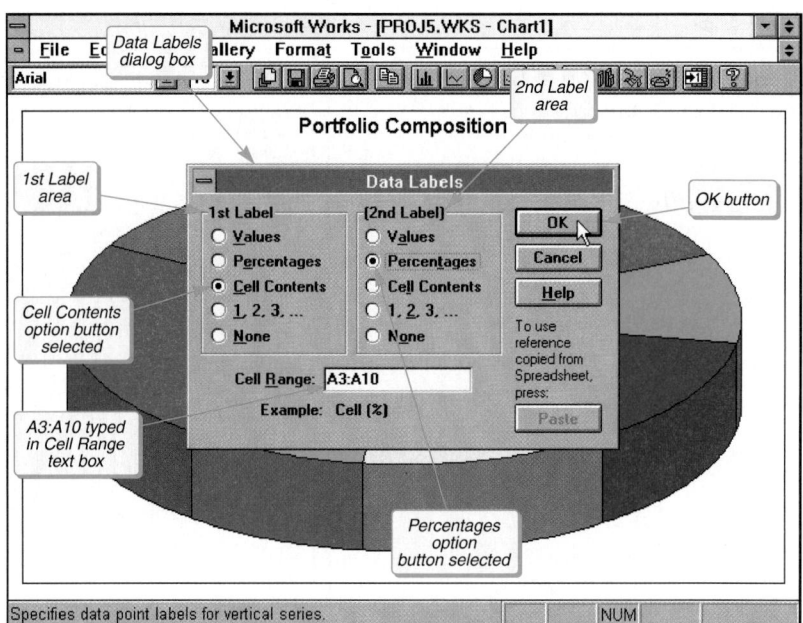

FIGURE 5-82

STEP 3 ▶

Choose the OK button in the Data Labels dialog box.

Works places the cell contents (Stock names) from cells A3:A10 as the 1st data labels (Figure 5-83). Notice that Works uses the stock name AT&T from the first row, row 3, for the number one slice of the Pie chart (the number 1 slice is in the upper right corner), then the stock name Boeing for the second slice of the pie on the chart, and so on. The percentage of the whole each stock represents displays within parentheses as the second label.

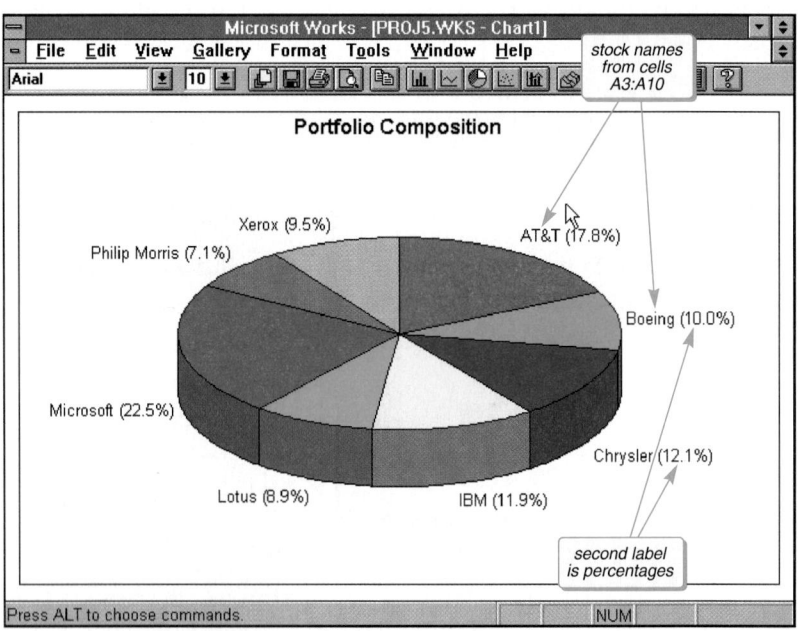

FIGURE 5-83

Formatting the Chart Title and Data Labels

The final task in preparing the chart is to format the title, Portfolio Composition, and the data labels. Complete the following steps to accomplish this task (see Figure 5-84).

TO FORMAT CHART TITLES AND DATA LABELS

Step 1: Highlight the chart title by clicking the title.

Step 2: Select the Format menu and choose the Font and Style command.

Step 3: In the Font and Style for Title dialog box that displays, select Bold, Italic, and Underline in the Style check boxes, select 18 in the Size list box, click the Color drop-down list box arrow and select Blue in the Color drop-down list box, and then choose the OK button.

Step 4: Click anywhere in the chart to remove the highlight.

Step 5: Select the Format menu and choose the Font and Style command.

Step 6: In the Font and Style for Subtitle and Labels dialog box that displays, select the Bold check box in the Style area, click the Color drop-down list box arrow and select Blue in the Color drop-down list box, and choose the OK button.

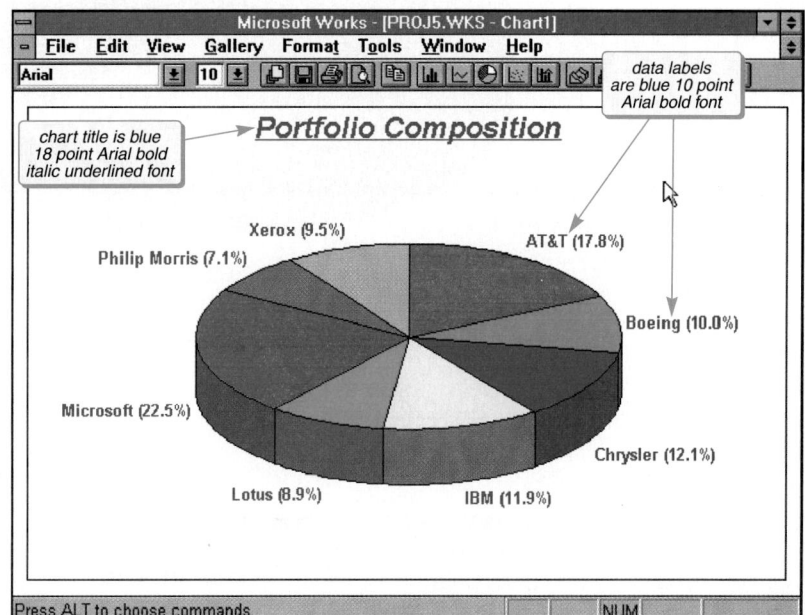

Works makes the format changes and displays the chart title and data labels with the selections you made (Figure 5-84).

FIGURE 5-84

Printing a Chart

You can print a Works chart by using the following steps.

TO PRINT A WORKS SPREADSHEET CHART

Step 1: Choose the Page Setup command from the File menu.

Step 2: Select the Source, Size and Orientation tab.

Step 3: Select the Landscape option button in the Orientation area of the Source, Size and Orientation screen.

Step 4: Choose the OK button in the Page Setup dialog box.

Step 5: Click the Print button on the Charting Toolbar.

The printout in landscape orientation is shown in Figure 5-85 on the next page.

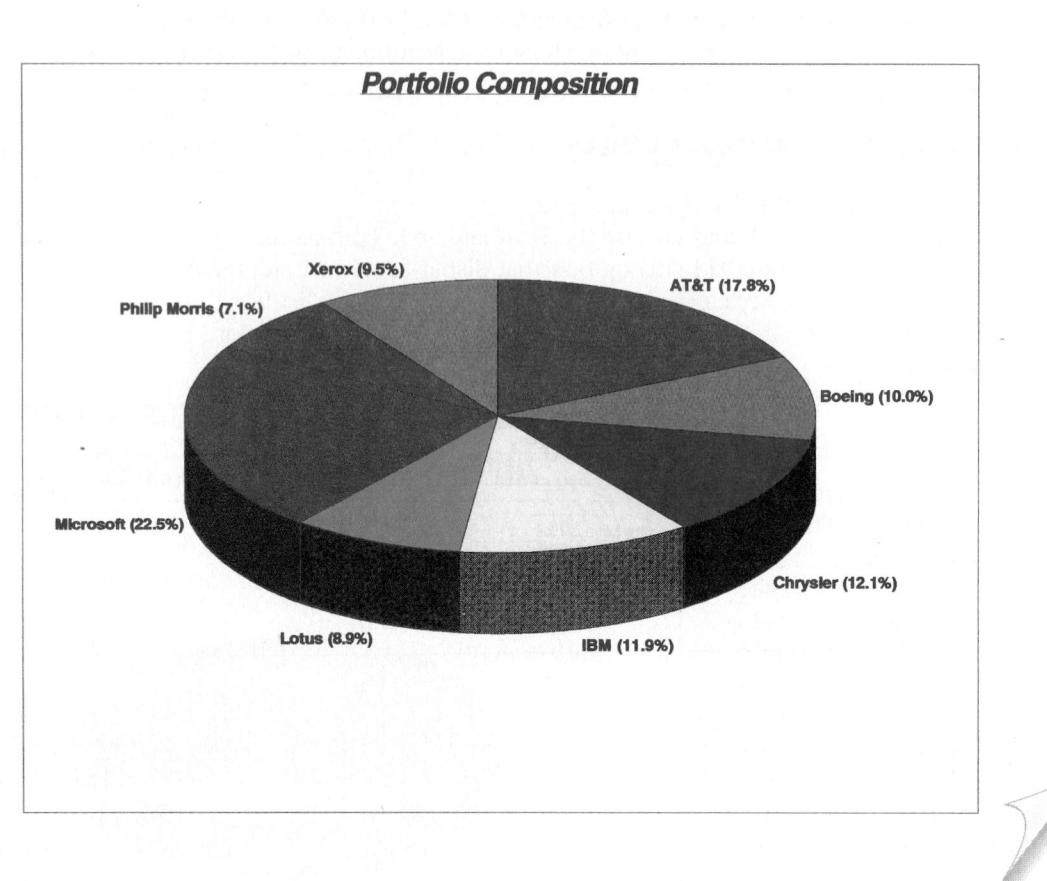

FIGURE 5-85

Saving the Spreadsheet and the Chart

To save the spreadsheet and the chart, click the Save button on the Toolbar. Both the spreadsheet and the chart will be saved on disk.

Quitting Works

After you have completed working on the Project 5 spreadsheet and chart, you can close them to work on another Works project or you can exit Works. To exit Works, complete the following steps.

TO EXIT WORKS

Step 1: Select the File menu.
Step 2: Choose the Exit Works command.

▶ PROJECT SUMMARY

In Project 5, you learned about Works formulas, operators, the sequence of operations in a formula, and how to enter a formula. You also learned how to format a spreadsheet and add color to a spreadsheet. The technique of sorting rows in the spreadsheet and printing the spreadsheet in landscape orientation was explained and illustrated.

Finally, you created a 3-D Pie chart that included labels in the chart from nonadjacent rows in the spreadsheet. You then learned how to format the chart title, format the data labels, and print the chart.

▶ KEY TERMS

algebraic rules *(W5.9)*
Alignment command *(W5.22)*
ascending *(W5.35)*
cell reference *(W5.9)*
descending *(W5.35)*
Fill Down command *(W5.15)*
Font and Style command
  (W5.29)

formula *(W5.9)*
landscape *(W5.38)*
Number command *(W5.25)*
operator *(W5.9)*
order of evaluation *(W5.9)*
Page Setup command *(W5.39)*
parentheses *(W5.9)*
Patterns command *(W5.30)*

Pie chart *(W5.4)*
Point mode *(W5.10)*
pointing method *(W5.12)*
portrait *(W5.38)*
solid pattern *(W5.30)*
sorting *(W5.35)*
Sort Rows command *(W5.35)*
wrap text *(W5.6)*

QUICK REFERENCE

In Microsoft Works, you can accomplish a task in a number of ways. The following table provides a quick reference to each task presented in this project with its available options. The commands listed in the Menu column can be executed using either the keyboard or mouse.

Task	Mouse	Menu	Keyboard Shortcuts
Add Color to Text		From Format menu choose Font and Style	
Add Color to Cells		From Format menu choose Patterns	
Add Data Labels		From chart Edit menu, choose Data Labels	
Change the Font	Click Font Name box arrow	From Format menu, choose Font and Style	
Change the Font Size	Click Font Size box arrow	From Format menu, choose Font and size	
Chart a Spreadsheet	Click New Chart button	From Tools menu, choose Create New Chart	
Create a 3-D Pie Chart	Click New Chart button, then select 3-D Pie in New Chart dialog box; or click 3-D Pie Chart button on Charting Toolbar	From chart Gallery menu, choose 3-D Pie	none
Confirm an Entry of Numeric Data	Click Enter box		Press ENTER or press arrow key

(continued)

QUICK REFERENCE (continued)

Task	Mouse	Menu	Keyboard Shortcuts
Confirm an Entry of Text Data	Click Enter box		Press ENTER or press arrow key
Format Chart Titles	Use buttons on Charting Toolbar	From chart Format menu, choose Font and Style	
Outline a Range with a Border		From Format menu, choose Border	
Percent Format		Form Format menu, choose Number	Press CTRL+5
Place a Cell Reference in a Formula	Click the cell		Type cell number or press arrow key
Place an Operator in a Formula			Type operator name
Print a Chart	Click Print button	From File menu, choose Print	Press CTRL+P
Print in a Landscape Orientation		From File menu, choose Page Setup	
Print in a Portrait Orientation		From File menu, choose Page Setup	
Print Preview	Click Print Preview button	From File menu, choose Print Preview	
Sort		From Tools menu, choose Sort Rows	

S T U D E N T   A S S I G N M E N T S

STUDENT ASSIGNMENT 1
True/False

Instructions: Circle T if the statement is true or F if the statement is false.

T F 1. A 3-D Pie chart is commonly used to compare three values over a period of time.

T F 2. When you enter text into a spreadsheet, the only way to confirm the entry is by pressing the ENTER key.

T F 3. In Works, a formula is an equation that calculates a new value from existing values in cells within the spreadsheet.

T F 4. A formula always begins with a plus (+) sign.

T F 5. The order of calculation within a formula is addition and subtraction first, followed by division and multiplication, and finally, exponentiation.

T F 6. The five operators used within a formula are =, +, -, \, and %.

T F 7. If cell C9 contains the value 7, cell D9 contains the value 2, and cell E9 contains the value 6, then the formula =C9+D9+E9/3 produces the answer 5.

T F 8. You can enter a formula into a cell by typing the entire formula, starting with an equal (=) sign.

T F 9. The Point mode means you point the block arrow mouse pointer at the command you want to execute and press the left mouse button.

T F 10. When you want to copy formulas in adjacent columns, you can copy all the formulas at one time.
T F 11. Selecting the Comma option button in the Number dialog box will always cause a number to display with two digits to the right of the decimal point.
T F 12. Works always displays negative numbers in a cell in red.
T F 13. Sorting allows you to place rows of spreadsheet data in a prescribed sequence.
T F 14. If you sort last names in ascending sequence, and the names Zebbi and Aaron are in the list, the name Zebbi will be nearer the top of the names than the name Aaron.
T F 15. Print Preview allows you to see the exact layout of your printed report prior to actually printing the report.
T F 16. When printing a report using landscape orientation, you print on a page considered 11 inches long and 8.5 inches wide.
T F 17. When you change a font size, you automatically have to change the font as well.
T F 18. To change the color of a font for a spreadsheet title, choose the Page Setup command from the File menu.
T F 19. To add color to cells, choose the Patterns command from the Format menu.
T F 20. To add data labels to a 3-D Pie chart, choose the Data Labels command from the Edit menu.

STUDENT ASSIGNMENT 2
Multiple Choice

Instructions: Circle the correct response.

1. To open a spreadsheet window labeled Sheet1, click the _____ .
   a. Create New File button on the Toolbar
   b. Microsoft Works program-item icon
   c. Create New File button in the Startup dialog box
   d. Spreadsheet button in the Startup dialog box
2. To confirm the entry of text data into a spreadsheet, you can _____ .
   a. press the ENTER key
   b. press an arrow key
   c. click the Enter box
   d. all of the above
3. A formula always begins with _____ .
   a. a plus sign
   b. a cell reference
   c. an equal sign
   d. a left parenthesis
4. If cell C3 contains 9, cell C4 contains 9, and cell C5 contains 6, the formula =(C3+C4+C5)/3 yields _____ .
   a.   8
   b. 24
   c. 20
   d. 72
5. To copy formulas in cells B3 and C3 to the range B4:C9, _____ .
   a. highlight the range B4:C9, then choose the Fill Right command from the Edit menu
   b. highlight the range B3:C9, then choose the Fill Down command from the Edit menu
   c. highlight cell B3, choose the Fill Down command from the Edit menu, highlight cell C3, and choose the Fill Down command from the Edit menu
   d. click the Copy button on the Toolbar

(continued)

STUDENT ASSIGNMENT 2 (continued)

6. To place an outline around the range B12:C15, _____ .
   a. highlight the range B12:B15 and click the Border button on the Toolbar
   b. highlight the range B12:C15, choose the Border command from the Format menu, select the Outline box, and choose the OK button
   c. highlight the range B12:C15, choose the Font and Style command from the Format menu, select the Border option button, and choose the OK button
   d. highlight the range B12:C15, choose the Outline command from the Insert menu, select the Outline box, and choose the OK button

7. Which of the following is sorted in ascending sequence?
   a. 3245, 76556, 23443, 90772, 5645
   b. Jones, Newmann, Opherey, Timmons, Waller
   c. Washington, Utah, Texas, South Dakota, California
   d. 9, 8, 7, 6, 5

8. When an entire spreadsheet will not print across an 8.5-inch wide page, one of your options to fit the spreadsheet on a single page is to _____ .
   a. print the report in portrait orientation
   b. print the report from the Print Preview screen
   c. print the report in landscape orientation
   d. sort the columns into a different sequence

9. To add color to a spreadsheet title, _____ .
   a. choose the Color button on the Toolbar
   b. choose the Options command from the Tools menu, select the color you want, and choose the OK button
   c. choose the Patterns command from the Format, select the solid pattern in the Foreground drop-down list box, and choose the OK button
   d. choose the Font and Style command from the Format menu, select the color you want from the Color drop-down list box, and choose the OK button

10. To add data labels to a chart, _____ .
    a. choose the Data Labels command from the Edit menu when the chart displays
    b. choose the Data Labels command from the Edit menu when the spreadsheet displays
    c. choose the chart type from the Gallery menu and then type the labels
    d. type the labels directly on the chart in the locations desired

STUDENT ASSIGNMENT 3
Formulas

Instructions: In the space provided, write the Works Spreadsheet formulas to accomplish the arithmetic specified.

1. Add the values in cells C3:C12 and divide the result by the value in cell F3.

   _____

2. Multiply the value in cell F6 by the sum of the values in cells C4 and L76, then subtract the result from the value in cell A5.

   _____

3. Square the value in cell G32 and then divide the result by the sum of the values in cells C4 and D21.

   _____

4. The formula to calculate the area of a circle is πR^2. Cell F7 contains the value of π and cell E5 contains the radius (R) of the circle. Write the formula to calculate the area of the circle.

   _____

STUDENT ASSIGNMENT 4
Evaluating Formulas

Instructions: Evaluate the formulas in the following problems given the values in the indicated cells.

Cell C5: 25	Cell C6: 34.5
Cell C7: 64	Cell C8: 4
Cell C9: 3	Cell C10: 8
Cell C11: .5	Cell C12: =C7/C8
Cell C13: 6	Cell C14: 4

1. =C5+C6 _____

2. =(C8+C9+C10)/3 _____

3. =C8+C9+C13/3 _____

4. =C10/C12 _____

5. =C8/C11−C13 _____

6. =(C7^(1/3)*C14)/C8 _____

STUDENT ASSIGNMENT 5
Correcting a Spreadsheet

Instructions: The spreadsheet in Figure SA5-5 contains an error. Identify the error and describe the method to correct the error in the space provided.

Error: _____

_____

_____

_____

_____

Correction: _____

_____

_____

_____

_____

_____

_____

	A	B	C	D	E	F	G	H
1			*Investment Club Report*					
2	Stock	Purchase Date	Shares	Purchase Price	Cost	Current Price	Current Value	Gain\Loss
3	AT&T	3/24/94	500	50.00	25,000.00	60.00	30,000.00	5,000.00
4	Boeing	1/23/94	300	49.50	14,850.00	56.25	16,875.00	2,025.00
5	Chrysler	3/22/94	300	60.00	18,000.00	68.00	20,400.00	2,400.00
6	IBM	4/18/94	400	55.00	22,000.00	50.00	20,000.00	(2,000.00)
7	Lotus	5/21/94	200	70.00	14,000.00	75.00	15,000.00	1,000.00
8	Microsoft	4/24/94	400	82.00	32,800.00	94.50	37,800.00	5,000.00
9	Philip Morris	1/17/94	200	50.00	10,000.00	60.00	12,000.00	2,000.00
10	Xerox	2/28/94	200	98.00	19,600.00	80.00	16,000.00	(3,600.00)
11	**Portfolio Performance**							
12	*Total Current Value*		168,075.00					
13	*Total Cost*		156,250.00					
14	*Net Gain\Loss*		(11,825.00)					
15	*Percentage Gain\Loss*		-7.57%					
16								
17								
18								

Microsoft Works - [SA5-5.WKS]

File Edit View Insert Format Tools Window Help

Arial 10

A18

Press ALT to choose commands. NUM

FIGURE SA5-5

STUDENT ASSIGNMENT 6
Entering and Copying Formulas

Instructions: In the spreadsheet in Figure SA5-6, the data has been entered. Cells E3, G3, and H3 contain the same formulas as in Project 5. In the space provided, list the steps to perform the following tasks.

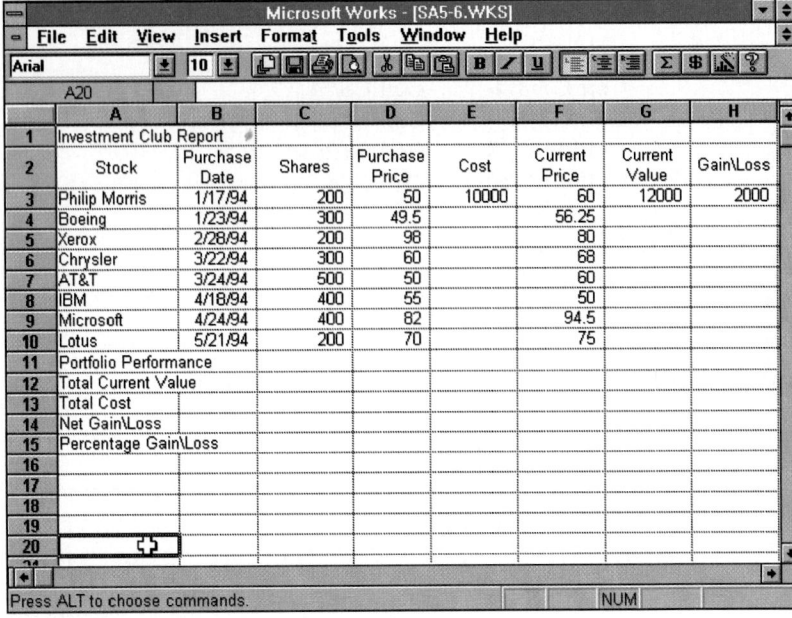

FIGURE SA5-6

Task 1: Copy the formula in cell E3 to the range E4:E10

Steps: _____

Task 2: Copy the formulas in cell G3 and cell H3 to the range G4:H10.

Steps: _____

_____

_____

Task 3: Enter the formula in cell C12 to calculate the Total Current Value.

Steps: _____

_____

_____

Task 4: Enter the formula in cell C13 to calculate the Total Cost.

Steps: _____

_____

_____

Task 5: Enter the formula in cell C14 to calculate the Net Gain/Loss.

Steps: _____

_____

_____

Task 6: Enter the formula in cell C15 to calculate the Percentage Gain/Loss.

Steps: _____

COMPUTER LABORATORY EXERCISE 1
Using the Help Menu

Instructions: Perform the following tasks using a personal computer.

1. Start the Microsoft Works Spreadsheet tool.
2. Select the Help menu.
3. Choose the Search for Help on command from the Help menu.
4. Type `show formulas`.
5. Select showing: formulas.
6. Choose the Show Topics button.
7. Choose the Go To button.
8. Read the Formulas command (View menu) screen and answer the following questions:
   a. Which menu contains the Formulas command? _____
   b. How do you turn on the Formulas command? _____
   c. How do you turn off the Formulas command? _____
   d. When the Formulas command is on, what do you see in the spreadsheet?

   _____

9. Click the Search button.
10. Type `zoom`.
11. Choose the Show Topics button.
12. Choose the Go To button.
13. Read the Zoom command (View menu) screen that displays and answer the following questions.
    a. Which menu contains the Zoom command? _____
    b. What happens when you choose the Zoom command? _____
    c. What sizes can you select for showing a document? _____
    d. When you print a document that has been reduced to 50% its normal size, what happens?

    _____

    e. What is the smallest you can reduce a document? _____
    f. What is the largest you can magnify a document? _____
14. To exit Help, from the Help File menu choose the Exit command.

COMPUTER LABORATORY EXERCISE 2
Formatting the Spreadsheet

Instructions: Start the Works Spreadsheet tool. Open the CLE5-2.WKS file on the Student Diskette that accompanies this book. The spreadsheet, shown in Figure CLE5-2, contains data and formulas, but none of the spreadsheet is formatted. Format the spreadsheet as illustrated in Figure 5-1 on page W5.3. When you have completed the formatting, print the formatted spreadsheet.

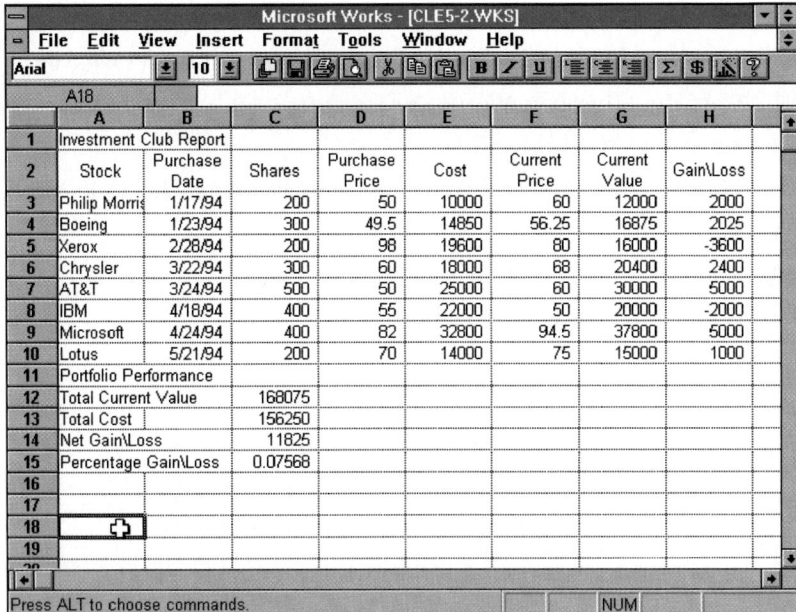

FIGURE CLE5-2

COMPUTER LABORATORY EXERCISE 3
Showing Formulas

Instructions: Start the Works Spreadsheet tool. Open the CLE5-3.WKS file on the Student Diskette that accompanies this book. The spreadsheet you will see on your screen is shown in Figure CLE5-3a.

FIGURE CLE5-3a

Select the View menu and choose the Formulas command. The screen will change. The columns become wider and formulas display in the cells. Change column widths as follows: A = 20, B = 6, C = 13, D = 8, E = 9, F = 8, G = 9, and H = 10. Your spreadsheet should now look like the spreadsheet in Figure CLE5-3b.

FIGURE CLE5-3b

All the formulas in the spreadsheet display on the screen. Print the spreadsheet using landscape orientation.

COMPUTER LABORATORY ASSIGNMENTS

COMPUTER LABORATORY ASSIGNMENT 1
Creating a Royalty Report

Purpose: To provide experience using the Works Spreadsheet to create a spreadsheet that requires entering text, numbers, and formulas, formatting text and numeric data, using the SUM function, adding color, sorting a spreadsheet, printing a spreadsheet, and creating a 3-D Pie chart with data labels and a formatted title.

Problem: Create a Royalty Report for artists at a recording company. The data for the spreadsheet is shown in the table on the right.

The spreadsheet is shown in Figure CLA5-1a on the next page.

ARTIST	TITLE	UNITS SOLD	UNIT PRICE
Elkone	Smiling Skies	198938	15.21
Tompson	Unchain Me	324786	8.42
Dessery	Loving You	333551	7.18
Elkone	Jazz It Up	643009	6.02
Tompson	Above Love	700923	5.56

COMPUTER LABORATORY ASSIGNMENT 1 (continued)

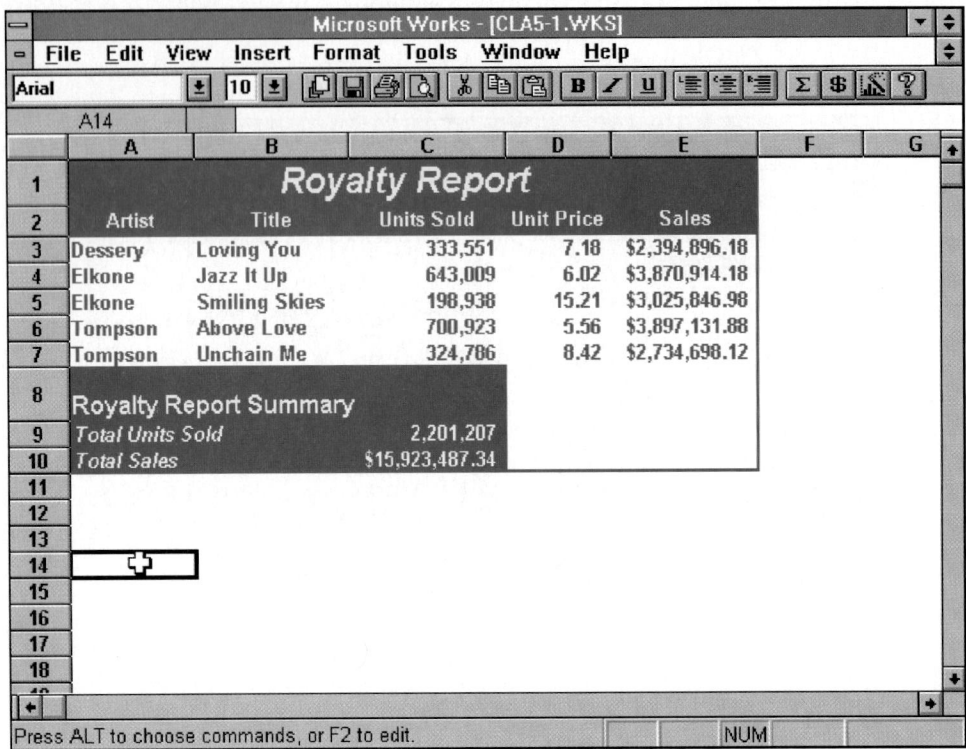

FIGURE CLA5-1a

Instructions:

1. Create a spreadsheet in the format shown in Figure CLA5-1a using the numbers and text from the table.
2. On the spreadsheet, calculate the Sales by multiplying the Units Sold by the Unit Price.
3. On the spreadsheet, calculate Total Units Sold and Total Sales.
4. Format the spreadsheet as shown. The entire spreadsheet is bold. The spreadsheet title displays in 18 point Arial italic font. The title at the bottom of the spreadsheet, Royalty Report Summary, displays in 12 point Arial font. The titles under the words Royalty Report Summary display in italic. The column widths are: A = 12; B = 15; C = 15; D = 10; and E = 14. Sales and Total Sales are formatted with the Currency format. The Units Sold and Total Units Sold are formatted with the Comma format with the number of decimals equal to zero. Color the spreadsheet title, column titles and Royalty Report Summary section titles yellow with the cells blue. Text and numeric data comprising the spreadsheet are blue. Place a blue border around the spreadsheet.
5. Sort the spreadsheet into ascending sequence by song title within Artist name.
6. Save the spreadsheet you create on a diskette. Use a filename consisting of the initials of your first and last names followed by the assignment number. Example: TC5-1.
7. Print the spreadsheet you have created. Ensure all columns will print on one page.
8. Create the 3-D Pie chart in Figure CLA5-1b from the Sales contained on the spreadsheet. The title is dark blue 18 point Arial bold italic underlined font. The data labels are dark blue 10 point Arial bold font.
9. Print the 3-D Pie chart in landscape orientation.
10. Sort the spreadsheet on song title alone.
11. Print the sorted spreadsheet.
12. Create a second 3-D Pie chart based on the Sales in the sorted spreadsheet and format it appropriately.
13. Print the 3-D Pie chart in landscape orientation.
14. Save the spreadsheet and new charts using a new filename.
15. Follow directions from your instructor for turning in this assignment.

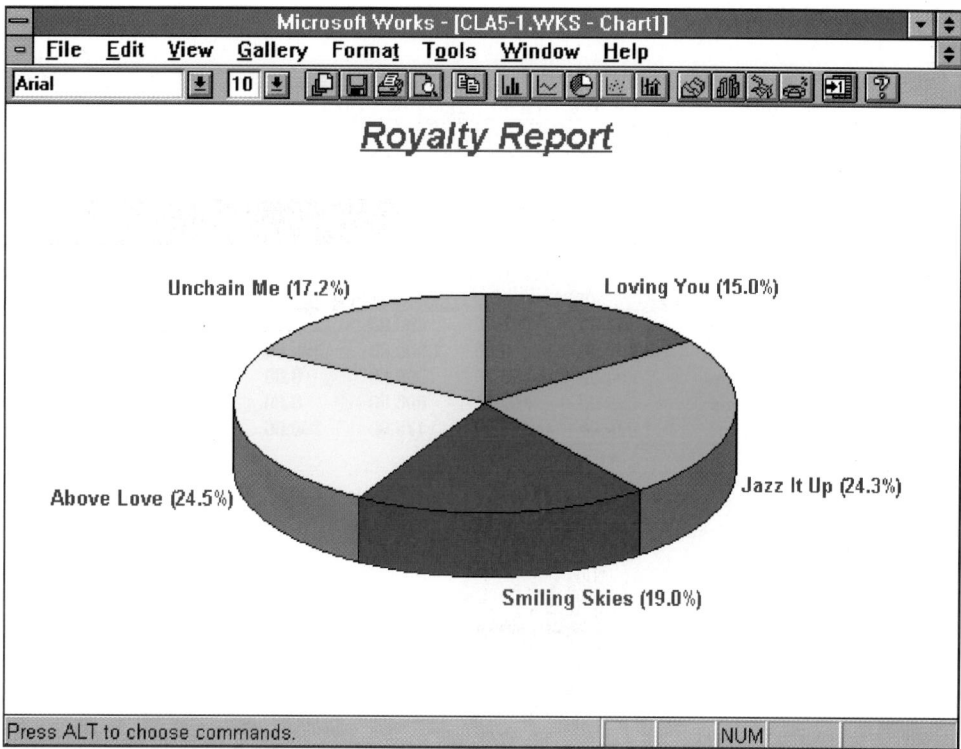

FIGURE CLA5-1b

COMPUTER LABORATORY ASSIGNMENT 2
Creating an Accounts Receivable Report

Purpose: To provide experience using the Works Spreadsheet to create a spreadsheet that requires entering text, numbers, and formulas, formatting text and numeric data, using the SUM function, adding color to the spreadsheet, sorting the spreadsheet, printing the spreadsheet, and creating a 3-D Pie chart with data labels and a formatted title.

Problem: Create an Accounts Receivable Report using the data in the following table.

CUSTOMER NUMBER	CUSTOMER NAME	BEGINNING BALANCE	PURCHASES	PAYMENTS	RETURNS
320-88	Simms	643.00	769.00	800.00	0.00
459-92	Adams	564.00	987.00	400.00	230.00
654-74	Taylor	1076.00	425.00	175.00	290.00
764-83	Hughes	290.00	158.50	300.00	0.00
864-91	Delman	2001.50	0.00	1500.00	190.00

The spreadsheet is shown in Figure CLA5-2a on the next page.

(continued)

COMPUTER LABORATORY ASSIGNMENT 2 (continued)

FIGURE CLA5-2a

Instructions:

1. Create a spreadsheet in the format shown in Figure CLA5-2a using the numbers and text from the table.
2. On the spreadsheet, calculate Service Charge by multiplying 2% times (Beginning Balance plus Purchases minus Payments minus Returns).
3. Calculate New Balance by the formula, Beginning Balance plus Purchases minus Payments minus Returns plus Service Charge.
4. Calculate the totals in the Accounts Receivable Summary section by summing the values in each of the respective columns.
5. Format the spreadsheet as shown. The entire spreadsheet is bold. All column widths are 10.
6. Add color to the spreadsheet as shown. The titles are white. The cell color is dark magenta for the spreadsheet and column titles and the Accounts Receivable Summary.
7. Sort the spreadsheet into ascending sequence by Customer Name.
8. Save the spreadsheet you create on a diskette. Use a filename consisting of the initials of your first and last names followed by the assignment number. Example: TC5-2.
9. Create the 3-D Pie chart in Figure CLA5-2b from the New Balance on the spreadsheet. The first data label is the Customer Name and the second data label is the Value in the New Balance field. The title is dark magenta 18 point Arial bold italic underlined font. The data labels are dark magenta 10 point Arial bold font.
10. Print the 3-D Pie chart.
11. Print the Accounts Receivable Report spreadsheet on a single page. Check whether the spreadsheet will fit on a single page by using Print Preview. If it will not fit, then use one of the techniques illustrated in Project 5 to print the spreadsheet on a single page.
12. Sort the spreadsheet on Customer Number.
13. Print the spreadsheet in Customer Number sequence on a single page.
14. Follow directions from your instructor for turning in this assignment.

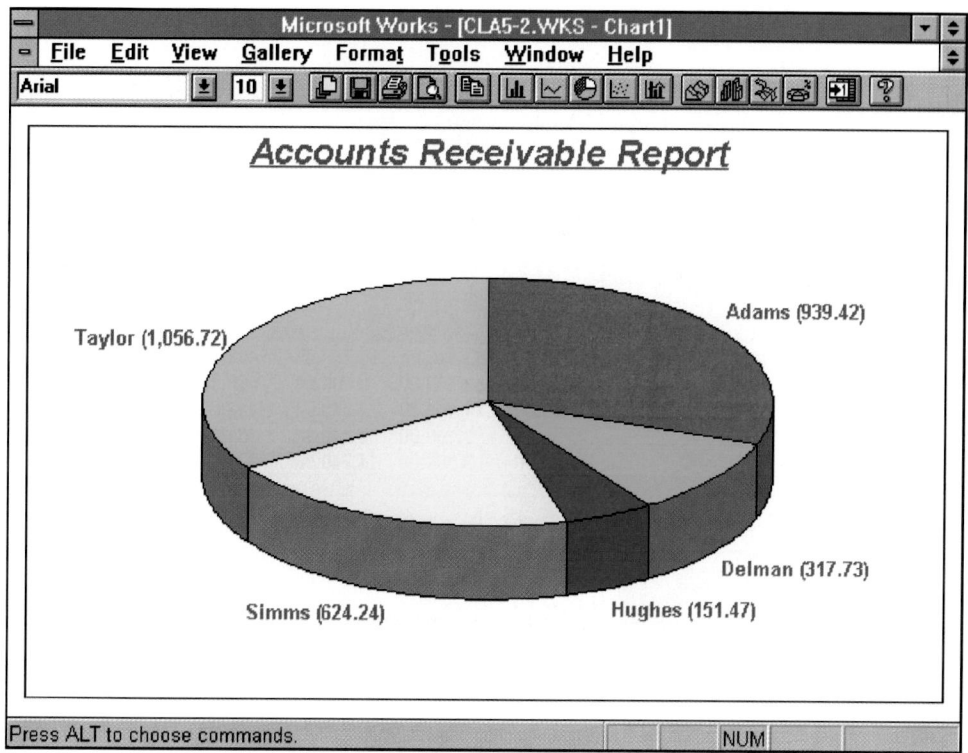

FIGURE CLA5-2b

COMPUTER LABORATORY ASSIGNMENT 3
Creating a Used Car Inventory Report

Purpose: To provide experience using the Works Spreadsheet to create a spreadsheet that requires entering text, numbers, and formulas, formatting text and numeric data, using the SUM function, adding color to a spreadsheet, sorting a spreadsheet, printing a spreadsheet, displaying and printing the formulas on the spreadsheet, and creating a 3-D Pie chart with data labels and a formatted title.

Problem: Create a Used Car Inventory Report using the data in the table on the right.

The spreadsheet is shown in Figure CLA5-3a on the next page.

AUTO	YEAR OF AUTO	ORIGINAL PRICE
Buick	1991	19,600.00
Cadillac	1992	35,400.00
Chevrolet	1994	17,800.00
Ford	1989	19,200.00
Nissan	1992	22,900.00

Instructions:

1. Create the spreadsheet in the format shown in Figure CLA5-3a using the numbers and text from the table.
2. For this spreadsheet, assume the current year is 1995. Obtain the Age of the auto by subtracting the Year of Auto from the value 1995.
3. Calculate the Lost Value, or depreciation, of the auto based on the fact that the auto loses 20% of its original price its first year and 10% of its original price for every year after the first year. Therefore, the Lost Value is equal to the Original Price times 20% plus the (Original Price times the Age less one year) times 10%.
4. Calculate Current Value equals the Original Price minus the Lost Value.
5. Calculate Profit equals 7% of the Current Value.
6. Calculate Sales Price equals Current Value plus the Profit.

(continued)

COMPUTER LABORATORY ASSIGNMENT 3 (continued)

Auto	Year of Auto	Age	Original	Lost Value	Current Value	Profit	Sales Price
\multicolumn{8}{c}{**Used Car Inventory Report**}							
Ford	1989	6	$19,200.00	$13,440.00	$5,760.00	$403.20	$6,163.20
Buick	1991	4	19,600.00	9,800.00	9,800.00	686.00	10,486.00
Cadilliac	1992	3	35,400.00	14,160.00	21,240.00	1,486.80	22,726.80
Nissan	1992	3	22,900.00	9,160.00	13,740.00	961.80	14,701.80
Chevrolet	1994	1	17,800.00	3,560.00	14,240.00	996.80	15,236.80

Inventory Summary

Projected Selling Price	$69,314.60
Current Inventory Value	$64,780.00
POTENTIAL PROFIT	$4,534.60

FIGURE CLA5-3A

7. In the Inventory Summary, the Projected Selling Price is the sum of the individual sales prices. Current Inventory Value equals the sum of the Current Values for all autos.
8. Potential Profit equals the sum of all the values in the Profit column.
9. Format the spreadsheet as shown. Add color and patterns in the spreadsheet to display as illustrated in Figure CLA 5-3a. The color for the cells where the spreadsheet title, column titles, and Inventory Summary sections display uses a non-solid pattern and combined foreground and background colors. Experiment with various patterns and color combinations to obtain the desired result. The titles display in white. Experiment to determine the background color for the text and numbers in the spreadsheet. The Potential Profit displays in dark green. The row 11 height is 23. Experiment to determine the proper column widths to display the entire spreadsheet on a single screen.
10. Sort the spreadsheet into ascending sequence by Year of Auto and by Auto name within the year.
11. Save the spreadsheet you create on a diskette. Use a filename consisting of the initials of your first and last names followed by the assignment number. Example: TC5-3.
12. Print the spreadsheet you have created on a single page.
13. Create the 3-D Pie chart in Figure CLA5-3b from the Current Value contained on the spreadsheet. The chart title is dark magenta 20 point Arial bold italic underlined font. The data labels are dark magenta 10 point Arial bold font.
14. Print the 3-D Pie chart.
15. Save the spreadsheet and chart.
16. Sort the spreadsheet in descending sequence based on the Profit field.
17. Format the spreadsheet so all formulas display. To do this, select the View menu and choose the Formulas command. Reduce the size of the spreadsheet and change the column widths so all formulas display. For further information on this process, see Computer Laboratory Exercise 1 on page W5.53 and Computer Laboratory Exercise 3 on page W5.54. Modify the column widths so all formulas are easily read on a single screen. The screen should resemble the screen in Figure CLA5-3c. Print the spreadsheet on a single page.
18. Follow directions from your instructor for turning in this assignment.

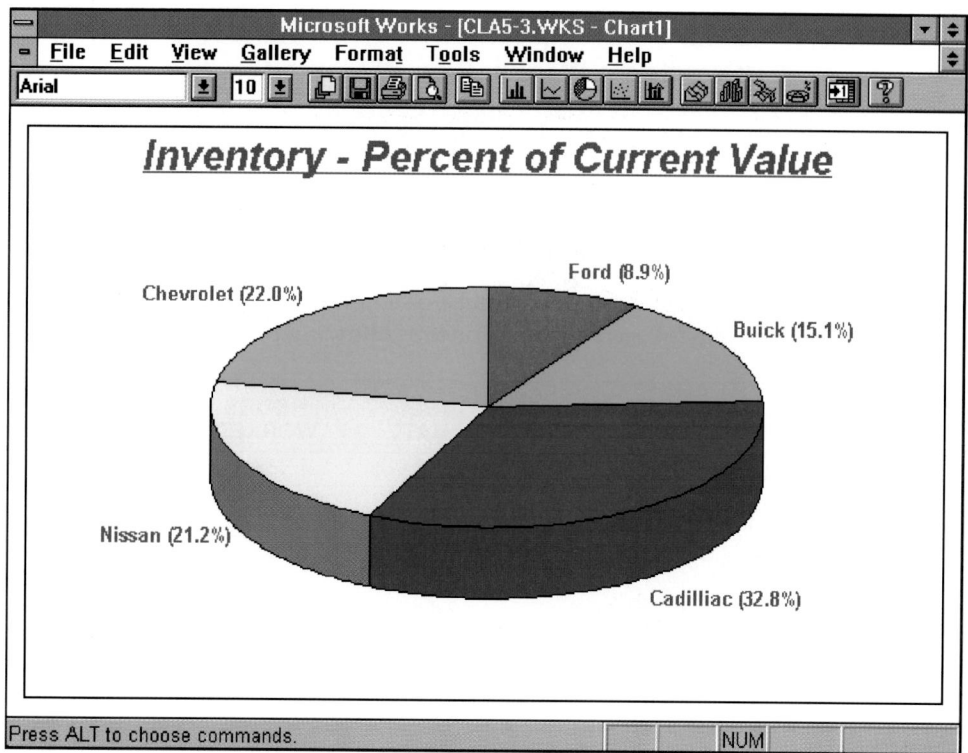

FIGURE CLA5-3b

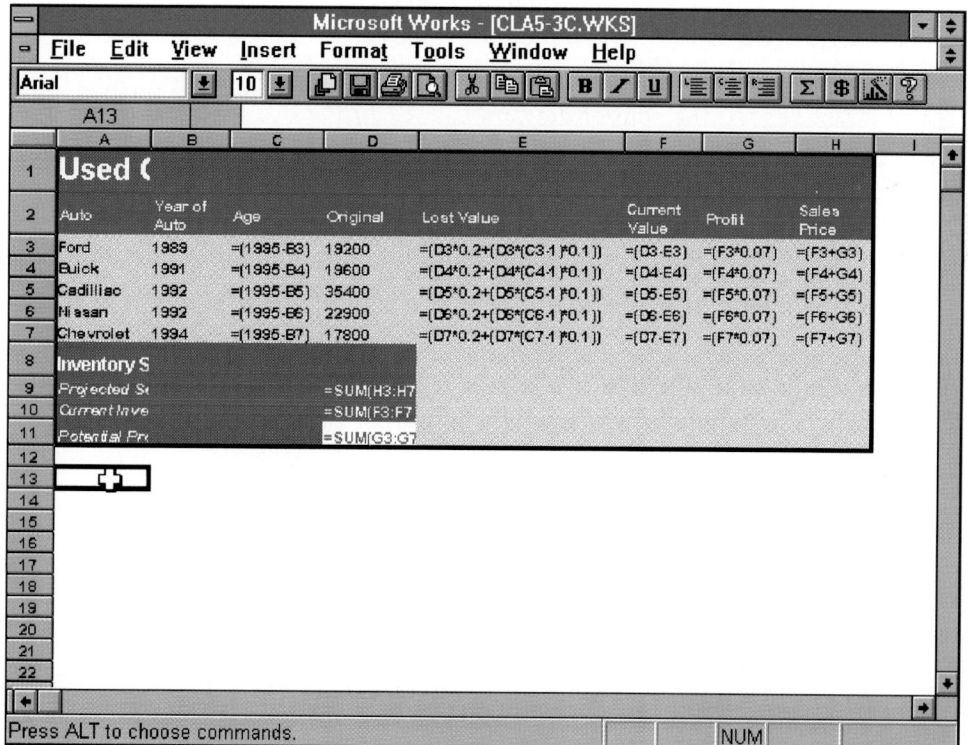

FIGURE CLA5-3c

COMPUTER LABORATORY ASSIGNMENT 4
Creating a Weekly Payroll Spreadsheet

Purpose: To provide experience using the Works Spreadsheet to create a spreadsheet that requires entering text, numbers, and formulas, formatting text and numeric data, using the SUM function, adding color, sorting a spreadsheet, printing a spreadsheet, displaying and printing the formulas on the spreadsheet, and creating a 3-D Pie chart with data labels and a formatted title.

Problem: You are employed in the payroll department of a computer assembly plant. Your manager asked you to prepare a weekly payroll spreadsheet for the following employees.

EMPLOYEE NUMBER	EMPLOYEE	HOURLY PAY RATE	HOURS WORKED	DEPENDENTS
221-7786	Hills, Marla	10.70	38	4
382-2153	Burrello, Anthony	15.60	40	2
560-5738	Peters, Ted	12.70	40	5
641-9074	Somme, Hilda	18.20	40	2
780-9805	Caruthers, Jake	9.10	38	1

Instructions:

1. Design and create a spreadsheet that includes the five fields listed in the table. In addition, you must include Gross Pay, Federal Tax, State Tax, and Net Pay. The formulas to use are:
   a. Gross Pay = Hourly Pay Rate * Hours Worked.
   b. Federal Tax = 24% * (Gross Pay - (Dependents * 40.00)).
   c. State Tax = 2.9% * (Gross Pay - (Dependents * 40.00)).
   d. Net Pay = Gross Pay - (Federal Tax + State Tax).
2. Calculate the totals for Gross Pay, Federal Tax, State Tax, and Net Pay and display them on the spreadsheet.
3. Format the spreadsheet appropriately. Add color to the spreadsheet to produce an attractive document.
4. Sort the spreadsheet in ascending sequence by Employee last name.
5. Save the spreadsheet you create on a diskette. Use a filename consisting of the initials of your first and last names followed by the assignment number. Example: TC5-4.
6. Print the spreadsheet you have created on a single page of paper.
7. Create a 3-D Pie chart based on Net Pay. Include an appropriate chart title. Use the Employee Number for the first data label and the Net Pay for the second data label. Format the chart title and data labels.
8. Sort the spreadsheet in ascending sequence by Employee Number.
9. Print the spreadsheet.
10. Follow directions from your instructor for turning in this assignment.

MICROSOFT WORKS 3.0 FOR WINDOWS

PROJECT SIX

▼

WHAT-IF ANALYSIS, FUNCTIONS, AND ABSOLUTE CELL REFERENCES

▼

WHAT-IF ANALYSIS, FUNCTIONS, AND ABSOLUTE CELL REFERENCES

OBJECTIVES You will have mastered the material in this project when you can:

- Enter spreadsheet titles
- Wrap text using the Alignment command
- Enter dates
- Identify the different date formats
- Change a column width by dragging
- Copy dates using the Fill Series command
- Specify day, weekday, month, and year options for copying dates
- Copy numeric cell contents using a formula
- Round cell contents using the ROUND function
- Explain the difference between the ROUND function and the rounding obtained using the Comma format

- Copy a function
- Enter a formula containing absolute cell references
- Copy a formula containing absolute and relative cell references
- Format a spreadsheet with color
- Perform what-if analysis on a spreadsheet with multiple variables
- Identify rounding discrepancies
- Add rows and columns to a spreadsheet
- Delete rows and columns from a spreadsheet

▶ INTRODUCTION

I n Project 4 and Project 5, you learned that a spreadsheet is useful for performing calculations and presenting data both as a spreadsheet and as a chart. You can also use spreadsheets to solve business, financial, and accounting problems that otherwise would be difficult to solve.

In particular, spreadsheets provide a means for asking **what-if questions** and obtaining immediate answers. For example, a business person might ask, What if we increased our sales twenty-two percent next year and our costs decreased twelve percent. What would be the net result to our profits? A Works Spreadsheet can easily provide the answer to this question.

▶ PROJECT SIX

T o illustrate the capability of Works to provide the answers to what-if questions, Project 6 produces the spreadsheet shown in Figure 6-1. The spreadsheet contains projections for a beginning publishing business. The business consists of publishing outstanding literary papers by university undergraduates and graduates in a literary newsletter.

In the spreadsheet in Figure 6-1, the Date is the date on which the newsletter will be published. The spreadsheet covers the first six months of publication. The Copies Printed column contains the number of copies the owners of the business have determined they will print on each of the publication dates. The number of Copies Printed for January 15, 1995 in cell B4 comes from the Copies Printed entry in cell B13 within the Assumptions section of the spreadsheet. Notice that for each succeeding month, the number of Copies Printed increases by ten percent.

The number of Copies Sold is a projection based upon the owner's previous experience that they never sell all the copies they print. In Figure 6-1, the owners project they will sell 90% of the copies they print. The percentage is stored in cell B14 in the Assumptions section. Copies Sold is determined by multiplying the number of Copies Printed (column B) times the % Printed Sold in cell B14. For example, for the January printing, the owners project they will sell 1,800 copies (2,000 * .90). It is to the owner's advantage to print only as many copies as they will sell, but they know this seldom happens.

The Income is determined by multiplying the number of Copies Sold (column C) times the Price per Copy in cell B11. The Price per Copy in Figure 6-1 is $1.00. Therefore, for the January 15 edition, the Income is $1,800.00 (1,800 * $1.00).

The Expense is calculated by multiplying the number of Copies Printed (column B) times the Expense per Copy in cell B12. The Expense per Copy in the spreadsheet shown is $0.50, so the Expense for January is $1,000.00 (2,000 * .50).

The Net is calculated by subtracting the Expense (column E) from the Income (column D). In Figure 6-1, the Net for the January 15, 1995 edition is $800.00 ($1,800.00 – $1,000.00).

The Assumptions section of the spreadsheet in Figure 6-1 contains the values used in the formulas in the spreadsheet. The owners can vary the values in the Assumptions section to ask what-if questions about their business. For example, they can ask, How much do Income and Net change if we change the Price per Copy from $1.00 to $1.25 while assuming all other variables remain the same? The result of this change is shown in Figure 6-2 on the next page.

Publishing Business Projections

Date	Copies Printed	Copies Sold	Income	Expense	Net
January 15, 1995	2,000	1,800	1,800.00	1,000.00	800.00
February 15, 1995	2,200	1,980	1,980.00	1,100.00	880.00
March 15, 1995	2,420	2,178	2,178.00	1,210.00	968.00
April 15, 1995	2,662	2,396	2,396.00	1,331.00	1,065.00
May 15, 1995	2,928	2,635	2,635.00	1,464.00	1,171.00
June 15, 1995	3,221	2,899	2,899.00	1,610.50	1,288.50

Assumptions

Price per Copy	$1.00
Expense per Copy	$0.50
Copies Printed	2,000
% Printed Sold	90.00%

FIGURE 6-1

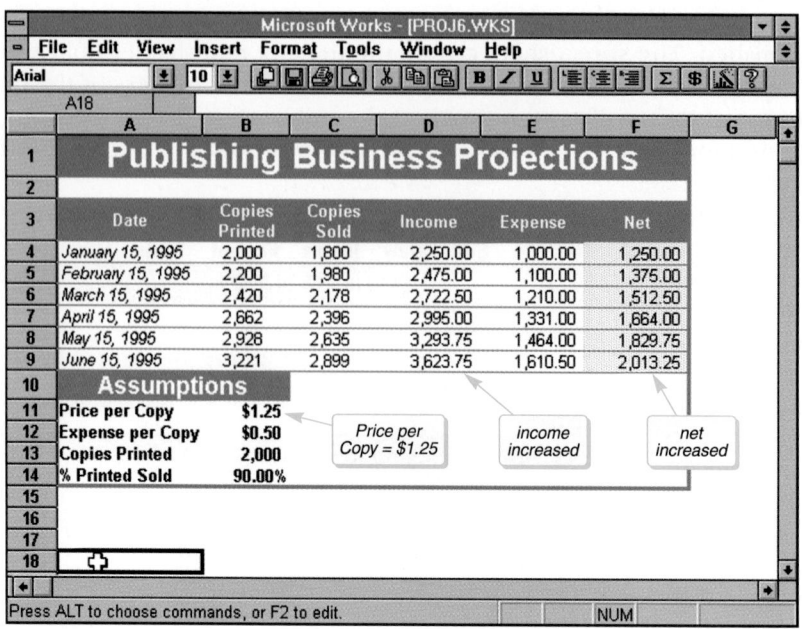

FIGURE 6-2

As you can see, changing the Price per Copy from $1.00 to $1.25 increases the Income and increases the Net. This spreadsheet can help the owners make decisions to maximize their profitability.

When a business starts out, the owners are often concerned with breaking even financially on their venture. Therefore, the owners of this publishing business want to determine answers to the following questions:

1. If we print 2,000 copies at an expense of $0.50 per copy and sell them for $1.00 apiece, what percentage of the copies we print must we sell to break even?
2. If our Expense per Copy is $0.36, we print 2,000 copies, and we sell 45% of the copies we print, at what price can we sell the newsletter and still break even?
3. If we sell the newsletter for $0.75 apiece, print 2,000 copies, and we are able to sell 40% of the copies we print, what is the maximum expense per newsletter we can pay and still break even?

These and other questions can be answered by the spreadsheet shown in Figure 6-1 on the previous page.

Spreadsheet Preparation Steps

The overall steps to prepare the spreadsheet in Figure 6-1 are listed below.

1. Start the Works Spreadsheet.
2. Enter the spreadsheet title (Publishing Business Projections) and the column titles (Date, Copies Printed, Copies Sold, Income, Expense, and Net). Format the column titles so they are easy to read.
3. Enter the dates in column A.
4. Enter the Assumptions section titles (Assumptions, Price per Copy, Expense per Copy, Copies Printed, and % Printed Sold).
5. Enter the assumed values shown in Figure 6-1.

6. Enter the formulas to calculate Copies Printed, Copies Sold, Income, Expense, and Net, and copy them for each of the six months.
7. Format the titles on the spreadsheet.
8. Format the numeric values on the spreadsheet.
9. Save the spreadsheet on disk.
10. Add color and a border to the spreadsheet.
11. Save the spreadsheet with color.
12. Print the spreadsheet.

The following pages contain a detailed explanation of each of these steps.

▶ STARTING THE WORKS SPREADSHEET

 o start the Works Spreadsheet, follow the steps you used in previous projects. These steps are reviewed below.

TO START THE WORKS SPREADSHEET

Step 1: From Program Manager, open the Microsoft Works for Windows group window.

Step 2: Double-click the Microsoft Works program-item icon.

Step 3: If necessary, choose the Start Works Now button and then point to the Spreadsheet button in the Works Startup dialog box.

Step 4: Choose the Spreadsheet button in the Works Startup dialog box.

Step 5: If the Microsoft Works window is not maximized, maximize it.

Step 6: Maximize the Sheet1 document window.

▶ ENTERING SPREADSHEET TITLES

 o enter the titles on the spreadsheet in Project 6, first highlight the cells in which the titles belong and then type the titles, as illustrated in the following steps.

TO ENTER SPREADSHEET TITLES ▼

STEP 1 ▶

Highlight the cell where you will enter the title – cell A1 (Figure 6-3).

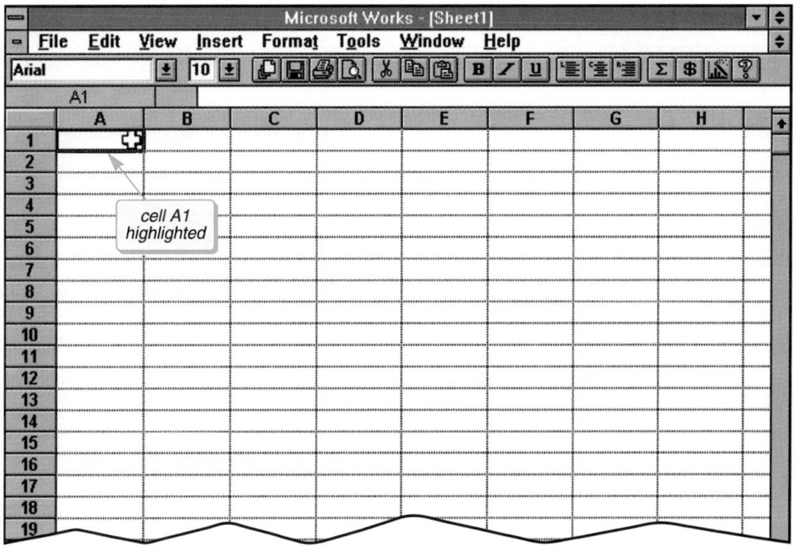

FIGURE 6-3

STEP 2 ▶

Type the spreadsheet title, Publishing Business Projections, **and either press the ENTER key or click the Enter box.**

Works enters the spreadsheet title into cell A1 (Figure 6-4).

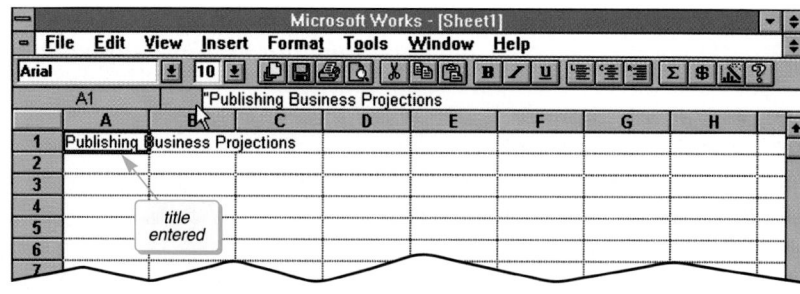

FIGURE 6-4

STEP 3 ▶

Type and enter the column titles in row 3.

The column titles display in row 3 (Figure 6-5). Because the column titles, Copies Printed and Copies Sold, contain more characters than can display in a cell, only the leftmost characters display. Row 2 was left blank to allow for a blank white line to appear between the spreadsheet title and the column titles.

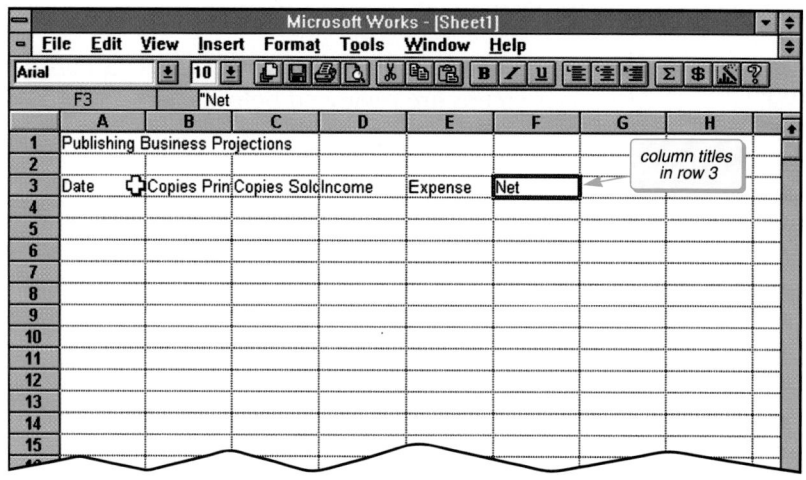

FIGURE 6-5

Wrapping Text

Because the columns titles, Copies Printed and Copies Sold, are difficult to read, it is recommended that you immediately format the column titles using Wrap Text. To wrap the text in the column titles, complete the following steps.

TO WRAP TEXT ▼

STEP 1 ▶

Highlight cells A3:F3. Select the Format menu and point to the Alignment command.

*Cells A3:F3 are highlighted, the Format menu displays, and the mouse pointer points to the **Alignment command** (Figure 6-6).*

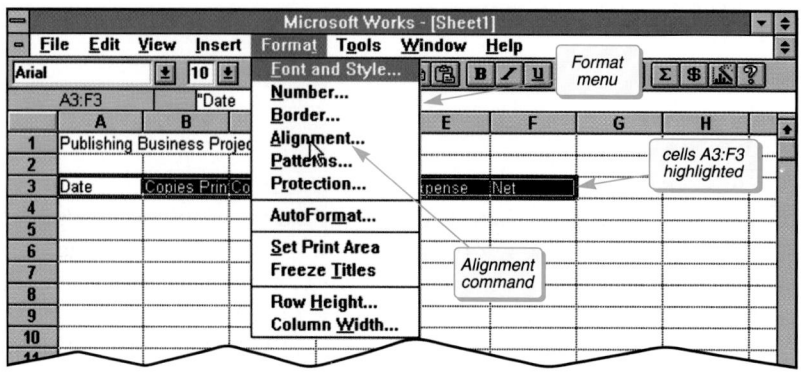

FIGURE 6-6

STEP 2 ▶

Choose the Alignment command from the Format menu. When the Alignment dialog box displays, select the Center option button in the Alignment area, select the Wrap text check box, select the Center option button in the Vertical area, and then point to the OK button.

The Alignment dialog box displays (Figure 6-7). The Center option button in the Alignment area is selected, the Wrap text check box is selected, the Center option button in the Vertical area is selected, and the mouse pointer points to the OK button.

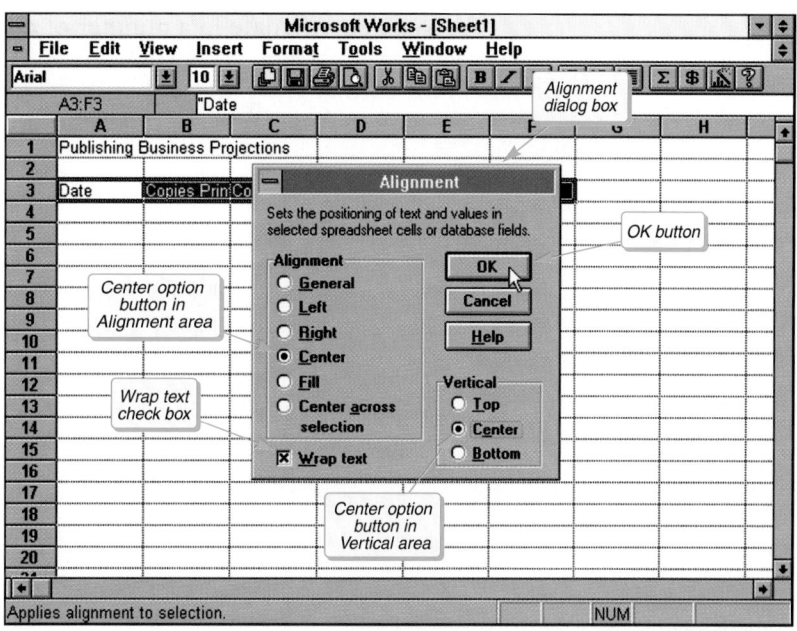

FIGURE 6-7

STEP 3 ▶

Choose the OK button in the Alignment dialog box.

The column titles, Copies Printed and Copies Sold, are centered horizontally and vertically and display on two lines (Figure 6-8). Works changes the row height to accommodate two lines. The other column titles are centered within their cells.

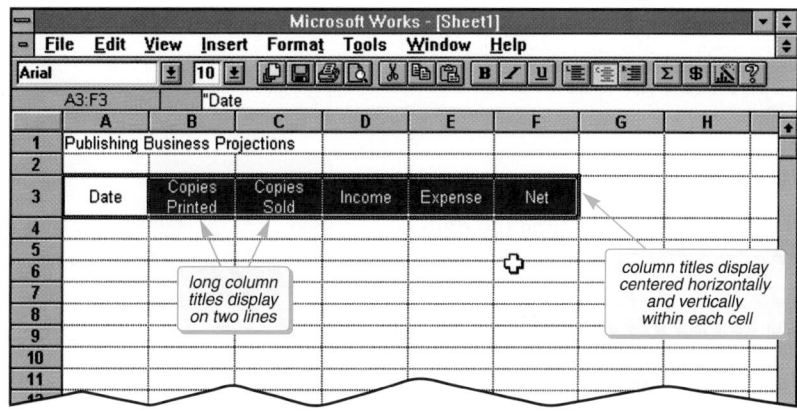

FIGURE 6-8

The column titles are now easy to read. To remove the highlight from row 3, click any cell in the spreadsheet.

▶ ENTERING DATES

A fter entering the column titles, the next step is to enter the dates in cells A4 through A9. When you enter a date, Works considers the date a numeric value. Therefore, a date is displayed right-aligned in the cell. After you type and confirm the entry of the date, if the date you enter contains more characters than can be stored in the cell, Works displays all # signs rather than continuing the characters into the next cell as it does with text characters.

You can enter a date in a number of different **date formats**. For example, the date, January 15, 1995, can also be entered as 1/15/95. Works initially displays the date in the format you enter it, but the date can be displayed in different formats as well. Table 6-1 contains the different formats in which a date can be displayed.

▶ **TABLE 6-1**

DATE ENTERED	FORMAT NAME	DATA DISPLAYED
January 15, 1995	Month, day, year - Long format	January 15, 1995
January 15, 1995	Month, day, year - Short format	1/15/95
January 15, 1995	Month, year - Long format	January 1995
January 15, 1995	Month, year - Short format	1/95
January 15, 1995	Month, day - Long format	January 15
January 15, 1995	Month, day - Short format	1/15
January 15, 1995	Month - Long format	January

In Project 6, the date is entered as January 15, 1995, so Works displays it in the Month, day, year – Long format. If you want to change the format of the date, choose the **Number command** from the Format menu, select the Date option button, and then select the format you want.

To enter the date in cell A4 in Project 6, perform the following steps.

TO ENTER A DATE ▼

STEP 1 ▶

Highlight cell A4 and type the date –
January 15, 1995.

Works displays a portion of the date you typed in the highlighted cell and the entire date in the formula bar (Figure 6-9).

FIGURE 6-9

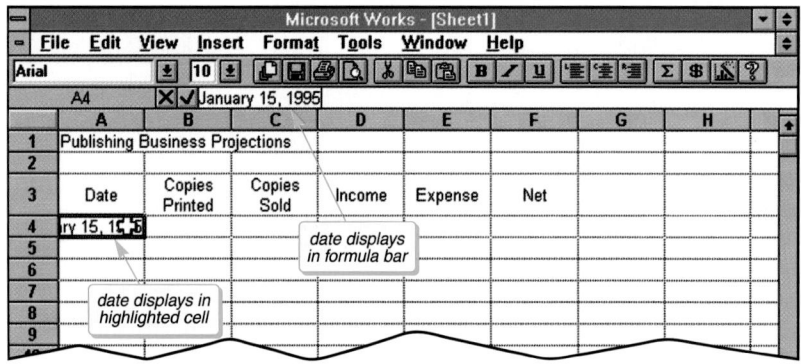

STEP 2 ▶

Confirm the entry by clicking the Enter box or pressing the ENTER key.

Because the date you entered contains more characters than Works can display in the cell, Works displays all # signs (Figure 6-10). To display the date entered, you must increase the width of column A.

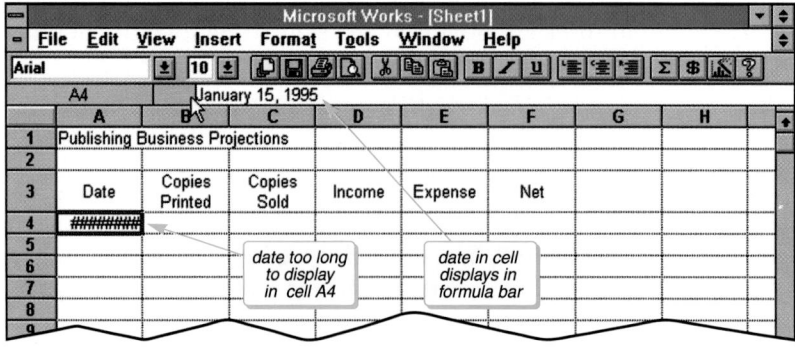

FIGURE 6-10

Works provides several methods of increasing column width. The following paragraphs describe how to increase the column width by dragging.

Increasing Column Width by Dragging

In previous projects you have seen how to change the **column width** through the use of the Column Width command on the Format menu. In this project, you will change the column width by dragging the column border, as shown in the following steps.

TO CHANGE COLUMN WIDTH BY DRAGGING THE COLUMN BORDER ▼

STEP 1 ▶

Place the mouse pointer on the border line that separates column A and column B in the column headings.

The mouse pointer changes to a symbol consisting of two vertical lines with arrowheads on the left and right sides and the word ADJUST below it (Figure 6-11). This indicates you can drag the column border left or right.

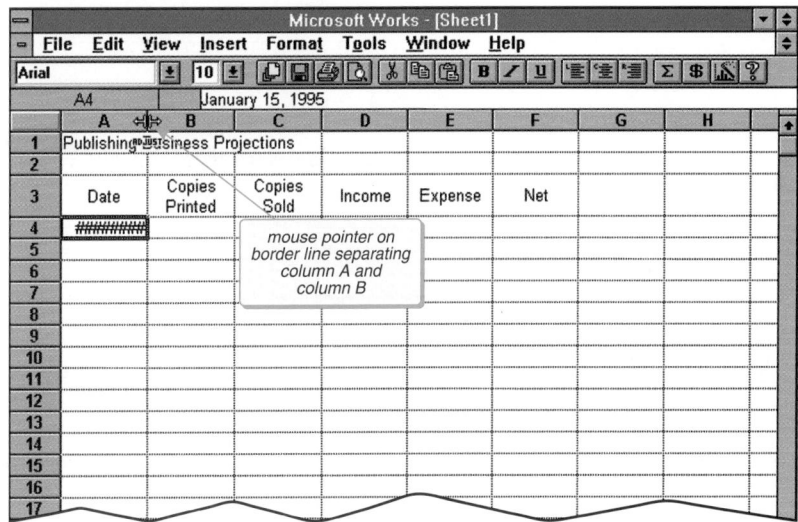

FIGURE 6-11

STEP 2 ▶

Drag the column border slowly to the right to approximately 3/4 the width of column B.

As you drag, the proposed column border represented by a gridline moves to the right (Figure 6-12). In some cases when you drag a border, you will not get the border the exact width you want and you may have to experiment to achieve the correct width.

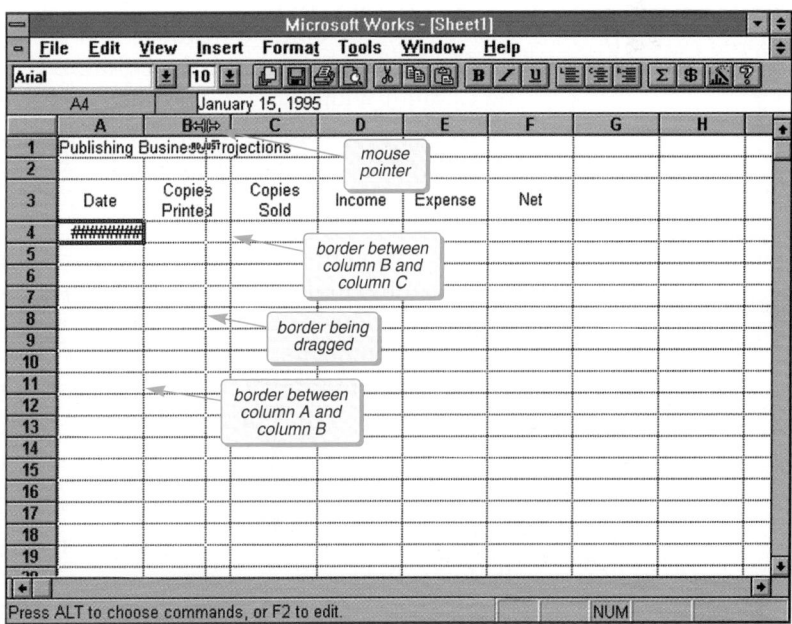

FIGURE 6-12

STEP 3 ▶

Release the left mouse button.

Works changes the width of column A to the width you selected by dragging the border and displays the date in the proper format (Figure 6-13).

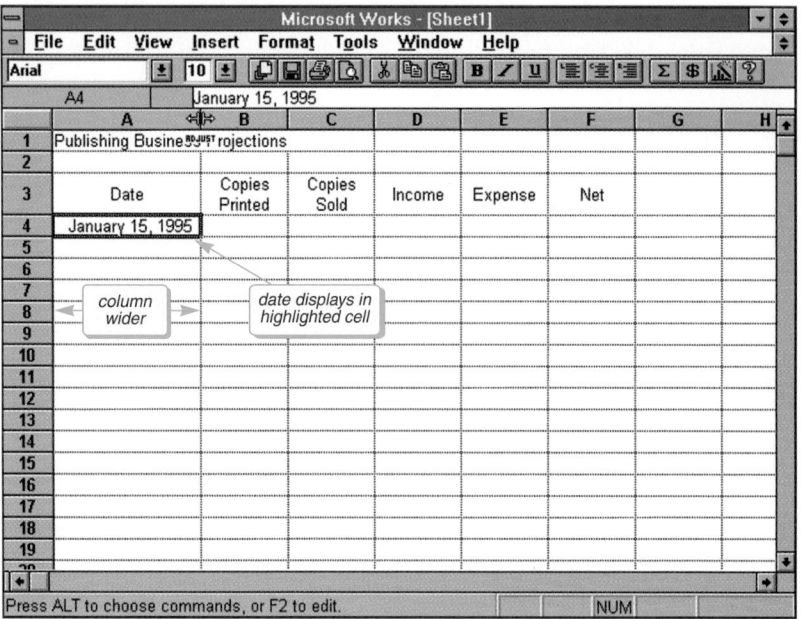

FIGURE 6-13

The technique of dragging a column border to change column width is an alternative to using the Column Width command from the Format menu. The advantage of dragging is that you can see the data on the screen and can visually fit the column width to the data without having to guess the correct column width. The major disadvantage occurs when you want to set the column width to an exact width, such as 17. Works does not display the actual column width as you drag the column border so the column width you set may not be the exact width you want and you will have to perform the process again.

Another technique you can use to fit the date, January 15, 1995, in a cell is to double-click the column heading. Works will change the column width to properly display the widest entry in the column. You can also select **best fit** by choosing the Column Width command from the Format menu and selecting the Best Fit check box in the Column Width dialog box.

Fill Series Command

After you enter the January date into the spreadsheet, the next task is to enter the remaining months. One method to accomplish this is to type each date in the manner previously explained. A more convenient method involves the use of the Fill Series command.

As noted in Project 4, the **Fill Series command** on the Edit menu allows you to copy certain types of data that Works will update for you. In this project, the dates, February 15, 1995 through June 15, 1995, are to be placed in cells A5 through A9, respectively. Works will automatically change the name of the month to the name of the following month when you copy the date in cell A4 to cells A5:A9 using the Fill Series command. To use the Fill Series command, complete the following steps.

TO COPY THE DATE USING THE FILL SERIES COMMAND ▼

STEP 1 ►

Highlight the cell containing the date to copy – cell A4 – and the range that will contain the copied dates – cells A5:A9 (Figure 6-14).

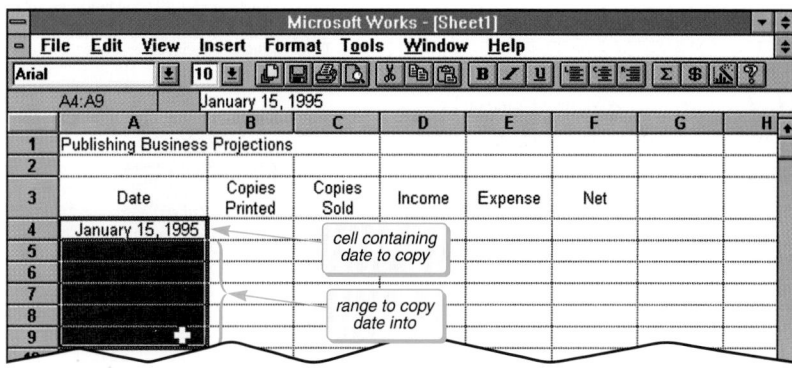

FIGURE 6-14

STEP 2 ►

Select the Edit menu and point to the Fill Series command.

The Edit menu displays and the mouse pointer points to the Fill Series command (Figure 6-15).

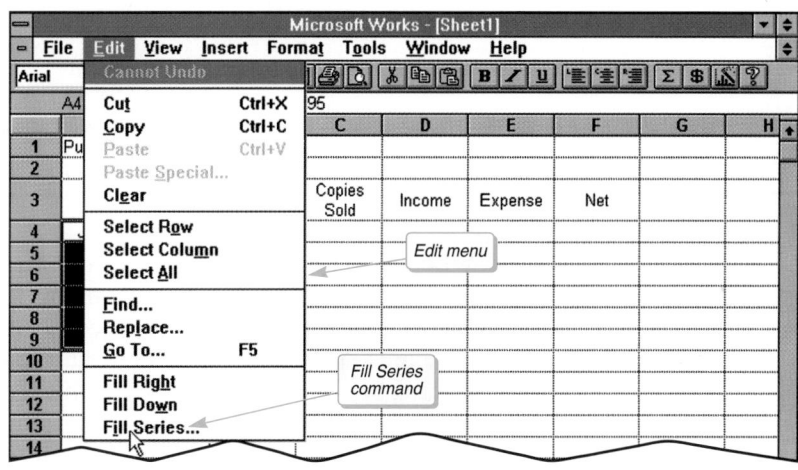

FIGURE 6-15

STEP 3 ►

Choose the Fill Series command from the Edit menu. When the Fill Series dialog box displays, select the Month option button. Point to the OK button.

Works displays the Fill Series dialog box (Figure 6-16). The Units area contains four options you can select to specify how Works will copy the date. The Month option button is selected and the mouse pointer points to the OK button.

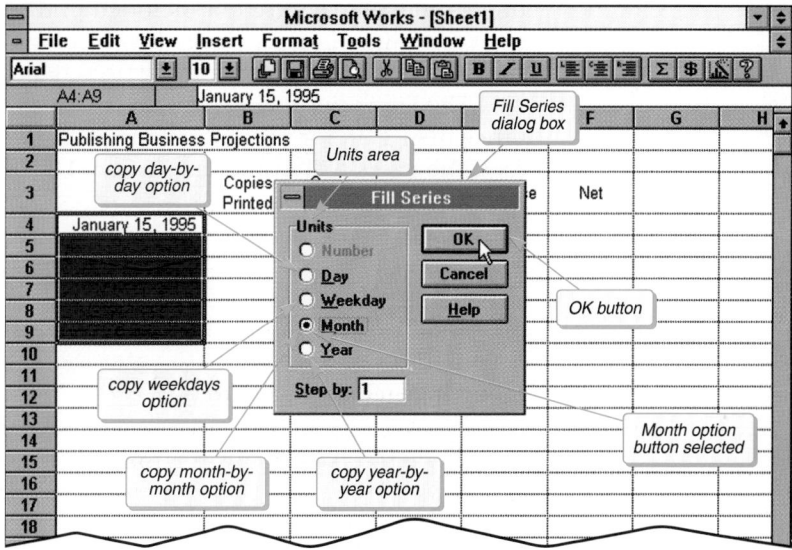

FIGURE 6-16

STEP 4 ▶

Choose the OK button in the Fill Series dialog box.

Works fills the highlighted cells A5:A9 with the dates (Figure 6-17). Each month name reflects the next successive month, that is, February, March, April, May, and June.

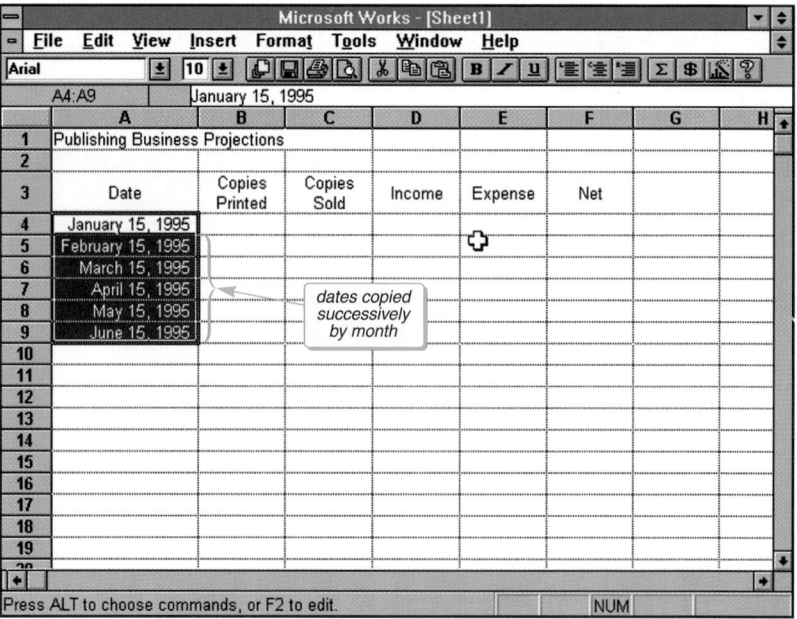

FIGURE 6-17

When the Fill Series command is completed, the range remains highlighted. To remove the highlight, click any cell in the spreadsheet.

You can also use the Fill Series command to increment values other than the month names. Notice in Figure 6-16 on the previous page that the Units area contains four other option buttons. The Number option button is available when a number is in a cell and the Fill Series command is used. This selection will allow the number in the original cell to be incremented in adjacent highlighted cells. The Day option will increment the day by one for each new cell. If you select that option, the dates will run January 15, 1995, January 16, 1995, January 17, 1995, and so on. The Weekday option means the date will increment by one day but Saturdays and Sundays are not included in the series. Finally, the Year option causes the year to increment by one. If you select Year, the dates will appear successively as January 15, 1995, January 15, 1996, January 15, 1997, and so on.

The Fill Series dialog box also allows you to increment by (Step by) a number other than 1. If, for example, you select the Year option and set the Step by entry to 3, the dates will display as January 15, 1995, January 15, 1998, January 15, 2001, and so on.

Entering Assumptions Section Titles

The next task in preparing the spreadsheet for Project 6 is to enter the Assumptions section titles. To enter the Assumptions section titles, complete the following steps (see Figure 6-18).

TO ENTER ASSUMPTION TITLES

Step 1: Highlight cell A10, type `Assumptions`, and press the DOWN ARROW key.

Step 2: Type `Price per Copy`, press the DOWN ARROW key, type `Expense per Copy`, press the DOWN ARROW key, type `Copies Printed`, press the DOWN ARROW key, type `% Printed Sold`, and press the ENTER key.

The spreadsheet after the titles are entered is shown in Figure 6-18.

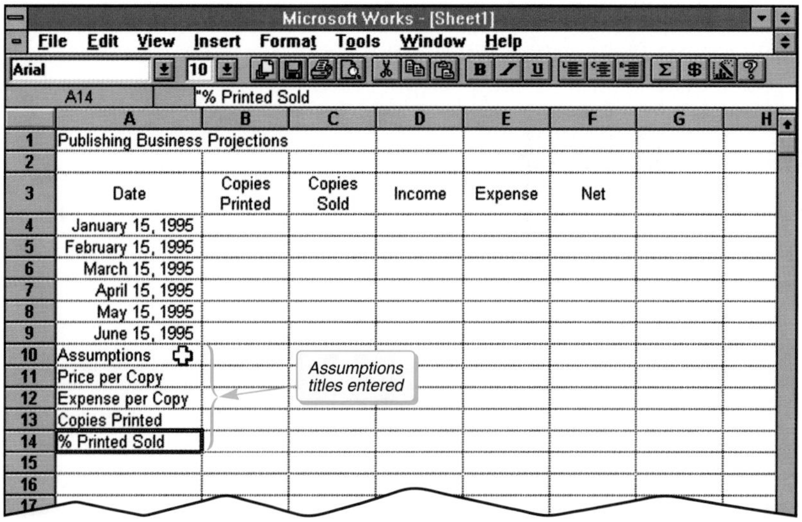

FIGURE 6-18

Entering Numeric Values

Before entering the formulas required to perform the calculations on the Publishing Business Projections spreadsheet, you will find it is useful to enter values in the Assumptions cells so you can more easily reference these cells when you enter the formulas. Complete the following step to enter the values in the Assumptions cells (see Figure 6-19).

TO ENTER NUMERIC DATA

Step 1: Highlight cell B11, type 1.00, and press the DOWN ARROW key. Type .50 and press the DOWN ARROW key. Type 2000 and press the DOWN ARROW key. Type .90 and press the ENTER key.

The Assumptions values display in cells B11:B14 (Figure 6-19).

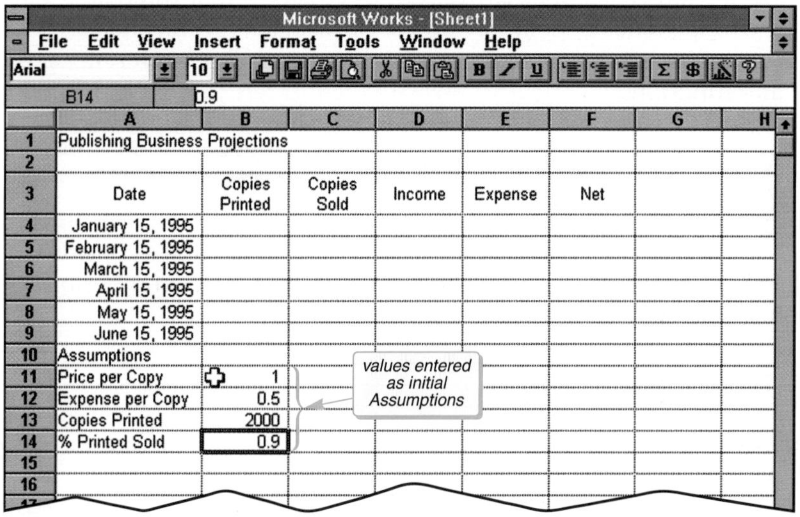

FIGURE 6-19

Notice that even though you type the Price per Copy in cell B11 as 1.00, the value displays as 1 when you confirm the entry. Also, if you enter a value without a zero to the left of the decimal point (for example, the Expense per Copy as .50), Works by default displays the value with a zero to the left of the decimal point (0.5). You will format these values later in the project.

▶ ENTERING FORMULAS

T he Copies Printed, Copies Sold, Income, Expense, and Net fields in the spreadsheet are calculated using formulas (Figure 6-20). Thus, to continue building the spreadsheet, you must enter the formulas in their respective cells.

	A	B	C	D	E	F	G	H
1	Publishing Business Projections							
2								
3	Date	Copies Printed	Copies Sold	Income	Expense	Net		
4	January 15, 1995	2000	1800	1800	1000	800		
5	February 15, 1995	2200	1980	1980	1100	880		
6	March 15, 1995	2420	2178	2178	1210	968		
7	April 15, 1995	2662	2396	2396	1331	1065		
8	May 15, 1995	2928	2635	2635	1464	1171		
9	June 15, 1995	3221	2899	2899	1610.5	1288.5		
10	Assumptions							
11	Price per Copy	1						
12	Expense per Copy	0.5						
13	Copies Printed	2000						
14	% Printed Sold	0.9						
15								
16								
17								
18								
19								

Copies Printed, Copies Sold, Income, Expense, and Net calculated from formulas

FIGURE 6-20

Recall from Project 5 that a **formula** is an equation that calculates a new value from existing values in cells within the spreadsheet. A formula always begins with an equal sign (=). It is followed by a combination of cell references, numbers, operators, and functions.

Copying Numeric Cell Contents Using a Formula

The Copies Printed field in column B is the first field to enter using a formula. This value reflects the number of copies of the newsletter that are printed each month. The value 2000 appears in cell B4 because that is the number of Copies Printed in January.

While you could enter the number 2000 in cell B4 as the number of Copies Printed in January and then use a formula to calculate the Copies Printed for subsequent months, the preferred way to design a spreadsheet is to place all values that can be varied in a specific location on the spreadsheet, such as the Assumptions section. Because the owners of the newsletter publishing business might want to examine the consequences if they publish a different number of newsletters in January, such as 3000 instead of 2000, the Copies Printed value should be placed in the Assumptions section of the spreadsheet and be incorporated into cell B4 through the use of a formula.

To copy the contents of cell B13 into cell B4 using a formula, complete the following steps.

TO COPY NUMERIC CELL CONTENTS USING A FORMULA ▼

STEP 1 ►

Highlight the cell to contain the formula – cell B4, type an equal sign, then highlight the cell containing the value to copy – cell B13.

The formula in cell B4 contains the equal sign and the cell reference for cell B13 (Figure 6-21). No other element in the formula is required because only cell B13 is used, so in effect the contents of cell B13 are copied into cell B4.

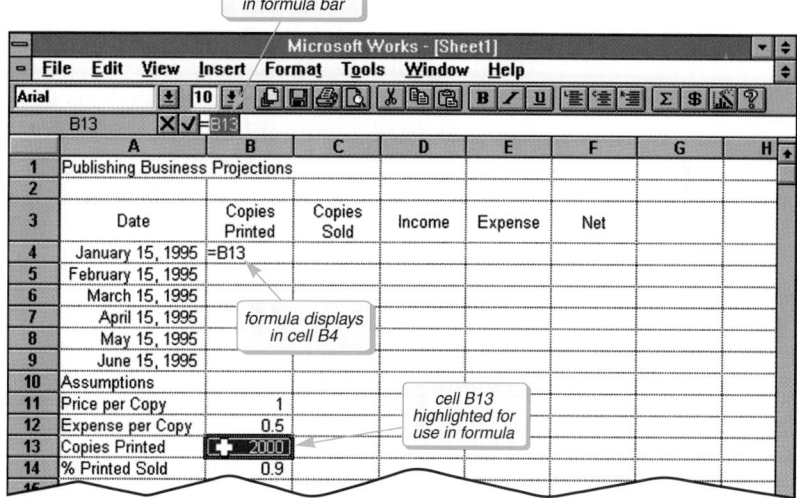

FIGURE 6-21

STEP 2 ►

Click the Enter box or press the ENTER key.

Works calculates the formula, which amounts to copying the contents of cell B13 into cell B4. The highlight returns to cell B4 (Figure 6-22).

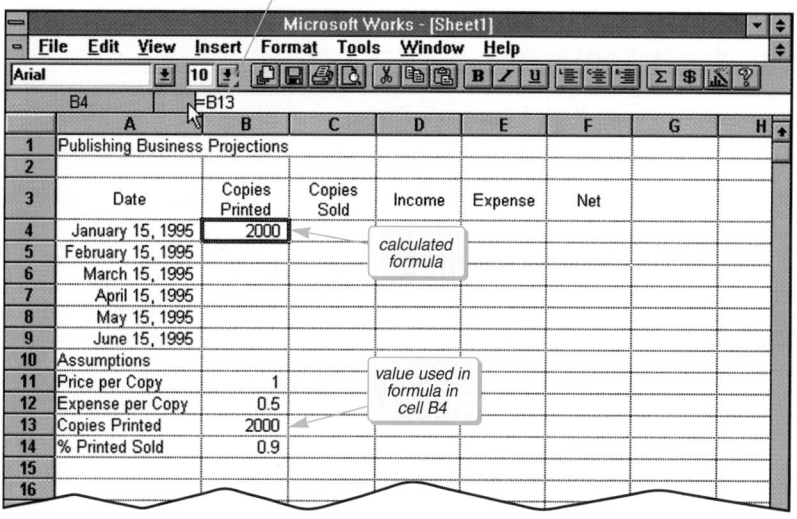

FIGURE 6-22

The next step in building the spreadsheet is to place the proper formula in the cells in the range B5:B9 to calculate the Copies Printed for the months February, March, April, May, and June. Recall that for each subsequent month, the number of Copies Printed is to increase by 10%. Therefore, in February 2200 copies will be printed, in March 2420 copies will be printed, and so on. The formula in cell B4 cannot merely be copied because it contains only the entry =B13. If you copied it, the change in the number of copies would not occur. Therefore, you must enter a new formula into cell B5.

▶ ROUNDING

T he formula required for cell B5 is =B4*1.1; that is, if the value in cell B4 (2000) is multiplied by the value 1.10, the value 2200 is obtained, which is a ten percent increase over the value 2000.

The Copies Printed in column B must always be a whole number because a fraction of a newsletter cannot be printed. Whenever you multiply a whole number by a number that contains positions to the right of a decimal point, however, the possibility exists that the answer will contain digits to the right of the decimal point. For example, if the value 2662 is multiplied by 1.10, the answer is 2928.2. Because 2928.2 cannot be the number of Copies Printed, you must change this number to a whole number.

Works provides two way to correct this situation. First, you can use the Comma format or the Fixed format and specify zero positions to the right of the decimal point. To do this, select the Format menu and choose the Number command from the menu. When the dialog box displays on the screen, select either the Fixed option button or the Comma option button and type zero in the Number of decimals text box. Then, choose the OK button in the dialog box. Works will round the displayed value in the cell. Therefore, in the example, the answer to the calculation 2662 * 1.10 would display as 2928, or 2,928 if the Comma format is used.

While this action takes care of the display issue, it does not completely solve the problem because even though the numbers are formatted correctly, the rounded values displayed in the cell are not the values Works uses in calculations. Thus, even though the value 2928 displays in the cell, the value 2928.2 would be used in calculations, resulting in answers on the spreadsheet that do not correspond. This condition is illustrated in Table 6-2.

▶ **TABLE 6-2**

Orignal Value	Product of Value *1.10	Display with Comma format, zero decimal positions	Result of Product * 10
2662	2928.2	2,928	29,282

In the table, the original value (2662) is multiplied by 1.10, giving a product of 2928.2. When the product is displayed using the Comma format and zero decimal positions, Works displays 2,928. When, however, the product appears in a formula, Works uses the value 2928.2. Therefore, the result of multiplying the product by 10 is 29,282, not 29,280 as would be expected when looking at the spreadsheet. By using formatting to produce a whole number on a spreadsheet, an error has been introduced.

Works offers a second method that works better. This method involves using the ROUND function. A **function** is a built-in equation you can use to calculate values in a spreadsheet. The **ROUND function** allows you to round any numeric value to the number of digits to the right or left of the decimal point you specify. For Copies Printed in the Publishing Business Projections spreadsheet, the rounded values should have no digits to the right of the decimal point.

The format of the round function is ROUND(x,NumberOfPlaces), where x is the value to round and NumberOfPlaces is a value specifying the number of positions to the right or left of the decimal point. If the value in NumberOfPlaces is positive, Works rounds the value x to the number of decimal places to the right of the decimal point. If NumberOfPlaces is negative, Works rounds to the number of places to the left of the decimal point. If the number is zero, x is rounded to the nearest integer.

The Copies Printed should be a whole number, so NumberOfPlaces should be zero.

The calculation in cell B5 to determine the Copies Printed is B4*1.1, which will multiply the value in cell B4 by 1.1, resulting in an increase in the number in cell B4 of 10%. The result of this calculation must be rounded to zero decimal places. Therefore, the formula containing the ROUND function should be =ROUND(B4*1.1,0), which states the value calculated by B4*1.1 should be rounded with zero positions to the right of the decimal point.

To enter the formula containing the ROUND function, complete the following steps.

TO ENTER A FORMULA CONTAINING THE ROUND FUNCTION ▼

STEP 1 ▶

Highlight the cell to contain the function – cell B5 – and type
`=round(`.

Works displays the data you typed in cell B5 and in the formula bar (Figure 6-23). The formula must begin with an equal sign. The word ROUND, which you can type in lowercase, uppercase, or a combination of the two, must be spelled properly, and be followed by a left parenthesis with no spaces in between.

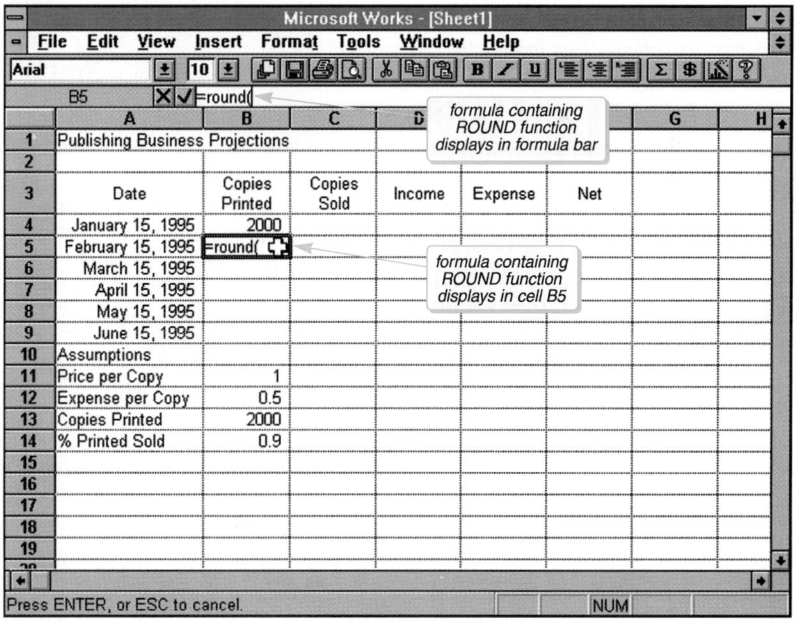

FIGURE 6-23

STEP 2 ►

Highlight cell B4 by clicking cell B4 or using the arrow keys.

Works highlights cell B4 with a black background and enters cell reference B4 into the function (Figure 6-24).

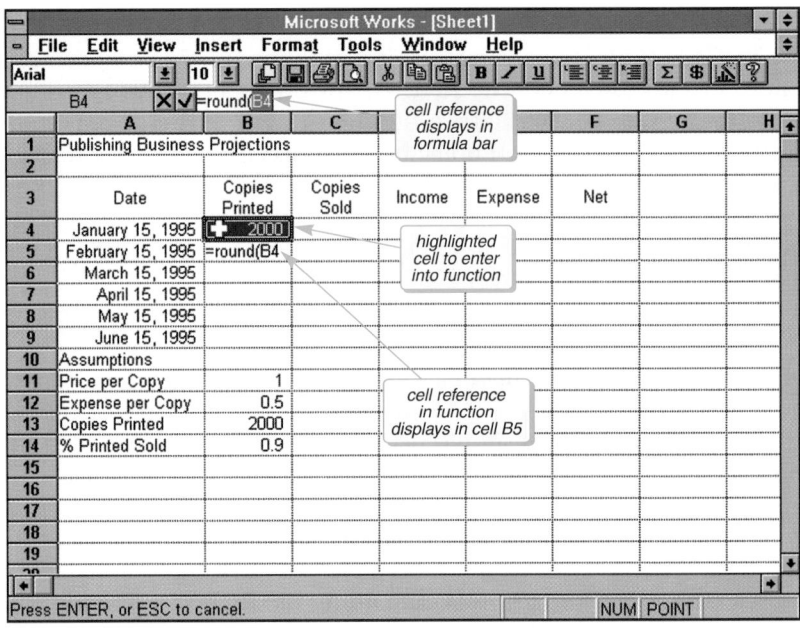

FIGURE 6-24

STEP 3 ►

Type *1.1,0).

Works enters the data you type into the function (Figure 6-25). The asterisk is the multiplication operator. The value 1.1, when multiplied by the value in cell B4, will yield a value ten percent greater than the value in cell B4. The comma is required, followed by the number zero, which is the number of places to the right of the decimal point to round. The right parenthesis is required to balance the left parenthesis.

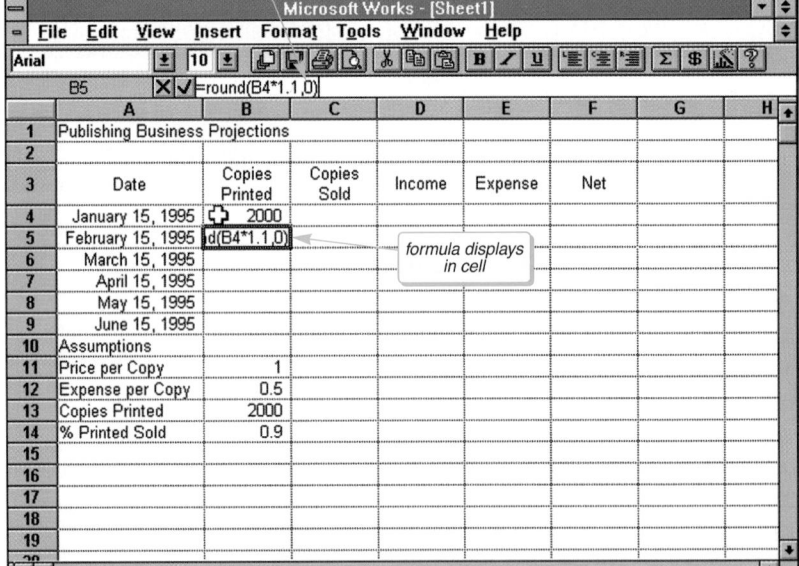

FIGURE 6-25

STEP 4 ▶

Click the Enter box or press the
ENTER key.

*Works enters the formula into cell
B5 and calculates the value
(Figure 6-26). The value in cell B5
(2200) is ten percent greater than
the value in cell B4 (2000).*

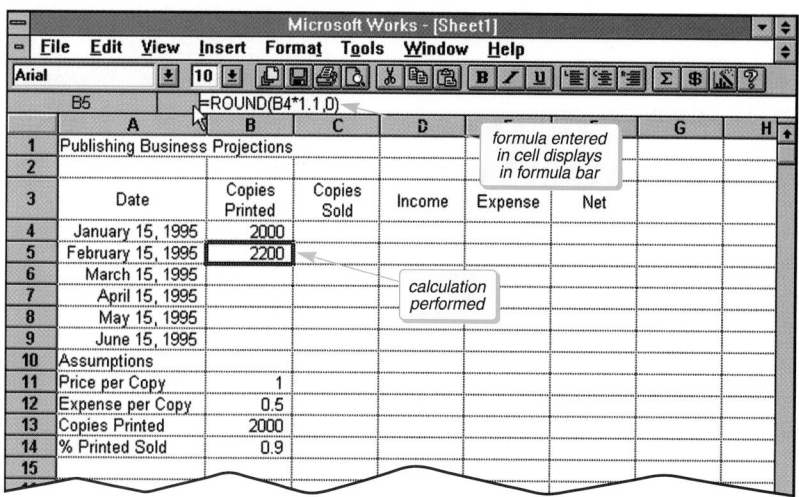

FIGURE 6-26

The ROUND function, as well as any function available in Works, also can be
inserted into a cell by choosing the Function command from the Insert menu.
When the Insert Function dialog box displays, select the function you want from
the Functions list box and choose the OK button in the Insert Function dialog box.
You must then enter the data for the particular function.

Copying a Formula Containing a Function

After you enter the formula containing the ROUND function into cell B5, you
must copy the formula into the range of cells B6:B9. To copy a formula containing
a function, perform the following steps.

TO COPY A FORMULA CONTAINING A FUNCTION ▼

STEP 1 ▶

Highlight the cell containing the
formula to copy – cell B5 – and the
range to copy into – cells B6:B9
(Figure 6-27).

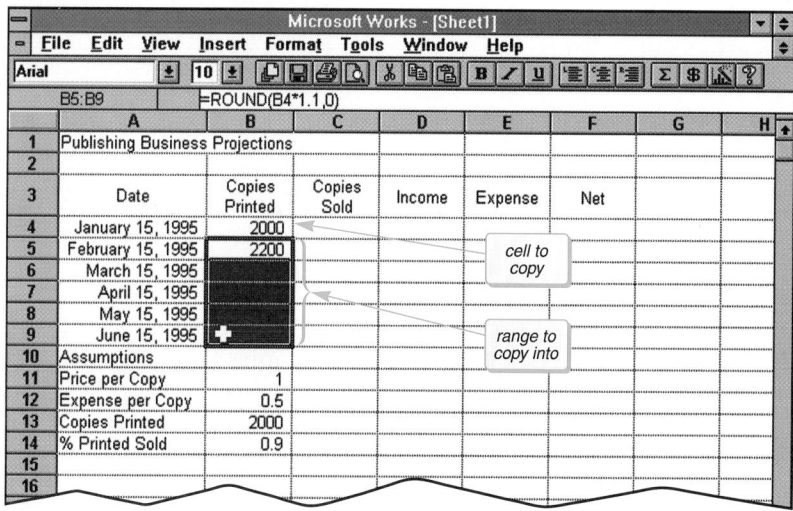

FIGURE 6-27

STEP 2 ▶

Select the Edit menu and point to
the Fill Down command.

*The Edit menu displays and the
mouse pointer points to the Fill
Down command (Figure 6-28).*

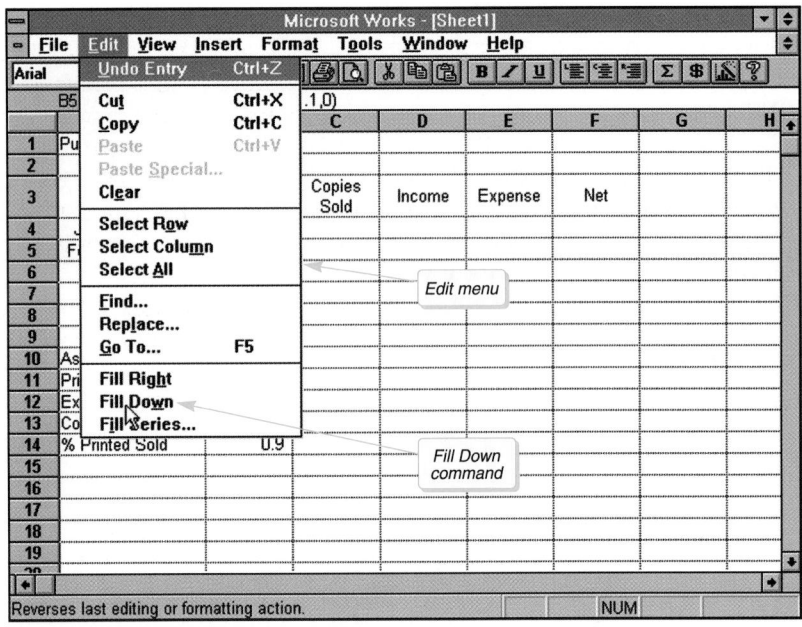

FIGURE 6-28

STEP 3 ▶

Choose the Fill Down command
from the Edit menu.

*Works copies the formula to the
range B6:B9 and calculates each
formula (Figure 6-29). Notice that
the value in cell B8 is 2928, which
is 2662 * 1.1 rounded.*

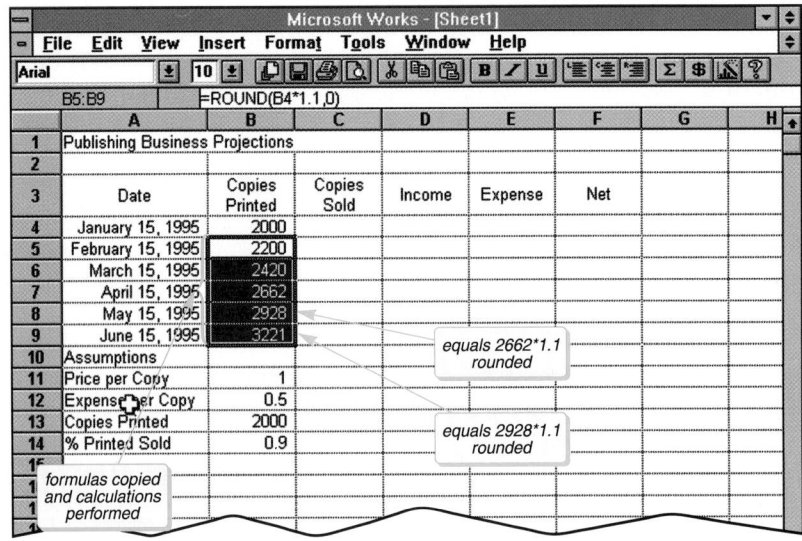

FIGURE 6-29

Absolute Cell References

The next step in preparing the spreadsheet in Project 6 is to enter the Copies
Sold formula. The Copies Sold value is calculated by multiplying the Copies
Printed (column B) times the % Printed Sold value in cell B14. Thus, the calcula-
tion to determine the Copies Sold for January is B4*B14.

Prior to entering the calculation to determine the Copies Sold, however, you
must become familiar with absolute cell references. Cell references used in a formula are one of two types — a relative cell reference or an absolute cell reference.

When you use a **relative cell reference**, the cell reference in the formula will change when you copy the formula from one cell to the next. Relative cell reference is the type used in Project 5 and in column B of this project to calculate the Copies Printed. For example, the cell reference within the ROUND function in the formula in cell B5 (=ROUND(B4*1.1,0)) is cell B4. When the formula is copied to cell B6, the cell reference is changed and becomes =ROUND(B5*1.1,0). The same process happens for the cell references in cells B7, B8, and B9. When the cell changes as the formula is copied from one cell to the next, it is termed a relative cell reference.

The % Printed Sold field (cell B14) in the calculation B4*B14, however, always remains the same. That is, the calculation for Copies Sold in January is B4*B14, the calculation for February is B5*B14, and the calculation for March is B6*B14. Notice that cell B14 is always used because it contains the % Printed Sold value. When a cell's reference does not change as the formula is copied from one cell to the next, the cell reference is called an **absolute cell reference**.

When you enter cell references into a formula, Works assumes they are relative cell references. To specify that a cell reference is an absolute cell reference, you must enter the cell number in the absolute cell reference format, which is a dollar sign preceding the column letter and a dollar sign preceding the row number. Thus, in a formula, the absolute cell reference for cell B14 is B14.

The following steps illustrate entering the formula that contains the ROUND function to calculate the Copies Printed. The formula uses both relative and absolute cell references.

TO ENTER A FORMULA CONTAINING RELATIVE AND ABSOLUTE CELL REFERENCES ▼

STEP 1 ▶

Highlight the cell to contain the formula – cell C4, and type =round(.

The formula containing the beginning of the ROUND function displays in both the highlighted cell and the formula bar (Figure 6-30).

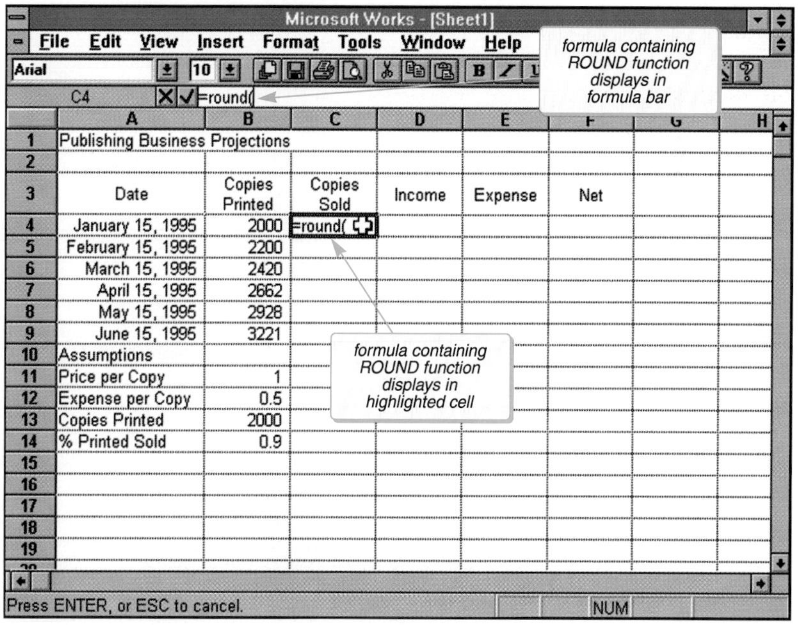

FIGURE 6-30

STEP 2 ▶

Highlight the first cell to enter into the function – cell B4 – by clicking the cell or pressing the LEFT ARROW key to move the highlight to the cell.

When you highlight cell B4, Works places a black background in the cell and also places the cell reference in the function (Figure 6-31).

FIGURE 6-31

STEP 3 ▶

Type the multiplication operator (*) and highlight the second cell in the function – cell B14.

Works displays the multiplication operator in both the formula bar and the cell where you are entering the formula and places the cell reference in the function (Figure 6-32).

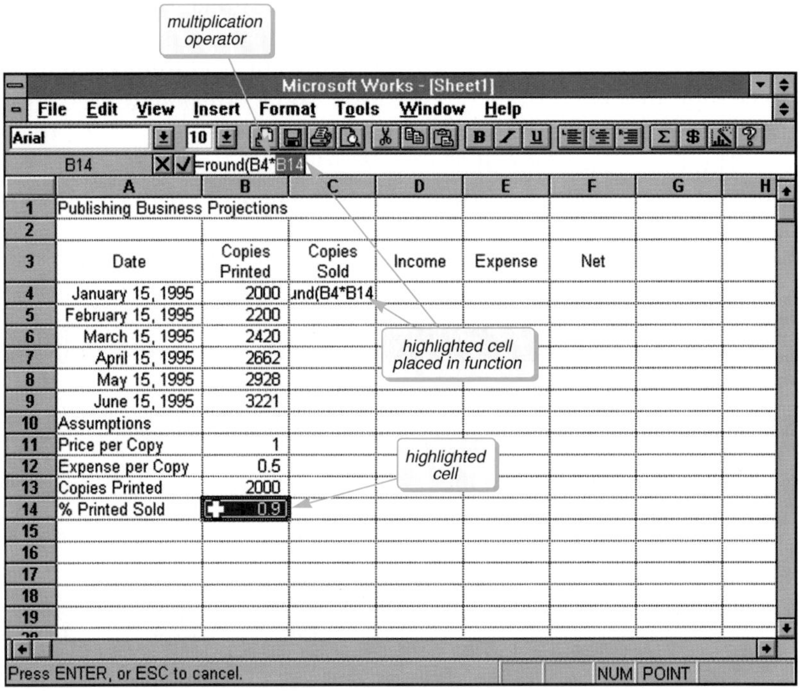

FIGURE 6-32

STEP 4 ▶

Press the F4 function key to change the B14 cell reference to an absolute cell reference.

Works places a dollar sign in front of the column letter and in front of the row number of the highlighted cell (Figure 6-33). The dollar signs tell Works that cell B14 is an absolute cell reference and should not be changed when the formula is copied.

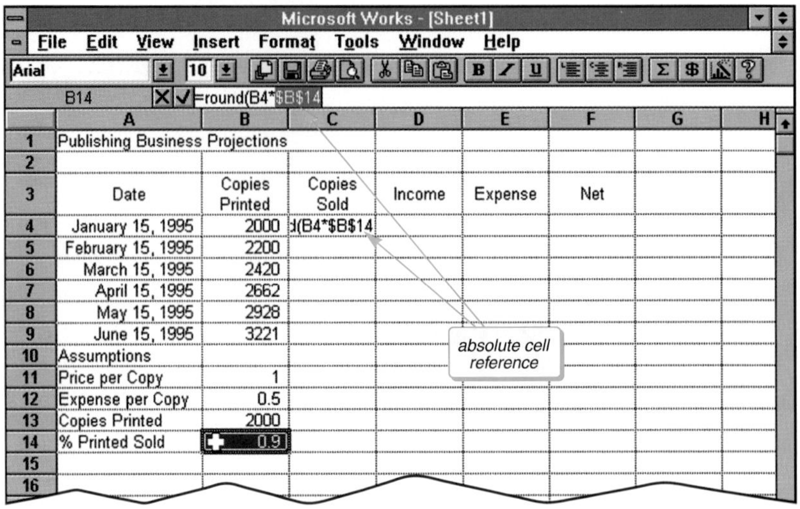

FIGURE 6-33

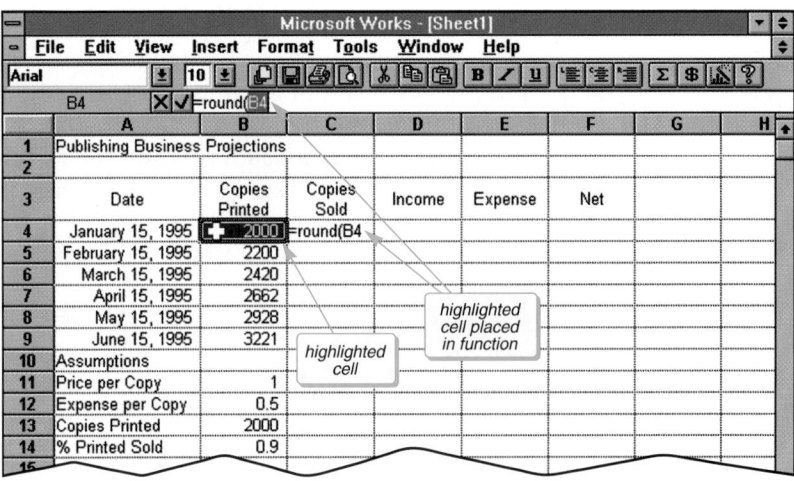

STEP 5 ▶

Type , 0) to complete the ROUND function (Figure 6-34).

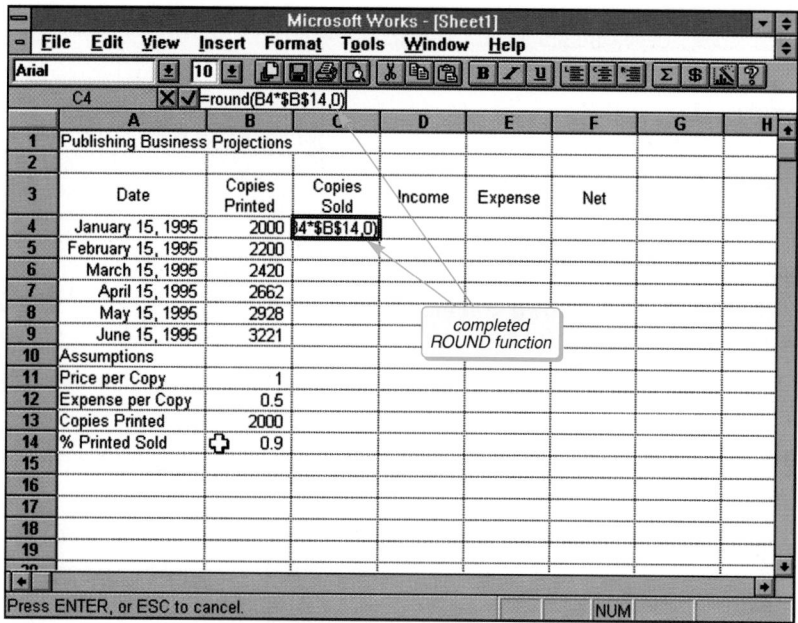

FIGURE 6-34

STEP 6 ▶

Click the Enter box or press the ENTER key.

Works enters the formula into the cell and performs the calculation (Figure 6-35). The result of the calculation is 1800 because the value in cell B4 (2000) times the value in cell B14 (.90) equals 1800. The calculation displays in the cell, but Works displays the formula in the formula bar.

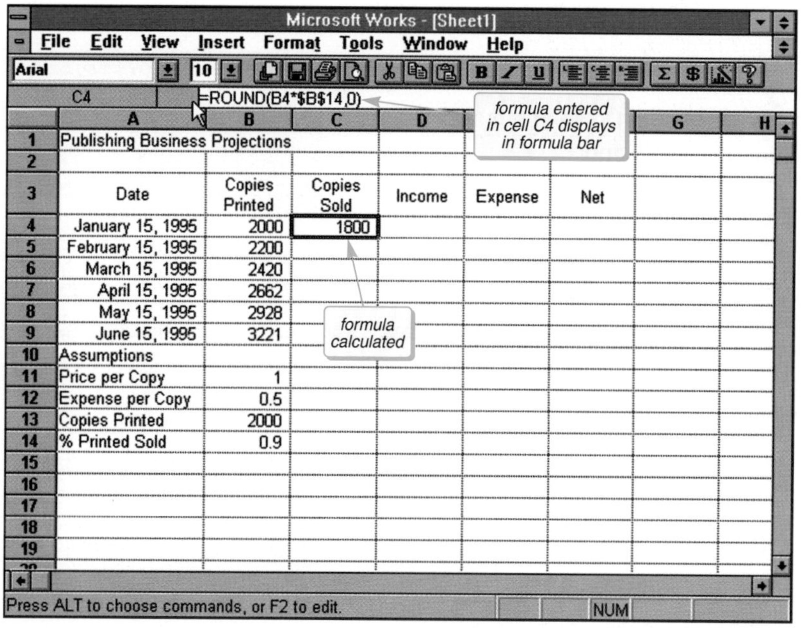

FIGURE 6-35

The next step in building the spreadsheet is to copy the formula containing the ROUND function in cell C4 to the range C5:C9. When you copy the formula, the reference to cell B4 will change to B5, B6, and so on while the reference to cell B14 will remain the same. To copy a formula containing a function with both relative and absolute cell references, complete the steps on the next page.

TO COPY A FORMULA WITH RELATIVE AND ABSOLUTE CELL REFERENCES ▼

STEP 1 ▶

Highlight the cell containing the formula to copy – cell C4 – and the range where it is to be copied – cells C5:C9. Then select the Edit menu and point to the Fill Down command.

The cell containing the formula to copy and the range where it is to be copied are highlighted (Figure 6-36). The Edit menu displays and the mouse pointer points to the Fill Down command.

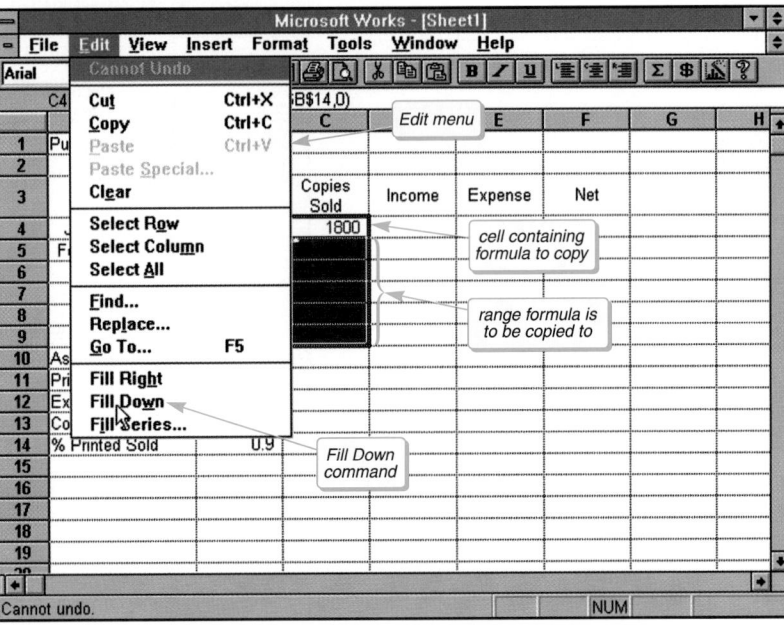

FIGURE 6-36

STEP 2 ▶

Choose the Fill Down command from the Edit menu.

Works copies the formula from cell C4 to the range C5:C9 (Figure 6-37). Works also performs the calculations, which includes rounding the results when required.

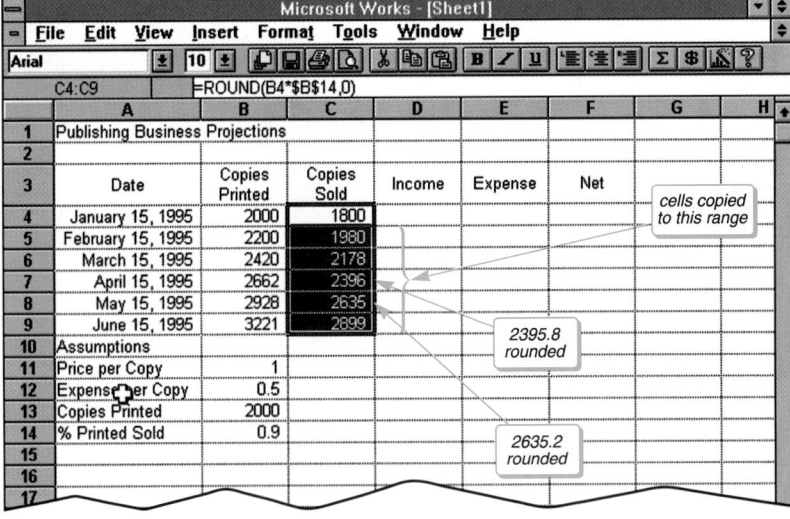

FIGURE 6-37

Entering Additional Functions and Formulas

After you enter the Copies Sold formula into the spreadsheet, the next step is to enter the Income formula. The Income is calculated by multiplying the Copies Sold by the Price per Copy. The Copies Sold for January is contained in cell C4 while the Price per Copy is in cell B11. Therefore, the calculation to determine the Income for January is C4*B11. Because the Price per Copy is contained in a single cell and should be used to calculate the Income for each of the months, cell B11 will be an absolute cell reference in the formula.

Perform the following steps to place the formula that calculates Income into the spreadsheet.

TO ENTER A FORMULA ▼

STEP 1 ▶

Highlight the cell to contain the formula – cell D4, type an equal sign, highlight the cell containing the Copies Sold – cell C4, type the multiplication operator (*), and highlight the cell containing the Price per Copy – cell B11.

Works inserts the cells you highlight and the multiplication operator into the formula (Figure 6-38).

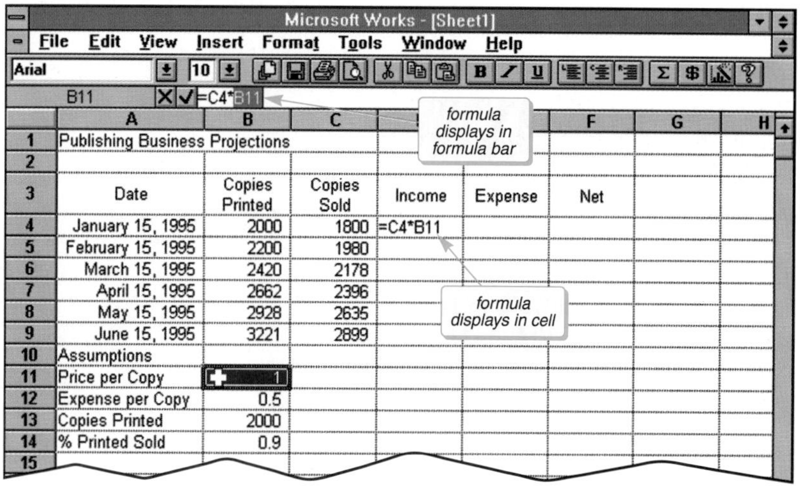

FIGURE 6-38

STEP 2 ▶

Press the F4 function key.

Works changes the relative cell reference in the formula (B11) to an absolute cell reference (B11) (Figure 6-39).

FIGURE 6-39

STEP 3 ▶

Click the Enter box or press the ENTER key.

*Works enters the formula into the cell and displays it in the formula bar (Figure 6-40). The calculated result 1800 (1800 * 1) displays in the cell.*

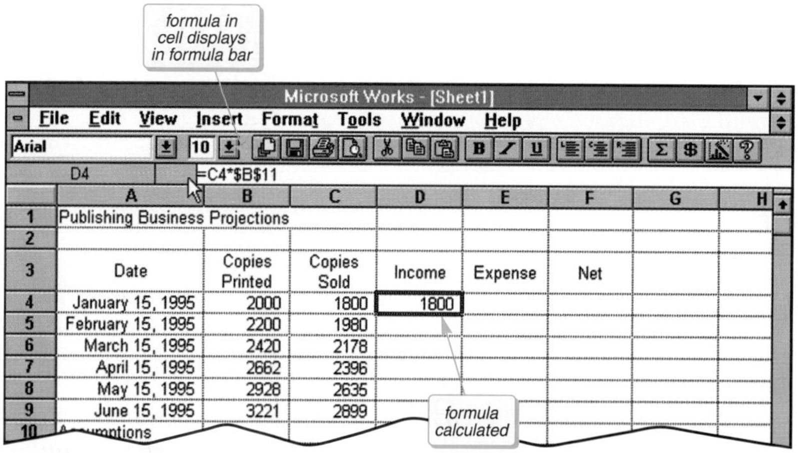

FIGURE 6-40

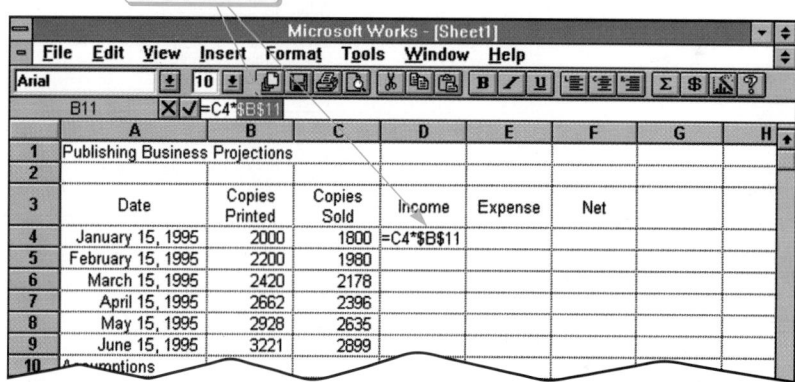

Notice that the Income displays as the value 1800. The reason the value does not contain a comma, a decimal point, and zeros to the right of the decimal point is because the value is not yet formatted using the Comma format. Formatting the values in the spreadsheet occurs after you have entered all the values.

Once you enter the formula to calculate the January Income in cell D4, you must copy the formula to the range D5:D9 so Works will calculate the Income for the months February through June. Copy the formula using the following procedure.

TO COPY A FORMULA ▼

STEP 1 ►

Highlight the cell containing the formula to copy – cell D4 – and the range to which to copy the formula – cells D5:D9, select the Edit menu, and choose the Fill Down command.

Works copies the formula from cell D4 to the range D5:D9 and performs the calculations specified in the copied formulas (Figure 6-41).

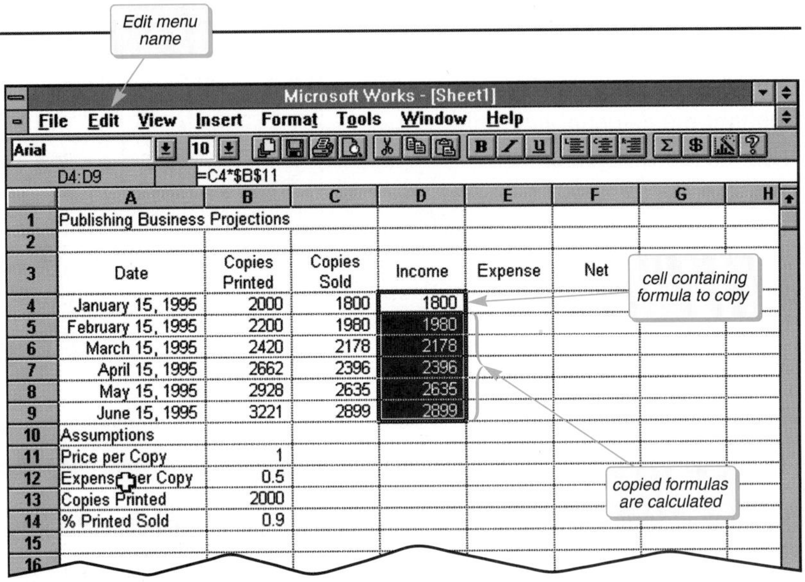

FIGURE 6-41

The next step is to enter the formula to calculate the Expense for January. The Expense is calculated by multiplying the Copies Printed (column B) times the Expense per Copy (cell B12). The formula for January is =B4*B12. The Expense per Copy cell is an absolute cell reference because it remains the same when calculating the Expense for February, March, and so on. To enter the formula, complete the following steps.

TO ENTER THE EXPENSE FORMULA ▼

STEP 1 ►

Highlight cell E4, type an equal sign, highlight cell B4 to place it in the formula, type the multiplication operator (*), highlight cell B12 to place it in the formula, and press the F4 function key.

The formula displays in the cell and in the formula bar (Figure 6-42).

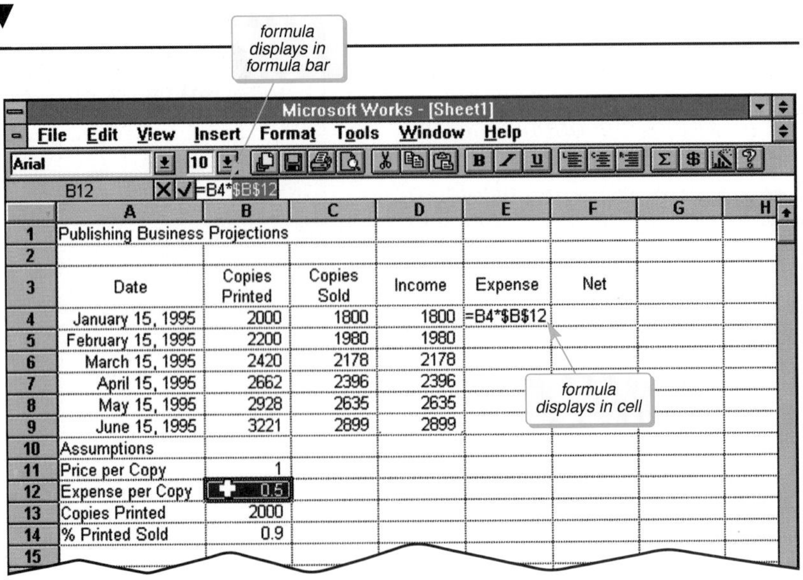

FIGURE 6-42

STEP 2 ►

Click the Enter box or press the ENTER key.

*Works enters the formula into cell E4 and calculates the Expense for January (2000 *. 5 = 1000) (Figure 6-43).*

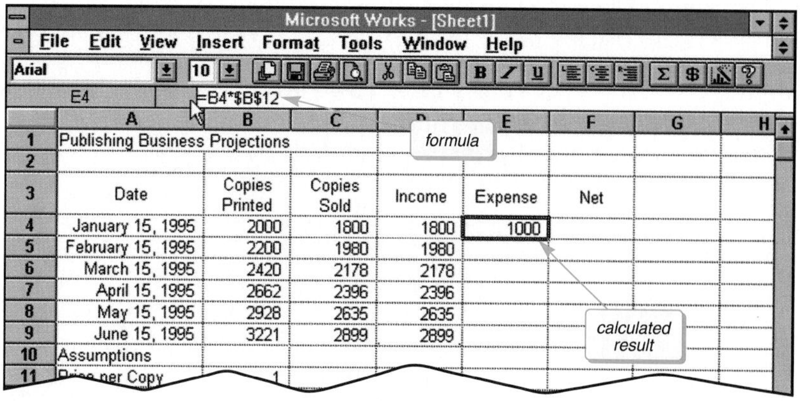

	A	B	C	D	E	F	G	H
1	Publishing Business Projections				*formula*			
2								
3	Date	Copies Printed	Copies Sold	Income	Expense	Net		
4	January 15, 1995	2000	1800	1800	1000			
5	February 15, 1995	2200	1980	1980				
6	March 15, 1995	2420	2178	2178				
7	April 15, 1995	2662	2396	2396				
8	May 15, 1995	2928	2635	2635		calculated result		
9	June 15, 1995	3221	2899	2899				
10	Assumptions							
11	Price per Copy	1						

E4   =B4*B12

FIGURE 6-43

Next, to copy the formula in cell E4 to cells E5:E9, do the following:

TO COPY A FORMULA

Step 1: Highlight cell E4 and the range E5:E9.
Step 2: Select the Edit menu and point to the Fill Down command.
Step 3: Choose the Fill Down command.

The spreadsheet after completing the steps above is shown in Figure 6-44.

A note of caution is in order when including decimal values in a spreadsheet. You must always be aware of the number of decimal places that will be generated when a multiplication or division operation takes place and plan for them, both in calculations and in formatting. While all the concerns have been addressed in the spreadsheet for Project 6, other problems could occur. For example, it is assumed that the Expense per Copy value in cell B12 of the spreadsheet will always be a whole cent figure, meaning two places to the right of the decimal point. As a result, because the Expense is calculated by multiplying a whole number (Copies Printed) times a value with two places to the right of the decimal point (Expense per Copy), the formula in cells E4:E9 to calculate the Expense does not require the ROUND function.

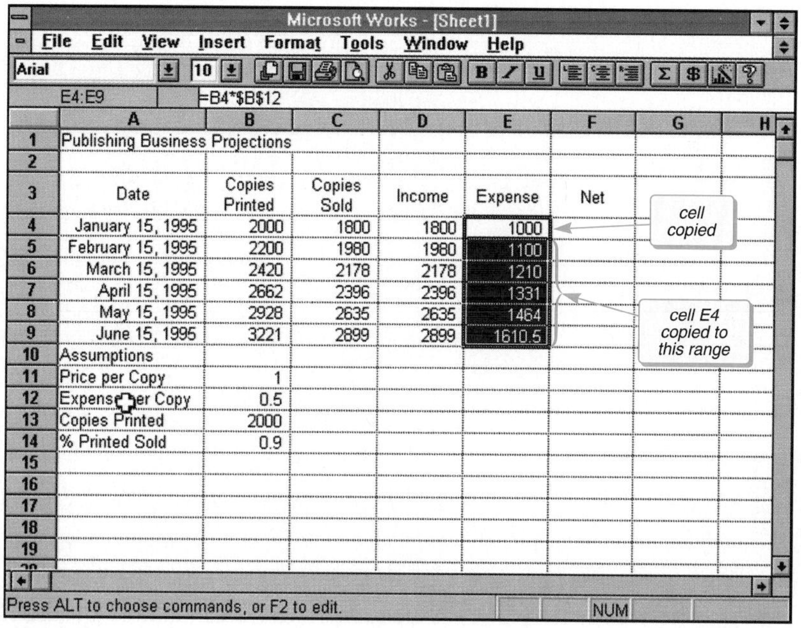

E4:E9   =B4*B12

	A	B	C	D	E	F	G	H
1	Publishing Business Projections							
2								
3	Date	Copies Printed	Copies Sold	Income	Expense	Net		
4	January 15, 1995	2000	1800	1800	1000		cell copied	
5	February 15, 1995	2200	1980	1980	1100			
6	March 15, 1995	2420	2178	2178	1210			
7	April 15, 1995	2662	2396	2396	1331			
8	May 15, 1995	2928	2635	2635	1464		cell E4 copied to this range	
9	June 15, 1995	3221	2899	2899	1610.5			
10	Assumptions							
11	Price per Copy	1						
12	Expense per Copy	0.5						
13	Copies Printed	2000						
14	% Printed Sold	0.9						
15								
16								
17								
18								
19								

Press ALT to choose commands, or F2 to edit.   NUM

FIGURE 6-44

If, however, a bid was made for an Expense per Copy of $0.515, the Expense column in the spreadsheet (column E) would be affected, because the formula in cells E4:E9 (=B4*B12, and so on) could produce a number with three digits to the right of the decimal point. To fix this problem, the Expense formula would have to be rounded.

Calculating Net Profit

The arithmetic to determine the Net (net profit) in column F of the spreadsheet is Income from column D minus Expense from column E. Therefore, the formula to calculate the Net for January is =D4-E4. The formulas for each of the ensuing months requires both cell D4 and cell E4 to be modified. Thus, this formula has no requirement for an absolute cell reference. To enter the formula in cells F4:F9, complete the following steps.

TO ENTER AND COPY A FORMULA

Step 1: Highlight cell F4, type an equal sign, highlight cell D4 to place it in the formula, type the subtraction operator (-), highlight cell E4 to place it in the formula, and click the Enter box or press the ENTER key.

Step 2: Highlight the cell containing the formula – cell F4 – and the range where it is to be copied – cells F5:F9.

Step 3: Select the Edit menu and choose the Fill Down command.

The spreadsheet after the steps above are complete is shown in Figure 6-45.

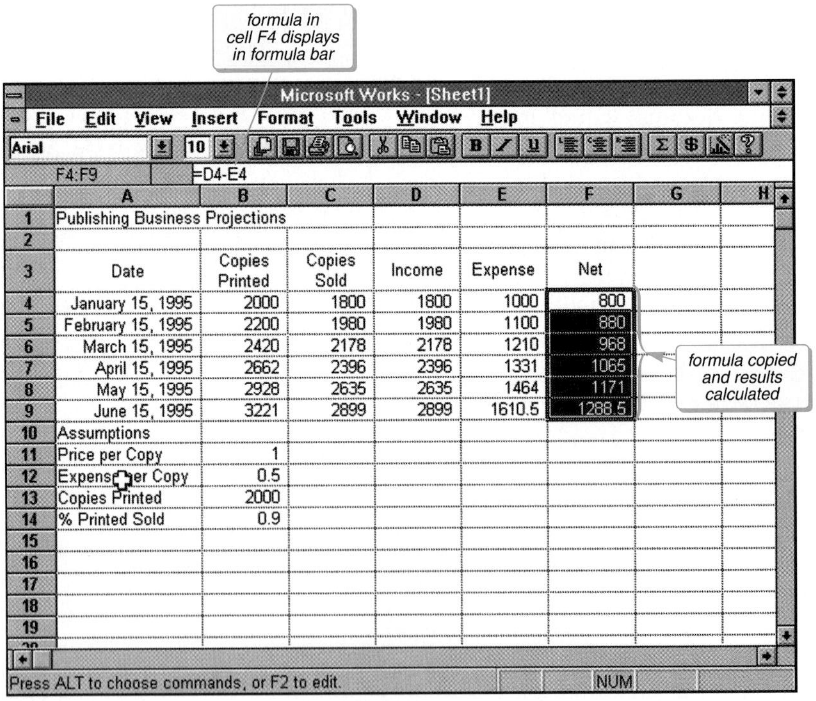

FIGURE 6-45

Moving Information Using Drag and Drop

It possible to move individual cells or groups of cells in the spreadsheet using the Works drag and drop feature. The following example illustrates how to move the Assumptions section of the spreadsheet to another location in the spreadsheet.

TO USE DRAG AND DROP TO MOVE CELLS ▼

STEP 1 ►

Highlight the range to be moved – cells A10:B14. Carefully position the mouse pointer on the border of the highlighted area until the mouse pointer becomes a block arrow with the word DRAG beneath it.

The mouse pointer displays within the highlighted range as a block arrow with the word DRAG beneath it (Figure 6-46).

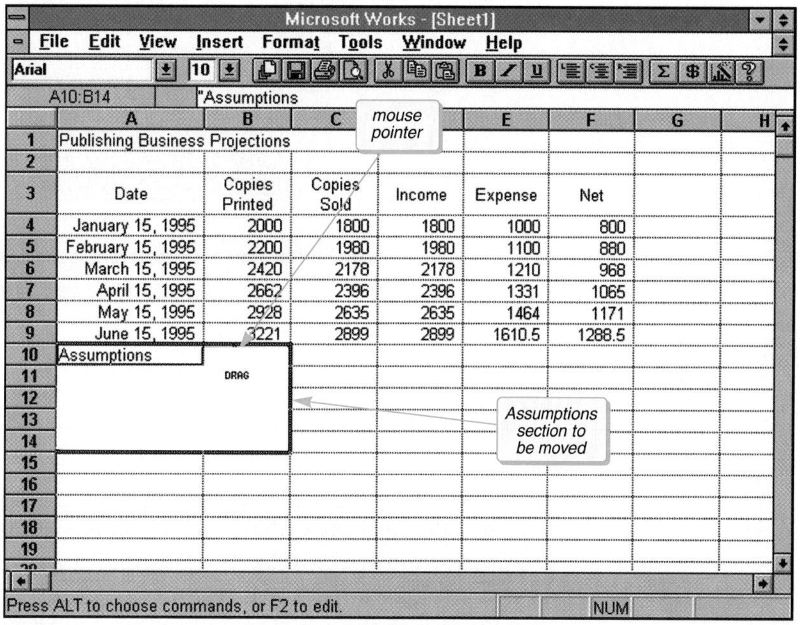

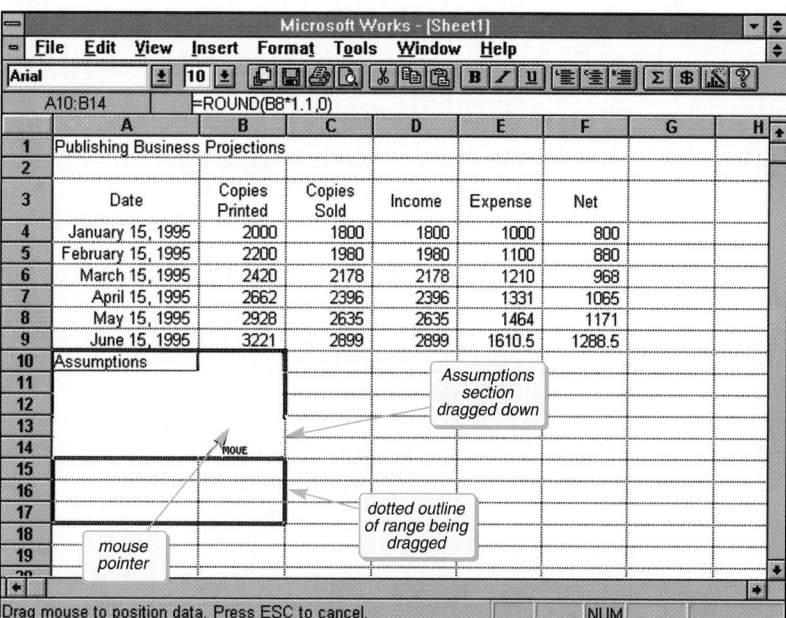

FIGURE 6-46

STEP 2 ►

Drag the highlighted range down until the bottom dotted line of the range you are dragging displays along the bottom of row 17.

Works displays the range being dragged as a dotted outline and the mouse pointer displays with the word MOVE beneath it (Figure 6-47).

FIGURE 6-47

STEP 3 ►

Release the left mouse button.

Works displays the highlighted range in cells A13:B17 (Figure 6-48).

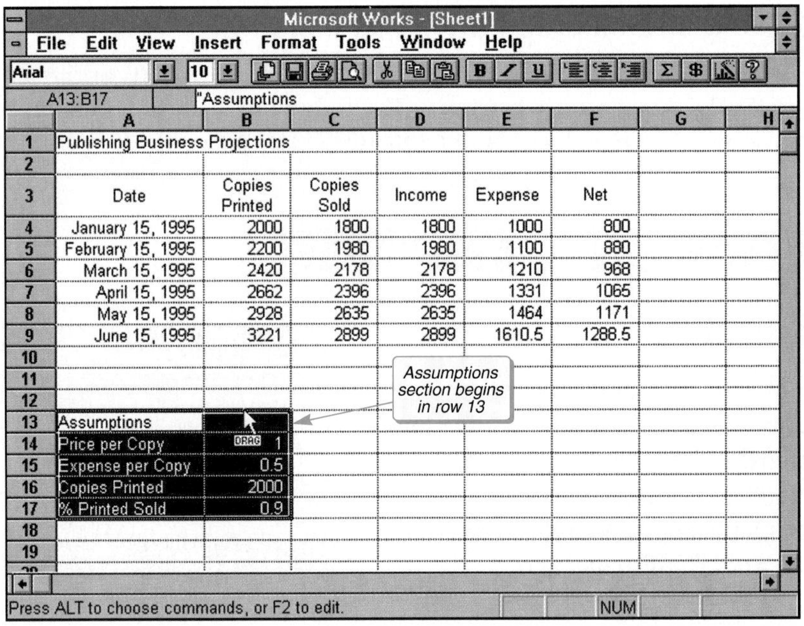

FIGURE 6-48

The range of cells are moved to a new location. To move cells in a spreadsheet, you can also highlight the range of cells to move and use the Cut and Paste buttons on the Toolbar or the Cut and Paste commands from the Edit menu.

You can copy, or duplicate, a cell or range of cells using drag and drop by using the following steps: (1) highlight the cell or range to copy; (2) position the mouse pointer on the border of the highlighted cell or range until the mouse pointer changes to a block arrow with the word DRAG beneath it; (3) hold down the CTRL key and at the same time drag the cell or range to the location in the spreadsheet where it is to be copied; and (4) release the CTRL key and the left mouse button. The copied cell or range will display in two locations within the spreadsheet.

You can also highlight a cell or range to be copied and use the Copy and Paste buttons on the Toolbar or the Copy and Paste commands from the Edit menu to copy a cell or range of cells.

Undo Drag and Drop Operations

If you decide you do not want the range of cells moved, you can undo the drag and drop operation by performing the following steps immediately after the drag and drop.

TO UNDO A DRAG AND DROP MOVE ▼

STEP 1 ►

Select the Edit menu and point to the Undo Drag and Drop command (Figure 6-49).

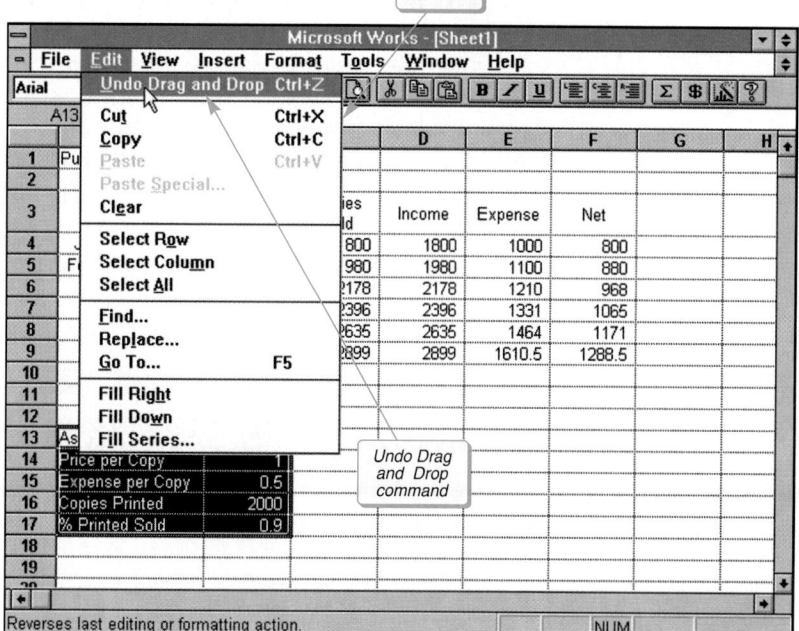

FIGURE 6-49

STEP 2 ►

Choose the Undo Drag and Drop command from the Edit menu.

Works places the range back into the original range (Figure 6-50).

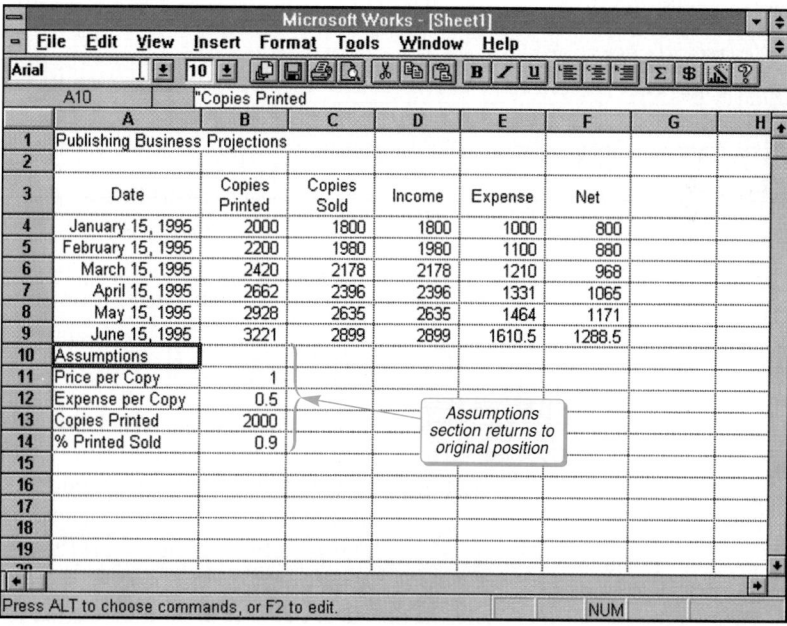

FIGURE 6-50

▶ FORMATTING THE SPREADSHEET

Formatting the spreadsheet in Project 6 includes changing font sizes and font styles, formatting the numeric data in the main portion of the spreadsheet with commas and decimal positions when required, and formatting the values in the Assumptions section as required. After the formatting is complete, color will be added to further enhance the appearance of the spreadsheet. When formatting is complete, excluding color, the spreadsheet will appear as shown in Figure 6-51.

Formatting the Spreadsheet Titles, Column Titles and Row Titles

FIGURE 6-51

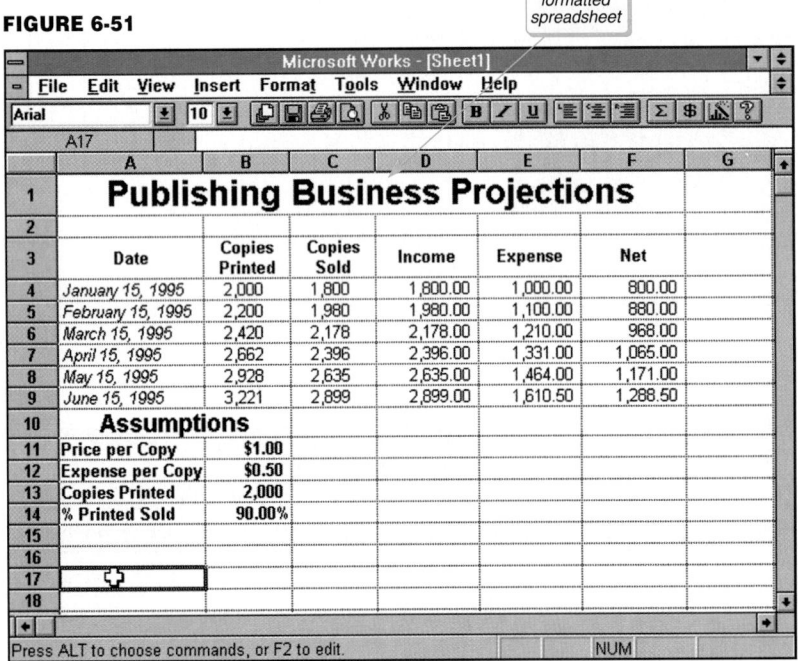

formatted spreadsheet

The following formatting of the spreadsheet titles is required.

1. The spreadsheet title, Publishing Business Projections, is to display in 20 point Arial bold font. The title is centered across the columns in the spreadsheet.
2. All column titles are bold.
3. The dates in the row titles are left-aligned and in italics.
4. The word Assumptions in cell A10 displays in 14 point Arial bold font and is centered across columns A and B.
5. The titles and values in rows 11 through 14 are bold.
6. The column width in columns D, E, and F is 12.

To accomplish the formatting, complete the following steps (see Figure 6-51).

TO FORMAT TITLES

Step 1: Highlight cell A1. Select the Font Size drop-down list box and select 20 point. Click the Bold button on the Toolbar to bold the spreadsheet title.

Step 2: Highlight cells A1:F1, select the Format menu and choose the Alignment command. When the Alignment dialog box displays, select the Center across selection option button and then choose the OK button in the Alignment dialog box.

Step 3: Highlight the column titles in cells A3:F3 and click the Bold button on the Toolbar.

Step 4: Highlight cells A4:A9 and click the Italic button and the Left Align button on the Toolbar.

Step 5: Highlight cell A10, select the Font Size drop-down list box and select 14 point. Click the Bold button on the Toolbar.

Step 6: Highlight cells A10:B10, select the Format menu and choose the Alignment command. When the Alignment dialog box displays, select the Center across selection option button and then choose the OK button in the Alignment dialog box.

Step 7: Highlight the range A11:B14 and click the Bold button on the Toolbar.

Step 8: Highlight columns D, E, and F by clicking cell D1 and dragging through cell F1. Select the Format menu and choose the Column Width command. When the Column Width dialog box displays, type 12 and choose the OK button.

Formatting the Numeric Values

The numeric values in the spreadsheet, even though they are generated by formulas, can still be formatted. The following formatting, as shown in Figure 6-51, is required.

1. The Copies Printed values in column B and the Copies Sold values in column C are centered and use the Comma format with zero positions to the right of the decimal point.
2. The Income, Expense, and Net values in columns D, E, and F, respectively, use the Comma format with two positions to the right of the decimal point. Any negative numbers in the Net column should display in red.
3. The Price per Copy value in cell B11 and the Expense per Copy value in cell B12 use the Currency format with two positions to the right of the decimal point.
4. The Copies Printed value in cell B13 uses the Comma format with zero positions to the right of the decimal point.
5. The % Printed Sold value in cell B14 uses the Percent format with two positions to the right of the decimal point.

To accomplish the formatting, complete the following steps:

TO FORMAT NUMERIC VALUES

Step 1: Highlight cells B4:C9 and click the Center Align button on the Toolbar. Select the Format menu and choose the Number command. When the Number dialog box displays, select the Comma option button, type zero in the Number of decimals text box, and choose the OK button.

Step 2: Highlight cells D4:F9. Select the Format menu and choose the Number command. When the Number dialog box displays, select the Comma option button, type 2 in the Number of decimals text box if necessary, select the Negative numbers in red check box, and choose the OK button.

Step 3: Highlight cells B11:B12 and click the Currency button on the Toolbar.

Step 4: Highlight cell B13. Select the Format menu and choose the Number command. When the Number dialog box displays, select the Comma option button, type zero in the Number of decimals text box, and choose the OK button.

Step 5: Highlight cell B14. Select the Format menu and choose the Number command. When the Number dialog box displays, select the Percent option button, type 2 in the Number of decimals text box if necessary, and choose the OK button.

The spreadsheet formatting is now complete. The final step is to add color to the spreadsheet. Before adding color to the spreadsheet, however, it is recommended that you save the spreadsheet in its present form.

Saving the Spreadsheet

To save the spreadsheet on drive A using the filename PROJ6, complete the following steps.

TO SAVE THE SPREADSHEET

Step 1: Click the Save button on the Toolbar.
Step 2: When the Save As dialog box displays, type `proj6` in the File Name text box.
Step 3: Select drive a: from the Drives drop-down list box.
Step 4: Choose the OK button in the Save As dialog box.

▶ ADDING COLOR TO THE SPREADSHEET

igure 6-1 on page W6.3 illustrates the Publishing Business Projections spreadsheet with color added to selected rows to enhance the appearance of the spreadsheet. The color used on the spreadsheet is:

1. The cells containing titles display in dark cyan.
2. The spreadsheet title, column titles, and the word Assumptions in row 10 display in white.
3. The lines under row 4 through row 9 display in dark cyan.
4. The cells in the Net column are shaded with a light gray pattern.
5. A dark cyan border displays around the entire spreadsheet.

When using white titles, it is recommended you first place color in the cells that contain the titles. The following steps explain how to add the required color to the spreadsheet.

TO ADD COLOR TO THE SPREADSHEET ▼

STEP 1 ▶

Highlight cells A1:F1, select the Format menu, and point to the Patterns command.

Cells A1:F1 are highlighted and the mouse pointer points to the Patterns command (Figure 6-52).

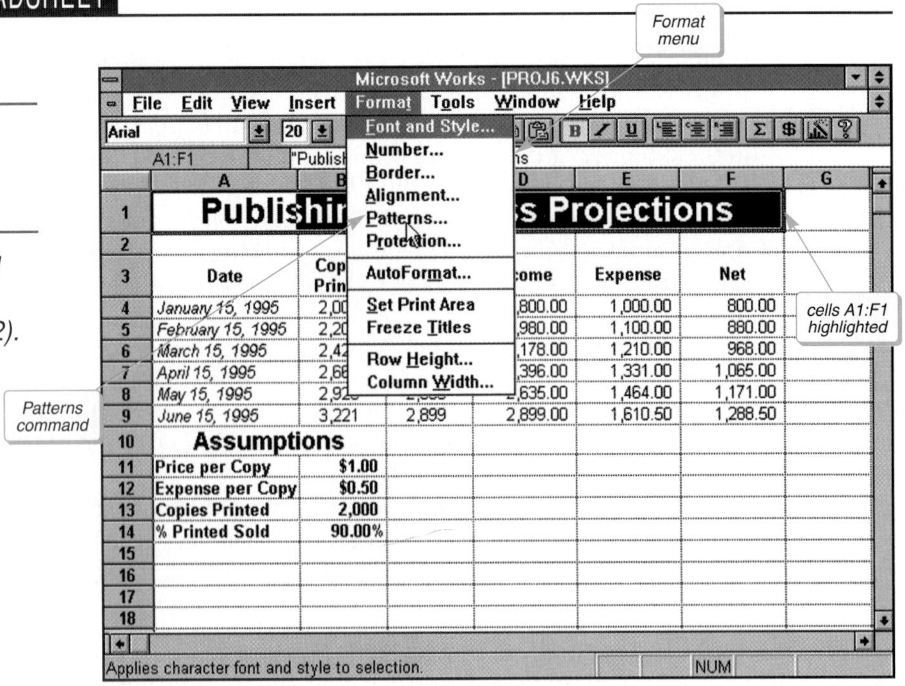

FIGURE 6-52

STEP 2 ▶

Choose the Patterns command. When the Patterns dialog box displays, click the Pattern drop-down list box arrow. Point to the solid pattern.

The Pattern drop-down list box displays within the Patterns dialog box (Figure 6-53). The mouse pointer points to the solid pattern.

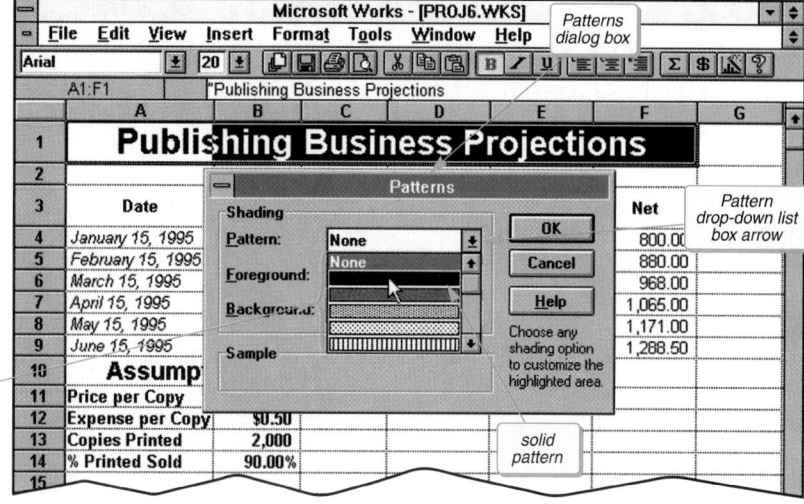

FIGURE 6-53

STEP 3 ▶

Select the solid pattern. Click the Foreground drop-down list box arrow. Scroll down and point to Dark Cyan.

The solid pattern displays in the Pattern drop-down list box (Figure 6-54). The Foreground drop-down list box displays and the mouse pointer points to Dark Cyan.

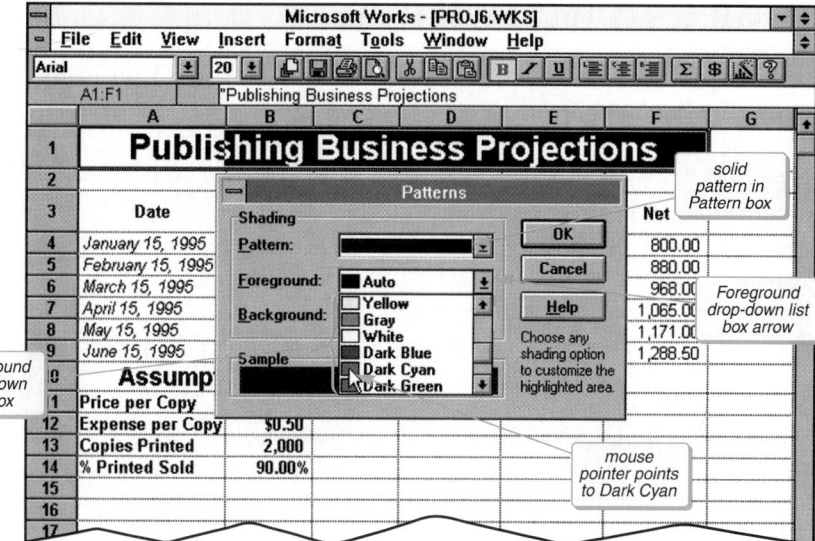

FIGURE 6-54

STEP 4 ▶

Select Dark Cyan. Point to the OK button.

Dark Cyan displays in the Foreground drop-down list box and the mouse pointer points to the OK button (Figure 6-55). The Sample area displays the selections you have made.

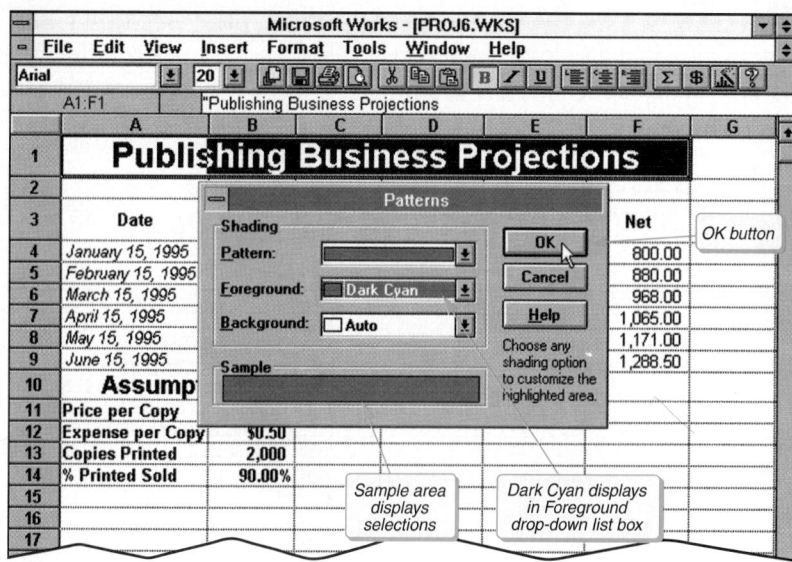

FIGURE 6-55

STEP 5 ▶

Choose the OK button. Highlight cell A1. Select the Format menu and point to the Font and Style command.

Works displays cells A1:F1 in dark cyan (Figure 6-56). The text is black. Cell A1 is high-lighted by a red heavy border. The Format menu displays and the mouse pointer points to the Font and Style command.

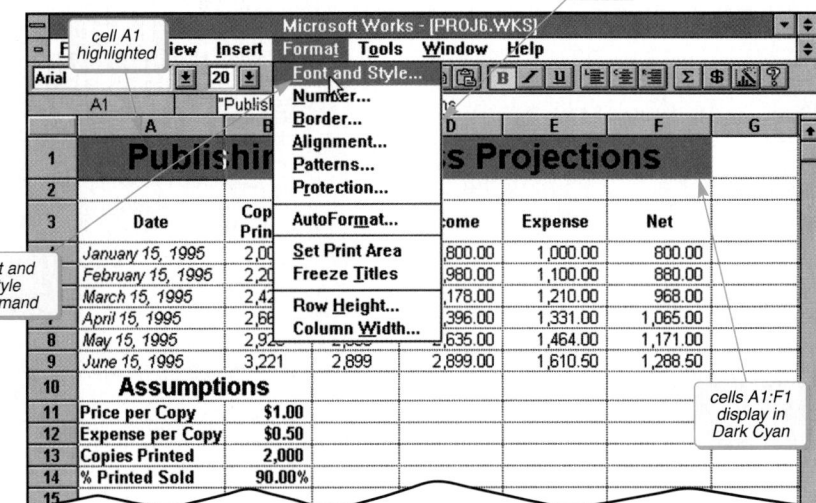

FIGURE 6-56

STEP 6 ▶

Choose the Font and Style command. When the Font and Style dialog box displays, click the Color drop-down list box arrow. Scroll to display the color White. Then, point to White.

The Font and Style dialog box dis-plays and the mouse pointer points to White in the Color drop-down list box (Figure 6-57).

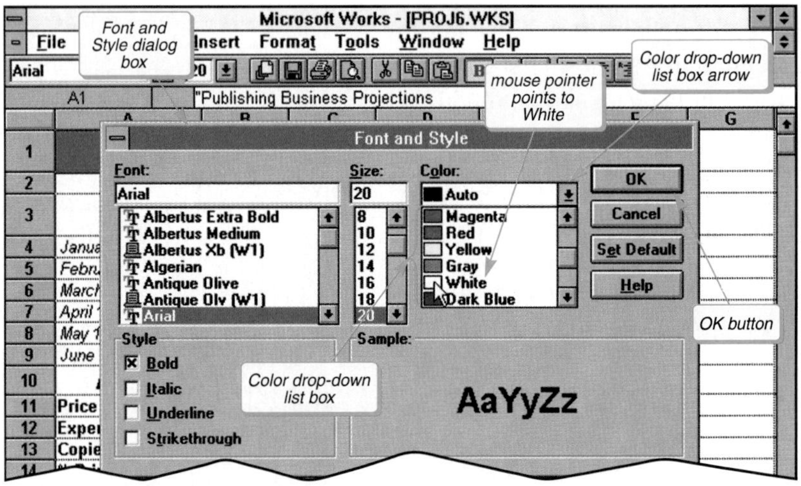

FIGURE 6-57

STEP 7 ▶

Select White in the Color drop-down list box. Then, choose the OK button in the Font and Style dialog box.

Works displays the font in white (Figure 6-58). The cell color is dark cyan.

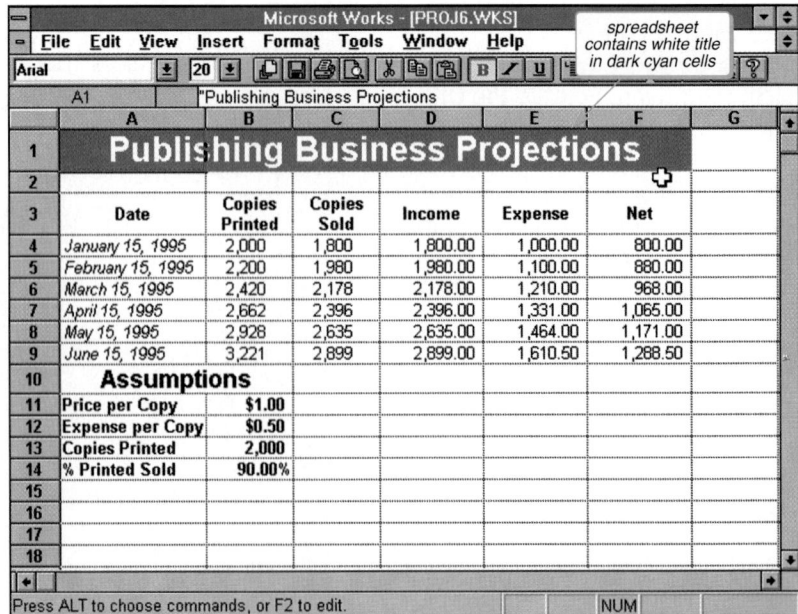

FIGURE 6-58

STEP 8 ▶

Highlight cells A3:F3. Select the Format menu and choose the Patterns command. Select the solid pattern in the Pattern drop-down list box, select the Dark Cyan color in the Color drop-down list box, and choose the OK button in the Patterns dialog box. Select the Format menu and choose the Font and Style command. Select White in the Color drop-down list box and choose the OK button in the Font and Style dialog box. Click any cell to remove the highlight.

The column titles display in white with a cell color of dark cyan (Figure 6-59).

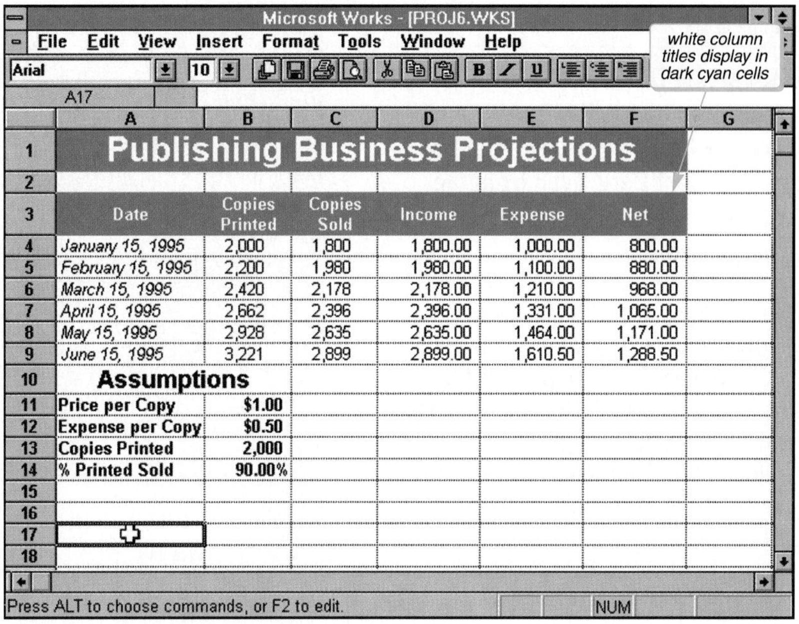

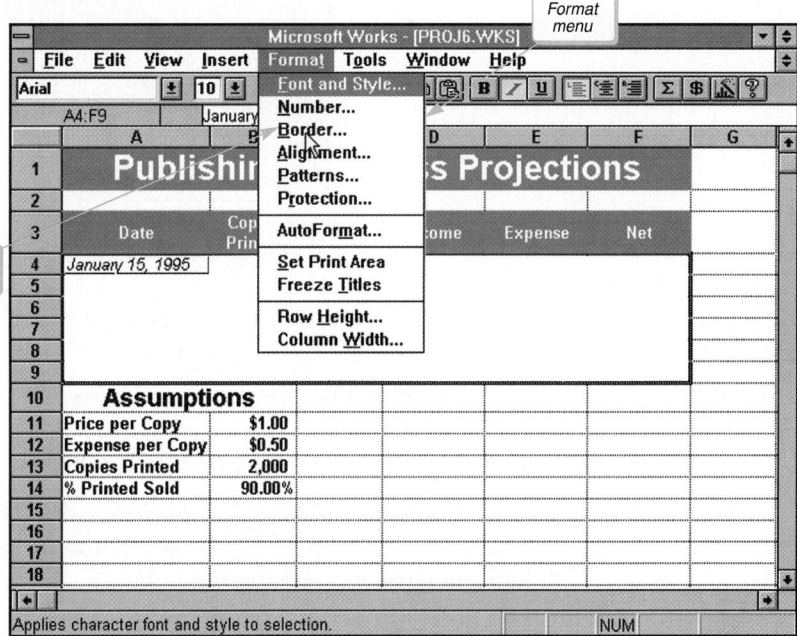

FIGURE 6-59

Adding Bottom Borders to the Spreadsheet

In the spreadsheet in Figure 6-1 on page W6.3, cells in the range A4:F9 contain a bottom border that displays in dark cyan. The following steps explain how to add a bottom border to selected cells.

TO ADD A BOTTOM BORDER TO SELECTED CELLS ▼

STEP 1 ▶

Highlight cells A4:F9, select the Format menu, and point to the Border command (Figure 6-60).

FIGURE 6-60

STEP 2 ▶

Choose the Border command. Select
the Bottom box in the Border area.
Click the Color drop-down list box
arrow. Select Dark Cyan from the
Color drop-down list box. Point to
the OK button.

*The Border dialog box displays
(Figure 6-61). A thin line displays
in the Bottom box because the thin
line is the Line Style default selection. Dark Cyan displays in the
Color drop-down list box and the
mouse pointer points to the OK
button.*

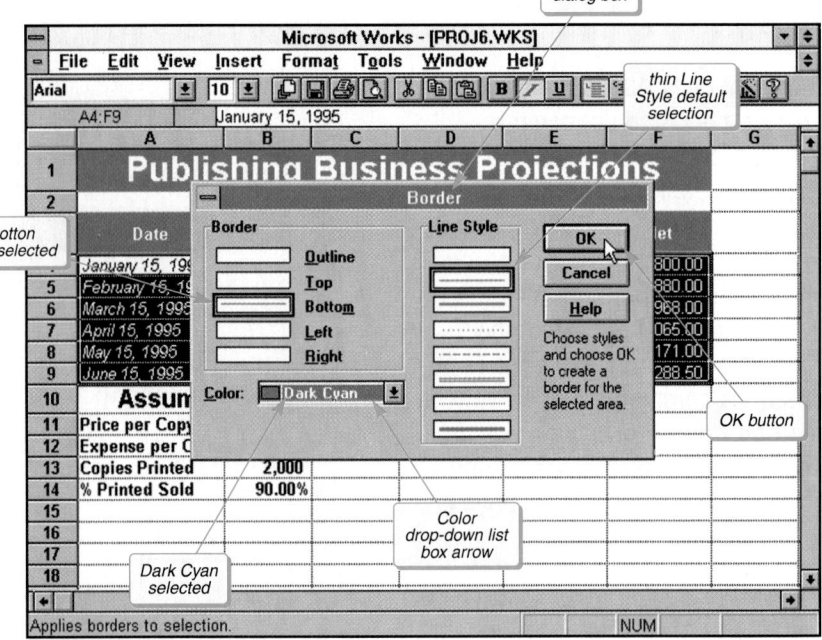

FIGURE 6-61

STEP 3 ▶

Choose the OK button. Click any cell
to remove the highlight.

*The spreadsheet displays with
dark cyan lines under cells in the
range A4:F9 (Figure 6-62).*

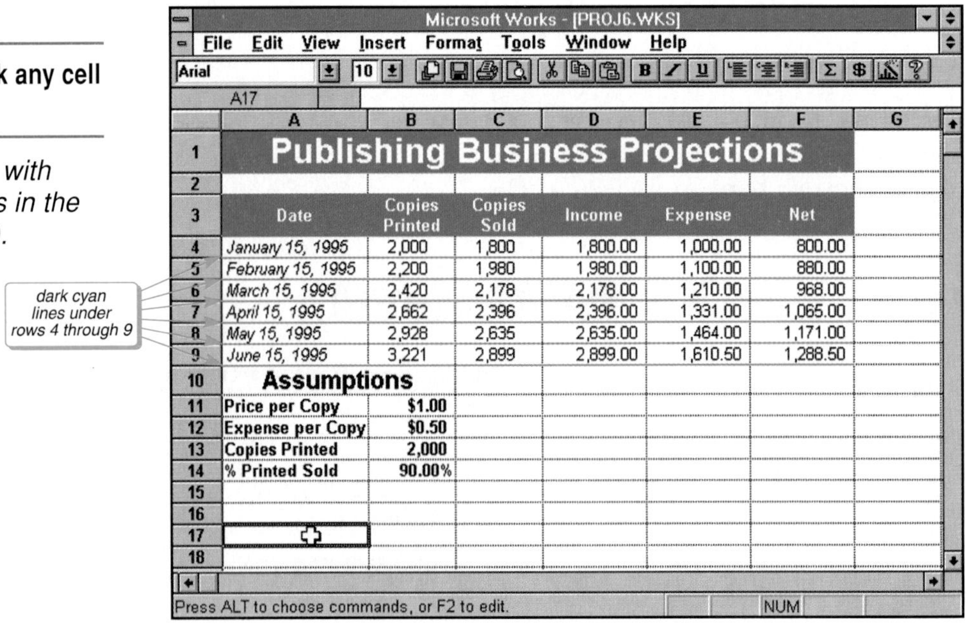

FIGURE 6-62

Adding a Pattern in Selected Cells

In Project 6, the cells in the range F4:F9 contain a light gray pattern to call
attention to the values in the Net column. Perform the following steps to add a
light gray pattern to selected cells.

TO ADD A PATTERN TO SELECTED CELLS ▼

STEP 1 ►

Highlight cells F4:F9. Select the Format menu and point to the Patterns command.

The range F4:F9 is highlighted, the Format menu displays, and the mouse pointer points to the Patterns command (Figure 6-63).

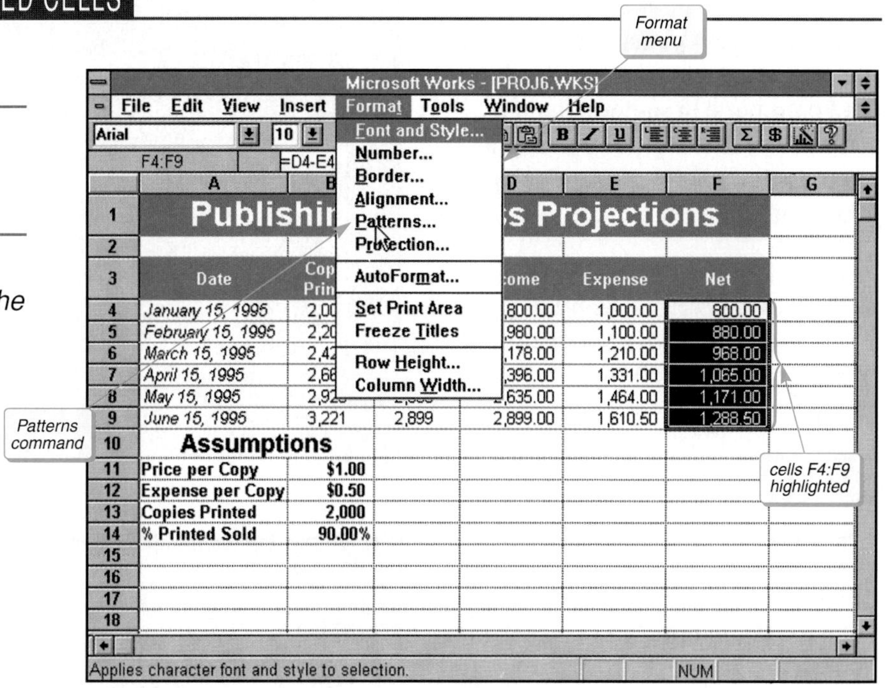

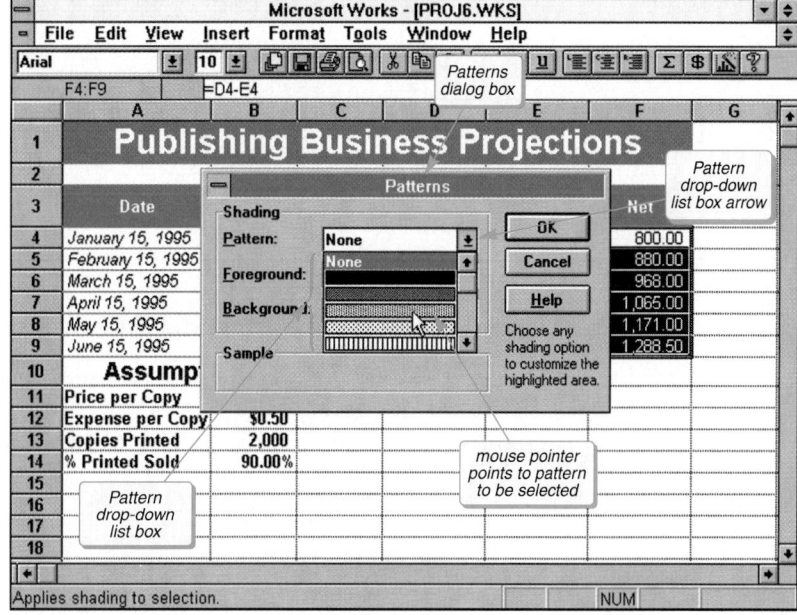

FIGURE 6-63

STEP 2 ►

Choose the Patterns command from the Format menu. When the Patterns dialog box displays, click the Pattern drop-down list box arrow and point to the fourth pattern in the drop-down list box.

The Patterns dialog box displays (Figure 6-64). The mouse pointer points to the fourth pattern in the Pattern drop-down list box.

FIGURE 6-64

STEP 3 ▶

Select the fourth pattern in the Patterns drop-down list box. Click the Foreground drop-down list box arrow, select the Light Gray color in the drop-down list box that displays, and point to the OK button.

The Sample area in the Patterns dialog box displays a sample of the pattern and light gray color that will display (Figure 6-65).

FIGURE 6-65

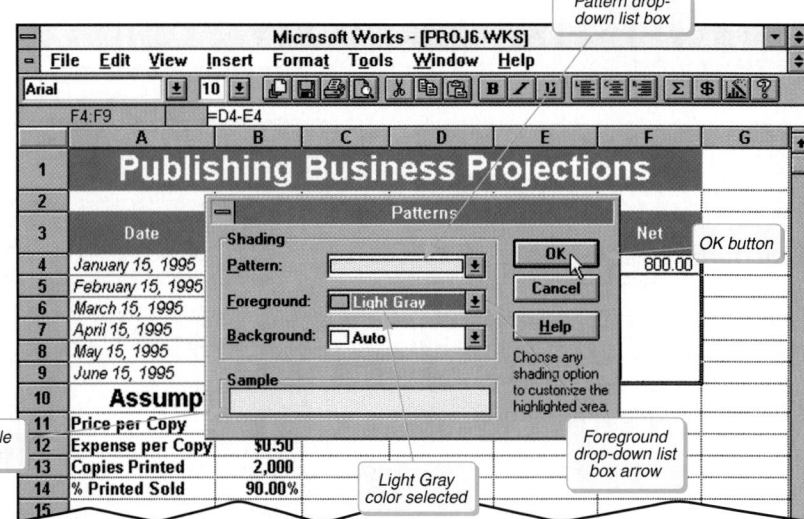

STEP 4 ▶

Choose the OK button in the Patterns dialog box. Click any cell to remove the highlight.

The spreadsheet displays with the light gray pattern in cells F4:F9 (Figure 6-66).

FIGURE 6-66

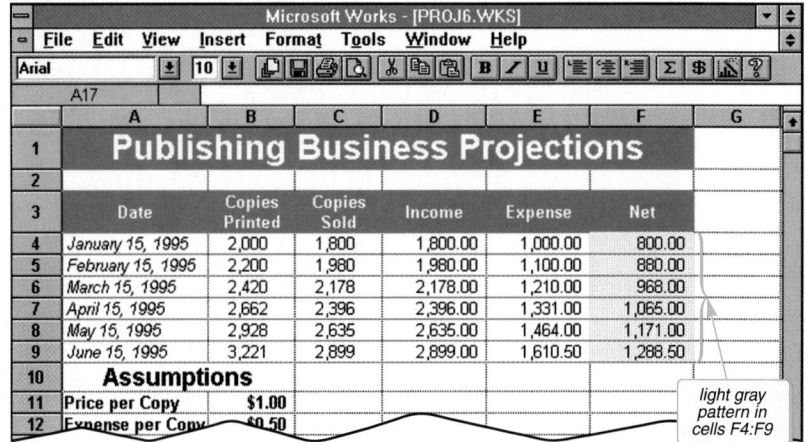

Adding Color to the Assumptions Section

Cell A10 contains the title Assumptions. This title is to display in white in cells with the dark cyan color (see Figure 6-1 on page W6.3). Complete the following steps to add color to this section of the spreadsheet.

TO ADD COLOR TO A TITLE

Step 1: Highlight cells A10:B10.

Step 2: Select the Format menu and choose the Patterns command.

Step 3: Select the solid pattern from the Pattern drop-down list box in the Patterns dialog box.

Step 4: Select Dark Cyan from the Foreground drop-down list box in the Patterns dialog box.

Step 5: Choose the OK button in the Patterns dialog box.

Step 6: Select the Format menu and choose the Font and Style command.

Step 7: Select White in the Color drop-down list box in the Font and Style dialog box.

Step 8: Choose the OK button in the Font and Style dialog box.

Adding a Border Around the Spreadsheet

The final step in adding color to the spreadsheet is to add a dark cyan border around the entire spreadsheet. To accomplish this task, perform the following steps.

TO ADD A COLOR BORDER AROUND THE ENTIRE SPREADSHEET ▼

STEP 1 ►

Highlight the spreadsheet in the range A1:F14. Select the Format menu and point to the Border command.

The range A1:F14 is highlighted and the mouse pointer points to the Border command (Figure 6-67).

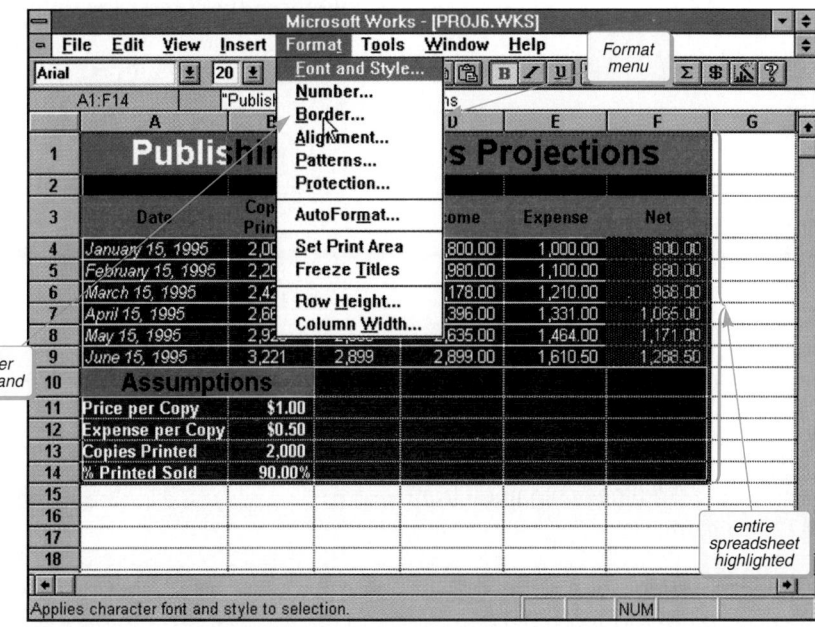

FIGURE 6-67

STEP 2 ►

Choose the Border command from the Format menu. When the Border dialog box displays, select the Outline box, click the Color drop-down list box arrow, select Dark Cyan, select the last box (thick line) in the Line Style area, and point to the OK button.

The Border dialog box displays (Figure 6-68). The Outline box in the Border area contains a thick line, the Color drop-down list box contains the words Dark Cyan, the last box in the Line Style area is selected, and the mouse pointer points to the OK button.

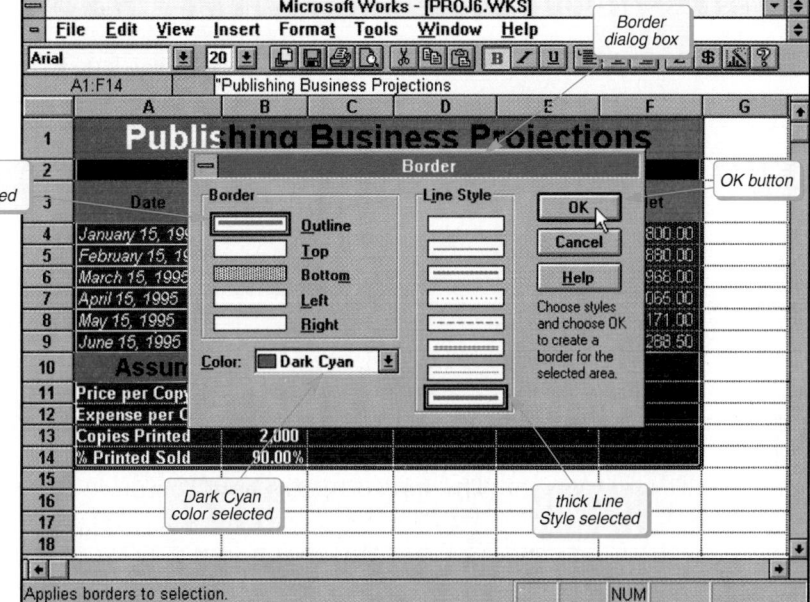

FIGURE 6-68

STEP 3 ▶

Choose the OK button. Select any cell to remove the highlight. Select the View menu and point to the Gridlines command (Figure 6-69).

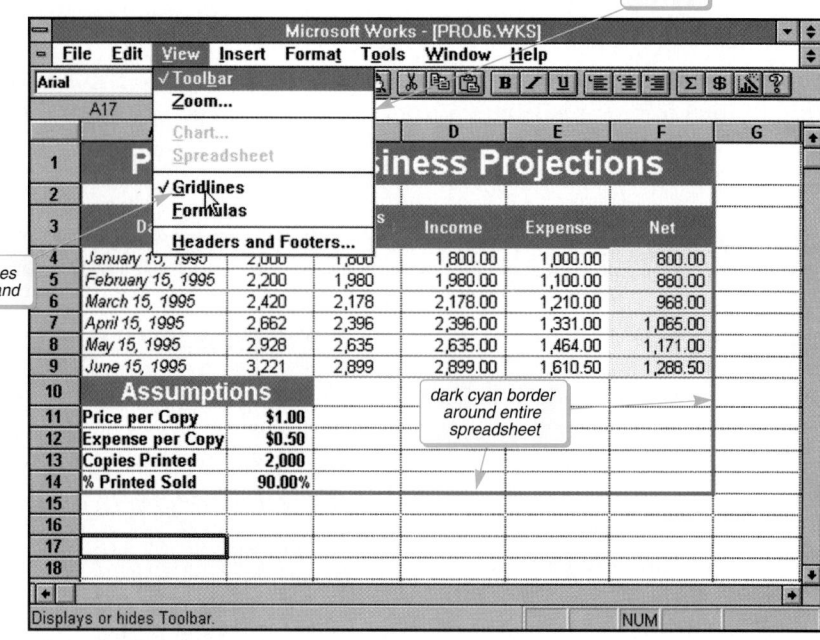

FIGURE 6-69

STEP 4 ▶

Choose the Gridlines command from the View menu.

The completed spreadsheet displays with color (Figure 6-70). Choosing the Gridlines command removes the gridlines from the spreadsheet and makes the border lines easier to see.

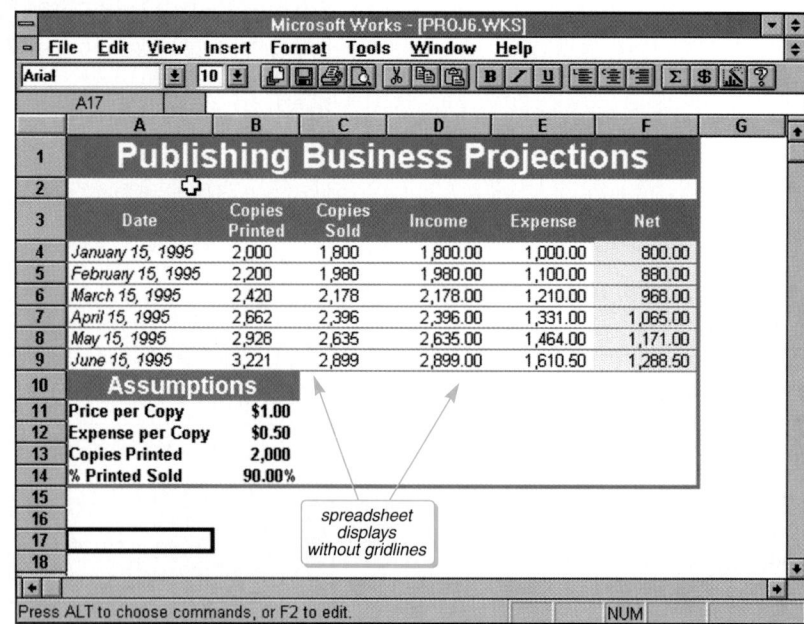

FIGURE 6-70

The spreadsheet is now complete.

Saving the Spreadsheet

You should once again save the spreadsheet using the Save button on the Toolbar. The spreadsheet will be saved with color.

▶ PRINTING A PORTION OF A SPREADSHEET

Often, your next step will be to print the spreadsheet. To print the entire spreadsheet, follow the steps explained in previous projects. It is also possible to print a portion of a spreadsheet. For example, in Project 6, you may want to print the spreadsheet but omit the Assumptions section on the printed output. To print a specific portion of a spreadsheet, do the following:

TO PRINT A PORTION OF A SPREADSHEET

Step 1: Highlight the range A1:F9, which is the portion of the spreadsheet you want to print.

Step 2: Select the Format menu.

Step 3: Choose the Set Print Area command.

Step 4: Choose the OK button in the Microsoft Works dialog box to confirm the print area.

Step 5: Select the File menu.

Step 6: Choose the Print command, make the desired selections in the Print dialog box, and choose the OK button.

Works prints the portion of the spreadsheet you designated as the print area (Figure 6-71).

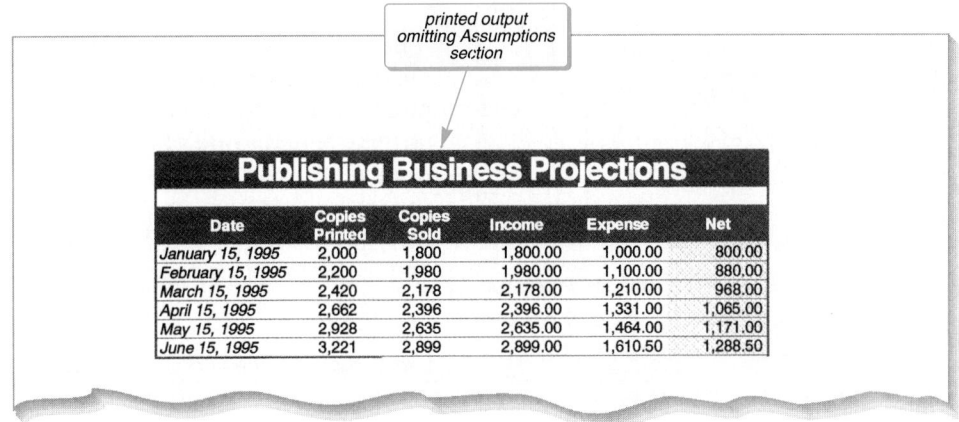

printed output omitting Assumptions section

Publishing Business Projections					
Date	Copies Printed	Copies Sold	Income	Expense	Net
January 15, 1995	2,000	1,800	1,800.00	1,000.00	800.00
February 15, 1995	2,200	1,980	1,980.00	1,100.00	880.00
March 15, 1995	2,420	2,178	2,178.00	1,210.00	968.00
April 15, 1995	2,662	2,396	2,396.00	1,331.00	1,065.00
May 15, 1995	2,928	2,635	2,635.00	1,464.00	1,171.00
June 15, 1995	3,221	2,899	2,899.00	1,610.50	1,288.50

FIGURE 6-71

If you want to print the entire spreadsheet after setting the print area, you must reset the print area by performing the following steps.

TO SET THE ENTIRE SPREADSHEET AS THE PRINT AREA

Step 1: Select the Edit menu.

Step 2: Choose the Select All command.

Step 3: Select the Format menu.

Step 4: Choose the Set Print Area command. When the Microsoft Works dialog box displays, choose the OK button.

Step 5: Click any cell to remove the highlight.

When you choose the Print command from the File menu or click the Print button on the Toolbar, the entire spreadsheet will print.

▶ WHAT-IF ANALYSIS

A major reason for creating the spreadsheet in this project is to perform a what-if analysis, which means asking the question, "What if such and such happened?" and then entering values into the spreadsheet to determine the answer.

In the Publishing Business Projections spreadsheet, the values you can enter display in the Assumptions section. These values include the Price per Copy, the Expense per Copy, the Copies Printed, and the % Printed Sold.

Based on the values you enter, different results will occur in the spreadsheet. For example, a projection might be that the newsletter sells for $1.00 per copy, the Expense per Copy is $0.50, the number of Copies Printed in January is 2,000, and sixty percent of the newsletters printed are actually sold. The results obtained from these values are shown in Figure 6-72.

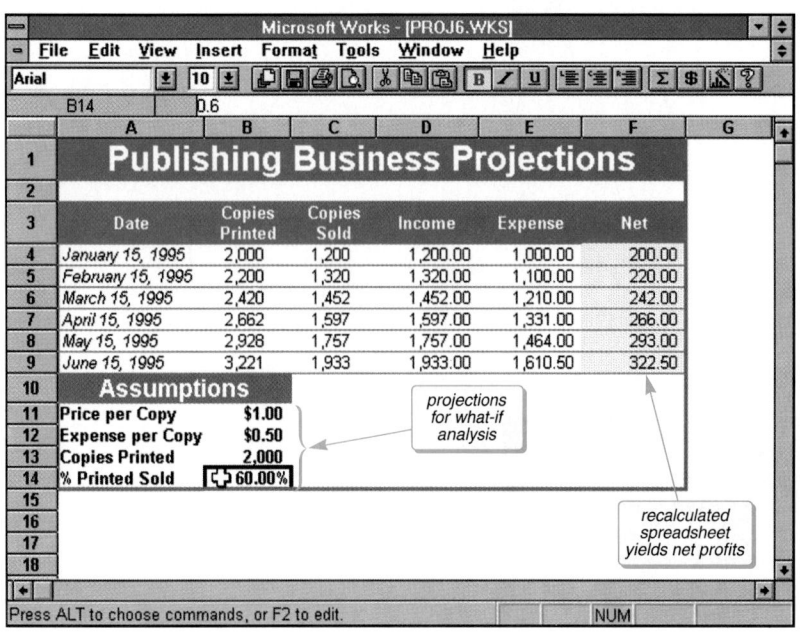

FIGURE 6-72

Notice that when you enter the new values, Works recalculates the spreadsheet. The recalculated values express the results that would be obtained if the assumptions all came true. In this example, the Net would increase each month until a profit of $322.50 occurred for the month of June.

Whenever you vary the contents of a cell used in formulas, by default Works recalculates the formulas. Therefore, each time you enter a value in one of the assumptions cells, Works will recalculate the entire spreadsheet. In most instances, this requires little time and is the proper procedure to use.

If, however, the spreadsheet is quite large and recalculation takes too long, you can stop this process by choosing the **Manual Calculation command** from the Tools menu. When you choose this command, Works places a checkmark next to the command in the menu. The formulas in the spreadsheet will not be calculated each time you change a value. To cause calculations to be performed, you can either turn off manual calculation by choosing the command again, or you can choose the **Calculate Now command** from the Tools menu. When you choose the Calculate Now command, Works recalculates all formulas in the spreadsheet.

In Project 6, a negative outlook can also be evaluated for the Publishing Business Projections. Assume the owners project they can only sell the newsletter for seventy-five cents per copy. Again they print 2,000 copies but the Expense per Copy is fifty-five cents and they are able to sell only seventy percent of the copies printed. The results are shown in Figure 6-73.

Notice that each month produces a negative net and that the negative number is displayed in red within parentheses. When using the Currency and Comma formats, Works displays negative numbers within parentheses. In the other numeric formats, negative numbers display with a minus sign appearing before the leftmost digit. The red color displays because you selected the Negative numbers in red check box when you formatted the numbers.

Clearly the values used as assumptions in Figure 6-72 produced a net profit and the values used in Figure 6-73 produced a net loss. On page W6.4 of this project, other questions were posed. To answer these questions, you must experiment with the values in the spreadsheet. The questions, and their answers, follow.

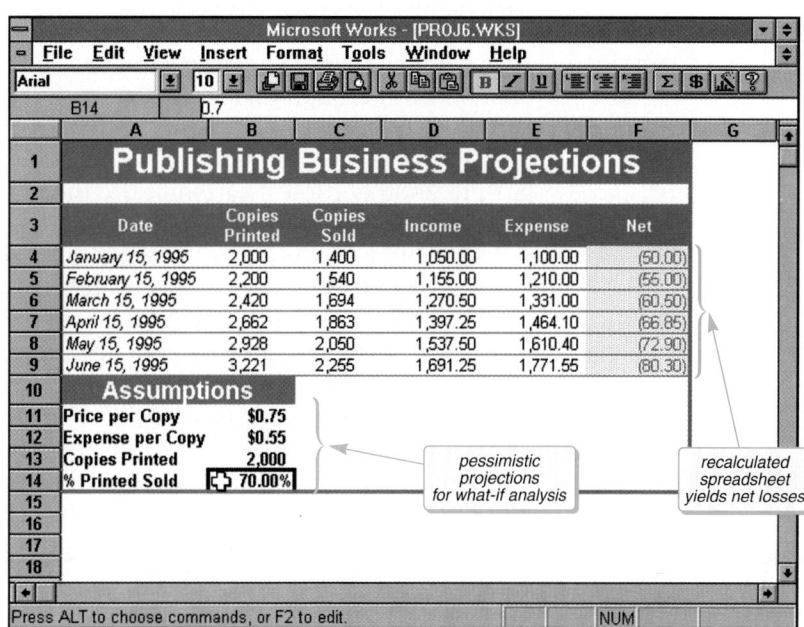

FIGURE 6-73

Question 1: If we print 2,000 copies at an expense of $0.50 per copy and sell them for $1.00 apiece, what percentage of the copies we print must we sell to break even?

Answer to Question 1: In this question, you know three of the four variables (Price per Copy = $1.00; Expense per Copy = $0.50; Copies Printed = 2,000). To determine the % Printed Sold to break even, that is, to obtain a Net of $0.00, you must enter different values in cell B14 until the Net in cell F4 equals zero. When the Net equals zero, the value in Income (cell D4) equals the value in Expense (cell E4) and the operation has broken even. After experimentation by entering different values in cell B14, it was found that the value 50% yielded a break-even condition where the Income equaled the Expense (Figure 6-74).

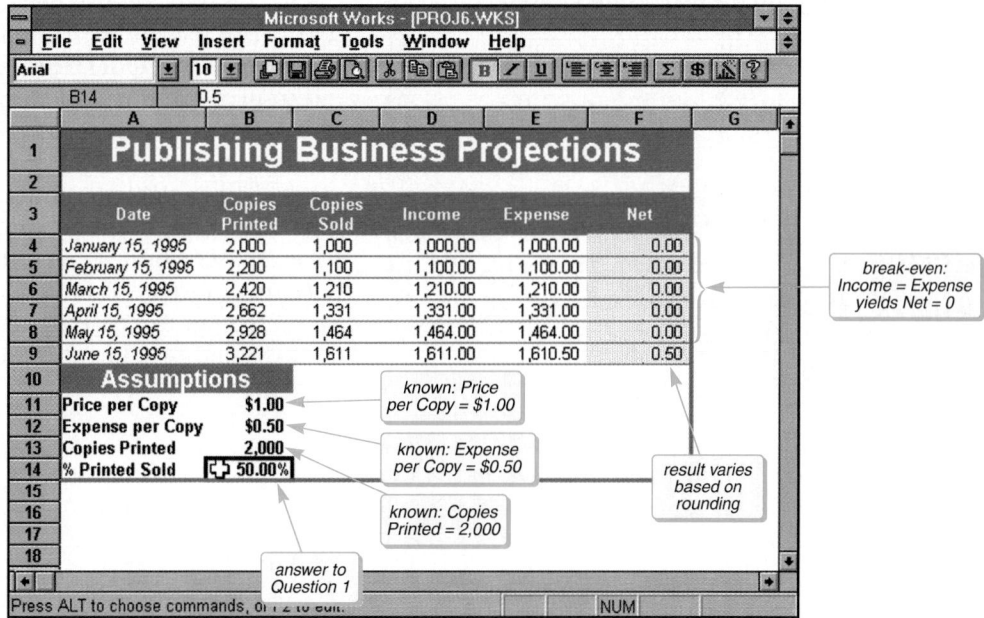

FIGURE 6-74

Rounding Discrepancies

Notice in Figure 6-74 on the previous page that row 9 does not contain a Net of 0.00 even though logically if one month produced a net of zero they all should. Nothing *wrong* is occurring. The difference is due to rounding.

In row 4, no rounding was required for the number of Copies Sold because 50% of 2000 is 1000. Therefore, the Income (1000 * 1.00 = 1000.00) equals the Expense (2000 * .50 = 1000.00).

In row 9, however, the formula to calculate Copies Sold (3221 * .50) yields an answer of 1610.5, which Works rounds to 1611 (cell C9). The Income calculated from the rounded value (1611 * 1.00 = 1611) is greater than if the unrounded number is used (1610.5 * 1.00 = 1610.50). Notice that the Income from the unrounded value (1610.50) is equal to the Expense (cell E9) and is the expected result. Because, however, the Copies Printed was rounded up, the Income will be slightly greater and therefore, the Net is positive.

You need to recognize that rounding can produce values that sometimes are not exact. Whenever you round within a spreadsheet, you must be aware of the effect it can have on answers obtained in your spreadsheet.

The second question asked on page W6.4 of this project is:

Question 2: If our Expense per Copy is $0.36, we print 2,000 copies, and we sell 45% of the copies we print, at what price can we sell the newsletter and still break even?

Answer to Question 2: For this question, you know the values for Expense per Copy ($0.36), Copies Printed (2,000), and % Printed Sold (45%). You must experiment by entering different values for Price per Copy to answer the question. After entering different values, the spreadsheet in Figure 6-75 shows the answer to be $0.80. That is, if the owners sell the newsletter for $0.80 per copy, the Net in cell F4 is zero and they have reached the break-even point.

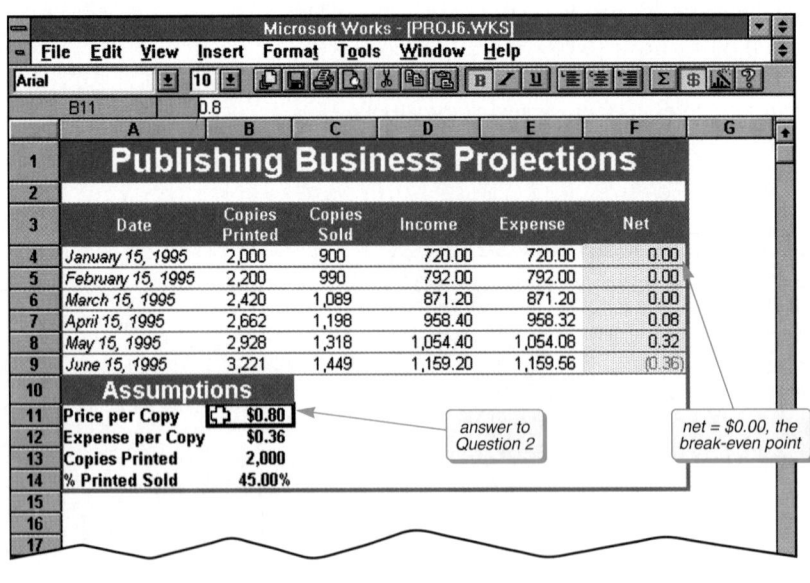

FIGURE 6-75

Notice again in column F that rounding discrepancies have occurred.

Question 3: If we sell the newsletter for $0.75 apiece, print 2,000 copies, and we are able to sell 40% of the copies we print, what is the maximum expense per newsletter we can pay and still break even?

Answer to Question 3: In this question, the known quantities are Price per Copy ($0.75), Copies Printed (2,000), and % Printed Sold (40%). The variable to enter in order to answer the question is the Expense per Copy. Again, after entering a variety of values, it was found that an Expense per Copy of $0.30 would produce the break-even point (Figure 6-76).

You can also ask questions in which two of the four variables would have to change. For example, you could ask, "If I sell the newsletter for seventy-five cents, and my Expense per Copy is thirty-five cents, how many newsletters must I print and what percentage of those I print must I sell to realize a profit of $900.00 in January given that the maximum I will print is 4,000 copies?"

A spreadsheet provides a means for examining many alternatives in a search to determine the optimum solution to a problem.

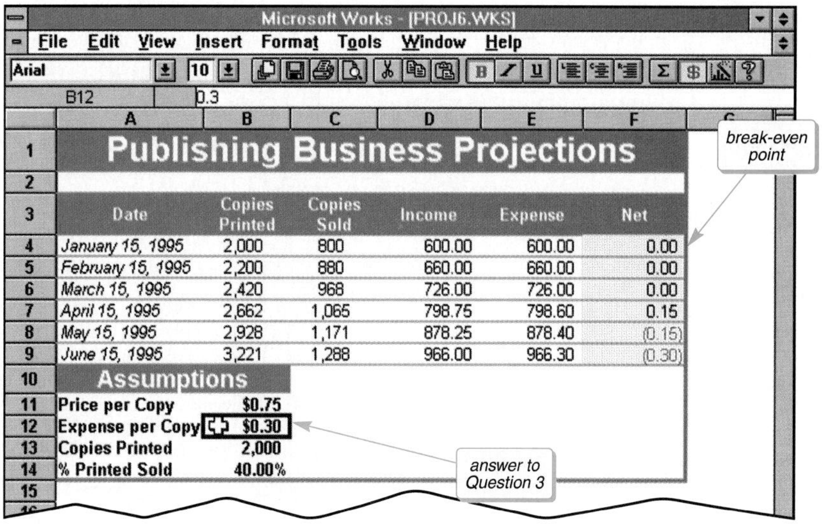

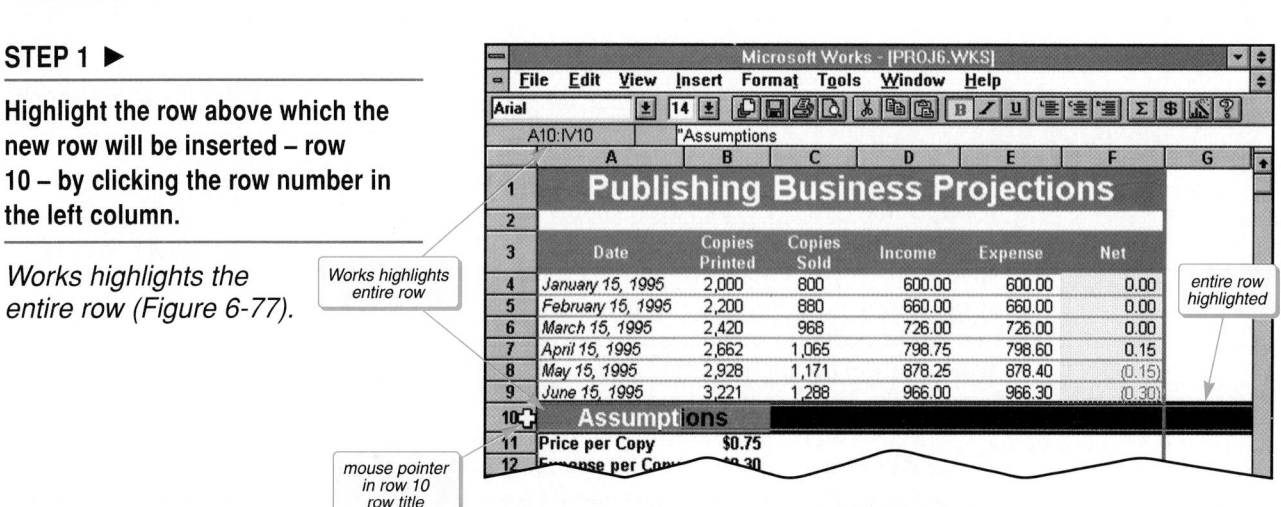

FIGURE 6-76

▶ MODIFYING A SPREADSHEET – INSERTING ROWS AND COLUMNS

T he first design of a spreadsheet, while useful, often requires modifications to become more useful. For example, in the Project 6 spreadsheet, while many of the questions asked can be answered, one question still remains: Over the six month period of time, how many copies were printed, how many copies were sold, what was the total income, what was the total expense, and what was the total net? To answer these questions, you must add a total row to the spreadsheet.

The totals should appear below row 9. However, row 10 in the spreadsheet is being used. To solve this problem, you must insert a new row above row 10 and place the totals in the new row. To insert a new row in a spreadsheet, perform the following steps.

TO INSERT A ROW ▼

STEP 1 ▶

Highlight the row above which the new row will be inserted – row 10 – by clicking the row number in the left column.

Works highlights the entire row (Figure 6-77).

FIGURE 6-77

STEP 2 ▶

Select the Insert menu and point to the Row/Column command (Figure 6-78).

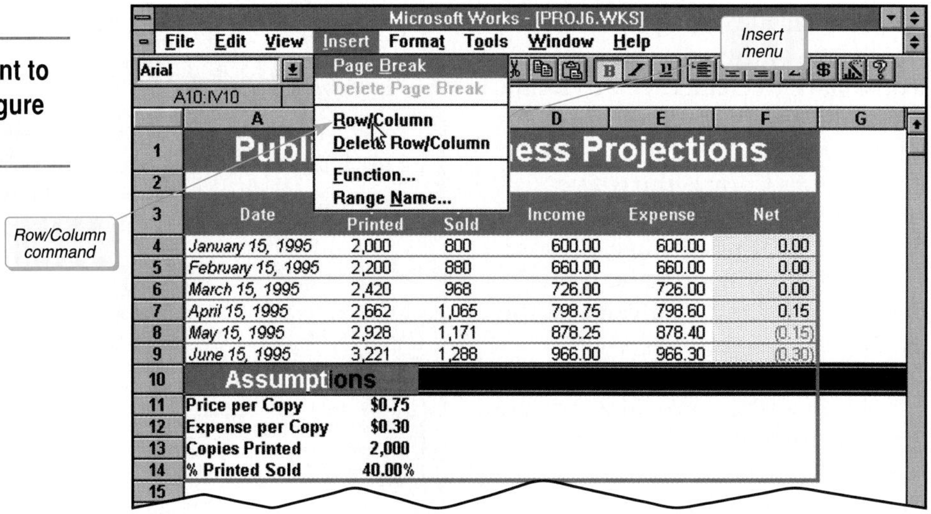

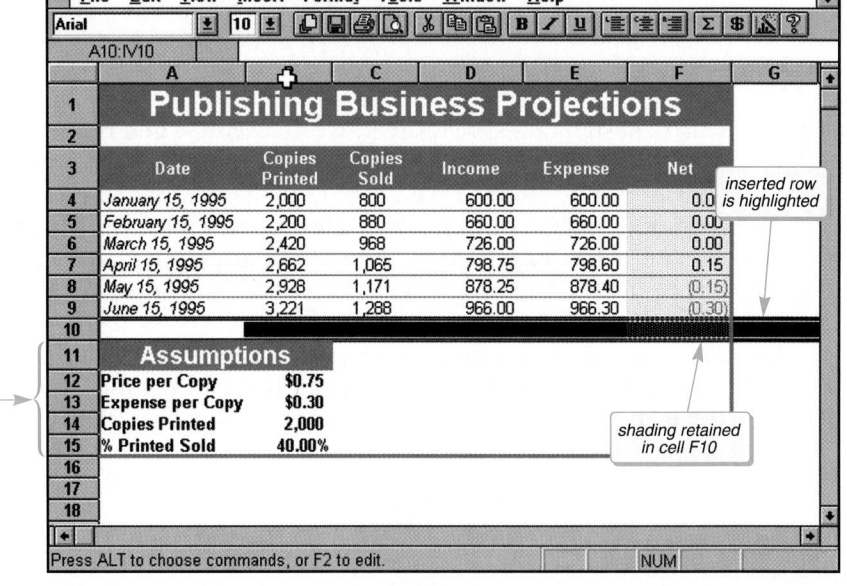

FIGURE 6-78

STEP 3 ▶

Choose the Row/Column command from the Insert menu.

Works inserts a row above the row that was highlighted, moves all the rows down one, and highlights the new row (Figure 6-79). The new row contains no data but retains the shading in cell F10.

FIGURE 6-79

If you want to insert more than one row, highlight the number of rows you want to insert, select the Insert menu, and choose the **Row/Column command**. For example, if you want to insert three rows, highlight three rows in the spreadsheet. When you choose the Row/Column command, three new inserted rows will appear above the highlighted rows.

An important consideration when inserting rows into a spreadsheet is that Works automatically modifies all formulas containing cell references that are changed because of the new row. In Figure 6-79, for example, notice that the Price per Copy value is contained in cell B12, whereas prior to inserting the row it was in cell B11 (see Figure 6-78). Works changes the cell reference in any formulas using cell B11 to the new reference B12.

You can also use the Row/Column command from the Insert menu to insert a column in a spreadsheet. To do so, highlight the column you want to move to the right. When you choose the Row/Column command from the Insert menu, Works moves all the columns, including the highlighted column to the right, inserts a new column to the left of the highlighted column, and highlights the new column.

Although not required in Project 6, Works also allows you to delete one or more rows or columns. To do so, complete the following steps:

TO DELETE A ROW OR COLUMN

Step 1: Highlight the row(s) or column(s) you want to delete.
Step 2: Choose the Delete Row/Column command from the Insert menu.

If you delete a row or column containing cells that are referenced in formulas, Works displays the letters ERR in those cells referencing the deleted cells. You must then correct the formulas.

Entering a Total Line

After the new row 10 is added to the spreadsheet, you should enter the Six Month Totals. The spreadsheet containing these totals is shown in Figure 6-80.

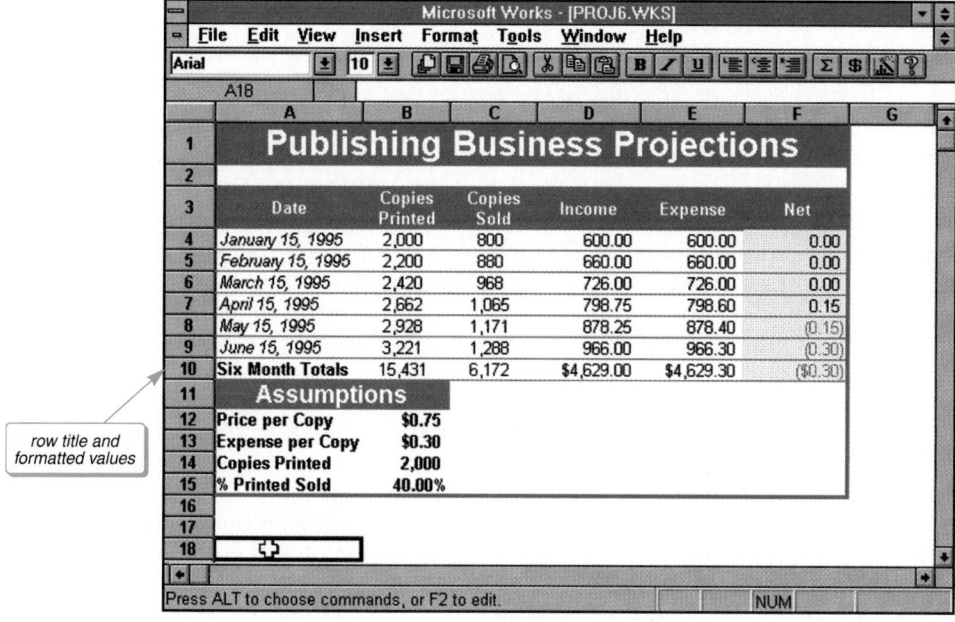

FIGURE 6-80

The steps to add the line are:

TO ENTER THE TOTAL LINE

Step 1: Highlight cell A10 and type the title, Six Month Totals, in cell A10.
Step 2: Press the RIGHT ARROW key to enter the title and highlight cell B10.
Step 3: Click the Autosum button on the Toolbar and drag the range B4:B9. Confirm the entry by clicking the Autosum button again, clicking the Enter box, or pressing the ENTER key.
Step 4: Highlight cell B10 and the range to copy to — cells C10:E10.
Step 5: From the Edit menu choose the Fill Right command.

Step 6: Select cell F10. Click the Autosum button, highlight the range F4:F9, and confirm the entry by clicking the Autosum button again, clicking the Enter box, or pressing the ENTER key. The reason you do not use the Fill Right command for the formula in cell F10 is Works will use the formatting of cell B10, which would eliminate the light gray pattern in cell F10 and also the right border of the cell.

Step 7: Select the Format menu, choose the Number command, select the Currency option button in the Format area of the Number dialog box, select the Negative number in red check box in the Currency area, and choose the OK button in the Number dialog box.

Step 8: Highlight cell A10 and click the Bold button on the Toolbar.

Step 9: Highlight cells B10:C10, click the Center Align button on the Toolbar, and then choose the Number command from the Format menu. When the Number dialog box displays, select the Comma option button, type zero in the Number of decimals text box, and then choose the OK button in the Comma dialog box.

Step 10: Highlight cells D10:E10 and click the Currency button on the Toolbar.

Figure 6-80 on the previous page displays the spreadsheet with the total line. Modifying a spreadsheet is a common occurrence. The ability to insert and delete rows and columns allows spreadsheets to be modified to fit your changing needs.

▶ PROJECT SUMMARY

In this project, you have learned to develop a spreadsheet that you can use to answer what-if questions. The project provided procedures to help you become familiar with entering functions into a spreadsheet. You saw the difference between relative cell references and absolute cell references, how to enter both into a formula, and how to copy both to adjacent cells. In addition, you reinforced your knowledge of formatting a spreadsheet, adding color to a spreadsheet, saving a spreadsheet, and printing a spreadsheet.

Using the steps and techniques presented, you learned about rounding values calculated by formulas and how to insert rows and columns in a spreadsheet for modification purposes.

▶ KEY TERMS

Alignment command *(W6.6)*
absolute cell reference *(W6.21)*
best fit *(W6.10)*
Calculate Now command *(W6.44)*
column width *(W6.9)*
date formats *(W6.8)*

Fill Series command *(W6.10)*
formula *(W6.14)*
function *(W6.17)*
Manual Calculation command *(W6.44)*
Number command *(W6.8)*
relative cell reference *(W6.21)*

ROUND function *(W6.17)*
Row/Column command *(W6.48)*
Undo Drag and Drop command *(W6.31)*
what-if questions *(W6.2)*

In Microsoft Works, you can accomplish a task in a number of ways. The following table provides a quick reference to each task presented in this project with its available options. The commands listed in the Menu column can be executed using either the keyboard or mouse.

Task	Mouse	Menu	Keyboard Shortcuts
Comma Format		From Format menu, choose Number	Press CTRL+COMMA
Copy Date / Increment Day		From Edit menu, choose Fill Series, select Day	
Copy Date / Increment Month		From Edit menu, choose Fill Series, select Month	
Copy Date / Increment Weekday		From Edit menu, choose Fill Series, select Weekday	
Copy Date / Increment Year		From Edit menu, choose Fill Series, select Year	
Delete a Column		From Edit menu, choose Delete Row/Column	
Delete a Row		From Insert menu, choose Delete Row/Column	
Highlight One Cell Down	Drag cell		Press SHIFT+DOWN ARROW
Highlight One Cell to the Left	Drag cell		Press SHIFT+LEFT ARROW
Highlight One Cell to the Right	Drag cell		Press SHIFT+RIGHT ARROW
Highlight One Cell Up	Drag cell		Press SHIFT+UP ARROW
Highlight to the Beginning of a Row	Drag to beginning of row		Press SHIFT+HOME
Highlight to the Beginning of the Spreadsheet	Drag to beginning of spreadsheet		Press CTRL+SHIFT+HOME
Highlight to the End of a Row	Drag to end of row		Press SHIFT+END
Highlight to the End of a Spreadsheet	Drag to end of spreadsheet		Press CTRL+SHIFT+END
Insert a Column		From Insert menu, choose Insert Row/Column	
Insert a Row		From Insert menu, choose Insert Row/Column	
Make Highlighted Cell an Absolute Cell Reference			Press F4
Percent Format		From Format menu, choose Number	Press CTRL+5
Place a Cell Reference in a Formula	Click cell		Type cell number or highlight cell using arrow key

STUDENT ASSIGNMENT 1
True/False

Instructions: Circle T if the statement is true or F if the statement is false.

T   F   1. You can use a spreadsheet to answer questions such as, "What must our revenues be for next year if our costs rise 10% and our profits rise 20%?"

T   F   2. Column titles should not be longer than the default width of a column.

T   F   3. When you enter a date into a spreadsheet, Works considers it text data and left-aligns it in the cell.

T   F   4. A date Works displays as January 15, 1995 is displayed in the Month, Day, Year – Short format.

T   F   5. To change the width of a column on the spreadsheet, drag the column border between the columns to the new location.

T   F   6. The Fill Down command will automatically update the name of the month when you copy a date.

T   F   7. A formula is an equation that calculates a new value from existing values in cells within the spreadsheet.

T   F   8. The formula =ROUND(C6*(D4+G9*F12),2) is a valid formula.

T   F   9. The ROUND function should always be used in a formula that references a cell containing a number with a decimal point.

T   F   10. A relative cell reference means a cell's reference does not change when a formula containing the cell reference is copied from one cell to another.

T   F   11. An absolute cell reference means a cell's reference does not change when a formula containing the cell reference is copied from one cell to another.

T   F   12. When you enter a cell reference, Works assumes it is a relative cell reference.

T   F   13. To change a cell reference to a relative cell reference, press the F4 function key.

T   F   14. Whenever you vary the contents of a cell used in a formula, by default Works recalculates the formula.

T   F   15. When you apply the Comma format, Works rounds the value formatted.

T   F   16. A function is a built-in equation you can use to calculate values in a spreadsheet.

T   F   17. You cannot format whole numbers using the Comma format.

T   F   18. What-if analysis is possible because Works recalculates formulas in a spreadsheet when you enter new values in cells used in formulas.

T   F   19. Rounding a number ensures that no arithmetic errors or discrepancies will occur in the spreadsheet.

T   F   20. You should avoid inserting a row or a column in a spreadsheet because you must then reenter all formulas.

STUDENT ASSIGNMENT 2
Multiple Choice Questions

Instructions: Circle the correct response.

1. When you set the column width of column C to twenty characters, highlight cell C3, type 1/13/95, and press the ENTER key, Works displays _____ in cell C3.
   a. January 13, 1995
   b. 1/13/95
   c. January, 1995
   d. 1/13

2. The entry ########## in a cell D6 means _____ .
   a. the numeric data in cell D6 is displayed in the date format
   b. the numeric data in cell D6 is a larger number than Works can display in cell D6
   c. the text data in cell D6 is longer than Works can display in cell D6
   d. Works cannot interpret the data entered into cell D6
3. To copy the date, February 16, 1995, from cell F2 to the range F3:F7, incrementing the day by one each time, so that cell F3 contains February 17, 1995, and so on, highlight the range and then _____ .
   a. from the Format menu, choose the Number command
   b. from the Edit menu, choose the Fill Down command, select Step 1 in the Fill Down dialog box, and choose the OK button in the Fill Down dialog box
   c. from the Edit menu, choose the Fill Series command, select Month in the Fill Series dialog box, and choose the OK button in the Fill Series dialog box
   d. from the Edit menu, choose the Fill Series command, select Day in the Fill Series dialog box, and choose the OK button in the Fill Series dialog box
4. Which of the following is NOT valid?
   a. =ROUND(F5*H12^3)
   b. =L21+K8*F12-23
   c. =((Q3-J26)*F27+B18)*E7
   d. =SUM(A6:C12)*F27
5. An absolute cell reference in a formula means _____ .
   a. the value in the cell will never change
   b. the cell reference will not change when the formula is copied to other cells
   c. the cell reference will change when the formula is copied to other cells
   d. the value in the cell will change when the formula is copied to other cells
6. If the value in cell F12 is 193.9982, and you specify the Comma format with two decimal positions for the cell, the value Works displays in the cell is _____ .
   a. 193.00
   b. 193.90
   c. 193.99
   d. 194.00
7. Cell F7 contains the formula =(ROUND(C4*H7,0)*D3)+G6. If cell C4 contains 2.25, cell H7 contains 3.1, cell D3 contains 3 and cell G6 contains 4, the result in cell F7 after the formula is calculated is _____ .
   a. 25
   b. 23.25
   c. 18
   d. 49
8. When performing a what-if analysis, you normally change the _____ in order to answer your question.
   a. value in one or more cells
   b. formulas in one or more cells
   c. titles in one or more cells
   d. all of the above
9. To add a row to a spreadsheet, _____ .
   a. click the Insert Row button on the Toolbar
   b. choose the Row/Column command from the Insert menu
   c. click the row number and press the ENTER key
   d. select the Row/Column command and type the row number
10. To delete a row, _____ .
   a. highlight the column A cell in the row to be deleted and press the DELETE key
   b. choose the Delete Row/Column command from the Insert menu
   c. choose the Replace command from the Edit menu
   d. highlight the row to be deleted and press the DELETE key

STUDENT ASSIGNMENT 3
Fill Series Command

Instructions: In the spaces provided, describe the steps required to perform the following tasks.

Task 1: Copy the date in cell A4 (1/22/95) into cells A5:A12. Each date should be the next day in the week. Display the dates in Month-Day – Long format

Steps: _____

_____

Task 2: Copy the date in cell F2 (2/19/95) into cells F3:F15. Each date should be the next day in the week except Saturdays and Sundays should not be included. Display the date in Month-Year – Short format.

Steps: _____

_____

Task 3: Copy the date in cell C2 (March 16, 1995) to the range D2:L2. Each date should be one week apart. Display the dates in Month-Day-Year – Long format.

Steps: _____

_____

Task 4: Copy the date in cell A12 (5/20/95) to the range A13:A40. The dates should be every other month, that is, May, July, September, and so on. Display the dates in Month-Year – Long format.

Steps: _____

_____

STUDENT ASSIGNMENT 4
Absolute Cell References

Instructions: The spreadsheet in Figure SA6-4 contains an error that results in erroneous data. Identify the error and state how the error can be corrected.

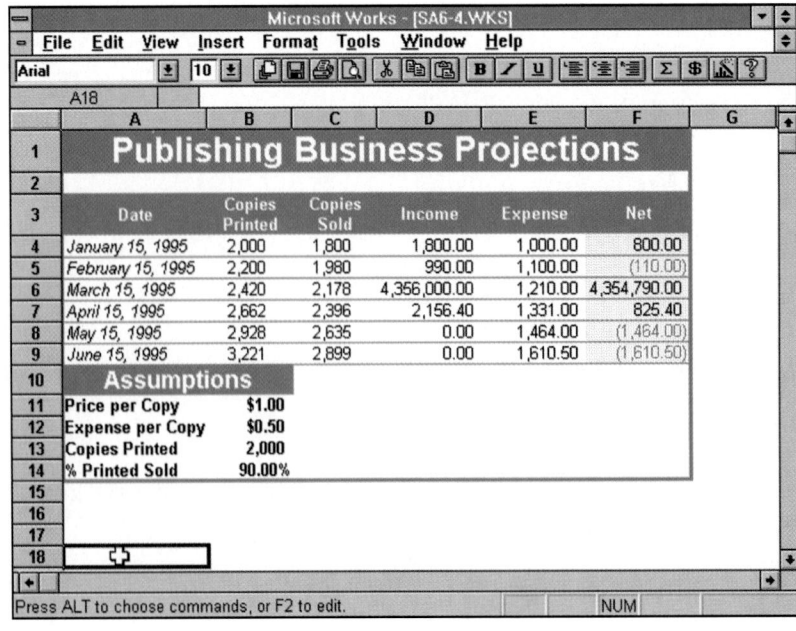

FIGURE SA6-4

Error: _____

_____

_____

Correction: _____

_____

_____

STUDENT ASSIGNMENT 5
Rounding

Instructions: In the spreadsheet in Figure SA6-5, which uses the same formulas as in the Project 6 spreadsheet, March, May, and June show a loss. In the space provided, explain the reason that the first two months are break-even and the other months are not.

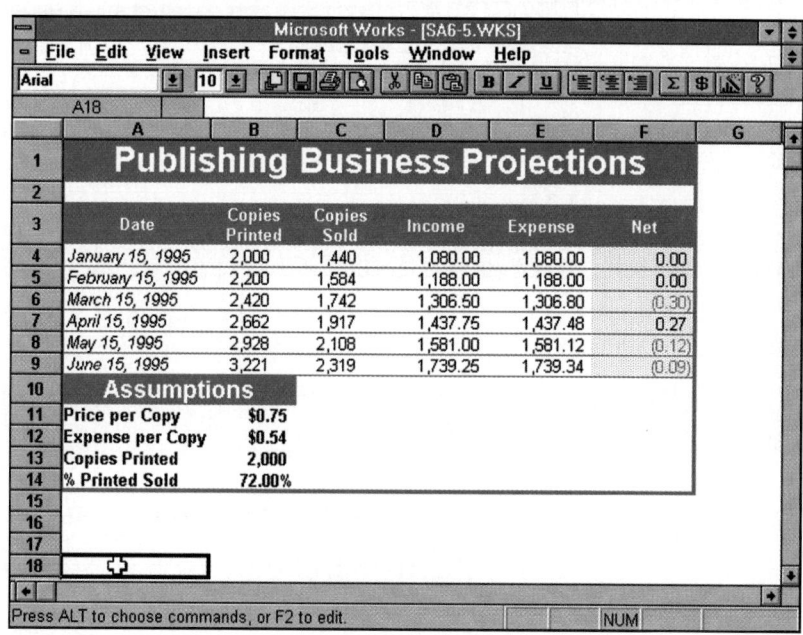

FIGURE SA6-5

Explanation: _____

_____

_____

_____

STUDENT ASSIGNMENT 6
Finding and Correcting Spreadsheet Errors

Instructions: The spreadsheet in Figure SA6-6 contains an error that results in erroneous data. In the space provided, identify the error and explain how the error can be corrected.

Error: _____

_____

_____

_____

Correction: _____

_____

_____

_____

FIGURE SA6-6

Microsoft Works - [SA6-6.WKS]

File Edit View Insert Format Tools Window Help

Arial   10   A18

Publishing Business Projections

	Date	Copies Printed	Copies Sold	Income	Expense	Net
4	January 15, 1995	2,000	1,800	1,800.00	1,000.00	800.00
5	February 15, 1995	2,200	1,980	1,980.00	1,100.00	880.00
6	March 15, 1995	2,420	2,178	2,178.00	1,210.00	968.00
7	April 15, 1995	2,662	2,396	2,395.80	1,331.00	1,064.80
8	May 15, 1995	2,928	2,635	2,635.20	1,464.00	1,171.20
9	June 15, 1995	3,221	2,899	2,898.90	1,610.50	1,288.40

Assumptions

11	Price per Copy	$1.00
12	Expense per Copy	$0.50
13	Copies Printed	2,000
14	% Printed Sold	90.00%

Press ALT to choose commands, or F2 to edit.   NUM

C O M P U T E R   L A B O R A T O R Y   E X E R C I S E S

COMPUTER LABORATORY EXERCISE 1
Using the Help Menu

Instructions: Perform the following tasks using a personal computer.

1. Start the Microsoft Works Spreadsheet tool.
2. Select the Help menu.
3. Choose Contents from the Help menu.
4. Choose Spreadsheet from the Works for Windows Help Contents screen.
5. Choose Changing spreadsheet information from the Spreadsheet: Step-by-step help screen.
6. Choose Deleting and clearing information from the Changing spreadsheet information screen.
7. Read Deleting and clearing information, print the topic, and answer the following questions:
   a. When you clear a cell, what happens to the cell formatting?

   _____

   _____

   b. What is the procedure to delete a single row from a spreadsheet?

   _____

c. How can you delete four columns from the spreadsheet?

_____

_____

d. If you delete a row from a spreadsheet and the letters ERR display in a cell, what causes this to occur and how can you fix it?

_____

_____

_____

8. Click the Back button two times. The Spreadsheet: Step-by-step help screen displays again.
9. Choose Spreadsheet basics.
10. From the Spreadsheet basics screen, choose Creating a Spreadsheet.
11. Read Creating a spreadsheet, print the topic, and answer the following questions:
   a. If cell B4 contains the entry January 15, 1995, cells B4 and B5 are highlighted, and from the Edit menu you choose the Fill Series command, select the Month option button in the Fill Series dialog box, enter a negative one in the Step By box, and choose the OK button in the Fill Series dialog box, what value will display in cell B5?

   _____

   b. If you want to enter a month name, such as November, as text rather than as a date value, what should you type before typing the month name? _____

12. At the end of the Creating a spreadsheet screen, choose Number formats.
13. Read the Number formats screen, print the topic, and answer the following question:
   a. List three ways you can cause Works to display a numeric value in the Currency format:

   (1) _____

   _____

   (2) _____

   _____

   (3) _____

   _____

14. Exit from the Help window.

COMPUTER LABORATORY EXERCISE 2
Entering Formulas

Instructions: Start the Works Spreadsheet tool. Open the CLE6-2.WKS file on the Student Diskette that accompanies this book. Using the spreadsheet on your screen as illustrated in Figure CLE6-2, enter the formulas to accomplish the same tasks as those in the Project 6 spreadsheet. When you have completed this task, format the numeric values in the spreadsheet, and then print the spreadsheet.

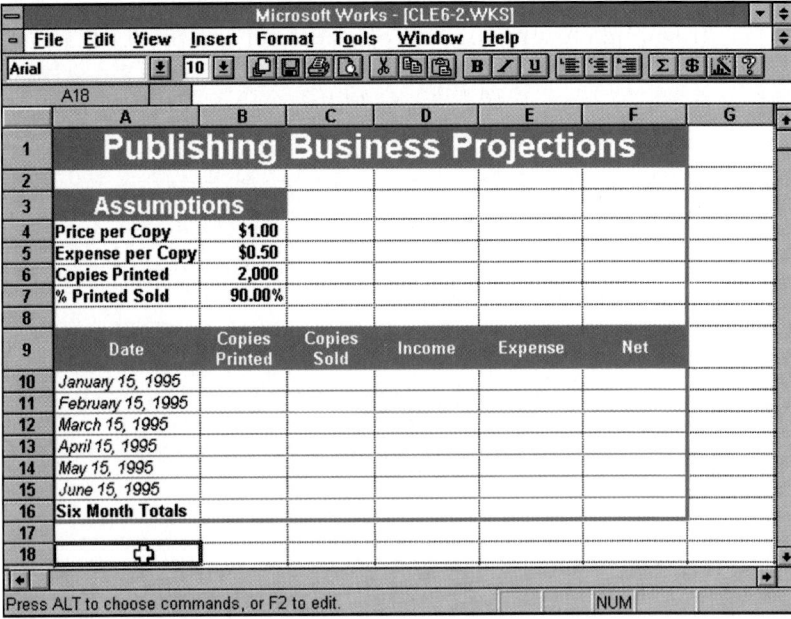

FIGURE CLE6-2

COMPUTER LABORATORY EXERCISE 3
What-If Analysis

Instructions: Start the Works Spreadsheet tool. Open the CLE6-3.WKS file on the Student Diskette that accompanies this book. Using the spreadsheet on your screen as illustrated in Figure CLE6-3, answer the following questions.

FIGURE CLE6-3

1. The assumptions in the spreadsheet are: Price per Copy: $1.00; Expense per Copy: $0.40; Copies Printed: 2,000; and, % Printed Sold: 100%. How many copies will be sold for the months, January through June?

What is the Net for all six months?

2. Using the CLE6-3.WKS spreadsheet, answer the following what-if questions:
   a. If you charge fifty cents per copy, sell 43% of the copies you print, and print 2,000 copies, what is the maximum Expense per Copy you can incur to make a minimum Net of $200.00 in January?

   b. If you charge eighty cents per copy, sell 45% of the copies you print, pay seventeen cents Expense per Copy, and print 2,000 copies, in which month do you first exceed a Net of $500.00 per month?

COMPUTER LABORATORY ASSIGNMENTS

COMPUTER LABORATORY ASSIGNMENT 1
Creating a Quarterly Budget Report

Purpose: To provide experience using the Works Spreadsheet to create a spreadsheet that requires entering text, dates, numbers, formulas, and functions, formatting, adding color, calculating sums, saving and printing the spreadsheet, and providing answers to what-if questions.

Problem: Create a Quarterly Budget Report where the Expenses are calculated as percentages of the Total Revenue. The Revenues are shown in the table on the right.

Revenue	January	February	March
Sales	125854.92	259036.28	199462.81
Other	23232.87	45454.00	37128.22

The spreadsheet without gridlines is shown in Figure CLA6-1.

Instructions:

1. Create a spreadsheet in the format shown in Figure CLA6-1 using the numbers from the table.

2. On the spreadsheet, calculate the Total for each item of Revenue (Sales and Other) by adding the Revenue for January, February, and March.

3. Calculate the Total Revenue by adding the Sales and Other values for January, February, March, and for the Total column.

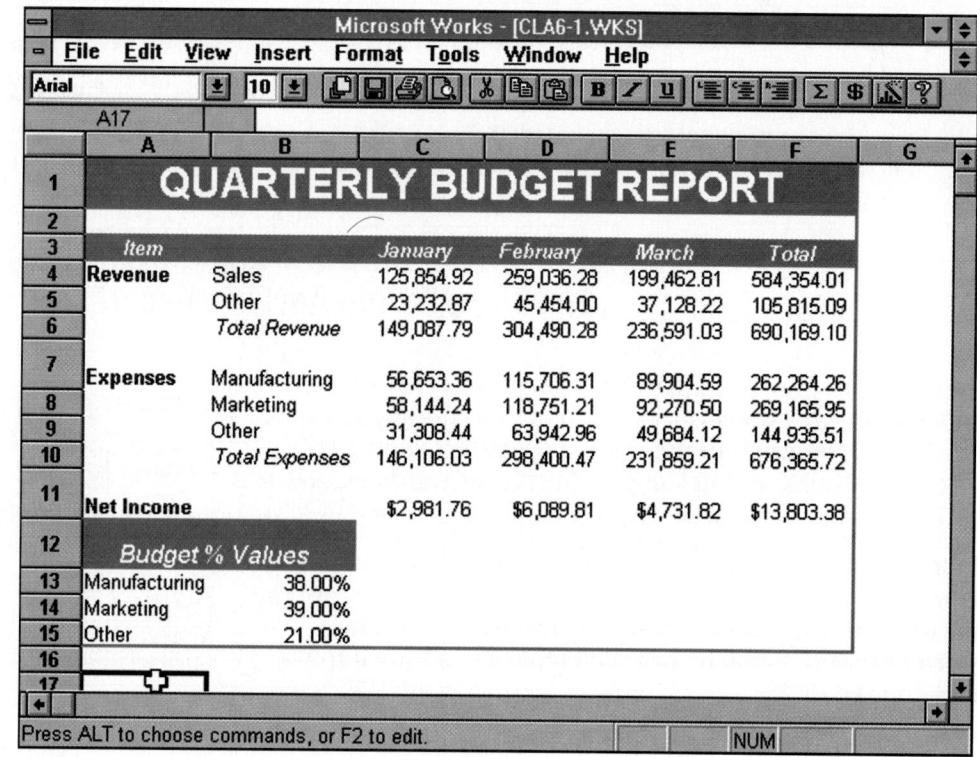

FIGURE CLA6-1

(continued)

COMPUTER LABORATORY ASSIGNMENT 1 (continued)

4. Calculate the Expenses for Manufacturing, Marketing, and Other by multiplying the Total Revenue for each month by the Manufacturing, Marketing, and Other percentages, respectively, found in the Budget % Values section of the spreadsheet. Perform rounding as required.
5. Calculate the Total Expenses for each month and the Total for all expenses by adding the Manufacturing, Marketing, and Other expenses for each month and for the Total column.
6. Calculate the Net Income for each month by subtracting the Total Expenses for each month from the Total Revenue for each month. Calculate the total Net Income by subtracting the Total Expenses from the Total Revenues.
7. Format the spreadsheet as shown. The column width for column A is 12, for column B is 14, and for columns C through F the width is 12.
8. Save the spreadsheet you create on a diskette. Use a filename consisting of the initials of your first and last names followed by the assignment number. Example: TC6-1.
9. Enter the following percentages for each of the Budget % Values and answer the following questions:
   Manufacturing: 35%
   Marketing: 47%
   Other: 19%
   a. What is the Total Net Income shown in the Quarterly Budget Report?

   _____

   b. What is the Manufacturing Expense for March?

   _____

10. Enter the following percentages for each of the Budget % Values and answer the following questions:
    Manufacturing: 31%
    Marketing: 38%
    Other: 26%
    a. What are the Total Expenses for January?

    _____

    b. What is the Net Income for February?

    _____

11. Print the spreadsheet you have created.
12. Follow directions from your instructor for turning in this assignment.

COMPUTER LABORATORY ASSIGNMENT 2
Creating a Payroll Analysis Report

Purpose: To provide experience using the Works Spreadsheet to create a spreadsheet that requires entering text, numbers, formulas, and functions, formatting, adding color, calculating sums, saving and printing the spreadsheet, and providing answers to what-if questions.

Problem: Create a Payroll Analysis Report where the Proposed Hourly Pay Rate and Proposed Weekly Pay Rate are calculated based upon a Proposed % Increase in pay. The Current Hourly Pay Rate for each employee is shown in the table on the right.

Employee Name	Current Hourly Pay Rate
Baker, Mary A.	7.50
Ehrhard, Douglas	9.26
Haynes, Hugh	8.75
Nelson, Peggy	9.52
Simpson, Hollis	7.84

The spreadsheet without gridlines is shown in Figure CLA6-2.

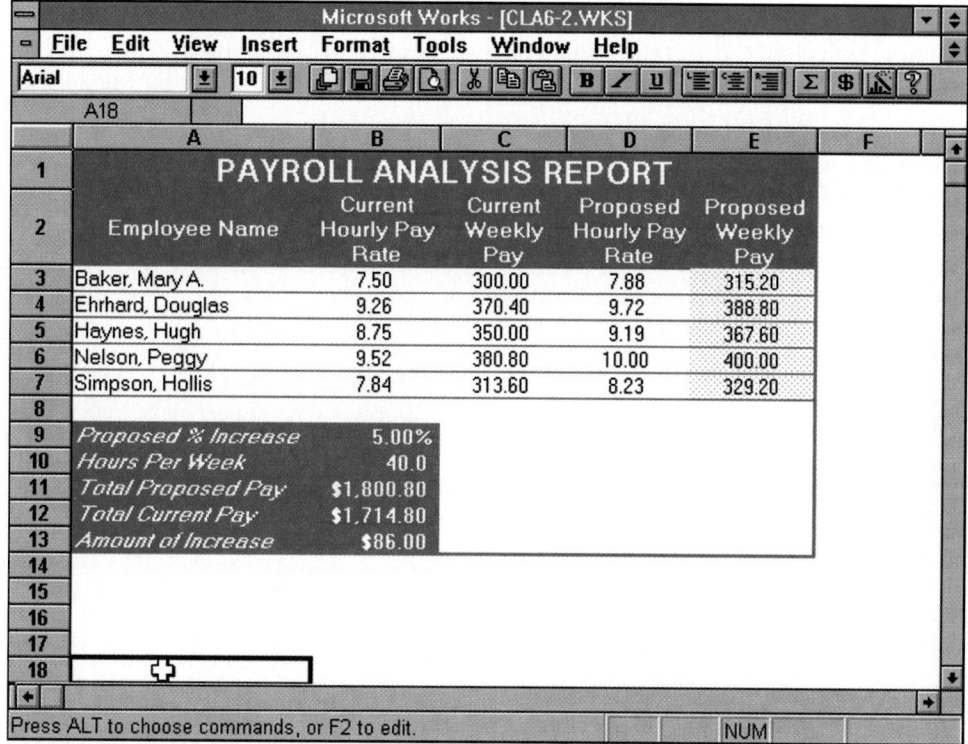

FIGURECLA6-2

Instructions:

1. Create a spreadsheet in the format shown in Figure CLA6-2 using the numbers from the table.
2. On the spreadsheet, calculate the Current Weekly Pay by multiplying the Current Hourly Pay Rate times the Hours Per Week.
3. Calculate the Proposed Hourly Pay Rate by the formula Current Hourly Pay Rate + (Current Hourly Pay Rate * Proposed % Increase).
4. Calculate the Proposed Weekly Pay by multiplying the Proposed Hourly Pay Rate times the Hours Per Week.
5. Calculate the Total Proposed Pay by summing the Proposed Weekly Pay for all employees.
6. Calculate the Total Current Pay by summing the Current Weekly Pay for all employees.
7. Calculate the Amount of Increase as follows: Total Proposed Pay minus the Total Current Pay.
8. Format the spreadsheet as shown. The width for column A is 23, and the width for the other columns is 12.
9. Save the spreadsheet you create on a diskette. Use a filename consisting of the initials of your first and last names followed by the assignment number. Example: TC6-2.
10. Answer the following questions based upon the spreadsheet:
    a. What is the total Amount of Increase if a Proposed % Increase of 12.5% is used?

    _____

    b. The employees have proposed that they will voluntarily switch to a thirty-six-hour work week with no increase in weekly pay. Because they will work fewer hours, an increase in the Current Hourly Pay Rate must occur to keep the Proposed Weekly Pay the same as the Current Weekly Pay. What is the minimum Percent Increase that can occur to ensure the Weekly Pay does not decrease ?

    _____

11. Print the spreadsheet you have created.
12. Follow directions from your instructor for turning in this assignment.

COMPUTER LABORATORY ASSIGNMENT 3
Creating an Above the Line Movie Budget

Purpose: To provide experience using the Works Spreadsheet to create a spreadsheet that requires entering text, dates, numbers, formulas, and functions, formatting, adding color, calculating sums, saving and printing the spreadsheet, and providing answers to what-if questions.

Problem: Create an Above the Line Movie Budget, which is a budget that includes costs for the writer, the producer, the director, and the principal actors as well as other fixed and variable costs. The fixed costs for the five month budget are specified in the table below.

Item	January	February	March	April	May
Story Rights	24,500	25,500	0	0	0
Producer's Unit	45,385	45,385	45,385	45,385	45,385
Director's Unit	0	25,600	48,900	48,900	48,900
Cast	0	0	340,900	340,900	340,900
Traveling	0	0	17,903	17,903	17,903
Fringe Benefits	22,250	22,250	22,250	22,250	22,250

The spreadsheet is shown in Figure CLA6-3.

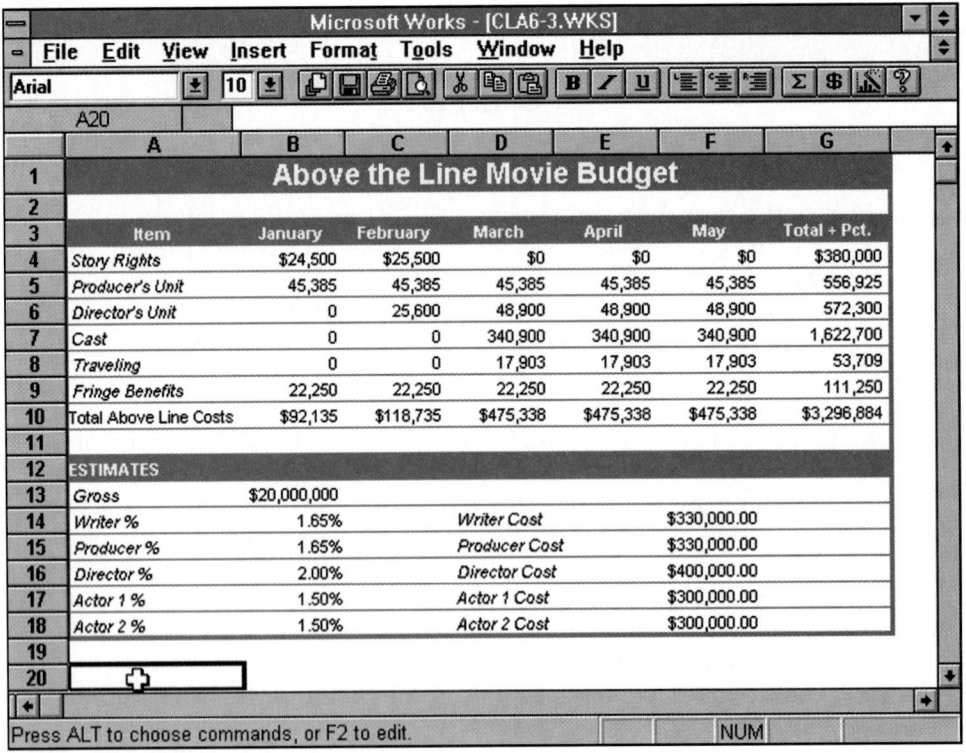

FIGURE CLA6-3

Instructions:

1. Create a spreadsheet in the format shown in Figure CLA6-3 using the numbers from the table.
2. On the spreadsheet, calculate the Total Above Line Costs for each month by adding each of the individual costs for the month.
3. Calculate the Total + Pct. for the Story Rights by adding the Story Rights costs in January through May (cells B4:F4) to the Writer Cost (cell F14) that you calculate by multiplying the estimated gross (cell B13) times the Writer % (cell B14).
4. Calculate the Total + Pct. for the Producer's Unit by adding the Producer's Unit costs for January through May (cells B5:F5) to the Producer Cost (cell F15) that you calculate by multiplying the estimated Gross (cell B13) times the Producer % (cell B15).
5. Calculate the Total + Pct. for the Director's Unit by adding the Director's Unit costs for January through May (cells B6:F6) to the Director Cost (cell F16) that you calculate by multiplying the estimated Gross (cell B13) times the Director % (cell B16).
6. Calculate the Total + Pct. for the Cast by adding the Cast costs for January through May (cells B7:F7) to the Actor 1 Cost (cell F17) and the Actor 2 Cost (cell F18). Calculate the Actor 1 Cost by multiplying the estimated Gross (cell B13) times the Actor 1 % (cell B17). Calculate the Actor 2 Cost by multiplying the estimated Gross (cell B13) times the Actor 2 % (cell B18).
7. Calculate the Total + Pct. for Traveling and Fringe Benefits by adding the costs for January through May (cells B9:F9 and B10:F10, respectively).
8. In all calculations, round when appropriate.
9. Format the spreadsheet as shown. Column A has a width of 17, columns B through F have a column width of 10, and column G has a width of 12.
10. Save the spreadsheet you create on a diskette. Use a filename consisting of the initials of your first and last names followed by the assignment number. Example: TC6-3.
11. Answer the following questions:
    a. If the movie grosses $14 million and the Director receives 3% of the gross, what is the Total + Pct. for Director's Unit?

    _____

    b. The producer has determined that the most likely gross for the film is $20 million. She has further determined that the maximum above the line costs are $3 million. The fixed costs in the spreadsheet cannot change. The two principle actors are demanding 1.5% of the gross receipts each and the director will not work for less than 2%. The Writer and Producer have agreed to take an equal percentage. What is the maximum percentage they each can take and keep the total above the line costs below $3 million?

    _____

12. Print the spreadsheet you have created. Be sure it will fit on one page. If it will not, use techniques from Project 5 to print the spreadsheet on one page.
13. Follow directions from your instructor for turning in this assignment.

COMPUTER LABORATORY ASSIGNMENT 4
Creating a Current and Projected Salaries Report

Purpose: To provide experience in planning and creating a spreadsheet using the skills learned in Project 6.

Problem: You have taken a part-time job in the Accounting department of a local company. They hired you because of your skills in developing spreadsheets. Your first assignment is to develop a spreadsheet that calculates the current and projected salaries for the company based on a percentage allocated to each department in the company.

Instructions: The company has told you the following facts:

   a. The projected salaries for all full-time employees in the period January through June is $3,900,800. The projected salaries for all full-time employees in the period July through December is the January through June amount plus an increase you should allow to be changed to answer what-if questions.
   b. The projected salaries for all part-time employees in the period January through June is $780,000. The projected salaries for all part-time employees in the period July through December is the January through June amount plus an increase you should allow to be changed to answer what-if questions.
   c. Company management wants to know the total projected salaries for both full-time and part-time employees for the entire year. They also want to know the combined totals for January through June and July through December for full-time and part-time employees.
   d. The company consists of four departments: Accounting, Production, Sales, and Administration. Each of these departments can be allocated a varying percentage of the total salary budget. For example, the Accounting department could have 28% of the salary budget, Production 32%, Sales 19%, and Administration 21%. The company has directed you to make these percentages variables so they can manipulate the percentages when answering what-if questions.
   e. For both the January through June and the July through December periods, you should calculate the salaries for each of the four departments and then determine an annual total for each of them.

Design and create a spreadsheet to accomplish the tasks specified. Format the spreadsheet appropriately. Save the spreadsheet you create on disk. Use a filename consisting of the initials of your first and last names followed by the assignment number. Example: TC6-4. Print the spreadsheet you have created. Follow directions from your instructor for turning in this assignment.

▼

CREATING A DATABASE

▼

CREATING A DATABASE

OBJECTIVES You will have mastered the material in this project when you can:

▸ Define the elements of a database
▸ Start the Works Database tool
▸ Identify all elements on the Works Database screen
▸ Enter a title in Form view using WordArt
▸ Enter a field name in Form view
▸ Enter the size for a field in Form view
▸ Correct errors when entering field names
▸ Save a database file
▸ Position fields in Form view
▸ Insert clip art into a form
▸ Use WordArt to format a title in Form view

▸ Add color to an object
▸ Format the field names in Form view
▸ Enter text and numeric data into a database
▸ Format numeric fields in a database in Form view
▸ Display the next record, previous record, first record, and last record in Form view
▸ Display the database in List view
▸ Format the database in List view
▸ Change font and font size in List view
▸ Set field widths in List view
▸ Print the database in both List view and Form view

fields

FIGURE 7-1

DATE	TITLE	FIRST NAME	LAST NAME	ADDRESS	CITY	STATE	ZIP	OCCUPATION
10/5/93	Mrs.	Tanya	Duncan	672 Lake Drive	Anaheim	CA	92634	Teacher
10/6/93	Dr.	Cara	Bailey	303 Sunrise Place	Irivne	CA	92628	Doctor
10/7/93	Ms.	Jane	Walters	1545 Elm Street	Fullerton	CA	92633	Teacher
10/9/93	Mrs.	Hillary	Fine	3233 Yule Drvie	Irvine	CA	92754	Teacher
10/15/93	Dr.	Juila	Lopez	12732 Clover Road	Fullerton	CA	92633	Doctor
10/18/93	Ms.	Rebecca	Tiong	87 Green Street	Olympia	WA	98506	Attorney
10/31/93	Mr.	Thomas	Henkle	1832 Yermo Place	Cerritos	CA	90701	Teacher
11/12/93	Mrs.	Lilla	Wilson	212 Tourny Street	Bellevue	WA	98005	Accountant
11/13/93	Dr.	Hugo	Weller	16 Burnside Drive	Seattle	WA	98109	Doctor
11/17/93	Mr.	Michael	Bolland	16 Carnation Way	Anaheim	CA	93834	Attorney
11/21/93	Miss	Linda	Cendajas	10 Park Avenue	Yorba	CA	92686	Accountant
11/30/93	Mr.	Steven	Smoldery	1200 Hill Street	Brea	CA	92621	Attorney
12/2/93	Mr.	Jeffery	Walen	987 Niagara Lane	Bellevue	WA	98004	Attorney
12/3/93	Dr.	Terry	Roberts	7655 Yale Drive	Seattle	WA	98103	Teacher
12/6/93	Mr.	Cody	Jefferson	142 Brookside Way	Fullerton	CA	92633	Attorney
12/7/93	Mr.	Tae	Nguyen	2396 Rock Drive	Yorba	CA	92686	Accountant

records

▶ INTRODUCTION

I n Projects 1 through 6 you have used the Microsoft Works Word Processor and Spreadsheet tools. In this project and in Project 8 and Project 9,
you will be learning about and using the Database tool.

The Works Database tool allows you to create, store, sort, and retrieve data.
Many people record data such as the names, addresses, and telephone numbers of
friends and business associates, records of investments, and records of expenses
for income tax purposes. These records must be arranged so the data can be
accessed easily when required.

The term **database** describes a collection of data organized in a manner that
allows access, retrieval, and use of that data. The Works Database tool allows you
to create a database; add, delete, and change data in the database; sort the data in
the database; retrieve the data in the database; and create reports using the data in
the database.

▶ PROJECT SEVEN

P roject 7 shows you how to create a database using Microsoft Works. The
database created in this project is shown in Figure 7-1. This database contains information about investors in an investment club called Global
Investments. The information for each member is stored in a record. A record contains all the information for a given person, product, or event. For example, the first
record in the database contains information about Mrs. Tanya Duncan.

A record consists of a series of fields. A **field** contains a specific piece of information within a record. For example, in the database shown in Figure 7-1, the first
field is the Date field, which contains the date on which the person invested. The
Title field identifies the person as Mr., Mrs., Miss, Ms., or Dr. The First Name and
Last Name fields contain the first and last names of each of the investors.

fields

INCOME	NET WORTH	FUND NAME	SHARES	PRICE PER SHARE
$46.300.00	$211,060.00	Growth	1,000	$11.00
$322.600.00	$1,325,700.00	Growth	2,500	$11.00
$51,970.00	$233,860.00	Fixed Income	600	$18.00
$47,650.00	$189,080.00	Fixed Income	200	$18.00
$129,800.00	$433,800.00	Options	1,200	$23.00
$112,800.00	$893,420.00	Options	1,000	$23.00
$41,200.00	$128,500.00	Growth	400	$11.00
$62,980.00	$198,750.00	Fixed Income	400	$18.00
$234,180.00	$995,400.00	Commodities	1,500	$15.00
$198,300.00	$633,800.00	Commodities	1,000	$15.00
$38,500.00	$143,980.00	Growth	800	$11.00
$210,332.00	$533,100.00	Options	1,400	$23.00
$567,500.00	$1,245,000.00	Commodities	2,000	$15.00
$67,210.00	$229,800.00	Growth	600	$11.00
$98,700.00	$278,930.00	Growth	700	$11.00
$43,760.00	$165,900.00	Growth	400	$11.00

records

The remaining fields in each of the records are:

1. Address: Street address of the investor.
2. City: City in which the investor lives.
3. State: State in which the investor lives.
4. Zip: Zip Code of the investor's city.
5. Occupation: The occupation of the investor.
6. Income: The yearly income of the investor. This value is required so the investment club can be sure the person is properly qualified to invest.
7. Net Worth: The estimated net worth of the investor. This field is required for the same reason as the Income field.
8. Fund Name: The name of the fund in which the investor placed money. Four funds are available through the investment club - Growth, Fixed Income, Options, and Commodities.
9. Shares: The number of shares the investor purchased in a particular fund.
10. Price per Share: The price per share the investor paid.

Each of these fields contains information for each investor record. Thus, for record one, the investor's first name is Tanya, the last name is Duncan, she lives at 672 Lake Drive, Anaheim, CA. In record two, the First Name field contains Cara and the Last Name field contains Bailey. Dr. Bailey lives in Irvine, CA, has an income of $322,600.00 and purchased 2,500 shares in the Growth fund.

It is important you understand that a record consists of one or more fields. When you define the database, you will define each field within a record. After you define the fields, you can enter data for as many records as are required in your database.

Creating a Database

To create the database shown in Figure 7-1 on pages W7.2 and W7.3, you will perform the following tasks:

1. Start Microsoft Works and choose the Database tool.
2. Enter the words Global Investments as a title on the screen that displays. This is the name of the investment club.
3. Enter the field names and field sizes required for the database. This step results in the **database structure**.
4. Save the database structure.
5. Position the fields in Form view, in which a single record displays on the screen.
6. Insert clip art in the title area of the form and format the title with special effects. Place a thin rectangular bar beneath the title in the form.
7. Color the clip art and the thin rectangle beneath the title. Place a color border around the field entries.
8. Enter the data for the records in the database.
9. Format the data fields in the database.
10. Save the database with the data you have entered.
11. Switch to List view where the entire database displays on the screen.
12. Format the database in List view.
13. Print the database in Form view.
14. Print the database in List view.

The following pages contain a detailed explanation of the steps and terms just listed.

▶ STARTING THE WORKS DATABASE

 o start the Works Database, follow the steps you used in previous examples, except choose the Database tool. These steps are summarized below.

TO START THE WORKS DATABASE

Step 1: From Program Manager open the Microsoft Works for Windows group window.

Step 2: Double-click the Microsoft Works program-item icon.

Step 3: If the Welcome to Microsoft Works dialog box displays, choose the Start Works Now button.

Step 4: Choose the Database button in the Startup dialog box.

Step 5: If the Microsoft Works application window is not maximized, maximize it.

Step 6: Maximize the Data1 window.

▶ WORKS DATABASE WINDOW

W hen you start the Microsoft Works Database tool, Works opens a document window called Data1 (Figure 7-2). The screen in Figure 7-2 is presented in Form view, which you can use to create fields in your database and also type entries into the fields. **Form view** means you are viewing the database as if each record in the database were recorded on a separate page of paper, or form. The screen is, in essence, the form.

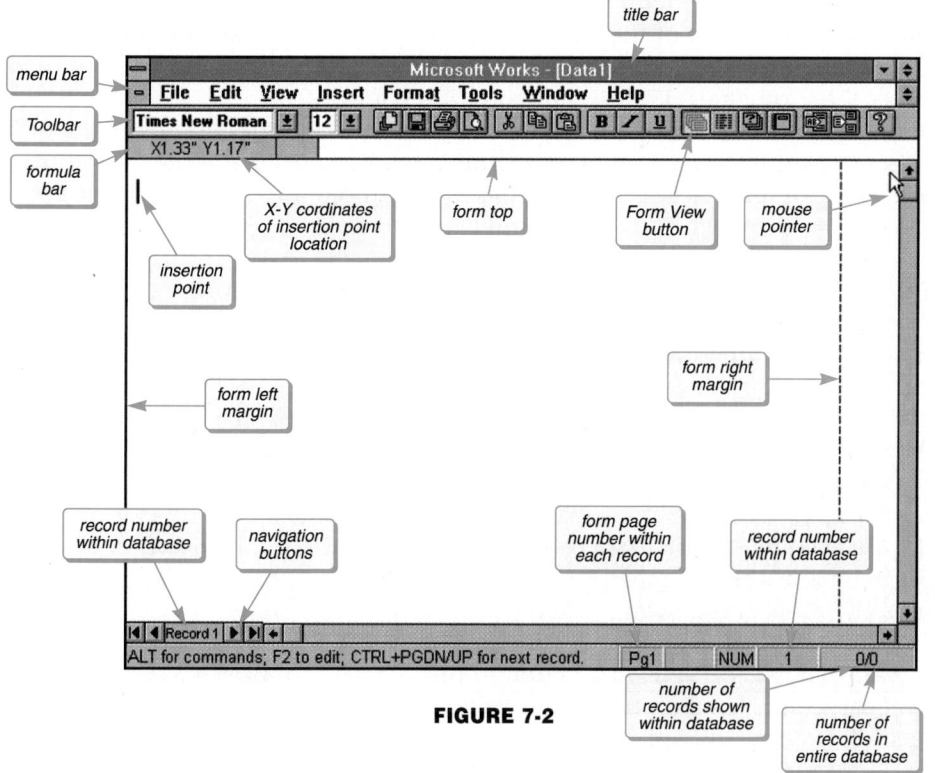

FIGURE 7-2

The left side of the screen is the left margin of the form. The form top is at the upper edge of the database window. A dotted vertical line indicates the right margin of the form.

Although you can see in Figure 7-2 that the Database window appears much the same as the Word Processing window and the Spreadsheet window, some important differences are present. The Database window consists of the elements listed on the next two pages.

TITLE BAR   The application name Microsoft Works and the default window name, Data1, display in the title bar.

MENU BAR   The menu bar in the Database is the same as the menu bar in the Spreadsheet. The menu names are: File, Edit, View, Insert, Format, Tools, Window, and Help. Most of the Database menus, however, contain additional or different commands than the corresponding Spreadsheet menu. These commands are explained as they are used.

TOOLBAR   The Toolbar contains many of the same buttons as the Word Processor and Spreadsheet Toolbars; however, the Database Toolbar also contains a number of unique buttons on the right side of the Toolbar. These buttons are explained as they are used. In Figure 7-2, the Form View button is light gray with red markings and is recessed, indicating the screen is showing the database in Form view.

FORMULA BAR   The Database formula bar functions in much the same manner as the Spreadsheet formula bar. When you type an entry into the database, the entry will display in the formula bar. The X and Y values shown in Figure 7-2 indicate the **X-Y coordinates** of the insertion point on the screen. The X value specifies the number of inches from the left edge of the form and the Y value specifies the number of inches from the top of the form. In Figure 7-2, the X-coordinate is 1.33" and the Y-coordinate is 1.17". This means the insertion point is located 1.33" from the left edge of the form and 1.17" from the top of the form.

Works Database automatically uses a left margin of 1.25" and a top margin of 1.00". These margins correspond to the left edge of the screen and the top of the Database window, respectively. Therefore, as you can see, the insertion point is located a little to the right of the left margin and a little down from the top margin.

INSERTION POINT   The **insertion point** specifies where on the form the next character you type will appear. As noted, the exact location of the insertion point, down to the hundredth of an inch, is indicated in the formula bar.

MOUSE POINTER   The **mouse pointer** in Figure 7-2 is shaped as a block arrow. As in all Works tools, the mouse pointer will change shape depending on its location on the screen and the task being accomplished.

RIGHT MARGIN MARKER   The dashed vertical line down the right side of the screen in Figure 7-2 marks the right margin on the form. The default setting is a 1.25" margin on the right of the form.

SCROLL BAR   The **scroll bar**, in addition to the normal scroll arrows, scroll box, and scroll bar, contains navigation buttons. You use **navigation buttons** to move from record to record in Form view. The function of each of the buttons is described in Figure 7-3. The use of these buttons with a loaded database will be illustrated later.

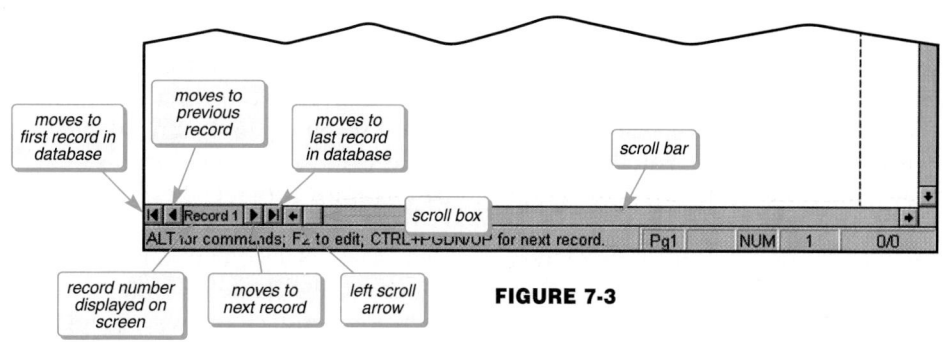

FIGURE 7-3

STATUS BAR   The **status bar** contains information regarding the database and the record currently displayed on the screen (see Figure 7-2 on page W7.5). The entry Pg1 states that the screen shows page one of the record on the screen. In some instances, a record may consist of more than one form page. The entry 1 following the NUM indicator states that record number 1 in the database is displayed on the screen. The next value, a number 0 (zero) separated from another number 0 (zero) by a slash, specifies the number of records currently available for display in the database and the total number of records stored in the database. These numbers can sometimes be different, as you will see in Project 9 where queries are explained. Works allows a maximum of 32,000 records in a database.

▶ CREATING A DATABASE

Once Works displays the empty Form view of the database on the screen, you can begin to create the database. The final Form view of the database in this project is shown in Figure 7-4. Notice that each of the fields in the database is arranged on the page for ease of reading.

Four different elements are displayed in the form in Figure 7-4 . The first is a clip art display of a globe in the upper left corner of the form. The second element contains the words Global Investments. Global Investments is the name of the investment club. The words Global Investments were created using a Works accessory called **WordArt**. WordArt allows you to display words in a database form in a variety of shapes and styles. You may also display a title on a database form using the standard fonts available as part of Works. In database terminology, when using standard font styles, the title would be called a **label**.

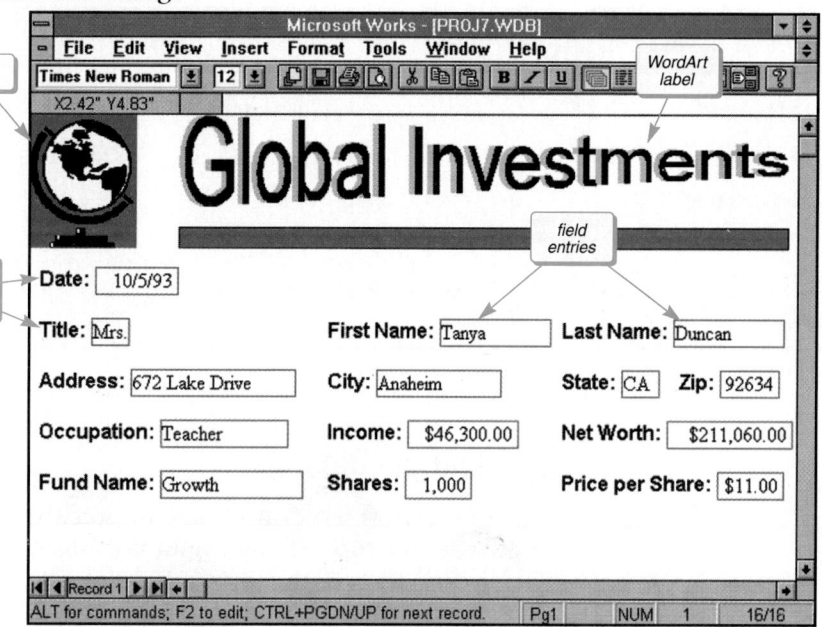

FIGURE 7-4

The third element on the form is the field name. A **field name** distinguishes a field from all other fields in the database. For example, in Figure 7-4 you can see that the field containing the date is called Date, the field name for first name is First Name, the field for last name is Last Name, and so on. A field name always ends with a colon (:). In Form view, you can format each of the field names in a style that makes the form easy to read. In the database for Project 7, each of the field names displays in 12 point Arial bold font.

The maximum number of characters in a field name is 15 characters, not including the colon. You should carefully choose each field name to indicate precisely the contents of the field. A field name can contain any character except a single quotation mark. You can enter up to 256 fields into your database.

The fourth element on the form is the field and the field entry. A **field entry** is the actual data in the field. In Figure 7-4, the field entry for the Date field is 10/5/93. The field entry for the Title field is Mrs., the field entry for the First Name field is Tanya, and so on. Field entries can contain any characters you want and can be a maximum of 256 characters. If the field contains only numeric data, Works considers it a numeric field and you can format it in the same manner as numeric fields when using the Spreadsheet. If the field contains any nonnumeric character, Works treats it as a text field.

An important design decision is to determine the width of the field. You want the field to be large enough to contain the largest field entry but no larger. In most cases, you will be able to determine the proper width based upon the maximum number of characters in the field entry, but the field width you specify when defining the field will not always correspond to the number of characters actually in the field because many fonts, such as Times New Roman, use variable width characters. For example, when using 12 point Times New Roman, to place twenty letter i's in a field requires a width of 10 while placing twenty letter m's in a field requires a width of 37. If you use a font with a fixed width for each character, such as Courier New, then the width you choose will correspond exactly with the number of characters in the field. When you choose the width, estimate as closely as you can while remembering you can easily change the width of a field at a later time.

The field widths for the Form view of the database in Project 7 are shown in Table 7-1.

▶ **TABLE 7-1**

FIELD NAME	FIELD WIDTH	FIELD NAME	FIELD WIDTH
date	11	Zip	8
Title	5	Occupation	17
First Name	15	Income	15
Last Name	15	Net Worth	17
Address	22	Fund Name	19
City	17	Shares	9
State	5	Price per Share	9

Building the Database

The steps you will complete to prepare the form illustrated in Figure 7-4 are: (1) change the top, left, and right margins using the Page Setup command from the File menu; (2) enter the form title, Global Investments, using WordArt; (3) enter the field names and specify the field widths; (4) insert clip art on the form; (5) format the WordArt title; (6) add color in the clip art and title area; (7) add a color border around the fields; (8) enter the field entries; and (9) format the field entries. These steps are explained on the following pages.

Changing Form Margins

In this project you must increase the area into which you will enter data to create the form in Figure 7-4. This requires setting the top margin, left margin, and right margin to .75 inch each. To change the margins, perform the following steps.

TO CHANGE THE MARGINS ▼

STEP 1 ►

Select the File menu and point to the Page Setup command (Figure 7-5).

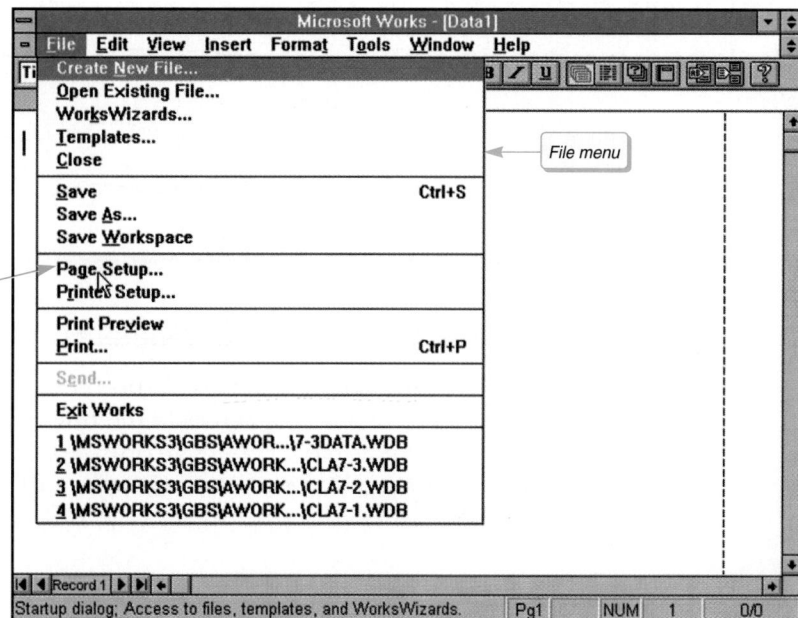

FIGURE 7-5

STEP 2 ►

Choose the Page Setup command from the File menu. When the Page Setup dialog box displays, change the Top margin to .75", the Left margin to .75", and the Right margin to .75". Point to the OK button.

Works displays the Page Setup dialog box (Figure 7-6). The top, left, and right margins have been changed to .75" and the mouse pointer points to the OK button.

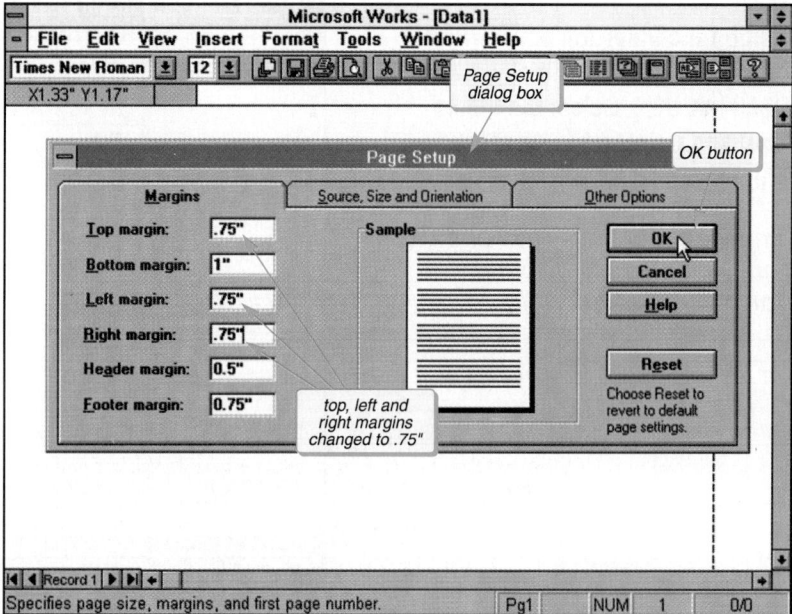

FIGURE 7-6

STEP 3 ▶

Choose the OK button in the Page Setup dialog box.

The Works database Form view document screen displays (Figure 7-7). The dotted right margin line is not visible because of the change in margins. Works also has moved the default X–Y coordinates to the new location of X0.83" Y0.92".

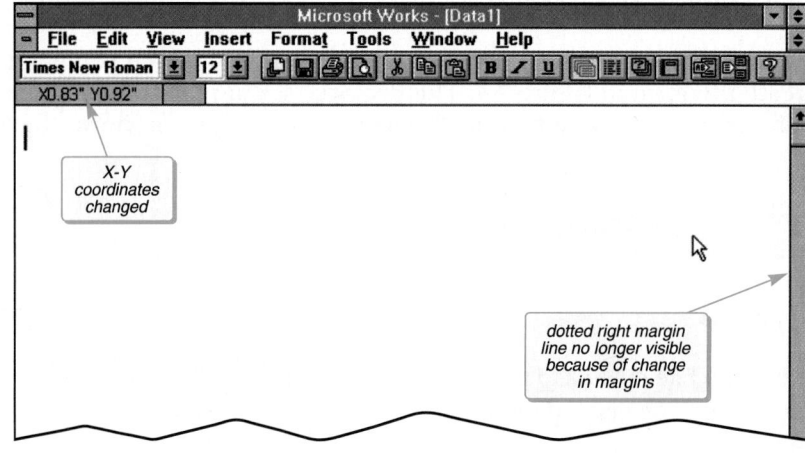

FIGURE 7-7

Entering a Title on a Database Form

The title on the database form, Global Investments, displays using special effects; that is, the characters in the title decrease in size from left to right and the title contains a shaded effect. To create a title with special effects, Works provides an accessory called **WordArt**. Complete the following steps to enter a title using WordArt.

TO ENTER A TITLE USING WORDART ▼

STEP 1 ▶

Position the insertion point where you want the title to initially display (X0.83" Y0.92"). Select the Insert menu and point to the WordArt command.

*The Insert menu displays and the mouse pointer points to the **WordArt command** (Figure 7-8).*

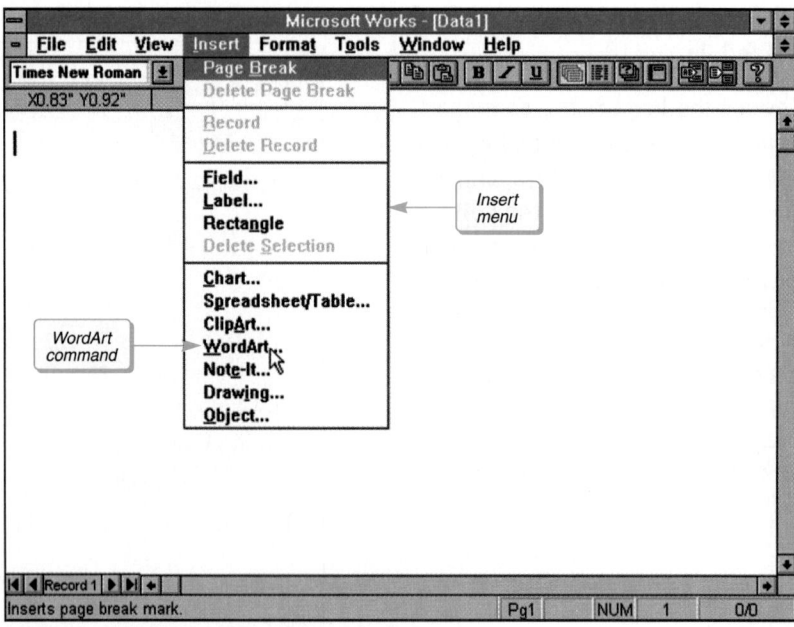

FIGURE 7-8

STEP 2 ▶

Choose the WordArt command from the Insert menu.

The Enter Your Text Here box displays (Figure 7-9). The default text, Your Text Here, is highlighted in the box. A shaded outline area containing the words Your Text Here displays above the window. After you type and display text, the text will display in the shaded outline area on the database form. A new menu bar and new Toolbar also display. The Toolbar contains a number of buttons unique to WordArt that assist in using WordArt. The buttons used in this project will be explained as needed. When you use WordArt, you are using the OLE 2.0 facilities of Works 3.0 as described in Project 3 of this book.

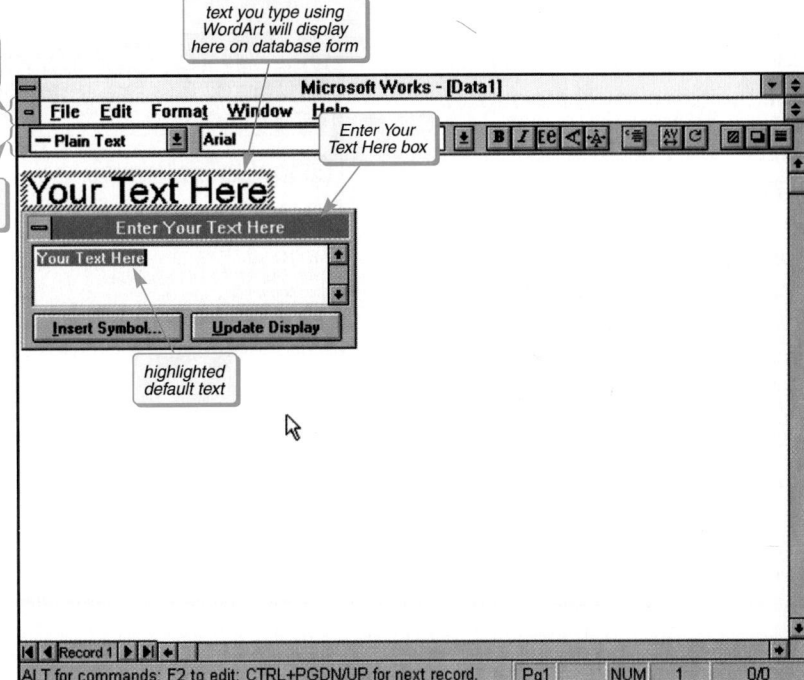

FIGURE 7-9

STEP 3 ▶

Type Global Investments **and then click the Update Display button in the box.**

Works displays the words Global Investments in the box as you type (Figure 7-10). When you click the Update Display button, the words Global Investments display in the shaded outline area on the database form. The window remains displayed with the mouse pointer pointing to the Update Display button.

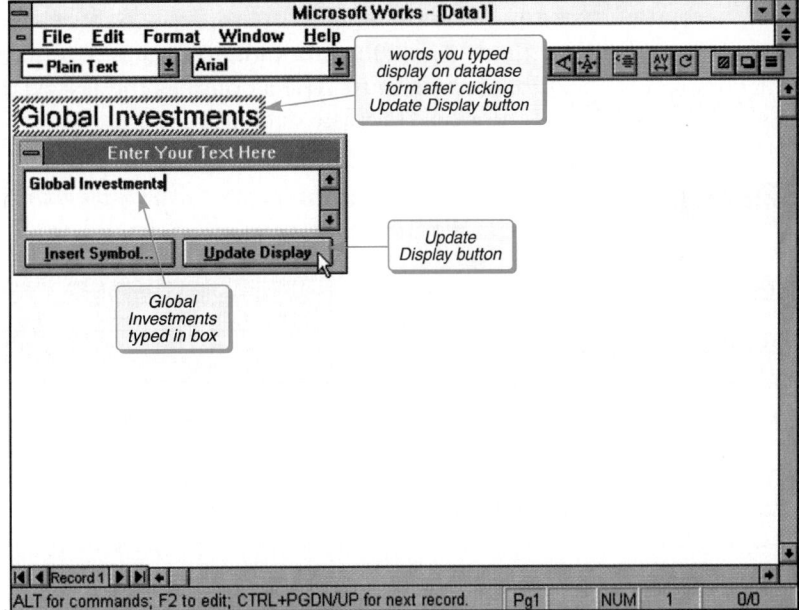

FIGURE 7-10

STEP 4 ▶

Click two times anywhere outside the Enter Your Text Here box.

Works displays the title, Global Investments, within a dotted rectangular box on the database form (Figure 7-11). The rectangular box is an embedded object with resize handles that allow you to change the size of the object. In the formula bar, the X-coordinate is 0.83" and the Y-coordinate is 0.92". These coordinates refer to the leftmost and topmost position of the object containing the words Global Investments.

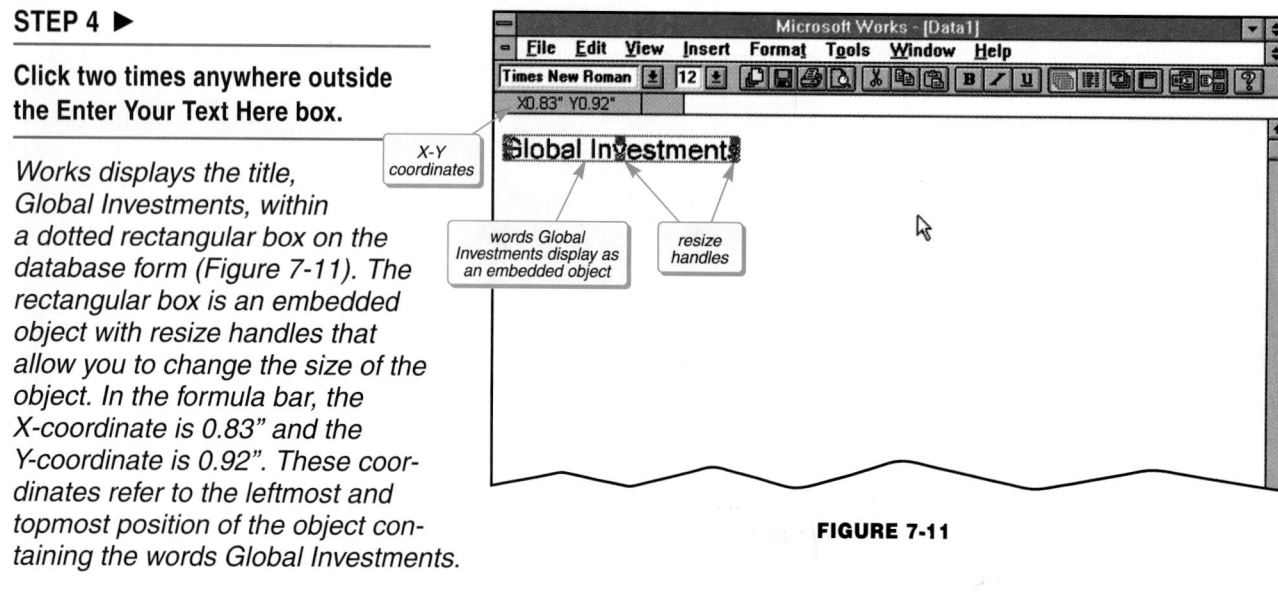

FIGURE 7-11

Later in this project you will format the title.

Entering Fields

After you enter the title, the next step is to enter the fields for the database. To enter the fields, you must enter the field names and also specify the size of each field. The field names identify each field in the database. When you enter a field name, you must type a colon as the last character. Complete the following steps to enter fields for the database record.

TO ENTER FIELDS ▼

STEP 1 ▶

Press the DOWN ARROW key to position the insertion point on the next line.

When you press the DOWN ARROW key, the insertion point moves down the form one-quarter inch (Figure 7-12). The Y-coordinate is now Y1.17" (Y-coordinate 1.17" minus Y-coordinate 0.92" = .25"). The distance the insertion point moves down depends on the font size. If the font size is greater than 12, then the insertion point will move down a greater distance than .25". The X-coordinate did not change, so the field name will line up vertically with the WordArt object you entered.

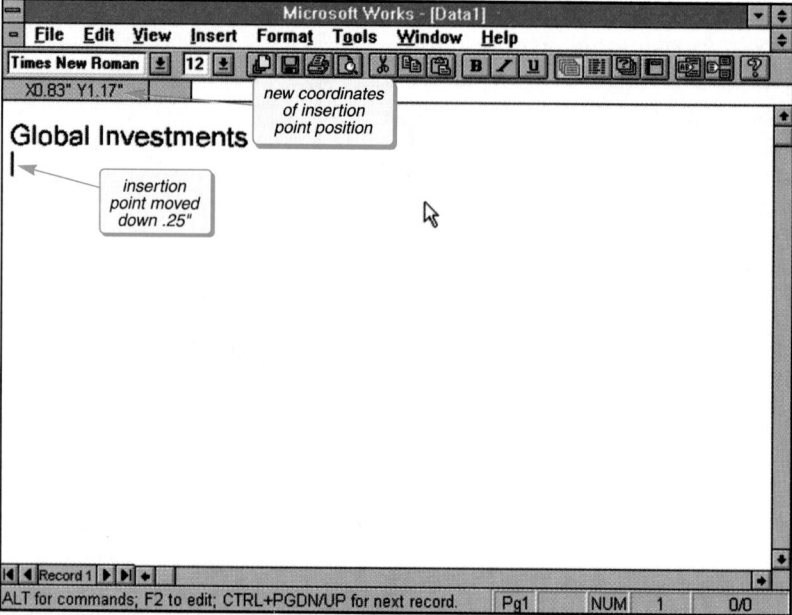

FIGURE 7-12

STEP 2 ▶

Type the field name followed immediately by a colon, `Date:`.

Works displays the field name you type on the form and in the formula bar (Figure 7-13). The field name on the form is highlighted with a dark background. It is important to remember that Works identifies a field name by the colon immediately following the name. You must always type the colon.

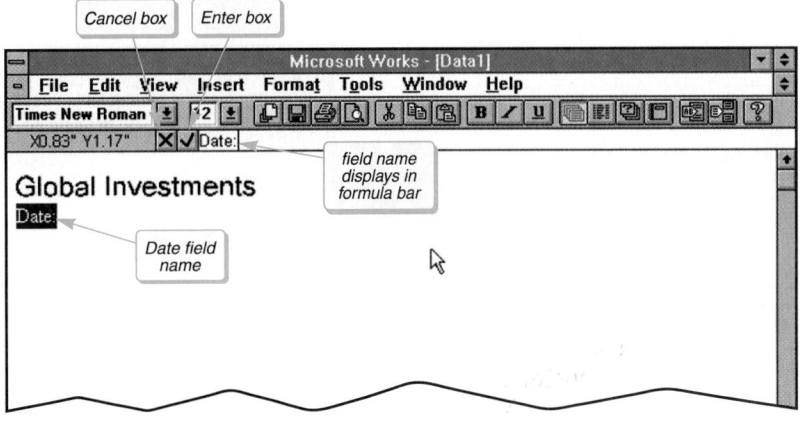

FIGURE 7-13

STEP 3 ▶

Press the ENTER key or click the Enter box.

Works displays the Field Size dialog box (Figure 7-14). Works automatically assigns a field width of 20 to each field. You can change the field width by typing a new number. Fields can also occupy more than one line (Height). The fields in the investment club database occupy only one line.

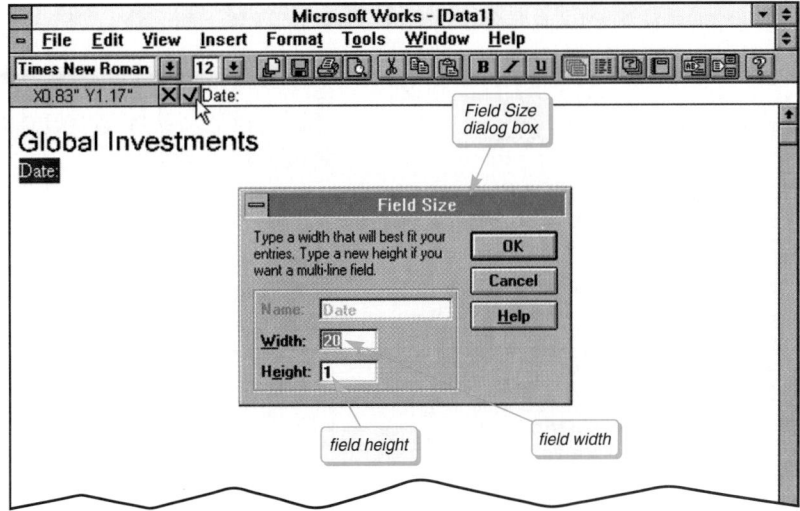

FIGURE 7-14

STEP 4 ▶

Type the field width for the Date field, `11`, **and point to the OK button.**

The field width for the Date field, 11, is entered in the Width text box (Figure 7-15). The height default, 1, is not changed. The mouse pointer points to the OK button.

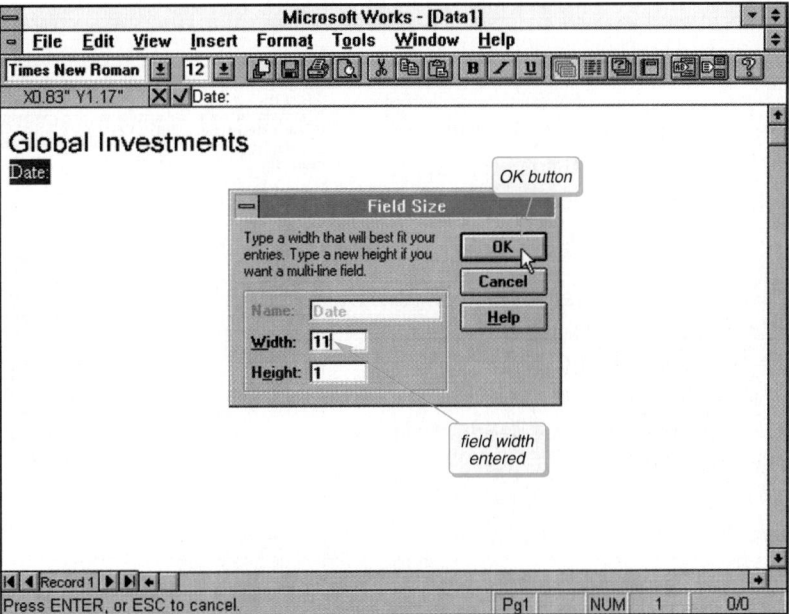

FIGURE 7-15

STEP 5 ►

Choose the OK button in the Field Size dialog box.

Works enters the Date field on the form (Figure 7-16). The field name, Date:, is displayed together with the field line, which indicates the width of the field and, when a field entry is made, will underline the field entry. In addition, Works moves the insertion point down one-quarter inch.

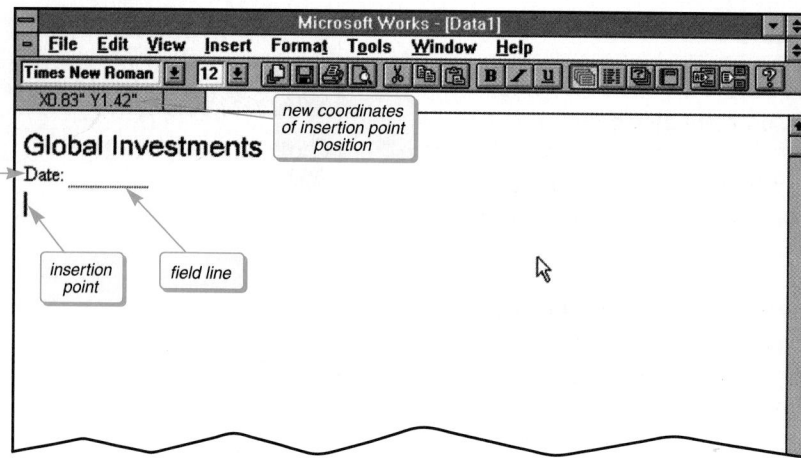

FIGURE 7-16

STEP 6 ►

Type the field name, Title:.

Works enters the field name you type on the form and in the formula bar (Figure 7-17). The field name remains highlighted with a dark background.

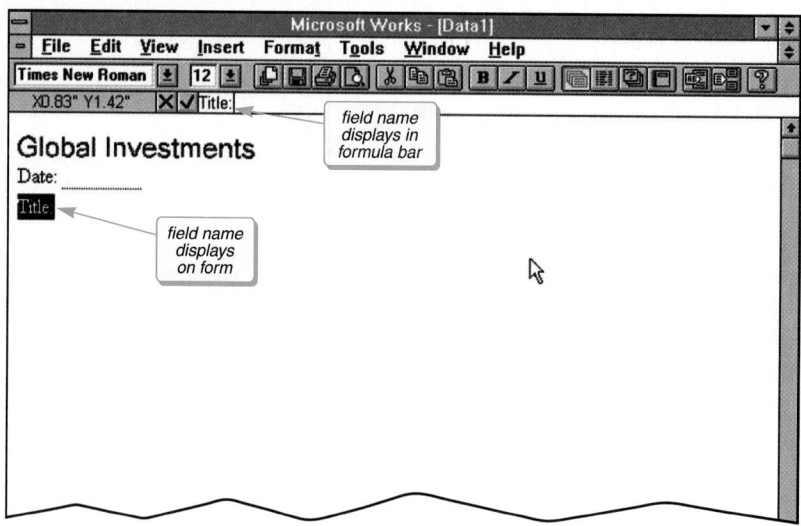

FIGURE 7-17

STEP 7 ►

Press the ENTER key or click the Enter box, type the field width, 5, and point to the OK button in the Field Size dialog box.

When you press the ENTER key or click the Enter box, Works displays the Field Size dialog box (Figure 7-18). After you type the field width, it displays in the Width text box. The mouse pointer points to the OK button.

FIGURE 7-18

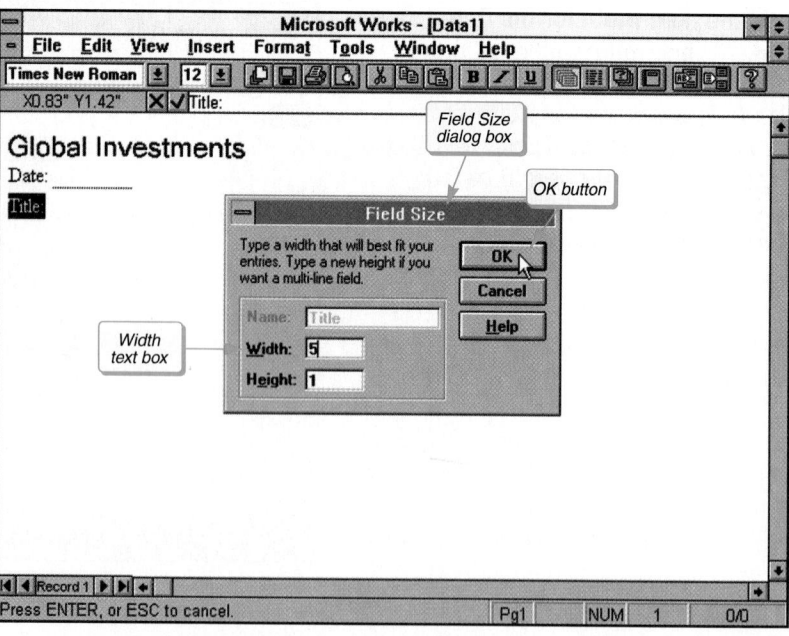

STEP 8 ►

Choose the OK button in the Field Size dialog box.

Works enters the Title field on the form and displays the field line (Figure 7-19). Works also moves the insertion point down one-quarter inch.

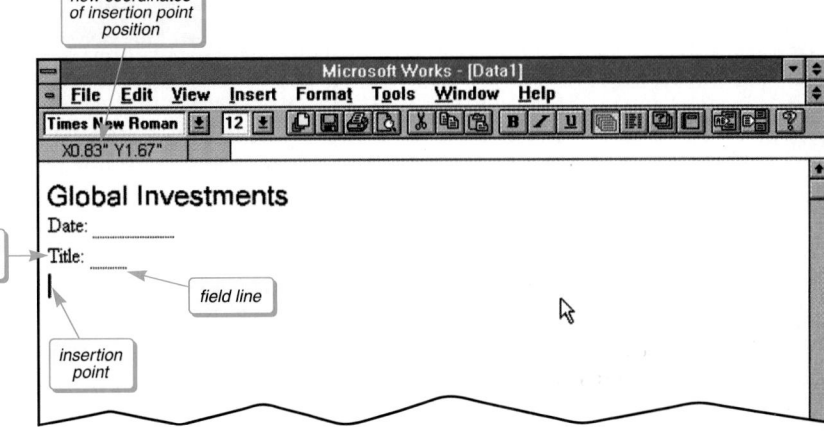

FIGURE 7-19

STEP 9 ►

Enter the remaining field names on the form, using the field widths specified previously on page W7.8 in Table 7-1.

All the fields in the database display on the form (Figure 7-20). Notice that the title, Global Investments, has scrolled off the top of the screen. You can use the scroll arrows, scroll buttons, and scroll bars to move around the database form.

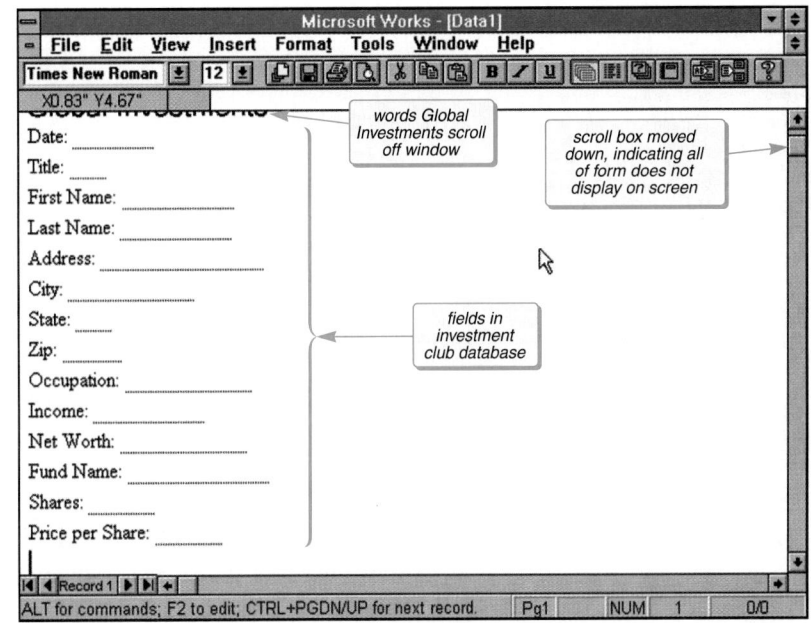

FIGURE 7-20

You should note several points when entering the fields for a database. First, choose the field names with care so they reflect the contents of the field. In all subsequent uses of the database, you will refer to the data in the fields by these names, so it is important to be able to easily identify the contents of the fields.

Second, if you make an error while typing a field name, you can correct the error in one of several ways. If you have not yet entered the field name on the form, then backspace to remove the error and type the correct characters. If you have entered the field name, you should highlight the field name by pointing to the field name in error and clicking the left mouse button. Works will highlight the field name and display it in the formula bar. You can then type the correct field name followed by a colon, and Works will change the field name.

You can also enter the Edit mode by either pressing the F2 function key or clicking in the formula bar after highlighting the field name. An edit insertion bar will appear in the formula bar and you can position it to make your correction.

Third, you should be aware that the location of the insertion point can be specified at any time by clicking the mouse pointer on the form. The insertion point appears at the location you clicked and the insertion point coordinates in the formula bar change to reflect the new location. In the steps to enter the field names, this technique was not required because Works automatically positions the insertion point one-quarter inch down when you choose the OK button in the Field Size dialog box. In subsequent examples, you will see the flexibility provided by using the mouse pointer when moving fields to different locations on the form.

Works also provides an **Insert Field button** on the Toolbar. Clicking the Insert Field button will display the Insert Field dialog box that allows you to enter both the field name and field width. After choosing the OK button in the dialog box, the field is entered on the form but you must position the insertion point using the mouse pointer for the entry of the next field.

You can also choose the Field command from the Insert menu to place a field at the location of the insertion point. The Insert Field dialog box will display the same as if you clicked the Insert Field button on the Toolbar.

▶ SAVING THE DATABASE

O nce you have defined the database by specifying all the field names and the field widths, you should normally save your work so an accidental loss of power does not destroy it. To save your work on a diskette in drive A using the filename PROJ7, complete the following steps.

TO SAVE THE DATABASE

Step 1: Click the Save button on the Toolbar.
Step 2: Type the filename, PROJ7, in the File Name text box of the Save As dialog box.
Step 3: If necessary, select drive A from the Drives drop-down list box.
Step 4: Choose the OK button in the Save As dialog box.

Works will save the file on the diskette in drive A and will place the name PROJ7.WDB in the title bar of the Works window. Works automatically adds the file extension .WDB to all database files.

▶ FORMATTING THE FORM

A fter you have entered the field names and saved the file, the next step is to format the form so it is easy to read and use. In most instances, you use the Form view of the database to enter the data into the database. Because someone might have to enter thousands of records into the database, the form should be easy to read and use.

Formatting the form consists of a number of separate tasks. The first is to position the fields on the form. The next is to insert clip art in the title area, position and format the title Global Investments on the database form, place a border beneath the title, and add color in the title area. You must then change font type and style of the field names. The final step is to add a color outline around the field entries. Figure 7-4 on page W7.7 illustrates the form for Project 7 after formatting. The technique for formatting is explained on the following pages.

Positioning Fields on the Form

The first task of positioning the fields in the proper location requires that you determine X-Y coordinates for each of the fields. You can do this by dragging the fields and field names to various locations until you are satisfied with their placement on the form. The coordinates in Table 7-2 are specified to assist in illustrating the technique of dragging fields in Form view. They were determined after moving the fields into various locations and then finally deciding on the best form layout.

These locations can be modified at a later time, as will be seen when the form title is formatted.

Perform the following steps to position the fields on the form.

▶ **TABLE 7-2**

LABEL OR FIELD	X-COORDINATE	Y-COORDINATE
Global Investments	X2.00"	Y0.75"
Date	X0.83"	Y1.17"
Title	X0.83"	Y1.58"
First Name	X3.25"	Y1.58"
Last Name	X5.25"	Y1.58"
Address	X0.83"	Y2.00"
City	X3.25"	Y2.00"
State	X5.25"	Y2.00"
Zip	X6.25"	Y2.00"
Occupation	X0.83"	Y2.42"
Income	X3.25"	Y2.42"
Net Worth	X5.25"	Y2.42"
Fund Name	X0.83"	Y2.83"
Shares	X3.25"	Y2.83"
Price per Share	X5.25"	Y2.83"

TO POSITION FIELDS ON THE FORM ▼

STEP 1 ▶

If necessary, scroll the screen up so the title Global Investments is visible. Highlight the Last Name field name by clicking the words Last Name.

Works highlights the field name Last Name with a dark background and the block arrow mouse pointer displays with the word DRAG below it (Figure 7-21). You will often find it easier to move fields out of sequence. The Last Name field is moved in this step because it occupies the rightmost position on the next line of the form.

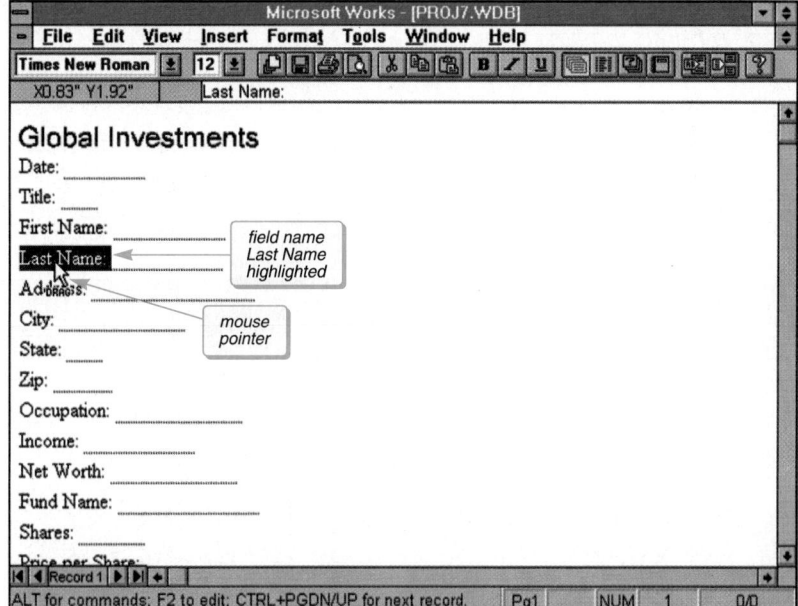

FIGURE 7-21

STEP 2 ▶

Drag the Last Name field toward its location.

As you drag the field, Works displays a dotted outline of both the field name and the field itself (Figure 7-22). The word MOVE displays under the mouse pointer. The coordinates of the outline are changed as you drag the outline. The field you drag remains highlighted and does not move while you drag.

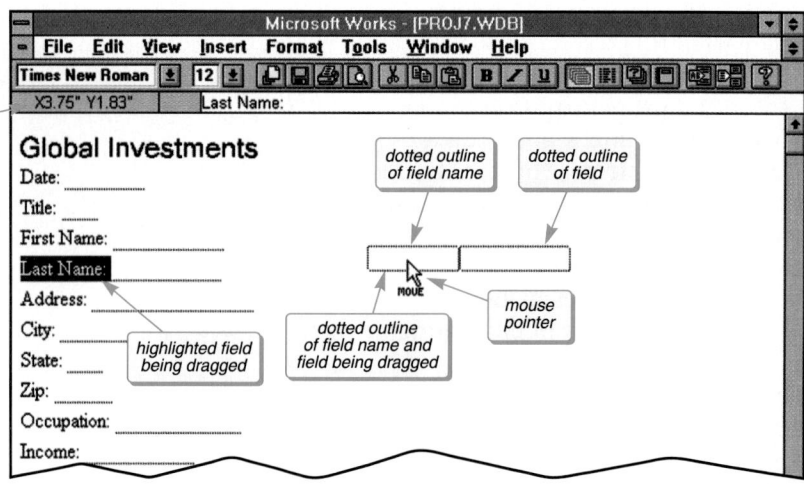

FIGURE 7-22

STEP 3 ▶

When the dotted outline is at the desired location (X5.25" Y1.58"), release the left mouse button.

Works moves the highlighted field to the location of the dotted outline (Figure 7-23). After being moved, the field name remains highlighted.

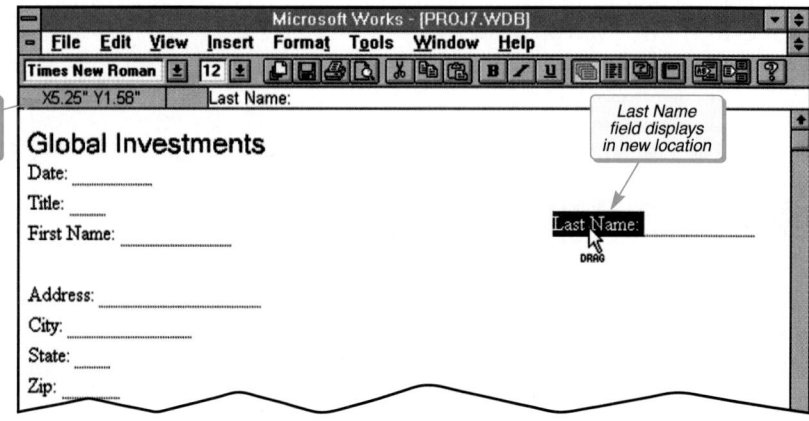

FIGURE 7-23

STEP 4 ▶

Using the same technique, move the First Name field to coordinates X3.25" Y1.58" and the Title field to X0.83" Y1.58".

The fields are moved to the prescribed locations (Figure 7-24). Each of the fields is on the same line (Y-coordinate 1.58").

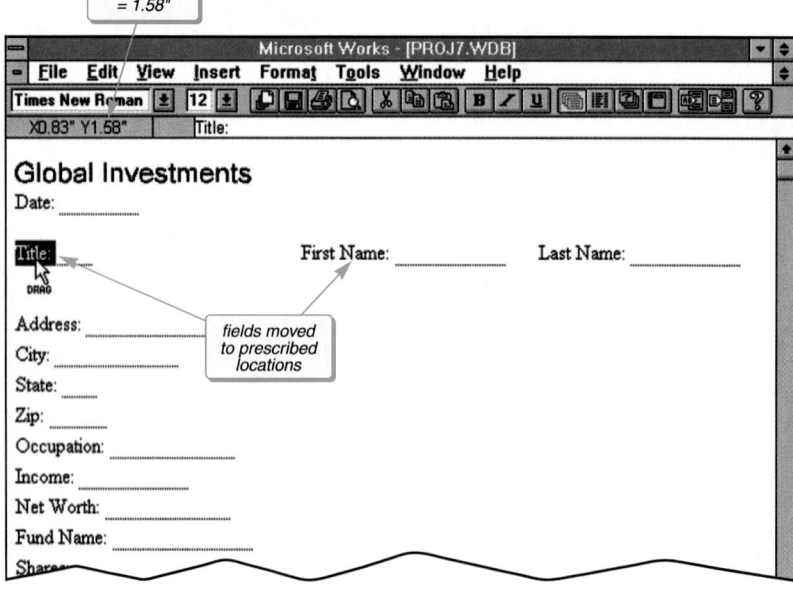

FIGURE 7-24

STEP 5 ▶

Drag the Zip, State, City, and Address fields to their proper locations, as specified in Table 7-2 on page W7.17.

Each of the fields is on the same line, Y-coordinate 2.00" (Figure 7-25).

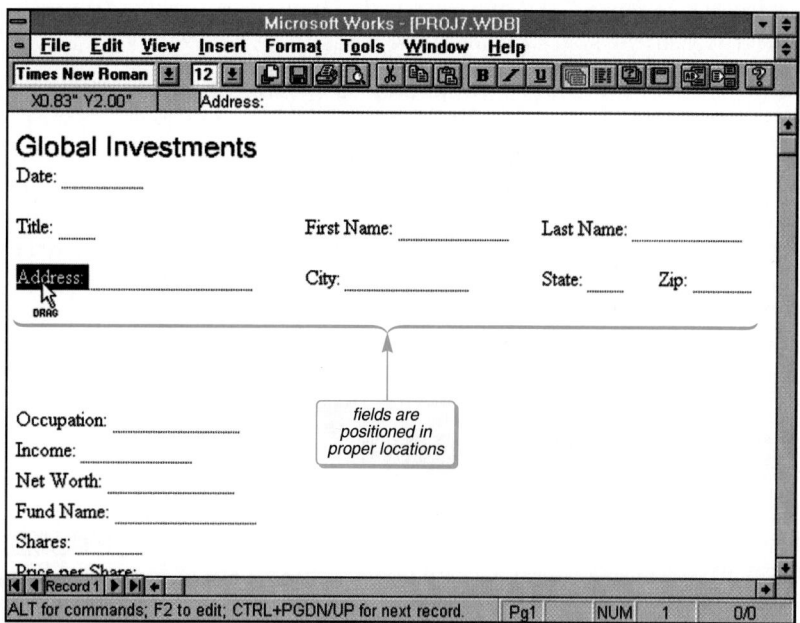

FIGURE 7-25

STEP 6 ▶

Drag the remaining fields to their proper locations as specified in Table 7-2.

All the fields are positioned in their proper locations (Figure 7-26).

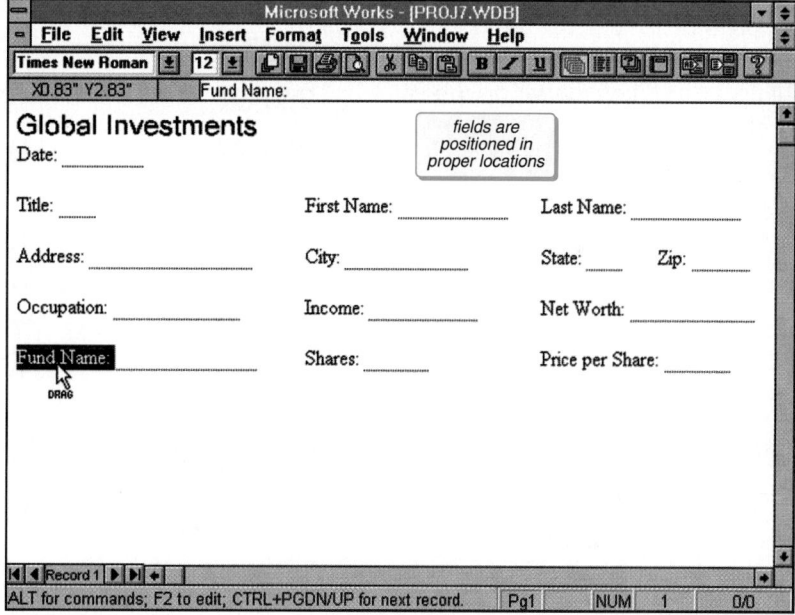

FIGURE 7-26

You should note that even after arranging the fields in the form, at any time you can move the fields to make the form more attractive and easier to read. The next step is to format the title of the database form.

Formatting the Title

To format the title, you must make room at the top of the form because the title will be increased in size and formatted using WordArt. The title will occupy an area of approximately one inch at the top of the form. To provide for this area at the top of the form, move the field names down approximately one inch. To move the field names down as a unit on the form, perform the following steps.

TO MOVE FIELD NAMES AS A UNIT ▼

STEP 1 ▶

Point to the Date field name and click. Hold down the CTRL key, point to the Title field name, and click. Continue this process until all fields on the database form are highlighted.

All fields are highlighted on the form (Figure 7-27).

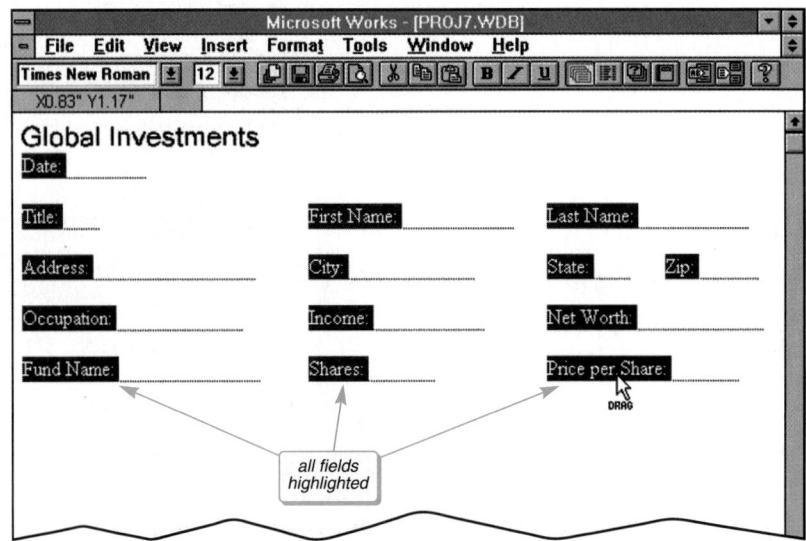

FIGURE 7-27

STEP 2 ▶

Point to the Date field name, hold down the left mouse button, and drag all fields down by dragging the Date field down.

After you highlight all field names, dragging a single field name will drag all field names as a unit (Figure 7-28).

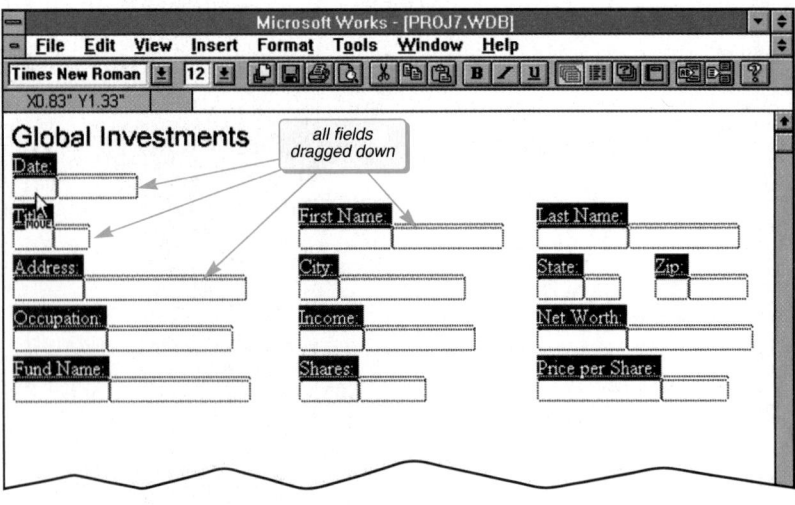

FIGURE 7-28

STEP 3 ▶

When the coordinates are X0.83"
Y2.00", release the left
mouse button.

*The fields are repositioned on the
database form (Figure 7-29). The
date is positioned at coordinates
X0.83" Y2.00". The other fields
retain their relative positions.*

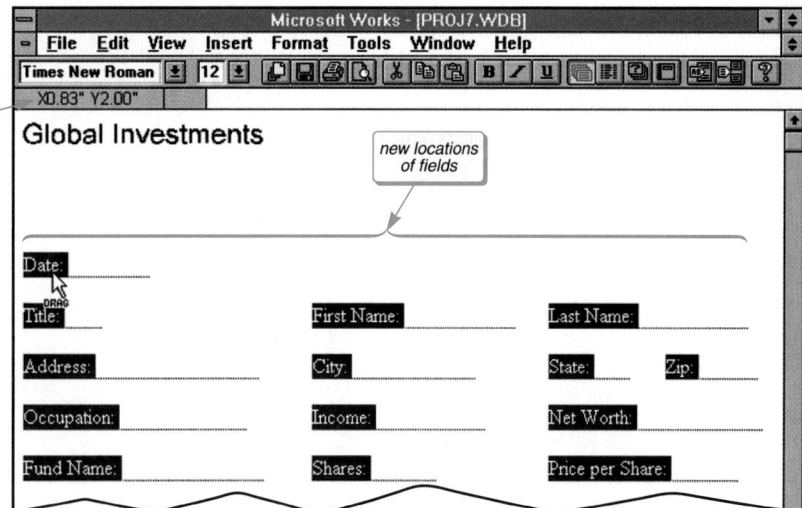

FIGURE 7-29

You can also use the **Position Selection command** on the Edit menu to
assist in moving fields. When this command is chosen, you can use the arrow keys
to move the field or use the mouse pointer to drag the field to a new location.

Formatting the Database Form Title Using Clip Art and WordArt

On the form in Figure 7-4 on page W7.7, **clip art** is displayed in the upper left
corner of the form and the title Global Investments is formatted with special
effects; that is, the letter G in Global is large and subsequent letters decrease in
size. Notice also that the letters contain a shadow and color is applied to the clip
art and to a rectangular bar that displays beneath the title. To insert clip art in the
form you must first move the title Global Investments to the right. To move the
title and insert the clip art, perform the following steps.

TO MOVE THE TITLE AND INSERT CLIP ART ▼

STEP 1 ▶

Highlight the embedded object
containing the words Global
Investments.

*Works places dotted lines around
the words Global Investments,
indicating the object is highlighted
(Figure 7-30). When an object is
highlighted, you can drag it to any
location on the form.*

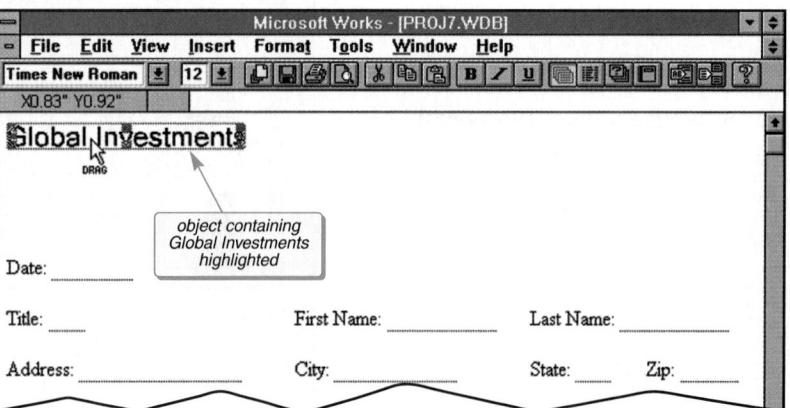

FIGURE 7-30

STEP 2 ▶

Drag the object containing the words Global Investments to its new location (X2.00" Y0.75"). Release the left mouse button.

The object containing the words Global Investments is positioned on the form to allow the clip art to be placed in the title area (Figure 7-31).

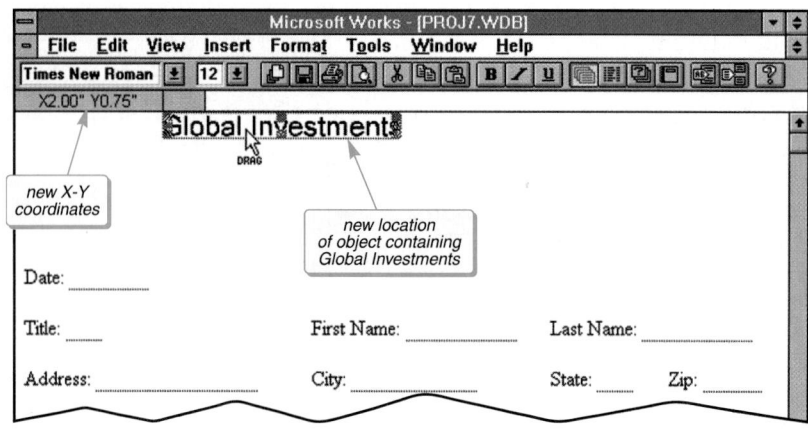

FIGURE 7-31

STEP 3 ▶

Position the Insertion point at the coordinates X0.75" Y0.75", which is the upper left corner of the form. Select the Insert menu and point to the ClipArt command.

*The insertion point displays in the upper left corner on the form, the Insert menu displays, and the mouse pointer points to the **ClipArt command**. (Figure 7-32). The formula bar displays the coordinates X0.75" Y0.75".*

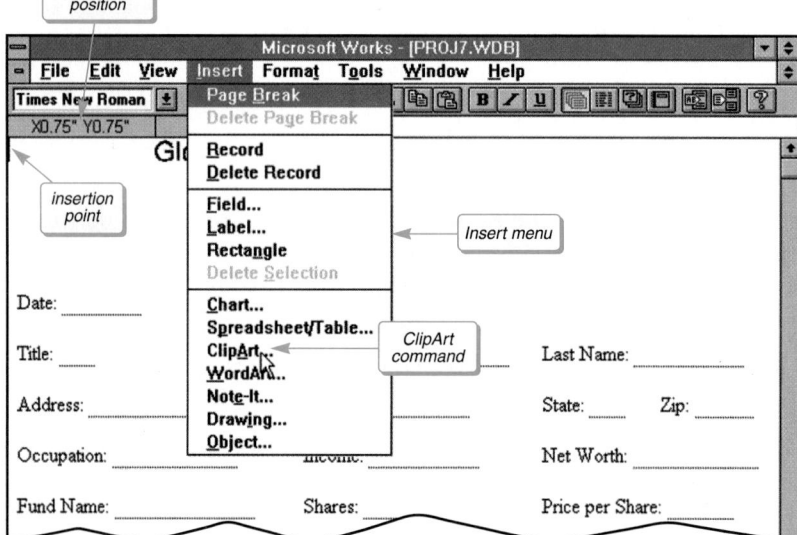

FIGURE 7-32

STEP 4 ▶

Choose the ClipArt command from the Insert menu. When the Microsoft ClipArt Gallery dialog box displays, select the clip art of the globe by pointing to the globe and clicking the left mouse button. Then point to the OK button.

The Microsoft ClipArt Gallery dialog box displays (Figure 7-33). When you select the clip art of the globe, Works places a blue border around the clip art. The mouse pointer points to the OK button.

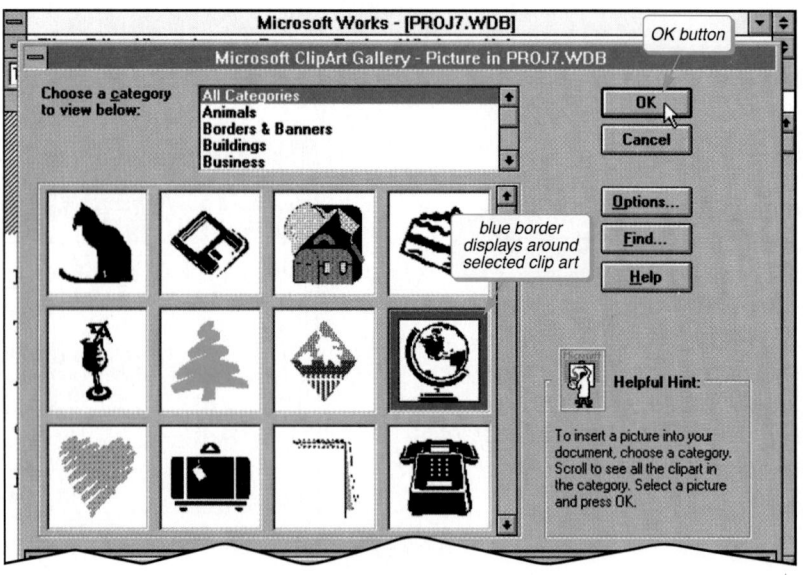

FIGURE 7-33

STEP 5 ►

Choose the OK button in the Microsoft ClipArt Gallery dialog box. Select the Format menu and point to the Picture/Object command

Works inserts the clip art of the Globe in the database form at the location of the insertion point (Figure 7-34). A rectangular box containing dotted lines and resize handles surrounds the clip art, indicating the clip art is an object and may be moved or resized. Because the clip art is too large for the title area, it must be resized. The Format menu displays and the mouse pointer points to the Picture/Object command.

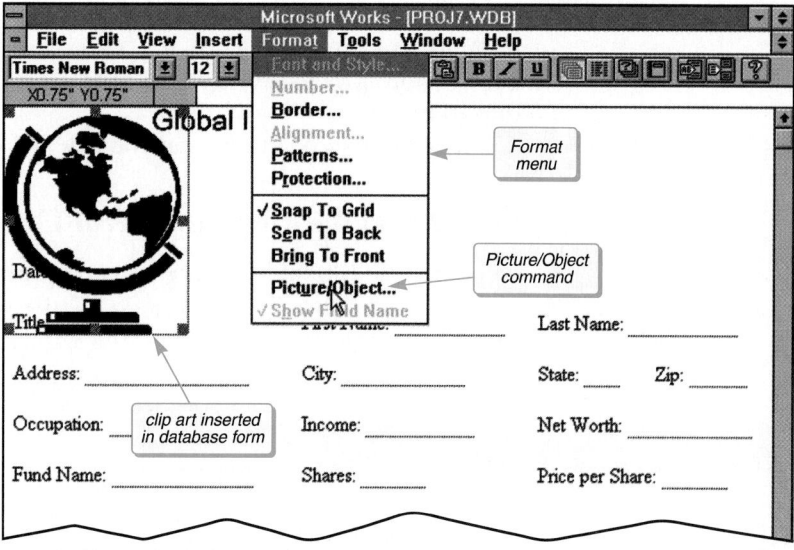

FIGURE 7-34

STEP 6 ►

Choose the Picture/Object command from the Format menu. When the Picture/Object dialog box displays, type 58 in the Width text box in the Scaling area and type 58 in the Height text box. Then, point to the OK button.

The Picture/Object dialog box allows you to precisely control the size of an object. The values you entered for width and height, 58, indicate you want the width and height to be 58% of the original size (Figure 7-35).

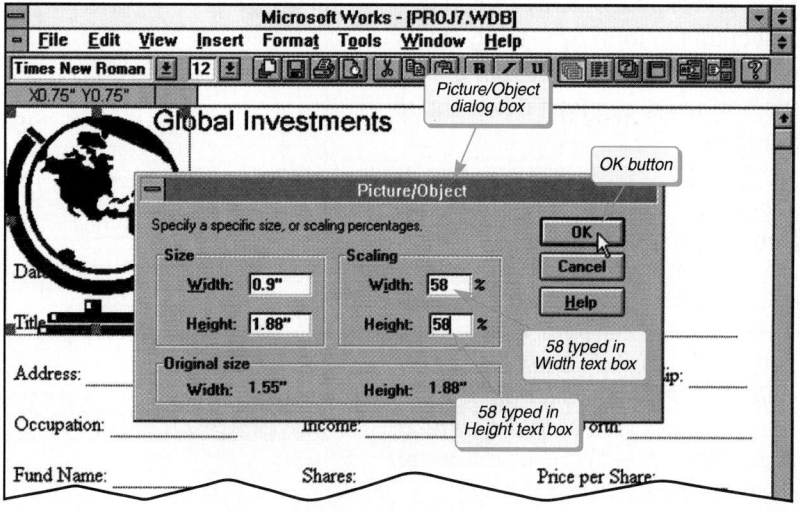

FIGURE 7-35

STEP 7 ►

Choose the OK button in the Picture/Object dialog box.

Works displays the clip art of the globe at 58% of the original size when it was placed on the form (Figure 7-36).

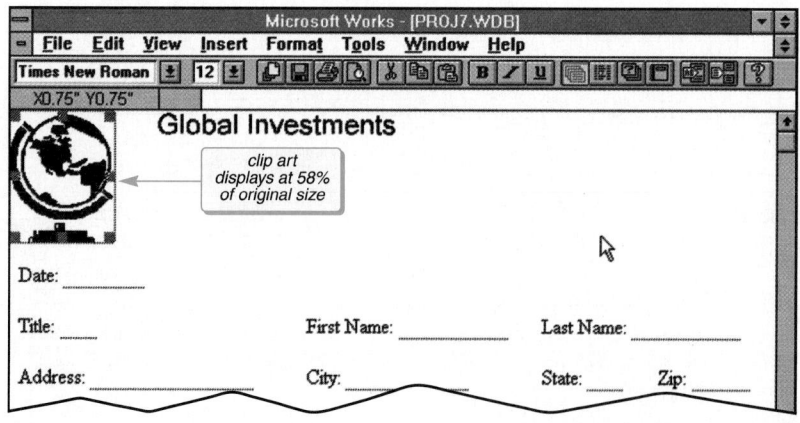

FIGURE 7-36

You can also use the resize handles that display in the rectangular box around the clip art to resize the clip art. Using the Picture/Object command, however, allows more precise control over the sizing in applications where the exact size is important.

The next step is to format the title, Global Investments, using WordArt.

Formatting the Title Using WordArt

The title Global Investments is to appear at the top of the database form as illustrated in Figure 7-4 on page W7.7. To accomplish this task, perform the following steps.

TO FORMAT THE TITLE USING WORDART ▼

STEP 1 ▶

Double-click the embedded object containing the title Global Investments. Move the Enter Your Text Here box away from the object on the form by placing the mouse pointer in the title bar of the box and dragging it down and to the right.

The Enter Your Text Here box displays when you double-click the embedded object containing the words Global Investments (Figure 7-37). It has been dragged away from the outlined object on the database form so it is easier to see the object area on the database form. The WordArt menu bar and WordArt Toolbar display.

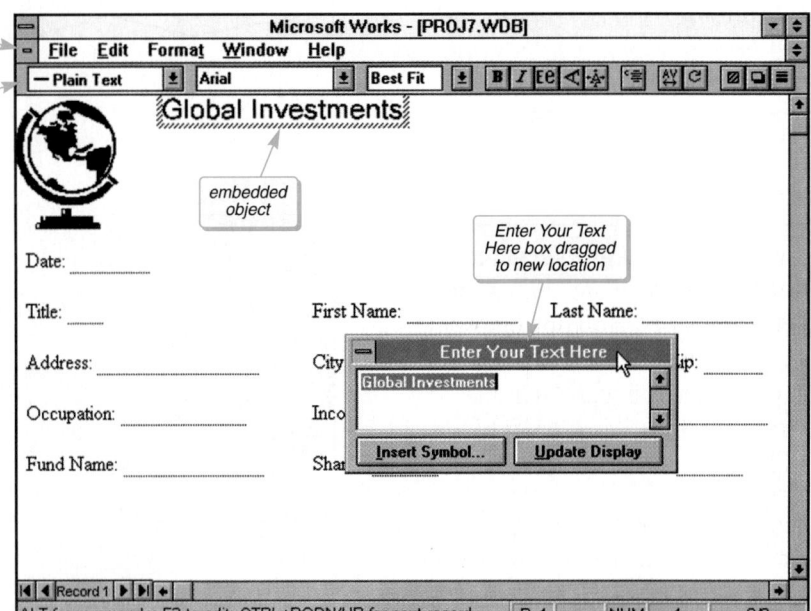

FIGURE 7-37

STEP 2 ▶

Click the Shape box arrow on the Toolbar. When the Shape drop-down box displays, point to the box in the lower left corner.

*The Shape drop-down box displays and the mouse pointer points to the **Fade Right** shape (Figure 7-38).*

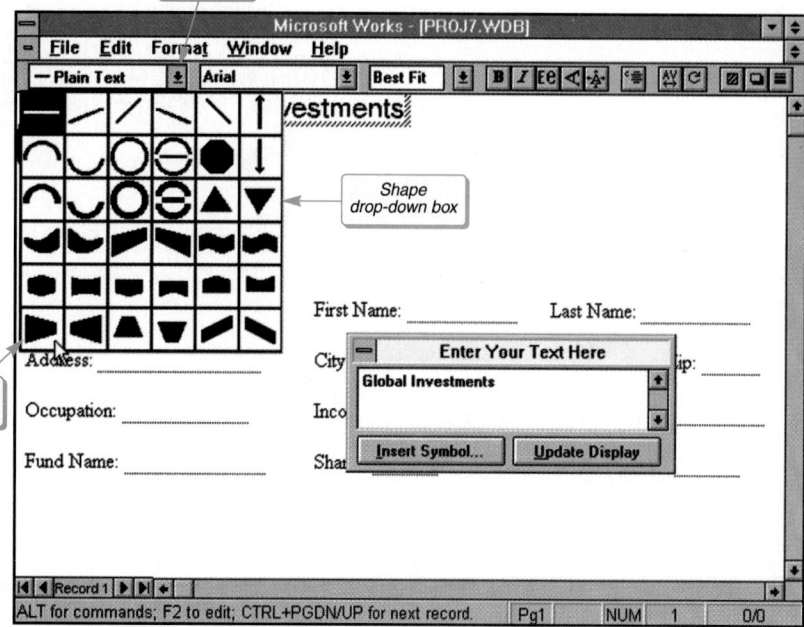

FIGURE 7-38

STEP 3 ▶

Choose the Fade Right shape by clicking the left mouse button. Point to the Stretch button on the Toolbar.

*The words Global Investments display in the object area on the form in compressed text (Figure 7-39). The mouse pointer points to the **Stretch button** on the Toolbar.*

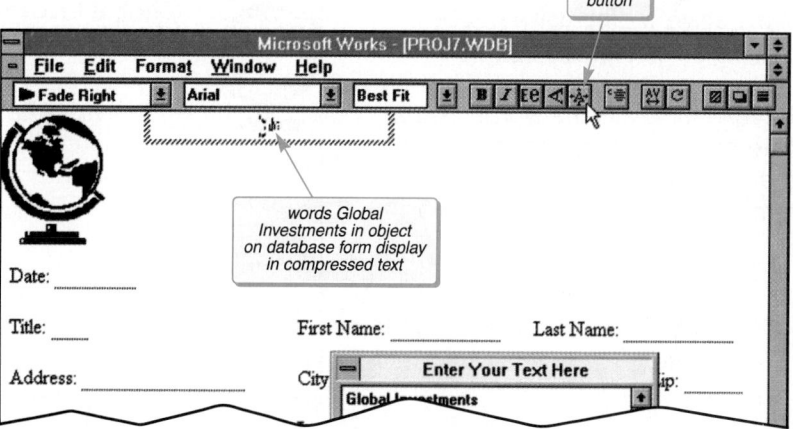

FIGURE 7-39

STEP 4 ▶

Click the Stretch button on the Toolbar. Then click the Shadow button on the Toolbar.

WordArt displays the words Global Investments with a fade right effect in the object area in the database form (Figure 7-40). The Shadow drop-down box displays. It allows the choice of one of nine special effects for shadows.

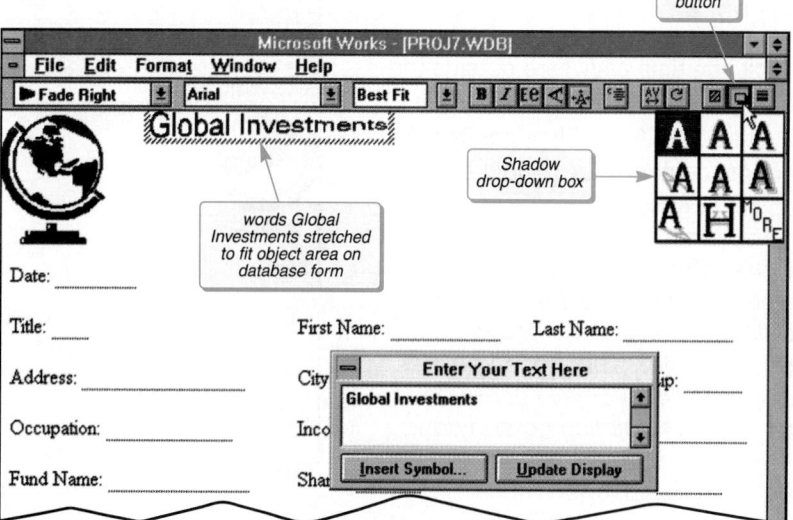

FIGURE 7-40

STEP 5 ▶

Point to the center box on the first line in the Shadow drop-down box (Figure 7-41).

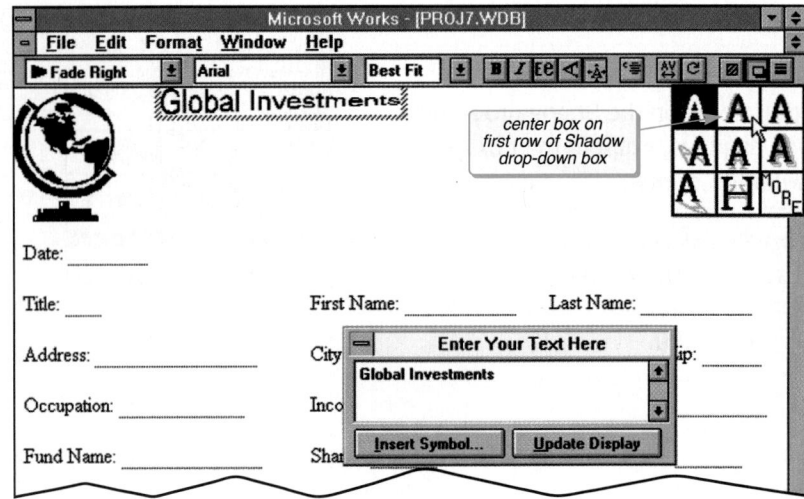

FIGURE 7-41

STEP 6 ▶

Select the center box on the first line in the Shadow drop-down box by clicking the left mouse button.

WordArt displays the words Global Investments with a shadow within the object area on the database form (Figure 7-42).

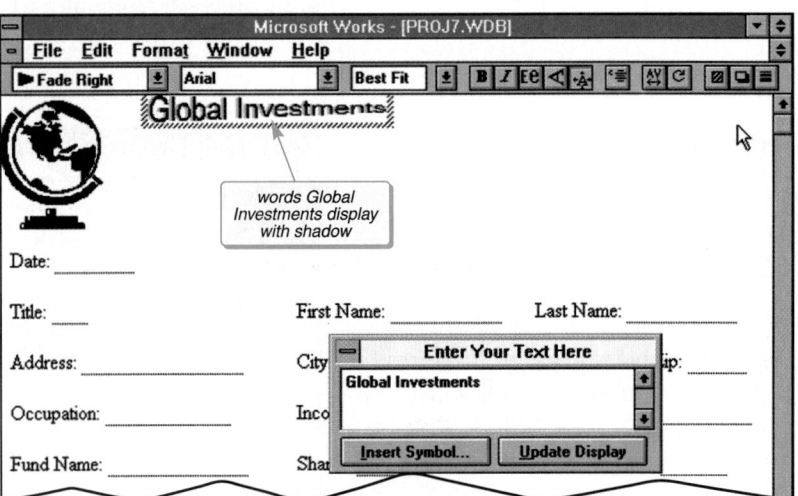

FIGURE 7-42

STEP 7 ▶

Click one time anywhere outside the Enter Your Text Here box to return to the database form. Then point to the bottom center resize handle on the object border.

Works displays the formatted words Global Investments on the database form in the object area (Figure 7-43). The mouse pointer displays with a small square box and arrows pointing up and down. The word RESIZE displays beneath the arrows.

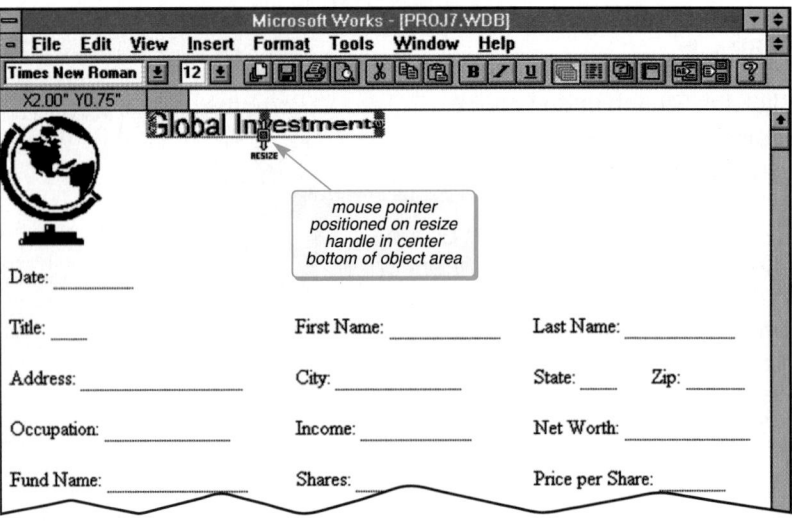

FIGURE 7-43

STEP 8 ▶

Drag the resize handle down to approximately the bottom of the globe. Then place the mouse pointer on the right center resize handle.

The object area containing the words Global Investments expands vertically (Figure 7-44). It is possible to drag the resize handle in the lower right corner to expand the rectangular box both vertically and horizontally at one time. For some individuals, a two-step approach makes it easier to control the vertical and horizontal expansion.

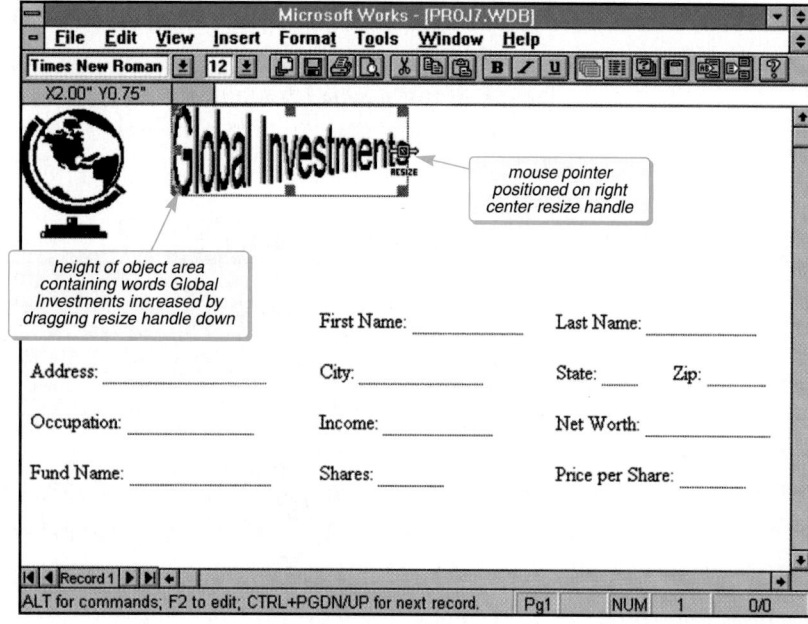

FIGURE 7-44

STEP 9 ▶

Drag the right center resize handle to the right approximately one-quarter of an inch from the edge of the screen.

The words Global Investments expand horizontally to fill the object area (Figure 7-45).

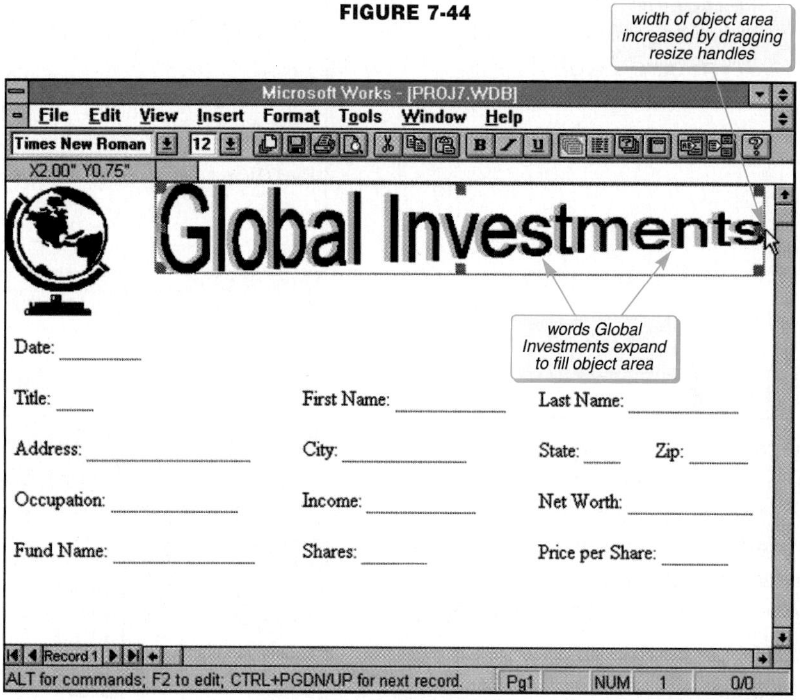

FIGURE 7-45

The words Global Investments have now been formatted as required. WordArt provides many special effects for text when using Microsoft Works.

Inserting a Rectangular Bar Beneath the Title

To further enhance the title area, the area is to contain a rectangular bar beneath the words Global Investments (see Figure 7-4 on page W7.7). Complete the following steps to insert the bar.

TO INSERT A RECTANGULAR BAR IN THE TITLE AREA ▼

STEP 1 ▶

Position the insertion point at the coordinates X2.00" Y1.67" by moving the mouse pointer to the area and clicking the left mouse button.

Works displays the insertion point beneath the words Global Investments and the formula bar displays the coordinates X2.00" Y1.67" (Figure 7-46).

FIGURE 7-46

STEP 2 ▶

Select the Insert menu and point to Rectangle command.

*The Insert menu displays and the mouse pointer points to the **Rectangle command** (Figure 7-47).*

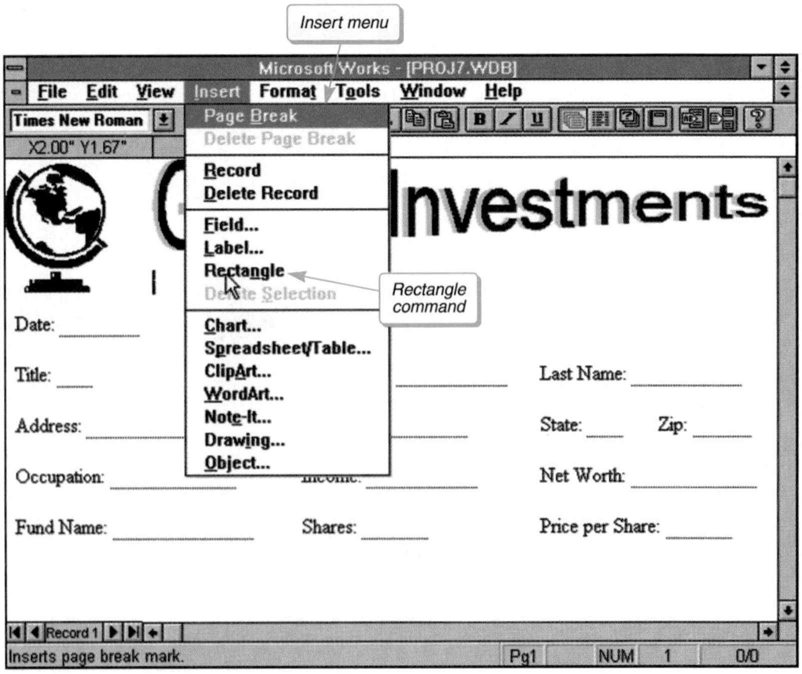

FIGURE 7-47

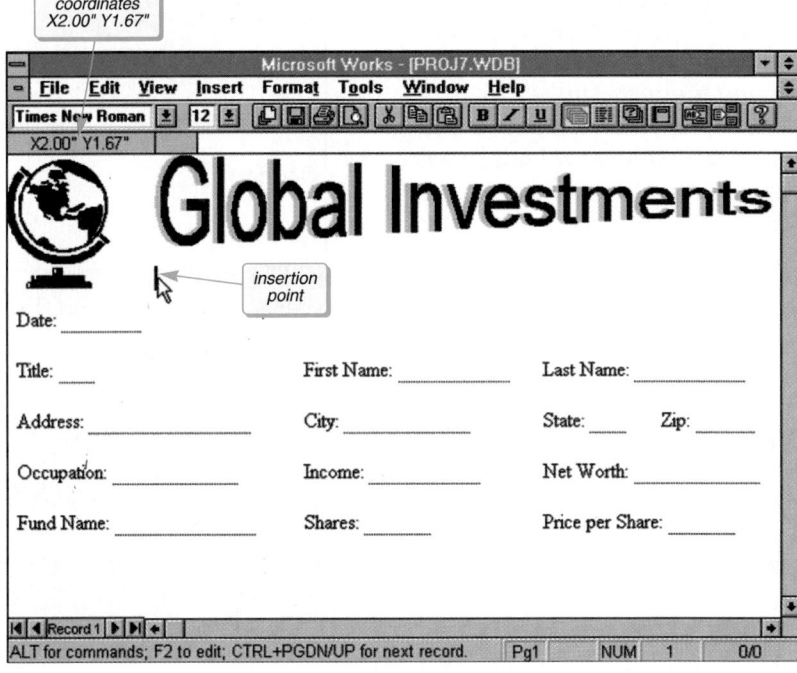

STEP 3 ▶

Choose the Rectangle command from the Insert menu and place the mouse pointer on the resize handle in the lower right corner of the rectangle that displays.

Works displays a box containing dotted lines and resize handles on the database form (Figure 7-48). The mouse points to the resize handle in the lower right corner.

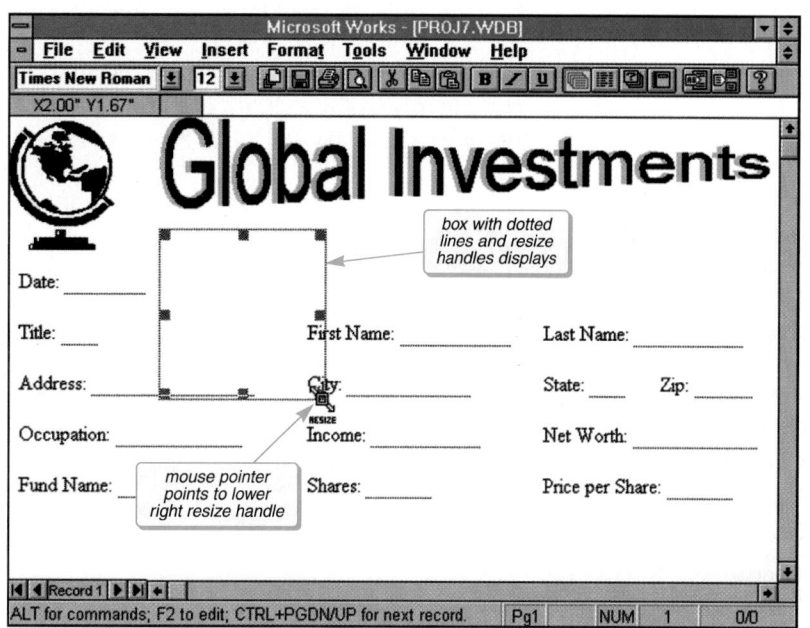

FIGURE 7-48

STEP 4 ▶

Drag the resize handle up to the bottom of the ClipArt and to the right edge of the screen.

Works displays the resized rectangular box beneath the words Global Investments (Figure 7-49).

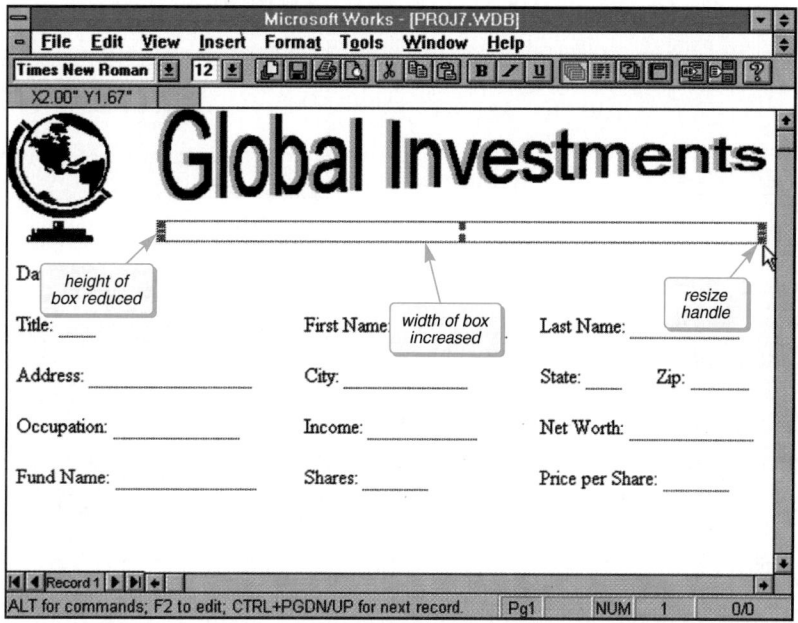

FIGURE 7-49

The format of the title area is now complete except for adding color. Adding color to the title area will be performed as one of the last steps in the database form design.

Formatting Field Names

To give further emphasis to the field names on the database form, each field name is to display in Arial bold font. The following steps explain how to change the field names from Times New Roman font to Arial bold font.

TO FORMAT THE FIELD NAMES

STEP 1 ▶

Point to the Date field name and click the left mouse button. Then, while holding down the CTRL key, click each field name on the database form to highlight them.

Each field name on the database form is now highlighted (Figure 7-50).

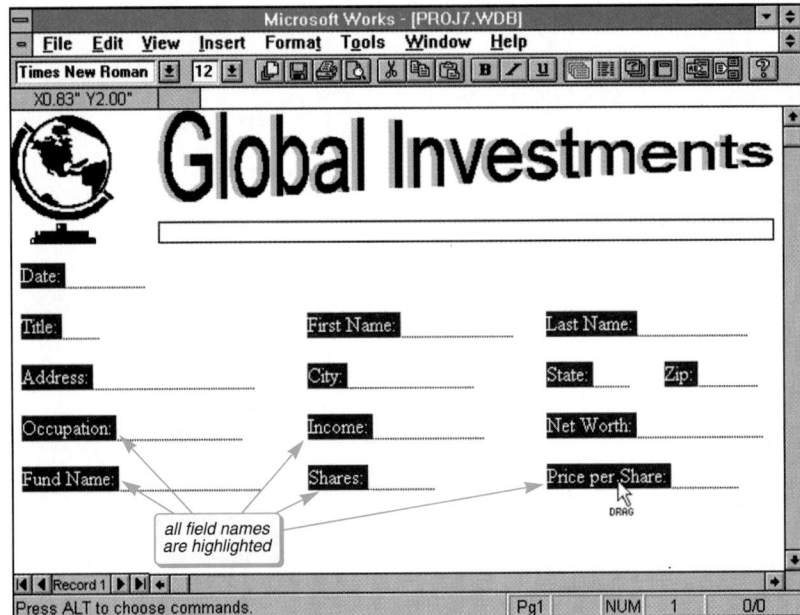

FIGURE 7-50

STEP 2 ▶

Click the Font Name box arrow on the Toolbar and scroll up until Arial displays in the Font Name drop-down list box. Point to Arial.

The Font Name drop-down list box displays and the mouse pointer points to Arial (Figure 7-51).

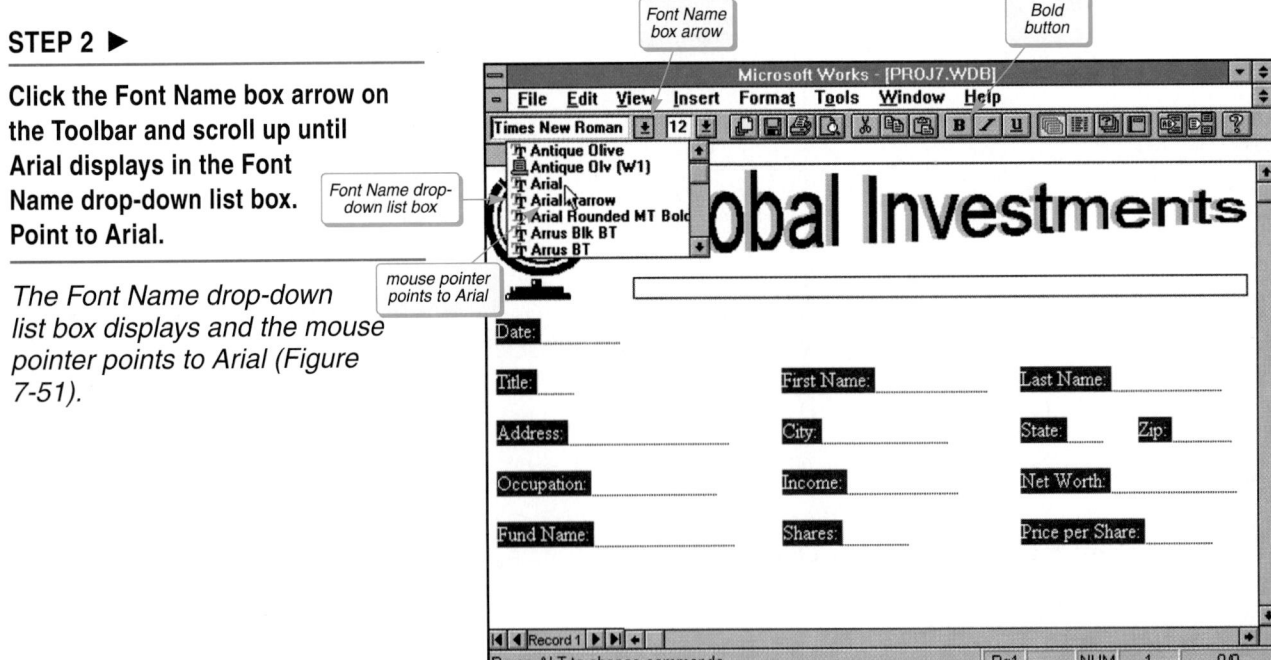

FIGURE 7-51

STEP 3 ▶

Select the Arial font by clicking the left mouse button. Then click the Bold button on the Toolbar.

Works displays the highlighted field names in Arial bold font (Figure 7-52).

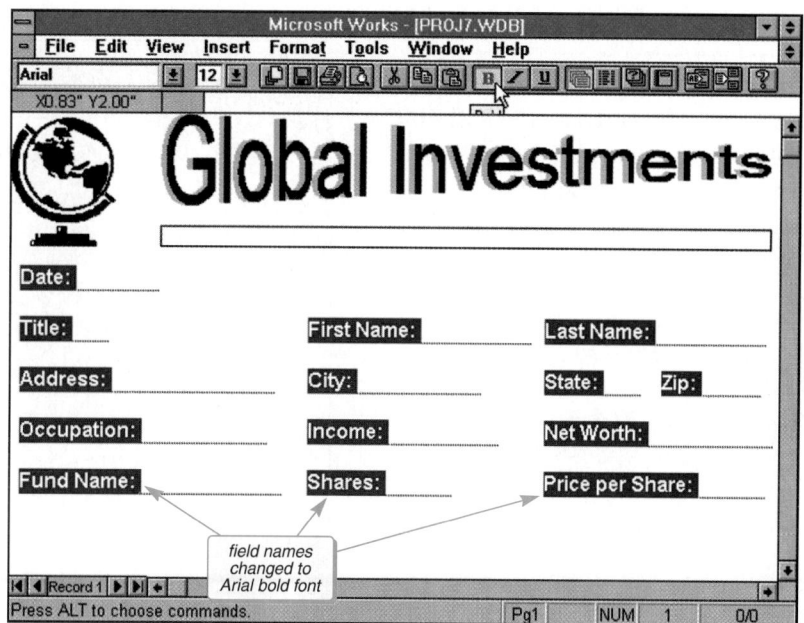

FIGURE 7-52

As you work, it is generally a good idea to save your database. Therefore, before adding color to the database form, save the database using the techniques previously explained.

Adding Color to the Database Form

The next step is to add color to the database form. A dark magenta color displays around the globe and in the rectangular bar beneath the words Global Investments. To add color, perform the following steps.

TO ADD COLOR TO THE DATABASE FORM ▼

STEP 1 ▶

Highlight the clip art by pointing to the clip art of the Globe and clicking the left mouse button. Hold down the CTRL key, point to the rectangle beneath the words Global Investments, and click the left mouse button. Select the Format menu and point to the Patterns command.

The clip art and the rectangle are highlighted, the Format menu displays, and the mouse pointer points to the Patterns command (Figure 7-53).

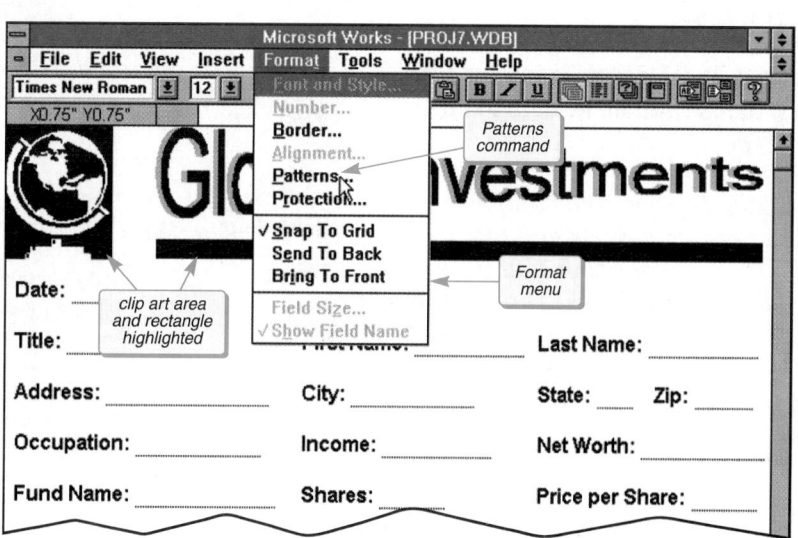

FIGURE 7-53

STEP 2 ▶

Choose the Patterns command from the Format menu. When the Patterns dialog box displays, click the Pattern box arrow and point to the solid pattern box in the drop-down list box that displays.

Works displays the Patterns dialog box and the Pattern drop-down list box (Figure 7-54). The mouse pointer points to the solid pattern in the Pattern drop-down list box.

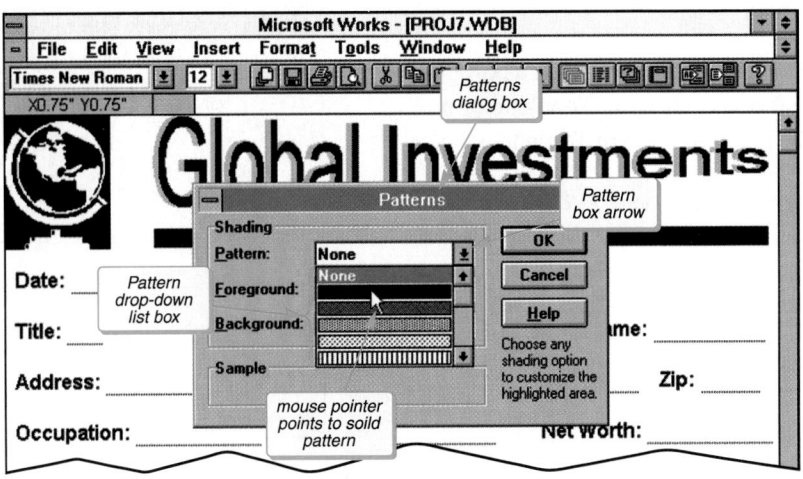

FIGURE 7-54

STEP 3 ▶

Select the solid pattern. Click the Foreground box arrow. When the Foreground drop-down list box displays, scroll down and then point to Dark Magenta (Figure 7-55).

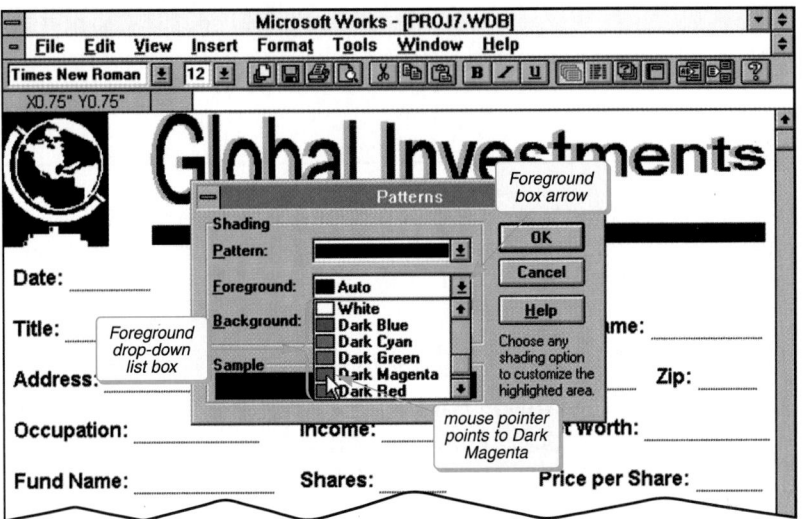

FIGURE 7-55

STEP 4 ▶

Select Dark Magenta by clicking the left mouse button. Point to the OK button.

Works displays Dark Magenta in the Foreground box and the mouse pointer points to the OK button (Figure 7-56). The Sample area displays a sample of the pattern and color that you have selected.

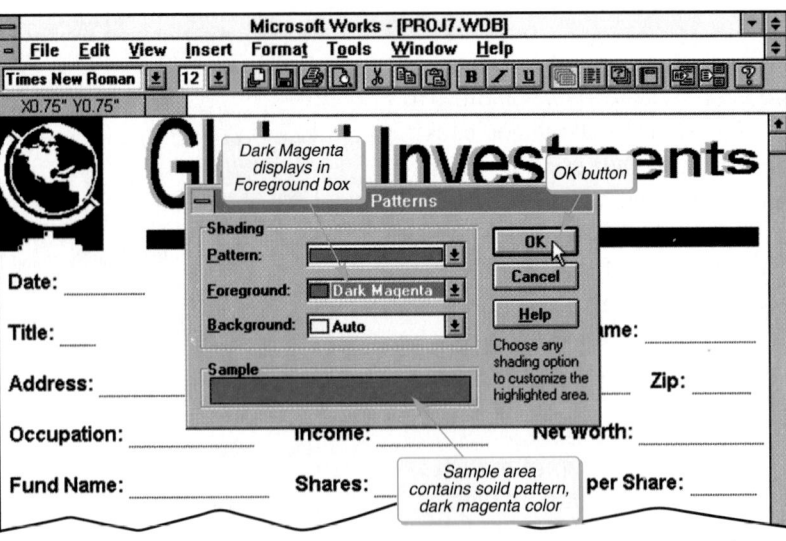

FIGURE 7-56

STEP 5 ▶

Choose the OK button in the Patterns dialog box. Click anywhere on the form to remove the highlight.

Works displays the area behind the clip art of the globe and the rectangular bar with a solid pattern, dark magenta color (Figure 7-57).

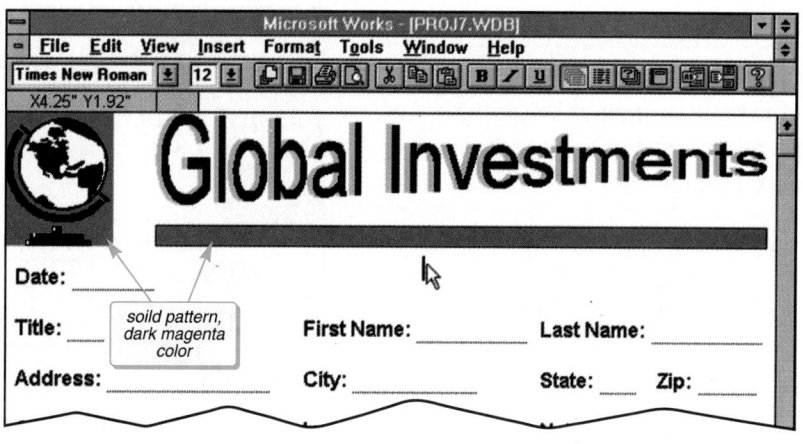

FIGURE 7-57

Most database forms in a modern computing environment use color to enhance the appearance of the form.

Adding a Border on Fields

The final step in developing the format of the database form is to add a color border around the fields. This technique precisely defines for the user where data is to appear. To accomplish this task, it is recommended that you first remove the field lines and then add the color borders. Perform the following steps to accomplish this task.

TO REMOVE FIELD LINES AND ADD A BORDER ON FIELDS ▼

STEP 1 ▶

Click the Date field. Then highlight all the fields by holding down the CTRL key and clicking each of the fields. Select the View menu and point to the Field Lines command.

*All fields are highlighted, the View menu displays, and the mouse pointer points to the **Field Lines command** (Figure 7-58).*

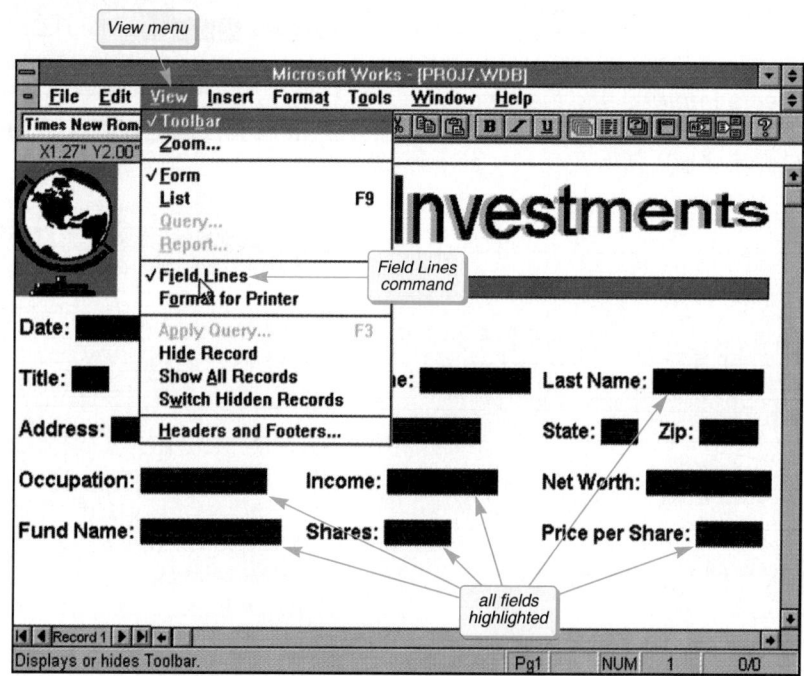

FIGURE 7-58

STEP 2 ►

Choose the Field Lines command from the View menu. Select the Format menu and point to the Border command.

Works no longer displays the field lines (Figure 7-59). The View menu displays and the mouse pointer points to the Border command.

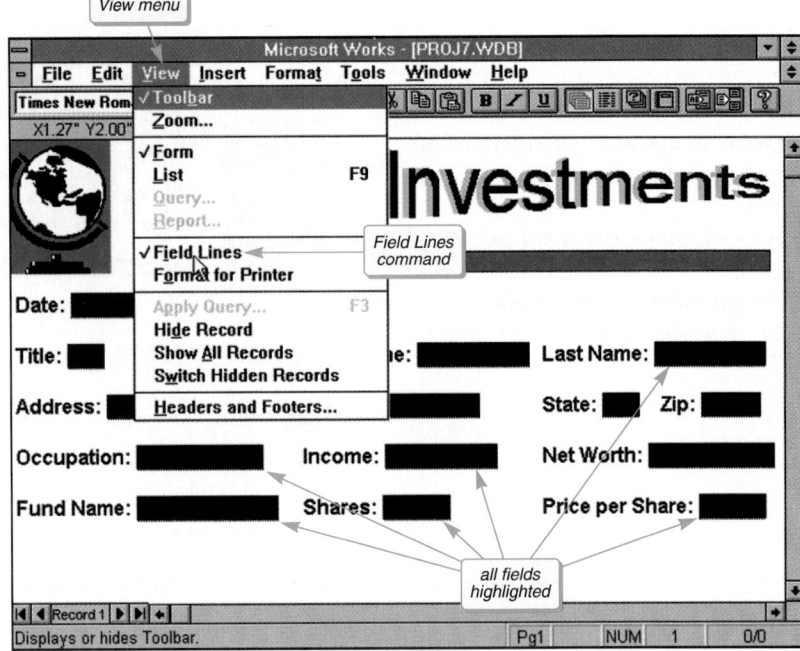

FIGURE 7-59

STEP 3 ►

Choose the Border command from the Format menu. When the Border dialog box displays, click the Outline box in the Border area, display the Color drop-down list box by clicking the Color box arrow, scroll down and select the Dark Magenta color from the Color drop-down list box, and then point to the OK button.

The Border dialog box displays the selected entries and the mouse pointer points to the OK button (Figure 7-60).

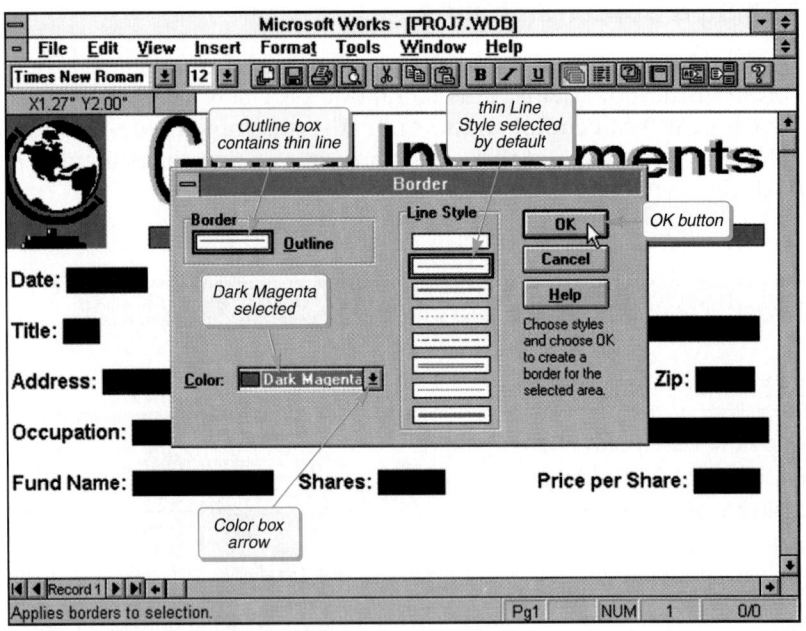

FIGURE 7-60

STEP 4 ▶

Choose the OK button in the Border dialog box. Then, click the form to remove the highlights from the fields.

Works removes the highlight from the fields and applies the dark magenta outline border to all fields (Figure 7-61).

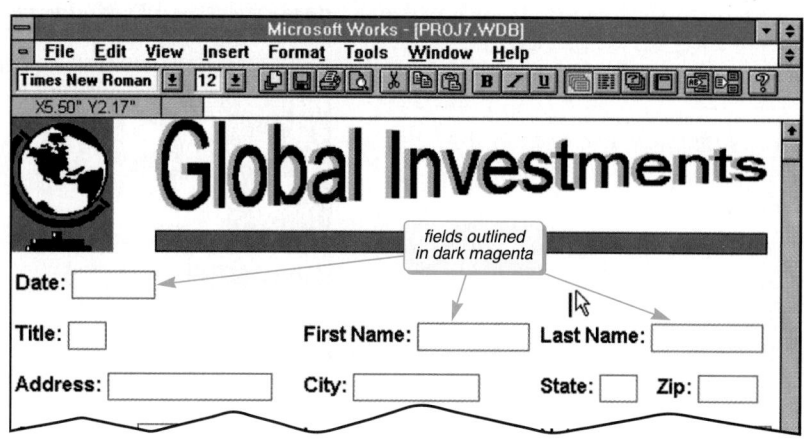

FIGURE 7-61

The format of the database form is now complete. In most cases, you should save the completed form on disk. To save the database, click the Save button on the Toolbar.

▶ ENTERING DATA INTO THE DATABASE

T
he fields contained within each record of the database constitute the structure of the database. The structure, however, merely defines the fields within the database. The whole purpose of a database is to enter data so the data is available for printing, sorting, querying, and other uses. Therefore, the next step is to enter data into the database. The data can consist of text, numbers, formulas, and even functions.

To enter data, highlight the field where you want to enter the data and then type the data. To enter the data for the first record in the database, complete the following steps.

TO ENTER DATA INTO THE DATABASE ▼

STEP 1 ▶

Highlight the Date field.

Works places a black background in the field and changes the mouse pointer to a block arrow with the word DRAG beneath it (Figure 7-62). Small shaded boxes that serve as resize handles display on the right and bottom borders of the highlighted field. These resize handles allow you to change the size of the field. The X-Y coordinates in the formula bar specify the location of the field, not the field name.

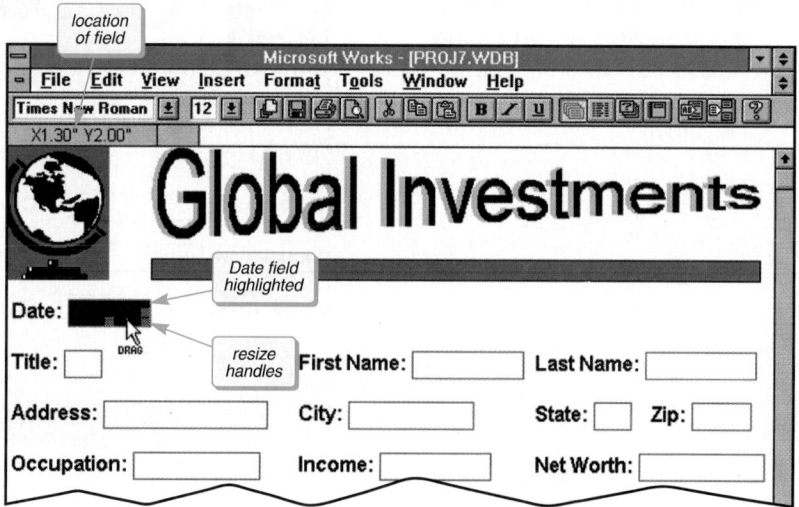

FIGURE 7-62

STEP 2 ▶

Type the date, 10/5/93.

Works displays the date in the formula bar and in the field (Figure 7-62a).

FIGURE 7-62a

STEP 3 ▶

Press the TAB key.

Works enters the date into the Date field and highlights the next field, Title (Figure 7-63). The TAB key causes both the data to be entered and the highlight to be moved from the previous field. If you press the ENTER key or click the Enter box, the data is entered but the highlight is not moved. Pressing the TAB key is the most efficient technique to enter data into a database.

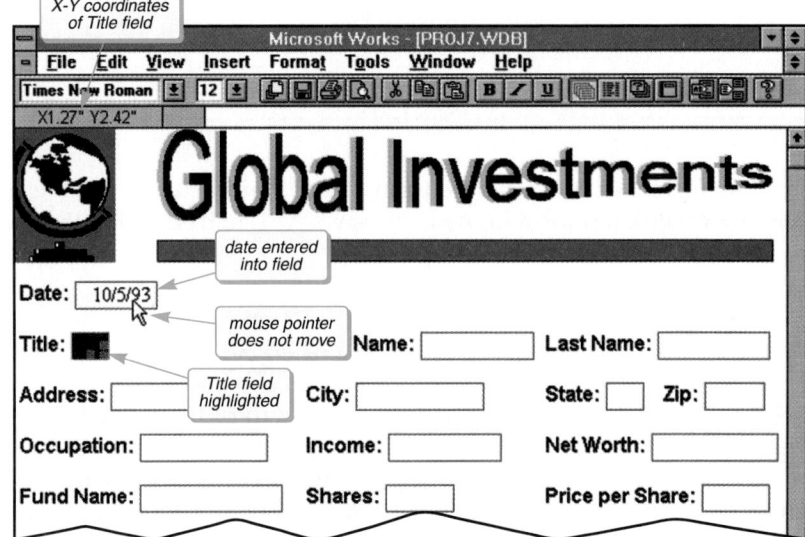

FIGURE 7-63

STEP 4 ▶

Type the title, Mrs., **and press the TAB key.**

Works enters the title, Mrs., into the Title field and highlights the next field, First Name (Figure 7-64).

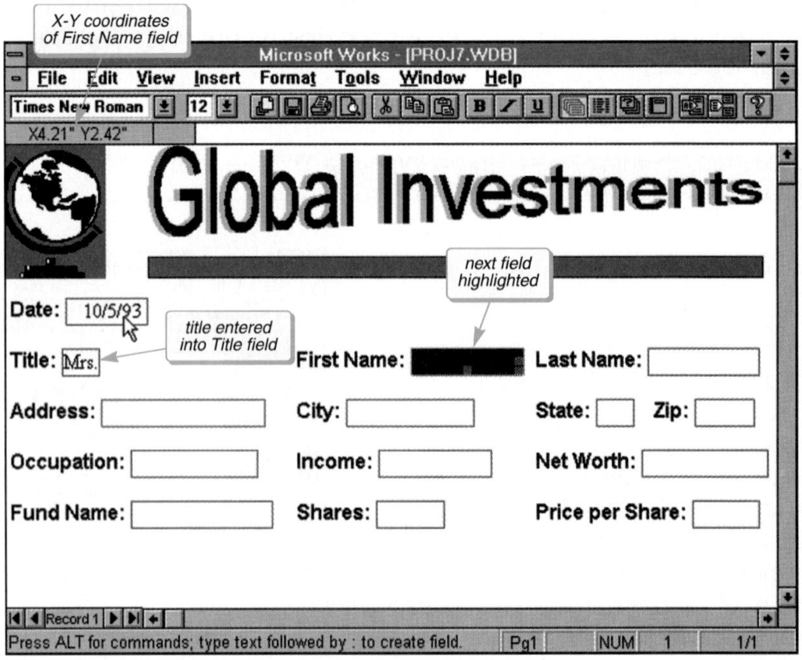

FIGURE 7-64

STEP 5 ►

Type and enter the remaining data for each of the fields in the first record. After typing the Price per Share, press the ENTER key or click the Enter box.

All the data for the first record is now entered (Figure 7-65). The Price per Share field is highlighted because you pressed the ENTER key or clicked the Enter box rather than pressing the TAB key. Pressing the TAB key would cause Works to highlight the Date field in the second record.

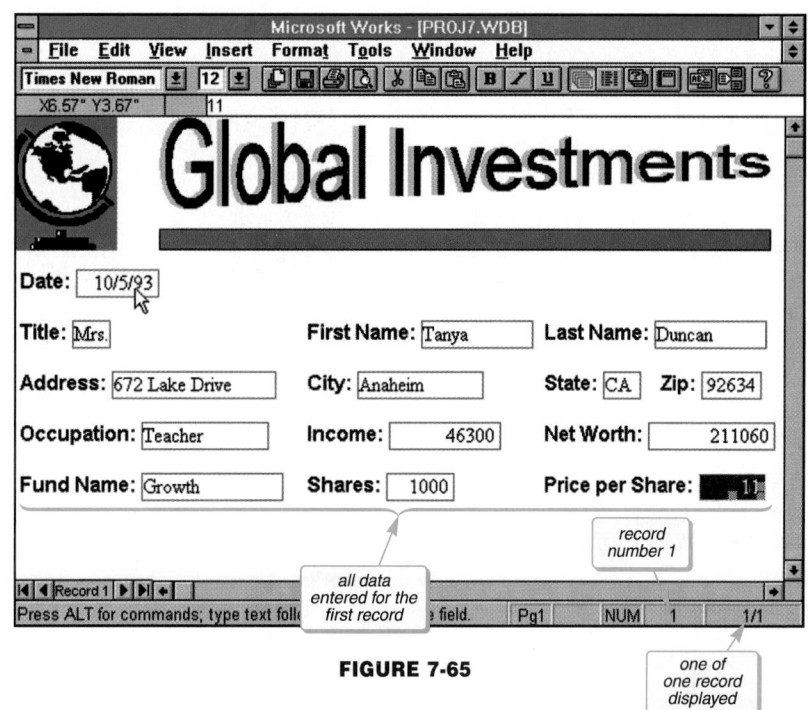

FIGURE 7-65

Notice several important items in the record shown in Figure 7-65. First, the Date field is considered a numeric field because Works considers dates numeric. Thus, the date is right-aligned in the field.

Second, the text fields, which are any fields containing one or more non-numeric characters, are left-aligned in their fields.

The Zip Code, Income, Net Worth, Shares, and Price per Share are numeric fields. The data is right-aligned in the fields.

If you accidentally enter erroneous data, you can correct the entry by highlighting the field containing the error and entering the correct data. Works will replace the erroneous data with the correct data.

Formatting Numeric Fields in a Database

The next step is to format the actual data in the fields in the first record in the database. The style includes: (1) formatting the Income field to a currency field with two digits to the right of the decimal point; (2) formatting the Net Worth field to a currency field with two digits to the right of the decimal point; (3) formatting the Shares field to a comma field with zero positions to the right of the decimal point; and (4) formatting the Price per Share field to a currency field with two digits to the right of the decimal point.

The steps to format the numeric data in the database are explained on the following pages.

TO FORMAT NUMERIC DATA IN A DATABASE ▼

STEP 1 ►

Highlight the Income field. Then, while holding down the CTRL key, click the Net Worth and Price per Share field entries. Select the Format menu and point to the Number command.

Works highlights the Income, Net Worth, and Price per Share field entries (Figure 7-66). The Format menu displays and the mouse pointer points to the Number command.

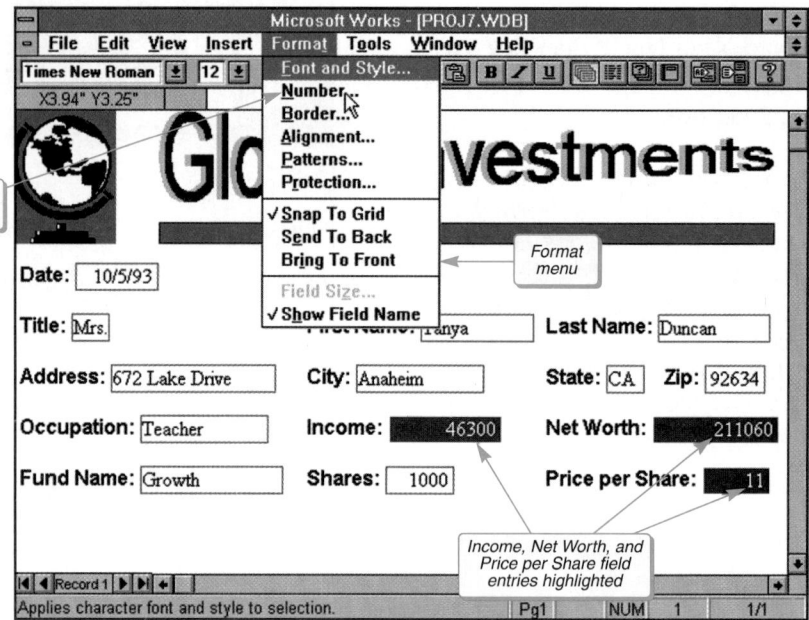

FIGURE 7-66

STEP 2 ►

Choose the Number command from the Format menu. When the Number dialog box displays, select the Currency option button, check to ensure the Number of decimals text box contains a 2, and then point to the OK button.

Works displays the Number dialog box (Figure 7-67). The Currency option button is selected, the Number of decimals text box contains a 2, and the mouse pointer points to the OK button.

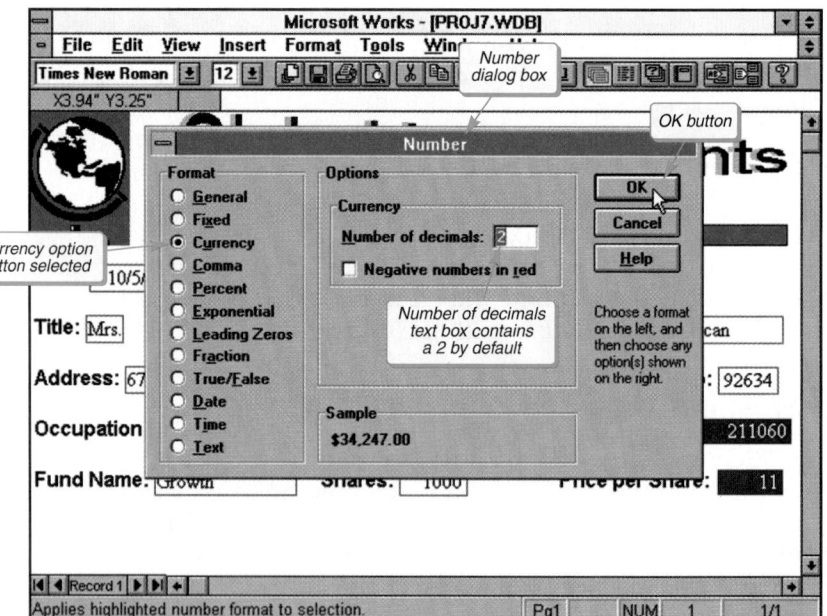

FIGURE 7-67

STEP 3 ▶

Choose the OK button in the Number dialog box. Highlight the Shares field entry, select the Format menu, and point to the Number command.

Works formats the Income, Net Worth, and the Price per Share fields in the currency format with dollar signs, commas if necessary, and decimal points (Figure 7-68). The Shares field entry is highlighted, the Format menu displays, and the mouse pointer points to the Number command.

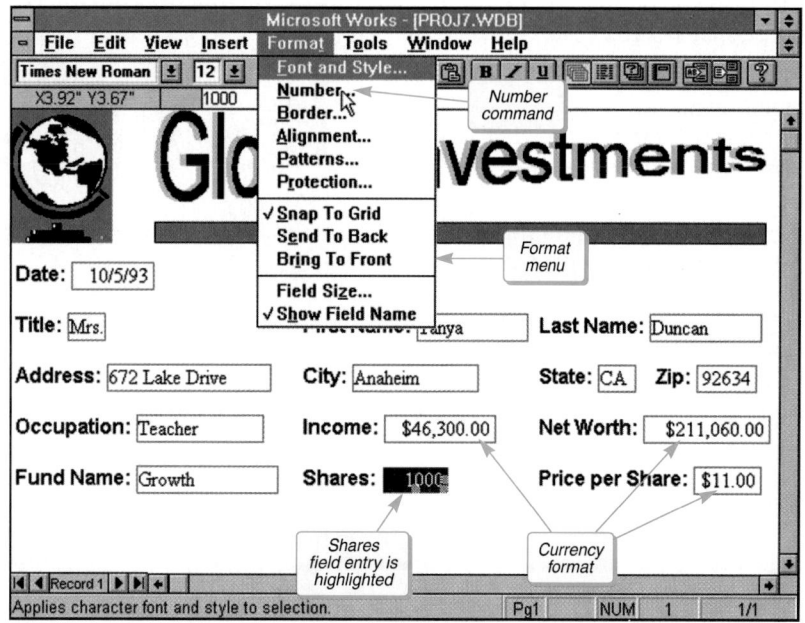

FIGURE 7-68

STEP 4 ▶

Choose the Number command. When the Number dialog box displays, select the Comma option button, type 0 in the Number of decimals text box, and point to the OK button.

Works displays the Number dialog box (Figure 7-69). The Comma option button is selected. The Number of decimals text box contains a zero. The zero indicates no positions to the right of the decimal point. The mouse pointer points to the OK button.

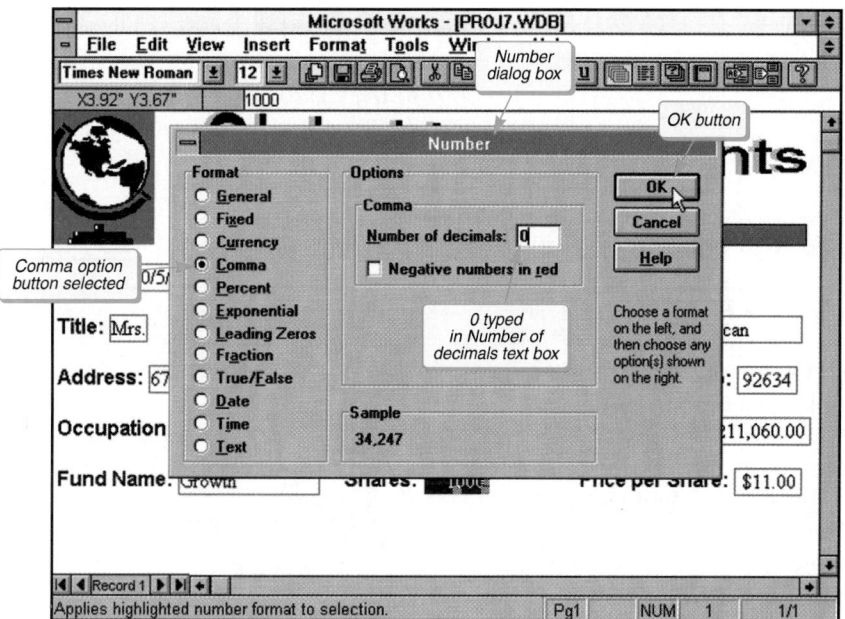

FIGURE 7-69

STEP 5 ▶

Choose the OK button in the Number dialog box.

Works formats the Shares field entry in the Comma format with zero positions to the right of the decimal point (Figure 7-70).

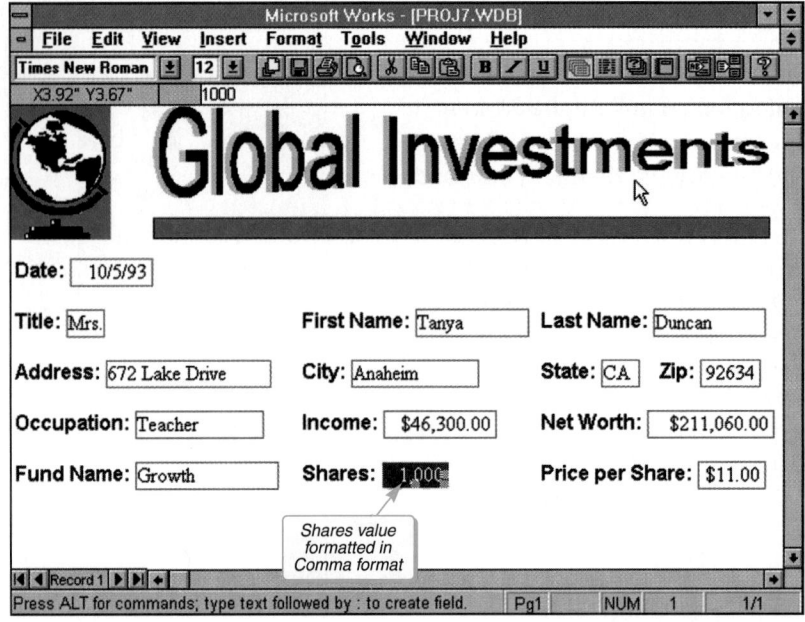

FIGURE 7-70

The first record in the database is now completely formatted. You will use the format specified for both the field names and field entries in record number 1 for every record in the database. To continue entering data into the database, you must display the form for record number 2 on the screen as shown in the next step.

TO DISPLAY THE NEXT RECORD IN FORM VIEW ▼

STEP 1 ▶

Highlight the Price per Share field and press the TAB key.

Works displays record number 2 (Figure 7-71). Notice that the Date field is highlighted. When you press the TAB key, Works highlights the next field, even if the next field is in the next record in the database.

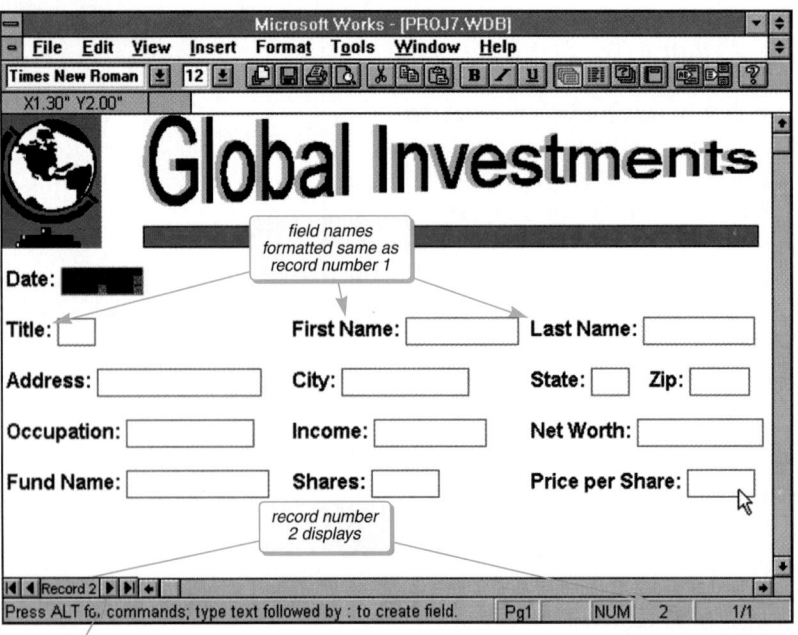

FIGURE 7-71

You can also move from one record to another using the navigation buttons on the scroll bar at the bottom of the screen (see Figure 7-71). When record number 1 is displayed and you click the next record navigation button, Works will display record number 2. The field highlighted, however, is the same field as on record number 1. Therefore, in the sequence from Figure 7-70 to Figure 7-71, if you click the next record navigation button, record number 2 will display on the screen with the Shares field highlighted. When you are entering data into the database, you normally want the first field in the next record highlighted. Therefore, pressing the TAB key is the preferred way to move from the last field in one record to the first field in the next record.

With record number 2 displayed, complete the following steps to enter the data for record number 2 (see Figure 7-72).

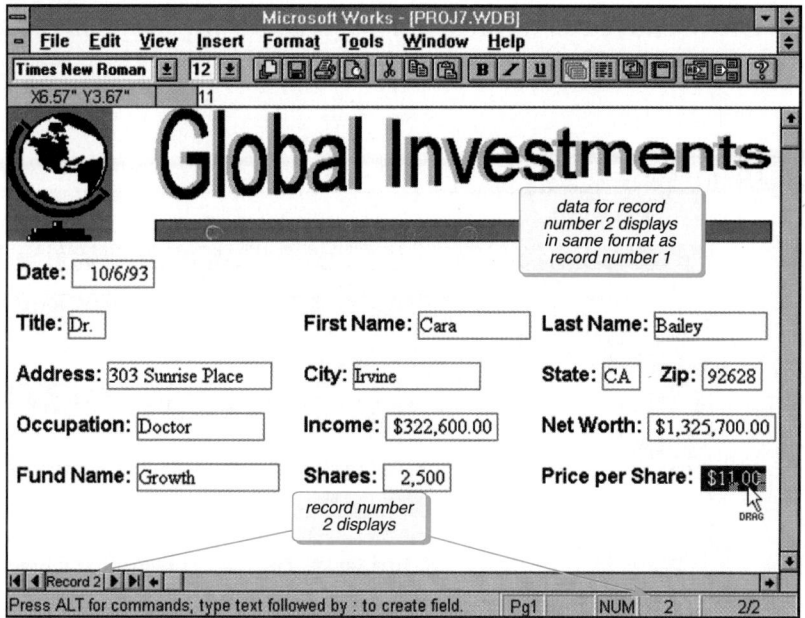

FIGURE 7-72

TO ENTER DATA FOR THE NEXT RECORD

Step 1: Type the date, 10/6/93, and press the TAB key.
Step 2: Type the title, Dr., and press the TAB key.
Step 3: Complete the remainder of the record using the data shown in Figure 7-72. When you type 11.00 for the Price per Share, press the ENTER key or click the Enter box to enter the value in the field.

The screen after you enter this data is shown in Figure 7-72. Notice that each of the fields is formatted in the same manner as record number 1; that is, the Income, Net Worth, and Price per Share fields display in the Currency format, while the Shares field displays in the Comma format. You do not need to perform any formatting after you have formatted one record. Each record in the database will assume the same formatting characteristics as the first record you formatted. In fact, if you want to change the formatting of a given field in the database, you can change the field in any record in the database and all other records will assume the new formatting.

Continue entering the data for the remaining records in the database as specified in the steps on the next page.

TO ENTER ALL DATA IN THE DATABASE

Step 1: With the Price per Share field in the second record highlighted, press the TAB key.

Step 2: Using the table in Figure 7-1 on pages W7.2 and W7.3 for data, enter the data for records 3 through 16. As you enter the data, you should periodically save the database so your work will not be lost in case of a power failure or other mishap. When you enter the data for the Price per Share field for record 16, press the ENTER key or click the Enter box.

Step 3: Click the Save button on the Toolbar.

The database contains sixteen records. The sixteenth record is shown in Figure 7-73.

After you have entered all records, you may want to display the first record in the database. To accomplish this, perform the following steps.

TO DISPLAY THE FIRST RECORD IN THE DATABASE ▼

STEP 1 ▶

Point to the first record navigation button on the scroll bar (Figure 7-73).

FIGURE 7-73

STEP 2 ▶

Click the first record navigation button.

Works displays the first record in the database (Figure 7-74).

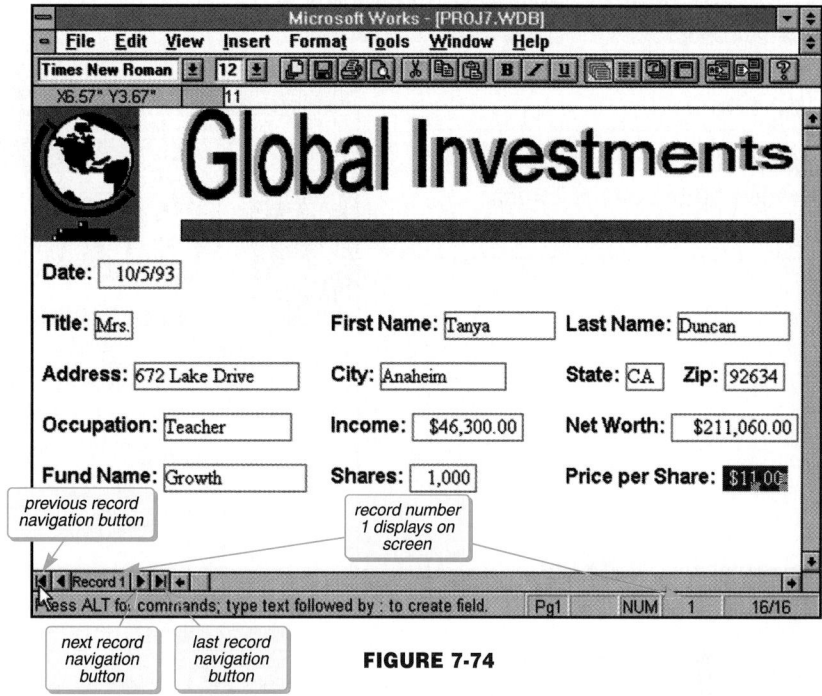

FIGURE 7-74

To move from record to record in the database, you can use the next record navigation button or the previous record navigation button (Figure 7-74). To move to the last record in the database, click the last record navigation button. Works always displays the last record in the database as a blank record. For example, in the database for this project, sixteen records have been entered. If you click the last record navigation button, Works will display the seventeenth record, a blank record.

You can also move to a specific record in the database by selecting the Edit menu and choosing the Go To command. In the Go to text box of the Go To dialog box, enter the record number you want to display and choose the OK button. In the Go To dialog box, you can also select the field you would like to highlight.

▶ LIST VIEW

I n all the examples thus far, you have viewed the database one record at a time in Form view. Works allows you to view multiple records at the same time using **List view**. To display the database in List view, perform the steps on the next page.

TO DISPLAY THE DATABASE IN LIST VIEW ▼

STEP 1 ►

Highlight the Date field. Point to the
List View button on the Toolbar
(Figure 7-75).

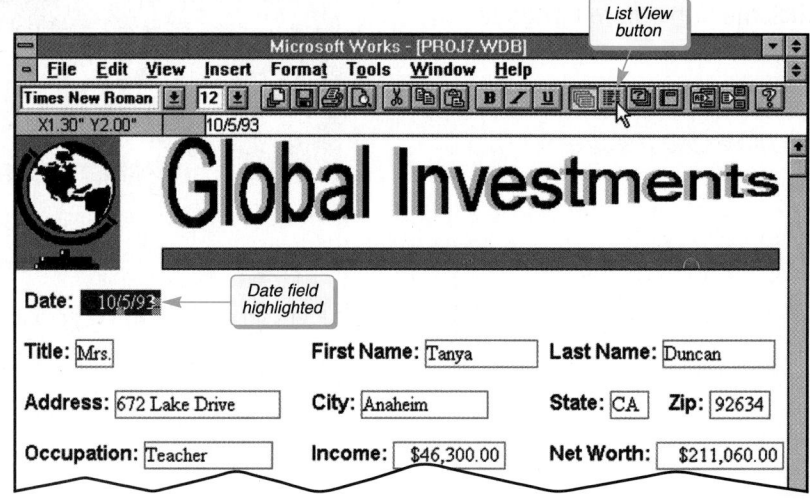

FIGURE 7-75

STEP 2 ►

Click the List View button
on the Toolbar.

Works displays the records in the
database in a grid that resembles
a spreadsheet (Figure 7-76). Note
that by default the type font
changes to Arial and the
point size to 10 in List
view. The field names
identify each column and the
record numbers identify each row.
All sixteen records in the database
are displayed, but each record is
not entirely displayed on the
screen because the records are
too long. Each column in Figure
7-76 is ten positions wide even
though the fields have different
sizes in Form view. Field sizes in
List view and Form view can be
different. Thefield sizes in Figure
7-76 must be adjusted because,
for example,the entire Address
field is not visible. The Date field
for record 1 is highlighted by a
dark border around the field.

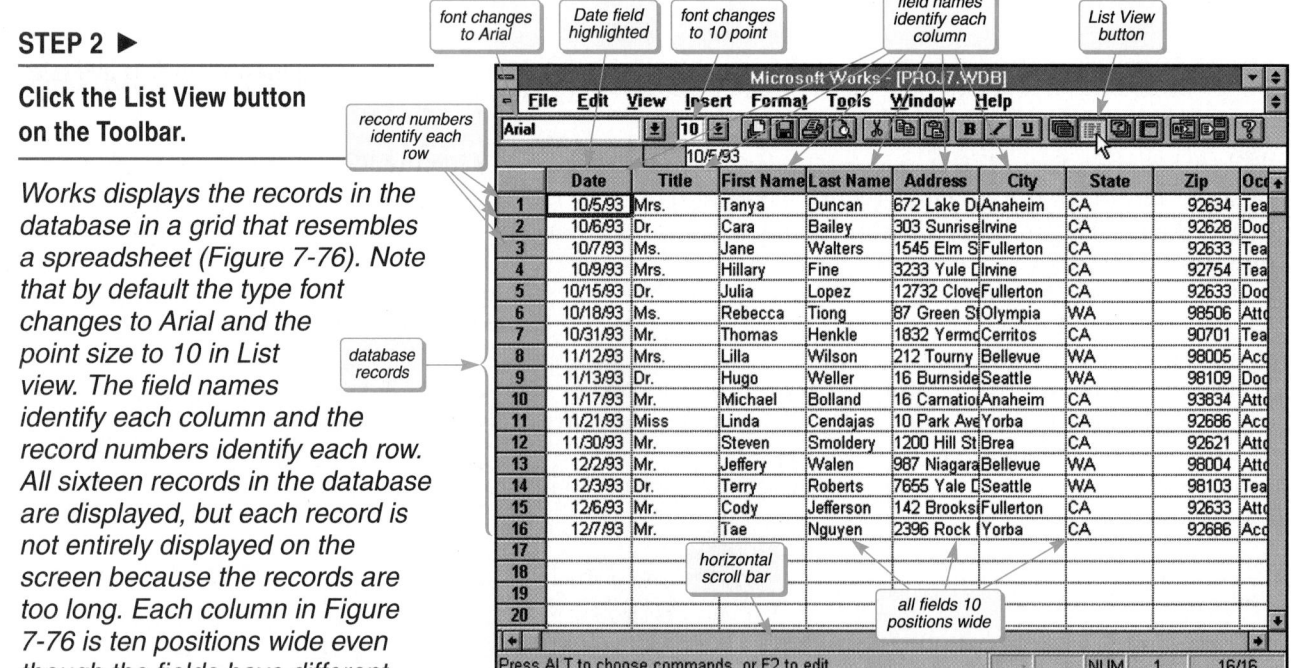

FIGURE 7-76

STEP 3 ▶

Click the horizontal scroll bar one time to display the remainder of each record.

Works displays the rightmost fields in the database records (Figure 7-77). Notice that some values in the Income field and all values in the Net Worth field do not fit in the ten positions-wide columns. These columns must be adjusted to display the values properly.

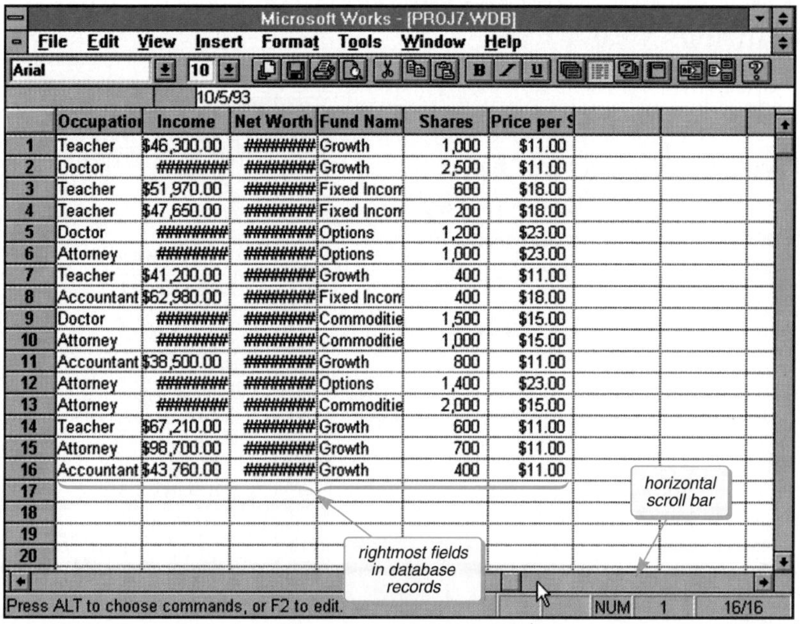

	Occupatio	Income	Net Worth	Fund Nam	Shares	Price per S			
1	Teacher	$46,300.00	########	Growth	1,000	$11.00			
2	Doctor	########	########	Growth	2,500	$11.00			
3	Teacher	$51,970.00	########	Fixed Incom	600	$18.00			
4	Teacher	$47,650.00	########	Fixed Incom	200	$18.00			
5	Doctor	########	########	Options	1,200	$23.00			
6	Attorney	########	########	Options	1,000	$23.00			
7	Teacher	$41,200.00	########	Growth	400	$11.00			
8	Accountant	$62,980.00	########	Fixed Incom	400	$18.00			
9	Doctor	########	########	Commoditie	1,500	$15.00			
10	Attorney	########	########	Commoditie	1,000	$15.00			
11	Accountant	$38,500.00	########	Growth	800	$11.00			
12	Attorney	########	########	Options	1,400	$23.00			
13	Attorney	########	########	Commoditie	2,000	$15.00			
14	Teacher	$67,210.00	########	Growth	600	$11.00			
15	Attorney	$98,700.00	########	Growth	700	$11.00			
16	Accountant	$43,760.00	########	Growth	400	$11.00			

rightmost fields in database records

horizontal scroll bar

Press ALT to choose commands, or F2 to edit.   NUM   1   16/16

FIGURE 7-77

Notice several important factors about the List view of the database. First, even though the field widths of the columns are not the same as the field widths in Form view, the formatting of the data in each field is the same. For example, in Figure 7-77, the Shares values display in the Comma format in the Shares column and the Price per Share values display in the Currency format.

Second, in Figure 7-77 when you clicked the scroll bar, the window display moved to the right one full window. If you click the scroll arrow, the window display moves one column at a time.

Third, when switching from Form view to List view, the record and field highlighted in Form view will be the record and field highlighted in List view. In Figure 7-75, the Date field in record 1 is highlighted. When you change to List view (Figure 7-76), the Date field in record 1 is still highlighted. This process works in the same manner when switching from List view to Form view.

Formatting the Database in List View

When you format the database in List view, you will normally not change the field entry formats, such as Currency or Comma formats. Instead, you normally change the field widths, font sizes, and other factors to accomplish three goals: (1) display the field names in their entirety; (2) display all the data in the fields; and (3) if possible, size the List view so an entire record can print on a single page.

To accomplish these goals you should proceed as follows: (1) change the font size from the default of 10 point to the smaller 8-point size; and (2) arrange the column widths to accomplish the goals. Complete the steps on the next two pages to format the database in List view.

TO CHANGE FONT SIZE ▼

STEP 1 ►

Click the horizontal scroll bar so the first fields in the database display. Select the Edit menu and point to the Select All command (Figure 7-78).

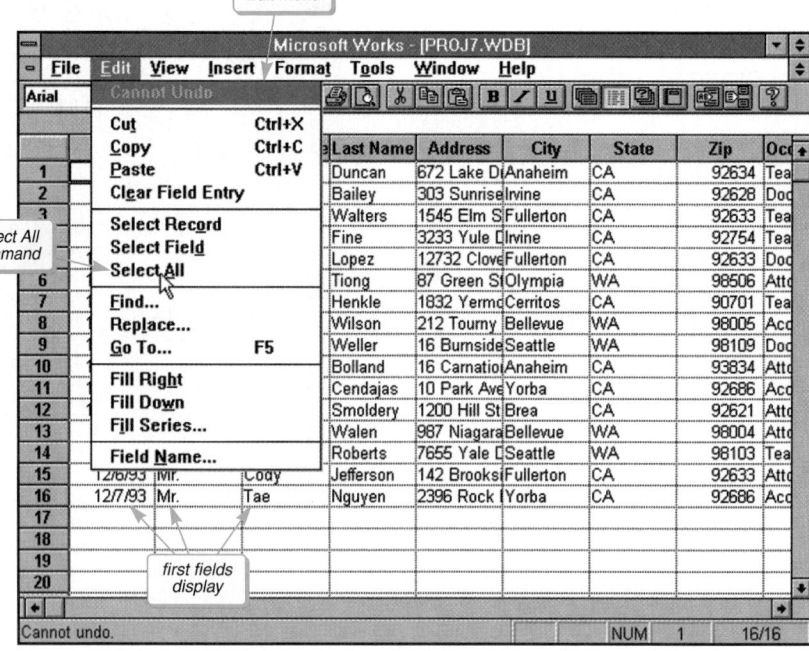

FIGURE 7-78

STEP 2 ►

Choose the Select All command from the Edit menu. Click the Font Size box arrow on the Toolbar. Point to the number 8 in the Font Size drop-down list box.

Works highlights the entire database (Figure 7-79). The Font Size drop-down list box displays and the mouse pointer points to the number 8.

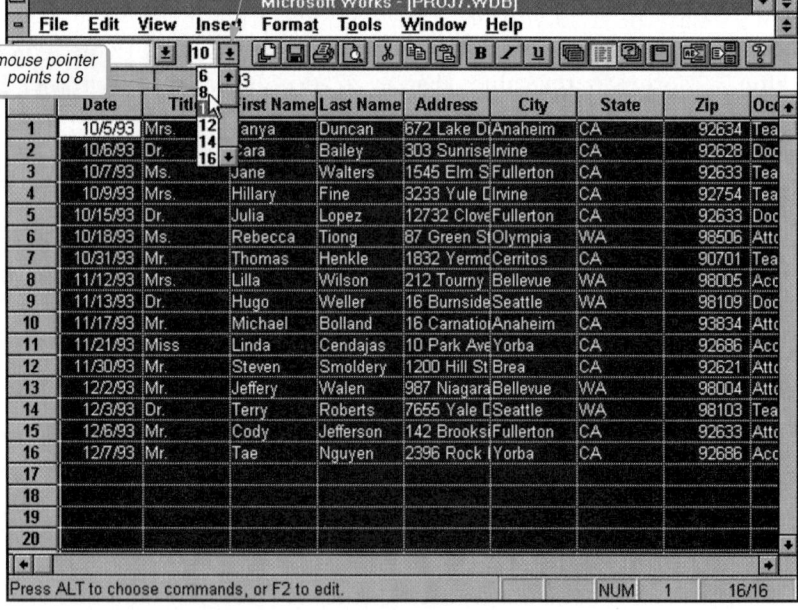

FIGURE 7-79

STEP 3 ▶

Click the left mouse button to select the 8 point font size.

The entire database, including the field names, the record numbers, and the actual data in the database display in 8 point Arial font (Figure 7-80). Eight point font is large enough to be readable but small enough to allow an entire record to print on one page in this project.

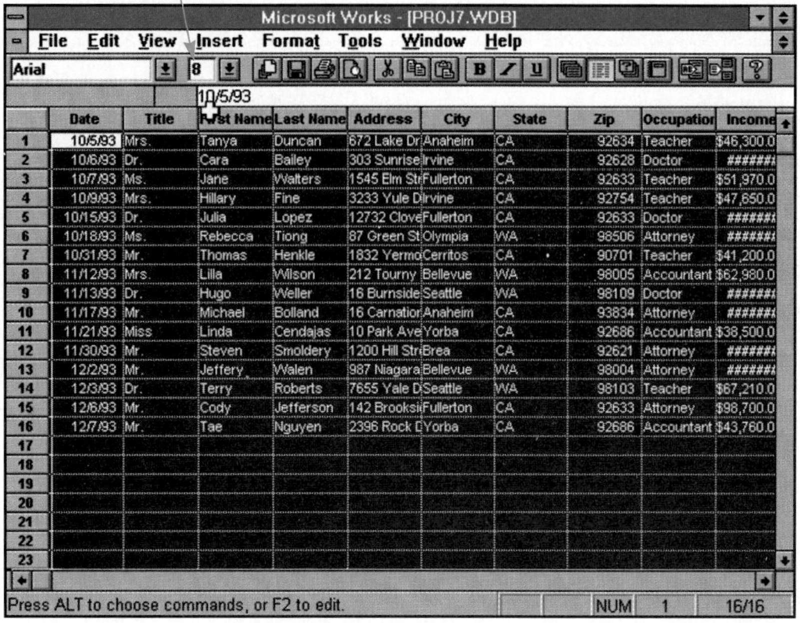

Font Size box contains 8

font size of entries in database changed to 8 point

	Date	Title	First Name	Last Name	Address	City	State	Zip	Occupation	Income
1	10/5/93	Mrs.	Tanya	Duncan	672 Lake Dr	Anaheim	CA	92634	Teacher	$46,300.0
2	10/6/93	Dr.	Cara	Bailey	303 Sunrise	Irvine	CA	92628	Doctor	#######
3	10/7/93	Ms.	Jane	Walters	1545 Elm Str	Fullerton	CA	92633	Teacher	$51,970.0
4	10/9/93	Mrs.	Hillary	Fine	3233 Yule Dr	Irvine	CA	92754	Teacher	$47,650.0
5	10/15/93	Dr.	Julia	Lopez	12732 Clove	Fullerton	CA	92633	Doctor	#######
6	10/18/93	Ms.	Rebecca	Tiong	87 Green St	Olympia	WA	98506	Attorney	#######
7	10/31/93	Mr.	Thomas	Henkle	1832 Yerma	Cerritos	CA	90701	Teacher	$41,200.0
8	11/12/93	Mrs.	Lilla	Wilson	212 Tourny	Bellevue	WA	98005	Accountant	$62,980.0
9	11/13/93	Dr.	Hugo	Weller	16 Burnside	Seattle	WA	98109	Doctor	#######
10	11/17/93	Mr.	Michael	Bolland	16 Carnation	Anaheim	CA	93834	Attorney	#######
11	11/21/93	Miss	Linda	Cendajas	10 Park Ave	Yorba	CA	92686	Accountant	$38,500.0
12	11/30/93	Mr.	Steven	Smoldery	1200 Hill Str	Brea	CA	92621	Attorney	#######
13	12/2/93	Mr.	Jeffery	Walen	987 Niagara	Bellevue	WA	98004	Attorney	#######
14	12/3/93	Dr.	Terry	Roberts	7655 Yale D	Seattle	WA	98103	Teacher	$67,210.0
15	12/6/93	Mr.	Cody	Jefferson	142 Brooksi	Fullerton	CA	92633	Attorney	$98,700.0
16	12/7/93	Mr.	Tae	Nguyen	2396 Rock D	Yorba	CA	92686	Accountant	$43,760.0

Press ALT to choose commands, or F2 to edit.   NUM   1   16/16

FIGURE 7-80

Setting Field Widths

The next step is to set the field widths for each of the fields in List view. Recall that the field widths set in List view will not necessarily be the same as those in Form view and changing the List view field widths will have no effect on the Form view field widths.

Setting field widths in List view may involve some experimentation to determine the proper widths to show the field names, show all data in all records, and yet keep the field widths to a minimum. Table 7-3 shows the field widths for the List view of the database.

▶ **TABLE 7-3**

FIELD NAME	FIELD WIDTH	FIELD NAME	FIELD WIDTH
Date	8	Zip	6
Title	5	Occupation	11
First Name	10	Income	12
Last Name	10	Net Worth	13
Address	16	Fund Name	11
City	8	Shares	7
State	5	Price per Share	15

You can set the field widths using either the **Field Width command** from the Format menu or by dragging the field border. Also, double-clicking the field name will apply the Best Fit feature of Works to the field. The method of changing field width using the Field Width command from the Format menu is shown in the steps on the next two pages.

TO SET FIELD WIDTHS IN LIST VIEW USING THE FIELD WIDTH COMMAND ▼

STEP 1 ▶

Highlight the Date field in any of the records by clicking the field. Then, select the Format menu from the menu bar and point to the Field Width command (Figure 7-81).

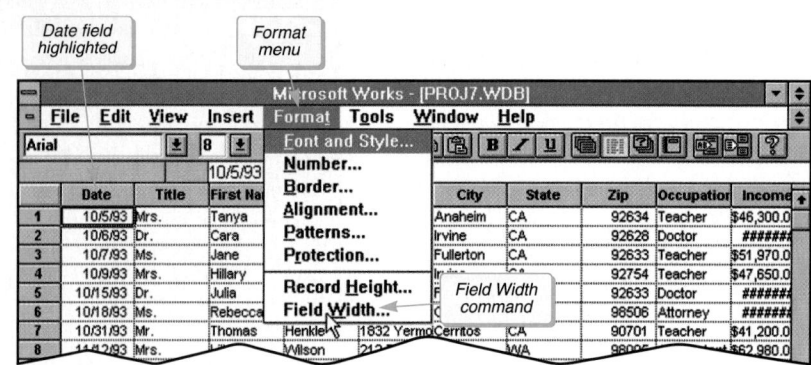

FIGURE 7-81

STEP 2 ▶

Choose the Field Width command from the Format menu. Type 8 in the Width text box and point to the OK button.

Works displays the Field Width dialog box (Figure 7-82). The number 8 displays in the Width text box and the mouse pointer points to the OK button.

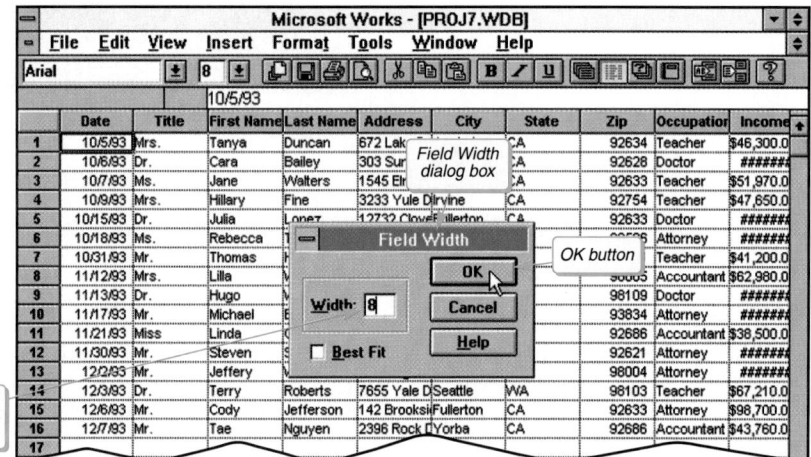

FIGURE 7-82

STEP 3 ▶

Choose the OK button in the Field Width dialog box.

Works changes the width of the Date field to 8 (Figure 7-83). All the values fit within the field.

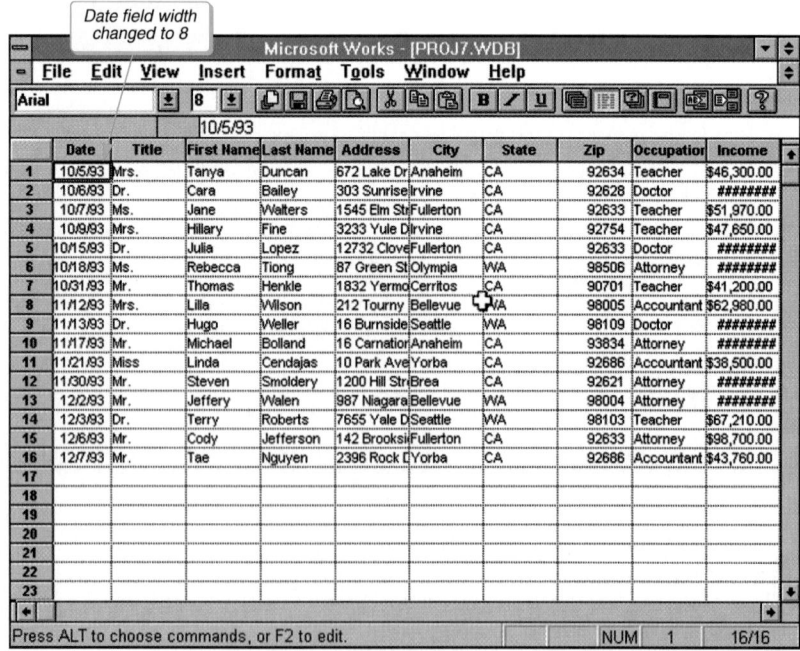

FIGURE 7-83

STEP 4 ▶

Using the techniques shown in Steps 1 through 3, set the remainder of the field columns to their proper widths as specified in Table 7-3 on page W7.47.

After setting the field sizes, each of the fields is just wide enough to display both the field name and all the data in each field (Figure 7-84).

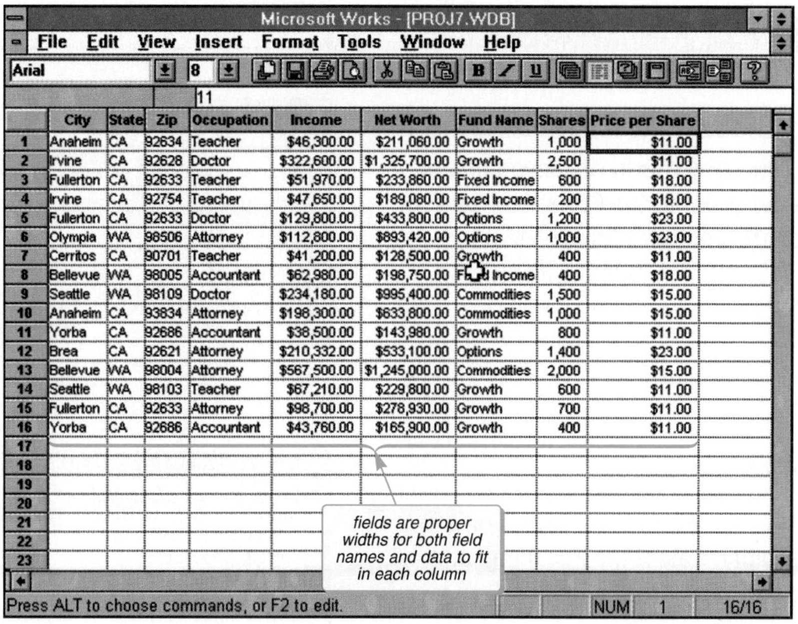

FIGURE 7-84

As previously stated, you can also drag the border to change the field width or use the Best Fit feature of Works. The method you choose when specifying the field width depends on your preference. Using the Field Width command from the Format menu is slower than dragging but you can specify the exact field width. Dragging allows you to see the actual field width, but because Works does not display the field width on the screen, the only way to determine the exact width is using the Field Width command from the Format menu.

Formatting the database in List view is now complete. Once the database is formatted, you should once again save the database. To save the database on drive A using the same filename (PROJ7.WDB), click the Save button on the Toolbar.

▶ PRINTING THE DATABASE

T he next step is to print the database. You can print the database from either Form view or List view. When you print from Form view, you will normally see one record per page, with the record appearing in the same format as it displays on the screen. When you print from List view, you can view up to twenty-three entire records per page, assuming the record is not too long to fit on one page. The next section of this project describes the steps to print the database from both Form view and List view.

Printing the Database in Form View

To print in Form view, you must first display the database in Form view on the screen. Then, after setting some choices for how the database should print, click the Print button on the Toolbar or choose the Print command from the File menu to print the database. The steps to perform these tasks are presented on the following pages.

TO PRINT A DATABASE IN FORM VIEW ▼

STEP 1 ►

If the database is displayed in List view, point to the Form View button on the Toolbar (Figure 7-85).

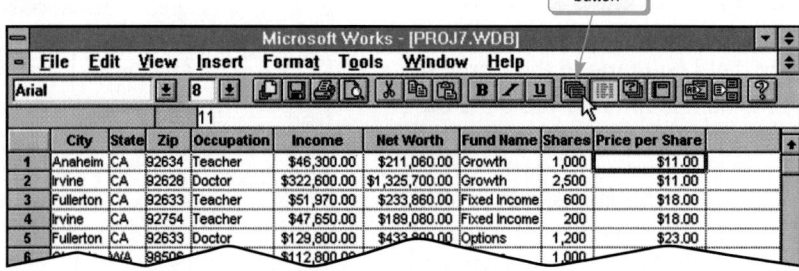

FIGURE 7-85

STEP 2 ►

Click the Form View button on the Toolbar. Select the File menu and point to the Print command.

Works displays the database in Form View (Figure 7-86). The record number displayed and the field highlighted will be the same as when the database was displayed in List view unless another field is selected.
The File menu displays and the mouse pointer points to the Print command.

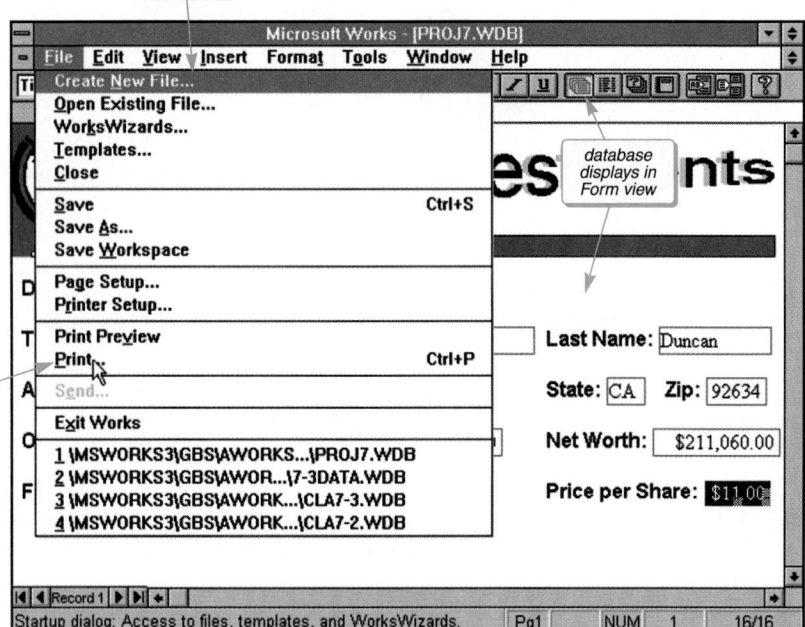

FIGURE 7-86

STEP 3 ►

Choose the Print command from the File menu. Make the appropriate entries in the Print dialog box, and then point to the OK button.

Works displays the Print dialog box (Figure 7-87). Make sure the All option button is selected. The mouse pointer points to the OK button.

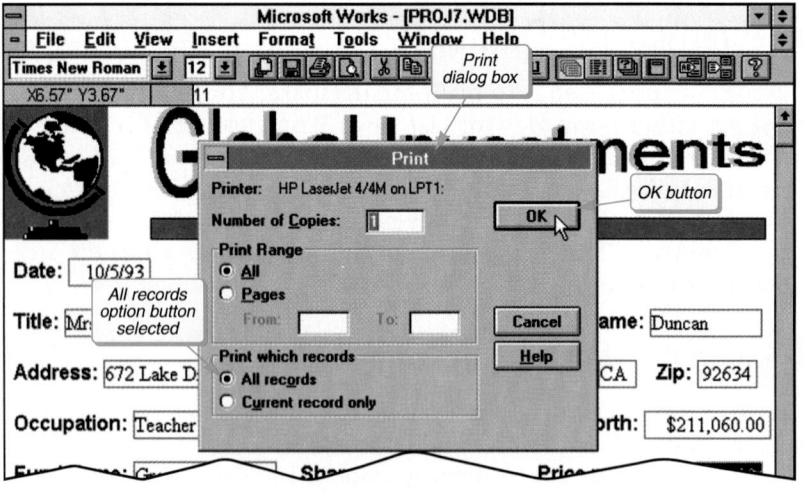

FIGURE 7-87

STEP 4 ▶

Choose the OK button in the Print dialog box.

The Form view records print (Figure 7-88).

FIGURE 7-88

If you know all the entries in the Print dialog box are properly set for printing, you can click the Print button on the Toolbar in place of Steps 2, 3, and 4 on the previous page.

Printing a Single Record in Form View

When working with Form view, you may want to print a single record. To print a single record, such as record 5, perform the following steps.

TO PRINT A SINGLE RECORD IN FORM VIEW ▼

STEP 1 ▶

Select the Edit menu and point to the Go To command (Figure 7-89).

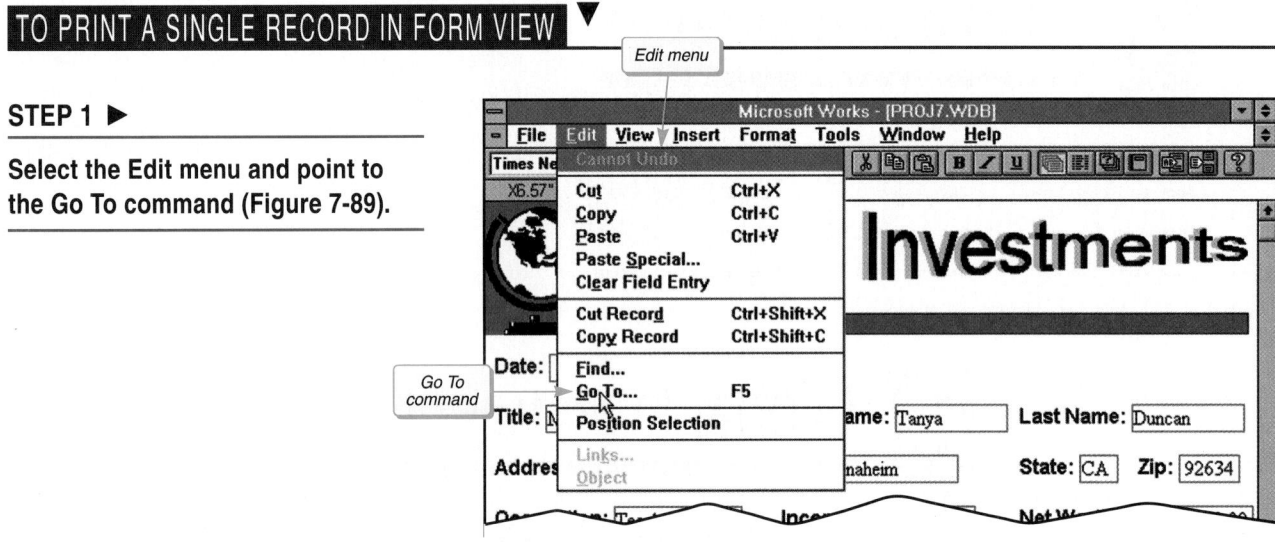

Edit menu

Go To command

FIGURE 7-89

STEP 2 ▶

Choose the Go To command. Type the number 5 in the Go to text box of the Go To dialog box, and then point to the OK button.

The Go To dialog box displays (Figure 7-90). The number 5 displays in the Go to text box, and the mouse pointer points to the OK button.

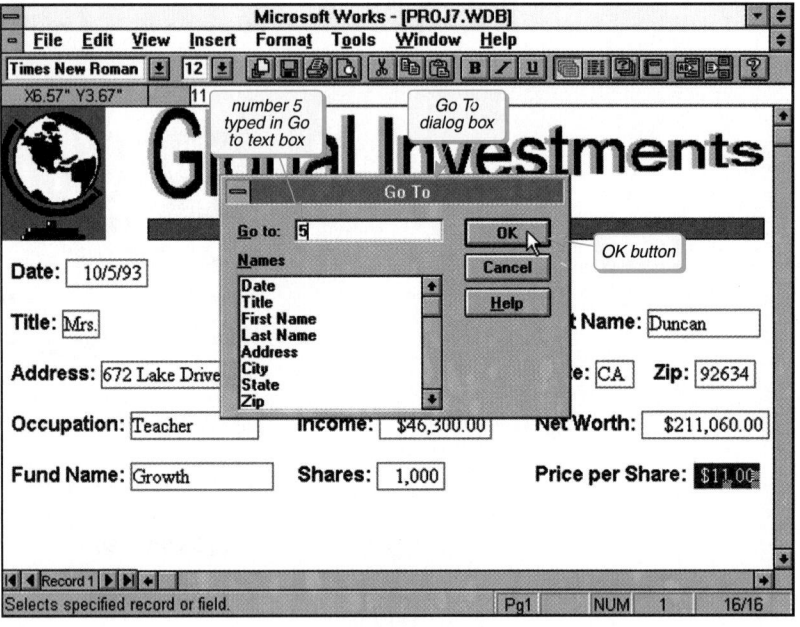

number 5 typed in Go to text box

Go To dialog box

OK button

FIGURE 7-90

STEP 3 ▶

Choose the OK button in the Go To dialog box. Select the File Menu and point to the Print command.

Record 5 displays in Form view (Figure 7-91). The File menu displays and the mouse pointer points to the Print command.

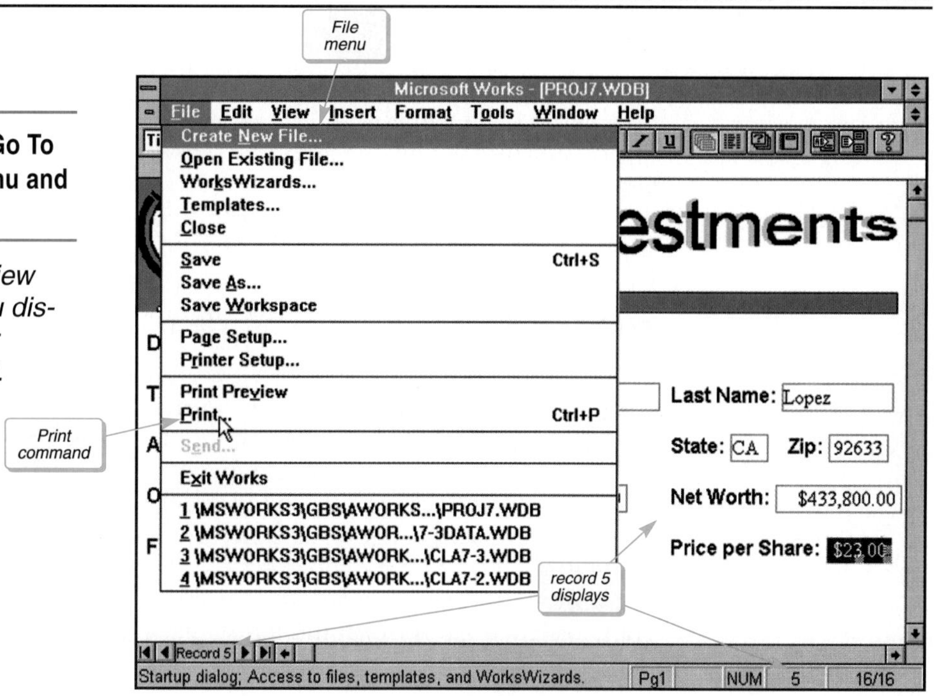

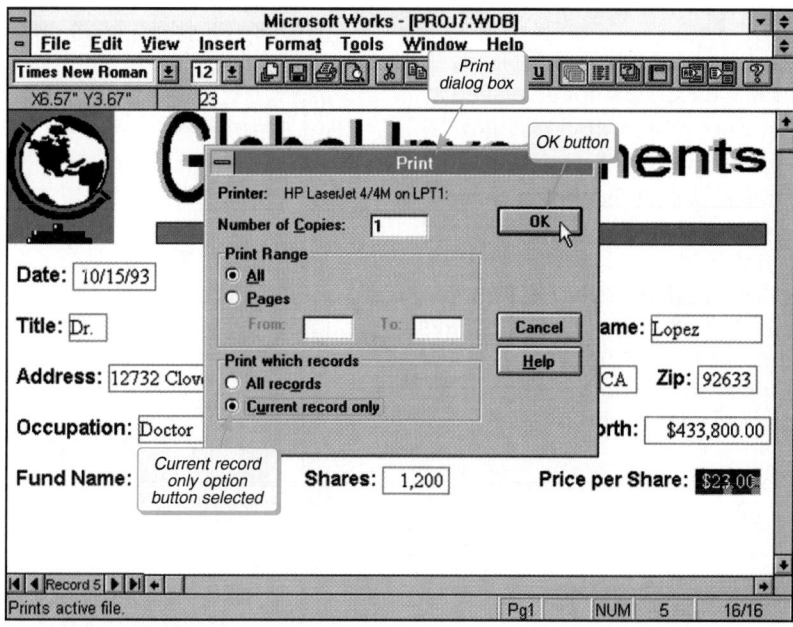

FIGURE 7-91

STEP 4 ▶

Choose the Print command from the File menu. When the Print dialog box displays, select the Current record only option button in the Print which records area. Point to the OK button.

The Print dialog box displays (Figure 7-92). The Current record only option button is selected and the mouse pointer points to the OK button.

STEP 5 ▶

Choose the OK button in the Print dialog box.

Record 5 in Form view will print on the printer.

FIGURE 7-92

You have additional control over how Form view records print by using the Page Setup command on the File menu. The dialog box that displays when using this command contains settings that allow you to control the printing of Field Lines and Field Entries.

It is also possible to print records in List view. The method to do this is explained in the following paragraphs.

Printing the Database in List View

Printing the database in List view allows you to print multiple records on one page. One of the concerns when printing in List view is to ensure the entire record fits on a single page. You can use the Print Preview feature of Works to determine if the record fits on one page. In this project, you must print the database using Landscape orientation in order to fit the entire record on a single page. Recall that to print using Landscape orientation, you must select Landscape orientation in the Page Setup dialog box.

To use Print Preview and then print the List view of the database using Landscape orientation, perform the following steps.

TO PRINT A DATABASE IN LIST VIEW ▼

STEP 1 ►

If the database is not displayed in List view, display it in List view by clicking the List View button on the Toolbar. Select the File menu and point to the Page Setup command.

Works displays the database in List view, the File menu displays, and the mouse pointer points to the Page Setup command (Figure 7-93).

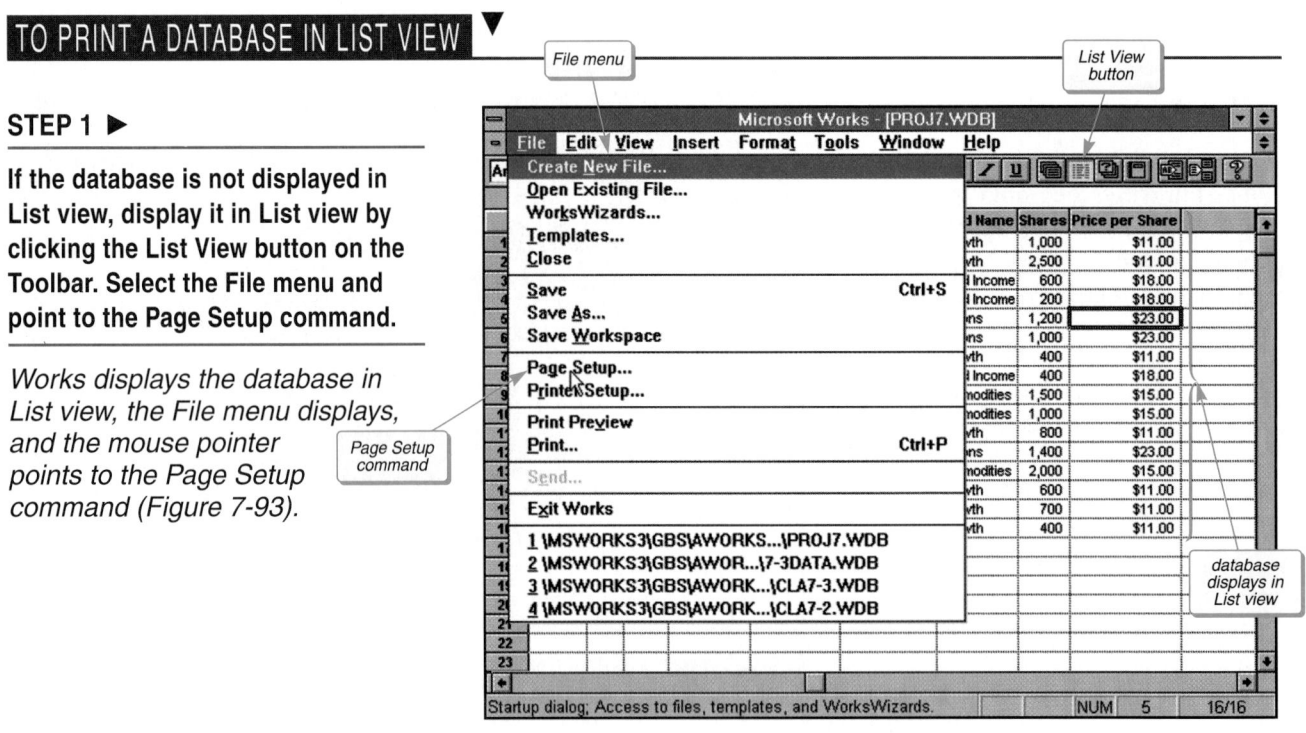

FIGURE 7-93

STEP 2 ►

Choose the Page Setup command from the File menu. When the Page Setup dialog box displays, select the Source, Size and Orientation tab. Select the Landscape option button in the Orientation area and point to the Other Options tab.

Works displays the Page Setup dialog box (Figure 7-94). Works automatically enters 11" in the Width text box and 8.5" in the Height text box when the Landscape option button is selected. The Sample section illustrates landscape orientation. The mouse pointer points to the Other Options tab.

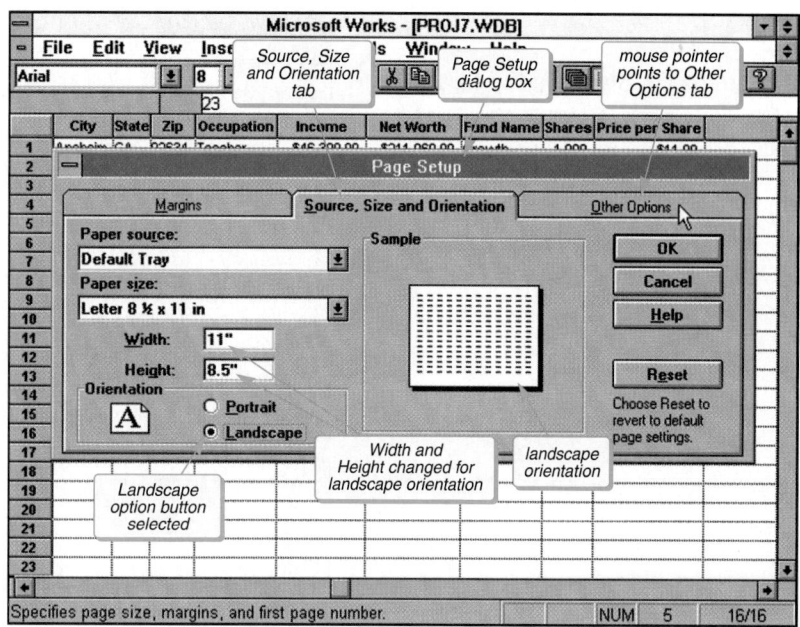

FIGURE 7-94

STEP 3 ►

Select the Other Options tab. When the Other Options screen displays, select the Print records and field labels check box, and then point to the OK button.

The Other Options screen displays (Figure 7-95). The Print record and field labels check box is selected, which means both the record numbers and the field labels will display on the report. If you leave this box unselected, only the field entries will appear on the report.

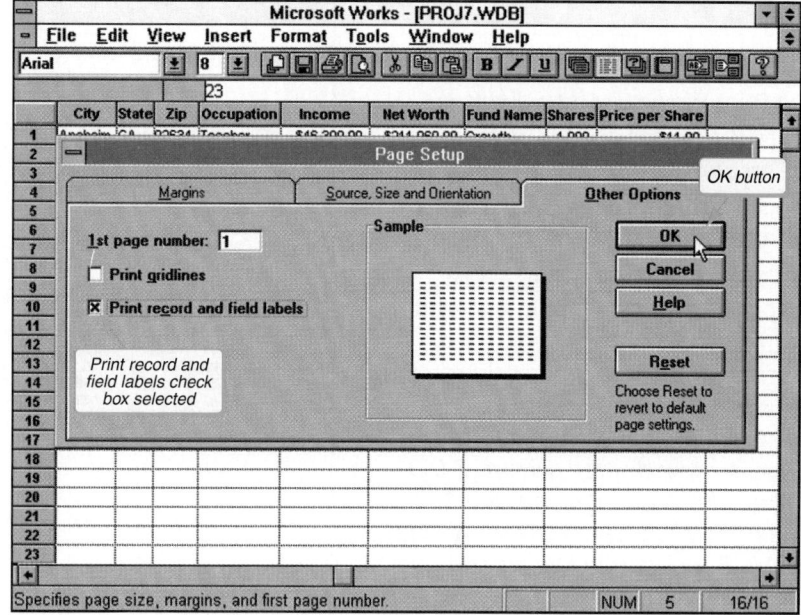

FIGURE 7-95

STEP 4 ►

Choose the OK button in the Page Setup dialog box. Point to the Print Preview button on the Toolbar.

The List view of the database displays and the mouse pointer points to the Print Preview button (Figure 7-96).

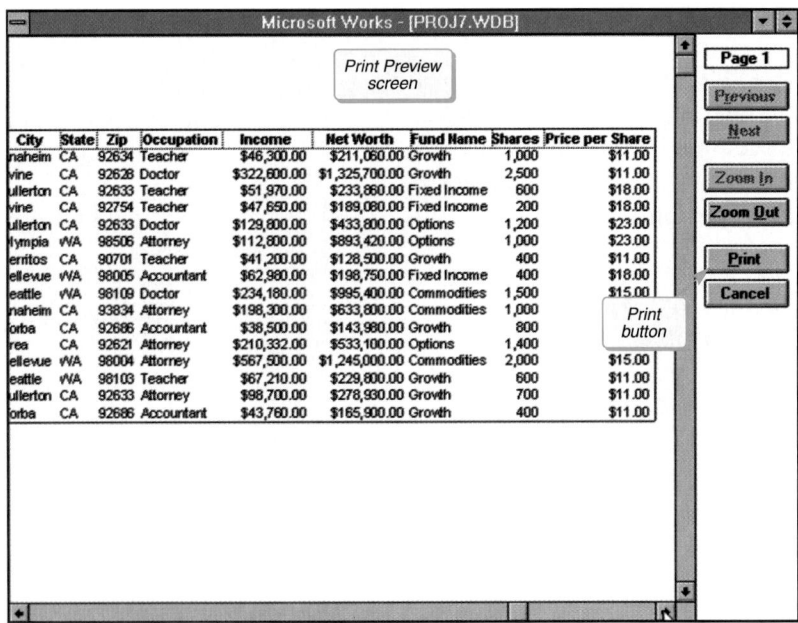

Print Preview button

	City	State	Zip	Occupation	Income	Net Worth	Fund Name	Shares	Price per Share
1	Anaheim	CA	92634	Teacher	$46,300.00	$211,060.00	Growth	1,000	$11.00
2	Irvine	CA	92628	Doctor	$322,600.00	$1,325,700.00	Growth	2,500	$11.00
3	Fullerton	CA	92633	Teacher	$51,970.00	$233,860.00	Fixed Income	600	$18.00
4	Irvine	CA	92754	Teacher	$47,650.00	$189,080.00	Fixed Income	200	$18.00
5	Fullerton	CA	92633	Doctor	$129,800.00	$433,800.00	Options	1,200	$23.00
6	Olympia	WA	98506	Attorney	$112,800.00	$893,420.00	Options	1,000	$23.00
7	Cerritos	CA	90701	Teacher	$41,200.00	$128,500.00	Growth	400	$11.00
8	Bellevue	WA	98005	Accountant	$62,980.00	$198,750.00	Fixed Income	400	$18.00
9	Seattle	WA	98109	Doctor	$234,180.00	$995,400.00	Commodities	1,500	$15.00
10	Anaheim	CA	93834	Attorney	$198,300.00	$633,800.00	Commodities	1,000	$15.00
11	Yorba	CA	92686	Accountant	$38,500.00	$143,980.00	Growth	800	$11.00
12	Brea	CA	92621	Attorney	$210,332.00	$533,100.00	Options	1,400	$23.00
13	Bellevue	WA	98004	Attorney	$567,500.00	$1,245,000.00	Commodities	2,000	$15.00
14	Seattle	WA	98103	Teacher	$67,210.00	$229,800.00	Growth	600	$11.00
15	Fullerton	CA	92633	Attorney	$98,700.00	$278,930.00	Growth	700	$11.00
16	Yorba	CA	92686	Accountant	$43,760.00	$165,900.00	Growth	400	$11.00

Press ALT to choose commands, or F2 to edit.   NUM   5   16/16

FIGURE 7-96

STEP 5 ►

Click the Print Preview button. When the Print Preview screen displays, place the mouse pointer on the report screen and click the left mouse button two times to magnify the view of the database. Scroll left and right to ensure the database displays properly. Point to the Print button.

Works magnifies the report to approximately the same size as the List view display (Figure 7-97). From this report you can see that the Price per Share field fits on the page. Because the Price per Share field is the rightmost field in the List view of the database and all the other fields are to the left, this means the entire record fits on one page.

Microsoft Works - [PROJ7.WDB]

Print Preview screen

City	State	Zip	Occupation	Income	Net Worth	Fund Name	Shares	Price per Share
naheim	CA	92634	Teacher	$46,300.00	$211,060.00	Growth	1,000	$11.00
vine	CA	92628	Doctor	$322,600.00	$1,325,700.00	Growth	2,500	$11.00
ullerton	CA	92633	Teacher	$51,970.00	$233,860.00	Fixed Income	600	$18.00
vine	CA	92754	Teacher	$47,650.00	$189,080.00	Fixed Income	200	$18.00
ullerton	CA	92633	Doctor	$129,800.00	$433,800.00	Options	1,200	$23.00
lympia	WA	98506	Attorney	$112,800.00	$893,420.00	Options	1,000	$23.00
erritos	CA	90701	Teacher	$41,200.00	$128,500.00	Growth	400	$11.00
ellevue	WA	98005	Accountant	$62,980.00	$198,750.00	Fixed Income	400	$18.00
eattle	WA	98109	Doctor	$234,180.00	$995,400.00	Commodities	1,500	$15.00
naheim	CA	93834	Attorney	$198,300.00	$633,800.00	Commodities	1,000	
orba	CA	92686	Accountant	$38,500.00	$143,980.00	Growth	800	
rea	CA	92621	Attorney	$210,332.00	$533,100.00	Options	1,400	
ellevue	WA	98004	Attorney	$567,500.00	$1,245,000.00	Commodities	2,000	$15.00
eattle	WA	98103	Teacher	$67,210.00	$229,800.00	Growth	600	$11.00
ullerton	CA	92633	Attorney	$98,700.00	$278,930.00	Growth	700	$11.00
orba	CA	92686	Accountant	$43,760.00	$165,900.00	Growth	400	$11.00

Page 1
Previous
Next
Zoom In
Zoom Out
Print
Cancel

Print button

FIGURE 7-97

STEP 6 ▼

Click the Print button in the Print Preview screen.

When you click the Print button in the Print Preview screen, Works momentarily displays the Printing dialog box, and then prints the report (Figure 7-98). Notice the entire database fits on one page.

	Date	Title	First Name	Last Name	Address	City	State	Zip	Occupation	Income	Net Worth	Fund Name	Shares	Price per Share
1	10/5/93	Mrs.	Tanya	Duncan	672 Lake Drive	Anaheim	CA	92634	Teacher	$46,300.00	$211,060.00	Growth	1,000	$11.00
2	10/6/93	Dr.	Cara	Bailey	303 Sunrise Place	Irvine	CA	92628	Doctor	$322,600.00	$1,325,700.00	Growth	2,500	$11.00
3	10/7/93	Ms.	Jane	Walters	1545 Elm Street	Fullerton	CA	92633	Teacher	$51,970.00	$233,860.00	Fixed Income	600	$18.00
4	10/9/93	Mrs.	Hillary	Fine	3233 Yule Drive	Irvine	CA	92754	Teacher	$47,650.00	$189,080.00	Fixed Income	200	$18.00
5	10/15/93	Dr.	Julia	Lopez	12732 Clover Road	Fullerton	CA	92633	Doctor	$129,800.00	$433,800.00	Options	1,200	$23.00
6	10/18/93	Ms.	Rebecca	Tiong	87 Green Street	Olympia	WA	98506	Attorney	$112,800.00	$893,420.00	Options	1,000	$23.00
7	10/31/93	Mr.	Thomas	Henkle	1832 Yermo Place	Cerritos	CA	90701	Teacher	$41,200.00	$128,500.00	Growth	400	$11.00
8	11/12/93	Mrs.	Lilla	Wilson	212 Tourny Street	Bellevue	WA	98005	Accountant	$62,980.00	$198,750.00	Fixed Income	400	$18.00
9	11/13/93	Dr.	Hugo	Weller	16 Burnside Drive	Seattle	WA	98109	Doctor	$234,180.00	$995,400.00	Commodities	1,500	$15.00
10	11/17/93	Mr.	Michael	Bolland	16 Carnation Way	Anaheim	CA	93834	Attorney	$198,300.00	$633,800.00	Commodities	1,000	$15.00
11	11/21/93	Miss	Linda	Cendajas	10 Park Avenue	Yorba	CA	92686	Accountant	$38,500.00	$143,980.00	Growth	800	$11.00
12	11/30/93	Mr.	Steven	Smoldery	1200 Hill Street	Brea	CA	92621	Attorney	$210,332.00	$533,100.00	Options	1,400	$23.00
13	12/2/93	Mr.	Jeffery	Walen	987 Niagara Lane	Bellevue	WA	98004	Attorney	$567,500.00	$1,245,000.00	Commodities	2,000	$15.00
14	12/3/93	Dr.	Terry	Roberts	7655 Yale Drive	Seattle	WA	98103	Teacher	$67,210.00	$229,800.00	Growth	600	$11.00
15	12/6/93	Mr.	Cody	Jefferson	142 Brookside Way	Fullerton	CA	92633	Attorney	$98,700.00	$278,930.00	Growth	700	$11.00
16	12/7/93	Mr.	Tae	Nguyen	2396 Rock Drive	Yorba	CA	92686	Accountant	$43,760.00	$165,900.00	Growth	400	$11.00

FIGURE 7-98

▶ EXITING WORKS

fter you have completed your work on the database, you can close the database file by choosing the Close command from the File menu, or you can exit works by choosing the Exit Works command from the File menu.

▶ PROJECT SUMMARY

In this project, you learned to define the structure of a database using the Works Database tool. Using WordArt, you entered the database title. In Form view, you entered field names, moved the fields to an appropriate location, formatted the field names, inserted clip art and a rectangle, and added color. Using techniques you learned in an earlier project, you saved the database on disk. Then you entered data into the database and formatted the data. Switching to the List view of the database, you specified the field widths for the fields. Finally, you printed the database using both Form view and List view.

▶ KEY TERMS

clip art *(W7.21)*
ClipArt command *(W7.22)*
database *(W7.3)*
database structure *(W7.4)*
Fade Right *(W7.25)*
field *(W7.3)*
field entry *(W7.8)*
field name *(W7.8)*
Field Lines command *(W7.33)*
Field Width command *(W7.47)*
Form view *(W7.5)*
Insert Field button *(W7.16)*

insertion point *(W7.6)*
label *(W7.7)*
List view *(W7.43)*
mouse pointer *(W7.6)*
navigation buttons *(W7.6)*
Patterns command *(W7.31)*
Picture/Object command *(W7.23)*
Position Selection command *(W7.21)*
record *(W7.3)*

Rectangle command *(W7.28)*
scroll bar *(W7.6)*
Shadow button *(W7.25)*
Shape drop-down list box *(W7.25)*
status bar *(W7.7)*
Stretch button *(W7.25)*
width of the field *(W7.47)*
WordArt *(W7.7, W7.10)*
WordArt command *(W7.10)*
X-Y coordinates *(W7.6)*

Q U I C K   R E F E R E N C E

In Microsoft Works, you can accomplish a task in a number of ways. The following table provides a quick reference to each task presented in this project with its available options. The commands listed in the Menu column can be executed using either the keyboard or the mouse

Task	Mouse	Menu	Keyboard Shortcuts
Cancel Field Entry	Click Cancel box in formula bar		Press ESC
Cancel Field Name	Click Cancel box in formula bar		Press ESC
Cancel Label	Click Cancel box in formula bar		Press ESC
Change Font	Click Font Name box arrow	From Format menu, choose Font and Style	
Change Font Size	Click Font Size box arrow	From Format menu, choose Font and Style	
Change Size of Field in Form View	Drag Field Size box	From Format menu, choose Field Size	
Change Width of Field in List View	Drag column border	From Format menu, choose Field Width	
Display First Record in Form View	Click first record navigation button	From Edit menu, choose Go To	
Display Last Record in Form View	Click last record navigation button	From Edit menu, choose Go To	
Display Next Record in Form View	Click next page navigation button	From Edit menu, choose Go To	
Display Previous Record in Form View	Click previous page navigation button	From Edit menu, choose Go To	
Enter Field Entry	Click Enter box in formula bar		Press ENTER, or press TAB, or press an arrow key

Task	Mouse	Menu	Keyboard Shortcuts
Enter Field Name	Click Enter box in formula bar		Press ENTER, or press TAB, or press an arrow key
Enter Label	Click Enter box in formula bar		Press ENTER, or press TAB, or press an arrow key
Enter Edit Mode	Click formula bar		Press F2
Format Field Entry	Click appropriate button on Toolbar	From Format menu, choose Number	Press CTRL+ appropriate key
Format Field Name	Click appropriate button on Toolbar	From Format menu, choose Font and Style	Press CTRL+ appropriate key
Format Label	Click appropriate button on Toolbar	From Format menu, choose Font and Style	Press CTRL+ appropriate key
Highlight Field	Click field		Press TAB if field highlighted
Highlight Name	Click field name		Press arrow keys
Highlight Label	Click label		Press arrow keys
Insert clip art		From Insert menu, choose ClipArt	
Insert WordArt		From Insert menu, choose WordArt	
Insert Rectangle		From Insert menu, choose Rectangle	
Position Field	Drag field name and field		
Position Field Name	Drag field name		
Position Label	Drag label		
Position Insertion Point	Click new location		Press arrow keys
Print Database in Form View	Click Print button	From File menu, choose Print	Press CTRL+P
Print Database in List View	Click Print button	From File menu, choose Print	Press CTRL+P
Switch to Form View	Click Form View button	From View menu, choose Form	Press F9
Switch to List View	Click List View button	From View menu, choose List	Press F9

STUDENT ASSIGNMENT 1
True/False

Instructions: Circle T if the statement is true or F if the statement is false.

T F 1. To create a new database, choose the Database button in the Startup dialog box.

T F 2. When you open a new database, Works automatically displays List view.

T F 3. Information in a database is divided into records and characters.

T F 4. A record is the name given to all the information in a database about one person, product, or event.

T F 5. Form view displays your database one record at a time.

T F 6. A field consists of a field name and the information you type into the field, called the field entry.

T F 7. WordArt must be used for field names.

T F 8. You can specify a maximum of twenty fields in a database.

T F 9. Each field entry in a database can contain up to 256 characters.

T F 10. You create a field name anywhere in Form view by typing a name for the field followed by a colon.

T F 11. You can use the same field name at several places in Form view.

T F 12. A field name can contain up to fifteen characters including the colon.

T F 13. When using the Works Database tool, the default field size is twenty positions wide and one-- inch high.

T F 14. You cannot display a multiple-line field.

T F 15. To move from one field to the next field, press the SHIFT+ENTER keys.

T F 16. Pressing the TAB key when a field entry is highlighted will cause the next field name on the form to be highlighted.

T F 17. List view displays multiple records on the screen at one time.

T F 18. When you print a database in Form view, you can choose to print a single record.

T F 19. When you print a database in List view, you can choose to print gridlines and to print record and field labels.

T F 20. To print records in List view, you must use landscape orientation.

STUDENT ASSIGNMENT 2
Multiple Choice

Instructions: Circle the correct response.

1. In a Works database, you can enter up to _____ records in the database.
   a. 20
   b. 256
   c. 32,000
   d. 4 million

2. Information in a database is divided into _____.
   a. records and fields
   b. fields and characters
   c. files and fields
   d. Form view and List view

3. You can define up to _____ fields in a database.
   a. 20
   b. 256
   c. 32,000
   d. 4 million
4. A field name may consist of up to _____.
   a. 256 characters followed by a colon
   b. 15 characters followed by a colon
   c. 20 characters followed by a colon
   d. 15 characters followed by five dotted lines for the field entry
5. When you define a field in Form view, the proposed field size is _____ positions.
   a. 8
   b. 12
   c. 15
   d. 20
6. When you have entered information into a field entry and you need to move to the next field entry, press _____.
   a. SHIFT+ENTER
   b. SHIFT+TAB
   c. TAB
   d. SPACEBAR
7. In a field entry you can enter _____.
   a. text only
   b. text or numbers only
   c. text, numbers, or a label
   d. none of the above
8. To move from the last record in the Form view of the database to the first record in the Form view of the database, _____.
   a. press the TAB key
   b. click the first record navigation button
   c. click the List View button
   d. click the vertical up scroll arrow
9. When using the database in List view, Works _____.
   a. displays fields in a record horizontally on the screen
   b. lets you view multiple records at a time
   c. lets you view the entire database on a single screen
   d. both a and c
10. When you print a database in Form view, _____.
   a. you must print all records
   b. you can print only the record in the screen window
   c. you can print all records or any single record
   d. you can choose to print all records in the database on one page

STUDENT ASSIGNMENT 3
Understanding Form View

Instructions: In the database screen shown in Figure SA7-3, arrows point to the major parts of a record displayed in Form view. Identify the parts of the database record in the spaces provided.

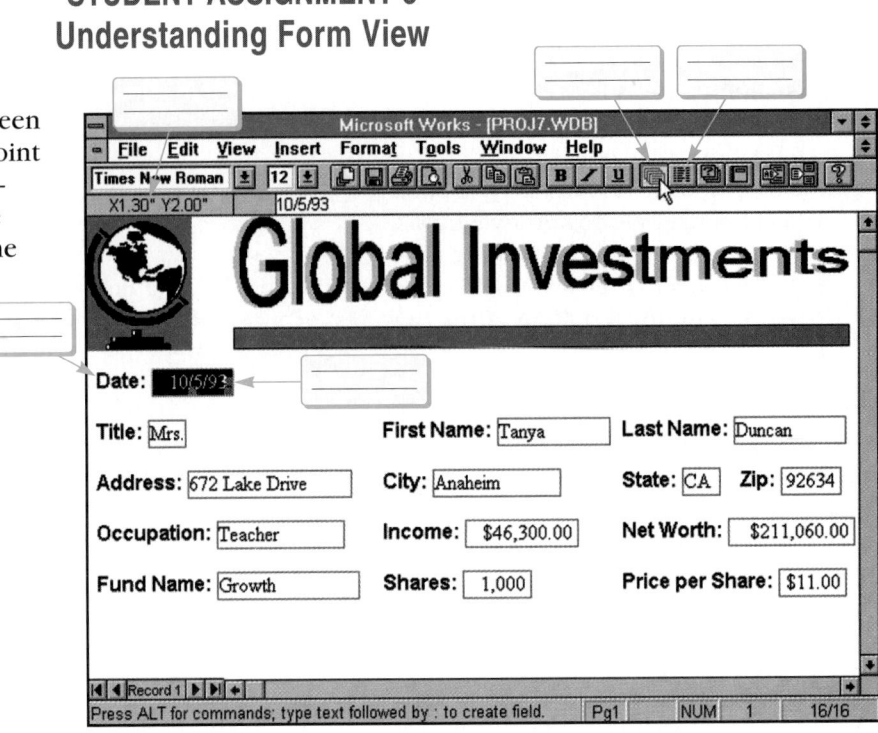

FIGURE SA7-3

STUDENT ASSIGNMENT 4
Understanding the Navigation Buttons

Instructions: Figure SA7-4 shows the navigation buttons used with the Form view of the database. In the spaces provided, briefly explain the function of the buttons identified by the pointing arrows.

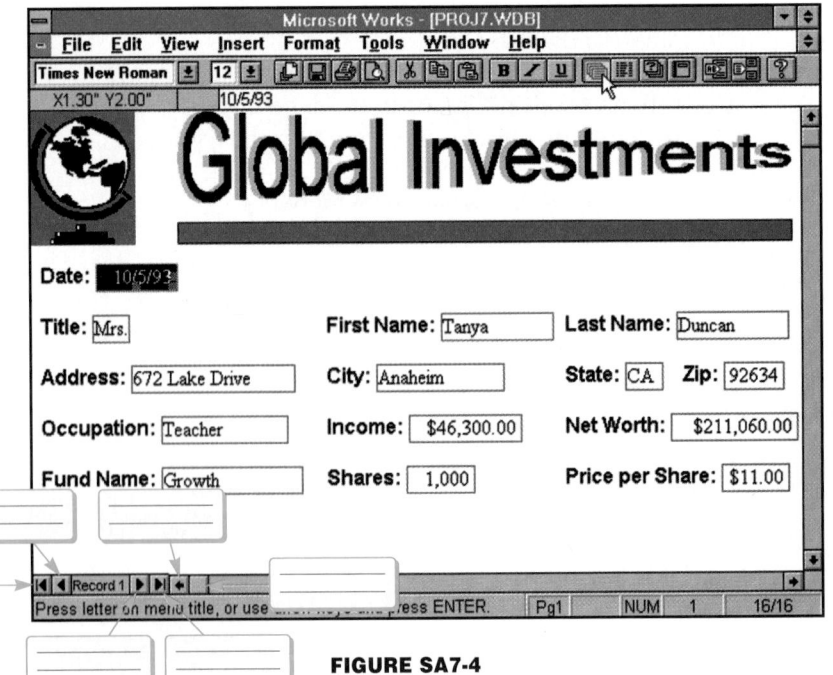

FIGURE SA7-4

STUDENT ASSIGNMENT 5
Highlighting

Instructions: Complete the following chart by explaining how to highlight using a mouse.

TO HIGHLIGHT	USING A MOUSE
Field name in Form view	_____
Entire field in List view	_____
Field in Form view	_____
Field entry in List view	_____
Record in List view	_____

STUDENT ASSIGNMENT 6
Modifying Field Locations, Field Sizes, and Field Widths

Instructions: Explain the steps to accomplish the following tasks.

Task 1: Change the field width for the Name field from 20 positions to 22 positions when displayed in Form view.

Steps: _____

_____

Task 2: Change the field width for the Name field from 20 positions to 18 positions when displayed in List view.

Steps: _____

_____

Task 3: Change the field width for the Price per Share field so the field name fits in the column with no extra space when displayed in List view.

Steps: _____

_____

Task 4: Move the First Name field from X-Y coordinates X1.33" Y1.50" to X-Y coordinates X2.50" Y3.75".

Steps: _____

_____

COMPUTER LABORATORY EXERCISE 1
Using the Help Menu

Instructions: Use Works online Help to solve the following problems.

Problem 1: How can you get help about WordArt while actually using WordArt?

Steps: _____

_____

Problem 2: When you find the information you need about WordArt, explain the purpose of the eleven rightmost buttons on the Toolbar when using WordArt.

1. _____
2. _____
3. _____
4. _____
5. _____
6. _____
7. _____
8. _____
9. _____
10. _____
11. _____

Problem 3: A single record in your database when displayed in List view will not fit on a single printed page even if you reduce the margins to 1/2 inch, reduce the font to 6 point, and print in landscape orientation. You have found four fields, however, that do not have to appear on the report and if they are not on the report, a record will fit on a single page. Explain the steps to hide these fields so they remain in the database but do not appear when you print the List view of the database.

Steps: _____

_____

COMPUTER LABORATORY EXERCISE 2
Understanding Form View and Form Formatting

Instructions: Start the Works Database tool. Open the CLE7-2.WDB file on the Student Diskette that accompanies this book. This file contains the Form view of the database before formatting (Figure CLE7-2). Follow the example in Project 7 and format the form as illustrated in Figure 7-4 on page W7.7. After formatting, print the form and turn in the form to your instructor.

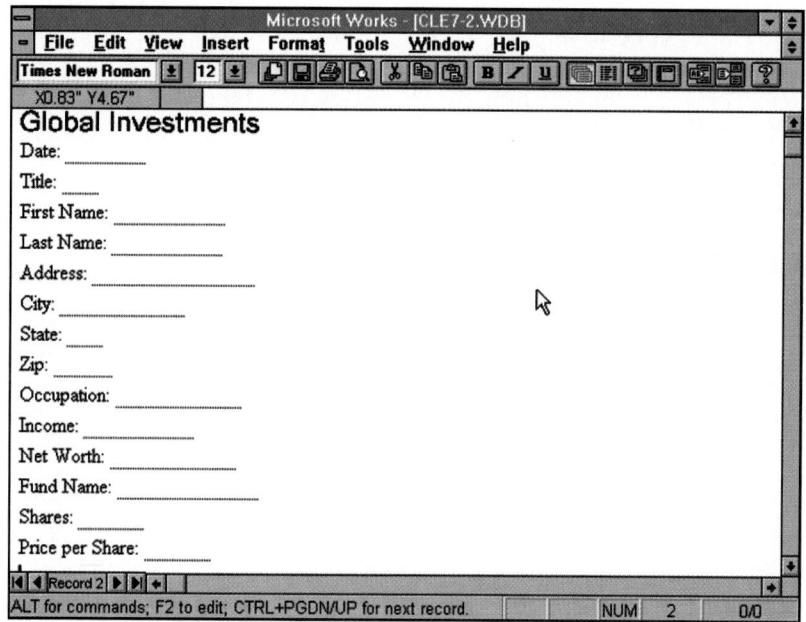

FIGURE CLE7-2

COMPUTER LABORATORY EXERCISE 3
Printing the Database

Instructions: Start the Works Database tool. Open the CLE7-3.WDB file on the Student Diskette that accompanies this book. This is a database created in the same format as the database in Project 7. Perform the following tasks:

1. Print the entire database using List view. Each record should appear in its entirety on one page. Turn in the printed report to your instructor.
2. Print the database in List view in 10 point Times New Roman font in the Portrait orientation. Do not print the Occupation, Income, Net Worth, Shares, or Price per Share fields (Hint: Search for Hiding fields in the Help menu). Turn in the printed report to your instructor.
3. Print record 8 and record 12 of the database in Form view. Turn in the printed copies of these records to your instructor.

COMPUTER LABORATORY ASSIGNMENT 1
Creating a Database

Purpose: To provide experience creating and displaying a database in both Form view and List view.

Problem: Create a database that contains information regarding scholarship donations given to the Woodland College Foundation. The contents of the database are shown in the following table.

Instructions: Perform the following tasks:

DATE JOINED	TITLE	FIRST NAME	M.I.	LAST NAME	SCHOLARSHIP	DONATION	CLASSIFICATION
10/15/94	Miss	Melissa	R.	Randall	Music	$1,000.00	President's Circle
10/16/94	Mr.	Robert	R.	Brown	Science	$500.00	Silver Circle
10/17/94	Ms.	Mary	C.	Crow	Business	$100.00	Donor
10/18/94	Dr.	Terrisa	A.	Mann	Athletics	$200.00	Donor
11/1/94	Mr.	William	B.	Gentry	Fine Arts	$700.00	Silver Circle
11/3/94	Ms.	Betty	L.	Bolton	Business	$3,000.00	President's Cirlce
11/7/94	Mr.	Jesse	J.	Ramos	Athletics	$750.00	Silver Circle
11/10/94	Mrs.	Wanda	G.	Grahame	Music	$100.00	Donor
11/22/94	Mrs.	Lynn	C.	Wong	Science	$2,000.00	President's Circle
11/28/94	Dr.	Susan	M.	Lopez	Science	$5,000.00	President's Circle

1. Create the database in the format shown in Figure CLA7-1. Experiment with the clip art size, title size, and field positions to obtain the desired format.

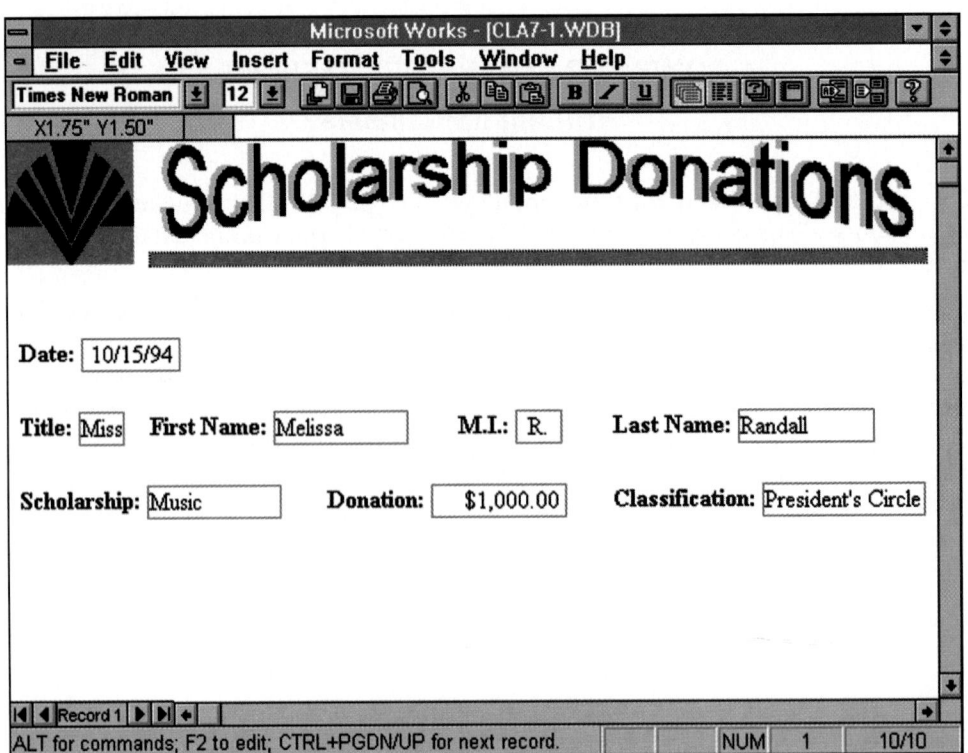

FIGURE CLA7-1

2. Format the field names as shown in Figure CLA7-1.
3. Enter the data from the table into the database.
4. Determine the proper field widths so that in List view the entire record in the database prints on a single page.
5. Save the database on a diskette. Use a filename consisting of the initials of your first and last names followed by the assignment number. Example: TC7-1.
6. Print the database in Form view.
7. Print the database in List view.
8. Follow the directions from your instructor for turning in this assignment.

COMPUTER LABORATORY ASSIGNMENT 2
Creating a Database

Purpose: To provide experience creating and displaying a database in both Form view and List view.

Problem: Create a database that contains the Inventory Listing of the Computer Reference Library. The contents of the database are shown below.

Instructions: Perform the following tasks:

1. Create the database in approximately the same format as shown in Figure CLA7-2. Experiment with the clip art size, title size, and field positions to obtain the desired format.

DATE ACQUIRED	BOOK NAME	AUTHOR	PUBLISHER
11/13/94	Basics of Spreadsheets	Simpson and Quincy	Hart and Timmons
11/14/94	Introduction to EasyCalc	Adams	Feldman Press
11/15/94	DataEase	Finer & Holloman	Computers Inc.
11/15/94	Local Area Networks	Morgan/Pressman	EastLink Press
11/15/94	Installing LANs	Morgan/Pressman	EastLink Press
12/2/94	Using Writelt	Krakowitz	Hart and Timmons
12/6/94	Learning Linker	Howell/Kimmins	Computers Inc.
12/7/94	WordWriter	Young and Bellows	WPS Publishers
12/19/94	Guide to FileMaster	Adams	Feldman Press
12/21/94	WhizWorks	Ruiz and Yang	WPS Publishers

YEAR PUBLISHED	CATEGORY	QUANTITY	UNIT COST
1994	Spreadsheet	6	$24.76
1994	Spreadsheet	3	$19.96
1993	Database	1	$27.83
1994	LAN	7	$43.51
1994	LAN	1	$76.91
1994	Word Processing	12	$23.74
1994	Integrated	3	$28.97
1994	Word Processing	3	$31.71
1993	Database	2	$21.56
1994	Integrated	2	$32.56

(continued)

COMPUTER LABORATORY ASSIGNMENT 2 (continued)

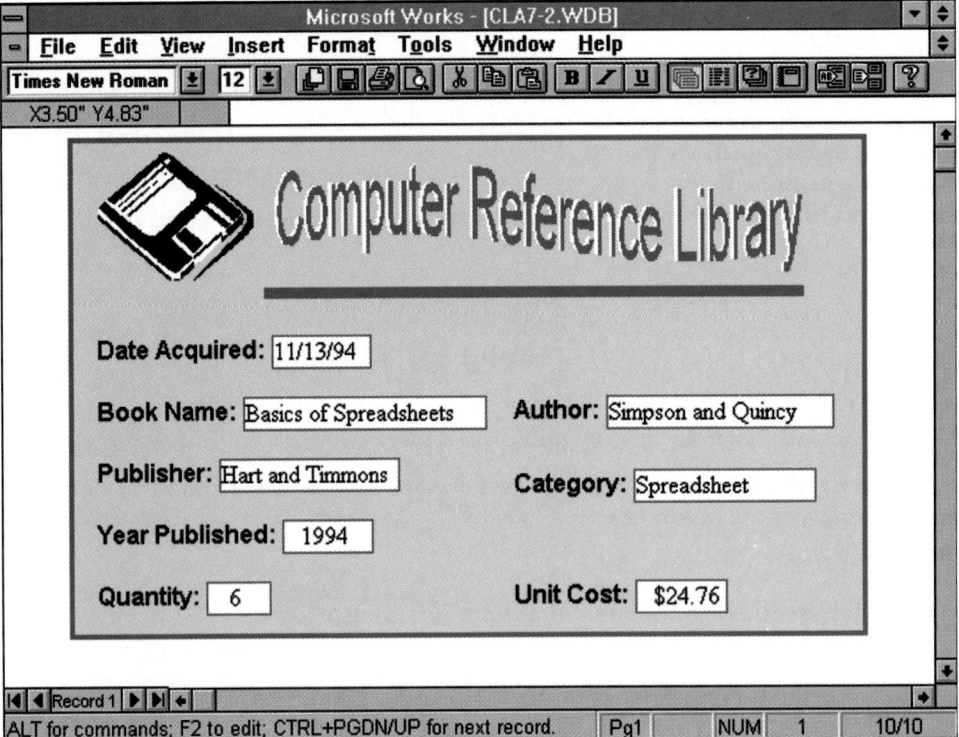

FIGURE CLA7-2

2. Enter the data from the table into the database.
3. Determine the proper field widths so that in List view the entire record in the database prints on a single page.
4. Save the database on a diskette. Use a filename consisting of the initials of your first and last names followed by the assignment number. Example: TC7-2.
5. Print the database in Form view.
6. Print the database in List view.
7. Follow the directions from your instructor for turning in this assignment.

COMPUTER LABORATORY ASSIGNMENT 3
Creating a Database

Purpose: To provide experience creating and displaying a database in both Form view and List view.

Problem: Create a database that contains the Membership Roster for your Computer Club. The contents of the database are shown in the following table.

DATE JOINED	FIRST NAME	M.I.	LAST NAME	ADDRESS	CITY	STATE
9/19/94	Julio	L.	Ferdez	211 Elliot Street	Cerritos	CA
9/19/94	Frankie	M.	Hughes	3323 Ashly Drive	Anaheim	CA
9/19/94	Marla	A.	McIntosh	999 Chapman Ave.	Fullerton	CA
9/20/94	Norma	J.	Genne	76 White Road	Anaheim	CA
9/21/94	Todd	A.	Walsh	5447 Whittier Dr.	La Habra	CA
9/21/94	Wilson	Q.	Phipps	671 Clay Terrace	Cerritos	CA
9/22/94	Joseph	I.	Yamma	93 Union Street	Fullerton	CA
9/22/94	Tricia	L.	Yung	7322 Teal Street	Anaheim	CA

ZIP	MAJOR	MEMBERSHIP	DUES
90701	Computer Science	Regular	$25.00
92822	Business	Regular	$25.00
92633	Biology	Associate	$15.00
92822	Computer Science	Regular	$25.00
92879	Chemistry	Associate	$15.00
90701	Computer Science	Regular	$25.00
92631	Computer Science	Regular	$25.00
92822	Business	Associate	$15.00

Instructions: Perform the following tasks:

1. Create the database using the fields and data shown in the table and in Figure CLA7-3. The Form View screen shown illustrates the fields in the database and a default field size of 20. Determine the location of each field in Form view and also the appropriate field size and formatting for each field. Create an attractive design using color in the Form View screen.
2. Enter the data from the table into the database.
3. Determine the proper field widths, font, font size, and page margins so that in List view the entire record in the database prints on a single page.
4. Save the database on a diskette. Use a filename consisting of the initials of your first and last names followed by the assignment number. Example: TC7-3.
5. Print the database in Form view.
6. Print the database in List view.
7. Follow the directions from your instructor for turning in this assignment.

(continued)

COMPUTER LABORATORY ASSIGNMENT 3 (continued)

```
┌──────────────────────────────────────────────────────────────┐
│ ▬              Microsoft Works - [CLA7-3.WDB]          ▼ ▲    │
│ ▬  File  Edit  View  Insert  Format  Tools  Window  Help   ▲ │
│ Times New Roman ± 12 ± □▤◈▣ ▓▦▨ B ∕ U ▣▤▨▢ ▨▤ ?          │
│  X1.33" Y4.42"                                              │
│ ┌────────────────────────────────────────────────────────┐▲│
│ │   Computer Club                                          │ │
│ │ Membership Roster                                        │ │
│ │ Date Joined: ......................................      │ │
│ │ First Name: .......................................      │ │
│ │ M.I.: ...............                                    │ │
│ │ Last Name: ........................................     │ │
│ │ Address: ...........................                     │ │
│ │ City: ............                                       │ │
│ │ State: ..........                                        │ │
│ │ Zip: ......................                              │ │
│ │ Major: .....................                             │ │
│ │ Membership: ......................                       │ │
│ │ Dues: .................                                  │ │
│ │ |                                                        │▼│
│ │◄ ◄ Record 1 ► ►│ ◄                                    ► │
│ ALT for commands; F2 to edit; CTRL+PGDN/UP for next record.│ NUM │ 1 │ 0/0 │
└──────────────────────────────────────────────────────────────┘
```

FIGURE CLA7-3

COMPUTER LABORATORY ASSIGNMENT 4
Creating a Database

Purpose: To provide experience creating and displaying a database in both Form view and List view.

Problem: Create a database that contains records of the music CDs (compact disks) and cassettes you own (or would like to own). The database should contain the following fields: date acquired, artist, CD or cassette title, record label, type (CD or cassette), favorite song on the CD or cassette, and amount paid. Enter a minimum of ten records.

Instructions:

1. Create the database. Be creative in your design of the Form View screen.
2. Save the database on a diskette. Use a filename consisting of the initials of your first and last names followed by the assignment number. Example: TC7-4.
3. Print the database in Form view.
4. Print the database in List view.
5. Follow the directions from your instructor for turning in this assignment.

▼

MAINTAINING A DATABASE

MAINTAINING A DATABASE

OBJECTIVES You will have mastered the material in this project when you can:

▸ Explain adding new records to a database
▸ Explain deleting records from a database
▸ Explain changing and updating records in a database
▸ Explain changing and updating the record structure in a database
▸ Open a currently existing database file
▸ Add a record to a database in Form view
▸ Add a record to a database in List view
▸ Delete a record from a database in Form view
▸ Delete a record from a database in List view
▸ Change data in a database record
▸ Insert a new field in a database in List view
▸ Add a new field in a database in Form view
▸ Add a field containing a formula

▸ Place data in a field added to a database
▸ Size and position an inserted field in Form view
▸ Delete a database field in Form view
▸ Delete a database field in List view
▸ Change a field name in Form view
▸ Change a field size in Form view
▸ Reformat the database form in Form view
▸ Add labels for a form in Form view
▸ Divide the List view of the database into panes
▸ Reformat a database
▸ Delete labels in Form view
▸ Use the Slide to left option
▸ Add headers and footers to a Form view report

▶ INTRODUCTION

T he database developed in Project 7 for an investment club called Global Investments can be used to provide a wide variety of information. Its use, however, is dependent upon current and correct data being stored in the database. For example, if the name of an investor is misspelled, or if someone moves and has a new address, or if a new person decides to invest, or if a current investor invests more money, the database must be updated to reflect these changes.

The process of ensuring a database contains current and correct data is called **database maintenance**. Database maintenance involves four main activities. These activities are explained on the following four pages.

1. **Adding new records to a database to reflect new activity**. If a new person invests in the investment club, this investor must be added to the database. In Figure 8-1, the investment club database contains 16 records before a record is added to the database. When a record for the new investor, Mr. Eugene McMurray, is added to the database, the database contains 17 records.

Adding New Records

Before Adding (List View)

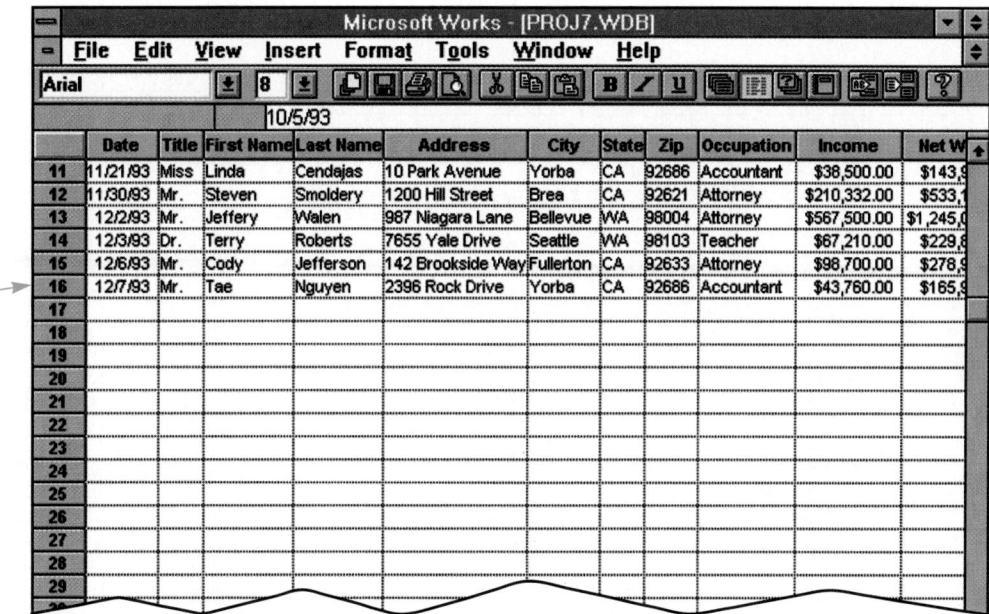

16 records in
Global Investments
database

After Adding (List View)

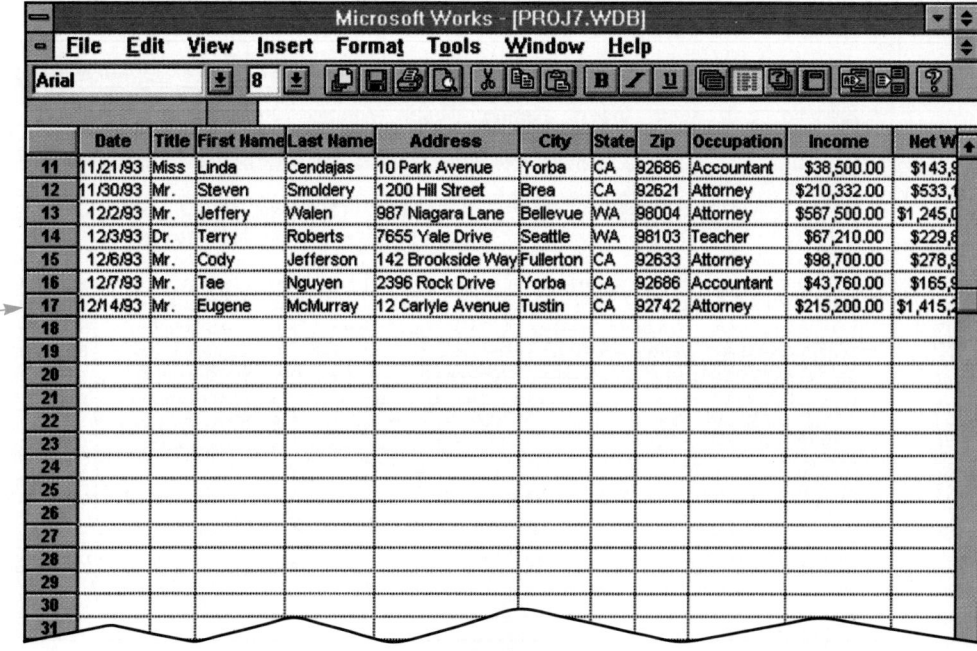

17th record
added to Global
Investments database

FIGURE 8-1

2. **Deleting records from a database**. If an investor decides to remove money and no longer invest in the investment club, his or her record must be removed from the database. In Figure 8-2, assume Michael Bolland has decided to remove his investment. The record for Michael Bolland, which is the tenth record in the database, must be deleted. When it is deleted, the investment club database contains 16 records instead of 17 records, and each record moves up one row.

Deleting Records

Before Deleting (List View)

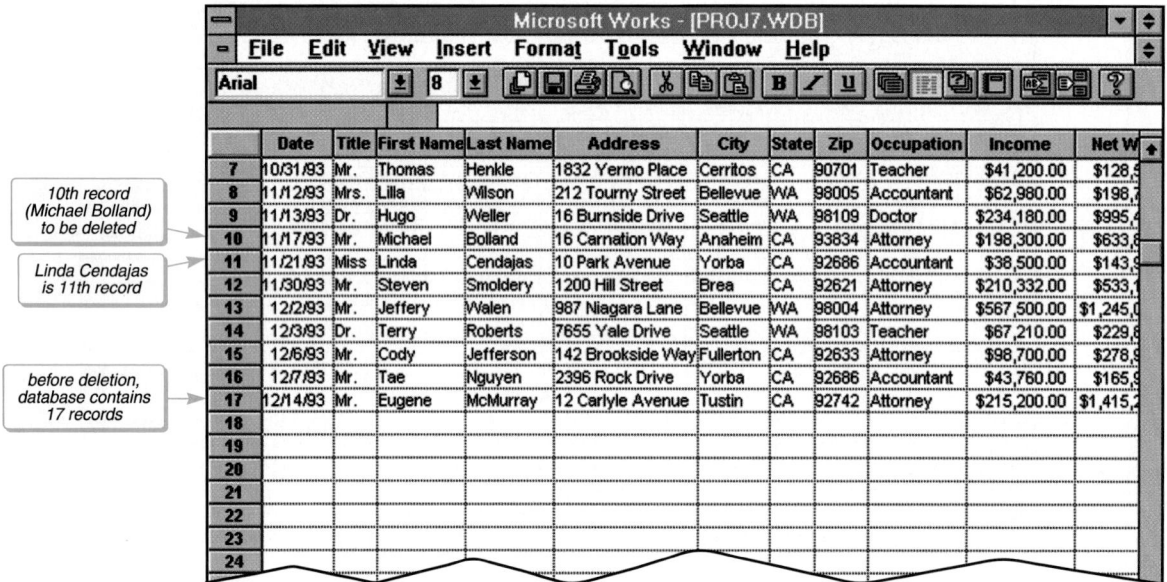

After Deleting (List View)

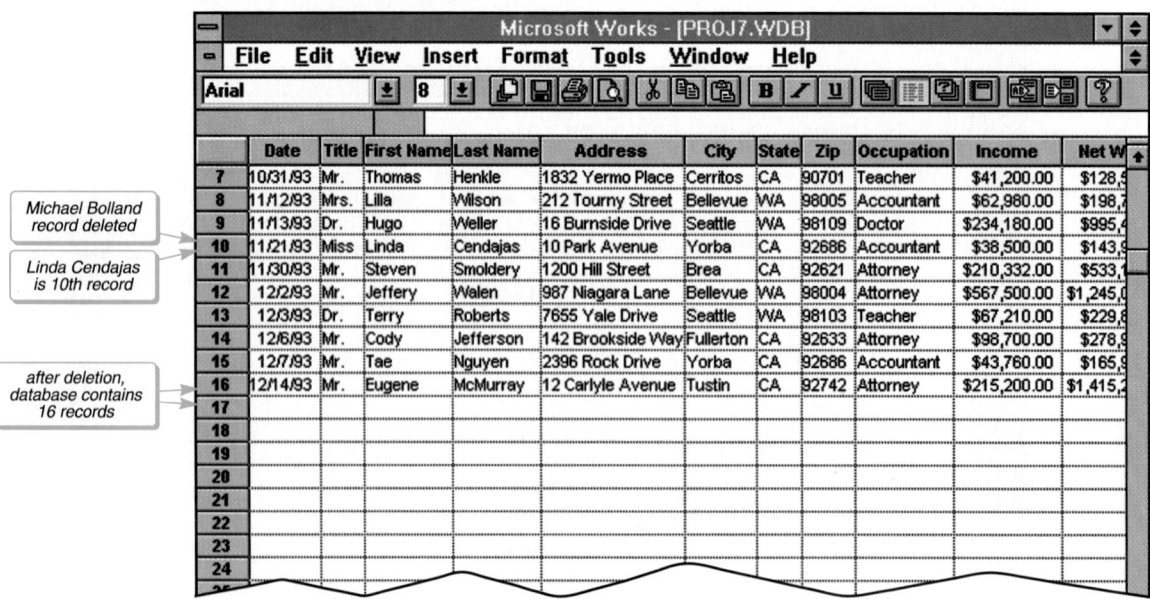

FIGURE 8-2

3. **Changing data in database records**. Whenever facts about records in a database change, the records in the database itself must be changed. For example, when an investor moves, the investor's record within the database must be changed to reflect the new address. In Figure 8-3, Steven Smoldery moved from Brea, California to Chino, California. Three fields (Address, City, and Zip) are changed.

Changing Records

Before Change (List View)

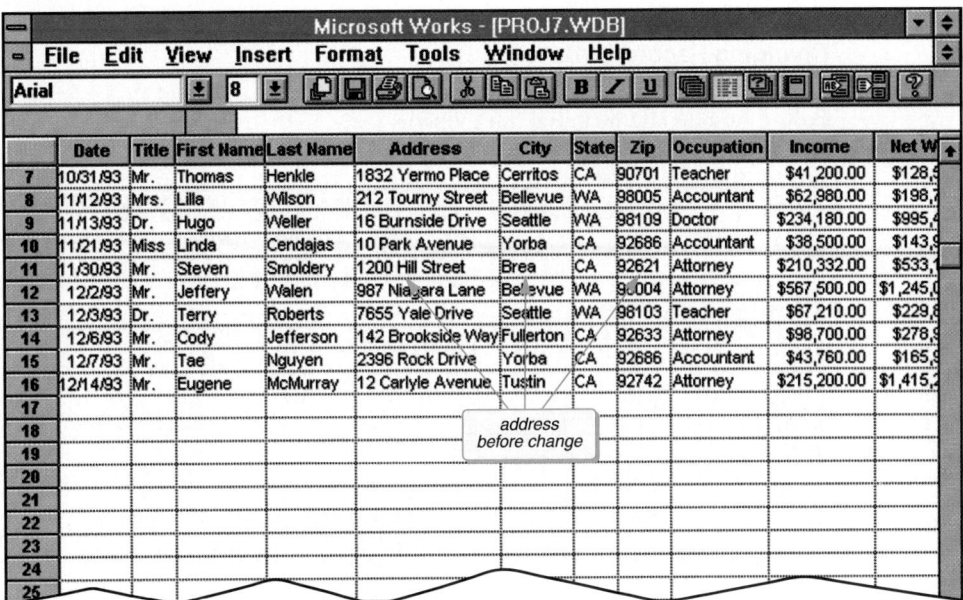

After Change (List View)

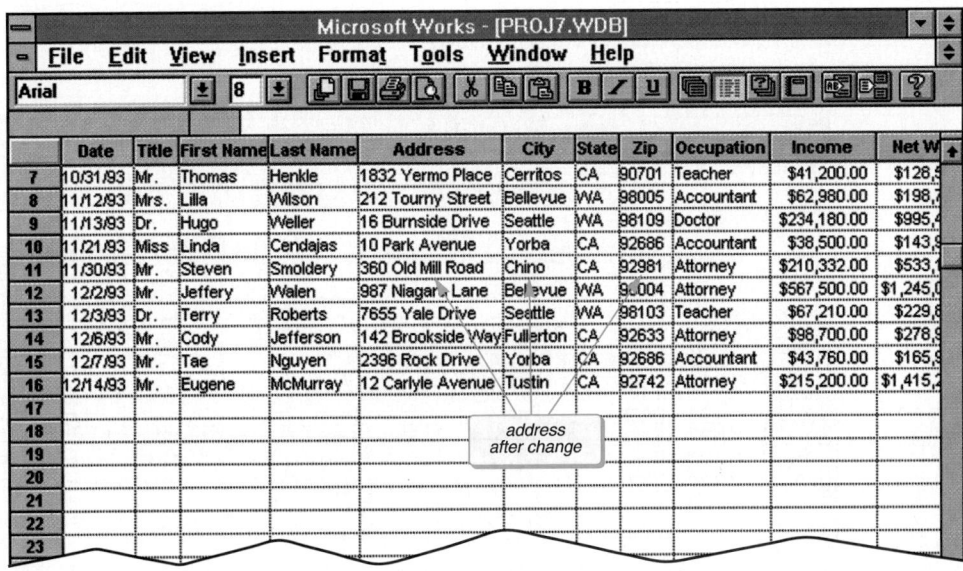

FIGURE 8-3

4. **Changing the record structure**. Sometimes the initial design of a record in a database must be changed to include additional data. For example, in the investment club database record, it may be determined that the middle initial should be added to the database record to more accurately identify each investor. This change is shown in Figure 8-4. Notice that the middle initial field has been added to the database and that data for each record has been placed in the field. Whenever a field is added to a database, data must also be placed in the field. You may also find an application where a field within the database must be deleted, where a field name must be changed, where the field size must be altered, or where the layout in Form view must be adjusted.

Changing Record Structure

Before Adding Middle Initial (List View)

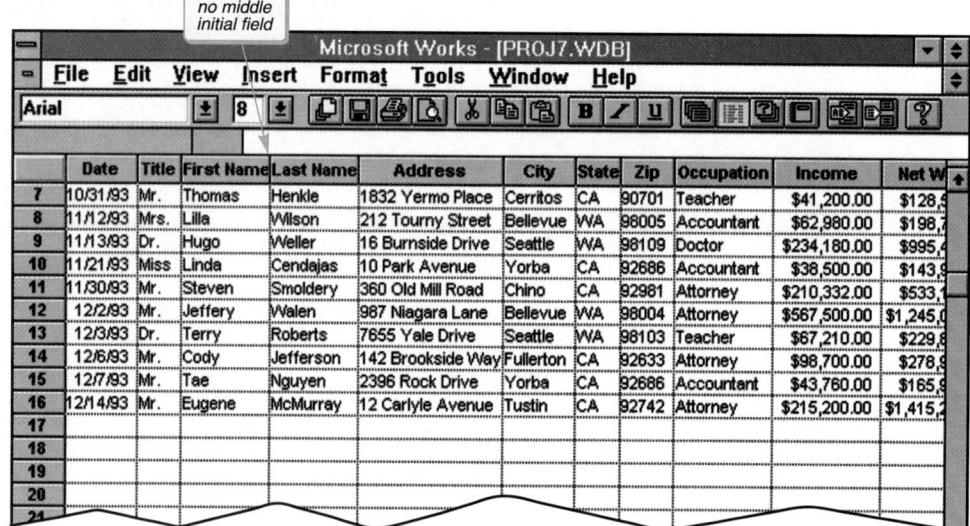

After Adding Middle Initial (List View)

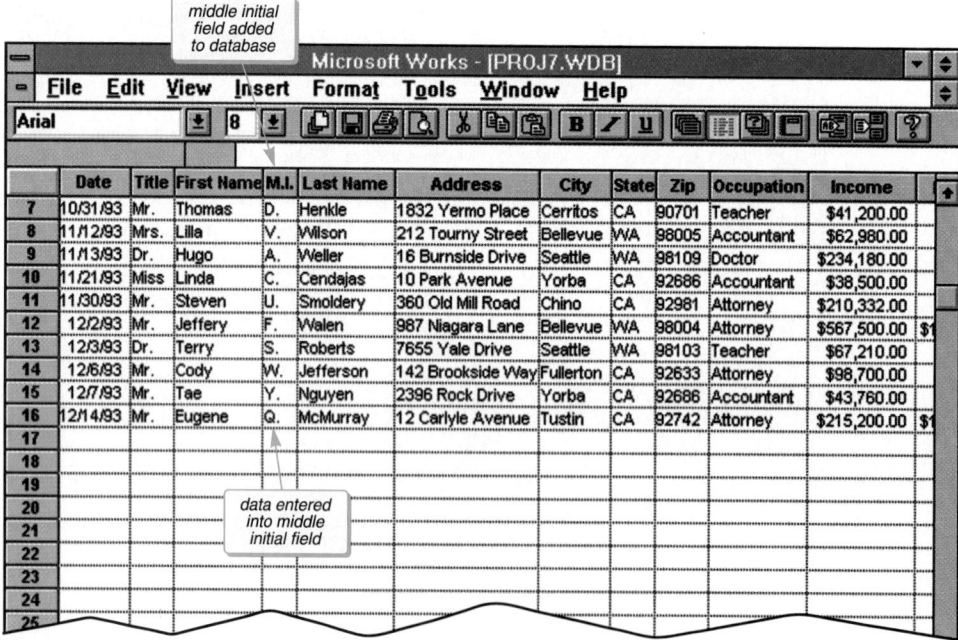

FIGURE 8-4

Each of the four activities for maintaining a database can be performed in either List view or Form view.

▶ PROJECT EIGHT

 o illustrate maintaining a database, in Project 8 the following tasks are performed on the investment club database created in Project 7:

1. A record for a new investor, Eugene McMurray, is added to the database in Form view.
2. A record for a new investor, Julie Zigasier, is added to the database in List view.
3. The record for Michael Bolland is deleted from the database in Form view.
4. The record for Jeffery Walen is deleted from the database in List view.
5. The method for changing the address of Steven Smoldery is explained.
6. The middle initial field is inserted into the database in List view, and data is added to the middle initial field of all records.
7. The Investment field, containing a formula, is inserted into the database in Form view.
8. The Income field is deleted from the database in Form view.
9. The Net Worth field is deleted from the database in List view.
10. The name of the Price per Share field is changed to Share Price in Form view.
11. The size of the Occupation field is changed from a width of 17 to a width of 12 in Form view.
12. The Fund Name, Shares, Share Price, and Investment fields are moved to a different location in Form view.
13. New labels are added to the Form view of the database.

In addition, the technique for viewing the database in panes is explained.

In some cases, a database can be changed to use the data for a different application. Figure 8-5 illustrates a database that contains only the names and addresses of the investors from the investment club database. The technique for changing an existing database and creating a report from that changed database is shown in this project.

Microsoft Works - [PROJ8RPT.WDB]

File   Edit   View   Insert   Format   Tools   Window   Help

Arial   8   "Mrs.

	Title	First Name	M.I.	Last Name	Address	City	State	Zip				
1	Mrs.	Tanya	I.	Duncan	672 Lake Drive	Anaheim	CA	92634				
2	Dr.	Cara	L.	Bailey	303 Sunrise Place	Irvine	CA	92628				
3	Ms.	Jane	R.	Walters	1545 Elm Street	Fullerton	CA	92633				
4	Mrs.	Hillary	P.	Fine	3233 Yule Drive	Irvine	CA	92754				
5	Dr.	Julia	W.	Lopez	12732 Clover Road	Fullerton	CA	92633				
6	Ms.	Rebecca	O.	Tiong	87 Green Street	Olympia	WA	98506				
7	Mr.	Thomas	D.	Henkle	1832 Yermo Place	Cerritos	CA	90701				
8	Mrs.	Lila	V.	Wilson	212 Tourny Street	Bellevue	WA	98005				
9	Dr.	Hugo	A.	Weller	16 Burnside Drive	Seattle	WA	98109				
10	Miss	Linda	C.	Cendajas	10 Park Avenue	Yorba	CA	92686				
11	Mr.	Steven	U.	Smoldery	360 Old Mill Road	Chino	CA	92981				
12	Dr.	Terry	S.	Roberts	7655 Yale Drive	Seattle	WA	98103				
13	Mr.	Cody	W.	Jefferson	142 Brookside Way	Fullerton	CA	92633				
14	Mr.	Tae	Y.	Nguyen	2396 Rock Drive	Yorba	CA	92686				
15	Mr.	Eugene	Q.	McMurray	12 Carlyle Avenue	Tustin	CA	92742				
16	Ms.	Julie	L.	Zigasier	1427 Soccer Road	Trent	CA	92544				
17												
18												

database records contain name and address only

FIGURE 8-5

The following pages contain a detailed explanation of the previous tasks.

▶ STARTING WORKS AND OPENING A DATABASE FILE

To start Works and open the PROJ7.WDB database file on which you will perform maintenance, follow the steps used in previous projects. These steps are summarized below.

TO START WORKS AND OPEN A DATABASE FILE

Step 1: From Program Manager open the Microsoft Works for Windows group window.

Step 2: Double-click the Microsoft Works program-item icon.

Step 3: If the Welcome to Microsoft Works dialog box displays, choose the Start Works Now button.

Step 4: Choose the Open Existing File button.

Step 5: In the Open dialog box, select the PROJ7.WDB file stored on the diskette in drive A.

Step 6: Choose the OK button in the Open dialog box.

Step 7: After Works opens the PROJ7.WDB file, maximize the Works application window if necessary, and then maximize the PROJ7.WDB document window.

The resulting Works window is shown in Figure 8-6.

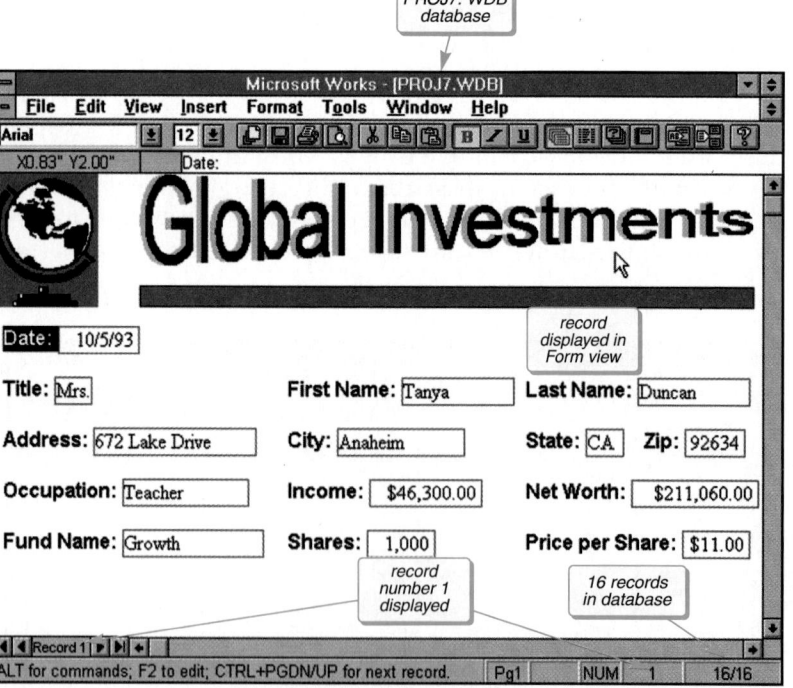

FIGURE 8-6

▶ Adding Records to a Database

T he first task in this project is to add two records to the investment club database. The first record is for an investor named Eugene McMurray, and the second record is for an investor named Julie Zigasier. You will add the McMurray record in Form view and the Zigasier record in List view.

Adding a Record in Form View

To add a record in Form view, perform the following steps.

TO ADD A RECORD TO A DATABASE IN FORM VIEW ▼

STEP 1 ▶

Point to the Last Record navigation button and click.

Works displays an empty form for record number 17 (Figure 8-7).

FIGURE 8-7

STEP 2 ▶

Highlight the Date field and type 12/14/93. Press the TAB key and type Mr. Press the TAB key and type Eugene, and then enter the remainder of the data. After you type the price per share (38.00), press the ENTER key, not the TAB key.

Works displays record 17 (Figure 8-8). When you enter data and a field already has been formatted, such as the Income, Net Worth, Shares, and Price per Share fields, Works automatically places the data in a new record into the same format as the other records in the database.

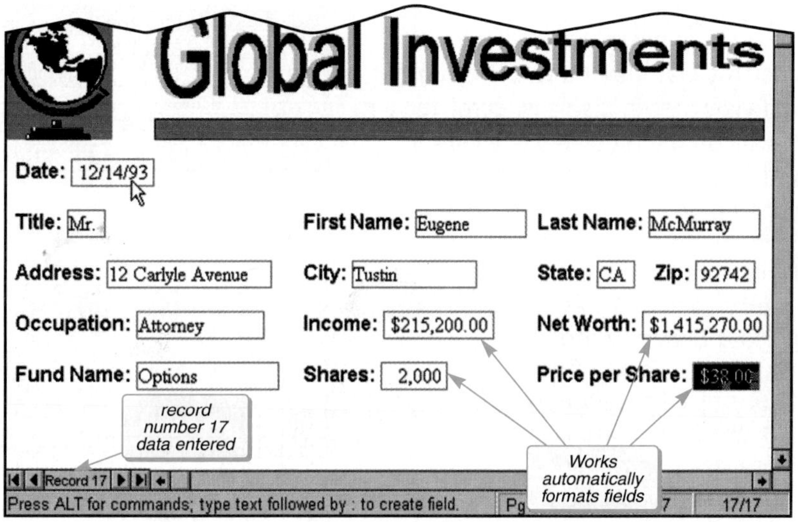

FIGURE 8-8

The record in Figure 8-8 is now added to the database. It is not, however, automatically saved on disk. Therefore, during the process of maintaining the database, you should periodically save the updated database on disk. To save the PROJ7.WDB database on the diskette in drive A, complete the following step.

TO SAVE AN UPDATED DATABASE USING THE SAME FILENAME

Step 1: Click the Save button on the Toolbar.

Works saves the updated database on the diskette placed in drive A using the PROJ7.WDB filename.

If you want to save the updated database using a different filename, use the Save As command from the File menu.

Adding a Record in List View

Works provides for adding a record to the database in List view as well as in Form view. To add a record to the database in List view, perform the following steps.

TO ADD A RECORD TO THE DATABASE IN LIST VIEW ▼

STEP 1 ▶

Point to the List View button on the Toolbar.

The mouse pointer points to the List View button on the Toolbar (Figure 8-9).

FIGURE 8-9

STEP 2 ▶

Click the List View button. When the List view screen displays, scroll to the left so the Date field is visible and highlight the Date field in the 18th record.

Works displays the database in List view (Figure 8-10). When you switch the display from Form view (Figure 8-9) to List view (Figure 8-10), the List view will have the Price per Share field highlighted because it was highlighted in Form view. When you scroll to the left using the left scroll arrow, the rightmost fields scroll off the screen and the Date field becomes visible.

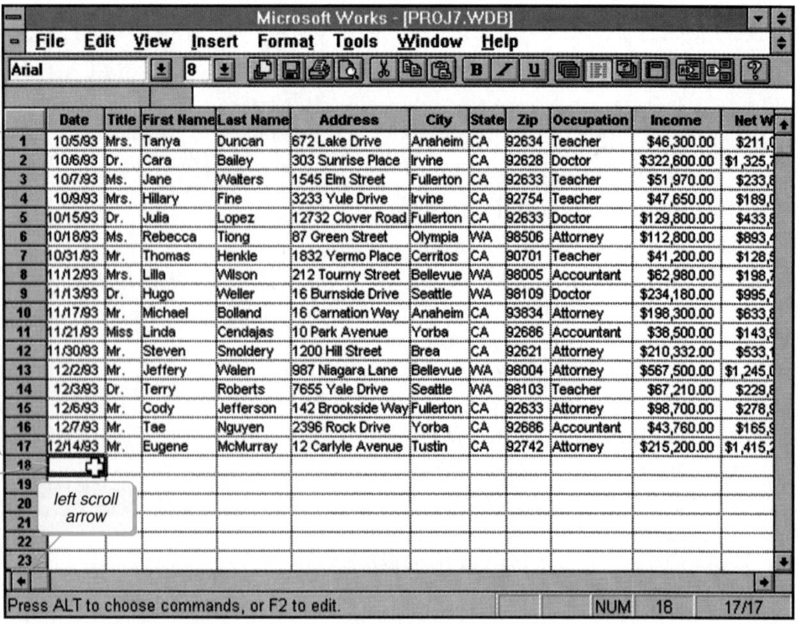

FIGURE 8-10

STEP 3 ►

Type the date, 12/17/93, **and press the TAB key.**

When you press the TAB key, Works enters the date you typed into the Date field and highlights the Title field (Figure 8-11).

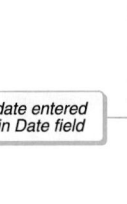

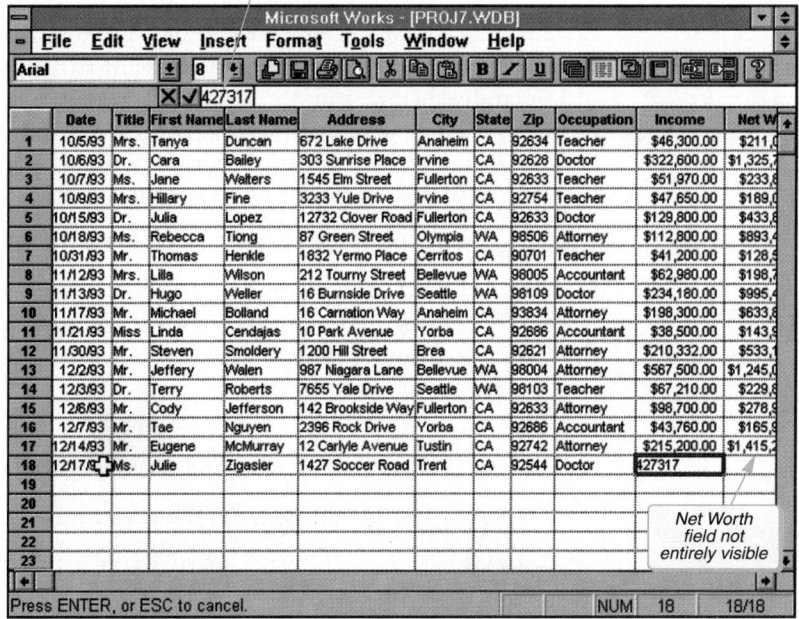

date entered
in Date field

Title field
highlighted

FIGURE 8-11

STEP 4 ►

Type the title, Ms., **press the TAB key, and continue entering data until you reach the Income field. Type the income,** 427317, **but do not press the TAB key.**

Works displays the data you type in each respective field (Figure 8-12). Notice that each field you enter follows the formatting of the data in the field for the previous records. Also, the Net Worth field, which is the field to the right of the Income field, is not entirely visible on the screen.

Income
typed but not
entered

Net Worth
field not
entirely visible

FIGURE 8-12

STEP 5 ▶

Press the TAB key. Then type the remaining data for the record. After you type the Price per Share, press the ENTER key instead of the TAB key.

As you type the data and press the TAB key, Works scrolls the List view of the database to the left, one field at a time until the Price per Share field is visible on the screen (Figure 8-13). The leftmost fields in the database scroll off the screen to the left. When you enter the data, the formatting is the same as for the data in the previous records.

	City	State	Zip	Occupation	Income	Net Worth	Fund Name	Shares	Price per Share	
1	Anaheim	CA	92634	Teacher	$46,300.00	$211,060.00	Growth	1,000	$11.00	
2	Irvine	CA	92628	Doctor	$322,600.00	$1,325,700.00	Growth	2,500	$11.00	
3	Fullerton	CA	92633	Teacher	$51,970.00	$233,860.00	Fixed Income	600	$18.00	
4	Irvine	CA	92754	Teacher	$47,650.00	$189,080.00	Fixed Income	200	$18.00	
5	Fullerton	CA	92633	Doctor	$129,800.00	$433,800.00	Options	1,200	$23.00	
6	Olympia	WA	98506	Attorney	$112,800.00	$893,420.00	Options	1,000	$23.00	
7	Cerritos	CA	90701	Teacher	$41,200.00	$128,500.00	Growth	400	$11.00	
8	Bellevue	WA	98005	Accountant	$62,980.00	$198,750.00	Fixed Income	400	$18.00	
9	Seattle	WA	98109	Doctor	$234,180.00	$995,400.00	Commodities	1,500	$15.00	
10	Anaheim	CA	93834	Attorney	$198,300.00	$633,800.00	Commodities	1,000	$15.00	
11	Yorba	CA	92686	Accountant	$38,500.00	$143,980.00	Growth	800	$11.00	
12	Brea	CA	92621	Attorney	$210,332.00	$533,100.00	Options	1,400	$23.00	
13	Bellevue	WA	98004	Attorney	$567,500.00	$1,245,000.00	Commodities	2,000	$15.00	
14	Seattle	WA	98103	Teacher	$67,210.00	$229,800.00	Growth	600	$11.00	
15	Fullerton	CA	92633	Attorney	$98,700.00	$278,930.00	Growth	700	$11.00	
16	Yorba	CA	92686	Accountant	$43,760.00	$165,900.00	Growth	400	$11.00	
17	Tustin	CA	92742	Attorney	$215,200.00	$1,415,270.00	Options	2,000	$38.00	
18	Trent	CA	92544	Doctor	$427,317.00	$986,420.00	Growth	1,000	$23.00	

leftmost fields scroll off the screen

Income field becomes visible as data is entered

formatting for new record is the same as for previous records

last field in record is complete

Press ALT to choose commands, or F2 to edit.

FIGURE 8-13

In the example just shown, the new record was entered at the end of the listing of database records. If you want to add the record at a particular place in the database (for example, as the 6th record), highlight the record number of the location where you want to insert the new record (for example, record 6), and click the **Insert Record button** on the Toolbar. Works will move all records down one line (that is, record 6 will become record 7 and so on) and leave an open record at the highlighted record (for example, at record 6). You can then enter the data for the record in same manner as shown in the previous example. You can also choose the Record/Field command from the Insert menu to insert a record.

Adding new records is a fundamental operation when maintaining a database. Works allows you to add new records in either Form view or List view.

▶ DELETING RECORDS FROM A DATABASE

A nother fundamental operation when maintaining a database is deleting records from the database. You must delete records from a database when the record contains data that no longer belongs in the database. In the sample project, records for investors are deleted when the investor decides to withdraw his or her money and no longer invest.

To illustrate the process of deleting records, assume Michael Bolland (record 10) and Jeffery Walen (record 13) decide to withdraw their money.

Deleting a Record in Form View

To delete a record in Form view, the record must first be displayed on the screen. The **Go To command** on the Edit menu allows you to display any record in the database when in Form view. Then you choose the **Delete Record command** from the Insert menu to delete the record. This process is shown in the following steps.

TO DELETE A RECORD IN FORM VIEW ▼

STEP 1 ▶

Return to Form view by clicking the Form View button on the Toolbar. Then select the Edit menu and point to the Go To command.

The Form view of the database displays on the screen (Figure 8-14). The Edit menu displays and the mouse pointer points to the Go To command.

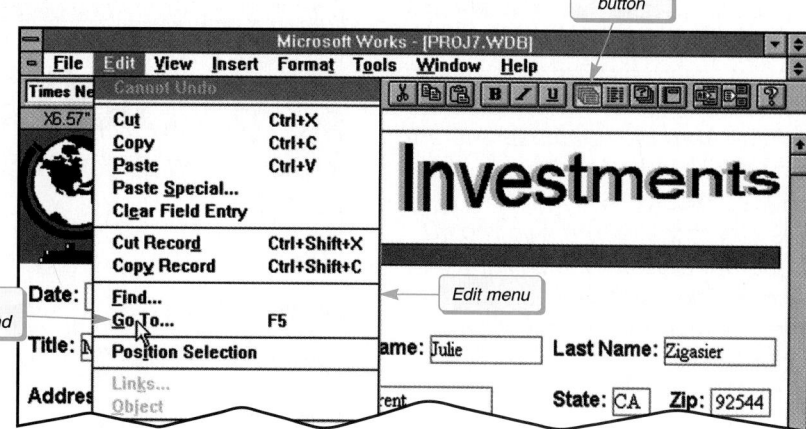

FIGURE 8-14

STEP 2 ▶

Choose the Go To command from the Edit menu. When the Go To dialog box displays, type 10 in the Go to text box. Then point to the OK button.

Works displays the Go To dialog box (Figure 8-15). Typing the number 10 in the Go to text box directs Works to display record 10. The mouse pointer points to the OK button.

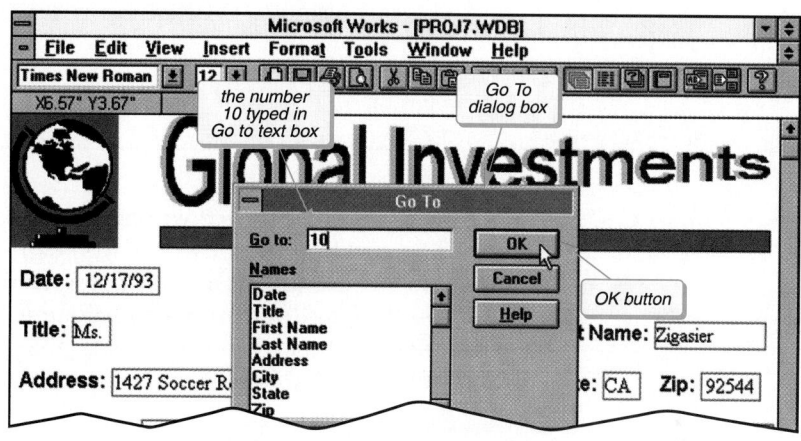

FIGURE 8-15

STEP 3 ▶

Choose the OK button in the Go To dialog box. When record number 10 displays, select the Insert menu and point to the Delete Record command.

Record number 10, for Michael Bolland, displays on the screen (Figure 8-16). This is the record you want to delete. The Insert menu displays and the mouse pointer points to the Delete Record command.

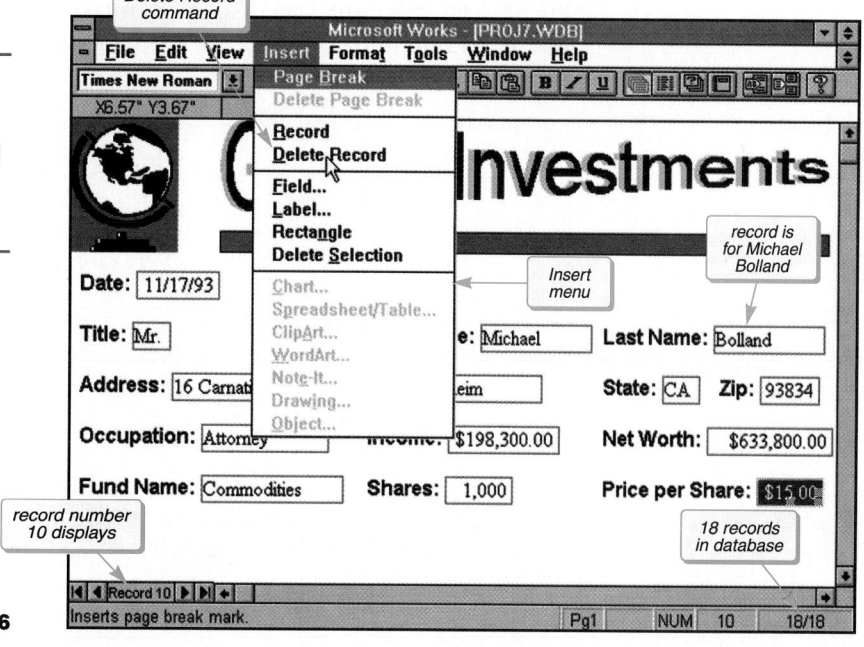

FIGURE 8-16

STEP 4 ▶

Choose the Delete Record command from the Insert menu.

The record for Michael Bolland is deleted from the database and the record for Linda Cendajas is identified as record 10 (Figure 8-17). The Cendajas record was record 11 before deleting the Bolland record. The database now contains 17 records instead of 18 records.

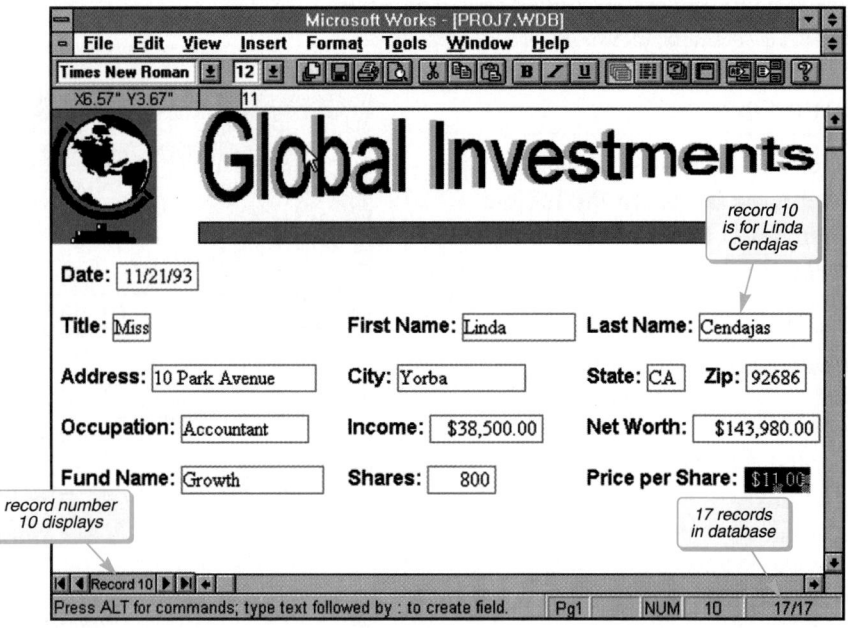

FIGURE 8-17

You should be positive you have identified the proper record to delete. If you delete a record in error, however, you can choose the **Undo Delete Record command** from the Edit menu to restore the deleted record to the database provided you have not performed subsequent operations. Before deleting records, it is recommended that you save the database file so that if you make a mistake, a correct file is available for use.

Deleting a Record in List View

Works also allows a record to be deleted in List view. To delete a record in List view, the database must be displayed in List view and the record to be deleted must be highlighted. Perform the following steps to delete record 12, for Jeffery Walen, in List view.

TO DELETE A RECORD IN LIST VIEW ▼

STEP 1 ▶

Click the List View button on the Toolbar to display the database in List view. If necessary, scroll to the left so the Date field is visible. Then point to record number 12 in the record number column and click the left mouse button.

The database displays in List view (Figure 8-18). The mouse pointer is located on record 12 in the record number column. When you click the record number, Works highlights the entire record.

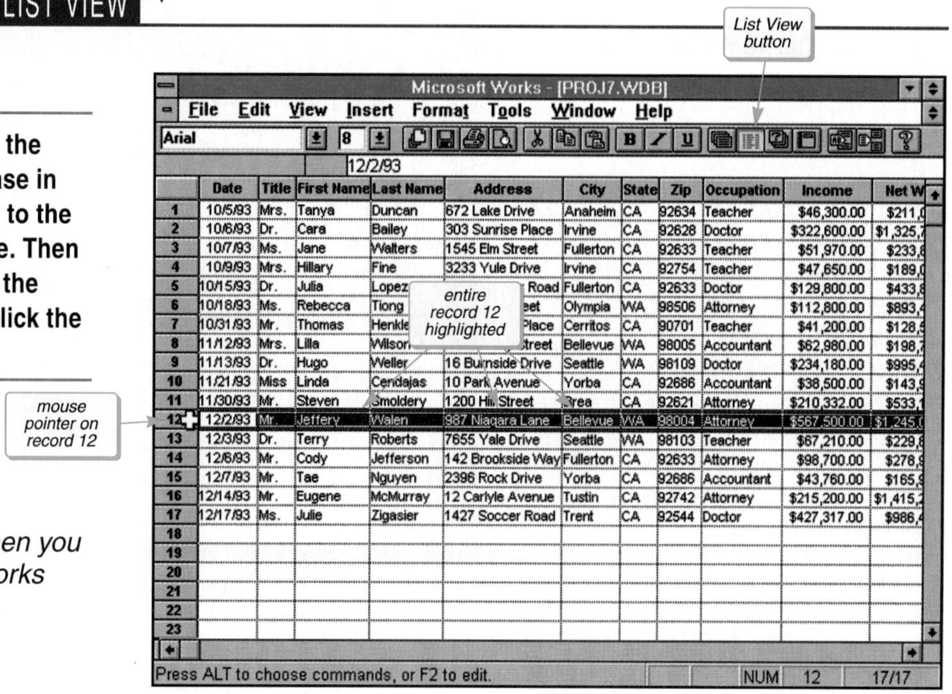

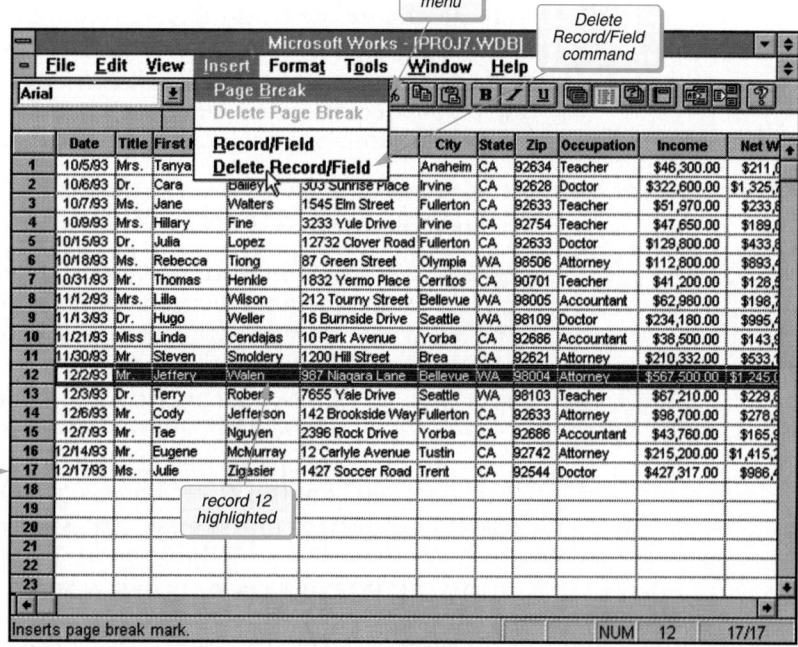

FIGURE 8-18

STEP 2 ▶

Select the Insert menu and point to the Delete Record/Field command.

*Works displays the Insert menu and the mouse pointer points to the **Delete Record/Field command** (Figure 8-19). Notice that record 12 is highlighted.*

FIGURE 8-19

STEP 3 ▶

Choose the Delete Record/Field command from the Insert menu.

Works deletes the highlighted record for Jeffery Walen (Figure 8-20). Although record 12 remains highlighted, the record is now for Terry Roberts, which before the deletion was record 13 (see Figure 8-19 on the previous page). Notice that the database now contains 16 records instead of the 17 records it contained before deleting the record.

record number 12 is now for Terry Roberts

database contains 16 records

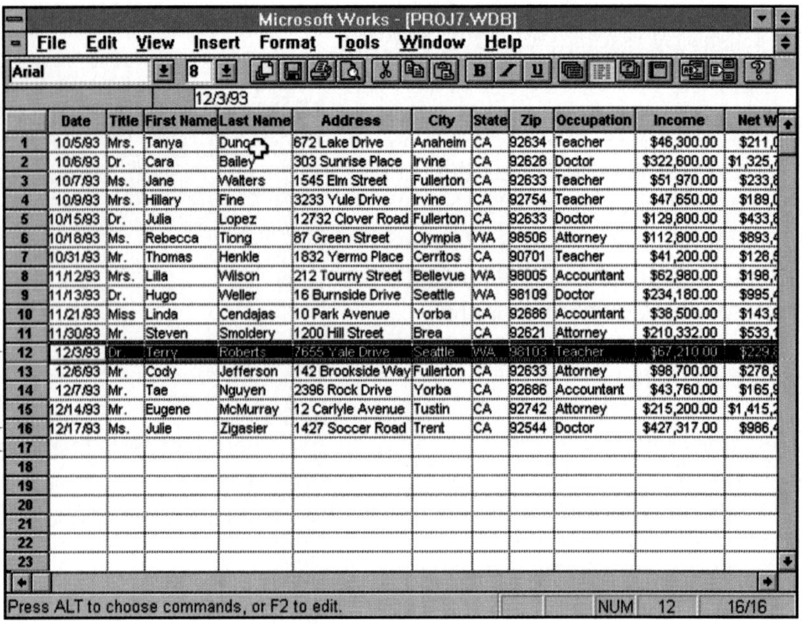

FIGURE 8-20

As when deleting records in Form view, when you delete a record in List view, you can choose the **Undo Delete Record command** from the Edit menu to restore the deleted record to the database provided no subsequent operations have been performed. Be careful when deleting records and always save a copy of the file before beginning the deletion process.

▶ CHANGING DATA IN A DATABASE FIELD

Perhaps the most frequent change to a database is changing data. For example, in the investment club database, if a person moves, the address must be changed. To change data in Form view, highlight the field in the record to be changed, type the new data, and press the ENTER key or click the Enter box. To change data in List view, highlight the field containing the data to change, type the new data, and press the ENTER key, click the Enter box, or press an arrow key. In Project 8, the address, city, and zip code of Steven Smoldery is changed from 1200 Hill Street, Brea, 92621 to 360 Old Mill Road, Chino, 92981. To make these changes in List View, complete the following steps.

TO CHANGE DATA IN A LIST VIEW FIELD

Step 1: Highlight the Address field for record number 11 in the database.
Step 2: Type 360 Old Mill Road.
Step 3: Press the RIGHT ARROW key.
Step 4: Type Chino.
Step 5: Press the RIGHT ARROW key two times.
Step 6: Type 92981 and press the ENTER key or click the Enter box.

This change is reflected in the contents of the database in future steps in this project.

▶ INSERTING A NEW FIELD IN A DATABASE

A relatively common requirement is to modify the structure of the database after it has been created. For example, you might have to insert a new field in the database. As with other database operations, a field can be inserted in the database using either List view or Form view.

When you insert a field in the database, you must accomplish four tasks: (1) insert the new field in the database; (2) give a name to the new field; (3) size the new field properly; and (4) place data in the new field. The examples on the following pages illustrate these four tasks for both List view and Form view.

Inserting a New Field in List View

For more complete identification of the investors, the records in the investment club database must contain the middle initial of each investor. To insert the middle initial field between the First Name and Last Name fields in the database in List view, name the field, size the field, and enter data into the field, perform the following steps.

TO INSERT A NEW FIELD IN LIST VIEW, NAME THE FIELD, SIZE THE FIELD, AND ENTER DATA ▼

STEP 1 ▶

Highlight the field (Last Name) to the right of the location for the new field by clicking the field name (Last Name) at the top of the column.

Works highlights the Last Name field column (Figure 8-21). The middle initial field will be inserted to the left of the highlighted field (Last Name).

Last Name field highlighted

mouse pointer

	Date	Title	First Name	Last Na	Address	City	State	Zip	Occupation	Income	Net W
1	10/5/93	Mrs.	Tanya	Duncan	672 Lake Drive	Anaheim	CA	92634	Teacher	$46,300.00	$211,0
2	10/6/93	Dr.	Cara	Bailey	303 Sunrise Place	Irvine	CA	92628	Doctor	$322,600.00	$1,325,7
3	10/7/93	Ms.	Jane	Walters	1545 Elm Street	Fullerton	CA	92633	Teacher	$51,970.00	$233,8
4	10/9/93	Mrs.	Hillary	Fine	3233 Yule Drive	Irvine	CA	92754	Teacher	$47,650.00	$189,0
5	10/15/93	Dr.	Julia	Lopez	12732 Clover Road	Fullerton	CA	92633	Doctor	$129,800.00	$433,8
6	10/18/93	Ms.	Rebecca	Tiong	87 Green Street	Olympia	WA	98506	Attorney	$112,800.00	$893,4
7	10/31/93	Mr.	Thomas	Henkle	1832 Yermo Place	Cerritos	CA	90701	Teacher	$41,200.00	$128,6
8	11/12/93	Mrs.	Lilla	Wilson	212 Tourny Street	Bellevue	WA	98005	Accountant	$62,980.00	$198,7
9	11/13/93	Dr.	Hugo	Weller	16 Burnside Drive	Seattle	WA	98109	Doctor	$234,180.00	$995,4
10	11/21/93	Miss	Linda	Cendajas	10 Park Avenue	Yorba	CA	92686	Accountant	$38,500.00	$143,9
11	11/30/93	Mr.	Steven	Smoldery	360 Old Mill Road	Chino	CA	92981	Attorney	$210,332.00	$533,1
12	12/3/93	Dr.	Terry	Roberts	7655 Yale Drive	Seattle	WA	98103	Teacher	$67,210.00	$229,8
13	12/6/93	Mr.	Cody	Jefferson	142 Brookside Way	Fullerton	CA	92633	Attorney	$98,700.00	$278,9
14	12/7/93	Mr.	Tae	Nguyen	2396 Rock Drive	Yorba	CA	92686	Accountant	$43,760.00	$165,9
15	12/14/93	Mr.	Eugene	McMurray	12 Carlyle Avenue	Tustin	CA	92742	Attorney	$215,200.00	$1,415,1
16	12/17/93	Ms.	Julie	Zigasier	1427 Soccer Road	Trent	CA	92544	Doctor	$427,317.00	$986,4
17											
18											
19											
20											
21											
22											
23											

Microsoft Works - [PROJ7.WDB]

File　Edit　View　Insert　Format　Tools　Window　Help

Arial

"Duncan

Press ALT to choose commands, or F2 to edit.　　NUM　1　16/16

FIGURE 8-21

STEP 2 ▶

Click the Insert Field button on the Toolbar.

Works inserts a new field to the left of the Last Name field (Figure 8-22). The new field is highlighted but does not contain a name.

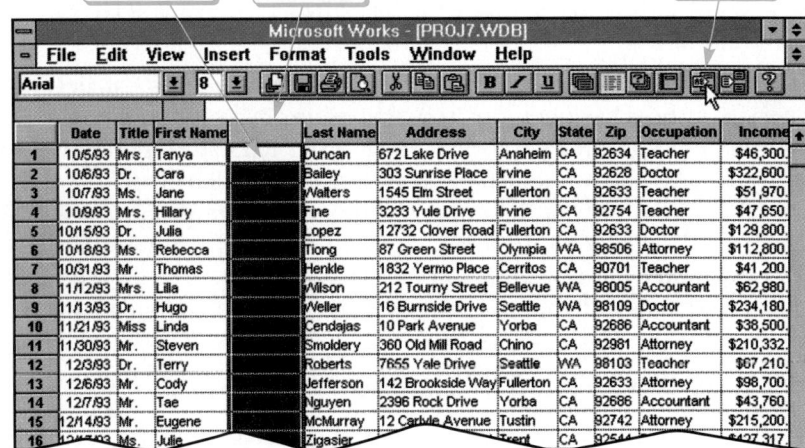

FIGURE 8-22

STEP 3 ▶

Select the Edit menu and point to the Field Name command.

*The Edit menu displays and the mouse pointer points to the **Field Name command** (Figure 8-23).*

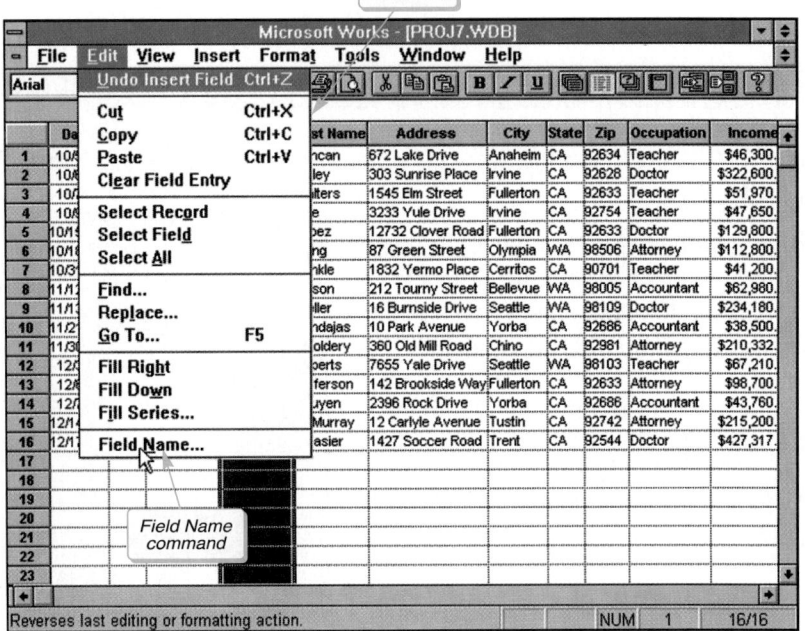

FIGURE 8-23

STEP 4 ▶

Choose the Field Name command from the Edit menu. When the Field Name dialog box displays, type the field name M.I. in the Name text box and point to the OK button.

Works displays the Field Name dialog box (Figure 8-24). The field name (M.I.) is typed in the Name text box. The mouse pointer points to the OK button.

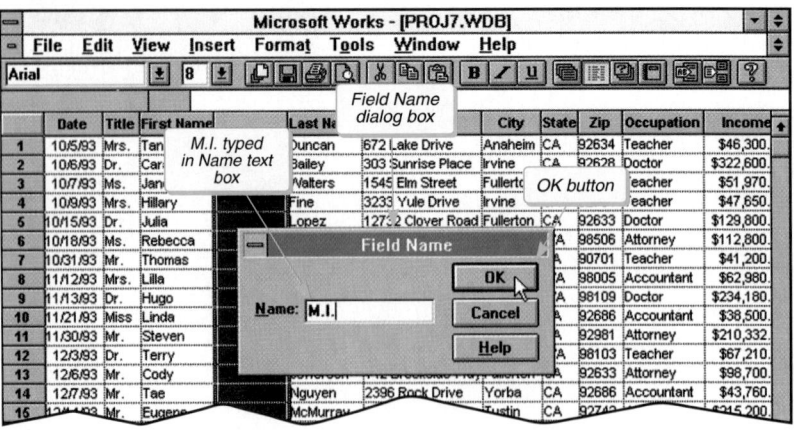

FIGURE 8-24

STEP 5 ▶

Choose the OK button in the Field Name dialog box. Then place the mouse pointer on the border line between the M.I. field name and the Last Name field name.

Works places the field name M.I. at the top of the middle initial field (Figure 8-25). The mouse pointer changes to a vertical line with arrowheads on the left and right and the word ADJUST beneath it, indicating you can drag the field border and resize the field.

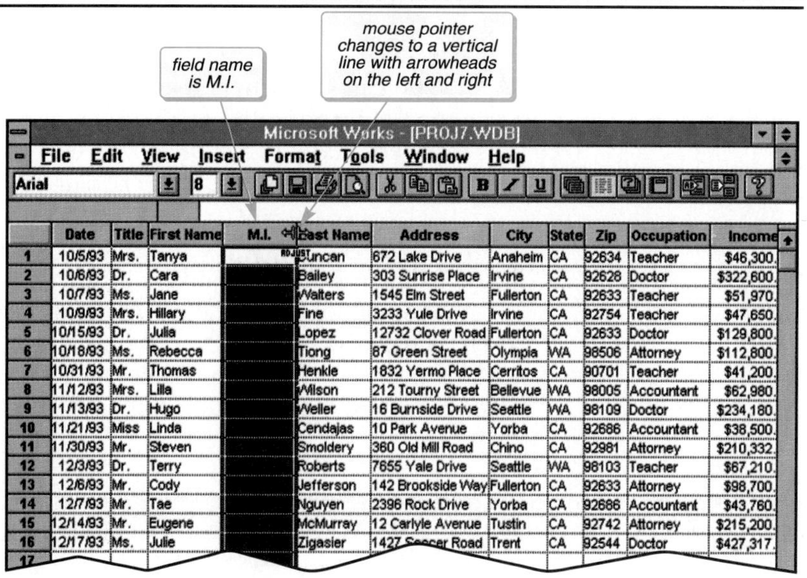

field name is M.I.

mouse pointer changes to a vertical line with arrowheads on the left and right

FIGURE 8-25

STEP 6 ▶

Drag the mouse pointer and column border to the left until there are no extra blank spaces and only the field name (M.I.) is visible. Release the mouse button.

The field size becomes smaller as you drag to the left (Figure 8-26). The proper size is obtained when the field name, M.I., displays in the field with no excess space. This is equal to a column width of 4.

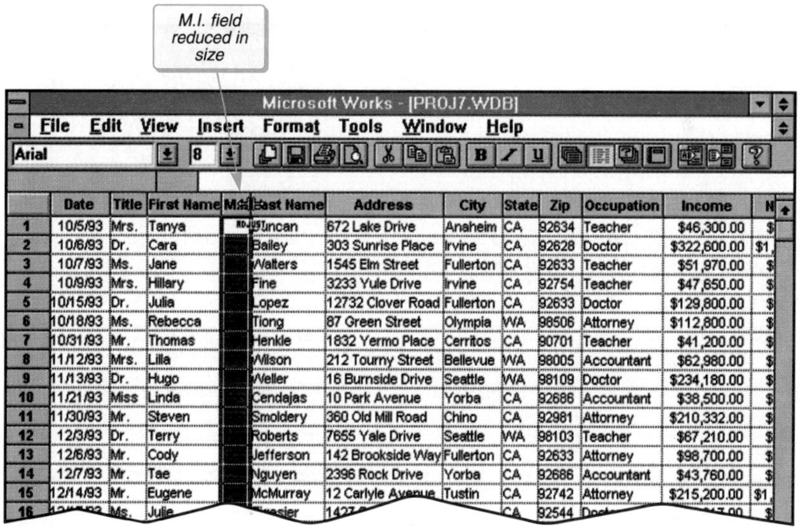

M.I. field reduced in size

FIGURE 8-26

STEP 7 ▶

Select the M.I. field for record 1 (Tanya Duncan) and type her middle initial, I.. Then press the DOWN ARROW key, and type the middle initial (L.) for Cara Bailey. Press the DOWN ARROW key and continue this process until you have entered all middle initials.

The middle initials for all investors in the database display in the M.I. field (Figure 8-27).

middle initials entered for all investors

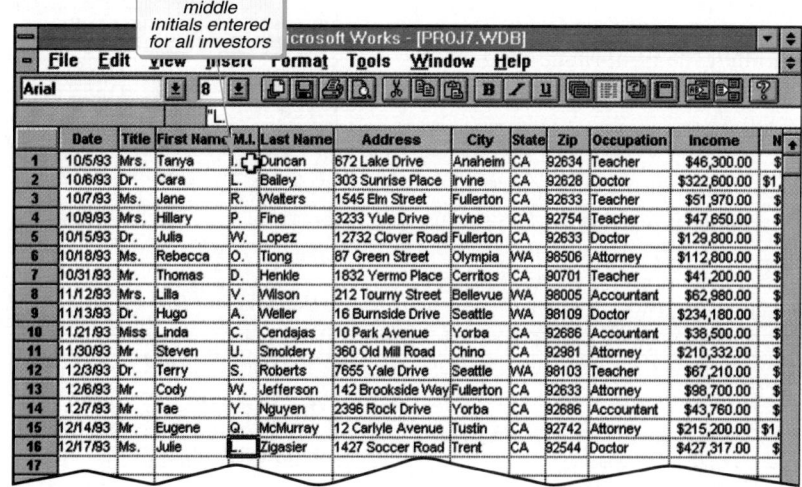

FIGURE 8-27

As you can see, when inserting a field in List view, you must insert the field, name the field, properly size the field, and enter the data for the field.

To insert a field in List view, you can also choose the **Record/Field command** from the Insert menu instead of clicking the Insert Field button on the Toolbar.

Sizing and Positioning an Inserted Field in Form View

When you insert a field in List view, the field is inserted into the database. As a result, it will also appear in Form view. The new field, however, is neither sized nor positioned properly on the form. To size and position the M.I. field in Form view, complete the following steps.

TO SIZE AND POSITION AN INSERTED FIELD IN FORM VIEW ▼

STEP 1 ►

Click the Form View button on the Toolbar.

Works displays the database in Form view (Figure 8-28). The record displayed and the field highlighted is the same as in List view (Figure 8-27). The inserted field name and field are highlighted and positioned in the upper left corner of the form. The field width is the Works Form view default value of 20.

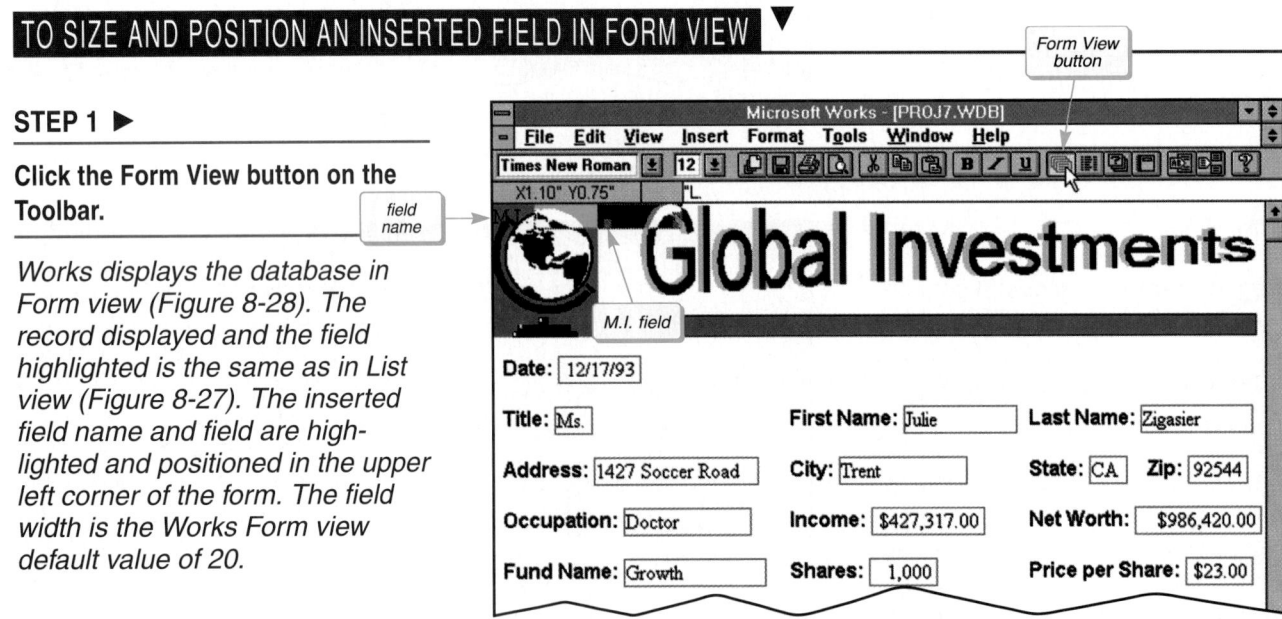

FIGURE 8-28

STEP 2 ►

Highlight the First Name field name and drag it left to coordinates X2.00" Y2.42".

The mouse pointer displays with the word MOVE below the pointer (Figure 8-29). As you drag, an outline shows where the field will be placed when you have completed the dragging operation.

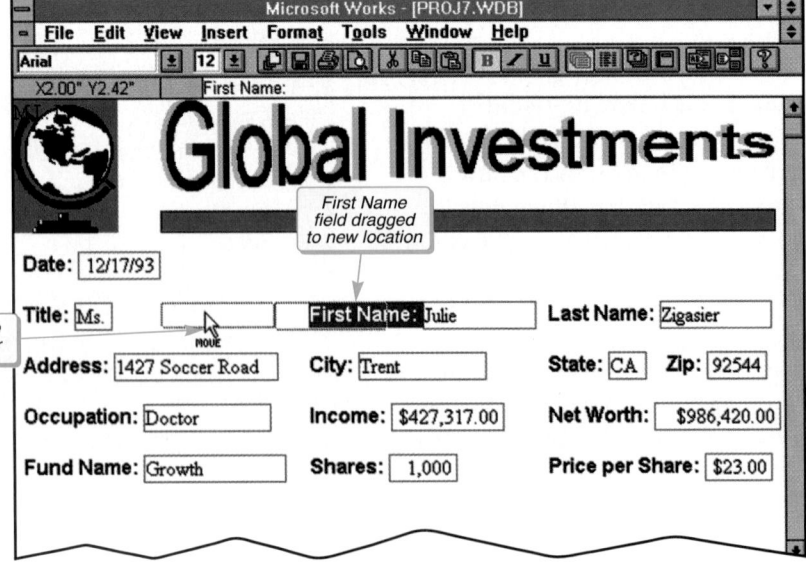

FIGURE 8-29

STEP 3 ▶

Release the left mouse button. Then highlight the M.I. field name in the upper left corner of the form and drag the M.I. field to coordinates X4.25" Y2.42".

As you drag the M.I. field, the outline displays (Figure 8-30). The outline also shows where the field will be placed when you have completed the dragging operation. Notice that part of the field overlaps the Last Name field. This will be corrected when the field width is reduced in size.

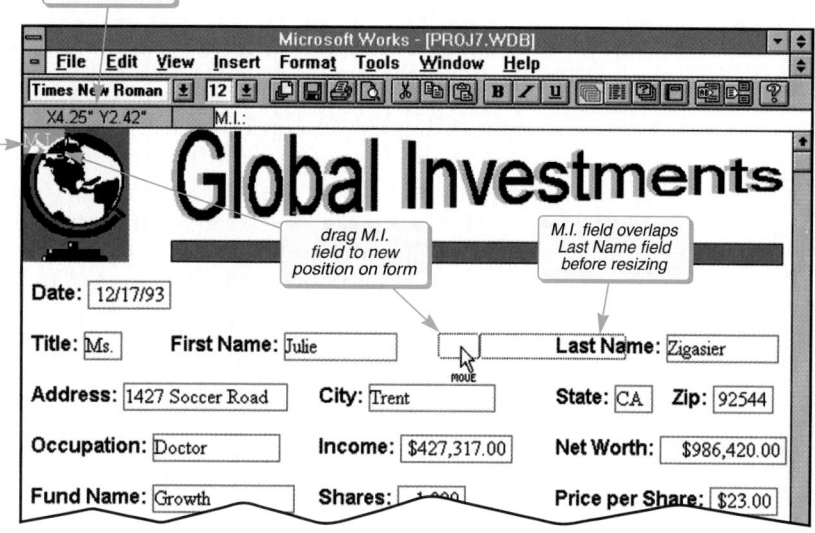

FIGURE 8-30

STEP 4 ▶

When the M.I. field is in the desired location, release the left mouse button. Format the Field name so that it displays as 12 point Arial bold font. Place a dark magenta outline border around the field. Position the mouse pointer on the resize handle at the right side of the M.I. field entry box. Drag the resize handle to the left to reduce the field size for the M.I. field so that only the middle initial and the period display. Release the left mouse button.

The M.I. field is positioned on the Form view screen, formatted, and resized to a width of 4 (Figure 8-31). You may check the size of the resized field by selecting the Format menu and choosing the Field Size command.

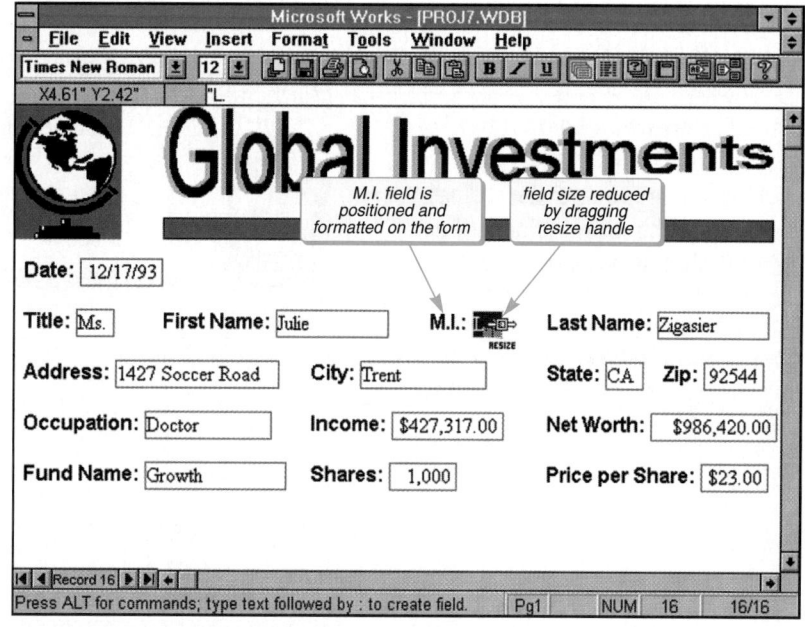

FIGURE 8-31

In virtually every case, whenever you insert a field using List view, you will have to resize and relocate the field in Form view.

After making changes to the database, it is suggested you save it by clicking the Save button on the Toolbar.

Adding a Field Containing a Formula in Form View

When you add a field in Form view, follow the same procedure as when you created the database in Project 7. This procedure is: (1) locate the position for the field on the form; (2) enter the field name; (3) enter the field size; (4) format the field name; (5) enter the field data; and (6) format the field data.

Works allows you to enter not only actual data but also **formulas** in a field. The formulas are similar to those you used when creating a spreadsheet. The formula begins with an equal sign and is followed by the names of the database fields that will be involved in the calculation.

In this project, a field called Investment is to be added to the database. The field width is 16. The value in the field is calculated by multiplying the Shares times the Price per Share. Thus, the formula is =Shares*Price per Share. The result of this calculation is the amount of money an investor invested. To add the Investment field to the database, perform the following steps.

TO ADD AND FORMAT A FIELD CONTAINING A FORMULA ▼

STEP 1 ▶

Place the insertion point at the coordinates X0.83" Y4.08" by clicking the mouse pointer at that location on the form. Point to the Insert Field button on the Toolbar.

The insertion point displays at the coordinates X0.83" Y4.08" and the mouse pointer points to the Insert Field button on the Toolbar (Figure 8-32).

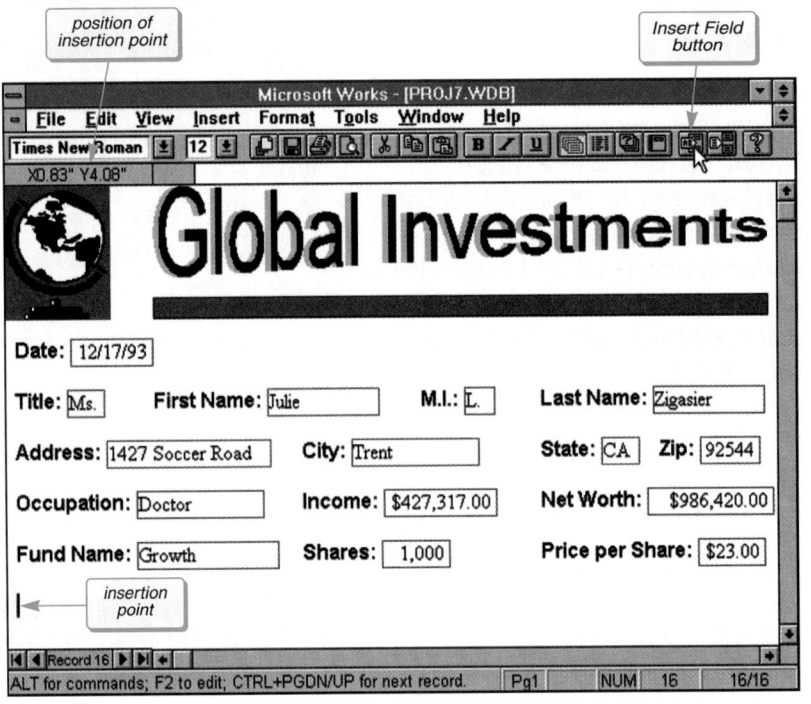

FIGURE 8-32

STEP 2 ►

Click the Insert Field button on the Toolbar. When the Insert Field dialog box displays, type the field name, Investment, in the Name text box, press the TAB key once, type 16 in the Width text box, and then point to the OK button.

Works displays the Insert Field dialog box (Figure 8-33). The word Investment is typed in the Name text box and the number 16 is typed in the Width text box. The mouse pointer points to the OK button.

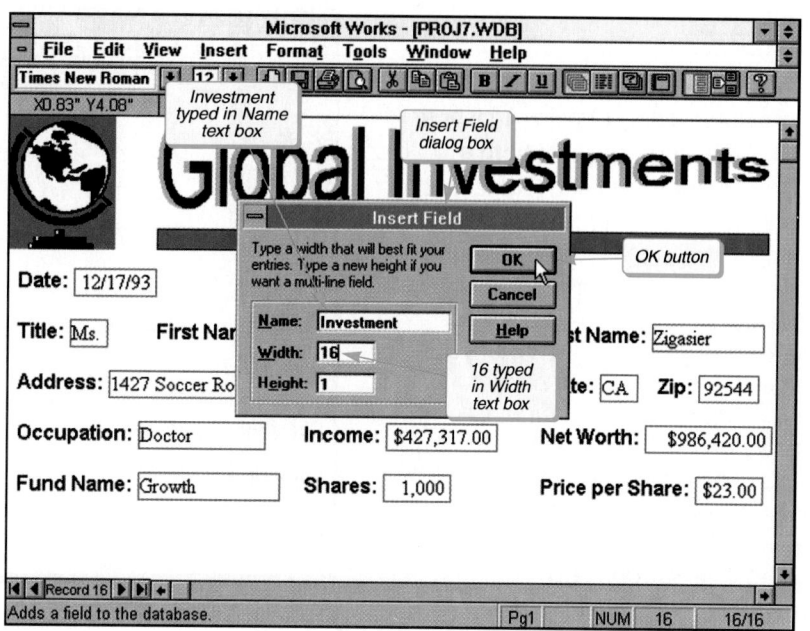

FIGURE 8-33

STEP 3 ►

Choose the OK button in the Insert Field dialog box.

When you choose the OK button, Works places the Investment field with a width of 16 on the database form in Form view (Figure 8-34).

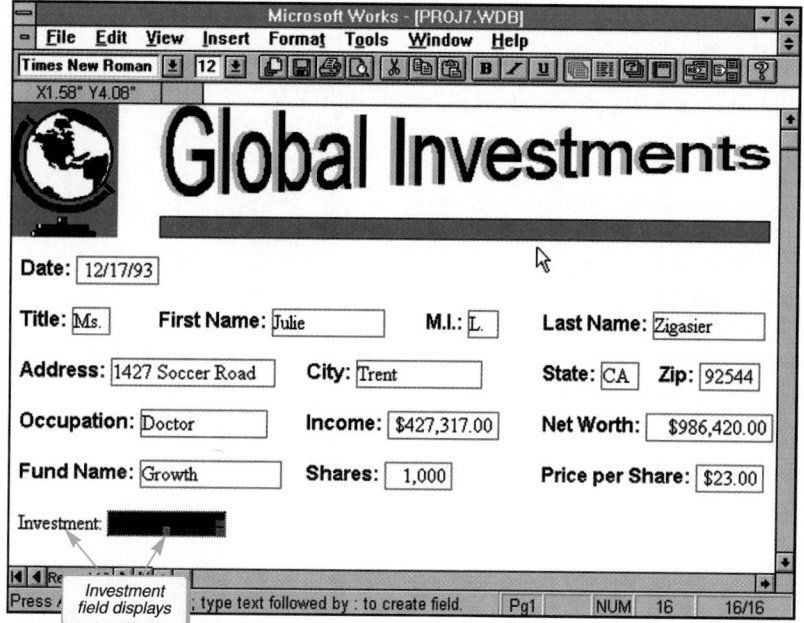

FIGURE 8-34

STEP 4 ▶

Highlight the Field Name. Format the Field Name using 12 point Arial bold font. Add a dark magenta border outline around the field. Highlight the Investment field and type the formula, `=Shares*Price per Share.`

The field name and field are formatted (Figure 8-35). When you type the equal sign and formula, they display in the formula bar and partially display in the Investment field. The equal sign informs Works you are entering a formula. The formula in the Investment field will multiply the value in the record's Shares field times the value in the record's Price per Share field.

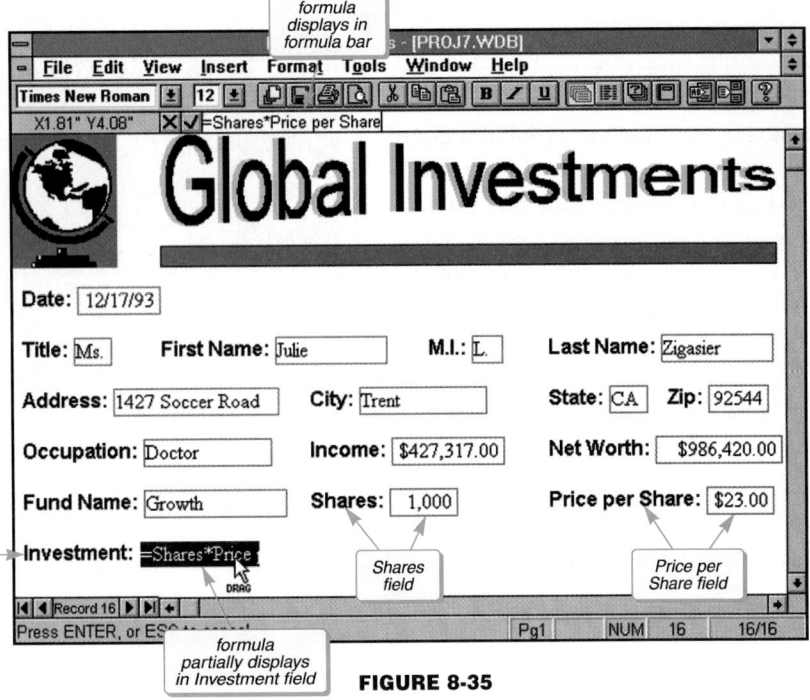

FIGURE 8-35

STEP 5 ▶

Press the ENTER key or click the Enter box.

Works calculates the formula and places the result in the Investment field (Figure 8-36). Because the Shares field contains the value 1,000 and the Price per Share field contains $23.00, the result in the Investment field is 23000.

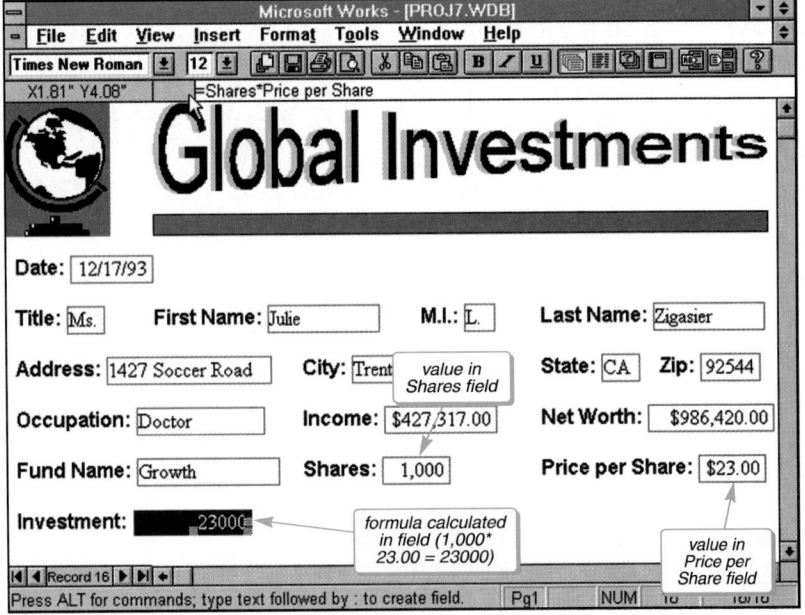

FIGURE 8-36

STEP 6 ▶

With the Investment field
highlighted, select the Format menu
and choose the Number command.
When the Number dialog box
displays, select the Currency option
button, check to ensure that the
number 2 displays in the Number of
decimals text box, and then choose
the OK button.

*The value in the Investment field
($23,000.00) is formatted as a cur-
rency field (Figure 8-37).*

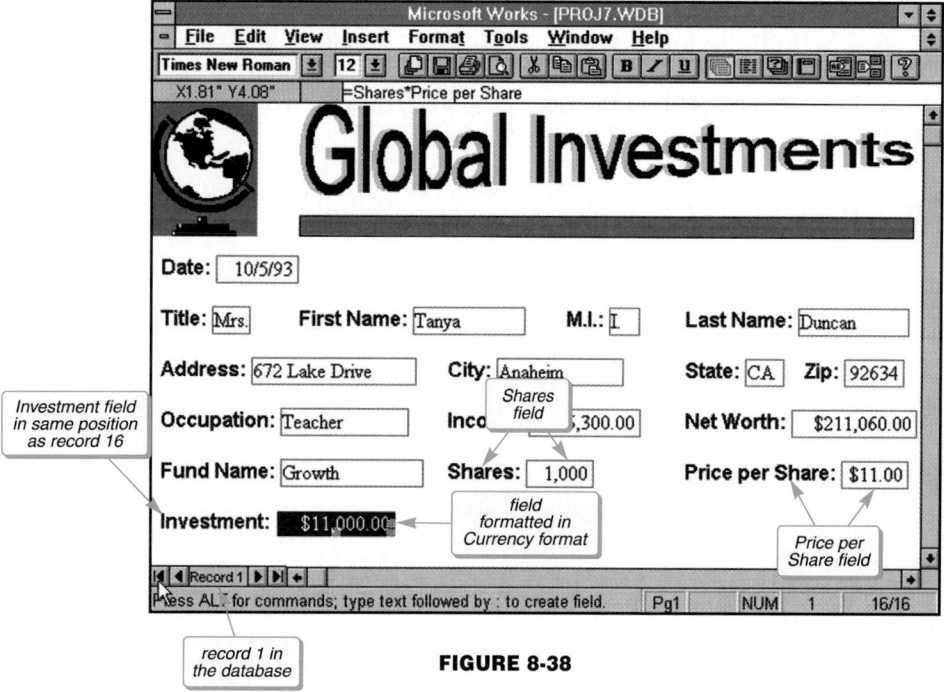

FIGURE 8-37

From Figure 8-37 you can see that the Investment field has been added to
record 16. When you add a field to one record in Form view, Works adds the field
to every other record in the database as well. This is illustrated Figure 8-38, where
record 1 in the database is displayed.

FIGURE 8-38

The Investment field in record 1 is located in the same position as in record 16 (see Figure 8-37 on the previous page). The value in the Investment field is displayed in the Currency format and the value, $11,000.00, is obtained by multiplying the record 1 Shares (1,000) times the record 1 Price per Share ($11.00). Each record in the database contains the Investment field, and in each record, the Investment is calculated by multiplying the Shares for that record times the Price per Share for that record.

The size of a field in List view that has been added in Form view will be 10, which is the List view default size. In Project 8, the field name Investment requires a width of 11 in List view to display properly. To change the Investment field width to 11 in List view, complete the following steps.

TO CHANGE THE FIELD WIDTH IN LIST VIEW

Step 1: Click the List View button on the Toolbar.
Step 2: Place the mouse pointer on the border between the Investment field name and the empty field to its right.
Step 3: Drag one position to the right. The Investment field name displays in its entirety.
Step 4: Click the Form View button on the Toolbar to return to Form view.

Adding or inserting fields in a database is an important procedure that occurs often when maintaining a database.

▶ DELETING DATABASE FIELDS

J ust as it is important to be able to add fields to records in a database, it is mandatory that you be able to delete fields from a database. You should delete fields from a database when they are no longer needed so they do not use valuable disk and memory space.

In Project 8, both the Income field and the Net Worth field are to be deleted from the database because they are no longer required for qualifying investors. The Income field will be deleted in Form view and the Net Worth field will be deleted in List view.

Deleting a Field in Form View

To delete the Income field when the database displays in Form view, complete the following steps.

TO DELETE A FIELD IN FORM VIEW ▼

STEP 1 ▶

With the database displayed in Form view, highlight the field name (Income) of the field to be deleted. Select the Insert menu and point to the Delete Selection command.

*The Income field name is highlighted and the Insert menu displays (Figure 8-39). The mouse pointer points to the **Delete Selection command**.*

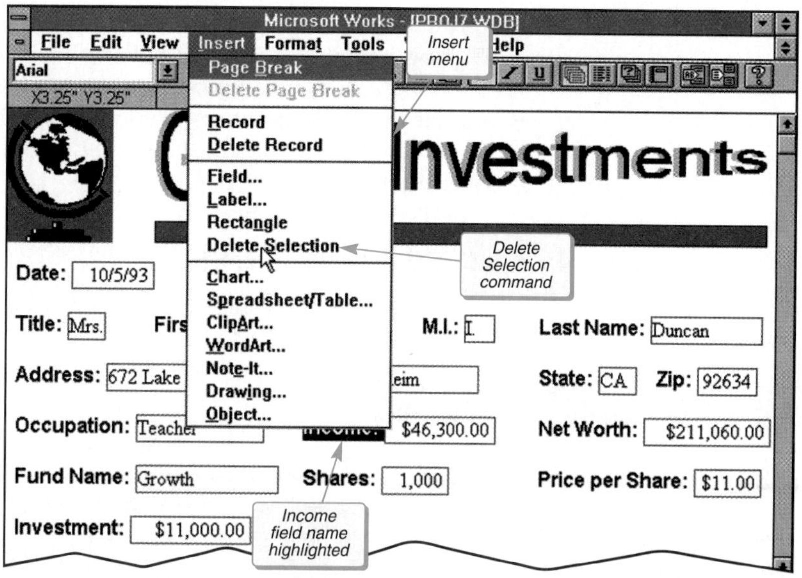

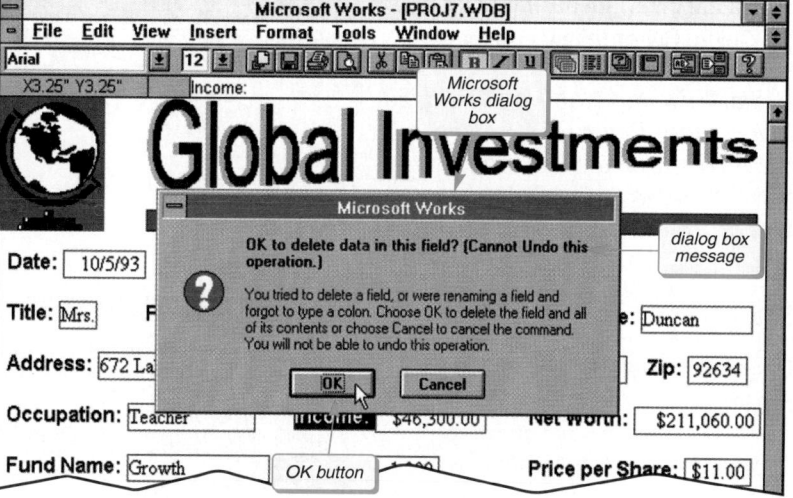

FIGURE 8-39

STEP 2 ▶

Choose the Delete Selection command. When the Microsoft Works dialog box displays, point to the OK button.

Works displays the Microsoft Works dialog box with the message, OK to delete data in this field? (Figure 8-40). This dialog box is intended to act as a safeguard so you do not accidentally delete a field you want to retain. If you did not want to delete this field, you would choose the Cancel button.

FIGURE 8-40

STEP 3 ▶

Choose the OK button in the Microsoft Works dialog box.

The Income field is deleted from the database (Figure 8-41).

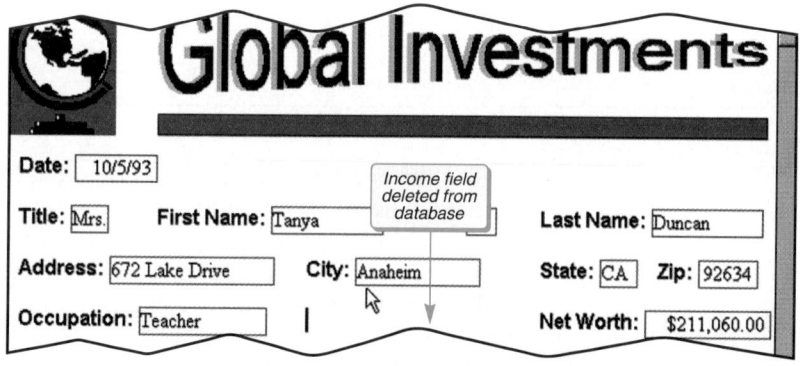

FIGURE 8-41

Note these two important points when deleting a field in a Works database. First, even though you delete the field from a single record, such as record 1 in Figure 8-41, the field is deleted from all records in the database. Thus, the Income field is deleted from all records in the database.

Second, when you are using Form view, once you have chosen the OK button in the Microsoft Works dialog box shown in Figure 8-40 on the previous page, the field is deleted and you cannot undo your action. Therefore, as a precaution it is normally a good idea to save the database before deleting fields so if you make a mistake, you can recover the data.

Deleting a Field in List View

To delete the Net Worth field in List view, perform the following steps.

TO DELETE A FIELD IN LIST VIEW ▼

STEP 1 ▶

Click the List View button on the Toolbar. Highlight the Net Worth field by clicking the field name (Net Worth). Select the Insert menu and point to the Delete Record/Field command.

*In List view, the Net Worth field is highlighted (Figure 8-42). This is the field to delete. The mouse pointer points to the **Delete Record/Field command** on the Insert menu.*

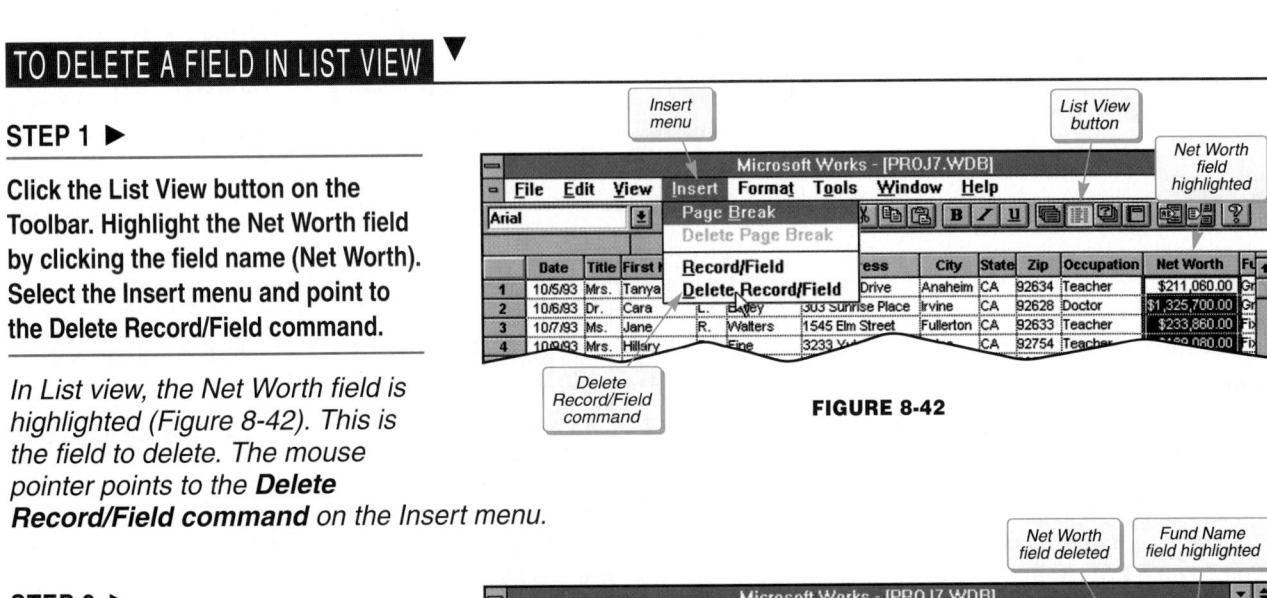

FIGURE 8-42

STEP 2 ▶

Choose the Delete Record/Field command.

Works deletes the highlighted field (Net Worth), moves fields left, and highlights the adjacent field to the right (Fund Name) (Figure 8-43).

FIGURE 8-43

Unlike Form view, when you delete a field in List view no dialog box displays as a safeguard to ensure you are deleting the correct field. When you choose the Delete Record/Field command from the Insert menu, the field deletion takes place with no further authorization. Thus, you should exercise care when deleting fields in List view to ensure you are deleting only those fields no longer intended to be part of the database.

However, unlike Form view, once you have deleted a field in List view you can use the Undo command on the Edit menu to restore the deleted field if you have performed no subsequent operations. You may have to resize the field after it has been deleted to properly display the values.

► CHANGING FIELD NAMES

O n some occasions, a field name used in a database must be changed. This can occur when the name is not as descriptive as possible, when there is a possible conflict with another field name in the database, or for a variety of other reasons. In the investment club database, you are to change the Price per Share field name to Share Price. To accomplish this task in Form view, complete the following steps.

TO CHANGE A FIELD NAME IN FORM VIEW ▼

STEP 1 ►

Click the Form View button on the Toolbar to return to Form view. Then highlight the Price per Share field name and type Share Price:.

The typed field name, Share Price:, displays in the formula bar and in the field name position on the form (Figure 8-44). When you begin typing the words Share Price:, the field entry disappears. Note that the Net Worth field, which was deleted in List view, no longer displays in Form view.

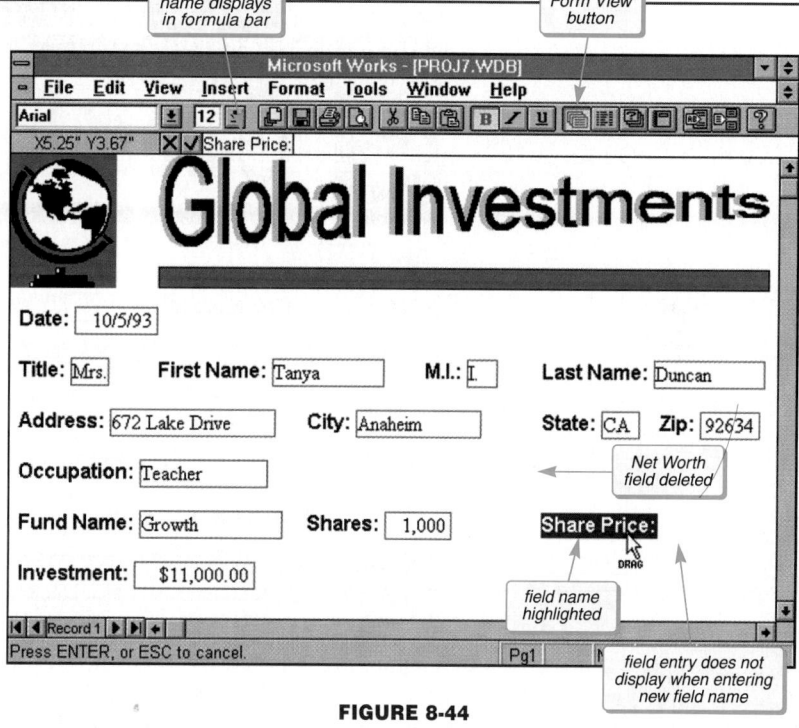

FIGURE 8-44

STEP 2 ►

Press the ENTER key or click the Enter box.

Share Price becomes the new field name (Figure 8-45).

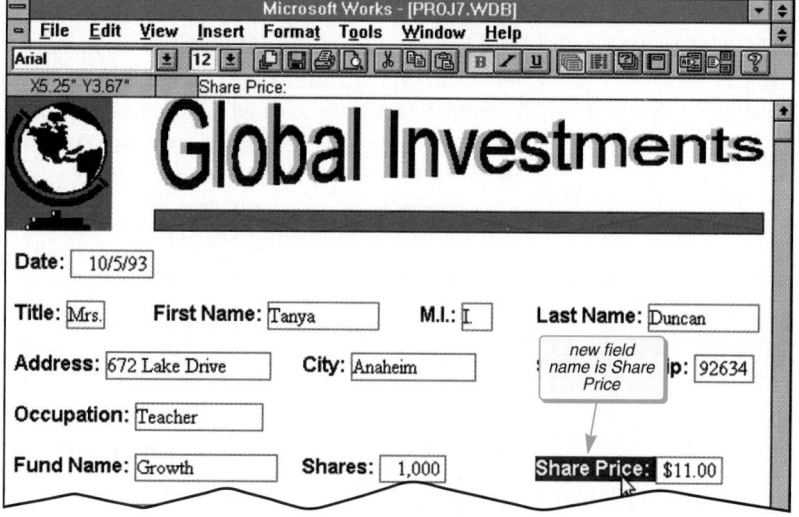

FIGURE 8-45

As you can see, the procedure for changing a field name in Form view is virtually the same as the procedure used for defining a field name in Project 7. When you view the database in List view, the name of the field will be Share Price, as well.

An important consideration when changing a field name is that Works also will change any reference to the field name in formulas. To illustrate this, in Figure 8-46, the Investment field is highlighted. Notice in the formula displayed in the formula bar that the field name used is Share Price, which is the new field name.

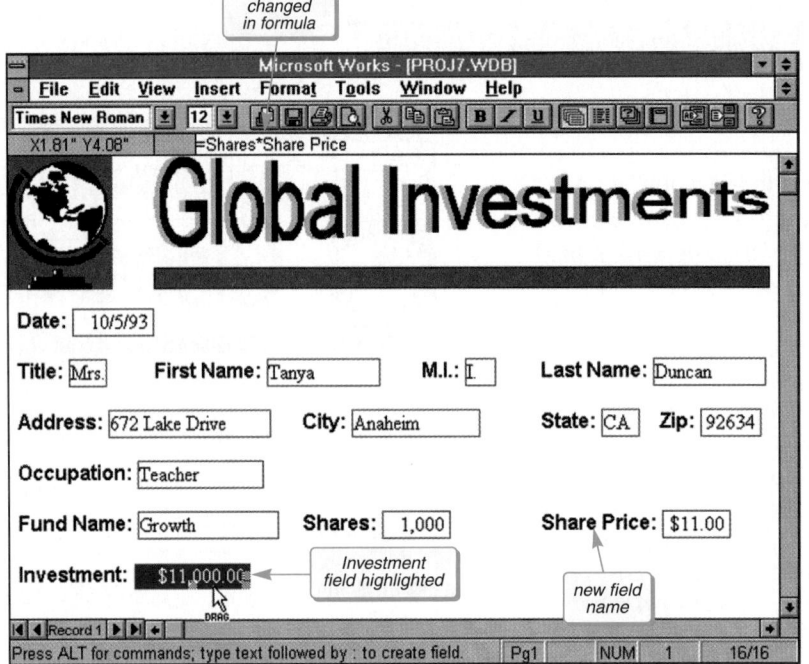

FIGURE 8-46

▶ CHANGING FIELD SIZE IN FORM VIEW

I n some applications, the size of the field should be changed because it is either too small to accommodate all entries or it is larger than it needs to be. In this project, the Occupation field size in Form view should be changed from a width of 17 to a width of 12.

In a previous example, you saw how to change the field size in Form view for the middle initial field by dragging a resize handle. The field size in Form view can also be changed by using the **Field Size command** from the Format menu, as shown in the following steps.

TO CHANGE FIELD SIZE IN FORM VIEW ▼

STEP 1 ▶

Highlight the Occupation field, select the Format menu, and point to the Field Size command.

The Occupation field is highlighted and the Format menu displays (Figure 8-47). The mouse pointer points to the Field Size command.

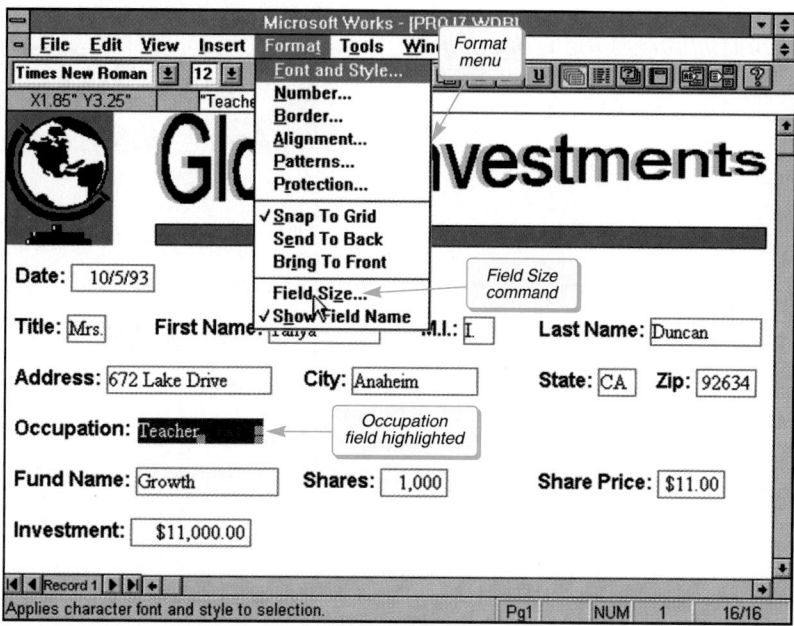

FIGURE 8-47

STEP 2 ▶

Choose the Field Size command from the Format menu. When the Field Size dialog box displays, type 12 in the Width text box and then point to the OK button.

Works displays the Field Size dialog box (Figure 8-48). The value 12, which is the new field size, displays in the Width text box. The mouse pointer points to the OK button.

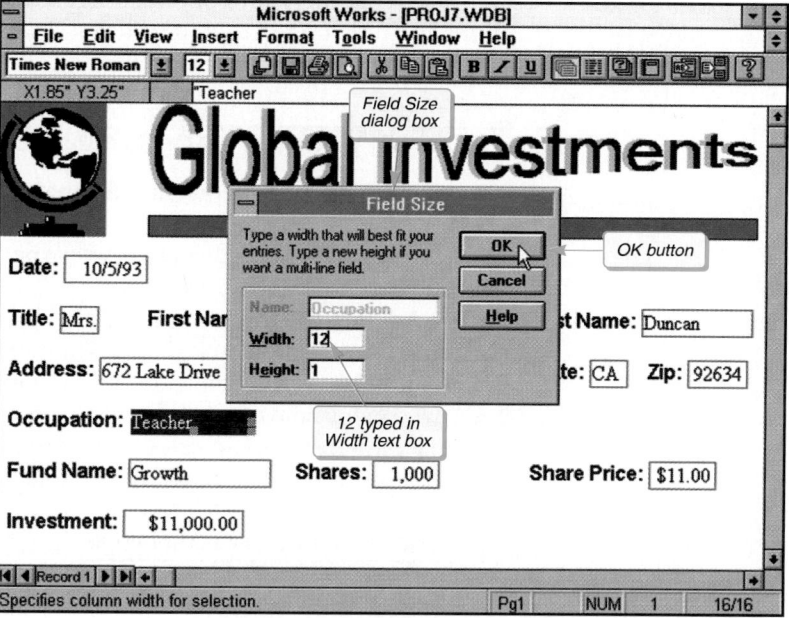

FIGURE 8-48

STEP 3 ▶

Choose the OK button.

Works changes the width of the Occupation field in all records to 12 (Figure 8-49).

FIGURE 8-49

Changing the width of a field already defined in the database is a process that should be fully understood because it is an important part of maintaining a database

▶ REFORMATTING THE FORM VIEW

W hen changes occur in a database record, you will often be required to modify the format of the record in Form view. In addition, after the form has been designed, you may determine a design that better suits your needs.

Redefining the format of the form could involve moving fields, adding labels, changing label or field styles, and other alterations. For the Form view of the investment club database, the changes are: (1) move the Fund Name, Shares, Share Price, and Investment fields to different locations on the form; (2) add several labels (an X and an =) to illustrate the calculation (Shares X Share Price = Investment).

To move the fields, perform the following steps (see Figure 8-50).

TO MOVE FIELDS IN FORM VIEW

Step 1: Highlight the Fund Name field name and drag to the coordinates X3.25" Y3.25".

Step 2: Highlight the Shares field name and drag to the coordinates X0.83" Y3.67".

Step 3: Highlight the Share Price field name and drag to the coordinates X3.25" Y3.67".

Step 4: Highlight the Investment field name and drag to the coordinates X5.25" Y3.67".

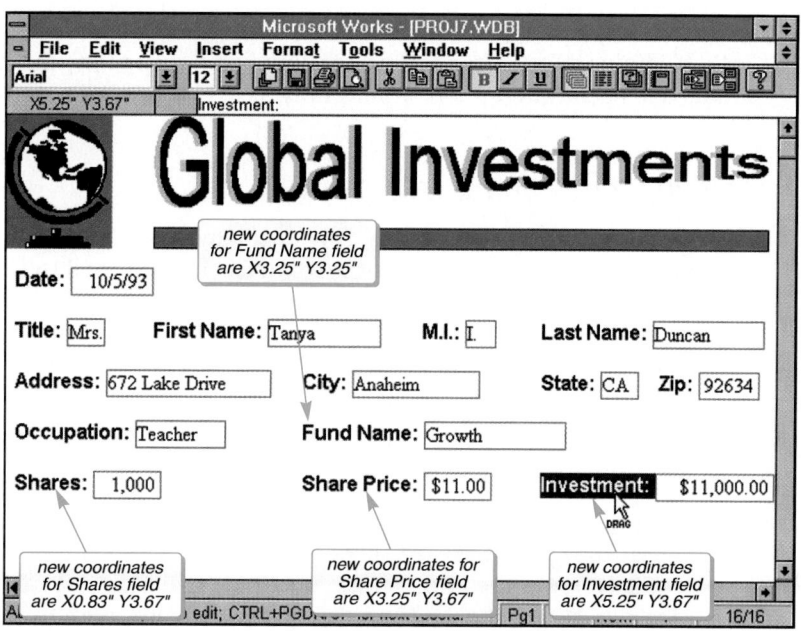

FIGURE 8-50

The Form view of the database after moving the fields to new positions is shown in Figure 8-50.

The next change to the format of the database in Form view is to add several labels to illustrate the calculation that produces the Investment value. A label is identifying information placed in a database form. Labels can be any words or numbers that provide the description or instructions you need. Labels can be any length. To make these changes, perform the following steps (see Figure 8-51).

TO ADD LABELS TO FORM VIEW

Step 1: Position the insertion point at the coordinates X2.58" Y3.67", type X, and click the Enter box or press the ENTER key. Do not type a colon following a label. Then change the label to Arial font and click the Bold button on the Toolbar.

Step 2: Position the insertion point at the coordinates X5.00" Y3.67", type =, and click the Enter box or press the ENTER key. Then change the equal sign to Arial font and click the Bold button on the Toolbar.

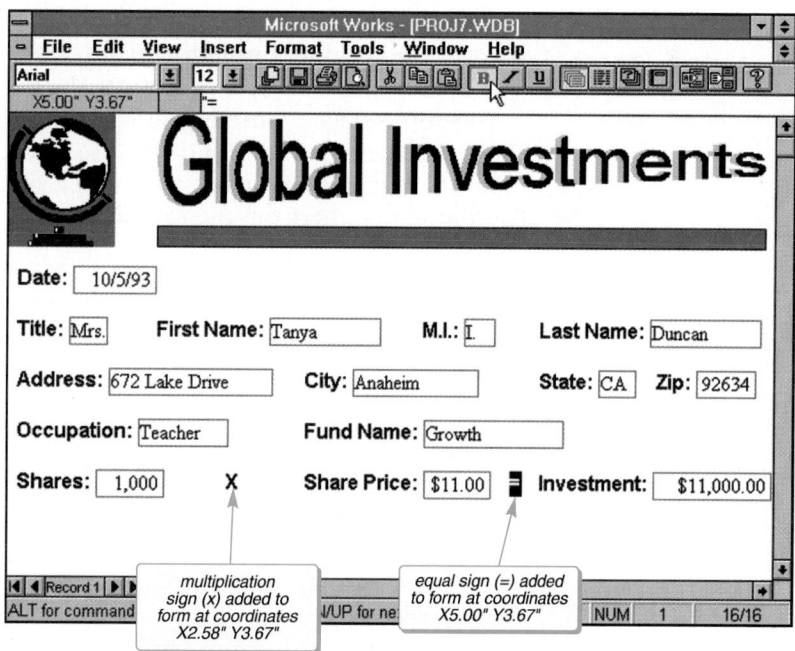

FIGURE 8-51

The database in Form view after adding the labels displays in Figure 8-51 on the previous page. After adding the labels to Form view, the maintenance of the database is complete. You should now save the revised database.

Saving a Revised Database

As you revise the database, it is normally a good practice to save the database periodically so your work is not lost in case of electrical or computer failure. If you are revising a database and want to keep the same name, then you should save the database by clicking the Save button on the Toolbar or by choosing the Save command from the File menu.

If you want to save the database using a different name, such as PROJ8, then use the Save As command shown in earlier projects. Perform the following steps to save the database with a new name.

TO SAVE A DATABASE FILE WITH A NEW NAME

Step 1: From the File menu, choose the Save As command.
Step 2: When the Save As dialog box displays, type `proj8` in the File Name text box.
Step 3: Select drive a: from the Drives drop-down list box.
Step 4: Choose the OK button in the Save As dialog box.

▶ VIEWING THE DATABASE IN LIST VIEW

When you work with a database in List view, quite often the records contain more fields than can display on the screen at one time. In some cases, it is advantageous to view records with the leftmost and rightmost fields visible, but with some fields between them not visible. Works allows you to do this by dividing the database work area into two or more panes. A **pane** is a part of the window through which you can view a portion of the database. The panes are separated by a **vertical split bar**, a **horizontal split bar**, or both.

Suppose, for example, you want to view the name of the investors in the database together with the Fund Name, Shares, Share Price, and Investment fields. To split the window into a left pane and a right pane and view these fields together on the screen, perform the following steps.

TO VIEW DATABASE IN PANES ▼

STEP 1 ►

If the database is not displayed in List view, click the List View button on the Toolbar. Position the mouse pointer on the vertical split box, which is a thin bar to the left of the left scroll arrow at the bottom of the screen.

*The database displays in List view (Figure 8-52). The mouse pointer, when positioned on the **vertical split box**, changes shape to two vertical bars and two horizontal arrows with the word ADJUST beneath it. The pointer indicates you can split the screen into two panes.*

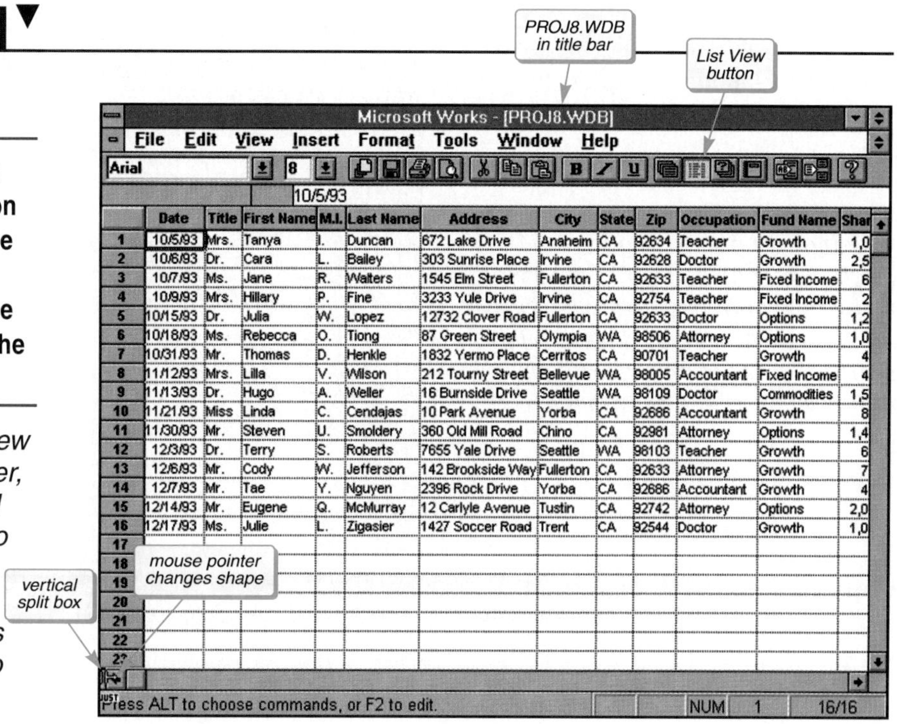

FIGURE 8-52

STEP 2 ►

Drag the mouse pointer and the vertical split bar to the right until the split bar rests in the first position of the Address field.

When you drag the mouse pointer positioned on the vertical split box, a wide vertical line called the vertical split bar accompanies the pointer (Figure 8-53). The split bar indicates where the window will be separated into panes. In Figure 8-53, the split bar is located at the beginning of the Address field. This location informs Works to make the Address field part of the right pane and the Last Name field part of the left pane.

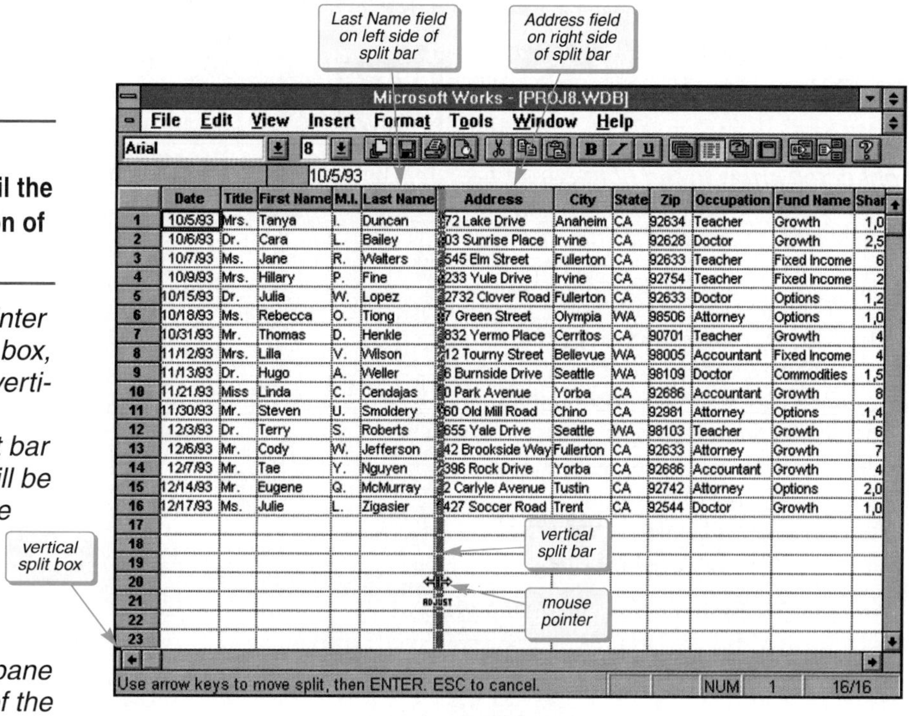

FIGURE 8-53

STEP 3 ►

Release the left mouse button and move the mouse pointer off the split bar.

Works divides the window into two side-by-side panes (Figure 8-54). Each pane has its own scroll bar, scroll box, and scroll arrows. This means you can scroll data in either pane left or right and the data in the other pane will not move.

FIGURE 8-54

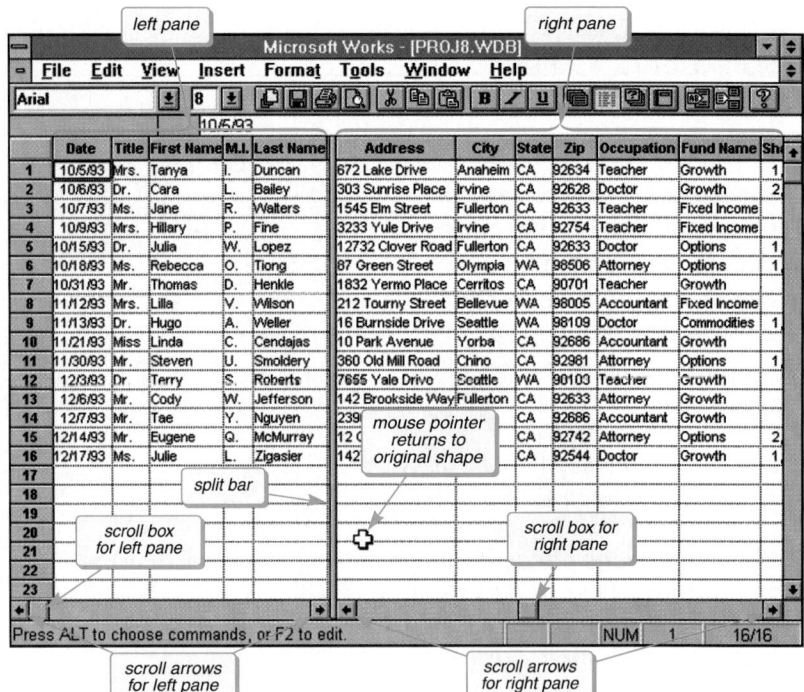

STEP 4 ►

Point to the right scroll arrow in the right pane and click the scroll arrow five times.

The mouse pointer points to the right scroll arrow in the right pane (Figure 8-55). Each time you click the right scroll arrow, the data in the right pane moves one field to the left, but the data in the left pane does not move. As a result, the left pane displays the Date, Title, First Name, M. I., and Last Name fields while the right pane displays the Fund Name, Shares, Share Price, and Investment fields. The fields between the Last Name and the Fund Name are hidden from view.

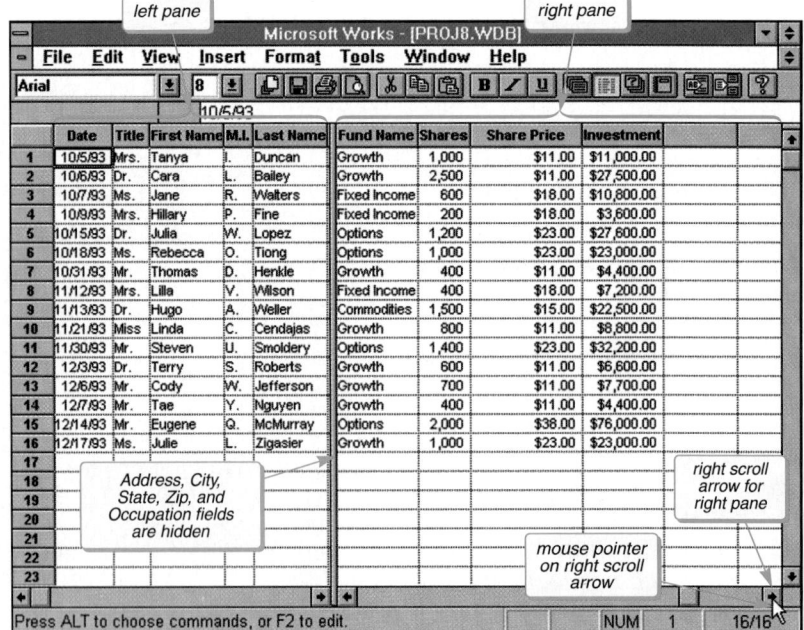

FIGURE 8-55

STEP 5 ▶

Through the use of the scroll arrows for the left and right panes, you can view any combination of fields you want. To remove the panes and return to a single window, position the mouse pointer on the split bar.

The mouse pointer changes shape and rests on the split bar (Figure 8-56).

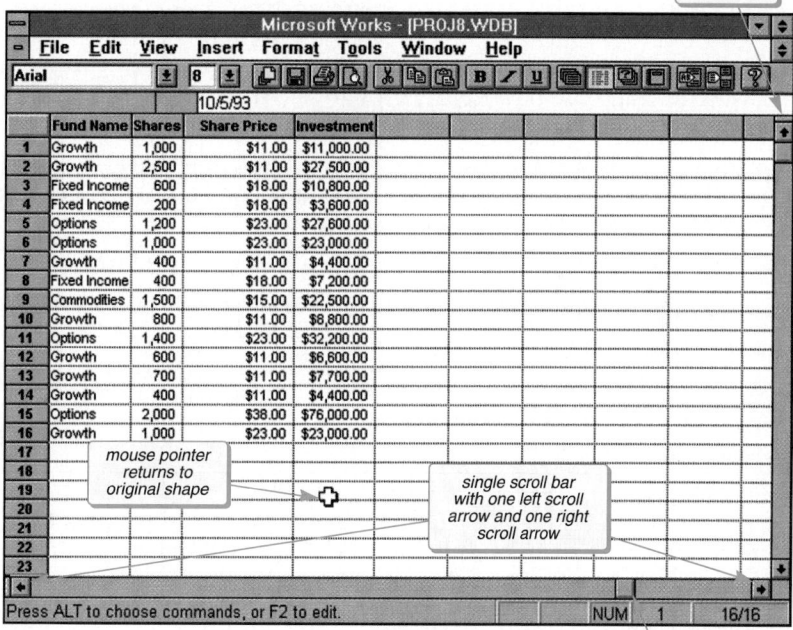

FIGURE 8-56

STEP 6 ▶

Double-click the left mouse button.

The split bar disappears and the separate panes no longer display (Figure 8-57). A single scroll bar, with a single scroll box and one set of scroll arrows displays at the bottom of the screen. The leftmost field (Fund Name) in the right pane (Figure 8-56) becomes the leftmost field in the window.

FIGURE 8-57

You can divide the List view window into an upper and lower pane by pointing to the **horizontal split box** (Figure 8-57 on the previous page) and dragging the split bar down to the desired location. This configuration is useful when your database consists of many records and you want to view records at the beginning of the database and other records in the middle or end of the database. For example, if the database contained 1,000 records, you could view record 1 through record 10 in the upper pane, and records 990 through 1,000 in the lower pane. When you split the window into upper and lower panes, each pane has a separate vertical scroll bar.

You can also split the window into four panes, each with its own scroll bar, using one of two methods: (1) drag the vertical split bar to the desired location, and then drag the horizontal split bar to the desired location; or (2) from the Window menu, choose the Split command.

When you choose the **Split command** from the Window menu, Works displays a horizontal and vertical split bar with a **split pointer** positioned at the intersection of the bars (Figure 8-58). You can drag the intersection around the window until you have selected the desired location, and then click the left mouse button to set the vertical and horizontal split bars in a permanent position.

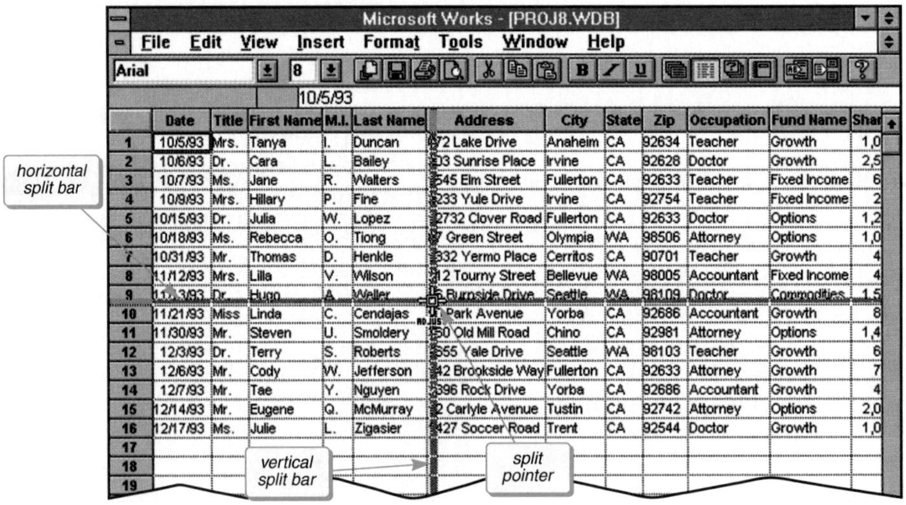

FIGURE 8-58

To return to a single window, place the mouse pointer at the intersection of the split bars, where it will once again change to the split pointer, and double-click the left mouse button.

▶ REFORMATTING A DATABASE

I n some applications a database may contain data which, when used in a different format, can produce a report or provide useful information. The PROJ8 database is such an application. To create the report in Figure 8-59, data in the PROJ8 database must be reformatted.

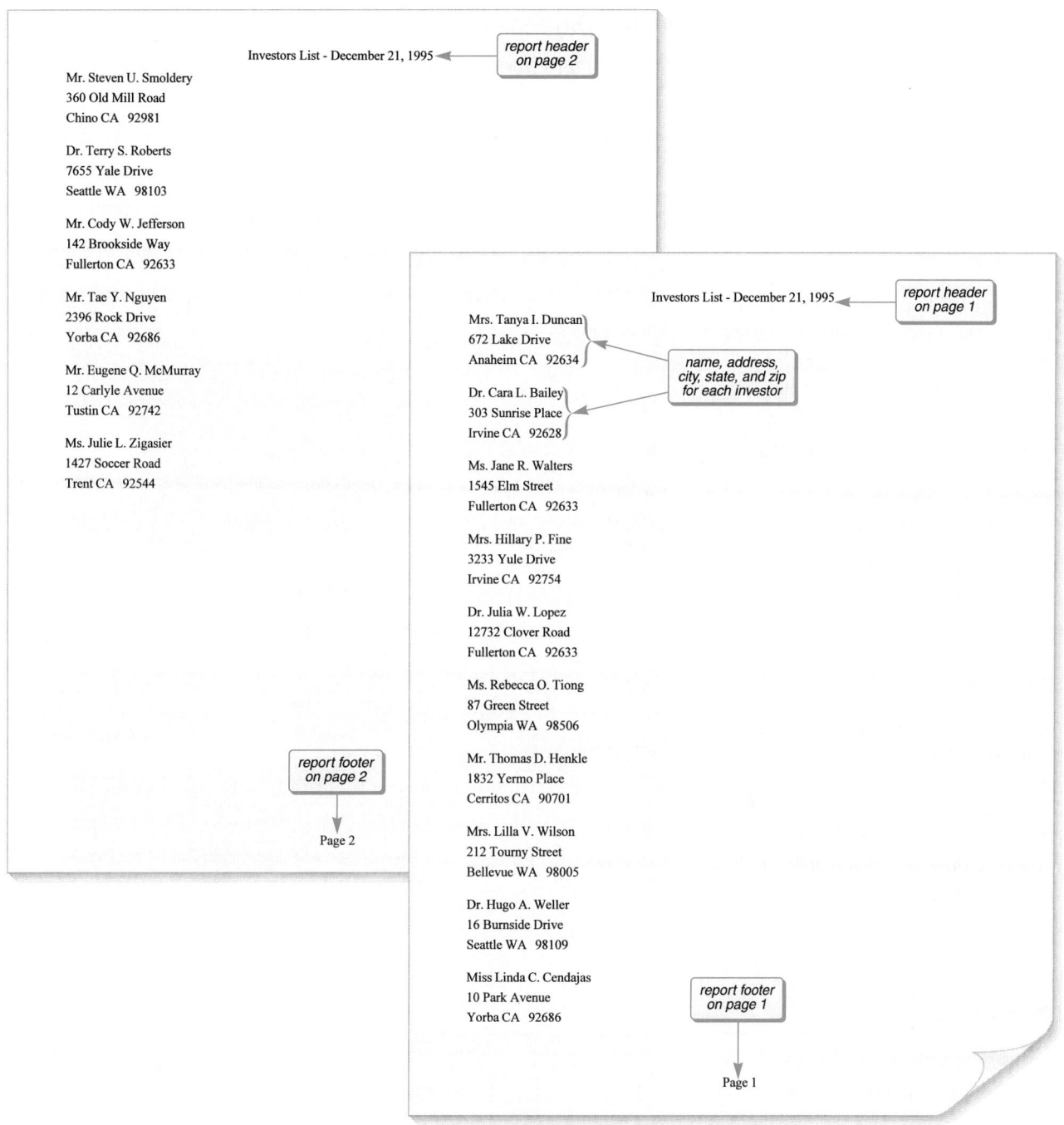

FIGURE 8-59

The reformatting process includes the following steps: (1) delete the fields in the PROJ8 database that are not needed for the report; (2) delete the clip art, WordArt title, and labels from the Form view of the database; (3) reformat the Form view of the database, including moving fields, removing field names, invoking the Slide to left option of the database, and changing settings in the Page Setup dialog box; (4) print the reformatted database in the new report format; and (5) save the reformatted database with a new name.

Each of these steps is explained in detail on the following pages.

Deleting Fields in a Database

The first task is to delete the fields not being used in the report. Complete the following steps to perform this task.

TO DELETE FIELDS IN LIST VIEW ▼

STEP 1 ►

With the PROJ8 database displayed in List view, scroll the window so the Occupation, Fund Name, Shares, Share Price, and Investment fields are visible. Then, drag the mouse pointer across these field names.

Works highlights the fields over which you dragged the mouse pointer (Figure 8-60).

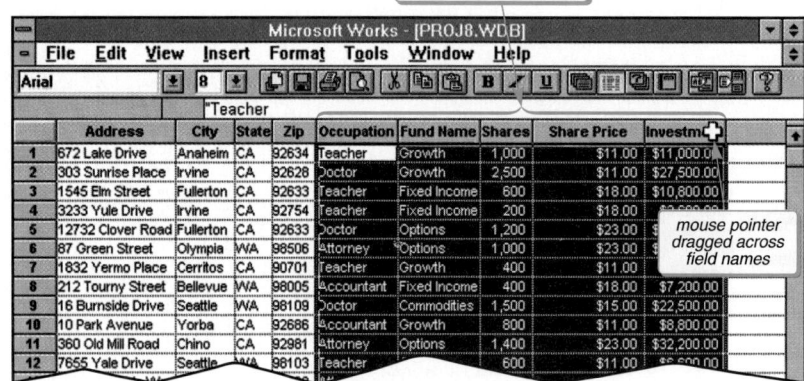

FIGURE 8-60

STEP 2 ►

Select the Insert menu and point to the Delete Record/Field command.

*The Insert menu displays and the mouse pointer points to the **Delete Record/Field command** (Figure 8-61).*

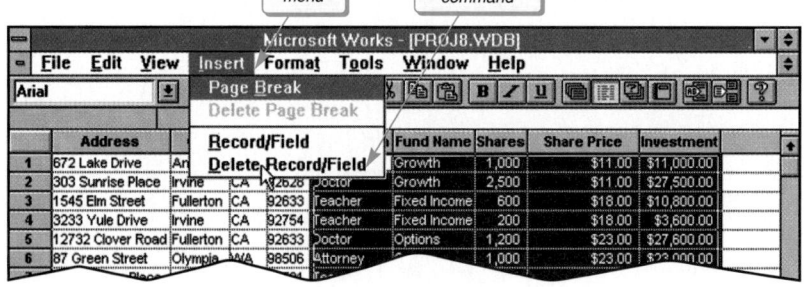

FIGURE 8-61

STEP 3 ►

Choose the Delete Record/Field command from the Insert menu.

Works deletes all the highlighted fields (Occupation, Fund Name, Shares, Share Price, and Investment) (Figure 8-62).

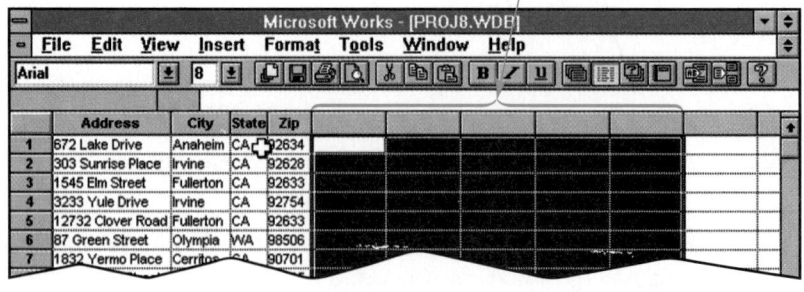

FIGURE 8-62

After deleting the fields in the List view, you must delete selected information in Form view.

Deleting Clip Art, WordArt, Fields, and Labels in Form View

The next task is to delete the clip art, the WordArt title, fields, and labels from Form view because this information is not used when producing the report. Complete the following steps to accomplish this task.

TO DELETE CLIP ART, WORDART, FIELDS, AND LABELS IN FORM VIEW ▼

STEP 1 ►

Click the Form View button on the Toolbar to display the database in Form view. Highlight the clip art of the globe by clicking it. Then, while holding down the CTRL key, click the object containing the words Global Investments, the rectangle, the Date field name, the X label, and the = label. Select the Insert menu and point to the Delete Selection command.

The database displays in Form view (Figure 8-63). The selected fields are highlighted. The mouse pointer points to the Delete Selection command on the Insert menu.

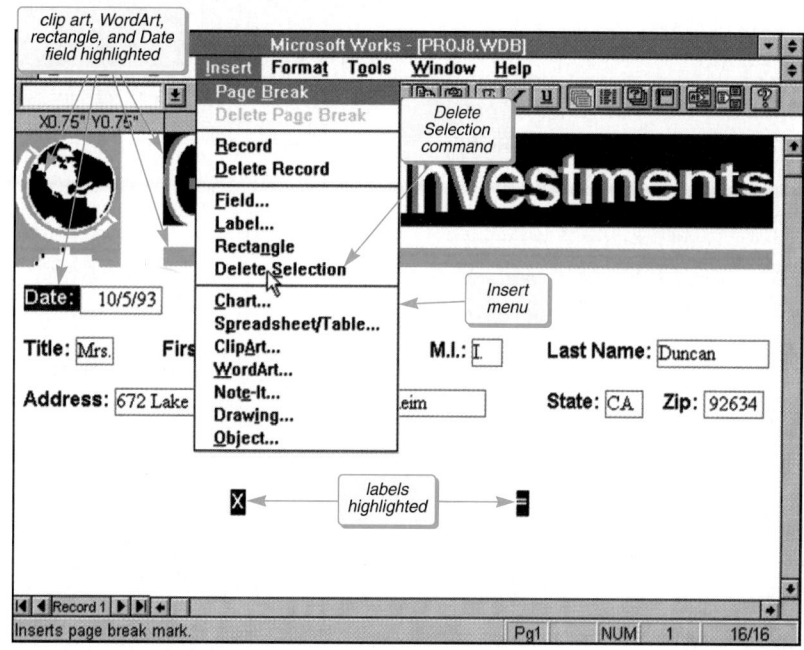

FIGURE 8-63

STEP 2 ►

Choose the Delete Selection command from the Insert menu. Choose the OK button in the Microsoft Works dialog box containing the question, OK to delete data in this field?

The clip art, the words Global Investments, the rectangle, the Date field, the X label, and = label are deleted (Figure 8-64).

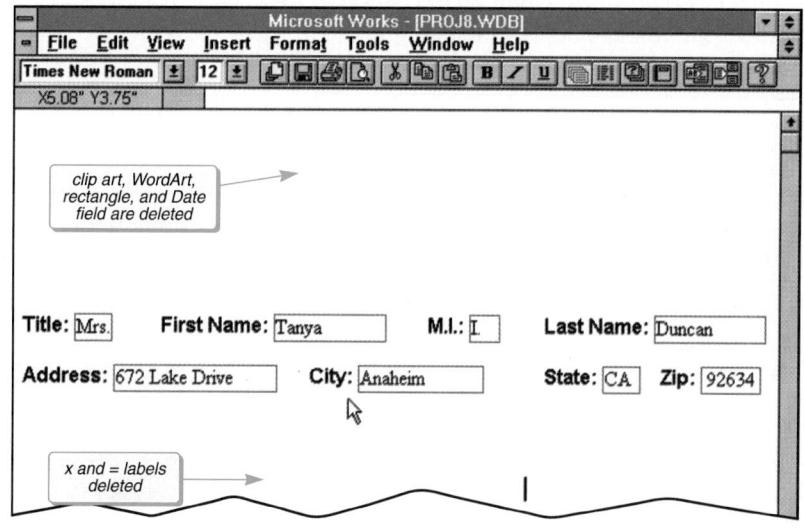

FIGURE 8-64

All the fields that are not needed to produce the output in Figure 8-59 on page W8.39 are now deleted from the database. The remaining fields, Title, First Name, M.I., Last Name, Address, City, State, and Zip are used to prepare the report.

Reformatting the Form View of the Database

The next task requires reformatting the Form view of the database. The first step is to rearrange the fields on the form, as shown in the following steps.

TO REARRANGE FIELDS IN FORM VIEW ▼

STEP 1 ▶

Click the Title field name. Then, while holding down the CTRL key, click the First Name, M.I., and Last Name field names.

The Title, First Name, M.I., and Last Name field names are highlighted (Figure 8-65).

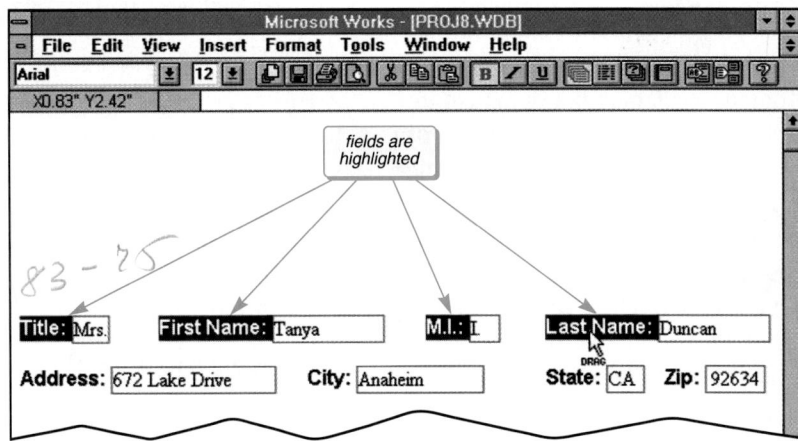

FIGURE 8-65

STEP 2 ▶

Drag the highlighted fields upward as a unit to the coordinates X0.83" Y0.75" and release the left mouse button.

The Title, First Name, M. I., and Last Name fields move upward as a unit and are positioned at the top left section of the form (Figure 8-66).

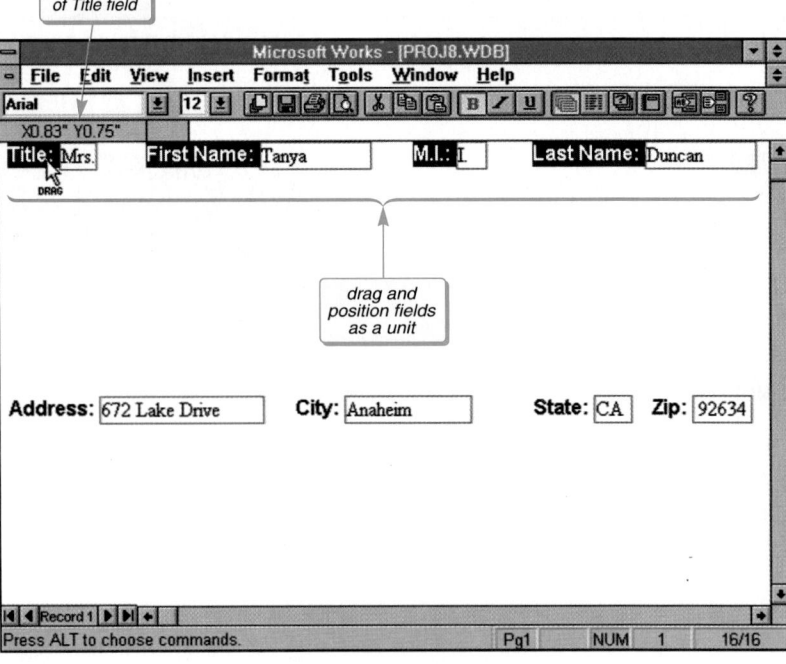

FIGURE 8-66

STEP 3 ▶

**Highlight the Address field name
and drag it to the coordinates
X0.83" Y1.00". Highlight the
City, State, and Zip fields
and drag the City, State, and
Zip fields as a unit to X0.83" Y1.25".**

*The fields are positioned in three
rows near the top of the form
(Figure 8-67).*

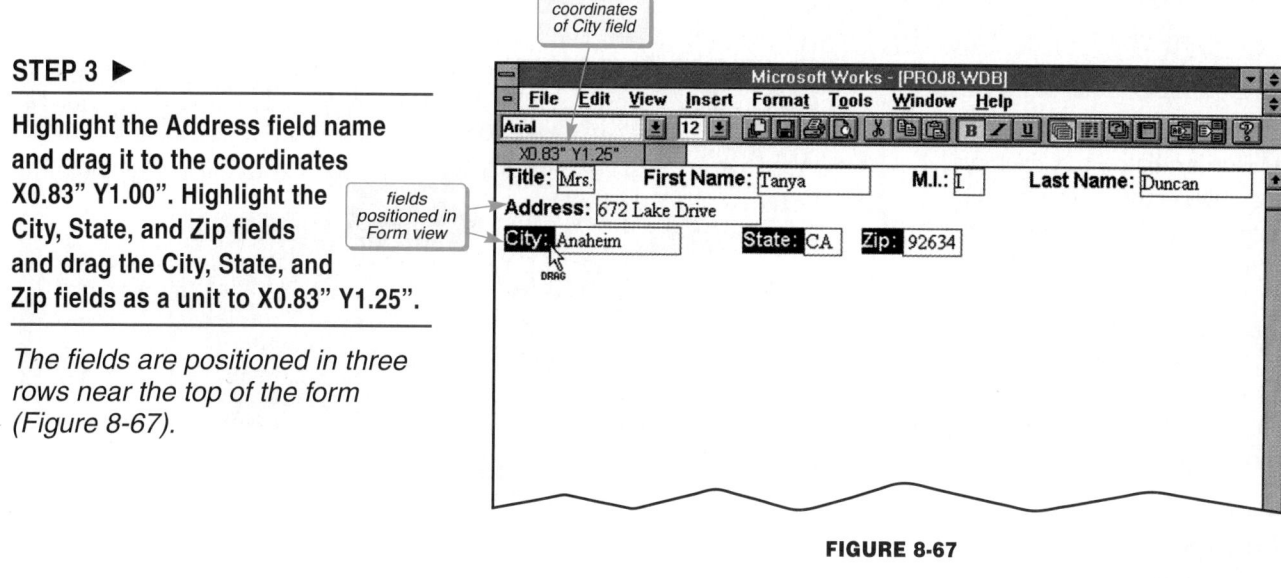

FIGURE 8-67

Removing the Border

After the fields are rearranged as shown in Figure 8-67, you must remove the
border surrounding the field entries and then inform Works that when the fields
print, they are to print next to each other. In addition, you must indicate to Works
that the field names are not to print (see Figure 8-59 on page W8.39). Perform the
following steps to remove the border.

TO REMOVE A BORDER AROUND THE FIELD ENTRIES ▼

STEP 1 ▶

**Highlight all the fields, select the
Format menu, and point to the
Border command (Figure 8-68).**

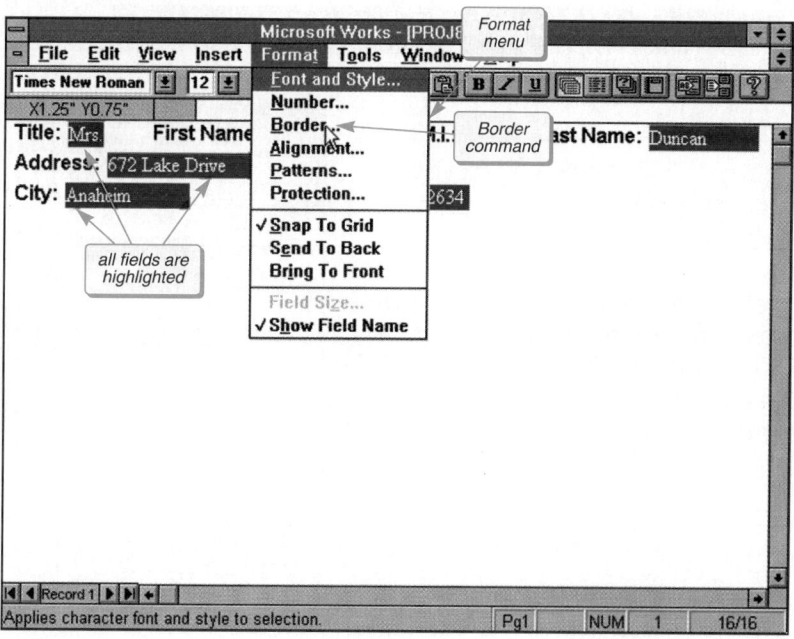

FIGURE 8-68

STEP 2 ▶

Choose the Border command. When the Border dialog box displays, select the empty box in the Line Style area and then point to the OK button.

The Border dialog box displays (Figure 8-69). The Outline box in the Border area displays no line because the empty box in the Line Style area was selected.

STEP 3 ▶

Choose the OK button in the Border dialog box.

Works removes the borders around the fields.

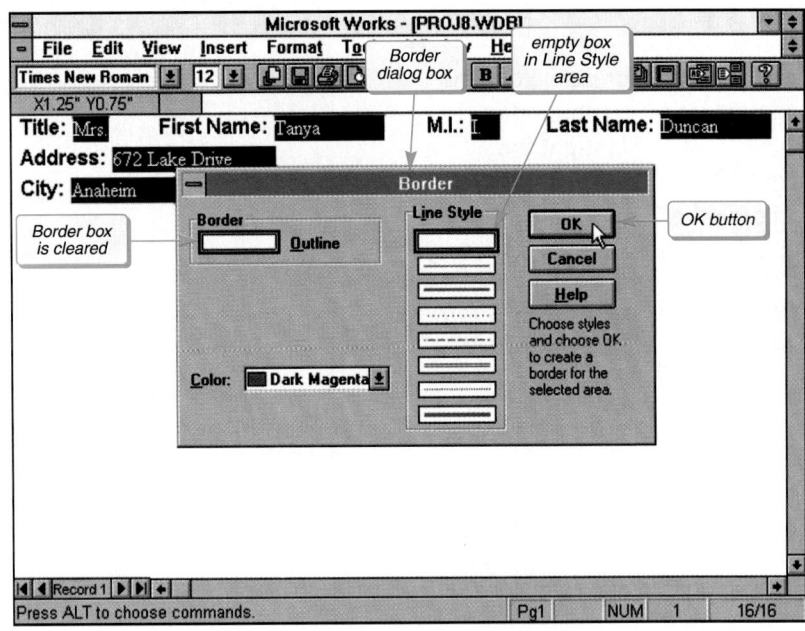

FIGURE 8-69

Sliding Fields to the Left and Hiding Field Names

The next step is to slide the fields to the left and hide the field names prior to printing. To accomplish this task, perform the following steps.

TO SELECT SLIDE TO LEFT AND HIDE FIELD NAMES ▼

STEP 1 ▶

Highlight all the fields in Form view, select the Format menu, and point to the Alignment command.

The Format menu displays and the mouse pointer points to the Alignment command (Figure 8-70). All the fields on the form are highlighted.

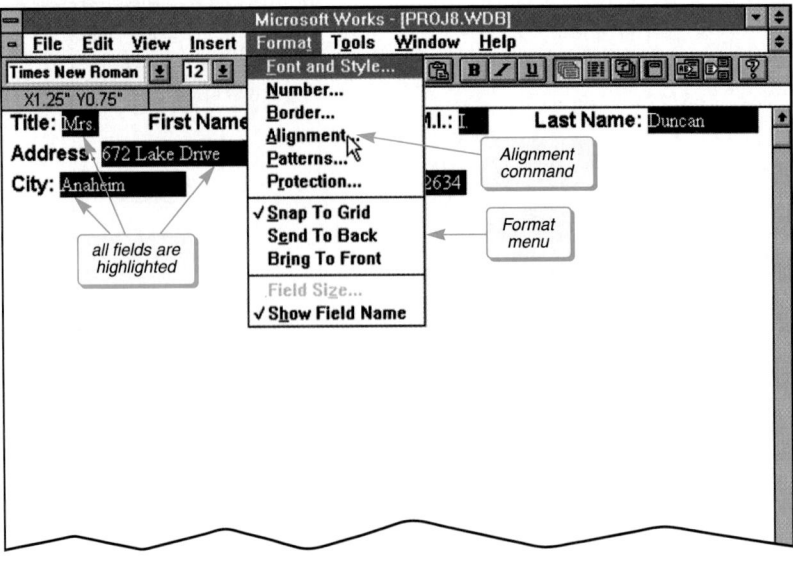

FIGURE 8-70

STEP 2 ▶

Choose the Alignment command. When the Alignment dialog box displays, select the Slide to left check box and point to the OK button.

*Works displays the Alignment dialog box (Figure 8-71). The **Slide to left check box** is selected and the mouse pointer points to the OK button. The Slide to left selection means that when the Form view of the database is printed, the highlighted fields will be moved to the left with only a single space separating them from the fields to their left, regardless of the amount of space separating them on the form itself. If a field is the leftmost field on a line, such as the Title field, it prints at the left margin. The Slide to left selection has no effect when the database displays in Form view on the screen.*

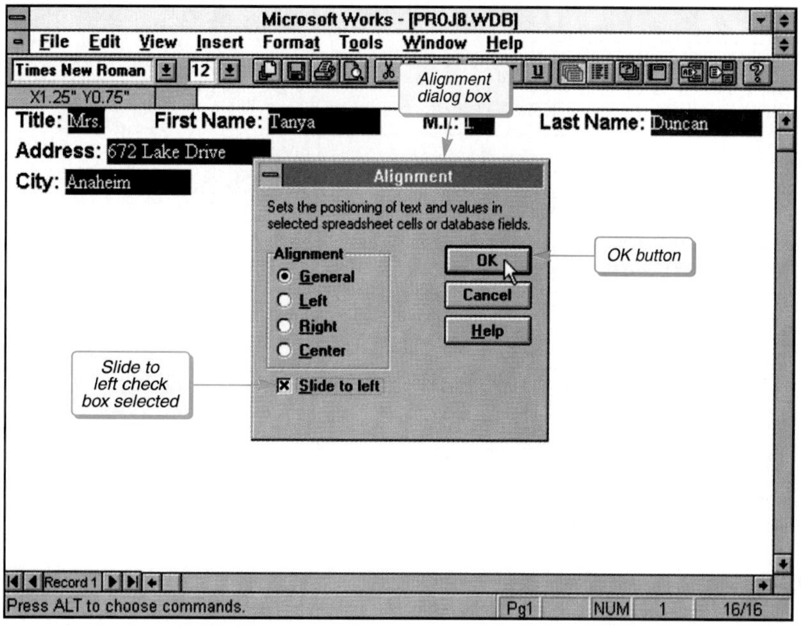

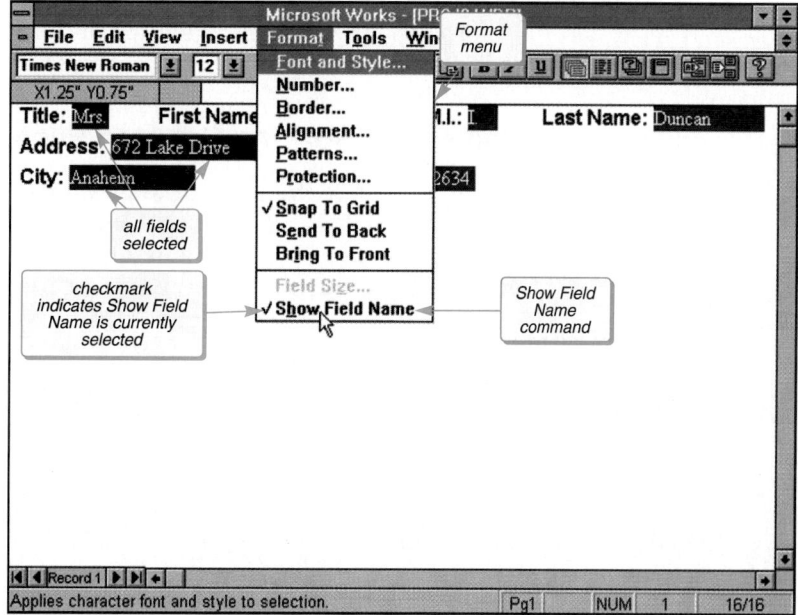

FIGURE 8-71

STEP 3 ▶

Choose the OK button in the Alignment dialog box. Then, with all the fields highlighted, select the Format menu and point to the Show Field Name command.

*Works displays the Format menu and the mouse pointer points to the **Show Field Name command** (Figure 8-72). The checkmark beside the Show Field Name command indicates the command is selected, which means the field names display in Form view and will print when the database is printed.*

FIGURE 8-72

STEP 4 ▶

Choose the Show Field Name command from the Format menu.

The field names no longer display in Form view (Figure 8-73). Notice that choosing the Show Field Name command when a check-mark appears next to it turns off the option. If you were to select the Format menu again and choose the Show Field Name command, the field name of the highlighted field would once again display in Form view.

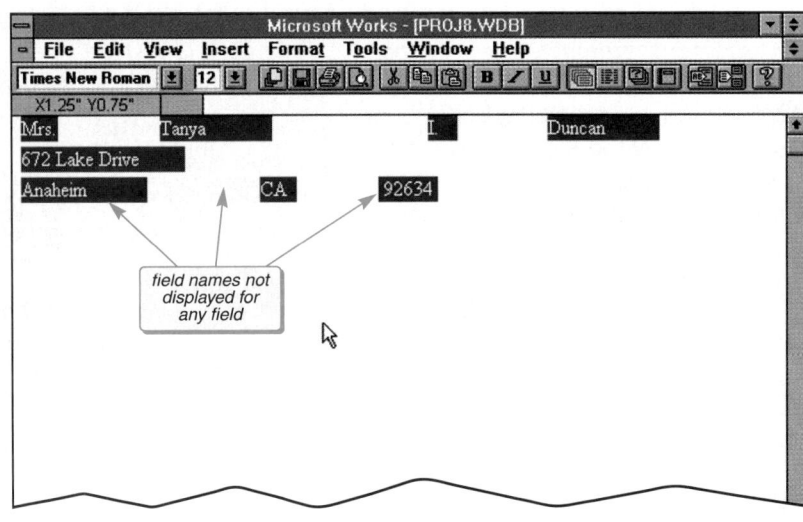

FIGURE 8-73

Notice two important aspects of the steps specified in Figure 8-72 and Figure 8-73. First, even though the field names do not display in Form view, the names are still associated with each field and the names do display in List view.

Second, although the fields on a single line are separated by multiple spaces in the Form view display, they will print with only one space between them because the Slide to left option in the Alignment dialog box has been selected for each field.

The use of the Slide to left feature of Works allows you to produce different styles of reports from the same database.

Controlling Spacing Between Records

To complete the preparation required to print the Investor List shown in Figure 8-59 on page W8.39, you must inform Works that multiple records are to print on the same page separated by a blank space. This requires the use of the **Page Setup command** on the File menu as illustrated in the following steps.

TO SPECIFY SPACE BETWEEN RECORDS AND NOT PRINT FIELD LINES ▼

STEP 1 ▶

Select the File menu and point to the Page Setup command.

*Works displays the File menu and the mouse pointer points to the **Page Setup command** (Figure 8-74).*

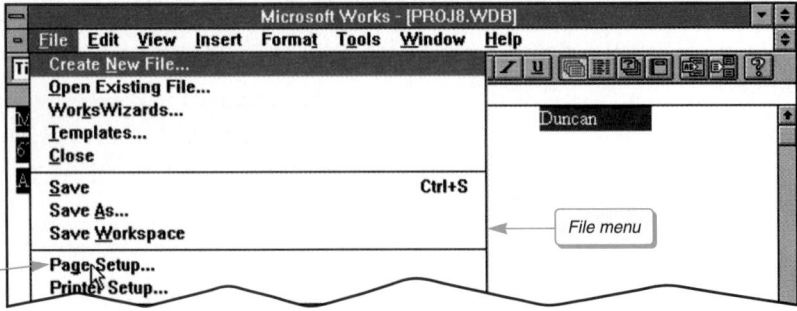

FIGURE 8-74

STEP 2 ▶

Choose the Page Setup command from the File menu. When the Page Setup dialog box displays, select the Other Options tab. Then ensure that the Print field lines and the Page breaks between records check boxes are not selected. Type .2" in the Space between records text box. Point to the OK button.

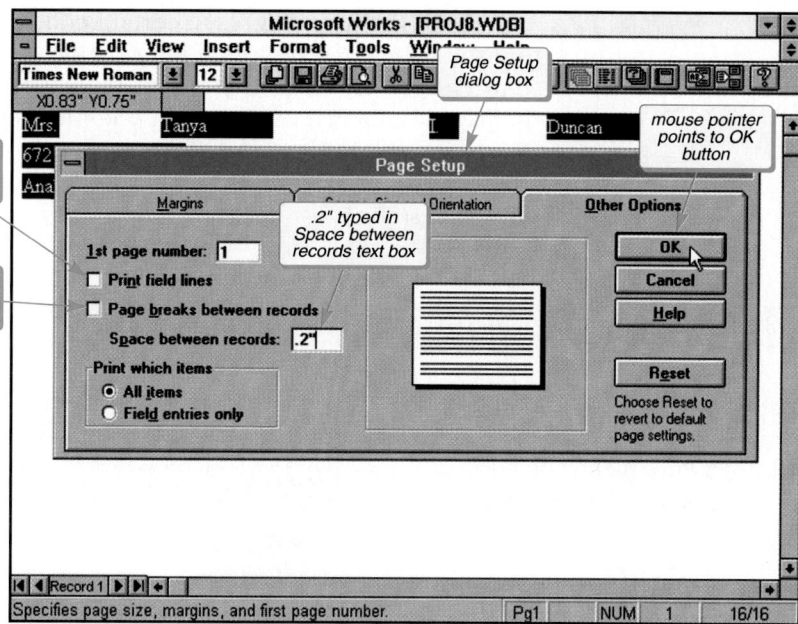

FIGURE 8-75

*Works displays the Page Setup dialog box (Figure 8-75). The **Print field lines check box** is not selected. The **Page breaks between records** check box is blank, informing Works not to place each record on a separate page. When multiple records print on the same page, you must indicate the space between each record. In Figure 8-75, the distance is specified as .2" in the **Space between records text box**. The mouse pointer points to the OK button.*

STEP 3 ▶

Choose the OK button in the Page Setup dialog box.

▲

Works returns to the Form view display of the database. Notice in Figure 8-75, in the Print which items area of the Page Setup dialog box, you can select either the All items option button or the Field entries only option button. It may appear that if you select the Field entries only option, you do not have to turn off the Show Field Names command on the Format menu. This is true if you are not using the Slide to left option. If you use the Slide to left option, however, Works prints only the field entry but leaves room on the report for the field name. Therefore, the only way to print the field entries next to each other is to turn off the Show Field Name command on the Format menu.

Headers and Footers

The last step before printing the database is to add a header and a footer to the report. The header contains the title, Investors List, together with the current date. The footer contains the page number. Headers and footers are displayed on Form view database reports in much the same way as shown for the Word Processor tool in Project 3 and as available for the Spreadsheet tool.

Recall that you can place certain codes in headers and footers to cause Works to display the corresponding information. In this project, use &n to direct Works to place the current date in the heading and &p in the footer so Works will place the page number in the footer. A complete listing of the codes you can use is shown in Table 3-1 on page W3.11.

To place a header and footer on a Form view database report, complete the following steps.

TO PLACE A HEADER AND FOOTER ON A FORM VIEW DATABASE REPORT ▼

STEP 1 ▶

Select the View menu and point to the Headers and Footers command.

*Works displays the View menu and the mouse pointer points to the **Headers and Footers command** (Figure 8-76).*

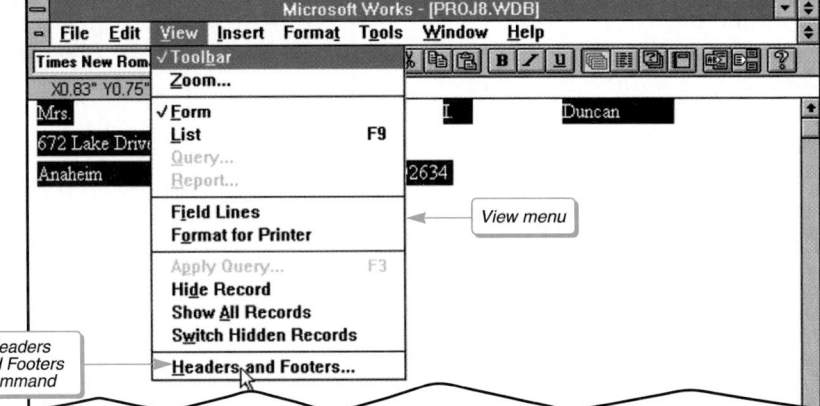

FIGURE 8-76

STEP 2 ▶

Choose the Headers and Footers command from the View menu. When the Headers and Footers dialog box displays, type Investors List - &n **in the Header text box and** Page &p **in the Footer text box. Then point to the OK button.**

Works displays the Headers and Footers dialog box (Figure 8-77). The Header and Footer text boxes contain the typed information. The mouse pointer points to the OK button.

STEP 3 ▶

Choose the OK button in the Headers and Footers dialog box.

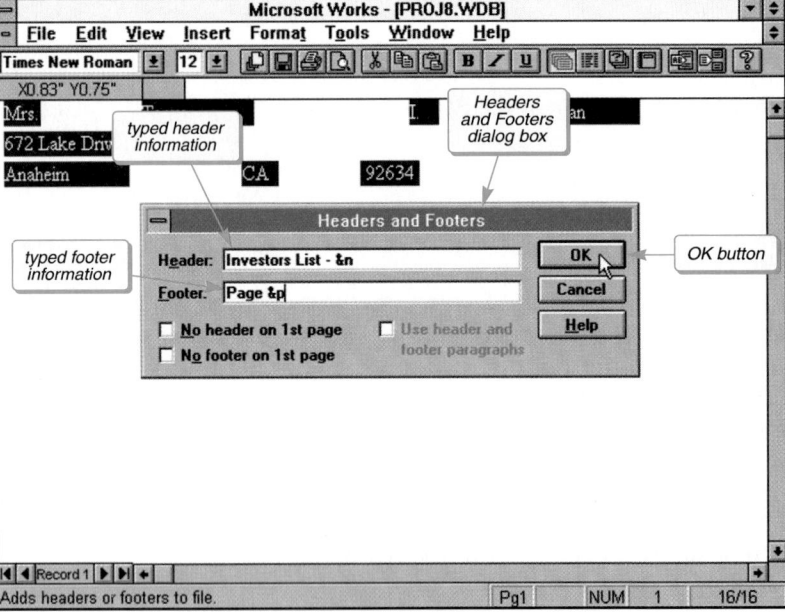

FIGURE 8-77

Works returns to the Form view display. No apparent change takes place in the display, but the headers and footers will print when the report is printed.

Printing the Revised Database

The preparation of the report is now complete. To ensure the document will print properly, you may have to make some alterations to the database settings. To ensure the database will print properly and then to print the database, complete the following steps.

TO ENSURE PROPER PRINTING AND PRINT THE REVISED DATABASE

Step 1: Select the File menu and choose the Page Setup command.
Step 2: Select the Source, Size and Orientation tab in the Page Setup dialog box.
Step 3: Ensure the Portrait option button in the Orientation area on the Source, Size and Orientation screen is selected.
Step 4: Choose the OK button in the Page Setup dialog box.
Step 5: Select the File menu and choose the Print command.
Step 6: Ensure the All records option button in the Print which records area is selected.
Step 7: Choose the OK button on the Print dialog box.

Works prints the report (see Figure 8-59 on page W8.39).

Saving the New Database

Once you have created the new database, save it using another name. To save the database using a different name, complete the following steps.

TO SAVE THE NEW DATABASE USING A DIFFERENT NAME

Step 1: From the File menu, choose the Save As command.
Step 2: When Works displays the Save As dialog box, type the new filename in the File Name text box.
Step 3: If necessary, select drive A from the Drives drop-down list box.
Step 4: Choose the OK button in the Save As dialog box.

▶ PROJECT SUMMARY

In this project you have learned about database maintenance. You added and deleted records from a database, learned how to change records in a database, added and deleted fields from the database, and changed the size of fields. You also changed the layout of the database in Form view and inserted a field containing a formula into the database. Finally, you derived a new database from a currently existing database and formatted a report.

▶ KEY TERMS

database maintenance *(W8.2)*
Delete Record command *(W8.12)*
Delete Record/Field command
   (W8.15, W8.28)
Delete Selection command
   (W8.27)
Field Name command *(W8.18)*
Field Size command *(W8.30)*
formulas *(W8.22)*
Go To command *(W8.12)*
Headers and Footers command
   (W8.48)

horizontal split bar *(W8.34)*
horizontal split box *(W8.38)*
Insert Field button *(W8.18)*
Insert Record button *(W8.12)*
Page breaks between records
   check box *(W8.47)*
Page Setup command *(W8.46)*
pane *(W8.34)*
Print field lines check box
   (W8.47)
Record/Field command (W8.20)

Show Field Name command
   (W8.45)
Slide to left check box *(W8.45)*
Space between records text box
   (W8.47)
split bar *(W8.35)*
Split command *(W8.38)*
split pointer *(W8.38)*
Undo Delete Record command
   (W8.14, W8.16)
vertical split bar *(W8.34)*
vertical split box *(W8.35)*

S T U D E N T   A S S I G N M E N T S

STUDENT ASSIGNMENT 1
True/False

Instructions: Circle T if the statement is true or F is the statement is false.

T F   1. To add a record to a database, you must first display the database in Form view.
T F   2. Once a database structure is defined, it cannot be changed.
T F   3. To open an existing database file, double-click the Open Existing File button in the Startup dialog box.
T F   4. When you add a record to the database, Works automatically saves it on a diskette.
T F   5. To delete a record in List view, highlight the entire record and click the Delete button on the Toolbar.
T F   6. A good practice is to save a database before deleting records because once you delete a record and perform subsequent operations, there is no way to undo the delete operation.
T F   7. To change data in List view, highlight the field containing the data to change, type the new data, and click the Enter box, press the ENTER key, or press an arrow key.
T F   8. To insert a new field in List view, you must first highlight the field to the left of the location of the new field. Then click the Insert Field button on the Toolbar.
T F   9. As a general rule, when you add a field in List view, the field is properly positioned and sized in Form view.
T F 10. When you add a field containing a formula to a database, the field name must begin with an equal sign.
T F 11. To delete a field in Form view, highlight the field name, choose the Delete Selection command from the Insert menu, and then choose the OK button when the Microsoft Works dialog box displays.
T F 12. In both Form view and List view, when you delete a field, Works gives you a chance to change your mind by asking the question, OK to delete data in this field?, in a dialog box.
T F 13. If you change a field name contained within a formula, you must change the formula to reflect the changed field name.
T F 14. To separate the List view of a database into a left pane and a right pane, choose the Pane command from the Window menu.
T F 15. To eliminate panes from the List view of a database, place the mouse pointer on the split bar and double-click.
T F 16. To delete a label in Form view, highlight the label and choose the Delete Selection command from the Insert menu.
T F 17. You can rearrange fields in the Form view of a database by dragging the fields to a new location.

T F   18. When you choose the Slide to left option in the Alignment dialog box, fields display in Form view with only a single space between them.

T F   19. To cause a field name to display on a printed report of a database displayed in Form view, select the Show Field Name option button in the Page Setup dialog box.

T F   20. To add a header to a printed report of a database displayed in Form view, choose the Headers and Footers command from the View menu, type the header in the Header text box, and choose the OK button in the Headers and Footers dialog box.

STUDENT ASSIGNMENT 2
Multiple Choice

Instructions: Circle the correct response.

1. The four primary activities when maintaining a database are _____.
   a. adding records, entering data, deleting records, and deleting fields
   b. adding records, deleting records, changing data in database records, and changing the record structure
   c. adding records, changing records, updating records, and designing new forms for existing databases
   d. adding and deleting records, changing records, saving records, and deleting fields

2. To save a database under a different name, _____.
   a. choose the Save As command from the File menu
   b. choose the Save command from the File menu
   c. choose the Close command from the File menu
   d. click the Save button on the Toolbar

3. To delete a record in Form view, display the record to be deleted and then _____.
   a. choose the Delete command from the File menu
   b. select the Delete Record option button in the File dialog box
   c. choose the Delete Selection command from the Insert menu
   d. choose the Delete Record command from the Insert menu

4. To delete a record in List view, highlight the record to be deleted and then _____.
   a. choose the Delete command from the File menu
   b. select the Delete Record option button in the File dialog box
   c. choose the Delete Record command from the Edit menu
   d. choose the Delete Record/Field command from the Insert menu

5. When in List view, clicking the Insert Field button will _____.
   a. insert a new field to the left of the highlighted field in List view
   b. insert a new field at the location of the insertion point in Form view
   c. insert a new field following the last field in Form view
   d. insert a new field to the right of the highlighted field in List view

6. To change the size of a field in Form view, _____.
   a. drag the resize handle associated with the field to the proper size
   b. choose the Field Size command from the Edit menu, enter the width in the Width text box, and choose the OK button in the Field Size dialog box
   c. choose the Field Width command from the Format menu, enter the width in the Width text box, and choose the OK button in the Field Width dialog box
   d. both a and c

7. To delete a field in Form view, _____.
   a. highlight the field to delete and press the DELETE key
   b. double-click the field name
   c. highlight the field to delete, choose the Delete Record/Field command from the Insert menu, and then choose the OK button in the dialog box that displays
   d. highlight the field name of the field to delete, choose the Delete Selection from the Insert menu, and then choose the OK button in the dialog box that displays

(continued)

STUDENT ASSIGNMENT 2 (continued)

8. To divide the List view of the database into four panes, _____.
   a. choose the Pane command from the Window menu
   b. drag the vertical split bar to the desired location
   c. drag the horizontal split bar to the desired location
   d. choose the Split command from the Window menu
9. To remove panes from a window that is divided into a left and right pane, _____.
   a. click in either the left or right pane
   b. double-click in either the left or right pane
   c. choose the Split command in the Window menu
   d. double-click the vertical split bar
10. The value &n appearing in the Header or Footer text box in the Headers and Footers dialog box will cause the _____ to print on the report.
   a. page number
   b. report title
   c. filename
   d. current date

STUDENT ASSIGNMENT 3
Inserting a Record in List View

Instructions: The List view of the investment club database displays in Figure SA8-3. In this assignment, you are to insert a record between record 5 (Julia Lopez) and record 6 (Rebecca Tiong). The new record is for Marlene Nellor. In the space provided, write the steps required to insert the record.

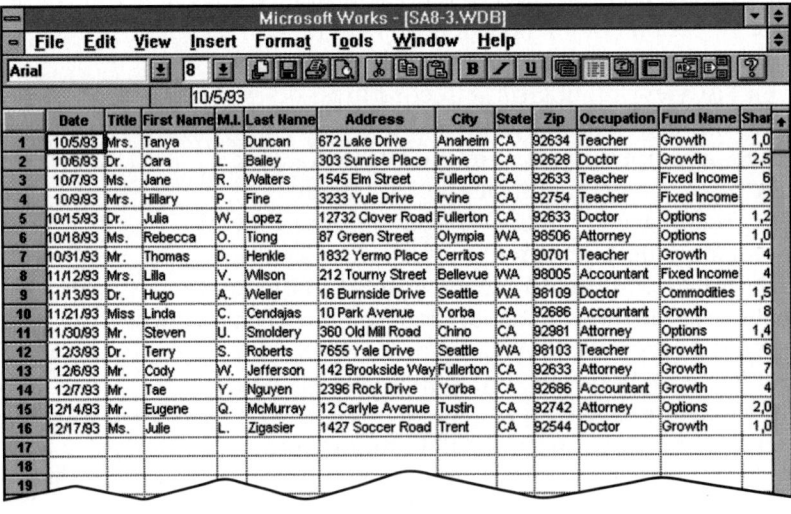

FIGURE SA8-3

Steps to insert a record in List view:

_____

_____

_____

_____

STUDENT ASSIGNMENT 4
Adding a Field in Form View

Instructions: Record 3 of the investment club database displays in Figure SA8-4. In this assignment, you are to add the Investment field to the database. The field should be located at the coordinates X0.83" Y4.08". The Investment field should contain a formula: =Shares*Price per Share. In the space provided, specify the steps required to add the Investment field to the database.

FIGURE SA8-4

Steps to add the Investment field:

_____

_____

_____

_____

STUDENT ASSIGNMENT 5
Maintaining a Database

Instructions: List the four primary activities when maintaining a database and give an example of each.

Activity 1: _____

_____

Activity 2: _____

_____

Activity 3: _____

_____

Activity 4:   _____

_____

STUDENT ASSIGNMENT 6
Maintenance Tasks

Instructions: In each of the following maintenance activities, give the reason and an example for each type of activity.

TASK	REASON AND EXAMPLE
1. Add a record	_____
2. Delete a record	_____
3. Change record data	_____
4. Add a field	_____
5. Delete a field	_____
6. Add a field with a formula	_____
7. Change a field name	_____
8. Change a field size	_____
9. Change the Form view format	_____
10. Add labels to Form view	_____
11. Delete labels from Form view	_____

COMPUTER LABORATORY EXERCISES

COMPUTER LABORATORY EXERCISE 1
Using the Help Menu

Instructions: Use the Works Help feature to solve the following problems.

Problem 1: You want to clear the field entries for the Price per Share field in record 2 and record 5 in Form view, but you want the Currency format to remain for the field. You do not want to delete the field from the database. In the space provided, explain how you would accomplish this task.

Explanation: _____

_____

Problem 2: Your database displays in List view. You want to add four new records to the database between record 9 and record 10. In the space provided, explain the procedure you should follow to accomplish this task.

Explanation: _____

_____

Problem 3: Assume you are working in List view with a large database that contains forty-three (43) fields. You know that somewhere in the 43 fields is a field named Customer City. Rather than scroll through all fields in the database, you would like to go directly to the field even though you do not know exactly where it is located in the database. In the space provided, explain how you would accomplish this task.

Explanation: _____

_____

Problem 4: You have entered a formula into the Investment field. You accidentally typed a numeric value into the Investment field in record 12 of your database. The number displays and the formula no longer calculates a value. How can you undo your mistake and restore the formula in the field? In the space provided, explain how you would accomplish this task.

Explanation: _____

_____

COMPUTER LABORATORY EXERCISE 2
Maintaining a Database

Instructions: In this exercise, you are to perform maintenance tasks on the investment club database. To perform the maintenance, start the Works Database tool and open the CLE8-2.WDB file on the Student Diskette that accompanies this book. Then perform the following maintenance:

1. Delete the Net Worth field.
2. Delete the Income field.
3. Add the Investment field. The Investment field contains the formula, =Shares*Price per Share.
4. Reformat the Form view of the database to a pleasing format.
5. Print the Form view of the database.
6. Print the List view of the database.
7. Follow directions from your instructor for turning in this exercise.

COMPUTER LABORATORY EXERCISE 3
Working with Panes in a Database

Instructions: Start the Works Database tool. Open the CLE8-3.WDB file on the Student Diskette that accompanies this book. Perform the following tasks:

1. Display the database in List view.
2. Split the database window into an upper and lower pane. Place the split bar between record 8 and record 9. Then display record 8 and record 14 next to one another.
3. Remove the upper and lower panes on the window.
4. Split the database window into four panes. Place the horizontal split bar between record 4 and record 5 and the vertical split bar between the Last Name field and the Address field.
5. Display the database so record 12 displays immediately below record 4 and the Fund Name field displays next to the Last Name field.
6. Remove the split panes from the database window.

COMPUTER LABORATORY ASSIGNMENTS

COMPUTER LABORATORY ASSIGNMENT 1
Maintaining a Database

Purpose: To provide experience maintaining a database, including adding and deleting records, changing data within records, and adding fields within records.

Problem: Perform maintenance on the Woodland College Foundation database created in Computer Laboratory Assignment 1 in Project 7.

Instructions:

1. Open the database you created in Computer Laboratory Assignment 1 in Project 7. If you did not create this database in Project 7, your instructor will provide you with the database file.
2. Add the two records shown in the following table to the database.

DATE	TITLE	FIRST NAME	M.I.	LAST NAME	SCHOLARSHIP	DONATION	CLASSIFICATION
12/16/94	Ms.	Rebecca	L.	Van de Swearengen	Fine Arts	$4,000.00	President's Circle
12/18/94	Dr.	Ronald	R.	Desmond	Science	$750.00	Silver Circle

3. When you add the Rebecca L. Van de Swearengen record, you discover the Last Name field in Form view is not large enough to display the entire name. Therefore, change the size of the field to accommodate the name.
4. Delete the record for Wanda G. Grahame.
5. Mr. William B. Gentry donated an additional $500.00 to the Fine Arts scholarship fund. Modify his record to reflect the additional donation and change his classification from Silver Circle to President's Circle.
6. The president of Woodland College has requested the database reflect the graduation year of each of the donors to the scholarship fund. If the donors are not graduates of Woodland College, place the entry NG in the field. Add the Graduation field to the Woodland College Foundation database. The table on the next page contains the last names of the donors and their graduation data.

7. The public relations director for Woodland College did not like the field name Classification. She suggested changing it to Honor Award. Make this change to the Classification field name.
8. Save the updated database on a diskette using a filename consisting of the initials of your first and last names followed by the assignment number. Example: TC8-1.
9. Print the updated database in Form view.
10. Print the updated database in List view. The entire record should print on a single page.
11. Follow the directions from your instructor for turning in this assignment.

LAST NAME	GRADUATION
Randall	1968
Brown	NG
Crow	1985
Mann	1988
Gentry	1955
Bolton	1979
Ramos	1992
Wong	1961
Lopez	1981
Van de Swearengen	1984
Desmond	1991

COMPUTER LABORATORY ASSIGNMENT 2
Maintaining a Database

Purpose: To provide experience maintaining a database, including adding and deleting records, changing data within records, adding and renaming fields within records, and reformatting the Form view of the database.

Problem: Perform maintenance on the Computer Reference Library database created in Computer Laboratory Assignment 2 in Project 7.

Instructions:

1. Open the database you created in Computer Laboratory Assignment 2 in Project 7. If you did not create this database in Project 7, your instructor will provide you with the database file.
2. The library has acquired two new books. The data for the books is shown in the following table.

DATE ACQUIRED	BOOK NAME	AUTHOR	PUBLISHER
12/22/94	SpeedWord	Krakowitz	Hart and Timmons
12/30/94	Using Integrated Application Packages	Young & Bellows	WPS Publishers

YEAR PUBLISHED	CATEGORY	QUANTITY	UNIT COST
1992	Word Processing	2	$28.99
1994	Integrated	1	$45.76

(continued)

3. When you add the second book, you find the entire title cannot display in the Book Name field in Form view. Change the field size in Form view so the entire title will display. When you change the Book Name field size in Form view, the Author field will no longer fit on the same line. Therefore, move the Author field to the next line and reposition other fields as required.
4. Display the database in List view. The book title does not entirely display in the Book Name field. Adjust the field size so the entire book title displays in the Book Name field.
5. The Computer Reference Library acquired three more copies of the book, *DataEase*, and two more copies of the book, *Installing LANs*. Update the Quantity field to reflect these acquisitions.
6. One copy of *WhizWorks* was loaned several months ago and has not been returned. The head librarian decided the book was not likely to be returned, so remove one copy of this book from the Quantity field.
7. The book, *Learning Linker*, has been recalled by the publisher from libraries because a large number of errors were accidentally incorporated into the book. The Computer Reference Library sent the copies in the library back to the publisher. Therefore, remove the book from the database.
8. The head librarian has decided he would like to know the total cost of the books in the library and have this data stored in the database. To accomplish these tasks, add a new field named TOTAL COST to the database. The data in the field is generated from the formula, Quantity times Unit Cost. Format the field as a currency field with two digits to the right of the decimal point.
9. Save the modified database on a diskette using a filename consisting of the initials of your first and last names followed by the assignment number. Example: TC8-2.
10. Print the updated database in Form view.
11. Print the updated database in List view. The entire record should print on a single page.
12. A report that contains the name of each book in the library, the publisher of the book, and the quantity of each book is required. Print the report so as many books as possible appear on each page. Do not print the Book Name or Publisher field names. Place a header containing the report title, Publisher Inventory, together with the current date on each page. Print the page number as a footer on each page. Reformat the Form view of the database so you can prepare the report. The Quantity field name and the Quantity field print on the first line for each book beginning 4.5 inches from the left edge of the paper. Modify the entries in the Page Setup dialog box to accomplish this task.
13. Save the format of the database generated in Step 12 using a filename consisting of the initials of your first and last names followed by the assignment number and the letters RPT. Example: TC8-2RPT.
14. Print the Publisher Inventory report.
15. Follow the directions from your instructor for turning in this assignment.

COMPUTER LABORATORY ASSIGNMENT 3
Maintaining a Database

Purpose: To provide experience maintaining a database, including adding and deleting records, changing data within records, adding and renaming fields within records, and reformatting the Form view of the database.

Problem Perform maintenance on the Computer Club Membership Roster database created in Computer Laboratory Assignment 3 in Project 7. The new school year has started and you have been assigned to delete members who graduated and add new members of the Computer Club.

Instructions:

1. Open the database you created in Computer Laboratory Assignment 3 in Project 7. If you did not create this database in Project 7, your instructor will provide you with the database file.
2. Two members of the Computer Club, Todd Walsh and Joseph Yamma, graduated. Remove their records from the database.
3. Four new members have joined the Computer Club. Their information is contained in the following table.

DATE JOINED	FIRST NAME	M.I.	LAST NAME	ADRESS	CITY
9/14/95	Maria	Q.	Ninez	322 Blue Ave.	Fullerton
9/15/95	Danny	L.	Sullivan	1211 Spice St.	Anaheim
9/16/95	Patricia	M.	Hillern	2 Indian Way, Apartment A2311	Cerritos
9/16/95	Thomas	K.	Runner	23 Swift Way	Anaheim

STATE	ZIP	MAJOR	MEMBERSHIP	DUES
CA	92633	Business	Regular	$25.00
CA	92823	English	Regular	$25.00
CA	90701	Biology	Associate	$15.00
CA	92822	Computer Science	Regular	$25.00

4. When you enter the address for Patricia Hillern, you find the entire address cannot display in the Address field in Form view. Change the field size in Form view so the entire field will display. If necessary, redesign the form by moving other fields so the form is easy to read.

5. If the Address field does not display entirely in List view, modify the width of the field so it will.

6. Marla McIntosh has moved for the new school year. Her new address is 1266 Glenn Drive, Anaheim, CA 92823. Wilson Phipps has changed majors from Computer Science to Business. Tricia Yung was married during the summer. Her new last name is Yung-Nguyen. Make the appropriate changes to the Computer Club database.

7. The Computer Club advisor has informed you of a new, fairer method of determining dues. Instead of paying a flat fee, students pay a fee based on the number of computer class units they are taking for the semester. The rate is $5.00 times the number of computer class units they are taking. The advisor has also asked you to add the class of each member. The number of units for each member of the club and their class are shown in Figure CLA8-3. Change the Dues field to use a formula to calculate the dues for each member, add the Class field, and redesign the Form as necessary.

8. Save the modified database on a diskette using a filename consisting of the initials of your first and last names followed by the assignment number. Example: TC8-3.

9. Print the updated database in Form view.

10. Print the updated database in List view. The entire record should print on a single page.

11. The advisor has requested a Name and Address list of all members of the Computer Club. She wants as many names as possible on a single page. The member's first name, middle initial, and last name should be on the first line, the address on the second line, and the city, state, and zip code on the third line. The report should have a heading consisting of the title, Computer Club Roster, and the current date, and the page number should appear at the bottom of the page. Place the heading and page number appropriately on the page.

LAST NAME	COMPUTER UNITS	CLASS
Ferdez	10	Sr.
Hughes	3	Jr.
McIntosh	3	So.
Genne	5	So.
Phipps	9	Sr.
Yung-Nguyen	4	So.
Ninez	5	Fr.
Sullivan	3	So.
Hillern	2	Fr.
Runner	4	Fr.

FIGURE CLA8-3

12. Save the form generated in Step 11 using a filename consisting of the initials of your first and last names followed by the assignment number and the letters RPT. Example: TC8-3RPT.

13. Print the Computer Club Roster.

14. Follow the directions from your instructor for turning in this assignment.

COMPUTER LABORATORY ASSIGNMENT 4
Maintaining a Database

Purpose: To provide experience maintaining a database, including adding and deleting records, changing data within records, adding and renaming fields within records, and reformatting the Form view of the database.

Problem: Perform maintenance on the Music database created in Computer Laboratory Assignment 4 in Project 7.

Instructions:

1. Open the database you created in Computer Laboratory Assignment 4 in Project 7.
2. Add four new cassettes or CDs you have purchased recently.
3. You gave your friend two of your cassettes. Remove them from your database.
4. You have found it difficult to determine your favorite song on a CD or cassette, so delete the field from your database.
5. You determine it would be helpful to know the number of songs on each cassette or CD you have in your database, so add a field for this data.
6. Print your updated database in Form view.
7. Print your updated database in List view.
8. Save your updated database using a filename consisting of the initials of your first and last names followed by the assignment number. Example: TC8-4.
9. You decide to create a report containing only the CD or cassette title, the artist, and the record label. Design and print the report.
10. Save the form for the report you created in Step 8. Use a filename consisting of the initials of your first and last names followed by the assignment number and the letters RPT. Example: TC8-4RPT.

▼

DATABASE QUERIES AND REPORTS

▼

DATABASE QUERIES AND REPORTS

OBJECTIVES You will have mastered the material in this project when you can:

- ▶ Define a query
- ▶ Perform a query to find records containing values equal to those you specify
- ▶ Show all records in the database
- ▶ Find records using a query based on conditional criteria
- ▶ Switch hidden records
- ▶ Use multiple fields in a query
- ▶ Perform a query using the AND and OR logical operators
- ▶ Apply a query to a database
- ▶ Define a report listing the database records

- ▶ Add fields to a report
- ▶ Modify a Works report definition
- ▶ Print a report
- ▶ Name a report
- ▶ Define a report with summary totals
- ▶ Insert rows and field entries into a report definition
- ▶ Select records for printing
- ▶ Define a report with sort breaks
- ▶ Sort a database on multiple fields in both ascending and descending sequence
- ▶ Duplicate a report definition

▶ INTRODUCTION

A database is designed to provide information. In addition to creating the database as shown in Project 7 and maintaining the database as shown in Project 8, you must also be able to obtain useful information from the database. Information is obtained from a database in two primary ways: (1) Queries; (2) Reports.

A **query** is a request for information from a database. For example, a query of the investment club database created in Project 7 and updated in Project 8 is, *Display all the investors in the Growth fund* (Figure 9-1). Notice in Figure 9-1 the only records that display are those for investors in the Growth fund. Works does not display the records for people who did not invest in the Growth fund. When you query a database, Works shows the records that match the query and hides the records that do not match the query. Most often, queries are performed by an individual using the computer and requesting specific information from the database.

The Works Database tool also provides the means for creating a variety of **reports**. For example, the report shown in Figure 9-2 was created from the investment club database. The report lists all the investors in the Global Investments investment club together with the number of shares they own and their investments. At the bottom of the report, totals appear for all the records in the database. As you can see, 16 investors own a total of 15,700 shares with an investment value of $296,300.00.

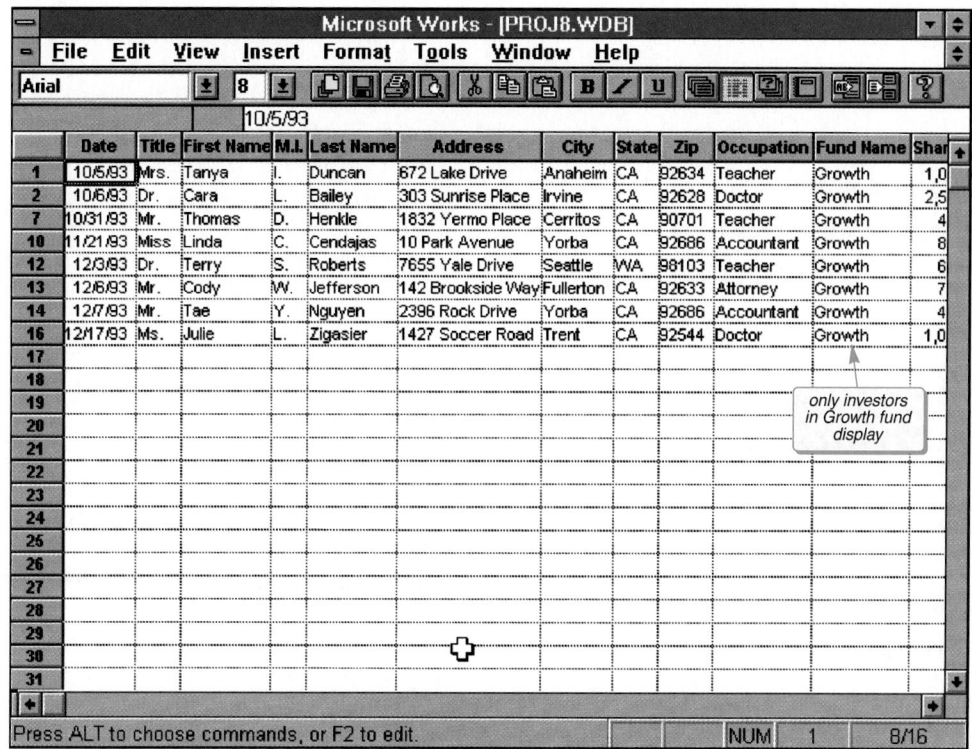

FIGURE 9-1

Investment Totals

Title	First Name	M.I.	Last Name	Shares	Investment
Dr.	Cara	L.	Bailey	2,500	$27,500.00
Miss	Linda	C.	Cendajas	800	$8,800.00
Mrs.	Tanya	I.	Duncan	1,000	$11,000.00
Mrs.	Hillary	P.	Fine	200	$3,600.00
Mr.	Thomas	D.	Henkle	400	$4,400.00
Mr.	Cody	W.	Jefferson	700	$7,700.00
Dr.	Julia	W.	Lopez	1,200	$27,600.00
Mr.	Eugene	Q.	McMurray	2,000	$76,000.00
Mr.	Tae	Y.	Nguyen	400	$4,400.00
Dr.	Terry	S.	Roberts	600	$6,600.00
Mr.	Steven	U.	Smoldery	1,400	$32,200.00
Ms.	Rebecca	O.	Tiong	1,000	$23,000.00
Ms.	Jane	R.	Walters	600	$10,800.00
Dr.	Hugo	A.	Weller	1,500	$22,500.00
Mrs.	Lilla	V.	Wilson	400	$7,200.00
Ms.	Julie	L.	Zigasier	1,000	$23,000.00

Total Investors 16
Total Shares 15,700
Total Investment $296,300.00

FIGURE 9-2

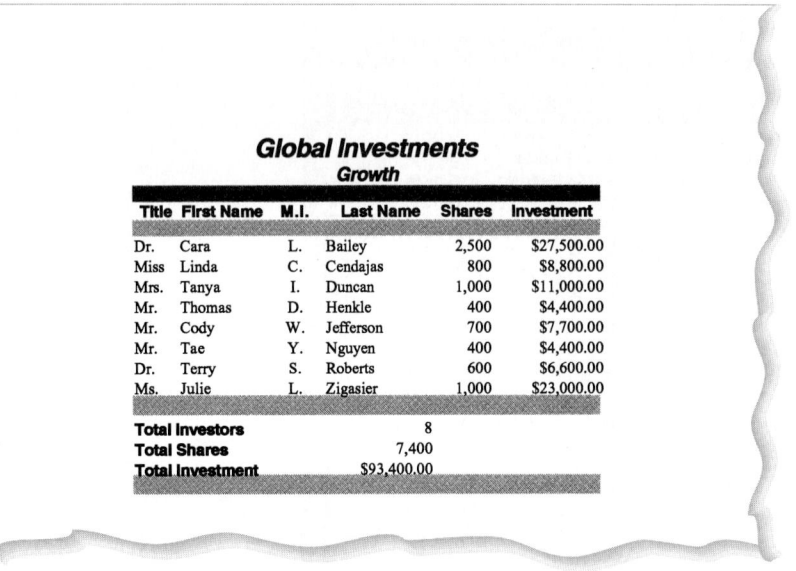

Global Investments
Growth

Title	First Name	M.I.	Last Name	Shares	Investment
Dr.	Cara	L.	Bailey	2,500	$27,500.00
Miss	Linda	C.	Cendajas	800	$8,800.00
Mrs.	Tanya	I.	Duncan	1,000	$11,000.00
Mr.	Thomas	D.	Henkle	400	$4,400.00
Mr.	Cody	W.	Jefferson	700	$7,700.00
Mr.	Tae	Y.	Nguyen	400	$4,400.00
Dr.	Terry	S.	Roberts	600	$6,600.00
Ms.	Julie	L.	Zigasier	1,000	$23,000.00

Total Investors	8
Total Shares	7,400
Total Investment	$93,400.00

FIGURE 9-3

Queries and reports can be performed in combination with one another. For example, a query can be performed to isolate specific data in the database and then a report can be printed using only that data. In Figure 9-3, the query requesting those individuals who invested in the Growth fund was performed. Then, a report was printed using only that data. The report lists the investors in the Growth fund, the number of shares they own, and the amount invested. The totals at the end of the report show eight investors in the Growth fund and they own 7,400 shares with an investment value of $93,400.00.

Obtaining information from a database is the reason for the existence of the database.

Queries and reports provide the two primary means of obtaining information from a database.

▶ PROJECT NINE

To learn how to obtain information from a database through the use of both queries and reports, you will accomplish the following tasks in Project 9:

1. Using a query, display all investors from the state of Washington.
2. Using a query, display all investors who have invested more than $20,000.00.
3. By switching hidden records, display all investors who have invested $20,000.00 or less.
4. Using a query, display all attorneys who have invested in the Options fund.
5. Using a query, display all individuals who have invested in the Growth fund or who have invested more than $50,000.00.
6. Using a query, display all investors who are teachers.
7. Using a query, display doctors who live in the cities Fullerton, Chino, or Yorba.
8. Create a report listing all investors in the investment club database.
9. Create a report listing all investors in the investment club database, the total investors in the investment club, the total number of shares owned, and the total dollars invested.

10. For each fund (Commodities, Fixed Income, Growth, and Options), create a report listing the investors in the fund, the shares they own, and the amount they have invested. At the end of the report, list the number of investors in the fund, the total number of fund shares, and the total dollars invested in each fund.
11. Create a single report listing the Fund Names in descending sequence, the investors in ascending alphabetical sequence within Fund Name, and the total dollars invested in each fund.

The steps to accomplish these tasks are explained on subsequent pages.

▶ STARTING WORKS AND OPENING A WORKS DATABASE FILE

T o accomplish the tasks just listed, you must first open the database that contains the data for the queries and reports. For Project 9, the database is the PROJ8.WDB database. To open the PROJ8.WDB database, follow the steps used in previous projects. These steps are summarized below.

TO START WORKS AND OPEN A DATABASE FILE

Step 1: From Program Manager, open the Microsoft Works for Windows group window.

Step 2: Double-click the Microsoft Works program-item icon.

Step 3: If the Welcome to Microsoft Works dialog box displays, choose the Start Works Now button.

Step 4: Choose the Open An Existing Document button.

Step 5: In the Open dialog box, select the PROJ8.WDB file stored on a diskette in drive A and choose the OK button.

Step 6: Maximize the Works application window if necessary, and then maximize the PROJ8.WDB document window.

Step 7: If necessary, click the List View button so the database displays in List view.

The resulting Works window with the PROJ8.WDB database displayed in List view is shown in Figure 9-4.

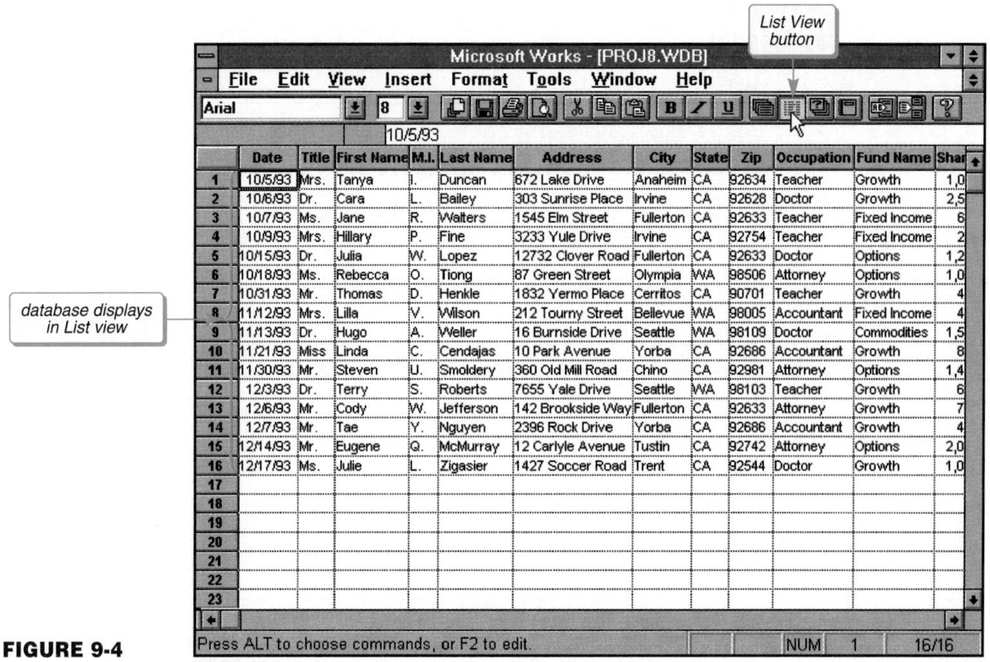

FIGURE 9-4

► QUERYING A WORKS DATABASE

A Works database query is a request to the database to find records whose fields satisfy a certain criteria. The criteria used in a query can vary depending on individual requirements. The following examples illustrate a variety of requests for information from the investment club database using queries.

Finding Records with Equal Fields

Quite often in a query you will ask to see records that have a value in a certain field or fields equal to a value you specify. For example, the first query in this project is to display all the investors who live in the state of Washington. Therefore, the criteria is that the value in the State field in the database must be equal to WA. To use a Works database query to find all investors who live in Washington, you use the **Create New Query command** from the Tools menu. Perform the following steps to create the query.

TO PERFORM A QUERY WITH AN EQUAL CONDITION ▼

STEP 1 ►

Select the Tools menu and point to the Create New Query command.

The Tools menu displays and the mouse pointer points to the Create New Query command (Figure 9-5).

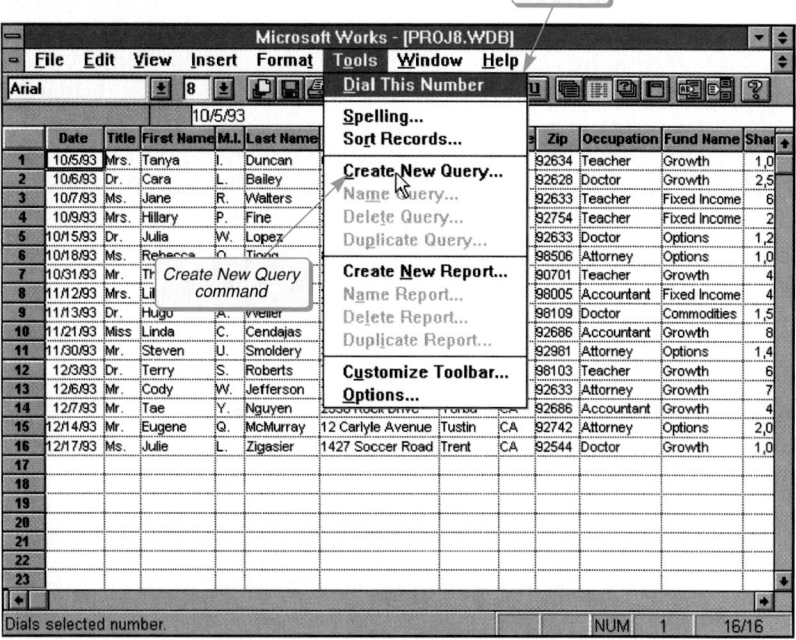

FIGURE 9-5

STEP 2 ▶

Choose the Create New Query command from the Tools menu.

Works displays the New Query dialog box (Figure 9-6). The words Query1 display in the Please give this query a name text box. The words Creates new query display in the status bar. Date appears in the Choose a field to compare drop-down list box, and is equal to displays in the How to compare the field drop-down list box.

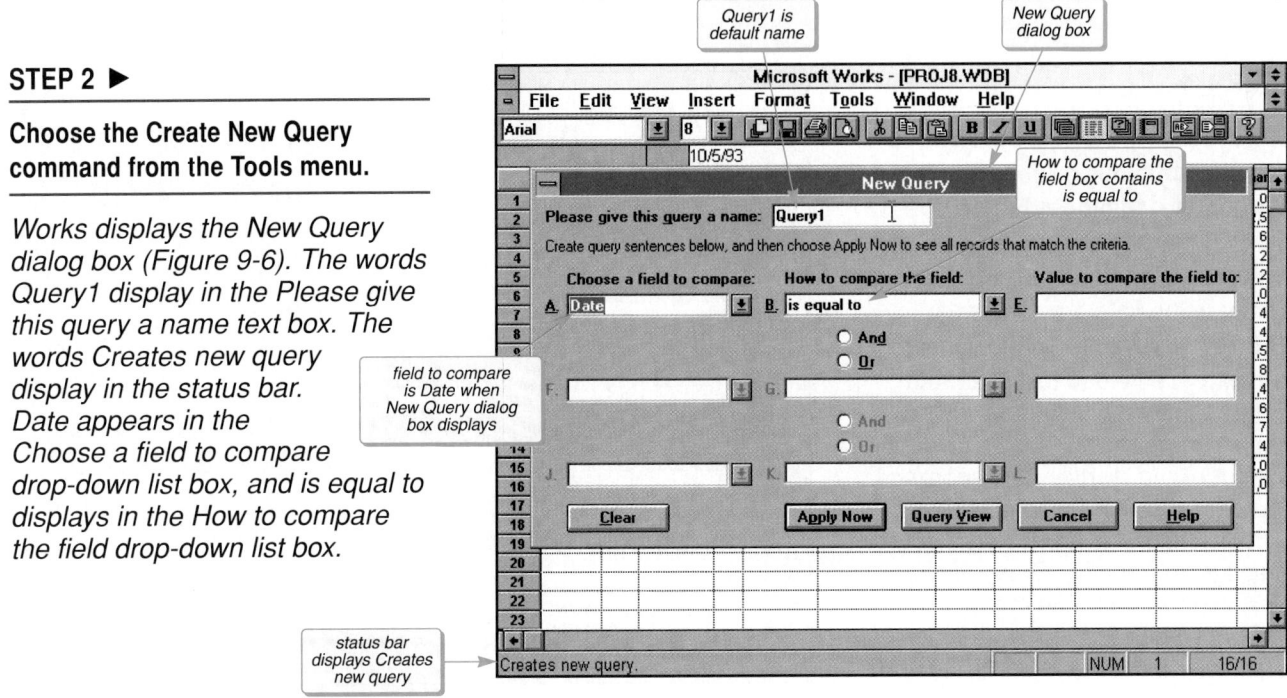

FIGURE 9-6

STEP 3 ▶

Highlight the word Query1 in the Please give this query a name text box and type Washington. **Click the Choose a field to compare drop-down list box arrow. Scroll down and point to the State field name.**

The Choose a field to compare drop-down list box contains the name of every field in the database (Figure 9-7). The mouse pointer points to the State field name. The name of the query you type in the Please give this query a name text box can be a maximum 15 characters.

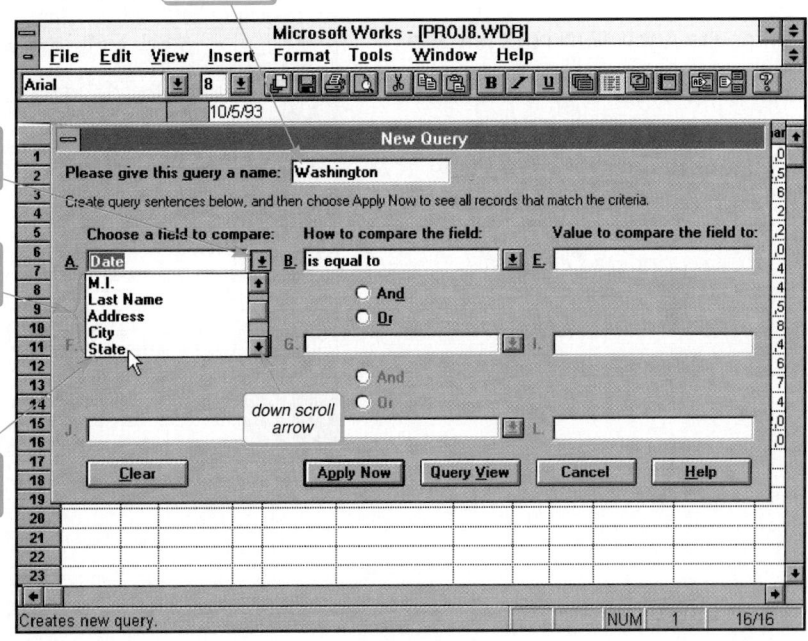

FIGURE 9-7

STEP 4 ▶

Select State in the Choose a field to compare drop-down list box by clicking the left mouse button. Press the TAB key and ensure the words is equal to appear in the How to compare the field box. Press the TAB key and type WA in the Value to compare the field to text box. Point to the Apply Now button.

*The query to display the records in the database for those investors who live in the state of Washington displays in the New Query dialog box (Figure 9-8). The mouse pointer points to the **Apply Now** button.*

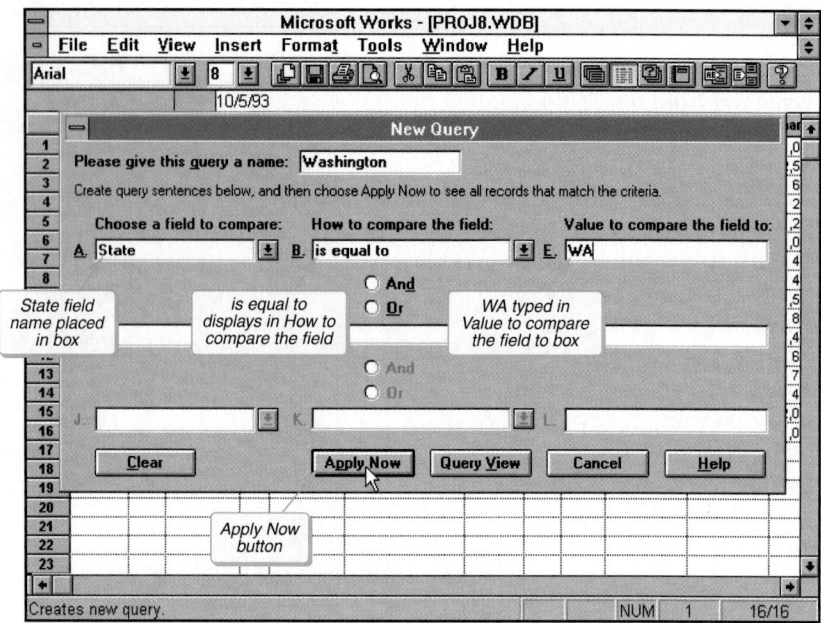

FIGURE 9-8

STEP 5 ▶

Choose the Apply Now button in the New Query dialog box.

Works displays in List view the records in the database of those investors whose State field contains WA (Figure 9-9). This is the list of investors who live in the state of Washington.

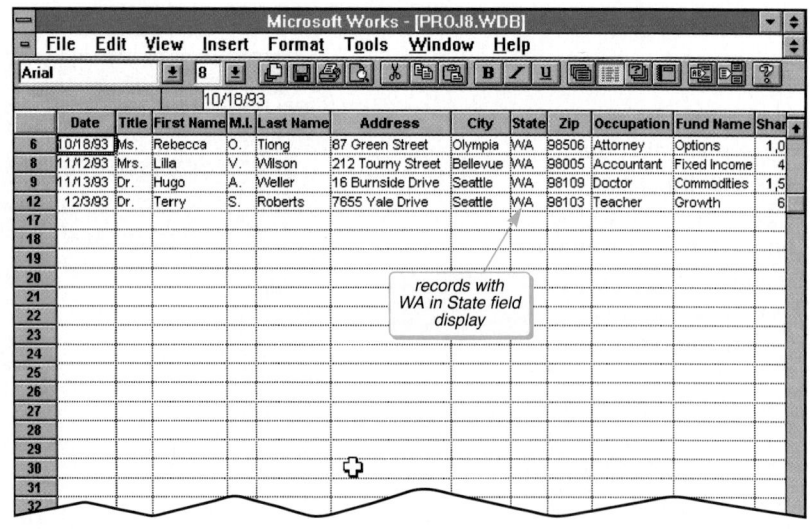

FIGURE 9-9

The query method shown in Figure 9-5 through Figure 9-9 can be used whenever you want to display only those records with a specific value in a field.

Other queries you might perform include displaying all the records for a given occupation such as teachers, or displaying all the records for investors who live in a certain city.

In Figure 9-9, the database displays in List view. You can also display the database in Form view after a query. In Form view, the selected records display one at a time on the screen. Thus, to see the four records in Figure 9-9 in Form view, you would display each of the four records one at a time. To move to the next record, you can click the next record navigation button.

Showing All Records in the Database

After performing a query, you might want to again display the entire database. To display all the records in the investment club database, perform the following steps.

TO SHOW ALL RECORDS IN A DATABASE ▼

STEP 1 ►

Select the View menu and point to the Show All Records command.

*Works displays the View menu and the mouse pointer points to the **Show All Records command** (Figure 9-10).*

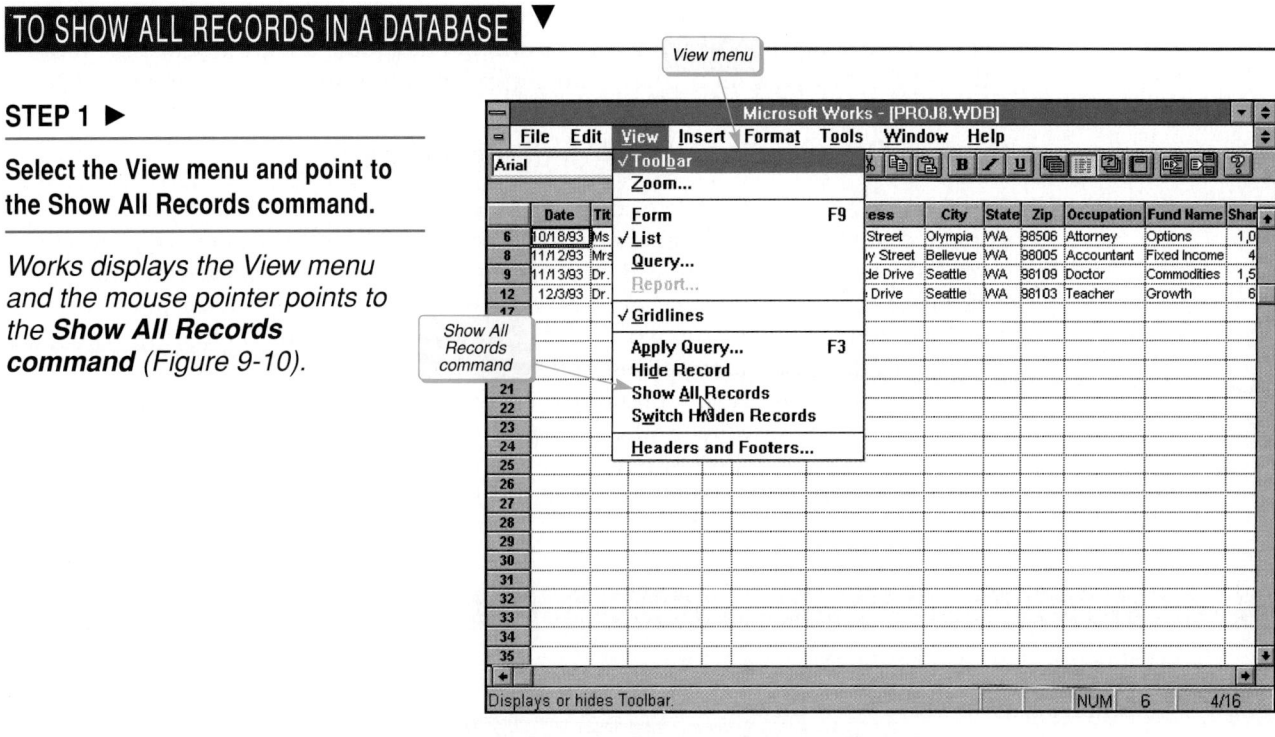

FIGURE 9-10

STEP 2 ►

Choose the Show All Records command from the View menu. Then scroll up until record 1 is visible.

Works displays the entire database in List view (Figure 9-11). Whenever you want to display all records in the database, you can use the Show All Records command.

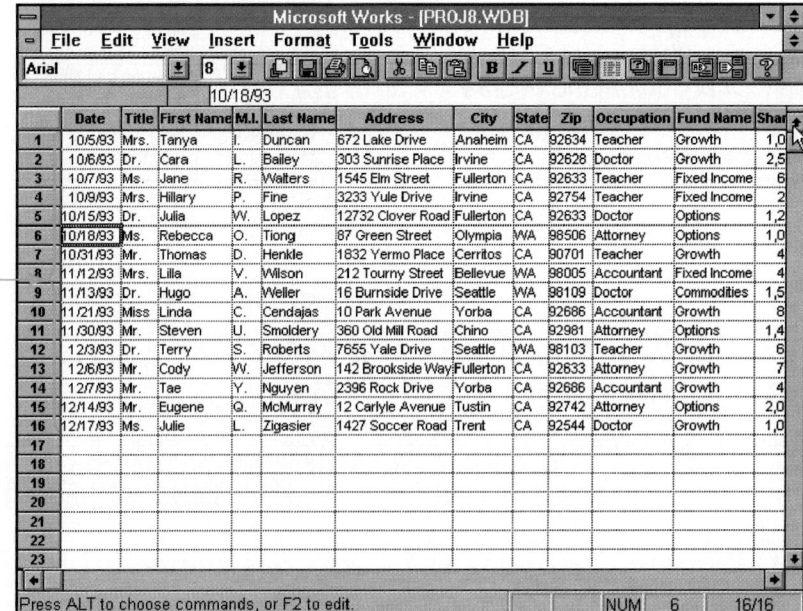

FIGURE 9-11

If you want to perform the same query again after you have displayed the entire database, you do not have to use the Create New Query command. Instead, you can select the View menu and choose the Apply Query command. When the Apply Query dialog box displays, select the name of the query you want to view (for example, Washington) and then choose the OK button in the Apply Query dialog box. You can choose the Apply Query command from the View menu in either List view or Form view.

You do not have to display the entire database by choosing the Show All Records command in order to create additional new queries, although some individuals prefer to view all records before applying the same or a new query.

Finding Records Based on Conditional Criteria

In the previous example of creating a new query, the words is equal to appeared in the How to compare the field box within the New Query dialog box. These words were the basis of the comparing operation. You can also specify other types of conditions that must be met in order for a record to display. You specify conditions using the words in the How to compare the field drop-down list box within the New Query dialog box.

To illustrate the use of conditional criteria other than is equal to when making queries using the New Query dialog box, the second task in this project is to display the records of all investors who invested more than $20,000.00 in the Global Investments investment club. To perform this query, complete the following steps.

TO DISPLAY RECORDS USING A QUERY BASED ON CONDITIONAL CRITERIA ▼

STEP 1 ►

Select the Tools menu and point to the Create New Query command.

The Tools menu displays and the mouse pointer points to the Create New Query command (Figure 9-12).

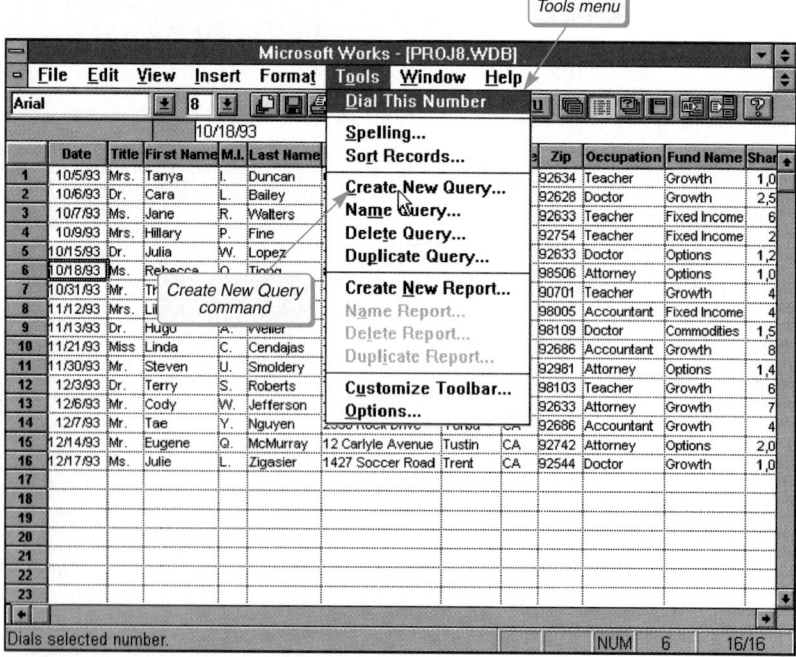

FIGURE 9-12

STEP 2 ▶

Choose the Create New Query command from the Tools menu. Type `Investment>20K` in the Please give this query a name text box. Click the Choose a field to compare drop-down list box arrow. Scroll down and select the field name Investment from the drop-down list box. Click the How to compare the field drop-down list box arrow. Point to the words is greater than in the drop-down list box.

The typed and selected entries display in the New Query dialog box (Figure 9-13). The field to be used as the basis of comparing is the Investment field. The mouse pointer points to the words is greater than.

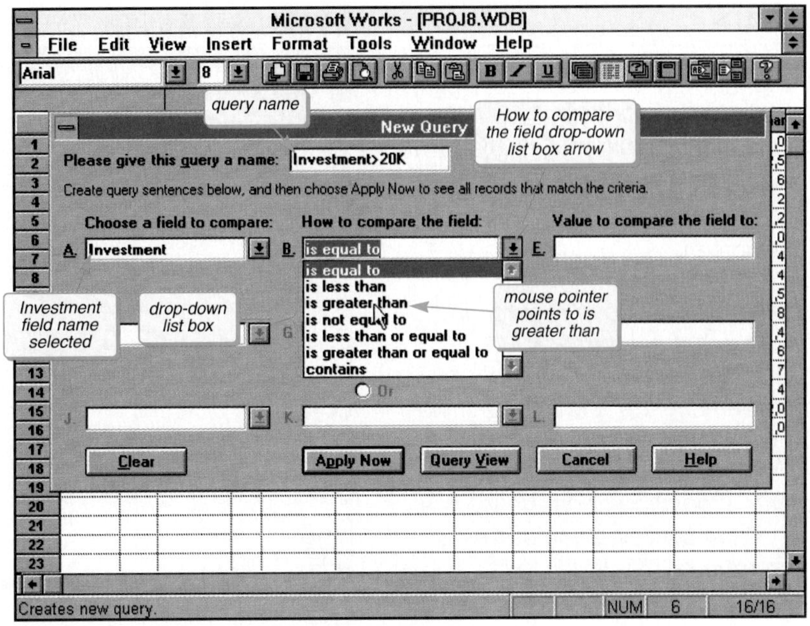

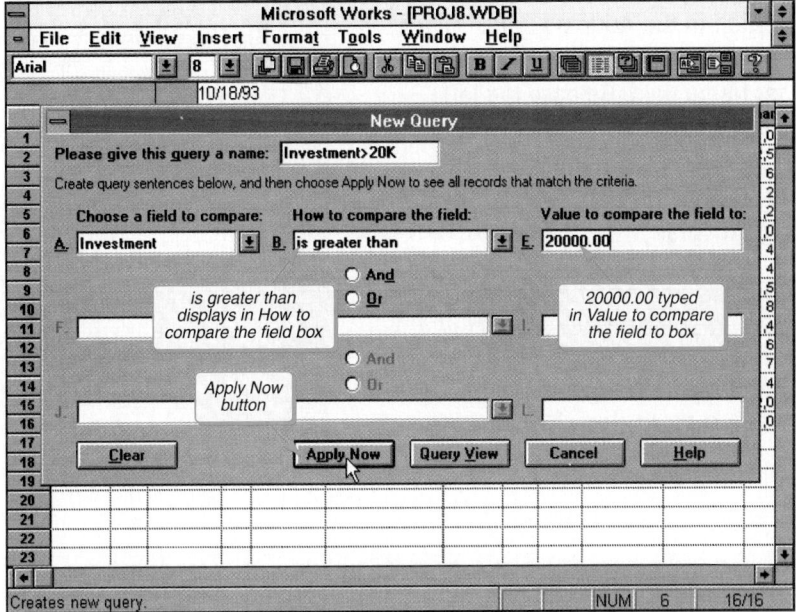

FIGURE 9-13

STEP 3 ▶

Select the words is greater than. Press the TAB key and type `20000.00` in the Value to compare the field to text box. Point to the Apply Now button.

The words is greater than display in the How to compare the field box and 20000.00 displays in the Value to compare the field to text box (Figure 9-14). This value is to be compared to the value in the Investment field in the database. The mouse pointer points to the Apply Now button. The query to be applied is: the value in the Investment field is greater than 20000.00.

FIGURE 9-14

STEP 4 ▶

Choose the Apply Now button to return to List view. Position the mouse pointer on the vertical split box in the lower left corner of the screen.

records display that have value in Investment field greater than 20,000.00

Works displays those records in List view that contain a value greater than 20000.00 in the Investment field (Figure 9-15). The List view displays the leftmost fields in the database. The mouse pointer is positioned on the vertical split box in the lower left corner of the screen.

mouse pointer points to vertical split box

	Date	Title	First Name	M.I.	Last Name	Address	City	State	Zip	Occupation	Fund Name	Shar
2	10/6/93	Dr.	Cara	L.	Bailey	303 Sunrise Place	Irvine	CA	92628	Doctor	Growth	2,5
5	10/15/93	Dr.	Julia	W.	Lopez	12732 Clover Road	Fullerton	CA	92633	Doctor	Options	1,2
6	10/18/93	Ms.	Rebecca	O.	Tiong	87 Green Street	Olympia	WA	98506	Attorney	Options	1,0
9	11/13/93	Dr.	Hugo	A.	Weller	16 Burnside Drive	Seattle	WA	98109	Doctor	Commodities	1,5
11	11/30/93	Mr.	Steven	U.	Smoldery	360 Old Mill Road	Chino	CA	92981	Attorney	Options	1,4
15	12/14/93	Mr.	Eugene	Q.	McMurray	12 Carlyle Avenue	Tustin	CA	92742	Attorney	Options	2,0
16	12/17/93	Ms.	Julie	L.	Zigasier	1427 Soccer Road	Trent	CA	92544	Doctor	Growth	1,0

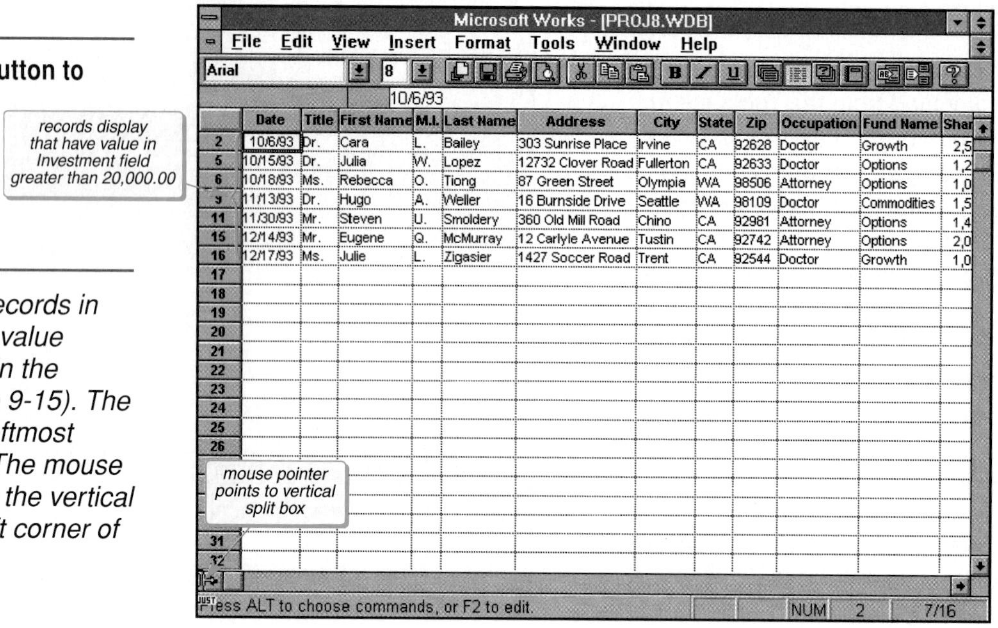

FIGURE 9-15

STEP 5 ▶

Drag the split bar to the first position in the Address field. This is the field immediately following the Last Name field. Release the left mouse button. Scroll the right pane until the Occupation, Fund Name, Shares, Share Price, and Investment fields display.

From the screen in Figure 9-16, you can see that investors Bailey, Lopez, Tiong, Weller, Smoldery, McMurray, and Zigasier each invested more than $20,000.00.

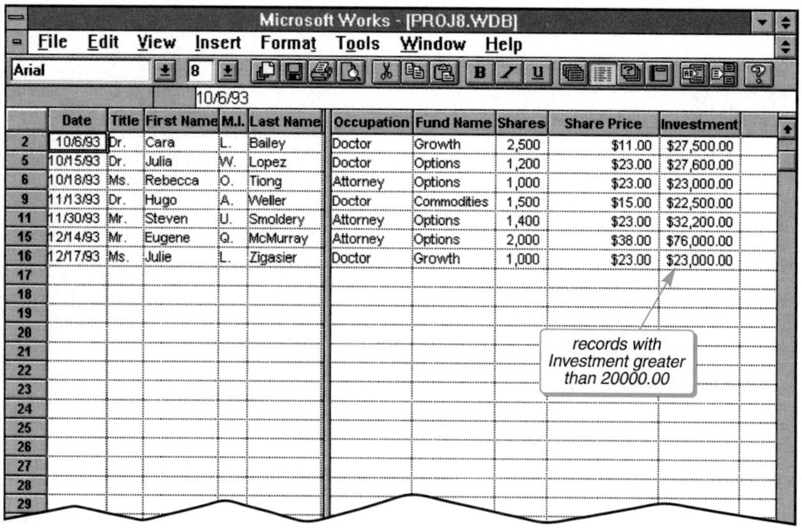

	Date	Title	First Name	M.I.	Last Name	Occupation	Fund Name	Shares	Share Price	Investment
2	10/6/93	Dr.	Cara	L.	Bailey	Doctor	Growth	2,500	$11.00	$27,500.00
5	10/15/93	Dr.	Julia	W.	Lopez	Doctor	Options	1,200	$23.00	$27,600.00
6	10/18/93	Ms.	Rebecca	O.	Tiong	Attorney	Options	1,000	$23.00	$23,000.00
9	11/13/93	Dr.	Hugo	A.	Weller	Doctor	Commodities	1,500	$15.00	$22,500.00
11	11/30/93	Mr.	Steven	U.	Smoldery	Attorney	Options	1,400	$23.00	$32,200.00
15	12/14/93	Mr.	Eugene	Q.	McMurray	Attorney	Options	2,000	$38.00	$76,000.00
16	12/17/93	Ms.	Julie	L.	Zigasier	Doctor	Growth	1,000	$23.00	$23,000.00

records with Investment greater than 20000.00

FIGURE 9-16

To display the Investment field in Figure 9-15, you could also scroll to the left until the Investment field displayed, but you would not be able to see the investor's name. Using window paning provides a convenient method of viewing different segments of a database while in List View.

Switching Hidden Records

When Works performs a query operation, it searches for the records in the database that satisfy the conditions in the query and displays those records. The other records in the database are hidden from view but they are still part of the database. These records are called **hidden records**. Works allows you to display all records that did not satisfy the query conditions (hidden records) through the use of the **Switch Hidden Records command.**

The third task specified on page W9.4 for this project is to display all investors who invested $20,000.00 or less. To accomplish this task, you could create a query that tests for a value less than or equal to 20000.00 in the Investment field. Because, however, the screen in Figure 9-16 displays all records for investors who invested more than 20,000.00, the hidden records are for investors who invested 20,000.00 or less. Therefore, a simpler method to display these investors is to use the Switch Hidden Records command, as shown in the following steps.

TO SWITCH HIDDEN RECORDS ▼

STEP 1 ►

Select the View menu and point to the Switch Hidden Records command.

Works displays the View menu and the mouse pointer points to the Switch Hidden Records command (Figure 9-17). Notice that the records currently displayed are for investments greater than $20,000.00.

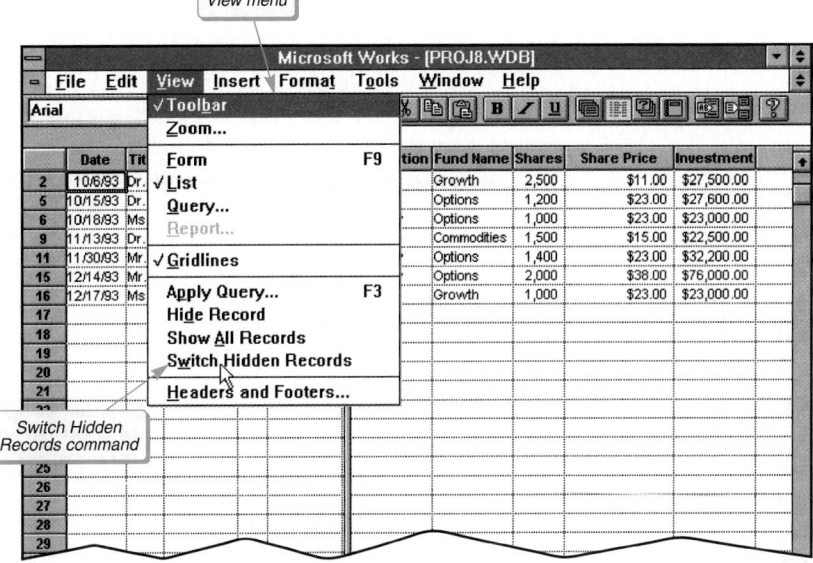

FIGURE 9-17

STEP 2 ►

Choose the Switch Hidden Records command from the View menu.

Works switches the hidden records by hiding the records whose investments are greater than $20,000.00 and displaying those records whose investments are less than or equal to $20,000.00 (Figure 9-18). Although the database contains no records with exactly $20,000.00 invested, if it did the records would display in Figure 9-18.

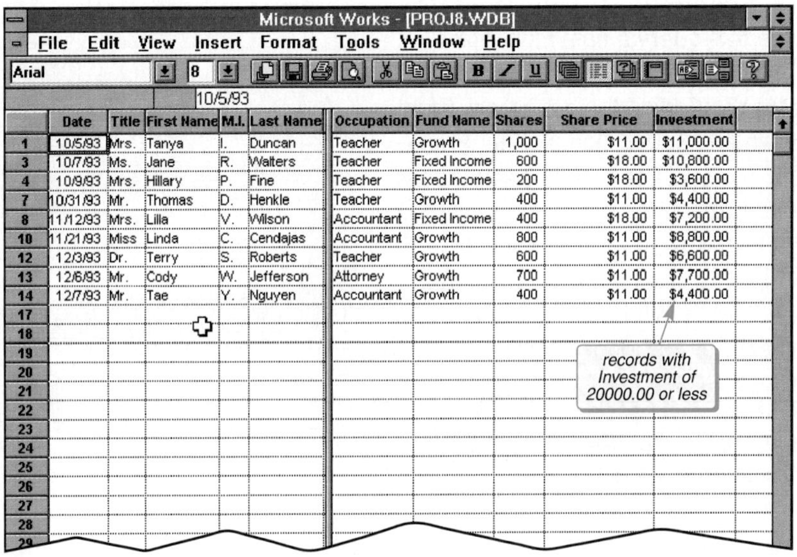

FIGURE 9-18

The Switch Hidden Records command is useful when performing queries because in effect it allows you to perform two queries by merely switching back and forth between the hidden records. In Figure 9-18, if you again choose the Switch Hidden Records command from the View menu, the records hidden in Figure 9-18 will display and the screen will be the same as in Figure 9-16 on the previous page.

Multiple Fields in Queries – The AND Logical Operator

Works allows queries in which more than one field is involved in determining the records to display. In the fourth task listed for Project 9 on page W9.4, you are to use a query to display all attorneys who have invested in the Options fund. To accomplish this task, Works must examine the Occupation field to find all records containing Attorney AND must search all Attorney records to find the word Options in the Fund Name field. In the query, the word AND is used. The word AND is called a **logical operator** in the query because it logically joins two different fields. When the **AND logical operator** is used in a query, both conditions must be true; that is, for a record to satisfy the query criteria, both the value Attorney must be in the Occupation field AND the value Options must be in the Fund Name field. To perform this query, complete the following steps.

TO PERFORM A QUERY USING MULTIPLE FIELDS ▼

STEP 1 ▶

Double-click the split bar in the List view display. Scroll left so the Date field displays. Select the Tools menu and choose the Create New Query command. When the New Query dialog box displays, type `Attorney/Option` in the Please give this query a name text box. Click the Choose a field to compare drop-down list box arrow. Scroll down and select Occupation. Press the TAB key. The How to compare the field box should contain is equal to. Press the TAB key and type `Attorney` in the Value to compare the field to text box. Point to and select the And option button.

The first part of the query is entered in the New Query dialog box (Figure 9-19).

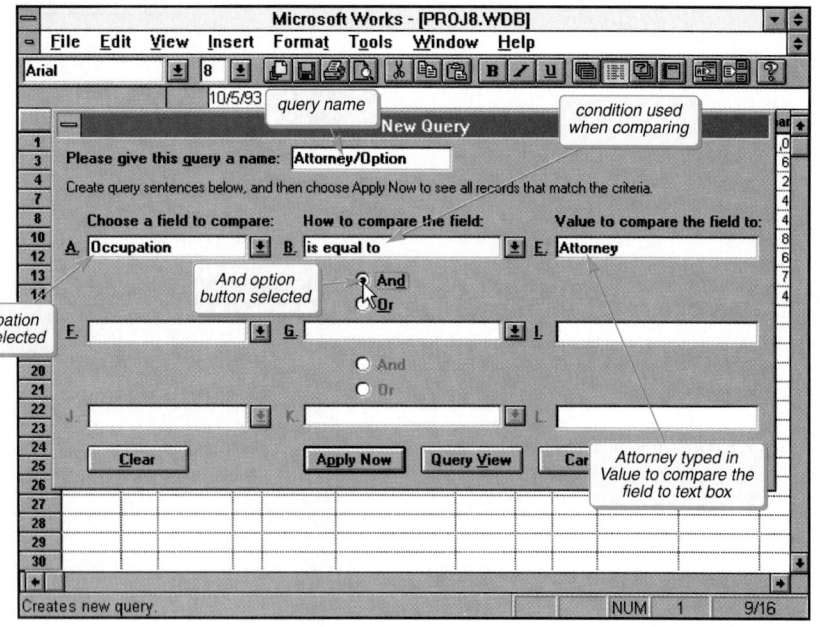

FIGURE 9-19

STEP 2 ►

In the Choose a field to compare drop-down list box marked F, click the box arrow, scroll down, and select Fund Name in the drop-down list box. Click the How to compare the field drop-down list box arrow and select is equal to in the drop-down list box. Press the TAB key and type Options in the Value to compare the field to text box. Point to the Apply Now button.

The next set of entries are made in the New Query dialog box and the mouse pointer points to the Apply Now button (Figure 9-20). The query to find records in the database with the Occupation field equal to Attorney AND the Fund Name equal to Options is entered into the New Query dialog box.

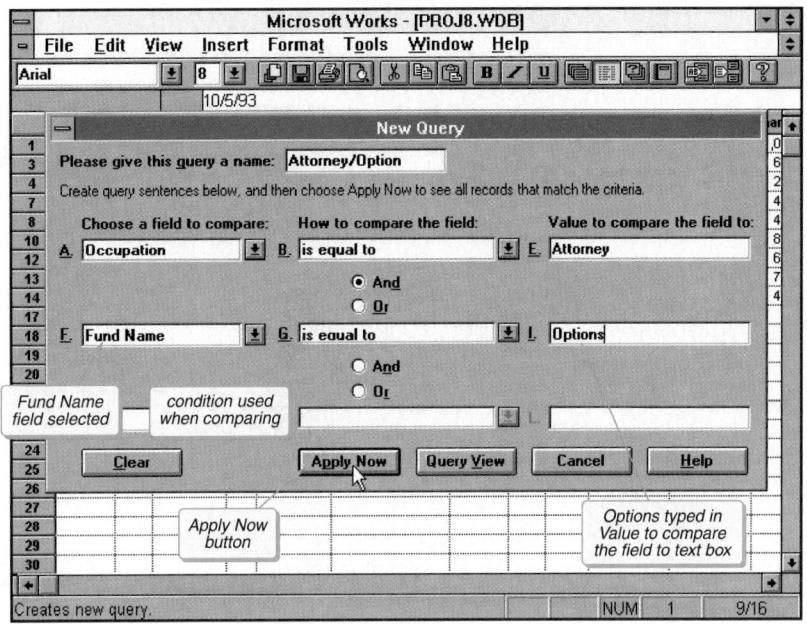

FIGURE 9-20

STEP 3 ►

Choose the Apply Now button in the New Query dialog box.

Works displays the records of individuals who are Attorneys AND have invested in Options (Figure 9-21).

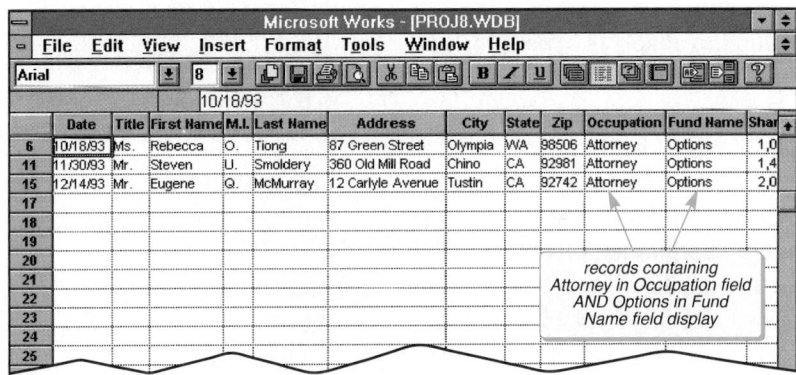

FIGURE 9-21

If necessary for your query, you can specify a third field also using the AND logical operator.

The OR Logical Operator in Queries

A second logical operator that can be used in queries is called the **OR logical operator**. When the OR logical operator is used, if either or both of the conditions stated are true, then the criteria is satisfied. For example, the fifth task in this project is to use a query to display all individuals who invested in the Growth fund OR whose investment is greater than $50,000.00. When you analyze this query, the condition can be stated as, display those records with the Fund Name equal to Growth OR the Investment field greater than 50000.00. The logical operator OR means either or both. To perform this query, complete the following steps.

TO PERFORM A QUERY USING THE OR LOGICAL OPERATOR ▼

STEP 1 ▶

Select the Tools menu and point to the Create New Query command.

The Tools menu displays and the mouse pointer points to the Create New Query command (Figure 9-22).

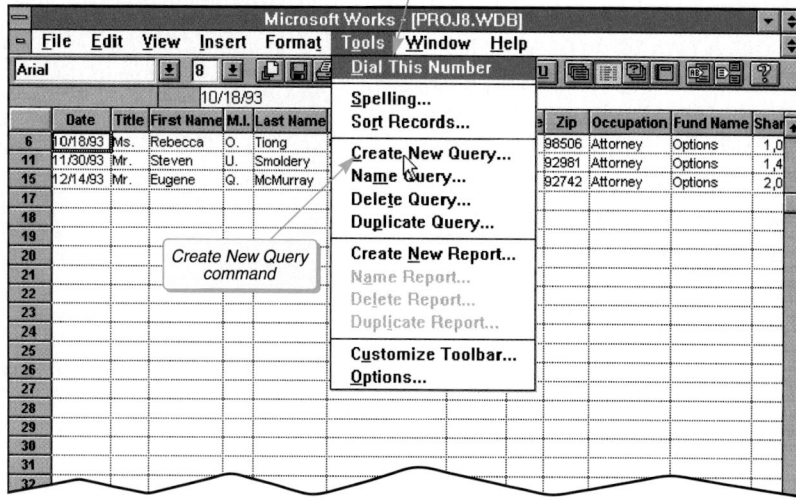

FIGURE 9-22

STEP 2 ▶

Choose the Create New Query command. When the New Query dialog box displays, type `Growth/ Invest` in the Please give this query a name text box. Click the Choose a field to compare drop-down list box arrow, scroll down and select Fund Name, press the TAB key two times, and type `Growth` in the Value to compare the field to text box. Select the Or option button. Click the Choose a field to compare drop-down list box arrow for the box marked F, scroll down and select Investment. Click the How to compare the field drop-down list box arrow in the second row and select is greater than in the drop-down list box. Press the TAB key and type `50000.00` in the Value to compare the field to text box in the second row. Point to the Apply Now button

The query in the New Query dialog box states Fund Name is equal to Growth Or Investment is greater than 50000.00 (Figure 9-23). The mouse pointer points to the Apply Now button.

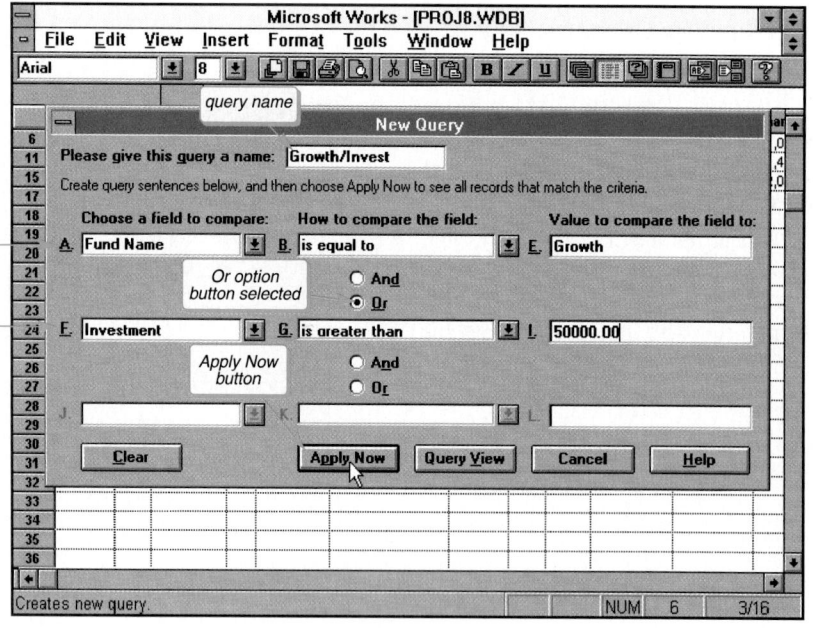

FIGURE 9-23

STEP 3 ►

Choose the Apply Now button in the New Query dialog box. Click the right scroll arrow five times to display the Investment field.

The List view of the data base displays records of individuals who invested in the Growth fund OR whose investment is greater than $50,000.00 (Figure 9-24).

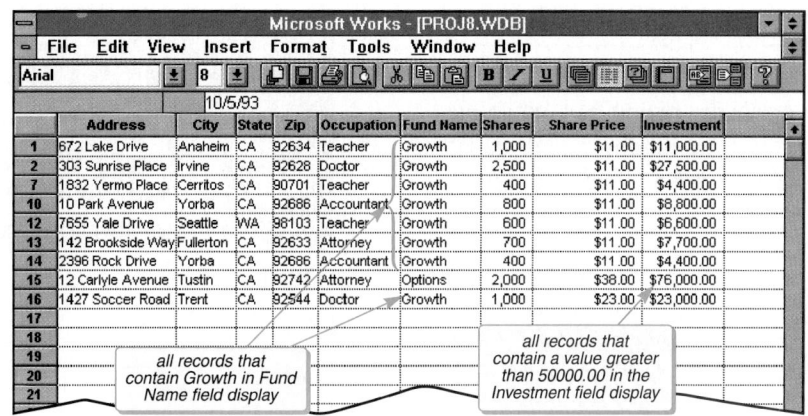

FIGURE 9-24

Works provides great flexibility in retrieving information from the database using its query capabilities and the AND and OR logical operators.

Query View

It is also possible to create queries using the **Query view** of a Works database. Query view displays a blank form that contains all the fields, as in Form view, but none of the data from the database unless entered as a part of the query. In Query view, you define the records you want to display by entering the appropriate query instructions in the fields. This technique can be used at any time, but must used when more than three conditions are stated in the query. The following steps explain how to use Query view to display records of individuals who are teachers.

TO USE QUERY VIEW ▼

STEP 1 ►

Select the Tools menu and choose the Create New Query command. When the New Query dialog box displays, type Teachers in the Please give this query a name text box, click Clear button, and point to the Query View button.

Works displays the New Query dialog box (Figure 9-25). Clicking the Clear button removes any previous queries in the Query view display. The mouse pointer points to the Query View button.

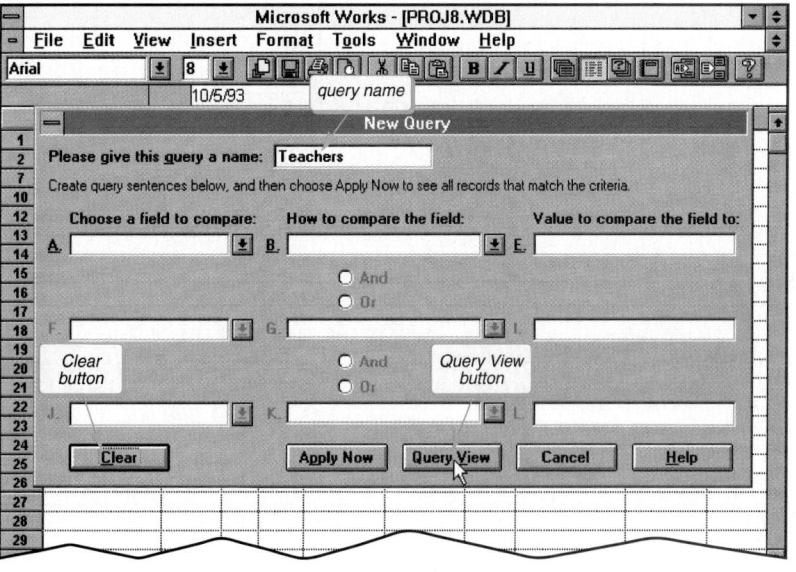

FIGURE 9-25

STEP 2 ▶

Choose the Query View button in the New Query dialog box. When the query view window displays, select the Occupation field and type Teacher.

The Query view window displays (Figure 9-26). The word Teacher displays in the Occupation field and also displays in the formula bar. In Query view, this entry tells Works to display all records that contain Teacher in the Occupation field.

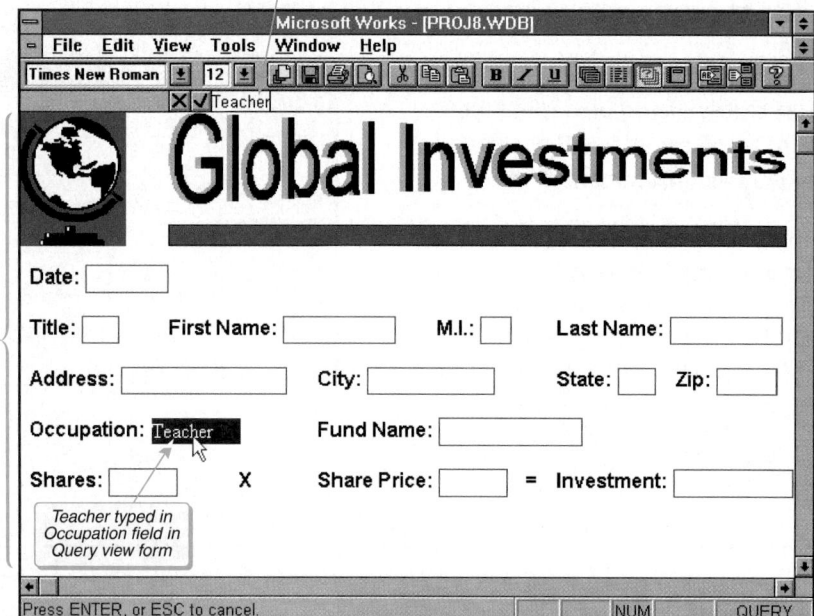

FIGURE 9-26

STEP 3 ▶

Press the ENTER key or click the Enter box. Then click the List View button on the Toolbar. Scroll left until the Date field is visible.

Works displays all records containing Teacher in the Occupation field (Figure 9-27).

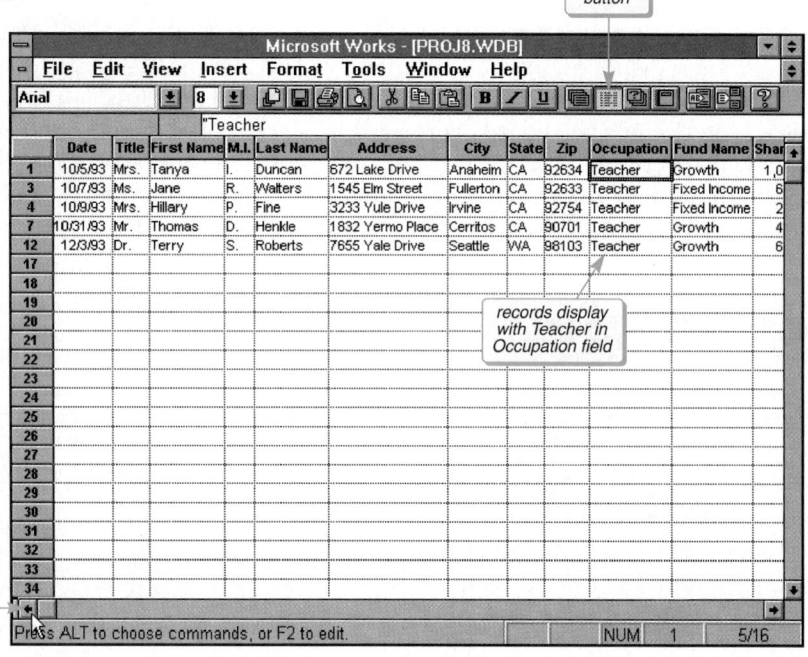

FIGURE 9-27

Conditional Operators

The Query view allows you to compare fields using conditional operators. A list of commonly used **conditional operators** and their meaning is shown in Table 9-1.

Performing a Query Using More Than Three Criteria

Is previously stated, when using the New Query dialog box to create queries, you are limited to using two logical operators. If you develop a query which requires more than two logical operators, you must use Query view.

The following example illustrates a query which is created to display investors who are doctors AND live in the cities of Fullerton OR Irvine OR Yorba. To create a query of this type, you must write a query instruction that is placed in one of the fields in the Query view form. The query instruction must begin with an equal sign and equal signs are used in the instruction to describe the query. Logical operators AND and OR are enclosed in pound signs (#). The query instruction to display investors who are doctors and live in Fullerton or Irvine or Yorba is:

=Occupation="Doctor"#AND#(City="Fullerton"#OR#City="Irvine"#OR#City="Yorba")

Note the use of parentheses. When using logical operators, Works evaluates fields joined by the AND logical operator first, and then the OR logical operator. This method of evaluation can be changed using parentheses. For example, if parentheses were not used in the previous example, Works would display the records of investors who were doctors AND lived in the City of Fullerton. Works would then evaluate the OR conditions and display records for any investor who lived in Irvine and any investor who lived in Yorba. Thus, any investor who lived in Irvine or Yorba would display in addition to doctors who lived in Fullerton. This would not produce the correct output. Care must be taken when using multiple logical operators to ensure that the correct query is created.

The steps to create the query described above are explained in the following paragraphs.

▸ **TABLE 9-1**

OPERATOR	MEANING
=	Equal
< >	Not Equal
>	Greater Than
<	Less Than
>=	Greater Than or Equal To
<=	Less Than or Equal To

TO CREATE A QUERY IN QUERY VIEW ▼

STEP 1 ▶

Select the Tools menu and choose the Create New Query command. When the New Query dialog box displays, type `Occupation/City` in the Please give this query a name text box, click the Clear button to remove previous queries from the Query view window, and then point to the Query View button.

The New Query dialog box displays and contains the query name, Occupation/City (Figure 9-28). The mouse pointer points to the Query View button.

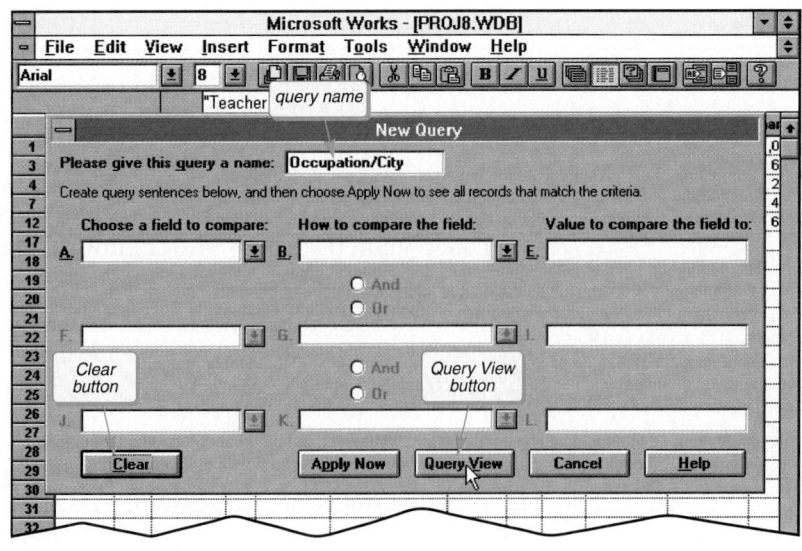

FIGURE 9-28

STEP 2 ▶

Choose the Query View button. When the Query view form displays, select the Occupation field. Then type =Occupation="Doctor" #AND#(City="Fullerton"# OR#City="Irvine"#OR# City="Yorba").

The first portion of the formula appears in the Occupation field and the complete formula displays in the formula bar (Figure 9-29).

FIGURE 9-29

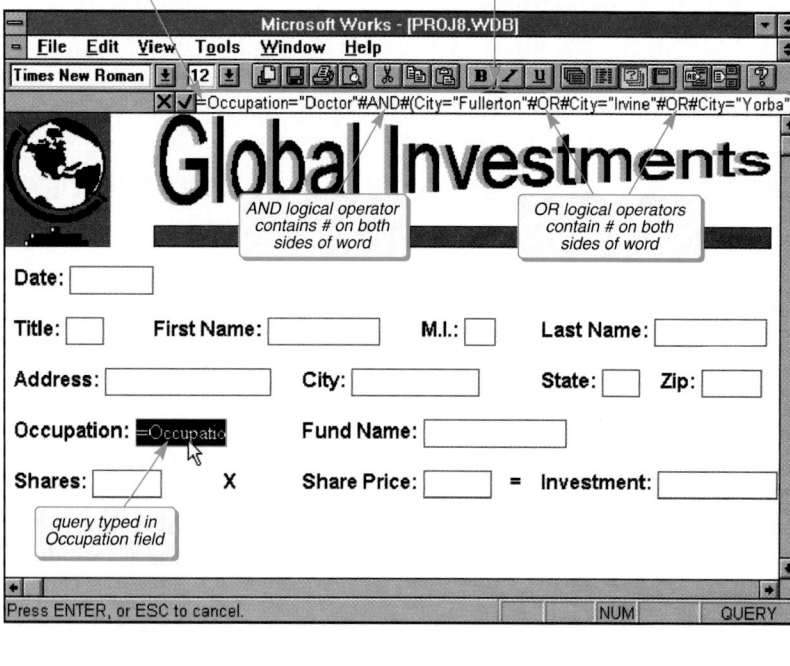

STEP 3 ▶

Press the ENTER key or click the Enter box. Then click the List View button on the Toolbar.

Works displays the records for the doctors who live in Fullerton or Irvine or Yorba (Figure 9-30).

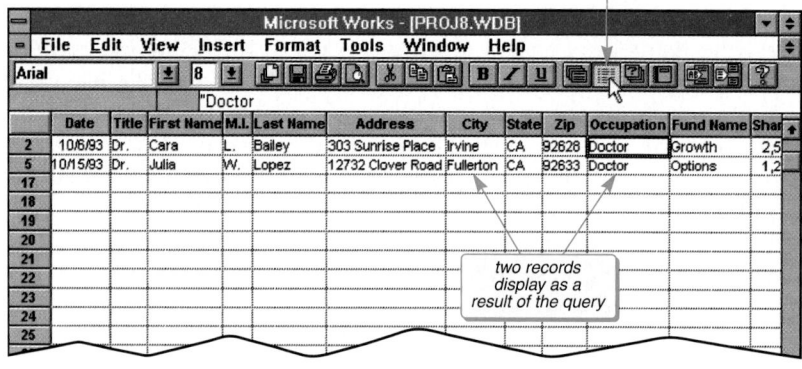

FIGURE 9-30

When developing queries that require multiple logical operators you must use great care when you type the entries.

Works also provides a **Query View button** on the Toolbar that you can click to move directly to Query view if a query has previously been named. Care must be taken when using this button, however, because if you have previously named a query and you click the Query View button on the Toolbar, the new query you enter will replace the previously named query.

Applying a Query

Once you name a query, you can apply the query to the database at a later time by choosing the **Apply Query command** from the View menu. To apply the Washington query created earlier, complete the following steps.

TO APPLY A QUERY ▼

STEP 1 ▶

Select the View menu and point to the Apply Query command.

The View menu displays and the mouse pointer points to the Apply Query command (Figure 9-31).

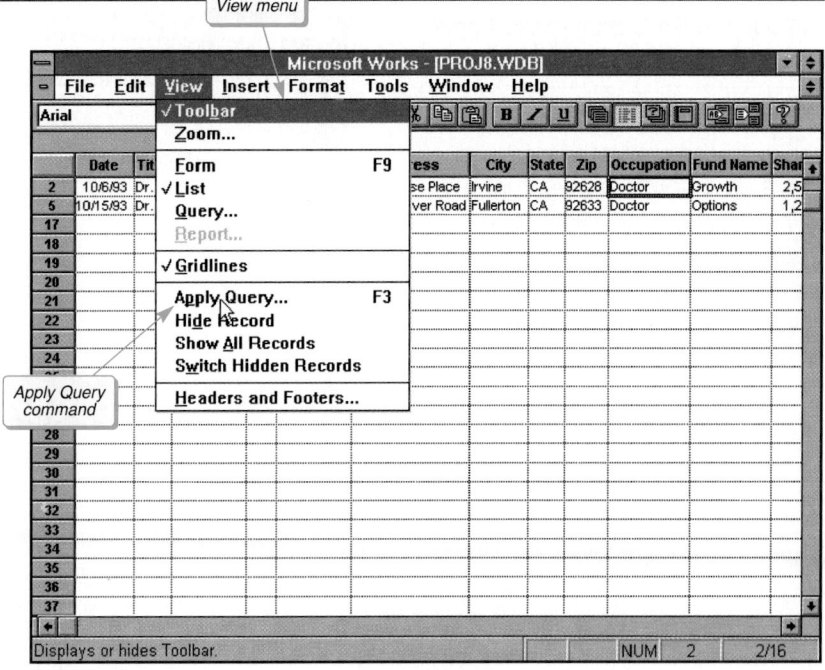

FIGURE 9-31

STEP 2 ▶

Choose the Apply Query command from the View menu. When the Apply Query dialog box displays, highlight the name Washington in the Query list box.

The Apply Query dialog box displays and the query name Washington is highlighted (Figure 9-32). The Query list box contains the names of all queries that have been defined for the database.

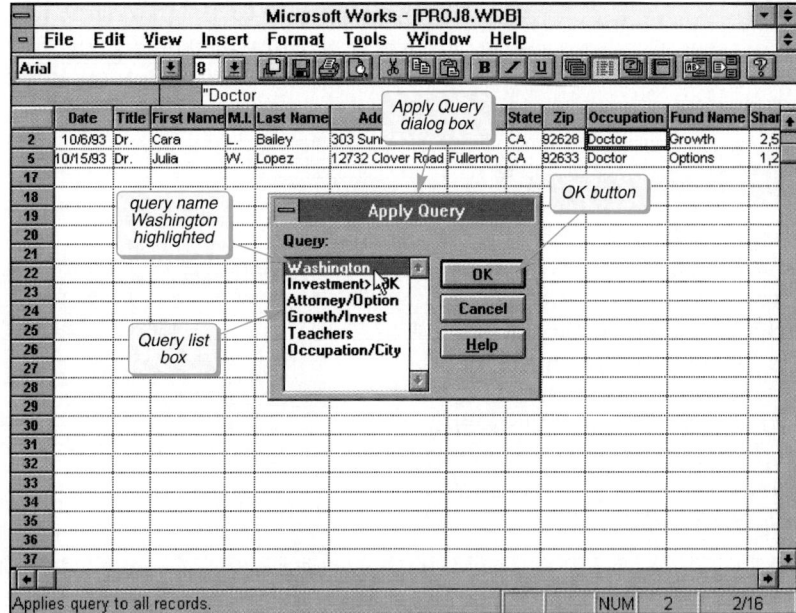

FIGURE 9-32

STEP 3 ▶

Choose the OK button in the Apply Query dialog box.

Works applies the Washington query to the database and displays all records of investors who live in the state of Washington (Figure 9-33).

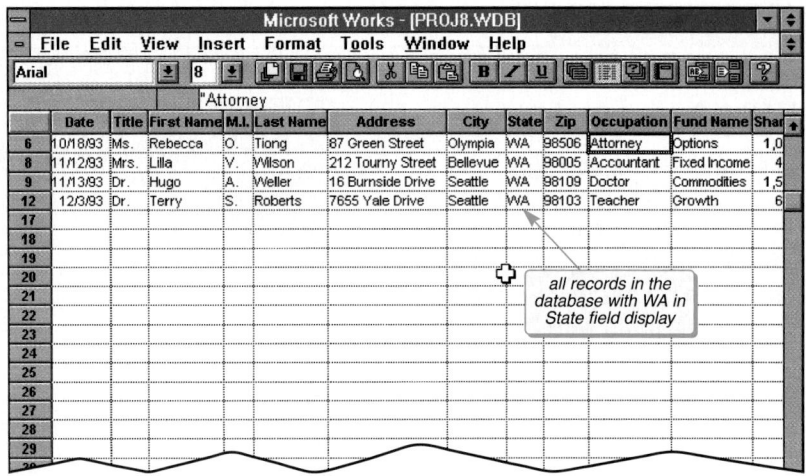

FIGURE 9-33

The Apply Query is an important command where there is a need to use a query more than one time.

Deleting a Query

Works allows you to assign a name to eight queries for any single database. You can delete previously named queries, however, to add another query. To delete a query, perform the following steps.

TO DELETE A QUERY ▼

STEP 1 ▶

Select the Tools menu and point to the Delete Query command.

Works displays the Tools menu and the mouse pointer points to the Delete Query command (Figure 9-34).

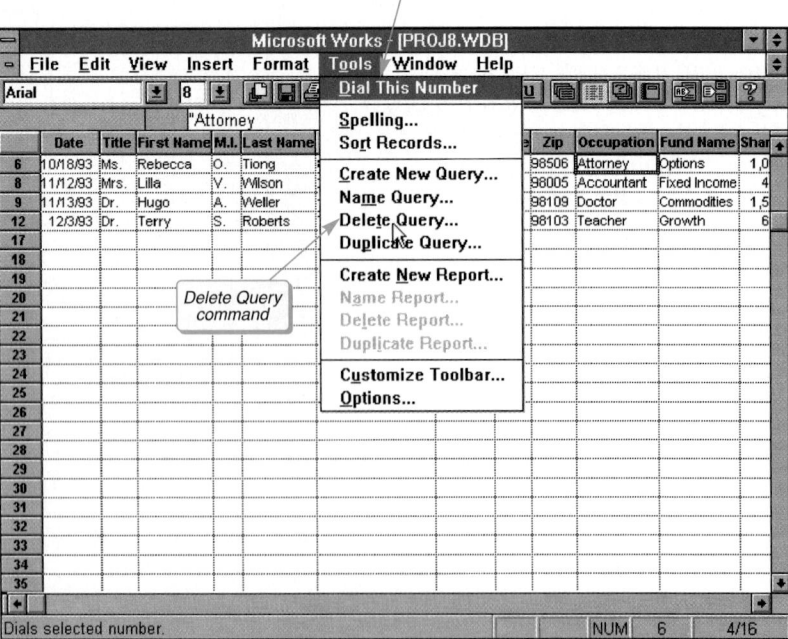

FIGURE 9-34

STEP 2 ▶

Choose the Delete Query command from the Tools menu. When the Delete Query dialog box displays, highlight the query name Occupation/City in the Queries list box. Then point to the Delete button.

Works displays the Delete Query dialog box (Figure 9-35). The query name Occupation/City is highlighted and the mouse pointer points to the Delete button.

STEP 3 ▶

Choose the Delete button and then choose the OK button in the Delete Query dialog box.

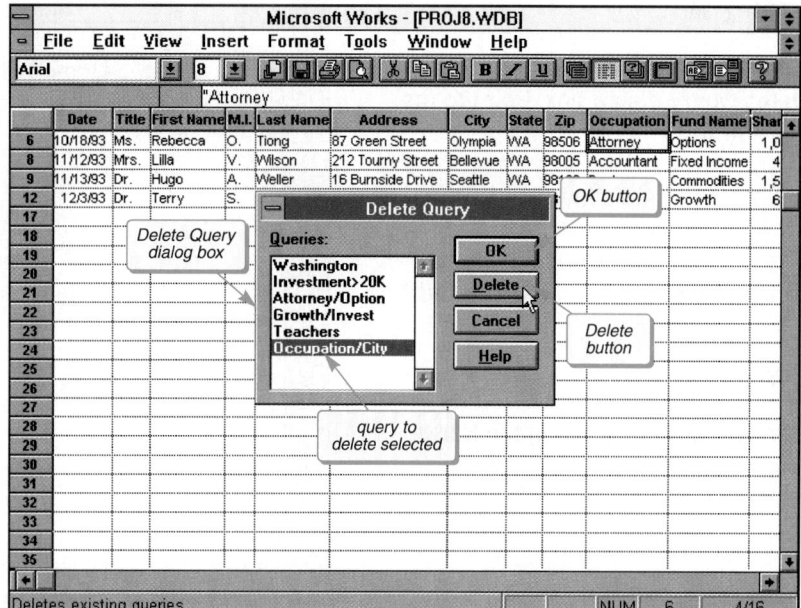

FIGURE 9-35

The query name Occupation/City is deleted and will no long display in the Apply Query dialog box when referenced.

Renaming a Query

You can rename any query you have previously named. To rename the Washington query to STofWashington, perform the following steps.

TO RENAME A QUERY ▼

STEP 1 ▶

Select the Tools menu and choose the Name Query command. When the Name Query dialog box displays, highlight the Washington query name in the Queries list box. Place the insertion point in the Name text box and type `STofWashington`. Point to the Rename button.

The Name Query dialog box displays (Figure 9-35a). The new query name, STofWashington, displays in the Name text box and the mouse pointer points to the **Rename button**.

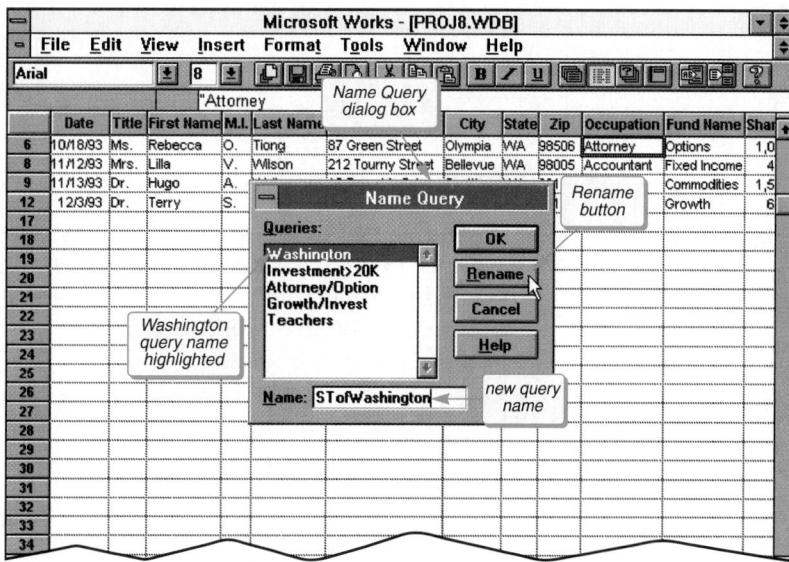

FIGURE 9-35a

STEP 2 ▶

Choose the Rename button in the Name Query dialog box. Point to the OK button.

Works changes the name of the highlighted Query name in the Queries list box from Washington to STofWashington (Figure 9-35b).

STEP 3 ▶

Choose the OK button in the Name Query dialog box.

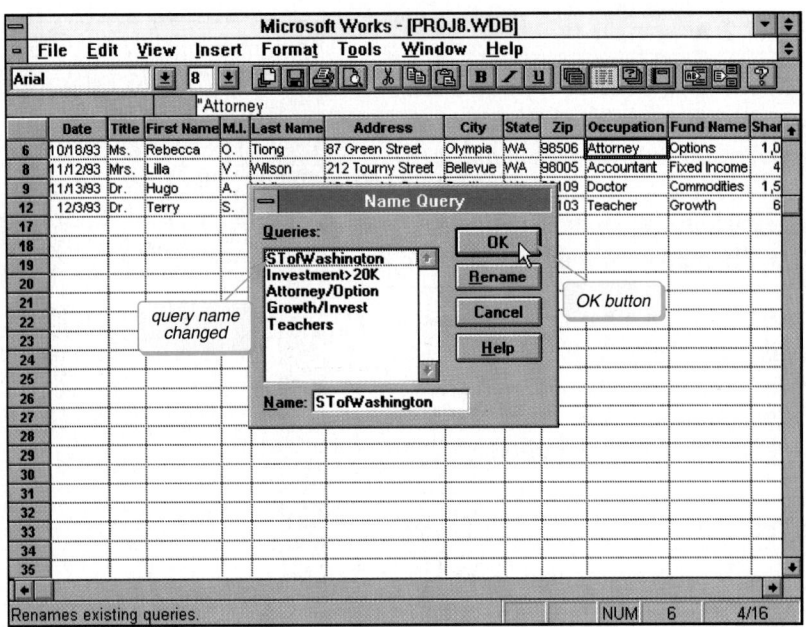

FIGURE 9-35b

Saving a Database with Queries

You can save the database with the queries. Then, you can apply the queries at a later time. To save the database containing queries using a different filename, complete the following steps.

TO SAVE A DATABASE WITH QUERIES

Step 1: Select the File menu.
Step 2: Choose the Save As command.
Step 3: Type `proj9` in the File Name text box of the Save As dialog box.
Step 4: Select drive A from the Drives drop-down list box.
Step 5: Choose the OK button in the Save As dialog box.

Database Query Summary

The Works Database query capability allows you to view records in the database based on virtually any condition or combination of conditions you can specify, ranging from simply finding records with a given value in a field to complex conditions involving conditional and logical operators.

In addition to allowing you to view records in either List or Form view on the screen, the query capability allows you to select certain records for use in reports. The database reporting capabilities of Works are explained next.

▶ WORKS DATABASE REPORTS

Works provides the means to create a variety of printed reports from the data in a database. These reports can range from simple listings to involved reports with calculations and summaries. This section of Project 9 demonstrates a variety of reports you can obtain using the Works Database tool and the methods for creating these reports.

Database Listing

The next task in this project is to create a report listing all investors in the database. The report is shown in Figure 9-36.

The title, first name, middle initial, last name, address, city, state, and zip code of each investor is listed in the report. Three different categories of lines appear on the report: (1) the report Title lines, which contain the word Investors on one line and a dark magenta bar on the next line; (2) the report Headings lines, which consist of the words Title, First Name, etc. on one line and a solid pattern, light gray bar on the next line; and (3) the Record lines (each individual record from the database). The record lines are followed by a solid pattern, light gray bar. It is important you understand these three categories of lines because you will use these categories when defining the report.

To create the database listing shown in Figure 9-36, you must identify the report title in the New Report dialog box and then select those fields that are to appear in the report. The headings are the field names of the fields you select. When you create a report, Works creates a report definition and displays it in Report view. The report definition defines the general format of the report. This definition may be modified to meet particular needs. To define the report listing all investors, complete the following steps.

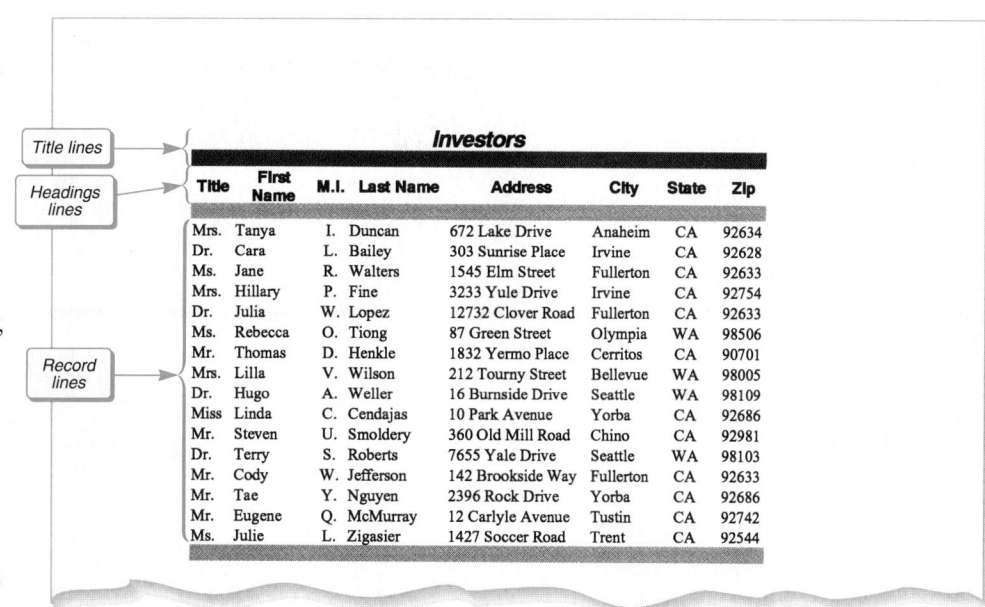

FIGURE 9-36

Title lines / Headings lines / Record lines

Title	First Name	M.I.	Last Name	Address	City	State	Zip
Mrs.	Tanya	I.	Duncan	672 Lake Drive	Anaheim	CA	92634
Dr.	Cara	L.	Bailey	303 Sunrise Place	Irvine	CA	92628
Ms.	Jane	R.	Walters	1545 Elm Street	Fullerton	CA	92633
Mrs.	Hillary	P.	Fine	3233 Yule Drive	Irvine	CA	92754
Dr.	Julia	W.	Lopez	12732 Clover Road	Fullerton	CA	92633
Ms.	Rebecca	O.	Tiong	87 Green Street	Olympia	WA	98506
Mr.	Thomas	D.	Henkle	1832 Yermo Place	Cerritos	CA	90701
Mrs.	Lilla	V.	Wilson	212 Tourny Street	Bellevue	WA	98005
Dr.	Hugo	A.	Weller	16 Burnside Drive	Seattle	WA	98109
Miss	Linda	C.	Cendajas	10 Park Avenue	Yorba	CA	92686
Mr.	Steven	U.	Smoldery	360 Old Mill Road	Chino	CA	92981
Dr.	Terry	S.	Roberts	7655 Yale Drive	Seattle	WA	98103
Mr.	Cody	W.	Jefferson	142 Brookside Way	Fullerton	CA	92633
Mr.	Tae	Y.	Nguyen	2396 Rock Drive	Yorba	CA	92686
Mr.	Eugene	Q.	McMurray	12 Carlyle Avenue	Tustin	CA	92742
Ms.	Julie	L.	Zigasier	1427 Soccer Road	Trent	CA	92544

TO DEFINE A LISTING REPORT ▼

STEP 1 ►

If necessary, in List view select the View menu and choose the Show All Records command. Scroll up so the first record is visible. Click the Report View button on the Toolbar. When the New Report dialog box displays, type `Investors` in the Report Title text box.

*Works displays the New Report dialog box (Figure 9-37). If no report is defined for the database, clicking the **Report View button** always results in Works displaying the New Report dialog box. The word Investors displays in the Report Title text box. The Field list box on the left contains the names of the fields in the database. The Fields in Report list box on the right shows all fields that have been selected to appear in the report. In Figure 9-37, no fields have been selected.*

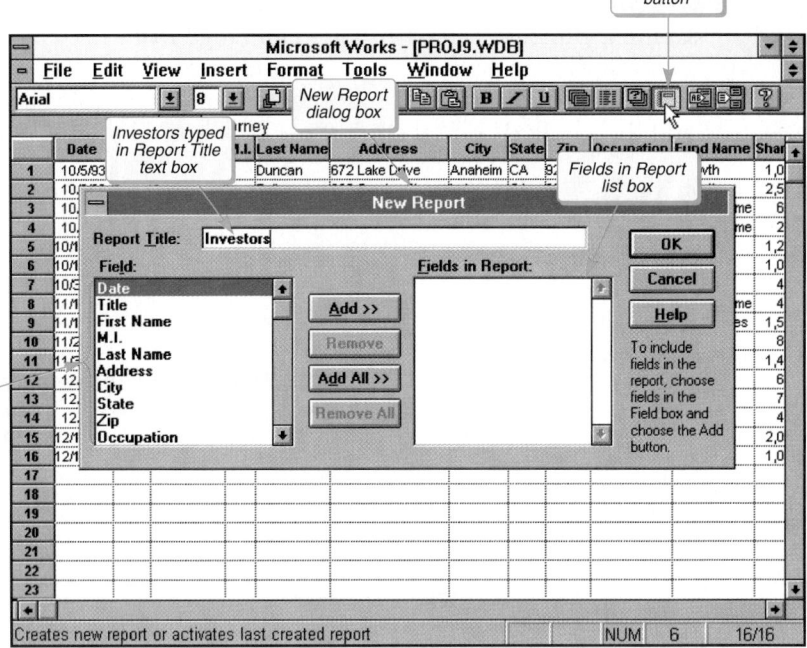

FIGURE 9-37

STEP 2 ►

Highlight the field name Title in the Field list box by clicking the word Title. Point to the Add button.

*The field name Title is highlighted and the mouse pointer points to the **Add button** (Figure 9-38).*

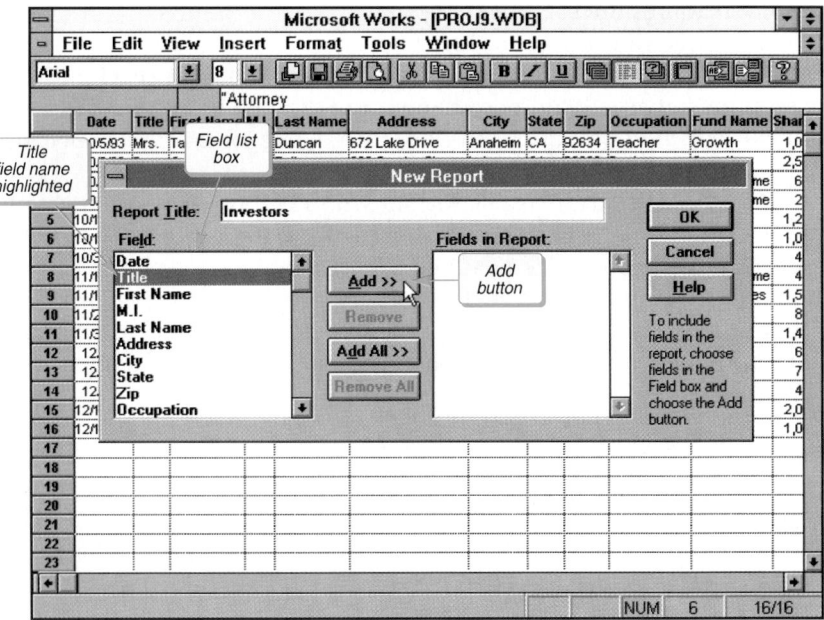

FIGURE 9-38

STEP 3 ▶

Choose the Add button to add the Title field to the Fields in Report list box. The highlight in the Field list box on the left automatically moves to the next field name (First Name) when you choose the Add button. Choose the Add button for each of the following fields: First Name, M.I., Last Name, Address, City, State, and Zip. Point to the OK button after all fields have been added to the Fields in Report list box.

Works places the field names you select in the Fields in Report list box (Figure 9-39). The Occupation field name is highlighted, but because it is not in the report the Add button should not be chosen. If you mistakenly place a field name in the Fields in Report list box that is not supposed to be in the report, highlight the incorrect field name in the Fields in Report list box and choose the Remove button. The field name will be removed from the Fields in Report list box. The mouse pointer points to the OK button.

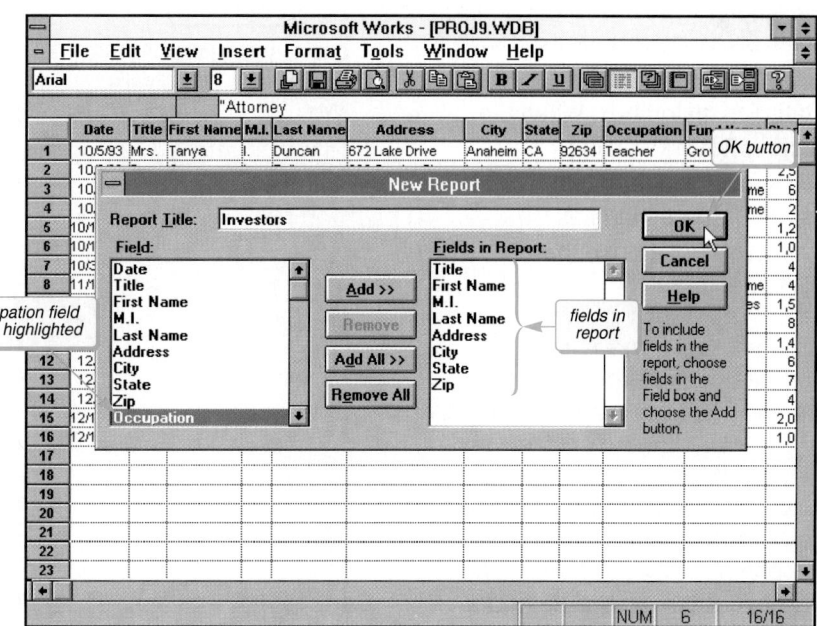

FIGURE 9-39

STEP 4 ▶

Choose the OK button in the New Report dialog box. When the Report Statistics dialog box displays, point to the OK button.

When you choose the OK button in the New Report dialog box, Works displays the Report Statistics dialog box (Figure 9-40). This dialog box is used to define summary statistics that can be included in a report. No statistics are required for the report in Figure 9-36, so no entries should be made in this section. A later report will demonstrate the use of the Statistics section. The mouse pointer points to the OK button.

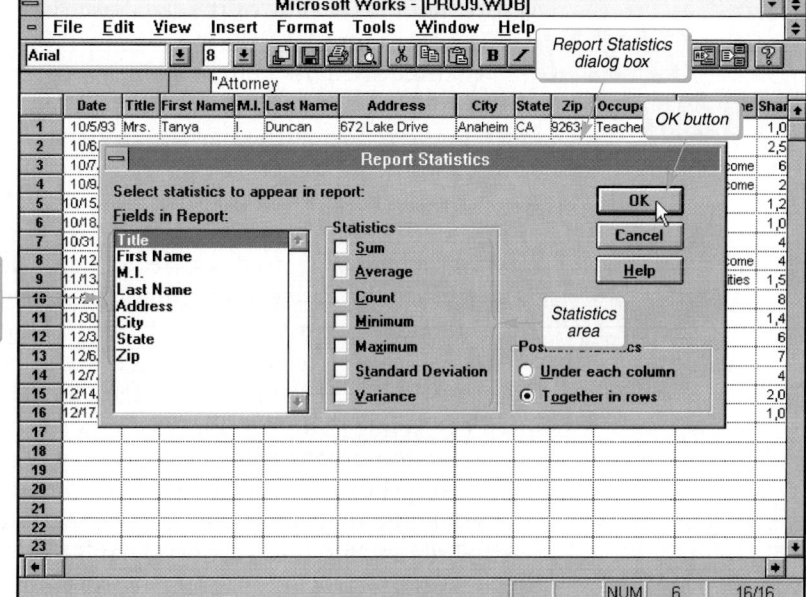

FIGURE 9-40

STEP 5 ▶

Choose the OK button in the Report Statistics dialog box. When the Microsoft Works dialog box displays stating that the report definition has been created, choose the OK button.

After you have made the choices and entries in the New Report dialog box and the Report Statistics dialog box, Works displays the Microsoft Works dialog box to inform you the report definition has been created. After choosing the OK button, Works displays the **report definition window** *(Figure 9-41).*

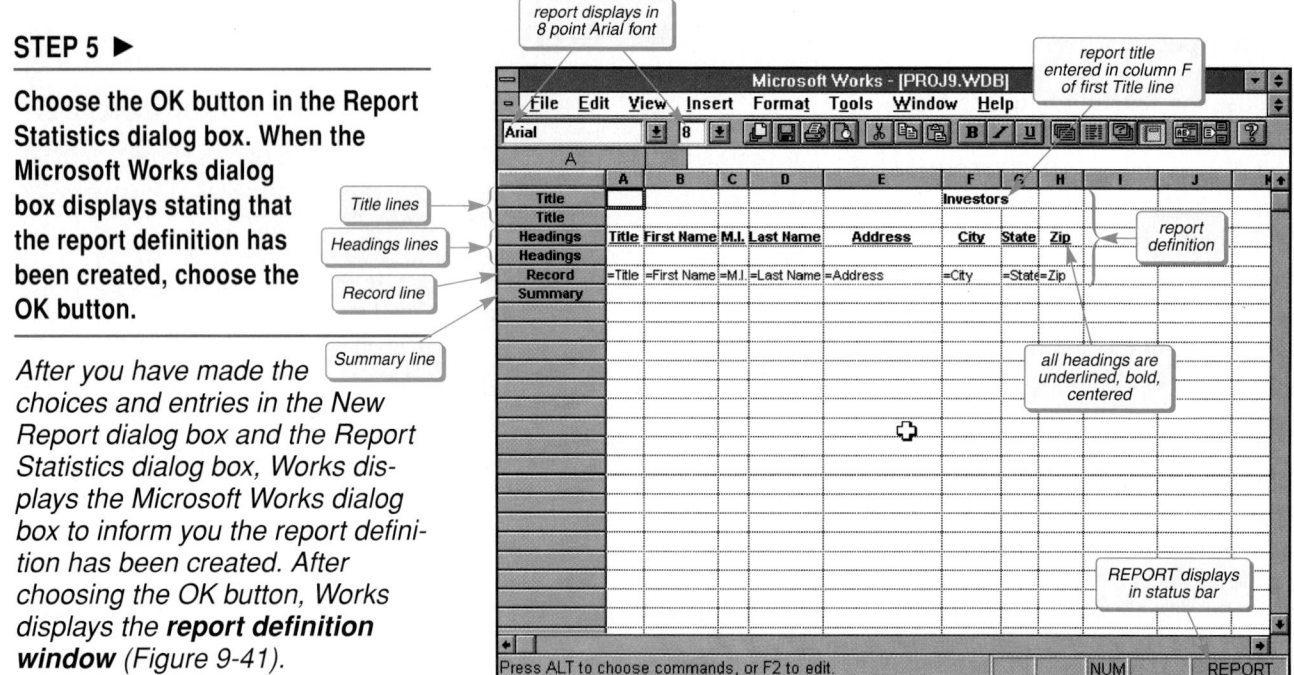

FIGURE 9-41

The report definition window in Figure 9-41 contains columns and rows much like the List view of the database. Each column is identified by column letters. The rows are identified by row titles at the left of the window. The first two rows are **Title rows**. Works always displays the title you entered in Step 1 (Investors) in a column to the right in the first title row. The title displays in 8 point Arial bold font. The second title row is blank. The next two rows are **Headings rows**. The field names you selected in Step 2 through Step 4 display in the columns of the first Headings row. By default, Works displays the headings in bold font, underlined and centered in each column. The font and size used for the headings is the same as used in the List view of the database (in this case, 8 point Arial font). The second Headings row is blank.

The **Record row** contains entries with an equal sign followed by the field names you selected for the report. This indicates Works will place the actual field entry in the report at the particular location. Although only one Record row appears in the report definition, one Record line will print on the report for each record in the database. The **Summary row** is blank. Each field in the report definition, and therefore the report itself, displays in the same font and size as the List view of the database. In this case, all fields display in 8 point Arial font. Fonts and font sizes can be changed for the fields on the report.

The Title line of a report will print at the top of the first page of the report and never again. The Headings lines print under the Title line on the first page of the report and at the top of the page on each subsequent page. As stated before, one Record line will print for each record in the database. Summary lines, if specified in the Report Statistics dialog box, will print on the report after all the Record lines have printed. In the listing report being created, no Summary lines will print.

While the report definition developed by Works provides the structure of the desired report, often the report default format is not the precise format you want for the report. Prior to changing the report definition, however, you can view the report as it will print. To view the report as it will print, perform the following steps (see Figure 9-41a).

TO VIEW A REPORT

Step 1: Click the Print Preview button on the Toolbar.

Step 2: Click the Zoom In button in the print preview window two times.

The report displays in the print preview window in Figure 9-41a.

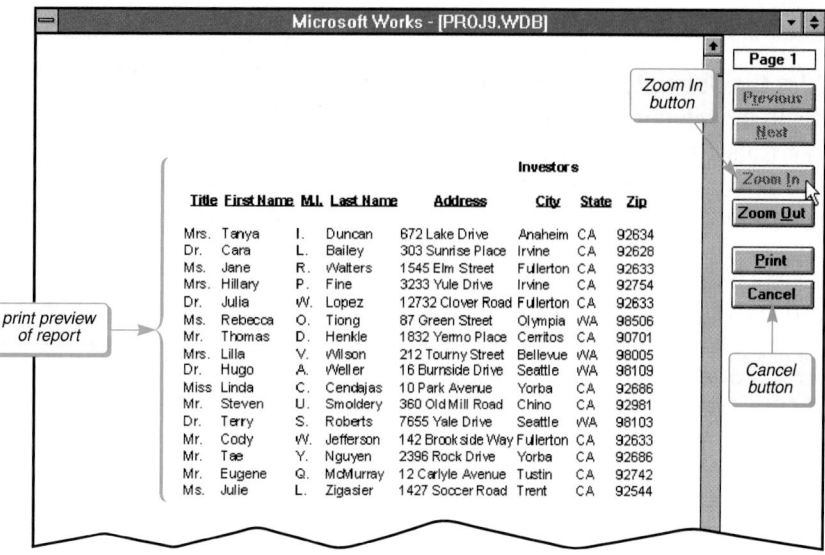

FIGURE 9-41a

▶ TO MODIFY A REPORT DEFINITION

I n Figure 9-41a it is apparent that several areas of the report must be modified to achieve the report format shown in Figure 9-36 on page W9.25. First, the title Investors, which will print to the right of the page in 8 point Arial bold font in its present format, must be changed to 14 point bold italic font and must be centered on the report. Second, the field headings, which will currently print in 8 point Arial bold and underlined font, must be changed to 10 point with the underline removed. The record lines should display in 10 point Times New Roman font. In addition, the fields should be increased in width to improve the appearance of the report. In Figure 9-36, a solid pattern, dark magenta line separates the report title from the report headings, and a solid pattern, light gray bar appears after the column titles and after all records have printed. To modify the current report definition to conform to the desired layout, perform the following steps.

TO MODIFY A REPORT DEFINITION ▼

STEP 1 ▶

Choose the Cancel button in the print preview window to return to the report definition window. Highlight column F in the first Title row. Point to the Cut button on the Toolbar.

*The cell containing the word Investors is highlighted and the mouse pointer points to the **Cut button** (Figure 9-42).*

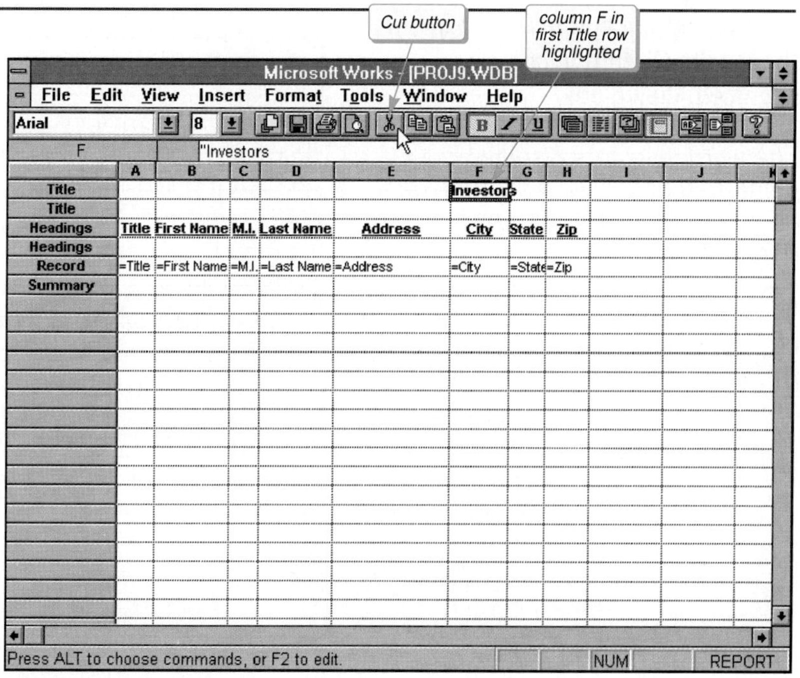

FIGURE 9-42

STEP 2 ►

Click the Cut button on the Toolbar. Highlight column A in the first Title row. Click the Paste button.

*Works cuts the word Investors in column F of the first Title row and places it on the Clipboard. When you click the **Paste button**, Works pastes the word Investors into column A of the first Title row (Figure 9-43).*

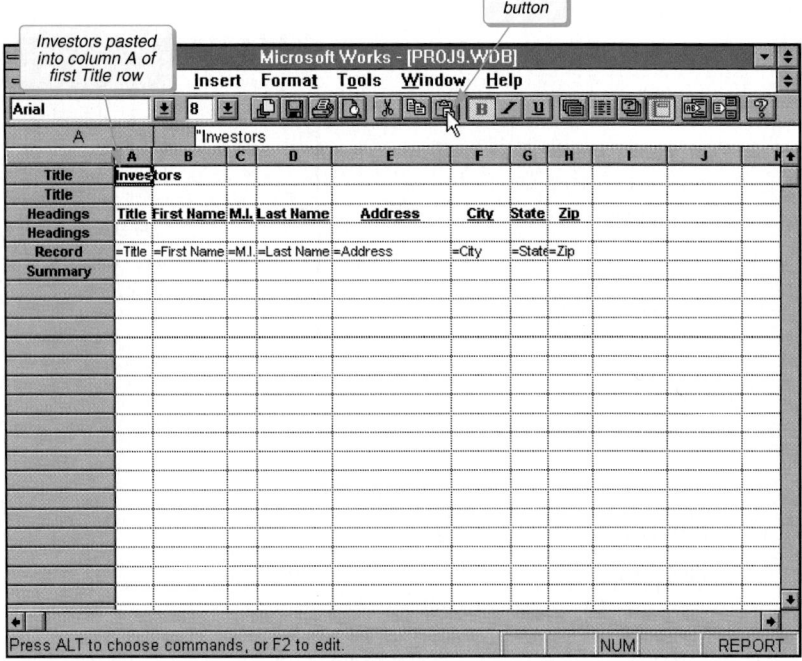

FIGURE 9-43

STEP 3 ►

Click the Font Size box arrow and select 14 from the drop-down list box. Click the Italic button on the Toolbar. Highlight columns A-H in the first Title row. Select the Format menu and choose the Alignment command. Select the Center across selection option button, and then choose the OK button in the Alignment dialog box.

The word Investors displays in 14 point Arial bold italic font, centered across columns A through H (Figure 9-44).

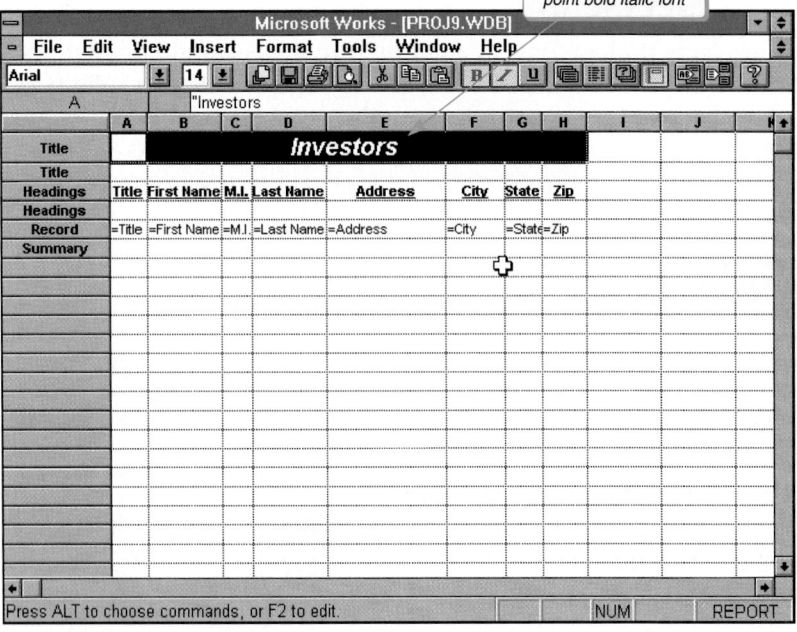

FIGURE 9-44

STEP 4 ▶

Highlight columns A-H in the first Headings row. Click the Under-line button on the Toolbar to remove the underline from the column headings. Increase the font size to 10. Select the Format menu and choose the Alignment command. Select the Wrap text check box, the Center option button in the Alignment area, and the Center option button in the Vertical area. Choose the OK button in the Alignment dialog box. Using the Column Width command from the Format menu, change the column widths as follows: Title (6); First Name (11); M.I. (5); Last Name (14); Address (19); City (9); State (9); and Zip (7).

The Headings row is formatted (Figure 9-45).

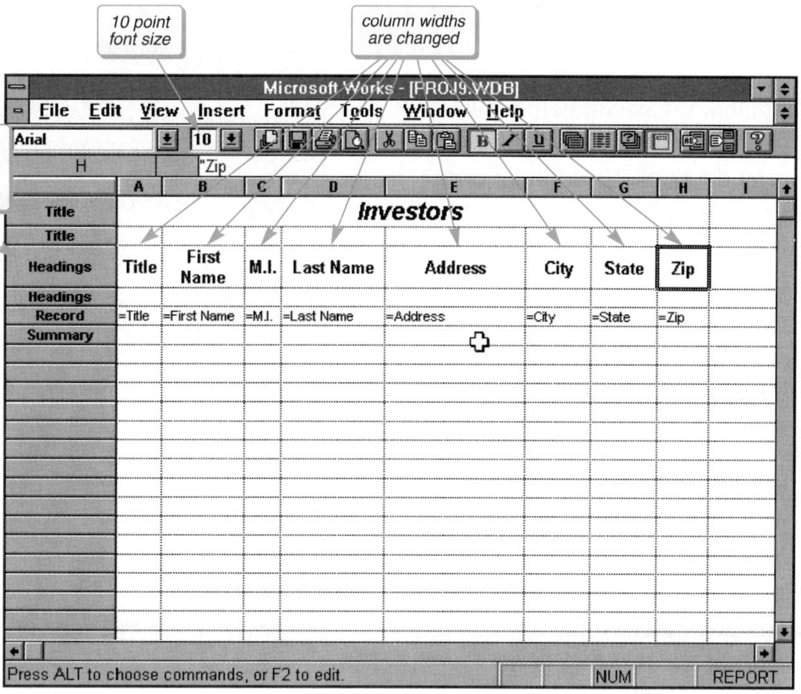

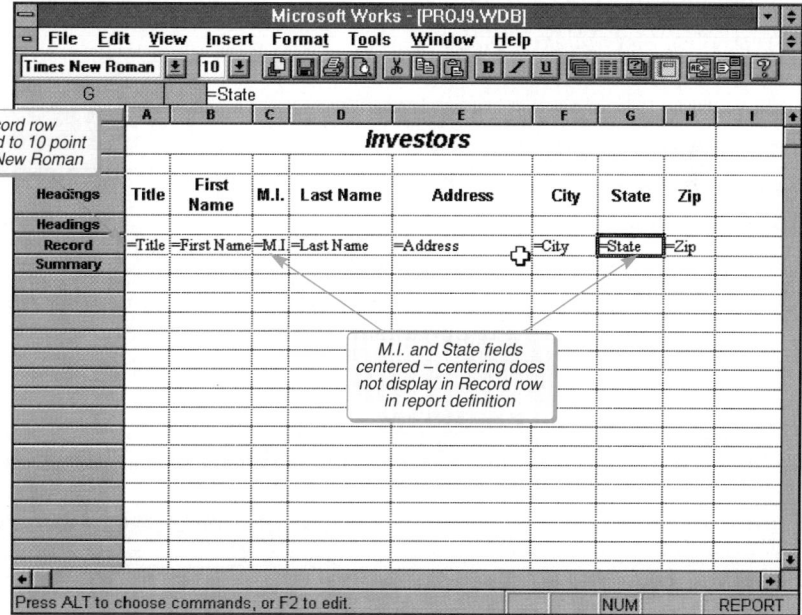

FIGURE 9-45

STEP 5 ▶

Highlight the Record row, column A through H. Change the font to 10 point Times New Roman. To center the M.I. field and the State field, highlight the field, choose the Alignment command from the Format menu, select the Center option button in the Alignment area of the Alignment dialog box, and choose the OK button in the Alignment dialog box. The centering will take place only on the printed report.

The record row is changed to 10 point Times New Roman (Figure 9-46).

FIGURE 9-46

STEP 6 ▶

Highlight the second Title row, columns A through H. This row is currently blank. Select the Format menu and choose the Patterns command. In the Patterns dialog box, select the solid pattern from the Pattern drop-down list box and select the Dark Magenta color from the Foreground drop-down list box. Choose the OK button in the Patterns dialog box. Highlight columns A through H in the second Headings row. Place a solid pattern, light gray color in this row using the Patterns command from the Format menu. Highlight columns A through H in the blank Summary row. Place a light gray solid pattern in the row by using the Patterns command from the Format menu.

The solid pattern, dark magenta line and the solid pattern, light gray lines are added to the report definition (Figure 9-47).

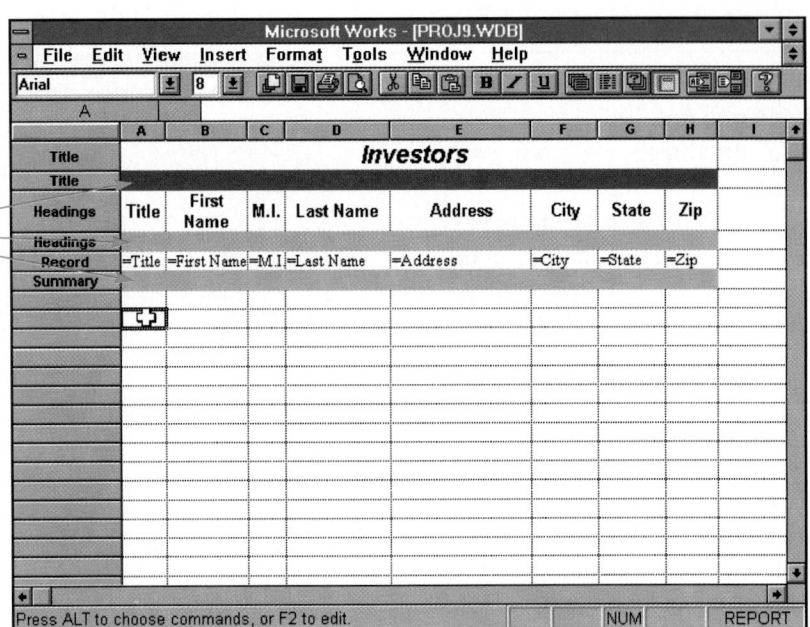

FIGURE 9-47

The report definition is now complete.

Previewing and Printing the Report

Before printing the report you should preview the report using the Print Preview command. To use the Print Preview to preview the report and print the report, perform the following steps.

TO USE PRINT PREVIEW AND PRINT THE REPORT ▼

STEP 1 ▶

Point to the Print Preview button on the Toolbar.

The Report form displays and the mouse pointer points to the Print Preview button (Figure 9-48).

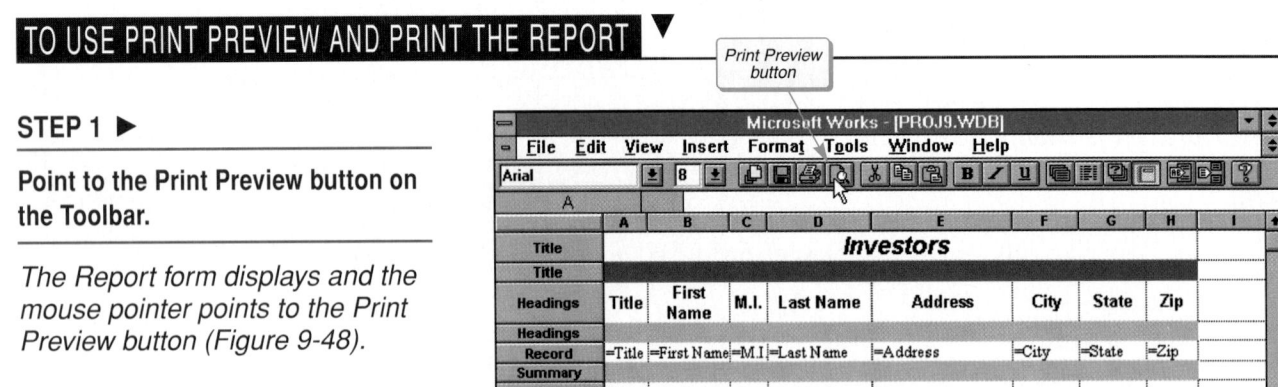

FIGURE 9-48

STEP 2 ▶

Click the Print Preview button. Click the Zoom In button in the print preview window two times. Click the right scroll arrow in the print preview window two times. Click the down scroll arrow one time.

The print preview window displays the report (Figure 9-49). When you click the Zoom In button, Works magnifies the report so it is easy to see. When using print preview, the screen will display in black and white unless you are using a color printer.

STEP 3 ▶

The report appears to be in the correct format, so click the Print button in the print preview window to print the report.

The report will print as shown in Figure 9-36.

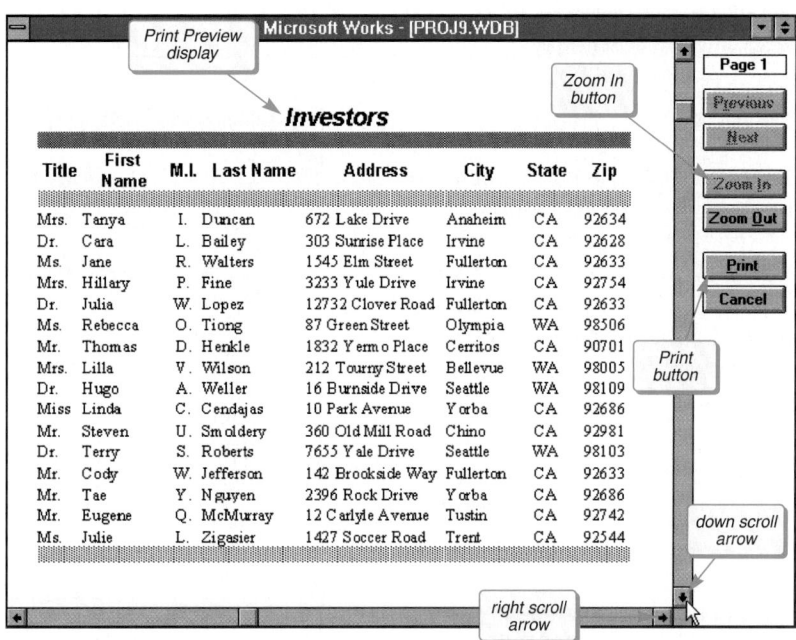

FIGURE 9-49

With the report defined and printed, the tasks for creating the Investor Report are complete.

Naming a Report

When you define a report, Works assigns the report a default name. The default name for the first report you define is Report1, the default name for the second report is Report2, and so on. A maximum eight reports can be defined for a single database. Quite often you will want to give your report a more meaningful name than the default name. To give the name Investor Report to the report you just created, complete the following steps.

TO NAME A REPORT ▼

STEP 1 ▶

Select the Tools menu and point to the Name Report command.

*Works displays the Tools menu (Figure 9-50). The mouse pointer points to the **Name Report command.***

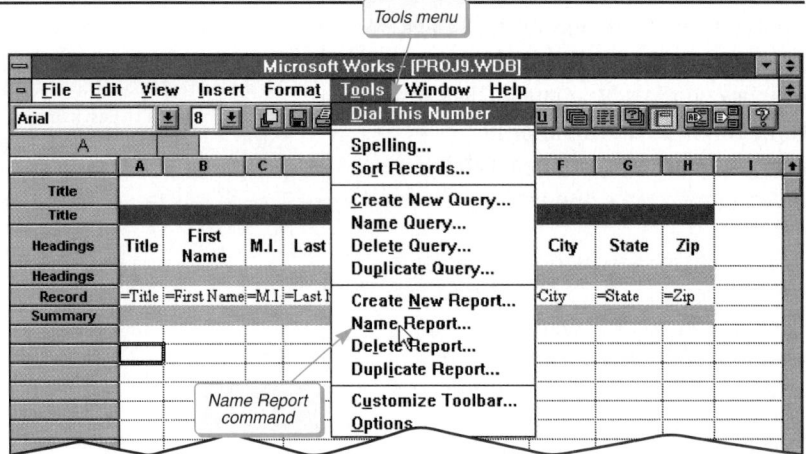

FIGURE 9-50

STEP 2 ▶

Choose the Name Report command from the Tools menu. Place the insertion point in the Name text box by pointing to the text box and clicking. Type Investor Report. Point to the Rename button.

*Works displays the Name Report dialog box (Figure 9-51). Report names are listed in the Reports list box. In Figure 9-51, the only report name is Report1, which is highlighted. In the Name text box, the new report name you typed, Investor Report, displays. The mouse pointer points to the **Rename button**.*

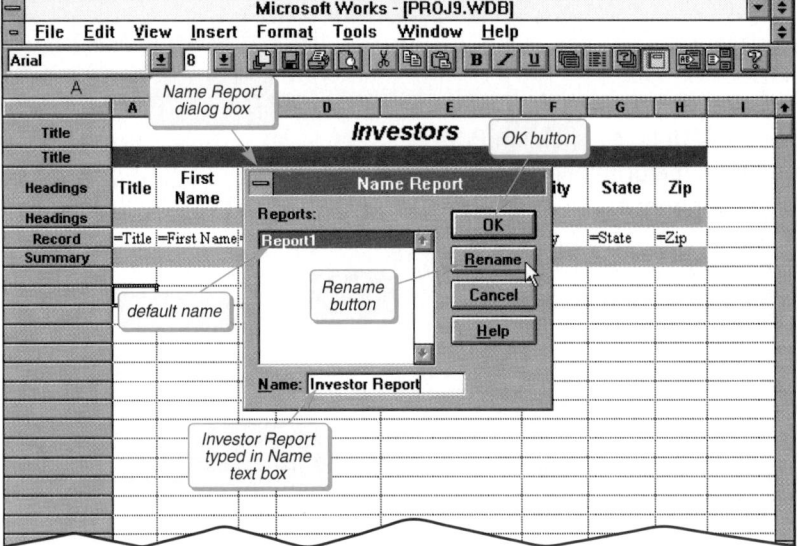

FIGURE 9-51

STEP 3 ▶

Choose the Rename button. Point to the OK button in the Name Report dialog box.

Works changes the highlighted report name in the Reports list box to the name in the Name text box (Figure 9-51a).

STEP 4 ▶

Choose the OK button in the Name Report dialog box.

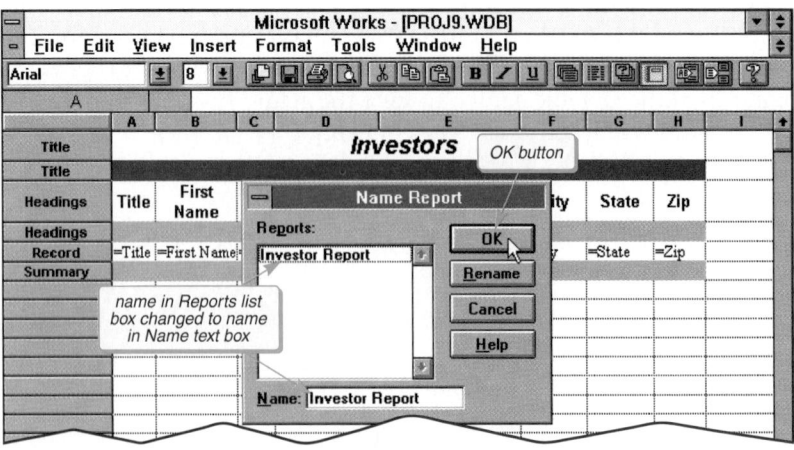

FIGURE 9-51a

Saving the Database with a Report

You should now save the database. When you save the database, the report definition will be saved with the database file. To save the database using the same name, perform the following step.

TO SAVE THE DATABASE

Step 1: Click the Save button on the Toolbar.

Viewing and Modifying a Report Definition

If you want to view, modify, or print the report at a later time, perform the following steps.

TO VIEW, MODIFY, OR PRINT A REPORT

Step 1: Display the database in List view or Form view.
Step 2: Select the View menu.
Step 3: Choose the **Report command**.
Step 4: When the Reports dialog box displays, in the Report list box highlight the name of the report you want to see.
Step 5: Choose the OK button in the Reports dialog box.
Step 6: Perform whatever tasks you require.
Step 7: Click the List view button on the Toolbar to return to List view or the Form view button on the Toolbar to return to Form view. You can always display a report definition through the use of the Report command from the View menu.

▶ SORTING RECORDS

W hen using the database tool, Works provides sorting capabilities similar to the spreadsheet tool. You can **sort** records alphabetically, numerically, or by date. The following steps explain how sort the investor club records so the records display in alphabetical order by the last name of the investors.

TO SORT RECORDS ▼

STEP 1 ▶

Display all records in List view. Select the Tools menu and point to the Sort Records command.

*The Tools menu displays and the mouse pointer points to the **Sort Records command** (Figure 9-52).*

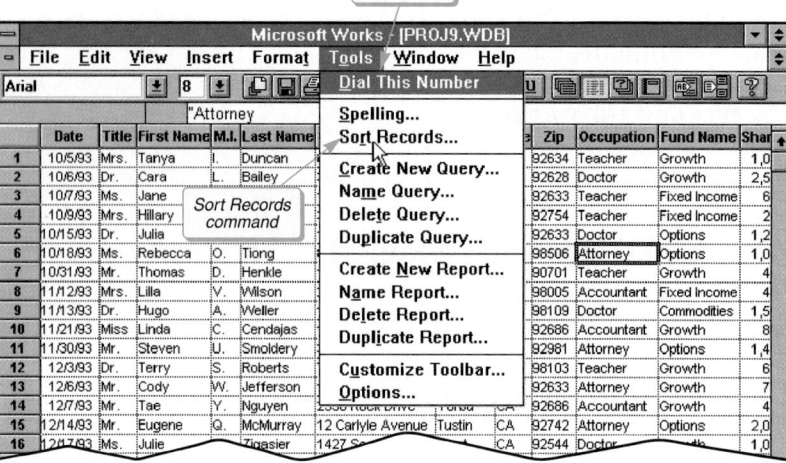

FIGURE 9-52

STEP 2 ▶

Choose the Sort Records command from the Tools menu. When the Sort Records dialog box displays, click the 1st Field drop-down list box arrow to display a list of field names. Select Last Name by scrolling down and clicking Last Name in the drop-down list box. If necessary, select the Ascend option button in the 1st Field area. Point to the OK button.

The Sort Records dialog box displays (Figure 9-53). The Last Name field is selected and the Ascend option button is selected. The mouse pointer points to the OK button.

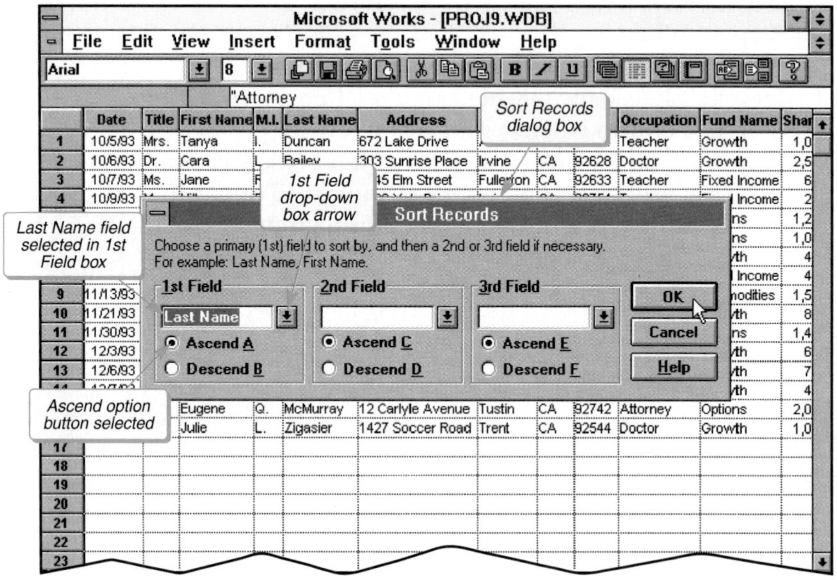

FIGURE 9-53

STEP 3 ▶

Choose the OK button in the Sort Records dialog box. When the List View of the database displays, point to the Report View button on the Toolbar.

The database records displayed in List view are sorted in alphabetical order, which is ascending sequence by last name (Figure 9-54). The mouse pointer points to the Report view button.

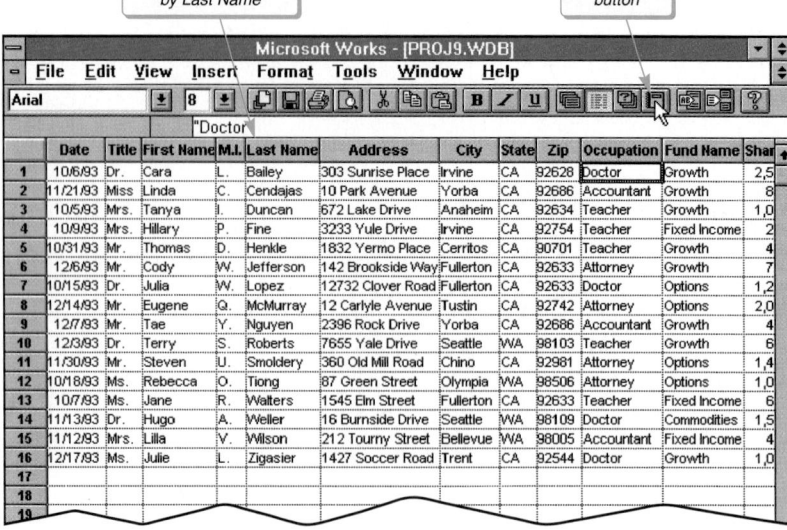

FIGURE 9-54

STEP 4 ▶

Click the Report View button. When the report definition screen displays, point to the Print button on the Toolbar.

The report view of the only named report (Investor Report) displays (Figure 9-55). The mouse pointer points to the Print button.

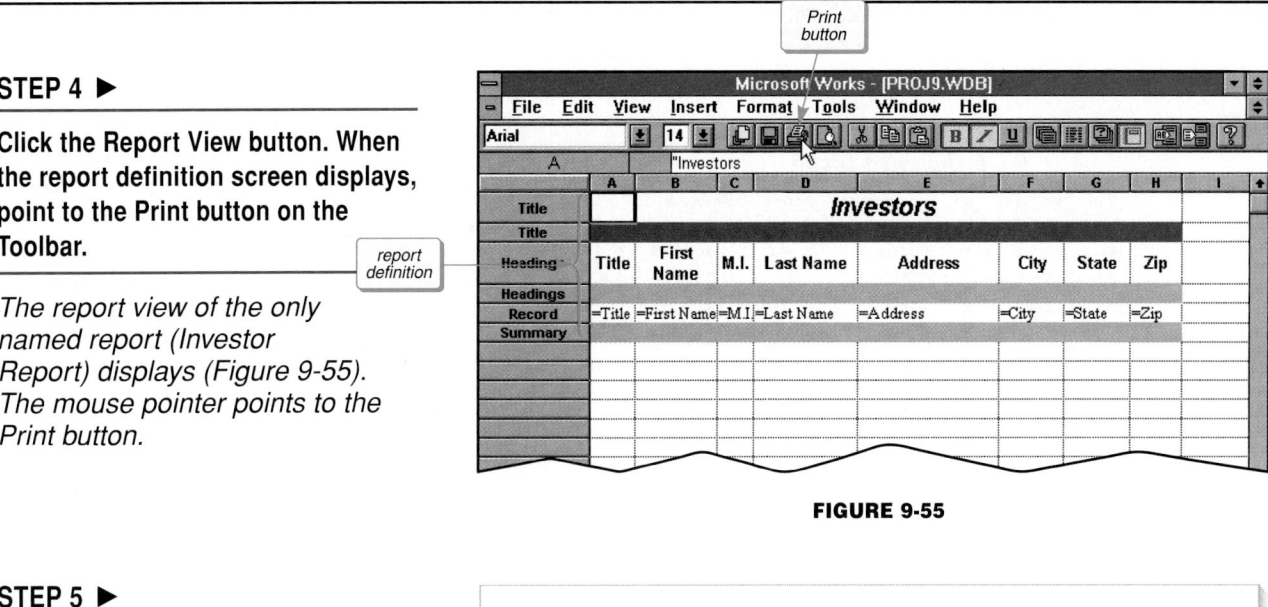

FIGURE 9-55

STEP 5 ▶

Click the Print button on the Toolbar.

Works prints the report in alphabetical order by last name (Figure 9-56).

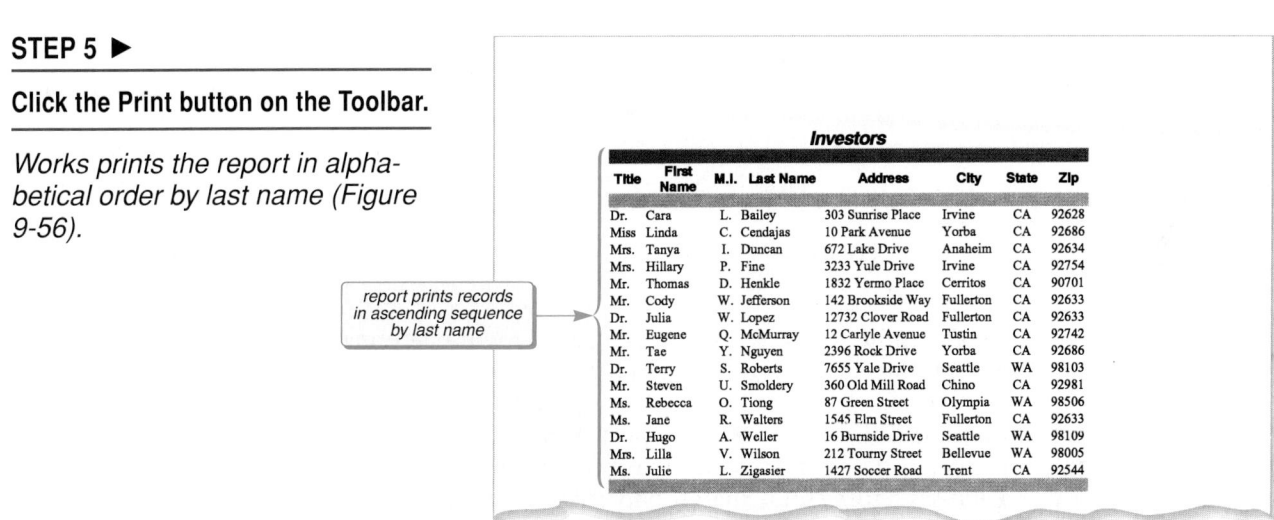

FIGURE 9-56

If you do not want the records in alphabetical order any longer, sort the records by date to arrange them in their original sequence. You can sort the database in any sequence you want.

In some applications, the original records might be in a sequence that cannot be recreated by sorting. If so, either save the sorted database using a different file name or close the sorted database without saving it. In this way, the database in the original sequence remains on disk.

Reports with Summary Totals

Works provides the ability to define reports that contain **summary totals** calculated from data in the database. Two common summary totals are counting the number of records in a database and summing the values in fields within the database.

Investment Totals

Title	First Name	M.I.	Last Name	Shares	Investment
Dr.	Cara	L.	Bailey	2,500	$27,500.00
Miss	Linda	C.	Cendajas	800	$8,800.00
Mrs.	Tanya	I.	Duncan	1,000	$11,000.00
Mrs.	Hillary	P.	Fine	200	$3,600.00
Mr.	Thomas	D.	Henkle	400	$4,400.00
Mr.	Cody	W.	Jefferson	700	$7,700.00
Dr.	Julia	W.	Lopez	1,200	$27,600.00
Mr.	Eugene	Q.	McMurray	2,000	$76,000.00
Mr.	Tae	Y.	Nguyen	400	$4,400.00
Dr.	Terry	S.	Roberts	600	$6,600.00
Mr.	Steven	U.	Smoldery	1,400	$32,200.00
Ms.	Rebecca	O.	Tiong	1,000	$23,000.00
Ms.	Jane	R.	Walters	600	$10,800.00
Dr.	Hugo	A.	Weller	1,500	$22,500.00
Mrs.	Lilla	V.	Wilson	400	$7,200.00
Ms.	Julie	L.	Zigasier	1,000	$23,000.00

Total Investors	16
Total Shares	15,700
Total Investment	$296,300.00

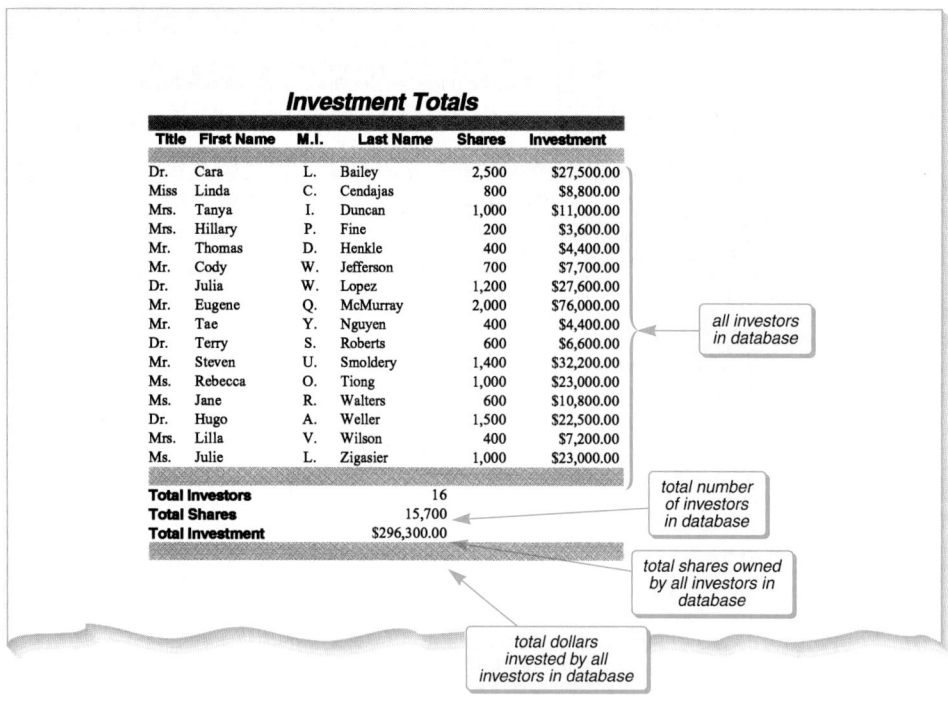

FIGURE 9-57

The next task in Project 9 is to create a report listing all investors in the investment club database, the total number of investors in the investment club, the total shares owned by all investors, and the total dollars invested. The report to be created is shown in Figure 9-57.

The report title is Investment Totals. This title should print at the top of every page of the report. As mentioned earlier, however, a value in the Title row of the report definition prints only on the first page of the report and never again. Therefore, the title Investment Totals on the report shown in Figure 9-57 will be defined in a Headings row so it will print on each page of the report. The fields on the report include the Title, First Name, M.I., Last Name, Shares, and Investment fields. The field names display in the Headings lines of the report. Fields from each record in the database are printed as Record lines on the report. At the bottom of the report are three totals: Total Investors, Total Shares, and Total Investment. These totals, each of which prints on a line by itself, are Summary lines.

To create the report definition for the report shown in Figure 9-57, complete the following steps.

TO DEFINE A REPORT WITH SUMMARY TOTALS ▼

STEP 1 ►

Click the List View button on the Toolbar to display the database in List view. Select the Tools menu and point to the Create New Report command.

Works displays the Tools menu and the mouse pointer points to the Create New Report command (Figure 9-58).

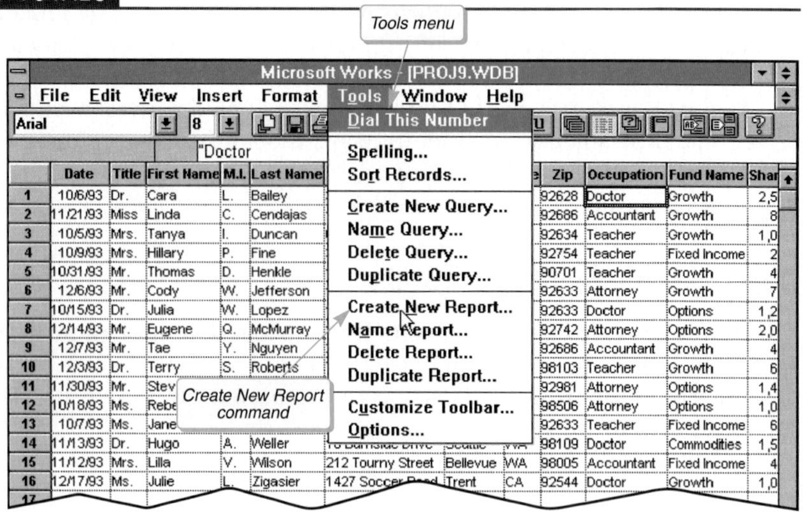

FIGURE 9-58

STEP 2 ▶

Choose the Create New Report command from the Tools menu. When the New Report dialog box displays, highlight Title in the Field list box, and choose the Add button.

Works displays the New Report dialog box (Figure 9-59). No report title is entered in the Report Title text box because the report title will be part of the Headings rows in the report definition. When you highlight the Title field name and choose the Add button, Works places the Title field name in the Fields in Report list box and high-lights the First Name field name in the Fields list box on the left.

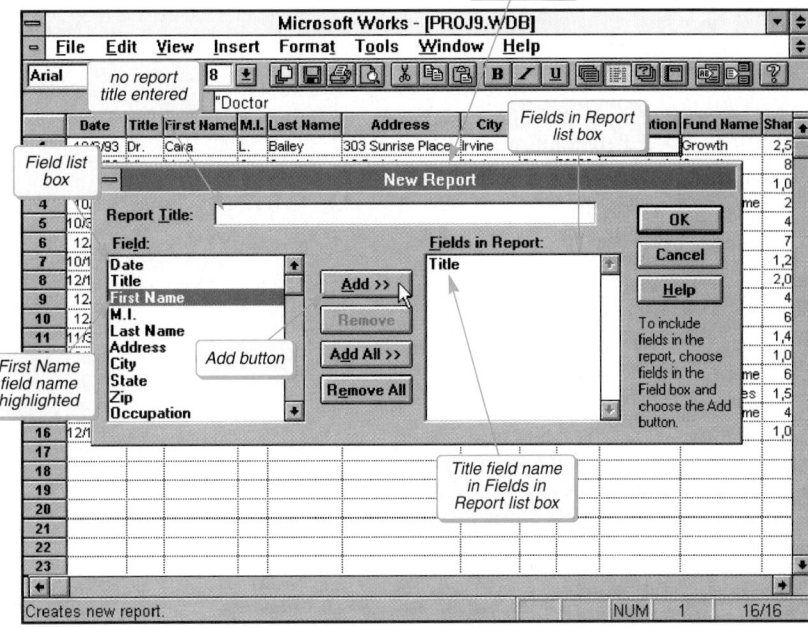

FIGURE 9-59

STEP 3 ▶

Choose the Add button for the First Name field. The highlight drops down to the M.I. field name. Choose the Add button for the M.I. field. The highlight drops down to the Last Name field. Choose the Add button for the Last Name field. Scroll down, highlight the Shares field name, and choose the Add button. Scroll down, highlight the Investment field name, and choose the Add button. Point to the OK button.

Each of the highlighted and added field names displays in the Fields in Report list box (Figure 9-60). When the last field name in the Field list box is added to the Fields in Report list box, the highlight moves to the first field name in the Field list box (Date). The mouse pointer points to the OK button.

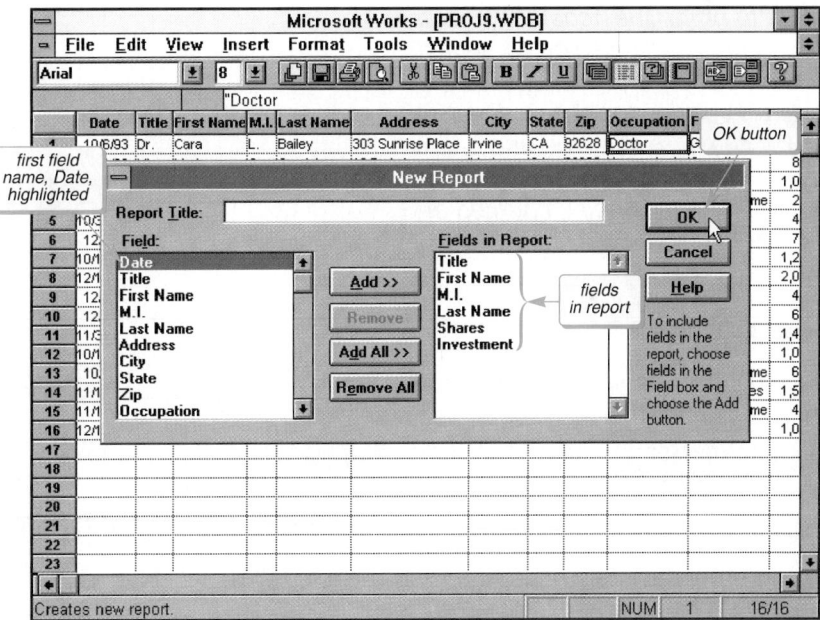

FIGURE 9-60

STEP 5 ▶

Choose the OK button in the New Report dialog box. When the Report Statistics dialog box displays, select the Count check box .

Works displays the Report Statistics dialog box (Figure 9-61). The Fields in Report list box on the left contains the field names of the fields in the report. The Title field name is highlighted. The Statistics area contains the types of statistics Works can generate for printing at the end of the report. By selecting the Count check box, you indicate the number of records containing the Title field should be counted. Because the database contains one record per investor, a count of the number of records gives the number of investors, which is the value to print. The Together in rows option button is selected by default in the Position Statistics area. This option specifies that totals should be printed in rows at the end of the report instead of under each column of the fields being counted or summed.

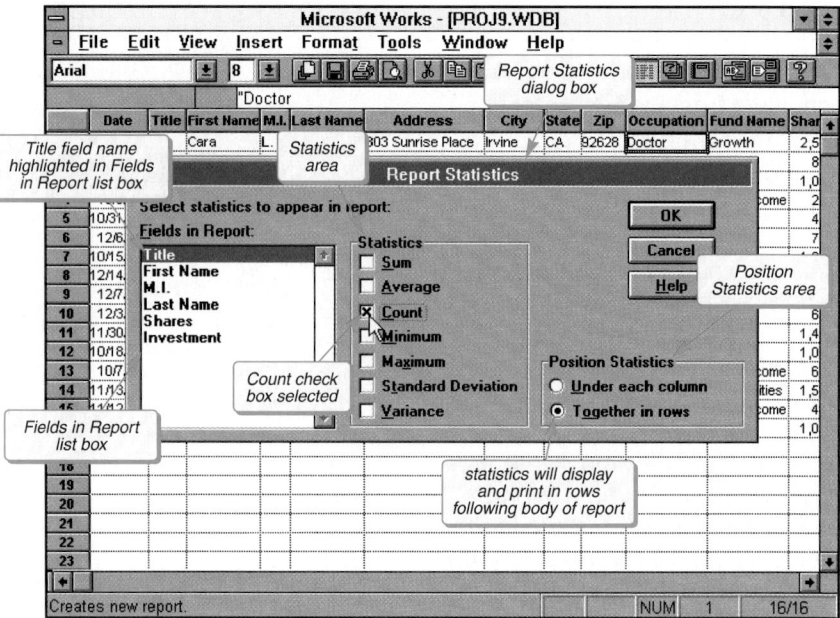

FIGURE 9-61

STEP 6 ▶

Highlight the Shares field name by clicking it in the Fields in Report list box, and then select the Sum check box in the Statistics area of the Report Statistics dialog box.

The Shares field name is highlighted and the Sum check box contains an X (Figure 9-62). Selecting the Sum check box instructs Works to sum the value in the Shares field in each of the database records. At the end of the report, this sum will print.

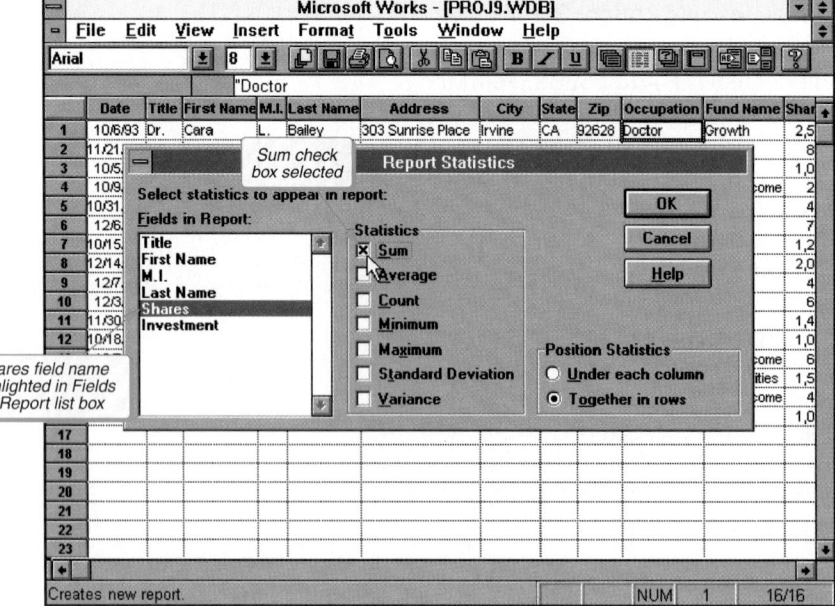

FIGURE 9-62

STEP 7 ▶

Highlight the Investment field name in the Fields in Report list box, and then select the Sum check box in the Statistics area of the Report Statistics dialog box.

The Investment field name is highlighted and the Sum check box contains an X (Figure 9-63). Selecting the Sum check box instructs Works to sum the value in the Investment field in each of the database records. At the end of the report, this sum will print.

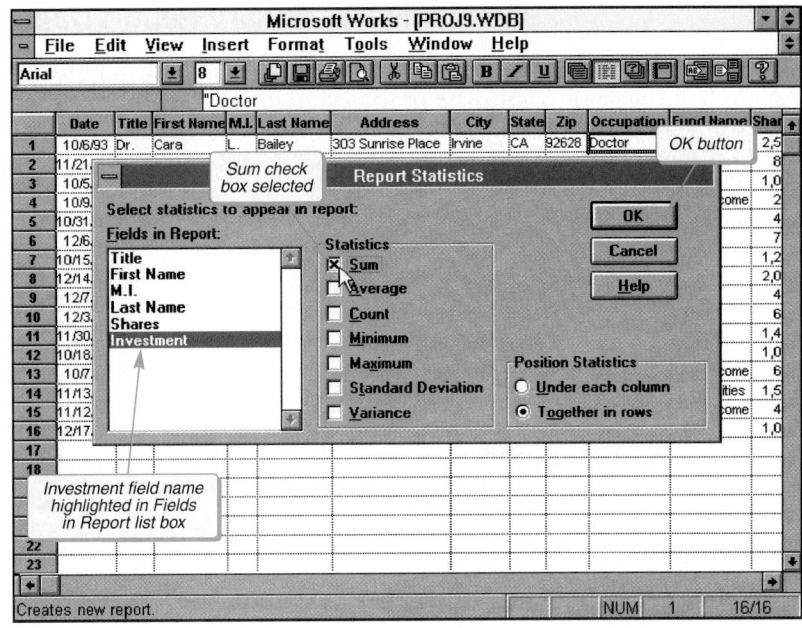

FIGURE 9-63

STEP 8 ▶

Choose the OK button in the Report Statistics dialog box. When the Microsoft Works dialog box displays that tells you the report definition has been created, choose the OK button.

*Works displays the report definition (Figure 9-64). Nothing displays in the Title row. The Headings row contains the field names of each field in the report in a bold, underlined format. The Record row contains each of the fields in the report. Four **Summary rows** are defined. The first Summary row is blank so a blank line will print between the body of the report and the total lines. The next three Summary rows contain summary titles in column A of each row. In column D, formulas display the count of the Title field, the sum of the Shares field, and the sum of the Investment field.*

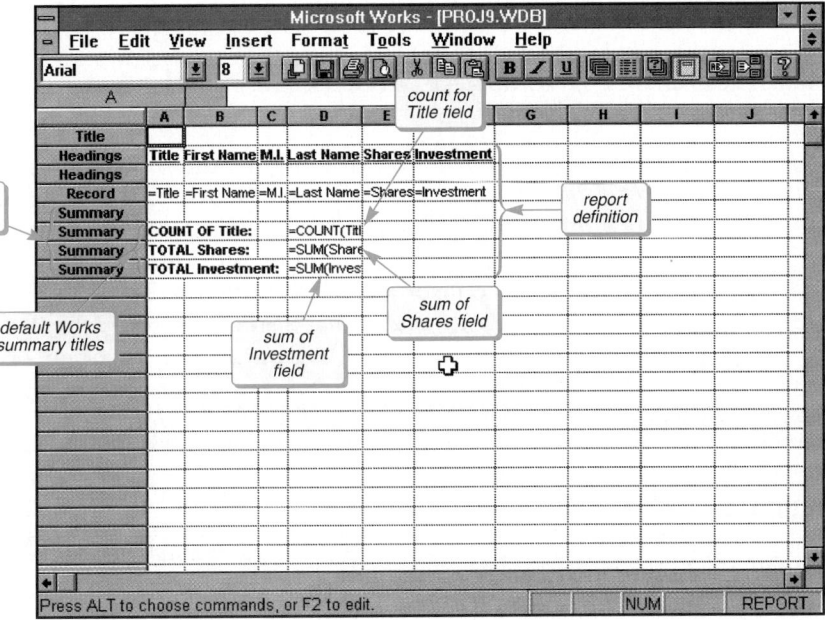

FIGURE 9-64

Modifying a Summary Report Definition

As with the previous report definitions, the definition of the summary report must be modified in order for it to produce the report shown in Figure 9-57 on page W9.38. To display the report with the current report definition in order to determine the modifications, complete the following steps (see Figure 9-64a).

FIGURE 9-64a

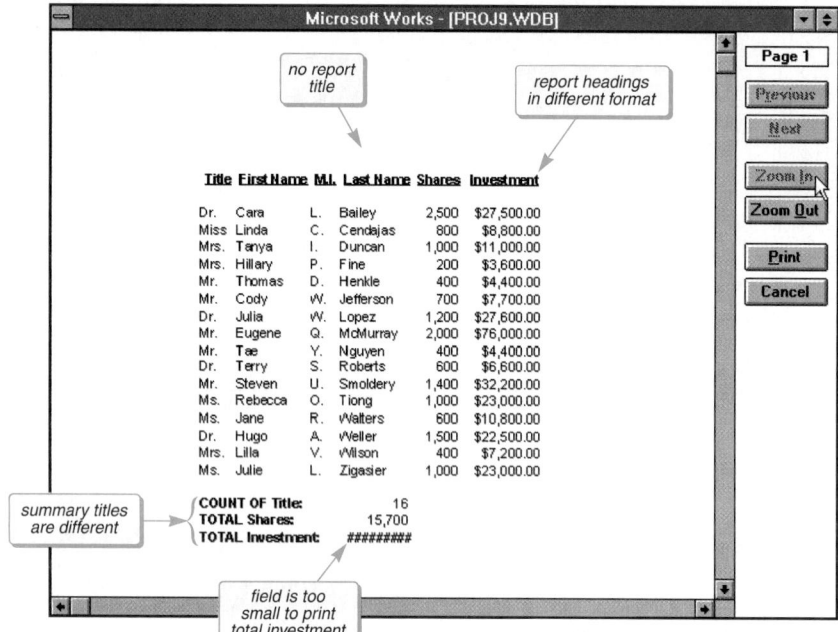

TO DISPLAY PRINT PREVIEW

Step 1: Click the Print Preview button on the Toolbar.

Step 2: Click the Zoom In button in the print preview window two times.

Step 3: Review the screen to determine the modifications that must be made (see Figure 9-64a). Note that no report title displays, the headings are in a different format, the summary titles are not the same, and the field is too small to display the total investment.

Step 4: Click the Cancel button in the print preview window.

To produce the report, the report definition must be modified using many of the techniques explained when creating the previous listing report. The two major tasks to accomplish are: (1) insert a report title; (2) format the summary report, including changing titles and adding color.

To insert the report title Investment Report in a heading line, you must first insert two additional headings rows in the report definition. To insert two blank rows in the report definition and add a report title, complete the following steps.

TO INSERT TWO BLANK HEADINGS ROWS AND ADD A TITLE ▼

STEP 1 ▶

Highlight the two Headings rows by pointing to the row title column in the first Headings row and dragging down through the second Headings row. Select the Insert menu and point to the Row/Column command.

When you drag the Headings rows, the two Headings rows are highlighted (Figure 9-65). Works displays the Insert menu and the mouse pointer points to the **Row/Column command.**

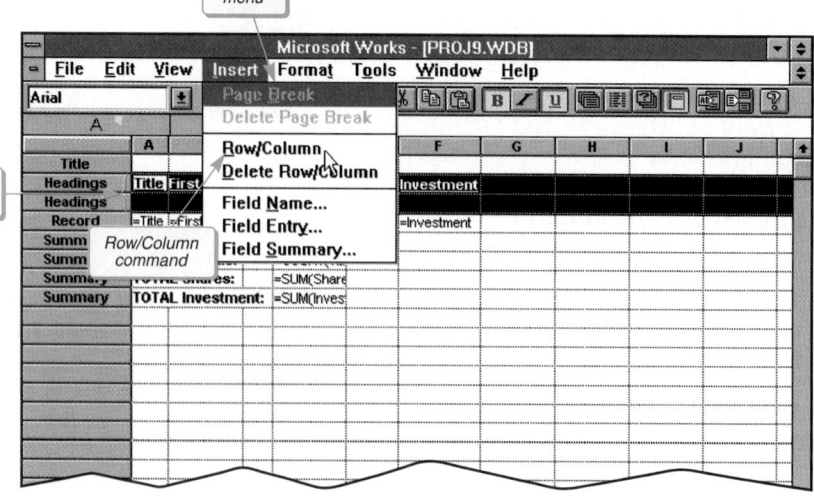

FIGURE 9-65

STEP 2 ▶

Choose the Row/Column command. When the Insert Row dialog box displays, point to the OK button.

Works displays the Insert Row dialog box (Figure 9-66). The word Headings is highlighted in the Type list box because you dragged and highlighted the Headings rows in Step 1. The Type list box indicates the type of row Works will insert. The mouse pointer points to the OK button.

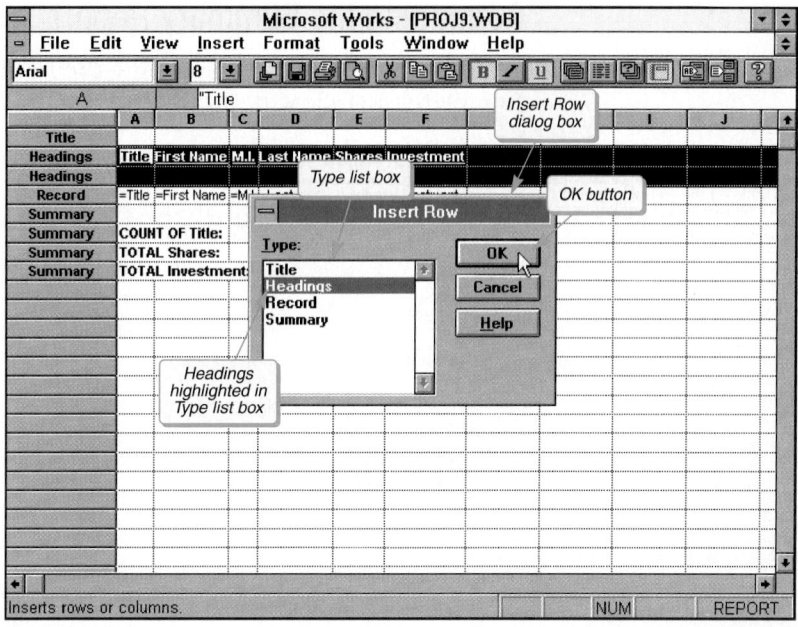

FIGURE 9-66

STEP 3 ▶

Choose the OK button in the Insert Row dialog box. When the two blank Headings rows display, highlight column A in the first Headings row, type `Investment Totals`, **and then press the ENTER key or click the Enter box.**

Works inserts two Headings rows above the two Headings rows you highlighted in Step 1 (Figure 9-67). Whenever you insert rows, the number of rows inserted always equals the number of rows highlighted, and the inserted rows always appear above the highlighted rows. The title Investment Totals is now included in the report definition in a heading line.

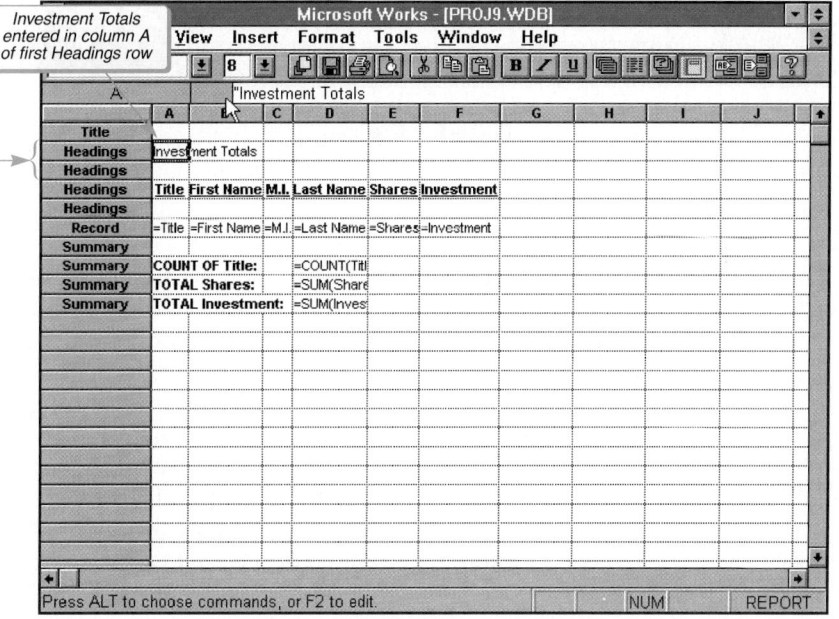

FIGURE 9-67

After entering the report title you must format the report.

Formatting the Summary Report

The techniques for formatting the report use techniques previously explained. Complete the following steps to format the report (see Figure 9-67a).

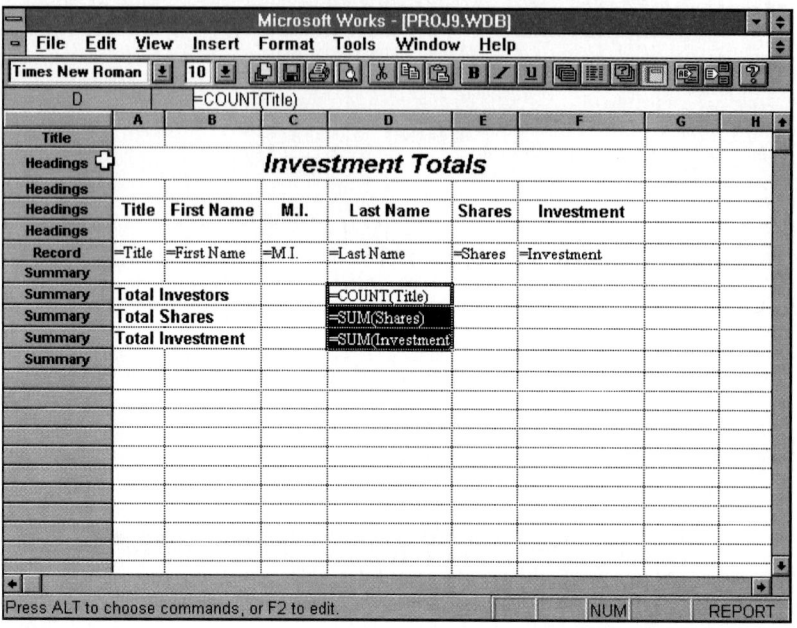

FIGURE 9-67a

TO FORMAT THE SUMMARY REPORT

Step 1: Highlight the title Investment Totals in column A of the first Headings row. Change the font to 16 point bold italic.

Step 2: Highlight columns A through F in the first Headings row. Select the Format menu. Choose the Alignment command. Select the Center across selection option button in the Alignment area of the Alignment dialog box. Choose the OK button in the Alignment dialog box.

Step 3: Highlight the column titles in the third Headings row and change them to 10 point. Click the Underline button on the Toolbar to remove the underline from the column titles.

Step 4: Highlight columns A through F beginning with the fourth Headings row through the row below the last summary row. Change the highlighted rows to 10 point size. After changing the point size, the word Summary will display on the left side of the last highlighted row.

Step 5: Highlight the columns A through F of the Record row. Change the font to Times New Roman.

Step 6: Using the Column Width command from the Format menu, change the column widths as follows: Title (7); First Name (13); M.I. (9); Last Name (17); Shares (9); Investment (17).

Step 7: Center the M.I. field on the report by selecting the M.I. field in the Record row, choosing the Alignment command from the Format menu, selecting the Center option button in the Alignment area, and choosing the OK button in the Alignment dialog box.

Step 8: Change the words COUNT OF Title: in the second Summary Row to the words Total Investors by highlighting the words COUNT OF Title: in column A of the second Summary row, typing Total Investors, and pressing the DOWN ARROW key.

Step 9: Type Total Shares and press the DOWN ARROW key.

Step 10: Type Total Investment and press the ENTER key or click the Enter box.

Step 11: Highlight column D of the three Summary rows that contain the formulas. Change the font to Times New Roman.

The Report is now formatted (Figure 9-67a). The next step is to add color to the report definition. To add color, perform the steps on the next page (see Figure 9-68).

TO ADD COLOR TO A REPORT DEFINITION

Step 1: Highlight columns A through F in the second Headings row, which is blank. Select the Format menu and choose the Patterns command. Select the solid pattern from the Pattern drop-down list box, and select Dark Cyan from the Foreground drop-down list box. Choose the OK button in the Patterns dialog box.

Step 2: Highlight columns A through F in the fourth Headings row, which is now blank. Select the Format menu and choose the Patterns command. Select the solid pattern from the Pattern drop-down list box and select the light gray color from the Foreground drop-down list box. Choose the OK button in the Patterns dialog box.

Step 3: Highlight columns A through F in the first Summary row. Select the Format menu and choose the Patterns command. Select the solid pattern from the Pattern drop-down list box and select the light gray color from the Foreground drop-down list box. Choose the OK button in the Patterns dialog box.

Step 4: Highlight columns A through F in the last Summary row. Select the Format menu and choose the Patterns command. Select the solid pattern from the Pattern drop-down list box and select the light gray color from the Foreground drop-down list box. Choose the OK button in the Patterns dialog box.

Formatting the report is now complete. Figure 9-68 illustrates the new report definition. Notice in the previous steps that the report was modified from the top to the bottom of the report; that is, the Headings rows were inserted and completed first, then the Summary rows were formatted and completed. While no set rules apply to the sequence in which a report definition should be modified, working from the top of the report definition to the bottom usually works well.

Again it should be pointed out that by placing the title in a Headings row, you ensure that the title will print at the top of each page of the report. Recall that if you place the title in the Title row of the report definition, it will print on the first page of the report only.

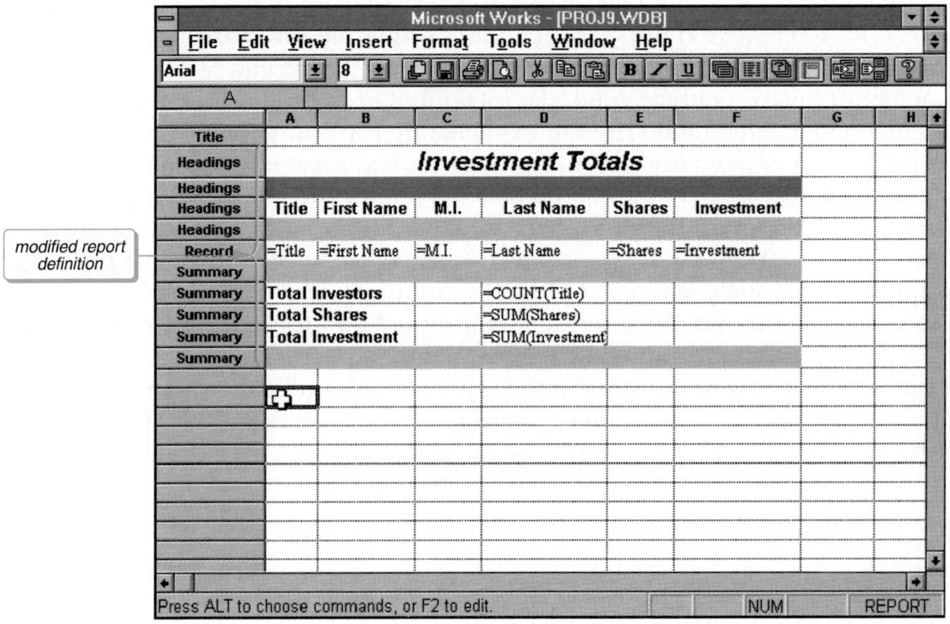

FIGURE 9-68

Naming and Printing the Modified Summary Report

To rename the report to the meaningful name Total Report, complete the following steps:

TO RENAME THE REPORT

Step 1: Select the Tools menu.
Step 2: Choose the Name Report command.
Step 3: Highlight Report1 in the Reports list box in the Name Report dialog box.
Step 4: Place the insertion point in the Name text box and type `Total Report`.
Step 5: Choose the Rename button in the Name Report dialog box.
Step 6: Choose the OK button in the Name Report dialog box.

After naming the report, the next step is to print the report. To print the report after displaying the print preview window, complete the following steps.

TO PRINT REPORT

Step 1: Click the Print Preview button on the Toolbar.
Step 2: Click the Zoom In button two times.
Step 3: Click the down scroll arrow two times.
Step 4: Click the right scroll arrow one time. Review the report to ensure it will print correctly.
Step 5: Click the Print button in the print preview window.

The report will print as shown in Figure 9-57 on page W9.38.

Creating a database report with summary totals is a common requirement. Be sure you thoroughly understand the procedure for creating and printing a database report with summary totals.

Duplicating a Report

All the records in the database have been used in the two reports defined thus far in this project. You can, however, print only selected records by using the query capability of Works to identify the records you want to print. The next task in Project 9 is to create a report for each fund, listing the investors in the fund, the shares they own, and the amount they have invested. At the end of the report, list the number of investors in the fund, the total number of fund shares, and the total dollars invested in each fund. The reports generated are shown in Figure 9-69.

A report is generated for each fund (Growth, Fixed Income, Options, and Commodities). Report totals for each report print after the individual report lines. Notice that the format of the reports in Figure 9-69 is virtually the same as the summary report in Figure 9-57 on page W9.38 except that the fund name prints in the report heading and the report heading is different.

To create the reports in Figure 9-69, you should duplicate the summary report called Total Report and name the new report Fund Report. You should then insert the heading line for the fund name in the report definition below the report title and modify the report. You can then perform one or more queries to display the records to print. To duplicate a report, perform the steps on page W9.48.

Global Investments
Growth

Title	First Name	M.I.	Last Name	Shares	Investment
Dr.	Cara	L.	Bailey	2,500	$27,500.00
Miss	Linda	C.	Cendajas	800	$8,800.00
Mrs.	Tanya	I.	Duncan	1,000	$11,000.00
Mr.	Thomas	D.	Henkle	400	$4,400.00
Mr.	Cody	W.	Jefferson	700	$7,700.00
Mr.	Tae	Y.	Nguyen	400	$4,400.00
Dr.	Terry	S.	Roberts	600	$6,600.00
Ms.	Julie	L.	Zigasier	1,000	$23,000.00

Total Investors	8
Total Shares	7,400
Total Investment	$93,400.00

Global Investments
Fixed Income

Title	First Name	M.I.	Last Name	Shares	Investment
Mrs.	Hillary	P.	Fine	200	$3,600.00
Ms.	Jane	R.	Walters	600	$10,800.00
Mrs.	Lilla	V.	Wilson	400	$7,200.00

Total Investors	3
Total Shares	1,200
Total Investment	$21,600.00

Global Investments
Options

Title	First Name	M.I.	Last Name	Shares	Investment
Dr.	Julia	W.	Lopez	1,200	$27,600.00
Mr.	Eugene	Q.	McMurray	2,000	$76,000.00
Mr.	Steven	U.	Smoldery	1,400	$32,200.00
Ms.	Rebecca	O.	Tiong	1,000	$23,000.00

Total Investors	4
Total Shares	5,600
Total Investment	$158,800.00

Global Investments
Commodities

Title	First Name	M.I.	Last Name	Shares	Investment
Dr.	Hugo	A.	Weller	1,500	$22,500.00

Total Investors	1
Total Shares	1,500
Total Investment	$22,500.00

FIGURE 9-69

TO DUPLICATE A REPORT ▼

STEP 1 ▶

Click the List View button on the
Toolbar. Select the Tools menu and
point to the Duplicate Report
command.

*Works displays the Tools menu
and the mouse pointer points to
the **Duplicate Report command**
(Figure 9-70).*

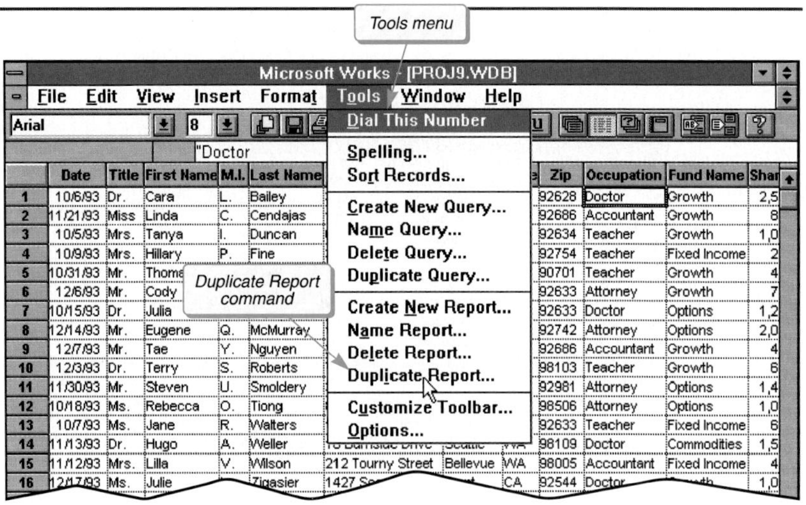

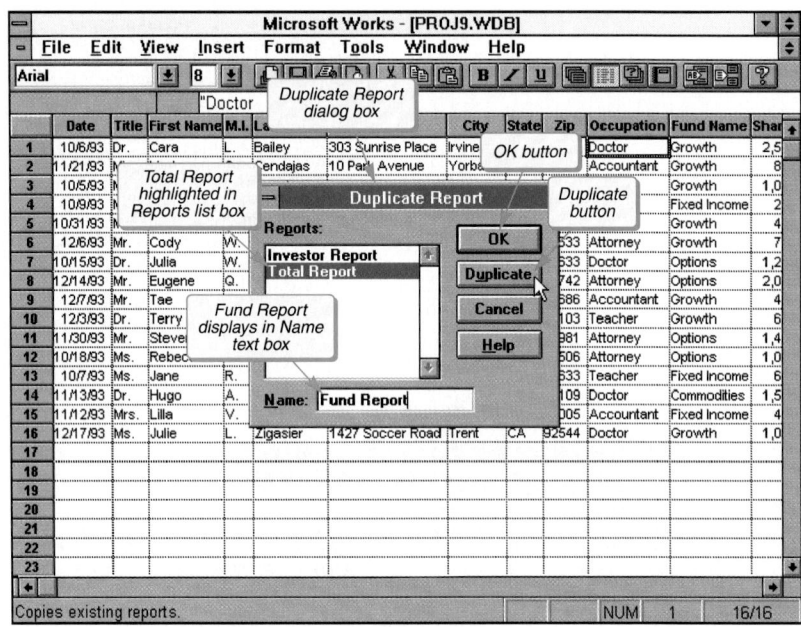

FIGURE 9-70

STEP 2 ▶

Choose the Duplicate Report
command from the Tools menu.
When the Duplicate Report dialog
box displays, ensure that the words
Total Report are highlighted in the
Reports list box. Select the Name
text box by clicking the box and type
Fund Report. **Point to the
Duplicate button.**

*Works displays the Duplicate
Report dialog box (Figure 9-71).
Fund Report, which is typed in the
Name text box, will be the name of
the new duplicate report definition.
The report definition will be a
duplicate of the report definition
referenced by the name Total
Report that is highlighted in the
Reports list box. The mouse
pointer points to the Duplicate
button.*

FIGURE 9-71

STEP 3 ▶

Choose the Duplicate button and
then the OK button in the Duplicate
Report dialog box.

A duplicate of the report definition referenced by the name Total Report is now available for use with the name Fund Report.

Displaying A Report Definition

To display the duplicate report definition given the name Fund Report and to modify that report definition, perform the following steps.

TO DISPLAY AND MODIFY THE REPORT DEFINITION ▼

STEP 1 ▶

Select the View menu and point to the Report command.

The View menu displays and the mouse pointer points to the Report command (Figure 9-72).

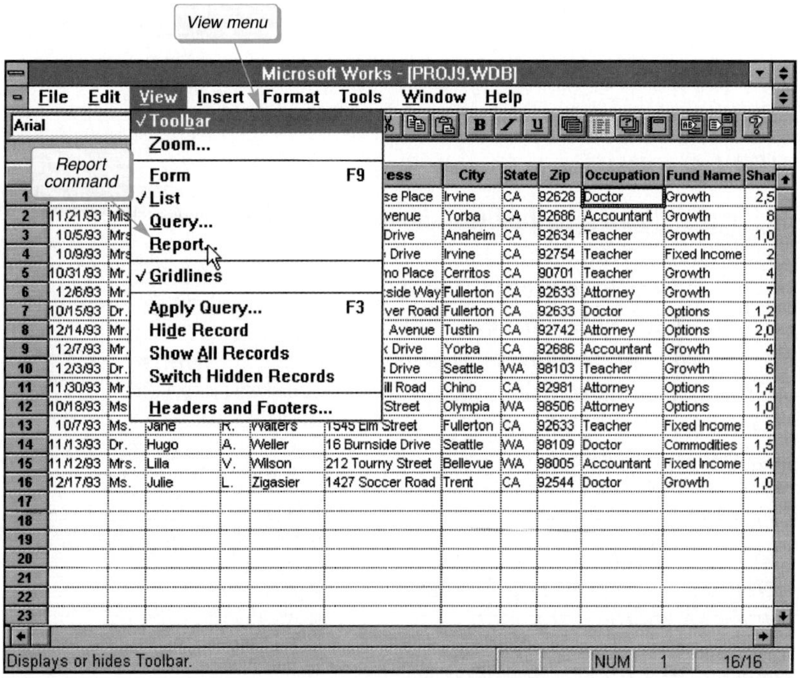

FIGURE 9-72

STEP 2 ▶

Choose the Report command from the View menu. When the Reports dialog box displays, if necessary highlight Fund Report in the Report list box. Point to the OK button.

Works displays the Reports dialog box (Figure 9-73). The report name Fund Report is highlighted. The mouse pointer points to the OK button.

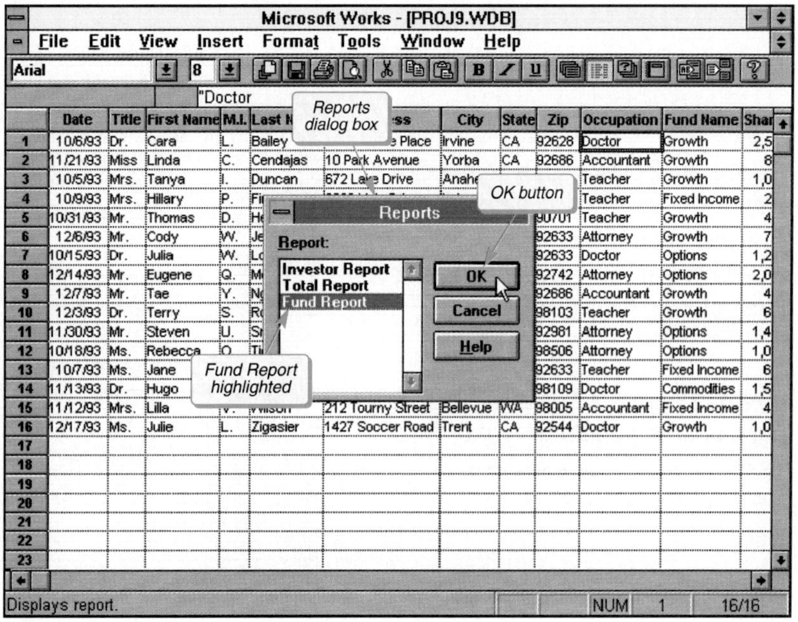

FIGURE 9-73

STEP 3 ▶

Choose the OK button in the Reports dialog box.

The duplicate report form named Fund Report displays (Figure 9-74).

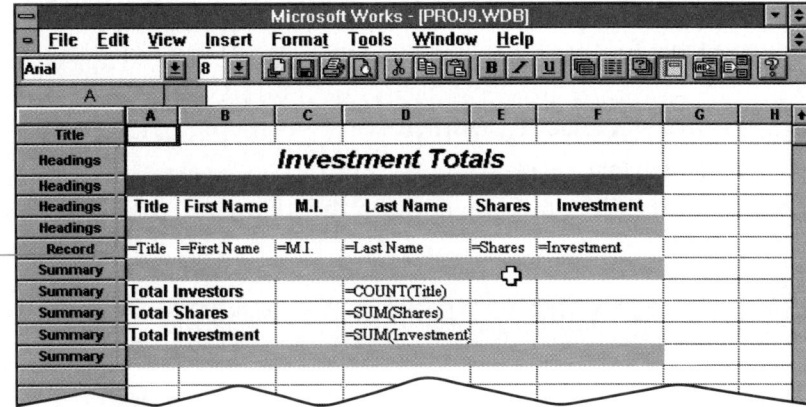

FIGURE 9-74

STEP 4 ▶

Highlight column A of the first Headings row, type `Global Investments`, and press the ENTER key or click the Enter box. Highlight the second Headings row by clicking the row title column. Select the Insert menu and point to the Row/Column command.

The second Headings row is high-lighted, the Insert menu displays, and the mouse pointer points to the Row/Column command (Figure 9-75). The new report heading, Global Investments, dis-plays in the first Headings row.

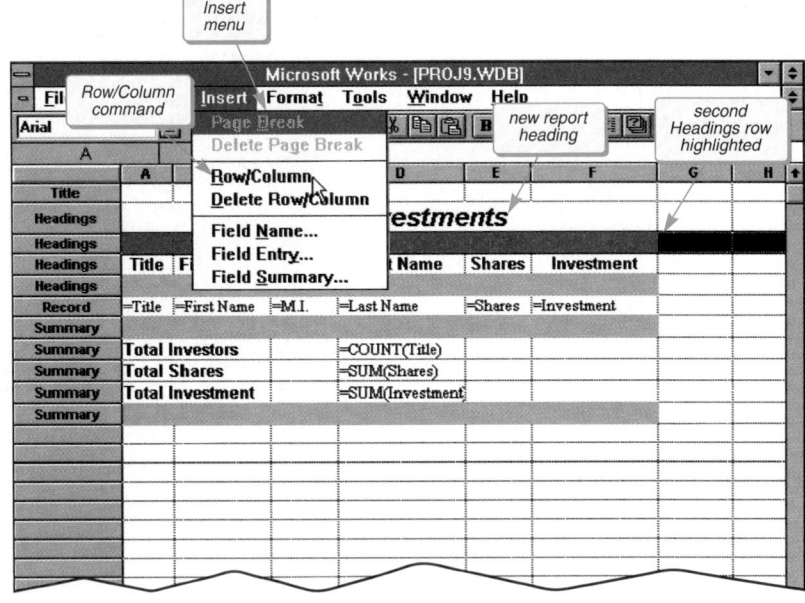

FIGURE 9-75

STEP 5 ▶

Choose the Row/Column command. When the Insert Row dialog box displays, ensure that Headings is highlighted in the Type list box, and then point to the OK button.

Works displays the Insert Row dia-log box (Figure 9-76). The Head-ings line is highlighted in the Type list box and the mouse pointer points to the OK button.

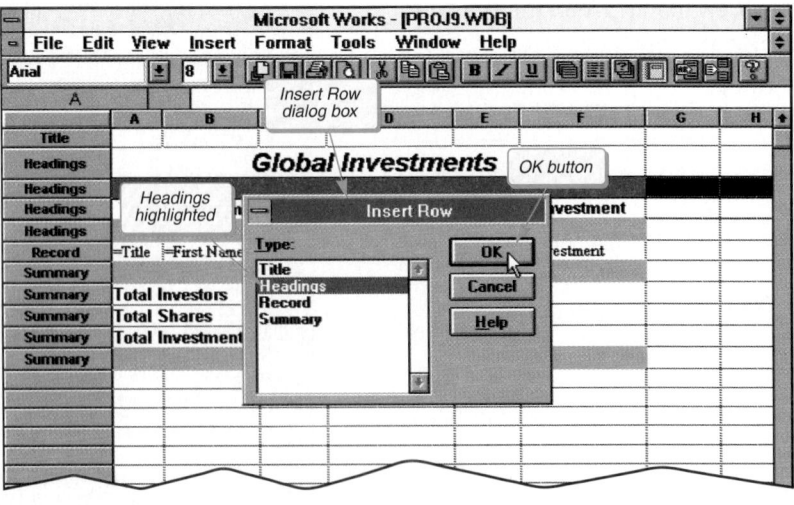

FIGURE 9-76

STEP 6 ▶

Choose the OK button in the Insert Row dialog box. Highlight column A in the inserted Headings row. Select the Insert menu and point to the Field Entry command.

*Works inserts a Headings row just above the highlighted row (Figure 9-77). Column A in the inserted (second) Headings row is highlighted, the Insert menu displays, and the mouse pointer points to the **Field Entry command**.*

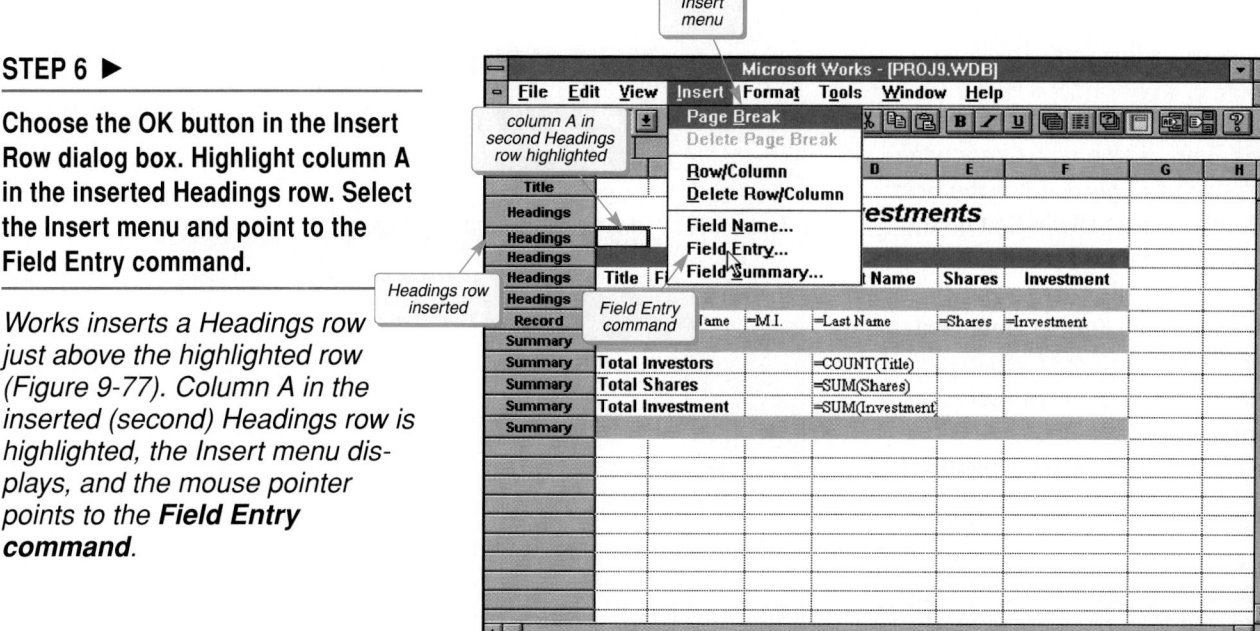

FIGURE 9-77

STEP 7 ▶

Choose the Field Entry command from the Insert menu. When the Insert Field Entry dialog box displays, scroll down the Fields list box and highlight Fund Name. Point to the OK button.

Works displays the Insert Field Entry dialog box (Figure 9-78). Fund Name is highlighted in the Fields list box and the mouse pointer points to the OK button.

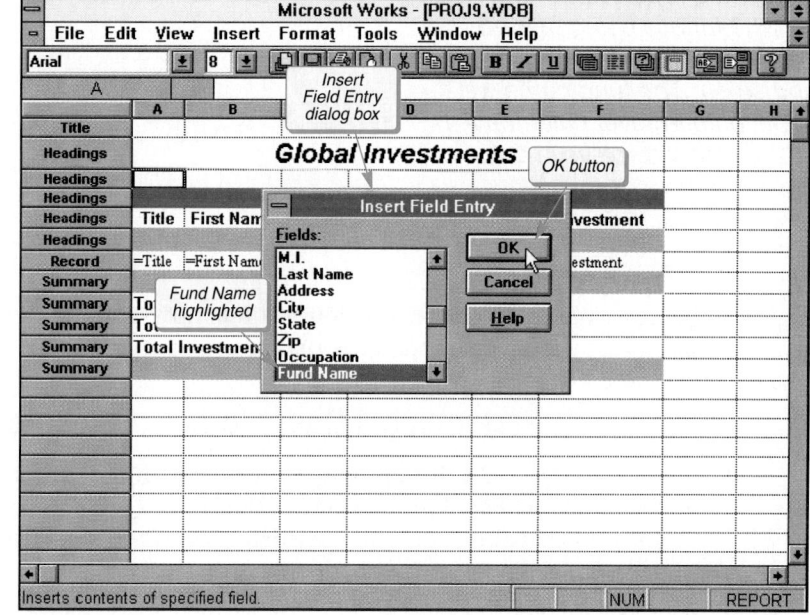

FIGURE 9-78

STEP 8 ▶

Choose the OK button in the Insert Field Entry dialog box. Change the font size to 12 point. Click the Bold button and the Italic button on the Toolbar. Highlight columns A through F on the second Headings row. Select the Format menu and choose the Alignment command. Select the Center across selection option button and choose the OK button in the Alignment dialog box.

The report definition window displays with the =Fund Name entry in column A of the second Headings row (Figure 9-79). The =Fund Name entry will cause the value in the Fund Name field to print in the report title. If the Growth fund is being printed, then Growth will print in the report title. If the Fixed Income fund is being printed, then Fixed Income will print in the field, and so on. The fund name will print centered over columns A-F but the entry displays in column A.

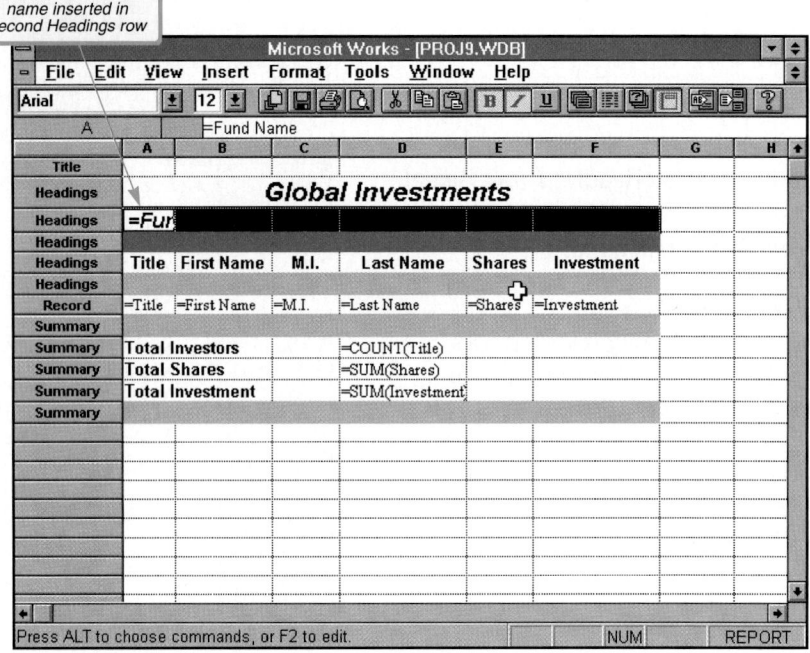

FIGURE 9-79

The report definition is now complete. You must now perform a query to select the records that you want to print.

Performing a Query to Select Records to Print

In this application you are to print the records of individuals who have invested in the each of the funds (see Figure 9-69 on page W9.47). To create this report, you must perform a query to select the records for each of the funds. To accomplish this for the Growth fund, and then to print the records in the Growth fund, perform the following steps.

TO SELECT RECORDS TO PRINT ▼

STEP 1 ▶

Select the Tools menu and choose the Create New Query command. When the New Query dialog box displays, type `Growth Fund` in the Please give this query a name text box, and make the required selections and entries so the query reads, Fund Name is equal to Growth. Point to the Apply Now button.

Works displays the New Query dialog box (Figure 9-80). The dialog box contains the query name Growth Fund and the appropriate entries in the dialog box to perform the query. The mouse pointer points to the Apply Now button.

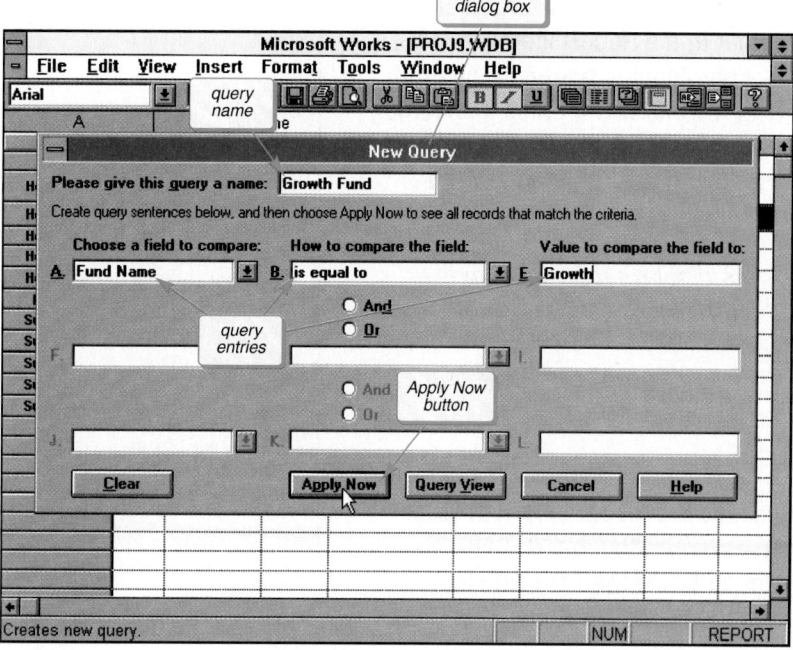

FIGURE 9-80

STEP 2 ▶

Choose the Apply Now button in the New Query dialog box. When the Report view displays, point to the Print Preview button.

After you apply the query, Works returns to the report view window (Figure 9-81). The mouse pointer points the Print Preview button. It is not necessary to view the screen in List view after applying the query but you should check the accuracy of the query using print preview.

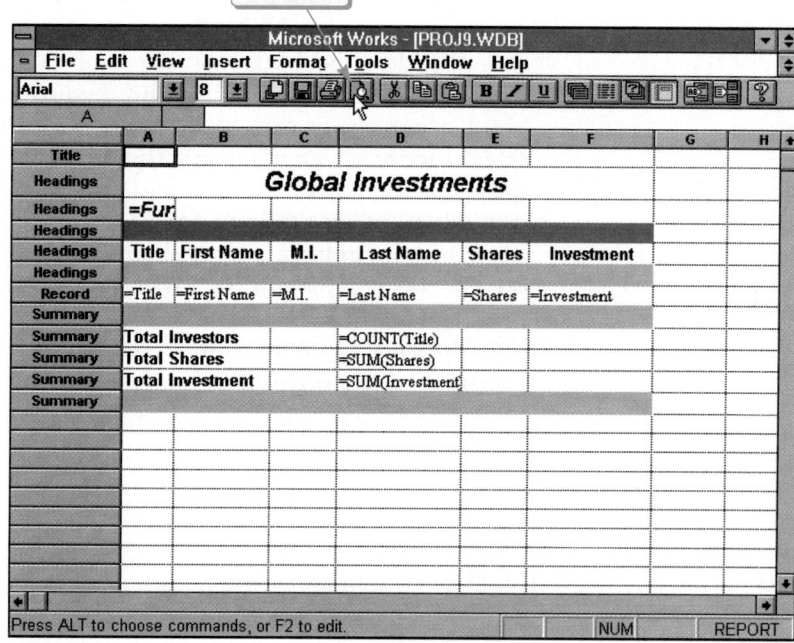

FIGURE 9-81

STEP 3 ▶

Click the Print Preview button on the Toolbar in the Report view window. Click the Zoom In button in the print preview window two times to enlarge the display. Click the right scroll arrow one time. Point to the Print button.

Works displays the report in the print preview window (Figure 9-82). Notice the Growth fund name centered in the heading.

STEP 4 ▶

Because the report is correct you can now print the report. Click the Print button in the Print Preview screen.

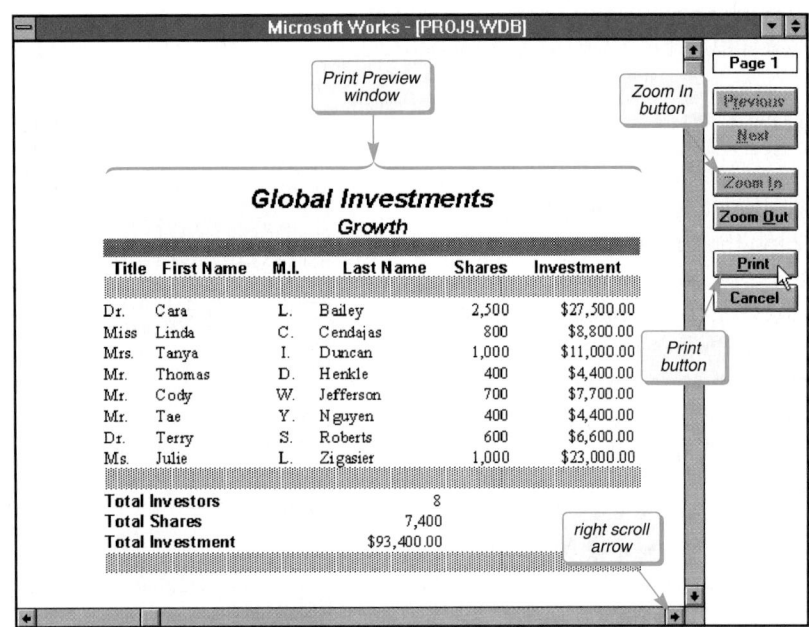

FIGURE 9-82

Works will print the Growth report shown in Figure 9-69 on page W9.47. To print the reports for the other funds, create a query for the fund you want to print, and click the Print button on the Toolbar, choose the Print button in the print preview window, or choose the Print command from the File menu.

If you have already created a query for the fund you want to print, in List view select the View menu, choose the Apply Query command, select the name of the query for the fund you want, and choose the OK button in the Apply Query dialog box. Then, select the View menu, choose the Report command, select the Fund Report in the Report list box, and choose the OK button in the Reports dialog box. Works will display the Fund Report report definition in Report view. Then, print the report.

Works allows a maximum 8 named queries. To create a query for each fund, you must delete one of the queries you created earlier. It is suggested you delete the Growth/Invest query.

▶ REPORTS WITH SORT BREAKS

The next task in this project is to create a single report listing the investors in sequence by each fund (Options, Growth, Fixed Income, and Commodities) and the total dollars invested in each fund. The report created for this task is shown in Figure 9-83. Notice that the records for each fund are grouped together. All the records for investors in the Options fund are together, followed by all the records for the Growth fund, and so on. For each fund, the investors are listed and then the Total Investments for that particular fund are printed. After all records have printed been, the total number of investors, totals shares in the investment club, and the total dollar investment is printed.

To create the report shown in Figure 9-83, the records in the database must be sorted on the Fund Name field in descending sequence and the Last Name field in ascending sequence.

Global Investments

Title	First Name	M.I.	Last Name	Shares	Investment	
Options						
Dr.	Julia	W.	Lopez	1,200	$27,600.00	
Mr.	Eugene	Q.	McMurray	2,000	$76,000.00	
Mr.	Steven	U.	Smoldery	1,400	$32,200.00	
Ms.	Rebecca	O.	Tiong	1,000	$23,000.00	
				Total Investments		$158,800.00
Growth						
Dr.	Cara	L.	Bailey	2,500	$27,500.00	
Miss	Linda	C.	Cendajas	800	$8,800.00	
Mrs.	Tanya	I.	Duncan	1,000	$11,000.00	
Mr.	Thomas	D.	Henkle	400	$4,400.00	
Mr.	Cody	W.	Jefferson	700	$7,700.00	
Mr.	Tae	Y.	Nguyen	400	$4,400.00	
Dr.	Terry	S.	Roberts	600	$6,600.00	
Ms.	Julie	L.	Zigasier	1,000	$23,000.00	
				Total Investments		$93,400.00
Fixed Income						
Mrs.	Hillary	P.	Fine	200	$3,600.00	
Ms.	Jane	R.	Walters	600	$10,800.00	
Mrs.	Lilla	V.	Wilson	400	$7,200.00	
				Total Investments		$21,600.00
Commodities						
Dr.	Hugo	A.	Weller	1,500	$22,500.00	
				Total Investments		$22,500.00

Totals For Investment Club

Total Investors	16
Total Shares	15,700
Total Investment	$296,300.00

FIGURE 9-83

When you sort database records in Report view, you can specify the fields on which to sort, the sequence in which to sort, and that a sort break is to occur. A **sort break** allows you to separate the data into groups and print intermediate rows and summary rows based on the data in the group. In Figure 9-83, a sort break occurs between each group of records in a given fund. Thus, a sort break occurs between the Options and Growth funds, between the Growth and Fixed Income funds, and between the Fixed Income and Commodities funds. By specifying a sort break in Report view, you can print an **Intermediate (INTR) row**, such as the row that contains the Fund Name prior to the records in the fund, and a **Summary (SUMM) row,** such as the Total Investments row for each of the funds.

This section explains how to create the report shown in Figure 9-83.

Creating a Sort Break Report

To create a sort break report, show all the records in the database so they will be used for the report. You must then create the report definition. While you can create a new report definition, the sort break report is quite similar to the Investment Totals report in Figure 9-57 on page W9.38. Therefore, you can create the report definition for the sort break report by duplicating the Investment Totals report, which was named Total Report. You can then sort the records in the database, change the heading, and modify the report definition.

To show all records and duplicate the report definition for use in the sort break report, complete the following steps.

TO SHOW ALL RECORDS AND DUPLICATE A REPORT DEFINITION

Step 1: If necessary, return to List view by clicking the List View button.
Step 2: Select the View menu and choose the Show All Records command. Scroll up so all the records in the database are visible.
Step 3: Select the Tools menu in List view.
Step 4: Choose the Duplicate Report command.
Step 5: In the Duplicate Report dialog box, highlight the Total Report in the Reports list box. Type `SortFundReport` in the Name text box.
Step 6: Choose the Duplicate button in the Duplicate Report dialog box.
Step 7: Choose the OK button in the Duplicate Report dialog box.

Step 8: Select the View menu in List view and choose the Report command.
Step 9: When the Reports dialog box displays, highlight the name SortFundReport in the Report list box. Choose the OK button in the Reports dialog box.

Works will display the duplicated report definition SortFundReport in the Report view window. You are then ready to specify the sorting for the report and modify the report format to produce the report shown in Figure 9-83.

Sorting Records in the Database and Creating Sort Breaks

To sort the records in the database and create sort breaks for the report, perform the following steps.

TO SORT THE DATABASE AND CREATE SORT BREAKS ▼

STEP 1 ▶

Select the Tools menu in Report view and point to the Sort Records command.

Works displays the Tools menu and the mouse pointer points to the Sort Records command (Figure 9-84).

FIGURE 9-84

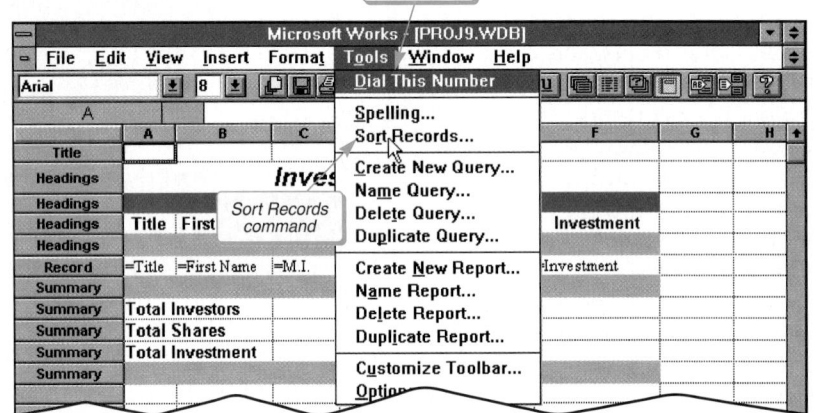

STEP 2 ▶

Choose the Sort Records command. When the Sort Records dialog box displays, select Fund Name from the 1st Field drop-down list box. Select the Descend option button in the 1st Field area, and select the Break check box in the 1st Field area. Select Last Name from the 2nd Field drop-down list box, and select the Ascend option button in the 2nd Field area. Point to the OK button.

Works displays the Sort Records dialog box (Figure 9-85). Fund Name displays in the 1st Field drop-down list box, specifying that

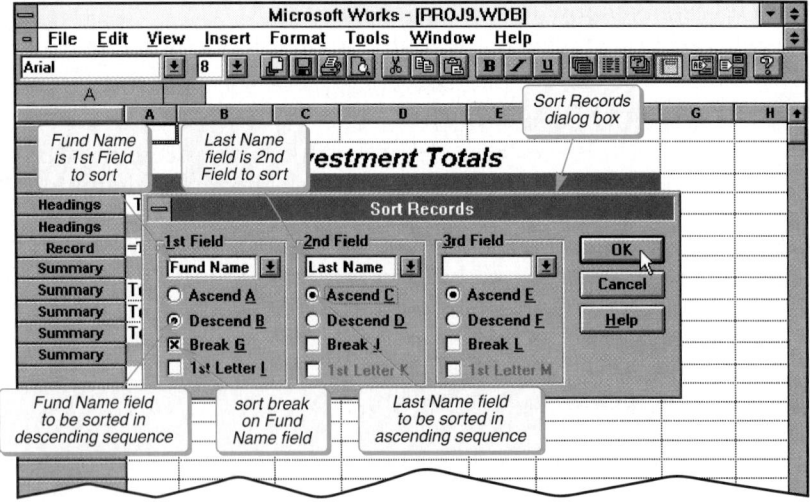

FIGURE 9-85

the first sort field is the Fund Name field. The selected Descend option button states the field is to be sorted in descending sequence. Selecting the Break check box tells Works to generate a sort break when the value in the Fund Name changes. Thus, when the value in the Fund Name field changes from Options to Growth, a sort break will occur. The Last Name field name displays in the 2nd Field drop-down list box, indicating that within Fund Name, the records are to be sorted in ascending sequence based on the value in the Last Name field. The mouse pointer points to the OK button.

STEP 3 ▶

Choose the OK button in the Sort Records dialog box.

The report view window displays with the Summ Fund Name row added to the report definition (Figure 9-86). This row is added because a sort break will occur on the Fund Name field. Works assumes you want to print totals for each field on the report in the Summ Fund Name row, so COUNT functions for each field that contains non-numeric data and SUM functions for each field that contains numeric data appear in the row. As in most cases, the Works report definition must be modified to produce the desired report.

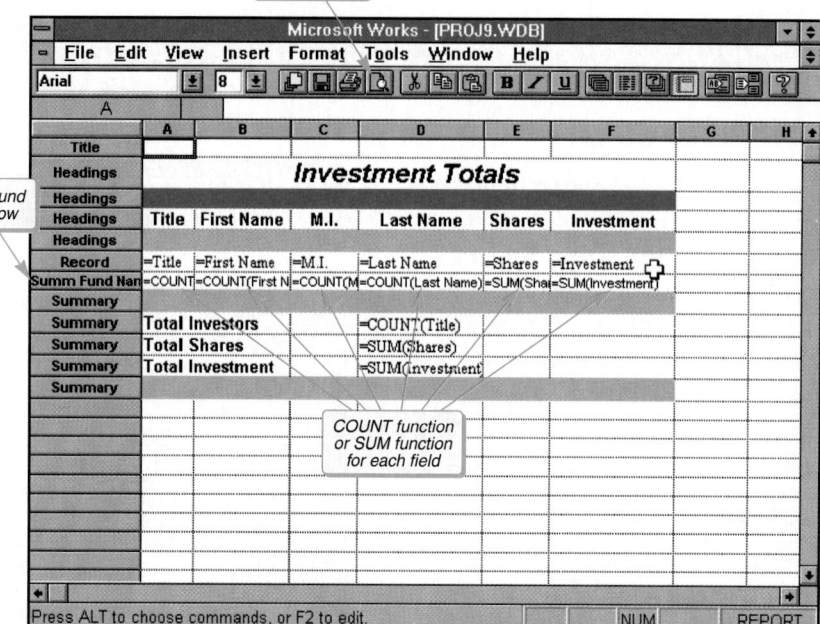

FIGURE 9-86

STEP 4 ▶

Point to and click the Print Preview button on the Toolbar and then choose the Zoom In button one time.

Works displays the print preview window (Figure 9-87). The count for each of the non-numeric fields and the sums for the numeric fields display.

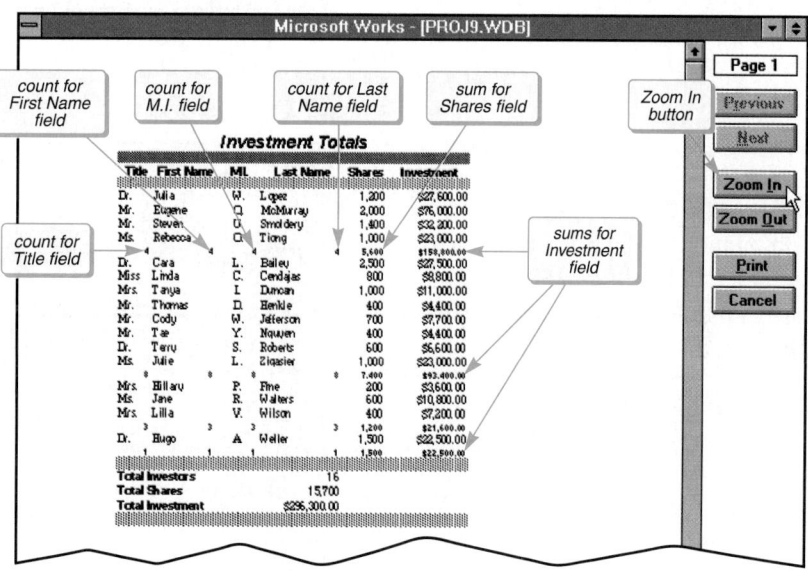

FIGURE 9-87

In Figure 9-87 you can see that several modifications must be made to the report definition so the report will print as shown in Figure 9-83 on page W9.55. The report heading must be changed. The excess count and sum fields must be cleared. The total investments value for each fund must be moved one column to the right and a title inserted in the row. The fund name must be placed on the report above the records for each fund, and the totals at the end of the report must be formatted properly.

To modify the report so it will print as shown in Figure 9-83, complete the following steps.

TO MODIFY A SORT BREAK REPORT AND INSERT AN INTERMEDIATE ROW ▼

STEP 1 ▶

Choose the Cancel button in the print preview window to return to the report definition window. Highlight column A in the first Headings row and type Global Investments. Highlight columns A through E in the Summ Fund Name row, select the Edit menu, and point to the Clear command.

*Works displays the report definition window (Figure 9-88). Columns A through E are highlighted, the Edit menu displays, and the mouse pointer points to the **Clear command**. This command can be used to clear the formulas from the Summ Fund Name row.*

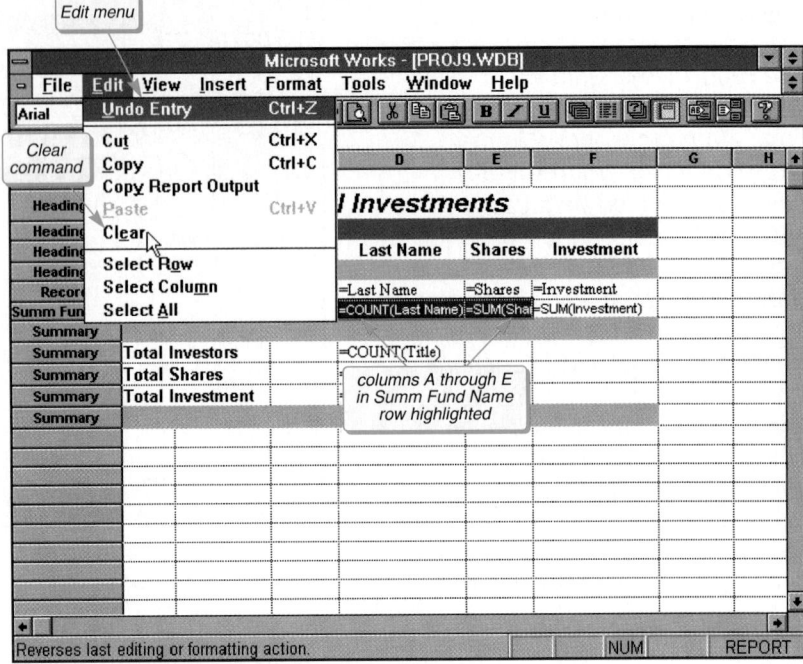

FIGURE 9-88

STEP 2 ▶

Choose the Clear command from the Edit menu. Highlight the formula in column F in the Summ Fund Name row, and point to the Cut button on the Toolbar.

Works clears the formulas from columns A through E of the Summ Fund Name row (Figure 9-89). The formula in column F is highlighted, and the mouse pointer points to the Cut button.

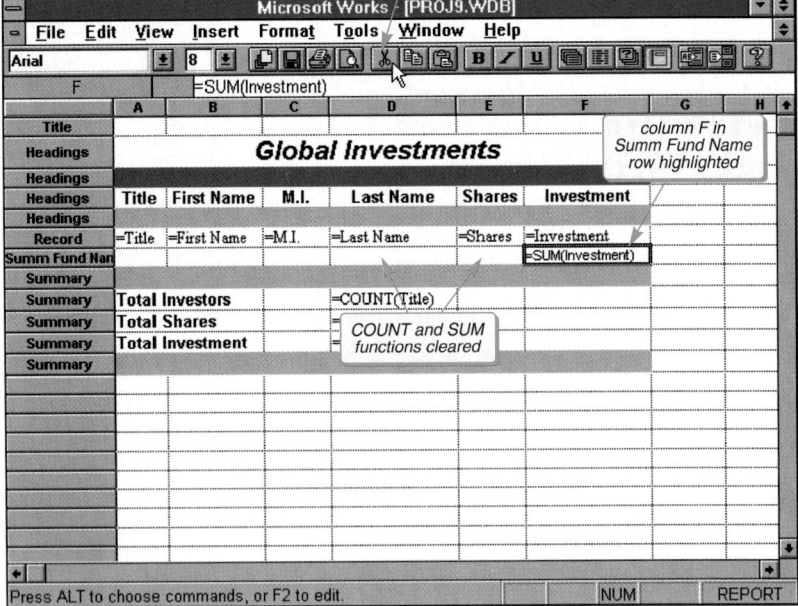

FIGURE 9-89

STEP 3 ▶

Click the Cut button on Toolbar. Highlight column G in the Summ Fund Name row, and click the Paste button on the Toolbar.

Works cuts the formula out of column F of the Summ Fund Name row and places the formula on the Clipboard (Figure 9-90). When you click the Paste button, the formula in the Clipboard is pasted in column G in the Summ Fund Name row.

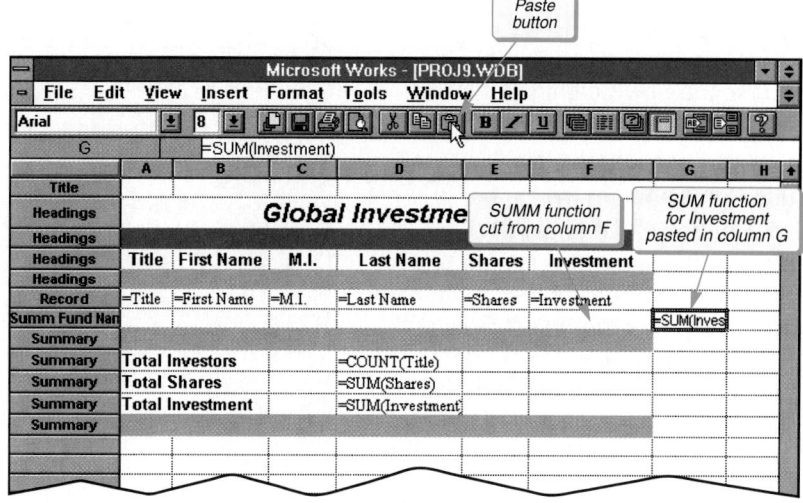

FIGURE 9-90

STEP 4 ▶

Change the entry in column G of the Summ Fund Name row to 10 point Times New Roman font. Place the mouse pointer on the border between column header G and column header H, drag the border to the right to increase the width of column G two positions, and then release the left mouse button. Highlight column E in the Summ Fund Name row, type Total Investments, **and press the ENTER key or click the Enter box. Change this entry to 10 point Arial bold font. Highlight the Record row, select the Insert menu, and point to the Row/Column command.**

The title Total Investments displays in 10 point Arial bold font beginning in column E of the Summ Fund Name row (Figure 9-91). Column G is wider. The Record row is highlighted because the Intermediate (INTR) row to be inserted will be inserted directly above the Record row. The Insert menu displays and the mouse pointer points to the Row/Column command.

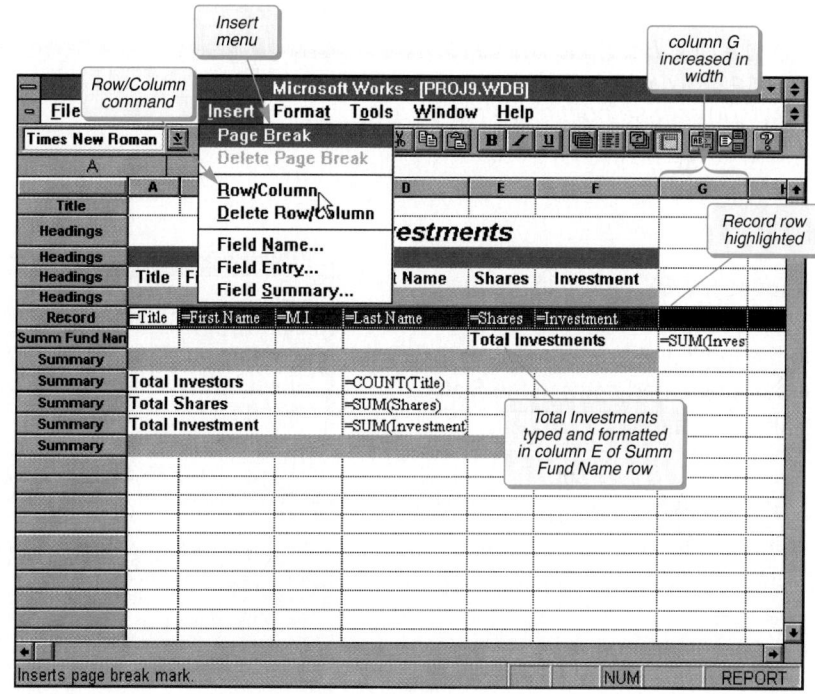

FIGURE 9-91

STEP 5 ▶

Choose the Row/Column command. When the Insert Row dialog box displays, highlight the Intr Fund Name entry in the Type list box. Point to the OK button in the Insert Row dialog box.

Works displays the Insert Row dialog box (Figure 9-92). The Intr Fund Name entry in the Type list box identifies the Intermediate row that can be inserted in a report. An Intermediate row can be inserted whenever a sort break is defined for the report. Because the Record row is highlighted, Works will place the inserted Intr Fund Name row immediately above the Record row. The mouse pointer points to the OK button.

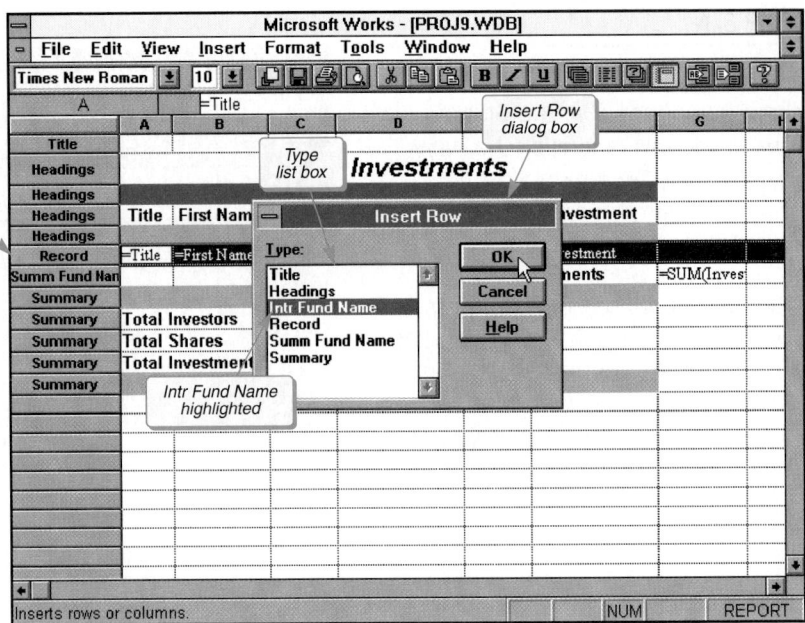

FIGURE 9-92

STEP 6 ▶

Choose the OK button in the Insert Row dialog box. Highlight column A in the Intr Fund Name row. Select the Insert menu and point to the Field Entry command.

Works inserts the Intr Fund Name row (Figure 9-93). This row will print each time the value in the Fund Name field changes. It will print before the first record for the new fund name. Column A in the Intr Fund Name row is highlighted. Works displays the Insert menu and the mouse pointer points to the Field Entry command.

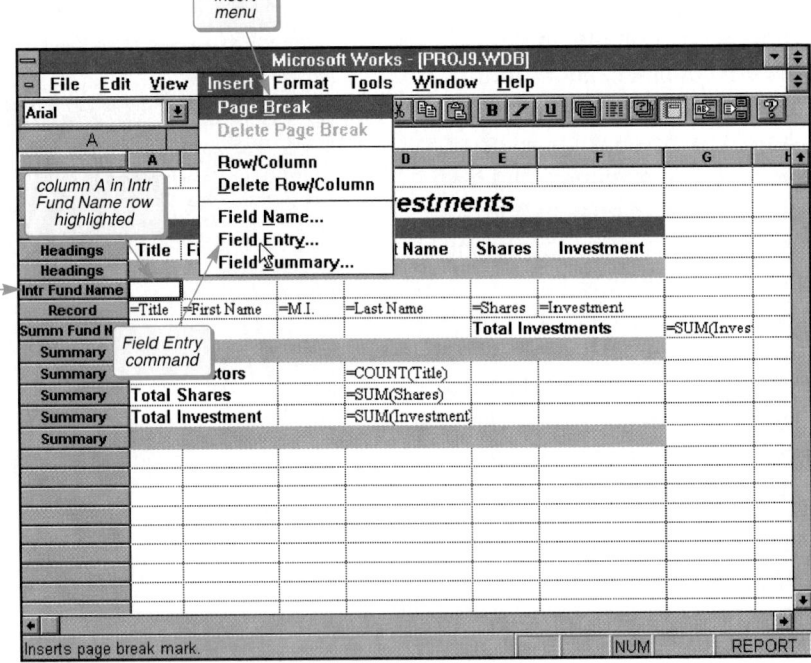

FIGURE 9-93

STEP 7 ▶

Choose the Field Entry command. When the Insert Field Entry dialog box displays, scroll down in the Fields list box, highlight the Fund Name field name, and point to the OK button.

The Insert Field Entry dialog box displays (Figure 9-94). The Fund Name field name in the Fields list box is highlighted and the mouse pointer points to the OK button.

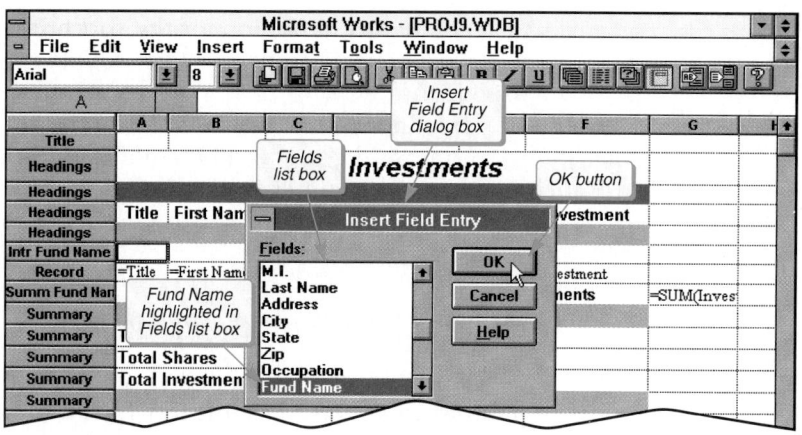

FIGURE 9-94

STEP 8 ▶

Choose the OK button in the Insert Field Entry dialog box. Change the field entry to 10 point bold italic font. Highlight the second Summary row, select the Insert menu, and point to the Row/Column command.

Works inserts the Fund Name field entry in column A in the Intr Fund Name row. The second Summary row is highlighted, the Insert menu displays, and the mouse pointer points to the Row/Column command (Figure 9-95).

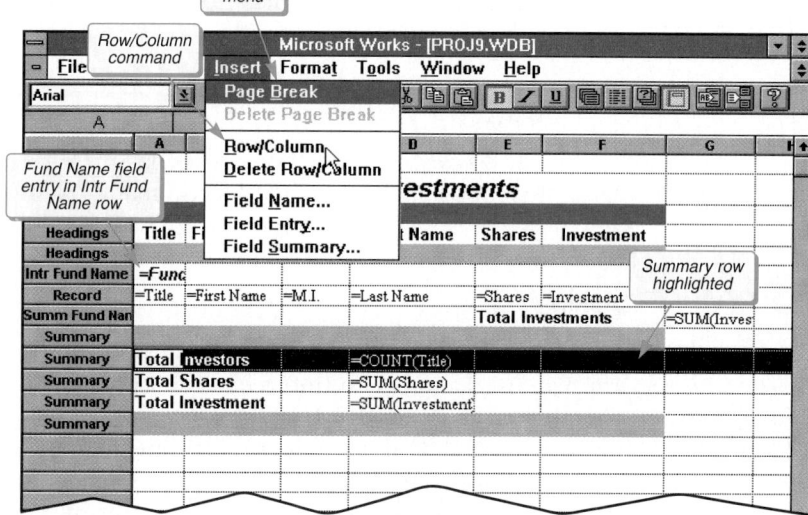

FIGURE 9-95

STEP 9 ▶

Choose the Row/Column command from the Insert menu. When the Insert Row dialog box displays, highlight Summary in the Type list box and choose the OK button. When the Report view displays, highlight column A in the second Summary row, type

Totals For
Investment Club,

press the ENTER key or click the Enter box, and change the font to 12 point Arial bold italic.

The title line for the report totals is entered and formatted (Figure 9-96).

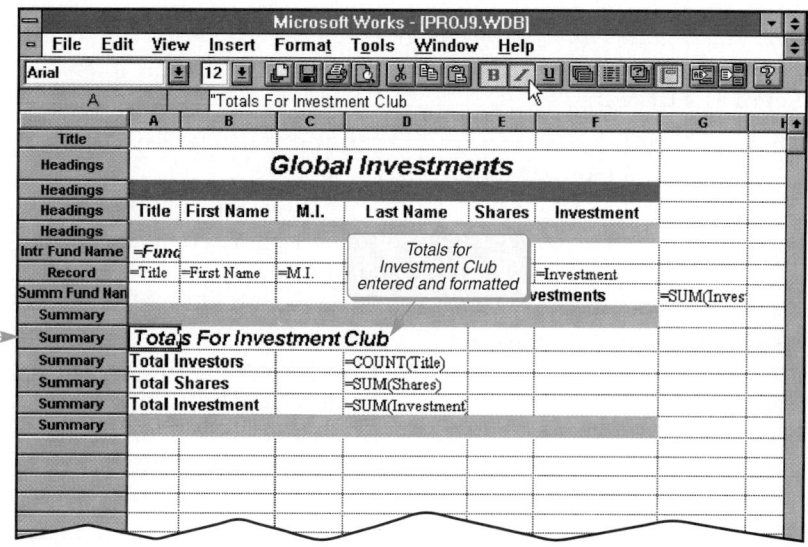

FIGURE 9-96

The report definition for the sort break report is now complete. You should use print preview to preview the report to make sure the correct output is produced.

Two incomplete tasks remain: (1) print the report; (2) save the database.

To print the report, click the Print button on the Toolbar. Works prints the report as shown in Figure 9-83 on page W9.55.

To save the database with the same name, click the Save button on the Toolbar.

Multiple Field Sort Break Reports

Works allows you to define reports with more than one sort break. For example, you can define a report in which two fields, State and Fund Name, are used for sort breaks. You can also define a report in which no Record row exists and the only rows that print are Summary rows. To prepare these types of reports, you must apply the concepts and techniques previously learned to create the new report formats.

Quitting Works

Now that all of the reports have been defined and printed, you can quit Works by choosing the Exit Works command from the File menu.

▶ PROJECT SUMMARY

In this project, you learned how to obtain information from the records in a database through the use of queries and reports. You used a query to find records with values in a field equal to values you specified, records with values greater than and less than values you specified, records with values in more than one field equal to values you specified, and you learned about the logical operators AND and OR.

In the Report view of Works, you learned about defining a report to list records in a database and to list records and print summary totals. You used a query to print only specific records in a database. Sorting and sort breaks were presented showing you how to create a report with sort break totals and summary totals.

▶ KEY TERMS

Add button *(W9.26)*
AND logical operator *(W9.14)*
Apply Now button *(W9.8)*
Apply Query command *(W9.20)*
Clear command *(W9.58)*
conditional operators *(W9.19)*
Create New Query command
   (W9.6)
Cut button *(W9.29)*
Delete Query command *(W9.22)*
Duplicate Report command
   (W9.48)
Field Entry command *(W9.51)*
Headings row *(W9.28)*
hidden records *(W9.12)*

Intermediate (INTR) row
   (W9.55)
logical operator *(W9.14)*
Name Report command *(W9.34)*
OR logical operator *(W9.15)*
Paste button *(W9.30)*
query *(W9.2)*
Query View *(W9.17)*
Query View button *(W9.20)*
Record row *(W9.28)*
Rename button *(W9.23, W9.34)*
Report command *(W9.35)*
reports *(W9.2)*
report definition window
   (W9.28)

Report View button *(W9.26)*
Row/Column command *(W9.42)*
Show All Records command
   (W9.9)
sort *(W9.35)*
sort break *(W9.55)*
Sort Records command *(W9.36)*
Summary (SUMM) row
   (W9.28, W9.55)
Summary rows *(W9.41)*
summary totals *(W9.37)*
Switch Hidden Records
   command *(W9.13)*
Title rows *(W9.28)*

STUDENT ASSIGNMENT 1
True/False

Instructions: Circle T if the statement is true or F if the statement is false.

T F 1. A query is a request for information from a database.

T F 2. The records that print on a report can be controlled through the use of queries.

T F 3. After you perform a query, Works automatically displays all the records in the database.

T F 4. To create a query, choose the Create New Query command from the Tools menu.

T F 5. Only one logical operator may be used when creating a query using the New Query dialog box.

T F 6. The entry =>25000 in the Investment field in a Query view window states that Works should find all records in which the value in the Investment field is less than or equal to 25000.

T F 7. When used in a query, the AND logical operator means both conditions must be true.

T F 8. The AND logical operator and the OR logical operator cannot be used in a single query.

T F 9. To be sure a report title prints at the top of every page of the report, place the report title in the Title row in the report definition.

T F 10. To change the report name Report1 to the report name Investors, use the Report command from the View menu.

T F 11. Selecting the Count check box in the Report Statistics dialog box when the Title field is highlighted in the Fields in Report list box tells Works to add the values in the Title field and print the sum at the end of the report.

T F 12. When you highlight two Headings rows, choose the Row/Column command from the Insert menu, and choose the OK button in the Insert Row dialog box, Works inserts two Headings rows directly below the two highlighted Headings rows.

T F 13. You can use the Cut button on the Toolbar to insert a row in the Report view.

T F 14. When you choose the Duplicate Report command from the Tools menu and then choose the Duplicate button in the Duplicate Report dialog box, Works duplicates the report whose name is highlighted in the Reports list box and then displays the report definition.

T F 15. A row with the name Summ Fund Name will print whenever the value in the Fund Name field changes from one database record to the next.

T F 16. A field sorted in alphabetic order is sorted in ascending sequence.

T F 17. When you create a sort break in a report, Works automatically assumes you want to print totals for each field in the report and generates entries to accomplish this task.

T F 18. A row with the name Intr State will print only if the value in the State field in a record is the same as the value in the State field in the previously printed record.

T F 19. The Switch Hidden Records command should be used after applying a query.

T F 20. Queries and reports cannot be saved as a part of a database.

STUDENT ASSIGNMENT 2
Multiple Choice

Instructions: Circle the correct response.

1. If you use Query view and you enter the value Dr. in the Title field and no other fields contain a value in Query view, when you click the List view button on the Toolbar, _____ .
   a. all records in the database display
   b. only those records with the value Dr. in the Title field display
   c. all records except those with the value Dr. in the Title field display
   d. no records display as this is not a valid query

(continued)

STUDENT ASSIGNMENT 2 (continued)

2. Which of the following is not a valid conditional criteria for a field in a database query?
   a. <25000
   b. >25000
   c. < >25000
   d. = < >25000

3. To delete a query, use the _____ .
   a. Delete Report command from the Tools menu
   b. Query command from the View menu
   c. Clear Field entry command from the Edit menu
   d. Delete Query command from the Tools menu

4. When you click the Report View button on the Toolbar and no reports have been defined for the database, _____ .
   a. Works displays the New Report dialog box
   b. Works displays the Report Statistics dialog box
   c. Works displays the Report view of the database
   d. Works displays a message in a Microsoft Works dialog box informing you no reports have been defined

5. The Title row of a report _____ .
   a. prints at the top of every page in the report
   b. prints at the top of the first page in the report only
   c. cannot be left blank in the report definition
   d. must contain the name of the report

6. To count the number of records in a database and print the total at the end of the report, select a field in the report and select the _____ check box in the Statistics area of the Report Statistics dialog box.
   a. Sum
   b. Maximum
   c. Count
   d. Records

7. The Row/Column command on the Insert menu _____ .
   a. inserts one row each time you choose the command
   b. inserts as many rows as you highlight each time you choose the command
   c. inserts one Summary row each time you choose the command
   d. inserts as many rows as you specify to insert in the Insert text box in the Insert Row dialog box

8. When you select Fund Name in the 1st Field drop-down list box of the Sort Records dialog box, and select the Break check box in the 1st Field area, _____ .
   a. Works places an Intr Fund Name row in the report definition
   b. Works places a Sort Fund Name row in the report definition
   c. Works places a Summary Fund Name row in the report definition
   d. Works places a Summ Fund Name row in the report definition

9. After you have created and named a query, you can execute the query again by choosing the

   _____ .
   a. Apply Query command from the View menu
   b. Query command from the View menu
   c. Name command from the Tools menu
   d. Create New Query command from the View menu

10. You must use Query view when the query requires the use of _____ .
    a. one or more logical operators
    b. two conditional operators
    c. three or more logical operators
    d. three or more query operators

STUDENT ASSIGNMENT 3
Queries

Instructions: The Query view of the database shown in Figure SA9-3 contains a query. Examine the query and then examine the List view of the database in Figure 9-4 on page W9.5. In the space provided, write the record number of each record that will display in List view when the query in Figure SA9-3 is executed.

Record Numbers: _____

_____

_____

_____

_____

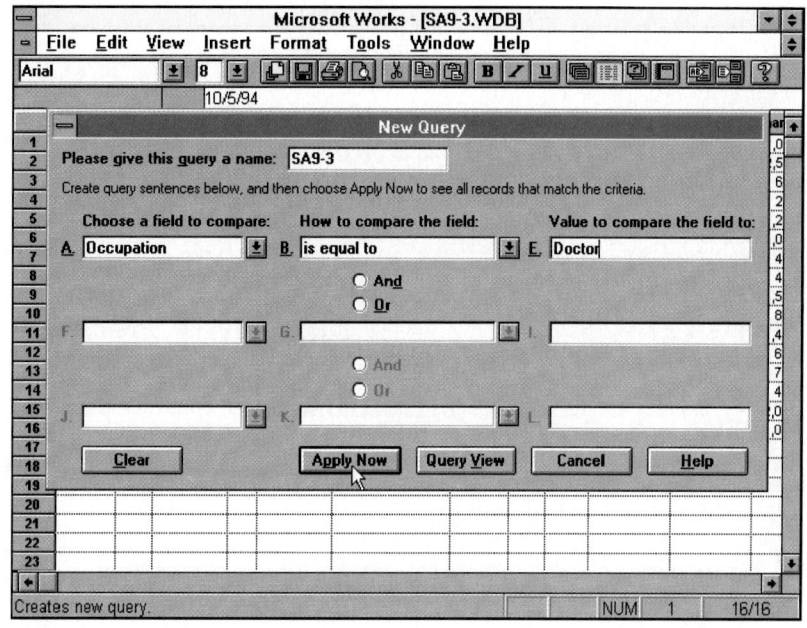

FIGURE SA9-3

STUDENT ASSIGNMENT 4
Adding Fields to a Report Definition

Instructions: The New Report dialog box displays in Figure SA9-4. In the space provided, write the steps required to add the Date, Last Name, City, State, and Occupation fields to the Fields in Report list box.

Steps: _____

_____

_____

_____

_____

_____

_____

FIGURE SA9-4

STUDENT ASSIGNMENT 5
Naming a Report

FIGURE SA9-5

Instructions: The Name Report dialog box displays in Figure SA9-5. In the space provided, write the steps required to change the name of the report from Report1 to Investors.

Steps: _____

_____

_____

_____

_____

_____

STUDENT ASSIGNMENT 6
Understanding Menus and Commands

Instructions: In the space provided in the MENU (VIEW) column, write the name of the menu and the database view for the menu that contains the command listed in the COMMAND column.

COMMAND	MENU (VIEW)
Create New Query	_____
Show All Records	_____
Apply Query	_____
Delete Query	_____
Clear Field Entry	_____
Show All Records	_____
Switch Hidden Records	_____
Cut	_____
Paste	_____
Name Report	_____
Create New Report	_____
Duplicate Report	_____
Sort Records	

COMPUTER LABORATORY EXERCISES

COMPUTER LABORATORY EXERCISE 1
Using the Help Menu

Instructions: Perform the following tasks using a computer.

1. Start the Microsoft Works Database tool.
2. Use the Help menu to answer the following questions. For each question, print the topic pages from the Help screens that explain your answer. When you are finished with this exercise, turn in the printed topic pages to your instructor.
   a. You have a database consisting of more than 30,000 records. One of the fields in this database is the Last Name field. You want a report which lists all the names in the database and provides a count of the number of Last Names that begin with each letter of the alphabet. You want a total for the number of last names that start with A, the number of last names that start with B, and so on, for all the records in the database. How can you do this?
   b. You have defined your report and discover you want to sort the report using four different fields. How can you do this?
   c. Your database contains 14,328 records, each record containing 14 fields. You know the Last Name of someone in the database begins with the characters SM, but you are not sure whether the spelling of the name is Smythe, Smithe, Smyth, or one of several dozen other spellings. You do not know the first name or any other information. How would you locate the record for this person?
   d. Your boss has asked you to search your database to discover how many people have the letter Z anywhere in their last name, which is found in the Last Name field. How can you display all the records at one time for people with Z in their last name?

COMPUTER LABORATORY EXERCISE 2
Queries

Instructions: Start the Works Database tool. Open the CLE9-2.WDB file on the Student Diskette that accompanies this book. This file contains the database that is used for all examples in Project 9. The screen in Figure CLE9-2 shows the database in List view. Perform the queries listed at the top of the next page. After each query, print the database in List view, showing all fields in the database. When you have completed this exercise, turn in the printouts to your instructor.

FIGURE CLE9-2

(continued)

W9.67

COMPUTER LABORATORY EXERCISE 2 (continued)

1. Display all records for people who invested in the month of December.
2. Display all records for doctors who live in the state of Washington.
3. Display all records for people whose zip code is greater than 92000 and who do not live in the state of Washington.
4. Display all records for teachers who live in Anaheim, California; Fullerton, California; or Yorba, California.
5. Display all records for teachers who live in California and invested more than $15,000.00.

COMPUTER LABORATORY EXERCISE 3
Defining a Sort Break Report

Instructions: Start the Works Database tool. Open the CLE9-3.WDB file on the Student Diskette that accompanies this book. This file contains the database that is used for all examples in Project 9. The screen in Figure CLE9-3 shows the Report view. The report to be printed should be sorted on Last Name within Fund Name and produce a sort break on the Fund Name field. The formatting of the report should be the same as shown in Figure 9-83 on page W9.55. Perform the steps necessary to create the report and then print the report. Turn in a copy of the report to your instructor.

FIGURE CLE9-3

COMPUTER LABORATORY ASSIGNMENT 1
Queries and Reports

Purpose: To provide experience performing queries and defining and printing database reports.

Problem: Obtain information from the Woodland College Foundation database created in Computer Laboratory Assignment 1 in Project 7 and maintained and updated in Computer Laboratory Assignment 1 in Project 8.

Instructions:

1. Open the database you created in Computer Laboratory Assignment 1 in Project 7 and maintained and updated in Computer Laboratory Assignment 1 in Project 8. If you do not have this updated database, your instructor will provide you with the database file.
2. Using a query, display all the people in the president's circle. Give the query a name of your choice. Print the List view of the database after the query.
3. Using a query, display all people who donated more than $2,000.00. Give the query a name of your choice. Print the List view of the database after the query.
4. Display all people who donated $2,000.00 or less. Print the List view of the database after the query.
5. Using a query, display all people who donated to the science scholarships and graduated before 1980. Give the query a name of your choice. Print the List view of the database after the query.
6. Using a query, display all people in the president's circle who donated to either the science or business scholarships. Give the query a name of your choice. Print the List view of the database after the query.
7. Using a query with a name of your choice, answer the following questions:
   a. How much money did the only nongraduate in the database contribute?
   b. What are the last names of the doctors in the database?
   c. How many people who graduated since 1990 contributed to the Woodland College Foundation scholarship fund?
8. Create a report listing all people in the Woodland College Foundation database. The report should contain the date, title, first name, middle initial, last name, and honor award. Format the report in a manner similar to the report shown in Figure 9-36 on page W9.25. Name the report a name of your choice.
9. Create a report listing all people in the Woodland College Foundation database, the total number of people, and the total dollars donated. The report should contain the title, first name, middle initial, last name, scholarship, and donation. Format the report in a manner similar to the report shown in Figure 9-57 on page W9.38. Name the report a name of your choice.
10. Create a report listing the donors in ascending sequence by scholarship. The fields on the report should be the same as the fields in the report created in number 9 above except scholarship should not print on each Record line. For each scholarship, print the number of donors and the total dollars donated to the scholarship. At the end of the report, print the total number of donors and the total dollars donated. Format the report in a manner similar to the report shown in Figure 9-83 on page W9.55. Name the report a name of your choice.
11. Save the database with the reports and queries on a diskette using a filename consisting of the initials of your first and last names followed by the assignment number. Example: TC9-1.
12. Follow the directions from your instructor for turning in this assignment.

COMPUTER LABORATORY ASSIGNMENT 2
Queries and Reports

Purpose: To provide experience performing queries and defining and printing database reports.

Problem: Obtain information from the Computer Reference Library database created in Computer Laboratory Assignment 2 in Project 7 and maintained and updated in Computer Laboratory Assignment 2 in Project 8.

Instructions:

1. Open the database you created in Computer Laboratory Assignment 2 in Project 7 and maintained and updated in Computer Laboratory Assignment 2 in Project 8. If you do not have this updated database, your instructor will provide you with the database file.
2. Using a query, display all books in the database published by Hart and Timmons. Give the query a name of your choice. Print the List view of the database after the query.
3. Using a query, display all books of which the library has 3 or more copies. Give the query a name of your choice. Print the List view of the database after the query.
4. Display all books of which the library has fewer than 3 copies. Print the List view of the database after the query.
5. Using a query, display all books about integrated software packages published by WPS Publishers. Give the query a name of your choice. Print the List view of the database after the query.
6. Using a query, display all books written by either Adams or Krakowitz. Give the query a name of your choice. Print the List view of the database after the query.
7. Using a query, display all word processing and database books published in either 1992 or 1993. Give the query a name of your choice. Print the List view of the database after the query.
8. Using a query with the name of your choice, answer the following questions.
   a. What is the most expensive book in the library?
   b. How many copies of the book, *Learning Linker*, are there in the library?
   c. What book was acquired on December 19, 1994?
   d. What books did Krakowitz write?
9. Create a report listing all books in the Computer Reference Library. The report should contain the book name, author, publisher, and year published. The listing should be in ascending sequence by book name. Format the report in a manner similar to the report shown in Figure 9-36 on page W9.25. Name the report a name of your choice.
10. Create a report listing all books in the Computer Reference Library, the total number of books in the library and the total cost of all books in the library. The report should contain the publisher, book name, author, category, quantity, unit cost, and total cost. Format the report in a manner similar to the report shown in Figure 9-57 on page W9.38. Name the report a name of your choice.
11. Create a report listing the books in ascending sequence by publisher. The fields on this report should be the same as the fields in the report created in number 10 above except the publisher should not print on each Record line. For each publisher, print the number of books in the library. At the end of the report, print the total number of books in the library and the total cost of all books in the library. Format the report in a manner similar to the report shown in Figure 9-83 on page W9.55. Name the report a name of your choice.
12. Create a report listing the author and the number of different titles written by the author in the library. The report should be in alphabetic sequence by author. At the end of the report, print the total number of different titles in the library. Format the report in a manner you think is appropriate. Name the report a name of your choice.
13. Save the database with the reports on a diskette using a filename consisting of the initials of your first and last names followed by the assignment number. Example: TC9-2.
14. Follow the directions from your instructor for turning in this assignment.

COMPUTER LABORATORY ASSIGNMENT 3
Queries and Reports

Purpose: To provide experience performing queries and defining and printing database reports.

Problem: Obtain information from the Computer Club Membership Roster database created in Computer Laboratory Assignment 3 in Project 7 and maintained and updated in Computer Laboratory Assignment 3 in Project 8.

Instructions:

1. Open the database you created in Computer Laboratory Assignment 3 in Project 7 and maintained and updated in Computer Laboratory Assignment 3 in Project 8. If you do not have this updated data-base, your instructor will provide you with the database file.
2. Using a query, display all the associate members. Give the query a name of your choice. Print the List view of the database after the query.
3. Using a query, display all the members who are taking five or more computer units. Give the query a name of your choice. Print the List view of the database after the query.
4. Display all the members who are taking less than five computer units. Print the List view of the data-base after the query.
5. Using a query, display all the regular members who are business majors. Give the query a name of your choice. Print the List view of the database after the query.
6. Using a query, display all junior and senior members of the Computer Club. Give the query a name of your choice. Print the List view of the database after the query.
7. Using a query, display all the freshman or sophomore members who are either business or computer science majors. Give the query a name of your choice. Print the List view of the database after the query.
8. Using a query with the name of your choice, answer the following questions.
   a. Which students live in Anaheim, California?
   b. Which student joined the club on September 20, 1994?
   c. Which students are paying more than $25.00 in dues?
   d. Which regular member is a freshman majoring in computer science?
9. Create a report listing all members of the Computer Club. The report should contain first name, mid-dle initial, last name, address, city, state, and zip code. The report should be in alphabetic sequence by last name. Format the report in a manner similar to the report shown in Figure 9-36 on page W9.25. Name the report a name of your choice.
10. Create a report listing all members of the Computer Club, the total number of members of the club, and the total dues paid by club members. The report should contain date joined, first name, middle initial, last name, major, membership, class, and dues. Format the report in a manner similar to the report shown in Figure 9-57 on page W9.38. Name the report a name of your choice.
11. Create a report listing the members in alphabetic sequence within major. The fields on this report should be the same as the fields in the report created in number 10 above except the major should not print on each Record line. For each major, print the number of members in that major and the total dues paid by everyone in that major. At the end of the report, print the total members in all majors and the total dues paid by all members. Format the report in a manner similar to the report shown in Figure 9-83 on page W9.55. Name the report a name of your choice.
12. Create a report listing majors within class. For each major, print the number of members in that major. For each class, print the number of members in that class. At the end of the report, print the total number of members in the club. Format the report in a manner you think is appropriate. Name the report a name of your choice.
13. Save the database with the reports on a diskette using a filename consisting of the initials of your first and last names followed by the assignment number. Example: TC9-3.
14. Follow the directions from your instructor for turning in this assignment.

COMPUTER LABORATORY ASSIGNMENT 4
Queries and Reports

Purpose: To provide experience performing queries and defining and printing database reports.

Problem: Obtain information from the Music database created in Computer Laboratory Assignment 4 in Project 7 and maintained and updated in Computer Laboratory Assignment 4 in Project 8.

Instructions:

1. Open the database you created in Computer Laboratory Assignment 4 in Project 7 and maintained and updated in Computer Laboratory Assignment 4 in Project 8.
2. You have been asked by your music professor to provide information about your cassette and CD collection. In order to provide as complete a picture of your collection as possible, design six different queries which would answer most of the questions someone might have about your collection. For each query, run the query and then print the List view of the database.
3. To further present your collection, design and print five different reports that most accurately provide information to someone wanting to know everything about your collection.
4. Follow the directions from your instructor for turning in this assignment.

▼

INTEGRATING THE MICROSOFT WORKS TOOLS

▼

INTEGRATING THE MICROSOFT WORKS TOOLS

OBJECTIVES You will have mastered the material in this project when you can:

▶ Create a letterhead template
▶ Open multiple document windows
▶ Use the Special Character command from the Insert menu
▶ Insert *longdate* in a word processing document
▶ Use the Database Field command from the Insert menu
▶ Insert database placeholders in a document
▶ Set tab stops for a table
▶ Use the Border command from the Format menu
▶ Outline a paragraph using the Border command
▶ Insert a linked chart in a word processing document

▶ Reduce the size of a chart in a word processing document
▶ Use the Picture/Object command from the Format menu
▶ Switch among open documents
▶ Use drag and drop to link a spreadsheet into a word processing document
▶ Use the Print command from the File menu to print form letters
▶ Print form letters using names and addresses from a database
▶ Print labels
▶ Print envelopes

▶ INTRODUCTION TO INTEGRATED SOFTWARE APPLICATIONS

I n Projects 1 through 9 you used the Microsoft Works Word Processor, Spreadsheet, and Database tools. In addition, you inserted clip art into a document and graphically illustrated spreadsheet data using the charting capabilities of the Spreadsheet tool.

In business applications you will often find it helpful to use information created by one of the Works tools in another Works application. For example, you might want to include a spreadsheet or a chart created by the Works Spreadsheet tool in a letter created by the Works Word Processor tool, or you might want to use the name and address fields in a database created using the Works Database tool to assist in creating form letters which you are going to send to a number of individuals. These tasks can be accomplished using Microsoft Works for Windows because Works is an integrated software package that allows the various software tools to be used together to solve business problems.

Within any of the three Works tools, you can cut and paste or copy and paste data from one application to another. Between the spreadsheet and the word processor you can use a special command that lets you create a link between a spreadsheet, its chart, and a word processing document so that when a change is made in the spreadsheet, information from the spreadsheet contained in the word processing document is updated. You can also drag a chart or spreadsheet to the word processing document and link them. This is called **Object Linking and Embedding (OLE)**. Project 10 illustrates these techniques.

▶ PROJECT TEN

I n Project 10 you are to send a form letter to selected members of the Global Investments investment club. Figure 10-1 contains the form letter.

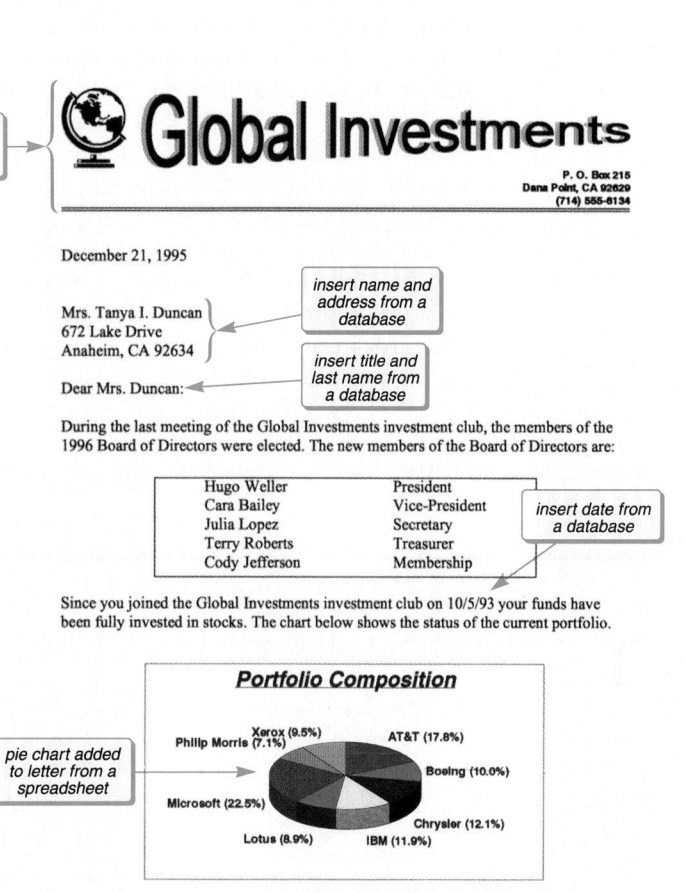

FIGURE 10-1

The letter is printed using a template created in the Works Word Processor using WordArt from the investor database form. The name and address in the inside address of the letter is obtained from the database of members of the investment club originally developed in Project 7 and later modified in Project 8. You will also use the names and addresses in the database to prepare mailing labels. The title and last name in the salutation of the letter is from the database. The date an individual joined the investment club, contained in each record in the database, appears in the second paragraph of the letter. Each form letter contains a 3-D Pie chart showing the percentage of funds the investment club has invested in various stocks. Each form letter also contains a spreadsheet which presents detailed information about the stocks. The chart and spreadsheet are those explained in Project 5 of this book. The database, spreadsheet, and pie chart used to produce the form letter are illustrated in Figure 10-2.

Database - PROJ8.WDB

DATE	TITLE	FIRST NAME	M.I.	LAST NAME	ADDRESS	CITY	STATE	ZIP	OCCUPATION	FUND NAME	SHARES	SHARE PRICE	INVESTMENT
10/5/93	Mrs.	Tanya	I.	Ducan	672 Lake Drive	Anaheim	CA	92634	Teacher	Growth	1,000	$11.00	$11,000.00
10/6/93	Dr.	Cara	L.	Bailey	303 Sunrise Place	Irvine	CA	92628	Doctor	Growth	2,500	$11.00	$27,500.00
10/7/93	Ms.	Jane	R.	Walters	1545 Elm Street	Fullerton	CA	92633	Teacher	Fixed Income	600	$18.00	$10,800.00
10/9/93	Mrs.	Hillary	P.	Fine	3233 Yule Drive	Irvine	CA	92754	Teacher	Fixed Income	200	$18.00	$3,600.00
10/15/93	Dr.	Julia	W.	Lopez	12732 Clover Road	Fullerton	CA	92633	Doctor	Options	1,200	$23.00	$27,600.00
10/18/93	Ms.	Rebecca	O.	Tiong	87 Green Street	Olympia	WA	98506	Attorney	Options	1,000	$23.00	$23,000.00
10/31/93	Mr.	Thomas	D.	Henkle	1832 Yermo Place	Cerritos	CA	90701	Teacher	Growth	400	$11.00	$4,400.00
11/12/93	Mrs.	Lilla	V.	Wilson	212 Tourny Street	Bellevue	WA	98005	Accountant	Fixed Income	400	$18.00	$7,200.00
11/13/93	Dr.	Hugo	A.	Weller	16 Burnside	Seattle	WA	98109	Doctor	Commodities	1,500	$15.00	$22,500.00
11/21/93	Miss.	Linda	C.	Cendajas	10 Park Avenue	Yorba	CA	92686	Accountant	Growth	800	$11.00	$8,800.00
11/30/93	Mr.	Steven	U.	Smoldery	360 Old Mill Road	Chino	CA	92981	Attorney	Options	1,400	$23.00	$32,200.00
12/3/93	Dr.	Terry	S.	Roberts	7655 Yale Drive	Seattle	WA	98103	Teacher	Growth	600	$11.00	$6,600.00
12/6/93	Mr.	Cody	W.	Jefferson	142 Brookside Way	Fullerton	CA	92633	Attorney	Growth	700	$11.00	$7,700.00
12/7/93	Mr.	Tae	Y.	Nguyen	2396 Rock Drive	Yorba	CA	92686	Accountant	Growth	400	$11.00	$4,400.00
12/14/93	Mr.	Eugene	Q.	McMurray	12 Carlyle Avenue	Tustin	CA	92742	Attorney	Options	2,000	$38.00	$76,000.00
12/17/93	Ms.	Juile	L.	Zigasier	1427 Soccer Road	Trent	CA	92544	Doctor	Growth	1,000	$23.00	$23,000.00

Spreadsheet - PROJ5.WKS

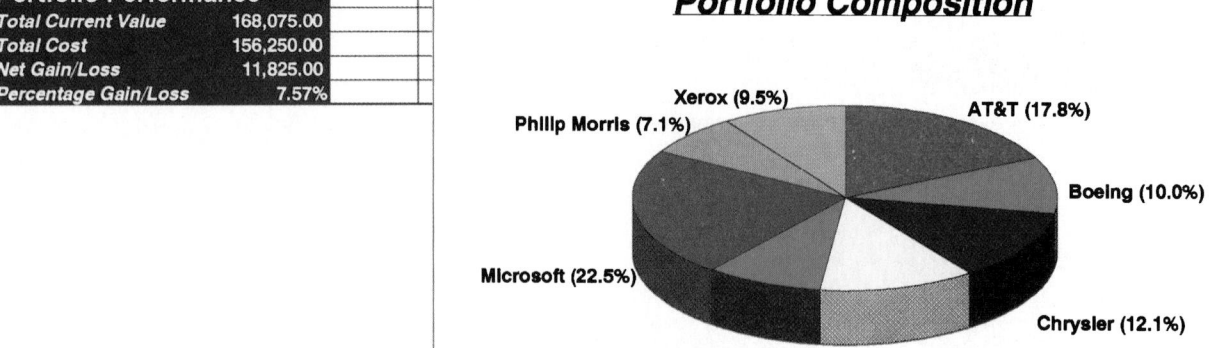

Chart - PROJ5.WKS

FIGURE 10-2

All individuals who invested in the Growth fund are to receive the letter.
Works will generate one letter for each such person in the database, as shown in
Figure 10-3.

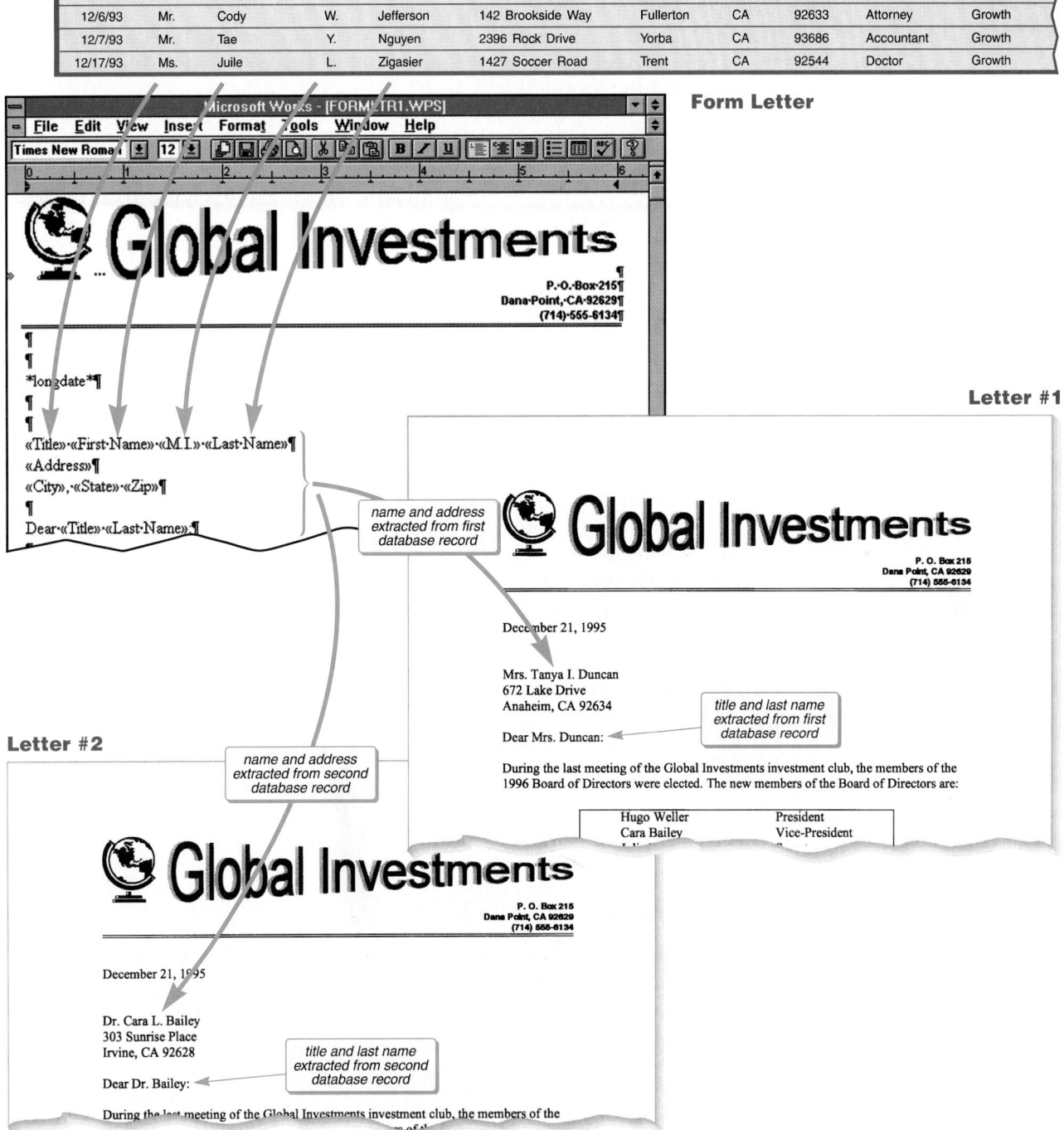

FIGURE 10-3

The form letter you create contains a **placeholder** for the Title, First Name, Middle Initial, Last Name, and so forth. A placeholder is the name of a database field surrounded by chevron marks (<< >>). When you print a letter, placeholders in the letter are replaced by the actual data contained in the database.

When you print the form letter, Works creates a separate letter for each record in the database that contains the word Growth in the Fund Name field. Thus, the first letter printed is addressed to Mrs. Tanya I. Duncan because her record is the first record in the database that contains the word Growth in the Fund Name field (see Figure 10-3 on the previous page). The second letter printed is to Dr. Cara L. Bailey because her record is the second record in the database that contains the word Growth in the Fund Name field.

After printing the form letters, you will also print a mailing label for each of the people who will receive a letter. You create the mailing labels using a process similar to creating the form letter.

General Steps to Prepare the Form Letters

The general steps to prepare the form letter illustrated in Figure 10-1 on page W10.3 are explained below.

1. Start Works.
2. Create the Global Investments letterhead template.
3. Open the PROJ8.WDB database file.
4. Open the PROJ5.WKS spreadsheet file.
5. Open a word processing document using the Global Investments letterhead template.
6. Enter a special character code in the letter to cause the current date to print in each letter.
7. Insert the placeholders of the fields from the database you will use for the inside address in the letter. When you print the letters, Works will replace these placeholders with the actual data from the database.
8. Type the salutation (Dear) and insert the Title field placeholder and Last Name field placeholder in the letter.
9. Type the body of the letter. Insert the Date field placeholder in the second paragraph.
10. Insert the pie chart and spreadsheet in the letter.
11. Save the letter on disk.
12. Print the form letters.
13. Create and print mailing labels for the form letters.
14. Exit Works.

The following pages contain a detailed explanation of each of these steps.

▶ STARTING WORKS AND OPENING FILES

 ou must first start Works to create the form letters. To start Works, complete the following steps.

TO START WORKS

Step 1: With the Microsoft Works for Windows group window open, double-click the Microsoft Works program-item icon.

Step 2: If necessary, choose the Start Works Now button.

Step 3: When the Startup dialog box displays, choose the Word Processor
button.
Step 4: If necessary, maximize the application window.
Step 5: Maximize the Word1 document window.

Creating the Letterhead Template

To prepare the form letter, you will first create the Global Investments letterhead template using methods shown in previous projects. Once the letterhead
template is created, it can be used for many letters. To create the letterhead template, complete the following steps (see Figure 10-4).

TO CREATE A LETTERHEAD TEMPLATE

Step 1: Select the Insert
menu and choose the
ClipArt command.
Step 2: Select the Globe clip
art in the chart of clip
art drawings and
choose the
OK button in
the Microsoft ClipArt
Gallery dialog box.
Step 3: Highlight the Globe
clip art, select the For-
mat menu, and
choose the Picture/Object command.

FIGURE 10-4

Step 4: Type 45 in the Width text box and 45 in the Height text box of the
Picture/Object dialog box. Choose the OK button in the
Picture/Object dialog box.
Step 5: Click to the right of the clip art object and press the SPACEBAR three
times.
Step 6: Select the File menu, choose the Open Existing File command, select
drive A if necessary, highlight the PROJ8.WDB filename in the File
Name list box, and choose the OK button in the Open dialog box.
You must open the database file because information from the data-
base form heading is used in the letterhead template.
Step 7: Display the database in Form view. Highlight the object containing the
words Global Investments and click the Copy button on the Toolbar.
Step 8: Select the Window menu. Choose Word1.
Step 9: Click the Paste button on the Toolbar. The Global Investments
WordArt displays in the word processing document.
Step 10: Position the insertion point following the Global Investments object.
Press the ENTER key and click the Right Align button on the Toolbar.
Step 11: Select 8 point Arial font. Click the Bold button on the Toolbar. Type
P. O. Box 215 and press the ENTER key. Type Dana Point, CA
92629 and press the ENTER key. Type (714) 555-6134 and press the
ENTER key. Click the Bold button on the Toolbar.
Step 12: Click the Left Align button on the Toolbar. Press the LEFT ARROW key.

Step 13: Select the Format menu and choose the Border command. Select the Bottom check box in the Border area of the Border dialog box and select the Double option button in the Line Style area. Choose the OK button in the Border dialog box.

Step 14: Position the mouse pointer following the border. Select 12 point Times New Roman font.

Step 15: Select the File menu, choose the Save As command, choose the Template button in the Save As dialog box, type `lethd1` in the Template Name text box, and choose the OK button in the Save As Template dialog box.

Step 16: Select the File menu and close the Word1 document. Do not save changes.

The PROJ8.WDB database displays in Form view. The LETHD1 template shown in Figure 10-4 on the previous page has been created and saved.

Opening the Spreadsheet File

The database file has been opened but before you can create the form letter, both the database file and the spreadsheet file must be open. To open the PROJ5.WKS spreadsheet file, perform the following steps (see Figure 10-5).

FIGURE 10-5

TO OPEN THE SPREADSHEET FILE

Step 1: Select the File menu and choose the Open Existing File command.

Step 2: Select drive A if necessary, highlight the PROJ5.WKS filename in the File Name list box, and choose the OK button in the Open dialog box.

The PROJ5.WKS spreadsheet file displays on the screen as shown in Figure 10-5.

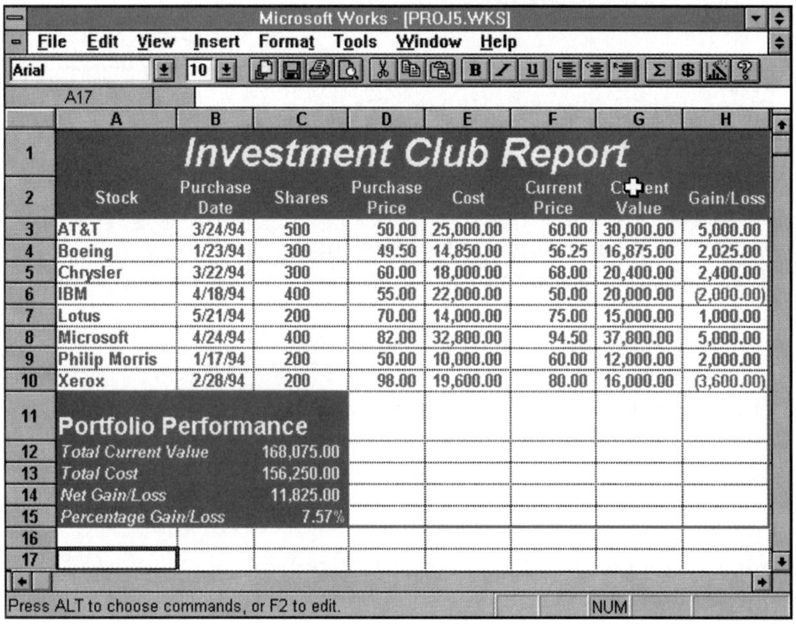

Opening the Word Processor

The form letter is prepared using the Word Processor tool of Microsoft Works. Therefore, the Word Processor must be opened, but in this application it will be opened by calling in the LETHD1 template you created earlier in this project. To open the Word Processor and use a template, complete the following steps (see Figure 10-6).

TO OPEN A WORD PROCESSOR TEMPLATE

Step 1: Click the Startup Dialog button on the Toolbar.

Step 2: Choose the Use A Template button in the Startup dialog box.

Step 3: Display the Custom template group.

Step 4: Select the LETHD1 template in the Choose a template list box.

Step 5: Choose the OK button in the Startup dialog box.

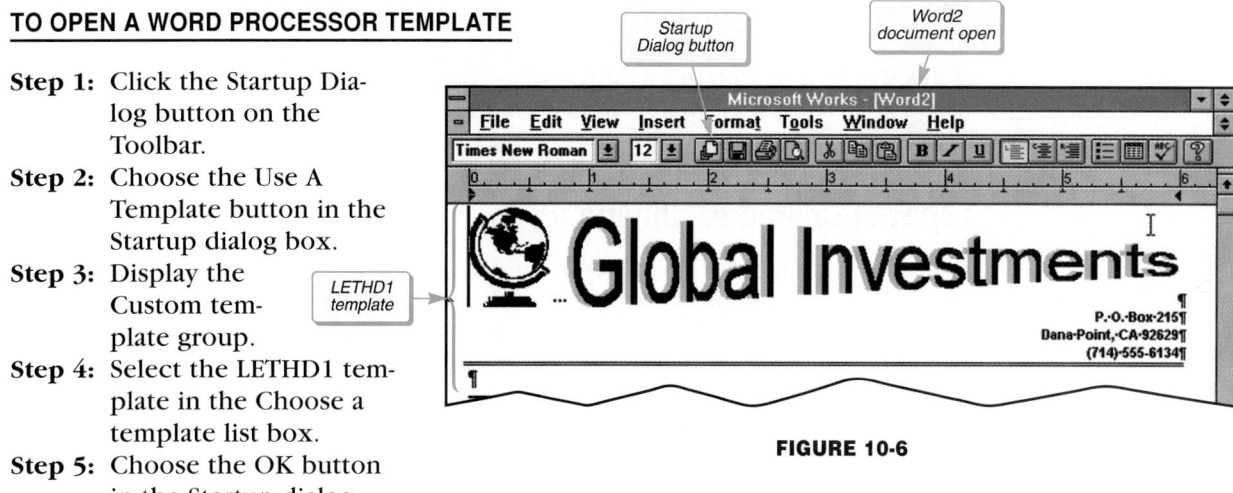

FIGURE 10-6

The LETHD1 template displays on the screen as part of the Word2 word processing document (Figure 10-6).

When you open the letterhead file, three documents are open - the word processor document (Word2), the spreadsheet document (PROJ5.WKS), and the database document (PROJ8.WDB). To display all three open documents at the same time, complete the following steps (see Figure 10-7).

TO DISPLAY MULTIPLE OPEN DOCUMENTS

Step 1: Select the Window menu.

Step 2: Choose the Tile command from the Window menu.

Each of the open documents displays alongside one another when the windows are tiled. The Word2 document is the active document as indicated by the green title bar. If you want to make another document the active document, click anywhere within the document window or, from the Window menu, choose the document name.

You can also display multiple open documents on top of one another by choosing the Cascade command from the Window menu.

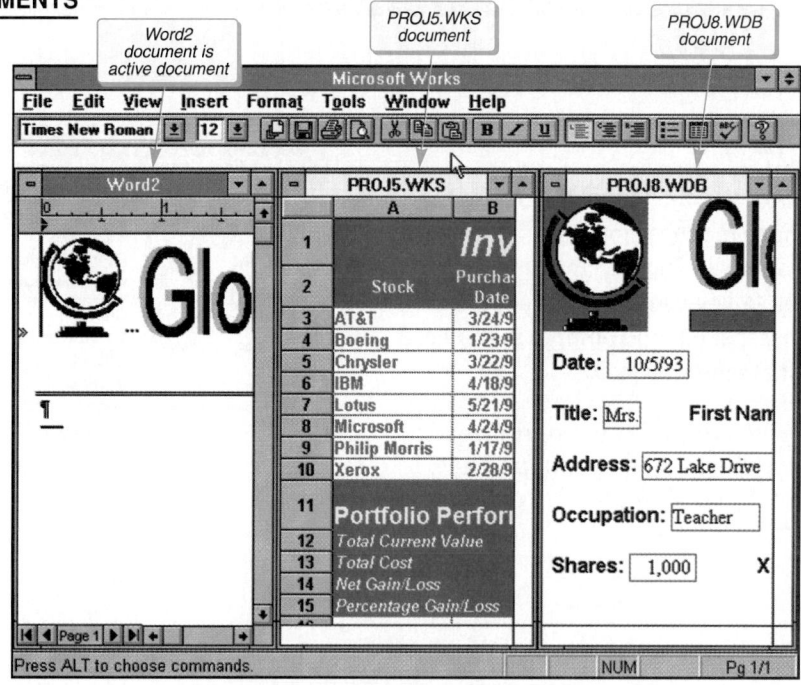

FIGURE 10-7

▶ CREATING THE FORM LETTER

 he first step in creating the form letter is to insert the current date using the Special Character command.

Special Character Command

In previous projects you entered the date in a document by typing the current date. You can also cause the current date to display or print in a document by using the Works Special Character command from the Insert menu.

The **Special Character command** inserts a code in the document that causes specific information associated with the code to appear when you print the document. For example, one of the Works special character codes is **longdate**. When you place the characters *longdate* in a document through the use of the Special Character command, and you print the document, the current date will print in the long format (for example, December 21, 1995). The current date is stored in the computer as part of the operating system. This technique is valuable if you are going to create form letters but are not certain of the exact date on which you will print the letters. No matter what day you print, the letter will contain the current date.

In this project *longdate* is used in the letter to print the date. To enter the special character *longdate* in the letter, perform the following steps.

TO ENTER THE DATE USING THE SPECIAL CHARACTER COMMAND ▼

STEP 1 ▶

Maximize the Word2 document. Place the insertion point below the double line border and press the ENTER key two times. Select the Insert menu and point to the Special Character command.

*Works displays the **Insert menu** and the mouse pointer points to the Special Character command (Figure 10-8).*

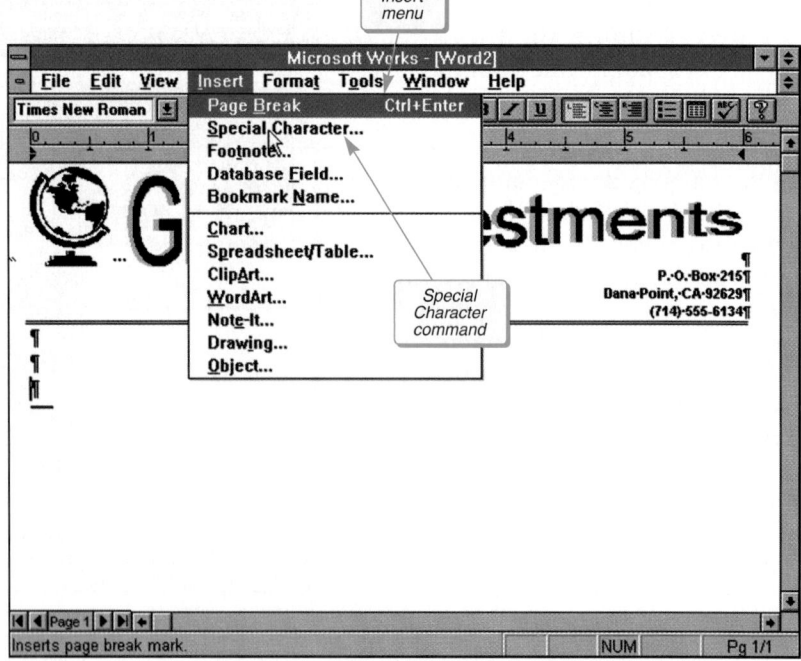

FIGURE 10-8

STEP 2 ▶

Choose the Special Character command from the Insert menu. When the Special Character dialog box displays, select the Print long date option button and then point to the OK button.

Works displays the Special Character dialog box (Figure 10-9). The Print long date option button is selected and the mouse pointer points to the OK button.

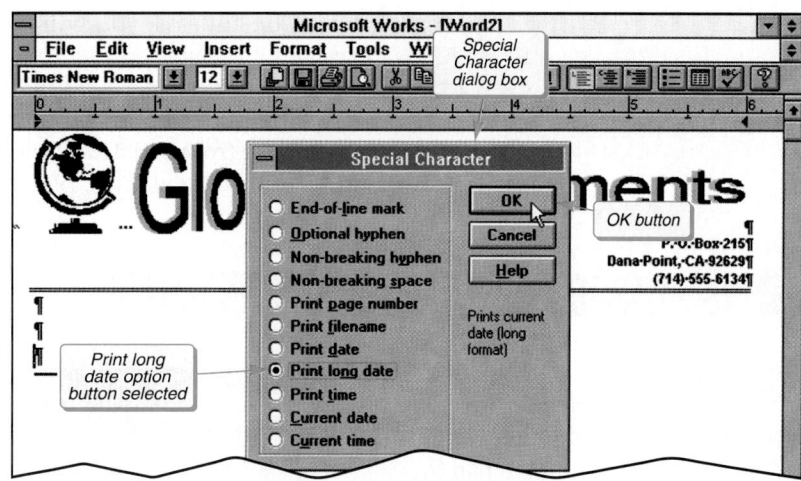

FIGURE 10-9

STEP 3 ▶

Choose the OK button in the Special Character dialog box.

Works inserts the *longdate* code into the letter (Figure 10-10). When you print the document, Works replaces *longdate* with the current date.

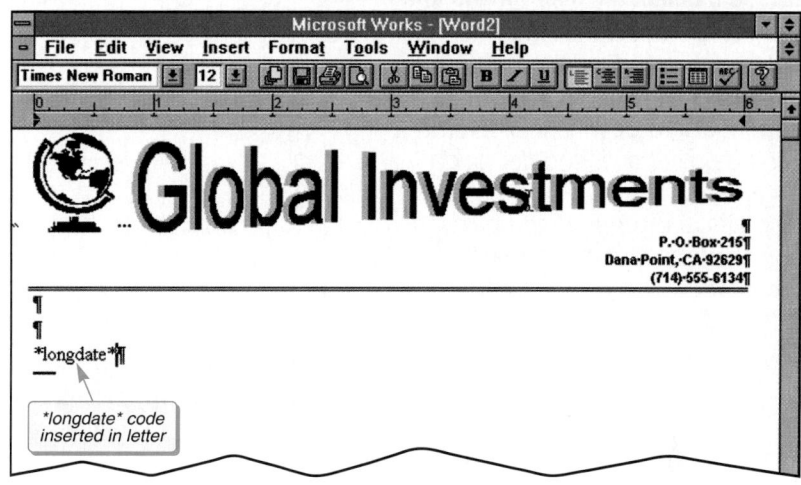

FIGURE10-10

The Special Character dialog box shown in Figure 10-9 offers two other styles in which to print the date. The Print date option will insert the *date* code in the document and print the date in the short format (for example, 12/21/95). The Current date option places the current date in the document as a fixed date. This option does not allow the date to change as the date on which the document is printed changes.

The Special Character dialog box provides other options as well. For a detailed explanation of these options, select Works online Help .

Entering the Inside Address

The next step is to enter the inside address of the letter, which contains the name and address of the individual to whom the letter will be sent. In this project, you are sending the same letter to many individuals. The names and addresses of the people who will receive the letter come from specific records in the PROJ8.WDB database (see Figure 10-3 on page W10.5).

To enter the inside address, you will use database placeholders, which are field names in the database surrounded by chevrons (<< >>). For example, <<Title>> is a placeholder for the Title field in the database. When Works prints a letter that contains the placeholder <<Title>>, it replaces the placeholder in the document with the data from the Title field in a record in the database. Perform the following steps to insert database placeholders in the form letter.

TO INSERT DATABASE PLACEHOLDERS IN A DOCUMENT ▼

STEP 1 ►

After inserting the *longdate* code, press the ENTER key three times to position the insertion point where you want to place the inside address. Select the Insert menu and point to the Database Field command.

*The insertion point is located three lines below the *longdate* code (Figure 10-11). The Insert menu displays and the mouse pointer points to the Database Field command.*

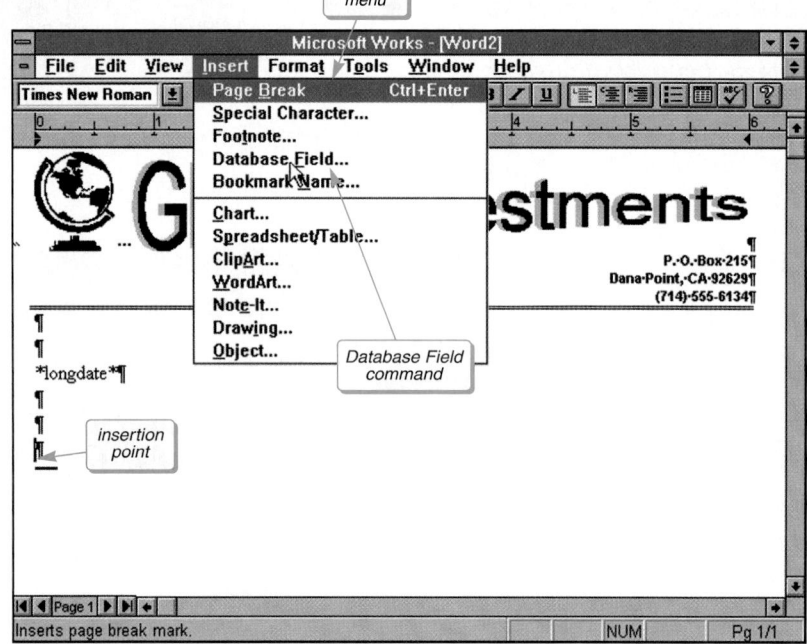

FIGURE 10-11

STEP 2 ►

Choose the Database Field command from the Insert menu. When the Insert Field dialog box displays, point to the Database button.

Works displays the Insert Field dialog box (Figure 10-12). The word None displays in the Current database box, indicating no database is currently being used for inserting fields. The mouse pointer points to the Database button.

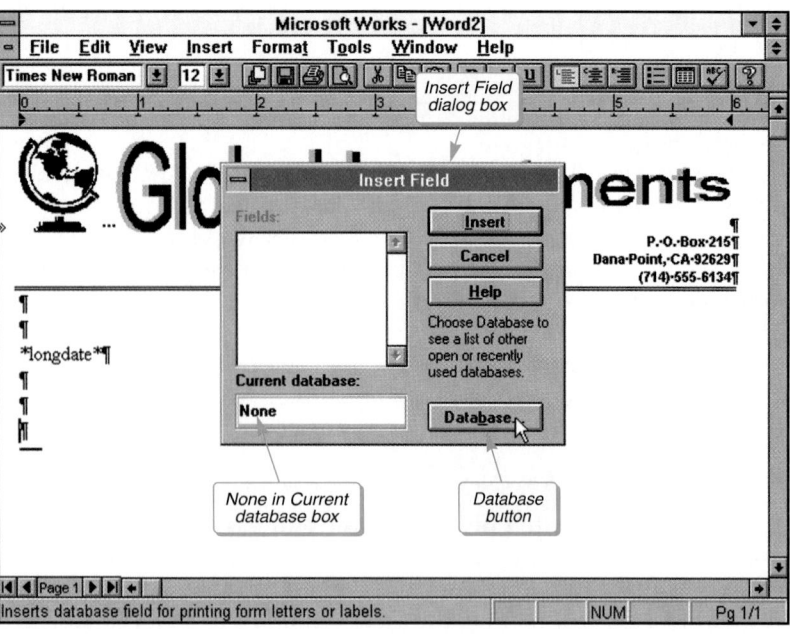

FIGURE 10-12

STEP 3 ▶

Choose the Database button in the Insert Field dialog box. When the Choose Database dialog box displays, highlight PROJ8.WDB in the Databases list box and point to the OK button.

Works displays the Choose Database dialog box (Figure 10-13). The PROJ8.WDB filename is highlighted and the mouse pointer points to the OK button. Notice in the Databases list box that two different icons display with the database names. The yellow storage drawer means the database is on disk and is not open. The rectangle with the blue top means the database is open.

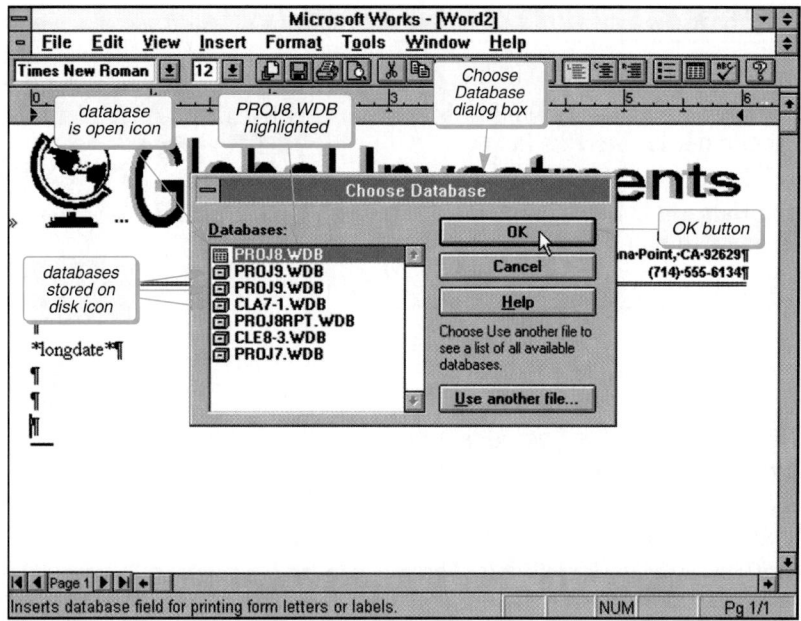

FIGURE 10-13

STEP 4 ▶

Choose the OK button in the Choose Database dialog box. When the Insert Field dialog box displays, select the Title field name in the Fields list box and point to the Insert button.

Works displays the Insert Field dialog box (Figure 10-14). Works displays the database name PROJ8.WDB in the Current database box because the PROJ8.WDB database was selected in Step 3. The field names in the PROJ8.WDB database display in the Fields list box. The Title field name is highlighted. The mouse pointer points to Insert button.

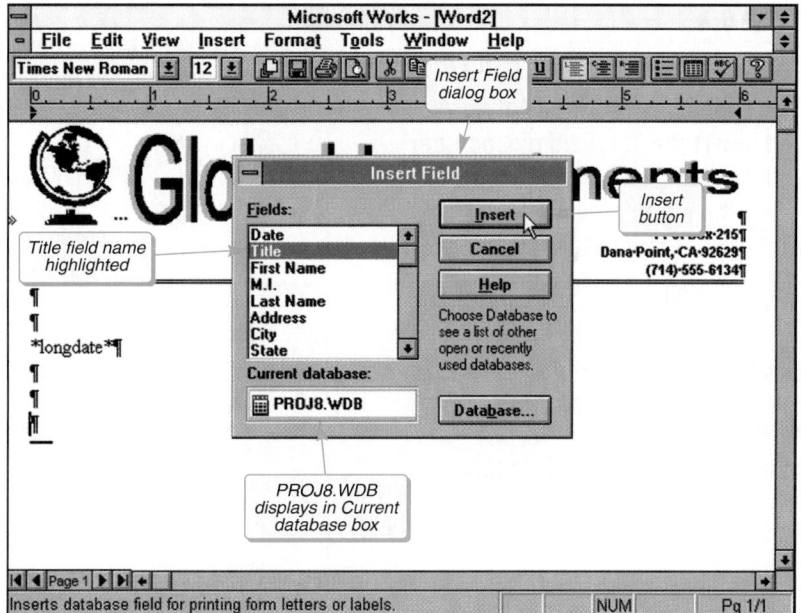

FIGURE 10-14

STEP 5 ▶

Choose the Insert button in the Insert Field dialog box to place the placeholder for the Title field (<<Title>>) in the letter. Select the First Name field name in the Fields list box and point to the Insert button.

Works places the Title field name enclosed in chevrons (<< >>) in the letter at the insertion point (Figure 10-15). The chevrons indicate the entry is a database placeholder and not regular text. The First Name field name in the Fields list box is highlighted. The mouse pointer points to the Insert button.

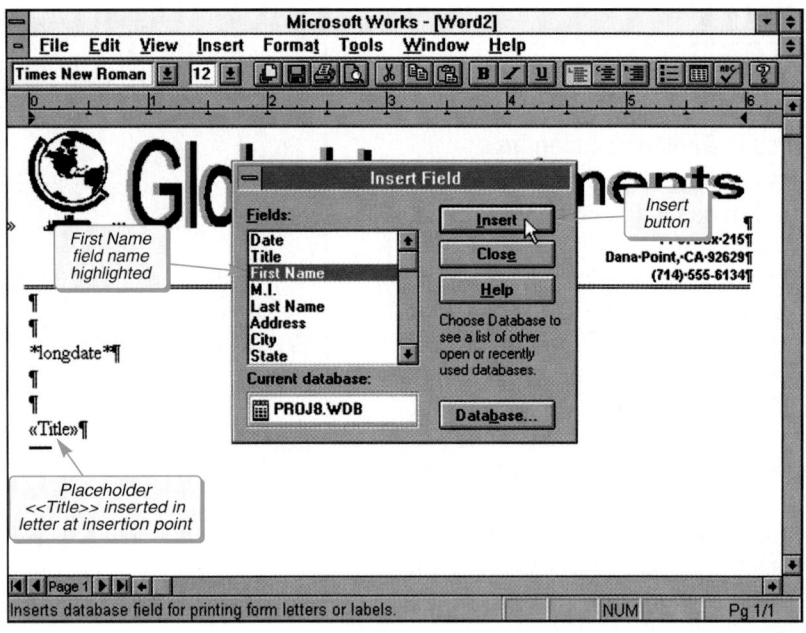

FIGURE 10-15

STEP 6 ▶

Choose the Insert button in the Insert Field dialog box. Highlight and insert the M.I. field placeholder and the Last Name field placeholder using the steps previously explained. Point to the Close button.

Works displays the placeholders for the Title, First Name, M.I. and Last Name fields in the letter and the mouse pointer points to the Close button (Figure 10-16). Notice that Works automatically places a single blank space between placeholders.

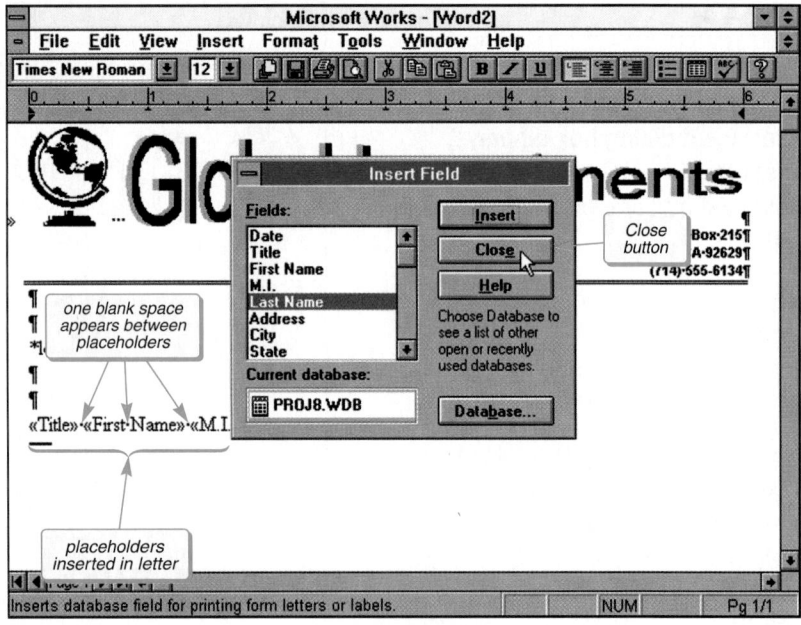

FIGURE 10-16

STEP 7 ▶

Choose the Close button from the Insert Field dialog box. Press the ENTER key.

Works removes the Insert Field dialog box from the screen (Figure 10-17). The insertion point is positioned on the second line of the inside address. You must close the Insert Field dialog box at the end of a line because you cannot press the ENTER key to move to the next line while the dialog box is open.

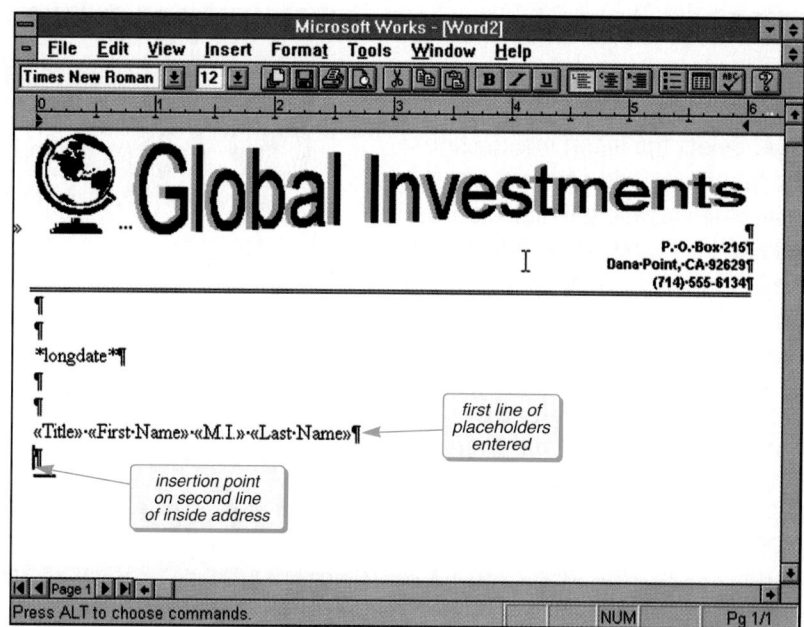

FIGURE 10-17

STEP 8 ▶

Select the Insert menu and choose the Database Field command. Continue inserting placeholders for the Address, City, State, and Zip fields using the techniques explained in the previous steps. To place a comma after the <<City>> placeholder, close the Insert Field dialog box, type a comma and a space. Select the Insert menu and choose the Database Field command to enter the placeholders for the State and Zip. After you enter the Zip placeholder, close the Insert Field dialog box.

Works inserts the placeholders for the inside address (Figure 10-18).

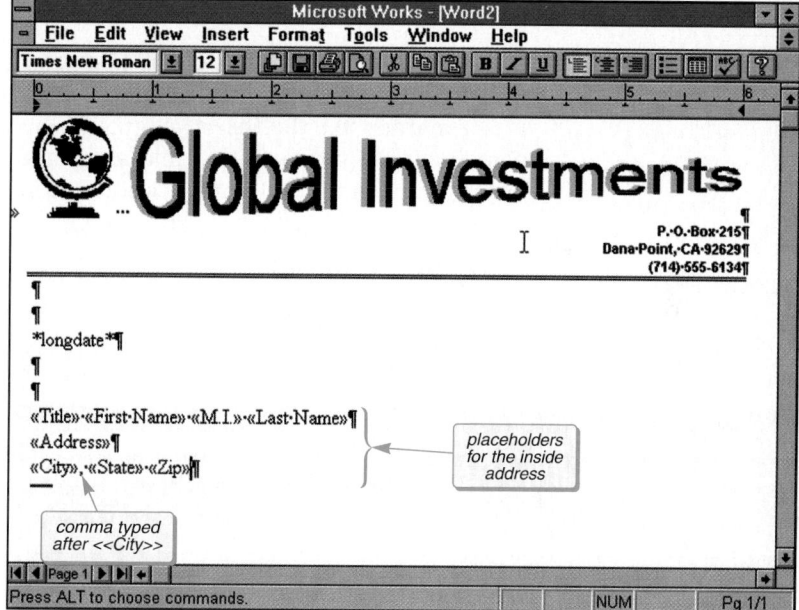

FIGURE 10-18

STEP 9 ▶

Press the ENTER key two times. Type `Dear` and press the SPACEBAR one time. Select the Insert menu, choose the Database Field command, and insert the placeholders for the Title field and the Last Name field. Close the Insert Field dialog box, type a colon (:), and press the ENTER key two times.

Works inserts the placeholders for the Title and Last Name (Figure 10-19). A colon displays following the Last Name placeholder.

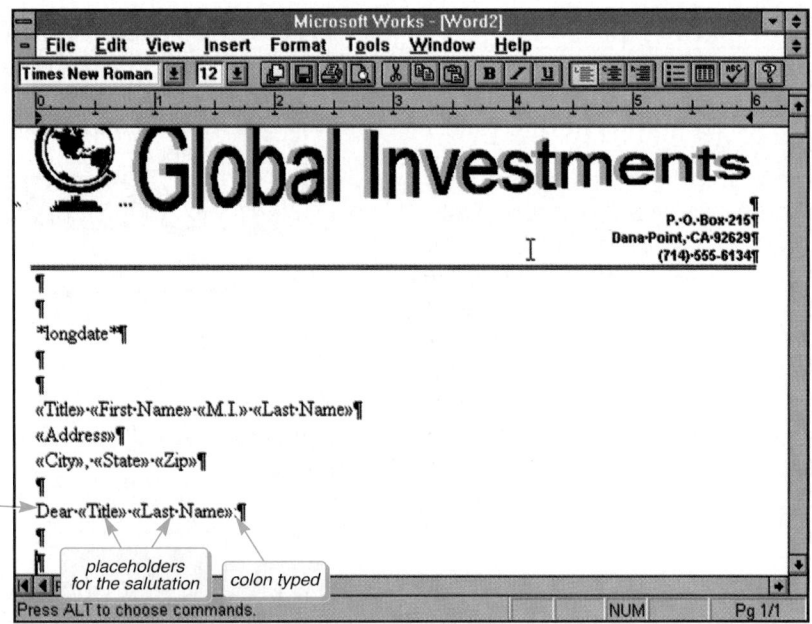

FIGURE 10-19

When using placeholders in a document you can type any text, spaces, or punctuation before or after the placeholders to produce the required output.

You must use the Insert menu and the Database Field command to insert a placeholder. If you type the field name and the chevrons yourself, Works will not insert the database field in the letter when it prints the letter.

Body of the Letter

The first paragraph of the body of the letter begins two lines below the salutation. To enter these lines, perform the following steps (see Figure 10-20).

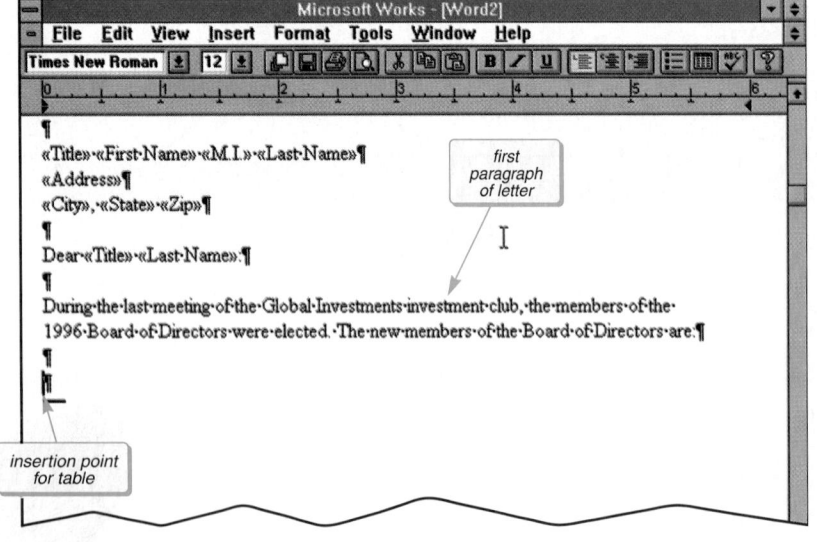

FIGURE 10-20

TO ENTER THE LETTER TEXT

Step 1: Type the first two lines of the letter.

Step 2: At the end of the second line, press the ENTER key two times.

Figure 10-20 illustrates the first paragraph of the letter. The first paragraph is followed by a table that lists the members of the Board of Directors for the Global Investments investment club in 1996.

Creating the Table

A **table** is a group of related columns in a document. In Project 3 you created a table using the Insert Spreadsheet/Table command from the Insert menu. Tables may also be created using the tab stops on the ruler. Tables created using tab stops should be relatively simple and not involve calculations within the table.

When you create a table, you must determine the general appearance of the table, how many columns you need, and the maximum width of each column in the table. The table you are to create in the letter is illustrated in Figure 10-21.

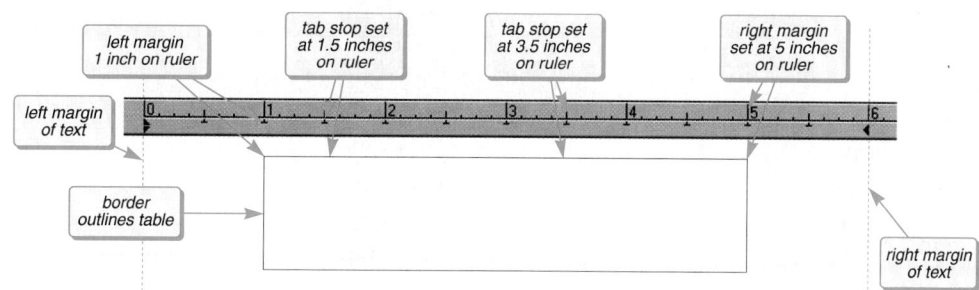

FIGURE 10-21

In the table in the form letter, a border outlines the table. The area set aside for the table is four inches wide. The left border line is one inch from the left margin. The names are indented one-half inch from the left border. A corresponding border on the right is one inch left of the right margin. Because the table is smaller than the six inch line used for text, you must change the left and right margins for the table area in the letter.

Setting Margins for the Table

To change the left and right margins in the table area of the letter, perform the following steps.

TO SET LEFT AND RIGHT MARGINS FOR THE TABLE ▼

STEP 1 ▶

Point to the left-margin indent marker on the ruler and drag both the left-margin indent marker and the first-line indent marker to the one-inch position.

The first-line indent marker and the left-margin indent marker are set at the one-inch mark on the ruler (Figure 10-22). Works also indents the paragraph mark and insertion point one inch.

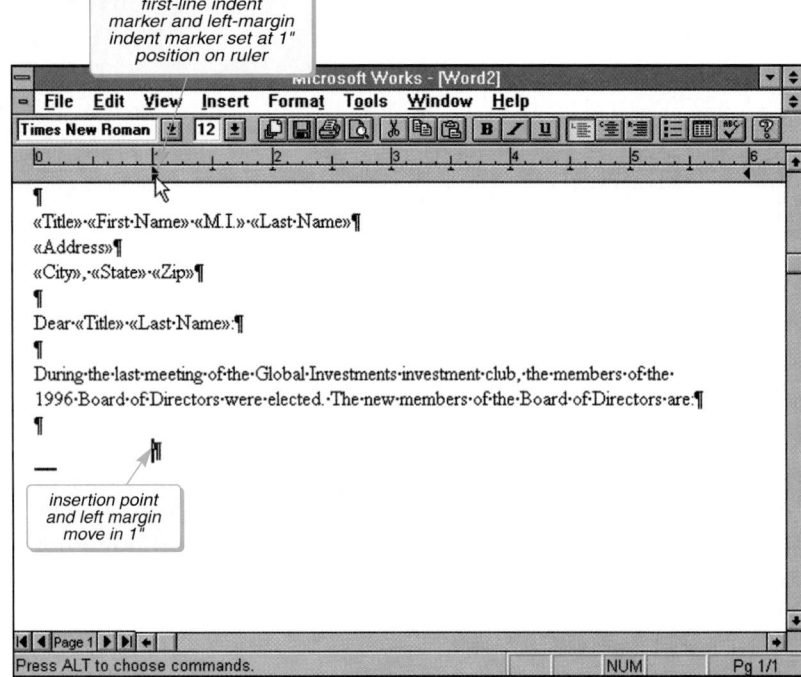

FIGURE 10-22

STEP 2 ▶

Point to the right-margin indent marker on the ruler and drag the right-margin indent marker to the five-inch position on the ruler.

The margins for the table are now set (Figure 10-23).

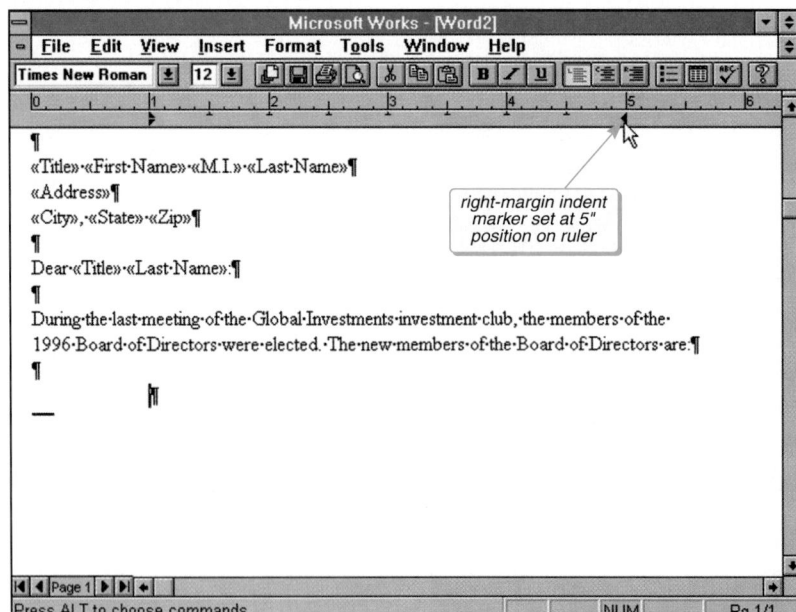

FIGURE 10-23

Setting Tab Stops

The next step is to set the required tab stops for the table. You use **tab stops** when you create tables so the columns in the table will be vertically aligned. You must use two left-aligned tab stops in the table in the form letter. Set these tab stops at the 1.5-inch position and the 3.5-inch position on the ruler by performing the following steps.

TO SET TAB STOPS ▼

STEP 1 ▶

Place the mouse pointer at the 1.5-inch position on the ruler and click the left mouse button. Then place the mouse pointer at the 3.5-inch position on the ruler and click the left mouse button.

Works displays a left-aligned tab stop at the 1.5-inch position on the ruler and at the 3.5-inch position on the ruler (Figure 10-24).

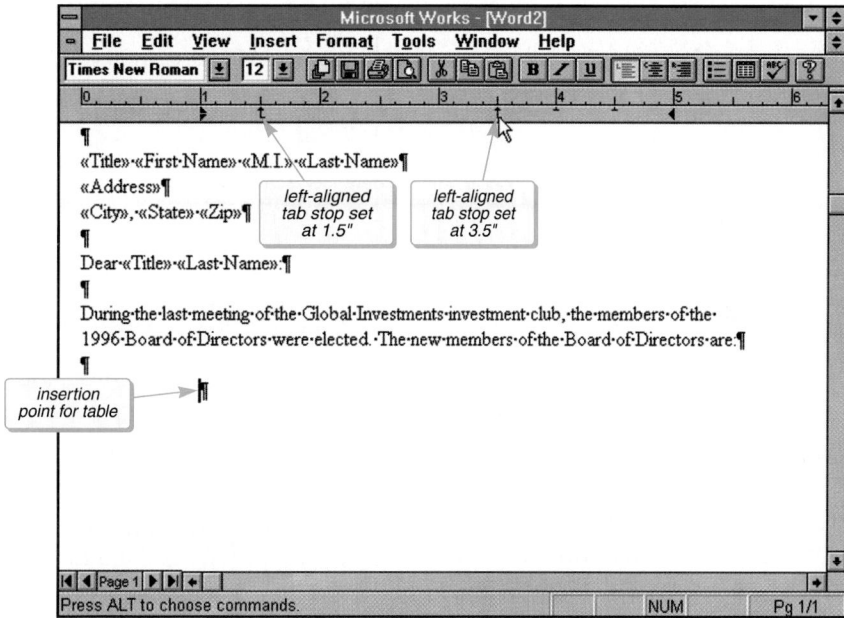

FIGURE 10-24

You can specify four types of tab stops when using the Works Word Processor. They are the left-aligned, right-aligned, center-aligned, and decimal-aligned tab stops. The **left-aligned tab stop** will cause text to print at the tab stop aligned to the left. This tab stop is commonly used when typing alphabetic information such as names. The **right-aligned tab stop** aligns data at the right margin set by the tab stop. The right-aligned tab stop is commonly used when typing numeric data. The **center-aligned tab stop** centers the typed characters beneath the tab stop position on the ruler. The **decimal-aligned tab stop** aligns numeric data on the decimal point in the number. Left-aligned tab stops are set by clicking the ruler. Other tab stops are set using the **Tabs command** from the Format menu and making appropriate entries in the Tabs dialog box.

Entering Text for the Table

The next step is to enter the names and titles of the newly elected members of the Board of Directors into the table. End each line in the table except the last line by holding down the SHIFT key while pressing the ENTER key. This allows the entire table to be treated by Works as a single paragraph. The steps on the next page illustrate how to enter text in the table.

TO ENTER TEXT IN A TABLE ▼

STEP 1 ▶

Ensure the insertion point is positioned at the beginning of the table. Press the TAB key. Type Hugo Weller.

The first entry in the table displays (Figure 10-25).

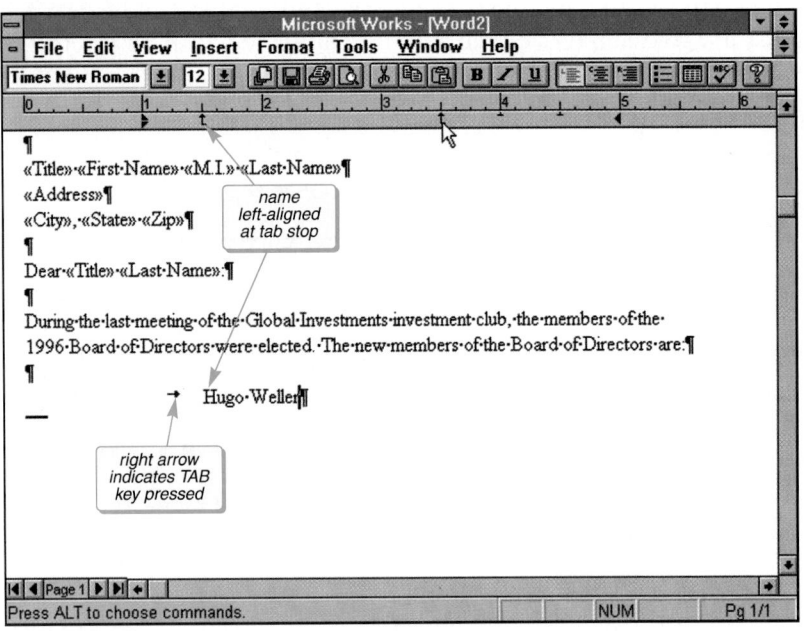

FIGURE 10-25

STEP 2 ▶

Press the TAB key again. Type President. **Hold down the SHIFT key and press the ENTER key to end the first line in the table.**

The first line of text displays in the table (Figure 10-26). The insertion point appears on the next line indented one inch from the zero position on the ruler. The end-of-line mark indicates the end of the line but not the end of the paragraph.

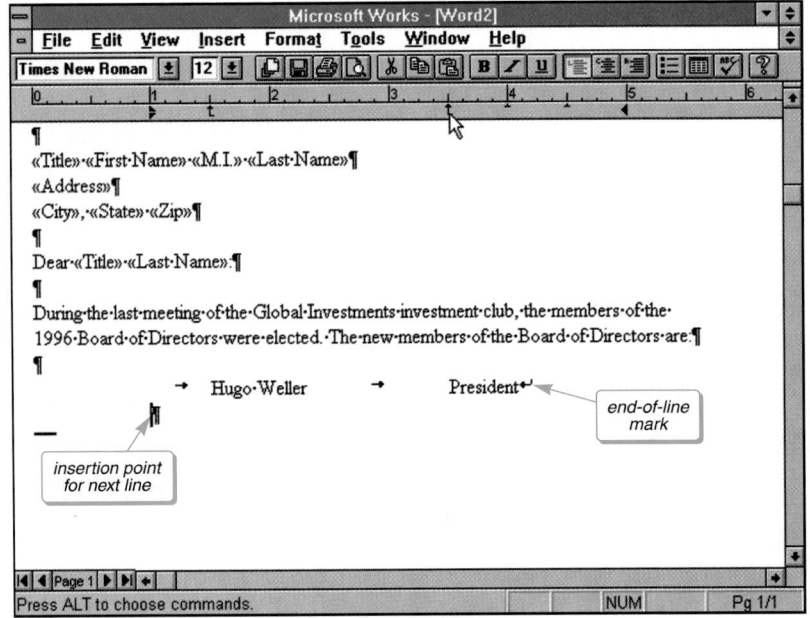

FIGURE 10-26

STEP 3 ▶

Press the TAB key and type the remaining names and titles. Press the TAB key at the beginning of each line in the table. Press the ENTER key at the end of the last line in the table.

The names and titles display left-aligned in the columns in the table (Figure 10-27).

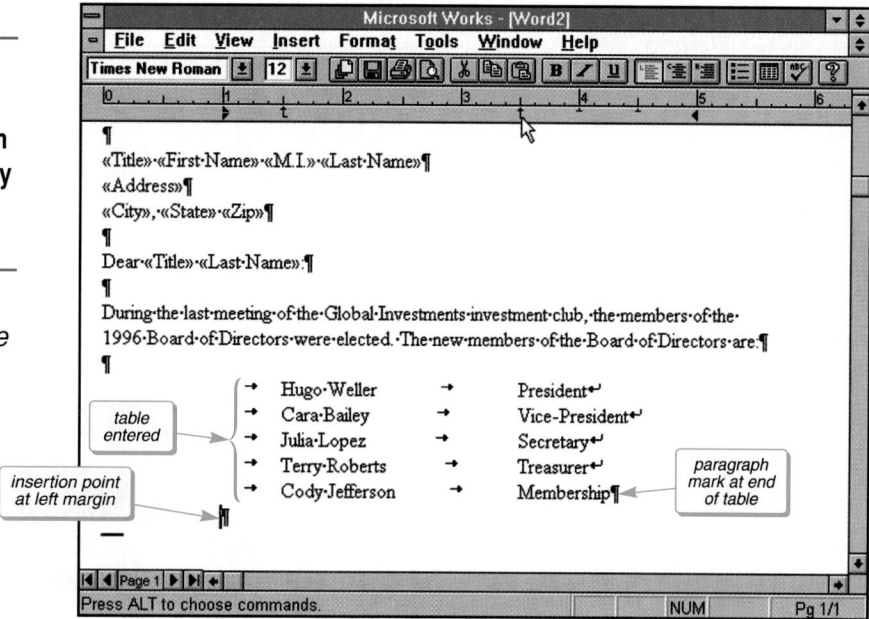

FIGURE 10-27

You use tables in applications that require data to be arranged in vertical columns. There can be two, three, or more columns in a table, and the columns in a table can use the left, right, center, or decimal-aligned tab stops or any combination of tab stops.

Creating a Border

Works allows you to add various types of borders to paragraphs. One or more paragraphs can be completely outlined or you can cause a border to display on only the top, bottom, left, or right of a paragraph by using options found in the Border dialog box associated with the **Border command** in the Format menu.

You can use three types of border line styles: normal, bold, or double. In the sample project, an outline border with a normal line style surrounds the table. Perform the steps on the next page to create a border around the table.

TO CREATE A BORDER ▼

STEP 1 ▶

Highlight the table by positioning the mouse in the left margin of the table and double-clicking.

Because Works considers the table to be a paragraph, double-clicking in the left margin highlights the entire table (Figure 10-28).

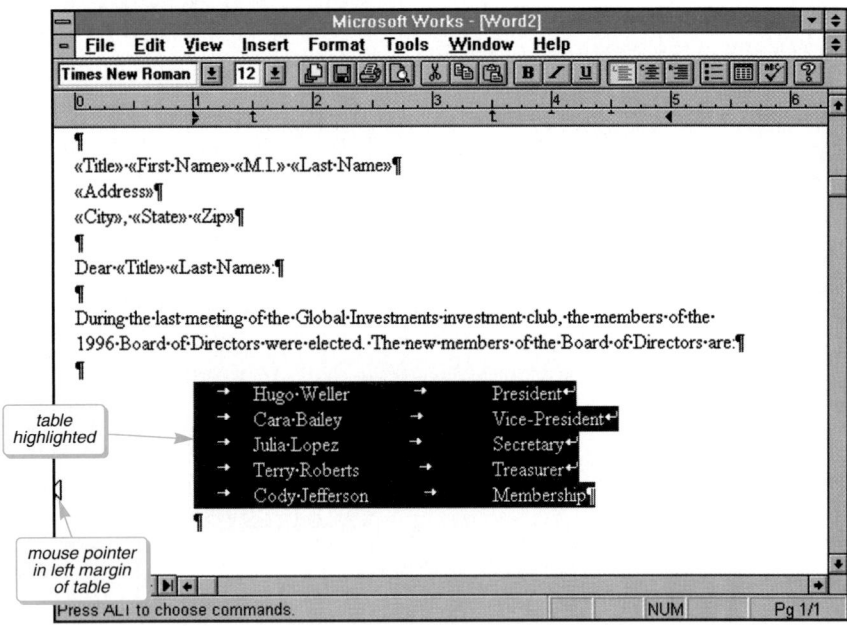

FIGURE 10-28

STEP 2 ▶

Select the Format menu and point to the Border command.

The Format menu displays and the mouse pointer points to the Border command (Figure 10-29).

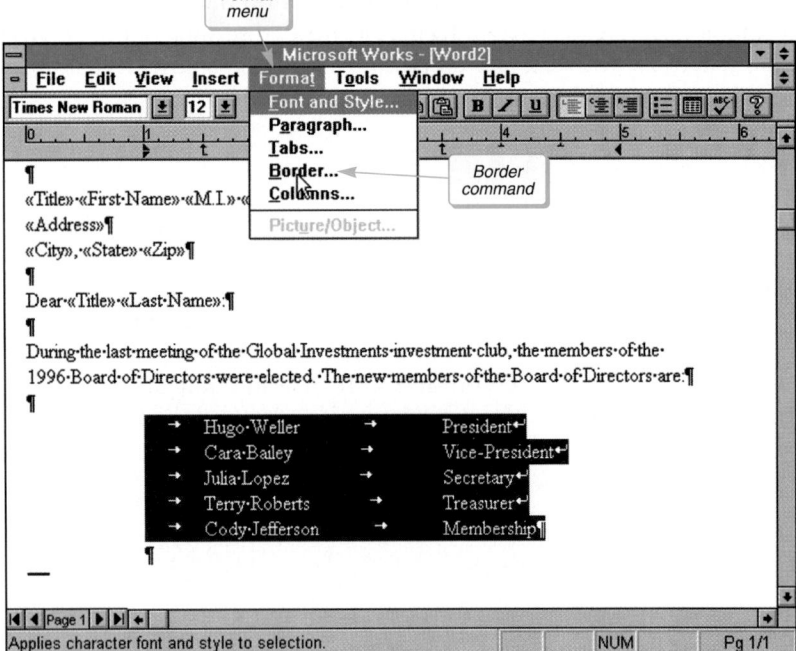

FIGURE 10-29

STEP 3 ▶

Choose the Border command from the Format menu. When the Border dialog box displays, select the Outline check box in the Border area. If necessary, select the Normal option button in the Line Style area. Point to the OK button.

The selections in the Border dialog box tell Works to place an outline with a normal line style around the highlighted paragraph (Figure 10-30). The mouse pointer points to the OK button.

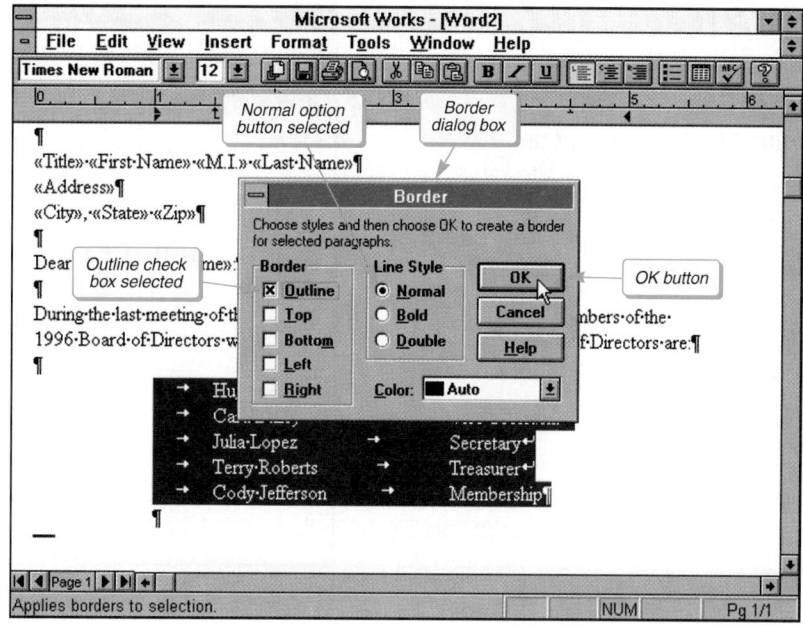

FIGURE 10-30

STEP 4 ▶

Choose the OK button in the Border dialog box. Position the insertion point in front of the paragraph mark outside the bottom left corner of the table.

Works places an outline border with a normal line around the table (Figure 10-31). The insertion point is located at the one-inch left margin.

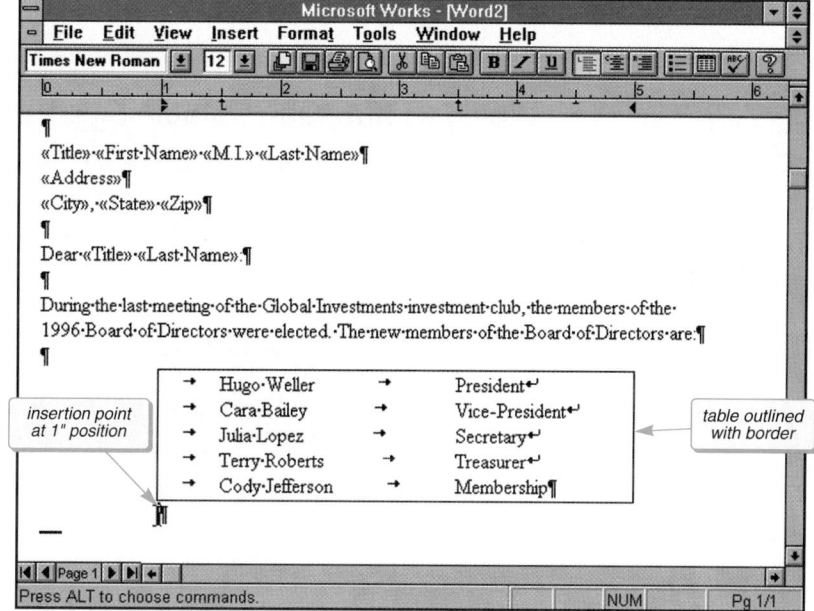

FIGURE 10-31

STEP 5 ►

Press the CTRL+Q keys to remove the paragraph formatting (margin and tab stops) associated with the table.

Works removes the paragraph formatting. The margin markers move to the zero position and the six-inch position on the ruler (Figure 10-32).

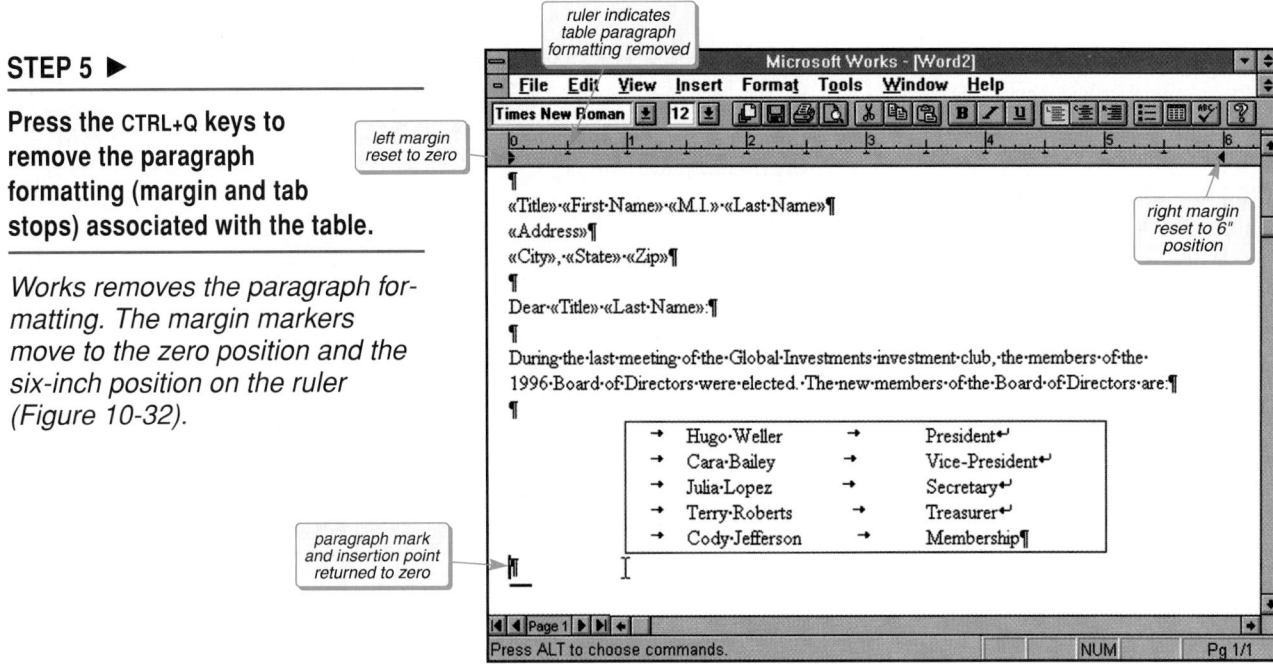

FIGURE 10-32

Typing a Paragraph Containing a Placeholder

In the next paragraph in the letter, the first sentence contains the words, Since you joined the Global Investments investment club on (Figure 10-33). This text is followed by the database placeholder <<Date>>, indicating the date from the database will be inserted in the text. Following the date placeholder is the remainder of the sentence contained in the paragraph.

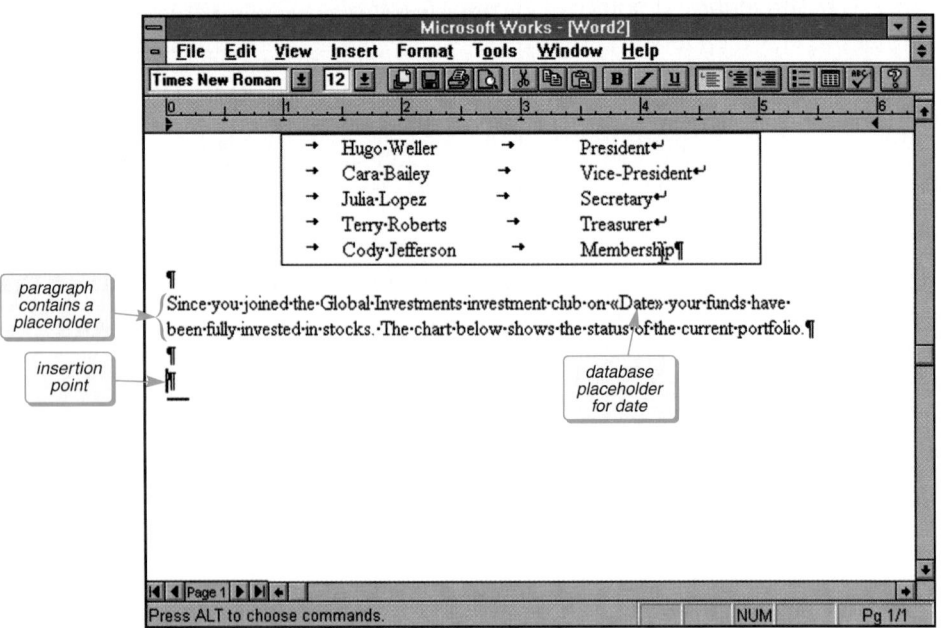

FIGURE 10-33

To type the sentence and enter the database placeholder in a paragraph, complete the following steps (see Figure 10-33).

TO INSERT A DATABASE PLACEHOLDER FOR THE DATE

Step 1: Press the ENTER key to add a blank line after the table. Type `Since you joined the Global Investments investment club on` . A blank space should follow the last word.

Step 2: Select the Insert menu and choose the Database Field command.

Step 3: The Current database box should display the database filename PROJ8.WDB

Step 4: Select the Date field name from the Fields list box.

Step 5: Choose the Insert button in the Insert Field dialog box.

Step 6: Choose the Close button in the Insert Field dialog box.

Step 7: Press the SPACEBAR one time, and then type the rest of the paragraph. Press the ENTER key twice.

When you print the letter, the date placeholder is replaced by the date from the Date field in the PROJ8.WDB database.

▶ ADDING A SPREADSHEET CHART TO THE LETTER

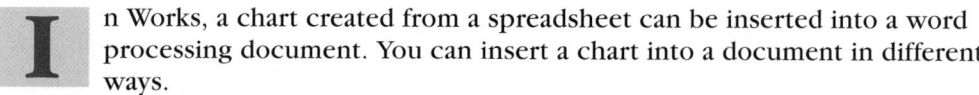

In Works, a chart created from a spreadsheet can be inserted into a word processing document. You can insert a chart into a document in different ways.

First, when the spreadsheet chart displays in the active window, you can click the **Copy button** on the Toolbar to place the chart on the Clipboard. Then, after making the word processing document the active window, you can click the **Paste button** on the Toolbar to paste the chart into the word processing document. You can also use the **Copy command** and the **Paste command** on the Edit menu. This method works well when you know that the information in the spreadsheet and related chart will never change.

A second method uses the Chart command from the Insert menu to insert and link a chart into a word processing document. When you use the Chart command, the chart from the spreadsheet that you insert in the word processing document remains linked to the spreadsheet. If you change a value in the spreadsheet, then the change will also be reflected in the chart inserted in the word processing document. You should link information in a document when you want to be sure that all associated documents have the latest version of the linked information.

Another method to link a chart into a word processing document is to use drag and drop.

In the form letter for this project, the 3-D Pie chart displays the percentage of the investment club funds invested in the various stocks. Perform the following steps to link this chart into the form letter using the Chart command from the Insert menu.

TO LINK A SPREADSHEET CHART TO A WORD PROCESSING DOCUMENT ▼

STEP 1 ▶

Be sure the spreadsheet file that contains the chart you are adding to the letter is open. In the example, it is open because it was opened together with the database and word processing files when you started Works (see Figure 10-7 on page W10.9). Center the insertion point by clicking the Center Align button on the Toolbar.

Works centers the insertion point (Figure 10-34).

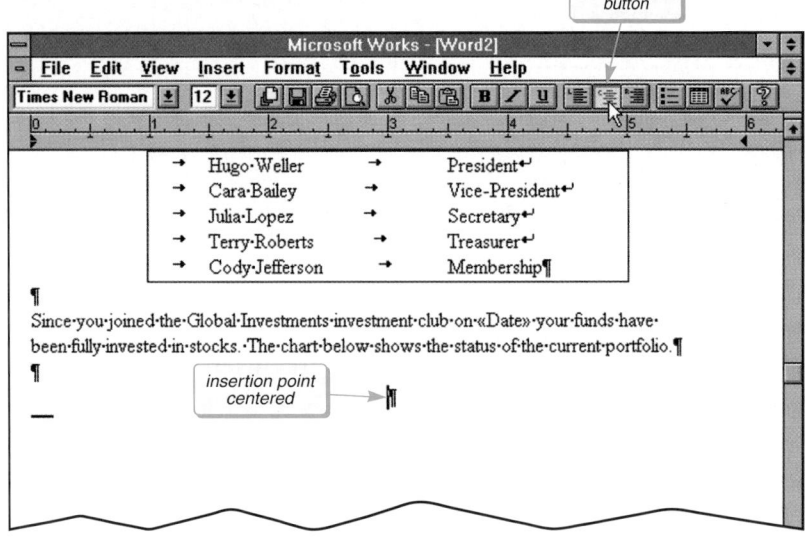

FIGURE 10-34

STEP 2 ▶

Select the Insert menu and point to the Chart command.

The Insert menu displays and the mouse pointer points to the Chart command (Figure 10-35).

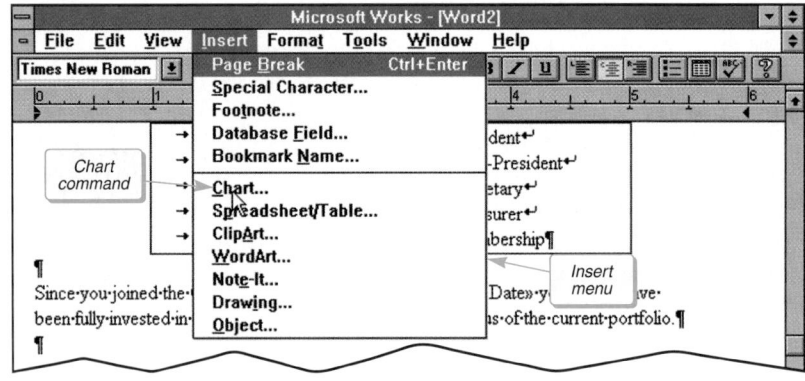

FIGURE 10-35

STEP 3 ▶

Choose the Chart command from the Insert menu. When the Insert Chart dialog box displays, if necessary select the Use existing chart option button, and then point to PROJ5.WKS in the Spreadsheets list box.

The Insert Chart dialog box displays (Figure 10-36). The Spreadsheets list box displays the names of the open spreadsheet files. The only open spreadsheet file is PROJ5.WKS. The mouse pointer points to PROJ5.WKS.

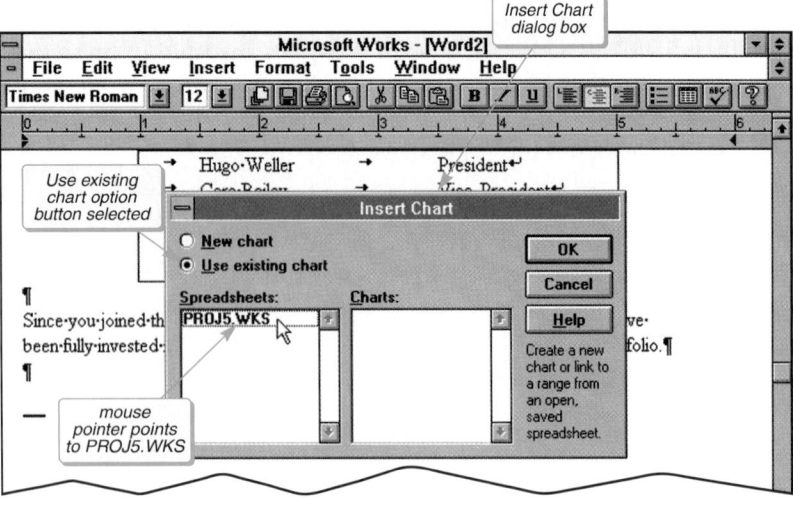

FIGURE 10-36

STEP 4 ▶

Highlight the spreadsheet filename containing the chart you want to add (PROJ5.WKS). Works displays the name Chart1 in the Charts list box. Highlight Chart1 in the Charts list box and point to the OK button.

When you select a spreadsheet, Works displays the names of all the charts associated with the spreadsheet (Figure 10-37). For the PROJ5.WKS spreadsheet, only one chart exists and the chart name is highlighted.

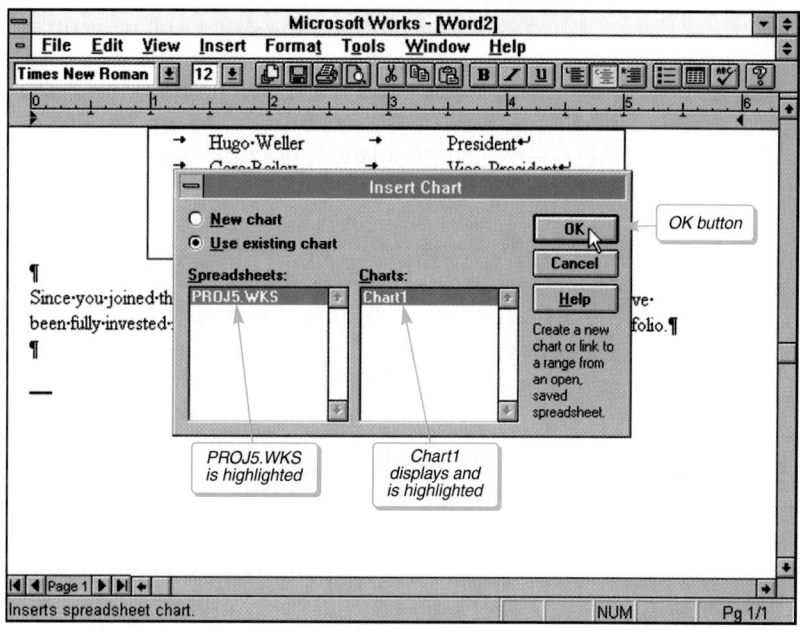

FIGURE 10-37

STEP 5 ▶

Choose the OK button in the Insert Chart dialog box. When the chart displays in the word processing document, scroll down so the entire chart displays on the screen.

Works inserts the chart at the insertion point. The entire chart displays after scrolling down (Figure 10-38).

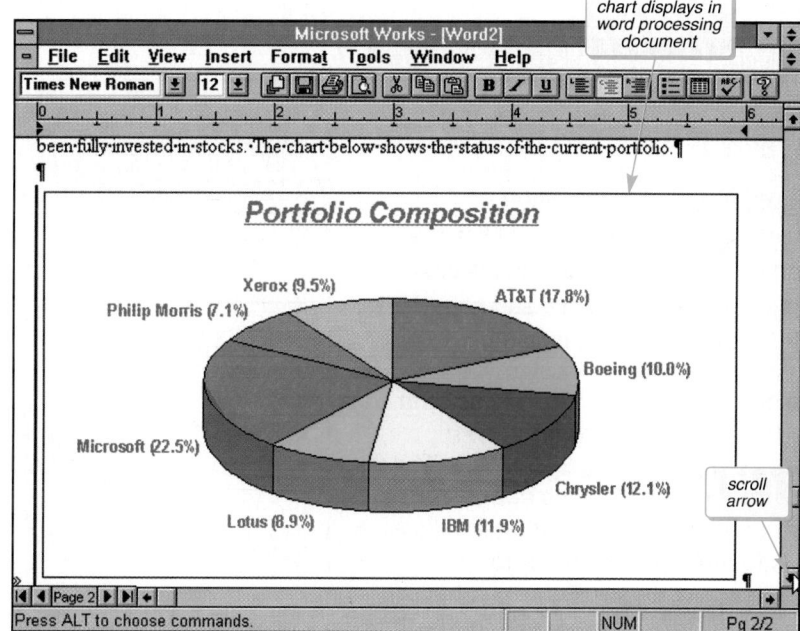

FIGURE 10-38

Because the spreadsheet chart is linked through the use of the Chart command, any change you make to the spreadsheet that changes the chart will automatically cause Works to update the chart in the word processing document. This process is illustrated later in this project.

A spreadsheet document must be named and saved before you can link information contained in it.

Notice that when you insert the chart in the word processing document, the spreadsheet document must be open. If you close all documents and want to print the letter at a later time, however, neither the spreadsheet file nor the database file must be open. When you open the word processing document, Works will inform you that linked information is contained within the document and will ask if you want to update the linked information. If you do, choose the Yes button in the dialog box; otherwise, choose the No button.

Changing the Size of a Chart in a Word Processing Document

When inserting a chart into a document, the chart retains its size unless it is higher or wider than the margins. If the chart is too large, Works scales it to fit within the margins. At times it may be desirable to reduce or enlarge the size of the chart you have placed in a word processing document. To change the size of the chart in the form letter, complete the following steps.

TO CHANGE THE SIZE OF A CHART ▼

STEP 1 ▶

Position the insertion point anywhere on the chart and click the left mouse button to select the chart. Select the Format menu and point to the Picture/Object command.

Works selects the chart by placing a border around the chart with resize handles (Figure 10-39). The Format menu displays and the mouse pointer points to the Picture/Object command.

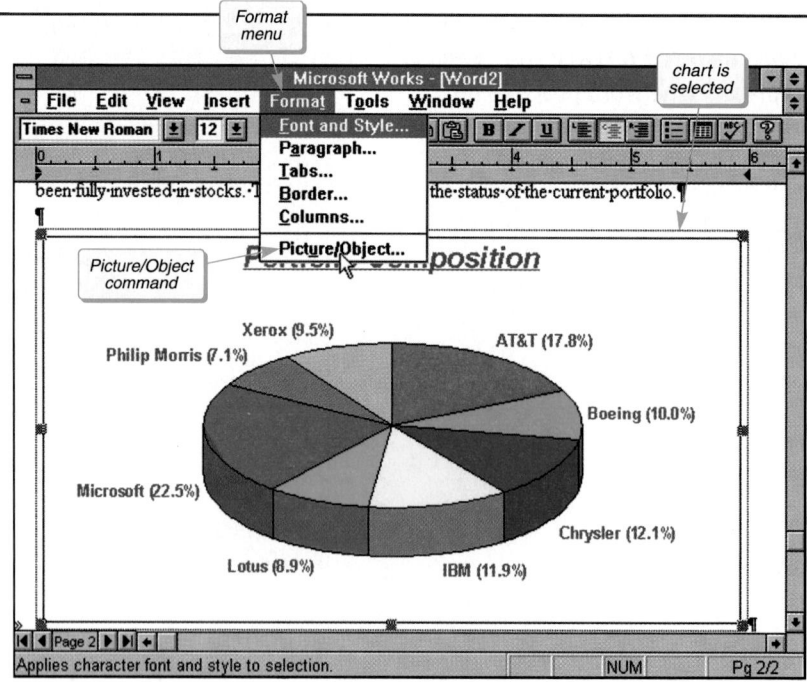

FIGURE 10-39

STEP 2 ▶

Choose the Picture/Object command. When the Picture/Object dialog box displays, type 70 in the Width text box, press the TAB key, type 70 in the Height text box, and then point to the OK button.

The Width and Height entries in the Width and Height text boxes contain 70, indicating the chart is to be reduced to 70% of its original width and height (Figure 10-40).

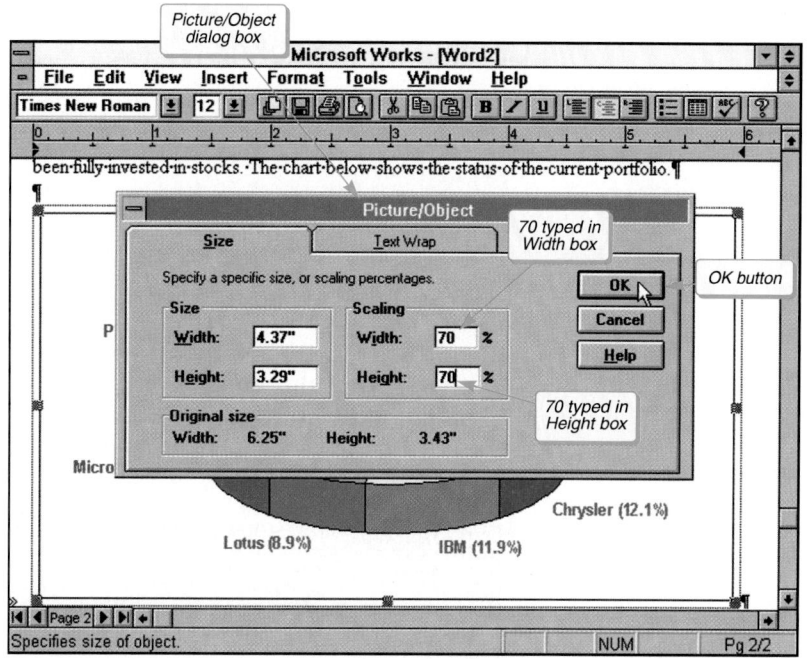

FIGURE 10-40

STEP 3 ▶

Choose the OK button from the Picture/Object dialog box. Position the mouse pointer on the paragraph mark in the lower right and click so the chart is no longer selected.

Works reduces the size of the chart in the letter to 70% of its original size (Figure 10-41). The insertion point displays to the right of the chart.

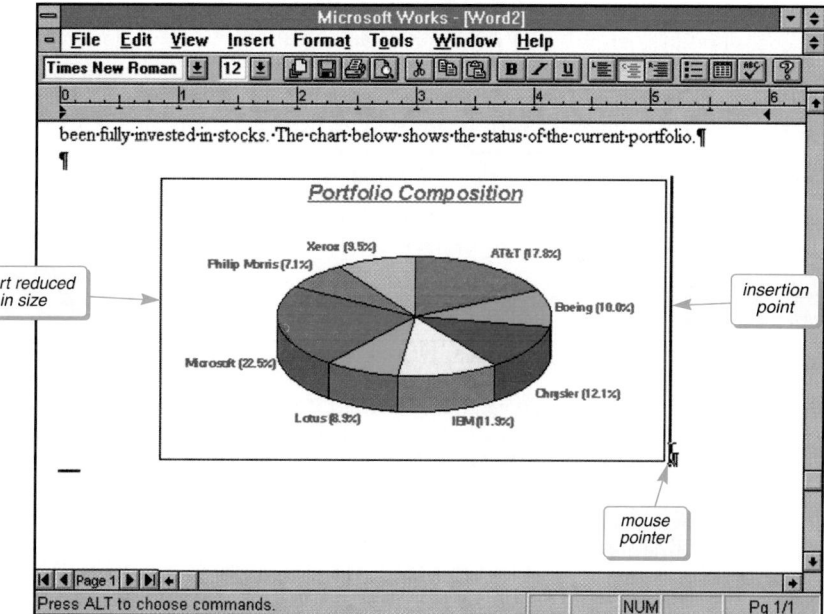

FIGURE 10-41

You can use the Picture/Object command to change the size of a chart or you can use the resize handles that display when the chart is selected to change a chart's size.

Continuing the Letter

After inserting the chart in the letter and positioning the insertion point at the right of the chart, perform the following steps to continue entering the letter (see Figure 10-42).

TO ENTER THE LETTER

Step 1: Press the ENTER key one time.
Step 2: Click the Left Align button on the Toolbar.
Step 3: Press the ENTER key one time.
Step 4: Type the next two paragraphs.
Step 5: Press the ENTER key two times.

You are now ready to insert the spreadsheet into the letter.

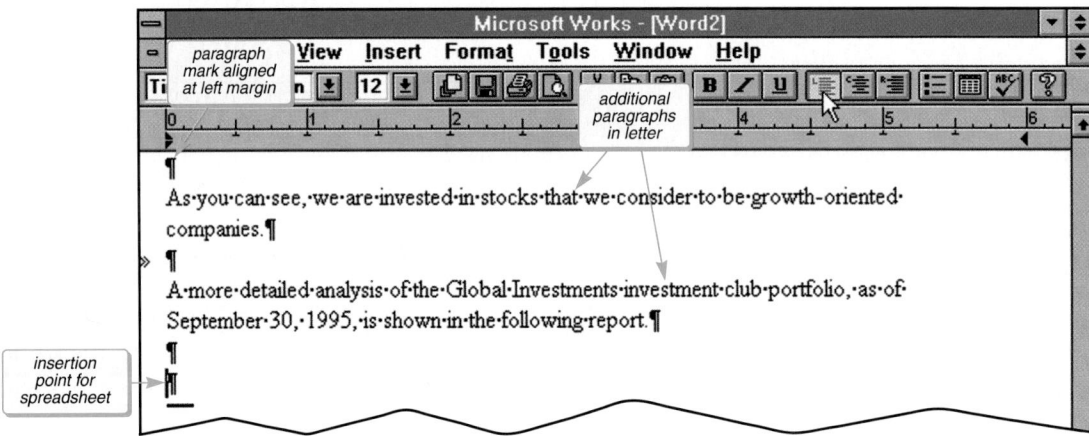

FIGURE 10-42

▶ LINKING A SPREADSHEET TO A WORD PROCESSING DOCUMENT

The next step is to add the spreadsheet to the letter. To link a spreadsheet into a word processing document, both the spreadsheet and the word processing files must be open. You can then use one of three methods to link the spreadsheet into the word processing document: (1) highlight the portion of the spreadsheet you want to place in the word processing document, click the Copy button on the Toolbar or choose the Copy command from the Edit menu to place the spreadsheet on the Clipboard, place the insertion point in the word processing document where you want the spreadsheet to be inserted, and choose the Paste Special command from the Edit menu to paste and link the spreadsheet into the word processing document; (2) highlight the range of the spreadsheet you want to insert in the word processing document, assign a name to that range using the Range command on the spreadsheet Insert menu, place the insertion point in the word processing document where you want the spreadsheet to be inserted, and choose the **Insert Spreadsheet/Table command** from the word processing Insert menu to insert and link the spreadsheet into the word processing document; (3) drag and drop.

To link a spreadsheet to a word processing document using drag and drop, perform the following steps.

TO LINK A SPREADSHEET TO A WORD PROCESSING DOCUMENT USING DRAG AND DROP ▼

STEP 1 ►

Select the Window menu and point to the PROJ5.WKS filename, which is the filename for the spreadsheet.

The Window menu displays and the mouse pointer points to the PROJ5.WKS filename (Figure 10-43).

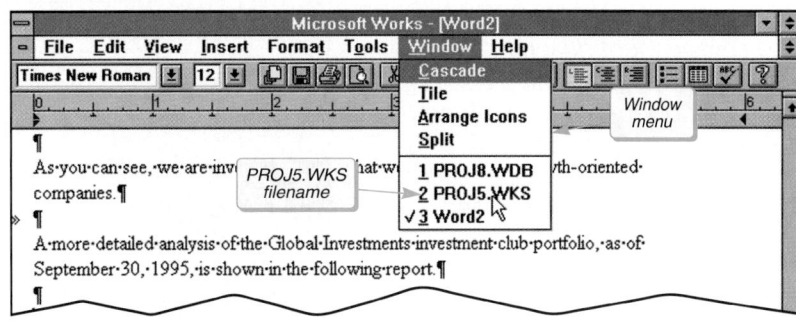

FIGURE 10-43

STEP 2 ►

Choose the PROJ5.WKS filename from the Window menu.

Works displays the PROJ5.WKS spreadsheet on the screen (Figure 10-44).

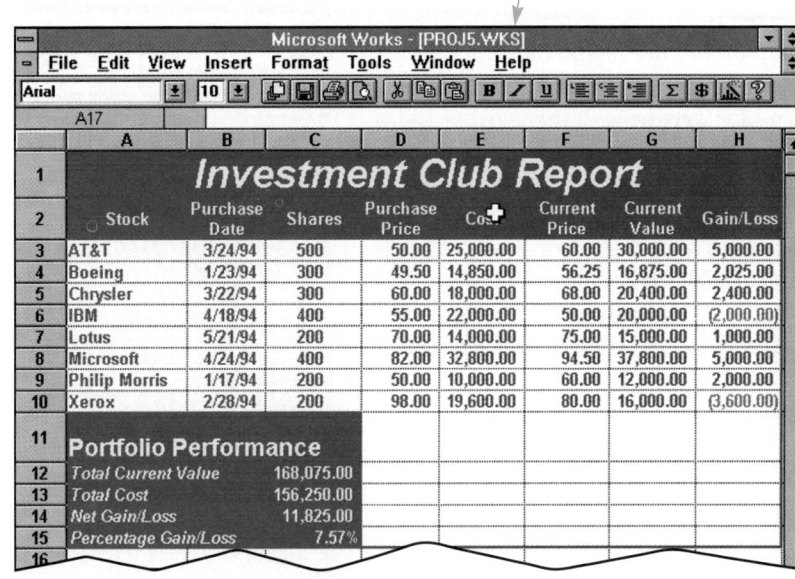

FIGURE 10-44

STEP 3 ►

Highlight the range A1:H15 in the spreadsheet, which is the range you want to insert into the word processing document. Select the Window menu and point to the Tile command.

*The range is highlighted, the Window menu displays, and the mouse pointer points to the **Tile command** (Figure 10-45).*

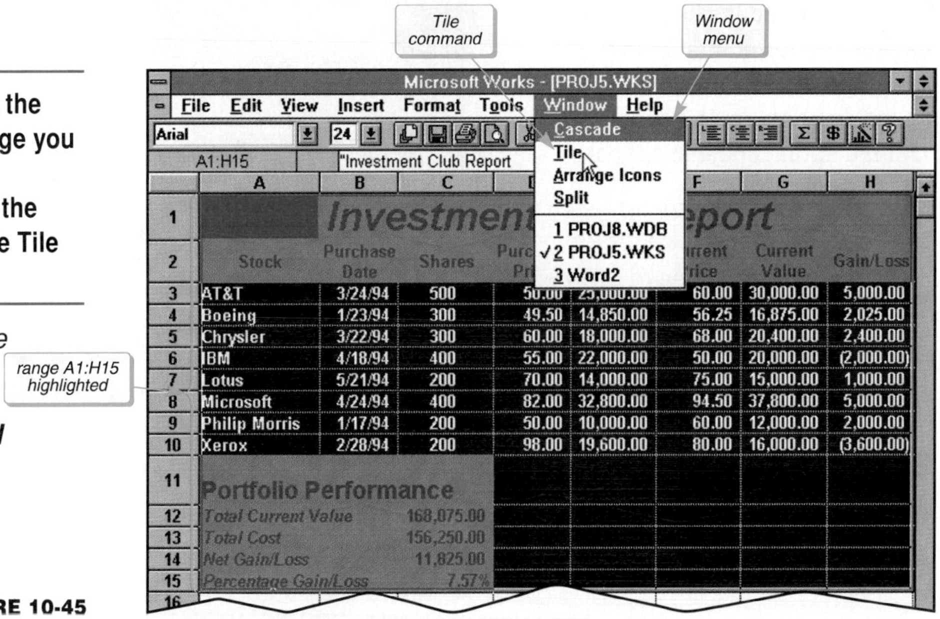

FIGURE 10-45

STEP 4 ▶

Choose the Tile command.

The spreadsheet document window, the word processing document window, and the database document window display side-by-side on the screen (Figure 10-46). The spreadsheet (PROJ5.WKS) is still the active window.

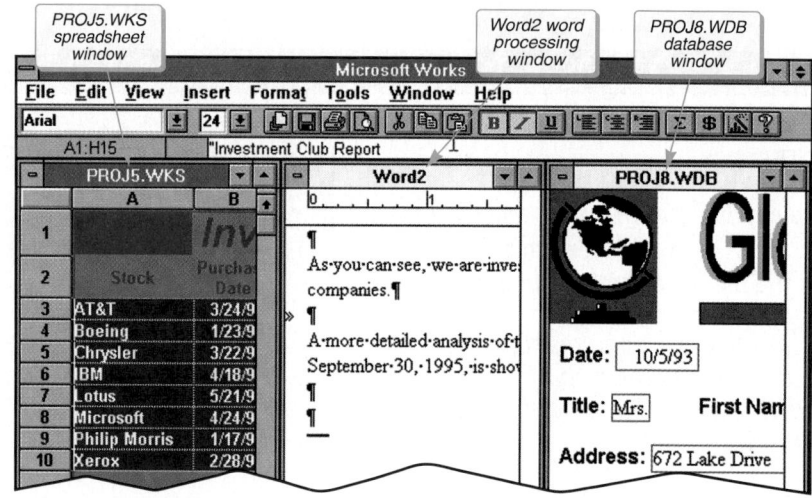

FIGURE 10-46

STEP 5 ▶

Position the mouse pointer near the top of cell A1 so the pointer changes to a block arrow with the word DRAG beneath it.

The mouse pointer in cell A1 changes to a block arrow with the word DRAG beneath it (Figure 10-47). The mouse pointer indicates you can drag the highlighted range of the spreadsheet.

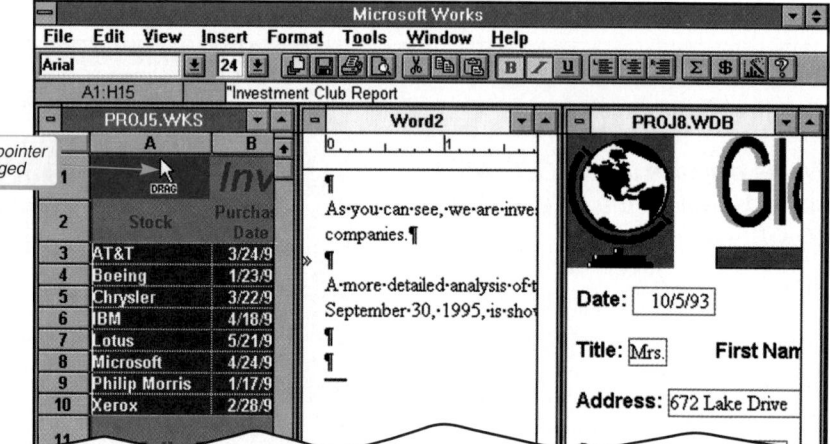

FIGURE 10-47

STEP 6 ▶

Press the left mouse button and drag the mouse pointer to the paragraph mark in the word processing document where you want the spreadsheet to appear.

When you press the left mouse button, the word beneath the mouse pointer changes to MOVE. When you drag the mouse pointer to the word processing document, the word changes to COPY, indicating you are going to copy the highlighted spreadsheet range into the word processing document (Figure 10-48).

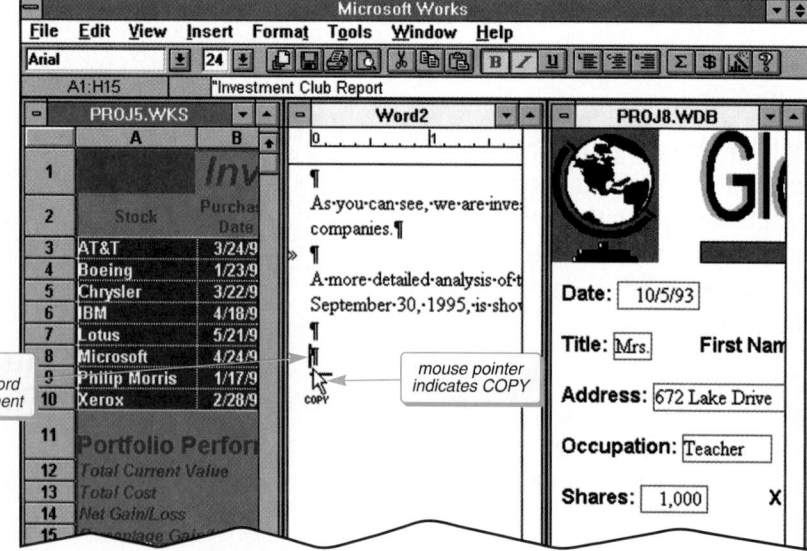

FIGURE 10-48

STEP 7 ▶

Release the left mouse button. Point to the Yes button in the Microsoft Works dialog box that asks if you want to link the copied data to the original data.

When you release the mouse button, Works displays a dialog box asking if you want to link the copied data to the original data (Figure 10-49). If you choose the Yes button, the spreadsheet will be linked with the word processing document. If you choose No, the spreadsheet becomes an embedded object in the word processing document.

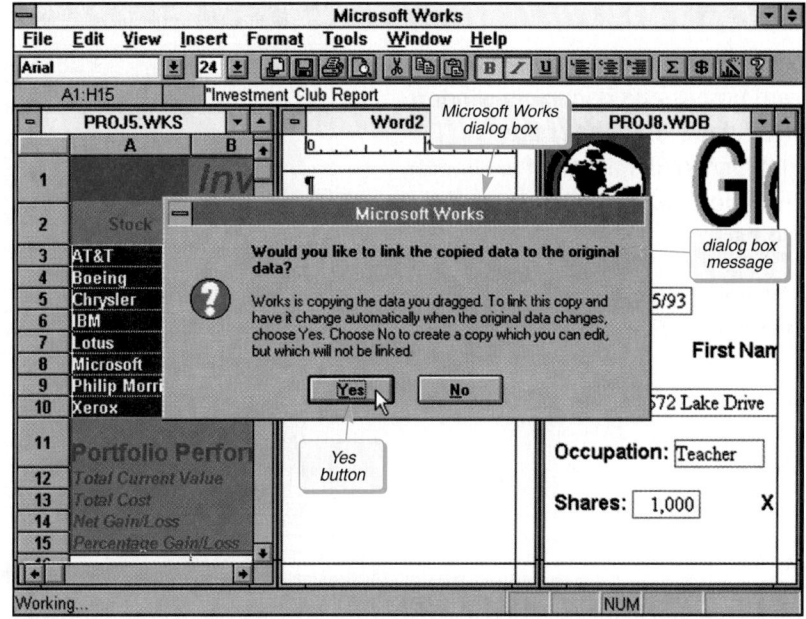

FIGURE 10-49

STEP 8 ▶

Choose the Yes button in the dialog box.

Works copies the highlighted range of the spreadsheet into the form letter (Figure 10-50). The spreadsheet in the form letter is linked to the PROJ5.WKS spreadsheet.

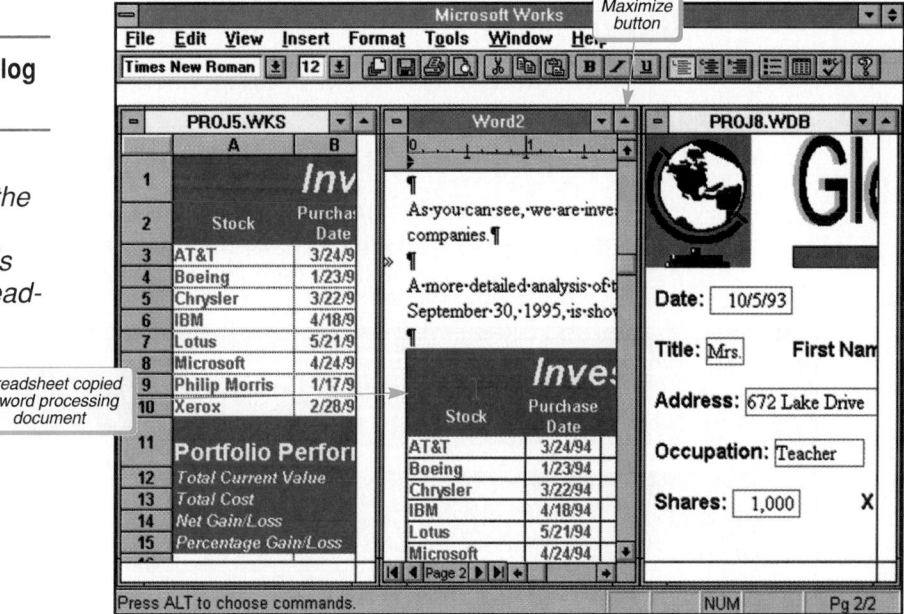

FIGURE 10-50

STEP 9 ▶

Click the Maximize button in the word processing document window. Scroll down until the entire spreadsheet displays in the window. Click the Center Align button on the Toolbar.

The spreadsheet is centered in the form letter (Figure 10-51).

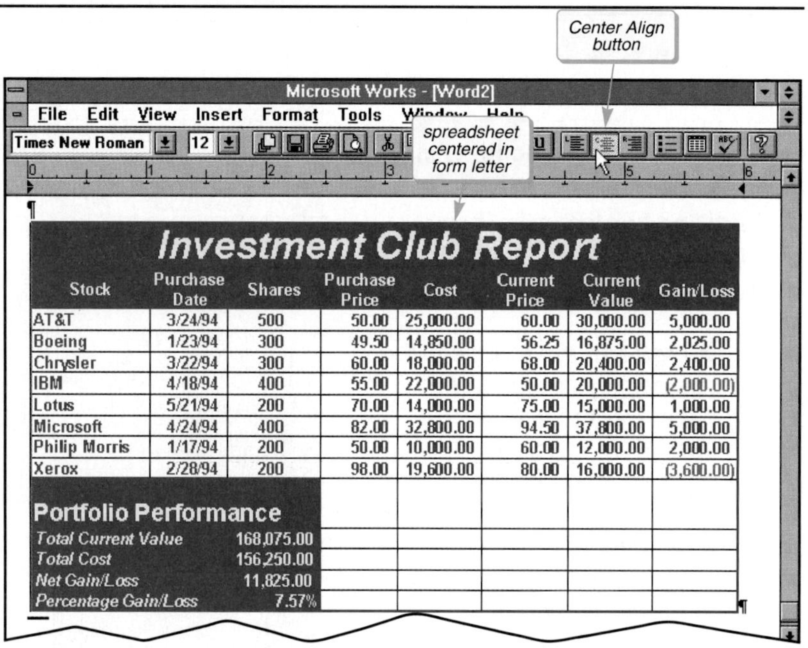

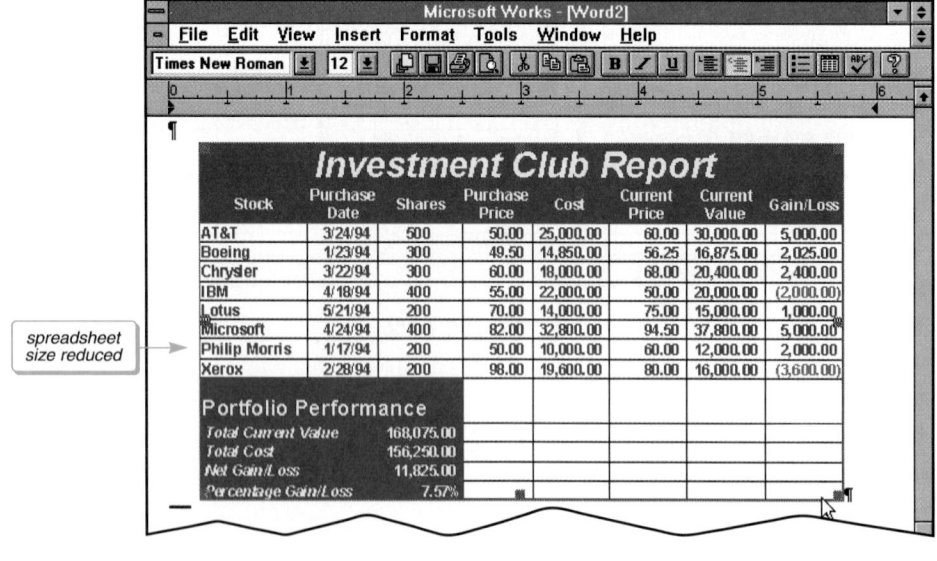

FIGURE 10-51

The spreadsheet is now linked to the word processing document. When a change is made to the original spreadsheet, Works automatically updates the spreadsheet in the word processing document.

Changing the Size of the Spreadsheet

To improve the appearance of the form letter you can reduce the size of the spreadsheet by dragging a resize handle. Complete the following steps to change the size of the spreadsheet (see Figure 10-52).

FIGURE 10-52

TO CHANGE THE SIZE OF A SPREADSHEET

Step 1: Select the spreadsheet by clicking the spreadsheet.

Step 2: Place the mouse pointer over the resize handle in the bottom right corner of the highlight border.

Step 3: Drag the resize handle up and left until the right border of the highlight rectangle is under the 5 1/2-inch mark on the ruler.

Step 4: Release the left mouse button.

The resized spreadsheet displays in the word processing document (Figure 10-52).

▶ COMPLETING THE LETTER

After inserting the spreadsheet in the letter and reducing its size, continue typing the remaining portion of the letter. To do this, perform the following steps (see Figure 10-53).

TO COMPLETE THE LETTER

Step 1: Position the mouse pointer at the lower right corner of the spreadsheet and click the left mouse button.
Step 2: Press the ENTER key one time.
Step 3: Click the Left Align button on the Toolbar.
Step 4: Press the ENTER key one time.
Step 5: Type the next paragraph, the complimentary closing, and the name and title of the person sending the letter.

The remaining portion of the letter is illustrated in Figure 10-53.

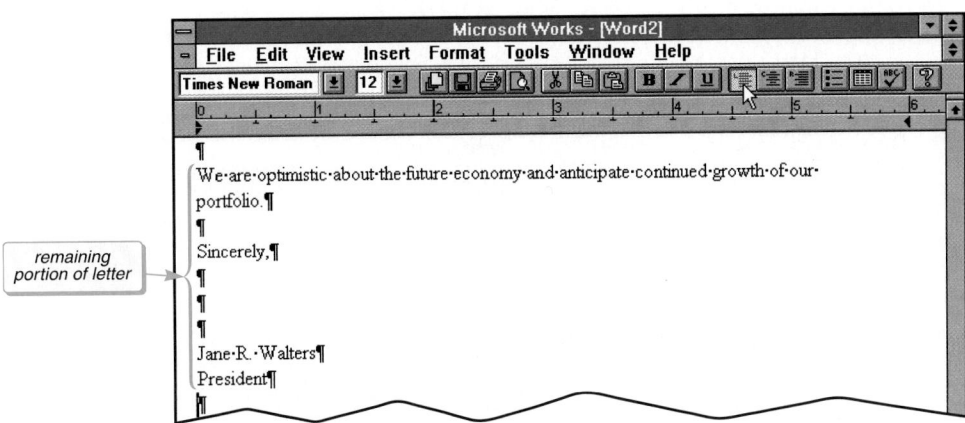

FIGURE 10-53

Entering Heading Information on the Second Page of a Letter

When writing a two-page form letter, the second page of the letter should contain a header that identifies the page number, the title, first name, middle initial and last name of the person to whom the letter is addressed, and the current date. You should enter each of these items at the top of the second page of the form letter. Each item should be on a separate line as shown in Figure 10-54.

Page 2
Mrs. Tanya I. Duncan
December 21, 1995

FIGURE 10-54

When creating a two-page letter that contains a chart or spreadsheet or both, you should create the letter first. Then, review the letter to determine the point at which you want the second page to begin and insert the header.

Works automatically creates a page break and begins a second page in a document when a full page has been entered. You can also press the CTRL+ENTER keys to have Works insert a page break at any point in a document. The beginning of a new page due to a page break is indicated by a page break mark (>>).

To display the page break mark in this project, perform the following steps (see Figure 10-55).

TO DISPLAY THE PAGE BREAK MARK AND SET THE INSERTION POINT

Step 1: Scroll the screen up until the page break mark displays.
Step 2: Place the insertion point in the first position of the line containing the page break mark.

This is the position at which you will insert the heading information (Figure 10-55).

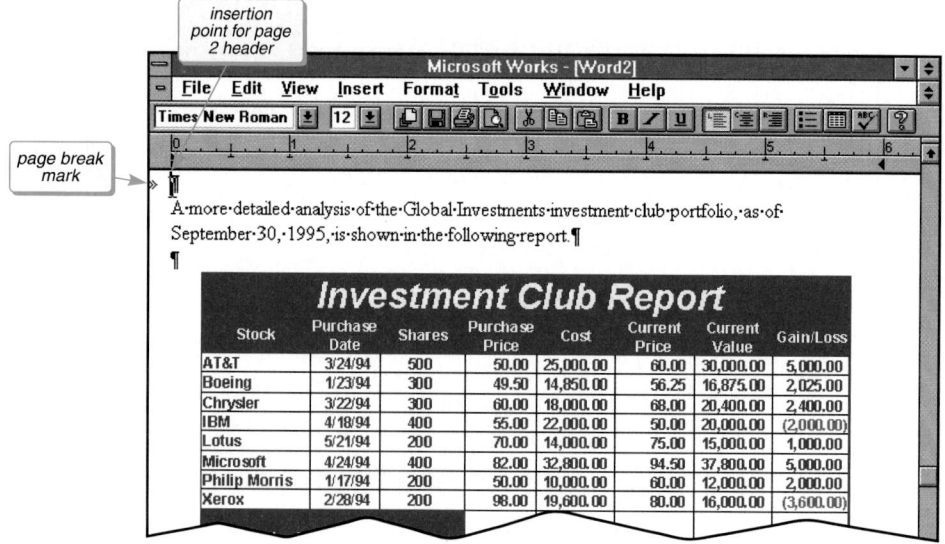

FIGURE 10-55

Because the form letter is being sent to a number of members of the investment club, you should use a database field name placeholder to insert an individual's title, first name, middle initial, and last name in the header to ensure that when you print each letter, the correct name will appear. You should also use the *longdate* special character code on the third line of the header to insert the current date in the header.

To enter the page 2 header, complete the following steps (see Figure 10-56).

TO ENTER THE PAGE NUMBER IN THE HEADER

Step 1: Ensure the insertion point is positioned at the page break mark in the document.
Step 2: Type Page 2 and press the ENTER key.

TO ENTER THE DATABASE FIELD NAME PLACEHOLDERS IN THE HEADER

Step 1: Select the Insert menu and choose the Database Field command.
Step 2: The Current database list box should contain the filename PROJ8.WDB. If not, choose the Database button and select the filename PROJ8.WDB from the Databases list box.
Step 3: Select the Title field name in the Fields list box and choose the Insert button to place the Title field placeholder into the letter. Following this same procedure, insert the First Name, M.I., and Last Name fields as placeholders into the letter.
Step 4: Choose the Close button.
Step 5: Press the ENTER key one time.

TO ENTER THE DATE IN THE HEADER

FIGURE 10-56

Step 1: Select the Insert menu and choose the Special Character command.
Step 2: Select the Print long date option button in the Special Character dialog box.
Step 3: Choose the OK button in the Special Character dialog box. Works inserts *longdate* in the document.

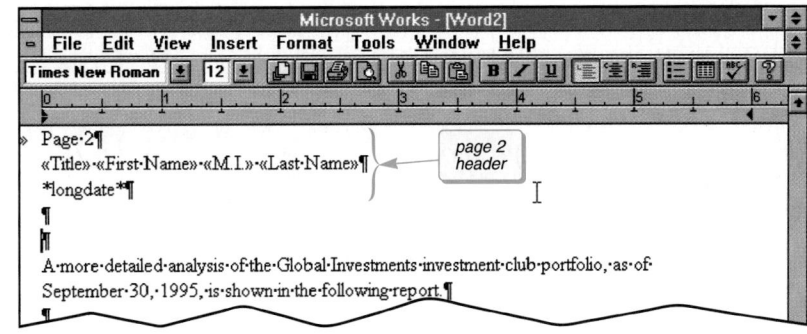

Step 4: Press the ENTER key two times to leave two blank lines after the date in the header.

The header and part of the second page of the form letter are illustrated in Figure 10-56.

Checking Spelling of a Letter

After you have completed the letter, you should check the letter for spelling errors. To check the spelling, perform the following steps.

TO CHECK THE FORM LETTER FOR SPELLING ERRORS

Step 1: Press the CTRL+HOME keys to move the insertion point to the beginning of the form letter.
Step 2: Click the Spelling Checker button on the Toolbar.
Step 3: Correct any spelling errors in the form letter.

Saving the Letter

To save the form letter, perform the following steps.

TO SAVE THE LETTER

Step 1: Click the Save button on the Toolbar.
Step 2: In the File Name text box in the Save As dialog box, type formltr1.
Step 3: If necessary, select drive A from the Drives drop-down list box and the subdirectory from the Directories box where you want to store the file.
Step 4: Choose the OK button in the Save As dialog box.

▶ SELECTING INDIVIDUALS TO RECEIVE THE FORM LETTER

A fter creating the form letter and saving the letter on a diskette, the next step is to print the letter. In this project, you are to send form letters to only those members of the Global Investments investment club whose investments are in the growth fund, which is indicated by the word Growth in the Fund Name field in the database (see Figure 10-3 on page W10.5).

To identify the records to be used for the printed form letter, you must perform a query. To perform the query, complete the following steps.

TO QUERY THE DATABASE ▼

STEP 1 ▶

Select the Window menu and point to PROJ8.WDB, the filename for the database.

The Window menu displays and the mouse pointer points to PROJ8.WDB (Figure 10-57).

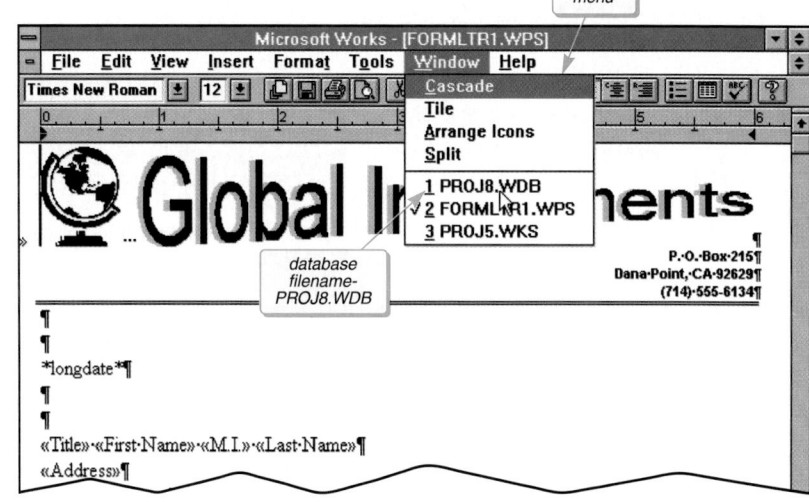

FIGURE 10-57

STEP 2 ▶

Choose the PROJ8.WDB filename from the Window menu and point to the List View button.

Works displays the database in Form view and the mouse pointer points to the List View button (Figure 10-58).

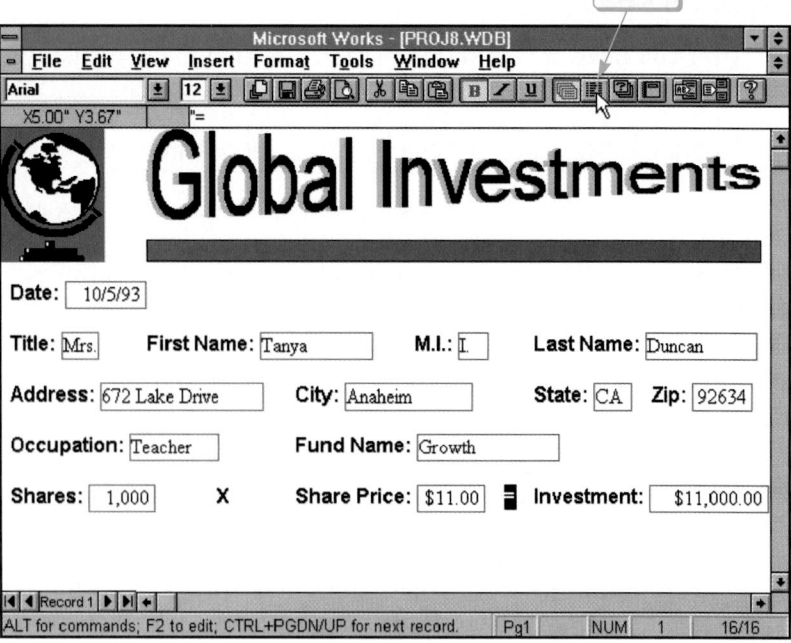

FIGURE 10-58

STEP 3 ▶

Click the List View button. When the database displays in List view, select the Tools menu and point to the Create New Query command.

The database displays in List view (Figure 10-59). Works displays the Tools menu and the mouse pointer points to the Create New Query command.

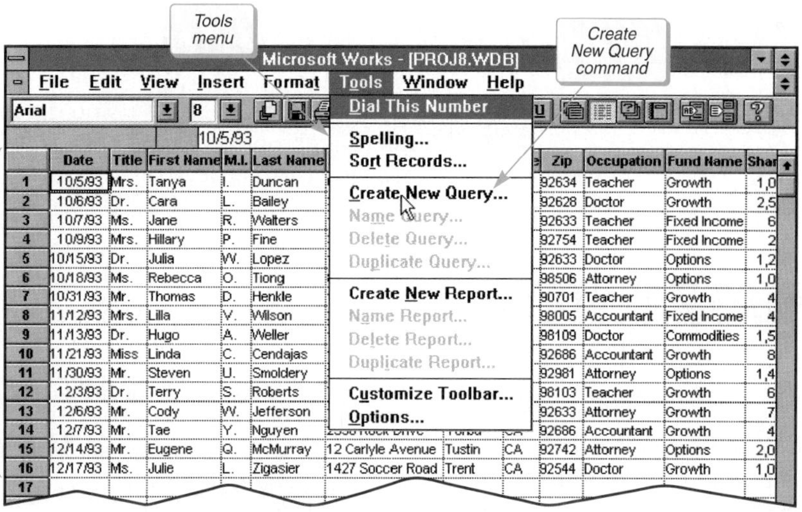

FIGURE 10-59

STEP 4 ▶

Choose the Create New Query command from the Tools menu. When the New Query dialog box displays, type Growth **in the Please give this query a name text box, select Fund Name in the Choose a field to compare drop-down list box, ensure the words is equal to display in the How to compare the field drop-down list box, and type** Growth **in the Value to compare the field to text box. Point to the Apply Now button.**

Works displays the New Query dialog box (Figure 10-60). The appropriate entries display in the dialog box. The mouse pointer points to the Apply Now button.

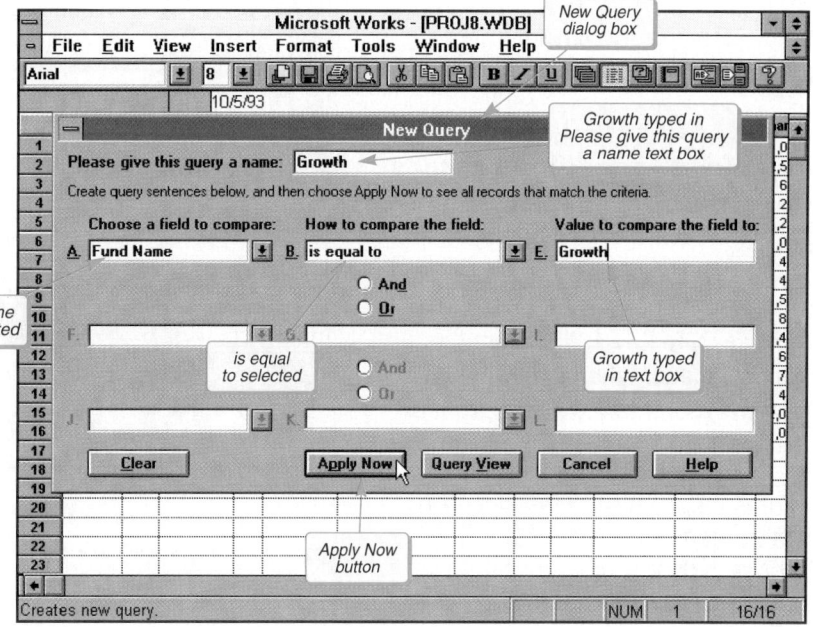

FIGURE 10-60

STEP 5 ▶

Choose the Apply Now button.

Works displays the records with the Fund Name equal to Growth (Figure 10-61). The records in the database you are to use in the form letter are now selected.

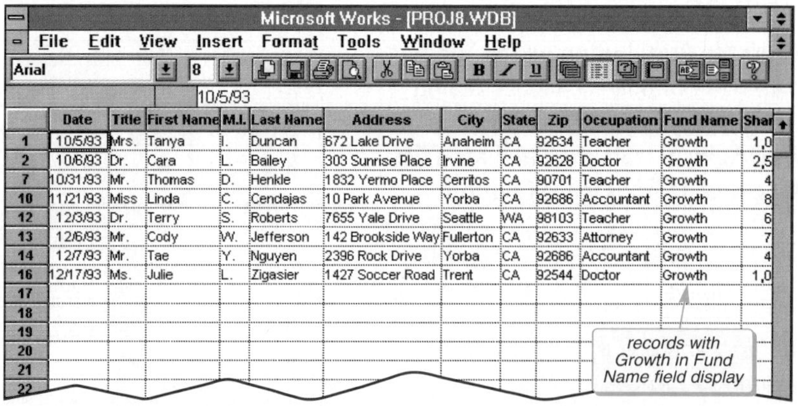

FIGURE 10-61

▶ PRINTING THE FORM LETTERS

 rinting the form letters using database fields in the records found by the query is the next step in this project. The following procedure illustrates printing form letters.

TO PRINT FORM LETTERS ▼

STEP 1 ▶

Select the Window menu and point to FORMLTR1.WPS, the filename for the form letter (Figure 10-62).

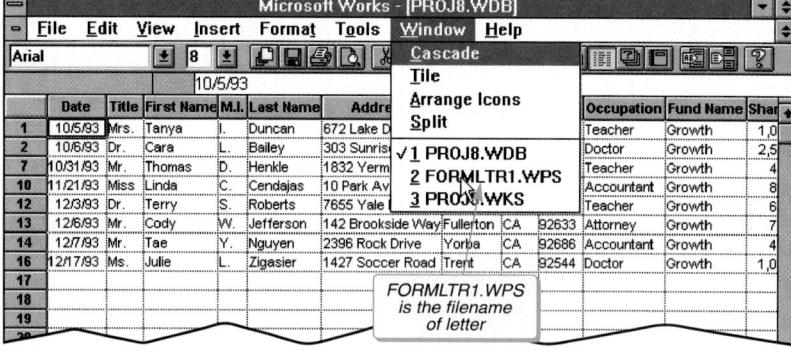

FIGURE 10-62

STEP 2 ▶

Choose FORMLTR1.WPS from the Window menu. When the form letter displays, point to the Print button on the Toolbar.

Works displays the form letter on the screen (Figure 10-63). The mouse pointer points to the Print button on the Toolbar.

FIGURE 10-63

STEP 3 ▶

Click the Print button on the Toolbar. When the Choose Database dialog box displays, if necessary select PROJ8.WDB from the Databases list box, and point to the OK button.

Works displays the Choose Database dialog box (Figure 10-64) The PROJ8.WDB filename is highlighted and the mouse pointer points to the OK button. This selection specifies the database from which the data will be taken for the form letters.

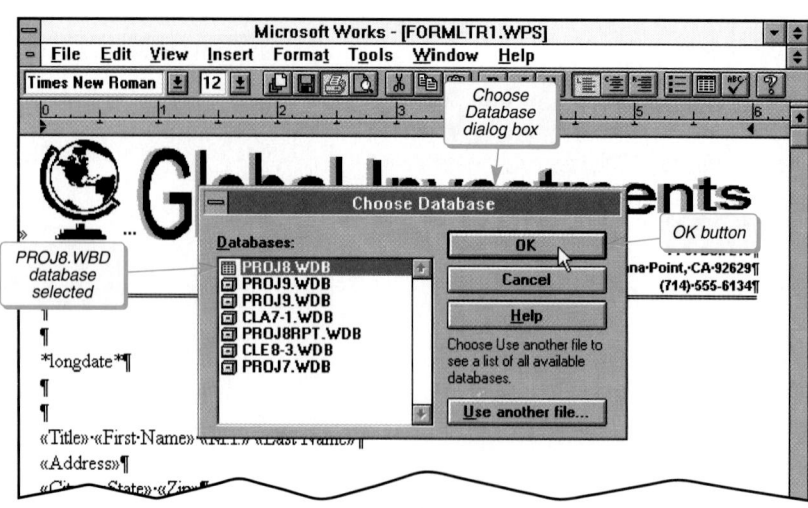

FIGURE 10-64

STEP 4 ▶

Choose the OK button in the Choose Database dialog box.

Works momentarily displays the Printing dialog box and then prints the form letters using fields from the database records. A total of eight letters would be printed because eight database records contain the word Growth in the Fund Name field. The first letter is shown in Figure 10-65.

Global Investments

P. O. Box 215
Dana Point, CA 92629
(714) 555-6134

December 21, 1995

Mrs. Tanya I. Duncan
672 Lake Drive
Anaheim, CA 92634

Dear Mrs. Duncan:

During the last meeting of the Global Investments investment club, the members of the 1996 Board of Directors were elected. The new members of the Board of Directors are:

Hugo Weller	President
Cara Bailey	Vice-President
Julia Lopez	Secretary
Terry Roberts	Treasurer
Cody Jefferson	Membership

Since you joined the Global Investments investment club on 10/5/93 your funds have been fully invested in stocks. The chart below shows the status of the current portfolio.

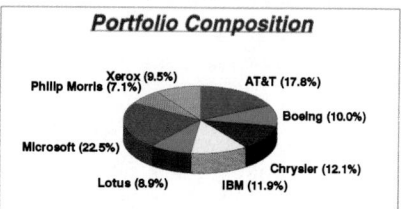

Portfolio Composition

Xerox (9.5%)
Philip Morris (7.1%)
AT&T (17.8%)
Boeing (10.0%)
Microsoft (22.5%)
Chrysler (12.1%)
Lotus (8.9%)
IBM (11.9%)

As you can see, we are invested in stocks that we consider to be growth-oriented companies.

Page 2
Mrs. Tanya I. Duncan
December 21, 1995

A more detailed analysis of the Global Investments investment club portfolio, as of September 30, 1995, is shown in the following report.

Investment Club Report

Stock	Purchase Date	Shares	Purchase Price	Cost	Current Price	Current Value	Gain/Loss
AT&T	3/24/94	500	50.00	25,000.00	60.00	30,000.00	5,000.00
Boeing	1/23/94	300	49.50	14,850.00	56.25	16,875.00	2,025.00
Chrysler	3/22/94	300	60.00	18,000.00	68.00	20,400.00	2,400.00
IBM	4/18/94	400	55.00	22,000.00	50.00	20,000.00	(2,000.00)
Lotus	5/21/94	200	70.00	14,000.00	75.00	15,000.00	1,000.00
Microsoft	4/24/94	400	82.00	32,800.00	94.50	37,800.00	5,000.00
Philip Morris	1/17/94	200	50.00	10,000.00	60.00	12,000.00	2,000.00
Xerox	2/28/94	200	98.00	19,600.00	80.00	16,000.00	(3,600.00)

Portfolio Performance	
Total Current Value	168,075.00
Total Cost	156,250.00
Net Gain/Loss	11,825.00
Percentage Gain/Loss	7.57%

We are optimistic about the future economy and anticipate continued growth of our portfolio.

Sincerely,

Jane R. Walters
President

FIGURE 10-65

The ability to insert a chart and spreadsheet into a letter, use fields in a database in a letter, and send form letters to individuals in a database based on certain criteria illustrates the power of Microsoft Works for Windows as an integrated software package.

Creating Mailing Labels

After you print the form letters, the final step is to prepare mailing labels. With Works you can print names and addresses on mailing labels and then attach each label to an envelope or package. You can also print names and addresses directly on envelopes.

To create mailing labels, you will use the same information that is in the inside address of the letters; that is, the title, first name, middle initial, last name, address, city, state, and zip code. Prior to creating the mailing labels, however, you must know the type and size of the mailing labels you are using. Mailing labels are commonly placed one, two, or three across a page and come in a variety of sizes. Works provides the manufacturer's name and dimensions of frequently used mailing labels.

To create the mailing labels, perform the following steps.

TO CREATE MAILING LABELS ▼

STEP 1 ▶

Select the Tools menu and point to the Envelopes and Labels command.

*The Tools menu displays and the mouse pointer points to the **Envelopes and Labels command** (Figure 10-66).*

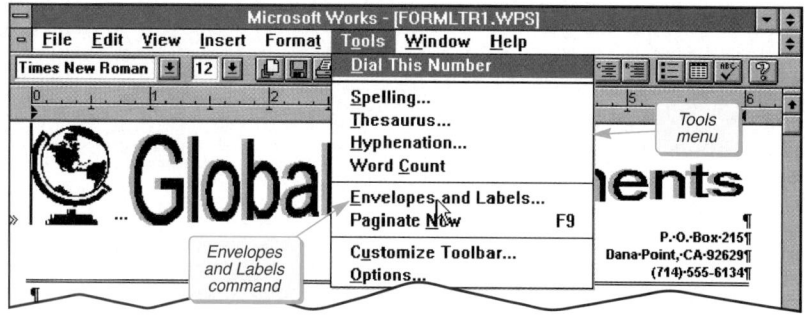

FIGURE 10-66

STEP 2 ▶

Choose the Envelopes and Labels command. When the Envelopes and Labels dialog box displays, select the Mailing Labels tab and point to the Fields>> button.

Works displays the Envelopes and Labels dialog box (Figure 10-67). The Mailing Labels screen displays. The default Label style is set to Avery 4143. Avery is the name of a widely used label. The mouse pointer points to the Fields>> button.

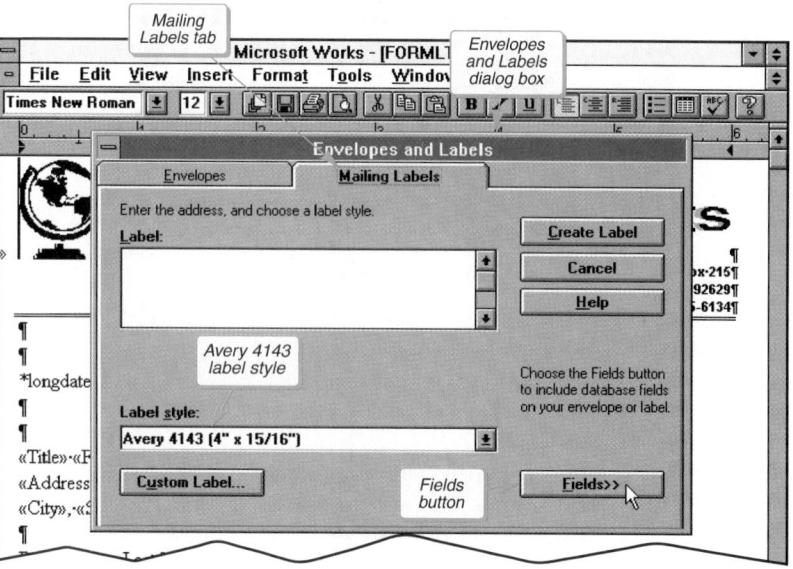

FIGURE 10-67

STEP 3 ►

Choose the Fields>> button. When the Fields list box displays, select Title from the Fields list box and point to the Insert button.

Works displays the Fields list box (Figure 10-68). The Title field name is highlighted in the Fields list box. The mouse pointer points to the Insert button. Notice that the Current database box contains the filename PROJ8.WDB.

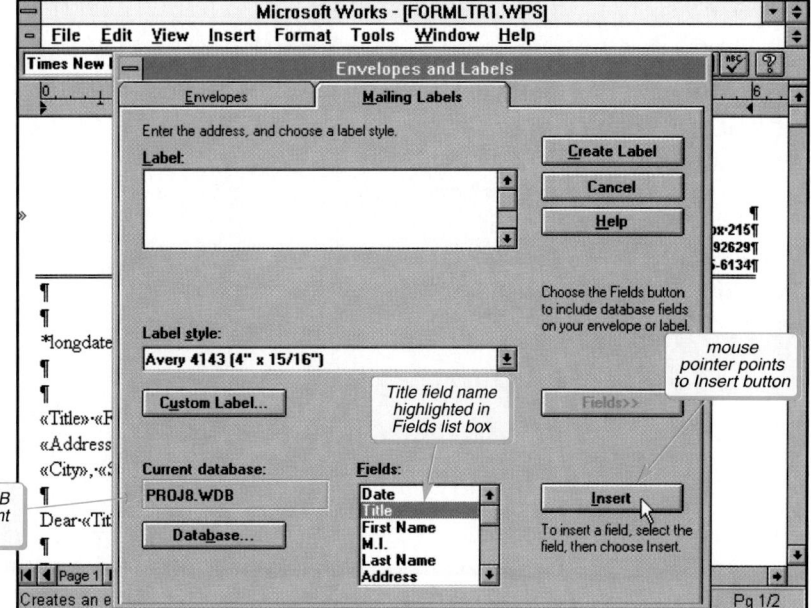

FIGURE 10-68

STEP 4 ►

Choose the Insert button. Select the First Name field name and choose the Insert button. Select the M.I. field name and choose the Insert button. Select the Last Name field name and choose the Insert button. Press the SHIFT+ENTER keys to end the line. Insert the remaining fields (Address, City, State, and Zip) using the techniques just described. Type a comma and a space after the City placeholder is entered. End each line by pressing the SHIFT+ENTER keys. Click the Label style drop-down list box arrow to display the drop-down list box of labels. Scroll down and point to Avery 5161 (1" x 4"). This is the label used for the form letter.

Works displays the placeholders in the Label box (Figure 10-69). You may type any text, spaces, or punctuation marks before or after the placeholders. The mouse pointer points to Avery 5161 (1" X 4") in the Label style drop-down list box.

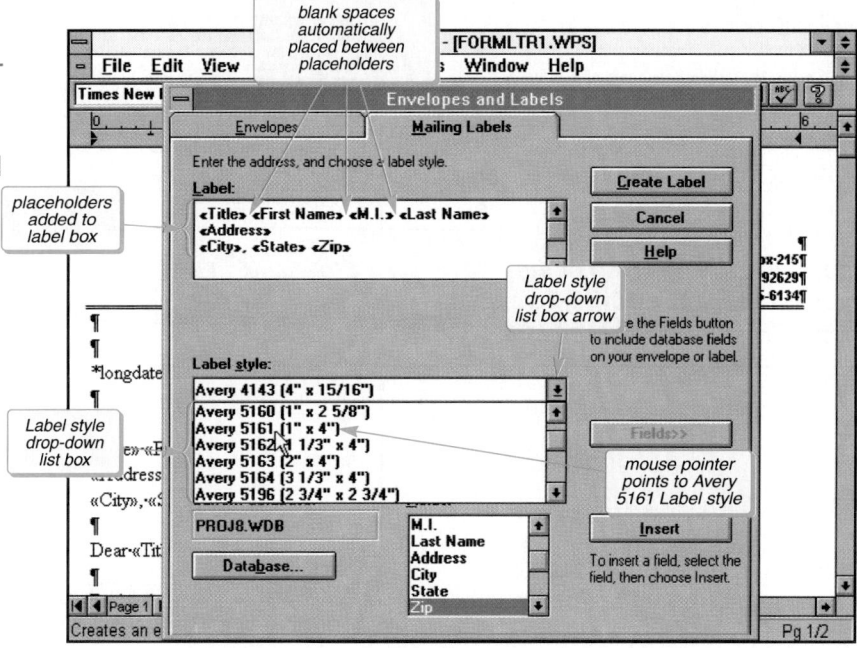

FIGURE 10-69

STEP 5 ▶

Select the Avery 5161 (1" x 4") entry in the Label style drop-down list box, and then point to the Create Label button.

Works highlights Avery 5161 (1" x 4") in the Label style box and the mouse pointer points to the Create Label button (Figure 10-70).

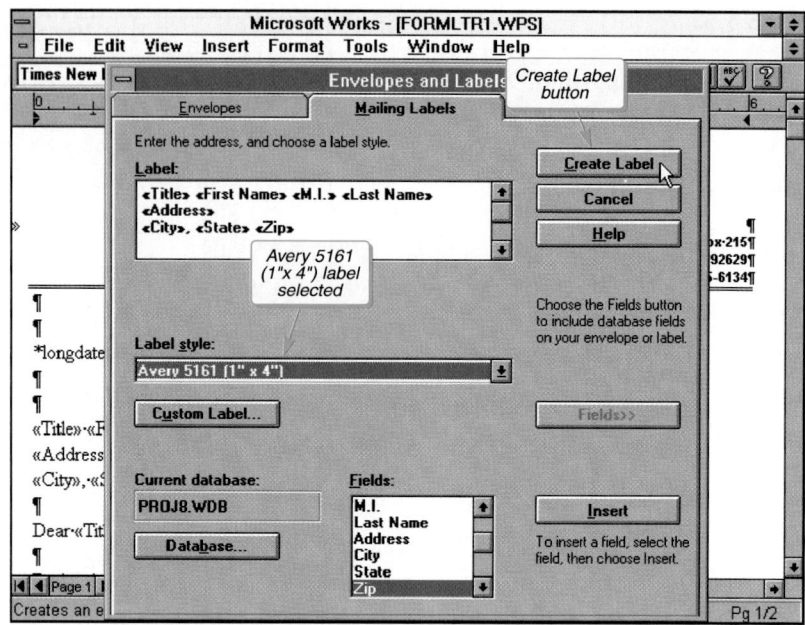

FIGURE 10-70

STEP 6 ▶

Choose the Create Label button.

Works displays the Word Processing document window and inserts the placeholders for the mailing labels at the beginning of the document (Figure 10-71). Works adds a manual page break to separate the label from the rest of the document.

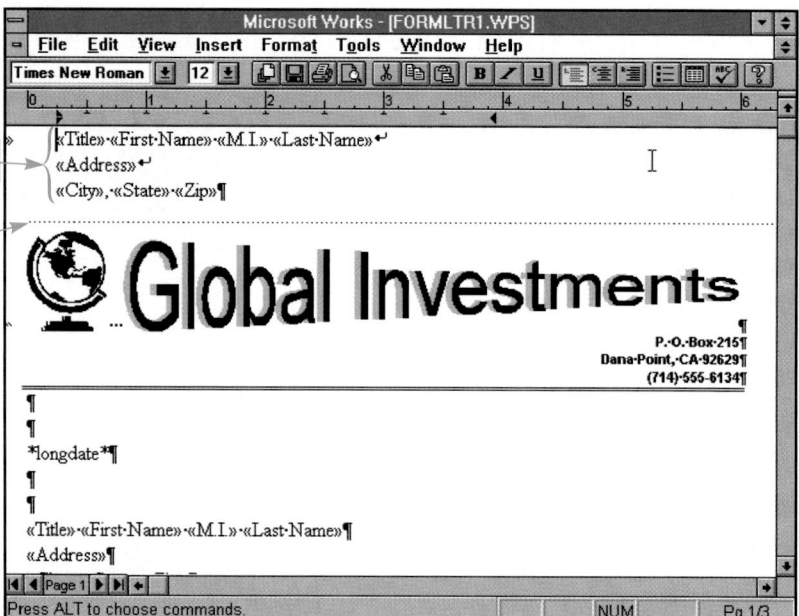

FIGURE 10-71

Printing the Mailing Labels

After creating the placeholders for the mailing labels, the next step is to print the mailing labels. The method to print mailing labels is presented in the following steps.

TO PRINT MAILING LABELS ▼

STEP 1 ►

Insert mailing labels in the printer.

STEP 2 ►

Select the File menu and point to the Print command (Figure 10-72).

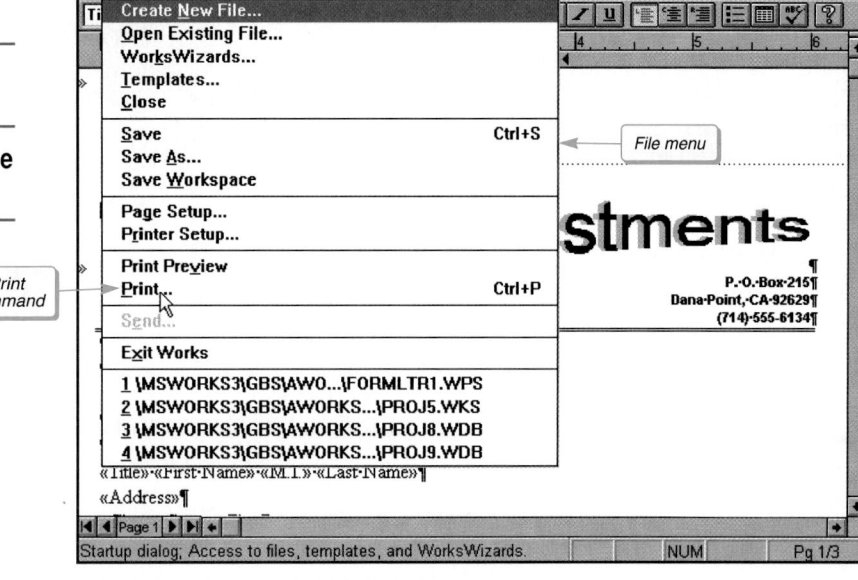

FIGURE 10-72

STEP 3 ►

Choose the Print command. When the Print dialog box displays, select the Mailing Labels option button and, if necessary, the Print merge check box. Point to the Preview button.

Works displays the Print dialog box (Figure 10-73). The Mailing Labels option button and Print merge check box are selected, and the mouse pointer points to the Preview button.

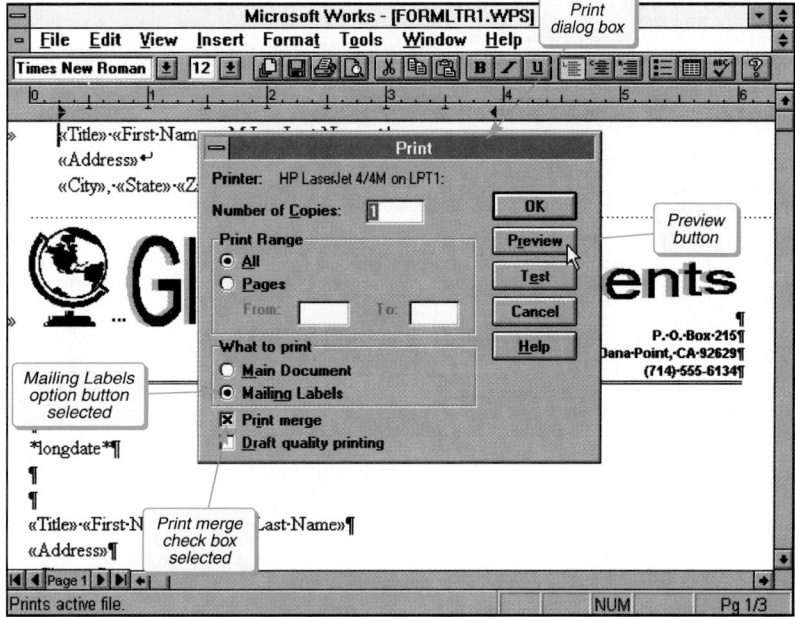

FIGURE 10-73

STEP 4 ▶

Choose the Preview button in the Print dialog box. When the Choose Database dialog box displays, ensure that PROJ8.WDB is highlighted in the Databases list box, and then point to the OK button.

Works displays the Choose Database dialog box (Figure 10-74). The current database, PROJ8.WDB, is highlighted in the Databases list box. The mouse pointer points to the OK button.

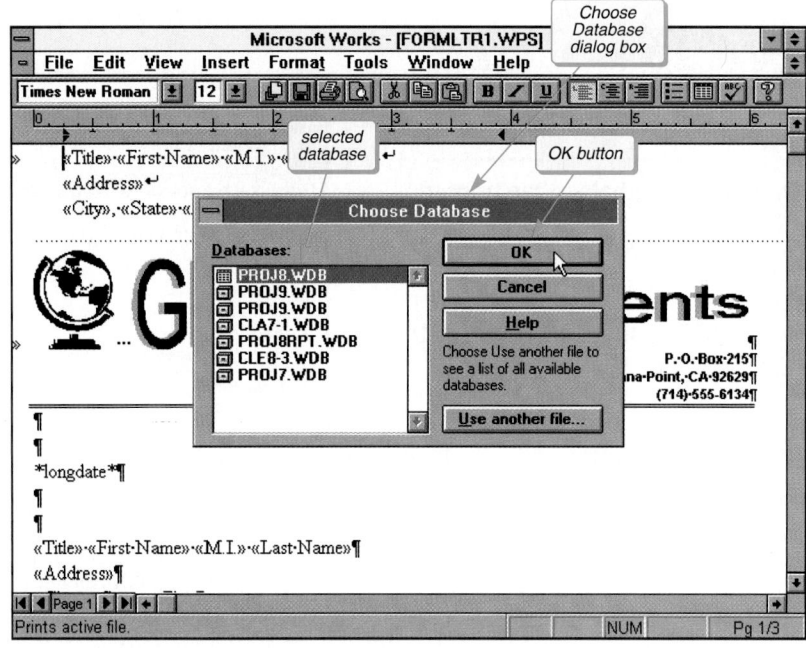

FIGURE 10-74

STEP 5 ▶

Choose the OK button in the Choose Database dialog box. When the preview screen displays, click the Zoom In button once and point to the Print button.

Works displays the preview screen and the mouse pointer points to the Print button (Figure 10-75). The labels display in the same format as they will print. This format is correct for Avery 5161 (1" x 4") labels.

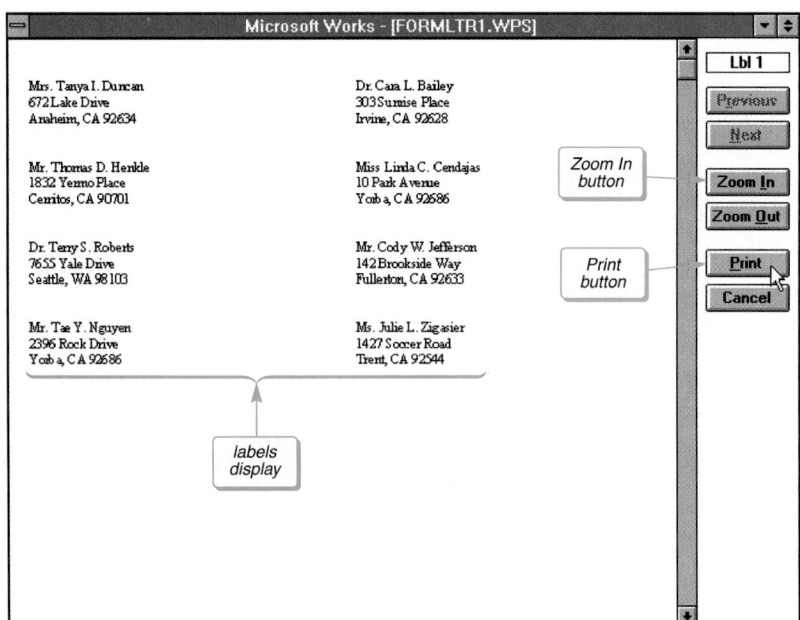

FIGURE 10-75

STEP 6 ▶

Choose the Print button. When the Print dialog box displays again, choose the OK button. When the Choose Database dialog box displays again, choose the OK button.

A Printing dialog box appears momentarily and then the mailing labels for the records print (Figure 10-76).

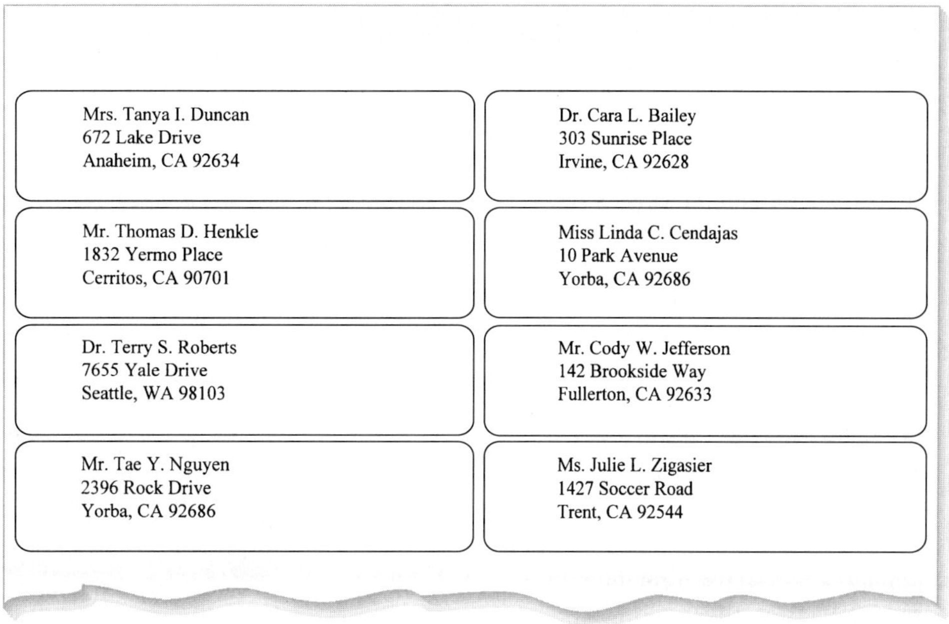

FIGURE 10-76

Mrs. Tanya I. Duncan
672 Lake Drive
Anaheim, CA 92634

Dr. Cara L. Bailey
303 Sunrise Place
Irvine, CA 92628

Mr. Thomas D. Henkle
1832 Yermo Place
Cerritos, CA 90701

Miss Linda C. Cendajas
10 Park Avenue
Yorba, CA 92686

Dr. Terry S. Roberts
7655 Yale Drive
Seattle, WA 98103

Mr. Cody W. Jefferson
142 Brookside Way
Fullerton, CA 92633

Mr. Tae Y. Nguyen
2396 Rock Drive
Yorba, CA 92686

Ms. Julie L. Zigasier
1427 Soccer Road
Trent, CA 92544

Printing Envelopes

In addition to printing mailing labels, you can print directly on envelopes. To do so, select the Envelopes tab in the Envelopes and Labels dialog box (see Figure 10-67 on page W10.42). You can select the size of envelope you will print in the same manner you used to select the label style. You add information for the address in the same way as with labels. You can also include a return address when you create an envelope.

To print an envelope, choose the Print command from the File menu. An Envelope option button displays in the Print dialog box when you have defined an envelope. Select the Envelope option button and then choose the OK button in the Print dialog box.

In order to print envelopes properly, you must have a printer with which you can insert and print envelopes.

Exiting Works

You have completed the form letter and the mailing labels. You can exit Works as explained in previous examples. Be sure to save the latest version of the form letter.

▶ CHANGING ENTRIES IN THE SREADSHEET

A t some later time you might want to send an updated letter to members of the Global Investments investment club reflecting changes in stock prices. As previously discussed, the spreadsheet and chart are linked to the word processing document, meaning that any change in the original spreadsheet will cause the spreadsheet and chart in the letter to be updated. To be sure these changes are occurring correctly, perform the steps on the next page.

TO CHANGE ENTRIES IN THE SPREADSHEET ▼

STEP 1 ▶

If you have exited Works, start Works. Then open the PROJ5.WKS spreadsheet file. Open the form letter FORMLTR1.WPS file and choose the Yes button in the Microsoft Works dialog box that asks if you want to update the links. Select the Window menu and choose the Tile command. Position the spreadsheet in the PROJ5.WKS window by scrolling so the names of the stocks display on the left of the screen. Position the form letter in the FORMLTR1.WPS window by scrolling so the left portion of the chart displays.

The spreadsheet and chart display in their respective tiled windows (Figure 10-77).

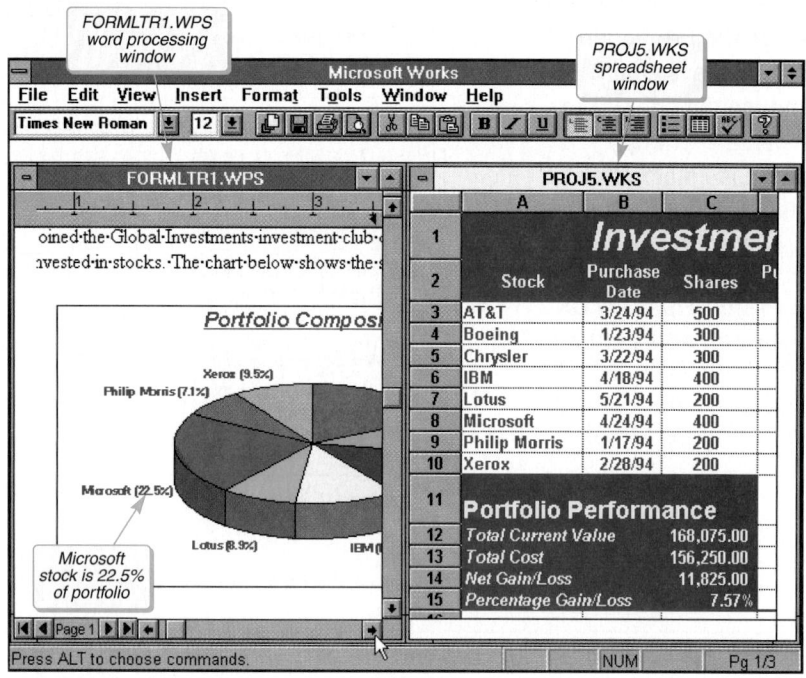

FIGURE 10-77

STEP 2 ▶

Click anywhere in the spreadsheet window. Drag the vertical split bar to the first position of column B. Scroll the right pane until you see the Current Price field and the Current Value field in the right pane. Change the Current Price of Microsoft to 180.00 by entering the number into the spreadsheet in column F.

The chart in the FORMLTR1.WPS document is updated (Figure 10-78). The Current Value of the Microsoft stock now comprises 35.6% of the value of the portfolio. Before the change in stock price, Microsoft stock comprised 22.5% of the stock as indicated in Figure 10-77. Notice that because of the change in the Current Price of the Microsoft stock, the percentages for the other stocks changed as well.

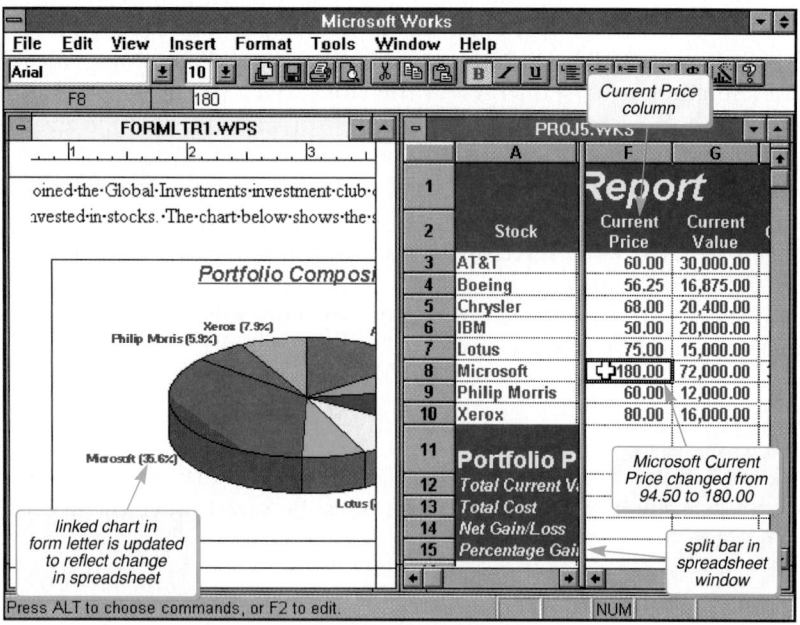

FIGURE 10-78

STEP 3 ▶

To determine if the spreadsheet in the letter has been updated, click anywhere in the word processing window and scroll down in the FORMLTR1 window to display the portion of the spreadsheet that contains the Current Price field.

The spreadsheet contains 180.00 in the Current Price field for Microsoft, indicating the spreadsheet has been updated (Figure 10-79).

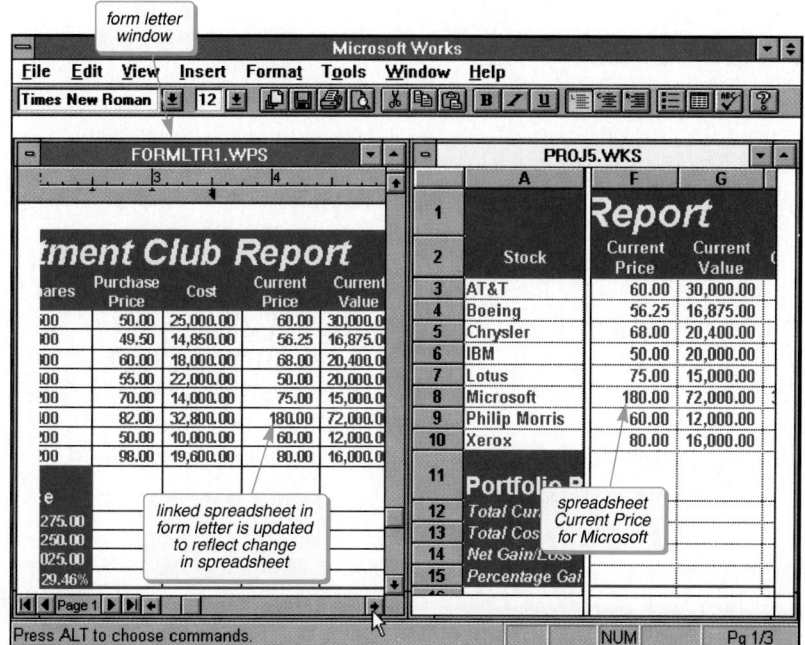

FIGURE 10-79

At this time, new updated form letters could be sent out or the updated spreadsheet saved for future use.

The capability to utilize the integrated features of Microsoft Works provides great flexibility and power to users of personal computers.

▶ PROJECT SUMMARY

In Project 10 you learned to use many of the integrated features of Microsoft Works for Windows. This project illustrates the use of Works integrated features using names and addresses from a database in a form letter, inserting a chart and a spreadsheet in a form letter, sending the form letters to selected individuals, and preparing mailing labels.

You are now able to use the special character *longdate* in a word processing document, use the Database Field command, make entries in the Insert Field dialog box, use database placeholders, and create tables in a document. In addition, you can use the Border command, make entries in the Border dialog box, use the Chart command, make entries in the Insert Chart dialog box, use the Picture/Object command, drag and link a spreadsheet into a word processing document, and print mailing labels.

You have seen how to share data between Works applications in three ways: (1) copy and paste; (2) inserting using commands from the Insert menu; (3) drag and drop.

▶ KEY TERMS

Border command *(W10.21)*
center-aligned tab stop *(W10.19)*
Chart command *(W10.26)*
Copy button *(W10.25)*
Copy command *(W10.25)*
Create New Query command *(W10.39)*
Database Field command *(W10.12)*
decimal-aligned tab stop *(W10.19)*
Envelopes and Labels command *(W10.42)*

Insert menu *(W10.10)*
Insert Spreadsheet/Table command *(W10.30)*
left-aligned tab stop *(W10.19)*
longdate *(W10.10)*
Object Linking and Embedding (OLE) *(W10.3)*
OLE *(W10.3)*
Paste button *(W10.25)*
Paste command *(W10.25)*
placeholder *(W10.6)*
Picture/Object command *(W10.28)*

Print command *(W10.45)*
right-aligned tab stop *(W10.19)*
Special Character command *(W10.10)*
tab stops *(W10.19)*
table *(W10.17)*
Tabs command *(W10.19)*
Tile command *(W10.9, W10.31)*
Window menu *(W10.9)*

Q U I C K   R E F E R E N C E

In Microsoft Works, you can accomplish a task in a number of ways. The following table provides a quick reference to each task presented in this project with its available options. The commands listed in the Menu column can be executed using either the keyboard or mouse.

Task	Mouse	Menu	Keyboard Shortcuts
Change the Chart Size in a Word Processing Document	drag resize handles	From Format menu, choose Picture/Object	
Copy	Click Copy button; drag and drop	From Edit menu, choose Copy	Press CTRL+C
Insert a Database Placeholder		From Insert menu, choose Database Field	
Insert a Special Character		From Insert menu, choose Special Character	
Left-Align Tab Stop	Click ruler	From Format menu, choose Tabs	
Link a Chart to a Word Processing Document	drag and drop	From Insert menu, choose Chart	
Link a Spreadsheet to a Word Processing Document	drag and drop	From Edit menu, choose Paste Special; or from Insert menu, choose Spreadsheet/Table	
Outline a Table		From Format menu, choose Border	
Paste	Click Paste button; drag and drop	From File menu, choose Paste	Press CTRL+V
Print Form Letters		From File menu, choose Print	
Print Labels		From File menu, choose Print	

Task	Mouse	Menu	Keyboard Shortcuts
Remove Paragraph Formatting		From Format menu, choose Paragraph	Press CTRL+Q
Switch Open Application Windows	Click title bar	From Window menu, choose filename	Press CTRL+F6

S T U D E N T   A S S I G N M E N T S

STUDENT ASSIGNMENT 1
True/False

Instructions: Circle T if the statement is true or F if the statement is false.

T F   1. To print the current date in a form letter, type *longdate* in the document, and then click the Print button on the Toolbar.
T F   2. The entry *longdate* in a document will cause the date to print in the form of 12/21/95.
T F   3. The Special Character command is found on the Tools menu.
T F   4. A database placeholder consists of a field name from a database with chevrons on each side of the field name.
T F   5. You may type a placeholder directly in a document.
T F   6. When a database placeholder is placed in a document, the placeholder is replaced with the actual data from a database when the document is printed.
T F   7. The Database Field command is used when creating placeholders.
T F   8. The Database Field command is located in the Window menu.
T F   9. Special characters such as a comma cannot be placed between placeholders.
T F 10. You cannot set special margins for a table.
T F 11. When creating a table that is more than one line long, press the SHIFT+ENTER keys at the end of each line except the last line.
T F 12. To outline a table, use the Border command from the Format menu.
T F 13. The four types of tab stops that can be used in Works are: left-aligned tab stop, right-aligned tab stop, decimal-aligned tab stop, and center-aligned tab stop.
T F 14. You can copy a spreadsheet to a word processing document using drag and drop.
T F 15. To link a spreadsheet chart to a word processing document, choose the Chart command from the Insert menu.
T F 16. To change the size of a chart in a word processing document, choose the Chart command from the View menu.
T F 17. You can use the Picture/Object command to insert a chart in a word processing document.
T F 18. You cannot link a spreadsheet to a word processing document.
T F 19. The Print command from the File menu is used to print form letters.
T F 20. The Print command from the File menu is used to print mailing labels.

STUDENT ASSIGNMENT 2
Multiple Choice

Instructions: Circle the correct response.

1. To insert *longdate* in a document, choose the _____.
   a. Page Setup command
   b. Special Character command
   c. Picture/Object command
   d. Paste Special command
2. Which of the following is a valid placeholder?_____.
   a. Last Name
   b. ^^LAST NAME^^
   c. *LAST NAME*
   d. <<Last Name>>
3. The Database Field command is used when _____.
   a. creating a database
   b. inserting *longdate* in a document
   c. creating a placeholder
   d. copying a database field to a word processing document
4. To outline a table, use the _____.
   a. Border command from the Format menu
   b. Headers & Footers command from the View menu
   c. Picture/Object command from the Format menu
   d. Outline command from the Insert menu
5. To create a table with a column that is to contain alphabetic data, use _____.
   a. a right-aligned tab stop
   b. a left-aligned tab stop
   c. the right-margin indent marker
   d. the Table command
6. To link a spreadsheet chart to a word processing document, use the _____.
   a. Database field command from the Insert menu
   b. Chart command from the Insert menu
   c. Picture/Object command from the Format menu
   d. Paste command from the Edit menu
7. The command to change the size of a chart in a word processing document is the _____.
   a. Page Setup command
   b. Picture/Object command
   c. Chart command
   d. Special Character command
8. To link a spreadsheet to a word processing document, use _____.
   a. the Paste command from the Edit menu
   b. the Chart command from the Insert menu
   c. the Picture/Object command from the Format menu
   d. drag and drop
9. To print a form letter, use the _____.
   a. Print command
   b. Print Form Letter command
   c. Print Preview command
   d. Form Letter command
10. To switch between open application windows, _____.
   a. choose a filename from the Window menu
   b. click the left mouse button in the open workspace area
   c. double-click the left mouse button in the open workspace area
   d. click in the left margin area

STUDENT ASSIGNMENT 3
Understanding Microsoft Works Menus

Instructions: In the space provided in the right column, record the name of the menu associated with the commands in the left column.

COMMAND	MENU
Border command	
Chart command	
Database Field command	
Special Character command	
Picture/Object command	
Print command	
Envelopes and Labels command	

STUDENT ASSIGNMENT 4
Inserting the Date in a Letter

Instructions: In the space provided, explain the steps necessary to place *longdate* in a letter at the insertion point in Figure SA10-4.

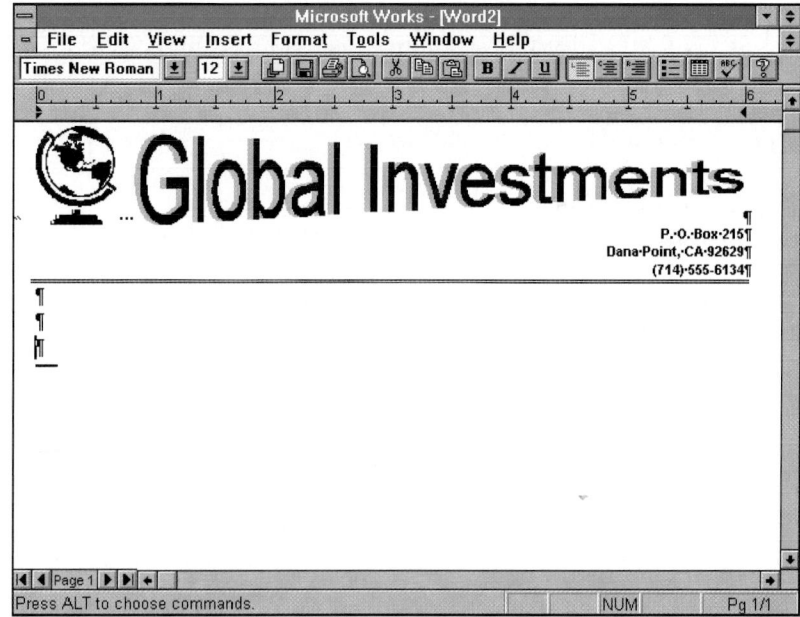

FIGURE SA10-4

STEPS:

1. _____

2. _____

3. _____

4. _____

5. _____

STUDENT ASSIGNMENT 5
Inserting a Placeholder in a Word Processing Document

Instructions: In the space provided below, explain the steps required to insert the <<Date>> placeholder as shown in the letter in Figure SA10-5. The database filename is PROJ8.WDB.

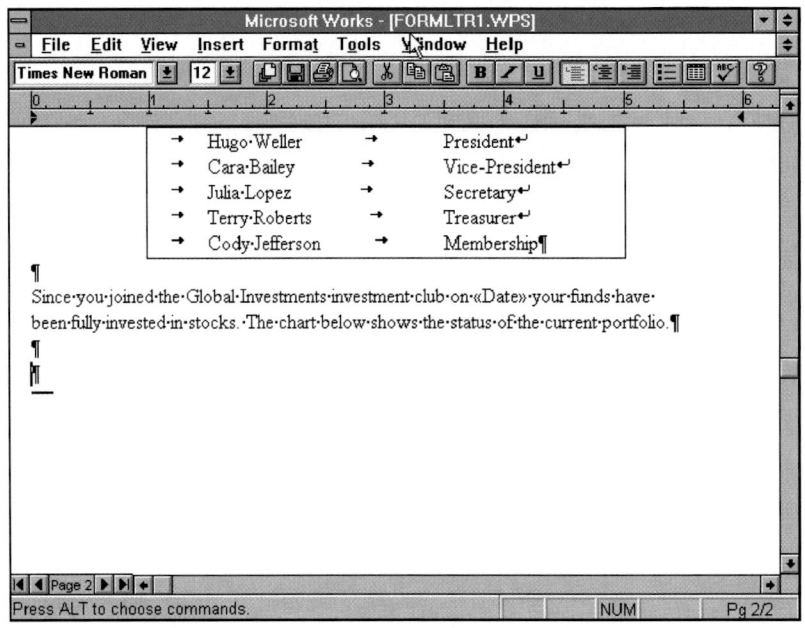

FIGURE SA10-5

STEPS:

1. _____

2. _____

3. _____

4. _____

5. _____

STUDENT ASSIGNMENT 6
Inserting a Spreadsheet in a Word Processing Document

Instructions: In the space provided below, explain the steps necessary to link a spreadsheet to a word processing document.

1. _____

2. _____

3. _____

4. _____

5. _____

COMPUTER LABORATORY EXERCISE 1
Using the Help Menu

Instructions: Perform the following tasks using a personal computer.

1. Start the Microsoft Works Word Processor Tool.
2. Select the Help menu.
3. Choose Search for Help on from the Help menu.
4. Type Special Character in the text box in the Search dialog box.
5. Choose the Show topics button.
6. Select Special Character command (Insert menu) WP in the list box at the bottom of the dialog box.
7. Choose the Go To button.
8. Review the screen display. Explain the following Dialog box options in the space provided.

DIALOG BOX OPTIONS	EXPLANATION
Print Page Number	
Print Filename	
Print Date	
Print Long Date	
Print Time	
Current Date	
Current Time	

9. Choose Exit from the Help file menu.

COMPUTER LABORATORY EXERCISE 2
Inserting a Chart in a Word Processing Document

Instructions: Start Works. Open the CLE10-2.WKS spreadsheet file and the CLE10-2.WPS word processing file on the Student Diskette that accompanies this book. The letter that is displayed is the letter in Figure 10-1 except the chart has not yet been inserted in the letter. At the proper location, insert the chart from the CLE10-2.WKS file. Reduce the chart to 70% of its original size. Complete Computer Laboratory Exercise 3 to insert the spreadsheet into the letter.

COMPUTER LABORATORY EXERCISE 3
Inserting a Spreadsheet in a Word Processing Document

Instructions: Insert the spreadsheet into the letter after the first paragraph on the second page. Print the document using the Print button on the Toolbar. This will print the document with the placeholders in the letter. Turn in the exercise to your instructor.

COMPUTER LABORATORY ASSIGNMENT 1
Creating and Printing Form Letters and Labels and Inserting a Chart in a Word Processing Document

Purpose: To provide experience using the Word Processor to create and print form letters and mailing labels and provide experience inserting a chart in a word processing document.

Problem: College Testing Service is a private educational group that tests students in English, mathematics, and verbal skills. After students are tested, a letter is sent advising them of the results of their test. Five students recently completed the testing program. A database of the students and their test scores is illustrated in Figure CLA10-1a.

DATE	LAST NAME	FIRST NAME	M.I.	ADDRESS	CITY	STATE
10/13/94	Adams	John	P.	231 S. Lambert Avenue	Brea	CA
10/13/94	Baker	Mary	A.	9845 Woodcrest Drive	Fullerton	CA
10/13/94	Jones	Carter	G.	17 Lake Terrace Lane	Yorba Linda	CA
10/13/94	Munoz	Theresa	A.	6523 Willow Lane	Fullerton	CA
10/13/94	Sanders	Carl	J.	890 S. Elm Street	Anaheim	CA

ZIP	ENGLISH	MATH	VERBAL	TEST SITE
92621	545	554	510	Brea College
92634	661	620	680	Brea College
92686	652	675	622	Brea College
92634	600	610	620	Brea College
92805	701	699	725	Brea College

FIGURE CLA 10-1a

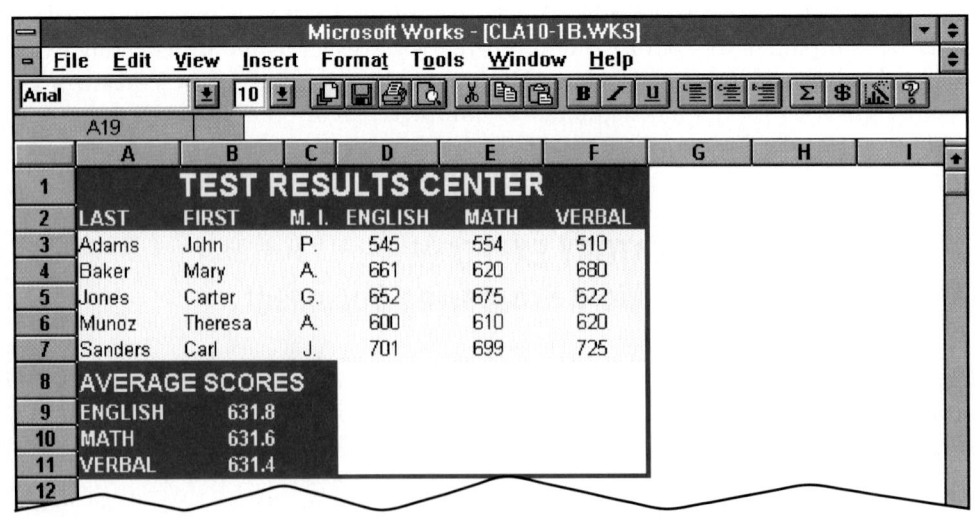

The spreadsheet in Figure CLA10-1b contains student test scores, and the average test scores in English, mathematics, and verbal skills for the five students taking the tests.

FIGURE CLA10-1b

After determining the test results, a letter is sent to each individual tested informing him or her of the results of the test. An example of the letter is illustrated in Figure CLA10-1c.

To establish the database, create the spreadsheet, and send letters to each individual, the College Testing Service has decided to utilize a personal computer.

Instructions: To complete this assignment, perform the following:

1. Create the database of the students in Figure CLA10-1a. Save the database on a diskette using an appropriate filename.

2. Create a spreadsheet and the associated chart for the average scores from the information in Figure CLA10-1b. Save the spreadsheet on a diskette using an appropriate filename.

3. Create and print form letters following the format in Figure CLA10-1c to be sent to each student taking the test. Insert the student's test scores in the letter from information in the database. The bar chart in the letter is from the chart for the average test scores associated with the spreadsheet. Save the form letter on a diskette using an appropriate filename.

4. Print a mailing label for each student.

College Testing Service

P.O. BOX 364 PRINCETON, NEW JERSERY 84592

December 21, 1995

John P. Adams
231 S. Lambert Avenue
Brea, CA 92621

Dear John:

The following are the results of the college entrance examinations which you took through College Testing Service on 10/13/94.

ENGLISH	545
MATH	554
VERBAL	510

The average scores for English, Math, and Verbal skills for all students who took the examination at Brea College on 10/13/94 are shown in the chart below.

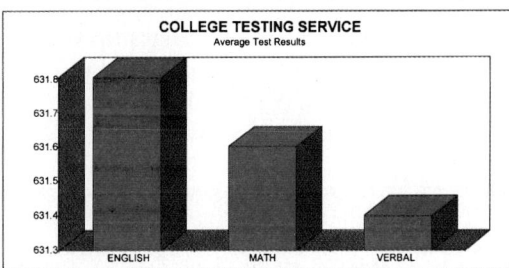

We hope this information will assist you in planning your college career.

Sincerely,

George Agrums
College Testing Service

FIGURE CLA10-1c

Turn in printed copies of the letters, spreadsheet, database in List View, and mailing labels to your instructor after completing the assignment.

COMPUTER LABORATORY ASSIGNMENT 2
Creating and Printing Form Letters and Labels and
Inserting a Chart and Spreadsheet in a Word Processing Document

Purpose: To provide experience using the Word Processor to create and print form letters and mailing labels and to provide experience inserting a chart and spreadsheet in a word processing document.

Problem: The Wakely College Foundation consists of friends of the college who solicit funds for scholarships. Funds donated may be designated for scholarships in Athletics, Business, Fine Arts, Humanities, or Math/Science. A database of foundation members is illustrated in Figure CLA10-2a.

TITLE	FIRST NAME	M.I.	LAST NAME	ADDRESS	CITY	STATE	ZIP	MEMBER TYPE
Mr.	Ernie	S.	Garcia	341 Harbor Ridge Road	Long Beach	CA	90808	Member
Mrs.	Maria	E.	Henderson	1745 Randolph Street	Cerritos	CA	90701	Member
Dr.	Darcy	A.	Hoban	5692 Willowbrook Avenue	Cerritos	CA	90701	Member
Mr.	Lyle	M.	Johnson	10461 Morado Drive	Long Beach	CA	90808	Associate
Ms.	Maureen	K.	McDaniels	5472 Highland Avenue	Cerritos	CA	90701	Associate
Ms.	Paula	S.	Miles	1934 Breakers Isle Road	Cerritos	CA	90701	Member
Dr.	Kevin	G.	Riley	1625 Brookdale Street	Long Beach	CA	90808	Associate
Mrs.	Catherine	J.	Thompson	7230 Fletcher Drive	Cerritos	CA	90701	Associate
Dr.	Harmon	V.	Ward	721 Monogram Lane	Long Beach	CA	90808	Member

FIGURE CLA10-2a

At the end of each academic year the Scholarship Chairman sends a letter to the members of the foundation showing the percentage of funds donated to the various academic areas, and the total amount donated to the scholarship program. A spreadsheet showing the scholarship funds donated in each area and the total amount of funds donated is shown in Figure CLA10-2b.

FIGURE CLA10-2b

A letter is sent to only those individuals who are identified in the database as a member in the Member Type field. An example of the letter sent to each member of the foundation is illustrated in Figure CLA10-2c. You have been directed to create the database, spreadsheet, chart, and letter using a personal computer.

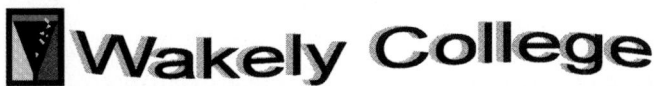

1321 COLLEGE DRIVE, WAKELY, CA 23956   (213) 555-4037

December 21, 1995

Mr. Ernie S. Garcia
341 Harbor Ridge Road
Long Beach, CA 90808

Dear Mr. Garcia:

The Officers for the Wakely College Foundation for 1995 are:

Catherine Thompson	President
Lyle Johnson	Vice President
Kevin Riley	Secretary
Maureen McDaniels	Treasurer
Darcy Hoban	Community Liason

We are pleased to announce that donations to our scholarship fund have increased for the fifth year. The chart below shows the percentage of funds donated to the various divisions of the college.

SCHOLARSHIP DONATIONS

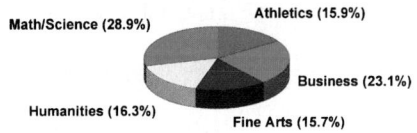

This year the business community made a number of large donations to our Math/Science scholarship program.

FIGURE CLA10-2c

Page 2
Mr. Ernie S. Garcia
December 21, 1995

The report below details the donations to our scholarship program.

Number of Donors	Scholarship Type	Total Amount
	WAKELY COLLEGE Scholarship Donations	
50	Athletics	$75,700.00
120	Business	$110,400.00
100	Fine Arts	$75,000.00
10	Humanities	$78,000.00
25	Math/Science	$138,000.00
Total Scholarships		**$477,100.00**

Thank you for your support.

Sincerely,

Kevin W. Conway
Scholarship Chairman

(continued)

COMPUTER LABORATORY ASSIGNMENT 2 (continued)

Instructions: To complete this assignment perform the following:

Part 1:

1. Create the database. Save the database on a diskette using an appropriate filename.
2. Create the spreadsheet and chart. Save the spreadsheet on a diskette using an appropriate filename.
3. Create and print form letters following the format in Figure CLA10-2c for each individual in the database identified as a member in the Member Type field. Insert the chart and spreadsheet created in Step 2 above. Save the form letter on a diskette using an appropriate filename.
4. Print a mailing label for each member.

Part 2:

1. The Wakely College Foundation just received a new $100,000.00 donation for Fine Arts scholarships. Update the spreadsheet to reflect this addition and print the updated letter and spreadsheet.

Turn in printed copies of the database, the spreadsheets, letters, and mailing labels to your instructor.

COMPUTER LABORATORY ASSIGNMENT 3
Creating and Printing Form Letters and Labels and Inserting a Chart and Spreadsheet in a Word Processing Document

Purpose: To provide experience using the Word Processor to create and print form letters and mailing labels and to provide experience inserting a chart and spreadsheet into a word processing document.

Problem: At the end of each month the North County Real Estate Association sends out letters to its broker members listing the total sales in various categories of real estate. A database of the members of the real estate association is illustrated in Figure CLA10-3a.

FIGURE CLA10-3a

TITLE	FIRST NAME	M.I.	LAST NAME	ADDRESS	CITY	STATE	ZIP	CLASS
Mr.	John	A.	Hunter	8534 Walnut Avenue	Placentia	CA	92670	Sales
Mrs.	Melissa	N.	Montgomery	123 W. Porter Drive	Fullerton	CA	92633	Broker
Mrs.	Nancy	I.	Lopez	3491 Gorden Avenue	La Habra	CA	90631	Sales
Mr.	Jim	B.	Chamberlain	9812 Lambert Road	Brea	CA	92621	Broker
Mr.	William	D.	Smith	1200 W. Brent Drive	La Habra	CA	90631	Sales
Ms.	Judy	K.	Tarbell	7602 Harbor Street	Placentia	CA	92670	Broker
Mr.	Anthony	D.	Owens	560 Dale Avenue	Fullerton	CA	92633	Sales
Ms.	Marcy	G.	Walker	620 S. Valley Street	Fullerton	CA	92633	Sales

A spreadsheet showing real estate sales in each major classification is illustrated in Figure CLA10-3b.

Microsoft Works - [CLA10-3B.WKS]

File   Edit   View   Insert   Format   Tools   Window   Help

Arial   10

A19

	A	B	C	D	E	F
1	*October Sales*					
3	*Division*	*Units Sold*	*Sales Total*			
4	Residential	40	$8,500,000.00			
5	Multi-Tenant	3	$5,500,000.00			
6	Commercial	5	$6,200,000.00			
7	Industrial	7	$3,500,000.00			
8	Office	10	$4,000,000.00			
9						
10	*Total Sales*		$27,700,000.00			
11						

FIGURE CLA10-3b

A letter is sent to only those individuals who are identified in the database as a broker in the Class field. An example of the letter sent to each broker is illustrated in Figure CLA10-3c. You have been directed to create the database, spreadsheet, chart, and letter using a personal computer.

North County Real Estate Association

1120 East Laguna Road, Fullerton, CA 92633 (714) 555-5027

December 21, 1995

Mr. John A. Hunter
8534 Walnut Avenue
Placentia, CA 92670

Dear Mr. Hunter:

Officers for the North County Real Estate Association Board of Directors for 1996 are:

President	John Hunter
Vice President	Marcy Walker
Secretary	Nancy Lopez
Treasurer	William Smith

Sales in all divisions of real estate increased for the third month in a row. The chart below shows the percentage of sales in each division for the month of October.

OCTOBER SALES
Real Estate

Office (14.4%)

Residential (30.7%)

Industrial (12.6%)

Commercial (22.4%)

Multi-Tenant (19.9%)

As you can see, residential sales have fallen off somewhat but that is more than offset by the increase in office sales.

FIGURE CLA10-3c

Page 2
Mr. John A. Hunter
December 21, 1995

A more detailed analysis is contained in the following chart.

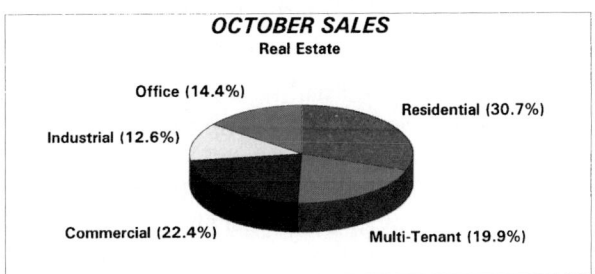

October Sales		
Division	**Units Sold**	**Sales Total**
Residential	40	$8,500,000.00
Multi-Tenant	3	$5,500,000.00
Commercial	5	$6,200,000.00
Industrial	7	$3,500,000.00
Office	10	$4,000,000.00
Total Sales		**$27,700,000.00**

We are optimistic that the real estate market will continue to expand.

Sincerely,

Kathy Baker
Executive Director

(continued)

COMPUTER LABORATORY ASSIGNMENT 3 (continued)

Instructions: To complete this assignment, perform the following:

Part 1:

1. Create the database. Save the database on a diskette using an appropriate filename.
2. Create the spreadsheet and chart. Save the spreadsheet on a diskette using an appropriate filename.
3. Create and print form letters following the format in Figure CLA10-3c on the previous page for each individual in the database identified as a broker in the Class field. Insert the chart and spreadsheet created in Step 2 in the letters. Save the form letter on a diskette using an appropriate filename.
4. Print a mailing label for each member.

Part 2:

1. An additional $2 million for October sales of 3 office properties should be added to the spreadsheet.
2. Print the updated letter and spreadsheet.

   Turn in printed copies of the database in List View, the spreadsheet, letters, and the mailing labels to your instructor after completing the assignment.

COMPUTER LABORATORY ASSIGNMENT 4
Creating and Printing Form Letters and Labels and Inserting a Chart and Spreadsheet in a Word Processing Document

Purpose: To provide experience using the Word Processor to create and print form letters and mailing labels and to provide experience inserting a chart and spreadsheet into a word processing document.

Instructions: Prepare a spreadsheet listing your projected total monthly expenses after you leave school in the following categories: Rent, Food, Clothing, Utilities, Automobile, Insurance, Entertainment, and Miscellaneous.

   Prepare a letter to be sent to five banks requesting a credit card. Include in the letter the spreadsheet showing your total monthly expenses and a chart showing the percentage of expenses in each category. The names and addresses of the bank should be established as a database. Print letters to each bank, along with a mailing label for each one.

   Turn in printed copies of the database in List View, the spreadsheet, the letters, and the mailing labels to your instructor after completing the assignment.

▼

Spreadsheet Charting

▼

SPREADSHEET CHARTING

You will have mastered the material in this project when you can:

- ▸ Specify the chart types you can create using Microsoft Works
- ▸ Explain the use of each chart type
- ▸ Create a 3-D Pie chart, add a title and subtitle, add slice titles, and change font, font size, and font style for titles
- ▸ Display values on a 3-D Pie chart
- ▸ Explode a 3-D pie slice
- ▸ Add a border to a chart
- ▸ Preview a chart before printing
- ▸ Print a chart

- ▸ Rotate a 3-D Pie chart
- ▸ Create a Bar chart
- ▸ Add legends to a Bar chart
- ▸ Change colors and patterns in a Bar chart
- ▸ Create a Line chart and add gridlines
- ▸ Add a right vertical (Y) axis
- ▸ Change the scale of an axis
- ▸ Create a Stacked Line chart
- ▸ Create a Combination chart
- ▸ Create an X-Y (Scatter) chart
- ▸ Create a logo using the Microsoft Draw tool

▶ INTRODUCTION

A chart is a graphical representation of the data in a spreadsheet. Charts can help you compare values, understand relationships among values, and see trends when comparing values. Charting is an important means of communicating information.

Project 4 and Project 5 introduced the use of the 3-D Bar chart and the 3-D Pie chart. Project 11 reviews the techniques used to create these charts and presents additional topics that allow you to produce other types of charts for a variety of applications.

▶ TYPES OF CHARTS

M icrosoft Works provides you with the capability of generating the following types of charts.

1. Pie chart
2. 3-D Pie chart
3. Bar chart
4. 3-D Bar chart
5. Line chart
6. 3-D Line chart

7. Area chart
8. 3-D Area chart
9. Stacked Line chart
10. Combination chart
11. X-Y (Scatter) chart
12. Radar chart

It is important to be able to analyze data in a spreadsheet and determine the appropriate chart type you should use to convey the contents of the spreadsheet in a meaningful manner. The following paragraphs explain the use of the various chart types.

Pie Charts

One of the more widely used charts is the Pie chart. Figure 11-1 illustrates a standard Pie chart.

A **Pie chart** is circular in form and is divided into wedges called **slices**. Each slice in the Pie chart represents a percentage, or portion, of the whole. The Pie chart in Figure 11-1 displays the amount of money spent on various forms of advertising by a company called Automobile Center. From the chart you can see that television advertising consumes the largest portion of the total advertising budget. One of the slices, for magazine advertising, is exploded, or slightly separated from the chart. This is done to emphasize one slice in the Pie chart. The values displayed within parentheses can be percentages as was shown in Project 5, or can be actual values found in the spreadsheet, as seen in Figure 11-1.

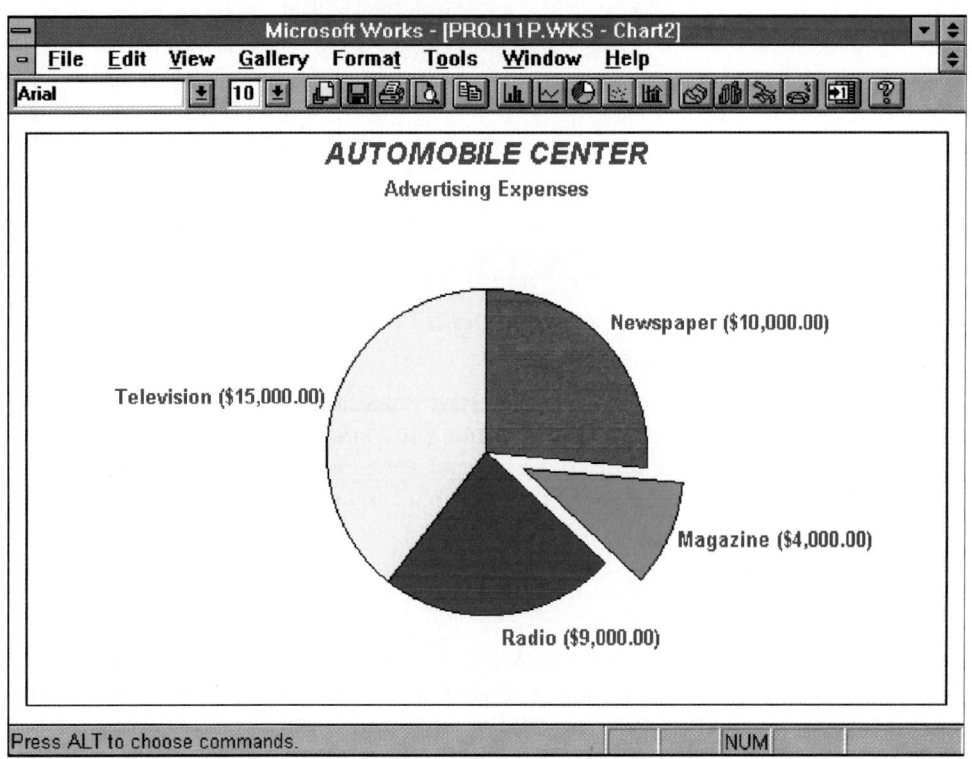

FIGURE 11-1

Figure 11-2 illustrates a **3-D Pie chart** displaying the same data as the Pie chart in Figure 11-1. Many individuals feel a 3-D Pie chart provides a more attractive form of presentation by giving added dimension to the chart.

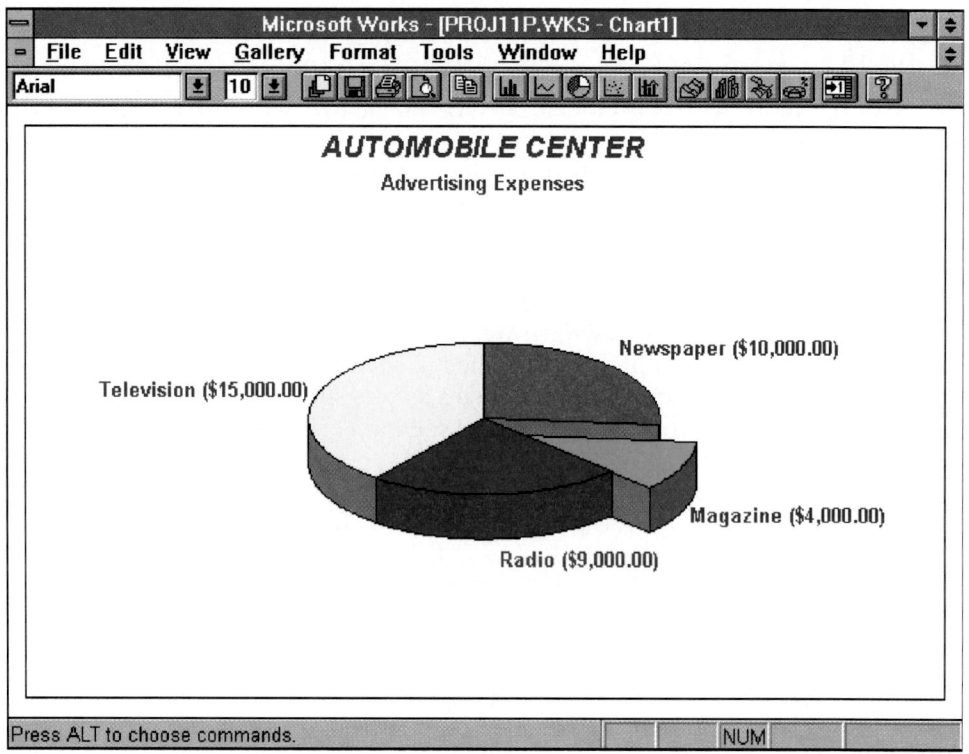

FIGURE 11-2

A disadvantage of the Pie chart is the chart does not display small percentages or amounts clearly because the slices become quite small. In addition, a Pie chart can effectively display only a limited number of slices, typically less than ten, and you can display only one category of data, such as advertising expense, in a single chart.

Bar Charts

The **Bar chart** displays data by drawing bars to represent values. The Bar chart is useful when comparing two or more values. The chart in Figure 11-3 illustrates the sale of tickets for children, adults, and seniors for the Showtime Theater during the days Monday through Friday. The red bars represent the number of tickets for children sold each day. The yellow bars represent the number of tickets for adults sold each day, and the blue bars show the number of tickets for seniors sold each day. From this chart it is easy to see that tickets for adults outsell tickets for children and seniors, and the greatest number of tickets for any single day are sold on Friday.

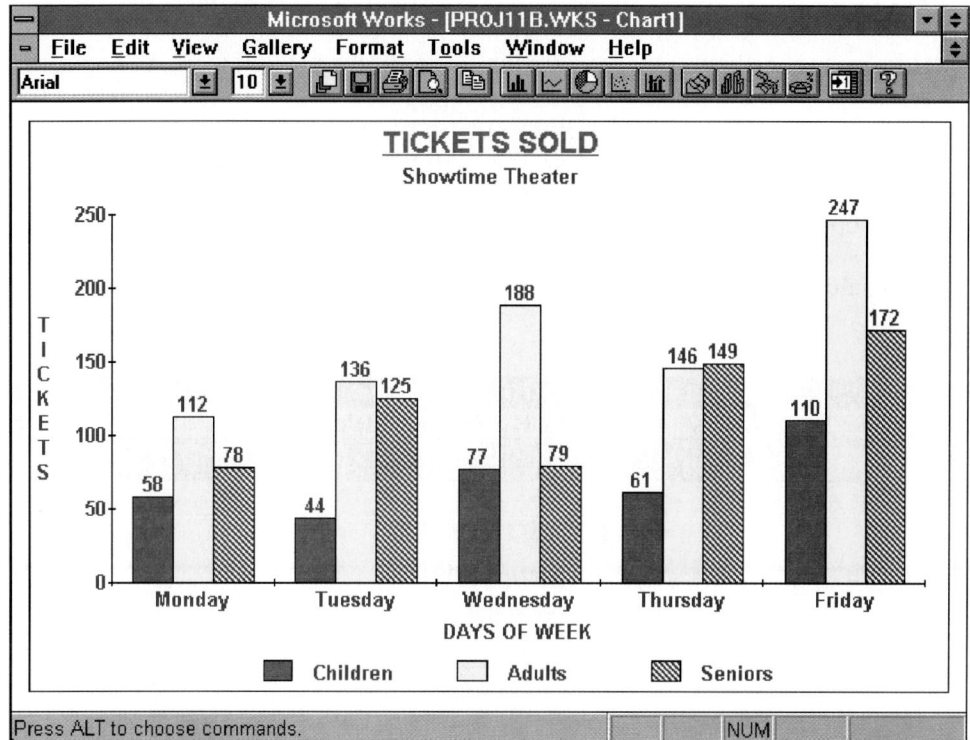

FIGURE 11-3

Notice that this Bar chart displays three values for each day. Because of this, you could not use a Pie Chart in this application.

Figure 11-4 illustrates a **3-D Bar chart** displaying the same data as the Bar chart in Figure 11-3. The numbers above each bar do not display in the 3-D Bar chart.

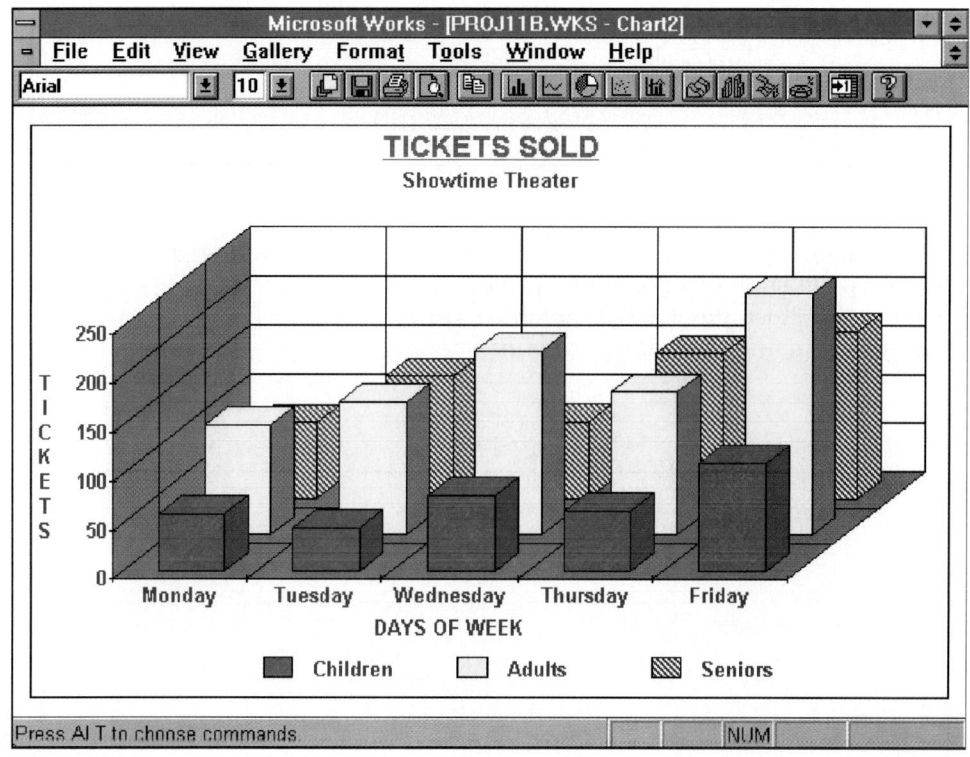

FIGURE 11-4

Line Charts

A **Line chart** displays data by drawing lines and/or placing markers horizontally across a page. Line charts are often used for showing trends over a period of time. The Line chart in Figure 11-5 shows projected software sales of a company called EZ Software over a period of six years for three products. From this chart you can see the trend in projected sales is upward for EZGraph, EZFind, and EZType except in the year 2000 where EZType trends downward. The small circles, squares, and diamonds on the chart are called **markers**. Markers represent individual values in spreadsheet cells based on the scale on the left and right sides of the chart.

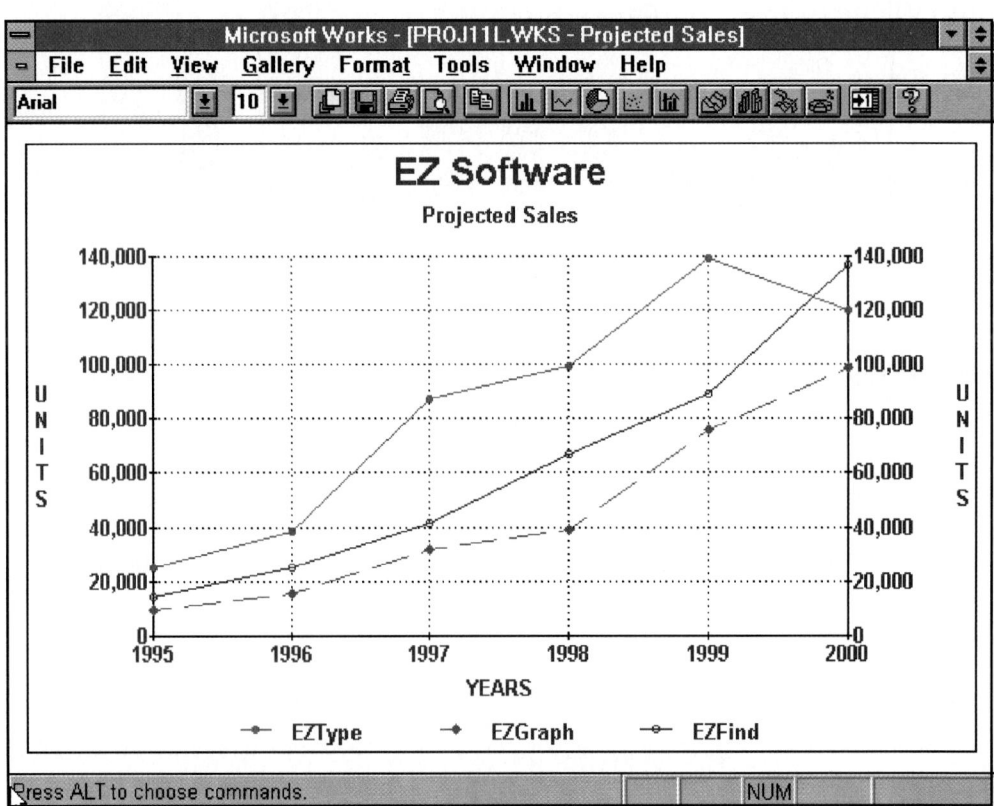

FIGURE 11-5

The Line chart in Figure 11-5 does not display precise values in a manner that is easy to see but shows trends over a period of time effectively.

Figure 11-6 illustrates a **3-D Line chart** with gridlines. 3-D Line charts represent the lines in a line chart as 3-D ribbons.

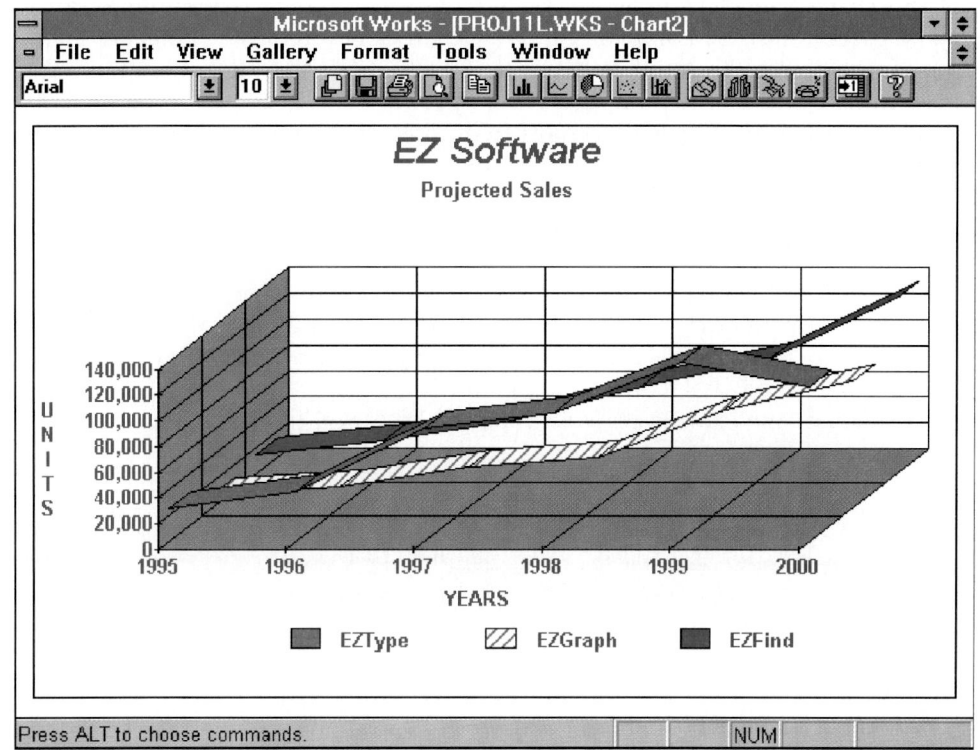

FIGURE 11-6

Stacked Line Charts

A **Stacked Line** chart illustrates the relationship between two or more values and their totals by drawing stacked lines and/or markers horizontally across a chart. In a Stacked Line chart, each line's values are added to those of the line below.

The Stacked Line chart in Figure 11-7 shows the number of computers produced on three shifts at a company called PCTech Computers. The magenta line represents the computers produced on the 7 am to 3 pm shift. For example, on Monday, approximately 100 computers were produced. The green line represents the combined total of computers produced on both the 7 am to 3 pm and 3 pm to 11 pm shifts. For Monday, the combined total of both shifts is a little more than 300 computers. The distance between the green line and the magenta line shows the number of computers produced on the 3 pm to 11 pm shift (a few more than 200 computers).

Similarly, the blue line on the chart in Figure 11-7 shows the number of computers produced on all three shifts. The distance between the blue line and the green line for each day shows the number of computers produced on the 11 pm to 7 am shift.

The Stacked Line chart is a special type of chart used to display totals over a period of time.

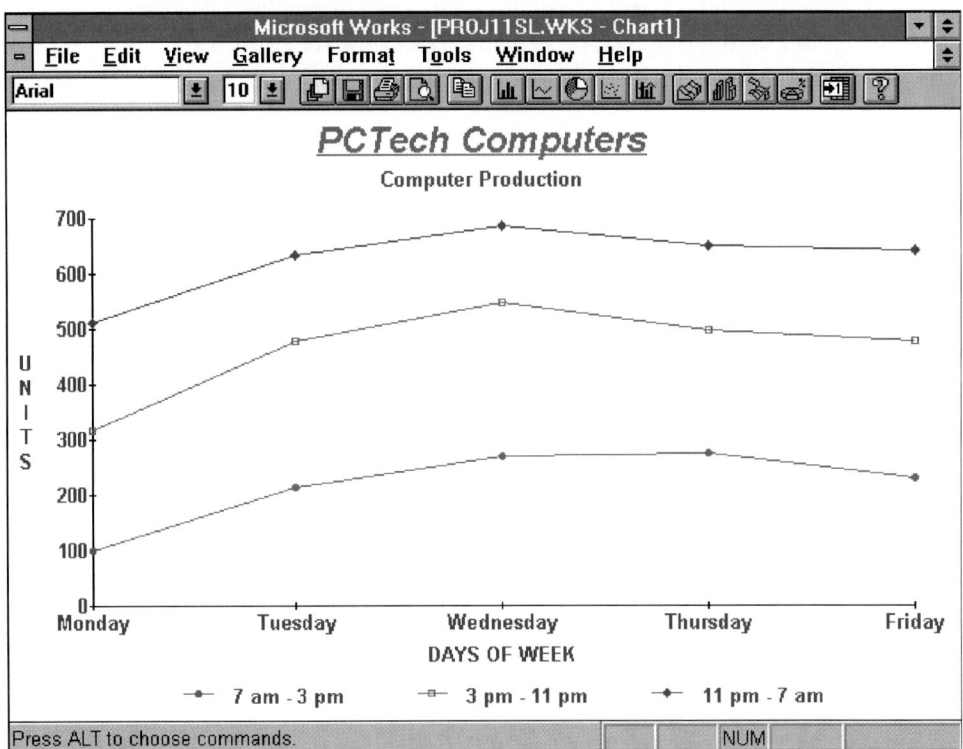

FIGURE 11-7

Area Charts

Figure 11-8 illustrates an **Area chart** displaying the same data as the Stacked Line chart previously explained. Area charts are similar to Line charts but tend to emphasize the amount or magnitude of change better than line charts.

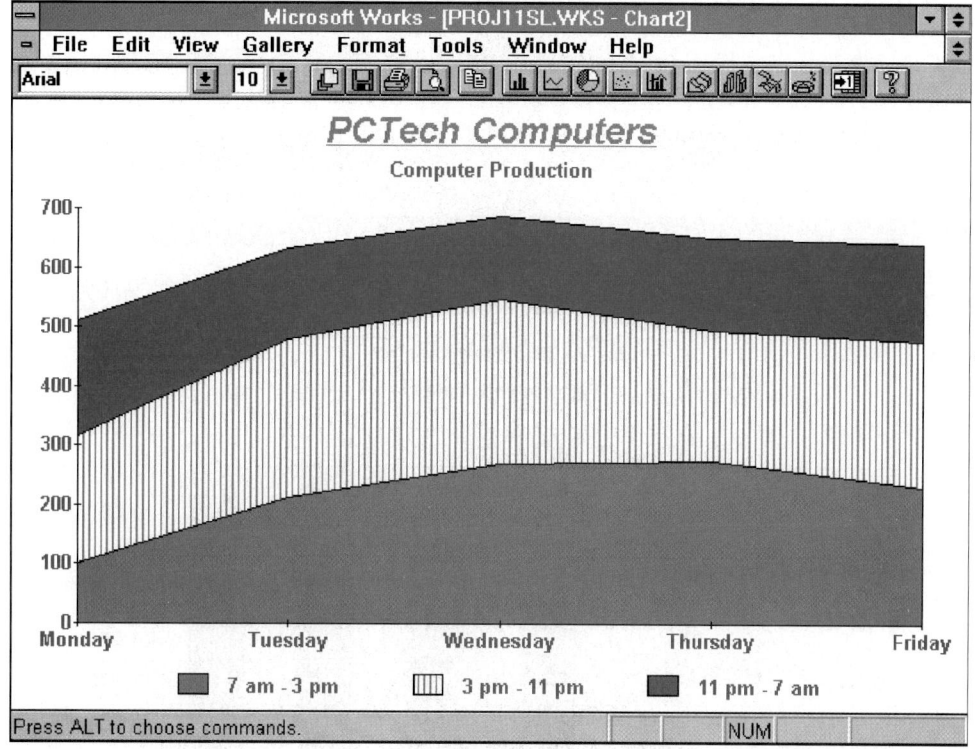

FIGURE 11-8

Figure 11-9 illustrates a **3-D Area chart**.

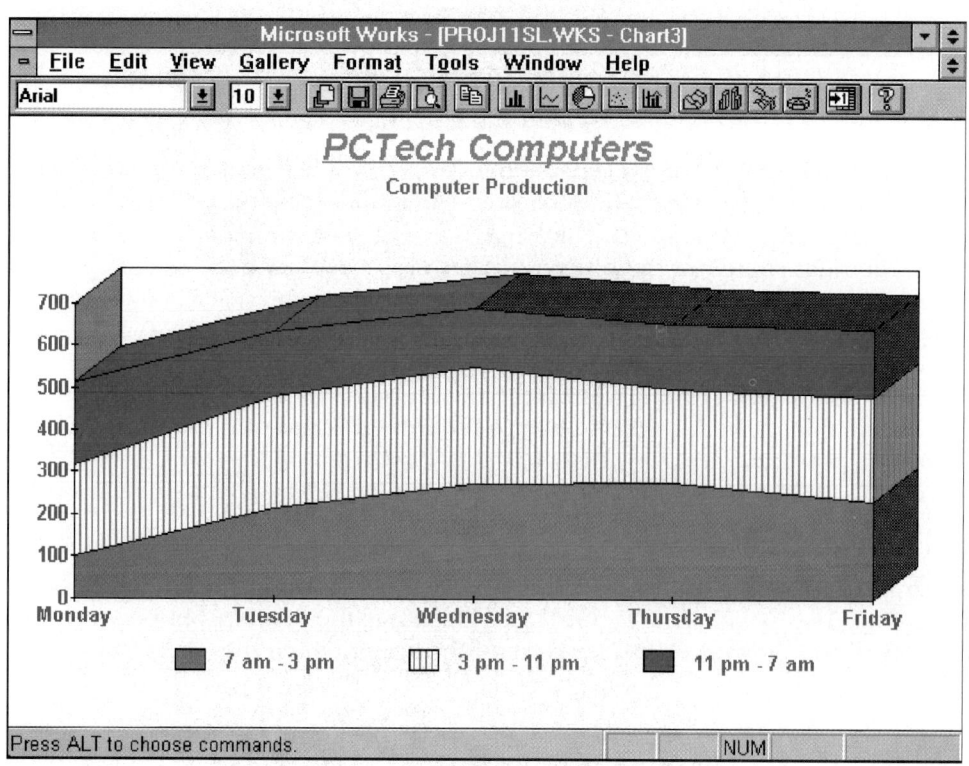

FIGURE 11-9

Combination Charts

A **Combination chart** mixes bars and lines on the same chart. The chart in Figure 11-10 shows the projected sales for two software products. The projected sales of EZType are indicated by the blue bars and the projected sales of EZGraph are indicated by the red line.

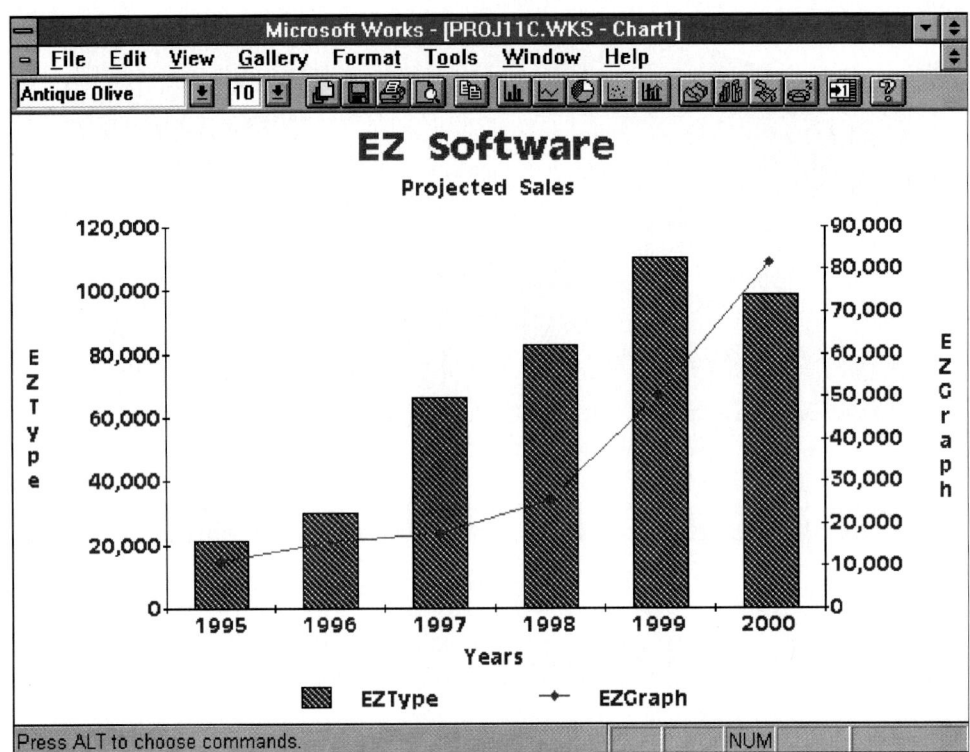

FIGURE 11-10

Notice in Figure 11-10 that the numbers for EZType on the left are different than the numbers for EZGraph on the right. The numbers on the left represent the projected sales of EZType and the blue bars are scaled to these numbers. The numbers on the right represent the projected sales of EZGraph and the red line is scaled to these numbers. As a result, the red diamond for the year 2000 represents a value of approximately 82,000, whereas the blue bar in the year 2000 represents a value of almost 100,000 even though it is lower than the red square.

The Combination chart serves essentially the same function as a Bar or Line chart. By combining both lines and bars, a different method of presentation and emphasis is possible.

X-Y (Scatter) Charts

An **X-Y chart**, also called a **Scatter chart**, shows relationships between related data. The X-Y chart in Figure 11-11 illustrates the relationship between the age of one hundred women in a survey and the age at which they were married.

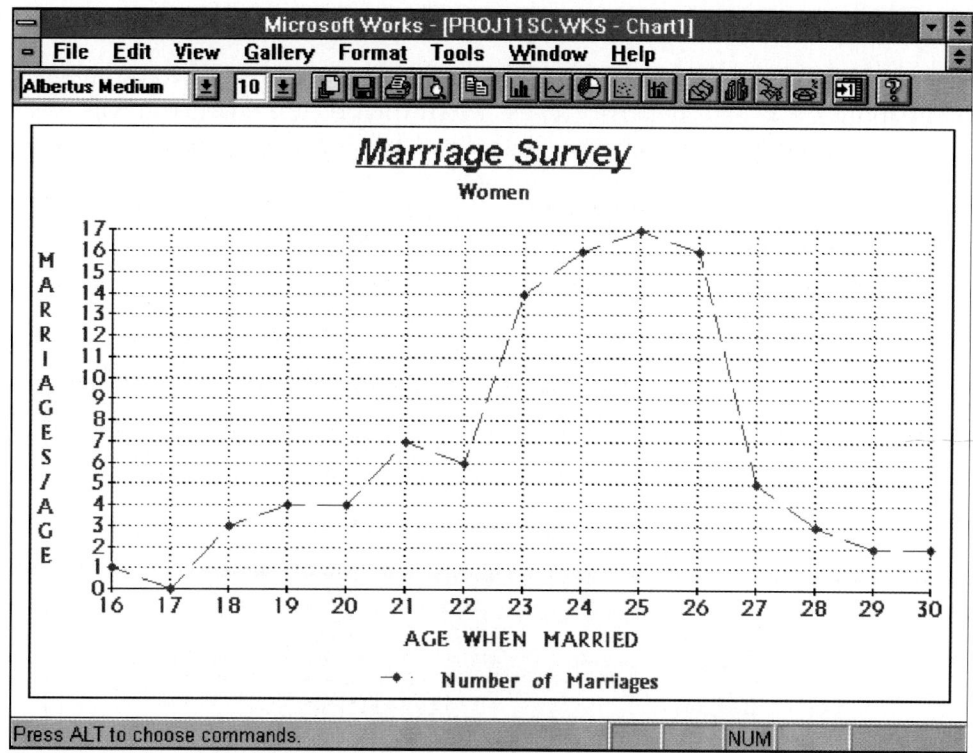

FIGURE 11-11

In Figure 11-11 you can see that one marriage occurred at age 16, zero marriages at age 17, and three marriages at age 18. The largest number of marriages occurred between 23 and 26 years of age.

Radar Chart

A chart type called a **Radar chart** may also be displayed using Works. The Radar chart shows changes in or frequencies of data relative to a center point and to each other. For additional information on the use of a Radar chart, see Works online Help.

Chart Variations

In addition to the basic format of the various charts, Works provides numerous variations on each of the chart types. When you create a chart, you will choose one of the basic chart types. Once the chart is created, you can change the chart type by clicking the Charting Toolbar (Figure 11-12). You can also choose from a variety of ways to display the chart within each chart type. For example, Figure 11-12 shows some of the variations of the 3-D Bar chart you can select.

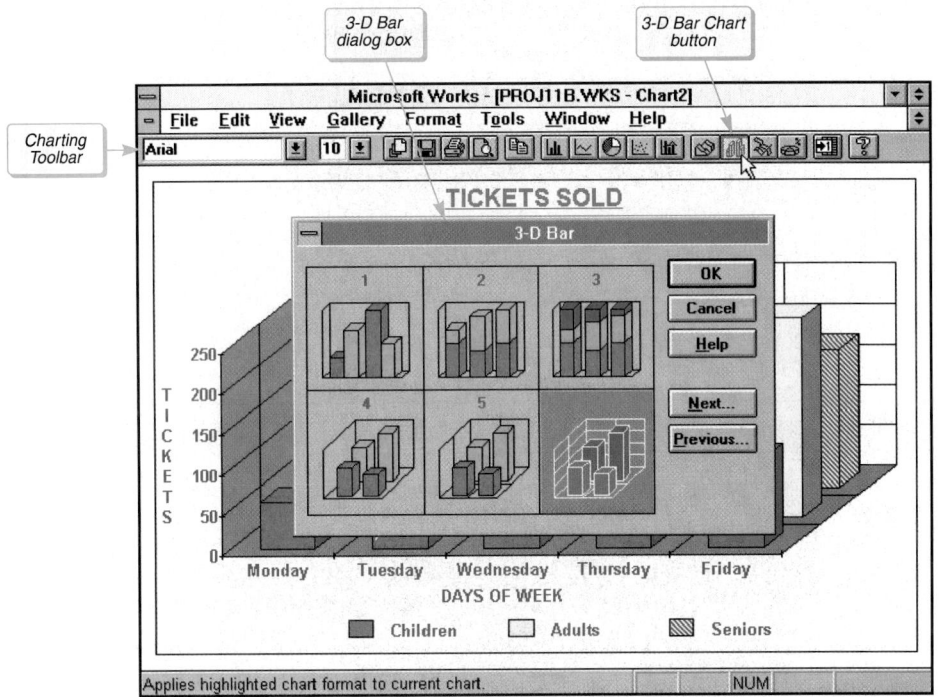

FIGURE 11-12

Selecting Option 1 in the 3-D Bar dialog box will display a standard 3-D representation of a Bar chart. Selecting Option 2 will display all values in each category as segments stacked in a single 3-D Bar. The combined segments represent the total values of that category. Selecting Option 3 will display all values in each category as a percentage stacked in a single 3-D Bar. Each segment represents a percentage of the 100 percent total of the category. Selecting Option 4 will display a 3-D Bar chart in which the bars of the same color display side-by-side, and the categories are represented in front-to-back rows. Selecting Option 5 shows the same representation as in Option 4 with vertical gridlines. Selecting Option 6 shows the same representation as in Option 4, with vertical and horizontal gridlines. The 3-D Bar chart in Figure 11-12 is an Option 6 chart.

Chart Summary

It is important to understand that you can chart spreadsheet data in a variety of ways using one or more of the charts available with Microsoft Works. The chart you use depends on the information you want to convey.

The remainder of this project shows the detailed steps required to construct many of the charts shown in Figure 11-1 through Figure 11-12.

▶ CREATING A 3-D PIE CHART

I n Project 5, you created a 3-D Pie chart. This project reviews the steps required to create a 3-D Pie chart and also explains how to add a subtitle, how to display labels containing amounts, how to explode a slice of the 3-D Pie chart, how to add a border around the chart, and how to print the chart in various sizes.

The spreadsheet and chart created in this project are illustrated in Figure 11-13. The spreadsheet contains the amount of money spent on newspaper, magazine, radio, and television media advertising by the Automobile Center. The same information is illustrated in chart form by the 3-D Pie chart.

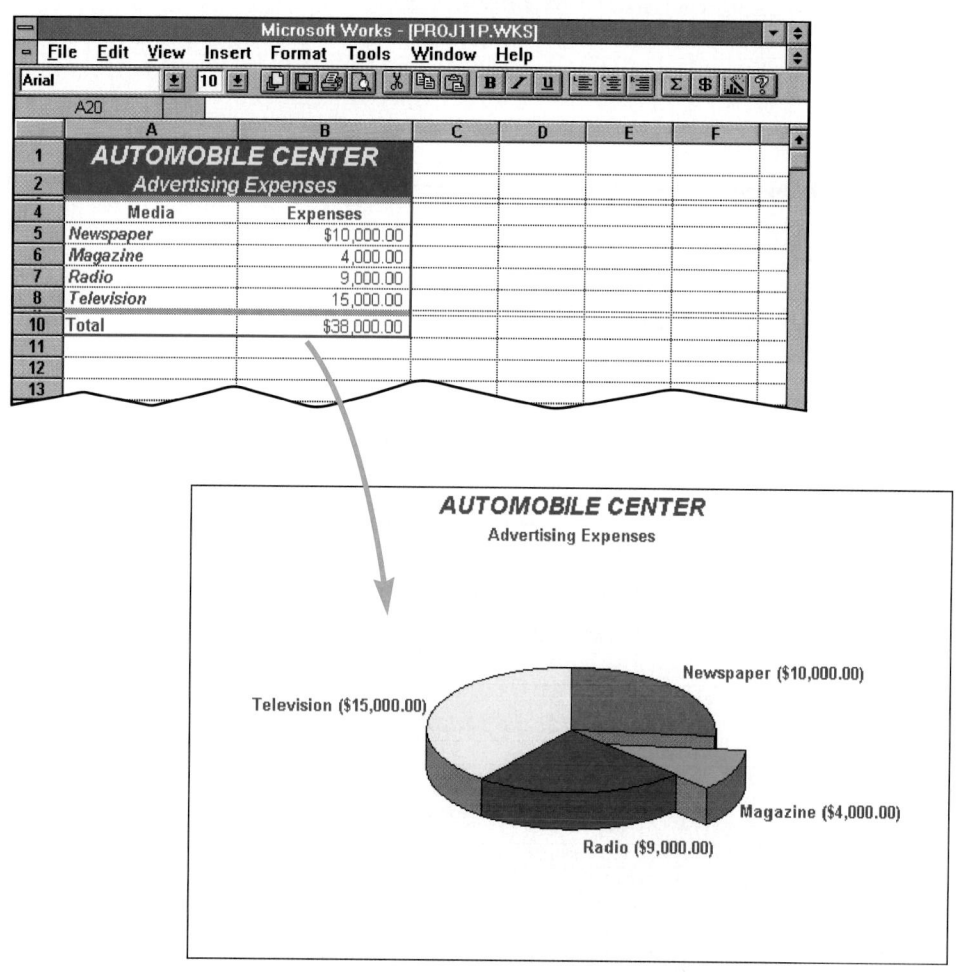

FIGURE 11-13

In the spreadsheet, the text in column A to the left of and adjacent to the cells containing numbers identifies each type of media. When you create a Pie chart, and there is text to the left of and adjacent to the cells containing the numbers to chart, Works can use the text for labels that identify each slice in the Pie chart.

To create the Pie chart in Figure 11-13, perform the steps on the next two pages. It is assumed the spreadsheet file is open and displays on the screen.

TO CREATE A PIE CHART ▼

STEP 1 ▶

Highlight the range to chart (cells A5:B8) in the spreadsheet and point to the New Chart button on the Toolbar (Figure 11-14).

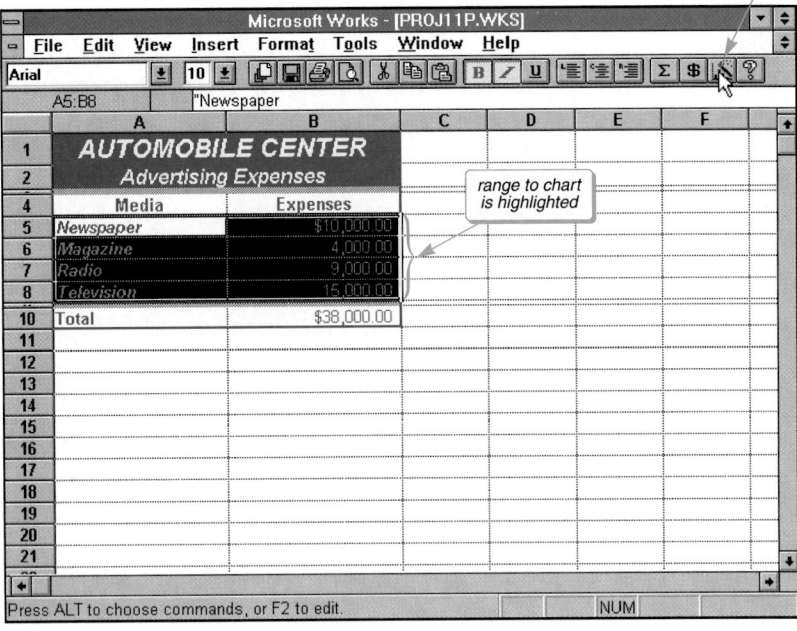

FIGURE 11-14

STEP 2 ▶

Click the New Chart button. When the New Chart dialog box displays, click the What type of chart do you want? drop-down list box arrow. Scroll down and select 3-D Pie. Type a1 in the Chart title text box, click the Add border check box, and point to the OK button.

Works displays the New Chart dialog box (Figure 11-15). 3-D Pie displays in the What type of chart do you want? drop-down list box. a1 displays in the Chart title text box. You can type the cell reference a1 in the Chart title text box if you want to display the title in the spreadsheet on the chart, or you can type a chart name in the text box. The Add border check box instructs Works to place a border around the chart. The mouse pointer points to the OK button.

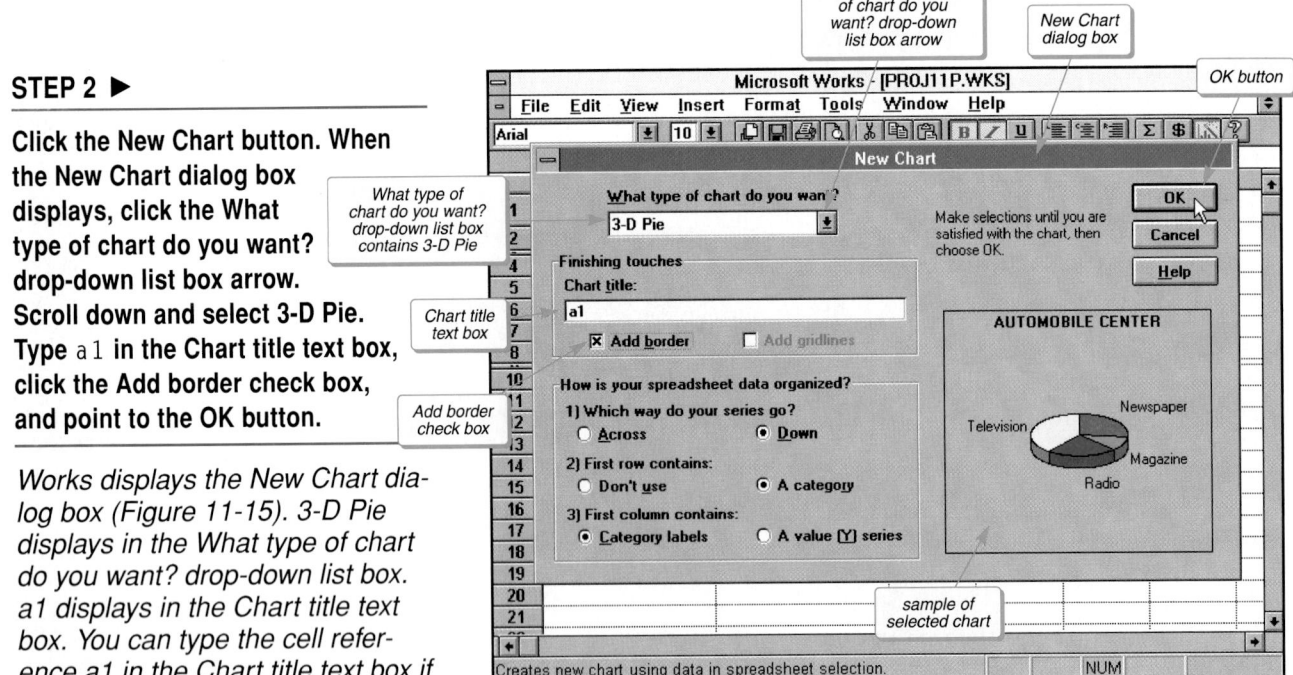

FIGURE 11-15

STEP 3 ▶

Choose the OK button in the New
Chart dialog box.

*Works displays a 3-D Pie chart
(Figure 11-16). Each pie slice contains a label called a **data label**
identifying each slice. The data
labels are from cells A5:A8
because you highlighted them in
Step 1. The name Chart1 displays
in the Title bar.*

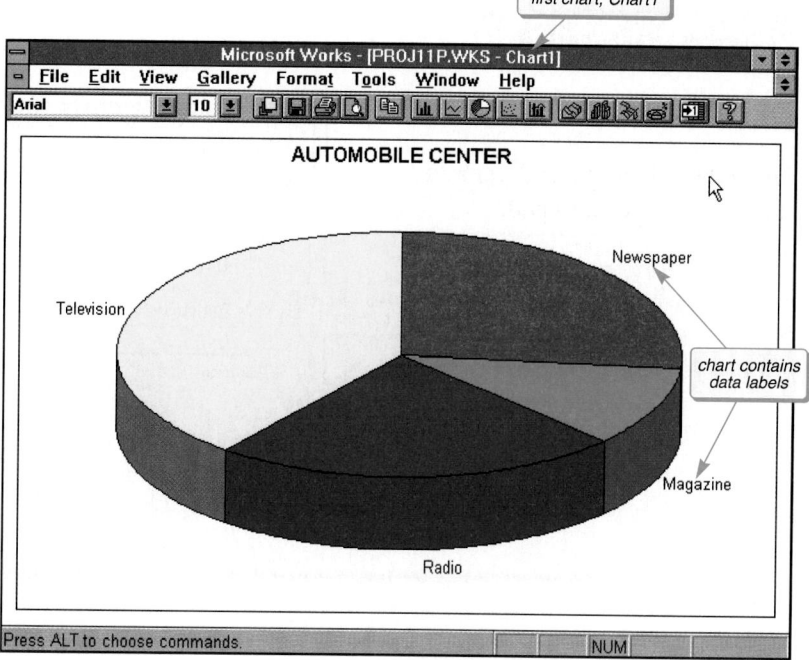

FIGURE 11-16

When you create a chart, Works names the first chart Chart1, places the chart
name in the title bar, and adds the name Chart1 to the Window menu and to the
list of charts created with data from the spreadsheet. You can view the chart when
needed by selecting the Window menu and choosing the chart name if the chart is
open. If the chart is not open, select the View menu and choose the Chart command. In the Charts dialog box, highlight the name of the chart you want to view
and choose the OK button.

Adding Data Labels

For each slice in the Pie chart, you can insert two **data labels**. The first data
label normally consists of text or sequential numbers used to identify each slice.
The second data label often consists of the percentage of each slice as related to
the whole or the actual numeric value in each cell you are charting. Text, actual
numeric values, percentages, or sequential numbers can be used in either or both
data labels. In the chart for this project, the first data labels (Newspaper, Magazine,
Radio, and Television) are in the chart because you selected range A5:B8 in the
spreadsheet and the labels describing the slices are in cells A5, A6, A7, and A8. To
add a second data label containing the values represented by each slice, perform
the steps on the next two pages.

TO ADD DATA LABELS ▼

STEP 1 ▶

Select the Edit menu and point to the Data Labels command.

*The Edit menu displays and the mouse pointer points to the **Data Labels command** (Figure 11-17).*

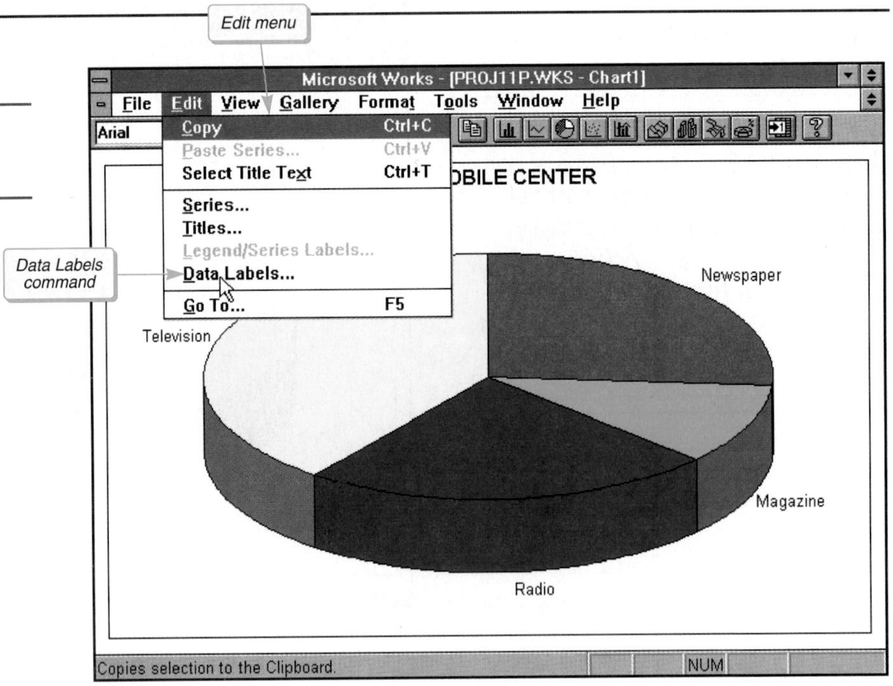

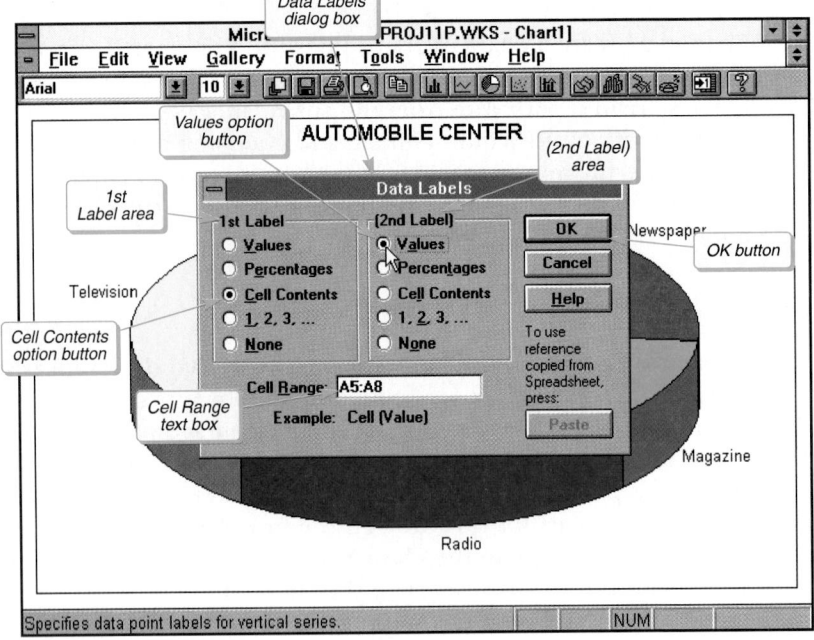

FIGURE 11-17

STEP 2 ▶

Choose the Data Labels command from the Edit menu. When the Data Labels dialog box displays, select the Values option button in the (2nd Label) area.

Works displays the Data Labels dialog box (Figure 11-18). In the 1st Label area, the Cell Contents option button is selected and the Cell Range text box contains A5:A8 because cells A5:A8 were highlighted together with the cells containing the values to chart (B5:B8) before creating the chart (see Figure 11-14 on page W11.14). Cells A5:A8 contain the text Newspaper, Magazine, Radio, and Television. In the 2nd Label area, the Values option button is selected. The Values option button specifies that the actual values charted should be displayed as the second data label.

FIGURE 11-18

STEP 3 ▶

Choose the OK button in the Data Labels dialog box.

Works displays the 3-D Pie Chart (Figure 11-19). The data labels in parentheses contain the values (actual amounts) represented by each slice.

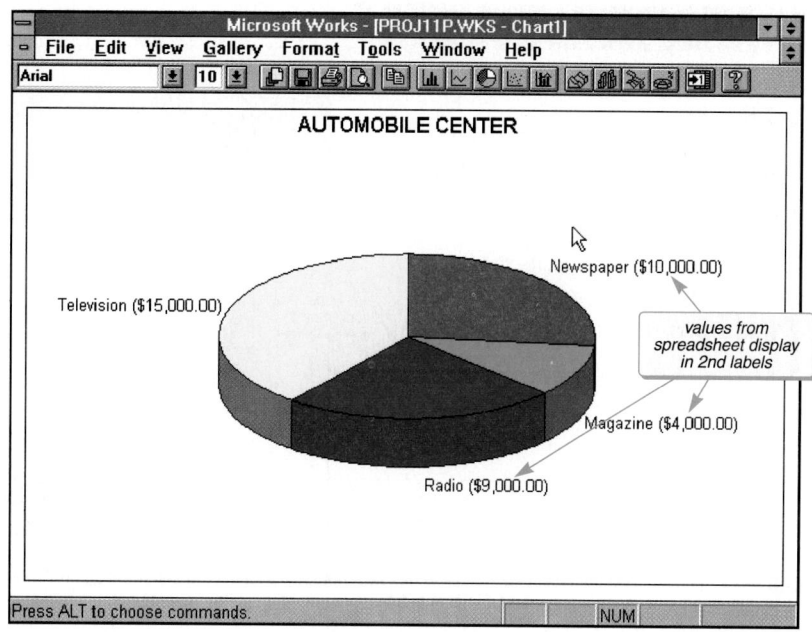

FIGURE 11-19

It is important to understand how to place data labels in a 3-D Pie chart. The method you use is dependent on whether text is adjacent to the cells you are to chart and what you want the 2nd Labels to contain. If you must add data labels to a Pie chart, use the Data Labels command from the Edit menu.

To delete data labels on a 3-D Pie chart, select the None option button in the 1st Label area or the 2nd Label area or both in the Data Labels dialog box, and then choose the OK button.

Adding a Subtitle to a Chart

In a Works chart, you can display a title and subtitle. In this project, the title is placed in the chart by entries in the New Chart dialog box. The title and subtitle can be the same title and subtitle contained on the spreadsheet or you can use other text to describe the chart. To add the subtitle, Advertising Expenses, to the chart, perform the steps on the next page.

TO ADD A SUBTITLE TO A CHART ▼

STEP 1 ▶

Select the Edit menu and point to
the Titles command.

*Works displays the Edit menu and
the mouse pointer points to the
Titles command (Figure 11-20).*

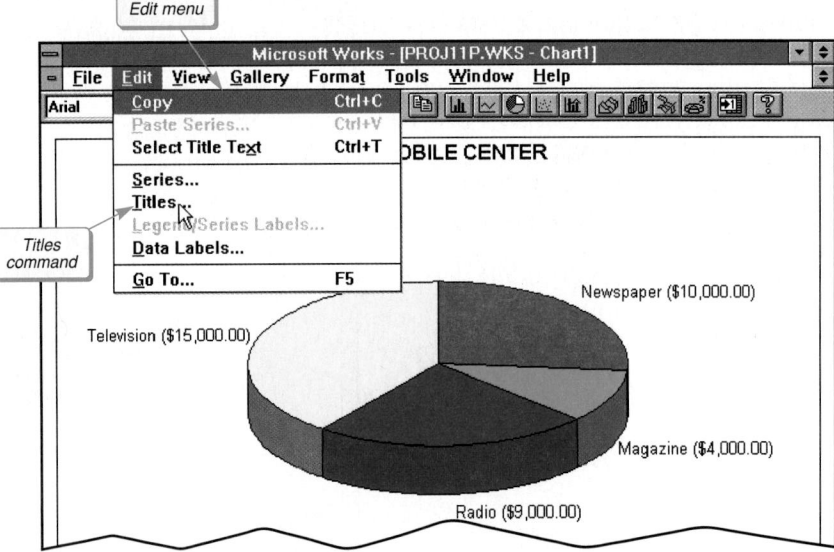

FIGURE 11-20

STEP 2 ▶

Choose the Titles command from the
Edit menu. When the Titles dialog
box displays, type a2 in the Subtitle
text box. A2 is the spreadsheet cell
that contains the subtitle to be
placed on the chart. Point to the OK
button.

*Works displays the Titles dialog
box (Figure 11-21). The Chart title
text box contains A1 because A1
was previously entered for the title
in the New Chart dialog box. The
Subtitle text box contains a2. The
mouse pointer points to the OK
button.*

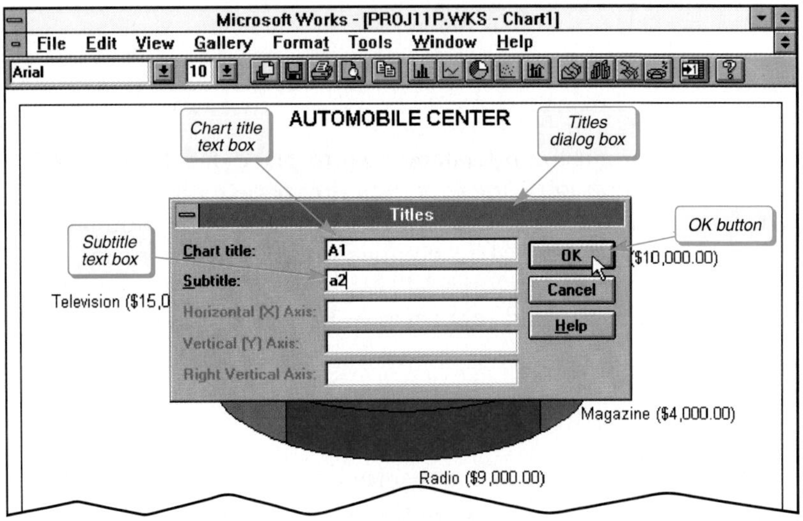

FIGURE 11-21

STEP 3 ▶

Choose the OK button in the Titles
dialog box.

*Works displays the subtitle
Advertising Expenses from cell A2
centered above the Pie chart
(Figure 11-22).*

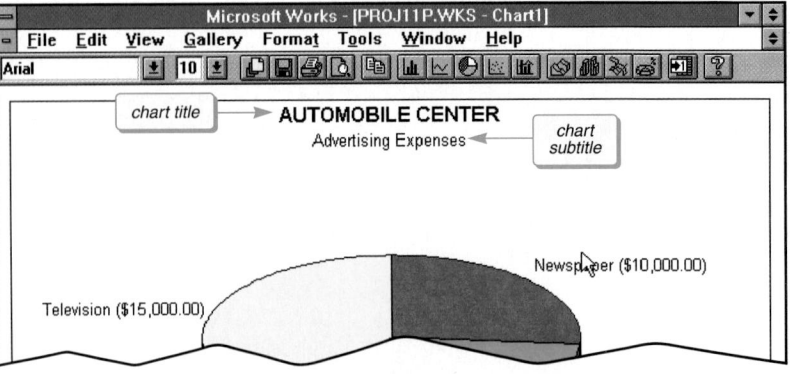

FIGURE 11-22

In the Subtitle text box in the Titles dialog box, you can type any text you want for the subtitle or you can type the spreadsheet cell reference that contains the subtitle you want to appear on the chart.

To delete a title or subtitle, select the Titles command from the Edit menu, in the Titles dialog box highlight the contents of the text box for the title or subtitle you want to delete, and press the DELETE key. Then choose the OK button.

Formatting the Chart Title

To further enhance the appearance of the chart, you can format the chart title, subtitle, and data labels by changing fonts, changing font size, changing color, and making the font bold, italic, or underlined. The following steps explain how to format the chart title in the 3-D Pie chart shown in Figure 11-22.

TO FORMAT THE CHART TITLE ▼

STEP 1 ►

Point to the chart title and click the left mouse button.

Works highlights the chart title (Figure 11-23).

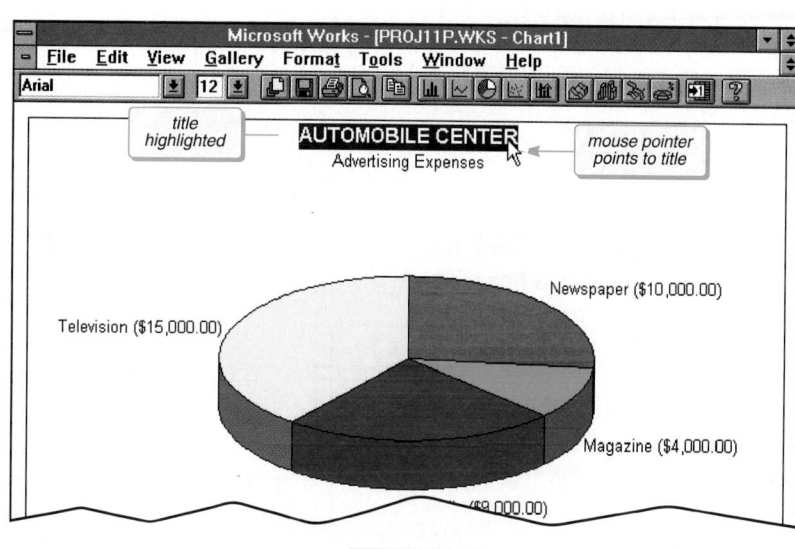

FIGURE 11-23

STEP 2 ►

Select the Format menu and point to the Font and Style command.

The Format menu displays and the mouse pointer points to the Font and Style command (Figure 11-24).

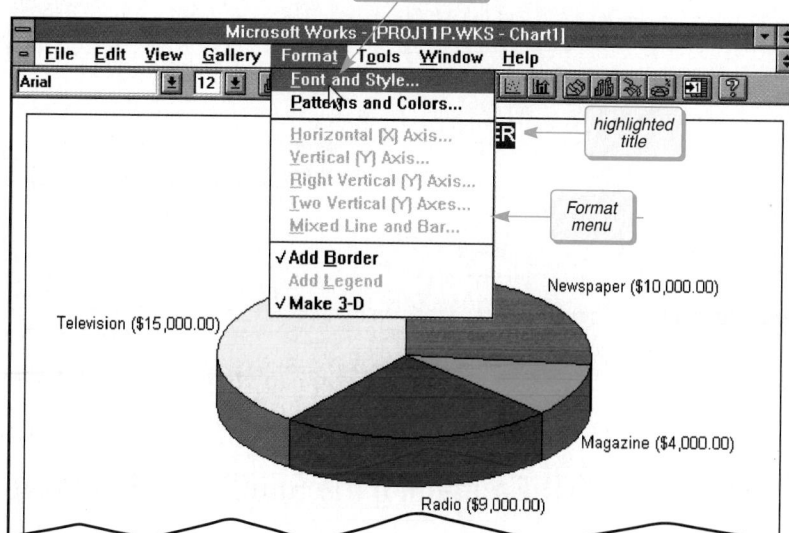

FIGURE 11-24

STEP 3 ▶

Choose the Font and Style command from the Format menu. When the Font and Style for Title dialog box displays, select 14 in the Size list box, select Blue from the Color drop-down list box, click the Italic check box in the Style area, and point to the OK button.

Works displays the Font and Style for Title dialog box (Figure 11-25). Arial is highlighted and displays in the Font list box, 14 is highlighted in the Size list box, Blue displays in the Color drop-down list box, an X displays in the Bold and Italic check boxes, and the mouse pointer points to the OK button.

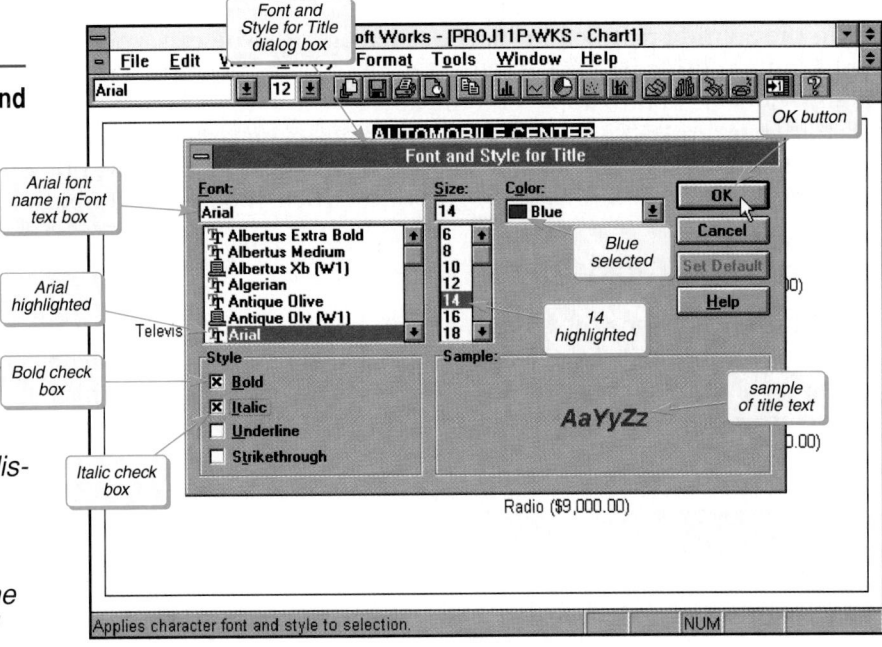

FIGURE 11-25

STEP 4 ▶

Choose the OK button in the Font and Style for Title dialog box. Click the chart anywhere except the chart title to remove the highlight.

Works displays the chart with the title AUTOMOBILE CENTER in blue 14 point Arial bold italic font (Figure 11-26).

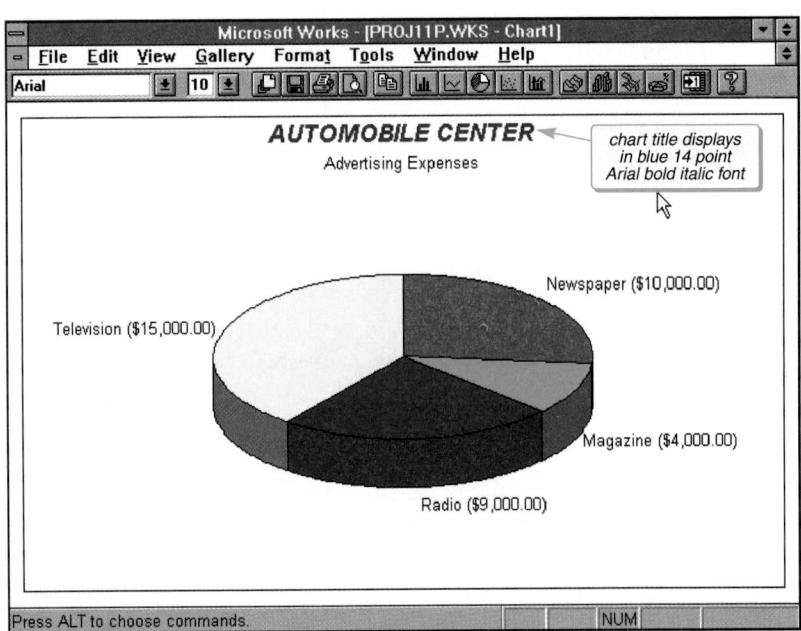

FIGURE 11-26

In Step 1, you can also select the chart title by selecting the Edit menu and choosing the Select Title Text command.

Formatting the Subtitle and Data Labels

The followings steps explain how to format the subtitle and data labels.

TO FORMAT A CHART SUBTITLE AND DATA LABELS ▼

STEP 1 ▶

Select the Format menu and point to the Font and Style command (Figure 11-27).

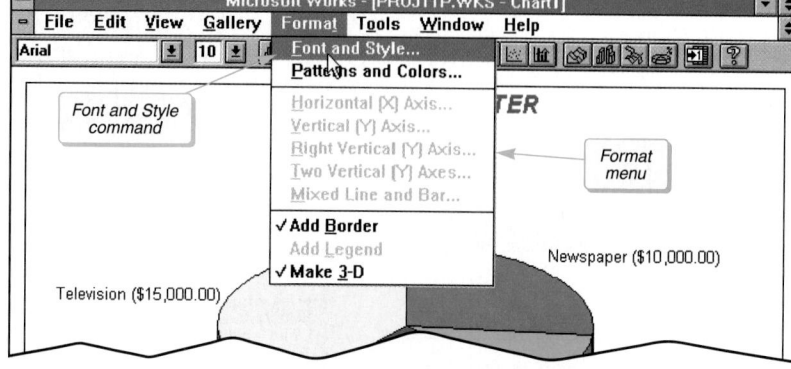

FIGURE 11-27

STEP 2 ▶

Choose the Font and Style command from the Format menu. Click the Bold check box in the Style area. Select Blue in the Color drop-down list box. Point to the OK button.

Works displays the Font and Style for Subtitles and Labels dialog box (Figure 11-28). Arial is contained in the Font list box, 10 (the default font size) is highlighted and displays in the Size list box, an X appears in the Bold check box, Blue displays in the Color drop-down list box, and the mouse pointer points to the OK button. A sample of the selected format displays in the Sample area.

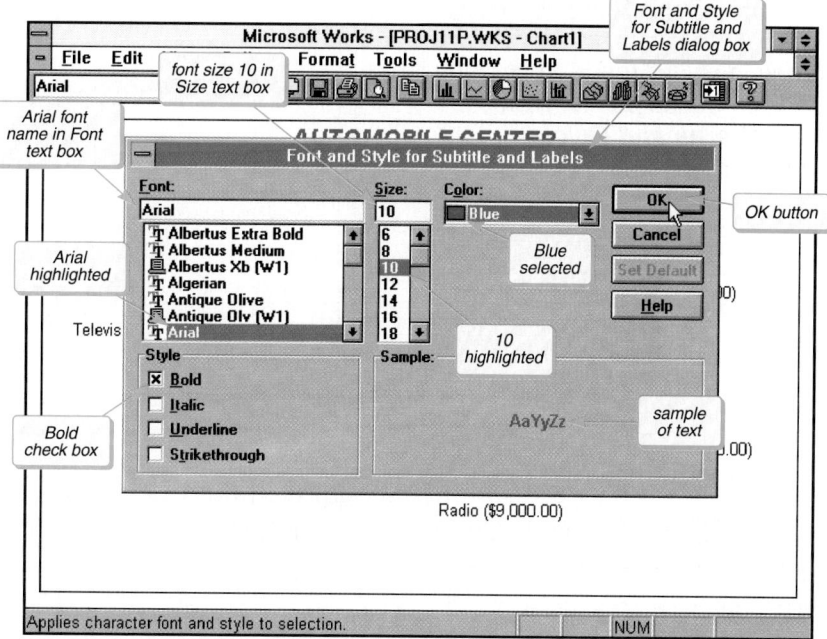

FIGURE 11-28

STEP 3 ▶

Choose the OK button in the Font and Style for Subtitle and Labels dialog box.

Works formats the subtitle and data labels based upon the entries in the Font and Style for Subtitles and Labels dialog box (Figure 11-28a).

FIGURE 11-28a

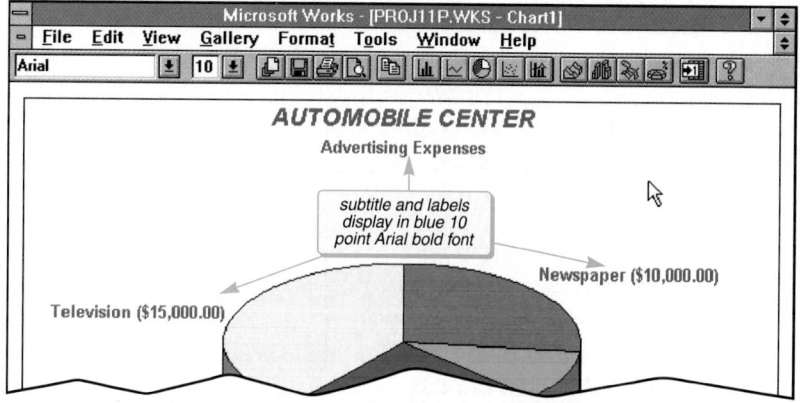

Exploding a Pie Slice

When you want to draw attention to a particular slice in a Pie chart, you can explode that **slice**, that is, separate the slice from the rest of the chart. Slices are numbered beginning in the upper right of the chart. In this project, the Magazine slice, which is the second slice when numbering clockwise from the upper right of the Pie chart, is exploded. Complete the following steps to explode the magazine pie slice.

TO EXPLODE A PIE SLICE ▼

STEP 1 ►

Select the Format menu and point to the Patterns and Colors command.

*Works displays the Format menu and the mouse pointer points to the **Patterns and Colors command** (Figure 11-29).*

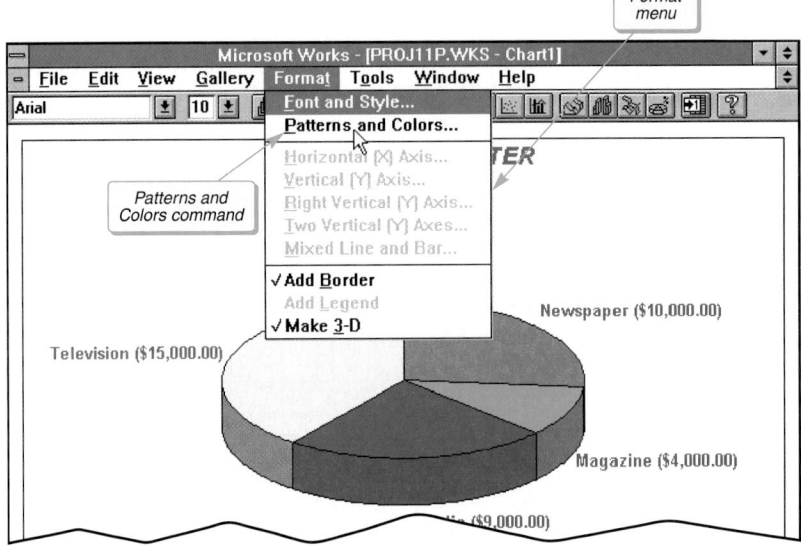

FIGURE 11-29

STEP 2 ►

Choose the Patterns and Colors command. When the Patterns and Colors dialog box displays, select 2 in the Slices list box, select the Explode Slice check box, and choose the Format button.

Works displays the Patterns and Colors dialog box (Figure 11-30). The number 2 is highlighted in the Slices list box, meaning that the selections in the dialog box will pertain to slice 2 of the Pie chart. The Explode Slice check box contains an X, which directs Works to explode slice 2 of the Pie chart. The mouse pointer points to the Format button. When you choose the Format button, Works formats the chart by exploding slice 2. The Patterns and Colors dialog box remains on the screen.

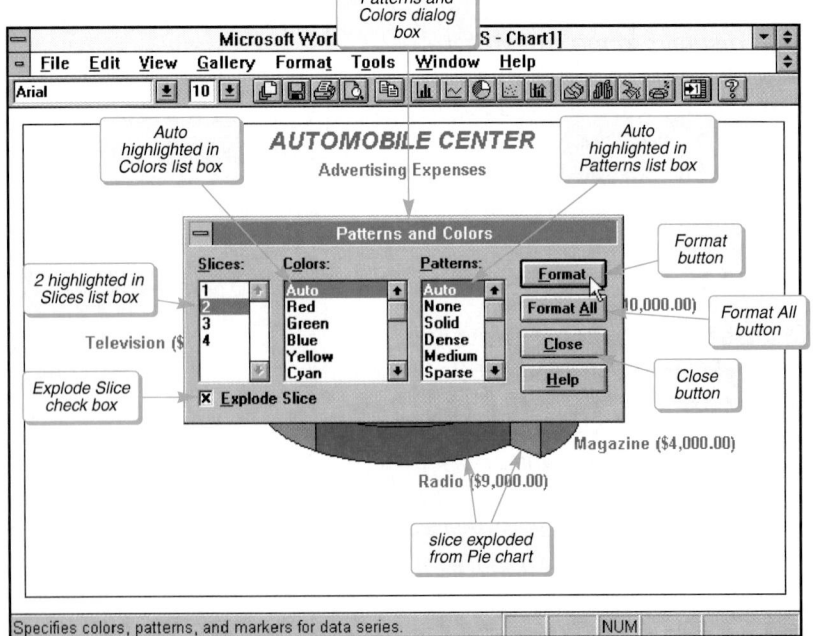

FIGURE 11-30

STEP 3 ▶

Choose the Close button in the Patterns and Colors dialog box.

Works displays the Pie chart with the second slice (Magazine) separated from the rest of the chart (Figure 11-31).

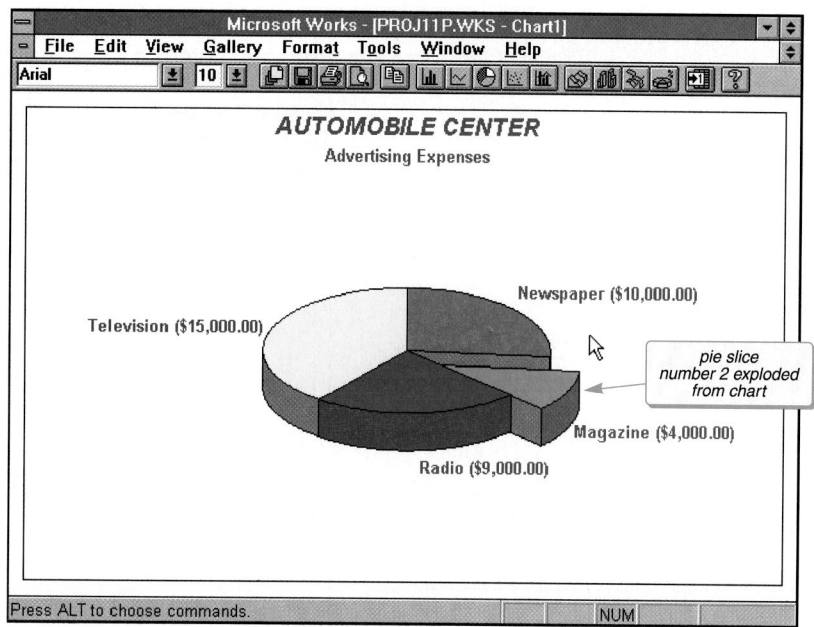

FIGURE 11-31

If you want to separate other slices, while the Patterns and Colors dialog box displays, select the slice number of the slice you want to explode, select the Explode Slice check box, and choose the Format command.

When the Patterns and Colors dialog box first displays on the screen (Step 2 on the previous page), the Close button appears as the Cancel button. You can choose the Cancel button to exit the Patterns and Colors dialog box without making any changes to the Pie chart. After choosing the Format button, however, the button name changes to Close, and the formatting has already taken place.

As shown in the previous steps, when you choose the Format button, the slice highlighted in the Slices list box is changed according to the selections in the dialog box. If you choose the Format All button, all the slices in the Pie chart are changed to the selections in the dialog box. Thus, for example, if you chose the Format All button in Figure 11-30 instead of the Format button, all slices of the Pie chart would be exploded.

Rotating a Chart

You can **rotate** 3-D charts by holding down the CTRL key and pressing the arrow keys. For Pie charts, you can press the UP ARROW key and the DOWN ARROW key while holding down the CTRL key. To rotate the Pie chart in Figure 11-31 to display as shown in Figure 11-32 on the next page, complete the steps on the next page.

TO ROTATE A 3-D PIE CHART ▼

STEP 1 ▶

While holding down the CTRL key, press the DOWN ARROW key three times.

Works rotates the chart so it displays with a different perspective (Figure 11-32).

STEP 2

While holding down the CTRL key, press the HOME key one time.

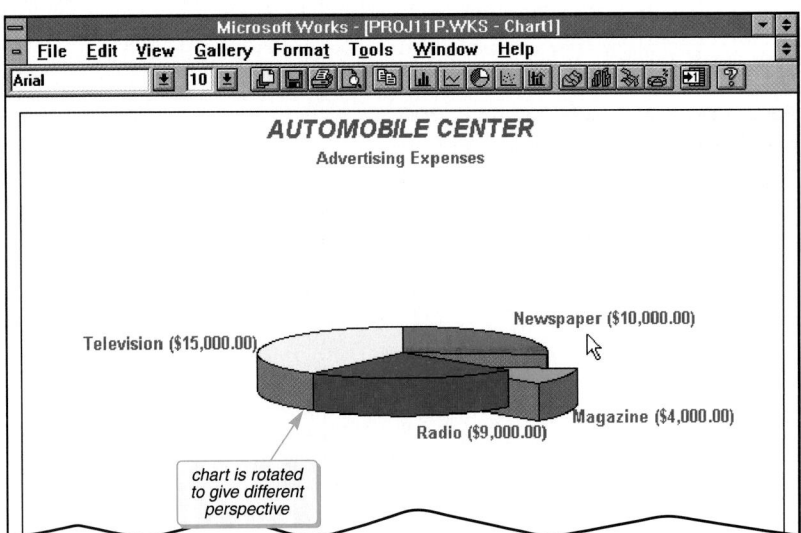

FIGURE 11-32

Pressing CTRL+HOME will always return a 3-D chart to its original position.

Saving a Chart

To save a spreadsheet that has already been saved with the same name and to include the chart, complete the following step.

TO SAVE A SPREADSHEET WITH THE SAME NAME AND INCLUDE THE CHART

Step 1: Click the Save button on the Toolbar or choose the Save command from the File menu.

As part of saving the spreadsheet, Works will save the chart with the name Chart1. Chart1 is the default name Works assigns to the first chart associated with a spreadsheet. You can create and save up to eight charts for each spreadsheet.

If you want to save the spreadsheet and chart with a name that is different from the name already used, choose the Save As command from the File menu.

Printing a Chart

When printing a chart, the Works default is full-page printing. To print a chart using full-page printing, click the Print button on the Charting Toolbar when the chart displays on the screen.

This approach, however, may produce unexpected results because Works attempts to utilize the full page. For example, when you print the chart created in the previous steps using full-page printing, the chart title and subtitle print at the top of the page, a space approximately three inches in size appears, and then the chart prints in the bottom portion of the page.

To override the Works default and print a more acceptable looking chart, use the **Page Setup command** on the File menu. The steps to specify the size of the chart on the printed page and to print the chart are explained on the next page.

TO USE THE PAGE SETUP COMMAND WHEN PRINTING A CHART ▼

STEP 1 ►

Select the File menu and point to the Page Setup command.

The File menu displays and the mouse pointer points to the Page Setup command (Figure 11-33).

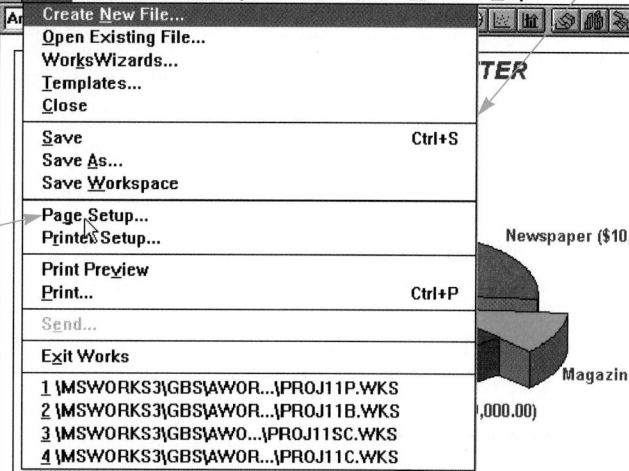

FIGURE 11-33

STEP 2 ►

Choose the Page Setup command from the File menu. When the Page Setup dialog box displays, select the Other Options tab and select the Full page, keep proportions option button in the Size area.

The Page Setup dialog box displays (Figure 11-34). The Other Options screen displays. The Full page, keep proportions option button is selected.

STEP 3 ►

Choose the OK button in the Page Setup dialog box.

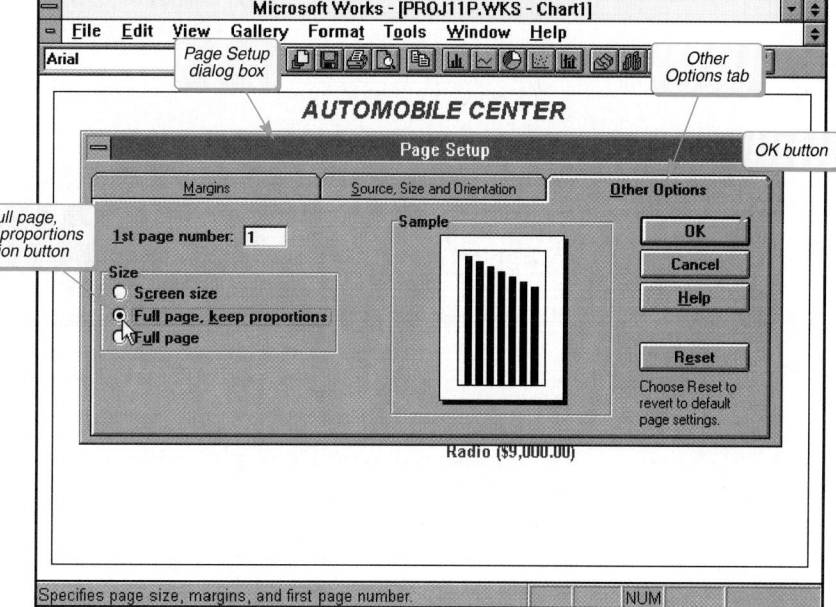

FIGURE 11-34

When you print the chart, Works will scale the width of the chart to the page width and change its height-to-width ratio as needed.

Selecting the Screen Size option button in the Size area of the Page Setup dialog box will cause Works to print the chart based on what Works determines is screen size. When you select this option button, Works prints the 3-D Pie chart approximately the same size as when the Full page, keep proportions option button is selected.

Previewing and Printing the Chart

You should use print preview to assure the chart will print as expected. To preview and then print the chart, complete the following steps (see Figure 11-35).

TO PREVIEW AND PRINT THE CHART

Step 1: Click the Print Preview button on the Toolbar. Review the chart in the print preview window that displays. If the chart displays in the form you want, you can print the chart.

Step 2: To print the chart, choose the Print button in the print preview window.

The printed chart is shown in Figure 11-35.

If you do not preview the chart, you can print it by clicking the Print button on the Toolbar or by choosing the Print command from the File menu.

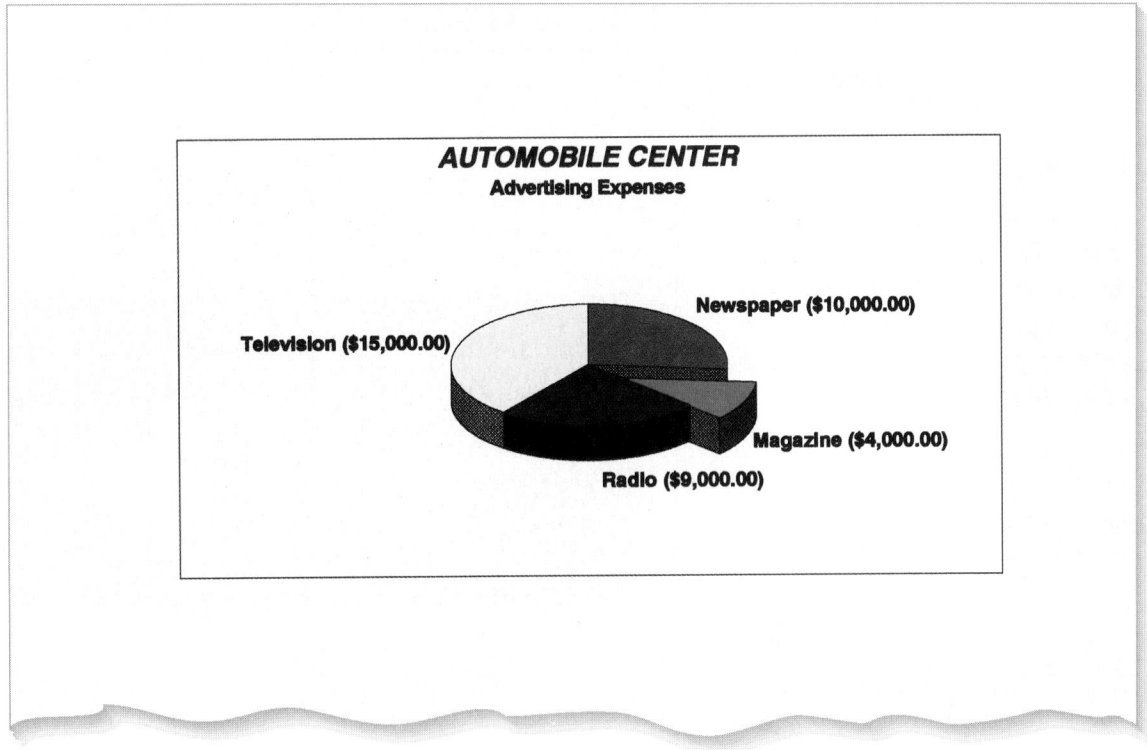

FIGURE 11-35

Displaying the Spreadsheet

After you print the chart, you can display the spreadsheet by performing the following steps.

TO DISPLAY THE SPREADSHEET ▼

STEP 1 ▶

Select the View menu and point to the Spreadsheet command.

Works displays the View menu and the mouse pointer points to the **Spreadsheet command** *(Figure 11-36).*

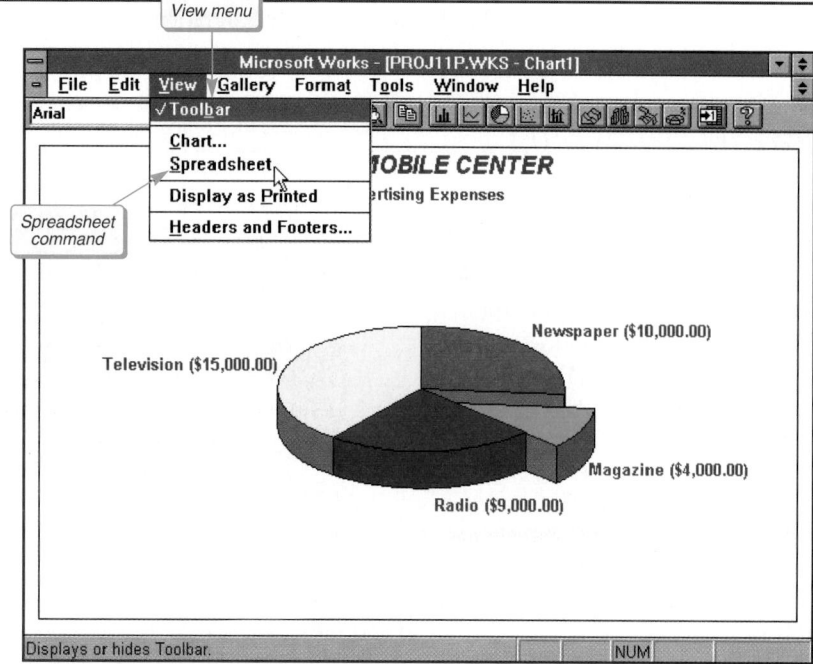

FIGURE 11-36

STEP 2 ▶

Choose the Spreadsheet command from the View menu.

Works displays the spreadsheet (Figure 11-37).

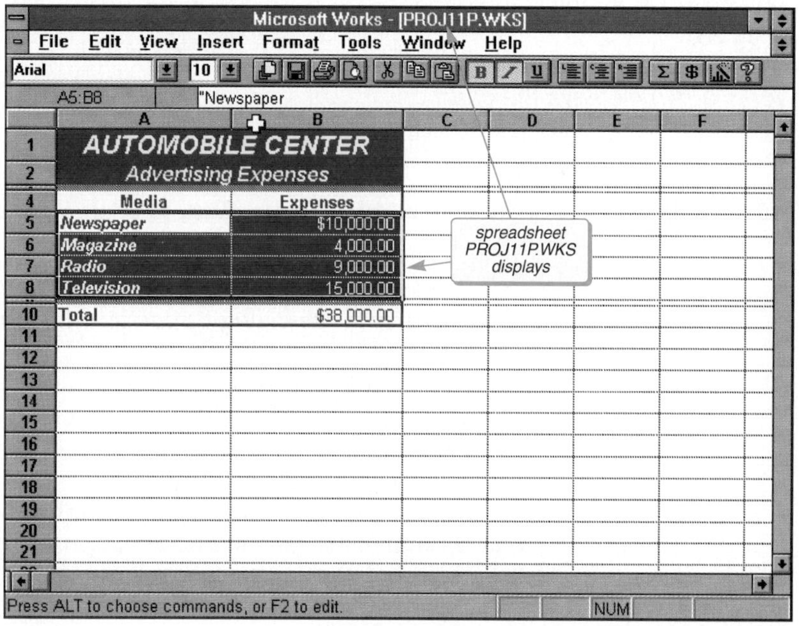

FIGURE 11-37

You can also select the Window menu and choose the name of the spreadsheet at the bottom of the menu to display the spreadsheet when the chart is displayed. If you have numerous documents open in Works, the Window menu can be crowded.

Displaying the Chart

To display the chart, perform the following steps.

TO DISPLAY THE CHART ▼

STEP 1 ▶

Select the View menu and choose the Chart command. When the Charts dialog box displays, select the chart name (Chart1) in the Chart list box and point to the OK button.

Works displays the Charts dialog box (Figure 11-38). The name of the chart to display (Chart1) is selected in the Chart list box. The mouse pointer points to the OK button.

STEP 2 ▶

Choose the OK button in the Charts dialog box.

Works again displays the chart on the screen.

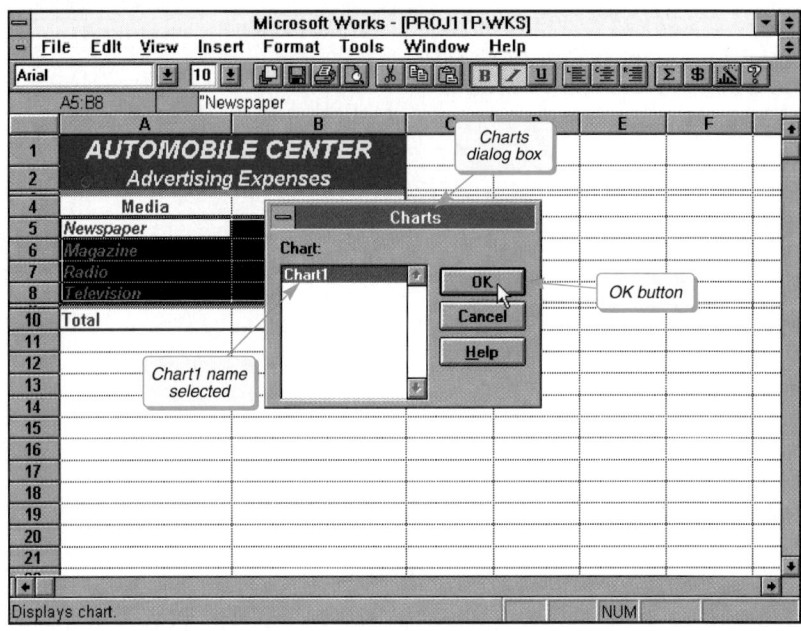

FIGURE 11-38

Works allows eight different charts for each spreadsheet. The chart names are listed in the Charts dialog box when the **Chart command** is chosen from the View menu.

If a chart is already open, you can also display the chart by selecting the Window menu and choosing the chart name at the bottom of the Window menu.

After you save and print the chart and have no more work to accomplish, you can quit Works by choosing the Exit Works command from the File menu.

This section has introduced techniques for creating and enhancing 3-D Pie charts. Many of these techniques apply to the other charts you can create with Works.

▶ THE BAR CHART

The Bar chart is another widely used chart. The Bar chart displays values in columns. The height of the column represents a given value. An advantage of the Bar chart as compared to the Pie chart is the Bar chart can display multiple values in a single category on one chart. Figure 11-39 illustrates a spreadsheet and the related Bar chart.

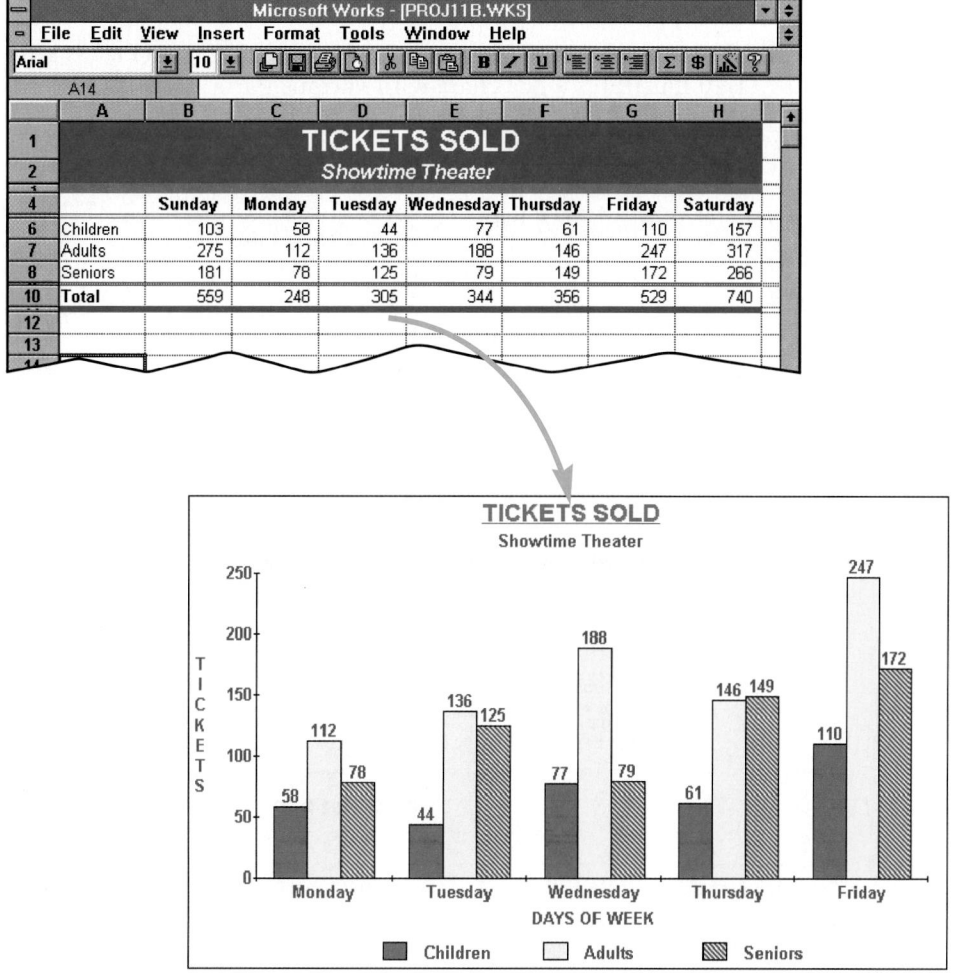

The following is the data table shown in the spreadsheet:

	Sunday	Monday	Tuesday	Wednesday	Thursday	Friday	Saturday
Children	103	58	44	77	61	110	157
Adults	275	112	136	188	146	247	317
Seniors	181	78	125	79	149	172	266
Total	559	248	305	344	356	529	740

FIGURE 11-39

The spreadsheet contains the Tickets Sold for the Showtime Theater during Sunday through Saturday. The three categories of tickets sold are for children, adults, and seniors. The Bar chart displays tickets sold for Monday through Friday to allow a comparison among the three categories of tickets sold during weekdays. Notice that the column and row titles are not adjacent to the numbers you are to chart. This project explains how to use the column titles and row titles in a chart when they are not adjacent to the data being charted.

A Bar chart is an appropriate choice of charts because it graphically illustrates the comparison of the three values on a daily basis.

Understanding Charting Terms

The following paragraphs review the terminology associated with charts. Figure 11-40 illustrates a Bar chart with various parts of the chart labeled.

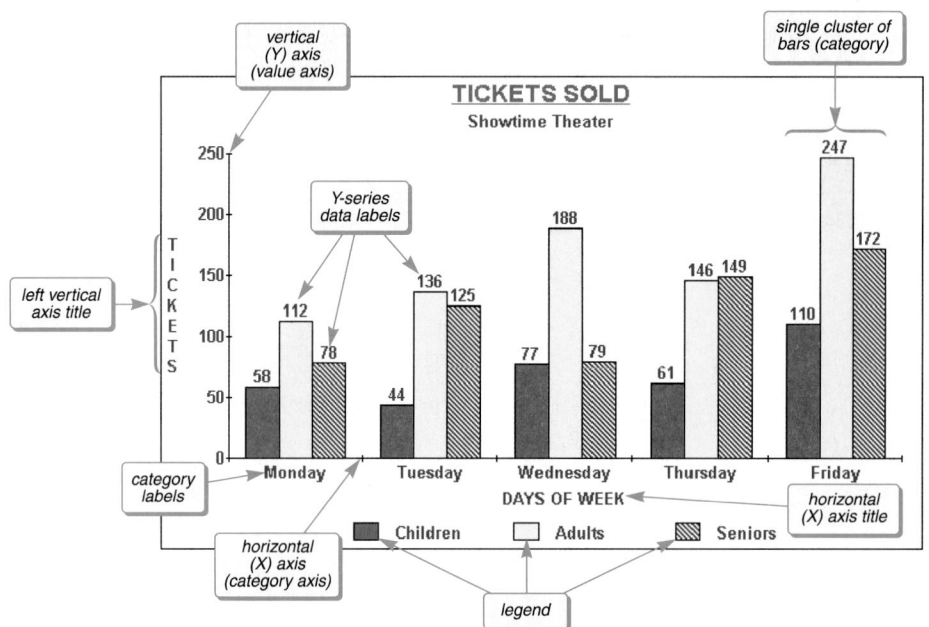

FIGURE 11-40

All charts except Pie charts have a horizontal axis called the **horizontal (X) axis**, or **category axis**, and a vertical axis called the **vertical (Y) axis**, or **value axis**.

The charted values are usually identified on the X axis (category axis) by **category labels**. In the chart in Figure 11-40, the category labels Monday, Tuesday, Wednesday, Thursday, and Friday are displayed below the X axis. A cluster of bars (representing tickets sold for children, adults, and seniors for one day) is called a **category**. All of the clusters of bars together (Monday, Tuesday, Wednesday, Thursday, and Friday) are called the **category (X) series**.

The vertical (Y) axis, or value axis, provides the measure against which values in the chart are plotted. In the example, the number of tickets sold is the value plotted. Works automatically divides the Y axis into units based on the lowest and highest values in the spreadsheet.

Works refers to each related group of values as a series. Each **series** (for example, tickets for children) has its own color. A set of bars of the same color, such as the red bars representing tickets for children, is called a **Y-series**, or **value-series**.

Works creates the category (X) series based on what you highlight in the spreadsheet. If you highlight more columns than rows, Works considers the columns as categories (Monday, Tuesday, Wednesday, and so on are categories). If you highlight more rows than columns, Works considers the rows as categories. If you include dates in a chart, Works always uses the dates as the category (X) series regardless of the number of rows or columns you highlight.

The numbers at the top of each bar, if present, are called data labels. Data labels for Bar charts show the spreadsheet values represented by each bar.

A **legend** in a chart tells you what the colors, patterns, and markers mean.

Creating the Bar Chart

This section of Project 11 explains the steps required to create the Bar chart in Figure 11-39 on page W11.29, including the category labels, a legend, a chart title and subtitle, and the colors and patterns in the bars.

To create the Bar chart, perform the following steps. It is assumed the spreadsheet file is open and displays on the screen.

TO CREATE A BAR CHART ▼

STEP 1 ▶

Highlight the range on the spreadsheet to chart (C6:G8) and point to the New Chart button on the Toolbar.

The cells containing the tickets sold for Monday through Friday for children, adults, and seniors are highlighted (Figure 11-41). The text in row 4 and the text in column A are not highlighted because they are not adjacent to the numbers you are charting.

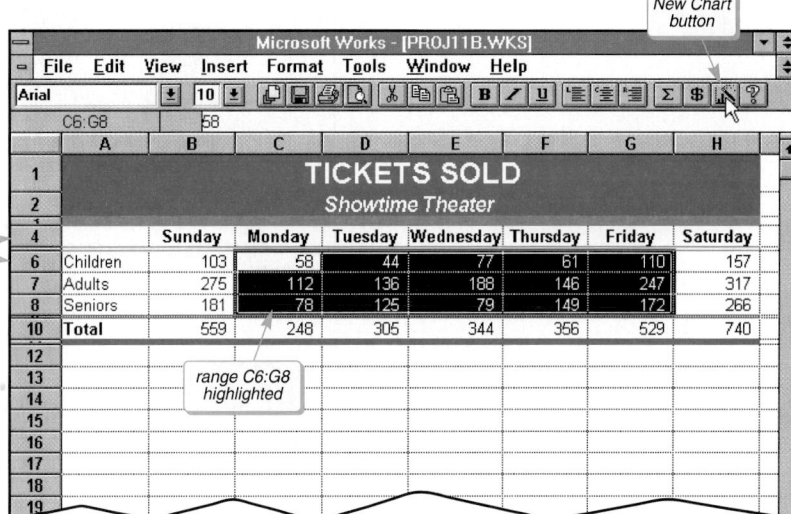

FIGURE 11-41

STEP 2 ▶

Click the New Chart button on the Toolbar. In the What type of chart do you want? drop-down list box, select Bar. Type a1 in the Chart title text box and select the Add border check box. Point to the OK button.

Works displays the New Chart dialog box (Figure 11-42). a1 displays in the Chart title text box. a1 is the spreadsheet cell containing the spreadsheet title that is also used as the chart title. Works displays the Bar chart in the lower right corner of the dialog box with a title and border as it will display when created.

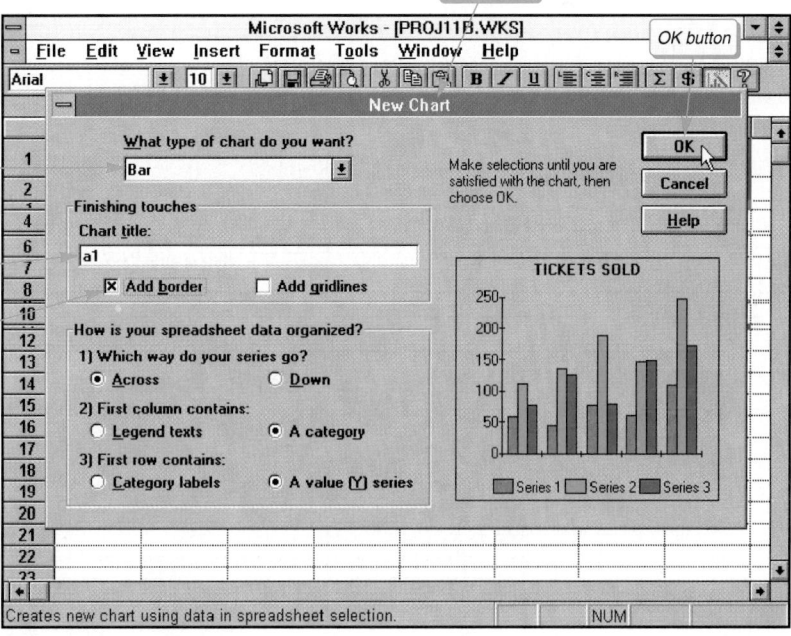

FIGURE 11-42

STEP 3 ▶

Choose the OK button in the New Chart dialog box.

Works displays the Bar chart (Figure 11-43). The default legend Series 1, Series 2, and Series 3 displays at the bottom of the chart.

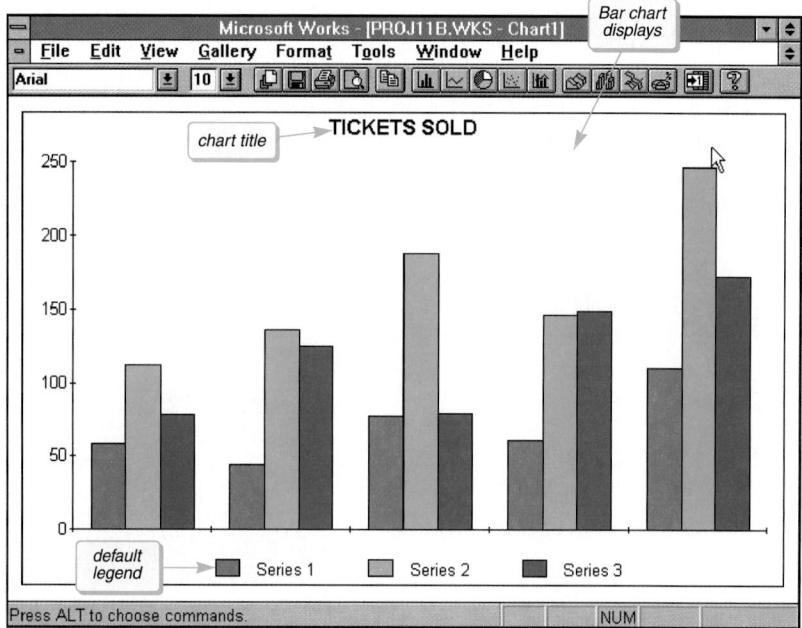

FIGURE 11-43

The next step is to add data labels to the chart.

Adding Data Labels

When displaying a Bar chart, it is possible to add data labels to the chart. With a Bar chart, data labels can display at the top of each bar and reflect the actual number represented by the bar. Perform the following steps to add data labels to the Tickets Sold Bar chart.

TO ADD DATA LABELS TO A BAR CHART ▼

STEP 1 ▶

Select the Edit menu and point to the Data Labels command (Figure 11-44).

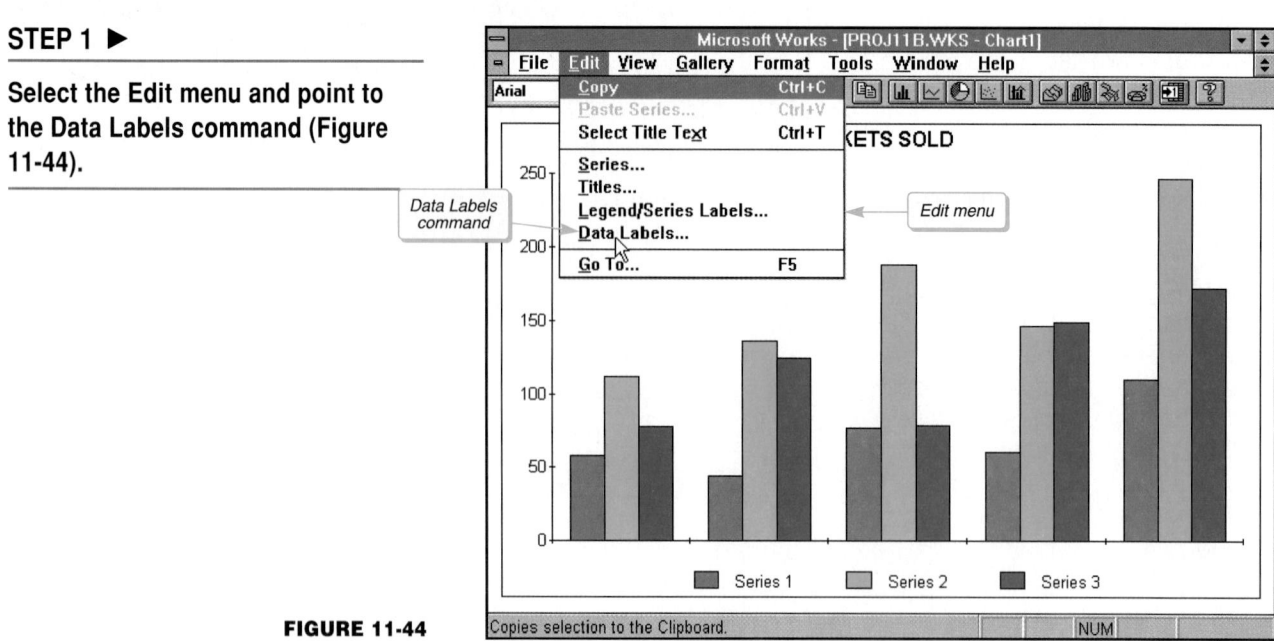

FIGURE 11-44

STEP 2 ▶

Choose the Data Labels command from the Edit menu. When the Data Labels dialog box displays, select the Use series data check box and point to the OK button.

The Data Labels dialog box displays (Figure 11-45). The Use series data check box is selected and the mouse pointer points to the OK button. The Use series check box tells Works to use the actual charted data as the data labels.

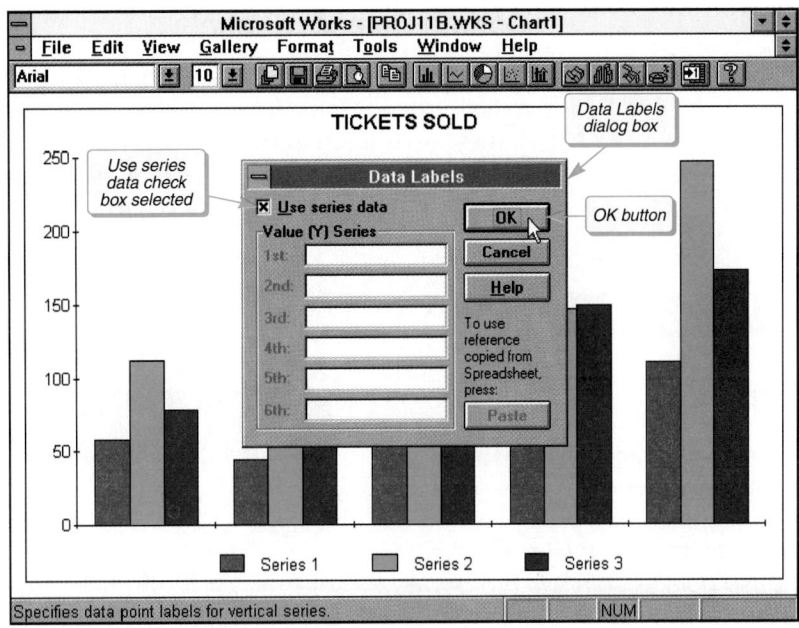

FIGURE 11-45

STEP 3 ▶

Choose the OK button in the Data Labels dialog box.

Works places data labels at the top of each bar (Figure 11-46). These labels specify the actual values represented by each bar.

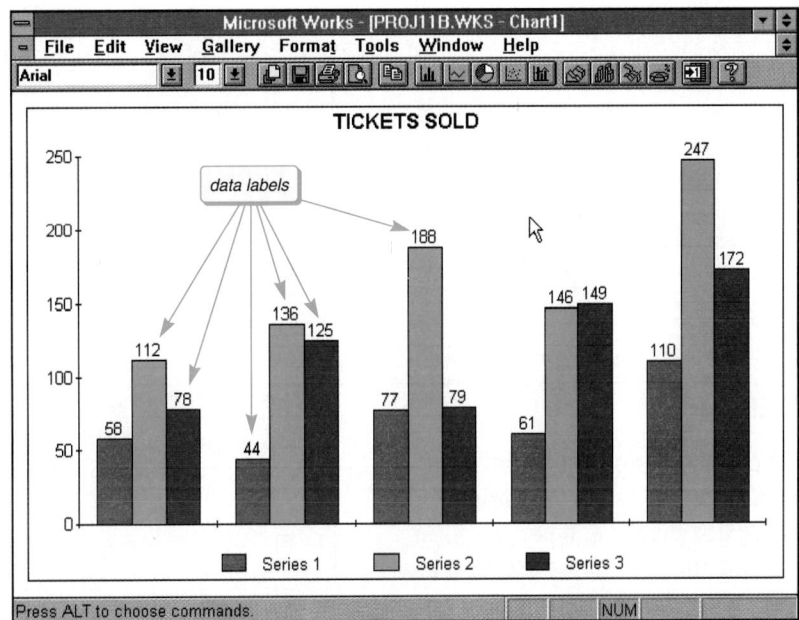

FIGURE 11-46

You can also use the Data Labels command from the Edit menu if you want to delete the labels at a later time. To remove the data labels, remove the check mark from the Use series data check box in the Data Labels dialog box and delete any information in the Value (Y) Series boxes.

Adding Category Labels

Category labels are words that identify information along the horizontal (X) axis. In the sample chart, the days of the week (Monday, Tuesday, Wednesday, Thursday, and Friday) are category labels. These labels are found in cells C4:G4 in the spreadsheet (see Figure 11-39 on page W11.29). Perform the following steps to add category labels to the Bar chart.

TO ADD CATEGORY LABELS ▼

STEP 1 ▶

Select the Edit menu and point to the Series command.

*The Edit menu displays and the mouse pointer points to the **Series command** (Figure 11-47).*

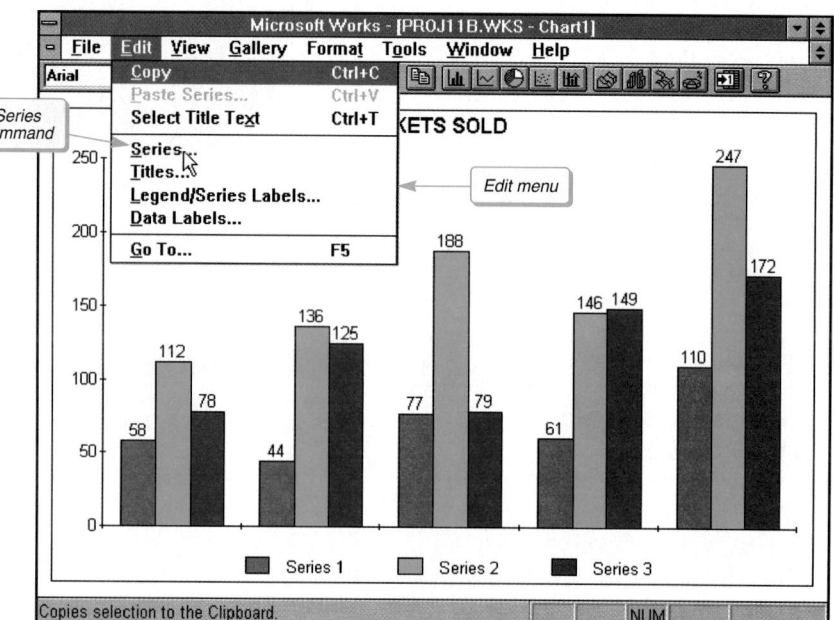

FIGURE 11-47

STEP 2 ▶

Choose the Series command from the Edit menu. When the Series dialog box displays, type c4:g4 in the Category (X) Series text box, and point to the OK button.

Works displays the Series dialog box (Figure 11-48). The typed entry c4:g4, which is the range of the category labels, displays in the Category (X) Series text box. The entries in the Value (Y) Series text boxes contain the ranges highlighted in the spreadsheet for the value (Y) series numbers (tickets sold for children, adults, and seniors).

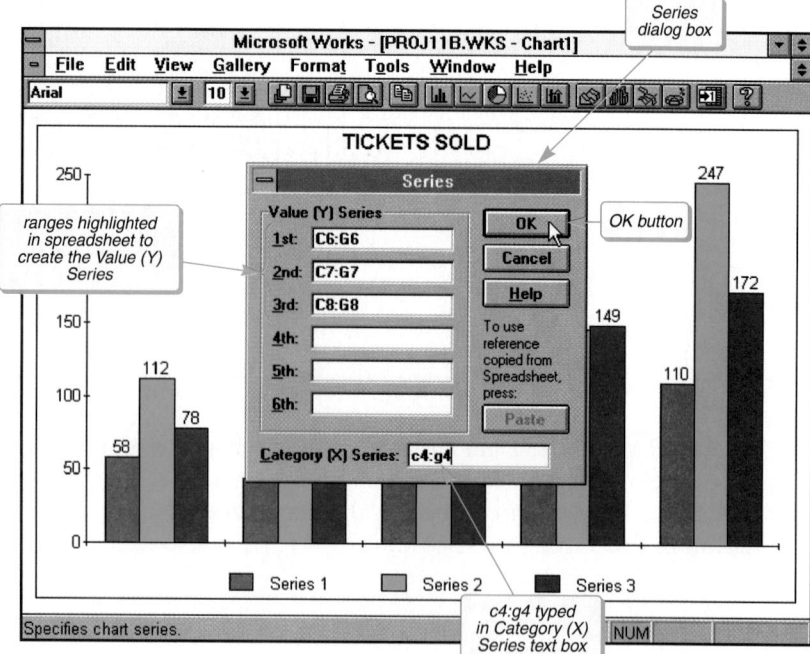

FIGURE 11-48

STEP 3 ▶

Choose the OK button in the Series dialog box.

Works displays the Bar chart with the category labels Monday, Tuesday, Wednesday, Thursday, and Friday at the bottom of the chart (Figure 11-49).

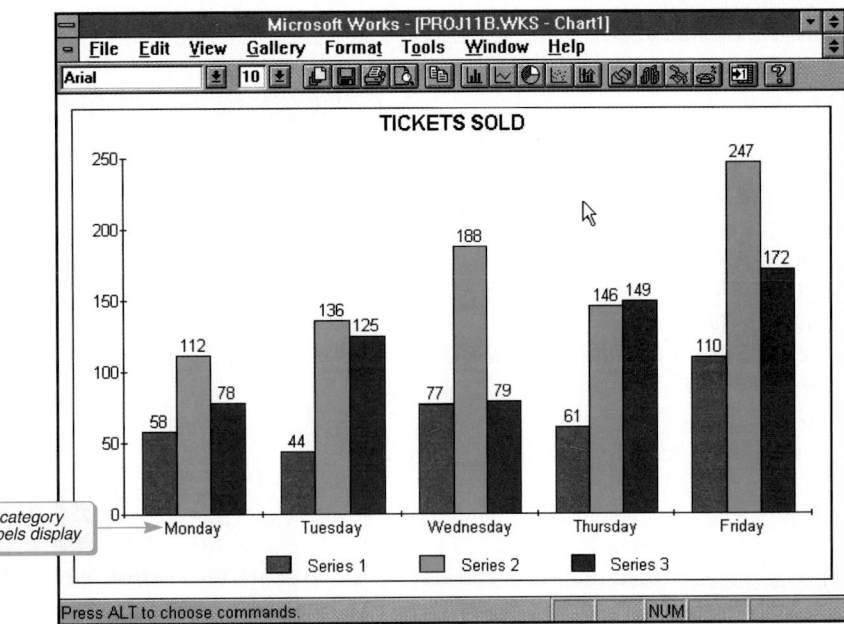

FIGURE 11-49

To delete category labels, highlight the Category (X) Series text box entry in the Series dialog box, press the DELETE key, and then choose the OK button in the Series dialog box.

When you create a Bar chart, if the category labels are adjacent to the values in the spreadsheet to be charted and the category labels are highlighted, Works will automatically display the labels on the Bar chart.

Adding a Legend

In the Bar chart developed for this project, the legend consists of the words Children (cell A6), Adults (cell A7), and Seniors (cell A8) together with a rectangular box for each that contains the related colors in the bars (see Figure 11-39 on page W11.29). A legend in a Bar chart tells you what the colors and/or patterns in the bars represent. When the Bar chart is created, Works inserts a default legend of Series 1, Series 2, and Series 3. To replace the default legend with the actual legend, complete the steps on the next two pages.

TO ADD A LEGEND ▼

STEP 1 ▶

Select the Edit menu and point to the Legend/Series Labels command.

*Works displays the Edit menu and the mouse pointer points to the **Legend/Series Labels command** (Figure 11-50).*

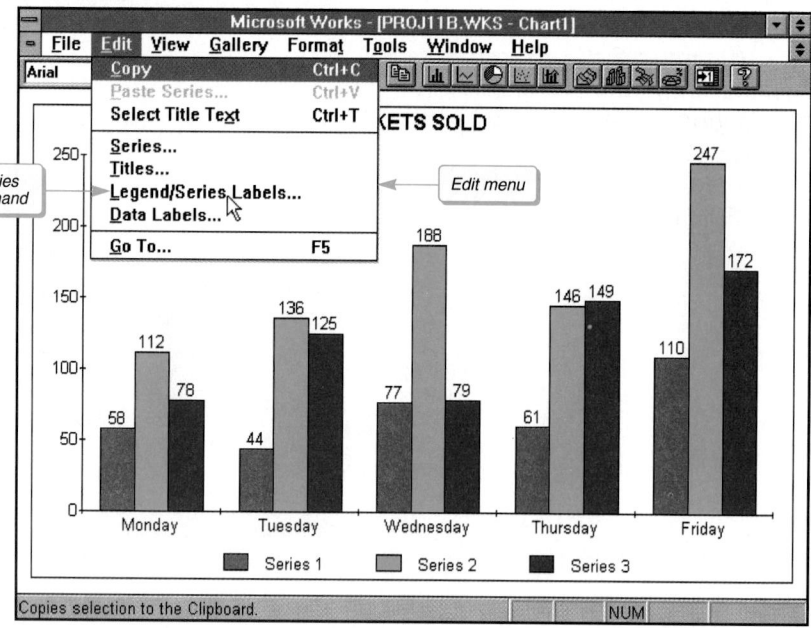

FIGURE 11-50

STEP 2 ▶

Choose the Legend/Series Labels command from the Edit menu. When the Legend/Series Labels dialog box displays, click the Auto series labels check box to turn off the automatic series label feature. Select the 1st Value Series text box by clicking it, and type a6. Press the TAB key and type a7 in the 2nd Value Series text box. Press the TAB key and type a8 in the 3rd Value Series text box. Point to the OK button.

Works displays the Legend/Series Labels dialog box (Figure 11-51). The Auto series label check box does not contain an X. The typed entry a6 (the cell referencing the word Children) displays in the 1st Value Series text box, the typed entry a7 (the cell referencing the word Adults) displays in the 2nd Value Series text box, and the typed entry a8 (the cell referencing the word Seniors) displays in the 3rd Value Series text box.

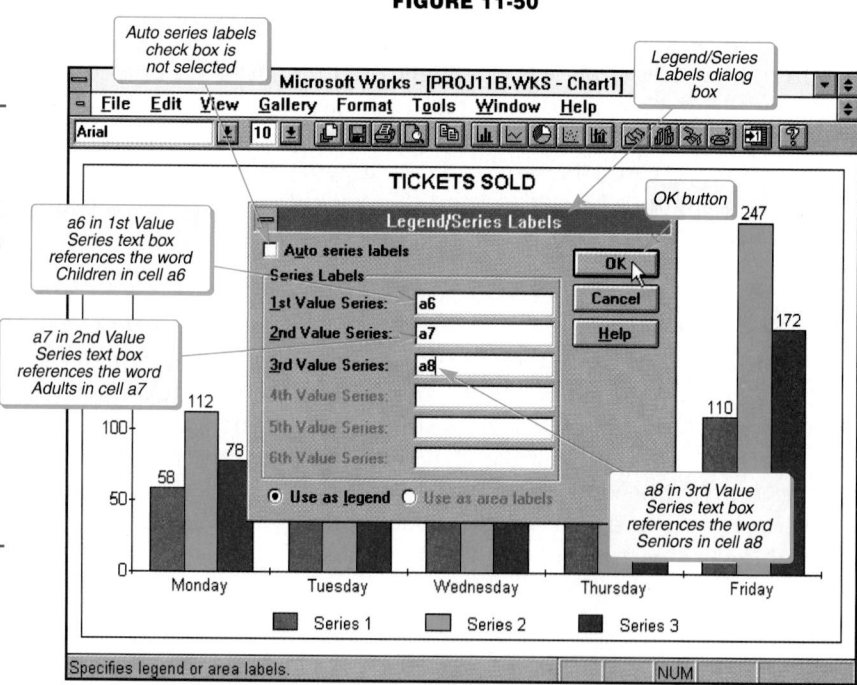

FIGURE 11-51

STEP 3 ▶

Choose the OK button in the Legend/Series Labels dialog box.

The Bar chart displays with the chart legend at the bottom of the chart (Figure 11-52).

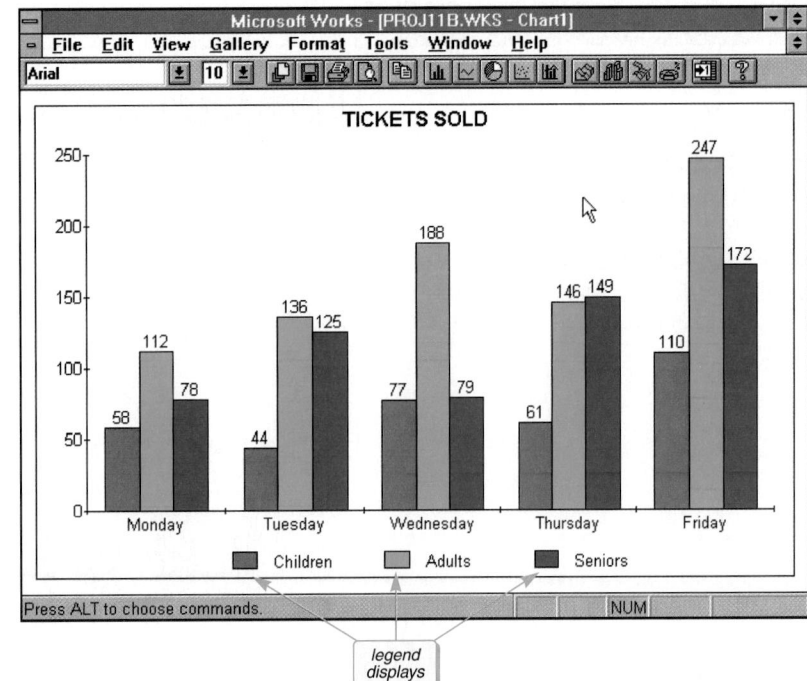

FIGURE 11-52

In the Legend/Series Labels dialog box (Figure 11-51), you can type a descriptive legend in the text boxes rather than a cell reference. Legend text can be up to 19 characters in length.

To delete a legend, highlight the cell reference or text in the appropriate text box in the Legend/Series Labels dialog box, press the DELETE key, and then choose the OK button.

You can further control displaying the legend by the Add Legend command on the Format menu. If the Add Legend command is chosen, a check mark displays beside the command on the menu and the legend displays in the chart. If the legend displays in the chart, you can remove the legend from the chart by choosing the Add Legend command again.

When you create a Bar chart, if the range you highlight in the spreadsheet includes the legend text adjacent to the numbers in the spreadsheet to be charted, Works automatically uses the text to create the legend. Thus, if the text Children, Adults, and Seniors had been adjacent to the numbers charted and had been highlighted, the correct legend instead of the default legend would have appeared automatically in the chart.

Adding Chart Titles to a Bar Chart

Chart titles can assist in making the chart easy to read and understand. Works allows you to add a title, subtitle, and titles on both the vertical and horizontal axes. In the Bar chart, the title is TICKETS SOLD and the subtitle is Showtime Theater. The left vertical (Y) axis area contains the word TICKETS, and below the horizontal (X) axis are the words, DAYS OF WEEK. The title was placed in the chart from the entry in the Chart title text box in the New Chart dialog box (see Figure 11-42 on page W11.31). To add the remaining titles to the Bar chart, perform the steps on the next two pages.

TO ADD TITLES TO A BAR CHART ▼

STEP 1 ►

Select the Edit menu and point to the Titles command.

Works displays the Edit menu and the mouse pointer points to the Titles command (Figure 11-53).

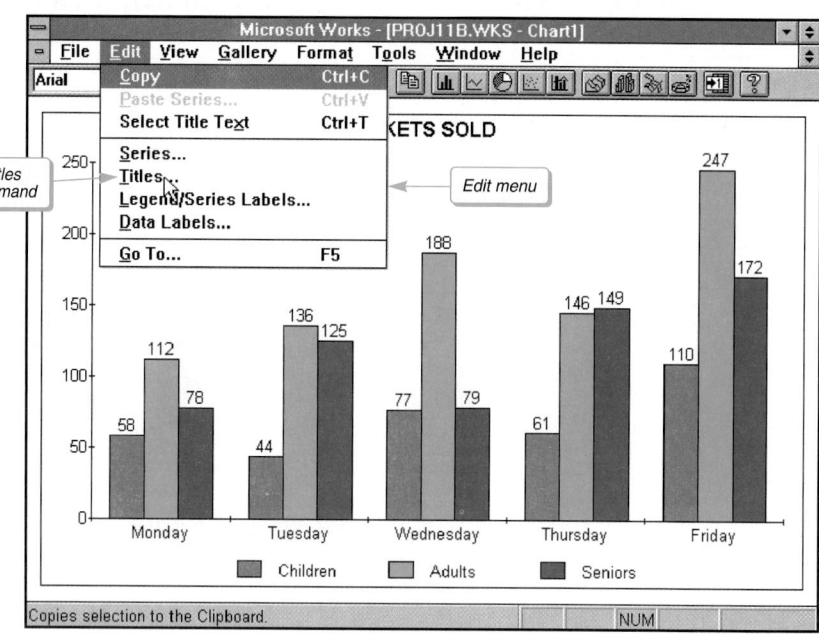

FIGURE 11-53

STEP 2 ►

Choose the Titles command from the Edit menu. When the Titles dialog box displays, type a2 in the Subtitle text box, type DAYS OF WEEK in the Horizontal (X) Axis text box, and type TICKETS in the Vertical (Y) Axis text box. Point to the OK button.

Works displays the Titles dialog box and the typed entries (Figure 11-54). The mouse pointer points to the OK button. The Titles text box contains A1 because a1 was entered in the New Chart dialog box in Figure 11-42.

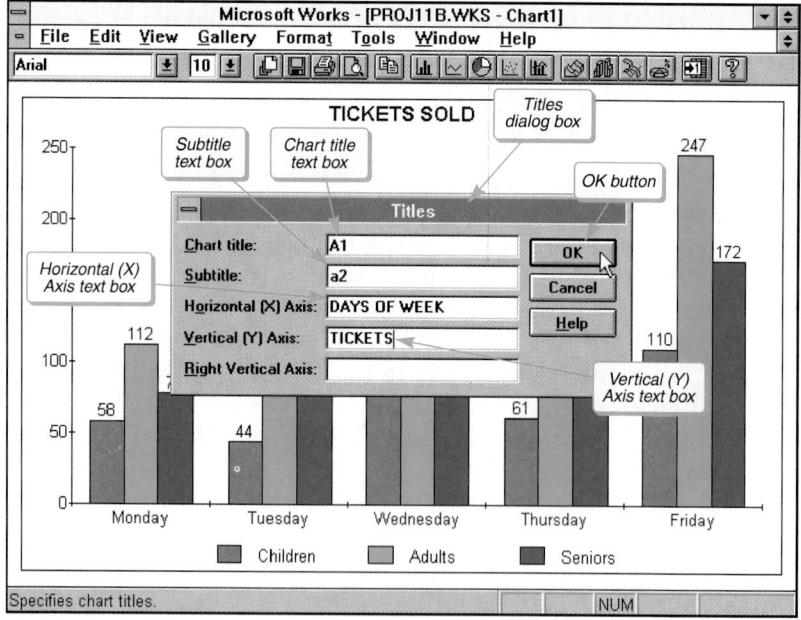

FIGURE 11-54

Choose the OK button in the Titles dialog box.

The Bar chart displays with the chart title, subtitle, vertical (Y) axis title, and horizontal (X) axis title (Figure 11-55).

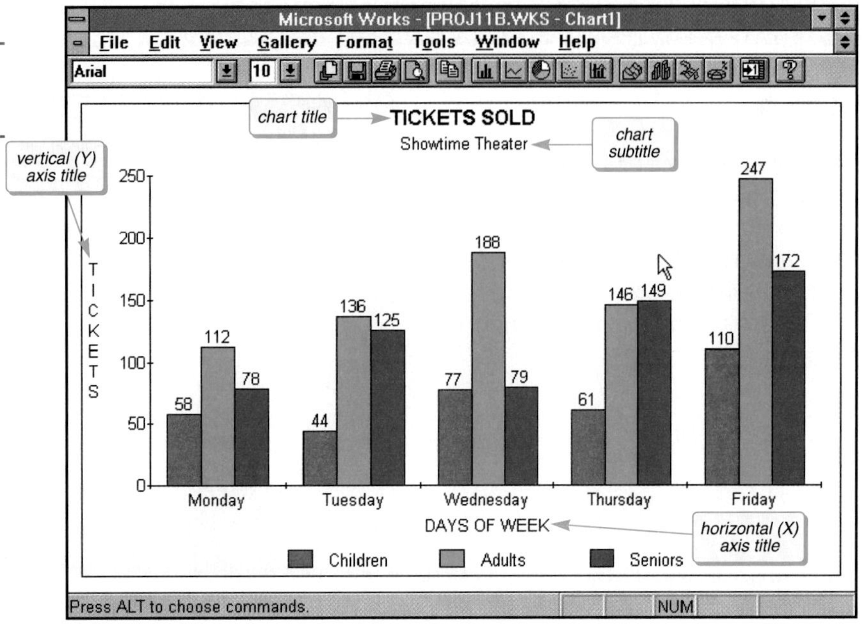

FIGURE 11-55

Instead of entering cell references you can type the actual chart title and subtitle or other text in the Titles dialog box. The information you type will display on the chart.

To delete a title, highlight the title to delete in the appropriate text box in the Titles dialog box, press the DELETE key, and then choose the OK button.

Changing the Color and Pattern of Bars

When you create a Bar chart, Works automatically assigns colors to the bars in the chart. In the example Bar chart, the red bar represents tickets sold for children, the green bar represents tickets sold for adults, and the blue bar represents tickets sold for seniors. You can change the colors of the bars in a chart, patterns within the bars, or both by using the Patterns and Colors command from the Format menu. To change the solid green bars representing tickets sold for adults to the color yellow and change the solid blue bars to striped blue bars, perform the steps on the next two pages.

TO CHANGE COLORS AND PATTERNS IN A BAR CHART ▼

STEP 1 ▶

Select the Format menu and point to the Patterns and Colors command.

Works displays the Format menu and the mouse pointer points to the Patterns and Colors command (Figure 11-56).

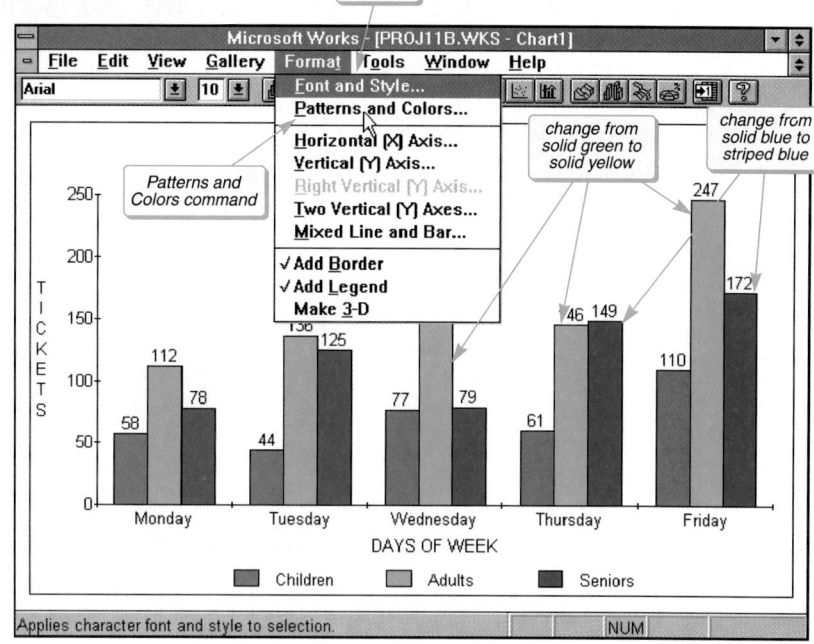

FIGURE 11-56

STEP 2 ▶

Choose the Patterns and Colors command from the Format menu.

The Patterns and Colors dialog box displays (Figure 11-57). The option button labeled 1st in the Series area is selected, indicating the entries in the Colors and Patterns list boxes describe the first series of values on the spreadsheet (tickets sold for Children). Auto is highlighted in the Colors list box and in the Patterns list box. Auto means Works automatically selects the color and pattern. For the first series values, the auto color is red and the pattern is solid.

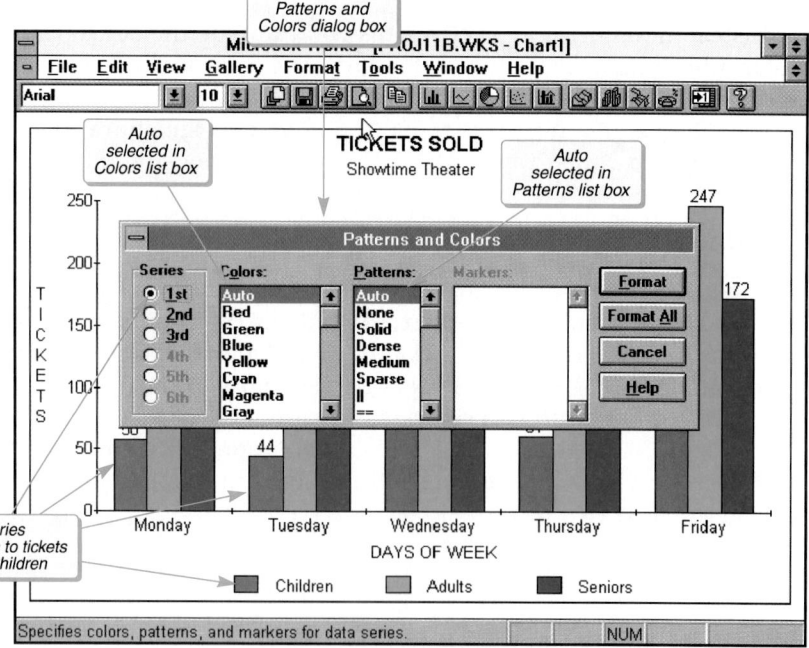

FIGURE 11-57

STEP 3 ▶

Select the 2nd option button in the Series area and highlight Yellow in the Colors list box. Choose the Format button.

The color for Adults, which corresponds to the 2nd option button in the Series area, changes to yellow (Figure 11-58). The Cancel button changes to a Close button.

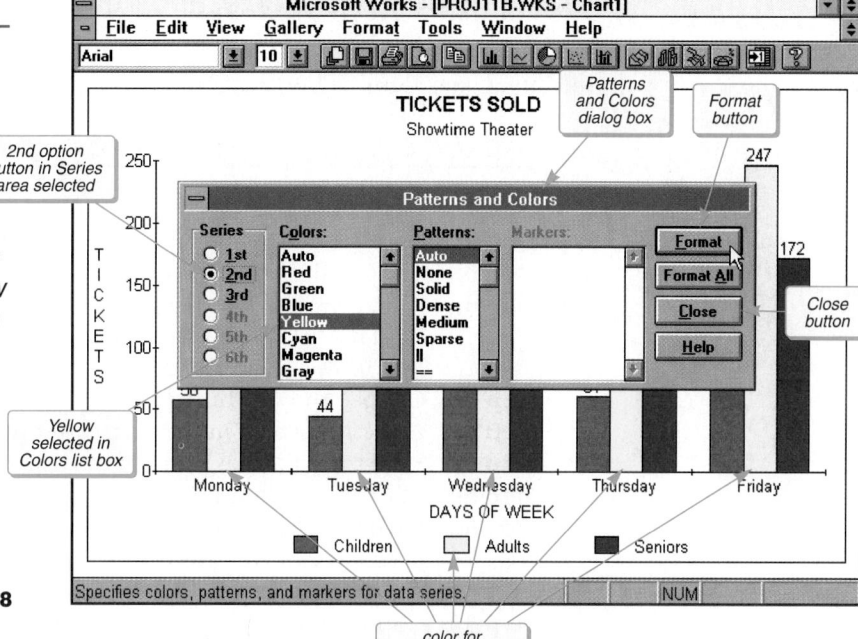

FIGURE 11-58

STEP 4 ▶

Select the 3rd option button in the Series area. Scroll down and highlight the \\ selection in the Patterns list box. Choose the Format button. Choose the Close button in the Patterns and Colors dialog box.

The third bar in the chart displays in blue with the selected pattern (Figure 11-59). The legends also change to reflect the changes in the chart bars.

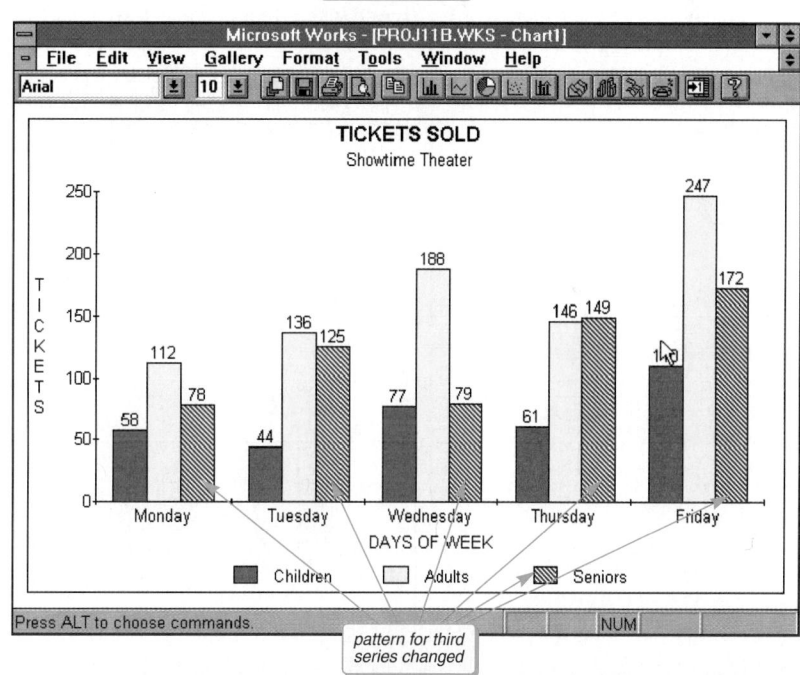

FIGURE 11-59

Changing Font, Font Size, and Font Style

To change the font, font size, and font style in the chart, complete the following steps (see Figure 11-60).

TO CHANGE FONT, FONT SIZE, AND FONT STYLE

Step 1: Click the chart title to highlight it.
Step 2: Select the Format menu.
Step 3: Choose the Font and Style command from the Format menu.
Step 4: When the Font and Style for Title dialog box displays, select 14 in the Size list. Select the Underline check box in the Style area. Select Red in the Color drop-down list box.
Step 5: Choose the OK button in the Font and Style for Title dialog box.
Step 6: Click anywhere in the chart except the chart title.
Step 7: Select the Format menu.
Step 8: Choose the Font and Style command.
Step 9: In the Font and Style for Subtitle and Labels dialog box, select the Bold check box in the Style area and select Blue in the Color drop-down list box.
Step 10: Choose the OK button in the Font and Style for Subtitle and Labels dialog box.

The formatted chart displays in Figure 11-60.

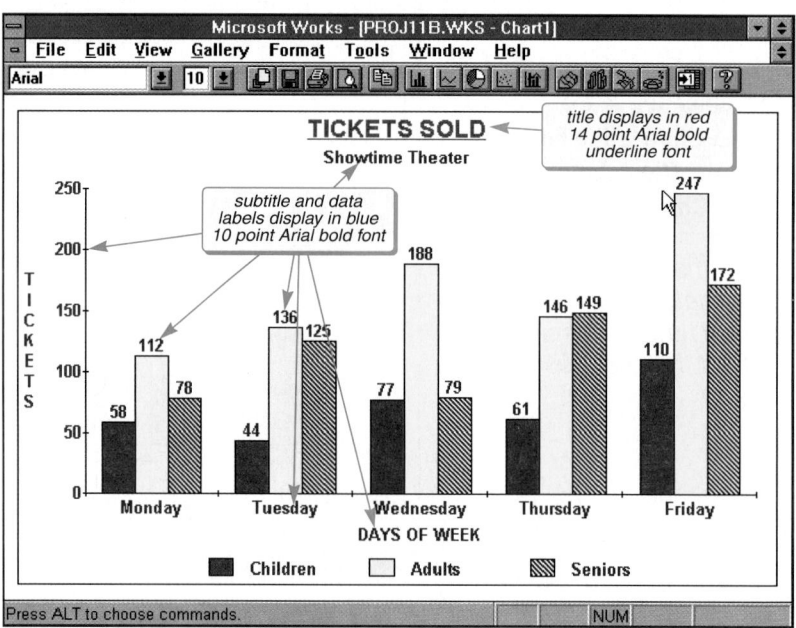

FIGURE 11-60

Previewing and Printing the Bar Chart

To preview and print the Bar chart, perform the following steps.

TO PREVIEW AND PRINT THE CHART

Step 1: Select the File menu.

Step 2: Choose the Page Setup command.

Step 3: If necessary, select the Other Options tab in the Page Setup dialog box.

Step 4: In the Size area of the Other Options screen, select the Full page, keep proportions option button.

Step 5: Choose the OK button in the Page Setup dialog box.

Step 6: Click the Print Preview button on the Toolbar.

Step 7: Review the print preview window to ensure the chart will print properly.

Step 8: Choose the Print button in the print preview window to print the chart.

Works prints the chart. If you have a color printer, the chart prints in color. If not, the chart prints in varying shades of gray.

If you do not want to preview the chart before printing it, you can click the Print button on the Toolbar or choose the Print command from the File menu to print the chart.

Saving the Spreadsheet and Chart

To save the spreadsheet together with the chart using the same filename, perform the following step.

TO SAVE THE SPREADSHEET AND CHART WITH THE SAME NAME

Step 1: Click the Save button on the Toolbar.

If you want to save the spreadsheet and chart with a different name, choose the Save As command from the File menu and enter the new filename in the Save As dialog box.

Creating a 3-D Bar Chart

After creating a standard Bar chart you can easily display the chart as a 3-D Bar chart. To change the standard Bar chart to a 3-D Bar chart, complete the steps on the next page.

TO CREATE A 3-D BAR CHART ▼

STEP 1 ▶

Select the Format menu and point to the Make 3-D command.

The Format menu displays and the mouse pointer points to the Make 3-D command (Figure 11-61).

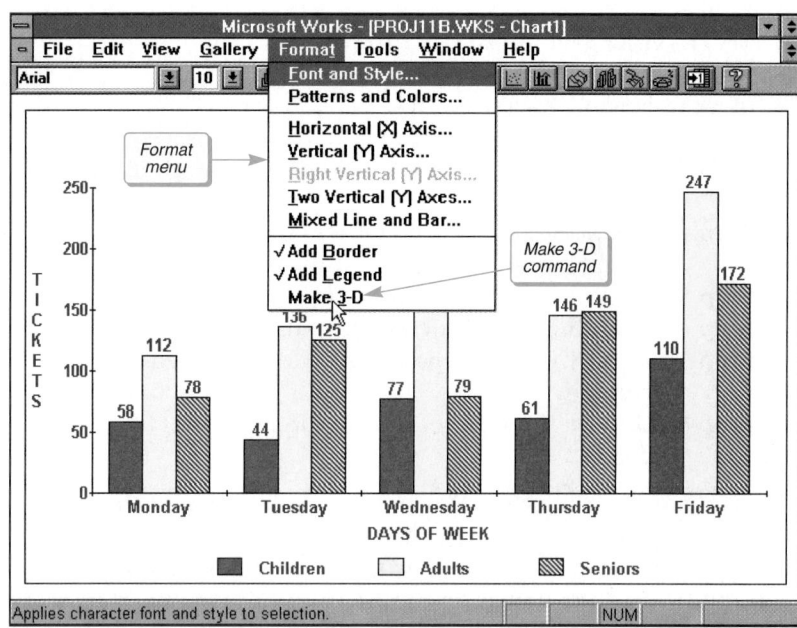

FIGURE 11-61

STEP 2 ▶

Choose the Make 3-D command from the Format menu.

Works displays the Bar chart as a 3-D Bar chart (Figure 11-62). Notice the data labels do not display.

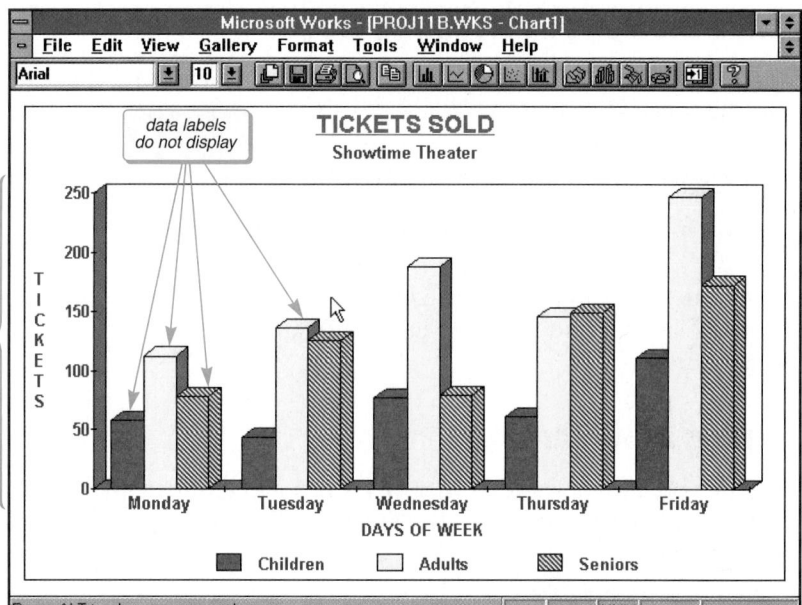

FIGURE 11-62

You can create a 3-D Bar chart without first creating a standard Bar chart. To create only a 3-D Bar chart, select 3-D Bar in the What type of chart do you want? drop-down list box in the Create New Chart dialog box when you initially create the chart.

You can rotate the 3-D Bar chart by holding down the CTRL key and pressing the arrow keys.

To return the chart to the standard Bar chart, once again select the Format menu and choose the Make 3-D command. Works will display the chart as the standard Bar chart.

Other Formats of 3-D Bar Charts

To view other types of 3-D Bar charts, complete the following steps.

STEP 1 ▶

Point to and click the 3-D Bar Chart button on the Toolbar.

Works displays the 3-D Bar dialog box (Figure 11-63). Six different options for 3-D Bar charts are available. Option 1 is highlighted, which means option 1 is currently displayed on the screen.

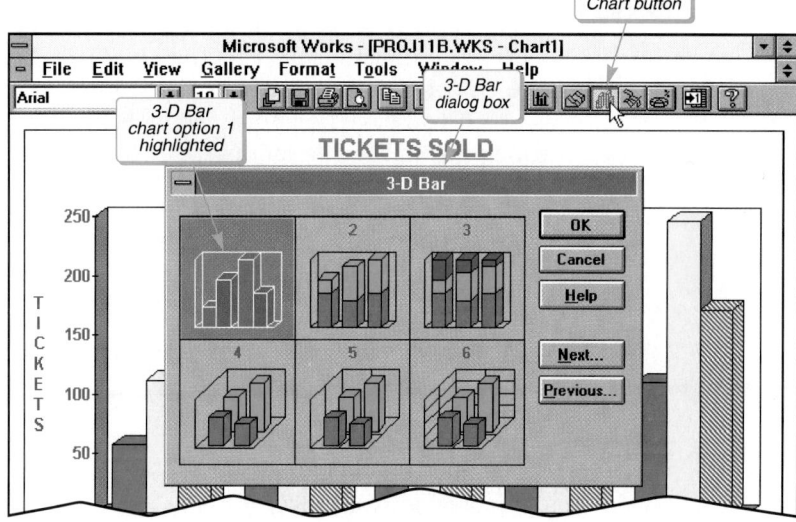

FIGURE 11-63

STEP 2 ▶

Highlight the option 6 box by clicking the box. Choose the OK button in the 3-D Bar dialog box.

Works displays the 3-D Bar chart in the option 6 format (Figure 11-64). The title and subtitle formatting remains the same, but the colors and patterns of the bars in the chart change to the Works defaults.

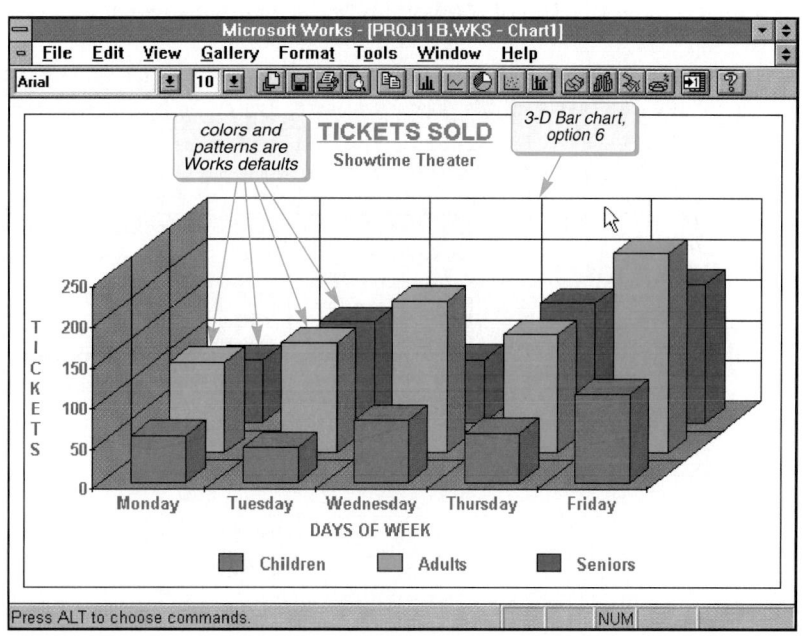

FIGURE 11-64

If you want to display the chart in Figure 11-64 with the same colors and patterns as the chart in Figure 11-63, select the Format menu, choose the Patterns and Colors command, and make the appropriate entries.

You should be aware that when you change the format of a chart, the previous format is replaced. If you have created a chart you want to keep, but would like to look at other formats for the chart as well, it is suggested you duplicate the chart before making changes. To duplicate a chart, select the Tools menu, choose the Duplicate Chart command, in the Charts list box of the Duplicate Chart dialog box highlight the name of the chart you want to duplicate, type the name of the new chart, choose the Duplicate button in the dialog box, and choose the OK button in the dialog box. To view the duplicate chart, select the View menu, choose the Chart command, select the name of the duplicate chart, and choose the OK button. Works will display the duplicate chart and you can change its format.

If you have no additional work, quit Works by choosing the Exit Works command from the File menu.

▶ LINE CHARTS

Another widely used chart is the Line chart. Line charts are valuable for showing trends over a period of time. In a Line chart, the values in a category are represented by a line, a marker, or a combination of a line and marker. A marker is a small circle, square, or diamond-shaped mark that identifies a particular point on a chart.

Figure 11-65 illustrates a spreadsheet containing projected unit sales for three types of software: EZType, EZGraph, and EZFind. Shown also is a Line chart illustrating the projected sales over the period of years 1995-2000. The markers display as small filled circles for EZType, small filled diamonds for EZGraph, and small hollow circles for EZFind. The red line for EZType and the blue line for EZFind are solid lines while the magenta line for EZGraph is dashed.

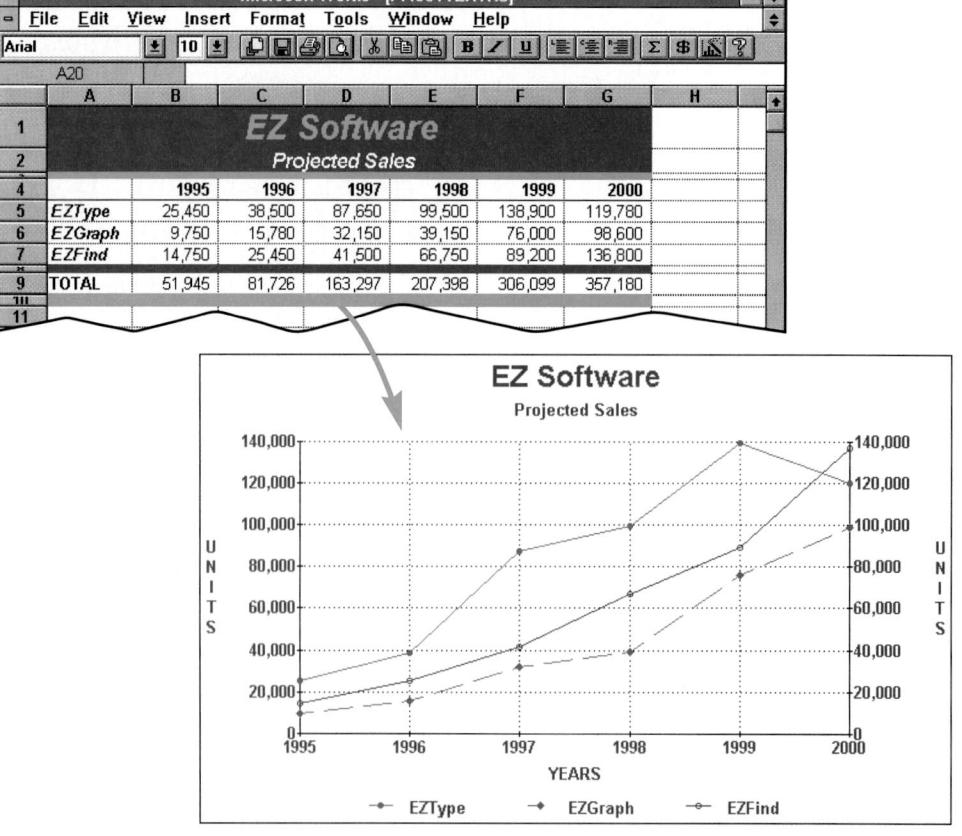

FIGURE 11-65

In the spreadsheet, the column titles (years) and the row titles (software names) are adjacent to the values being charted. This simplifies the task of including category labels (years) and legends (software names) on the chart because Works will automatically place category labels and legends on a chart if the adjacent columns and rows containing the labels and legends are highlighted prior to creating the chart. In the chart, the vertical (Y) axis label, UNITS, and the unit sales numbers display on both the left and right sides of the chart. The technique for accomplishing this is explained in this section of Project 11.

Creating a Line Chart

To create a Line chart, perform the following steps. It is assumed the spreadsheet file is open and displays on the screen.

TO CREATE A LINE CHART ▼

STEP 1 ▶

Highlight the range to chart (cells A4:G7) and point to the New Chart button on the Toolbar (Figure 11-66).

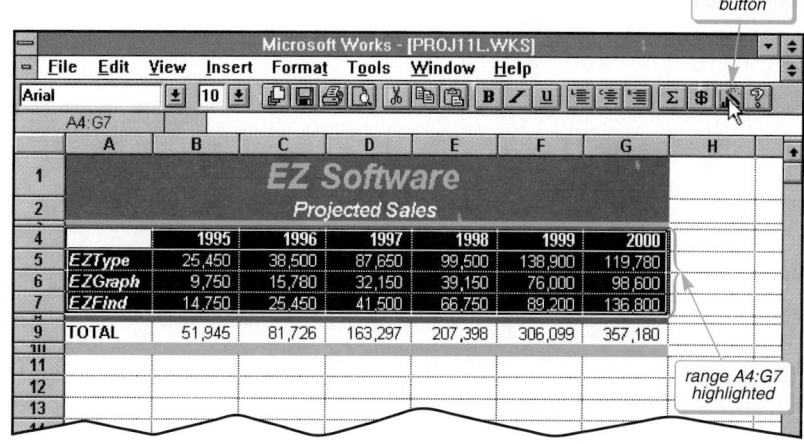

FIGURE 11-66

STEP 2 ▶

Click the New Chart button on the Toolbar. When the New Chart dialog box displays, select Line from the What type of chart do you want? drop-down list box. Type a1 in the Chart title text box and select the Add border check box. Point to the OK button.

Works displays the New Chart dialog box (Figure 11-67). A sample of the chart as it will display with the current selections displays on the right side of the dialog box.

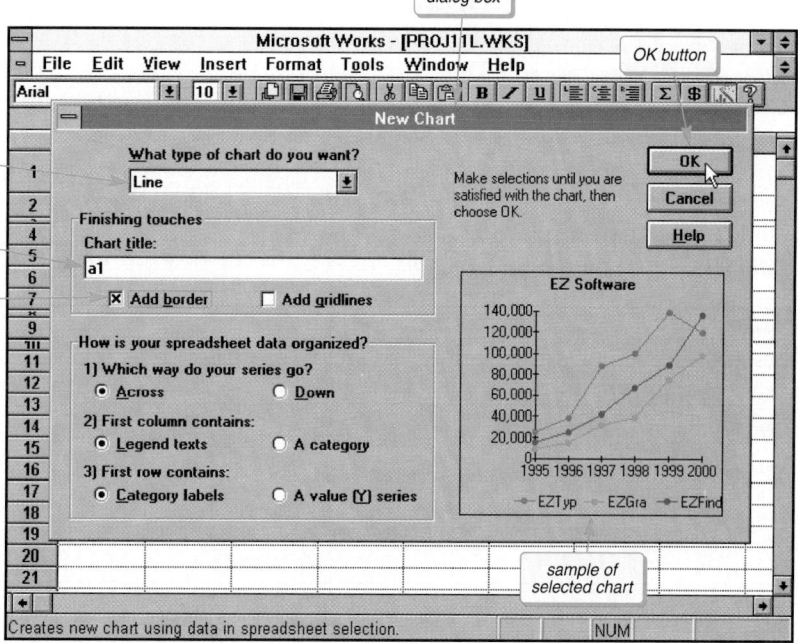

FIGURE 11-67

STEP 3 ▶

Choose the OK button in the New Chart dialog box.

Works displays the Line chart (Figure 11-68). The values for EZType, EZGraph, and EZFind software are charted. Small circle markers identify specific values from the spreadsheet for each year based on the numbers in the vertical (Y) axis. The category labels (years) and the legend for EZType, EZGraph, and EZFind display below the horizontal axis because the adjacent text for the category labels and legend was highlighted prior to creating the chart.

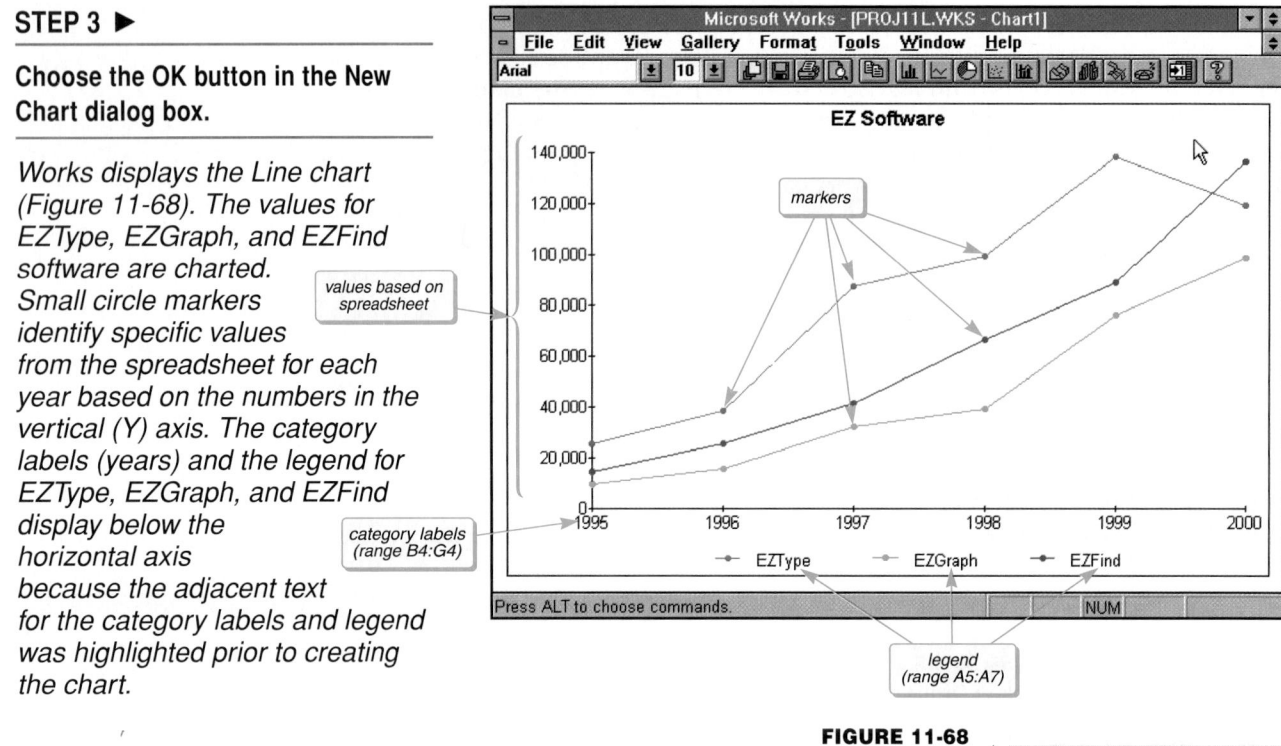

FIGURE 11-68

Works determines the range of numbers on the left vertical axis based on the values in the charted range of the spreadsheet. The maximum value on the vertical axis is 140,000 because the greatest value in the spreadsheet is near 140,000. The interval between numbers on the chart is 20,000.

Adding Gridlines

When creating a Line chart, gridlines often assist in making the chart easier to read. To add gridlines to the X and Y axes, perform the following steps.

TO ADD GRIDLINES ▼

STEP 1 ▶

With the Line chart displayed, point to the Line Chart button on the chart Toolbar.

The mouse pointer points to the Line Chart button on the chart Toolbar (Figure 11-69).

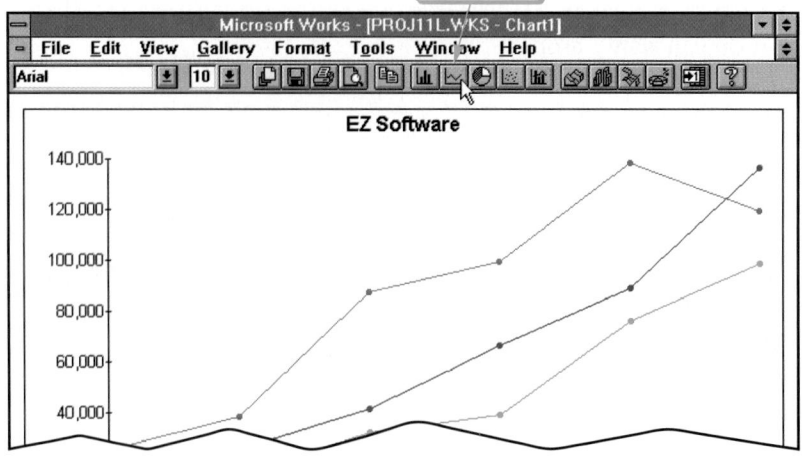

FIGURE 11-69

STEP 2 ▶

Click the Line Chart button on the chart Toolbar. When the Line dialog box displays, select option 5 by pointing to the square and clicking the left mouse button. Point to the OK button in the Line dialog box.

Works displays the Line dialog box (Figure 11-70). Option 5 is selected as shown by the dark-ened background in the option five square. Option 5 will display a chart with both horizontal and ver-tical gridlines. The mouse pointer points to the OK button.

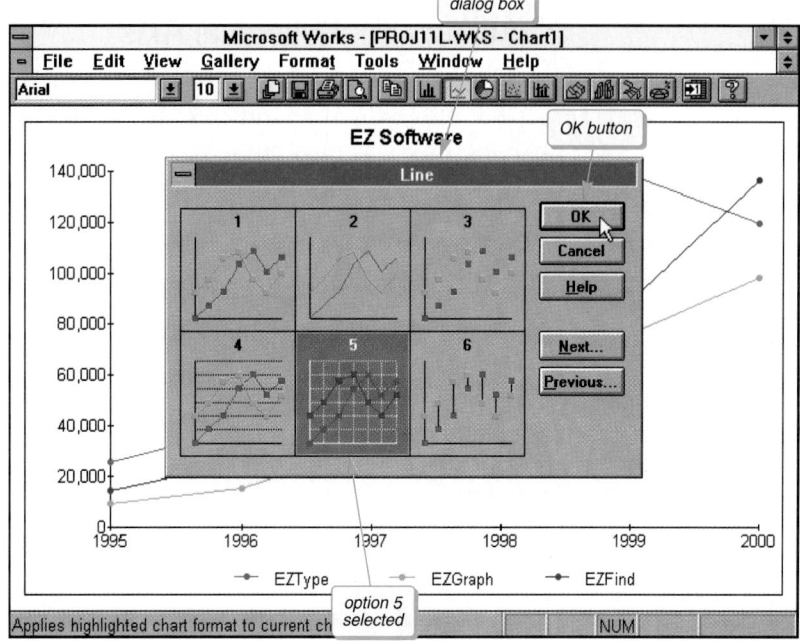

FIGURE 11-70

STEP 3 ▶

Choose the OK button in the Line dialog box.

Works displays the Line chart with both horizontal and vertical gridlines (Figure 11-71).

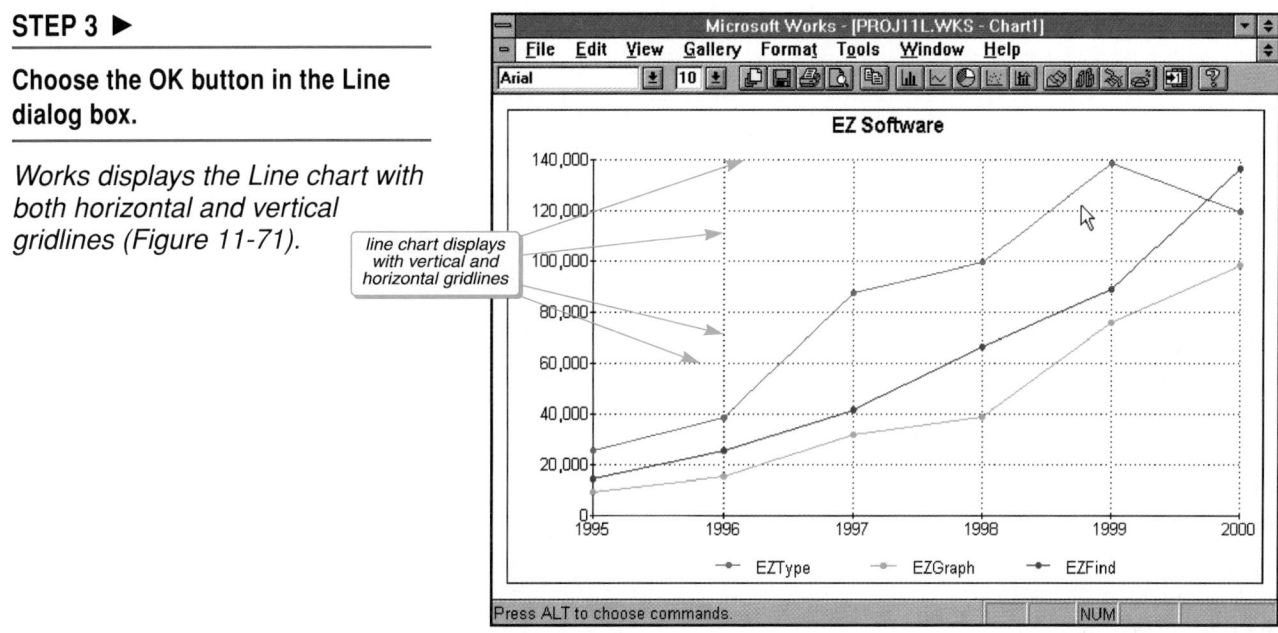

FIGURE 11-71

You can also insert horizontal gridlines by choosing the **Horizontal (X) Axis command** from the chart Format menu and selecting the Show Gridlines check box in the Horizontal Axis dialog box. Similarly, you can insert vertical gridlines by choosing the **Vertical (Y) Axis command** from the chart Format menu and selecting the Show Gridlines check box in the Vertical Axis dialog box.

Adding a Right Vertical Axis

In a Line chart, you can add a right vertical axis and place values on the axis. To do this, you must indicate that values are to appear on the right axis as well as the left axis, as illustrated in the following steps.

TO ADD A RIGHT VERTICAL AXIS ▼

STEP 1 ▶

Select the Format menu and point to the Two Vertical (Y) Axes command.

*Works displays the Format menu (Figure 11-72). The mouse pointer points to the **Two Vertical (Y) Axes command.***

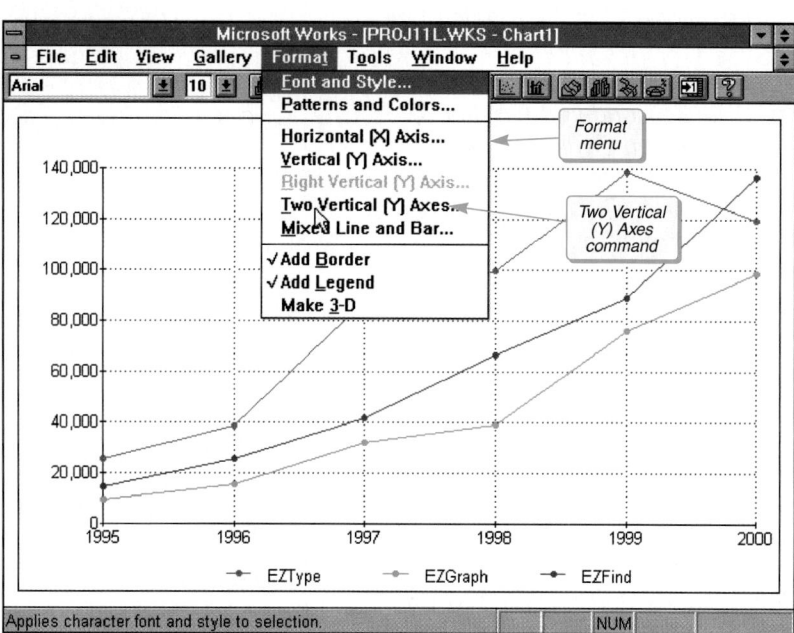

FIGURE 11-72

STEP 2 ▶

Choose the Two Vertical (Y) Axes command from the Format menu. When the Two Vertical Axes dialog box displays, select the Right option buttons in the 1st Value Series, 2nd Value Series, and 3rd Value Series areas. Point to the OK button.

The Right option button for each of the three series is selected (Figure 11-73). These selections inform Works that the right vertical axis values should be the same as the left vertical axis values. The mouse pointer points to the OK button.

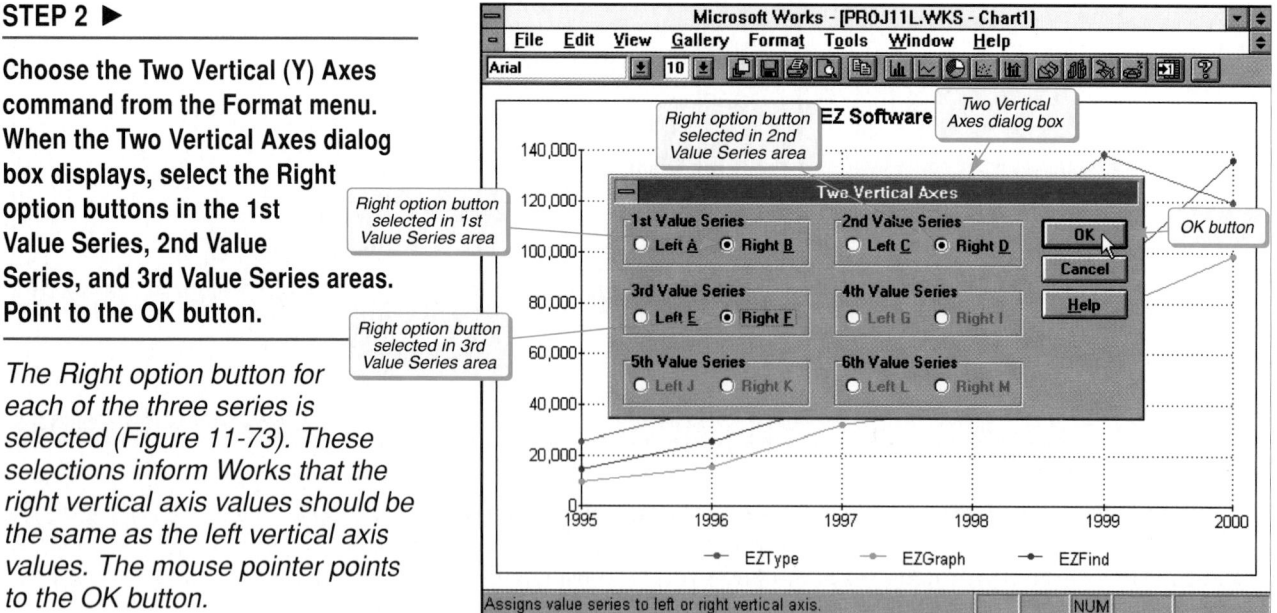

FIGURE 11-73

STEP 3 ▶

Choose the OK button in the Two Vertical Axes dialog box.

Works displays the Line chart (Figure 11-74). The chart contains values on the right vertical (Y) axis.

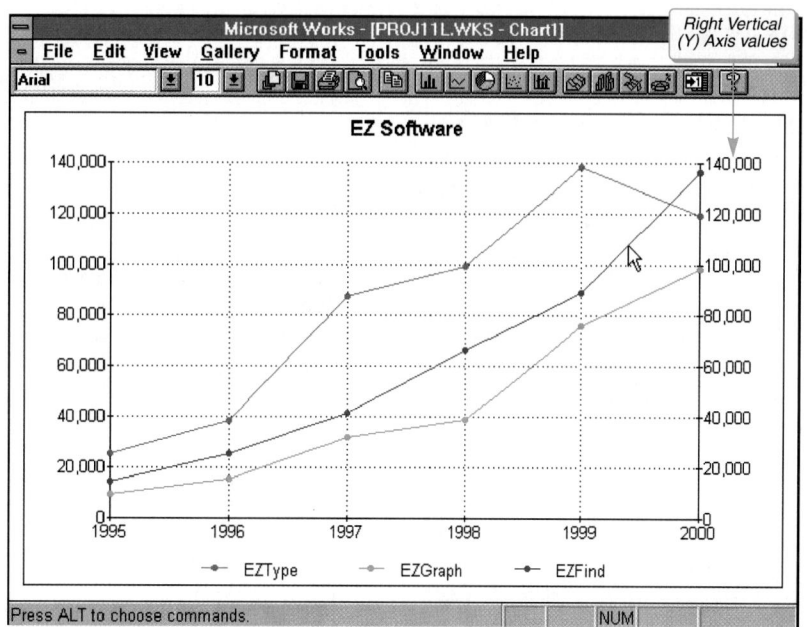

FIGURE 11-74

To make the values on the right vertical (Y) axis the same as those on the left vertical axis, the Right option buttons in the Value Series areas in the Two Vertical Axes dialog box must be selected for all values represented in the chart.

Changing the Type of Lines and Markers

On a Line chart, you can change the type of lines, the color of the lines, and the shape of the markers. In the example problem, to change the 2nd value (EZGraph) to a magenta dashed line with solid, diamond-shaped markers and the 3rd value (EZFind) to a hollow circle marker, perform the following steps.

TO CHANGE THE TYPE OF LINES AND MARKERS ▼

STEP 1 ▶

Select the Format menu and point to the Patterns and Colors command.

*The Format menu displays and the mouse pointer points to the **Patterns and Colors command** (Figure 11-75).*

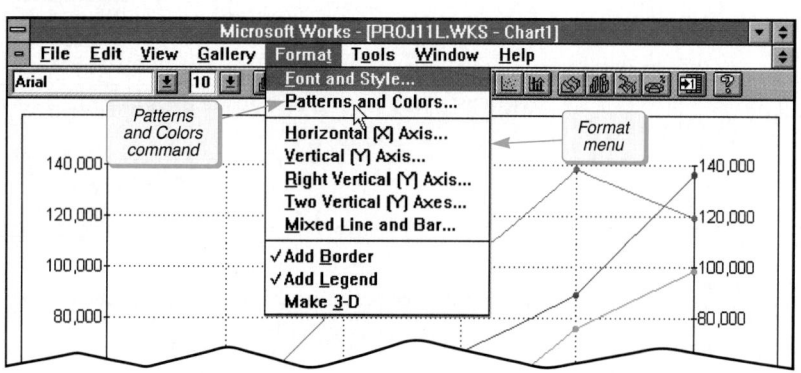

FIGURE 11-75

STEP 2 ►

Choose the Patterns and Colors command from the Format menu. When the Patterns and Colors dialog box displays, select the 2nd option button in the Series area, highlight Magenta in the Colors list box, highlight Dashed in the Patterns list box, and highlight Filled diamond in the Markers list box. Choose the Format button.

The Patterns and Colors dialog box contains the selected entries (Figure 11-76). When you choose the Format button, the Cancel button changes to the Close button and the lines are formatted according to the selections.

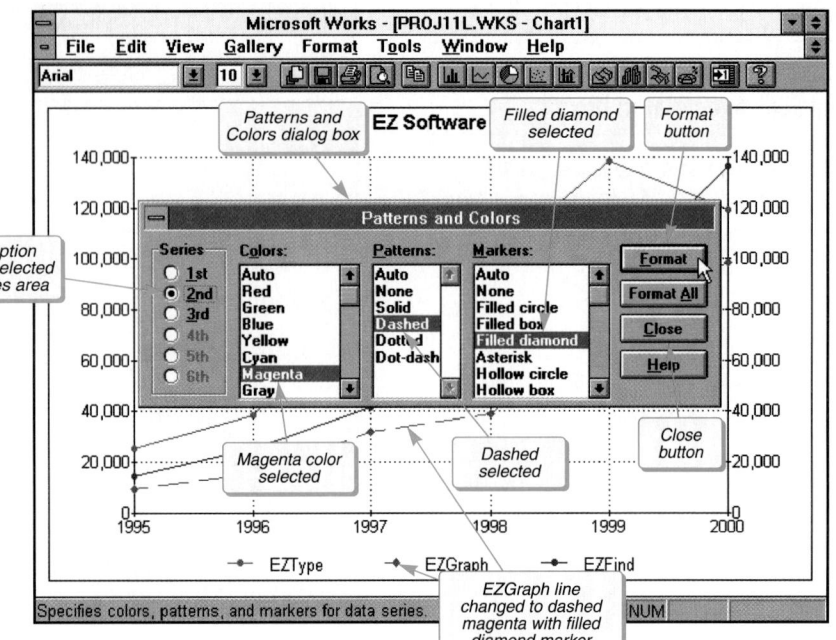

FIGURE 11-76

STEP 3 ►

Select the 3rd option button in the Series area, highlight Hollow circle in the Markers list box, and choose the Format button. Choose the Close button in the Patterns and Colors dialog box.

Works displays the chart (Figure 11-77). The line for EZGraph is now dashed and magenta, and the marker is a filled diamond shape. The marker for EZFind is a hollow circle. The legends for the entries are also changed.

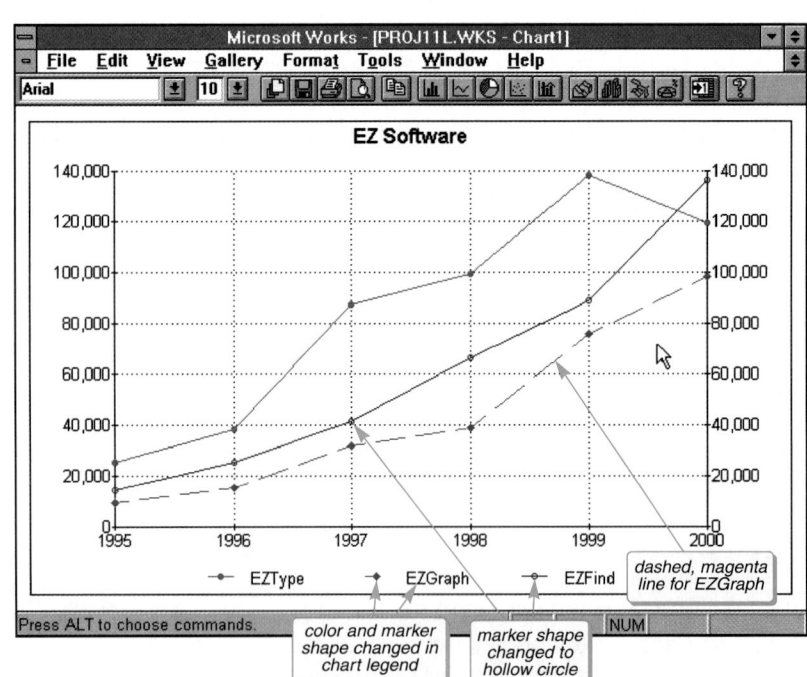

FIGURE 11-77

The Patterns and Colors command and related dialog box can be used with all charts you create using Works.

Adding Titles to the Chart

To add the titles to the chart, including a chart subtitle, a title on the horizontal (X) axis, the left vertical (Y) axis and right vertical (Y) axis, perform the following steps.

TO ADD TITLES TO A LINE CHART ▼

STEP 1 ►

Select the Edit menu and point to the Titles command.

Works displays the Edit menu and the mouse pointer points to the Titles command (Figure 11-78).

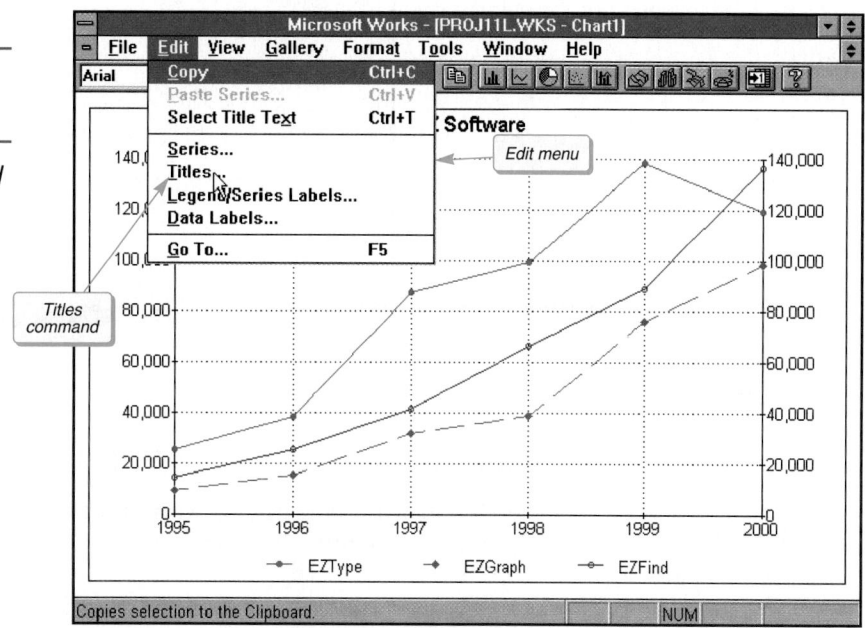

FIGURE 11-78

STEP 2 ►

Choose the Titles command from the Edit menu. Type a2 in the Subtitle text box (the cell reference for the words Projected Sales), type YEARS in the Horizontal (X) Axis text box, type UNITS in the Vertical (Y) Axis text box, and type UNITS in the Right Vertical Axis text box. Point to the OK button.

Works displays the Titles dialog box (Figure 11-79). Cell references are contained in the Chart title and Subtitle text boxes and the remaining text boxes contain actual titles. The cell reference for the Chart title was entered when you created the chart.

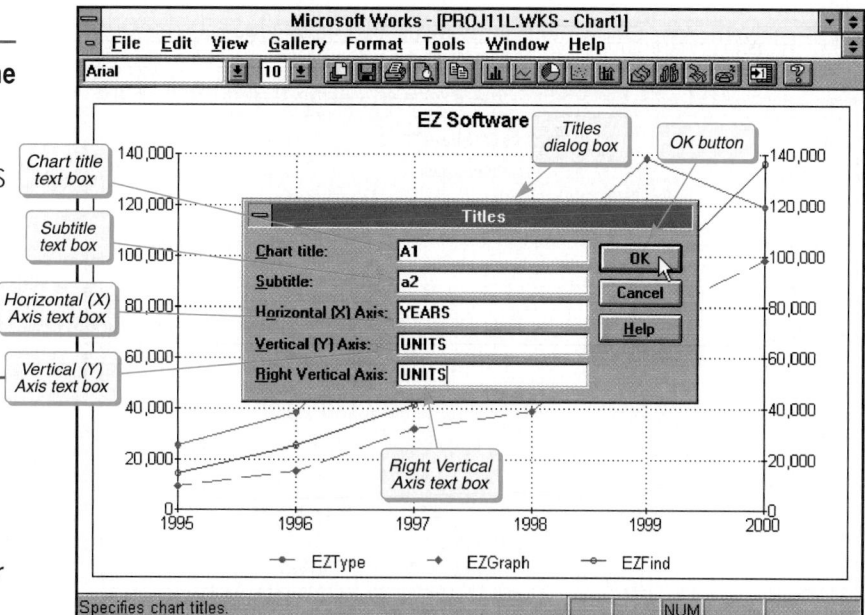

FIGURE 11-79

STEP 3 ▶

Choose the OK button in the Titles dialog box.

Works displays the chart with titles (Figure 11-80).

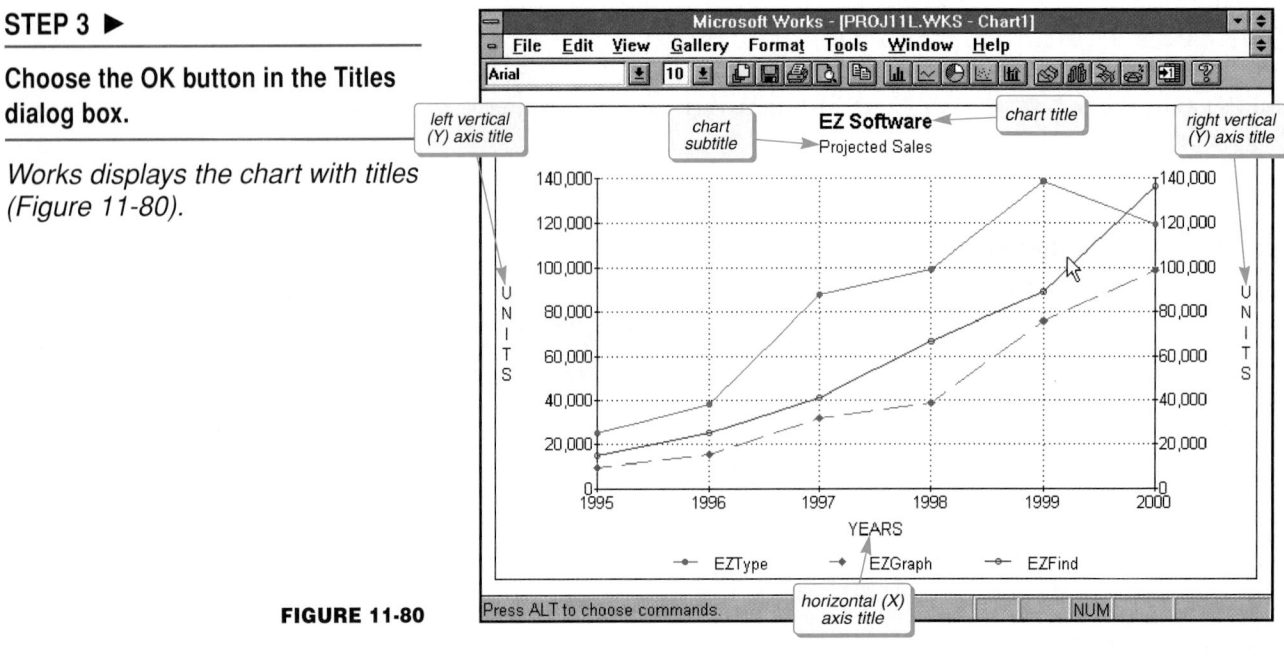

FIGURE 11-80

Changing Font, Font Size, and Font Style

To change the font, font size, and font style of the chart title, perform the following steps (see Figure 11-81).

TO CHANGE THE CHART TITLE FORMATTING

Step 1: Select the chart title by clicking the title.
Step 2: Select the Format menu.

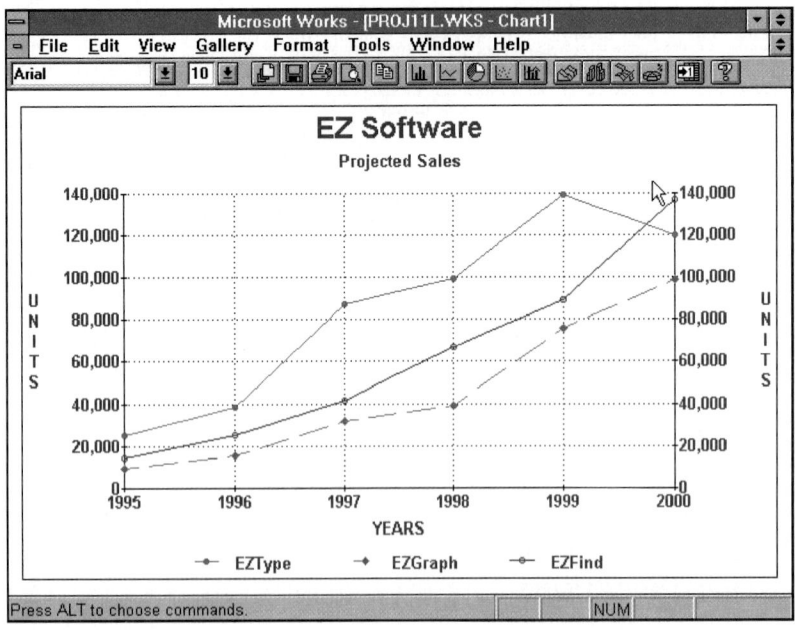

FIGURE 11-81

Step 3: Choose the Font and Style command.
Step 4: When Works displays the Font and Style for Title dialog box, select 18 in the Size list box and select Dark Blue in the Color drop-down list box.
Step 5: Choose the OK button in the Font and Style for Title dialog box.

To change the subtitle and labels on the chart, perform the steps on the next page (see Figure 11-81).

TO CHANGE SUBTITLE AND LABEL FORMATTING

Step 1: Click the chart anywhere except the chart title.
Step 2: Select the Format menu.
Step 3: Choose the Font and Style command.
Step 4: When the Font and Style for Subtitle and Labels dialog box displays, select the Bold check box in the Style area and select Dark Blue in the Color drop-down list box.
Step 5: Choose the OK button in the Font and Style for Subtitle and Labels dialog box.

The formatted chart displays in Figure 11-81.

Naming a Chart

Works allows you to give meaningful names to charts rather than the default names Chart1, Chart2, and so on. To give the name Projected Sales to the Line chart shown in Figure 11-81, perform the following steps.

TO NAME A CHART ▼

STEP 1 ▶

Select the Tools menu and point to the Name Chart command.

Works displays the Tools menu and the mouse pointer points to the Name Chart command (Figure 11-82).

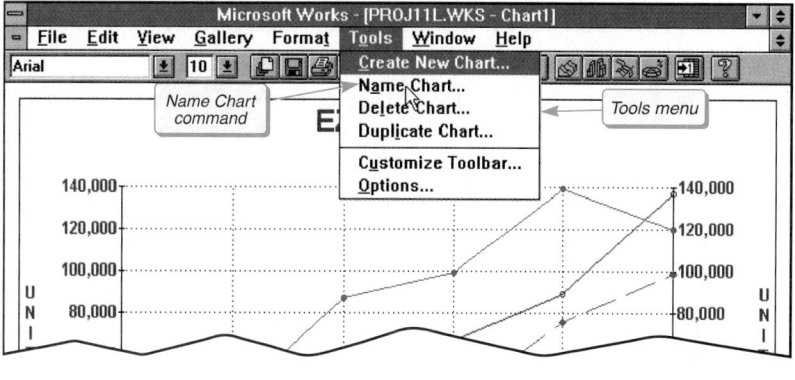

FIGURE 11-82

STEP 2 ▶

Choose the Name Chart command from the Tools menu. When the Name Chart dialog box displays, type `Projected Sales` in the Name text box. Point to the Rename button.

Works displays the Name Chart dialog box (Figure 11-83). The current chart name, Chart1, is highlighted in the Charts list box. The name Projected Sales displays in the Name text box and the mouse pointer points to the Rename button.

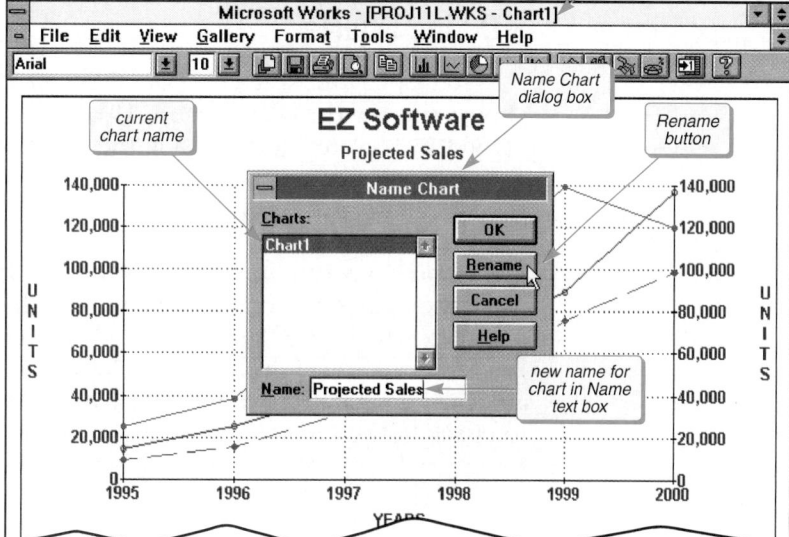

FIGURE 11-83

STEP 3 ▶

Choose the Rename button and point to the OK button.

Works changes the name of the chart in the Title bar of the Works application window and in the Charts list box (Figure 11-84). The mouse pointer points to the OK button.

STEP 4

Choose the OK button to remove the Name Chart dialog box from the screen.

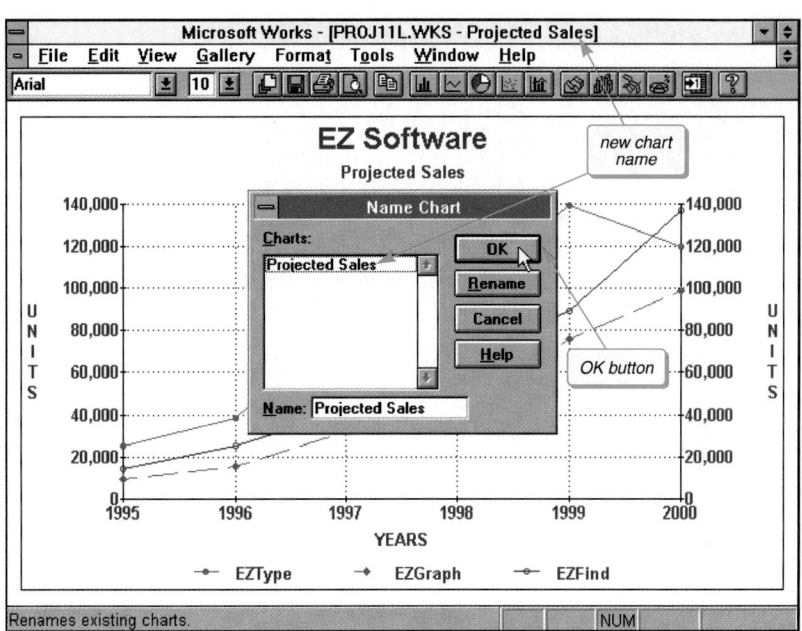

FIGURE 11-84

Two other commands are available on the Tools menu (see Figure 11-82 on the previous page). The Delete Chart command allows you to delete a chart from the spreadsheet file. To delete a chart, choose the Delete Chart command from the Tools menu, highlight the name of the chart you want to delete in the Charts list box of the Delete Chart dialog box, choose the Delete button in the Delete Chart dialog box, and then choose the OK button.

To duplicate a chart, choose the Duplicate Chart command from the Tools menu. Select the chart you want to duplicate in the Charts list box of the Duplicate Chart dialog box, choose the Duplicate button in the Duplicate Chart dialog box, and then choose the OK button. Works will duplicate the chart you select and name the new ChartX, where X is the next number in sequence.

3-D Line Charts

To display the Line chart as a 3-D Line chart, select the Format menu and choose the Make 3-D command. The 3-D Line chart can be rotated by holding down the CTRL key and pressing the arrow keys.

Printing the Line Chart

In previous examples, the size of the chart you print has been controlled by using the Page Setup command and selecting the Full page, keep proportions option button in the Other Options screen of the Page Setup dialog box. Sometimes this will result in a printed chart that is not in the proportions you desire and can eliminate important information. You should use the Print Preview feature to check how a Line chart will display before printing the Line chart.

You can control the size of a printed chart by choosing the Page Setup command from the File menu and making entries in the Top, Bottom, Left, and Right margin text boxes in the Margins screen of the Page Setup dialog box. Perform the following steps to create the printed chart in Figure 11-85.

TO PRINT A CHART WITH THE FULL PAGE OPTION

Step 1: Select the File menu.
Step 2: Choose the Page Setup command from the File menu.
Step 3: Select the Margins tab.
Step 4: Type 5" in the Bottom margin text box, type 1" in the Left margin text box, and type 1" in the Right margin text box.
Step 5: Select the Other Options tab in the Page Setup dialog box.
Step 6: Select the Full page option button in the Size area of the Other Options screen.
Step 7: Choose the OK button in the Page Setup dialog box.

To print the chart, choose the Print button in the print preview window, click the Print button on the Toolbar, or choose the Print command from the File menu. The printed chart is shown in Figure 11-85.

When you print charts, you may find it necessary to experiment with the entries in the Page Setup dialog box to obtain the printed chart in the size that meets your needs.

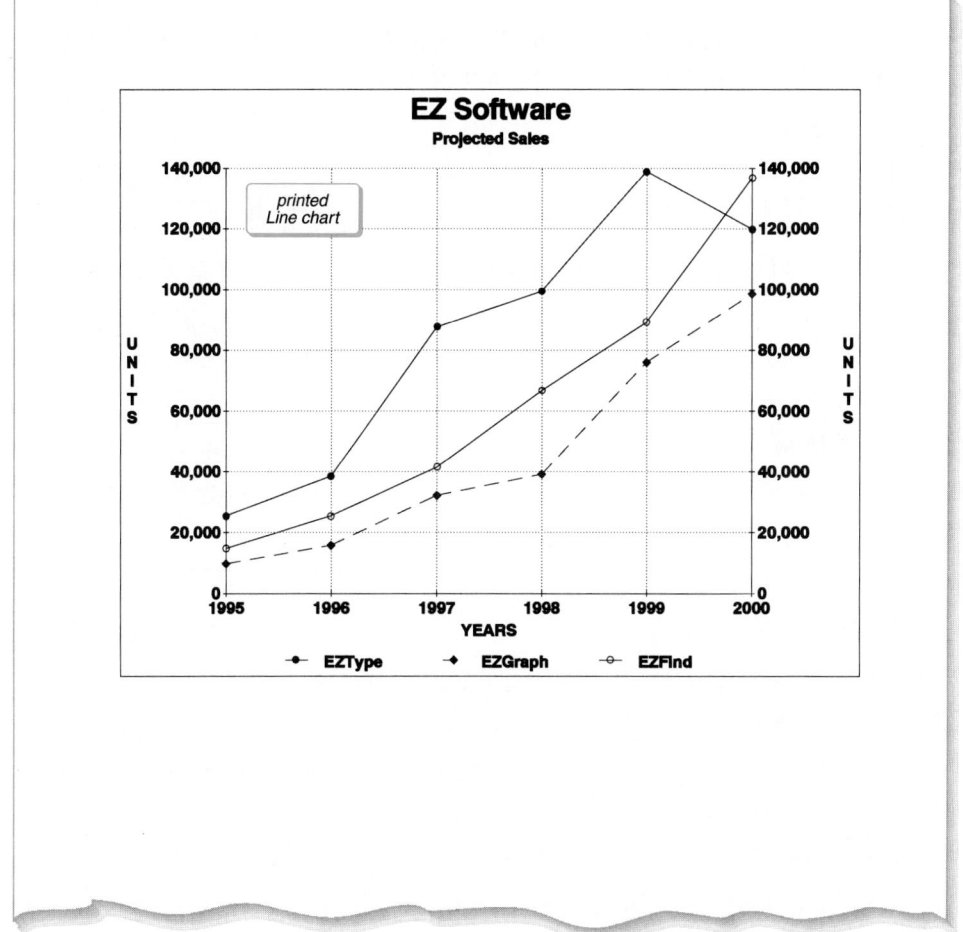

FIGURE 11-85

▶ STACKED LINE CHARTS

Stacked Line charts show the relationships between the values of several categories and their totals by drawing stacked lines; that is, each line's values are added to those of the line below.

Figure 11-86 illustrates a spreadsheet that contains the number of personal computers manufactured by PCTech Computers on three shifts: 7 am - 3 pm, 3 pm - 11 pm, and 11 pm - 7 am, for Monday through Friday. Also shown is the Stacked Line chart derived from the spreadsheet.

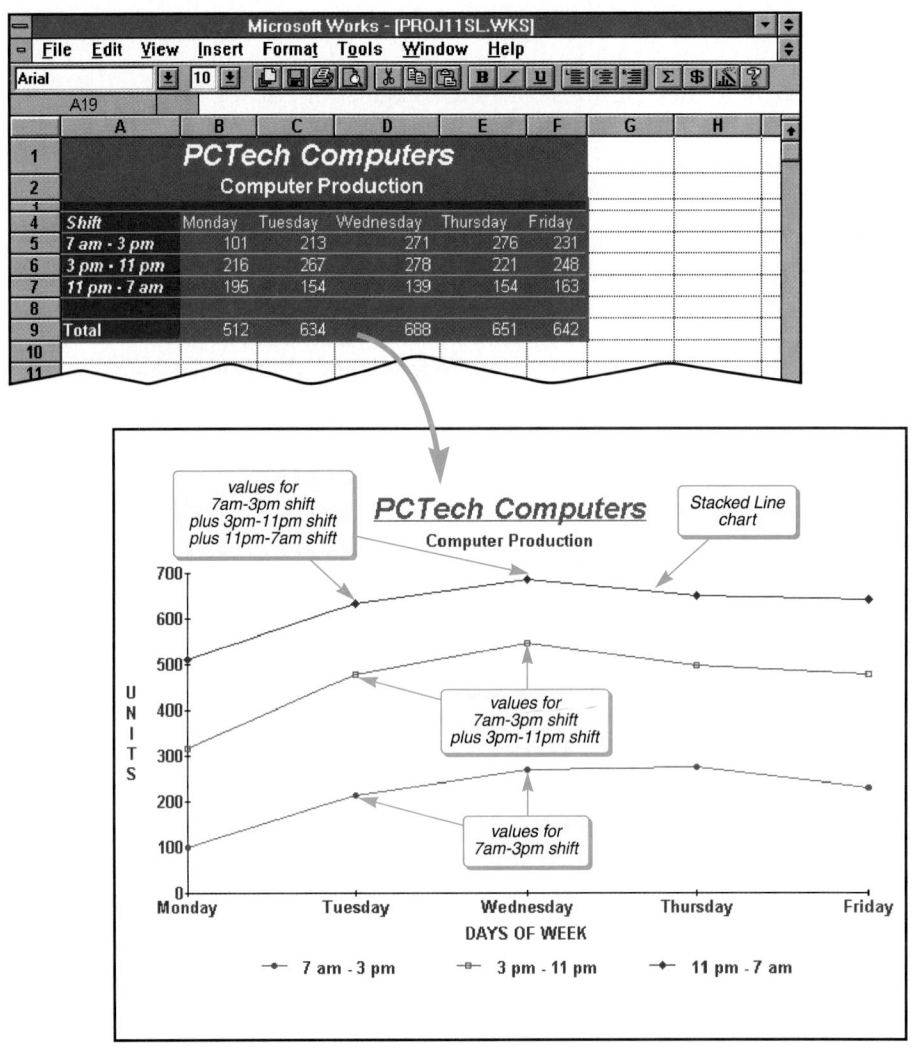

FIGURE 11-86

Notice in the chart that the first line has a marker on Monday near the 100 unit mark. This is the production of the 7 am - 3 pm shift. The next marker for Monday is just above the 300 unit mark. This marker represents the production of both the 7 am – 3 pm shift (101 units) and the 3 pm – 11 pm shift (216 units). The third marker on Monday is just above the 500 unit mark (101 units on the 7 am – 3 pm shift plus 216 units on the 3 pm – 11 pm shift plus 195 units on the 11 pm – 7 am shift). Thus, you can see that the lines on the Stacked Line chart are cumulative.

To create the Stacked Line chart, follow the steps previously explained for creating other charts by highlighting the cells on the spreadsheet you want to chart, clicking the New Chart button and making the appropriate entries in the New Chart dialog box. The techniques for adding a legend, title, subtitle, changing fonts, and so forth are the same as explained in previous sections of this project.

▶ 3-D AREA CHARTS

3-D Area chart can be used in place of the Stacked Line chart to display the same type of data with a different perspective. The 3-D Area chart for the spreadsheet in Figure 11-86 is shown in Figure 11-87.

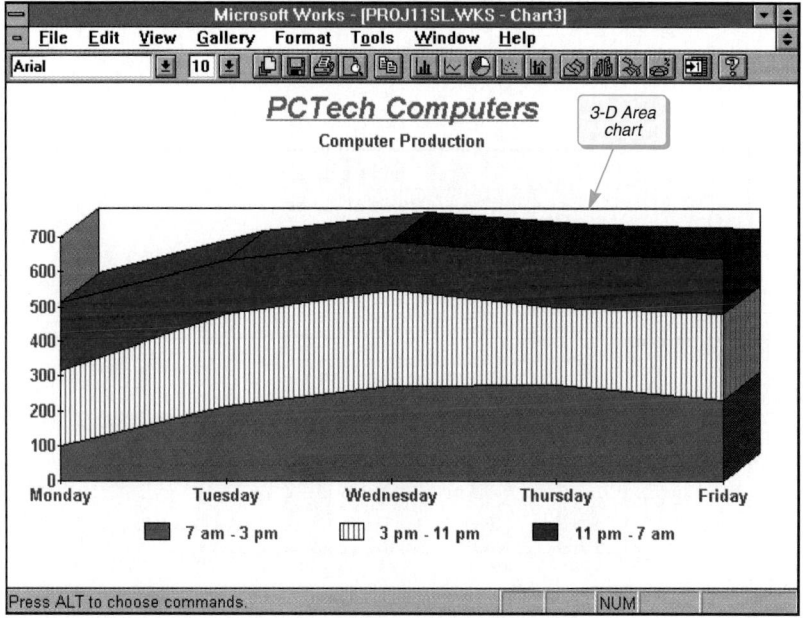

FIGURE 11-87

You can create a 3-D Area chart by selecting 3-D Area chart in the What type of chart do you want? drop-down list box in the New Chart dialog box when you originally create the chart, or you can click the 3-D Area Chart button on the Charting Toolbar to convert an existing chart to a 3-D Area chart.

▶ COMBINATION CHARTS

Combination charts allow you to combine bars and lines in a single chart. Figure 11-88 illustrates a spreadsheet and related Combination chart that displays the projected sales for EZType software as bars and EZGraph software as a line. Notice that the values on the left vertical axis are different than the values on the right vertical axis. The values on the left correspond to the bars for EZType and the values on the right correspond to the lines for EZGraph.

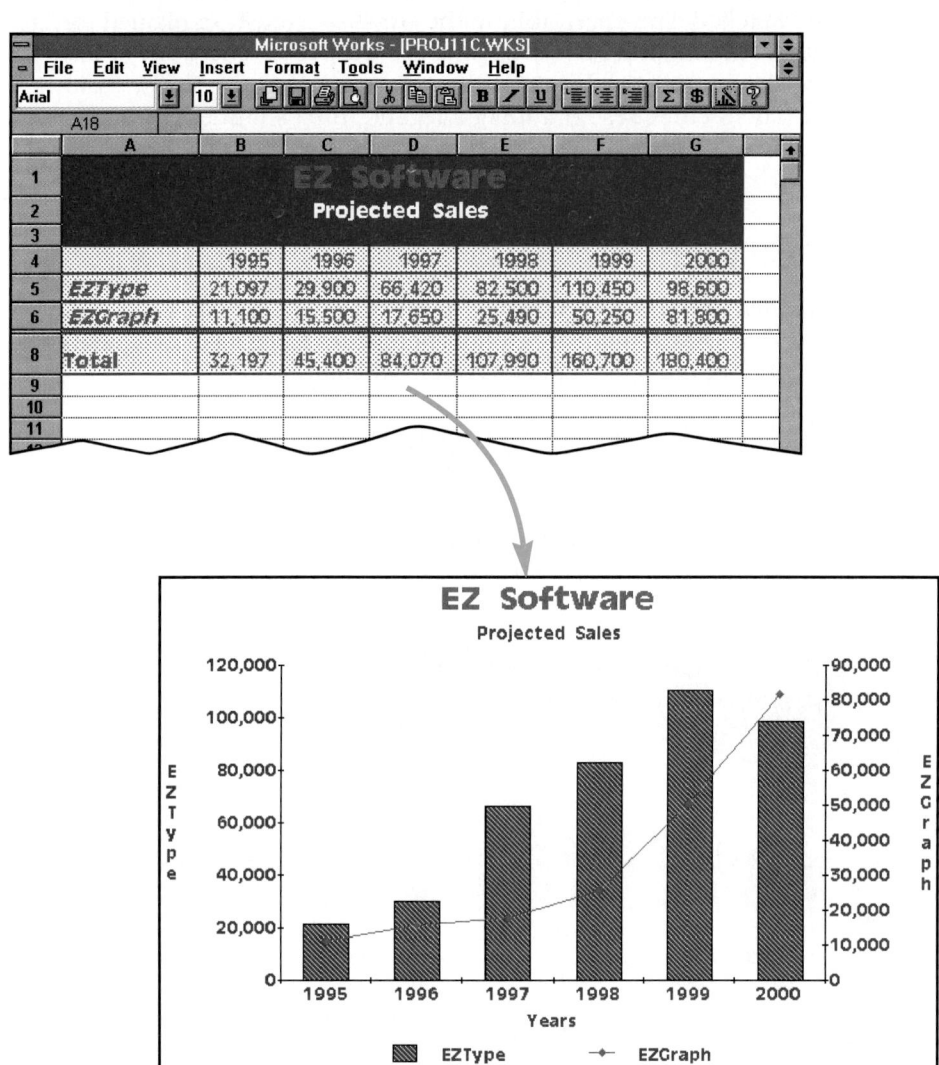

FIGURE 11-88

To create the Combination chart for EZ Software, designate two vertical axes, and specify different values on the left and right vertical axes, perform the following steps (see Figure 11-88).

TO CREATE A COMBINATION CHART WITH
DIFFERENT LEFT AND RIGHT VERTICAL AXES VALUES

Step 1: In the spreadsheet, highlight the data you want to chart.
Step 2: Click the New Chart button on the Toolbar.
Step 3: Select Combination in the What type of chart do you want? drop-down list box in the New Chart dialog box.
Step 4: Type a1 in the Chart title text box in the New Chart dialog box.
Step 5: Choose the OK button in the New Chart dialog box.
Step 6: Select the Format menu.
Step 7: Choose the Two Vertical (Y) Axes command from the Format menu.
Step 8: In the Two Vertical Axes dialog box, select the Right option button in the Second Value Series area.
Step 9: Choose the OK button in the Two Vertical Axes dialog box.
Step 10: Using techniques described previously, format the chart.

The formatted Combination chart with different left and right vertical axes values displays in Figure 11-88.

Notice in Figure 11-88 that the left vertical axis shows the range 0-120,000, while the right vertical axis shows the range 0-90,000. Works automatically calculates these ranges based on values in the spreadsheet. You can change the ranges and the intervals between values on the axes by choosing the Vertical Axis command from the Format menu and making the appropriate entries.

To switch which value (Y) series is the bar and which value (Y) series is the line, you can choose the **Mixed Line and Bar command** from the Format menu and make appropriate selections.

▶ X-Y (SCATTER) CHARTS

X-Y (Scatter) charts show relationships between two categories of related data and are commonly used for charting irregularly occurring data. The X-Y (Scatter) chart in Figure 11-89 on the next page displays the relationship of the age when women marry and the number of marriages that occur at each age.

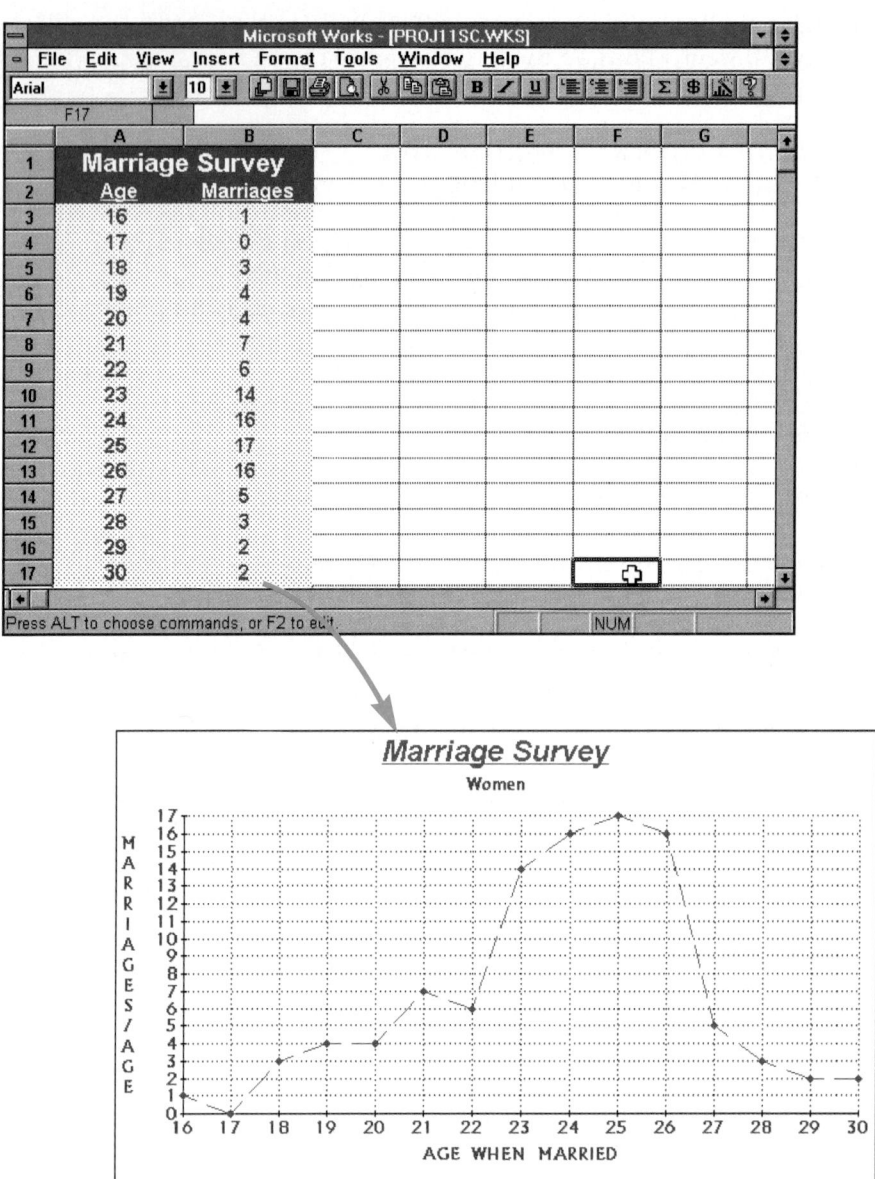

FIGURE 11-89

To create the X-Y (Scatter) chart shown in Figure 11-89, perform the following steps.

TO CREATE AN X-Y (SCATTER) CHART

Step 1:   In the spreadsheet, highlight the data you want to chart. In the example, the data is the number of marriages in cells B3:B17. But to include chart labels, highlight the range A3:B17.

Step 2:   Click the New Chart button on the Toolbar.

Step 3:   In the New Chart dialog box, select X-Y (Scatter) from the What type of chart do you want? drop-down list box. Type a1 in the Chart title text box and select the Add border check box. Choose the OK button in the New Chart dialog box.

Step 4: Select the Format menu, choose the Horizontal (X) Axis command, type 16 in the Minimum text box, type 1 in the Interval text box, and choose the OK button in the Horizontal Axis dialog box.

Step 5: Select the Format menu, choose the Vertical (Y) Axis command, type 1 in the Interval text box, and choose the OK command in the Vertical Axis dialog box.

Step 6: Select the Edit menu and choose the Titles command. When the Titles dialog box displays, type Women in the Subtitle text box, type AGE WHEN MARRIED in the Horizontal (X) Axis text box, type MARRIAGES/AGE in the Vertical (Y) Axis dialog box, and choose the OK button in the Titles dialog box.

Step 7: Format the chart using techniques described previously.

An X-Y (Scatter) chart provides another means for graphically presenting data in a Works spreadsheet.

▶ MICROSOFT DRAW

Works provides Microsoft Draw to create and modify pictures you can insert in various Works documents. For example, using **Microsoft Draw** you can create a company logo, art work for a company letterhead, or other illustrations to enhance the appearance of your documents.

To illustrate the use of Microsoft Draw, the steps to create and insert a logo in the Automobile Center 3-D Pie chart that was created in this project will be explained. The chart with the logo is illustrated in Figure 11-90.

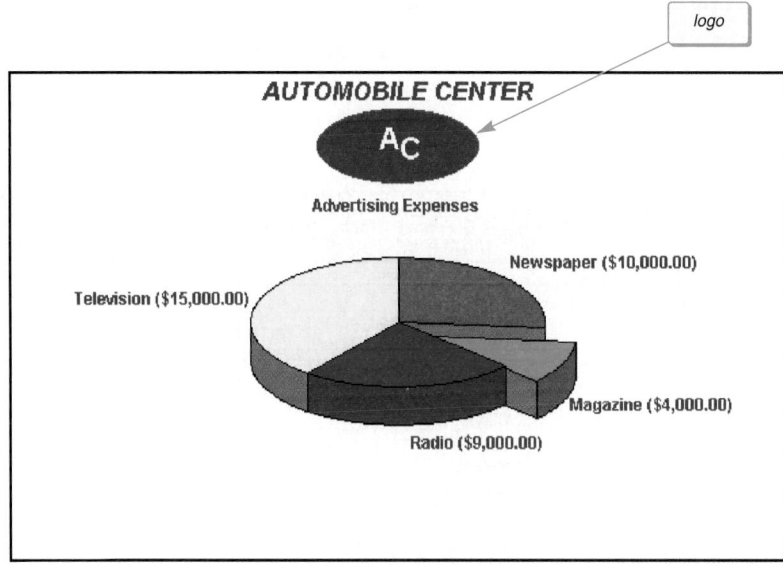

FIGURE 11-90

Using Microsoft Draw

To create and insert a logo into the 3-D Pie chart, you must first copy the 3-D Pie chart to a word processing document. To accomplish this task, perform the following steps.

TO COPY A CHART TO A WORD PROCESSING DOCUMENT ▼

STEP 1 ▶

Open the Automobile Center spreadsheet (PROJ11P.WKS). When the spreadsheet displays on the screen, select the View menu and choose the Chart command. When the Charts dialog box displays, if necessary highlight Chart1 in the Chart list box and then choose the OK button. When the 3-D Pie chart displays on the screen, point to the Copy button on the Toolbar.

The 3-D Pie chart displays on the screen (Figure 11-91). The mouse pointer points to the Copy button on the Toolbar.

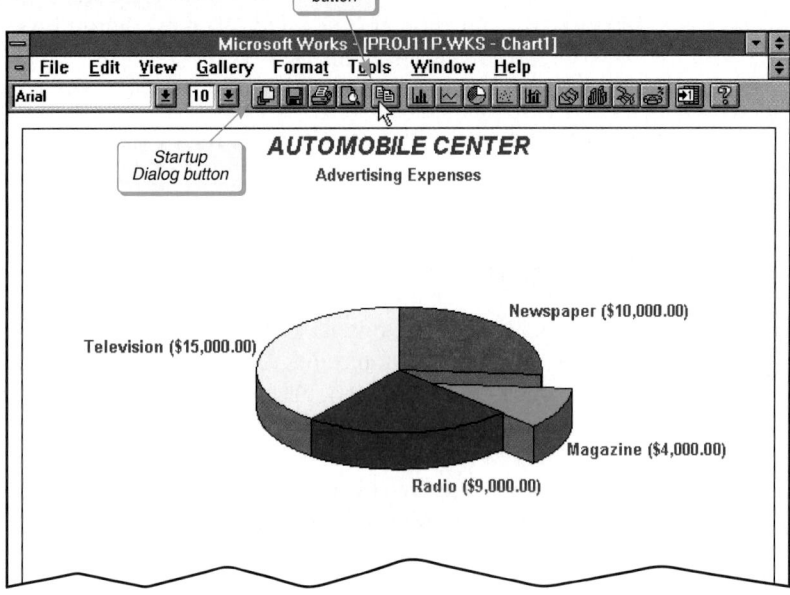

FIGURE 11-91

STEP 2 ▶

Click the Copy button on the Toolbar. The chart will be copied to the Clipboard.

STEP 3 ▶

Click the Startup Dialog button on the Toolbar. When the Startup dialog box displays, choose the Word Processor button. When the Microsoft Works Word1 application window displays, maximize the window. Then select the Insert menu and point to the Drawing command.

Works displays the Word1 word processing application window (Figure 11-92). The Insert menu displays and the mouse pointer points to the Drawing command.

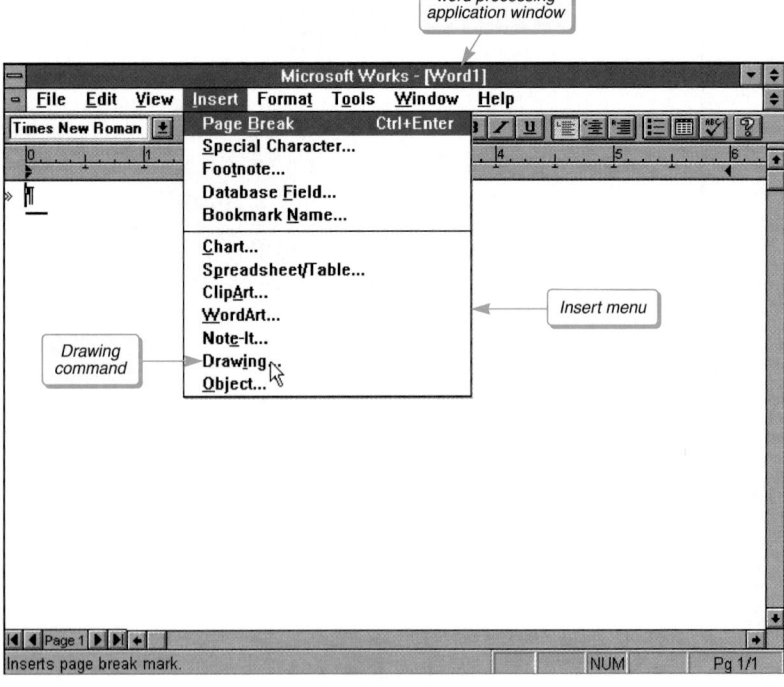

FIGURE 11-92

STEP 4 ▶

Choose the Drawing command from the Insert menu. When the Microsoft Draw - Drawing in Word1 window displays, maximize the Draw window. Then select the Edit menu and point to the Paste command.

The Microsoft Draw window displays (Figure 11-93). The mouse pointer points to the Paste command in the Edit menu. The Microsoft Draw tools display in the MS Draw Toolbox on the left side of the window.

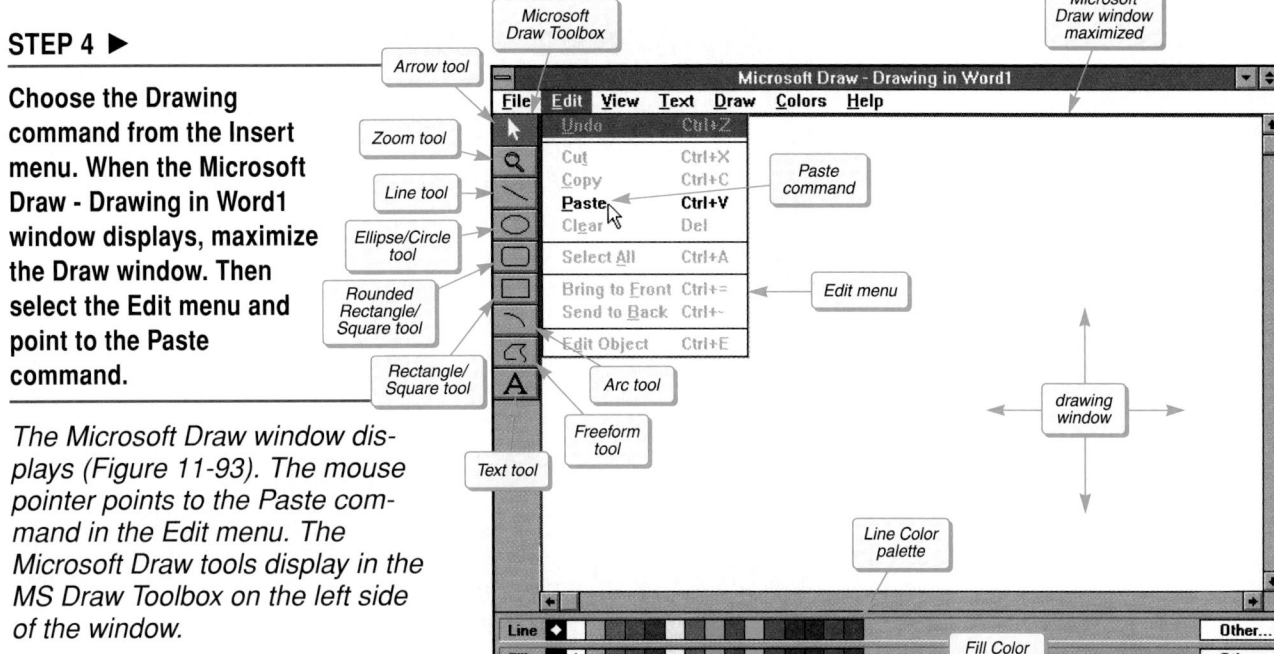

FIGURE 11-93

STEP 5 ▶

Choose the Paste command from the Edit menu. After the chart is pasted into the window, select the View menu and point to the 200% Size command.

The chart is pasted into the Microsoft Draw window (Figure 11-94). Microsoft Draw places resize handles around all the objects in the chart. The View menu displays and the mouse pointer points to the 200% Size command.

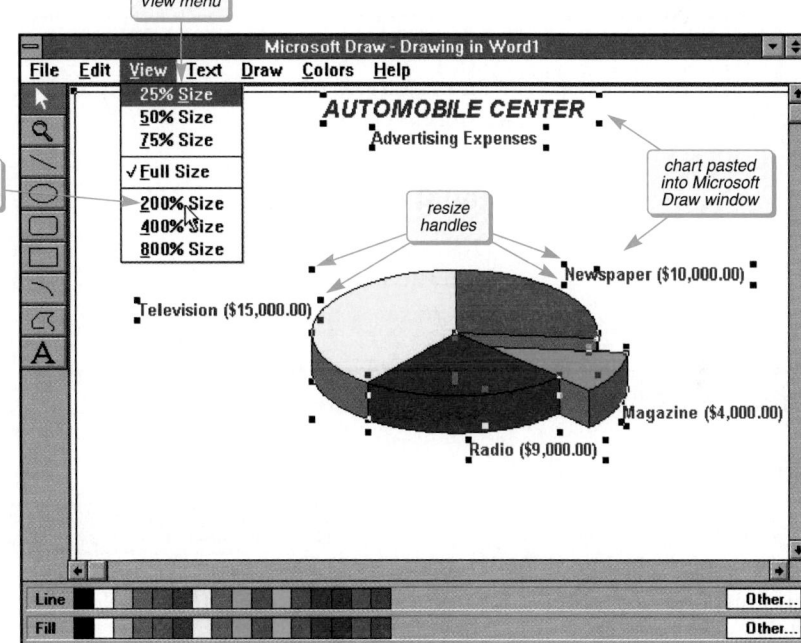

FIGURE 11-94

STEP 6 ▶

Choose the 200% Size command from the Edit menu. Scroll to the top of the document. Click anywhere on the chart to remove the resize handles surrounding each object.

The enlarged chart displays (Figure 11-95).

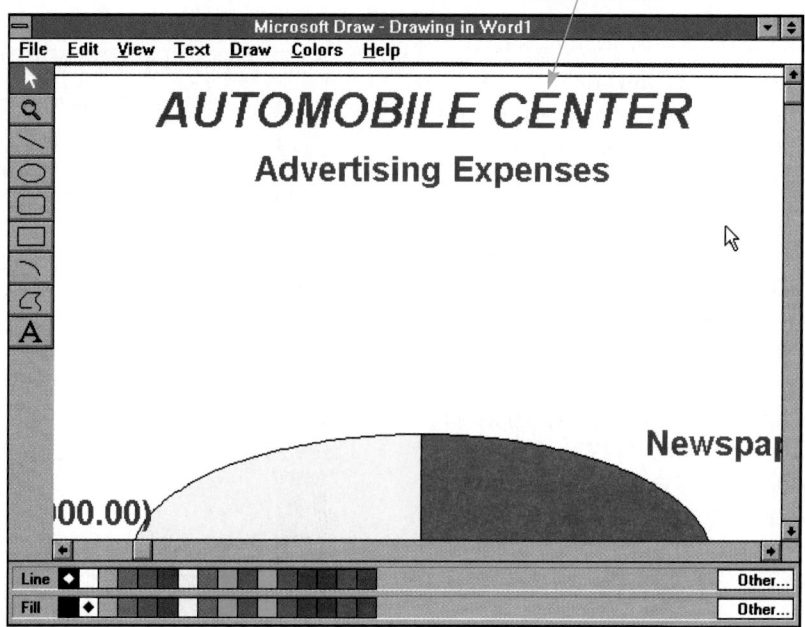

FIGURE 11-95

You are now ready to create the logo to be placed below the words Automobile Center.

Creating a Logo Using Draw

To create and insert the logo for the automobile center in the 3-D Pie chart, perform the following steps.

TO CREATE A LOGO USING MICROSOFT DRAW ▼

STEP 1 ▶

Highlight the subtitle Advertising Expenses by clicking within the text. Carefully drag the subtitle down to allow room for the logo. Point to and click the Text tool in the MS Draw Toolbox.

The words Advertising Expense are moved down the chart (Figure 11-96). The mouse pointer points to the Text tool, which is highlighted.

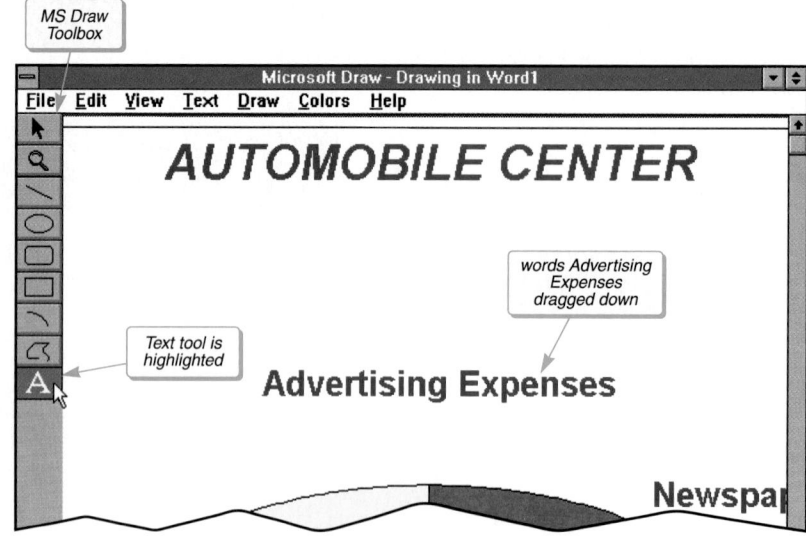

FIGURE 11-96

STEP 2 ▶

Position the mouse pointer in the approximate location on the screen where you want to place the letter of the alphabet A in the logo. Click the left mouse button to position the insertion point. Hold down the SHIFT key and type A.

Selecting the Text tool allows you to type in the Draw window. The letter A displays in the window (Figure 11-97).

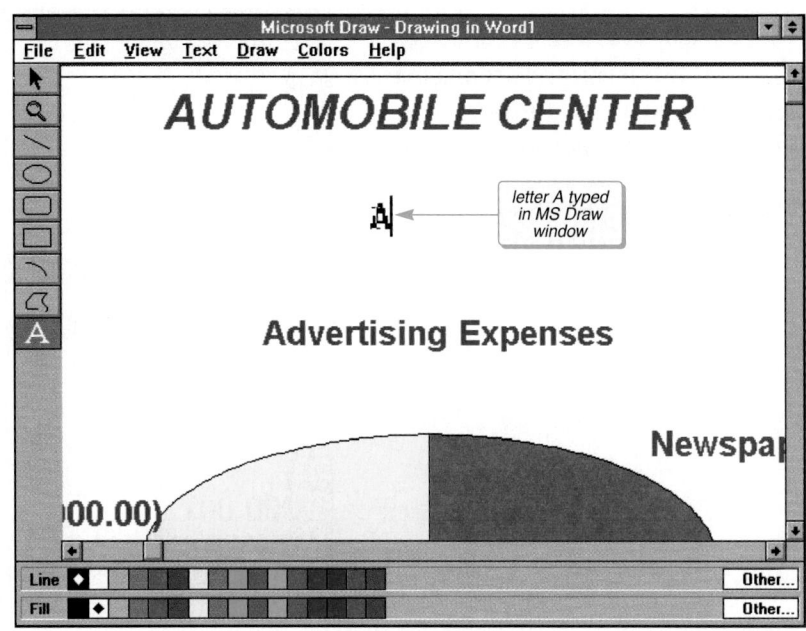

FIGURE 11-97

STEP 3 ▶

Click anywhere on the screen so the Text tool is no longer selected. Select the Text tool in the MS Draw Toolbox by pointing to the Text tool and clicking the left mouse button. Position the mouse pointer in the approximate location where the C is to display. Hold down the SHIFT key and type C. When the C is typed in the required location, click to deselect the Text tool. Then hold down the SHIFT key and click the letter A so both letters are selected.

The letters A and C are surrounded by resize handles and are now objects that can be positioned and manipulated as a group (Figure 11-98).

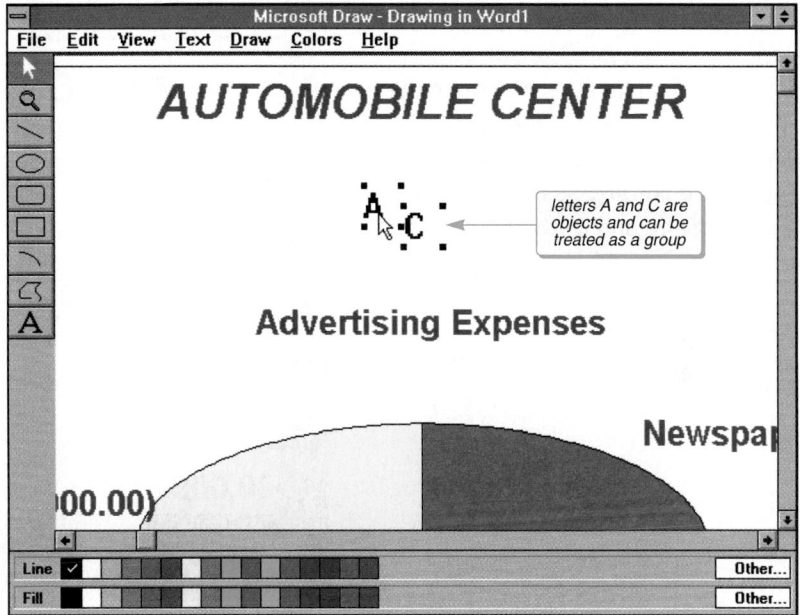

FIGURE 11-98

STEP 4 ▶

Select the Text menu and choose the Size command. When the Size submenu displays, point to 18.

A submenu displays as a part of the Text menu (Figure 11-99).

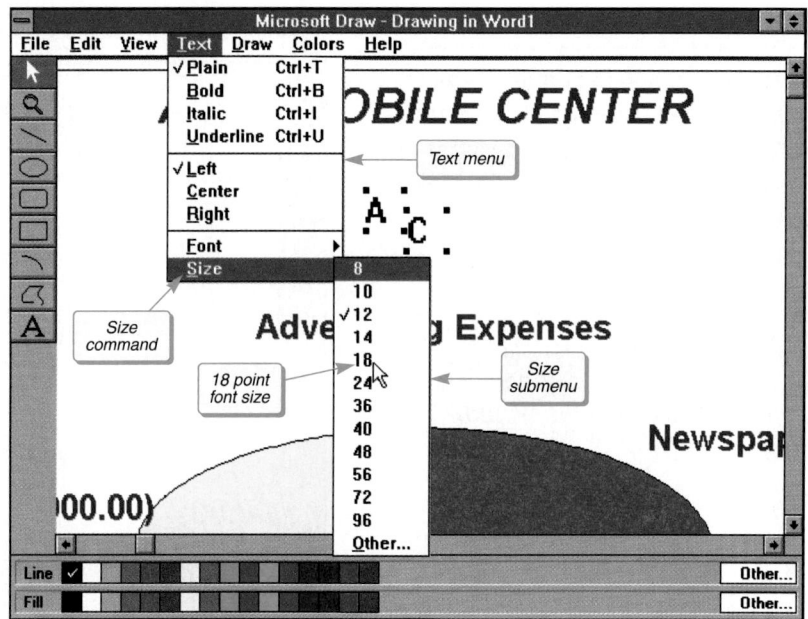

FIGURE 11-99

STEP 5 ▶

Choose 18 from the Size submenu. Select the Text menu and choose the Font command. When the list of fonts displays, select Arial and release the left mouse button. Select the Text menu and choose the Bold command.

The characters A and C display in 18 point Arial bold font (Figure 11-100).

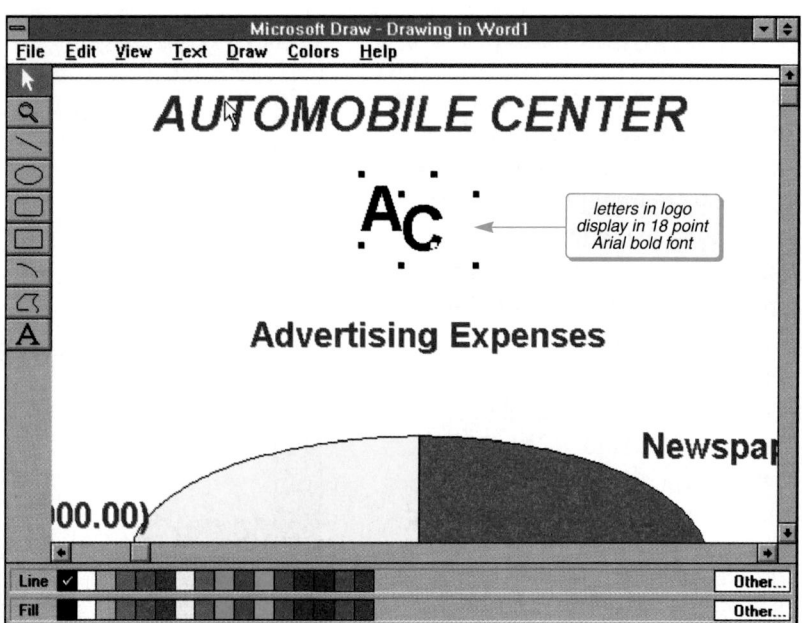

FIGURE 11-100

STEP 6 ▶

Horizontally center the A and C by dragging them until the space between the A and the C is above the line that separates the yellow and red in the chart. Vertically center the A and C approximately half way between the title and subtitle. Click the Ellipse/Circle tool in the MS Draw Toolbox and place the mouse pointer above and to the left of the A and C characters. Drag the mouse pointer down and to the right to create an ellipse in front the text. You may have to experiment to achieve the correct shape and location for the ellipse. If the ellipse is drawn incorrectly, press the DELETE key while the ellipse is selected.

The ellipse displays with a black line and white fill. It displays in front of the text (Figure 11-101).

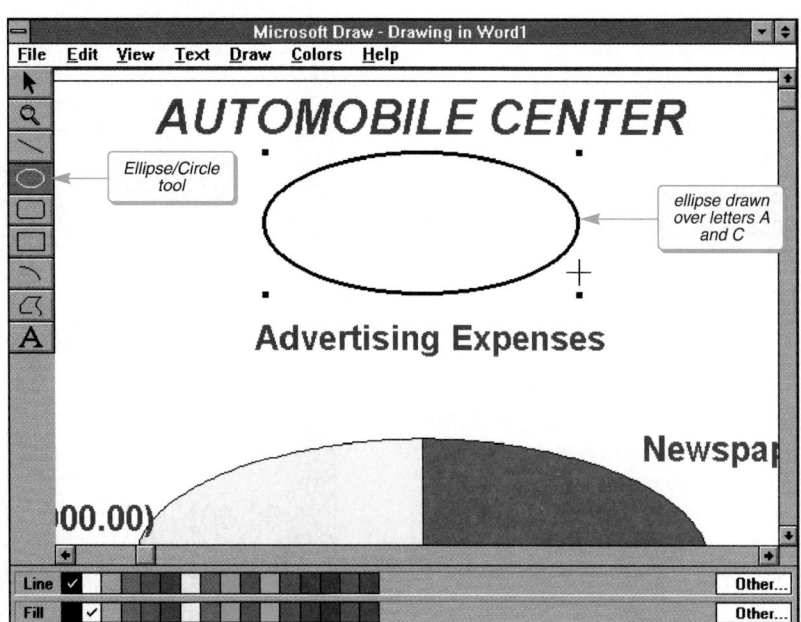

FIGURE 11-101

STEP 7 ▶

Select the Edit menu and point to the Send to Back command.

The Edit menu displays and the mouse pointer points to the Send to Back command (Figure 11-102).

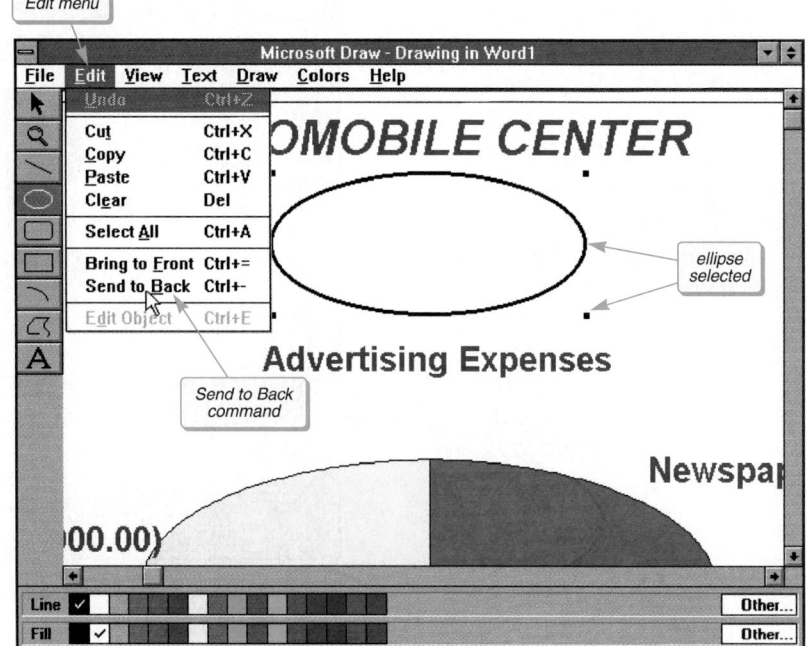

FIGURE 11-102

STEP 8 ▶

Choose the Send to Back command from the Edit menu. With the ellipse selected, select the Dark Magenta box on the Line Color palette by clicking it. Then select the Dark Blue box on the Fill Color palette by clicking it.

The logo displays on the screen (Figure 11-103). The ellipse is a sold dark blue color with a dark magenta outline. The letters within the logo display in black. The selected colors on the palettes contain a white checkmark.

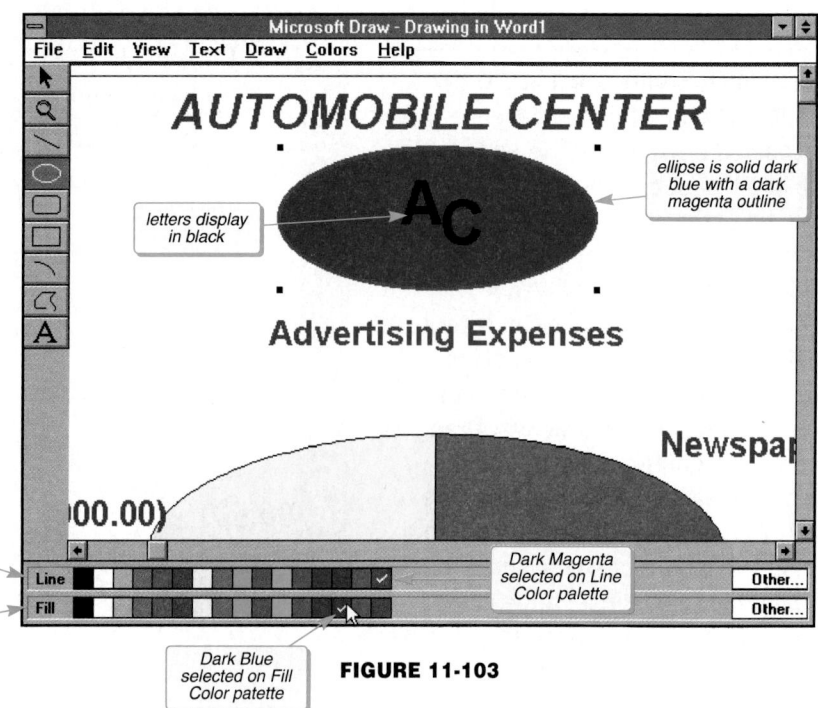

FIGURE 11-103

STEP 9 ▶

Click anywhere in the window deselect the ellipse. Select the A and C by holding down the SHIFT key, pointing to each character, and clicking the left mouse button. Select the White box on the Line Color palette. Select the File menu and point to the Exit and Return to Word1 command.

*The logo displays with the letters in white (Figure 11-104). The mouse pointer points to the **Exit and Return to Word1 command**.*

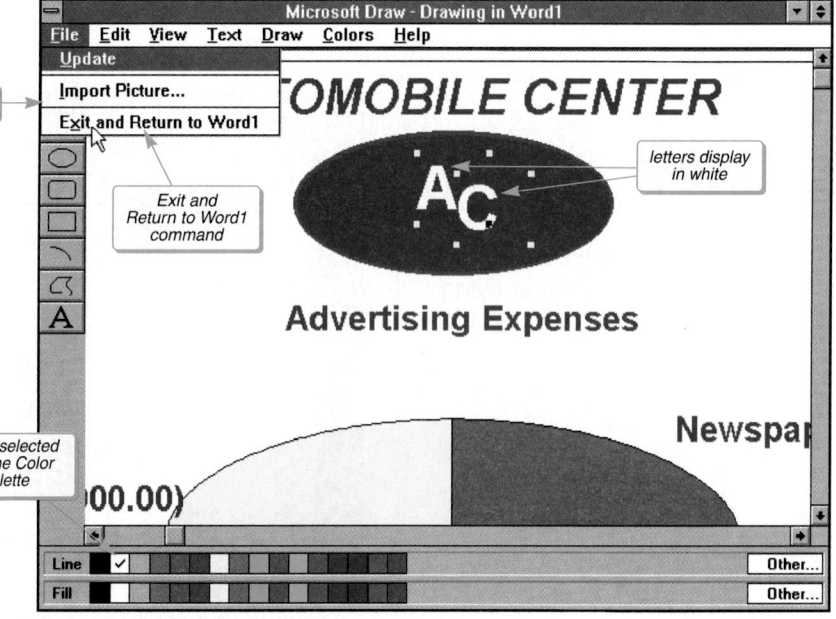

FIGURE 11-104

STEP 10 ►

Choose the Exit and Return to Word1 command. When the Microsoft Draw dialog box displays asking, Update Word1?, choose the Yes button.

The chart with the logo is placed in the Word Processing document (Figure 11-105).

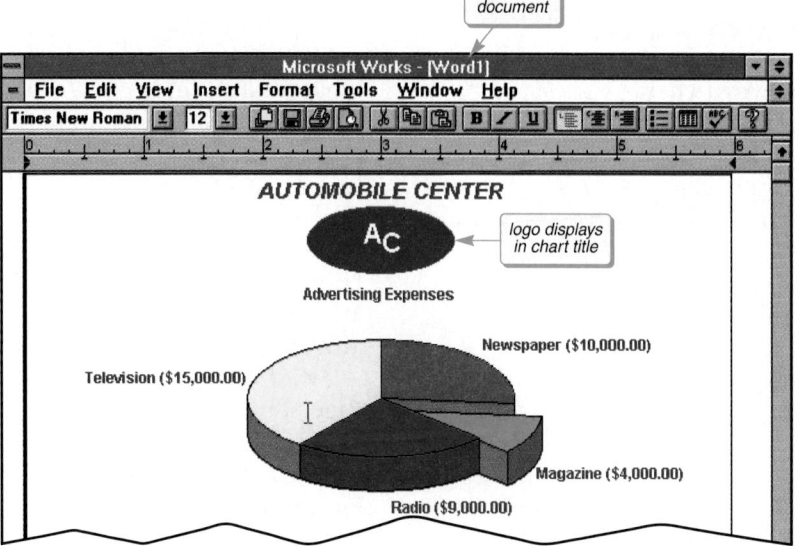

FIGURE 11-105

You can now print the chart with the logo and you can save the document just as you would any other word processing document. To save the document, complete the following steps.

TO SAVE THE CHART AND LOGO DOCUMENT

Step 1: Click the Save button on the Toolbar.
Step 2: Type ACLOGO in the File Name text box of the Save As dialog box.
Step 3: If necessary, select drive A in the Drives drop-down list box.
Step 4: Choose the OK button in the Save As dialog box.

In this project you should save the file because in Project 12 this file will be transmitted over communications lines to the sales manager at a remote location using the Works Communications tool.

► PROJECT SUMMARY

In Project 11, you learned about basic types of charts you can create when using Works: the Pie chart, the 3-D Pie chart, the Bar chart, the 3-D Bar chart, the Line chart, the Stacked Line chart, the Area chart, the Combination chart, and the X-Y (Scatter) chart. As a part of each chart, you learned how to add legends, titles, subtitles, and category labels; how to change fonts, font size and style, and patterns and colors; and how to preview and print charts in varying sizes. Using the techniques explained in this project, you are able to create of variety of professional charts for business or personal use.

You also learned the basic elements of Microsoft Draw. Microsoft Draw allows you to create drawings for use in various Works documents.

▶ KEY TERMS

3-D Area chart *(W11.9)*
3-D Bar chart *(W11.5)*
3-D Line chart *(W11.6)*
3-D Pie chart *(W11.3)*
Area chart *(W11.8)*
Bar chart *(W11.4)*
category *(W11.30)*
category axis *(W11.30)*
category label *(W11.30)*
category (X) series *(W11.30)*
Chart command *(W11.28)*
Combination chart *(W11.10)*
data labels *(W11.15)*
Data Labels command *(W11.16)*
Exit and Return to Word1
   command *(W11.70)*

horizontal (X) axis *(W11.30)*
Horizontal (X) Axis command
   (W11.49)
legend *(W11.30)*
Legend/Series Labels command
   (W11.36)
Line chart *(W11.6)*
Microsoft Draw *(W11.63)*
Mixed Line and Bar command
   (W11.61)
Page Setup command *(W11.24)*
Patterns and Colors command
   (W11.22)
Pie chart *(W11.3)*
Radar chart *(W11.11)*
rotate *(W11.23)*

Scatter chart *(W11.10)*
Series *(W11.30)*
Series command *(W11.34)*
slice *(W11.3, W11.22)*
Spreadsheet command *(W11.27)*
Stacked Line chart *(W11.7)*
Two Vertical (Y) Axes command
   (W11.50)
value axis *(W11.30)*
value-series *(W11.30)*
vertical (Y) axis *(W11.30)*
Vertical (Y) Axis command
   (W11.49)
X-Y chart *(W11.10)*
Y-series *(W11.30)*

Q U I C K   R E F E R E N C E

In Microsoft Works, you can accomplish a task in a number of ways. The following table provides a quick
reference to each task presented in this project with its available options. The commands listed in the
Menu column can be executed using either the keyboard or mouse.

Task	Mouse	Menu	Keyboard Shortcuts
Add Category Labels		From chart Edit menu, choose Series	
Add a Chart Title		From chart Edit menu, choose Titles or in New Chart dialog box, type title	
Add Data Labels		From chart Edit menu, choose Data Labels	
Add Horizontal Gridlines		From chart Format menu, choose Horizontal (X) Axis	
Add Legends		From chart Edit menu, choose Legend/Series Labels	
Add a Right Vertical Axis		From chart Format menu, choose Two Vertical (Y) Axes	
Change the Chart Print Size		From chart File menu, choose Page Setup	
Change the Chart Subtitles Font		From chart Format menu, choose Font and Style	
Change the Chart Title Font		From chart Edit menu, choose Select Title Text	
Change Colors and/or Patterns		From chart Format menu, choose Patterns and Colors	

Task	Mouse	Menu	Keyboard Shortcuts
Change the Vertical Axis Scale		From chart Format menu, choose Vertical (Y) Axis	
Create a 3-D Area Chart	Click 3-D Area Chart button on Charting Toolbar	From chart Gallery menu, choose 3-D Area or in New Chart dialog box, select 3-D Area	
Create a 3-D Bar Chart	Click 3-D Bar Chart button on Charting Toolbar	From chart Gallery menu, choose 3-D Bar or in New Chart dialog box, select 3-D Bar	
Create a 3-D Line Chart	Click 3-D Line Chart button on Charting Toolbar	From chart Gallery menu, choose 3-D Line or in New Chart dialog box, select 3-D Line	
Create a 3-D Pie Chart	Click 3-D Pie Chart button on Charting Toolbar	From chart Gallery menu, choose 3-D Pie or in New Chart dialog box, select 3-D Pie	
Create a Bar Chart	Click Bar Chart button on Charting Toolbar	From chart Gallery menu, choose Bar, or in New Chart dialog box, select Bar	
Create a Combination Chart	Click Mixed Chart button on Charting Toolbar	From chart Gallery menu, choose Combination or in New Chart dialog box, select Combination	
Create a Line Chart	Click Line Chart button on Charting Toolbar	From chart Gallery menu, choose Line or in New Chart dialog box, select Line	
Create a New Chart	Click New Chart button on Toolbar	From Tools menu, choose Create New Chart	
Create a Pie Chart	Click Pie Chart button on Charting Toolbar	From chart Gallery menu, choose Pie or in New Chart dialog box, select Pie	
Create a Stacked Line Chart		From chart Gallery menu, choose Stacked Line or in New Chart dialog box, select Stacked Line	
Delete a Chart		From Tools menu, choose Delete Chart	
Duplicate a Chart		From Tools menu, choose Duplicate Chart	
Explode a Pie Slice		From chart Format menu, choose Patterns and Colors	
Name a Chart		From Tools menu, choose Name Chart	
Print a Chart	Click Print button on Charting Toolbar or in print preview screen	From chart File menu, choose Print	

(continued)

QUICK REFERENCE (continued)

Task	Mouse	Menu	Keyboard Shortcuts
Print Preview	Click Print Preview button	From File menu, choose Print Preview	
Return to a Chart from a Spreadsheet		From Window menu, choose chart name; or from View menu, choose Chart	Press CTRL+F6
Return to a Spreadsheet from a Chart		From Window menu, choose spreadsheet name or from View menu, choose Spreadsheet	Press CTRL+F6
Use Microsoft Draw		From Insert menu, choose Drawing	

S T U D E N T   A S S I G N M E N T S

STUDENT ASSIGNMENT 1
True/False

Instructions: Circle T if the statement is true or F if the statement is false.

T F 1. After highlighting the range to chart in a spreadsheet, clicking the New Chart button on the Toolbar will display the New Chart dialog box.

T F 2. Each slice in a Pie chart represents a percentage, or portion, of a whole.

T F 3. A Bar chart cannot be used effectively to compare two or more values.

T F 4. Line charts are widely used for showing trends over a period of time.

T F 5. A Stacked Line chart is any line chart that contains two or more charted values in the form of lines or lines and markers.

T F 6. A Combination chart mixes bars and lines on the same chart.

T F 7. When you create a Pie chart, Works automatically names the chart PIE1.

T F 8. To add data labels to a Pie chart, you can use the Data Labels command on the chart Edit menu.

T F 9. The title that displays at the top of a chart must be the same title that is contained on the spreadsheet.

T F 10. To explode a slice in a Pie chart, use the Patterns and Colors command from the chart Format menu.

T F 11. Once a border has been added to a chart, it cannot be removed unless you close the file.

T F 12. Works saves any chart you create when you save the associated spreadsheet.

T F 13. You can save only one chart per spreadsheet.

T F 14. When you print a chart, Works automatically prints the chart the same size as the chart on the screen.

T F 15. To delete a chart, choose the Delete Chart command from the Tools menu.

T F 16. The horizontal, or X, axis is also called the category axis.

T F 17. To add category labels to a chart, use the Title command from the chart Format menu.

T F 18. You can use the Patterns and Colors command to change colors only on a Bar chart.

T F 19. To add a Right Vertical Axis to a chart, you must use the Two Vertical Axes command.

T F 20. When a chart displays, you can return to the spreadsheet by choosing the Spreadsheet command from the View menu.

STUDENT ASSIGNMENT 2
Multiple Choice

Instructions: Circle the correct response.

1. After highlighting a range to chart, clicking the New Chart button on the Toolbar will display _____.
   a. the New Chart dialog box
   b. a blank chart window with a Charting Toolbar
   c. a Bar chart
   d. a Line chart

2. In a spreadsheet that contains five columns and two rows, if text is highlighted and is to the left of and adjacent to the highlighted numeric data, the text will be used as _____ in a Bar chart.
   a. a chart title
   b. category labels
   c. data labels
   d. legends

3. When you create the first chart for a spreadsheet, Works automatically names the chart _____.
   a. Chart1
   b. Chart1.wks
   c. Chart1.chrt
   d. Bar1

4. You can save up to _____ charts for each spreadsheet.
   a. two (2)
   b. four (4)
   c. six (6)
   d. eight (8)

5. When you print a chart, the default option in the Other Options screen of the Page Setup dialog box is _____.
   a. Screen size   c. Full page, keep proportions
   b. Full page   d. Full page, landscape

6. To change a chart type, _____.
   a. on the Charting Toolbar, click the chart type button you want
   b. from the Gallery menu, choose the chart type you want
   c. return to the spreadsheet and click the New Chart button
   d. both a and b

7. The labels for each cluster of bars in a Bar chart are called the _____.
   a. value series   c. Y series
   b. category labels   d. chart legends

8. To change the scale of the left vertical (Y) axis in a Line chart, use the _____.
   a. Series command from the Edit menu
   b. Legend command from the Edit menu
   c. Vertical (Y) Axis command from the Format menu
   d. Left Vertical Axis command from the Format menu

9. To change the shape of markers in a Line chart, use the _____.
   a. Patterns and Colors command from the Format menu
   b. Legend command from the Edit menu
   c. Titles command from the Edit menu
   d. Font and Style command from the Format menu

10. To combine lines and bars in a single chart, use a _____.
    a. Line chart, option 5
    b. Combination chart
    c. Stacked Line chart
    d. X-Y (Scatter) chart

STUDENT ASSIGNMENT 3
Understanding the Charting Toolbar

Instructions: In the space provided, identify each of the buttons on the Charting Toolbar shown in Figure SA11-3.

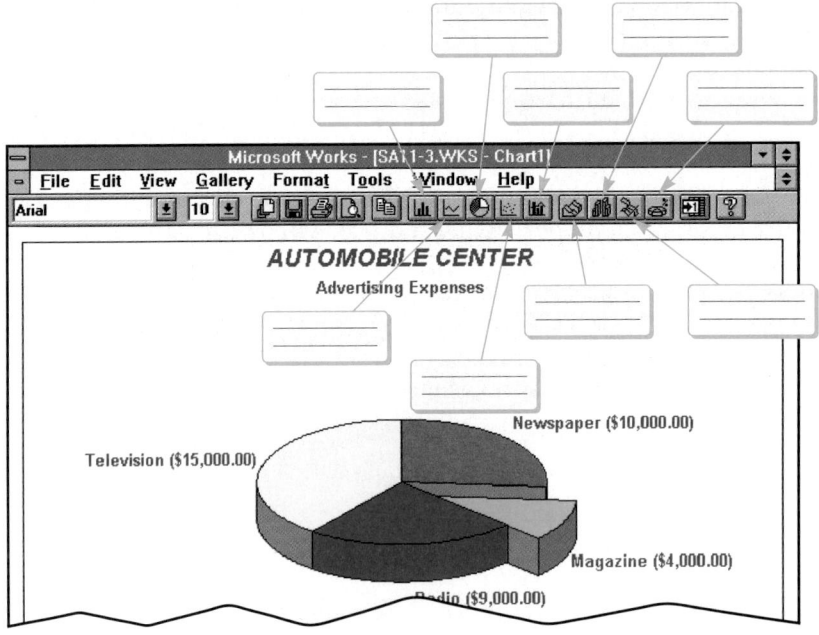

FIGURE SA11-3

STUDENT ASSIGNMENT 4
Understanding the 3-D Pie Dialog Box

Instructions: In the space provided, describe the chart that displays when you select each of the six options from the 3-D Pie dialog box shown in Figure SA11-4. Assume only numeric values are highlighted in the related spreadsheet.

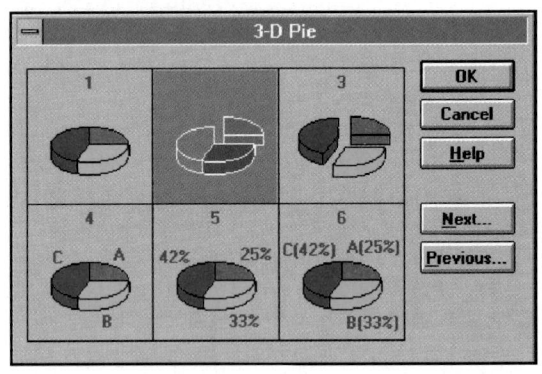

FIGURE SA11-4

Option 1: _____

Option 2: _____

Option 3: _____

Option 4: _____

Option 5: _____

Option 6: _____

STUDENT ASSIGNMENT 5
Understanding the 3-D Bar Dialog Box

Instructions: In the space provided, describe the chart that displays when you select each of the six options from the 3-D Bar dialog box shown in Figure SA11-5. Assume only numeric values are highlighted in the related spreadsheet.

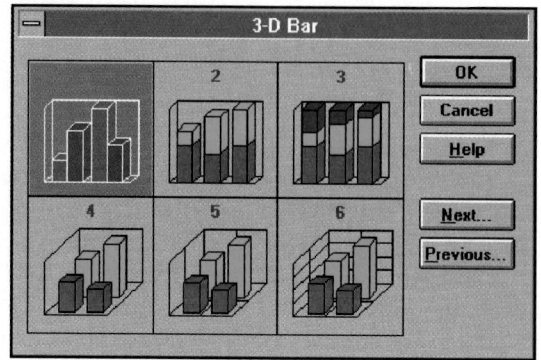

FIGURE SA11-5

Option 1: _____

Option 2: _____

Option 3: _____

Option 4: _____

Option 5: _____

Option 6: _____

STUDENT ASSIGNMENT 6
Understanding Microsoft Works Menus

Instructions: In the spaces provided in the right column, record the name of the menu associated with the commands in the left column.

COMMAND	MENU
Data Labels	
Horizontal (X) Axis	
Page Setup	
Patterns and Colors	
Series	
Add Legend	
Add Border	
Titles	
Two Vertical (Y) Axes	
Vertical (Y) Axis	

COMPUTER LABORATORY EXERCISE 1
Using the Help Menu

Instructions: Perform the following tasks using a personal computer.

1. Start the Microsoft Works Spreadsheet tool and use the Help menu to answer the following questions.
2. You have created a Bar chart for Weekly Sales Projections. You would like to print this chart with both a page header that identifies the chart and a page footer that contains the page number. How can you do this? Print the topic pages from the Help screens that explain your answer.
3. Provide an explanation and example of the use of logarithmic scales when charting. Print the topic pages from the Help screens that explain your answer.
4. Your chart does not have room to print all the category labels. How would you print only selected category labels? Print the topic pages from the Help screens that explain your answer.
5. You are not sure what cells are used on your chart as labels. How can you determine the cells used as labels? Print the topic pages from the Help screens that explain your answer.

COMPUTER LABORATORY EXERCISE 2
Formatting a Chart

Instructions: Start Works. Open the CLE11-2.WKS spreadsheet file on the Student Diskette that accompanies this book. Display Chart1 and then perform the following tasks:

1. Remove the data labels at the top of each bar.
2. Change the color of the first bar in each category to dark magenta and the second bar in each category to dark red.
3. Print a copy of the chart.
4. Close the file. Do not save the chart you have changed.
5. Follow directions from your instructor for turning in this exercise.
6. Quit Works.

COMPUTER LABORATORY EXERCISE 3
Displaying and Printing 3-D Bar and 3-D Line Charts

Instructions: Start Works. Open the CLE11-2.WKS spreadsheet file on the Student Diskette that accompanies this book. Display Chart1 and then perform the following tasks:

1. Duplicate Chart1, giving it the name Chart 2. Display Chart2.
2. Display the 3-D Bar dialog box by clicking the 3-D Bar Chart button on the Toolbar.
3. Select option 2 in the 3-D Bar dialog box and display the chart. Change the colors and patterns to match those in Chart1.
4. Print Chart2 using the screen size option.
5. Duplicate Chart2, giving it the name Chart3.
6. Display Chart3. Click the 3-D Line Chart button on the Toolbar. Select option 2 in the 3-D Line dialog box. Rotate the chart until you find a view you like.
7. Print the 3-D Line chart in the rotated view you select.
8. Follow directions from your instructor for turning in this assignment.
9. Quit Works.

COMPUTER LABORATORY ASSIGNMENT 1
Creating a 3-D Pie Chart

Purpose: To provide experience creating a spreadsheet and related 3-D Pie chart.

Problem: The Chi Delta sorority recently had an open house party for new members. As chairperson, you have been asked to prepare a report regarding expenses for presentation at the next meeting of the sorority officers. A report and 3-D Pie chart from last year's party are shown in Figure CLA11-1.

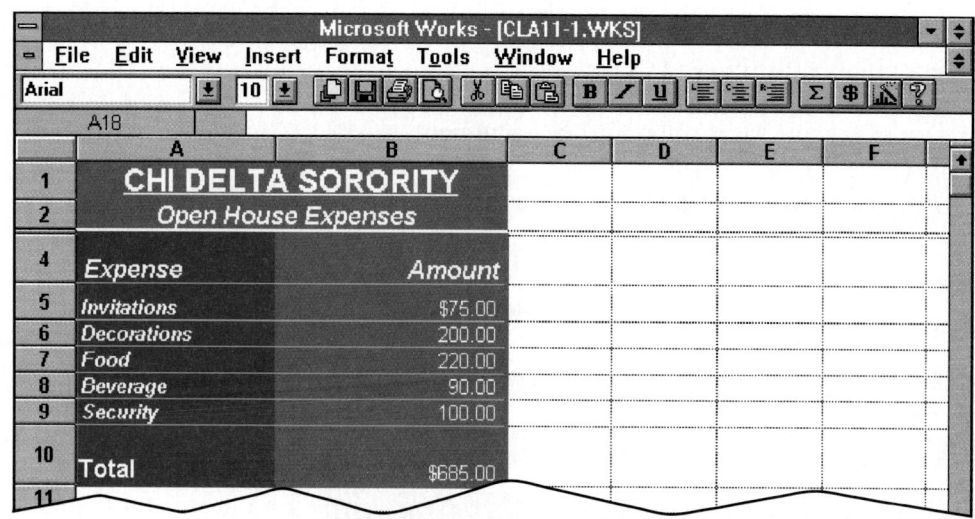

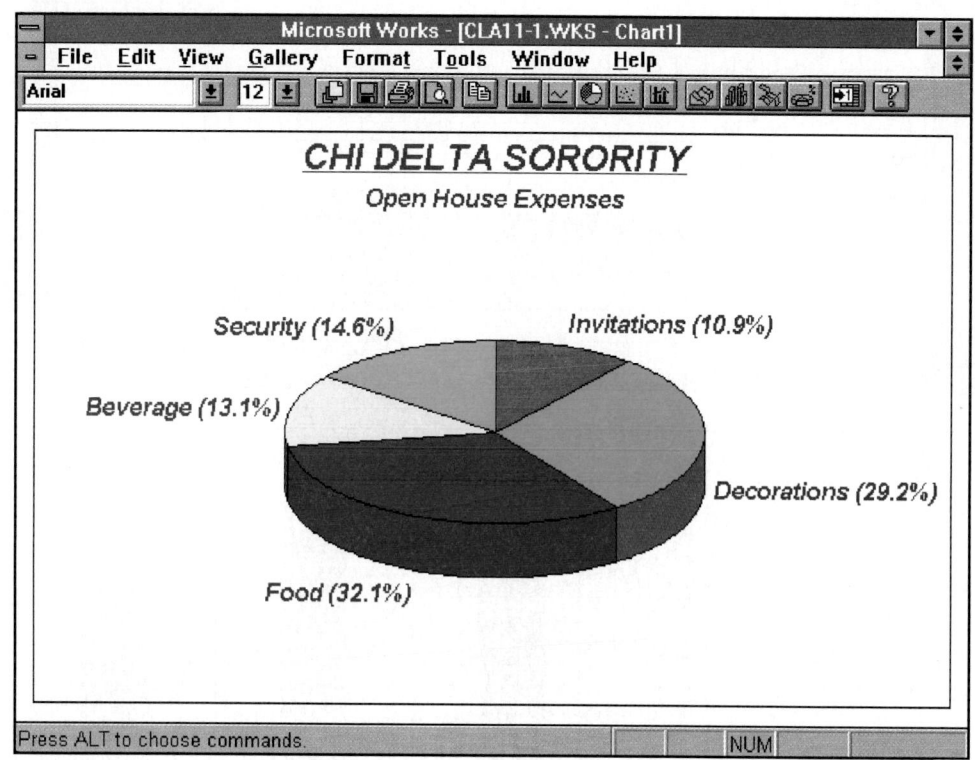

FIGURE CLA11-1

(continued)

COMPUTER LABORATORY ASSIGNMENT 1 (continued)

Instructions:

1. Create and format a spreadsheet with the following values: Invitations $125.00; Decorations $250.00; Entertainment $300.00; Refreshments $200.00; and Security $100.00.
2. Create two 3-D Pie charts. One chart should display the percentage that each slice represents. The second chart should display the actual expense each slice represents.
3. Format the 3-D Pie charts as shown in Figure CLA11-1. The title is dark blue 18 point Arial bold italic underlined font. The other labels are dark blue 12 point Arial bold italic font.
4. Explode the slice that contains the largest percentage of expense amount. Include a diagonal pattern (//) in the slice.
5. Save the spreadsheet and charts using a filename consisting of the initials of your first and last names followed by the assignment number. Example: TC11-1.
6. Print the spreadsheet and print both charts.
7. Follow directions from your instructor for turning in this assignment.

COMPUTER LABORATORY ASSIGNMENT 2
Creating a Bar Charts

Purpose: To provide experience creating a spreadsheet and related Bar charts.

Problem: You have been asked to prepare a spreadsheet and Bar chart detailing the enrollment for the fall semester of Bradley College. Last year's report and Bar chart are illustrated in Figure CLA11-2.

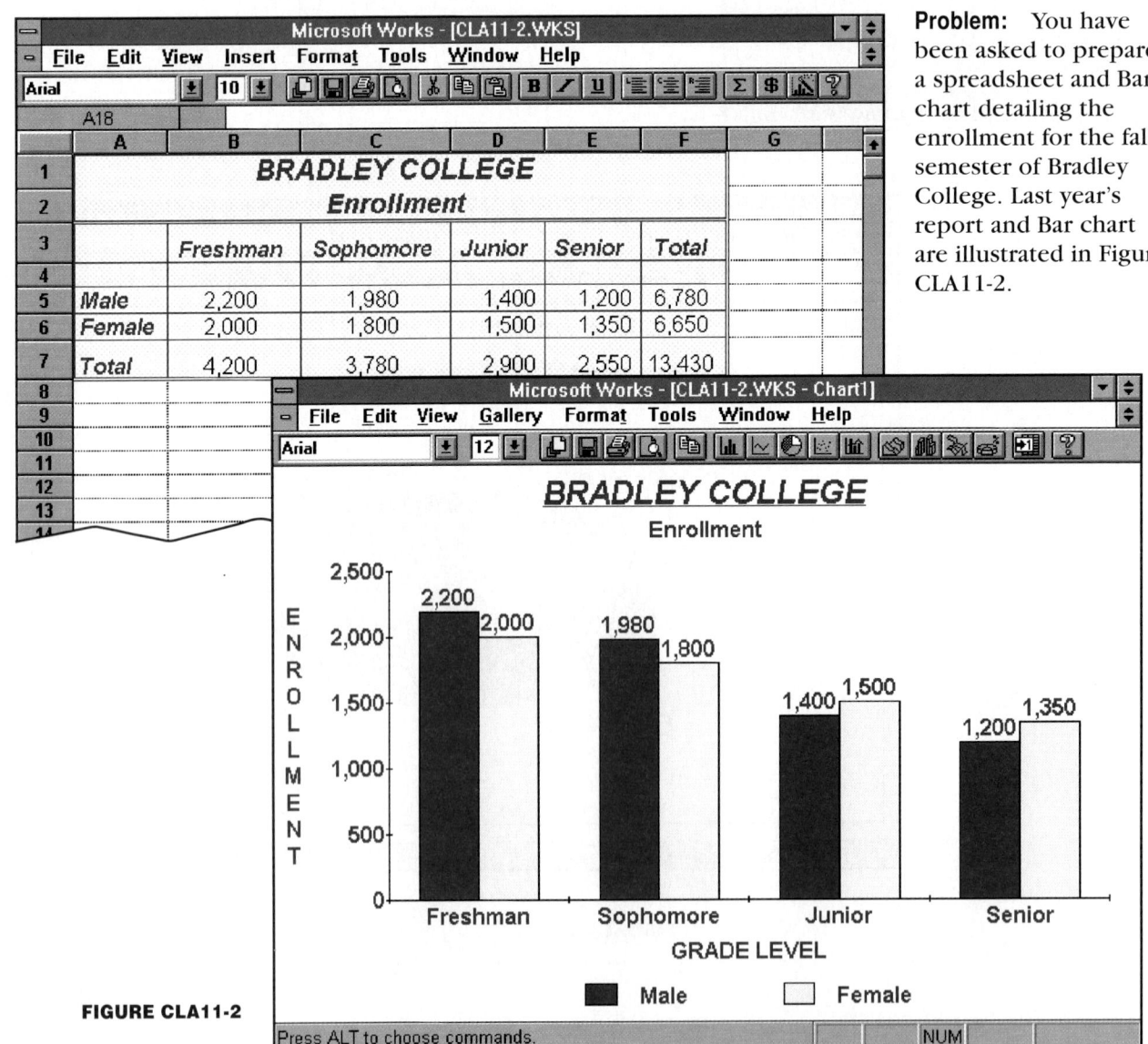

FIGURE CLA11-2

COMPUTER LABORATORY ASSIGNMENTS   **W11.81**

Instructions:

Part 1:

1. Create and format a new spreadsheet with the following values:

Freshman Males	1,200
Freshman Females	1,750
Sophomore Males	1,100
Sophomore Females	1,400
Junior Males	950
Junior Females	1,100
Senior Males	900
Senior Females	1,050

2. Create a Bar chart showing the enrollment of both males and females for the four grade levels at Bradley College.
3. Change the bars representing Males to dense yellow.
4. Change the bars representing Females to dark blue.
5. Format the Bar chart as you see fit.
6. Print the spreadsheet and the Bar chart.
7. Save the spreadsheet and chart using a filename consisting of the initials of your first and last names followed by the assignment number. Example: TC11-2.

Part 2:

1. Duplicate Chart1 and create a new 3-D Bar chart using option 2 in the 3-D Bar dialog box in the chart window.
2. Format the Bar chart using the same colors and patterns as in Part 1.
3. Print the Bar chart.
4. Save the spreadsheet and chart using the same filename as in Part 1.

Part 3:

1. Duplicate Chart2 and create a 3-D Bar chart using option 3 in the 3-D Bar dialog box in the chart window.
2. Format the Bar chart using different colors and patterns than in Part 2.
3. Name the chart Percentages.
4. Print the Bar chart.
5. Save the spreadsheet and chart using the same filename as in Part 1.
6. Follow directions from your instructor for turning in this assignment.

COMPUTER LABORATORY ASSIGNMENT 3
Creating a Line Chart

Purpose: To provide experience creating a spreadsheet and related Line chart.

Problem: Prepare a chart illustrating growth in the actual and estimated hourly compensation of manufacturing industries in Germany, the United States, and Japan since 1985. Base the chart on the information shown in the following table.

▸ **HOURLY COMPENSATION IN MANUFACTURING**

	1985	1990	1995	2000
Germany	$13.00	$19.00	$22.00	$25.00
United States	$10.00	$12.00	$15.00	$17.00
Japan	$5.00	$5.50	$13.00	$15.00

(continued)

COMPUTER LABORATORY ASSIGNMENT 3 (continued)

Instructions:

Part 1:

1. Create and format the spreadsheet.
2. Create a Line chart showing the trend in wages from 1985 to 2000 for Germany, the United States, and Japan.
3. Format the chart, including a right vertical (Y) axis and labels on the axis.
4. Print the spreadsheet and Line chart.
5. Save the chart using a filename consisting of the initials of your first and last names followed by the assignment number. Example: TC11-3.
   (Hint: In the subsequent parts, you should duplicate a chart before creating a new chart).

Part 2:

1. Create a 3-D Bar chart using option 6 for 3-D Bar charts. The bars representing Germany should be cyan in color, the United States bars should be blue, and the Japan bars red.
2. Format the 3-D Bar chart in an attractive style.
3. Print the Bar chart.
4. Name the chart Rate Chart.
5. Save the spreadsheet and chart using the same filename as in Part 1.

Part 3:

1. Create a 3-D Area chart from the data in the spreadsheet.
2. Format the chart in an attractive style.
3. Print the chart.
4. Name the chart Country.
5. Save the spreadsheet and chart using the same filename as in Part 1.

Part 4:

1. Create a Combination chart from the data in the spreadsheet.
2. The United States should be represented by a line while Germany and Japan are represented by bars.
3. Format the chart in an attractive style.
4. Print the chart.
5. Name the chart Comparison.
6. Save the spreadsheet and chart using the same filename as in Part 1.
7. Follow directions from your instructor for turning in this assignment.

COMPUTER LABORATORY ASSIGNMENT 4
Creating Charts

Purpose: To provide experience creating a spreadsheet and related chart.

Problem: Prepare a spreadsheet and chart illustrating the average cost of one ounce of gold for the twelve months of the year based on the following information: January $357.00, February $365.00, March $372.00, April $380.00, May $374.00, June $370.00, July $362.00, August $370.00, September $375.00, October $360.00, November $340.00, December $325.00.

Instructions:

1. Analyze the data, and create a spreadsheet and four different charts that display the data so you can completely analyze the changes in the price of one ounce of gold for each month.
2. Format the spreadsheet and charts.
3. Print the spreadsheet and charts.
4. Save the spreadsheet and charts using a filename consisting of the initials of your first and last names followed by the assignment number. Example: TC11-4.
5. Follow directions from your instructor for turning in this assignment.

USING THE COMMUNICATIONS TOOL

USING THE COMMUNICATIONS TOOL

OBJECTIVES You will have mastered the material in this project when you can:

- ▸ Define data communications
- ▸ Describe the basic components of a data communications system
- ▸ Explain the purpose of a modem
- ▸ Use the Works Communications tool to connect to another computer

- ▸ Use the Works Communications tool to access a local bulletin board system
- ▸ Use the Works Communications tool to access information using the Internet
- ▸ Transfer a file from one computer to another

▶ INTRODUCTION

For many years computers have been used to perform complex mathematical calculations and to process business data at rapid speeds. Today, computers are also recognized as important communication devices. Using a computer, it is possible for you to communicate with other computers and people anywhere in the world. This capability allows you to access data instantly and obtain information that would otherwise be unavailable or difficult to acquire.

Computers as communication devices can be used for both business and personal applications. Banks, retail stores, airlines, hotels, and many other businesses use computers for sending and receiving information. As a personal computer user, you can access databases available on large computers quickly and conveniently to perform research and obtain information such as stock market reports, news stories, airline schedules, weather reports and even theater and movie reviews. You can *chat* with other computer users, play games, send electronic mail, send files such as spreadsheets and word processing documents, and conduct a wide variety of other activities.

The purpose of this project is to provide an overview of how personal computers communicate with other computers and how to use the Works Communications tool. You will be shown how to access an electronic bulletin board, how to access vast sources of information through a large network of computers called the Internet, and how to perform a file-to-file transfer from one computer to another.

W12.2

▶ DATA COMMUNICATIONS CONCEPTS

T he term data communications is frequently used when describing computer-to-computer communications. **Data communications** is defined as the transmission of data and information over a communications channel, such as standard telephone lines, from one computer to another computer. Figure 12-1 shows the basic model for a data communications system.

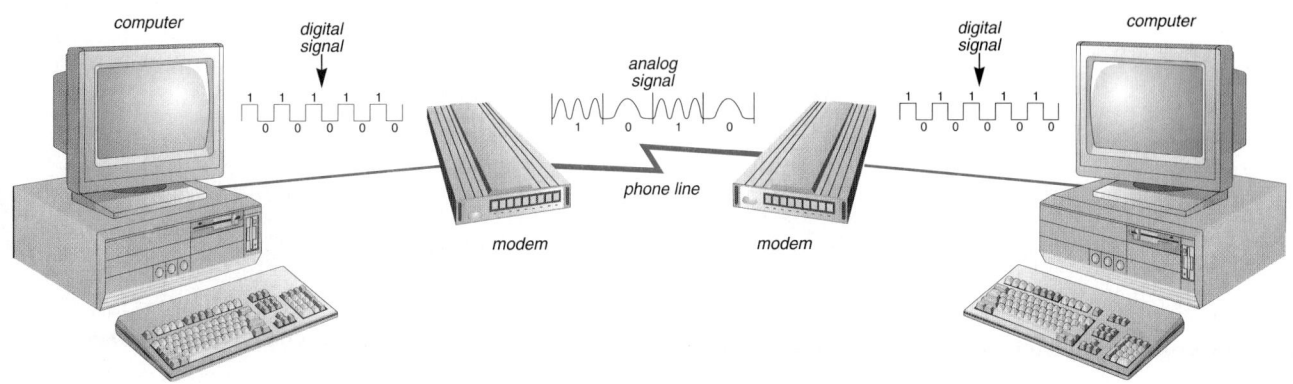

FIGURE 12-1

In this diagram of a simple communications system, each computer is attached to a device called a modem. Data is transmitted from one computer through the modem, over telephone lines, to another modem that is attached to another computer. The following paragraphs explain the use of the modem and basic data communications concepts.

Modems

Computer equipment is designed to process data in the form of **digital signals**. With digital signals, electronic impulses are used to represent bits that are grouped together to form characters. Bits may be thought of as small electronic spots that are either on or off.

Telephones commonly uses continuous electrical wave forms called **analog signals** to transmit information. Thus, to use telephone lines to transmit digital computer signals, a special piece of equipment called a **modem** must be used. Modems convert digital signals to analog signals and analog signals to digital signals so telephone lines can transmit computer data. A modem is needed at both the sending and receiving ends of a communications channel.

An **external modem** is a separate, or stand-alone, device that is attached to the computer by a cable. These modems are contained in a relatively small housing that can be placed adjacent to the computer. A cord from the modem plugs directly into a standard telephone jack to allow communication over telephone lines. An advantage of an external modem is that it can be moved easily from one computer to another.

An **internal modem** is a circuit board that is installed inside a computer. An advantage of the internal modem is that no computer-to-modem cable is required, and there is no extra electronic unit connected externally to the computer. In addition, internal modems are generally less expensive than comparable external modems. A disadvantage of the internal modem is that after an internal modem is installed, the modem is not easily removed for use on another computer.

Modems can send and receive data at different speeds. Personal computer modems commonly transmit data at rates of 2,400, 9,600 or 14,400 bits per second (bps). Businesses and heavy volume users often use faster modems.

Data Transmission and Communications Methods

In modern communications systems, transmission media other than telephone lines can be used when data is transmitted over long distances. Often, several different transmission methods are used. Figure 12-2 illustrates some of the various transmission methods used to transmit data from a personal computer on the West coast of the United States to another computer on the East coast. An example of the steps that could occur in Figure 12-2 are listed on the next page.

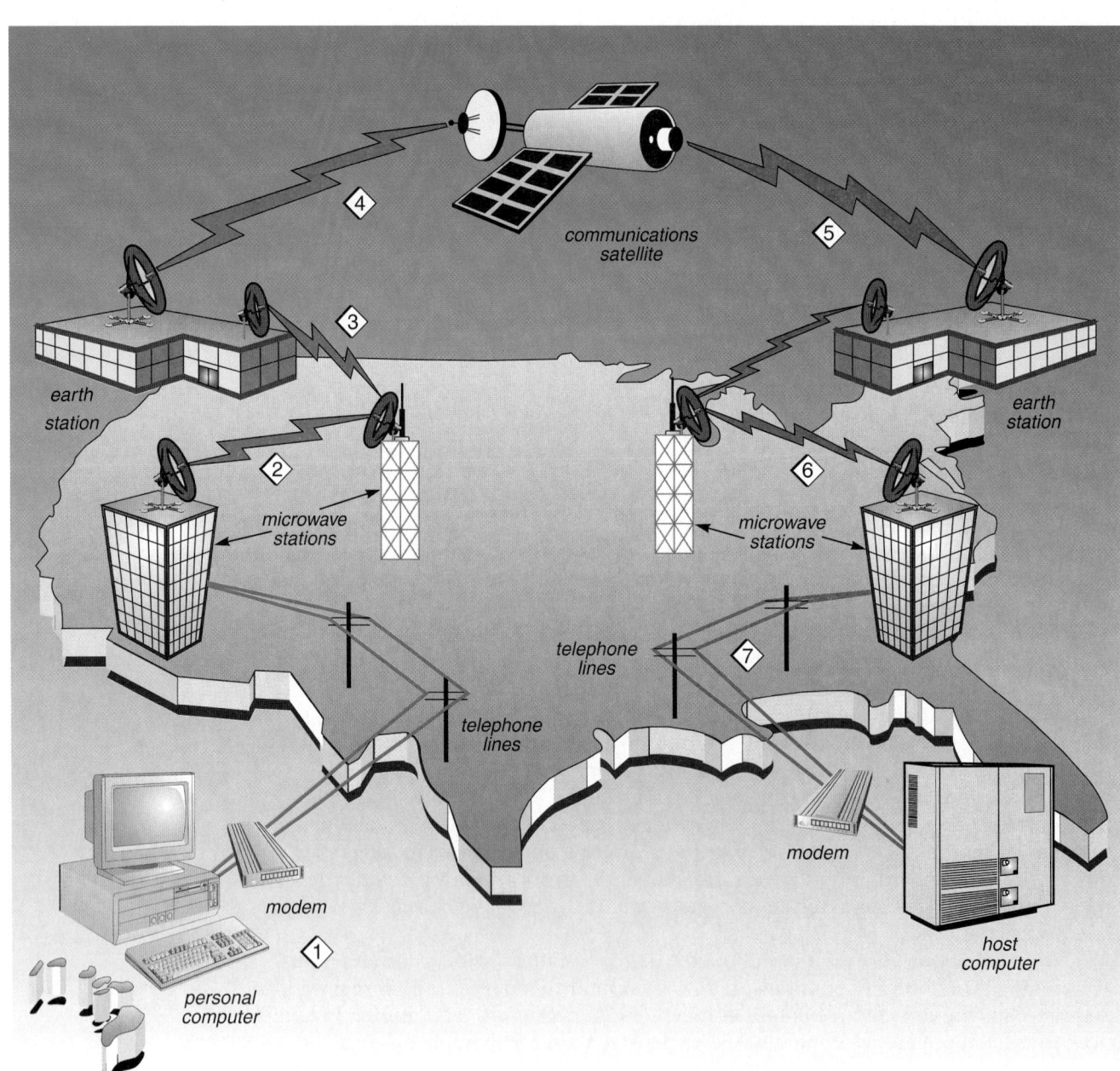

FIGURE 12-2

1. Data from a personal computer is sent over telephone lines from the computer to a microwave station.
2. Microwave stations transmit data through open space much like radio or television signals. The data is then transmitted from one microwave station to another.
3. The data is transmitted from the last microwave station to an earth station.
4. An earth station is a communication facility that contains a very large antenna that can transmit data to a communications satellite. Satellites positioned approximately 22,000 miles above the earth can relay signals from one earth station to another. The earth station transmits the data to the communications satellite.
5. The satellite relays the data to another earth station on the other side of the country.
6. The data received at the earth station is transmitted to microwave stations.
7. The data is sent over the telephone lines to the computer on the East coast, which can then transmit data back to the computer on the West coast.

The entire transmission process would take less than one second. Not all data transmission is as complex as this example, but such sophisticated communications systems do exist to meet the needs of users.

▶ COMMUNICATIONS SERVICES

Many business activities use computers and data communications. When you make an airline reservation at the local travel agent, the agent will normally use a computer to access a database at some remote location to obtain information about available flight schedules. Using an ATM machine at the bank is a form of data communications involving computer-to-computer communications.

Computers and data communications are an important part of our daily lives. Some of the commonly used data communications services are briefly described in the following paragraphs.

Bulletin Board Systems

Today, thousands of bulletin board systems exist. These **bulletin board systems** (BBS) allow users to communicate computer-to-computer over data communication channels for the purpose of sharing programs, reading bulletins left by others, and exchanging ideas concerning current issues.

Many bulletin board systems serve special-interest groups. Bulletin boards are used by computer clubs, professional associations, teachers, and other individuals or groups that share common interests. Most bulletin board systems are free or low in cost. A system operator (sysop) maintains the bulletin board and assists members. A listing of bulletin board systems in your area is often published in local papers or can be found by contacting a local computer store.

The steps to access a bulletin board are explained later in this project.

Commercial On-line Information Services

Many commercial **on-line information services** are currently available. Companies providing these services normally require users to pay a fixed monthly subscription charge. Many of the information services can be accessed by a local telephone call.

Widely used services include Prodigy, CompuServe, and America Online. On-line information services provide for airline, hotel, and car rental reservations, access to information on stock prices, weather reports, headline news, movie reviews, games, and many other sources of information. An important element of these services is the opportunity to chat with other computer users. You can send and receive messages in a real-time manner so you are carrying on a conversation using your computer. You can also send electronic mail to anyone using the service.

The Internet

The Internet is a web of interconnecting computer networks that provides computer-to-computer communications for millions of users. The Internet provides access to vast amounts of information stored on databases in computers throughout the world. There are now more than one million computers connected to the Internet.

The Internet services are designed to support research for individuals, educational institutions and government agencies, and others who need access to information. As a system, the Internet is governed and regulated cooperatively by individuals and groups interested in promoting on-line access to information.

All types of people use the Internet, including students, librarians, scientists, engineers, university researchers, and individuals in governmental agencies. Their purpose is to communicate, exchange ideas, and gain access to knowledge. The Internet is now comprised of more than 7,500 networks operating in more than 40 countries throughout the world. The Internet is used by approximately 25 million people a day.

Through the Internet, you can send and receive messages to other computer users throughout the world, effectively leaving electronic mail for everyone.

The Works Communications tool can be used to assist you in connecting to the Internet.

▶ INTRODUCTION TO THE WORKS COMMUNICATIONS TOOL

To communicate with another computer, you need a modem and a **communications software package**. The communications software package consists of computer instructions required for computer-to-computer communications. Works includes a Communications tool that allows you to communicate with other computers through a modem and telephone lines or other communications channels.

To connect to a bulletin board, on-line information service, or another computer, you must provide Works with the information needed to make the connection to another computer. This information is provided in a **Communications file** that you create by clicking the Communications button in the Startup dialog box and making appropriate entries in dialog boxes that display.

When you first tell Works to make a connection to another computer, Works uses standard communications settings used by many information services. If the settings do not match the computer or service you want to connect to, difficulties may arise; therefore, it is suggested that you review the Works default communications settings as one of the first steps in a communications session.

Communications Settings

As previously explained, before you can connect to another computer, certain communication settings must be set. In Works, a Settings dialog box displays these settings. These settings control how fast your computer transmits or receives data, and other information related to the communication of data using a computer.

Before attempting to communicate with another computer, bulletin board or information service, you must know the settings required by the computer with which your computer will be communicating.

Table 12-1 briefly explains some important communications settings and terminology. These settings display in the Works Settings dialog box.

▶ **TABLE 12-1**

TYPE OF SETTING	INITIAL SETTING	DESCRIPTION
Port	COM1	The port your modem or cable is connected to.
Baud Rate	9600	The rate at which data is transferred. Use the highest rate your modem and the other computer's modem can use.
Parity	None	Check for transmission errors. Match the other computer's setting.
Ignore Parity	None	If you need to use a parity setting, clear this check box and then use the parity setting you need.
Data Bits	8	The number of bits used to represent a character. Match the other computer's setting.
Handshake	Xon/Xoff	Controls how data flows from one computer to the other. Xon/Xoff is the standard for communicating through modems.
Stop bits	1	The number of bits used to represent the end of each character. Match the other computer's setting.

A thorough understanding of the settings in Table 12-1 requires an in-depth knowledge of data communications. From a users point of view, all that is necessary to know is that certain settings must be made to meet the requirements of the modem and computer you are using and the modem and computer at the remote site. For a more detailed explanation of communications settings, use Works On-Line Help.

Communications Window Toolbar

When using the Works Communications tool, you will be working in a Communications Window. This window contains a Toolbar with a number of specialized buttons. These buttons are identified in Figure 12-3 on the next page.

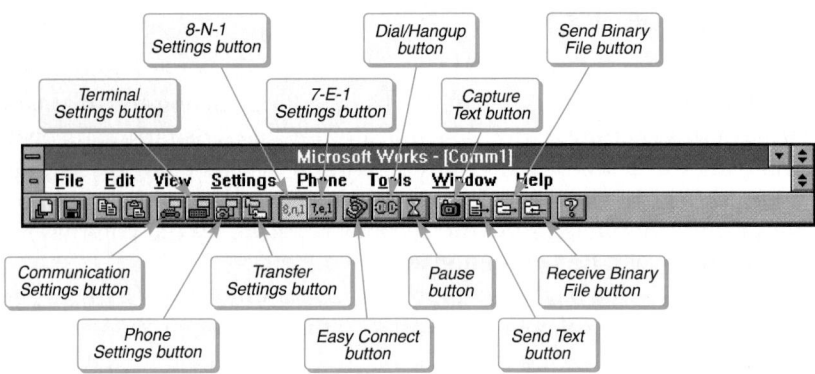

FIGURE 12-3

The buttons will be explained as they are used.

Communications Settings

In the first communication session in Project 12, you will access a bulletin board. To access the bulletin board, you should review the Works communications settings and make the changes to conform with the required settings of the bulletin board, as explained in the following steps.

TO SET THE COMMUNICATIONS SETTINGS ▼

STEP 1 ▶

Start Works. When the Startup Dialog box displays, point to the Communications button.

*The Startup dialog box displays (Figure 12-4). The mouse pointer points to the **Communications button**.*

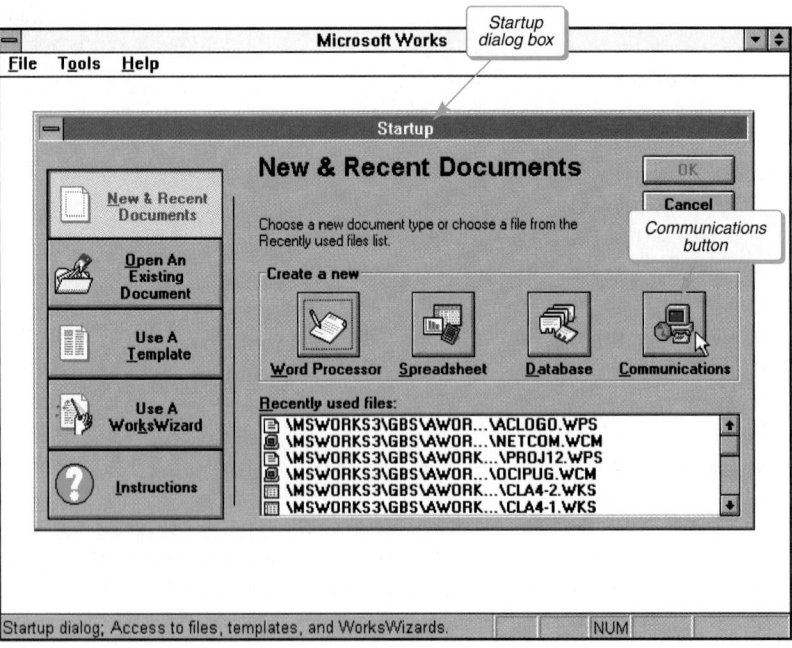

FIGURE 12-4

STEP 2 ▶

Choose the Communications button in the Startup dialog box. When the Easy Connect dialog box displays, point to the Cancel button because you are not connecting to another computer at this time.

The Easy Connect dialog box displays within the Microsoft Works Comm1 window (Figure 12-5). The mouse pointer points to the Cancel button. The menu bar and the Toolbar are unique for use by the Communications tool.

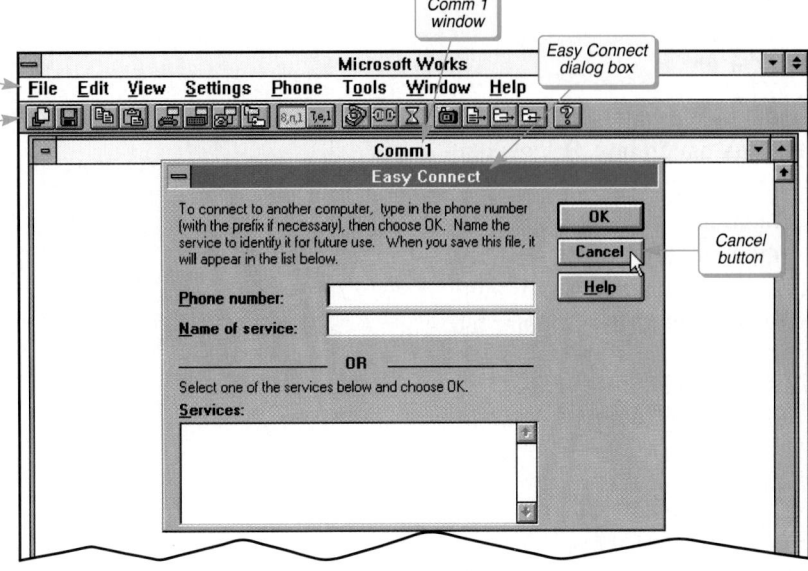

FIGURE 12-5

STEP 3 ▶

Choose the Cancel button in the Easy Connect dialog box. When the Easy Connect dialog box disappears from the screen, click the Maximize button in the Comm1 window. Then click the Communication Settings button on the Toolbar. Review the entries in the dialog box.

The Settings dialog box displays within the maximized Comm1 window (Figure 12-6). The entries on the Communication screen display. **Port** *refers to the computer port to which the modem is connected. The port selected is COM2. The* **Baud rate** *is the speed of data transfer between computers. Standard rates range from 300 to 19,200 bits per seconds (bps). The larger the number, the faster*

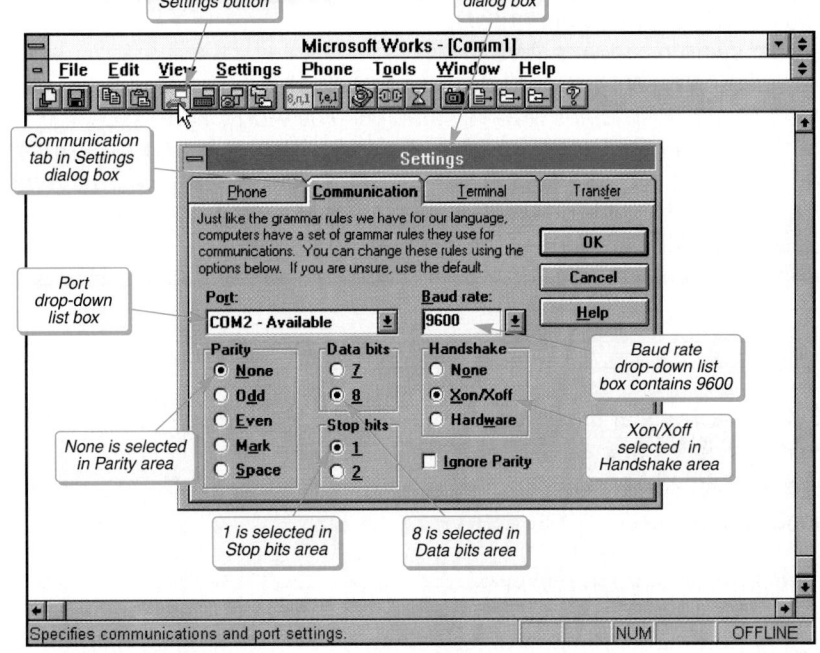

FIGURE 12-6

the transfer speed. Works has selected 9600 bps. **Parity** *is a mathematical technique used to check for errors in transmission. Works uses a default setting of None, which effectively allows the Works Communications tool to communicate regardless of the parity setting for the other computer.* **Data bits** *refers to the number of bits required to represent characters. Characters are represented by 7 or 8 bits. If you're not sure about the other computer's setting, select 8. Works has selected the 8 option button by default. Stop bits signify the end of each character. Works has selected the 1 option button.* **Handshake** *refers to the technique used to establish the communication connection. Works has selected the Xon/Xoff option button, which specifies software handshaking. This is the standard for communicating through modems. Some of these settings may need to be changed depending upon the computer and the modem used.*

STEP 4 ▶

Select the Terminal tab in the
Settings dialog box. Review the
settings. Highlight ANSI in the
Terminal list box. This is the
Terminal setting recommended by
the bulletin board sysop in this
project. Point to the Transfer tab.

*The Terminal screen displays
(Figure 12-7). The information in
the Terminal screen allows you to
make choices about how your
computer displays and responds
to data that is received from
another computer. **TTY** is the
default setting in the Terminal list
box. **ANSI** is selected in the Terminal list box because the bulletin
board system requires ANSI to be
specified. The Normal option but-*

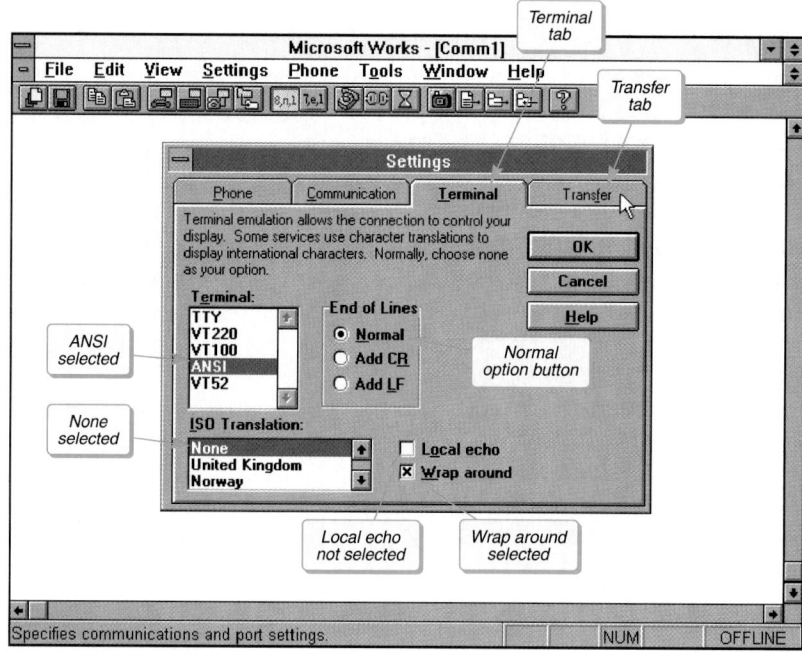

FIGURE 12-7

*ton in the End of Lines area is selected. The Add CR or Add LF options should be selected if incom-
ing text appears on only one line. None is selected in the ISO Translation list box. If you receive
international information, chose an appropriate country setting in the ISO Translation list box. Select
the Local echo check box if you are typing during a communications session and you want the typing
to display. Turn Wrap around off only if you do not want text to wrap to the next line at the Window's
edge. For a more detailed explanation of these entries, see Works On-Line Help.*

STEP 5 ▶

Select the Transfer tab in the
Settings dialog box. Select Kermit in
the Transfer protocol list box. Point
to the Phone tab.

*The Transfer screen displays
(Figure 12-8). The **Transfer protocol** determines the method used
by computers when transferring
data from one computer to
another. The Transfer protocol is
set to **Kermit**. Both computers
should be using the same protocol. Some protocols are faster
than others but less reliable. Kermit protocol is slow but reliable.
When you are sending an ASCII
text file, type a number in the Line
Delay text box if the computer cannot process the text as quickly as
it is being sent. Works will pause
that many tenths of a second
between each line of text it sends.
The Line Delay text box contains 0 by default.*

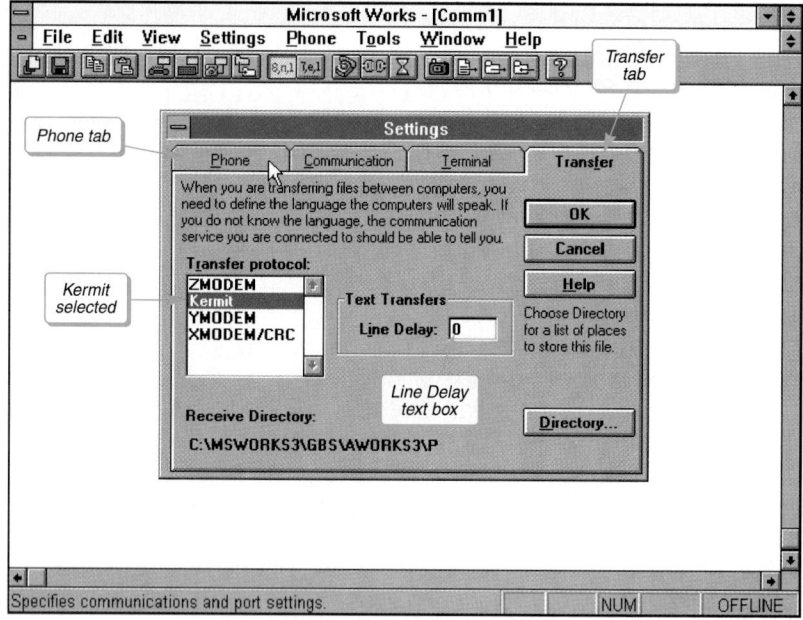

FIGURE 12-8

STEP 6 ▶

Select the Phone tab. Type 843-9248, the telephone number of the computer you are connecting to, in the Phone number text box. This number may be different from the number you use when you connect to your local bulletin board system. Press the TAB key and type Orange Coast BBS, the name of the bulletin board system, in the Name of service text box. Point to the OK button.

The Phone screen displays (Figure 12-9). The telephone number and the name of the bulletin board system display in their respective text boxes. If necessary, include the area code if you normally dial an area code with the number. Dial once is selected in the Connect option area and Tone is selected in the Dial type area. If you have a touch tone phone, Tone should be selected. The mouse pointer points to the OK button.

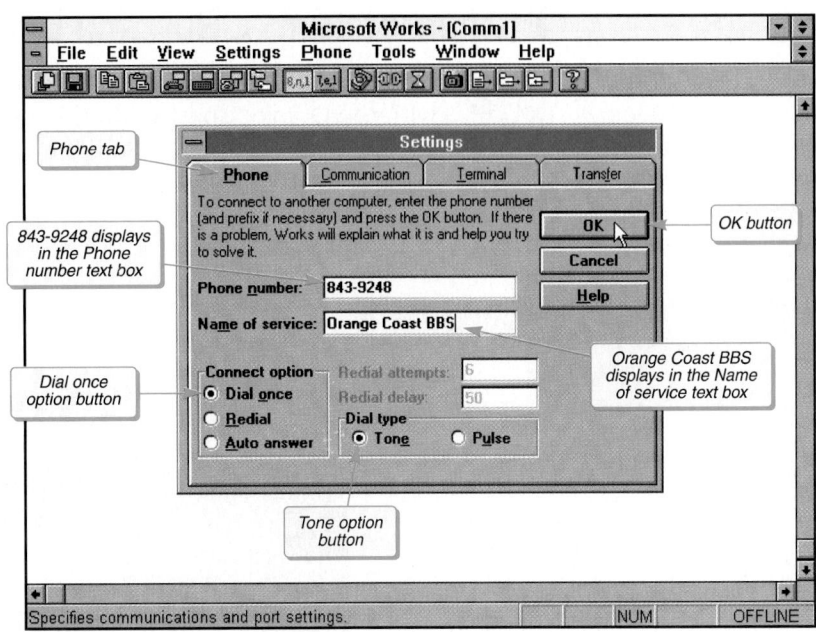

FIGURE 12-9

STEP 7

Choose the OK button in the Settings dialog box.

You can display any of the individual settings in the Settings dialog box by clicking the **Communication Settings button**, **Terminal Settings button**, **Phone Settings button**, or **Transfer Settings button** on the Toolbar, or by selecting the Settings menu and choosing the appropriate command from this menu.

It is important to make any required communications settings before beginning a communications session; otherwise, incorrect data may be sent or received.

Now that the communications settings have been reviewed and set, you can access the bulletin board system.

▶ CONNECTING TO A BULLETIN BOARD SYSTEM

The steps below and on the following pages illustrate how to communicate with the Orange Coast IBM PC User Group bulletin board (OCIPUG). You should be aware that the bulletin board procedures to connect to a bulletin board in your area and the data you enter, such as your name, may differ from those shown here.

TO CONNECT TO A BULLETIN BOARD ▼

STEP 1 ▶

Click the Dial/Hang-Up button on the Toolbar.

Works momentarily displays the Dial Status dialog box to inform you of the progress as the connection is being made (Figure 12-10). When Works dials, with most modems you hear Works dial the number and you hear the phone at the other end ring. When the connection is made, one or more bursts of static indicate the two computers are communicating.

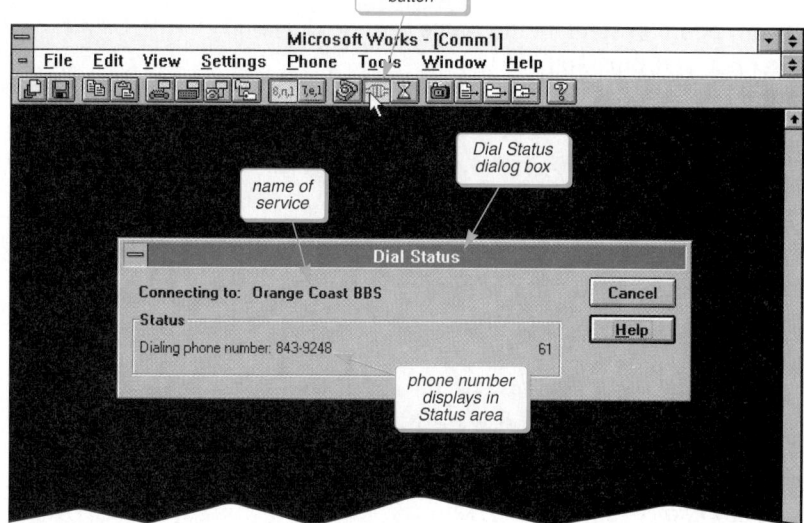

FIGURE 12-10

STEP 2 ▶

Once you have established the connection, the opening bulletin board screen displays.

The opening screen contains the title of the bulletin board system and other information about the system (Figure 12-11). At the bottom of the screen you can type C, N, or S in the response area. The response area is contained within brackets ([ ]). Type N for nonstop display of screens, or S for Stop. The letter C currently displays in the response area.

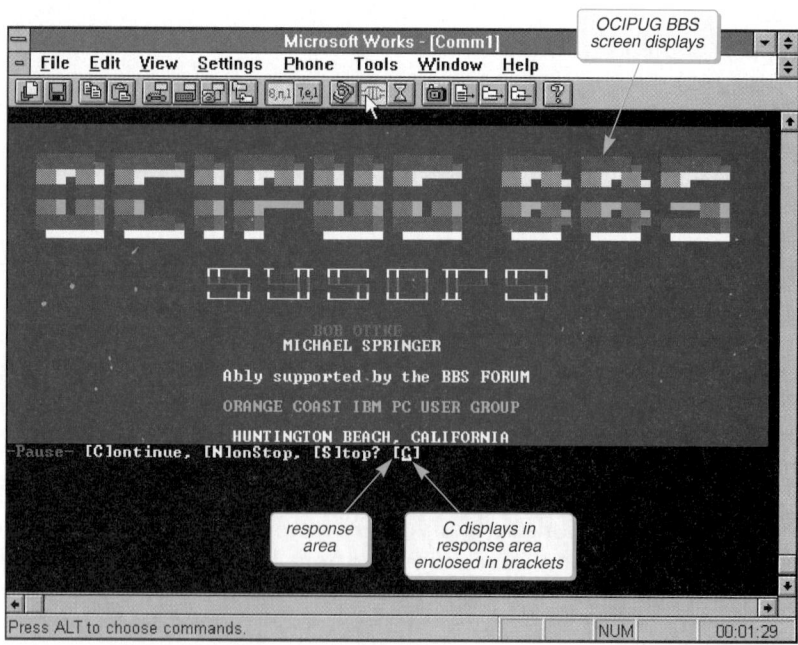

FIGURE 12-11

STEP 3 ▶

Ensure a C displays in the response area and then press the ENTER key to display the next screen.

The next screen displays and contains information about the next general meeting (Figure 12-12). The letter C remains in the response area.

FIGURE 12-12

STEP 4 ▶

Press the ENTER key repeatedly until the line asking, What is your first name? displays. Type michael. **Press the ENTER key. When the line displays, What is your last name?, type** boland. **Press the ENTER key. When Password? displays, type the unique word or words you have selected as your password. Your password must be prearranged with the bulletin board sysop.**

The first name and the last name of the user are entered (Figure 12-13). Asterisks (********) display in the Password section of the screen. For security reasons, the password does not display when it is typed. The names used and the password used must be prearranged with the bulletin board sysop. If you do not enter a valid name or a valid password, you will not be able to use the bulletin board system.

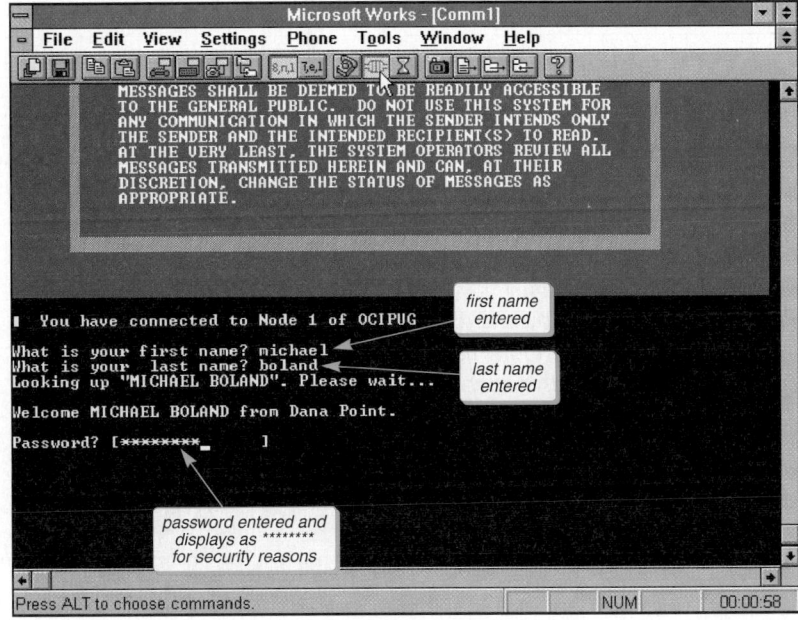

FIGURE 12-13

STEP 5 ►

Press the ENTER key repeatedly until a screen displays that contains the message, Would you like to view the bulletin menu? Type Y.

The screen displays that asks, Would you like to view the bulletin menu? (Figure 12-14). The letter Y you typed in the response area indicates yes.

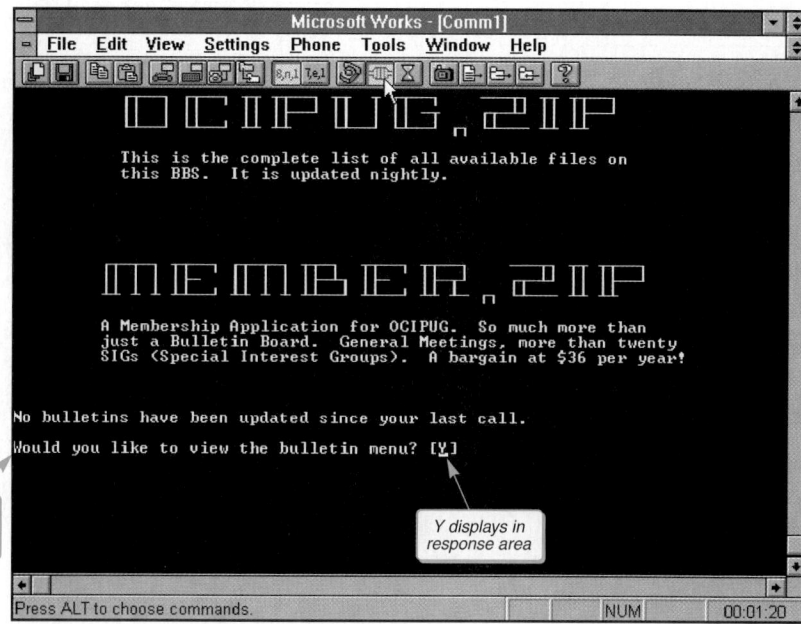

message displays on screen

Y displays in response area

FIGURE 12-14

STEP 6 ►

Press the ENTER key to continue.

The screen with the title, BULLETIN MENU, displays (Figure 12-15). This screen contains a list of menu selections you can select to display information that might be of interest. Pressing the ENTER key will display additional menu items when there is a C in the response area.

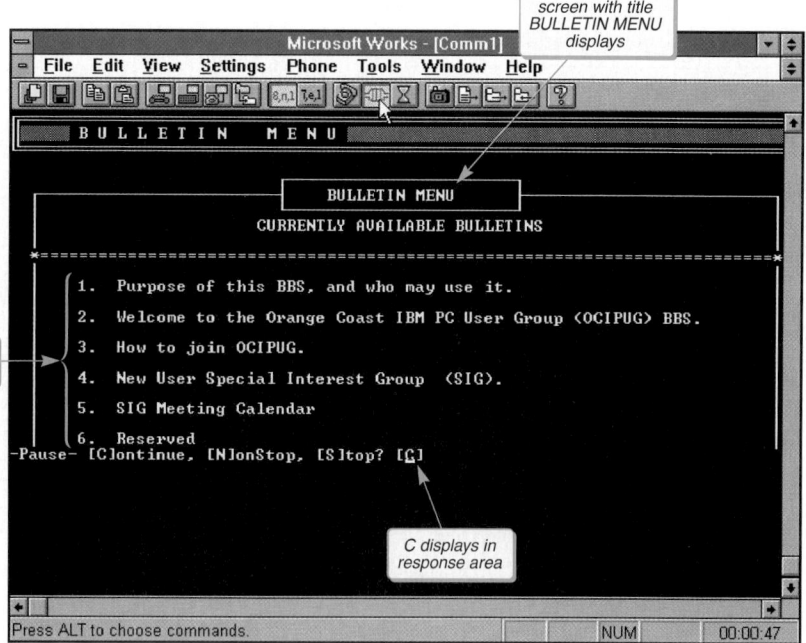

screen with title BULLETIN MENU displays

menu selections

C displays in response area

FIGURE 12-15

STEP 7 ▶

Press the ENTER key repeatedly until the last menu item displays. The last line of the screen displays, Enter bulletin number # [1..30]. Type 5 in the response area to display menu selection number 5, the SIG Meeting Calendar (see Figure 12-15).

The last Bulletin Menu item displays (Figure 12-16). The number 5 is typed in the response area.

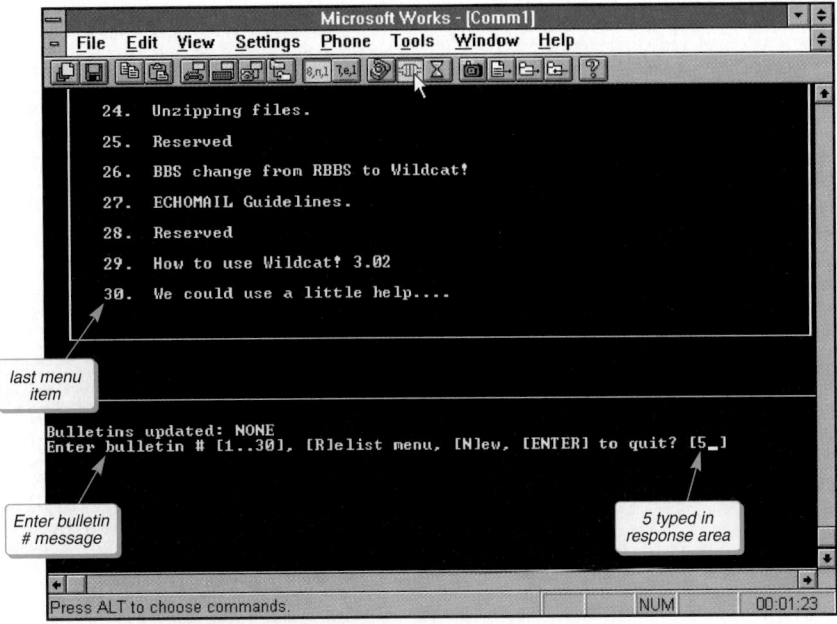

FIGURE 12-16

STEP 8 ▶

Continually press the ENTER key to display the meeting calendar.

The meeting calendar information displays (Figure 12-17).

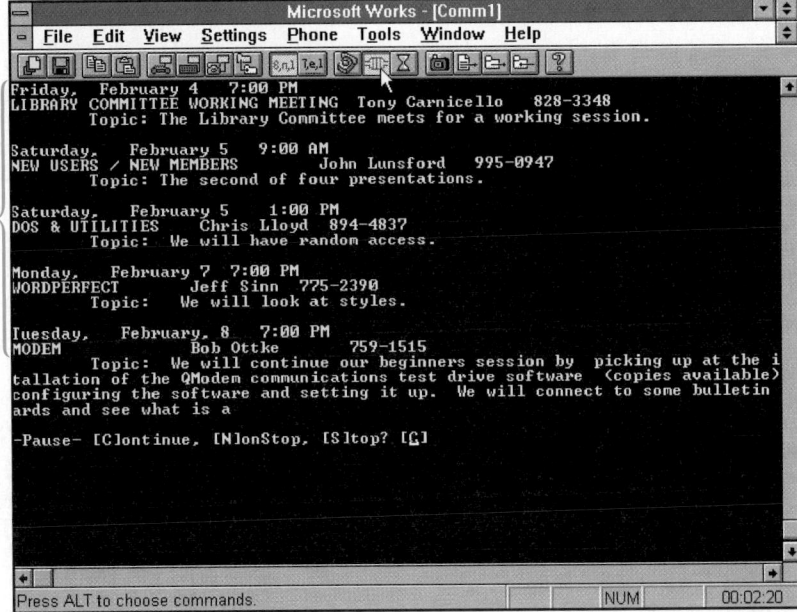

FIGURE 12-17

Quitting the Bulletin Board System

You should quit a communications session by following the instructions that display on your screen. The following steps explain how to quit the OCIPUG BBS.

TO QUIT THE BBS ▼

STEP 1 ▶

Type S **and press the** ENTER **key.**

The screen displays the message [ENTER] to quit? [ ] on the right side of the last line (Figure 12-18).

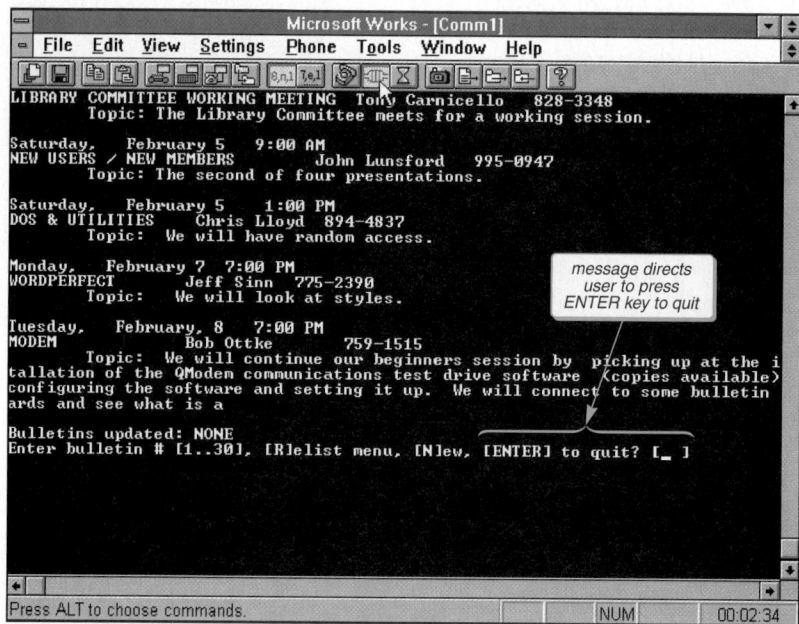

FIGURE 12-18

STEP 2 ▶

Press the ENTER **key to quit. Press the** ENTER **key again. When the main menu screen displays, type** G **in the Your Selection? response area.**

The Main Menu screen displays (Figure 12-19). The Main Menu indicates you should type G to Goodbye and Log Off. G displays in the response area.

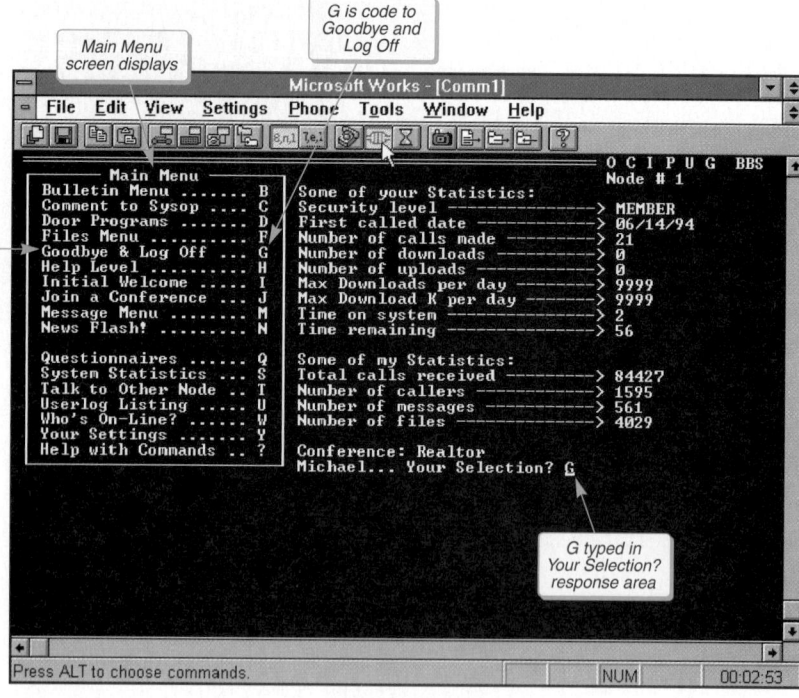

FIGURE 12-19

STEP 3 ▶

Press the ENTER key. When the message, Are you sure you wish to logoff? displays, ensure the letter Y displays in the response area.

The message displays - Are you sure you want to logoff? at the bottom of the screen (Figure 12-20). The letter Y displays in the response area.

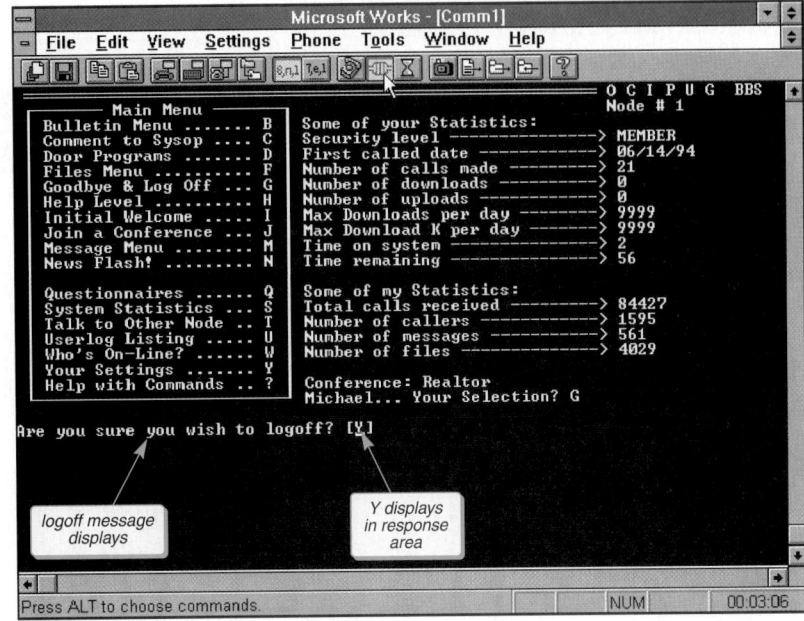

FIGURE 12-20

STEP 4 ▶

Press the ENTER key to log off the bulletin board. Click the Dial/Hangup button on the Toolbar.

A screen displays specifying the total time logged onto the bulletin board. When you click the Dial/Hangup button on the Toolbar, a Microsoft Works dialog box displays asking, OK to disconnect? (Figure 12-21).

STEP 5

Choose the OK button in the Microsoft Works dialog box. The communications session is ended.

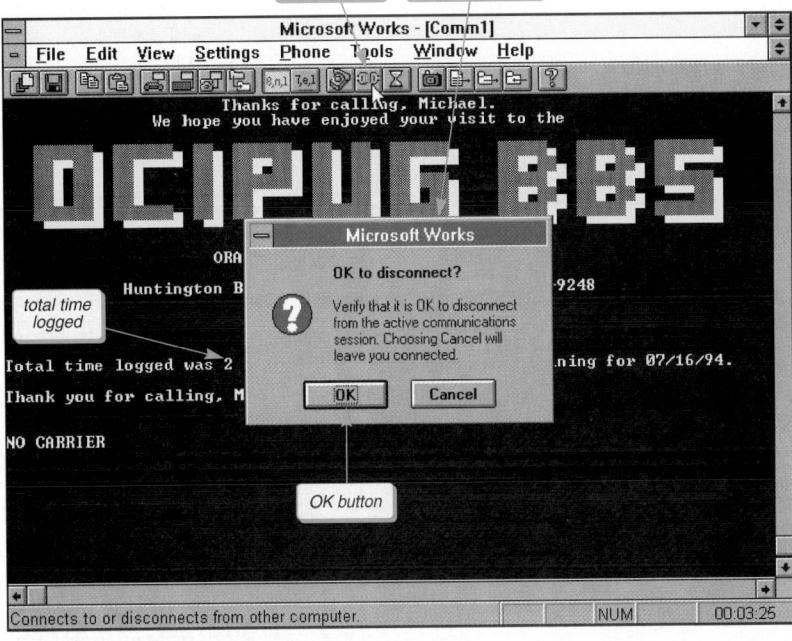

FIGURE 12-21

Saving a Communications File

The communications file you created contains the telephone number of the bulletin board system you accessed, the communications settings, and the name Orange Coast BBS. To save this file so you do not have to type the settings, telephone number, and the bulletin board name again, perform the following steps.

TO SAVE A COMMUNICATIONS FILE ▼

STEP 1 ►

With the Comm1 window displayed, point to the Save button on the Toolbar.

The mouse pointer points to the Save button (Figure 12-22).

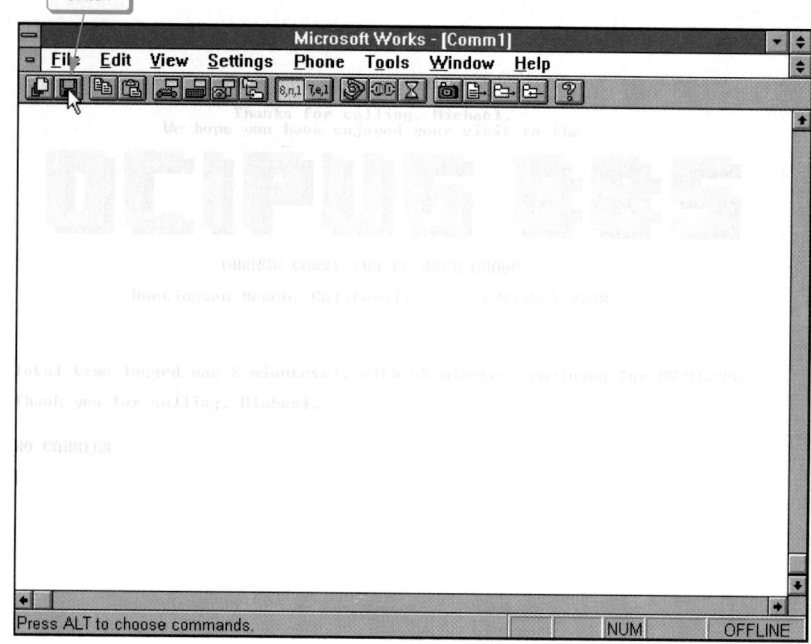

FIGURE 12-22

STEP 2 ►

Click the Save button. When the Save As dialog box displays, type `ocipug` in the File Name text box and if necessary select drive A in the Drives drop-down list box. Point to the OK button.

Works displays the Save As dialog box (Figure 12-23). Drive A is selected. ocipug displays in the File Name text box. The mouse pointer points to the OK button.

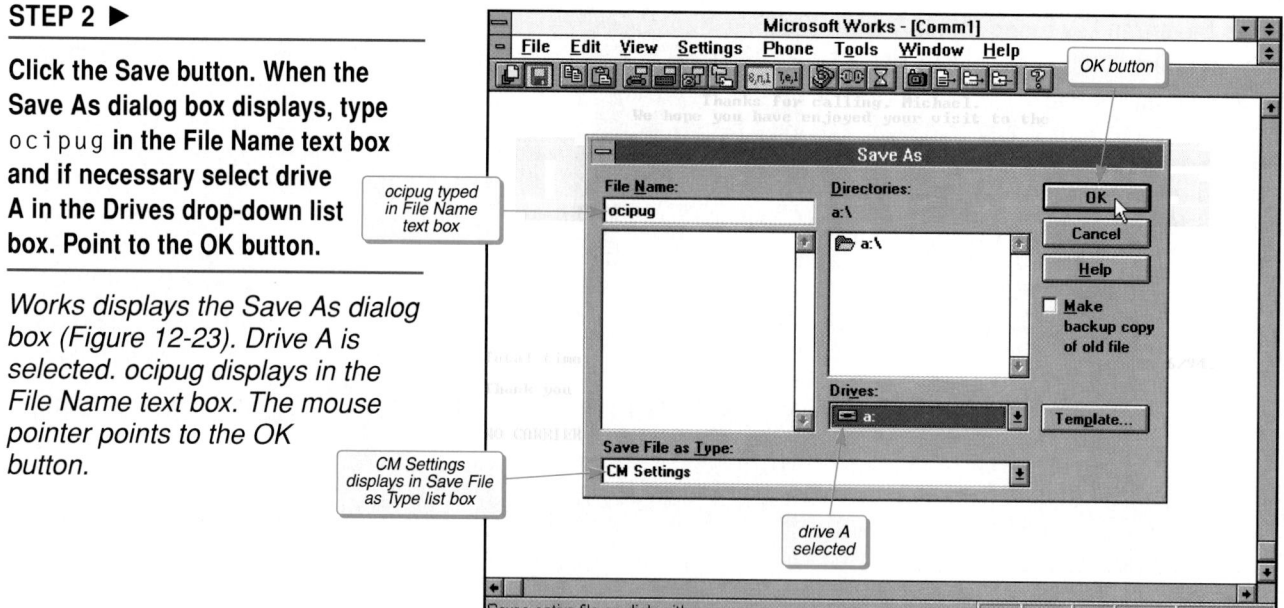

FIGURE 12-23

STEP 3 ▶

Choose the OK button in the Save As dialog box. Select the File menu and point to the Close command.

Works save the communications settings as a communications file called OCIPUG.WCM. Works adds the extension .WCM to all communications files. The File menu displays and the mouse pointer points to the Close command (Figure 12-24).

STEP 4

Choose the Close command.

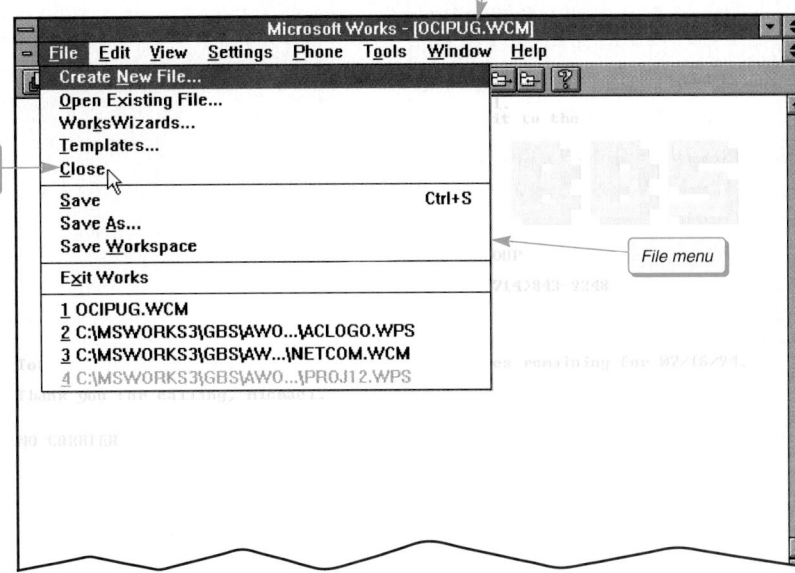

FIGURE 12-24

The communications session is now closed and the communications settings are saved for use in the future. If you have no more work, you should exit Works.

▶ RECONNECTING TO A BULLETIN BOARD SYSTEM

To reconnect to the bulletin board system, perform the following steps.

TO RECONNECT TO THE BULLETIN BOARD ▼

STEP 1 ▶

Start Works. When the Startup dialog box displays, point to the Communications button.

The Startup dialog box displays and the mouse pointer points to the Communications button (Figure 12-25).

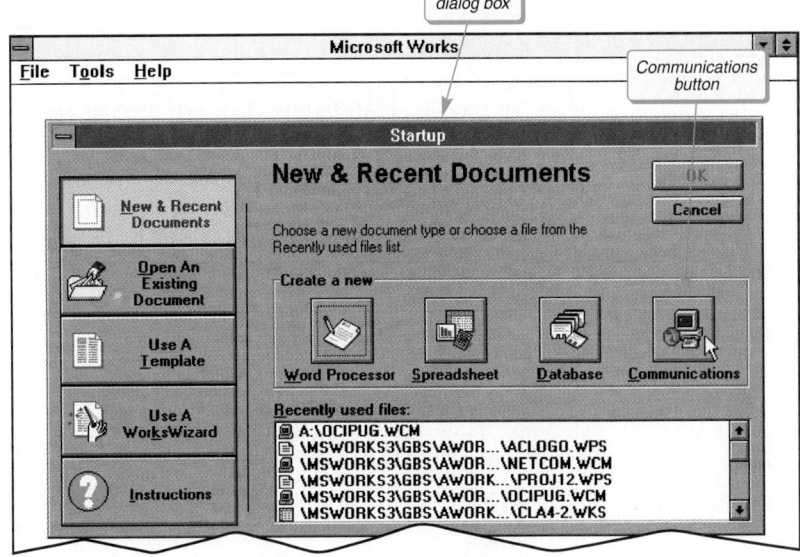

FIGURE 12-25

STEP 2 ▶

Choose the Communications button in the Startup dialog box. When the Easy Connect dialog box displays, if necessary highlight Orange Coast BBS in the Services list box. Point to the OK button.

Orange Coast BBS displays in the Services list box as a result of saving the communications file (Figure 12-26). The mouse pointer points to the OK button.

FIGURE 12-26

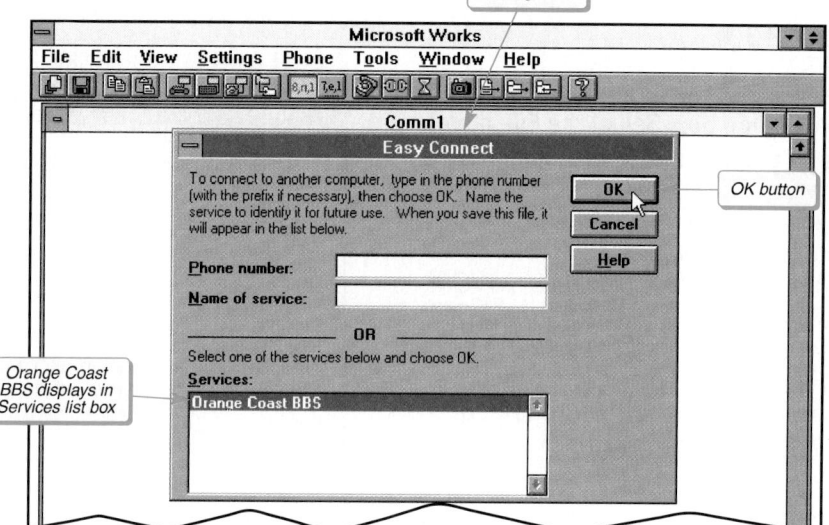

STEP 3 ▶

Choose the OK button in the Easy Connect dialog box. When the Microsoft Works dialog box displays, point to the OK button.

The Microsoft Works dialog box displays asking, Connect to other computer? (Figure 12-27). The mouse pointer points to the OK button.

STEP 4

Choose the OK button in the Microsoft Works dialog box.

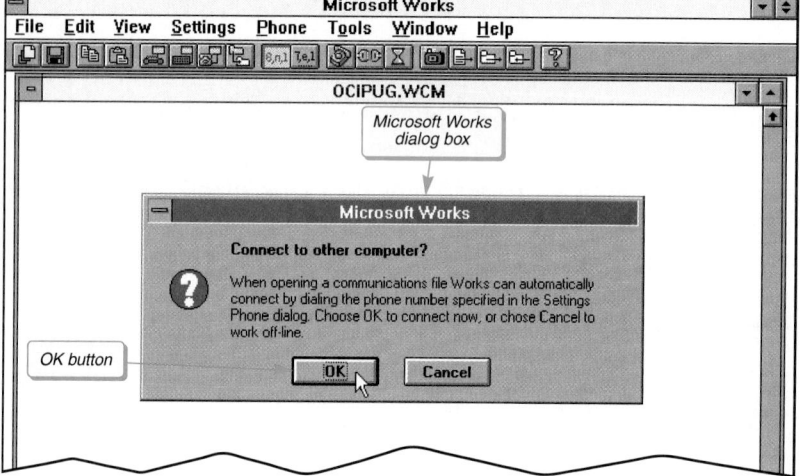

FIGURE 12-27

Works will dial the bulletin board system and connect you to the bulletin board again. After completing the session, you should close the communications file.

Exploring the services provided by bulletin board systems can be an enjoyable and rewarding experience and provide access to information that would otherwise be time consuming and difficult to obtain. When using bulletin boards, you can also print information that displays, download files such as games and utilities that are stored on the bulletin board system's computer, and, with many systems, send and receive electronic mail.

▶ THE INTERNET

he Internet provides computer users with the ability to access thousands of bulletin boards and databases throughout the world. The databases are located in universities, state and federal government agencies, and in numerous other locations that store information that might be of interest to a diverse group of millions of users.

To use the Internet, you must have access to a server that will allow you to connect to the Internet. Many schools have developed procedures to allow students to use the Internet. In addition, commercial servers are available that charge a monthly fee. These servers charge in the range of $20.00 per month for unlimited access through local telephone service. In this project, a commercial server company called NETCOM is used.

The communications file created in this project illustrates how to use the commercial server NETCOM to connect to the Internet and obtain information from NASA using the resources of Yale University. The purpose is to retrieve the schedule of future space shuttle launchings from NASA.

Communications Settings

With the computer used in this project, VT100 is the recommended Terminal setting when using NETCOM. Thus, the only setting which must be changed from the previous settings used when accessing the bulletin board is to change the Terminal setting to VT100. To make this setting, perform the following steps.

TO CHANGE TERMINAL SETTINGS ▼

STEP 1 ▶

Start Works. When the Works Startup dialog box displays, choose the Communications button. The Comm1 window will display. The Comm1 window contains the Easy Connect dialog box. Choose the Cancel button in the Easy Connect dialog box to remove this dialog box from the window. Maximize the Comm1 window. Click the Terminal Settings button on the Toolbar. When the Settings dialog box displays, highlight VT100 in the Terminal list box. All other selections are default selections and need not be changed. Point to the OK button.

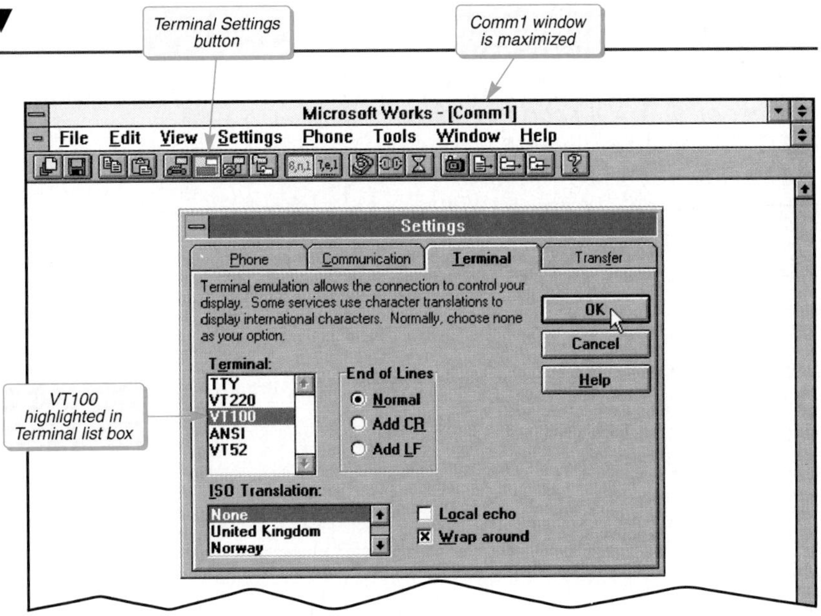

Terminal Settings button

Comm1 window is maximized

VT100 highlighted in Terminal list box

FIGURE 12-28

The Settings dialog box displays in the Comm1 window (Figure 12-28). VT100 is highlighted in the Terminal area of the Terminal screen in the Settings dialog box. The mouse pointer points to the OK button.

STEP 2

Choose the OK button in the Settings dialog box.

It is important to understand that the Terminal settings may vary depending on the computer, modem, and server you are using.

Accessing the Internet Using NETCOM

The next step is to access the Internet using NETCOM. Perform the following steps to accomplish this task.

TO ACCESS THE INTERNET USING NETCOM ▼

STEP 1 ▶

With the Comm1 window displayed, click the Easy Connect button on the Toolbar. When the Easy Connect dialog box displays, type 708-3801 **in the Phone number text box, press the TAB key once, and type** NETCOM **in the Name of service text box.**

The Easy Connect dialog box displays (Figure 12-29). The phone number of NETCOM and the entry NETCOM display as typed in the appropriate text boxes. In this example, the Easy Connect button was selected to allow entry of the telephone number and the name of the service. In the previous example of accessing a bulletin board, the Phone screen in the Settings dialog box was used to enter the telephone number and name of service. Either method can be used.

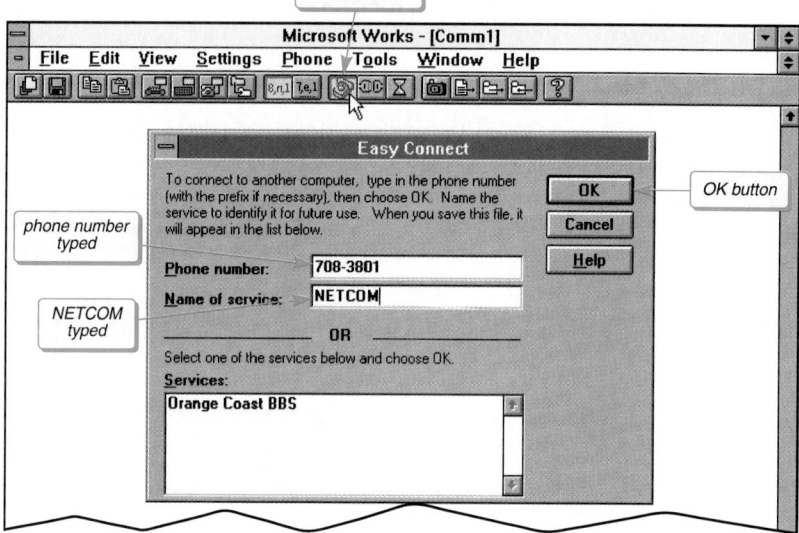

FIGURE 12-29

STEP 2 ▶

Choose the OK button in the Easy Connect dialog box.

Works momentarily displays the Dial Status dialog box to inform you of the progress as the communications connection is made (Figure 12-30). With most modems, when Works dials, you hear Works dial the number and you hear the phone at the other end ring. When the connection is made, you will hear one or more bursts of static indicating the two computers are connected.

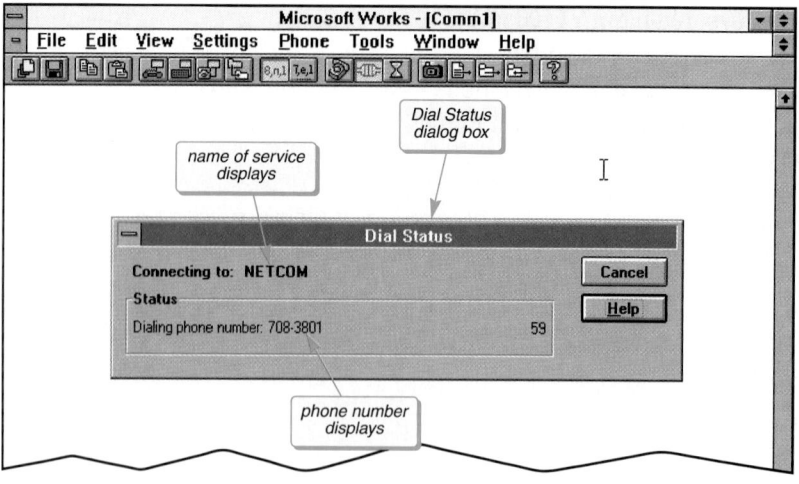

FIGURE 12-30

STEP 3 ►

When the Dialing Status dialog box disappears from the Comm1 window, a screen displays that allows you to login.

After the connection is made, CONNECT 9600/REL-LAPM-COMP displays on the first line in the upper left corner of the Comm1 window (Figure 12-31). The 9600 indicates the baud rate at which the communication is to take place. The next line displays netcom3 login:. This display is followed by a blinking cursor. At this time you must type a user ID.

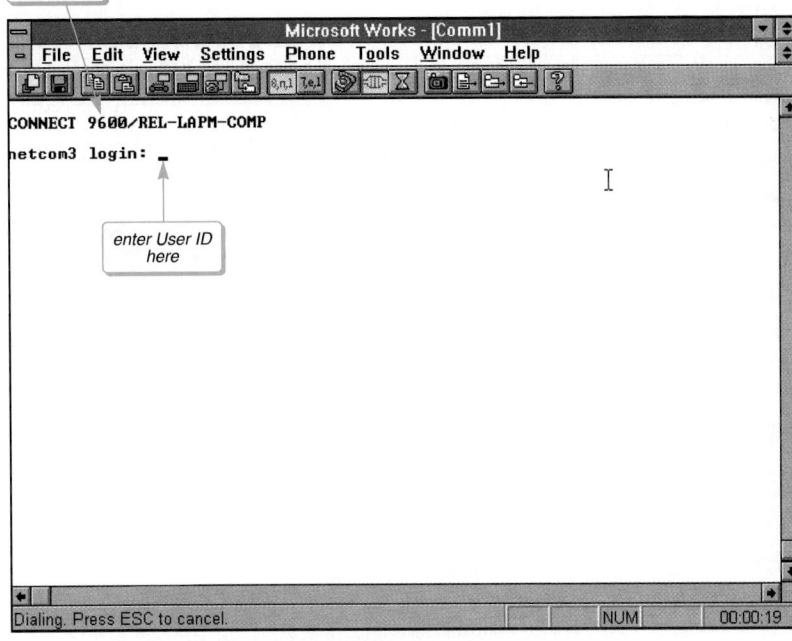

FIGURE 12-31

STEP 4 ►

Type boland **in lower case. This is the user ID in this example. Press the ENTER key.**

The word boland displays following login: (Figure 12-32). The user ID boland must be a name agreed upon with NETCOM. On the next line, Password: displays, followed by a blinking cursor.

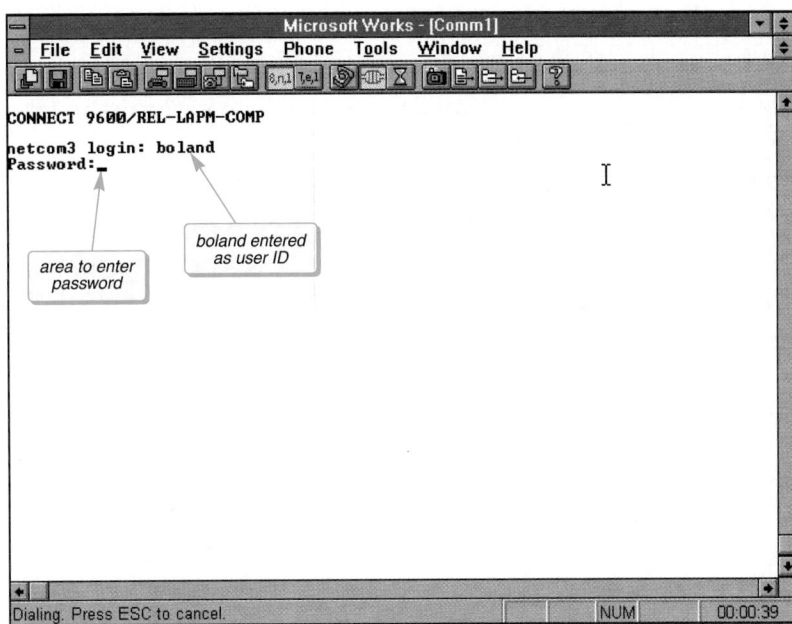

FIGURE 12-32

STEP 5 ▶

Type the password of the user. The password is a word agreed upon by the user and NETCOM. You must enter a valid password to connect to the Internet through NETCOM. The password that is typed does not display on the screen. After typing the password, press the ENTER key. When the next screen displays, type menu following the entry (netcom3:1) on the last line on the screen.

The NETCOM opening screen displays (Figure 12-33). The word menu displays as the last word on the screen.

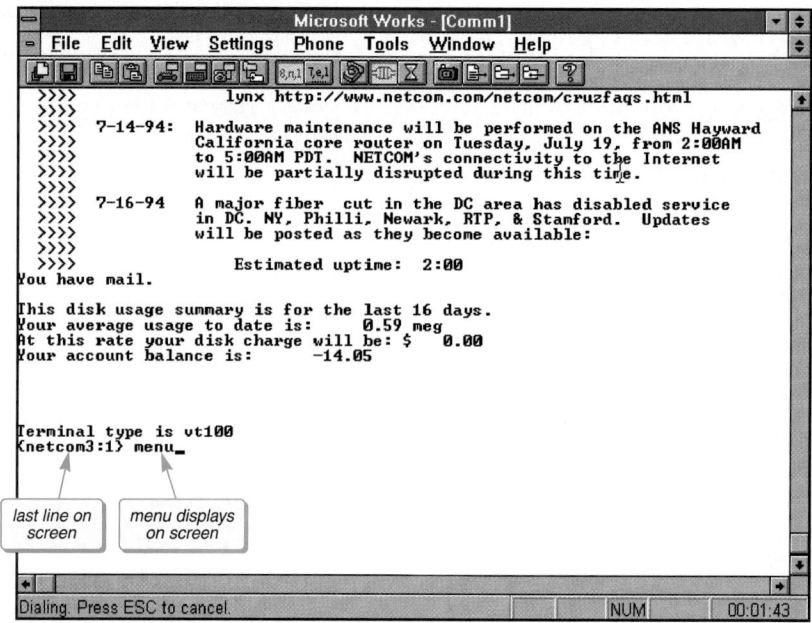

FIGURE 12-33

You are now ready to navigate the Internet to retrieve and display the information you need.

Navigating the Internet

The Internet consists of many thousands of sources of information. This information may be stored on private bulletin boards, on computer databases at the world's leading libraries and universities, on computer databases at many state and federal government agencies, and on databases from many other sources.

There are a number of ways to access this information. Some methods involve typing a series of addresses which specify how to get to the information. Other methods use menus to assist you in obtaining the information you need. The Gopher system uses a series of menus that allows you to conveniently explore the many sources of information available through the Internet. The Gopher system is used in this project and is available for use on most computers that connect to the Internet.

In Project 12, you are to navigate through the Internet to obtain the schedule of space shuttle launchings from NASA. NASA may be accessed through the resources of Yale University in the state of Connecticut. To navigate the Internet, perform the following steps.

TO NAVIGATE THE INTERNET ▼

STEP 1 ►

Press the ENTER key after typing `menu`. **Read the instructions on the screen that displays. Highlight the word Gopher on the left side of the screen under the word OPTIONS by pressing the 'd' key seven times.**

The first Internet screen displays (Figure 12-34). The instructions indicate you use the 'u' and 'd' keys to move up and down through the list of items on THIS SCREEN. The word Gopher is highlighted in the OPTIONS column.

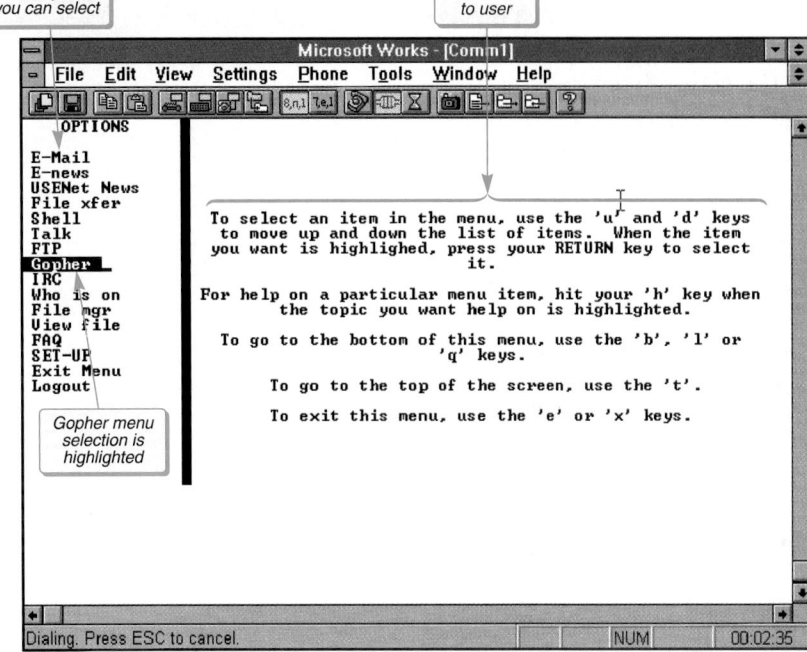

FIGURE 12-34

STEP 2 ►

Press the ENTER key when the word Gopher is highlighted. A menu displays listing ten selections you can make. Press the DOWN ARROW key until the right pointing arrow and the cursor are next to 6. Other Internet Gopher Servers (via U.C. Santa Cruz)/ in the menu.

The right pointing arrow and cursor are next to menu selection 6 (Figure 12-35). Pressing the DOWN ARROW key or UP ARROW key moves the right pointing arrow and cursor down and up on this screen. Pressing the 'u' key when THIS AND SUBSEQUENT SCREENS display will cause the previous screen to display. You should note that items are frequently added to the menu in the Internet. Therefore, when you are connected to the Internet, the menu selection numbers and entries may not be identical to those shown in Figure 12-35.

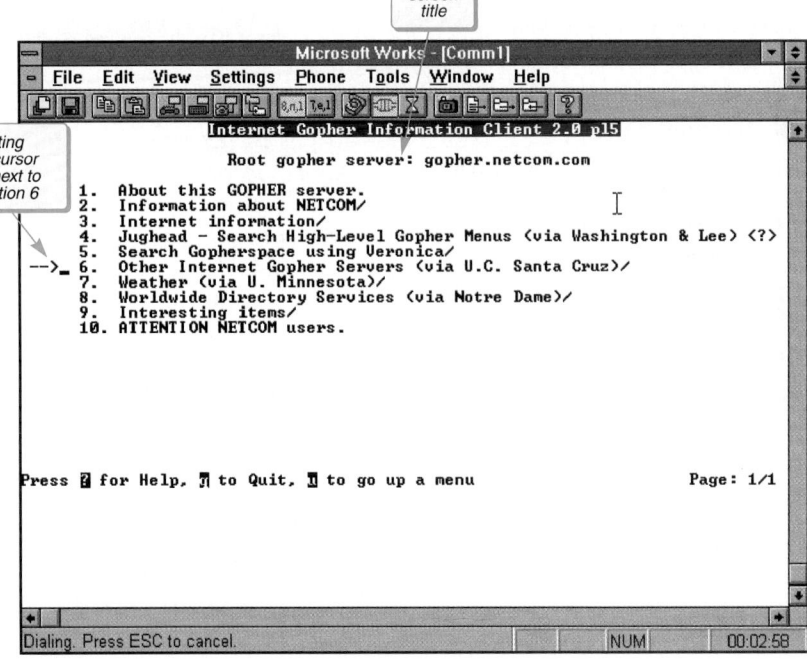

FIGURE 12-35

STEP 3 ▶

Press the ENTER key. When the next screen displays, press the DOWN ARROW key until the right pointing arrow and the cursor are next to 10. North America/ in the menu.

The screen titled Other Internet Gopher Servers (via U.C. Santa Cruz) displays (Figure 12-36). The right pointing arrow and the cursor are next to menu selection 10.

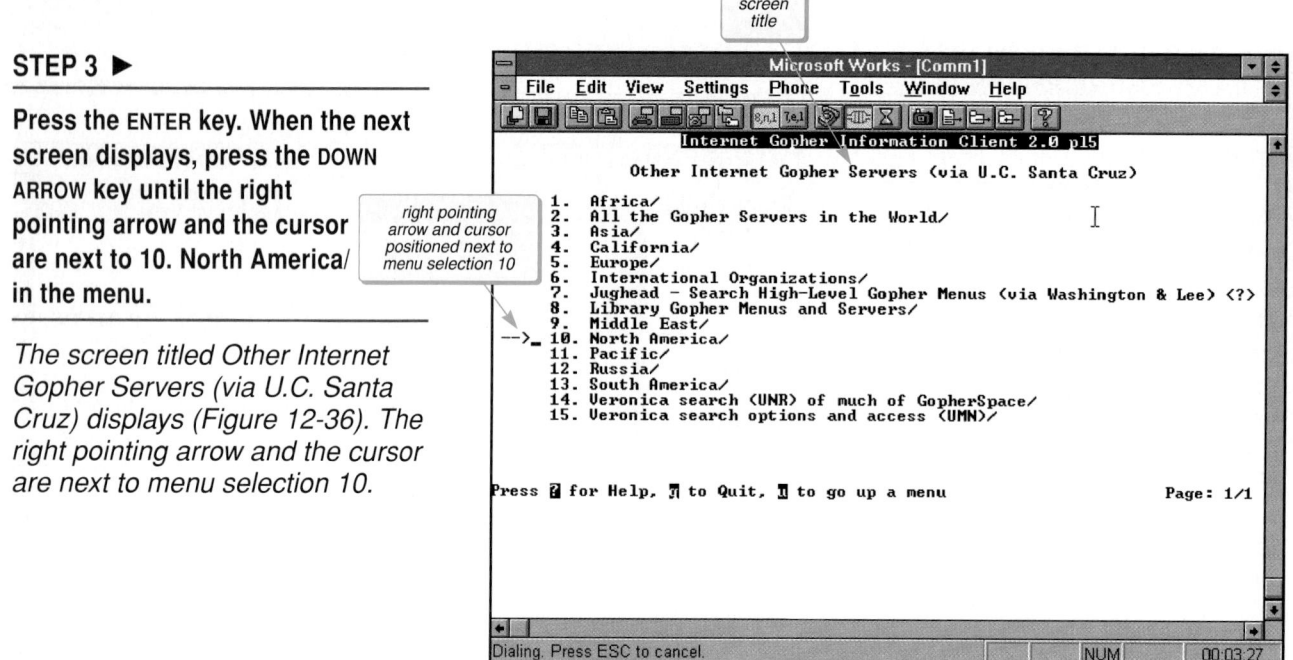

FIGURE 12-36

STEP 4 ▶

Press the ENTER key. When the next screen displays, press the DOWN ARROW key until the right pointing arrow and the cursor are next to 4. USA/ in the menu.

The screen titled North America displays (Figure 12-37). The right pointing arrow and the cursor are next to menu selection 4.

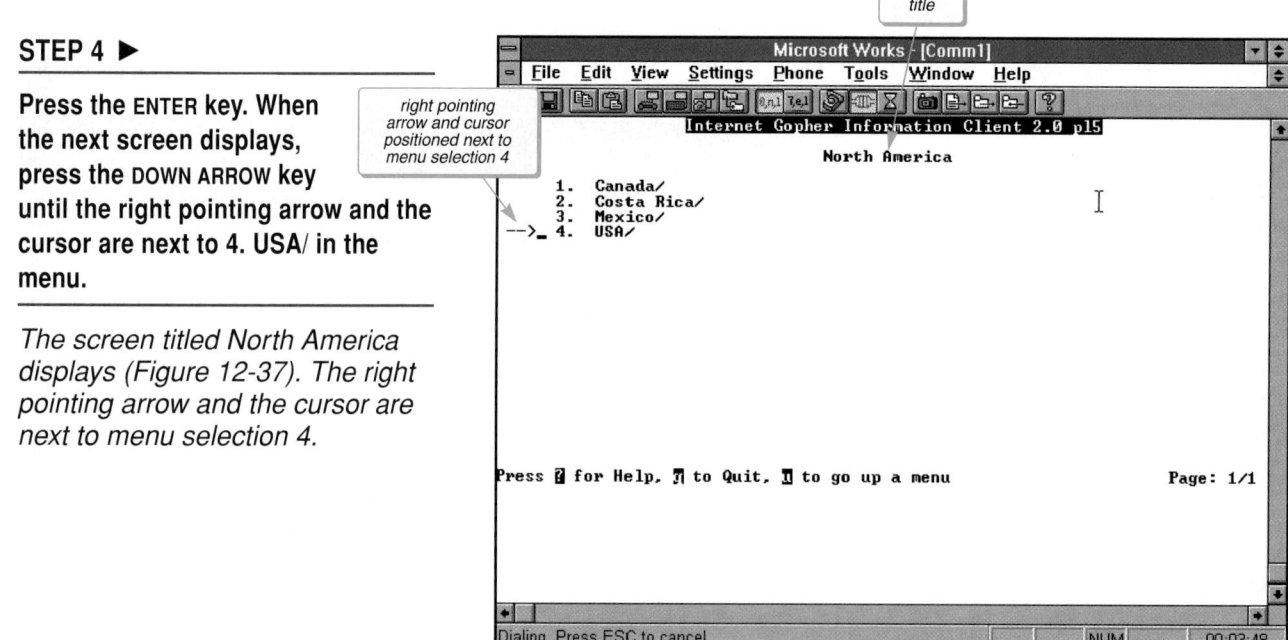

FIGURE 12-37

STEP 5 ▶

Press the ENTER key. When the next screen displays, press the DOWN ARROW key until the right pointing arrow and the cursor are next to 9. connecticut/ in the menu.

The screen titled USA displays (Figure 12-38). The right pointing arrow and the cursor are next to menu selection 9.

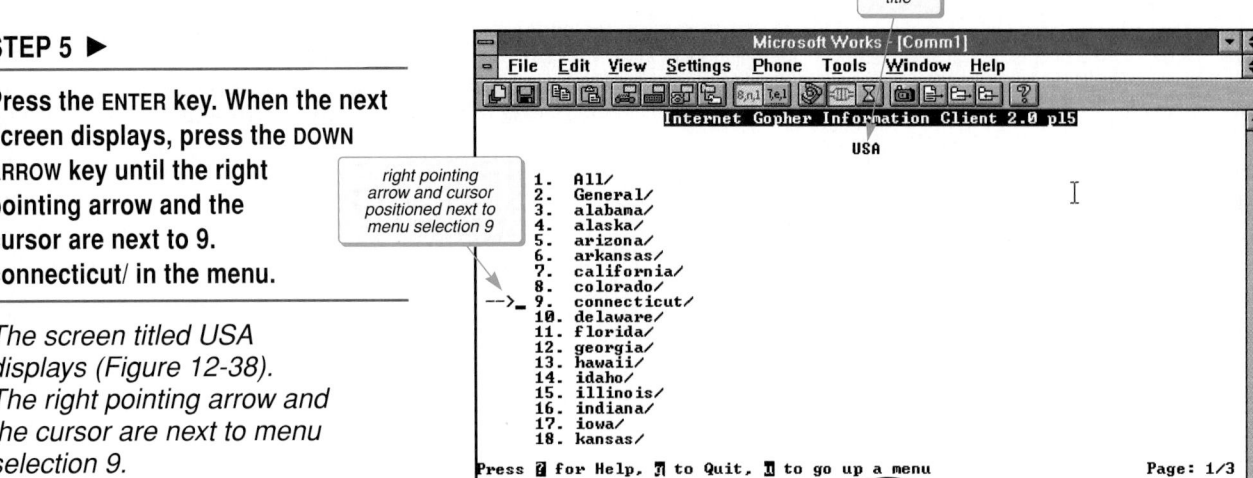

FIGURE 12-38

STEP 6 ▶

Press the ENTER key. When the next screen displays, press the DOWN ARROW key until the right pointing arrow and the cursor are next to 15. Yale University/ in the menu.

The screen titled connecticut displays (Figure 12-39). The right pointing arrow and the cursor are next to menu selection 15.

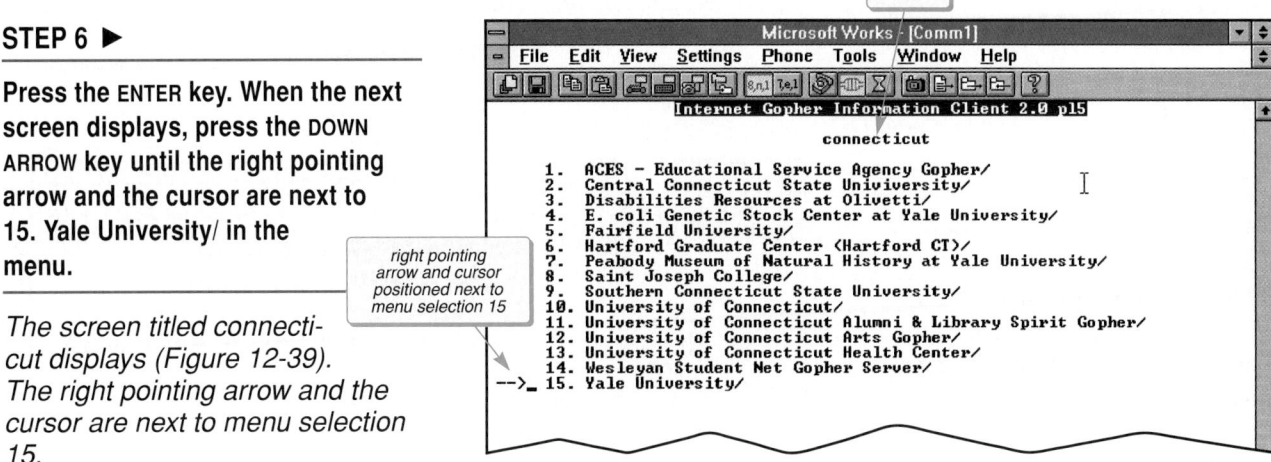

FIGURE 12-39

STEP 7 ▶

Press the ENTER key. When the next screen displays, press the DOWN ARROW key until the right pointing arrow and the cursor are next to 5. The Internet (additional information and services)/ in the menu.

The screen titled Yale University displays (Figure 12-40). The right pointing arrow and the cursor are next to menu selection 5.

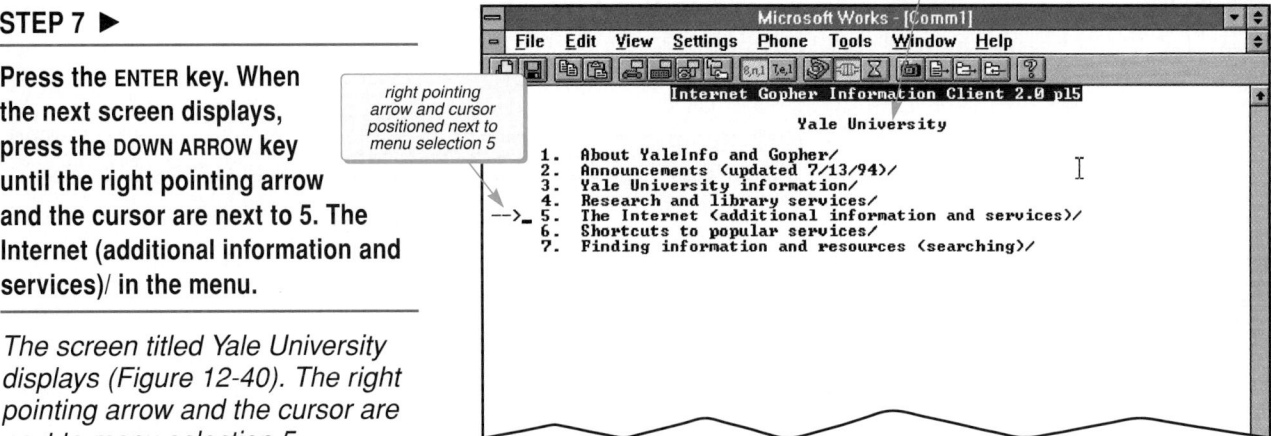

FIGURE 12-40

STEP 8 ▶

**Press the ENTER key. When the
next screen displays, press
the DOWN ARROW key until the
right pointing arrow and the
cursor are next to 6. News and
weather/ in the menu.**

*The screen titled The Internet
(additional information and services) displays (Figure 12-41). The
right pointing arrow and the cursor
are next to menu selection 6.*

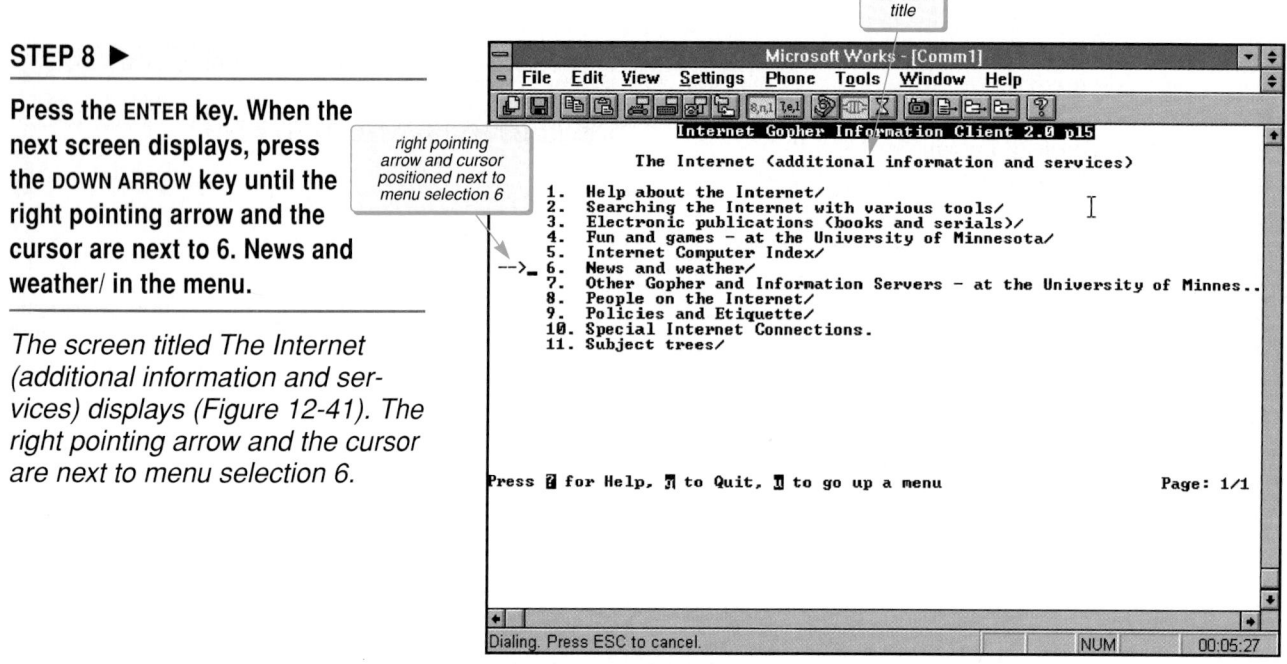

FIGURE 12-41

STEP 9 ▶

**Press the ENTER key. When the
next screen displays, press
the DOWN ARROW key until the
right pointing arrow and the
cursor are next to 6. United States
Government/ in the menu.**

*The screen titled News and
weather displays (Figure 12-42).
The right pointing arrow and
the cursor are next to menu
selection 6.*

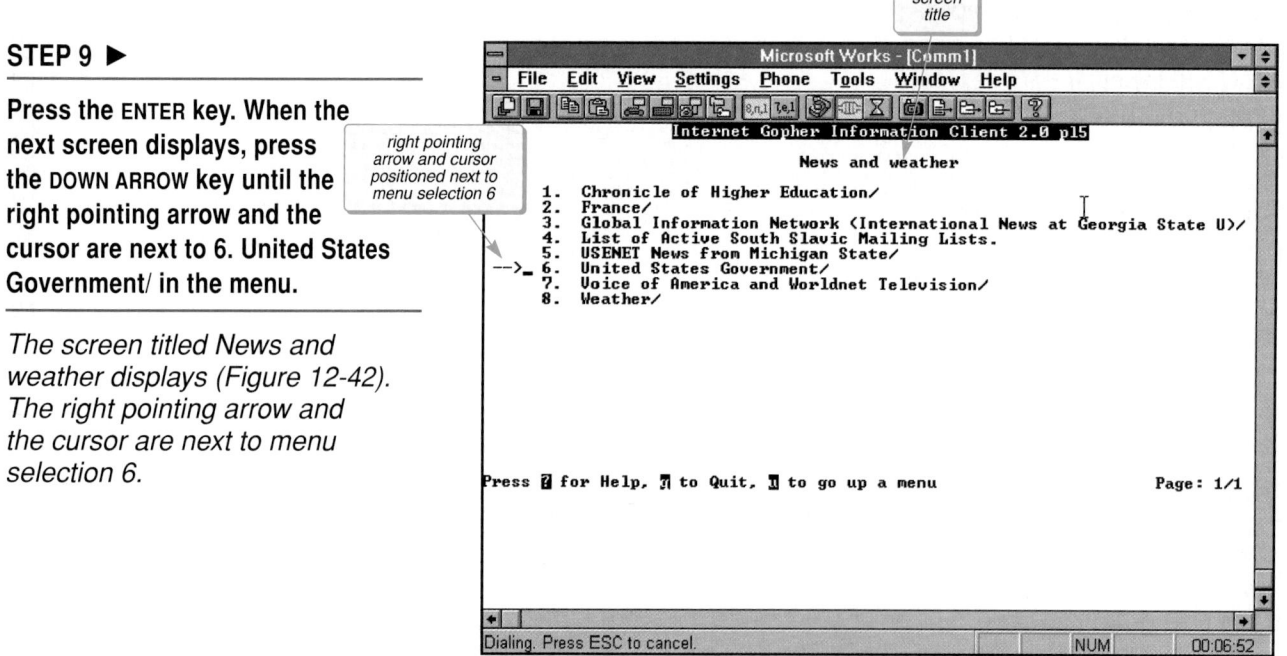

FIGURE 12-42

STEP 10 ▶

Press the ENTER key. When the next screen displays, press the DOWN ARROW key until the right pointing arrow and the cursor are next to 4. United States GOVERNMENT Gophers/ in the menu.

The screen titled United States Government displays (Figure 12-43). The right pointing arrow and the cursor are next to menu selection 4.

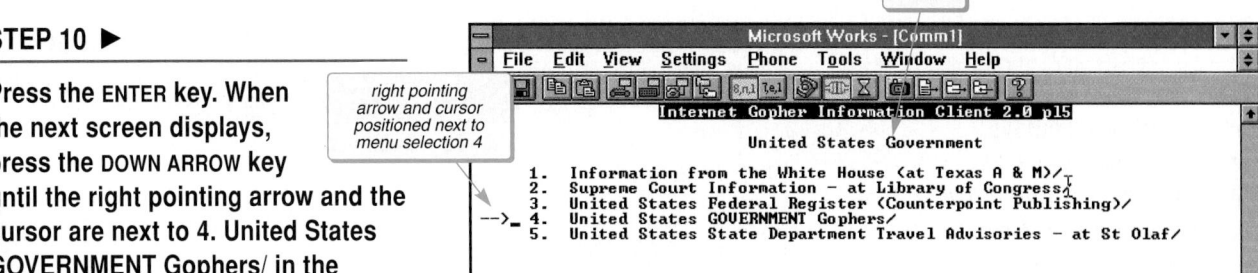

FIGURE 12-43

STEP 11 ▶

Press the ENTER key. When the United States GOVERNMENT Gophers screen displays, review the menu selections.

The screen titled United States GOVERNMENT Gophers displays (Figure 12-44). Because none of the menu items provides the information needed, no menu selections are made on this screen.

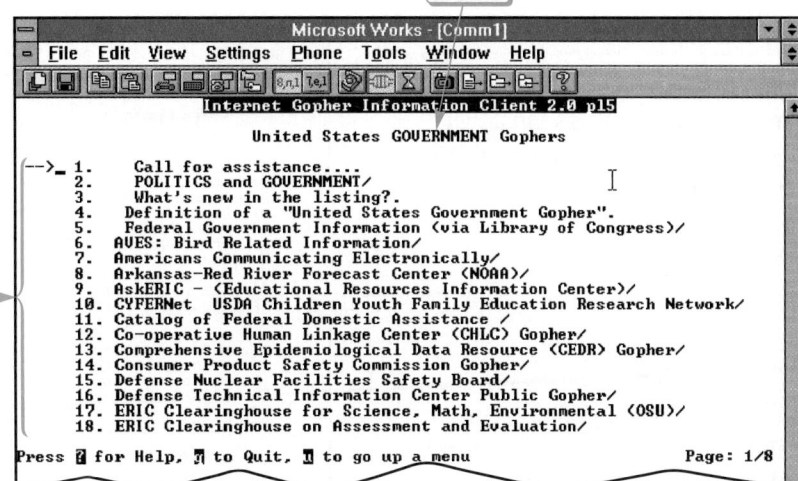

FIGURE 12-44

STEP 12 ▶

Press the DOWN ARROW key until the screen with the title United States GOVERNMENT Gophers displays with menu items 37 through 54. Press the DOWN ARROW key until the right pointing arrow and the cursor are next to 50. NASA Goddard Space Flight Center/ in the menu.

The screen titled United States GOVERNMENT Gophers with menu items 37-54 displays (Figure 12-45). The right pointing arrow and the cursor are next to menu selection 50.

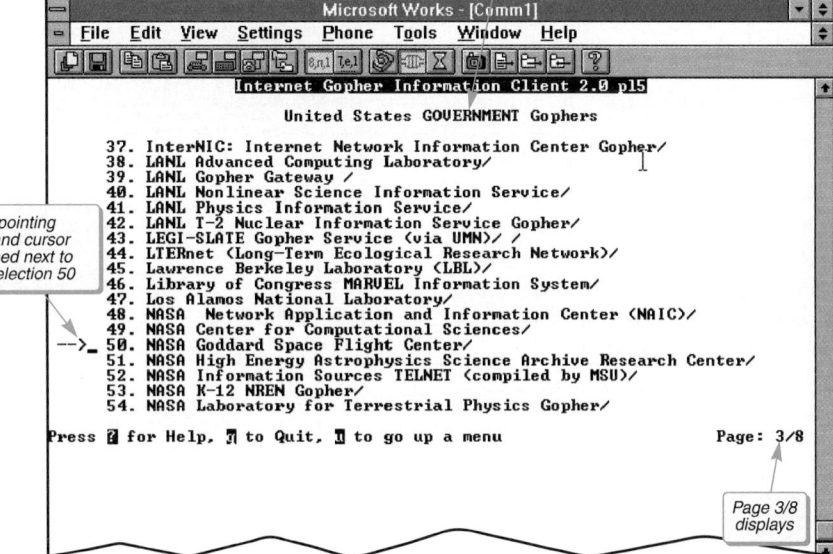

FIGURE 12-45

STEP 13 ▶

Press the ENTER key. When the next screen displays, press the DOWN ARROW key until the right pointing arrow and the cursor are next to 4. NASA information/ in the menu.

The screen titled NASA Goddard Space Flight Center displays (Figure 12-46). The right pointing arrow and the cursor are next to menu selection 4.

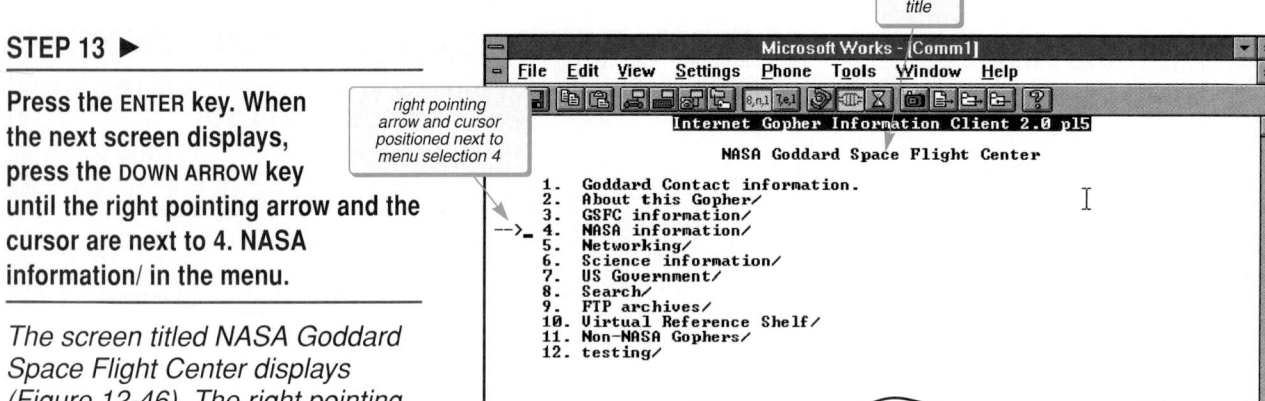

FIGURE 12-46

STEP 14 ▶

Press the ENTER key. When the next screen displays, press the DOWN ARROW key until the right pointing arrow and the cursor are next to 14. NASA Space Shuttle Launch Schedule. in the menu.

The screen titled NASA information displays (Figure 12-47). The right pointing arrow and the cursor are next to menu selection 14.

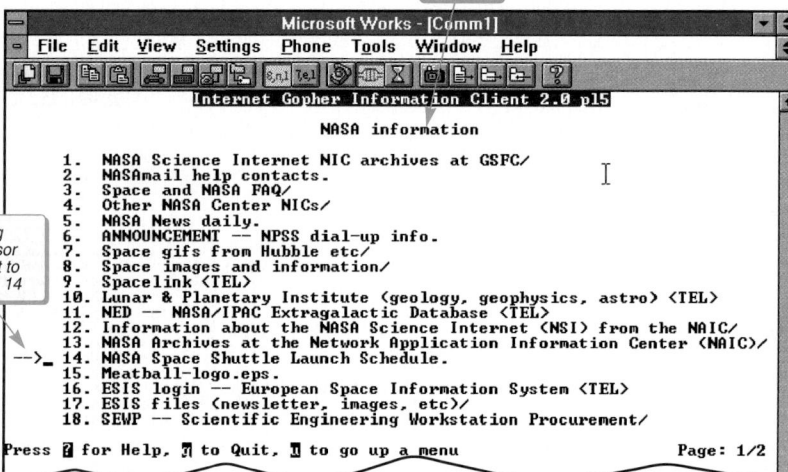

FIGURE 12-47

STEP 15 ▶

Press the ENTER key.

The NASA Space Shuttle Launch Schedule displays (Figure 12-48). The current NASA Space Shuttle Launch Schedule includes the Mission, Launch Date, Inclination of orbit (deg), and Prime Payload information. The last line displays some options for the next operation.

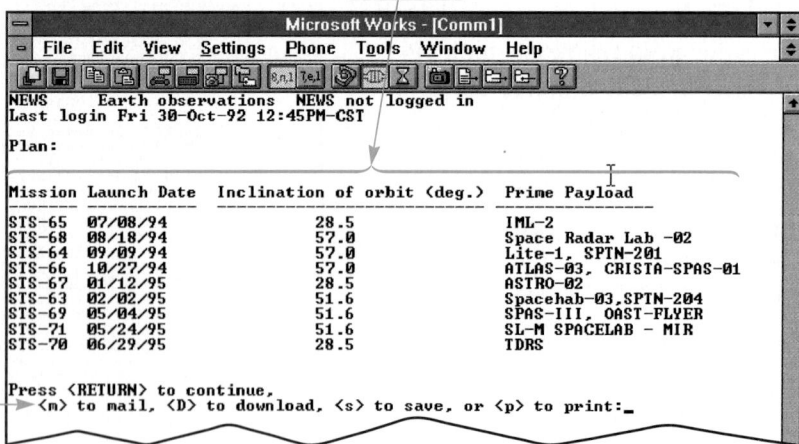

FIGURE 12-48

It is possible to print the information accessed through the Internet. The following paragraph explains one method of printing information on the screen using Works.

Printing Information When Connected to the Internet

To print information that displays on the screen when connected to the Internet, perform the following steps.

TO PRINT INFORMATION WHEN CONNECTED TO THE INTERNET

Step 1: When connected to the Internet, click the Pause button on the Communications Toolbar.

Step 2: Highlight the text you want to print.

Step 3: From the Edit menu, choose the Copy Text command.

Step 4: Click the Start Dialog button on the Toolbar.

Step 5: When the Startup dialog box displays, choose the Word Processor button. When the word processing document window displays, position the insertion point where you want the text to display.

Step 6: Click the Paste button on the Toolbar. The text will display in the word processing document window. Click the Print button to print the information.

Step 7: Switch to the communications document by choosing the communications document name from the Window menu. Click the Pause button again to continue the communications session.

Quitting The Internet

To quit the Internet, perform the following steps.

TO QUIT THE INTERNET

Step 1: Press the ENTER key to return to the previous screen.

Step 2: Type q. The Internet displays the message, Really Quit?.

Step 3: If necessary, type y.

Step 4: Press the ENTER key twice.

Step 5: When the OPTIONS menu displays, use the "d" key to scroll down to the Logout command.

Step 6: Press the ENTER key.

Step 7: NETCOM displays the message, "Thanks for choosing NETCOM." You will exit Internet and NETCOM.

Step 8: Disconnect from the modem by clicking the Dial/Hangup button on the Toolbar and choosing the OK button in the Microsoft Works dialog box that displays.

You can save the communications settings and phone number for NETCOM in a communications file so you do not have to enter the telephone number each time you want to connect to the Internet. To save the communications file, click the Save button on the Toolbar and make the necessary entries in the Save As dialog box that displays.

You have now navigated the Internet. As previously mentioned, thousands of databases can be accessed using the techniques just described. A number of books are available that specify where various types of information can be found on the Internet. If these books are not available, you can explore the Internet on your own using the techniques explained in this project.

▶ TRANSMITTING FILES

As you become experienced using computer-to-computer communications, you might want to send a file you have created to an individual at another computer. In the following example, you have been requested to transmit the Automobile Center 3-D Pie Chart with the logo you created in Project 11 to the national sales manager, who is located in a different state, using computer-to-computer communication. Figure 12-49 illustrates the 3-D Pie chart you are to transmit to the national sales manager.

To transmit a file from one computer to another, the person sending the file and the person receiving the file must make specific communications settings prior to transmitting the file. With the computers used in this example, the communications settings for the sending and receiving computers must include selecting the Local echo check box, setting the Transfer protocol to XMODEM/CRC, setting the Baud rate to 9600, and setting the Terminal type to ANSI. The following steps explain how to prepare the computers to perform a file-to-file transfer.

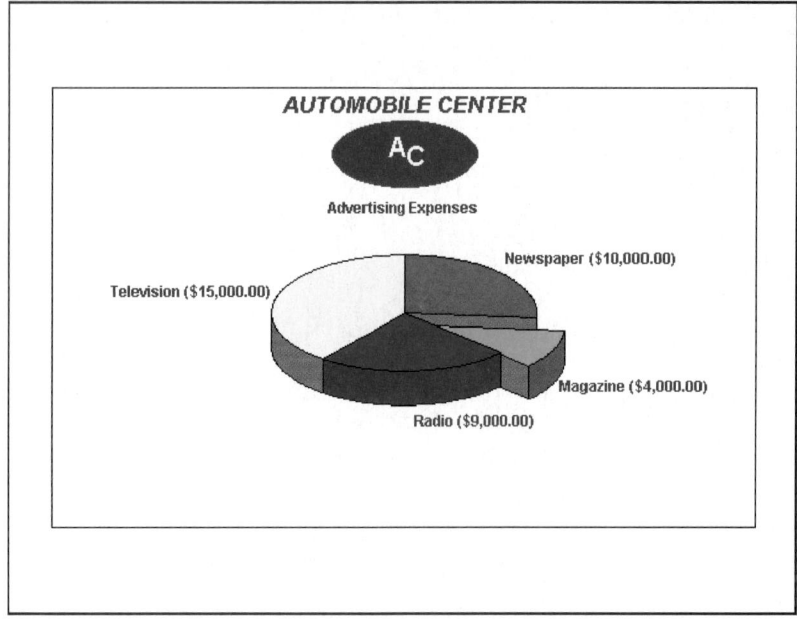

FIGURE 12-49

TO PERFORM A FILE-TO-FILE TRANSFER

ON THE COMPUTER RECEIVING THE FILE

Step 1: Start Works

Step 2: Choose the Communications button in the Startup dialog box.

Step 3: Choose the Cancel button in the Easy Connect dialog box. Maximize the Comm1 window.

Step 4: Click the Phone Settings button on the Toolbar. When the Settings dialog box displays, if necessary clear the Phone number text box and Name of service text box. Then select the Auto Answer option button.

Step 5: Select the Communication tab in the Settings dialog box. Set the Baud rate to 9600.

Step 6: Select the Terminal tab in the Settings dialog box. When the Terminal screen displays, select ANSI in the Terminal list box. Select the Local echo check box.

Step 7: Select the Transfer tab in the Settings dialog box. Highlight XMODEM/CRC in the Transfer protocol list box. Choose the Directory button. When the Choose A Directory dialog box displays, set it to receive the transmitted file on the diskette in drive A. Choose the OK button in the Choose A Directory dialog box.

Step 8: When the Transfer screen displays again, choose the OK button in the Settings dialog box.

Step 9: Click the Dial/Hangup button on the Toolbar. Works displays a series of characters in the upper left corner of the Comm1 window. This means the computer is connected and ready to receive data.

ON THE COMPUTER SENDING THE FILE

Step 1: Start Works

Step 2: Choose the Communications button in the Startup dialog box.

Step 3: Choose the Cancel button in the Easy Connect dialog box. Maximize the Comm1 window.

Step 4: Click the Phone Settings button on the Toolbar. When the Settings dialog box displays, type 555-9699 (or the actual number you are using) in the Phone number text box. If necessary, clear the Name of service text box.

Step 5: Select the Communication tab in the Settings dialog box. Set the Baud rate to 9600.

Step 6: Select the Terminal tab in the Settings dialog box. When the Terminal screen displays, select ANSI in the Terminal list box. Select the Local echo check box.

Step 7: Select the Transfer tab in the Settings dialog box. Highlight XMODEM/CRC in the Transfer protocol list box.

Step 8: Choose the OK button in the Settings dialog box.

Step 9: Click the Dial/Hangup button.

Step 10: When the computers are connected, type Prepare for file transfer. This message will display on both computer screens, letting the receiver know you are ready to send a file.

Once the computers have connected, the receiving computer user must immediately perform the following steps. A delay can cause a timeout and terminate the communications session. If done in any other sequence, the file transfer may not take place successfully.

ON THE COMPUTER RECEIVING THE FILE

Step 1: Click the **Receive Binary File button** on the Toolbar.

Step 2: When the Receive File dialog box displays, enter the name ACLOGO.WPS in the File Name text box and choose the OK button.

ON THE COMPUTER SENDING THE FILE

Step 1: The letters CK display on the screen of the computer sending the file when the receiving computer is ready.

Step 2: Click the **Send Binary File button** on the Toolbar.

Step 3: When the Send File dialog box displays, select the file you want to send (ACLOGO.WPS), which is the name of the file that contains the chart with a logo.

Step 4: Choose the OK button in the Send File dialog box.

The transmission of the file from the sending computer to the receiving computer will take place. A dialog box displays on the sending and receiving computers' screens. The dialog boxes display the number of bytes received as they are being transmitted. After the file is transmitted, the file does not display on the receiving computer's screen but the file is stored on a diskette in drive A of the receiving computer. The file may be printed by opening it as a word processing file and printing it.

Logging Off

Once the file is transmitted, the two computers must logoff by performing the following steps.

TO LOGOFF

Step 1: Both computer users should type Bye and then click the Dial/Hangup button on the Toolbar.
Step 2: Works displays a dialog box asking if it is OK to disconnect. Choose the OK button.

The communications session is now complete. You should continue with another application or quit Works.

▶ PROJECT SUMMARY

In this project, you learned basic data communications concepts, including the purpose of a modem and how computer-to-computer communication takes place. Bulletin board systems and on-line communication services were described, and you were briefly introduced to the use and scope of the Internet.

The first project involved the use of the Works Communications tool to access a bulletin board system. To access the bulletin board, you were required to review basic communications settings and make required changes in the settings. The actual steps to access the bulletin board were then explained. After accessing the bulletin board, you saved the communications file so you could easily access the file when you wanted to contact the bulletin board in the future.

In the next project, you learned to use the server NETCOM to connect to the Internet. When connected to the Internet, the use of the menu system called Gopher was explained.

The last application explained how to perform a file-to-file transfer. A knowledge of these basic application areas should provide the skills necessary to effectively use the Works Communications tool in a variety of areas.

▶ KEY TERMS

ANSI (W12.10)
analog signals (W12.3)
bulletin board system (W12.5)
baud rate (W12.9)
Communications button (W12.8)
Communications Settings button (W12.11)
communications software package (W12.6)
Communications file (W12.6)
Data bits (W12.9)
data communications (W12.3)

digital signals (W12.3)
external modem (W12.3)
Handshake (W12.9)
internal modem (W12.3)
The Internet (W12.6)
Kermit (W12.10)
modem (W12.3)
on-line information services (W12.5)
Parity (W12.9)
Phone Settings button (W12.11)
Port (W12.9)

Receive a Binary File button (W12.33)
Send a Binary File button (W12.33)
Terminal Settings button (W12.11)
Transfer Settings button (W12.11)
Transfer protocol (W12.10)
TTY (W12.10)

In Microsoft Works, you can accomplish a task in a number of ways. The following table provides a quick reference to each task presented in this project with its available options. The commands listed in the Menu column can be executed using either the keyboard or mouse.

Task	Mouse	Menu	Keyboard Shortcuts
Change Communications Settings	Click the Communication Settings button	From the Settings menu, choose Communication	
Change Terminal Settings	Click the Terminal Settings button	From the Settings menu, choose Terminal	
Change Phone Settings	Click the Phone Settings button	From the Settings menu, choose Phone	
Change Transfer Settings	Click the Transfer Settings button	From the Settings menu, choose Transfer	
Receive Binary File	Click the Receive Binary File button	From the Tools menu, choose Receive Files	
Reconnect after Saving a File	Click the Easy Connect button	From the Phone menu, choose Easy Connect	
Send Binary File	Click the Send Binary File button	From the Tool menu choose Receive File	
Terminate a cell	Click the Dial/Hangup button	From the Phone menu, choose Hangup	

S T U D E N T   A S S I G N M E N T S

STUDENT ASSIGNMENT 1
True/False

Instructions: Circle T if the statement is true or F if the statement is false.

T F 1. Data communications is defined as the transmission of data and information over a communications channel, such as standard telephone lines, from one computer to another computer.

T F 2. Computer equipment is designed to process data in the form of analog signals.

T F 3. Analog signals are commonly used to transmit data over telephone lines.

T F 4. A modem can be used to convert analog signals to digital signals.

T F 5. A modem is only necessary on the receiving end of a file-to-file transfer.

T F 6. Internal modems are faster than external modems.

T F 7. The baud rate is the speed of data transfer between computers.

T F 8. The Internet is the name of a communications software package.

T F 9. It is not important to know required communications settings before beginning a communications session because Works automatically adjusts all settings depending on the computers and modems used.

T F 10. The Port setting COM2 refers to the name of the communications channel in the modem.

T F 11. You should normally transmit data at the slowest rate possible.

(continued)

STUDENT ASSIGNMENT 1 (continued)

T F 12. The term Parity check refers to a technique that checks for transmission errors.

T F 13. Selecting the Xon/Xoff option button in the Settings dialog box specifies software handshaking, which is the standard for communicating through modems.

T F 14. Data bits refers to the number of bits used to represent each character. You should match the other computer's setting.

T F 15. The Local echo check box in the Terminal screen of the Settings dialog box should be selected if you do not want typing to appear on the screen.

T F 16. The Transfer protocol determines the type of modem and the speed of the modem you are using.

T F 17. ANSI must be selected in the Terminal tab of the Settings dialog box for all data communications.

T F 18. You should click the Phone Settings button to terminate a communications session.

T F 19. It is not possible to save communications settings.

T F 20. To transmit a file from one computer to another, use the Copy and Paste commands.

STUDENT ASSIGNMENT 2
Multiple Choice

Instructions: Circle the correct response.

1. A modem is an electronic device _____.
   a. that increases the speed at which data can be transmitted over telephone lines
   b. that uses continuous electrical wave forms called analog signals to transmit data from one computer to another
   c. that converts the analog signals of the computer to digital signals that can be transmitted over telephone lines
   d. that converts the digital signals of the computer to analog signals that can be transmitted over telephone lines

2. To communicate with another computer, you must have _____.
   a. a modem and communications software on the sending computer only
   b. a modem and communications software on the receiving computer only
   c. a modem and communications software on both the sending and receiving computer
   d. a modem and communications software on both the sending and receiving computer only if you are transmitting data over long distances that requires microwave transmission

3. A typical data transmission speed using a personal computer modem is _____.
   a. 960 bits per second
   b. 9600 bits per second
   c. 96000 bits per second
   d. 9600 bits per minute

4. To start the Works Communications tool, _____.
   a. select the Communications command from the word processing File menu
   b. click the Communications icon in the Microsoft Works for Windows group window
   c. double-click the Communications icon in the Program Manager
   d. choose the Communications button in the Startup dialog box

5. To display the Settings dialog box, _____.
   a. click the Communication Settings button on the Toolbar
   b. click the Easy Connect button on the Toolbar
   c. click the Dial/Hangup button on the Toolbar
   d. click the Send Binary File button on the Toolbar

6. _____ refers to the mathematical technique used to check for errors in transmission.
   a. Handshake
   b. Protocol
   c. Parity
   d. Xon/Xoff

7. Stop bits are bits _____.
   a. used to represent the end of each character
   b. used to represent the end of transmission
   c. used to represent the end of a paragraph
   d. that terminate transmission of data
8. When two computers are connected and either party types a message that does not display, you should _____.
   a. disconnect from the modem and start over with the same settings
   b. set the baud rate to a slower setting
   c. set the Port to COM2
   d. select the Local echo check box in the Terminal screen of the Settings dialog box
9. Saving a communications file will allow you to _____.
   a. print the information accessed through a bulletin board or the Internet
   b. transmit information from one computer to another
   c. perform a file-to-file transfer
   d. reconnect to a communications service without entering the telephone number and name of service each time
10. When using the Internet, the word Gopher refers to _____.
   a. the name of the service used to connect to the Internet
   b. the address of a database within the Internet
   c. a series of menus that assist you in navigating the Internet
   d. the method used to terminate an Internet session

STUDENT ASSIGNMENT 3
Understanding the Communications Toolbar

Instructions: In Figure SA12-3, identify each of the buttons on the Toolbar in the space provided.

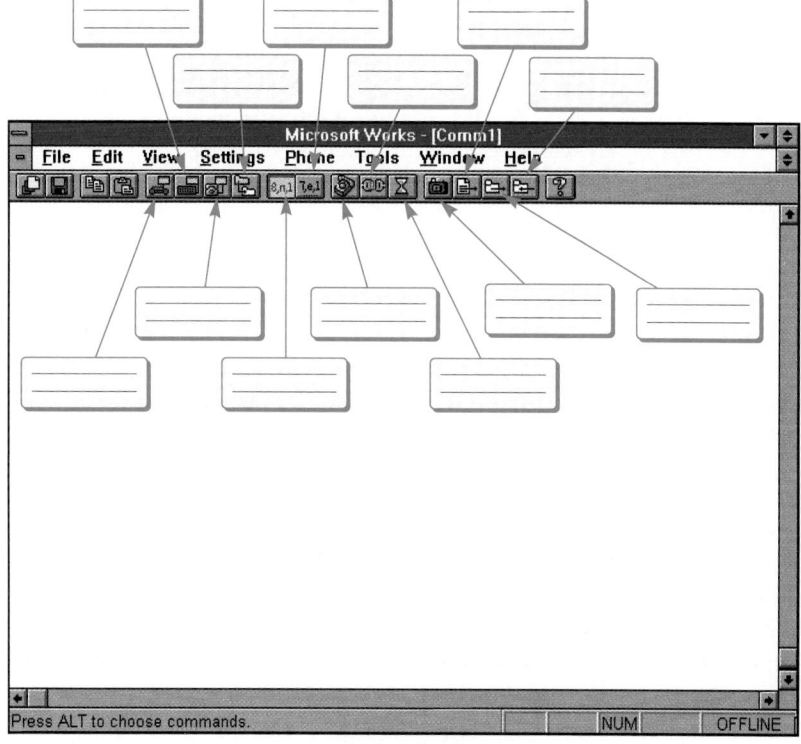

FIGURE SA12-3

STUDENT ASSIGNMENT 4
Understanding the Communications Settings

Instructions: The following table lists the Works initial communications settings. In the space provided, describe the purpose of each setting.

TYPE OF SETTING	INITIAL SETTING	DESCRIPTION
1. Port	COM1	1. _____ _____
2. Baud Rate	9600	2. _____ _____
3. Parity	None	3. _____ _____
4. Ignore Parity	On	4. _____ _____
5. Data Bits	8	5. _____ _____
6. Handshake	Xon/Xoff	6. _____ _____
7. Stop Bits	1	7. _____ _____

C O M P U T E R   L A B O R A T O R Y   E X E R C I S E S

COMPUTER LABORATORY EXERCISE 1
Using Works Online Help

Instructions: Perform the following tasks using a computer.

1. Start Works. Open the Comm1 Window.
2. Select the Help menu. Choose the Search for Help on ... command.
3. When the Search dialog box displays, type `communication` in the text box.
4. Choose the Show Topics button.
5. In the list box at the bottom of the screen, Communication command [Settings menu] CM is highlighted.
6. Choose the Go To button.
7. When the Communication command (Settings menu) screen displays, read the screen and print a copy of the screen. Then, click the words Adjusting settings overview at the bottom of the screen.
8. When the Adjusting settings overview screen displays, read and print the screen. Then, click the words Terminal settings at the bottom of the screen.
9. When the Terminal settings screen displays, click the words Terminal command (Settings menu) at the bottom of the screen.
10. Print a copy of the Terminal command (Settings menu) screen.
11. Exit Help.
12. Turn in the printed reports to your instructor.

COMPUTER LABORATORY ASSIGNMENT 1
Accessing the Internet

Purpose: To provide experience using the Works Communications tool to connect to and navigate the Internet.

Problem: You are to connect to and navigate the Internet to display information about the state of Alaska.

Instructions: Determine the communications settings required by the computer and the server you are using. Then perform the following steps.

Step 1: Start Works. Use the Works Communications tool to connect to the server available at your location that allows you to connect to the Internet.

Step 2: When connected to the Internet, display the OPTIONS menu. Highlight the word Gopher on the left side of the screen under the word OPTIONS by pressing the 'd' key as many times as required.

Step 3: Press the ENTER key when the word Gopher is highlighted. A menu displays listing selections you can make. Press the DOWN ARROW key until the right pointing arrow and the cursor are next to the number that references menu selection Other Internet Gopher Servers (via U.C. Santa Cruz)/.

Step 4: Press the ENTER key. When the next screen displays, press the DOWN ARROW key until the right pointing arrow and the cursor are next to the number that references menu selection North America/.

Step 5: Press the ENTER key. When the next screen displays, press the DOWN ARROW key until the right pointing arrow and the cursor are next to the number that references menu selection USA/.

Step 6: Press the ENTER key. When the next screen displays, press the DOWN ARROW key until the right pointing arrow and the cursor are next to the number that references menu selection alaska/.

Step 7: Press the ENTER key. When the next screen displays, press the DOWN ARROW key until the right pointing arrow and the cursor are next to the number that references menu selection University of Alaska Info/.

Step 8: Press the ENTER key. When the next screen displays, press the DOWN ARROW key until the right pointing arrow and the cursor are next to the number that references menu selection Information About Alaska/.

Step 9: Press the ENTER key. When the next screen displays, press the DOWN ARROW key until the right pointing arrow and the cursor are next to the number that references menu selection About Alaska/.

Step 10: Press the ENTER key. Read the report about Alaska and answer the following questions
Question 1: Who did the United States purchase Alaska from? _____
Question 2: What did the United States pay for Alaska? _____
Question 3: When did the United States purchase Alaska? _____
Question 4: Alaska has about _____ times as many pilots per capita as the rest of the United States.
Question 5: Farmers in the Matanuska Valley grow cabbages weighing more than _____ pounds.

Step 11: Quit the Internet and end the communications session.

Turn in the answers to these questions to your instructor.

COMPUTER LABORATORY ASSIGNMENT 2
Accessing the Internet

Purpose: To provide experience using the Works Communications tool to connect to and navigate the Internet.

Problem: You are to connect to and navigate the Internet to obtain a list of the members of the United States Senate Budget Committee.

Instructions: Determine the communications settings required by the computer and the server you are using. Then perform the following steps.

Step 1: Start Works. Use the Works Communications tool to connect to the server available at your location that allows you to connect to the Internet.

Step 2: When connected to the Internet, display the OPTIONS menu. Highlight the word Gopher on the left side of the screen under the word OPTIONS by pressing the 'd' key as many times as required.

Step 3: Press the ENTER key when the word Gopher is highlighted. A menu displays listing selections you can make. Press the DOWN ARROW key until the right pointing arrow and the cursor are next to the number that references menu selection Other Internet Gopher Servers (via U.C. Santa Cruz)/ .

Step 4: Press the ENTER key. When the next screen displays, press the DOWN ARROW key until the right pointing arrow and the cursor are next to the number that references menu selection North America/.

Step 5: Press the ENTER key. When the next screen displays, press the DOWN ARROW key until the right pointing arrow and the cursor are next to the number that references menu selection USA/.

Step 6: Press the ENTER key. When the next screen displays, press the DOWN ARROW key until the right pointing arrow and the cursor are next to the number that references menu selection Michigan/.

Step 7: Press the ENTER key. When the next screen displays, press the DOWN ARROW key until the right pointing arrow and the cursor are next to the number that references menu selection University of Michigan Libraries/.

Step 8: Press the ENTER key. When the next screen displays, press the DOWN ARROW key until the right pointing arrow and the cursor are next to the number that references menu selection Social Sciences Resources/.

Step 9: Press the ENTER key. When the next screen displays, press the DOWN ARROW key until the right pointing arrow and the cursor are next to the number that references menu selection Government and Politics/.

Step 10: Press the ENTER key. When the next screen displays, press the DOWN ARROW key until the right pointing arrow and the cursor are next to the number that references menu selection US Government Resources: Legislative Branch/.

Step 11: Press the ENTER key. When the next screen displays, press the DOWN ARROW key until the right pointing arrow and the cursor are next to the number that references menu selection US Congress: Committee Assignments (Mich)/.

Step 12: Press the ENTER key. When the next screen displays, press the DOWN ARROW key until the right pointing arrow and the cursor are next to the number that references menu selection US Congress: Senate Committee Assignments (UMich)/.

Step 13: Press the ENTER key. When the next screen displays, press the DOWN ARROW key until the right pointing arrow and the cursor are next to the number that references menu selection Budget (Mich).

Step 14: Press the ENTER key. When the next screen displays, press the space bar to list all of the members.

Step 15: Print a copy of the text.

Step 16: Quit the Internet and end the communications session.

Turn in a copy of the members of the budget committee to your instructor.

COMPUTER LABORATORY ASSIGNMENT 3
Accessing The Internet

Purpose: To provide experience using the Works Communications tool to connect to and navigate the Internet.

Problem: You are to connect to and navigate the Internet to obtain a news story concerning the computer industry.

Instructions: Determine the communications settings required by the computer and the server you are using. Then perform the following steps.

Step 1: Start Works. Use the Works Communications tool to connect to the server available at your location that allows you to connect to the Internet.

Step 2: When connected to the Internet, display the OPTIONS menu. Highlight the word E-News on the left side of the screen under the word OPTIONS by pressing the 'd' key as many times as necessary.

Step 3: Press the ENTER key when the word E-News is highlighted. A menu displays listing selections you can make. Press the DOWN ARROW key until the right pointing arrow and the cursor are next to the number that references menu selection Computer Industry News.

Step 4: Press the ENTER key. When the next screen displays, select a magazine or newspaper of your choice.

Step 5: Press the ENTER key. When the next screen displays, select a story of your choice.

Step 6: Press the ENTER key. When the story displays, print the story.

Step 7: Quit the Internet and end the communications session.

Turn in a copy of the story to your instructor.

COMPUTER LABORATORY ASSIGNMENT 4
Accessing The Internet

Purpose: To provide experience using the Works Communications tool to connect to and navigate the Internet.

Problem: You are to connect to and navigate the Internet to find information that is of interest to you.

Instructions: Capture and print information of interest to you that you have found using the Internet. Turn in a copy of the information to your instructor.

WORKS FUNCTIONS

▼

WORKS FUNCTIONS

▶ INTRODUCTION

 Works function is a built-in equation you can use in Works spreadsheets or databases. Works has 76 functions that allow you to perform a variety of calculations.

The general format of a function consists of the function name, a set of parentheses, and arguments, as illustrated in Figure A-1.

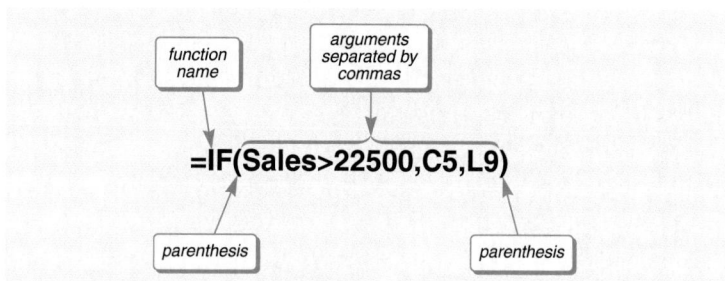

FIGURE A-1

Most Works functions use one or more arguments, which are values the function uses in its calculations. For instance, in the function SQRT(25), SQRT is the function and 25 is the argument. This function gives the result, 5, which is the square root of 25.

Functions and their arguments must be written in a specific way, called the function syntax. Some of the rules for function syntax are:

1. An argument can be a number or an expression that results in a number. This means an argument can be a number, a cell, a range reference, a range name, another function, a field name, or any allowable combination. Some arguments can also contain text, or string, data.
2. The arguments must be separated by a comma.
3. The arguments of a function must be inside parentheses.
4. Some functions can only use a range reference, range name, or field name as an argument. Some functions have no arguments.

A numeric function can be placed inside any mathematical formula that allows a numeric value in that place. For example, the following is a valid use of a function.

=45-SQRT(25)*200

The following pages contain a list of the names of all Works functions, their syntax, the result they produce, and an example of the function. In some cases, a special note about the function is included as well. To see the result of each function when using Works, enter each example that follows in a spreadsheet cell.

▶ WORKS FUNCTIONS

FUNCTION NAME:	**ABS**
Syntax:	ABS(x)
Result:	Gives the absolute (positive) value of x
Example:	=ABS(-8) equals 8

FUNCTION NAME:	**ACOS**
Syntax:	ACOS(x)
Result:	Gives the arccosine of x
Example:	=ACOS(-0.5) equals 2.094

FUNCTION NAME:	**AND**
Syntax:	AND(Logical0,Logical1,...)
Result:	Gives 1 (TRUE) if all of the arguments are TRUE (nonzero) and gives 0 (FALSE) if one or more arguments are false (zero)
Example:	=AND(2+2=4,2+3=5) equals 1 (TRUE)

FUNCTION NAME:	**ASIN**
Syntax:	ASIN(x)
Result:	Gives the arcsine of x
Example:	=ASIN(-0.5) equals -0.524

FUNCTION NAME:	**ATAN**
Syntax:	ATAN(x)
Result:	Gives the arctangent of x
Example:	=ATAN(1) equals 0.785

FUNCTION NAME:	**ATAN2**
Syntax:	ATAN2(x-coordinate,y-coordinate)
Result:	Gives the arctangent of an angle defined by the x- and y-coordinates
Example:	=ATAN2(1.1) equals 0.785

FUNCTION NAME:	**AVG**
Syntax:	AVG(RangeReference0,RangeReference1,...)
Result:	Gives the average of values in RangeReferences
Example:	=AVG(2,25,9,16,8) equals 12
Special Note:	RangeReferences can be numbers, cell references, range references, or formulas

FUNCTION NAME:	**CHOOSE**
Syntax:	CHOOSE(Choice,Option0,Option1,...)
Result:	If Choice is equal to 0, Option0 appears in the cell; if choice is equal to 1, option1 appears in the cell, and so on
Example:	=CHOOSE(A1,5,10,15,20) If cell A1 = 0, then the cell where the function was entered will contain a 5; if cell A1 = 1, then the cell where the function was entered will contain a 10, and so on
Special Note:	If Choice is less than zero or greater than the number of options in the list, Choose gives the error value ERR

FUNCTION NAME:	**COLS**
Syntax:	COLS(RangeReference)
Result:	Gives the number of columns in RangeReference
Example:	=COLS(A5:F7) equals 6

FUNCTION NAME:	**COS**
Syntax:	COS(x)
Result:	Gives the cosine of x (an angle measured in radians)
Example:	=COS(1.047) equals 0.5

FUNCTION NAME:	**COUNT**
Syntax:	Count(RangeReference0,RangeReference1,...)
Result:	Gives the number of cells contained in RangeReferences
Example:	=COUNT(A5:A10,B1:B20) equals 26
Special Note:	Count adds 1 for every cell that contains a number, formula, text, ERR, and N/A

FUNCTION NAME:	**CTERM**
Syntax:	CTERM(Rate,FutureValue,PresentValue)
Result:	Gives the number of compounding periods needed for an investment, earning a fixed Rate per compounding period, to grow from a PresentValue to a FutureValue
Example:	=CTERM(.10,2000,1000) equals 7.273
Special Note:	Rate must be expressed as an interest rate either as a percentage or as a percentage in a decimal form

FUNCTION NAME:	**DATE**
Syntax:	DATE(Year,Month,Day)
Result:	Gives a date number ranging from 1 to 65534 for the date specified by Year, Month, and Day
Example:	=DATE(94,7,4) equals 34519
Special Note:	This function is usually used in calculations with values for other dates

FUNCTION NAME:	**DAY; MONTH; YEAR**
Syntax:	DAY(DateNumber); MONTH(DateNumber); YEAR(DateNumber)
Result:	Day, Month, and Year give the number of the day, month, or year specified by DateNumber
Example:	=DAY(34519) equals 4; =MONTH(34519) equals 7; YEAR(34519) equals 94

FUNCTION NAME:	**DDB**
Syntax:	DDB(Cost,Salvage,Life,Period)
Result:	Uses the double-declining balance method to find the amount of depreciation in a specific Period
Example:	=DDB(20000,1000,10,2) equals $3,200.00
Special Note:	Cost is the amount paid for the asset. Salvage is the value of the asset at the end of its life. Life is the number of years you expect the asset to be in use. Period is the time period for which you want to find the depreciation amount

FUNCTION NAME:	**ERR**
Syntax:	ERR()
Result:	ERR gives the error value ERR
Example:	=(IF(A1=0,ERR(),A1)) equals ERR when cell A1 contains 0
Special Note:	Use to force a cell to display ERR whenever a specified condition exists

FUNCTION NAME: **EXACT**
Syntax: EXACT(TextValue0,TextValue1)
Result: Compares two strings of characters and gives 1 (TRUE) if they are exactly the same, 0 (FALSE) if they are not
Example: =EXACT("Fred","Thomas") equals 0 (FALSE)

FUNCTION NAME: **EXP**
Syntax: EXP(x)
Result: Gives e to the power of x, where e is 2.71828, which is the base number of natural logarithms
Example: =EXP(1) equals 2.718
Special Note: To compute powers of other bases, use the exponential operator (^)

FUNCTION NAME: **FALSE**
Syntax: FALSE()
Result: FALSE gives the logical value 0 (FALSE)
Example: =IF(A1>10,TRUE(),FALSE()) equals FALSE if A1 contains 5
Special Note: You can use FALSE() instead of 0 to create more readable logical formulas

FUNCTION NAME: **FIND**
Syntax: FIND(FindText,SearchText,Offset)
Result: Finds one string of text (FindText) within another string of text (SearchText) and returns the number of the character at which FindText occurs. The search begins at the offset number (0 is the first character, one is the second character, etc.)
Example: =FIND("eat","The Beatles",0) equals 5

FUNCTION NAME: **FV**
Syntax: FV(Payment,Rate,Term)
Result: Gives the future value of an ordinary annuity of equal Payments, earning a fixed Rate of interest per Term, compounded over several Terms
Example: =FV(2000,5.75%,20) equals $71624.26

FUNCTION NAME: **HLOOKUP**
Syntax: HLOOKUP(LookupValue,RangeReference,RowNumber)
Result: Searches the top row of RangeReference until it finds the number that matches LookupValue. Then it goes down the column the number of rows indicated by RowNumber to get the entry
Example: =HLOOKUP(1995,C4:G7,2)
Special Note: Arrange numbers in top row in ascending order

FUNCTION NAME: **HOUR; Minute; Second**

Syntax: HOUR(TimeNumber); MINUTE(TimeNumber);
SECOND(TimeNumber)

Result: Hour gives the number for the hour represented by
TimeNumber as an integer ranging from 0 through 23;
Minute gives the number for the minute represented by
TimeNumber as an integer ranging from 0 through 59;
Second gives the number for the second represented by
TimeNumber as an integer ranging from 0 through 59

Example: =HOUR(0.70035) equals 16; =MINUTE(0.70035) equals
48; =SECOND(0.70035) equals 30

FUNCTION NAME: **IF**

Syntax: IF(Condition,ValueIfTrue,ValueIfFalse)

Result: Determines whether Condition is true or false, then gives
either ValueIfTrue or ValueIfFalse

Example: IF(A1>100,D1,E1)

FUNCTION NAME: **INDEX**

Syntax: INDEX(RangeReference,Column,Row)

Result: Gives the value in a cell in RangeReference at the intersection of the Column and Row

Example: =INDEX(A2:C5,2,1)

Special Note: Column and row numbering begins with zero

FUNCTION NAME: **INT**

Syntax: INT(X)

Result: Gives the integer part of x

Example: =INT(7.9) equals 7

Special Note: INT deletes the digits to the right of the decimal point
without rounding to the nearest integer

FUNCTION NAME: **IRR**

Syntax: IRR(Guess,RangeReference)

Result: Gives the internal rate of return for the cash flow series in
RangeReference

Example: =IRR(10%,B1:H1)

FUNCTION NAME: **ISERR**

Syntax: ISERR(x)

Result: Gives the logical value 1 (TRUE) if x is the error value
ERR, otherwise, it gives the logical value 0 (FALSE)

Example: =ISERR(3/0) equals 1

FUNCTION NAME: **ISNA**

Syntax: ISNA(x)

Result: Gives the logical value 1 (TRUE) if x is the value N/A, otherwise, it gives the logical value 0 (FALSE)

Example: =IF(ISNA(A1),2,1) equals 2 if A1 contains the value N/A

FUNCTION NAME: **LEFT**

Syntax: LEFT(TextValue,Length)

Result: Gives the first (or leftmost) character (or characters) in a phrase

Example: =LEFT("Works Word Processor",5) gives Works

FUNCTION NAME: **LENGTH**

Syntax: LENGTH(TextValue)

Result: Gives the number of characters and spaces in a string of text

Example: =LENGTH("spreadsheet tool") gives 16

FUNCTION NAME: **LN**

Syntax: LN(x)

Result: Gives the natural logarithm of x

Example: =LN(EXP(3)) equals 3

Special Note: X must be a positive number

FUNCTION NAME: **LOG**

Syntax: LOG(x)

Result: Gives the base 10 logarithm of x

Example: =LOG(10) equals 1

Special Note: X must be a positive number

FUNCTION NAME: **LOWER**

Syntax: LOWER(TextValue)

Result: Converts all uppercase letters of text to lowercase

Example: =LOWER("ABCDEF") gives abcdef

FUNCTION NAME: **MAX**

Syntax: MAX(RangeReference0,RangeReference1,...)

Result: Gives the largest number contained in RangeReferences

Example: =MAX(B2:F2)

FUNCTION NAME: **MID**

Syntax: MID(TextValue,Offset,Length)

Result: Gives a specific number of characters from a text string, starting at the position you specify

Example: =MID("The Beatles",5,3) equals eat

FUNCTION NAME:	**MIN**
Syntax:	MIN(RangeReference0,RangeReference1,...)
Result:	Gives the smallest number contained in RangeReferences
Example:	=MIN(B2:F2)

FUNCTION NAME:	**MINUTE**
Syntax:	MINUTE(TimeSerialNumber)
Result:	Gives the number for the minute of the time represented by TimeSerialNumber
Example:	=MINUTE(.7253) equals 24

FUNCTION NAME:	**MOD**
Syntax:	MOD(Numerator,Denominator)
Result:	Gives the remainder (modulus) of a Denominator divided into a Numerator
Example:	=MOD(10,4) equals 2

FUNCTION NAME:	**MONTH**
Syntax:	MONTH(DateSerialNumber)
Result:	Gives the number for the month specified in DateSerialNumber
Example:	=MONTH(33706) equals 4

FUNCTION NAME:	**N**
Syntax:	N(RangeReference)
Result:	Gives the entry in the first cell in the range as a value; if the cell contains text, N returns zero
Example:	If cell A1 contains the text JANUARY and cell A2 contains 123.32, then =N(A1:A2) equals 0 (zero)

FUNCTION NAME:	**NA**
Syntax:	NA()
Result:	Gives the value N/A
Example:	=IF(A10,NA(),A1) equals NA if A1 contains 0
Special Note:	N/A is treated as numeric

FUNCTION NAME:	**NOT**
Syntax:	NOT(Logical)
Result:	Reverses the value of its argument
Example:	=NOT(1+1=3) equals 1 (TRUE)

FUNCTION NAME: **NOW**
Syntax: NOW()
Result: Gives the date and time number for the current date and time
Example: =NOW()
Special Note: Time number is updated at every recalculation

FUNCTION NAME: **NPV**
Syntax: NPV(Rate,RangeReference)
Result: Gives the net present value of a series of cash flow payments represented by numbers in RangeReference, discounted at a fixed Rate per period
Example: =NPV(10%,B2:F2)-B1 equals $1,784.82

FUNCTION NAME: **OR**
Syntax: OR(Logical0,Logical1,...)
Result: Gives 1 (TRUE) if one or more arguments are TRUE; gives 0 (FALSE) if all the arguments are false
Example: =OR(1+1=3, 2+2=7) equals 0

FUNCTION NAME: **PI**
Syntax: PI()
Result: Gives the number 3.14159...
Example: =PI()

FUNCTION NAME: **PMT**
Syntax: PMT(Principal,Rate,Term)
Result: Gives the periodic payment for a loan or an investment of Principal based on a fixed interest Rate per compounding period over a given Term
Example: =PMT(15000,9%/12,24) equals 685.27

FUNCTION NAME: **PROPER**
Syntax: PROPER(TextValue)
Result: Capitalizes the first letter of each word and any text that follows any character other than a letter
Example: =PROPER("this is a string") equals This Is A String

FUNCTION NAME: **PV**
Syntax: PV(Payment,Rate,Term)
Result: Gives the present value of an ordinary annuity of equal Payments, earning a fixed interest Rate per period, over several periods (Term)
Example: =PV(5000,9%,10) equals $32,088.29

FUNCTION NAME: RAND
Syntax: RAND()
Result: Gives a random number from 0 up to, but not including 1
Example: =RAND()

FUNCTION NAME: RATE
Syntax: RATE(FutureValue,PresentValue,Term)
Result: RATE gives the fixed interest rate per compounding period needed for an investment of PresentValue to grow to a FutureValue over several compounding periods (Terms)
Example: =RATE(1500000,500000,6) equals 20.09%

FUNCTION NAME: REPEAT
Syntax: REPEAT(TextValue,Count)
Result: Repeats text as many times as you specify
Example: =REPEAT("book",5) equals bookbookbookbookbook

FUNCTION NAME: REPLACE
Syntax: REPLACE(OldText,Offset,Length,NewText)
Result: Exchange one string of text for another
Example: =REPLACE("abcdefffi",6,2,"gh") equals abcdefghi

FUNCTION NAME: RIGHT
Syntax: RIGHT(TextValue,Length)
Result: Returns the last (or rightmost) characters or characters in a phrase
Example: =RIGHT("uvwxyz",3) equals xyz

FUNCTION NAME: ROUND
Syntax: ROUND(x,NumberOfPlaces)
Result: Rounds x to the specifed NumberOfPlaces to the left or right of the decimal point
Example: =ROUND(9.15,1) equals 9.2
Special Note: If NumberOf Places is positive, x is rounded to the number of decimal places to the right of the decimal point; if Number of Places is 0, x is rounded to the nearest integer

FUNCTION NAME: ROWS
Syntax: ROWS(RangeReference)
Result: Gives the number of rows in RangeReference
Example: =ROWS(C2:E5) equals 4

FUNCTION NAME: **S**
Syntax: S(RangeReference)
Result: Gives the text in the first cell in a range
Example: If cell A1 contains CA and cell A2 contains WY, =S(A1:A2) equals CA

FUNCTION NAME: **SECOND**
Syntax: SECOND(TimeSerialNumber)
Result: Gives the number for the second of the time represented by TimeSerialNumber
Example: =SECOND(0.7253) equals 26

FUNCTION NAME: **SIN**
Syntax: SIN(x)
Result: Gives the sine of x
Example: =SIN(1.047)equals 0.866
Special Note: X is an angle measured in radians

FUNCTION NAME: **SLN**
Syntax: SLN(Cost,Salvage,Life)
Result: Uses the straight-line depreciation method to find the amount of depreciation in one period
Example: =SLN(10000,2000,4) equals $2,000

FUNCTION NAME: **SQRT**
Syntax: SQRT(x)
Result: Gives the square root of x
Example: =SQRT(25) equals 5
Special Note: If x is negative, Works gives the value ERR

FUNCTION NAME: **STD**
Syntax: STD(RangeReference0,RangeReference1,...)
Result: Gives the population standard deviation of RangeReferences
Example: =STD(B2:G2)

FUNCTION NAME: **STRING**
Syntax: STRING(x,DecimalPlaces)
Result: Gives the value converted to text, with the specified number of decimal places
Example: =STRING(256,2) equals 250.00 as text

FUNCTION NAME: **SUM**
Syntax: SUM(RangeReference0,RangeReference1,...)
Result: Gives the total in all values in RangeReferences
Example: =SUM(B2:G2)

FUNCTION NAME: **SYD**
Syntax: SYD(Cost,Salvage,Life,Period)
Result: Uses the sum-of-the-years digits method to find the amount of depreciation in a specific Period
Example: =SYD(50000,8000,10,7) equals $3054.55
Special Note: Cost is the amount paid for the asset; Salvage is the amount you expect to obtain when you sell the asset at the end of its life; Life is the number of periods you expect to use the asset; Period is the period for which you want to find the depreciation

FUNCTION NAME: **TAN**
Syntax: TAN(x)
Result: Gives the tangent of x
Example: =TAN(0.785) equals

FUNCTION NAME: **TERM**
Syntax: TERM(Payment,Rate.,FutureValue)
Result: Gives the number of compounding periods necessary for a series of equal Payments, earning a fixed interest Rate per period, to grow to a FutureValue
Example: =TERM(200,7.75%/12,5000) equals 23.25

FUNCTION NAME: **TIME**
Syntax: TIME(Hour,Minute,Second)
Result: Gives a time number for the time specified by Hour, Minute, and Second
Example: =Time(16,48,0) equals 0.7 (time number of 4.48:00 p.m.)
Special Note: The time number is a fraction ranging from 0.0 through 0.999, representing times from 0:00:00 or 12:00:00 p.m. through 23.59.59 or 11:59:59 p.m; Hour is generally a number ranging from 0 through 23; Minute and Second are generally numbers ranging from 0 through 59

FUNCTION NAME: **TRIM**
Syntax: TRIM(TextValue)
Result: Removes all spaces from TextValue except for single spaces between words
Example: If cell A1 contains A   Pretty   Morning, then =TRIM(A1) equals A Pretty Morning

FUNCTION NAME: **TRUE**
Syntax: TRUE( )
Result: Gives the logical value 1 (TRUE). You can use TRUE( ) instead of 1 to create more readable logical formulas
Example: =IF(A1>10,TRUE( ),FALSE( ))

FUNCTION NAME: **UPPER**
Syntax: UPPER(TextValue)
Result: Converts all text in TextValue to uppercase
Example: =UPPER("appendix a") equals APPENDIX A

FUNCTION NAME: **VALUE**
Syntax: VALUE(TextValue)
Result: Converts a number entered as text to its corresponding numeric value
Example: =VALUE("$578.04") equals 578.04

FUNCTION NAME: **VAR**
Syntax: VAR(RangeReference0,RangeReference1,...)
Result: Calculates the variance of the numbers in RangeReferences
Example: =VAR(B2:F2)

FUNCTION NAME: **VLOOKUP**
Syntax: VLOOKUP(LookupValue,RangeReference,ColumnNumber)
Result: Searches the leftmost column of RangeReference until it finds the number that matches the LookupValue; then it goes to the right by the number of columns indicated by ColumnNumber to get the entry
Example: =VLOOKUP(1995,B10:E14,2)
Special Note: Arrange numbers in column in ascending order